PRENTICE HALL
LITERATURE

TEACHER'S EDITION • GRADE 7

COMMON CORE EDITION ©

ISBN-13: 978-0-13-319056-4
ISBN-10: 0-13-319056-0
5 6 7 8 9 10 V011 15 14 13 12

ALWAYS LEARNING

PEARSON

Preparing Students for College and Career

Literature opens minds. It should also open doors to a student's future. *Prentice Hall Literature Common Core Edition* is a comprehensive literacy program that teaches the new standards and helps students become better readers, better writers, and better thinkers so they're better prepared for college, careers, and beyond. You can be confident that what you are teaching meets the Common Core framework.

Common Core in *Prentice Hall Literature*

- Leveled support and scaffolding for understanding increasingly complex texts
- Informational texts across content areas
- Emphasis on writing argumentative, informative/explanatory, and narrative texts
- Critical thinking and higher-order thinking skills presented in instruction
- Traditional and performance-based assessments
- Best-in-class digital resources
- Teacher training to implement the new standards

Builds Better Readers

Prentice Hall Literature provides a scaffolded approach to rigorous instruction, enabling students to build a solid literary foundation that is necessary for success in college and careers.

Exposure to rich literature selections with increasing text complexity across genres builds students' literary and cultural knowledge, so they become comfortable reading different text structures and understand the elements that appear in the selections.

Leveled Selection Pairs in the Student Edition let you choose the right text without skipping essential skills.

Text Complexity Rubrics guide you in choosing the selection that's appropriate for your students' abilities.

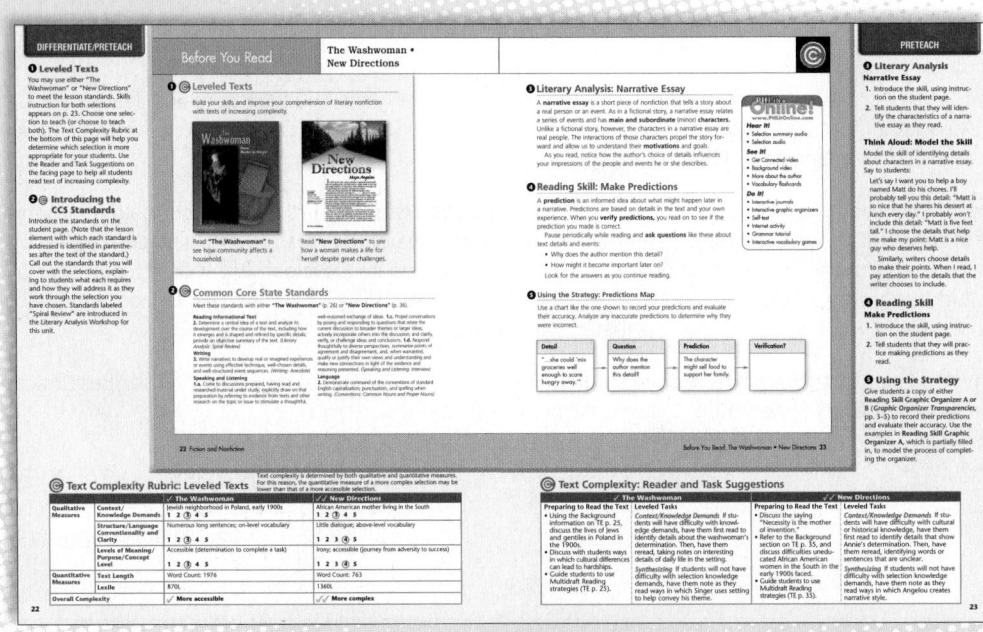

Reader and Task Suggestions offer support to ensure all readers meet achievable challenges.

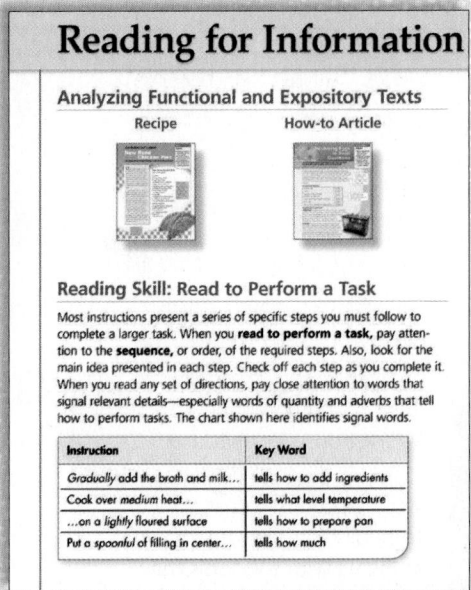

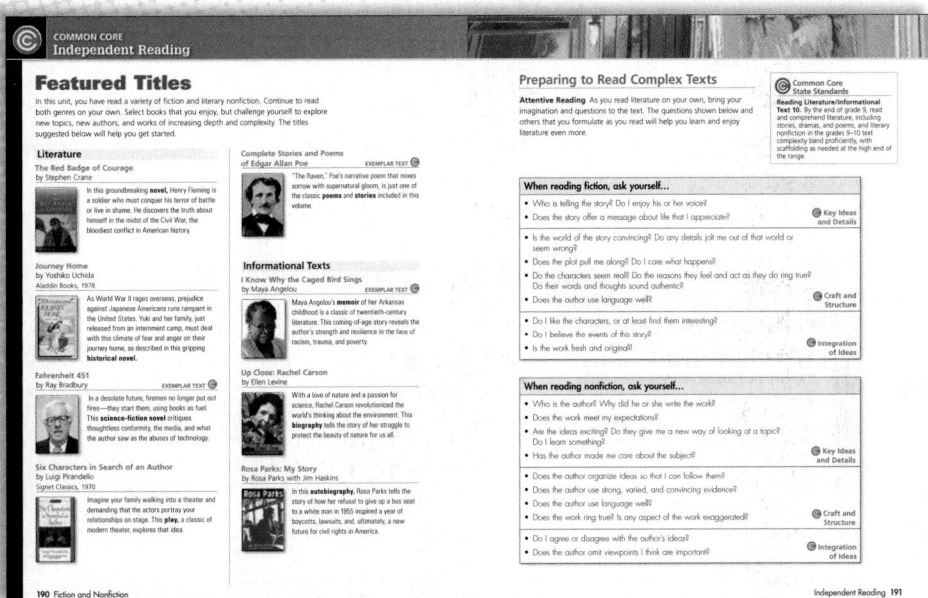

Informational texts provide context for learning and allow for the application of knowledge across science, social studies, and math.

Wide and deep independent readings of increasing complexity challenge learners. Support for reading complex texts is aligned to the Common Core.

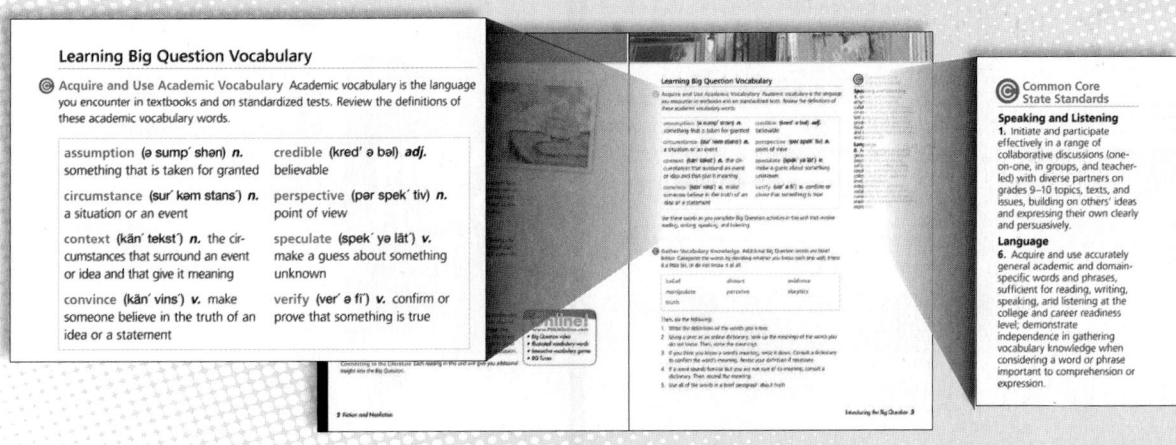

Extensive practice with general and domain-specific vocabulary builds vocabulary knowledge and prepares students for success.

Digital Resources Target Practice with Customized Instruction

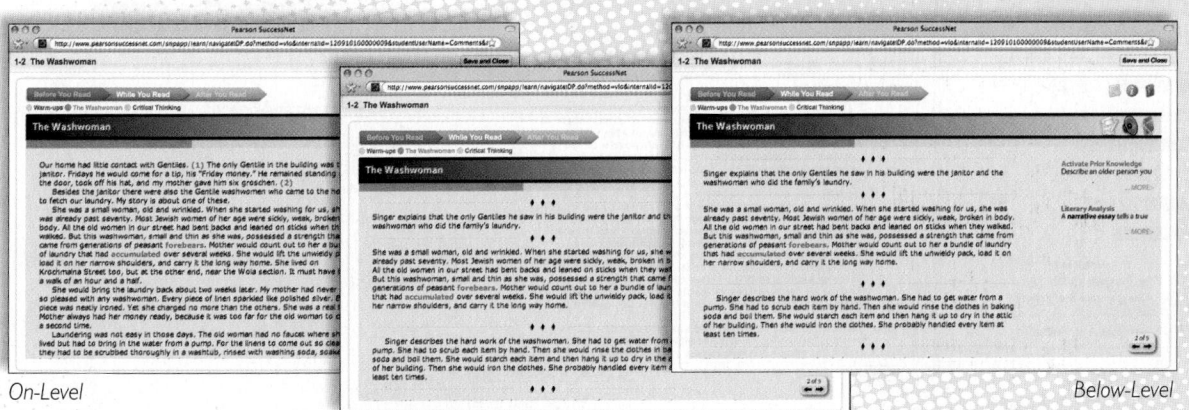

On-Level

English Learner

Below-Level

Online instruction instantly responds to students' needs with precise practice and scaffolding. PHLitOnline automatically assigns learner levels based on Diagnostic Test results.

Better Writers, Better Thinkers

Writing, speaking, and listening are integrated throughout *Prentice Hall Literature* with rigorous, robust skill instruction that takes students to the next level of mastery.

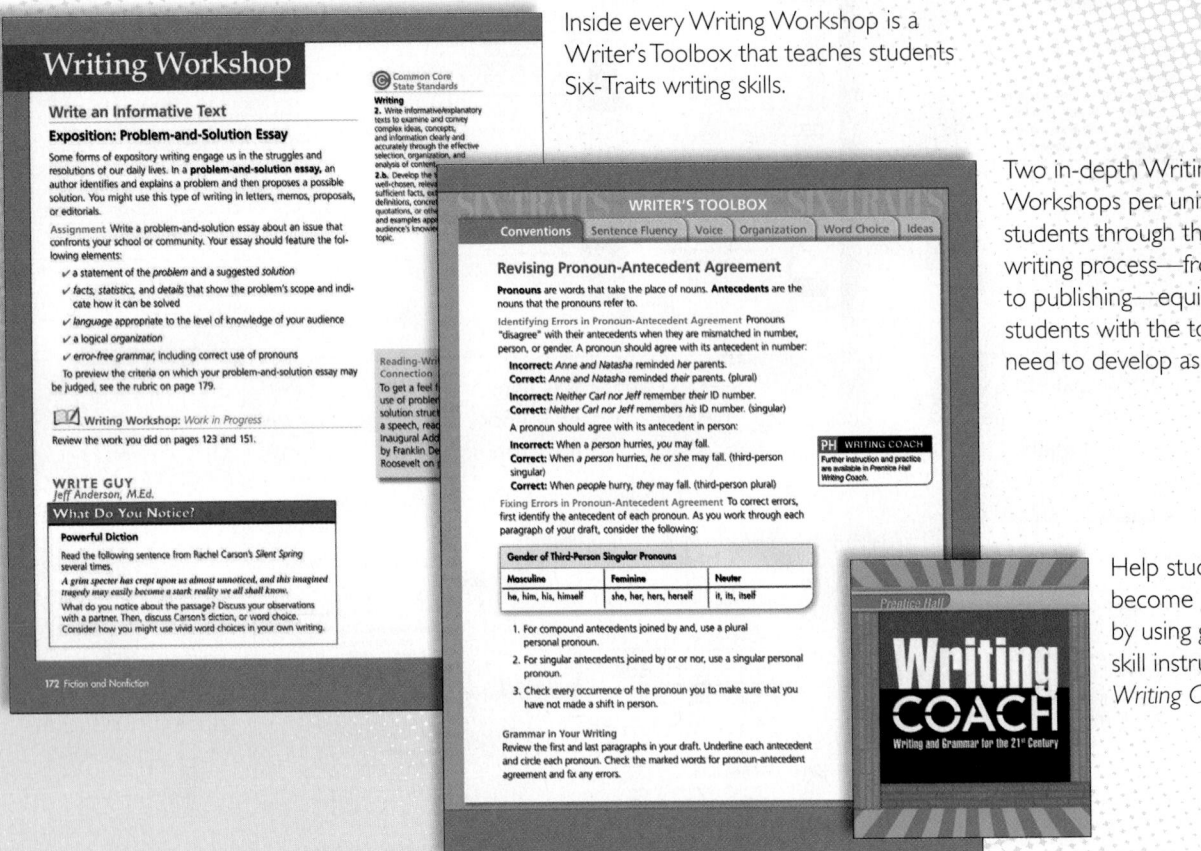

Inside every Writing Workshop is a Writer's Toolbox that teaches students Six-Traits writing skills.

Two in-depth Writing Workshops per unit take students through the complete writing process—from drafting to publishing—equipping students with the tools they need to develop as writers.

Help students become great writers by using guided writing skill instruction from *Writing Coach*.

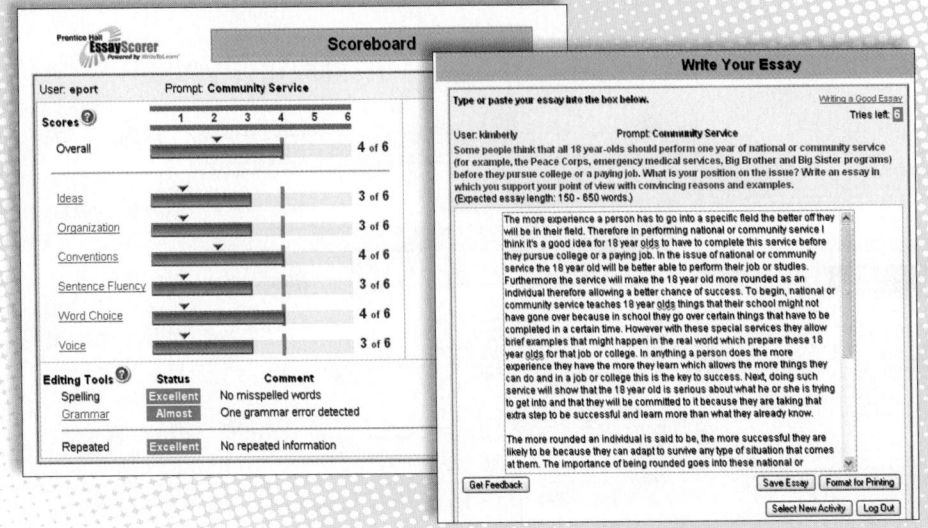

EssayScorer saves you hundreds of hours grading papers by providing students instant feedback on their writing.

Vocabulary and Communications Workshops build essential college and career-ready skills. Practical, valuable applications are used to help students become more fluent in these skills.

Speaking and Listening are emphasized to help students develop the career-ready skills they need for life and work.

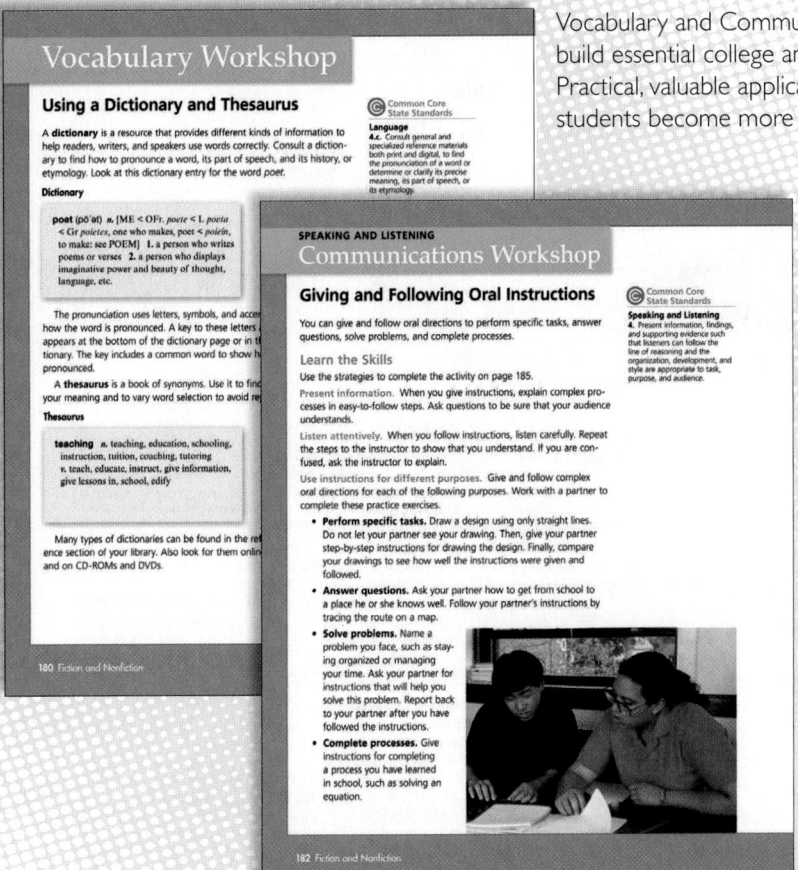

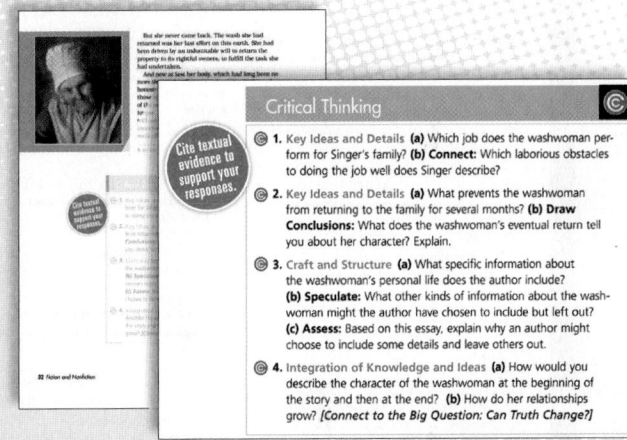

Critical Thinking questions build learning skills by helping students apply their reading.

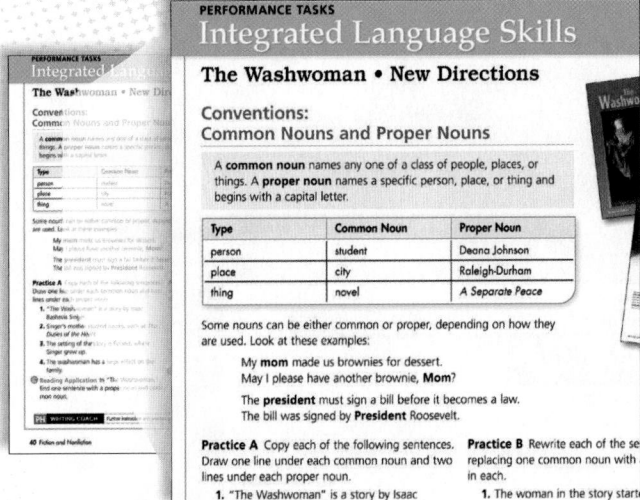

Integrated Language Skills offers full coverage of grammar, writing, speaking and listening, and research.

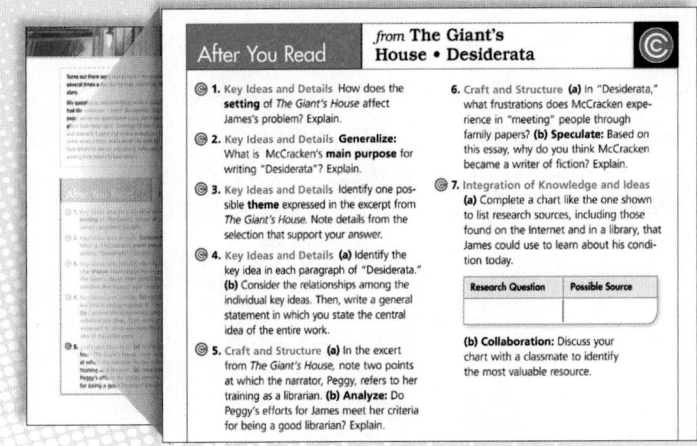

Every selection is followed by critical thinking questions aligned to the organizational structure of the Common Core Reading Domain.

Ensure Mastery

The new standards require new assessments. *Prentice Hall Literature* provides traditional assessments along with new performance-based assessments as called for by the Common Core. Students are given opportunities to apply critical thinking to demonstrate mastery of the standards.

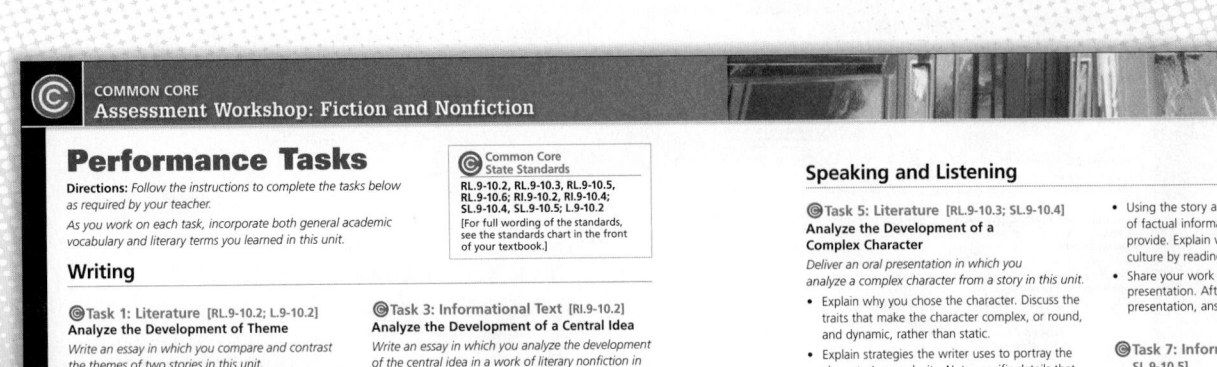

COMMON CORE
Assessment Workshop: Fiction and Nonfiction

Performance Tasks

Directions: *Follow the instructions to complete the tasks below as required by your teacher.*

As you work on each task, incorporate both general academic vocabulary and literary terms you learned in this unit.

Common Core State Standards
RL.9-10.2, RL.9-10.3, RL.9-10.5,
RL.9-10.6; RI.9-10.2, RI.9-10.4;
SL.9-10.4, SL.9-10.5; L.9-10.2
[For full wording of the standards, see the standards chart in the front of your textbook.]

Writing

Task 1: Literature [RL.9-10.2; L.9-10.2]
Analyze the Development of Theme

Write an essay in which you compare and contrast the themes of two stories in this unit.

- Analyze the development of the theme in each story and discuss similarities and differences in the message each expresses.
- Note specific strategies each author uses to introduce and develop the theme.
- Discuss specific details that contribute to the development of each theme. Explain what each detail adds.
- To ensure that readers understand your analysis, include an objective summary of each story.
- Capitalize proper nouns, including characters' and authors' names, correctly.

Task 2: Literature [RL.9-10.5]
Analyze the Effects of Structure in a Story

Write an essay in which you explain how the structure of a story in this unit leads to a specific emotional effect, such as tension or suspense.

- Identify the story's main conflict and summarize the narrative.
- Describe specific structural choices the writer makes. For example, discuss how much exposition the author provides and how he or she introduces the conflict. Also describe any use of plot devices, such as foreshadowing.
- Finally, explain how the story affects you as a reader and how the author's choices regarding structure contribute to that effect.
- Cite textual evidence to support your assertions.

Task 3: Informational Text [RI.9-10.2]
Analyze the Development of a Central Idea

Write an essay in which you analyze the development of the central idea in a work of literary nonfiction in this unit.

- Clearly explain the central idea of the work and discuss how it emerges or is introduced by the author.
- Identify specific details that shape and refine the central idea. Consider various types of evidence and explain what each adds to the development of the central idea.
- To ensure that readers understand your analysis, include an objective summary of the work.

Task 4: Informational Text [RI.9-10.6]
Analyze an Author's Purpose and Use of Rhetoric

Write an essay in which you determine an author's purpose and point of view and analyze his or her uses of rhetoric in a work of nonfiction in this unit.

- Explain the topic of the work and determine both the author's general and specific purposes for writing.
- Analyze the author's perspective or point of view on the topic. For example, explain whether the author has a positive or negative perspective or expresses a particular attitude toward the topic.
- Note specific examples of the author's uses of rhetoric. For example, identify examples of parallel structure or repetition. Then, explain how those uses of rhetoric work to advance the author's purpose and point of view.

Speaking and Listening

Task 5: Literature [RL.9-10.3; SL.9-10.4]
Analyze the Development of a Complex Character

Deliver an oral presentation in which you analyze a complex character from a story in this unit.

- Explain why you chose the character. Discuss the traits that make the character complex, or round, and dynamic, rather than static.
- Explain strategies the writer uses to portray the character's complexity. Note specific details that add to the character's portrayal as the story develops.
- Describe how the character's complexity, including his or her emotions, motivations, actions, and reactions, advances the plot and contributes to the story's theme.
- Present your analysis and evidence logically so that listeners can follow your line of reasoning. Make sure your overall approach, including both content and style, is appropriate for a classroom presentation on an academic topic.

Task 6: Literature [RL.9-10.6; SL.9-10.5]
Analyze a Cultural Perspective

Present a visual essay in which you analyze a cultural perspective reflected in a story in this unit.

- A visual essay combines images and text to explain an idea. The visual part of your essay may take the form of a slideshow, poster, or other format.
- Choose a story from this unit that reflects a cultural perspective from outside the United States. Explain how that cultural perspective is reflected in the setting and events as well as in characters' thoughts, emotions, actions, and reactions.

- Using the story as an example, discuss the kinds of factual information a work of fiction can provide. Explain what you learned about another culture by reading this story.
- Share your work with the class in an informal presentation. After you have delivered your presentation, answer questions from classmates.

Task 7: Informational Text [RI.9-10.4; SL.9-10.5]
Analyze the Effect of Word Choice on Tone

Write and present an essay in which you analyze the cumulative effect of word choice on tone in a work of literary nonfiction in this unit.

- Choose a work of literary nonfiction from this unit that offers a clear and distinct tone. Explain your choice.
- Identify specific word choices that contribute to the creation of that tone.
- Illustrate your analysis by creating a graphic organizer or chart that captures your ideas visually.
- Present your essay, including charts or graphic organizers, to the class. Use technology to display graphics, or distribute them as handouts.

 Can truth change?
At the beginning of Unit 1, you participated in a discussion about the Big Question. Now that you have completed the unit, write a response to the question. Discuss how your initial ideas have either changed or been reinforced. Cite specific examples from the literature in this unit, from other subject areas, and from your own life to support your ideas. Use Big Question vocabulary words (see page 3) in your response.

188 Fiction and Nonfiction

Assessment Workshop **189**

Performance Tasks in the unit Assessment Workshops call for the application of higher-level thinking skills.

Students are assessed across the key Common Core domains of reading, writing, speaking and listening, and language.

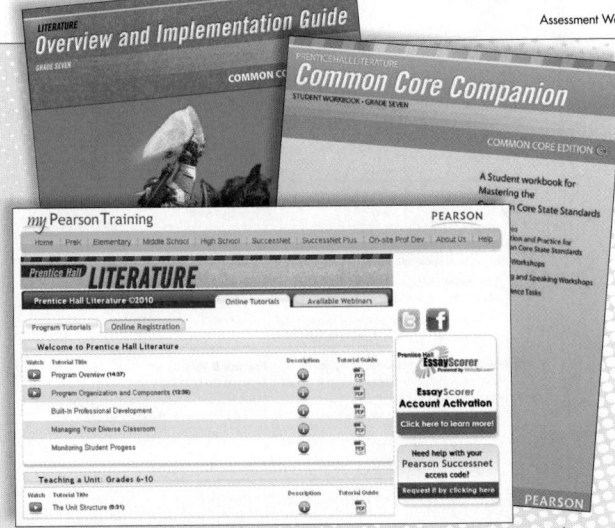

Prentice Hall Literature offers additional resources to ensure a successful implementation.

Cumulative Review

I. Reading Literature

Directions: *Read the passage. Then, answer each question that follows.*

Common Core
State Standards

RL.9-10.2, RL.9-10.3, RL.9-10.5; L.9-10.4.a
[For the full wording of the standards, see the standards chart in the front of your textbook.]

I was born in Brooklyn, New York and lived there until I was eleven. I had never really been outside the city. Sure, I had been to Long Island for beach days with my family, but I had never been to the country. My mother got a job Upstate, and suddenly my parents were planning the move. They said that living in the country would be a great experience for all of us, but I was miserable. In August, as we drove the long winding country roads to our new home, I barely said a word.

Many things were lacking in the country. There was no basketball game to pick up. There was no Thai food. There was no skateboarding. There was no sitting on the stoop. Most importantly, there were no old friends. I was so lonely—and bored. It was just my mom, my dad, and me. We were in the middle of nowhere with the closest neighbor over a mile away. Life as I had known it came to an end that August day.

Dad tried to get me to go fishing, but I thought the whole idea was disgusting. Mom tried to get me to walk in the woods, but I didn't like all the bugs, and the brambles scratched my legs. I wanted to go back to Brooklyn in the worst way. All of that would soon change.

I was petrified when I walked into my homeroom. Everyone there knew everyone else, and I did not know anyone. I was set apart from all the other boys by my pale skin and long hair. I sat in the back, and no one said anything to me. The teacher came in and introduced herself.

"Class, we have two new students with us this year." My ears perked up at the word *two*, and I scanned the room for another outsider.

"First, I want to introduce Dave from Brooklyn." The teacher pointed to me. My face flushed as I said "Hi."

"Next, meet Alexis from Washington, D.C."

"Call me Al," she said to the class, looking as lost as I felt.

I had been staring at the back of her head. Her hair was as short as mine was long. I knew immediately that this was not only the year of the Big Move, but it was also the year of the New Best Friend.

1. From which **point of view** is this story told?
   A. first person
   B. second person
   C. third-person limited
   D. third-person omniscient

2. Which element from the passage helped you determine the **point of view**?
   A. The narrator directly addresses his audience, the reader.
   B. The narrator refers to himself as *I* and *me*.
   C. The narrator knows only one person's thoughts.
   D. The narrator has insight into all the people's thoughts.

3. Which word best describes the **author's voice**?
   A. formal
   B. casual
   C. friendly
   D. sarcastic

4. Which of the following sentences is an example of **foreshadowing**?
   A. All of that would soon change.
   B. I had never really been outside of the city.
   C. I wanted to go back to Brooklyn in the worst way.
   D. The teacher pointed to me.

5. Which event occurs during the **rising action** of the narrative?
   A. Dave is born in Brooklyn.
   B. Dave makes a new friend.
   C. Dave's mom gets a job Upstate.
   D. Dave meets Alexis.

6. Which event is the turning point, or **climax,** of the narrative?
   A. Dave moves in August.
   B. Dave wants to move back to Brooklyn.
   C. Dave refuses to go fishing.
   D. Dave hears the teacher say "two."

7. **Vocabulary** Which word is closest in meaning to the underlined word *petrified*?
   A. angry
   B. terrified
   C. annoyed
   D. disturbed

8. How is the conflict in the story resolved?
   A. Dave makes a new friend in the city.
   B. Dave wants to return to Brooklyn.
   C. Dave's mom does not like her job.
   D. Dave goes fishing with his dad.

9. In what way does the choice of narrator affect the description of the country in paragraph 2?
   A. Life in the country seems frightening.
   B. The country appears to offer lots of fun activities.
   C. Moving to the country sounds like a good idea.
   D. The country seems to lack a lot of things that life in the city has to offer.

⏱ **Timed Writing**

10. In a well-developed essay, **identify** the conflict in this story. **Explain** how the author of the text establishes the conflict. Cite evidence from the text to support your analysis. [20 minutes]

GO ON ➡

Traditional Cumulative Review prepares students for high-stakes testing.

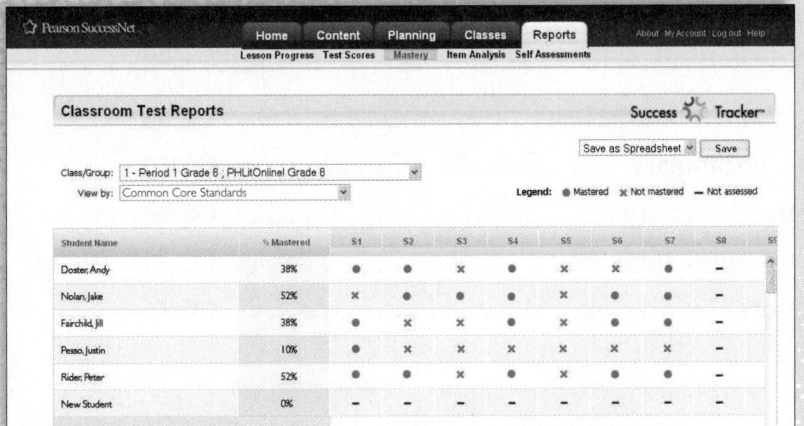

SuccessTracker® includes reporting tools to make progress monitoring easier.

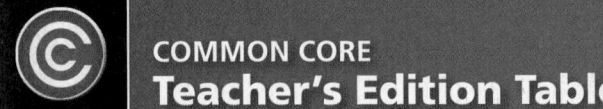

Research Bibliography

▶ Reading and Concept-Driven Instruction

Alexander, Patricia A., and Tamara Jetton. "Learning from Text: A Multidimensional and Developmental Perspective." *Handbook of Reading Research*, vol. 3. Ed. M. L. Kamil, P. B. Mosenthal, P. D. Pearson, and R. Barr, 285–310. Mahwah, NJ: Lawrence Erlbaum Associates, 2000.

Blau, Sheridan. *The Literature Workshop: Teaching Texts and Their Readers*. Portsmouth: Heinemann Press, 2003.

Buehl, Doug, Judith L. Irvin, and Ronald M. Klemp. *Reading and the High School Student: Strategies to Enhance Literacy*. Boston: Allyn and Bacon, 2007.

Buehl, Doug, Judith L. Irvin, and Barbara J. Radcliffe. *Strategies to Enhance Literacy and Learning in Middle School Content Area Classrooms*. Boston: Allyn and Bacon, 2007.

Daniels, Harvey. *Literature Circles: Voice and Choice in Book Clubs and Reading Groups*. Portland: Stenhouse Publishers, 2002.

———*Mini-Lessons for Literature Circles*. Portsmouth: Heinemann Press, 2005.

Gallagher, Kelly. *Reading Reasons: Motivational Mini-Lessons for the Middle and High School*. Portland: Stenhouse Publishers, 2003.

Guthrie, John T. and Allan Wigfield. "Engagement and Motivation in Reading." *Handbook of Reading Research*, vol. 3, eds. M. L. Kamil, P. B. Mosenthal, P. D. Pearson, and R. Barr, 403–422. Mahwah: Lawrence Erlbaum Associates, 2000.

Harvey, Stephanie, and Anne Goudvis. "Determining Importance in Text: The Nonfiction Connection." *Strategies That Work: Teaching Comprehension to Enhance Understanding*. Portland: Stenhouse Publishers, 2000.

Langer, Judith. "Beating the Odds: Teaching Middle and High School Students to Read and Write Well," 1999. Center on English Learning and Achievement. May 2003.<http://cela.albany.edu/eie2/main.html>

National Reading Panel. *Teaching Children to Read: An Evidence-Based Assessment of the Scientific Research on Reading and Its Implications for Reading Instruction*. NIH Publication 00–4769. Bethesda: U.S. Department of Health and Human Services, 2000.

Pressley, Michael. "What Should Comprehension Instruction Be the Instruction Of?" *Handbook of Reading Research*, vol. 3, eds. M. L. Kamil, P. B. Mosenthal, P. D. Pearson, and R. Barr, 545–562. Mahwah: Lawrence Erlbaum Associates, 2000.

Scieszka, Jon. *Guys Write for Guys Read*. New York: Penguin Group, 2005.

Wiggins, Grant P., and Jay McTighe. *Understanding by Design*. Alexandria: Association for Supervision and Curriculum Development, 2006.

▶ Vocabulary, Writing, and Grammar

Anderson, Jeff. *Mechanically Inclined: Building Grammar, Usage, and Style into Writer's Workshop*. Portland: Stenhouse Publishers, 2005.

Baumann, J. F., and E. J. Kame'enui. *Vocabulary Instruction: From Research to Practice*. New York: Guilford Press, 2004.

Blachowicz, Camille, and Peter Fisher. *Teaching Vocabulary in All Classrooms*, Second Edition. Upper Saddle River: Merrill, 2002.

Feber, Jane. *Creative Book Reports: Fun Projects With Rubrics for Fiction and Nonfiction*. Gainesville: Maupin House Publishing, Inc., 2004.

———*Active Word Play*. Gainesville: Maupin House Publishing, Inc., 2008.

Kinsella, Kate. "Strategies to Teach Academic Vocabulary." *Strategies to Promote Academic Literacy for Second Language Learners Within the English Language Arts Classroom*. 2005.

Kinsella, Kate and Kevin Feldman. *Narrowing the Language Gap: The Case for Explicit Vocabulary Instruction*. New York: Scholastic, 2005.

Marzano, Robert J. "The Developing Vision of Vocabulary Instruction." In Baumann and Kame'enui, *Vocabulary Instruction: From Research to Practice*. New York: Guilford Press, 2004.

▶ Differentiated Instruction for Universal Access

Allington, Richard L. *What Really Matters for Struggling Readers: Designing Research Based Programs*. New York: Longman, 2001.

Armbruster, Bonnie, and Thomas H. Anderson. "On Selecting 'Considerate' Content Area Textbooks." *Remedial and Special Education*, 9.1 (1988): 47–52.

Balderrama, María V., and Lynne T. Díaz-Rico. *Teacher Performance Expectations for Educating English Learners*. Boston: Allyn and Bacon, 2006.

Ball, Arnetha F. and Ted Lardner. *African American Literacies Unleashed: Vernacular English and the Composition Classroom*. Carbondale: Southern Illinois University Press, 2005.

Carnie, Douglas, Jerry Silbert, and Edward J. Kame'enui. *Direct Instruction Reading*. 3rd ed. Upper Saddle River: Prentice Hall, 1997.

Deshler, Donald D., Keith B. Lenz, and Brenda R. Kissam. *Teaching Content to All: Evidence-Based Inclusive Practices in Middle and Secondary Schools*. Boston: Allyn and Bacon, 2004.

Francis, David, Mabel Rivera, Nonie Lesaux, Michael Kieffer, and Hector Rivera. *Practical Guidelines for the Education of English Language Learners*. Portsmouth: RMC Research Corporation, Center on Instruction, 2006.

Vaughn, Sharon, Candace S. Bos, and Jeanne Shay Schumm. *Teaching Exceptional, Diverse, and At-Risk Students in the General Education Classroom*. Boston: Allyn and Bacon, 2002.

Pearson Prentice Hall Literature:
A Rich Tradition of Learning Success

▶ The Research Process

Since 1988, *Pearson Prentice Hall Literature* has been at the forefront of language arts instruction, providing teachers and their students with quality instruction and assessment tools to ensure success. Each successive edition builds on the strong heritage of the program. Our research comprised these three design stages:

1. EXPLORATORY NEEDS ASSESSMENT

In conjunction with Pearson Prentice Hall authors, we conducted research proven to explore educational reading methodologies. This research was incorporated into our instructional strategy and pedagogy to create a more effective literature program. This stage included:

- reading research
- review of state standards
- teacher interviews

2. FORMATIVE RESEARCH, DEVELOPMENT, AND FIELD-TESTING

During this phase of the research, we developed and field-tested prototype material with students and teachers. Results informed revisions to the final design and pedagogy. Formative research included:

- field-testing of prototypes in classroom pilots
- classroom observations
- teacher reviews
- supervisor reviews
- educator advisory panels

3. SUMMATIVE RESEARCH AND VALIDATION RESEARCH

Finally, we have conducted and will continue to conduct longer-term research under actual classroom conditions. Research at this phase includes:

- pilot-testing
- prepublication learner verification research
- postpublication validation studies, including validation of test questions
- evaluation of results on standardized tests

Harvey Daniels
Voice and Choice

Excerpts from "Using Leveled Selections" and "Leveled Reading Selections, A Key to Differentiation" by Harvey Daniels

> "With leveled texts, all students can understand their selection—and no one is left behind."

Harvey Daniels is known for his passionate work on literacy and student-led book clubs. He is the author of *Literature Circles: Voice and Choice in Book Clubs and Reading Groups* and *Mini-lessons for Literature Circles.* He has been a classroom teacher, writing project director, author, and university professor.

Read the full text of Harvey Daniels's articles at PHLitOnline.

We have all watched it unfold. You select a wonderful book or article for your class to read. You hand it out to the students and what happens? The text is way too hard for some kids, far too easy for others, and "bor-ing" to still others. Not a good feeling.

Using Leveled Readings. Happily, research on differentiated instruction shows us a better way: leveled selections. **Prentice Hall Literature** offers two levels of text. All students can understand and enjoy their selection and still learn same required skills—and no one is left behind.

Why are leveled selections so important?

- If we expect kids to grow as readers, they must spend part of each day reading *text they can read.* As the Common Core State Standards put it: "Students need opportunities to stretch their reading abilities but also to experience the satisfaction and pleasure of easy, fluent reading, both of which the Standards allow for."
- A *choice* of texts means that more students will have the background knowledge to understand and enjoy the chosen selection.
- All students need to read increasingly challenging text as the school year unfolds, but every student does not need to read the same texts. As the Common Core standards explain: "Teachers who have had success using particular texts that are easier than those required for a given grade band should feel free to continue to use them, so long as the general movement during a given school year is toward texts of higher levels of complexity."

These are the reasons *Prentice Hall Literature* offers two leveled selections for almost every lesson—one more accessible and one more challenging. Every student can be challenged at his or her own level, from lesson to lesson, throughout the school year.

> "When we make accommodations like leveled selections, we often find that such accommodations make learning work better for everyone."

Grant Wiggins
Better Big Questions

Excerpts from "Teaching Literature by Design: Introducing the Big Questions" by Grant Wiggins

A Big Question is different from many of the questions teachers typically ask students in class.

A Big Question is more of a *why?* or a *so what?* question rather than a *what?* or a *where?* question. We are not looking for an answer, really; we are inviting inquiry and reflection. The Big Questions awaken curiosity and thus provide a purpose for reading.

What Makes a Question "Big"?

"Big" connotes "substantial"—occupying a considerable amount of space and time. A question is "big" or "weighty" if it has significant depth and breadth—occupying a good deal of our psychic space, such as our thoughts and feelings. Another aspect of "bigness" is the time it consumes. Vital issues and inquiries remain alive over days, months, and years, unlike simple or superficial queries. Important questions recur over and through time, as we rethink and reflect on our present and past experiences. **Prentice Hall Literature** provides Big Questions that meet the criteria in ways that others do not.

- The questions cannot be answered with a list or a single answer.
- The questions are designed to allow answers to change to accommodate new information or experience.
- The questions are designed to encourage answers that change over time.

Why Ask Big Questions?
The teacher has a different intent when asking a "big" as opposed to an "academic" question. If we want students to end up asking Big Questions on their own, then our courses have to be designed "backward" from that goal. If we want students to learn from their reading, our methods have to foster that questioning and meaning-making.

" . . . our methods have to foster that questioning and meaning-making."

Grant Wiggins is the co-author of *Understanding By Design*, published by ASCD. He is also the president of Authentic Education in Hopewell, New Jersey. He consults with schools, districts, and state education departments on a variety of reform issues. His work has been supported by the Pew Charitable Trusts, the Geraldine R. Dodge Foundation, and the National Science Foundation.

Read the full text of Grant Wiggins's article at PHLitOnline.

" Important questions occur over and through time."

Kelly Gallagher
Multidraft Reading

Excerpts from "The Value of Second Draft Reading" and "Powerful, Purposeful Reading" by Kelly Gallagher

> " In our classrooms, we are the 'tour guides.' "

Kelly Gallagher is a full-time English teacher at Magnolia High School in Anaheim, California, where he has taught for twenty-two years. He is the author of several books:

- *Reading Reasons: Motivational Mini-Lessons for the Middle and High School*
- *Deeper Reading: Comprehending Challenging Texts*
- *Teaching Adolescent Writers*
- *Readicide*

Read the full text of Kelly Gallagher's article at PHLitOnline.

Where do adolescents get the idea that they can read complex text one time and get it?

More importantly, how can we help our students to understand that much of our deepest thinking comes when we reread? How can we teach our students to recognize the value of second-draft reading?

The Importance of Rereading

The principal strategy that good readers employ when confronted by difficult text is to reread it. If the text is particularly difficult, you might have students read the text first with the sole purpose of monitoring where they were confused. Use the blue dots in the student edition of **Prentice Hall Literature** to help students "chunk" the text into passages with logical pause points to stop, reread, and clarify.

Multi-Lens Reading

Students often read difficult text better when they have been provided a purpose for their reading. In our classrooms, we are the "tour guides." We create student tours by first determining the purpose for each reading. Providing students with a specific purpose gives them a more focused, meaningful reading experience.

Prentice Hall Literature provides the tools for multiple reading purposes.

When students read with a purpose in mind, their anxiety is lowered, their comprehension deepens, and they are given the confidence to approach works they might have otherwise shunned.

> " Providing students with a specific purpose gives them a more focused, meaningful reading experience."

Elfrieda H. Hiebert
What Is Text Complexity?

The Common Core State Standards cite research that shows that the difficulty of texts used in elementary and secondary classrooms in the United States has decreased over the past 50 years, while the difficulty of college texts has not. As a result, students entering post-secondary education are not prepared for the level of text complexity required to be successful.

To address this issue, the Standards have identified text complexity grade bands (K–1, 2–3, 4–5, 6–8, 9–10, 11–12), in which students read increasingly complex texts within a defined spectrum. Ultimately, greater focus on text complexity will help close the gap that exists between secondary and post-secondary education and prepare students for the increasing demands of required reading in college and the workplace.

The Common Core State Standards identify a three-part model for measuring a text's complexity. This model, as detailed below, includes quantitative and qualitative measures as well as variables of individual readers.

Quantitative Dimensions
Quantitative dimensions are aspects of text complexity that can be measured with traditional readability formulas, such as the Lexile measure. These formulas measure such aspects of a text as word length and frequency, total number of words, average sentence length, and text cohesion.

Qualitative Dimensions
Qualitative dimensions consist of "those aspects of text complexity best measured or only measurable by an attentive human reader." Qualitative measures include categories such as a student's familiarity with a text's structure, levels of meaning, language clarity and conventionality, and knowledge demands, or what the reader needs to know to access the text.

Reader and Task Considerations
Reader and task considerations include an evaluation of student variables, such as the reader's motivation, background knowledge, experience, and cognitive abilities. Evaluating text complexity is best done by the classroom teacher who brings to bear professional judgments concerning subject matter and individual students.

> " . . . greater focus on text complexity will help . . . prepare students for the increasing demands of required reading in college and the workplace."

Dr. Elfrieda "Freddy" H. Hiebert is the President and CEO of TextProject, Inc. Her model of accessible texts for beginning and struggling readers—TExT—has been used to develop several reading programs. Most recently, Dr. Hiebert served on the Common Core State Standards development team focused on text complexity. Dr. Hiebert has published more than 130 research articles, chapters in edited volumes, and books. In particular, Hiebert's interests lie in how fluency, vocabulary, and knowledge can be fostered through appropriate texts.

> " . . . students read increasingly complex texts . . ."

Text Complexity: Building Capacity for All Students

To better gauge a text's difficulty, Dr. Elfrieda Hiebert has created a Text Complexity Multi-Index. In this model, four comprehensive measures and considerations are taken into account to determine a text's appropriateness for a student or group of students.

The four parts of Dr. Hiebert's model expand upon the Common Core State Standards' three-part model for measuring text complexity. A critical component of both models is that qualitative measures and reader-task considerations are balanced with quantitative measures to achieve an overall text complexity recommendation. By measuring text complexity, both quantitative and qualitative, teachers can challenge students to read more complex texts as they move toward college and career readiness.

In Dr. Hiebert's Multi-Index, quantitative measures consist of Overall Text Difficulty and Specifics of Text Difficulty. Qualitative Measures include Themes and Knowledge Demands. Reader and Task in the Common Core aligns with Purpose and Task in Dr. Hiebert's index. These four parts of Dr. Hiebert's Text Complexity Multi-Index are explained below.

Text Complexity Multi-Index

❶ Themes and Knowledge Demands

- The reader's familiarity with the theme of a text and the concept presented must be considered as part of the assessment of text complexity.

- Knowledge demands are based on the background knowledge students need to bring to a given text. Teachers can assess background knowledge through informal classroom discussions.

❷ Specifics of Text Difficulty

- Readability scores are based on quantitative variables, such as average sentence length and overall word frequency.

- Sentence length is determined by averaging the number of words in each sentence in a selection. Formulaically speaking, shorter sentences should mean easier reading. However, teachers must consider conceptual and thematic complexity of a selection to accurately assess a text's difficulty.

- Word frequency refers to how often the same words appear in a text. A low score indicates that the text most likely has words that students may not have encountered. This is especially true when dealing with informational texts that may address unfamiliar content and concepts.

❸ Overall Quantitative Text Difficulty

- Overall quantitative text difficulty can be determined by a readability formula. Frequently used readability formulas include Lexile, Dale-Chall, and Spache.

❹ Purpose and Task

- Purpose and task refer to the why and what of reading—questions such as "Why am I reading this text?" and "What tasks are involved before, during, and after reading to build knowledge?"

- To address purpose and task, teachers use professional judgment to assess reader and task compatibility.

The Text Complexity Rubric in *Prentice Hall Literature*

The following rubric is a sample from the Grade 9, Unit 1 Teacher's Edition. The leveled texts "The Washwoman" and "New Directions" are featured in Unit 1 of this grade level. The leveling of these selections relies on many factors as depicted in the measures outlined here.

Analyze the Qualitative and Quantitative measures to determine the complexity of these texts.

© Text Complexity Rubric: Leveled Texts

Text complexity is determined by both qualitative and quantitative measures. For this reason, the quantitative measure of a more complex selection may be lower than that of a more accessible selection.

		✓ The Washwoman	✓✓ New Directions
1 Qualitative Measures	Context/ Knowledge Demands	Jewish neighborhood in Poland, early 1900s 1 2 ③ 4 5	African American mother living in the South 1 2 ③ 4 5
	Structure/Language Conventionality and Clarity	Numerous long sentences; on-level vocabulary 1 2 ③ 4 5	Little dialogue; challenging vocabulary 1 2 3 ④ 5
	Levels of Meaning/ Purpose/Concept Level	Accessible concept (determination to complete a task) 1 2 ③ 4 5	Irony; accessible concept (journey from adversity to success) 1 2 3 ④ 5
2 Quantitative Measures	Text Length	Word Count: 1,976	Word Count: 763
	Lexile	870L	1360L
3 Overall Complexity		✓ More accessible	✓✓ More complex

❶ Themes and Knowledge Demands

Context/Knowledge Demands: The accessibility of texts is dependent in part on the range of students' experiences and their background knowledge.

Structure/Language Conventionality and Clarity: Conventional and unconventional structures as well as domain-specific language and vocabulary all affect the ability of students to access text.

Levels of Meaning/Purpose/Concept Level: An author's use of either single or multiple levels of meaning impacts the accessibility of a text's concepts.

❷ Specifics of Text Difficulty

Pearson has provided two quantitative measures of text complexity—text length and Lexile score. Use these measures in tandem with qualitative measures to make informed choices.

❸ Overall Quantitative Text Difficulty

Based on the criteria cited above for Themes and Knowledge Demands and Specifics of Text Difficulty, texts can be deemed either more accessible or more complex.

© Text Complexity: Reader and Task Suggestions

✓ The Washwoman		✓✓ New Directions	
Preparing to Read the Text	**Leveled Tasks**	**Preparing to Read the Text**	**Leveled Tasks**
• Using the Background information on TE p. 25, discuss the lives of Jews and gentiles in Poland in the 1900s. • Discuss with students ways in which cultural differences can lead to hardships. • Guide students to use Multidraft Reading strategies (TE p. 25).	*Knowledge Demands* If students will have difficulty with knowledge demands, have them first read to identify details about the washwoman's determination. Then, have them reread, taking notes on interesting details of daily life in the setting. *Synthesizing* If students will not have difficulty with selection knowledge demands, have them note as they read ways in which Singer uses setting to help convey his theme.	• Refer to the Background section on TE p. 35, and discuss difficulties uneducated African American women in the South in the early 1900s faced. • Discuss the saying "Necessity is the mother of invention." • Guide students to use Multidraft Reading strategies (TE p. 35).	*Knowledge Demands* If students will have difficulty with cultural or historical knowledge, have them first read to identify details that show Annie's determination. Then, have them reread, identifying words or sentences that are unclear. *Synthesizing* If students will not have difficulty with selection knowledge demands, have them note as they read ways in which Angelou creates narrative style.

❹ Purpose and Task

Specific pre-reading suggestions are given in "Preparing to Read the Text." These are followed by "Leveled Tasks" that will help you guide students' comprehension as they analyze, synthesize, or evaluate the concept development of selections. Teachers may adapt the leveled tasks, as needed, to suit the needs of their students.

Jim Cummins
Second Language Learning

Excerpts from "The Challenge of Learning Academic English" by Jim Cummins

> " Students who gain a sense of control over language will want to use it for powerful purposes."

Jim Cummins's research focuses on literacy development in multilingual school contexts as well as English Language Learners' academic trajectories. He has been a recipient of the International Reading Association's Albert J. Harris award, and has published in *Educational Researcher, International Education Journal, NABE Journal*, and *TESOL Quarterly.*

Read the full text of Jim Cummins's article at PHLitOnline.

Learning difficulties faced by struggling readers can derive from a variety of sources. This is true regardless of whether their home language is English or a language other than English. Intervention should address the specific difficulties they are experiencing.

Scaffold Instruction We can promote literacy engagement among ELL students and struggling readers by using "scaffolds" or supports to make the input more comprehensible (e.g., through graphic organizers, demonstrations, etc.). It is also important to scaffold students' use of language.

Build Background Effective instruction for ELL students and struggling readers will also activate students' prior knowledge and build background knowledge as needed. Learning can be defined as the integration of new knowledge or skills with the knowledge or skills we already possess. Therefore, it is crucial to activate ELL students' preexisting knowledge so that they can relate new information to what they already know.

Validate Culture Identity affirmation is also crucial for literacy engagement. Students who feel their culture and identity validated in the classroom are much more likely to engage with literacy than those who perceive their culture and identity ignored or devalued.

Literacy engagement among ELL students and struggling readers also requires that teachers across the curriculum explain how language works and stimulate students' curiosity about language. Students who gain a sense of control over language will want to use it for powerful purposes.

> " Students who feel their culture and identity validated in the classroom are much more likely to engage with literacy. . . ."

Sharroky Hollie
Culturally Responsive Instruction

Excerpts from "Expanding Academic Home Language" and "Navigating Cultural Discourse Styles" by Sharroky Hollie

Students entering the classroom bring with them a variety of experiences, traditions, interpretive frameworks, and learning styles. Culturally responsive instruction begins when a teacher acknowledges this variety as a positive resource for education. By capitalizing on the student's own resources, a teacher ensures success.

What is Culturally Responsive Instruction?

To make academic progress, a student must build on one success to another. How do we ensure that we are teaching to and through students' personal and cultural strengths and prior accomplishments?

- Build bridges from what students already know or have experienced to new knowledge and skills.
- Create a cooperative learning environment rich in affirmations of students' heritages.
- Build not just on individual strengths, but on the new strength that emerges when individuals join together in a community that respects their diversity.

> " By capitalizing on the student's own resources, a teacher ensures success."

Sharroky Hollie is the Executive Director of the Center for Culturally Responsive Teaching and Learning. He is an assistant professor at California State University and a visiting professor at Webster University in St. Louis. His work focuses on African American education and on second language methodology. In addition to his university teaching, Dr. Hollie also teaches professional development courses, and he is the co-founding director of the Culture and Language Academy of Success, an independent charter school in Los Angeles.

Read the complete texts of Sharroky Hollie's articles on PHLitOnline.

Building on Strength

A key premise for culturally responsive pedagogy is that education proceeds from students' strengths and not students' weaknesses. **Prentice Hall Literature** consistently supports culturally responsive instruction with each selection in the anthology. Integrated throughout each lesson plan are the strategies for using what students bring with them into the classroom to enrich learning and foster success.

> " . . . education proceeds from students' strengths and not students' weaknesses."

William G. Brozo
Response to Intervention

" Within RTI, the frontline of prevention is Tier 1, or the general education classroom, where every student regardless of ability is to receive high-quality instruction. What's revolutionary about these new standards is that they situate literacy and language development squarely within the content areas...Common core proponents assert that prevailing literacy curriculum needs to shift from a focus on developing reading skills and building fluency with simple narratives toward reading and writing to gain knowledge and express new understandings with informational text."

William G. Brozo, "The Role of Content Literacy in an Effective RTI Program,"
The Reading Teacher, (64)2, pp. 147–150

Donald J. Leu
21st-Century Solutions

" The good news about the Common Core State Standards is that we are going to increasingly support higher-level thinking, reasoning, and comprehension. Locating, evaluating, integrating, and communicating information – all these skills are essential to students' success in the future. We need to help students think in deeper, more complex ways as they read a wider variety of texts, both print and digital."

Karen K. Wixson
The Goal: College and Career Readiness

" The ELA Common Core State Standards are meant to be read as an integrated English Language Arts program beginning with College and Career Readiness Anchor Standards. It is absolutely essential that teachers and administrators look first at the anchor standards, next the appendices, and lastly at the grade-level standards."

Expanded essays by these authors are available at PHLitOnline.com.

Master Teacher Board

Heather Barnes
Language Arts Instructor
Central Crossing High School
Grove City, Ohio

Lee Bromberger
English Department Chairperson
Mukwonago High School
Mukwonago, Wisconsin

Cathy Cassy
Communication Arts Curriculum Supervisor 6-12
St. Louis Public Schools
St. Louis, Missouri

Judy Castrogiavanni
English Teacher
Abington Heights School
Clarks Summit, Pennsylvania

Ann Catrillo
Sr. English & AP Teacher; Department Chairperson
East Stroudsburg High School South
East Stroudsburg, Pennsylvania

Susan Cisna
Instructor Middle School Education
Eastern Illinois University
Charleston, Illinois

Linda Fund
Reading Specialist
Ezra L. Nolan Middle School #40
Jersey City, New Jersey

Gail Hacker
Adjunct Professor
Springfield College School of Human Services
North Charleston, South Carolina

Patricia Matysik
English Department Chairperson
Belleville West Middle School
Belleville, Illinois

Gail Phelps
Literacy Intervention Coach
Oak Grove High School
Little Rock, Arkansas

Julie Rucker
Literacy Coach/English Teacher
Tift County High School
Tifton, Georgia

Kathy Ryan
Curriculum Coordinator
Rockwood Schools
St. Louis, Missouri

Matthew Scanlon
Vice Principal
Kinnelon High School
Kinnelon, New Jersey

Renee Trotier
Freshman Principal
Lafayette High School
Wildwood, Missouri

Carolyn Waters
Language Arts Supervisor
Cobb County Schools
Marietta, Georgia

Martha Wildman
Social Studies Teacher
Las Cruces Public Schools
Las Cruces, New Mexico

Melissa Williams
District Supervisor
Delsea Regional Schools
Franklinville, New Jersey

Charles Youngs
English Language Arts Facilitator
Bethel Park High School
Bethel Park, Pennsylvania

Student Edition Pages

Contributing Authors

The contributing authors guided the direction and philosophy of Pearson Prentice Hall Literature. *Working with the development team, they helped to build the pedagogical integrity of the program and to ensure its relevance for today's teachers and students.*

Grant Wiggins, Ed.D., is the President of Authentic Education in Hopewell, New Jersey. He earned his Ed.D. from Harvard University and his B.A. from St. John's College in Annapolis. Grant consults with schools, districts, and state education departments on a variety of reform matters; organizes conferences and workshops; and develops print materials and Web resources on curricular change. He is the coauthor, with Jay McTighe, of *Understanding by Design* and *The Understanding by Design Handbook,* the award-winning and highly successful materials on curriculum published by ASCD. His work has been supported by the Pew Charitable Trusts, the Geraldine R. Dodge Foundation, and the National Science Foundation. *The Association for Supervision of Curriculum Development (ASCD), publisher of the "Understanding by Design Handbook" co-authored by Grant Wiggins and registered owner of the trademark "Understanding by Design," has not authorized, approved, or sponsored this work and is in no way affiliated with Pearson or its products.*

Jeff Anderson has worked with  struggling writers and readers for almost 20 years. Anderson's specialty is the integration of grammar and editing instruction into the processes of reading and writing. He has published two books, *Mechanically Inclined: Building Grammar, Usage, and Style into Writer's Workshop* and *Everyday Editing: Inviting Students to Develop Skill and Craft in Writer's Workshop,* as well as a DVD, *The Craft of Grammar.* Anderson's work has appeared in *English Journal.* Anderson won the NCTE Paul and Kate Farmer Award for his *English Journal* article on teaching grammar in context.

Arnetha F. Ball, Ph.D., is a  Professor at Stanford University. Her areas of expertise include language and literacy studies of diverse student populations, research on writing instruction, and teacher preparation for working with diverse populations. Dr. Ball has also served as an academic specialist for the United States Information Services Program in South Africa. She is the author of *African American Literacies Unleashed* with Dr. Ted Lardner, and *Multicultural Strategies for Education and Social Change.*

Sheridan Blau is Professor of  Education and English at the University of California, Santa Barbara, where he directs the South Coast Writing Project and the Literature Institute for Teachers. He has served in senior advisory roles for such groups as the National Board for Professional Teaching Standards, the College Board, and the American Board for Teacher Education. Blau served for twenty years on the National Writing Project Advisory Board and Task Force, and is a former president of NCTE. Blau is the author of *The Literature Workshop: Teaching Texts and Their Readers,* which was named by the Conference on English Education as the 2004 Richard Meade Award winner for outstanding research in English education.

William G. Brozo, Ph.D., is  a Professor of Literacy at George Mason University in Fairfax, Virginia. He has taught reading and language arts in junior and senior high school and is the author of numerous texts on literacy development. Dr. Brozo's work focuses on building capacity among teacher leaders, enriching the literate culture of schools, enhancing the literate lives of boys, and making teaching more responsive to the needs of all students. His recent publications include *Bright Beginnings for Boys: Engaging Young Boys in Active Literacy* and the *Adolescent Literacy Inventory.*

Doug Buehl is a teacher, author, and  national literacy consultant. He is the author of *Classroom Strategies for Interactive Learning* and coauthor of *Reading and the High School Student: Strategies to Enhance Literacy;* and *Strategies to Enhance Literacy and Learning in Middle School Content Area Classrooms.*

Jim Cummins, Ph.D, is a profes-  sor in the Modern Language Centre at the University of Toronto. He is the author of numerous publications, including *Negotiating Identities: Education for Empowerment in a Diverse Society.* Cummins coined the acronyms BICS and CAPT to help differentiate the type of language ability students need for success.

Harvey Daniels, Ph.D., has been  a classroom teacher, writing project director, author, and university professor. "Smokey" serves as an international consultant to schools, districts, and educational agencies. He is known for his work on student-led book clubs, as recounted in *Literature Circles: Voice and Choice in Book Clubs & Reading Groups* and *Mini Lessons for Literature Circles.* Recent works include *Subjects Matter: Every Teacher's Guide to Content-Area Reading* and *Content Area Writing: Every Teacher's Guide.*

Jane Feber taught language arts in  Jacksonville, Florida, for 36 years. Her innovative approach to instruction has earned her several awards, including the NMSA Distinguished Educator Award, the NCTE Edwin A. Hoey Award, the Gladys Prior Award for Teaching Excellence, and the Florida Council of Teachers of English Teacher of the Year Award. She is a National Board Certified Teacher, past president of the Florida Council of Teachers of English and is the author of *Creative Book Reports* and *Active Word Play*.

Danling Fu, Ph.D., is Professor  of Language and Culture in the College of Education at the University of Florida. She researches and provides inservice to public schools nationally, focusing on literacy instruction for new immigrant students. Fu's books include *My Trouble is My English* and *An Island of English* addressing English language learners in the secondary schools. She has authored chapters in the *Handbook of Adolescent Literacy Research* and in *Adolescent Literacy: Turning Promise to Practice*.

Kelly Gallagher is a full-time English  teacher at Magnolia High School in Anaheim, California. He is the former co-director of the South Basin Writing Project at California State University, Long Beach. Gallagher wrote *Reading Reasons: Motivational Mini-Lessons for the Middle and High School, Deeper Reading: Comprehending Challenging Texts 4-12,* and *Teaching Adolescent Writers.* Gallagher won the Secondary Award of Classroom Excellence from the California Association of Teachers of English—the state's top English teacher honor.

Sharroky Hollie, Ph.D., is an  assistant professor at California State University, Dominguez Hills, and an urban literacy visiting professor at Webster University, St. Louis. Hollie's work focuses on professional development, African American education, and second language methodology. He is a contributing author in two texts on culturally and linguistically responsive teaching. He is the Executive Director of the Center for Culturally Responsive Teaching and Learning and the co-founding director of the Culture and Language Academy of Success, an independent charter school in Los Angeles.

Dr. Donald J. Leu, Ph.D., teaches  at the University of Connecticut and holds a joint appointment in Curriculum and Instruction and in Educational Psychology. He directs the New Literacies Research Lab and is a member of the Board of Directors of the International Reading Association. Leu studies the skills required to read, write, and learn with Internet technologies. His research has been funded by groups including the U.S. Department of Education, the National Science Foundation, and the Bill & Melinda Gates Foundation.

Jon Scieszka founded GUYS READ,  a nonprofit literacy initiative for boys, to call attention to the problem of getting boys connected with reading. In 2008, he was named the first U.S. National Ambassador for Young People's Literature by the Library of Congress. Scieszka taught from first grade to eighth grade for ten years in New York City, drawing inspiration from his students to write *The True Story of the 3 Little Pigs!, The Stinky Cheese Man*, the *Time Warp Trio* series of chapter books, and the *Trucktown* series of books for beginning readers.

Sharon Vaughn, Ph.D., teaches  at the University of Texas at Austin. She is the previous Editor-in-Chief of the *Journal of Learning Disabilities* and the co-editor of *Learning Disabilities Research and Practice.* She is the recipient of the American Education Research Association SIG Award for Outstanding Researcher. Vaughn's work focuses on effective practices for enhancing reading outcomes for students with reading difficulties. She is the author of more than 100 articles and numerous books designed to improve research-based practices in the classroom.

Karen K. Wixson is Dean of the  School of Education at the University of North Carolina, Greensboro. She has published widely in the areas of literacy curriculum, instruction, and assessment. Wixson has been an advisor to the National Research Council and helped develop the National Assessment of Educational Progress (NAEP) reading tests. She is a past member of the IRA Board of Directors and co-chair of the IRA Commission on RTI. Recently, Wixson served on the English Language Arts Work Team that was part of the Common Core State Standards Initiative.

COMMON CORE
Contents in Brief

Each unit addresses a BIG Question to enrich exploration of literary concepts and reading strategies.

Six units per grade explore specific genres while focusing on a Big Question.

Robust Literary Analysis Workshops enable students to perform in-depth exploration of genres and standards.

? What is the best way to find the *truth*?

Theme in Fiction
Theme in Fiction
Central Idea in Nonfiction
Central Idea in Nonfiction

Context Clues
Narrative Text

Context Clues
Point of View

Leveled selection pairs let you choose text that is appropriate for your students' abilities without skipping essential skills.

INFORMATIONAL TEXT HIGHLIGHTED

Student Edition Pages

Locate Types of
Information

Reading for
Information texts
appear twice per unit.

Comparing Fiction
and Nonfiction

Author's Purpose
Setting

Author's Purpose
Historical Context

www.PHLitOnline.com

Interactive resources provide
personalized instruction and
activities online.

All program resources are
available online for classroom
presentation or individual study.

COMMON CORE
Unit 1 ▪ Fiction and Nonfiction

Assessment practice includes writing on demand activities.

Professional authors model their own revision strategies.

Vocabulary Workshops provide robust instruction and multiple practice opportunities.

The Assessment Workshops provide both multiple choice tests and performance tasks.

x Contents

Student Edition Pages

Skills at a Glance

This page provides a quick look at the skills you will learn and practice in Unit 1.

Reading Skills

> Each unit develops reading and literary skills, teaching them to mastery.

Context Clues

  Unlock Meaning

  Reread or Read Ahead to Confirm Meaning

Author's Purpose

  Recognize Details

  Use Background Information

Reading for Information

Locate Types of Information

Analyze Structure and Purpose

Literary Analysis

Theme

Central Idea

Narrative Writing

Point of View

Comparing Fiction and Nonfiction

Setting

Historical Context

Comparing Characters

Vocabulary

Big Question Vocabulary

Prefixes: *re-, in-, trans-, ac-*

Roots: *-vita-, -man-, -dict-, -sper-*

Using a Dictionary and Thesaurus

Conventions

Common and Proper Nouns

Possessive Nouns

Revising Incorrect Forms of Plural Nouns

Personal Pronouns

Possessive Pronouns

Checking Pronoun-Antecedent Agreement

Writing

Writing About the Big Question

Essay

Description

News Report

Letter

Timed Writing

Writing Workshop: Informative Text: Descriptive Essay

Writing Workshop: Narrative Text: Autobiographical Narrative

Speaking and Listening

Dramatic Reading

Discussion

Interview

Delivering a Narrative Presentation

Research and Technology

Biographical Report

 Common Core State Standards Addressed in This Unit

Reading Literature RL.7.1, RL.7.2, RL.7.3, RL.7.6, RL.7.10

Reading Informational Text RI.7.1, RI.7.2, RI.7.3, RI.7.5, RI.7.6, RI.7.10

Writing W.7.2, W.7.2.a–e, W.7.3, W.7.3.a–e, W.7.5, W.7.7, W.7.9.a, W.7.9.b, W.7.10

Speaking and Listening SL.7.1.a–c, SL.7.3, SL.7.4, SL.7.6

Language L.7.1, L.7.2, L.7.2.b, L.7.3, L.7.3.a, L.7.4, L.7.4.a–d, L.7.5, L.7.5.b, L.7.6

[For the full wording of the standards, see the standards chart in the front of your textbook.]

> The Common Core State Standards are addressed throughout the unit.

Contents **xi**

❓ Does every *conflict* have a winner?

INFORMATIONAL TEXT HIGHLIGHTED

Comparing Idioms

Writing Workshops provide step-by-step instruction in the writing process.

Make Inferences
Conflict and Resolution

Make Inferences
Theme

Literature in Context notes provide point-of-use cross curricular nonfiction links to selections.

PHLit Online!
www.PHLitOnline.com
Interactive resources provide personalized instruction and activities online.

The "What Do You Notice?" feature leads to in-depth exploration of ways in which authors use language.

Independent Reading suggestions offer opportunities for students to read complex texts independently.

Skills at a Glance

This page provides a quick look at the skills you will learn and practice in Unit 2.

Reading Skills

Make Predictions
  Use Prior Knowledge to Make Predictions
  Read Ahead to Verify Predictions
Make Inferences
  Recognize Details
  Read Between the Lines
    by Asking Questions

Reading for Information

Understand Text Structure and Purpose
Connecting Ideas to Make Inferences
  and Generalizations

Literary Analysis

Plot and Plot Devices
Point of View
Character
Comparing Idioms
Conflict and Resolution
Theme
Comparing Irony

> Key vocabulary skills are taught throughout the program.

Vocabulary

Big Question Vocabulary
Prefixes: *mal-, per-*
Suffixes: *-ance, -tion, -ment, -ious*
Roots: *-tract-, -spir-*
Word Origins

Conventions

Verbs
The Principal Parts of Verbs
Word Choice
Adjectives
Adverbs
Revising for Correct Verb Tense

Writing

Writing About the Big Question
Informative Article
Journal Entry
Anecdote
Letter to the Editor
Timed Writing
Writing Workshop: Argumentative Text:
  Response to Literature
Writing Workshop: Narrative Text: Short Story

Speaking and Listening

Informal Debate
News Story
Delivering an Oral Summary

Research and Technology

Outline

 Common Core State Standards Addressed in This Unit

Reading Literature RL.7.1, RL.7.2, RL.7.3, RL.7.4, RL.7.6, RL.7.10

Reading Informational Text RI.7.1, RI.7.4, RI.7.5, RI.7.9, RI.7.10

Writing W.7.1, W.7.1.a–e, W.7.2, W.7.2.a, W.7.2.d–f, W.7.3, W.7.3.a–e, W.7.5, W.7.7, W.7.9, W.7.9.a

Speaking and Listening SL.7.1, SL.7.1.a, SL.7.3, SL.7.5, SL.7.6

Language L.7.1, L.7.2.a, L.7.2.b, L.7.3, L.7.4.b, L.7.4.c, L.7.5.a, L.7.5.c, L.7.6

[For the full wording of the standards, see the standards chart in the front of your textbook.]

> The Common Core State Standards are addressed throughout the unit.

Contents **xv**

xvi Contents

INFORMATIONAL TEXT HIGHLIGHTED

Student Edition Pages

Comparing Biography and Autobiography

The Writer's Toolbox focuses on six traits.

Classifying Fact and Opinion
Persuasive Essay

Classifying Fact and Opinion
Word Choice and Diction

Leveled selection pairs let you choose text that is appropriate for your students' abilities without skipping essential skills.

PHLit Online!
www.PHLitOnline.com

Interactive resources provide personalized instruction and activities online.

All program resources are available online for classroom presentation or individual study.

A perfect mix of classic and contemporary selections provides a rich variety of choices.

Professional authors model their own revision strategies.

Independent Reading suggestions offer opportunities for students to read complex texts independently.

Skills at a Glance

This page provides a quick look at the skills you will learn and practice in Unit 3.

Reading Skills

Each unit develops reading and literary skills, teaching them to mastery.

Main Idea

Adjust Your Reading Rate to Recognize Main Ideas and Key Points

Make Connections Between Key Points and Supporting Details

Classifying Fact and Opinion

Recognize Clues That Indicate an Opinion

Use Resources to Check Facts

Reading for Information

Analyze Author's Argument

Understand Structure and Purpose

Literary Analysis

Point of View and Purpose

Development of Ideas

Word Choice and Tone

Expository Essay

Reflective Essay

Comparing Biography and Autobiography

Persuasive Essay

Word Choice and Diction

Comparing Humor

Vocabulary

Big Question Vocabulary

Suffixes: *-ness, -able*

Roots: *-rupt-, -leg-, -peti-, -vers-, -sol-*

Words With Multiple Meanings

Conventions

Conjunctions

Prepositions and Prepositional Phrases

Revising to Combine Sentences Using Conjunctions

Subjects and Predicates

Compound Subjects and Predicates

Revising Errors in Adjective and Adverb Usage

Writing

Writing About the Big Question

Analogy

Outline

Persuasive Letter

Adaptation

Timed Writing

Writing Workshop: Explanatory Text: How-to Essay

Writing Workshop: Informative Text: Comparison-and-Contrast Essay

Speaking and Listening

Response

Public Service Announcement

Oral Summary

Evaluating a Persuasive Presentation

Research and Technology

Help-Wanted Ad

Ⓒ Common Core State Standards Addressed in This Unit

Reading Literature RL.7.3, RL.7.10

Reading Informational Text RI.7.1, RI.7.2, RI.7.3, RI.7.4, RI.7.5, RI.7.6, RI.7.7, RI.7.8, RI.7.9, RI.7.10

Writing W.7.1.a, W.7.1.b, W.7.2, W.7.2.a–e, W.7.3.d, W.7.4, W.7.5, W.7.8, W.7.9, W.7.9.b

Speaking and Listening SL.7.1, SL.7.1.b, SL.7.2, SL.7.3, SL.7.4

Language L.7.1, L.7.1.a, L.7.1.c, L.7.2.b, L.7.3, L.7.3.a, L.7.4, L.7.4.b–d, L.7.5.b, L.7.6

[For the full wording of the standards, see the standards chart in the front of your textbook.]

Common Core State Standards are integrated throughout the units.

Contents **xix**

What is the best way to *communicate?*

Robust Literary Analysis Workshops enable students to perform in-depth exploration of genres and standards.

Figurative Language

Poetic Form and Structure

Drawing Conclusions
Forms of Poetry

Poetry is organized in collections to allow students to practice skills with either group.

Draw Conclusions
Figurative Language

INFORMATIONAL TEXT HIGHLIGHTED

Student Edition Pages

A robust mix of literary and informational texts provides a wide range of reading.

Grammar, Writing, Speaking and Listening, and Research activities link to selection content.

Contents **xxi**

> Assessment practice includes writing on demand activities.

> Communications Workshops enable students to practice speaking and listening skills for the twenty-first century.

Skills at a Glance

This page provides a quick look at the skills you will learn and practice in Unit 4.

Reading Skills

Drawing Conclusions

Asking Questions

Connecting the Details

Paraphrase

Read Poetry Aloud, According to Punctuation

Restate Passages

Reading for Information

Follow Technical Directions

Determine the Main Idea

Literary Analysis

Poetic Form and Structure

Forms of Poetry

Figurative Language

Comparing Narrative Poems

Sound Devices

Rhythm and Rhyme

Comparing Imagery

> Each unit develops reading and literary skills, teaching them to mastery.

Vocabulary

Big Question Vocabulary

Prefixes: *un-, im-*

Suffixes: *-ly, -y, -ancy or -ency, -less*

Roots: *-gram-, -leg-, -peti-, -vers-, -sol-*

Connotation and Denotation

Conventions

Infinitives and Infinitive Phrases

Appositives and Appositive Phrases

Revising Sentences Using Participles

Independent and Subordinate Clauses

Sentence Structures

Revising Fragments and Run-on Sentences

Writing

Writing About the Big Question

Lyric Poem, Concrete Poem, or Haiku

Metaphor

Paraphrase

Poem

Timed Writing

Writing Workshop: Argumentative Text: Problem-and-Solution Essay

Writing Workshop: Argumentative Text: Persuasive Essay

Speaking and Listening

Presentation

Poetry Reading

Evaluating Media Messages and Advertisements

Research and Technology

Scientific Explanation

Survey

 Common Core State Standards Addressed in This Unit

Reading Literature RL.7.1, RL.7.4, RL.7.5, RL.7.6, RL.7.7, RL.7.10

Reading Informational Text RI.7.1, RI.7.4, RI.7.5, RI.7.10

Writing W.7.1, W.7.1.a, W.7.1.b–e, W.7.2, W.7.2.a, W.7.2.b, W.7.2.d–f, W.7.4, W.7.5, W.7.7, W.7.9, W.7.9.a, W.7.10

Speaking and Listening SL.7.1, SL.7.1.c, SL.7.2, SL.7.3, SL.7.4, SL.7.5, SL.7.6

Language L.7.1, L.7.1.a–c, L.7.2, L.7.2.b, L.7.4.b, L.7.4.c, L.7.5.b, L.7.5.c, L.7.6

[For the full wording of the standards, see the standards chart in the front of your textbook.]

> The Common Core State Standards are addressed throughout the unit.

Contents **xxiii**

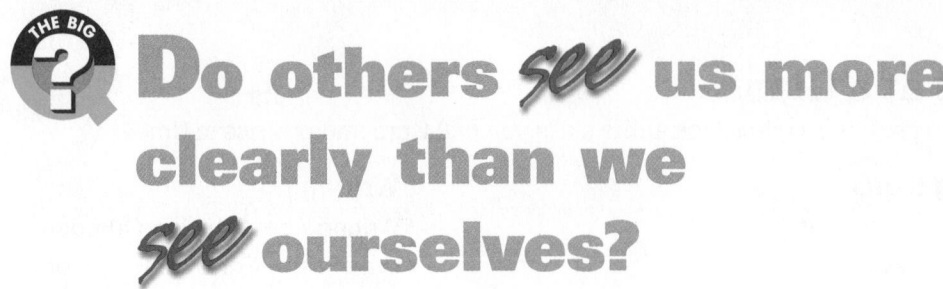

Do others *see* us more clearly than we *see* ourselves?

INFORMATIONAL TEXT HIGHLIGHTED

Student Edition Pages

Reading for Information texts appear twice per unit.

The Writer's Toolbox focuses on six traits.

PHLit Online!
www.PHLitOnline.com
Interactive resources provide personalized instruction and activities online.

Professional authors model their own revision strategies.

Vocabulary Workshops provide robust instruction and multiple practice opportunities.

Skills at a Glance

This page provides a quick look at the skills you will learn and practice in Unit 5.

Reading Skills

Purpose for Reading

Adjust Your Reading Rate

Preview a Text Before Reading

Summarize

Distinguish Between Important and Unimportant Details

Reading for Information

Identify Author's Perspective

Identify Bias and Stereotyping

Literary Analysis

Conflict

Character

Elements of Drama

Stage Directions

Dialogue

Comparing Characters

Characters' Motives

Comparing Dramatic Speeches

Vocabulary

Big Question Vocabulary

Prefixes: *inter-*

Roots: *-grat-, -sist-*

Borrowed and Foreign Words

Conventions

Interjections

Double Negatives

Revising to Avoid Common Usage Problems

Sentence Functions and Endmarks

Correcting Subject-Verb Agreement With Compound Subjects

Writing

Writing About the Big Question

Letter

Tribute

Summary

Timed Writing

Writing Workshop: Informative Text: Multimedia Report

Writing Workshop: Explanatory Text: Cause-and-Effect Essay

Speaking and Listening

Dramatic Monologue

Conducting an Interview

Research and Technology

Costume Plans

Film Version

 Common Core State Standards Addressed in This Unit

Reading Literature RL.7.1, RL.7.2, RL.7.3, RL.7.5, RL.7.6, RL.7.7, RL.7.10

Reading Informational Text RI.7.1, RI.7.6, RI.7.9, RI.7.10

Writing W.7.1, W.7.1.a–c, W.7.2, W.7.2.a–c, W.7.4, W.7.7, W.7.8, W.7.9, W.7.9.a

Speaking and Listening SL.7.1, SL.7.1.a–c, SL.7.5, SL.7.6

Language L.7.1, L.7.2, L.7.2.b, L.7.3, L.7.4.b–d, L.7.6

[For the full wording of the standards, see the standards chart in the front of your textbook.]

The Common Core State Standards are addressed throughout the unit.

Contents **xxvii**

INFORMATIONAL TEXT HIGHLIGHTED

Student Edition Pages

Writing Workshops provide step-by-step instruction in the writing process.

Exemplar texts appear throughout the program.

PHLit Online!
www.PHLitOnline.com
Interactive resources provide personalized instruction and activities online.

All program resources are available online for classroom presentation or individual study.

Contents **xxix**

The "What Do You Notice?" feature leads to in-depth exploration of ways in which authors use language.

Independent Reading suggestions offer opportunities for students to read complex texts independently.

Student Edition Pages

Skills at a Glance

This page provides a quick look at the skills you will learn and practice in Unit 6.

Reading Skills

Cause and Effect

Ask Questions to Analyze
Cause-and-Effect Relationships

Reread to Look for Connections

Compare and Contrast

Using Your Prior Knowledge
to Compare and Contrast

Using a Venn Diagram

Reading for Information

Analyze Cause-and-Effect Organization

Analyze Point of View

Literary Analysis

> Each unit develops reading and literary skills, teaching them to mastery.

Theme

Structure and Theme

Myth

Legend and Fact

Comparing Universal Themes

Cultural Context

Folk Tale

Comparing Tone and Themes

Vocabulary

Big Question Vocabulary

Prefixes: *out-, uni-*

Suffixes: *-ity*

Roots: *-vac-, -dom-, -myst-, -know-*

Figurative Language

Conventions

Punctuation Marks

Commas

Revising Incorrect Use of Commas

Capitalization

Abbreviations

Revising to Correct Use of Pronoun Case

Writing

Writing About the Big Question

Myth

Description and Comparison

Plot Summary

Review

Timed Writing

Writing Workshop: Informative Text:
Business Letter

Writing Workshop: Informative Text:
Research Report

Speaking and Listening

Debate

Persuasive Speech

Story

Television News Report

Research Presentation

 **Common Core State Standards
Addressed in This Unit**

Reading Literature RL.7.1, RL.7.2, RL.7.3, RL.7.5, RL.7.9, RL.7.10

Reading Informational Text RI.7.1, RI.7.5, RI.7.6, RI.7.9, RI.7.10

Writing W.7.1, W.7.1.a, W.7.1.b, W.7.1.e, W.7.2, W.7.2.a–c, W.7.2.e, W.7.2.f, W.7.3, W.7.3.a, W.7.3.b, W.7.4, W.7.5, W.7.7, W.7.8, W.7.9, W.7.9.a

Speaking and Listening SL.7.1, SL.7.1.a–c, SL.7.4, SL.7.5, SL.7.6

Language L.7.1, L.7.2, L.7.2.a, L.7.2.b, L.7.3.a, L.7.4.b, L.7.5, L.7.5.a, L.7.5.b, L.7.6

[For the full wording of the standards, see the standards chart in the front of your textbook.]

> Common Core State Standards are integrated throughout the units.

Contents **xxxi**

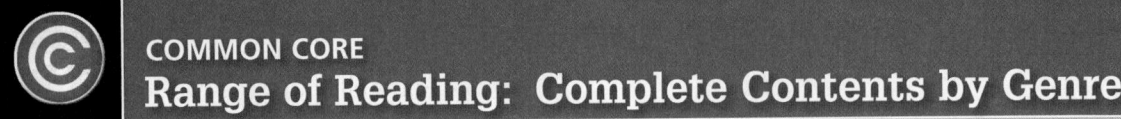
Literature

▶ Poetry

Informational Text—Literary Nonfiction

Student Edition Pages

▶ Functional Text

▶ Literature in Context—Reading
in the Content Areas

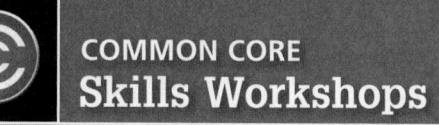

▶ Writing Workshops

▶ Vocabulary Workshops

▶ Communications Workshop

Building Academic Vocabulary

Academic vocabulary is the language you encounter in textbooks and on standardized tests and other assessments. Understanding these words and using them in your classroom discussions and writing will help you communicate your ideas clearly and effectively.

There are two basic types of academic vocabulary: general and domain-specific. **General academic vocabulary** includes words that are not specific to any single course of study. For example, the general academic vocabulary word *analyze* is used in language arts, math, social studies, art, and so on. **Domain-specific academic vocabulary** includes words that are usually encountered in the study of a specific discipline. For example, the words *factor* and *remainder* are most often used in mathematics classrooms and texts.

 Common Core State Standards

Language 6. Acquire and use accurately grade-appropriate general academic and domain-specific words and phrases; gather vocabulary knowledge when considering a word or phrase important to comprehension or expression.

General Academic Vocabulary

Word	Definition	Related Words	Word in Context
analyze (AN uh lyz) *v.*	break down into parts and examine carefully	analytical	Our assignment is to analyze the story's ending.
appreciate (uh PREE shee ayt) *v.*	be thankful for	appreciative appreciating	Once I read Frost's poem, I learned to appreciate his use of symbols.
assumption (uh SUHMP shuhn) *n.*	belief or acceptance that something is true	assume assuming	The assumption in the essay is well supported by facts.
attitude (AT uh tood) *n.*	mental state involving beliefs, feelings, and values	attitudes	The writer's attitude toward his subject was respectful and full of admiration.
awareness (uh WAIR nehs) *n.*	knowledge gained from one's own perceptions or from information	aware	It is important to develop an awareness of the writer's message.
bias (BY uhs) *n.*	tendency to see things from a slanted or prejudiced viewpoint	biased	You must consider if an advertisement contains bias or tries to mislead the reader.
culture (KUHL chuhr) *n.*	collected customs of a group or community	cultural	Folk tales reveal the values of a culture and teach a lesson.
challenge (CHAL uhnj) *v.*	dare; a calling into question	challenging challenged	Ted invited me to challenge him to a debate.

Ordinary Language:
I **like** poems with strong rhymes and rhythms.

Academic Language:
I **appreciate** poems with strong rhymes and rhythms.

Ⅰ Introductory Unit

Student Edition Pages

Word	Definition	Related Words	Word in Context
characteristic (kar ihk tuh RIHS tihk) *n.*	trait; feature	character characteristically	One characteristic of poetry is figurative language.
common (KOM uhn) *adj.*	ordinary; expected	commonality	It is common for an essay to contain humor.
communicate (kuh MYOO nuh kayt) *v.*	share thoughts or feelings, usually in words	communication communicating	It is important to be able to communicate thoughts and feelings in writing.
communication (kuh myoo nuh KAY shuhn) *n.*	activity of sharing information or speaking	communicate	There seemed to be a lack of communication between the mother and daughter.
community (kuh MYOO nuh tee) *n.*	group of people who share an interest or who live near each other	communities	Local newspapers serve the community where the paper is published.
conclude (kuhn KLOOD) *v.*	bring to a close; end	concluding conclusion	The writer was able to conclude the essay with a positive memory.
contribute (kuhn TRIHB yut) *v.*	add to; enrich	contribution	Editorials contribute to a public discussion about an issue.
convince (kuhn VIHNS) *v.*	persuade; cause to accept a point of view	convincing	It is important to convince readers of the character's dream.
debate (dih BAYT) *v.*	argue in an attempt to convince	debated debating	The two students tried to debate whether or not the new website was helpful.
define (dih FYN) *v.*	determine the nature of or give the meaning of	defined definition	I was able to define the story's plot quickly.
discover (dihs KUHV uhr) *v.*	find or explore	discovering discovery	The reader tries to discover the reasons for the character's behavior.
diversity (duh VUR suh tee) *n.*	variety, as of groups or cultures	diverse	Reading works from different writers provides diversity.

> **Ordinary Language:**
> In this essay, I will **tell the meaning** of key terms.
>
> **Academic Language:**
> In this essay, I will **define** key terms.

Word	Definition	Related Words	Word in Context
environment (ehn VY ruhn muhnt) *n.*	surroundings; the natural world	environs environmentally	The essay described the beautiful environment where the writer lived.
evaluate (ih VAL yoo ayt) *v.*	judge; determine the value or quality of	evaluated evaluation	The girl was unable to evaluate her friend's work without bias.
examine (ehg ZAM uhn) *v.*	study in depth; look at closely	examining examination	In order to examine the evidence, it was necessary to research the subject.
explain (ehk SPLAYN) *v.*	make plain or clear	explaining explanation	I will explain three key factors in the story's success.
explore (ehk SPLAWR) *v.*	investigate; look into	explored exploration	I wrote a research report to explore my ideas.
facts (fakts) *n.*	accepted truths or reality	factual	I supported my statement with facts and details.
focus (FOH kuhs) *n.*	central point or topic of investigation	focused focusing	The focus of the essay was to provide information about water safety.
generate (JEN uhr ayt) *v.*	create	generated generating	Before researching, I tried to generate a list of topics to explore.
identify (ahy- DEHN tuh fy) *v.*	recognize as being	identification	How do you identify the meaning of this poem?
ignore (ihg NAWR) *v.*	refuse to notice; disregard	ignored ignoring	If we ignore the message, we miss the purpose of the writing.
image (IHM ihj) *n.*	picture; representation	images imaging	The image in the book helped me to visualize the story.
individual (ihn duh VIHJ oo uhl) *n.*	single person or thing	individuals	The story is told from the perspective of one individual.
inform (ihn FORM) *v.*	tell; give information about	information	The purpose of the research paper was to inform the reader about whales.
inquire (ihn KWYR) *v.*	ask in order to learn about	inquiring inquired	We were assigned to inquire about weather patterns and present our findings.
insight (IHN syt) *n.*	ability to see the truth; an understanding	insightful	My teacher shared her insight about the characters with us.
investigate (ihn VEHS tuh gayt) *v.*	examine thoroughly	investigated investigation	As a team, we were able to investigate each aspect of the problem.

lii Introductory Unit

Word	Definition	Related Words	Word in Context
media (MEE dee uh) n.	collected sources of information, including newspapers, television, and the Internet		The media are an everyday source of information and entertainment for the public.
opposition (op uh ZIHSH uhn) n.	state of being against	oppose opposing	The villain in the story presented the opposition to the hero's happiness.
outcome (OWT kuhm) n.	way something turns out		We found the outcome of the problem to be a favorable solution.
perceive (puhr SEEV) v.	be aware of; see	perceived perception	I was able to perceive Jenny's character through her actions and words.
perception (puhr SEHP shuhn) n.	the act of becoming aware of through one or more of the senses	perceive perceptive	My perception of the character changed over the course of the story.
perspective (puhr SPEHK tihv) n.	point of view		I did not agree with the writer's perspective.
produce (pruh DOOS) v.	make; create	produced producing	In order to produce a new show, the writing team must provide a script.
reaction (ree AK shuhn) n.	response to an influence, action, or statement	react	I had a strong reaction to the claims made in the commercial.
reflect (rih FLEHKT) v.	think about; consider	reflected reflection	In order to reflect on what had been said, I took some quiet time.
resolution (rehz uh LOO shuhn) n.	end of a conflict in which one or both parties is satisfied	resolved resolving	The resolution of the story helped me to see how a compromise can help many people.
team (teem) n.	group united in a common goal		Our team prepared a report, and each member presented a part of it.

Word	Definition	Related Words	Word in Context
technology (tehk NOL uh jee) *n.*	practical application of science to business or industry	technologies	At one time, the computer was considered a new technology.
tradition (truh DIHSH uhn) *n.*	custom, as of a social group or culture	traditional	A tradition is often handed down to a new generation though storytelling.
transmit (trans MIHT) *v.*	send or give out	transmitted transmission	We were able to transmit our message over the school's radio station.
understanding (uhn duhr STAN dihng) *n.*	agreement; end of conflict	understand	The students came to an understanding of how best to organize the club.
unify (YOO nuh fy) *v.*	bring together as one	unified unifying	It is important to unify details so that they support the central idea.
unique (yoo NEEK) *adj.*	one of a kind	uniqueness uniquely	Each writer has a unique way of telling a story.

Practice

Examples of various kinds of domain-specific academic vocabulary appear in the charts below. Some chart rows are not filled in. In your notebook, look up the definitions of the remaining words, provide one or two related words, and use each word in context.

Social Studies: Domain-Specific Academic Vocabulary

Word	Definition	Related Words	Word in Context
communism (KOM yuh niz uhm) *n.*	an economic and social system where the land and all products of industry belong to the government as a whole	commune communist	Communism failed in Eastern Europe.
dissent (dih SENT) *n.*	difference of feeling or opinion	dissention dissenter	There was much dissent and disagreement in the government.
neutrality (noo TRAL i tee) *n.*	the state of being neutral; not taking sides in a conflict	neutral	Switzerland kept its neutrality during World War II.
segregation (seg ri GEY shuhn) *n.*	the separation of people because of race, color, or gender	segregate segregated	The Civil Rights Movement helped to end segregation in the South.
socialism (SOH shuh liz uhm) *n.*	a theory or system of organization in which major sources of production are owned or controlled by the community or government	social socialist	Socialism stresses the community rather than the individual.
adaptation (ad uhp TEY shuhn) *n.*			
emigration (em I GREY shuhn) *n.*			
colonization (KOL uh nih ZAY shuhn) *n.*			
nobility (noh BIL i tee) *n.*			
urbanization (UR buh nuh ZAY shuhn) *n.*			

Mathematics: Domain-Specific Academic Vocabulary

Word	Definition	Related Words	Word in Context
negative number (NEG ah tiv NUHM ber) *n.*	a number below zero on a number line; indicated by a minus sign	positive number	The number −4 is a negative number, while 4 is a positive number.
odds (oddz) *n.*	the probability that something will happen	odd oddity	What are the odds that I will win the lottery?
proportion (pruh PAWR shuhn) *n.*	a statement of the equality of two ratios, or the mathematical relationship of a part to the whole	proportionate	The teacher said that the proportion should be written as 4/2 = 10/5.
range (reynj) *n.*	the difference between the largest and smallest values in a group of numbers	ranging	Find the range in the following number set: 2, 3, 4, 5, and 6.
ratio (REY shee oh) *n.*	proportionate relationship between two numbers	ratios	The ratio of 5 to 2 is written as 5:2.
minimum (MIN uh muhm) *n.*			
property (PROP er tee) *n.*			
rate (reyt) *n.*			
reliability (ri LY uh bil i tee) *n.*			
sequence (SEE kwuhns) *n.*			

Science: Domain-Specific Academic Vocabulary

Word	Definition	Related Words	Word in Context
hypothesis (hy POTH uh sis) *n.*	something not proved but assumed to be true for the purpose of further study or argument	hypothesize	The hypothesis that the earth was flat was later proven to be false.
erosion (ih ROH zhuhn) *n.*	the process by which the surface of the earth is worn away by the action of water and other natural events	erode	The hurricane caused beach erosion.
metamorphic (met uh MAWR fik) *adj.*	changing in form or structure	metamorphosis	Metamorphic rock is formed by heat and pressure within the earth.
solubility (sol yuh BIL i tee) *n.*	the ability of a substance to dissolve	soluble	We tested the solubility of salt in a science lab.
synthesize (SIN thuh syz) *v.*	form by combining parts or elements	synthetic	Scientists synthesize compounds by combining two or more substances.

lvi Introductory Unit

Student Edition Pages

Science: Domain-Specific Academic Vocabulary (continued)

Word	Definition	Related Words	Word in Context
energy (EN er jee) n.			
evidence (EV i iduhns) n.			
gene (jeen) n.			
heredity (huh RED i tee) n.			
substance (SUHB stuhns) n.			

Art: Domain-Specific Academic Vocabulary

Word	Definition	Related Words	Word in Context
intensity (in TEN si tee) n.	the quality of a color's brightness and purity	intense	The intensity of the red paint was stronger than the artist wanted.
linear (LIN ee er) adj.	having to do with a line	line	The sculpture of the building was linear and rigid.
saturation (sach uh REY shuhn) n.	the degree of purity of a color	saturate	The saturation of the pink paint gave the room a lively feel.
texture (TEKS cher) n.	the way things feel, or look as if they might feel, when touched	textured	The carpet had a thick and fluffy texture.
unity (YOO ni tee) n.	the look and feel of wholeness in a work of art	unite, unified	The mural had good balance and unity.
definition (def uh NISH uhn) n.			
form (fawrm) n.			
motion (MOH shuhn) n.			
space (speys) n.			
value (VAL yoo) n.			

Technology: Domain-Specific Academic Vocabulary

Word	Definition	Related Words	Word in Context
database (DEY tuh beys) *n.*	a collection of related information stored in a computerized format	databases	The library has a database of all its books.
digital (DIJ i tl) *adj.*	available in an electronic format	digit, digitize	I have a digital version of that book on my computer.
login (LOG in) *n.*	information related to an electronic account name and its password	logging in	I use my login to access my account on a secure Web site.
network (NET work) *n.*	a group of computers connected together to share information	networking, networked	The Internet is the largest network in the world.
platform (PLAT fawrm) *n.*	a group of compatible computers that can share software	platforms	PC is the computer platform used in our school.
bookmark (BOOK mahrk) *n.*			
copy (KOP ee) *n., v.*			
download (DOUN lohd) *v.*			
input (IN poot) *n., v.*			
output (OUT poot) *n., v.*			

Student Edition Pages

Increasing Your Word Knowledge

Increase your word knowledge and chances of success by taking an active role in developing your vocabulary. Here are some tips for you.

To own a word, follow these steps:

Steps to Follow	Model
1. Learn to identify the word and its basic meaning.	The word *examine* means "to look at closely."
2. Take note of the word's spelling.	*Examine* begins and ends with an *e*.
3. Practice pronouncing the word so that you can use it in conversation.	The *e* on the end of the word is silent. Its second syllable gets the most stress.
4. Visualize the word and illustrate its key meaning.	When I think of the word *examine*, I visualize a doctor checking a patient's health.
5. Learn the various forms of the word and its related words.	*Examination* and *exam* are forms of the word *examine*.
6. Compare the word with similar words.	*Examine, peruse,* and *study* are synonyms.
7. Contrast the word with similar words.	*Examine* suggests a more detailed study than *read* or *look at*.
8. Use the word in various contexts.	"I'd like to *examine* the footprints more closely." "I will *examine* the use of imagery in this poem."

Building Your Speaking Vocabulary

Language gives us the ability to express ourselves. The more words you know, the better able you will be to get your points across. There are two main aspects of language: reading and speaking. Using the steps above will help you to acquire a rich vocabulary. Follow these steps to help you learn to use this rich vocabulary in discussions, speeches, and conversations.

Steps to Follow	Tip
1. Practice pronouncing the word.	Become familiar with pronunciation guides, which will help you to sound out unfamiliar words. Listening to audio books as you read the text will help you learn pronunciations of words.
2. Learn word forms.	Dictionaries often list forms of words following the main word entry. Practice saying word families aloud: "generate," "generated," "generation," "regenerate," "generator."
3. Translate your thoughts.	Restate your own thoughts and ideas in a variety of ways, to inject formality or to change your tone, for example.
4. Hold discussions.	With a classmate, practice using academic vocabulary words in discussions about the text. Choose one term to practice at a time, and see how many statements you can create using that term.
5. Tape-record yourself.	Analyze your word choices by listening to yourself objectively. Note where your word choice could be strengthened or changed.

Building Academic Vocabulary **lix**

Writing an Objective Summary

The ability to write objective summaries is key to success in college and in many careers. Writing an effective objective summary involves recording the key ideas of a text while demonstrating your understanding.

**Common Core
State Standards**

Literature 2. Determine a theme or central idea of a text and analyze its development over the course of the text; provide an objective summary of the text.
Informational Text 2. Determine two or more central ideas in a text and analyze their development over the course of the text; provide an objective summary of the text.

What Is an Objective Summary?

An effective objective summary is a concise, complete, accurate, and objective overview of a text. The following are key characteristics of an objective summary:

- A good summary focuses on the main theme, or central idea, of a text and specific, relevant details that support that theme, or central idea. Unnecessary supporting details are left out.
- An effective summary is usually brief. However, the writer must be careful not to misrepresent the text by leaving out key elements.
- A successful summary accurately captures the essence of the longer text it is describing.
- An effective summary remains objective—the writer refrains from inserting his or her own opinions, reactions, or personal connections into the summary.

What to Avoid in an Objective Summary

- An objective summary is not a collection of sentences or paragraphs copied from the original source.
- It is not a long recounting of every event, detail, or point in the original text.
- A good summary does not include evaluative words or comments, such as the reader's overall opinion of or reaction to the piece. An objective summary is not the reader's interpretation or critical analysis of the work.

Model Objective Summary

Review the elements of an effective objective summary, which are pointed out in the sidenotes that appear next to the summary. Then, write an objective summary of a selection you recently read. Review your summary, and delete any unnecessary details, personal opinions, or evaluations of the text.

Summary of "Mowgli's Brothers"

"Mowgli's Brothers" is one of the stories in *The Jungle Book,* written by Rudyard Kipling. The setting of the story is a jungle in India, and the ~~enchanting~~ story tells the tale of Mowgli, a young boy who is raised by wolves.

One night Mother and Father Wolf woke from their rest to find Tabaqui, a jackal, at the mouth of their cave, begging for food. No one in the jungle liked Tabaqui. However, the wolves gave him a bone to eat in spite of the fact that he upset Mother Wolf ~~by complimenting her on her four young cubs. The wolves thought it was unlucky to compliment children to their faces.~~ Tabaqui further upset the wolves by bringing the news that Shere Khan, a tiger, was moving into their hunting grounds.

After Tabaqui left, Father Wolf set out on his hunt. He heard Shere Khan's roar and then saw him rolling around on the ground. The tiger had landed in a woodcutter's fire while trying to catch his prey.

Soon after that, something approached the wolves' cave. Father Wolf was ready to pounce until he saw what it was—a smiling, happy baby boy. Father Wolf gently picked up the man's cub and brought him to Mother Wolf. The man's cub was not at all afraid, and he snuggled right up with the wolf cubs.

Before long, Shere Khan stuck his big head into the cave. He wanted the man's cub, which had been his prey. The wolves wouldn't give him up, which angered the tiger. But Mother Wolf was even angrier. She said, "The man's cub is mine…He shall not be killed. He shall live to run with the Pack and to hunt with the Pack; and in the end. . .he shall hunt thee."

Mother Wolf named the man's cub Mowgli, and he was brought before the Wolf Pack for approval. With the help of Baloo the bear and Bagheera the black panther, Mowgli was accepted into the Pack. Shere Khan slinked away into the night, roaring his disapproval.

A one-sentence synopsis, or brief overview, highlighting the theme, or central idea, of the story can be an effective start to a summary.

The adjective *enchanting* indicates an opinion and should not be included in an objective summary.

Unnecessary details should be eliminated.

Transition words and phrases show chronological order and enable readers to easily follow the order of events.

If actual sentences from the story are used to show the essence of a text, they must be placed within quotation marks.

Writing an Objective Summary **lxi**

Comprehending Complex Texts

Common Core State Standards

Literature 10. By the end of the year, read and comprehend literature, including stories, dramas, and poems, in the grades 6–8 text complexity band proficiently, with scaffolding as needed at the high end of the range.

Over the course of your school years, you will be required to read increasingly complex texts as preparation for college and a career. A complex text is a text that contains challenging vocabulary; long, complex sentences; figurative language; multiple levels of meaning; or unfamiliar settings and situations.

The selections in this textbook provide you with a range of readings, from short stories to autobiographies, poetry, drama, myths, and even science and social studies texts. Some of these texts will fall within your comfort zone; others will most likely be more challenging.

Strategy 1: Multidraft Reading

Most successful readers know that to fully understand a text, you must reread it several times. Get in the habit of reading a text or portions of a text two to three times in order to ensure that you get the most out of your reading experience. To fully understand a text, try this multidraft reading strategy:

1st Reading

On your first reading, look for the basics. If, for example, you are reading a story, look for who does what to whom, what conflicts arise, and how conflicts are resolved. If the text is nonfiction, look for the main ideas and the ways they are presented. If you are reading a lyric poem, read first to get a sense of who the speaker is. Also take note of the poem's setting and main focus.

2nd Reading

During your second reading of a text, focus on the artistry or the effectiveness of the writing. Look for text structures and think about why the author chose those organizational patterns. Then, examine the author's creative uses of language and the effects of that language. For example, has the author used metaphor, simile, or hyperbole? If so, what effect did that use of figurative language create?

3rd Reading

After your third reading, compare and contrast the text with other similar selections you have read. For example, if you read a haiku, think of other haiku you have read and ways the poems are alike or different. Evaluate the text's overall effectiveness and its central idea, or theme.

lxii Introductory Unit

Independent Practice

As you read this poem, practice the multidraft reading strategy by completing a chart like the one below. Use a separate piece of paper.

"Prayers of Steel" by Carl Sandburg

Lay me on an anvil, O God.

Beat me and hammer me into a crowbar.

Let me pry loose old walls;

Let me lift and loosen old foundations.

Lay me on an anvil, O God.

Beat me and hammer me into a steel spike.

Drive me into the girders that hold a skyscraper together.

Take red-hot rivets and fasten me into the central girders.

Let me be the great nail holding a skyscraper through blue

     nights into white stars.

Multidraft Reading Chart

	My Understanding
1st Reading Look for key ideas and details that unlock basic meaning.	
2nd Reading Read for deeper meanings. Look for ways in which the author used text structures and language to create effects.	
3rd Reading Read to integrate your knowledge and ideas. Connect the text to others of its kind and to your own experience.	

Strategy 2: Close Read the Text

To comprehend a complex text, perform a close reading—a careful analysis of the words, phrases, and sentences within the text. As you close read, use the following tips to comprehend the text:

Tips for Close Reading
1. **Break down long sentences** into parts. Look for the subject of the sentence and its verb. Then, identify which parts of the sentence modify, or give more information about, the subject.
2. **Reread difficult passages** to confirm that you understand their meaning.

3. **Look for context clues,** such as
 	
  a. restatement of an idea. For example, in this sentence, "defeated" restates the verb *vanquished.*
    The army **vanquished,** or <u>defeated</u>, its enemy.
 	
  b. definition of sophisticated words. In this sentence, the underlined information defines the word *girder.*
    A **girder's** <u>long beam provides support for the floor above.</u>
 	
  c. examples of concepts and topics. In the following passage, the underlined text provides an example of the adjective *voracious.*
    <u>Eating his entire dinner, two apples, and a banana</u> finally satisfied Rob's **voracious** appetite.
 	
  d. contrasts of ideas and topics. The following sentence points out a difference between Lori and Ellen.
    Lori was **vivacious,** <u>unlike her shy, quiet</u> sister Ellen.

4. **Identify pronoun antecedents.** If long sentences or passages contain pronouns, reread the text to make sure you know to whom or what the pronouns refer. In the following passage, the underlined pronouns all have the antecedent *freedom.*   **Freedom** is precious. Through <u>it</u> we prosper. In <u>its</u> absence we doubt, quake, rage, and suffer; <u>it</u> is just as necessary to life as is the air we breathe. For, without <u>it</u>, we surely perish.
5. **Look for conjunctions,** such as *and, or,* and *yet,* to help understand relationships between ideas.
6. **Paraphrase,** or restate in your own words, passages of difficult text in order to check your understanding. Remember that a paraphrase is a word-for-word restatement of an original text; it is not a summary.

Close-Read Model

As you read this document, take note of the sidenotes that model ways to unlock meaning in the text.

---

from "Speech to the Constitutional Convention" by Benjamin Franklin

I confess that I do not entirely approve of this Constitution at present; but, sir, I am not sure I shall never approve of it, for, having lived long, I have experienced many instances of being obliged, by better information or fuller consideration, to change opinions even on important subjects, which I once thought right, but found to be otherwise. It is therefore that, the older I grow, the more apt I am to doubt my own judgment of others. Most men, indeed, as well as most sects in religion think themselves in possession of all truth, and that wherever others differ with them, it is so far error. . . . .

In these sentiments, sir, I agree to this Constitution with all its faults—if they are such—because I think a general government necessary for us, and there is no form of government but what may be a blessing to the people if well administered; and I believe, further, that this is likely to be well administered for a course of years, and can only end in despotism, as other forms have done before it, when the people shall become so corrupted as to need a despotic government, being incapable of any other. I doubt, too, whether any other convention we can obtain may be able to make a better Constitution; for, when you assemble a number of men, to have the advantage of their joint wisdom, you inevitably assemble with those men all their prejudices, their passions, their errors of opinion, their local interests, and their selfish views. From such an assembly can a perfect production be expected?

It therefore astonishes me, sir, to find this system approaching so near to perfection as it does. . . .

Break down this long sentence into parts. The text highlighted in yellow conveys the basic meaning of the sentence. The text highlighted in blue provides additional information.

Look for antecedents. In this sentence, the noun *faults* is replaced by the pronoun *they*. The conjunction *because,* highlighted in blue, indicates a cause-and-effect relationship.

Search for context clues. The words in blue are context clues that help you figure out the meaning of the word that appears in yellow.

Comprehending Complex Texts **lxv**

Strategy 3: Ask Questions

Be an attentive reader by asking questions as you read. Throughout this textbook, we have provided questions for you following each selection. These questions are sorted into three basic categories that build in sophistication and lead you to a deeper understanding of the texts you read.

Here is an example from this text:

Some questions are about Key Ideas and Details in the text. To answer these questions, you will need to locate and cite explicit information in the text or draw inferences from what you have read.

Some questions are about Craft and Structure in the text. To answer these questions, you will need to analyze how the author developed and structured the text. You will also look for ways in which the author artfully used language and how those word choices impacted the meaning and tone of the work.

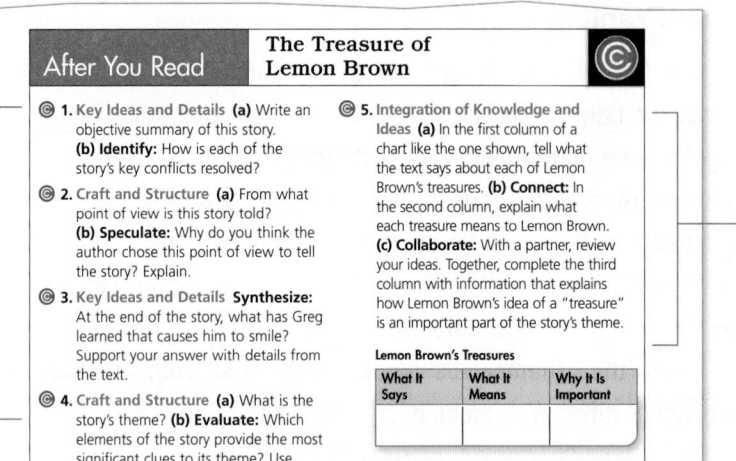

After You Read

The Treasure of Lemon Brown

1. Key Ideas and Details (a) Write an objective summary of this story. **(b) Identify:** How is each of the story's key conflicts resolved?

2. Craft and Structure (a) From what point of view is this story told? **(b) Speculate:** Why do you think the author chose this point of view to tell the story? Explain.

3. Key Ideas and Details Synthesize: At the end of the story, what has Greg learned that causes him to smile? Support your answer with details from the text.

4. Craft and Structure (a) What is the story's theme? **(b) Evaluate:** Which elements of the story provide the most significant clues to its theme? Use specific details to support your answer.

5. Integration of Knowledge and Ideas (a) In the first column of a chart like the one shown, tell what the text says about each of Lemon Brown's treasures. **(b) Connect:** In the second column, explain what each treasure means to Lemon Brown. **(c) Collaborate:** With a partner, review your ideas. Together, complete the third column with information that explains how Lemon Brown's idea of a "treasure" is an important part of the story's theme.

Lemon Brown's Treasures

What It Says	What It Means	Why It Is Important

Some questions are about the Integration of Knowledge and Ideas in the text. These questions ask you to evaluate a text in many different ways, such as comparing texts, looking at arguments in the text, and many other methods of analyzing a text's ideas.

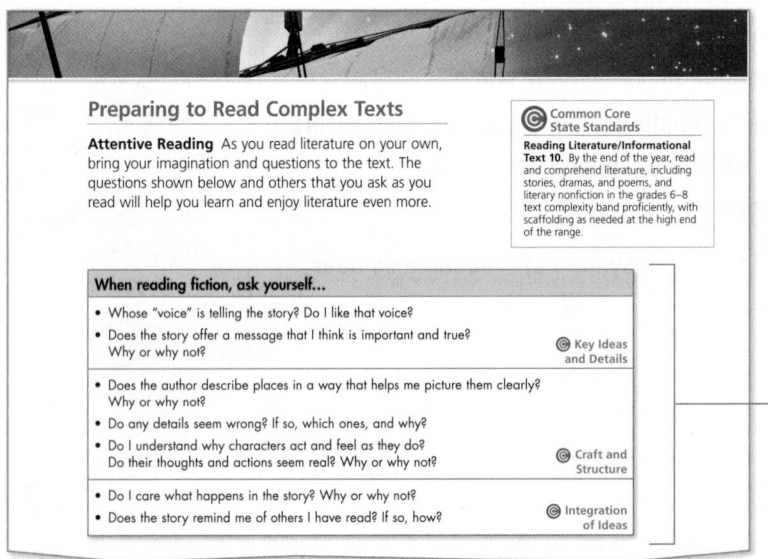

Preparing to Read Complex Texts

Attentive Reading As you read literature on your own, bring your imagination and questions to the text. The questions shown below and others that you ask as you read will help you learn and enjoy literature even more.

Common Core State Standards

Reading Literature/Informational Text 10. By the end of the year, read and comprehend literature, including stories, dramas, and poems, and literary nonfiction in the grades 6–8 text complexity band proficiently, with scaffolding as needed at the high end of the range.

When reading fiction, ask yourself...

- Whose "voice" is telling the story? Do I like that voice?
- Does the story offer a message that I think is important and true? Why or why not?

Key Ideas and Details

- Does the author describe places in a way that helps me picture them clearly? Why or why not?
- Do any details seem wrong? If so, which ones, and why?
- Do I understand why characters act and feel as they do? Do their thoughts and actions seem real? Why or why not?

Craft and Structure

- Do I care what happens in the story? Why or why not?
- Does the story remind me of others I have read? If so, how?

Integration of Ideas

As you read independently, ask similar types of questions to ensure that you fully enjoy and comprehend texts you read for school and for pleasure. We have provided sets of questions for you on the Independent Reading pages at the end of each unit.

INFORMATIONAL TEXT

Model

Following is an example of a complex text. The sidenotes show sample questions that an attentive reader might ask while reading.

Sample questions:

from "Owning Books" by William Lyon Phelps

in a radio broadcast on April 6, 1933:

The habit of reading is one of the greatest resources of mankind; and we enjoy reading books that belong to us much more than if they are borrowed. . . your own books belong to you; you treat them with that affectionate intimacy that annihilates formality. Books are for use, not for show; you should own no book that you are afraid to mark up, or afraid to place on the table wide open and face down. A good reason for marking favorite passages in books is that this practice enables you to remember more easily the significant sayings, to refer to them quickly, and then in later years, it is like visiting a forest where you once blazed a trail. You have the pleasure of going over the old ground, and recalling both the intellectual scenery and your own earlier self.

Key Ideas and Details
Does the first sentence state facts or express an opinion? Who is meant by *we* and *us*?

Craft and Structure
What parallel structures does the writer use in this passage? What effect does that use have on readers?

Integration of Knowledge and Ideas
To what extent do you agree with the author's viewpoint? Explain.

INFORMATIONAL TEXT

Independent Practice

Write three to five questions you might ask yourself as you read this passage from a speech delivered by Theodore Roosevelt at the Grand Canyon in 1903.

from "Speech at the Grand Canyon" by Theodore Roosevelt

. . . In the Grand Canyon, Arizona has a natural wonder which, so far as I know, is, in kind, absolutely unparalleled throughout the rest of the world. I want to ask you to do one thing in connection with it, in your own interest and in the interest of the country—to keep this great wonder of nature as it now is. I was delighted to learn of the wisdom of the Santa Fe railroad people in deciding not to build their hotel on the brink of the canyon. I hope you will not have a building of any kind, not a summer cottage, a hotel, or anything else, to mar the wonderful grandeur, the sublimity, the great loneliness and beauty of the canyon. Leave it as it is. You cannot improve on it. The ages have been at work on it, and man can only mar it. What you can do is to keep it for your children, your children's children and for all who come after you, as one of the great sights which every American, if he can travel at all, should see. . . .

Comprehending Complex Texts **lxvii**

Analyzing Arguments

Common Core State Standards

Informational Text 8. Trace and evaluate the argument and specific claims in a text, assessing whether the reasoning is sound and the evidence is relevant and sufficient to support the claims.

Language 6. Acquire and use accurately general academic and domain-specific words and phrases.

The ability to evaluate an argument, as well as to make one, is an important skill for success in college and in the workplace.

What Is an Argument?

Chances are, you have used the word *argument* to refer to a disagreement between people. This type of argument involves trading opinions and evidence in a conversational way, with both sides contributing to the discussion. A formal argument, however, presents one side of a controversial or debatable issue. Through this type of argument, the writer logically supports a particular belief, conclusion, or point of view. A good argument is supported with reasoning and evidence.

Purposes of Argument

There are three main purposes for writing a formal argument:
- to change the reader's mind about an issue
- to convince the reader to accept what is written
- to motivate the reader to take action, based on what is written

Elements of an Argument

Claim (assertion)—what the writer is trying to prove
Example: *Sports programs should be funded by private individuals, not schools.*

Grounds (evidence)—the support used to convince the reader
Example: *Because students who participate in sports get the benefits of that activity, the students should do fund-raising to pay for the use of equipment and training.*

Justification—the link between the grounds and the claim; why the grounds are credible
Example: *For example, participants in sports often get college scholarships—money that is paid to them. Since those students benefit personally from the sports experience, they should help fund the cost of the sports activities.*

Evaluating Claims

When reading or listening to an argument, critically assess the claims that are made. Analyze the argument to identify claims that are based on fact or that can be proved true. Also evaluate evidence that supports the claims. If there is little or no reasoning or evidence provided to support the claims, the argument may not be sound or valid.

lxviii Introductory Unit

Student Edition Pages

Model Argument

from "Speech Supporting Women's Suffrage"
by Robert L. Owen

Women compose one-half of the human race. . . A full half of the work of the world is done by women. A careful study of the matter has demonstrated the vital fact that these working women receive a smaller wage for equal work than men do, and that the smaller wage and harder conditions imposed on the woman worker are due to the lack of the ballot. . . . Equal pay for equal work is the first great reason justifying this change of governmental policy.

There are other reasons which are persuasive: First, women, take it all in all, are the equals of men in intelligence, and no man has the hardihood to assert the contrary. . . .

Every evil prophecy against granting the suffrage has failed. The public men of Colorado, Wyoming, Utah, and Idaho give it a cordial support.

The testimony is universal:

First, it has not made women mannish; they. . .are better able to protect themselves and their children because of the ballot.

Second, they have not become office-seekers. . . It [suffrage] has made women broader and greatly increased the understanding of the community at large of the problems of good government. . . .

It has not absolutely regenerated society, but it has improved it. It has raised the . . .moral standard of the suffrage, because there are more criminal men than criminal women. . . .

The great doctrine of the American Republic that "all governments derive their just powers from the consent of the governed" justifies the plea on one-half of the people, the women, to exercise the suffrage. The doctrine of the American Revolutionary War that taxation without representation is unendurable justifies women in exercising the suffrage.

Claim: Smaller wages and poor working conditions for women are caused by the fact that women cannot vote.

Grounds: Equal pay should be given for equal work.

Grounds: Women are just as intelligent as men.

An opposing argument is acknowledged and refuted.

Justification: Women should have the right to vote because government derives its powers from the consent of the governed, and women are half of the governed population. Also, taxation without representation is against U.S. principles. If women are to be taxed, they should have a vote.

A strong conclusion does more than simply restate the claim.

Analyzing Arguments **lxix**

The Art of Argument: Rhetorical Devices and Persuasive Techniques

Rhetorical Devices

Rhetoric is the art of using language in order to make a point or to persuade listeners. Rhetorical devices such as the ones listed below are accepted elements of argument. Their use does not weaken an argument. Rather, the use of rhetorical devices is regarded as a key part of an effective argument.

Rhetorical Devices	Examples
Repetition The repeated use of words, phrases, or sentences	It is not **fair** to expect this treatment. Nor is it **fair** to pay for this decision.
Parallelism The repeated use of similar grammatical structures	Good students learn <u>to read, to question, and to respond</u>.
Rhetorical Question Calls attention to the issue by implying an obvious answer	Shouldn't consumers get what they pay for?
Sound Device The use of alliteration, assonance, rhyme, or rhythm	The invention is both **p**ractical and **p**rofitable.
Simile and Metaphor Compares two seemingly unlike things or asserts that one thing *is* another	**Teachers** are <u>like sparks</u> igniting the curiosity of their students.

Persuasive Techniques

Persuasive techniques are often found in advertisements and in other forms of informal persuasion. Although techniques like the ones below are sometimes found in informal arguments, they should be avoided in formal arguments.

Persuasive Techniques	Examples
Bandwagon Approach/Anti-Bandwagon Approach Appeals to a person's desire to belong; encourages or celebrates individuality	Anyone with any sense will vote for Richard Rock. Vote your conscience; an election is not a popularity contest.
Emotional Appeal Evokes people's fear, anger, or desire	Without working smoke detectors, your family is in danger.
Endorsement/Testimony Employs a well-known person to promote a product or idea	"I use this toothpaste, and it brightens my movie-star smile."
Loaded Language The use of words that are charged with emotion	The heroic firefighters bravely battled the raging inferno.
Hyperbole Exaggeration to make a point	Our candidate does the work of ten people.

lxx Introductory Unit

Student Edition Pages

INFORMATIONAL TEXT

Model Speech

The excerpted speech below includes examples of rhetorical devices and persuasive techniques.

---

from "Inaugural Address" by Dwight D. Eisenhower

My fellow citizens:

... Since this century's beginning, a time of tempest has seemed to come upon the continents of the earth. Masses of Asia have awakened to strike off shackles of the past. Great nations of Europe have fought their bloodiest wars. Thrones have toppled and their vast empires have disappeared. New nations have been born.

> The use of alliteration makes these phrases memorable.

For our own country, it has been a time of recurring trial. We have grown in power and in responsibility. We have passed through the anxieties of depression and of war to a summit unmatched in man's history. Seeking to secure peace in the world, we have had to fight through the forests of the Argonne, to the shores of Iwo Jima, and to the cold mountains of Korea...

> Eisenhower uses parallelism and repetition to emphasize his main points.

How far have we come in man's long pilgrimage from darkness toward light? Are we nearing the light—a day of freedom and of peace for all mankind? Or are the shadows of another night closing in upon us?...

> Rhetorical questions call attention to the speaker's point.

. . . we know that the virtues most cherished by free people—love of truth, pride of work, devotion to country—all are treasures equally precious in the lives of the most humble and of the most exalted. The men who mine coal and fire furnaces and balance ledgers and turn lathes and pick cotton and heal the sick and plant corn—all serve as proudly, and as profitably, for America as the statesmen who draft treaties and the legislators who enact laws.

> Additional examples of parallel structure enable the audience to follow Eisenhower's ideas and to be moved by his words.

...We must be willing, individually and as a Nation, to accept whatever sacrifices may be required of us. A people that values its privileges above its principles soon loses both.

> Sound devices, such as alliteration, are a way to emphasize a phrase.

These basic precepts are not lofty abstractions, far removed from matters of daily living... Patriotism means equipped forces and a prepared citizenry. Moral stamina means more energy and more productivity...Love of liberty means the guarding of every resource that makes freedom possible...

No person, no home, no community can be beyond the reach of this call. We are summoned to act in wisdom and in conscience, to work with industry, to teach with persuasion, to preach with conviction, to weigh our every deed with care and with compassion. For this truth must be clear before us: whatever America hopes to bring to pass in the world must first come to pass in the heart of America.

> The parallelism created by repeated grammatical structures gives the speech rhythm.

The Art of Argument: Rhetorical Devices and Persuasive Techniques **lxxi**

Composing an Argument

 Common Core State Standards

Writing 1.a. Introduce claim(s), acknowledge alternate or opposing claims, and organize the reasons and evidence logically.

Writing 1.b. Support claim(s) with logical reasoning and relevant evidence, using accurate, credible sources and demonstrating an understanding of the topic or text.

Writing 1.e. Provide a concluding statement or section that follows from and supports the argument presented.

Choosing a Topic

You should choose a topic that matters to people—and to you. Brainstorm topics you would like to write about, and then choose the topic that most interests you.

Once you have chosen a topic, check to be sure you can make an arguable claim. Ask yourself:

1. What am I trying to prove? What ideas do I need to get across?

2. Are there people that would disagree with my claim? What alternate, or opposing, opinions might they have?

3. Do I have evidence to support my claim? Is my evidence sufficient or relevant?

If you are able to put into words what you want to prove and answered "yes" to numbers 2 and 3, you have an arguable claim.

Introducing the Claim and Establishing Its Significance

Before you begin writing, think about your audience and what they probably know about the topic. Then, provide only as much background information as necessary. Remember that you are not writing a summary of the issue—you are crafting an argument. Once you have provided context for your argument, clearly state your claim, or thesis. A written argument's claim often, but not always, appears in the first paragraph.

Developing Your Claim with Reasoning and Evidence

Now that you have made your claim, you must support it with evidence, or grounds. A good argument should have at least three solid pieces of evidence to support the claim. Evidence can range from personal experience to researched data or expert opinion. Knowing your audience's knowledge level, concerns, values, and possible biases can help you decide what kind of evidence will have the strongest impact. Make sure your evidence is up to date and comes from a credible source. Don't forget to credit your sources and address the opposing counterclaim.

Writing a Concluding Statement or Section

Restate your claim in the conclusion of your argument, and synthesize, or pull together, the evidence you have provided. Make your conclusion strong enough to be memorable to the reader; leave him or her with something to think about.

Student Edition Pages

Practice

Complete an outline like the one below to help you plan your own argument.

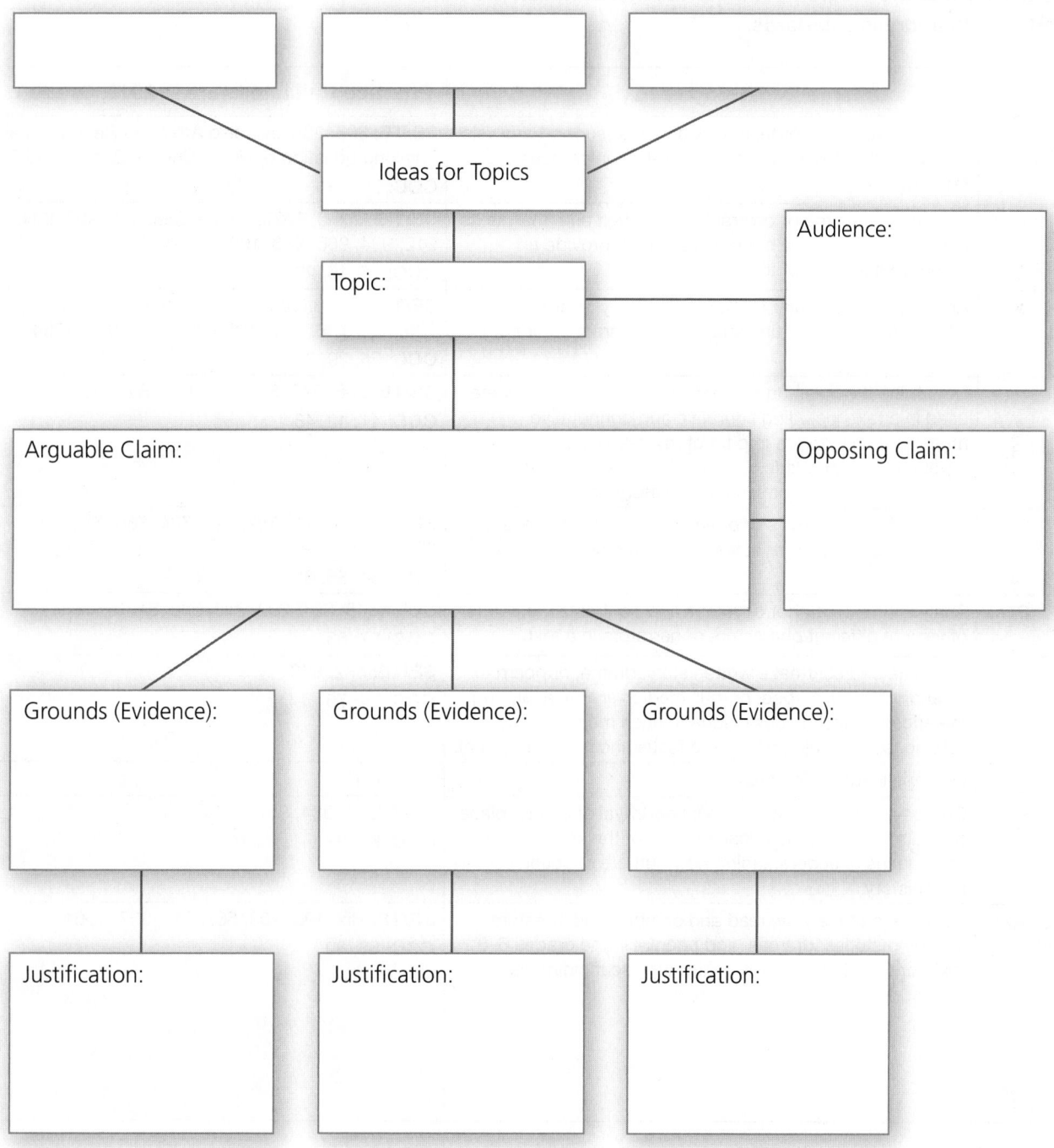

Correlation to Prentice Hall Literature © 2012

The following correlation shows points at which focused, sustained instruction is provided in the Student Edition. The standards are spiraled and revisited throughout the program, and the Teacher's Edition provides further opportunity to address standards.

Key
SE/TE: Student Edition/Teacher's Edition
CCC: Common Core Companion

	Grade 7 Reading Standards for Literature		Prentice Hall Literature © 2012, Grade 7
Key Ideas and Details	**RL.1**	Cite several pieces of textual evidence to support analysis of what the text says explicitly as well as inferences drawn from the text.	**SE/TE:** 308, 336; see also After You Read Critical Thinking question banks in Units 1, 2, 4, 5, and 6. **CCC:** 2, 3, 9
	RL.2	Determine a theme or central idea of a text and analyze its development over the course of the text; provide an objective summary of the text.	**SE/TE:** xlix, 5, 6, 22, 48, 98, 336, 830, 903, 904, 912, 934, 966, 988, 1005, 1034 **CCC:** 15, 16, 22
	RL.3	Analyze how particular elements of a story or drama interact (e.g., how setting shapes the characters or plot).	**SE/TE:** 78, 98, 160, 201, 202, 216, 370, 536, 723, 724, 736, 772, 818, 830, 966, 1006, 1034 **CCC:** 28, 29, 35
Craft and Structure	**RL.4**	Determine the meaning of words and phrases as they are used in a text, including figurative and connotative meanings; analyze the impact of rhymes and other repetitions of sounds (e.g., alliteration) on a specific verse or stanza of a poem or section of a story or drama.	**SE/TE:** 288, 573, 574, 600, 628, 646, 664, 692 **CCC:** 41, 42, 48
	RL.5	Analyze how a drama's or poem's form or structure (e.g., soliloquy, sonnet) contributes to its meaning.	**SE/TE:** 573, 575, 582, 723, 724, 736, 772, 830, 866, 1034 **CCC:** 54, 55, 61
	RL.6	Analyze how an author develops and contrasts the points of view of different characters or narrators in a text.	**SE/TE:** 48, 201, 202, 248, 628, 818 **CCC:** 67, 68
Integration of Knowledge and Ideas	**RL.7**	Compare and contrast a written story, drama, or poem to its audio, filmed, staged, or multimedia version, analyzing the effects of techniques unique to each medium (e.g., lighting, sound, color, or camera focus and angles in a film).	**SE/TE:** 582, 830 **CCC:** 74, 75
	RL.8	(Not applicable to literature)	
	RL.9	Compare and contrast a fictional portrayal of a time, place, or character and a historical account of the same period as a means of understanding how authors of fiction use or alter history.	**SE/TE:** 21, 934, 957 **CCC:** 81, 82
Range of Reading and Level of Text Complexity	**RL.10**	By the end of the year, read and comprehend literature, including stories, dramas, and poems, in the grades 6–8 text complexity band proficiently, with scaffolding as needed at the high end of the range.	**SE/TE:** xlix, 195, 403, 567, 717, 897, 1061 **CCC:** 88, 89

Grade 7 Reading Standards for Informational Text		Prentice Hall Literature © 2012, Grade 7
Key Ideas and Details	**RI.1** Cite several pieces of textual evidence to support analysis of what the text says explicitly as well as inferences drawn from the text.	**SE/TE:** 128, 364; see also After You Read Critical Thinking question banks in Units 1, 3, and 6 **CCC:** 96, 97, 103
	RI.2 Determine two or more central ideas in a text and analyze their development over the course of the text; provide an objective summary of the text.	**SE/TE:** xlix, 5, 7, 48, 128, 420, 440 **CCC:** 109, 110, 116
	RI.3 Analyze the interactions between individuals, events, and ideas in a text (e.g., how ideas influence individuals or events, or how individuals influence ideas or events).	**SE/TE:** 78, 128, 160, 409, 411, 440 **CCC:** 122, 123
Craft and Structure	**RI.4** Determine the meaning of words and phrases as they are used in a text, including figurative, connotative, and technical meanings; analyze the impact of a specific word choice on meaning and tone.	**SE/TE:** 409, 411, 506, 622 **CCC:** 129, 130, 136
	RI.5 Analyze the structure an author uses to organize a text, including how the major sections contribute to the whole and to the development of the ideas.	**SE/TE:** 72, 154, 282, 409, 410, 420, 468, 490, 530, 622, 686, 960 **CCC:** 142, 143
	RI.6 Determine an author's point of view or purpose in a text and analyze how the author distinguishes his or her position from that of others.	**SE/TE:** 48, 154, 409, 410, 440, 468, 812, 862, 1028 **CCC:** 149, 150, 156
Integration of Knowledge and Ideas	**RI.7** Compare and contrast a text to an audio, video, or multimedia version of the text, analyzing each medium's portrayal of the subject (e.g., how the delivery of a speech affects the impact of the words).	**SE/TE:** 420, 439, 440, 459 **CCC:** 162, 163
	RI.8 Trace and evaluate the argument and specific claims in a text, assessing whether the reasoning is sound and the evidence is relevant and sufficient to support the claims.	**SE/TE:** xlix, 462, 490 **CCC:** 169, 170
	RI.9 Analyze how two or more authors writing about the same topic shape their presentations of key information by emphasizing different evidence or advancing different interpretations of facts.	**SE/TE:** 282, 530, 862, 1028 **CCC:** 176, 177
Range of Reading and Level of Text Complexity	**RI.10** 10. By the end of the year, read and comprehend literary nonfiction in the grades 6–8 text complexity band proficiently, with scaffolding as needed at the high end of the range.	**SE/TE:** 195, 403, 567, 717, 897, 1061 **CCC:** 183, 184

Grade 7 Writing Standards		Prentice Hall Literature © 2012, Grade 7
W.1	Write arguments to support claims with clear reasons and relevant evidence.	**SE/TE:** 302, 640, 642, 692, 698, 736, 771, 1006, 1025 **CCC:** 191, 192, 193, 194, 195, 196, 197, 198
W.1.a	Introduce claim(s), acknowledge alternate or opposing claims, and organize the reasons and evidence logically.	**SE/TE:** xlix, 304, 336, 361, 462, 490, 505, 640, 698, 736, 771, 934, 957, 1006, 1025, 1028 **CCC:** 191, 192, 193, 194, 195, 196, 197, 198
W.1.b	Support claim(s) with logical reasoning and relevant evidence, using accurate, credible sources and demonstrating an understanding of the topic or text.	**SE/TE:** xlix, 247, 302, 304, 336, 361, 490, 505, 640, 698, 736, 771, 812, 934, 957, 1006, 1025, 1028 **CCC:** 191, 192, 193, 194, 195, 196, 197, 198
W.1.c	Use words, phrases, and clauses to create cohesion and clarify the relationships among claim(s), reasons, and evidence.	**SE/TE:** 302, 642, 700, 702, 736, 771 **CCC:** 191, 192, 193, 194, 195, 196, 197, 198
W.1.d	Establish and maintain a formal style.	**SE/TE:** 302, 700 **CCC:** 191, 192, 193, 194, 195, 196, 197, 198
W.1.e	Provide a concluding statement or section that follows from and supports the argument presented.	**SE/TE:** xlix, 304, 642, 700, 1028 **CCC:** 191, 192, 193, 194, 195, 196, 197, 198
W.2	Write informative/explanatory texts to examine a topic and convey ideas, concepts, and information through the selection, organization, and analysis of relevant content.	**SE/TE:** 22, 48, 98, 127, 247, 468, 548, 600, 619, 772, 809, 824, 866, 878, 934, 957, 966, 982, 988, 1005, 1040 **CCC:** 202, 203, 204, 205, 206, 207, 208, 209, 210, 211, 212
W.2.a	Introduce a topic clearly, previewing what is to follow; organize ideas, concepts, and information, using strategies such as definition, classification, comparison/contrast, and cause/effect; include formatting (e.g., headings), graphics (e.g., charts, tables), and multimedia when useful to aiding comprehension.	**SE/TE:** 78, 92, 94, 160, 288, 308, 335, 370, 440, 459, 484, 486, 548, 550, 824, 826, 880, 960, 982, 1006, 1025, 1042 **CCC:** 202, 203, 204, 205, 206, 207, 208, 209, 210, 211, 212
W.2.b	Develop the topic with relevant facts, definitions, concrete details, quotations, or other information and examples.	**SE/TE:** 22, 47, 94, 128, 151, 486, 548, 550, 830, 859, 866, 880, 934, 957, 984, 988, 1005, 1006, 1025, 1034, 1042 **CCC:** 202, 203, 204, 205, 206, 207, 208, 209, 210, 211, 212
W.2.c	Use appropriate transitions to create cohesion and clarify the relationships among ideas and concepts.	**SE/TE:** 94, 128, 151, 486, 550, 826, 830, 859, 882, 960, 984, 1044 **CCC:** 202, 203, 204, 205, 206, 207, 208, 209, 210, 211, 212
W.2.d	Use precise language and domain-specific vocabulary to inform about or explain the topic.	**SE/TE:** 48, 69, 92, 216, 247, 484, 486, 548, 600, 619, 622 **CCC:** 202, 203, 204, 205, 206, 207, 208, 209, 210, 211, 212
W.2.e	Establish and maintain a formal style.	**SE/TE:** 92, 216, 247, 308, 335, 548, 552, 984 **CCC:** 202, 203, 204, 205, 206, 207, 208, 209, 210, 211, 212
W.2.f	Provide a concluding statement or section that follows from and supports the information or explanation presented.	**SE/TE:** 247, 288, 984, 988, 1005, 1006, 1025, 1042 **CCC:** 202, 203, 204, 205, 206, 207, 208, 209, 210, 211, 212
W.3	Write narratives to develop real or imagined experiences or events using effective technique, relevant descriptive details, and well-structured event sequences.	**SE/TE:** 176, 178, 308, 335, 384, 912, 988, 1005 **CCC:** 214, 215, 216, 217, 218, 219, 220, 221, 222, 223, 224

(left margin) Text Types and Purposes

Text Types and Purposes	W.3.a	Engage and orient the reader by establishing a context and point of view and introducing a narrator and/or characters; organize an event sequence that unfolds naturally and logically.	**SE/TE:** 176, 178, 180, 248, 279, 384, 386, 912, 933, 988, 1005 **CCC:** 214, 215, 216, 217, 218, 219, 220, 221, 222, 223, 224
	W.3.b	Use narrative techniques, such as dialogue, pacing, and description, to develop experiences, events, and/or characters.	**SE/TE:** 180, 248, 279, 388, 912, 933, 988, 1005 **CCC:** 214, 215, 216, 217, 218, 219, 220, 221, 222, 223, 224
	W.3.c	Use a variety of transition words, phrases, and clauses to convey sequence and signal shifts from one time frame or setting to another.	**SE/TE:** 180, 386 **CCC:** 214, 215, 216, 217, 218, 219, 220, 221, 222, 223, 224
	W.3.d	Use precise words and phrases, relevant descriptive details, and sensory language to capture the action and convey experiences and events.	**SE/TE:** 178, 180, 386, 388, 506, 527 **CCC:** 214, 215, 216, 217, 218, 219, 220, 221, 222, 223, 224
	W.3.e	Provide a conclusion that follows from and reflects on the narrated experiences or events.	**SE/TE:** 178, 308, 335 **CCC:** 214, 215, 216, 217, 218, 219, 220, 221, 222, 223, 224
Production and Distribution of Writing	W.4	Produce clear and coherent writing in which the development, organization, and style are appropriate to task, purpose, and audience.	**SE/TE:** 468, 484, 506, 527, 550, 552, 582, 599, 880, 982 **CCC:** 225, 226
	W.5	With some guidance and support from peers and adults, develop and strengthen writing as needed by planning, revising, editing, rewriting, or trying a new approach, focusing on how well purpose and audience have been addressed.	**SE/TE:** 92, 94, 180, 388, 484, 527, 552, 1044 **CCC:** 232, 233, 239
	W.6	Use technology, including the Internet, to produce and publish writing and link to and cite sources as well as to interact and collaborate with others, including linking to and citing sources.	**SE/TE:** 582, 599, 664, 683, 826, 828, 830, 859, 986 **CCC:** 245, 246, 252
Research to Build and Present Knowledge	W.7	Conduct short research projects to answer a question, drawing on several sources and generating additional related, focused questions for further research and investigation.	**SE/TE:** 48, 69, 248, 279, 336, 361, 600, 619, 640, 664, 683, 736, 771, 824, 878, 1040, 1042 **CCC:** 258, 259, 262
	W.8	Gather relevant information from multiple print and digital sources, using search terms effectively; assess the credibility and accuracy of each source; and quote or paraphrase the data and conclusions of others while avoiding plagiarism and following a standard format for citation.	**SE/TE:** 506, 824, 1040, 1044, 1048 **CCC:** 265, 266, 267, 268, 269, 270, 271, 272, 273, 274, 275, 276
	W.9	Draw evidence from literary or informational texts to support analysis, reflection, and research.	**SE/TE:** 302, 304, 420, 439, 536, 628, 772, 809, 812, 818, 859, 1042 **CCC:** 279, 280, 283, 284
	W.9.a	Apply grade 7 Reading standards to literature (e.g., "Compare and contrast a fictional portrayal of a time, place, or character and a historical account of the same period as a means of understanding how authors of fiction use or alter history.").	**SE/TE:** 304, 400, 564, 646, 663, 714, 818, 830, 859, 1058 **CCC:** 279, 280, 283, 284
	W.9.b	Apply grade 7 Reading standards to literary nonfiction (e.g., "Trace and evaluate the argument and specific claims in a text, assessing whether the reasoning is sound and the evidence is relevant and sufficient to support the claims.").	**SE/TE:** 439, 1058 **CCC:** 279, 280, 283, 284

Grade 7 Writing Standards			Prentice Hall Literature © 2012, Grade 7
Range of Writing	W.10	Write routinely over extended time frames (time for research, reflection, and revision) and shorter time frames (a single sitting or a day or two) for a range of discipline-specific tasks, purposes, and audiences.	**SE/TE:** 72, 154, 619; also see these features in Units 1, 2, 3, 4, 5, and 6: Integrated Language Skills; Reading for Information: Comparing Informational Texts; Comparing Literary Works; Writing Workshops. **CCC:** 287, 288, 289, 290, 293, 294, 295, 296

Grade 7 Speaking and Listening Standards			Prentice Hall Literature © 2012, Grade 7
Comprehension and Collaboration	SL.1	Engage effectively in a range of collaborative discussions (one-on-one, in groups, and teacher-led) with diverse partners on grade 7 topics, texts, and issues, building on others' ideas and expressing their own clearly.	**SE/TE:** 3, 127, 199, 247, 571, 721, 901 **CCC:** 298, 299, 300, 301, 302, 303, 304
	SL.1.a	Come to discussions prepared, having read or researched material under study; explicitly draw on that preparation by referring to evidence on the topic, text, or issue to probe and reflect on ideas under discussion.	**SE/TE:** 98, 127, 216, 888, 912, 933 **CCC:** 298, 299, 300, 301, 302, 303, 304
	SL.1.b	Follow rules for collegial discussions, track progress toward specific goals and deadlines, and define individual roles as needed.	**SE/TE:** 98, 127, 407, 888 **CCC:** 298, 299, 300, 301, 302, 303, 304
	SL.1.c	Pose questions that elicit elaboration, and respond to others' questions and comments with relevant observations and ideas that bring the discussion back on topic as needed.	**SE/TE:** 98, 127, 128, 151, 664, 683, 888, 912, 933 **CCC:** 298, 299, 300, 301, 302, 303, 304
	SL.1.d	Acknowledge new information expressed by others and, when warranted, modify their own views.	**SE/TE:** 98, 127, 582, 599 **CCC:** 298, 299, 300, 301, 302, 303, 304
	SL.2	Analyze the main ideas and supporting details presented in diverse media and formats (e.g., visually, quantitatively, orally) and explain how the ideas clarify a topic, text, or issue under study.	**SE/TE:** 420, 439, 558, 708 **CCC:** 305, 306
	SL.3	Delineate a speaker's argument and specific claims, evaluating the soundness of the reasoning and the relevance and sufficiency of the evidence.	**TE/SE:** 216, 247, 558, 708 **CCC:** 309, 310, 313
Presentation of Knowledge and Ideas	SL.4	Present claims and findings, emphasizing salient points in a focused, coherent manner with pertinent descriptions, facts, details, and examples; use appropriate eye contact, adequate volume, and clear pronunciation.	**SE/TE:** 186, 394, 420, 439, 394, 490, 505, 646, 663, 934, 957, 988, 1005, 1006, 1025, 1052 **CCC:** 316, 317, 320
	SL.5	Include multimedia components and visual displays in presentations to clarify claims and findings and emphasize salient points.	**SE/TE:** 336, 361, 600, 619, 826, 1052 **CCC:** 323, 324
	SL.6	Adapt speech to a variety of contexts and tasks, demonstrating command of formal English when indicated or appropriate.	**SE/TE:** 22, 47, 308, 335, 646, 663, 772, 809, 1052 **CCC:** 325, 326, 329

Ⓒ Grade 7 Language Standards			Prentice Hall Literature © 2012, Grade 7
Conventions of Standard English	L.1	Demonstrate command of the conventions of standard English grammar and usage when writing or speaking.	**SE/TE:** 128, 151, 247, 248, 279, 336, 361, 420, 439, 736, 771, 772, 809, 826, 882, 1044 **CCC:** 333, 334, 335, 336, 337, 338
	L.1.a	Explain the function of phrases and clauses in general and their function in specific sentences.	**SE/TE:** 440, 459, 582, 599, 600, 619, 646, 663 **CCC:** 333, 334
	L.1.b	Choose among simple, compound, complex, and compound-complex sentences to signal differing relationships among ideas.	**SE/TE:** 646, 663, 664, 683 **CCC:** 335, 336
	L.1.c	Place phrases and clauses within a sentence, recognizing and correcting misplaced and dangling modifiers.	**SE/TE:** 552, 642 **CCC:** 337, 338
	L.2	Demonstrate command of the conventions of standard English capitalization, punctuation, and spelling when writing.	**SE/TE:** 22, 47, 702, 736, 771, 772, 809, 830, 859, 912, 933, 934, 957, 988, 1005, 1006, 1025 **CCC:** 339, 340, 341, 342
	L.2.a	Use a comma to separate coordinate adjectives (e.g., *It was a fascinating, enjoyable movie,* but not *He wore an old[,] green shirt*).	**SE/TE:** 308, 335, 934, 957, 984 **CCC:** 339, 340
	L.2.b	Spell correctly.	**SE/TE:** 96, 306, 488, 644, 884, 986 **CCC:** 341, 342
Knowledge of Language	L.3	Use knowledge of language and its conventions when writing, speaking, reading, or listening.	**SE/TE:** 486, 886 **CCC:** 343, 344
	L.3.a	Choose language that expresses ideas precisely and concisely, recognizing and eliminating wordiness and redundancy.	**SE/TE:** 94, 486, 552, 984, 1006, 1025 **CCC:** 343, 344
Vocabulary Acquisition and Use	L.4	Determine or clarify the meaning of unknown and multiple-meaning words and phrases based on grade 7 reading and content, choosing flexibly from a range of strategies.	**SE/TE:** 22, 48, 556 **CCC:** 345, 346, 347, 348, 349, 350, 351, 352
	L.4.a	Use context (e.g., the overall meaning of a sentence or paragraph; a word's position or function in a sentence) as a clue to the meaning of a word or phrase.	**SE/TE:** 22, 48, 72, 556 **CCC:** 345, 346
	L.4.b	Use common, grade-appropriate Greek or Latin affixes and roots as clues to the meaning of a word (e.g., *belligerent, bellicose, rebel*).	**SE/TE:** 98, 127, 216, 248, 279, 308, 335, 336, 361, 392, 420, 439, 462, 490, 505, 506, 530, 736, 772, 809, 830, 859, 912, 933, 934, 1006 **CCC:** 347, 348
	L.4.c	Consult general and specialized reference materials (e.g., dictionaries, glossaries, thesauruses), both print and digital, to find the pronunciation of a word or determine or clarify its precise meaning or its part of speech.	**SE/TE:** 184, 364, 392, 556, 646, 663, 706, 886, 960 **CCC:** 349, 350
	L.4.d	Verify the preliminary determination of the meaning of a word or phrase (e.g., by checking the inferred meaning in context or in a dictionary).	**SE/TE:** 184, 407, 530, 556, 886 **CCC:** 351, 352
	L.5	Demonstrate understanding of figurative language, word relationships, and nuances in word meanings.	**SE/TE:** 22, 48, 1050 **CCC:** 353, 354, 355, 356, 357, 358

		Grade 7 Language Standards	Prentice Hall Literature © 2012, Grade 7
Vocabulary Acquisition and Use	L.5.a	Interpret figures of speech (e.g., literary, biblical, and mythological allusions) in context.	**SE/TE:** 392, 1050 **CCC:** 353, 354
	L.5.b	Use the relationship between particular words (e.g., synonym/antonym, analogy) to better understand each of the words.	**SE/TE:** 22, 47, 48, 69, 440, 646, 663, 664, 988, 1005, 1050 **CCC:** 355, 356
	L.5.c	Distinguish among the connotations (associations) of words with similar denotations (definitions) (e.g., *refined, respectful, polite, diplomatic, condescending*).	**SE/TE:** 302, 706 **CCC:** 357, 358
	L.6	Acquire and use accurately grade-appropriate general academic and domain-specific words and phrases; gather vocabulary knowledge when considering a word or phrase important to comprehension or expression.	**SE/TE:** xlix, 3, 22, 47, 98, 127, 128, 151, 154, 199, 216, 248, 279, 282, 308, 335, 336, 361, 364, 407, 440, 459, 462, 490, 505, 506, 530, 571, 582, 599, 600, 622, 664, 686, 721, 736, 772, 809, 812, 862, 901, 960, 988, 1005 **CCC:** 359, 360

The following skills are particularly likely to require continued attention in higher grades as they are applied to increasingly sophisticated writing and speaking.

		Grade 7 Language Progressive Skills	Prentice Hall Literature © 2012, Grade 7
Conventions of Standard English	L.6.1.c	Recognize and correct inappropriate shifts in pronoun number and person.	151, 181
	L.5.1.d	Recognize and correct inappropriate shifts in verb tense.	305, 526, 883
	L.6.1.d	Recognize and correct vague pronouns (i.e., ones with unclear or ambiguous antecedents).	181
	L.6.1.e	Recognize variations from standard English in their own and others' writing and speaking, and identify and use strategies to improve expression in conventional language.	700, 808, 984
	L.3.1.f	Ensure subject-verb and pronoun-antecedent agreement.	526, 883
	L.4.1.f	Produce complete sentences, recognizing and correcting inappropriate fragments and run-ons.	489, 682, 703
	L.4.1.g	Correctly use frequently confused words (e.g., *to/too/two; there/their*).	97, 827, 829
	L.5.2.a	Use punctuation to separate items in a series.	956, 985
	L.6.2.a	Use punctuation (commas, parentheses, dashes) to set off nonrestrictive/parenthetical elements.	618, 705, 932
Knowledge of Language	L.3.3.a	Choose words and phrases for effect.	69, 93, 507, 700, 770
	L.6.3.a	Vary sentence patterns for meaning, reader/listener interest, and style.	93, 487, 552, 702
	L.4.3.b	Choose punctuation for effect.	599, 858
	L.6.3.b	Maintain consistency in style and tone.	984

Key Features of the Standards

The following summary of key features is from the Introduction to the Common Core State Standards for English Language Arts © 2010, National Governors Association for Best Practices and Council of Chief State School Officers. All rights reserved.

Reading
Text Complexity and the Growth of Comprehension

The Reading standards place equal emphasis on the sophistication of what students read and the skill with which they read. Standard 10 defines a grade-by-grade "staircase" of increasing text complexity that rises from beginning reading to the college and career readiness level. Whatever they are reading, students must also show a steadily growing ability to discern more from and make fuller use of text, including making an increasing number of connections among ideas and between texts, considering a wider range of textual evidence, and becoming more sensitive to inconsistencies, ambiguities, and poor reasoning in texts.

Writing
Text Types, Responding to Reading, and Research

The Standards acknowledge the fact that whereas some writing skills, such as the ability to plan, revise, edit, and publish, are applicable to many types of writing, other skills are more properly defined in terms of specific writing types: arguments, informative/explanatory texts, and narratives. Standard 9 stresses the importance of the writing-reading connection by requiring students to draw upon and write about evidence from literary and informational texts. Because of the centrality of writing to most forms of inquiry, research standards are prominently included in this strand, though skills important to research are infused throughout the document.

Speaking and Listening
Flexible Communication and Collaboration

Including but not limited to skills necessary for formal presentations, the Speaking and Listening standards require students to develop a range of broadly useful oral communication and interpersonal skills. Students must learn to work together, express and listen carefully to ideas, integrate information from oral, visual, quantitative, and media sources, evaluate what they hear, use media and visual displays strategically to help achieve communicative purposes, and adapt speech to context and task.

Language
Conventions, Effective Use, and Vocabulary

The Language standards include the essential "rules" of standard written and spoken English, but they also approach language as a matter of craft and informed choice among alternatives. The vocabulary standards focus on understanding words and phrases, their relationships, and their nuances and on acquiring new vocabulary, particularly general academic and domain-specific words and phrases.

Introductory Unit	Standards Addressed
• Building Academic Vocabulary	Language 6
• Writing an Objective Summary	Informational Text 2, Literature 2
• Comprehending Complex Texts	Literature 10
• Analyzing Arguments	Informational Text 8, Writing 1.a, Writing 1.b, Writing 1.e, Language 6

	Literary Analysis Workshop	Writing Workshop	Vocabulary Workshop
Unit 1	Literary Analysis Workshop: **Fiction and Nonfiction**	**Informative Text: Descriptive Essay,** pp. 92–97 **Work in Progress:** pp. 47, 69 **Narrative Text: Autobiographical Narrative,** pp. 176–183 **Work in Progress:** pp. 127, 151	**Using a Dictionary and Thesaurus,** pp. 184–185
Unit 2	Literary Analysis Workshop: **Short Stories**	**Argument: Response to Literature,** pp. 302–307 **Work in Progress:** pp. 247, 279 **Narrative Text: Short Story,** pp. 384–391 **Work in Progress:** pp. 335, 361	**Word Origins,** pp. 392–393
Unit 3	Literary Analysis Workshop: **Types of Nonfiction**	**Explanatory Text: How-to Essay,** pp. 484–489 **Work in Progress:** pp. 439, 459 **Informative Text: Comparison-and-Contrast Essay,** pp. 548–555 **Work in Progress:** pp. 505, 527	**Words With Multiple Meanings,** pp. 556–557
Unit 4	Literary Analysis Workshop: **Poetry**	**Argument: Problem-and-Solution,** pp. 640–645 **Work in Progress:** pp. 600, 619 **Argument: Persuasive Essay,** pp. 698–705 **Work in Progress:** pp. 663, 683	**Connotation and Denotation,** pp. 706–707
Unit 5	Literary Analysis Workshop: **Drama**	**Informative Text: Multimedia Report,** pp. 824–829 **Work in Progress:** p. 809 **Explanatory Text: Cause-and-Effect Essay** pp. 878–885 **Work in Progress:** p. 859	**Borrowed and Foreign Words,** pp. 886–887
Unit 6	Literary Analysis Workshop: **Themes in the Oral Tradition**	**Informative Text: Business Letter,** pp. 982–987 **Work in Progress:** pp. 933, 957 **Informative Text: Research Report,** pp. 1040–1049 **Work in Progress:** pp. 1005, 1025	**Figurative Language,** pp. 1050–1051

Ⓒ Common Core State Standards appear in red throughout the Skills Navigator.

Communications Workshop	Independent Reading	Assessment Practice
Delivering a Narrative Presentation, pp. 186–187	**Independent Reading,** pp. 194–195	**Test Practice: Cumulative Review,** pp. 188–191 **Performance Tasks,** pp. 192–193
Delivering an Oral Summary, pp. 394–395	**Independent Reading,** pp. 402–403	**Test Practice: Cumulative Review,** pp. 396–399 **Performance Tasks,** pp. 400–401
Evaluating a Persuasive Presentation, pp. 558–559	**Independent Reading,** pp. 566–567	**Test Practice: Cumulative Review,** pp. 560–563 **Performance Tasks,** pp. 564–565
Evaluating Media Messages and Advertisements, pp. 708–709	**Independent Reading,** pp. 716–717	**Test Practice: Cumulative Review,** pp. 710–713 **Performance Tasks,** pp. 714–715
Conducting an Interview, pp. 888–889	**Independent Reading,** pp. 896–897	**Test Practice: Cumulative Review,** pp. 890–893 **Performance Tasks,** pp. 894–895
Research Presentation, pp. 1052–1053	**Independent Reading,** pp. 1060–1061	**Test Practice: Cumulative Review,** pp. 1054–1057 **Performance Tasks,** pp. 1058–1059

		Selection	Page	Reading Skill	Literary Analysis	Word Study
LITERARY ANALYSIS WORKSHOP		*from* **The Tale of the Mandarin Ducks** © Katherine Paterson	9–10		**Determining Theme in Fiction,** p. 6 **RL.2** **Determining Central Ideas in Nonfiction,** p. 7 **RI.2** **Close Read: Theme in Fiction,** pp. 8–17 **Close Read: Central Ideas in Nonfiction,** pp. 18–20	**Introducing the Big Question,** pp. 2–3 **L.6**
		The Three-Century Woman Richard Peck	11–17			
		from **The Great Fire** Jim Murphy ©	19			
		The Fall of the Hindenburg Michael Morrison	20			
READING FOCUS CONTEXT CLUES	MA MC	**Papa's Parrot** Cynthia Rylant	26	**Use Context Clues,** pp. 23, 28, 31, 35, 37, 43, 45; **UR** pp. 35, 53 **L.4, L.4.a**	**Narrative Text,** pp. 23, 27, 28, 31, 37, 38, 40, 41, 43, 45; **UR** pp. 36, 54 Spiral Review, pp. 30, 40	**Latin prefix** *re-,* pp. 24, 31 **Latin prefix** *in-,* pp. 32, 45
	MA	**mk** Jean Fritz	34			
	MA	*from* **An American Childhood** Annie Dillard	52	**Reread and Read Ahead to Confirm the Meaning: Using Context Clues,** pp. 49, 55, 57, 59, 63, 67; **UR** pp. 74, 92	**Point of View,** pp. 49, 53, 58, 59, 65, 66, 67; **UR** pp. 75, 93 **RL.6, RI.6** Spiral Review, pp. 57, 66	**Latin prefix** *trans-,* pp. 50, 59 **Latin prefix** *ac-,* pp. 60, 67
	MC	**The Luckiest Time of All** Lucille Clifton	62			
		Reading for Information Atlas/Public Document	72	**Locate Types of Information,** pp. 72–76 **RI.5**		
		Comparing Literary Works *from* **Barrio Boy** Ernesto Galarza	80		**Comparing Literary Works: Fiction and Nonfiction,** pp. 78–79, 91; **UR** p. 113 **RL.3, RI.3** Spiral Review, pp. 84, 90	
		A Day's Wait Ernest Hemingway	86			
READING FOCUS AUTHOR'S PURPOSE	MA MC	**All Summer in a Day** Ray Bradbury	102	**Recognize Details That Indicate the Author's Purpose,** pp. 99, 103, 107, 110, 111, 116, 118, 122, 124, 125; **UR** pp. 139, 157	**Setting,** pp. 99, 103, 105, 109, 111, 118, 121, 125; **UR** pp. 140, 158 **RL.3** Spiral Review, pp. 109, 120	**Latin root** *-vit-* **and** *-viv-,* pp. 100, 111 **Latin root** *-manere-,* pp. 112, 125 **L.4.b**
	MC	**Suzy and Leah** Jane Yolen	114			
	MA	**My First Free Summer** Julia Alvarez	132	**Use Background Information to Determine the Author's Purpose,** pp. 129, 133, 135, 136, 137, 141, 142, 144, 146, 149; **UR** pp. 178, 196 **RI.1**	**Historical Context,** pp. 129, 132, 134, 137, 144, 149; **UR** pp. 179, 197 **RI.3** Spiral Review, pp. 136, 148	**Latin root** *-dict-,* pp. 130, 137 **Latin root** *-sper-* **and** *-spes-,* pp. 138, 149
	MC	*from* **Angela's Ashes** Frank McCourt	140			
		Reading for Information Application/Contract	154	**Analyze Structure and Purpose,** p. 154 **RI.5, RI.6**		
		Comparing Literary Works **The Night the Bed Fell** James Thurber	162		**Comparing Literary Works:** Characters, pp. 160, 163, 165, 166, 167, 170, 171, 172, 173, 175; **UR** p. 217 **RL.3, RI.3** Spiral Review, pp. 167, 170	
		Stolen Day Sherwood Anderson	168			

Key: UR: *Unit Resources*   **MA:** More Accessible   **MC:** More Challenging   © Indicates an Exemplar Text

Writing	Conventions	Extension Activity	Assessment
Informative Text: Compare-and-Contrast Essay, p. 47; **UR** p. 58 **W.2.b** **Writing Workshop: Work in Progress:** Prewriting for Descriptive Essay, p. 47	**Common and Proper Nouns,** p. 46; **UR** p. 57 **L.2**	• **Speaking and Listening: Dramatic Reading,** p. 47; **UR** p. 59 **SL.6**	Selection Tests, UR pp. 42–47, 63–68
Explanatory Text: Description That Includes Hyperbole, p. 69; **UR** p. 97 **W.2.d** **Writing Workshop: Work in Progress:** Prewriting for Description, p. 69	**Possessive Nouns,** p. 68; **UR** p. 96	• **Research and Technology: Biographical Report,** p. 69; **UR** p. 98 **W.7**	**Test Practice: Reading: Context Clues,** pp. 70–71 **Selection Tests, UR** pp. 81–86, 102–107
Timed Writing: Informative Text: Letter, p. 77 **W.2**			
Timed Writing: Explanatory Text: Essay, p. 91; **UR** p. 115 **W.2.a**			Selection Tests, UR pp. 119–124
Informative Text: News Report, p. 127; **UR** p. 162 **W.2** **Writing Workshop: Work in Progress:** Prewriting for Narration, p. 127	**Personal Pronouns,** p. 126; **UR** p. 161	• **Speaking and Listening:** Discussion, p. 127; **UR** p. 163 **SL.1.a–d**	Selection Tests, UR pp. 146–151, 167–172
Informative Text: Letter, p. 151; **UR** p. 201 **W.2.b** **Writing Workshop: Work in Progress:** Prewriting for Autobiography, p. 151	**Possessive Pronouns,** p. 150; **UR** p. 200 **L.1**	• **Speaking and Listening:** Interview, p. 151; **UR** p. 202 **SL.1.c**	**Test Practice: Reading: Author's Purpose,** pp. 152–153 **Selection Tests, UR** pp. 185–190, 206–211
Timed Writing: Explanatory Text: Chart, p. 159 **W.2.b**			
Timed Writing: Explanatory Text: Essay p. 175; **UR** p. 219 **W.2.a**			Selection Tests, UR pp. 223–228 **Cumulative Review,** pp. 188–191 **Performance Tasks,** pp. 192–193

All selections are supported in the *Reader's Notebooks*.

	Selection	Page	Reading Skill	Literary Analysis	Word Study
LITERARY ANALYSIS WORKSHOP	**The Dinner Party** Mona Gardner	205		**Analyzing How Elements Interact,** p. 202–203 **RL.3, RL.6**	**Introducing the Big Question,** pp. 198–199 **L.6**
	The Treasure of Lemon Brown Walter Dean Myers	205		**Close Read: Analyzing Story Elements,** p. 204–205	
READING FOCUS PREDICTING	MA — **The Bear Boy** Joseph Bruchac	220	**Use Prior Knowledge to Make Predictions,** pp. 217, 221, 225, 230, 233, 239, 245; **UR** pp. 28, 46	**Plot,** pp. 217, 222, 223, 224, 225, 229, 232, 235, 236, 238, 240, 241, 242, 243, 245; **UR** pp. 29, 47 **RL.3** Spiral Review, p. 241	**Latin suffix -ance,** pp. 218, 225 **Latin suffix -tion,** pp. 226, 245 **L.4.b**
	MC — **Rikki-tikki-tavi** Rudyard Kipling	228			
	MA — *from* **Letters from Rifka** Karen Hesse	252	**Read Ahead to Verify Predictions,** pp. 249, 253, 257, 263, 266, 270, 272, 274, 275, 277; **UR** pp. 67, 85	**Character,** pp. 249, 253, 257, 261, 262, 265, 267, 277; **UR** pp. 68, 86 **RL.6** Spiral Review, pp. 255, 270	**Latin root -tract-,** pp. 250, 257 **Latin root -spir-,** pp. 258, 277 **L.4.b**
	MC — **Two Kinds** Amy Tan	260			
	Reading for Information Magazine Article/ Encyclopedia Entry	282	**Understand Text Structure and Purpose,** p. 282 **RI.5, RI.9**		
	Comparing Literary Works **Seventh Grade** Gary Soto	290		**Comparing Literary Works: Comparing Idioms,** pp. 288, 292, 295, 299, 301; **UR** p. 106 **RL.4** Spiral Review, pp. 295, 297	
	Melting Pot Anna Quindlen	296			
READING FOCUS MAKING INFERENCES	MA — **The Third Wish** Joan Aiken	312	**Recognize Details to Make Inferences,** pp. 309, 315, 318, 319, 322, 324, 327, 329, 330, 333; **UR** pp. 131, 149 **RL.1** Spiral Review, pp. 314, 328	**Conflict and Resolution,** pp. 309, 312, 315, 317, 319, 323, 325, 330, 333; **UR** pp. 132, 150	**Latin prefix mal-,** pp. 310, 319 **Latin prefix per-,** pp. 320, 333 **L.4.b**
	MC — **Amigo Brothers** Piri Thomas	322			
	MA — **Zoo** Edward Hoch	340	**Read Between the Lines by Asking Questions to Make Inferences,** pp. 337, 341, 343, 348, 349, 352, 358, 359; **UR** pp. 170, 188 **RL.1**	**Theme,** pp. 337, 341, 343, 351, 357, 359; **UR** pp. 171, 189 **RL.2** Spiral Review, pp. 342, 353	**Latin suffix -ment,** pp. 338, 343 **Latin suffix -ious,** pp. 344, 359 **L.4.b**
	MC — **Ribbons** Laurence Yep	346			
	Reading for Information Government Publication/ Web Site	364	**Connecting Ideas to Make Inferences and Generalizations,** p. 364 **RI.1**		
	Comparing Literary Works **After Twenty Years** O. Henry	372		**Comparing Literary Works: Irony,** pp. 370, 374, 375, 377, 379, 380, 381, 383; **UR** p. 209 **RL.3** Spiral Review, p. 377	
	He—y, Come on O—ut! Shinichi Hoshi	378			

Key: UR: *Unit Resources* **MA:** More Accessible **MC:** More Challenging Ⓔ Indicates an Exemplar Text

Writing	Conventions	Extension Activity	Assessment
Informative Text: Informative Article, p. 247; **UR** p. 51 **W.1.b, W.2, W.2.d** **Writing Workshop: Work in Progress:** Preview for Response to Literature, p. 247	**Verbs,** p. 246; **UR** p. 50 **L.1**	• **Speaking and Listening: Informal Debate,** p. 247; **UR** p. 52 **SL.1, SL.3**	**Selection Tests, UR** pp. 35–40, 56–61
Narrative Text: Journal Entry, p. 279; **UR** p. 90 **W.3.a, W.3.b** **Writing Workshop: Work in Progress:** Prewriting for Response to Literature, p. 279	**The Principal Parts of Verbs,** p. 278; **UR** p. 89 **L.1**	• **Research and Technology: Outline,** p. 279; **UR** p. 91 **W.7**	**Test Practice: Reading,** pp. 280–281 **Selection Tests, UR** pp. 74–79, 95–100
Timed Writing: Informative Text: Description, p. 287 **W.2.b**			
Timed Writing: Explanatory Text: Essay, p. 301; **UR** p. 108 **W.2.a**			**Selection Tests, UR** pp. 112–117
Narrative Text: Anecdote, p. 335; **UR** p. 154 **W.3, W.3.e** **Writing Workshop: Work in Progress:** Prewriting for Narration p. 335	**Adjectives,** p. 334; **UR** p. 153 **L.2.a**	• **Speaking and Listening: News Story,** p. 335, **UR** p. 155 **SL.6; W.2.a, W.2.e**	**Selection Tests, UR** pp. 139–143, 159–164
Argument: Letter to the Editor, p. 361; **UR** p. 193 **W.1.a, W.1.b** **Writing Workshop: Work in Progress:** Prewriting for Narration p. 361	**Adverbs,** p. 360; **UR** p. 192 **L.1**	• **Research and Technology: Poster,** p. 361; **UR** p. 194 **W.7**	**Test Practice: Reading,** pp. 362–363 **Selection Tests, UR** pp. 177–182, 198–203
Timed Writing: Explanatory Text: Directions, p. 369 **W.2**			
Timed Writing: Explanatory Text: Essay, p. 383; **UR** p. 211 **W.2.a**			**Selection Tests, UR** pp. 215–220 **Cumulative Review,** pp. 396–399 **Performance Tasks,** pp. 400–401

All selections are supported in the *Reader's Notebooks*.

		Selection	Page	Reading Skill	Literary Analysis	Word Study
LITERARY ANALYSIS WORKSHOP		*from* Freedom Walkers: The Story of the Montgomery Bus Boycott Russell Freedman ©	413		**Analyzing Structure in Literary Nonfiction,** p. 410 **RI.5, RI.6** **Analyzing Relationships in Literary Nonfiction,** p. 411 **RI.3, RI.4** **Close Read: Determining Author's Purpose,** pp. 412–419	**Introducing the Big Question,** pp. 406–407 **L.4.d, L.6**
		What Makes a Rembrandt a Rembrandt? Richard Mühlberger	415			
READING FOCUS MAIN IDEA	MA	**Life Without Gravity** Robert Zimmerman	424	**Adjust Your Reading Rate to Recognize the Main Idea,** pp. 421, 426, 429, 433, 436, 437; **UR** pp. 28, 46 **RI.2**	**Expository Essay,** pp. 421, 425, 429, 432, 437; **UR** pp. 29, 47 **RI.5** Spiral Review, p. 425, 433	**Old English suffix -ness,** pp. 422, 429 **Latin suffix -able,** pp. 430, 437 **L.4.b**
	MC	**Conversational Ballgames** Nancy Masterson Sakamoto	432			
	MA	**I Am a Native of North America** Chief Dan George	444	**Make Connections to Identify Main Idea,** pp. 441, 447, 449, 454, 457; **UR** pp. 67, 85 **RI.2**	**Reflective Essay,** pp. 441, 444, 447, 449, 457; **UR** pp. 68, 86 **RI.3, RI.6** Spiral Review, pp. 446, 456	**Latin root -just-,** pp. 442, 449 **Latin root -rupt-,** pp. 450, 457
	MC	**Volar: To Fly** Judith Ortiz Cofer	452			
		Reading for Information Textbook Article/Magazine Article	462	**Analyze Author's Argument,** p. 462 **RI.8**		
		Comparing Literary Works **A Special Gift—The Legacy of "Snowflake" Bentley** Barbara Eaglesham	470		**Comparing Literary Works: Comparing Biography and Autobiography,** pp. 468, 472, 476, 478, 479, 481, 482, 483; **UR** p. 106 **RI.5, RI.6** Spiral Review, pp. 471, 476	
		No Gumption Russell Baker	474			
READING FOCUS FACT AND OPINION	MA	**All Together Now** Barbara Jordan	494	**Classify Fact and Opinion by Recognizing Clues That Indicate an Opinion,** pp. 491, 495, 497, 501, 503; **UR** pp. 132, 150	**Persuasive Essay,** pp. 495, 497, 503; **UR** pp. 133, 151 **RI.8** Spiral Review, pp. 495	**Latin root -leg-,** pp. 492, 497 **Latin root -peti-,** pp. 498, 503 **L.4.b**
	MC	**The Eternal Frontier** Louis L'Amour	500			
	MA	**The Real Story of a Cowboy's Life** Geoffrey C. Ward	510	**Classifying Fact and Opinion by Using Resources to Check Facts,** pp. 507, 511, 515, 519, 522, 525; **UR** pp. 171, 189	**Word Choice and Diction,** pp. 507, 512, 515, 522, 524, 525; **UR** pp. 172, 190 **RI.4** Spiral Review, pp. 519	**Latin root -vers-,** pp. 508, 515 **Latin root -sol-,** pp. 516, 525 **L.4.b**
	MC	**Rattlesnake Hunt** Marjorie Kinnan Rawlings	518			
		Reading for Information Instruction Manual/Signs	530	**Structure and Purpose,** p. 530 **RI.5, RI.9**		
		Comparing Literary Works **Alligator** Bailey White	538		**Comparing Literary Works: Humor,** pp. 536, 540, 541, 547; **UR** p. 210 **RL.3** Spiral Review, p. 540, 544	
		The Cremation of Sam McGee Robert Service	542			

Key: UR: *Unit Resources*   **MA:** More Accessible   **MC:** More Challenging   © Indicates an Exemplar Text

Writing	Conventions	Extension Activity	Assessment
Explanatory Text: Analogy, p. 439; **UR** p. 51 **W.9, W.9.b** **Writing Workshop: Work in Progress:** Prewriting for Exposition, p. 439	**Conjunctions,** p.438; **UR** p. 50 **L.1**	• **Speaking and Listening: Oral Summary,** p. 439; **UR** p. 52 **SL.2, SL.4**	**Selection Tests,** pp. 35–40, 56–61
Informative Text: Outline, p. 459; **UR** p. 90 **W.2.a** **Writing Workshop: Work in Progress:** Prewriting for Exposition, p. 459	**Prepositions and Prepositional Phrases,** p. 458; **UR** p. 89 **L.1.a**	• **Speaking and Listening: Response,** p. 459; **UR** p. 91 **SL.3**	**Test Practice: Reading: Main Idea,** pp. 460–461 **Selection Tests, UR** pp. 74–79, 95–100
Timed Writing: Informative Text: Propose a Solution, p. 467 **W.2**			
Timed Writing: Explanatory Text: Essay, p. 483; **UR** p. 108 **W.2, W.4**			**Selection Tests, UR** pp. 112–117
Argument: Persuasive Letter, p. 505; **UR** p. 155 **W.1.a, W.1.b** **Writing Workshop: Work in Progress:** Prewriting for Exposition, p. 505	**Subjects and Predicates,** p. 504; **UR** p. 154	• **Speaking and Listening: Public Service Announcement,** p. 505; **UR** p. 156 **SL.4**	**Selection Tests, UR** pp. 139–144, 160–165
Informative Text: Adaptation, p. 527; **UR** p. 194 **W.3.d, W.4** **Writing Workshop: Work in Progress:** Prewriting for Exposition, p. 527	**Compound Subjects and Predicates,** p. 526; **UR** p. 193	• **Research and Technology: Help-Wanted Ad,** p. 527; **UR** p. 195 **W.8**	**Test Practice: Reading: Fact and Opinion,** pp. 528–529 **Selection Tests, UR** pp. 178–183, 199–204
Timed Writing: Explanatory Text: Essay, p. 535 **W.2**			
Timed Writing: Explanatory Text: Essay, p. 547; **UR** p. 212			**Selection Tests, UR** pp. 216–221 **Cumulative Review,** pp. 560–563 **Performance Tasks,** pp. 564–565

All selections are supported in the *Reader's Notebooks.*

		Selection	Page	Reading Skill	Literary Analysis	Word Study
LITERARY ANALYSIS WORKSHOP		**The Railway Train** © Emily Dickinson	577		**Analyzing Poetic Language,** p. 574 **RL.4** **Analyzing Poetic Form and Structure,** p. 575 **RL.5** **Close Read: Analyzing Structure and Meaning,** pp. 576–581	**Introducing the Big Question,** pp. 570–571 **L.6**
		Maestro, The Desert Is My Mother, Bailando Pat Mora	578, 579, 580			
READING FOCUS — DRAWING CONCLUSIONS	**MA** / **MA MC**	**Poetry Collection 1**	586	**Asking Questions to Draw Conclusions,** pp. 583, 590, 591, 594, 597; **UR** pp. 28, 46	**Forms of Poetry,** p. 583; **UR** pp. 29, 47 **RL.5** Spiral Review, p. 590	**Latin root -lum-,** pp. 584, 591 **Greek root, -gram-** pp. 592, 597
		Poetry Collection 2	594			
	MA / **MC**	**Poetry Collection 3**	604, 606, 608	**Connecting the Details to Draw Conclusions,** pp. 601, 608, 609, 613, 615, 617; **UR** pp. 67, 85	**Figurative Language,** pp. 601, 607, 609, 613, 615, 617; **UR** pp. 68, 86 **RL.4** Spiral Review, p. 607	**Latin suffix -ly,** pp. 602, 609 **Greek suffix -y,** pp. 610, 617
		Poetry Collection 4	612, 614, 616			
		Reading for Information Technical Directions/Product Warranty	622	**Follow Technical Directions,** p. 622 **RI.4, RI.5**		
		Comparing Literary Works **The Highwayman** Alfred Noyes	630		**Comparing Literary Works: Narrative Poems,** pp. 628, 630, 631, 632, 633, 634, 637, 638, 639 **RL.4, RL.5, RL.6** Spiral Review, pp. 632, 638	
		How I Learned English Gregory Djanikian	636			
READING FOCUS — PARAPHRASE	**MA** / **MC**	**Poetry Collection 5**	650, 652, 654	**Reading Aloud According to Punctuation to Paraphrase,** pp. 647, 652, 655, 658, 661; **UR** pp. 132, 150	**Sound Devices,** pp. 647, 651, 654, 655, 661; **UR** pp. 133, 151 **RL.4** Spiral Review, p. 651	**Latin suffix -ancy and -ency,** pp. 648, 655 **Old English suffix -less,** pp. 656, 661
		Poetry Collection 6	658, 659, 660			
	MA / **MC**	**Poetry Collection 7**	668, 670, 672	**Reread and Restate to Paraphrase,** pp. 665, 669, 673, 677, 681; **UR** pp. 171, 189	**Sound Devices: Rhythm and Rhyme,** pp. 665, 668, 673, 679, 680, 681; **UR** pp. 172, 190 **RL.4** Spiral Review, pp. 672, 677	**Latin prefix im-,** pp. 666, 673 **Old English prefix un-,** pp. 674, 681
		Poetry Collection 8	676, 679, 680			
		Reading for Information Magazine Article/Educational Song	686	**Determine the Main Idea,** pp. 686 **RI.5**		
		Comparing Literary Works **Miracles** Walt Whitman **in Just—** E.E. Cummings	694 696		**Comparing Literary Works: Imagery,** pp. 692, 695, 697; **UR** p. 210 **RL.4** Spiral Review, p. 695	

Key: UR: *Unit Resources*   **MA:** More Accessible   **MC:** More Challenging   © Indicates an Exemplar Text

Writing	Conventions	Extension Activity	Assessment
Poetry: Poem, p. 599; **UR** p. 51 **W.4, W.6** **Writing Workshop: Work in Progress:** Prewriting for Exposition, p. 599	**Infinitives and Infinitive Phrases,** p. 598; **UR** p. 50 **L.1.a**	• **Speaking and Listening: Presentation,** p. 599; **UR** p. 52 **RL.7, SL.1.d**	**Selection Tests, UR** pp. 35–40, 56–61
Explanatory Text: Metaphor, p. 619 **W.2.d** **Writing Workshop: Work in Progress:** Prewriting for Exposition, p. 619	**Appositives and Appositive Phrases,** p. 618; **UR** p. 89 **L.1.a**	• **Research and Technology: Scientific Explanation,** p. 619; **UR** p. 91 **W.7, SL.5**	**Test Practice: Reading: Drawing Conclusions,** pp. 620–621 **Selection Tests, UR** pp. 74–79, 95–100
Timed Writing: Explanatory Text: Directions, p. 627 **W.2.d**			
Timed Writing: Explanatory Text: Essay, p. 639; **UR** p. 108 **W.9**			**Selection Tests, UR** pp. 112–117
Informative Text: Paraphrase, p. 663; **UR** p. 155 **W.9.a, L.4.c, L.5.b** **Writing Workshop: Work in Progress:** Prewriting for Persuasion, p. 663	**Independent and Subordinate Clauses,** p. 662; **UR** p. 154 **L.1.a, L.1.b**	• **Speaking and Listening: Presentation,** pp. 583, 587; **UR** p. 156 **RL.7, SL.1.d**	**Selection Tests, UR** pp. 139–143, 159–164
Poetry: Poem, p. 683; **UR** p. 194 **W.6** **Writing Workshop: Work in Progress:** Prewriting for Persuasion, p. 683	**Sentence Structures,** p. 682; **UR** p. 193 **L.1.b**	• **Research and Technology: Survey,** p. 683; **UR** p. 195 **W.7, SL.1.c**	**Test Practice: Reading: Paraphrasing,** pp. 684–685 **Selection Tests, UR** pp. 178–183, 199–204
			Timed Writing: Explanatory Text: Paraphrase, p. 691 **W.2**
Timed Writing: Argument: Recommendation, p. 383; **UR** p. 211 **W.1**			**Selection Tests, UR** pp. 216–221 **Cumulative Review,** pp. 710–713 **Performance Tasks,** pp. 714–715

All selections are supported in the *Reader's Notebooks*.

	Selection	Page	Reading Skill	Literary Analysis	Word Study
LITERARY ANALYSIS WORKSHOP	*from* **Sorry, Wrong Number** ⓒ Lucille Fletcher	727		**Analyzing Drama,** pp. 724–725 **RL.3, RL.5** **Close Read: Understanding Elements of Drama,** pp. 726–735	**Introducing the Big Question,** pp. 720–721 **L.6**
	from **Dragonwings** Laurence Yep	728, 730			
PURPOSE FOR READING (READING FOCUS) — MC	**A Christmas Carol: Scrooge and Marley, Act 1** Israel Horovitz	740	**Preview a Text to Set a Purpose for Reading,** pp. 737, 741, 752, 754, 756, 761, 768, 769; **UR** p. 28	**Dialogue,** pp. 737, 742, 745, 746, 751, 753, 757, 758, 760, 762, 764, 765, 767, 769; **UR** p. 29 **RL.3, RL.5** Spiral Review, p. 757	**Latin root -grat-,** pp. 738, 769 **L.4.b**
MC	**A Christmas Carol: Scrooge and Marley, Act 2** Israel Horovitz	775	**Adjust Your Reading Rate to Set the Purpose for Reading,** pp. 773, 776, 778, 780, 786, 792, 796, 799, 802; **UR** p. 49	**Stage Directions,** pp. 773, 775, 779, 782, 784, 788, 789, 791, 793, 794, 798, 801, 804, 805; **UR** p. 50 **RL.3, RL.5** Spiral Review, p. 785	**Latin prefix inter-,** pp. 774, 807 **L.4.b**
	Reading for Information Review(s)/Radio Interview	812	**Identify the Author's Perspective,** p. 812 **RI.6**		
	Comparing Literary Works *from* **A Christmas Carol: Scrooge and Marley, Act 1, Scene 2** Israel Horovitz	820		**Comparing Literary Works: Character,** pp. 818, 820, 821, 823; **UR** p. 70 **RL.3**	
	from **A Christmas Carol: Scrooge and Marley, Act 1, Scene 5** Israel Horovitz	821			
SUMMARIZING (READING FOCUS) — MA	**The Monsters Are Due on Maple Street** Rod Serling	834	**Distinguish Between Important and Unimportant Details to Summarize,** pp. 831, 836, 841, 842, 844, 845, 846, 851, 853, 854, 857; **UR** p. 96 **RL.2**	**Characters' Motives,** pp. 831, 837, 839, 840, 845, 847, 849, 850, 852, 857; **UR** p. 97 **RL.3** Spiral Review, pp. 843, 846	**Latin root -sist-,** pp. 832, 857 **L.4.b**
	Reading for Information Editorials	862	**Identify Bias and Stereotyping,** p. 862 **RI.6, RI.9**		
	Comparing Literary Works *from* **Grandpa and the Statue** Arthur Miller	868		**Comparing Literary Works: Comparing Dramatic Speeches,** pp. 866, 870, 873, 875, 876, 877; **UR** p. 117 **RL.5** Spiral Review, pp. 869, 875	
	My Head Is Full of Starshine Peg Kehret	874			

Key: UR: *Unit Resources*   **MA:** More Accessible   **MC:** More Challenging   ⓒ Indicates an Exemplar Text

Writing	Conventions	Extension Activity	Assessment
Argument: Letter, p. 771; **UR** p. 33 W.1, W.1.a, W.1.b, W.1.c **Writing Workshop: Work in Progress:** Prewriting for Research; p. 771	**Interjections,** p. 770; **UR** p. 32 L.1, L.2	• **Research and Technology:** **Costume Plans,** p. 771; **UR** p. 34 W.7	**Selection Tests** **UR** p. 38–43
Argument: Tribute, p. 809; **UR** p. 54 **Writing Workshop: Work in Progress:** Prewriting for Research p. 809 W.2, W.9	**Double Negatives,** p. 808; **UR** p. 53 L.1	• **Speaking and Listening:** **Dramatic Monologue,** p. 809; **UR** p. 55 W.7, SL.5	**Test Practice:** **Reading: Purpose for Reading,** pp. 810–811 **Selection Tests,** **UR** pp. 59–64
Timed Writing: Analytic Text: Essay, p. 817 W.1.b, W.9			
Timed Writing: Explanatory Text: Essay, p. 823; **UR** p. 72 W.9, W.9.a			**Selection Tests,** **UR** pp. 76–81
Informative Text: Summary, p. 859; **UR** p. 101 W.2.b, W.2.c, W.6, W.9.a **Writing Workshop: Work in Progress:** Prewriting for Exposition, p. 859	**Sentence Functions and End Marks,** p. 858; **UR** p. 100 L.2	• **Research and Technology:** **Film Version,** p. 859; **UR** p. 102 RL.7	**Test Practice:** **Reading: Summary,** pp. 860–861 **Selection Tests,** **UR** pp. 106–111
Timed Writing: Argumentative Text: Evaluation, p. 865 W.1			
Timed Writing: Explanatory Text: Essay, p. 877; **UR** p. 119 W.2, W.2.b			**Selection Tests,** **UR** pp. 123–128 **Cumulative Review,** pp. 890–893 **Performance Tasks,** pp. 894–895

All selections are supported in the *Reader's Notebooks*.

		Selection	Page	Reading Skill	Literary Analysis	Word Study
LITERARY ANALYSIS WORKSHOP		The Travelers and the Bear retold by Jerry Pinkney	907		**Determining Themes in Folk Literature,** p. 904 **RL.2** **Examining Structure and Theme,** p. 905	**Introducing the Big Question,** pp. 900–901 **L.6**
		Grasshopper Logic, The Other Frog Prince, Duckbilled Platypus vs. Beefsnakstik® Jon Scieszka and Lane Smith	908, 909, 910		**Close Read: Story Development and Theme,** pp. 906–911	
READING FOCUS CAUSE AND EFFECT	MA	Icarus and Daedalus Josephine Preston Peabody	916	**Ask Questions to Analyze Cause and Effect,** pp. 913, 918, 920, 921, 931; **UR** pp. 28, 46	**Myth,** pp. 913, 916, 918, 921, 927, 931; **UR** pp. 29, 47 **RL.2** Spiral Review, p. 918	**Latin root -vac-,** pp. 914, 921 **Latin root -dom-,** pp. 922, 931 **L.4.b**
	MC	Demeter and Persephone Anne Terry White	924			
	MA	Tenochtitlan: Inside the Aztec Capital Jacqueline Dineen	938	**Reread to Look for Connections Between Cause and Effect,** pp. 935, 940, 943, 948, 949, 955; **UR** pp. 67, 85	**Legend and Fact,** pp. 935, 939, 943, 951, 954, 955; **UR** pp. 68, 86 **RL.9** Spiral Review, p. 941	**Old English prefix out-,** pp. 936, 943 **Latin prefix uni-,** pp. 944, 955 **L.4.b**
	MC	Popocatepetl and Ixtlaccihuatl Juliet Piggott Wood	946			
		Reading for Information Textbook Article/Question and Answer	960	**Analyze Cause-and-Effect Organization,** p. 960 **RI.5**		
		Comparing Literary Works **The Voyage** Mary Pope Osborne	968		**Comparing Literary Works: Universal Themes,** pp. 966, 970, 971, 975, 976, 978, 980, 981; **UR** p. 106 **RL.2, RL.3** Spiral Review, pp. 970, 976	
		To the Top of Everest Samantha Larson	973			
READING FOCUS COMPARE AND CONTRAST	MA	Sun and Moon in a Box Alfonso Ortiz and Richard Erdoes	992	**Use Your Prior Knowledge to Compare and Contrast,** pp. 989, 995, 997, 1002, 1003; **UR** pp. 132, 150 **RL.9**	**Cultural Context,** pp. 989, 994, 997, 1003; **UR** pp. 133, 151 **RL.2** Spiral Review, p. 993	**Latin suffix -ity,** pp. 990, 997, 998, 1003
	MC	How the Snake Got Poison Zora Neale Hurston	1000			
	MA	The People Could Fly Virginia Hamilton	1010	**Use a Venn Diagram to Compare and Contrast,** pp. 1007, 1012, 1014, 1015, 1021, 1023; **UR** pp. 171, 189	**Folk Tale,** pp. 1007, 1010, 1015, 1020, 1023; **UR** pp. 172, 190 **RL.3** Spiral Review, p. 1022	**Greek root -myst-,** pp. 1008, 1015 **Old English root -know-,** pp. 1016, 1023 **L.4.b**
	MC	All Stories Are Anansi's Harold Courlander	1018			
		Reading for Information Editorials	1028	**Analyze Point of View,** p. 1028 **RI.6, RI.9**		
		Comparing Literary Works **The Fox Outwits the Crow** William Cleary	1036		**Comparing Literary Works: Tone and Theme,** pp. 1034, 1037, 1039; **UR** p. 210 **RL.2, RL.3, RL.5**	
		The Fox and the Crow Aesop	1038			

Key: UR: *Unit Resources*   **MA:** More Accessible   **MC:** More Challenging   ⒸIndicates an Exemplar Text

Writing	Conventions	Extension Activity	Assessment
Narrative Text: Myth, p. 933; **UR** p. 51 **W.3, W.3.a, W.3.b** **Writing Workshop: Work in Progress:** Prewriting for Workplace Writing, p. 933	**Punctuation Marks,** p. 932; **UR** p. 50 **L.2**	• **Speaking and Listening: Debate,** p. 933; **UR** p. 52 **SL.1.a, SL.1.c**	**Selection Tests, UR** pp. 35–40, 56–61
Informative Text: Description, p. 957; **UR** p. 90 **W.2, W.2.b** **Writing Workshop: Work in Progress:** Prewriting for Workplace Writing, p. 957	**Commas,** p. 956; **UR** p. 89 **L.2, L.2.a**	• **Speaking and Listening: Persuasive Speech,** p. 957; **UR** p. 91 **SL.4**	**Test Practice: Reading: Cause and Effect,** pp. 958–959 **Selection Tests, UR** pp. 74–79, 95–100
Timed Writing: Explanatory Text: Essay, p. 965 **W.2a, W.2c**			
Timed Writing: Explanatory Text: Essay, p. 981; **UR** p. 108 **W.2**			**Selection Tests, UR** pp. 112–117
Informative Text: Plot Summary, p. 1005; **UR** p. 155 **W.2, W.2.b, W.2.f** **Writing Workshop: Work in Progress:** Prewriting for Research, p. 1005	**Capitalization,** p. 1004; **UR** p. 154 **L.2**	• **Speaking and Listening: Story,** p. 1005; **UR** p. 156 **SL.4**	**Selection Tests, UR** pp. 139–144, 160–165
Argument: Review, p. 1025; **UR** p. 194 **W.1, W.1.a, W.1.b** **Writing Workshop: Work in Progress:** Prewriting for Research, p. 1025	**Abbreviations,** p. 1024; **UR** p. 193 **L.2**	• **Speaking and Listening: Television News Report,** p. 1025; **UR** p. 195 **SL.4**	**Test Practice: Reading: Compare and Contrast,** pp. 1026–1027 **Selection Tests, UR** pp. 178–183, 199–204
Timed Writing: Argument: Editorial, p. 1033 **W.1.a, W.1.b, W.1.e**			
Timed Writing: Explanatory Text: Essay, p. 1039; **UR** p. 212 **W.2.b**			**Selection Tests, UR** pp. 216–221 **Cumulative Review,** pp. 1054–1057 **Performance Tasks,** pp. 1058–1059

All selections are supported in the *Reader's Notebooks.*

1   Where Do I Start?

Right here! These pages will guide you through the program's unique organization and describe the many resources that will enrich your teaching.

2   How Do I Teach the Unit?

Begin each unit with **Introducing the Big Question** to present an overarching big idea that will guide students' reading. Have students use the academic vocabulary to think, talk, and write about this question throughout the unit.

Assign the related question in the Performance Tasks feature at the end of each unit. This assignment will help students explore how their ideas about the Big Question have deepened or changed as a result of their reading.

What is the best way to find the truth?

At the beginning of Unit 1, you wrote a response to the Big Question. Now that you have completed the unit, write a new response. Discuss how your initial ideas have been changed or reinforced. Cite specific examples from the literature in this unit, from other subject areas, and from your own life to support your ideas. Use Big Question vocabulary words (see page 3) in your response.

Each of the six units focuses on a different genre. The **Literary Analysis Workshops** provide in-depth exploration of each genre by introducing important characteristics, key concepts, and literary terms.

Then, in the **Model Selection,** students are shown how to apply their understanding of the literary forms and concepts. The Independent Practice selections that follow the models enable students to immediately practice what they have learned. The standards that are introduced and modeled in the introductions are developed and reinforced through spiraled instruction throughout the unit.

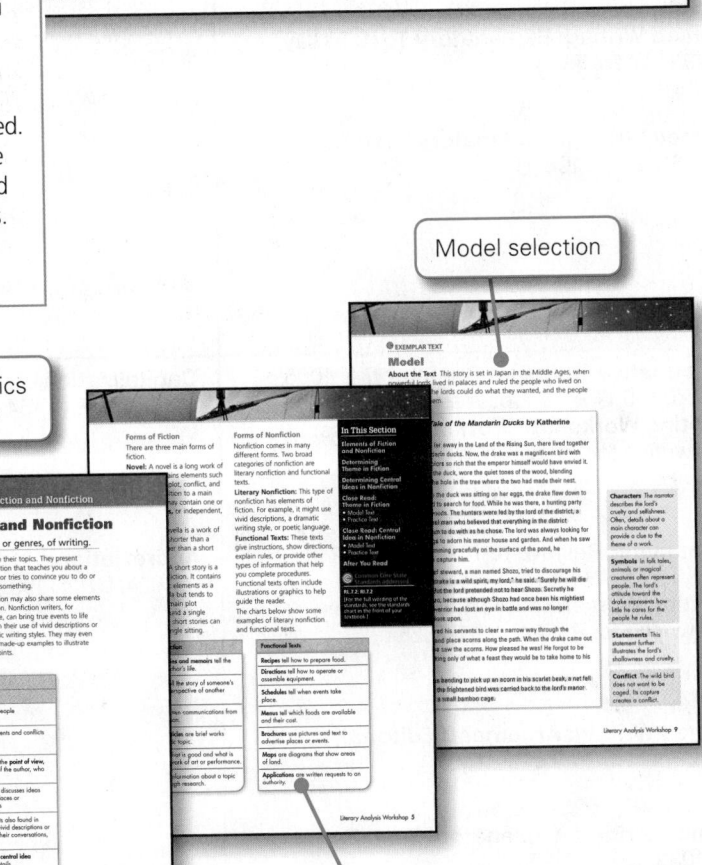

Model selection

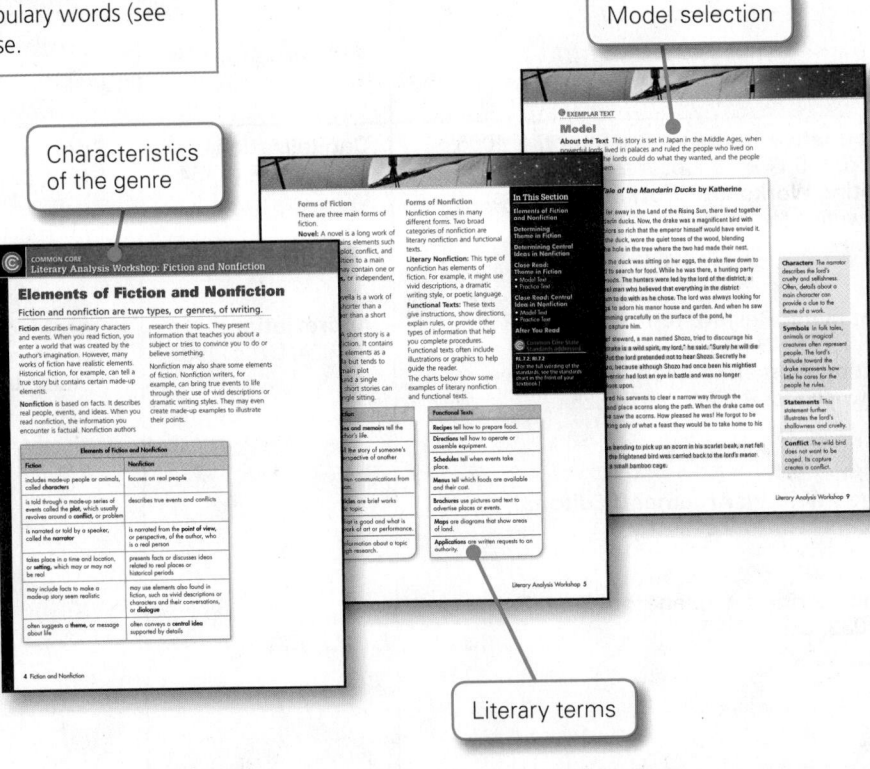

Characteristics of the genre

Literary terms

3   What Should I Use to Plan and Prepare?

Start your planning with the **Pacing Plan** at the beginning of each unit and the **Time and Resource Manager** that precedes every leveled selection pairing.

The Time and Resource Manager provides

- a detailed lesson plan.
- a list of the standards covered in the lesson.
- suggestions for incorporating program resources into your instruction.

For an at-a-glance look at selection resources, see the **Visual Guide to Featured Selection Resources** that precedes each leveled selection pairing.

Lesson Pacing Guide
Suggested pacing information

Meeting Common Core State Standards
Standard-coverage information

Resources
Suggested resources for differentiated instruction

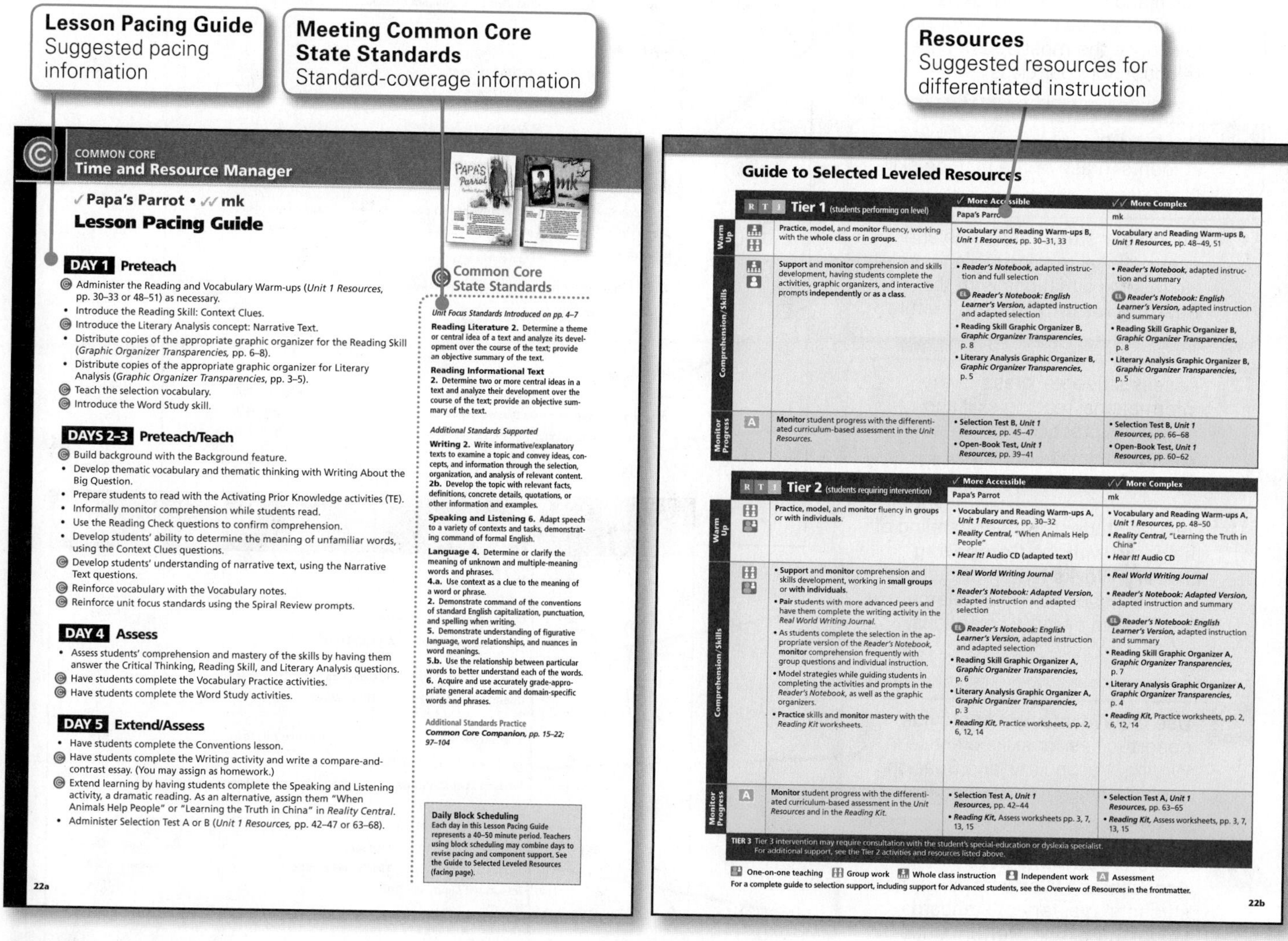

COMMON CORE
Time and Resource Manager

✓ Papa's Parrot • ✓✓ mk
Lesson Pacing Guide

DAY 1 Preteach

- Administer the Reading and Vocabulary Warm-ups (*Unit 1 Resources*, pp. 30–33 or 48–51) as necessary.
- Introduce the Reading Skill: Context Clues.
- Introduce the Literary Analysis concept: Narrative Text.
- Distribute copies of the appropriate graphic organizer for the Reading Skill (*Graphic Organizer Transparencies*, pp. 6–8).
- Distribute copies of the appropriate graphic organizer for Literary Analysis (*Graphic Organizer Transparencies*, pp. 3–5).
- Teach the selection vocabulary.
- Introduce the Word Study skill.

DAYS 2–3 Preteach/Teach

- Build background with the Background feature.
- Develop thematic vocabulary and thematic thinking with Writing About the Big Question.
- Prepare students to read with the Activating Prior Knowledge activities (TE).
- Informally monitor comprehension while students read.
- Use the Reading Check questions to confirm comprehension.
- Develop students' ability to determine the meaning of unfamiliar words, using the Context Clues questions.
- Develop students' understanding of narrative text, using the Narrative Text questions.
- Reinforce vocabulary with the Vocabulary notes.
- Reinforce unit focus standards using the Spiral Review prompts.

DAY 4 Assess

- Assess students' comprehension and mastery of the skills by having them answer the Critical Thinking, Reading Skill, and Literary Analysis questions.
- Have students complete the Vocabulary Practice activities.
- Have students complete the Word Study activities.

DAY 5 Extend/Assess

- Have students complete the Conventions lesson.
- Have students complete the Writing activity and write a compare-and-contrast essay. (You may assign as homework.)
- Extend learning by having students complete the Speaking and Listening activity, a dramatic reading. As an alternative, assign them "When Animals Help People" or "Learning the Truth in China" in *Reality Central*.
- Administer Selection Test A or B (*Unit 1 Resources*, pp. 42–47 or 63–68).

22a

Common Core
State Standards

Unit Focus Standards Introduced on pp. 4–7

Reading Literature 2. Determine a theme or central idea of a text and analyze its development over the course of the text; provide an objective summary of the text.

Reading Informational Text
2. Determine two or more central ideas in a text and analyze their development over the course of the text; provide an objective summary of the text.

Additional Standards Supported

Writing 2. Write informative/explanatory texts to examine a topic and convey ideas, concepts, and information through the selection, organization, and analysis of relevant content.
2b. Develop the topic with relevant facts, definitions, concrete details, quotations, or other information and examples.

Speaking and Listening 6. Adapt speech to a variety of contexts and tasks, demonstrating command of formal English.

Language 4. Determine or clarify the meaning of unknown and multiple-meaning words and phrases.
4.a. Use context as a clue to the meaning of a word or phrase.
2. Demonstrate command of the conventions of standard English capitalization, punctuation, and spelling when writing.
5. Demonstrate understanding of figurative language, word relationships, and nuances in word meanings.
5.b. Use the relationship between particular words to better understand each of the words.
6. Acquire and use accurately grade-appropriate general academic and domain-specific words and phrases.

Additional Standards Practice
Common Core Companion, pp. 15–22; 97–104

Daily Block Scheduling
Each day in this Lesson Pacing Guide represents a 40–50 minute period. Teachers using block scheduling may combine days to revise pacing and component support. See the Guide to Selected Leveled Resources (facing page).

Guide to Selected Leveled Resources

Tier 1 (students performing on level)

R T		✓ More Accessible Papa's Parrot	✓✓ More Complex mk
Warm-Up	**Practice, model,** and **monitor** fluency, working with the **whole class** or in **groups**.	Vocabulary and Reading Warm-ups B, *Unit 1 Resources*, pp. 30–31, 33	Vocabulary and Reading Warm-ups B, *Unit 1 Resources*, pp. 48–49, 51
Comprehension/Skills	**Support** and **monitor** comprehension and skills development, having students complete the activities, graphic organizers, and interactive prompts **independently** or **as a class**.	• *Reader's Notebook*, adapted instruction and full selection RL *Reader's Notebook: English Learner's Version*, adapted instruction and adapted selection • **Reading Skill Graphic Organizer B**, *Graphic Organizer Transparencies*, p. 8 • **Literary Analysis Graphic Organizer B**, *Graphic Organizer Transparencies*, p. 5	• *Reader's Notebook*, adapted instruction and summary RL *Reader's Notebook: English Learner's Version*, adapted instruction and summary • **Reading Skill Graphic Organizer B**, *Graphic Organizer Transparencies*, p. 8 • **Literary Analysis Graphic Organizer B**, *Graphic Organizer Transparencies*, p. 5
Monitor Progress	**Monitor** student progress with the differentiated curriculum-based assessment in the *Unit Resources*.	• **Selection Test B,** *Unit 1 Resources*, pp. 45–47 • **Open-Book Test,** *Unit 1 Resources*, pp. 39–41	• **Selection Test B,** *Unit 1 Resources*, pp. 60–62 • **Open-Book Test,** *Unit 1 Resources*, pp. 60–62

Tier 2 (students requiring intervention)

R T		✓ More Accessible Papa's Parrot	✓✓ More Complex mk
Warm-Up	**Practice, model,** and **monitor** fluency in **groups** or with **individuals**.	• Vocabulary and Reading Warm-ups A, *Unit 1 Resources*, pp. 30–32 • *Reality Central,* "When Animals Help People" • **Hear It!** Audio CD (adapted text)	• Vocabulary and Reading Warm-ups A, *Unit 1 Resources*, pp. 48–50 • *Reality Central,* "Learning the Truth in China" • **Hear It!** Audio CD
Comprehension/Skills	• **Support** and **monitor** comprehension and skills development, working in **small groups** or with **individuals**. • **Pair** students with more advanced peers and have them complete the writing activity in the *Real World Writing Journal*. • As students complete the selection in the appropriate version of the *Reader's Notebook*, **monitor** comprehension frequently with group questions and individual instruction. • **Model** strategies while guiding students in completing the activities and prompts in the *Reader's Notebook*, as well as the graphic organizers. • **Practice** skills and **monitor** mastery with the *Reading Kit* worksheets.	• *Real World Writing Journal* • *Reader's Notebook: Adapted Version*, adapted instruction and adapted selection RL *Reader's Notebook: English Learner's Version*, adapted instruction and adapted selection • **Reading Skill Graphic Organizer A**, *Graphic Organizer Transparencies*, p. 6 • **Literary Analysis Graphic Organizer A**, *Graphic Organizer Transparencies*, p. 3 • *Reading Kit*, Practice worksheets, pp. 2, 6, 12, 14	• *Real World Writing Journal* • *Reader's Notebook: Adapted Version*, adapted instruction and summary RL *Reader's Notebook: English Learner's Version*, adapted instruction and summary • **Reading Skill Graphic Organizer A**, *Graphic Organizer Transparencies*, p. 7 • **Literary Analysis Graphic Organizer A**, *Graphic Organizer Transparencies*, p. 4 • *Reading Kit*, Practice worksheets, pp. 2, 6, 12, 14
Monitor Progress	**Monitor** student progress with the differentiated curriculum-based assessment in the *Unit Resources* and in the *Reading Kit*.	• **Selection Test A,** *Unit 1 Resources*, pp. 42–44 • *Reading Kit*, Assess worksheets pp. 3, 7, 13, 15	• **Selection Test A,** *Unit 1 Resources*, pp. 63–65 • *Reading Kit*, Assess worksheets pp. 3, 7, 13, 15

TIER 3 Tier 3 intervention may require consultation with the student's special-education or dyslexia specialist. For additional support, see the Tier 2 activities and resources listed above.

🗣 One-on-one teaching   👥 Group work   🖥 Whole class instruction   ✏ Independent work   A Assessment
For a complete guide to selection support, including support for Advanced students, see the Overview of Resources in the frontmatter.

22b

---

4   How Does the Program Help Me With Pacing?

The program is organized into three-week instructional blocks, with each block focusing on core skills and standards. This consistent organization ensures thorough skills coverage presented in manageable chunks. A benchmark test is provided at the middle and end of each unit, allowing you to administer assessment at 3-, 6-, or 9-week intervals. This systematic, logical organization with built-in progress monitoring allows you to make sound instructional choices for your class without skipping or missing any skills or standards.

5 | # How Do I Use Each Feature in a Unit?

A Use the **Literary Analysis Workshop** to provide rigorous study of a genre and related Common Core standards.

B Choose a selection from the **leveled selection pairing** to teach and practice core skills and strategies. See p. CC 107 for how to choose the most appropriate selection for your class.

C Use **Test Practice** to assess students' grasp of the reading skill.

D Show your students how to apply informational reading skills to real-life reading situations with the **Reading for Information** feature.

E Assess students' grasp of the informational reading skill and give them practice with timed writing.

F Deepen students' understanding of the genre with the **Comparing Literary Works** feature. Students analyze a specific literary element at work in two or more selections.

G Use the **Workshops** to provide opportunities for skills practice in Writing, Vocabulary, and Speaking and Listening.

H Use the **Common Core Assessment Workshops** to check students' mastery of standards taught in the unit. Performance Tasks allow for hands-on application of skills as called for by the Common Core framework.

I Develop students' abilities to read independently through this end-of-unit feature. Selected titles include Exemplar Texts and strategies for reading complex texts.

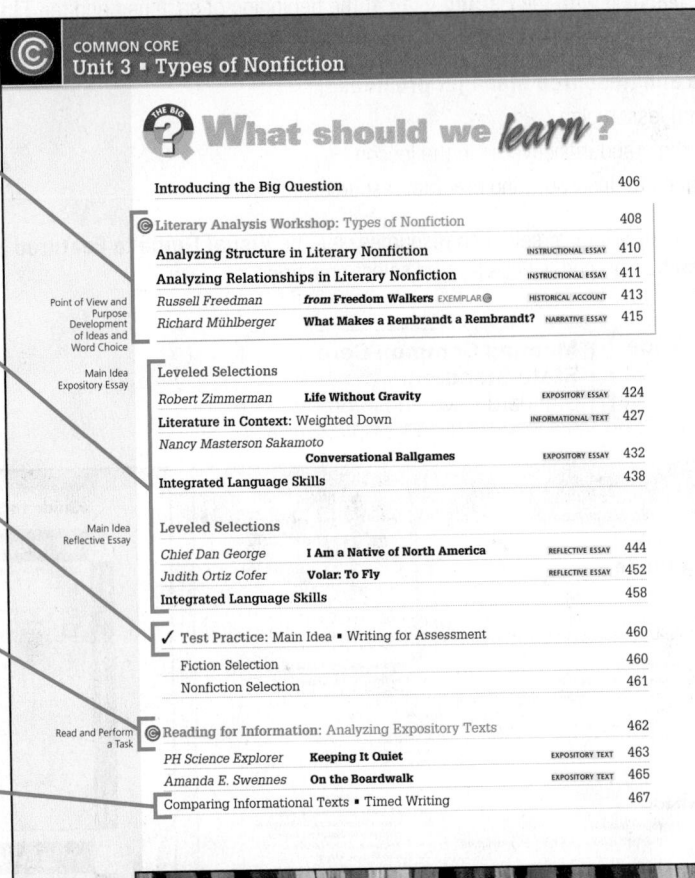

6 How Do I Use the Leveled Selection Pairs?

Pearson Prentice Hall Literature addresses the challenges of today's mixed-ability classrooms through its unique combination of differentiated instruction, online activities, and skills support. When planning lessons for a diverse group of students, consult the **Text Complexity** rubric on the Before You Read pages. (See pages CC 16 and CC 17 for more information.) Take advantage of the following useful features:

The rubric provides a **Lexile** score. Lexile uses factors such as sentence length and vocabulary difficulty to determine a score that can help you predict student comprehension.

This rubric also provides a variety of qualitative measures to help you make informed choices about literature assignments.

Text complexity is determined by both qualitative and quantitative measures. For this reason, the quantitative measure of a more complex selection may be lower than that of a more accessible selection.

Ⓒ Text Complexity Rubric: Leveled Texts

		✓ The Washwoman	✓✓ New Directions
Qualitative Measures	**Context/ Knowledge Demands**	Jewish neighborhood in Poland, early 1900s 1 2 ③ 4 5	African American mother living in the South 1 2 ③ 4 5
	Structure/Language Conventionality and Clarity	Numerous long sentences; on-level vocabulary 1 2 ③ 4 5	Little dialogue; challenging vocabulary 1 2 3 ④ 5
	Levels of Meaning/ Purpose/Concept Level	Accessible concept (determination to complete a task) 1 2 ③ 4 5	Irony; accessible concept (journey from adversity to success) 1 2 3 ④ 5
Quantitative Measures	**Text Length**	Word Count: 1,976	Word Count: 763
	Lexile	870L	1360L
Overall Complexity		✓ **More accessible**	✓✓ **More complex**

Use the **Overall Complexity** as the final tool for deciding which selection to assign to your students.

7 How Do I Differentiate Instruction?

Pearson Prentice Hall Literature provides unprecedented opportunities for differentiated instruction:

- **Teacher's Edition:** Use the strategies and techniques geared toward a variety of reading levels and learning styles.
- **Reader's Notebooks:** Customize instruction with reading support for struggling readers and English learners.
- **Leveled Vocabulary and Reading Warm-ups:** For each selection, build background, fluency, and vocabulary.
- **Leveled Selection Tests:** Choose from two tests for each selection, according to your students' ability levels.
- **Graphic Organizers:** Give struggling readers additional support with completed versions of all organizers in the Student Edition.

Differentiated Instruction for Universal Access

Strategy for Less Proficient Readers
Display **Reading Skill Graphic Organizer B** (*Graphic Organizer Transparencies*, p. 5), and review the process of making and verifying predictions. Fill in the first box of the organizer with the following sentences from this page: "But to return to the washwoman. That winter was a harsh one."

Guide students as they list questions that they might ask about the second sentence. For example, How will the harsh winter affect the washwoman? Will the cold weather get even worse? With students' input, choose a question for the second box of the organizer.

Next, tell students to think about what they have read and what they know about older people. Have students brainstorm for predictions and write them on sheets of paper. At the end of the selection, have students confirm or revise their predictions.

PHLitOnline provides a customized learning experience for students. Learner levels are assigned to students based on Diagnostic Test results. All selections and support provided are based on that level, creating a truly personalized learning experience!

8

When Do I Teach Writing?

This program incorporates opportunities in every unit for both process writing and writing for assessment.

Writing Process: To help students prepare for every **Writing Workshop,** *Work in Progress* features appear with each leveled selection pair. These focused prewriting activities encourage students to practice prewriting strategies such as these:

- choosing and narrowing a topic
- gathering details
- preparing a thesis statement

Twice per unit, a **Writing Workshop** with step-by-step instruction guides students to develop their ideas into full-length compositions, addressing these key stages in the writing process:

- Prewriting
- Drafting
- Revising
- Editing and Proofreading
- Publishing and Presenting

Timed Writing: To address the call for writing in the Common Core State Standards, the program provides several opportunities for students to practice writing for assessment. Each **Reading for Information** and **Comparing Literary Works** feature concludes with an annotated timed-writing prompt that includes a step-by-step planner to help students complete the assignment.

Finally, to facilitate your teaching of writing, **Prentice Hall EssayScorer** provides instant scoring and feedback, plus tips for revision. You save time, and your students become better writers!

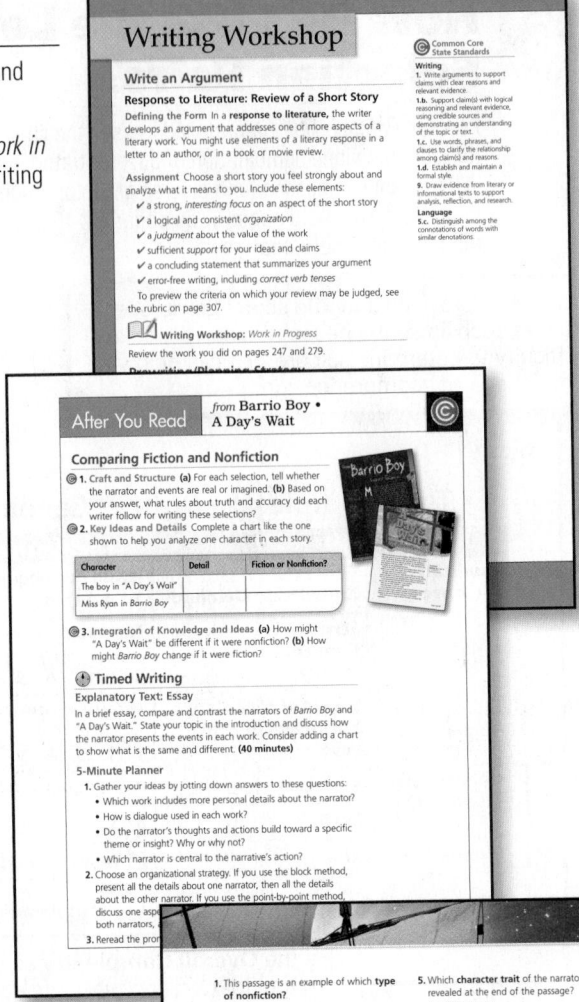

9

How Do I Monitor Student Progress?

Pearson Prentice Hall makes progress monitoring easy with frequent opportunities to evaluate student progress and to reteach material. For more information on the program's assessments, see the Assessment Roadmap in PHLitOnline under Resources & Downloads.

- The **Beginning-of-Year Benchmark Test** assesses students' skills and deficiencies at the onset of the year. Test results allow you to tailor your instruction to students.

- Use the **Diagnostic Tests** at the beginning of the school year to determine entry-level reading skills. You will find frequent **reading checks** and suggestions in the Teacher's Edition for monitoring student progress during reading. If tests are taken online, learner levels are assigned automatically, based on test results.

- After reading selections, use the **Open Book Tests** and leveled **Selection Tests** to assess comprehension and mastery of the literary, reading, and vocabulary skills.

- As you teach the unit, use the **Cumulative Review** pages in standardized-test format to give students practice in applying core unit skills and in writing for assessment under test-taking conditions.

- Use the **Benchmark Tests** to monitor progress at regular, frequent intervals. For your convenience, both mid-unit and end-of-unit tests are provided. If taken online, remediation for skills missed is assigned automatically!

- **Mid-Year Tests** and **End-of-Year Summative Tests** provide a measure of student achievement over a longer period of time.

Use the electronic test generator to customize assessment.

10 How Can I Use Technology in My Classroom?

PHLitOnline allows you to teach the entire program without using the print products. Here, you will find the components of the program in one central location—PLUS integrated videos, animations, interactive practice activities, songs, and audio. You will navigate through the program by using the Table of Contents, exactly as you would in the textbook.

You can choose to use PHLitOnline only, or you may choose to use it in conjunction with the print program. Supporting resources such as videos, audio, online assessments, lesson planning, and reporting are just what you need to teach literature to your 21st Century students!

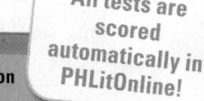

All tests are scored automatically in PHLitOnline!

Enriched Online Student Edition
- Full narration of selections
- Interactive graphic organizers
- Linked Get Connected and Background videos
- All worksheets and other student resources

Professional Development
- The *Professional Development Guidebook* online
- Additional professional development essays by program authors

Planning, Assigning, and Monitoring
- Software for online assignment of work to students, individually or to the whole class
- A system for tracking and grading student work

11 How Can PHLitOnline Help Me in the Classroom?

The **PHLitOnline Teacher Center** has digital and print tools you can use to reach your students, manage your teaching resources, and meet the Common Core State Standards. You can

- provide personalized diagnosis, instruction, and remediation to all students.
- tailor instruction for the right level of support for each student's specific needs.
- create customized assignments.
- correlate lessons to the Common Core State Standards.
- plan with easy-to-use tools.
- access all print resources online.

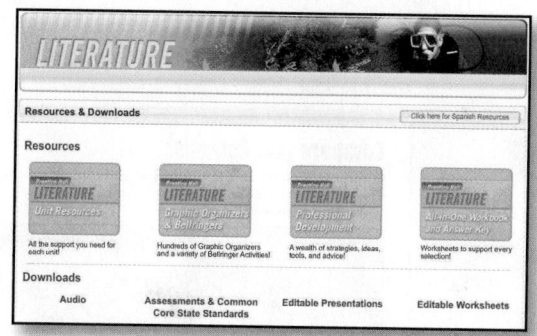

The **PHLitOnline Student Center** allows students to access the complete program from computers in the classroom or at home. In addition to all print and activity-based materials, the PHLitOnline Student Center offers videos, animations, interactive practice activities, "sticky" notes, songs, and audio features.

12 How Can PHLitOnline Help Me Personalize Instruction?

PHLitOnline provides personalized differentiated support with **Diagnostic** and **Benchmark** tests. The program can assess, diagnose, and auto-assign reading materials and practice at each student's level. And, since you know your students better than anyone, you have the flexibility to change the learner level as needed!

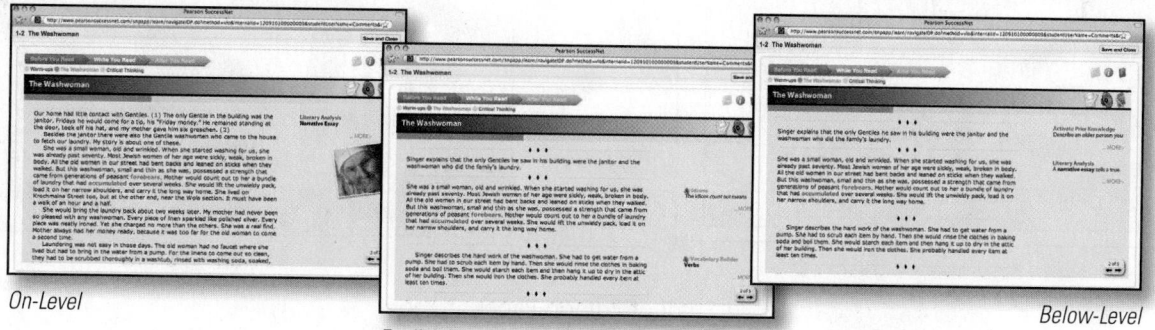

On-Level

English Learner

Below-Level

Students are assigned a learner level—On-Level, Below-Level, or English Learner.

Full-size versions of these Picture It! pages can be found in the Student Edition.

PICTURE IT!
A Comprehension Handbook

Author's Purpose
An author writes for many purposes, some of which are to inform, to entertain, to persuade, or to express. An author may have more than one purpose for writing.

Inform

Entertain

Persuade

Express

lxxiv

Cause and Effect
An effect is something that happens. A cause is why that thing happens. An effect sometimes has more than one cause. A cause sometimes has more than one effect. Clue words such as *because, as a result, therefore,* and *so that* can signal causes and effects.

Cause

Effect

lxxv

Student Edition Pages

Compare and Contrast
To compare and contrast is to look for similarities and differences in things. Clue words such as *like* or *as* show similarities. Clue words such as *but* or *unlike* show differences.

lxxvi

Context Clues
You can use context clues—the words and phrases around an unfamiliar word—to determine the meaning of an unfamiliar word.

I can tell by the grossed-out look on your face that you think my marshmallow meatloaf is repugnant.

Grossed-out + Marshmallow Meatloaf = Repugnant

lxxvii

Student Edition Pages

Draw Conclusions

When we draw conclusions, we make sensible decisions or form reasonable opinions after thinking about the facts and details in what we are reading.

lxxviii

Fact and Opinion

A fact is something that can be proved. Facts are based on evidence. Opinions express ideas and are based on interpretation of evidence.

lxxix

Main Idea and Details

lxxx

Making Predictions

To make predictions, use text, graphics, and prior knowledge to predict what might happen in a story or what you might learn from a text. As you read, new information can lead to new or revised predictions.

lxxxi

Making Inferences

When we make inferences, or infer something, we come to a conclusion based on a detail an author provides in the text.

lxxxii

Paraphrasing

Paraphrasing is restating a sentence or an idea in your own words. Paraphrasing can lead to a better understanding of what we read.

lxxxiii

Setting a Purpose for Reading

When we set a purpose for reading, we approach a text with a specific goal or question that we would like answered. Setting a purpose for reading guides comprehension by focusing our attention on specific information.

lxxxiv

Summarizing

To summarize, we restate the main ideas of a text or the main events of a plot. In a summary, we leave out the supporting details.

lxxxv

Full-size versions of these Media Literacy Handbook pages can be found in the Student Edition.

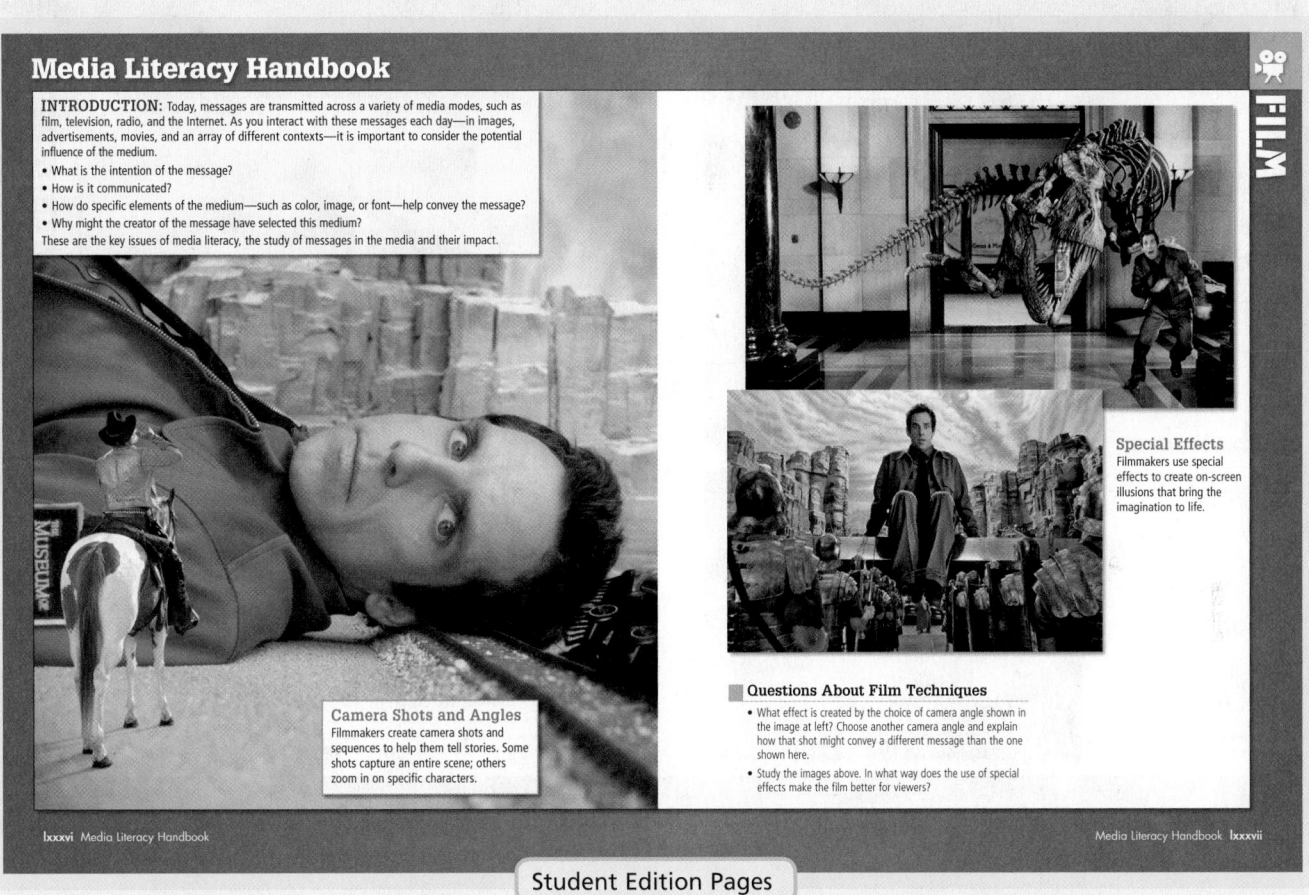

Student Edition Pages

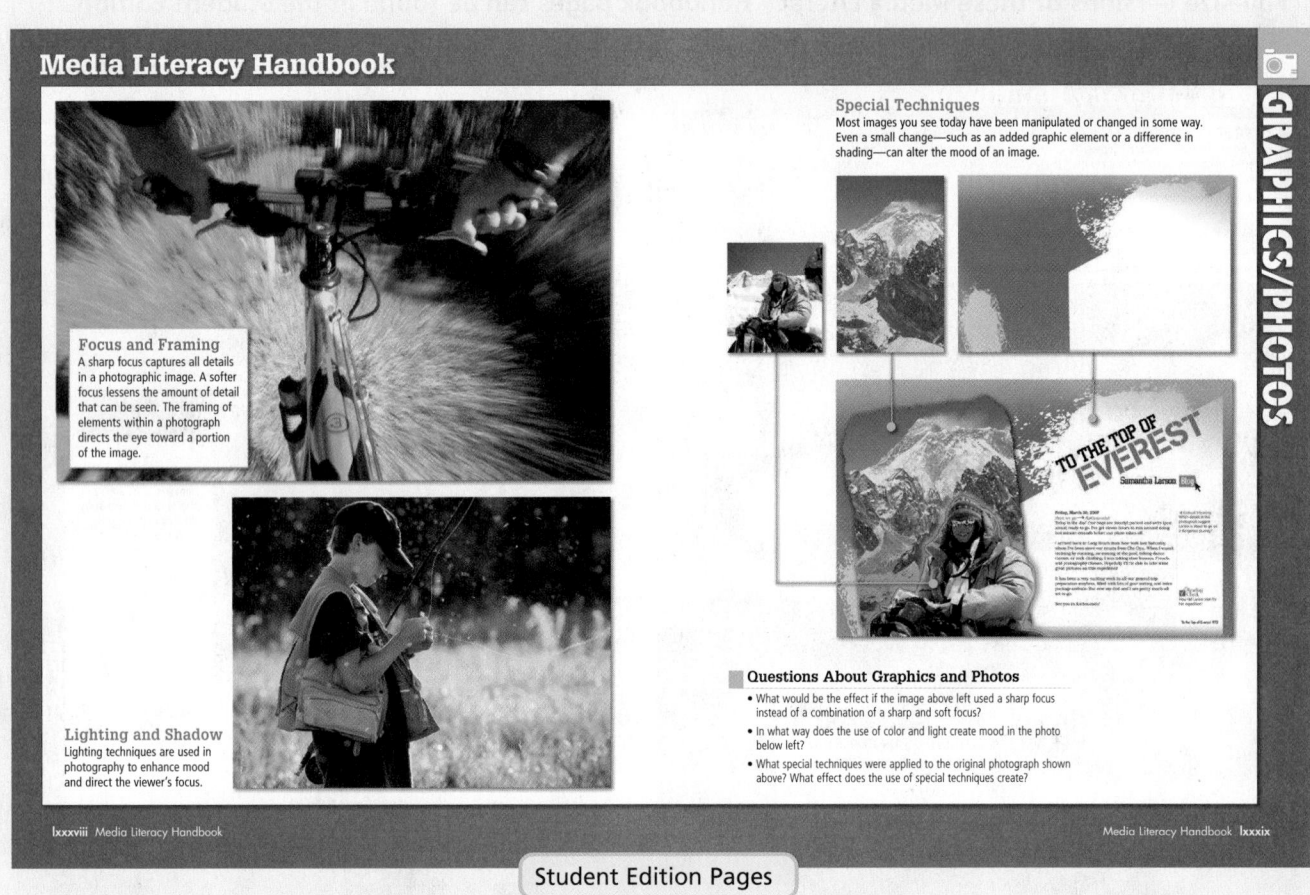

Media Literacy Handbook

Focus and Framing
A sharp focus captures all details in a photographic image. A softer focus lessens the amount of detail that can be seen. The framing of elements within a photograph directs the eye toward a portion of the image.

Lighting and Shadow
Lighting techniques are used in photography to enhance mood and direct the viewer's focus.

Special Techniques
Most images you see today have been manipulated or changed in some way. Even a small change—such as an added graphic element or a difference in shading—can alter the mood of an image.

Questions About Graphics and Photos
- What would be the effect if the image above left used a sharp focus instead of a combination of a sharp and soft focus?
- In what way does the use of color and light create mood in the photo below left?
- What special techniques were applied to the original photograph shown above? What effect does the use of special techniques create?

Student Edition Pages

Persuasive Techniques
Advertisements use carefully selected visual elements and specific language to appeal to the viewer's emotions.

Text and Graphics
Newspaper and magazine layouts are constructed to capture the eye and quickly convey the important ideas of a story. The use of type fonts, imagery, and page space direct the eye to portions of the printed page.

Questions About Print Media
- What image or graphic dominates the advertisement at left? In what way does the use of language in the ad enhance its message?
- Which of the above grabs your attention: the image or the graphic on the magazine cover? Explain.
- What do you notice first on the newspaper's front page? What overall effect does the use of type size and fonts create?

Student Edition Pages

How is this book organized?

- There are six units, each focusing on a specific genre.
- Each unit has a Big Question to get you thinking about important ideas and to guide your reading.
- A Literary Analysis Workshop begins each unit, providing instruction and practice for essential skills.

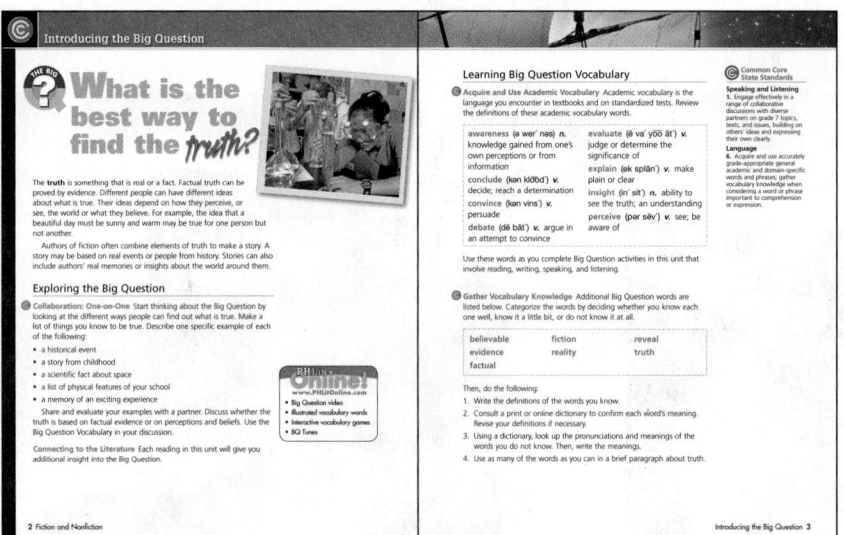

◀ At the beginning of the unit, **Introducing the Big Question** provides a reading focus for the entire unit. Use **academic vocabulary** to think, talk, and write about this question.

A **Literary Analysis Workshop** provides an overview of the unit genre, an in-depth exploration of Common Core State Standards, as well as models and practice opportunities. ▶

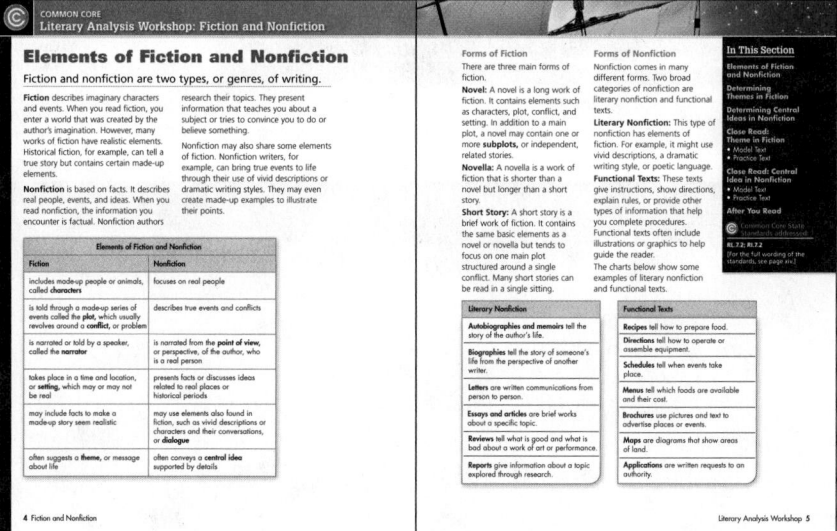

How are the literary selections organized?

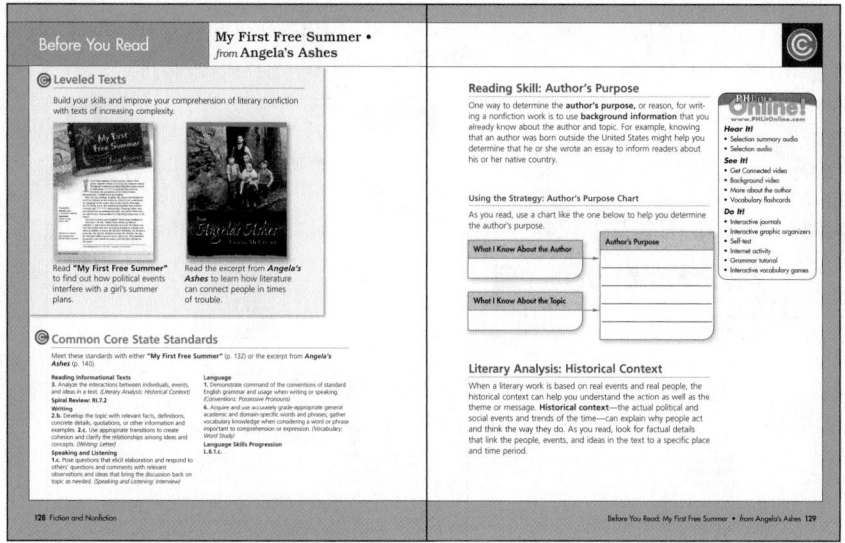

◄ **Before You Read** introduces two selection choices that both teach the same skills. Your teacher will help you choose the selection that is right for you.

Writing About the Big Question is a quick-writing activity that helps you connect the Big Question to the selection you are about to read.

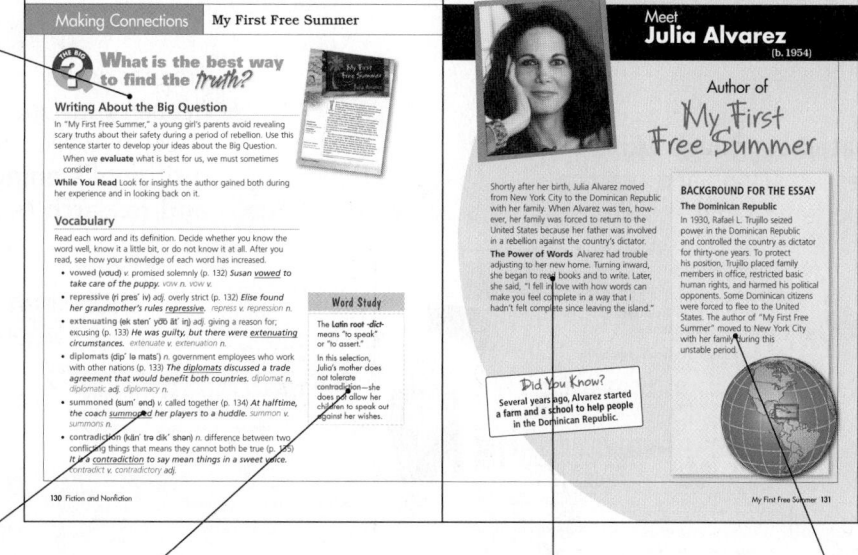

Vocabulary and Word Study introduce important selection vocabulary words and teach you about prefixes, suffixes, and roots.

Meet the Author and Background teach you about the author's life and provide information that will help you understand the selection.

How to Use This Book **xciii**

How are the literary selections organized? *(continued)*

After You Read helps you practice the skills you have learned. ▼

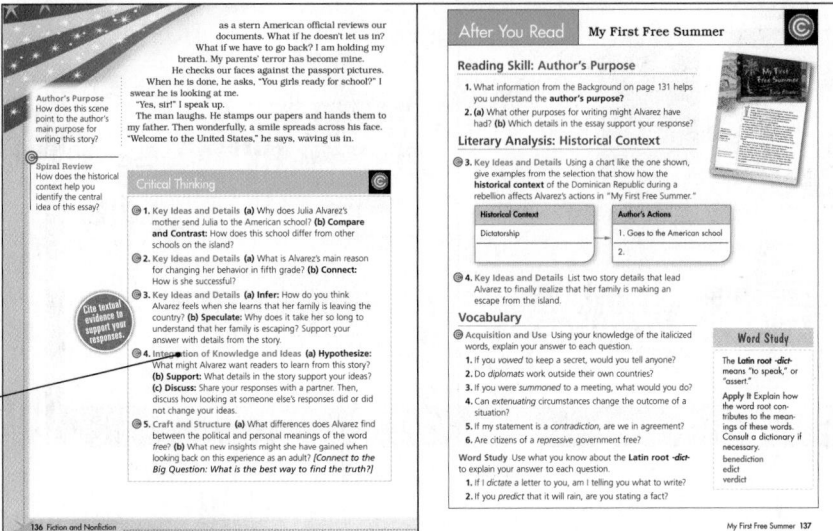

Critical Thinking questions help you reflect on what you have read and apply the Big Question to the selection.

Projects and activities help you deepen your understanding of the selection while strengthening your **writing, listening, speaking, and research skills.**

Integrated Language Skills provides instruction and practice for important grammar skills.

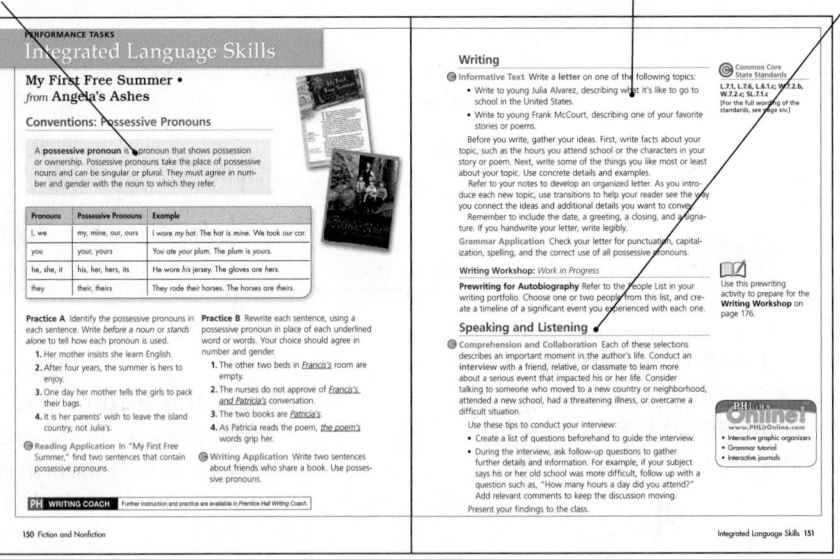

What special features will I find in this book?

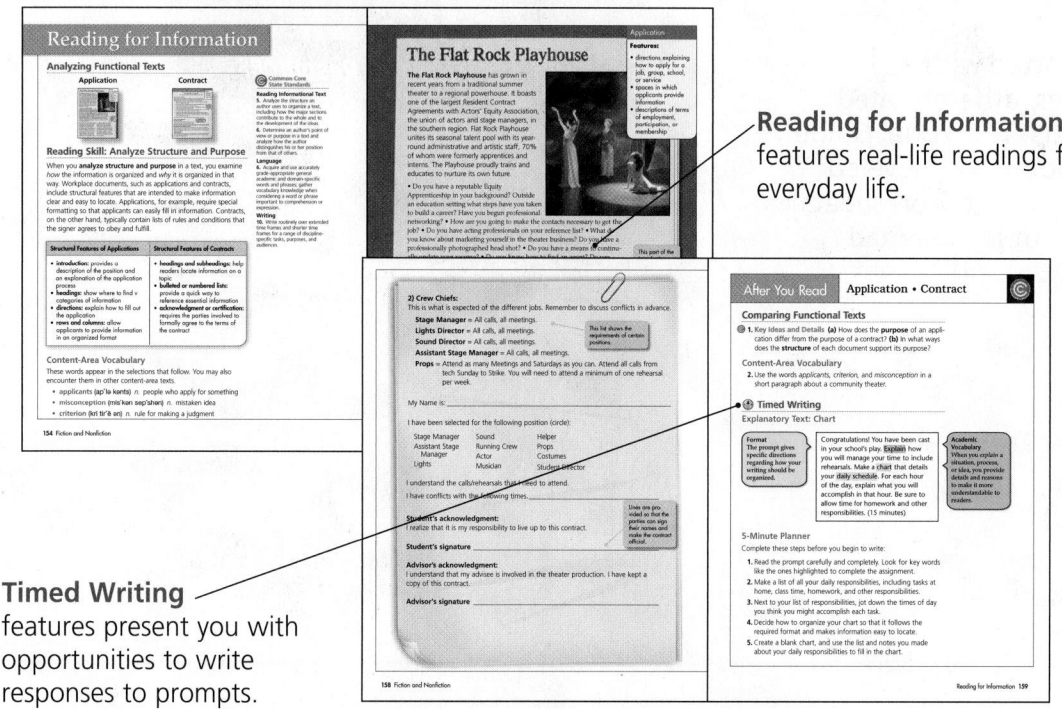

Reading for Information features real-life readings from everyday life.

Timed Writing features present you with opportunities to write responses to prompts.

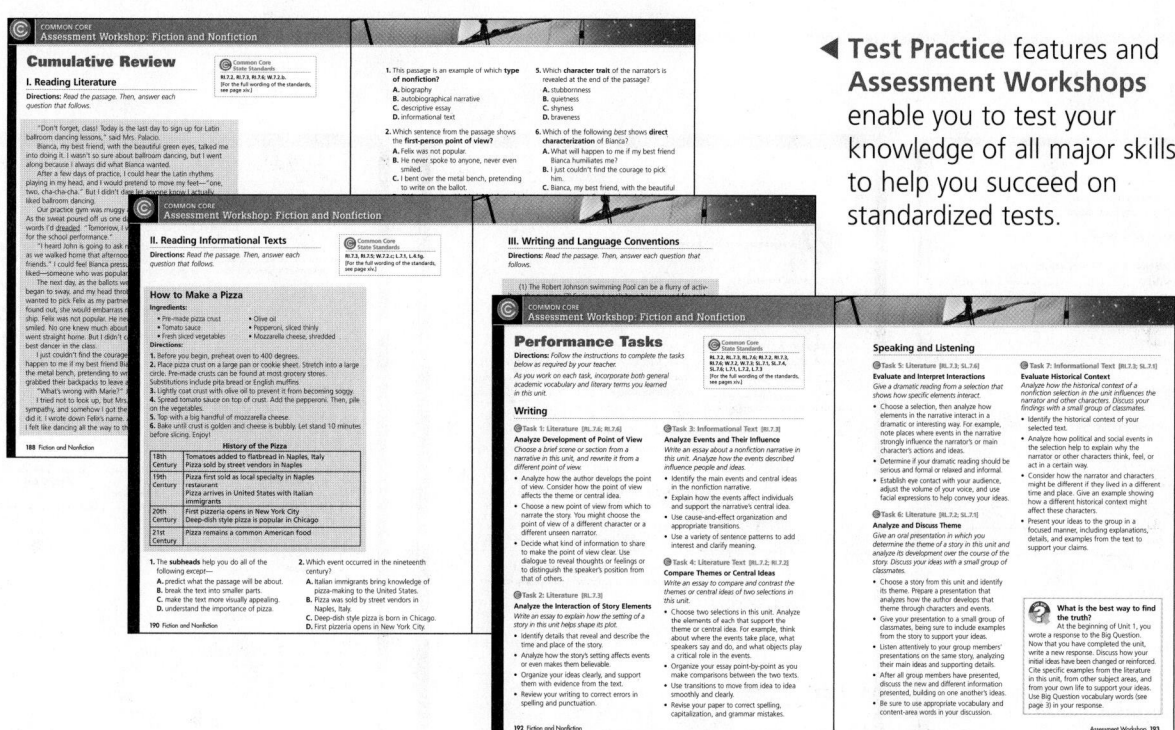

◀ **Test Practice** features and **Assessment Workshops** enable you to test your knowledge of all major skills to help you succeed on standardized tests.

How to Use This Book **xcv**

Selection and Skills Support

Every selection is fully supported with worksheets in *Unit Resources*, differentiated for various groups of learners. The Visual Guide to Selected Resources preceding each leveled selection pair gives a sample of the worksheets available. The full complement is presented on these pages.

RESOURCES FOR:

L1 Special-Needs Students

L2 Below-Level Students (Tier 2)

L3 On-Level (Tier 1)

L4 Advanced Students (Tier 1)

EL English Learners

All All Students

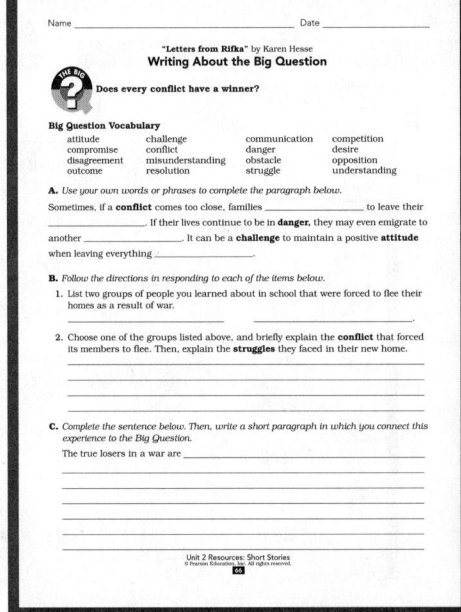

EL L1 L2 Vocabulary Warm-ups A and B

vocabulary and reading practice for lower-level students and English learners

All Writing About the Big Question

thematic vocabulary and thought-provoking activities centered around the unit Big Question

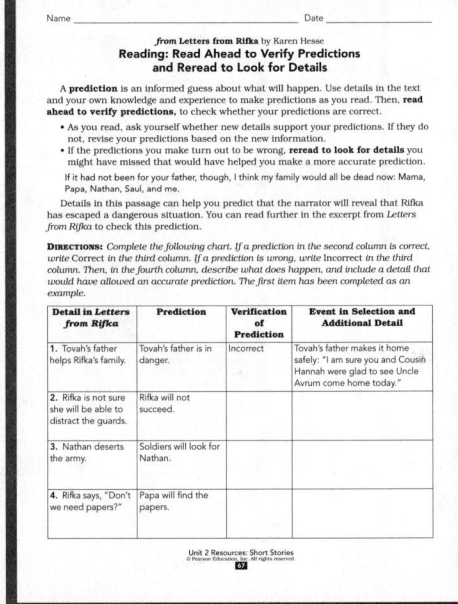

All Reading

a full page of support for the Reading Skill taught with the selection

All teacher resources are available online at www.PHLitOnline.com

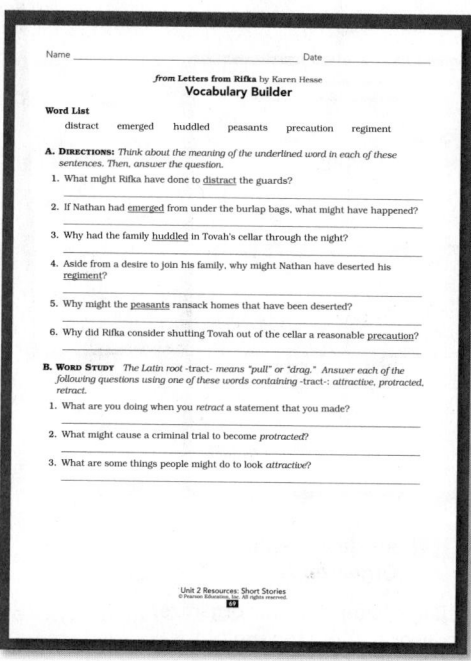

All Literary Analysis

a full page of support for the Literary Analysis concept taught with the selection

All Vocabulary Builder

selection vocabulary and Word Study skill practice

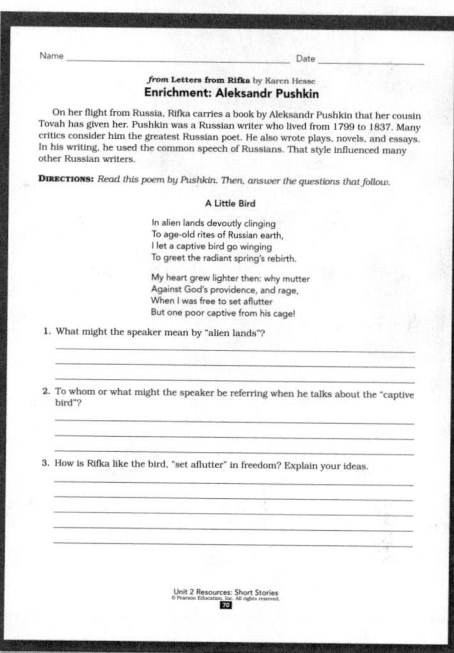

L4 Enrichment

a selection-related challenge for advanced learners

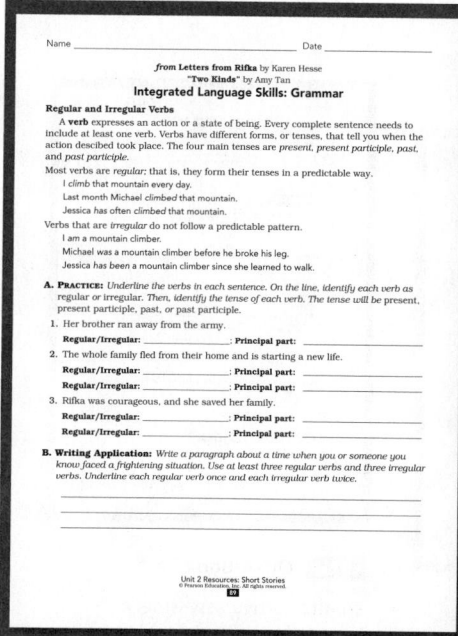

L3 L4 Grammar

more practice with the grammar skill taught with the selection

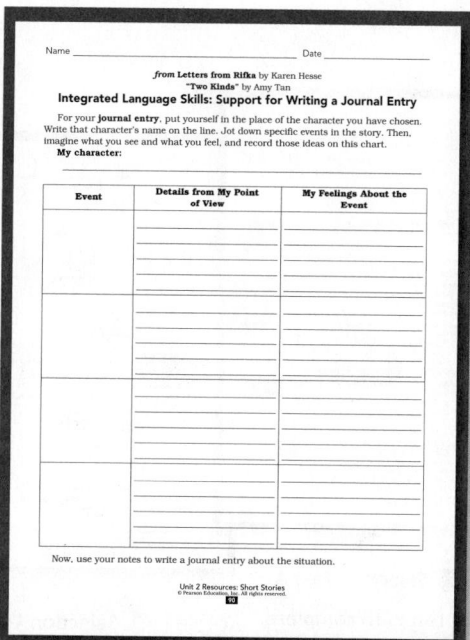

L3 L4 Writing

support for the writing activity accompanying the selection

L3 L4 Extend Your Learning

customized support for the Listening and Speaking or Research and Technology activity related to the selection

Selection Support

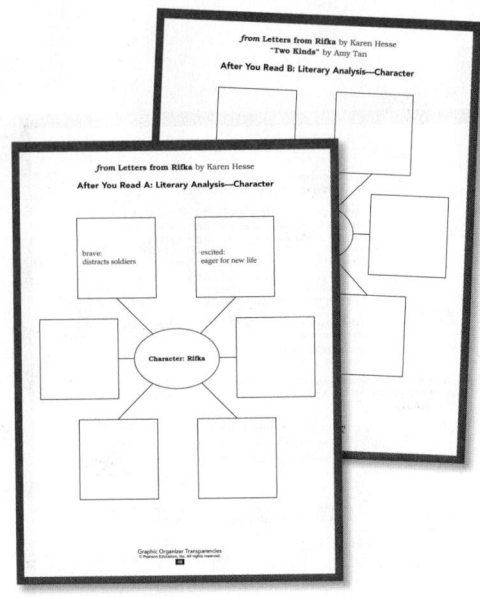

EL L1 L2 Reading Graphic Organizer A

a partially filled-in graphic organizer to model or scaffold the use of the organizer

L3 Reading Graphic Organizer B

the blank version of the organizer

EL L1 L2 Literary Analysis Graphic Organizer A

a partially filled-in graphic organizer to model or scaffold the use of the organizer

L3 Literary Analysis Organizer B

the blank version of the organizer

Assessment

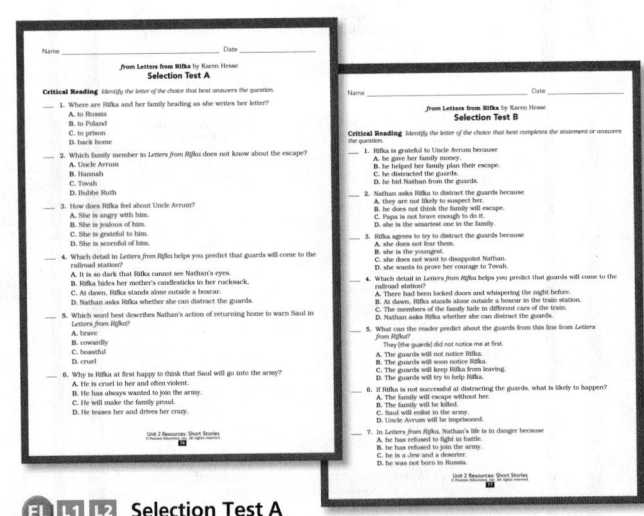

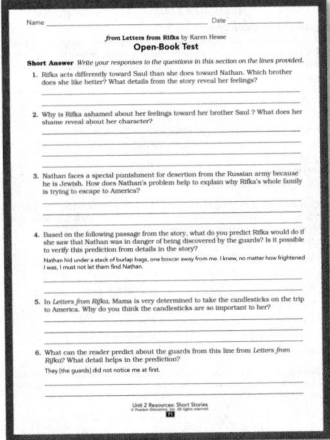

EL L1 L2 Selection Test A

selection test with complete skills coverage, adapted for lower-level students and English learners

EL L3 L4 Selection Test B

selection test with complete skills coverage, including multiple choice and essay items

L3 L4 Open-Book Test

an alternative assessment format for on-level and advanced students

Common Core Companion

The Common Core Companion
student workbook provides
instruction and practice for all
Common Core State Standards.
Here is a closer look at this
workbook.

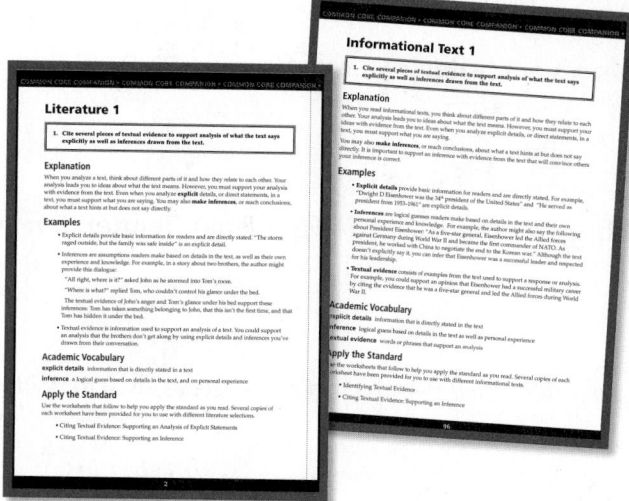

All Literature and Informational Text

Direct instruction and practice for each Common
Core State Standard. Standards requiring writing
or presentation outcomes are supported through
process workshops.

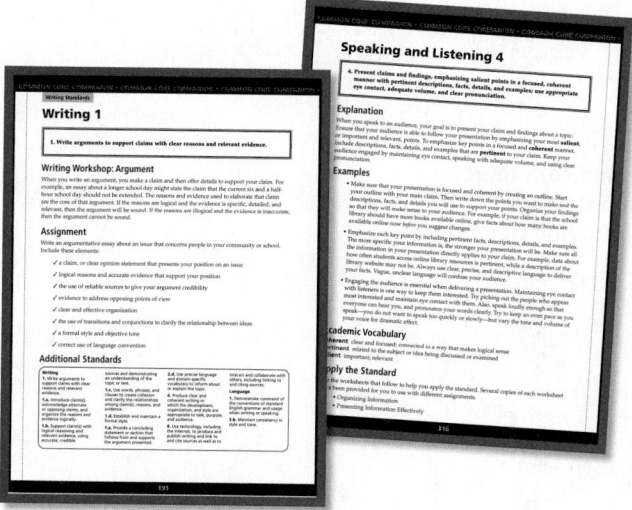

All Writing and Speaking and Listening

Full writing process workshops are supported with direct
instruction and worksheets. Writing process standards are
integrated with Speaking and Listening activities.

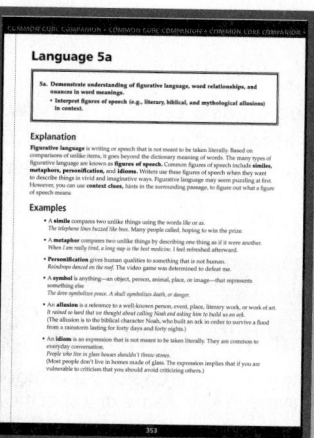

All Language

Explicit instruction supports
each Language standard.
Practice worksheets and graphic
organizers provide additional
opportunities for mastery.

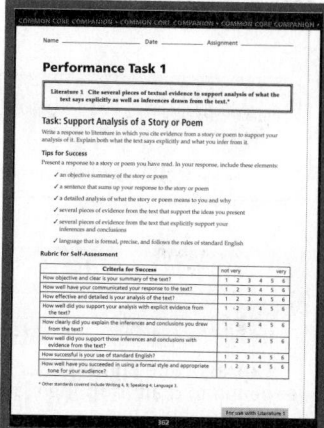

All Performance Tasks

Assessment opportunities are
provided for each reading
standard, along with tips for
success and rubrics.

Classroom Strategies

Each unit in this Teacher's Edition begins with a professional development essay by a program author. For more professional development essays, visit www.PHLitOnline.com.

Log on as a teacher at www.PHLitOnline.com to access a library of all Professional Development articles by the Contributing Authors of *Pearson Prentice Hall Literature*.

PROFESSIONAL DEVELOPMENT Jeff Anderson

APPLY THE STRATEGY

Express-Lane Editing After students have begun to draft, stop them after they have written about half a page. Say:

Readers expect us to follow certain patterns when we write letters. One convention that really helps communicate to our readers in business letters is capitalization. Let's do an express-lane edit of what we've written in our draft so far.

First, let's review the rules of capitalization. What do writers show with capitalization?

(Capitalization shows that a word is the name of a specific place or person—like a company or brand.)

As the discussion continues, have students record this information on their shopping lists. During revising, they will focus on the items they have listed.

For more of Jeff Anderson's strategies, see his Professional Development essay, pp. 900c–900d.

Authors give concrete applications for the strategies they discuss in their essays at point of use in the Teacher's Edition.

PRENTICE HALL

LITERATURE

GRADE 7

COMMON CORE EDITION

Upper Saddle River, New Jersey

Boston, Massachusetts

Chandler, Arizona

Glenview, Illinois

ALWAYS LEARNING

PEARSON

Student Edition Pages

Cover: (C) ©Steve Satushek/Stone/Getty Images, (R) ©Don Farrall/Getty Images, (C) ©Datacraft/imagenavi/Getty Images, (Bkgd) ©Peter Griffith/Getty Images, (C) ©Jan Greune/LOOK/Getty Images

Acknowledgments appear on page R61, which constitutes an extension of this copyright page.

PEARSON

ISBN-13: 978-0-13-319553-8
ISBN-10:   0-13-319553-8

2 3 4 5 6 7 8 9 10 VO92 15 14 13 12 11

Student Edition Pages

PRENTICE HALL

LITERATURE

TEACHER'S EDITION • GRADE 7

COMMON CORE EDITION

PEARSON

Unit 1 Features Overview

Unit Genre and Big Question

In this unit, students will analyze both fiction and nonfiction. As they read they will discuss responses to the unit Big Question: What is the best way to find the truth?

Unit 1 Selections

Teach Selections are presented in leveled pairs. To teach the skills and meet the objectives, you need to assign only one selection in each pair.

Differentiate and Reinforce Choose the selection in a pair that is best suited for your students, based on the Text Complexity box shown on the next page. You may use the other selection to reinforce skills or provide enrichment.

Integrate Skills Each selection presents students with a reading strategy, a literary analysis concept, a vocabulary skill, and grammar instruction. Students can extend learning in the writing and extension activities.

Additional Unit Features

Ⓒ Literary Analysis Workshop Teach and model the Unit Focus standards. Spiral Review notes enable students to revisit these skills over the course of the unit.

Reading for Information Students analyze functional, expository, and argumentative texts and complete Timed Writing activities.

Comparing Literary Works Students study two literary works either within or across genres.

Test Practice: Reading This feature provides extra practice in utilizing reading skills to master assessments.

Writing Workshops Two writing workshops appear in each unit, along with rubrics and instruction in the writing process.

Assessment Workshop Cumulative Skill Review and Performance Tasks provide a range of assessment opportunities.

Independent Reading Students broaden their knowledge as they read longer works of increasing complexity.

THE BIG ? What is the best way to find the *truth*?

www.PHLitOnline.com

Teaching From Technology

Enriched Online Student Edition
- full narration of selections
- interactive graphic organizers
- linked **Get Connected** and **Background** videos
- all worksheets and other student resources

Professional Development
- the *Professional Development Guidebook* online
- additional professional development essays by program authors

Planning, Assigning, and Monitoring
- software for online assignment of work to students, individually or to the whole class
- a system for tracking and grading student work

Fiction and Nonfiction

Unit 1

Instructional Resources

Unit 1 Resources supports Unit skills with pages of the following types:

▶ **Benchmark Tests** assess and monitor student progress at mid-Unit and at Unit's end.

▶ **Vocabulary and Reading Warm-ups** provide additional vocabulary support, based on Lexile rankings of words, for each selection. "A" **Warm-ups** are for students reading two grades below level. "B" **Warm-ups** are for students reading one grade below level.

▶ **Selection Support** These practice pages are available for each selection:

- Reading Skill
- Literary Analysis
- Writing About the Big Question
- Vocabulary
- Support for Writing
- Support for Extend Your Learning
- Enrichment

PHLit Online!
www.PHLitOnline.com

Hear It!
- Selection summary audio
- Selection audio
- BQ Tunes

See It!
- Author videos
- Big Question video
- Get Connected videos
- Background videos
- More about the authors
- Illustrated vocabulary words
- Vocabulary flashcards

Do It!
- Interactive journals
- Interactive graphic organizers
- Grammar tutorials
- Interactive vocabulary games
- Test practice

PHLit Online!
All worksheets and other student resources are also available online at **www.PHLitOnline.com**.

1

Text Complexity: Accessibility for Various Ability Levels

This chart gives a general text complexity rating to help you decide which selection in each leveled pair is more appropriate for your students. **Choose one selection in each pair, or choose to teach both.** You will meet the objectives for the pair when you teach either of the two selections. For additional guidance on factors that affect the complexity of each selection, see the Leveled Texts page for each selection set.

Accessibility for English Learners

 This icon indicates support for English learners at point of use in this Teacher's Edition.

	✓ More Accessible	✓✓ More Complex
Pair 1	Papa's Parrot	mk
Pair 2	*from* An American Childhood	The Luckiest Time of All
Pair 3	All Summer in a Day	Suzy and Leah
Pair 4	My First Free Summer	*from* Angela's Ashes

Common Core State Standards

Unit 1 Focus Standards
• Reading Literature 1
• Reading Informational Text 2

Additional Activities and Assessments
• Writing 2, 7
• Speaking and Listening 1, 6
• Language 1, 2, 4, 5, 6
• Reading Literature 3, 6
• Reading Informational Text 3
• Reading Informational Text 6
• Language 6

	Week 1					Week 2					Week 3				
	1	2	3	4	5	1	2	3	4	5	1	2	3	4	5
Administer the Diagnostic Test (*Unit 1 Resources,* pp. 1–6).	●														
Introduce the Unit Big Question (pp. 2–3).	●														
Introduce the unit forms, fiction and nonfiction, using the Literary Analysis Workshop (pp. 4–7).		●													
Introduce the focus CCS standards for the unit and lead students in a close reading of exemplar texts. (pp. 6–21).		●	●												
Teach one selection from Pairing 1 (pp. 22–47).				●	●	●	●	●							
Teach one selection from Pairing 2 (pp. 48–69).							●	●	●	●	●				
Complete the Test Practice: Reading (pp. 70–71).										●					
Teach Reading for Information (pp. 72–77).											●				
Teach Comparing Literary Works (pp. 78–91).												●	●		
Have students complete the Writing Workshop (pp. 92–97).											●	●	●	●	●
Administer **Benchmark Test 1** (*Unit 1 Resources,* pp. 127–137).														●	
Reteach skills, judging which skills to reteach by evaluating students' performance on **Benchmark Test 1.**															●

Independent Reading

Have students choose a full-length work from the Independent Reading feature at the end of the unit and read it while working on this unit.

Pacing Suggestions
• Have students read their chosen work for homework.
• Devote parts of class periods in each school week to Literature Circles in which students reading the same work discuss it.

	Week 4					Week 5					Week 6				
	1	2	3	4	5	1	2	3	4	5	1	2	3	4	5
Teach one selection from Pairing 3 (pp. 98–127).	●	●	●	●	●										
Teach one selection from Pairing 4 (pp. 128–151).					●	●	●	●	●						
Complete the Test-Practice: Reading (pp. 152–153).								●							
Teach Reading for Information (pp. 154–159).									●						
Teach Comparing Literary Works (pp. 160–175).										●	●				
Have students complete the Writing Workshop (pp. 176–183).									●	●	●	●	●		
Have students complete the Vocabulary Workshop (pp. 184–185).												●			
Have students complete the Communications Workshop (pp. 186–187).													●		
Have students complete the first three sections of the Assessment Workshop: Fiction and Nonfiction (pp. 188–191).													●	●	●
Have students complete the selected Performance Tasks in the Assessment Workshop (pp. 192–193).														●	
Administer Benchmark Test 2 (*Unit 1 Resources,* pp. 234–242).														●	
Reteach skills, judging which skills to reteach by evaluating students' performance on **Benchmark Test 2.**															●

- Cover the focus standards with independent readings and abbreviate review of the focus standards with student-edition selections.
- Do not assign extension activities for selections (day 5 of main selection lessons), except as needed for full standards coverage.
- If students demonstrate reading proficiency, consider omitting Test Practice: Reading features in the unit.

Block and Daily Scheduling

The assignments and activities in this Unit planner are organized by week. You may adjust them to your daily or block schedule. The Time and Resource Manager for each selection set gives specific pacing suggestions, or you may use the comprehensive lesson planning support online at **www.PHLitOnline.com.**

Monitoring Progress

Diagnose Each main selection pairing in the Unit contains a more accessible and a more complex selection. To determine which selection to assign to students, administer the **Diagnostic Test, *Unit 1 Resources,*** pp. 5–10. Use the **Interpretation Guide** to interpret the results of the diagnostic portion of the test.

Preteach and Prepare As indicated by the diagnostic, prepare students for reading by assigning the **Vocabulary Practice** and **Reading Warm-ups** for the selections you assign.

Teach Follow this Pacing Plan and use the resources to teach the skills and selections. For specific pacing suggestions and a list of resources, see the Time and Resource Manager and the Visual Guide to Featured Selection Resources preceding each selection pairing.

Classroom Management
For classroom management suggestions for using leveled texts in a mixed-ability classroom, see Harvey Daniels's professional development essay "Leveled Reading Selections," online at **www.PHLitOnline.com.**

Assess After students have completed the first half of the Unit, administer **Benchmark Test 1.** Administer **Benchmark Test 2** at the end of the Unit. **Note:** For the most accurate diagnosis of students who score in the middle range of the diagnostic portion of the test, administer the additional diagnostic questions online at **www.PHLitOnline.com.**

Intervention and Reteach After administering each test, use the **Interpretation Guide** for the tests to determine which reteaching pages, if any, you should assign from the *Reading Kit.* The appropriate pages are also available through the online Progress Monitoring software.

CLASSROOM STRATEGIES

Teaching Vocabulary at Middle Grades **Sharon Vaughn**

> "Many of our students have underdeveloped vocabularies for the texts they are reading as well."

"My students can read the words, they just don't know what they mean." Have you had similar thoughts? Of course, students can't understand if they can't read the words—but they surely can't understand if they don't know what the words mean either. It is why many of us struggle with reading and understanding a foreign language; we have underdeveloped vocabularies in the language we are reading. Many of our students have underdeveloped vocabularies for the texts they are reading as well. We know that asking them to look up words in the dictionary does not help students know the word. So what can you do to further develop and enhance the vocabulary of your students?

Improving Vocabulary Learning

There are so many words to choose from, how do we know which words to teach? In their book *Bringing Words to Life,* the authors (Beck & McKeown, 2002) discuss the fact that we have many types of words in our listening and speaking vocabulary and that these words can be thought of as consisting of levels or tiers.

1. **Tier 1 are common words** that can be readily learned by listening and talking to others. These words include *automobile, school, fire, run, happy,* and other very readily recognized words that do not need to be taught.
2. **Tier 2 are academic words** that students need to learn through instruction. These are more complex words that occur in academic listening or reading: for example, words like *clarify, context, reveal, significance* and *verify.* Most of your time will be spent teaching Tier 2 words.
3. **Tier 3 are more content-specific words** that are highly specialized and relate to the discipline students are studying—for example, *narrative, literary analysis, context clues,* and *reading strategy.*

Teaching Academic Vocabulary

The following vocabulary learning practices are likely to pay high dividends for improving students' knowledge of Tier 2 words (Denton, Bryan, Wexler, Reed, & Vaughn, 2007).

Promoting Word Consciousness When students are more "word conscious," they pay attention to how words are used, new meanings of words, words they have heard before but don't really know, and new words. You can promote word consciousness by:

- creating a word-rich environment in which you use the academic vocabulary words you are teaching and recognize students when they use these words either orally or in writing.
- promoting word learning and use within the class and at home by "looking" for new, unusual, unknown, or interesting words.

- teaching metalinguistic awareness in which students learn to "monitor" words they know and don't know while they are reading. Ask students to keep a list of new and unusual words.

- making connections among words by describing how they are the same, different, or similar in meaning.

Selecting Words to Teach and Teaching Specific Word Meanings We are challenged by the number of words students need to know and by how many we can readily teach and students can remember. You can promote word learning by

- recognizing the key vocabulary words that are highlighted for you. Consider whether there are additional words that need to be taught.

- teaching several new words each day and reviewing previously learned words regularly.

- teaching students to use context clues by reading the sentence before the unknown word and after the unknown word (as well as the sentence the unknown word is in) to figure out its meaning.

- providing vocabulary word walls where key words are listed, and asking students to maintain vocabulary journals.

Using Morphology to Promote Word Meaning

Teaching students critical aspects of morphology such as prefixes, suffixes, and common root words and derivations will help them readily discern the meaning of words. Consider promoting morphology by

- teaching students common meanings of prefixes and suffixes such as the prefix *re-*, meaning "again," and then demonstrating how this can be applied to word meaning by using examples from text and also by illustrating that some words, such as *reason*, do not incorporate the prefix, despite appearances.

- teaching students how to recognize roots which are meaningful units that cannot stand alone but can be used to form meaningful words. For example, knowing that *-cred-* means "belief" will help you know the meaning of words like *credible, incredible,* and *credulous.*

- showing students how key words relate to other words, how they are the same and different, and how they can be used is a big step toward making words spring to life in students' everyday use.

Modeled Strategy

See pp. 35 and 104 for point-of-use notes modeling these strategies.

Teacher Resources

- *Professional Development Guidebook*
- *Classroom Strategies and Teaching Routines cards*

Log on as a teacher at **www.PHLitOnline.com** to access a library of all Professional Development articles by the Contributing Authors of Pearson Prentice Hall *Literature.*

Sharon Vaughn, Ph.D.

Sharon Vaughn is the H.E. Hartfelder/ Southland Corporation Regents Chair of Human Development and Professor, University of Texas at Austin. She is the author of numerous books and articles on practices for enhancing reading outcomes for students with reading difficulties.

Supporting Research

Beck, I.L., & McKeown, M.G. (2002). *Bringing words to life: Robust vocabulary instruction.* New York: Guilford.

Denton, C., Bryan, D., Wexler, J., Reed, D., & Vaughn, S. (2007). *Effective instruction for middle school students with reading difficulties: The reading teacher's sourcebook.* University of Texas System/Texas Education Agency.

❶ Introducing the Big Question

1. Have students read the introductory section on the student page.

2. **Ask:** How would you go about proving or disproving a statement of fact? (**Possible responses:** go to outside print or online sources; consult an expert on the subject.)

3. **Ask** students the Big Question: "What is the best way to find the truth?" (**Possible answers:** Look for evidence; ask someone reliable.)

4. Note that the works in this Unit explore different ways of finding the truth. As students read, they should consider whether the stories support or challenge their first answers to the Big Question.

❷ Exploring the Big Question

Collaboration: One-on-One

1. Introduce the activity, using the instruction on the student page.

2. Have students work individually to think of examples. Then, have them work in pairs to determine which of their examples are based on factual evidence and which are based on perceptions and beliefs. If students have difficulty with the first and third bullet points, prompt ideas with questions:
   - What is an important date in our history? (**Sample response:** 1776)
   - What is the name of a planet in our solar system? (**Sample response:** Mercury)

3. Review the Big Question vocabulary on page 3, following the teaching suggestions. Have students use the vocabulary as they complete the activity on page 2.

Connecting to the Literature

Explain the Big Question strand in the unit, referring to the box at right.

---

❶ What is the best way to find the *truth?*

The **truth** is something that is real or a fact. Factual truth can be proved by evidence. Different people can have different ideas about what is true. Their ideas depend on how they perceive, or see, the world or what they believe. For example, the idea that a beautiful day must be sunny and warm may be true for one person but not another.

Authors of fiction often combine elements of truth to make a story. A story may be based on real events or people from history. Stories can also include authors' real memories or insights about the world around them.

❷ Exploring the Big Question

Collaboration: One-on-One Discussion Start thinking about the Big Question by looking at the different ways people can find out what is true. Make a list of things you know to be true. Describe one specific example of each of the following:

- a historical event
- a story from childhood
- a scientific fact about space
- a list of physical features of your school
- a memory of an exciting experience

Share and evaluate your examples with a partner. Discuss whether the truth is based on factual evidence or on perceptions and beliefs. Use the Big Question Vocabulary in your discussion.

Connecting to the Literature Each reading in this unit will give you additional insight into the Big Question.

www.PHLitOnline.com
- Big Question video
- Illustrated vocabulary words
- Interactive vocabulary games
- BQ Tunes

2 Fiction and Nonfiction

Applying Understanding by Design Principles

The Big Question
Explain to students that they will continue to consider the Big Question as they work through Unit 1.
- At the beginning of each selection, they will write a response to a Writing About the Big Question sentence frame.
- As they read the selection, they will look for details related to the Big Question.

- At the end of the selection, they will answer a Critical Thinking Question that is related to the Big Question.
- Tell students that their goal will be to gain a deeper understanding of literature and a more sophisticated way of discussing the Big Question.

③ Learning Big Question Vocabulary

ⓒ Acquire and Use Academic Vocabulary Academic vocabulary is the language you encounter in textbooks and on standardized tests. Review the definitions of these academic vocabulary words.

awareness (ə wer´ nəs) *n.* knowledge gained from one's own perceptions or from information

conclude (kən klōōd´) *v.* decide; reach a determination

convince (kən vins´) *v.* persuade

debate (dē bāt´) *v.* argue in an attempt to convince

evaluate (ē val´ yōō āt´) *v.* judge or determine the significance of

explain (ek splān´) *v.* make plain or clear

insight (in´ sīt´) *n.* ability to see the truth; an understanding

perceive (pər sēv´) *v.* see; be aware of

Use these words as you complete Big Question activities in this unit that involve reading, writing, speaking, and listening.

ⓒ Gather Vocabulary Knowledge Additional Big Question words are listed below. Categorize the words by deciding whether you know each one well, know it a little bit, or do not know it at all.

believable	fiction	reveal
evidence	reality	truth
factual		

Then, do the following:

1. Write the definitions of the words you know.
2. Consult a print or online dictionary to confirm each word's meaning. Revise your definitions if necessary.
3. Using a dictionary, look up the pronunciations and meanings of the words you do not know. Then, write the meanings.
4. Use as many of the words as you can in a brief paragraph about truth.

Introducing the Big Question **3**

ⓒ Common Core State Standards

Speaking and Listening
1. Engage effectively in a range of collaborative discussions with diverse partners on grade 7 topics, texts, and issues, building on others' ideas and expressing their own clearly.

Language
6. Acquire and use accurately grade-appropriate general academic and domain-specific words and phrases; gather vocabulary knowledge when considering a word or phrase important to comprehension or expression.

③ Learning Big Question Vocabulary

Acquire and Use Academic Vocabulary

1. Introduce the academic vocabulary words in the first word bank on the student page. Have students preview the words.
2. For each word, have students say the word aloud. Then, use the word in a sentence that defines the word.

Gather Vocabulary Knowledge

1. With the class, review the steps in the activity on the student page. Have students complete the activity independently, with partners, or in small groups.
2. Before students complete the last step, review the words and their meanings as a class. (Definitions appear below on the left.) Then, have students complete their paragraphs.

Gather Vocabulary Knowledge: Definitions

believable (bə lēv´ ə bəl) *adj.* able to be believed; possibly true

evidence (ev´ə dəns) *n.* proof in support of a claim or statement

factual (fak´ chōō əl) *adj.* based on or limited to fact

fiction (fik´ shən) *n.* something invented or imagined

reality (rē al´ə tē) *n.* state or quality of being real or true

reveal (ri vēl´) *v.* make known; show

truth (trōōth) *n.* what is the case

Show the Big Question video, online at **www.PHLitOnline.com.**

3

❶ Elements of Fiction and Nonfiction

1. Introduce the forms, fiction and nonfiction, using the instruction on the student page.

2. Clarify that the chart on the student page compares and contrasts elements of fiction and nonfiction. **Ask:** What elements does the first row contrast, and what contrast does it point out?

   Answer: It contrasts characters in fiction with people in nonfiction, pointing out that fictional characters are made up while people in nonfiction are real.

3. Point out that the chart uses bold print for elements that are literary terms, which are terms that students will learn about and use in studying literature. **Ask:** What literary term and its explanation appears in the first row?

   Answer: The term is *characters,* explained as "made-up people or animals."

4. **Ask:** What comparison or similarity does the fifth row show?

   Answer: It shows that each form may contain elements associated with the other—facts are associated with nonfiction, but sometimes fiction contains them; dialogue is an element of fiction, but sometimes nonfiction has dialogue.

5. Discuss each of the other rows on the chart, the elements they compare or contrast, and any literary terms they introduce.

❶ Elements of Fiction and Nonfiction

Fiction and nonfiction are two types, or genres, of writing.

Fiction describes imaginary characters and events. When you read fiction, you enter a world that was created by the author's imagination. However, many works of fiction have realistic elements. Historical fiction, for example, can tell a true story but contains certain made-up elements.

Nonfiction is based on facts. It describes real people, events, and ideas. When you read nonfiction, the information you encounter is factual. Nonfiction authors research their topics. They present information that teaches you about a subject or tries to convince you to do or believe something.

Nonfiction may also share some elements of fiction. Nonfiction writers, for example, can bring true events to life through their use of vivid descriptions or dramatic writing styles. They may even create made-up examples to illustrate their points.

Elements of Fiction and Nonfiction	
Fiction	**Nonfiction**
includes made-up people or animals, called **characters**	focuses on real people
is told through a made-up series of events called the **plot**, which usually revolves around a **conflict**, or problem	describes true events and conflicts
is narrated or told by a speaker, called the **narrator**	is narrated from the **point of view**, or perspective, of the author, who is a real person
takes place in a time and location, or **setting**, which may or may not be real	presents facts or discusses ideas related to real places or historical periods
may include facts to make a made-up story seem realistic	may use elements also found in fiction, such as vivid descriptions or characters and their conversations, or **dialogue**
often suggests a **theme**, or message about life	often conveys a **central idea** supported by details

4 Fiction and Nonfiction

Teaching Resources

All *Common Core Companion,* pp. 15–27, 109–121

All *Unit 1 Resources,* pp. 13–29

All *Professional Development Guidebook,* pp. 33, 42

All *See It!* DVD
Patricia McKissack, Segments 1 and 2

All *Graphic Organizer Transparencies,* pp. 1, 2

All **Enriched Online Student Edition**

L2 L3 *Reader's Notebook*

L1 *Reader's Notebook: Adapted Version*

EL *Reader's Notebook: English Learner's Version*

L2 EL *Hear It!* Audio CD

L1 EL *Hear It!* Audio CD (adapted text)

All resources, including print and video, are available online at **www.PHLitOnline.com.**

Forms of Fiction

There are three main forms of fiction.

Novel: A novel is a long work of fiction. It contains elements such as characters, plot, conflict, and setting. In addition to a main plot, a novel may contain one or more **subplots,** or independent, related stories.

Novella: A novella is a work of fiction that is shorter than a novel but longer than a short story.

Short Story: A short story is a brief work of fiction. It contains the same basic elements as a novel or novella but tends to focus on one main plot structured around a single conflict. Many short stories can be read in a single sitting.

Forms of Nonfiction ❸

Nonfiction comes in many different forms. Two broad categories of nonfiction are literary nonfiction and functional texts.

Literary Nonfiction: This type of nonfiction has elements of fiction. For example, it might use vivid descriptions, a dramatic writing style, or poetic language.

Functional Texts: These texts give instructions, show directions, explain rules, or provide other types of information that help you complete procedures. Functional texts often include illustrations or graphics to help guide the reader.

The charts below show some examples of literary nonfiction and functional texts.

❹ In This Section

Elements of Fiction and Nonfiction

Determining Theme in Fiction

Determining Central Ideas in Nonfiction

Close Read: Theme in Fiction
• Model Text
• Practice Text

Close Read: Central Idea in Nonfiction
• Model Text
• Practice Text

After You Read

 Common Core State Standards addressed:

RL.7.2; RI.7.2
[For the full wording of the standards, see the standards chart in the front of your textbook.]

Literary Nonfiction
Autobiographies and memoirs tell the story of the author's life.
Biographies tell the story of someone's life from the perspective of another writer.
Letters are written communications from person to person.
Essays and articles are brief works about a specific topic.
Reviews tell what is good and what is bad about a work of art or performance.
Reports give information about a topic explored through research.

Functional Texts
Recipes tell how to prepare food.
Directions tell how to operate or assemble equipment.
Schedules tell when events take place.
Menus tell which foods are available and their cost.
Brochures use pictures and text to advertise places or events.
Maps are diagrams that show areas of land.
Applications are written requests to an authority.

Literary Analysis Workshop **5**

❷ Forms of Fiction

1. Introduce the forms, using the instruction on the student page.
2. Explore students' knowledge of the three forms of fiction by having students name novels, novellas, and stories that they have read. If they name no novellas, mention that the original version of *A Christmas Carol* by Charles Dickens is a novella; a drama based on the novella appears in students' texts.

❸ Forms of Nonfiction

1. Introduce the forms, using the instruction and the chart on the student page.
2. **Ask** students to categorize these two types of nonfiction: a biography of a leader of the American Revolution; a medical pamphlet explaining the symptoms and treatment of an illness.

   Answer: The biography is literary nonfiction; the medical pamphlet is a functional text.

❹ In This Section

Explain that in the remainder of this Literary Analysis Workshop, students will analyze an important element of each form: theme in the case of fiction, and central idea in the case of nonfiction. After reviewing the concept, they will then see it applied in an analysis of two Model texts. Finally, they will apply what they have learned to two Independent Practice texts.

Differentiated Instruction   for Universal Access

Support for Special-Needs Students
Have students read the **Learning About Fiction and Nonfiction** pages for these selections in the *Reader's Notebook: Adapted Version.* This version provides a basic-level introduction to fiction and nonfiction.

Support for Less Proficient Readers
Have students read the **Learning About Fiction and Nonfiction** pages for these selections in the *Reader's Notebook.* This version provides a basic-level introduction to fiction and nonfiction.

EL Support for English Learners
Have students read the **Learning About Fiction and Nonfiction** pages for these selections in the *Reader's Notebook: English Learner's Version.* This version provides a basic-level introduction to fiction and nonfiction.

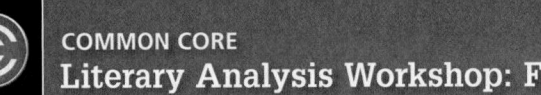

 **Common Core State Standards**

Unit 1 Focus Standards

• Reading Literature 2
• Reading Informational Text 2

These standards spiral through the unit.

❶ Determining Theme in Fiction

1. Introduce the concept of theme, using the instruction on the student page.

2. Stress the idea that a theme is usually implied through story details, rather than stated directly in the story.

3. Review with students the concepts of universal and multiple themes, which are both defined on the student page.

4. Discuss the three interpretations of the theme in the example about Daedalus and Icarus. **Ask:** In what ways do the details in the myth support each theme?

   Sample response: Icarus's failure to limit his flight in spite of his father's warning points to the first interpretation. The disaster brought on by his failure to recognize the power of the sun, a force of nature, points to the second. His ambitious effort to fly, rather than simply escape, points to the third.

5. Remind students that in this Workshop they will read a model analysis of the theme of a passage and then perform their own analysis of a second passage.

❶ Determining Theme in Fiction

Works of fiction express themes— messages or insights about life.

 **Common Core State Standards**

Reading Literature 2. Determine a theme or central idea of a text and analyze its development over the course of the text; provide an objective summary of the text.

The **theme** is a central message in a literary work. When you read a work of fiction, remember that theme and subject are not the same. The subject is what the story is about. The theme is the writer's message about a particular subject.

Subject	Theme
Competition	Winning isn't everything.
Forces of Nature	Humans can't control the forces of nature.
Failure	Failure may teach more than success teaches.

In some works of fiction, the writer will state the theme directly. More often, however, a fiction writer *implies,* or suggests, a theme through the words and experiences of characters or through events in the story.

Universal Themes A **universal theme** is a message about life that is expressed in many different cultures and time periods. The value of friendship and the power of love are two examples of universal themes. Ideas like these address experiences that are common to many people. Such universal themes can be found in a variety of works, such as tales from ancient Greece or modern novels.

Multiple Themes Some works of fiction express more than one theme. Novels, full-length plays, and some long poems may have multiple themes, while a short story usually expresses a single theme.

Interpreting Themes Different people may interpret the theme of a story in different ways. Consider, for example, the classic myth of Daedalus and Icarus.

> **Example:**
> Daedalus constructs wings with feathers held together by wax to help his son Icarus and himself escape an island prison. Daedalus warns Icarus not to fly too close to the sun because the sun's heat could melt the wax. Thrilled by the adventure of flying, Icarus ignores his father's warning. The wax melts, causing Icarus's wings to fall apart, and Icarus falls to his death.

> **Possible Interpretations of Theme:**
> • Know your limitations.
> • Defying nature leads to disaster.
> • Ambition can be costly.

These themes are all different, but each reflects the events of the story.

6 Fiction and Nonfiction

Think Aloud

Determining Theme

To model the skill of determining theme, use the following "think aloud." Say to students:

To figure out a story's theme, I pay attention to the story's details and especially the outcome. For instance, suppose a story is about a seventh grader who is so shy about expressing her opinions that people treat her like a doormat. Then, her best friend tells her to start telling people what she thinks in order to do better in school and in life. However, when she tells her friend that a new outfit makes the friend look absolutely awful, the friend's feelings are hurt and the two stop being best friends.

Thinking about what the story events and outcome say about life in general, I can see that one theme is about expressing opinions; for example, *It is important to express your opinions, but you need to do so in a tactful way.* The events and outcome also express a theme about giving advice, such as *Good advice can have bad consequences* or *People may not like the consequences of the advice they give.*

❷ Determining Central Ideas in Nonfiction

Works of literary nonfiction express central, or main, ideas.

Common Core State Standards

Reading Information 2. Determine two or more central ideas in a text and analyze their development over the course of the text; provide an objective summary of the text.

The **central,** or **main, idea** is the key point in a work of literary nonfiction. All nonfiction works express one or more central ideas. Sometimes the author directly states the central idea, then supports it with key details. In many cases, however, the author *implies*, or suggests, the central idea. Readers can determine the central idea by analyzing the key details and supporting evidence the author provides.

Topic Sentences and Supporting Details In many works of nonfiction, the author conveys one central idea for the entire work, which is supported by central ideas in individual paragraphs. The central idea of a paragraph can often be found in the **topic sentence,** which is usually the first sentence.

The example below shows three paragraphs with topic sentences that support the central idea of the entire work.

> **Example: Topic Sentences**
> **Central Idea:** Breakfast is the most important meal of the day.
> **Paragraph 1:** Children who eat breakfast do better in school.
> **Paragraph 2:** People who skip breakfast may make unhealthy snack choices.
> **Paragraph 3:** People who eat breakfast are likely to maintain a healthy weight.

In the same way that each paragraph supports the central idea of the entire work, supporting details support the topic sentence of each paragraph. The following example shows a supporting detail for Paragraph 1.

> **Example: Supporting Detail**
> In a recent study, children who ate breakfast made fewer mistakes and worked faster on math tests than children who skipped breakfast.

Author's Purpose and Central Idea An **author's purpose** is his or her main reason for writing. The three most common purposes are to **entertain,** to **inform,** or to **persuade** the reader. An author may have more than one purpose in a single work. The author will also have a *specific* purpose that relates to his or her topic. The central idea is what the author wants readers to believe about that topic.

Author's Purpose	To persuade
Specific Purpose	To persuade citizens to vote to build a wind farm in their town
Central Idea	A wind farm will benefit people in the community.

Literary Analysis Workshop **7**

❷ Determining Central Ideas in Nonfiction

1. Introduce the concept of central, or main, idea, using the instruction on the student page.

2. Review the material on topic sentences and supporting details, making sure students understand the relationship between the central idea of a work and the central ideas in its paragraphs. **Ask:** In the example shown on the first chart, how do the topic sentences of the three paragraphs all support the central idea of the entire work?

   Answer: They all state reasons why breakfast is the most important meal of the day.

3. Lead a discussion on the relationship between the author's purpose and the central idea. Remind students that a central idea may be stated or implied. **Ask:** If the author's purpose is to inform, is the author more likely to state or imply the central idea? Why?

   Sample response: The author is more likely to state the central idea because it is an important piece of information, and providing information is his or her purpose in writing.

4. Remind students that in this Workshop they will read a model analysis of the central idea of a passage and then perform their own analysis of a second passage.

❸ Close Read: Theme in Fiction

1. Remind students that the theme of a work is its message or insight about life.

2. Review the Clues to Theme chart, making sure students understand each clue. Clarify that a symbol literally exists within a story but also represents something else. For instance, in the myth of Icarus on page 6, the sun is literally the sun in the story but also represents nature.

3. Divide the class into groups. Write this theme on the board: *Kindness will be rewarded.* Have each group devise clues to theme in one of the six different chart categories. Then, have groups share their clues.

   Sample responses: *Title*—The Good Deed; *Characters*— twelve-year-old Luis and an old hermit; *Conflict*—Luis struggles with peers who try to get him to join in tormenting an old hermit; *Statements and Observations*— "That ol' hermit never hurt me; why should I hurt him?"; *Symbols*—the hermit's fortune, which Luis is surprised to inherit when the hermit dies

4. Refer students to the Model text on page 9. Explain that details in the text that illustrate each category on the chart are highlighted in the same color and that corresponding side-column annotations use corresponding colors.

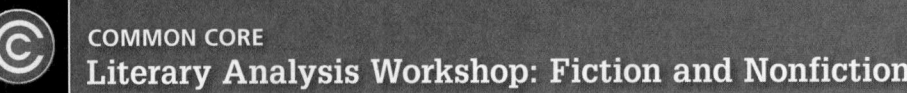

❸ Close Read: Theme in Fiction

All the elements of a story, from the title to the characters to individual words, work together to support the theme.

Authors of fiction seldom directly state the theme, or central message about life. Instead, they often present the theme indirectly. To discover a theme that is implied, or presented indirectly, pay attention to details in the selection by asking yourself the questions in the chart below. They may provide clues that will help you discover what the work reveals about people or life.

Clues to Theme		
Title The **title** is the name of the story. • Do the words in the title prompt ideas or stir emotions? • Do the words include any "universal theme" words (*love, friendship, nature, time*)?	**Conflict** A **conflict** is a struggle between opposing forces. • What is the main conflict in the story? • How does the conflict affect the characters? • What message about life might the conflict suggest?	**Setting** The **setting** is the time and place of the action. • How does the setting affect the characters? • Could this story take place in a different setting?
Characters A **character** is a person or an animal that takes part in the action of the story. • What is each character's main problem or conflict? • Do the characters change or learn anything about life?	**Statements and Observations** A **statement** or **observation** expresses an idea. • What do the characters say about themselves and each other? • Which of the narrator's statements pertain to life or human nature? • What sentences stand out in your mind? Why?	**Symbols** A **symbol** is something that stands for or represents something else. • What objects are important in the story? • How do characters react to particular objects, people, or words?

Vocabulary Development   ©️ CCSS Language 6

Domain-Specific Words: Literature
Reinforce comprehension of the literary terms on the page by having students complete these "show-you-know" sentences, which also include information about the story that begins on page 9. Ask students to explain how the context clues in the sentences help them determine the literary term to use.

1. The _____ of the story is Japan, or the Land of the Rising Sun, during the Middle Ages.

Answer: setting; **Explanation**—The context gives the time and place of the story, and setting is the time and place of a story.

2. In the story, the drake, or male duck, may be a _____ of oppressed people, or it may stand for beauty or nature.

Answer: symbol; **Explanation**—The context discusses what the drake stands for, and a symbol is something that stands for something else.

© EXEMPLAR TEXT

❹ Model

About the Text This story is set in Japan in the Middle Ages, when powerful lords lived in palaces and ruled the people who lived on their estates. The lords could do what they wanted, and the people had to obey them.

from *The Tale of the Mandarin Ducks* by Katherine Paterson

Long ago and far away in the Land of the Rising Sun, there lived together a pair of mandarin ducks. Now, the drake was a magnificent bird with plumage of colors so rich that the emperor himself would have envied it. But his mate, the duck, wore the quiet tones of the wood, blending exactly with the hole in the tree where the two had made their nest.

One day while the duck was sitting on her eggs, the drake flew down to a nearby pond to search for food. While he was there, a hunting party entered the woods. The hunters were led by the lord of the district, a proud and cruel man who believed that everything in the district belonged to him to do with as he chose. The lord was always looking for beautiful things to adorn his manor house and garden. And when he saw the drake swimming gracefully on the surface of the pond, he determined to capture him.

The lord's chief steward, a man named Shozo, tried to discourage his master. "The drake is a wild spirit, my lord," he said. "Surely he will die in captivity." But the lord pretended not to hear Shozo. Secretly he despised Shozo, because although Shozo had once been his mightiest samurai, the warrior had lost an eye in battle and was no longer handsome to look upon.

The lord ordered his servants to clear a narrow way through the undergrowth and place acorns along the path. When the drake came out of the water he saw the acorns. How pleased he was! He forgot to be cautious, thinking only of what a feast they would be to take home to his mate.

Just as he was bending to pick up an acorn in his scarlet beak, a net fell over him, and the frightened bird was carried back to the lord's manor and placed in a small bamboo cage.

❺ Characters The narrator describes the lord's cruelty and selfishness. Often, details about a main character can provide a clue to the theme of a work.

❻ Symbols In folk tales, animals or magical creatures often represent people. The lord's attitude toward the drake represents how little he cares for the people he rules.

❼ Statements This statement further illustrates the lord's shallowness and cruelty.

❽ Conflict The wild bird does not want to be caged. Its capture creates a conflict.

Literary Analysis Workshop **9**

❹ Reading the Model

1. Discuss the About the Text paragraph. Explain that the story features a steward, a servant who cares for the lord's estate and who was once a samurai, or Japanese warrior. It also features a drake, or male duck.

2. Have students read the passage (pp. 9–10). Discuss it, clarifying as needed, before reviewing the annotations.

❺ Characters

Read aloud the Characters annotation. **Ask:** Based on the lord's behavior, what human qualities is the theme likely to be about?

Possible response: It is likely to be about cruelty and selfishness.

❻ Symbols

Read aloud the Symbols annotation. **Ask:** Based on the symbol's meaning, what kind of human relationship might the theme be about?

Possible response: It might be about the relationship between those in power and those they rule.

❼ Statements

Read aloud the highlighted statement and the Statements annotation. **Ask:** How does the statement show the lord's shallowness?

Possible response: Only a shallow person would place such value on physical appearance and show no respect for someone who was once his mightiest warrior.

❽ Conflict

Read aloud the Conflict annotation. **Ask:** What does the bird seem to value?

Possible response: It values freedom.

❾ Setting

Read aloud the Setting annotation after students review the highlighted passage. **Ask:** Why does the lord invite other wealthy landowners to see the duck, instead of just showing it off to those he rules on his estate?

Possible response: He wants people of his own class to envy him.

❿ Conflict

1. Have a student read aloud the Conflict annotation. **Ask:** Who is responsible for the bird's illness? Why?

   Possible response: The lord is responsible, since he insisted on capturing it.

⓫ Conflict

1. Have students read more about the conflict in the first sentence of the last paragraph. **Ask:** How is the lord's attitude toward the drake like his attitude toward the steward?

   Possible response: In both cases, he shows no sympathy for those who lose their looks.

⓬ Theme

1. Read aloud the Theme annotation. Explain that the interpretation of the story's theme will depend in part on the interpretation of the symbol of the drake. **Ask:** If the drake is a symbol of beauty or nature, what themes might the story express?

   Possible response: Beauty can never be fully captured. The wild creatures of nature are destroyed if confined.

 EXEMPLAR TEXT

Model continued

❾ Setting In the society in which the story takes place, the lord has a high position. He likes to show off in front of others.

❿ Conflict The conflict builds as grief causes the captured drake to become ill.

❾ The lord was delighted with his new pet. He ordered a feast to be prepared and invited all the wealthy landowners from miles around, so that he could show off the drake and brag about his wonderful plumage, which was indeed more beautiful than the finest brocade.

But the drake could think only of his mate sitting alone on her eggs, not knowing what had happened to her husband.

❿ As the days wore on, his crested head began to droop. His lovely feathers lost their luster. His proud, wild cry became first a weary *cronk* and then he fell silent. No matter what delicacies the kitchen maid brought him, he refused to eat. He is grieving for his mate, the girl thought, for she was wise in the customs of wild creatures.

⓫ The lord, who liked things only so long as they were beautiful and brought him honor, grew angry when he saw that the drake was ailing. "Perhaps we should let him go," Shozo suggested, "since he no longer pleases you, my lord." But the lord did not like anyone to tell him what to do, much less a one-eyed servant. He refused to release the drake, ordering instead that the cage be put out of sight so that he would no longer be annoyed by the bird's sad appearance.

⓬ **Theme** The story continues, but based on details you have learned so far, you can determine one or more possible themes. For example, based on the lord's cruelty, one theme might be that selfish people can do terrible harm to others. Based on the drake's grief, another theme might be that separation from a loved one can cause great pain.

Vocabulary Development

 CCSS Language 6

Thematic Vocabulary: The Big Question

As students discuss the selection from *The Tale of the Mandarin Ducks,* encourage them to use the thematic vocabulary presented in Introducing the Big Question, pages 2–3. Help them with sentence starters such as these:

1. At first, the drake has no *awareness* that he is in danger when he . . .
2. The lord fails to *perceive* that his own actions have . . .
3. The steward shows *insight* when he suggests . . .

⑬ Independent Practice

About the Selection During a visit to a nursing home, a young girl sees a whole new side of her 102-year-old great-grandmother.

"The Three-Century Woman" by Richard Peck

"I guess if you live long enough," my mom said to Aunt Gloria, "you get your fifteen minutes of fame."

Mom was on the car phone to Aunt Gloria. The minute Mom rolls out of the garage, she's on her car phone. It's state-of-the-art and better than her car.

We were heading for Whispering Oaks to see my great-grandmother Breckenridge, who's lived there since I was a little girl. They call it an Elder Care Facility. Needless to say, I hated going.

The reason for Great-grandmother's fame is that she was born in 1899. Now it's January 2001. If you're one of those people who claim the new century begins in 2001, not 2000, even you have to agree that Great-grandmother Breckenridge has lived in three centuries. This is her claim to fame.

We waited for a light to change along by Northbrook Mall, and I gazed fondly over at it. Except for the Multiplex, it was closed because of New Year's Day. I have a severe mall habit. But I'm fourteen, and the mall is the place without homework. Aunt Gloria's voice filled the car.

"If you take my advice," she told Mom, "you'll keep those Whispering Oaks people from letting the media in to interview Grandma. Interview her my foot! Honestly. She doesn't know where she is, let alone how many centuries she's lived in. The poor old soul. Leave her in peace. She's already got one foot in the—"

"Gloria, your trouble is you have no sense of history." Mom gunned across the intersection. "You got a C in history."

"I was sick a lot that year," Aunt Gloria said.

"Sick of history," Mom mumbled.

"I heard that," Aunt Gloria said.

They bickered on, but I tuned them out. Then when we turned in at Whispering Pines, a sound truck from IBC-TV was blocking the drive.

"Good grief," Mom murmured. "TV."

---

⑭ Conflict Why might the narrator hate visiting Whispering Oaks?

⑮ Character What do Aunt Gloria's words tell you about her attitude toward her grandmother?

Literary Analysis Workshop **11**

---

⑬ Introducing the Independent Practice

1. Explain to students that they will determine the theme of the Independent Practice selection.

2. Discuss the About the Selection note, and have students read the selection. Then, direct them to go back through and respond to the side-column prompts. Conclude by having students answer the After You Read questions on page 21.

⑭ Conflict

1. Read aloud the third paragraph, including the highlighted text. **Ask:** What conflict involving the narrator does the third paragraph introduce?

   Possible response: She must visit her great-grandmother at the nursing home but hates going.

2. Have a student read the remainder of the bracketed text. **Ask** the Conflict question.

   Possible response: She is bored by visiting her great-grandmother and would rather be at the mall.

⑮ Character

1. Read aloud Aunt Gloria's comments in the sixth paragraph, including the highlighted remarks. Refer students to the story's title and fourth paragraph to explain the media's presence. **Ask:** Why are the media coming?

   Answer: They want to interview a woman who has lived in three centuries.

2. **Ask** the Character question.

   Possible response: She considers her grandmother too feeble or senile to be interviewed.

---

16 Setting

1. Have a student read aloud the bracketed passage. **Ask:** Which detail in this passage gives the most positive impression of Whispering Oaks?

   Possible response: The real Christmas tree gives the most positive impression.

2. **Ask:** What does the detail of the red button and use of the word *inmates* show about Megan's view of the nursing-home residents?

   Possible response: She finds their lives very restricted, like prison inmates' lives.

3. **Ask** the Setting question.

   Possible response: By showing the situation in which elderly people find themselves, the narrator's statement may suggest a theme about the elderly.

17 Character

1. Have two students read aloud the exchange between the mother and newswoman, including the text highlighted in blue.
   Ask: What attitude does the mother have toward her grandmother?

   Possible response: She is fiercely protective of her grandmother, who she believes is in a diminished state.

2. **Ask** the Character question.

   Possible response: She is physically weak and somewhat senile.

Practice continued

"I told you," Aunt Gloria said, but Mom switched her off. She parked in a frozen rut.

"I'll wait in the car," I said. "I have homework."

"Get out of the car," Mom said.

16 Setting How might the narrator's description of Whispering Oaks help develop a theme?

16 If you get so old you have to be put away, Whispering Oaks isn't that bad. It smells all right, and a Christmas tree glittered in the lobby. A real tree. On the other hand, you have to push a red button to unlock the front door. I guess it's to keep the inmates from escaping, though Great-grandmother Breckenridge wasn't going anywhere and hadn't for twenty years.

When we got to her wing, the hall was full of camera crews and a woman from the suburban newspaper with a notepad.

Mom sighed. It was like that first day of school when you think you'll be okay until the teachers learn your name. Stepping over a cable, we stopped at Great-grandma's door, and they were on to us.

"Who are you people to Mrs. Breckenridge?" the newspaperwoman said. "I want names."

These people were seriously pushy. And the TV guy was wearing more makeup than Mom. It dawned on me that they couldn't get into Great-grandma's room without her permission. Mom turned on them.

17 Character Based on these comments, what is your impression of Great-grandma?

17 "Listen, you're not going to be interviewing my grandmother," she said in a quiet bark. "I'll be glad to tell you anything you want to know about her, but you're not going in there. She's got nothing to say, and . . . she needs a lot of rest."

"Is it Alzheimer's?"[1] the newswoman asked. "Because we're thinking Alzheimer's."

"Think what you want," Mom said. "But this is as far as you get. And you people with the camera and the light, you're not going in there either. You'd scare her to death, and then I'd sue the pants off you."

They pulled back.

But a voice came wavering out of Great-grandma's room. Quite an eerie, echoing voice.

---

1. **Alzheimer's** (älts´ hī´ mərz) *n.* a progressive disease in which brain cells degenerate, leading to severe dementia.

Vocabulary Development   © CCSS Language 6

Media Terminology

Great-grandma's family is concerned about "the media" interviewing her. You might wish to clarify with students terms related to the media, particularly those used in the selection.

- *media:* sources through which news is communicated such as television, newspapers, radio, and magazines
- *anchor:* the main newscaster or newsreader on a television news program; in this story, the anchor is also doing the interviewing
- *cameraman:* the person who operates a video camera and tapes scenes to be aired on television
- *close-up:* a camera view of a subject from up close
- *pan:* move the camera horizontally to get a wider view of a scene
- *"that's a wrap":* a phrase meaning that a session is concluded

"Let them in!" the voice said.

It had to be Great-grandma Breckenridge. Her roommate had died. "Good grief," Mom muttered, and the press surged forward.

Mom and I went in first, and our eyes popped. Great-grandma was usually flat out in the bed, dozing, with her teeth in a glass and a book in her hand. Today she was bright-eyed and propped up. She wore a fuzzy pink bed jacket. A matching bow was stuck in what remained of her hair.

18

"Oh, for pity's sake," Mom said. "They've got her done up like a Barbie doll."

Great-grandma peered from the bed at Mom. "And who are you?" she asked.

"I'm Ann," Mom said carefully. "This is Megan," she said, meaning me.

"That's right," Great-grandma said. "At least you know who you are. Plenty around this place don't."

The guy with the camera on his shoulder barged in. The other guy turned on a blinding light.

Great-grandma blinked. In the glare we noticed she wore a trace of lipstick. The TV anchor elbowed the woman reporter aside and stuck a mike in Great-grandma's face. Her claw hand came out from under the covers and tapped it.

"Is this thing on?" she inquired.

"Yes, ma'am," the TV anchor said in his broadcasting voice. "Don't you worry about all this modern technology. We don't understand half of it ourselves." He gave her his big, fivethirty news smile and settled on the edge of the bed. There was room for him. She was tiny.

19

"We're here to congratulate you for having lived in three centuries—for being a Three-Century Woman! A great achievement!"

Great-grandma waved a casual claw. "Nothing to it," she said. "You sure this mike's on? Let's do this in one take."

The cameraman snorted and moved in for a closer shot. Mom stood still as a statue, wondering what was going to come out of Great-grandma's mouth next.

18

Statements What does Megan's use of the word "claw" say about her feelings toward aging?

19

Character Does Great-grandma appear to have a good understanding of what is going on? Explain.

Literary Analysis Workshop **13**

18 Statements

1. Have students reread Megan's statements in the third paragraph on this page. **Ask:** What contrast in Great-grandma's appearance and behavior does this statement reveal?

   Possible response: Usually when Megan visits, Great-grandma is sluggish and does nothing to prepare for visitors, but today she is alert and dressed up.

2. **Ask:** Why is Great-grandma different today?

   Possible response: She is excited about the interview and wants to look her best.

3. Have students reread the first highlighted statement. **Ask** the Statements question.

   Possible response: She finds the changes caused by aging to be unpleasant.

19 Character

1. Have two students read aloud the exchange between Great-grandma and the TV anchor, including the part highlighted in blue. **Ask:** What does the remark about modern technology show about the TV anchor's view of Great-grandma?

   Possible response: He believes she is too old to be familiar with modern technology.

2. **Ask** the Character question.

   Possible response: Yes, she obviously knows what the microphone is and is even familiar with broadcast jargon like "take."

3. **Ask:** How do Great-grandma's remarks and behavior contradict what others have thought about her so far?

   Possible response: Others have thought her feeble and somewhat senile, but she is alert and interested in being interviewed.

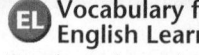

Differentiated Instruction for Universal Access

EL Vocabulary for English Learners

Teach students the following idiomatic expressions from the selection.

- *pushy* (p. 12): bold and rude when trying to get what one wants
- *dawned on me* (p. 12): became clear to me
- *scare to death* (p. 12): frighten someone so much the person feels he or she might die
- *sue the pants off you* (p. 12): start a lawsuit against someone for everything he or she owns (including the pants that person is wearing)
- *eyes popped* (p. 13): eyes opened wide in surprise
- *look for an angle* (p. 14): look for a way to approach a task to get a particular result
- *put one's nose out of joint* (p. 17): cause someone to feel annoyed, disappointed, or ill-tempered

13

20 Character

1. Have students recall their impression of Great-grandma before she appeared in the story. **Ask:** Before you met Great-grandma, what state did you think she would be in when reporters tried to interview her?

   Possible response: She seemed likely to be too weak and senile to participate fully.

2. **Ask:** Why did you get that impression?

   Possible response: Megan's attitude and the remarks of Aunt Gloria and Megan's mom all conveyed that impression.

3. Have students review the highlighted text. **Ask** the Character questions.

   Possible response: Yes, the initial impression of a senile old lady has changed. Her remarks show that she is up to date, knows how to give a colorful interview, and has a sense of humor.

21 Character

1. Have students review Megan's impressions of the TV anchor in the bracketed passage. **Ask:** Which details might lead Megan to conclude that the anchor has no sense of humor?

   Possible response: He does not laugh when Great-grandma says that she lived long because her husband died young or that she fell off the bed pan.

2. **Ask:** What does the portrayal of the TV anchor poke fun at? Explain.

   Possible response: It pokes fun at the media by showing a stereotypical TV anchor with no sense of humor who barrels ahead regardless of what happens. It also pokes fun at self-centered people and people who make false assumptions about the elderly.

Practice continued

20

Character Based on her remarks, has your impression of Great-grandma changed since you began reading this story? Why or why not?

20 "Mrs. Breckenridge," the anchor said, "to what do you attribute[2] your long life?"

"I was only married once," Great-grandma said. "And he died young."

The anchor stared. "Ah. And anything else?"

"Yes. I don't look back. I live in the present."

The camera panned around the room. This was all the present she had, and it didn't look like much.

"You live for the present," the anchor said, looking for an angle, "even now?" Great-grandma nodded. "Something's always happening. Last night I fell off the bed pan."

Mom groaned.

21 The cameraman pulled in for a tighter shot. The anchor seemed to search his mind. You could tell he thought he was a great interviewer, though he had no sense of humor. A tiny smile played around Great-grandma's wrinkled lips.

"But you've lived through amazing times, Mrs. Breckenridge. And you never think back about them?"

Great-grandma stroked her chin and considered. "You mean you want to hear something interesting? Like how I lived through the San Francisco earthquake—the big one of oh-six?"

Beside me, Mom stirred. We were crowded over by the dead lady's bed. "You survived the 1906 San Francisco earthquake?" the anchor said.

22 Great-grandma gazed at the ceiling, lost in thought.

"I'd have been about seven years old. My folks and I were staying at that big hotel. You know the one. I slept in a cot at the foot of their bed. In the middle of the night, that room gave a shake, and the chiffonier walked right across the floor. You know what a chiffonier is?"

"A chest of drawers?" the anchor said.

"Close enough," Great-grandma said. "And the pictures flapped on the walls. We had to walk down twelve flights because the elevators didn't

---

2. **attribute** (ə trib′ yo͞ot) *v.* think of as caused by.

14 Fiction and Nonfiction

Vocabulary Development   CCSS Language 6

THE BIG ? **Thematic Vocabulary: The Big Question**

As students are discussing "The Three-Century Woman," encourage them to use the thematic vocabulary presented in Introducing the Big Question, pages 2–3. You might use sentence starters such as these:

1. Great-grandma shows her *awareness* of the world around her by . . .

2. Mom is quick to *perceive* that Great-grandma is . . .

3. The news anchor does not bother to *evaluate* . . .

4. Great-grandma's stories sound *believable* because . . .

5. Great-grandma's behavior during the interview helps to *reveal* that she is . . .

work. When we got outside, the streets were ankle-deep in broken glass. You never saw such a mess in your life."

Mom nudged me and hissed: "She's never been to San Francisco. She's never been west of Denver. I've heard her say so."

"Incredible!" the anchor said.

"Truth's stranger than fiction," Great-grandma said, smoothing her sheet.

"And you never think back about it?"

Great-grandma shrugged her little fuzzy pink shoulders. "I've been through too much. I don't have time to remember it all. I was on the *Hindenburg* when it blew up, you know."

Mom moaned, and the cameraman was practically standing on his head for a close-up.

"The *Hindenburg*!"

"That big gas thing the Germans built to fly over the Atlantic Ocean. It was called a zeppelin.[3] Biggest thing you ever saw—five city blocks long. It was in May of 1937, before your time. You wouldn't remember. My husband and I were coming back from Europe. No, wait a minute."

Great-grandma cocked her head and pondered for the camera.

"My husband was dead by then. It was some other man. Anyway, the two of us were coming back on the *Hindenburg*. It was smooth as silk. You didn't know you were moving. When we flew in over New York, they stopped the ball game at Yankee Stadium to see us passing overhead."

Great-grandma paused, caught up in the memories.

"And then the *Hindenburg* exploded," the anchor said, prompting her.

She nodded. "We had no complaints about the trip till then. The luggage was all stacked, and we were coming in at Lakehurst, New Jersey. I was wearing my beige coat—beige or off-white, I forget. Then whoosh! The gondola[4] heated up like an oven, and people peeled out of the windows. We hit the ground and bounced. When we hit again, the door fell off, and I walked out and kept going. When they caught up to me in the parking

---

3. **zeppelin** (zep´ ə lin) *n.* a large, cigar-shaped airship with separate compartments filled with gas; used from 1900 to 1937.
4. **gondola** (gän´ dō lə) *n.* a cabin attached to the underside of an airship to hold the motors, instruments, passengers, etc.

22 **Statements** How might Great-grandma know so much about the San Francisco earthquake if she has never been to San Francisco?

22 **Statements**

1. Have two volunteers perform the interview between the TV anchor and Great-grandma in the brackets passage beginning on page 14.

2. Read aloud the mother's statement about Great-grandma's remarks, highlighted on this page. Clarify that the 1906 San Francisco earthquake is one of the best-known events of the early twentieth century.

3. **Ask:** Why do you think Great-grandma pretends to have been in San Francisco at the time of the 1906 earthquake?

   Possible response: She wants to make herself more interesting to the anchor by giving him the sort of information he wants to hear.

4. **Ask** the Statements question.

   Possible response: She probably read about it.

5. **Ask:** In making up her stories, do you think Great-grandma is making fun of the TV anchor? If so, why?

   Possible response: She probably is, since he is so self-important and has no sense of humor.

Differentiated Instruction for Universal Access

Strategy for Special-Needs Students
Check students' understanding of the literary terms used to discuss fiction by applying the terms to a more familiar or comfortable context, such as a current film students have seen. Ask students to identify the characters and the main events in the plot of the film. Then, guide them in stating the main conflict. After students have read or listened to "The Three-Century Woman," have them identify the characters, main plot events, and conflict.

Enrichment for Advanced Readers
Explain that conflicts in a story keep the plot moving from one event to the next and usually lead to changes in an important character. Guide students to identify Megan's conflict (she does not want to visit her grandmother but knows she should). Have them use the clues on pages 13–16 to explain how she might be feeling now that she is in her grandmother's room (her grandmother is more interesting than she thought). Have students look for the way Megan's conflict is finally resolved at the end of the story and ways in which she changes.

㉓ Statements

1. Have three students each read one of Great-grandma's first three predictions in the bracketed passage. **Ask:** What is funny about the first two predictions?

   Possible response: They are very likely to happen, so saying they will is not much of a prediction. Not finding parking places is also a very trivial topic.

2. **Ask** the first Statements question.

   Possible response: It suggests a theme about the way we view and treat elderly people.

㉔ Statements

1. Read aloud Great-grandma's final prediction (the second highlighted passage). **Ask:** What does the prediction show about Great-grandma's knowledge or awareness?

   Possible response: She is well aware of current technology.

2. **Ask** the second Statements question.

   Possible response: She may want to tease him in her humorous way. She also may feel he is a bad reporter, since he has taken her claims at face value, without investigation, and paid little attention to her as a person.

Practice continued

lot, they wanted to put me in the hospital. I looked down and thought I was wearing a lace dress. The fire had about burned up my coat. And I lost a shoe."

"Fantastic!" the anchor breathed. "What detail!" Behind him the woman reporter was scribbling away on her pad.

"Never," Mom muttered. "Never in her life."

"Ma'am, you are living history!" the anchor said. "In your sensational span of years you've survived two great disasters!"

"Three." Great-grandma patted the bow on her head. "I told you I'd been married."

"And before we leave this venerable lady," the anchor said, flashing a smile for the camera, "we'll ask Mrs. Breckenridge if she has any predictions for this new twenty-first century ahead of us here in the Dawn of the Millennium."

㉓ Statements How might this statement relate to a possible theme?

㉓ "Three or four predictions," Great-grandma said, and paused again, stretching out her airtime. "Number one, taxes will be higher. Number two, it's going to be harder to find a place to park. And number three, a whole lot of people are going to live as long as I have, so get ready for us."

"And with those wise words," the anchor said, easing off the bed, "we leave Mrs. B—"

㉔ Statements Why does Great-grandma say this to the reporter?

㉔ "And one more prediction," she said. "TV's on the way out. Your network ratings are already in the basement. It's all web-sites now. Son, I predict you'll be looking for work."

And that was it. The light went dead. The anchor, looking shaken, followed his crew out the door. When TV's done with you, they're done with you. "Is that a wrap?" Great-grandma asked.

But now the woman from the suburban paper was moving in on her. "Just a few more questions, Mrs. Breckenridge."

"Where you from?" Great-grandma blinked pink-eyed at her.

"The Glenview Weekly Shopper."

"You bring a still photographer with you?" Great-grandma asked.

"Well, no."

"And you never learned shorthand[5] either, did you?"

"Well, no."

"Honey, I only deal with professionals. There's the door."

So then it was just Mom and Great-grandma and I in the room. Mom planted a hand on her hip. "Grandma. Number one, you've never been to San Francisco. And number two, you never saw one of those zeppelin things."

Great-grandma shrugged. "No, but I can read." She nodded to the pile of books on her nightstand with her spectacles folded on top. "You can pick up all that stuff in books."

"And number three," Mom said, "Your husband didn't die young. I can remember Grandpa Breckenridge."

"It was that TV dude in the five-hundred-dollar suit who set me off," Great-grandma said. "He dyes his hair, did you notice? He made me mad, and it put my nose out of joint. He didn't notice I'm still here. He thought I was nothing but my memories. So I gave him some."

Now Mom and I stood beside her bed.

"I'll tell you something else," Great-grandma said. "And it's no lie."

We waited, holding our breath to hear. Great-grandma Breckenridge was pointing her little old bent finger right at me. "You, Megan," she said. "Once upon a time, I was your age. How scary is that?"

Then she hunched up her little pink shoulders and winked at me. She grinned and I grinned. She was just this little withered-up leaf of a lady in the bed. But I felt like giving her a kiss on her little wrinkled cheek, so I did.

"I'll come and see you more often," I told her.

"Call first," she said. "I might be busy." Then she dozed.

---

5. shorthand (shôrt´ hand´) *n.* a system of speed writing using symbols to represent letters, words, and phrases.

25 **Statements** What has Great-grandma proved to everyone?

26 **Character** How has Megan's attitude toward her great-grandmother changed?

27 **Theme** What is one possible theme of this story?

25 Statements

1. Have students reread the bracketed passage. **Ask:** What do Great-grandma's comments reveal about her reasons for deceiving the TV anchor?

   Possible response: She felt he was a vain TV personality who did not respect her and was interested only in getting a story.

2. **Ask** the Statements question.

   Possible response: She has proved that she is an interesting person.

26 Character

1. Have a student read the bracketed passage aloud. **Ask:** How is Megan's description here different from her earlier detail about Great-grandma's "claw"?

   Possible response: It is physically appealing and affectionate.

2. **Ask** the Character question.

   Possible response: She now feels affection and admiration for Great-grandma and wants to visit again.

27 Theme

1. Remind students to consider the clues discussed on page 8 in deciding on a story's theme. **Ask:** What does the story's title suggest its theme may be about?

   Possible response: It may be about people who have lived a very long time.

2. **Ask** the Theme question, and solicit several responses.

   Possible response: Despite their physical state, old people can be interesting, humorous, and perceptive. We should respect the elderly as individuals.

㉘ Close Read: Central Idea in Nonfiction

1. Be sure students understand that the central idea of a nonfiction work is the main point the author wishes to convey. The key point of each paragraph supports the central idea.

2. Explain that when a central idea is implied, students must examine the key points and draw a conclusion about the central idea.

3. Provide these key points, and ask students to state the central idea:

Point 1: *Most ballet dancers begin training in childhood.*

Point 2: *Ballet students must practice for hours every day.*

Point 3: *Ballet training is often painful.*

Possible response: Ballet dancing requires years of intensive, often painful training.

4. Review the Types of Supporting Details chart. **Ask** what type of detail each of these examples is:

The word restaurant *comes from French.*

Answer: fact

Being a chef is like being a general in the army.

Answer: analogy

5. Refer students to the Model text on page 19. Explain that passages in the text that illustrate a type of detail on the chart are highlighted in the color of that detail in the chart and that the corresponding side-column annotations use corresponding colors.

㉘ Close Read: Central Idea in Nonfiction

The central idea is often stated early in the work. Supporting details develop that idea.

A nonfiction work has an overall central idea, but each paragraph in the work also has its key point. The details in each paragraph support its key point, and the paragraphs support the central idea of the whole work.

Stated Central Idea In some cases, an author tells the reader the central idea. The idea can often be found in a topic sentence in the opening paragraph.

> **Example:**
> Movie versions of popular novels are almost always disappointments. They can never match the pictures in readers' imaginations and often leave out popular moments from the story.

Implied Central Idea Sometimes authors do not directly state the central idea. Instead, they imply, or suggest, it through a series of related details.

> **Example:**
> Restaurant kitchens require a great deal of expensive equipment. They constantly need to maintain a supply of fresh food. A bad location can doom even the best restaurant.

Each sentence points out a difficulty in running a restaurant. The central idea might be stated as follows: It is difficult to run a successful restaurant.

Types of Supporting Details

Authors use different kinds of details to develop their central ideas. As you read, notice the types of details authors choose, and think about why they were selected.

Facts are statements that can be proved. *Example: Polar bears can swim as fast as 6.2 miles per hour.*	**Observations** are reports from eyewitnesses. *Example: During a one-hour period, sixteen cars did not even pause at the stop sign.*
Statistics are facts in the form of numbers. *Example: Only 40% of those polled could remember last year's Best Picture winner.*	**Personal experiences** come from life. *Example: I learned that shoes really matter when I finished the hike with blistered feet.*
Expert statements come from authoritative sources. *Example: Dr. Flynn said the virus could not affect humans.*	**Anecdotes** are stories that make a point. *Example: To encourage me to keep trying, my coach said, "I made many mistakes myself in my first year of playing soccer."*
Examples are concrete illustrations of a concept. *Example: Shoppers have choices. Supermarkets devote entire aisles to ethnic foods.*	**Analogies** use comparisons to make a point. *Example: Baking a cake is like building a house. You need the right tools and materials.*

18 Fiction and Nonfiction

Vocabulary Development
ⓒ **CCSS Language 6**

Thematic Vocabulary: The Big Question
As students discuss the selection from *The Great Fire,* encourage them to use the thematic vocabulary presented in Introducing the Big Question, pages 2–3. Help them with sentence starters such as these:

1. *Evidence* suggests that the Chicago Fire spread rapidly because . . .

2. Patrick and Catherine O'Leary probably had no *awareness* that . . .

3. From the details in the selection, I can *conclude* that wood . . .

㉙ Model

About the Text This is an excerpt from a book about the Great Chicago Fire of 1871. The fire started in Patrick O'Leary's barn on the night of October 8 and lasted until the 10th, when rain helped put it out. It caused property damage that totaled almost 200 million dollars.

from *The Great Fire* by Jim Murphy

Chicago in 1871 was a city ready to burn. The city boasted having 59,500 buildings, many of them—such as the Courthouse and the Tribune Building—large and ornately decorated. The trouble was that about two-thirds of all these structures were made entirely of wood. Many of the remaining buildings (even the ones proclaimed to be "fireproof") looked solid, but were actually jerry-built affairs; the stone or brick exteriors hid wooden frames and floors, all topped with highly flammable tar or shingle roofs. It was also a common practice to disguise wood as another kind of building material. The fancy exterior decorations on just about every building were carved from wood, then painted to look like stone or marble. Most churches had steeples that appeared to be solid from the street, but a closer inspection would reveal a wooden framework covered with cleverly painted copper or tin.

The situation was worst in the middle-class and poorer districts. Lot sizes were small, and owners usually filled them up with cottages, barns, sheds, and outhouses—all made of fast-burning wood, naturally. Because both Patrick and Catherine O'Leary worked, they were able to put a large addition on their cottage despite a lot size of just 25 by 100 feet. Interspersed in these residential areas were a variety of businesses—paint factories, lumberyards, distilleries, gasworks, mills, furniture manufacturers, warehouses, and coal distributors.

Wealthier districts were by no means free of fire hazards. Stately stone and brick homes had wood interiors, and stood side by side with smaller wood-frame houses. Wooden stables and other storage buildings were common, and trees lined the streets and filled the yards.

㉚ **Statistics** The number of flammable structures supports the statement that the city was ready to burn.

㉛ **Facts** This fact explains how even more buildings had flammable parts.

㉜ **Examples** This example shows how tightly packed the small lots were.

㉝ **Central Idea** The author states the central idea in the opening sentence, then uses facts to support the idea that Chicago was ready to burn.

Literary Analysis Workshop **19**

㉙ **Reading the Model**

1. Discuss the About the Text note. Explain that at the time of the Great Fire, Chicago was a young but growing city, the hub of Midwestern transportation and commerce.

2. Have students read the passage. Discuss it, clarifying as needed, before reviewing the annotations.

㉚ **Statistics**

Read aloud the Statistics annotation. **Ask:** What two statistics does the first highlighted passage contain?

Answer: The number of buildings in 1871 Chicago and the fraction of that number that were made of wood.

㉛ **Facts**

Read aloud the Facts annotation. **Ask:** From the facts in the first paragraph, what can you conclude about the dangers of wood?

Possible response: It is very flammable.

㉜ **Examples**

Read aloud the highlighted example and the Examples annotation. **Ask:** Why is the small lot size an important factor?

Answer: The smaller the lot, the closer the structures are to each other, and the easier for fire to spread.

㉝ **Central Idea**

Read aloud the Central Idea annotation. **Ask:** What three key ideas does each paragraph convey in support of the central idea?

Possible response: Most Chicago structures were made of wood. Structures in middle-class and poorer districts were even more likely to catch fire because they were close together. Wealthier districts also had fire hazards.

③④ Introducing the Independent Practice

1. Explain to students that they will determine the central idea of the Independent Practice selection.

2. Discuss the About the Selection note, and have students read the selection. Then, direct them to go back through and respond to the side-column prompts. Conclude by having students answer the After You Read questions on page 21.

③⑤ Facts

Read the first highlighted passage aloud. Then, **ask** the Facts question.

Possible response: They are key facts that stress the scope of the disaster.

③⑥ Statistics

Have students reread the second highlighted passage. **Ask** the Statistics question.

Answer: The *Hindenburg* was very big.

③⑦ Observations

Have a student read aloud the text highlighted in green. **Ask** the Observations questions.

Possible response: It expresses horror at the many deaths. It supports the idea that the *Hindenburg* explosion was a tragedy.

③⑧ Expert Statements

Have students reread the last paragraph, including the highlighted text. **Ask** the Expert Statements question.

Possible response: It stresses the preventability of the disaster.

③⑨ Central Idea

Ask the Central Idea question.

Possible response: The *Hindenburg* explosion was a great tragedy.

---

③④ Independent Practice

About the Selection Michael Morrison's article tells the story of the *Hindenburg* disaster described in "The Three-Century Woman."

"The Fall of the Hindenburg" by Michael Morrison

③⑤ On May 6, 1937, the German airship *Hindenburg* burst into flames 200 feet over its intended landing spot at New Jersey's Lakehurst Naval Air Station. Thirty-five people on board were killed (13 passengers and 22 crewmen), along with one crewman on the ground.

③⑥ **803 Feet Long and 242 Tons** The giant flying vessel measured 803.8 feet in length and weighed approximately 242 tons. Its mostly metal frame was filled with hydrogen. It came complete with sleeping quarters, a library, dining room, and a magnificent lounge, but still managed a top speed of just over 80 miles per hour. The zeppelin had just crossed the Atlantic Ocean after taking off from Frankfurt, Germany, $2\frac{1}{2}$ days prior on its first transatlantic voyage of the season. Thirty-six passengers and a crew of 61 were on board.

Disaster Strikes As it reached its final destination in New Jersey, it hovered over its landing spot and was beginning to be pulled down to the ground by landing lines by over 200 crewmen when disaster struck. A burst of flame started just forward of the upper fin, then blossomed into an inferno that engulfed the *Hindenburg*'s tail.

"Oh, the Humanity!" Many jumped from the burning craft, landed on the soft sand of the naval base below, and lived to tell about it; others weren't so lucky. ③⑦ Herb Morrison, a reporter for WLS Radio in Chicago, happened to be covering the event and cried out the now famous words, "Oh, the Humanity!" The majestic ship turned into a ball of flames on the ground in only 34 seconds.

Unknown Cause The cause of the disaster is still uncertain. At the time, many thought the ship had been hit by lightning. Many still believe that the highly flammable hydrogen was the cause. Some Germans even cried foul play, suspecting sabotage intended to sully the reputation of the Nazi regime. ③⑧ NASA research, however, has shown that the highly combustible varnish treating the fabric on the outside of the vessel most likely caused the tragedy.

20 Fiction and Nonfiction

Side column prompts

③⑤ **Facts** Why might the author have opened the article with these facts?

③⑥ **Statistics** What idea do these statistics convey?

③⑦ **Observations** What emotion does this quotation express? How does it support a central idea?

③⑧ **Expert Statements** How does this detail relate to the entire article?

③⑨ **Central Idea** What is the central idea of this article?

Think Aloud

Analyzing Cause-and-Effect Relationships
To help students analyze these cause-and-effect relationships, use the following "think aloud":

To find out the cause of the *Hindenburg* crash, I read the last paragraph, which has the heading "Unknown Cause."

I notice that there are several causes included in this paragraph. I see the author has included some clues to tell me which cause is the most likely.

First, the phrase "at the time" in the second sentence indicates that lightning was once believed to have been a cause—but that no one believes this explanation anymore. When the author says some "even" suspected sabotage, he is using the word *even* to show that he thinks this explanation is unlikely or hard to believe.

I realize that he is probably leading up to the explanation. The word *however* suggests that the writer thinks NASA's explanation is the best one, since he is using it to contradict all the others.

Common Core
State Standards

Reading Literature 9. Compare and contrast a fictional portrayal of a time, place, or character and a historical account of the same period as a means of understanding how authors of fiction use or alter history.

After You Read

The Three-Century Woman • The Fall of the Hindenburg

1. Key Ideas and Details (a) In "The Three-Century Woman," find two statements that show details about Megan's character. **(b) Speculate:** Why do you think the author chose to tell the story in Megan's voice?

2. Key Ideas and Details (a) Speculate: Why do you think the reporter believes Great-grandma's version of the truth? **(b) Infer:** What are clues that Great-grandma is not telling the truth?

3. Key Ideas and Details (a) Infer: Why does Great-grandma make up these stories? **(b) Analyze:** What does Great-grandma's storytelling reveal about her character?

4. Key Ideas and Details Analyze: What is Michael Morrison's main **purpose** for writing "The Fall of the Hindenburg"? Explain.

5. Key Ideas and Details (a) Compare: How does the fictional account of the *Hindenburg* disaster differ from the historical account? **(b) Connect:** How does the purpose of each text help determine what key information is presented? Support your answers with details from the texts.

6. Integration of Knowledge and Ideas (a) In the first column of a chart like the one below, write three of Great-grandma's reactions to the reporters. **(b) Infer:** In the second column, explain what Great-grandma's reactions reveal about her character. **(c) Interpret:** In the third column, explain a possible theme or message these reactions might convey.

Her Reaction	Her Character	Message/ Theme

(d) Collaborate: Discuss your chart with a classmate to identify the **theme** that best fits the story.

7. Key Ideas and Details (a) Write an objective summary of "The Three-Century Woman." Remember that an objective summary should contain only the most important events or ideas. It should not include your personal opinions. **(b)** Write an objective summary of "The Fall of the Hindenburg."

Literary Analysis Workshop **21**

✓ Papa's Parrot • ✓✓ mk
Lesson Pacing Guide

DAY 1 | Preteach

- © Administer the Reading and Vocabulary Warm-ups (*Unit 1 Resources*, pp. 30–33 or 48–51) as necessary.
- • Introduce the Reading Skill: Context Clues.
- © Introduce the Literary Analysis concept: Narrative Text.
- • Distribute copies of the appropriate graphic organizer for the Reading Skill (*Graphic Organizer Transparencies*, pp. 6–8).
- • Distribute copies of the appropriate graphic organizer for Literary Analysis (*Graphic Organizer Transparencies*, pp. 3–5).
- © Teach the selection vocabulary.
- © Introduce the Word Study skill.

DAYS 2–3 | Preteach/Teach

- © Build background with the Background feature.
- • Develop thematic vocabulary and thematic thinking with Writing About the Big Question.
- • Prepare students to read with the Activating Prior Knowledge activities (TE).
- • Informally monitor comprehension while students read.
- • Use the Reading Check questions to confirm comprehension.
- • Develop students' ability to determine the meaning of unfamiliar words, using the Context Clues questions.
- © Develop students' understanding of narrative text, using the Narrative Text questions.
- © Reinforce vocabulary with the Vocabulary notes.
- © Reinforce unit focus standards using the Spiral Review prompts.

DAY 4 | Assess

- • Assess students' comprehension and mastery of the skills by having them answer the Critical Thinking, Reading Skill, and Literary Analysis questions.
- © Have students complete the Vocabulary Practice activities.
- © Have students complete the Word Study activities.

DAY 5 | Extend/Assess

- • Have students complete the Conventions lesson.
- © Have students complete the Writing activity and write a compare-and-contrast essay. (You may assign as homework.)
- © Extend learning by having students complete the Speaking and Listening activity, a dramatic reading. As an alternative, assign them "When Animals Help People" or "Learning the Truth in China" in *Reality Central*.
- • Administer Selection Test A or B (*Unit 1 Resources*, pp. 42–47 or 63–68).

© Common Core State Standards

Reading Literature 2. Determine a theme or central idea of a text and analyze its development over the course of the text; provide an objective summary of the text.

Writing 2. Write informative/explanatory texts to examine a topic and convey ideas, concepts, and information through the selection, organization, and analysis of relevant content.
2b. Develop the topic with relevant facts, definitions, concrete details, quotations, or other information and examples.

Speaking and Listening 6. Adapt speech to a variety of contexts and tasks, demonstrating command of formal English.

Language 2. Demonstrate command of the conventions of standard English capitalization, punctuation, and spelling when writing.
4. Determine or clarify the meaning of unknown and multiple-meaning words and phrases.
4.a. Use context as a clue to the meaning of a word or phrase.
5. Demonstrate understanding of figurative language, word relationships, and nuances in word meanings.
5.b. Use the relationship between particular words to better understand each of the words.
6. Acquire and use accurately grade-appropriate general academic and domain-specific words and phrases.

Additional Standards Practice
***Common Core Companion*, pp. 15–22; 97–104**

Daily Block Scheduling
Each day in this Lesson Pacing Guide represents a 40–50 minute period. Teachers using block scheduling may combine days to revise pacing. In addition, teachers may differentiate and support core instruction by integrating components for extended and intensive support, as students require. See the Guide to Selected Leveled Resources (facing page).

Guide to Selected Leveled Resources

R T I **Tier 1** (students performing on level)	✓ **More Accessible**	✓✓ **More Complex**
	Papa's Parrot	mk
Warm Up — Practice, model, and monitor fluency, working with the whole class or in groups.	Vocabulary and Reading Warm-ups B, *Unit 1 Resources*, pp. 30–31, 33	Vocabulary and Reading Warm-ups B, *Unit 1 Resources*, pp. 48–49, 51
Comprehension/Skills — Support and monitor comprehension and skills development, having students complete the activities, graphic organizers, and interactive prompts independently or as a class.	• *Reader's Notebook,* adapted instruction and full selection EL *Reader's Notebook: English Learner's Version,* adapted instruction and adapted selection • Reading Skill Graphic Organizer B, *Graphic Organizer Transparencies,* p. 8 • Literary Analysis Graphic Organizer B, *Graphic Organizer Transparencies,* p. 5	• *Reader's Notebook,* adapted instruction and summary EL *Reader's Notebook: English Learner's Version,* adapted instruction and summary • Reading Skill Graphic Organizer B, *Graphic Organizer Transparencies,* p. 8 • Literary Analysis Graphic Organizer B, *Graphic Organizer Transparencies,* p. 5
Monitor Progress A — Monitor student progress with the differentiated curriculum-based assessment in the *Unit Resources.*	• Selection Test B, *Unit 1 Resources,* pp. 45–47 • Open-Book Test, *Unit 1 Resources,* pp. 39–41	• Selection Test B, *Unit 1 Resources,* pp. 66–68 • Open-Book Test, *Unit 1 Resources,* pp. 60–62

R T I **Tier 2** (students requiring intervention)	✓ **More Accessible**	✓✓ **More Complex**
	Papa's Parrot	mk
Warm Up — Practice, model, and monitor fluency in groups or with individuals.	• Vocabulary and Reading Warm-ups A, *Unit 1 Resources*, pp. 30–32 • *Reality Central,* "When Animals Help People" • *Hear It!* Audio CD (adapted text)	• Vocabulary and Reading Warm-ups A, *Unit 1 Resources*, pp. 48–50 • *Reality Central,* "Learning the Truth in China" • *Hear It!* Audio CD
Comprehension/Skills — • Support and monitor comprehension and skills development, working in small groups or with individuals. • Pair students with more advanced peers and have them complete the writing activity in the *Real World Writing Journal.* • As students complete the selection in the appropriate version of the *Reader's Notebook,* monitor comprehension frequently with group questions and individual instruction. • Model strategies while guiding students in completing the activities and prompts in the *Reader's Notebook,* as well as the graphic organizers. • Practice skills and monitor mastery with the *Reading Kit* worksheets.	• *Real World Writing Journal* • *Reader's Notebook: Adapted Version,* adapted instruction and adapted selection EL *Reader's Notebook: English Learner's Version,* adapted instruction and adapted selection • Reading Skill Graphic Organizer A, *Graphic Organizer Transparencies,* p. 6 • Literary Analysis Graphic Organizer A, *Graphic Organizer Transparencies,* p. 3 • *Reading Kit,* Practice worksheets, pp. 2, 6, 12, 14	• *Real World Writing Journal* • *Reader's Notebook: Adapted Version,* adapted instruction and summary EL *Reader's Notebook: English Learner's Version,* adapted instruction and summary • Reading Skill Graphic Organizer A, *Graphic Organizer Transparencies,* p. 7 • Literary Analysis Graphic Organizer A, *Graphic Organizer Transparencies,* p. 4 • *Reading Kit,* Practice worksheets, pp. 2, 6, 12, 14
Monitor Progress A — Monitor student progress with the differentiated curriculum-based assessment in the *Unit Resources* and in the *Reading Kit.*	• Selection Test A, *Unit 1 Resources,* pp. 42–44 • *Reading Kit,* Assess worksheets pp. 3, 7, 13, 15	• Selection Test A, *Unit 1 Resources,* pp. 63–65 • *Reading Kit,* Assess worksheets, pp. 3, 7, 13, 15

TIER 3 Tier 3 intervention may require consultation with the student's special-education or dyslexia specialist. For additional support, see the Tier 2 activities and resources listed above.

One-on-one teaching   Group work   Whole class instruction   Independent work   A Assessment

For a complete guide to selection support, including support for Advanced students, see the Overview of Resources in the frontmatter.

✓Papa's Parrot
✓✓mk

RESOURCES FOR:

- **L1** Special-Needs Students
- **L2** Below-Level Students (Tier 2)
- **L3** On-Level Students (Tier 1)
- **L4** Advanced Students (Tier 1)
- **EL** English Learners
- **All** All Students

Vocabulary/Fluency/Prior Knowledge

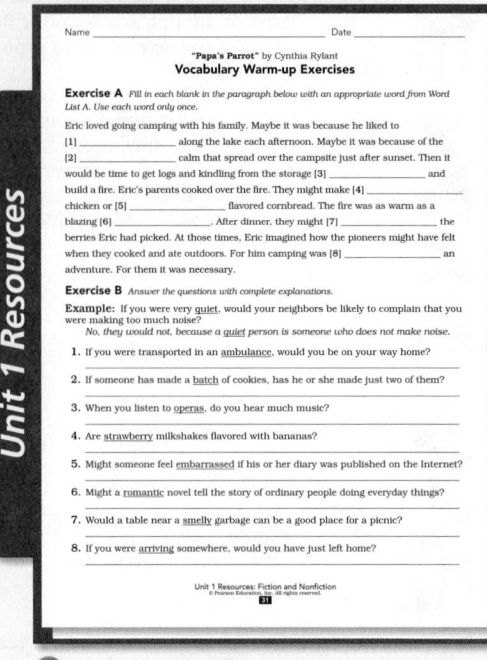

EL L1 L2 **Vocabulary Warm-ups A and B,** pp. 30–31, 48–49

Also available for these selections:

EL L1 L2 **Reading Warm-ups A and B,** pp. 32–33, 50–51

All **Writing About the Big Question,** pp. 34, 52

All **Vocabulary Builder,** pp. 37, 55

Reader's Notebooks

Pre- and postreading pages for both selections, as well as "Papa's Parrot," appear in an interactive format in the *Reader's Notebooks.* Each *Notebook* is differentiated for a different group of learners. The selections in the Adapted and English Learner's versions are abridged.

- **L2 L3** *Reader's Notebook*
- **L1** *Reader's Notebook: Adapted Version*
- **EL** *Reader's Notebook: English Learner's Version*
- **EL** *Reader's Notebook: Spanish Version*

© *Common Core Companion*

Additional instruction and practice for each Common Core State Standard

Selection Support

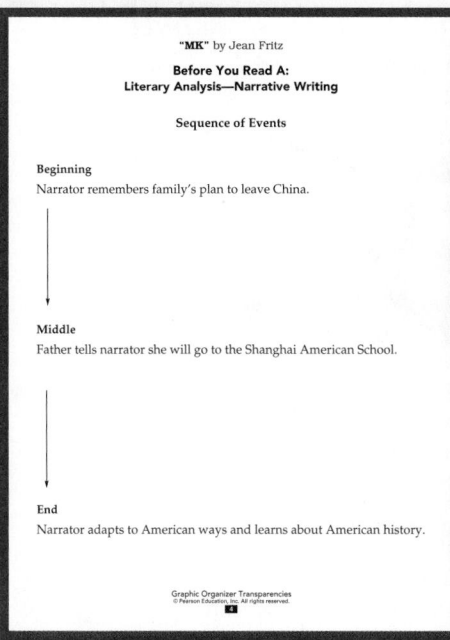

"MK" by Jean Fritz

Before You Read A:
Literary Analysis—Narrative Writing

Sequence of Events

Beginning

Narrator remembers family's plan to leave China.

Middle

Father tells narrator she will go to the Shanghai American School.

End

Narrator adapts to American ways and learns about American history.

EL **L1** **L2** **Literary Analysis: Graphic Organizer A** pp. 3, 4 (partially filled in)

Also available for these selections:

EL **L3** Literary Analysis: Graphic Organizer B p. 5

EL **L1** **L2** Reading: Graphic Organizer A, pp. 6, 7 (partially filled in)

EL **L3** Reading: Graphic Organizer B p. 8

Skills Development/Extension

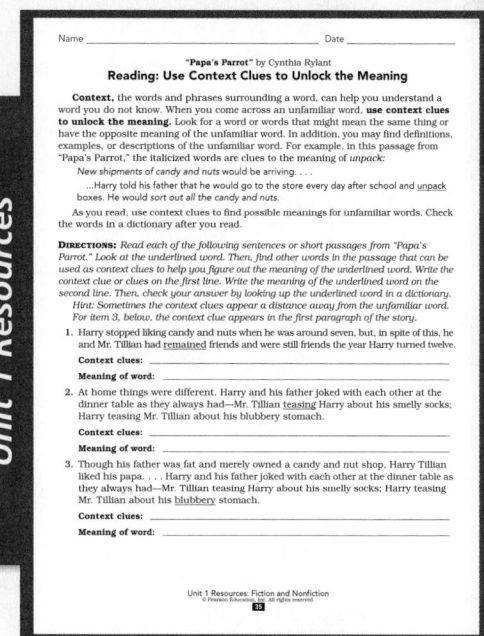

Name _____ Date _____

"Papa's Parrot" by Cynthia Rylant
Reading: Use Context Clues to Unlock the Meaning

Context, the words and phrases surrounding a word, can help you understand a word you do not know. When you come across an unfamiliar word, **use context clues to unlock the meaning.** Look for a word or words in the passage that might mean the same thing or have the opposite meaning of the unfamiliar word. In addition, you may find definitions, examples, or descriptions of the unfamiliar word. For example, in this passage from "Papa's Parrot," the italicized words are clues to the meaning of *unpack:*

New shipments of candy and nuts would be arriving. . . .
...Harry told his father that he would go to the store every day after school and *unpack* boxes. He would sort out all the candy and nuts.

As you read, use context clues to find possible meanings for unfamiliar words. Check the words in a dictionary after you read.

DIRECTIONS: *Read each of the following sentences or short passages from "Papa's Parrot." Look at the underlined word. Then, find other words in the passage that can be used as context clues to help you figure out the meaning of the underlined word. Write the context clue or clues on the first line. Write the meaning of the underlined word on the second line. Then, check your answer by looking up the underlined word in a dictionary. Hint: Sometimes the context clues appear a distance away from the unfamiliar word. For item 3, below, the context clue appears in the first paragraph of the story.*

1. Harry stopped liking candy and nuts when he was around seven, but, in spite of this, he and Mr. Tillian had <u>remained</u> friends and were still friends the year Harry turned twelve.

Context clues: _____

Meaning of word: _____

2. At home things were different. Harry and his father joked with each other at the dinner table as they always had—Mr. Tillian <u>teasing</u> Harry about his smelly socks; Harry teasing Mr. Tillian about his blubbery stomach.

Context clues: _____

Meaning of word: _____

3. Though his father was fat and merely owned a candy and nut shop, Harry Tillian liked his papa. . . . Harry and his father joked with each other at the dinner table as they always had—Mr. Tillian teasing Harry about his smelly socks; Harry teasing Mr. Tillian about his <u>blubbery</u> stomach.

Context clues: _____

Meaning of word: _____

All **Reading: Context Clues, pp.** 35, 53

Also available for these selections:

All Literary Analysis: Narrative Texts, pp. 36, 54

L4 Enrichment, pp. 38, 56

EL **L3** **L4** Grammar, p. 57

EL **L3** **L4** Support for Writing, p. 58

L3 **L4** Support for Extend Your Learning, p. 59

Assessment

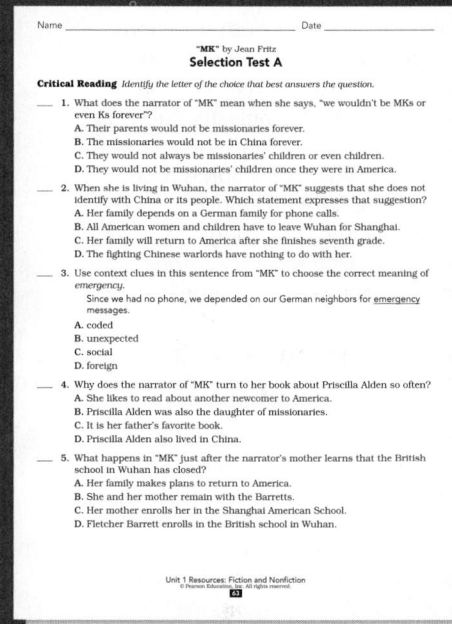

Name _____ Date _____

"MK" by Jean Fritz
Selection Test A

Critical Reading *Identify the letter of the choice that best answers the question.*

___ 1. What does the narrator of "MK" mean when she says, "we wouldn't be MKs or even Ks forever"?
A. Their parents would not be missionaries forever.
B. The missionaries would not be in China forever.
C. They would not always be missionaries' children or even children.
D. They would not be missionaries' children once they were in America.

___ 2. When she is living in Wuhan, the narrator of "MK" suggests that she does not identify with China or its people. Which statement expresses that suggestion?
A. Her family depends on a German family for phone calls.
B. All American women and children have to leave Wuhan for Shanghai.
C. Her family will return to America after she finishes seventh grade.
D. The fighting Chinese warlords have nothing to do with her.

___ 3. Use context clues in this sentence from "MK" to choose the correct meaning of emergency.
Since we had no phone, we depended on our German neighbors for <u>emergency</u> messages.
A. coded
B. unexpected
C. social
D. foreign

___ 4. Why does the narrator of "MK" turn to her book about Priscilla Alden so often?
A. She likes to read about another newcomer to America.
B. Priscilla Alden was also the daughter of missionaries.
C. It is her father's favorite book.
D. Priscilla Alden also lived in China.

___ 5. What happens in "MK" just after the narrator's mother learns that the British school in Wuhan has closed?
A. Her family makes plans to return to America.
B. She and her mother remain with the Barretts.
C. Her mother enrolls her in the Shanghai American School.
D. Fletcher Barrett enrolls in the British school in Wuhan.

EL **L1** **L2** **Selection Test A, pp.** 42–44, 63–65

Also available for these selections:

EL **L3** **L4** Selection Test B, pp. 45–47, 66–68

L3 **L4** Open-Book Test, pp. 39–41, 60–62

PHLit Online!
www.PHLitOnline.com

Online Resources: All print materials are also available online.

- complete narrated selection text
- a thematically related video with writing prompt
- an interactive graphic organizer
- highlighting feature
- access to all student print resources, adapted to individual student needs
- Spanish and English summaries
- adapted selection translations in Spanish

Background Video

Also available:

Get Connected! (thematic video with writing prompt)
All videos are available in Spanish.

Vocabulary Central (tools, activities, and songs for studying vocabulary)

Also available:

Writer's Journal (with graphics feature)

❶ Leveled Texts

You may use either "Papa's Parrot" or "mk" to meet the lesson objectives. Skills instruction for both selections appears on p. 23. Choose one selection to teach (or choose to teach both). The Text Complexity Rubric at the bottom of this page will help you determine which selection is more appropriate for your students. Use the Reader and Task Suggestions on the facing page to help all students read text of increasing complexity.

❷ ⓒ Introducing the CCS Standards

Introduce the standards on the student page. (Note that the lesson element with which each standard is addressed is identified in parentheses after the text of the standard.) Call out the standards that you will cover with the selections, explaining to students what each requires and how they will address it as they work through the selection you have chosen. Standards labeled "Spiral Review" are introduced in the Literary Analysis Workshop for this unit.

Before You Read | Papa's Parrot • mk

❶ ⓒ Leveled Texts

Build your skills and improve your comprehension of fiction and nonfiction with texts of increasing complexity.

Read "**Papa's Parrot**" to find out how a parrot helps a boy understand his father's feelings.

Read "**mk**" to learn how a young girl raised in China tries to find her identity as an American.

❷ ⓒ Common Core State Standards

Meet these standards with either "**Papa's Parrot**" (p. 26) or "**mk**" (p. 34).

Reading Literature
2. Determine a theme or central idea of a text and analyze its development over the course of the text; provide an objective summary of the text. (*Literary Analysis: Spiral Review*)

Writing
2. Write informative/explanatory texts to examine a topic and convey ideas, concepts, and information through the selection, organization, and analysis of relevant content. **2.b.** Develop the topic with relevant facts, definitions, concrete details, quotations, or other information and examples. (*Writing: Compare-and-Contrast Essay*)

Speaking and Listening
6. Adapt speech to a variety of contexts and tasks, demonstrating command of formal English when indicated or appropriate. (*Speaking and Listening: Dramatic Reading*)

Language
2. Demonstrate command of the conventions of standard English capitalization, punctuation, and spelling when writing. (*Conventions: Common and Proper Nouns*)

4. Determine or clarify the meaning of unknown and multiple-meaning words and phrases based on grade 7 reading and content, choosing flexibly from a range of strategies. **4.a.** Use context as a clue to the meaning of a word or phrase. (*Reading Skill: Context Clues*)

5. Demonstrate understanding of figurative language, word relationships, and nuances in word meanings. **5.b.** Use the relationship between particular words to better understand each of the words. (*Vocabulary: Synonyms*)

6. Acquire and use accurately grade-appropriate general academic and domain-specific words and phrases; gather vocabulary knowledge when considering a word or phrase important to comprehension or expression. (*Vocabulary: Word Study*)

22 Fiction and Nonfiction

ⓒ Text Complexity Rubric: Leveled Texts

Text complexity is determined by both qualitative and quantitative measures. For this reason, the quantitative measure of a more complex selection may be lower than that of a more accessible selection.

		✓ Papa's Parrot	✓✓ mk
Qualitative Measures	**Context/Knowledge Demands**	Boy and his father in small-town U.S.A.; contemporary 1 2 ③ 4 5	American missionary child; China and U.S.; 1920s 1 2 3 ④ 5
	Structure/Language Conventionality and Clarity	On-level vocabulary; some longer sentences or clauses; straightforward structure; some implicit events 1 ② 3 4 5	Challenging vocabulary; more sophisticated diction; sentence fragments 1 2 3 ④ 5
	Levels of Meaning/ Purpose/Concept Level	Some implicit meaning (Papa misses Harry); accessible concept (changes that occur as children grow) 1 2 ③ 4 5	Symbolism and allegory (Priscilla is Jean); challenging concept (individual and national identity) 1 2 3 4 ⑤
Quantitative Measures	**Text Length**	Word Count: 1,104	Word Count: 2,910
	Lexile	770L	820L
Overall Complexity		✓ **More accessible**	✓✓ **More complex**

❸ Reading Skill: Context Clues

Context, the words and phrases surrounding a word, can help you understand a word you do not know. When you come across an unfamiliar word, **use context clues** to unlock the meaning.

- **Restatement:** The population, or number of people in the country, is stable.
- **Opposite, or contrast:** Average rainfall has not declined, it has increased.
- **Example:** Modes of transportation, such as car, train, and airplane, are available.

You can also use syntactic clues—the word's position or function in the sentence—to determine an unfamiliar word. As you read, use context clues to find possible meanings for unfamiliar words. Verify your understanding by consulting a dictionary.

❹ Literary Analysis: Narrative Text

Narrative text is writing that tells a story. The act or process of telling a story is also called **narration.**

- A narrative is usually told in *chronological order*—the order in which events occurred in time.
- A narrative may be presented in fiction, nonfiction, or poetry.

As you read, think about how the sequence of events is important to the story.

❺ Using the Strategy: Narration Chart

As you read, record the sequence of story events in a chart like this:

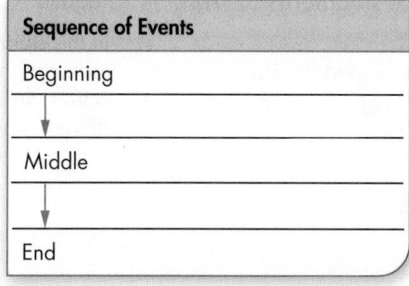

Sequence of Events
Beginning
Middle
End

PHLit Online!
www.PHLitOnline.com

Hear It!
- Selection summary audio
- Selection audio

See It!
- Get Connected video
- Background video
- More about the author
- Vocabulary flashcards

Do It!
- Interactive journals
- Interactive graphic organizers
- Self-test
- Internet activity
- Grammar tutorial
- Interactive vocabulary games

❸ Reading Skill
Context Clues
1. Introduce the skill, using the instruction on the student page.
2. Tell students that they will use context clues as they read.

❹ Literary Analysis
Narrative Text
1. Introduce the skill, using the instruction on the student page.
2. Tell students that they will note narrative elements as they read.

Think Aloud: Model the Skill

Model a way of understanding narrative writing. Say to students:

To help me understand narrative writing, I think of a simple story, such as "The Three Little Pigs." At the beginning, the pigs build their houses. In the middle, the wolf destroys two of the houses. At the end, the third pig outsmarts the wolf. Usually the beginning, middle, and end of a story tell events in the order they happened. Identifying the parts of a story helps me appreciate the whole story.

❺ Using the Strategy
Give students a copy of either **Literary Analysis Graphic Organizer A or B** (*Graphic Organizer Transparencies,* pp. 3–5) to record events as they read. Use the examples in **Literary Analysis Graphic Organizer A,** which is partially filled in, to model the process of completing the organizer.

© Text Complexity: Reader and Task Suggestions

✓ Papa's Parrot		✓✓ mk	
Preparing to Read the Text	**Leveled Tasks**	**Preparing to Read the Text**	**Leveled Tasks**
• Using the Background information on p. 25, discuss the speech abilities of parrots. • Discuss with students the importance of good communication with parents. • Guide students to use Multidraft Reading strategies to deepen their comprehension.	*Levels of Meaning* If students will have difficulty with meaning, have them first read to identify the boy's changing experiences in his father's store. Then, have them reread, identifying descriptions of the parrot's contribution to the story. *Evaluating* If students will not have difficulty with meaning, have them note as they read the implied content Rylant conveys through the parrot's dialogue.	• Using the Background note on TE p. 33, have students discuss what they know about China. • Discuss ways that moving to a new country might intensify the process of growing up. • Guide students to use Multidraft Reading strategies to deepen their comprehension.	*Levels of Meaning* If students will have difficulty with meaning, have them first read to identify familiar aspects of Jean's daily life. Then, have them reread, identifying fragments and imaginary parts of Jean's experience. *Analyzing* If students will not have difficulty with meaning, have them note as they read ways in which Priscilla's imagined comments symbolize Jean's hopes for her future in America.

❶ Writing About the Big Question

1. Review the assignment with the class.

2. Lead students in discussing how misunderstandings can arise when people conceal their true feelings.

3. Have students complete the sentence starter. Review responses as a class. (**Sample answer:** Sometimes we can discover the truth by accident. When we reveal our feelings, others may reach out to us with sympathy.)

4. Remind students that their answers will help them think about the Big Question, "What is the best way to find the truth?"

While You Read

Tell students that as they read, they should look for details that show how Harry's relationship with his father changes as he learns the truth.

❷ Vocabulary

1. Have students preview the selection vocabulary.

2. For each word, have students say the word aloud.

3. Then, use the word in a sentence that defines the word.

4. Finally, repeat your definitional sentence or a similar sentence with the word missing and have the class "fill in the blank" chorally. Here are some examples:

If something resumed, it started again after a pause. After a short time-out, the game [students say "resumed"].

Clusters are bunches or groups that are tightly connected. Grapes are a fruit that grow in bunches or [students say "clusters"].

❸ Word Study

1. Introduce the skill, using the instruction in the box.

2. Ask students to name a re- word that means "to write again." (**Answer:** rewrite)

---

❶ What is the best way to find the truth?

Writing About the Big Question

In "Papa's Parrot," the truth about a father's feelings toward his son are revealed through an unlikely source—his parrot. Use this sentence starter to develop your ideas about the Big Question.

Sometimes we can discover the **truth** by _____.

When we **reveal** our feelings, others _____.

While You Read Look for details that show how Harry's relationship with his father changes as he learns the truth.

❷ Vocabulary

Read each word and its definition. Decide whether you know the word well, know it a little bit, or do not know it at all. After you read, see how your knowledge of each word has increased.

- **merely** (mir´ lē) *adv.* no more than; simply (p. 26) *The child who fell down was merely scared, not injured.* mere *adj.*

- **clusters** (klus´ tərz) *n.* numbers of things of the same sort that are grouped together; bunches (p. 27) *Grapes grow in clusters on vines.* cluster *n.* clustering *v.*

- **ignored** (ig nôrd´) *v.* paid no attention to (p. 27) *I ignored his rude comment and went on talking.* ignore *v.* ignorance *n.*

- **shipments** (ship´ mənts) *n.* deliveries or acts of sending goods (p. 27) *A freak snowstorm delayed the shipments of fruit.* ship *v.* shipping *adj.*

- **resumed** (ri zoomd´) *v.* began again; continued (p. 29) *The campers resumed the hike after stopping for lunch.* resume *v.* resuming *v.* resumption *n.*

- **perch** (pʉrch) *n.* roost for a bird; seat (p. 30) *The robin found a perch on a high branch of the tree.* perch *v.* perched *v.*

❸ Word Study

The **Latin prefix** *re-* means "back" or "again."

In this story, Harry took care of the parrot, then **resumed**, or went back to, his task of sorting candy in his father's store.

24 Fiction and Nonfiction

Vocabulary Development

Vocabulary Knowledge Rating

Create a **Vocabulary Knowledge Rating Chart** (*Professional Development Guidebook,* p. 33) for this selection. Include the selection vocabulary and the Big Question words that appear in the Writing About the Big Question sentence starters on this page. (The Big Question vocabulary is introduced on pp. 2–3.)

Give students a copy of the chart. Read the words aloud, and have students mark their rating in the Before Reading column. Urge them to be alert to these words as they read and discuss the selection.

Tally how many students think they know a word to gauge how much instruction to provide. As students read and discuss the selection, point out the words and their context.

Vocabulary Central, featuring tools, activities, and songs for studying vocabulary, is available online at www.PHLitOnline.com.

Meet
Cynthia Rylant
(b. 1954)

Author of

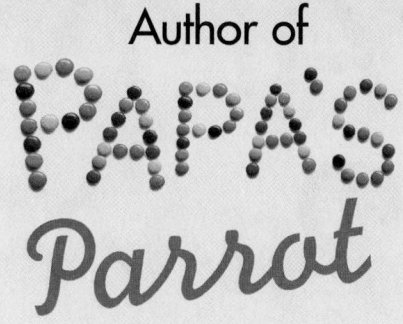
PAPA'S Parrot

Growing up in a small mountain town in West Virginia, Cynthia Rylant never thought about becoming a writer. Aside from comic books, she did not do much reading, and the only writing she did was for school assignments. A future career as an author was the farthest thing from her mind.

A Change of Plans When Rylant entered college, her plan was to become a nurse. Then, in a required English course, she read a story by Langston Hughes. The story "just knocked me off my feet," Rylant has said. She decided to change her major to English. It was a good choice, as she has found great success as a writer.

> ## DID YOU KNOW?
> Rylant, an animal lover with many pet dogs, often includes animals in her stories.

❹ BACKGROUND FOR THE STORY

Parrots

Parrots can learn to say words that are repeated over and over to them. Most of a parrot's "vocabulary" is taught on purpose, but a parrot may learn words accidentally. In "Papa's Parrot," the bird's accidental vocabulary plays a key part in the story.

Papa's Parrot **25**

➤ Daily Bellringer
For each class during which you teach this selection, have students complete one of the five Quick Write activities for Week 1 in the *Daily Bellringer Activities* booklet.

❹ Background

Parrots

Parrots, such as the one in Cynthia Rylant's story, are tropical or subtropical birds that have curved, hooked bills and often boast crests and brightly colored feathers. Cockatoos, macaws, and parakeets are kinds of parrots. Parrot owners find their birds to be intelligent, social animals and affectionate companions. Parrots require much attention and care. Some parrots live as long as eighty years.

Multidraft Reading

This icon ● marks natural pauses in the selection. To assist struggling readers and to deepen reading for all, assign the text in "chunks," following the icons, and apply multidraft reading protocols. For each reading, have students set the purpose indicated:

- **First reading**—identifying key ideas and details and answering any Reading Checks.
- **Second reading**—analyzing craft and structure and responding to the side-column prompts.
- **Third reading**—integrating knowledge and ideas, connecting to other texts and the world, and answering the end-of-selection questions.

For more guidance, refer to the *Classroom Strategies and Teaching Routines* card on multidraft reading.

Differentiated Instruction Additional Daily Instruction

EL Extended Support— English Learners
Have students complete the **Reading and Vocabulary Warm-ups**, *Unit 1 Resources*, pp. 30–33, before they read. Assign the prereading pages in the *Reader's Notebook: English Learner's Version*. Then, have students listen to portions of the selection on the *Hear It! Audio CD*.

L1 L2 Extended Support— Struggling Readers
Have students complete the **Reading and Vocabulary Warm-ups**, *Unit 1 Resources*, pp. 30–33, before they read. Assign the prereading pages in the *Reader's Notebook: Adapted Version*. Then, have students listen to portions of the selection on the *Hear It! Audio CD* (adapted text).

Extended Support— Reluctant Readers
To build motivation and engagement before assigning the selection, have students read "When Animals Help People," a thematically related selection in *Reality Central*. Then, use the questions at the conclusion of the related selection to guide discussion.

PHLit Online!
For more about the author, practice with the selection vocabulary, or more background, go online at **www.PHLitOnline.com**.

25

❶ Activating Prior Knowledge

1. Prepare an **Anticipation Guide** (*Professional Development Guidebook*, p. 38) with the following statements:

   • It is normal for teenagers to want to spend more time with their friends than with their family.

   • Family responsibilities are as important as responsibilities to friends.

   • One aspect of becoming an adult is learning to balance one's own wishes with the needs of others.

2. Give students a copy of the pre-pared **Anticipation Guide** and have them respond in the Me column. Have students discuss the statements in groups and respond again in the Group column.

3. For further guidance, use the *Classroom Strategies and Teaching Routines* card for **Anticipation Guides.**

Concept Connector ➡

Tell students that after reading the selection, they will return to their ideas.

Individual Activity

Tell students that the story they are about to read deals with a boy's changing relationship with his father. Have students write a brief story or a nonfiction essay about how children's relationships with parents change as the children grow. Invite volunteers to share their writings with the class.

❷ About the Selection

Harry Tillian's father owns and oper-ates a nut and candy store, where Harry once spent a good deal of time. As Harry gets older, however, he spends less time at the store. When Mr. Tillian falls ill, Harry learns—with the help of a pet parrot—how much his father misses him.

❸ Critical Viewing

Answer: Parrots' colorful feathers and intelligent gazes make them appealing pets.

PAPA'S Parrot
Cynthia Rylant

❶
❷

❸ ▲ **Critical Viewing**
Based on the picture, why might people find parrots appeal-ing as pets? **[Apply Prior Knowledge]**

Vocabulary
merely (mir´ lē) *adv.* no more than; simply

Though his father was fat and merely owned a candy and nut shop, Harry Tillian liked his papa. Harry stopped liking candy and nuts when he was around seven, but, in spite of this, he and Mr. Tillian had remained friends and were still friends the year Harry turned twelve.

For years, after school, Harry had always stopped in to see his father at work. Many of Harry's friends stopped there, too, to spend a few cents choosing penny candy from the giant bins or to sample Mr. Tillian's latest batch of roasted peanuts. Mr. Tillian looked forward to seeing his son and his son's friends every day. He liked the company.

26 Fiction and Nonfiction

Vocabulary Development   © CCSS Language 6

Thematic Vocabulary: The Big Question
As students are discussing "Papa's Parrot," encourage them to use the the-matic vocabulary presented in Introducing the Big Question, pp. 2–3. You might encourage them with sentence starters like these:

1. Harry does not *perceive* his father's . . .
2. When Papa gets the parrot, Harry *concludes* . . .
3. Working in the shop while his father is ill, Harry begins to gain *insight* . . .
4. Finally, the parrot *convinces* Harry that . . .

When Harry entered junior high school, though, he didn't come by the candy and nut shop as often. Nor did his friends. They were older and they had more spending money. They went to a burger place. They played video games. They shopped for records.[1] None of them were much interested in candy and nuts anymore.

A new group of children came to Mr. Tillian's shop now. But not Harry Tillian and his friends.

The year Harry turned twelve was also the year Mr. Tillian got a parrot. He went to a pet store one day and bought one for more money than he could really afford. He brought the parrot to his shop, set its cage near the sign for maple clusters, and named it Rocky.

Harry thought this was the strangest thing his father had ever done, and he told him so, but Mr. Tillian just ignored him.

Rocky was good company for Mr. Tillian. When business was slow, Mr. Tillian would turn on a small color television he had sitting in a corner, and he and Rocky would watch the soap operas. Rocky liked to scream when the romantic music came on, and Mr. Tillian would yell at him to shut up, but they seemed to enjoy themselves.

The more Mr. Tillian grew to like his parrot, and the more he talked to it instead of to people, the more embarrassed Harry became. Harry would stroll past the shop, on his way somewhere else, and he'd take a quick look inside to see what his dad was doing. Mr. Tillian was always talking to the bird. So Harry kept walking.

At home things were different. Harry and his father joked with each other at the dinner table as they always had— Mr. Tillian teasing Harry about his smelly socks; Harry teasing Mr. Tillian about his blubbery stomach. At home things seemed all right.

But one day, Mr. Tillian became ill. He had been at work, unpacking boxes of caramels, when he had grabbed his chest and fallen over on top of the candy. A customer had found him, and he was taken to the hospital in an ambulance.

Mr. Tillian couldn't leave the hospital. He lay in bed, tubes in his arms, and he worried about his shop. New shipments of candy and nuts would be arriving. Rocky would be hungry.

---

1. **records** (rek´ erdz) *n.* thin grooved discs on which music is recorded and played on a phonograph, or record player.

Narration
What details make this fictional narrative seem realistic?

Vocabulary
clusters (klus´ tərz)
n. numbers of things of the same sort that are grouped together; bunches
ignored (ig nôrd´)
v. paid no attention to
shipments (ship´ mənts)
n. deliveries or acts of sending goods

5 Reading Check
Why is Harry embarrassed by his father?

---

4 Narration

1. Before students begin reading the bracketed text, explain that "Papa's Parrot" is a straightforward narrative—the events move forward from beginning to end. After students have read the bracketed passage, point out that the background information it provides is important for setting up the story's main events.

2. **Ask** students how they might complete the Beginning section of their graphic organizers.
   Answer: Harry grows away from his father, and Mr. Tillian buys a parrot.

3. **Ask** students to respond to the Narration question.
   Answer: After Harry and his friends enter junior high school, their interests change from a childish interest in candy to a teenage interest in video games and music. These details reflect a change that real children undergo when they become teenagers.

5 Reading Check

Answer: Harry is embarrassed because his father talks to the parrot.

This selection is available in interactive format in the **Enriched Online Student Edition**, at **www.PHLitOnline.com,** which includes a thematically related video with writing prompt and an interactive graphic organizer.

❻ Narration

1. Read the bracketed text together as a class. Then, **ask** students which segment of the narrative they have just read in this passage (beginning, middle, or end), and ask how they know they are no longer reading background information.
Answer: This passage falls in the middle of the narrative. It is the middle of the story because Harry must respond to something serious that has happened.

2. **Ask** students to answer the Narration question.
Answer: Harry organizes the candy and nuts and cares for Rocky.

❼ Context Clues

1. Remind students that context clues are hints to the meanings of unfamiliar words. Point out that context clues are not always in the same sentence as the unfamiliar word. Sometimes students must look back or read further.

2. **Ask** students what is in the boxes Harry opens.
Answer: The boxes contain different types of candy.

3. Point out that the candies belong in their respective containers, and Harry is putting the candies where they belong.

4. **Ask** students the Context Clues question.
Answer: The mention of different kinds of candies, and the fact that Harry travels from one to the next to put them where they belong, suggests the meaning of the word *bin*: "container."

Narration
What does Harry do after school to help his father?

❻

Context Clues
What clues point to the meaning of the word *bin*?

❼

28 Fiction and Nonfiction

Who would take care of things?

Harry said he would. Harry told his father that he would go to the store every day after school and unpack boxes. He would sort out all the candy and nuts. He would even feed Rocky.

So, the next morning, while Mr. Tillian lay in his hospital bed, Harry took the shop key to school with him. After school he left his friends and walked to the empty shop alone. In all the days of his life, Harry had never seen the shop closed after school. Harry didn't even remember what the CLOSED sign looked like. The key stuck in the lock three times, and inside he had to search all the walls for the light switch.

The shop was as his father had left it. Even the caramels were still spilled on the floor. Harry bent down and picked them up one by one, dropping them back in the boxes. The bird in its cage watched him silently.

Harry opened the new boxes his father hadn't gotten to. Peppermints. Jawbreakers. Toffee creams. Strawberry kisses. Harry traveled from bin to bin, putting the candies where they belonged.

"Hello!"

Harry jumped, spilling a box of jawbreakers.

"Hello, Rocky!"

Harry stared at the parrot. He had forgotten it was there. The bird had been so quiet, and Harry had been thinking only of the candy.

"Hello," Harry said.

Vocabulary Development

Vocabulary Knowledge Rating
When students have completed reading and discussing "Papa's Parrot," have them take out their **Vocabulary Knowledge Rating Chart** for this selection. Read the words aloud once more, and have students write their own definitions or examples in the appropriate column. Then, have students complete the Vocabulary Practice at the end of the selection. Encourage students to use the words in further discussion and written work about this selection. Remind them that they will be accountable for these words on the **Selection Test**, *Unit 1 Resources*, pp. 42–44 or pp. 45–47.

"Hello, Rocky!" answered the parrot.

Harry walked slowly over to the cage. The parrot's food cup was empty. Its water was dirty. The bottom of the cage was a mess.

Harry carried the cage into the back room.

"Hello, Rocky!"

"Is that all you can say, you dumb bird?" Harry mumbled. The bird said nothing else.

Harry cleaned the bottom of the cage, refilled the food and water cups, and then put the cage back in its place and **resumed** sorting the candy.

"Where's Harry?"

Harry looked up.

"Where's Harry?"

Harry stared at the parrot.

"Where's Harry?"

Chills ran down Harry's back. What could the bird mean? It was something from "The Twilight Zone."[2]

"Where's Harry?"

Harry swallowed and said, "I'm here. I'm here, you stupid bird."

"You stupid bird!" said the parrot.

Well, at least he's got one thing straight, thought Harry.

"Miss him! Miss him! Where's Harry? You stupid bird!"

Harry stood with a handful of peppermints.

---

2. **"The Twilight Zone"** science-fiction television series from the 1960s.

Papa's Parrot **29**

❽ LITERATURE IN CONTEXT

Science Connection

Do parrots like Rocky understand language?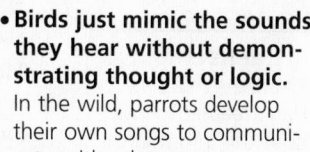
Here are two sides of the scientific debate:

- **Birds just mimic the sounds they hear without demonstrating thought or logic.** In the wild, parrots develop their own songs to communicate with other parrots.

- **Parrots can be taught language.** A Harvard University researcher taught a parrot named Alex to recognize items by name and to identify seven different colors. Alex learned to understand concepts like bigger versus smaller.

Connect to the Literature

Which side of the debate do you think the story supports? Explain your answer.

Vocabulary
resumed (ri zoomd´)
v. began again; continued

❽ Literature in Context

Science Connection The very colorful species of parrots called amazons are especially good at imitating sounds in the human world. However, these birds have not been observed mimicking in their natural environments. There is also no scientific evidence to support the argument that talking parrots understand what they are saying.

Connect to the Literature
Have students read the Literature in Context feature, and present the additional background information above. Then, **ask** students to recall the words that the parrot in the story spoke and whether they feel that Rocky was actually talking to Harry.

Possible response: Rocky said things that Mr. Tillian said many times as well as repeating what Harry said to him, so he was probably repeating and not actually talking to Harry.

Next, **ask** the Connect to the Literature question: Which side of the debate do you think the story supports? Explain your answer.

Possible response: In the story, Rocky says things—such as "Hello, Rocky!"—that sound as if he is talking to himself. Also, Harry understands that his father has been saying certain things in front of the bird for a long time. Both examples suggest that parrots do not understand what they say.

❾ ？ Connecting to the Big Question

1. Point out that sometimes we don't know the truth of people's feelings, even when we live with those people.

2. Have students reread the bracketed text on page 29. **Ask** students: How does Harry react when he hears Rocky asking, "Where's Harry?"

Possible response: He gets chills down his back.

3. **Ask:** How does Harry learn the truth about his father's feelings?

Possible response: Harry learns the truth by hearing Rocky repeat words that his father must have said often.

Concept Connector

Literary Analysis Graphic Organizer
Ask students to review the graphic organizers on which they listed the sequence of events in the story. Then, have students share the details that they listed on their graphic organizers.

？ Writing About the Big Question
Have students compare their responses to the sentence starters they completed before reading the story with their thoughts afterward. Ask them to explain whether their thoughts have changed.

Anticipation Guide
Have students return to their Anticipation Guides and respond to the statements again in the After Reading column. They may do this individually or in their original groups. Then lead a class discussion, probing for what students have learned that confirms or invalidates each statement. Encourage students to cite specific details, quotations, or other evidence from the text to support their responses to each statement.

Spiral Review

Theme

1. Remind students that they studied the concept of theme in the Unit 1 Literary Analysis Workshop (pp. 4–21).

2. **Ask** students the first Spiral Review question.

   Possible response: Harry has learned that his father misses him.

3. **Ask** students the second Spiral Review question.

   Possible response: He has learned the truth about his father's feelings.

ASSESS

Answers

Critical Thinking

Remind students to support their answers with evidence from the text.

1. (a) Harry and his friends visited Mr. Tillian after school because the children wanted to buy candy and sample the nuts. (b) They are older, have more spending money, and want to do other things.

2. (a) Rocky is Mr. Tillian's parrot. (b) He buys the parrot for company after Harry and his friends stop coming by the store.

3. (a) He throws peppermints at the bird and shouts insults at him. (b) He is angry with himself for neglecting his father.

4. (a) Harry needs to realize that Mr. Tillian still needs his company and Mr. Tillian needs to understand that Harry is growing up. (b) Harry has a greater responsibility to be understanding because he has been neglecting his father. (c) Students should explain whether or not their responses changed.

5. **Possible responses:** (a) Rocky reveals that Mr. Tillian feels hurt by Harry's absence from the store. (b) It is better for Harry to learn the truth from the parrot. His father would not have been comfortable explaining his own feelings.

Vocabulary
perch (pʉrch) *n.* roost for a bird; seat

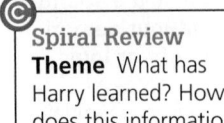

Spiral Review
Theme What has Harry learned? How does this information point to a possible theme?

"What?" he asked.

"Where's Harry?" said the parrot.

"I'm here, you stupid bird! I'm here!" Harry yelled. He threw the peppermints at the cage, and the bird screamed and clung to its perch.

Harry sobbed, "I'm here." The tears were coming.

Harry leaned over the glass counter.

"Papa." Harry buried his face in his arms.

"Where's Harry?" repeated the bird.

Harry sighed and wiped his face on his sleeve. He watched the parrot. He understood now: someone had been saying, for a long time, "Where's Harry? Miss him."

Harry finished his unpacking and then swept the floor of the shop. He checked the furnace so the bird wouldn't get cold. Then he left to go visit his papa.

Critical Thinking

1. **Key Ideas and Details (a)** In the past, why did Harry and his friends visit Mr. Tillian after school? **(b) Infer:** Why have Harry and his friends stopped visiting Harry's father?

2. **Key Ideas and Details (a)** Who is Rocky? **(b) Analyze Cause and Effect:** Why does Mr. Tillian buy Rocky?

3. **Key Ideas and Details (a)** Explain how Harry reacts when Rocky says "Where's Harry?" and "Miss him!" **(b) Analyze:** Why does Harry react as he does?

4. **Integration of Knowledge and Ideas (a) Analyze:** What does each main character need to understand about the other? **(b) Make a Judgment:** Which character has a greater responsibility to be understanding? Why? **(c) Discuss:** Share your response with a partner. Then, explain how understanding someone else's response did or did not change your opinion.

5. **Integration of Knowledge and Ideas (a)** What truth does Rocky reveal about Mr. Tillian's feelings toward Harry? **(b)** Would it have been better for Harry to learn the truth from his father? Explain. *[Connect to the Big Question: What is the best way to find the truth?]*

Cite textual evidence to support your responses.

Assessment Resources

Unit 1 Resources

L1 L2 EL **Selection Test A,** pp. 42–44. Administer Test A to less advanced readers.

L3 L4 EL **Selection Test B,** pp. 45–47. Administer Test B to on-level and more advanced students.

L3 L4 **Open-Book Test,** pp. 39–41. As an alternative, give the Open-Book Test.

All **Customizable Test Bank**

All **Self-tests**
Students may prepare for the **Selection Test** by taking the **Self-test** online.

All assessment resources are available at **www.PHLitOnline.com.**

Reading Skill: Context Clues

1. In a chart like this, write the italicized word in the left column. Then, write the **context clues** and what the word means. Check your response in a dictionary. **(a)** Harry would *stroll* past the pet shop on his way to somewhere else . . . Mr. Tillian was always talking to the bird. So Harry kept on walking. **(b)** He checked the *furnace* so the bird wouldn't get cold.

Unfamiliar Word	Context Clues	Possible Meaning

Literary Analysis: Narrative Text

2. Craft and Structure Identify a reason that the story is called a **narrative.**

3. Craft and Structure The order of events is important in narration. **(a)** Did Mr. Tillian buy his parrot before or after Harry stopped coming to the store? **(b)** Why is this detail important?

Vocabulary

Acquisition and Use Explain your answer to each question.

1. Would you *resume* a meeting before taking a break?

2. If children play in a *cluster,* are they playing together?

3. If *shipments* are ready for delivery, have they already arrived?

4. What part of a bird holds onto a *perch?*

5. If something is *merely* a chance, is it likely to happen?

6. If you *ignored* your friend, would you respond to him?

Word Study Use the context of the sentences and what you know about the **Latin prefix re-** to explain your answers.

1. If a person *rejoins* a group, has he or she been there before?

2. Can you *recall* something you have not learned yet?

Word Study

The **Latin prefix re-** means "back" or "again."

Apply It Explain how the prefix *re-* contributes to the meanings of these words. Consult a dictionary if necessary.
relocate
recede
remove

Papa's Parrot **31**

Word Study:
Sample answers:

1. Yes, the prefix *re-* means "again," and *rejoins* means "join again."

2. No, the prefix *re-* means "again," so you can only *recall* something you already know, and so can think of again.

Word Study: Apply It
Sample answers:

To *relocate* is to locate again. To *recede* is to go back to an earlier point or level. To *remove* is to move something again, or put it farther away.

---

1. (a) Unfamiliar Word—*stroll*; Context Clues—Harry kept walking; Possible Meaning—"walk" (b) Unfamiliar Word—*furnace*; Context Clues—the furnace is important for keeping the bird warm; Possible Meaning—"heater"

For other sample answers, see *Graphic Organizer Transparencies,* **Reading Skill Graphic Organizer A,** p. 6, and the **Additional Answers** section.

Literary Analysis

2. "Papa's Parrot" is called a narrative because it tells a story with events happening in chronological order.

3. (a) Mr. Tillian bought his parrot after Harry stopped coming to the store. (b) This is important to the story because Mr. Tillian needed the parrot to keep him company once Harry no longer visited.

Vocabulary
Acquisition and Use
Sample answers:

1. You would <u>resume</u>, or continue, a meeting after taking a break.

2. If children play in a <u>cluster</u>, they are playing in a group.

3. No, if <u>shipments</u> are ready for delivery, they still need to be delivered.

4. A bird's feet hold it onto a <u>perch</u>.

5. If something is <u>merely</u> a chance, there is only a small chance it will happen.

6. No, if I <u>ignored</u> my friend, I would not pay attention or respond.

❶ 🅱 Writing About the Big Question

1. Review the assignment with the class.

2. Ask students for examples of made-up stories that people believe. Explore why people continue to believe these stories.

3. Have students complete the sentence starters. Review responses as a class. (**Sample answer:** Sometimes we <u>believe</u> in things that are not true because it helps us feel strong. We find what is <u>real</u> by experiencing it.)

4. Remind students that their answers will help them think about the Big Question, "What is the best way to find the truth?"

While You Read

Tell students that as they read, they should look for ways that Jean discovers who she is.

❷ Vocabulary

1. Have students preview the selection vocabulary.

2. For each word, have students say the word aloud.

3. Then, use the word in a sentence that defines the word.

4. Finally, repeat your definitional sentence or a similar sentence with the word missing and have the class "fill in the blank" chorally. Here are some examples:

   When something is <u>adequate</u>, it is just enough. The essay Helen wrote received a grade just above passing because it was only [students say "adequate"].

   When you <u>deceive</u> people, you trick them. If you tell your friends that you are home sick when you are at the beach, you [students say "deceive"] them.

❸ Word Study

1. Introduce the skill, using the instruction in the box.

2. Have students suggest another word beginning with *in-* and explain its meaning. (**Sample answer:** *inability*; "lack of ability")

Making Connections | mk

🅱 THE BIG ❓ What is the best way to find the *truth*?

❶ Writing About the Big Question

In "mk," a real historical figure becomes a fictional friend to a young girl. Use these sentence starters to develop your ideas about the Big Question.

Sometimes we **believe** in things that are not true because it helps us _____.

We find what is **real** by _____.

While You Read Look for ways that Jean discovers who she is through her experiences as an American who lives overseas.

❷ Vocabulary

Read each word and its definition. Decide whether you know the word well, know it a little bit, or do not know it at all. After you read, see how your knowledge of each word has increased.

- **relation** (ri lā´ shən) *n.* connection between two or more things (p. 34) *Kim chose a seat based on its <u>relation</u> to her friends.* relationship *n.* relative *adj.* relate *v.* related *adj.*

- **quest** (kwest) *n.* long search for something (p. 35) *The pirates set out on a <u>quest</u> for treasure.* request *n.* question *n.*

- **adequate** (ad´ i kwət) *adj.* enough (p. 36) *The small sandwich was not an <u>adequate</u> lunch for a growing girl.* adequately *adv.* adequacy *n.* inadequate *n.*

- **deceive** (dē sēv´) *v.* make someone believe something that is not true (p. 39) *Sadly, Annie tried to <u>deceive</u> her friend by making up a story.* deceived *v.* deceiving *v.* deception *n.*

- **transformation** (trans´ fər mā´ shən) *n.* change (p. 39) *Lily's <u>transformation</u> from soccer star to prom queen was amazing.* transform *v.* transformative *adj.*

- **ignorant** (ig´ nə rənt) *adj.* not knowing facts or information (p. 43) *The traveler was <u>ignorant</u> of the country's customs and had to ask a lot of questions.* ignorance *n.* ignore *v.* ignored *v.*

❸ Word Study

The **Latin prefix *in-*** means "not."

In this story, Jean thought her greeting to Mrs. Barrett was **adequate**, or enough. However, Mrs. Barrett was displeased because she found it *inadequate*.

32 Fiction and Nonfiction

Vocabulary Development

Vocabulary Knowledge Rating

Create a **Vocabulary Knowledge Rating Chart** (*Professional Development Guidebook,* p. 33) for this selection. Include the selection vocabulary and the Big Question words that appear in the Writing About the Big Question sentence starters on this page. (The Big Question vocabulary is introduced on pp. 2–3.)

Give students a copy of the chart. Read the words aloud, and have students mark their rating in the Before Reading column. Urge them to be alert to these words as they read and discuss the selection.

Tally how many students think they know a word to gauge how much instruction to provide. As students read and discuss the selection, point out the words and their context.

PHLit Online! **Vocabulary Central**, featuring tools, activities, and songs for studying vocabulary, is available online at www.PHLitOnline.com.

Meet
Jean Fritz
(b. 1915)

Author of

mk

Missionary Kid An only child of missionary parents, Jean Fritz grew up in China. Although she had not yet been in the United States, she read and heard from her father about American heroes, such as George Washington and Teddy Roosevelt. Her fascination with these heroes inspired her career as a writer of American history.

Fritz fills her biographies with unusual but true details about her subjects, which she researches thoroughly. "History is full of gossip; it's real people and emotion," she says. The details make her books about historical figures such as Pocahontas or Sam Adams spring to life.

> ### DID YOU KNOW?
> As a child, Fritz kept a journal to help her feel less lonely.

❹ BACKGROUND FOR THE SELECTION

Overseas Schools

When American parents live and work outside the United States, their children often attend American schools overseas. At most of these schools, students are taught in English and study many of the things that students study in the United States. International schools, like the one described in this selection, are located all over the world.

mk **33**

❹ Daily Bellringer
For each class during which you teach this selection, have students complete one of the five Quick Write activities for Week 1 in the *Daily Bellringer Activities* booklet.

❹ Background
The Chinese Revolution

In the 1920s in China, there was no strong central government. Local leaders, called warlords, fought with each other over territory. Two groups, the Nationalist Party and the Communist Party, tried to form a central government and fought not only the warlords, but sometimes each other. In 1949, under the leadership of Mao Zedong, the Communist Party took over. Nationalist Party members and their leader, Chiang Kai-Shek, fled to an island off the coast of mainland China, where they formed the Republic of Taiwan.

Multidraft Reading

This icon ◗ marks natural pauses in the selection. To assist struggling readers and to deepen reading for all, assign the text in "chunks," following the icons, and apply multidraft reading protocols. For each reading, have students set the purpose indicated:

- **First reading**—identifying key ideas and details and answering any Reading Checks.
- **Second reading**—analyzing craft and structure and responding to the side-column prompts.
- **Third reading**—integrating knowledge and ideas, connecting to other texts and the world, and answering the end-of-selection questions.

For more guidance, refer to the *Classroom Strategies and Teaching Routines* card on multidraft reading.

Differentiated Instruction   Additional Daily Instruction

EL Extended Support— English Learners
Have students complete the **Reading and Vocabulary Warm-ups**, *Unit 1 Resources,* pp. 48–51, before they read. Assign the prereading pages in the *Reader's Notebook: English Learner's Version*. Then, have students listen to portions of the selection on the *Hear It!* **Audio CD.**

L1 L2 Extended Support— Struggling Readers
Have students complete the **Reading and Vocabulary Warm-ups**, *Unit 1 Resources,* pp. 48–51, before they read. Assign the prereading pages in the *Reader's Notebook: Adapted Version*. Then, have students listen to portions of the selection on the *Hear It!* **Audio CD** (adapted text).

Extended Support— Reluctant Readers
To build motivation and engagement before assigning the selection, have students read "Learning the Truth in China," a thematically related selection in *Reality Central.* Then, use the questions at the conclusion of the related selection to guide discussion.

PHLit Online!
For more about the author, practice with the selection vocabulary, or more background, go online at www.PHLitOnline.com.

33

❶ Activating Prior Knowledge

1. Prepare an **Anticipation Guide** (*Professional Development Guidebook,* p. 38) with the following statements:

   • Children who are raised overseas do not feel completely at home in any country.

   • Everyone spends time in life deciding where they belong.

   • Getting something we want does not always make us happy.

   • Where a person comes from is always an important part of who that person is.

2. Give students a copy of the prepared **Anticipation Guide** and have them respond in the Me column. Have students discuss the statements in groups and respond again in the Group column.

3. For further guidance, use the *Classroom Strategies and Teaching Routines* card for **Anticipation Guides.**

Concept Connector ➡️

Students will return to the **Anticipation Guide** after completing the story.

Individual Activity

Tell students to think of a time when they knew something important was going to happen to them, such as moving to a new town or school. Have them write a paragraph that describes how they expected to feel when the event took place and how they actually felt when it happened. Allow volunteers to share their experiences with the class.

❷ About the Selection

In "mk," the Anglo-American author recalls her last months in China, her family's move to the United States, and her ongoing search for a national identity. She is disappointed when attending certain schools does not make her feel like a "real" American, as though that were the one place she belonged. Fritz later realizes that no matter where she lives, China, a significant part of her history, will be with her forever.

mk
Jean Fritz

Vocabulary
relation (ri lā′ shən) *n.* connection between two or more things

I suspect for most of us MKs[1] China not only sharpened our sense of time but our sense of place. We always knew where we were in relation to the rest of the world. And we noticed. Perhaps because we knew we would be leaving China sometime (we wouldn't be MKs or even Ks forever), we developed the habit of observing our surroundings with care. We have strong memories, which explains why as an adult, walking along a beach in Maine, I suddenly found myself on the verge of tears. In front of me, pushing up from the crevice of a rock, was a wild bluebell[2] like the wild bluebells I had known in my summers at Kuling.[3] Suddenly I was a child again. I was back in China, welcoming bluebells back in my life.

---

1. **MKs** (em′ kāz′) *n.* Missionary Kids; the children of missionaries.
2. **bluebell** (blo͞o′ bel′) *n.* plant with blue, bell-shaped flowers.
3. **Kuling** (ko͞ol′ iŋ) *n.* now called Lushan, a hill resort south of the Yangtze River in China.

34 Fiction and Nonfiction

Vocabulary Development   ©️ CCSS Language 6

Thematic Vocabulary: The Big Question
As students are discussing "mk," encourage them to use the thematic vocabulary presented in Introducing the Big Question, pp. 2–3. You might encourage them with sentence starters like these:

1. As Jean gets older, her *awareness* of being American becomes . . .

2. Fletcher and Jean *debate* about . . .
3. Jean interacts with *fiction* when she . . .
4. Her time at the Shanghai American School helps Jean *evaluate* . . .
5. As she travels across America, Jean begins to *perceive* . . .

For a long time it was hard for me to unscramble the strings that made up my quest. I have noticed, however, that those MKs who were born in China and stayed there through their high school years were more likely to commit their lives in some way to China. After finishing their higher education in the States, they would return to China as consuls, as teachers, as businessmen and women, as writers, as historians.

I wouldn't be staying through high school. My family planned to return to America when I had finished seventh grade, whether I was finished with China or not. Of course I knew I had to become an American, the sooner the better. So far away from America, I didn't feel like a real American. Nor would I, I thought, until I had put my feet down on American soil.

I had just finished sixth grade at the British School in Wuhan,[4] so I would have one more year to go. Nothing would change that. I knew that there was fighting up and down the Yangtze River, but the Chinese were always fighting—warlord against warlord.[5] That had nothing to do with me. But as soon as I saw the servant from next door racing toward our house with a message for my mother, I knew something was happening. Since we had no phone, we depended on our German neighbors for emergency messages. My father had called, the servant explained. All American women and children had to catch the afternoon boat to Shanghai.[6] The army, which had done so much damage to Nanjing (just down the river), was on its way here.

As I helped my mother pack, my knees were shaking. I had only felt this once before. My mother and I had been in a ricksha on the way to the racecourse when farmers ran to the road, calling hateful words at us and throwing stones.

---

4. **Wuhan** (wōō´ hän´) *n.* city in the central part of China, near the Yangtze River.
5. **warlord** (wôr´ lôrd´) *n.* local leader.
6. **Shanghai** (shaŋ´ hī´) *n.* seaport in eastern China.

Context Clues
Identify examples in this paragraph that help you define *commit*.

Vocabulary
quest (kwest) *n.* long search for something

④ ▼ **Critical Viewing**
Does a ricksha offer much protection to the riders? Explain. **[Speculate]**

✔ **Reading Check**
⑤ As a child, where did the narrator live?

mk **35**

❸ **Context Clues**

1. Briefly review the use of example context clues as a strategy for decoding unfamiliar words while reading.

2. Tell students that the clues do not always appear in the same sentence in which the word itself appears. Explain that to infer its meaning, students will need to read the sentences before and after the one in which the word appears.

3. After reading the bracketed section, **ask** students to complete the Context Clues task.
   Possible response: The example of MKs born in China and returning there to work suggests the meaning of the word *commit*: "give over to" or "make a serious pledge or promise of."

❹ **Critical Viewing**

Possible response: The enclosed ricksha in the picture appears to afford very little protection to the riders since the large window openings leave their upper bodies exposed.

❺ **Reading Check**

Answer: As a child, the narrator of "mk" lived in China.

PROFESSIONAL DEVELOPMENT | **Sharon Vaughn, Ph.D.**

▼ **Apply the Strategy**

Tier 2 Vocabulary Before reading the story, direct students to the paragraphs that have the following Tier 2 vocabulary words: *verge* (p. 34), *continent* (p. 41), *fading* (p. 43), *hometown* (p. 43). Start with the word *verge*. Ask students to read the paragraph in which the word appears and determine if they can "figure out" what *verge* means. Give students an opportunity to explain its meaning. Then, wrap up by providing a clear definition.

Follow this same procedure with the other words. Give several students an opportunity to report to the class their understanding of the word meaning, and then clarify for each word. Also provide examples of what the word does "not" mean. With the word *fading,* ask students what it does "not" mean: "getting stronger or bolder."
For more of Sharon Vaughn's strategies, see her Professional Development essay, p. 2c–2d.

Connect

1. Remind students that people often use experiences from their past to help them understand experiences in the present.

2. Have students read the first sentence of the bracketed text on page 36 and recall the entire incident as Jean describes it on page 35. **Ask** them what experience from her past Jean describes.
Answer: She describes a frightening ricksha ride, on which she and her mother are stoned by farmers shouting angry words.

3. Have students read the rest of the bracketed text on page 36. **Ask** them what connection Jean makes between the ricksha ride and her current situation.
Answer: She compares the nervousness she feels currently with her feeling on the ricksha ride.

7 Critical Viewing

Answer: This type of boat might be used for fishing or for transporting a few passengers at a time.

Vocabulary
adequate
(ad´ i kwət) *adj.* enough

7 ▼ Critical Viewing
Jean probably saw boats like this on the Yangtze River. What purpose do you think these boats served? **[Hypothesize]**

---

6 The ricksha-pullers were fast runners, so we weren't hurt, but I told myself this was like Stephen in the Bible who was stoned to death. He just didn't have a ricksha handy. By the time we reached the boat that afternoon, my knees were normal. So was I. And I knew what our plans were. My father and other American men would work in the daytime, but for safety at night they would board one of the gunboats anchored in the river. The women and children going to Shanghai would be protected from bullets by steel barriers erected around the deck. And when we reached Shanghai, then what? I asked my mother. ●

We would be staying with the Barretts, another missionary family, who had one son, Fletcher, who was two years younger than I and generally unlikable. Mr. Barrett met us in Shanghai and drove us to their home, where his wife was on the front porch. My mother greeted her warmly but I just held out my hand and said, "Hello, Mrs. Barrett," which I thought was adequate. She raised her eyebrows. "Have you become so grown up, Jean," she said, "that I'm no longer your 'Auntie Barrett'?"

I didn't say that I'd always been too grown up for the "auntie" business. I just smiled. In China all MKs called their parents' friends "auntie" or "uncle." Not me. Mrs. B. pushed Fletcher forward.

36 Fiction and Nonfiction

Think Aloud

Vocabulary: Context Clues
Direct students' attention to the words *rummy* and *patience* on page 37. Using a think-aloud process, model how to use context to figure out these unfamiliar words. Say to students:

I'm going to think aloud to show you how I would figure out the meanings of *rummy* and *patience* from their context.

In this sentence, *rummy* and *patience* are used as nouns and are something that Jean and Fletcher play. If I reread the sentence before, I see that Jean says "Fletcher had a lot of games." I think that *patience* and *rummy* must be kinds of games. If I read on to the last sentence in the paragraph, I see a reference to another game, called Uncle Wiggley. Yes, *rummy* and *patience* are examples of games that Fletcher wants to play.

"Fletcher has been so excited about your visit, Jean," she said. "He has lots of games to show you. Now, run along, children."

Fletcher did have a lot of games. He decided what we'd play—rummy, then patience, while he talked a blue streak. I didn't pay much attention until, in the middle of an Uncle Wiggley game, he asked me a question.

"Have you ever been in love, Jean?" he asked.

What did he think I was? I was twelve years old, for heaven's sakes!

Ever since first grade I'd been in love with someone. The boys never knew it, of course.

Fletcher hadn't finished with love. "I'm in love now," he said. "I'll give you a hint. She's an MK."

"Naturally."

"And she's pretty." Then he suddenly shrieked out the answer as if he couldn't contain it a second longer. "It's you," he cried. "Y-O-U."

Well, Fletcher Barrett was even dumber than I'd thought. No one had ever called me "pretty" before. Not even my parents. Besides, this conversation was making me sick. "I'm tired," I said. "I think I'll get my book and lie down."

At the last minute I had slipped my favorite book in my suitcase. It was one my father and I had read last year—*The Courtship of Miles Standish*[7]—all about the first settlers in America. I knew them pretty well now and often visited with Priscilla Alden.

Settled on the bed in the room I'd been told was mine, I opened the book and let the Pilgrims step off the Mayflower into Shanghai. Priscilla was one of the first.

"You're still a long way from Plymouth," I told her, "but you'll get there. Think you'll like it?"

"I know I will," she answered promptly. "Everything will be better there."

"How do you know?"

"It's a new country. It will be whatever we make it."

"It may be hard," I warned her.

"Maybe," she admitted. "But I'll never give up. Neither will John," she added.

---

7. ***The Courtship of Miles Standish*** *n.* narrative poem by Henry Wadsworth Longfellow, written in 1858. One character in the poem is Priscilla Alden.

Context Clues
Which word restates the meaning of *shrieked* here?

Narration
What problems does reading help Jean solve?

 **Reading Check**
Why is it necessary for Jean and her mother to travel to Shanghai?

mk **37**

---

❽ Context Clues

1. Remind students that some context clues will restate an unfamiliar word by including another word with the same meaning.

2. Have students reread the bracketed section. Point out that the way Fletcher speaks is described twice in the paragraph.

3. **Ask** them which words describe how Fletcher says these lines to Jean.

4. **Answer:** The words *shrieked* and *cried* tell how Fletcher speaks.

5. Then, **ask** them the Context Clues question.
   Answer: *Cried* restates the meaning of *shrieked.*

❾ Narration

1. Review the early events from the narrative, such as Jean living in China with her missionary parents, fleeing to Shanghai to escape the violence in her town, and imagining that she is talking with the Pilgrims from a book she is reading. Have students list these events on their graphic organizers.

2. **Ask** students where Jean is preparing to go and how she might feel about going there.
   Answer: She is moving to America and is probably a little nervous.

3. Have students read the second bracketed passage. Point out that Jean is interacting with a character in a book. Jean's talk with Priscilla is a way of considering her own thoughts and problems. Then, **ask** students the Narration question.
   Answer: Reading helps Jean work out her feelings about moving to America.

❿ Reading Check

Answer: Wuhan became unsafe for Americans because the Chinese army was coming there.

⓫ Critical Viewing

Answer: The children's clothing and hair styles are different from children of today, but their expressions and the way they are arranged for the picture are similar to most children today.

⓬ Narration

1. Tell students that the sequence of events is important for understanding why Jean's school closed. Recall that, first, Americans learned that the army was on its way to Wuhan.

2. **Ask** how some of the foreign businesses in China responded to the scare.
   Answer: They chose to close and not reopen.

3. Then, **ask** students how this affected the British School in Wuhan.
   Answer: The school closed.

4. Have students reread the bracketed text. **Ask** students the Narration question.
   Answer: The author is affected by the threat of violence and the closing of foreign businesses in China.

⓫ ▶ **Critical Viewing**
In what ways do the children in this picture look similar to and different from children of today? **[Compare and Contrast]**

Narration ⓬
What world events affect the author of this nonfiction narrative?

I was being called for supper. I waited for the Pilgrims to get back on the Mayflower. Then I closed the book and went downstairs.

The days that followed, I spent mostly with Fletcher, whether I liked it or not. Fletcher was fussing now that the summer was almost over and he'd have to go back to school soon.

"I thought you'd like it," I said. "After all, it's an American school and you're an American."

"So what?"

"Don't you feel like an American when you're in school?"

"What's there to feel?"

He was impossible. If he had gone to a British school, the way I had all my life, he might realize how lucky he was. The Shanghai American School was famous. Children from all over China were sent there to be boarders. Living in Shanghai, Fletcher was just a day student. But even so!

Then one day my mother got a letter from my father. The danger was mostly over, he thought, but some foreign businesses were not reopening. The British School had closed down. (Good news!)

The Yangtze River boats went back in service the next week, so my mother went downtown to buy our tickets back to Wuhan. Fletcher was back in school now, and as soon as he came home, he rushed to see me, his face full of news.

"Your mother is only buying one ticket," he informed me. "You're not going. You're going to the Shanghai American School as a boarder."

"My mother would never do that. You're crazy," I replied. "Where did you get such an idea?"

"I overheard our mothers talking. It's true, Jean."

"Yeah, like cows fly."

When my mother came back, I could see that she was upset. Fletcher did a disappearing act; I figured he didn't want to be caught in a lie.

"Oh, I'm sorry, Jean," my mother said, her eyes filling with tears. She put her arms around me. "Since the British School is closed," she said, "I've arranged

38 Fiction and Nonfiction

Vocabulary Development © **CCSS Language 6**

Word Form Chart
Expand students' vocabulary by helping them learn related forms of the selection vocabulary words. Four of the selection vocabulary words for "mk" have related forms. Give students a blank **Word Form Chart** (*Professional Development Guidebook*, pp. 41–42), with *adequate, deceive, transformation,* and *ignorant* in the correct columns. Work with the class, or have students work with a partner, to determine the related forms. The final chart should look like the one shown.

Hold students accountable for integrating the related forms of the words into their speaking and writing.

Noun	Verb	Adjective	Adverb
adequacy		**adequate**	adequately
deceit	**deceive**	deceitful	deceitfully
transformation	transform		
ignorance		**ignorant**	ignorantly

⓭ **Connecting to the Big Question**

1. Point out that sometimes we take actions that we think lead toward one truth and are surprised to learn another truth.

2. Have students reread the bracketed text on page 39. **Ask** students: What does Jean discover about herself at this moment? **Possible response:** She discovers that she's very happy to be going to the Shanghai American School, that she's willing to deceive her mother to protect her, and that she doesn't feel like an American just because she goes to an American place.

3. **Ask:** What will probably be the best way for Jean to understand the truth of what being an American means to her? **Possible response:** She probably won't know this truth fully until she gets to America.

⓮ **Reading Check**

Answer: Jean is excited because she expects the new school to help make her feel like an American.

for you to be a boarder at the American School. It won't be for long. We may even go back to America early. At least I'll know you're safe."

I knew my mother was worried that I'd be homesick, so I couldn't let on how I really felt. (Just think, I told myself, I'd have almost a year to practice being an American.) I buried my head on her shoulder. "I'll be okay," I said, sniffing back fake tears. Sometimes it's necessary to deceive your parents if you love them, and I did love mine. ●

After my mother left on the boat, Mr. Barrett took me to the Shanghai American School (SAS for short). I guess I expected some kind of immediate transformation. I always felt a tingling when I saw the American flag flying over the American consulate. Surely it would be more than a tingling now; surely it would overwhelm me. But when we went through the iron gates of the school grounds, I didn't feel a thing. On the football field a group of high school girls were practicing cheerleading. They were jumping, standing on their hands, yelling rah, rah, rah. It just seemed like a lot of fuss about football. What was the matter with me?

Vocabulary
deceive (dē sēv′) v. make someone believe something that is not true

transformation (trans′ fər mā′ shən) n. change

⓮ **Reading Check**
Why is Jean excited about going to the American school?

mk **39**

Differentiated Instruction for Universal Access

Culturally Responsive Instruction
Culture Focus Point out that Jean looks eagerly at the American flag as she drives to the American consulate and its school. Like people everywhere, she associates the flag with her nation and hopes it will create a sense of belonging for her. Most nations have flags, but many people feel a stronger connection to a culture than they do to a political nation. Invite students to reflect on their own allegiances to nation and culture. Urge them to consider and identify the feelings they associate with the American flag, the flag of other countries that are important to their family, and other symbols of cultures or groups to which they belong. Invite volunteers to share their thoughts, first stressing that it is possible to feel connected to and part of many different political and cultural groups.

⑮ Narration

1. Tell students that one main idea in this narrative is that Jean wants very much to feel like an American. Point out that appearances are important ways for people to express who they are. In the story, Jean's roommate appears very grown-up and acts as though she knows how an American should look.

2. Have students read the bracketed passage. **Ask** them what Paula seems to think of Jean when they first meet.
Answer: Paula seems to think that Jean looks too much like an MK.

3. Explain that it is likely that Paula does not think Jean looks "American" enough.

4. Have students fill in the appropriate events in their graphic organizers.

5. Then, **ask** them to answer the Narration question.
Answer: She decides to cut Jean's hair to look more American.

Spiral Review

Central Idea

1. Remind students that they studied the concept of central idea in the Unit 1 Literary Analysis Workshop (pp. 4–21).

2. **Ask** students the Spiral Review question.
Possible response: Jean wants to be more American.

Narration ⑮
What is the first thing Jean's roommate decides to do for her?

Spiral Review
Central Idea How does Jean's agreement to get a haircut support a central idea of this narrative?

The dormitory where I'd be living was divided in half by a swinging door. The high school girls were on one side of the door; the junior high (which included me) were on the other. On my side there were two Russian girls and two American MKs, the Johnson sisters, who had long hair braided and wound around their heads like Sunday school teachers. And there was Paula, my American roommate, who looked as though she belonged on the other side of the door. Hanging in our shared closet I noticed a black velvet dress. And a pair of high heeled shoes. She wore them to tea dances, she explained, when one of her brother's friends came to town. She was squinting her eyes as she looked at me, sizing up my straight hair and bangs.

"I happen to know you're an MK," she said, "but you don't have to look like one." The latest style in the States, she told me, was a boyish bob.[8] She'd give me one, she decided.

So that night she put a towel around my shoulders and newspaper on the floor, and she began cutting. This might make all the difference, I thought, as I watched my hair travel to the floor.

It didn't. My ears might have felt more American, but not me. After being in hiding all their lives, my ears were suddenly outdoors, looking like jug handles on each side of my face. I'd get used to them, I told myself. Meanwhile I had to admit that SAS was a big improvement over the British School. Even without an American flag feeling, I enjoyed the months I was there.

What I enjoyed most were the dances, except they weren't dances. There were too many MKs in the school, and the Ms didn't approve of dancing. Instead, we had "talk parties." The girls were given what looked like dance cards and the boys were supposed to sign up for the talk sessions they wanted. Of course a girl could feel like a wallflower[9] if her card wasn't filled up, but mine usually was. These parties gave me a chance to look over the boys in case I wanted to fall in love, and actually I was almost ready to make a choice when my parents suddenly appeared. It was early spring. Just as my mother had suspected, we were going to America early. ●

⑰ I knew that three weeks crossing the Pacific would be different from five days on the Yangtze but I didn't know how

---

8. **bob** (bäb) *n.* woman's or child's short haircut.
9. **wallflower** (wôl´ flou´ ər) *n.* person who stands against the wall and watches at a dance due to shyness or lack of popularity.

Vocabulary Development
© **CCSS Language 6**

Expressive Vocabulary
To help students broaden their expressive vocabulary, encourage them to use the following words as they discuss the selection: *discover, explore, imitate,* and *observe.* Have them complete these sentence starters:
After moving to America, Jean will probably *discover . . .*

Jean uses reading to *explore . . .*
Jean wants to *imitate . . .*
While living in China, Jean was able to *observe . . .*

16 Critical Viewing

Possible response: Jean probably felt very excited about arriving in San Francisco Bay, though it's also possible that she was unsure of whether she belonged there.

17 Narration

1. After reading the first paragraph on this page, which begins on page 40, **ask** students why Jean looks forward to crossing the Pacific.
   Answer: She imagines that she will enjoy lounging on the deck drinking tea under a warm rug.

2. Point out that during the trip she learns just how different crossing the ocean is from a boat ride on the Yangtze River.

3. Have students reread the bracketed passage, and **ask** them the Narration question.
   Answer: The trip was rough and unpleasant. Passengers on the steamer were seasick and spent most of their time confined to their cabins.

18 Reading Check

Answer: It takes Jean three weeks to cross the Pacific.

different. My father had given me a gray-and-green plaid steamer rug that I would put over me when I was lying on my long folding deck chair. At eleven o'clock every morning a waiter would come around with a cup of "beef tea." I loved the idea of drinking beef tea under my steamer rug but it didn't happen often. The captain said this was the roughest crossing he'd ever made, and passengers spent most of their time in their cabins. If they came out for a meal, they were lucky if they could get it down before it came back up again. I had my share of seasickness, so of course I was glad to reach San Francisco.

I couldn't wait to take my first steps on American soil, but I expected the American soil to hold still for me. Instead, it swayed as if we were all still at sea, and I lurched about as I had been doing for the last three weeks. I noticed my parents were having difficulty, too. "Our heads and our legs aren't ready for land," my father explained. "It takes a little while." We spent the night in a hotel and took a train the next day for Pittsburgh where our relatives were meeting us.

It was a three-day trip across most of the continent, but

16 ▲ Critical Viewing
How do you think Jean might have felt as she appoached the Golden Gate Bridge in San Francisco by ship? **[Speculate]**

Narration
Why is Jean excited about the end of the crossing?

18 ✓ Reading Check

How long does it take Jean and her family to cross the Pacific?

mk **41**

41

Interpret

1. Remind students that a character's words, actions, and reactions are clues to emotion.

2. Have students read the bracketed text on page 42 and describe what Jean is doing.
   Answer: She is riding a train across America to her grandmother's house.

3. **Ask** students what Jean sees on her train ride.
   Answer: She sees the size and variety of the American landscape. She sees Americans living their daily lives.

4. **Ask:** How does Jean feel about being an American after her journey across the country?
   Answer: She finally feels like an American and feels that she belongs.

5. Finally, **ask** students: Why does the journey have this effect on Jean? Explain.
   Possible response: America is a vast and varied land. Perhaps seeing that variety makes Jean realize that there is no right way to be an American and she can be American no matter who she is.

⑳ **Critical Viewing**

Answer: The mountains may be higher but similar to the hills where Jean spent time in the summers in China.

⑳ ▼ **Critical Viewing**
How does this landscape of the United States compare with Jean's description of where she lived in China? **[Compare and Contrast]**

⑲ it didn't seem long. Every minute America was under us and rushing past our windows—the Rocky Mountains, the Mississippi river, flat ranch land, small towns, forests, boys dragging school bags over dusty roads. It was all of America at once splashed across where we were, where we'd been, where we were going. How could you not feel American? How could you not feel that you belonged? By the time we were settled at my grandmother's house, I felt as if I'd always been a part of this family. And wasn't it wonderful to have real aunts and uncles, a real grandmother, and yes, even a real bathroom, for heaven's sakes?

I wanted to talk to Priscilla, so I took my book outside, and when I opened it, out tumbled the Pilgrims, Priscilla first. I smiled. Here we were, all of us in America together, and it didn't matter that we came from different times. We all knew that America was still an experiment and perhaps always

42 Fiction and Nonfiction

would be. I was one of the ones who had to try to make the experiment work. •

"You'll have disappointments," Priscilla said. "But it will help if you get to know Americans who have spent their lives working on the experiment."

I wasn't sure just what she meant, but I knew it was important. "I'll try," I said.

"Try!" Priscilla scoffed. "If you want to be a real American, you'll have to do more than that." Her voice was fading. Indeed, the Pilgrims themselves were growing faint. Soon they had all slipped away.

I learned about disappointment as soon as I went to school. Of course I was no longer an MK, but I was certainly a curiosity. I was the Kid from China. "Did you live in a mud hut?" one boy asked me. "Did you eat rats and dogs? Did you eat with sticks?"

I decided that American children were ignorant. Didn't their teachers teach them anything? After a while, as soon as anyone even mentioned China, I shut up. "What was the name of your hometown?" I was asked, but I never told. I couldn't bear to have my hometown laughed at.

"Not all American children are ignorant," my mother pointed out. "Just a few who ask dumb questions."

Even in high school, however, I often got the same questions. But now we were studying about the American Revolution and George Washington. Of course I'd always known who Washington was, but knowing history and understanding it are two different things. I had never realized how much he had done to make America into America. No matter how much he was asked to do for his country, he did it, even though he could hardly wait to go back home and be a farmer again. Of course there were disappointments on the way; of course he became discouraged. "If I'd known what I was getting into," he said at the beginning of the Revolution, "I would have chosen to live in an Indian teepee all my life." He never took the easiest way. When he thought his work was over at the end of the Revolution, he agreed to work on the Constitution. When the country needed a president, he took the oath of office. When his term was over, he was persuaded to run once again. Everyone had confidence that as long as he was there, the new government would work.

Context Clues
Which clues in this paragraph help you to understand the meaning of *fading*?

Vocabulary
ignorant (igʹ nə rənt) *adj.* not knowing facts or information

Narration
What does Jean learn in high school that she did not understand before?

Reading Check
How does Jean feel about living in the United States?

mk **43**

Concept Connector

Literary Analysis Graphic Organizer
Ask students to review the graphic organizers on which they listed the sequence of events. Have students share the details that they listed on their graphic organizers.

Writing About the Big Question
Have students compare their responses to the sentence starters they completed before reading the story with their ideas afterward. Ask them to explain whether their thoughts have changed.

Anticipation Guide
Have students return to their **Anticipation Guides** and respond to the statements again in the After Reading column. They may do this individually or in their original pairs or groups. Then, lead a class discussion, probing for what students have learned that confirms or invalidates each statement. Encourage students to cite specific details, quotations, or other evidence from the text to support their responses to each statement.

㉑ Context Clues

1. Remind students once again that context clues can appear in more than one sentence and can restate the meaning of an unfamiliar word.

2. Have students reread the first bracketed paragraph. Point out that the meaning of the word *fading* is restated twice in this paragraph.

3. Then, **ask** students the Context Clues question.
   Answer: The words "growing faint" and "slipped away" help explain the meaning of *fading*.

▶ **Monitor Progress:** Make sure students are able to identify clues to the meaning of the word *fading*.

▶ **Reteach:** If students have difficulty, remind them that clues to the meaning of difficult words often appear in the surrounding words and sentences. Then, have students begin with the sentence, "Her voice was fading," and reread the remainder of the paragraph. Remind them that Priscilla was a Pilgrim and tell them that, in Jean's mind, the Pilgrims grew faint and slipped away.

㉒ Narration

1. Read the bracketed text with students. Then, **ask** them what Jean mentions studying in high school.
   Answer: She mentions studying the American Revolution and George Washington.

2. Point out that she says she had always known about George Washington but understands somethings about him better now.

3. **Ask** students the Narration question.
   Answer: She learns how much George Washington had done to make America into America.

㉓ Reading Check

Answer: Jean feels proud and not sure that she can live up to her idea of an American. She feels disappointed that some Americans are ignorant and don't accept her as they should.

Critical Thinking

Before students respond, you may wish to have them write a brief objective summary of the selection. As they answer the questions below, remind them to support their answers with evidence from the text.

1. **Possible response:** The story's first setting is China. This creates the situation where the narrator feels like she isn't a "real" American.

2. (a) They are in danger in Wuhan and will be safe in Shanghai. (b) At first the school does not live up to Jean's expectations, because she doesn't feel anything special when she enters it. However, she does enjoy her time there and says it is better than the British School.

3. **Possible responses:** Pro—A person can learn more about the world by living in a different country. For example, Jean had a better understanding of life in China than her American classmates. Con—A person who lives outside the United States may not feel perfectly at home in any country. For example, Jean spends many years on a quest for who she really is.

4. **Possible responses:**
(a) Connecting to Priscilla Alden helps Jean see that being an American is a journey toward the unknown, one that many others have made before her. (b) Jean concludes that it takes courage and adventurousness to be a real American, but mostly that there is room for all kinds of Americans.

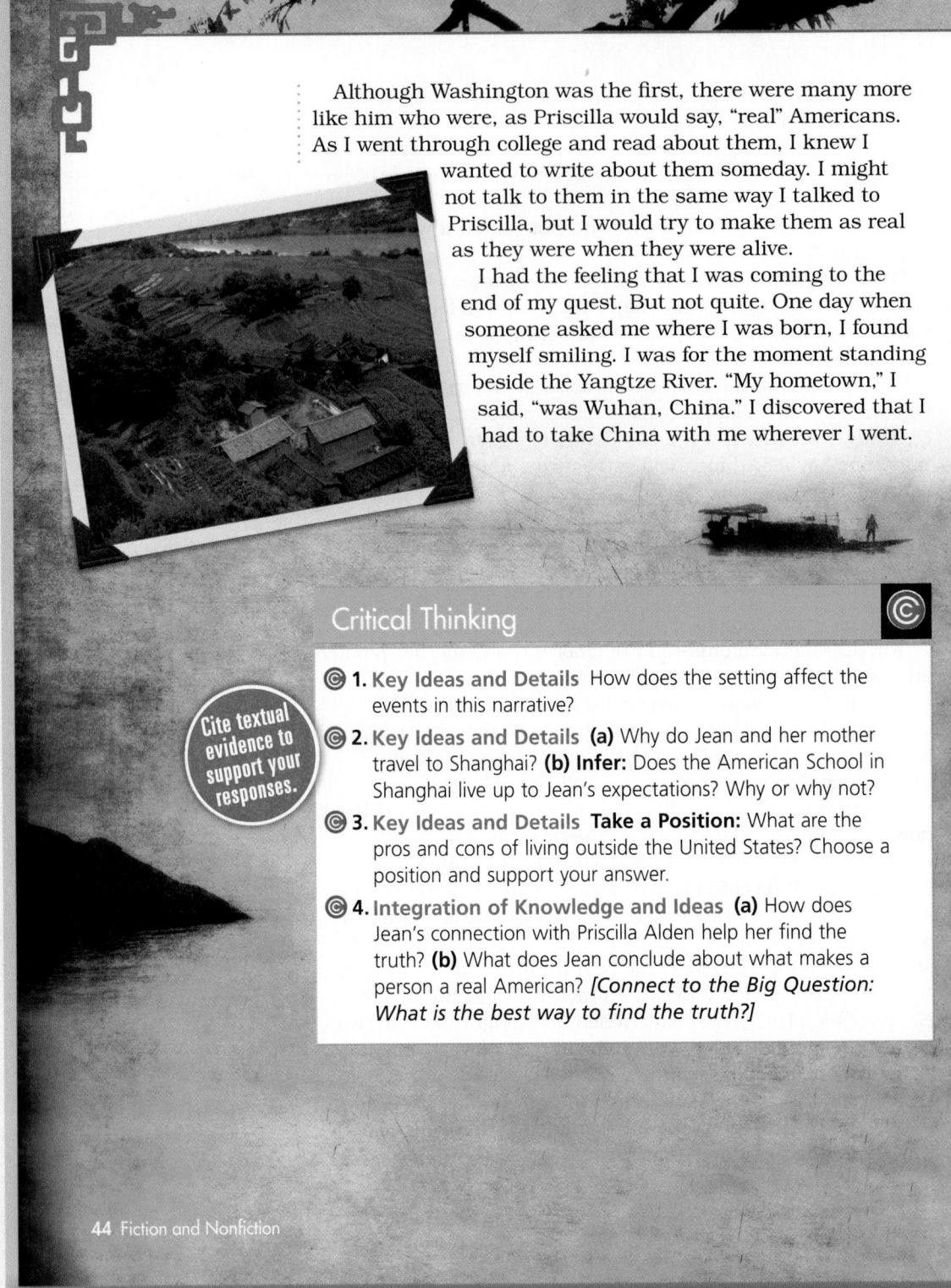

Although Washington was the first, there were many more like him who were, as Priscilla would say, "real" Americans. As I went through college and read about them, I knew I wanted to write about them someday. I might not talk to them in the same way I talked to Priscilla, but I would try to make them as real as they were when they were alive.

I had the feeling that I was coming to the end of my quest. But not quite. One day when someone asked me where I was born, I found myself smiling. I was for the moment standing beside the Yangtze River. "My hometown," I said, "was Wuhan, China." I discovered that I had to take China with me wherever I went.

Critical Thinking

Cite textual evidence to support your responses.

1. **Key Ideas and Details** How does the setting affect the events in this narrative?

2. **Key Ideas and Details** (a) Why do Jean and her mother travel to Shanghai? (b) **Infer:** Does the American School in Shanghai live up to Jean's expectations? Why or why not?

3. **Key Ideas and Details Take a Position:** What are the pros and cons of living outside the United States? Choose a position and support your answer.

4. **Integration of Knowledge and Ideas** (a) How does Jean's connection with Priscilla Alden help her find the truth? (b) What does Jean conclude about what makes a person a real American? *[Connect to the Big Question: What is the best way to find the truth?]*

44 Fiction and Nonfiction

Assessment Resources

Unit 1 Resources

L1 L2 EL Selection Test A, pp. 63–65. Administer Test A to less advanced readers.

L3 L4 EL Selection Test B, pp. 66–68. Administer Test B to on-level and more advanced students.

L3 L4 Open-Book Test, pp. 60–62. As an alternative, give the Open-Book Test.

All Customizable Test Bank

All Self-tests
Students may prepare for the **Selection Test** by taking the **Self-test** online.

PHLit Online! All assessment resources are available at **www.PHLitOnline.com**.

Reading Skill: Context Clues

1. In a chart like this, write the italicized word in the left column. Then, write the **context clues** and what the word means. Check your response in a dictionary. **(a)** I was no longer an MK, but I was certainly a *curiosity*. I was the Kid from China. **(b)** I expected the American soil to hold still for me. Instead, it *swayed* as if we were all still at sea.

Unfamiliar Word	Context Clues	Possible Meaning

Literary Analysis: Narrative Text

2. **Craft and Structure** Identify the main reason that "mk" is classified as a **narrative.**

3. **Craft and Structure** The order of events is important in **narration. (a)** What is the first thing Jean sees as she goes through the iron gates of the Shanghai American School? **(b)** Why is this information important to the story?

Vocabulary

Acquisition and Use Rewrite each sentence, replacing each underlined word with a **synonym,** or word with a similar meaning.

1. The travelers were on a <u>quest</u> for adventure.
2. They brought <u>adequate</u> supplies for a week of camping.
3. When you smile, your face undergoes a <u>transformation</u>.
4. The <u>relation</u> between extreme sports and injuries is high.
5. Do not try to <u>deceive</u> me with that silly mask and fake voice!
6. The players were <u>ignorant</u> of the new rules of the game.

Word Study Use the context of the sentences and what you know about the **Latin prefix in-** to explain each answer.

1. If something is *inaccurate,* is it correct or incorrect?
2. Would an *insensitive* person cry during a sad part of a movie?

Word Study

The **Latin prefix in-** means "not."

Apply It Explain how the prefix in- contributes to the meanings of these words. Consult a print dictionary if necessary.

invisible
inactive
incomplete

mk **45**

Reading Skill

1. **Possible responses:**
   (a) Unfamiliar Word—*curiosity*; Context Clue—"the Kid from China" suggests something foreign or unfamiliar; Possible meaning—"something unusual"
   (b) Unfamiliar Word—*swayed*; Context Clue—"instead" suggests the ground did not hold still; Possible meaning—"rocked back and forth"

   For other sample answers, see *Graphic Organizer Transparencies,* **Reading Skill Graphic Organizer A, p. 7,** and the **Additional Answers** section.

Literary Analysis

2. "mk" is a narrative because it has characters and tells a story with a beginning, middle, and end.

3. (a) The first thing Jean sees is a group of girls practicing cheerleading on the football field.
   (b) Cheerleading seems very American, but Jean is not impressed by it. Jean wants very badly to feel American, and she thinks there is something wrong with her for finding cheerleading uninteresting. She does not yet understand that feeling like an American means different things to different people.

Vocabulary
Acquisition and Use
Sample answers:

1. search
2. enough
3. change
4. connection
5. trick
6. uninformed

Word Study
Sample answers:

1. The prefix *in-* means "not." If something is *inaccurate,* it is <u>not</u> accurate, or it is wrong.

2. No. The prefix *in-* means "not," so an *insensitive* person would <u>not</u> be sensitive to or cry at a sad movie.

Word Study: Apply It
Sample answers:

To be *invisible* is to be <u>not</u> visible. To be *inactive* is to be <u>not</u> active. To be *incomplete* is to be <u>not</u> complete.

45

Conventions

1. Introduce the skill, using the instruction on the student page.
2. Discuss the examples in the chart.

Think Aloud: Model the skill

Model the skill of identifying common and proper nouns. Say to students:

To decide whether a noun is common or proper, I ask myself if the noun is a name. Let's say I read the noun *college*. This noun could identify *any* college. That tells me it is a common noun. Now let's say I read the noun *Harvard*. This noun names a particular college. That fact tells me the word is a proper noun.

PH **WRITING COACH** Grade 7

Students will find further instruction on and practice with common and proper nouns in Chapter 13, Section 1.

Practice A

1. parrot (c); Mr. Tillian (p)
2. Harry (p); father (c); fun (c)
3. Mr. Tillian (p); boxes (c)
4. Harry (p); store (c)
5. parrot (c); Harry (p)
6. Harry (p); lesson (c); Rocky (p)

Reading Application

Sample answer: Common—At <u>home</u> <u>things</u> were different; New <u>shipments</u> of <u>candy</u> and <u>nuts</u> would be arriving; Proper—So <u>Harry</u> kept walking; <u>Harry</u> said he would.

Practice B

Sample answers:

1. kids, country; Jean, Fletcher, and Paula knew they would leave China someday.
2. book, settlers; Jean's favorite, *The Courtship of Miles Standish,* was about the Pilgrims.
3. children, world, school; Sandra and Ling, from America and China, attended the Shanghai American School.
4. students, country, her, questions; The Americans, John and Miguel, asked Jean silly questions.

Writing Application

Sample answer: It would be hard to go to school (c) in China (p). All the books (c) would be in Chinese (p).

46

Integrated Language Skills

Papa's Parrot • mk

Conventions: Common and Proper Nouns

All nouns can be classified as either **common nouns** or **proper nouns.**

- A common noun names a person, place, or thing.
- A proper noun names a specific person, place, or thing.

Common nouns are not capitalized unless they begin a sentence or a title. Proper nouns are always capitalized.

Common Nouns	Proper Nouns
singer	Jennifer Johnson
city	Phoenix
dog	Prince

Practice A Identify the nouns in each sentence. Then, label each as a common or proper noun.

1. The parrot was good for Mr. Tillian.
2. Harry and his father had fun together.
3. Mr. Tillian fell onto the candy boxes.
4. Harry helped in the store.
5. That parrot talked to Harry.
6. Harry learned a lesson from Rocky.

ⓔ **Reading Application** In "Papa's Parrot," find two sentences with common nouns and two sentences with proper nouns.

Practice B Revise each sentence to replace common nouns with proper nouns.

1. The missionary kids knew they would leave the country someday.
2. Jean's favorite book was about the first settlers.
3. Children from around the world attended that school.
4. Many students in her new country asked her silly questions.

ⓔ **Writing Application** Write two sentences describing what it might be like to go to school in another country. Use at least one common noun and one proper noun in your description. Capitalize the proper nouns.

PH **WRITING COACH** Further instruction and practice are available in *Prentice Hall Writing Coach.*

Writing

Informative Text Write a brief **compare-and-contrast essay.** If you write about "Papa's Parrot," compare and contrast Harry's behavior before and after he entered junior high school. Before you write, gather details from the story in a two-column chart.

- In the first column, list details that show what Harry was like before junior high school.
- In the second column, list details that show his behavior and thoughts once he entered junior high school.

If you write about "mk," compare and contrast Jean's feelings about America before and after she arrives in the United States. Before you write, gather story details in a two-column chart.

- In the first column, list details that show her thoughts and feelings about America when she was living in China.
- In the second column, list details that show her thoughts and feelings when she lived and went to school in the United States.

Grammar Application Capitalize all the proper nouns in your essay.

Writing Workshop: *Work in Progress*

Prewriting for Descriptive Essay Think of a memorable place. List five qualities or features that make it special for you. Pick one or two items from this list, and jot down sensory details that you associate with each one. Describe the sight, sound, and smell of the places. Save this Place List in your writing portfolio.

Speaking and Listening

Comprehension and Collaboration With a partner, perform a **dramatic reading** of either "Papa's Parrot" or "mk." Read the story and choose a section that is especially moving, emotional, or funny. Divide the text so that each partner can present a portion. As you rehearse, focus on these points:

- Speak clearly so that each word can be heard.
- Raise and lower your voice to express emotion.
- Slow down and stress certain words for effect.
- Make eye contact with your listeners as you read.

Common Core State Standards

L.7.2, L.7.5.b, L.7.6; W.7.2.b; SL.7.6
[For the full wording of the standards, see page 22.]

Use this prewriting activity to prepare for the **Writing Workshop** on page 92.

PHLit Online!
www.PHLitOnline.com

- Interactive graphic organizers
- Grammar tutorial
- Interactive journals

Integrated Language Skills **47**

Teaching Resources

Unit 1 Resources
L3 L4 EL **Integrated Language Skills: Grammar,** p. 57
L3 L4 EL **Support for Writing,** p. 58
L3 L4 **Support for Extend Your Learning,** p. 59
L4 **Enrichment,** pp. 38, 56

Enriched Online Student Edition
Available under After You Read for this selection:
All **Interactive Grammar Tutorial**
L3 L4 **Internet Research Activity**

Professional Development Guidebook
Rubrics for Self-Assessment: Comparison-Contrast Essay, pp. 234–235

PHLit Online! All print and digital resources are available online at **www.PHLitOnline.com.**
Online resources accessible to students are noted on the student page.

Writing

1. Review the assignment, using the instruction on the student page.
2. To guide students in writing a compare-and-contrast essay, give them **Support for Writing,** p. 58 in *Unit 1 Resources.*
3. To evaluate students' informative texts, use the rubrics for **Comparison-Contrast Essay,** pp. 234–235 in the *Professional Development Guidebook.* In addition, you might evaluate how clearly students describe the details of their chosen character's behavior or feelings.

Grammar Application

Have students check their drafts to make sure they have capitalized all proper nouns.

Six Traits Focus

✓ Ideas	Word Choice	
✓ Organization	Sentence Fluency	
Voice	Conventions	

PH WRITING COACH Grade 7

Students will find further instruction on and practice with expository writing in Chapter 8.

Writing Workshop
Work in Progress

Have students save their completed Place Lists in their portfolios. They will use the lists later as they continue this Work-in-Progress assignment (see p. 69). These assignments prepare them to complete the Writing Workshop assignment (see pp. 92–97).

Speaking and Listening

1. Review the assignment, using the instruction on the student page.
2. Have students complete the **Support for Extend Your Learning** page (*Unit 1 Resources,* p. 59).

47

In this two-page Test Practice, students apply the reading skill for the first half of Unit 1 to a passage of fiction and a passage of nonfiction.

Review this skill, using context clues, and then administer the test. For more guidance, consult the *Classroom Strategies and Teaching Routines* card, *Formally Assessing Students.*

ASSESS

Answers

Answers With Explanations

1. **B**—People typically look at things in a gift shop. *Incorrect answers:* A—People are usually prohibited from opening things in shops; C—The second sentence makes it clear that the characters were not initially buying things; D—A shop is not a place for testing things.

2. **C**—The contrast between this sentence and the narrator's desire to buy is the clue. *Incorrect answers:* A—This happened before they browsed in the shop; B—The people who browsed is not a clue to the verb's meaning; D—This phrase is not a clue.

3. **A**—Things found in King Tut's tomb would be very ancient objects. *Incorrect answers:* B—The act of digging up would not be "found" in a tomb. C—Objects found in a tomb would not be newly made; D—This is not the meaning of the word.

4. **B**—The narrator overcomes her <u>uncertainty</u> after her aunt promises not to tell. *Incorrect answers:* A—The narrator is worried, not excited; C—Fear is too strong an emotion for this context; D—Nothing has happened to make Megan angry.

5. **B**—Her aunt's lips are sealed, but Megan is the one who overcomes her hesitation. *Incorrect answers:* A—The expression means the gift will stay a secret; C—Saying this is the way Aunt Margaret promises to keep quiet; D—This phrase means the same thing.

Writing for Assessment

Students should demonstrate an understanding of the words they choose and of context clues.

Test Practice: Reading

Context Clues

Fiction Selection

Directions: *Read the selection. Then, answer the questions.*

After we toured the Egyptian wing at the museum, my Aunt Margaret and I <u>browsed</u> in the gift shop. I had only planned to look, but I found the perfect birthday gift for my mother. It was a <u>replica</u> of a piece of jewelry that was found when King Tut's tomb was discovered. My mother is very interested in archaeology and the Egyptian <u>antiquities</u> found in King Tut's tomb. I really wanted to buy the necklace for her, but then I remembered that my aunt was with me. I did not know if I could trust her to keep my gift a secret. But I overcame my <u>hesitation</u> after my aunt promised to keep quiet. "My lips are <u>sealed</u>, Megan," she said. "I will not tell a soul."

1. What does the word *browsed* mean in this passage?
   A. opened things
   B. looked over things
   C. bought things
   D. tested things

2. What context clue helps you clarify the meaning of *browsed*?
   A. we toured the Egyptian wing
   B. my Aunt Margaret and I
   C. I had only planned to look
   D. the perfect birthday gift

3. What does the word *antiquities* mean?
   A. ancient objects
   B. the act of digging up
   C. newly-made jewelry
   D. the rooms inside a tomb

4. What is the meaning of the word *hesitation*?
   A. excitement
   B. uncertainty
   C. fear
   D. anger

5. In the passage, which words do *not* help you understand the expression *my lips are sealed*?
   A. keep my gift a secret
   B. overcame my hesitation
   C. promised to keep quiet
   D. will not tell a soul

Writing for Assessment

Write a paragraph of your own in which you correctly use two of the words from this selection. As you write, build in context clues to help readers figure out the meanings of those words.

Strategies for Test Taking

Remind students to look for different kinds of context clues to the meanings of unfamiliar words. Sometimes a writer will give an example that defines the word. For instance, in the sentence, "The candidate was guilty of minor *transgressions* such as failing to pay parking tickets," the example helps you figure out that *transgressions* are illegal acts. Sometimes the context clue is a familiar antonym. In the sentence, "The stray cat used to be *emaciated*, but now she is plump," it is clear that *emaciated* means the opposite of plump, or "thin." In some cases, context clues are spread throughout an entire sentence or even paragraph. In the sentence, "Marisol apologized to me; she felt *penitent* about losing my sneakers," the reference to an apology and the explanation of what Marisol did combine to suggest that *penitent* means "sorry."

Nonfiction Selection

Directions: *Read the selection. Then, answer the questions.*

In 1922, an Egyptologist named Howard Carter discovered a buried staircase that led to a <u>sealed</u> tomb. When the tomb was opened, Carter found fantastic treasures—items made of gold, <u>alabaster</u>, ebony, and precious stones. It was the greatest collection of Egyptian artifacts ever discovered. The mummified body of King Tutankhamen, the 18-year-old Egyptian boy king, had been buried with jewelry and other items that indicated his importance. He had clearly been of <u>noble</u> birth. Many people had tried to find the tomb of King Tutankhamen, also known as King Tut, but Carter was the first to discover the tomb. It was no easy task. Carter searched for almost eight years before he and his crew discovered the boy king's final resting place.

1. What does the word *sealed* mean in the context of this selection?
   - **A.** open
   - **B.** missing
   - **C.** tightly closed
   - **D.** damp

2. What context clue helps you clarify the meaning of *sealed*?
   - **A.** a buried staircase
   - **B.** when the tomb was opened
   - **C.** Howard Carter discovered a buried staircase
   - **D.** Carter found fantastic treasures

3. Which phrase helps you clarify the meaning of the word *noble*?
   - **A.** mummified body
   - **B.** Egyptian boy king
   - **C.** buried staircase
   - **D.** fantastic treasures

4. In the selection, which word does *not* hint at the meaning of *alabaster*?
   - **A.** gold
   - **B.** treasures
   - **C.** precious
   - **D.** opened

Writing for Assessment

Connecting Across Texts
Explain how the meaning of the word *sealed* differs in each passage. Write a brief paragraph, using details from both passages to support your answer.

- Online practice
- Instant feedback

Answers With Explanations

1. **C**—Since the sealed tomb had to be opened, sealed must mean "tightly closed." *Incorrect answers:* A—Something open would not have to be opened; B—A tomb that was missing could not be opened; D—There is no mention of this in the passage.

2. **B**—The fact that the tomb had to be opened is the clue to the meaning of *sealed*. *Incorrect answers:* A—This detail does not tell what kind of tomb it was; C—same explanation as for A; D—same explanation as for A.

3. **B**—The fact that the mummy was that of a king is a clue to the meaning of *noble*. *Incorrect answers:* A—This detail is not a clue to the meaning of *noble*; C— same explanation as for A; D—same explanation as for A.

4. **D**—The word *opened* does not help the reader understand the significance of the items found after this action occurred. *Incorrect answers:* A—Gold is precious and is listed with alabaster, so alabaster is probably another precious material; B—*Treasures* is the category under which *alabaster* falls; C—*Precious* suggests that alabaster is also valuable.

Writing for Assessment

In their responses, students should explain that in the first passage, *sealed* has a figurative meaning. The aunt will not open her lips to tell a secret. In the second passage, *sealed* has a literal meaning: the door is closed so tightly that it has to be physically forced open.

Differentiated
Instruction *for Universal Access*

EL Strategies for English Learners

Remind English learners that one of the first steps to take when using context clues to figure out the meaning of an unfamiliar word is to determine the word's part of speech. Knowing if a word is a noun, verb, pronoun, preposition, or modifier will help the reader figure out its precise meaning. For example, item 3 asks about the meaning of the word *noble*. This word appears in the fifth sentence, "He had clearly been of *noble* birth." The word *of* is a familiar preposition. A preposition is always followed by its object, a noun. In this sentence, the object of the preposition is *birth*. Point out that the word *noble* comes before *birth*, and remind them that in English, adjectives come before the nouns they modify. Therefore, the reader should be able to figure out that *noble* is an adjective telling "what kind of" birth. Using this information, the reader can reread the sentences before and after sentence 5 to look for clues to what kind of birth Tutankhamen had.

Students may take the test in interactive format with instant feedback online at **www.PHLitOnline.com.**

71

Common Core State Standards

- Reading Informational Text 5
- Writing 10
- Language 4.a

Reading Skill

1. Introduce the skill.
2. Tell students that they will use text features to locate information.

Think Aloud: Model the Skill

Say to students:

If I am reading a text that has visual elements such as photographs and charts, I read the captions. If the text includes maps, I look for scale bars and legends, or keys. All of these text features help me understand the information these visual elements are providing. As I read the text, I look for headings and boldfaced words and terms. These text features indicate the most important information.

Multidraft Reading

Have students follow a multidraft reading protocol.

- **First reading**—Have students read to identify key ideas and details.
- **Second reading**—Have students read to identify the structure of the text.
- **Third reading**—Have students read to integrate knowledge and ideas by connecting the text to the world, their own experiences, and other texts.

Content-Area Vocabulary

1. Have students say each word.
2. Next, use each word in a sentence that defines it.
3. Finally, repeat your definitional sentence or a similar sentence with the word missing and have the class "fill in the blank" chorally.

Reading for Information

Analyzing Functional and Expository Texts

Atlas Entry	Public Document

Reading Skill: Locate Types of Information

When you read informational texts, such as consumer, workplace, and public documents, use structural features to **locate specific types of information**. Features such as headings can help you to quickly find information about a particular subject. Captions for photographs and other graphic elements can help you to find information that is provided visually. As you read, remember that you can locate useful information both in the body of the text and in supporting visuals. This chart shows some features that will help you locate information in atlases and public documents.

Features in Atlases	Features in Public Documents
• headings • bold print • map keys or legends • captions for graphs	• headings • images and captions • direct quotations

Content-Area Vocabulary

These words appear in the selections that follow. You may also encounter them in other content-area texts.

- **industrial** (in dus´ trē əl) *adj.* having highly developed forms of business, trade, or manufacture
- **decipher** (di sī´ fər) *v.* make out the meaning of
- **interrogations** (in ter´ə gā´ shənz) *n.* formal examinations that involve questioning the subject

 What is the best way to find the truth?

Have students look for facts and other truths as they read.

Common Core State Standards

Reading Informational Text
5. Analyze the structure an author uses to organize a text, including how the major sections contribute to the whole and to the development of the ideas.

Language
4.a. Use context as a clue to the meaning of a word or phrase.

Writing
10. Write routinely over extended time frames and shorter time frames for a range of discipline-specific tasks, purposes, and audiences.

Differentiated Instruction   for Universal Access

Reading Support
Give students reading support with the appropriate version of the *Reader's Notebooks*:

L2 L3 *Reader's Notebook*

L1 *Reader's Notebook: Adapted Version*

EL *Reader's Notebook: English Learner's Version*

EAST ASIA

China, Mongolia, Taiwan

China is the world's third-largest country and its most populous—over one billion people live there. Under its communist government, which came to power in 1949, China has became a major **industrial** nation, but most of its people still live and work on the land as they have for thousands of years. Taiwan also has a booming economy and exports its products around the world. Mongolia is a vast, remote country with a small population, many of whom are nomads.

Features:

- maps that give an overview of geographic locations
- articles that provide information about places shown in maps
- legends, or keys, that explain symbols and colors used in maps
- reference material for a general audience

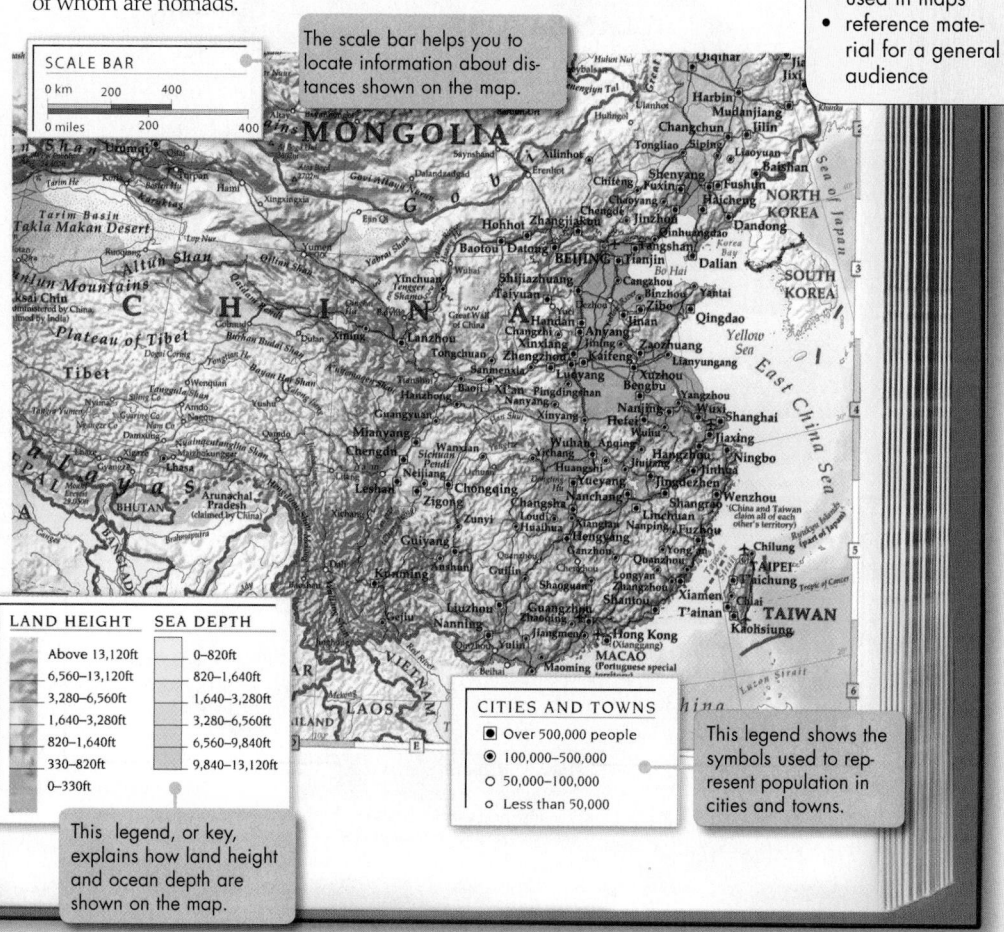

The scale bar helps you to locate information about distances shown on the map.

SCALE BAR

| 0 km | 200 | 400 |
| 0 miles | 200 | 400 |

LAND HEIGHT

Above 13,120ft	
6,560–13,120ft	
3,280–6,560ft	
1,640–3,280ft	
820–1,640ft	
330–820ft	
0–330ft	

SEA DEPTH

0–820ft	
820–1,640ft	
1,640–3,280ft	
3,280–6,560ft	
6,560–9,840ft	
9,840–13,120ft	

This legend, or key, explains how land height and ocean depth are shown on the map.

CITIES AND TOWNS

- ■ Over 500,000 people
- ◉ 100,000–500,000
- ○ 50,000–100,000
- ○ Less than 50,000

This legend shows the symbols used to represent population in cities and towns.

Reading for Information: Atlas **73**

About Atlases

1. Introduce the features listed in the Atlas box on page 73. **Ask** a volunteer to explain what a *symbol* on a map is.
   Possible response: A symbol on a map is a shape, color, or mark used to show a political or geographical feature.

2. Ask volunteers to identify the scale bar and the two legends, or keys, on the student page. Discuss the function of these different text features, pointing out the notes on the student page.

3. Tell students that they may use atlases in social studies classes. **Ask** volunteers to give examples of other situations in which you might use an atlas.
   Possible response: You might use an atlas when you travel.

Locate Types of Information

1. Tell students to scan the two pages of the atlas and the notes about its text features.

2. Point out the text above the map on this page. **Ask:** What types of information might an atlas include in addition to the information shown on maps?
   Possible response: An atlas might also provide information about the people, government, and economy of different countries or regions.

3. Direct students' attention to the scale bar. **Ask:** What type of information does this text feature help you figure out about the countries shown on the map?
   Possible response: The scale bar helps you figure out the size of the countries and the distance between specific places.

4. Direct students' attention to the two legends at the bottom of the page. **Ask** a volunteer to give an example of a piece of information that he or she could figure out from one of the legends.
   Possible response: Using the cities and towns legend, I could figure out how many cities in China have a population greater than 500,000.

Locate Types of Information

1. Give students an opportunity to look at the map and read the atlas text and notes about the keys. Draw a compass rose on the board to make sure that all students can identify the "eastern part" of China, referred to in the text.

2. Direct students' attention to the two-part key on this page. **Ask** a volunteer to give an example of something on the map that the key explains.
   Possible response: You can tell that Beijing is a capital city because it is marked by a red square, and the key on the left explains that red squares are used to indicate capital cities.

3. Have students refer back to the map on page 73 so that they can connect the information shown on the two maps. **Ask:** Which cities are the capitals of China, Mongolia, and Taiwan?
   Answer: Beijing is the capital of China, Ulan Bator is the capital of Mongolia, and Taipei is the capital of Taiwan.

4. Direct students' attention to the circle graph. Point out that sometimes a key may include information that is not shown on the map. In this case, the information relates to the text. Help students see a connection between the statistics in the text and those in the key.

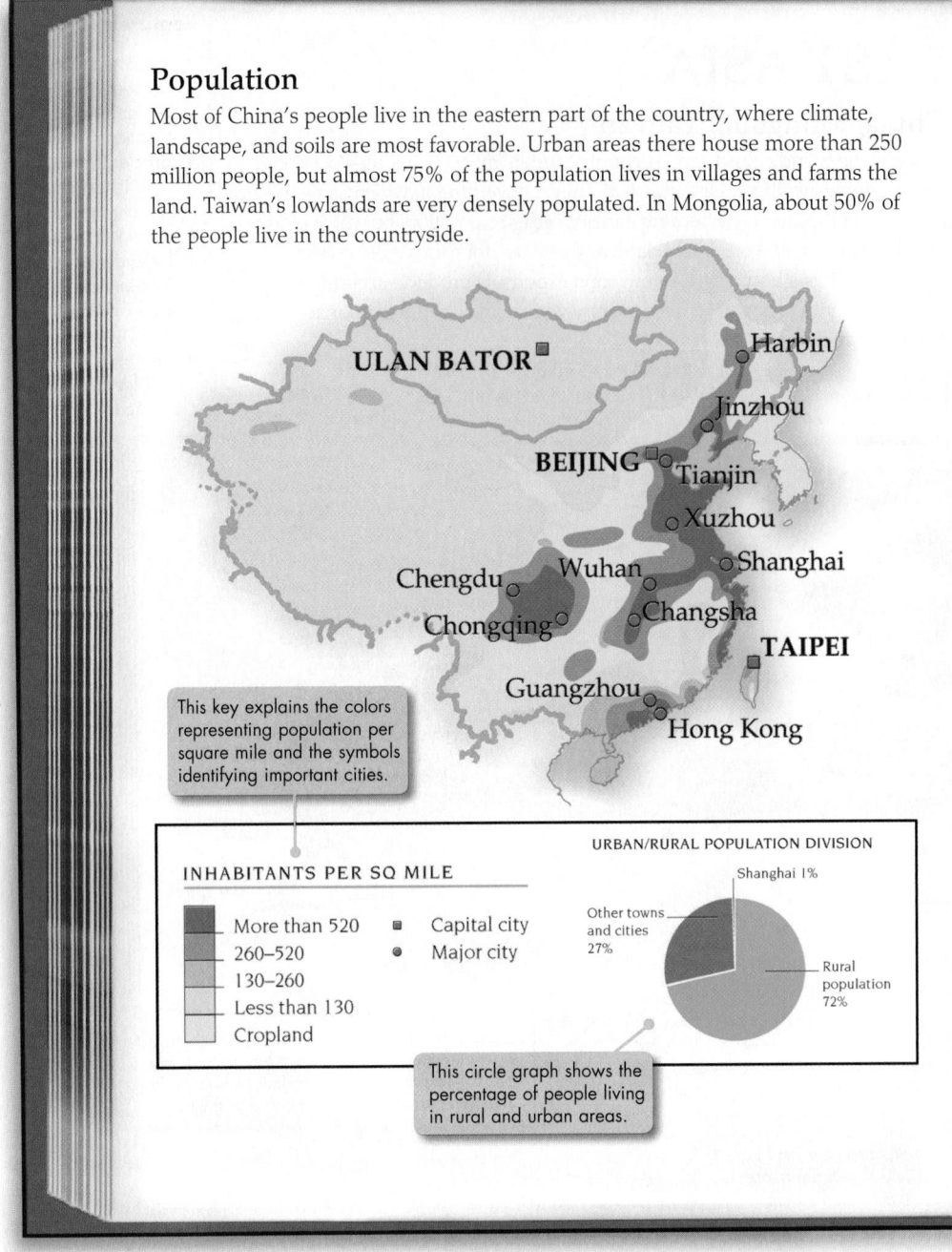

Population

Most of China's people live in the eastern part of the country, where climate, landscape, and soils are most favorable. Urban areas there house more than 250 million people, but almost 75% of the population lives in villages and farms the land. Taiwan's lowlands are very densely populated. In Mongolia, about 50% of the people live in the countryside.

This key explains the colors representing population per square mile and the symbols identifying important cities.

INHABITANTS PER SQ MILE

- More than 520
- 260–520
- 130–260
- Less than 130
- Cropland
- ■ Capital city
- ● Major city

URBAN/RURAL POPULATION DIVISION

Shanghai 1%
Other towns and cities 27%
Rural population 72%

This circle graph shows the percentage of people living in rural and urban areas.

Vocabulary Development

© **CCSS** Language 6

Content-Area Vocabulary: Social Studies

Students might benefit from identifying unfamiliar or difficult terms in the atlas that relate to social studies topics. For example, students might need help with these terms: *populous, communist, industrial, exports, products, nomads, urban, rural,* and *lowlands.* Have students work with a partner to identify all the social studies terms in the atlas. Then, have partners list these terms in a three-column chart. In column 1, they should list any terms they can confidently define. In column 2, they should list terms whose definitions they need to clarify. In column 3, they should list any terms that they cannot define. Encourage students to use context clues to infer the meaning of the terms they have listed in columns 2 and 3. Then, have them check their inferences by using a dictionary.

Public Document

Features:

- information published for the benefit of the public
- text that educates citizens about a subject
- photos or other informative visuals

The Statue of Liberty - Ellis Island Foundation, Inc.

Byron Yee: Discovering a Paper Son

For actor Byron Yee, family history provides the inspiration for his one-man show. "My name is Byron Yee. I am the second son of Bing Quai Yee. I am the son of a paper son.

"My father was an immigrant. He came to America to escape the Japanese invasion of China in 1938. He was 15 years old and he didn't know a word of English. He didn't have a penny in his pocket and he was living in a crowded apartment in New York City with relatives he had never met. I know nothing about my father's history, about his past."

Most Chinese immigrants came through Angel Island in San Francisco Bay.

This photo shows where Byron Yee first searched for his father's immigration records.

With little to go on, Byron set out to **decipher** his father's story. He started at Angel Island, located in the middle of San Francisco Bay. "Angel Island has been called the Ellis Island of the West and for the most part, all the Chinese who came to the United States came through here, from a period of 1910 to 1940. But the rules were a little bit different. European settlers, Russian settlers were processed within an hour. The Japanese were kept for one day. But the Chinese were detained anywhere from three weeks to two years for their **interrogations**. So this was not so much the Ellis Island of the West for the Chinese; it was more like Alcatraz."

In 1882, Congress passed a law prohibiting Chinese laborers from immigrating to the United States. The Chinese Exclusion Act was the only immigration law ever based

Reading for Information: Public Document **75**

About Public Documents

1. Review with students the features of public documents listed in the box on page 75. Explain that a public document is a text that informs people about some issue, event, or topic of public interest.

2. **Ask** the class to brainstorm for examples of public documents relating to their school or community.
   Possible response: The minutes of a school council meeting and a policy statement by the mayor are examples of public documents.

3. Tell students that the document they are about to read is from the "Family Histories" section of the Web site of the Statue of Liberty–Ellis Island Foundation (**www.ellisisland.org**). This section of the site presents several stories of Americans from different backgrounds who have researched their ancestry. As students read, encourage them to think about the public function of such histories.

Locate Types of Information

1. Tell students to scan the selection and the notes about its features.

2. Direct students' attention to the photographs and captions on this page and page 76. **Ask** students to predict what the selection will be about on the basis of the information in these text features.
   Possible response: The selection will probably have something to do with Chinese immigration to the United States.

3. Tell students to check their predictions as they read the selection and locate more information. Encourage them to use self-stick notes to mark places in the text that provide the most important pieces of information.

Differentiated Instruction   for Universal Access

Support for Less Proficient Readers
Students may need help understanding Yee's comment that Angel Island "was not so much the Ellis Island of the West for the Chinese; it was more like Alcatraz." **Ask:** What do you know about Ellis Island? (**Possible responses:** Immigrants who came to America had to stop at Ellis Island before they could enter the United States; some people who arrived at Ellis Island were not permitted to enter the United States, and they had to go back to the places from which they came.) **Ask:** What do you know about Alcatraz? (**Possible responses:** It was a famous prison; it was an island.) **Ask:** What does Yee mean when he says that the Angel Island "was not so much the Ellis Island of the West for the Chinese; it was more like Alcatraz"? (**Answer:** Unlike Ellis Island, which was a relatively quick stop for immigrants, Angel Island became a prison like Alcatraz for the Chinese immigrants who were detained there for long periods of time.)

1. Point out that although this selection is not a first-person account by Byron Yee, it includes lots of quotations by him. Tell students to notice the way the writer integrates Yee's quotations into the selection.

2. **Ask:** How is the information presented in the quotations different from the information presented in the rest of the selection?
Possible response: The quotations elaborate on the facts presented in the rest of the selection by presenting Yee's personal experiences and impressions.

3. As they read, encourage students to consider how the account would be different if it did not include so many quotations.

on race alone. But people found ways around the act: US law states that children of American citizens are automatically granted citizenship themselves, no matter where they were born. Taking advantage of that opening, some immigrants claimed to be legitimate offspring of U.S. citizens when in fact they were not. These individuals, mostly male, were called paper sons.

Byron's next step was to find his father's immigration file. The National Archives regional office in San Bruno, California contains thousands of files related to Angel Island. While Byron did not find his father's records there, he did find those of his grandfather, Yee Wee Thing. In one of the documents in his grandfather's file, Byron found a cross reference to his father, Yee Bing Quai. To avoid the scrutiny of Angel Island, Byron's father had sailed through Boston. Byron found his file at the National Archives in Massachusetts.

The Chinese Exclusion Act prohibited the immigration of Chinese laborers.

This caption highlights a key fact provided in the text.

"My father at 15. He is asked 197 questions: 'When did your alleged father first come to the United States?' 'Have you ever seen a photograph of your alleged father?' 'How many trips to China has your alleged father made since first coming to the United States?'" The lengthy interrogation made Byron suspect that his father was in fact a paper son. Maybe this was why he never knew his father's story.

Though Byron's mother knew very little about her husband's past, she did have an old photo, which she sent to Byron—a portrait of his father's family back in China. Byron learned that the baby on the left was his father. The boy in the middle was Yee Wee Thing, not Byron's grandfather at all, but his uncle.

"It kind of floored me because all of a sudden it made a lot of sense—why he was the way he was, why he never really talked about his past, why he was very secretive. It explained a lot about him and about his history.

"You see my story is no different from anyone else's. . . In all of our collective past, we've all had that one ancestor that had the strength to break from what was familiar to venture into the unknown. I can never thank my father and uncle enough for what they had to do so that I could be here today. One wrong answer between them and I would not be here."

Think Aloud

Vocabulary: Context
Model the use of context clues to determine the meaning of an unfamiliar word. Say to students:

The author uses the term "paper sons" and explains that it means "immigrants [who] claimed to be legitimate offspring of U.S. citizens when in fact they were not," but doesn't explain why the term means that. A literal meaning of the term— "sons who are made of paper"—doesn't make sense in this context. I know that people sometimes use the phrase "on paper" when they mean that something's official status isn't the same as its true status. For example, a job applicant who has strong references might "look good on paper" but might not really possess the skills necessary for the job. I can put these clues together and decide that the term "paper sons" refers to the difference between these immigrants' official status (sons of United States citizens) and their true status (sons of people who are not United States citizens).

Comparing Functional and Expository Texts

1. Key Ideas and Details (a) Which text presents more information in the form of visual elements? **(b)** Which text presents more information through quotations? **(c)** How do visuals and quotations each help you to understand a topic? Explain.

Content-Area Vocabulary

2. (a) Explain how context clues in the selections suggest the meanings of *industrial, decipher,* and *interrogations.* **(b)** Use each word in a sentence that shows its meaning.

⏱ Timed Writing

Informative Text: Letter

> **Format and Audience**
> The prompt gives instructions to write a letter. Because the letter will be addressed to family members, it can be informal.

> Write a letter from the perspective of a "paper son," like Byron Yee's father, arriving in America for the first time. Write to your family and describe your experiences. Use the public document you have read to add details to your letter. (15 minutes)

> **Academic Vocabulary**
> When you *describe* something, you use words that appeal to the senses to create a vivid picture in your reader's mind.

5-Minute Planner

Complete these steps before you begin to write:

1. Read the prompt carefully and completely. Notice key words like the ones highlighted.

2. Reread the public document to locate information related to the assignment. Look for details that help you understand the experience of Chinese immigrants arriving in America during the early twentieth century. **TIP:** Quotations in public documents often include detailed information about people's experiences.

3. Make a list of the people, places, events, and experiences that you want to describe in your letter. Next to each, jot down a few details you can provide in your description, based on text information and on your own imagination.

4. Refer to your list as you draft your letter.

Comparing Functional and Expository Texts

1. (a) The atlas presents more information in the form of visual elements. (b) The public document presents more information through quotations. (c) **Possible response:** Photographs and illustrations show what something looks like that might be hard to visualize just through a written description. Maps and charts present information in a clear, simple way that is often easier to understand than a list of statistics or facts. Quotations provide opinions, insights, and details about personal experiences, and therefore help to clarify a topic by adding to the plain facts.

2. (a) The atlas entry says China is an industrial nation but most of the people still work on the land. That suggests that industrial means not just farming. The sentences around the word *decipher* in the public document describe not knowing something and trying to figure it out. That suggests that *decipher* means something like "figure out." The sentences around *interrogations* describe people being "processed" before they come into the United States. They were probably being asked questions. That suggests that interrogations are processes in which people are questioned. (b) **Sample response:** My grandfather had an industrial job in a factory. I can't quite decipher your handwriting. The try-outs took an hour, but the coach's interrogations took all day.

⏱ Timed Writing

1. Before students complete the activity, guide them in identifying and analyzing key words and phrases in the prompt, which are highlighted on the student page.

2. Work with students to draw up guidelines for their essays based on the key words, as in this example:

   • **Main Impression** The writer should create a clear main impression, or overall feeling, in the letter.

   • **Balance** The writer should present descriptive details about his or her experiences, sharing personal emotions about leaving home and arriving in America.

   • **Elaboration** The writer should provide details and explanations that make those experiences and emotions seem real.

   • **Style** The writer should write in an informal style appropriate to communicating with family members.

3. Have students use the 5-Minute Planner to structure their time.

4. Allow students 15 minutes to complete the assignment. Evaluate their work using the guidelines they have developed.

Common Core State Standards

• Reading Literature 3
• Reading Informational Text 3
• Writing 2.a

❶ Comparing Fiction and Nonfiction

1. Introduce the skill, using the instruction on the student page.
2. Give students a copy of **Comparing Fiction and Nonfiction Graphic Organizer B** (*Graphic Organizer Transparencies,* p. 16). Tell them they will fill it in as they read.

Think Aloud: Model the Skill

Model a way to understand fictional and nonfictional narratives. Say:

When a friend says, "Let me tell you a story," I know that he is going to tell me a narrative. I do not know if the narrative will be fiction or nonfiction, but I do know that there will be a narrator, characters, events, and dialogue. If the narrative is fiction, the characters, dialogue, and events will be imaginary. If the narrative is nonfiction, they will be real.

Comparing Literary Works

from **Barrio Boy •
A Day's Wait**

❶ Comparing Fiction and Nonfiction

Fiction is prose writing that tells about imaginary characters and events. Novels, novellas, and short stories are types of fiction.
Literary nonfiction is prose writing that tells about real people, places, objects, or events. Biographies, memoirs, and historical accounts are types of nonfiction.

While one is fiction and the other nonfiction, the selections here are both examples of **narrative writing** that include the following elements:

• a *narrator* who tells the story
• *characters,* or people living the story
• *dialogue,* or the conversations that the characters have
• story *events* that make up the action
• a *theme* or *central idea*

These elements work together to develop the narratives. For example, both writers use dialogue to convey the impact that a specific event or situation has upon the characters.

Narrators are another important element of fiction and literary nonfiction. The narrator in the excerpt from *Barrio Boy* tells about an important real event in the writer's life. In contrast, the narrator in "A Day's Wait" tells the story of an imagined boy on a single day. As you read, use a chart like the one shown to note ways in which the elements and features of the works are similar and different.

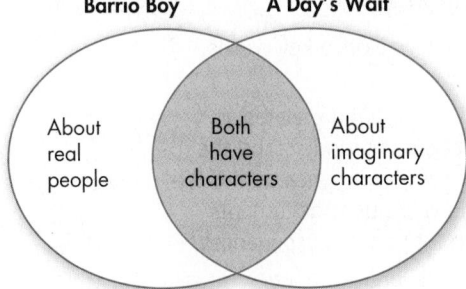

Barrio Boy   A Day's Wait

About real people

Both have characters

About imaginary characters

www.PHLitOnline.com

• Vocabulary flashcards
• Interactive journals
• More about the authors
• Selection audio
• Interactive graphic organizers

Common Core State Standards

Reading Literature
3. Analyze how particular elements of a story or drama interact.

Reading Informational Texts
3. Analyze the interactions between individuals, events, and ideas in a text.

Writing
2.a. Introduce a topic clearly, previewing what is to follow; organize ideas, concepts, and information, using strategies such as definition, classification, comparison/contrast, and cause/effect; include formatting, graphics, and multimedia when useful to aiding comprehension.

Vocabulary Development

Vocabulary Knowledge Rating

Create a **Vocabulary Knowledge Rating Chart** (*Professional Development Guidebook,* p. 33) featuring the words glossed in the selections:

reassuring (p. 80)	*epidemic* (p. 87)
contraption (p. 80)	*flushed* (p. 88)
formidable (p. 82)	*evidently* (p. 89)

Give students a copy of the chart, and read the words aloud. Have students mark their rating of each in the Before You Read column. To gauge how much instruction to provide, tally the students who think they know each word.

Explain that the words are defined in the margin at the point where they appear in the selection. Urge students to be alert to these words as they read the selections. They will rate their knowledge again when they finish.

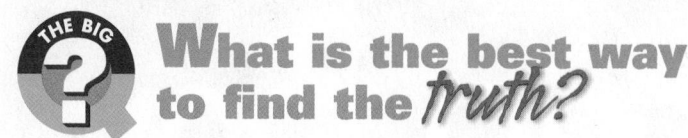

What is the best way to find the *truth?*

❷ Writing About the Big Question

In each of these narratives, a boy faces a situation—real or imagined—that he perceives as frightening. Use this sentence starter to develop your ideas.

When something is **explained** to us, it makes us less afraid because _____.

Meet the Authors

Ernesto Galarza (1905–1984)

Author of "Barrio Boy"

When he was seven years old, Ernesto Galarza moved from Mexico to California. There, his family harvested crops in the fields of Sacramento and struggled to make ends meet. Galarza learned English quickly and won a scholarship for college.

Helping Farm Workers From 1936 to 1947, Galarza served as chief of the Division of Labor and Social Information for the Pan-American Union, dealing with education and labor in Latin America. When he returned to California, he worked to gain rights for farm workers.

Ernest Hemingway (1899–1961)

Author of "A Day's Wait"

A true adventurer, Ernest Hemingway based much of his writing on his own experiences. He served as an ambulance driver in World War I, worked as a journalist, traveled the world, and enjoyed outdoor sports.

Writing About the Familiar Hemingway's fiction celebrates his spirit of adventure. The story "A Day's Wait" captures the quiet bravery of many of his characters.

from Barrio Boy/A Day's Wait **79**

Teaching Resources

- **All** *Unit 1 Resources,* pp. 108–115
- **All** *Graphic Organizer Transparencies* pp. 15–18
- **All** *Common Core Companion,* pp. 28–35; 122–123; 202–212
- **All** Enriched Online Student Edition
- **All** **EL** *Hear It!* Audio CD

All resources, including print and audio, are available online at **www.PHLitOnline.com**.

Daily Bellringer

For each class during which you will teach this selection, have students complete one of the five Vocabulary activities for Week 3 in the *Daily Bellringer Activities* booklet.

❷ Writing About the Big Question

1. Introduce the assignment.
2. Ask students for examples of situations when they were younger where they initially misunderstood what was happening.
3. Have students complete the sentence starter. Review the responses as a class. (**Sample response:** When something is explained to us, it makes us less afraid because we understand the situation better.)
4. Remind students that their answers will help them think about the Big Question, "What is the best way to find the truth?" As they read, they should look for ways that characters find out the truth.

Concept Connector ➤

Students will return to their sentence starters after reading.

Multidraft Reading

To assist struggling readers and to deepen reading for all, apply multidraft reading protocols. For each reading, have students set the purpose indicated:

- **First reading**—identifying key ideas and details and answering any Reading Checks.
- **Second reading**—analyzing craft and structure and responding to the side-column prompts.
- **Third reading**—integrating knowledge and ideas, connecting to other texts and the world, and answering the end-of-selection questions.

For more guidance, see the *Classroom Strategies and Teaching Routines* card on multidraft reading.

PHLit Online!

For more about the authors and practice with the selection vocabulary, go online at www.PHLitOnline.com.

❶ Background

Moving from Home Ernesto Galarza lived in Mazatlán before moving to California. Mazatlán is a seaport on the western coast of Mexico, located almost directly across the gulf from Baja California. It is known for exporting metal ores, tobacco, hides, and shrimp. Most Americans know it as a beach resort.

❷ Activating Prior Knowledge

Ask students to consider the difficulties a child might face who moves to the United States from another country, enters a new school, and speaks no English. Have them describe difficulties the child might experience in communicating to other children and teachers, making friends with children who speak different languages, and learning new customs.

Concept Connector ⟶

Students will follow up on this activity after reading the excerpt.

❸ About the Selection

Young Ernesto from Mexico has just arrived in the United States, where he will attend Lincoln School. On his first day, the principal and her interpreter greet Ernesto and his mother. His teacher welcomes him to his new country and helps him with his new language. Ernesto and the other immigrant children form a bond as they learn English and adapt to their new lives. The school staff guides them to take pride in their diverse backgrounds.

❹ Critical Viewing

Answer: Yes. The boy looks lonely, as someone entering a new school might.

❺ Nonfiction

Have a volunteer read the bracketed passage on page 80 aloud.
Ask students the Nonfiction question.
Answer: This is nonfiction, so the author is the narrator. He is telling a story about himself, shown in his use of the words *I, me, we,* and *us.*

❶
❷
❸

from Barrio Boy
Ernesto Galarza

❹ ▶ **Critical Viewing**
Does this picture convey the emotions that a child might feel as he enrolls in a new school? Explain. **[Evaluate]**

Vocabulary
reassuring
(rē ə shoor′ iŋ)
adj. having the effect of restoring confidence

contraption
(kən trap′ shən)
n. strange device or machine

Nonfiction
Who is the narrator of this work? How can you tell?

My mother and I walked south on Fifth Street one morning to the corner of Q Street and turned right. Half of the block was occupied by the Lincoln School. It was a three-story wooden building, with two wings that gave it the shape of a double-T connected by a central hall. It was a new building, painted yellow, with a shingled roof that was not like the red tile of the school in Mazatlán. I noticed other differences, none of them very reassuring. We walked up the wide staircase hand in hand and through the door, which closed by itself. A mechanical contraption screwed to the top shut it behind us quietly.

Up to this point the adventure of enrolling me in the school had been carefully rehearsed. Mrs. Dodson had told us how to find it and we had circled it several times on our walks. Friends in the barrio[1] explained that the director was called a principal, and that it was a lady and not a man. They assured us that there was always a person at the school who could speak Spanish.

Exactly as we had been told, there was a sign on the door in both Spanish and English: "Principal." We crossed the hall and entered the office of Miss Nettie Hopley.

Miss Hopley was at a roll-top desk to one side, sitting in a swivel chair that moved on wheels. There was a sofa against the opposite wall, flanked by two windows and a door that opened on a small balcony. Chairs were set around a table and framed pictures hung on the walls of a man with long white hair and another with a sad face and a black beard. The principal half turned in the swivel chair to look at us

1. **barrio** (bär′ ē ō) *n.* part of a town or city where most of the people are Hispanic.

80 Fiction and Nonfiction

❺

Ⓒ Text Complexity Rubric

Barrio Boy

Qualitative Measures	Context/Knowledge Demands	Immigrant boy in new elementary school; Some knowledge of the immigrant experience 1 ② 3 4 5
	Structure/Language Conventionality and Clarity	Numerous long sentences and figurative descriptive passages; several footnoted words 1 2 3 ④ 5
	Levels of Meaning/ Purpose/Concepts	Accessible concept (main character's move to a new school) 1 2 ③ 4 5
Quantitative Measures	Text Length	Word Count: 1,500
	Lexile	1110L

from *Barrio Boy* 81

Whole-Class Activity

1. **Ask** students to describe what they see in the picture.
   Sample response: I see a young boy looking out a window. He seems to be thinking deeply about something.

2. Then, tell students to consider what they've read in the story so far. Lead them in a discussion of what the boy might be thinking. Elicit that he may be thinking about how unfamiliar his new school is.

3. **Ask** students how they would get along in an unfamiliar school, and who they would rely on for information.
   Sample response: I would ask the teachers for help, and talk to other students when I needed to know things.

Small-Group Activity

1. Divide the class into small groups. Have students take turns describing what they think the boy in the picture is feeling, and making predictions about the story based on those feelings.

2. Ask one person from each group to summarize the group's ideas.

3. To model the process of making connections to an image, choose one of the groups' ideas and explain how those ideas are supported by the picture.

Individual Activity

1. As a class, briefly discuss the picture.

2. Ask students to write a paragraph predicting how the story will progress based on the picture.

3. In class, or as homework, have students edit and proofread their paragraphs.

4. Post the paragraphs around the room. Have students compare their predictions about the story to the selection from *Barrio Boy* as they read.

PHLit Online!

This selection is available in interactive format in the **Enriched Online Student Edition,** which includes an interactive graphic organizer.

© **Text Complexity: Reader and Task Suggestions**

from **Barrio Boy**

Preparing to Read the Text	Leveled Tasks
• Using the Activating Prior Knowledge note on TE p. 80, discuss the difficulties people might face moving to a different country with a new language. • Explain that the story includes figurative language. Guide students in how to determine the meanings of metaphors and similes. • Guide students in using Multidraft Reading strategies to deepen their comprehension (TE p. 79).	*Structure/Language* If students will have difficulty with figurative language, have them first read to recognize familiar details in Ernesto's experience at a new school. Have them reread, noting figurative language that is confusing. *Synthesizing* If students will not have difficulty with language, have them note as they read ways that the author uses language to convey personal and universal emotions about new places. Have students discuss what they have found as a class.

⑦ Critical Viewing

Possible response: He would probably feel comfortable in a classroom like the one in the picture because the teacher looks friendly and kind, and the children look happy. He might also enjoy looking at the pictures in the book the teacher is holding even though he could not understand the story she is reading.

⑧ Connecting to the Big Question

1. Remind students of the Big Question (What is the best way to find the truth?) and point out that people find the truth in many ways. They learn from what others tell them and from their own experiences.

2. **Ask:** What has the narrator learned so far about the experience of going to school in the United States? How has he learned it?
   Answer: He has learned from direct observation that his new school looks very different from his school in Mexico. He has learned from Mrs. Dodson how to find the school. He has learned from friends that the director is a lady and that there will be someone there who speaks Spanish.

3. Have students reread the bracketed passage. **Ask:** What does Ernesto learn from Miss Hopley's eyes?
   Answer: He learns that he is welcome.

4. **Ask:** As a child in a new country, what are some of the ways Ernesto relies on adults to help him interpret his new experiences?
   Answer: If no one had told him the principal would be a woman, he might not have understood that Miss Hopley was the principal. Miss Hopley's expression tells him he is welcome.

5. Tell students as they read to look for ways in which the adults in the selection help Ernesto understand his new experiences.

⑦ ▲ **Critical Viewing**
Do you think the narrator would feel comfortable in a classroom like this one? Why or why not? **[Speculate]**

Vocabulary
formidable
(fôr′ mə də bəl) *adj.*
impressive

over the pinch glasses crossed on the ridge of her nose. To do this she had to duck her head slightly as if she were about to step through a low doorway.

What Miss Hopley said to us we did not know but we saw in her eyes a warm welcome and when she took off her glasses and straightened up she smiled wholeheartedly, like Mrs. Dodson. We were, of course, saying nothing, only catching the friendliness of her voice and the sparkle in her eyes while she said words we did not understand. She signaled us to the table. Almost tiptoeing across the office, I maneuvered myself to keep my mother between me and the gringo lady. In a matter of seconds I had to decide whether she was a possible friend or a menace.[2] We sat down.

Then Miss Hopley did a formidable thing. She stood up. Had she been standing when we entered she would have seemed tall. But rising from her chair she soared. And what she carried up and up with her was a buxom superstructure,[3] firm shoulders, a straight sharp nose, full cheeks slightly molded by a curved line along the nostrils, thin lips that moved like steel springs, and a high forehead topped by hair gathered in a bun. Miss Hopley was not a giant in body but when she mobilized[4] it to a standing position she seemed

---

2. **menace** (men′ əs) *n.* danger; threat.
3. **buxom superstructure** full figure.
4. **mobilized** (mō′ bə līzd′) *v.* put into motion.

82 Fiction and Nonfiction

Think Aloud

Think Aloud: Using Context
Direct students' attention to the word *withering* on page 83. Using a think-aloud process, model how to use context to infer the meaning of an unknown word. Say to students:

   I'm going to think aloud to show you how I would figure out the meaning of *withering* from its context.

   In this sentence, *withering* is used to describe Miss Ryan's height. The narrator calls himself skinny and runty, which means that he is small.

   He also says that Miss Ryan patrolled the class, making her sound like an intimidating authority figure. Miss Ryan probably seemed very tall to her young students. Something that seems big will often make us feel smaller than we are, so I think that *wither* means to become smaller and *withering* describes Miss Ryan's height and shows that it made Ernesto feel smaller.

a match for giants. I decided I liked her.

She strode to a door in the far corner of the office, opened it and called a name. A boy of about ten years appeared in the doorway. He sat down at one end of the table. He was brown like us, a plump kid with shiny black hair combed straight back, neat, cool, and faintly obnoxious.

Miss Hopley joined us with a large book and some papers in her hand. She, too, sat down and the questions and answers began by way of our interpreter. My name was Ernesto. My mother's name was Henriqueta. My birth certificate was in San Blas. Here was my last report card from the Escuela Municipal Numero 3 para Varones of Mazatlán,[5] and so forth. Miss Hopley put things down in the book and my mother signed a card.

As long as the questions continued, Doña[6] Henriqueta could stay and I was secure. Now that they were over, Miss Hopley saw her to the door, dismissed our interpreter and without further ado took me by the hand and strode down the hall to Miss Ryan's first grade. Miss Ryan took me to a seat at the front of the room, into which I shrank—the better to survey her. She was, to skinny, somewhat runty me, of a withering height when she patrolled the class. And when I least expected it, there she was, crouching by my desk, her blond radiant face level with mine, her voice patiently maneuvering me over the awful idiocies of the English language.

During the next few weeks Miss Ryan overcame my fears of tall, energetic teachers as she bent over my desk to help me with a word in the pre-primer. Step by step, she loosened me and my classmates from the safe anchorage of the desks for recitations at the blackboard and consultations at her desk. Frequently she burst into happy announcements to the whole class. "Ito can read a sentence," and small Japanese Ito, squint-eyed and shy, slowly read aloud while the class listened in wonder: "Come, Skipper, come. Come and run." The Korean, Portuguese, Italian, and

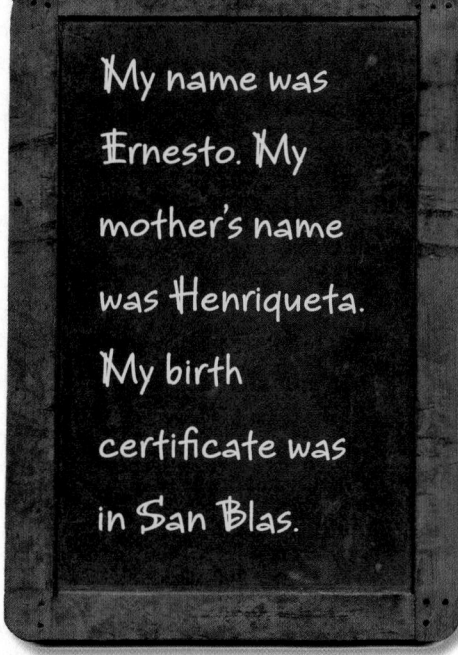

My name was Ernesto. My mother's name was Henriqueta. My birth certificate was in San Blas.

Reading Check
How did the principal welcome the narrator and his mother?

5. **Escuela Municipal Numero 3 para Varones of Mazatlán** (es kwä lä mōō nē sē päl′ nōō′ me rō träs pä′ rä bä rō′ nes mä sät län′) Municipal School Number 3 for Boys of Mazatlán.
6. **Doña** (dō′ nyä) Spanish title of respect meaning "lady" or "madam."

from Barrio Boy **83**

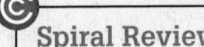
⓫ Nonfiction

1. Have students read the first bracketed passage. **Ask** them to summarize the information in this passage.
   Answer: The passage explains that Miss Ryan works individually with each student who needs to learn English.

2. Next, **ask** students the Nonfiction question.
   Possible responses: The fact that the teacher feels such devotion to her students that she gives some of them private lessons in a closet and the fact that the teacher is very dedicated to teaching English.

⓬ Nonfiction

1. Tell students that writers of both fiction and nonfiction narratives reveal only the details they need to tell a good story.

2. Have students read the second bracketed passage. Summarize that Ernesto is describing the children in his class. **Ask** students what they learn about Ernesto's classmates.
   Answer: They come from many backgrounds and speak different languages.

3. **Ask** students the Nonfiction question.
   Answer: The details reveal the nationalities of the children and the physical characteristics of a couple of the children.

Ⓒ
Spiral Review

Central Idea

1. Remind students that they studied the concept of central idea in the Unit 1 Literary Analysis Workshop (pp. 4–21).

2. **Ask** students the Spiral Review question.

   Possible response: Galarza remembers students from all over the world who all get along and respect each other.

Nonfiction
What details in this section help you appreciate the importance of the author's actual experience?

 ⓫

Nonfiction
What details in this passage tell about each character in the narrative?

 ⓬

Ⓒ **Spiral Review**
Central Idea How do Galarza's memories of Lincoln School relate to a central idea?

---

⑨ Polish first graders had similar moments of glory, no less shining than mine the day I conquered "butterfly," which I had been persistently pronouncing in standard Spanish as boo-ter-flee. "Children," Miss Ryan called for attention. "Ernesto has learned how to pronounce *butterfly*!" And I proved it with a perfect imitation of Miss Ryan. From that celebrated success, I was soon able to match Ito's progress as a sentence reader with "Come, butterfly, come fly with me."

Like Ito and several other first graders who did not know English, I received private lessons from Miss Ryan in the closet, a narrow hall off the classroom with a door at each end. Next to one of these doors Miss Ryan placed a large chair for herself and a small one for me. Keeping an eye on the class through the open door she read with me about sheep in the meadow and a frightened chicken going to see the king, coaching me out of my phonetic ruts in words like *pasture, bow-wow-wow, hay,* and *pretty,* which to my Mexican ear and eye had so many unnecessary sounds and letters. She made me watch her lips and then close my eyes as she repeated words I found hard to read. When we came to know each other better, I tried interrupting to tell Miss Ryan how we said it in Spanish. It didn't work. She only said "oh" and went on with *pasture, bow-wow-wow,* and *pretty.* It was as if in that closet we were both discovering together the secrets of the English language and grieving together over the tragedies of Bo-Peep. The main reason I was graduated with honors from the first grade was that I had fallen in love with Miss Ryan. Her radiant, no-nonsense character made us either afraid not to love her or love her so we would not be afraid, I am not sure which. It was not only that we sensed she was with it, but also that she was with us. Like the first grade, the rest of the Lincoln School was a sampling of the lower part of town where many races made their home. My pals in the second grade were Kazushi, whose parents spoke only Japanese; Matti, a skinny Italian boy; and Manuel, a fat Portuguese who would never get into a fight but wrestled you to the ground and just sat on you. Our assortment of nationalities included Koreans, Yugoslavs, Poles, Irish, and home-grown Americans.

At Lincoln, making us into Americans did not mean scrubbing away what made us originally foreign. The teachers called us as our parents did, or as close as they could pronounce our names in Spanish or Japanese. No one was ever scolded or punished for speaking in his native tongue on

---

Vocabulary Development   Ⓒ **CCSS** Language 6

Words From Social Studies
Several words on this page are related to the children in the story who are learning English. Discuss the meanings of each word or phrase with students before reading to help ensure understanding of the passage. *Races:* groups of people with common characteristics such as hair or skin color or nationality. *Nationalities:* memberships in particular groups of people, each under one government. *Home-grown:* raised in the place in which one was born. *Originally foreign:* belonging first to a different country. *Native tongue:* language of one's first homeland.

the playground. Matti told the class about his mother's down quilt, which she had made in Italy with the fine feathers of a thousand geese. Encarnación acted out how boys learned to fish in the Philippines. I astounded the third grade with the story of my travels on a stagecoach, which nobody else in the class had seen except in the museum at Sutter's Fort. After a visit to the Crocker Art Gallery and its collection of heroic paintings of the golden age of California, someone showed a silk scroll with a Chinese painting. Miss Hopley herself had a way of expressing wonder over these matters before a class, her eyes wide open until they popped slightly. It was easy for me to feel that becoming a proud American, as she said we should, did not mean feeling ashamed of being a Mexican.

 ▲ **Critical Viewing**
What do you think it would be like to travel in a stagecoach like the one in this picture? **[Speculate]**

Critical Thinking ©

Cite textual evidence to support your responses.

© **1. Key Ideas and Details Summarize:** Describe Galarza's experiences as a newcomer in school.

© **2. Key Ideas and Details (a)** Why is Galarza afraid of Miss Ryan at first? **(b) Interpret:** What does Galarza mean when he says Miss Ryan "was with it" and "with us"?

© **3. Integration of Knowledge and Ideas Analyze:** What experiences in Lincoln School help Galarza realize his dream of "becoming a proud American"?

© **4. Integration of Knowledge and Ideas (a)** What is the unknown that frightens Galarza in this story? **(b)** How does Galarza use his experience at school to discover the truth about those around him? *[Connect to the Big Question: What is the best way to find the truth?]*

from Barrio Boy **85**

Possible response: It would probably be uncomfortable and slow to travel in the stagecoach. The stagecoach must be pulled by a horse, which cannot go very fast. The wheels would probably make for a bumpy ride.

Concept Connector
After reading the story, have students reconsider the difficulties a child might face when moving from another country to the U.S. Then, have them compare their Writing About the Big Question responses with their ideas after reading.

◄

ASSESS

Answers

Critical Thinking
Remind students to support their answers with evidence from the text.

1. **Possible response:** Ernesto is afraid and wants to hide behind his mother. Miss Hopley seems very large to him, but he can sense that she is kind. His teacher. Miss Ryan also seems large, but she is patient and kind, and soon he starts to get good at speaking English.

2. **(a)** He is suspicious of tall, energetic teachers who loom over students. **(b)** He means that Miss Ryan understands the children's difficulties and that she uses her knowledge to help them.

3. The people at the Lincoln School helped Galarza remain proud of his heritage while preparing him for life in the United States.

4. **Possible response:**
(a) Galarza is frightened by the unknown of a new teacher, a new language, and a new class. **(b)** Galarza uses his experience at school to discover that he can learn from and about his classmates, who were of an assortment of nationalities. He also discovers that he is not alone in learning about a new language and culture.

⑭ ⑮ ⑯

⑭ Background
Facing Fear

Restless for excitement, Ernest Hemingway left home after high school. Just before his nineteenth birthday, he was wounded in World War I. While hospitalized in Italy, he received a medal for heroism. These experiences became the basis for several short stories and the novel *A Farewell to Arms.* Hemingway's writing celebrates heroes and explores the nature of courage. In much of his writing, he dramatizes the importance of bravery in the face of death and everyday problems. "A Day's Wait" deals with the quiet courage needed to face fear.

⑮ Activating Prior Knowledge

Tell students that most of us spend some time each day waiting. Ask students what kind of waiting they have done recently. Point out that lying in bed when we are sick can be the worst kind of waiting. In addition to feeling ill and being bored, you have time to worry. Then, ask students what they think is the worst kind of waiting: for example, waiting in a doctor's office or waiting for a punishment.

Concept Connector ➡

Students will return to their ideas about waiting after reading "A Day's Wait."

⑯ About the Selection

In "A Day's Wait," a young boy is terrified by his illness but hides his fears. Unaware of the boy's true feelings, his father leaves the house to go for a walk. Returning, the father realizes how tormented the boy has been all day. The simple misunderstanding and source of the boy's fears is finally revealed. The boy's quiet resolve shows how some people face distressing situations with courage and concern for others.

⑰ Critical Viewing

Possible response: The adult's hand and the boy's withdrawn expression suggest that the boy probably feels ill—weak, tired, achy, and feverish.

⑰ ▲ **Critical Viewing** Describe how you think the boy in this picture might feel. **[Connect]**

⑱

H e came into the room to shut the windows while we were still in bed and I saw he looked ill. He was shivering, his face was white, and he walked slowly as though it ached to move.

"What's the matter, Schatz[1]?"

"I've got a headache."

"You better go back to bed."

"No. I'm all right."

"You go to bed. I'll see you when I'm dressed."

But when I came downstairs he was dressed, sitting by the fire, looking a very sick and miserable boy of nine years. When I put my hand on his forehead I knew he had a fever.

"You go up to bed," I said, "you're sick."

"I'm all right," he said.

When the doctor came he took the boy's temperature.

"What is it?" I asked him.

"One hundred and two."

Downstairs, the doctor left three different medicines in different colored capsules with instructions for giving them. One was to bring down the fever, another a purgative, the

---

1. **Schatz** (shäts) German term of affection, used here as a loving nickname.

© Text Complexity Rubric

A Day's Wait		
Qualitative Measures	Context/Knowledge Demands	A boy's misunderstanding of his illness 1 2 ③ 4 5
	Structure/Language Conventionality and Clarity	Straightforward narrative; mostly short sentences and on-level vocabulary 1 2 ③ 4 5
	Levels of Meaning/ Purpose/Concepts	Accessible concept (courage in the face of fear) 1 2 ③ 4 5
Quantitative Measures	Text Length	Word Count: 1,063
	Lexile	900L

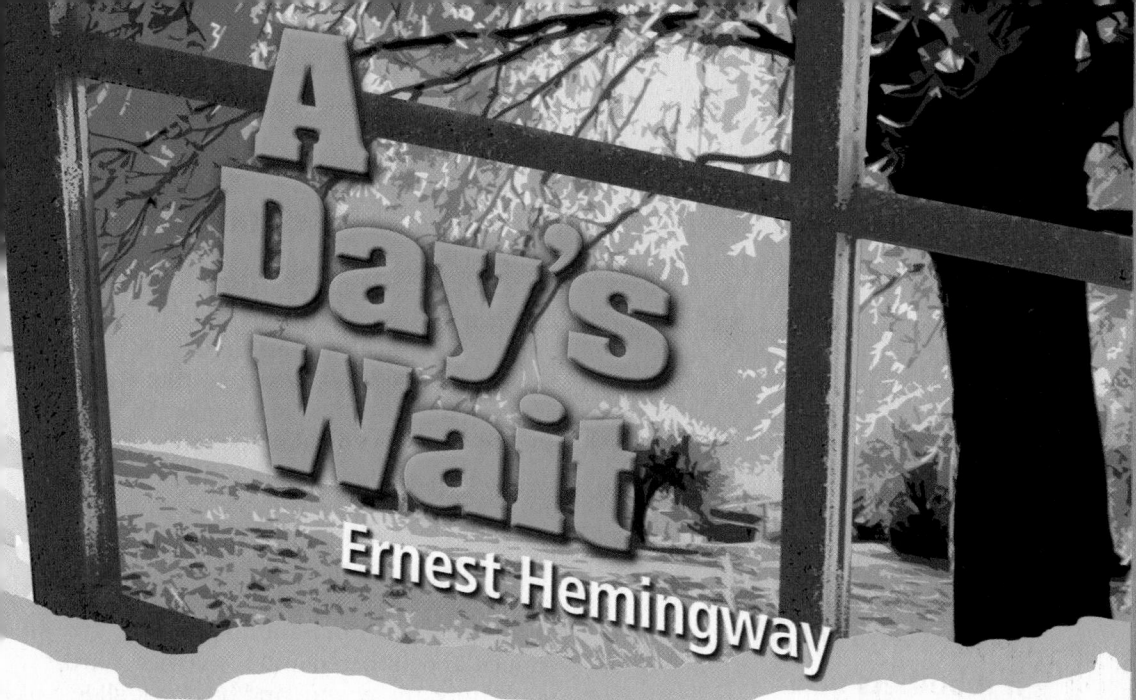

A Day's Wait

Ernest Hemingway

third to overcome an acid condition. The germs of influenza can only exist in an acid condition, he explained. He seemed to know all about influenza and said there was nothing to worry about if the fever did not go above one hundred and four degrees. This was a light epidemic of flu and there was no danger if you avoided pneumonia.

Back in the room I wrote the boy's temperature down and made a note of the time to give the various capsules.

"Do you want me to read to you?"

"All right. If you want to," said the boy. His face was very white and there were dark areas under his eyes. He lay still in the bed and seemed very detached from what was going on.

I read aloud from Howard Pyle's *Book of Pirates*; but I could see he was not following what I was reading.

"How do you feel, Schatz?" I asked him.

"Just the same, so far," he said.

I sat at the foot of the bed and read to myself while I waited for it to be time to give another capsule. It would have been natural for him to go to sleep, but when I looked up he was looking at the foot of the bed, looking very strangely.

"Why don't you try to go to sleep? I'll wake you up for the medicine."

Vocabulary
epidemic (ep´ ə dem´ ik)
n. outbreak of a
contagious disease

A Day's Wait **87**

18 **Connecting to the Big Question**

1. Remind students that the Big Question asks about the best way to find the truth. Point out that one way to find out the truth is to get information from experts.

2. **Ask** students: What information does the father have in this situation that the boy does not have? Why?
Answer: The father knows the doctor's diagnosis (influenza), the purposes of the various pills, and the fact that there is no need to worry as long as the boy's fever does not rise above one hundred and four degrees. The boy does not know these details because the doctor conveyed this information to the father downstairs while the boy was upstairs in bed.

3. **Ask:** How does the boy's lack of medical information about his condition limit his ability to understand the truth of his situation?
Answer: The boy does not know exactly what is wrong with him, how he is being treated, and what dangers his father has been instructed to watch for. He can only judge his situation based on the way he feels.

4. Tell students that as they continue to read the story, they should look for ways in which the boy might not understand the truth of his situation.

© Text Complexity: Reader and Task Suggestions

A Day's Wait

Preparing to Read the Text
- Discuss fears that people sometimes have, using the Background note on TE p. 86. Guide students in applying this knowledge to help them interpret the boy's words and actions.
- Discuss differences between metric and customary temperature scale, referring to the Literature in Context notes on SE/TE p. 89.
- Guide students in using Multidraft Reading strategies to deepen their comprehension (TE p. 79).

Leveled Tasks
Levels of Meaning If students will have difficulty with levels of meaning, have them first read to identify details about the boy's illness. Then, have them reread to identify and contrast how the boy and his father respond to those details. Discuss and clarify the contrast.

Analyzing If students will not have difficulty interpreting levels of meaning, have them note as they read ways that the author uses descriptive detail to highlight the contrast between the experiences of the boy and his father.

This selection is available in interactive format in the **Enriched Online Student Edition,** which includes an interactive graphic organizer.

⑲ Fiction

1. Remind students that both fiction and nonfiction narratives can be written from the first-person point of view.

2. As students read the bracketed section, have them look for pronouns that reveal the point of view. Discuss why the pronouns in the dialogue do not necessarily indicate who is telling the story.

3. **Ask** students the Fiction question.
   Answer: The father of the sick boy is the narrator, because he uses the pronoun *I* and refers to his sick child as *he*.

"You don't have to stay in here with me, Papa, if it bothers you."

Vocabulary
flushed (flusht) *v.* drove from hiding

Fiction
Who is the narrator of this work? How do you know? ⑲

"I'd rather stay awake."

After a while he said to me, "You don't have to stay in here with me, Papa, if it bothers you."

"It doesn't bother me."

"No. I mean you don't have to stay if it's going to bother you."

I thought perhaps he was a little lightheaded and after giving him the prescribed capsules at eleven o'clock I went out for a while. It was a bright, cold day, the ground covered with a sleet that had frozen so that it seemed as if all the bare trees, the bushes, the cut brush and all the grass and the bare ground had been varnished with ice. I took the young Irish setter for a little walk up the road and along a frozen creek, but it was difficult to stand or walk on the glassy surface and the red dog slipped and slithered and I fell twice, hard, once dropping my gun and having it slide away over the ice.

We flushed a covey of quail under a high clay bank with overhanging brush and I killed two as they went out of sight over the top of the bank. Some of the covey lit in trees but most of them scattered into brush piles and it was necessary to jump on the ice-coated mounds of brush several times before they would flush. Coming out while you were poised unsteadily on the icy, springy brush they made difficult shooting, and I killed two, missed five, and started back pleased to have found a covey close to the house and happy there were so many left to find on another day.

At the house they said the boy had refused to let anyone come into the room.

"You can't come in," he said. "You mustn't get what I have."

I went up to him and found him in exactly the position I had left him, white-faced, but with the tops of his cheeks flushed by the fever, staring still, as he had stared at the foot of the bed.

I took his temperature.

"What is it?"

"Something like a hundred," I said. It was one hundred and two and four tenths.

Think Aloud

Fiction
Draw students' attention to the section of the story describing the narrator's walk with his dog, beginning with "I thought perhaps . . ." and ending with ". . . refused to let anyone come into the room." Use the following "think aloud" to model the process of analyzing the events in a piece of fiction.

When I read about the father's walk, I notice several things. I notice that the narrator is in a good mood and enjoying his walk; he clearly is not worried about his son. I think about the story's title, "A Day's Wait," and I think that the father is not waiting for anything; he is just going on with his life. I notice that when he returns to the house, he learns that his son is acting strangely. I see a contrast between the father's pleasant experience out in the fresh air and the boy's experience as he waits in his room alone. I decide to keep reading to learn why the narrator and the boy have such different attitudes.

"It was a hundred and two," he said.

"Who said so?"

"The doctor."

"Your temperature is all right," I said. "It's nothing to worry about."

"I don't worry," he said, "but I can't keep from thinking."

"Don't think," I said. "Just take it easy."

"I'm taking it easy," he said and looked straight ahead. He was *evidently* holding tight on to himself about something.

"Take this with water."

"Do you think it will do any good?"

"Of course it will."

I sat down and opened the *Pirate* book and commenced to read, but I could see he was not following, so I stopped.

"About what time do you think I'm going to die?" he asked.

"What?"

"About how long will it be before I die?"

"You aren't going to die. What's the matter with you?"

"Oh, yes, I am. I heard him say a hundred and two."

A Day's Wait 89

Vocabulary
evidently (ev´ ə dent´ lē) *adv.* clearly; obviously

21 Reading Check

How does the boy know his temperature?

20 Literature in Context

Science Connection Many illnesses result in a fever, which is the body's method of fighting an infection. A person's temperature does not necessarily indicate the severity of the illness, but a very high temperature can be a serious health threat.

The average body temperature on the Fahrenheit scale is 98.6°. This is the equivalent of 37° Celsius. A body temperature of up to 105°F or 40.55°C can be uncomfortable, but it is not always considered dangerous, except in small children. Fevers that result in higher temperatures, especially 108°F or 42.22°C or more, can be deadly.

Connect to the Literature

1. Point out to students that a doctor took the boy's temperature, the father took note of it, and the boy asked about it. **Ask** them what the doctor tells the father about the boy's fever.
   Answer: The doctor tells the father not to worry unless the fever goes above 104 degrees.

2. Then, **ask** them the Connect to the Literature question.
   Answer: The boy's temperature is important to him and his father because it indicates to them that he is ill and will show whether or not he is in any immediate danger.

21 Reading Check

Answer: The boy overhears the doctor read his temperature and later asks his father about it.

Theme

1. Remind students that they studied the concept of theme in the Unit 1 Literary Analysis Workshop (pp. 4–21).

2. **Ask** students the first Spiral Review question.

   Possible response: He has learned that he is not going to die.

3. Then, **ask** students the second Spiral Review question.

   Possible response: He becomes his old self, which shows that fear changes how we view things.

ASSESS

Answers

Critical Thinking

Remind students to support their answers with evidence from the text.

1. (a) The boy is worried that he may die and that his father will catch the illness. (b) It reveals that he is brave and caring.

2. (a) His temperature is 102°F. In France, he was told that people die with a temperature above 44°C. He doesn't understand that the numbers have a different meaning on each type of thermometer. (b) The boy waits the whole day to die.

3. (a) Comments such as *Just the same, so far, I can't keep from thinking,* and *Do you think it will do any good?* show that he thinks something is wrong. Also, he is very detached from what is going on, and he does not care about being read to. (b) **Possible response:** The story is about the boy's bravery because he does not break down, even though he is afraid. (c) The boy's father probably would have explained the difference between the two types of thermometers and relieved the boy's fears earlier in the day.

4. **Possible response:** The boy may learn that even though he is brave, he does not need to hide his fears. Sometimes it is okay to show weakness.

"People don't die with a fever of one hundred and two. That's a silly way to talk."

"I know they do. At school in France the boys told me you can't live with forty-four degrees. I've got a hundred and two."

He had been waiting to die all day, ever since nine o'clock in the morning.

"You poor Schatz," I said. "Poor old Schatz. It's like miles and kilometers. You aren't going to die. That's a different thermometer. On that thermometer thirty-seven is normal. On this kind it's ninety-eight."

"Are you sure?"

"Absolutely," I said. "It's like miles and kilometers. You know, like how many kilometers we make when we do seventy miles in the car?"

"Oh," he said.

But his gaze at the foot of the bed relaxed slowly. The hold over himself relaxed too, finally, and the next day it was very slack and he cried very easily at little things that were of no importance.

> "At school in France the boys told me you can't live with forty-four degrees. I've got a hundred and two."

Spiral Review

Theme What critical information has the boy learned from this conversation with his father? How does his reaction relate to a possible theme?

Cite textual evidence to support your responses.

Critical Thinking

1. **Key Ideas and Details (a)** Why does the boy tell his father to leave the sickroom? **(b) Infer:** What does this reveal about the boy?

2. **Key Ideas and Details (a)** Why does the boy think he will die? Use details from the story to support your response. **(b) Interpret:** What is the meaning of the story's title?

3. **Key Ideas and Details (a) Analyze:** Which of the boy's words and actions give clues that he believes something terrible is wrong? **(b) Evaluate:** Do you think the story is about the boy's bravery or about the boy's fear? Explain. **(c) Speculate:** What might have happened if the boy had shared his fears?

4. **Integration of Knowledge and Ideas** When the truth of the boy's illness is explained to him, what truth has he learned about his character? *[Connect to the Big Question: What is the best way to find the truth?]*

90 Fiction and Nonfiction

Vocabulary Development

Vocabulary Knowledge Rating
When students have completed reading and discussing the excerpt from *Barrio Boy* and "A Day's Wait," have them take out their **Vocabulary Knowledge Rating Chart.** Read the words aloud once more, and have students rate their knowledge of the words again in the After Reading column. Clarify any words that are still problematic. Have students write their own definition and example or sentence in the

appropriate column. Then, have students complete the Vocabulary Practice activities at the end of this selection. Encourage students to use the words in further discussion and written work about this selection. Remind them that they will be accountable for these words on the **Selection Test,** *Unit 1 Resources,* pp. 119–121 or 122–124.

Comparing Fiction and Nonfiction

© **1. Craft and Structure (a)** For each selection, tell whether the narrator and events are real or imagined. **(b)** Based on your answer, what rules about truth and accuracy did each writer follow for writing these selections?

© **2. Key Ideas and Details** Complete a chart like the one shown to help you analyze one character in each story.

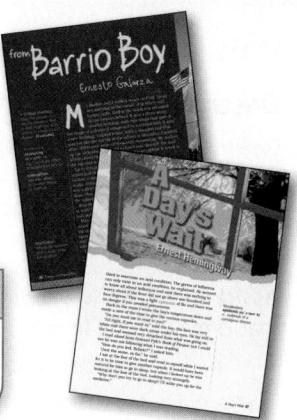

Character	Detail	Fiction or Nonfiction?
The boy in "A Day's Wait"		
Miss Ryan in *Barrio Boy*		

© **3. Integration of Knowledge and Ideas (a)** How might "A Day's Wait" be different if it were nonfiction? **(b)** How might *Barrio Boy* change if it were fiction?

 Timed Writing

Explanatory Text: Essay

In a brief essay, compare and contrast the narrators of *Barrio Boy* and "A Day's Wait." State your topic in the introduction and discuss how the narrator presents the events in each work. Consider adding a chart to show what is the same and different. **(40 minutes)**

5-Minute Planner

1. Gather your ideas by jotting down answers to these questions:
   - Which work includes more personal details about the narrator?
   - How is dialogue used in each work?
   - Do the narrator's thoughts and actions build toward a specific theme or insight? Why or why not?
   - Which narrator is central to the narrative's action?

2. Choose an organizational strategy. If you use the block method, present all the details about one narrator, then all the details about the other narrator. If you use the point-by-point method, discuss one aspect of both narrators, then another aspect of both narrators, and so on.

3. Reread the prompt and then draft your essay.

from Barrio Boy • A Day's Wait **91**

Comparing Fiction and Nonfiction

1. **(a)** The narrator and events in the excerpt from *Barrio Boy* are real. In "A Day's Wait," the narrator and events are imagined. **(b)** In the excerpt from *Barrio Boy*, the author probably tried to tell a truthful and accurate tale. In "A Day's Wait," the author used his imagination to create a story that seems realistic.

2. **Possible response:** [in the Detail column] waits patiently to die; is caring and helpful; [in the Fiction or Nonfiction column] fiction; nonfiction.

   Other sample answers can be found in *Graphic Organizer Transparencies,* **Comparing Fiction and Nonfiction Transparency A (Apply the Skills),** p. 17, and in the **Additional Answers** section.

3. **(a)** It might include less dialogue and more personal details such as the narrator's feelings. **(b)** It might include fewer personal details and more dialogue and interaction among the characters.

Timed Writing

1. Review the prompt with students.

2. Have students use the 5-Minute Planner to structure their time. Guide them in answering the bulleted questions. For example, point out that the second bulleted item might lead them to focus on how the dialogue, or lack of dialogue, affects the narration of each story.

3. Allow students 40 minutes to complete the assignment.

4. As students prewrite and draft, have them refer to their completed **Comparing Fiction and Nonfiction Graphic Organizer.**

Six Traits Focus

✔	Ideas		Word Choice
✔	Organization		Sentence Fluency
	Voice		Conventions

 **Common Core State Standards**

• Writing 2.a, b, c, d, e; 5
• Language 2.b

Introducing the Writing Assignment

Review the assignment and the criteria, using the instruction on the student page.

Connecting to Real-Life Writing

Explain to students that description occurs in almost every type of writing.

 Writing Workshop
Work in Progress

If students have completed the Work-in-Progress assignments on pp. 47 and 69, suggest that they try to develop their Work-in-Progress ideas in a descriptive essay.

Prewriting/Planning Strategy

1. Introduce the prewriting strategy, using the instruction and the graphic organizer.

2. Have students apply the strategy to gather details.

Six Traits Focus

✓ Ideas	Word Choice	
✓ Organization	Sentence Fluency	
Voice	Conventions	

Writing Workshop

Write an Informative Text

Description: Descriptive Essay

Defining the Form A **descriptive essay** creates a picture of a person, place, thing, or event. Descriptive language engages your attention by creating vivid images that help you "see" the action. You might use descriptive language in short stories, poems, and journals.

Assignment Write a descriptive essay about a place or an event that is meaningful to you. Your essay should feature these elements:

✔ vivid *sensory details* to appeal to the five senses
✔ a *main impression* supported by each detail
✔ clear, *consistent organization*
✔ links between details and the feelings or thoughts they inspire
✔ effective *transitions*
✔ error-free writing, including *correct spelling of plural nouns*

To preview the criteria on which your descriptive essay may be judged, see the rubric on page 97.

📖✏ Writing Workshop: *Work in Progress*

Review the work you did on pages 47 and 69.

Prewriting/Planning Strategy

Use cubing to gather details. Follow these steps to "cube" your subject and uncover information that will bring your description to life for readers.

1. Describe it. Explain how it looks, sounds, feels, tastes, or smells.
2. Associate it. List feelings or stories it calls to mind.
3. Apply it. Show how your topic can be used.
4. Analyze it. Divide it into parts.
5. Compare and contrast it. Compare it with a related subject.
6. Argue for or against it. Show its good and bad points.

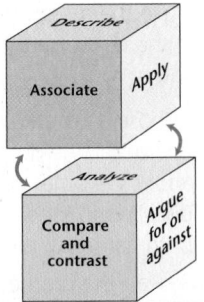

 Common Core State Standards

Writing
2.a. Introduce a topic clearly, previewing what is to follow; organize ideas, concepts, and information, using strategies such as definition, classification, comparison/contrast, and cause/effect.
2.d. Use precise language and domain-specific vocabulary to inform about or explain the topic.
2.e. Establish and maintain a formal style.
5. With some guidance and support from peers and adults, develop and strengthen writing as needed by planning, revising, editing, rewriting, or trying a new approach, focusing on how well purpose and audience have been addressed.

Teaching Resources

The following resources can be used to enrich or extend the instruction.

All *Unit 1 Resources*
Writing Workshop, pp. 125, 126

All *Common Core Companion,*
pp. 190–201; 220–221

All *Professional Development Guidebook*
Rubrics for Self-Assessment: Descriptive Essay, pp. 220–221

All *Graphic Organizers Transparencies*
Rubric for Self-Assessment: Descriptive Essay, p. 19

PHLit Online! All resources are available online at **www.PHLitOnline.com.**

| Voice | Organization | Word Choice | Ideas | Conventions | Sentence Fluency |

Find Your Voice

Voice describes a writer's distinctive style and can be influenced by word choice, sentence structure, and tone—the writer's attitude toward his or her subject. A professional writer usually has a distinct voice that makes his or her writing instantly recognizable. For example, think of how a jazz musician and a hip-hop artist might play "The Star-Spangled Banner" completely differently. Developing a unique voice can take time. These tips and activities will help get you started.

Learning from the Professionals Next time you are reading a descriptive passage that you enjoy, think about the writer's voice. Filling in a chart like the one shown will help you analyze voice. This chart refers to Ernest Hemingway's "A Day's Wait," which appears on pages 86–90, but you can use it for any text that you enjoy.

Word Choice	*Varnished with ice; glassy surface; covey of quail*
Sentence Structure	*Long sentences; many short phrases joined together*
Tone	*Sentence structure makes narrator sound breathless, rushed.*

Checking Your Voice As you write your descriptive essay, review your draft for word choice, sentence structure, and tone. Remember to consider your purpose and audience. Decide if your style of writing should be formal or informal. Are you happy with the voice you are using? If not, try changing some of these elements to change your voice. Ask yourself these questions:

- *Word Choice*: What kinds of words have I chosen? Have I used precise language to create a strong impression?
- *Sentence Structure*: How did I arrange the words in my sentences? What type of sentences do I typically create?
- *Tone*: How do I feel about my subject?

Then, ask a partner to read your draft and give feedback. By adjusting the elements above, you can adjust your voice. Many writers refer to this process as "finding their voice."

PH WRITING COACH

Further instruction and practice are available in *Prentice Hall Writing Coach*.

Applying Understanding by Design Principles

Clarifying Expected Outcomes: Using Rubrics

- Before students begin work on this assignment, have them preview the Rubric for Self-Assessment (p. 97) to learn what qualities their descriptive essay must have. A copy of this rubric appears in the *Graphic Organizer Transparencies,* p. 19.

- Review the criteria in the Rubric with the class. Before students use the Rubric to assess their own writing, work with them to rate the Student Model (p. 96) using the Rubric.
- If you wish to assess students' descriptive essays with either a 4-point or a 6-point scoring rubric, see the *Professional Development Guidebook,* pp. 220–221.

TEACH

Find Your Voice

1. Introduce the writing skill, using the instructions on the student page.
2. Discuss the examples in the chart.
3. Have students follow the instructions to check and adjust their voice.

Teaching the Writing Skill

1. Explain to the students that, just as each person looks unique and has a distinct personality, each person also has a unique writing voice. That voice is created by the writer's choice of words and the way the writer puts words together in a sentence.
2. Explain to the class that tone is created by using positive and negative words, by word sound, and by the general picture that each word creates. **Ask** students to tell you if the following descriptions have a positive or negative tone.

   It is dark and gloomy. The rain is constant. (**Answer:** negative)

   The raindrops made steady tat-a-tat-tat on the roof, as distant lightning brightened the dark sky. (**Answer:** positive)

3. Review the chart on the student page with the class, and ask the students to fill in a chart for another descriptive passage.
4. Have students exchange their drafts. Ask students to apply the questions on the student page to their partners' drafts and to identify the general voice of the draft. Then, have them circle a sentence that does not convey voice, or that is inconsistent with the voice of the rest of the draft. Have them propose a rewrite of the circled sentence to add consistent voice, changing the word choice and sentence structure as necessary. Afterwards, partners should discuss the proposed revisions.

PH WRITING COACH Grade 7

Students will find additional support for writing a descriptive essay in chapter 7.

Prentice Hall EssayScorer

A writing prompt for this mode of writing can be found on the *Prentice Hall EssayScorer* at www.PHLitOnline.com.

Drafting Strategies

1. Introduce the drafting strategies.
2. Have students apply the strategies as they draft their essays.

Teaching the Strategies

Have students practice using spatial order with partners. Suggest they describe the classroom in various orders, moving from left to right or up and down.

Think Aloud: Model Using Sensory Details

Say to students:

> Just sitting in my friend's classroom, I can practice creating a main impression with sensory details. I see the posters on the walls and the crazy quotes she has pasted all over the door, so I write those sensory details down. The sensory details I include help my reader understand the classroom's inviting atmosphere.

Six Traits Focus

✔	Ideas		Word Choice
✔	Organization		Sentence Fluency
	Voice		Conventions

Revising Strategies

1. Introduce the revising strategies.
2. Have students apply the strategies as they revise.

Teaching the Strategies

Use the following example to show students how precise adjectives help bring a scene to life:

> **Vague:** <u>Some</u> <u>nice</u> passengers boarded the train for a <u>great</u> trip through the western states.

> **Precise:** <u>Four</u> <u>smiling</u> passengers boarded the train for a <u>week-long</u> <u>sightseeing</u> trip through the western states.

Six Traits Focus

✔	Ideas	✔	Word Choice
✔	Organization	✔	Sentence Fluency
	Voice		Conventions

Drafting Strategies

Organize your ideas. Present your details in a pattern that will make sense to readers. Use a chart like the one shown to select a general organizational plan for your essay. Keep in mind that you may use elements of more than one plan as you write. For example, you may use chronological order as your *overall* organization to describe an event. You may also use elements of spatial order to describe the setting.

Spatial Order	Chronological Order	Order of Importance
If you are writing about a place or object, use a form of spatial order, such as near to far, left to right, front to back, or bottom to top.	If you are describing an event, present details in the order they happen.	If you are describing to show the significance of your subject, begin with your least important details and build up to the most important.

Elaborate to create a main impression. Set a mood or use an idea to unify your essay. For example, you might create a feeling of suspense, a calm atmosphere, or a flurry of activity. Include sensory details that support and strengthen this overall impression.

Revising Strategies

Revise for organization and transition. Review your draft with a partner to find places you can improve the organization of your composition in order to fit your purpose and audience. Add transition words and phrases to show the connections between details and ideas.

Revise word choice. Highlight vague or empty adjectives like *nice* and *good*, which do not add information to your description. Then, use a print or digital **thesaurus** to help you find words that have the same basic meaning but are more precise.

> **Vague Adjective:** A *bad* wind blew.
> **Precise Adjective:** A *ferocious* wind blew.

> **Vague Adverb:** He sang *well.*
> **Precise Adverb:** He sang *angelically.*

 **Common Core State Standards**

Writing

2.a. Introduce a topic clearly, previewing what is to follow; organize ideas, concepts, and information, using strategies such as definition, classification, comparison/contrast, and cause/effect.

2.b. Develop the topic with relevant facts, definitions, concrete details, quotations, or other information and examples.

2.c. Use appropriate transitions to create cohesion and clarify the relationships among ideas and concepts.

5. With some guidance and support from peers and adults, develop and strengthen writing as needed by planning, revising, editing, rewriting, or trying a new approach, focusing on how well purpose and audience have been addressed.

Language

3.a. Choose language that expresses ideas precisely and concisely.

Revising Incorrect Forms of Plural Nouns

The plural form of a noun indicates that more than one person, place, or thing is named. Plural forms are either regular or irregular.

Identifying Incorrect Forms of Plural Nouns To identify and fix incorrect forms of plural nouns, you must first know how to create plural nouns. Regular nouns form their plurals by adding -s or -es.

Regular Plural Nouns

Singular:	bus	monkey	radio
Plural:	bus**es**	monkey**s**	radio**s**

Sometimes the singular and plural forms of a noun are the same.

Irregular Plural Nouns

Singular:	ox	goose	woman	mouse	deer	clothes
Plural:	oxen	geese	women	mice	deer	clothes

Forming Regular Plural Nouns

Word Ending	Rule
-o or -y preceded by a vowel -ff	Add -s
-s, -ss, -x, -z, -zz, -sh, -ch -o preceded by a consonant	Add -es (exceptions: solo and other musical terms)
-y preceded by a consonant	Change y to i and add -es
-fe	Change f to v and add -es
-f	Add -s OR change f to v and add -es

PH WRITING COACH

Further instruction and practice are available in *Prentice Hall Writing Coach*.

Fixing Incorrect Forms of Plural Nouns To fix an incorrect form of a plural noun, verify the spelling using one of these methods:

1. **Review the rules for forming regular plural nouns.** First, write the singular form of the noun and circle the last two letters. Then, find the corresponding rule in the chart.

2. **Use a dictionary to look up the correct spelling.**

Grammar in Your Writing

Choose two paragraphs in your draft and circle each plural noun. If the spelling is faulty, correct it using one of the methods described.

Writing Workshop **95**

Strategies for Using Technology in Writing

Many word processing programs are equipped with thesauruses that list synonyms and antonyms. Explain to students that this tool will help them use more precise language and allow them to find more interesting and descriptive words, which will improve the overall quality of their compositions. Students can also use the Vague Adjectives Revision Checker in the **Writing and Grammar Interactive Textbook Online** at **www.pearsonsuccessnet.com**. Emphasize that students should check a dictionary before using an unfamiliar word to make sure it is appropriate in the context of their writing.

Revising Incorrect Forms of Plural Nouns

1. Introduce the grammar skill, using the instruction on the student page.

2. Discuss the rules and examples, as well as the strategies for fixing incorrect usage.

3. Have students follow the instruction under Grammar in Your Writing to correct errors in their drafts.

Teaching the Grammar Skill

1. Remind students of the general rule that singular nouns are made plural by adding an *s* to the end of the word.

2. Point out that plurals of irregular nouns such as *child, man, goose* vary. Students should memorize them or consult a dictionary.

3. Some words have two plural forms: *scarfs/scarves, dwarfs/dwarves.*

4. Have students form the plurals of the following nouns:

bureau (**Answer:** bureaus)

fly (**Answer:** flies)

elf (**Answer:** elves)

potato (**Answer:** potatoes)

territory (**Answer:** territories)

box (**Answer:** boxes)

tattoo (**Answer:** tattoos)

trout (**Answer:** trout)

Think Aloud: Model Forming Plural Nouns

Say to students:

When I want to figure out whether the plural of a word takes -s or -es, I make my decision based on the sound of the word. If the noun ends in a letter that easily combines with the s sound, it takes -s. If the noun ends in an s sound or a letter, such as sh, j, x, or z, that doesn't combine easily with s, it ends in -es. The word *boy* easily combines with the s sound, so it takes -s to become *boys.* The word *boss* ends in an s sound that does not combine easily with s. I add -es to form the plural *bosses.*

PH WRITING COACH | Grade 7

Students will find practice with and guidance on plural nouns in Chapter 23.

Student Model

Review the Student Model with the class, using the annotations to analyze the writer's successful use of the elements of a descriptive essay.

Teaching From the Student Model

1. Explain that the student model is a sample and essays may be longer.

2. **Ask** students how Charity orders the description of details in the first paragraph. (**Answer:** day to evening: time or chronological order)

3. Note that the writer makes particularly effective use of chronological order by inviting readers to pretend they are taking a walk during springtime. Discuss the use of words that signal chronological order. Ask the students to identify transitional words and phrases. (**Answer:** *During the rest of the season, shortly after, later, when the grass grows . . .*)

4. Discuss how Charity conveys her overall sense of spring as a time of lightness by inviting the reader to imagine certain sensations, such as shedding their winter coats. Have students provide other examples from the text that support this impression. (**Possible responses:** imagining you are on a brisk walk, "you'll feel uplifted and energized," the breeze ruffling your hair.)

5. Discuss the use of adjectives and colorful words that add life to the writing, including: "purple-gray dusk," "high-pitched monotonous chirping sound," and "shrill and persistent."

Connecting to Real-Life Writing

Tell students that descriptive writing will be useful in a variety of jobs. For example, journalists must use description in every story or article they write. In addition, those in the business world need good descriptive writing skills to convey their ideas and needs effectively. Marketing and sales representatives need to describe products and services to make them appealing to their clients. Discuss with students other work situations in which descriptive writing might be needed and why.

Student Model: Charity Jackson, Fort Wayne, IN

Spring Into Spring

Spring is the perfect time to get outdoors and get active. The spring season brings the freshness of a new beginning. If you've been cooped up all winter, the perfect start to spring is a brisk walk. If you walk during the day, you will feel the sunshine warming up the pavement; a breeze may ruffle your hair; you'll hear the songs of birds that you'd almost forgotten about over the winter. If you walk in the early evening, in the purple-gray dusk, you may even hear the "spring peepers," little frogs that become suddenly vocal around April. You might mistake them for crickets, because they have that same high-pitched monotonous chirping sound, but peepers are more shrill and persistent. Any one of these sensations by itself is enough to raise a little hope that winter is over. If you're lucky enough to experience them all at once on your first spring walk, you'll feel uplifted and energized by the knowledge that soon that stuffy old winter coat can be put in storage for many months.

During the rest of the season, if you continue to walk, you will experience new additions to the spring line-up. Not long after you've heard the peepers, you'll start to smell the earth. As the ground warms up, it gives off a soft, distinct "spring-like" smell. The scent of warm earth says "spring" the way the scent of pine says "winter." Because the ground is warming up, the smell of flowers can't be far behind! The first flowers of spring, though, are more a treat for the eyes than the nose. The brilliant yellow forsythia don't have much of an aroma, but they're so bright, they don't really need one to announce their arrival! The shy hyacinth, which blooms shortly after, is not as easily spotted, but your nose will tell you that the strong perfume in the air means a hyacinth is hiding somewhere nearby. Neighbors working their gardens—some of whom you may not have seen all winter—will call a friendly hello. Everyone seems friendlier at the beginning of spring.

Later in the season, when you begin to hear the growl and grumble of lawnmowers around the neighborhood, you'll know that spring has done its work. When the grass grows tall enough to need mowing, it's time to start thinking about those summer sensations!

> Sensory details about sunshine, breezes, birdsongs, and the colors of dusk appeal to the senses of touch, hearing, and sight.

> Charity reinforces the overall impression of lightness and energy to contrast with the stuffy winter coat.

> The description is organized in time order—new details are introduced in the order in which they appear as spring progresses.

> Here, and at various points in the essay, Charity includes her feelings and reactions to what she is describing.

> Transitions that indicate time help readers follow the chronological organization of the description.

Strategies for Test Taking

When taking a test that includes a descriptive writing prompt, students should pay attention to the organization of their writing. Students must understand that the readability of their essays depends heavily on organization. Before students begin writing, they should consider the topic, which is often provided, and decide which organization will work best. Then, they should consider the best transition words to use in order to make the organization clear. Before students turn in their writing, they should take time to review the writing for overall coherence and unity.

Editing and Proofreading

Proofread your essay to fix errors in grammar and punctuation.

Focus on Spelling: Troublesome Words Use a dictionary to confirm the spelling of troublesome words in your essay. If you used a word-processor to draft, use the spell-check function to search for errors. Then, review each word because spell-check will not catch **homophones** such as *there* and *their*—words that are spelled correctly but have several correct spellings and meanings. Use **mnemonic devices**, or memory aids, to help you remember which spelling to use. For example, to distinguish between *there* and *their,* notice that the word that is the opposite of *here* also contains the word *here.*

Publishing and Presenting

Consider one of the following ways to share your writing.

Tape-record your essay. Read your description aloud on tape. Add sound effects or background music that reinforces the main impression of your description. Play the tape for your classmates.

Post your composition. Put your description on a class bulletin board or post it on a school Web site. Add photos or art if possible.

Reflecting on Your Writing

Writer's Journal Jot down your answer to this question:

Which strategy was most useful for creating vivid details?

Rubric for Self-Assessment

Find evidence in your writing to address each category. Then, use the rating scale to grade your work.

Criteria	Rating Scale
	not very very
Focus: How clear is the main impression?	1 2 3 4 5
Organization: How clear and consistent is the organization?	1 2 3 4 5
Support/Elaboration: How effectively do you use sensory details in your description?	1 2 3 4 5
Style: How effective are your transitions?	1 2 3 4 5
Conventions: How correct is your grammar, especially your use of plural nouns?	1 2 3 4 5
Voice: How consistent is the style of your writing?	1 2 3 4 5

Spiral Review

Earlier in the unit, you learned about **common and proper nouns** (p. 46) and **possessive nouns** (p. 68). Check the capitalization of the common and proper nouns in your narrative. Review your descriptive essay to be sure you have placed apostrophes correctly in possessive nouns.

PH WRITING COACH

Further instruction and practice are available in *Prentice Hall Writing Coach.*

Editing and Proofreading

1. Introduce the editing and proofreading focus, using the instruction on the student page.

2. Have students edit and proofread their narratives, correcting grammar, spelling, punctuation, and word choice. Make sure they check for errors of the type noted in the lesson focus and the Spiral Review.

Teaching the Editing Focus

Students may make homophone errors when they are working quickly or they are distracted. Review some common examples of homophones, such as the following:

> I <u>ate eight</u> bananas.

> I can <u>see</u> the <u>sea</u> from my window.

> If you pass <u>by</u> the store, <u>buy</u> some milk.

> They took <u>their</u> mother <u>there</u> for dinner.

Six Traits Focus

Ideas	Word Choice
Organization	Sentence Fluency
Voice	✔ Conventions

ASSESS

Publishing and Presenting

1. Suggest that students who choose to play their audiotapes for family members or classmates ask the audience to close their eyes as they listen. Have them note their audience's feedback about what they saw, felt, and heard to help them evaluate how successful their descriptions were.

2. Suggest that students look in magazines for photos to illustrate their descriptions.

Reflecting on Your Writing

Suggest that students refer to their cubing diagrams to review their associations.

PH WRITING COACH Grade 7

Students will find more information on the writing process in Chapter 3.

Differentiated Instruction for Universal Access

Strategy For Less Proficient Writers

Suggest to students that they choose to write about a place that is convenient for them to revisit, a person with whom they still have contact, or a thing that is in their possession. Explain to students that using these topics will make it easier for them to come up with descriptive details.

EL Strategy For English Learners

If possible, have students visit the place they are going to write about or view a photograph of the person or thing that is the subject of their writing. Then, have them write a list of sensory details in their first languages. Have students work with partners to translate the details into English.

Enrichment For Advanced Writers

Challenge students to choose topics that they have never written about before. Then, as students gather details about their topics, have them make a list of synonyms for each detail. Tell students to choose the most specific and vivid words to use in their descriptions. Students may use a thesaurus if necessary.

✓ All Summer in a Day • ✓✓ Suzy and Leah
Lesson Pacing Guide

DAY 1 Preteach

- © Administer the Reading and Vocabulary Warm-ups (*Unit 1 Resources*, pp. 134–137 or 152–155) as necessary.
- Introduce the Reading Skill: Author's Purpose.
- © Introduce the Literary Analysis concept: Setting.
- Distribute copies of the graphic organizer for the Reading Skill (*Graphic Organizer Transparencies*, pp. 20–22).
- Distribute copies of the graphic organizer for Literary Analysis (*Graphic Organizer Transparencies*, pp. 23–25).
- © Teach the selection vocabulary.
- © Introduce the Word Study skill.

DAYS 2–3 Preteach/Teach

- © Build background with the Background feature.
- Develop thematic vocabulary and thematic thinking with Writing About the Big Question.
- Prepare students to read with the Activating Prior Knowledge activities (TE).
- Informally monitor comprehension while students read.
- Use the Reading Check questions to confirm comprehension.
- Develop students' ability to determine the author's purpose using the Author's Purpose questions.
- © Develop students' understanding of setting using the Setting questions.
- © Reinforce vocabulary with the Vocabulary notes.
- © Reinforce unit focus standards using the Spiral Review prompts.

DAY 4 Assess

- Assess students' comprehension and mastery of the skills by having them answer the Critical Thinking, Reading Skill, and Literary Analysis questions.
- © Have students complete the Vocabulary Practice activities.
- © Have students complete the Word Study activities.

DAY 5 Extend/Assess

- Have students complete the Conventions lesson.
- © Have students complete the Writing activity and write a news report. (You may assign as homework.)
- © Extend learning by having students complete the Speaking and Listening activity, a discussion. As an alternative, assign them "The Word on Bullies" or "Campers Give Peace a Chance" in *Reality Central*.
- Administer Selection Test A or B (*Unit 1 Resources*, pp. 146–151 or 167–172).

© Common Core State Standards

Reading Literature 2. Determine a theme or central idea of a text and analyze its development over the course of the text; provide an objective summary of the text.
3. Analyze how particular elements of a story or drama interact.

Writing 2. Write informative/explanatory texts to examine a topic and convey ideas, concepts, and information through the selection, organization, and analysis of relevant content.

Speaking and Listening 1.a. Come to discussions prepared, having read or researched material under study; explicitly draw on that preparation by referring to evidence on the topic, text, or issue to probe and reflect on ideas under discussion.
1.b. Follow rules for collegial discussions, track progress toward specific goals and deadlines, and define individual roles as needed.
1.c. Pose questions that elicit elaboration and respond to others' questions and comments with relevant observations and ideas that bring the discussion back on topic as needed.
1.d. Acknowledge new information expressed by others and, when warranted, modify their own views.

Language 4.b. Use common, grade-appropriate Greek or Latin affixes and roots as clues to the meaning of a word.
6. Acquire and use accurately grade-appropriate general academic and domain-specific words and phrases.

Additional Standards Practice
Common Core Companion, pp. 15–22; 97–104

Daily Block Scheduling
Each day in this Lesson Pacing Guide represents a 40–50 minute period. Teachers using block scheduling may combine days to revise pacing and component support. In addition, teachers may differentiate and support core instruction by integrating components for extended and intensive support, as students require. See the Guide to Selected Leveled Resources (facing page).

Guide to Selected Leveled Resources

R T I **Tier 1** (students performing on level)		✓ **More Accessible** All Summer in a Day	✓✓ **More Complex** Suzy and Leah
Warm Up	**Practice, model,** and **monitor** fluency, working with the whole class or in groups.	Vocabulary and Reading Warm-ups B, *Unit 1 Resources,* pp. 134–135, 137	Vocabulary and Reading Warm-ups B, *Unit 1 Resources,* pp. 152–153, 155
Comprehension/Skills	**Support** and **monitor** comprehension and skills development, having students complete the activities, graphic organizers, and interactive prompts **independently** or **as a class.**	• *Reader's Notebook,* adapted instruction and summary **EL** *Reader's Notebook: English Learner's Version,* adapted instruction and summary • Reading Skill Graphic Organizer B, *Graphic Organizer Transparencies,* p. 22 • Literary Analysis Graphic Organizer B, *Graphic Organizer Transparencies,* p. 25	• *Reader's Notebook,* adapted instruction and full selection **EL** *Reader's Notebook: English Learner's Version,* adapted instruction and adapted selection • Reading Skill Graphic Organizer B, *Graphic Organizer Transparencies,* p. 22 • Literary Analysis Graphic Organizer B, *Graphic Organizer Transparencies,* p. 25
Monitor Progress [A]	**Monitor** student progress with the differentiated curriculum-based assessment in the *Unit Resources.*	• Selection Test B, *Unit 1 Resources,* pp. 149–151 • Open-Book Test, *Unit 1 Resources,* pp. 143–145	• Selection Test B, *Unit 1 Resources,* pp. 170–172 • Open-Book Test, *Unit 1 Resources,* pp. 164–166

R T I **Tier 2** (students requiring intervention)		✓ **More Accessible** All Summer in a Day	✓✓ **More Complex** Suzy and Leah
Warm Up	**Practice, model,** and **monitor** fluency **in groups** or **with individuals.**	• Vocabulary and Reading Warm-ups A, *Unit 1 Resources,* pp. 134–136 • *Reality Central,* "The Word on Bullies" • *Hear It!* Audio CD	• Vocabulary and Reading Warm-ups A, *Unit 1 Resources,* pp. 152–154 • *Reality Central,* "Campers Give Peace a Chance" • *Hear It!* Audio CD (adapted text)
Comprehension/Skills	• **Support** and **monitor** comprehension and skills development, working **in small groups** or **with individuals.** • **Pair** students with more advanced peers and have them complete the writing activity in the *Real-World Writing Journal.* • As students complete the selection in the appropriate version of the *Reader's Notebook,* **monitor** comprehension frequently with group questions and individual instruction. • **Model** strategies while guiding students in completing the activities and prompts in the *Reader's Notebook,* as well as the graphic organizers. • **Practice** skills and **monitor** mastery with the *Reading Kit* worksheets.	• *Real-World Writing Journal,* Lesson 5, pp. 18–21 • *Reader's Notebook: Adapted Version,* adapted instruction and summary **EL** *Reader's Notebook: English Learner's Version,* adapted instruction and summary • Reading Skill Graphic Organizer A, *Graphic Organizer Transparencies,* p. 20 • Literary Analysis Graphic Organizer A, *Graphic Organizer Transparencies,* p. 23 • *Reading Kit,* Practice worksheets, pp. 26, 30, 36, 38, 46	• *Real-World Writing Journal,* Lesson 6, pp. 22–25 • *Reader's Notebook: Adapted Version,* adapted instruction and adapted selection **EL** *Reader's Notebook: English Learner's Version,* adapted instruction and adapted selection • Reading Skill Graphic Organizer A, *Graphic Organizer Transparencies,* p. 21 • Literary Analysis Graphic Organizer A, *Graphic Organizer Transparencies,* p. 24 • *Reading Kit,* Practice worksheets, pp. 26, 30, 36, 38, 46
Monitor Progress [A]	**Monitor** student progress with the differentiated curriculum-based assessment in the *Unit Resources* and in the *Reading Kit.*	• Selection Test A, *Unit 1 Resources,* pp. 146–148 • *Reading Kit,* Assess worksheets pp. 27, 31, 37, 39, 47	• Selection Test A, *Unit 1 Resources,* pp. 167–169 • *Reading Kit,* Assess worksheets, pp. 27, 31, 37, 39, 47

TIER 3 Tier 3 intervention may require consultation with the student's special-education or dyslexia specialist. For additional support, see the Tier 2 activities and resources listed above.

One-on-one teaching   Group work   Whole class instruction   Independent work   [A] Assessment

For a complete guide to selection support, including support for Advanced students, see the Overview of Resources in the frontmatter.

✓ All Summer in a Day
✓✓ Suzy and Leah

RESOURCES FOR:
- **L1** Special-Needs Students
- **L2** Below-Level Students (Tier 2)
- **L3** On-Level Students (Tier 1)
- **L4** Advanced Students (Tier 1)
- **EL** English Learners
- **All** All Students

Vocabulary/Fluency/Prior Knowledge

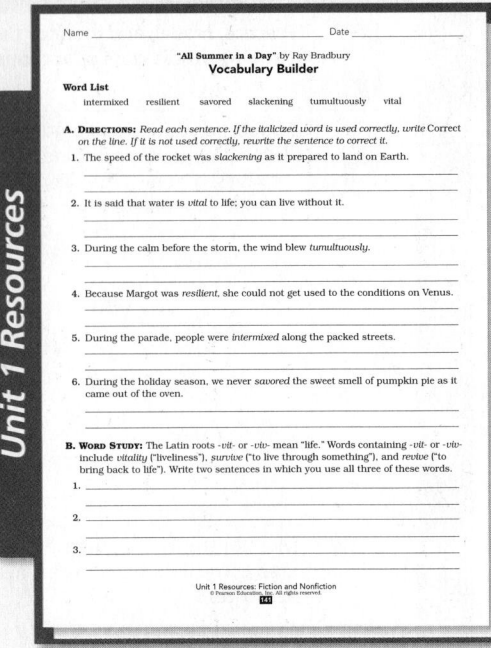

All Vocabulary Builder, pp. 141, 159

Also available for these selections:
- **EL** **L1** **L2** Vocabulary Warm-ups A and B, pp. 134–135, 152–153
- **EL** **L1** **L2** Reading Warm-ups A and B, pp. 136–137, 154–155
- **All** Writing About the Big Question, pp. 138, 156

Reader's Notebooks

Pre- and postreading pages for both selections, as well as "Suzy and Leah," appear in an interactive format in the *Reader's Notebooks.* Each *Notebook* is differentiated for a different group of learners. The selections in the Adapted and English Learner's versions are abridged.

- **L2** **L3** *Reader's Notebook*
- **L1** *Reader's Notebook: Adapted Version*
- **EL** *Reader's Notebook: English Learner's Version*
- **EL** *Reader's Notebook: Spanish Version*

© *Common Core Companion*

Additional instruction and practice for each Common Core State Standard

Selection Support

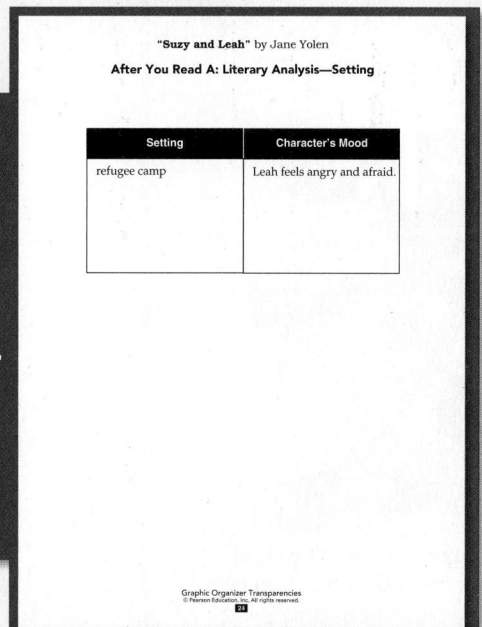

"Suzy and Leah" by Jane Yolen

After You Read A: Literary Analysis—Setting

Setting	Character's Mood
refugee camp	Leah feels angry and afraid.

EL L1 L2 Literary Analysis: Graphic Organizer A, pp. 23, 24

Also available for these selections:

EL L1 L2 Reading: Graphic Organizer A, pp. 20, 21 (partially filled in)

EL L3 Reading: Graphic Organizer B, p. 22

EL L3 Literary Analysis: Graphic Organizer B, p. 25

Skills Development/Extension

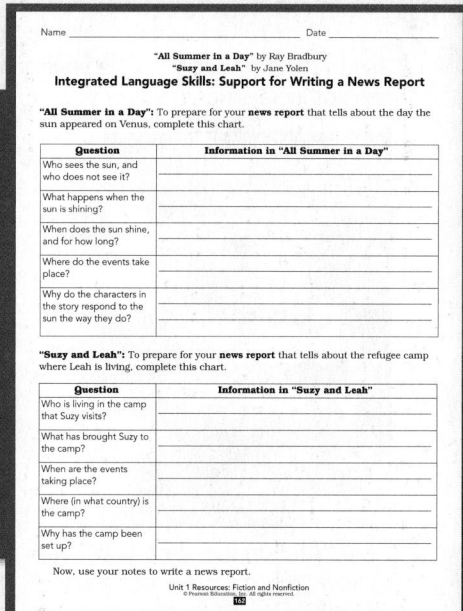

Name _____ Date _____

"All Summer in a Day" by Ray Bradbury
"Suzy and Leah" by Jane Yolen
Integrated Language Skills: Support for Writing a News Report

"All Summer in a Day": To prepare for your **news report** that tells about the day the sun appeared on Venus, complete this chart.

Question	Information in "All Summer in a Day"
Who sees the sun, and who does not see it?	
What happens when the sun is shining?	
When does the sun shine, and for how long?	
Where do the events take place?	
Why do the characters in the story respond to the sun the way they do?	

"Suzy and Leah": To prepare for your **news report** that tells about the refugee camp where Leah is living, complete this chart.

Question	Information in "Suzy and Leah"
Who is living in the camp that Suzy visits?	
What has brought Suzy to the camp?	
When are the events taking place?	
Where (in what country) is the camp?	
Why has the camp been set up?	

Now, use your notes to write a news report.

EL L3 L4 Support for Writing, p. 162

Also available for these selections:

All Reading: Author's Purpose, pp. 139, 157

All Literary Analysis: Setting pp. 140, 158

L4 Enrichment, pp. 142, 160

EL L3 L4 Grammar, p. 161

L3 L4 Support for Extend Your Learning, p. 163

Assessment

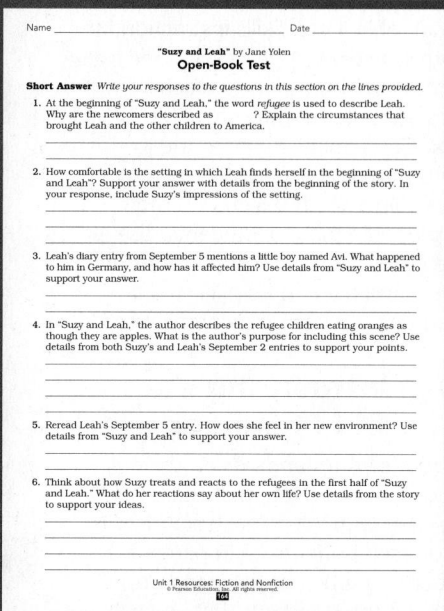

Name _____ Date _____

"Suzy and Leah" by Jane Yolen
Open-Book Test

Short Answer *Write your responses to the questions in this section on the lines provided.*

1. At the beginning of "Suzy and Leah," the word *refugee* is used to describe Leah. Why are the newcomers described as ___? Explain the circumstances that brought Leah and the other children to America.

2. How comfortable is the setting in which Leah finds herself in the beginning of "Suzy and Leah"? Support your answer with details from the beginning of the story. In your response, include Suzy's impressions of the setting.

3. Leah's diary entry from September 5 mentions a little boy named Avi. What happened to him in Germany, and how has it affected him? Use details from "Suzy and Leah" to support your answer.

4. In "Suzy and Leah," the author describes the refugee children eating oranges as though they are apples. What is the author's purpose for including this scene? Use details from both Suzy's and Leah's September 2 entries to support your points.

5. Reread Leah's September 5 entry. How does she feel in her new environment? Use details from "Suzy and Leah" to support your answer.

6. Think about how Suzy treats and reacts to the refugees in the first half of "Suzy and Leah." What do her reactions say about her own life? Use details from the story to support your ideas.

All Open-Book Test, pp. 143–145, 164–166

Also available for these selections:

EL L1 L2 Selection Test A, pp. 146–148, 167–169

EL L3 L4 Selection Test B, pp. 149–151, 170–172

PHLit Online!
www.PHLitOnline.com

Online Resources: All print materials are also available online.

- complete narrated selection text
- a thematically related video with writing prompt
- an interactive graphic organizer
- highlighting feature
- access to all student print resources, adapted to individual student needs
- Spanish and English summaries
- adapted selection translations in Spanish

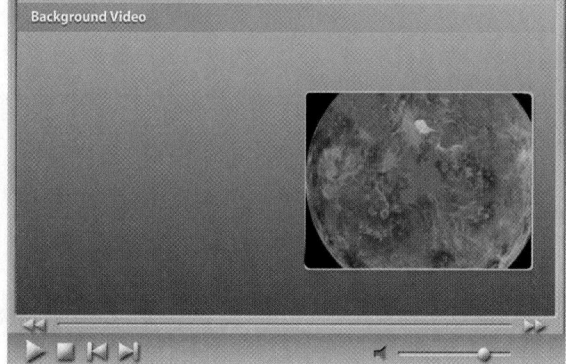

Background Video

Also available:

Get Connected! (thematic video with writing prompt)
All videos are available in Spanish.

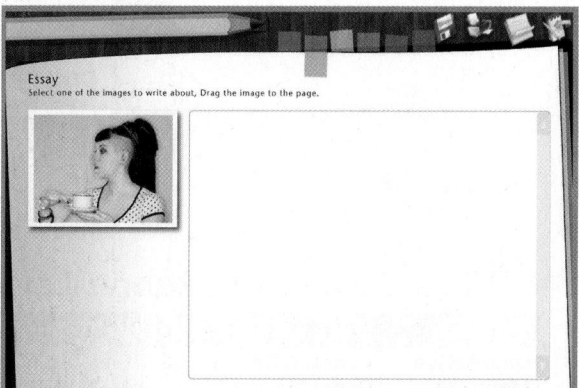

Writer's Journal (with graphics feature)

Also available:

Vocabulary Central (tools, activities, and songs for studying vocabulary)

❶ Leveled Texts

You may use either "All Summer in a Day" or "Suzy and Leah" to meet the lesson objectives. Skills instruction for both selections appears on p. 99. Choose one selection to teach (or choose to teach both). The Text Complexity Rubric at the bottom of this page will help you determine which selection is more appropriate for your students. Use the Reader and Task Suggestions on the facing page to help all students read text of increasing complexity.

❷ ⓒ Introducing the CCS Standards

Introduce the standards on the student page. (Note that the lesson element with which each standard is addressed is identified in parentheses after the text of the standard.) Call out the standards that you will cover with the selections, explaining to students what each requires and how they will address it as they work through the selection you have chosen. Standards labeled "Spiral Review" are introduced in the Literary Analysis Workshop for this unit.

Before You Read

All Summer in a Day • Suzy and Leah

❶ ⓒ Leveled Texts

Build your skills and improve your comprehension of fiction with texts of increasing complexity.

Read **"All Summer in a Day"** to learn about a day when the sun shines briefly on the wet, dark planet Venus.

Read **"Suzy and Leah"** to find out what happens when two girls from very different backgrounds struggle to be friends.

❷ ⓒ Common Core State Standards

Meet these standards with either **"All Summer in a Day"** (p. 102) or **"Suzy and Leah"** (p. 114).

Reading Literature
3. Analyze how particular elements of a story or drama interact. *(Literary Analysis: Setting)*
Spiral Review: RL.7.2
Writing
2. Write informative/explanatory texts to examine a topic and convey ideas, concepts, and information through the selection, organization, and analysis of relevant content. *(Writing: News Report)*
Speaking and Listening
1.a. Come to discussions prepared, having read or researched material under study; explicitly draw on that preparation by referring to evidence on the topic, text, or issue to probe and reflect on ideas under discussion.
1.b. Follow rules for collegial discussions, track progress toward specific goals and deadlines, and define individual

roles as needed. **1.c.** Pose questions that elicit elaboration and respond to others' questions and comments with relevant observations and ideas that bring the discussion back on topic as needed. **1.d.** Acknowledge new information expressed by others and, when warranted, modify their own views. *(Speaking and Listening: Discussion)*
Language
4.b. Use common, grade-appropriate Greek or Latin affixes and roots as clues to the meaning of a word. *(Vocabulary: Word Study)*
6. Acquire and use accurately grade-appropriate general academic and domain-specific words and phrases; gather vocabulary knowledge when considering a word or phrase important to comprehension or expression. *(Vocabulary: Word Study)*

98 Fiction and Nonfiction

ⓒ Text Complexity Rubric: Leveled Texts

Text complexity is determined by both qualitative and quantitative measures. For this reason, the quantitative measure of a more complex selection may be lower than that of a more accessible selection.

		✓ All Summer in a Day	✓✓ Suzy and Leah
Qualitative Measures	Context/Knowledge Demands	Futuristic; human colonists on Venus 1 2 ③ 4 5	Refugee camp; 1940s; World War II persecution of Jews 1 2 3 ④ 5
	Structure/Language Conventionality and Clarity	Straightforward narrative; some long, impressionistic sentences; on-level vocabulary 1 2 ③ 4 5	Some British English usage; stream-of-consciousness syntax; on-level vocabulary 1 2 3 4 ⑤
	Levels of Meaning/ Purpose/Concept Level	Accessible concept (consequences of cruel behavior) 1 2 ③ 4 5	Accessible concept (learning from those who are different) 1 2 ③ 4 5
Quantitative Measures	Text Length	Word Count: 1,937	Word Count: 2,699
	Lexile	940L	590L
Overall Complexity		✓ **More accessible**	✓✓ **More complex**

❸ Reading Skill: Author's Purpose

Fiction writers may write for a variety of **purposes.** To achieve their purpose, writers use details that entertain, teach, call readers to action, or reflect on experiences. **Recognizing details that indicate the author's purpose** can give you a rich understanding of a literary work.

❹ Using the Strategy: Details Chart

As you read, use a **details chart** like the one below. Record details in the story that help you identify the author's purpose for writing.

Entertain	Teach	Reflect
Funny details or details that create interest	Explanations	Details that create a mood

❺ Literary Analysis: Setting

The **setting** of a story is the time and place of the action. In this example, the details in italics help establish the story's setting:

As *night fell,* the hungry raccoons roamed the *forest* for food.

- In some stories, setting is just a backdrop. The same story events could take place in a completely different setting.
- In other stories, setting is very important. It develops a specific atmosphere or mood in the story. The setting may even relate directly to the story's central **conflict,** or problem.

As you read, notice the details and information that build the setting. Then, decide whether the time and place of the story shapes the story's characters or events.

❸ Reading Skill
Author's Purpose

1. Introduce the skill, using the instruction on the student page.
2. Tell students that they will identify author's purpose as they read.

❹ Using the Strategy

Give students a copy of either **Reading Skill Graphic Organizer A** or **B** (*Graphic Organizer Transparencies,* pp. 20–22) to record details that help fulfill author's purpose as they read. Use the examples in **Reading Skill Graphic Organizer A,** which is partially filled in, to model the process of completing the organizer.

❺ Literary Analysis
Setting

1. Introduce the skill, using the instruction on the student page.
2. Tell students that they will note elements of setting as they read.

Think Aloud: Model the Skill

Model a way of understanding setting. Say to students:

As I read, I pay attention to clues the author presents about *where* and *when* the story takes place. As the author answers these questions, I think about how the setting affects the story. For example, the suspense in *Hansel and Gretel* is greater because it takes place in a forest that is dark and scary. The setting adds a tense layer to the mood or atmosphere that would not exist if the children were lost at noon on the street where they live.

Before You Read: All Summer in a Day • Suzy and Leah **99**

© Text Complexity: Reader and Task Suggestions

✓ All Summer in a Day		✓✓ Suzy and Leah	
Preparing to Read the Text	**Leveled Tasks**	**Preparing to Read the Text**	**Leveled Tasks**
• Refer to the Background on TE/SE p. 101 to discuss the conditions on Venus. • Discuss irony, pointing out that when readers know something characters do not, it adds a layer of complexity to a story. • Guide students to use Multidraft Reading strategies to deepen their comprehension.	*Levels of Meaning* If students will have difficulty with meaning, have them first read to identify details about the children's cruelty to Margot. Then, have them reread, taking notes about the unusual story setting. *Synthesizing* If students will not have difficulty with meaning, have them note as they read ways in which Bradbury uses setting to emphasize his theme of cruelty to outsiders. Discuss as a class.	• Using the Background note on SE p. 113, discuss challenges of making friends with someone with different experiences. • Discuss how alternating narrators might affect a story. • Guide students to use Multidraft Reading strategies to deepen their comprehension.	*Structure/Language* If students will have difficulty with narrative structure, have them read to recognize setting details. Then, have them reread, noting the contrast in how each girl's entries describe that setting. *Analyzing* If students will not have difficulty with narrative structure, have them note the ways in which the author varies language for each narrator to help convey the challenges of connecting across cultures.

① Writing About the Big Question

1. Review the assignment with the class.

2. Have students discuss how a person from the past might react to a description of a cell phone. Discuss why it may be difficult to convince a person of a truth the person has no experience of.

3. Have students complete the sentence starter. Review responses as a class. (**Sample response:** When we have <u>evidence</u> that something exists, but others don't believe us, we can try to convince them.)

4. Remind students that their answers will help them think about the Big Question, "What is the best way to find the truth?"

While You Read

Tell students that as they read, they should consider how Margot's special knowledge causes others to treat her.

② Vocabulary

1. Have students preview the selection vocabulary.

2. For each word, have students say the word aloud.

3. Then, use the word in a sentence that defines the word.

4. Finally, repeat your definitional sentence or a similar sentence with the word missing and have the class "fill in the blank" chorally. Here are some examples:

If something is <u>vital</u>, it is necessary and very important. For people everywhere, having food and shelter is [students say "vital"].

When something is <u>resilient</u>, it keeps its shape after being stretched. A rubber band that stretches without breaking is [students say "resilient"].

③ Word Study

1. Introduce the skill, using the instruction in the box.

2. Point out the related word *vitamin* in the definition of *vital* on the student page. Ask students to explain how the root contributes to the meaning of *vitamin*. (**Answer:** Vitamins are substances necessary for life.)

100

What is the best way to find the *truth?*

RAY BRADBURY · ALL Summer in a Day

① Writing About the Big Question

In "All Summer in a Day," a group of students live on a planet where it rains all the time. Only one girl remembers seeing the sun because she once lived on Earth. Use this sentence starter to develop your ideas about the Big Question.

When we have **evidence** that something exists, but others don't believe us, we can _____.

While You Read Look for ways the author shows that Margot is treated differently by the others because of what she knows.

② Vocabulary

Read each word and its definition. Decide whether you know the word well, know it a little bit, or do not know it at all. After you read, see how your knowledge of each word has increased.

- **intermixed** (in´ tər mikst´) *adj.* mixed together (p. 103) *All of the puzzle pieces were <u>intermixed</u>.* intermix *v.* intermixing *v.*

- **slackening** (slak´ ən iŋ) *adj.* easing; becoming less active (p. 104) *The dying man's strength was <u>slackening</u>.* slacken *v.* slacker *n.* slack *adj.*

- **vital** (vīt´ 'l) *adj.* extremely important or necessary (p. 106) *Food and water are <u>vital</u> for survival.* vitally *adv.* vitality *n.* vitamin *n.*

- **tumultuously** (tōō mul´ chōō əs lē) *adv.* noisily and violently (p. 108) *The angry crows protested <u>tumultuously</u>.* tumult *n.* tumultuous *adj.*

- **resilient** (ri zil´ yənt) *adj.* able to spring back into shape (p. 108) *Rubber is a <u>resilient</u> material.* resilience *n.* resiliency *n.*

- **savored** (sā´ vərd) *v.* tasted or experienced with delight (p. 109) *Eric <u>savored</u> his hot fudge sundae.* savor *v.* savory *adj.*

100 Fiction and Nonfiction

③ Word Study

The **Latin root -*vit*-** or -*viv*- means "life."

In this story, Margot's parents believe it is **vital**, or extremely important for her life, for Margot to return to Earth.

Vocabulary Development

Vocabulary Knowledge Rating
Create a **Vocabulary Knowledge Rating Chart** (*Professional Development Guidebook*, p. 33) for this selection. Include the selection vocabulary and the Big Question word that appears in the Writing About the Big Question sentence starter on this page. (The Big Question vocabulary is introduced on pp. 2–3).

Give students a copy of the chart. Read the words aloud, and have students mark their rating in the Before Reading column. Urge them to be alert to these words as they read and discuss the selection.

Tally how many students think they know a word to gauge how much instruction to provide. As students read and discuss the selection, point out the words and their context.

 **Vocabulary Central,** featuring tools, activities, and songs for studying vocabulary, is available online at **www.PHLitOnline.com.**

Meet
Ray Bradbury
(b. 1920)

Author of
ALL SUMMER IN A DAY

As a boy, Ray Bradbury loved magicians, circuses, and science-fiction stories. He began writing his own imaginative tales and by age seventeen had his first story published in a magazine called *Imagination!*

A Science-Fiction Wonder In 1950, Bradbury won fame for his book of science-fiction stories called *The Martian Chronicles.* One story describes how a group of Earthlings struggle on the rainy world of Venus. Bradbury began to wonder how a child might react to the sun's brief appearance on Venus. Four years later, he answered his own question by writing "All Summer in a Day."

DiD YOU KNOW?
Many of Bradbury's stories were adopted for the television series *The Twilight Zone.*

❹ BACKGROUND FOR THE STORY

Venus

"All Summer in a Day" is set on Venus, the second planet from the sun. Today, we know that Venus has a surface temperature of almost 900° Fahrenheit. In 1950, when Ray Bradbury wrote this story, some scientists believed that the clouds of Venus concealed a watery world. That information may have led Bradbury to create a setting of soggy jungles and constant rain.

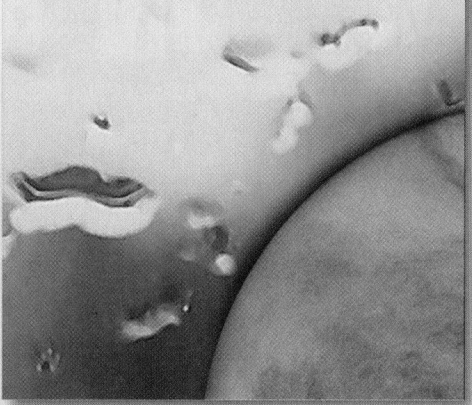

All Summer in a Day **101**

⑭ Critical Viewing

Possible response: The bright colors express the excitement of the children as they play outside for the first time.

⑮ Critical Thinking

Evaluate

1. Have students read the bracketed text, continuing on to p. 109.

2. **Ask:** Why do you think the author uses the word *animals* to describe the children?
Possible responses: He may use the word to emphasize how free the children feel and how their bodies are responding to this freedom. He may use the word to remind readers of the children's cruelty toward Margot.

3. **Ask:** In your opinion, does thinking of the children as *animals* help justify or excuse their cruel behavior, or does it make them seem more guilty?
Possible responses: It helps excuse their behavior because it is natural for animals to turn on weaker animals in a frenzy. It makes them seem even more guilty, because they have chosen to do something less than human.

Vocabulary

tumultuously
(tōō mul´ chōō əs lē) *adv.* noisily and violently

resilient
(ri zil´ yənt) *adj.* able to spring back into shape

⑭ ▼ **Critical Viewing**
Do you think this picture illustrates emotions that the children feel while playing outside? Why or why not? **[Connect]**

They stopped running and stood in the great jungle that covered Venus, that grew and never stopped growing, tumultuously, even as you watched it. It was a nest of octopi, clustering up great arms of fleshlike weed, wavering, flowering in this brief spring. It was the color of rubber and ash, this jungle, from the many years without sun. It was the color of stones and white cheeses and ink, and it was the color of the moon.

The children lay out, laughing, on the jungle mattress, and heard it sigh and squeak under them, resilient and alive. They ran among the trees, they slipped and fell, they pushed each other, they played hide-and-seek and tag, but most of all they squinted at the sun until tears ran down their faces, they put their hands up to that yellowness and that amazing blueness and they breathed of the fresh, fresh air and listened and listened to the silence which suspended them in a blessed sea of no sound and no motion. They looked

⑮

108 Fiction and Nonfiction

Vocabulary Development

Vocabulary Knowledge Rating
When students have finished reading and discussing "All Summer in a Day," have them take out their **Vocabulary Knowledge Rating Chart** for this selection. Read the words aloud once more and have students rate their knowledge of the words again in the After Reading column. Clarify any words that are still problematic. Have students write their own definition and example or sentence in the appropriate column. Then have students complete the Vocabulary Practice activities at the end of the selection. Encourage students to use the words in further discussion and written work about the selection. Remind them that they will be accountable for these words on the **Selection Test,** *Unit 1 Resources,* pp. 146–148 or 149–151.

at everything and savored everything. Then, wildly, like animals escaped from their caves, they ran and ran in shouting circles. They ran for an hour and did not stop running.

And then—

In the midst of their running one of the girls wailed.

Everyone stopped.

The girl, standing in the open, held out her hand.

"Oh, look, look," she said, trembling.

They came slowly to look at her opened palm.

In the center of it, cupped and huge, was a single raindrop.

She began to cry, looking at it.

They glanced quietly at the sky.

"Oh, Oh."

A few cold drops fell on their noses and their cheeks and their mouths. The sun faded behind a stir of mist. A wind blew cool around them. They turned and started to walk back toward the underground house, their hands at their sides, their smiles vanishing away.

A boom of thunder startled them and like leaves before a new hurricane, they tumbled upon each other and ran. Lightning struck ten miles away, five miles away, a mile, a half mile. The sky darkened into midnight in a flash.

They stood in the doorway of the underground for a moment until it was raining hard. Then they closed the door and heard the gigantic sound of the rain falling in tons and avalanches, everywhere and forever. ●

"Will it be seven more years?"

"Yes. Seven."

Then one of them gave a little cry.

"Margot!"

"What?"

"She's still in the closet where we locked her."

"Margot."

They stood as if someone had driven them, like so many stakes, into the floor. They looked at each other and then looked away. They glanced out at the world that was raining now and raining and raining steadily. They could not meet each other's glances. Their faces were solemn and pale. They looked at their hands and feet, their faces down.

Vocabulary
savored (sā′ vərd)
v. tasted or experienced with delight

Setting
How does the change in the weather affect the children's mood?

Spiral Review
Theme What details hint at the importance of the setting to the story? How does the setting relate to a possible theme?

17 ✓ **Reading Check**
What do the children do when the sun comes out?

16 Setting

1. Have a volunteer read aloud the second bracketed passage.

   Remind students that the setting often develops a specific atmosphere or mood in a story. Have students think about the physical sensations Bradbury describes as the rain begins to fall.

2. **Ask** the Setting question on this page.
   Answer: The change in the weather dampens the children's mood. It makes them sad and miserable.

Spiral Review

Theme

1. Remind students that they studied the concept of theme in the Unit 1 Literary Analysis Workshop (pp. 4–21).

2. **Ask** students the first Spiral Review question.

   Possible response: The author writes a lot about how the rain sounds and how different the world is when the sun comes out.

3. **Ask** students the second Spiral Review question.

   Possible response: If the story were not set on Venus, Margot would not be so different from the other children.

17 Reading Check

Possible response: They play enthusiastically and wildy, like animals.

Concept Connector

Anticipation Guide
Have students return to their **Anticipation Guides** and respond to the statements again in the After Reading column. They may do this individually or in their original pairs or groups. Then, lead a class discussion to probe for ideas that students have learned that confirm or invalidate each statement. Encourage students to cite specific details, quotations, or other evidence from the text to support their responses to each statement.

Reading Skill Graphic Organizer
Ask students to review the graphic organizers they completed to identify the author's purpose while reading. Show them **Reading Skill Graphic Organizer A** (*Graphic Organizer Transparencies,* p. 20) as an example. Then, have students share their graphic organizers.

? **Writing About the Big Question**
Have students compare their responses to the sentence starter they completed before reading the story with their ideas afterward. Ask them to explain whether their thoughts have changed.

Author's Purpose

Have students read the bracketed passage. **Ask** students the Author's Purpose question. **Possible response:** Details include the children's whispers, their slow motions, the sound of the thunder, and the blue reflections of lightning on their faces. These details suggest that the author's purpose is to show readers the terrible consequences of being insensitive or cruel to those who seem different.

ASSESS

Answers

Critical Thinking

Before students respond, you may wish to have them write a brief objective summary of the selection. As they answer the questions below, remind them to support their answers with evidence from the text.

1. (a) Margot lived on Earth. (b) The children reject Margot's description of it because they have never seen the sun.

2. (a) The children want the teacher to let them outside. (b) William is the "leader" of the class. (c) The children go along because they dislike Margot. They may feel less responsibility because it was William's idea, not theirs.

3. (a) The children cannot look at each other. (b) They feel bad when they realize that Margot, who longed for the sun more than any of them, didn't get to see it. (c) **Possible response:** The children learn that people should try to accept each other's differences and treat each other kindly.

4. (a) **Possible responses:** She may withdraw from them even further. (b) Her frail, quiet nature suggests this. (c) Encourage students to consider different responses before they decide on one.

5. **Possible response:** Margot would have been able to see the sun and the children would not have felt guilty for locking her in the closet.

Author's Purpose
What details here help to reveal the author's purpose? Explain.

"Margot."

One of the girls said, "Well . . .?"

No one moved.

"Go on," whispered the girl.

They walked slowly down the hall in the sound of cold rain. They turned through the doorway to the room in the sound of the storm and thunder, lightning on their faces, blue and terrible. They walked over to the closet door slowly and stood by it.

Behind the closet door was only silence.

They unlocked the door, even more slowly, and let Margot out.

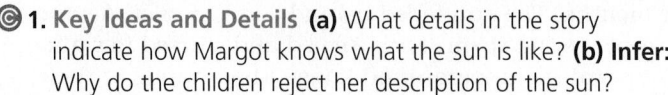

Critical Thinking

Cite textual evidence to support your responses.

1. **Key Ideas and Details (a)** What details in the story indicate how Margot knows what the sun is like? **(b) Infer:** Why do the children reject her description of the sun?

2. **Key Ideas and Details (a)** Why do the children want the teacher to hurry back to the classroom at the beginning of the story? **(b) Infer:** Who is the "leader" of the class when the teacher is out of the room? **(c) Draw Conclusions:** Why do the children go along with the prank that is played on Margot?

3. **Key Ideas and Details (a)** How do the children react when they realize that Margot missed the sun because of their prank? **(b) Draw Conclusions:** Why do you think they react as they do? **(c) Generalize:** What might the children have learned from their experiences?

4. **Integration of Knowledge and Ideas (a) Speculate:** How do you think Margot will respond to the children after the incident? **(b) Support:** Why do you think so? **(c) Discuss:** In a small group, discuss your responses. As a group, choose one answer to share with the class.

5. **Integration of Knowledge and Ideas** How would the story be different if the children had believed Margot when she told them about the sun? *[Connect to the Big Question: What is the best way to find the truth?]*

Assessment Resources

Unit 1 Resources

L1 L2 EL **Selection Test A,** pp. 146–148. Administer Test A to less advanced readers.

L3 L4 EL **Selection Test B,** pp. 149–151. Administer Test B to on-level and more advanced students.

L3 L4 **Open-Book Test,** pp. 143–145. As an alternative, give the Open-Book Test.

All Customizable Test Bank

All Self-tests
Students may prepare for the **Selection Test** by taking the **Self-test** online.

 All assessment resources are available at www.PHLitOnline.com.

Reading Skill: Author's Purpose

1. What are two things the author might have wished to teach his audience through this story?

2. (a) In your own words, what was the author's main **purpose** in writing this story? **(b)** Which details support your answer?

Literary Analysis: Setting

3. Key Ideas and Details How does the **setting** of this story affect the characters and events?

4. Key Ideas and Details Using a chart like the one shown, give two examples from the story to show how setting affects the story's mood.

Setting	Story's Mood

Vocabulary

Acquisition and Use An **analogy** shows a relationship between a pair of words or phrases. Use a word from the vocabulary list on page 100 to complete each analogy. Your choice should create a word pair whose relationship matches the relationship between the first two words or phrases.

1. *More* is to *increasing* as *less* is to _____.

2. *Beautiful day* is to *enjoyed* as *good meal* is to _____.

3. *Singing* is to *optional* as *breathing* is to _____.

4. *Quickly* is to *rapidly* as *noisily* is to _____.

5. *One person* is to *separate* as *crowd* is to _____.

6. *Steel* is to *unbreakable* as *rubber* is to _____.

Word Study Use the context of the sentences and what you know about the **Latin root -vit- or -viv-** to explain your answer to each question.

1. If a doctor *revitalizes* a patient, does the patient live or die?

2. Would a *vivacious* dog lie down when you enter the room?

Word Study

The **Latin root -vit-** or **-viv-** means "life."

Apply It Explain how the root contributes to the meanings of these words. Consult a dictionary if necessary.
survive
vitamin
revive

ASSESS/EXTEND
Answers

Reading Skill

1. Possible response: The author might have wished to teach his audience to be sensitive to people who seem different and to consider the possible outcomes of an action before taking that action.

2. (a) Possible response: The author's main purpose may have been to entertain his audience with a story that also teaches a lesson. (b) The rainy environment, the suspense about the sun's arrival, the children's eagerness, and their treatment of Margot all create interest.

Literary Analysis

3. Possible response: The rainy setting contributes to the way the children behave, which is similar to the actions of animals trapped in a cage and eager to be free.

4. Possible response: *Setting*—the classroom in the underground house on Venus, in the rain; before the sun comes out for the first time in seven years; *Story's Mood*—The children are eager to see the sun; the mood is one of excitement; *Setting*—the outdoors when the sun finally comes out on Venus; *Story's Mood*—The children are excited and happy, but also feel guilty and ashamed about Margot's imprisonment and absence; the mood is heavy and sad.

For other sample answers, see *Graphic Organizer Transparencies,* **Literary Analysis Graphic Organizer A, p. 23,** and the **Additional Answers** section.

Vocabulary
Acquisition and Use
Sample answers:

1. slackening
2. savored
3. vital
4. tumultuously
5. intermixed
6. resilient

Word Study
Sample answers:

1. If a doctor in an emergency room *revitalizes* her patient, the patient is given new energy and <u>lives</u>.

2. No, a <u>vivacious</u> dog would be full of <u>life</u> and energy so would not lie down when you enter the room.

Word Study: Apply It
Sample answers: To *survive* is to stay <u>alive</u>. A *vitamin* is a substance that helps you <u>live</u> and be healthy. To *revive* someone is to bring him or her back to <u>life</u>.

111

Skills instruction for the **Reading Skill** and the **Literary Analysis** concepts for this selection appears on p. 99.

❶  Writing About the Big Question

1. Review the assignment with the class.

2. Lead students in discussing ways in which good or bad experiences shape the way people react to others. Have them explore the misunderstandings that can result when people's past experiences guide their reactions in a new and different situation.

3. Have students complete the sentence starter. Review responses as a class. (**Sample response:** When we have <u>insight</u> about someone's life, we can understand their feelings and actions.)

4. Remind students that their answers will help them think about the Big Question, "What is the best way to find the truth?"

While You Read

Tell students that as they read, they should look for ways that the author reveals truth about each character and ways that she weaves historical details into the story.

❷ Vocabulary

1. Have students preview the selection vocabulary.

2. For each word, have students say the word aloud.

3. Then, use the word in a sentence that defines the word.

4. Finally, repeat your definitional sentence or a similar sentence with the word missing and have the class "fill in the blank" chorally. Here is one example:

   When something is <u>permanent</u>, it will last forever. The color of your eyes will never change; it is [students say "permanent"].

❸ Word Study

1. Introduce the skill, using the instruction in the box.

2. Ask students to use the meaning of *manere* to explain why chemical and long-lasting curling of a person's hair is called a <u>permanent</u>. (**Possible response:** A permanent helps hair "remain" in place.)

112

❶ What is the best way to find the *truth?*

Writing About the Big Question

In "Suzy and Leah," two girls struggle to understand each other until the truth is revealed about one of their lives. Use this sentence starter to develop your ideas about the Big Question.

   When we have **insight** about someone's life, we can _____.

While You Read Look for ways that Yolen reveals the truth about each of these characters—and the way she weaves true historical details into the story.

❷ Vocabulary

Read each word and its definition. Decide whether you know the word well, know it a little bit, or do not know it at all. After you read, see how your knowledge of each word has increased.

- **refugee** (ref´ yoo jē´) *n.* person who flees home or country to seek shelter from war or cruelty (p. 115) *The refugee crossed the border into safety. refugees n. refuge n.*

- **penned** (pend) *v.* locked up in a small enclosure (p. 115) *The horses were penned in a corral. pen v. pen n.*

- **porridge** (pôr´ ij) *n.* soft food made of cereal boiled in water or milk (p. 116) *Oatmeal is a type of porridge.*

- **cupboard** (kub´ ərd) *n.* cabinet with shelves for cups, plates, and food (p. 117) *Her grandmother built a special cupboard for her collection of teacups. cupboards n.*

- **falsely** (fôls´ lē) *adv.* incorrectly; untruthfully (p. 118) *Vicky insisted she had been falsely accused. false adj. falsehood n.*

- **permanent** (pur´ mə nənt) *adj.* lasting for all time (p. 120) *His accident left a permanent scar. permanently adj. permanence n.*

❸ Word Study

The **Latin root word** *manere* means to "remain" or "dwell."

In this story, Suzy describes Leah as having a **permanent** frown, or a frown that remains on her face always.

112 Fiction and Nonfiction

Vocabulary Development

Vocabulary Knowledge Rating

Create a **Vocabulary Knowledge Rating Chart** (*Professional Development Guidebook,* p. 33) for this selection. Include the selection vocabulary and the Big Question word that appears in the Writing About the Big Question sentence starter on this page. (The Big Question vocabulary is introduced on pp. 2–3.)

Give students a copy of the chart. Read the words aloud, and have students mark their rating in the Before Reading column. Urge them to be alert to these words as they read and discuss the selection.

Tally how many students think they know a word to gauge how much instruction to provide. As students read and discuss the selection, point out the words and their context.

PHLit Online! **Vocabulary Central,** featuring tools, activities, and songs for studying vocabulary, is available online at **www.PHLitOnline.com.**

Author of
Suzy and Leah

Jane Yolen has written more than two hundred books. "I am a person in love with story and with words," says Yolen. "I wake up, and I have to write."

Finding Inspiration Yolen is never at a loss for ideas. Whenever an idea strikes her, she jots it down and places it in an "idea file" that she keeps. Then, when searching for a new story to write, she simply consults the file. "I don't care whether the story is real or fantastical," she explains. "I tell the story that needs to be told."

A Personal Interest Although Yolen is known primarily for her fantasy stories, her Jewish heritage inspired her to write "Suzy and Leah," the story of a Holocaust survivor. Yolen wrote about the Holocaust so that her own children could understand and remember what happened to Jews in Europe during World War II.

Did You Know?
Jane Yolen's storytelling career began in first grade, when she wrote a class musical about vegetables.

④ BACKGROUND FOR THE STORY

War Refugee Board
"Suzy and Leah" is based on actual events. The United States established the War Refugee Board in January 1944. The goal of the Board was to rescue victims of Nazi persecution from death in German-occupied Europe. In one rescue effort, 982 people from eighteen countries were brought to a refugee camp in Oswego, New York.

Suzy and Leah 113

❹ Background

Nazi Germany

The Nazi party took power in Germany in 1933, when Adolf Hitler became the head of the German government. The Nazis proclaimed the Germans to be the "master race" and blamed specific groups of people for the country's earlier economic problems, as well as Germany's defeat in World War I. Europe's Jews bore the brunt of this blame, suffering most and dying in the largest numbers. Jewish families such as Leah's were terrorized, taken from their homes, forced into labor, or sent to concentration camps, where millions were gassed or died of starvation and disease.

◉ Multidraft Reading

This icon ● marks natural pauses in the selection. To assist struggling readers and to deepen reading for all, assign the text in "chunks," following the icons, and apply multidraft reading protocols. For each reading, have students set the purpose indicated:

- **First reading**—identifying key ideas and details and answering any Reading Checks.
- **Second reading**—analyzing craft and structure and responding to the side-column prompts.
- **Third reading**—integrating knowledge and ideas, connecting to other texts and the world, and answering the end-of-selection questions.

For more guidance, refer to the *Classroom Strategies and Teaching Routines* card on multidraft reading.

For more about the author, practice with the selection vocabulary, or more background, go online at **www.PHLitOnline.com.**

21

1

1.

2.

3.

Cri
Bef...
to h...
sum...
ans...
the...
evic...

1.

2.

3.

Co
Stu...
An...
the...

Sn
Ha...
alo...
cha...
ner...
the...
exa...
pu...

2

Thi...
dia...
Jew...
in ...
19...
reli...
oth...
in I...
wh...
gir...
the...
pat...
be...
gro...

11   12

Conventions

1. Introduce the skill, using the instruction on the student page.
2. Discuss the examples in the chart.

Think Aloud: Model the Skill

Model the skill of choosing personal pronouns. Say to students:

> Let's say I want to replace a subject noun, such as *girl* in *The girl caught the frisbee.* I would use the subject pronoun *she: She caught the frisbee.* Now I want to replace an object noun, such as *girl* in *Mrs. Harris helped the girl,* I would use the object pronoun *her: Mrs. Harris helped her.* When I am unsure of which personal pronoun to use, I figure out if it will function as a subject or an object in the sentence. This helps me choose the correct pronoun in speaking and writing.

PH WRITING COACH | Grade 7

Students will find further instruction on and practice personal pronouns in Chapter 13, Section 2, and Chapter 22, Section 1.

Practice A

1. she; Margot
2. them; children
3. her; Margot
4. it; sun

Speaking Application
Sample answer: <u>She</u> was a very frail girl who looked as if <u>she</u> had been lost . . . .; "All a joke!" said the boy, and seized <u>her</u> roughly.

Practice B
Sample answers:

1. them; object; I saw them running across the field.
2. her; object; We saw her recently.
3. they; subject; They loved the movie.
4. she; subject; She sent me a hat and scarf.

Writing Application
Sample answer: Accept all reasonable responses.

Integrated Language Skills

All Summer in a Day • Suzy and Leah

Conventions: Personal Pronouns

A **personal pronoun** takes the place of a noun that names a person. Some personal pronouns take the place of the **subject**—the person doing the action. Other personal pronouns take the place of the **object**—the one receiving the action.

Pronouns, such as those listed in the chart below, are used every day in conversation. Writers use pronouns to avoid the awkwardness of repeating the same noun over and over.

Subject Pronouns	Object Pronouns
I, we, you, he, she, it, they	me, us, you, him, her, it, them

Practice A Identify the personal pronoun in each sentence. Then, identify the noun it replaces.

1. When Margot talked about the sun, she came to life.
2. The children waited for the sun to shine on them.
3. The students locked Margot in the closet and forgot about her.
4. When the sun came out, it made the children happy.

© Speaking Application Read "All Summer in a Day" to find two sentences with personal pronouns. Recite these sentences to a partner and identify the personal pronouns.

Practice B Identify the personal pronoun in each sentence. Then, tell whether it is a subject or object pronoun. Use each personal pronoun in a sentence of your own.

1. Suzy gave them oranges as a gift.
2. Leah did not like her at first.
3. They were in the same class.
4. Eventually, she began to understand Leah.

© Writing Application Write a dialogue in which two characters from the story you read discuss their experiences. Use at least two subject pronouns and two object pronouns.

PH WRITING COACH | Further instruction and practice are available in *Prentice Hall Writing Coach*.

Writing

 **Informative Text** Write a **news report** based on the story you read. Your report should describe either **(a)** the day the sun appeared on Venus, or **(b)** conditions at the refugee camp where Leah is living.

- First, list questions that your news report will answer. Write questions that ask *who, what, where, when, why,* and *how.*
- Before you write your report, answer each question. Use story details to help you gather information.
- Present the most important information in your opening paragraph. Then, write the rest of your report, based on the information you have collected.

Grammar Application Review your news report, looking for places where you can replace repeated nouns with personal pronouns.

Writing Workshop: *Work in Progress*

Prewriting for Narration Jot down a list of five people whom you know. Keep this People List in your portfolio. Refer to this list when you write your autobiographical narrative.

Speaking and Listening

 Comprehension and Collaboration With a partner, hold a **discussion** about the underlying message of the story you read. If you read "All Summer in a Day," discuss a lesson the selection taught you about treating others. If you read "Suzy and Leah," discuss how reading the story affected your understanding of the Holocaust.

Follow these steps to complete the assignment:

- Prepare by rereading the selection, keeping in mind the topic of your discussion. Jot down points that support your position.
- Listen carefully to your partner's points.
- Ask your partner questions to clarify his or her position. Look for evidence to support these ideas.
- Write down key points that you and your partner make.
- Identify the strongest points, and share them with the class.
- As a group, identify two lessons readers might learn from the story you read.

Common Core State Standards

W.7.2; SL.7.1.a–d; L.7.4.b, L.7.6
[For the full wording of the standards, see page 98.]

Use this prewriting activity to prepare for the **Writing Workshop** on page 176.

PHLit Online!
www.PHLitOnline.com
- Interactive graphic organizers
- Grammar tutorial
- Interactive journals

Integrated Language Skills **127**

Writing

1. Review the assignment, using the instruction on the student page.
2. To guide students in writing a news report, give them **Support for Writing,** p. 162 in *Unit 1 Resources.*
3. To evaluate students' informative texts, use the rubrics for **Generic (Holistic) Writing,** pp. 256–257 in *Professional Development Guidebook.* In addition, you might evaluate reports on their treatment of the questions *who, what, when, where, why,* and *how.*

Grammar Application

Have students check their drafts to make sure they have correctly replaced repeated nouns with the appropriate personal pronoun.

Six Traits Focus

✔ Ideas	Word Choice
✔ Organization	Sentence Fluency
Voice	Conventions

PH WRITING COACH Grade 7

Students will find further instruction on and practice with expository writing in Chapter 8.

Writing Workshop
Work in Progress

Have students save their completed People Lists in their portfolios. They will use the lists later as they continue this Work-in-Progress assignment (p. 151). These assignments prepare them to complete the Writing Workshop assignment (see pp. 176–183).

Speaking and Listening

1. Review the assignment, using the instruction on the student page.
2. Have students complete the **Support for Extend Your Learning** page (*Unit 1 Resources,* p. 163).

Teaching Resources

Unit 1 Resources
L3 L4 EL Integrated Language Skills: Grammar, p. 161
L3 L4 EL Support for Writing, p. 162
L3 L4 Support for Extend Your Learning, p. 163
L4 Enrichment, pp. 142, 160

Enriched Online Student Edition
Available under After You Read for this selection:
All Interactive Grammar Tutorial
L3 L4 Internet Research Activity

Professional Development Guidebook
Rubrics for Self-Assessment: Generic (Holistic) Writing, pp. 256–257

PHLit Online! All print and digital resources are available online at **www.PHLitOnline.com.** Online resources accessible to students are noted on the student page.

✓ My First Free Summer • ✓✓ *from* Angela's Ashes
Lesson Pacing Guide

DAY 1 Preteach

- © Administer the Reading and Vocabulary Warm-ups (*Unit 1 Resources*, pp. 174–176 or 192–194) as necessary.
- • Introduce the Reading Skill: Author's Purpose.
- © Introduce the Literary Analysis concept: Historical Context.
- • Distribute copies of the graphic organizer for the Reading Skill (*Graphic Organizer Transparencies*, pp. 26–28).
- • Distribute copies of the graphic organizer for Literary Analysis (*Graphic Organizer Transparencies*, pp. 29–31).
- © Teach the selection vocabulary.
- © Introduce the Word Study skill.

DAYS 2–3 Preteach/Teach

- © Build background with the Background feature.
- • Develop thematic vocabulary and thematic thinking with Writing About the Big Question.
- • Prepare students to read with the Activating Prior Knowledge activities (TE).
- • Informally monitor comprehension while students read.
- • Use the Reading Check questions to confirm comprehension.
- • Develop students' ability to determine the author's purpose using the Author's Purpose questions.
- © Develop students' understanding of historical context using the Historical Context questions.
- © Reinforce vocabulary with the Vocabulary notes.
- © Reinforce unit focus standards using the Spiral Review prompts.

DAY 4 Assess

- • Assess students' comprehension and mastery of the skills by having them answer the Critical Thinking, Reading Skill, and Literary Analysis questions.
- © Have students complete the Vocabulary Practice activities.
- © Have students complete the Word Study activities.

DAY 5 Extend/Assess

- • Have students complete the Conventions lesson.
- © Have students complete the Writing activity and write a letter. (You may assign as homework.)
- © Extend learning by having students complete the Speaking and Listening activity, an interview. As an alternative, assign them "Return to Humanity" or "Luol Deng: A True Winner" in *Reality Central*.
- • Administer Selection Test A or B (*Unit 1 Resources*, pp. 185–190 or 206–211).

© Common Core State Standards

Reading Informational Text 1. Cite several pieces of textual evidence to support analysis of what the text says explicitly as well as inferences drawn from the text.
2. Determine two or more central ideas in a text and analyze their development over the course of the text; provide an objective summary of the text.
3. Analyze the interactions between individuals, events, and ideas in a text.

Writing 2.b. Develop the topic with relevant facts, definitions, concrete details, quotations, or other information and examples.
2.c. Use appropriate transitions to create cohesion and clarify the relationships among ideas and concepts.

Speaking and Listening 1.c. Pose questions that elicit elaboration and respond to others' questions and comments with relevant observations and ideas.

Language 1. Demonstrate command of the conventions of standard English grammar and usage.
6. Acquire and use accurately grade-appropriate general academic and domain-specific words and phrases; gather vocabulary knowledge when considering a word or phrase important to comprehension or expression.

Additional Standards Practice
Common Core Companion, pp. 15–22; 97–104

Daily Block Scheduling
Each day in this Lesson Pacing Guide represents a 40–50 minute period. Teachers using block scheduling may combine days to revise pacing. In addition, teachers may differentiate and support core instruction by integrating components for extended and intensive support, as students require. See the Guide to Selected Leveled Resources (facing page).

Guide to Selected Leveled Resources

Tier 1 (students performing on level)

R T I Tier 1 (students performing on level)	✓ **More Accessible** **My First Free Summer**	✓✓ **More Complex** *from* Angela's Ashes
Warm Up — Practice, model, and monitor fluency, working with the whole class or in groups.	Vocabulary and Reading Warm-ups B, *Unit 1 Resources,* pp. 173–174, 176	Vocabulary and Reading Warm-ups B, *Unit 1 Resources,* pp. 191–192, 194
Comprehension/Skills — Support and monitor comprehension and skills development, having students complete the activities, graphic organizers, and interactive prompts independently or as a class.	• *Reader's Notebook,* adapted instruction and full selection • EL *Reader's Notebook: English Learner's Version,* adapted instruction and adapted selection • Reading Skill Graphic Organizer B, *Graphic Organizer Transparencies,* p. 28 • Literary Analysis Graphic Organizer B, *Graphic Organizer Transparencies,* p. 31	• *Reader's Notebook,* adapted instruction and summary • EL *Reader's Notebook: English Learner's Version,* adapted instruction and summary • Reading Skill Graphic Organizer B, *Graphic Organizer Transparencies,* p. 28 • Literary Analysis Graphic Organizer B, *Graphic Organizer Transparencies,* p. 31
Monitor Progress — Monitor student progress with the differentiated curriculum-based assessment in the *Unit Resources.*	• Selection Test B, *Unit 1 Resources,* pp. 188–190 • Open-Book Test, *Unit 1 Resources,* pp. 182–184	• Selection Test B, *Unit 1 Resources,* pp. 209–211 • Open-Book Test, *Unit 1 Resources,* pp. 203–205
Assess/Screen — • Assess student progress using Benchmark Test 2. • Preassess instructional needs using the Vocabulary in Context section of the test.	• Benchmark Test 2, *Unit 1 Resources,* pp. 235–242, including Vocabulary in Context diagnostic items	• Benchmark Test 2, *Unit 1 Resources,* pp. 235–242, including Vocabulary in Context diagnostic items

Tier 2 (students requiring intervention)

R T I Tier 2 (students requiring intervention)	✓ **More Accessible** **My First Free Summer**	✓✓ **More Complex** *from* Angela's Ashes
Warm Up — Practice, model, and monitor fluency in groups or with individuals.	• Vocabulary and Reading Warm-ups A, *Unit 1 Resources,* pp. 173–175 • *Reality Central,* "Return to Humanity" • *Hear It!* Audio CD (adapted text)	• Vocabulary and Reading Warm-ups A, *Unit 1 Resources,* pp. 191–193 • *Reality Central,* "Luol Deng: A True Winner" • *Hear It!* Audio CD
Comprehension/Skills — • Support and monitor comprehension and skills development, working in small groups or with individuals. • Pair students with more advanced peers and have them complete the writing activity in the *Real-World Writing Journal.* • As students complete the selection in the appropriate version of the *Reader's Notebook,* monitor comprehension frequently with group questions and individual instruction. • Model strategies while guiding students in completing the activities and prompts in the *Reader's Notebook,* as well as the graphic organizers. • Practice skills and monitor mastery with the *Reading Kit* worksheets.	• *Real-World Writing Journal,* Lesson • *Reader's Notebook: Adapted* Version, adapted instruction and adapted selection • EL *Reader's Notebook: English Learner's Version,* adapted instruction and adapted selection • Reading Skill Graphic Organizer A, *Graphic Organizer Transparencies,* p. 26 • Literary Analysis Graphic Organizer A, *Graphic Organizer Transparencies,* p. 29 • *Reading Kit,* Practice worksheets, pp. 26, 32, 36, 40	• *Real-World Writing Journal,* Lesson • *Reader's Notebook: Adapted* Version, adapted instruction and summary • EL *Reader's Notebook: English Learner's Version,* adapted instruction and summary • Reading Skill Graphic Organizer A, *Graphic Organizer Transparencies,* p. 27 • Literary Analysis Graphic Organizer A, *Graphic Organizer Transparencies,* p. 30 • *Reading Kit,* Practice worksheets, pp. 26, 32, 36, 40
Monitor Progress — Monitor student progress with the differentiated curriculum-based assessment in the *Unit Resources* and in the *Reading Kit.*	• Selection Test A, *Unit 1 Resources,* pp. 185–187 • *Reading Kit,* Assess worksheets pp. 27, 33, 37, 41	• Selection Test A, *Unit 1 Resources,* pp. 206–208 • *Reading Kit,* Assess worksheets, pp. 27, 33, 37, 41
Assess/Screen — • Assess student progress using Benchmark Test 2. • Preassess instructional needs using the Vocabulary in Context section of the test.	• Benchmark Test 2, *Unit 1 Resources,* pp. 235–242, including Vocabulary in Context diagnostic items	• Benchmark Test 2, *Unit 1 Resources,* pp. 235–242, including Vocabulary in Context diagnostic items

TIER 3 Tier 3 intervention may require consultation with the student's special-education or dyslexia specialist. For additional support, see the Tier 2 activities and resources listed above.

 One-on-one teaching   Group work   Whole class instruction   Independent work   A Assessment

For a complete guide to selections support, including support for Advanced students, see the Overview of Resources in the frontmatter.

❶ Leveled Texts

You may use either "My First Free Summer" or the excerpt from *Angela's Ashes* to meet the lesson objectives. Skills instruction for both selections appears on p. 128. Choose one selection to teach (or choose to teach both). The Text Complexity Rubric at the bottom of this page will help you determine which selection is more appropriate for your students. Use the Reader and Task Suggestions on the facing page to help all students read text of increasing complexity.

❷ ©️ Introducing the CCS Standards

Introduce the standards on the student page. (Note that the lesson element with which each standard is addressed is identified in parentheses after the text of the standard.) Call out the standards that you will cover with the selections, explaining to students what each requires and how they will address it as they work through the selection you have chosen. Standards labeled "Spiral Review" are introduced in the Literary Analysis Workshop for this unit.

Before You Read

My First Free Summer • *from* Angela's Ashes

❶ ©️ Leveled Texts

Build your skills and improve your comprehension of literary nonfiction with texts of increasing complexity.

Read **"My First Free Summer"** to find out how political events interfere with a girl's summer plans.

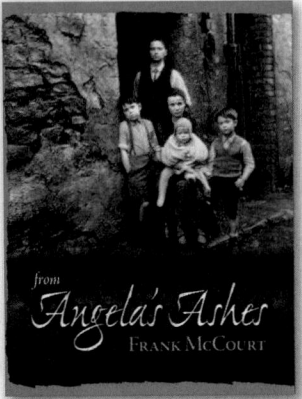

Read the excerpt from **Angela's Ashes** to learn how literature can connect people in times of trouble.

❷ ©️ Common Core State Standards

Meet these standards with either **"My First Free Summer"** (p. 132) or the excerpt from **Angela's Ashes** (p. 140).

Reading Informational Texts
1. Cite several pieces of textual evidence to support analysis of what the text says explicitly as well as inferences drawn from the text. *(Reading Skill: Author's Purpose)*
3. Analyze the interactions between individuals, events, and ideas in a text. *(Literary Analysis: Historical Context)*
Spiral Review: RI.7.2

Writing
2.b. Develop the topic with relevant facts, definitions, concrete details, quotations, or other information and examples. **2.c.** Use appropriate transitions to create cohesion and clarify the relationships among ideas and concepts. *(Writing: Letter)*

Speaking and Listening
1.c. Pose questions that elicit elaboration and respond to others' questions and comments with relevant observations and ideas that bring the discussion back on topic as needed. *(Speaking and Listening: Interview)*

Language
1. Demonstrate command of the conventions of standard English grammar and usage when writing or speaking. *(Conventions: Possessive Pronouns)*
6. Acquire and use accurately grade-appropriate general academic and domain-specific words and phrases; gather vocabulary knowledge when considering a word or phrase important to comprehension or expression. *(Vocabulary: Word Study)*

128 Fiction and Nonfiction

©️ Text Complexity Rubric: Leveled Texts

Text complexity is determined by both qualitative and quantitative measures. For this reason, the quantitative measure of a more complex selection may be lower than that of a more accessible selection.

		✓ **My First Free Summer**	✓✓ *from* **Angela's Ashes**
Qualitative Measures	**Context/Knowledge Demands**	Dominican Republic dictatorship; 1960s 1 2 3 ④ 5	Irish children's hospital; 1940s; disease and poverty 1 2 3 4 ⑤
	Structure/Language Conventionality and Clarity	Straightforward narrative; on-level vocabulary; some nested clauses; youthful diction and expressions 1 2 ③ 4 5	Unpunctuated dialogue; foreign dialect; stream-of-consciousness syntax; challenging vocabulary 1 2 3 4 ⑤
	Levels of Meaning/ Purpose/Concept Level	Accessible concepts (wish for freedom; confusion about adult activities) 1 2 ③ 4 5	Challenging concepts (illness and death; isolation from caring adults) 1 2 3 ④ 5
Quantitative Measures	**Text Length**	Word Count: 1,279	Word Count: 2,477
	Lexile	760L	1270L
Overall Complexity		✓ **More accessible**	✓✓ **More complex**

❸ Reading Skill: Author's Purpose

One way to determine the **author's purpose,** or reason, for writing a nonfiction work is to use **background information** that you already know about the author and topic. For example, knowing that an author was born outside the United States might help you determine that he or she wrote an essay to inform readers about his or her native country.

Another way to determine author's purpose is to look for details in the text that help you make inferences about author's purpose. For example, if an author provides detailed descriptions about a historical setting, you might infer that the author's purpose is to educate the reader.

❹ Using the Strategy: Author's Purpose Chart

As you read, use a chart like the one below to help you determine the author's purpose.

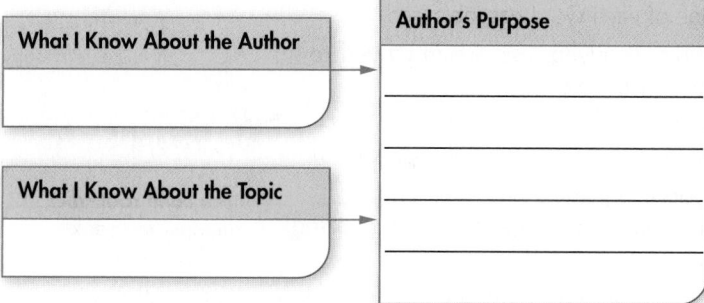

❺ Literary Analysis: Historical Context

When a literary work is based on real events and real people, the historical context can help you understand the action as well as the theme or message. **Historical context**—the actual political and social events and trends of the time—can explain why people act and think the way they do. As you read, look for factual details that link the people, events, and ideas in the text to a specific place and time period.

Before You Read: My First Free Summer • *from* Angela's Ashes **129**

PHLit Online!
www.PHLitOnline.com

Hear It!
• Selection summary audio
• Selection audio

See It!
• Get Connected video
• Background video
• More about the author
• Vocabulary flashcards

Do It!
• Interactive journals
• Interactive graphic organizers
• Self-test
• Internet activity
• Grammar tutorial
• Interactive vocabulary games

---

❸ Reading Skill
Author's Purpose
1. Introduce the skill, using the instruction on the student page.
2. Tell students that they will identify author's purpose as they read.

❹ Using the Strategy
Give students a copy of either **Reading Skill Graphic Organizer A** or **B** (*Graphic Organizer Transparencies,* pp. 26–28) to record details that will help them determine the author's purpose. Use the examples in **Reading Skill Graphic Organizer A,** which is partially filled in, to model the process of completing the organizer.

❺ Literary Analysis
Historical Context
1. Introduce the skill, using the instruction on the student page.
2. Tell students that they will note historical context as they read.

Think Aloud: Model the Skill

Model a way to interpret historical context. Say to students:

> To help me relate a narrative to its historical context, I first identify that context. I ask where and when in history the narrative takes place. I think of important events from that time and place. For example, if I read a story about the United States in the 1950s, I would think about the first space rocket launches and the birth of rock music. Thinking about these events might help me understand why the writer thinks of this time as a time of beginnings. They might also help me determine the narrative's main message.

ⓒ Text Complexity: Reader and Task Suggestions

✓ **My First Free Summer**		✓✓ *from* **Angela's Ashes**	
Preparing to Read the Text	**Leveled Tasks**	**Preparing to Read the Text**	**Leveled Tasks**
• Refer to Background note (TE/SE p. 131) to clarify historical events in Julia's community. • Discuss different ways that people can be free, referring to About the Selection (TE p. 132). • Guide students to use Multidraft Reading strategies to deepen their comprehension.	*Levels of Meaning* If students will have difficulty with meaning, have them read to identify details about Julia's personal progress toward a summer free of school. Then, have them reread, taking notes about how history changes her understanding of freedom. *Analyzing* If students will not have difficulty with meaning, have them note the ways in which Alvarez crafts young Julia's voice to reflect a country's wish for political freedom.	• Using the note on TE p. 139, discuss poverty in 1940s Ireland. • With students, practice strategies for reading unpunctuated dialogue and stream-of-consciousness syntax. • Guide students to use Multidraft Reading strategies to deepen their comprehension.	*Structure/Language* If students will have difficulty with dialogue formatting, have them read to discover Frank's and Patricia's friendship. Then, have them reread the dialogue aloud and identify changes in speaker. *Analyzing* If students will not have difficulty with formatting, have them note the ways in which the author's use of stream-of-consciousness syntax enhances the experience of being inside Frank's head.

❶ Writing About the Big Question

1. Review the assignment with the class.

2. Remind students that young children sometimes don't have all the information about their situation, so it can be difficult to find the truth.

3. Have students complete the sentence starter. Review responses as a class. (**Sample response:** When we evaluate what is best for us, we must sometimes consider that we don't have all the information.)

4. Remind students that their answers will help them think about the Big Question, "What is the best way to find the truth?"

While You Read

Tell students that as they read, they should look for insights the author gained during her experience and in looking back on it.

❷ Vocabulary

1. Have students preview the selection vocabulary.

2. For each word, have students say the word aloud.

3. Then, use the word in a sentence that defines the word.

4. Finally, repeat your definitional sentence or a similar sentence with the word missing and have the class "fill in the blank" chorally. Here are some examples:

> When people are _summoned_, they are called together, usually for an important reason. When the king called all his advisors into a special meeting, he [students say "summoned"] them.

> If someone _vowed_, he or she made a solemn promise. If a witness promised to tell the truth, she [students say "vowed"].

❸ Word Study

1. Call students' attention to the Word Study box on the page. Introduce the skill, using the instruction in the box.

2. Ask students to name another -dict- word that means "a collection of definitions." (dictionary)

130

---

❶ What is the best way to find the *truth*?

❶ Writing About the Big Question

In "My First Free Summer," a young girl's parents avoid revealing scary truths about their safety during a period of rebellion. Use this sentence starter to develop your ideas about the Big Question.

> When we **evaluate** what is best for us, we must sometimes consider _____.

While You Read Look for insights the author gained both during her experience and in looking back on it.

❷ Vocabulary

Read each word and its definition. Decide whether you know the word well, know it a little bit, or do not know it at all. After you read, see how your knowledge of each word has increased.

- **vowed** (voud) v. promised solemnly (p. 132) *Susan vowed to take care of the puppy.* vow n. vow v.

- **repressive** (ri pres´ iv) adj. overly strict (p. 132) *Elise found her grandmother's rules repressive.* repress v. repression n.

- **extenuating** (ek sten´ yōō āt´ iŋ) adj. giving a reason for; excusing (p. 133) *He was guilty, but there were extenuating circumstances.* extenuate v. extenuation n.

- **diplomats** (dip´ lə mats´) n. government employees who work with other nations (p. 133) *The diplomats discussed a trade agreement that would benefit both countries.* diplomat n. diplomatic adj. diplomacy n.

- **summoned** (sum´ ənd) v. called together (p. 134) *At halftime, the coach summoned her players to a huddle.* summon v. summons n.

- **contradiction** (kän´ trə dik´ shən) n. difference between two conflicting things that means they cannot both be true (p. 135) *It is a contradiction to say mean things in a sweet voice.* contradict v. contradictory adj.

❸ Word Study

The **Latin root -dict-** means "to speak" or "to assert."

In this selection, Julia's mother does not tolerate **contradiction**—she does not allow her children to speak out against her wishes.

130 Fiction and Nonfiction

Vocabulary Development

Vocabulary Knowledge Rating

Create a **Vocabulary Knowledge Rating Chart** (*Professional Development Guidebook*, p. 33) for this selection. Include the selection vocabulary and the Big Question word that appears in the Writing About the Big Question sentence starter on this page. (The Big Question vocabulary is introduced on pp. 2–3.)

Give students a copy of the chart. Read the words aloud, and have students mark their rating in the Before Reading column. Urge them to be alert to these words as they read and discuss the selection.

Tally how many students think they know a word to gauge how much instruction to provide. As students read and discuss the selection, point out the words and their context.

PHLit Online! **Vocabulary Central**, featuring tools, activities, and songs for studying vocabulary, is available online at **www.PHLitOnline.com**.

Meet
Julia Alvarez
(b. 1954)

Author of
My First Free Summer

Shortly after her birth, Julia Alvarez moved from New York City to the Dominican Republic with her family. When Alvarez was ten, however, her family was forced to return to the United States because her father was involved in a rebellion against the country's dictator.

The Power of Words Alvarez had trouble adjusting to her new home. Turning inward, she began to read books and to write. Later, she said, "I fell in love with how words can make you feel complete in a way that I hadn't felt complete since leaving the island."

Did You Know?
Several years ago, Alvarez started a farm and a school to help people in the Dominican Republic.

❹ BACKGROUND FOR THE ESSAY
The Dominican Republic

In 1930, Rafael L. Trujillo seized power in the Dominican Republic and controlled the country as dictator for thirty-one years. To protect his position, Trujillo placed family members in office, restricted basic human rights, and harmed his political opponents. Some Dominican citizens were forced to flee to the United States. The author of "My First Free Summer" moved to New York City with her family during this unstable period.

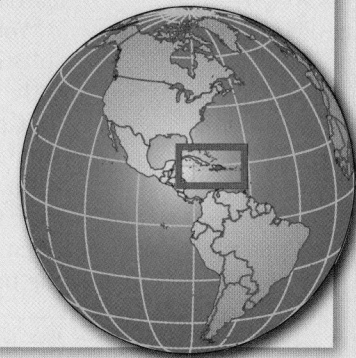

My First Free Summer **131**

❹ Background
The Dominican Republic

The Dominican Republic is located on the Island of Hispaniola, in the Caribbean Sea. At the time that this story takes place, it had been ruled by a ruthless dictator named Rafael Trujillo for about thirty years. Not long after this story ends, Trujillo was assassinated.

About 700,000 immigrants from the Dominican Republic now live in the United States; the majority of Dominicans live in New York City and other urban areas in the Northeast. Many Dominicans have distinguished themselves in the fields of entertainment, fashion, and sports. Nearly 400 people who played professional baseball in the United States during the years 1960–2005 were born in the Dominican Republic. They include outfielder Sammy Sosa and pitcher Pedro Martinez.

Multidraft Reading

This icon ● marks natural pauses in the selection. To assist struggling readers and to deepen reading for all, assign the text in "chunks," following the icons, and apply multidraft reading protocols. For each reading, have students set the purpose indicated:

- **First reading**—identifying key ideas and details and answering any Reading Checks.
- **Second reading**—analyzing craft and structure and responding to the side-column prompts.
- **Third reading**—integrating knowledge and ideas, connecting to other texts and the world, and answering the end-of-selection questions.

For more guidance, refer to the *Classroom Strategies and Teaching Routines* card on multidraft reading.

❶ Activating Prior Knowledge

Explain that according to scientific laws of motion, an object in motion will continue moving until stopped by an outside force. For example, an apple that falls from a tree stops only when it hits the ground. Next, propose that this principle can apply to human behaviors, too. Once someone has decided on a course of action, it is difficult to change direction. Ask students to think about a time when they set upon a course of action that was interrupted by an outside event or person. Discuss their experiences as a class.

Individual Activity

After students read "My First Free Summer," have them retell three of its important moments in the form of journal entries. Tell students to write their entries from Julia's point of view, and ask them to include important historical details.

❷ About the Selection

This autobiographical narrative is based on events from the author's childhood in the Dominican Republic. While her father participates in a rebellion against the government, Julia faces her own challenge: learning English. Every year, she must attend summer school. In the fifth grade, she finally becomes motivated, and earns, at long last, a free summer. But when the revolution is exposed, Julia's summer is interrupted as the family flees to the United States. By exploring two different meanings of the word *free*—the personal and the political—the essay shows how historical events affect people's lives in concrete ways.

❸ Historical Context

1. Remind students to pay attention to factual details in order to have a better understanding of the time and place in which the text takes place. Then, read the bracketed text aloud.

2. **Ask** the Historical Context question on this page.
   Answer: He has been in power for thirty years.

My First Free Summer

Julia Alvarez

I never had summer—I had summer school. First grade, summer school. Second grade, summer school. Thirdgrade-summerschoolfourthgradesummerschool. In fifth grade, I vowed I would get interested in fractions, the presidents of the United States, Mesopotamia; I would learn my English.

That was the problem. English. My mother had decided to send her children to the American school so we could learn the language of the nation that would soon be liberating us. For thirty years, the Dominican Republic had endured a bloody and repressive dictatorship. From my father, who was involved in an underground plot, my mother knew that los américanos[1] had promised to help bring democracy to the island.

"You have to learn your English!" Mami kept scolding me.

"But why?" I'd ask. I didn't know about my father's activities. I didn't know the dictator was bad. All I knew was that my friends who were attending Dominican schools were often on holiday to honor the dictator's birthday, the dictator's saint day, the day the dictator became the dictator, the day the dictator's oldest son was born, and so on. They marched in parades and visited the palace and had their picture in the paper.

---

1. **los américanos** (lōs ä me´ ri kä´ nōs) *n.* Spanish for "the Americans."

Vocabulary
vowed (voud)
v. promised solemnly

repressive
(ri pres´ iv) *adj.*
overly strict

Historical Context
How long has the dictator been in power?

Vocabulary Development

© **CCSS** Language 6

Thematic Vocabulary: The Big Question
As students are discussing "My First Free Summer," encourage them to use the thematic vocabulary presented in Introducing the Big Question, pp. 2–3. You might encourage them with sentence starters like these:

1. The narrator has limited *awareness* of . . .
2. Because she is a young child, she does not *perceive* . . .
3. The adults do not *explain* that . . .
4. As she recalls this important summer, the author gains *insight* about . . .

Meanwhile, I had to learn about the pilgrims with their funny witch hats, about the 50 states and where they were on the map, about Dick and Jane[2] and their tame little pets, Puff and Spot, about freedom and liberty and justice for all—while being imprisoned in a hot classroom with a picture of a man wearing a silly wig hanging above the blackboard. And all of this learning I had to do in that impossibly difficult, rocks-in-your-mouth language of English!

Somehow, I managed to scrape by. Every June, when my prospects looked iffy, Mami and I met with the principal. I squirmed in my seat while they arranged for my special summer lessons.

"She is going to work extra hard. Aren't you, young lady?" the principal would quiz me at the end of our session.

My mother's eye on me, I'd murmur, "Yeah."

"Yes, what?" Mami coached.

"Yes." I sighed. "Sir."

It's a wonder that I just wasn't thrown out, which was what I secretly hoped for. But there were **extenuating** circumstances, the grounds on which the American school stood had been donated by my grandfather. In fact, it had been my grandmother who had encouraged Carol Morgan to start her school. The bulk of the student body was made up of the sons and daughters of American **diplomats** and business people, but a few Dominicans—most of them friends or members of my family—were allowed to attend.

"You should be grateful!" Mami scolded on the way home from our meeting. "Not every girl is lucky enough to go to the Carol Morgan School!"

In fifth grade, I straightened out. "Yes, ma'am!" I learned to say brightly. "Yes, sir!" To wave my hand in sword-wielding swoops so I could get called on with the right answer. What had changed me? Gratitude? A realization of my luckiness? No, sir! The thought of a fun summer? Yes, ma'am! I wanted to run with the pack of cousins and friends in the common yard that connected all our properties. To play on the

---

2. **Dick and Jane** characters in a reading book commonly used by students in the 1950s.

Author's Purpose
What evidence shows that the author's purpose was to add humor in this paragraph?

Vocabulary
extenuating
(ek sten´ yoo āt´ iŋ)
adj. giving a reason for; excusing

diplomats
(dip´ lə mats´) *n.* government employees who work with other nations

6 **Reading Check**

Why does Julia have to go to summer school?

Differentiated Instruction for Universal Access

Author's Purpose
1. Have a volunteer read aloud the bracketed paragraph.
2. **Ask** the Author's Purpose question on this page.
   Possible responses: She describes the pilgrims' hats as "funny witch hats"; George Washington as a man with a "silly wig"; and English as a "rocks-in-your-mouth" language.
3. **Ask** what purpose the author might have had for making light of important figures in American history. **Possible response:** She may want to emphasize how little these things mattered to her at that time.

Connecting to the Big Question
1. Point out the truth that we are sometimes motivated by our own self-interest.
2. Have students reread the bracketed text on page 133. **Ask** students: What insight motivates the narrator to change her behavior in fifth grade? **Possible response:** She realizes that it's the only way to avoid summer school and get a fun summer of play.
3. **Ask:** Is doing what will make you happy the best way to find the truth? Explain. **Possible response:** Not usually. Usually we discover truth better through facing challenges instead of through choosing what makes us feel good.

Reading Check
Answer: She did not master her English lessons during the year.

Strategy for Less Proficient Readers
As students discuss the Author's Purpose question on this page, show them **Reading Skill Graphic Organizer A** (*Graphic Organizer Transparencies,* p. 26). The partially filled-in graphic organizer will help students understand how to use knowledge they already have to identify the author's purpose. Have students use the completed chart as a model as they work to determine the author's purpose at different points throughout "My First Free Summer."

EL Pronunciation for English Learners
Point out the word *father* on page 132 and the word *family* on page 133. Pronounce them clearly, and have students echo you. Then, write these words on the board: *fan / pan / ban* and *fin / pin / bin.* Call out the words at random. Have the class direct a volunteer at the board to point to the correct word each time. Discuss results. Conclude by leading students in pronouncing the words *father* and *family* again.

PHLit Online!
This selection is available in interactive format in the **Enriched Online Student Edition,** at www.PHLitOnline.com, which includes a thematically related video with writing prompt and an interactive graphic organizer.

133

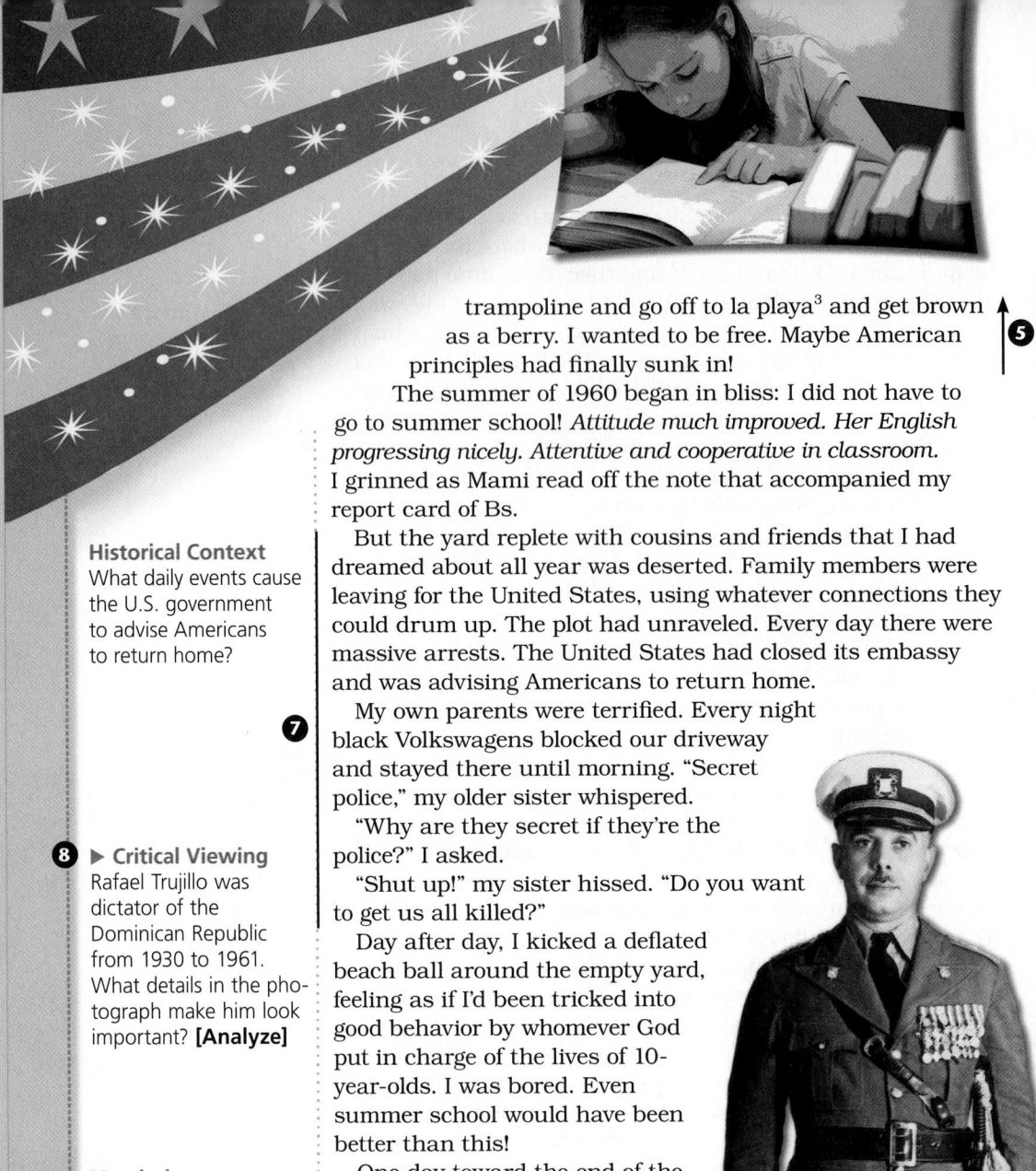

➐ Historical Context

1. Remind students that the political events of a particular time can explain why characters act and think the way they do. Have a student read the bracketed text.

2. **Ask** the Historical Context question on this page.
   Answer: The United States has closed its embassy, and people thought to be involved in the rebellion are being arrested. Alvarez's own home is being monitored by the secret police.

▶ **Monitor Progress: Ask** students how the narrative's historical context relates to Julia's life.

▶ **Reteach:** If students have difficulty with this question, point out the two historical events described on this page and show how these events affect Julia: the plot to overthrow the dictator has failed, so Julia's father's life is in danger; the United States has closed its embassy and advised all Americans to return home. These events dictate what the family must do: leave the country as quickly as possible.

➑ Critical Viewing

Possible responses: The military uniform, the medals, his posture, and the stern look on his face all make Trujillo look important.

Historical Context
What daily events cause the U.S. government to advise Americans to return home?

➐

➑ ▶ **Critical Viewing**
Rafael Trujillo was dictator of the Dominican Republic from 1930 to 1961. What details in the photograph make him look important? **[Analyze]**

Vocabulary
summoned (sum′ ənd) *v.* called together

---

trampoline and go off to la playa[3] and get brown as a berry. I wanted to be free. Maybe American principles had finally sunk in!

The summer of 1960 began in bliss: I did not have to go to summer school! *Attitude much improved. Her English progressing nicely. Attentive and cooperative in classroom.* I grinned as Mami read off the note that accompanied my report card of Bs.

But the yard replete with cousins and friends that I had dreamed about all year was deserted. Family members were leaving for the United States, using whatever connections they could drum up. The plot had unraveled. Every day there were massive arrests. The United States had closed its embassy and was advising Americans to return home.

My own parents were terrified. Every night black Volkswagens blocked our driveway and stayed there until morning. "Secret police," my older sister whispered.

"Why are they secret if they're the police?" I asked.

"Shut up!" my sister hissed. "Do you want to get us all killed?"

Day after day, I kicked a deflated beach ball around the empty yard, feeling as if I'd been tricked into good behavior by whomever God put in charge of the lives of 10-year-olds. I was bored. Even summer school would have been better than this!

One day toward the end of the summer, my mother summoned my sisters and me. She wore that

---

3. **la playa** (lä plä′ yä) *n.* Spanish for "the beach."

---

too-bright smile she sometimes pasted on her terrified face.

"Good news, girls! Our papers and tickets came! We're leaving for the United States!"

Our mouths dropped. We hadn't been told we were going on a trip anywhere, no less to some place so far away.

I was the first to speak up, "But why?"

My mother flashed me the same look she used to give me when I'd ask why I had to learn English.

I was about to tell her that I didn't want to go to the United States, where summer school had been invented and everyone spoke English. But my mother lifted a hand for silence. "We're leaving in a few hours. I want you all to go get ready! I'll be in to pack soon." The desperate look in her eyes did not allow for contradiction. We raced off, wondering how to fit the contents of our Dominican lives into four small suitcases.

Our flight was scheduled for that afternoon, but the airplane did not appear. The terminal lined with soldiers wielding machine guns, checking papers, escorting passengers into a small interrogation room. Not everyone returned.

"It's a trap," I heard my mother whisper to my father.

This had happened before, a cat-and-mouse game the dictator liked to play. Pretend that he was letting someone go, and then at the last minute, their family and friends conveniently gathered together—wham! The secret police would haul the whole clan away.

Of course, I didn't know that this was what my parents were dreading. But as the hours ticked away, and afternoon turned into evening and evening into night and night into midnight with no plane in sight, a light came on in my head. If the light could be translated into words, instead, they would say: Freedom and liberty and justice for all . . . I knew that ours was not a trip, but an escape. We had to get to the United States.

The rest of that night is a blur. It is one, then two the next morning. A plane lands, lights flashing. We are walking on the runway, climbing up the stairs into the cabin. An American lady wearing a cap welcomes us. We sit down, ready to depart. But suddenly, soldiers come on board. They go seat by seat, looking at our faces. Finally, they leave, the door closes, and with a powerful roar we lift off and I fall asleep.

Next morning, we are standing inside a large, echoing hall

Author's Purpose
How does your background knowledge of Julia and her mother help you understand the look described here?

Vocabulary
contradiction
(kän´ trə dik´ shən) *n.* difference between two conflicting things that means they cannot both be true

⑩ ▼ Critical Viewing
Describe Julia based on this passport photo and what you have read. **[Infer]**

⑪ ✓ Reading Check
Where did many of Julia's relatives go during the summer of 1960?

---

⑨ Author's Purpose
1. Review with students the information they already have on Julia and her relationship with her mother. In the "Meet Julia Alvarez" section, we learn that Julia's family is forced to leave the Dominican Republic when Julia is ten. On pp. 132–133, we see that Julia and her mother are in conflict over Julia's learning English. Julia resists her mother's scolding and discipline. Have students fill in this information on their graphic organizer.

2. Have a volunteer read aloud the bracketed paragraph. Then **ask** the Author's Purpose question. **Possible response:** It helps the reader understand that the look was stern and authoritative.

⑩ Critical Viewing
Possible response: Julia looks calm and serious. At the time the photo was taken, she may not have known that she and her family would be risking their lives when they leave the country.

⑪ Reading Check
Possible response: Julia's relatives have fled to the United States.

Concept Connector

Anticipation Guide
Have students compare the sentences they wrote before reading with their thoughts about interrupted plans after reading "My First Free Summer." Ask them to explain whether their thoughts have changed and, if so, how.

Reading Skill Graphic Organizer
Ask students to review the graphic organizers they completed to identify the author's purpose while reading. Show them **Reading Skill Graphic Organizer A** *(Graphic Organizer Transparencies, p. 29)* as an example.

Then, have students share the graphic organizers they completed and discuss the author's purposes they identified.

? Writing About the Big Question
Have students compare their responses to the sentence starter before they completed reading the story with their ideas afterward. Ask them to explain whether their thoughts have changed.

Author's Purpose

Ask students the Author's Purpose question on this page.

Possible response: The American official asks about school, and Alvarez uses the phrase "Yes, sir." By highlighting school and English, which caused her problems before, the author shows how her experience changed her.

© **Spiral Review**

Central Idea

1. Remind students that they studied the concept of central idea in the Unit 1 Literary Analysis Workshop (pp. 4–21).

2. **Ask** students the Spiral Review question.

    Possible response: The historical context explains why the family has to leave the country to be free.

ASSESS

Answers

Critical Thinking

Remind students to support their answers with evidence from the text.

1. (a) She wants Julia to learn the language of the people who might liberate the country. (b) The American school teaches English and the history of the United States. The other schools have holidays to honor the dictator.

2. (a) Julia doesn't want to go to summer school. (b) She raises her grades.

3. (a) She is surprised because she has not heard anything about a vacation. (b) She is concerned with her own problems and does not realize what is going on around her.

4. (a) **Possible responses:** She might want readers to appreciate living in a democracy. (b) She sees the desperate look in her mother's eyes and the terror that they experience at the airport. (c) Encourage students to find different ideas.

5. **Possible responses:** (a) Political freedom is necessary for safety while personal freedom is more related to happiness. (b) Adults should make young children more aware of their political surroundings.

136

---

as a stern American official reviews our documents. What if he doesn't let us in? What if we have to go back? I am holding my breath. My parents' terror has become mine.

He checks our faces against the passport pictures. When he is done, he asks, "You girls ready for school?" I swear he is looking at me.

"Yes, sir!" I speak up.

The man laughs. He stamps our papers and hands them to my father. Then wonderfully, a smile spreads across his face. "Welcome to the United States," he says, waving us in.

Author's Purpose
How does this scene point to the author's main purpose for writing this story?

© **Spiral Review**
Central Idea
How does the historical context help you identify the central idea of this essay?

Cite textual evidence to support your responses.

Critical Thinking

© 1. **Key Ideas and Details (a)** Why does Julia Alvarez's mother send Julia to the American school? **(b) Compare and Contrast:** How does this school differ from other schools on the island?

© 2. **Key Ideas and Details (a)** What is Alvarez's main reason for changing her behavior in fifth grade? **(b) Connect:** How is she successful?

© 3. **Key Ideas and Details (a) Infer:** How do you think Alvarez feels when she learns that her family is leaving the country? **(b) Speculate:** Why does it take her so long to understand that her family is escaping? Support your answer with details from the story.

© 4. **Integration of Knowledge and Ideas (a) Hypothesize:** What might Alvarez want readers to learn from this story? **(b) Support:** What details in the story support your ideas? **(c) Discuss:** Share your responses with a partner. Then, discuss how looking at someone else's responses did or did not change your ideas.

© 5. **Craft and Structure (a)** What differences does Alvarez find between the political and personal meanings of the word *free*? **(b)** What new insights might she have gained when looking back on this experience as an adult? *[Connect to the Big Question: What is the best way to find the truth?]*

136 Fiction and Nonfiction

Assessment Resources

Unit 1 Resources

L1 L2 EL **Selection Test A,** pp. 185–187. Administer Test A to less advanced readers.

L3 L4 EL **Selection Test B,** pp. 188–190. Administer Test B to on-level and more advanced students.

L3 L4 **Open-Book Test,** pp. 182–184. As an alternative, give the Open-Book Test.

All Customizable Test Bank

All Self-tests
Students may prepare for the **Selection Test** by taking the **Self-test** online.

PHLit Online! All assessment resources are available at www.PHLitOnline.com.

Reading Skill: Author's Purpose

1. What information from the Background on page 131 helps you understand the **author's purpose?**

2. **(a)** What other purposes for writing might Alvarez have had? **(b)** Which details in the essay support your response?

Literary Analysis: Historical Context

3. **Key Ideas and Details** Using a chart like the one shown, give examples from the selection that show how the **historical context** of the Dominican Republic during a rebellion affects Alvarez's actions in "My First Free Summer."

Historical Context		Author's Actions
Dictatorship	→	1. Goes to the American school
		2.

4. **Key Ideas and Details** List two story details that lead Alvarez to finally realize that her family is making an escape from the island.

Vocabulary

Acquisition and Use Using your knowledge of the italicized words, explain your answer to each question.

1. If you *vowed* to keep a secret, would you tell anyone?
2. Do *diplomats* work outside their own countries?
3. If you were *summoned* to a meeting, what would you do?
4. Can *extenuating* circumstances change the outcome of a situation?
5. If my statement is a *contradiction*, are we in agreement?
6. Are citizens of a *repressive* government free?

Word Study Use what you know about the **Latin root** *-dict-* to explain your answer to each question.

1. If I *dictate* a letter to you, am I telling you what to write?
2. If you *predict* that it will rain, are you stating a fact?

Word Study

The **Latin root** *-dict-* means "to speak," or "assert."

Apply It Explain how the word root contributes to the meanings of these words. Consult a dictionary if necessary.

benediction
edict
verdict

My First Free Summer **137**

Word Study
Sample answers:

1. Yes. The root *-dict-* means "to speak," and *dictate* means "to speak what must be written."

2. No. The root *-dict-* means "to assert," and *predict* means "to assert what you think will happen next."

Word Study: Apply It
Sample answers: A *benediction* includes words spoken as a blessing. An *edict* is a formal rule asserted by a leader or government. A *verdict* is a decision spoken by a jury.

Reading Skill

1. **Possible response:** The information about the political events in the Dominican Republic, as well as the biographical information about Alvarez's moving to the United States, help the reader understand the author's purpose.

2. (a) **Possible response:** Other purposes might include entertaining readers with a story about a girl who achieves a goal.
(b) **Possible response:** Humorous details and details that show Julia's changing attitude help fulfill the purpose of entertaining.

Literary Analysis

3. **Possible response:** Historical Context—failed coup; Author's Actions—quickly packs bags to leave country; travels to the United States.

   For other sample answers, see *Graphic Organizer Transparencies,* **Literary Analysis Graphic Organizer A**, p. 29, and the **Additional Answers** section.

4. **Possible response:** The presence of soldiers at the airport and the fact that people enter but do not return from the interrogation room help Julia realize what is happening.

Vocabulary
Acquisition and Use

1. No, if I <u>vowed</u> to keep a secret, I would have made a solemn promise not to tell anyone.
2. Yes, <u>diplomats</u> need to travel to other countries to represent their own nations.
3. If I were <u>summoned</u> to an important meeting, I would go.
4. Yes, <u>extenuating</u> circumstances can lead others to forgive rather than blame you.
5. No, my <u>contradiction</u> would disagree with your statement.
6. No, citizens of a <u>repressive</u> government are bound by overly strict rules.

Skills instruction for the Reading Skill and Literary Analysis concepts appears on p. 129.

① Writing About the Big Question

1. Review the assignment with the class.

2. Discuss how discovering a new interest, whether a hobby or a friend, can lead to a new way of seeing the world—a new truth.

3. Have students complete the sentence starter. Review responses as a class. (**Sample response:** A difficult experience can increase our awareness of what matters most because in such an experience we have no time and energy for unimportant details.)

4. Remind students that their answers will help them think about the Big Question, "What is the best way to find the truth?"

While You Read

Tell students that as they read, they should look for places where the author uses humor and true facts to describe his stay in the hospital.

② Vocabulary

1. Have students preview the selection vocabulary.

2. For each word, have students say the word aloud.

3. Then, use the word in a sentence that defines the word.

4. Finally, repeat your definitional sentence or a similar sentence with the word missing and have the class "fill in the blank" chorally. Here is one example:

When a situation is desperate, it is very serious and difficult. The boy's illness got worse and worse until it was [students say "desperate"].

③ Word Study

1. Introduce the skill, using the instruction in the box.

2. Have students use *desperate* in a sentence. Ask them to explain how the root's meaning—hope—relates to the sentence.

138

① **What is the best way to find the *truth*?**

① Writing About the Big Question

In this excerpt from *Angela's Ashes*, a young boy discovers the joy of language while recovering from a serious illness. Use this sentence starter to develop your ideas about the Big Question.

A difficult experience can increase our **awareness** of _____ _____ because _____.

While You Read Look for places where the author uses humor and truth to describe his childhood stay in the hospital.

② Vocabulary

Read each word and its definition. Decide whether you know the word well, know it a little bit, or do not know it at all. After you read, see how your knowledge of each word has increased.

- **miracle** (mir´ ə kəl) *n.* remarkable event or thing; marvel (p. 141) *It was a miracle that he survived the fall. miraculous adj.*

- **saluting** (sə lσσt´ iŋ) *v.* honoring by performing an act or gesture (p. 142) *The soldiers were saluting as they passed the general. salute v. salutation n.*

- **desperate** (des´ pər it) *adj.* without hope; having a great desire or need (p. 143) *John was desperate for a new pair of shoes. desperation n. desperately adv.*

- **patriotic** (pā trē ät´ ik) *adj.* showing love and support for one's own country (p. 143) *The crowds waved the American flag in a patriotic show. patriot n. patriotism n.*

- **ban** (ban) *n.* order forbidding something (p. 146) *The theater has a ban on cell phone use while a film is playing. ban v. banned v. banish v.*

- **guzzled** (guz´ əld) *v.* drank greedily (p. 147) *Ted guzzled water while hiking in the desert. guzzle v. guzzler n.*

138 Fiction and Nonfiction

③ Word Study

The **Latin root -sper-** or **-spes-** means "hope."

In this story, Frank has recovered from a **desperate**, or nearly hopeless, illness.

Vocabulary Development

Vocabulary Knowledge Rating
Create a **Vocabulary Knowledge Rating Chart** (*Professional Development Guidebook*, p. 33) for this selection. Include the selection vocabulary and the Big Question word that appears in the Writing About the Big Question sentence starter on this page. (The Big Question vocabulary is introduced on pp. 2–3.)

Give students a copy of the chart. Read the words aloud, and have students mark their rating in the Before Reading column. Urge them to be alert to these words as they read and discuss the selection.

Tally how many students think they know a word to gauge how much instruction to provide. As students read and discuss the selection, point out the words and their context.

Vocabulary Central, featuring tools, activities, and songs for studying vocabulary, is available online at **www.PHLitOnline.com.**

Author of
Angela's Ashes

Frank McCourt was born in Brooklyn, New York, but he was raised in Ireland. His father struggled to keep a job, and the family often went hungry. Because of the family's squalid living conditions, McCourt nearly died of typhoid fever when he was ten years old. At age thirteen, McCourt left school and worked at a series of odd jobs in an effort to help feed his family. At age nineteen, he sailed for America, where he eventually enrolled at New York University and became an English teacher. *Angela's Ashes*, McCourt's Pulitzer Prize-winning memoir, describes the author's youth in Ireland.

Did You Know?
McCourt taught English for twenty-seven years in New York City high schools before becoming a writer.

❹ BACKGROUND FOR THE SELECTION

Infectious Diseases in Ireland
In Ireland during the 1940s, infectious diseases such as typhoid and diphtheria claimed the lives of many children. This was especially true in poor and working-class districts where conditions could be very unsanitary. In some neighborhoods, entire blocks of houses shared a single outhouse, or outdoor toilet, which often overflowed and attracted rats and flies. These pests would then make their way into surrounding homes, and spread disease by tainting food and water.

from Angela's Ashes **139**

❹ Daily Bellringer
For each class during which you teach this selection, have students complete one of the five Research activities for Week 5 in the *Daily Bellringer Activities* booklet.

❹ Background
Limerick, Ireland
Limerick, Ireland, where Frank McCourt's family lived in the 1940s, neighbors Ireland's poorest regions in the west and southwest. Largely agricultural until recent years, these regions lacked the fertile soil that allowed eastern counties to thrive. While Frank McCourt survived his bout with typhoid, three of his siblings died of diseases related to the family's poverty.

Multidraft Reading

This icon ● marks natural pauses in the selection. To assist struggling readers and to deepen reading for all, assign the text in "chunks," following the icons, and apply multidraft reading protocols. For each reading, have students set the purpose indicated:

- **First reading**—identifying key ideas and details and answering any Reading Checks.
- **Second reading**—analyzing craft and structure and responding to the side-column prompts.
- **Third reading**—integrating knowledge and ideas, connecting to other texts and the world, and answering the end-of-selection questions.

For more guidance, refer to the *Classroom Strategies and Teaching Routines* card on multidraft reading.

For more about the author, practice with the selection vocabulary, or more background, go online at **www.PHLitOnline.com**.

❶ Activating Prior Knowledge

1. Prepare an **Anticipation Guide** (*Professional Development Guidebook,* p. 38) with the following statements:

   • Children should follow the direction of adults in positions of authority.

   • It is okay to do something that is wrong to help a friend.

   • It is always better to know the truth, even if that truth is unpleasant.

   • Feeling happy will help you be strong physically.

2. Give students a copy of the prepared **Anticipation Guide** and have them respond in the *Me* column. Have them discuss the statements in groups and mark the Guides again in the *Group* column.

3. For further guidance, use the *Classroom Strategies and Teaching Routines* card for Anticipation Guides.

Concept Connector ➡

Students will return to the **Anticipation Guide** after completing the selection from *Angela's Ashes.*

Individual Activity

Challenge students to recall a time when they were ill. Have them write a brief journal entry about that time, recalling and exploring what caused their illness, where they stayed while recovering, what they did to pass the time, and about how long it took to get better.

❷ About the Selection

Angela's Ashes is a memoir of Frank McCourt's childhood in Limerick, Ireland. The selection focuses on Frank's time at Fever Hospital, where he is recovering from typhoid. At the hospital, which is run very strictly by Roman Catholic nurses, Frank meets a young girl. Despite the nurse's disapproval, the two sick children become friends, and Patricia introduces Frank to great poetry.

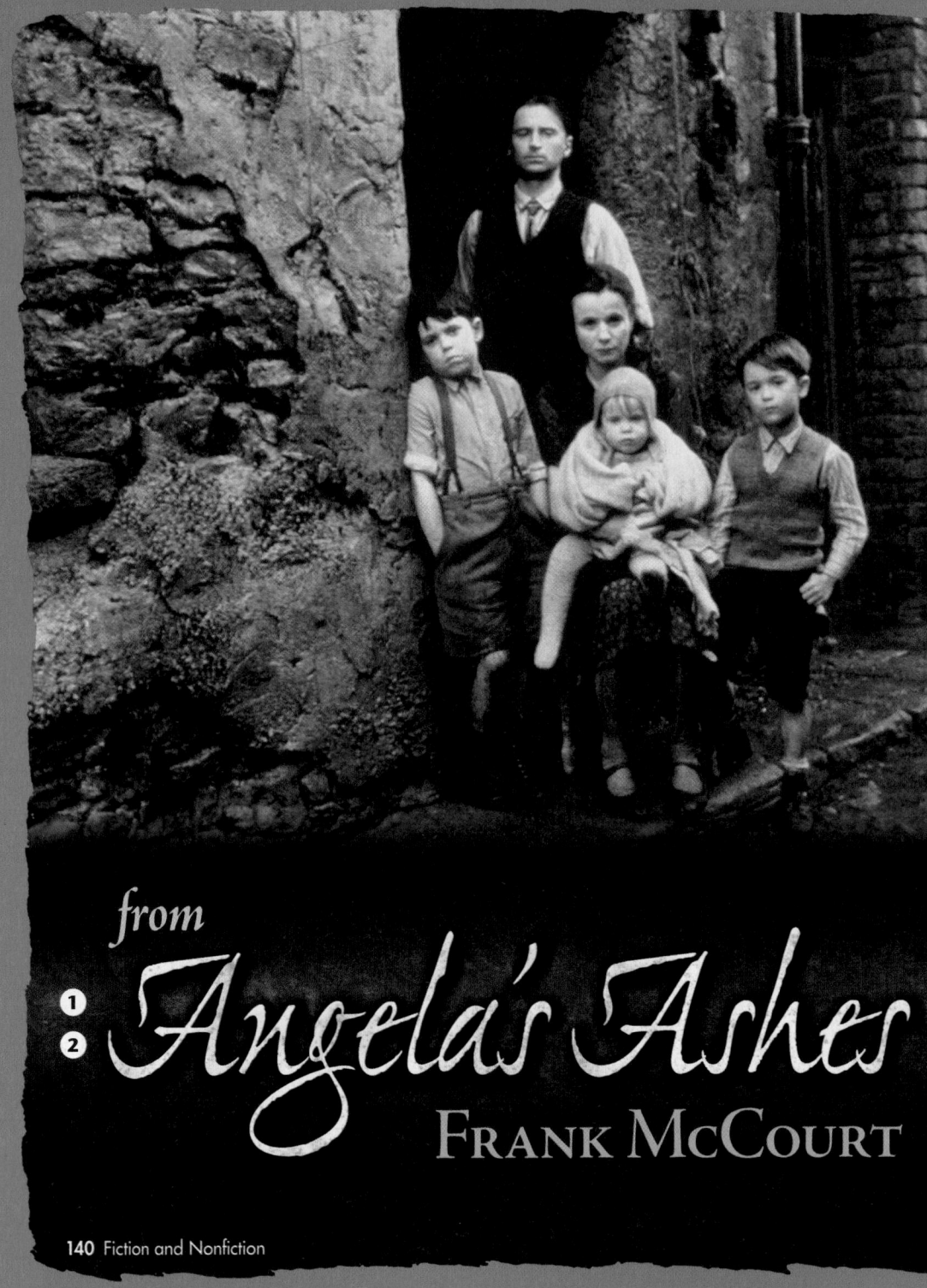

from

❶❷ Angela's Ashes

FRANK McCOURT

140 Fiction and Nonfiction

Vocabulary Development

© **CCSS Language 6**

Thematic Vocabulary: The Big Question

As students are discussing the selection from *Angela's Ashes,* encourage them to use the thematic vocabulary presented in Introducing the Big Question, pp. 2–3. You might encourage them with sentence starters like these:

1. Frank has limited *awareness* of . . .
2. Patricia has to *explain* to Frank about . . .
3. The nuns cannot be *convinced* that . . .
4. Meeting Patricia gives Frank *insight* about . . .
5. Young Frank doesn't *perceive* that Patricia . . .

The other two beds in my room are empty. The nurse says I'm the only typhoid[1] patient and I'm a miracle for getting over the crisis.

The room next to me is empty till one morning a girl's voice says, Yoo hoo, who's there?

I'm not sure if she's talking to me or someone in the room beyond.

Yoo hoo, boy with the typhoid, are you awake?

I am.

Are you better?

I am.

Well, why are you here?

I don't know. I'm still in the bed. They stick needles in me and give me medicine.

What do you look like?

I wonder, What kind of a question is that? I don't know what to tell her.

Yoo hoo, are you there, typhoid boy?

I am.

What's your name?

Frank.

That's a good name. My name is Patricia Madigan. How old are you?

Ten.

Oh. She sounds disappointed.

But I'll be eleven in August, next month.

Well, that's better than ten. I'll be fourteen in September. Do you want to know why I'm in the Fever Hospital?

I do.

I have diphtheria[2] and something else.

What's something else?

They don't know. They think I have a disease from foreign parts because my father used to be in Africa. I nearly died. Are you going to tell me what you look like?

I have black hair.

You and millions.

I have brown eyes with bits of green that's called hazel.

---

1. **typhoid** (tī´ foid´) *n.* severe infectious disease causing fever and intestinal disorders.
2. **diphtheria** (dif thir´ ē ə) *n.* severe infectious disease causing high fever and leading to the blockage of breathing passages.

Vocabulary

miracle (mir´ ə kəl) *n.* remarkable event or thing; marvel

Author's Purpose
How can you tell that the author is describing a personal experience?

④ ✓ Reading Check

Why is Frank in the hospital?

from Angela's Ashes **141**

③ Author's Purpose

1. **Remind** students that the selection comes from a memoir about the author's real experiences.

2. **Ask** students what they already know about McCourt's memoir and its main topic.
   Possible response: The memoir is about McCourt's poor childhood in Ireland and his brush with death from typhoid at age ten. Many children died from diseases brought on by their poor living conditions.

3. Have students reread the bracketed passage. **Ask** them why the narrator is in the hospital, what his name is, and how old he is.
   Answer: The narrator is in the hospital for typhoid, his name is Frank, and he is ten.

4. **Ask** students the Author's Purpose question on the student page.
   Possible response: The author is Frank McCourt and the narrator's name is Frank. Also, the passage is about being in the hospital for typhoid, which happened to the author when he was ten.

5. Have students list the details they identified in **Reading Skill Graphic Organizer B** (*Graphic Organizer Transparencies,* p. 28).

④ Reading Check

Answer: Frank is in the hospital for typhoid.

Fluency

Distribute copies of page 141 and pair students. Have partners take turns reading lines or paragraphs aloud. Listeners should mark words or sections with which readers struggle. Circulate to monitor the fluency of students' reading. Collect students' marked-up copies of the page and review difficult words and passages as a group.

If students have difficulty reading the unpunctuated dialogue on page 141, begin by reading the page aloud fluently. Use your voice to show the different characters' voices and to indicate when the narrator is thinking to himself ("She sounds disappointed."). Have students track the text as you read. Then, ask the group to read the page chorally in order to find the rhythm of McCourt's style.

This selection is available in interactive format in the **Enriched Online Student Edition,** at **www.PHLitOnline.com,** which includes a thematically related video with writing prompt and an interactive graphic organizer.

⑤ Author's Purpose

1. Clarify that the author, Frank McCourt, is from an Irish Catholic family. His narrative contains references to the Catholic Church, such as that the nurses in the hospital are nuns. Nuns are women who have dedicated their lives to the Church and are referred to as "Sister." They may wear special clothing called a habit and a rosary, a long string of beads for counting prayers. *The Little Messenger of the Sacred Heart* is a religious book, such as a book of prayers.

2. Read aloud the bracketed passage. **Ask** students to describe Sister Rita.
   Possible response: She takes her job very seriously and doesn't want the children to have any fun.

3. **Ask** students how Patricia responds to Sister Rita's scolding.
   Possible response: She mimics Sister Rita.

4. **Ask** students the Author's Purpose question.
   Possible response: The details that describe Sister Rita wagging her finger and Patricia mimicking her are humorous and help readers imagine the situation.

Vocabulary
saluting (sə lōōt´ iŋ) *v.* honoring by performing an act or gesture

You and thousands.

I have stitches on the back of my right hand and my two feet where they put in the soldier's blood.

Oh, . . . did they?

They did.

You won't be able to stop marching and saluting.

There's a swish of habit[3] and click of beads and then Sister Rita's voice. Now, now, what's this? There's to be no talking between two rooms especially when it's a boy and a girl. Do you hear me, Patricia?

I do, Sister.

Do you hear me, Francis?

I do, Sister.

⑤ You could be giving thanks for your two remarkable recoveries. You could be saying the rosary. You could be reading *The Little Messenger of the Sacred Heart* that's beside your beds. Don't let me come back and find you talking.

She comes into my room and wags her finger at me. Especially you, Francis, after thousands of boys prayed for you at the Confraternity. Give thanks, Francis, give thanks.

She leaves and there's silence for a while. Then Patricia whispers, Give thanks, Francis, give thanks, and say your rosary, Francis, and I laugh so hard a nurse runs in to see if I'm all right. She's a very stern nurse from the County Kerry[4]

Author's Purpose
What humorous details here help you understand the situation better?

---

3. **habit** (hab´ it) *n.* the costume traditionally worn by nuns.
4. **County Kerry** (ker´ ē) southwestern county of Ireland.

142 Fiction and Nonfiction

Think Aloud

Author's Purpose
Draw students' attention to the paragraph on page 143 beginning "She plods out. . . ." Model the skill of analyzing author's purpose, using the following "think aloud":

> When I read this paragraph, I realize that Patricia is making fun of the nun. She imitates the sister's accent, and she repeats "internal apparatus," the sister's phrase for the inner organs. The scene is funny, and I see that the author's purpose is to entertain me.

When I think about the circumstances in the story, though, I realize that the author may have another purpose, too. Both Patricia and the narrator have deadly diseases. Yet, they are having fun just as any children might. Even when death is near, the author seems to be saying, people can enjoy life. This idea makes me think about how precious and fragile life is. I think part of the author's purpose here is to show me this truth. As I read further, I will look for details that also fulfill this purpose.

and she frightens me. What's this, Francis? Laughing? What is there to laugh about? Are you and that Madigan girl talking? I'll report you to Sister Rita. There's to be no laughing for you could be doing serious damage to your internal apparatus.

She plods out and Patricia whispers again in a heavy Kerry accent, No laughing, Francis, you could be doin' serious damage to your internal apparatus. Say your rosary, Francis, and pray for your internal apparatus.

Mam visits me on Thursdays. I'd like to see my father, too, but I'm out of danger, crisis time is over, and I'm allowed only one visitor. Besides, she says, he's back at work at Rank's Flour Mills and please God this job will last a while with the war on and the English desperate for flour.[5] She brings me a chocolate bar and that proves Dad is working. She could never afford it on the dole.[6] He sends me notes. He tells me my brothers are all praying for me, that I should be a good boy, obey the doctors, the nuns, the nurses, and don't forget to say my prayers. He's sure St. Jude pulled me through the crisis because he's the patron saint of desperate cases and I was indeed a desperate case. ●

Patricia says she has two books by her bed. One is a poetry book and that's the one she loves. The other is a short history of England and do I want it? She gives it to Seamus, the man who mops the floors every day, and he brings it to me. He says, I'm not supposed to be bringing anything from a dipteria room to a typhoid room with all the germs flying around and hiding between the pages and if you ever catch dipteria on top of the typhoid they'll know and I'll lose my good job and be out on the street singing patriotic songs with a tin cup in my hand, which I could easily do because there isn't a song ever written about Ireland's sufferings I don't know. . . .

Oh, yes, he knows Roddy McCorley. He'll sing it for me right

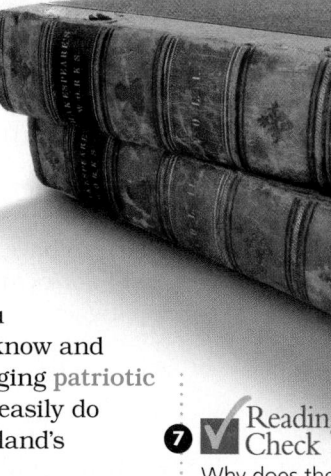

Vocabulary
desperate (des´ pər it) *adj.* without hope; having a great desire or need
patriotic (pā trē ät´ ik) *adj.* showing love and support for one's own country

❼ **Reading Check**
Why does the nurse run into Frank's room?

---

5. **with the war on and the English desperate for flour** (1939–1945) The Second World War caused shortages of food and other basic supplies in England.
6. **on the dole** unemployed and receiving money from the government in compensation.

from Angela's Ashes **143**

❻ **Connecting to the Big Question**

1. Point out that times of crisis often reveal the truth about people's character.

2. Have students reread the bracketed text on page 143. **Ask** students: What truth does the narrator reveal about his father in this passage?
Possible response: His father is often out of work. He seems to love his son and be concerned for his health.

3. **Ask:** How did young Frank feel about his father? How do the memories described in this passage help Frank McCourt find the truth of these feelings?
Possible response: Young Frank loved his father despite the man's shortcomings as a provider. Remembering that he wanted to see his father but that he knew his father had visited him during the crisis and sent him notes to show his ongoing concern helps Frank find the truth of his feelings.

❼ **Reading Check**

Answer: The nurse runs into Frank's room because Frank and Patricia are laughing. The nurse doesn't think they should be talking or laughing.

❽ Author's Purpose

1. Read the first bracketed passage aloud, emphasizing the different characters' dialogue with changes in your voice.

2. To help compare the oral version with the text as they read it silently, **ask:** Whose voice or voices do you hear in the oral version? Whose voice or voices do you hear in the written version?
Possible responses: Students should hear all the voices clearly in the oral version but Frank's voice most clearly in the written version.

3. **Ask** the Author's Purpose question on the page.
Possible response: Omitting quotation marks when people speak makes it seem that the entire conversation is happening inside Frank's head.

❾ Historical Context

1. Have a volunteer read aloud the second bracketed passage on the page.

2. **Ask** students to describe the book that Seamus gives to Frank. If necessary, direct them to reread page 143 beginning "Patricia says she has two books. . . ."
Answer: The book is a history of England.

3. Have a volunteer **paraphrase** Seamus's remark about the book he is bringing to Frank.
Possible response: I'm sorry that you're reading about England because England has not treated Ireland well. You should be reading about your own country, Ireland.

4. **Ask** students the Historical Context question.
Possible response: Seamus's comments reveal that Ireland and England have been in conflict and that he believes England has treated Ireland badly.

144

Author's Purpose
What is the effect of the author's choice to omit quotation marks to show when people are speaking?

Historical Context
What historical information about Ireland do you learn from Seamus's comments about the book he gives Frank?

❾

---

enough but he's barely into the first verse when the Kerry nurse rushes in. What's this, Seamus? Singing? Of all the people in this hospital you should know the rules against singing. I have a good mind to report you to Sister Rita.

Ah, . . . don't do that, nurse.

Very well, Seamus. I'll let it go this one time. You know the singing could lead to a relapse in these patients.

When she leaves he whispers he'll teach me a few songs because singing is good for passing the time when you're by yourself in a typhoid room. He says Patricia is a lovely girl the way she often gives him sweets from the parcel her mother sends every fortnight. He stops mopping the floor and calls to Patricia in the next room, I was telling Frankie you're a lovely girl, Patricia, and she says, You're a lovely man, Seamus. He smiles because he's an old man of forty and he never had children but the ones he can talk to here in the Fever Hospital. He says, Here's the book, Frankie. Isn't is a great pity you have to be reading all about England after all they did to us, that there isn't a history of Ireland to be had in this hospital.

The book tells me all about King Alfred and William the Conqueror and all the kings and queens down to Edward, who had to wait forever for his mother, Victoria, to die before he could be king. The book has the first bit of Shakespeare I ever read.

I do believe, induced by potent circumstances
That thou art mine enemy.

The history writer says this is what Catherine, who is a wife of Henry the Eighth, says to Cardinal Wolsey, who is trying to have her head cut off. I don't know what it means and I don't care because it's Shakespeare and it's like having jewels in my mouth when I say the words. If I had a whole book of Shakespeare they could keep me in the hospital for a year. ● Patricia says she doesn't know what induced means or potent circumstances and she doesn't care about Shakespeare, she has her poetry book and she reads to me from beyond the wall a poem about an owl and a pussycat that went to sea in a green boat with honey and money and it makes no sense and when I say that Patricia gets huffy and says that's the last poem she'll ever read to me. She says I'm always reciting the lines from Shakespeare and they make no sense either. Seamus stops mopping again

144 Fiction and Nonfiction

Vocabulary Development © CCSS Language 6

Archaic Words

Point out that the poems and writings that Patricia shares include archaic words no longer in common use. Students may benefit from identifying and defining these words. Challenge partners to identify archaic words from the italicized text on pages 144–145, such as *thou, art, galleon, claret, breeches, doe-skin,* and *rapier hilt.* Help students use context to speculate on the meaning of these words, and then provide these definitions to confirm meanings:

thou: you
art: are
galleon: a large sailing ship
claret: a dark, purplish red color
breeches: knee-length pants
doe-skin: leather made from deer
rapier hilt: sword handle

Have students demonstrate understanding by writing new sentences with the words.

and tells us we shouldn't be fighting over poetry because we'll have enough to fight about when we grow up and get married. Patricia says she's sorry and I'm sorry too so she reads me part of another poem[7] which I have to remember so I can say it back to her early in the morning or late at night when there are no nuns or nurses about,

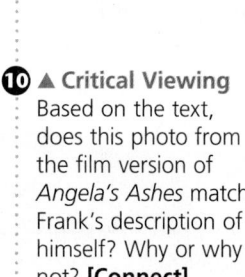

> *The wind was a torrent of darkness among the gusty trees,*
> *The moon was a ghostly galleon tossed upon cloudy seas,*
> *The road was a ribbon of moonlight over the purple moor,*
> *And the highwayman came riding*
> *Riding riding*
> *The highwayman came riding, up to the old inn-door.*
>
> *He'd a French cocked-hat on his forehead, a bunch of lace at his chin,*
> *A coat of the claret velvet, and breeches of brown doe-skin,*
> *They fitted with never a wrinkle, his boots were up to the thigh.*
> *And he rode with jeweled twinkle,*
> *His pistol butts a-twinkle,*
> *His rapier hilt a-twinkle, under the jewelled sky.*

Every day I can't wait for the doctors and nurses to leave me alone so I can learn a new verse from Patricia and find out what's happening to the highwayman and the landlord's red-lipped daughter. I love the poem because it's exciting and almost as good as my two lines of Shakespeare. The redcoats are after the highwayman because they know he told her, I'll come to thee by moonlight. . . .

I'd love to do that myself, come by moonlight for Patricia in the next room. . . . She's ready to read the last few verses

⑩ ▲ Critical Viewing
Based on the text, does this photo from the film version of *Angela's Ashes* match Frank's description of himself? Why or why not? **[Connect]**

⑪ ✓ Reading Check
Who wrote the first piece of poetry that Frank read?

---

7. **another poem** The passage following is from the famous poem "The Highwayman" by Alfred Noyes (1880–1958). A highwayman is a robber in past times who held up travelers.

from Angela's Ashes **145**

⑩ Critical Viewing
Possible response: The photo shows a young boy who looks kind of dreamy and unhappy. Frank's description of himself—that he is ten and from a poor family—could match this photo, though the boy in the picture looks healthy while Frank is ill and probably less healthy looking even without typhoid. Frank says that he has black hair and brown eyes with bits of green in them, but this boy has brown hair and green eyes.

⑪ Reading Check
Answer: Shakespeare wrote the first piece of poetry he read.

Differentiated
Instruction for Universal Access

Support for Less Proficient Readers
McCourt's style of interweaving thoughts and descriptions can be confusing without the visual cues of quotation marks. As a way to keep the characters straight and clarify which statements are conversation and which are description, recommend that students read the scenes on pages 144–146 as though they were from a play. Choose students to read the roles of Frank, Patricia, Seamus, Sister Rita, and the stern nurse from County Kerry.

EL Strategy for English Learners
Point out that McCourt writes in dialect for some of his characters, sometimes spelling words in unusual ways to reflect the dialectical pronunciation. In addition, the poems he quotes feature archaic words. To help students figure out dialect and archaic words in text, tell them to read the sentence containing the word and think about a familiar word that would make sense in the context and that sounds like the word that is used. Together, practice this strategy with the word *thee* on page 145.

⑫ Author's Purpose

1. **Read** the bracketed text aloud to students.

2. **Ask** students to paraphrase the text. **Possible answer:** "Reading poetry is harmless." "I want you to take the boy upstairs right now."

3. **Ask:** Who is speaking? **Possible answer:** Seamus and the nurse from County Kerry are speaking to each other.

4. **Ask** the Author's Purpose question on the student page. **Possible response:** The word *by* (her pronunciation of *boy*) reflects the nurse's Irish accent, which helps McCourt describe her.

▶ **Monitor Progress: Ask** students to summarize what they know about the nurse. **Answer:** She's from County Kerry and speaks with a Kerry accent. She is very stern and thinks laughing is bad for the children. She has been shouting at the children and at Seamus.

▶ **Reteach:** If students have difficulty describing the nurse, direct them to the passage at the bottom of page 142 in which Frank says the nurse frightens him and to the passage at the top of page 143 in which Patricia mimics the nurse's Kerry accent. Then, review the Background and Meet the Author section to remind students of what they know about the author, such as that he is writing to recall experiences from his childhood in Ireland. Point out that McCourt can share those experiences most effectively by including accents that vividly capture people such as the nurse from County Kerry.

⑫

Author's Purpose
How does the author's use of the word "by" help describe the nurse? Explain.

Vocabulary
ban (ban) *n.* order forbidding something

when in comes the nurse from Kerry shouting at her, shouting at me, I told ye there was to be no talking between rooms. Diphtheria is never allowed to talk to typhoid and visa versa. I warned ye. And she calls out, Seamus, take this one. Take the by. Sister Rita said one more word out of him and upstairs with him. We gave ye a warning to stop the blathering but ye wouldn't. Take the by, Seamus, take him.

Ah, now, nurse, sure isn't he harmless. 'Tis only a bit o'poetry.

Take that by, Seamus, take him at once.

He bends over me and whispers, Ah, . . . I'm sorry, Frankie. Here's your English history book. He slips the book under my shirt and lifts me from the bed. He whispers that I'm a feather. I try to see Patricia when we pass through her room but all I can make out is a blur of dark head on a pillow.

Sister Rita stops us in the hall to tell me I'm a great disappointment to her, that she expected me to be a good boy after what God had done for me, after all the prayers said by hundreds of boys at the Confraternity, after all the care from the nuns and nurses of the Fever Hospital, after the way they let my mother and father in to see me, a thing rarely allowed, and this is how I repaid them lying in the bed reciting silly poetry back and forth with Patricia Madigan knowing very well there was a **ban** on all talk between typhoid and diphtheria. She says I'll have plenty of time to reflect on my sins in the big ward upstairs and I should beg God's forgiveness for my disobedience reciting a pagan English poem about a thief on a horse and a maiden with red lips who commits a terrible sin when I could have been praying or reading the life of a saint. She made it her business to read that poem so she did and I'd be well advised to tell the priest in confession.

The Kerry nurse follows us upstairs gasping and holding on to the banister. She tells me I better not get the notion she'll be running up to this part of the world every time I have a little pain or a twinge.

There are twenty beds in the ward, all white, all empty. The nurse tells Seamus put me at the far end of the ward against

146 Fiction and Nonfiction

Vocabulary Development

Vocabulary Knowledge Rating
When students have completed reading and discussing the selection from *Angela's Ashes*, have them take out their **Vocabulary Knowledge Rating Chart** for the selection. Read the words aloud and have students rate their knowledge of words again in the After Reading column. Clarify any words that are still problematic. Have students write their own definition and example or sentence in the appropriate column. Then, have students complete the Vocabulary Practice activities at the end of the selection. Encourage students to use the words in further discussion and written work about the selection. Remind them that they will be accountable for these words on the **Selection Test,** *Unit 1 Resources,* pp. 206–208 or 209–211.

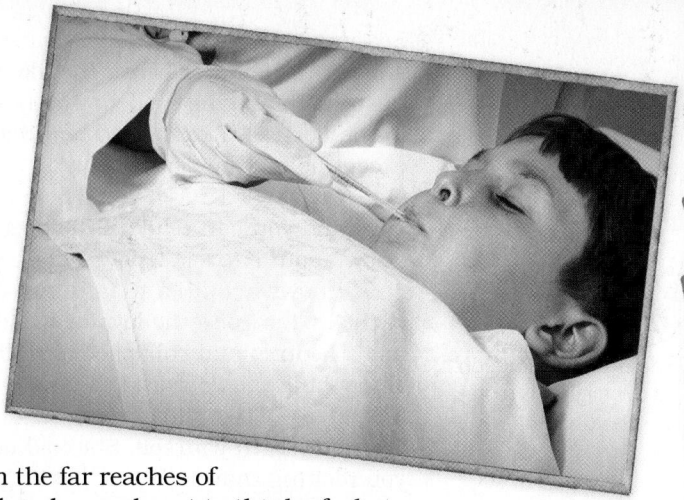

the wall to make sure I don't talk to anyone who might be passing the door, which is very unlikely since there isn't another soul on this whole floor. She tells Seamus this was the fever ward during the Great Famine[8] long ago and only God knows how many died here brought in too late for anything but a wash before they were buried and there are stories of cries and moans in the far reaches of the night. She says 'twould break your heart to think of what the English did to us, that if they didn't put the blight on the potato they didn't do much to take it off. No pity. No feeling at all for the people that died in this very ward, children suffering and dying here while the English feasted on roast beef and guzzled the best of wine in their big houses, little children with their mouths all green from trying to eat the grass in the fields beyond, God bless us and save us and guard us from future famines.

Seamus says 'twas a terrible thing indeed and he wouldn't want to be walking these halls in the dark with all the little green mouths gaping at him. The nurse takes my temperature, 'Tis up a bit, have a good sleep for yourself now that you're away from the chatter with Patricia Madigan below who will never know a gray hair.

She shakes her head at Seamus and he gives her a sad shake back.

Nurses and nuns never think you know what they're talking about. If you're ten going on eleven you're supposed to be simple like my uncle Pat Sheehan who was dropped on his head. You can't ask questions. You can't show you understand what the nurse said about Patricia Madigan, that she's going to die, and you can't show you want to cry over this girl who taught you a lovely poem which the nun says is bad.

The nurse tells Seamus she has to go and he's to sweep the lint from under my bed and mop up a bit around the ward.

Vocabulary
guzzled (guz´ əld)
v. drank greedily

 Reading Check

What does Seamus make sure that Frank is able to keep?

---

8. **Great Famine** severe food shortage in Ireland beginning in 1845 caused by the failure of the potato crop. Roughly one million Irish died of starvation in the famine.

from Angela's Ashes **147**

Spiral Review

Central Idea

1. Remind students that they studied the concept of central idea in the Unit 1 Literary Analysis Workshop (pp. 4–21).

2. **Ask** students the first Spiral Review question.

   Possible response: The author regrets not telling Patricia that his getting moved wasn't her fault.

3. **Ask** students the second Spiral Review question.

   Possible response: Life can be short, and it is important to share and communicate while we are able.

ASSESS

Answers

Critical Thinking

Remind students to support their answers with evidence from the text.

1. (a) He has typhoid fever.
   (b) **Possible response:** Yes, the stern nurse frightens him, and he seems very alone.

2. (a) They both face serious physical illness. They also both face fear of death, helplessness under the nuns' authority, and loneliness away from their families. (b) **Possible response:** They believed it was inappropriate for boys and girls to talk to one another.

3. (a) She sends a book of English history. (b) **Possible response:** The book helps Frank by getting him interested in something other than his illness, and it introduces him to Shakespeare's poetry.

4. **Possible response:** Strangers can keep each other company in difficult circumstances, but most of all they can help people feel that they are not alone.

5. **Possible response:** He uses truth to show how difficult the moment was and humor to make the story bearable to write and read. Understanding the past helps us understand the present.

Seamus tells me . . . that you can't catch a disease from a poem. . . . He never heard the likes of it, a little fella shifted upstairs for saying a poem and he has a good mind to go to the *Limerick Leader* and tell them print the whole thing except he has this job and he'd lose it if ever Sister Rita found out. Anyway, Frankie, you'll be outa here one of these fine days and you can read all the poetry you want though I don't know about Patricia below, I don't know about Patricia. . . .

He knows about Patricia in two days because she got out of the bed to go to the lavatory when she was supposed to use a bedpan and collapsed and died in the lavatory. Seamus is mopping the floor and there are tears on his cheeks and he's saying, 'Tis a dirty rotten thing to die in a lavatory when you're lovely in yourself. She told me she was sorry she had you reciting that poem and getting you shifted from the room, Frankie. She said 'twas all her fault.

It wasn't Seamus.

I know and didn't I tell her that.

Spiral Review
Central Idea What does the author regret? How might his regret relate to a central idea?

Critical Thinking

Cite textual evidence to support your responses.

1. **Key Ideas and Details** **(a)** Why is Francis in the hospital? **(b) Infer:** Do you think the experience is frightening for him? Why or why not?

2. **Key Ideas and Details** **(a)** What challenges, both emotional and physical, do Francis and Patricia face while in the hospital? **(b) Speculate:** Why do the nuns forbid Francis and Patricia to speak to each other?

3. **Key Ideas and Details** **(a)** What special gift does Patricia send to Francis? **(b) Speculate:** How does this gift help him? Support your answer with details from the story.

4. **Integration of Knowledge and Ideas** **(a) Discuss:** In a group, consider the ways that strangers facing difficult circumstances, like Francis and Patricia, can help each other. Choose a point person to share your group's ideas with the class.

5. **Craft and Structure** How does the author use both truth and humor to express his view? Explain. *[Connect to the Big Question: What is the best way to find the truth?]*

148 Fiction and Nonfiction

Assessment Resources

148

Reading Skill: Author's Purpose

1. What information from the Background on page 139 helps you understand the **author's purpose**?

2. **(a)** What other purposes for writing might McCourt have had? **(b)** Which details in the passage support your response?

Literary Analysis: Historical Context

3. **Key Ideas and Details** Use a chart like the one shown to record factual details that give clues about the work's historical context.

Historical Context		Details
Widespread disease	→	1. Many children die from typhoid and diphtheria.
		2.

4. **Key Ideas and Details** How does the historical context help you understand Seamus's actions in the selection?

Vocabulary

Acquisition and Use Use your understanding of the italicized words to explain your answer to each question.

1. If you *guzzled* your lemonade, did you drink it slowly?

2. In what professions is *saluting* most common?

3. Is a *miracle* an everyday occurrence?

4. If you feel *desperate,* are you happy?

5. Does a *patriotic* person care about his or her country?

6. If your parents *ban* television, are you allowed to watch it?

Word Study Use the context of the sentences and what you know about the **Latin root -*spes*-** to explain your answer to each question.

1. Does a *prosperous* person have trouble paying bills?

2. If you feel *despair,* have you lost all hope?

Word Study

The **Latin root -*sper*-** or -*spes*- means "hope."

Apply It Explain how the root contributes to the meanings of these words. Consult a print or digital dictionary if necessary.

despair
prosper
prosperous

Reading Skill

1. **Possible response:** The Background describes difficult living conditions in the past, which seems to indicate that the selection will involve the author's past experiences with these conditions.

2. **Possible responses:** (a) He might have wanted to entertain people by sharing his experience. (b) The humorous details in the passage, such as the description of Patricia mimicking Sister Rita, support a purpose of entertaining.

Literary Analysis

3. **Possible responses:** Historical Context—Roman Catholic hospital and staff; Details—boys and girls not supposed to talk to one another.

   For other sample answers, see *Graphic Organizers Transparencies*, **Literary Analysis Graphic Organizer A, p. 30**, and the **Additional Answers** section.

4. **Possible response:** The context that many children have died from disease helps me understand why Seamus wants to make life better for these children. He knows that the odds are against them and wants them to enjoy what they can.

Vocabulary
Acquisition and Use
Sample answers:

1. No, if you guzzled your lemonade, you drank it very quickly.

2. Saluting is most common in military professions.

3. No, a miracle is an unusual and unexplained occurrence.

4. No, if you feel desperate, you feel unhappy and hopeless.

5. Yes, a patriotic person loves and supports his or her country.

6. No, if your parents ban television, they forbid you to watch it.

Word Study
Sample answers:

1. No, a *prosperous* person has achieved his or her hopes, so is successful and can pay bills.

2. Yes, if you feel *despair*, you are without hope.

Word Study: Apply It
Sample answers: To *despair* is to feel hopeless. To *prosper* is to succeed and achieve your hopes. To be *prosperous* is to have succeeded and achieved your hopes.

Conventions

1. Introduce the skill, using the instruction on the student page.
2. Discuss the examples in the chart.

Think Aloud: Model the Skill

Model the skill of identifying possessive pronouns and checking agreement. Say to students:

> Remember that possessive pronouns replace nouns. They show ownership just as do possessive nouns. Let's say I write the sentence "Jenna likes Jenna's new book." I can create a smoother sentence by replacing the possessive noun *Jenna's* with the possessive pronoun *her*: "Jenna likes her new book." Because *her* refers to *Jenna*, which is a third-person feminine noun, I chose a third-person feminine pronoun.

PH WRITING COACH | Grade 7

Students will find further instruction on and practice with possessive pronouns in Chapter 22, Section 1.

Practice A

1. Her; before a noun
2. hers; stands alone
3. her; before a noun; their; before a noun
4. her; before a noun

Reading Application

Sample answer: <u>My</u> mother had decided to send <u>her</u> children to the American school. . . . You have to learn <u>your</u> English!

Practice B

Sample answers:

1. The other two beds in his room are empty.
2. The nurses do not approve of their conversation.
3. The two books are hers.
4. As Patricia reads the poem, its words grip her.

Writing Application

Sample answer: Helena offered to lend her book to Maria. Maria shook her head and said, "Thanks, but I have my own."

Integrated Language Skills

My First Free Summer •
from Angela's Ashes

Conventions: Possessive Pronouns

A **possessive pronoun** is a pronoun that shows possession or ownership. Possessive pronouns take the place of possessive nouns and can be singular or plural. They must agree in number and gender with the noun to which they refer.

Pronouns	Possessive Pronouns	Examples
I, we	my, mine, our, ours	I wore *my* hat. The hat is *mine*. We took *our* car.
you	your, yours	You ate *your* plum. The plum is *yours*.
he, she, it	his, her, hers, its	He wore *his* jersey. The gloves are *hers*.
they	their, theirs	They rode *their* horses. The horses are *theirs*.

Practice A Identify the possessive pronouns in each sentence. Write *before a noun* or *stands alone* to tell how each pronoun is used.

1. Her mother insists that she learn English.
2. After four years, the summer is hers to enjoy.
3. One day her mother tells the girls to pack their bags.
4. It is her parents' wish to leave the island country, not Julia's.

© Reading Application In "My First Free Summer," find two sentences that contain possessive pronouns.

Practice B Rewrite each sentence, using a possessive pronoun in place of each underlined word or words. Your choice should agree in number and gender.

1. The other two beds in <u>*Francis's*</u> room are empty.
2. The nurses do not approve of <u>*Francis's and Patricia's*</u> conversation.
3. The two books are <u>*Patricia's*</u>.
4. As Patricia reads the poem, <u>*the poem's*</u> words grip her.

© Writing Application Write two sentences about friends who share a book. Use possessive pronouns.

PH WRITING COACH | Further instruction and practice are available in *Prentice Hall Writing Coach*.

Extend the Lesson

Sentence Modeling

Choose the sentence given from the selection students have read:

> *I squirmed in my seat while they arranged for my special summer lessons.* ("My First Free Summer")

> *I don't know what it means and I don't care because it's Shakespeare and it's like having jewels in my mouth when I say the words.* (from *Angela's Ashes*)

Have students identify the possessive pronoun(s) in the sentence. Then, ask them what else they notice about the sentence. ("My First Free Summer": Contrast between the physical *squirmed* and *seat* and the intangible or abstract *arranged* and *lessons*; *Angela's Ashes:* A run-on sentence in which the word *jewels* takes the reader by surprise after a string of pronouns.)

Have students imitate the sentence by writing a sentence on a topic of their own choosing, matching each grammatical and stylistic feature discussed. Collect the sentences, and share them with the class.

Writing

 **Informative Text** Write a **letter** on one of the following topics:

- Write to young Julia Alvarez, describing what it's like to go to school in the United States.
- Write to young Frank McCourt, describing one of your favorite stories or poems.

Before you write, gather your ideas. First, write facts about your topic, such as the hours you attend school or the characters in your story or poem. Next, write some of the things you like most or least about your topic. Use concrete details and examples.

Refer to your notes to develop an organized letter. As you introduce each new topic, use transitions to help your reader see the way you connect the ideas and additional details you want to convey.

Remember to include the date, a greeting, a closing, and a signature. If you handwrite your letter, write legibly.

Grammar Application Check your letter for punctuation, capitalization, spelling, and the correct use of all possessive pronouns.

Writing Workshop: *Work in Progress*

Prewriting for Autobiography Refer to the People List in your writing portfolio. Choose one or two people from this list, and create a timeline of a significant event you experienced with each one.

Speaking and Listening

 Comprehension and Collaboration Each of these selections describes an important moment in the author's life. Conduct an **interview** with a friend, relative, or classmate to learn more about a serious event that impacted his or her life. Consider talking to someone who moved to a new country or neighborhood, attended a new school, had a threatening illness, or overcame a difficult situation.

Use these tips to conduct your interview:

- Create a list of questions beforehand to guide the interview.
- During the interview, ask follow-up questions to gather further details and information. For example, if your subject says his or her old school was more difficult, follow up with a question such as, "How many hours a day did you attend?" Add relevant comments to keep the discussion moving.

Present your findings to the class.

© **Common Core State Standards**

L.7.1, L.7.6; W.7.2.b, W.7.2.c; SL.7.1.c

[For the full wording of the standards, see page 128.]

Use this prewriting activity to prepare for the **Writing Workshop** on page 176.

PHLit Online!
www.PHLitOnline.com
- Interactive graphic organizers
- Grammar tutorial
- Interactive journals

Integrated Language Skills **151**

Writing

1. Review the assignment, using the instruction on the student page.
2. To guide students in writing a letter, give them **Support for Writing**, p. 201 in *Unit 1 Resources*.
3. To evaluate students' informative texts, use the rubrics for **Business Letter**, pp. 265–266 in the *Professional Development Guidebook*. You might also evaluate how well students use factual details to paint a complete picture of the context their letter describes.

PH WRITING COACH Grade 7

Students will find further instruction on and practice with letter writing in Chapter 12.

Six Traits Focus

Ideas	Word Choice
✔ Organization	Sentence Fluency
✔ Voice	✔ Conventions

Grammar Application

Have students check their drafts and make sure that the punctuation, capitalization, spelling, and use of possessive pronouns are correct.

Writing Workshop
Work in Progress

Have students save their completed People Lists in their portfolios. They will use the lists later as they complete the Writing Workshop assignment (see pp. 176–183).

Speaking and Listening

1. Review the assignment, using the instruction on the student page.
2. Have students complete the **Support for Extend Your Learning** page (*Unit 1 Resources*, p. 202).

Teaching Resources

Unit 1 Resources

L3 L4 EL **Integrated Language Skills: Grammar,** p. 200
L3 L4 EL **Support for Writing,** p. 201
L3 L4 **Support for Extend Your Learning,** p. 202
L4 **Enrichment,** pp. 181, 199

Enriched Online Student Edition

Available under After You Read for this selection:
All **Interactive Grammar Tutorial**
L3 L4 **Internet Research Activity**

Professional Development Guidebook
Rubrics for Self-Assessment: Business Letter, pp. 265–266

PHLit Online! All print and digital resources are available online at **www.PHLitOnline.com.** Online resources accessible to students are noted on the student page.

ASSESS

Answers

Answers With Explanations

1. **C**—The author includes many amusing details to entertain the reader. Incorrect answers: A—The author does not inform the reader about anything; B—The author does not try to persuade the reader to do or believe anything; D—The author does not teach the reader anything.

2. **B**—The fact that the author has sisters does not support the passage's purpose. Incorrect answers: A—This is one of the entertaining details; C—same explanation as for A; D—same explanation as for A.

3. **D**—The details are a series of amusing jokes. Incorrect answers: A—There is nothing serious about the pranks described; B—No details indicate that the father is nervous; C—The jokes are amusing, not thoughtful.

4. **C**—The author indicates affection for her father. Incorrect answers: A—The author's tone is not full of yearning; B—The author's tone is not full of mean-spirited irony; D—The author's tone is not marked by fear or surprise.

Writing for Assessment

Students should point out that the author supports her purpose of entertaining the reader by describing many of her father's amusing April Fools' Day pranks.

Test Practice: Reading

Author's Purpose

Fiction Selection

Directions: *Read the selection. Then, answer the questions.*

My dad loves to play pranks on April Fools' Day. He started many years ago by shaking our hands with a hidden buzzer that tickled us. My sisters and I loved that joke. Each year, he would think of creative ways to make us laugh for weeks before April 1st. Over time, the pranks got funnier and more creative. One April 1st, we awoke to find the furniture in our house rearranged! He liked to think of ways to surprise each of us with a special prank. Mom's favorite joke was when Dad wrote her a big check and told her to cash it the next day. That's when she discovered it had been written in disappearing ink!

1. What is the author's purpose for writing this passage?
   A. to inform
   B. to persuade
   C. to entertain
   D. to teach

2. Which of the following details does *not* support the author's purpose?
   A. Dad shakes hands with a tickling buzzer.
   B. The narrator has sisters.
   C. Dad rearranges the furniture.
   D. Mom gets a check written with disappearing ink.

3. Which word *best* describes the narrator's father?
   A. serious
   B. nervous
   C. thoughtful
   D. playful

4. Which of these words *best* describes the author's tone—her feelings about her father and his April Fools' Day tradition?
   A. wistful
   B. sarcastic
   C. loving
   D. alarmed

Writing for Assessment

Reread the passage, and write a paragraph in which you describe the author's purpose. Cite specific details from the passage that help the author achieve her purpose for writing.

Strategies for Test Taking

Remind students that one way to determine an author's purpose for writing a passage is to become aware of the effect of the passage on the reader. For example, if a passage makes a reader laugh or smile, the author's purpose was probably to entertain. If the reader knows a lot more about a certain subject after finishing a passage, the author's purpose was most likely to inform. If the reader wants to do or try something described in the passage, or comes up with a new opinion on a subject covered in the passage, the author's purpose was most likely to persuade. Point out, however, that because readers' reactions are individual and subjective, students will sometimes have a different reaction from the one the author intended. For example, a student might read a joke and think that it's not funny, even though the author's purpose was to entertain.

Nonfiction Selection

Directions: *Read the selection. Then, answer the questions.*

Ready to laugh and make others laugh? The annual International Clown Convention will take place November 3rd through 5th at the Civic Center in downtown Portland. Register now for side-splitting classes taught by clowning professionals from around the world. It is never too late to try something new! Learn how to juggle, ride a unicycle, apply clown makeup like a pro, and more! While you're here, be sure to visit our huge costume and gift shop on the second floor of the Civic Center, where you'll find hilarious gag gifts as well as Portland's widest selection of wacky costumes and accessories. The convention runs every day from 10 a.m. to 10 p.m. Space is limited, so register now before this circus leaves town!

1. What is the author's purpose for writing this passage?
 A. The author wants to stress the importance of humor.
 B. The author wants to inform readers that the Civic Center is crowded.
 C. The author wants to persuade readers to register for the clown convention.
 D. The author wants to entertain readers with facts about clowning.

2. Which possible title would *best* support the author's purpose?
 A. The Clowns Are Coming
 B. Register Now for Clown Classes
 C. Learn Something New
 D. Clowns Are No Joke

3. Why does the author include information about the costume and gift shop?
 A. to encourage readers to visit the shop
 B. to mention the store hours
 C. to appeal to people who do not like classes
 D. to convince people to be funny

4. What words from the article *best* support the author's purpose?
 A. side-splitting; clowning professionals; Portland's widest selection
 B. International Clown Convention; juggle; gift shop
 C. November 3rd through 5th; Civic Center; downtown Portland
 D. around the world; try something new; circus leaves town

Writing for Assessment

Connecting Across Texts

If the father in the first passage read the second passage in his local newspaper, do you think the author of the second passage would partly achieve his purpose for writing? Write a brief response, using details from the two passages to support your answer.

PHLit Online!
www.PHLitOnline.com
• Online practice
• Instant feedback

Test Practice Reading **153**

PHLit Online!
Students may take the test in interactive format with instant feedback online at www.PHLitOnline.com.

153

Common Core State Standards

- Reading Informational Text 5, 6
- Writing 10
- Language 6

Reading Skill

1. Introduce the skill and chart.
2. Tell students that they will analyze the structure and purpose of an application and a contract.

Think Aloud: Model the Skill

Say to students:

When I read an application, I pay close attention to the directions, because I know that they will tell me what information I need to provide and how I am supposed to fill out the form. When I read a contract, I always look for a bulleted or numbered list of conditions or terms, because I want to know exactly what I am agreeing to do (or not do).

Multidraft Reading

Have students follow a multidraft reading protocol.

- **First reading**—Have students read to identify key ideas and details.
- **Second reading**—Have students read to identify the structure of the text.
- **Third reading**—Have students read to integrate knowledge and ideas by connecting the text to the world, their own experiences, and other texts.

Content-Area Vocabulary

1. Have students say each word.
2. Next, use each word in a sentence that defines it.
3. Finally, repeat your definitional sentence or a similar sentence omitting the word, and have the class "fill in the blank" chorally.

Reading for Information

Analyzing Functional Texts

Application

Contract

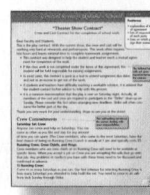

Reading Skill: Analyze Structure and Purpose

When you **analyze structure and purpose** in a text, you examine *how* the information is organized and *why* it is organized in that way. Workplace documents, such as applications and contracts, include structural features that are intended to make information clear and easy to locate. Applications, for example, require special formatting so that applicants can easily fill in information. Contracts, on the other hand, typically contain lists of rules and conditions that the signer agrees to obey and fulfill.

Structural Features of Applications	Structural Features of Contracts
• **introduction:** provides a description of the position and an explanation of the application process • **headings:** show where to find categories of information • **directions:** explain how to fill out the application • **rows and columns:** allow applicants to provide information in an organized format	• **headings and subheadings:** help readers locate information on a topic • **bulleted or numbered lists:** provide a quick way to reference essential information • **acknowledgment or certification:** requires the parties involved to formally agree to the terms of the contract

Content-Area Vocabulary

These words appear in the selections that follow. You may also encounter them in other content-area texts.

- **applicants** (ap´lə kənts) *n.* people who apply for something
- **misconception** (mis´kən sep´shən) *n.* mistaken idea
- **criterion** (krī tir´ē ən) *n.* rule for making a judgment

154 Fiction and Nonfiction

Common Core State Standards

Reading Informational Text
5. Analyze the structure an author uses to organize a text, including how the major sections contribute to the whole and to the development of the ideas.
6. Determine an author's point of view or purpose in a text and analyze how the author distinguishes his or her position from that of others.

Language
6. Acquire and use accurately grade-appropriate general academic and domain-specific words and phrases; gather vocabulary knowledge when considering a word or phrase important to comprehension or expression.

Writing
10. Write routinely over extended time frames and shorter time frames for a range of discipline-specific tasks, purposes, and audiences.

What is the best way to find the truth?

As students read, have them look for the kinds of factual information that the application and contract request. Ask them to consider why it is important to be completely truthful when filling out forms.

The Flat Rock Playhouse

The Flat Rock Playhouse has grown in recent years from a traditional summer theater to a regional powerhouse. It boasts one of the largest Resident Contract Agreements with Actors' Equity Association, the union of actors and stage managers, in the southern region. Flat Rock Playhouse unites its seasonal talent pool with its year-round administrative and artistic staff, 70% of whom were formerly apprentices and interns. The Playhouse proudly trains and educates to nurture its own future.

• Do you have a reputable Equity Apprenticeship in your background? Outside an education setting what steps have you taken to build a career? Have you begun professional networking? • How are you going to make the contacts necessary to get the job? • Do you have acting professionals on your reference list? • What do you know about marketing yourself in the theater business? Do you have a professionally photographed head shot? • Do you have a means to continually update your resume? • Do you know how to find an agent? Do you know how to get call backs at a cattle-call audition? • Would you feel comfortable in a professional environment? • Are you ready to join a union? Are you a triple-threat talent?

> This part of the introduction describes the application process.

We will be attending SETC (Southeastern Theatre Conference) in March and will be happy to contact all serious **applicants** who have already initiated contact regarding their audition numbers. Applicants can, of course, call and set up personal auditions at the Playhouse if they are not attending SETC. However, if one's schedule or geographic distance from the Playhouse makes a personal audition impossible, one may send a videotaped audition consisting of two monologues and if applicable examples of singing and dance work. Also to expedite our selection and registration process, be sure to include two reference letters with the return correspondence. An application form and descriptive material about the program are subject to change due to variations in the talents and needs of each student class. Please complete and return the application at your earliest convenience if you wish to be considered among this year's candidates.

TEACH

About Applications

1. Review with students the features listed in the Application box on page 155. **Ask** volunteers to give an example of an application a middle school student might have to complete.
   Possible response: A middle school student might have to fill out an application to be an editor on the school newspaper or to run for class office.

2. **Ask** volunteers to give examples of other kinds of applications that they anticipate filling out as they get older.
   Possible response: Students might mention job, college, financial aid, driver's license, and mortgage applications.

3. Tell students that they are about to read an application for a theater apprenticeship program at the Flat Rock Playhouse in North Carolina. Those accepted into the program become members of the theater's apprentice troupe, called the Vagabond Players.

Analyze Structure and Purpose

1. Tell students to let their eyes run over the page. **Ask** them what features of the text stand out.
   Possible response: The image stands out most. The bulleted questions stand out as well.

2. **Ask** students why these particular text features stand out.
   Possible response: The image stands out because it is colorful and different from the rest of the page. The questions stand out because of the bullets and because they are in a different typeface.

3. Direct students' attention to the bulleted questions. Discuss what they think the typeface indicates about this portion of the text. Lead them to understand that the typeface indicates that this text serves a different purpose than the surrounding text. The surrounding text gives readers information about the Flat Rock Playhouse. The bulleted text leads readers to think about themselves and how the Flat Rock Playhouse can help them.

Fluency

Distribute copies of page 155, and pair students. Partners should take turns reading aloud. Have listeners mark text with which reading partners struggle. Circulate to monitor students' fluency; then, collect the marked-up pages. Review difficult words. Some potential trouble spots include:

- If students have trouble with *SETC*, remind them that this is an acronym. Acronyms are a kind of abbreviation in which letters represent words, and they are generally spelled using only uppercase letters. Usually acronyms are pronounced one letter at a time, as in *FBI* (Federal Bureau of Investigation), *ETA* (Estimated Time of Arrival), and *LA* (Los Angeles).
- If students struggle to correctly pronounce the word *audition*, remind them that the suffix *-tion* is pronounced the same way as in the words *position, addition,* and *solution.*

Analyze Structure and Purpose

1. **Ask** the class what they would read first on this page and why.
   Possible response: I would read the title first, because it is at the top and it is biggest.

2. **Ask** the class what they would read next, and why.
   Possible response: I would read the directions next, because they are next on the page and they are written in uppercase letters.

3. Discuss with students how the organization of this page mirrors the steps you should take when filling out an application. The title is first and largest, so that you can make sure you are filling out the correct application. The directions are next, and some of them are in uppercase letters. This helps you remember to read them and make sure you understand them before you fill out the application.

Apprentice Application Form for the Vagabond School of Drama

TO ENROLL: PLEASE PRINT THIS FORM, COMPLETE IT, AND RETURN IT WITH A HEADSHOT OR SNAP SHOT, as well as any other information you deem necessary. Videotapes are welcome. Auditions and/or interviews by the Executive Director or his appointee are required.

Student Name		Social Security
Address		
City	State	Zip
Home Phone	Work Phone	E-mail
Age Date of Birth / /	Weight Height	Hair Color

Instruction

| Song | Dance | Instruments |

| Theater Training |
| Parent/Guardian Name |
| Address |
| City | State | Zip |
| Home Phone | Work Phone | E-mail |

Please provide a character reference

| Name |
| Address |
| City | State | Zip |
| Home Phone | Work Phone | E-mail |

The Vagabond School of the Drama, Inc. is a not-for-profit educational institution that admits students of any race, creed, sex, national, or ethnic origin.

The directions at the top of the page explain what applicants are required to do.

The application provides spaces for applicants to give information about themselves.

Vocabulary Development

CCSS Language 6

Words From Business

Tell students that when they fill out applications they may encounter new words specific to businesses and other organizations. Guide them to understand the meaning of the following business-related words on this application:

- *enroll:* When you join a school, class, or program, you are said to *enroll* in it.
- *executive:* This word refers to a person or group that has authority to manage people or resources.
- *Social Security:* On an application, this usually refers to the applicant's Social Security Number, which is a unique number that the government uses for tax purposes.

Crystal Springs Uplands School

"Theater Show Contract"
Crew and Cast Contract for the completion of school work.

Features:
- explanation of terms of agreement
- lists of responsibilities of each party
- lines on which parties sign their names

Dear Faculty and Students,

This is the play contract. With the current show, the crew and cast will be working very hard at rehearsals and performances. This work often requires late hours and leaves minimal time to complete homework assignments.

- This contract was designed to help the student and teacher reach a mutual agreement for completion of the work.
- If the class work is not completed under the terms of this agreement, the student will be held responsible for missing assignments.
- In most cases, this contract is used as a tool to *extend* assignment due dates and not as an excuse to get out of the work.
- If students and teachers have difficulty reaching a workable solution, it is advised that the student contact his/her advisor to help with this process.
- It is a common misconception that the play is over on Saturday night. Actually, all members of the cast and crew are required to participate in the "Strike" clean-up on Sunday. Please consider this fact when arranging new deadlines. Strike will often consume the better part of the day.

Thank you very much for your understanding. Hope to see you at the show!

> The bulleted list calls out some important terms of the contract.

Crew Commitments

> This subheading introduces the section dealing with crew responsibilities.

Saturday Set Crew
Anyone can come and help on Saturdays. You can come as often as you like and stay for any amount of time you can spare. {The Crew members, who come to the most Saturdays, have the best chance of being on Running Crew.} Lunch is usually at 1 pm and typically costs $5.

Running Crew, Crew Chiefs, and Props
Crew members who are crew chiefs or on Running Crew will need to be available at specific times. When you accept a job on Crew you are accepting the calls that go with that job. Any problems or conflicts you have with these times need to be discussed and confirmed in advance.

1) Running Crew:
Come to as many Saturdays as you can. Our first criterion for selecting Running Crew is how many Saturdays you attended to help build the set. You need to come to all calls from tech Sunday through Strike.

Differentiated Instruction — for Universal Access

Strategy for Less Proficient Readers

If students are confused by the large amounts of information presented in the contract, encourage them to break it into parts and understand each one individually. For example, the beginning of the contract, starting with "Dear Faculty and Students," and ending with "Hope to see you at the show!" can be read alone, as if it were a letter.

Strategy for Advanced Readers

Divide the group into pairs. In each pair, assign one student the role of a director and the other the role of a crew member working on a play. Have each pair draw up a contract regarding the responsibilities of the crew member and the director, and the schedule they will follow, using the student text as a model.

TEACH

About Contracts

1. Review with students the features listed in the Contract box on page 157. **Ask** volunteers to give an example of agreements they've entered into in the past. **Possible response:** Students may recall times they agreed to do chores in exchange for a reward, or agreed to help a friend in exchange for a favor.

2. Discuss how examples students mention are like contracts. Similarities include a definition of terms and explanations of what's expected of each party.

3. Tell students that they are about to read a contract for the cast and crew of the Crystal Springs Uplands School theater show. The contract defines the responsibilities for students participating in the show, then provides a place for students and their advisors to sign.

Analyze Structure and Purpose

1. **Ask** students what text features stand out on this page. **Possible response:** The bullets in the first section stand out, as do the large headers and the boldface number.

2. Lead students in a discussion of how the bullets in the first section help the reader understand the different points being made. Lead students to understand that each bullet represents a single idea or topic.

3. **Ask** students what part of the contract defines to whom this contract applies. **Possible response:** The boldface heads saying "Saturday Set Crew" and "Running Crew, Crew Chiefs, and Props" call out these groups.

4. Discuss with students how the structure of the page directs readers to the important information, such as to whom the contract applies and what their responsibilities are.

Analyze Structure and Purpose

1. Draw students' attention to the indented list at the top of the page, under "Crew Chiefs." **Ask** students what the indentation indicates about the list.
   Possible response: The indentation indicates that this list is related to the text above it. It calls out more specific information related to that topic.

2. Remind students that the lines on this page represent a place for parties to write in information or sign their names. Draw a distinction between these lines and other lines they may see on contracts and other documents, which serve to divide the document into different parts.

3. **Ask** students which features of this text they find most and least useful for understanding important information.
   Possible response: I think the indented bullets on the first page are the most useful, because they call out specific ideas. I thought the boldface heads with numbers were less useful, because I wasn't sure whether if they were more or less important than the other boldface heads.

---

2) Crew Chiefs:

This is what is expected of the different jobs. Remember to discuss conflicts in advance.

Stage Manager = All calls, all meetings.

Lights Director = All calls, all meetings.

Sound Director = All calls, all meetings.

Assistant Stage Manager = All calls, all meetings.

Props = Attend as many Meetings and Saturdays as you can. Attend all calls from tech Sunday to Strike. You will need to attend a minimum of one rehearsal per week.

> This list shows the requirements of certain positions.

My Name is: _____

I have been selected for the following position (circle):

Stage Manager	Sound	Helper
Assistant Stage Manager	Running Crew	Props
	Actor	Costumes
Lights	Musician	Student Director

I understand the calls/rehearsals that I need to attend.

I have conflicts with the following times. _____

Student's acknowledgment:

I realize that it is my responsibility to live up to this contract.

Student's signature _____

> Lines are provided so that the parties can sign their names and make the contract official.

Advisor's acknowledgment:

I understand that my advisee is involved in the theater production. I have kept a copy of this contract.

Advisor's signature _____

Think Aloud

Vocabulary: Using Context

To model the skill of using context clues, direct students to the line "Attend all calls from tech Sunday to Strike." Then, say to students:

> When the contract states that Props crew members should "attend all calls from tech Sunday to Strike," it is using a familiar word, *strike*, in an unfamiliar way. To figure out what the contract means by *strike*, I use contexts clues. *Strike* is contrasted with *tech Sunday*, and they are presented as being two different points in time. I think that *Strike* is probably something that happens at the end of the play. To check, I skim back over the document. On page 157, I see that the final bullet on the page refers to the "Strike" clean-up that occurs the day after the play. I think this must be the *Strike* the contract refers to: a clean-up after the show. I can then check my reasoning using a dictionary.

Comparing Functional Texts

 1. Key Ideas and Details (a) How does the **purpose** of an application differ from the purpose of a contract? **(b)** In what ways does the **structure** of each document support its purpose?

Content-Area Vocabulary

2. Use the words *applicants, criterion,* and *misconception* in a short paragraph about a community theater.

🕐 Timed Writing

Explanatory Text: Chart

> **Format**
> The prompt gives specific directions regarding how your writing should be organized.

> Congratulations! You have been cast in your school's play. Explain how you will manage your time to include rehearsals. Make a chart that details your daily schedule. For each hour of the day, explain what you will accomplish in that hour. Be sure to allow time for homework and other responsibilities. (15 minutes)

> **Academic Vocabulary**
> When you *explain* a situation, process, or idea, you provide details and reasons to make it more understandable to readers.

5-Minute Planner

Complete these steps before you begin to write:

1. Read the prompt carefully and completely. Look for key words like the ones highlighted to complete the assignment.

2. Make a list of all your daily responsibilities, including tasks at home, class time, homework, and other responsibilities.

3. Next to your list of responsibilities, jot down the times of day you think you might accomplish each task.

4. Decide how to organize your chart so that it follows the required format and makes information easy to locate.

5. Create a blank chart, and use the list and notes you made about your daily responsibilities to fill in the chart.

Comparing Functional Texts

1. (a) **Possible response:** An application introduces someone who wants a position to the people deciding who will be given that position, while a contract defines responsibilities for parties entering into an agreement. (b) **Possible response:** An application contains directions for completion, as well as designated areas for responses to questions, to help the candidate introduce him- or herself. A contract contains information defining to whom the contract applies, information on the responsibilities of all parties involved in the contract, and lines for parties to sign to show that they agree to the contract.

2. **Sample response:** My Dad was one of the applicants to be director of the play at the local community theater. However, he had a misconception about who should apply. He thought previous experience was unnecessary. In fact, it was the main criterion for the job.

🕐 Timed Writing

1. Before students complete the activity, guide them in identifying and analyzing key words and phrases in the prompt, which are highlighted on the student page.

2. Work with students to draw up guidelines for their essays based on the key words, as in this example:

• **Focus** The writer should clearly present his or her schedule and explain how rehearsals will fit into it.

• **Organization** The writer should make a chart that is easy to read and presents his or her schedule in chronological order.

• **Elaboration** The writer should make sure that all important elements of his or her daily schedule are included and that the explanations are thorough.

• **Style** The audience is not specified, so a formal style is appropriate.

3. Have students use the 5-Minute Planner to structure their time.

4. Allow students 15 minutes to complete the assignment. Evaluate their work using the guidelines they have developed.

❶ Comparing Characters

1. Introduce the skill to students, using the instruction on the student page.

2. Give students a copy of **Comparing Characters Graphic Organizer B** (*Graphic Organizer Transparencies,* p. 33). Tell them they will fill it in as they read.

Think Aloud: Model the Skill

Model the skill of distinguishing between direct and indirect characterization. Say to students:

To remember the difference between direct and indirect characterization, I think of the story "Cinderella." When the writer tells me that Cinderella is a sweet, obedient girl, he is using direct characterization. He tells me directly what Cinderella is like. When I read that Cinderella's stepmother makes her stay home during the ball, the writer is using indirect characterization. He doesn't have to tell me that the stepmother is mean—her action shows that she is.

Comparing Literary Works

The Night the Bed Fell • Stolen Day

❶ Comparing Characters

A **character** is a person, animal, or being that takes part in the action of a literary work. In literature, you will find characters with a range of personalities and attitudes. For example, a character might be dependable and smart but also stubborn. The qualities that make each character unique are called **character traits.** Writers use the process of **characterization** to create and develop characters. There are two types of characterization:

- **Direct characterization:** The writer directly states or describes the character's traits.

- **Indirect characterization:** The writer reveals a character's personality through his or her words and actions, and through the thoughts, words, and actions of others.

A character's responses may be internal or external. An **internal response** reveals a character's thoughts, while an **external response** consists of a character's actions or deeds. Writers use the internal and external responses of characters to **develop the plot** of a literary work. For example, the characters' responses can strongly influence the conflict—the problem or struggle that increases the tension in a story.

As you read, look for character traits that show each narrator's qualities, attitudes, and values. Use a chart like the one below to analyze how the writer develops the narrator's character.

	"The Night the Bed Fell"	"Stolen Day"
Main character		
Direct descriptions		
Character's words and actions		
What others say about character		

- Vocabulary flashcards
- Interactive journals
- More about the authors
- Selection audio
- Interactive graphic organizers

www.PHLitOnline.com

160 Fiction and Nonfiction

Vocabulary Development

Vocabulary Knowledge Rating

Create a **Vocabulary Knowledge Rating Chart** (*Professional Development Guidebook,* p. 33) featuring the vocabulary words glossed in the selections:

ominous (p. 162)	perilous (p. 164)
culprit (p. 167)	solemn (p. 170)

Give students a copy of the chart, and read the words aloud. Have students mark their rating of each in the Before You Read column. To gauge how much instruction to provide, tally the number of students who think they know each word.

Explain that the words are defined in the margin at the point where they appear in the selection. Urge students to be alert to these words as they read and discuss the selections. They will rate their knowledge again when they finish.

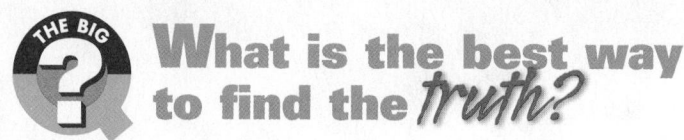

What is the best way to find the *truth?*

Writing About the Big Question

Each of these stories describes a misunderstanding that happened when people's own beliefs got in the way of what is true. Use this sentence starter to develop your ideas.

When people **misunderstand** a situation, it creates confusion because _____.

Meet the Authors

James Thurber (1894–1961)

Author of "The Night the Bed Fell"

According to James Thurber, if you had lived in his Ohio home, you would have observed absurd events. He wrote of such events—but always showed affection for his quirky relatives.

Understanding Humor To Thurber, humor results from the contrast between the confusion of a moment and the insight gained later. In "The Night the Bed Fell," Thurber calmly recounts and makes sense of an instance of total confusion— and the result is laughter. Thurber's literary home was *The New Yorker* magazine, where he wrote essays that gently poked fun at the world. He often did line drawings for his essays, even when his sight began to fail him.

Sherwood Anderson (1876–1941)

Author of "Stolen Day"

As a teenager, Sherwood Anderson worked as a newsboy, housepainter, and stable groom. Later, he fought in Cuba in the Spanish-American War. Even though Anderson did not begin to write professionally until he was forty years old, he is considered an important writer of the twentieth century.

A Powerful Influence Anderson's novel *Winesburg, Ohio* was published in 1919. In it, Anderson used simple, everyday language to capture the sense of loneliness and lost hope of characters living in a small town.

The Night the Bed Fell/Stolen Day **161**

Teaching Resources

- **All** *Unit 1 Resources,* pp. 212–219
- **All** *Graphic Organizer Transparencies,* pp. 32–35, 213
- **All** *Common Core Companion,* pp. 28–35; 122–123; 202–212
- **All** **Enriched Online Student Edition**
- **L2** **EL** *Hear It!* **Audio CD**

All resources, including print and audio, are available online at **www.PHLitOnline.com**.

❶ Background
James Thurber
An early accident left writer and cartoonist James Thurber blind in one eye from childhood. He joined the staff of *The New Yorker* magazine in 1927 where, despite limited and deteriorating eyesight, he worked for many years as an editor, staff writer, and cartoonist.

❷ Focusing Reading

Ask six or more volunteers to stand in front of the class and participate in a game of "telephone." Tell the first person to whisper a message into the next person's ear, and so on down the line. Ask the last student to say the message out loud. Compare this message with the original message, and discuss as a group the often humorous ways in which a message can become garbled or misunderstood. Tell students that in this essay, a series of misunderstandings causes some comical events to unfold.

Concept Connector ➤

Tell students they will discuss ways in which their game of telephone resembles the characters' experiences in "The Night the Bed Fell" after they read.

❸ About the Selection

In this essay, characters' mistaken ideas set off a chain reaction that produces total confusion. As the narrator's bed overturns during the night, each character responds in his or her own bizarre way. One reason the essay is so satisfying is that, prior to the action proper, Thurber describes the quirkiness of other family members, laying the groundwork for the odd ideas and actions of the characters.

The Night the Bed Fell
James Thurber

I suppose that the high-water mark of my youth in Columbus, Ohio, was the night the bed fell on my father. It makes a better recitation (unless, as some friends of mine have said, one has heard it five or six times) than it does a piece of writing, for it is almost necessary to throw furniture around, shake doors, and bark like a dog, to lend the proper atmosphere and verisimilitude[1] to what is admittedly a somewhat incredible tale. Still, it did take place.

It happened, then, that my father had decided to sleep in the attic one night, to be away where he could think. My mother opposed the notion strongly because, she said, the old wooden bed up there was unsafe: it was wobbly and the heavy headboard would crash down on father's head in case the bed fell, and kill him. There was no dissuading him, however, and at a quarter past ten he closed the attic door behind him and went up the narrow twisting stairs. We later heard ominous creakings as he crawled into bed. Grandfather, who usually slept in the attic bed when he was with us, had disappeared some days before. On these occasions he was usually gone six or eight days and returned growling and out of temper, with the news that the

Vocabulary
ominous (ăm´ ə nəs)
adj. threatening

---

1. **verisimilitude** (ver´ ə si mil´ ə tōōd) *n.* appearance of truth or reality.

162 Fiction and Nonfiction

Ⓒ Text Complexity Rubric

The Night the Bed Fell		
Qualitative Measures	**Context/Knowledge Demands**	Unusual extended family with quirky ideas and behaviors; some references to culture of early 1900s America 1 2 3 ④ 5
	Structure/Language Conventionality and Clarity	Numerous long, ornate sentences and lengthy descriptive passages; some slightly archaic vocabulary 1 2 3 ④ 5
	Levels of Meaning/ Purpose/Concepts	Humorous exaggeration and contrast (confusion and later insight) 1 2 ③ 4 5
Quantitative Measures	**Text Length**	Word Count: 1,738
	Lexile	1170L

Federal Union[2] was run by a passel of blockheads and that the Army of the Potomac[3] didn't have a chance.

We had visiting us at this time a nervous first cousin of mine named Briggs Beall, who believed that he was likely to cease breathing when he was asleep. It was his feeling that if he were not awakened every hour during the night, he might die of suffocation. He had been accustomed to setting an alarm clock to ring at intervals until morning, but I persuaded him to abandon this. He slept in my room and I told him that I was such a light sleeper that if anybody quit breathing in the same room with me, I would wake instantly. He tested me the first night—which I had suspected he would—by holding his breath after my regular breathing had convinced him I was asleep. I was not asleep, however, and called to him. This seemed to allay his fears a little, but he took the precaution of putting a glass of spirits of camphor[4] on a little table at the head of his bed. In case I didn't arouse him until he was almost gone, he said, he would sniff the camphor, a powerful reviver. Briggs was not the only member of his family who had his crotchets.[5] Old Aunt Melissa Beall (who could whistle like a man, with two fingers in her mouth) suffered under the premonition that she was destined to die on South High Street, because she had been born on South High Street and married on South High Street. Then there was Aunt Sarah Shoaf, who never went to bed at night without the fear that a burglar was going to get in and blow chloroform[6] under her door through a tube. To avert this calamity—for she was in greater dread of anesthetics than of losing her household goods—she always piled her money, silverware, and other valuables in a neat stack just outside her bedroom, with a note reading: "This is all I have. Please take it and do not use your chloroform, as this is all I have." Aunt Gracie Shoaf also had a burglar phobia, but she met it with more fortitude. She was confident that burglars had been getting into her house every night for forty years. The fact that she never missed anything was to her no proof to the contrary. She always claimed that she scared them off before they could take anything, by throwing shoes down the hallway. When she went to bed she piled, where she could get at them handily, all the shoes

---

2. **Federal Union** northern side during the Civil War of the 1860s. He is under the illusion that the Civil War has not yet ended.
3. **Army of the Potomac** one of the northern armies during the Civil War.
4. **spirits of camphor** liquid with a powerful odor.
5. **crotchets** (kräch´ its) *n.* peculiar ideas.
6. **chloroform** (klôr´ ə fôrm´) *n.* substance used at one time as an anesthetic.

Character
What details about this character are probably exaggerated?

Character
What are the contrasts between the aunts' beliefs and reality?

6 **Reading Check**
What kind of a story does the narrator say he is going to tell?

The Night the Bed Fell **163**

---

❹ Character

1. Have a volunteer read aloud the first bracketed section of the text.
2. Remind students that they have already been introduced to one eccentric member of Thurber's family: his grandfather. **Ask** if they think there is anything about Grandfather's character that might have been exaggerated. **Answer:** It is possible that Grandfather, although a bit confused, did not really believe that the Civil War was still raging.
3. Then, **ask** the first Character question: What details about this character are probably exaggerated? **Answer:** Although it is believable that Briggs Beall was very nervous and even that he feared that he would stop breathing during the night, it is unlikely that he set his alarm clock to ring every single hour of every night, as Thurber implies. It is also unlikely that Beall really believed that the smell of camphor would be sufficient to revive him if he were about to die of suffocation.

❺ Character

1. Continue discussing how each of Thurber's characters appears to suffer from a delusion. Point out that the grandfather, for example, has an idea of reality that bears no relation to the truth: He thinks the country is still fighting the Civil War.
2. **Ask** the second Character question on this page. **Answer:** Aunt Melissa Beall is convinced she is going to die on the street on which she had been born and married, but there is no rational or logical basis for this belief. There is no evidence to support Aunt Sarah Shoaf's belief that one night a burglar will get into her house and blow chloroform into her room. Aunt Gracie Shoaf believes burglars enter her house every night, even though none of her possessions has ever been stolen.

❻ Reading Check

Answer: He says that he is going to tell an incredible but true tale from his childhood.

ⓒ Text Complexity: Reader and Task Suggestions

The Night the Bed Fell

Preparing to Read the Text
- Have students review Thurber's drawings in the selection. Ask what they add to the story.
- Explain that the story contains many long, complex sentences. Discuss examples of this. Model how to break down long sentences into manageable chunks.
- Guide students in using Multidraft Reading strategies to deepen their comprehension (TE p. 161).

Leveled Tasks
Structure/Language If students will have difficulty with sentence complexity, have them first read to identify each family member's part in the confusion. Then, have them reread, noting long or confusing sentences.

Evaluating If students will not have difficulty with sentence complexity, have them note as they read ways that Thurber uses sentence complexity to create a humorous mood and frantic pace. For example, complex sentences may read as if they are tumbling forward much like the story's events tumble into chaos.

163

Some nights she threw them all. by James Thurber

❼ ▲ **Critical Viewing**
How would Gracie Shoaf defend the actions shown in this drawing? **[Analyze]**

Vocabulary
perilous (per´ ə ləs)
adj. dangerous

there were about her house. Five minutes after she had turned off the light, she would sit up in bed and say "Hark!" Her husband, who had learned to ignore the whole situation as long ago as 1903, would either be sound asleep or pretend to be sound asleep. In either case he would not respond to her tugging and pulling, so that presently she would arise, tiptoe to the door, open it slightly and heave a shoe down the hall in one direction, and its mate down the hall in the other direction. Some nights she threw them all, some nights only a couple of pair.

But I am straying from the remarkable incidents that took place during the night that the bed fell on father. By midnight we were all in bed. The layout of the rooms and the disposition[7] of their occupants is important to an understanding of what later occurred. In the front room upstairs (just under father's attic bedroom) were my mother and my brother Herman, who sometimes sang in his sleep, usually "Marching Through Georgia" or "Onward, Christian Soldiers." Briggs Beall and myself were in a room adjoining this one. My brother Roy was in a room across the hall from ours. Our bull terrier, Rex, slept in the hall.

My bed was an army cot, one of those affairs which are made wide enough to sleep on comfortably only by putting up, flat with the middle section, the two sides which ordinarily hang down like the sideboards of a drop-leaf table. When these sides are up, it is perilous to roll too far toward the edge, for then the cot is likely to tip completely over, bringing the whole bed down on top of one, with a tremendous banging crash. This, in fact, is precisely what happened about two o'clock in the morning. (It was my mother who, in recalling the scene later, first referred to it as "the night the bed fell on your father.")

---

7. disposition (dis´ pə zish´ ən) *n.* arrangement.

164 Fiction and Nonfiction

Always a deep sleeper, slow to arouse (I had lied to Briggs), I was at first unconscious of what had happened when the iron cot rolled me onto the floor and toppled over on me. It left me still warmly bundled up and unhurt, for the bed rested above me like a canopy. Hence I did not wake up, only reached the edge of consciousness and went back. The racket, however, instantly awakened my mother, in the next room, who came to the immediate conclusion that her worst dread was realized: the big wooden bed upstairs had fallen on father. She therefore screamed, "Let's go to your poor father!" It was this shout, rather than the noise of my cot falling, that awakened Herman, in the same room with her. He thought that mother had become, for no apparent reason, hysterical. "You're all right, Mamma!" he shouted, trying to calm her. They exchanged shout for shout for perhaps ten seconds: "Let's go to your poor father!" and "You're all right!" That woke up Briggs. By this time I was conscious of what was going on, in a vague way, but did not yet realize that I was under my bed instead of on it. Briggs, awakening in the midst of loud shouts of fear and apprehension, came to the

8 ▼ Critical Viewing
What part of the story does this picture show? **[Connect]**

Character
How does the mother's reaction make this situation humorous?

 Reading Check
10 What type of bed does the narrator sleep on this night?

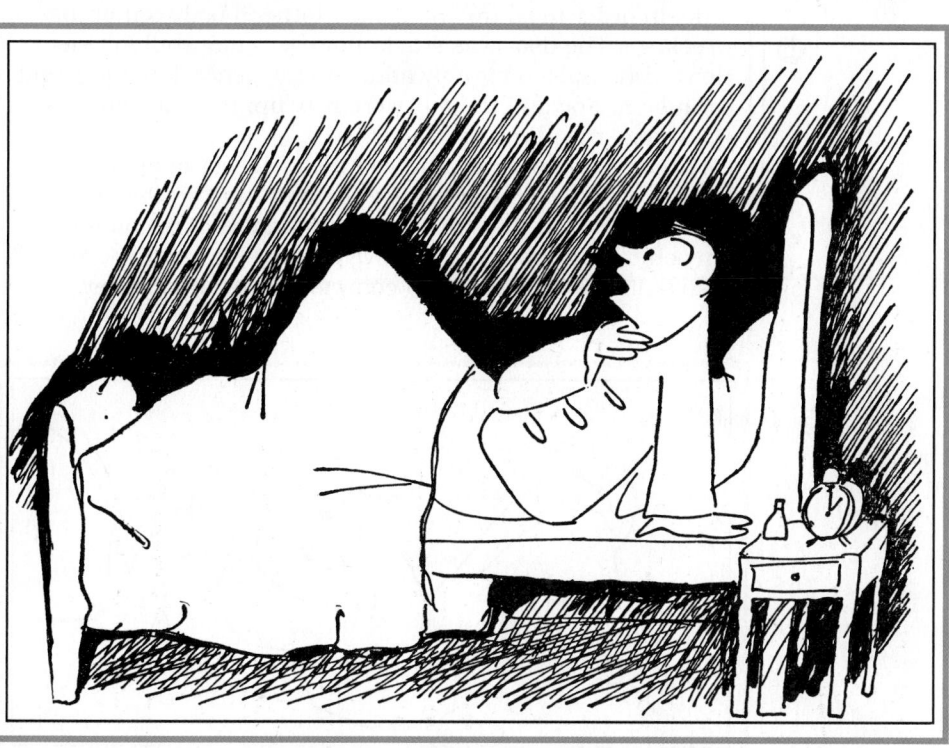

The Night the Bed Fell **165**

8 Critical Viewing

Answer: It shows Briggs being afraid that he is suffocating.

9 Character

1. Have students reread the bracketed passage. Then, **ask** them what they have already learned about the narrator's mother, through both direct and indirect characterization.
   Answer: The mother opposed her husband's plan of sleeping in the attic because she was afraid the wobbly headboard would fall on his head and kill him. We also learn on page 164 that she has her own view of reality: In the future she will refer to this event as "the night the bed fell on your father" when in fact the bed fell on her son.

2. Then, **ask** the Character question: How does the mother's reaction make this situation humorous?
   Answer: Because nobody has actually been injured and because the mother has misinterpreted which bed fell, her hysterical over-reaction is amusing. Also, the fact that her over-reaction provokes a chain of other, equally irrational responses from the other members of the family compounds the humor.

10 Reading Check

Answer: The narrator sleeps in an army cot with the sideboards up.

Differentiated Instruction *for Universal Access*

Strategy for Special-Needs Students
Students may have difficulty remembering the sequence of events in this humorous story because things happen quickly. As students read, have them identify significant events in the narrative. Help students use the **Series-of-Events Chain** on p. 213 in *Graphic Organizer Transparencies.*

Strategy for Less Proficient Readers
This selection includes unfamiliar words that are not defined in the text. Examples include *dissuading, passel, hark,* and *presently.* Help students use a dictionary to find the meanings of difficult words they encounter and create informal glossaries to accompany the story.

PHLit Online!
This selection is available in interactive format in the **Enriched Online Student Edition,** online at www.PHLitOnline.com, which includes an interactive graphic organizer.

165

166

⑪ Character

1. Have a volunteer read aloud the bracketed section.

2. **Ask** the Character question.
Answer: Briggs is so nervous that instead of sniffing the camphor he poured it over himself.

⑫ Connecting to the Big Question

1. Remind students that the truth is not always obvious, and the characters in Thurber's story have strong tendencies to ignore or bend reality.

2. **Ask:** Identify each character who has a mistaken idea of what is happening at this point in the story.
Answer: The narrator knows he is somehow trapped, but he is too groggy to know that his bed has fallen. Briggs thinks that he is suffocating. The mother thinks the bed in the attic has fallen and killed her husband. Herman thinks the mother is shouting for no reason.

3. Then, **ask** how everyone could find out the truth.
Answers: Briggs could fully wake the narrator and tell him that his bed has fallen; the narrator could wake up and tell Briggs there is nothing wrong with him; the mother should stop screaming and call up to the attic to see if her husband is all right. Herman should ask his mother why she is screaming. Everybody could find out the truth if they stopped yelling, turned on some lights, and looked around.

⑬ Critical Viewing

Possible response: The dog jumping on a helpless man captures the essay's mood of mounting chaos.

Character
⑪ What action does Briggs perform that helps to reveal his nervous personality?

⑬ ▶ **Critical Viewing**
How does the action in this drawing capture the mood of the story? **[Analyze]**

166 Fiction and Nonfiction

---

⑪ quick conclusion that he was suffocating and that we were all trying to "bring him out." With a low moan, he grasped the glass of camphor at the head of his bed and instead of sniffing it poured it over himself. The room reeked of camphor. "Ugf, ahfg," choked Briggs, like a drowning man, for he had almost succeeded in stopping his breath under the deluge of pungent spirits. He leaped out of bed and groped toward the open window, but he came up against one that was closed. With his hand, he beat out the glass, and I could hear it crash and tinkle on the alleyway below. It was at this juncture that I, in trying to get up, had the uncanny sensation of feeling my bed above me! Foggy with sleep, I ⑫ now suspected, in my turn, that the whole uproar was being made in a frantic endeavor to extricate me from what must be an unheard-of and perilous situation. "Get me out of this!" I bawled. "Get me out!" I think I had the nightmarish belief that I was entombed in a mine. "Gugh," gasped Briggs, floundering in his camphor.

By this time my mother, still shouting, pursued by Herman, still shouting, was trying to open the door to the attic, in order to go up and get my father's body out of the ⑭ wreckage. The door was stuck, however, and wouldn't yield. Her frantic pulls on it only added to the general banging and confusion. Roy and the dog were now up, the one shouting questions, the other barking.

Father, farthest away and soundest sleeper of all, had by this time been awakened by the battering on the attic door. He decided that the house was on fire. "I'm coming, I'm coming!" he wailed in a slow, sleepy voice—it took him many minutes to regain full consciousness. My mother,

Roy had to throw Rex. by James Thurber

Vocabulary Development
CCSS Language 6

 Thematic Vocabulary: The Big Question
As students are discussing "The Night the Bed Fell," ask them to use the thematic vocabulary presented in Introducing the Big Question, pp. 2–3. You might encourage them with sentence starters like these, using the words or their variants:

1. Not one of the characters has a clear *awareness* . . .

2. Gracie Shoaf's husband does not find it *believable* that . . .

3. The narrator might have had more *insight* into what had happened to him if . . .

4. Briggs Beall's weak grip on *reality* is demonstrated by . . .

5. Mother *perceives* the loud crash as coming from . . .

still believing he was caught under the bed, detected in his "I'm coming!" the mournful, resigned note of one who is preparing to meet his Maker. "He's dying!" she shouted.

"I'm all right!" Briggs yelled to reassure her. "I'm all right!" He still believed that it was his own closeness to death that was worrying mother. I found at last the light switch in my room, unlocked the door, and Briggs and I joined the others at the attic door. The dog, who never did like Briggs, jumped for him—assuming that he was the culprit in whatever was going on—and Roy had to throw Rex and hold him. We could hear father crawling out of bed upstairs. Roy pulled the attic door open, with a mighty jerk, and father came down the stairs, sleepy and irritable but safe and sound. My mother began to weep when she saw him. Rex began to howl. "What in the name of heaven is going on here?" asked father.

The situation was finally put together like a gigantic jigsaw puzzle. Father caught a cold from prowling around in his bare feet but there were no other bad results. "I'm glad," said mother, who always looked on the bright side of things, "that your grandfather wasn't here."

Character
What characteristics make the mother amusing?

Vocabulary
culprit (kul´ prit)
n. guilty person

Spiral Review
Central Idea What are two central ideas in this humorous essay?

Critical Thinking

1. Key Ideas and Details (a) Who is in the house on the night Thurber describes? **(b) Compare:** What quality or qualities do these characters share? **(c) Support:** What examples illustrate the shared qualities?

2. Key Ideas and Details (a) Describe the layout of the rooms. **(b) Analyze:** Why is the placement of the rooms in the house important to the events?

3. Key Ideas and Details (a) What do Briggs, Aunt Sarah Shoaf, and Aunt Gracie Shoaf do before going to bed? **(b) Infer:** What do you suppose the author, looking back, thinks of this behavior? **(c) Make a Judgment:** Do you think the author treats his relatives fairly in the essay? Why or why not?

4. Integration of Knowledge and Ideas (a) How do the misunderstandings in this essay help reveal each character's beliefs? **(b)** How can we use a misunderstanding to bring us closer to the truth? *[Connect to the Big Question: What is the best way to find the truth?]*

Cite textual evidence to support your responses.

The Night the Bed Fell **167**

⓮ Character
Ask the Character question.
Possible response: The mother always believes the worst is happening, so she misinterprets events and words.

Spiral Review
Central Idea

1. Students studied the concept of central idea in the Unit 1 Literary Analysis Workshop (pp. 4–21).

2. **Ask** students the Spiral Review question.

   Possible response: People's preconceived ideas can lead them to misunderstand a situation, and the world is not as scary as some people think it is.

ASSESS

Answers

Critical Thinking
Remind students to support their answers with evidence from the text.

1. (a) Mr. and Mrs. Thurber, James, Herman, Roy, Briggs Beall, and Rex are in the house. (b) They have peculiar ideas and are excitable. (c) Briggs's fear is peculiar, and so is Mrs. Thurber's.

2. (a) Mr. Thurber is in the attic. Herman is with Mrs. Thurber in her room below the attic room. James and Briggs are in the bedroom next to Mrs. Thurber's. Roy is in his bedroom across the hall. (b) The rooms are so close that Mrs. Thurber mistakes which room the crash comes from.

3. (a) Briggs puts camphor by his bed in case he stops breathing. Aunt Sarah Shoaf piles her valuables outside the door. Aunt Gracie Shoaf piles all the shoes in the house where she can reach them. (b) He thinks his relatives are crazy. (c) Yes; he factually reports on their actions. No; he withholds information that would help readers understand his relatives better.

4. (a) The misunderstandings reveal the characters' biggest fears: Mrs. Thurber fears that the bed will fall on her husband, and Briggs fears that he will suffocate in his sleep. (b) A misunderstanding can inspire us to work hard at communicating to avoid confusing or misleading others.

167

In "Stolen Day," the main character convinces himself that he has "inflammatory rheumatism." Today this condition is called rheumatoid arthritis. It is a kind of inflammatory arthritis that attacks the membranes surrounding the fluid in the joints.

⑯ Activating Prior Knowledge

Use the **Vocab-o-Gram** strategy (*Professional Development Guidebook,* p. 40) to introduce students to the selection and to provide information that will allow them to make predictions about the reading. Put these words on the board or on a transparency:

actor	bite
ache	whopper
limp	hero
swell	laughed
fishing	cried

Then, give students the Vocab-o-Gram chart (*Professional Development Guidebook,* p. 40), and have them work with a partner or group to place the words in appropriate categories and to make predictions about the story. Have students discuss or explain their word placements and their predictions.

Concept Connector ➤

Tell students they will return to their predictions after they read the selection.

⑰ About the Selection

On the way to school, a boy sees Walter, a classmate who has an illness bad enough to keep him out of school but not serious enough to keep him from fishing and walking about. Intrigued by Walter's freedom, the boy fakes having the same illness in order to stay at home from school and to go fishing, too.

It must be that *all children* are actors.

168 Fiction and Nonfiction

ⓒ Text Complexity Rubric

Stolen Day		
Qualitative Measures	**Context/Knowledge Demands**	Early 20th-century small town setting; fishing; childhood illness 1 2 ③ 4 5
	Structure/Language Conventionality	Short sentences and on-level vocabulary, but some colloquial phrases 1 2 ③ 4 5
	Levels of Meaning/ Purpose/Concept Level	Accessible concept (a boy wants attention) 1 2 ③ 4 5
Quantitative Measures	**Text Length**	Word Count: 1,746
	Lexile	690L

⑮
⑯
⑰

Stolen Day

Sherwood Anderson

It must be that all children are actors. The whole thing started with a boy on our street named Walter, who had inflammatory rheumatism.[1] That's what they called it. He didn't have to go to school.

Still he could walk about. He could go fishing in the creek or the waterworks pond. There was a place up at the pond where in the spring the water came tumbling over the dam and formed a deep pool. It was a good place. Sometimes you could get some big ones there.

I went down that way on my way to school one spring morning. It was out of my way but I wanted to see if Walter was there.

He was, inflammatory rheumatism and all. There he was, sitting with a fish pole in his hand. He had been able to walk down there all right.

⑱ It was then that my own legs began to hurt. My back too. I went on to school but, at the recess time, I began to cry. I did it when the teacher, Sarah Suggett, had come out into the schoolhouse yard.

She came right over to me.

"I ache all over," I said. I did, too.

---

1. **inflammatory rheumatism** (in flam′ ə tôr′ ē rōō′ mə tiz′ əm) *n.* a disease which causes the joints to swell painfully and gradually break down.

Character
What can you tell about the narrator based on the pain he experiences?

⑱ **Character**
1. Have a volunteer read aloud the bracketed selection.
2. **Ask** the Character question. **Answer:** The narrator seems to be someone who feels pain easily; just thinking about Walter's pain makes the narrator's own legs and back begin to hurt. He is probably hopeful that the pain will allow him to get out of school, like Walter, showing that he is capable of putting on a show.

© Text Complexity: Reader and Task Suggestions

Stolen Day

Preparing to Read the Text
- Use the Background note on TE p. 168 to discuss arthritis.
- Have students discuss the reasons why someone might want to fake an illness.
- Guide students in using Multidraft Reading strategies to deepen their comprehension (TE p. 161).

Leveled Tasks

Levels of Meaning If students will have difficulty with levels of meaning, have them first read to recognize details about the boy's desire for attention. Then, have them reread, noting when he pretends illness to get attention.

Analyzing If students will not have difficulty with levels of meaning, have them note as they read ways that Anderson uses contrasting perceptions to develop character and humor. For example, the narrator's description of his family's reaction to his death highlights his childish view of the world.

PHLit Online!
This selection is available in interactive format in the **Enriched Online Student Edition**, at **www.PHLitOnline.com,** which includes an interactive graphic organizer.

1. Have students reread the bracketed passage.

2. **Ask** the Character question.
   Answer: The narrator's pain goes away because he only imagined it. The narrator wants to believe he has inflammatory rheumatism so that he can get out of school.

3. Explain to students that when an author uses indirect characterization, readers may have to make assumptions or inferences about the character. **Ask** what assumption they can make about the narrator.
   Answer: He is deceiving himself and others to get something he wants.

Spiral Review

Theme

1. Remind students that they studied the concept of theme in the Unit 1 Literary Analysis Workshop (pp. 4–21).

2. **Ask** students the Spiral Review question.
   Possible response: When the boy wished to be sick, he started to feel pain. This relates to the theme that imagination is a very powerful thing.

Character
Why does the narrator's pain suddenly disappear? **19**

Spiral Review
Theme How might the narrator's so-called pain relate to a possible theme?

Vocabulary
solemn (säl′ əm) *adj.*
serious; somber

I kept on crying and it worked all right.

"You'd better go on home," she said.

So I went. I limped painfully away. I kept on limping until I got out of the schoolhouse street.

Then I felt better. I still had inflammatory rheumatism pretty bad but I could get along better.

I must have done some thinking on the way home.

"I'd better not say I have inflammatory rheumatism," I decided. "Maybe if you've got that you swell up."

I thought I'd better go around to where Walter was and ask him about that, so I did—but he wasn't there.

"They must not be biting today," I thought.

I had a feeling that, if I said I had inflammatory rheumatism, Mother or my brothers and my sister Stella might laugh. They did laugh at me pretty often and I didn't like it at all.

"Just the same," I said to myself, "I have got it." I began to hurt and ache again.

I went home and sat on the front steps of our house. I sat there a long time. There wasn't anyone at home but Mother and the two little ones. Ray would have been four or five then and Earl might have been three.

It was Earl who saw me there. I had got tired sitting and was lying on the porch. Earl was always a quiet, solemn little fellow.

He must have said something to Mother for presently she came.

"What's the matter with you? Why aren't you in school?" she asked.

I came pretty near telling her right out that I had inflammatory rheumatism but I thought I'd better not. Mother and Father had been speaking of Walter's case at the table just the day before. "It affects the heart," Father had said. That frightened me when I thought of it. "I might die," I thought. "I might just suddenly die right here; my heart might stop beating."

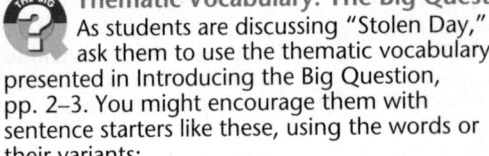

170 Fiction and Nonfiction

Vocabulary Development ©**CCSS** Language 6

Thematic Vocabulary: The Big Question
As students are discussing "Stolen Day," ask them to use the thematic vocabulary presented in Introducing the Big Question, pp. 2–3. You might encourage them with sentence starters like these, using the words or their variants:

1. When the narrator sees that Walter can still go fishing, he *concludes* that . . .

2. *Evidence* that the narrator is really quite healthy is . . .

3. The narrator is afraid that if he tells his mother the *truth* about why he is not in school . . .

4. The narrator starts to believe in his own *fiction* so much that . . .

5. At the end of the story, the main character gains *insight* into . . .

I kept on crying and it worked all right.

On the day before I had been running a race with my brother Irve. We were up at the fairgrounds after school and there was a half-mile track.

"I'll bet you can't run a half-mile," he said. "I bet you I could beat you running clear around the track."

And so we did it and I beat him, but afterwards my heart did seem to beat pretty hard. I remembered that lying there on the porch. "It's a wonder, with my inflammatory rheumatism and all, I didn't just drop down dead," I thought. The thought frightened me a lot. I ached worse than ever.

"I ache, Ma," I said. "I just ache."

She made me go in the house and upstairs and get into bed.

It wasn't so good. It was spring. I was up there for perhaps an hour, maybe two, and then I felt better.

I got up and went downstairs. "I feel better, Ma," I said.

Mother said she was glad. She was pretty busy that day and hadn't paid much attention to me. She had made me get into bed upstairs and then hadn't even come up to see how I was.

I didn't think much of that when I was up there but when I got downstairs where she was, and when, after I had said I felt better and she only said she was glad and went right on with her work, I began to ache again.

I thought, "I'll bet I die of it. I bet I do."

I went out to the front porch and sat down. I was pretty sore at Mother.

"If she really knew the truth, that I have the inflammatory rheumatism and I may just drop down dead any time, I'll bet

⓴ ▲ Critical Viewing
Does this boy look genuinely upset, or do you think he is making himself cry, as the story's narrator does? Explain. **[Evaluate]**

Character
What character trait do the narrator's thoughts suggest?

⓶⓶  **Reading Check**
What does the narrator believe is wrong with him?

Stolen Day **171**

⓴ Critical Viewing
Possible response: Details such as his frown and the fact that he clutches his head with one hand and his knee with the other look genuine, but they might also be put on for show.

㉑ Character
1. Have students reread the bracketed passage. Point out that this section focuses on the thoughts and actions of the main character, who is also the narrator. **Ask** students to sum up what the narrator is doing and thinking at this point in the story.
   Answer: The narrator tells his mother that he aches, and she sends him to bed. After a while he gets up and goes downstairs. When his mother ignores him, he feels sick again and decides that he'll probably die.

2. **Ask** the Character question.
   Answer: The narrator's thoughts suggest that he feels ignored and thinks his mother doesn't really care about him. He has the trait of feeling sorry for himself.

3. Tell students to use these details to fill in their graphic organizers comparing characters.

㉒ Reading Check
Answer: The narrator believes that he has inflammatory rheumatism and might drop dead at any time.

Differentiated Instruction for Universal Access

Support for Special-Needs Students
Some students may be puzzled by the narrator's ambiguous attitude toward his "illness." They may want to know if the narrator is just playing a part or if he really feels ill. Explain that both are true. He really feels aches and pains, but he pretends to limp while his teacher is watching him leave the school, and he feels fine after lying down at home until he realizes his mother isn't acting sympathetic enough. Ask students if they have ever made up a story and then convinced themselves that it was true.

Strategy for Less Proficient Readers
Because the vocabulary in this selection is mostly very simple and the sentences are short, "Stolen Day" can provide a good opportunity for less proficient readers to practice their oral reading skills. Have a group of such readers prepare several pages to read aloud, first circling any long or unfamiliar words and making sure they know what the words mean and how to pronounce them. Then, have the group take turns reading a section at a time and correcting each other's errors, if any.

171

1. Have students reread the bracketed passage. Make sure students
understand that the narrator is
imagining what would happen if
his heart were suddenly to stop
beating and he were to fall into
the pond.

2. **Ask** the Character question.
Possible response: Students
may suggest that the narrator is
silly, thoughtless, or selfish.

3. **Ask** students why, given the narrator's daydream, it is humorous
when he says "When I got there I
thought I'd better not sit too near
the edge of the high bank."
Answer: The line is humorous
because although the narrator
had just had a very satisfying daydream about how sad everyone
would be if he were to die, he
really does not want to die.

4. Tell students to use these details
to fill in their graphic organizers
comparing characters.

she wouldn't care about that either," I thought.

I was getting more and more angry the more thinking I did.

"I know what I'm going to do," I thought; "I'm going to go
fishing."

I thought that, feeling the way I did, I might be sitting on
the high bank just above the deep pool where the water
went over the dam, and suddenly my heart would stop
beating.

And then, of course, I'd pitch forward, over the bank into
the pool and, if I wasn't dead when I hit the water, I'd drown
sure.

They would all come home to supper and they'd miss
me.

"But where is he?"

Then Mother would remember that I'd come home
from school aching.

She'd go upstairs and I wouldn't be there. One
day during the year before, there was a child
got drowned in a spring. It was one of the Wyatt
children.

Right down at the end of the street there was
a spring under a birch tree and there had been a
barrel sunk in the ground.

Everyone had always been saying the spring
ought to be kept covered, but it wasn't.

So the Wyatt child went down there, played
around alone, and fell in and got drowned.

Mother was the one who had found the drowned
child. She had gone to get a pail of water and there
the child was, drowned and dead.

This had been in the evening when we were all at home,
and Mother had come running up the street with the dead,
dripping child in her arms. She was making for the Wyatt
house as hard as she could run, and she was pale.

She had a terrible look on her face, I remembered then.

"So," I thought, "they'll miss me and there'll be a search
made. Very likely there'll be someone who has seen me sitting
by the pond fishing, and there'll be a big alarm and all the
town will turn out and they'll drag the pond."

I was having a grand time, having died. Maybe, after they
found me and had got me out of the deep pool, Mother would
grab me up in her arms and run home with me as she had
run with the Wyatt child.

Character
Based on this imagi-
nary scene, what words
would you use to
describe the narrator?

Think Aloud

Point of View
Using the following "think aloud," model the
skill of analyzing point of view, introduced on
page 49. Say to students:

The narrator of this story uses the words I
and my to refer to himself. That means that
this story is told from the first-person point of
view. Because I know that a first-person narrator can directly reveal only his or her own
thoughts and feelings, I pay close attention
to these thoughts and feelings. I learn that
the narrator both wants to be sick so that he

can skip school and win his mother's sympathy, and wants not to have an illness that
could kill him. Because the narrator's emotions and thoughts are confused and childish, I realize that I must figure out when he is
describing actual events and when he is
caught up in a fantasy. I decide that when he
reports dialogue, he is recording reality.
However, when he records his thoughts, he
is just daydreaming.

I got up from the porch and went around the house. I got my fishing pole and lit out for the pool below the dam. Mother was busy—she always was—and didn't see me go. When I got there I thought I'd better not sit too near the edge of the high bank.

By this time I didn't ache hardly at all, but I thought. "With inflammatory rheumatism you can't tell," I thought.

"It probably comes and goes," I thought.

"Walter has it and he goes fishing," I thought.

I had got my line into the pool and suddenly I got a bite. It was a regular whopper. I knew that. I'd never had a bite like that.

I knew what it was. It was one of Mr. Fenn's big carp.

Mr. Fenn was a man who had a big pond of his own. He sold ice in the summer and the pond was to make the ice. He had bought some big carp and put them into his pond and then, earlier in the spring when there was a freshet,[2] his dam had gone out.

So the carp had got into our creek and one or two big ones had been caught—but none of them by a boy like me.

The carp was pulling and I was pulling and I was afraid he'd break my line, so I just tumbled down the high bank holding onto the line and got right into the pool. We had it out, there in the pool. We struggled. We wrestled. Then I got a hand under his gills and got him out.

He was a big one all right. He was nearly half as big as I was myself. I had him on the bank and I kept one hand under his gills and I ran.

I never ran so hard in my life. He was slippery, and now and then he wriggled out of my arms; once I stumbled and fell on him, but I got him home.

So there it was. I was a big hero that day. Mother got a washtub and filled it with water. She put the fish in it and all the neighbors came to look. I got into dry clothes and went

---

"I know what I'm going to do," I thought; "I'm going to go fishing."

Character
What do the narrator's actions with the carp reveal about his physical condition?

25 ✔ Reading Check
What happened to the Wyatt child?

2. **freshet** (fresh´ it) a great rise or overflowing of a stream caused by heavy rains or melted snow.

ASSESS

Answers

Critical Thinking

Remind students to support their answers with evidence from the text.

1. (a) He notices that Walter is too sick to go to school but is sometimes well enough to go fishing. (b) He would be able to go fishing instead of going to school. (c) Students may think that it is a bad idea to wish that you had a serious illness, or they may appreciate the logic of the narrator's thinking.

2. (a) He sits on the porch for a while. Eventually his mother sends him to bed. When he gets bored with being there, he goes fishing. (b) She is busy working. Her behavior suggests that she knows that he is not really sick.

3. (a) They laugh. (b) Students may think that the family is too harsh and should be more sympathetic to the worries the boy had been dealing with all day. They may also suggest that the family laughs because the boy could not possibly have landed the big fish if he really had inflammatory rheumatism.

4. **Possible responses:** We sometimes need to realize that we have been imagining something before we can learn the truth.

---

down to supper—and then I made a break that spoiled my day.

There we were, all of us, at the table, and suddenly Father asked what had been the matter with me at school. He had met the teacher, Sarah Suggett, on the street and she had told him how I had become ill.

"What was the matter with you?" Father asked, and before I thought what I was saying I let it out.

"I had the inflammatory rheumatism," I said—and a shout went up. It made me sick to hear them, the way they all laughed.

It brought back all the aching again, and like a fool I began to cry.

"Well, I *have* got it—I *have*, I *have*," I cried, and I got up from the table and ran upstairs.

I stayed there until Mother came up. I knew it would be a long time before I heard the last of the inflammatory rheumatism. I was sick all right, but the aching I now had wasn't in my legs or in my back.

I was a **BIG** *hero that day.*

Critical Thinking

Cite textual evidence to support your responses.

1. **Key Ideas and Details (a)** What inspires the narrator to think he has inflammatory rheumatism? **(b) Infer:** Why does the narrator think this would be an appealing disease to have? **(c) Respond:** What do you think of his idea? Explain.

2. **Key Ideas and Details (a)** What does the narrator do after he gets home? **(b) Infer:** Why does his mother pay him little attention?

3. **Integration of Knowledge and Ideas (a)** How does his family respond when the narrator says he has inflammatory rheumatism? **(b) Defend:** Do you think the narrator's family should have been more understanding? Why or why not?

4. **Integration of Knowledge and Ideas** How does discovering what is *not* real help us determine what is real? Explain. *[Connect to the Big Question: What is the best way to find the truth?]*

Vocabulary Development

Vocabulary Knowledge Rating
When students have completed reading and discussing "The Night the Bed Fell" and "Stolen Day," have them take out their **Vocabulary Knowledge Rating Chart**. Read the words aloud once more, and have students rate their knowledge of words again in the After Reading column. Clarify any words that are still problematic. Have students write their own definition and example or sentence in the appropriate column. Then, have students complete the Vocabulary Practice activities on page 175. Encourage them to use the words in further discussion and written work about these selections. Remind students that they will be accountable for these words on the **Selection Test,** *Unit 1 Resources,* pp. 223–225 or 226–228.

Comparing Characters

 1. Key Ideas and Details Identify one example of **direct characterization** and one example of **indirect characterization** in each selection.

2. Key Ideas and Details (a) What happens to the narrator's army cot in "The Night the Bed Fell"? **(b)** What does his mother think happened?

3. Key Ideas and Details (a) What does the narrator of "Stolen Day" do that causes his teacher to send him home? **(b)** Why does he do this?

4. Integration of Knowledge and Ideas Use the chart below to compare how the narrators of both stories are alike and how they are different.

	How similar?	How different?
Narrator: "Stolen Day"	A boy	Believes he is sick
Narrator: "The Night the Bed Fell"		

⏱ Timed Writing

Explanatory Text: Essay

In an essay, compare and contrast the narrators in these selections. Describe ways in which the narrators' internal and external responses to conflict affect the development of the plot. Cite evidence from the texts to support your analysis. **(30 minutes)**

5-Minute Planner

1. Read the prompt carefully and completely.

2. Answer these questions to help you gather your ideas.

- What are a few traits of each narrator? How does each respond to conflict?
- To what extent do the narrators' responses affect the plot of each selection?
- Which narrator do you think will learn the most from his experiences? Why?

3. Create an outline in which you organize the details of your essay.

4. Reread the prompt, and then use your outline to draft your essay.

Assessment Resources

The following resources can be used to assess students' knowledge and skills.

Unit 1 Resources

L1 L2 EL **Selection Test A,** pp. 223–225

L3 L4 EL **Selection Test B,** pp. 226–228

L3 L4   **Open Book Test,** pp. 220–222

 All assessment resources are available at **www.PHLitOnline.com.**

Comparing Characters

1. **Possible responses:** In "The Night the Bed Fell," the narrator uses direct characterization in describing Briggs Beall as "a nervous first cousin of mine." Roy's decisiveness is shown through indirect characterization when he stops the dog from attacking Briggs and then jerks open the stuck attic door. In "Stolen Day," an example of direct characterization is the narrator's description of his brother Earl as "a quiet, solemn little fellow." The mother's matter-of-fact nature is shown through indirect characterization when she calmly tells the narrator to go to bed and then says she is glad when he feels better.

2. (a) The cot tips over. (b) The mother thinks the attic bed's headboard fell on her husband.

3. (a) The narrator cries and says he aches all over. (b) He does this because he wants to skip school as Walter does.

4. In their charts, students may note that both narrators are confused about events but that Thurber's narrator is confused by the chaos around him while Anderson's is confused by his own desires.

For other sample answers, see **Comparing Literary Works Graphic Organizer A (After You Read),** *Graphic Organizer Transparencies,* p. 34.

⏱ Timed Writing

1. Review the prompt with students.

2. Have students use the 5-Minute Planner to structure their time. Guide them in answering the bulleted questions. For example, point out the second bullet point and help students list each character's responses before they try to answer the question.

3. Allow students 30 minutes to complete the assignment.

4. As students prewrite and draft, have them refer to their completed **Comparing Characters Graphic Organizer.**

Six Traits Focus

✓ Ideas	Word Choice
Organization	Sentence Fluency
Voice	Conventions

Common Core
State Standards

• Writing 3, 3.a, b, c, d, e; 5

Introducing the Writing Assignment

Review the assignment and the criteria.

Richard Peck on Fiction

Show students Segment 3 on Richard Peck on *See It!* DVD or from this page in the **Enriched Student Online Edition** at **www.PHLitOnline.com.** Discuss his statement that all fiction is based on contrast, and ask students to consider how it might apply to their autobiographical narratives.

Writing Workshop
Work in Progress

If students have completed the Work-in-Progress assignments on pp. 127 and 151, suggest that they consider developing their Work-In-Progress ideas into an autobiographical narrative.

What Do You Notice?

1. Have a volunteer read the quotation aloud. **Ask** students the first question: What do you notice about the structure of these sentences? (**Possible response:** The sentences contain interruptions.)

2. Guide students to the first sentence. **Ask** What effect does the dash have? (**Possible response:** It signals a digression from the action of the story to reveal the narrator's thoughts.)

3. How does the structure add interest or increase action in the story? (**Possible response:** It allows the reader to follow the character's thoughts. It also makes the dramatic "whoosh" in her next statement more surprising.)

Writing Workshop

Write a Narrative

Narration: Autobiographical Narrative

Defining the Form Stories that tell of real events in a writer's life are called **autobiographical narratives.**

Assignment Write an autobiographical narrative about an event in your life that helped you grow or changed your outlook. Include

✔ a clear *sequence of events* involving you, the writer

✔ a problem or *conflict,* or a clear contrast between past and present viewpoints

✔ a *plot* line that includes a beginning, rising action, climax, and resolution, or *denouement*

✔ *pacing* that effectively builds the action

✔ *specific details and quotations*

✔ well-developed *major and minor characters*

✔ error-free writing, including *correct use of pronouns*

To preview the criteria on which your autobiographical narrative may be judged, see the rubric on page 183.

Writing Workshop: *Work in Progress*

Review the work you did on pages 127 and 151.

WRITE GUY
Jeff Anderson, M.Ed.

What Do You Notice?

Structure and Style

These sentences are from Richard Peck's "The Three-Century Woman." Read them several times.

"I was wearing my beige coat—beige or off-white, I forget. Then whoosh! The gondola heated up like an oven, and people peeled out of the windows. We hit the ground and bounced."

Discuss these questions with a partner:

• What do you notice about the structure of these sentences?
• How does the sentence style add interest or increase action?

Think about ways to use structure to add interest to your writing.

Common Core
State Standards

Writing
3. Write narratives to develop real or imagined experiences or events using effective technique, relevant descriptive details, and well-structured event sequences.
3.a. Engage and orient the reader by establishing a context and point of view and introducing a narrator and/or characters; organize an event sequence that unfolds naturally and logically.

Reading-Writing Connection

To get the feel for narrative nonfiction, read *An American Childhood* by Annie Dillard (p. 52) and *Angela's Ashes* by Frank McCourt (p. 140)

Teaching Resources

The following resources can be used to enrich or extend the instruction.

All *Unit 1 Resources*
Writing Workshop, pp. 229, 230

All *Common Core Companion,*
pp. 202–212; 220–221

All *Professional Development Guidebook*
Rubrics for Self-Assessment:
Autobiographical Narrative, pp. 222–223

All *Graphic Organizer Transparencies*
Rubric for Self-Assessment:
Autobiographical Narrative,
p. 36

All *See It!* DVD
Richard Peck, Segments 3 and 4

All resources, including video, are also available online at www.PHLitOnline.com.

Prewriting/Planning Strategies

Choose a topic. To choose the right event from your life to narrate, use one of the following strategies:

- **Freewriting** Write for five minutes about whatever comes to mind on these general topics: *funny times, sad times,* and *lessons I have learned*. When you are finished, review what you have written and circle any ideas that could make a good topic for your purpose and audience.

- **Listing** Fill in a chart like the one below. In each column, list names or descriptions of memorable people and things that you know or have a particular viewpoint about from home, school, or travel. Review your chart to find connections between the items. For each connection you find, circle the two items and draw an arrow between them. Finally, review the connections you have found, and jot down ideas for engaging stories that they suggest.

People	Places	Things	Events

Make a timeline. Once you have decided on a topic, begin to gather the details that you will use in your narrative. Fill out a timeline like the one shown to organize your details in time order.

Timeline

Event 1: I meet Mark.

Event 2: We decide to join the swim team.

Event 3: Mark and I compete in the freestyle.

Detail 1: Mark has red hair, carries his knapsack everywhere.

Detail 2: Cold day—everybody lines up nervously by the pool waiting for the coach.

Detail 3: I feel funny about trying to beat Mark. He is probably my best friend.

Applying Understanding by Design Principles

Clarifying Expected Outcomes: Using Rubrics

- Before students begin work on this assignment, have them preview the Rubric for Self-Assessment (p.183) to learn what qualities their autobiographical narrative must have. A copy of this rubric appears in the *Graphic Organizer Transparencies*, p. 36.

- Review the criteria in the Rubric with the class. Before students use the Rubric to assess their own writing, work with them to rate the Student Model (p. 182) using the Rubric.

- If you wish to assess student's autobiographical narratives with either a 4-point or a 6-point scoring rubric, see *Professional Development Guidebook*, pp. 222–223.

Prewriting/Planning Strategies

1. Introduce the prewriting strategies.
2. Have students apply the strategies to choose a topic and gather details.

Teaching the Strategies

1. Help students decide which prewriting technique will work best for them. Tell students to look at the topics under Freewriting. Which groups of words spark their interest? Do they prefer to write freely or to make lists?

2. Remind students who choose freewriting that this is a way to generate ideas. Students should write continuously without thinking about organization, grammar, spelling, or other mechanics. Emphasize that an event, rather than a description of a person or place, should be the basis of the narrative.

3. Once students have generated some ideas and have come up with a topic, have them plot the details they uncovered on a timeline. A timeline will help them arrange the events of their narratives in the correct sequence.

4. Students who choose listing should use the chart on the student page to organize their ideas.

Six Traits Focus

✔ Ideas		Word Choice
✔ Organization		Sentence Fluency
Voice		Conventions

PH WRITING COACH Grade 7

Students will find additional information on autobiographical narratives in Chapter 5.

Prentice Hall EssayScorer

A writing prompt for this mode of writing can be found on the *Prentice Hall EssayScorer* at www.PHLitOnline.com.

Drafting Strategies

1. Introduce the drafting strategies.
2. Have students apply the strategies as they draft.

Teaching the Strategies

1. To help students focus on the conflict, have them create a conflict chart like the one shown. You may wish to guide them in identifying and stating a conflict.

2. Instruct students to hint at the conflict in the opening of their drafts before telling how it began, developed, and was resolved. To conclude, students should reflect or comment on what they learned from the experience.

3. Encourage students to picture a setting and sketch it, and then itemize the visual details in the setting. Ask students to add the other senses by asking themselves these questions:

   What sounds do I hear constantly in this setting?

   What objects or props do the characters use in the setting?

   Are there smells that evoke a response in the reader?

   Are there tastes associated with this setting?

4. Challenge students to include at least one vivid or precise word or phrase to describe each person, place, or thing in the narrative.

Think Aloud: Model Dialogue

Say to students:

   Suppose I have written, *Joanie was nervous about her first day in a new school.* The character will come through much more clearly if I have Joanie say, *"Mom, my friend Alexi isn't sure about where her classroom is. Could you walk with us to school and help her out? I'm fine, but I think she's a little nervous today."* Dialogue gives your character a "voice."

Six Traits Focus

✔	Ideas	✔	Word Choice
✔	Organization		Sentence Fluency
	Voice		Conventions

Drafting Strategies

Map out your story. Make a conflict chart like the one below. In the center, write a brief description of the conflict. Fill in linked circles with specific narrative action related to the conflict. Number the circles to help put the events of your story in order. As you draft, refer to your chart to help connect details to your central conflict.

Develop the plot line. Once you have mapped out the plot, make sure that you arrange the pace in the story so that the conflict intensifies during the **rising action.** The climax should be the highest point of interest in your story. The **resolution,** or **denouement,** should be the conclusion in which your conflict is resolved.

Develop a setting. A vivid setting can bring your story to life and help readers understand your characters. When describing a setting, try to appeal to several of your readers' senses. Draw a word picture of the place with precise and colorful nouns, adjectives, verbs, and adverbs.

> **Vague Description:** We lived in a small town.
>
> **Vivid Description:** Main Street smelled like pine trees because the woods were only steps away.

Develop characters through dialogue. Bring people to life by using dialogue—quoting what people said as they said it. Do not report everything a character says. Instead, create conversations that vividly show the character's feelings, gestures, and expressions as he or she reacts to events.

Background
Mark and I were best friends.

Event 1:
Mark and I are matched in an important race.

Central Conflict
My friendship with Mark vs. my desire to win.

Event 2:
As the race approaches, Mark and I stop talking to each other.

Final Change:
Mark and I tied! We're still friends.

Common Core State Standards

Writing
3. Write narratives to develop real or imagined experiences or events using effective technique, relevant descriptive details, and well-structured event sequences.

3.a. Engage and orient the reader by establishing a context and point of view and introducing a narrator and/or characters; organize an event sequence that unfolds naturally and logically.

3.d. Use precise words and phrases, relevant descriptive details, and sensory language to capture the action and convey experiences and events.

3.e. Provide a conclusion that follows from and reflects on the narrated experiences or events.

Strategies for Using Technology in Writing

- If students are using word processing software, suggest that they make their writing more precise by consulting the thesaurus. Tell students to select words that seem vague and use the thesaurus to identify more precise words to replace them. Advise students always to check the meanings of synonyms in a dictionary before substituting them for words in their compositions.

- Students can also use features of the **Writing and Grammar Interactive Text** *Online* at **www.pearsonsuccessnet.com** to revise their narratives.

Writers on Writing

Richard Peck On Conflict in Fiction

Richard Peck is the author of "The Three-Century Woman" (p. 11).

My novel *Fair Weather* is about a farm girl named Rosie Beckett who's never been anywhere until she and her family have the adventure of their lives. They visit the World's Columbian Exposition, the great Chicago World's Fair of 1893. It's in the Women's Building at the fair where Rosie finds her future. But the story begins down on the farm because all fiction is based on contrast: young, old; male, female; country, city. . . .

"I wrote 'The Three-Century Woman' twelve times. . . ."
— Richard Peck

Professional Model:

from *Fair Weather*

It was the last day of our old lives and we didn't even know it.

I didn't. It looked like any old day to me, a sultry, summer morning hot enough to ruffle the roofline. But then, any little thing could come as a surprise to us. We were just plain country people. I suppose we were poor, but we didn't know it. Poor, but proud. There wasn't a ~~scrap~~ blister of paint in the house, but there were no hogs under the porch, ~~and no rust on the implements~~.

I was sitting out in the old rope swing at the back of our place because the house was too full of Mama and my sister Lottie. I wasn't swinging. I thought I was pretty nearly too old to ~~be swinging~~ swing. In the fall I'd be fourteen, with only one more year of school to go.

Strangely, this book was published on September 10, 2001.

I decided to leave it with hogs. The detail about the rust wasn't necessary, as further evidence of the family's pride.

I wanted to suggest a conflict here between sister and mother, but to let the reader wonder what the problem is.

Writing Workshop **179**

Revising Strategies

1. Introduce the revising strategies, using the instruction on the student page.

2. Have students apply the strategies as they revise.

Teaching the Strategies

1. Remind students that the climax is the moment when the central conflict of the story takes its most dramatic turn and determines the outcome of the plot. The character is changed by the conflict regardless of whether he or she solves the problem.

2. To help students link details to their central conflict, have them write a sentence that sums up the central conflict of their story. They should then check each paragraph of their narrative for connections to this statement. Suggest that they write a note next to each paragraph indicating its connection to the conflict. The connection can be a character, the setting, or an action taken. When they've finished, they should consider deleting any paragraph that does not connect to the conflict.

Think Aloud: Model Revising for Specific, Precise Nouns

Model the strategy of revising for word choice, using the following "think aloud." Say to students:

I revise my writing to make sure that each word used is the most specific and precise available. Suppose I have written the word *boy*. I can tell the reader much more about the character by replacing *boy* with *toddler* or *teenager*. Here is another example: If I have originally chosen the word *house*, I might replace it with *cottage* or *apartment building*. By choosing specific words, I give the reader a better picture. I also check the dictionary to make sure the new words mean precisely what I intend.

Six Traits Focus

	Ideas	✔	Word Choice
✔	Organization	✔	Sentence Fluency
	Voice		Conventions

Revising Strategies

Review sequence of events. Read through your narrative to make sure that the events you describe are in chronological order. Add transition words, such as *first, next, later,* and *finally,* to clarify the sequence of events.

Check your pacing. A good story builds to a single most exciting moment, called the **climax.** The secret of building to a climax is **pacing**—the speed at which your story moves along. Pace your story to build suspense. To improve the pacing of your story, use the following strategies:

- Cut details and events that do not build suspense or heighten readers' interest.
- Revise or delete any paragraph that is not clearly connected to the central conflict.
- Make clear connections between other events to show readers how events relate to each other.

Use specific, precise nouns. Look for nouns that are vague or general and might leave the reader wondering *what kind*. Replace general and vague nouns with specific and precise ones. Review your draft, circling any nouns that do not answer the questions *What exactly?* and *What kind?* Replace these nouns with specific, precise nouns that convey a lively picture. Use a dictionary to confirm the precise meaning of the words you are using.

Vague	**Precise**
stuff ⟶	souvenirs
General	**Specific**
decorations ⟶	party streamers and balloons

Peer Review

Give your draft to one or two classmates to read. Ask them to highlight details that slow the story down or ideas that are unconnected to the central conflict. Use the feedback to eliminate any unnecessary details from your draft. As you review comments and revise your draft, adjust your writing to your purpose and audience as needed.

 **Common Core State Standards**

Writing

3.a. Engage and orient the reader by establishing a context and point of view and introducing a narrator and/or characters; organize an event sequence that unfolds naturally and logically.

3.b. Use narrative techniques, such as dialogue, pacing, and description, to develop experiences, events, and/or characters.

3.c. Use a variety of transition words, phrases, and clauses to convey sequence and signal shifts from one time frame or setting to another.

3.d. Use precise words and phrases, relevant descriptive details, and sensory language to capture the action and convey experiences and events.

5. With some guidance and support from peers and adults, develop and strengthen writing as needed by planning, revising, editing, rewriting, or trying a new approach, focusing on how well purpose and audience have been addressed.

Strategies for
Improving Word Choice

Tell students that just as they check their use of nouns to make sure they are specific, they can also check their use of verbs, specifically the verb *to be.*

Have students circle forms of *be,* such as *am, is, are, was, were, be, being,* and *been.* Tell them to challenge themselves to change some of them to more vivid action verbs. They may need to rewrite sentences when they change the verb.

Then, have them do the same thing with vague, empty or weak words like *very, a lot,* and *nice.* Have students remove or replace these words with more precise words.

Checking Pronoun-Antecedent Agreement

Incorrect pronoun-antecedent agreement occurs when a personal pronoun disagrees with its antecedent in person, number, or gender.

Identifying Incorrect Pronoun-Antecedent Agreement An **antecedent** is the word or words for which a pronoun stands. A pronoun's antecedent may be a noun, a group of words acting as a noun, or another pronoun.

Antecedent	Pronoun

Example: I told <u>Alexis</u> to bring a bathing suit with <u>her</u>.

In this example, the pronoun *her* is third person and singular. It agrees with its feminine antecedent, *Alexis*, which is also third person (the person spoken about) and singular.

Fixing Agreement Errors To fix an incorrect pronoun-antecedent agreement, identify both the pronoun and the antecedent for which it stands. Then use one of the following methods.

1. **Identify the person of the antecedent** as first, second, or third. Choose a pronoun that matches the antecedent in person.

2. **Identify the number of the antecedent** as singular or plural. Choose a pronoun that matches the antecedent in number.

3. **Identify the gender of the antecedent** as masculine or feminine. Choose a pronoun that matches the antecedent in gender.

Personal Pronouns		
	Singular	**Plural**
First Person	I, me, my, mine	we, us, our, ours
Second Person	you, your, yours	you, your, yours
Third Person	**Feminine:** she, her, hers **Masculine:** he, him, his **Neutral:** it, its	they, them, their, theirs

PH WRITING COACH

Further instruction and practice are available in *Prentice Hall Writing Coach.*

Grammar in Your Writing

Read your draft. Draw an arrow from each personal pronoun to its antecedent. If the agreement is incorrect, fix it using one of the methods above.

Checking Pronoun-Antecedent Agreement

1. Introduce the grammar skill, using the instruction on the student page.

2. Discuss the rules and examples as well as the strategies for fixing incorrect usage.

3. Have students follow the instruction under Grammar in Your Writing to correct errors in their drafts.

Teaching the Grammar Skill

1. Instruct students to check that the pronouns in their narratives agree with their antecedents in person, number, and gender. Students often make errors , for example, when the antecedent is an indefinite pronoun, such as in the following situations:

   Each boy must get <u>his</u> parents' permission.

   All the children returned to <u>their</u> seats.

   Everybody placed <u>his (or her)</u> test on the teacher's desk.

2. Have students complete the following sentences with the correct pronoun.

   Everyone should go to _____ seat. (**Answer:** his or her)

   All of her classmates had completed _____ assignments. (**Answer:** their)

PH WRITING COACH   Grade 7

Students will find practice with and guidance on pronoun-antecedent agreement in Chapter 23, Section 2.

181

Student Model

Review the Student Model with the class, using the annotations to analyze the writer's use of the elements of a narrative.

Teaching from the Student Model

1. Explain that the Student Model is a sample and that narratives may be longer.

2. **Ask** students to identify the transitional words and phrases that the writer uses to sequence events in the second and third paragraphs.
(**Answer:** *Then, After, while, As we headed toward home*)

3. After noting the effectiveness of the precise word *grumbling* to describe the sound of the motor in the fourth paragraph, **ask** students to suggest other effective alternatives. (**Possible responses:** *rumbling, sputtering, clattering*)

4. Have students identify other examples of precise descriptive language. (**Possible responses:** "new, metallic green bike," "jumble of parts")

Connecting to Real-Life Writing

Explain that students may be asked to tell about a significant event in their lives on a college or a job application. Point out that a problem or change that a student has faced is often an excellent focus for such an essay. Discuss why a school or company might ask a potential student or employee to write about an important event in his or her life. Then, have students imagine that they are applying for admission to a college or for a job. What event would they choose to write about, and why? Invite students to share their ideas.

182

Student Model: Alexander Baker, Palos Verdes, CA

Bicycle Braking Blues

Crash! Once again, I found myself flying off my bike and toward the grass. At age eight, crashes were an everyday occurrence, and I reminded myself that it was better to practice braking here by the lawn than to risk another episode like "The Club Hill Clobbering."

> With this hint, Alexander clearly connects his introduction to the central conflict of his story.

It all started when I arrived at my grandparents' house in Galesburg to spend the summer. I made many friends in their neighborhood, but they spent most of their time riding bikes, and I didn't have one. Then, my step-grandmother gave me the almost new, metallic green bike that her grandson had outgrown. I was overjoyed to have a bike. . . . I learned to ride it well enough—what I didn't learn was how to use the brakes. On the flat ground near my grandparents' house, I just let the bike slow down until I could put my feet down.

> Adding this detail helps move the story along—it shows why a bike is so important to Alexander.

One day my babysitter took me for lunch at the club grill. She rode my grandfather's golf cart while I rode my bike. When we had to climb the big hill leading up to the club, I walked my bike alongside the cart. After lunch, I mounted my bike while Erika drove Grandpa's golf cart. As we headed toward home, neither of us gave a thought to . . . the HILL.

> Alexander narrates events in clear sequence.

As we came around the corner of the bike path, I started picking up speed. By the time I realized what was happening, it was too late. "The hill!" I yelled to Erika. "Your brakes! Use your brakes!" she shouted. With the wind rushing in my ears, I could hardly hear her. Looking down the hill, I saw a golf cart was blocking the path. It seemed to be getting bigger and closer by the second. "Well," I thought to myself, "it's now or never." I steered my speeding bike toward the grass alongside the path and jumped off sideways. I leapt off and BAM! The world turned upside down and inside out. The next sound I heard was the grumbling of a golf cart engine. It sounded annoyed about the jumble of parts in its path. The next thing I saw was Erika's face. She was so scared that her face was stiff and pale. I stood up to show Erika that I was fine. The only damage I sustained was some dirt on my jeans, and the bike survived without too many scratches too. Also, my pride was hurt. How can you ride a bike if you can never go down hill? So every day, Erika took me to the hill and we'd go a little further up. That way, I learned to brake on a hill, little by little, rather than getting clobbered again!

> Using this precise noun helps vividly convey the scene to readers.

> Details such as *stiff* and *pale* help readers vividly imagine Erika's expression.

Editing and Proofreading

Review your draft to correct errors in spelling, grammar, and punctuation.

Focus on the Dialogue: As you proofread your story, pay close attention to the correct punctuation of **dialogue**—the actual words spoken by a character. Use the examples as a guide. All dialogue should be enclosed in quotation marks. A **split dialogue** is when a quotation is split up with additional information in the middle, such as identifying the speaker.

"She went home," I said.

"Wow!" I yelled. "I love it."

Publishing and Presenting

Consider one of the following ways to share your writing:

Present an oral narrative. Practice telling your story, using notes rather than reading from your draft, until you can deliver it smoothly and naturally. Practice using gestures to emphasize key points. Tell your story to the class.

Make a poster. Arrange photos, artwork, or small souvenirs, along with a neat copy of your narrative, on posterboard to display in class.

Reflecting on Your Writing

Writer's Journal Jot down your answer to this question:

As you wrote, what new insights into your story did you have?

Rubric for Self-Assessment

Find evidence in your writing to address each category. Then, use the rating scale to grade your work.

Criteria	Rating Scale
	not very / very
Focus: How clearly does the narrative present the problem or conflict?	1 2 3 4 5
Organization: How clearly is the sequence of events presented?	1 2 3 4 5
Support/Elaboration: How vivid are details and quotations?	1 2 3 4 5
Style: How effectively is the action of the story paced?	1 2 3 4 5
Conventions: How correct is your grammar, especially your use of pronouns and antecedents?	1 2 3 4 5

Spiral Review

Earlier in the unit, you learned about **personal pronouns** (p. 126) and **possessive pronouns** (p. 150). Check the use of possessive pronouns in your narrative. Review your autobiographical narrative to be sure you have avoided inappropriate shifts in pronoun number (singular or plural) and person.

> **PH WRITING COACH**
> Further instruction and practice are available in *Prentice Hall Writing Coach.*

Strategies for Test-Taking

A writing prompt on a test may assess students' ability to write narratives. Explain that although prompts usually specify the audience, purpose, and topic for a narrative, students may still have to narrow the topic by focusing on a specific conflict or change. Recommend that students use a conflict graphic like the one on page 178 to organize their ideas. Before writing, students should put events in chronological order and then describe them. Narratives need a clear beginning, middle, and end. Remind students to review their drafts, add details, and substitute precise words.

Editing and Proofreading

1. Introduce the editing and proofreading focus, using the instruction on the student page.

2. Have students edit and proofread their essays, correcting grammar, spelling, punctuation, and word choice. Make sure they look for errors of the type noted in the lesson focus and the Spiral Review.

Teaching the Editing Focus

1. Review the rules of punctuating dialogue.

2. Emphasize that when quoted speech is interrupted or followed by a phrase such as *said Bob*, the phrase is set off in commas and not included in the quote.

   "I never expected to win first prize," she insisted.

   "The party is at my house," she said, "next Thursday evening."

3. Point out that indirect discourse, or a summary of what the character said, should not be enclosed in quotation marks.

   She told us to come after dinner.

Six Traits Focus

Ideas		Word Choice	
Organization		✔	Sentence Fluency
Voice			Conventions

ASSESS

Publishing and Presenting

1. Have students identify other audiences besides their classmates. Elicit from students that they might share their narratives with family members or friends.

2. Model the process of presenting a narrative for students, using appropriate gestures and expression.

Reflecting on Your Writing

Suggest that students evaluate their conflict charts and their initial notes to see which strategies elicited new connections and insights.

> **PH WRITING COACH** Grade 7
>
> Students will find more information on the writing process in Chapter 3.

Common Core
State Standards

• Language 4.c, d

Using a Dictionary and Thesaurus

1. Introduce the skill, using the instruction on the student page.

2. In conjunction with the first paragraph of instruction, review the example of the dictionary entry. Note that abbreviations in the entry, such as *n.* for "noun," are explained in a key near the front or back of the dictionary. Symbols used in phonetic respellings are usually explained in a separate pronunciation key that appears near the front or back and also at the bottom of each right-hand page.

3. In conjunction with the second and third paragraphs of instruction, review the example of the thesaurus entry. Mention that thesauruses often provide antonyms as well as synonyms. Point out the cross-reference at the end of the entry, and explain that print thesauruses typically avoid repetition by providing long entries for certain words only; in this case, the synonym *explain* apparently has a longer entry where one can find more possible synonyms for *clarify*.

Think Aloud: Model the Skill

Model the skill of using a dictionary and thesaurus. Say to students:

A dictionary can help me understand the meaning or meanings of words I encounter in my reading or want to use in my writing. It can also tell me how to spell and pronounce words, although I have to have some idea of how to spell a word in order to look it up.

A thesaurus can help me use synonyms to improve my writing. If I am not sure how to use one of the synonyms it provides, I can check the word in a dictionary.

Vocabulary Workshop

Using a Dictionary and Thesaurus

If you need to know the meaning, the pronunciation, or the part of speech of a word, you can find that information in a **dictionary.** In addition, a dictionary can show you a word's **etymology,** or origin. Etymologies explain how words come into the English language and how they change over time. Check the front or back of a dictionary for a guide to the symbols and abbreviations used in etymologies.

Here is an example of a dictionary entry. Notice what it tells you about the word *anthology*.

Dictionary

> **anthology** (an ·äl´ ß jè) *n.*, *pl.* **-gies** [Gr. *anthologia*, a garland, collection of short poems < *anthologos*, gathering flowers < *anthos*, flower + *legein*, to gather] a collection of poems, stories, songs, excerpts, etc., chosen by the compiler

In a **thesaurus,** you will find a list of a word's synonyms, or words with similar meanings. You can use a thesaurus when you are looking for alternate word choices in your writing. Look at this example of a thesaurus entry.

Thesaurus

> **clarify** *v.* interpret, define, elucidate, see EXPLAIN.

Note that a thesaurus does not provide definitions of words. Before you use a word you find in a thesaurus, check a dictionary to be sure you understand the word's meaning.

Where to Find a Dictionary and Thesaurus
You can find these resources in book form at your school or library. You can also use *digital tools*, such as *online dictionaries* and *thesauruses*, to find the most precise words to express your ideas. Ask your teacher to recommend the best online word study resources.

Common Core
State Standards

Language
4.c. Consult general and specialized reference materials, both print and digital, to find the pronunciation of a word or determine or clarify its precise meaning or its part of speech.
4.d. Verify the preliminary determination of the meaning of a word or phrase.

Teaching Resources

Unit 1 Resources
Using a Dictionary and Thesaurus, pp. 231, 232

PHLit Online! **Vocabulary Central,** featuring definitions, audio pronunciations, Word Families, and activities, is online at **www.PHLitOnline.com.**

Practice A Find each of the following words in a print or online dictionary. Write down the first pronunciation, part of speech, and definition of each word. Then, use each word in a sentence that shows its meaning.

1. voyage   **2.** robust   **3.** engulf   **4.** intricate

Practice B Use a print or online thesaurus to find an alternate word for the italicized word in each sentence. Choose a more expressive word that means the same thing as the original. Verify the meaning of the word you choose in a dictionary.

1. I had to *run* down the street to catch the school bus on time.

2. After soccer practice, all we wanted to do was *sit* on the couch.

3. On our class trip to the nature trail, our assignment was to *find* as many bugs as possible.

4. After the storm, Damian had to *make* his storage shed again.

5. We had to *push* the trash down to make it fit in the can.

Activity Create a quick-reference thesaurus of some commonly used words. Make notecards like the one shown for the words *big*, *nice*, and *interesting*. Share your notecards with classmates and collect more synonyms. Then, with a partner, distinguish the shades of meaning that each word conveys. Use cards like these to help you find precise words when you write.

Word:
Part of Speech:
Definition:
Synonym 1:
Synonym 1 Definition:
Shades of Meaning:
Synonym 2:
Synonym 2 Definition:
Shades of Meaning:

PHLit Online!
www.PHLitOnline.com
- Illustrated vocabulary words
- Interactive vocabulary games
- Vocabulary flashcards

Comprehension and Collaboration

With a partner, look up the meanings of the words *bolt* and *preserve*. Note that each word can be used as both a noun and a verb. For each word, write one sentence using the word as a noun and another sentence using the word as a verb.

Practice A
Answers:

1. voyage (voi'ij) *n.,* a relatively long journey, especially by ship, plane, or spacecraft; We went on a <u>voyage</u> to Alaska.

2. robust (rō bust') *adj.* strong and healthy; After the rain, the vine showed <u>robust</u> growth.

3. engulf (en gulf') *v.* to swallow up or overwhelm; We feared the huge waves would <u>engulf</u> the small raft.

4. intricate (in'tri kit) *adj.* full of puzzling parts and thus hard to follow; The design was too <u>intricate</u> to copy.

Practice B
Answers:

1. race
2. sprawl
3. locate
4. construct
5. press

Activity

Supply students with notecards to complete the activity. Point out that unlike a typical thesaurus entry, students' notecards are to include definitions for the synonyms they suggest. Have students choose partners with whom to discuss the shades of meaning of the synonyms. Remind students that shades of meaning for synonyms may be clarified in dictionary entries for those words.

Comprehension and Collaboration

Provide students with dictionaries in which to look up the two words. Note that the words will have more than two meanings and that students should illustrate just one noun and one verb meaning of each word. Evaluate sentences based on the accuracy with which they reflect a particular meaning.

Instruction   **for Universal Access**

Strategy for Special-Needs Students

Students may need special help in working with dictionary and thesaurus entries. Slowly go over the key parts of the sample dictionary entry, pointing out the entry word, *anthology,* in boldface; the pronunciation in parentheses; the part-of-speech label in italics; and the etymology, or word history, in brackets; and reading aloud the definition. Similarly, go over the parts of the sample thesaurus entry, pointing out the entry word, *clarify,* in boldface; the part-of-speech label in italics; the three synonyms; and the cross-reference to *explain.*

EL Strategy for English Learners

English learners may need special help in using dictionary pronunciation keys and phonetic respellings. Direct students to the pronunciation key of a dictionary you use in class. Carefully pronounce the letters and sample words in the key, and have students repeat them. Once students have mastered a particular sound in the key, have them apply that sound to the pronunciation of a longer word; for example, after mastering the short *a* in the sample words in the key, they should attempt to say the same sound in the first syllable of *anthology.*

185

Common Core State Standards

• Speaking and Listening 4

Learn the Skills

1. Introduce the workshop, including the activity on page 187.

2. Have students plan their narratives and begin to write.

3. Review the basic elements of an effective story, such as vivid descriptions of character and setting, an engaging plot, and realistic dialogue. Students should identify the story's conflict first, and then build the plot around it.

4. Remind students that the intended audience should determine not only the tone of a speech, but also its content.

Deliver Your Narrative

Suggest that students mark their narrative scripts with directions about facial expression, volume, pitch, and tone. Remind them to allow ample time for rehearsal.

SPEAKING AND LISTENING

Communications Workshop

Delivering a Narrative Presentation

A **narrative presentation** is similar to a written narrative. In a presentation, however, you can add interest by using your voice, gestures, and facial expressions. These techniques and strategies will help make your presentation effective and interesting.

Learn the Skills

Use these strategies to complete the activity on page 187.

Develop a plot line. A narrative presentation tells events in order. Begin by introducing a conflict. Then, develop rising action leading to a climax. Consider adding suspense to keep your audience engaged. Finally, provide a clear resolution. Determine the point of view from which the story will be told and write your narrative from that perspective.

Establish setting and characters. Think about how you will describe the setting—the time and place of your narrative. Describe major and minor characters and bring them to life through dialogue and descriptions of their actions.

Consider your audience. As you write, think about your audience. Choose words and a tone, such as serious or playful, that will appeal to that audience.

Deliver Your Narrative

Rehearse your delivery. Read through your narrative to become familiar with it. If you plan to use a script, remember to look up frequently, use clear pronunciation, and make eye contact with your audience.

- **Vary the volume.** For example, you might speak loudly to express how a coach peps up her team or softly to describe how a baby falls asleep.

- **Switch the pitch.** For example, you might use a high voice to show panic and a low voice to show sternness or tiredness.

- **Use clear pronunciation.** For example, be careful to pronounce each sound that a letter makes in a word and make sure not to drop sounds that appear at the ends of words.

Common Core State Standards

Speaking and Listening

4. Present claims and findings, emphasizing salient points in a focused, coherent manner with pertinent descriptions, facts, details, and examples; use appropriate eye contact, adequate volume, and clear pronunciation.

Presentation Tips for Specific Audiences

Younger Audience	Older Audience
• Exaggerate reactions with dramatic facial expressions.	• Use more realistic voices and facial expressions.
• Use short sentences and simple vocabulary.	• Use varied sentences and sophisticated vocabulary level.
• Insert questions that invite audience participation. Make frequent eye contact.	• Maintain audience attention by changing your position and moving about as you speak. Make frequent eye contact.

Strategies for
Delivering an Oral Presentation

Explain to students that spending enough time rehearsing is the key to a successful presentation. Give students these additional strategies for delivering a presentation:

- Tell them to practice their material until they don't have to frequently look at their paper.
- Explain that students should vary their pace. Make sure they avoid speaking too slowly or too quickly.
- Instruct them to avoid unnecessary pauses and filler words like *um, you know,* and *like.*

- Tell students to practice pronouncing new or unfamiliar words.
- Guide students in practicing natural gestures and effective body language as they deliver their speeches.
- Recommend that students rehearse their speeches with a partner. Partners can evaluate one another using the Presentation Checklist on page 187.

Practice the Skills

© **Presentation of Knowledge and Ideas** Use what you have learned in this workshop to perform the following task.

ACTIVITY: Prepare and Deliver a Narrative

Choose a fictional story to present to your class. It may be either a story you write yourself or a story written by another author. Use the strategies in this workshop to organize and practice your presentation. Finally, deliver your presentation. Answer the following questions as you prepare:
- Who is my audience?
- From whose point of view will I tell the story?
- What descriptions and details can I include to add interest to my story?
- How can I build drama or suspense to engage my audience?
- What is the tone of the story, and how can I convey that tone during my presentation?
- How will I use my voice effectively?

Practice your presentation, using the checklist below to help you prepare. Try using different tones of voice and different speaking rates until you find the most effective delivery. When you feel you are ready, present your story to your classmates.

Presentation Checklist

Presentation Delivery
- ❏ Is the overall presentation suitable for the audience?
- ❏ Does the speaker's style of speaking fit the characters and plot?
- ❏ Is the tone of the story clearly communicated through the speaker's volume, pitch, facial expressions, and gestures?
- ❏ Does the pace of the presentation fit the story's action?
- ❏ Does the speaker pronounce words clearly and precisely?
- ❏ Does the speaker make frequent eye contact with the audience?
- ❏ What could the speaker do to improve the presentation?

© **Comprehension and Collaboration** After your presentation, ask your classmates to give you feedback by completing the Presentation Checklist. Then use the checklist to provide feedback on your classmates' presentations.

Practice the Skills

1. Review the assignment with students. Make sure they understand that the way they use their voice should convey information about the meaning of the story. It is important they understand the story well before they begin to prepare the presentation.

2. Explain to students that they should use a copy of the Presentation Checklist to evaluate their own presentation and the presentations made by classmates.

3. Before students give their presentations to the class, remind listeners to ask questions if any points are unclear. To maintain order, encourage them to raise their hands and wait to be acknowledged by the presenter before stating their questions. Suggest that students making presentations scan the classroom from time to time so they will notice any students who have questions.

Evaluate the Activity

1. Evaluate students' presentations on the basis of the speaker's style, pace of delivery, and their use of questions and responses to ensure listeners' comprehension.

2. When the class discusses the presentations that were most effective, encourage students to make note of the features of those presentations that made them effective and to incorporate those techniques in their future presentations.

Differentiated
Instruction   for Universal Access

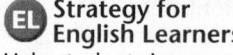

EL Strategy for English Learners

Help students improve their narrative presentations by having them focus on creating vivid images with words. Have students collect pictures of different environments and people engaged in various activities. Supply students with sensory words that describe the pictures, such as *warm, sweet, smooth,* or *shout.*

Then, encourage them to list their own vivid words. Ask students to use some of these words in their narratives. Allow students time to practice the words they are not familiar with before they give their presentations.

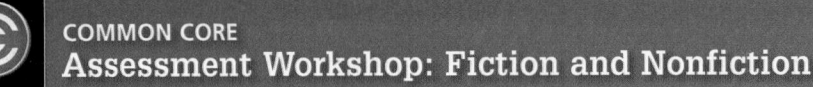

Cumulative Review

In this Common Core Assessment Workshop (pp. 188–193), students apply and reinforce their mastery of the Common Core Standards and the skills taught in Unit 1. The practice is divided into four sections, including a section of Performance Tasks addressing CCSS Reading standards.

1. Before assigning each section, review the relevant Common Core Standards and unit skills with students.

2. Set a time limit for the multiple choice items in each section, allowing a little over one minute per question. Allow twenty minutes for any Timed Writing questions.

3. Administer each of the first three sections of the Cumulative Review (pp. 188–191).

4. Use the Performance Tasks on pages 192–193 to assess the depth of students' mastery of standards taught in the unit. Follow the suggestions on teacher pages 192–193 for assigning tasks and for supporting and evaluating student performance.

Reteaching Skills

1. For each practice, use the Reteach chart on the same page as the answers to determine which skills require reteaching, given the items students answered incorrectly.

2. Reteach these skills prior to assigning the **Benchmark Test** for the second half of *Unit 1 (Resources*, pp. 234–239). The Benchmark Test concludes instruction in the Unit skills.

Cumulative Review

I. Reading Literature

 Common Core State Standards

RI.7.2, RI.7.3, RI.7.6; W.7.2.b.
[For the full wording of the standards, see the standards chart in the front of your textbook.]

Directions: *Read the passage. Then, answer each question that follows.*

"Don't forget, class! Today is the last day to sign up for Latin ballroom dancing lessons," said Mrs. Palacio.

Bianca, my best friend, with the beautiful green eyes, talked me into doing it. I wasn't so sure about ballroom dancing, but I went along because I always did what Bianca wanted.

After a few days of practice, I could hear the Latin rhythms playing in my head, and I would pretend to move my feet—"one, two, cha-cha-cha." But I didn't dare let anyone know I actually liked ballroom dancing.

Our practice gym was muggy and lit only by faint sunlight. As the sweat poured off us one day, Mrs. Palacio said the terrible words I'd <u>dreaded</u>. "Tomorrow, I want you to select your partner for the school performance."

"I heard John is going to ask me," Bianca said with excitement as we walked home that afternoon. "You should choose one of his friends." I could feel Bianca pressuring me to choose someone she liked—someone who was popular.

The next day, as the ballots were passed out, the gym walls began to sway, and my head throbbed. I had a huge secret. I wanted to pick Felix as my partner. But I figured that if Bianca found out, she would embarrass me, maybe even end our friendship. Felix was not popular. He never spoke to anyone, never even smiled. No one knew much about him except that after practice, he went straight home. But I didn't care. Felix was handsome and the best dancer in the class.

I just couldn't find the courage to pick him. I froze. What will happen to me if my best friend Bianca humiliates me? I bent over the metal bench, pretending to write on the ballot. The other kids grabbed their backpacks to leave as I sat there with tears welling up.

"What's wrong with Marie?" John asked on his way out.

I tried not to look up, but Mrs. Palacio caught my eye. I felt her sympathy, and somehow I got the courage to make my decision. I did it. I wrote down Felix's name. A weight was suddenly lifted, and I felt like dancing all the way to the moon—on my own two feet.

Differentiated Instruction   for Universal Access

Strategy for Special-Needs Students
Remind students that writing assignments often ask students to state a main idea or concept and then support it with specific examples. Give a simple model: A dog can be a great pet. [main idea] You can take walks with a dog. [supporting example] Next, read item 8 aloud to students. The main idea of the student's paragraph should be how the writer uses indirect characterization to describe the narrator of the story. The student should include supporting details: examples of indirect characterization that describe the narrator.

Strategy for Less Proficient Readers
Review skills and warm up for the test by walking through item 8. Read item 8 and ask for a volunteer to remind the rest of the group what *indirect characterization* means. Then, read the passage aloud, asking students to raise their hands whenever they hear an example of *indirect characterization*. Have students underline each example and refer to the underlined sections to write their answers to the question.

1. This passage is an example of which **type of nonfiction?**

   A. biography
   B. autobiographical narrative
   C. descriptive essay
   D. informational text

2. Which sentence from the passage shows the **first-person point of view?**

   A. Felix was not popular.
   B. He never spoke to anyone, never even smiled.
   C. I bent over the metal bench, pretending to write on the ballot.
   D. "What's wrong with Marie?" John asked on his way out.

3. Which sentence from the passage describes the **setting?**

   A. But I didn't dare let anyone know I actually liked ballroom dancing.
   B. Felix was not popular.
   C. I tried not to look up, but Mrs. Palacio caught my eye.
   D. Our practice gym was muggy and lit only by faint sunlight.

4. Which of the following statements *best* describes the **central idea** of the passage?

   A. Do what you feel is right, no matter what others may think.
   B. If you practice hard, you will improve.
   C. If you like something, practice after school.
   D. It is important to do what your friends think is right in order to fit in.

5. Which **character trait** of the narrator's is revealed at the end of the passage?

   A. stubbornness
   B. quietness
   C. shyness
   D. braveness

6. Which of the following *best* shows **direct characterization** of Bianca?

   A. What will happen to me if my best friend Bianca humiliates me?
   B. I just couldn't find the courage to pick him.
   C. Bianca, my best friend, with the beautiful green eyes, talked me into doing it.
   D. But I figured that if Bianca found out, she would embarrass me, maybe even end our friendship.

7. **Vocabulary** Which word or phrase is closest in meaning to the underlined word <u>dreaded</u>?

   A. feared
   B. hoped for
   C. practiced
   D. forgotten

 Timed Writing

8. In a paragraph, explain how the writer uses **indirect characterization** to describe the narrator. **Support** your ideas with at least three specific examples from the passage.

 GO ON

Assessment Workshop **189**

Reteach

Question	Pages to Reteach
1	7, 23, 78, 176
2	49
3	99
4	6
5	160
6	160
7	23, 49
8	160

Answers continued
C—The narrator does not practice the terrible words; someone else speaks them; D—*Forgotten* is not a synonym for *dreaded*.

🕐 **Timed Writing**

8. In their responses, students should describe the narrator's personality and refer to at least three examples from the text.

I. Literary Skills
Answers With Explanations

1. **B**—The author describing events about her life makes this an autobiographical narrative. *Incorrect answers:* A—The author writes about herself, so this is not a biography; C—The passage contains no detailed descriptions; D—The passage is a narrative, not an informational text.

2. **C**—The personal pronoun *I* reveals the first-person point of view. *Incorrect answers:* A—This sentence contains no first-person pronouns; B—same explanation as for A; D—same explanation as for A.

3. **D**—The gym is where the story takes place, or its setting. *Incorrect answers:* A—This sentence describes a character, not the setting; B—same explanation as for A; C—This sentence describes an event, not the setting.

4. **A**—The narrator writes down Felix's name even though her friend might not approve. *Incorrect answers:* B—The story does not mention that the narrator improves through hard work; C—The character secretly likes ballroom dancing, but she does not practice for this reason; D—The story shows that you should do what you think is right even if you do not fit in.

5. **D**—The narrator states that she finds courage to make her decision. *Incorrect answers:* A—The narrator shows no stubbornness; B—The narrator is writing at the end; there is no need for her to speak; C—No details support this answer.

6. **C**—The phrase "my best friend with the beautiful green eyes" is direct characterization of Bianca. *Incorrect answers:* A—This sentence indirectly shows that Bianca can be mean; B—This sentence is about the narrator, not Bianca; D—This sentence indirectly shows that Bianca is not a good friend.

7. **A**—The narrator *dreads*, or <u>fears</u>, the terrible words. *Incorrect answers:* B—It would not make sense to hope for "terrible" words;

189

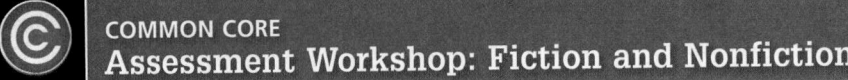

II. Reading Informational Texts

Answers With Explanations

1. **D**—The subheads highlight ingredients for pizza, directions on how to make pizza, and the history of pizza. There are no subheads that would help readers understand the importance of pizza. *Incorrect answers:* A—Subheads allow the reader to skim the passage and predict what it will be about since each subhead summarizes part of the content; B—One function of subheads is to break the text into smaller parts; C—One function of subheads is to make text more visually appealing by presenting it in manageable chunks rather than as a single, possibly overwhelming, block of text.

2. **A**—According to the table, pizza arrived in the United States in the nineteenth century. *Incorrect answers:* B—Pizza was sold by street vendors in Naples in the eighteenth century; C—Deep-dish style pizza was born in Chicago in the twentieth century; D—The first pizzeria opened in New York City in the twentieth century.

Reteach

Question	Pages to Reteach
1	72
2	72

II. Reading Informational Texts

Directions: *Read the passage. Then, answer each question that follows.*

Common Core
State Standards

RI.7.3, RI.7.5; W.7.2.c; L.7.1, L.4.1.g
[For the full wording of the standards, see the standards chart in the front of your textbook.]

How to Make a Pizza

Ingredients:

- Pre-made pizza crust
- Tomato sauce
- Fresh sliced vegetables
- Olive oil
- Pepperoni, sliced thinly
- Mozzarella cheese, shredded

Directions:

1. Before you begin, preheat oven to 400 degrees.
2. Place pizza crust on a large pan or cookie sheet. Stretch into a large circle. Pre-made crusts can be found at most grocery stores. Substitutions include pita bread or English muffins.
3. Lightly coat crust with olive oil to prevent it from becoming soggy.
4. Spread tomato sauce on top of crust. Add the pepperoni. Then, pile on the vegetables.
5. Top with a big handful of mozzarella cheese.
6. Bake until crust is golden and cheese is bubbly. Let stand 10 minutes before slicing. Enjoy!

History of the Pizza

18th Century	Tomatoes added to flatbread in Naples, Italy Pizza sold by street vendors in Naples
19th Century	Pizza first sold as local specialty in Naples restaurant Pizza arrives in United States with Italian immigrants
20th Century	First pizzeria opens in New York City Deep-dish style pizza is popular in Chicago
21st Century	Pizza remains a common American food

1. The **subheads** help you do all of the following *except*—
   A. predict what the passage will be about.
   B. break the text into smaller parts.
   C. make the text more visually appealing.
   D. understand the importance of pizza.

2. Which event occurred in the nineteenth century?
   A. Italian immigrants bring knowledge of pizza-making to the United States.
   B. Pizza was sold by street vendors in Naples, Italy.
   C. Deep-dish style pizza is born in Chicago.
   D. First pizzeria opens in New York City.

190 Fiction and Nonfiction

Strategies for Test Taking

Often the anxiety surrounding test taking causes students to skim (or even skip) the instructions. Tell students that carefully reading the instructions for each section is essential to performing well. A misreading might cause them to answer every question in a section incorrectly.

III. Writing and Language Conventions

Directions: *Read the passage. Then, answer each question that follows.*

(1) The Robert Johnson swimming Pool can be a flurry of activity in the summer. (2) Swimming pools have been around for centuries. (3) The squealing children jump repeatedly into the turquoise water. (4) Across the pool you can hear faint voices engaged in a "Marco Polo" game. (5) Childrens beach balls fly across the pool. (6) When the swimmers finally get out, the scorching pavement burns there feet. (7) Labor Day comes. (8) That unique feeling of summer ends when the lifeguard locks the gate, closing the pool until next year.

1. How could the writer revise sentence 3 to appeal to the **sense** of touch?

　A. The squealing children smell the chlorine in the pool water.

　B. The squealing children jump repeatedly into the water, making loud splashes.

　C. The squealing children eat candy and chips by the turquoise water.

　D. The squealing children jump into the chilly water to escape the summer heat.

2. How could the writer *best* revise sentence 7 to include a **transition?**

　A. Labor Day comes.

　B. By the way, Labor Day comes.

　C. Finally, Labor Day comes.

　D. After all, Labor Day comes.

3. Which sentence should the writer remove from the passage because it does not add to the **main impression?**

　A. sentence 1

　B. sentence 2

　C. sentence 7

　D. sentence 8

4. What is the correct way to capitalize the **proper nouns** in sentence 1?

　A. The Robert Johnson swimming pool can be a flurry of activity in the summer.

　B. The Robert Johnson Swimming Pool can be a flurry of activity in the summer.

　C. The Robert Johnson Swimming pool can be a flurry of activity in the summer.

　D. The Robert johnson swimming pool can be a flurry of activity in the summer.

5. What is the correct way to punctuate the **possessive noun** in sentence 5?

　A. Childrens beach ball's fly across the pool.

　B. Childrens' beach ball fly across the pool.

　C. Children's beach balls' fly across the pool.

　D. Children's beach balls fly across the pool.

6. How can the writer revise sentence 6 to correctly spell a **troublesome word?**

　A. Change *there* to *their*.

　B. Change *there* to *they're*.

　C. Change *there* to *they*.

　D. The sentence is correct.

STOP

Assessment Workshop **191**

Reteach

Question	Pages to Reteach
1	92
2	94
3	94
4	46
5	68
6	150

Benchmark

Reteach skills as indicated by students' performance, following the Reteach charts included on pp. 189–191. Then, administer the end-of-Unit **Benchmark Test** (*Unit 1 Resources*, pp. 234–242). The Benchmark Test concludes instruction in the Unit skills. Follow the **Interpretation Guide** for the test (*Unit 1 Resources*, p. 246) to assign reteaching pages as necessary in the *Reading Kit*. Use the built-in tracking software at www.PHLitOnline.com to automatically assign these pages.

III. Writing and Language Conventions

Answers With Explanations

1. **D**—*Chilly water* and *summer heat* appeal to the sense of touch. *Incorrect answers:* A—*Smell the chlorine* appeals to the sense of smell; B—*Making loud splashes* appeals to hearing; C—*Eat candy and chips* appeals to taste.

2. **C**—*Finally* suggests the last event in a series. *Incorrect answers:* A—This sentence does not include a transition; B—*Because* implies a cause-and-effect relationship that is not stated in the text; D—*After all* suggests something that contradicts, as opposed to something that simply follows what came before.

3. **B**—This passage is about a specific pool; Sentence 2 is about pools in general. *Incorrect answers:* A—This sentence introduces the main topic: the pool in summer; C—This sentence sets up the paragraph's conclusion; D—This sentence provides the conclusion: what happens when summer ends.

4. **B**—All words in the pool's official name should be capitalized. *Incorrect answers:* A—*swimming pool* should be capitalized; C—*pool* should be capitalized because it is part of a proper noun; D—A person's last name is always capitalized.

5. **D**—To make *children* possessive, you add *'s* after the *n*. *Incorrect answers:* A—There should be an apostrophe in *childrens*, not *balls*; B—With a regular plural noun that ends in *s*, the apostrophe indicating possession goes after the *s*. However, *children* is an irregular plural; C—*Balls* should not be possessive in this sentence.

6. **A**—*Their* is the correct spelling of the possessive. *Incorrect answers:* B—*They're* is a contraction of *they are*, which does not make sense in this sentence; C—*They* does not make sense in this sentence; D—This sentence is not correct.

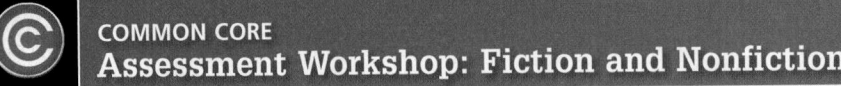
Performance Tasks

Assigning Tasks/Reteaching Skills

Use the chart below to choose appropriate Performance Tasks by identifying which tasks assess lessons in the textbook that you have taught. Use the same lessons for reteaching when students' performance indicates a failure to fully master a standard. For additional instruction and practice, assign the *Common Core Companion* pages indicated for each task.

Task	Where Taught/ Pages to Reteach	*Common Core Companion* Pages
1	6–7, 49, 154	67–73, 149–161
2	78, 99, 160	28–40
3	18, 129	122–128
4	6–7, 18, 47	15–27, 109–121
5	8, 160	28–40, 325–331
6	6–8, 98	15–27, 298–304
7	8, 47, 128, 160	122–128, 298–304

Assessment Pacing

In assigning the Writing Tasks on this student page, allow a class period for the completion of a task. As an alternative, assign tasks as homework. In assigning the Speaking and Listening Tasks on the facing page, consider having students do any required preparation as a homework assignment. Then, allow a class period for the presentations themselves.

Evaluating Performance Tasks

Use the rubric at the bottom of this Teacher Edition page to evaluate students' mastery of the standards as demonstrated in their Performance Task responses. Review the rubric with students before they begin work so they know the criteria by which their work will be evaluated.

Performance Tasks

Directions: *Follow the instructions to complete the tasks below as required by your teacher.*

As you work on each task, incorporate both general academic vocabulary and literary terms you learned in this unit.

Common Core
State Standards

RL.7.2, RL.7.3, RL.7.6; RI.7.2, RI.7.3;
W.7.2, W.9.a, W.9.b; SL.7.1, SL.7.4,
SL.7.6; L.7.1, L.7.2, L.7.3
[For the full wording of the standards,
see the standards chart in the front of
your textbook.]

Writing

Task 1: Literature [RL.7.6]

Analyze Point of View

Analyze how the author develops the points of view of two different characters in a story from this unit.

- Choose a story in which two characters clearly display their points of view.
- Write an analysis that tells how the author develops these distinct points of view through the characters' words and actions.
- Include examples from the story that show how the author makes each character's point of view clear to readers. Explain how one character's perspective is similar to or different from the perspective of the other character.

Task 2: Literature [RL.7.3]

Analyze the Interaction of Story Elements

Write an essay to explain how the setting of a story in this unit helps shape its plot.

- Identify details that reveal and describe the time and place of the story you chose.
- Analyze how the story's setting affects events or even makes them believable.
- Organize your ideas clearly, and support them with evidence from the text.
- Review your writing to correct errors in spelling and punctuation.

Task 3: Informational Text [RI.7.3]

Analyze Events and Their Influence

Write an essay about a nonfiction narrative in this unit. Analyze how the events described influence people and ideas.

- Identify the main events and central ideas in the nonfiction narrative.
- Explain how the events affect individuals and support the narrative's central idea.
- Use cause-and-effect organization and appropriate transitions.
- Use a variety of sentence patterns to add interest and clarify meaning.

Task 4: Literature [RL.7.2; RI.7.2]

Compare Themes or Central Ideas

Write an essay to compare and contrast the themes or central ideas of two selections in this unit.

- Choose two selections in this unit. Analyze the elements of each that support the theme or central idea. For example, think about where the events take place, what speakers say and do, and what objects play a critical role in the events.
- Organize your essay point-by-point to clearly show comparisons between the two texts.
- Use transitions to move smoothly from one idea to the next.
- Revise your essay to correct spelling, capitalization, and grammar mistakes.

192 Fiction and Nonfiction

Performance Task Rubric: Standards Mastery	Rating Scale				
	not very				*very*
Critical Thinking: How clearly and consistently does the student pursue the specific mode of reasoning or discourse required by the standard, as specified in the prompt (e.g., comparing and contrasting, analyzing, explaining)?	1	2	3	4	5
Focus: How well does the student understand and apply the focus concepts of the standard, as specified in the prompt (e.g., development of theme or of complex characters, effects of structure, and so on)?	1	2	3	4	5
Support/Elaboration: How well does the student support points with textual or other evidence? How relevant, sufficient, and varied is the evidence provided?	1	2	3	4	5
Insight: How original, sophisticated, or compelling are insights the student achieves by applying the standard to the text(s)?	1	2	3	4	5
Expression of Ideas: How well does the student organize and support ideas? How well does the student use language, including word choice and conventions, in the expression of ideas?	1	2	3	4	5

Speaking and Listening

ⓒ Task 5: Literature [RL.7.3; SL.7.6]

Evaluate and Interpret Interactions

Give a dramatic reading from a selection in this unit that shows how specific elements interact.

- Choose a selection, then analyze how elements in the narrative interact in a dramatic or interesting way. For example, note places where events in the narrative strongly influence the narrator's or main character's actions and ideas.

- Determine if your dramatic reading should be serious and formal or relaxed and informal.

- Begin by explaining to your audience how the elements interact. Then, read one or two passages of the text that clearly illustrate this interaction.

- Establish eye contact with your audience, adjust the volume of your voice, and use facial expressions to help convey your ideas.

ⓒ Task 6: Literature [RL.7.2; SL.7.1]

Analyze and Discuss Theme

Give an oral presentation in which you determine the theme of a story in this unit and analyze its development over the course of the story.

- Choose a story from this unit and identify its theme. Prepare a presentation that analyzes how the author develops that theme through characters and events.

- Give your presentation to a small group of classmates, being sure to include examples from the story to support your ideas.

- Listen attentively to your group members' presentations, analyzing their main ideas and supporting details.

- Be sure to use appropriate vocabulary and content-area words in your discussion.

ⓒ Task 7: Informational Text [RI.7.3; SL.7.1]

Evaluate Historical Context

Analyze how the historical context of a nonfiction selection in this unit influences the narrator and other characters. Discuss your findings with a small group of classmates.

- Identify the historical context of your selected text.

- Analyze how political and social events in the selection help to explain why the narrator or other characters think, feel, or act in a certain way.

- Consider how the narrator and characters might be different if they lived in a different time and place. Give an example showing how a different historical context might affect these characters.

- Present your ideas to the group in a focused manner, including explanations, details, and examples from the text to support your claims.

> **THE BIG ?**
>
> ### What is the best way to find the truth?
>
> At the beginning of Unit 1, you wrote a response to the Big Question. Now that you have completed the unit, write a new response. Discuss how your initial ideas have been changed or reinforced. Cite specific examples from the literature in this unit, from other subject areas, and from your own life to support your ideas. Use Big Question vocabulary words (see page 3) in your response.

Supporting Speaking and Listening

1. Consider having students work with partners or in groups to complete Performance Tasks involving speaking and listening. For tasks that you assign for individual work, you may still wish to have students rehearse with partners, who can provide constructive feedback.

2. As students rehearse, have them keep in mind these tips:
   - Present findings and evidence clearly and concisely.
   - Observe conventions of standard English grammar and usage.
   - Be relaxed and friendly but maintain a formal tone.
   - Make eye contact with the audience, pronounce words clearly, and vary your pace.
   - When working with a group, respond thoughtfully to others' positions, modifying your own in response to new evidence.

Linking Performance Tasks to Independent Reading

If you wish to cover the standards with students' independent reading, adapt Performance Tasks of your choice to the works they have selected. (Independent reading suggestions appear on the next page.)

> **THE BIG ?**
>
> ### What is the best way to find the truth?
>
> 1. Remind students that the unit Big Question is "What is the best way to find the truth?"
>
> 2. Have students complete their responses to the prompt on the student page. Point out that they have read selections in this unit about different ways to look for truth and that they should draw on these selections in their responses. Remind them that they can also draw on their own experiences and what they have learned in other subject areas in formulating their answers.

Differentiated Instruction for Universal Access

Strategy for Less Proficient Readers

Assign a Performance Task, and then have students meet in groups to review the standard assessed in that task. Remind students of the selections or independent readings to which they have previously applied the standard. Have groups summarize what they learned in applying the standard and then present their summaries. Discuss, clarifying any points of confusion. After students have completed their tasks, have groups meet again to evaluate members' work. Encourage members to revise their work based on the feedback they receive.

EL Strategy for English Learners

For each assigned Performance Task, review the instructions with students. Clarify the meaning of any unfamiliar vocabulary, emphasizing routine classroom words such as *narrator*, *context*, and *claims* and academic vocabulary such as *organize*.

Next, have students note ideas for their responses. Pair students, and have them review each other's notes, asking questions to clarify meaning and suggesting improvements. Encourage students to ask for your assistance in supplying English words or expressions they may require.

Independent Reading

Titles featured on the Independent Reading pages at the end of each unit represent a range of reading, including stories, dramas, and poetry, as well as literary nonfiction and other types of informational text. Throughout, labels indicate the works that are CCSS Exemplar Texts. Choosing from among these featured titles will help students read works at increasing levels of text complexity in the grades 6–8 text complexity band.

Independent Reading and Pacing

See the Unit Overview and Pacing Plan, pp. 2a–2b, for suggestions on integrating independent reading with work in the Student Edition.

Using Literature Circles

A literature circle is a temporary group in which students independently discuss a book.

Use the guidance in the *Professional Development Guidebook*, pp. 47–49, as well as the teaching notes on the facing page, for additional suggestions for literature circles.

Ⓒ Meeting Unit 1 CCS Focus Standards

Students can use books listed on this page to apply and to reinforce their mastery of the CCS Focus Standards covered in this unit. (The Focus Standards are introduced on pp. 4–9.)

Introducing Featured Titles

Have students choose a book or books for independent reading. Assist them by previewing the titles, noting their subject matter and level of difficulty. **Note:** Before recommending a work to students, preview it, taking into account the values of your community as well as the maturity of your students.

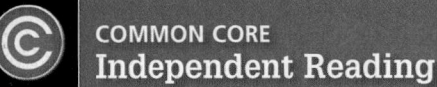

Featured Titles

In this unit, you have read a variety of fiction and literary nonfiction. Continue to read on your own. Select books that you enjoy, but challenge yourself to explore new topics, new authors, and works of increasing depth and complexity. The titles suggested below will help you get started.

Literature

Amanda/Miranda
by Richard Peck

In this long, fictional story, or **novel,** a servant girl trades identities with her look-alike mistress during the real-life sinking of the ship *Titanic.*

Letters from Rifka
by Karen Hesse

This work of **fiction** is set in Russia after World War II, an era in which Jews were brutally treated. Many, like 12-year-old Rifka and her family, fled the country. Rifka's story unfolds in a series of **letters** that describe her separation from her family and her ultimate reunion with them in America.

Little Women
by Louisa May Alcott   **EXEMPLAR TEXT** Ⓒ

Based on the author's life, this classic **novel** tells the story of the four March sisters—Meg, Joe, Beth, and Amy—who are growing up during the Civil War. The sisters face great challenges but never lose their determination.

A Fire in My Hands
by Gary Soto   **EXEMPLAR TEXT** Ⓒ

This collection of free-verse **poems,** including "Oranges" and "That Girl," reflects on Soto's experiences as a young Mexican American. The book also includes **essays** by Soto about his writing process.

Blessing the Boats: New and Selected Poems
by Lucille Clifton

In this collection, celebrated poet Lucille Clifton describes both ordinary life and extraordinary experiences. Her **poems** use few words to achieve great beauty and power.

Informational Texts

The Emperor's Silent Army
by Jane O'Connor
Viking, 2002

In 1974, farmers digging in China uncovered an army of life-sized clay soldiers buried for over 2,000 years. This work of **historical nonfiction** tells that story.

Discoveries: Truth Is Stranger Than Fiction

Find out new information in this book, which contains **essays** about different subject areas. You will read "The Wonders of the World," "Snakes in the Sky!," "Reel Time," and "Math Tricks."

A Night to Remember
by Walter Lord   **EXEMPLAR TEXT** Ⓒ

This work of **historical nonfiction,** based on true accounts by survivors of the *Titanic*, details the sinking of the famous ship.

Ⓒ Text Complexity: Aligning Texts With Readers and Tasks

TEXTS	READERS AND TASKS
• *Letters from Rifka* (Lexile: 660L) • *A Fire in My Hands*	**Below-Level Readers** Allow students to focus on reading for content, and challenge them to interpret multiple perspectives.
• *Amanda/Miranda* (Lexile: 790L) • *Little Women* (Lexile: 790L) • *Discoveries: Truth Is Stranger Than Fiction* (Lexile: 870L)	**Below-Level Readers** Challenge students as they read for content. **On-Level Readers** Allow students to focus on reading for content, and challenge them to interpret multiple perspectives. **Advanced Readers** Allow students to focus on interpreting multiple perspectives.
• *Blessing the Boats: New and Selected Poems* • *A Night to Remember* (Lexile: 950L)	**On-Level Readers** Challenge students as they read for content. **Advanced Readers** Allow students to focus on reading for content, and challenge them to interpret multiple perspectives.

Preparing to Read Complex Texts

Attentive Reading As you read literature on your own, bring your imagination and questions to the text. The questions shown below and others that you ask as you read will help you learn and enjoy literature even more.

 **Common Core State Standards**

Reading Literature/Informational Text 10. By the end of the year, read and comprehend literature, including stories, dramas, and poems, and literary nonfiction in the grades 6–8 text complexity band proficiently, with scaffolding as needed at the high end of the range.

When reading fiction, ask yourself...

- Whose "voice" is telling the story? Do I like that voice?
- Does the story offer a message that I think is important and true? Why or why not?

Key Ideas and Details

- Does the author describe places in a way that helps me picture them clearly? Why or why not?
- Do any details seem wrong? If so, which ones, and why?
- Do I understand why characters act and feel as they do? Do their thoughts and actions seem real? Why or why not?

Craft and Structure

- Do I care what happens in the story? Why or why not?
- Does the story remind me of others I have read? If so, how?

Integration of Ideas

When reading nonfiction, ask yourself...

- Who is the author? Why did he or she write the work?
- Has the author made me care about the subject? Why or why not?

Key Ideas and Details

- Does the author organize ideas well, or is the text hard to follow?
- Does the author use evidence that helps me understand the ideas?
- Does the author support his or her claims with solid evidence?

Craft and Structure

- Does the author leave out ideas I think are important?
- Do I agree with some of the author's ideas, but not with others? If so, why?
- What else have I read about this topic? How is this work similar to or different from those other works?
- What have I learned from this text?

Integration of Ideas

Independent Reading **195**

Text Complexity: Reader and Task Support Suggestions

INDEPENDENT READING

Increased Support Suggest that students choose a book that they feel comfortable reading and one that is a bit more challenging. Pair a more proficient reader with a less proficient reader and have them work together on the more challenging text. Partners can prepare to read the book by reviewing questions on this student page. They can also read difficult passages together, sharing questions and insights. They can use the questions on the student page to guide after-reading discussion.

Increased Challenge Encourage students to integrate knowledge and ideas by combining the Big Question and the Unit Focus concepts in their approach to two or more featured titles.

For example, students might consider how individuals search for truth in *Letters from Rifka* and *A Night to Remember*. In addition, students can focus on similarities and differences in the ways authors develop a theme in fiction and a central idea in nonfiction.

Preparing to Read Complex Texts

1. Tell students they can be attentive readers by bringing their experience and imagination to the texts they read and by actively questioning those texts. Explain that the questions they see on the student page are examples of types of questions to ask about works of fiction and nonfiction.

2. Point out that, like writing, reading is a "multidraft" process, involving several readings of complete works or passages, revising and refining one's understanding each time.

Key Ideas and Details

3. As an example, review and amplify the second bulleted item in the fiction section. **Ask:** What key ideas and details could you cite as evidence that a story's message is important and true?

   Possible response: You might point out that the theme is universal or that the characters seem believable.

Craft and Structure

4. **Ask:** What details of craft and structure would you cite as evidence that the author describes places vividly?

   Possible response: You might point to an author's effective use of specific details or of language that appeals to the five senses.

Integration of Ideas

5. **Ask:** How would you determine whether an author left out important ideas?

   Possible response: You would have to consult other sources and possibly reread the text to make sure no important ideas were missing.

6. Finally, explain to students that they should cite key ideas and details, examples of craft and structure, or instances of the integration of ideas as evidence to support their points during a book discussion. After hearing the evidence, the group might reach a consensus or might agree to disagree.

195

Unit 2 Features Overview

Unit Genre and Big Question

In this unit, students will analyze short stories. As they read they will discuss responses to the unit Big Question: Does every conflict have a winner?

Unit 2 Selections

Teach Selections are presented in leveled pairs. To teach the skills and meet the objectives, you need to assign only one selection in each pair.

Differentiate and Reinforce Choose the selection in a pair that is best suited for your students, based on the Text Complexity box shown on the next page. You may use the other selection to reinforce skills or provide enrichment.

Integrate Skills Each selection presents students with a reading strategy, a literary analysis concept, a vocabulary skill, and grammar instruction. Students can extend learning in the writing and extension activities.

Additional Unit Features

© Literary Analysis Workshop Teach and model the Unit Focus standards. Spiral Review notes enable students to revisit these skills over the course of the unit.

Reading for Information Students analyze functional, expository, and argumentative texts and complete Timed Writing activities.

Comparing Literary Works Students study two literary works either within or across genres.

Test Practice: Reading This feature provide extra practice in utilizing reading skills to master assessments.

Writing Workshops Two writing workshops appear in each unit, along with rubrics and instruction in the writing process.

Assessment Workshop Cumulative Skills Review and Performance Tasks provide a range of assessment opportunities.

Independent Reading Students broaden their knowledge as they read longer works of increasing complexity.

THE BIG ? Does every *conflict* have a winner?

196 Short Stories

PHLit Online!
www.PHLitOnline.com

Teaching From Technology

Enriched Online Student Edition
- full narration of selections
- interactive graphic organizers
- linked **Get Connected!** and **Background** videos
- all worksheets and other student resources

Professional Development
- the *Professional Development Guidebook* online
- additional professional development articles by program authors

Planning, Assigning, and Monitoring
- software for online assignment of work to students, individually or to the whole class
- a system for tracking and grading student work

Unit 2

PHLit Online!
www.PHLitOnline.com

Hear It!
• Selection summary audio
• Selection audio
• BQ Tunes

See It!
• Author videos
• Big Question video
• Get Connected videos
• Background videos
• More about the authors
• Illustrated vocabulary words
• Vocabulary flashcards

Do It!
• Interactive journals
• Interactive graphic organizers
• Grammar tutorials
• Interactive vocabulary games
• Test practice

197

Instructional Resources

The booklet *Unit 2 Resources* supports Unit skills with pages of the following types:

▶ **Benchmark Tests** assess and monitor student progress at mid-Unit and at Unit's end. Diagnostic questions are included at intervals five times a year.

▶ **Vocabulary and Reading Warm-ups** provide additional vocabulary support, based on Lexile rankings of words, for each selection. "A" Warm-ups are for students reading two grades below level. "B" Warm-ups are for students reading one grade below level.

▶ **Selection Support** These practice pages are available for each selection:
  • Reading Skill
  • Literary Analysis
  • Writing About the Big Question
  • Vocabulary Builder
  • Support for Writing
  • Support for Extend Your Learning
  • Enrichment

PHLit Online!
All worksheets and other student resources are also available online at www.PHLitOnline.com.

© **Text Complexity: Accessibility for Various Ability Levels**

This chart gives a general text complexity rating to help you decide which selection in each leveled pair is more appropriate for your students. **Choose one selection in each pair, or choose to teach both.** You will meet the objectives for the pair when you teach either of the two selections. For additional guidance on factors that affect the complexity of each selection, see the Leveled Texts page for each selection set.

Accessibility for English Learners

 EL This icon indicates support for English learners at point of use in this Teacher's Edition.

	✓ **More Accessible**	✓✓ **More Complex**
Pair 1	The Bear Boy	Rikki-tikki-tavi
Pair 2	*from* Letters from Rifka	Two Kinds *from* The Joy Luck Club
Pair 3	The Third Wish	Amigo Brothers
Pair 4	Zoo	Ribbons

Common Core State Standards

Unit 2 Focus Standards
• Reading Literature 2, 3, 6

Additional Activities and Assessments
• Writing 1, 2, 3, 7
• Reading Literature 1
• Speaking and Listening 1, 3, 5
• Language 1, 2, 4, 6

	Week 1					Week 2					Week 3				
	1	2	3	4	5	1	2	3	4	5	1	2	3	4	5
Introduce the Unit Big Question (pp. 198–199).	●														
Introduce the unit form, short stories, using the Literary Analysis Workshop (pp. 200–203).	●														
Introduce the focus CCS standards for the unit and lead students in a close reading of exemplar texts. (pp. 202–215).	●	●													
Teach one selection from Pairing 1 (pp. 216–247).		●	●	●	●	●									
Teach one selection from Pairing 2 (pp. 248–279).							●	●	●	●	●				
Complete the Test Practice: Reading (pp. 280–281).									●						
Teach Reading for Information (pp. 282–287).										●					
Teach Comparing Literary Works (pp. 288–301).												●	●		
Have students complete the Writing Workshop (pp. 302–307).										●	●	●	●	●	
Administer **Benchmark Test 3** (*Unit 2 Resources*, pp. 120–124).														●	
Reteach skills, judging which skills to reteach by evaluating students' performance on **Benchmark Test 3**.															●

Independent Reading

Have students choose a full-length work from the Independent Reading feature at the end of the unit and read it while working on this unit.

Pacing Suggestions
• Have students read their chosen work for homework.
• Devote parts of class periods in each school week to Literature Circles in which students reading the same work discuss it.

Acknow
every rea
poetry. S
mystery n
what kinc
like most.
what they
self-motiv
enthusiast
opinions.
preferenc
readers a
reading (

Offering
book for
is importc
itself does
stories, it
Have you
objective
the order.
them mos
them a gr

Presenti
that all ki
just a ver
narrative
and every
& Thomps
teacher, c
ers, local
machine,
what kinc
them abc

Activity	W4 1	W4 2	W4 3	W4 4	W4 5	W5 1	W5 2	W5 3	W5 4	W5 5	W6 1	W6 2	W6 3	W6 4	W6 5
Teach one selection from Pairing 3 (pp. 308–335).	●	●	●	●	●										
Teach one selection from Pairing 4 (pp. 336–361).						●	●	●	●	●					
Complete the Test-Practice: Reading (pp. 362–363).						●									
Teach Reading for Information (pp. 364–369).							●								
Teach Comparing Literary Works (pp. 370–383).								●	●						
Have students complete the Writing Workshop (pp. 384–391).							●	●	●	●	●				
Have students complete the Vocabulary Workshop (pp. 392–393).											●				
Have students complete the Communications Workshop (pp. 394–395).												●			
Have students complete the first three sections of the Assessment Workshop: Short Stories (pp. 396–399).											●	●	●		
Have students complete the selected Performance Tasks in the Assessment Workshop (pp. 400–401).													●		
Administer Benchmark Test 4 (*Unit 2 Resources,* pp. 226–233).													●		
Reteach skills, judging which skills to reteach by evaluating students' performance on **Benchmark Test 4.**															●

- Cover the focus standards with independent readings and abbreviate review of the focus standards with student-edition selections.
- Do not assign extension activities for selections (day 5 of main selection lessons), except as needed for full standards coverage.
- If students demonstrate reading proficiency, consider omitting Test Practice: Reading features in the unit.

Support

Brozo, William
To be a boy
(pp. 11–20
Internationa
Gee, James Pa
What video
about learni
45–50). Ne

Block and Daily Scheduling

The assignments and activities in this Unit planner are organized by week. You may adjust them to your daily or block schedule. The Time and Resource Manager for each selection set gives specific pacing suggestions, or you may use the comprehensive lesson planning support online at **www.PHLitOnline.com.**

Monitoring Progress

Diagnose Each main selection pairing in the Unit contains a more accessible and a more complex selection. To determine which selection in each pairing to assign, refer to students' results on the **Vocabulary in Context** section of **Benchmark Test 2, Unit 1 Resources,** pp. 240–242 (administered at the end of the previous Unit). Use the **Interpretation Guide** to interpret the results of this diagnostic portion of the test. **Note:** For the most accurate diagnosis of students who score in the middle range, administer the additional diagnostic questions online at **www.PHLitOnline.com.**

Preteach and Prepare As indicated by the diagnostic, prepare students for reading by assigning the **Vocabulary** and **Reading Warm-ups** for the selections you assign.

Teach Follow this Pacing Plan and use the resources to teach the skills and selections. For specific pacing suggestions and a list of resources, see the Time and Resource Manager and the Visual Guide to Selected Resources preceding each selection pairing.

Classroom Management
For classroom management suggestions for using leveled texts in a mixed-ability classroom, see Harvey Daniels's professional development essay "Leveled Reading Selections," online at **www.PHLitOnline.com.**

Assess After students have completed the first half of the Unit, administer **Benchmark Test 3.** Administer **Benchmark Test 4** at the end of the Unit.

Intervention and Reteach After administering each test, use the **Interpretation Guide** for the tests to determine which reteaching pages, if any, you should assign from the *Reading Kit.* The appropriate pages are also available through the online Progress Monitoring software.

❷ Close Read: Analyzing Story Elements

1. Remind students that story elements work together to develop theme.

2. Review the chart, making sure students understand each clue. Clarify that a story's title may help pinpoint a key symbolic meaning related to its theme. For example, if a story titled "The Past" features a photo of the main character's best friend from the past, the photo may be a symbol of past friendship, and the theme may be whatever the main character learns, or the resolution reveals, about past friendship.

3. Divide the class into groups. Assign a single theme, *Dishonesty never pays.* Have groups each outline a different story in which examples of the six story elements work together to convey this theme.

   Sample response: *Characters*— Lia, her older brother Bud, the headmaster of a private school; *Conflict*—Lia badly wants to get into the school; *Plot*—Lia hates the essay she wrote for the school application, asks Bud if she can use his college-application essay instead, steals his essay from his computer after he refuses, and does not get in to the school because the headmaster happens to be on the college board too and recognizes Bud's essay; *Setting*—a contemporary suburb; *Point of View*—third-person omniscient; *Symbols*—Bud's essay, symbol of individual achievement

4. Refer students to the model text beginning on page 205. Explain that details in the text that illustrate each element on the chart are highlighted in the same color and that corresponding side-column annotations use corresponding colors.

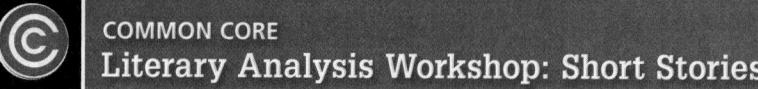

COMMON CORE
Literary Analysis Workshop: Short Stories

❷ Close Read: Analyzing Story Elements

Authors use all the elements of a short story to develop a theme.

A good story does more than capture a reader's interest and stir deep feelings—it also develops a **theme,** or insight about life. Readers can analyze a variety of clues to determine how the theme is revealed through a story's key elements.

Clues That Show How Story Elements Interact to Develop Theme	
Characters Characters' actions, decisions, and dialogue can highlight a story's theme. As you read, consider • characters' words, actions, and interactions with other characters; • the motivations, or reasons, for characters' actions; • changes that characters undergo.	**Conflict** A story's central conflict fuels the plot and often ties directly to the theme. Identify • external or internal conflicts in the story; • what each side in the conflict has at stake and is willing to fight for; • whether the main character changes or learns something as a result of the conflict.
Plot Consider the sequence of events in a story to infer a story's theme. As you read, note • key background information in the exposition; • what happens to the characters at the plot's climax, or turning point; • the use of plot devices, such as foreshadowing or flashback; • the way events are wrapped up in the resolution, or conclusion, of the story.	**Setting** The time and place of a story can influence the theme directly or indirectly. As you read, think about • the role setting plays in the conflicts and in the characters' motivations; • whether the same story could take place in a different setting; • the emotional associations of setting details, including the cultural and social context in which events occur.
Point of View The perspective from which a story is told can help reveal theme. As you read, notice • who is telling the story and what this narrator knows or does not know; • observations made by the narrator; • how the narrator's point of view affects what readers know; • how the author develops and contrasts different characters' points of view.	**Symbols** Some stories include symbols that may point to a theme by representing important ideas. As you read, look for • people, objects, or events that may stand for something greater than themselves; • ideas mentioned in the title of the story that might have symbolic meanings.

204 Short Stories

Think Aloud

Vocabulary: Using Context
Model the use of context clues for students. Direct their attention to the word *veranda,* used twice on the facing page. Say to students:

    If I were unfamiliar with the word *veranda,* I could use context clues to figure out the meaning. The first paragraph describes the setting of "The Dinner Party"—the dining room of a British couple in colonial India. The last sentence says that the room has a marble floor, open rafters, or ceiling beams, and "wide glass doors opening onto a

veranda." From the context I can tell that a *veranda* is a place just outside the doors, like a porch or patio or lawn or backyard.

    The word is used again in the fifth paragraph, in which a servant places a bowl of milk "on the veranda just outside the open doors." The context here tells me that a *veranda* is a place with flooring on which you could place a bowl. So it isn't a lawn or backyard; it must be something like a porch or patio.

❸ Model

About the Text This story is set during India's colonial period, when the country was ruled by England.

"The Dinner Party" by Mona Gardner

The country is India. A colonial official and his wife are giving a large dinner party. They are seated with their guests—army officers, and government attachés with their wives, and a visiting American naturalist—in their spacious dining room. It has a bare marble floor, open rafters, and wide glass doors opening onto a veranda.

A spirited discussion springs up between a young girl who insists that women have outgrown the jumping-on-a-chair-at-the-sight-of-a-mouse era and a colonel who says that they haven't.

❹ "A woman's unfailing reaction in any crisis," the colonel says, "is to scream. And while a man may feel like it, he has that ounce more of nerve control than a woman has. And that last ounce more is what counts."

❺ The American does not join in the argument but watches the other guests. As he looks, he sees a strange expression come over the face of the hostess. She is staring straight ahead, her muscles contracting slightly. With a slight gesture, she summons the native boy standing behind her chair and whispers to him. The boy's eyes widen, and he quickly leaves the room.

❻ Of the guests, none except the American notices this or sees the boy place a bowl of milk on the veranda just outside the open doors.

❼ The American comes to with a start. In India, milk in a bowl means only one thing—bait for a snake. He realizes there must be a cobra in the room. He looks up at the rafters—the likeliest place—but they are bare. Three corners of the room are empty, and in the fourth the servants are waiting to serve the next course. There is only one place left—under the table. ❽

His first impulse is to jump back and warn the others, but he knows the commotion would frighten the cobra into striking. He speaks quickly, the tone of his voice so arresting that it sobers everyone.

---

❹ **Characters** The colonel believes that women lack self-control. Characters' opinions and beliefs may be clues to theme.

❺ **Point of View** The narrator's point of view is limited to what the American notices. This heightens suspense by leaving the cause of the hostess's expression unknown.

❻ **Plot** The author uses foreshadowing. Readers sense there is something significant about the bowl of milk but do not yet know what it is.

❼ **Setting** The setting of this story is crucial to the plot. In India, the bowl of milk has a special significance.

❽ **Conflict** The American faces an internal conflict. He wants to warn the others, but does not want to endanger them. He must exercise *self-control*, which begins to emerge as a central idea in the story.

Literary Analysis Workshop **205**

---

❸ Reading the Model

1. Discuss the About the Text note. Explain that when Britain ruled India, British officials and army officers often socialized together.

2. Have students read the story (pp. 205–206). Discuss it, clarifying as needed, before reviewing the annotations.

❹ Characters

Have a student read the colonel's statement and the Characters annotation. **Ask:** What does this statement tell you about the colonel?

Possible responses: He has strong opinions. He is old-fashioned.

❺ Point of View

Read aloud the Point of View annotation. Clarify that the point of view is third person, but limited to the American's impressions.

❻ Plot

Have students read the Plot annotation. **Ask:** What might the milk foreshadow?

Possible response: It might foreshadow a crisis in which milk will be used as bait.

❼ Setting

Read aloud the Setting annotation. Explain that snakes are common in India, and many are poisonous.

❽ Conflict

Read aloud the Conflict annotation. **Ask:** Why is it significant to the plot and conflict that the American is a naturalist, or scientist who studies nature?

Possible response: He recognizes what the milk signifies and knows to avoid a commotion that would startle the cobra.

205

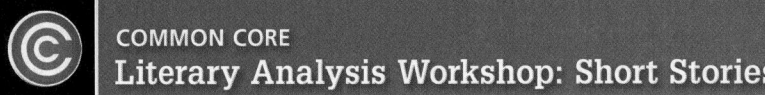
❾ Characters

1. Have students reread the first two paragraphs on the page. Clarify that *rupees* refers to the money used in India. Then, **ask:** What do you think of the naturalist's plan? Why?

   Possible response: It seems like a good way to keep the people from moving and endangering themselves and also keep them from knowing why and creating a commotion that would endanger them too.

2. **Ask:** What does the naturalist's plan show you about him?

   Possible response: He is quick-thinking in a crisis.

3. Read the host's comment and the Character annotation about it. **Ask:** Does the naturalist's behavior prove the colonel's point?

   Possible response: Yes and no. It does show that one man did indeed display self-control and handle a crisis well. However, it does not show anything about how other men would handle a crisis, nor does the naturalist's behavior show that a woman would handle it differently, as the colonel indicated.

❿ Plot

1. Read aloud the first sentence in the Plot annotation. Have a student summarize how Mrs. Wynnes's behavior has disproved the colonel's earlier statement about women.

   Possible response: The cobra was crawling on her foot, but she did not panic or scream, as the colonel indicated women do in a crisis. Instead, she calmly dealt with the crisis.

2. Read aloud the second sentence of the annotation, which shows the theme that the plot and its resolution help convey. **Ask:** What is amusing or appealing about the resolution?

   Possible response: The opinionated colonel gets his comeuppance in a surprising way.

Model continued

❾ Characters The host's statement recalls the argument at the beginning of the story. A repeated idea may point to the theme of a story.

❿ Plot In the resolution, we discover that Mrs. Wynnes has shown more self-control than any other character. The final sentence suggests the theme: *Courage and self-control are not specific to a gender.*

"I want to know just what control everyone at this table has. I will count to three hundred—that's five minutes—and not one of you is to move a muscle. Those who move will forfeit fifty rupees¹. Ready!"

❾ The twenty people sit like stone images while he counts. He is saying "two hundred and eighty" when, out of the corner of his eye, he sees the cobra emerge and make for the bowl of milk. Screams ring out as he jumps to slam the veranda doors safely shut.

"You were right, Colonel!" the host exclaims. "A man has just shown us an example of perfect control."

"Just a minute," the American says, turning to his hostess. "Mrs. Wynnes, how did you know the cobra was in the room?"

❿ A faint smile lights up the woman's face as she replies, "Because it was crawling across my foot."

---

1. rupee (rōō pē´) *n.* the unit of money of several Asian countries such as India, Pakistan, and Sri Lanka.

Vocabulary Development

Ⓒ **CCSS Language 6**

Thematic Vocabulary: The Big Question
As students discuss "The Dinner Party" (pp. 205–206), encourage them to use the thematic vocabulary presented in Introducing the Big Question, pp. 198–199. Help them with sentence starters such as these:

1. At the dinner party in the story, a *disagreement* arises about . . .
2. The *attitude* of the colonel is that . . .
3. At first the naturalist has no *understanding* of . . .
4. After the hostess's *communication* with the servant, the servant brings . . .
5. The naturalist recognizes the *danger* to the guests when he sees . . .
6. The naturalist proposes a *competition* in which . . .
7. The real aim of the naturalist's *challenge* to the dinner guests is . . .
8. The *outcome* contradicts the colonel's belief by showing . . .

① Independent Practice

About the Text Walter Dean Myers bases much of his work on his childhood experiences growing up in New York City's Harlem.

"The Treasure of Lemon Brown" by Walter Dean Myers

The dark sky, filled with angry, swirling clouds, reflected Greg Ridley's mood as he sat on the stoop of his building. His father's voice came to him again, first reading the letter the principal had sent to the house, then lecturing endlessly about his poor efforts in math.

"I had to leave school when I was thirteen," his father had said, "that's a year younger than you are now. If I'd had half the chances that you have, I'd . . ."

Greg had sat in the small, pale green kitchen listening, knowing the lecture would end with his father saying he couldn't play ball with the Scorpions. He had asked his father the week before, and his father had said it depended on his next report card. It wasn't often the Scorpions took on new players, especially fourteen-year-olds, and this was a chance of a lifetime for Greg. He hadn't been allowed to play high school ball, which he had really wanted to do, but playing for the Community Center team was the next best thing. Report cards were due in a week, and Greg had been hoping for the best. But the principal had ended the suspense early when she sent that letter saying Greg would probably fail math if he didn't spend more time studying.

"And you want to play *basketball*?" His father's brows knitted over deep brown eyes. "That must be some kind of a joke. Now you just get into your room and hit those books."

That had been two nights before. His father's words, like the distant thunder that now echoed through the streets of Harlem, still rumbled softly in his ears.

It was beginning to cool. Gusts of wind made bits of paper dance between the parked cars. There was a flash of nearby lightning, and soon large drops of rain splashed onto his jeans. He stood to go upstairs, thought of the lecture that probably awaited him if he did anything except shut himself in his room with his math book, and started walking down the street instead. Down the block there was an old tenement[1] that had been abandoned for some months. Some of the guys had held an impromptu checker tournament there the week before, and Greg had noticed that the door, once boarded over, had been slightly ajar.

---

1. **tenement** (ten´ ə mənt) *n.* old, run-down apartment house.

Literary Analysis Workshop **207**

---

⑫ **Plot** What conflict does this flashback reveal?

⑬ **Characters** What is Greg's motivation for staying out in the bad weather rather than going home?

---

⑪ Introducing the Independent Practice

1. Explain to students that they will analyze story elements in the Independent Practice selection.

2. Discuss the About the Text note.

   Explain that Harlem has for over a century been an important center of African American culture. One important tradition in that culture is blues music, born in the South but brought north with the waves of African Americans who moved to cities like Chicago and New York in the first half of the twentieth century. Blues music figures prominently in the background of one character in Myers's story.

⑫ Plot

1. Have students reread the highlighted flashback. **Ask:** What makes this scene a flashback?

   Answer: It interrupts the chronological order of plot events to portray a scene from an earlier time.

2. Remind students that the events of a plot center on a conflict the main character faces. **Ask** the Plot question.

   Possible response: Greg wants to play basketball with the Scorpions, a real honor for a fourteen-year-old, but his father will not allow it because Greg is failing math.

⑬ Characters

1. Have students read the highlighted passage. **Ask** the Character question.

   Possible response: He does not want to study and wants to avoid his father's lecture.

2. **Ask:** What does this behavior show about Greg?

   Possible response: He resents his father's lectures and likes to avoid unpleasantness, but he also wants to do as he pleases.

PHLit Online!

Enriched Online Student Edition
To have students read the selection in interactive format, with narration and point-of-use interactive graphic organizers, go online at www.PHLitOnline.com.

Differentiated Instruction   for Universal Access

Support for Special-Needs Students
Have students read the adapted version of "The Treasure of Lemon Brown" in the *Reader's Notebook: Adapted Version.* They may also listen to the adapted version on the *Hear It!* Audio CD, which includes adapted text. Then, have them complete the questions and activities in the student edition.

Support for Less Proficient Readers
Have students read "The Treasure of Lemon Brown" in the *Reader's Notebook.* After students finish the selection in the *Reader's Notebook,* have them complete the questions and activities in the Student Edition.

EL Support for English Learners
Have students read "The Treasure of Lemon Brown" in the *Reader's Notebook: English Learner's Version.* English learners may also read the selection as they listen to the recorded version on the *Hear It!* Audio CD. Then, have them complete the questions and activities in the student edition.

⑭ Setting

1. Some setting details in the story may be unfamiliar to students. Explain, if necessary, that a *tenement* is a rundown apartment building, a *bodega* is a small Latino grocery store, and a *parlor* is similar to a living room. Note that *graffiti* refers to signatures, slogans, or sketches painted or drawn, usually without permission, on public spaces such as the sides of buildings, buses, and subway cars.

2. Have a student read aloud the highlighted Setting passage. **Ask** the Setting question.

   Possible response: It echoes his stormy resentment of his father's lectures and his turmoil about playing basketball.

3. **Ask:** What do you predict Greg may encounter in this setting?

   Possible response: He may encounter the treasure mentioned in the title.

⑮ Conflict

1. Have a student read aloud the bracketed text. **Ask** the Conflict question.

   Possible response: His feelings reflect his conflict with his father over Greg's playing basketball, which his father will not allow while Greg is failing math.

2. **Ask:** What does his lack of interest in his father's story show about Greg?

   Possible response: He is somewhat self-centered and unappreciative of loved ones.

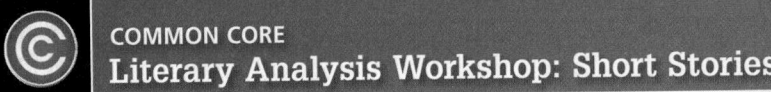

Practice continued

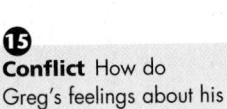

⑭ **Setting** How does the weather echo Greg's state of mind?

⑮ **Conflict** How do Greg's feelings about his father reflect a conflict?

⑭ Pulling his collar up as high as he could, he checked for traffic and made a dash across the street. He reached the house just as another flash of lightning changed the night to day for an instant, then returned the graffiti-scarred building to the grim shadows. He vaulted over the outer stairs and pushed tentatively on the door. It was open, and he let himself in.

The inside of the building was dark except for the dim light that filtered through the dirty windows from the streetlamps. There was a room a few feet from the door, and from where he stood at the entrance, Greg could see a squarish patch of light on the floor. He entered the room, frowning at the musty smell. It was a large room that might have been someone's parlor at one time. Squinting, Greg could see an old table on its side against one wall, what looked like a pile of rags or a torn mattress in the corner, and a couch, with one side broken, in front of the window.

He went to the couch. The side that wasn't broken was comfortable enough, though a little creaky. From the spot he could see the blinking neon sign over the bodega[2] on the corner. He sat awhile, watching the sign blink first green then red, allowing his mind to drift to the Scorpions, then to his father. His father had been a postal worker for all Greg's life, and was proud of it, often telling Greg how hard he had worked to pass the test. Greg had heard the story too many times to be interested now. ⑮

For a moment Greg thought he heard something that sounded like a scraping against the wall. He listened carefully, but it was gone.

Outside the wind had picked up, sending the rain against the window with a force that shook the glass in its frame. A car passed, its tires hissing over the wet street and its red taillights glowing in the darkness.

Greg thought he heard the noise again. His stomach tightened as he held himself still and listened intently. There weren't any more scraping noises, but he was sure he had heard something in the darkness—something breathing!

He tried to figure out just where the breathing was coming from; he knew it was in the room with him. Slowly he stood, tensing. As he turned, a flash of lightning lit up the room, frightening him with its sudden brilliance. He saw nothing, just the overturned table, the pile of rags and an old newspaper on the floor. Could he have been imagining the sounds? He continued listening, but heard nothing and thought that it might have just been rats. Still, he thought, as soon as the rain let up he would leave. He went to the window and was about to look when he heard a voice behind him.

---

2. **bodega** (bō dā′ gə) *n.* small grocery store serving a Latino neighborhood.

Vocabulary Development

Vocabulary Knowledge Rating

Create a **Vocabulary Knowledge Rating Chart** (*Professional Development Guidebook,* p. 33) with these words from the selection:

impromptu   ajar   tentatively

Give students a copy of the chart. Read the words aloud, and have students mark their rating in the Before Reading column. Urge them to be alert to these words as they read and discuss "The Treasure of Lemon Brown" because they will rate their knowledge of the words again after they finish.

Tally how many students think they know a word to gauge how much instruction to provide. As students read, point out the words and their context.

"Don't try nothin' 'cause I got a razor here sharp enough to cut a week into nine days!"

Greg, except for an involuntary tremor[3] in his knees, stood stock still. The voice was high and brittle, like dry twigs being broken, surely not one he had ever heard before. There was a shuffling sound as the person who had been speaking moved a step closer. Greg turned, holding his breath, his eyes straining to see in the dark room.

The upper part of the figure before him was still in darkness. The lower half was in the dim rectangle of light that fell unevenly from the window. There were two feet, in cracked, dirty shoes from which rose legs that were wrapped in rags.

"Who are you?" Greg hardly recognized his own voice.

"I'm Lemon Brown," came the answer. "Who're you?"

"Greg Ridley."

"What you doing here?" The figure shuffled forward again, and Greg took a small step backward.

"It's raining," Greg said.

"I can see that," the figure said.

The person who called himself Lemon Brown peered forward, and Greg could see him clearly. He was an old man.

His black, heavily wrinkled face was surrounded by a halo of crinkly white hair and whiskers that seemed to separate his head from the layers of dirty coats piled on his smallish frame. His pants were bagged to the knee, where they were met with rags that went down to the old shoes. The rags were held on with strings, and there was a rope around his middle. Greg relaxed. He had seen the man before, picking through the trash on the corner and pulling clothes out of a Salvation Army box. There was no sign of the razor that could "cut a week into nine days."

"What are you doing here?" Greg asked.

"This is where I'm staying," Lemon Brown said. "What you here for?"

"Told you it was raining out," Greg said, leaning against the back of the couch until he felt it give slightly.

"Ain't you got no home?"

"I got a home," Greg answered.

3. **involuntary** (in väl′ ən ter′ ē) **tremor** (trem′ ər) *n.* automatic trembling or shaking.

16 **Characters** What do you learn about Lemon Brown based on his own words? What do you learn based on the narrator's description?

17 **Point of View** What character's perspective does the narrator share?

18 **Plot** How does the tension of the story lessen when Greg sees Lemon Brown?

---

16 **Characters**

1. Have a student read aloud Lemon Brown's first words to Greg and the author's description of Brown's high voice. **Ask** the two Characters questions.

   Possible response: (a) His words tell that he is frightened of strangers and willing to attack anyone who threatens him. **(b)** The narrator's description suggests Brown is old and feeble and unlikely to be strong enough to carry out his threat.

17 **Point of View**

1. Have students reread the yellow highlighted text. **Ask** the Point of View question.

   Possible response: The narrator shares Greg's perspective.

2. **Ask** students to provide examples explaining or showing that the narrative is limited to Greg's perspective.

   Possible response: The reader never knows that Lemon Brown is there until Greg does. The narrative provides Greg's thoughts and impressions and details that only he can know—"holding his breath, his eyes straining to see"—but it never gives the thoughts and impressions of other characters.

18 **Plot**

1. Have students reread the description of "the person who called himself Lemon Brown" once Greg can see him clearly. **Ask:** What can you conclude about this man?

   Possible response: He is an elderly homeless man.

2. **Ask** the Plot question.

   Possible response: Greg realizes that he has little to fear from the man, since he has seen him before and knows him to be weak and elderly and also since he sees no sign of a weapon.

Differentiated Instruction for Universal Access

Strategy for Special-Needs Students
To make sure that students fully comprehend the selection, have them listen to the *Hear It!* **Audio CD.** Have students keep track of the events in the story as they listen. They may wish to use a storyboard or timeline to take notes.

Enrichment for Gifted/Talented Students
Have students reread the passage that describes the inside of the tenement building. Then, challenge artistically gifted students to render the description using the medium of their choice (pastels, acrylics, charcoal, collage, or even digital software). Students should base their artworks on the descriptions in the text. After students have completed their works, allow them to display their work in the classroom. Discuss how each piece of artwork captures the atmosphere of the scene.

⑲ Symbols

1. Refer students to the portion of the conversation between Greg and Lemon Brown that is highlighted in pale orange. **Ask** the Symbols question.

   Possible response: *Treasure* connotes something valuable and rare, especially valued by the person who possesses it.

⑳ Characters

1. Have two different students read aloud the portion of the conversation between Greg and Brown that is highlighted in blue. **Ask** the Characters question.

   Possible response: He was once a blues musician—well known, he claims—who performed mainly in the South. He then encountered a reversal of fortune, or "hard times," and has known misfortune ever since.

2. Explain that Sweet Lemon Brown is obviously a nickname and that blues singers traditionally have had such nicknames—Mississippi John Hurt, Big Mama Thornton, Howlin' Wolf, and so on. Mention that there was even a famous blues musician nicknamed Blind Lemon Jefferson.

㉑ Characters

1. Read aloud the bracketed text. **Ask** the two Characters questions.

   Possible response: (a) Brown feels affection for his own son and sees similarities in Greg. **(b)** These feelings might point to a theme about not taking relationships with loved ones for granted, as Greg has been doing.

Practice continued

⑲ **Symbols** Lemon Brown mentions the treasure of the story's title. What ideas and associations are conveyed by the word *treasure*?

⑳ **Characters** What do you learn about Lemon Brown through this dialogue?

㉑ **Characters** What does this dialogue reveal about Brown's feelings toward both his son and Greg? How might these feelings connect to a possible theme?

"You ain't one of them bad boys looking for my treasure, is you?" Lemon Brown cocked his head to one side and squinted one eye. "Because I told you I got me a razor."

"I'm not looking for your treasure," Greg answered, smiling. "If you have one."

⑲ "What you mean, if I have one," Lemon Brown said. "Every man got a treasure. You don't know that, you must be a fool!"

"Sure," Greg said as he sat on the sofa and put one leg over the back. "What do you have, gold coins?"

"Don't worry none about what I got," Lemon Brown said. "You know who I am?"

"You told me your name was orange or lemon or something like that."

"Lemon Brown," the old man said, pulling back his shoulders as he did so, "they used to call me Sweet Lemon Brown."

"Sweet Lemon?" Greg asked.

"Yes sir. Sweet Lemon Brown. They used to say I sung the blues so sweet that if I sang at a funeral, the dead would commence to rocking with the beat. Used to travel all over Mississippi and as far as Monroe, Louisiana, and east on over to Macon, Georgia. You mean you ain't never heard of Sweet Lemon Brown?"

⑳ "Afraid not," Greg said. "What . . . what happened to you?"

"Hard times, boy. Hard times always after a poor man. One day I got tired, sat down to rest a spell and felt a tap on my shoulder. Hard times caught up with me."

"Sorry about that."

"What you doing here? How come you didn't go on home when the rain come? Rain don't bother you young folks none."

"Just didn't." Greg looked away.

"I used to have a knotty-headed boy just like you." Lemon Brown had half walked, half shuffled back to the corner and sat down against the wall. "Had them big eyes like you got, I used to call them moon eyes. Look into them moon eyes and see anything you want."

㉑ "How come you gave up singing the blues?" Greg asked.

"Didn't give it up," Lemon Brown said. "You don't give up the blues; they give you up. After a while you do good for yourself, and it ain't nothing but foolishness singing about how hard you got it. Ain't that right?"

"I guess so."

"What's that noise?" Lemon Brown asked, suddenly sitting upright.

Greg listened, and he heard a noise outside. He looked at Lemon Brown and saw the old man pointing toward the window.

Greg went to the window and saw three men, neighborhood thugs, on the stoop. One was carrying a length of pipe. Greg looked back toward Lemon Brown, who moved quietly across the room to the window. The old man looked out, then beckoned frantically for Greg to follow him. For a moment Greg couldn't move. Then he found himself following Lemon Brown into the hallway and up darkened stairs. Greg followed as closely as he could. They reached the top of the stairs, and Greg felt Lemon Brown's hand first lying on his shoulder, then probing down his arm until he finally took Greg's hand into his own as they crouched in the darkness.

"They's bad men," Lemon Brown whispered. His breath was warm against Greg's skin.

"Hey! Rag man!" A voice called. "We know you in here. What you got up under them rags? You got any money?"

Silence.

"We don't want to have to come in and hurt you, old man, but we don't mind if we have to."

Lemon Brown squeezed Greg's hand in his own hard, gnarled fist.

There was a banging downstairs and a light as the men entered. They banged around noisily, calling for the rag man.

"We heard you talking about your treasure." The voice was slurred. "We just want to see it, that's all."

"You sure he's here?" One voice seemed to come from the room with the sofa.

"Yeah, he stays here every night."

"There's another room over there; I'm going to take a look. You got that flashlight?"

"Yeah, here, take the pipe too."

Greg opened his mouth to quiet the sound of his breath as he sucked it in uneasily. A beam of light hit the wall a few feet opposite him, then went out.

"Ain't nobody in that room," a voice said. "You think he gone or something?"

"I don't know," came the answer. "All I know is that I heard him talking about some kind of treasure. You know they found that shopping bag lady with that money in her bags."

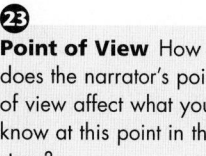

Plot During this rising action, how does the relationship between Greg and Lemon Brown change?

Point of View How does the narrator's point of view affect what you know at this point in the story?

22 Plot

1. Have students reread the highlighted passage that corresponds to the Plot question. **Ask:** What do the word *thugs* and the presence of the length of pipe suggest about the three men outside?

   Possible response: They are violent men who may use the pipe as a weapon.

2. **Ask:** How does Greg feel when he sees the thugs, and what does he do?

   Possible response: He is frightened and follows Lemon Brown, hoping to find safety. He takes Brown's hand.

3. **Ask** the Plot question.

   Possible response: Greg grows closer with Brown, the two becoming a bit like father and son.

23 Point of View

1. Read aloud the highlighted conversation of the thugs and Greg's reaction to it. **Ask:** What does the conversation that Greg overhears show about the motivation of the three thugs?

   Possible response: They are looking for money. They heard Lemon Brown talk about some kind of treasure and have come to steal it.

2. **Ask** the Point of View question.

   Possible response: We do not know what the treasure is or if it really exists.

3. **Ask:** How might this passage be different if it were told from an omniscient point of view?

   Possible response: We would probably know Brown's thoughts on hearing the men talk about his treasure.

211

㉔ Plot

1. Have a student read aloud the purple highlighted text, using appropriate tones for the voices of the thugs and sound effects for Greg's howl. **Ask:** Why does Greg howl?

   Possible response: He hopes to frighten the thugs off and prevent them from doing harm.

2. **Ask:** What does Greg's decision to howl show about him?

   Possible response: He is quick thinking and willing to risk harm to help another person.

3. **Ask** the Plot question.

   Possible response: The point of view puts the reader in Greg's shoes to experience Greg's panic and also to appreciate his quick thinking and wonder whether the ploy will work.

Practice continued

"Yeah. You think he's upstairs?"

"Hey, old man, are you up there?"

Silence.

"Watch my back, I'm going up."

There was a footstep on the stairs, and the beam from the flashlight danced crazily along the peeling wallpaper. Greg held his breath. There was another step and a loud crashing noise as the man banged the pipe against the wooden banister[4]. Greg could feel his temples throb as the man slowly neared them. Greg thought about the pipe, wondering what he would do when the man reached them—what he *could* do.

Then Lemon Brown released his hand and moved toward the top of the stairs. Greg looked around and saw stairs going up to the next floor. He tried waving to Lemon Brown, hoping the old man would see him in the dim light and follow him to the next floor. Maybe, Greg thought, the man wouldn't follow them up there. Suddenly, though, Lemon Brown stood at the top of the stairs, both arms raised high above his head.

"There he is!" A voice cried from below.

"Throw down your money, old man, so I won't have to bash your head in!"

Lemon Brown didn't move. Greg felt himself near panic. The steps came closer, and still Lemon Brown didn't move. He was an eerie sight, a bundle of rags standing at the top of the stairs, his shadow on the wall looming over him. Maybe, the thought came to Greg, the scene could be even eerier.

Greg wet his lips, put his hands to his mouth and tried to make a sound. Nothing came out. He swallowed hard, wet his lips once more and howled as evenly as he could.

"What's that?"

As Greg howled, the light moved away from Lemon Brown, but not before Greg saw him hurl his body down the stairs at the men who had come to take his treasure. There was a crashing noise, and then footsteps. A rush of warm air came in as the downstairs door opened, then there was only an ominous silence.

Greg stood on the landing. He listened, and after a while there was another sound on the staircase.

"Mr. Brown?" he called.

"Yeah, it's me," came the answer. "I got their flashlight."

Plot How does the narrator's point of view increase tension and suspense as the story nears its climax?

4. **banister** (ban′ is tər) *n.* railing along a staircase.

Vocabulary Development

© **CCSS Language 6**

Thematic Vocabulary: The Big Question

As students are discussing "The Treasure of Lemon Brown," encourage them to use the thematic vocabulary presented in Introducing the Big Question, pp. 198–199. You might use sentence starters such as these:

1. Greg's *disagreement* with his father occurred because . . .
2. Greg feels a sense of *danger* when . . .
3. Lemon Brown's *attitude* toward the thugs is . . .
4. The *conflict* with the thugs is resolved when . . .
5. By the end of the story, Greg has a new *understanding* of . . .

Greg exhaled in relief as Lemon Brown made his way slowly back up the stairs.

25

"You OK?"

"Few bumps and bruises," Lemon Brown said.

"I think I'd better be going," Greg said, his breath returning to normal. "You'd better leave, too, before they come back."

"They may hang around outside for a while," Lemon Brown said, "but they ain't getting their nerve up to come in here again. Not with crazy old rag men and howling spooks. Best you stay a while till the coast is clear. I'm heading out west tomorrow, out to East St. Louis."

"They were talking about treasures," Greg said. "You *really* have a treasure?"

26

"What I tell you? Didn't I tell you every man got a treasure?" Lemon Brown said. "You want to see mine?"

"If you want to show it to me," Greg shrugged.

"Let's look out the window first, see what them scoundrels be doing," Lemon Brown said.

They followed the oval beam of the flashlight into one of the rooms and looked out the window. They saw the men who had tried to take the treasure sitting on the curb near the corner. One of them had his pants leg up, looking at his knee.

"You sure you're not hurt?" Greg asked Lemon Brown.

"Nothing that ain't been hurt before," Lemon Brown said. "When you get as old as me all you say when something hurts is, 'Howdy, Mr. Pain, sees you back again.' Then when Mr. Pain see he can't worry you none, he go on mess with somebody else."

27

Greg smiled.

"Here, you hold this." Lemon Brown gave Greg the flashlight.

He sat on the floor near Greg and carefully untied the strings that held the rags on his right leg. When he took the rags away, Greg saw a piece of plastic. The old man carefully took off the plastic and unfolded it. He revealed some yellowed newspaper clippings and a battered harmonica.

"There it be," he said, nodding his head. "There it be."

Greg looked at the old man, saw the distant look in his eye, then turned to the clippings. They told of Sweet Lemon Brown, a blues singer and harmonica player who was appearing at different theaters in the South.

25 **Plot** What happens at the climax of the story? What clues suggest that the story has now entered the falling action?

26 **Symbols** Lemon Brown once again says that "every man got a treasure." What possible theme might this idea support?

27 **Characters** How have Greg's feelings toward Lemon Brown changed since the two first met?

25 Plot

1. Read aloud the bracketed text. Then, **ask** the two Plot questions.

 Possible responses: (a) Brown attacks the thugs, and they run off. **(b)** Greg's exhaling in relief shows that the mounting tension has ended and the story may have entered the falling action.

26 Symbols

1. Have students reread the high-lighted exchange about the trea-sure. **Ask:** How does Greg seem to feel about the treasure?

 Possible response: He seems curious to discover whether it exists and what it might be.

2. **Ask** the Symbols question.

 Possible response: Everyone has something they value, and different people treasure different things.

27 Characters

1. Have students reread the blue highlighted passage. **Ask:** What does Lemon Brown reveal about his attitude toward life with comments like the one about "Howdy, Mr. Pain"?

 Possible response: He is philo-sophical and accepting. He is not one to complain.

2. **Ask** the Characters question, and have students explain their response.

 Possible response: Greg has come to feel affection and con-cern for Lemon Brown. Even though they are heading to the treasure, he pauses to find out how Brown feels.

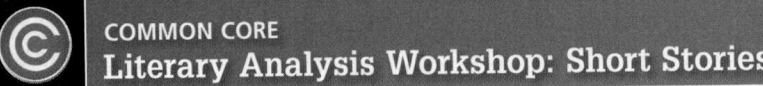
㉘ Plot

1. Have students reread the high-lighted section in which Brown explains what happened to his wife and son. Explain that "mouth fiddle" is a rare slang term for a harmonica. **Ask:** How did you react to learning this information about Lemon Brown?

   Possible response: I found it very sad and moving.

2. **Ask:** By keeping the clippings and mouth fiddle, what did the son show about his feelings for his father?

   Possible response: He was proud of his father and missed him.

3. **Ask** the two Plot questions.

   Possible responses: (a) Brown treasures these items because they show how much his son treasured him and because he has tragically lost his wife and son. **(b)** One theme is that family ties are valuable and should not be taken for granted.

㉙ Conflict

1. Read aloud the exchange between Brown and Greg that is highlighted in pink. **Ask** the two Conflict questions.

   Possible responses: (a) Greg knows that no matter how valu-able the items are to Lemon Brown, he risked his life to keep it from those thugs with the lead pipe. **(b)** Brown's response rein-forces the value of family ties.

2. **Ask:** What does the treasure symbolize, or represent, to Lemon Brown?

   Possible response: It represents the pride and love his son felt for him, the pride he takes in his son's feelings, and the love he feels for his son. It represents his memory of family love.

Practice continued

㉘ **Plot** What do these past events reveal about Lemon Brown's treasure? What theme does the author develop here?

㉘

㉙ **Conflict** Why does Greg ask if the treasure was worth fighting for? How does Lemon Brown's response reinforce the developing theme?

One of the clippings said he had been the hit of the show, although not the headliner. All of the clippings were reviews of shows Lemon Brown had been in more than 50 years ago. Greg looked at the harmonica. It was dented badly on one side, with the reed holes on one end nearly closed.

"I used to travel around and make money for to feed my wife and Jesse—that's my boy's name. Used to feed them good, too. Then his mama died, and he stayed with his mama's sister. He growed up to be a man, and when the war come he saw fit to go off and fight in it. I didn't have nothing to give him except these things that told him who I was, and what he come from. If you know your pappy did something, you know you can do something too.

"Anyway, he went off to war, and I went off still playing and singing. 'Course by then I wasn't as much as I used to be, not without somebody to make it worth the while. You know what I mean?"

"Yeah," Greg nodded, not quite really knowing.

"I traveled around, and one time I come home, and there was this letter saying Jesse got killed in the war. Broke my heart, it truly did.

"They sent back what he had with him over there, and what it was is this old mouth fiddle and these clippings. Him carrying it around with him like that told me it meant something to him. That was my treasure, and when I give it to him he treated it just like that, a treasure. Ain't that something?"

"Yeah, I guess so," Greg said.

"You *guess* so?" Lemon Brown's voice rose an octave as he started to put his treasure back into the plastic. "Well, you got to guess 'cause you sure don't know nothing. Don't know enough to get home when it's raining."

"I guess . . . I mean, you're right."

"You OK for a youngster," the old man said as he tied the strings around his leg, "better than those scalawags[5] what come here looking for my treasure. That's for sure."

"You really think that treasure of yours was worth fighting for?" Greg asked. "Against a pipe?"

"What else a man got 'cepting what he can pass on to his son, or his daughter, if she be his oldest?" Lemon Brown said. "For a big-headed boy you sure do ask the foolishest questions."

Lemon Brown got up after patting his rags in place and looked out the window again.

5. **scalawags** (skal´ ə wagz´) *n.* people who cause trouble; scoundrels.

214 Short Stories

Vocabulary Development

Vocabulary Knowledge Rating

When students have completed reading and discussing "The Treasure of Lemon Brown," have them take out their **Vocabulary Knowledge Rating Chart** for this selection. Read the words aloud once more, and have students rate their knowledge of words again in the After Reading column. Clarify any words that are still problematic. Have students write their own definitions or examples in the appro-priate column. Encourage students to use the words in further discussion and written work about the selection.

"Looks like they're gone. You get on out of here and get yourself home. I'll be watching from the window so you'll be all right."

Lemon Brown went down the stairs behind Greg. When they reached the front door the old man looked out first, saw the street was clear and told Greg to scoot on home.

"You sure you'll be OK?" Greg asked.

"Now didn't I tell you I was going to East St. Louis in the morning?" Lemon Brown asked. "Don't that sound OK to you?"

"Sure it does," Greg said. "Sure it does. And you take care of that treasure of yours."

"That I'll do," Lemon said, the wrinkles about his eyes suggesting a smile. "That I'll do."

30 The night had warmed and the rain had stopped, leaving puddles at the curbs. Greg didn't even want to think how late it was. He thought ahead of what his father would say and wondered if he should tell him about Lemon Brown. He thought about it until he reached his stoop, and decided against it. Lemon Brown would be OK, Greg thought, with his memories and his treasure.

31 Greg pushed the button over the bell marked Ridley, thought of the lecture he knew his father would give him, and smiled.

30 **Setting** How does a change in the setting echo a change that has taken place in Greg?

31 **Conflict** How might Greg's experience with Lemon Brown have changed his attitude toward his father?

After You Read	The Treasure of Lemon Brown	

© **1. Key Ideas and Details (a)** Write an objective summary of this story. **(b) Identify:** How is each of the story's key conflicts resolved?

© **2. Craft and Structure (a)** From what point of view is this story told? **(b) Speculate:** Why do you think the author chose this point of view to tell the story? Explain.

© **3. Key Ideas and Details Synthesize:** At the end of the story, what has Greg learned that causes him to smile? Support your answer.

© **4. Craft and Structure (a)** What is the story's theme? **(b) Evaluate:** Which elements of the story provide the most significant clues to its theme? Explain.

© **5. Integration of Knowledge and Ideas (a)** In the first column of a chart like the one shown, tell what the text says about each of Lemon Brown's treasures. **(b) Connect:** In the second column, explain what each treasure means to Lemon Brown. **(c) Collaborate:** With a partner, review your ideas. Together, complete the third column with information that explains how Lemon Brown's idea of a "treasure" is an important part of the story's theme.

Lemon Brown's Treasures

What It Says	What It Means	Why It Is Important

Literary Analysis Workshop **215**

Assessment Resources

The following resources can be used to assess students' knowledge and skills.

Unit 2 Resources

L1 L2 EL **Selection Test A,** pp. 17–19

L3 L4 EL **Selection Test B,** pp. 20–22

L3 L4 **Open Book Test,** pp. 14–16

PHLit Online! Students may use the **Self-test,** online at www.PHLitOnline.com, to prepare for the **Selection Test.**

✓ **The Bear Boy** • ✓✓ **Rikki-tikki-tavi**
Lesson Pacing Guide

DAY 1 Preteach

- Ⓒ Administer the Reading and Vocabulary Warm-ups (*Unit 2 Resources*, pp. 23–26 or 41–44) as necessary.
- Introduce the Reading Skill: Making Predictions.
- Ⓒ Introduce the Literary Analysis concept: Plot.
- Distribute copies of the graphic organizer for the Reading Skill (*Graphic Organizer Transparencies*, pp. 42–44).
- Distribute copies of the graphic organizer for Literary Analysis (*Graphic Organizer Transparencies*, pp. 39–41).
- Ⓒ Teach the selection vocabulary.
- Ⓒ Introduce the Word Study skill.

DAYS 2–3 Preteach/Teach

- Ⓒ Build background with the Background feature.
- Develop thematic vocabulary and thematic thinking with Writing About the Big Question.
- Prepare students to read with the Activating Prior Knowledge activities (TE).
- Informally monitor comprehension while students read.
- Use the Reading Check questions to confirm comprehension.
- Develop students' ability to make predictions using the Making Predictions questions.
- Ⓒ Develop students' understanding of Plot using the Plot questions.
- Ⓒ Reinforce vocabulary with the Vocabulary notes.
- Ⓒ Reinforce unit focus standards using the Spiral Review prompts.

DAY 4 Assess

- Assess students' comprehension and mastery of the skills by having them answer the Critical Thinking, Reading Skill, and Literary Analysis questions.
- Ⓒ Have students complete the Vocabulary Practice activities.
- Ⓒ Have students complete the Word Study activities.

DAY 5 Extend/Assess

- Have students complete the Conventions lesson.
- Ⓒ Have students complete the Writing activity and write an informative article. (You may assign as homework.)
- Ⓒ Extend learning by having students complete the Speaking and Listening activity, an informal debate. As an alternative, assign them "Athletes as Role Models" or "Coyotes on the Go" in *Reality Central.*
- Administer Selection Test A or B (*Unit 2 Resources,* pp. 35–40 or 56–61).

Ⓒ Common Core State Standard

Reading Literature 3. Analyze how particular elements of a story or drama interact (e.g., how setting shapes the characters or plot).

Writing 2.d. Use precise language and domain-specific vocabulary to inform about or explain the topic.
2.e. Establish and maintain a formal style.

Speaking and Listening 1.a. Come to discussions prepared, having read or researched material under study; explicitly draw on that preparation by referring to evidence on the topic, text, or issue to probe and reflect on ideas under discussion.
3. Delineate a speaker's argument and specific claims, evaluating the soundness of the reasoning and the relevance and sufficiency of the evidence.

Language
4.b. Use common, grade-appropriate Greek or Latin affixes and roots as clues to the meaning of a word.
6. Acquire and use accurately grade-appropriate general academic and domain-specific words and phrases; gather vocabulary knowledge when considering a word or phrase important to comprehension or expression.

Additional Standards Practice
Common Core Companion, pp. 15–35, 67–68

Daily Block Scheduling
Each day in this Lesson Pacing Guide represents a 40–50 minute period. Teachers using block scheduling may combine days to revise pacing. In addition, teachers may differentiate and support core instruction by integrating components for extended and intensive support, as students require. See the Guide to Selected Leveled Resources (facing page).

Guide to Selected Leveled Resources

Tier 1 (students performing on level)

		✓ **More Accessible** The Bear Boy	✓✓ **More Complex** Rikki-tikki-tavi
Warm Up	Practice, model, and monitor fluency, working with the whole class or in groups.	Vocabulary and Reading Warm-ups B, *Unit 2 Resources*, pp. 23–24, 26	Vocabulary and Reading Warm-ups B, *Unit 2 Resources*, pp. 41–42, 44
Comprehension/Skills	Support and monitor comprehension and skills development, having students complete the activities, graphic organizers, and interactive prompts independently or as a class.	• *Reader's Notebook,* adapted instruction and full selection **EL** *Reader's Notebook: English Learner's Version,* adapted instruction and adapted selection • Reading Skill Graphic Organizer B, *Graphic Organizer Transparencies,* p. 44 • Literary Analysis Graphic Organizer B, *Graphic Organizer Transparencies,* p. 41	• *Reader's Notebook,* adapted instruction and summary **EL** *Reader's Notebook: English Learner's Version,* adapted instruction and summary • Reading Skill Graphic Organizer B, *Graphic Organizer Transparencies,* p. 44 • Literary Analysis Graphic Organizer B, *Graphic Organizer Transparencies,* p. 41
Monitor Progress	Monitor student progress with the differentiated curriculum-based assessment in the *Unit Resources.*	• Selection Test B, *Unit 2 Resources,* pp. 38–40 • Open-Book Test, *Unit 2 Resources,* pp. 32–34	• Selection Test B, *Unit 2 Resources,* pp. 59–61 • Open-Book Test, *Unit 2 Resources,* pp. 53–55

Tier 2 (students requiring intervention)

		✓ **More Accessible** The Bear Boy	✓✓ **More Complex** Rikki-tikki-tavi
Warm Up	Practice, model, and monitor fluency in groups or with individuals.	• Vocabulary and Reading Warm-ups A, *Unit 2 Resources,* pp. 23–25 • *Reality Central,* "Athletes as Role Models" • *Hear It!* Audio CD (adapted text)	• Vocabulary and Reading Warm-ups A, *Unit 2 Resources,* pp. 41–43 • *Reality Central,* "Coyotes on the Go" • *Hear It!* Audio CD
Comprehension/Skills	• Support and monitor comprehension and skills development, working in small groups or with individuals. • Pair students with more advanced peers and have them complete the writing activity in the *Real-World Writing Journal.* • As students complete the selection in the appropriate version of the *Reader's Notebook,* monitor comprehension frequently with group questions and individual instruction. • Model strategies while guiding students in completing the activities and prompts in the *Reader's Notebook,* as well as the graphic organizers. • Practice skills and monitor mastery with the *Reading Kit* worksheets.	• *Real-World Writing Journal,* Lesson 1, pp. 36–39 • *Reader's Notebook: Adapted Version,* adapted instruction and adapted selection **EL** *Reader's Notebook: English Learner's Version,* adapted instruction and adapted selection • Reading Skill Graphic Organizer A, *Graphic Organizer Transparencies,* p. 42 • Literary Analysis Graphic Organizer A, *Graphic Organizer Transparencies,* p. 39 • *Reading Kit,* Practice worksheets, pp. 52, 56, 62, 64, 68	• *Real-World Writing Journal,* Lesson 2, pp. 40–43 • *Reader's Notebook: Adapted Version,* adapted instruction and summary **EL** *Reader's Notebook: English Learner's Version,* adapted instruction and summary • Reading Skill Graphic Organizer A, *Graphic Organizer Transparencies,* p. 43 • Literary Analysis Graphic Organizer A, *Graphic Organizer Transparencies,* p. 40 • *Reading Kit,* Practice worksheets, pp. 52, 56, 62, 64, 68
Monitor Progress	Monitor student progress with the differentiated curriculum-based assessment in the *Unit Resources* and in the *Reading Kit.*	• Selection Test A, *Unit 2 Resources,* pp. 35–37 • *Reading Kit,* Assess worksheets, pp. 53, 57, 63, 65, 69	• Selection Test A, *Unit 2 Resources,* pp. 56–58 • *Reading Kit,* Assess worksheets, pp. 53, 57, 63, 65, 69

TIER 3 Tier 3 intervention may require consultation with the student's special-education or dyslexia specialist. For additional support, see the Tier 2 activities and resources listed above.

🔲 One-on-one teaching   🔲 Group work   🔲 Whole class instruction   🔲 Independent work   🅰 Assessment

For a complete guide to selection support, including support for Advanced students, see the Overview of Resources in the frontmatter.

✓ The Bear Boy
✓✓ Rikki-tikki-tavi

RESOURCES FOR:

L1 Special-Needs Students

L2 Below-Level Students (Tier 2)

L3 On-Level Students (Tier 1)

L4 Advanced Students (Tier 1)

EL English Learners

All All Students

Vocabulary/Fluency/Prior Knowledge

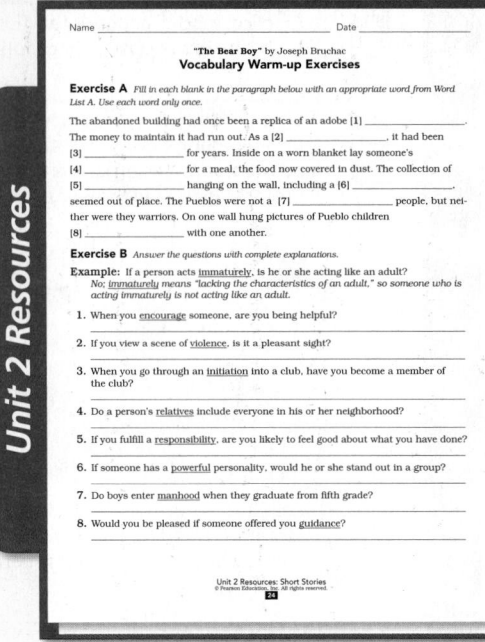

EL **L1** **L2** **Vocabulary Warm-ups A and B,** pp. 23–24, 41–42

Also available for these selections:

L2 **Reading Warm-ups A and B,** pp. 25–26, 43–44

All **Writing About the Big Question,** pp. 27, 45

All **Vocabulary Builder,** pp. 30, 48

Reader's Notebooks

Pre- and postreading pages for both selections, as well as the selection "The Bear Boy," appear in an interactive format in the *Reader's Notebooks.* Each *Notebook* is differentiated for a different group of learners. The selections in the Adapted and English Learner's versions are abridged.

L2 **L3** *Reader's Notebook*

L1 *Reader's Notebook: Adapted Version*

EL *Reader's Notebook: English Learner's Version*

EL *Reader's Notebook: Spanish Version*

© *Common Core Companion*

Additional instruction and practice for each Common Core State Standard

Selection Support

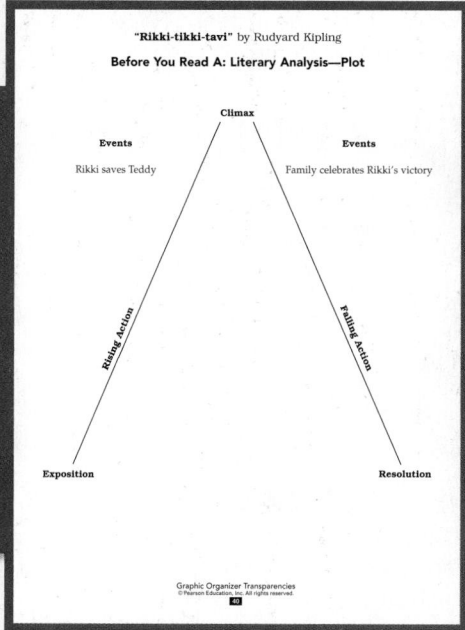

Graphic Organizer Transparencies

"Rikki-tikki-tavi" by Rudyard Kipling

Before You Read A: Literary Analysis—Plot

Climax

Events — Rikki saves Teddy

Events — Family celebrates Rikki's victory

Rising Action

Falling Action

Exposition

Resolution

EL **L1** **L2** **Literary Analysis: Graphic Organizer A,** pp. 39, 40 (partially filled in)

Also available for these selections:

EL **L3** Literary Analysis: Graphic Organizer B, p. 41

EL **L1** **L2** Reading: Graphic Organizer A, pp. 42, 43 (partially filled in)

EL **L3** Reading: Graphic Organizer B, p. 44

Skills Development/Extension

Unit 2 Resources

Name _____ Date _____

"The Bear Boy" by Joseph Bruchac
Enrichment: Initiation Into Adulthood

In "The Bear Boy," Kuo-Haya stays with the bears in order to learn the things he must know to become a man. In many cultures around the world, young people go through initiation ceremonies to become adults. They learn lessons and often have to pass a test of some kind to become full members of their society.

A. DIRECTIONS: *List eight things young people should know before they become adults in our society.*

1. _____
2. _____
3. _____
4. _____
5. _____
6. _____
7. _____
8. _____

B. DIRECTIONS: *Now, write three responsibilities that adults in our society have.*

1. _____
2. _____
3. _____

L4 **Enrichment,** pp. 31, 49

Also available for these selections:

All Reading: Makes Predictions, pp. 28, 46

All Literary Analysis: Plot, pp. 29, 47

EL **L3** **L4** Grammar, p. 50

EL **L3** **L4** Support for Writing, p. 51

L3 **L4** Support for Extend Your Learning, p. 52

Assessment

Name _____ Date _____

"Rikki-tikki-tavi" by Rudyard Kipling
Selection Test B

Critical Reading *Identify the letter of the choice that best completes the statement or answers the question.*

___ 1. Read the following quotation from "Rikki-tikki-tavi." Then, based on the quotation and your prior knowledge, choose the most likely outcome from the choices below.
"No," said his mother; "let's take him in and dry him. Perhaps he isn't really dead."
A. Rikki-tikki will soon die.
B. Rikki-tikki will survive.
C. Rikki-tikki will survive and attack the boy's mother.
D. The mother will become Rikki-tikki's only friend.

___ 2. After Teddy's father beats the dead Karait, Rikki-tikki thinks, "What is the use of that? . . . I have settled it all." This thought shows that Rikki-tikki feels
A. proud.
B. annoyed.
C. jealous.
D. defeated.

___ 3. Using prior knowledge and the information contained in the following passage from "Rikki-tikki-tavi," what can you predict will happen?
Darzee and his wife only cowered down in the nest without answering, for from the thick grass at the foot of the bush there came a low hiss.
A. Rikki-tikki will run away.
B. Rikki-tikki will be killed.
C. A snake will appear.
D. Rikki-tikki will be killed.

___ 4. Using prior knowledge and the information contained in the following passage from "Rikki-tikki-tavi," what can you predict will happen?
Though Rikki-tikki had never met a live cobra before, his mother had fed him on dead ones, and he knew that all a grown mongoose's business in life was to fight and eat snakes. Nag knew that, too, and at the bottom of his cold heart he was afraid.
A. Rikki-tikki will return to his mother and again eat dead cobras.
B. Nag will defeat Rikki-tikki in battle.
C. Rikki-tikki will defeat Nag in battle.
D. Rikki-tikki and Nag will settle their differences peacefully.

___ 5. The central conflict in "Rikki-tikki-tavi" is between
A. the English family and the snakes.
B. Darzee and the cobras.
C. Rikki-tikki and the cobras.
D. Rikki-tikki and Karait.

EL **L3** **L4** **Selection Test B,** pp. 38–40, 59–61

Also available for these selections:

L3 **L4** Open-Book Test, pp. 32–34, 53–55

EL **L1** **L2** Selection Test A, pp. 35–37, 56–58

PHLit Online!
www.PHLitOnline.com

Online Resources: All print materials are also available online.

- complete narrated selection text
- a thematically related video with writing prompt
- an interactive graphic organizer
- highlighting feature
- access to all student print resources, adapted to individual student needs
- Spanish and English summaries
- adapted selection translations in Spanish

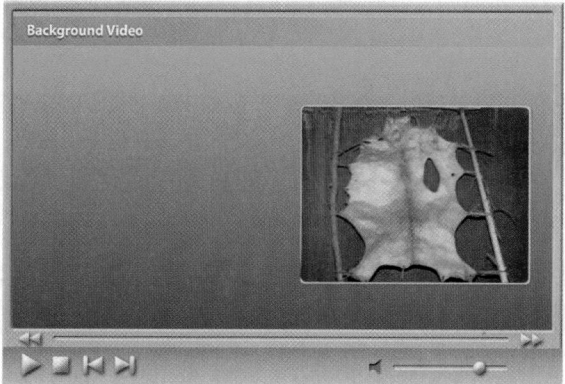

Background Video

Also available:

Get Connected! (thematic video with writing prompt)
All videos are available in Spanish.

Vocabulary Central (tools, activities, and songs for studying vocabulary)

Also available:

Writer's Journal (with graphics feature)

❶ Leveled Texts

You may use either "The Bear Boy" or "Rikki-tikki-tavi" to meet the lesson objectives. Skills instruction for both selections appears on page 217. Choose one selection to teach (or choose to teach both). The Text Complexity Rubric at the bottom of this page will help you determine which selection is more appropriate for your students. Use the Reader and Task Suggestions on the facing page to help all students read text of increasing complexity.

❷ ⓒ Introducing the CCS Standards

Introduce the standards on the student page. (Note that the lesson element with which each standard is addressed is identified in parentheses after the text of the standard.) Call out the standards that you will cover with the selections, explaining to students what each requires and how they will address it as they work through the selection you have chosen. Standards labeled "Spiral Review" are introduced in the Literary Analysis Workshop for this unit.

---

❶ ⓒ Leveled Texts

Build your skills and improve your comprehension of short stories with texts of increasing complexity.

Read **"The Bear Boy"** to discover how a father and son learn an important lesson from bears.

Read **"Rikki-tikki-tavi"** to meet a brave mongoose who battles a deadly family of cobras.

❷ ⓒ Common Core State Standards

Meet these standards with either **"The Bear Boy"** (p. 220) or **"Rikki-tikki-tavi"** (p. 228).

Reading Literature
3. Analyze how particular elements of a story or drama interact. *(Literary Analysis: Plot)*

Writing
2.d. Use precise language and domain-specific vocabulary to inform about or explain the topic. *(Writing: Informative Article)*
2.e. Establish and maintain a formal style. *(Writing: Informative Article)*

Speaking and Listening
1.a. Come to discussions prepared, having read or researched material under study; explicitly draw on that preparation by referring to evidence on the topic, text, or issue to probe and reflect on ideas under discussion. *(Speaking and Listening: Informal Debate)*

3. Delineate a speaker's argument and specific claims, evaluating the soundness of the reasoning and the relevance and sufficiency of the evidence. *(Speaking and Listening: Informal Debate)*

Language
4.b. Use common, grade-appropriate Greek or Latin affixes and roots as clues to the meaning of a word. *(Vocabulary: Word Study)*
6. Acquire and use accurately grade-appropriate general academic and domain-specific words and phrases; gather vocabulary knowledge when considering a word or phrase important to comprehension or expression. *(Vocabulary: Word Study)*

216 Short Stories

ⓒ Text Complexity Rubric: Leveled Texts

Text complexity is determined by both qualitative and quantitative measures. For this reason, the quantitative measure of a more complex selection may be lower than that of a more accessible selection.

		✓ The Bear Boy	✓✓ Rikki-tikki-tavi
Qualitative Measures	**Context/Knowledge Demands**	Boy and his father in Native-American pueblo village 1 2 ③ 4 5	India, 1800s; animals personified 1 2 ③ 4 5
	Structure/Language Conventionality and Clarity	Simple diction with some longer but direct sentences; structure reflects some skipped events 1 ② 3 4 5	Some subject-specific words; some long, very complex sentences; some implied events 1 2 3 ④ 5
	Levels of Meaning/ Purpose/Concept Level	Accessible concept (lessons about family connections) 1 2 ③ 4 5	Accessible concept (war between natural enemies) 1 ② 3 4 5
Quantitative Measures	**Text Length**	Word Count: 1,269	Word Count: 5,699
	Lexile	710L	1010L
Overall Complexity		✓ **More accessible**	✓✓ **More complex**

Reading Skill: Make Predictions

Predicting means making an intelligent judgment about what will happen next in a story based on details in the text. You can also **use prior knowledge to make predictions.** For example, if a character in a story sees dark clouds, you can predict that there will be a storm. That is because your prior knowledge tells you that dark clouds often mean stormy weather.

As you read, use details from the story and your prior knowledge to make predictions about what characters will do.

Literary Analysis: Plot

Plot is the related sequence of events in a short story and other works of fiction. Each event serves to move the story forward. Some plot events drop hints about what might happen next. Such events create **foreshadowing.** A plot has the following elements:

- **Exposition:** introduction of the setting, the characters, and the basic situation
- **Rising Action:** events that introduce a **conflict,** or struggle, and increase the tension; events that explain character's past actions
- **Climax:** the story's high point, at which the eventual outcome becomes clear
- **Falling Action:** events that follow the climax
- **Resolution:** the final outcome and tying up of loose ends

Using the Strategy: Plot Diagram

Record story details on a **plot diagram** like this one.

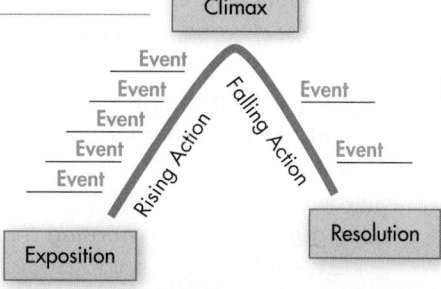

PHLit Online!
www.PHLitOnline.com

Hear It!
- Selection summary audio
- Selection audio

See It!
- Get Connected video
- Background video
- More about the author
- Vocabulary flashcards

Do It!
- Interactive journals
- Interactive graphic organizers
- Self-test
- Internet activity
- Grammar tutorial
- Interactive vocabulary games

❸ Reading Skill
Make Predictions

1. Introduce the skill, using the instruction on the student page.
2. Tell students that they will make predictions as they read.

❹ Literary Analysis
Plot

1. Introduce the skill, using the instruction on the student page.
2. Tell students that they will note elements of plot as they read.

Think Aloud: Model the Skill

Model a way of understanding plot elements. Say to students:

> To help me remember plot elements, I think of a simple story, such as "The Three Little Pigs." The first sentence, "Once upon a time there were three little pigs," is the exposition. The events of the middle, when the pigs each build their house and have it destroyed by the wolf, form the rising action. The climax, or turning point, comes when the wolf falls down the chimney—the outcome becomes clear. The rest of the events are the falling action, before the resolution—the pigs win.

❺ Using the Strategy

Give students a copy of either **Literary Analysis Graphic Organizer A** or **B** (*Graphic Organizer Transparencies,* pp. 39, 41) to record plot elements and events as they read. Use the examples in **Graphic Organizer A,** which is partially filled in, to model the process of completing the organizer.

Before You Read: The Bear Boy • Rikki-tikki-tavi **217**

Text Complexity: Reader and Task Suggestions

✓ The Bear Boy		✓✓ Rikki-tikki-tavi	
Preparing to Read the Text	**Leveled Tasks**	**Preparing to Read the Text**	**Leveled Tasks**
• Using the Background information on p. 219, discuss the role of bears and other animals in Native American culture. • Use the plot diagram on SE p. 217 to discuss story structure. • Guide students to use Multidraft Reading strategies (TE p. 219).	*Structure/Language* If students will have difficulty with skipped plot events, have them first read to identify the boy's relationship to his father. Then, have them reread, listing plot events in sequence to identify any jumps. *Analyzing* If students will not have difficulty with structure, have them note ways that each character changes during the story's explicit and implicit events.	• Using the Background information on p. 227, discuss the traditional enmity between mongooses and cobras. • Review strategies for reading long and complex sentences, such as breaking sentences into parts. • Guide students to use Multidraft Reading strategies (TE p. 219).	*Structure/Language* If students will have difficulty with sentence structure, have them first read to understand the battle between Rikki and the cobras. Then, have them reread, identifying sentences that are confusing. *Synthesizing* If students will not have difficulty with sentence structure, have them note as they read ways in which the author varies language and syntax to create vivid characters.

❶ Writing About the Big Question

1. Review the assignment with the class.

2. Lead students in discussing the importance of people caring for one another. Have them consider how lack of care can lead to conflict, as when a neglected person becomes angry.

3. Have students complete the sentence starter. Review responses as a class. (**Sample response:** When a person does not <u>understand</u> how to care for others, closeness and love can be lost.)

4. Remind students that their answers will help them think about the Big Question, "Does every conflict have a winner?"

While You Read

Tell students that as they read, they should think about who benefits from the boy's encounter with the bears.

❷ Vocabulary

1. Have students preview the selection vocabulary.

2. For each word, have students say the word aloud.

3. Then, use the word in a sentence that defines the word.

4. Finally, repeat your definitional sentence or a similar sentence with the word missing and have the class "fill in the blank" chorally. Here are some examples:

If a person <u>neglected</u> something, he or she did not take care of it. When we left the bicycle out in the rain for a week, we [students say "neglected"] it.

<u>Guidance</u> is advice that tells someone what to do or think. Jill didn't know what to do, so she asked for [students say "guidance"].

❸ Word Study

1. Introduce the skill, using the instruction in the box.

2. Point out that *guide* is the base word in *guidance*. **Ask** students to add the suffix *-ance* to the base word *admit* and to define the resulting word. (**Answer:** *admittance;* "the act of admitting")

❓ THE BIG **Does every *conflict* have a winner?**

❶ Writing About the Big Question

In "The Bear Boy," a family of bears help resolve a conflict by teaching a father how to care for his son. Use this sentence starter to develop your ideas about the Big Question.

When a person does not **understand** how to care for others, _____ can be lost.

While You Read Think about who benefits from the boy's encounter with the bears.

❷ Vocabulary

Read each word and its definition. Decide whether you know the word well, know it a little bit, or do not know it at all. After you read, see how your knowledge of each word has increased.

- **timid** (tim´ id) *adj.* shy; fearful (p. 220) *The <u>timid</u> child was afraid of me. timidity n. timidly adv.*

- **initiation** (i nish´ ē ā´ shən) *n.* process that makes a person a member of a group (p. 220) *Jo looked forward to her <u>initiation</u> into the Honor Society. initiate v. initiated v. initiating v.*

- **canyon** (kan´ yən) *n.* long narrow valley between high cliffs (p. 221) *Many tourists hike from the rim to the valley of the Grand <u>Canyon</u>.*

- **approvingly** (ə proov´ iŋ lē) *adv.* with acceptance (p. 221) *The coach clapped <u>approvingly</u> at the pitcher's strikeout. approve v. approved v. approval n.*

- **neglected** (ni glekt´ əd) *v.* failed to take care of (p. 221) *The cat <u>neglected</u> her kittens, so we raised them. neglect v. neglectful adj.*

- **guidance** (gīd´ 'ns) *n.* advice or assistance (p. 222) *Students need <u>guidance</u> when choosing their classes. guide n. guide v. guided v.*

❸ Word Study

The **Latin suffix *-ance*** means "the act of" and indicates a noun form.

In this story, Kuo-Haya's father asks for **guidance**, or the act of providing direction, in dealing with the mother bear.

Vocabulary Development

Vocabulary Knowledge Rating

Create a **Vocabulary Knowledge Rating Chart** (*Professional Development Guidebook,* p. 33) for this selection. Include the selection vocabulary and the Big Question word that appears in the Writing About the Big Question sentence starter on this page. (The Big Question vocabulary is introduced on pp. 198–199.)

Give students a copy of the chart. Read the words aloud, and have students mark their rating in the Before Reading column. Urge them to be alert to these words as they read and discuss the selection.

Tally how many students think they know a word to gauge how much instruction to provide. As students read and discuss the selection, point out the words and their context.

PHLit Online! **Vocabulary Central,** featuring tools, activities and songs for studying vocabulary, is available online at www.PHLitOnline.com.

Meet
Joseph Bruchac
(b. 1942)

Author of
THE BEAR BOY

Joseph Bruchac was raised by his grandparents in the foothills of the Adirondack Mountains in New York State. There, his grandfather, who was of Abenaki Indian descent, taught Bruchac to appreciate the forest. From his grandmother, a law school graduate, Bruchac inherited a love of books and writing. Bruchac has written more than seventy books for children and has performed worldwide as a teller of Native American folk tales.

Respect for Tradition Bruchac respects the role that storytelling plays in Native American cultures. Like "The Bear Boy," many of his stories are based on traditional folk tales and on his ancestors' way of life. He has said, "I always go back to what I have heard, what I have seen, what I have experienced. And whatever I imagine or create new always comes out of that life experience."

DID YOU KNOW?
Bruchac's younger sister and his two sons, James and Jesse, work for the preservation of Abenaki culture.

❹
BACKGROUND FOR THE STORY
Animals in Native American Folk Tales

In early times, Native Americans depended on animals for food, clothing, and shelter. As a result, Native Americans felt gratitude toward animals and included them as important characters in their oral stories. "The Bear Boy" is a Native American story that focuses on a mother bear and her cubs.

The Bear Boy **219**

🔖 Daily Bellringer
For each class during which you will teach this selection, have students complete one of the five Quick Write activities for Week 7 in the *Daily Bellringer Activities* booklet.

❹ Background
Animals in Native American Folk Tales

Although there are many differences among the cultures of Native Americans, all Native American groups feature animals in their myths and stories. In some cultures, Raven and Coyote are popular heroes. The reason animals have such importance is that followers of Native American religions believe that the same life force flows through all creatures. This element of kinship with animals appears in "The Bear Boy" when the medicine man says that bears are his relatives. The medicine man is recognizing the connection between the spirits of animals and humans.

🔖 Multidraft Reading

This icon ● marks natural pauses in the selection. To assist struggling readers and to deepen reading for all, assign the text in "chunks," following the icons, and apply multidraft reading protocols. For each reading, have students set the purpose indicated:

- **First reading**—identifying key ideas and details and answering any Reading Checks.

- **Second reading**—analyzing craft and structure and responding to the side-column prompts.

- **Third reading**—integrating knowledge and ideas, connecting to other texts and the world, and answering the end-of-selection questions.

For more guidance, refer to the *Classroom Strategies and Teaching Routines* card on multidraft reading.

For more about the author, practice with the selection vocabulary, or more background, go online at www.PHLitOnline.com.

THE Bear BOY

❶
❷

Joseph Bruchac

Vocabulary
timid (tim´ id) *adj.* shy; fearful

initiation (i nish´ ē ā´ shən) *n.* process that makes a person a member of a group

220 Short Stories

Long ago, in a Pueblo village, a boy named Kuo-Haya lived with his father. But his father did not treat him well. In his heart he still mourned the death of his wife, Kuo-Haya's mother, and did not enjoy doing things with his son. He did not teach his boy how to run. He did not show him how to wrestle. He was always too busy.

As a result, Kuo-Haya was a timid boy and walked about stooped over all of the time. When the other boys raced or wrestled, Kuo-Haya slipped away. He spent much of his time alone.

Time passed, and the boy reached the age when his father should have been helping him get ready for his initiation into manhood. Still Kuo-Haya's father paid no attention at all to his son.

One day Kuo-Haya was out walking far from the village, toward the cliffs where the bears lived. Now the people of the village always knew they must stay away from these cliffs, for the bear was a very powerful animal. It was said that if someone saw a bear's tracks and followed them, he might never come

back. But Kuo-Haya had never been told about this. When he came upon the tracks of a bear, Kuo-Haya followed them along an arroyo, a small canyon cut by a winding stream, up into the mesas.[1] The tracks led into a little box canyon below some caves. There, he came upon some bear cubs.

When they saw Kuo-Haya, the little bears ran away. But Kuo-Haya sat down and called to them in a friendly voice.

"I will not hurt you," he said to the bear cubs. "Come and play with me." The bears walked back out of the bushes. Soon the boy and the bears were playing together. As they played, however, a shadow came over them. Kuo-Haya looked up and saw the mother bear standing above him.

"Where is Kuo-Haya?" the people asked his father.

"I do not know," the father said.

"Then you must find him!"

So the father and other people of the pueblo began to search for the missing boy. They went through the canyons calling his name. But they found no sign of the boy there. Finally, when they reached the cliffs, the best trackers found his footsteps and the path of the bears. They followed the tracks along the arroyo and up into the mesas to the box canyon. In front of a cave, they saw the boy playing with the bear cubs as the mother bear watched them approvingly, nudging Kuo-Haya now and then to encourage him.

The trackers crept close, hoping to grab the boy and run. But as soon as the mother bear caught their scent, she growled and pushed her cubs and the boy back into the cave.

"The boy is with the bears," the trackers said when they returned to the village.

"What shall we do?" the people asked.

"It is the responsibility of the boy's father," said the medicine man. Then he called Kuo-Haya's father to him.

"You have not done well," said the medicine man. "You are the one who must guide your boy to manhood, but you have neglected him. Now the mother bear is caring for your boy as you should have done all along. She is teaching him to be strong as a young man must be strong. If you love your son, only you can get him back."

Every one of the medicine man's words went into the

---

1. **mesas** (mā′ səz) *n.* plateaus (or flat-topped hills) with steep sides.

Vocabulary
canyon (kan′ yən) *n.* long narrow valley between high cliffs

Make Predictions
Based on your knowledge of bears, what do you think will happen to Kuo-Haya?

4 ▲ Critical Viewing
What does this artifact show about the relationship between Pueblo people and bears? **[Connect]**

Vocabulary
approvingly
(ə prōōv′ iŋ lē) *adv.* with acceptance.

neglected
(ni glekt′ əd) *v.* failed to take care of

5 ✓ Reading Check

How does Kuo-Haya end up living with the bears?

---

3 Make Predictions

1. Have students read the bracketed text at the top of this page.

2. Remind students that predictions are judgments based on what they know. Have them share what they know about bears. As needed, explain that bears are wild animals. Usually, they do not bother or attack people. However, if a mother bear thinks a person is going to hurt her cubs, she may attack and possibly kill the person.

3. **Ask** the Make Predictions question.
   Possible responses: The mother bear will attack Kuo-Haya because she is afraid he will hurt her cubs. The mother bear will see that Kuo-Haya is not hurting her cubs, so she will not hurt him.

4. After students read further, have them confirm or revise their predictions.

4 Critical Viewing

Answer: It shows that people and bears usually do not get along—they seem to be engaged in a fight.

5 Reading Check

Possible answer: Kuo-Haya begins playing with the bear cubs, and the mother bear approves. She treats Kuo-Haya like one of her cubs and protects him when people approach.

The Bear Boy **221**

PHLit Online!

This selection is available in interactive format in the **Enriched Online Student Edition**, at www.PHLitOnline.com, which includes a thematically related video with writing prompt and an interactive graphic organizer.

father's heart like an arrow. He began to realize that he had been blind to his son's needs because of his own sorrow.

"You are right," he said. "I will go and bring back my son."

Kuo-Haya's father went along the arroyo and climbed the cliffs. When he came to the bears' cave, he found Kuo-Haya wrestling with the little bears. As the father watched, he saw that his son seemed more sure of himself than ever before.

"Kuo-Haya," he shouted. "Come to me."

The boy looked at him and then just walked into the cave. Although the father tried to follow, the big mother bear stood up on her hind legs and growled. She would not allow the father to come any closer.

So Kuo-Haya's father went back to his home. He was angry now. He began to gather together his weapons, and brought out his bow and his arrows and his lance.[2] But the medicine man came to his lodge and showed him the bear claw that he wore around his neck.

"Those bears are my relatives!" the medicine man said. "You must not harm them. They are teaching your boy how we should care for each other, so you must not be cruel to them. You must get your son back with love, not violence."

Kuo-Haya's father prayed for guidance. He went outside and sat on the ground. As he sat there, a bee flew up to him, right by his face. Then it flew away. The father stood up. Now he knew what to do!

"Thank you, Little Brother," he said. He began to make his preparations. The medicine man watched what he was doing and smiled.

Kuo-Haya's father went to the place where the bees had their hives. He made a fire and put green branches on it so that it made smoke. Then he blew the smoke into the tree where the bees were. The bees soon went to sleep.

Carefully Kuo-Haya's father took out some honey from their hive. When he was done, he placed pollen and some small pieces of turquoise[3] at the foot of the tree to thank the bees for their gift. The medicine man, who was watching all this, smiled again. Truly the father was beginning to learn.

Kuo-Haya's father traveled again to the cliffs where the bears

---

2. **lance** (lans) *n.* long spear.
3. **turquoise** (tʉr′ koiz′) *n.* greenish-blue gemstone.

lived. He hid behind a tree and saw how the mother bear treated Kuo-Haya and the cubs with love. He saw that Kuo-Haya was able to hold his own as he wrestled with the bears.

He came out from his hiding place, put the honey on the ground, and stepped back. "My friends," he said, "I have brought you something sweet."

The mother bear and her cubs came over and began to eat the honey. While they ate, Kuo-Haya's father went to the boy. He saw that his little boy was now a young man.

"Kuo-Haya," he said, putting his hands on his son's shoulders, "I have come to take you home. The bears have taught me a lesson. I shall treat you as a father should treat his son."

"I will go with you, Father," said the boy. "But I, too, have learned things from the bears. They have shown me how we must care for one another. I will come with you only if you promise you will always be friends with the bears." The father promised, and that promise was kept. Not only was he friends with the bears, but he showed his boy the love a son deserves.

Plot
Is this scene part of the rising action? Explain your answer.

⑩ ✓ Reading Check
Why did Kuo-Haya's father gather the honey?

LITERATURE IN CONTEXT

Social Studies Connection

The Pueblo
The word pueblo refers to the village-dwelling Native Americans of the southwestern United States. Pueblo villages, like this one, are made of adobe and contain hundreds of rooms.

▶ *Pueblo pottery is known for the beauty of its shape and decoration.*

▶ *This is the entrance to a kiva, or sacred ceremonial room.*

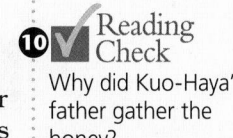
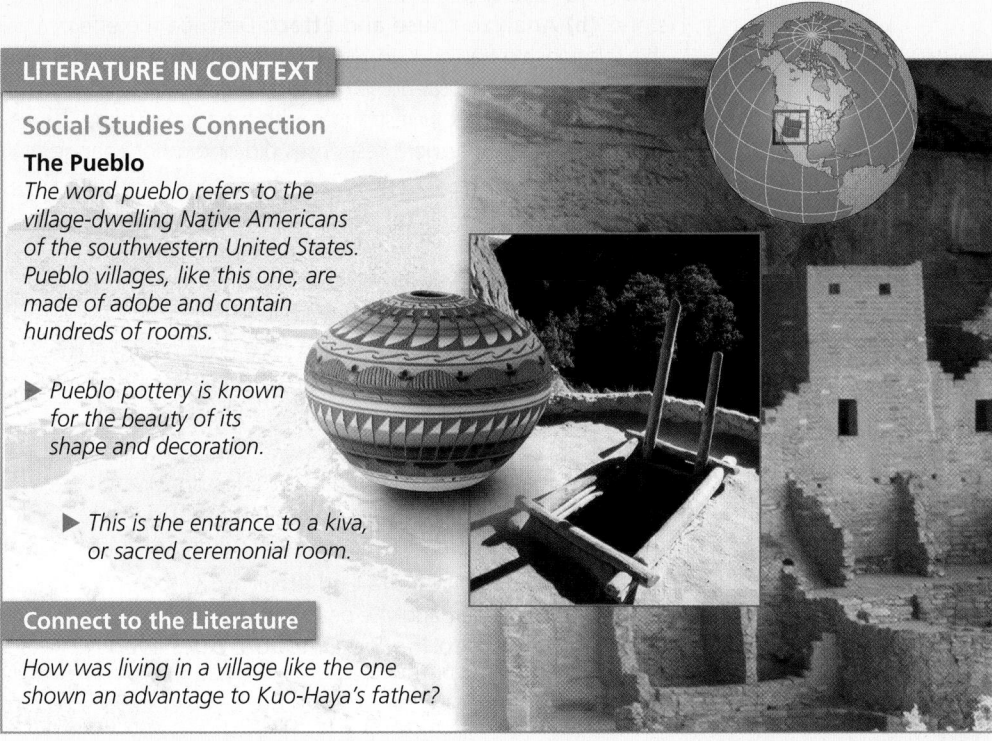

Connect to the Literature

How was living in a village like the one shown an advantage to Kuo-Haya's father?

The Bear Boy **223**

Ask students the Plot question.
Answer: Kuo-haya returns to the village; he has become a good wrestler. The father has changed, too; he gives his son the love and teaching he needs.

ASSESS

Answers

Critical Thinking

Before students respond, you may wish to have them write a brief objective summary of the selection. As they answer the questions below, remind them to support their answers with evidence from the text.

1. (a) Kuo-Haya and his father, who has neglected him, are not close. (b) Kuo-Haya has not learned what his father should have taught him. (c) Kuo-Haya spends time alone because he is timid and does not feel that he fits in with boys his age. (d) Students will say that they were or were not influenced by their partners.

2. (a) He approaches the small bears and begins to play with them. (b) The mother bear encourages him and teaches him to be strong. Kuo-Haya feels as if he belongs with the bears. In the village, he was neglected by his father and felt like an outsider. He was timid and spent much time alone.

3. (a) He tells Kuo-Haya's father that he must bring back his son, but in a way that does not harm the bears. (b) Seeing the bee gives the father the idea to use honey as part of his plan to talk to his son.

4. **Possible answers:** (a) Parents have a responsibility to love their children and to teach them all the things they will need to know. (b) Yes, children everywhere need loving attention and guidance.

5. **Possible response:** Kuo-Haya becomes a good wrestler. His father learns to pay attention to his son. The bears get honey and the respect of Kuo-Haya's people.

Plot **12**
Which details in this paragraph show how the story's conflict is resolved?

And he taught him all the things a son should be taught.

Everyone in the village soon saw that Kuo-Haya, the bear boy, was no longer the timid little boy he had been. Because of what the bears had taught him, he was the best wrestler among the boys. With his father's help, Kuo-Haya quickly became the greatest runner of all. To this day, his story is told to remind all parents that they must always show as much love for their children as there is in the heart of a bear.

Critical Thinking

Cite textual evidence to support your responses.

1. **Key Ideas and Details (a)** What kind of relationship does Kuo-Haya have with his father at the beginning of the story? **(b) Analyze Cause and Effect:** Describe the effect this relationship has on Kuo-Haya. **(c) Interpret:** Why does Kuo-Haya choose to spend so much time alone? **(d) Discuss:** Share your responses with a partner. Then, discuss how your partner's responses did or did not change your interpretation.

2. **Key Ideas and Details (a)** What does Kuo-Haya do when he first sees the bear cubs? **(b) Compare and Contrast:** How is Kuo-Haya's life with the bears different from his life in the village? Support your answer with details from the story.

3. **Key Ideas and Details (a)** What advice does the medicine man offer the father? **(b) Connect:** How does seeing a bee help the father decide how to get his son back?

4. **Integration of Knowledge and Ideas (a) Analyze:** Native American folk tales often teach a lesson. What lesson does this folk tale teach? **(b) Evaluate:** Do you think the lesson applies to people of all cultures? Explain.

5. **Integration of Knowledge and Ideas** How do Kuo-Haya, his father, and the bears all benefit from conflict? *[Connect to the Big Question: Does every conflict have a winner?]*

224 Short Stories

Assessment Resources

Unit 2 Resources

L1 L2 EL **Selection Test A**, pp. 35–37. Administer Test A to less advanced readers.

L3 L4 EL **Selection Test B**, pp. 38–40. Administer Test B to on-level and more advanced students.

L3 L4 **Open-Book Test**, pp. 32–34. As an alternative, give the Open-Book Test.

All **Customizable Test Bank**

All **Self-tests**
Students may prepare for the **Selection Test** by taking the **Self-test** online.

PHLit Online! All assessment resources are available at www.PHLitOnline.com.

After You Read   The Bear Boy

Reading Skill: Make Predictions

1. What **prior knowledge** did you have from reading the Background note on page 219 that helped you **predict** that Kuo-Haya would be accepted by the bears?

2. Choose another prediction based on prior knowledge that you made as you read this story. Use a graphic organizer like the one here to show how you made your prediction.

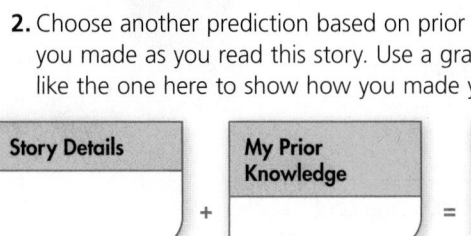

Story Details		My Prior Knowledge		Prediction
	+		=	

THE BEAR BOY
Joseph Bruchac

Literary Analysis: Plot

3. Key Ideas and Details Identify two **plot** events that increase the tension of the story.

4. Key Ideas and Details Identify two or three events that move the plot toward the **climax,** when Kuo-Haya's father asks his son to come home.

Vocabulary

Acquisition and Use Answer each question. Then, explain your answer.

1. Would a *timid* child enjoy performing for a crowd?

2. Does an *initiation* mark a new beginning?

3. Is a *canyon* considered a wide open space?

4. If someone looks at you *approvingly,* does he or she dislike what you are doing?

5. If you *neglected* a houseplant, what would happen to it?

6. Do you ask for *guidance* if you know what to do?

Word Study Use the context of the sentences and what you know about the **Latin suffix -ance** to explain your answer.

1. If someone is asking for *assistance,* does she need help?

2. If you have no *tolerance* for your noisy neighbors, do you put up with them?

Word Study

The **Latin suffix -ance** means "the act of."

Apply It Explain how the suffix *-ance* contributes to the meanings of these words. Consult a dictionary if necessary.

utterance

disturbance

reliance

The Bear Boy **225**

Reading Skill

1. Possible response: Knowing that Native Americans have a special relationship with wild animals helps readers predict that the bears will accept Kuo-Haya.

2. Possible response: Students may have predicted that Kuo-Haya's father would succeed in getting the bears to accept his gift of honey. They may have made this prediction based on prior knowledge that bears are especially fond of honey.

For other sample answers, see *Graphic Organizer Transparencies,* **Reading Skill Graphic Organizer A,** p. 42, and the **Additional Answers** section.

Literary Analysis

3. One event that increases tension occurs when Kuo-Haya follows the bear's tracks even though, as the narrator points out, a person following a bear's tracks might never return; another is the first approach of the mother bear. Another is the father's becoming angry and gathering his weapons.

4. Kuo-Haya's father is prevented by the bears from speaking with his son. He begins to gather his weapons, but the medicine man advises him to use love, not violence. The appearance of a bee inspires him to collect honey to bring to the bears.

Vocabulary
Acquisition and Use
Sample answers:

1. No, a <u>timid</u> child is probably too shy to enjoy performing for a crowd.

2. Yes, an <u>initiation</u> marks the beginning of a new phase of life.

3. No, a <u>canyon</u> is a deep gap in the land with high walls.

4. No, if someone looks at you <u>approvingly</u>, or with acceptance, he or she likes what you are doing.

5. If you <u>neglected</u> a houseplant, it might wither and lose its leaves because you would not be giving it enough water.

6. No, you would not ask for <u>guidance</u>, or help, if you already knew what to do.

Word Study
Sample answers:

1. Yes, someone asking for *assistance* is asking for <u>an act of</u> help.

2. No, when you have no *tolerance,* you do not perform <u>the act of</u> accepting.

Word Study: Apply It
Sample answers:

Utterance means "<u>the act of</u> uttering." *Disturbance* means "<u>the act of</u> disturbing." *Reliance* means "<u>the act of</u> relying on."

Teaching notes introducing the **Reading Skill** *and the* **Literary Analysis** *concept for this selection appear on p. 217.*

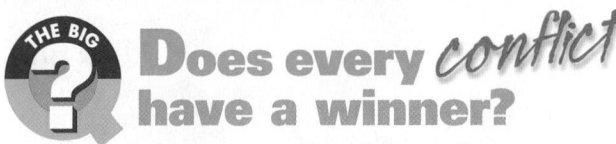

❶ ⍰ Writing About the Big Question

1. Review the assignment with the class.

2. Elicit from students a definition of the term *innocent victim* (someone who comes to harm through no fault of his or her own). Lead them in thinking of examples of conflict that results in innocent victims (war; a factory closing).

3. Have students complete the sentence starter. Review responses as a class. (**Sample response:** Sometimes in a conflict, innocent victims get hurt or suffer.)

4. Remind students that their answers will help them think about the Big Question, "Does every conflict have a winner?"

While You Read

Tell students that as they read, they should consider who suffers in the conflict between Rikki-tikki-tavi and the cobras.

❷ Vocabulary

1. Have students preview the selection vocabulary.

2. For each word, have students say the word aloud.

3. Then, use the word in a sentence that defines the word.

4. Finally, repeat your definitional sentence or a similar sentence with the word missing and have the class "fill in the blank" chorally. Here is an example:

Immensely means "a great deal," or "very much." Joe sat with a huge grin on his face, having enjoyed his Thanksgiving dinner [students say "immensely"].

❸ Word Study

1. Introduce the skill, using the instruction in the box.

2. Have students generate a sentence that uses *consolation*. (**Sample answer:** Giving someone a hug can be an act of *consolation*.)

⍰ Does every *conflict* have a winner?

❶ Writing About the Big Question

"Rikki-tikki-tavi" tells the story of a fierce battle between a mongoose and two cobras. Use this sentence starter to develop your ideas about the Big Question.

Sometimes in a **conflict**, innocent victims _____.

While You Read Consider who suffers as a result of the conflict between Rikki-tikki-tavi and the cobras.

❷ Vocabulary

Read each word and its definition. Decide whether you know the word well, know it a little bit, or do not know it at all. After you read, see how your knowledge of each word has increased.

- **revived** (ri vīvd´) *v.* came back to life or consciousness (p. 229) *A brave bystander revived the man who almost drowned.* revive *v.* reviving *v.* revival *n.*

- **immensely** (i mens´ lē) *adv.* a great deal; very much (p. 230) *We enjoyed ourselves immensely at the circus.* immense *adj.* immensity *n.*

- **veranda** (və ran´də) *n.* an open porch, usually with a roof (p. 230) *In the summer, we like to eat dinner on the veranda.*

- **mourning** (môr´ niŋ) *adj.* expressing grief, especially after someone dies (p. 239) *The young widow was in mourning.* mourning *n.* mourn *v.* mourner *n.* mournful *adj.*

- **consolation** (kän´ sə lā´ shən) *n.* something that comforts a disappointed person (p. 240) *The sick boy got a toy as consolation for missing the party.* console *v.* consolable *adj.* consolingly *adv.*

- **cunningly** (kun´ iŋ lē) *adv.* cleverly (p. 240) *He cunningly took the plate with the largest slice of pizza.* cunning *adj.*

226 Short Stories

❸ Word Study

The **Latin suffix -tion** is an ending that turns a verb into a noun, meaning "the thing that is."

In this story, Nagaina suggests that Teddy's death will be a **consolation**, or something that is consoling or comforting, for Darzee's wife.

Vocabulary Development

Vocabulary Knowledge Rating
Create a **Vocabulary Knowledge Rating Chart** (*Professional Development Guidebook,* p. 33) for this selection. Include the selection vocabulary and the Big Question word that appears in the Writing About the Big Question sentence starter on this page. (The Big Question vocabulary is introduced on pp. 198–199.)

Give students a copy of the chart. Read the words aloud, and have students mark their rating in the Before Reading column. Urge them to be alert to these words as they read and discuss the selection.

Tally how many students think they know a word to gauge how much instruction to provide. As students read and discuss the selection, point out the words and their context.

Meet
Rudyard Kipling
(1865–1936)

Author of
RIKKI-TIKKI-TAVI

Rudyard Kipling was born in Bombay, India, to English parents. Although he moved to England when he was five, Kipling remained attached to the land of his birth. In 1882, he returned there as a journalist and began writing the stories that would make him famous.

International Popularity Kipling's stories became an immediate success when they were published in England because they brought the details of Indian life to an eager audience. Soon after, the stories became popular in the U.S., too. Kipling traveled a great deal and wrote several books of stories and poems, including *The Jungle Book* and *Captains Courageous*. In 1907, Kipling became the first English writer to win the Nobel Prize in Literature.

Did You Know?
Organizations such as the Boy Scouts and Girl Scouts grew out of ideas found in Kipling's Jungle Book.

BACKGROUND FOR THE STORY

Mongoose *vs.* Cobra

In this story, a brave mongoose takes on a family of snakes known as Indian cobras. Cobras feed on small animals. The mongoose is a brown, furry animal about fifteen inches long—the perfect size for a cobra's meal. However, the fast, fierce mongoose usually wins a battle with a cobra.

Rikki-tikki-tavi **227**

PRETEACH

Daily Bellringer
For each class during which you will teach this selection, have students complete one of the five Quick Write activities for Week 7 in the *Daily Bellringer Activities* booklet.

❹ **Background**
Mongooses Around the World

Mongooses, which live in Africa, Asia, and southern Europe, come in more than forty varieties. They can be small (a little over one foot long) or large (as long as four feet). Mongooses usually feed on insects, lizards, frogs, eggs, and fruit. As the title character in "Rikki-tikki-tavi" illustrates, mongooses are known for their ability to fight snakes. A mongoose kills a snake by using its teeth to break the snake's spine at the back of its neck. Mongooses move very quickly, and they have a high tolerance for snake venom.

Multidraft Reading

This icon ● marks natural pauses in the selection. To assist struggling readers and to deepen reading for all, assign the text in "chunks," following the icons, and apply multidraft reading protocols. For each reading, have students set the purpose indicated:

• **First reading**—identifying key ideas and details and answering any Reading Checks.
• **Second reading**—analyzing craft and structure and responding to the side-column prompts.
• **Third reading**—integrating knowledge and ideas, connecting to other texts and the world, and answering the end-of-selection questions.

For more guidance, refer to the *Classroom Strategies and Teaching Routines* card on multidraft reading.

Differentiated
Instruction   Additional Instruction

EL Extended Support—
English Learners
Have students complete the **Reading and Vocabulary Warm-ups**, *Unit 2 Resources*, pp. 41–44, before they read. Assign the prereading pages for the selection in the *Reader's Notebook: English Learner's Version*. Then, have students listen to portions of the selection on the *Hear It!* Audio CD.

L1 L2 Extended Support—
Struggling Readers
Have students complete the **Reading and Vocabulary Warm-ups**, *Unit 2 Resources*, pp. 41–44, before they read. Assign the prereading pages for the selection in the *Reader's Notebook: Adapted Version*. Then, have students listen to portions of the selection on the *Hear It!* Audio CD (adapted text).

Extended Support—
Reluctant Readers
To build motivation and engagement before assigning the selection, have students read "Coyotes on the Go," a thematically related selection in *Reality Central*. Then, use the questions at the conclusion of the related selection to guide discussion.

For more about the author, practice with the selection vocabulary, or more background, go online at www.PHLitOnline.com.

RIKKI-TIKKI

Rudyard Kipling

his is the story of the great war that Rikki-tikki-tavi fought, single-handed, through the bathrooms of the big bungalow in Segowlee cantonment.[1] Darzee, the tailorbird bird, helped him, and Chuchundra (chōō chun´ drə) the muskrat, who never comes out into the middle of the floor, but always creeps round by the wall, gave him advice; but Rikki-tikki did the real fighting.

He was a mongoose, rather like a little cat in his fur and his tail, but quite like a weasel in his head and his habits. His eyes and the end of his restless nose were pink; he could scratch himself anywhere he pleased, with any leg, front or back, that he chose to use; he could fluff up his tail till it looked like a bottle brush, and his war cry as he scuttled through the long grass, was: "*Rikk-tikk-tikki-tikki-tchk!*"

One day, a high summer flood washed him out of the burrow where he lived with his father and mother, and carried him, kicking and clucking,

1. **Segowlee cantonment** (sē gou´ lē kan tän´ mənt) *n.* living quarters for British troops in Segowlee, India.

228 Short Stories

-TAVI

down a roadside ditch. He found a little wisp of grass floating there, and clung to it till he lost his senses. When he revived, he was lying in the hot sun on the middle of a garden path, very draggled² indeed, and a small boy was saying: "Here's a dead mongoose. Let's have a funeral."

"No," said his mother; "let's take him in and dry him. Perhaps he isn't really dead."

They took him into the house, and a big man picked him up between his finger and thumb and said he was not dead but half choked; so they wrapped him in cotton wool, and warmed him, and he opened his eyes and sneezed.

"Now," said the big man (he was an Englishman who had just moved into the bungalow); "don't frighten him, and we'll see what he'll do."

It is the hardest thing in the world to frighten a mongoose, because he is eaten up from nose to tail with curiosity. The motto of all the mongoose family is, "Run and find out"; and Rikki-tikki was a true mongoose. He looked at the cotton wool, decided that it was not good to eat, ran all round the table, sat up and put his fur in order, scratched himself, and jumped on the small boy's shoulder.

"Don't be frightened, Teddy," said his father. "That's his way of making friends."

"Ouch! He's tickling under my chin," said Teddy.

Rikki-tikki looked down between the boy's collar and neck, snuffed at his ear, and climbed down to the floor, where he sat rubbing his nose.

"Good gracious," said Teddy's mother, "and that's a wild creature! I suppose he's so tame because we've been kind to him."

"All mongooses are like that," said her husband. "If Teddy

2. **draggled** (drag′ əld) *adj.* wet and dirty.

Vocabulary
revived (ri vīvd′)
v. came back to life or consciousness

Plot
What important details about the mongoose are revealed in the exposition on the previous page?

④ ✓ Reading Check
Who is Rikki-tikki-tavi, and how does he meet Teddy?

---

③ Plot

1. Remind students that the exposition introduces the setting, characters, and basic situation.

2. Read the bracketed passage on page 228. Point out that it introduces the main character, the mongoose Rikki-tikki-tavi. It tells readers what the story is about—a war that the mongoose fights.

3. **Ask** the Plot question.
   Answer: The exposition reveals both physical characteristics of the mongoose and character traits: The mongoose is physically like a cat and a weasel; it is war-like.

④ Reading Check

Answer: Rikki-tikki-tavi is a young mongoose. He meets Teddy after floodwaters wash him out of his nest and into Teddy's garden. Teddy finds the nearly drowned mongoose in his garden.

Differentiated Instruction for Universal Access

Strategies for Less Proficient Readers
As students read, encourage them to jot down on self-sticking notes questions they have about the story. They should affix the notes to passages in the story to indicate when the question occurred to them. As they discover answers, either in reading further or in class discussion, they should return to their notes and record the answers.

EL Support for English Learners
Point out the term *cotton wool* on page 229. Explain that because Teddy and his family are English, they use some words in ways Americans do not. Cotton wool is material that feels like cotton balls. In this case, the material is spread out like a piece of fabric. Help students identify and interpret other British usages in the story, such as *horrid* (p. 231), *chap* (p. 238), and *rubbish* (p. 239).

PHLit Online!
This selection is available in interactive format in the **Enriched Online Student Edition**, at **www.PHLitOnline.com**, which includes a thematically related video with writing prompt and an interactive graphic organizer.

229

1. Have students read the passage that begins "Teddy's mother and father came in." Then **ask** students how Teddy's mother feels about Rikki-tikki. **Answer:** She thinks of the mongoose as a wild animal, and she is worried that it will bite her son.

2. **Ask** students how Teddy's father portrays Rikki-tikki. **Answer:** He considers Rikki-tikki to be a guardian, not a threat to Teddy.

3. Remind students that good readers base their predictions about a story on clues from the text. Then, **ask** students the Make Predictions question.
Possible response: Students may predict that Rikki-tikki will save Teddy from a snake.

Vocabulary
immensely
(i mens´ lē) *adv.* a great deal; very much

veranda (və ran´də) *n.* an open porch, usually with a roof

❺
Make Predictions
Based on the parents' thoughts about Rikki, what do you predict will happen in the story?

doesn't pick him up by the tail, or try to put him in a cage, he'll run in and out of the house all day long. Let's give him something to eat."

They gave him a little piece of raw meat. Rikki-tikki liked it immensely, and when it was finished he went out into the veranda and sat in the sunshine and fluffed up his fur to make it dry to the roots. Then he felt better.

"There are more things to find out about in this house," he said to himself, "than all my family could find out in all their lives. I shall certainly stay and find out."

He spent all that day roaming over the house. He nearly drowned himself in the bathtubs, put his nose into the ink on a writing table, and burned it on the end of the big man's cigar, for he climbed up in the big man's lap to see how writing was done. At nightfall he ran into Teddy's nursery to watch how kerosene lamps were lighted, and when Teddy went to bed Rikki-tikki climbed up too; but he was a restless companion, because he had to get up and attend to every noise all through the night, and find out what made it. Teddy's mother and father came in, the last thing, to look at their boy, and Rikki-tikki was awake on the pillow. "I don't like that," said Teddy's mother; "he may bite the child." "He'll do no such thing," said the father. "Teddy's safer with that little beast than if he had a bloodhound to watch him. If a snake came into the nursery now—"

But Teddy's mother wouldn't think of anything so awful.

Early in the morning Rikki-tikki came to early breakfast in the veranda riding on Teddy's shoulder, and they gave him banana and some boiled egg; and he sat on all their laps one after the other, because every well-brought-up mongoose always hopes to be a house mongoose some day and have rooms to run about in, and Rikki-tikki's mother (she used to live in the General's house at Segowlee) had carefully told Rikki what to do if ever he came across Englishmen.

Then Rikki-tikki went out into the garden to see what was to be seen. It was a large garden, only half cultivated, with bushes as big as summer houses of Marshal Niel roses, lime and orange trees, clumps of bamboos, and thickets of high grass. Rikki-tikki licked his lips. "This is a splendid hunting ground," he said, and his tail grew bottlebrushy at the thought of it, and he scuttled up and down the garden,

Think Aloud

Vocabulary: Context
Direct students' attention to the word *cowered* on p. 231. Use the following "think aloud" to model the use of context clues to infer the meaning of an unknown word. Say to students:

I'm going to show you how I would figure out the meaning of *cowered*. In this sentence, *cowered* expresses an action: Darzee and his wife "cowered down." The clue word *for* lets me know that the sentence will tell me why they are cowering—they hear a snake's hiss. Darzee and his wife must be afraid of snakes, because a snake ate one of their babies.

Whatever *cowered* is, it involves fear or self-defense. The birds are cowering down "in the nest," so I know that *cowered* doesn't mean "ran away" or "flew away."

When I picture this scene, I see two birds in a nest set in a bush and a snake below. I think the birds might hide by making their bodies small and keeping themselves low in the nest. I decide that *cowered* probably means "shrink one's body in fear." I can check my definition in a dictionary to be sure.

snuffing here and there till he heard very sorrowful voices in a thornbush.

It was Darzee, the tailorbird, and his wife. They had made a beautiful nest by pulling two big leaves together and stitching them up the edges with fibers, and had filled the hollow with cotton and downy fluff. The nest swayed to and fro, as they sat on the rim and cried.

"What is the matter?" asked Rikki-tikki.

"We are very miserable," said Darzee.

"One of our babies fell out of the nest yesterday and Nag ate him."

"H'm!" said Rikki-tikki, "that is very sad—but I am a stranger here. Who is Nag?"

Darzee and his wife only cowered down in the nest without answering, for from the thick grass at the foot of the bush there came a low hiss—a horrid cold sound that made Rikki-tikki jump back two clear feet. Then inch by inch out of the grass rose up the head and spread hood of Nag, the big black cobra, and he was five feet long from tongue to tail. When he had lifted one third of himself clear of the ground, he stayed balancing to and fro exactly as a dandelion tuft balances in the wind, and he looked at Rikki-tikki with the wicked snake's eyes that never change their expression, whatever the snake may be thinking of.

"Who is Nag?" he said. "*I* am Nag. The great god Brahm[3] put his mark upon all our people when the first cobra spread his hood to keep the sun off Brahm . . . as he slept. Look, and be afraid!"

He spread out his hood more than ever, and Rikki-tikki saw the spectacle mark on the back of it that looks exactly like the eye part of a hook-and-eye fastening. He was afraid for the minute; but it is impossible for a mongoose to stay frightened for any length of time, and though Rikki-tikki had never met a live cobra

Rikki-tikki licked his lips.

"This is a splendid hunting ground," he said...

❼ ✓ Reading Check

How do Teddy's parent's feel about Rikki-tikki-tavi staying at their house?

---

3. **Brahm** (bräm) short for Brahma, the name of the chief god in the Hindu religion.

❻ ❓ **Connecting to the Big Question**

1. Remind students that there are two sides to any conflict.

2. Have students read the bracketed passage. **Ask:** Who suffers as a result of Nag's presence in the garden?
   Possible response: Darzee and his wife suffer because Nag eats one of their babies.

3. **Ask** students: Does anyone benefit from the conflict between Nag and the birds?
   Possible response: Nag benefits by getting food to eat.

4. Finally, **ask** students whether they would consider Darzee's baby an innocent victim.
   Possible response: Yes; the baby did not enter the conflict willingly.

❼ Reading Check

Answer: Teddy's parents are happy to have Rikki-tikki-tavi staying at their house, though his mother worried at first that Rikki-tikki-tavi might bite Teddy.

❽ Plot

1. Review with students the definition of *conflict*—"a struggle between opposing forces."

2. Have a volunteer read the bracketed passage. Then, **ask** the Plot question on the student page. **Possible response:** Details such as Nagaina sneaking up on Rikki-tikki-tavi intensify the conflict because they make readers wonder who will win the battle and because they show that Nagaina and Nag are both threats.

❾ Critical Viewing

Possible answer: Based on the photograph, the mongoose should win a match with a cobra. The mongoose looks very fierce, with angry eyes and sharp teeth.

Plot
What details intensify the conflict here?

❽

❾ ▼ **Critical Viewing**
Based on this photograph, which animal would you expect to win a match to the death—the cobra or the mongoose? Why? **[Speculate]**

---

before, his mother had fed him on dead ones, and he knew that all a grown mongoose's business in life was to fight and eat snakes. Nag knew that too, and at the bottom of his cold heart he was afraid.

"Well," said Rikki-tikki, and his tail began to fluff up again, "marks or no marks, do you think it is right for you to eat fledglings out of a nest?"

Nag was thinking to himself, and watching the least little movement in the grass behind Rikki-tikki. He knew that mongooses in the garden meant death sooner or later for him and his family; but he wanted to get Rikki-tikki off his guard. So he dropped his head a little, and put it on one side.

"Let us talk," he said. "You eat eggs. Why should not I eat birds?"

"Behind you! Look behind you!" sang Darzee.

Rikki-tikki knew better than to waste time in staring. He jumped up in the air as high as he could go, and just under him whizzed by the head of Nagaina (nə gī′nə), Nag's wicked wife. She had crept up behind him as he was talking, to make an end of him; and he heard her savage hiss as the stroke missed. He came down almost across her back, and if he had been an old mongoose he would have known that then was the time to break her back with one bite; but he was afraid of the terrible lashing return stroke of the cobra. He bit, indeed, but did not bite long enough, and he jumped clear of the whisking tail, leaving Nagaina torn and angry.

"Wicked, wicked Darzee!" said Nag, lashing up high as he could reach toward the nest in the thornbush; but Darzee had built it out of reach of snakes; and it only swayed to and fro.

232 Short Stories

Word Forms

Expand students' vocabulary by helping them learn related forms of the selection vocabulary words. Give students a blank **Word Form Chart** (*Professional Development Resources*, p. 42) with the words *revived, immensely,* and *consolation* in the correct columns. Work with the class, or have students work with a partner, to determine

the related forms. The final chart should look like the one shown.

Hold students accountable for integrating the related forms of the words into their speaking and writing.

Noun	Verb	Adjective	Adverb
revival	revive	**revived**, reviving	
immensity		immense	**immensely**
consolation	console	consoling	consolingly

232

Rikki-tikki felt his eyes growing red and hot (when a mongoose's eyes grow red, he is angry), and he sat back on his tail and hind legs like a little kangaroo, and looked all around him, and chattered with rage. But Nag and Nagaina had disappeared into the grass. When a snake misses its stroke, it never says anything or gives any sign of what it means to do next. Rikki-tikki did not care to follow them, for he did not feel sure that he could manage two snakes at once. So he trotted off to the gravel path near the house, and sat down to think. It was a serious matter for him. **10**

If you read the old books of natural history, you will find they say that when the mongoose fights the snake and happens to get bitten, he runs off and eats some herb that cures him. That is not true. The victory is only a matter of quickness of eye and quickness of foot—snake's blow against mongoose's jump—and as no eye can follow the motion of a snake's head when it strikes, that makes things much more wonderful than any magic herb. Rikki-tikki knew he was a young mongoose, and it made him all the more pleased to think that he had managed to escape a blow from behind. It gave him confidence in himself, and when Teddy came running down the path, Rikki-tikki was ready to be petted. **11**

Make Predictions
What do you predict will be the outcome of the conflict? What prior knowledge helps you make that prediction?

Reading Check
Who is Nagaina and what does she do to Rikki-tikki-tavi?

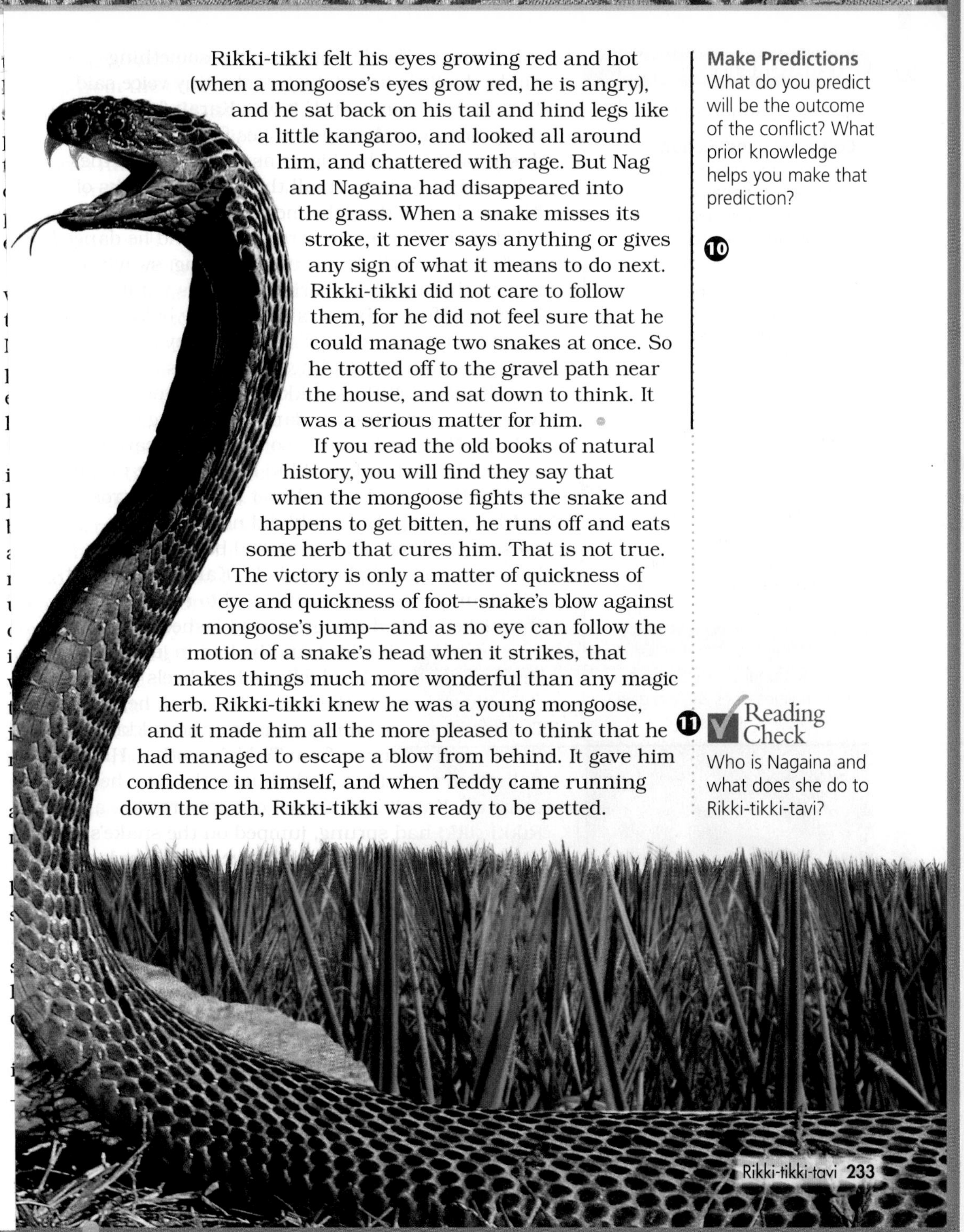

Differentiated Instruction for Universal Access

Strategy for Special-Needs Students
Kipling personifies, or assigns human characteristics to, animal characters. To help students track the human traits of the nonhuman characters, have them complete a diagram like the **Web** on p. 219 of ***Graphic Organizer Transparencies.*** In the large center circle, have students write *Animal Characters.* As students encounter new animal characters, they should draw smaller circles and write the characters' names and traits in them. Have students use this organizer to analyze characters as they read.

EL Strategy for English Learners
Kipling's story offers readers insight into the natural world of India. Students acquiring English may have trouble distinguishing names of animals and plants in this story. Have student partners work together to create a two-column chart in which they list the names of plants and animals mentioned in the story so far. Encourage students to add to the lists as they continue to read.

10 Make Predictions

1. Have students reread the paragraph that begins "Rikki-tikki felt his eyes growing red. . . ." Then, **ask** students the first part of the Make Predictions question.
Answer: Students may predict that Rikki-tikki will plan to attack the cobras, but separately.
2. Next, **ask** the second part of the Make Predictions question.
Possible response: Some students may say that it is Rikki-tikki's nature to fight the cobras. They might also interpret Rikki-tikki's realization that he can't attack both of them at once to mean that he intends to attack them separately.

11 Reading Check

Answer: Nagaina is a cobra who lives in Teddy's garden. She sneaks up on Rikki-tikki and attacks him, but her stroke misses.

12

Sc
th
"R
Ki
m
te
qu
or
sta
ev
tic

C
H
C
ac
ab
Lit
ch
Ki
A
ab
su

Spiral Review
Setting

1. Remind students that they studied the concept of setting in the Unit 2 Literary Analysis Workshop (pp. 200–215).

2. **Ask** the Spiral Review question.
Possible response: The reader can't "see" into the hole, so doesn't know whether Rikki has killed Nagaina or not.

26 Plot

1. Read aloud the bracketed passage. Discuss Darzee's role in the story so far.
Answer: He tells Rikki-tikki about Nag, but otherwise is not very helpful. He sings of Nag's death while Rikki-tikki is still dealing with the dangerous Nagaina. He does not want Rikki-tikki to destroy Nagaina's eggs. Now he is singing of Rikki-tikki's death before he knows for sure whether Rikki-tikki has been killed.

2. **Ask** students the Plot question.
Answer: The comment adds to the tension because it is not clear that Rikki-tikki will survive the fight. Rikki-tikki has taken a great risk by following Nagaina into a hole. However, Darzee is foolish and doesn't really know what has happened. Rikki-tikki may survive.

3. **Ask** students what part of the plot this passage is.
Answer: This scene is part of the climax.

Nagaina gathered herself together, and flung out at him. Rikki-tikki jumped up and backward. Again and again and again she struck, and each time her head came with a whack on the matting of the veranda and she gathered herself together like a watchspring. Then Rikki-tikki danced in a circle to get behind her, and Nagaina spun round to keep her head to his head, so that the rustle of her tail on the matting sounded like dry leaves blown along by the wind. •

He had forgotten the egg. It still lay on the veranda, and Nagaina came nearer and nearer to it, till at last, while Rikki-tikki was drawing breath, she caught it in her mouth, turned to the veranda steps, and flew like an arrow down the path, with Rikki-tikki behind her. When the cobra runs for her life, she goes like a whiplash flicked across a horse's neck.

Rikki-tikki knew that he must catch her, or all the trouble would begin again. She headed straight for the long grass by the thornbush, and as he was running Rikki-tikki heard Darzee still singing his foolish little song of triumph. But Darzee's wife was wiser. She flew off her nest as Nagaina came along, and flapped her wings about Nagaina's head. If Darzee had helped they might have turned her; but Nagaina only lowered her hood and went on. Still, the instant's delay brought Rikki-tikki up to her, and as she plunged into the rat hole where she and Nag used to live, his little white teeth were clenched on her tail, and he went down with her—and very few mongooses, however wise and old they may be, care to follow a cobra into its hole. It was dark in the hole; and Rikki-tikki never knew when it might open out and give Nagaina room to turn and strike at him. He held on savagely, and struck out his feet to act as brakes on the dark slope of the hot, moist earth.

Then the grass by the mouth of the hole stopped waving, and Darzee said: "It is all over with Rikki-tikki! We must sing his death song. Valiant Rikki-tikki is dead! For Nagaina will surely kill him underground."

So he sang a very mournful song that he made up all on the spur of the

Spiral Review
Setting How does the setting of the cobra's hole introduce uncertainty into the plot?

Plot
How does Darzee's comment here add to the tension? **26**

27

242 Short Stories

Vocabulary Development

Vocabulary Knowledge Rating
When students have completed reading and discussing "Rikki-tikki-tavi," have them take out their **Vocabulary Knowledge Rating Chart** for this selection. Read the words aloud and have students rate their knowledge of words again in the After Reading column. Clarify any words that are still problematic. Have students write their own definition and example or sentence in the appropriate column. Then, have students complete the Vocabulary Practice activities at the end of the selection. Encourage students to use the words in further discussion and written work about the selection. Remind them that they will be accountable for these words on the **Selection Test**, *Unit 2 Resources,* pp. 56–58 or 59–61.

minute, and just as he got to the most touching part the grass quivered again, and Rikki-tikki, covered with dirt, dragged himself out of the hole leg by leg, licking his whiskers. Darzee stopped with a little shout. Rikki-tikki shook some of the dust out of his fur and sneezed. "It is all over," he said. "The widow will never come out again." And the red ants that live between the grass stems heard him, and began to troop down one after another to see if he had spoken the truth.

Rikki-tikki curled himself up in the grass and slept where he was—slept and slept till it was late in the afternoon, for he had done a hard day's work.

"Now," he said, when he awoke, "I will go back to the house. Tell the Coppersmith, Darzee, and he will tell the garden that Nagaina is dead."

The Coppersmith is a bird who makes a noise exactly like the beating of a little hammer on a copper pot; and the reason he is always making it is because he is the town crier to every Indian garden, and tells all the news to everybody who cares to listen. As Rikki-tikki went up the path, he heard his "attention" notes like a tiny dinner gong; and then the steady "*Ding-dong-tock! Nag is dead—dong! Nagaina is dead! Ding-dong-tock!*" That set all the birds in the garden singing, and the frogs croaking; for Nag and Nagaina used to eat frogs as well as little birds.

When Rikki got to the house, Teddy and Teddy's mother and Teddy's father came out and almost cried over him; and that night he ate all that was given him till he could eat no more, and went

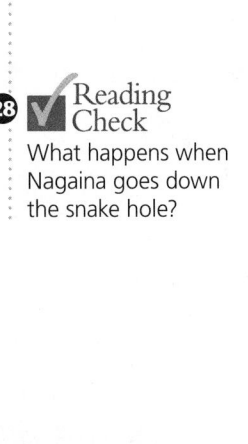

Rikki-tikki-tavi **243**

Plot
What part of the plot does Rikki's comment illustrate?

28 ✓ Reading Check
What happens when Nagaina goes down the snake hole?

27 Plot

1. After students have read the bracketed paragraph, **ask** them what happened.
   Answer: Rikki-tikki has killed Nagaina and survived the fight.

2. Point out that some suspense still lingers about the outcome of the story until Rikki-tikki says, "It is all over . . . . The widow will never come out again." **Ask** the Plot question.
   Answer: The comment illustrates the end of the climax. The outcome of the story is clear: Rikki-tikki has beaten the cobras.

3. Have students note the end of the climax on their plot diagrams.

28 Reading Check

Answer: Darzee sings a song to mourn Rikki-tikki's death, but Rikki-tikki comes out triumphant, having killed Nagaina.

Concept Connector

Literary Analysis Graphic Organizer
Ask students to review the graphic organizers they completed to diagram the plot while reading. Then, have students share the graphic organizers they completed and compare how they plotted the story.

Writing About the Big Question
Have students compare their responses to the sentence starter they completed before reading the story with their ideas afterward. Ask them to explain whether their thoughts have changed.

Anticipation Guide
Have students return to their **Anticipation Guides** and respond to the statements again in the After Reading column. They may do this individually or in their original groups. Then, lead a class discussion, probing for what students have learned that confirms or invalidates each statement. Encourage students to cite specific details, quotations, or other evidence from the text to support their responses to each statement.

Critical Thinking

Before students respond, you may wish to have them write a brief objective summary of the selection. As they answer the questions below, remind them to support their answers with evidence from the text.

1. (a) Rikki-tikki feels a great dislike for the snakes, especially when they threaten the family. The snakes despise Rikki-tikki for protecting the family. They are also afraid of him. (b) Rikki-tikki is lovable, considerate, and caring, shown in his defense of the family. He is also a good planner, a quick thinker, and an athletic fighter, shown in his successful war against the snakes. The cobras are proud, power-hungry, and murderous. They take offense easily and are vengeful, shown in Nagaina's last attack on the family.

2. (a) Nag and Nagaina are husband and wife. (b) Nagaina plans to attack the family, which makes Rikki-tikki determined to kill the snakes. (c) Nagaina's plan makes her a villain because she plans to kill innocent people simply so she can rule the garden.

3. (a) Darzee's gossip helps explain who the characters are and provides humor and suspense. (b) Rikki-tikki's approach to life is effective, because he thinks seriously about consequences before taking action or making claims.

4. (a) Students may say that the story is popular because its plot is suspenseful and exciting. Also, its hero is likable, and its villains are evil. (b) Students should be able to support their opinions with examples from the story. (c) Students should explain whether or not they were influenced by their partners.

5. **Possible response:**
   (a) Rikki-tikki-tavi destroys Nagaina's eggs even though the snakes within the eggs have done nothing to Rikki, so they are innocent victims. (b) Teddy and his family suffer from the conflict by being threatened and terrified by the snakes and worrying about Rikki.

---

to bed on Teddy's shoulder, where Teddy's mother saw him when she came to look late at night.

"He saved our lives and Teddy's life," she said to her husband. "Just think, he saved all our lives."

Rikki-tikki woke up with a jump, for all the mongooses are light sleepers.

"Oh, it's you," said he. "What are you bothering for? All the cobras are dead; and if they weren't, I'm here."

Rikki-tikki had a right to be proud of himself; but he did not grow too proud, and he kept that garden as a mongoose should keep it, with tooth and jump and spring and bite, till never a cobra dared show its head inside the walls.

Critical Thinking

Cite textual evidence to support your responses.

1. **Key Ideas and Details** **(a)** How does Rikki feel about the cobras? How do they feel about Rikki? **(b) Compare:** Using details from the story, compare Rikki's and the cobras' personalities.

2. **Key Ideas and Details** **(a)** What is the relationship between Nag and Nagaina? **(b) Analyze:** What does Nagaina do to make matters worse for Nag and herself? **(c) Draw Conclusions:** Why does this plan make her a villain?

3. **Key Ideas and Details** **(a) Analyze:** What role does Darzee play in the story? **(b) Compare and Contrast:** Whose approach to life, Darzee's or Rikki's, do you think is more effective? Why?

4. **Integration of Knowledge and Ideas** **(a) Analyze:** "Rikki-tikki-tavi" is among the most widely read short stories ever written. Why do you think it is so popular? **(b) Evaluate:** Do you think the story deserves this standing? Explain. **(c) Discuss:** Share your responses with a partner. Then, discuss how looking at someone else's responses did or did not change your evaluation.

5. **Integration of Knowledge and Ideas** **(a)** In what way are Nagaina's eggs innocent victims of the conflict? **(b)** How do Teddy and his family suffer? *[Connect to the Big Question: Does every conflict have a winner?]*

244 Short Stories

Assessment Resources

Reading Skill: Make Predictions

1. What **prior knowledge** did you have from reading the Background note on page 227 that helped you **predict** that Rikki-tikki-tavi would be able to defeat the cobras?

2. Choose another prediction based on prior knowledge that you made as you read this story. Use a graphic organizer like the one here to show how you made your prediction.

 + 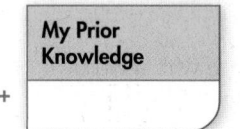 =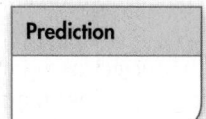

Literary Analysis: Plot

© 3. **Key Ideas and Details** Identify two **plot** events that increase the tension between Rikki and Nag.

© 4. **Key Ideas and Details** Identify two or three events that move the plot toward the **climax,** when Rikki and Nagaina battle.

Vocabulary

© **Acquisition and Use** Answer each question. Then, explain your response.

1. Is someone who has just been *revived* ready to run a race?

2. If you like a man *immensely,* how do you feel about him?

3. When you sit on a *veranda,* are you inside the house?

4. If you are *mourning* someone, are you smiling?

5. Is missing dinner *consolation* for getting home late?

6. If you are *cunningly* disguised, can you be recognized?

Word Study Use the context of the sentences and what you know about the **Latin suffix *-tion*** to explain your answer.

1. If a painting is an *imitation,* is it the original?

2. If someone offers a *suggestion,* is he being helpful?

Word Study

The **Latin suffix *-tion*** is an ending that turns a verb into a noun, meaning "the thing that is."

Apply It Explain how the suffix *-tion* contributes to the meanings of these words. Consult a dictionary if necessary.

infection
creation
restoration

Rikki-tikki-tavi **245**

Word Study
Sample answers:
1. No, an *imitation* is not the original. It is a thing that imitates, or pretends to be, something else.
2. Yes, a *suggestion* is helpful. It is a thing that suggests, or proposes, an idea.

Word Study: Apply It
Sample answers:
An *infection* is the thing that infects you.
A *creation* is the thing that has been created.
A *restoration* is the thing that is restored or the act that restores.

Reading Skill
1. **Possible response:** Students may say that the Background note helped them predict that Rikki-tikki would be able to defeat the cobras because mongooses are good at killing snakes.

2. **Possible response:** Students' predictions will vary, but each prediction should be supported by a reasonable explanation of how prior knowledge helped or did not help in making the prediction.

   For other sample answers, see *Graphic Organizer Transparencies,* Reading Skill Graphic Organizer A, p. 43, and the **Additional Answers** section.

Literary Analysis
3. **Possible response:** The tension between Rikki-tikki and Nag increases after Rikki-tikki bites Nagaina and after Rikki-tikki overhears Nag and Nagaina plotting to kill Teddy and his family.

4. **Possible response:** Nag threatens Rikki-tikki. The cobras plan to kill the family. Rikki-tikki and Nag battle. Rikki-tikki destroys all the eggs but one.

Vocabulary
Acquisition and Use
Sample answers:
1. No, someone who has just been <u>revived</u> has just regained consciousness and can't run a race.

2. If you like a man <u>immensely</u>, you like him a great deal.

3. No, when you sit on a <u>veranda,</u> you are sitting on a porch outside the house.

4. No, if you are <u>mourning</u> someone, you are sad, so you are not smiling.

5. No, missing dinner is punishment for getting home late, not <u>consolation</u>, or comfort.

6. No, if you are <u>cunningly,</u> or cleverly, disguised, your disguise will fool people.

245

Conventions

1. Introduce the skill, using the instruction on the student page.
2. Discuss the examples in the chart.

Think Aloud: Model the Skill

Say to students:

> One way I figure out whether a verb is an action verb or a linking verb is by deciding whether the subject of the sentence is being described. If the words after the verb are a description of the subject, I know that the verb is probably a linking verb. Suppose a friend tells me, "Ben grew tall." Because *tall* is a description of Ben, I know *grew* is a linking verb in this sentence. Then, let's say that someone tells me, "Maria grew flowers." I know that *flowers* is not a description of Maria, so in this sentence, *grew* must be an action verb.

PH WRITING COACH | Grade 7

Students will find further instruction on and practice with action and linking verbs in Chapter 14, Sections 1 and 2.

Practice A

1. felt (linking)
2. followed (action)
3. searched (action)
4. was (linking)

Reading Application
Sample answer:

Action: So Kuo-Haya's father went back to his home. (p. 222)
Linking: He was angry now. (p. 222)

Practice B
Sample answers:

1. looked; Carlos looked sad today.
2. felt; Helen felt glad after finishing her homework.
3. appeared; The dog appeared friendly.
4. turned; The sky turned cloudy.

Writing Application
Sample answers:

1. Linking: The mongoose looks fierce.
2. Action: The mongoose snarls fiercely.

Integrated Language Skills

The Bear Boy • Rikki-tikki-tavi

Conventions: Verbs

A **verb** is a word that expresses an action or a state of being. Every complete sentence must have at least one verb.

- An **action verb** tells what action someone or something is doing.
- A **linking verb** joins the subject of a sentence with a word or phrase that describes or renames the subject. The most common linking verbs are forms of *be*, such as *am, is, was, were, has been,* and *will be.* Other linking verbs include *seem, become, stay, feel, taste,* and *look.*

Action Verbs	Linking Verbs
John *rode* his bike. Let's *skate* in the park.	Jessica *seems* happy. James *is* a member of the club. The theater *will be* crowded.

Practice A Identify the verb or verbs in each sentence, and indicate whether they are action verbs or linking verbs.

1. Kuo-Haya felt shy in front of the other boys.
2. Kuo-Haya followed bear tracks into a canyon.
3. Kuo-Haya's father searched for Kuo-Haya among the cliffs.
4. Kuo-Haya's father was angry at the mother bear.

© **Reading Application** In "The Bear Boy," find one sentence with a linking verb and one with an action verb.

Practice B Identify the action verb in each sentence. Then, write a new sentence for each, using the verb as a linking verb.

1. Rikki-tikki-tavi looked all around the bungalow.
2. Rikki-tikki-tavi felt the soft pillow on Teddy's bed.
3. Karait, the dusty brown snakeling, appeared in the dust.
4. Nagaina turned to see her only remaining egg.

© **Writing Application** Choose a photo from pages 228–244 and write two sentences: one using a linking verb, and one using an action verb.

PH WRITING COACH | Further instruction and practice are available in *Prentice Hall Writing Coach*.

Writing

© **Informative Text** Write an **informative article** based on the story you read.

- If you read "Bear Boy," write about how a mother bear raises cubs.
- If you read "Rikki-tikki-tavi," write about cobras or mongooses.

An informative article teaches readers about a topic and contains these elements:

- an introduction, a body, and a conclusion
- details that tell *when, how much, how often,* or *to what extent*
- a formal style that avoids slang and incomplete sentences
- terms specific to your topic, such as *den, venom, predator*

Grammar Application Check your writing to make sure your use of action and linking verbs is correct.

Writing Workshop: *Work in Progress*

Preview for Response to Literature Answer the following: *What stories have I read that I enjoyed or did not enjoy? What characters stand out?* Save this Story List in your writing portfolio.

Speaking and Listening

© **Comprehension and Collaboration** With a partner, engage in an **informal debate** based on the story you read. Each of you should pick an opposing viewpoint to present.

- If you read "The Bear Boy," debate whether it is ethical to train wild animals for entertainment purposes, such as circuses or shows.
- If you read "Rikki-tikki-tavi," defend the actions of either the mongoose or the cobras in the story. Explain your position.

Follow these steps to complete the assignment.

- Convince your partner of your viewpoint by supporting your ideas with valid arguments based on credible research.
- Respect your partner's time to talk. Do not interrupt.
- As you listen to your partner, take note of his or her argument. When it is your turn to talk, do one of three things:

  (1) Explain why there is not enough evidence to support your partner's argument. (2) Explain why the evidence contradicts your partner's argument. (3) Find an inconsistency with one of your partner's earlier arguments.

Common Core State Standards

W.7.2.d, W.7.2.e, SL.1.a, SL.3
[For the full wording of the standards, see page 216.]

Use this prewriting activity to prepare for the **Writing Workshop** on page 302.

PHLit Online!
www.PHLitOnline.com

- Interactive graphic organizers
- Grammar tutorial
- Interactive journals

Integrated Language Skills **247**

Writing

1. Review the assignment, using the instruction on the student page.
2. To guide students in writing an informative text, give them **Support for Writing**, p. 51 in *Unit 2 Resources.*
3. To evaluate students' articles, use the rubrics for **Research Report**, pp. 242–243 in *Professional Development Guidebook.* In addition, you might evaluate how effectively students use simple language to explain their topic.

Grammar Application

Have students check their drafts to make sure they have used action and linking verbs correctly.

Six Traits Focus

	Ideas	✔	Word Choice
✔	Organization		Sentence Fluency
	Voice		Conventions

PH WRITING COACH | Grade 7

Students will find further instruction on and practice with expository text in Chapter 8.

📖 Writing Workshop
Work in Progress

Have students save their completed Story Lists in their portfolios. They will use the lists later as they continue this Work-in-Progress assignment (see p. 279). These assignments prepare them to complete the Writing Workshop assignment (see pp. 302–307).

Speaking and Listening

1. Review the assignment, using the instruction on the student page.
2. Have students complete the **Support for Extend Your Learning** page (*Unit 2 Resources*, p. 52).

Teaching Resources

Unit 2 Resources

- L3 L4 EL **Integrated Language Skills: Grammar,** p. 50
- L3 L4 EL **Support for Writing,** p. 51
- L3 L4 **Support for Extend Your Learning,** p. 52
- L4 **Enrichment,** p. 49

Enriched Online Student Edition

Available under After You Read for this selection:

- All **Interactive Grammar Tutorial**
- L3 L4 **Internet Research Activity**

Professional Development Guidebook

Rubrics for Self-Asssessment: Research, pp. 242–243

PHLit Online! All print and digital resources are available online at **www.PHLitOnline.com**. Online resources accessible to students are noted on the student page.

247

Lesson Pacing Guide

DAY 1 Preteach

- Ⓒ Administer the Reading and Vocabulary Warm-ups (*Unit 2 Resources*, pp. 62–65, 80–83) as necessary.
- Introduce the Reading Skill: Make Predictions.
- Ⓒ Introduce the Literary Analysis concept: Character.
- Distribute copies of the graphic organizer for the Reading Skill (*Graphic Organizer Transparencies*, pp. 45–47).
- Distribute copies of the graphic organizer for Literary Analysis (*Graphic Organizer Transparencies*, pp. 48–50).
- Ⓒ Teach the selection vocabulary.
- Ⓒ Introduce the Word Study skill.

DAYS 2–3 Preteach/Teach

- Ⓒ Build background with the Background feature.
- Develop thematic vocabulary and thematic thinking with Writing About the Big Question.
- Prepare students to read with the Activating Prior Knowledge activities (TE).
- Informally monitor comprehension while students read.
- Use the Reading Check questions to confirm comprehension.
- Develop students' ability to make predictions using the Make Predictions questions.
- Ⓒ Develop students' understanding of character using the Character questions.
- Ⓒ Reinforce vocabulary with the Vocabulary notes.
- Ⓒ Reinforce unit focus standards using the Spiral Review prompts.

DAY 4 Assess

- Assess students' comprehension and mastery of the skills by having them answer the Critical Thinking, Reading Skill, and Literary Analysis questions.
- Ⓒ Have students complete the Vocabulary Practice activities.
- Ⓒ Have students complete the Word Study activities.

DAY 5 Extend/Assess

- Have students complete the Conventions lesson.
- Ⓒ Have students complete the Writing activity and write a journal entry. (You may assign as homework.)
- Ⓒ Extend learning by having students complete the Research and Technology activity, an outline. (You may assign as homework.) As an alternative, assign them "Moms and Dads in the Military" or "Sports Parents" in *Reality Central*.
- Administer Selection Test A or B (*Unit 2 Resources*, pp. 74–79 or 95–100).

Common Core State Standards

Reading Literature 6. Analyze how an author develops and contrasts the points of view of different characters or narrators in a text.

Writing 3.a. Engage and orient the reader by establishing a context and point of view and introducing a narrator and/or characters; organize an event sequence that unfolds naturally and logically.
3.b. Use narrative techniques, such as dialogue, pacing, and description, to develop experiences, events, and/or characters.
7. Conduct short research projects to answer a question, drawing on several sources and generating additional related focused questions for further research and investigation.

Language 1. Demonstrate command of the conventions of standard English grammar and usage when writing or speaking.
4.b. Use common, grade-appropriate Greek or Latin affixes and roots as clues to the meaning of a word.
6. Acquire and use accurately grade-appropriate general academic and domain-specific words and phrases; gather vocabulary knowledge when considering a word or phrase important to comprehension or expression.

Additional Standards Practice
Common Core Companion, pp. 15–35, 67–68

Daily Block Scheduling
Each day in this Lesson Pacing Guide represents a 40–50 minute period. Teachers using block scheduling may combine days to revise pacing. In addition, teachers may differentiate and support core instruction by integrating components for extended and intensive support, as students require. See the Guide to Selected Leveled Resources (facing page).

Guide to Selected Leveled Resources

Tier 1 (students performing on level)

			✓ **More Accessible**	✓✓ **More Complex**
			from **Letters from Rifka**	**Two Kinds** *from* **The Joy Luck Club**
Warm Up		Practice, model, and monitor fluency, working with the whole class or in groups.	Vocabulary and Reading Warm-ups B, *Unit 2 Resources*, pp. 62–63, 65	Vocabulary and Reading Warm-ups B, *Unit 2 Resources*, pp. 80–81, 83
Comprehension/Skills		Support and monitor comprehension and skills development, having students complete the activities, graphic organizers, and interactive prompts independently or as a class.	• *Reader's Notebook,* adapted instruction and full selection EL *Reader's Notebook: English Learner's Version,* adapted instruction and adapted selection • Reading Skill Graphic Organizer B, *Graphic Organizer Transparencies,* p. 47 • Literary Analysis Graphic Organizer B, *Graphic Organizer Transparencies,* p. 50	• *Reader's Notebook,* adapted instruction and summary EL *Reader's Notebook: English Learner's Version,* adapted instruction and summary • Reading Skill Graphic Organizer B, *Graphic Organizer Transparencies,* p. 47 • Literary Analysis Graphic Organizer B, *Graphic Organizer Transparencies,* p. 50
Monitor Progress	A	Monitor student progress with the differentiated curriculum-based assessment in the *Unit Resources.*	• Selection Test B, *Unit 2 Resources,* pp. 77–79 • Open-Book Test, *Unit 2 Resources,* pp. 71–73	• Selection Test B, *Unit 2 Resources,* pp. 98–100 • Open-Book Test, *Unit 2 Resources,* pp. 92–94
Assess/ Screen	A	Assess student progress using Benchmark Test 3.	• Benchmark Test 3, *Unit 2 Resources,* pp. 120–124	• Benchmark Test 3, *Unit 2 Resources,* pp. 120–124

Tier 2 (students requiring intervention)

			✓ **More Accessible**	✓✓ **More Complex**
			from **Letters from Rifka**	**Two Kinds** *from* **The Joy Luck Club**
Warm Up		Practice, model, and monitor fluency in groups or with individuals.	• Vocabulary and Reading Warm-ups A, *Unit 2 Resources,* pp. 62–64 • *Reality Central,* "Moms and Dads in the Military" • *Hear It!* Audio CD (adapted text)	• Vocabulary and Reading Warm-ups A, *Unit 2 Resources,* pp. 80–82 • *Reality Central,* "Sports Parents" • *Hear It!* Audio CD
Comprehension/Skills		• Support and monitor comprehension and skills development, working in small groups or with individuals. • Pair students with more advanced peers and have them complete the writing activity in the *Real-World Writing Journal.* • As students complete the selection in the appropriate version of the *Reader's Notebook,* monitor comprehension frequently with group questions and individual instruction. • Model strategies while guiding students in completing the activities and prompts in the *Reader's Notebook,* as well as the graphic organizers. • Practice skills and monitor mastery with the *Reading Kit* worksheets.	• *Real-World Writing Journal, Lesson 3,* pp. 44–47 • *Reader's Notebook: Adapted Version,* adapted instruction and adapted selection EL *Reader's Notebook: English Learner's Version,* adapted instruction and adapted selection • Reading Skill Graphic Organizer A, *Graphic Organizer Transparencies,* p. 45 • Literary Analysis Graphic Organizer A, *Graphic Organizer Transparencies,* p. 48 • *Reading Kit,* Practice worksheets, pp. 52, 58, 62, 64, 70	• *Real-World Writing Journal, Lesson 4,* pp. 48–51 • *Reader's Notebook: Adapted Version,* adapted instruction and summary EL *Reader's Notebook: English Learner's Version,* adapted instruction and summary • Reading Skill Graphic Organizer A, *Graphic Organizer Transparencies,* p. 46 • Literary Analysis Graphic Organizer A, *Graphic Organizer Transparencies,* p. 49 • *Reading Kit,* Practice worksheets, pp. 52, 58, 62, 64, 70
Monitor Progress	A	Monitor student progress with the differentiated curriculum-based assessment in the *Unit Resources* and in the *Reading Kit.*	• Selection Test A, *Unit 2 Resources,* pp. 74–76 • *Reading Kit,* Assess worksheets pp. 53, 59, 63, 65, 71	• Selection Test A, *Unit 2 Resources,* pp. 95–97 • *Reading Kit,* Assess worksheets, pp. 53, 59, 63, 65, 71
Assess/ Screen	A	Assess student progress using Benchmark Test 3.	• Benchmark Test 3, *Unit 2 Resources,* pp. 120–124	• Benchmark Test 3, *Unit 2 Resources,* pp. 120–124

TIER 3 Tier 3 intervention may require consultation with the student's special-education or dyslexia specialist. For additional support, see the Tier 2 activities and resources listed above.

One-on-one teaching   Group work   Whole class instruction   Independent work   A Assessment

For a complete guide to selections support, including support for Advanced students, see the Overview of Resources in the frontmatter.

248b

1. Have students read the bracketed passage. Challenge them to imagine and describe what both the narrator and the narrator's mother are thinking and feeling after the talent show.
Possible answers: The mother may feel humiliated by her daughter's poor performance. The narrator is devastated because she has let her mother down.

2. **Ask** students the Predict question.
Possible response: The mother may voice her disappointment and shame to her daughter, or she may punish her.

▶ **Monitor Progress:** Review students' prediction graphic organizers to see whether their predictions are logical.

▶ **Reteach:** If students struggle to predict how the mother will react, point to her earlier reactions: "my mother's disappointed face" (p. 263), "My mother slapped me" (p. 265), "her stricken face" (p. 270). Ask students what these reactions have in common and why they think the mother reacts the way she does.

Vocabulary
devastated (dev´ ə stāt´ əd) v. destroyed; completely upset

nonchalantly (nän´ shə länt´ lē) adv. seemingly uninterested **25**

Predict
What do you predict the mother will say to her daughter now that the piano recital is over?

But my mother's expression was what **devastated** me: a quiet, blank look that said she had lost everything. I felt the same way, and it seemed as if everybody were now coming up, like gawkers at the scene of an accident, to see what parts were actually missing. When we got on the bus to go home, my father was humming the busy-bee tune and my mother was silent. I kept thinking she wanted to wait until we got home before shouting at me. But when my father unlocked the door to our apartment, my mother walked in and then went to the back, into the bedroom. No accusations. No blame. And in a way, I felt disappointed. I had been waiting for her to start shouting, so I could shout back and cry and blame her for all my misery. ●

老師

I assumed my talent-show fiasco meant I never had to play the piano again. But two days later, after school, my mother came out of the kitchen and saw me watching TV.
"Four clock," she reminded me as if it were any other day. I was stunned, as though she were asking me to go through the talent-show torture again. I wedged myself more tightly in front of the TV.
"Turn off TV," she called from the kitchen five minutes later.
I didn't budge. And then I decided. I didn't have to do what my mother said anymore. I wasn't her slave. This wasn't China. I had listened to her before and look what happened. She was the stupid one.
She came out from the kitchen and stood in the arched entryway of the living room. "Four clock," she said once again, louder.
"I'm not going to play anymore," I said **nonchalantly**. "Why should I? I'm not a genius."
She walked over and stood in front of the TV. I saw her chest was heaving up and down in an angry way.
"No!" I said, and I now felt stronger, as if my true self had finally emerged. So this was what had been inside me all along.

272 Short Stories

Vocabulary Development

© **CCSS** Language 6

Selection Vocabulary Reinforcement

To reinforce and assess students' comprehension of selection vocabulary words, give them sentences in which the word may or may not be used correctly. Students must tell whether the use is correct and explain their answer. Use these sentences:

1. The dog deserved *reproach* for its perfect performance at the dog show. **Answer:** No, *reproach* is not used correctly. It means "blame or disgrace." A dog that performs perfectly deserves praise, not reproach.

2. The choir members *conspired* to present the conductor with a gift after the concert. **Answer:** Yes, *conspired* is used correctly. *Conspired* means "planned together." The choir members worked together to plan the gift for the conductor.

3. The slow economy *devastated* local businesses, and many closed. **Answer:** Yes, *devastated* is used correctly. *Devastated* means "destroyed or completely upset." A slow economy could ruin local businesses.

"No! I won't!" I screamed.

She yanked me by the arm, pulled me off the floor, snapped off the TV. She was frighteningly strong, half pulling, half carrying me toward the piano as I kicked the throw rugs under my feet. She lifted me up and onto the hard bench. I was sobbing by now, looking at her bitterly. Her chest was heaving even more and her mouth was open, smiling crazily as if she were pleased I was crying.

"You want me to be someone that I'm not!" I sobbed. "I'll never be the kind of daughter you want me to be!"

"Only two kinds of daughters," she shouted in Chinese. "Those who are obedient and those who follow their own mind! Only one kind of daughter can live in this house. Obedient daughter!"

"Then I wish I wasn't your daughter. I wish you weren't my mother," I shouted. As I said these things I got scared. It felt like worms and toads and slimy things crawling out of my chest, but it also felt good, as if this awful side of me had surfaced, at last.

"Too late change this," said my mother shrilly.

And I could sense her anger rising to its breaking point. I wanted to see it spill over. And that's when I remembered the babies she had lost in China, the ones we never talked about. "Then I wish I'd never been born!" I shouted. "I wish I were dead! Like them."

It was as if I had said the magic words. Alakazam!—and her face went blank, her mouth closed, her arms went slack, and she backed out of the room, stunned, as if she were blowing away like a small brown leaf, thin, brittle, lifeless.

It was not the only disappointment my mother felt in me. In the years that followed, I failed her so many times,

"You want me to be someone that I'm not!" I sobbed. "I'll never be the kind of daughter you want me to be!"

27 ✓ Reading Check

How does the narrator feel about her performance at the talent show?

26 **Critical Thinking**
Connect
1. Have students read the bracketed passage. Point out that the mother's response explains the title of the story. One kind of daughter is rebellious and follows her own mind; the other kind is obedient.
2. **Ask** students what character traits contribute to the daughter's outburst.
   Answer: The daughter's rebelliousness, anger, and pride contribute to her outburst. She wants to hurt her mother and show her independence.
3. **Ask** students which kind of daughter the narrator is and why they think so.
   Answer: The narrator is clearly a rebellious daughter. She yells at her mother and says that she wishes she were not her mother's daughter.

27 **Reading Check**
Answer: The narrator is angry and ashamed of her performance at the talent show.

Differentiated Instruction for Universal Access

Strategy for Less Proficient Readers
To help students understand the multiple and conflicting feelings that the narrator experiences, have them focus on her outburst and her reaction to it on this page and the next. Ask students why the narrator reacts so strongly to her mother and why she becomes scared by the things she says to her mother. Students should contrast the narrator's immediate feeling of release with later feelings of shame or regret. Challenge students to talk about ways the narrator and her mother might resolve their differences.

Enrichment for Gifted/Talented Students
Have students represent the cultural and generational conflicts of "Two Kinds" in various ways. Point out that people and cultures may be composed of two sides that coexist in harmony or two sides in conflict like the mother and daughter in this story. Have students choose a medium or method in which to present "two kinds." Students might choose from the following: a dance duet, recordings or musical performances, a collage, a videotape of a person's actions, or a poem. Have students share their representations with the class.

㉘ Critical Thinking
Interpret

1. Before students read the bracketed passage, have them reread the last paragraph that begins on page 273. Point out to students that at this point the story "flashes," or moves, forward in time. The narrator is now an adult looking back in time.

2. **Ask** students to share what they learn about the narrator in this passage. **Answer:** Students should understand that the narrator disappointed her mother many times in the course of growing up.

3. Read aloud the following sentence: "For unlike my mother, I did not believe I could be anything I wanted to be. I could only be me." **Ask** students to explain what this statement says about the mother and the narrator. **Answer:** The mother was an optimist who believed her daughter could be anything. The daughter was more of a realist; she never really believed she was destined for greatness.

㉙ Predict

1. Ask students to read the first sentence of the passage that begins "For after our struggle at the piano . . . ." **Ask** students to predict what happens to the piano. **Possible response:** The mother sells it or gives it away.

2. After students finish reading the passage, **ask** the Predict question. **Possible response:** She may become angry or ashamed; she may not want to be reminded of that troubled period in her life. She may wish to give the piano another chance.

Vocabulary
expectations (ek´ spekt tā´ shənz) ㉘ *n.* things looked forward to

> *For unlike my mother, I did not believe I could be anything I wanted to be. I could only be me.*

Predict
How do you predict the narrator will respond to the gift of the piano?

each time asserting my own will, my right to fall short of expectations. I didn't get straight A's. I didn't become class president. I didn't get into Stanford. I dropped out of college.

For unlike my mother, I did not believe I could be anything I wanted to be. I could only be me.

And for all those years, we never talked about the disaster at the recital or my terrible accusations afterward at the piano bench. All that remained unchecked, like a betrayal that was now unspeakable. So I never found a way to ask her why she had hoped for something so large that failure was inevitable.

And even worse, I never asked her what frightened me the most: Why had she given up hope?

For after our struggle at the piano, she never mentioned my playing again. The lessons stopped. The lid to the piano was closed, shutting out the dust, my misery, and her dreams.

So she surprised me. A few years ago, she offered to give me the piano, for my thirtieth birthday. I had not played in all those years. I saw the offer as a sign of forgiveness, a tremendous burden removed. ㉙

"Are you sure?" I asked shyly. "I mean, won't you and Dad miss it?"

"No, this your piano," she said firmly. "Always your piano. You only one can play."

"Well, I probably can't play anymore," I said. "It's been years."

"You pick up fast," said my mother, as if she knew this was certain. "You have natural talent. You could been genius if you want to."

"No I couldn't."

"You just not trying," said my mother. And she was neither angry nor sad. She said it as if to announce a fact that could never be disproved. "Take it," she said.

But I didn't at first. It was enough that she had offered it to me. And after that, every time I saw it in my parents'

274 Short Stories

Vocabulary Development

Vocabulary Knowledge Rating

When students have completed reading and discussing "Two Kinds," have them take out their **Vocabulary Knowledge Rating Chart** for this selection. Read the words aloud and have students rate their knowledge of words again in the After Reading column. Clarify any words that are still problematic. Have students write their own definition and example or sentence in the appropriate column. Then have students complete the Vocabulary Practice activities at the end of the selection. Encourage students to use the words in further discussion and written work about the selection. Remind them that they will be accountable for these words on the **Selection Test**, *Unit 2 Resources*, pp. 95–97 or 98–100.

living room, standing in front of the bay windows, it made me feel proud, as if it were a shiny trophy I had won back.

Last week I sent a tuner over to my parents' apartment and had the piano reconditioned, for purely sentimental reasons. My mother had died a few months before and I had been getting things in order for my father, a little bit at a time. I put the jewelry in special silk pouches. The sweaters she had knitted in yellow, pink, bright orange—all the colors I hated—I put those in moth-proof boxes. I found some old Chinese silk dresses, the kind with little slits up the sides. I rubbed the old silk against my skin, then wrapped them in tissue and decided to take them home with me.

After I had the piano tuned, I opened the lid and touched the keys. It sounded even richer than I remembered. Really, it was a very good piano. Inside the bench were the same exercise notes with handwritten scales, the same secondhand music books with their covers held together with yellow tape.

I opened up the Schumann book to the dark little piece I had played at the recital. It was on the left-hand side of

Vocabulary

sentimental (sen´ tə ment´ əl) *adj.* emotional; showing tender feeling

Predict

What do you think the narrator will do now that the piano has been tuned after so many years?

**Reading Check**

What gift does the narrator receive for her 30th birthday? Why?

30 Predict

1. Read aloud the passage that begins "Last week I sent a tuner . . . ." **Ask** students why the narrator is having the piano tuned.
   Possible response: She may be planning to play. She may be simply trying to repair past neglect to the piano and to her mother's dreams.

2. **Ask** students the Predict question.
   Possible response: The narrator may try to play again. She may take lessons and really apply herself.

31 Reading Check

Possible response: The mother gives the narrator the piano for her thirtieth birthday. The narrator believes it is a sign of forgiveness.

Concept Connector

Reading Skill Graphic Organizer
Ask students to review the graphic organizers they completed to form and verify predictions while reading. Then, have students share the graphic organizers they completed and compare their predictions.

Writing About the Big Question
Have students compare their responses to the sentence starters they completed before reading the story with their thoughts afterwards. Ask them to explain whether their thoughts have changed.

Anticipation Guide
Have students return to their **Anticipation Guides** and respond to the statements again in the After Reading column. They may do this individually or in their original pairs or groups. Then, lead a class discussion, probing for what students have learned that confirms or invalidates each statement. Encourage students to cite specific details, quotations, or other evidence from the text to support their responses to each statement.

Critical Thinking

Before students respond, you may wish to have them write a brief objective summary of the selection. As they answer the questions below, remind them to support their answers with evidence from the text.

1. (a) The mother pushes her daughter, tests her, and arranges for piano lessons without consulting her. (b) The daughter believes she can never meet her mother's expectations, and the mother is angry because her daughter refuses to try. Supporting details include the daughter's unwillingness to try to learn the piano and the mother's slapping the daughter.

2. (a) The titles are "Pleading Child" and "Perfectly Contented." (b) The grownup author realizes that the two piano pieces are two parts of the same whole, just as the parts of her character make up the same whole. The "dark little piece," "Pleading Child," is like her as a child, but "Perfectly Contented," with its lighter, faster melody, is like her as an adult.

3. (a) Students may agree that many people believe they can be anything they want, but it is not easy to become anything you want. (b) Students may suggest that the mother pushed her daughter too hard. The mother's efforts backfired. Her daughter believed she would never be good enough and stopped trying.

4. Answers will vary. Accept all reasonable responses.

5. **Possible response:** No one wins. The mother never achieves the life she wants for her daughter, and the daughter doesn't develop the self-esteem she might have had if she had followed her mother's path to success.

---

the page, "Pleading Child." It looked more difficult than I remembered. I played a few bars, surprised at how easily the notes came back to me.

And for the first time, or so it seemed, I noticed the piece on the right-hand side. It was called "Perfectly Contented." I tried to play this one as well. It had a lighter melody but the same flowing rhythm and turned out to be quite easy. "Pleading Child" was shorter but slower; "Perfectly Contented" was longer, but faster. And after I played them both a few times, I realized they were two halves of the same song.

老師

Critical Thinking

Cite textual evidence to support your responses.

1. **Key Ideas and Details (a)** In what ways does the mother pressure her daughter for change? **(b) Draw Conclusions:** How does the difference in their attitudes create problems? Support your answer with details from the text.

2. **Key Ideas and Details (a)** What are the titles of the two pieces in the Schumann book that the daughter plays at the end of the story? **(b) Connect:** In what ways do the titles and pieces reflect the daughter's feelings about herself?

3. **Integration of Knowledge and Ideas (a) Evaluate:** Do you agree that people can be anything they want to be? Why or why not? **(b) Make a Judgment:** Should the narrator's mother have pushed the daughter as she did? Explain.

4. **Craft and Structure** How might the story be different if it were told from the mother's point of view?

5. **Integration of Knowledge and Ideas** In this story, conflict results when a mother pushes her daughter to become a success. Is there a winner in this conflict? Explain. *[Connect to the Big Question: Does every conflict have a winner?]*

Assessment Resources

Unit 2 Resources

L1 L2 EL **Selection Test A**, pp. 95–97. Administer Test A to less advanced readers.

L3 L4 EL **Selection Test B**, pp. 98–100. Administer Test B to on-level and more advanced students.

L3 L4 **Open-Book Test**, pp. 92–94. As an alternative, give the Open-Book Test.

All **Customizable Test Bank**

All **Self-tests**
Students may prepare for the **Selection Test** by taking the **Self-test** online.

PHLit Online! All assessment resources are available at www.PHLitOnline.com.

Reading Skills: Make Predictions

1. **(a)** What **predictions** did you make about how well the narrator would play at the recital? **(b)** Did reading ahead cause you to change your prediction?

2. **(a)** At what point in the story were you able to **predict** that the daughter would eventually refuse to play the piano? **(b)** Did your prediction change as you read? Explain.

Literary Analysis: Character

© 3. **Key Ideas and Details** Using a diagram like this one, list the daughter's **character traits,** supporting your answers with story details.

© 4. **Key Ideas and Details** What **motives** does this daughter have to rebel against her mother finally?

Vocabulary

© **Acquisition and Use** Make up an answer to each question. Use a complete sentence that includes the italicized vocabulary word.

1. Who *conspired* to make the party a surprise?
2. Why did the *reproach* bother him?
3. What kind of weather *devastated* the crops?
4. What instruments does the musical *prodigy* play?
5. How did the audience respond to the singer's *debut?*
6. How did the *obedient* child behave at the lecture?

Word Study Use the context of the sentences and what you know about the **Latin root -spir-** to explain each answer.

1. Is a *spirited* person lively or dull?
2. If something *inspires* you, does it make you feel excitement?

Word Study

The **Latin root -spir-** means "breath."

Apply It Explain how the root *-spir-* contributes to the meanings of these words. Consult a dictionary if necessary.

perspire
transpire
respiration

Two Kinds **277**

Reading Skill

1. **(a) Possible response:** I predicted that the narrator would not do well at the talent show because she is not interested in playing well and her teacher is no longer effective. (b) Most students probably had their predictions validated when they read ahead in the story.

2. **(a)** Students may say that as soon as they read that piano lessons were in store for the daughter they knew that at some point she would stop playing. By then, they had read about her track record of failure. Other students may say that after reading about the author's humiliating performance at the talent show they assumed that she would refuse to play the piano any more. (b) Students may point to the narrator's reaction to her mother's tests and her uncaring attitude toward the piano lessons as details that led to their guess.

Literary Analysis

3. **Possible response:** The daughter is rebellious, insecure, proud, and arrogant. The narrator shows that she is rebellious when she refuses to practice and when, after the recital, she refuses to continue playing the piano. She shows that she is arrogant and proud when she assumes that she will perform acceptably at the recital even without proper practice. She shows that she is insecure when she becomes upset over her failures at her mother's "tests."

For other sample answers, see *Graphic Organizer Transparencies,* Literary Analysis Graphic Organizer A, p. 49, and the **Additional Answers** section.

4. The daughter's motives are to get her mother to accept her as she is, not as her mother wants her to be.

Vocabulary
Acquisition and Use

1. The children conspired with their father to make the mother's party a surprise.
2. The reproach bothered him because he did not like being blamed for something he did not do.
3. The endless heat devastated the crops.
4. The musical prodigy plays violin, cello, and piano.
5. The audience responded to the singer's debut with applause and loud cheers.
6. The obedient child behaved respectfully.

Word Study
Sample answers:

1. A spirited person is lively—full of spirit, or life.
2. Yes, something that inspires you breathes life into you and excites you.

Word Study: Apply It
Sample answers:

To *perspire* is to "breathe out" perspiration, or sweat. To *transpire* is to occur, but it is also to "breathe out" waste products, as through the skin. *Respiration* is the act of breathing. All three connect to the act of taking in and giving out.

277

Conventions

1. Introduce the skill, using the instruction on the student page.

2. Discuss the examples in the chart.

Think Aloud: Model the Skill

Say to students:

> I think of the principal parts of a verb as interlocking blocks. Once you hook them to other words, they make tenses. For example, if I join the present participle *running* with the helping verb *is,* I get a verb in a present tense: *is running.* It expresses action that is going on right now. However, if I join that present participle to the helping verb was, I get a verb in a past tense: *was running.*

PH WRITING COACH Grade 7

Students will find further instruction on and practice with the principle parts of verbs in Chapter 21, Section 1.

Practice A
Sample answers:
1. searched; past
2. had boarded; past participle
3. writes; present
4. was hiding; past participle

Reading Application
Sample answer: We <u>made</u> it. (past); Saul <u>says</u> I <u>am</u> too little. . . . (present); Those who <u>have helped</u> him . . . . (past participle); "Come," Papa said, <u>leading</u> us through the woods to the train station. (present participle)

Practice B
Sample answers:
1. The narrator's mother <u>hopes</u> her daughter will become a prodigy; The action is now present tense.
2. The mother <u>was buying</u> Jing-mei a piano for her lessons; The action is now in process, but in the past.
3. The narrator, Jing-mei, <u>performed</u> in the recital; The action is now in the past.
4. She <u>has trouble</u> pleasing her mother; The action is now in process in the present.

Writing Application
Sample answer: I <u>found</u> this picture yesterday. In it a young girl <u>is playing</u> the piano. She <u>looks</u> happy. She <u>has</u> probably <u>practiced</u> a lot.

Integrated Language Skills

from Letters from Rifka • Two Kinds

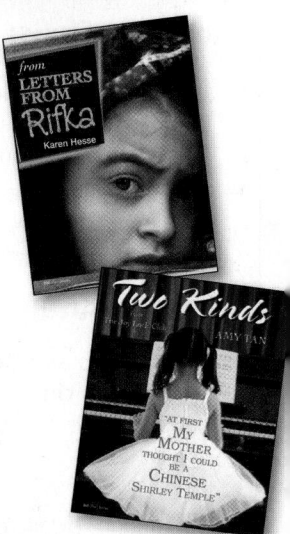

Conventions: The Principal Parts of Verbs

A verb has four **principal parts**: *present, present participle, past,* and *past participle.*

Verb tenses indicate when something occurred. Tenses are formed using the principal parts of verbs. In the chart below, you will find the four principal parts of the verb *talk.* Notice that when you use both the present and past participle, you also include helping verbs. Common helping verbs include *has, have, had, am, is, are, was,* and *were.* A verb and its helping verb is called a "verb phrase."

	Present	Present Participle	Past	Past Participle
Regular	Today I **talk**.	I am **talking** now.	Yesterday we **talked**.	We have **talked** often.
Irregular	He **sits** down.	He is **sitting** down.	Yesterday he **sat** down.	He has often **sat** there.

Practice A Locate the verb or verb phrase in the following sentences and indicate which of the four main tenses they are.
1. The Army searched for Nathan.
2. The family had boarded the train quickly and quietly.
3. Rifka writes a letter to Tovah describing her escape.
4. Rifka was hiding from the guards.

© **Reading Application** In "Letters from Rifka," locate at least three of the principal parts of verbs.

Practice B Rewrite each sentence, using a different principal part. Explain how your choice changes the meaning of the sentence.
1. The narrator's mother had hoped her daughter would become a prodigy.
2. The mother bought her daughter, Jing-mei, a piano for her lessons.
3. Jing-mei is performing in the recital.
4. She had trouble pleasing her mother.

© **Writing Application** Choose a photograph featured in "Two Kinds" and write four sentences about it. Use at least two of the four principal parts of verbs.

PH WRITING COACH Further instruction and practice are available in *Prentice Hall Writing Coach.*

278 Short Stories

Writing

Common Core State Standards

L.7.1, L.7.4.b, L.7.6; W.7.3.a, W.7.3.b, W.7.7
[For the full wording of the standards, see page 248.]

Narrative Text Write a **journal entry** as a character from either *Letters from Rifka* or "Two Kinds."

- Choose a character and a specific situation from your story.
- Write from the character's point of view, using the word *I*.
- Describe the situation by presenting a clear sequence of events.
- Use dialogue and descriptive details to relay the character's thoughts and feelings.

Grammar Application Check your writing to be sure you have used verb tenses correctly.

Writing Workshop: *Work in Progress*

Prewriting for Response to Literature Review the Story List in your portfolio. For each story you describe, create a two-column chart with the labels "What I Liked" and "What I Disliked." Then, note specific scenes, characters, images, or actions that fit in each column. Keep this Response Chart in your portfolio.

Use this prewriting activity to prepare for the **Writing Workshop** on page 302.

Research and Technology

Build and Present Knowledge Write an **outline** that provides background.

- If you read *Letters from Rifka*, find out more about the unfair treatment of Jews in twentieth-century Russia.
- If you read "Two Kinds," research traditional Chinese beliefs and customs about the relationship between parents and children.

Follow these steps to complete the assignment:

- Generate a list of questions on your topic to guide your research.
- Consult a variety of library or Internet resources to answer your questions.
- Organize your thoughts by jotting down notes.
- In outline form, state briefly and in your own words the main points and key details of what you learned.
- Group your notes by category. Use Roman numerals (I, II, III) to number your most important points. Under each Roman numeral, use capital letters for each supporting detail.
  TIP: Look at the Outline Format model on page 1042.
- Share your findings with other students.

PHLit Online!
www.PHLitOnline.com
- Interactive graphic organizers
- Grammar tutorial
- Interactive journals

Integrated Language Skills **279**

Writing

1. Review the assignment, using the instruction on the student page.
2. To guide students in writing a narrative text, give them **Support for Writing**, p. 90 in *Unit 2 Resources.*
3. To evaluate students' journal entries, use the rubrics for **Response to Literature,** pp. 224–225 in the *Professional Development Guidebook.* In addition, you might evaluate how well students respond to the narrator's feelings and how many details from the story they incorporate in their entries.

Grammar Application

Have students check their drafts for correct use of verb tenses.

Six Traits Focus

Ideas		✔ Word Choice
Organization		Sentence Fluency
Voice		Conventions

PH WRITING COACH   Grade 7

Students will find further instruction on and practice with the principle parts of verbs in Chapter 21, Section 1.

Writing Workshop
Work in Progress

Have students save their completed charts in their portfolios. They will use the charts later as they complete the Writing Workshop (see pp. 302–307).

Research and Technology

1. Review the assignment, using the instruction on the student page.
2. To support students' work on the assignment, have them complete the **Support for Extend Your Learning** page *Unit 2 Resources,* p. 91).

Teaching Resources

Unit 2 Resources

L3 L4 EL **Integrated Language Skills: Grammar,** p. 89

L3 L4 EL **Support for Writing,** p. 90

L3 L4 **Support for Extend Your Learning,** p. 91

L4 **Enrichment,** p. 88

Enriched Online Student Edition
Available under After You Read for this selection:

All **Interactive Grammar Tutorial**

L3 L4 **Internet Research Activity**

Professional Development Guidebook
Rubrics for Self–Assessment: Response to Literature, pp. 224–225

PHLit Online! All print and digital resources are available online at **www.PHLitOnline.com.** Online resources accessible to students are noted on the student page.

279

Using the Test Practice

In this two-page Test Practice, students apply the reading skill for the first half of Unit 2 to a passage of fiction and a passage of nonfiction.

Review this skill, making predictions, and then administer the test. For more guidance, consult the *Classroom Strategies and Teaching Routines* card **Formally Assessing Students.**

ASSESS

Answers

Answers With Explanations

1. **B**—Dark clouds are a sign of a coming storm. *Incorrect answers:* A—There is no reference to soccer in this paragraph; C—Characters can go indoors for many reasons; D—The fact that Jenna had taken Weather Safely does not indicate a storm is coming.

2. **B**—The weather safety course probably taught what to do during a storm. *Incorrect answers:* A—Jenna's age does not indicate that she knows what to do in a storm; C—The fact that Jenna wants to check the news is not evidence that she will know what to do; D—The clouds indicate a coming storm, not how Jenna will behave.

3. **C**—Lights that go off during a storm usually come on after it passes. *Incorrect answers:* A—The lights suggest that the storm has ended, not that it will intensify; B—The lights suggest that the storm is ending, not continuing; D—The return of the lights does not indicate that there is much lightning.

4. **A**—Their mother is on her way home. She is the likeliest person to pull into the driveway. *Incorrect answers:* B—The story contains no mention of a neighbor; C—The story contains no mention of a soccer coach; D—There is no reason for a reporter to arrive.

Test Practice: Reading

Make Predictions

Fiction Selection

Directions: *Read the selection. Then, answer the questions.*

Outdoors, Jenna and her little brother Tim noticed dark clouds building on the horizon. They decided to go indoors. Jenna had taken a weather safety course, and she knew that there was danger from lightning, even if a storm seemed far away.

Earlier, Mom had called to say she would be a little late getting home. Tim suggested to Jenna that they get dinner started. The two were cutting up vegetables when a loud crack of thunder shook the house. Startled, Jenna went to see the news on television. Just then, there was a flash of lightning and the house lost power. Jenna grabbed Tim by the hand and led him to a hall in the center of the house. Then, the lights came on, and Jenna heard the sound of a car pulling into the driveway.

1. What information in the first paragraph helps you predict that a storm is brewing?
  A. Jenna and Tim are playing soccer.
  B. There are dark clouds on the horizon.
  C. Jenna and Tim go indoors.
  D. Jenna had taken a weather safety course.

2. What detail helps you predict that Jenna will know what to do when the lights go out?
  A. She is Tim's older sister.
  B. She has taken a weather safety course.
  C. She wants to check the news.
  D. She sees dark clouds on the horizon.

3. Which prediction might you make when you learn that the lights have come on?
  A. The storm will become stronger.
  B. The storm will continue.
  C. The storm will soon end.
  D. Lightning will strike their house.

4. Based on details in the story, who do you predict is in the car?
  A. Jenna and Tim's mother is in the car.
  B. A neighbor is in the car.
  C. The town soccer coach is in the car.
  D. A television reporter is in the car.

Writing for Assessment

Based on your prior knowledge and details in the story, write two or three sentences predicting what Jenna will say when her mother gets home. Use details from the story to support your answer.

Writing for Assessment

In their responses, students should create a conclusion to the story that follows logically from the storm, the brief loss of lights, and the fact that Jenna took good care of Tim. For example, students may predict that the mother and the children will discuss the storm as they make dinner.

Strategies for Test Taking

Remind students that writers may plant clues in their stories to help readers figure out what will happen next. When reading a test passage, students should use these clues plus their own knowledge and experience to make predictions. For example, if the writer describes a character in a certain situation, readers should think about how they and the people they know would think, feel, and act in a similar situation. Then, they can make logical predictions about the character's future actions.

Nonfiction Selection

Directions: *Read the selection. Then, answer the questions.*

Several severe thunderstorms raced through Connecticut last Wednesday, producing damaging winds and cloud-to-ground lightning. Winds reached as high as 60 miles per hour in some areas, knocking down trees and power lines.

One Connecticut man saw a tree crash through the roof of his home. Another family escaped unharmed through their back door after a power surge caused a fire to erupt in their basement. Approximately 61,000 homes lost power.

As soon as weather conditions allowed, utility crews began removing downed trees and restoring electricity. By the next day, the utility company had restored power to more than half of the homes.

1. What detail in the first paragraph helps you predict that people lost electricity during the storm?
   A. There were several different storms.
   B. The storm took place in the summer.
   C. There was cloud-to-ground lightning.
   D. Winds knocked down power lines.

2. Based on details in the passage, what might you predict would happen two days after the storm?
   A. Another severe storm would sweep through the state.
   B. Power would have been restored for most residents.
   C. Most power lines would remain down.
   D. Many families would order pizza.

3. What do you predict happened after the tree crashed through the man's home?
   A. Rain poured in through the roof.
   B. The wind stopped.
   C. Lightning caused a power outage.
   D. Trees fell on all the neighbors' homes.

4. Based on details in the passage, what do you predict will happen as a result of the storm?
   A. Many branches will need to be cleaned up.
   B. People will move to a safer area.
   C. People will be without power for weeks.
   D. Many houses will be repainted.

Writing for Assessment

Connecting Across Texts

If Jenna and Tim experienced a storm like the one in Connecticut, how might that change your prediction about what Jenna would say when her mother got home? Write a brief response, using details from the two passages to support your answer.

PHLit Online!
www.PHLitOnline.com
- Online practice
- Instant feedback

Strategy for Less Proficient Readers

To help students answer item 1 on this page, discuss their prior knowledge of the causes of power outages during severe storms. Then, point out that item 1 asks which detail "in the first paragraph" helps them predict that people will lose electricity.

Reread the first paragraph with students. Point out that there is no reference to "summer" (answer B), nor does the occurrence of "several storms" (answer A) mean that the storms were strong enough to knock out electrical equipment. Therefore, choices A and B can be eliminated.

Students must now choose between C and D. The first sentence of the paragraph mentions "cloud-to-ground lightning" (answer C) but does not state that the lightning damaged any electrical equipment. The second sentence states that the winds knocked down power lines (answer D). Damage to power lines is a clear source of power failure, so D is the best choice.

Answers With Explanations

1. **D**—Knocked-down power lines often cause people to lose electricity. *Incorrect answers:* A—The severity of a storm, not the number of storms, is a predictor of loss of electricity; B—The paragraph contains no details indicating the season; C—High winds, not lightning, downed the power lines.

2. **B**—Because it took crews one day to restore electricity to half of the homes, they should be able to restore power to the rest one day later. *Incorrect answers:* A—No details suggest another storm is coming; C—Half of the power lines are repaired just a day after the storm; D—If the power is restored two days later, families have no special reason to order out.

3. **A**—Rain will enter a hole in a roof. *Incorrect answers:* B—Nothing suggests that wind will stop immediately after it blows down a tree; C— The downing of a tree by wind is not a predictor of a lightning strike; D—One tree falling on one home does not indicate that trees will fall on all homes.

4. **A**—Many trees fell down; therefore, many branches will need to be cleaned up. *Incorrect answers:* B—Severe thunderstorms seldom cause people to relocate; C—Power was restored quickly; D—Storms do not usually cause people to repaint their homes.

Writing for Assessment

In their responses, students should cite details showing that the storm in Connecticut was more severe than the one experienced by Jenna and Tim. They might then revise their predictions about what Jenna might say. For example, they might predict that the family will lose power again, have a tree land on the house, or experience a dangerous power surge.

PHLit Online!
Students may take the test in interactive format with instant feedback online at www.PHLitOnline.com.

281

Reading Skill

1. Introduce the skill and point out examples of each text feature.
2. Tell students that they will analyze text features to better understand the text's purpose.

Think Aloud: Model the Skill

Model the skill of understanding text structure. Say to students:

The purpose of any informational text is to provide information. The purpose of an encyclopedia, for example, is to give facts about a wide range of topics. If I am researching one specific topic, then I must use the structure of the encyclopedia as a guide. An encyclopedia is not meant to be read from beginning to end; it is meant to be read one topic at a time, as needed. Entries are organized alphabetically, so that they can be found quickly. Because an encyclopedia has a structure that makes information easy to find, I know that it achieves its purpose and will be useful for my research.

▶ Multidraft Reading

Have students follow a multidraft reading protocol.

- **First reading**—Have students read to identify key ideas and details.
- **Second reading**—Have students read to identify the structure of the text.
- **Third reading**—Have students read to integrate knowledge and ideas by connecting the text to the world, their own experiences, and other texts.

Content-Area Vocabulary

1. Have students say each word.
2. Next, use each word in a sentence that defines it.
3. Finally, repeat your definitional sentence or a similar sentence, omitting the word, and have the class "fill in the blank" chorally.

Reading for Information

Analyzing Expository and Functional Texts

Magazine Article

Encyclopedia Entry

Reading Skill: Understand Text Structure and Purpose

Your **purpose,** or reason, for reading affects the way you approach informational texts. When you read to learn about a specific topic, you may consult a variety of texts. Although they share a common topic, each text may present different facts on the topic, or the texts may present evidence in different ways.

Understanding the text structure will help you decide if a specific text suits your purpose for reading. Text structure includes the special features of each type of writing, as shown in the chart below.

Text Features	Description
Title	The name of the article, which often gives clues about the topic
Subheadings	Boldface words that identify the main idea of each section
Photographs, illustrations, captions	Images and their labels that give additional information about the topic
Charts, graphs, diagrams	Information that is presented visually
Maps, legends	Art that shows geographic information

Content-Area Vocabulary

These words appear in the selections that follow. You may also encounter them in other content-area texts.

- **predators** (pred´ ə tərz) *n.* people or animals that exist by eating other animals
- **burrows** (bur´ ōz) *n.* tunnels or holes dug into the ground by animals, for shelter

Does every conflict have a winner?

Sometimes our solutions to conflicts are short-lived. Have students discuss the importance of seeing the long-term effects of our solutions.

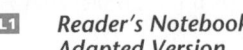

Mongoose
on the Loose
Larry Luxner

Magazine Article

Features:

- text meant for leisure reading
- products published at regular intervals
- text published along with photos, ads, and articles by different writers

The **introduction** to the magazine article sets up the topic.

In 1872 a Jamaican sugar planter imported nine furry little mongooses from India to eat the rats which were devouring his crops. They did such a good job, the planter started breeding his exotic animals and selling them to eager farmers on neighboring islands.

Population Explodes

Boldface **subheadings** give clues to the content in each section.

With no natural **predators**—like wolves, coyotes, or poisonous snakes—the mongoose population exploded, and within a few years, they were killing not just rats but pigs, lambs, chickens, puppies, and kittens. Dr. G. Roy Horst, a U.S. expert on mongooses, says that today mongooses live on seventeen Caribbean islands as well as Hawaii and Fiji, where they have attacked small animals, threatened endangered species, and have even spread minor rabies epidemics.

In Puerto Rico there are from 800,000 to one million of them. That is about one mongoose for every four humans. In St. Croix, there are 100,000 mongooses, about twice as many as the human population. "It's impossible to eliminate the mongoose population, short of nuclear war," says Horst. "You can't poison them, because cats, dogs, and chickens get poisoned, too. I'm not a prophet crying in the wilderness, but the potential for real trouble is there," says Horst.

According to Horst, great efforts have been made to rid the islands of mongooses, which have killed off

Reading for Information: Magazine Article **283**

283

1. **Ask** students to name the text features they notice on this page of the magazine article.
   Answer: Features include the subhead "Scientist Studies Problem," the photograph, and the caption.

2. **Ask** them to explain why the caption is useful in understanding the photograph.
   Possible response: According to the caption, the photograph shows a man tagging a mongoose. Without the caption, a reader might guess that he is performing a medical procedure.

3. **Ask** students to explain what the subhead on the page suggests about the photograph and about the act it shows.
   Possible response: The subhead, "Scientist Studies Problem," suggests that the reason the man in the photograph is tagging the mongoose is to study the mongoose population problem. This connection indicates that tagging is a way of studying population.

4. **Ask** students what purpose this page serves.
   Possible response: This page would serve the purpose of showing readers what scientists are doing to study the mongoose population problem.

a number of species including the Amevia lizard on St. Croix, presumed extinct for several decades. On Hawaii, the combination of mongooses and sports hunting has reduced the Hawaiian goose, or nene, to less than two dozen individuals.

> A **conclusion** gives a final summary and brings closure to the text.

Scientist Studies Problem

The fifty-nine-year-old biology professor, who teaches at Potsdam College in upstate New York, recently finished his third season at the 500-acre Cabo Rojo National Wildlife Refuge in southwestern Puerto Rico, using microchips to study the life cycle and reproductive habits of the Caribbean mongoose. (He is also doing similar work at the Sandy Point Fish and Wildlife Refuge on St. Croix in the U.S. Virgin Islands.) "I want to know what happens when you take a small animal and put him in an area with no competition. This is a model that doesn't exist anywhere else in the world."

Horst's five-year, $60,000 study is being sponsored by Earthwatch Incorporated, a non-profit group that has funded some 1,300 research projects in eighty-seven countries. Volunteers pay $1,500 each (not including airfare) to come to Puerto Rico for ten days and help Horst set out mongoose traps, study the animals, and keep records. Often he and his volunteers spend a sweaty day walking about ten miles while setting out mongoose traps in the wilderness. Later, they perform surgery on their unwilling subjects to implant the electronic devices that will allow them to track the animal's habits.

Horst has tagged more than 400 mongooses with

> **Photographs and captions** give additional information about the content of the magazine article.

PITs (permanently implanted transponders), a new microchip technology, which he says has changed his work dramatically. "You couldn't do this with ear tags. It was very hard to permanently mark these animals until this technology came along," he said.

Horst has caught thousands of mongooses and has reached some interesting conclusions. Among them: mongooses have a life expectancy of six to ten years, much longer than the previously accepted figure of three years. Horst says his research will provide local and federal health officials with extremely valuable information if they ever decide to launch a campaign against rabies in Puerto Rico or the U.S. Virgin Islands.

A mongoose gets tagged.

Think Aloud

Making Connections

To model the skill of making connections, read the quotation in the first paragraph under the subhead on this page. Then, use the following "think aloud." Say to students:

When Professor Horst says that "This is a model that doesn't exist anywhere else in the world," I realize that he means that the mongoose's situation on the islands is unusual. I think about the facts that I have already learned. On the previous page, I read that there are no animals on these islands that hunt for mongooses. I realize

that if no animals are eating mongooses, then it makes sense that mongooses would grow in numbers. In many other places in the world, though, animal populations are in balance. There is the right number of animals of each kind—one kind keeps another kind from spreading too much and eating too many other animals. The mongooses' situation is unusual because nothing is stopping their population from growing. As I read, I will look for other details to connect to these facts.

Indian Grey Mongoose

from WildInfo

The **title** tells you what the encyclopedia entry is about.

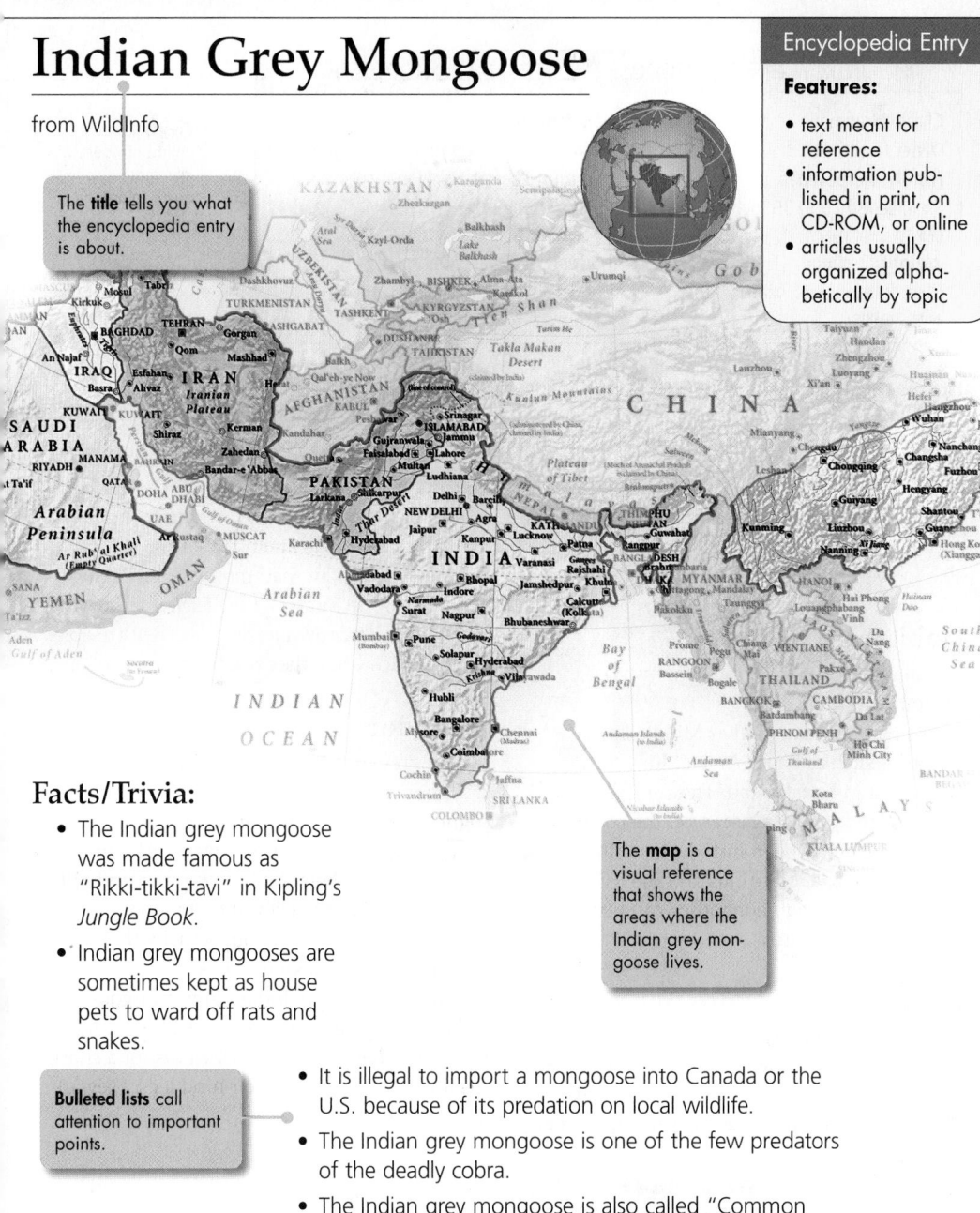

The **map** is a visual reference that shows the areas where the Indian grey mongoose lives.

Facts/Trivia:

• The Indian grey mongoose was made famous as "Rikki-tikki-tavi" in Kipling's *Jungle Book*.

• Indian grey mongooses are sometimes kept as house pets to ward off rats and snakes.

Bulleted lists call attention to important points.

• It is illegal to import a mongoose into Canada or the U.S. because of its predation on local wildlife.

• The Indian grey mongoose is one of the few predators of the deadly cobra.

• The Indian grey mongoose is also called "Common mongoose" and "Edward's mongoose."

• Mongooses are related to civets, genets and meerkats.

Reading for Information: Encyclopedia Entry **285**

About Encyclopedia Entries

1. Review the list of encyclopedia features on the student page with the class. Make sure that students understand the alphabetical organization of topics in an encyclopedia, reminding them that the key terms used are general ideas or proper nouns (not descriptive phrases) and that initial articles such as *a* and *the* are ignored for purposes of alphabetizing.

2. **Ask** students to list occasions when they use encyclopedia entries. Then, **ask** them to explain why encyclopedia entries are helpful on these occasions.
Sample answers: Students may say that they use encyclopedia entries when they need to write research reports because the information is easy to find and because all of the important information on a topic is included in one entry.

Understand Text Structure and Purpose

1. Review the text structure of the magazine article, which includes subheads and photographs.

2. Next, tell students to let their eyes wander over the student page and to make mental notes of the features they notice first. **Ask** volunteers to share their reactions.
Answer: Students may suggest that they noticed the map highlighting the mongoose habitat first.

3. **Ask** students to list ways in which the encyclopedia entry looks different from the magazine article.
Answer: Students may say that the magazine article contains more text and fewer visual representations of information. In contrast, the encyclopedia entry breaks apart the text with bullets and gives a map for quick reference.

4. **Ask** students what purpose the entry might serve.
Answer: Students may say that the structure of the encyclopedia entry makes it suitable for a reader searching for answers to specific questions.

Differentiated Instruction for Universal Access

Less Proficient Readers

As students read the entry, have them identify sections of the text that are difficult to understand. Encourage them to use self-sticking notes to mark trouble spots, jotting down a question for clarification on each note. This technique will help students organize their questions for later discussion and clarification. When students have finished reading the entry, discuss the problem spots they identified. Distribute the **KWL Chart**, *Professional Development Guidebook,* p. 75, and have them enter what they know and what they have questions about. Next, ask students to reread the entry with their questions in mind.

Enrichment for Advanced Readers

Challenge students to find out information about another animal. They might visit the school library to examine more encyclopedia entries and magazine articles and to look up information on the Internet. Distribute the **KWL Chart**, *Professional Development Guidebook,* p. 75, and direct them to fill it in as they gather information. When they have completed their research, have students write their own short encyclopedia entry on the animal they chose.

285

1. **Ask** students to identify features listed in the chart on p. 282 that appear on this page.
   Answer: Features include subheads and a chart.

2. Then, **ask** them how they would use the subheads on the page if their purpose was to find out what a mongoose eats.
   Answer: Information about what a mongoose eats will appear under the subhead "Feeding Habits," so a reader should read that section for the information.

INDIAN GREY MONGOOSE (*HERPESTES EDWARDSI*)

Class: Mammalia
Order: Carnivora
Family: Herpestidae
Size: Length: 9 to 26 inches (23 to 65 cm)
Weight: 3 pounds (1.4 kg)
Diet: Rats, insects, lizards, eggs and snakes

Distribution: Asia
Young: 2 to 4, up to 3 times a year
Animal Predators: None (cobras kill young mongooses)
Terms: No special terms
Lifespan: 7 to 12 years in the wild and 20 or more years in captivity

Charts visually call out important information for quick reference.

Description

Indian grey mongooses resemble weasels, with grey-brown fur; a long, slender body; a pointed face and a long, bushy tail. Their fur is dense, providing protection from cobras' fangs. Indian grey mongooses have amazing stamina, and are able to overpower cobras.

Habitat

Indian grey mongooses are found in India, Sri Lanka and Nepal as well as Middle Eastern countries such as Saudi Arabia, Iraq, Iran, Pakistan and Kazakhstan. They are also found on the island of Madagascar, off the coast of Africa. They have been introduced to Italy, the Malay Peninsula, Mauritius and the Ryukyu Islands. Indian grey mongooses can usually be found in wooded areas.

Paragraphs help break up the article into smaller sections of information.

Feeding Habits

Indian grey mongooses tend to prey on small mammals such as rats, but will also eat insects, lizards, eggs, fruit and the occasional snake. They search for prey by sniffing the ground and turning over rocks and stones.

Encyclopedia entries present factual information about many aspects of the mongoose.

Reproduction

Females undergo a two-month pregnancy before giving birth to two to four young. The young are born with some hair but are unable to see for the first few days. Young mongooses are early developers and after several weeks begin hunting with their mother. Once they become skillful hunters, they leave their mother to establish their own territories. They are able to reproduce when they reach two years of age.

Behavior

Indian grey mongooses live alone, but pair up during mating season. They sleep in **burrows** at night and come out during the day to hunt and bask in the sun. They are active, quick hunters. Because of their ability to capture and kill cobras, it was once believed that mongooses were immune to venom, but actually they are so quick when attacking a snake that they manage not to get bitten. Indian grey mongooses are extremely agile animals, capable of climbing walls and trees, running backwards for a short distance, and by using their hind legs, they are able to leap high in the air.

Vocabulary Development

© CCSS Language 6

Relevant Content-Area Vocabulary: Natural Science

Students may benefit from identifying words in the entry that relate to the topics of geography, animal classification, and other natural sciences. Have students work with a partner to create a list of unfamiliar technical words that appear in the entry. After students have created their lists, challenge them to look up and define the words by using a dictionary. Possible words students might be unfamiliar with are: *class, order, family, distribution, stamina, immune,* and *agile.*

Comparing Expository and Functional Texts

1. Key Ideas and Details (a) What are two differences between the **structure** of a magazine article and the structure of an encyclopedia entry? **(b)** What type of information did you find in the encyclopedia article that was not in the magazine article?

Content-Area Vocabulary

2. (a) Add the suffix *-y* to the base word *predator*. Explain how the suffix alters the meaning of the base word. **(b)** Use two of these words in a sentence that shows you understand the meaning of each word: *predator, predatory, burrows.*

🕐 Timed Writing

Informative Text: Description

> **Format**
> The prompt gives specific directions about what to focus on in your description. Narrow your descriptive details to these two items.

> Describe a mongoose. Include specific details from the magazine article and encyclopedia entry that describe its appearance and behavior. Include vivid words and phrases that create strong images for readers.
> (20 minutes)

> **Academic Vocabulary**
> When you *describe* something, you give information and details about it.

5-Minute Planner

Complete these steps before you begin to write:

1. Read the prompt carefully, noting key highlighted words.

2. To prepare your response, fold a piece of paper in half lengthwise, making two columns. Write "Appearance" on one side and "Behavior" on the other.

3. Review the different information about mongooses in the magazine article and the encyclopedia entry. In each column, jot down facts, quotations, or other relevant information from the texts.

4. For each fact you record, write a descriptive word or phrase that will make your writing more vivid.

5. Use your notes to write your description.

Comparing Expository and Functional Texts

1. (a) **Sample answer:** The magazine article is divided into fewer sections and has fewer subheads. The encyclopedia divides information into basic topics and presents each under a new subhead, without transitions between them. The magazine article tells a story, starting with an event, then explaining the problems it led to, and then explaining what one man is doing about the problems today.
(b) **Sample answer:** The encyclopedia article tells where a certain kind of mongoose lives around the world. The magazine article deals only with the Caribbean. The encyclopedia article covers basic facts about this type of mongoose, providing a map of all the places it lives, details about what it eats, and facts about its behavior.

2. (a) When you add the *-y* suffix to the word *predator,* you get the word *predatory.* Adding the suffix changes the noun to an adjective.
(b) **Sample response:** The predatory eagle waits for the rabbits to come out of their burrows.

🕐 Timed Writing

1. Before students complete the activity, guide them in identifying and analyzing key words and phrases in the prompt, highlighted on the student page.

2. Work with students to draw up guidelines for their descriptions based on the key words in the prompt:

   • **Focus** The essay should focus on a description of a mongoose's appearance and behavior.

   • **Organization** Related details should be grouped together; details unrelated to the topic should not be included.

   • **Elaboration** The essay should include specific details from the magazine article and encyclopedia entry. Descriptions should be vivid.

   • **Word Choice** The essay should include vivid words to convey each detail.

3. Have students use the 5-Minute Planner to structure their time.

4. Allow students 20 minutes to complete the assignment. Evaluate their work using the guidelines they have developed.

Common Core State Standards

- Reading Literature 4
- Writing 2.a, f

❶ Comparing Idioms

1. Introduce the skill, using the instruction on the student page.

2. Give students a copy of **Comparing Idioms Graphic Organizer B** (*Graphic Organizer Transparencies,* p. 52). Tell them they will fill it in with examples of idioms as they read.

Think Aloud: Model the Skill

Say to students:

We use idioms in conversation all of the time. If I say I need to hit the road, I don't mean I should strike the pavement with my fist! I mean that it is time for me to leave. If I read an unfamiliar phrase that does not make literal sense to me, I realize there's a good chance it's an idiom. To determine its meaning, I ask myself, "What meaning makes the most sense here?" Then, I check my idea by looking up the idiom in a dictionary under the main word in the phrase.

Comparing Literary Works

Seventh Grade Melting Pot

❶ Comparing Idioms

Figurative language is writing or speech that is not meant to be understood literally. An **idiom** is one type of figurative language. It is an expression with a meaning that is different from the meanings of the actual words. For example, if your friend asks if you "need a hand," he is not asking if you need an actual hand. Instead, he wants to know if you need help. The meaning of an idiom comes from common use of the expression, which is often unique to a language, region, or community. We are so used to hearing idioms that we forget that they do not make sense if we take them literally.

Writers use idioms to make their writing more interesting and colorful, and to reflect the ways that people actually talk. Both "Seventh Grade" and "Melting Pot" contain idioms. Use a chart like the one shown to record the idioms you find in each story. Then, explain how the use of idioms enables the writers to achieve specific effects.

Story	Idiom	Literal Meaning	Actual Meaning
"Seventh Grade"			
"Melting Pot"			

- Vocabulary flashcards
- Interactive journals
- More about the authors
- Selection audio
- Interactive graphic organizers

www.PHLitOnline.com

288 Short Stories

Common Core State Standards

Reading Literature
4. Determine the meaning of words and phrases as they are used in at text, including figurative and connotative meanings.

Writing
2.a. Introduce a topic clearly, previewing what is to follow; organize ideas, concepts, and information, using strategies such as definition, classification, comparison/contrast, and cause/effect. *(Timed Writing)*

2.f. Provide a concluding statement or section that follows from and supports the information or explanation presented.

Vocabulary Development

Vocabulary Knowledge Rating

Create a **Vocabulary Knowledge Rating Chart** (*Professional Development Guidebook,* p. 33) featuring the words glossed in the selections:

elective (p. 290)	*fluent* (p. 296)
scowl (p. 291)	*bigots* (p. 294)
conviction (p. 291)	

Give students a copy of the chart, and read the words aloud. Have students mark their

rating of each in the Before You Read column. To gauge how much instruction to provide, tally the students who think they know each word.

Explain that the words are defined in the margin at the point where they appear in the selection. Urge students to be alert to these words as they read the selections. They will rate their knowledge again when they finish.

Vocabulary Central, featuring tools, activities, and songs for studying vocabulary, is available online at **www.PHLitOnline.com**.

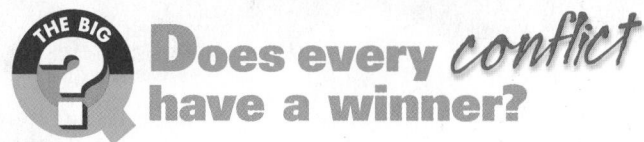

Does every *conflict* have a winner?

Writing About the Big Question

In both of these selections, characters face a conflict when they try to figure out how to fit in with people that seem different from them. Use this sentence starter to develop your ideas about the Big Question.

Sometimes it is a **struggle** to fit in because _____.

Meet the Authors

Gary Soto (b. 1952)

Author of "Seventh Grade"

Like the characters in many of his works, Gary Soto grew up in Fresno and once harvested crops in the fields of California.

A Sense of Belonging Soto began writing while in college. In the fiction and poetry he has written since, he reaches back to the sense of belonging he felt in Fresno. He often writes for young adults, who he knows are also searching for their own community and their own place. When he is not writing, Soto enjoys basketball, karate, and Aztec dance.

Anna Quindlen (b. 1953)

Author of "Melting Pot"

Anna Quindlen spent five years reporting for *The New York Times*, covering issues relating to her family and her neighborhood. "Melting Pot" originally appeared in "Life in the 30's," a popular column that Quindlen wrote for the *Times* from 1986 to 1988.

Building on Success In 1992 Quindlen's regular columns earned her a Pulitzer Prize. Later, she left the newspaper to write novels. She has published several bestsellers, including *One True Thing, Black and Blue,* and *Blessings*.

Seventh Grade • Melting Pot **289**

Teaching Resources

All *Unit 2 Resources*, pp. 101–108

All *Graphic Organizer Transparencies* pp. 51–54

All *Common Core Companion,* 41–48; 202–212

All Enriched Online Student Edition

L2 **EL** *Listening to Literature* Audio CD

All resources, including print and video, are available online at www.PHLitOnline.com.

❷ Writing About the Big Question

1. Review the assignment with the class.
2. Have students discuss the challenges that people may face in fitting in with a group. Remind them that struggles within oneself are conflicts, just as much as struggles with others are.
3. Have students complete the sentence starter. Review responses as a class. (**Sample response:** Sometimes it is a <u>struggle</u> to fit in because you want others to like you but do not want to compromise your values.)
4. Tell students that as they read, they should identify characters who are struggling and analyze their struggles.

Concept Connector ➡

Students will return to their ideas after they have concluded reading.

Multidraft Reading

To assist struggling readers and to deepen reading for all, apply multidraft reading protocols. For each reading, have students set the purpose indicated:

• **First reading**—identifying key ideas and details and answering any Reading Checks.

• **Second reading**—analyzing craft and structure and responding to the side-column prompts.

• **Third reading**—integrating knowledge and ideas, connecting to other texts and the world, and answering the end-of-selection questions.

For more guidance, see the *Classroom Strategies and Teaching Routines* card, **Using Multidraft Reading Strategy.**

For more about the authors and practice with the selection vocabulary, go online at www.PHLitOnline.com.

❶ Background

In some countries, many people grow up speaking two or more languages. In the United States, most people speak just one language fluently: English. Many American students encounter foreign-language instruction for the first time when they enter junior high school. Most language experts argue that foreign language instruction should begin as early as possible.

❷ Activating Prior Knowledge

Use the **Vocab-o-Gram** strategy (*Professional Development,* p. 40) to provide information that will allow students to make predictions about the reading. Put the following words on the board or on transparency:

cute
homeroom
scowl
lingered
impress
embarrassed
shame
pretending
love

Then, give students the **Vocab-o-Gram** chart (*Professional Development,* p. 40), and have them work with a partner or group to place the words in appropriate categories and to make predictions about the story.

Concept Connector ➡

Tell students they will return to their predictions after they read the selection.

❸ About the Selection

On the first day of seventh grade, Victor and his friend Michael try to hide their insecurities and impress the girls in their class. With his sights on Teresa, Victor signs up for French class to be near her. In that class, Victor takes a risk, impulsively implying that he knows French when he really does not. Victor's enthusiasm leads him to an embarrassing situation, but the sensitive teacher saves Victor from losing the respect of his classmates. Victor learns that teachers can be kind, that girls are approachable, and that taking a risk to fit in can pay off.

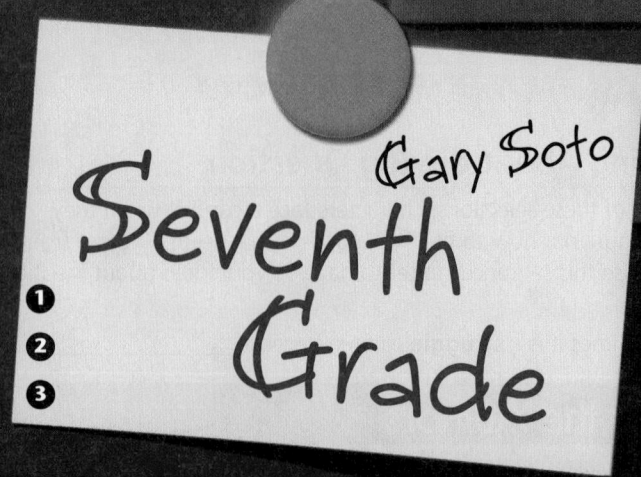

Seventh Grade
Gary Soto

❶
❷
❸

Vocabulary
elective (ē lek´ tiv)
n. optional course

On the first day of school, Victor stood in line half an hour before he came to a wobbly card table. He was handed a packet of papers and a computer card on which he listed his one elective, French. He already spoke Spanish and English, but he thought some day he might travel to France, where it was cool; not like Fresno, where summer days reached 110 degrees in the shade. There were rivers in France and huge churches, and fair-skinned people everywhere, the way there were brown people all around Victor.

Besides, Teresa, a girl he had liked since they were in catechism classes at Saint Theresa's, was taking French, too. With any luck they would be in the same class. Teresa is going to be my girl this year, he promised himself as he left the gym full of students in their new fall clothes. She was cute. And good in math, too, Victor thought as he walked down the hall to his homeroom. He ran into his friend, Michael Torres, by the water fountain that never turned off.

They shook hands, *raza*-style, and jerked their heads at one another in a *saludo de vato.*[1] "How come you're making a face?" asked Victor.

"I ain't making a face, *ese.*[2] This is my face." Michael said his face had changed during the summer. He had read a *GQ*

---

1. **raza-style . . . saludo de vato** (sä lōō´ dō dä bä´ tō) Spanish gestures of greeting between friends.
2. **ese** (es´ ā) *n.* Spanish word for "man."

© Text Complexity Rubric

Seventh Grade		
Qualitative Measures	**Context/Knowledge Demands**	Contemporary, urban U.S.; familiar situation 1 ② 3 4 5
	Structure/Language Conventionality	Mostly short sentences and on-level vocabulary; some idioms 1 ② 3 4 5
	Levels of Meaning/ Purpose/Concepts	Accessible concept (young adults fitting in) 1 2 ③ 4 5
Quantitative Measures	**Text Length**	Word Count: 1,885
	Lexile	730L

magazine that his older brother had borrowed from the Book Mobile and noticed that the male models all had the same look on their faces. They would stand, one arm around a beautiful woman, and *scowl*. They would sit at a pool, their rippled stomachs dark with shadow, and *scowl*. They would sit at dinner tables, cool drinks in their hands, and *scowl*.

"I think it works," Michael said. He scowled and let his upper lip quiver. His teeth showed along with the ferocity of his soul. "Belinda Reyes walked by a while ago and looked at me," he said.

Victor didn't say anything, though he thought his friend looked pretty strange. They talked about recent movies, baseball, their parents, and the horrors of picking grapes in order to buy their fall clothes. Picking grapes was like living in Siberia,[3] except hot and more boring.

"What classes are you taking?" Michael said, scowling.

"French. How 'bout you?"

"Spanish. I ain't so good at it, even if I'm Mexican."

"I'm not either, but I'm better at it than math, that's for sure."

 **A tinny, three-beat bell** propelled students to their homerooms. The two friends socked each other in the arm and went their ways, Victor thinking, man, that's weird. Michael thinks making a face makes him handsome.

On the way to his homeroom, Victor tried a scowl. He felt foolish, until out of the corner of his eye he saw a girl looking at him. Umm, he thought, maybe it does work. He scowled with greater conviction.

In homeroom, roll was taken, emergency cards were passed out, and they were given a bulletin to take home to their parents. The principal, Mr. Belton, spoke over the crackling loudspeaker, welcoming the students to a new year, new experiences, and new friendships. The students squirmed in their chairs and ignored him. They were anxious to go to first period. Victor sat calmly, thinking of Teresa, who sat two rows away, reading a paperback novel. This would be his lucky year. She was in his homeroom, and would probably be in his English and math classes. And, of course, French.

The bell rang for first period, and the students herded noisily through the door. Only Teresa lingered, talking with the homeroom teacher.

---

3. **Siberia** (sī bir′ ē ə) *n.* region in northern Asia known for its harsh winters.

Vocabulary
scowl (skoul) *v.* look at someone or something in an angry or disapproving way

Vocabulary
conviction
(kən vik′ shən) *n.* belief

⑤ ✓ Reading Check

Why does Victor choose to study French?

Seventh Grade **291**

---

❹ Critical Thinking

Compare

1. Tell students that authors often include characters in their stories who provide contrast to the main character. They usually do this in order to highlight a particular characteristic of the main character.

2. After students read the bracketed passage, **ask** them how Victor and Michael are similar and different.

3. **Possible response:** Both Victor and Michael want girls to like them. Michael has decided that scowling is the way to get girls' attention. Unlike Michael, Victor is already interested in one particular girl, Teresa. Michael's plan, to attract girls by scowling, is funny and seems less likely to succeed than Victor's plan of taking a class in order to increase his chances that he will see Teresa often.

❺ Reading Check

Answer: Victor decides to study French because he would like to visit France one day, because he already speaks English and Spanish, and because a girl he likes is taking French.

ⓒ Text Complexity: Reader and Task Suggestions

Seventh Grade	
Preparing to Read the Text	**Leveled Tasks**
• Using the Background information on p. 290, discuss the role of foreign language instruction in the story. • In the story, Victor wants to impress a girl. Discuss actions young people take in such situations. Help students make predictions about the results of the boy's actions. For example, ask how girls will likely respond to bragging. • Guide students in using Multidraft Reading strategies (TE p. 289).	***Levels of Meaning*** If students will have difficulty with levels of meaning, have them first read to identify familiar aspects of Victor's crush on Teresa. Have them reread to identify untruthful actions Victor takes to impress Teresa. Clarify the actions and discuss their unpredictable outcome. ***Evaluating*** If students will not have difficulty interpreting levels of meaning, have them note as they read ways that the author uses humor to convey his message.

292 Short Stories

"So you think I should talk to Mrs. Gaines?" she asked the teacher. "She would know about ballet?"

"She would be a good bet," the teacher said. Then added, "Or the gym teacher, Mrs. Garza."

Victor lingered, keeping his head down and staring at his desk. He wanted to leave when she did so he could bump into her and say something clever.

He watched her on the sly. As she turned to leave, he stood up and hurried to the door, where he managed to catch her eye. She smiled and said, "Hi, Victor."

He smiled back and said, "Yeah, that's me." His brown face blushed. Why hadn't he said, "Hi, Teresa," or "How was your summer?" or something nice?

As Teresa walked down the hall, Victor walked the other way, looking back, admiring how gracefully she walked, one foot in front of the other. So much for being in the same class, he thought. As he trudged to English, he practiced scowling.

In English they reviewed the parts of speech. Mr. Lucas, a portly man, waddled down the aisle, asking, "What is a noun?"

"A person, place, or thing," said the class in unison.

"Yes, now somebody give me an example of a person—you, Victor Rodriguez."

"Teresa," Victor said automatically. Some of the girls giggled. They knew he had a crush on Teresa. He felt himself blushing again.

"Correct," Mr. Lucas said. "Now provide me with a place."

Mr. Lucas called on a freckled kid who answered, "Teresa's house with a kitchen full of big brothers."

After English, Victor had math, his weakest subject. He sat in the back by the window, hoping that he would not be called on. Victor understood most of the problems, but some of the stuff looked like the teacher made it up as she went along. It was confusing, like the inside of a watch.

After math he had a fifteen-minute break, then social studies, and, finally, lunch. He bought a tuna casserole with buttered rolls, some fruit cocktail, and milk. He sat with Michael, who practiced scowling between bites.

Girls walked by and looked at him.

"See what I mean, Vic?" Michael scowled. "They love it."

"Yeah, I guess so."

They ate slowly, Victor scanning the horizon for a glimpse of Teresa. He didn't see her. She must have brought lunch, he

thought, and is eating outside. Victor scraped his plate and left Michael, who was busy scowling at a girl two tables away.

The small, triangle-shaped campus bustled with students talking about their new classes. Everyone was in a sunny mood. Victor hurried to the bag lunch area, where he sat down and opened his math book. He moved his lips as if he were reading, but his mind was somewhere else. He raised his eyes slowly and looked around. No Teresa.

He lowered his eyes, pretending to study, then looked slowly to the left. No Teresa. He turned a page in the book and stared at some math problems that scared him because he knew he would have to do them eventually. He looked to the right. Still no sign of her. He stretched out lazily in an attempt to disguise his snooping.

Then he saw her. She was sitting with a girlfriend under a plum tree. Victor moved to a table near her and daydreamed about taking her to a movie. When the bell sounded, Teresa looked up, and their eyes met. She smiled sweetly and gathered her books. Her next class was French, same as Victor's.

They were among the last students to arrive in class, so all the good desks in the back had already been taken. Victor was forced to sit near the front, a few desks away from Teresa, while Mr. Bueller wrote French words on the chalkboard. The bell rang, and Mr. Bueller wiped his hands, turned to the class, and said, "*Bonjour.*"[4]

"*Bonjour,*" braved a few students.

"*Bonjour,*" Victor whispered. He wondered if Teresa heard him. Mr. Bueller said that if the students studied hard, at the end of the year they could go to France and be understood by the populace.

One kid raised his hand and asked, "What's 'populace'?"

"The people, the people of France."

Mr. Bueller asked if anyone knew French. Victor raised his hand, wanting to impress Teresa. The teacher beamed and said, "*Très bien. Parlez-vous français?*"[5]

---

4. **Bonjour** (bōn zhōōr´) French for "hello;" "good day."
5. **Très bien. Parlez-vous français?** (trā byan pär lā vōō´ frän sā´) French for "Very well. Do you speak French?"

> He sat in the back by the window, hoping that he would not be called on.

⑧ ✓ Reading Check

Who or what is Victor thinking of during lunch?

⑧ Reading Check

Answer: Victor is thinking about finding Teresa and hoping to get her attention.

Differentiated Instruction · for Universal Access

EL **Strategy for English Learners**

Explain that one use of hyphens in English is to combine two words to form one concept. Point out the following phrases: "three-beat bell" (p. 291), "fifteen-minute break" (p. 292), and "triangle-shaped campus" (p. 293). Each pair of hyphenated words is a compound adjective that describes the following noun. A "fifteen-minute break" is a break that lasts fifteen minutes. Have students practice creating compound adjectives.
Ask: What kind of jacket has a fleece lining?
Answer: A fleece-lined jacket.

Culturally Responsive Instruction

Culture Focus Refer students to the encounter between Victor and Michael on page 290. They shake hands *raza*-style and jerk their heads in the *saludo de vato,* gestures that reflect their cultural backgrounds, and Michael calls Victor *ese.* Discuss with students the benefit the boys get from using these gestures and this word. Then, discuss the benefit Victor tries to get out of pretending he speaks French. Have students compare the social value of knowing French with the value of knowing community language.

⑨ Literature in Context

Vocabulary Connection

1. Have a volunteer read the Literature in Context feature. If students are not familiar with the terms, have them check the footnotes that appear on p. 290. If you have Spanish speakers in your class, they may provide further insight.

2. Lead the class in a discussion of how students feel when they read stories or nonfiction articles that contain unfamiliar words and phrases from other languages. Students may suggest that they are interested in learning words from other languages. Others may feel impatient at having to look up new words.

3. Invite students to think of other words that originated in Spanish that are used frequently in English. Make a list of the words on the board.

4. If time allows, have students think of words from other languages that have made their way into English. Challenge students to think of a generalization about the words they have gathered. For example, do most of the words in the list seem to be related to food or leisure activities?

Connect to the Literature

Ask the Connect to the Literature question.
Possible response: Soto's use of Spanish helps readers "hear" the characters speak. It reminds readers that the characters share the bond of speaking two languages.

⑩ Critical Thinking

Analyze

1. After students read p. 294, **ask** them to recall what has happened to Victor.
   Answer: Victor tells his teacher he speaks French, because he wants to impress Teresa, but when the teacher speaks to him in French, Victor can only make up nonsense phrases.

2. **Ask** students to explain Victor's motivation.
   Answer: Victor is so eager to impress Teresa that he does not stop to think that he might have to say something in French.

294

---

⑨

LITERATURE IN CONTEXT

Vocabulary Connection

New English Words
At the beginning of the story, Victor and Michael shake hands *raza-style* and give each other a *saludo de vato*. These Spanish terms may be unfamiliar to many English speakers. However, the following words also originated in Spanish and are now very familiar in English.

- **tortilla:** a thin, flat, round bread made of cornmeal or flour and cooked on a griddle

- **fiesta:** a celebration or holiday

- **siesta:** a brief nap or rest taken after the noon meal

Connect to the Literature

How does Soto use Spanish to help him develop characters in the story?

294 Short Stories

Victor didn't know what to say. The teacher wet his lips and asked something else in French. The room grew silent. Victor felt all eyes staring at him. He tried to bluff his way out by making noises that sounded French.

"La me vave me con le grandma," he said uncertainly.

Mr. Bueller, wrinkling his face in curiosity, asked him to speak up.

Great rosebushes of red bloomed on Victor's cheeks. A river of nervous sweat ran down his palms. He felt awful. Teresa sat a few desks away, no doubt thinking he was a fool. Without looking at Mr. Bueller, Victor mumbled, "Frenchie oh wewe gee in September."

Mr. Bueller asked Victor to repeat what he had said.

"Frenchie oh wewe gee in September," Victor repeated.

Mr. Bueller understood that the boy didn't know French and turned away. He walked to the blackboard and pointed to the words on the board with his steel-edged ruler.

"*Le bateau,*" he sang.

"*Le bateau,*" the students repeated.

"*Le bateau est sur l'eau,*"[6] he sang.

"*Le bateau est sur l'eau.*"

Victor was too weak from failure to join the class. He stared at the board and wished he had taken Spanish, not French. Better yet, he wished he could start his life over. He had never been so embarrassed. He bit his thumb until he tore off a sliver of skin.

The bell sounded for fifth period, and Victor shot out of the room, avoiding the stares of the other kids, but had to return for his math book. He looked sheepishly at the teacher, who was erasing the board, then widened his eyes in terror at Teresa who stood in front of him. "I didn't know you knew French," she said. "That was good."

Mr. Bueller looked at Victor, and Victor looked back. Oh please, don't say anything, Victor pleaded with his eyes. I'll wash your car, mow your lawn, walk your dog—anything! I'll be your best student and I'll clean your erasers after school.

---

6. *Le bateau est sur l'eau* (lə bä tō′ ā sŏŏr lō) French for "The boat is on the water."

Vocabulary Development

ⓒ CCSS Language 6

Vocabulary Reinforcement
Students will benefit from additional examples and practice with the selection vocabulary words. Reinforce their comprehension with "show-you-know" sentences. The first part of the sentence uses the vocabulary word in an appropriate context. The second part of the sentence—the "show-you-know" part—clarifies the first. Model the strategy with this example using the selection vocabulary word *elective*:

> *I decided to sign up for drama as my elective; even though I did not have to take it, I am interested in the theater.*

Then give students sentence prompts like this one, and coach them in creating the clarification part.

> As she walked along the corridor, the woman *scowled* at the children who were running; _____.

Sample answer: she disapproved of running in the halls and showed it with her frowning face.

Mr. Bueller shuffled through the papers on his desk. He smiled and hummed as he sat down to work. He remembered his college years when he dated a girlfriend in borrowed cars. She thought he was rich because each time he picked her up he had a different car. It was fun until he had spent all his money on her and had to write home to his parents because he was broke.

Victor couldn't stand to look at Teresa. He was sweaty with shame. "Yeah, well, I picked up a few things from movies and books and stuff like that." They left the class together. Teresa asked him if he would help her with her French.

"Sure, anytime," Victor said.

"I won't be bothering you, will I?"

"Oh no, I like being bothered."

"*Bonjour*," Teresa said, leaving him outside her next class. She smiled and pushed wisps of hair from her face.

"Yeah, right, *bonjour*," Victor said. He turned and headed to his class. The rosebushes of shame on his face became bouquets of love. Teresa is a great girl, he thought. And Mr. Bueller is a good guy.

He raced to metal shop. After metal shop there was biology, and after biology a long sprint to the public library, where he checked out three French textbooks.

He was going to like seventh grade.

Idiom
What does the expression "he was broke" mean?

Spiral Review
Setting Does the setting help make this story appealing to readers? Explain.

Critical Thinking

 1. Key Ideas and Details (a) Why do you think Michael scowls? **(b) Compare and Contrast:** What is similar about Michael's scowling and Victor's pretending to speak French?

 2. Key Ideas and Details (a) Infer: How does Victor view Teresa? **(b) Support:** What examples from the story indicate his feelings?

 3. Integration of Knowledge and Ideas (a) Analyze: What does Victor probably learn from his experiences in seventh grade? **(b) Apply:** How can you apply this lesson to your own life?

 4. Integration of Knowledge and Ideas (a) How does Mr. Bueller help Victor avoid a conflict when he does not correct Victor's French skills? **(b)** How does this action help Victor be accepted by Teresa? *[Connect to the Big Question: Does every conflict have a winner?]*

Cite textual evidence to support your responses.

Seventh Grade **295**

⓫ Idiom

1. Read aloud the bracketed passage.

2. Remind students that Mr. Bueller is remembering a past experience that makes him sympathize with Victor's situation. Point out that he had fun until he "spent all his money on" the girl he liked.

3. **Ask** students the Idiom question. **Answer:** "He was broke" means that he did not have any money.

Spiral Review

Setting

1. Remind students that they studied the concept of setting in the Unit 2 Literary Analysis Workshop (pp. 200–215).

2. **Ask** students the Spiral Review question. **Possible response:** Yes, the setting is appealing to readers because everyone has been to school, so it is a familiar place.

ASSESS

Answers

Critical Thinking

Remind students to support their answers with evidence from the text.

1. (a) He thinks it will impress the girls. (b) Both characters pretend to be something they are not in order to impress girls.

2. (a) He thinks she is pretty and smart. (b) He is taken with her looks, her personality, and her mathematical ability.

3. (a) Victor learns that he needs to be careful about pretending, because he came so close to getting caught. (b) **Possible response:** It is important for me to be myself, because pretending to be someone else can cause trouble.

4. **Possible responses:** (a) Mr. Bueller helped Victor avoid an internal conflict between his desire to impress and feelings of embarrassment and regret. (b) By not exposing Victor's lie, Mr. Bueller helped Victor keep Teresa's respect. Students may point out that the outcome of the story suggests that everyone wins in this conflict.

295

MELTING POT

Anna Quindlen

⓬ Background

Melting Pot In Israel Zangwill's 1908 play, *The Melting Pot,* America was first called "The great Melting Pot where all the races of Europe are melting and reforming!" Over time, those people in the "melting pot" came to include immigrants from every part of the world. Although the phrase originally described a welcome breakdown of racial and national prejudices in order to form a homogeneous culture, it now suggests to some an unwelcome loss of ethnic identity. Some people prefer to refer to America as a mosaic—in which each piece retains its own identity while forming a united whole with others—instead of a melting pot.

⓭ Activating Prior Knowledge

Explain to students that in "Melting Pot," the author uses her childhood experiences to help make sense of the world in which she lives.
Ask students about stories they heard or experiences they had as children that have influenced them.
Possible response: Students may mention lessons children learn in nursery school or on the playground that prove valuable in later years.

Concept Connector ➡

Tell students they will return to the discussion of childhood lessons after they read the article.

⓮ About the Selection

The speaker of "Melting Pot" describes her changing urban neighborhood both from the viewpoint of an outsider who has arrived only recently and from the viewpoint of an insider who is the daughter of immigrants. She considers the idea of being accepted in a multicultural community:—how people regard their neighbors as "us" or "them," and how they may hold broad prejudices against some ethnic groups as a whole but relax the prejudices as they get to know individual members of those groups.

Vocabulary
fluent (flo͞o′ ənt) *adj.* able to write or speak easily and smoothly

My children are upstairs in the house next door, having dinner with the Ecuadorian family that lives on the top floor. The father speaks some English, the mother less than that. The two daughters are fluent in both their native and their adopted languages, but the youngest child, a son, a close friend of my two boys, speaks almost no Spanish. His parents thought it would be better that way. This doesn't surprise me; it was the way my mother was raised, American among Italians. I always suspected, hearing my grandfather talk about the "No Irish Need Apply" signs outside factories, hearing my mother talk about the

296 Short Stories

ⓒ Text Complexity Rubric

Melting Pot		
Qualitative Measures	Context/Knowledge Demands	1980s New York City; familiar situation 1 2 3 ④ 5
	Structure/Language Conventionality	Informal and conversational language; some idioms 1 2 ③ 4 5
	Levels of Meaning/ Purpose/Concepts	Challenging concept (broad historical perspective on community) 1 2 3 ④ 5
Quantitative Measures	Text Length	Word Count: 959
	Lexile	1070L

296

neighborhood kids, who called her greaseball, that the American fable of the melting pot was a myth. Here in our neighborhood it exists, but like so many other things, it exists only person-to-person.

The letters in the local weekly tabloid[1] suggest that everybody hates everybody else here, and on a macro level they do. The old-timers are angry because they think the new moneyed professionals are taking over their town. The professionals are tired of being blamed for the neighborhood's rising rents, particularly since they are the ones paying them. The old immigrants are suspicious of the new ones. The new ones think the old ones are bigots. Nevertheless, on a micro level most of us get along. We are friendly with the Ecuadorian family, with the Yugoslavs across the street, and with the Italians next door, mainly by virtue of our children's sidewalk friendships. It took awhile. Eight years ago we were the new people on the block, filling dumpsters with old plaster and lath, . . . (sitting) on the stoop with our demolition masks hanging around our necks like goiters.[2] We thought we could feel people staring at us from behind the sheer curtains on their windows. We were right.

---

1. **tabloid** (tab´ loid´) *n.* small newspaper.
2. **goiters** (goit´ ərz) *n.* swellings in the lower front of the neck caused by an enlarged thyroid gland.

Spiral Review
Setting What type of neighborhood does Quindlen live in? What details helped you answer?

Vocabulary
bigots (big´ əts) *n.* narrow-minded, prejudiced people

15 ✓ Reading Check
What attitude does Quindlen say most people have toward others who are new or different?

Spiral Review
Setting

1. Remind students that they studied the concept of setting in the Unit 2 Literary Analysis Workshop (pp. 200–215).

2. **Ask** students the first Spiral Review question.

   Possible response: She lives in a very diverse neighborhood.

3. **Ask** students the second Spiral Review question.

   Possible response: She describes all the different types of people who live in her neighborhood.

15 Reading Check

Answer: Many people mistrust strangers who are new to the neighborhood or have a background different from theirs.

Melting Pot **297**

© Text Complexity: Reader and Task Suggestions

Melting Pot

Preparing to Read the Text

- Use the Background information on p. 296 to introduce the melting pot and mosaic models for American culture.
- Explain that the essay hints at economic pressures causing changes in urban communities. Help students draw on prior knowledge to understand these pressures. For example, ask students why raising rents in a neighborhood might lead some older residents to move.
- Guide students in using Multidraft Reading strategies (TE p. 289).

Leveled Tasks

Knowledge Demands If students will have difficulty with context, have them read to identify familiar places and experiences in Quindlen's community. Have them reread to identify references to economic or cultural context that they find confusing.

Synthesizing If students will not have difficulty with context, have them note as they read ways that the author uses language to vividly describe the cultures of her community. For example, students may note descriptions of food and architecture.

This selection is available in interactive format in the **Enriched Online Student Edition**, online at **www.PHLitOnline.com**, which includes an interactive graphic organizer.

Infer

1. Have a volunteer read the bracketed paragraph aloud, pausing after each sentence.

2. Remind students of the elderly men's position in the neighborhood. On page 297, Quindlen wrote, "The old-timers are angry because they think the new money-eyed professionals are taking over their town."

3. **Ask:** students to infer how the men feel as they watch work being done on the new restaurant. Support your inference with details from the passage.
   Possible response: The men doubt that the new restaurant will last long and seem to hope it will fail. The details that they have grown up in this neighborhood, sit watching the construction, and place bets on how long the glass and the building will last support this inference.

4. Then, **ask:** Why do the men comment on the prices in the restaurant?
   Answer: They resent the people who can afford the expensive prices in the restaurant, which stands for the end of their ownership of the neighborhood.

My first apartment in New York was in a gritty warehouse district, the kind of place that makes your parents wince. A lot of old Italians lived around me, which suited me just fine because I was the granddaughter of old Italians. Their own children and grandchildren had moved to Long Island and New Jersey. All they had was me. All I had was them.

I remember sitting on a corner with a group of half a dozen elderly men, men who had known one another since they were boys sitting together on this same corner, watching a glazier install a great spread of tiny glass panes to make one wall of a restaurant in the ground floor of an old building across the street. The men laid bets on how long the panes, and the restaurant, would last. Two years later two of the men were dead, one had moved in with his married daughter in the suburbs, and the three remaining sat and watched dolefully as people waited each night for a table in the restaurant. "Twenty-two dollars for a piece of veal!" one of them would say, apropos of nothing.[3] But when I ate in the restaurant they never blamed me. "You're not one of them," one of the men explained. "You're one of me." It's an argument familiar to members of almost any embattled race or class: I like you, therefore you aren't like the rest of your kind, whom I hate.

Change comes hard in America, but it comes constantly. The butcher whose old shop is now an antiques store sits day after day outside the pizzeria here like a lost child. The old people across the street cluster together and discuss what kind of money they might be offered if the person who bought their building

"You're not one of them..."

3. **apropos** (ap´ rə pō´) **of nothing** without connection.

298 Short Stories

Vocabulary Development © CCSS Language 6

Words About Buildings and Construction

To describe her neighborhood, Quindlen uses terminology related to architecture and the building trade. Call out the following terms, and ask students to define them: *plaster* (p. 297), *lath* (p. 297), *warehouse* (p. 298), *glazier* (p. 298), *condominium* (p. 299), and *storefront* (p. 299). Write students' definitions on the board, and then have students check them in a dictionary. Then, ask students to explain in each case how full knowledge of the word's meaning helps them better appreciate the scene it is used to describe. For example, knowing that a *lath* is a strip of wood used as a foundation for plaster helps readers understand that when Quindlen throws out "plaster and lath," she is involved in ripping out old walls, a task that is difficult and dirty and that requires her to wear a mask.

wants to turn it into condominiums. The greengrocer stocks yellow peppers and fresh rosemary for the gourmands, plum tomatoes and broad-leaf parsley for the older Italians, mangoes for the Indians. He doesn't carry plantains, he says, because you can buy them in the bodega.[4]

Sometimes the baby slips out with the bath water. I wanted to throw confetti the day that a family of rough types who propped their speakers on their station wagon and played heavy metal music at 3:00 A.M. moved out. I stood and smiled as the seedy bar at the corner was transformed into a slick Mexican restaurant. But I liked some of the people who moved out at the same time the rough types did. And I'm not sure I have that much in common with the singles who have made the restaurant their second home.

Yet somehow now we seem to have reached a nice mix. About a third of the people in the neighborhood think of squid as calamari, about a third think of it as sushi, and about a third think of it as bait. Lots of the single people who have moved in during the last year or two are easygoing and good-tempered about all the kids. The old Italians have become philosophical about the new Hispanics, although they still think more of them should know English. The firebrand community organizer with the storefront on the block, the one who is always talking about people like us as though we stole our houses out of the open purse of a ninety-year-old blind widow, is pleasant to my boys.

---

4. **bodega** (bō dä´ gə) *n.* small, Hispanic grocery store.

> **Idiom**
> What do you think the expression "baby slips out with the bath water" really means?

Melting Pot **299**

⓱ Idiom

1. Have a volunteer read the bracketed section aloud.

2. Discuss the situation that Quindlen is describing in this section and analyze her emotional reaction to it. Point out to students that although she felt like celebrating when some of her "rough" neighbors moved out and also when a seedy bar was replaced by a slick new restaurant, she also felt sad when others had to leave the neighborhood. She doesn't really identify with the patrons of the slick new restaurant.

3. Then, **ask** students the Idiom question.
   Answer: It means that sometimes something valuable is accidentally thrown away along with something useless.

Fluency

Distribute copies of pages 298 and 299. Have students mark each comma with a highlighter. Remind students that when reading aloud, they should make a short pause for a comma and a longer pause for a period, a question mark, or an exclamation mark at the end of a sentence. Have students each read one paragraph. If a student does not pause at a period, or pauses too long, interrupt him or her and reread the sentence, modeling appropriate fluency. Then, have the student reread the sentence and continue to the end of the paragraph. After completing the pages, select several commas and discuss why they are used. For example, in the sentence on page 298 that begins, "Two years later," commas are used to separate elements in a series. Read the sentence aloud to the class, and discuss how the pauses provide an audible separation between distinct elements. They make it easier for the listener to follow what is being said.

Critical Thinking

Before students respond, you may wish to have them write a brief objective summary of the selection. As they answer the questions below, remind them to support their answers with evidence from the text.

1. (a) Groups include: new arrivals and long-time residents; children of past immigrants; and families and singles. (b) Most of the residents have seen a lot of changes in their neighborhood. (c) **Possible response:** The residents are united by common problems and by the ways in which they adapt to the changing neighborhood. Change can also divide them, as when old-time immigrants look on new arrivals as outsiders.

2. **Possible response:** Quindlen would suggest that being tolerant and interested in people from all backgrounds will help people get along.

3. (a) She is one of them—an interloper—because she is one of the young professionals who has moved into a neighborhood and changed its character; she is one of us—the oldtimers—because she is of immigrant Italian descent. (b) **Possible responses:** You can if you work at respecting both groups; You cannot, because you can't be two things at the same time. (c) **Possible response:** It suggests that there is a great mix of people in city neighborhoods.

4. **Possible response:** (a) They come from different backgrounds, sometimes speak different languages, have different financial resources, and have different attitudes and beliefs. These differences lead some groups to mistrust or dislike the others. (b) The author finds some aspect of almost each member of the community to relate to: the older Italian immigrants remind her of her grandparents and the new, moneyed professionals are similar to her professionally.

We MELT together, then draw apart.

Drawn in broad strokes, we live in a pressure cooker: oil and water, us and them. But if you come around at exactly the right time, you'll find members of all these groups gathered around complaining about the condition of the streets, on which everyone can agree. We melt together, then draw apart. I am the granddaughter of immigrants, a young professional—either an interloper[5] or a longtime resident, depending on your concept of time. I am one of them, and one of us.

---

5. **interloper** (in′ tər lō′ pər) *n.* one who intrudes on another.

Critical Thinking

Cite textual evidence to support your responses.

1. **Key Ideas and Details (a)** Identify the different groups in Quindlen's neighborhood. **(b) Connect:** What experiences do most of the residents share? **(c) Interpret:** How do these shared experiences both unite and divide the residents?

2. **Key Ideas and Details Draw Conclusions:** What advice would Quindlen give about how people of different cultures can get along?

3. **Integration of Knowledge and Ideas (a) Analyze:** How is Quindlen both "one of them" and "one of us"? **(b) Make a Judgment:** Do you think it is possible to belong to both groups? **(c) Apply:** What does this essay suggest about the way people live in city neighborhoods in the United States?

4. **Integration of Knowledge and Ideas (a)** How were the people in this neighborhood in conflict with one another? **(b)** How did the author find a way to be successful within the different cultural environments? *[Connect to the Big Question: Does every conflict have a winner?]*

300 Short Stories

Vocabulary Development

© CCSS Language 6

Vocabulary Knowledge Rating

When students have completed reading and discussing "Seventh Grade" and "Melting Pot," have them take out their **Vocabulary Knowledge Rating Chart.** Read the words aloud once more, and have students rate their knowledge of words again in the After Reading column. Clarify any words that are still problematic. Have students write their own definition and example or sentence in the appropriate column. Then, have students complete the Vocabulary Practice activities at the end of the selection. Encourage them to use the words in further discussion and written work about these selections. Remind students that they will be accountable for these words on the **Selection Test,** *Unit 2 Resources,* pp. 112–114 or 115–117.

Comparing Idioms

1. **Key Ideas and Details (a)** Identify two **idioms** in "Seventh Grade." **(b)** Explain the difference between the literal and intended meaning of each idiom.

2. **Key Ideas and Details** Identify and explain at least one idiom in "Melting Pot."

3. **Integration of Knowledge and Ideas** Choose an idiom from each selection. Then, think about how each idiom helps you either understand or enjoy the selection. Record your ideas in a chart like the one below.

	"Seventh Grade"	"Melting Pot"
Idiom		
How it helps my understanding or enjoyment		

Timed Writing

Explanatory Text: Essay

In an essay, compare and contrast to explain how idioms added to your interest as you read "Seventh Grade" and "Melting Pot." **(25 minutes)**

5-Minute Planner

1. Read the prompt carefully and completely.

2. Choose at least one idiom from each selection to support your response. Discuss both the literal and actual meaning of each idiom.

3. Explain how the writer's use of each idiom adds interest to the description of a character or situation. For example, think about how the idioms help you get to know the narrator in each selection.

4. Reread the prompt, and then draft your essay. Provide a concluding statement in which you make a judgment about which writer uses idioms more effectively.

Assessment Resources

Unit 2 Resources

L1 L2 EL Selection Test A, pp. 112–114. Administer Test A to less advanced students and English learners.

L3 L4 EL Selection Test B, pp. 115–117. Administer Test B to on-level and more advanced students.

L3 L4 Open-Book Test, pp. 109–111. As an alternative, give the Open-Book Test.

All Customizable Test Bank

All Self-tests
Students may prepare for the **Selection Test** by taking the **Self-test** online.

PHLit Online! All assessment resources are available at **www.PHLitOnline.com.**

Comparing Idioms

1. **Sample response:** (a) "This would be his <u>lucky year</u>"; "He watched her <u>on the sly</u>." (b) The literal meaning of the first idiom is that the year itself was lucky; the actual meaning is that he will be fortunate this year. The literal meaning of the second idiom is that a boy watched a girl on a "sly." The true meaning is, "He watched her sneakily."

2. **Sample response:** One idiom in "Melting Pot" is "Change comes hard." It means that change is painful and difficult.

3. **Sample response:**

"bump in into"	This idiom helps me enjoy the selection because it suggests a casual meeting, but I know Victor will turn such a meeting into a big deal.
"melting pot"	This idiom helps me understand the concept of many different people melting into one new nation.

Timed Writing

1. Review the prompt with students.

2. Have students use the 5-Minute Planner to structure their time. Guide them through the numbered points. For example, have students think about the difference between "bump into" and "meet."

3. Allow students 25 minutes to complete the assignment.

4. As students prewrite and draft, have them refer to their completed Comparing Idioms Graphic Organizer.

Six Traits Focus

✓ Ideas	Word Choice
✓ Organization	Sentence Fluency
Voice	Conventions

301

Introducing the Writing Assignment

Review the assignment and the criteria on the student page.

Connecting to Real-Life Writing

Point out to students that the basic elements of a response to literature appear in book and movie reviews.

 **Writing Workshop**
Work in Progress

If students have completed the Work-in-Progress assignments on pp. 247 and 279, suggest that they try to develop their Work-in-Progress ideas in a response to literature.

Prewriting/Planning Strategy

Introduce the prewriting strategy. Have students apply the strategy to choose a topic.

Six Traits Focus

✔ Ideas	Word Choice
✔ Organization	Sentence Fluency
Voice	Conventions

Writing Workshop

Write an Argument

Response to Literature: Review of a Short Story

Defining the Form In a **response to literature,** the writer develops an argument that addresses one or more aspects of a literary work. You might use elements of a literary response in a letter to an author, or in a book or movie review.

Assignment Choose a short story you feel strongly about and analyze what it means to you. Include these elements:

✔ a strong, *interesting focus* on an aspect of the short story

✔ a logical and consistent *organization*

✔ a *judgment* about the value of the work

✔ sufficient *support* for your ideas and claims

✔ a concluding statement that summarizes your argument

✔ error-free writing, including *correct verb tenses*

To preview the criteria on which your review may be judged, see the rubric on page 307.

 Writing Workshop: *Work in Progress*

Review the work you did on pages 247 and 279.

Prewriting/Planning Strategy

Find connections. After you have decided on a story, read or review the selection carefully to find a topic for your essay. Complete a chart like the one shown. Fill in each column by answering the corresponding question. Look over what you have written and highlight details that connect in ways that interest you. To create a focused topic, sum up the highlighted details in a sentence.

Characters	Settings	Actions	Motivations
Who did the action?	When or where was it done?	What was done?	Why was it done?

 Common Core State Standards

Writing
1. Write arguments to support claims with clear reasons and relevant evidence.
1.b. Support claim(s) with logical reasoning and relevant evidence, using credible sources and demonstrating an understanding of the topic or text.
1.c. Use words, phrases, and clauses to clarify the relationship among claim(s) and reasons.
1.d. Establish and maintain a formal style.
9. Draw evidence from literary or informational texts to support analysis, reflection, and research.
Language
5.c. Distinguish among the connotations of words with similar denotations.

Teaching Resources

The following resources can be used to enrich or extend the instruction.

All *Unit 2 Resources*
Writing Workshop, pp. 118, 119

All *Common Core Companion,*
pp. 191–198, 279–284; 339–342, 353–358

All *Professional Development Guidebook*
Rubrics for Self-Assessment: Response to Literature, pp. 224–225

All *Graphic Organizer Transparencies*
Rubric for Self-Assessment: Review of a Short Story, p. 55

 All resources are also available online at **www.PHLitOnline.com.**

WRITER'S TOOLBOX

| **Word Choice** | Ideas | Conventions | Sentence Fluency | Voice | Organization |

Finding the Perfect Word

Word choice is the specific language a writer selects in order to create a strong impression. Critics choose memorable words and phrases to emphasize their arguments and to grab readers' attention. Follow these tips as you write your review.

Developing Tone The tone of your writing reveals your attitude toward your audience or subject. Ask yourself:

- How did the plot of this short story make me feel?
- Did I like the characters or dislike them? Why?
- Would I recommend this story to others?

Write your answers to these questions in complete sentences. Then use your responses as you draft your review, using a formal style that is appropriate for a review.

Choosing Language As you write, use language that helps you develop your arguments and that accurately captures your feelings about an aspect of the story. Include colorful words, phrases, and comparisons. Consider the **connotations** of words, or the feelings and associations they convey, as well as their **denotations,** or meanings. For example, if you liked the climax of a story, you might describe it as *dramatic*. If you did not like it, you might describe it as *exaggerated*. Add examples and quotations to support your descriptions. The chart shows descriptive words that you might use.

> **PH WRITING COACH**
> Further instruction and practice are available in *Prentice Hall Writing Coach*.

Plot	Characters	Dialogue	Description
suspenseful predictable confusing	hideous flat intriguing	unrealistic engaging humorous	unique extensive uninteresting

Supporting Claims With Reasons Choose words that support your claims. For example, if you claim that a character is overly dramatic, you might use words that emphasize the character's hysterical reactions to an ordinary event.

Checking Language With a partner, review your word choices for fairness, accuracy, and consistency.

Applying Understanding by Design Principles

Clarifying Expected Outcomes: Using Rubrics

- Before students begin work on this assignment, have them preview the Rubric for Self-Assessment (p. 307) to know what is expected. A copy of this rubric appears in *Graphic Organizer Transparencies*, p. 72.

- Review the criteria in the Rubric with the class. Before students use the Rubric to assess their own writing, work with them to rate the Student Model (p. 306) using the Rubric.
- If you wish to assess students' descriptive essays with either a 4-point or a 6-point scoring rubric, see the *Professional Development Guidebook*, pp. 224–225.

Finding the Perfect Word

1. Introduce the writing skill, using the instruction on the student page.
2. Discuss the definitions, as well as the strategies for improving style.

Teaching the Writing Skill

1. To emphasize the difference between "word use" and "word choice," ask students to complete this sentence with the first word that comes to mind:

   The school was _____.

   Now, ask them to think of the one idea they want to convey about the school and then complete the sentence again. Emphasize that the first sentence is word use and may not have conveyed the same idea that the second sentence does.

2. Remind students that words make negative or positive impressions on the reader. Words such as *ridiculous, monstrous,* and *lazy* convey a negative tone, or feeling. Words such as *silly, huge* and *laid-back* can have the same basic definition but convey a more positive tone.

3. To help students check word choice, put students in groups of three or four. Have each student pass his or her paper to the person on his or her left, and set a timer for two minutes. Tell the class that they need to write five suggested changes in word choice on the paper they have in the two minutes. At the end of the time each person should pass the draft he or she has marked to the next person. This person has to choose another five words and suggest word changes. Continue until each paper has been returned to its original owner.

4. Tell students that as a reviewer, they must be both accurate and interesting. Remind students that using a thesaurus will help them find a precise or colorful word.

> **PH WRITING COACH**   Grade 7
>
> Students will find additional support for responding to literature in chapter 10.

❶ Activating Prior Knowledge

1. Prepare an **Anticipation Guide** (*Professional Development Guidebook*, pp. 36–38) with the following statements:

   • There are no free gifts.

   • Kind people are usually happy.

   • If you love someone, you do what he or she wants.

2. Give students a copy of the pre-pared **Anticipation Guide** and have students mark their responses in the Me column. Have students discuss the statements and mark the Guide again in the Group column.

3. For further guidance, use the *Classroom Strategies and Teaching Routines* card for **Anticipation Guides**.

Concept Connector ➡

Students will return to the **Anticipation Guide** after reading.

Individual Activity

Ask students to recall other literary works that feature swans, such as Hans Christian Andersen's "The Ugly Duckling." Urge students to read one or more of these works and note the swan's symbolic meaning.

❷ About the Selection

In "The Third Wish," Mr. Peters frees a swan entangled in the brush. When the swan changes into the King of the Forest, Mr. Peters receives three wishes. First, he wishes for a wife and marries Leita. Mr. Peters soon learns that Leita used to be a swan and misses her earlier life. Seeing his wife unhappy, Mr. Peters must decide how to use his wishes.

❸ Critical Viewing

Possible response: Details such as the purple trees and the designs in the water suggest that this story has elements of fantasy in it.

❹ Conflict and Resolution

Ask the Conflict and Resolution question. **Answer:** Mr. Peters tries to rescue the swan without it injuring him.

The Third Wish

Joan Aiken

❶
❷

❸ ▶ **Critical Viewing**
What details of this picture could help you predict that this story has elements of fantasy? **[Connect]**

Conflict and Resolution ❹
What external conflict does Mr. Peters face after he finds the swan?

ONCE THERE WAS A MAN WHO WAS DRIVING IN HIS CAR AT DUSK ON A SPRING EVENING THROUGH PART OF THE FOREST OF SAVERNAKE. HIS NAME WAS MR. PETERS. THE PRIMROSES WERE JUST BEGINNING BUT THE TREES WERE STILL BARE, AND IT WAS COLD; THE BIRDS HAD STOPPED SINGING AN HOUR AGO.

As Mr. Peters entered a straight, empty stretch of road he seemed to hear a faint crying, and a struggling and thrashing, as if somebody was in trouble far away in the trees. He left his car and climbed the mossy bank beside the road. Beyond the bank was an open slope of beech trees leading down to thorn bushes through which he saw the gleam of water. He stood a moment waiting to try and discover where the noise was coming from, and presently heard a rustling and some strange cries in a voice which was almost human—and yet there was something too hoarse about it at one time and too clear and sweet at another. Mr. Peters ran down the hill and as he neared the bushes he saw something white among them which was trying to extricate[1] itself; coming closer he found that it was a swan that had become entangled in the thorns growing on the bank of the canal.

The bird struggled all the more frantically as he approached, looking at him with hate in its yellow eyes, and when he took hold of it to free it, it hissed at him, pecked him, and thrashed dangerously with its wings which were powerful enough to break his arm. Nevertheless he managed to release it from the thorns, and carrying it tightly with one arm, holding the snaky head well away with

1. **extricate** (eks′ tri kāt′) *v.* set free.

312 Short Stories

Thematic Vocabulary: The Big Question

As students are discussing "The Third Wish," encourage them to use the thematic vocabulary presented in Introducing the Big Question, pp. 198–199. You might guide them with sentence starters like these:

1. The *challenge* that Mr. Peters faces in making three wishes is . . .

2. One *obstacle* to Leita's happiness is . . .

3. In order to give Leita what she seems to *desire,* Mr. Peters must . . .

4. The *compromise* that Mr. Peters and Leita make requires them to . . .

5. Mr. Peters' *understanding attitude* about Leita's situation suggests that he . . .

The Third Wish 313

Swan Imagery
Swans are a common feature of myths, fairytales, and fiction from across the globe. Swans that transform into young women or men appear in the folklore of many countries in Europe, and even as far away as Japan. In Celtic mythology, Aengus was the Irish god of love who fell in love with a young woman named Caer who was magically turned into a swan. Aengus turned into a swan as well so that he could be with her. In the ballet *Swan Lake* by Russian composer Pyotr Ilich Tchaikovsky, a Prince falls in love with a girl named Odette who has been enchanted to turn into a swan during the daytime and return to human form at night. Many cultures have their own stories of humans who transform into swans, with the swan often acting as a representation of love and loyalty.

Differentiated
Instruction   for Universal Access

Strategy for Special-Needs Students
To give students a context for the story and help them see how to make inferences about characters, show them **Reading Skill Graphic Organizer A** (*Graphic Organizer Transparencies*, p. 56) for "The Third Wish." The partially filled-in graphic organizer will help students understand the process of making inferences. They can use it as a model for making their own inferences about characters as they read.

Strategy for Less Proficient Readers
Have students clarify events by constructing flowcharts of the story's progression. Tell students that they should record only main events in their charts. Encourage students to add to their flowcharts as they read. Consider having them work in pairs and check each other's work as they proceed.

PHLit Online!

This selection is available in interactive format in the **Enriched Online Students Edition**, online at **www.PHLitOnline.com**, which includes a thematically related video with writing prompt and an interactive graphic organizer.

❻ Critical Thinking

Analyze

1. Read the bracketed passage aloud. **Ask** students what mysterious event occurs.
   Answer: The swan changes into a little man dressed in green and wearing a golden crown.

2. **Ask** students to identify elements in the story that hint at this mysterious event before it occurs.
   Possible response: Students may suggest that the description of the swan's cries as sounding almost human alludes to the swan's having magical power.

Spiral Review

Plot

1. Students studied plot in the Unit 2 Literary Analysis Workshop (pp. 200–215).

2. **Ask** the first Spiral Review question. **Possible response:** The wishes will be the rising action of the story.

3. **Ask** the second Spiral Review question. **Possible response:** The warning lets readers know that there will be a problem later in the story.

❼ Connecting to the Big Question

1. Point out that when a conflict is internal, the person experiencing it may end up as both winner and loser. People often experience internal conflicts between the urge to do something and the knowledge of possible risks in the action.

2. Have students read the bracketed passage. **Ask:** How does pricking himself with the thorn reveal Mr. Peters' internal conflict about how to use his wishes?
   Possible response: By pricking himself, Mr. Peters shows he knows how hard it will be to keep from using the wishes rashly.

3. **Ask** students: How does Mr. Peters "win" in this small conflict? How does he lose?
   Possible response: He wins by controlling his urge to be rash. He loses by getting a pricked tongue.

314

❻

Vocabulary
verge (vʉrj)
n. edge; brink

dabbling (dab´ ling)
v. wetting by dipping, splashing, or paddling in the water

presumptuous
(prē zump´ cho̅o̅ əs)
adj. overconfident; lacking respect

Spiral Review
Plot The King of the Forest grants Mr. Peters three wishes, but not without a warning. How does granting the wishes advance the plot? How does the warning hint at how the plot might develop?

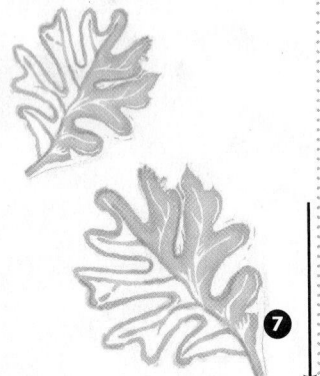

❼

---

the other hand (for he did not wish his eyes pecked out), he took it to the verge of the canal and dropped it in.

The swan instantly assumed great dignity and sailed out to the middle of the water, where it put itself to rights with much dabbling and preening, smoothing its feathers with little showers of drops. Mr. Peters waited, to make sure that it was all right and had suffered no damage in its struggles. Presently the swan, when it was satisfied with its appearance, floated in to the bank once more, and in a moment, instead of the great white bird, there was a little man all in green with a golden crown and long beard, standing by the water. He had fierce glittering eyes and looked by no means friendly.

"Well, Sir," he said threateningly, "I see you are presumptuous enough to know some of the laws of magic. You think that because you have rescued—by pure good fortune—the King of the Forest from a difficulty, you should have some fabulous reward."

"I expect three wishes, no more and no less," answered Mr. Peters, looking at him steadily and with composure.[2]

"Three wishes, he wants, the clever man! Well, I have yet to hear of the human being who made any good use of his three wishes—they mostly end up worse off than they started. Take your three wishes then"—he flung three dead leaves in the air—"don't blame me if you spend the last wish in undoing the work of the other two."

Mr. Peters caught the leaves and put two of them carefully in his briefcase. When he looked up, the swan was sailing about in the middle of the water again, flicking the drops angrily down its long neck.

Mr. Peters stood for some minutes reflecting on how he should use his reward. He knew very well that the gift of three magic wishes was one which brought trouble more often than not, and he had no intention of being like the forester who first wished by mistake for a sausage, and then in a rage wished it on the end of his wife's nose, and then had to use his last wish in getting it off again. Mr. Peters had most of the things which he wanted and was very content with his life. The only thing that troubled him was that he was a little lonely, and had no companion for his old age. He decided to use his first wish and to keep the other two in case of an emergency. Taking a thorn he pricked his tongue with

---

2. **composure** (kəm pō´ zhər) *n.* calmness of mind.

314 Short Stories

Selection Vocabulary Reinforcement
Students will benefit from additional examples and practice with the selection vocabulary words. Reinforce their comprehension with "show-you-know" sentences. The first part of the sentence uses the vocabulary word in an appropriate context. The second part of the sentence—the "show-you-know" part—clarifies the first. Model the strategy with this example for *presumptuous*. Say to students:

A movie star we saw in Hollywood was really *presumptuous;* he acted like we were just dying for his autograph.

Then, give students these sentence prompts, and coach them in creating the clarification part.

1. Her decision was quite *rash;* _____.
   Sample answer: she walked out of school with no thought for the consequences.

2. A *remote* location has some advantages; _____.
   Sample answer: it's never crowded, and you have a lot of privacy.

it, to remind himself not to utter **rash** wishes aloud. Then holding the third leaf and gazing round him at the dusky undergrowth, the primroses, great beeches and the blue-green water of the canal, he said:

"I wish I had a wife as beautiful as the forest."

A tremendous quacking and splashing broke out on the surface of the water. He thought that it was the swan laughing at him. Taking no notice he made his way through the darkening woods to his car, wrapped himself up in the rug and went to sleep.

When he awoke it was morning and the birds were beginning to call. Coming along the track towards him was the most beautiful creature he had ever seen, with eyes as blue-green as the canal, hair as dusky as the bushes, and skin as white as the feathers of swans.

"Are you the wife that I wished for?" asked Mr. Peters.

"Yes, I am," she replied. "My name is Leita."

She stepped into the car beside him and they drove off to the church on the outskirts of the forest, where they were married. Then he took her to his house in a **remote** and lovely valley and showed her all his treasures—the bees in their white hives, the Jersey cows, the hyacinths, the silver candlesticks, the blue cups and the luster bowl for putting primroses in. She admired everything, but what pleased her most was the river which ran by the foot of his garden.

"Do swans come up there?" she asked.

"Yes, I have often seen swans there on the river," he told her, and she smiled.

Leita made him a good wife. But as time went by Mr. Peters began to feel that she was not happy. She seemed restless, wandered much in the garden, and sometimes when he came back from the fields he would find the house empty and she would return after half an hour or so with no explanation of where she had been. On these occasions she was always especially tender and would put out his slippers to warm and cook his favorite dish—Welsh rarebit[3] with wild strawberries—for supper.

One evening he was returning home along the river path when he saw Leita in front of him, down by the water. A swan had sailed up to the verge and she had her arms round its neck and the swan's head rested against her cheek. She was

---

3. **Welsh rarebit** a dish of melted cheese served on crackers or toast.

The Third Wish **315**

Vocabulary

rash (rash) *adj.* too hasty

remote (ri mōt´) *adj.* far away from anything else

Conflict and Resolution
What inner conflict is resolved for Mr. Peters when he gets a wife?

Make Inferences On what details does Mr. Peters base his inference that Leita is not happy?

 **Reading Check**
⑩ What happens after Mr. Peters makes his first wish?

---

❽ Conflict and Resolution

1. Have students **review** what they know about inner conflict.
   Answer: An inner conflict happens within a character; it is a struggle to overcome opposing feelings, beliefs, needs, or desires.

2. Remind students that when you resolve a conflict, you settle it in some way. Then, **ask** students what single dissatisfaction Mr. Peters has in life.
   Answer: He wants a companion.

3. Read the bracketed passage aloud. **Ask** students to answer the Conflict and Resolution question.
   Answer: He stops feeling lonely and stops worrying about growing old without a companion. He has someone to share his treasures with.

❾ Make Inferences

1. Have students read the bracketed paragraph. **Ask** students to list details about Leita in the paragraph.
   Possible response: She seems restless and sometimes disappears without explanation. When she returns, she is especially nice to him.

2. **Ask** the Make Inferences question on the student page.
   Answer: Mr. Peters bases his inference on her restlessness and her disappearances. Her restlessness shows that she wants to be somewhere else; she is not content.

▶ **Monitor Progress:** Review students' graphic organizers to ensure that they are making reasonable inferences.

▶ **Reteach:** If students have difficulty following Mr. Peters' inference, have a volunteer act out restless behavior. Guide students in understanding that such behavior indicates discontent.

❿ Reading Check

Answer: He goes to sleep, and the next morning Leita appears from the forest prepared to marry him.

Fluency

Distribute copies of pages 314 and 315. Have students take turns reading paragraphs aloud as a partner marks areas of difficulty, paying particular attention to mispronounced words. Collect students' marked-up copies of the pages, and review problem words or passages with the class. Focus on these possible problems: If students have mispronounced words such as *angrily* and *forester* (p. 314) and *dusky* (p. 315), point out that these words are similar to, but not the same as, the words *angry*, *forest*, and *dusty*. Cover up the letters *il* in *angrily* and *er* in *forester* to highlight the difference. Write the word *dusky* on the board, then write the letter *t* on a sticky note. Add and remove the sticky note from *dusky* to form *dusty* and highlight the difference. Lead students in pronouncing each word correctly.

⓫ Literature in Context

Mythology Connection The constellation Cygnus (Latin for "swan") is often pictured flying south, down the Milky Way. It may be observed from both the northern and southern hemispheres. Cygnus has another name, the Northern Cross, that comes from the cross shape formed by its brightest stars. From the late Middle Ages through the Early Modern period, people in Europe sometimes called the constellation Galina ("hen"). It was also known as the Cross of Calvary, at a time when Church authorities sought to rid the sky of pagan imagery.

Connect to the Literature
Have students read the Literature in Context feature, and present the additional background information above. Then, remind students that fairy tales, such as "The Third Wish," often include magic, spells, and charms. Point out that, in "The Third Wish," Leita and her sister were unhappily separated. Finally, **ask** students the Connect to the Literature question.

Answer: In both stories, humans are changed into swans (or swans into humans). Each story involves separation, and each includes a fierce and powerful character (Zeus and the King of the Forest).

⓫ **LITERATURE IN CONTEXT**

Mythology Connection

A Star Is Born The graceful, noble swan has been celebrated in the myths and literature of many cultures. It is also visible in the skies as a constellation, Cygnus the Swan.

In one version of how the constellation came to be, Phaethon, a human son of Apollo the sun god, borrowed his father's chariot. Phaethon drove dangerously, and to stop him, Zeus hurled a thunderbolt at him. It killed him instantly, and he fell from the sky.

Phaethon's friend Cygnus searched the river for him. As Apollo watched him dive in, he thought Cygnus resembled a swan. When Cygnus died of grief, Apollo took pity and changed him into a swan, placing him forever among the stars.

Connect to the Literature

What similarities can you find between the story of Cygnus and "The Third Wish"?

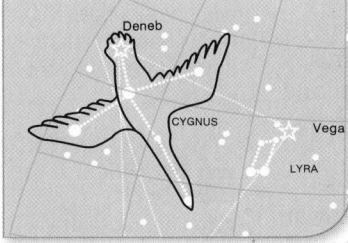

---

weeping, and as he came nearer he saw that tears were rolling, too, from the swan's eyes.

"Leita, what is it?" he asked, very troubled.

"This is my sister," she answered. "I can't bear being separated from her."

Now he understood that Leita was really a swan from the forest, and this made him very sad because when a human being marries a bird it always leads to sorrow.

"I could use my second wish to give your sister human shape, so that she could be a companion to you," he suggested.

"No, no," she cried, "I couldn't ask that of her."

"Is it so very hard to be a human being?" asked Mr. Peters sadly.

"Very, very hard," she answered.

"Don't you love me at all, Leita?"

"Yes, I do, I do love you," she said, and there were tears in her eyes again. "But I missed the old life in the forest, the cool grass and the mist rising off the river at sunrise and the feel of the water sliding over my feathers as my sister and I drifted along the stream."

"Then shall I use my second wish to turn you back into a swan again?" he asked, and his tongue pricked to remind him of the old King's words, and his heart swelled with grief inside him.

"Who will take care of you?"

"I'd do it myself as I did before I married you," he said, trying to sound cheerful.

She shook her head. "No, I could not be as unkind to you as that. I am partly a swan, but I am also partly a human being now. I will stay with you."

Poor Mr. Peters was very distressed on his wife's account and did his best to make her life happier, taking her for drives in the car, finding beautiful music for her to listen to on the radio, buying clothes for her and even suggesting a trip round the world. But she said no to that; she would prefer to stay in their own house near the river.

He noticed that she spent more and more time baking wonderful cakes—jam puffs, petits fours, eclairs and meringues. One day he saw her take a basketful down to the

---

Vocabulary Development

Vocabulary Knowledge Rating
When students have completed reading and discussing "The Third Wish," have them take out their **Vocabulary Rating Chart** for this selection. Read the words aloud once more and have students rate their knowledge of the words again in the After Reading column. Clarify any words that are still problematic. Have students write their own definition and example or sentence in the appropriate

column. Then, have students complete the Vocabulary Practice activities at the end of the selection. Encourage students to use the words in further discussion and written work about this selection. Remind them that they will be accountable for these words on the **Selection Test,** *Unit 2 Resources,* pp. 138–140 or 141–143.

river and he guessed that she was giving them to her sister.

He built a seat for her by the river, and the two sisters spent hours together there, communicating in some wordless manner. For a time he thought that all would be well, but then he saw how thin and pale she was growing.

One night when he had been late doing the account he came up to bed and found her weeping in her sleep and calling:

"Rhea! Rhea! I can't understand what you say! Oh, wait for me, take me with you!"

Then he knew that it was hopeless and she would never be happy as a human. He stooped down and kissed her goodbye, then took another leaf from his notecase, blew it out of the window, and used up his second wish.

Next moment instead of Leita there was a sleeping swan lying across the bed with its head under its wing. He carried it out of the house and down to the brink of the river, and then he said, "Leita! Leita!" to waken her, and gently put her into the water. She gazed round her in astonishment for a moment, and then came up to him and rested her head lightly against his hand; next instant she was flying away over the trees towards the heart of the forest.

He heard a harsh laugh behind him, and turning round saw the old King looking at him with a malicious expression.

"Well, my friend! You don't seem to have managed so wonderfully with your first two wishes, do you? What will you do with the last? Turn yourself into a swan? Or turn Leita back into a girl?"

"I shall do neither," said Mr. Peters calmly. "Human beings and swans are better in their own shapes."

But for all that he looked sadly over towards the forest where Leita had flown, and walked slowly back to his house.

Next day he saw two swans swimming at the bottom of the garden, and one of them wore the gold chain he had given Leita after their marriage; she came up and rubbed her head against his hand.

Mr. Peters and his two swans came to be well known in that part of the country; people used to say that he talked to swans and they understood him as well as his neighbors. Many people were a little frightened of him. There was a story that once when thieves tried to break into his house they were set upon by two huge white birds which carried them off bodily and dropped them into the river.

Conflict and Resolution

Beyond what he has already done to resolve his wife's conflict, what else do you suggest Mr. Peters could do?

Vocabulary

malicious (mə lish′ əs) *adj.* hateful; spiteful

13 ✓ Reading Check

Why does Leita want to be a swan again?

The Third Wish **317**

12 **Conflict and Resolution**

1. Review with students the definition of *internal conflict*—"a struggle between opposing forces within a person." Then, **ask** students to restate Leita's conflict. **Possible response:** She misses her swan sister Rhea terribly, but she also loves Mr. Peters and wants to stay with him as a human being.

2. Have a volunteer read the bracketed passage. **Ask** students to list the steps Mr. Peters has already taken to resolve Leita's conflict. **Possible response:** He offers to wish to turn her back into a swan, takes her for drives, plays beautiful music for her, buys clothes for her, suggests a trip, and builds a seat by the river.

3. **Ask** the Conflict and Resolution question on the student page. **Possible response:** Mr. Peters could change Leita back into a swan without her consent. He could wish that she forget her life as a swan. He could change Rhea into a human.

13 **Reading Check**

Answer: She misses her swan sister Rhea.

Concept Connector

Anticipation Guide

Have students return to their **Anticipation Guides** and respond to the statements again in the After Reading column. They may do this individually or in their original pairs or groups. Then, lead a class discussion, probing for what students have learned that confirms or invalidates each statement. Encourage students to cite specific details, quotations, or other evidence from the text to support their responses to each statement.

Writing About the Big Question

Have students compare their responses to the sentence starters they completed before reading the story with their ideas afterward. Ask them to explain whether their thoughts have changed.

Reading Skill Graphic Organizer

Ask students to review the graphic organizers they completed to make inferences about characters while reading. Then, have students share their graphic organizers and the inferences they made about other characters.

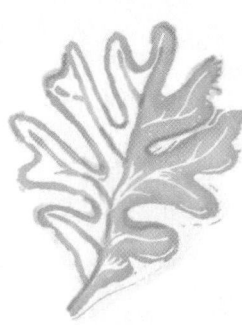

Make Inferences
What inferences can you make from ⓮ knowing what Mr. Peters held in his hands when he died?

As Mr. Peters grew old everyone wondered at his contentment. Even when he was bent with rheumatism[4] he would not think of moving to a drier spot, but went slowly about his work, with the two swans always somewhere close at hand.

Sometimes people who knew his story would say to him: "Mr. Peters, why don't you wish for another wife?"

"Not likely," he would answer serenely. "Two wishes were enough for me, I reckon. I've learned that even if your wishes are granted they don't always better you. I'll stay faithful to Leita."

One autumn night, passers-by along the road heard the mournful sound of two swans singing. All night the song went on, sweet and harsh, sharp and clear. In the morning Mr. Peters was found peacefully dead in his bed with a smile of great happiness on his face. In his hands, which lay clasped on his breast, were a withered leaf and a white feather.

---

4. **rheumatism** (roo′ mə tiz′ əm) *n.* pain and stiffness of the joints and muscles.

Critical Thinking

Cite textual evidence to support your responses.

ⓒ 1. **Key Ideas and Details** (a) How does Mr. Peters get the opportunity to ask for three wishes? (b) **Reflect:** How did you think Mr. Peters's wishing would turn out? Was your prediction correct?

ⓒ 2. **Key Ideas and Details** (a) How does Mr. Peters use his first wish? (b) **Speculate:** Why do you think he does not wish for riches?

ⓒ 3. **Key Ideas and Details** (a) **Make a Judgment:** Do you think Mr. Peters used his wishes wisely? (b) **Support:** What evidence from the story makes you feel that way?

ⓒ 4. **Integration of Knowledge and Ideas** **Apply:** Many cultures have traditional tales about wishes that do not work out. Why do you think this kind of story is so common?

ⓒ 5. **Integration of Knowledge and Ideas** (a) Do you think Mr. Peters made the right decision to help him resolve his internal conflict? (b) What story details support your response? *[Connect to the Big Question: Does every conflict have a winner?]*

318 Short Stories

Reading Skill: Make Inferences

1. List details that support the **inference** that Mr. Peters loves Leita more than he loves himself.

2. List details that support the inference that Leita still loves Mr. Peters even after changing back to a swan.

3. List details that suggest that Mr. Peters is not afraid to die.

Literary Analysis: Conflict and Resolution

© **4. Key Ideas and Details (a)** What **conflict** does Mr. Peters's first wish introduce? **(b)** What **resolution** does Mr. Peters find for the conflict?

© **5. Key Ideas and Details** On a chart like the one shown, identify two smaller conflicts that build toward Mr. Peters's main conflict, and tell how each is resolved.

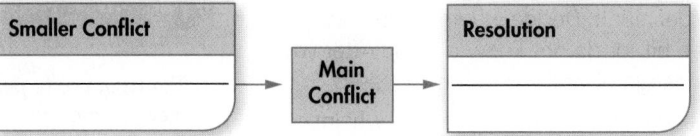

Vocabulary

© **Acquisition and Use** Answer each question, and explain your response.

1. To people in your school, does Australia seem *remote*?
2. Does it take a long time to make a *rash* decision?
3. What would you do if you faced a *malicious* person?
4. Is it safe to stand on the *verge* of a steep cliff?
5. Is it *presumptuous* of a host to invite guests to a party?
6. If you see someone *dabbling* in a pool, is he in danger?

Word Study Use what you know about the **Latin prefix mal-** to explain your answer to each question.

1. If something is *malodorous*, does it smell good?
2. What kind of physical *malady* might a player have after a football game?

Word Study

The **Latin prefix mal-** means "bad."

Apply It Explain how the prefix contributes to the meanings of these words. Consult a dictionary if necessary.

malfunction
maladjusted
malnutrition

The Third Wish **319**

Word Study
Sample answers:
1. No, if something is *malodorous*, it has a <u>bad</u> odor.
2. A football player might have a *malady*, or <u>bad</u> physical condition, such as sore muscles, after playing a game.

Word Study: Apply It
Sample answers:
A *malfunction* is a <u>bad</u> or improper function. Someone who is *maladjusted* has adjusted <u>badly</u>. Someone with *malnutrition* suffers from <u>bad</u> nutrition.

Answers

Reading Skill

1. He uses his second wish for her benefit instead of for his own. He declines to take another wife.

2. She spends much time with him. She protects him and mourns his death.

3. He does not use his last wish to avoid death. He dies with a smile on his face.

Literary Analysis

4. (a) Conflict arises when Leita reveals that she misses being a swan. (b) Mr. Peters resolves the conflict by giving Leita her old life back.

5. Two smaller conflicts are introduced: Mr. Peters suffers from loneliness; Leita doesn't want to leave Mr. Peters. The resolution of the first conflict is that Mr. Peters wishes for and receives a wife. The second conflict is resolved by Mr. Peters reassuring Leita that he will be all right.

   For other sample answers, see *Graphic Organizer Transparencies*, **Literary Analysis Graphic Organizer A, p. 59,** and the **Additional Answers** section.

Vocabulary
Acquisition and Use
Sample answers:

1. Yes, Australia seems <u>remote</u> to people in the Americas because it is very far away.

2. No, a <u>rash</u> decision takes very little time because it is made without consideration.

3. I would get away from a <u>malicious</u> person, who would probably be mean.

4. No, it is not safe to stand on the <u>verge</u> of a cliff because you might fall off the edge.

5. No, it's not <u>presumptuous</u> for a host to invite guests. Inviting guests is what a host does.

6. No, <u>dabbling</u> in a pool is just splashing about, so it is not dangerous, unlike taking a deep dive.

319

Skills instruction for the Reading Skill and the Literary Analysis concept for this selection appears on p. 309.

❶ Writing About the Big Question

1. Review the assignment with the class.

2. Remind students that even close friends can have conflicts, whether in emotional or even in physical form.

3. Have students complete the sentence starters. Review responses as a class. (**Sample answers:** When close friends <u>compete</u>, they may be unsure if they want to win or lose. <u>Conflicts</u> between friends can create feelings of confusion and frustration.)

4. Remind students that their answers will help them think about the Big Question, "Does every conflict have a winner?"

While You Read

Tell students that as they read, they should look for internal conflicts that each character faces.

❷ Vocabulary

1. Have students preview the selection vocabulary.

2. For each word, have students say the word aloud.

3. Then, use the word in a sentence that defines the word.

4. Finally, repeat your definitional sentence or a similar sentence with the word missing and have the class "fill in the blank" chorally. Here is one example:

   Something that is <u>perpetual</u> is constant and unending. A hummingbird flits so restlessly from flower to flower that it appears to be in [students say "perpetual"] motion.

❸ Word Study

1. Introduce the skill, using the instruction in the box.

2. Ask students to guess the meaning of the word *pervaded* in this sentence, given their knowledge of *per-*: The smell of roses <u>pervaded</u> the room. (**Answer:** spread throughout)

Making Connections | Amigo Brothers

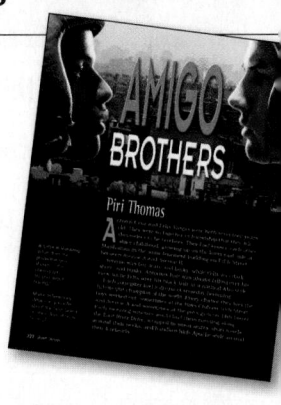

Does every *conflict* have a winner?

❶ Writing About the Big Question

In "Amigo Brothers," two good friends compete against each other in a boxing match. Use these sentence starters to develop your ideas about the Big Question.

When close friends **compete**, _____.

Conflicts between friends can create feelings of _____.

While You Read Look for internal conflicts in each character as the story builds up to the big fight.

❷ Vocabulary

Read each word and its definition. Decide whether you know the word well, know it a little bit, or do not know it at all. After you read, see how your knowledge of each word has increased.

- **devastating** (dev′ ə stāt iŋ) *adj.* destructive; overwhelming (p. 323) *A devastating storm destroyed the town. devastate v. devastation n. devastating v.*

- **perpetual** (pər pech′ ōō əl) *adj.* constant; unending (p. 326) *Toddlers are in perpetual motion, never standing still. perpetually adv. perpetuate v. perpetuity n.*

- **dignitaries** (dig′ nə tər′ ēz) *n.* people holding high positions or offices (p. 327) *The people honored the dignitaries by giving them the best seats. dignitary n. dignify v. dignified adj.*

- **improvised** (im′ prə vīzd) *v.* composed or performed on the spur of the moment (p. 327) *Working without a script, they improvised the entire play. improvisation n. improvising v.*

- **dispelled** (di speld′) *v.* driven away; made to disappear (p. 329) *Luckily, my worries were dispelled by the good news. dispel v. dispelling v.*

- **evading** (ē vād′ iŋ) *v.* avoiding (p. 330) *We hid behind the fence, evading the bullies. evade v. evasive adj. evasively adv.*

320 Short Stories

❸ Word Study

The **Latin prefix *per-*** means "through" or "completely."

In this story, Antonio imagines **perpetual** boxing motions, motions that are unending throughout the night.

Vocabulary Development

Vocabulary Knowledge Rating

Create a **Vocabulary Knowledge Rating Chart** (*Professional Development Guidebook*, p. 33) for this selection. Include the selection vocabulary and the Big Question words that appear in the Writing About the Big Question sentence starters on this page. (The Big Question vocabulary is introduced on pp. 198–199.)

Give students a copy of the chart. Read the words aloud, and have students mark their rating in the Before Reading column. Urge them to be alert to these words as they read and discuss the selection.

Tally how many students think they know a word to gauge how much instruction to provide. As students read and discuss the selection, point out the words and their context.

Vocabulary Central, featuring tools, activities, and songs for studying vocabulary, is available online at www.PHLitOnline.com.

Meet
Piri Thomas
(b. 1928)

Author of
AMIGO BROTHERS

Growing up on the streets of New York City's Spanish Harlem, Piri Thomas faced tough challenges like poverty, gangs, and racism. He later related those struggles in his best-selling autobiographical novel, *Down These Mean Streets*. The book introduced many non-Hispanics to the world of *el barrio*—"the neighborhood."

An Avid Reader When he was young, Thomas tried to avoid the difficult world around him by surrounding himself with books. "My one island of refuge in *el barrio* was the public library," Thomas has recalled. "I gorged myself on books. . . . Reading helped me to realize that there was a world out there far vaster than the narrow confines of *el barrio*."

DID YOU KNOW?
Thomas has written many magazine articles reflecting on ways for people everywhere to achieve peace and justice.

❹ BACKGROUND FOR THE STORY

Amateur Boxing

In "Amigo Brothers," two teenage boys want to compete in the annual Golden Gloves tournament. This competition is probably the most famous amateur boxing event in the United States. Each year, local and regional elimination bouts lead to final championship matches.

For each class during which you teach this selection, have students complete one of the five Revision activities for Week 10 in the *Daily Bellringer Activities* booklet.

❹ Background
Amateur Boxing

"Amigo Brothers" is about two friends who dream of becoming championship boxers. The seed that grew into the Golden Gloves Tournament of Champions was planted by the *Chicago Tribune,* which sponsored an amateur boxing contest in 1927 to test the anti–boxing law in Illinois. The tournament was a huge success, ultimately leading to the legalization of boxing and the establishment of a nationwide tournament. The event is now international, with competitions between boxers from the United States and other countries.

Multidraft Reading

To assist struggling readers and to deepen reading for all, apply multidraft reading protocols. For each reading, have students set the purpose indicated:

- **First reading**—identifying key ideas and details and answering any Reading Checks.
- **Second reading**—analyzing craft and structure and responding to the side-column prompts.
- **Third reading**—integrating knowledge and ideas, connecting to other texts and the world, and answering the end-of-selection questions.

For more guidance, refer to the *Classroom Strategies and Teaching Routines* card on multidraft reading.

Differentiated
Instruction   Additional Instruction

🔵EL Extended Support— English Learners
Have students complete the **Reading and Vocabulary Warm-ups,** *Unit 2 Resources,* pp. 144–147, before they read. Assign the prereading pages for the selection in the *Reader's Notebook: English Learner's Version.* Then, have students listen to portions of the selection on the *Hear It!* Audio CD.

L1 L2 Extended Support— Struggling Readers
Have students complete the **Reading and Vocabulary Warm-ups,** *Unit 2 Resources,* pp. 144–147, before they read. Assign the prereading pages for the selection in the *Reader's Notebook: Adapted Version.* Then, have students listen to portions of the selection on the *Hear It!* Audio CD (adapted text).

Extended Support— Reluctant Readers
To build motivation and engagement before assigning the selection, have students read "Sister Champions," a thematically related selection in *Reality Central.* Then, use the questions at the conclusion of the related selection to guide discussion.

For more about the author, practice with the selection vocabulary, or more background, go online at **www.PHLitOnline.com.**

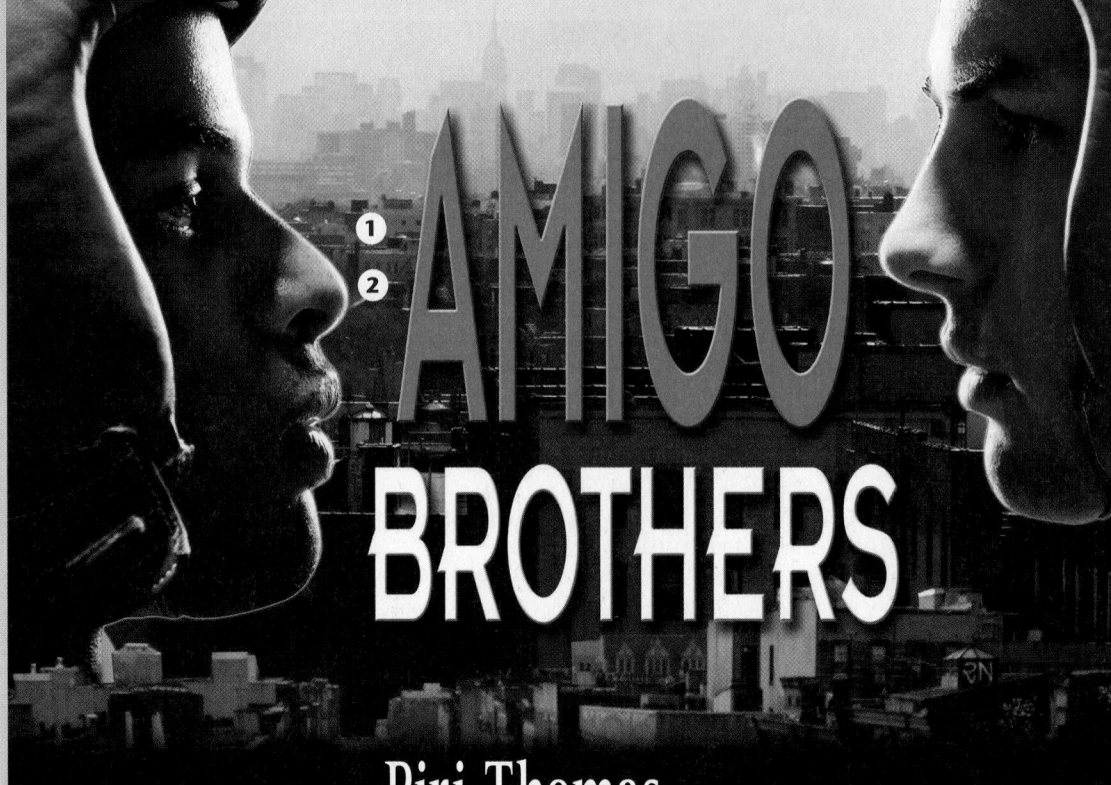

❶ Activating Prior Knowledge

1. Prepare an **Anticipation Guide** (*Professional Development Guidelines,* p. 38) with the following statements:
   - An athlete will do anything to win.
   - All challenges are physical.
   - Only one person can win a conflict.

2. Give students a copy of the prepared **Anticipation Guide** and have students mark their responses in the Me column. Have students discuss the statements in groups and mark the Guide again in the Group column.

3. For further guidance, use the *Classroom Strategies and Teaching Routines* card for **Anticipation Guides.**

Concept Connector ➡

Students will return to the **Anticipation Guide** after completing the story.

Whole-Class Activity

Ask volunteers familiar with boxing to demonstrate techniques such as *feinting, haymaker, bob and weave, straight left, jab,* and *countered.*

❷ About the Selection

Antonio and Felix are good friends who dream of becoming champion boxers. They must learn to resolve the problems raised by competition between friends.

❸ Critical Viewing

Answer: The gear suggests that boxers must protect themselves from serious injury.

❹ Make Inferences

1. Have students use their graphic organizers to record details about the boys' dedication to boxing.

2. Then, **ask** students the Make Inferences question. Encourage them to use the details they recorded to make inferences. **Possible response:** The boys are disciplined, determined, and well–informed about boxing.

AMIGO BROTHERS

Piri Thomas

Antonio Cruz and Felix Vargas were both seventeen years old. They were so together in friendship that they felt themselves to be brothers. They had known each other since childhood, growing up on the lower east side of Manhattan in the same tenement building on Fifth Street between Avenue A and Avenue B.

Antonio was fair, lean, and lanky, while Felix was dark, short, and husky. Antonio's hair was always falling over his eyes, while Felix wore his black hair in a natural Afro style.

Each youngster had a dream of someday becoming lightweight champion of the world. Every chance they had the boys worked out, sometimes at the Boys Club on 10th Street and Avenue A and sometimes at the pro's gym on 14th Street. Early morning sunrises would find them running along the East River Drive, wrapped in sweat shirts, short towels around their necks, and handkerchiefs Apache style around their foreheads.

❸ **▲ Critical Viewing**
What does the protective gear shown in this photograph tell you about boxing?

Make Inferences
What can you infer about the boys based on their dedication to boxing?

322 Short Stories

Vocabulary Development

© **CCSS** Language 6

Thematic Vocabulary: The Big Question
As students are discussing "Amigo Brothers," encourage them to use the thematic vocabulary presented in Introducing the Big Question, pp. 198–199. You might encourage them with sentence starters like these:
1. The biggest *challenge* that Antonio and Felix face is . . .
2. Each boy feels a tremendous *conflict* between . . .
3. As they prepare for the *competition,* both boys . . .
4. The crowd perhaps has a *misunderstanding* of . . .
5. The *outcome* of the story proves that . . .

While some youngsters were into street negatives, Antonio and Felix slept, ate, rapped, and dreamt positive. Between them, they had a collection of *Fight* magazines second to none, plus a scrapbook filled with torn tickets to every boxing match they had ever attended, and some clippings of their own. If asked a question about any given fighter, they would immediately zip out from their memory banks divisions, weights, records of fights, knock-outs, technical knock-outs, and draws or losses.

Each had fought many bouts representing their community and had won two gold-plated medals plus a silver and bronze medallion. The difference was in their style. Antonio's lean form and long reach made him the better boxer, while Felix's short and muscular frame made him the better slugger. Whenever they had met in the ring for sparring sessions, it had always been hot and heavy.

Now, after a series of elimination bouts, they had been informed that they were to meet each other in the division finals that were scheduled for the seventh of August, two weeks away—the winner to represent the Boys Club in the Golden Gloves Championship Tournament.

The two boys continued to run together along the East River Drive. But even when joking with each other, they both sensed a wall rising between them.

One morning less than a week before their bout, they met as usual for their daily work-out. They fooled around with a few jabs at the air, slapped skin, and then took off, running lightly along the dirty East River's edge.

Antonio glanced at Felix who kept his eyes purposely straight ahead, pausing from time to time to do some fancy leg work while throwing one-twos followed by upper cuts to an imaginary jaw. Antonio then beat the air with a barrage of body blows and short devastating lefts with an overhand jaw-breaking right. After a mile or so, Felix puffed and said, "Let's stop a while, bro. I think we both got something to say to each other." Antonio nodded. It was not natural to be acting as though nothing unusual was happening when two ace-boon buddies were going to be blasting each other within a few short days.

They rested their elbows on the railing separating them from the river. Antonio wiped his face with his short towel. The sunrise was now creating day.

Felix leaned heavily on the river's railing and stared across to the shores of Brooklyn. Finally, he broke the silence.

---

1. superimp

Conflict and Resolution
What external conflict is introduced in this part of the story?

Vocabulary
devastating (dev´ ə stāt´ iŋ) *adj.* destructive; overwhelming

 **6 Reading Check**
What dream do Antonio and Felix share?

Amigo Brothers **323**

323

❼ Make

1. Have tw
   of Anton
   aloud th

2. **Ask** stu
   the con
   them m
   the boy

Possibl
refer to
"*herma*
easily co
about co
other.

3. Have st
   organiz
   to reco

4. **Ask** stu
   question

Possibl
are such
are alm

❽ Criti

Make a J

1. Have st
   passage
   boys' p
   Felix pr

Answe
friends
they m
they are
that the
of the f

2. **Ask** stu
   the solu
   whethe
   ever be
   strange
   support

Possib
dents w
will hel
pare to
might c
the boy
friendsh
the figh

⑫ Literature in Context

Spanish Terms Young children learn their native language easily by listening to and imitating their parents and those around them. Many studies have indicated that children aged ten and under can learn a foreign language more easily and quickly than older students. For this reason, some schools begin foreign language instruction in the early grades.

Connect to the Literature

1. Have students read the Literature in Context feature, and present the additional background information above. Then, **ask** a volunteer to identify the story setting.
   Answer: The story is set in a Puerto Rican neighborhood in New York City.

2. **Ask** students what two languages people most likely speak in that area.
   Answer: English and Spanish.

3. **Ask** students the Connect to the Literature question.
   Possible response: The author uses Spanish words because Felix and Antonio live in a Puerto Rican neighborhood where many people's first language is Spanish. He wants to reflect the reality of their world.

⑬ Critical Thinking

Draw Conclusions

1. Have students read the bracketed paragraph. Then, **ask** them to summarize what is happening.
   Answer: As Felix walks at night, some gang members size him up, and Felix displays some boxing moves.

2. **Ask** students why they think Felix behaves this way.
   Possible answer: He wants the kids to know that he is not an easy target.

3. Then, **ask** them why the kids do not bother Felix but go about their own business.
   Answer: The kids do not bother Felix because they see him making boxing moves and are impressed and dissuaded by his apparent ability to fight.

---

⑫ LITERATURE IN CONTEXT

Language Connection

Spanish Terms

amigo (ə mē´ gō) *n.* Spanish for "friend"

panín (pä nēn´) *n.* Spanish for "pal"

cheverote (che bē rō´ tā) Spanish for "the greatest"

hermano (er mä´ nō) *n.* Spanish for "brother"

suavecito (swä vä sē´ tō) Spanish for "take it easy"

sabe (sä´ bā) *v.* Spanish for "understand?"

salsa (säl´ sä) *n.* a style of Latin American music

señores y señoras (se nyō´ res ē se nyō´ räs) Spanish for "Gentlemen and Ladies"

mucho corazón (mōō´ chō kô rä sôn´) Spanish for "much courage"

Connect to the Literature

Why do you think the author uses Spanish words in this story?

Vocabulary
perpetual (pər pech´ ōō əl) *adj.* constant; unending

---

to psyche himself for tomorrow's fight. It was Felix the Champion vs. Antonio the Challenger.

He walked up some dark streets, deserted except for small pockets of wary-looking kids wearing gang colors. Despite the fact that he was Puerto Rican like them, they eyed him as a stranger to their turf. Felix did a fast shuffle, bobbing and weaving, while letting loose a torrent of blows that would demolish whatever got in its way. It seemed to impress the brothers, who went about their own business.

Finding no takers, Felix decided to split to his aunt's. Walking the streets had not relaxed him, neither had the fight flick. All it had done was to stir him up. He let himself quietly into his Aunt Lucy's apartment and went straight to bed, falling into a fitful sleep with sounds of the gong for Round One.

Antonio was passing some heavy time on his rooftop. How would the fight tomorrow affect his relationship with Felix? After all, fighting was like any other profession. Friendship had nothing to do with it. A gnawing doubt crept in. He cut negative thinking real quick by doing some speedy fancy dance steps, bobbing and weaving like mercury.[2] The night air was blurred with perpetual motions of left hooks and right crosses. Felix, his *amigo* brother, was not going to be Felix at all in the ring. Just an opponent with another face. Antonio went to sleep, hearing the opening bell for the first round. Like his friend in the South Bronx, he prayed for victory, via a quick clean knock-out in the first round.

Large posters plastered all over the walls of local shops announced the fight between Antonio Cruz and Felix Vargas as the main bout.

The fight had created great interest in the neighborhood. Antonio and Felix were well liked and respected. Each had his own loyal following. Antonio's fans counted on his boxing skills. On the other side, Felix's admirers trusted in his dynamite-packed fists.

Felix had returned to his apartment early in the morning of August 7th and stayed there, hoping to avoid seeing Antonio.

---

2. mercury (mɥr´ kyōōr ē) *n.* the element mercury, also known as quicksilver because it is so quick and fluid.

Vocabulary Development

ⓒ **CCSS Language 6**

Word Forms

Expand students' vocabulary by helping them learn related forms of the selection vocabulary words. Three of the selection vocabulary words for "Amigo Brothers" have related forms. Give students a blank **Word Form Chart** (*Professional Development Resources*, p. 42), with *devastating, perpetual,* and *evading* in the correct columns. Work with the class, or have students work with a

partner, to determine the related forms. The final chart should look like the one shown.

Hold students accountable for integrating the related forms of the words into their writing and speaking.

Noun	Verb	Adjective	Adverb
devastation	devastate	**devastating**	devastatingly
perpetuity	perpetuate	**perpetual**	
evasion	evade	**evading**, evasive	

He turned the radio on to *salsa* music sounds and then tried to read while waiting for word from his manager.

The fight was scheduled to take place in Tompkins Square Park. It had been decided that the gymnasium of the Boys Club was not large enough to hold all the people who were sure to attend. In Tompkins Square Park, everyone who wanted could view the fight, whether from ringside or window fire escapes or tenement rooftops.

The morning of the fight Tompkins Square was a beehive of activity with numerous workers setting up the ring, the seats, and the guest speakers' stand. The scheduled bouts began shortly after noon and the park had begun filling up even earlier.

The local junior high school across from Tompkins Square Park served as the dressing room for all the fighters. Each was given a separate classroom with desk tops, covered with mats, serving as resting tables. Antonio thought he caught a glimpse of Felix waving to him from a room at the far end of the corridor. He waved back just in case it had been him.

The fighters changed from their street clothes into fighting gear. Antonio wore white trunks, black socks, and black shoes. Felix wore sky blue trunks, red socks, and white boxing shoes. Each had dressing gowns to match their fighting trunks with their names neatly stitched on the back.

The loudspeakers blared into the open windows of the school. There were speeches by dignitaries, community leaders, and great boxers of yesteryear. Some were well prepared, some improvised on the spot. They all carried the same message of great pleasure and honor at being part of such a historic event. This great day was in the tradition of champions emerging from the streets of the lower east side.

Amigo Brothers **327**

Vocabulary

dignitaries (dig´ nə tər´ ēz) *n.* people holding high positions or offices

improvised (im´ prə vīzd) *v.* composed or performed on the spur of the moment

Make Inferences
What does Antonio's wave from the dressing room suggest about his feelings for Felix?

15 ✓ **Reading Check**
Why are so many people in the neighborhood interested in watching the fight?

16 ▼ **Critical Viewing**
How do you think the boxers feel as they wait for the bell to start the match? **[Connect]**

---

14 **Make Inferences**

1. Review with students the fact that Felix and Antonio have not seen each other in a week. **Ask** students to speculate about doubts the boys might feel about each other at this point.
   Answer: Each boy might fear that the fight will hurt their friendship.

2. Have students reread the bracketed passage on the page. Then, **ask** them to explain why Antonio waves.
   Answer: He thinks he sees Felix waving to him.

3. **Ask** students the Make Inferences question on the page.
   Answer: The wave suggests that Antonio still views Felix as a friend, even though they will be opponents.

▶ **Monitor Progress:** Confirm that the inferences students have made while reading and their answer to the Make Inferences question are reasonable.

▶ **Reteach:** If students have difficulty making inferences, point out that being separated before the fight has put a strain on the two boys. Then, reread the bracketed paragraph aloud. Help students to see that Antonio hoped it was Felix waving and so waved back.

15 **Reading Check**

Answer: People in the neighborhood are interested in watching the fight because both boys grew up there and have many friends there.

16 **Critical Viewing**

Possible response: The boys probably feel nervous as they wait for the bell to start.

Spiral Review

Plot

1. Remind students that they studied the concept of plot in the Unit 2 Literary Analysis Workshop (pp. 200–215).

2. **Ask** the first Spiral Review question. **Possible response:** This sequence of events adds tension because the reader is wondering how the boys will treat each other in the ring.

3. **Ask** the second Spiral Review question. **Possible response:** These events happen while the tension is still building and before the climax. This is the rising action section of the story.

⑰ Critical Thinking

Analyze

1. As one student reads aloud the bracketed passage, have two others pantomime the fighters' expressions and movements. **Ask** students to explain what happened when the boys made eye contact. **Possible response:** When they looked into each other's eyes, each boy saw the friend that he knew.

2. **Ask:** Why do the boys quickly turn away from each other? **Possible response:** The boys know they must force themselves to think of each other as strangers.

⑱ Connecting to the Big Question

1. Direct students to reread the bracketed passage, then **ask:** What internal conflicts do Antonio and Felix reveal by looking at each other and then looking away? **Possible response:** They reveal their conflicts between wanting to win the fight and wanting to stay friends.

2. **Ask** students: Is there any way for either boy to be the winner of the conflict between them? Explain. **Possible response:** There is no way for either to win. Whichever boy wins the fight will know that he has caused pain and disappointment for his friend.

328

Spiral Review
Plot How does the sequence of events that begins with the boxers entering the ring and builds to the bell ringing increase the tension of the plot? Why are these events part of the rising action of the plot?

⑰
⑱

⑲

328 Short Stories

Interwoven with the speeches were the sounds of the other boxing events. After the sixth bout, Felix was much relieved when his trainer Charlie said, "Time change. Quick knockout. This is it. We're on."

Waiting time was over. Felix was escorted from the classroom by a dozen fans in white T-shirts with the word FELIX across their fronts.

Antonio was escorted down a different stairwell and guided through a roped-off path.

As the two climbed into the ring, the crowd exploded with a roar. Antonio and Felix both bowed gracefully and then raised their arms in acknowledgment.

Antonio tried to be cool, but even as the roar was in its first birth, he turned slowly to meet Felix's eyes looking directly into his. Felix nodded his head and Antonio responded. And both as one, just as quickly, turned away to face his own corner.

Bong—bong—bong. The roar turned to stillness.

"Ladies and Gentlemen. *Señores y Señoras.*"

The announcer spoke slowly, pleased at his bilingual efforts.

"Now the moment we have all been waiting for— the main event between two fine young Puerto Rican fighters, products of our lower east side. In this corner, weighing 134 pounds, Felix Vargas. And in this corner, weighing 133 pounds, Antonio Cruz. The winner will represent the Boys Club in the tournament of champions, the Golden Gloves. There will be no draw. May the best man win."

The cheering of the crowd shook the window panes of the old buildings surrounding Tompkins Square Park. At the center of the ring, the referee was giving instructions to the youngsters.

"Keep your punches up. No low blows. No punching on the back of the head. Keep your heads up. Understand. Let's have a clean fight. Now shake hands and come out fighting."

Both youngsters touched gloves and nodded. They turned and danced quickly to their corners. Their head towels and dressing gowns were lifted neatly from their shoulders by their trainers' nimble fingers. Antonio crossed himself. Felix did the same.

BONG! BONG! ROUND ONE. Felix and Antonio turned and faced each other squarely in a fighting pose. Felix wasted no time. He came in fast, head low, half hunched toward his right shoulder, and lashed out with

---

Vocabulary Development

CCSS Language 6

Selection Vocabulary Reinforcement

Students will benefit from additional examples and practice with the selection vocabulary words. Reinforce their comprehension using the Yes/No—Why? format. Model the strategy with this example for *devastating*:

Would it be *devastating* to achieve a goal? No, you would be happy and proud. Devastating things make you feel bad.

Then give students these sentences, and coach them in explaining yes/no, and why.

1. Is winter in the United States *perpetual*? **Sample answer:** No, winter does not last all year.

2. Would a fear of heights be *dispelled* by going underwater? **Sample answer:** No, you cannot get rid of a fear of heights by going underwater.

3. Is *evading* whomever is "it" a successful strategy in a game of tag? **Sample answer:** Yes, avoiding getting tagged by "it" is the point of the game.

a straight left. He missed a right cross as Antonio slipped the punch and countered with one-two-three lefts that snapped Felix's head back, sending a mild shock coursing through him. If Felix had any small doubt about their friendship affecting their fight, it was being neatly dispelled.

Antonio danced, a joy to behold. His left hand was like a piston pumping jabs one right after another with seeming ease. Felix bobbed and weaved and never stopped boring in. He knew that at long range he was at a disadvantage. Antonio had too much reach on him. Only by coming in close could Felix hope to achieve the dreamed-of knockout.

Antonio knew the dynamite that was stored in his *amigo* brother's fist. He ducked a short right and missed a left hook. Felix trapped him against the ropes just long enough to pour some punishing rights and lefts to Antonio's hard midsection. Antonio slipped away from Felix, crashing two lefts to his head, which set Felix's right ear to ringing.

Bong! Both *amigos* froze a punch well on its way, sending up a roar of approval for good sportsmanship.

Felix walked briskly back to his corner. His right ear had not stopped ringing. Antonio gracefully danced his way toward his stool none the worse, except for glowing glove burns, showing angry red against the whiteness of his midribs.

"Watch that right, Tony." His trainer talked into his ear. "Remember Felix always goes to the body. He'll want you to drop your hands for his overhand left or right. Got it?"

Antonio nodded, spraying water out between his teeth. He felt better as his sore midsection was being firmly rubbed.

Felix's corner was also busy.

"You gotta get in there, fella." Felix's trainer poured water over his curly Afro locks. "Get in there or he's gonna chop you up from way back."

Bong! Bong! Round two. Felix was off his stool and rushed Antonio like a bull, sending a hard right to his head. Beads of water exploded from Antonio's long hair.

Antonio, hurt, sent back a blurring barrage of lefts and rights that only meant pain to Felix, who returned with a short left to the head followed by a looping right to the body. Antonio countered with his own flurry, forcing Felix to give ground. But not for long.

Felix bobbed and weaved, bobbed and weaved, occasionally

Vocabulary
dispelled (di speld′)
v. driven away; made to disappear

Make Inferences
What do their actions here tell you about Felix and Antonio as boxers?

㉑ ✓ Reading Check
Why can't the fight be a tie?

Amigo Brothers **329**

---

⑲ Critical Thinking

Evaluate

1. Have students read the bracketed passage. Then, **ask:** Based on what you've read so far, which boy do you think is the better fighter?
   Answer: Some students will say Antonio; others will say Felix.

2. Point out that this is only the first round. Have students speculate about how the fight will continue. **Ask** if they think it will be easy for Antonio or Felix to achieve a knockout. Why or why not?
   Possible response: No. It will probably be a close fight. Both boys have sparred together often, so they know each other's strengths and weaknesses.

⑳ Make Inferences

1. Have students reread the referee's instructions on p. 328. **Ask** students to summarize them.
   Answer: No low blows, no punching on the back of the head, and fight fair.

2. **Ask:** What does it mean to "have a clean fight"?
   Answer: It means to play by the rules and don't do anything outside the rules to harm your opponent.

3. Direct students' attention to the bracketed passage. Have students identify details that describe the boys' actions.
   Answer: Telling details include the blows they land and avoid as well as the boys' stopping in mid–punch when the bell rings.

4. **Ask** the Make Inferences question.
   Answer: Felix and Antonio are fierce, skilled fighters, but they respect the art of boxing. They play by the rules and are good sports.

㉑ Reading Check

Answer: The fight cannot be a tie because there are no draws in elimination bouts.

Fluency

Distribute copies of pages 328 and 329. Have partners take turns reading paragraphs aloud. Listeners should mark any words or phrases that readers struggle with. Circulate to monitor students' fluency, then collect students' marked up copies of the pages. Review difficult words and passages, including these problem spots.

• If students have difficulty with the phrase *bong—bong—bong* (p. 328) and *BONG! BONG!* (p. 328), explain that these are sound

words. They imitate the sound that the bell makes. Demonstrate how to say the phrases so that they convey the ringing of a bell.

• If students read the action passages on pages 328 and 329 in a choppy or laborious manner, review the meaning and pronunciation of any action words. Then, use echo reading to help students develop fluency—read a sentence with expression, then have the student read it back, imitating your phrasing.

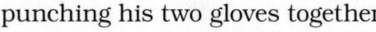

22 Conflict and Resolution

1. Have students summarize the action in round two so far.
   Answer: Felix endures a painful blur of lefts and rights, forcing him to give ground. Then, Antonio throws a left to his chin, causing Felix to buckle.

2. Direct students' attention to the bracketed paragraph and **ask** the Conflict and Resolution question.
   Possible response: The author increases the external conflict by suggesting that Felix could be faking injury and waiting to knock out Antonio the instant Antonio moves in closer.

▶ **Monitor Progress: Ask** students why the bracketed paragraph would increase the external conflict.
   Answer: It adds uncertainty about the outcome.

▶ **Reteach:** If students have difficulty explaining why the conflict is increased, read the two-sentence paragraph aloud and explain that interest in a conflict increases when we don't know the outcome. Point out that Felix seems to be hurt, but if he is exaggerating the extent of his pain, Antonio could face "the powerful bombs he carried in each fist."

23 Make Inferences

1. Ask a volunteer to read aloud the second bracketed paragraph. Then, **ask** students to name the details that show how Felix is feeling.
   Possible responses: Felix doesn't hear something very important—the count. He does hear the crowd but only through a fog. He is glad when the round ends.

2. **Ask** students the Make Inferences question.
   Possible response: Felix is becoming exhausted and may not be able to keep fighting much longer.

3. **Ask:** Do you think Felix is ready to give up? Why or why not?
   Possible response: No. Felix got up quickly. Even though he was groggy, he was still game to fight.

4. Remind students to add their responses to their graphic organizers.

330

---

22 Conflict and Resolution

How does the author increase the external conflict here?

Vocabulary

evading (ē vād´ iŋ) *v.* avoiding

23 Make Inferences

What can you infer from the fact that Felix is groggy and glad to sit down?

330 Short Stories

---

punching his two gloves together.

Antonio waited for the rush that was sure to come. Felix closed in and feinted[3] with his left shoulder and threw his right instead. Lights suddenly exploded inside Felix's head as Antonio slipped the blow and hit him with a pistonlike left catching him flush on the point of his chin.

Bedlam[4] broke loose as Felix's legs momentarily buckled. He fought off a series of rights and lefts and came back with a strong right that taught Antonio respect.

Antonio danced in carefully. He knew Felix had the habit of playing possum when hurt, to sucker an opponent within reach of the powerful bombs he carried in each fist.

A right to the head slowed Antonio's pretty dancing. He answered with his own left at Felix's right eye that began puffing up within three seconds.

Antonio, a bit too eager, moved in too close and Felix had him entangled into a rip-roaring, punching toe-to-toe slugfest that brought the whole Tompkins Square Park screaming to its feet.

Rights to the body. Lefts to the head. Neither fighter was giving an inch. Suddenly a short right caught Antonio squarely on the chin. His long legs turned to jelly and his arms flailed out desperately. Felix, grunting like a bull, threw wild punches from every direction. Antonio, groggy, bobbed and weaved, evading most of the blows. Suddenly his head cleared. His left flashed out hard and straight catching Felix on the bridge of his nose.

Felix lashed back with a haymaker,[5] right off the ghetto streets. At the same instant, his eye caught another left hook from Antonio. Felix swung out trying to clear the pain. Only the frenzied screaming of those along ringside let him know that he had dropped Antonio. Fighting off the growing haze, Antonio struggled to his feet, got up, ducked, and threw a smashing right that dropped Felix flat on his back.

Felix got up as fast as he could in his own corner, groggy but still game. He didn't even hear the count. In a fog, he heard the roaring of the crowd, who seemed to have gone insane. His head cleared to hear the bell sound at the end of the round. He was very glad. His trainer sat him down on the stool.

In his corner, Antonio was doing what all fighters do when they are hurt. They sit and smile at everyone.

3. **feinted** (fānt´ ed) *v.* pretended to make a blow.
4. **Bedlam** (bed´ ləm) *n.* condition of noise and confusion.
5. **haymaker** punch thrown with full force.

Vocabulary Development

Vocabulary Knowledge Rating
When students have completed reading and discussing "Amigo Brothers," have them take out their **Vocabulary Rating Chart** for this selection. Read the words aloud once more, and have students rate their knowledge of the words again in the After Reading column. Clarify any words that are still problematic. Have students write their own definition and example or sentence in the appropriate column. Then, have students complete the Vocabulary Practice activities at the end of the selection. Encourage students to use the words in further discussion and written work about this selection. Remind them that they will be accountable for these words on the **Selection Test**, *Unit 2 Resources,* pp. 159–161 or 162–164.

Neither Fighter WAS GIVING AN INCH.

The referee signaled the ring doctor to check the fighters out. He did so and then gave his okay. The cold water sponges brought clarity to both *amigo* brothers. They were rubbed until their circulation ran free.

Bong! Round three—the final round. Up to now it had been tic-tac-toe, pretty much even. But everyone knew there could be no draw and this round would decide the winner.

This time, to Felix's surprise, it was Antonio who came out fast, charging across the ring. Felix braced himself but couldn't ward off the barrage of punches. Antonio drove Felix hard against the ropes.

The crowd ate it up. Thus far the two had fought with *mucho corazón.* Felix tapped his gloves and commenced his attack anew. Antonio, throwing boxer's caution to the winds, jumped in to meet him.

Both pounded away. Neither gave an inch and neither fell to the canvas. Felix's left eye was tightly closed. Claret red blood poured from Antonio's nose. They fought toe-to-toe.

The sounds of their blows were loud in contrast to the silence of a crowd gone completely mute. The referee was stunned by their savagery.

Bong! Bong! Bong! The bell sounded over and over again. Felix and Antonio were past hearing. Their blows continued to pound on each other like hailstones.

Finally the referee and the two trainers pried Felix and Antonio apart. Cold water was poured over them to bring

24 ▲ Critical Viewing
Why do you think that competitors in boxing matches wear contrasting colors such as the blue and red shown here? **[Hypothesize]**

25 ✓ Reading Check
Does Felix or Antonio fall to the mat first?

Amigo Brothers **331**

---

24 Critical Viewing

Possible response: It helps the judges and the fans tell who is who and makes it easier for them to focus on a particular competitor.

25 Reading Check

Answer: Antonio falls to the mat first.

Concept Connector

Anticipation Guide
Have students return to their **Anticipation Guides** and respond to the statements again in the After Reading column. They may do this individually or in their original groups. Then, lead a class discussion, probing for what students have learned that confirms or invalidates each statement. Encourage students to cite specific details, quotations, or other evidence from the text to support their responses to each statement.

Reading Skill Graphic Organizer
Ask students to review the graphic organizers they completed to make inferences about characters while reading. Then, have students share their graphic organizers and the inferences they made.

? Writing About the Big Question
Have students compare their responses to the sentence starters they completed before reading the story with their thoughts afterwards. Ask them to explain whether their thoughts have changed.

Possible response: According to Mom, a bride's beauty would help her attract a rich man to marry.

㉑ **Critical Thinking**
Compare and Contrast

1. Have students read the bracketed passage and identify the object that is the focus of the passage and in the story in general.
   Answer: The silk ribbons are the main object discussed.

2. **Ask** students to compare the significance of the ribbons to Stacy and to Grandmother.
   Answer: To Stacy, the ribbons represent dance, which is her way of expressing herself, as well as enjoying herself and feeling free. To Grandmother, the ribbons represent oppression through foot binding.

3. **Ask:** How do the ribbons make each character feel?
   Answer: For Stacy, the ribbons are a delight and source of pride; for Grandmother, they are a source of pain and oppression.

㉒ 🌐 **Connecting to the Big Question**

1. Point out to students that conflicts often have a resolution. If the people in a conflict settle their disagreement or solve their problem, then the conflict is said to be resolved.

2. Have students reread the bracketed passage on this page. Remind them that Stacy caught a glimpse of her grandmother's feet in the bathroom earlier. **Ask:** In what way does Stacy's conflict with Grandmother in the bathroom benefit Stacy?
   Possible response: Her distress over seeing Grandmother's feet finally leads her mother to explain what happened to Grandmother. Stacy realizes why her grandmother objects to her toe-shoe ribbons—Grandmother mistook them for foot-binding bandages.

3. **Ask** students what this scene suggests about who will win in the conflict between Stacy and her Grandmother.
   Possible response: If Stacy understands her grandmother, she may be able to get on her grandmother's good side and so "win."

356

⓴
▼ **Critical Viewing**
According to Mom's explanation, why was a bride's beauty important in China? **[Analyze]**

356 Short Stories

beautiful. When a girl was about five, her mother would gradually bend her toes under the sole of her foot."

"Ugh." Just thinking about it made my own feet ache. "Her own mother did that to her?"

Mom smiled apologetically. "Her mother and father thought it would make their little girl attractive so she could marry a rich man. They were still doing it in some of the back areas of China long after it was outlawed in the rest of the country."

I shook my head. "There's nothing lovely about those feet."

"I know. But they were usually bound up in silk ribbons."

Mom brushed some of the hair from my eyes. "Because they were a symbol of the old days, Paw-paw undid the ribbons as soon as we were free in Hong Kong—even though they kept back the pain."

I was even more puzzled now. "How did the ribbons do that?"

Mom began to brush my hair with quick, light strokes. "The ribbons kept the blood from circulating freely and bringing more feeling to her feet. Once the ribbons were gone, her feet ached. They probably still do."

I rubbed my own foot in sympathy. "But she doesn't complain."

"That's how tough she is," Mom said.

Finally the truth dawned on me. "And she mistook my toe-shoe ribbons for her old ones."

Mom lowered the brush and nodded solemnly. "And she didn't want you to go through the same pain she had."

I guess Grandmother loved me in her own way. When she came into the bedroom with Ian later that evening, I didn't leave. However, she tried to ignore me—as if I had become tainted by her secret.

Vocabulary Development

Vocabulary Knowledge Rating
When students have completed reading and discussing "Ribbons," have them take out their **Vocabulary Knowledge Rating Chart** for this selection. Read the words aloud once more and have students rate their knowledge of the words again in the After Reading column. Clarify any words that are still problematic. Have students write their own definition and example or sentence in the appropriate

column. Then, have students complete the Vocabulary Practice activities at the end of the selection. Encourage students to use the words in further discussion and written work about this selection. Remind them that they will be accountable for these words on the **Selection Test**, *Unit 2 Resources*, pp. 198–200 or 201–203.

When Ian demanded a story, I sighed. "All right. But only one."

Naturally, Ian chose the fattest story he could, which was my old collection of fairy tales by Hans Christian Andersen. Years of reading had cracked the spine so that the book fell open automatically in his hands to the story that had been my favorite when I was small. It was the original story of "The Little Mermaid"—not the cartoon. The picture illustrating the tale showed the mermaid posed like a ballerina in the middle of the throne room.

"This one," Ian said, and pointed to the picture of the Little Mermaid.

When Grandmother and Ian sat down on my bed, I began to read. However, when I got to the part where the Little Mermaid could walk on land, I stopped.

Ian was impatient. "Come on, read," he ordered, patting the page.

"After that," I went on, "each step hurt her as if she were walking on a knife." I couldn't help looking up at Grandmother.

This time she was the one to pat the page. "Go on. Tell me more about the mermaid."

So I went on reading to the very end, where the Little Mermaid changes into sea foam. "That's a dumb ending," Ian said. "Who wants to be pollution?"

"Sea foam isn't pollution. It's just bubbles," I explained. "The important thing was that she wanted to walk even though it hurt."

"I would rather have gone on swimming," Ian insisted.

"But maybe she wanted to see new places and people by going on the land," Grandmother said softly. "If she had kept her tail, the land people would have thought she was odd. They might even have made fun of her."

When she glanced at her own feet, I thought she might be talking about herself—so I seized my chance. "My satin ribbons aren't like your old silk ones. I use them to tie my toe shoes on when I dance." Setting the book down, I got out my other shoe. "Look."

Grandmother fingered the dangling ribbons and then pointed at my bare feet. "But you already have calluses there."

I began to dance before Grandmother could stop me. After a minute, I struck a pose on half-toe. "See? I can move fine."

She took my hand and patted it clumsily. I think it was the first time she had showed me any sign of affection. "When I

Theme
What details in this paragraph support a theme of understanding cultural differences?

 Reading Check
What happened to Grandmother's feet when she was a child?

Ribbons **357**

---

② Theme

1. Remind students that readers must often figure out the theme of a story from details that the writer provides, such as an object that seems especially important to a character.

2. Have students summarize the misunderstanding about the ribbons.
   Answer: Stacy uses the ribbons for ballet, but Grandmother thinks she uses them to bind her feet.

3. Read aloud the bracketed paragraph as students follow along. Then, **ask** the Theme question.
   Possible response: Stacy's awareness that Grandmother sees the satin ribbons as a source of shame—not as a symbol of freedom or self-expression—expresses the theme of understanding cultural differences. An important detail is Stacy's noticing Grandmother's glancing at her feet. Stacy uses the opportunity to educate Grandmother about how the ribbons are used for ballet.

4. **Ask:** What object, repeated throughout the story, symbolizes this theme?
   Answer: The ribbons symbolize the theme.

② Reading Check

Answer: Grandmother's mother bound her feet according to ancient Chinese custom.

Concept Connector

Anticipation Guide
Have students return to their **Anticipation Guides** and respond to the statements again in the After Reading column. They may do this individually or in their original pairs or groups. Then, lead a class discussion, probing for what students have learned that confirms or invalidates each statement. Encourage students to cite specific details, quotations, or other evidence from the text to support their responses to each statement.

Reading Skill Graphic Organizer
Ask students to review the graphic organizers they completed to make inferences while reading. Then, have students share their graphic organizers and the inferences they made.

Writing About the Big Question
Have students compare the sentence starters they completed before reading the story with their ideas afterward. Ask them whether their thoughts have changed.

357

1. Have students describe the relationship between Stacy and Grandmother up until the point where Stacy reads a story to Ian. **Answer:** Their relationship is tense.

2. Have students read the bracketed passage. **Ask** the Make Inferences question.
Answer: Grandmother and Stacy are crying with joy because they understand each other and have strengthened their relationship.

ASSESS
Answers

Critical Thinking

Remind students to support their answers with evidence from the text.

1. **Possible responses:** The differences are revealed through the misunderstanding about the ribbons. Grandmother thinks the ribbons will be used to bind Stacy's feet because she does not know about ballet shoes. Stacy wants to show grandmother the ribbons because she does not know about foot binding.

2. (a) **Possible responses:** Stacy and Ian must be quiet around the house; they cannot watch their favorite television programs. (b) Stacy has a lot of energy and resents having to be quiet; she might be frustrated that she cannot watch her TV shows. (c) **Possible responses:** Many students will sympathize with Stacy and point out that Grandmother does not seem to care about Stacy. Some may point out that Grandmother needs time to adapt to a new situation. Students should explain how their views changed after discussion.

3. (a) Stacy accidentally sees Grandmother's feet when Grandmother is soaking them. (b) Stacy begins to understand Grandmother's behavior.

4. **Possible response:** (a) The story of Grandmother's bound feet comes out, and they begin to understand each other. (b) Stacy learns that her Grandmother cares about her despite their differences. Grandmother learns that she must let go of some of her old ideas.

358

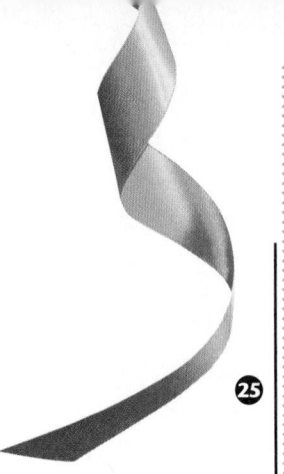

Make Inferences
Why do you think the narrator and her grandmother are crying?

saw those ribbons, I didn't want you feeling pain like I do."

I covered her hands with mine. "I just wanted to show you what I love best—dancing."

"And I love my children," she said. I could hear the ache in her voice. "And my grandchildren. I don't want anything bad to happen to you."

Suddenly I felt as if there were an invisible ribbon binding us, tougher than silk and satin, stronger even than steel; and it joined her to Mom and Mom to me.

I wanted to hug her so badly that I just did. Though she was stiff at first, she gradually softened in my arms.

"'Let me have my ribbons and my shoes," I said in a low voice. "Let me dance."

"Yes, yes," she whispered fiercely.

I felt something on my cheek and realized she was crying, and then I began crying, too.

"So much to learn," she said, and began hugging me back. "So much to learn."

Critical Thinking

1. Key Ideas and Details How are differences in generation and culture revealed in this story? Support your answer.

2. Key Ideas and Details (a) Identify two examples from the story that show how Stacy's life changes when Grandmother arrives. **(b) Analyze Cause and Effect:** For each, tell how you would expect Stacy to feel about these changes. **(c) Evaluate:** Discuss with a partner whether or not you sympathize with Stacy. Then discuss how hearing your partner's responses did or did not change your view.

3. Key Ideas and Details (a) How does Stacy learn the secret of Grandmother's feet? **(b) Connect:** How does Stacy's attitude change after her mother explains older Chinese customs?

4. Integration of Knowledge and Ideas (a) How do Grandmother and Stacy finally overcome their conflict and begin to understand and appreciate one another? **(b)** What lessons does each character learn? *[Connect to the Big Question: Does every conflict have a winner?]*

Cite textual evidence to support your responses.

358 Short Stories

Assessment Resources

Unit 2 Resources
L1 L2 EL **Selection Test A,** pp. 198–200. Administer Test A to less advanced readers.
L3 L4 EL **Selection Test B,** pp. 201–203. Administer Test B to on-level and more advanced students.
L3 L4 **Open-Book Test,** pp. 195–197. As an alternative, give the Open-Book Test.

All **Customizable Test Bank**
All **Self-tests**
Students may prepare for the **Selection Test** by taking the **Self-test** online.

PHLit Online!
All assessment resources are available at **www.PHLitOnline.com.**

After You Read | Ribbons

Reading Skill: Make Inferences

1. The author describes Grandmother's arrival by saying, "The rear car door opened, and a pair of carved black canes poked out like six-shooters." Why do you think he includes those details instead of simply introducing the character by name?

2. Grandmother carried her daughter on her back to Hong Kong to escape her enemy. What questions might you ask to help you make an **inference** about Grandmother's life?

Literary Analysis: Theme

Ⓒ 3. **Key Ideas and Details** What **theme** does the story convey about understanding between grandparents and grandchildren? In a graphic organizer like this one, list details about the setting and characters that support the theme.

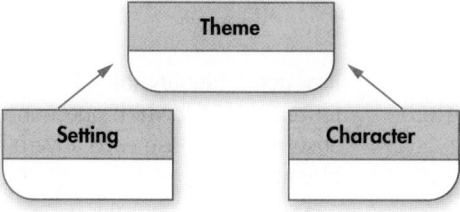

Vocabulary

Ⓒ **Acquisition and Use** Use your knowledge of the italicized words to answer each question. Explain your responses.

1. If a girl is *meek*, how might she answer questions in class?
2. How would you *coax* someone to go somewhere with you?
3. What subject in school is the most *laborious* for you?
4. What is your least favorite type of *exertion*?
5. If your forehead is *furrowed*, how might you feel?
6. If someone is *sensitive,* is it a good idea to tease him?

Word Study Use the context of the sentences and what you know about the **Latin suffix -ious** to explain your answer to each question.

1. If a meal is *nutritious*, what kinds of foods does it include?
2. Who do you know who has *ambitious* goals?

Word Study

The **Latin suffix -ious** means "full of."

Apply It Explain how the suffix -**ious** contributes to the meanings of these words. Consult a dictionary if necessary.

glorious
gracious
hilarious

Ribbons **359**

Word Study
Sample answers:

1. A *nutritious* meal includes healthful foods <u>full of</u> nutrition.

2. My sister is <u>full of</u> ambition, so she has the *ambitious* goal to become class president.

Word Study: Apply It
Sample answers:

Something that is *glorious* is <u>full of</u> glory;
Someone who is *gracious* is <u>full of</u> grace;
Something that is *hilarious* is <u>full of</u> hilarity.

Reading Skill

1. **Possible response:** This method of introducing Grandmother is dramatic and presents her as a powerful, unknown force. The author also wants to establish that Grandmother has trouble walking and will be hard to get along with. The image of "six-shooters" foreshadows the conflict between Grandmother and Stacy.

2. **Possible response:** Why does the author include the detail about Grandmother carrying her daughter on her back? Why does he include the detail about Grandmother walking such a great distance?

Literary Analysis

3. **Possible response:** *Theme:* Grandparents and grandchildren can form strong bonds by understanding each other's perspectives; *Setting:* A very traditional grandmother from China comes to live with her American family; *Character:* Grandmother becomes upset when she sees toe-shoe ribbons. Stacy learns that ribbons were used to bind Grandmother's feet.

For other sample answers, see *Graphic Organizer Transparencies,* **Literary Analysis Graphic Organizer A,** p. 66, and the **Additional Answers** section.

Vocabulary
Acquisition and Use
Sample answers:

1. If a girl is <u>meek</u>, she would answer hesitantly out of shyness.

2. I would ask really nicely in order to <u>coax</u>, or convince, someone to come with me.

3. Math is most <u>laborious</u> for me because it takes the most work.

4. Running is my least favorite type of <u>exertion</u> because it takes so much effort.

5. If your forehead is <u>furrowed</u>, or creased, you might feel confused.

6. If someone is <u>sensitive</u>, the person is easily affected, so he or she might be very upset by your teasing.

Conventions

1. Introduce the skill, using the instruction on the student page.
2. Discuss the examples in the chart.

Think Aloud: Model the Skill

Model the skill of identifying adverbs. Say to students:

> Adverbs help me picture what I read by adding details about verbs, adjectives, or other adverbs. To identify adverbs in reading, I look for words that answer the questions *How? When? Where? How often?* and *To what extent?* For example, in the sentence *The robin flew away,* the adverb *away* answers a *Where?* question: "Where did the robin fly?" The word tells me more about the verb *flew.*

PH WRITING COACH   Grade 7

Students will find further instruction on and practice with adverbs in Chapter 15, Section 2.

Practice A

1. anxiously; *modifies:* waited
2. slowly; *modifies:* walked
3. annually; *modifies:* brought
4. thoroughly; *modifies:* explained
5. never; *modifies:* been

Reading Application
Sample answers:

"And the crowds <u>slowly</u> filed by. . . .";
"The citizens of Earth clustered <u>around</u>. . . ."

Practice B

1. courteously; *How?; Sample sentence:* Al greeted me <u>courteously</u>.
2. usually; *How often?; Sample sentence:* I <u>usually</u> practice piano after dinner.
3. finally; *When?; Sample sentence:* After several hours, we <u>finally</u> bought tickets to the movie.
4. badly; *To what extent?; Sample sentence:* I needed a bike so <u>badly</u> that I worked every day.

Writing Application
Sample answers: Adverbs include *often, rarely, quickly, loudly,* and *seldom.*

Integrated Language Skills

Zoo • Ribbons

Conventions: Adverbs

> An **adverb** is a word that modifies or describes a verb, an adjective, or another adverb.

Adverbs provide information by answering the question *how? when? where? how often?* or *to what extent?* Many adverbs end in the suffix *-ly.* The chart shows examples:

How?	When?	Where?	How Often?	To What Extent?
She paced *nervously.*	I will finish it *later.*	The robins flew *away.*	Linda *always* laughs.	Luke moved *slightly.*

Practice A Identify the adverb in each sentence. Then, tell which word the adverb modifies.

1. The people waited anxiously for the Professor to lift the sides of the spaceship.
2. The crowds slowly walked by the creatures' cages.
3. Professor Hugo brought the creatures to Chicago annually.
4. When returning home, the little creature thoroughly explained the adventure to his mother.
5. She had never been on an interplanetary trip.

© **Reading Application** In "Zoo," find two sentences with adverbs.

Practice B Identify the adverb in each sentence. Next, tell which question the adverb answers. Then, use each adverb in a sentence of your own.

1. Ian greeted his grandmother courteously when she arrived.
2. Grandmother usually chose to play with Ian instead of showing interest in Stacy.
3. Stacy's mother finally explained Grandmother's strong reaction to the ribbons.
4. I wanted to hug her so badly that I just did.

© **Writing Application** List at least five adverbs that can be used to revise this sentence: *They sometimes talked to each other.* Discuss the effect of each change.

PH WRITING COACH   Further instruction and practice are available in *Prentice Hall Writing Coach.*

360 Short Stories

Writing

 **Argument** Write a **letter to the editor** of a local newspaper as a response to either "Zoo" or "Ribbons." If you write in response to "Zoo," take a position about whether zoo animals should live in natural habitats instead of cages. If you write in response to "Ribbons," take a position about whether young people should participate in extra schooling by taking art classes or participating in sports.

- First, consider both sides of the issue and list at least one reason in support of each one. Then, choose which position to support.
- As you draft, state and support your position. Consult credible sources to find logical reasons and evidence that will convince readers to take your side.
- E-mail your letter to the editor of a newspaper.

Grammar Application Use adverbs correctly in your writing.

Writing Workshop: *Work in Progress*

Prewriting for Narration Choose two ideas from the Conflict List in your writing portfolio and jot down ideas about how each might be resolved. Save the Resolution Ideas List for later development.

Research and Technology

 **Build and Present Knowledge** Create a **poster** based on the story you read.

- If you read "Zoo," your poster should focus on a zoo in your town, city, or state. Provide zoo hours, admission fees, special exhibits, and the animals you would recommend others visit.
- If you read "Ribbons," your poster should give information about the basic arm and foot positions used in ballet and the benefits of learning to dance.

Follow these steps to complete the assignment:

- Identify the topic of your poster. Then, jot down questions to guide your research.
- Develop a search plan. Then, use the Internet and library resources to conduct your research. Use photos, drawings, and diagrams to illustrate your poster.
- Present your poster and research to the class. Add music or sound effects to emphasize key points.

Common Core State Standards

L.7.1, L.7.4.b, L.7.6; W.7.1.a, W.7.1.b, W.7; SL.7.5
[For the full wording of the standards, see page 336.]

 Use this prewriting activity to prepare for the **Writing Workshop** on page 384.

 **PHLit Online!**
www.PHLitOnline.com

- Interactive graphic organizers
- Grammar tutorial
- Interactive journals

Writing

1. Review the assignment, using the instruction on the student page.
2. To guide students in writing an argument, give them **Support for Writing**, p. 193 in *Unit 2 Resources*. In addition, review conventions for writing e-mails.
3. To evaluate students' letters, use the rubrics for **Writing: Persuasive Essay**, pp. 230–231 in *Professional Development Guidebook.* You might also evaluate how clearly students state their position and how well they support it with evidence.

Grammar Application

Have students check their drafts for correct use of adverbs.

Six Traits Focus

✔ Ideas	Word Choice	
✔ Organization	Sentence Fluency	
Voice	Conventions	

PH WRITING COACH Grade 7

Students will find guidance on letter writing on pp. 790–791.

Writing Workshop
Work in Progress

Have students save the ideas based on their Conflicts Lists in their portfolios. They will use the ideas later as they complete the Writing Workshop assignment (see pp. 384–391).

Research and Technology

1. Review the assignment, using the instruction on the student page.
2. Have students complete the **Support for Extend Your Learning** page (*Unit 2 Resources*, p. 194).

Teaching Resources

Unit 2 Resources

- L3 L4 EL **Integrated Language Skills: Grammar,** p. 192
- L3 L4 EL **Support for Writing,** p. 193
- L3 L4 **Support for Extend Your Learning,** p. 194
- L4 **Enrichment,** p. 191

Enriched Online Student Edition

Available under After You Read for this selection:

- All **Interactive Grammar Tutorial**
- L3 L4 **Internet Research Activity**

Professional Development Guidebook

Rubrics for Self–Assessment: Persuasive Essay, pp. 230–231

PHLit Online! All print and digital resources are available online at **www.PHLitOnline.com.** Online resources accessible to students are noted on the student page.

Using the Test Practice

In this two-page Test Practice, students apply the reading skill for the second half of Unit 2 to a passage of fiction and a passage of nonfiction.

Review this skill, making inferences, and then administer the test. For more guidance, consult the *Classroom Strategies and Teaching Routines* card, **Administering Timed Tests.**

ASSESS

Answers

Answers With Explanations

1. **B**—A boardwalk, sand, waves, dune grass, and shells indicate a beach. *Incorrect answers:* A—Parks do not usually have sand and waves; C—Sand and waves do not suggest mountains; D—There are no details to suggest that this beach is on an island.

2. **D**—Being away from home for two weeks suggests a vacation. *Incorrect answers:* A—Many people live in warm places year-round; People can hum at any time; B—Skipping and picking up shells show that Tina is having fun but not that she is on vacation; C—Tina could do these things without being on vacation.

3. **A**—One carefully wraps delicate things. *Incorrect answers:* B—Something can be hard to find but still sturdy; C—Something can be colorful without needing to be wrapped carefully; D—Tina wraps the shells carefully because they might break, not because they are popular.

4. **A**—Skipping and humming are actions people take when they are contented. *Incorrect answers:* B—Tina's actions indicate happiness, not nervousness; C—Quiet humming and browsing for shells suggest that she is contented rather than overjoyed; D—Tina is clearly interested in collecting shells, so she is not bored.

Test Practice: Reading

Make Inferences

Fiction Selection

Directions: *Read the selection. Then, answer the questions.*

Tina skipped down the boardwalk and onto the sand. The morning sun glistened on the waves, and a warm breeze stirred the dune grass. Humming quietly to herself, Tina walked along, picking up interesting shells as she went. She was assembling a collection for her grandmother, who liked to use them in craft projects. Later, Tina would wrap the shells carefully to prevent them from breaking. Then, she would put them in a box and mail them off to her grandmother. In the meantime, she would enjoy her beautiful surroundings, because tomorrow her family would head back home. She would be glad to see her friends after a two-week absence, but Tina really hated to think of leaving.

1. From details in the first two sentences, what can you infer about the story's setting?
   A. The story is set in a park.
   B. The story is set at the beach.
   C. The story is set near the mountains.
   D. The story is set on an island.

2. Which two details *best* help you infer that Tina is on vacation?
   A. She is in a place with warm breezes, and she hums to herself.
   B. She skips down the boardwalk, and she picks up shells.
   C. She is on the sand, and she mails a package to her grandmother.
   D. She will go home tomorrow, and she has been away for two weeks.

3. What can you infer about shells from the way Tina packs them to send to her grandmother?
   A. Shells are delicate.
   B. Shells are hard to find.
   C. Shells come in many colors.
   D. Shells are popular keepsakes.

4. Based on details in the passage, which word *best* describes how Tina feels at the beginning of the story?
   A. contented
   B. nervous
   C. overjoyed
   D. bored

Writing for Assessment

Write a paragraph explaining whether you think that Tina enjoyed her vacation. Use details from the story to support your inference.

Writing for Assessment

Students should infer from the last sentence and other details that Tina enjoyed her vacation. In two sentences, they should state this inference and support it with relevant details.

Strategies for Test Taking

Remind students that when a test question asks about information that is not directly stated in the passage, they should make an inference, not just guess. To make a valid inference, they should reread the part of the passage that the question relates to and look for the clues that lead to the answer.

Nonfiction Selection

Directions: *Read the selection. Then, answer the questions.*

People collect seashells for many reasons—to decorate their homes, to make crafts, or to impress their friends. Some people find shells while walking along the seashore. Others buy shells at souvenir shops, which are often located in seaside communities.

These souvenir shops offer a variety of small, medium, and large seashells for sale. The shops also sell coral, starfish, sea horses, and sand dollars. Craftspeople can often find mini craft shells as small as a quarter-inch long. The stores usually sell these shells by the pound.

Prices for seashells can vary greatly. A half-inch starfish might cost as little as thirty cents, while a 400-pound Tridacna Gigas clam shell might cost over six hundred dollars.

1. Which of the following details helps you infer that customers can buy large quantities of shells from souvenir shops?
   A. The shops sell large shells.
   B. The shops sell shells by the pound.
   C. The shops sell very expensive shells.
   D. The shops sell starfish.

2. Based on details in the passage, what is a souvenir shop's main reason for collecting and selling shells?
   A. to clean up the seashore
   B. to create an attractive display
   C. to help craftspeople
   D. to make money

3. What inferences can you make based on details in the passage?
   A. People like to collect one type of shell.
   B. It is easy to find shells on the sand.
   C. People buy many types of shells.
   D. Shells are only bought by tourists.

4. Which of the following inferences is *not* supported by details in the passage?
   A. Seashells come in many shapes and sizes.
   B. Some people enjoy making crafts with seashells.
   C. Some people think seashells are beautiful.
   D. People who collect seashells like to swim in the ocean.

Writing for Assessment

Connecting Across Texts
Write a description of how Tina's grandmother might react if she were to visit a souvenir shop like the one in the passage. Use details from both passages to support your ideas.

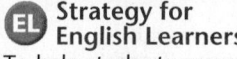

www.PHLitOnline.com
• Online practice
• Instant feedback

Differentiated Instruction   *for Universal Access*

EL **Strategy for English Learners**

To help students answer the items on this page, remind them to read each question, or item stem, very carefully. For example, items 2 and 3 instruct students to answer questions "based on details in the passage." Tell students that this phrase means that they must use information in the passage to select the correct answer, rather than just using common sense or their own prior experience. Tell students to cover this phrase in item 3. There could be many answers to the question, "What inferences can you make about shell collecting?" However, there is just one correct answer to the question if students base their choice on details in the passage.

Answers With Explanations

1. **B**—"By the pound" suggests large quantities of shells, most of which do not weigh much by themselves. *Incorrect answers:* A—Selling large items is not the same as selling large quantities; C—Selling expensive items is not the same as selling large quantities; D—The shops might sell just a few starfish.

2. **D**—A shop's main reason for selling items is to make money. *Incorrect answers:* A—No details support this answer; B—Craftspeople, not souvenir shops, use shells to create displays. C—A shop owner's *main* motive is to make money rather than to help people.

3. **C**—The fact that the store carries a variety of shells suggests that collectors buy different kinds. *Incorrect answers:* A—same explanation as for C; B—The fact that people buy shells suggests that they are not always easy to find; D—The passage does not indicate whether the buyers are tourists or local residents.

4. **D**—There is no evidence that shell collectors like to swim in the ocean. *Incorrect answers:* A—The passage refers to shells of different sizes; the word *variety* implies that there are different shapes; B—The people who make crafts with shells most likely enjoy doing so; C—People decorate their homes with shells, so they must think shells are beautiful.

Writing for Assessment

Students should write a paragraph that refers to the fact that Tina's grandmother uses shells in craft projects and that souvenir shops sell different types of shells. They should make a logical prediction about the grandmother's reaction based on these details, such as the prediction that she will enjoy the visit.

Students may take the test in interactive format with instant feedback online at **www.PHLitOnline.com.**

363

© Common Core
State Standards

• Reading Informational Text 1
• Language 4.c, 6

Reading Skill

1. Introduce the skill and review the chart.

2. Tell students they will connect ideas to make inferences and generalizations as they read.

Think Aloud: Model the Skill

Say to students:

> When I read informational materials, I actively connect ideas in order to make inferences and generalizations. If I read that almonds, pecans, and pistachios are healthful snacks, I can make the generalization that many nuts are good snacks. If I read that a region had very low rainfall during the growing season and a poor harvest in the fall, I infer that the poor rainfall resulted in fewer crops.

Multidraft Reading

Have students follow a multidraft reading protocol.

- **First reading**—Have students read to identify key ideas and details.

- **Second reading**—Have students read to identify the structure of the text.

- **Third reading**—Have students read to integrate knowledge and ideas by connecting the text to the world, their own experiences, and other texts.

Content-Area Vocabulary

1. Have students say each word.

2. Next, use each word in a sentence that defines it.

3. Finally, repeat your definitional sentence or a similar sentence, omitting the word, and have the class "fill in the blank" chorally.

Reading for Information

Analyzing Expository Texts

Government Publication

Web Site

© Common Core
State Standards

Reading Informational Text
1. Cite several pieces of textual evidence to support analysis of what the text says explicitly as well as inferences drawn from the text.

Language
4.c. Consult general and specialized reference materials, both print and digital, to find the pronunciation of a word or determine or clarify its precise meaning or its part of speech.
6. Acquire and use accurately grade-appropriate general academic and domain-specific words and phrases; gather vocabulary knowledge when considering a word or phrase important to comprehension or expression.

Reading Skill: Connecting Ideas to Make Inferences and Generalizations

An **inference** is a logical conclusion about information that is not directly stated. It is based on details in the text that are stated explicitly, or directly, and your own knowledge and experience. When you apply an inference in a general or nonspecific way, you are making a generalization. A **generalization** is a broad statement that applies to many examples and is supported by evidence. For example, a person who has successfully trained many dogs might make the generalization that all dogs are trainable. Use a chart like the one shown to record evidence that supports a generalization.

 **Evidence** +  **Evidence** +  **Evidence** = **Generalization**

Content-Area Vocabulary

These words appear in the selections that follow. You may also encounter them in other content-area texts.

- **exertion** (eg zʉr´ shən) *n.* physical or mental effort

- **calories** (kal´ ə rēz) *n.* units used for measuring the energy produced by food

- **infrastructure** (in´ frə struk´ chər) *n.* systems, such as roads, schools, power plants, and so on, that allow a community to continue to exist and grow

364 Short Stories

 Does every conflict have a winner?

Have students discuss how some solutions to problems can have long-term benefits.

Differentiated
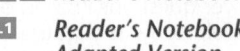
Instruction   for Universal Access

Reading Support
Give students reading support with the appropriate version of the *Reader's Notebooks:*

L2 L3 *Reader's Notebook*

L1   *Reader's Notebook: Adapted Version*

EL   *Reader's Notebook: English Learner's Version*

Walking for Exercise and Pleasure

Government Publication

Features:

- information provided by a government office or agency free of charge
- content published in print or online
- material available to all people

The President's Council on Physical Fitness and Sports

Walking: An Exercise for All Ages

Walking is easily the most popular form of exercise. Other activities generate more conversation and media coverage, but none of them approaches walking in number of participants. Approximately half of the 165 million American adults (18 years of age and older) claim they exercise regularly, and the number who walk for exercise is increasing every year.

Walking is the only exercise in which the rate of participation does not decline in the middle and later years. In a national survey, the highest percentage of regular walkers (39.4%) for any group was found among men 65 years of age and older.

Unlike tennis, running, skiing, and other activities that have gained great popularity fairly recently, walking has been widely practiced as a recreational and fitness activity throughout recorded history.

Classical and early English literature seems to have been written largely by men who were prodigious walkers, and Emerson and Thoreau helped carry on the tradition in America. Among American presidents, the most famous walkers included Jefferson, Lincoln, and Truman.

Walking: The Slower, Surer Way to Fitness

People walk for many reasons: for pleasure . . . to rid themselves of tensions . . . to find solitude . . . or to get from one place to another. Nearly everyone who walks regularly does so at least in part because of a conviction that it is good exercise.

Often dismissed in the past as being "too easy" to be taken seriously, walking recently has gained new respect as a means of improving

> This subheading contains a **generalization** about exercise.

> The information in this passage supports an **inference** that walking is popular among older men.

> This line tells you which office of the government published the document.

> Topic sentences such as this one can often serve as evidence to support an **inference** or **generalization**.

Reading for Information: Government Publication **365**

About Government Publications

1. Have students read the examples of government publications, and **ask** them to think about how the information in these publications might affect their lives.
   Possible response: Students might mention current Internet file-sharing legislation or other laws that affect their interests.

2. Generate discussion of the importance of government publications. **Ask** students what types of government publications they expect to read in the future.
   Possible responses: Students might want to study state driving booklets, learn about educational loans or training programs, or find out about summer jobs and internships.

3. Discuss how knowing the purpose and structure of government publications will help students find and interpret the information found in these documents.

Make Inferences and Generalizations

1. Explain that making generalizations helps people use a limited amount of information to explain a large number of cases.

2. Have students read the first section of the publication: "Walking for Exercise and Pleasure." Have them give examples of sentences in the selection that give details about how widespread walking for exercise is.
   Possible response: Sentences include "Other activities generate more conversation and media coverage, but none of them approaches walking in number of participants."

3. Then, **ask** students to find a generalization in the article that is supported by this information.
   Answer: "Walking is easily the most popular form of exercise."

4. **Ask** for other generalizations supported by this section.

5. Remind students that an inference is not an idea directly stated in the text. Instead, it is a logical conclusion based on the stated information.

365

Make Inferences and Generalizations

1. Review with students the facts about calorie-burning presented on this page. Then, **ask** them to make an inference about the effects of walking.
Possible response: Because walking burns calories—and burns more calories the heavier the person—it can help people lose weight.

2. **Ask** students to make or find generalizations supported by the second section of the publication: "Walking: The Slower, Surer Way to Fitness."
Possible responses: Walking offers the same fitness and health benefits as other forms of exercise, but is more convenient and easier. Walking also puts less strain on the body than other activities.

physical fitness. Studies show that, when done briskly on a regular schedule, it can improve the body's ability to consume oxygen during **exertion**, lower the resting heart rate, reduce blood pressure, and increase the efficiency of the heart and lungs. It also helps burn excess **calories**.

Walking burns approximately the same amount of calories per mile as does running, a fact particularly appealing to those who find it difficult to sustain the jarring effects of long distance jogging. Briskly walking one mile in 15 minutes burns just about the same number of calories as jogging an equal distance in 8½ minutes. In weight-bearing activities like walking, heavier individuals will burn more calories than lighter persons. For example, studies show that a 110-pound person burns about half as many calories as a 216-pound person walking at the same pace for the same distance.

In addition to the qualities it has in common with other activities, walking has several unique advantages. Some of these are:

Almost everyone can do it.
You don't have to take lessons to learn how to walk. Probably all you need to do to become a serious walker is step up your pace and distance and walk more often.

> Given the details listed here, you might **infer** that the writer enjoys walking.

You can do it almost anywhere.
All you have to do to find a place to walk is step outside your door. Almost any sidewalk, street, road, trail, park, field, or shopping mall will do. The variety of settings available is one of the things that makes walking such a practical and pleasurable activity.

You can do it almost anytime.
You don't have to find a partner or get a team together to walk, so you can set your own schedule. Weather doesn't pose the same problems and uncertainties that it does in many sports. Walking is not a seasonal activity, and you can do it in extreme temperatures that would rule out other activities.

It doesn't cost anything.
You don't have to pay fees or join a private club to become a walker. The only equipment required is a sturdy, comfortable pair of shoes.

Listen to Your Body

Listen to your body when you walk. If you develop dizziness, pain, nausea, or any other unusual symptom, slow down or stop. If the problem persists, see your physician before walking again.

> The information in the final paragraph presents a **generalization.**

The most important thing is simply to set aside part of each day and walk. No matter what your age or condition, it's a practice that can make you healthier and happier.

Vocabulary Development

© CCSS Language 6

Health and Fitness Terms
Tell students that when reading government publications, they may encounter new words specific to the content of those publications. Guide them to understand the meaning of the following health- and fitness-related words that appear in this publication. Point out the term *resting heart rate.* Explain that this term refers to how fast a person's heart pumps when he or she is not exercising. Then, talk about other terms on the page that might be unfamiliar to students, such as *blood pressure* or *excess calories.* Have students discuss what they think these terms mean.

Safe Routes to School
It's Happening in Metro Atlanta

Web site

Features:

- full color, interactive presentation of information
- a home page links to other documents
- content available to all with Internet access

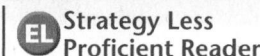

This photo allows you to infer that many students in Atlanta are walking to school.

Many of us over 30 remember walking or biking to school as an important part of childhood—a time to stretch our legs, explore our neighborhoods, make friends, feel the wind.... Many children today no longer have those opportunities. Safe Routes to School programs are developing in many parts of the world to bring that experience back to kids.

The Metro Atlanta Safe Routes to School Demonstration Project is the first comprehensive program to promote walking and biking to school in the state of Georgia. Our pilot project is making environments around schools safer so that more and more kids— and adults!—can walk and bike on their journeys

to and from school. Our research will be compiled into a guidebook that will help other communities establish Safe Routes to School programs across Georgia.

The Atlanta Bicycle Campaign is now in its third year of this 4-year project. Many thanks to our partners of the Metro Atlanta Safe Routes to School Coalition and to our funders, the Georgia Department of Transportation/Federal Highway Administration!

Click here to learn more about the Safe Routes to School program.

Click here to learn about some of the tools we have used to implement our program.

This sentence supports the inference that the bicycle campaign has been successful.

Reading for Information: Web Site **367**

About Web Sites

1. Review the list of features in the box on page 367 with students. Make sure they understand that the word *interactive* means the Web site responds to a visitor's choices and input by providing further choices and related information in various formats.

2. **Ask** students to give examples of occasions when they have used the Internet to locate information.
   Possible responses: Students may report conducting online research for school reports or in order to compare prices of consumer items.

3. Point out that students are about to read information from a Web site detailing a project in metropolitan Atlanta that promotes walking and biking to school.

Make Inferences and Generalizations

1. Have students imagine someone entered the classroom carrying a dripping umbrella. Observe that they would use their prior knowledge of when people carry wet umbrellas to make the inference that it was raining outside.

2. **Ask** students what generalization can be made from the text.
   Possible response: Young people and adults who walk or bike to school face potential safety hazards.

3. Next **ask** them to make an inference about community response to this problem based on the Web site.
   Possible responses: Two groups—the Metro Atlanta Safe Routes to School Coalition and the Atlanta Bicycle Campaign— would like to decrease the number of accidents involving pedestrians and cyclists on their way to and from school.

Differentiated Instruction for Universal Access

Strategy for Special-Needs Students

If there are students in the class with visual or hearing impairments or who require a wheelchair, have them lead the class in a discussion of additional challenges to safety. These might include the danger in not hearing vehicle horns, clearly seeing traffic lights or road signs, and the need to seek out access ramps. Conclude by having students note problem areas in their own community that should be called to the attention of community leaders.

EL Strategy Less Proficient Readers

Some students may experience difficulty with some of the language used in the Web site, including *comprehensive, environments,* and *implement.* Observe that one strategy for increasing knowledge of individual words is to keep a dictionary handy and to look up unfamiliar words when they are encountered. Note that students should also keep a small notepad with them in which they can write unfamiliar words to look up later on.

Make Inferences and Generalizations

1. Complete the reading of the Web site, reading aloud as students follow along silently in their texts.

2. **Ask:** What generalization can you make about the Safe Routes to School program based on its third stated goal?
   Possible response: The Atlanta program is to be a pilot or model for a statewide program.

3. **Ask:** What inference can you make about why the founders of the program chose to refer to the approach they were promoting as using the "4 E's"?
   Possible response: Using a memory device makes it easier for people to remember these four principles.

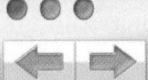

The word *Demonstration* supports the inference that other communities will use Atlanta as a model.

The Metro Atlanta Safe Routes to School Demonstration Project

What are the goals of the Metro Atlanta Demonstration Project?

The project has 3 specific goals:

1. To improve the safety of children who walk and bicycle to and from school;

2. To increase the numbers of school community members who walk and/or bicycle safely to and from school;

3. To prepare a guidebook for Safe Routes to School in Georgia.

How is the project carried out?

The project uses the "4 E's" approach:

Engineering—focusing on **infrastructure** improvements around the school that support walking and bicycling;

Enforcement—focusing on legal enforcement of traffic laws as well as school policies that support walking and bicycling;

Education—focusing on bicycle and pedestrian safety training of children and adults in the school community;

Encouragement—focusing on fun, educational, and motivational activities and events that promote safe walking and bicycling.

Where and when is the project taking place?

This project is working at four school sites, two in DeKalb County, representing an urban environment, and two in Gwinnett County, representing a suburban environment.

What will the demonstration project accomplish?

This is a demonstration project for the state of Georgia. At the conclusion of our work with the schools, we will produce a guidebook for use by others interested in establishing a Safe Routes to School program in their communities in Georgia.

Do you want to start a Safe Routes to School program in your neighborhood?

Click here to find out how.

368 Short Stories

Think Aloud

Vocabulary: Using Context
Direct students' attention to the word *pedestrian* in the first column on this page. Using the following "think aloud," model the use of context to infer the meaning of an unknown word. Say to students:

> I'm going to show you how I would figure out the meaning of *pedestrian* from its general and specific context. First I notice that the general or main theme of the Web site is walking to school and a special program to increase the safety of walkers. Next,

I look at the specific context—nearby words and phrases. In the same list as the word, the phrase *walking and bicycling* occurs three times. The word *pedestrian* occurs in the phrase *bicycle and pedestrian safety*. Since these phrases are given parallel treatment, I can assume that *walking and pedestrian* have meanings that are close. From these clues, I can assume that *pedestrian* means "a person who is walking," which I can verify by checking the dictionary.

Comparing Expository Texts

⊚ **1. Key Ideas and Details (a)** Make one **inference** and one **generalization** about walking based on each text. Use the graphic organizer on page 364 to support your generalizations with evidence. **(b)** How are the generalizations you made about walking from each text similar to and different from each other?

Content-Area Vocabulary

2. (a) Remove the suffix *-ion* from the word *exertion*. Using a print or online dictionary, explain how removing the suffix alters the meaning of the word and its part of speech. **(b)** Use the word *exert* in a sentence that shows its meaning.

🕐 Timed Writing

Explanatory Text: Directions

Format
To draw a map, first consider the scale by estimating distances between points. Provide a legend, or key, to explain your color coding.

Suppose that you are organizing a Walk to School Week for the students in your neighborhood. Decide on a meeting place, and write clear directions from that spot to the front door of your school. Identify the streets, landmarks, and distances between points in your directions. In addition, draw a detailed map with important information clearly labeled. (30 minutes)

Academic Vocabulary
When you *identify* something, you recognize and bring attention to it.

5-Minute Planner

Complete these steps before you begin to write:

1. Read the prompt carefully, noting that there are two assignments that you must complete—a set of directions and a map.

2. In a rough sketch, map out the location of the school, the meeting place, and streets and landmarks between them.

3. Determine the walking path. Note where you turn left or right and where you cross streets. Estimate the distances between key points. **TIP** If possible, use a map of your town or city to help identify street names and estimate distances.

4. Use your notes and rough map as you draft your directions.

Comparing Expository Texts

1. (a) Sample response: "Walking for Exercise and Pleasure"— Walking is a good choice as a form of exercise. Supporting evidence includes the fact that walking is easy, inexpensive, and accessible and that it burns calories. "Safe Routes to School"—Supporting walking contributes to the quality of life in a community. Evidence includes the following: If more people walk, and if their neighbors support them, then there will be safer drivers and fewer traffic accidents.
(b) Sample response: Both generalizations relate to the benefits of walking, but the first focuses on the benefits of the exercise itself and the second focuses on the secondary benefits to a community and the individuals within it.

2. (a) When you take the *-ion* suffix away from the word *exertion*, you get the word *exert*. It is a verb that means "to put (something) to use," instead of a noun that means "an effort." **(b) Sample response:** She exerted all her strength to throw the shot put.

🕐 Timed Writing

1. Before students complete the activity, guide them in identifying and analyzing key words and phrases in the prompt, highlighted on the student page.

2. Work with students to draw up guidelines for their directions based on the key words:

- **Focus** The set of directions should contain all information necessary to get from one place to the other, with no extraneous details.

- **Organization** The directions should be organized in the correct sequence, with a logical ordering of directions and information about distances and landmarks.

- **Details** The directions should include key instructions, such as whether to turn right or left, and estimated distances.

3. Have students use the 5-Minute Planner to structure their time.

4. Allow students 30 minutes to complete the assignment. Evaluate their work using the guidelines they have developed.

© Common Core
State Standards

• Reading Literature 3
• Writing 2.a

Comparing Literary Works

After Twenty Years
He—y, Come On Ou

❶ Comparing Irony

1. Introduce the skill, using the instruction on the student page.

2. Give students a copy of **Comparing Irony Graphic Organizer B** (*Graphic Organizer Transparencies*, p. 69). Tell them they will fill it in with ironic details as they read.

Think Aloud: Model the Skill

Say to students:

> We notice irony in real life all of the time. When someone comments that the weather is lovely on a cold, rainy, windy day, I know she can't be saying what she really means. Calling bad weather lovely is an example of verbal irony. If I work all night to prepare for a big meeting and then oversleep and miss the meeting entirely, this situation is full of situational irony. What happened was exactly the opposite of my intention. In literature, writers use irony to entertain and to convey messages.

❶ Comparing Irony

Irony is a literary element that involves a contradiction or contrast of some kind. In literature, writers often use irony to entertain and to convey a theme, or message.

- In **situational irony**, something takes place that is the opposite of what we expect to happen. For example, people note the irony when a fire station burns down.

- In **verbal irony,** a speaker or character says something that contradicts what he or she actually means. A jealous runner-up who says to a rival, "You deserved the medal" is speaking ironically if she really means, "You deserved the *second-place* medal."

As you read these stories, ask yourself questions like these to help you understand the author's use of situational irony:

- What details lead me to expect a certain outcome?
- What happened instead of the outcome I expected?
- Does irony in the story help convey a message or insight about life?

Use a chart like this to record your observations.

Story		
Expected Outcome		
Actual Ending		
Clues in Story		

© Common Core
State Standards

Reading Literature
3. Analyze how particular elements of a story or drama interact.
Writing
2.a. Introduce a topic clearly, previewing what is to follow; organize ideas, concepts, and information, using strategies s as definition, classification, comparison/contrast, and caus effect; include formatting, graphics, and multimedia whe useful to aiding comprehensio *(Timed Writing)*

- Vocabulary flashcards
- Interactive journals
- More about the authors
- Selection audio
- Interactive graphic organizers

www.PHLitOnline.com

Vocabulary Development

Vocabulary Knowledge Rating

Create a **Vocabulary Knowledge Rating Chart** (*Professional Development Guidebook*, p. 33) featuring the words glossed in the selections:

spectators (p. 373)   simultaneously (p. 376)
intricate (p. 373)   apparent (p. 380)
destiny (p. 374)   plausible (p. 380)
proposal (p. 380)

Give students a copy of the chart, and read

the words aloud. Have students mark their rating of each in the Before You Read column. To gauge how much instruction to provide, tally the students who think they know each word.

Explain that the words are defined in the margin at the point where they appear in the selection. Urge students to be alert to these words as they read the selections. They will rate their knowledge again when they finish.

 **Vocabulary Central**, featuring tools, activities, and songs for studying vocabulary, is available online at **www.PHLitOnline.com**.

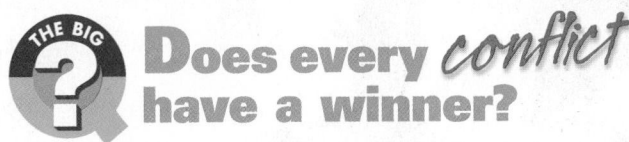

Does every *conflict* have a winner?

Writing About the Big Question

Both of these stories have events that take characters—and readers—by surprise. Use this sentence starter to develop your ideas.

Unexpected events can **challenge** people by _____.

Meet the Authors

O. Henry (1862–1910)

Author of "After Twenty Years"

O. Henry is the pen name of William Sydney Porter. He is known for his warm, witty short stories featuring ordinary people. Porter held many jobs, including working on a sheep ranch, in a bank, in a newspaper office, and as the publisher of a humor magazine. Later, Porter was sentenced to prison for stealing bank funds, a crime he may not have committed.

Finding a New Identity While serving time, Porter wrote short stories. On his release, he moved to New York City and started a career as a writer. He used the name O. Henry to shield his identity. Many of his 300 stories are inspired by his time in prison, where he gained an understanding of people on both sides of the law.

Shinichi Hoshi (1926–1997)

Author of "He—y, Come On Ou—t!"

Shinichi Hoshi, a Japanese writer, is best known for his "short-short stories," in which he makes observations about human nature and society. Hoshi wrote more than a thousand short-short stories as well as longer fantasy stories, detective stories, biographies, and travel articles. In addition, he was one of the first Japanese science-fiction writers. Hoshi's stories have been translated into many languages, and devoted readers enjoy their unexpected plot turns.

Teaching Resources

- 🄰 *Unit 2 Resources*, pp. 204–211
- 🄰 *Graphic Organizer Transparencies*, pp. 68–71
- 🄰 *Common Core Companion*, pp. 28–35; 202–212
- 🄰 **Enriched Online Student Edition**
- 🄰 🄴🄻 *Hear It!* **Audio CD**

PHLit Online! All resources, including print and audio, are available online at www.PHLitOnline.com.

 Daily Bellringer

For each class during which you will teach this selection, have students complete one of the five Sentence Combining activities for Week 12 in the *Daily Bellringer Activities* booklet.

② Writing About the Big Question

1. Review the assignment with the class.
2. Ask students for examples of unexpected events in their lives, asking them to explain whether these events challenged them.
3. Then, have students complete the sentence starter. Review responses as a class. (**Sample response:** Unexpected events can <u>challenge</u> people by forcing them to step outside their usual routines.)
4. Tell students that as they read, they should identify conflicts caused or revealed by unexpected events.

Concept Connector ➡

Students will return to their sentence starters after they have concluded reading.

Multidraft Reading

To assist struggling readers and to deepen reading for all, apply multidraft reading protocols. For each reading, have students set the purpose indicated:

- **First reading**—identifying key ideas and details and answering any Reading Checks.
- **Second reading**—analyzing craft and structure and responding to the side-column prompts.
- **Third reading**—integrating knowledge and ideas, connecting to other texts and the world, and answering the end-of-selection questions.

For more guidance, see the *Classroom Strategies and Teaching Routines* card on multidraft reading.

For more about the authors and practice with the selection vocabulary, go online at www.PHLitOnline.com.

❶ Background

Surprise Endings Tell students that O. Henry was known for his surprise endings. Through them he helped establish the popularity of the American short story. Today, the best short stories published every year are given the "O. Henry Award." O. Henry knew that a surprise ending should be startling, but for it to be most successful and satisfying for readers, it also had to make sense.

❷ Activating Prior Knowledge

Ask students whether they think they would recognize someone they know today from a photograph taken many years before. To connect this discussion to the story, obtain twenty-year-old photographs of adults with whom all students are familiar, such as yourself, other teachers, or celebrities. Present these photographs to groups. Challenge students to identify the person in each photograph. Lead students to the story by telling them that it concerns a meeting between two friends who have not seen each other for twenty years.

Concept Connector ➡

Students will follow up on this activity after completing the story.

❸ About the Selection

"After Twenty Years" shows how people change over time. Two old friends, one now a shady character wanted by the law, the other now a police officer, meet after a twenty-year separation. Neither the reader nor the criminal realizes that the uniformed officer is the criminal's old friend. The officer, however, recognizes the man, both as his old friend and as one being sought for crimes committed elsewhere. Although he cannot bring himself to make the arrest, the duty-bound cop engages a plainclothes colleague to do so.

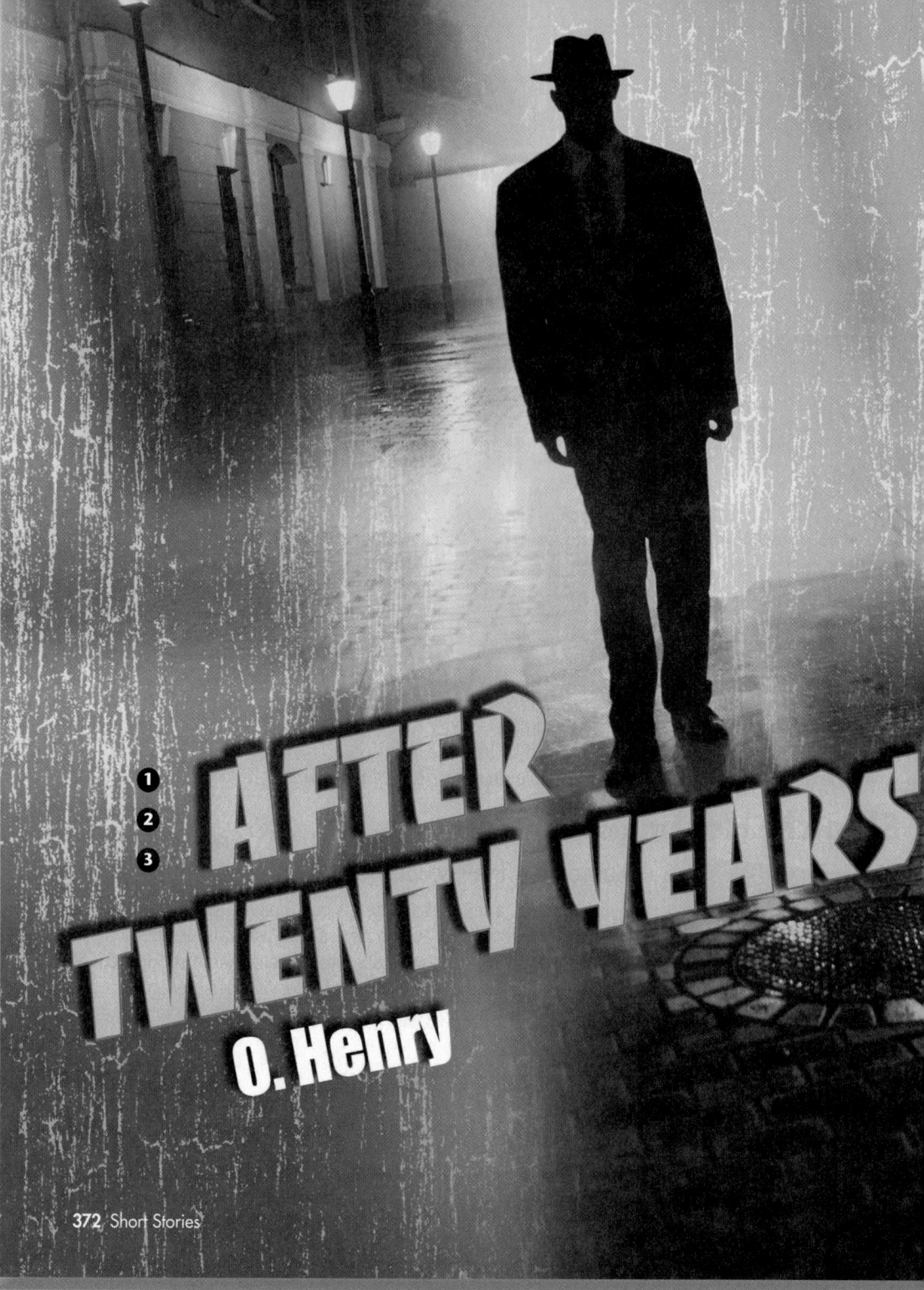

❶
❷
❸

AFTER TWENTY YEARS
O. Henry

372 Short Stories

ⓒ Text Complexity Rubric

After Twenty Years		
Qualitative Measures	**Context/Knowledge Demands**	New York City neighborhood, circa 1900 1 ② 3 4 5
	Structure/Language Conventionality	Vocabulary is challenging and somewhat dated 1 2 3 ④ 5
	Levels of Meaning/ Purpose/Concepts	Accessible concept (irony; unexpected outcome) 1 2 ③ 4 5
Quantitative Measures	**Text Length**	Word Count: 1,261
	Lexile	860L

The policeman on the beat moved up the avenue impressively. The impressiveness was habitual and not for show, for spectators were few. The time was barely 10 o'clock at night, but chilly gusts of wind with a taste of rain in them had well nigh[1] depeopled the streets.

Trying doors as he went, twirling his club with many intricate and artful movements, turning now and then to cast his watchful eye down the pacific thoroughfare,[2] the officer, with his stalwart form and slight swagger, made a fine picture of a guardian of the peace. The vicinity was one that kept early hours. Now and then you might see the lights of a cigar store or of an all-night lunch counter; but the majority of the doors belonged to business places that had long since been closed.

When about midway of a certain block the policeman suddenly slowed his walk. In the doorway of a darkened hardware store a man leaned, with an unlighted cigar in his mouth. As the policeman walked up to him the man spoke up quickly.

"It's all right, officer," he said, reassuringly. "I'm just waiting for a friend. It's an appointment made twenty years ago. Sounds a little funny to you, doesn't it? Well, I'll explain if you'd like to make certain it's all straight. About that long ago there used to be a restaurant where this store stands—'Big Joe' Brady's restaurant."

"Until five years ago," said the policeman. "It was torn down then."

The man in the doorway struck a match and lit his cigar. The light showed a pale, square-jawed face with keen eyes, and a little white scar near his right eyebrow. His scarfpin was a large diamond, oddly set.

"Twenty years ago tonight," said the man, "I dined here at 'Big Joe' Brady's with Jimmy Wells, my best chum, and the finest chap in the world. He and I were raised here in New York, just like two brothers, together. I was eighteen and Jimmy was twenty. The next morning I was to start for the

---

1. **well nigh** *adv.* very nearly.
2. **pacific thoroughfare** calm street.

Vocabulary

spectators
(spek´ tāt´ erz) *n.*
people who watch

intricate (in´ tri kit) *adj.*
complex; detailed

5 ◀ Critical Viewing
Based on this picture, what are three words that might describe the story you are about to read? **[Predict]**

6 ✓ Reading Check
What is the officer doing?

---

4 Critical Thinking

Analyze

1. Have two volunteers read the first two paragraphs aloud in turn.

2. Have students list descriptions in the first two paragraphs related to the emptiness of the streets. **Answer:** Details include the absence of spectators, the wind that has driven people indoors, and the fact that most businesses are closed.

3. Then, have students list descriptions related to the patrolman. **Answer:** The patrolman is described as moving impressively, as twirling his club artfully, and as watchful.

4. **Ask** students what main impression is created by the first two paragraphs. **Possible response:** The paragraphs paint a picture of empty streets under the watch of an impressive patrolman.

5. Have a third volunteer read the third paragraph aloud. **Ask** students why the appearance of the leaning man at this point in the story is dramatic. **Possible response:** Many details in the first two paragraphs emphasize the emptiness of the streets, so his appearance is surprising. When he appears, the emphasis on the patrolman makes readers wonder whether the new person will cause trouble or perhaps need help.

5 Critical Viewing

Answer: Students may mention the words *eerie, ominous,* and *mysterious.*

6 Reading Check

Answer: He is patrolling the block.

© Text Complexity: Reader and Task Suggestions

After Twenty Years

Preparing to Read the Text
- Using the Background information on p. 372, prepare students for the possibility of a surprise ending to the story.
- Explain that the story contains many instances of irony, when characters and/or readers are surprised. Have students give examples of irony from stories they have read.
- Guide students in using Multidraft Reading strategies (TE p. 371).

Leveled Tasks

Levels of Meaning If students will have difficulty with levels of meaning, have them first read to identify the history of Bob and Jimmy's relationship. Then, have them reread to look for clues to the story's outcome. Discuss what each clue suggests to students.

Analyzing If students will not have difficulty interpreting levels of meaning, have them note as they read ways that the author uses setting to set up the story's surprise ending. Discuss as a class.

PHLit Online!
This selection is available in interactive format in the Enriched Online Student Edition, online at at **www.PHLitOnline.com**, which includes an interactive graphic organizer.

1. Remind students that irony always involves something unexpected. A character may be surprised or the reader may be surprised—or both.

2. Have a volunteer read the bracketed passage aloud. Note how sure the speaker is that his friend Jimmy will show up. **Ask** students whether they also think Jimmy will show up and why they think so.
   Possible responses: He won't show up because he has died. He will show up, but it won't be the happy reunion that the friend is expecting.

3. **Ask** the Irony question.
   Possible responses: The situation is suspicious. The man waiting has a scar on his face and a diamond pin and watch. These details make him sound like a shady character. Also, the streets are empty and it's windy and rainy. These details do not foreshadow a happy ending. There is little indication in the story to suggest whether they will or will not reunite.

4. Have students fill in their graphic organizers with details from their responses that suggest a particular outcome.

Vocabulary
destiny (des´ tə nē) *n.* preplanned course of events

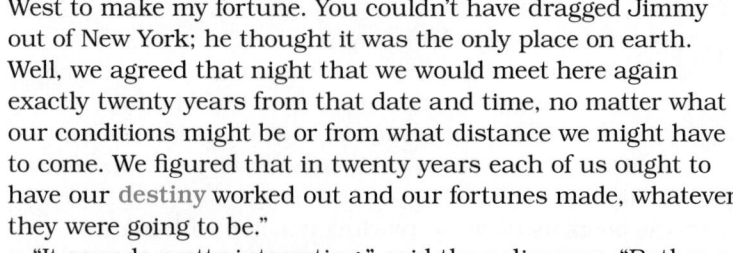

Irony
Based on the story so far, do you expect the old friends to reunite? Explain your answer.

West to make my fortune. You couldn't have dragged Jimmy out of New York; he thought it was the only place on earth. Well, we agreed that night that we would meet here again exactly twenty years from that date and time, no matter what our conditions might be or from what distance we might have to come. We figured that in twenty years each of us ought to have our destiny worked out and our fortunes made, whatever they were going to be."

"It sounds pretty interesting," said the policeman. "Rather a long time between meets, though, it seems to me. Haven't you heard from your friend since you left?"

"Well, yes, for a time we corresponded," said the other. "But after a year or two we lost track of each other. You see, the West is a pretty big proposition, and I kept hustling around over it pretty lively. But I know Jimmy will meet me here if he's alive, for he always was the truest, stanchest old chap in the world. He'll never forget. I came a thousand miles to stand in this door tonight, and it's worth it if my old partner turns up."

The waiting man pulled out a handsome watch, the lids of it set with small diamonds.

"Three minutes to ten," he announced. "It was exactly ten o'clock when we parted here at the restaurant door."

"Did pretty well out West, didn't you?" asked the policeman.

"You bet! I hope Jimmy has done half as well. He was a kind of plodder, though, good fellow as he was. I've had to compete with some of the sharpest wits going to get my pile. A man gets in a groove in New York. It takes the West to put a razor-edge on him."

The policeman twirled his club and took a step or two.

"I'll be on my way. Hope your friend comes around all right. Going to call time on him sharp?"

"I should say not!" said the other. "I'll give him half an hour at least. If Jimmy is alive on earth he'll be here by that time. So long, officer."

"Good-night, sir," said the policeman, passing on along his beat, trying doors as he went.

There was now a fine, cold drizzle falling, and the wind

Vocabulary Development

© **CCSS** Language 6

Thematic Vocabulary: The Big Question
As students are discussing "After Twenty Years," encourage them to use the thematic vocabulary presented in Introducing the Big Question, pp. 198–199. You might guide them with sentence starters like these:

1. The waiting man has a strong *desire* to . . .
2. The waiting man's *attitude* toward is Jimmy Wells is . . .
3. The *competition* the waiting man faced out West was . . .
4. Bob's *misunderstanding* of the situation becomes clear when . . .

had risen from its uncertain puffs into a steady blow. The few foot passengers astir in that quarter hurried dismally and silently along with coat collars turned high and pocketed hands. And in the door of the hardware store the man who had come a thousand miles to fill an appointment, uncertain almost to absurdity,[3] with the friend of his youth, smoked his cigar and waited.

About twenty minutes he waited, and then a tall man in a long overcoat, with collar turned up to his ears, hurried across from the opposite side of the street. He went directly to the waiting man.

"Is that you, Bob?" he asked, doubtfully.

"Is that you, Jimmy Wells?" cried the man in the door.

"Bless my heart!" exclaimed the new arrival, grasping both the other's hands with his own. "It's Bob, sure as fate. I was certain I'd find you here if you were still in existence. Well, well, well!—twenty years is a long time. The old restaurant's gone, Bob; I wish it had lasted, so we could have had another dinner there. How has the West treated you, old man?"

"Bully;[4] it has given me everything I asked it for. You've changed lots, Jimmy. I never thought you were so tall by two or three inches."

"Oh, I grew a bit after I was twenty."

"Doing well in New York, Jimmy?"

"Moderately. I have a position in one of the city departments. Come on, Bob; we'll go around to a place I know of, and have a good long talk about old times."

The two men started up the street, arm in arm. The man from the West, his egotism enlarged by success, was

---

3. **absurdity** (ab sur´də tē) *n.* nonsense.
4. **bully** *interj.* very good.

8 ▲ **Critical Viewing**
Would it be hard to identify an old friend in a setting like this one? Why? **[Explain]**

Irony
Did you expect Jimmy to show up for the meeting? Why or why not?

10  Reading Check
Why did Jimmy and Bob agree to meet in twenty years?

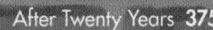

⓫ Humanities

Nighthawks, 1942
by Edward Hopper

Edward Hopper (1882–1967) led a simple and unremarkable life devoted to his art. Best known for his paintings of ordinary urban scenes, houses, and bleak, lonely streets and rooms, he claimed that he did not intend his paintings to show the grim emotions and moods they often do. Rather, he saw them as attempts to capture color and the quality of light. Lead a discussion about the painting using the following questions.

• How can you tell that this city scene is from the past?
  Possible response: Students might refer to the old-fashioned look of the diner and the clothes the people are wearing.

• How does the artist create a sense of detachment, or loneliness, in the painting?
  Possible response: The solitary figures, the lack of decoration in the diner, and the darkness behind the windows create such a feeling.

⓬ Critical Viewing

Answer: The setting is clearly urban, possibly a street corner in New York City, just as in the story. It is night outside the diner, as in the story. Across the street from the diner is a recessed doorway similar to the one described in the story.

⓫   Nighthawks, Edward Hopper, The Art Institute of Chicago

▲ **Critical Viewing**
What details in this painting match the setting of the story? **[Connect]**

Vocabulary
simultaneously
(sī′ məl tā′ nē əs lē) *adv.*
at the same time

beginning to outline the history of his career. The other, submerged in his overcoat, listened with interest.

At the corner stood a drug store, brilliant with electric lights. When they came into this glare each of them turned simultaneously to gaze upon the other's face.

The man from the West stopped suddenly and released his arm.

"You're not Jimmy Wells," he snapped. "Twenty years is a long time, but not long enough to change a man's nose from a Roman to a pug."[5]

"It sometimes changes a good man into a bad one," said the tall man. "You've been under arrest for ten minutes, 'Silky' Bob. Chicago thinks you may have dropped over our way and wires us she wants to have a chat with you. Going quietly are you? That's sensible. Now, before we go to the station here's a

---

5. **change a man's nose from a Roman to a pug** A Roman nose has a high, prominent bridge, but a pug nose is short, thick, and turned up at the end.

Think Aloud

Vocabulary: Using Context
Direct students' attention to the word *submerged* on this page. Using the following "think aloud," model how to use context and prior knowledge to infer the meaning of a word used in an unusual way.

    I'm going to think aloud to show you how I would figure out the meaning of *submerged* in this context.

    In this sentence, *submerged* is used to describe the way a man looks in his long

overcoat. When something is literally *submerged,* it is underwater, but since this man is not in water, the word clearly means something else here. I ask myself how a person in an overcoat could resemble something underwater. I realize that both are covered up, or hidden. I try replacing *submerged* with the phrase *covered up* and it makes sense: "The other, covered up in his overcoat, listened with interest."

note I was asked to hand to you. You may read it here at the window. It's from Patrolman Wells."

The man from the West unfolded the little piece of paper handed him. His hand was steady when he began to read, but it trembled a little by the time he had finished. The note was rather short.

Bob,
I was at the appointed place on time.
When you struck the match to light your
cigar I saw it was the face of the man
wanted in Chicago. Somehow I couldn't
do it myself, so I went around and got a
plain clothes man to do the job.
Jimmy.

Irony
How does the patrolman's name indicate the irony of the conversation with the policeman at the beginning of this story?

 Spiral Review
Conflict What conflict do you think each man felt when Bob was taken to jail?

Critical Thinking

1. **Key Ideas and Details (a)** Where is the story set? **(b) Analyze:** Describe the atmosphere, or mood, using two details from the story.

2. **Key Ideas and Details (a)** How does Bob describe Jimmy's strengths and weaknesses? **(b) Infer:** How did Bob spend his time away from his hometown after he left?

3. **Key Ideas and Details (a)** What evidence shows that both Bob and Jimmy are proud of their accomplishments? **(b) Make a Judgment:** Who has been more successful? Explain your answer.

4. **Integration of Knowledge and Ideas (a)** Do you think Bob's expectations of Jimmy were fulfilled? **(b)** Was there a "winner" in this story? Support your answer with details from the story. *[Connect to the Big Question: Does every conflict have a winner?]*

Cite textual evidence to support your responses.

Differentiated Instruction for Universal Access

Strategy for Less Proficient Readers
After students have finished reading, ask them to review the story and the information they put in their graphic organizers to find details that hint at the outcome. Show students the partially filled-in **Comparing Irony Graphic Organizer Transparency A** (*Graphic Organizer Transparencies,* p. 68) to help them complete their charts. Help students find details that hint at the situational irony of the story's ending.

Enrichment for Advanced Readers
After students have finished reading, ask them to brainstorm about alternative ironic endings, and then write those endings for the story. Explain that students may need to change details in the story to fit the new ending, but that they should keep the same premise—the meeting after 20 years. Explain to students that an unexpected ending does not mean an ending that is not supported by details in the story. Their new endings must still make sense. Remind students to foreshadow their endings throughout their stories.

⓭ Irony

1. **Ask** students if it seems as though the men know each other. **Answer:** No, they don't seem to know each other.

2. **Ask** the Irony question. **Answer:** The first few paragraphs indicate that the patrolman and the man in the doorway are strangers. When the reader finds out that the patrolman is Jimmy Wells, the irony becomes clear.

 Spiral Review

Conflict

1. Students studied conflict in the Unit 2 Literary Analysis Workshop (pp. 200–215).

2. **Ask** the Spiral Review question.

   Possible response: Jimmy probably felt a conflict between his loyalty to his old friend and his duty to uphold the law. Bob probably felt a conflict between his anger at being caught and his shame at being seen as a criminal by his friend.

ASSESS

Answers

Critical Thinking

Remind students to support their answers with evidence from the text.

1. (a) On a New York City street. (b) The atmosphere is suspenseful and gloomy, because the streets are deserted and a chilly wind is blowing.

2. (a) Bob describes Jimmy as a good person but not very motivated. (b) Committing crimes.

3. (a) Jimmy's loyalty to his job shows his pride. Bob's bragging shows his pride. (b) Some students might say Jimmy, because he has stayed on the right side of the law.

4. (a) **Possible responses:** Yes, because Jimmy did show up for the appointment and did not arrest his friend himself. He shows the respect for their old friendship that Bob expected. (b) **Possible responses:** Some students may say there was no winner because both men lost a friend.

⑭
⑮
⑯

He-y, Come On Ou-t!

Shinichi Hoshi
Translated by Stanleigh Jones

⑰ ▲ **Critical Viewing**
In what ways do people who live in towns like the one shown have to depend on their environment? **[Analyze]**

The typhoon had passed and the sky was a gorgeous blue. Even a certain village not far from the city had suffered damage. A little distance from the village and near the mountains, a small shrine had been swept away by a landslide.

"I wonder how long that shrine's been here."

"Well, in any case, it must have been here since an awfully long time ago."

"We've got to rebuild it right away."

While the villagers exchanged views, several more of their number came over.

"It sure was wrecked."

"I think it used to be right here."

"No, looks like it was a little more over there."

Just then one of them raised his voice. "Hey what in the world is this hole?"

Where they had all gathered there was a hole about a meter in diameter. They peered in, but it was so dark nothing could be seen. However, it gave one the feeling that it was so deep it went clear through to the center of the earth.

378 Short Stories

ⓒ Text Complexity Rubric

He-y, Come On O-ut!		
Qualitative Measures	**Context/Knowledge Demands**	Japan, late 1900s; contemporary situation 1 2 ③ 4 5
	Structure/Language Conventionality and Clarity	On-level vocabulary; conversational syntax; simple and compound sentences 1 2 ③ 4 5
	Levels of Meaning/ Purpose/Concept Level	Accessible concept (irony; multiple meanings; ambiguous ending) 1 2 3 ④ 5
Quantitative Measures	**Text Length**	Word Count: 1,364
	Lexile	890L

There was even one person who said, "I wonder if it's a fox's hole."

"He—y, come on ou—t!" shouted a young man into the hole. There was no echo from the bottom. Next he picked up a pebble and was about to throw it in.

"You might bring down a curse on us. Lay off," warned an old man, but the younger one energetically threw the pebble in. As before, however, there was no answering response from the bottom. The villagers cut down some trees, tied them with rope and made a fence which they put around the hole. Then they repaired to the village.

"What do you suppose we ought to do?"

"Shouldn't we build the shrine up just as it was over the hole?"

A day passed with no agreement. The news traveled fast, and a car from the newspaper company rushed over. In no time a scientist came out, and with an all-knowing expression on his face he went over to the hole. Next, a bunch of gawking curiosity seekers showed up; one could also pick out here and there men of shifty glances who appeared to be concessionaires.[1] Concerned that someone might fall into the hole, a policeman from the local substation kept a careful watch.

One newspaper reporter tied a weight to the end of a long cord and lowered it into the hole. A long way down it went. The cord ran out, however, and he tried to pull it out, but it would not come back up. Two or three people helped out, but when they all pulled too hard, the cord parted at the edge of the hole. Another reporter, a camera in hand, who had been watching all of this, quietly untied a stout rope that had been wound around his waist.

The scientist contacted people at his laboratory and had them bring out a high-powered bull horn, with which he was going to check out the echo from the hole's bottom. He tried switching through various sounds, but there was no echo. The scientist was puzzled, but he could not very well give up with everyone watching him so intently. He put the bull horn right up to the hole, turned it to its highest volume, and let it sound continuously for a long time. It was a noise that would

Irony
What expectations does the author create in the reader's mind about the hole?
18

19 ✓ Reading Check

What is unusual about the hole where the shrine used to be?

---

1. concessionaires (kən sesh′ ə nerz′) *n.* business people.

© Text Complexity: Reader and Task Suggestions

He-y, Come On O-ut!	
Preparing to Read the Text	**Leveled Tasks**
• Using the Background information on p. 378, discuss the role that Japanese culture and history play in the story. • Have students discuss an event in their lives that had unanticipated consequences. • Guide students in using Multidraft Reading strategies (TE p. 371).	*Levels of Meaning* If students will have difficulty with levels of meaning, have them first read to identify the physical changes to the hole during the story. Then, have them reread to look for ways that characters react to the hole. Clarify these reactions as needed. *Evaluating* If students will not have difficulty interpreting levels of meaning, have them note as they read ways that the author uses description to contrast science and spiritual approaches to the hole. Discuss how the ambiguous ending reflects this contrast.

1. Explain that one way authors use irony is to have something happen that is not what the reader would have predicted.

2. Then, **ask** the Irony question.
Answer: No. One would expect the site to be treated with more respect, perhaps honored with a commemorative plaque.

3. Have students discuss whether ironies like this one are common in modern life.
Possible responses: Some students may point out that old buildings and even entire neighborhoods may be eliminated by developers without an effort to preserve the past. Others may point out that people often make strong efforts to preserve landmarks and other signs of heritage.

Vocabulary
apparent (ə par´ ənt)
adj. seeming
plausible (plô´ zə bəl)
adj. believable
proposal (prə pōz´ əl)
n. plan; offer

20

Irony
Is this how you would expect the former site of a shrine to be treated? Explain.

have carried several dozen kilometers above ground. But the hole just calmly swallowed up the sound.

In his own mind the scientist was at a loss, but with a look of apparent composure he cut off the sound and, in a manner suggesting that the whole thing had a perfectly plausible explanation, said simply, "Fill it in."

Safer to get rid of something one didn't understand.

The onlookers, disappointed that this was all that was going to happen, prepared to disperse. Just then one of the concessionaires, having broken through the throng and come forward, made a proposal.

"Let me have that hole. I'll fill it in for you."

"We'd be grateful to you for filling it in," replied the mayor of the village, "but we can't very well give you the hole. We have to build a shrine there."

"If it's a shrine you want, I'll build you a fine one later. Shall I make it with an attached meeting hall?"

Before the mayor could answer, the people of the village all shouted out.

"Really? Well, in that case, we ought to have it closer to the village."

"It's just an old hole. We'll give it to you!"

So it was settled. And the mayor, of course, had no objection.

The concessionaire was true to his promise. It was small, but closer to the village he did build for them a shrine with an attached meeting hall.

About the time the autumn festival was held at the new shrine, the hole-filling company established by the concessionaire hung out its small shingle at a shack near the hole.

The concessionaire had his cohorts mount a loud campaign in the city. "We've got a fabulously deep hole! Scientists say it's at least five thousand meters deep! Perfect for the disposal of such things as waste from nuclear reactors."

Government authorities granted permission. Nuclear power plants fought for contracts. The people of the village were a bit worried about this, but they consented when it was explained that there would be absolutely no above-ground contamination[2] for several thousand years and that they would share in the profits. Into the bargain, very shortly a

---

2. **contamination** (kən tam´ ə nā´ shən) *n.* pollution by poison or other dangerous substances.

380 Short Stories

Vocabulary Development   © **CCSS** Language 6

Expressive Vocabulary
As students discuss the use of the hole as a place to dispose of nuclear waste, encourage them to use the following expressive vocabulary words: *reveal, affect,* and *anticipate.* You might encourage them with sentence starters like these:

1. When the concessionaire first offers to fill in the hole, he does not *reveal* . . .
Possible response: his plans for nuclear waste disposal.

2. The villagers are briefly concerned about how nuclear waste will *affect* . . .
Possible response: their health and community.

3. The villagers do not fully *anticipate* the consequences of . . .
Possible response: giving the hole to the concessionaire.

magnificent road was built from the city to the village.

Trucks rolled in over the road, transporting lead boxes. Above the hole the lids were opened, and the wastes from nuclear reactors tumbled away into the hole.

From the Foreign Ministry and the Defense Agency boxes of unnecessary classified documents were brought for disposal. Officials who came to supervise the disposal held discussions on golf. The lesser functionaries, as they threw in the papers, chatted about pinball.

The hole showed no signs of filling up. It was awfully deep, thought some; or else it might be very spacious at the bottom. Little by little the hole-filling company expanded its business.

Bodies of animals used in contagious disease experiments at the universities were brought out, and to these were added the unclaimed corpses of vagrants. Better than dumping all of its garbage in the ocean, went the thinking in the city, and plans were made for a long pipe to carry it to the hole.

The hole gave peace of mind to the dwellers of the city. They concentrated solely on producing one thing after another. Everyone disliked thinking about the eventual consequences. People wanted only to work for production companies and sales corporations; they had no interest in becoming junk dealers. But, it was thought, these problems too would gradually be resolved by the hole.

Young girls whose betrothals[3] had been arranged discarded old diaries in the hole. There were also those who were inaugurating new love affairs and threw into the hole old photographs of themselves taken with former sweethearts. The police felt comforted as they used the hole to get rid of accumulations of expertly done counterfeit bills. Criminals breathed easier after throwing material evidence into the hole.

Whatever one wished to discard, the hole accepted it all.

---

3. betrothals (bē trōth′ əlz) *n.* promises of marriage.

㉑ ▲ Critical Viewing
What feelings do you think people would have after visiting a shrine like the one shown? **[Connect]**

Irony
Does this use of the hole seem like a good idea? Why or why not?

㉔ ✓ Reading Check
In what ways has the concessionaire used the hole to his advantage?

He—y, Come On Ou—t! **381**

381

25 Critical Viewing

Answer: The man might be looking up to see where the voice came from.

ASSESS

Answers

Critical Thinking

Before students respond, you may wish to have them write a brief objective summary of the selection. As they answer the questions below, remind them to support their answers with evidence from the text.

1. (a) A shrine had once stood on the site where the hole appeared. It had been there longer than anyone could remember. (b) The author may want the reader to think of the place as important or even sacred.

2. (a) The concessionaire offers to fill the hole, making it go away, if the village gives it to him. (b) People dispose of unwanted and disgusting objects in the hole. The city seems to flourish and grow as a result, which leads to more and more dumping.

3. (a) The author may be maligning people who put profit before the health of the environment. (b) The author may be suggesting that we cannot trust overly easy ways of getting rid of our problems. The voice and pebble indicate that everything is interconnected, and that the result of an action always returns to the doer of the action.

4. ❓ (a) The hole provides an easy way for the community to dispose of items, but at the end of the story the author implies that the community will suffer. (b) **Possible responses:** The ending implies that there is a conflict between people's desire for easy solutions and their reluctance to face the consequences of such solutions. (c) **Possible answers:** People who do not think through their actions must lose; there are no winners here.

The hole cleansed the city of its filth; the sea and sky seemed to have become a bit clearer than before.

Aiming at the heavens, new buildings went on being constructed one after the other.

One day, atop the high steel frame of a new building under construction, a workman was taking a break. Above his head he heard a voice shout:

"He—y, come on ou—t!"

But, in the sky to which he lifted his gaze there was nothing at all. A clear blue sky merely spread over all. He thought it must be his imagination. Then, as he resumed his former position, from the direction where the voice had come, a small pebble skimmed by him and fell on past.

The man, however, was gazing in idle reverie[4] at the city's skyline growing ever more beautiful, and he failed to notice.

---

4. **idle reverie** (rev′ ə rē) *n.* daydreaming.

---

25 ▲ **Critical Viewing** Based on the story, why might the man in this picture be looking up? **[Hypothesize]**

Cite textual evidence to support your responses.

Critical Thinking

© 1. **Key Ideas and Details (a)** What had stood before the hole appeared, and for how long? **(b) Infer:** What is the author suggesting about the site?

© 2. **Key Ideas and Details (a)** What does the concessionaire offer to do with the hole? **(b) Analyze Causes and Effects:** What is the result of his action?

© 3. **Integration of Knowledge and Ideas (a) Synthesize:** What comment do you think the author may be making about people and the environment? **(b) Generalize:** What message does the author suggest when a voice and a pebble apparently come out of the hole?

© 4. **Integration of Knowledge and Ideas (a)** Do you think the author believes that the hole provides a good solution for the community? **(b)** What conflicts do you think the author wants you to see in the ending of the story? **(c)** Do these conflicts have winners and losers? Explain, using details from the story. *[Connect to the Big Question: Does every conflict have a winner?]*

382 Short Stories

Vocabulary Development   © CCSS Language 6

Vocabulary Knowledge Rating
When students have completed reading and discussing "After Twenty Years" and "He—y, Come On O—ut!" have them take out their **Vocabulary Knowledge Rating Chart.** Read the words aloud once more and have students rate their knowledge of the words again in the After Reading column. Clarify any words that are still problematic. Have students write their own definition and example or sentence in the appropriate column. Then, have students complete the Vocabulary Practice activities at the end of the selection. Encourage students to use these words in further discussion and written work about this selection. Remind them that they will be accountable for these words on the **Selection Test,** *Unit 2 Resources,* pp. 215–217 or 218–220.

Comparing Irony

1. **Craft and Structure** Did the end of O. Henry's story entertain or shock you? Explain.
2. **Craft and Structure** Did the ending of "He—y, Come on Ou—t!" change your mind or confirm your thinking about a social issue? Explain.
3. **Integration of Knowledge and Ideas** Create a chart to compare irony. **(a)** In the first column, identify the irony you found. **(b)** In the second column, explain what the irony tells you about the characters. **(c)** In the third column, explain what message the author delivers through the use of irony.

	What It Says	What It Means	Why It Is Important
After Twenty Years			
He—y, Come on Ou—t!			

⏱ Timed Writing

Explanatory Text: Essay

In an essay, compare and contrast your responses to the two stories based on the authors' use of irony. Support your ideas with details from the texts. **(40 minutes)**

5-Minute Planner

1. Read the prompt carefully and completely.
2. Gather your ideas in a Venn diagram or by jotting down answers to these questions:
   - Is believability important to you when you respond to ironic stories? Why or why not?
   - Which story's ironic message did you understand more easily?
3. Use a compare-and-contrast organizational strategy. For example, compare and contrast your reactions to a surprising aspect in each story.
4. Reread the prompt, and then draft your essay.

Assessment Resources

The following resources can be used to assess students' knowledge and skills.

Unit 2 Resources

L1 L2 EL **Selection Test A,** pp. 215–217

L3 L4 EL **Selection Test B,** pp. 218–220

L3 L4 **Open Book Test,** pp. 212–214

Students may use the **Self-test,** online at **www.PHLitOnline.com,** to prepare for the Selection Test.

Comparing Irony

1. Students might say that the ending entertained them because they enjoyed the surprise.
2. The ending may have reminded students that we cannot throw problems away.
3. O. Henry: (a) Bob and Jimmy want to meet again as friends, but one has become a criminal and the other a policeman. (b) It means that people's roles in life can be more important than friendship. (c) It's important because friend-ship may not last forever.
   Hoshi: (a) People think they can throw their garbage away forever, but it will return. (b) It means that actions have consequences that their doers must face. (c) It's important because people put a curse on their future when they think only of immediate needs.

   For other sample answers, see *Graphic Organizer Transparencies,* **Comparing Irony Transparency A,** (Apply the Skills), p. 70.

⏱ Timed Writing

1. Review the prompt with students.
2. Have students use the 5-Minute Planner to structure their time. Guide them through the bul-leted points. For example, to help students focus on the first bullet point, ask them to think about their reaction when they discov-ered the identity of the patrolman in "After Twenty Years."
3. Allow students 40 minutes to complete the assignment.
4. As students prewrite and draft, have them refer to their com-pleted Comparing Idioms Graphic Organizer.

Six Traits Focus

✔	Ideas		Word Choice
✔	Organization		Sentence Fluency
	Voice		Conventions

383

Common Core
State Standards

• Writing 3.a, c, d

Introducing the Writing Assignment

Review the assignment and the criteria, using the instruction on the student page.

Walter Dean Myers on Short Stories

Show students Segment 3 on Walter Dean Myers on *See It!* DVD or from this page in the **Enriched Online Student Edition,** at www.PHLitOnline.com. Discuss Myers's comments about how he learned to "tell" short stories.

Writing Workshop
Work in Progress

If students have completed the Work-in-Progress assignments on pp. 335 and 361, suggest that they examine their recorded ideas as they begin prewriting. They may wish to develop these ideas in a short story.

What Do You Notice?

1. Read the passage aloud. **Ask** students the first question: What do you notice about this passage? (**Possible response:** The tone of the passage is somber but not depressing.)

2. **Ask** the second question: How does the word choice contribute to the tone? (**Possible responses:** The word choice adds a light, peaceful feeling to the passage, creating a tone of acceptance.)

3. Encourage students to choose words as they draft that will convey exactly the right tone in their stories.

384

Writing Workshop

Write a Narrative

Narration: Short Story

Defining the Form A **short story** is a brief, creative fictional narrative. You might use elements of this type of writing in an autobiographical essay, a drama, a feature article, or a biography.

Assignment Write a short story about an interesting or original situation that will capture readers' attention. Include these elements:

✔ well-developed *major and minor characters*

✔ a *conflict* that keeps the reader asking, "What will happen next?"

✔ a clear story line or sequence told from a *consistent point of view*

✔ effective *pacing*

✔ narrative that develops *dialogue, suspense, descriptive details,* and other literary elements and devices

✔ a *title* that catches the reader's attention

✔ precise vocabulary and *effective word choice*

✔ error-free writing, including *correct use of comparatives*

To preview the criteria on which your short story may be judged, see the rubric on page 391.

 Writing Workshop: *Work in Progress*

Review the work you did on pages 335 and 361.

WRITE GUY
Jeff Anderson, M.Ed.

What Do You Notice?

Tone

The following sentences are from Joan Aiken's "The Third Wish."

In the morning, Mr. Peters was found peacefully dead in his bed with a smile of great happiness on his face. In his hands, which lay clasped on his breast, were a withered leaf and a white feather.

Discuss these questions with a partner:

• What do you notice about this passage?
• How does the word choice contribute to the tone?

Think about ways you might use word choice to contribute to the tone of your work.

384 Short Stories

 Common Core
State Standards

Writing
3. Write narratives to develop real or imagined experiences or events using effective technique, relevant descriptive details, and well-structured event sequences.
3.a. Engage and orient the reader by establishing a context and point of view and introducing a narrator and/or characters; organize an event sequence that unfolds naturally and logically.

Reading-Writing Connection

To get the feel for short story, review "Zoo" by Edward Hoch on page 340 or "Ribbons" by Laurence Yep on page 346.

Teaching Resources

The following resources can be used to enrich or extend the instruction.

All *Unit 2 Resources*
Writing Workshop, pp. 221, 222

All *Common Core Companion,*
pp. 214–224; 232–239

All *Professional Development Guidebook*
Rubrics for Self-Assessment: Short Story,
pp. 226–227

All *Graphic Organizer Transparencies*
Rubric for Self-Assessment: Short Story,
p. 72

All *See It! DVD*
Walter Dean Myers, Segments 3 and 4

 All resources, including print and video, are also available online at www.PHLitOnline.com.

Prewriting/Planning Strategies

Use a "what if" strategy. To help you choose the characters and situation for your story, fill in the blanks of a sentence such as the one shown here. Try a number of situations and choose the one that interests you the most.

> What if _____ (describe a person)
> suddenly _____ (describe a problem)?

Identify the conflict. A **conflict** is a struggle between opposing forces. A character's conflict may be *external,* as when a sheriff has a conflict with an outlaw, or *internal,* as when that outlaw struggles with his conscience. Identify the conflict to focus your topic and get your story moving. Ask yourself these questions:

• Who is the main character of my story?
• What does the main character want?
• What is preventing him or her from getting it?

Use listing and itemizing. Your next step is to gather details to include in your story. Review the model shown here and follow these steps to try this strategy:

1. Quickly jot down a list of everything that comes to mind about a general idea.
2. Circle the most interesting item on the list.
3. Itemize that detail—create another list of everything that comes to mind about it.
4. After you have generated several lists, look for connections among all the circled items. These connections will help you decide which details to include in your story.

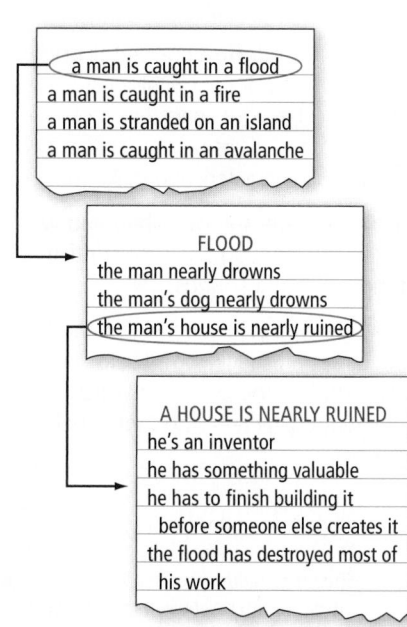

a man is caught in a flood
a man is caught in a fire
a man is stranded on an island
a man is caught in an avalanche

FLOOD
the man nearly drowns
the man's dog nearly drowns
the man's house is nearly ruined

A HOUSE IS NEARLY RUINED
he's an inventor
he has something valuable
he has to finish building it
  before someone else creates it
the flood has destroyed most of
his work

Applying Understanding by Design Principles

Clarifying Expected Outcomes: Using Rubrics
• Before students begin work on this assignment, have them preview the Rubric for Self-Assessment (p. 391) to learn what qualities their short stories must have.
• Review the criteria in the Rubric with the class. Before students use the Rubric to assess their own writing, work with them to rate the Student Model (p. 390) using the Rubric.

• If you wish to assess students' short stories with either a 4-point or a 6-point scoring rubric, see the *Professional Development Guidebook,* pp. 226–227.

Prewriting/Planning Strategies

1. Introduce the prewriting strategies, using the instruction on the student page.
2. Have students apply the strategies to choose a topic.

Teaching the Strategies

1. For the "What If?" strategy, have students brainstorm for several situations and record these in their notebooks. Tell each student to choose the most interesting situation for his or her story.
2. Use the example in the "What if?" strategy to explain how students might construct a conflict. Point out that the conflict might be external or internal. Students should also consider possible ways to resolve the conflict.
3. Ask students to work in pairs, "telling" their stories to their partner.

Think Aloud: Model Listing

Model the strategy, using the following "think aloud":

> To start off listing, I just start writing down whatever comes into my head: "mall, shopping, birthday gift, party." Then, I look over what I've written and circle the most interesting idea. I'm going to circle "birthday gift" because I'm starting to think of some funny ones. Now, I list some of them: a digital potato peeler and a glow-in-the-dark sombrero. I'm going to circle the words *digital potato peeler* on my list because I think I can tell a funny story involving one.

Six Traits Focus

✔ Ideas		Word Choice
Organization		Sentence Fluency
Voice		Conventions

PH WRITING COACH Grade 7

Students will find additional information on writing a short story in Chapter 6.

Prentice Hall EssayScorer

A writing prompt for this mode of writing can be found in the *Prentice Hall EssayScorer* at www.PHLitOnline.com.

Drafting Strategies

1. Introduce the drafting strategies, using the instruction on the student page.
2. Have students apply the strategies as they draft.

Teaching the Strategies

1. Tell students that as they review their plot maps, they should make sure that events are not clustered in a single section and that there are no long stretches where nothing occurs.
2. Review the concepts of foreshadowing and suspense with students. Explain that both devices involve telling readers just enough to involve them while at the same time holding back crucial information.
3. Encourage students to include descriptive details about the setting so readers know where and when the action takes place.
4. Read the following pairs of sentences to review how using precise details to show rather than tell helps to bring a scene to life.

> *Maya was upset.* **Hot tears streamed down Maya's face.**
>
> *Alicia said she wouldn't.* **"No way!" Alicia cried, stamping her foot.**

Think Aloud: Model Characterization

Model the strategy, using the following "think aloud":

Let's say that I want everyone to see that my character is a fun person to be around. Here's what I might write: "Maya was fun to be around." That doesn't make a clear picture for a reader, so I add some details about others' reactions: "When she walked into the room, everyone brightened up. 'Hey, Maya,' said José, 'we're glad to see you.'" Now, I know my readers will see her as a friendly, sunny person. If I also add details about her sunny smile and cute laugh, the picture really starts to come to life.

Six Traits Focus

✔	Ideas	✔	Word Choice
✔	Organization		Sentence Fluency
	Voice		Conventions

386

Drafting Strategies

 Common Core State Standards

Writing

3.c. Use a variety of transition words, phrases, and clauses to convey sequence and signal shifts from one time frame or setting to another.

3.d. Use precise words and phrases, relevant descriptive details, and sensory language to capture the action and convey experiences and events.

Create a plot. Begin by mapping out a **plot,** the arrangement of actions in the story. In most stories, the plot follows this pattern:

- The **exposition** introduces the main characters and their basic situation, including the central conflict or problem.
- The **conflict** intensifies during the rising action.
- The **climax** is the high point of interest.
- The story's falling action leads to the **resolution,** or denouement, in which the conflict is resolved in some way.

As you write, use transitional words and phrases, such as *next, then,* and *later* to show how one event in your plot leads to the next.

Use literary elements and devices. A good story builds to a single exciting moment. To achieve this, writers rely on literary elements and devices. For example, **foreshadowing** is the use of clues hinting at future plot events. This creates **suspense,** a technique that makes the reader wonder what will happen next.

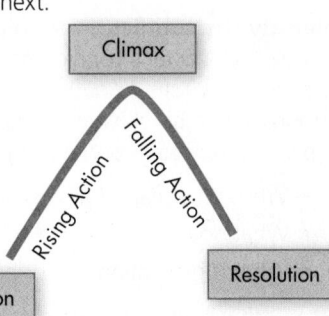

Use details to define character and setting. As you draft your story, add details that reveal what your characters look like, how they act, what they think, and how others react to them. By adding these details, you develop your characters and make them more interesting.

Make sure readers know when and where the action is taking place. Use sensory language and descriptive details to describe how your setting looks and sounds.

Show; do not tell. Although it can be useful to tell readers something directly, usually you should show them rather than tell them. As you draft, choose precise words and use narrative techniques to show your characters' thoughts, feelings, actions, and reactions.

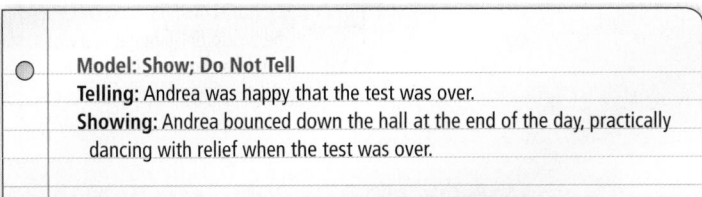

> **Model: Show; Do Not Tell**
> **Telling:** Andrea was happy that the test was over.
> **Showing:** Andrea bounced down the hall at the end of the day, practically dancing with relief when the test was over.

Differentiated Instruction for Universal Access

Strategy for Less Proficient Writers
Have students draw sketches of the setting, characters, and events in their stories. Then, have them write sentences explaining what they have drawn in each case. As they draft, have them draw on these sentences for ideas and words to elaborate on their descriptions.

EL Strategy for English Learners
To help students elaborate on their descriptions of characters and setting, encourage students to write five words that describe their settings and five words to describe their main character. Have them draw on their word lists as they draft.

Strategy for Advanced Writers
The events in a story must be ordered in a way that will not be confusing. Suggest that students use the **Series of Events Chain** in the resources online at **www.PHLitOnline.com** to plot their stories. Challenge students to start their stories in the middle and include earlier events as flashbacks.

Writers on Writing

Walter Dean Myers On Revising to Heighten Tension

> Walter Dean Myers is the author of "The Treasure of Lemon Brown" (p. 207).

As a child listening to the stories from the Old Testament, I formed images in my mind of what exactly was going on. At first I only sympathized with the character Joseph, but as I grew older I wondered how his eldest brother, Reuben, must have felt. So, I explored Reuben's feelings in a short story entitled "Reuben and Joseph." This section from my draft of the story shows how I revise to heighten tension.

"Often the minor characters interest me the most."

—Walter Dean Myers

Professional Model:

from "Reuben and Joseph"

~~Joseph lives~~. My brother lives. Like a man risen from the dead, he has appeared from the ashes of memory. ~~We are bid~~ He tells us that we are to go home tomorrow and tell our father the good news. But ~~those glad tidings~~ that good news, the joyous celebration he envisions, ~~will also speak of my disgrace~~ is filled with danger and disgrace for the messengers. Grief and fear sit in the pit of my stomach like two huge rocks. If I could scream silently, I would do so. If my tears could speak, I would let them.

~~Tonight I spent hours waiting for sleep and then, when sleep finally came, I awoke with a start, my heart pounding.~~ I have been tossing and turning all night. Sleep comes now and again, but then I quickly wake, my heart pounding. The room is too warm, and I hear the breathing of my brothers who lie on mats around me. . . .

It was more important to establish that he is talking about his brother than to give his brother's name. I want the reader to wonder, *Why does he worry that his brother lives?*

Okay, so I'm into what I imagine to be the jargon of the day, but I need to get on with my story.

Saying that there is danger here immediately heightens the tension. "Also speak of my disgrace" is too stiff.

"I have been tossing and turning all night" is more direct than the sentence I crossed out and creates more drama.

Writing Workshop **387**

Strategies for Elaboration

To help students elaborate on their drafts, suggest the "Exploding the Moment" strategy. As they draft, have them pause at the end of each paragraph and circle the sentence that describes the most important event. Have them affix a self-stick note at the end of the paragraph, jotting additional descriptions of the event. They might imagine the event unwinding in slow motion so that they can capture the full details. After they have finished drafting, have them review their notes for details that will enhance their stories and then add the selected details to their drafts.

Walter Dean Myers on Revising

Review the passage on the student page with the class, using Walter Dean Myers's comments to deepen students' understanding of the process of writing a short story.

Teaching From the Professional Model

1. Show students Segment 4 on Walter Dean Myers on the *See It!* **DVD** or from this page in the **Enriched Online Student Edition.** Discuss the techniques he uses to create his characters, and compare them to the techniques students used in prewriting.

2. Point out how Myers uses incidents from his own life and the Bible, as well as stories told by relatives, as inspiration for his own writing. Discuss with students various sources that might inspire them, such as music, movies, or news stories.

3. Discuss Myers's use of vivid, precise details in the passage on the student page. Point out that many of his revisions are intended to keep the reader's interest.

Show or assign the video online at **www.PHLitOnline.com.**

387

Revising Strategies

1. Introduce the revision strategies, using the instruction on the student page.

2. Have students apply the strategies as they revise their short stories.

Teaching the Strategies

1. Suggest that students concentrate on one character at a time as they use the star. As they review their drafts, they should play through the story from each character's perspective, imagining the character's actions and reactions.

2. Remind students that readers read passive voice sentences more slowly than they read active voice sentences, so passive voice slows the sense of action. If the writer wants the reader to be involved in the action, then he or she should use active voice.

   Ask the class to tell you whether they would primarily use active or passive voice for the following story events:

   • *A high-speed car chase.* (**Possible response:** Active voice to keep the action moving.)

   • *The beginning of a race.* (**Possible response:** Active voice helps the reader share in the excitement of the beginning of a race.)

   • *A person reflecting on his or her childhood.* (**Possible response:** Passive voice would slow the reader and add to the sense of reflection.)

3. Instruct students that when reviewing their partner's characterization, they should note the type of detail—looks, actions, feelings, reactions, or conversation—that is needed to more fully develop the characters. They should also look for verbs in the passive voice and recommend replacing them with verbs in the active voice.

Six Traits Focus

✔ Ideas	✔ Word Choice	
✔ Organization	Sentence Fluency	
Voice	Conventions	

Revising Strategies

Improve your characterization. Cut a five-pointed star out of construction paper and label the points *Dialogue, Movement, Gestures, Feelings,* and *Expressions.* Slide the star down your draft as you look for places where you can add details that reveal more about your characters. When you find a place to include more precise information, make notes in the margin and start over.

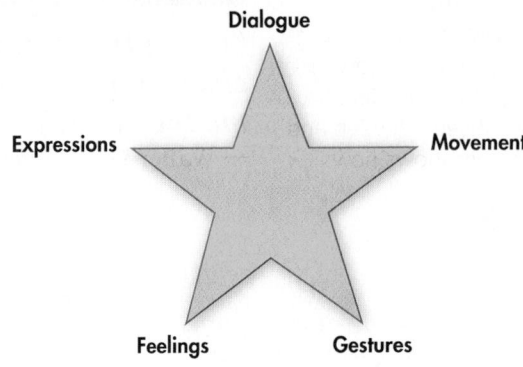

Follow these suggestions as you add information to develop character:

Dialogue: Write conversations that show how the character speaks, using the words and phrasing he or she might use.

Movement: Describe a character's movements using precise words like *rushed, timid,* or *excited.*

Gestures: Tell how the characters stand, move, and act.

Feelings: Consider the way events will make your characters feel, and include relevant descriptive details to reveal these emotions.

Expressions: Describe the facial expressions your characters make to convey their ideas and feelings without words.

Use active voice. A verb in active voice shows that the subject is performing the action: *Ana bought the computer.* A verb in passive voice shows that the subject receives the action: *The computer was bought by Ana.* Sentences written in active voice are less wordy and are usually stronger and more effective.

Peer Review

Give your draft to a few classmates to read. Ask them to highlight places where you can include details to develop stronger characters. Then, revise your draft, focusing on your purpose and audience.

388 Short Stories

Writing
3.b. Use narrative techniques, such as dialogue, pacing, and description, to develop experiences, events, and/or characters.
3.d. Use precise words and phrases, relevant descriptive details, and sensory language to capture the action and convey experiences and events.
5. With some guidance and support from peers and adults, develop and strengthen writing as needed by planning, revising, editing, rewriting, or trying a new approach, focusing on how well purpose and audience have been addressed.

Strategies for Improving Word Choice

Color-Coding Verbs Have students circle each verb in the first three paragraphs of their stories, using a green pencil. Then, have them draw a red square around any verb that seems vague or boring or that they have used too frequently. Suggest that they replace as many of these verbs as possible with a better choice.

Comparison of Adjectives and Adverbs

Most adjectives and adverbs have three degrees of comparison: the *positive*, the *comparative*, and the *superlative*.

Identifying Degrees of Adjectives and Adverbs The positive is used when no comparison is made. The comparative is used when two things are being compared. The superlative is used when three or more things are being compared.

Positive: Hannah is a *fast* runner.

Comparative: Eva is a *faster* runner than Hannah.

Superlative: Emmy is the *fastest* runner on the team.

Forming Comparative and Superlative Degrees	
Use *-er* or *more* to form the comparative degree.	faster, taller, narrower, sunnier, more intelligent, more expressive
Use *-est* or *most* to form the superlative degree.	fastest, tallest, sunniest, most nutritious, most sorrowful
Use *more* and *most* with modifiers of three or more syllables.	more popular, more intelligently, most popular, most intelligently

PH WRITING COACH

Further instruction and practice are available in *Prentice Hall Writing Coach*.

Fixing Incorrect Use of Comparative and Superlative Degrees
To fix the incorrect use of comparative and superlative degrees of adjectives and adverbs, use one or more of the following methods:

1. **Identify the number of things being compared.** Review the rules for comparison and use the correct word or word ending.

2. **Identify the number of syllables in the modifier.** Review the rules for modifiers with a specific number of syllables and use the correct word or word ending.

3. **Read the words aloud.** If the words sound awkward, combine the modifier with a different word or word ending.

Grammar in Your Writing
Choose two paragraphs in your draft. Underline every sentence that compares two or more things. If the use of a comparative or superlative degree of any adjective or adverb is faulty, fix it.

Comparison of Adjectives and Adverbs

1. Introduce the grammar skill, using the instruction on the student page.

2. Discuss the examples, the rules given in the box, and the strategies for fixing incorrect usage.

3. Have students follow the instruction under Grammar in Your Writing to correct errors in their drafts.

Teaching the Grammar Skill

1. Students may have trouble using the comparative and superlative degrees of adjectives and adverbs correctly, particularly those that do not add *–er* or *–est*. Provide the following examples of comparative and superlative forms: *easy (easier, easiest); smart (smarter, smartest); young (younger, youngest); politely (more politely, most politely); wonderful (more wonderful, most wonderful); stunning (more stunning, most stunning).*

2. Review the use of *more* and *most* with students. Remind them that for one- or two-syllable adjectives, there is no general rule. Tell students to pay attention to how the word sounds. If adding these suffixes makes the word sound awkward, the comparative and superlative forms probably require the use of *more* and *most.*

3. Have students change the underlined adjective or adverb to the form noted in parentheses in the following examples:

   The sun was shining brightly. (comparative)
   (**Answer:** more brightly)

   She is the lazy one. (superlative)
   (**Answer:** laziest)

   The king was a just ruler. (comparative).
   (**Answer:** more just)

   The quick runner will win the race. (superlative)
   (**Answer:** quickest)

   He is the eager member of the group. (superlative)
   (**Answer:** most eager)

PH WRITING COACH | Grade 7

Students will find practice with and guidance on the comparison of adjectives and adverbs in Chapter 24, Section 1.

Student Model

Review the Student Model with the class, using the annotations to analyze the writer's use of the elements of a short story.

Teaching From the Student Model

1. Explain that the Student Model is a sample and that short stories may be longer.

2. Note how the writer's use of precise sensory details in the first paragraph—cuffs flapping in the biting wind, the sharp chill down his spine—bring the setting to life.

3. Have students identify the conflict. **Answer:** The conflict is the struggle between the narrator and the storm.

4. Note that as the action rises toward the climax, the writer builds suspense along the way with foreshadowing. **Ask** students for examples.
   Possible responses: Examples include the references to a chill down his spine, the warning voice in his head, the date of Friday the 13th, and the feeling that something is wrong.

Connecting to Real-Life Writing

Let students know that there are many careers and activities that call on short story writing skills. News reporters use literary elements to tell stories that are true. Magazines and newspapers often have story writing contests, and many high schools and colleges have literary magazines that print student work. In addition, the skills used to write stories can be transferred easily to writing for the stage, television, and movies.

Student Model: K.C. Marker, Portland, OR

The Leaky Boat

It was a cold September evening. My linen cuffs flapped uncontrollably in a biting wind baring its white teeth of snow. The sun had long since set, and all was quiet on the sea. A cool mist had settled around the bay, sending a sharp chill down my spine. I continued to row; I had seen worse. I could still hear the voice ringing through my head:

"This is it, son. Either you're ready or you're not."

I was ready. The fire in my lantern flickered as another wind blew across the bay, carrying more frightening sounds from the distance. I gripped my father's pendant for reassurance, clenching the jade cross and willing myself to be strong. I was ready.

No one dared go out on such a night. Tonight was Friday—the 13th. I was the only one traveling the waters, or so I thought. Ever since the coast guard had shown us out, no one dared go fishin' even if it was for a big fish; I mean a big fish, a legend, and a monster! But it wasn't a fish anyone in my family could bring themselves to kill. It was ancient, and it had, in a distant time, saved one of my ancestors from being swallowed by the sea.

Now, I had survived many a boating trip before, but what happened next would become a remarkable memory for the rest of my life.

As I shifted in my seat I could feel it. Something was wrong. I shifted once more and that's when I heard it. The wind blew hard against my face, the cold stinging my eyes. Rushing water all around me—a storm! It had come slowly at first. I had not thought much of it, but now it was at its nastiest, and I was in the middle of it! The waves crashed against my boat like hail pounding on a window. I was violently thrown back and forth in my boat! I turned to the side. How close was I to the rocky shore?

Another wave hit, revealing a large rock off the starboard side. A wave came from the opposite side, drenching me with water, but that was not all. The wave sent me hurtling toward the rock! I slammed into the rock with full force! I was swept aside by another, smaller wave as water poured into my boat! What was I to do? Thunder roared overhead.

As I struggled to keep upright, a massive wave came up from behind, plunging me into the water. I swam with all my strength to the surface, taking in a big breath of air and holding tight to my father's pendant.

The water churned around me fiercely, tossing to and fro. The foam swirled around me, and the salt stung my eyes as it hit me. I was plunged under again. I swam up for air with my strength rapidly leaving me. Disaster struck! I felt a wave come. I could not see it. I felt the necklace being ripped from my neck, leaving the sanctuary of my head and spiraling down to the murky depths. I looked down for it, squinting to open my burning eyes; I saw an eye and a long slender body, and then all went dark.

I awoke the next morning on an unfamiliar shore, not knowing where I was. I felt something cold against my neck—the pendant! How had it been retrieved? How had I survived? The fish. The family fish had saved my family again. I still don't know how I obtained the pendant or where I had to go, for that is another story.

> K.C. uses descriptive language to set the scene for the story.

> The story is told from a first-person point of view. Readers learn about the narrator from what he thinks and experiences.

> K.C. develops suspense by foreshadowing something dangerous.

> The varied sentence structure and length make the pacing of the story's conflict suspenseful.

> Vivid details and tension make the reader want to know what is going to happen next.

Strategies for Test Taking

When taking a test that includes a narrative writing prompt, students should be careful to use realistic dialogue. To make characters sound like real people, writers use contractions, colloquialisms, interrupted speech, and other types of language that occur frequently in conversation. Have students practice using these techniques in timed writing assignments to gain the skills required for taking tests.

Editing and Proofreading

Review your draft to find and eliminate errors in grammar, spelling, and punctuation.

Focus on dialogue. Enclose a character's exact words in quotation marks. If dialogue comes *before* the words announcing speech, use a comma, question mark, or exclamation point at the end of the quotation—not a period. If dialogue comes *after* the words announcing speech, use a comma before the quotation.

"I heard the siren," Benjamin said.

Sally jumped and shouted, "So did I, but it still surprised me!"

Publishing and Presenting

Share your writing with a wider audience:

Submit your story. Submit your story to a school literary magazine, a national publication, an online journal, or a contest.

Give a reading. Read your story aloud to your class or to a group of friends. Prepare posters announcing your reading and distribute signed copies of your story at the event.

Reflecting on Your Writing

Writer's Journal Jot down your answer to this question:

How has your writing experience changed the way you read short stories?

Rubric for Self-Assessment

Find evidence in your writing to address each category. Then, use the rating scale to grade your work.

Criteria	Rating Scale
	not very very
Focus: How well-developed are your characters?	1 2 3 4 5
Organization: How clearly organized is the story line or sequence of events?	1 2 3 4 5
Support/Elaboration: How well do the dialogue and suspense support the plot?	1 2 3 4 5
Style: How precise is your word choice?	1 2 3 4 5
Conventions: How correct is your grammar, especially your use of comparative adjectives and adverbs?	1 2 3 4 5

Spiral Review

Earlier in the unit, you learned about **adjectives** (p. 334) and **adverbs** (p. 360). Review your short story to be sure you have used adjectives and adverbs correctly to achieve your intended effect.

Editing and Proofreading

1. Introduce the editing and proofreading focus, using the instruction on the student page.

2. Have students edit and proofread their essays, correcting grammar, spelling, punctuation, and word choice. Make sure they look for errors of the type noted in the lesson focus and the Spiral Review.

Teaching the Editing Focus

Remind students of the rules for punctuating dialogue. Then, ask them to read their stories and highlight each section that contains dialogue. Students should check the highlighted sections against the rules of punctuation on the student page, putting a check mark next to each section of dialogue they have revised. Have students exchange papers and verify their partner's corrections.

Six Traits Focus

Ideas	Word Choice
Organization	Sentence Fluency
Voice	✔ Conventions

ASSESS

Publishing and Presenting

1. Find out whether the town newspaper or other local publications accept student fiction, and encourage students to submit to these venues. Guide students in writing a cover letter to the editor introducing themselves and their work.

2. Suggest that before giving a reading, students practice reading their stories aloud using appropriate gestures and expression. If possible, videotape or tape-record their performances so students can critique themselves.

Reflecting on Your Writing

Suggest that students choose a story from the Unit and in light of their own writing experience, determine what specific challenges the writer had to solve in writing it.

Word Origins

1. Introduce the skill, using the instruction on the student page.

2. Review the definitions and examples.

Think Aloud: Model the Skill

Model the skill of using knowledge of a word's origins to understand its meaning. Say to students:

> Once I know the meaning of a prefix, suffix, or root, I can use it to figure out the meaning of many unfamiliar words. I might come across the word *misinterpret* in a story. I know that the word *interpret* means "to understand or explain." I know that the prefix *mis-* means "wrong." Using this information, I figure out that *misinterpret* means "understand wrongly."

> Sometimes, knowing the origins of a word can add interest to my reading. Everyone knows that March is the third month of the year, but I find it interesting that it is named after the Roman god of war.

Practice A

Sample answers

1. *construction;* The root *-struct-* means "to build," and *construction* means "the process of building."

2. *interrupts;* The prefix *inter-* means "between"; to interrupt someone is to speak "between" his or her words.

3. *careful;* The suffix *-ful* means "full of," and to be careful is to be "full of care."

4. *auditorium;* The root *-aud-* means "to hear," and an auditorium is a place where you go to hear things.

5. *miscounted;* The prefix *mis-* means "wrong," and when something is miscounted, it is counted wrong.

392

Vocabulary Workshop

Word Origins

A word's **origin,** or **etymology,** tells the history of the word. Knowing the history of a word or word part can help you understand its meaning. This chart gives the meanings of several Latin, Greek, Old English, and Middle English word parts.

Latin and Greek Word Parts			
Roots	**Origin**	**Meaning**	**Examples**
-aud-	Latin	to hear	audio, audience
-struct-	Latin	to build	structure, instruct
-port-	Latin	to carry	portable, transport
Prefixes	**Origin**	**Meaning**	**Examples**
inter-	Latin	among, between	internet, international
mis-	Old English	wrong, not	misbehave, misfortune
tele-	Greek	distant	telephone, telescope
Suffixes	**Origin**	**Meaning**	**Examples**
-ful	Middle English	full of	joyful, fearful
-less	Middle English	without	careless, thoughtless

Practice A For each word in italics, underline the root, prefix, or suffix. Then, explain how the the meaning of the word part contributes to the meaning of the word. If necessary, consult a print or online dictionary.

1. The *construction* of the new bank building is on schedule.

2. When Samuel *interrupts* me, I can't remember what I have been saying.

3. When the roads are slick, signs alert drivers to be *careful.*

4. The *auditorium* was full of people eager to hear the symphony.

5. The losing candidate suspected that the votes were *miscounted.*

Teaching Resources

Unit 2 Resources
   Word Origins, pp. 223–224

PHLit Online!   **Vocabulary Central,** featuring definitions, audio pronunciations, word families, and activities, is online at **www.PHLitOnline.com.**

Many words and phrases in English come from **Latin, Greek, and Anglo-Saxon mythology.** Study the chart below to learn the origins of some of these words and phrases.

Words and Phrases From Mythology		
Word or Phrase	**Origin**	**Meaning**
January	Janus, a Roman god, had two faces — one looking forward and one looking backward.	The first month of our calendar year
Achilles heel	Achilles, a great Greek warrior, was known to be weak only in his foot.	A weakness or weak point
Herculean effort	The Greek hero Hercules was known for his strength and for completing twelve difficult tasks.	A difficult task requiring great strength
high horse	In medieval England, nobles were given tall horses to show their importance. The phrase "get off your high horse" developed from this practice.	A superior attitude

Practice B Identify the word or phrase from the chart that is associated with each sentence.

1. When Byron bragged about his new car we told him <u>not to be too proud of himself</u>.
2. It is always good to have a fresh start in <u>the new year</u>.
3. I can usually stick to a healthy diet, but my <u>weakness</u> is brownies
4. Beating the other team will require <u>us to be stronger than ever</u>.

Activity An **allusion** is a reference to a well-known person, event, literary work, or work of art. Many works of literature contain allusions. For example, a writer might describe a long or difficult journey as an "odyssey." This is an allusion to *The Odyssey*, a long epic poem that was written sometime between 600 and 800 B.C. In the poem, the ancient Greek hero Odysseus takes a long, difficult voyage to reach his home. Another ancient Greek hero is Hercules, who was famous for completing amazingly difficult tasks. Write a short tale about an odyssey in which the hero must make a Herculean effort. Your story can be set in the past or present.

Comprehension and Collaboration

Trade your odyssey story with a partner. Rewrite your partner's story to include three new words based on word parts from the chart on the previous page. You may use words that appear in this Vocabulary Workshop, other words you know, or new words you find in a dictionary.

Practice B
Answers
1. high horse
2. January
3. Achilles heel
4. Herculean effort

Activity
Give students time in class to brainstorm for ideas for their stories. Then, assign writing the story as homework. In their stories, students should tell of a hero who makes a long and difficult journey involving a great effort. Evaluate students' stories on the basis of their originality.

Comprehension and Collaboration

Provide dictionaries for students to use in identifying words based on the Latin and Greek word parts listed on page 394. You might also suggest that students search the Web for sites that provide lists of words containing specific word parts.

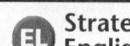

Differentiated Instruction for Universal Access

EL **Strategy for English Learners**
Point out that languages other than English also draw on Latin and Greek roots. For example, the Spanish word *abajo,* meaning "below," and the English word *base,* meaning "lowest part," both come from the Latin word *basis,* which comes from a Greek word for step. If students' home language is a Romance language, have them use a dictionary to find three English words similar to words in their home language. Then, have them use the word origins given in the dictionary to determine whether it is likely that the words share a common root.

Strategy for Advanced Learners
Divide the class into groups. Give the students time to prepare a list and define twelve words using the prefixes *inter-, mis-,* and *tele-.* Some of the words should be genuine; others should be made up. The definition of each made-up word should reflect the meaning of the prefix it includes. Each group should take a turn reading words with their definitions. Members of the other groups should respond by guessing whether the word is genuine or made up. Correct guesses earn the guessing team one point. Successful bluffs earn the team that made up the word two points.

Common Core
State Standards

• Speaking and Listening 4

Learn the Skills

1. Introduce the workshop, including the activity on page 395.

2. Remind students to focus on main ideas and significant details.

3. Urge students to use transitional words such as *then*, *therefore*, *however*, and *because*.

4. Remind students that their audience cannot revisit points as they would if they were reading. Encourage students to repeat important points during the presentation.

Planning Your Delivery

1. Tell students that varying their sentence structure will help them hold the interest of the audience.

2. Remind students to avoid speaking too quickly or in a monotone voice.

3. Suggest that students rehearse their presentations in front of family members and friends.

SPEAKING AND LISTENING

Communications Workshop

Delivering an Oral Summary

An **oral summary** shares many of the characteristics of a written summary. The guidelines below will help you plan what you want to say and help you say it with confidence.

Learn the Skills

Use these strategies to complete the activity on page 395.

Summarize. Like its written counterpart, an oral summary should briefly state the main idea of a work, with only as many details as needed to give a complete, but concise, picture of the work.

Organize your points in sequence. To create a summary to use in an oral presentation, organize your ideas and record them on note cards.

Write the "main idea"—the overall statement of the work's content—on your first note card. Include one or two key details that support the main idea. Make additional cards to present points from the beginning, middle, and end of the work. Write your conclusion on a separate card. Refer to your note cards as you deliver your presentation.

Show a comprehensive understanding. As you prepare your presentation, do not just string together fact after fact. Ask yourself, "What does all this mean?" Try to convey a genuine understanding of what you have seen or read, not just the surface details.

Consider your audience. Include enough information so that your audience can follow the summary accurately.

Plan your delivery. Try to project confidence and a positive attitude. Plan and practice your delivery so that you stay focused when presenting.

- **Vary your sentence structure.** To add interest, vary your sentence structure just as you do when you write. Listen to your words and monitor yourself for errors in grammar.

- **Use your voice well.** Be energetic, but speak clearly and precisely. Enunciate every word. Vary the pitch and speed of your voice to keep your listeners engaged. Make sure that you are speaking loudly enough to be heard clearly.

- **Make eye contact.** Memorize as much of your summary as you can to enable you to make eye contact with listeners.

Common Core
State Standards

Speaking and Listening
4. Present claims and findings, emphasizing salient points in a focused, coherent manner with pertinent descriptions, facts, details, and examples; use appropriate eye contact, adequate volume, and clear pronunciation.

Main Idea

Giant pandas have become rare because hunters kill them.
Facts: There are only about 2,500 living in the wild. There are only about 150 in zoos.

Conclusion

If we can support the efforts to save pandas, maybe there will be more pandas in the world of our children and grandchildren.

Strategies for
Delivering an Oral Summary

Give students these additional strategies for developing an oral summary:

- Tell students they may need to reread the source material several times. They cannot expect to create an effective summary until they fully understand the material.

- Encourage students to think about the aspects of the source they found most interesting. Explain that the audience is likely to find those points interesting, too.

- Guide students in creating effective paraphrases. Ask them to write one paragraph that covers the most important points in the source material.

- Caution them against reading long excerpts from the source. Explain that the purpose of a summary is to provide an overview, rather than to explain details.

Practice the Skills

Ⓒ Presentation of Knowledge and Ideas Use what you have learned in this workshop to complete the following activity.

ACTIVITY: Prepare and Deliver an Oral Summary

Choose an article, at least three pages long, from a magazine or Web site. Present an oral summary of the article to your class. Use the instruction on page 394 and the following steps to guide you:

- Begin with a strong opening statement. You might use a rhetorical question—a question asked for effect: *Does anyone wonder what happened to the plans for the new park?* You might use an impressive fact contained in the article: *It has been two years since the plans were first approved.*
- Use formal English.
- When presenting, project your voice so that everyone can hear. Pronounce words clearly. Do not rush.
- End with a strong closing statement that relates to your opening statement. *So, that is what has happened to the park plans: repeated budget cuts.*

Ⓒ Comprehension and Collaboration Ask your classmates to give you feedback by saying how they rated you on the Presentation Evaluation Checklist shown here. While your classmates give their presentations, use the checklist to rate their work.

Presentation Evaluation Checklist

Presentation Content
Was the summary clear and easy to follow?
Check all that apply.

- ❑ It had a strong beginning and ending.
- ❑ It included all key points.
- ❑ I understood the main points of the work based on this summary.

Presentation Delivery
Did the speaker deliver the summary effectively?
Check all that apply.

- ❑ The speaker established good eye contact.
- ❑ The speaker enunciated clearly and maintained good volume.
- ❑ The speaker varied rate and pitch of voice.
- ❑ The speaker used formal English.

Communications Workshop **395**

Differentiated Instruction   for Universal Access

Strategy for Special-Needs Students
Some students might have difficulty identifying the main ideas and significant details in a text. Explain that the first paragraph of a news article usually contains the main idea. Also, each paragraph typically contains a significant detail that supports the main idea. Present students with a news article and help them identify the topic sentence of each paragraph. Then, work with them to create a summary of the entire article.

EL Strategy for English Learners
Have students write their summaries. Ask them to practice reading with partners. Partners should use the Presentation Checklist to provide constructive comments on pronunciation, delivery, and grammar. Allow students time to incorporate the suggestions into their revisions before they present their oral summaries to the class.

Practice the Skills

1. Review the assignment with students. Make sure they understand that the summary should focus on the most important points from the article or Web site. Remind students of the importance of holding the audience's interest. Explain that the audience will not absorb the summary if they do not pay attention to the presentation.

2. Explain to students that they should use a copy of the Presentation Checklist to evaluate their own presentation and the presentations made by classmates.

3. Before students give their presentations to the class, remind listeners to ask questions if any points are unclear. To maintain order, encourage them to raise their hands and wait to be acknowledged by the presenter before stating their questions. Suggest that students making presentations scan the classroom from time to time so they will notice any students who have questions.

Evaluate the Activity

1. Evaluate students' presentations on the basis of the strength of the introduction and conclusion, the inclusion of important points, the delivery of the presentation, and students' use of questions and responses to ensure listeners' comprehension.

2. When the class discusses the presentations that were easiest to follow, encourage students to make note of the features of those presentations that made them effective and to incorporate those techniques in their future presentations.

Cumulative Review

In this Common Core Assessment Workshop (pp. 396–401), students apply and reinforce their mastery of the Common Core State Standards and the skills taught in Unit 2. The practice is divided into four sections, including a section of Performance Tasks addressing CCS Reading standards.

1. Before assigning each section, review the relevant Common Core State Standards and unit skills with students.

2. Set a time limit for the multiple-choice items in each section, allowing a little over one minute per question. Allow twenty minutes for any Timed Writing questions.

3. Administer each of the first three sections of the Cumulative Review (pp. 396–399).

4. Use the Performance Tasks on pages 400–401 to assess the depth of students' mastery of standards taught in the unit. Follow the suggestions on teacher pages 396–399 for assigning tasks and for supporting and evaluating student performance.

Reteaching Skills

1. For each practice, use the Reteach chart on the same page as the answers to determine which skills require reteaching, given the items students answered incorrectly.

2. Reteach these skills prior to assigning the **Benchmark Test** for the second half of Unit 2 (*Unit 2 Resources,* pp. 226–233). The Benchmark Test concludes instruction in the Unit skills.

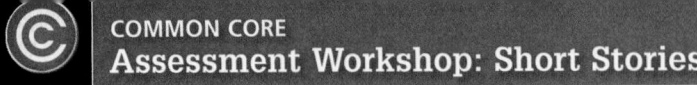

COMMON CORE
Assessment Workshop: Short Stories

Cumulative Review

I. Reading Literature

Common Core
State Standards

RL.7.2, RL.7.3, RL.7.6; W.7.10
[For the full wording of the standards, see the standards chart in the front of your textbook.]

Directions: *Read the story. Then, answer each question that follows.*

"They say that if you are lost in the Everglades, you die. That is, of course, if you have no food, no shelter, and no survival skills," Alicia said as she stared at the sawgrass prairie stretching before her. Her gaze swept along the distant horizon, where the flat grasslands touched the sky. There was not a mini-mart in sight.

"We're not lost," Petra assured her. "I know exactly where we are." Then she whispered, "I just don't know how to get to where we *were.*"

Petra was feeling more guilty than scared. The ride into the sawgrass prairie had been her idea, and she had planned well, packing food, water, and a first-aid kit. All the supplies were loaded on the rented horse that carried both girls along the trail. It was not her fault that the horse had wandered off while she and Alicia explored one of the side trails on foot.

"We should stay where we are," Petra said casually, without a trace of care. "The horse will probably return soon. It knows the trail that will take us back."

Alicia shaded her eyes and searched the western region for the missing horse. The bright sun was blinding and hot. That is why they had decided to explore the marsh, where the ground was soggy but the temperature was cooler. Alicia had never ventured into a marsh before. Her boldness had surprised her, but then she had second thoughts. She felt the presence of unknown creatures and wished she had some way to protect herself against those alligators and poisonous snakes that were surely eyeing her soft flesh. All at once her boldness had evaporated. Her skin felt suddenly clammy, and she had run back to the main trail—into a worse nightmare: the horse was gone.

All at once, Alicia's thoughts were interrupted by the sound of Petra's voice. "The horse!" yelled Petra, pointing excitedly. "It's coming back!"

"Ah!" sighed Alicia. "We live for another day."

Differentiated Instruction   for Universal Access

Strategy for Less Proficient Readers

Review skills and warm up for the test by walking through item 2. Read the passage with students, helping them summarize it. Then, ask a volunteer to read item 2 aloud. Help students define *climax* (the moment of greatest tension in a story, when the outcome is determined). Next, guide students in eliminating incorrect answer choices.

- A—Alicia does *not* find a mini-mart in the passage. (Eliminate.)
- B—The horse *does* wander away, and its disappearance creates the moment of greatest tension in the story.

- C—Although Alicia does become scared, her fear is not the moment of *greatest* tension. It also does not determine the outcome. (Eliminate.)
- D—Petra *does* pack up the first-aid kit, but she does so *early* in the story, not at the climax. (Eliminate.)

Guide students in seeing that **B** is the best choice. Have them complete the remaining items, encouraging them to apply a similar strategy to each: First, define key terms in the prompt, then eliminate incorrect choices.

1. Which event in the story's **plot** happens first?

   A. Alicia and Petra decide to explore the marsh.
   B. The horse comes back to Alicia and Petra.
   C. Petra decides to wait for the horse.
   D. A snake scares the horse.

2. Which event marks the **climax** of the story?

   A. Alicia finds a mini-mart.
   B. Petra yells that the horse is coming back.
   C. Alicia becomes scared in the marsh.
   D. Petra packs up the first-aid kit.

3. What part of the **plot** reveals that Petra had packed food, water, and a first aid kit?

   A. the exposition
   B. the rising action
   C. the falling action
   D. the resolution

4. Which of the following **character traits** does Petra possess?

   A. She is easily scared.
   B. She does not enjoy hiking.
   C. She stays calm in emergencies.
   D. She does not get along with others.

5. Which of the following story details contributes most to the **external conflict?**

   A. The horse wanders off.
   B. There is no mini-mart.
   C. Petra feels guilty.
   D. The girls have food and water.

6. What is Alicia's **motive** for exploring the marsh?

   A. She wants to get out of the hot sun.
   B. She wants to hide from alligators.
   C. She is looking for her first-aid kit.
   D. She wants to capture a snake.

7. What happens in the **resolution** of the story?

   A. Petra begins feeling guilty.
   B. The horse wanders off.
   C. Petra shows bravery.
   D. The horse returns.

8. Which sentence best conveys the **theme** of the story?

   A. Preparation can save your life.
   B. Staying calm can help in a scary situation.
   C. Friendships are invaluable.
   D. Life can be full of hardships.

 Timed Writing

9. Write an essay in which you **explain** whether you think the **main conflict** of this story is internal or external. Cite evidence from the text to support your analysis.

 GO ON

Reteach

Question	Pages to Reteach
1	217
2	217
3	217
4	249
5	309
6	249
7	309
8	309
9	309

Answers continued

8. **B**—The story turns out well, showing that even a scary situation can turn out fine. *Incorrect answers:* A—The story does not support this message, since the girls do bring food and water; C—This statement does not convey a theme, or message about life; D—No details in the story support this idea.

 Timed Writing

9. Students should indicate that the main conflict in the story is external, supporting their answer with details from the story.

I. Reading Literature

Answers With Explanations

1. **A**—Their decision to explore the marsh comes first in time. *Incorrect answers:* B—The horse returns at the end of the story; C—Petra makes this decision after they have already entered the marsh; D—The event does not occur in the story.

2. **B**—The horse's reappearance is the turning point of the story. *Incorrect answers:* A—This event does not occur in the story; C—Alicia's fear is not the moment of greatest tension; D—Petra packs up the kit early in the story.

3. **A**—The exposition provides this background information. *Incorrect answers:* B—The event occurs early and does not increase the tension; C—The event occurs before, not after the climax; D—The event does not settle the conflict.

4. **C**—Petra stays calm even after the horse wanders away, showing that she is not easily scared. *Incorrect answers:* A—Petra is not frightened; B—Petra does enjoy hiking; D—Petra gets along with Alicia, showing that she does get along with others.

5. **A**—The disappearance of the horse is the main element of the girls' conflict with nature. *Incorrect answers:* B—This detail is not part of the conflict; C—Petra's guilt is part of an internal conflict; D—This does not cause a conflict.

6. **A**—The story explains that her desire to get out of the sun is her reason for exploring the marsh. *Incorrect answers:* B—She thinks the marsh is where alligators might live, not a place to hide from them; C—They have brought the first-aid kit with them; D—No details support this answer.

7. **D**—The return of the horse solves the girls' problem. *Incorrect answers:* A—Petra's guilt is part of the rising action; B—The horse's disappearance causes the conflict; C—Petra shows bravery during the conflict, not after its resolution.

397

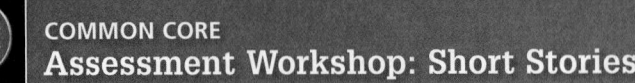

II. Reading Informational Text

Answers With Explanations

1. **B**—Both the "Appearance" section and the "Average Size" chart provide physical descriptions. *Incorrect answers:* A—"The American Alligator" refers to the entire excerpt; C—"Diet" gives details that would not appear in a physical description; D—same explanation as for C.

2. **C**—Both "Appearance" and "Diet" name a section of the entry. *Incorrect answers:* A—"The American Alligator" is the title of the excerpt, not a subhead; B—"Average Size" is the title of the chart, not a subhead; D—same explanation as for C.

3. **C**—No details indicate whether or not alligators live in the ocean. *Incorrect answers:* A—The chart shows that males are generally larger than females; B—Details about alligators swimming and hunting suggest that they spend much time in water; D—The fact that alligators swim with their eyes above the surface suggests that they use sight for hunting.

4. **A**—The strong jaws, sharp teeth, powerful bodies, and good hunting abilities of alligators clearly suggest that they are dangerous. *Incorrect answers:* B—There is no information in the passage about where alligators are found; C—There is no information in the passage about training alligators; D—There is no information in the passage about their lifespan.

II. Reading Informational Text

Directions: *Read the excerpt from an encyclopedia entry. Then, answer each question that follows.*

Common Core
State Standards

RI.7.1, RI.7.5; W.7; L.7.1., L.7.3
[For the full wording of the standards, see the standards chart in the front of your textbook.]

The American Alligator

Appearance

Alligators look like large lizards with thick bodies and tails. They have strong jaws and many sharp teeth. An alligator's eyes stick up above its skull, allowing it to see above the water while its body is beneath the surface. It swims by moving its powerful tail from side to side.

Average Size				
Length when hatched	Length for adult male	Length for adult female	Weight for adult male	Weight for adult female
9 inches	11–12 feet	9 feet or less	450–550 pounds	160 pounds

Diet

Alligators are meat-eating reptiles that eat birds, fish, snakes, turtles, frogs, and mammals. Alligators are good hunters, partly because they are not easily seen by their prey. That is because they swim with only their eyes and tough, scaly backs visible above the surface. To an unsuspecting creature, an alligator can look like a dead log floating in the water.

1. If you wanted to write a physical description of an American alligator, in which sections of the encyclopedia entry would you look for information?

   A. The American Alligator *and* Appearance
   B. Appearance *and* Average Size
   C. Appearance *and* Diet
   D. Average Size *and* Diet

2. What are the **subheads** in this encyclopedia entry?

   A. The American Alligator *and* Appearance
   B. Appearance *and* Average Size
   C. Appearance *and* Diet
   D. Average Size *and* Diet

3. Which **generalization** is *not* supported by information in the encyclopedia entry?

   A. Male alligators are bigger than females.
   B. Alligators spend much of their time in the water.
   C. Alligators do not live in the ocean.
   D. Alligators use their sense of sight for hunting.

4. What can you **infer** from the information about alligators?

   A. Alligators are dangerous.
   B. Alligators are found in the South.
   C. Alligators are easy to train.
   D. Alligators live a long time.

398 Short Stories

Reteach

Question	Pages to Reteach
1	282
2	282
3	364
4	364

Strategies for Test Taking

Tell students that they may make mistakes on standardized tests if they do not read the questions correctly and completely. They should pay particular attention to those small words, such as *not* and *except*, that can play a critical part in determining the meaning of a question.

III. Writing and Language Conventions

Directions: *Read the passage below. Then, answer each question that follows.*

(1) "Seventh Grade" is a funny and believable story. (2) In it, a boy named Victor likes a girl named Teresa. (3) To impress her, Victor pretends to speak French in class. (4) Although he seems smart, he did not really know French. (5) Victor's teacher knows Victor is faking. (6) However, the teacher is very cool. (7) He does not tell the class that Victor's answers are wrong. (8) That is because he remembers what it is like to be a teenager.

1. What sentence states the writer's **claim** about "Seventh Grade"?

A. sentence 1
B. sentence 3
C. sentence 5
D. sentence 7

2. Which additional sentence would *best* **support** the writer's opinion?

A. Victor's secret is safe with his teacher.
B. Gary Soto is the author of "Seventh Grade."
C. You can tell that the story's author, Gary Soto, remembers being young.
D. You should read other stories by the author, Gary Soto.

3. Which word is the **best** replacement for the word **cool** in sentence 6?

A. cold
B. intelligent
C. prepared
D. understanding

4. How would you revise the verb in sentence 6 to use the **future tense?**

A. will be
B. is not
C. was not
D. understand

5. What is the tense of the **principal part** of the verb *tell* in sentence 7?

A. present
B. present participle
C. past
D. past participle

6. How could the writer revise sentence 4 to change the verb to the **present tense?**

A. Although he was smart, he did not really know French.
B. Although he seemed smart, he does not really know French.
C. Although he seems smart, he does not really know French.
D. The sentence is already in the present tense.

Assessment Workshop **399**

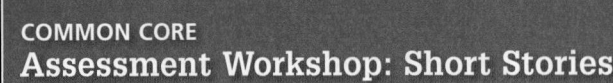

Performance Tasks

Assigning Tasks/Reteaching Skills

Use the chart below to choose appropriate Performance Tasks by identifying which tasks assess lessons in the textbook that you have taught. Use the same lessons for reteaching when students' performance indicates a failure to fully master a standard. For additional instruction and practice, assign the *Common Core Companion* pages indicated for each task.

Task	Where Taught/ Pages to Reteach	Common Core Companion Pages
1	204, 249, 302, 388	28–40, 279–286
2	200–204, 302–303, 337	67–73, 279–286
3	200–204, 217, 309, 337	2–14, 279–286
4	200–203, 337, 370	15–27, 325–331
5	200–204, 217, 249, 309, 394	28–40, 325–331
6	200–204, 335, 385–386	28–40, 323–324

Assessment Pacing

In assigning the Writing Tasks on this student page, allow a class period for the completion of a task. As an alternative, assign tasks as homework. In assigning the Speaking and Listening Tasks on the facing page, consider having students do any required preparation as a homework assignment. Then, allow a class period for the presentations themselves.

Evaluating Performance Tasks

Use the rubric at the bottom of this Teacher Edition page to evaluate students' mastery of the standards as demonstrated in their Performance Task responses. Review the rubric with students before they begin work so they know the criteria by which their work will be evaluated.

Performance Tasks

Common Core
State Standards
RL.7.1, RL.7.2, RL.7.3, RL.7.6; W.7.9.a;
SL.7.5, SL.7.6; L.7.1, L.7.2, L.7.3, L.7.6
[For the full wording of the standards, see the standards chart in the front of your textbook.]

Directions: *Follow the instructions to complete the tasks below as required by your teacher.*

As you work on each task, incorporate both general academic vocabulary and literary terms you learned in this unit.

Writing

Task 1: Literature [RL.7.3; W.7.9.a]
Analyze Setting and Character
Write an essay about a story in this unit in which you discuss how the setting shapes the characters.

- Choose a story with a distinct setting. Remember that time, place, climate, and common beliefs of the time are all part of the setting.
- Analyze how the setting shapes the characters. Describe how it affects their beliefs, thoughts, feelings, actions, and reactions.
- Use appropriate transitions to clarify the relationships between ideas in your essay.
- Use a dictionary to check your spelling of commonly confused words, such as *there*, *their*, and *they're*.

Task 2: Literature [RL.7.6; W.7.9.a]
Analyze Characters' Points of View
Write an essay in which you identify at least two characters' points of view from a story in this unit. Analyze how the author develops and contrasts the points of view of these characters.

- Identify the points of view of at least two characters from a story. Describe what the characters believe and how they feel. Discuss their motives.
- Analyze how the author develops each character's point of view through narration, dialogue, and action. Include concrete

400 Short Stories

details from the text to develop and support your analysis.
- Then, discuss how the author *contrasts* the points of view of your chosen characters through their dialogue, actions, and reactions.
- As you revise, check your writing for correct spelling and punctuation.

Task 3: Literature [RL.7.1; W.7.9.a]
Evaluate Plot
Write an essay in which you evaluate the plot in one of the stories in this unit.

- Choose a story with a plot that you feel is developed in a particularly effective way. Then, write an opening sentence that expresses your view.
- Analyze how well the parts of the plot work together to move the story forward. Focus on the exposition, rising action and conflict, climax, falling action, and resolution.
- Use details from the text to support your evaluation. For example, point out examples of effective narrative techniques such as the use of foreshadowing, descriptive language, or specific details that build tension or suspense.
- Use transitional words or phrases, such as *furthermore, likewise, however, and in addition to*, to create unity between the ideas in sentences or paragraphs.
- Add a conclusion that sums up your main points and ties your essay together.

Performance Task Rubric: Standards Mastery	Rating Scale				
	not very				*very*
Critical Thinking: How clearly and consistently does the student pursue the specific mode of reasoning or discourse required by the standard, as specified in the prompt (e.g., comparing and contrasting, analyzing, explaining)?	1	2	3	4	5
Focus: How well does the student understand and apply the focus concepts of the standard, as specified in the prompt (e.g., development of theme or of complex characters, effects of structure, and so on)?	1	2	3	4	5
Support/Elaboration: How well does the student support points with textual or other evidence? How relevant, sufficient, and varied is the evidence provided?	1	2	3	4	5
Insight: How original, sophisticated, or compelling are insights the student achieves by applying the standard to the text(s)?	1	2	3	4	5
Expression of Ideas: How well does the student organize and support ideas? How well does the student use language, including word choice and conventions, in the expression of ideas?	1	2	3	4	5

Speaking and Listening

© Task 4: Literature [RL.7.2; SL.7.6]
Analyze and Develop Theme

Write a brief narrative in which you develop the theme of a story from this unit in a different way. Read your story aloud to a group of classmates.

- Determine the theme of a story in this unit and analyze its development over the course of the story.
- Decide on a different way to develop the same theme. Then, write a brief narrative to develop imagined experiences that express the theme.
- As you write, choose language that expresses your ideas clearly and effectively.
- Read your story aloud to a group of classmates.

© Task 5: Literature [RL.7.3; SL.7.6]
Analyze Story Elements

Give an oral presentation in which you analyze the ways that literary elements interact in a story in this unit.

- Determine the ways that literary elements work together in your chosen story. For example, consider how the characters and setting affect the plot.
- Explain the impact of these elements on the story as a whole. Determine how the story would be different if it took place in a different setting or if a character had been developed in a different way.
- In your oral presentation, capture your audience's attention by beginning with a powerful opening statement. Vary your volume, pitch, and pacing and establish eye contact as you speak.

© Task 6: Literature [RL.7.3; SL.7.5]
Analyze Conflict Development

Give a presentation in which you use multimedia or visual displays to clarify your analysis of how particular story elements interact to develop the conflict of a story in this unit.

- Prepare a presentation that identifies the internal or external conflict faced by the main character in a story of your choice. Analyze how particular story elements, such as setting, plot, and other characters, interact to develop the conflict.
- Create a story map, a cause-and-effect chart, or another graphic to visually display the conflict and the progress of its development.
- Accurately use appropriate vocabulary and content-area words in your presentation.

 Does every conflict have a winner?

At the beginning of Unit 2, you wrote a response to the Big Question. Now that you have completed the unit, write a new response. Discuss how your initial ideas have either been changed or reinforced. Cite specific examples from the literature in this unit, from other subject areas, and from your own life to support your ideas. Use Big Question vocabulary words (see p. 199) in your response.

Assessment Workshop **401**

Supporting Speaking and Listening

1. Consider having students work with partners or in groups to complete Performance Tasks involving speaking and listening. For tasks that you assign for individual work, you may still wish to have students rehearse with partners, who can provide constructive feedback.

2. As students rehearse, have them keep in mind these tips:
   - Present findings and evidence clearly and concisely.
   - Observe conventions of standard English grammar and usage.
   - Be relaxed and friendly but maintain a formal tone.
   - Make eye contact with the audience, pronounce words clearly, and vary your pace.
   - When working with a group, respond thoughtfully to others' positions, modifying your own in response to new evidence.

Linking Performance Tasks to Independent Reading

If you wish to cover the standards with students' independent reading, adapt Performance Tasks of your choice to the works they have selected. (Independent reading suggestions appear on the next page.)

Does every conflict have a winner?

1. Remind students that the unit Big Question is "Does every conflict have a winner?"

2. Have students complete their responses to the prompt on the student page. Point out that they have read selections in this unit about different ways to examine conflicts and that they should draw on these selections in their responses. Remind them that they can also draw on their own experiences and what they have learned in other subject areas in formulating their answers.

Differentiated Instruction   for Universal Access

Strategy for Less Proficient Readers

Assign a Performance Task, and then have students meet in groups to review the standard assessed in that task. Remind students of the selections or independent readings to which they have previously applied the standard. Have groups summarize what they learned in applying the standard and then present their summaries. Discuss, clarifying any points of confusion. After students have completed their tasks, have groups meet again to evaluate members' work. Encourage members to revise their work based on the feedback they receive.

Strategy for English Learners

For each assigned Performance Task, review the instructions with students. Clarify the meaning of any unfamiliar vocabulary, emphasizing routine classroom words such as *narrative*, *elements*, and *statement*, and academic vocabulary such as *evaluate*.

Next, have students note ideas for their responses. Pair students, and have them review each other's notes, asking questions to clarify meaning and suggesting improvements. Encourage students to ask for your assistance in supplying English words or expressions they may require.

401

Independent Reading

Titles featured on the Independent Reading pages at the end of each unit represent a range of reading, including stories, dramas, and poetry, as well as literary nonfiction and other types of informational text. Throughout, labels indicate the works that are CCSS Exemplar Texts. Choosing from among these featured titles will help students read works at increasing levels of text complexity in the grades 6–8 text complexity band.

Independent Reading and Pacing

See the Unit Overview and Pacing Plan, pp. 198a–198b, for suggestions on integrating independent reading with work in the Student Edition.

Using Literature Circles

A literature circle is a temporary group in which students independently discuss a book.

Use the guidance in the *Professional Development Guidebook*, pp. 47–49, as well as the teaching notes on the facing page, for additional suggestions for literature circles.

Ⓒ Meeting Unit 2 CCS Focus Standards

Students can use books listed on this page to apply and to reinforce their mastery of the CCS Focus Standards covered in this unit. (The Focus Standards are introduced on pp. 200–203.)

Introducing Featured Titles

Have students choose a book or books for independent reading. Assist them by previewing the titles, noting their subject matter and level of difficulty. **Note:** Before recommending a work to students, preview it, taking into account the values of your community as well as the maturity of your students.

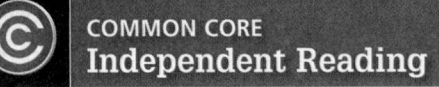

COMMON CORE
Independent Reading

Featured Titles

In this unit, you have read a variety of short stories. Continue to read on your own. Select works that you enjoy, but challenge yourself to explore new authors and works of increasing depth and complexity. The titles suggested below will help you get started.

Literature

The Dark Is Rising

by Susan Cooper
Aladdin, 1973   **EXEMPLAR TEXT** Ⓒ

On his eleventh birthday, Will Stanton learns that he is the Sign-Seeker, an immortal who must fight the Dark to keep the world safe from evil. This **novel** is the first in a series of five books that draw inspiration from ominous Welsh and Celtic myths, as well as the action-packed legends of King Arthur.

The Collected Poems of Langston Hughes

by Langston Hughes
Vintage, 1994   **EXEMPLAR TEXT** Ⓒ

Langston Hughes was just nineteen when his first poem, "The Negro Speaks of Rivers," was published. Critics were soon raving about his original voice, which combined the rhythms of jazz and blues with the words and speech patterns of his African American heritage. This collection of **poetry** spans Hughes's long and brilliant career.

White Fang and The Call of the Wild

by Jack London

White Fang tells the first-person story of a wolf whom a man adopts after enduring a series of hardships. *The Call of the Wild* is about a pampered dog stolen from his home and forced to endure harsh Yukon winters and cruel masters as a sled dog. In both **novels,** the animals rely on instinct to survive in a brutal environment.

Heat

by Mike Lupica
Philomel, 2006

Michael Arroyo is such a skilled pitcher that coaches of rival baseball teams demand proof of his age. In this **novel,** Michael must struggle to find a way to play the game that he loves and to cope with his difficult home life.

The Devil's Arithmetic

by Jane Yolen

In this **historical novel,** a girl finds herself whisked back in time to a Polish village to experience firsthand the horrors her relatives experienced. She learns the history of the Holocaust in a way that no history lesson could teach.

Informational Texts

Geeks: How Two Lost Boys Rode the Internet out of Idaho

by Jon Katz
Villard Books, 2000   **EXEMPLAR TEXT** Ⓒ

In this **nonfiction** book, Jesse and Eric, two computer "geeks" with few social skills or future prospects, meet the reporter Jon Katz, who convinces them that they can use their computer savvy to create a better life.

Discoveries: Working It Out

What role does conflict play in social studies, science, music, and mathematics? The **essays** and **stories** in this book explore different types of conflicts and how they are worked out.

Ⓒ Text Complexity: Aligning Texts With Readers and Tasks

TEXTS	READERS AND TASKS
• *Discoveries: Working It Out* (Lexile: 665L) • *The Devil's Arithmetic* (730L)	**Below-Level Readers** Allow students to focus on reading for content, and challenge them to interpret multiple perspectives.
• *The Dark Is Rising* (Lexile: 920L) • *Heat* (Lexile: 940L) • *White Fang and the Call of the Wild* (Lexile: 970L)	**Below-Level Readers** Challenge students as they read for content. **On-Level Readers** Allow students to focus on reading for content, and challenge them to interpret multiple perspectives. **Advanced Readers** Allow students to focus on interpreting multiple perspectives.
• *Geeks: How Two Lost Boys Rode the Internet out of Idaho* (Lexile: 1070L)	**On-Level Readers** Challenge students as they read for content. **Advanced Readers** Allow students to focus on reading for content, and challenge them to interpret multiple perspectives.

Preparing to Read Complex Texts

Attentive Reading As you read on your own, ask yourself questions about the text. The questions below, along with others that you ask as you read, will enrich your reading experience.

Common Core State Standards

Reading Literature/Informational Text
10. By the end of the year, read and comprehend literature, including stories, dramas, and poems, and literary nonfiction in the grades 6–8 text complexity band proficiently, with scaffolding as needed at the high end of the range.

When reading short stories, ask yourself...

- Can I clearly picture the setting of the story? Which details help me do so?
- Can I picture the characters clearly in my mind? Why or why not?
- Do the characters speak and act like real people? Why or why not?
- Which characters do I like? Why? Which characters do I dislike? Why?
- Do I understand why the characters act as they do? Why or why not?
- What does the story mean to me? Does it express a meaning or an insight I find important and true?

Ⓒ **Key Ideas and Details**

- Does the story grab my attention right from the beginning? Why or why not?
- Do I want to keep reading? Why or why not?
- Can I follow the sequence of events in the story? Am I confused at any point? If so, what information would make the sequence clearer?
- Do the characters change as the story progresses? If so, do their changes seem believable?
- Are there any passages that I find especially moving, interesting, or well written? If so, why?

Ⓒ **Craft and Structure**

- How is this story similar to and different from other stories I have read?
- Do I care what happens to the characters? Do I sympathize with them? Why or why not?
- How do my feelings toward the characters affect my experience of reading the story?
- Did the story teach me something new or cause me to look at something in a new way? If so, what did I learn?
- Would I recommend this story to others? Why or why not?
- Would I like to read other works by this author? Why or why not?

Ⓒ **Integration of Ideas**

Ⓒ Text Complexity: Reader and Task Support Suggestions

INDEPENDENT READING

Increased Support Suggest that students choose a book that they feel comfortable reading and one that is a bit more challenging. Pair a more proficient reader with a less proficient reader and have them work together on the more challenging text. Partners can prepare to read the book by reviewing questions on this student page. They can also read difficult passages together, sharing questions and insights. They can use the questions on the student page to guide after-reading discussion.

Increased Challenge Encourage students to integrate knowledge and ideas by combining the Big Question and the Unit Focus concepts in their approach to two or more featured titles.

For example, students might consider who the "winners" and "losers" are in the conflicts described in *The Dark is Rising* and *White Fang and the Call of the Wild*. In addition, students can focus on similarities and differences in plot elements in different works of fiction.

Preparing to Read Complex Texts

1. Tell students they can be attentive readers by bringing their experience and imagination to the texts they read and by actively questioning those texts. Explain that the questions they see on the student page are examples of types of questions to ask about short stories.

2. Point out that, like writing, reading is a "multidraft" process, involving several readings of complete works or passages, revising and refining one's understanding each time.

Ⓒ **Key Ideas and Details**

3. As an example, review and amplify the third bulleted item. **Ask:** What key ideas and details would you cite as evidence that the characters speak and act like real people?

   Possible response: You might describe the ways in which a character reminds you of someone you know or point to the author's use of diction.

Ⓒ **Craft and Structure**

4. **Ask:** What details of craft and structure would you evaluate to determine if a story grabs your attention from the beginning?

   Possible response: You might point to an exciting action that opens the story or to a strong image in the first paragraph.

Ⓒ **Integration of Ideas**

5. **Ask:** How would you decide if you sympathize with a character?

   Possible response: You might consider whether the character seems likeable or whether you can relate to the character's experience.

6. Finally, explain to students that they should cite key ideas and details, examples of craft and structure, or instances of the integration of ideas as evidence to support their points during a book discussion. After hearing the evidence, the group might reach a consensus, or might agree to disagree.

Unit 3 Features Overview

Unit Genre and Big Question

In this unit, students will analyze nonfiction. As they read they will discuss responses to the unit Big Question: What should we learn?

Unit 3 Selections

Teach Selections are presented in leveled pairs. To teach the skills and meet the objectives, you need to assign only one selection in each pair.

Differentiate and Reinforce Choose the selection in a pair that is best suited for your students, based on the Text Complexity box shown on the next page. You may use the other selection to reinforce skills or provide enrichment.

Integrate Skills Each selection presents students with a reading strategy, a literary analysis concept, a vocabulary skill, and grammar instruction. Students can extend learning in the writing and extension activities.

Additional Unit Features

ⓒ Literary Analysis Workshop Teach and model the Unit Focus standards. Spiral Review notes enable students to revisit these skills over the course of the unit.

Reading for Information Students analyze functional, expository, and argumentative texts and complete Timed Writing activities.

Comparing Literary Works Students study two literary works either within or across genres.

Test Practice: Reading This feature provide extra practice in utilizing reading skills to master assessments.

Writing Workshops Two writing workshops appear in each unit, along with rubrics and instruction in the writing process.

Assessment Workshop Cumulative Skills Review and Performance Tasks provide a range of assessment opportunities.

Independent Reading Students broaden their knowledge as they read longer works of increasing complexity.

THE BIG **?** **What should we** *learn* **?**

404

Teaching From Technology

Enriched Online Student Edition
- full narration of selections
- interactive graphic organizers
- linked **Get Connected** and **Background** videos
- all worksheets and other student resources

Professional Development
- the *Professional Development Guidebook* online
- additional professional development articles by program authors

Planning, Assigning, and Monitoring
- software for online assignment of work to students, individually or to the whole class
- a system for tracking and grading student work

Types of Nonfiction

Unit
3

405

Instructional Resources

The booklet *Unit 3 Resources* supports Unit skills with pages of the following types:

▶ **Benchmark Tests** assess and monitor student progress at mid-Unit and at Unit's end.

▶ **Vocabulary and Reading Warm-ups** provide additional vocabulary support, based on Lexile rankings of words, for each selection.
"A" Warm-ups are for students reading two grades below level.
"B" Warm-ups are for students reading one grade below level.

▶ **Selection Support** These practice pages are available for each selection:
- Reading Skill
- Literary Analysis
- Writing About the Big Question
- Vocabulary
- Support for Writing
- Support for Extend Your Learning
- Enrichment

PHLit Online!
www.PHLitOnline.com

All worksheets and other student resources are also available online at www.PHLitOnline.com.

PHLit Online!
www.PHLitOnline.com

Hear It!
- Selection summary audio
- Selection audio
- BQ Tunes

See It!
- Author video
- Big Question video
- Get Connected videos
- Background videos
- More about the authors
- Illustrated vocabulary words
- Vocabulary flashcards

Do It!
- Interactive journals
- Interactive graphic organizers
- Grammar tutorials
- Interactive vocabulary games
- Test practice

© Text Complexity: Accessibility for Various Ability Levels

This chart gives a general text complexity rating to help you decide which selection in each leveled pair is more appropriate for your students. **Choose one selection in each pair, or choose to teach both.** You will meet the objectives for the pair when you teach either of the two selections. For additional guidance on factors that affect the complexity of each selection, see the Leveled Texts page for each selection set.

Accessibility for English Learners

 This icon indicates support for English learners at point of use in this Teacher's Edition.

	✓ More Accessible	✓✓ More Complex
Pair 1	Life Without Gravity	Conversational Ballgames
Pair 2	I Am a Native of North America	Volar: To Fly
Pair 3	All Together Now	The Eternal Frontier
Pair 4	The Real Story of a Cowboy's Life	Rattlesnake Hunt

Unit 3 Focus Standards
- Reading Informational Text 3, 5, 6

Additional Activities and Assessments
- Reading Informational Text 2, 4, 8
- Writing 1, 2, 4, 8, 9
- Speaking and Listening 2, 3, 4
- Language 1, 4, 5, 6

	Week 1					Week 2					Week 3				
	1	2	3	4	5	1	2	3	4	5	1	2	3	4	5
Introduce the Unit Big Question (pp. 406–407).	●														
Introduce the unit form, nonfiction, using the Literary Analysis Workshop (pp. 408–411).	●														
Introduce the focus CCS standards for the unit and lead students in a close reading of exemplar texts. (pp. 410–419).	●	●													
Teach one selection from Pairing 1 (pp. 420–439).			●	●	●	●									
Teach one selection from Pairing 2 (pp. 440–459).							●	●	●	●	●				
Complete the Test Practice: Reading (pp. 460–461).									●						
Teach Reading for Information (pp. 462–467).										●					
Teach Comparing Literary Works (pp. 468–483).											●	●			
Have students complete the Writing Workshop (pp. 484–489).											●	●	●	●	●
Administer **Benchmark Test 5** (*Unit 3 Resources*, pp. 120–125).														●	
Reteach skills, judging which skills to reteach by evaluating students' performance on **Benchmark Test 5.**															●

Independent Reading

Have students choose a full-length work from the Independent Reading feature at the end of the unit and read it while working on this unit.

Pacing Suggestions

- Have students read their chosen work for homework.
- Devote parts of class periods in each school week to Literature Circles in which students reading the same work discuss it.

	Week 4					Week 5					Week 6				
	1	2	3	4	5	1	2	3	4	5	1	2	3	4	5
Teach one selection from Pairing 3 (pp. 490–505).	•	•	•	•	•										
Teach one selection from Pairing 4 (pp. 506–527).					•	•	•	•	•						
Complete the Test-Practice: Reading (pp. 528–529).								•							
Teach Reading for Information (pp. 530–535).									•						
Teach Comparing Literary Works (pp. 536–547).										•	•				
Have students complete the Writing Workshop (pp. 548–555).									•	•	•	•	•		
Have students complete the Vocabulary Workshop (pp. 556–557).												•			
Have students complete the Communications Workshop (pp. 558–559).												•			
Have students complete the first three sections of the Assessment Workshop: Nonfiction (pp. 560–563).												•	•	•	
Have students complete the selected Performance Tasks in the Assessment Workshop (pp. 564–565).														•	
Administer Benchmark Test 6 (*Unit 3 Resources,* pp. 227–234).														•	
Reteach skills, judging which skills to reteach by evaluating students' performance on Benchmark Test 6.															•

- Cover the focus standards with independent readings and abbreviate review of the focus standards with student-edition selections.

- Do not assign extension activities for selections (day 5 of main selection lessons), except as needed for full standards coverage.

- If students demonstrate reading proficiency, consider omitting Test Practice: Reading features in the unit.

Block and Daily Scheduling

The assignments and activities in this Unit planner are organized by week. You may adjust them to your daily or block schedule. The Time and Resource Manager for each selection set gives specific pacing suggestions, or you may use the comprehensive lesson planning support online at **PHLitOnline.com**

Monitoring Progress

Diagnose Each main selection pairing in the Unit contains a more accessible and a more complex selection. To determine which selection in each pairing to assign, refer to students' results on the **Vocabulary in Context** section of **Benchmark Test 4,** *Unit 2 Resources,* pp. 226–233 (administered at the end of the previous Unit). Use the **Interpretation Guide** to interpret the results of this diagnostic portion of the test. **Note:** For the most accurate diagnosis of students who score in the middle range, administer the additional diagnostic questions online at **www.PHLitOnline.com.**

Preteach and Prepare As indicated by the diagnostic, prepare students for reading by assigning the **Vocabulary** and **Reading Warm-ups** for the selections you assign.

Teach Follow this Pacing Plan and use the resources to teach the skills and selections. For specific pacing suggestions and a list of resources, see the Time and Resource Manager and the Visual Guide to Featured Selection Resources preceding each selection pairing.

Classroom Management
For classroom management suggestions for using leveled texts in a mixed-ability classroom, see Harvey Daniels's professional development essay "Leveled Reading Selections," online at **www.PHLitOnline.com.**

Assess After students have completed the first half of the Unit, administer **Benchmark Test 5.** Administer **Benchmark Test 6** at the end of the Unit.

Intervention and Reteach After administering each test, use the **Interpretation Guide** for the tests to determine which reteaching pages, if any, you should assign from the *Reading Kit.* The appropriate pages are also available through the online Progress Monitoring software.

CLASSROOM STRATEGIES

Bringing All Students Into the Conversation **William G. Brozo**

> We need to reconsider our roles during typical class discussions.

"Over 200 years ago, Samuel Johnson captured the essential role social discourse plays in promoting learning when he said "The seeds of knowledge may be planted in solitude, but must be cultivated in public" (Boswell, 1979, p. 121). We know from important research (Fielding & Pearson, 1994) that students need ample time to discuss with others what they are reading in order to process it more deeply and make it more memorable. We also know that discussion strategies work best in a classroom environment where student input is desired and respected (Alvermann, O'Brien, & Dillon, 1990).

Increasing Student Engagement in Class Discussions

We need to reconsider our roles during typical class discussions. In order to maximize participation, we need to make time for students to reflect, converse, share, and critique in an atmosphere of mutual respect. Underlying effective discussion strategies is the idea that plumbing the depths of a text or topic by inviting students to explore interpretations and challenge their various points of view can stimulate critical thinking and engender motivation for reading and learning (Green, 2000). This goal can be achieved through these teacher strategies:

- Maintaining deliberate silence instead of immediately answering a question or providing terminal feedback
- Modeling good listening habits to avoid dominating classroom talk
- Encouraging students to ask and answer questions posed to the teacher and to one another
- Allowing for small-group brainstorming first before opening the discussion to the whole class

Four Effective Classroom Discussion Strategies

English/language arts teachers can use many other simple discussion techniques to energize student learning and heighten enthusiasm for texts and topics. Each of these practices transforms students from passive observers and listeners to engaged and active discussants

- ***Turn to Your Neighbor*** Before eliciting responses to the questions asked of the whole group, tell students to turn to their neighbor and talk for 60 seconds about possible answers. When time is up, invite students to share with the whole class what they discussed with their partners. As compared with the teacher's single respondent to her questions, this approach is likely to elicit input from a variety of class

members. Furthermore, the teacher will know from eavesdropping on the conversations among the student pairs, that even though some remained silent during the question discussions, these individuals had done some good thinking and expressed relevant ideas and responses, too.

- **Inside-Outside Circles** For this discussion strategy, clear some space in the middle of the room, and organize the class into two concentric circles. Students in the smaller inner circle face outward, and those in the larger outer circle face inward. Next, pose a question that will help the class think more personally about the text. Ask students to discuss interpretations and reactions with the person standing most directly in front of them. After a minute or so, have the inner circle rotate to the right until a new pair of students is facing each other. Then, start the discussion anew. After a few more rotations, randomly call on students to share with the rest of the class what they discussed with the various persons from their circles. This strategy instigates numerous responses and counter-responses, as well as a great deal of valuable and meaningful discussion.

- **Value Lines** Leave a row of desks in the middle of the classroom while clearing out space on either side. Present students with an assertion about the text. Tell the class to move to the right of the row of desks if they agree with the assertion or to the left if they disagree. Once taking their sides, ask them to talk with someone nearby about why they agree or disagree. After a minute or so, ask students to discuss their opinions with someone across the row of desks. Periodically, interrupt opposing conversants to elicit opinions and ideas and to make sure pairs of students are respectfully arguing their points.

- **Fishbowl** This discussion strategy is well labeled because it involves one group of students looking in on another smaller group of students in a manner not unlike watching fish through the clear glass of an aquarium. To set it up, organize a closed circle of 4–5 desks in the middle of the room. Randomly call on students and ask them to sit in the specially arranged desks. Direct the remaining class members to gather around the group seated in the middle, and then pose a question related to the text for the seated group. While the students in the "fishbowl" discuss responses to the question among themselves, the others should watch and listen quietly. When the discussion concludes, elicit reactions from those students watching from the outside. Afterward, a new group of students can be asked to sit in the "fishbowl" and discuss the same or another question about the reading.

Modeled Strategy

See pp. 463 and 494 for a point-of-use note modeling these strategies.

Teacher Resources

- **Professional Development Guidebook**
- **Classroom Strategies and Teaching Routines cards**

Log on as a teacher at **www.PHLitOnline.com** to access a library of all Professional Development articles by the Contributing Authors of Pearson Prentice Hall *Literature*.

William G. Brozo

William G. Brozo writes the "Strategic Moves" column for the journal *Thinking Classroom* and co-authors the "Content Literacy" column for *The Reading Teacher*. His work focuses on enhancing the literate lives of boys and making teaching more responsive to the needs of all students.

Supporting Research

Alvermann, D., O'Brien, D., & Dillon, D. (1990). What teachers do when they say they're having discussions of content area reading assignments. *Reading Research Quarterly, 25,* 296–322.

Boswell, J. (1979). *The life of Samuel Johnson.* New York: Viking Press.

Brozo, W.G., & Simpson, M.L. (2003). *Readers, teachers, learners: Expanding literacy across the content areas* (4th ed.).

Upper Saddle River, NJ: Merrill/ Prentice Hall.

Fielding, L.P., & Pearson, P.D. (1994). Reading comprehension: What works. *Educational Leadership, 51,* 62–68.

Green, T. (2000). Responding and sharing: Techniques for energizing classroom discussions. *The Clearing House, 73,* 331–334.

Common Core State Standards
- Speaking and Listening 1.b
- Language 4.d, 6

❶ Introducing the Big Question

1. **Read aloud** the introductory section as students follow along silently. Emphasize the different forms knowledge can take, including lessons from others. **Ask:** What are some examples of these lessons? (**Possible responses:** right from wrong, respect for others and their property)

2. **Ask** students the Big Question, "What should we learn?" (**Possible responses:** things we are interested in; different kinds of things)

3. Tell students that literature can be one of the most powerful teachers of life lessons and other forms of learning. As students read, they should consider how the selections affect their answers to the Big Question.

❷ Exploring the Big Question

Collaboration: Group Discussion

1. Introduce the activity, using the instruction on the student page.

2. Have students work individually to list examples. If students have difficulty with the last two bullets, prompt ideas with questions:

   - What is a problem that needs to be solved, and how could we solve it? (**Sample response:** world hunger; We could solve it by growing more food.)

   - What is your favorite thing to do? (**Sample response:** play video games.)

3. Review the Big Question vocabulary on page 407, following the teaching suggestions. Have students use the vocabulary as they complete the activity on page 406.

Connecting to the Literature

Explain the Big Question strand in the unit, referring to the box at right.

406

---

❶ What should we learn?

Everyone has their own ideas about what is important to learn. Some people believe we should learn information that helps us develop practical skills. Others believe we should explore topics driven by our curiosity and talents.

When you think about what we should learn, remember that knowledge includes skills you learn in school and lessons you learn from others. It also includes information that helps you understand other cultures, and ideas that inspire you to investigate the world around you. No matter what is most important to you, the drive to discover new things is something we all have in common.

❷ Exploring the Big Question

Collaboration: Group Discussion Start thinking about the Big Question by making a list of things you believe are important to learn. Describe an example for each of the following:

- A skill that could save someone's life
- A subject you would like to study in school
- A job that requires specific knowledge
- An idea that might make the world a better place
- A personal interest of yours

With a small group, discuss why you think some of these items are more important to learn than others. During your discussion, speak when it is your turn and listen to others without interrupting. Assign a discussion leader to keep ideas moving forward and a group recorder to list the items in the order of importance the group agrees to support. Ask a timekeeper to monitor your discussion and limit it to fifteen minutes. Finally, choose a speaker to present your group's ideas to the class.

Connecting to the Literature Each reading in this unit will give you additional insight into the Big Question.

406 Fiction and Nonfiction

PHLit
Online!
www.PHLitOnline.com
- Big Question video
- Illustrated vocabulary words
- Interactive vocabulary games
- BQ Tunes

Applying Understanding by Design Principles

The Big Question

Explain to students that they will continue to consider the Big Question as they work through Unit 3.

- At the beginning of each selection, they will write a response to a Writing About the Big Question sentence starter.
- As they read the selection, they will look for details related to the Big Question.

- At the end of the selection, they will answer a Critical Thinking question that is related to the Big Question.
- Tell students that their goal will be to gain a deeper understanding of literature and a more sophisticated way of discussing the Big Question.

"Understanding by Design" is registered as a trademark with the Patent and Trademark Office by the Association for Supervision of Curriculum Development (ASCD). ASCD has not authorized, approved, or sponsored this work and is in no way affiliated with Pearson or its products.

Learning Big Question Vocabulary

Acquire and Use Academic Vocabulary Academic vocabulary is the language you encounter in textbooks and on standardized tests. Review the definitions of these academic vocabulary words.

Common Core State Standards

Speaking and Listening
1.b. Follow rules for collegial discussions, track progress toward specific goals and deadlines, and define individual roles as needed.

Language
4.d. Verify the preliminary determination of the meaning of a word or phrase.
6. Acquire and use accurately grade-appropriate general academic and domain-specific words and phrases; gather vocabulary knowledge when considering a word or phrase important to comprehension or expression.

analyze (anʹə līzʹ) v. break into parts in order to study closely

discover (di skuvʹər) v. find something hidden or previously unknown

evaluate (ē valʹyo͞o ātʹ) v. judge or rate

examine (eg zamʹ ən) v. study in depth in order to find or check something

explore (ek splôrʹ) v. travel through an unfamiliar area to find out what it is like; thoroughly discuss a topic

facts (fakts) n. true information about a topic

inquire (in kwīrʹ) v. ask someone for information

investigate (in vesʹ tə gātʹ) v. work to find out the truth

Use these words as you complete Big Question activities in this unit that involve reading, writing, speaking, and listening.

Gather Vocabulary Knowledge Additional Big Question words are listed below. Categorize the words by deciding whether you know each one well, know it a little bit, or do not know it at all.

curiosity	interview	question
experiment	knowledge	understand
information		

Then, do the following:

1. Write the definitions of the words you know.
2. Verify the definitions by looking up each word in a print or online dictionary. Revise your definitions as needed.
3. Continue to use the dictionary to look up the meanings and pronunciations of the unknown words.
4. Then, write a paragraph, using all the vocabulary words, about the types of things you think are important to learn.

Gather Vocabulary Knowledge: Definitions

curiosity (kyo͞orʹē äsʹə tē) n. desire to know more about something

experiment (ek sperʹə mənt) n. a test to find out something

information (inʹfər māʹshən) n. knowledge given or received

interview (inʹtər vyo͞oʹ) v. talk with a person who shares information

knowledge (nälʹij) n. learning; awareness

question (kwesʹchən) v. doubt; wonder about

understand (unʹdər standʹ) v. get knowledge about

---

❸ Learning Big Question Vocabulary

Acquire and Use Academic Vocabulary

1. Introduce the academic vocabulary words in the first word bank on the student page. Have students preview the words.

2. For each word, have students say the word aloud. Then, use the word in a sentence that defines the word.

Gather Vocabulary Knowledge

1. With the class, review the steps in the activity on the student page. Have students complete the activity independently, with partners, or in small groups.

2. Before students complete the last step, review the words and their meanings as a class. (Definitions appear below on the left.) Then, have students complete their paragraphs.

Show the Big Question video, online at **www.PHLitOnline.com**.

❶ Elements of Nonfiction

1. Introduce the form, nonfiction, using the instruction on the student page.

2. To clarify the two categories of nonfiction, cite directions, applications, and recipes as examples of functional texts; cite biographies, letters, and essays as examples of literary nonfiction. **Ask:** Into which of the two categories does a bus schedule fall? Into which does a book review fall?

   Answer: The schedule is a functional text; the review is literary nonfiction.

3. Go over the five nonfiction structures. **Ask:** Which pattern of organization would work best for a review of two different film versions of a novel? Which would work best for a physical description of the Oval Office?

   Answer: A comparison-and-contrast structure would work best for the review; a spatial structure would be best for the description.

4. Review the definition of narrative nonfiction. **Ask:** What are some common types of narrative nonfiction?

   Possible response: Types include biography, autobiography, and memoir.

5. Clarify that the chart explains storytelling elements in narrative nonfiction by comparing it to fiction. Note that the elements are similar except for one thing. **Ask:** What is the one main difference?

   Answer: The elements of narrative nonfiction are real.

6. Review with students each specific characteristic of narrative nonfiction listed on the chart.

❶ Elements of Nonfiction

Nonfiction is writing about actual people, ideas, and events.

Nonfiction writing presents information that is true or thought to be true. Two broad categories of nonfiction are **functional texts,** which are practical documents that help readers perform everyday tasks, and **literary nonfiction,** which features some of the same literary elements and techniques as fiction.

Authors of nonfiction write with one or more **purposes,** or goals, in mind. Usually, these are to inform, describe, or persuade. To fulfill his or her purpose, the writer organizes information in a logical **structure,** or arrangement of parts, using patterns of organization such as these:

- **Chronological,** which presents events in the order in which they happened
- **Spatial,** which describes items as they appear in space—for example, left to right

- **Comparison-and-contrast,** which groups ideas based on their similarities and differences
- **Cause-and-effect,** which explains how one event causes, or leads to, another
- **Problem-and-solution,** which examines a problem and proposes ways to solve it

Literary Nonfiction In addition to informing, describing, or persuading, literary nonfiction may have an additional purpose: to entertain. When a work of literary nonfiction tells a story, it is called **narrative nonfiction.** It may include the elements listed in the right-hand column of the chart below.

Comparison of Storytelling Elements

In Fiction	In Narrative Nonfiction
Characters are developed through • **direct characterization,** or statements about what the characters are like; • **indirect characterization,** or descriptions of what the characters do, say, and think.	**Direct** and **indirect characterization** reveal the personalities of **real people.**
Setting is revealed through • **vivid descriptions** of **time, place,** and **customs;** • **figurative language,** or unusual comparisons, such as similes.	**Vivid descriptions** and **figurative language** describe **real places, real historical eras,** and **real customs.**
Plot, or the sequence of fictional events in a story, is **artfully paced and organized** to sustain readers' interest.	**Artful pacing and organization** describe **actual events.**

408 Types of Nonfiction

Teaching Resources

All *Common Core Companion,* pp. 122–161

All *Unit 3 Resources,* pp. 7–22

All *Professional Development Guidebook,* p. 33

All *See It!* DVD
Richard Mühlberger, Segments 1 and 2

All *Graphic Organizer Transparencies* pp. 73, 74

All Enriched Online Student Edition

L2 L3 *Reader's Notebook*

L1 *Reader's Notebook: Adapted Version*

EL *Reader's Notebook: English Learner's Version*

L2 EL *Hear It!* Audio CD

L1 EL *Hear It!* Audio CD (adapted text)

PHLit Online! All resources, including print and video, are available online at **www.PHLitOnline.com.**

2 Forms of Literary Nonfiction

In addition to narrative nonfiction, three common forms of literary nonfiction are articles, essays, and speeches.

Articles are short prose works that present facts about a subject. They may appear in print sources, such as newspapers, or in online sources, such as Web sites.

Essays are also short prose works that focus on a particular subject. They may be more personal than articles, however. The author of an essay often has a deep emotional connection to the subject.

Speeches are written texts that are delivered orally to an audience. Like an essay, a speech expresses the speaker's point of view, or perspective, on a topic.

Types of Nonfiction 3

Just as there are different *forms* of nonfiction, there are also different *types*—each with its own general purpose. The chart below shows the most common types of nonfiction and gives examples of ways that a work of each type might address the same general subject: pets.

Types and Purposes of Nonfiction

Type	Purpose	Examples
Expository	to present facts and ideas or to explain a process	an online article that explores ways to keep your dog healthy
Persuasive	to convince readers to take an action or to adopt a point of view	a speech urging the audience to adopt a pet
Narrative	to tell the story of a real-life experience	an essay about a dog who saved a person's life
Descriptive	to provide a vivid picture of something	an essay about the writer's favorite pet
Reflective	to explain the writer's insights about an event or experience	an essay describing lessons about life the writer learned from owning a pet
Humorous	to entertain and amuse	an article about the challenges of training a very frisky puppy
Analytical	to break a large idea into parts to show how the parts work as a whole	an article that discusses the criteria used for judging champion show dogs

Literary Analysis Workshop **409**

2 Forms of Literary Nonfiction

1. Introduce the forms, using the instruction on the student page.

2. Discuss the three forms of literary nonfiction mentioned on this page. Clarify that articles and essays can be narrative nonfiction if they tell a story but are not when they have other purposes—an expository essay aims to inform, for example; a reflective essay gives insights into a subject.

3. **Ask** students to identify examples of literary nonfiction that they have read or heard and the purpose of each.

   Possible response: State of the Union speech, to persuade; science textbook section on the tides, to inform; James Thurber essay in Unit 1, to entertain and amuse.

3 Types of Nonfiction

1. Introduce the types, using the chart on the student page.

2. **Ask** students to categorize these two nonfiction works into one of the seven types: an essay about how elements of a poem work together to create a mood; an article about the causes of eclipses.

   Answer: The essay is analytical; the article is expository.

4 In This Section

Explain that in the remainder of this Literary Analysis Workshop, students will analyze an important element of nonfiction: structure. After reviewing the concept, they will then see it applied in an analysis of the author's purpose in a Model text. Finally, they will apply what they have learned to an Independent Practice text.

Differentiated Instruction for Universal Access

Support for Special-Needs Students
Have students read **Learning About Types of Nonfiction** in the *Reader's Notebook: Adapted Version.* This version provides a basic-level introduction to nonfiction.

Support for Less Proficient Readers
Have students read **Learning About Types of Nonfiction** in the *Reader's Notebook.* This version provides a basic-level introduction to nonfiction.

EL Support for English Learners
Have students read **Learning About Types of Nonfiction** in the *Reader's Notebook: English Learner's Version.* This version provides a basic-level introduction to nonfiction.

Common Core State Standards

Unit 3 Focus Standards

- Reading Informational Text 3, 4, 5, 6

These standards spiral through the unit.

❶ Analyzing Structure in Literary Nonfiction

1. Introduce the concept of structure, using the instruction on the student page.

2. Define structure as the way a work is organized. Note that structure helps an author achieve his or her purpose and that, by examining structure, students can get a good idea of the author's purpose.

3. Stress that structure includes text features such as headings, graphics, and lists. Direct students' attention to the chart on text features. **Ask:** How are steps and dates often presented in text?

   Possible response: Steps often appear in numbered lists or boxes; dates often appear in chronological lists or timelines.

4. Review the examples that show how opening sentences and section headings state or hint at key ideas, point of view, and/or the author's purpose. **Ask** students to identify the key idea, point of view, and author's purpose in this example:

   The Development of Skyscrapers

   Modern skyscrapers developed in the late 1800s. Before these amazing structures could be safely built, many other inventions had to take place.

   Possible response: Key Idea— Modern skyscrapers developed in the late 1800s. **Point of View—** They were amazing. **Author's Purpose—** to trace the development of skyscrapers.

5. Remind students that in this Workshop, they will read a model analysis of the structure of a passage and then perform their own analysis of a second passage.

---

❶ Analyzing Structure in Literary Nonfiction

The structure of a nonfiction work provides clues to the author's purpose.

Common Core State Standards

Reading Informational Text 5. Analyze the structure an author uses to organize a text, including how the major sections contribute to the whole and to the development of the ideas.

Reading Informational Text 6. Determine an author's point of view or purpose in a text and analyze how the author distinguishes his or her position from that of others.

Writers of nonfiction deliberately arrange their words, sentences, paragraphs, and sections in ways that clearly develop their key ideas.

Text Features You can often tell how a nonfiction work is organized by looking at its arrangement on the page. Text features, such as subheads and charts, can provide clues about the author's purpose.

If a text has . . .	It is probably organized . . .	Its purpose may be . . .
steps or dates	in time order	• to tell a story • to explain a process
section headings	by topic	• to inform • to describe

Key Ideas All nonfiction works communicate one or more key ideas. The opening sentences of a work usually state or suggest the key idea and hint at the author's purpose:

> I was only three when I first smelled the fresh, damp soil of Grandma's garden. Somewhere inside me, a seed of love sprouted and began to grow.

These sentences convey the key idea that the writer began gardening at a very young age. The author's purpose might be to reflect on a personal experience.

410 Types of Nonfiction

Point of View The author's point of view is his or her basic beliefs about a subject. The opening sentences in the previous example tell you that the author has a passion for gardening. Her point of view is that gardening is a worthwhile pursuit.

Major Sections Nonfiction may be organized into sections arranged under headings. Each section supports a key idea and helps fulfill the author's purpose. Consider the section headings in an article about New York City:

Example: Section Headings
How to Get Around
What to See and Do
Where to Eat

↓

Unstated Key Idea
New York City is a good place to visit.

↓

Author's Purpose
To inform tourists

The structure, key idea, and purpose of a text are interrelated. The headings suggest that there are a lot of things to do in New York City. The information presented indicates that the article is meant for visitors. These elements combine to express the author's purpose to offer guidance to tourists.

Think Aloud

Theme

To model the skill of analyzing structure, use the following "think aloud." Say to students:

When I want to analyze structure to determine the author's purpose and point of view in literary nonfiction, I look first at text features like headings, major sections, and graphics. I then look at the opening sentences of the work or its sections. These structural elements usually give me a good idea of the author's purpose and his or her point of view. For instance, suppose an article called *Career Choices* is divided into two major sections called *The Arts* and *The Sciences,* has a graph called *Rapid Job Growth in Health and Medicine,* and opens with these sentences: *Planning a career as a visual artist? Take a course in medical illustration.* I can tell from these structural elements that the author's purpose is to discuss career opportunities in the arts and sciences and that his or her point of view is that there are more opportunities in science, especially health and medicine.

❷ Analyzing Relationships in Literary Nonfiction

Works of **literary nonfiction** show relationships between people, events, and ideas.

Common Core State Standards

Reading Informational Text 3. Analyze the interactions between individuals, events, and ideas in a text.

Reading Informational Text 4. Determine the meaning of words and phrases as they are used in a text, including figurative, connotative, and technical meanings; analyze the impact of a specific word choice on meaning and tone.

Logical Relationships Nonfiction works show their subjects in relationship to the larger world. For instance, they may show cause-and-effect relationships, such as ways in which people are affected by events and ideas—and vice versa. Here are some specific examples.

If a text is about . . .	It might show . . .
the Civil War	• what events and ideas caused the war • who suffered during the war
the author's life as a spy	• what caused her career choice • how her actions affected others
social networks	• how they have impacted users' lives • why they have become so popular

People do not always agree about the causes or effects of an event. Two writers, given the same facts, may express different opinions. Each writer's point of view affects his or her interpretation of information. In some nonfiction works, the writer may be *biased,* expressing a one-sided opinion. However, a writer is not necessarily biased just because he or she has a particular point of view.

Word Choice Looking closely at an author's choice of words can help you detect his or her point of view. Word choice can also help reveal an author's **tone,** or attitude toward his or her subject and audience. In particular, notice words with positive or negative **connotations,** or emotional associations. For example, the words *curious* and *nosy* have the same basic meaning. However, calling someone "curious" conveys positive connotations, while calling that same person "nosy" conveys negative connotations.

Figurative Language In literary nonfiction, writers often use figurative language, or unusual comparisons, to bring an idea to life and to create a certain tone. Look at the example, in which a girl is described in three very different ways.

Example	Lily is compared to . . .	Tone
"Cyclone Lily" strikes again.	a cyclone	sarcastic
Lily sheds her things like a tree sheds leaves.	a tree	matter-of-fact
Lily is bursting with life. She can't help but drop petals along the way.	a flower	adoring

Literary Analysis Workshop **411**

---

❷ Analyzing Relationships in Literary Nonfiction

1. Introduce the concept of relationships, using the instruction on the student page.

2. Review the section and chart on logical relationships. **Ask:** In addition to cause-and-effect relationships, what are some other logical relationships in nonfiction?

   Possible response: Relationships include chronological, comparison-and-contrast, spatial, problem-and-solution, and category-and-examples.

3. Stress the significance of word choice, including connotations of words, in conveying a writer's tone. Offer these sentences and **ask:** How is the tone affected by the connotations of the words chosen?

   The landlord was sly and tight-fisted.

   The landlord was clever and thrifty.

   Possible response: In the first sentence, the negative connotations of *sly* and *tightfisted* create a critical tone; in the second, the positive connotations of *clever* and *thrifty* create an admiring tone.

4. Review the chart illustrating how figurative language helps convey tone. Clarify that figurative language makes comparisons not meant to be taken literally; the second column of the chart shows the comparison being made in each example.

5. Remind students that in this Workshop, they will read a model analysis of the relationships in a passage and then perform their own analysis of a second passage.

411

❸ Close Read: Determining Author's Purpose

1. Remind students that the author's purpose is the main reason he or she is writing.

2. Review the Clues to Author's Purpose chart, making sure students understand each clue. Clarify how literary elements can be clues to the author's purpose. For example, if an author creates vivid, positive portraits of real-life characters who work on the real-life setting of a wind farm, the author's purpose may be to stress the value of wind farms.

3. Divide the class into groups. Assign each group the same topic, the school cafeteria, but a different purpose in writing about it: to get the cafeteria remodeled; to make it less noisy; to praise the staff or food; to demand healthier food; to criticize sloppy students; and so on. Have group members work together on a list of clues that would help achieve their purpose if they were writing a news article about the cafeteria.

   Possible response: *Purpose*—to get the cafeteria remodeled; *Key Idea*—school cafeteria needs remodeling; *Point of View*—cafeteria is too dark and small; *Text Structure*—include diagram stressing small size; *Relationships*—problem-and-solution; *Connotation and Tone*—negative words *(cramped, dingy)* for current conditions; positive *(spacious, bright)* for remodeled version; *Literary Elements*—setting.

4. Refer students to the Model text beginning on page 413. Explain that details in the text that illustrate each category on the chart are highlighted in the same color and corresponding side-column annotations use corresponding colors.

❸ Close Read: Determining Author's Purpose

To discover the purpose or purposes of a work of literary nonfiction, look closely at key elements of the text.

Literary nonfiction contains elements of nonfiction writing *and* elements of "literary," or creative, writing. Literary nonfiction may please the reader with its graceful use of language. However, it may also persuade, inform, explain, describe, tell a story, or amuse. You can discover an author's purpose by looking closely at the following key elements of a text.

Clues to Author's Purpose

Key Ideas are main points that the author wants readers to understand and remember. To find key ideas and use them as clues, ask yourself:

- Does the beginning of the work directly state a key idea? If so, what is it?
- Do details in the text suggest key ideas? If so, what are those ideas?
- Why does the author include these key ideas?

Relationships are the logical connections between ideas, such as cause-and-effect relationships. To find relationships and use them as clues, ask yourself:

- How does one detail connect to other details?
- How do these connections point to a key idea?
- What do the relationships between ideas suggest about the author's purpose?

Point of View is the author's position and beliefs about a subject. To identify point of view and use it as a clue, ask yourself:

- What are the author's beliefs about his or her subject?
- Which details reveal those beliefs?
- What is the author's reason for expressing this point of view?

Connotation and Tone Connotations are the positive or negative feelings associated with a word. Tone is the author's attitude toward his or her subject and audience. To identify connotations and tone and use them as clues, ask yourself:

- Which words, if any, convey a strongly positive or negative attitude?
- What larger purpose do the words or attitude support?

Text Structure refers to the various parts of the text and their organization. To identify text structure and use it as a clue, ask yourself:

- What overall pattern of organization does the author use?
- Why does the author use that pattern?

Literary Elements are storytelling elements such as characters, setting, and plot, and the techniques associated with them. To use these elements as clues, ask yourself:

- What is the literary element?
- What is the writer's aim in using this element?

412 Types of Nonfiction

Vocabulary Development

© **CCSS Language 6**

Domain-Specific Words: Social Studies

To help students with comprehension of the selection from *Freedom Walkers* (pp. 413–414), explain these terms related to the Civil Rights Movement, most of which appear in the selection.

- *civil rights:* the rights guaranteed to citizens in the U.S. Constitution or related laws
- *racial segregation:* separation of people of different races

- *"Jim Crow" laws:* laws once in place throughout the American South that kept African Americans from exercising their civil rights
- *discriminate against:* to single out for negative treatment; to show prejudice against
- *white supremacy:* the situation in society in which whites had the most rights and powers
- *poll tax:* a tax charged for voting

© EXEMPLAR TEXT

❹ Model

About the Text This excerpt is from a nonfiction book about a famous boycott. A boycott is a form of protest in which people refuse to buy a particular product or use a particular service. The first part of the excerpt is the book's introduction. The second part tells the story of a woman who decided to participate in the boycott.

from *Freedom Walkers: The Story of the Montgomery Bus Boycott* by Russell Freedman

Not so long ago in Montgomery, Alabama, the color of your skin determined where you could sit on a public bus. If you happened to be an African American, you had to sit in the back of the bus, even if there were empty seats up front.

Back then, racial segregation was the rule throughout the American South. Strict laws—called "Jim Crow" laws—enforced a system of white supremacy that discriminated against blacks and kept them in their place as second-class citizens.

People were separated by race from the moment they were born in segregated hospitals until the day they were buried in segregated cemeteries. Blacks and whites did not attend the same schools, worship in the same churches, eat in the same restaurants, sleep in the same hotels, drink from the same water fountains, or sit together in the same movie theaters.

In Montgomery, it was against the law for a white person and a Negro to play checkers on public property or ride together in a taxi.

Most southern blacks were denied their right to vote. The biggest obstacle was the poll tax, a special tax that was required of all voters but was too costly for many blacks and for poor whites as well. Voters also had to pass a literacy test to prove that they could read, write, and understand the U.S. Constitution. These tests were often rigged to disqualify even highly educated blacks. Those who overcame the obstacles and insisted on registering as voters faced threats, harassment, and even physical violence. As a result, African Americans in the South could not express their grievances in the voting booth, which, for the most part, was closed to them. But there were other ways to protest, and one day a half century ago, the black citizens in Montgomery rose up in protest and united to demand their rights—by walking peacefully.

It all started on a bus.

❺ Point of View This sentence announces that the author will view his subject through the eyes of African Americans.

❻ Relationships These sentences show how the "Jim Crow" laws affected people's daily lives.

❼ Text Structure This paragraph builds up to the key idea of the entire book: black citizens finally refused to stay "in their place."

❽ Literary Elements This sentence sums up, in an intriguing and provocative way, how the protest started.

Literary Analysis Workshop **413**

❹ Reading the Model

1. Discuss the About the Text note. Explain that the Montgomery, Alabama, bus boycott of 1955–1956 was a landmark event in the Civil Rights Movement.

2. Have students read the selection (pp. 413–414). Discuss it, clarifying as needed, before reviewing the annotations.

❺ Point of View

Read aloud the Point of View annotation and the sentence to which it applies. **Ask:** How does the author feel about the situation?

Possible response: He feels angry and considers it unjust.

❻ Relationships

Read aloud the Relationships annotation. **Ask:** What is the relationship between the highlighted sentences and the statement in the previous paragraph?

Answer: The sentences give examples of a general statement or category ("Jim Crow" laws) in the previous paragraph.

❼ Text Structure

Read aloud the highlighted sentence and Text Structure annotation. **Ask:** What earlier element of text structure also helps make this key idea clear?

Possible response: The title and subtitle also help make it clear.

❽ Literary Elements

Read aloud the Literary Elements annotation. **Ask:** What storytelling element does this statement begin?

Answer: It begins the plot.

⑨ Key Ideas

Read aloud the Key Ideas annotation. **Ask:** How will this key idea probably relate to the selection's central idea?

Possible response: The experience probably will involve a violation of Jo Ann's civil rights.

⑩ Text Structure

Read aloud the Text Structure annotation. **Ask:** What literary element does the chronological structure help create?

Possible response: It helps create a plot.

⑪ Point of View

Have a student read aloud the Point of View annotation. **Ask:** How does the author feel about the bus driver's behavior?

Possible response: He finds it unjust.

⑫ Literary Elements

Read aloud the Literary Elements annotation. **Ask:** To what part of a plot does the tense narrative build?

Possible response: It builds to a climax.

⑬ Relationships

Read aloud the Relationships annotation. **Ask:** How does this last quotation relate to the first paragraph on the page?

Possible response: It shows Jo Ann's "deep hurt."

⑭ Author's Purpose

Read aloud the Author's Purpose annotation. **Ask:** How do the selection's two sections each convey part of the author's purpose?

Possible response: The first shows the informational purpose; the second shows the human side.

© EXEMPLAR TEXT

Model continued

⑨ Key Ideas This section begins with a key idea: Jo Ann Robinson suffered a very upsetting experience.

⑩ Text Structure Transitions signal that the story is being told in chronological order.

⑪ Point of View This quotation reveals the bus driver's biased point of view.

⑫ Literary Elements The description and quotation build tension.

⑬ Relationships The quotation connects this section to the introduction by explaining why this incident caused Robinson to later join the bus boycott.

⑭ Author's Purpose Details suggest that the author's purpose is to inform readers about the Montgomery bus boycott while also giving the human side of the story.

Jo Ann Robinson

⑨ Looking back, she remembered it as the most humiliating experience of her life, "a deep hurt that would not heal." It had happened just before Christmas in 1949. She was about to visit relatives in Cleveland, Ohio, where she would spend the holidays.

⑩ Earlier that day she had driven out to Dannelly Field, the Montgomery, Alabama, airport, and checked her luggage for the flight to Cleveland. Then she drove back to the campus of Alabama State, an all-black college where she had been hired that fall as a professor of English. After parking her car in the campus garage, she took her armful of Christmas gifts, walked to the nearest bus stop, and waited for a ride back to the airport.

Soon a Montgomery City Lines bus rolled into view and pulled up at the stop. Balancing her packages, Jo Ann Robinson stepped aboard and dropped her dime into the fare box. She saw that the bus was nearly empty. Only two other passengers were aboard—a black man in a seat near the back and a white woman in the third seat from the front. Without thinking, Robinson took a seat two rows behind the white woman.

"I took the fifth-row seat from the front and sat down," she recalled, "immediately closing my eyes and envisioning, in my mind's eye, the wonderful two-week vacation I would have with my family and friends in Ohio."

Jolted out of her reverie by an angry voice, she opened her eyes and sat upright. The bus driver had come to a full stop and turned in his seat. He was ⑪ speaking to her. "If you can sit in the fifth row from the front seat of the other buses in Montgomery," he said, "suppose you get off and ride in one of them."

The driver's message didn't register at first. Robinson was still thinking about her holiday trip. Suddenly the driver rose from his seat, went over to ⑫ her, and stood with his arm drawn back, as if to strike her. "Get up from there!" he yelled. "Get up from there!"

Shaken and alarmed, Robinson bolted to her feet and stumbled off the bus in tears, packages falling from her arms. She had made the mistake of sitting in one of the front ten seats, which were reserved for white riders only.

"I felt like a dog," she wrote later. "And I got mad, after this was over, and I ⑬ realized I was a human being, and just as intelligent and far more [educationally] trained than that bus driver was. But I think he wanted to hurt me, and he did. . . . I cried all the way to Cleveland."

414 Types of Nonfiction

Vocabulary Development

Vocabulary Knowledge Rating

Create a **Vocabulary Knowledge Rating Chart** (*Professional Development Guidebook,* p. 33) with these words from the selection:

realism   contrast   color   impression

Give students a copy of the chart. Read the words aloud. Have them mark their rating in the Before Reading column. Urge them to be alert to these words as they read and discuss "What Makes a Rembrandt a Rembrandt?" because they will rate their knowledge of the words again after they have finished.

To gauge how much instruction to provide, tally how many students think they know a word. As students read, point out the words and their context.

⑮ Independent Practice

About the Selection In this article, author and educator Richard Mühlberger discusses a famous painting by Rembrandt, a Dutch painter who lived and worked during the 1600s. Rembrandt is generally considered one of the greatest painters of all time.

⑯ | **from *What Makes a Rembrandt a Rembrandt?***
by Richard Mühlberger

Citizen Soldiers

A Dutch poet of Rembrandt's day wrote, "When the country is in danger, every citizen is a soldier." That was the idea behind the militia, or civic guard companies, which trained citizens how to fight and shoot in case their city was attacked. Each company drilled in archery, the crossbow, or the musket. By Rembrandt's time, militia companies were as much social clubs as military organizations.

⑰ Captain Frans Banning Cocq, out to impress everyone, chose Rembrandt to paint his militia company, with members of the company paying the artist to have their portraits included in the painting. The huge canvas was to be hung in the new hall of the militia headquarters, where it would be seen at receptions and celebrations along with other militia paintings.

By the mid-seventeenth century, there were more than one hundred big militia paintings hanging in public halls in the important cities of the Netherlands. In all of these group portraits, the men were evenly lined up so that each face got equal attention, just as they had been in traditional anatomy lesson paintings. Rembrandt did not like this way of presenting the scene. He had seen militia companies in action, and there were ⑱ always people milling about who were not militiamen but who took part in their exercises and parades. To add realism to the piece, he decided to include some of these people, as well as a dog. There was room on the wall for a canvas about sixteen feet wide, large enough for Rembrandt to do what no other painter had ever done before. His idea was to show the exciting commotion before a parade began.

⑯ **Key Ideas** What does the title suggest the text will be about? How might the subhead support that key idea?

⑰ **Literary Elements** Who is the central character of the painting? Do you think he will also be the central "character" of the article? Explain.

⑱ **Relationships** How will Rembrandt's painting differ from earlier militia paintings by other artists?

Literary Analysis Workshop **415**

⑮ Introducing the Independent Practice

1. Explain to students that they will analyze structural elements to determine the author's purpose in the Independent Practice selection.

2. Discuss the About the Selection note, and have students read the selection. Then, direct them to go back through and respond to the side-column prompts. Conclude by having students answer the After You Read questions on page 419.

⑯ Key Ideas

Explain that Rembrandt is especially famous for portraits, including group portraits and self-portraits. Then **ask** the two Key Ideas questions.

Possible responses: The title suggests a text about the qualities that make Rembrandt's paintings great and typically his. The subhead may be about a group portrait he painted.

⑰ Literary Elements

Have students reread the second highlighted passage. **Ask** the two Literary Elements questions.

Possible responses: The painting's central character is Captain Frans Banning Cocq. Given the article's title, he is probably not its central character.

⑱ Relationships

1. Have students reread the third paragraph, including the highlighted passage. **Ask** the Relationships question.

   Possible response: He will make the scene more realistic, showing an "exciting commotion" rather than an even line of men.

2. **Ask:** How is the highlighted information related to the article's title?

   Possible response: It shows what makes Rembrandt's work different from that of more traditional artists.

415

⑲ Text Structure

1. Have students reread the first paragraph. Point out that the second sentence uses comparison-and-contrast structure to illustrate the contrasts mentioned in the first sentence. **Ask:** What does the contrast show to be Rembrandt's goal?

   Possible response: He wants to honor the citizen soldiers and their work by literally showing them in the best possible light.

2. Have a student read aloud the first highlighted passage. **Ask** the two Text Structure questions.

   Possible responses: It is organized spatially. The phrase "Standing next to him" indicates this organization.

3. Have students reread the first three sentences of the next paragraph. **Ask:** What do the spatial details show about the painting's two key characters?

   Possible response: They show the men's relationship as a captain speaking and a lieutenant listening.

⑳ Key Ideas

1. Have a student read aloud the highlighted sentence in the last paragraph. **Ask** the Key Ideas question.

   Possible response: The sentence and the section both stress the respect Rembrandt had for the people he painted and the realism and illuminating humanity of his portraits.

2. **Ask:** What does the highlighted sentence show about the author's point of view and purpose?

   Possible response: It shows his view of Rembrandt as a great painter and his purpose of explaining Rembrandt's greatness to readers.

Practice continued

⑲
Text Structure How is this section organized? What words or phrases tell you this?

⑳
Key Ideas How does this sentence—and the entire section—help answer the title question?

Two Handsome Officers

Everywhere in the painting, Rembrandt used sharp contrasts of dark and light. Everything that honors the citizen soldiers and their work is illuminated; everything else is in shadow. Captain Frans Banning Cocq is the man dressed in black with a red sash under his arm, striding forward in the center. Standing next to him is the most brightly lighted man in the painting, Lieutenant Willem van Ruytenburgh, attired in a glorious gold and yellow uniform, silk sash, soft leather cavalry boots, and a high hat with white ostrich plumes. His lancelike weapon, called a partisan, and the steel gorget[1] around his neck—a leftover from the days when soldiers wore full suits of armor—are the only hints that he is a military man. Rembrandt links him to Banning Cocq by contrasting the colors of their clothing and by painting the shadow of Banning Cocq's hand on the front of van Ruytenburgh's coat. The captain is giving orders to his lieutenant for the militia company to march off.

Banning Cocq is dressed in a black suit against a dark background, yet he does not disappear. Rembrandt made him the most important person in the composition. Van Ruytenburgh turns to listen to him, which shows his respect for his commander. Banning Cocq's face stands out above his bright red sash and white collar. How well Rembrandt knew that darkness makes faces shine! The captain's self-assured pace, the movement of the tassels at his knees, and the angle of his walking staff are proof of the energy and dignity of his stride.

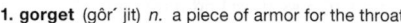

1. **gorget** (gôr´ jit) *n.* a piece of armor for the throat.

416 Types of Nonfiction

Muskets and Mascots

On either side of these two handsome officers, broad paths lead back into the painting

 Rembrandt knew that when the huge group scene was placed above eye level on the wall of the militia headquarters, these empty areas would be the first to be seen. He wanted them to lead the eyes of viewers to figures in the painting who did not have the advantage of being placed in the foreground. In the middle of one of these paths is a man in red pouring gunpowder into the barrel of his musket. Behind the captain, only partially seen, another man shoots his gun into the air, and a third militiaman, to the right of van Ruytenburgh, blows on his weapon to clean it. Loading, shooting, and cleaning were part of the standard drill for musketeers, and so they were included in the painting to demonstrate the men's mastery of their weapons.

Walking in a stream of bright light down the path on the left is a blond girl dressed in yellow with a dead chicken tied to her waist. She has a friend in blue behind her. In their public shows, the militia would choose two young girls to carry the emblems[2] of their company, here the claws of a bird. The yellow and blue of the girls' costumes are the militia's colors. In the parade that is being organized, these mascots will take a prominent place, the fair-haired girl holding aloft the chicken's claws.

Many of the background figures stand on stairs so that their faces can be seen. The man above the girl in yellow is Jan Corneliszoon Visscher, after Banning Cocq and van Ruytenburgh the highest-ranking person in the militia company. He waves a flag that combines the colors of the militia company with the three black crosses of Amsterdam. While Rembrandt did not pose him in bright light, he made him important by placing him high up on the stairs, by showing the sheen in his costume, and by giving him the large flag to unfurl.

21 Connotation and Tone Does the word *mastery* have positive or negative connotations? How does this word relate to the essay's key idea about Rembrandt?

22 Connotation and Tone Why do you think the author chose the word *unfurl* instead of *hold* or *wave*?

---

2. **emblems** *n.* objects that stand for something else; symbols.

---

21 Connotation and Tone

1. Refer students to the opening statement in this section. **Ask:** How do the connotations of words in this statement convey a particular tone?

   Possible response: Using *handsome* and *broad* to describe the painting helps convey an admiring tone.

2. Have students reread the next paragraph, including the highlighted portion. **Ask** the two Connotation and Tone questions in the first box.

   Possible responses: *Mastery* has a positive connotation. It stresses the idea that Rembrandt respected the people he painted and painted them in a positive, yet realistic, light that captured their achievements and individuality.

22 Connotation and Tone

1. Have students reread the last paragraph on the page, including the highlighted portion. **Ask:** What connotation does the word *sheen* have? What does it help convey about Visscher?

   Possible response: It has a positive connotation. It helps convey his individuality and achievement.

2. **Ask** the Connotation and Tone question in the second box.

   Possible response: *Unfurl* connotes more effort and importance than merely *holding* or *waving*, stressing the importance Rembrandt conveyed on Visscher and the honor of holding the flag.

Differentiated
Instruction   for Universal Access

Enrichment for Gifted/Talented Students

After students have read the selection, lead a discussion about the author's analysis of the painting. Then, challenge each student to choose a painting they have seen and write an analytical article using the same techniques and style that the author uses. Have students bring in copies of their paintings to show the rest of the class.

Students can print copies from the Internet or bring in an art book displaying their paintings. Allow students time to show their paintings and to read their articles to the class. Then, hold a class discussion about the ways the students' articles capture the significance of the paintings.

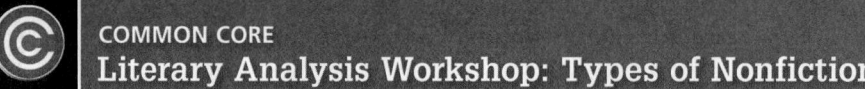

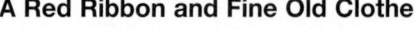

23 Literary Elements

1. Have students reread the first two sentences on the page. **Ask** the Literary Elements question.

   Possible response: It reminds readers of the sometimes dangerous job of being in the militia.

2. **Ask:** In addition to suspense, what other literary elements do these two sentences contain? Explain.

   Possible response: They contain aspects of character and plot. They help convey the character of the drummer and hint at a story behind his relationship with the dog.

24 Key Ideas

1. Have students reread the second paragraph, including the highlighted portion. **Ask** the Key Ideas question.

   Possible response: It stresses the key idea that Rembrandt tries to dignify the achievement of the people he paints.

2. **Ask:** What effects described earlier are similar to the effect of the elegant clothing? Explain.

   Possible response: The lighting described on page 416 and the placement described on page 417 also aim to bring honor to the people Rembrandt paints.

25 Point of View

Read aloud the last highlighted statement. **Ask** the Point of View question.

Possible response: Yes, the author has devoted pages to explaining why the painting is so wonderful and why Rembrandt is such a great painter.

Practice continued

23 Literary Elements
How does this detail create suspense?

24 Key Ideas What does this fact tell you about the details of Rembrandt's paintings?

25 Point of View Do you think the author shares this opinion? Explain.

A Red Ribbon and Fine Old Clothes

23 In spite of his partial appearance, the drummer on the right seems ready to come forward to lead a march with his staccato beat. The sound seems to bother the dusty dog below. Behind the drummer, two men appear to be figuring out their places in the formation. The one in the white collar and black hat outranks many of the others in the scene. His prestige is signaled in an unusual way: A red ribbon dangles over his head, tied to the lance of the man in armor behind van Ruytenburgh. Additional lances can be counted in the darkness, some leaning against the wall, others carried by militiamen. Their crisscross patterns add to the feeling of commotion that Rembrandt has captured everywhere on the huge canvas.

24 The costumes worn in this group portrait are much more ornate and colorful than what Dutchmen ordinarily wore every day. Some, like the breeches and helmet of the man shooting his musket behind Banning Cocq, go back a hundred years to the beginnings of the militia company. In the eyes of many Dutchmen, clothing associated with a glorious past brought special dignity to the company. What an opportunity for Rembrandt, perhaps the greatest lover of old clothes in Amsterdam!

Not a Night Watch

Night Watch is a mistaken title that was given to the painting over a hundred years after Rembrandt died, but it has stuck, and is what the painting is almost universally called. Although the exaggerated chiaroscuro[3] does give an impression of night time, there is daylight in the scene. It comes from the left, as the shadows under Banning Cocq's feet prove. And it is clear that no one in the painting is on watch, alert to the approach of an enemy. The official title of the painting is *Officers and Men of the Company of Captain Frans Banning Cocq and Lieutenant Willem van Ruytenburgh.*

Rembrandt completed the painting in 1642, when he was thirty-six years old. He probably had no idea that it would be the most famous Dutch painting of all time. In 1678, one of his former students wrote that it would "outlive all its rivals," and 25 within another century the painting was considered one of the wonders of the world.

---

3. **chiaroscuro** (kē är´ ə skoor´ ō) *n.* a dramatic style of light and shade in a painting or drawing.

Vocabulary Development

Vocabulary Knowledge Rating

When students have completed reading and discussing "What Makes a Rembrandt a Rembrandt?" have them take out their **Vocabulary Knowledge Rating Chart** for this selection. Read the words aloud once more and have students rate their knowledge of the words again in the After Reading column.

Clarify any words that are still problematic. Have students write their own definitions or examples in the appropriate column. Encourage students to use the words in further discussion and written work about this selection.

After You Read

from What Makes a Rembrandt a Rembrandt?

© 1. **Key Ideas and Details** **(a)** Why was Rembrandt hired to paint Captain Banning Cocq's militia company? **(b) Analyze:** How did Rembrandt change the way military group portraits were painted?

© 2. **Key Ideas and Details (a) Interpret:** According to the article, what techniques does Rembrandt use to emphasize higher-ranking figures? **(b) Support:** How does the painter make the background figures visible? **(c) Summarize:** What details reveal that a parade is being organized?

© 3. **Integration of Knowledge and Ideas** Based on your reading of the essay, what title would you give Rembrandt's painting? Why?

© 4. **Craft and Structure (a) Describe:** How is this essay organized? **(b) Infer:** Why do you think the author chose to organize it this way?

© 5. **Key Ideas and Details (a)** What might Rembrandt be trying to teach through his artwork? **(b)** How does reading about art help you learn more about it?

© 6. **Integration of Knowledge and Ideas (a)** Use a chart like the one shown to analyze the types of writing Mühlberger uses in the essay.

Examples of Description	Examples of Exposition

(b) Collaborate: With a partner, review your charts. Together, discuss the **author's purpose(s)** for writing the essay. Share your ideas with the class.

Literary Analysis Workshop **419**

1. **Possible response: (a)** Banning Cocq wanted to impress everyone with a huge painting of his company for the new militia headquarters being built. **(b)** Earlier military group portraits were painted with the men evenly lined up so everyone got equal attention. Rembrandt wanted to make his painting more realistic and to show the excitement before a parade, so he included people moving about and doing things.

2. **Possible response: (a)** The two highest-ranking men are in the front, the captain's face lit against a dark background, the lieutenant's whole body in bright colors. **(b)** Rembrandt painted broad paths to lead the viewer's eye to the background figures. **(c)** A parade is indicated by the girls serving as mascots, the officer waving a flag, and the men standing around preparing their weapons for drill.

3. **Possible response:** *Citizen Soldiers* because the militia men are the most important aspect of the painting

4. **Possible response: (a)** It has an introductory section, a body organized spatially, and a conclusion. **(b)** The spatial arrangement helps readers picture the painting.

5. **Possible response: (a)** Rembrandt might be teaching that art should reflect life as it is, not an ideal version. **(b)** After reading the article, the painting comes to life.

6. **Possible response: (a)** Description of Banning Cocq, van Ruytenburgh, the blonde girl, and Visscher. Exposition: how the background images are made visible by painting the paths; the use of color to create contrasts between light and dark. For other sample answers, see *Graphic Organizer Transparencies, Graphic Organizer A*, p. 73, and Additional Answers section. **(b)** Partners should use their examples from the article to support their analysis of the author's purpose.

❶ Leveled Texts

You may use either "Life Without Gravity" or "Conversational Ballgames" to meet the lesson objectives. Skills instruction for both selections appears on page 421. Choose one selection to teach (or choose to teach both). The Text Complexity Rubric at the bottom of this page will help you determine which selection is more appropriate for your students. Use the Reader and Task Suggestions on the facing page to help all students read text of increasing complexity.

❷ ⓒ Introducing the CCS Standards

Introduce the standards on the student page. (Note that the lesson element with which each standard is addressed is identified in parentheses after the text of the standard.) Call out the standards that you will cover with the selections, explaining to students what each requires and how they will address it as they work through the selection you have chosen. Standards labeled "Spiral Review" are introduced in the Literary Analysis Workshop for this unit.

Before You Read

Life Without Gravity • Conversational Ballgames

❶ ⓒ Leveled Texts

Build your skills and improve your comprehension of literary nonfiction with texts of increasing complexity.

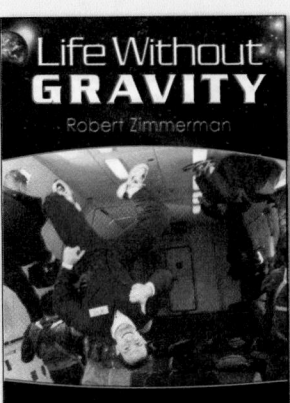

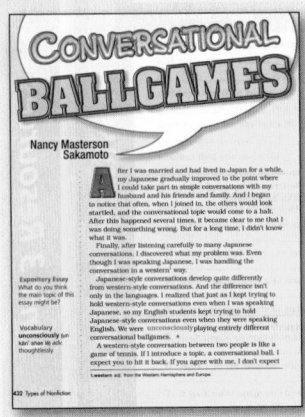

Read **"Life Without Gravity"** to find out about the weightlessness that astronauts experience in space.

Read **"Conversational Ballgames"** to learn how cultural differences can affect the way people talk to one another.

❷ ⓒ Common Core State Standards

Meet these standards with either **"Life Without Gravity"** (p. 424) or **"Conversational Ballgames"** (p. 432).

Reading Informational Text
2. Determine two or more central ideas in a text and analyze their development over the course of the text; provide an objective summary of the text. *(Reading Skill: Main Idea)*

5. Analyze the structure an author uses to organize a text, including how the major sections contribute to the whole and to the development of the ideas. *(Literary Analysis: Expository Essay)*

7. Compare and contrast a text to an audio, video, or multimedia version of the text, analyzing each medium's portrayal of the subject. *(Speaking and Listening: Oral Summary)*

Writing
9. Draw evidence from literary or informational texts to support analysis, reflection, and research. **9.b.** Apply *grade 7 Reading standards* to literary nonfiction. *(Writing: Analogy)*

Speaking and Listening
2. Analyze the main ideas and supporting details presented in diverse media and formats and explain how the ideas clarify a topic, text, or issue under study. *(Speaking and Listening: Oral Summary)*

4. Present claims and findings, emphasizing salient points in a focused, coherent manner with pertinent descriptions, facts, details, and examples; use appropriate eye contact, adequate volume, and clear pronunciation. *(Speaking and Listening: Oral Summary)*

Language
1. Demonstrate command of the conventions of standard English grammar and usage when writing or speaking. *(Conventions: Conjunctions)*

4.b. Use common, grade-appropriate Greek or Latin affixes and roots as clues to the meaning of a word. *(Vocabulary: Word Study)*

420 Types of Nonfiction

ⓒ Text Complexity Rubric: Leveled Texts

Text complexity is determined by both qualitative and quantitative measures. For this reason, the quantitative measure of a more complex selection may be lower than that of a more accessible selection.

		✓ Life Without Gravity	✓✓ Conversational Ballgames
Qualitative Measures	**Context/Knowledge Demands**	Weightlessness and the effects of gravity on the body 1 2 ③ 4 5	Comparison of Japanese and Western styles of conversation; sports rules; Japanese culture 1 2 3 ④ 5
	Structure/Language Conventionality and Clarity	Explained scientific vocabulary; comparison/contrast structure 1 2 ③ 4 5	Subject-specific vocabulary; some long, complex sentences; extended figurative comparisons 1 2 3 ④ 5
	Levels of Meaning/ Purpose/Concepts	Accessible (description of life in weightlessness) 1 ② 3 4 5	Challenging (observation of cultural differences) 1 2 3 ④ 5
Quantitative Measures	**Text Length**	Word Count: 1,035	Word Count: 1,459
	Lexile	980L	940L
Overall Complexity		✓ **More accessible**	✓✓ **More complex**

Reading Skill: Main Idea

The **main idea** is the central point of a nonfiction text. While most texts focus on one main idea, some may address two or more closely related central ideas. The main idea of a paragraph is often stated in a topic sentence. The rest of the paragraph presents **supporting details** that give examples, explanations, or reasons.

When reading nonfiction, **adjust your reading rate to recognize main ideas.**

- **Skim,** or look over the text quickly, to get a sense of the main ideas before you begin reading.
- **Read closely** to learn what the central ideas are.
- **Scan,** or run your eyes over the text, to find answers to questions, to clarify, or to find supporting details.

Using the Strategy: Main Idea Chart

Refer to the chart below as you look for central ideas.

Reading Rate	What to Look For
Skimming before reading	Organization, topic sentences, repeated words
Close reading	Key points, supporting details
Scanning	Particular word or idea

Literary Analysis: Expository Essay

An **expository essay** is a short piece of nonfiction in which an author explains, defines, or interprets ideas, events, or processes. The organization, or structure, of the information depends on the topic and on the author's purpose, or reason for writing. Ideas may be developed in sections or in related paragraphs. Transitional words, such as *finally* and *since,* may clarify the development of ideas.

As you read, analyze the structure the author uses to present ideas.

Before You Read: Life Without Gravity • Conversational Ballgames 421

PHLit Online!
www.PHLitOnline.com

Hear It!
- Selection summary audio
- Selection audio

See It!
- Get Connected video
- Background video
- More about the author
- Vocabulary flashcards

Do It!
- Interactive journals
- Interactive graphic organizers
- Self-test
- Internet activity
- Grammar tutorial
- Interactive vocabulary games

❸ Reading Skill
Main Idea

1. Introduce the skill, using the instruction on the student page.
2. Tell students that they will identify main idea and key points as they read.

❹ Using the Strategy

Give students a copy of either **Reading Skill Graphic Organizer A** or **B** (*Graphic Organizer Transparencies,* pp. 75–77). Have them use the chart to identify details. Use the examples in **Reading Skill Graphic Organizer A,** which is partially filled in, to model the process of completing the organizer.

❺ Literary Analysis
Expository Essay

1. Introduce the skill, using the instruction on the student page.
2. Tell students that they will analyze expository essay structure as they read.

Think Aloud: Model the Skill

Model a way of approaching expository essays. Say to students:

> To read expository essays effectively, I recall that their purpose may be to explain. Suppose an author wants to explain how she trains for a marathon. How might she organize information to fit this topic? Since authors often connect related ideas, I look at the sequence of key points. So, in an article comparing training methods, I'll watch for information about one method to be followed by related information about another method. This reading approach helps me follow the key points.

© Text Complexity: Reader and Task Suggestions

✓ Life Without Gravity		✓✓ Conversational Ballgames	
Preparing to Read the Text	**Leveled Tasks**	**Preparing to Read the Text**	**Leveled Tasks**
• Using the Background information on p. 423, preview the scientific force of gravity. • Use Literature in Context on p. 428 to help explain the pros and cons the author associates with life without gravity. • Guide students to use Multidraft Reading strategies (TE p. 423).	***Structure/Language*** If students will have difficulty with structure, have them read to identify familiar tasks that astronauts will undertake. Then, have them list positive and negative effects of weightlessness. ***Evaluating*** If students will not have difficulty with structure, have them note ways in which the author infuses the essay with humor. Discuss how this humor helps the author clarify the setting for readers.	• Using the Background information on p. 431, discuss key differences between Japanese and American culture. • Review strategies for applying extended figurative comparisons. • Guide students to use Multidraft Reading strategies (TE p. 431).	***Structure/Language*** If students will have difficulty with figurative language, have them first read for familiar details about conversation. Then, have them reread, identifying figurative comparisons that are confusing. ***Analyzing*** If students will not have difficulty with language, have them note as they read ways in which the author uses language to convey her opinions about different conversational styles. Discuss as a class.

❶ Writing About the Big Question

1. Review the assignment with the class.

2. Remind students that one way to learn about the world and about themselves is by responding to other people's experiences.

3. Have students complete the sentence starters. Review responses as a class. (**Sample responses:** Reading about other people's experiences can help us <u>explore</u> our ideas about the world. When we are <u>curious</u> about unfamiliar experiences, we can find out more by studying other people's thoughts about those experiences.)

4. Remind students that their answers will help them think about the Big Question, "What should we learn?"

While You Read

Tell students that as they read, they should look for information that tells about the astronauts' experiences, such as how a lack of gravity affects the human body.

❷ Vocabulary

1. Have students preview the selection vocabulary.

2. For each word, have students say the word aloud.

3. Then, use the word in a sentence that defines the word.

4. Finally, repeat your definitional sentence or a similar sentence with the word missing and have the class "fill in the blank" chorally. Here are some examples:

   People's <u>spines</u> are their backbones. People who do not sit up straight may damage their backbones, or [students say "spines"].

   When you are <u>feeble,</u> you are weak or ill. After a week in bed with the flu, Mercedes was weak and [students say "feeble"].

❸ Word Study

1. Introduce the skill, using the instruction in the box.

2. Ask students for another *-ness* word that means "the condition of being friendly." *(friendliness)*

❶ Writing About the Big Question

In "Life Without Gravity," the author describes the ways that astronauts adjust to being weightless in space. Use these sentence starters to develop your ideas about the Big Question.

Reading about other people's experiences can help us **explore** our ideas about _____.

When we are **curious** about unfamiliar experiences, we can find out more by _____.

While You Read Look for information that helps you learn about the astronauts' experiences. For example, identify details that show how a lack of gravity can affect the human body.

❷ Vocabulary

Read each word and its definition. Decide whether you know the word well, know it a little bit, or do not know it at all. After you read, see how your knowledge of each word has increased.

- **manned** (mand) *adj.* having human operators on board (p. 425) *Robotic spacecraft are often cheaper to build than manned ships.* man *v.*

- **spines** (spīnz) *n.* backbones (p. 425) *Sitting up straight is good for our spines.* spiny *adj.* spinal *adj.*

- **feeble** (fē´ bəl) *adj.* weak (p. 426) *The injured bird made a feeble attempt to fly.* feebleness *n.* feebly *adv.*

- **blander** (bland´ ər) *adj.* more tasteless (p. 426) *The lack of spices made the chili blander than the cornbread.* bland *adj.* blandest *adj.*

- **globules** (gläb´ yoolz) *n.* drops of liquid (p. 427) *Globules of water made her hair wet.* globule *n.*

- **readapted** (rē ə däpt´ əd) *v.* gradually adjusted again (p. 428) *After returning from camp, he readapted to life at home.* readapt *v.* adapt *v.* adapted *v.* adaptor *n.* adaptive *adj.*

❸ Word Study

The **Old English suffix -ness** means "the condition or quality of being." It usually indicates the word is a noun.

In this essay, the author explains that **feebleness**, a weakened condition, can be brought on by a lack of gravity.

422 Types of Nonfiction

Vocabulary Development

Vocabulary Knowledge Rating

Create a **Vocabulary Knowledge Rating Chart** (*Professional Development Guidebook,* p. 33) for this selection. Include the selection vocabulary and forms of the Big Question words that appear in the Writing About the Big Question sentence starters on this page. (The Big Question vocabulary is introduced on pp. 406–407.)

Give students a copy of the chart. Read the words aloud, and have students mark their rating in the Before Reading column. Urge them to be alert to these words as they read and discuss the selection.

Tally how many students think they know a word to gauge how much instruction to provide. As students read and discuss the selection, point out the words and their context.

Vocabulary Central, featuring tools, activities, and songs for studying vocabulary, is available online at **www.PHLitOnline.com**.

Meet
Robert Zimmerman
(b. 1953)

Author of
Life Without
GRAVITY

As a boy, Robert Zimmerman became fascinated with science-fiction books. They appealed to him because "the time was the early 1960s, when the first humans were going into space, and these books had an optimistic and hopeful view of that endeavor, as well as the future."

Influence of TV Today, Zimmerman watches little television, but as a child, he remembers viewing the blastoff of *Mercury*, NASA's first manned spacecraft. He recalls thinking, "This is the United States. We can do anything if we put our minds to it!"

DID YOU KNOW?
Zimmerman spent twenty years in the movie business as a screenwriter and producer.

❹ BACKGROUND FOR THE ESSAY
Gravity and Weightlessness

Here on Earth, gravity is the force that holds people and objects down and gives them weight. Beyond Earth's atmosphere, however, gravity is weaker. This causes people and things to weigh less. For astronauts in space, the weak gravity environment affects how they eat, drink, and move. It can even affect their bones and muscles, as "Life Without Gravity" points out.

Life Without Gravity **423**

 Daily Bellringer

For each class during which you teach this selection, have students complete one of the five Quick Write activities for Week 13 in the *Daily Bellringer Activities* booklet.

❹ Background

Gravity and Weightlessness
Gravity is the force that keeps the sun, Earth, and moon in their proper orbits in space. Through gravity, the sun, Earth, and moon affect each other. For example, the sun's gravity helps keep Earth in orbit around the sun. Earth's gravity in turn helps keep the moon in orbit around Earth. Even though the moon's gravity is much weaker than Earth's, it affects the rise and fall of the oceans' tides.

Multidraft Reading

This icon ● marks natural pauses in the selection. To assist struggling readers and to deepen reading for all, assign the text in "chunks," following the icons, and apply multidraft reading protocols. For each reading, have students set the purpose indicated:

- **First reading**—identifying key ideas and details and answering any Reading Checks.
- **Second reading**—analyzing craft and structure and responding to the side-column prompts.
- **Third reading**—integrating knowledge and ideas, connecting to other texts and the world, and answering the end-of-selection questions.

For more guidance, refer to the *Classroom Strategies and Teacher's Routines* card on multidraft reading.

Differentiated
Instruction   Additional Daily Instruction

EL Extended Support— English Learners
Have students complete the **Reading and Vocabulary Warm-ups**, *Unit 3 Resources*, pp. 23–26, before they read. Assign the prereading pages and the adapted selection in the *Reader's Notebook: English Learner's Version.* Then, have students listen to portions of the selection on the *Hear It!* **Audio CD.**

L1 L2 Extended Support- Struggling Readers
Have students complete the **Reading and Vocabulary Warm-ups**, *Unit 3 Resources*, pp. 23–26, before they read. Assign the prereading pages and the adapted selection in the *Reader's Notebook: Adapted Version.* Then, have students listen to portions of the selection on the *Hear It!* **Audio CD** (adapted text).

Extended Support— Reluctant Readers
To build motivation and engagement before assigning the selection, have students read "Travel to Mars," a thematically related selection in *Reality Central.* Then, use the questions at the conclusion of the related selection to guide discussion.

PHLit Online!
For more about the author, practice with the selection vocabulary, or more background, go online at www.PHLitOnline.com.

423

❶ Activating Prior Knowledge

1. Organize student groups. Give them a copy of a **KWL chart** (see **Professional Development Guidebook**, p. 75), with the topic identified as "Life Without Gravity."

2. Ask students to work together to complete the first two columns. In the Know column, students may write what they know about living without gravity. In the Want to Know column, they should write questions they have about living in a weightless environment.

Concept Connector ➡️

Students will return to the **KWL** charts after reading "Life Without Gravity." At that point, they may complete the final column, What I Learned.

Whole-Class Activity

Invite students to imagine and act out ordinary movements as they might appear if they were performed in space, where there is no gravity. Students may suggest through their gestures and movements that physical actions in space are slow, graceful, and fluid. After students read the selection and learn about how astronauts feel after they return to Earth after months in a gravity-free environment, ask them to demonstrate what the returning astronauts' movements might look like.

❷ About the Selection

"Life Without Gravity," by Robert Zimmerman, describes the effects of weightlessness on the bodies and behavior of astronauts living in space. The author explains that although living without gravity looks like fun, the human body needs time in order to adjust to weightlessness. Weightlessness affects people's blood flow, digestion, bone density, and muscle strength. The author explains that it is important to understand the effects of life without gravity if we ever hope to send astronauts on the long journey through space to Mars and beyond.

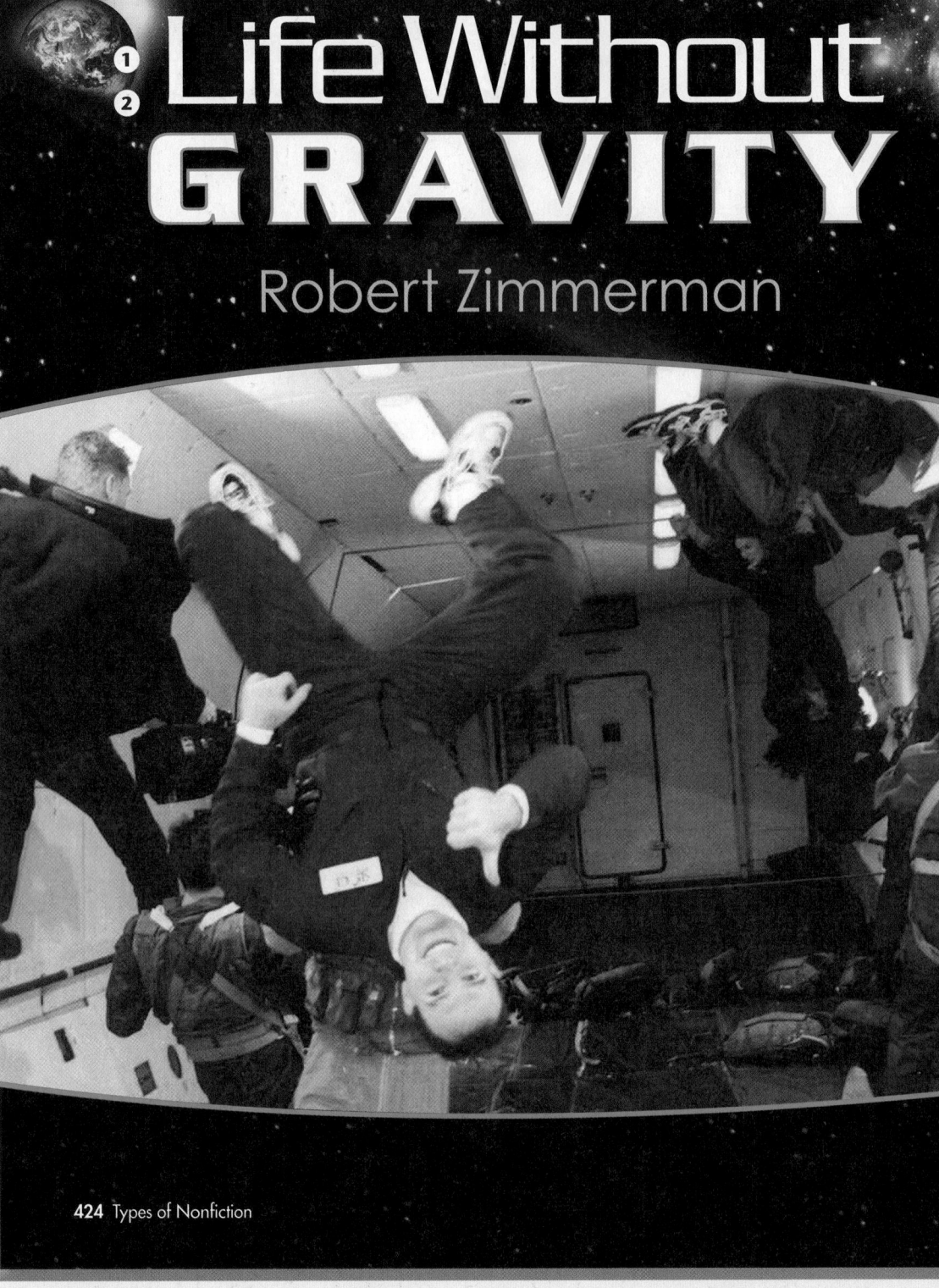

Life Without GRAVITY

Robert Zimmerman

424 Types of Nonfiction

Vocabulary Development   © **CCSS** Language 6

Thematic Vocabulary: The Big Question

As students are discussing "Life Without Gravity," encourage them to use the thematic vocabulary presented in Introducing the Big Question, pp. 406–407. You might encourage them with sentence starters like these:

1. The author *analyzes* the experience of . . .
2. The *information* he provides allows readers to *analyze* . . .
3. Readers learn that in space it is difficult to *evaluate* or *explore* one's surroundings because . . .
4. Astronauts can gather *information* and *facts*, but they also . . .
5. This raises *questions* about the value of space exploration, such as . . .

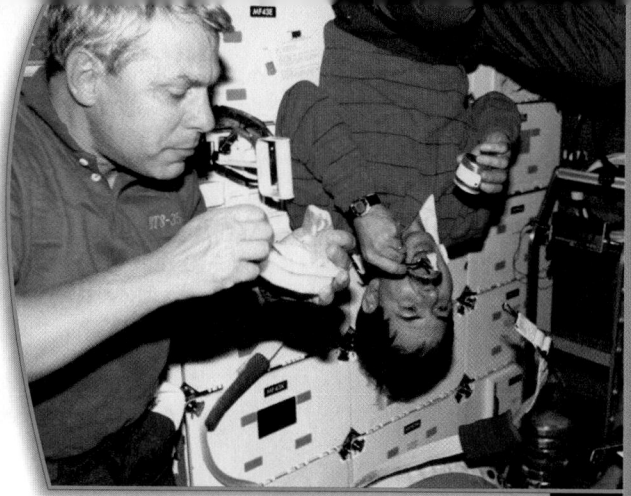

Being weightless in space seems so exciting. Astronauts bounce about from wall to wall, flying! They float, they weave, they do somersaults and acrobatics without effort. Heavy objects can be lifted like feathers, and no one ever gets tired because nothing weighs anything. In fact, everything is fun, nothing is hard.

NOT! Since the first manned space missions in the 1960s, scientists have discovered that being weightless in space isn't just flying around like Superman. Zero gravity is alien stuff. As space tourist Dennis Tito said when he visited the international space station, "Living in space is like having a different life, living in a different world."

Worse, weightlessness can sometimes be downright unpleasant. Your body gets upset and confused. Your face puffs up, your nose gets stuffy, your back hurts, your stomach gets upset, and you throw up. If astronauts are to survive a one-year journey to Mars—the shortest possible trip to the Red Planet—they will have to learn how to deal with this weird environment.

Our bodies are adapted to Earth's gravity. Our muscles are strong in order to overcome gravity as we walk and run. Our inner ears[1] use gravity to keep us upright. And because gravity wants to pull all our blood down into our legs, our hearts are designed to pump hard to get blood up to our brains.

In space, the much weaker gravity makes the human body change in many unexpected ways. In microgravity,[2] your blood is rerouted, flowing from the legs, which become thin and sticklike, to the head, which swells up. The extra liquid in your head also makes you feel like you're hanging upside down or have a stuffed-up nose.

The lack of gravity causes astronauts to routinely "grow" between one and three inches taller. Their spines straighten

---

1. **inner ears** (in´ ər irz) *n.* internal parts of the ears that give people a sense of balance.
2. **microgravity** (mī´ krō grav´ i tē) *n.* state of near-weightlessness that astronauts experience as their spacecraft orbits Earth.

Vocabulary

manned (mand) *adj.* having human operators on board

spines (spīnz) *n.* backbones

Expository Essay
What information do you learn about the human body in these paragraphs?

 Spiral Review
Author's Point of View How does the author regard space travel? Explain your answer.

❹ ☑ Reading Check
What are some disadvantages of weightlessness?

Life Without Gravity **425**

Answer: Without gravity, liquids do not flow. Instead, they separate into globules like this red one and float all around.

❻ Connecting to the Big Question

1. Point out that learning about unfamiliar environments, such as space, gives us a chance to learn about new ways that people respond to familiar challenges.

2. Have students reread the bracketed text. **Ask** students: How does the human sense of balance respond to lack of gravity? What happens over time?
   Possible response: The sense of balance is disturbed, so astronauts are often nauseous. Over time, astronauts' balance adjusts and they feel better.

3. **Ask:** Is it useful to know this information? Explain.
   Possible response: Yes, because we may find ourselves in other situations where our bodies must adjust to new surroundings. Knowing that this is often temporary can help us understand and gain confidence.

❼ Main Idea

1. Ask students to read the bracketed paragraph that begins on this page and ends on page 427.

2. **Ask** students the Main Idea question.
   Answer: The main idea is that without gravity every direction is equally accessible, including up, so every surface can be used, including the ceiling.

▶ **Monitor Progress:** Review that the purpose of this expository essay is to inform readers. **Ask** students to explain what information the essay "Life Without Gravity" provides.
   Answer: The essay explains the effects of life without gravity on the human body.

▶ **Reteach:** If students have trouble identifying information from the essay, ask them to review the questions they wrote in the second column of their **KWL** chart. **Ask** what the questions all have in common.
   Answer: All the questions focus on life without gravity, which is the topic of the expository essay.

Vocabulary

feeble (fē´ bəl)
adj. weak

blander (bland´ ər)
adj. more tasteless

globules (gläb´ yo͞olz)
n. drops of liquid

out. The bones in the spine and the disks between them spread apart and relax.

But their bones also get thin and spongy. The body decides that if the muscles aren't going to push and pull on the bones, it doesn't need to lay down as much bone as it normally does. Astronauts who have been in space for several months can lose 10 percent or more of their bone tissue. If their bones got much weaker, they would snap once the astronauts returned to Earth.

And their muscles get weak and flabby. Floating about in space is too easy. If astronauts don't force themselves to exercise, their muscles become so feeble that when they return to Earth they can't even walk.

Worst of all is how their stomachs feel. During the first few days in space, the inner ear—which gives people their sense of balance—gets confused. Many astronauts become nauseous. They lose their appetites. Many throw up. Many throw up a lot! ●

Weightlessness isn't all bad, however. After about a week people usually get used to it. Their stomachs settle down. Appetites return (though astronauts always say that food tastes blander in space). The heart and spine adjust.

Then, flying around like a bird becomes fun! Rooms suddenly seem much bigger. Look around you: The space above your head is pretty useless on Earth. You can't get up there to work, and anything you attach to the ceiling is simply something you'll bump your head on.

In space, however, that area is useful. In fact, equipment can be installed on every inch of every wall. In weightlessness you choose to move up or down and left or right simply by

▲ **Critical Viewing**
Why do you think the red liquid in this picture is floating around? Explain. **[Analyze]**

Main Idea
What is the main idea in this paragraph?

426 Types of Nonfiction

Vocabulary Development

Vocabulary Knowledge Rating
When students have completed reading and discussing the excerpt from "Life Without Gravity," have them take out their **Vocabulary Knowledge Rating Chart** for this selection. Read the words aloud and have students rate their knowledge of words again in the After Reading column. Clarify each word that is still problematic. Have students write their own definition and example or sentence in the appropriate column. Then have students complete the Vocabulary Practice activities at the end of the selection. Encourage students to use the words in further discussion and written work about the selection. Remind them that they will be accountable for these words on the **Selection Test**, *Unit 3 Resources*, pp. 35–37 or 38–40.

pointing your head. If you turn yourself upside down, the ceiling becomes the floor.

And you can't drop anything! As you work you can let your tools float around you. But you'd better be organized and neat. If you don't put things back where they belong when you are finished, tying them down securely, they will float away. Air currents will then blow them into nooks and crannies, and it might take you days to find them again.

In microgravity, you have to learn new ways to eat. Don't try pouring a bowl of cornflakes. Not only will the flakes float all over the place, the milk won't pour. Instead, big balls of milk will form. You can drink these by taking big bites out of them, but you'd better finish them before they slam into a wall, splattering apart and covering everything with little tiny milk globules.

Some meals on the space station are eaten with forks and knives, but scooping food with a spoon doesn't work. If the food isn't gooey enough to stick to the spoon, it will float away.

Everyone in space drinks through a straw, since liquid simply refuses to stay in a glass. The straw has to have a clamp at one end, or else when you stop drinking, the liquid will continue to flow out, spilling everywhere.

To prevent their muscles and bones from becoming too weak for life on Earth, astronauts have to follow a boring two-hour exercise routine every single day. Imagine having to run on a treadmill for one hour in the morning and then ride an exercise bicycle another hour before dinner. As Russian astronaut Valeri Ryumin once said, "Ye-ech!"

Even after all this exercise, astronauts who spend more than two months in space are usually weak and uncomfortable when they get back to Earth. Jerry Linenger, who spent more than four months on the Russian space station, *Mir*[3] struggled to walk after he returned. "My

---

3. *Mir* (mēr) *n.* Russian space station.

---

❽ Science Connection

Weighted Down Your weight in pounds is actually the measure of the downward force of gravity upon your body. How much force gravity puts on you depends on the size and mass of the planet on which you are standing.

Imagine that on Earth you weigh 100 pounds. Because the surface gravity of Jupiter is 2.64 times that of Earth, you would weigh 264 pounds on Jupiter without eating a forkful more. On the other hand, surface gravity on the moon is one-sixth of Earth's gravity. That means your moon weight would be just under 17 pounds, though you would look exactly the same.

Of course, when you are not on a planet or moon, you are out of gravity's pull, so you weigh nothing at all.

Connect to the Literature

Is weightlessness as described in "Life Without Gravity" something you would like to experience? Why or why not?

Life Without Gravity **427**

---

❽ Literature in Context

Science Connection Point out to students that they can calculate weights on the planet Jupiter and on the Earth's moon by using simple equations:

Jupiter weight = Earth weight x 2.64.
Moon weight = Earth weight ÷ 6.

Have students estimate the weights of objects around the room and figure those weights on Jupiter and the moon.

Have students read the Literature in Context feature, and present the additional background information above. Then, **ask** the Connect to the Literature question.

Possible responses: Students may be interested in the sensation of floating and moving easily, but they may be put off by the idea of feeling queasy and dizzy.

Concept Connector

KWL
Have students complete the last column of their KWL charts. As a class, discuss what questions have been answered and what new questions have emerged.

Reading Skill Graphic Organizer
Ask students to review the graphic organizer in which they monitored their reading rates. Then, have students share the graphic organizers they completed and compare their findings.

Writing About the Big Question
Have students compare their responses to the sentence starters they completed before reading the essay with their ideas afterward. Ask them to explain whether their thoughts have changed.

Critical Thinking

Before students respond, you may wish to have them write a brief objective summary of the selection. As they answer the questions below, remind them to support their answers with evidence from the text.

1. Students might think that having an upset stomach or a swollen head would be difficult.

2. (a) Unpleasant effects include: dizziness, a stuffed-up head, weak muscles, and an upset stomach. (b) Without gravity to keep fluids down, blood and other fluids rise to the head, making it swell. Without gravity to tell the inner ear which way is up, people get dizzy and feel sick to their stomachs. Without gravity to work against, people's muscles get weak.

3. (a) Fun aspects include: being able to reach the ceiling, and not worrying about dropping tools. (b) An astronaut can choose to move up or down, left or right, just by moving his or her head. He or she can choose to let tools float nearby while working.

4. (a) Students might warn the astronauts about the importance of doing exercise to keep their bones and muscles strong. They might also remind the astronauts that they may feel sick for the first few days, but will feel better quickly. (b) Students should work together to identify pieces of advice.

5. **Possible responses:** (a) Reading about the experiences of the astronauts in this essay helps us to discover the world of outer space and to understand how that environment affects people. (b) We can learn how the new information, environment, or idea might affect all people.

body felt like a 500 pound barbell," he said. He even had trouble lifting and holding his fifteen-month-old son, John.

When Linenger went to bed that first night, his body felt like it was being smashed into the mattress. He was constantly afraid that if he moved too much, he would float away and out of control.

And yet, Linenger recovered quickly. In fact, almost two dozen astronauts have lived in space for more than six months, and four have stayed in orbit for more than a year. These men and women faced the discomforts of weightlessness and overcame them. And they all **readapted** to Earth gravity without problems, proving that voyages to Mars are possible . . . Even if it feels like you are hanging upside down the whole time!

**Vocabulary
readapted** (rē ə däpt´ əd) *v.* gradually adjusted again

Critical Thinking

Cite textual evidence to support your responses.

1. **Key Ideas and Details** What is difficult about living in a weightless environment? Support your answer.

2. **Craft and Structure (a)** List three unpleasant effects of weightlessness that are explained in the essay. **(b) Cause and Effect:** Describe the cause of each unpleasant effect.

3. **Key Ideas and Details (a)** What are some of the fun aspects of weightlessness? **(b) Connect:** What new choices does living in a weightless environment give an astronaut?

4. **Integration of Knowledge and Ideas (a) Synthesize:** If the astronauts quoted in the article were offered another trip in space, what advice would you give them about the wisdom of taking the trip again? **(b) Discuss:** Talk about your advice in a small group. As a group, choose three important pieces of advice to share with the class.

5. **Integration of Knowledge and Ideas (a)** How do the experiences of other people—such as those of the astronauts in this essay—help us to discover the world? Explain. **(b)** What can we learn from people who experiment with something new? *[Connect to the Big Question: What should we learn?]*

428 Types of Nonfiction

Assessment Resources

Unit 3 Resources

L1 L2 EL **Selection Test A,** pp. 35–37. Administer Test A to less advanced students.

L3 L4 EL **Selection Test B,** pp. 38–40. Administer Test B to on-level and more advanced students.

L3 L4 **Open-Book Test,** pp. 32–34. As an alternative, give the Open-Book Test.

All **Customizable Test Bank**

All **Self-tests** Students may prepare for the **Selection Test** by taking the **Self-test** online.

 All assessment resources are available at **www.PHLitOnline.com.**

Reading Skill: Main Idea

1. What ideas did you identify from **skimming** the article before you read it?

2. **(a)** What are three **main ideas** in the article? **(b)** What **supporting details** does the author provide for each idea?

3. Is one main idea more important than the others? Explain.

Literary Analysis: Expository Essay

4. **Craft and Structure** Explain why "Life Without Gravity" is an **expository essay.** Give examples from the text to support your answer.

5. **Craft and Structure** Fill out a chart like the one shown to organize the information provided in the essay.

What Is Weightlessness?	What Are Its Advantages?	What Are Its Disadvantages?	Author's Conclusion

Vocabulary

Acquisition and Use Rewrite each sentence so that it includes a word from the vocabulary list on page 422 that conveys the same basic meaning as the italicized word or phrase.

1. I could barely hear her *weak* voice over the noise of the radio.

2. My cold makes this food seem *less tasty.*

3. Space flights *with humans aboard* took place in the 1960s.

4. When the thermometer broke, *tiny drops* of mercury spilled onto the table.

5. With no *bones in our backs*, we would not be able to stand.

6. After vacation, we *have gotten used to* being home again.

Word Study Use what you know about the **Old English** suffix **-ness** to explain your answer to each question.

1. If Sara is known for her *nastiness,* does she treat people well?

2. Could *laziness* prevent someone from being productive?

Word Study

The **Old English suffix -ness** means "the condition or quality of being."

Apply It Explain how the suffix **-ness** contributes to the meanings of these words. Consult a dictionary if necessary.

dreariness
togetherness
greatness

Reading Skill

1. Students' skimming should have revealed that the selection describes the drawbacks and the fun of living without gravity.

2. (a) Main ideas include: Living without gravity has negative effects on the body. Weightlessness is fun once you get used to it. Even with preparation, the body needs time to readjust when it returns to Earth and to gravity. (b) The negative effects of weightlessness include upset stomach, thinning bones, and weakening muscles. The fun effects include flying like a bird and the fact that you cannot drop anything. Readjustment involves weakness and feeling very heavy.

3. Yes, the main idea that weightlessness has its negative effects but can be overcome seems to be the most important idea in the article.

Literary Analysis

4. "Life Without Gravity" is an expository essay because it gives information: It defines weightlessness, explains the effects of weightlessness on the human body, and discusses aspects of weightlessness.

5. **Possible responses:** [col. 1]—It is life without gravity, or the force that holds people and objects down on Earth. [col. 2]—It is fun to float around. You can float up to the ceiling. You can change direction just by moving your head. [col. 3]—Weightlessness can make you feel dizzy and sick to your stomach; it causes your head to swell and your muscles and bones to weaken. [col. 4]—Weightlessness can be fun, and its effects are quickly reversed back on Earth. Astronaut's experiences with weightlessness prove that journeys to Mars are possible.

For other sample answers, see *Graphic Organizer Transparencies,* **Literary Analysis Graphic Organizer A,** p. 78, and the **Additional Answers** section.

Vocabulary
Acquisition and Use
Sample answers:

1. I could barely hear her <u>feeble</u> voice over the noise of the radio.

2. My cold makes food taste <u>blander</u>.

3. <u>Manned</u> space flights took place in the 1960s.

4. When the thermometer broke, <u>globules</u> of mercury spilled onto the table.

5. Without <u>spines</u>, we would not be able to stand.

6. After vacation, we have <u>readapted</u> to being home again.

Word Study
Sample answers:

1. No; The suffix -*ness* means "quality of being." A person with the <u>quality of being</u> nasty treats people badly.

2. Yes; The suffix -*ness* means "quality of being." A person with the <u>quality of being</u> lazy is not productive.

Word Study: Apply It
Sample answers: *Dreariness* is the <u>quality of being</u> dreary. *Togetherness* is the <u>condition of being</u> together. *Greatness* is the <u>quality of being</u> great.

*Skills instruction for the **Reading Skill** and **Literary Analysis** concept for this selection appear on p. 421.*

❶ Writing About the Big Question

1. Review the assignment with the class.

2. Discuss why a conversation might need rules, such as the rule "don't interrupt," which helps people hear each other clearly.

3. Have students complete the sentence starter. Review responses as a class. (**Sample response:** <u>Understanding</u> conversational "rules" can be helpful because then we can exchange ideas more effectively.)

4. Remind students that their answers will help them think about the Big Question, "What should we learn?"

While You Read

Tell students that as they read, they should look for insights about how communication between people is affected by cultural beliefs and practices.

❷ Vocabulary

1. Have students preview the selection vocabulary.

2. For each word, have students say the word aloud.

3. Then, use the word in a sentence that defines the word.

4. Finally, repeat your definitional sentence or a similar sentence with the word missing and have the class "fill in the blank" chorally. Here are some examples:

If someone is <u>murmuring,</u> he or she is speaking in a soft, musical way. When mothers speak to their babies in a quiet, soothing way, they are [students say "murmuring"].

Something that is <u>indispensable</u> is absolutely necessary. Some students cannot study without music and find it to be truly [students say "indispensable"].

❸ Word Study

1. Introduce the skill, using the instruction in the box.

2. Ask students to name another word that ends with the *-able* suffix and tell what it means.

430

---

❶

What should we *learn?*

Writing About the Big Question

In "Conversational Ballgames," we learn that Japanese and western cultures have different "rules" for conversation. Use this sentence starter to develop your ideas about the Big Question.

Understanding conversational "rules" can be helpful

because _____.

While You Read Look for insights about how communication between people may be affected by cultural beliefs and practices.

❷ Vocabulary

Read each word and its definition. Decide whether you know the word well, know it a little bit, or do not know it at all. After you read, see how your knowledge of each word has increased.

- **unconsciously** (un kän′ shəs lē) *adv.* thoughtlessly (p. 432) *The dog <u>unconsciously</u> scratched his ear. unconscious adj. conscious adj.*

- **elaboration** (ē lab′ ə rā′ shən) *n.* addition of more details (p. 433) *His <u>elaboration</u> of the main idea helped me grasp his point. elaborate v. elaborately adv. elaborateness n.*

- **murmuring** (mʉr′ mər iŋ) *v.* making low sounds that cannot be heard clearly (p. 433) *My parents were <u>murmuring</u> in the hallway to each other. murmur v. murmur n.*

- **parallel** (par′ ə lel′) *adj.* extending in the same direction and at the same distance apart (p. 434) *The train tracks ran <u>parallel</u> to the highway. parallelism n. parallelogram n.*

- **suitable** (sōōt′ ə bəl) *adj.* appropriate (p. 434) *The movie was <u>suitable</u> for children. suitability n. suitably adv. suit v.*

- **indispensable** (in′ di spen′ sə bəl) *adj.* absolutely necessary (p. 435) *Sunscreen is <u>indispensable</u> in the strong summer sun. indispensably adv. dispensable adj.*

430 Types of Nonfiction

❸ Word Study

The **Latin suffix *-able*** means "capable" or "worthy of being."

In Japanese culture, there is always a **suitable**, or appropriate, pause between speakers.

Vocabulary Development

Vocabulary Knowledge Rating

Create a **Vocabulary Knowledge Rating Chart** (*Professional Development Guidebook,* p. 33) for this selection. Include the selection vocabulary and the form of the Big Question word that appears in the Writing About the Big Question sentence starter on this page. (The Big Question vocabulary is introduced on pp. 406–407.)

Give students a copy of the chart. Read the words aloud, and have students mark their rating in the Before Reading column. Urge them to be alert to these words as they read and discuss the selection.

Tally how many students think they know a word to gauge how much instruction to provide. As students read and discuss the selection, point out the words and their context.

Vocabulary Central, featuring tools, activities, and songs for studying vocabulary, is available online at **www.PHLitOnline.com.**

Meet
Nancy Masterson Sakamoto
(b. 1931)

Author of
CONVERSATIONAL BALLGAMES

Nancy Masterson Sakamoto graduated from UCLA with an English degree. She married a Japanese artist and Buddhist priest, and the couple lived in Japan for twenty-four years. There, Sakamoto was a visiting professor at the University of Osaka, where she trained Japanese teachers who taught English to middle school and high school students.

Cultural Differences While living in Japan, Sakamoto was able to observe conversations from both the Japanese and American perspectives.

DID YOU KNOW?
Sakamoto was a professor of American Studies at Shitennoji Gakuen University in Hawaii.

④ BACKGROUND FOR THE ESSAY
Cultural Diversity

While people around the world have much in common, they also have cultural differences. Some of the ways people express these differences are through the foods they eat and the ways they dress. In this essay, you will learn that a way of talking that may seem normal to you might be considered strange, or even rude, to a person from another culture.

Conversational Ballgames **431**

④ Background
Cultural Diversity

Japanese and American cultures have very different approaches to communication. Americans value direct and clear sentences that express what a person thinks or wants. Japanese speakers frequently use incomplete sentences or hint at an idea rather than state it outright. They trust that the listener is aware enough to know what the speaker means. In the United States, speakers are more likely to approach a conversation as though all participants are equals. In Japan, people are more aware of the status or social standing of each person in a group.

Multidraft Reading

This icon ● marks natural pauses in the selection. To assist struggling readers and to deepen reading for all, assign the text in "chunks," following the icons, and apply multidraft reading protocols. For each reading, have students set the purpose indicated:

• **First reading**—identifying key ideas and details and answering any Reading Checks.

• **Second reading**—analyzing craft and structure and responding to the side-column prompts.

• **Third reading**—integrating knowledge and ideas, connecting to other texts and the world, and answering the end-of-selection questions.

For more guidance, refer to the *Classroom Strategies and Teaching Routines* card on multidraft reading.

❶ Activating Prior Knowledge

1. Organize students in groups. Give them a copy of a **KWL chart** (see *Professional Development Guidebook*, p. 75), with the topic identified as "Conversational Ballgames."

2. In the Know column, students may write what they know about rules of conversation. In the Want to Know column, they should write questions they have about speaking with people from Japan.

Concept Connector ➡

Students will return to the **KWL** charts after reading "Conversational Ballgames," and then may complete the chart's final column.

Individual Activity

Have students draw sketches of the different sports in the essay to show the spatial relationships among the players. Students should understand that volleyball and tennis are interactive sports while bowling is individual. Help students link their observations to the author's comments about communication.

❷ About the Selection

In the essay "Conversational Ballgames," Nancy Masterson Sakamoto compares the approaches American and Japanese speakers have toward conversation with different sports. She discusses how these cultural differences affect social and learning situations.

❸ Expository Essay

1. Review that an essay's main topic is usually stated in the topic sentence of an early paragraph. The Think Aloud note on page 432 can also help students use the topic to identify the essay's purpose.

2. **Ask** students the Expository Essay question.
   Possible response: Japanese and American speakers have different conversational styles.

CONVERSATIONAL ❶ ❷ BALLGAMES

Nancy Masterson Sakamoto

After I was married and had lived in Japan for a while, my Japanese gradually improved to the point where I could take part in simple conversations with my husband and his friends and family. And I began to notice that often, when I joined in, the others would look startled, and the conversational topic would come to a halt. After this happened several times, it became clear to me that I was doing something wrong. But for a long time, I didn't know what it was.

Finally, after listening carefully to many Japanese conversations, I discovered what my problem was. Even though I was speaking Japanese, I was handling the conversation in a western[1] way.

Japanese-style conversations develop quite differently from western-style conversations. And the difference isn't only in the languages. I realized that just as I kept trying to hold western-style conversations even when I was speaking Japanese, so my English students kept trying to hold Japanese-style conversations even when they were speaking English. We were unconsciously playing entirely different conversational ballgames. •

A western-style conversation between two people is like a game of tennis. If I introduce a topic, a conversational ball, I expect you to hit it back. If you agree with me, I don't expect

❸ **Expository Essay**
What do you think the main topic of this essay might be?

Vocabulary
unconsciously (un kän´ shəs lē) *adv.* thoughtlessly

---
1. **western** *adj.* from the Western Hemisphere and Europe.

432 Types of Nonfiction

Think Aloud

Author's Purpose

You may wish to use the Expository Essay question on the student page to model the process of identifying author's purpose (introduced on p. 99). Focus on an essay's topic as a clue to its author's purpose. Say to students:

When I read the first paragraph of the essay, I see that it identifies a question that the author wants to answer: "What goes wrong when she tries to join in Japanese conversations?" I realize that this question offers a clue to the author's purpose, or reason, for writing. She probably wants to answer her question, or to explain the problem she has had.

When I read the next paragraph, I see that the author begins to identify her topic. She will explain the difference between Japanese and western styles of conversation. Yes, my idea about author's purpose is correct: The author is writing to explain.

you simply to agree and do nothing more. I expect you to add something—a reason for agreeing, another example, or an elaboration to carry the idea further. But I don't expect you always to agree. I am just as happy if you question me, or challenge me, or completely disagree with me. Whether you agree or disagree, your response will return the ball to me.

And then it is my turn again. I don't serve a new ball from my original starting line. I hit your ball back again from where it has bounced. I carry your idea further, or answer your questions or objections, or challenge or question you. And so the ball goes back and forth, with each of us doing our best to give it a new twist, an original spin, or a powerful smash.

And the more vigorous the action, the more interesting and exciting the game. Of course, if one of us gets angry, it spoils the conversation, just as it spoils a tennis game. But getting excited is not at all the same as getting angry. After all, we are not trying to hit each other. We are trying to hit the ball. So long as we attack only each other's opinions, and do not attack each other personally, we don't expect anyone to get hurt. A good conversation is supposed to be interesting and exciting.

If there are more than two people in the conversation, then it is like doubles in tennis, or like volleyball. There's no waiting in line. Whoever is nearest and quickest hits the ball, and if you step back, someone else will hit it. No one stops the game to give you a turn. You're responsible for taking your own turn.

But whether it's two players or a group, everyone does his best to keep the ball going, and no one person has the ball for very long.

A Japanese-style conversation, however, is not at all like tennis or volleyball. It's like bowling. You wait for your turn. And you always know your place in line. It depends on such things as whether you are older or younger, a close friend or a relative stranger to the previous speaker, in a senior or junior position, and so on.

When your turn comes, you step up to the starting line with your bowling ball, and carefully bowl it. Everyone else stands back and watches politely, murmuring encouragement. Everyone waits until the ball has reached the end of the alley, and watches to see if it knocks down all the pins, or only some of them, or none of them. There is a pause, while everyone registers your score.

Main Idea
What details in this paragraph support the idea that conversation is like tennis?

Vocabulary
elaboration (ē lab´ ə rā´ shən) *n.* addition of more details
murmuring (mur´ mər iŋ) *v.* making low sounds that cannot be heard clearly

Spiral Review
Author's Point of View How does the author seem to feel about communication across cultures? Explain your answer.

❺ Reading Check
What happens when the author tries to join Japanese conversations?

Conversational Ballgames 433

❹ **Main Idea**

1. Remind students that the main idea of a paragraph is supported by details in the sentences that surround the topic sentence. Ask students to read the bracketed paragraph. Review the graphic organizer on page 421 and tell students to choose an appropriate reading rate to recognize the main idea and key points.

2. **Ask** students the Main Idea question.
Answer: Each comment in the conversation is like the ball in a game of tennis. It goes back and forth, with each person or player trying to give it a twist, spin, or smash.

3. Later, after students read the author's comparison of Japanese conversational style to bowling on pages 433–434, invite students to identify the details that support that idea.
Answer: Each person takes a turn in bowling and in Japanese conversation. The others watch respectfully. Then the next person takes a turn.

Spiral Review

Author's Point of View

1. Students studied author's point of view in the Unit 3 Literary Analysis Workshop (pp. 408–419).

2. **Ask** the Spiral Review question.

Possible response: The author thinks that communication is not just about language but also about culture. She explains that western conversations are like tennis, while Japanese conversations are like bowling.

❺ **Reading Check**
Answer: The Japanese speakers look confused and the conversations stop.

PHLit Online!
This selection is available in interactive format in the **Enriched Online Student Edition**, online at www.PHLitOnline.com, which includes a thematically related video with writing prompt and an interactive graphic organizer.

❻ Critical Viewing

Possible response: The picture shows a tennis player using a dialogue bubble as a racket. She will serve her excitement about the topic, which is suggested by the exclamation point in place of a ball. The image reflects the author's description of Western conversation, in which each player serves an idea with excitement to the other player.

❼ Critical Thinking

Summarize

1. Read aloud the bracketed passage, continuing on to page 435, as students read along silently. Point out that in this section of the essay, the author uses the game of volleyball to illustrate how students reacted in her English classes.

2. **Ask** students to summarize what happened when the author tried to initiate conversation in English with her Japanese students.
   Answer: She would serve a topic, like a volleyball, but none of the students would return it or elaborate on it. They would just murmur. Then someone would start speaking about another topic.

3. **Ask** students to comment on the author's use of the image "the other person tries to bowl with my tennis ball." What does the author mean?
   Possible response: The Japanese students do not interact in conversation as if they are playing tennis. Instead, they act as though they are bowling, with no one hitting back the teacher's topic (which she has served, like a tennis ball), but instead sending another topic down the lane while the others listen.

Vocabulary

parallel (par´ ə lel´) *adj.* extending in the same direction and at the same distance apart

suitable (sŏŏt´ ə bəl) *adj.* appropriate

❻ ▼ **Critical Viewing**
How does this image fit the author's description of a conversation between someone from Japan and someone from the west? **[Connect]**

There is no back and forth at all. All the balls run parallel.

434 Types of Nonfiction

Then, after everyone is sure that you have completely finished your turn, the next person in line steps up to the same starting line, with a different ball. He doesn't return your ball, and he does not begin from where your ball stopped. There is no back and forth at all. All the balls run parallel. And there is always a suitable pause between turns. There is no rush, no excitement, no scramble for the ball. No wonder everyone looked startled when I took part in Japanese conversations. I paid no attention to whose turn it was, and kept snatching the ball halfway down the alley and throwing it back at the bowler. Of course the conversation died. I was playing the wrong game.

This explains why it is almost impossible to get a western-style conversation or discussion going with English students in Japan. I used to think that the problem was their lack of English language ability. But I finally came to realize that the biggest problem is that they, too, are playing the wrong game.

Whenever I serve a volleyball, everyone just stands back and watches it fall, with occasional murmurs of encouragement. No one hits it back. Everyone waits until I call on someone to take a turn. And when that person speaks, he doesn't hit my ball back. He serves a new ball. Again, everyone just watches it fall. So I call on someone else. This person does not refer to what the previous speaker has said. He also serves a new ball. Nobody seems to have paid any attention to what anyone

else has said. Everyone begins again from the same starting line, and all the balls run parallel. There is never any back and forth. Everyone is trying to bowl with a volleyball.

And if I try a simpler conversation, with only two of us, then the other person tries to bowl with my tennis ball. No wonder foreign English teachers in Japan get discouraged.

Now that you know about the difference in the conversational ballgames, you may think that all your troubles are over. But if you have been trained all your life to play one game, it is no simple matter to switch to another, even if you know the rules. Knowing the rules is not at all the same thing as playing the game.

Even now, during a conversation in Japanese I will notice a startled reaction, and belatedly realize that once again I have rudely interrupted by instinctively trying to hit back the other person's bowling ball. It is no easier for me to "just listen" during a conversation than it is for my Japanese students to "just relax" when speaking with foreigners. Now I can truly sympathize with how hard they must find it to try to carry on a western-style conversation.

If I have not yet learned to do conversational bowling in Japanese, at least I have figured out one thing that puzzled me for a long time. After his first trip to America, my husband complained that Americans asked him so many questions and made him talk so much at the dinner table that he never had a chance to eat. When I asked him why he couldn't talk and eat at the same time, he said that Japanese do not customarily think that dinner, especially on fairly formal occasions, is a suitable time for extended conversation.

Since westerners think that conversation is an indispensable part of dining, and indeed would consider it impolite not to converse with one's dinner partner, I found this Japanese custom rather strange. Still, I could accept it as a cultural difference even though I didn't really understand it. But when my husband added, in explanation, that Japanese consider it extremely rude to talk with one's mouth full, I

▲ **Critical Viewing**
9 Does this image illustrate the author's ideas about Japanese conversation? Explain. **[Analyze]**

Vocabulary
indispensable (in´ di spen´ sə bəl) *adj.* absolutely necessary

Reading Check
10 To what two sports does the author compare western-style conversation?

8 **Connecting to the Big Question**

1. Point out that if we learn about the way that others approach interaction with us, we will understand that interaction better.

2. Have students reread the bracketed text on page 435. **Ask** students: What insight does the author share about the way cultural experience affects communication?
Possible response: She reveals that cultural experience influences our training in conversation, so that even if we know another culture's rules, we often forget to follow those rules.

3. **Ask:** Should we learn about the conversational rules of other cultures? Explain.
Possible response: Yes, knowing these rules can help us avoid misunderstandings with friends from other cultures.

9 **Critical Viewing**
Possible response: Yes. It shows a person bowling. Bowling is a game in which each person takes a turn while the others watch and wait. The ball is not passed to other players, and a new ball is thrown from the same starting place each time.

10 **Reading Check**
Answer: She compares Western-style conversation to tennis and volleyball.

Concept Connector

KWL
Have students complete the last column of their KWL charts. As a class, discuss what questions have been answered and what new questions have emerged.

Reading Skill Graphic Organizer
Ask students to review the graphic organizers they completed while reading at different rates. Then, have students share the graphic organizers they completed and compare their findings.

Writing About the Big Question
Have students compare their responses to the sentence starter they completed before reading the essay with their thoughts afterwards. Ask them to explain whether their thoughts have changed.

1. Have students read the bracketed passage on page 435. Have students compare the American approach to mealtime conversation with the Japanese one.

2. **Ask** the Main Idea question. **Answer:** Westerners can talk during dinner—even though they think talking while you have food in your mouth is rude—because their conversational style gives them the chance to talk between bites.

Critical Thinking

Before students respond, you may wish to have them write a brief objective summary of the selection. As they answer the questions below, remind them to support their answers with evidence from the text.

1. (a) People would become confused, and the conversations would suddenly stop. (b) The author did not understand that she should wait her turn to speak and that she should not respond to others' comments.

2. (a) She compares Western-style conversation to tennis and volleyball and compares Japanese-style conversation to bowling. (b) **Possible response:** The Japanese friends should understand that the author may often interrupt but does not mean to be rude. The author should understand that Japanese speakers think it is rude to respond to their ideas in conversation.

3. (a) They do not engage in extended conversation at the dinner table. (b) Westerners enjoy conversation at dinner.

4. **Possible responses:** (a) If we are aware of other cultures, we can respect cultural practices of communicating, and avoid confusion or misunderstanding. (b) If we understand how people from other cultures communicate, we will be better able to find common ground with them.

436

---

got confused. Talking with one's mouth full is certainly not an American custom. We think it very rude, too. Yet we still manage to talk a lot and eat at the same time. How do we do it?

For a long time, I couldn't explain it, and it bothered me. But after I discovered the conversational ballgames, I finally found the answer. Of course! In a western-style conversation, you hit the ball, and while someone else is hitting it back, you take a bite, chew, and swallow. Then you hit the ball again, and then eat some more. The more people there are in the conversation, the more chances you have to eat. But even with only two of you talking, you still have plenty of chances to eat.

Maybe that's why polite conversation at the dinner table has never been a traditional part of Japanese etiquette.[2] Your turn to talk would last so long without interruption that you'd never get a chance to eat.

Main Idea
State the main idea of this paragraph in your own words.

---

2. **etiquette** (et´ i kit) *n.* formal rules for polite behavior in society or in a particular group.

Critical Thinking

Cite textual evidence to support your responses.

1. **Key Ideas and Details (a)** What happened at first when the author joined in during conversations in Japan? **(b) Draw Conclusions:** What misunderstandings took place during those initial conversations? Use examples from the essay to support your response.

2. **Key Ideas and Details (a)** To what sports or games does the author compare Japanese-style and western-style conversations? **(b) Apply:** What do the author and her family and friends need to understand about each other?

3. **Key Ideas and Details (a)** How do the Japanese feel about conversing during dinner? **(b) Compare and Contrast:** How does their behavior compare with westerners' behavior during a meal?

4. **Integration of Knowledge and Ideas (a)** How does awareness of other cultures help us to communicate with people? **(b)** How does it help us to understand the world better? *[Connect to the Big Question: What should we learn?]*

436 Types of Nonfiction

Assessment Resources

Unit 3 Resources

L1 L2 EL **Selection Test A**, pp. 56–58. Administer Test A to less advanced students.

L3 L4 EL **Selection Test B**, pp. 59–61. Administer Test B to on-level and more advanced students.

L3 L4 **Open-Book Test**, pp. 53–55. As an alternative, give the Open-Book Test.

All **Customizable Test Bank**

All **Self-tests** Students may prepare for the **Selection Test** by taking the **Self-test** online.

PHLit Online! All assessment resources are available at **www.PHLitOnline.com**.

After You Read

Conversational Ballgames

Reading Skill: Main Idea

1. What ideas did you identify from **skimming** the article?

2. **(a)** What are three **main ideas** in the article? **(b)** What **supporting details** does the author provide for each idea?

3. Is one main idea more important than the others? Explain.

Literary Analysis: Expository Essay

ⓒ 4. **Craft and Structure** Explain why "Conversational Ballgames" is an **expository essay.** Give examples from the text to support your answer.

ⓒ 5. **Craft and Structure** Fill out a chart like the one shown to organize the information provided in the essay.

Describe Polite Conversation in the United States	Describe Polite Conversation in Japan	Author's Conclusion

Vocabulary

ⓒ **Acquisition and Use** Rewrite each sentence so that it includes a word from the vocabulary list on page 430 that conveys the same basic meaning as the italicized words or phrases.

1. The lines in the parking lot are *side by side.*

2. I could hear people *talking softly* in the next room.

3. Your descriptive essay should include *many details.*

4. A pencil sharpener is *completely necessary* in a classroom.

5. *Unaware of her actions,* she twirled her hair as she read.

6. Be sure to wear something *appropriate* for the award ceremony at school.

Word Study Use the context of the sentences and what you know about the **Latin suffix -able** to explain your answer to each question.

1. If something is *noticeable,* can you easily see it?

2. Do you reuse a *disposable* camera?

Word Study

The **Latin suffix -able** means "capable" or "worthy of being."

Apply It Explain how the suffix **-able** contributes to the meanings of these words. Consult a dictionary if necessary.

lovable
enjoyable
preferable

Reading Skill

1. Students may say they learned that the two conversational styles were like different sports.

2. (a) First main idea: Western- and Japanese-style conversations are different. Second main idea: Western-style conversations are like interactive sports, while Japanese-style conversations are like parallel sports. Third main idea: Westerners and Japanese have different ideas about dinner time conversation. (b) The author's own attempts to speak with Japanese people support the first idea. The author's own observations of the two types of conversation support the second and third ideas.

3. Yes, the idea that Western- and Japanese-style conversations are very different is the most important point that the author is making.

Literary Analysis

4. The essay is expository because it explains the differences between the two conversational styles.

5. **Possible responses:** [col. 1]—It includes passing the topic back and forth, like a tennis ball or volleyball; it is exciting and fun; it occurs during meal times; it involves all the members of the conversation in no particular order. [col. 2]—It allows only one speaker at a time, according to his or her social standing. While the speaker talks, the others listen quietly. When it is time for a new speaker, he or she starts with a new topic. [col. 3]—Western-style conversation is like tennis or volleyball, and Japanese-style conversation is like bowling, but both are valid forms of conversation.

For other sample answers, see *Graphic Organizers Transparencies,* **Literary Analysis Graphic Organizer A,** p. 79, and the **Additional Answers** section.

Vocabulary
Acquisition and Use
Sample answers:

1. The lines in the parking lot are <u>parallel</u>.

2. I could hear people <u>murmuring</u> in the next room.

3. Your descriptive essay should include <u>elaboration</u>.

4. A pencil sharpener is <u>indispensable</u> in a classroom.

5. She twirled her hair <u>unconsciously</u> as she read.

6. Be sure to wear something <u>suitable</u> for the award ceremony at school.

Word Study
Sample answers:

1. Yes. You are <u>capable of</u> seeing, or noticing, something *noticeable.*

2. No. A *disposable* camera is <u>worthy of being</u> disposed, not reused.

Word Study: Apply It
Sample answers: Something *lovable* is <u>worthy of being</u> loved. Something *enjoyable* is <u>worthy of being</u> enjoyed. Something *preferable* is <u>worthy of being</u> preferred.

Conventions

Introduce the skill, using the instruction on the student page.

Think Aloud: Model the Skill

Writers use coordinating conjunctions to show the connections between their ideas. Let's say I'm writing an e-mail to a friend about a camping trip. I might write "I'll bring a canoe. The weather may be too stormy to go on the lake." I realize that the relationship between these two ideas is contrast or opposition. One idea works against the other. To make this relationship clear, I can write, "I'll bring a canoe, *but* the weather may be too stormy to go on the lake." The coordinating conjunction *but* shows the connection between ideas clearly.

PH WRITING COACH | Grade 7

Students will find instruction on and practice with conjunctions in Chapter 17, Section 1.

Practice A

1. *and; advantages* and *disadvantages*
2. *but; You are able to fly* and *you also lose your balance*
3. *so; You have to exercise* and *your muscles don't get too weak*
4. *nor; I would not like losing my appetite* and *would I like chasing my food*

Reading Application

Sample answer: But their bones also get *thin* <u>and</u> *spongy*; Some meals on the space station are eaten with *forks and knives,* <u>but</u> *scooping food with a spoon doesn't work.*

Practice B

Sample answers:

1. *but;* My oldest brother is very tall, <u>but</u> my middle brother is the same height as I am.
2. *so;* Henry wanted to visit Japan, <u>so</u> he studied Japanese for two years.
3. *or;* Alana could not find her socks <u>or</u> her shoes.
4. *yet;* Jed tried every day not to forget something, <u>yet</u> he somehow managed to miss an item at school.

Writing Application

Sample answer: Students' paragraphs should describe conversational styles and contain three different circled coordinating conjunctions.

Life Without Gravity • Conversational Ballgames

Conventions: Conjunctions

Conjunctions connect words or groups of words.
Coordinating conjunctions, such as *but* and *so,* connect words or groups of words that are similar in form. Conjunctions show the relationship between those two parts.

In the following examples, the coordinating conjunctions are boldface. The words or groups of words they connect are italicized.

Example: **Nouns:** The *pen* **and** *paper* contained fingerprints.
Verbs: Shall we *walk* **or** *ride* our bicycles?
Groups of words: *He ran out the door,* **but** *the bus had already left.*

Coordinating Conjunctions						
but	or	yet	so	for	and	nor

Practice A Circle the coordinating conjunction in each sentence. Underline the words or groups of words connected by the conjunction.

1. Being weightless has both advantages and disadvantages.
2. You are able to fly, but you also lose your balance.
3. You have to exercise so your muscles don't get too weak.
4. I would not like losing my appetite, nor would I like chasing my food!

© **Reading Application** In "Life Without Gravity," find two sentences, each with a different coordinating conjunction, and identify the words or groups of words the conjunctions connect.

Practice B Identify the coordinating conjunction in each sentence. Then, use the conjunction in a sentence of your own.

1. Conversations stopped when Sakamoto joined in, but she did not know why.
2. She wanted to solve the problem, so she listened carefully to other conversations.
3. She learned that she should not interrupt or challenge a speaker.
4. She tried not to interrupt, yet sometimes she could not help herself.

© **Writing Application** Write a paragraph about how people converse, using three different coordinating conjunctions. Then, circle the words that the conjunctions connect.

PH WRITING COACH | Further instruction and practice are available in *Prentice Hall Writing Coach.*

Extend the Lesson

Sentence Modeling

Choose the sentence given from the selection students have read:

Everyone in space drinks through a straw, since liquid simply refuses to stay in a glass. ("Life Without Gravity")
Everyone else stands back and watches politely, murmuring encouragement. ("Conversational Ballgames")

First, ask students to identify the coordinating conjunctions and the words or phrases they connect. ("Life Without Gravity"—*since;*

Everyone in space drinks through a straw and *liquid simply refuses to stay in a glass.* "Conversational Ballgames"— *and: stands back* and *watches politely.*) Then, ask students what else they notice about the conjunctions. ("Life Without Gravity"—The conjunction shows contrast; "Conversational Ballgames"—The conjunction shows similarity in the two actions.)

Have students imitate the sentence, matching each feature discussed.

Writing

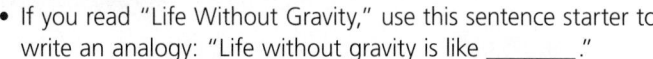 **Explanatory Text** An **analogy** makes a comparison between two or more things that are alike in some ways but otherwise different. For example: A follower without a leader is like a planet without a sun.

- If you read "Life Without Gravity," use this sentence starter to write an analogy: "Life without gravity is like _____."

- If you read "Conversational Ballgames," use this sentence starter to write an analogy: "Communicating with someone from another culture is like _____."

Write several sentences to develop your analogy. Support your statements with details from the selection that you chose. Also use anecdotes (personal stories), examples from real life, and facts or statistics to explain your ideas.

Grammar Application Reread your analogy to make sure you have used conjunctions correctly.

Writing Workshop: *Work in Progress*

Prewriting for Exposition To prepare for a how-to essay that you may write, make a list of five everyday tasks. These tasks can be anything you do, from brushing your teeth to opening your locker. Then, save this Everyday Task List in your writing portfolio.

Speaking and Listening

 Presentation of Ideas As your teacher directs, listen to the audio version of either Zimmerman's or Sakamoto's expository essay. Access the audio of the selection by visiting www.PHLitOnline. In a small group, compare and contrast the audio and text versions of your chosen selection. Discuss the ways in which you find each version compelling. Then, prepare and deliver an **oral summary** of the essay.

- Be objective. In your own words, outline the main ideas and supporting details.

- Gather visual aids, such as photographs, illustrations, or charts that support your summary.

- Show each visual aid as you talk about the point it illustrates.

- Provide a clear summarizing concluding statement. Then, as a class, discuss how visual aids clarified each presentation.

 **Common Core State Standards**

L.7.1, L.7.4.b; RI.7.7; W.7.9, W.7.9.b; RI.7.7; SL.7.2, SL.7.4
[For the full wording of the standards, see page 420.]

Use this prewriting activity to prepare for the **Writing Workshop** on page 484.

PHLit Online!
www.PHLitOnline.com

- Interactive graphic organizers
- Grammar tutorial
- Interactive journals

Integrated Language Skills **439**

Writing

1. Review the assignment, using the instruction on the student page.

2. To guide students in writing an explanatory text, give them **Support for Writing,** p. 51 in *Unit 3 Resources.*

3. To evaluate students' analogies, use the **Generic (Holistic) Writing Rubric,** pp. 256–257 in *Professional Development Guidebook.* In addition, you might evaluate how imaginative students are in connecting dissimilar ideas.

Grammar Application

Have students check their drafts to make sure they have used conjunctions correctly.

Six Traits Focus

✔	Ideas		Word Choice
✔	Organization		Sentence Fluency
	Voice		Conventions

PH WRITING COACH Grade 7

Students will find further instruction on and practice with explanatory text in Chapter 12.

Writing Workshop
Work in Progress

Have students save their completed Everyday Task Lists in their portfolios. They will use the lists later as they continue this Work-in-Progress assignment (see p. 459). These assignments prepare them to complete the Writing Workshop assignment (see pp. 484–489).

Speaking and Listening

1. Review the assignment, using the instruction on the student page.

2. To support students' work on the assignment, have them complete the **Support for Extend Your Learning** page (*Unit 3 Resources,* p. 52).

Teaching Resources

Unit 3 Resources

L3 L4 EL Integrated Language Skills: Grammar, p. 50

L3 L4 EL Support for Writing, p. 51

L3 L4 Support for Extend Your Learning, p. 52

L4 Enrichment, pp. 31, 49

Enriched Online Student Edition
Available under After You Read for this selection:

All Interactive Grammar Tutorial
L3 L4 Internet Research Activity

Professional Development Guidebook
Rubrics for Self-Assessment: Generic (Holistic) Writing), pp. 256–257

PHLit Online! All print and digital resources are available online at **www.PHLitOnline.com.** Online resources accessible to students are noted on the student page.

439

✓ I Am a Native of North America •
✓✓ Volar: To Fly
Lesson Pacing Guide

DAY 1 Preteach

- ⓒ Administer the Reading and Vocabulary Warm-ups (*Unit 3 Resources,* pp. 62–65 or 80–83) as necessary.
- • Introduce the Reading Skill: Main Idea.
- ⓒ Introduce the Literary Analysis concept: Reflective Essay.
- • Distribute copies of the graphic organizer for the Reading Skill (*Graphic Organizer Transparencies,* pp. 81–83).
- • Distribute copies of the graphic organizer for Literary Analysis (*Graphic Organizer Transparencies,* pp. 84–86).
- ⓒ Teach the selection vocabulary.
- ⓒ Introduce the Word Study skill.

DAYS 2–3 Preteach/Teach

- ⓒ Build background with the Background feature.
- • Develop thematic vocabulary and thematic thinking with Writing About the Big Question.
- • Prepare students to read with the Activating Prior Knowledge activities (TE).
- • Informally monitor comprehension while students read.
- • Use the Reading Check questions to confirm comprehension.
- • Develop students' ability to determine the main idea using the Main Idea questions.
- ⓒ Develop students' understanding of reflective essays using the Reflective Essay questions.
- ⓒ Reinforce vocabulary with the Vocabulary notes.
- ⓒ Reinforce unit focus standards using the Spiral Review prompts.

DAY 4 Assess

- • Assess students' comprehension and mastery of the skills by having them answer the Critical Thinking, Reading Skill, and Literary Analysis questions.
- ⓒ Have students complete the Vocabulary Practice activities.
- ⓒ Have students complete the Word Study activities.

DAY 5 Extend/Assess

- • Have students complete the Conventions lesson.
- ⓒ Have students complete the Writing activity and write an outline. (You may assign as homework.)
- ⓒ Extend learning by having students complete the Speaking and Listening activity, a response. As an alternative, assign them "Making Sport of Tradition" or "In Your Dreams" in *Reality Central.*
- • Administer Selection Test A or B (*Unit 3 Resources,* pp. 74–79 or 95–100).

ⓒ Common Core State Standards

Reading Informational Text
2. Determine two or more central ideas in a text and analyze their development over the course of the text; provide an objective summary of the text. *(Reading Skill: Main Idea)*
3. Analyze the interactions between individuals, events, and ideas in a text. *(Literary Analysis: Reflective Essay)*
6. Determine an author's point of view or purpose in a text and analyze how the author distinguishes his or her position from that of others. *(Literary Analysis: Spiral Review)*
7. Compare and contrast a text to an audio, video, or multimedia version of the text, analyzing each medium's portrayal of the subject. *(Listening and Speaking: Response)*

Writing 2.a. Introduce a topic clearly, previewing what is to follow; organize ideas, concepts, and information, using strategies such as definition, classification, comparison/contrast, and cause/effect.

Speaking and Listening 3. Delineate a speaker's argument and specific claims, evaluating the soundness of the reasoning and the relevance and sufficiency of the evidence.

Language 1.a. Explain the function of phrases and clauses in general and their function in specific sentences.
5.b. Use the relationship between particular words to better understand each of the words.
6. Acquire and use accurately grade-appropriate general academic and domain-specific words and phrases.

Additional Standards Practice
Common Core Companion, pp. 122–123, 142–156

Daily Block Scheduling
Each day in this Lesson Pacing Guide represents a 40–50 minute period. Teachers using block scheduling may combine days to revise pacing. In addition, teachers may differentiate and support core instruction by integrating components for extended and intensive support, as students require. See the Guide to Selected Leveled Resources (facing page).

Guide to Selected Leveled Resources

RTI Tier 1 (students performing on level)			✓ More Accessible I Am a Native of North America	✓✓ More Complex Volar: To Fly
Warm Up	Whole class instruction; Group work	**Practice, model,** and **monitor** fluency, working **with the whole class** or **in groups.**	**Vocabulary** and **Reading Warm-ups B,** ***Unit 3 Resources,*** pp. 62–63, 65	**Vocabulary** and **Reading Warm-ups B,** ***Unit 3 Resources,*** pp. 80–81, 83
Comprehension/Skills	Whole class instruction; Independent work	**Support** and **monitor** comprehension and skills development, having students complete the activities, graphic organizers, and interactive prompts **independently** or **as a class.**	• ***Reader's Notebook,*** adapted instruction and full selection EL ***Reader's Notebook: English Learner's Version,*** adapted instruction and adapted selection • **Reading Skill Graphic Organizer B,** ***Graphic Organizer Transparencies,*** p. 83 • **Literary Analysis Graphic Organizer B,** ***Graphic Organizer Transparencies,*** p. 86	• ***Reader's Notebook,*** adapted instruction and summary EL ***Reader's Notebook: English Learner's Version,*** adapted instruction and summary • **Reading Skill Graphic Organizer B,** ***Graphic Organizer Transparencies,*** p. 83 • **Literary Analysis Graphic Organizer B,** ***Graphic Organizer Transparencies,*** p. 86
Monitor Progress	A	**Monitor** student progress with the differentiated curriculum-based assessment in the *Unit Resources.*	• **Selection Test B,** ***Unit 3 Resources,*** pp. 77–79 • **Open-Book Test,** ***Unit 3 Resources,*** pp. 71–73	• **Selection Test B,** ***Unit 3 Resources,*** pp. 98–100 • **Open-Book Test,** ***Unit 3 Resources,*** pp. 92–94
Assess/Screen	A	**Assess** student progress using Benchmark Test 5.	• **Benchmark Test 5,** ***Unit 3 Resources,*** pp. 120–125	• **Benchmark Test 5,** ***Unit 3 Resources,*** pp. 120–125

RTI Tier 2 (students requiring intervention)			✓ More Accessible I Am a Native of North America	✓✓ More Complex Volar: To Fly
Warm Up	Group work; One-on-one teaching	**Practice, model,** and **monitor** fluency **in groups** or **with individuals.**	• **Vocabulary and Reading Warm-ups A,** ***Unit 3 Resources,*** pp. 62–64 • ***Reality Central,*** "Making Sport of Tradition" • ***Hear It!*** **Audio CD (adapted text)**	• **Vocabulary and Reading Warm-ups A,** ***Unit 3 Resources,*** pp. 80–82 • ***Reality Central,*** "In Your Dreams" • ***Hear It!*** **Audio CD**
Comprehension/Skills	Group work; One-on-one teaching	• **Support** and **monitor** comprehension and skills development, working **in small groups** or **with individuals.** • **Pair** students with more advanced peers and have them complete the writing activity in the *Real-World Writing Journal*. • As students complete the selection in the appropriate version of the *Reader's Notebook,* **monitor** comprehension frequently with group questions and individual instruction. • **Model** strategies while guiding students in completing the activities and prompts in the *Reader's Notebook,* as well as the graphic organizers. • **Practice** skills and **monitor** mastery with the *Reading Kit* worksheets.	• ***Real-World Writing Journal,*** Lesson 3, pp. 78–81 • ***Reader's Notebook: Adapted Version,*** adapted instruction and adapted selection EL ***Reader's Notebook: English Learner's Version,*** adapted instruction and adapted selection • **Reading Skill Graphic Organizer A,** ***Graphic Organizer Transparencies,*** p. 81 • **Literary Analysis Graphic Organizer A,** ***Graphic Organizer Transparencies,*** p. 84 • ***Reading Kit,*** Practice worksheets, pp. 100, 106, 110, 114, 120	• ***Real-World Writing Journal,*** Lesson 4, pp. 82–85 • ***Reader's Notebook: Adapted Version,*** adapted instruction and summary EL ***Reader's Notebook: English Learner's Version,*** adapted instruction and summary • **Reading Skill Graphic Organizer A,** ***Graphic Organizer Transparencies,*** p. 82 • **Literary Analysis Graphic Organizer A,** ***Graphic Organizer Transparencies,*** p. 85 • ***Reading Kit,*** Practice worksheets, pp. 100, 106, 110, 114, 120
Monitor Progress	A	**Monitor** student progress with the differentiated curriculum-based assessment in the *Unit Resources* and in the *Reading Kit.*	• **Selection Test A,** ***Unit 3 Resources,*** pp. 74–76 • ***Reading Kit,*** Assess worksheets, pp. 101, 107, 111, 115, 121	• **Selection Test A,** ***Unit 3 Resources,*** pp. 95–97 • ***Reading Kit,*** Assess worksheets, pp. 101, 107, 111, 115, 121
Assess/Screen	A	**Assess** student progress using the Benchmark Test 5.	• **Benchmark Test 5,** ***Unit 3 Resources,*** pp. 120–125	• **Benchmark Test 5,** ***Unit 3 Resources,*** pp. 120–125

TIER 3 Tier 3 intervention may require consultation with the student's special-education or dyslexia specialist. For additional support, see the Tier 2 activities and resources listed above.

One-on-one teaching | Group work | Whole class instruction | Independent work | A Assessment

For a complete guide to selection support, including support for Advanced students, see the Overview of Resources in the frontmatter.

✓ I Am a Native of North America
✓ Volar: To Fly

RESOURCES FOR:

- **L1** Special-Needs Students
- **L2** Below-Level Students (Tier 2)
- **L3** On-Level Students (Tier 1)
- **L4** Advanced Students (Tier 1)
- **EL** English Learners
- **All** All Students

Vocabulary/Fluency/Prior Knowledge

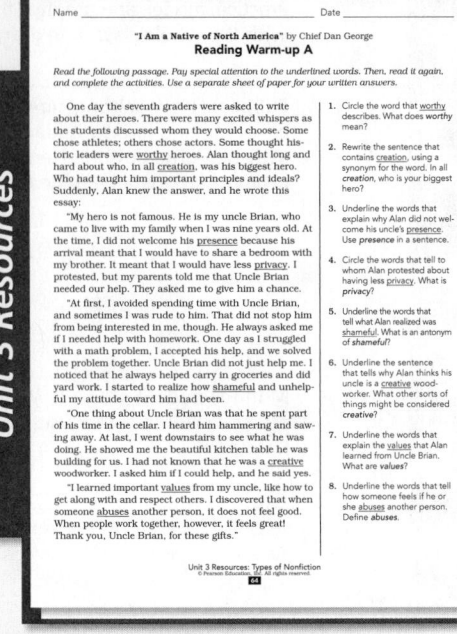

EL **L1** **L2** **Reading Warm-ups A and B,** pp. 64–65, 82–83

Also available for these selections:

EL **L1** **L2** **Vocabulary Warm-ups A and B,** pp. 62–63, 80–81

All **Writing About the Big Question,** pp. 66, 84

All **Vocabulary Builder,** pp. 69, 87

Reader's Notebooks

Pre- and postreading pages for both selections, as well as the selection "I Am a Native of North America," appear in an interactive format in the *Reader's Notebooks*. Each *Notebook* is differentiated for a different group of learners. The selections in the Adapted and English Learner's versions are abridged.

- **L2** **L3** *Reader's Notebook*
- **L1** *Reader's Notebook: Adapted Version*
- **EL** *Reader's Notebook: English Learner's Version*
- **EL** *Reader's Notebook: Spanish Version*

© *Common Core Companion*

Additional instruction and practice for each Common Core State Standard

Selection Support

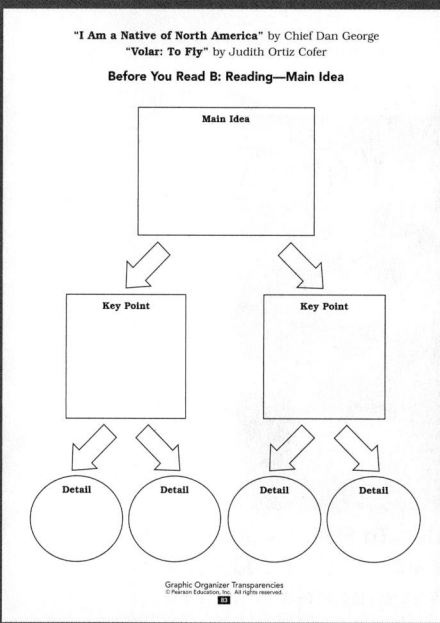

"I Am a Native of North America" by Chief Dan George
"Volar: To Fly" by Judith Ortiz Cofer
Before You Read B: Reading—Main Idea

Graphic Organizer Transparencies

EL **L3** **Reading: Graphic Organizer B,** p. 83

Also available for these selections:
EL **L1** **L2** **Reading: Graphic Organizer A,**
pp. 81, 82 (partially filled in)

EL **L1** **L2** **Literary Analysis: Graphic**
Organizer A, pp. 84, 85 (partially
filled in)

EL **L3** **Literary Analysis: Graphic Organizer B,**
p. 86

Skills Development/Extension

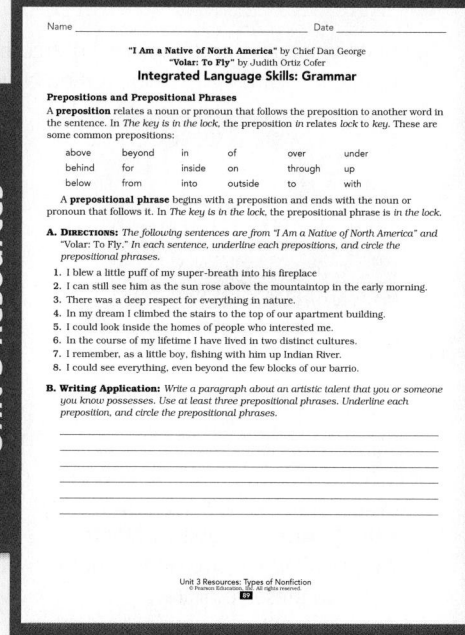

"I Am a Native of North America" by Chief Dan George
"Volar: To Fly" by Judith Ortiz Cofer
Integrated Language Skills: Grammar

Unit 3 Resources

EL **L3** **L4** **Grammar,** p. 89

Also available for these selections:
All **Reading: Main Idea,** pp. 67, 85

All **Literary Analysis: Reflective Essay,**
pp. 68, 86

L4 **Enrichment,** pp. 70, 88

EL **L3** **L4** **Support for Writing,** p. 90

L3 **L4** **Support for Extend Your Learning,**
p. 91

Assessment

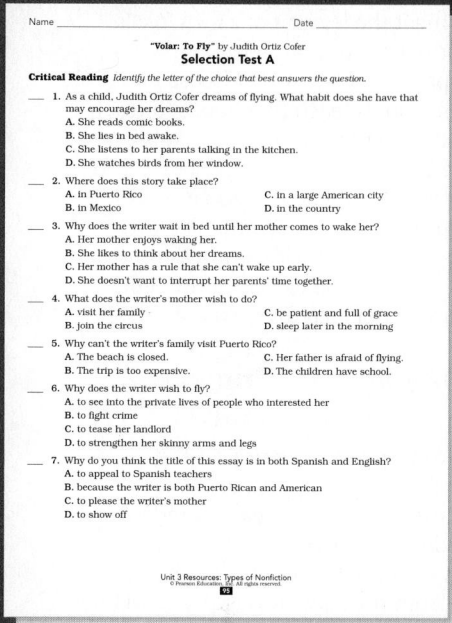

"Volar: To Fly" by Judith Ortiz Cofer
Selection Test A

EL **L1** **L2** **Selection Test A,** pp. 74–46, 95–97

Also available for these selections:
All **Open-Book Test,** pp. 71–73, 92–94

EL **L3** **L4** **Selection Test B,** pp. 77–79, 98–100

![PHLit Online! www.PHLitOnline.com]

Online Resources: All print materials are also available online.

- complete narrated selection text
- a thematically related video with writing prompt
- an interactive graphic organizer
- highlighting feature
- access to all student print resources, adapted to individual student needs
- Spanish and English summaries
- adapted selection translations in Spanish

Get Connected! (thematic video with writing prompt)

Also available:
Background Video
All videos are available in Spanish.

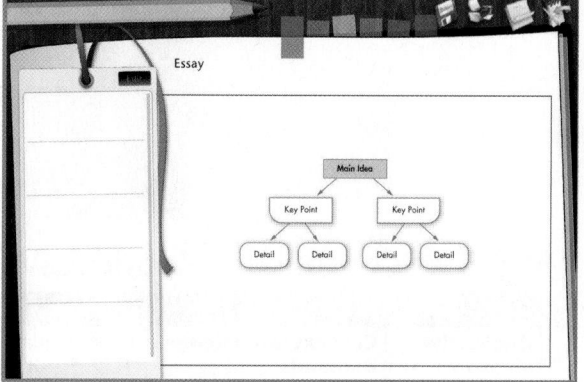

Writer's Journal (with graphics feature)

Also available:
Vocabulary Central (tools, activities, and songs for studying vocabulary)

❶ Leveled Texts

You may use either "I Am a Native of North America" or "Volar: To Fly" to meet the lesson objectives. Skills instruction for both selections appears on page 441. Choose one selection to teach (or choose to teach both). The Text Complexity Rubric at the bottom of this page will help you determine which selection is more appropriate for your students. Use the Reader and Task Suggestions on the facing page to help all students read text of increasing complexity.

❷ ⓒ Introducing the CCS Standards

Introduce the standards on the student page. (Note that the lesson element with which each standard is addressed is identified in parentheses after the text of the standard.) Call out the standards that you will cover with the selections, explaining to students what each requires and how they will address it as they work through the selection you have chosen. Standards labeled "Spiral Review" are introduced in the Literary Analysis Workshop for this unit.

Before You Read

I Am a Native of North America • Volar: To Fly

❶ ⓒ Leveled Texts

Build your skills and improve your comprehension of literary nonfiction with texts of increasing complexity.

Read **"I Am a Native of North America"** to discover the author's desire to preserve his Native American culture.

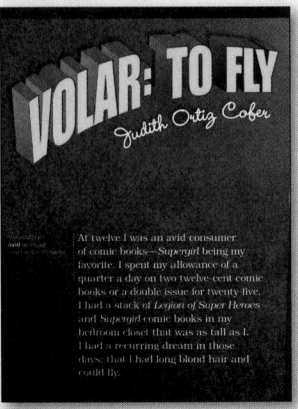

Read **"Volar: To Fly"** to learn about the author's childhood wish to escape her life and fly.

❷ ⓒ Common Core State Standards

Meet these standards with either **"I Am a Native of North America"** (p. 444) or **"Volar: To Fly"** (p. 452).

Reading Informational Text

2. Determine two or more central ideas in a text and analyze their development over the course of the text; provide an objective summary of the text. *(Reading Skill: Main Idea)*

3. Analyze the interactions between individuals, events, and ideas in a text. *(Literary Analysis: Reflective Essay)*

6. Determine an author's point of view or purpose in a text and analyze how the author distinguishes his or her position from that of others. *(Literary Analysis: Spiral Review)*

7. Compare and contrast a text to an audio, video, or multimedia version of the text, analyzing each medium's portrayal of the subject. *(Speaking and Listening: Response)*

Writing

2.a. Introduce a topic clearly, previewing what is to follow; organize ideas, concepts, and information, using strategies

such as definition, classification, comparison/contrast, and cause/effect. *(Writing: Outline)*

Language

1.a. Explain the function of phrases and clauses in general and their function in specific sentences. *(Conventions: Prepositions and Prepositional Phrases)*

5.b. Use the relationship between particular words to better understand each of the words. *(Vocabulary: Synonyms and Antonyms)*

6. Acquire and use accurately grade-appropriate general academic and domain-specific words and phrases; gather vocabulary knowledge when considering a word or phrase important to comprehension or expression. *(Vocabulary: Word Study)*

440 Types of Nonfiction

ⓒ Text Complexity Rubric: Leveled Texts

Text complexity is determined by both qualitative and quantitative measures. For this reason, the quantitative measure of a more complex selection may be lower than that of a more accessible selection.

		✓ I Am a Native of North America	✓✓ Volar: To Fly
Qualitative Measures	**Context/Knowledge Demands**	Understanding of Native American culture 1 2 ③ 4 5	Understanding of U.S. Puerto Rican culture 1 2 ③ 4 5
	Structure/Language Conventionality and Clarity	On-level vocabulary; some long sentences; culturalisms; footnoted unfamiliar terms; essay structure 1 2 3 ④ 5	On-level vocabulary; complex sentences; Spanish phrases; structural digression 1 2 3 ④ 5
	Levels of Meaning/ Purpose/Concept Level	Accessible concept (conflict between Native American and modern cultures) 1 ② 3 4 5	Challenging concept (what it takes to feel at home) 1 2 3 ④ 5
Quantitative Measures	**Text Length**	Word Count: 1,187	Word Count: 1,030
	Lexile	940L	675L
Overall Complexity		✓ **More accessible**	✓✓ **More complex**

Reading Skill: Main Idea

The **main, or central, idea** is the most important idea in a work or a passage of text. A single main idea may grow out of two or more important ideas that develop throughout the text. Sometimes the author directly states the main idea and then provides the key points that support it. These key points are supported in turn by details such as examples and descriptions.

Other times, the main idea is unstated. The author provides only the key points or supporting details that add up to the main idea. To understand the main idea, **make connections between key points and supporting details.**

- Notice how the writer groups details.
- Look for sentences that pull details together.

Using the Strategy: Main Idea Chart

Use a chart like this one to help you make connections as you read.

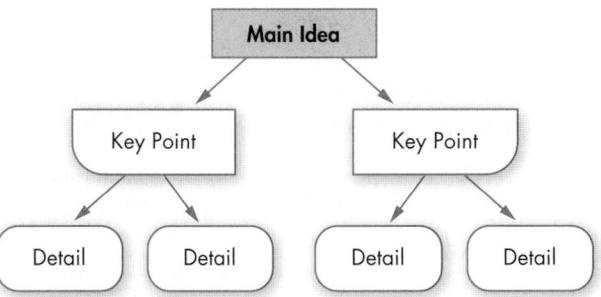

Literary Analysis: Reflective Essay

A **reflective essay** is a brief prose work that presents a writer's thoughts and feelings—or reflections—about an experience or idea. The purpose is to communicate these thoughts and feelings so that readers will respond with thoughts and feelings of their own. As you read a reflective essay, think about the ideas the writer is sharing and analyze the interactions between individuals, events, and ideas in the text.

Before You Read: I Am a Native of North America • Volar: To Fly **441**

❸ Reading Skill
Main Idea

1. Introduce the skill, using the instruction on the student page.
2. Tell students that they will practice linking key points and main ideas as they read.

❹ Using the Strategy

Give students a copy of either **Reading Skill Graphic Organizer A** or **B** (*Graphic Organizer Transparencies*, pp. 81–83) to record and connect key points, details, and main ideas as they read. Use the examples in **Reading Skill Graphic Organizer A**, which is partially filled in, to model the process of completing the organizer.

❺ Literary Analysis
Reflective Essay

1. Introduce the skill using the instruction on the student page.
2. Tell students that they will note elements of reflective essays as they read.

Think Aloud: Model the Skill

Model a way of approaching reflective essays. Say to students:

To read reflective essays effectively, I recall that their purpose is to explore thoughts and feelings. For example, an author may write about a childhood event and its impact. It will likely be an important event, such as the birth of a new sibling. That's because authors often reflect on events or topics about which they feel strongly. So, to read reflective essays, I first identify the topic. Then, I identify the author's view of the topic. Finally, I decide what I think about it.

ⓒ Text Complexity: Reader and Task Suggestions

✓ I Am a Native of North America		✓✓ Volar: To Fly	
Preparing to Read the Text	**Leveled Tasks**	**Preparing to Read the Text**	**Leveled Tasks**
• Using the Background information on p. 443, preview the history of the Coast Salish Indians. • Model strategies for breaking down long sentences and defining culturalisms, such as reading sentence parts and paraphrasing. • Guide students to use Multidraft Reading strategies (TE p. 443).	*Structure/Language* If students will have difficulty with subject-specific language, have them read to identify the author's positive feelings for his culture. Have them reread, noting sentences or culturalisms they find confusing. *Evaluating* If students will not have difficulty with language, have them note ways in which the author's perspective on white culture comes through in the essay. Ask students to describe that perspective.	• Using the Background information on p. 451, explore how Puerto Rican history might affect a young immigrant girl. • Use the Differentiated Instruction note on p. 453 to help students identify real and dream elements. • Guide students to use Multidraft Reading strategies (TE p. 451).	*Structure/Language* If students will have difficulty with structure, have them read for details of the narrator's home life. Have them reread, charting real and "dream" elements. *Analyzing* If students will not have difficulty with structure, have them note as they read ways in which the author structurally contrasts dreams and reality to show a difference between her young and adult selves.

441

❶ Writing About the Big Question

1. Review the assignment with the class.

2. Explain that different cultures have different priorities, or values, about what people need to learn.

3. Have students complete the sentence starter. Review responses as a class. (**Sample response:** It is important to <u>discover</u> the traditions and beliefs of people from different cultures because we both learn new ideas and also recognize common ground.)

4. Remind students that their answers will help them think about the Big Question, "What should we learn?"

While You Read

Tell students that as they read, they should consider how Native Americans' values influenced the way they lived and the choices they made.

❷ Vocabulary

1. Have students preview the selection vocabulary.

2. For each word, have students say the word aloud.

3. Then, use the word in a sentence that defines the word.

4. Finally, repeat your definitional sentence or a similar sentence with the word missing and have the class "fill in the blank" chorally. Here are some examples:

   When something is <u>distinct</u>, it is separate and different. Someone who speaks Japanese may struggle to understand English because the two languages are so entirely [students say "distinct"].

   When something is <u>communal</u>, it is shared by the members of a community. If many families live together in one house, the house is [students say "communal"].

❸ Word Study

1. Introduce the skill, using the instruction in the box.

2. Ask students to name another *-just-* word that means the same as *fairness*. (*justice*)

❶ What should we *learn?*

Writing About the Big Question

In "I Am a Native of North America," Chief Dan George recalls the traditions that his Native American culture valued above all. Use this sentence starter to develop your ideas about the Big Question.

It is important to **discover** the traditions and beliefs of people from different cultures because _____.

While You Read Learn how Native Americans' values influenced the way they lived and the choices they made.

❷ Vocabulary

Read each word and its definition. Decide whether you know the word well, know it a little bit, or do not know it at all. After you read, see how your knowledge of each word has increased.

- **distinct** (di stiŋkt´) *adj.* separate and different (p. 444) *Sparrows and owls are two <u>distinct</u> groups of birds.* *distinctive adj. distinctly adv. distinction n. indistinct adj.*

- **communal** (kə myo͞on´ əl) *adj.* shared by all (p. 444) *Campers ate together in a <u>communal</u> lunchroom.* *communally adv. commune n. commune v. community n.*

- **justifies** (jus´ tə fīz´) *v.* excuses; explains (p. 446) *Her fear <u>justifies</u> her strange behavior.* *justify v. justifiable adj. justification n.*

- **promote** (prə mōt´) *v.* encourage; contribute to the growth of (p. 447) *The teacher tried to <u>promote</u> her students' good habits. promotion n. promotional adj.*

- **hoarding** (hôr´ diŋ) *v.* accumulating and storing a supply as a reserve (p. 447) *After the war, <u>hoarding</u> food made her feel safer. hoard v. hoarder n.*

- **integration** (in´ tə grā´ shən) *n.* the end of separation of cultural or racial groups (p. 448) *<u>Integration</u> allowed students of all races to attend school together. integrate v. integrating v.*

442 Types of Nonfiction

❸ Word Study

The **Latin root** *-just-* means "law" or "fair and right."

In this essay, Chief Dan George cannot understand a culture that **justifies**, or defends as right, the killing of others in a war.

Vocabulary Development

Vocabulary Knowledge Rating
Create a **Vocabulary Knowledge Rating Chart** (*Professional Development Guidebook*, p. 33) for this selection. Include the selection vocabulary and the Big Question word that appears in the Writing About the Big Question sentence starter on this page. (The Big Question vocabulary is introduced on pp. 406–407.)

Give students a copy of the chart. Read the words aloud, and have students mark their rating in the Before Reading column. Urge them to be alert to these words as they read and discuss the selection.

Tally how many students think they know a word to gauge how much instruction to provide. As students read and discuss the selection, point out the words and their context.

PHLit Online! **Vocabulary Central**, featuring tools, activities, and songs for studying vocabulary, is available online at **www.PHLitOnline.com**.

Meet
Chief Dan George
(1899–1981)

Author of
I Am a Native of North America

Chief Dan George, the son of a tribal chief, was named "Tes-wah-no" but was also known as Dan Slaholt. At age five, he was sent to a mission boarding school, where his last name was changed to George.

At seventeen, Dan George left school and began working. While he was working as a bus driver, he won the role of an aging Indian in a TV series.

Life as an Actor George was called one of the "finest natural actors anywhere." He won acting awards in Canada and earned parts in major motion pictures. With fame, George became a spokesman for Native Americans.

DID YOU KNOW?

Chief Dan George was more than sixty years old when he became a movie actor.

❹ BACKGROUND FOR THE ESSAY

Vancouver-Area Native Americans

Chief Dan George was a member of the Coast Salish Indians in western Canada. His ancestors organized their lives according to a cycle of hunting, food gathering, and cultural activities. During winter, the people stayed in large villages near sheltered bays. In spring, they moved to the beaches, where they fished, hunted, and gathered berries. Then, in the fall, groups met along the rivers to fish. Their cycle of living connected them closely to the natural world.

I Am a Native of North America **443**

🔔 Daily Bellringer

For each class during which you teach this selection, have students complete one of the five Sentence Modeling activities for Week 14 in the *Daily Bellringer Activities* booklet.

❹ Background

Vancouver-Area Native Americans

The Coast Salish people are a group of Native American Indians who have traditionally lived in the Pacific Northwest regions of the United States and Canada. They are part of a larger group of people who speak a dialect of the Salish language. The Coast Salish people built permanent houses along the water and lived in them with their extended families. Each family had its own house, and several houses combined to make a village. Members of each village worked together to gather and store food for winter. Today, many of the Salish people live on reservations, where many features of their culture have lost relevance in the modern world. Members of some Pacific Northwest tribes are working to restore some of their traditions and rights.

Multidraft Reading

This icon ● marks natural pauses in the selection. To assist struggling readers and to deepen reading for all, assign the text in "chunks," following the icons, and apply multidraft reading protocols. For each reading, have students set the purpose indicated:

- **First reading**—identifying key ideas and details and answering any Reading Checks.

- **Second reading**—analyzing craft and structure and responding to the side-column prompts.

- **Third reading**—integrating knowledge and ideas, connecting to other texts and the world, and answering the end-of-selection questions.

For more guidance, refer to the *Classroom Strategies and Teaching Routines* card on multidraft reading.

For more about the author, practice with the selection vocabulary, or more background, go online at **www.PHLitOnline.com**.

❶ Activating Prior Knowledge

1. Prepare an **Anticipation Guide** (*Professional Development Guidebook,* p. 38), with the following statements:

   • Modern American culture poses a great threat to Native American traditions and culture.

   • One thing that makes America great is its ability to absorb people of all cultures and traditions.

2. Give students a copy of the prepared **Anticipation Guide,** and have them mark their responses in the Me column. Have students discuss the statements in pairs or groups and mark the Guides again in the Group column.

3. For further guidance, use the **Classroom Strategies and Teaching Routines** card for **Anticipation Guides.**

Concept Connector ➡

Students will follow up on their **Anticipation Guides** after reading.

Individual Activity

Ask students to write a journal entry in which they reflect on their family's or community's cultures and traditions. Do they cherish the traditions or feel the need to break from them? Invite volunteers to share their responses during the lesson.

❷ About the Selection

In this essay, Chief Dan George recalls the traditional ways of his people. He questions certain contemporary values and choices and anticipates the vanishing of his culture. He pleads for love and tolerance as the hope for a peaceful future.

❸ Reflective Essay

1. Remind students that a reflective essay contains the writer's thoughts about his or her own experiences.

2. Read the bracketed text aloud, and **ask** the Reflective Essay question.
   Answer: Chief Dan George reflects on his people's love and respect for each other and for nature.

Vocabulary
distinct (di stiŋkt´) *adj.* separate and different
communal (kə myōōn´ əl) *adj.* shared by all

Reflective Essay
What experience or idea is the author reflecting on here?

n the course of my lifetime I have lived in two **distinct** cultures. I was born into a culture that lived in **communal** houses. My grandfather's house was eighty feet long. It was called a smoke house, and it stood down by the beach along the inlet.[1] All my grandfather's sons and their families lived in this large dwelling. Their sleeping apartments were separated by blankets made of bull rush reeds, but one open fire in the middle served the cooking needs of all. In houses like these, throughout the tribe, people learned to live with one another; learned to serve one another; learned to respect the rights of one another. And children shared the thoughts of the adult world and found themselves surrounded by aunts and uncles and cousins who loved them and did not threaten them. My father was born in such a house and learned from infancy how to love people and be at home with them.

And beyond this acceptance of one another there was a deep respect for everything in nature that surrounded them.

1. inlet (in´ let´) *n.* narrow strip of water jutting into a body of land from a river, a lake, or an ocean.

444 Types of Nonfiction

Vocabulary Development　　　© **CCSS** Language 6

Thematic Vocabulary: The Big Question
As students are discussing "I Am a Native of North America," encourage them to use the thematic vocabulary presented in Introducing the Big Question, pp. 406–407. You might encourage them with sentence starters like these:

1. Chief Dan George *explores* ways that his culture and modern American culture . . .

2. He *investigates* how Native American culture teaches . . .

3. He *questions* how modern American culture . . .

4. He *analyzes* each culture's priorities and *discovers* . . .

5. Ultimately, Chief George hopes readers will *understand* that . . .

❶❷ I Am a NATIVE of North America

Chief Dan George

❹ **Critical Viewing**
Possible response: The photograph suggests the author's idea that it is important to appreciate nature and its beauty.

❺ **Connecting to the Big Question**

1. Remind students that parents will teach their children the lessons they feel the children should learn.

2. Have students reread the bracketed text on page 445. **Ask:** What does Chief Dan George's father tell him about fishing for fun? How do the values of Native American culture influence the father's direction of his son's actions?
Possible response: Chief Dan George's father tells his son not to fish for fun, only for food. Native American values influence this directive because these values say that the earth and everything it contains is a gift to be respected and loved.

3. **Ask:** Is it important for parents to teach their children such cultural values? Explain.
Possible response: Yes. It is important to pass on to children the values that parents and cultures hold true. In this way, these values can be passed on to future generations.

My father loved the earth and all its creatures. The earth was his second mother. The earth and everything it contained was a gift from See-see-am² . . . and the way to thank this great spirit was to use his gifts with respect. ●

I remember, as a little boy, fishing with him up Indian River and I can still see him as the sun rose above the mountain top in the early morning . . . I can see him standing by the water's edge with his arms raised above his head while he softly moaned . . . "Thank you, thank you." It left a deep impression on my young mind.

And I shall never forget his disappointment when once he caught me gaffing for fish³ "just for the fun of it." "My Son," he said, "the Great Spirit gave you those fish to be your brothers, to feed you when you are hungry. You must respect them. You must not kill them just for the fun of it."

This then was the culture I was born into and for some years the only one I really knew or tasted. This is why I find

❹ ▲ **Critical Viewing**
What ideas expressed by Chief Dan George does this photograph suggest? **[Connect]**

❻ ✓ **Reading Check**
What did Chief Dan George's father teach him about the Earth?

❻ **Reading Check**
Answer: He taught him to respect and love the Earth and give thanks to the Great Spirit for the gifts of the Earth.

2. **See-see-am** the name of the Great Spirit, or "The Chief Above," in the Salishan language of Chief George's people.
3. **gaffing for fish** using a barbed spear to catch river fish.

I Am a Native of North America **445**

Differentiated Instruction for Universal Access

Culturally Responsive Instruction
Culture Focus Point out that this essay describes not only the differences between two cultures but also the many qualities that are common to all people. Invite students to share knowledge about the values of their own home culture or family's culture of origin. Discuss ways that these values are similar to or different from those that Chief Dan George describes in Native American culture and in modern

American culture. Help students create a three-way Venn diagram, or offer them one (see *Graphic Organizer Transparencies*, p. 215) to show the similarities and differences among the three cultures. Students should label one section *Chief Dan George's Native Culture*, one section *Modern American Culture*, and one section *My Home Culture*.

PHLit Online!
This selection is available in interactive format in the **Enriched Online Student Edition**, at www.PHLitOnline.com, which includes a thematically related video with writing prompt and an interactive graphic organizer.

❼ Critical Viewing

Possible response: The people in the photograph are giving thanks for the bounty of the water.

❽ Critical Thinking

Draw Conclusions

1. Read aloud the bracketed paragraph as students read along silently. Challenge them to identify the topic sentence in the paragraph.
   Answer: The first sentence is the topic sentence.

2. Then, discuss the details and examples the author uses to support the idea.
   Answer: He gives examples of the attacks on nature, citing the building of cities; the stripping of mountains for wood, minerals, and other resources; and the poisoning of the water and air.

3. **Ask** students to identify the culture the author describes.
   Answer: He is describing the culture of modern North America.

4. Finally, **ask** students to draw a conclusion about the author's attitude toward modern America in this paragraph.
   Possible response: The author feels anger and confusion when he thinks about what the "white brother" has done to the environment.

Spiral Review

Author's Point of View

1. Remind students that they studied the concept of author's point of view in the Unit 3 Literary Analysis Workshop (pp. 408–419).

2. **Ask** the Spiral Review question.

   Possible response: Chief Dan Gorge cares a great deal about his subject and it upsets him. He writes with detail and emotion. For example, he uses phrases such as "deep hate," "tearing things from the bosom of mother earth," and "chokes the air."

❼ ▲ **Critical Viewing** Based on what you have read, describe what the people in these boats might be doing. **[Speculate]**

Vocabulary
justifies (jus´ tə fīz´)
v. excuses; explains

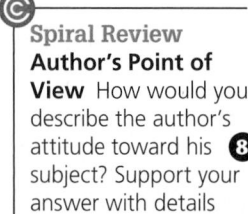

Spiral Review
Author's Point of View How would you describe the author's attitude toward his ❽ subject? Support your answer with details from the essay.

it hard to accept many of the things I see around me.

I see people living in smoke houses hundreds of times bigger than the one I knew. But the people in one apartment do not even know the people in the next and care less about them.

It is also difficult for me to understand the deep hate that exists among people. It is hard to understand a culture that justifies the killing of millions in past wars, and is at this very moment preparing bombs to kill even greater numbers. It is hard for me to understand a culture that spends more on wars and weapons to kill, than it does on education and welfare to help and develop.

It is hard for me to understand a culture that not only hates and fights its brothers but even attacks nature and abuses her. I see my white brother going about blotting out nature from his cities. I see him strip the hills bare, leaving ugly wounds on the face of mountains. I see him tearing things from the bosom of mother earth as though she were a monster, who refused to share her treasures with him. I see him throw poison in the waters, indifferent to the life he kills there; and he chokes the air with deadly fumes.

My white brother does many things well for he is more clever than my people but I wonder if he knows how to love well. I wonder if he has ever really learned to love at all. Perhaps he only loves the things that are his own but never

❾

446 Types of Nonfiction

Vocabulary Development

Vocabulary Knowledge Rating
When students have completed reading and discussing "I Am a Native of North America," have them take out their **Vocabulary Knowledge Rating Chart** for this selection. Read the words aloud once more, and have students rate their knowledge of words again in the After Reading column. Clarify any words that are still problematic. Have students write their own definitions and examples or sentences in the appropriate column. Then, have students complete the Vocabulary Practice activities at the end of the selection. Encourage students to use the words in further discussion and written work about this selection. Remind them that they will be accountable for these words on the **Selection Test**, *Unit 3 Resources*, pp. 74–76 or 77–79.

learned to love the things that are outside and beyond him. And this is, of course, not love at all, for man must love all creation or he will love none of it. Man must love fully or he will become the lowest of the animals. It is the power to love that makes him the greatest of them all . . . for he alone of all animals is capable of love.

Love is something you and I must have. We must have it because our spirit feeds upon it. We must have it because without it we become weak and faint. Without love our self-esteem weakens. Without it our courage fails. Without love we can no longer look out confidently at the world. Instead we turn inwardly and begin to feed upon our own personalities and little by little we destroy ourselves.

You and I need the strength and joy that comes from knowing that we are loved. With it we are creative. With it we march tirelessly. With it, and with it alone, we are able to sacrifice for others.

There have been times when we all wanted so desperately to feel a reassuring hand upon us . . . there have been lonely times when we so wanted a strong arm around us . . . I cannot tell you how deeply I miss my wife's presence when I return from a trip. Her love was my greatest joy, my strength, my greatest blessing. ●

I am afraid my culture has little to offer yours. But my culture did prize friendship and companionship. It did not look on privacy as a thing to be clung to, for privacy builds up walls and walls promote distrust. My culture lived in big family communities, and from infancy people learned to live with others.

My culture did not prize the hoarding of private possessions; in fact, to hoard was a shameful thing to do among my people. The Indian looked on all things in nature as belonging to him and he expected to share them with others and to take only what he needed.

Everyone likes to give as well as receive. No one wishes only to receive all the time. We have taken much from your culture . . . I wish you had taken something from our culture . . . for there were some beautiful and good things in it.

I Am a Native of North America **447**

Main Idea
What key words or sentences so far have helped you determine the essay's main idea?

Reflective Essay
What experiences does the author reflect on here?

Vocabulary
promote (prə mōt′) *v.* encourage; contribute to the growth of
hoarding (hôr′ diŋ) v. accumulating and storing a supply as a reserve

❾ Main Idea

1. Explain to students that writers reinforce their main ideas by using key words, phrases, or sentences over and over.

2. Have students reread the bracketed passage that begins on page 446 and skim the previous pages. Then, **ask** the Main Idea question.
Possible response: Students should identify the words *love* and *man*, which are repeated several times. From earlier in the essay, students may identify: *acceptance, respect, the great spirit, my white brothers,* "It is difficult for me to understand . . . ," "love is something we must have," and "without love . . ."

3. Have students add their ideas to their graphic organizers.

❿ Reflective Essay

1. Read aloud the second bracketed passage while students read along silently.

2. **Ask** students the Reflective Essay question.
Answer: The author reflects on his experiences as a man who misses his wife's love and strength.

3. Challenge students to think of a time when they have had feelings similar to those expressed by the author here. Invite volunteers to share their experiences.

▶ **Monitor Progress: Ask** students how they know that "I Am a Native of North America" is a reflective essay.
Answer: The essay presents the author's thoughts and feelings about how Native American culture is changing and disappearing in the modern world.

▶ **Reteach:** If students have difficulty identifying the elements that make the selection a reflective essay, review the essay with them, pointing out moments where the author shares his feelings and thoughts about his culture and his past.

Concept Connector

Anticipation Guide
Have students return to their **Anticipation Guides** and respond to the statements again in the After Reading column. They may do this individually or in their original pairs or groups. Then, lead a class discussion, probing for what students have learned that confirms or invalidates each statement. Encourage them to cite specific details, quotations, or other evidence from the text to support their responses.

Reading Skill Graphic Organizer
Ask students to review the graphic organizer in which they documented the main idea, key points, and details. Then, have students share the graphic organizers they completed and compare their findings.

Writing About the Big Question
Have students compare the sentence starter they completed before reading the essay with their ideas afterward. Ask them whether their thoughts have changed.

Critical Thinking

Before students respond, you may wish to have them write a brief objective summary of the selection. As they answer the questions below, remind them to support their answers with evidence from the text.

1. (a) They learn to live together, to serve one another, and to respect the rights of others. (b) **Possible response:** Modern culture is more focused on personal rights and possessions than on the communal ties valued by Native American culture, and its members are less conscious of their relationship to the land than are members of Native American culture.

2. (a) He cannot understand why people hate one another, why they mistreat nature and the earth, and how they can show so little love for one another. (b) He means that his "white brother" has been more successful in spreading his values than George's culture has been. George also feels that his "white brother" has been more clever at inventing new technologies.

3. (a) By "brotherhood," he means love, patience, trust, acceptance, peace, and forgiveness among all people. (b) **Possible response:** Brotherhood is extremely important. It represents the best human qualities—love, mutual respect, and the ability to live in peace.

4. **Possible response:** Students may suggest that people of different cultures can live together and maintain their cultures while also respecting other cultures. Some students may feel that some cultures tend to dominate others or that people often lose touch with their original culture when in a new culture.

5. **Possible responses:** (a) It is important to know the beliefs and traditions of those who came before because they can teach us values that offer guidance and because they can help us feel connected to a larger community. (b) If we ignore the past, we may miss the opportunity to learn from people's successes and failures.

Soon it will be too late to know my culture, for *integration* is upon us and soon we will have no values but yours. Already many of our young people have forgotten the old ways. And many have been shamed of their Indian ways by scorn and ridicule. My culture is like a wounded deer that has crawled away into the forest to bleed and die alone.

The only thing that can truly help us is genuine love. You must truly love us, be patient with us and share with us. And we must love you—with a genuine love that forgives and forgets . . . a love that forgives the terrible sufferings your culture brought ours when it swept over us like a wave crashing along a beach . . . with a love that forgets and lifts up its head and sees in your eyes an answering love of trust and acceptance.

This is brotherhood . . . anything less is not worthy of the name.

I have spoken.

Vocabulary

integration (in′ tə grā′ shən) *n.* the end of separation of cultural or racial groups

Critical Thinking

Cite textual evidence to support your responses.

1. **Key Ideas and Details (a)** Name three things that people learn from growing up in communal homes. Use examples from the essay to support your answer. **(b) Compare and Contrast:** Identify several differences between the "two distinct cultures" in which Chief Dan George lived.

2. **Craft and Structure (a)** What three things puzzle Chief Dan George about his "white brother"? **(b) Interpret:** When Chief Dan George says, "My white brother . . . is more clever than my people," what does he mean by *clever*?

3. **Integration of Knowledge and ideas (a) Analyze:** What is the "brotherhood" that Chief Dan George talks about in the essay? **(b) Evaluate:** Is this brotherhood important? Why or why not?

4. **Integration of Knowledge and Ideas Make a Judgment:** Can people maintain a sense of cultural identity while interacting with another group that does not have the same culture? Explain.

5. **Integration of Knowledge and Ideas (a)** Why it is important to know the beliefs and traditions of those who came before us? **(b)** What could happen if we ignore the past? *[Connect to the Big Question: What should we learn?]*

448 Types of Nonfiction

Assessment Resources

Unit 3 Resources

L1 L2 EL **Selection Test A,** pp. 74–76. Administer Test A to less advanced readers.

L3 L4 EL **Selection Test B,** pp. 77–79. Administer Test B to on-level and more advanced students.

L3 L4 **Open-Book Test,** pp. 71–73. As an alternative, give the Open-Book Test.

All **Customizable Test Bank**

All **Self-tests**
Students may prepare for the **Selection Test** by taking the **Self-test** online.

PHLit Online! All assessment resources are available at **www.PHLitOnline.com**.

Reading Skill: Main Idea

1. (a) What details does Chief Dan George provide about his father's relationship with nature? **(b)** Find a sentence from the work that pulls these details together.

2. What is the **main idea** of the essay?

Literary Analysis: Reflective Essay

3. Craft and Structure Analyze the **reflective essay** in a chart like the one shown. In the first column, write George's reflections on three points. Then, write your response. Trade charts with a partner and discuss your responses. In the third column of your chart, explain whether your responses changed based on your discussion.

George's Reflections	My Responses	After Discussion
Father gives thanks on fishing trip.		

Vocabulary

Acquisition and Use An **antonym** is a word that is opposite in meaning to another word. For the first word in each item, choose the word that is its antonym. Explain your answers.

1. distinct: **(a)** similar **(b)** different **(c)** decided

2. communal: **(a)** busy **(b)** private **(c)** organized

3. justifies: **(a)** supports **(b)** opposes **(c)** excuses

4. promote: **(a)** encourage **(b)** advance **(c)** prevent

5. hoarding: **(a)** storing **(b)** distributing **(c)** saving

6. integration: **(a)** segregation **(b)** assimilation **(c)** mixing

Word Study Use the context of the sentences and what you know about the **Latin root -just-** to explain your answer to each question.

1. If a decision is *unjust,* is it fair?

2. If there is no *justification* for your error, are you to blame?

Word Study

The **Latin root -just-** means "law" or "fair and right."

Apply It Explain how the word root *-just-* contributes to the meanings of these words. Consult a dictionary if necessary.

justice
adjust
injustice

Word Study
Sample answers:
1. No; The root *-just-* means "fair" and *unjust* means "not <u>fair</u>."
2. Yes; The root *-just-* means "fair," and *justification* means "reason or explanation." If there is no <u>fair</u> reason or explanation for an error, you are to blame for it.

Word Study: Apply It
Sample answers: *Justice* is <u>fair</u>ness in how people are treated. To *adjust* is to make changes that can make a situation <u>right</u> or <u>fair</u>. An *injustice* is a situation that is un<u>fair</u>.

Answers continued
5. b; *Hoarding* means "storing a reserve." *Distributing* means "giving away."
6. a; *Integration* means "interaction between cultural or racial groups." *Segregation* means "separation of cultural or racial groups."

Reading Skill

1. (a) The author recalls seeing his father thanking the Great Spirit. He also remembers his father's anger when he caught the author killing fish for fun. (b) **Possible response:** "My father loved the earth and all its creatures."

2. **Possible response:** The author believes it is important for all Americans to love, respect, care for, and forgive one another and to live in peace.

Literary Analysis

3. **Possible response:** (George's Reflection) <u>Point:</u> George's father gives thanks on a fishing trip. <u>Reflection:</u> George is impressed by his father's respect for the natural world. (My Response) I can relate to how a parent's values can be passed down to a child. (George's Reflection) <u>Point:</u> George wonders what his culture can offer American society. <u>Reflection:</u> His culture does not value "the hoarding of private possessions." (My Response) There is too much commercialism today. (George's Reflection) <u>Point:</u> George is concerned that his culture will vanish. <u>Reflection:</u> George feels that many young Native Americans are ashamed of their culture. He feels that love and acceptance can remedy this. (My Response) This concern is understandable because young people often feel pressure to fit in. (Students should share their responses.)

Vocabulary
Acquisition and Use
Sample answers:
1. a; Things that are <u>distinct</u> are different. Things that are <u>similar</u> are nearly the same.
2. b; *Communal* means "shared by all." *Private* means "just for some."
3. b; *Justifies* means "finds reasons for something." *Opposes* means "finds reasons against something."
4. c; *Promote* means "encourage." *Prevent* means "stop."

❶ ⬛ Writing About the Big Question

1. Review the assignment with the class.

2. Suggest to students that learning about ourselves can be extremely important.

3. Have students complete the sentence starter. Review responses as a class. (**Sample response:** Our hopes and dreams help us to <u>examine</u> what is important in our lives because they show us what we wish for most.)

4. Remind students that their answers will help them think about the Big Question, "What should we learn?"

While You Read

Tell students that as they read, they should look for details that reveal the wishes of the author and her mother.

❷ Vocabulary

1. Have students preview the selection vocabulary.

2. For each word, have students say the word aloud.

3. Then, use the word in a sentence that defines the word.

4. Finally, repeat your definitional sentence or a similar sentence with the word missing and have the class "fill in the blank" chorally. Here are some examples:

Something that is <u>dismal</u> is depressing or gloomy. When it rains for days on end, we say that the weather is [students say "dismal"].

<u>Refuse</u> is garbage. Every Tuesday, we separate items for recycling from the trash, and then throw away the remaining [students say "refuse"].

❸ Word Study

1. Introduce the skill, using the instruction in the box.

2. Have students create a meaningful sentence with the word *interrupted.* (**Sample answer:** Despite being *interrupted,* I was still able to complete my homework.)

450

---

❶ 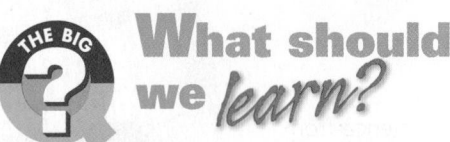 **What should we *learn?***

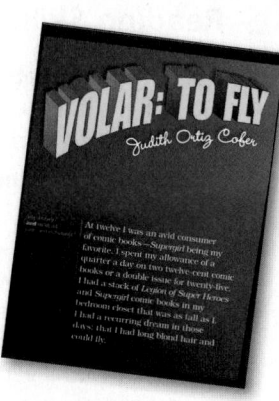

Writing About the Big Question

In "Volar: To Fly," a daughter learns of her mother's deepest wish. Use this sentence starter to develop your ideas about the Big Question.

> Our hopes and dreams help us to **examine** what is important in our lives because they show us _____.

While You Read Look for details that reveal the wishes of the author and her mother. Consider what the author learns from knowing these dreams.

❷ Vocabulary

Read each word and its definition. Decide whether you know the word well, know it a little bit, or do not know it at all. After you read, see how your knowledge of each word has increased.

- **avid** (av´ id) *adj.* eager and enthusiastic (p. 452) *Julia was an <u>avid</u> reader of adventure stories. avidly adv.*

- **obsession** (əb sesh´ ən) *n.* extreme interest in something (p. 455) *Her <u>obsession</u> with soccer keeps her from playing other sports. obsess v. obsessive adj. obsessed adj.*

- **interrupted** (in´ tə rupt´ əd) *v.* briefly stopped someone from speaking or completing a task (p. 455) *Tim <u>interrupted</u> me as I was speaking. interrupt v. interruptive adj. interruption n.*

- **dismal** (diz´ məl) *adj.* dark and gloomy (p. 456) *The grey skies and rainy weather made the day appear <u>dismal</u>. dismally adv.*

- **refuse** (ref´ yo͞oz) *n.* trash; waste (p. 456) *The garbage truck collected all the <u>refuse</u>.*

❸ Word Study

The **Latin root -*rupt*-** means "break" or "burst."

The essay's author knows her parents will be disappointed if their morning talk is **interrupted,** or if their private time is broken.

450 Types of Nonfiction

Vocabulary Development

Vocabulary Knowledge Rating
Create a **Vocabulary Knowledge Rating Chart** (*Professional Development Guidebook*, p. 33) for this selection. Include the selection vocabulary and the Big Question word that appears in the Writing About the Big Question sentence starter on this page. (The Big Question vocabulary is introduced on pp. 406–407.)

Give students a copy of the chart. Read the words aloud, and have students mark their rating in the Before Reading column. Urge them to be alert to these words as they read and discuss the selection.

Tally how many students think they know a word to gauge how much instruction to provide. As students read and discuss the selection, point out the words and their context.

Vocabulary Central, featuring tools, activities, and songs for studying vocabulary, is available online at **www.PHLitOnline.com.**

Meet
Judith Ortiz Cofer
(b. 1952)

Author of
VOLAR: TO FLY

Judith Ortiz Cofer was born in Puerto Rico, but moved to Paterson, New Jersey, with her family when she was very young. Her family made frequent trips between Paterson and Hormigueros, Puerto Rico, where Cofer spent time with her extended family and listened to her grandmother's family stories. In the late 1960s, Cofer's family moved to Augusta, Georgia, where she attended high school and college.

Writing About Cultures Cofer's writing includes fiction, nonfiction, and poetry for both children and adults. Much of Cofer's work addresses differences between the cultures of the United States and Puerto Rico. She is currently a professor of English and creative writing at the University of Georgia.

DID YOU KNOW?
Cofer's first novel, *In The Line of the Sun*, was nominated for the Pulitzer Prize.

❹ BACKGROUND FOR THE ESSAY

Puerto Rico

Puerto Rico is a U.S. territory located between the Caribbean Sea and the North Atlantic Ocean, about 1,000 miles from Miami, Florida. It is approximately three times the size of Rhode Island. Although residents of Puerto Rico were granted U.S. citizenship in 1917, they do not vote in American presidential elections or pay federal taxes. They have their own local government and constitution. Still, as U.S citizens, they can be drafted into military service and must obey federal laws. The dominant language of Puerto Rico is Spanish; however, both English and Spanish are considered official languages.

Volar: To Fly **451**

🕮 Daily Bellringer
For each class during which you teach this selection, have students complete one of the five Sentence Modeling activities for Week 14 in the *Daily Bellringer Activities* booklet.

❹ Background
Puerto Rico

Judith Ortiz Cofer's experience is not uncommon among Puerto Rican families. Many come to live in parts of the United States. In 2002, there were 37.4 million people of Latin or Hispanic origin living in the United States, nearly 10% of them Puerto Rican. More than half of the Puerto Ricans live in the Northeast, such as Paterson, New Jersey, where Ortiz Cofer's family settled. More than half live in urban areas, like the one Ortiz Cofer describes in her essay.

Multidraft Reading

To assist struggling readers and to deepen reading for all, assign the text in "chunks," and apply multidraft reading protocols. For each reading, have students set the purpose indicated:

- **First reading**—identifying key ideas and details and answering any Reading Checks.
- **Second reading**—analyzing craft and structure and responding to the side-column prompts.
- **Third reading**—integrating knowledge and ideas, connecting to other texts and the world, and answering the end-of-selection questions.

For more guidance, refer to the *Classroom Strategies and Teaching Routines* card on multidraft reading.

Differentiated
Instruction   Additional Instruction

ⒺⓁ Extended Support— English Learners
Have students complete the **Reading and Vocabulary Warm-ups**, *Unit 3 Resources*, pp. 80–83, before they read. Assign the prereading pages in the *Reader's Notebook: English Learner's Version*. Then, have students listen to portions of the selection on the *Hear It! Audio CD.*

L1 L2 Extended Support- Struggling Readers
Have students complete the **Reading and Vocabulary Warm-ups**, *Unit 3 Resources*, pp. 80–83, before they read. Assign the prereading pages in the *Reader's Notebook: Adapted Version.* Then, have students listen to portions of the selection on the *Hear It! Audio CD* (adapted text).

Extended Support— Reluctant Readers
To build motivation and engagement before assigning the selection, have students read "In Your Dreams," a thematically related selection in *Reality Central.* Then, use the questions at the conclusion of the related selection to guide discussion.

PHLit Online!
For more about the author, practice with the selection vocabulary, or more background, go online at www.PHLitOnline.com.

451

❶ Activating Prior Knowledge

1. Slowly read the following list of words, giving students time to think carefully about each word and how it relates to the list: *swooping, graceful, lightness, airy, swiftness, freedom, wings, sky, feathers, clouds,* and *whoosh.*

2. Ask for a show of hands to see how many students were able to determine the topic of the list, which is "flying." Have volunteers tell which word gave them the final clue for their correct guess. Ask students to brainstorm for additional words they might add to the list. Explain that writers use vivid words to allow readers to imagine a scene or an idea.

3. Explain that the selection suggests that flight stands for freedom and independence. Suggest that students pay close attention to the author's choice of words.

Concept Connector ➡

Students will follow up on this activity after reading "Volar: To Fly."

Individual Activity

Invite students to write a sentence that describes the three images on p. 453. Ask them to consider what these images tell them about the selection's author, Judith Ortiz Cofer. What are her interests? Where does she live? What might she hope for in her life? Have them keep their ideas in mind as they read.

❷ About the Selection

Judith Ortiz Cofer recounts her experience as a twelve-year-old struggling to shape her identity. She connects her experience to that of her Puerto Rican family, which is struggling to make a life in New Jersey, far from family in Puerto Rico. Ortiz Cofer recalls that, as a comic book fan, she hoped for superpowers that would help her climb to the top of her building, break away from gravity, and fly wherever she wanted.

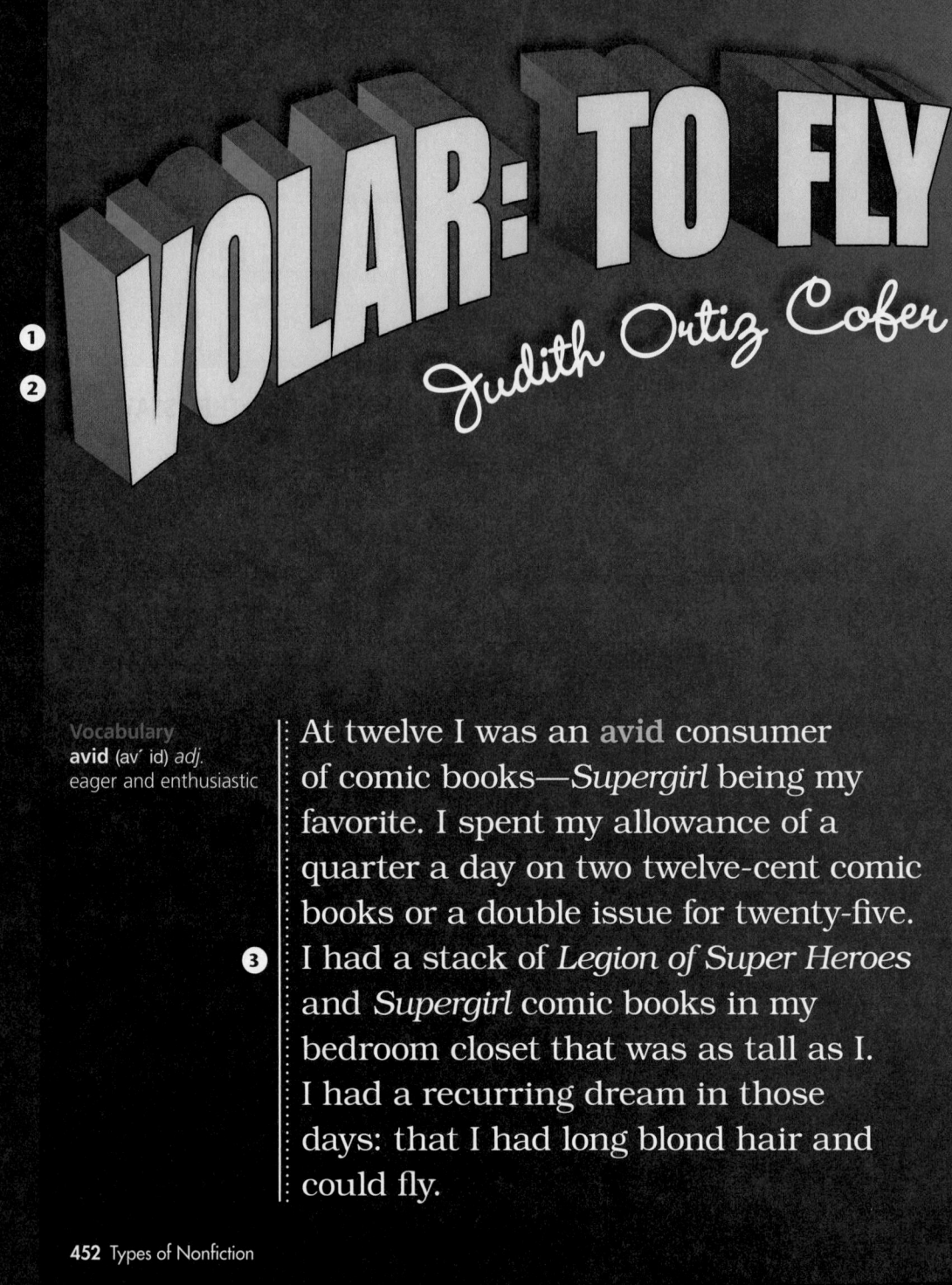

VOLAR: TO FLY

Judith Ortiz Cofer

❶
❷

Vocabulary
avid (av´ id) *adj.*
eager and enthusiastic

❸ At twelve I was an avid consumer of comic books—*Supergirl* being my favorite. I spent my allowance of a quarter a day on two twelve-cent comic books or a double issue for twenty-five. I had a stack of *Legion of Super Heroes* and *Supergirl* comic books in my bedroom closet that was as tall as I. I had a recurring dream in those days: that I had long blond hair and could fly.

452 Types of Nonfiction

Vocabulary Development

Vocabulary Knowledge Rating
When students have completed reading and discussing "Volar: To Fly," have them take out their **Vocabulary Knowledge Rating Chart** for this selection. Read the words aloud and have students rate their knowledge of words again in the After Reading column. Clarify any words that are still problematic. Have students write their own definition and example or sentence in the appropriate column. Then have students complete the Vocabulary Practice activities at the end of the selection. Encourage students to use the words in further discussion and written work about the selection. Remind them that they will be accountable for these words on the **Selection Test,** *Unit 3 Resources,* pp. 95–97 or 98–100.

Volar: To Fly **453**

1. Point out that growing up involves learning about who we are and deciding what we want in life.

2. Have students reread the brack-eted text on p. 452 and study the images on p. 453. **Ask:** What details in the text and images reveal what the author wishes for?
   Possible response: The text and images reveal that she wishes for blond hair and to escape her surroundings by flying. The images show a city neighborhood with a blond superhero flying above, and comic books, which offer another kind of escape. The text says that the author dreams over and over that she has blond hair and can fly.

3. **Ask:** Should we learn about peo-ple's hopes and dreams? Should we learn about our own hopes and dreams? Explain.
   Possible response: Yes, it is important to learn about others' hopes and dreams so that we can understand their actions. It is important to learn about our own hopes and dreams so that we can find ways of achieving them or of reshaping them into more realistic goals.

Differentiated Instruction for Universal Access

Strategy for Less Proficient Readers
Students should understand that most of the essay's first paragraph (pp. 452–455) is a description of the author's dream of being a flying superhero. To help distinguish fact from fiction, have students draw a two-column chart, labeling the columns "Author's Dream" and "Author's Real Life." Have students jot down details from the selection about the author's dream life as a superhero and her real life, which includes waking up in bed and waiting for her parents to call her. Help students compare and contrast the two sides of the girl's world.

Enrichment for Gifted/Talented Students
Point out that the author's dream of being a superhero borrows heavily from superheroes in comic books. Invite students to draw a comic strip that illustrates the author's metamorphosis from ordinary girl to superhero with nighttime flying adventures and back again. Students should include thought and speech bubbles and provide dialogue. Ask students to present their comic strip to the class and to summarize the events it depicts.

PHLit Online!

This selection is available in inter-active format in the **Enriched Online Student Edition**, online at **www.PHLitOnline.com**, which includes a thematically related video with writing prompt and an interactive graphic organizer.

453

❹ Main Idea

1. Have students reread the text on p. 454, and then read the paragraph on p. 452. **Ask** them to summarize the author's description. **Possible response:** She describes loving to read comic books. She describes wishing she were blond and could fly, and imagining becoming this way as she prepares to fly off her building. Once airborne, she would see her neighborhood and beyond to the larger world.

2. Have students list details from the author's description in their graphic organizers. Then, **ask** them what key point the author has made so far and how the details support that point. **Possible response:** The author has made the key point that she wishes for a different life. Supporting details include her description of wishing she were blond and wishing she could fly away from her home.

3. **Ask** the Main Idea question. **Possible response:** The main idea of the essay is that the author wishes to be different.

❺ Critical Thinking

Compare and Contrast

1. Review the bracketed passage with the class.

2. Point out that the author is looking back at how she was when she was twelve. Explain that the author most likely thinks about life differently now than when she was a girl. **Ask** students to identify the traits of the author when she was twelve. **Possible response:** She likes to read, she is curious about others, and she is imaginative.

3. Then, explain that the author is different in her superhero dreams than she is in real life. **Ask** students to compare and contrast the person whom the author dreamed of being with who she really was. **Possible response:** In her dreams, the girl has straight blond hair, long muscular arms and legs, and can fly. In life, she has tight curly hair, skinny arms and legs, and cannot fly.

Main Idea
Based on what the author has described so far, what do you think is the main idea of this essay?
❹

...and my hair would magically go straight and turn a golden color...

❺

In my dream I climbed the stairs to the top of our apartment building as myself, but as I went up each flight, changes would be taking place. Step by step I would fill out: my legs would grow long, my arms harden into steel, and my hair would magically go straight and turn a golden color. . . Once on the roof, my parents safely asleep in their beds, I would get on tip-toe, arms outstretched in the position for flight and jump out my fifty-story-high window into the black lake of the sky. From up there, over the rooftops, I could see everything, even beyond the few blocks of our barrio; with my X-ray vision I could look inside the homes of people who interested me. Once I saw our landlord, whom I knew my parents feared, sitting in a treasure-room dressed in an ermine coat and a large gold crown. He sat on the floor counting his dollar bills. I played a trick on him. Going up to his building's chimney, I blew a little puff of my super-breath into his fireplace, scattering his stacks of money so that he had to start counting all over again. I could more or less program my Supergirl dreams in those days by focusing on the object

454 Types of Nonfiction

Think Aloud

Vocabulary: Context Clues

Direct students' attention to the word *incongruous* on p. 455. Model how to use context to infer the meaning of an unknown word. Say to students:

> I'm going to think aloud to show you how I would figure out the meaning of *incongruous* from its context.

> In the sentence, the author says that she would "wake up in my tiny bedroom with the *incongruous*—at least in our tiny apartment—white 'princess' furniture my mother

had chosen for me. . . ." The word *incongruous* is used to describe the furniture. The phrase *at least* suggests that the furniture is *incongruous* in relation to the tiny apartment—it might not be *incongruous* in a large apartment. The word *princess* suggests luxury, while the idea of a tiny apartment suggests a lack of luxury. My guess is that *incongruous* means "not fitting in."

of my current obsession. This way I "saw" into the private lives of my neighbors, my teachers, and in the last days of my childish fantasy and the beginning of adolescence, into the secret room of the boys I liked. In the mornings I'd wake up in my tiny bedroom with the incongruous—at least in our tiny apartment—white "princess" furniture my mother had chosen for me, and find myself back in my body: my tight curls still clinging to my head, skinny arms and legs . . . •

In the kitchen my mother and father would be talking softly over a café con leche. She would come "wake me" exactly forty-five minutes after they had gotten up. It was their time together at the beginning of each day and even at an early age I could feel their disappointment if I interrupted them by getting up too early. So I would stay in my bed recalling my dreams of flight, perhaps planning my next flight. In the kitchen they would be discussing events in the barrio. Actually, he would be carrying that part of the conversation; when it was her turn to speak she would, more often than not, try shifting the topic toward her desire to see her *familia* on the Island: *How about a vacation in Puerto Rico together this year, Querido? We could rent a car, go to the beach. We could . . .* And he would answer patiently, gently, *Mi amor, do*

Vocabulary
obsession
(əb sesh´ ən) *n.* extreme interest in something
interrupted
(in´ tə rupt´ əd) *v.* briefly stopped someone from speaking or completing a task

❻ Critical Thinking

Compare and Contrast

1. Have a volunteer read the second bracketed paragraph on p. 455, continuing to its completion on p. 456. **Ask** students to describe the author's mother.
   Possible response: The mother misses her family in Puerto Rico and wants to see them. She agrees with her husband that traveling is too expensive. She wishes she could fly.

2. **Ask** students how the mother and daughter are similar and how they are different.
   Answer: Both the mother and the daughter wish they could fly. The mother is older and more experienced. She misses her family and wants to see them. The daughter is young and feeling awkward. She wishes she could fly so she could be special and have special powers.

3. **Ask** students to speculate about how the author feels now as an adult. For example, do they think she feels differently about wanting to fly?
   Possible response: Students may suggest that as the author grew up, she turned her creativity toward writing instead of fantasizing about being able to fly. The author is probably more comfortable with herself now than when she was younger.

Volar: To Fly 455

Concept Connector

Reading Skill Graphic Organizer
Ask students to review the graphic organizers they completed to identify details, key points, and main ideas while reading. Then, have students share the graphic organizers they completed and share their details, points, and ideas.

Writing About the Big Question
Have students compare the sentence starter they completed before reading the story with their ideas afterward. Ask them whether their thoughts have changed.

Activating Prior Knowledge
Have students return to the list of words they created for the topic of flying and add any new words suggested by the selection. Then, recall the discussion of how flight may stand for freedom and independence. Ask students if they find this connection of ideas to be convincing. Encourage students to cite specific details, quotations, or other evidence from the text to support their position, or to suggest other images or ideas that they associate with freedom or independence.

Spiral Review

Author's Point of View

1. Remind students that they studied the concept of author's point of view in the Unit 3 Literary Analysis Workshop (pp. 408–419).

2. **Ask** the Spiral Review question.

   Possible response: Reality is ugly and difficult, but dreams are freeing and like flying.

ASSESS

Answers

Critical Thinking

Remind students to support their answers with evidence from the text.

1. (a) The author dreams about having long blond hair and being able to fly away from her neighborhood. (b) **Possible response:** Her dreams reveal that she wishes she had different life.

2. **Possible responses:** (a) She doesn't want to interrupt her parents' special time. (b) Her mother and father want privacy so they can discuss topics not meant for the author's ears.

3. **Possible response:** The daughter wants to fly so that she can get away from her life and feel special. The mother wants to fly so that she can visit her family.

4. (a) The author's father says that they cannot visit Puerto Rico because it is too expensive to fly there and he cannot take time off work. (b) **Possible response:** This reveals that the family's life in the barrio is a financial struggle.

5. **Possible responses:** (a) No, the mother will not go to Puerto Rico. In the final paragraph, she sighs and shows that she is resigned to staying. (b) Students should identify a place and provide specific reasons for their wish to go there.

6. **Possible responses:** (a) The author learns that she cannot change who she is but that she can explore new horizons. (b) Our imaginations help us visualize ourselves in new situations.

456

Vocabulary

dismal (diz´ məl) *adj.* dark and gloomy

refuse (ref´ yo͞oz) *n.* trash; waste

Spiral Review ⑥

Author's Point of View In what way do these details about a simple morning routine help convey the author's perspective on the contrast between dreams and reality?

---

you know how much it would cost for the all of us to fly there? It is not possible for me to take the time off . . . Mi vida, please understand. . . . And I knew that soon she would rise from the table. Not abruptly. She would . . . look out the kitchen window. The view was of a **dismal** alley that was littered with **refuse** thrown from windows. The space was too narrow for anyone larger than a skinny child to enter safely, so it was never cleaned. My mother would check the time on the clock over her sink, the one with a prayer for patience and grace written in Spanish. A birthday gift. She would see that it was time to wake me. She'd sigh deeply and say the same thing the view from her kitchen window always inspired her to say: *Ay, si yo pudiera volar.**

---

* Oh, if only I could fly.

Critical Thinking

Cite textual evidence to support your responses.

1. **Key Ideas and Details (a)** What does the author dream about at night? Use details to support your answer. **(b) Analyze:** What do you think her dreams reveal about her life?

2. **Craft and Structure (a) Infer:** Why does the author wait in bed in the morning? **(b) Interpret:** Why do you think the mother and father want time to talk?

3. **Craft and Structure Connect:** Why do both the daughter and mother long to fly? Explain each of their reasons.

4. **Craft and Structure (a)** What reasons does the author's father give her mother for why they cannot visit Puerto Rico? **(b) Infer:** What does this reveal about their life in the barrio?

5. **Integration of Knowledge and Ideas (a) Predict:** Do you think that the mother will go to Puerto Rico? Why or why not? **(b) Discuss:** If you were able to fly, where would you go? In a small group, discuss your responses. As a group, choose one idea to share with the class.

6. **Integration of Knowledge and Ideas (a)** What does the author learn from her dreams? **(b)** How do our imaginations help us to create new possibilities in our lives? *[Connect to the Big Question: What should we learn?]*

456 Types of Nonfiction

Assessment Resources

Unit 3 Resources

L1 L2 EL **Selection Test A,** pp. 95–97. Administer Test A to less advanced readers.

L3 L4 EL **Selection Test B,** pp. 98–100. Administer Test B to on-level and more advanced students.

L3 L4 **Open-Book Test,** pp. 92–94. As an alternative, give the Open-Book Test.

All **Customizable Test Bank**

All **Self-tests**
Students may prepare for the **Selection Test** by taking the **Self-test** online.

PHLit Online! All assessment resources are available at **www.PHLitOnline.com**.

Reading Skill: Main Idea

1. (a) What details does Cofer provide about her desire to fly?
(b) Give an example of a sentence from the work that pulls these details together.

2. What is the **main idea** of the essay?

Literary Analysis: Reflective Essay

3. Craft and Structure Analyze this **reflective essay** in a chart like the one shown. In the first column, write Cofer's reflections on three points, including the one provided. Then, write your responses. Trade charts with a partner and discuss your responses. In the third column, explain whether your responses changed based on your discussion.

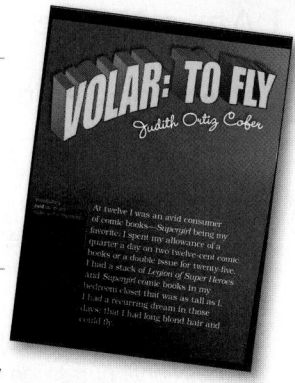

Cofer's Reflections	My Responses	After Discussion
Mother longs to visit her family.		

Vocabulary

Acquisition and Use A **synonym** is a word that is the same or similar in meaning to another word. For the first word in each numbered item, choose the word that is its synonym. Explain your answers.

1. avid: **(a)** apathetic **(b)** eager **(c)** lukewarm

2. interrupted: **(a)** stopped **(b)** appeased **(c)** soothed

3. obsession: **(a)** indifference **(b)** fixation **(c)** coldness

4. refuse: **(a)** treasure **(b)** gift **(c)** rubbish

5. dismal: **(a)** gloomy **(b)** cheerful **(c)** bright

Word Study Use the context of the sentences and what you know about the **Latin root -rupt-** to explain your answer to each question.

1. Would a noisy audience *disrupt* a piano recital?

2. If your appendix *ruptured,* would you need to see a doctor?

Word Study

The **Latin root -rupt-** means "break or burst."

Apply It Explain how the word root **-rupt-** contributes to the meanings of these words. Consult a dictionary if necessary.

corrupt
abrupt
erupt

Word Study
Sample answers:

1. Yes. The root -rupt- means "break or burst." A noisy audience would <u>break</u> the flow of music at a recital.

2. Yes. The root -rupt- means "break or burst." If your appendix *ruptured,* or <u>burst</u>, only a doctor could fix it.

Word Study: Apply It
Sample answers: To *corrupt* is to <u>break,</u> or destroy, someone's honesty. Something that is *abrupt* is sudden and <u>breaks</u> the pattern of what is expected. To *erupt* is to <u>burst</u> out suddenly.

Reading Skill

1. **Possible responses:** (a) She provides details about becoming strong and blond, and altogether different. (b) Step by step I would fill out: my legs would grow long, my arms harden into steel, and my hair would magically go straight and turn a golden color . . .

2. **Possible response:** The main idea of the essay is that dreams help us survive the present and build for the future.

Literary Analysis

3. **Possible responses:** Point 1— (col 1) Mother longs to visit her family; (col 2) I understand how she feels; (col 3) She should find a way to go. Point 2—(col 1) Author longs to be different; (col 2) I often feel that way, too; (col 3) She should try to get comfortable with who she is. Point 3— (col 1) The author sees that her mother will not pursue her dreams; (col 2) The mother is giving up too easily; (col 3) The author should understand how difficult her mother's situation is.

For other sample answers, see *Graphic Organizer Transparencies,* **Literary Analysis Graphic Organizer A, p. 85,** and the **Additional Answers** section.

Vocabulary
Acquisition and Use
Sample answers:

1. b; *Avid* means "enthusiastic," as does <u>eager</u>.

2. a; *Interrupted* means "briefly <u>stopped</u>."

3. b; An *obsession* is an extreme interest in something, as is a <u>fixation</u>.

4. c; *Refuse* is garbage, which is another word for <u>rubbish</u>.

5. a; *Dismal* means "dark and <u>gloomy</u>."

Conventions

1. Introduce the skill, using the instruction on the student page.
2. Discuss the examples in the chart.

Think Aloud: Model the Skill

Say to students:

To help identify prepositions, I look for words that answer *where, what,* and *when*. In the sentence "Anton put his shoes near the door," I look for words that answer *where, what,* or *when* about shoes. The prepositional phrase *near the door* answers *where*. The word *near* is a preposition and relates *door* to *shoes*. The word *door* is the object of the preposition and tells *near what*.

PH WRITING COACH Grade 7

Students will find instruction on and practice with prepositions and prepositional phrases in Chapter 16 and in Chapter 19, Section 1.

Practice A

1. <u>in</u> (P) <u>big family communities</u> (Obj)
2. <u>with</u> (P) <u>one another</u> (Obj)
3. <u>for</u> (P) <u>nature's gifts</u> (Obj)
4. <u>Among</u> (P) <u>their people</u> (Obj)

Reading Application
Sample answers:

"In the course of my lifetime I have lived <u>in two distinct cultures</u>"; "I was born <u>into a culture</u> that lived in communal houses"; "It was called a smoke house, and it stood <u>down by the beach</u> along the inlet."

Practice B
Sample answers:

1. The skates <u>in (P) her bedroom closet</u> (Obj) showed her Olympic ambitions.
2. <u>During (P) the night</u> (Obj), she dreamt of a gold medal.
3. (Obj); She imagined flying <u>through (P) the cloudless sky</u> (Obj) to the Olympic city.
4. Then, she would travel back <u>across (P) the ocean</u> (Obj) to be greeted by fans.

Writing Application

Students should use three prepositions from "Volar: To Fly" to write a paragraph about a dream.

458

Integrated Language Skills

I Am a Native of North America • Volar: To Fly

Conventions: Prepositions and Prepositional Phrases

A **preposition** relates a noun or a pronoun that follows the preposition to another noun or pronoun in the sentence. In the sentence *The book is on the table*, the preposition *on* shows the relationship between *table* and *book*.

A **prepositional phrase** begins with a preposition and ends with a noun or pronoun—called the **object of the preposition.** In the prepositional phrase *on the table*, the preposition is *on*, and the object of the preposition is *table*.

Some Commonly Used Prepositions			
above	below	in	over
across	beneath	into	through
after	between	near	to
against	by	of	toward
along	down	on	under
at	during	onto	until
before	for	out	up
behind	from	outside	with

Practice A Identify the prepositional phrase in each sentence. Then, identify the preposition and the object of the preposition.

1. Native Americans lived in big family communities.
2. They learned to live with one another.
3. They had a great respect for nature's gifts.
4. Among their people, hoarding was considered shameful.

ⓒ Reading Application In "I Am a Native of North America," find three sentences with prepositional phrases.

Practice B Identify the preposition and the object of the preposition in each prepositional phrase. Then, use the prepositional phrase to write a sentence about hopes and dreams.

1. in her bedroom closet
2. during the night
3. through the cloudless sky
4. across the ocean

ⓒ Writing Application Choose three prepositions from "Volar: To Fly." Then, write a paragraph about a dream you have using the prepositions.

PH WRITING COACH Further instruction and practice are available in *Prentice Hall Writing Coach*.

Extend the Lesson

Sentence Modeling

Choose the sentence given from the selection students have read.

> *My culture lived in big family communities, and from infancy people learned to live with others.* ("I Am a Native of North America")

> *The view was of a dismal alley that was littered with refuse thrown from windows.* ("Volar: To Fly")

Have students *identify* the prepositional phrases from the sentence you chose. ("I Am a Native...": *in big family communities; from infancy; with others*; "Volar: To Fly": *with refuse; from windows*).

Next, ask students what they notice about the sentence, eliciting that in the first sentence, the placement and wording of the phrase "from infancy" adds emphasis. In the second sentence, Cofer builds a scene by adding detail as the sentence unfolds, culminating in "thrown from windows."

Finally, have students imitate the sentence by writing a sentence on a topic of their own choosing, matching the grammatical and stylistic feature discussed. Have volunteers share their sentences.

Writing

Informative Text Make an **outline** to show the main idea and supporting details of either "I Am a Native of North America" or "Volar: To Fly." Build your outline using this format:

At the top of your outline, write a sentence stating the main ideas of the essay in your own words. Then, list subtopics for each main idea, and finally, list details.

- Use Roman numerals to identify each key point.
- Use capital letters to identify supporting details.

Grammar Application Check your writing to be sure you have used prepositions and prepositional phrases correctly.

Writing Workshop: *Work in Progress*

Prewriting for Exposition Specific details tell readers exactly how a step should be performed. Review your Everyday Task List for the process you described earlier. Consider what additional details would be useful to readers and include them at the appropriate steps.

Speaking and Listening

Presentation of Ideas In a small group, present a **response** to an audio version of either "I Am a Native of North America" or "Volar: To Fly." Access the audio of the selection by visiting www.PHLitOnline. Once you have listened to the audio version of your chosen selection, follow these steps to complete your response.

- Listen to the audio version of the selection as a group, taking notes on the impact of the selection as it is read aloud. For example, note whether the audio version brings certain words and phrases to life or if the audio version emphasizes a serious or humorous tone that is not evident in the printed version.
- Then, discuss with the group ways in which the audio version enhanced or detracted from the meaning and tone of the printed version. Replay the audio as needed to confirm the group's ideas.
- After your discussion, plan a presentation to the class in which you share your response.
- Assign presenter roles, and rehearse your presentation.
- At the conclusion of your presentation, invite questions and comments from your audience.

Common Core State Standards

L.7.1.a, L.7.6; RI.7.7; W.7.2.a
[For the full wording of the standards, see page 440.]

Use this prewriting activity to prepare for the **Writing Workshop** on page 484.

www.PHLitOnline.com
- Interactive graphic organizers
- Grammar tutorial
- Interactive journals

Integrated Language Skills **459**

ASSESS / EXTEND

Writing

1. Review the assignment, using the instruction on the student page.
2. To guide students in writing an informative text, give them **Support for Writing**, p. 90 in *Unit 3 Resources.*
3. To evaluate students' outlines, make sure that their outlines include at least two key points and two supporting details for each point. Remind students that the main idea should incorporate all the information in the outline.

Grammar Application

Have students check their drafts to make sure they have used prepositions and prepositional phrases correctly.

Six Traits Focus

✔	Ideas		Word Choice
✔	Organization		Sentence Fluency
	Voice	✔	Conventions

PH WRITING COACH Grade 7

Students will find further instruction on and practice with informative text in Chapter 8.

Writing Workshop
Work in Progress

Have students save their completed Everyday Task Lists in their portfolios. They will use the Lists later as they complete the Writing Workshop assignment (see pp. 484–489).

Speaking and Listening

1. Review the assignment, using the instruction on the student page.
2. To support students' work on the assignment, have them complete the **Support for Extend Your Learning** page (*Unit 3 Resources*, p. 91).

Teaching Resources

Unit 3 Resources

L3 L4 EL **Integrated Language Skills: Grammar,** p. 89

L3 L4 EL **Support for Writing,** p. 90

L3 L4 **Support for Extend Your Learning,** p. 91

L4 **Enrichment,** pp. 70, 88

Enriched Online Student Edition
Available under After You Read for this selection:
All **Interactive Grammar Tutorial**
L3 L4 **Internet Research Activity**

Professional Development Guidebook
Rubrics for Self-Assessment: Generic (Holistic Writing), pp. 256–257

PHLit Online! All print and digital resources are available online at **www.PHLitOnline.com**.
Online resources accessible to students are noted on the student page.

459

Using the Test Practice

In this two-page Test Practice, students apply the reading skill for the first half of Unit 3 to a passage of fiction and a passage of nonfiction.

Review this skill, main idea, and then administer the test. For more guidance, consult the *Classroom Strategies and Teaching Routine* card, *Formally Assessing Students.*

ASSESS

Answers

Answers With Explanations

1. **C**—The change in her back yard upsets the writer at first but ultimately has a good outcome. *Incorrect answers:* A—The writer realizes that her father has cut down the tree for a good reason; B—Though the view looks different, that is not the main idea; D—Family togetherness is not the main idea of the story.

2. **A**—The act of cutting down the tree does not support the main idea. *Incorrect answers:* B—This detail supports the idea that change can be hard; C—This detail supports the idea that sometimes change can be good; D—same explanation as for C.

3. **B**—*Change* appears in the first and second paragraphs, and *amazing* appears in the second and third paragraphs. *Incorrect answers:* A—Each of these words appears once; C—same explanation as for A; D—same explanation as for A.

4. **A**—A new view and hobby lead the narrator to see the advantages of change. *Incorrect answers:* B—This lesson fits bird-watching but does not grow out of the first two paragraphs; C—This is partly true, but is not the main lesson; D—The writer never names the birds that she watches.

Writing for Assessment

In their responses, students should list three details related to the way the writer's attitude changes from the beginning of the story to the end.

Test Practice: Reading

Main Idea

Fiction Selection

Directions: *Read the selection. Then, answer the questions.*

When Dad chopped down the pear tree in our back yard, I cried. I loved its short gnarly branches and its pretty white flowers. I was sure I would miss seeing it from my bedroom window. Then Dad transplanted some bushes, and I got upset again. I guess I don't like change very much.

All winter long, I moped about the changes. I especially missed seeing my little tree covered in snow. But a funny thing happened in the spring. When I looked out my window, I realized I could see wetlands in the distance and some rolling hills beyond that. Dad had opened up an amazing view!

Now I spend hours looking through my binoculars. I watch beavers swim in the water. Sometimes I see a large bird with long, slender legs and a long beak fly back and forth. It is amazing how much time my family now spends outside together while bird watching.

1. What is the main idea of this passage?
   A. It is wrong to chop down trees.
   B. Everything looks different in springtime.
   C. Change can be hard, but sometimes it is good.
   D. Spending time together as a family is important.

2. What detail does *not* support the main idea?
   A. The writer's father chopped down a tree.
   B. The writer does not like change.
   C. Without the tree, the writer has an amazing view.
   D. The family now spends hours together outside.

3. Which two words are repeated in the text and hint at the main idea?
   A. chopped and transplanted
   B. change and amazing
   C. upset and missed
   D. spring and family

4. What lesson did the writer learn?
   A. She learned that change can lead to something good.
   B. She learned to enjoy simple things.
   C. She learned to appreciate nature.
   D. She learned to identify different birds.

Writing for Assessment

In a paragraph, identify three details in the passage that show how the writer's attitude changes.

460 Types of Nonfiction

Strategies for Test Taking

Remind students that finding the main idea of a fiction selection can sometimes be more challenging than finding the main idea of a piece of nonfiction. In nonfiction, the author often states the main idea explicitly at the beginning of the passage. All or most of the details that follow support this idea. In fiction, readers need to read between the lines to identify the main idea. Many of the details support it, but some details have another purpose.

The main idea of a piece of fiction is often an important life lesson or a truth about life that applies to many people—not just the characters in the story. A story may take place in a dangerous mine, but that does not mean that the story's main idea is that mines are dangerous. The mine is simply the setting that the author has chosen to teach a lesson. The main idea may be that courage helps people face challenges.

Nonfiction Selection

Directions: *Read the selection. Then, answer the questions.*

You can learn a lot about a bird by looking at its beak, or bill. Birds such as cardinals, sparrows, and finches have strong, thick, cone-shaped beaks. These beaks are perfect for cracking seeds. Bird lovers place feeders filled with seeds in their yards for songbirds. Woodpeckers, on the other hand, have long, chisel-shaped beaks. They use their beaks to peck holes in trees. Tiny hummingbirds have long, tubular bills that they use in much the same way we use a straw.

Herons walk on long, slender legs and often live near wetlands. They have long, straight bills with sharp edges that keep slippery fishes from escaping. Other fish-eaters, like cormorants, have hooks on the end of their beaks for holding fishes. Wading birds with long, narrow bills use their beaks to probe deep in the sand for tasty insects or worms.

1. What is the main idea of this selection?
   A. A bird's beak gives clues about what it eats.
   B. Birds eat a wide variety of foods.
   C. Fish-eaters live near the shore.
   D. It does not really matter what type of beak a bird has.

2. Which detail does *not* directly support the main idea of paragraph 1?
   A. Cone-shaped beaks can crack seeds.
   B. Bird lovers feed songbirds.
   C. Woodpeckers peck holes in trees.
   D. A hummingbird uses its beak like a straw.

3. What is the main idea of paragraph 2?
   A. Herons are fish-eaters.
   B. You can guess a shore bird's diet by looking at its beak.
   C. Most shore birds have long legs.
   D. Shore birds' beaks are different from those of birds that live in the woods.

4. Which detail in paragraph 2 directly supports the main idea of that paragraph?
   A. Herons have long, slender legs.
   B. Fish can be slippery.
   C. A hooked beak can hold a fish.
   D. Birds think insects and worms are tasty.

Writing for Assessment

Connecting Across Texts
Based on information in both passages, write a paragraph describing which birds the writer of the first passage might see through her binoculars.

PHLit
Online!
www.PHLitOnline.com
• Online practice
• Instant feedback

Answers With Explanations

1. **A**—The first sentence states that you can learn about a bird from its beak, and the subsequent sentences show that you learn about the bird's diet. *Incorrect answers:* B—This answer leaves out the importance of the beak; C—Though true, it is not the main idea of the passage; D—This is untrue.

2. **B**—This detail is irrelevant to the idea that bills give clues about diet. *Incorrect answers:* A—This detail shows the relationship of the bird's bill to its diet; C—This shows how woodpeckers use their beaks to find insects; D—This detail supports the relationship of the beak to the diet.

3. **B**—The specific details about the birds' bills all support this idea. *Incorrect answers:* A—This is a detail, not a main idea; C—There is no mention of birds other than herons having long legs; D—This comparison is not made in paragraph 2.

4. **C**—This detail relates beak shape to diet. *Incorrect answers:* A—This detail relates to a bird's legs rather than its bill; B—This detail explains why fish eaters need special bills, but it does not mention birds that eat fish; D—This detail does not involve birds' beak shapes.

Writing for Assessment

In their responses, students should include birds found in the wetlands and possibly the hills in the distance—environments visible to the writer.

Differentiated

Instruction   for Universal Access

EL **Strategy for English Learners**

Point out to students that the writer of this passage switches back and forth between the synonyms *bills* and *beaks.* The four items use the word *beak* only. Students should not be confused by the fact that the passage refers to hummingbirds' *bills* whereas item 2 refers to their *beaks*. The two words express the same meaning. Students should keep this example in mind when taking standardized tests. They should understand that a writer may, for example, use one word in the main idea statement in a passage and a synonym in a test question about the main idea. Students should focus on the meaning of a passage or item rather than overly focusing on specific vocabulary.

PHLit
Online!
Students may take the test in interactive format with instant feedback online at www.PHLitOnline.com.

461

Common Core State Standards

- Reading Informational Text 8
- Writing 1.a
- Language 4.b, 6

Reading Skill

1. Introduce the skill.
2. Tell students they will analyze texts to assess authors' arguments and support.

Think Aloud: Model the Skill

Say to students:

When I read a text in which an author appears to be making an argument, I read with a number of ideas in mind. First, I assess whether the subject of the argument is clearly stated and supported by evidence. Then, I ask myself if the argument makes sense.

Multidraft Reading

Have students follow a multidraft reading protocol.

- **First reading**—Have students read to identify key ideas and details.
- **Second reading**—Have students read to identify the structure of the text.
- **Third reading**—Have students read to integrate knowledge and ideas by connecting the text to the world, their own experiences, and other texts.

Content-Area Vocabulary

1. Have students say each word.
2. Next, use each word in a sentence that defines it.
3. Finally, repeat your definitional sentence or a similar sentence, omitting the word, and have the class "fill in the blank" chorally.

Reading for Information

Analyzing Expository Texts

Textbook Article

Magazine Article

Common Core State Standards

Reading Informational Text
8. Trace and evaluate the argument and specific claims in a text, assessing whether the reasoning is sound and the evidence is relevant and sufficient to support the claims.

Writing
1.a. Write arguments to support claims with clear reasons and relevant evidence.

Language
4.b. Use common, grade-appropriate Greek or Latin affixes and roots as clues to the meaning of a word.
6. Acquire and use accurately grade-appropriate general academic and domain-specific words and phrases; gather vocabulary knowledge when considering a word or phrase important to comprehension or expression.

Reading Skill: Analyze Author's Argument

When you read a text that explains a problem and proposes a solution, **analyze the author's argument** to be sure you understand it. Look for a clear statement of the problem and evidence that supports the proposed solution. The evidence that the author presents should come from trustworthy sources and should include facts and statistics. The author's evidence should also be focused, relating directly to his or her claim.

As you read, use a checklist like the one shown to help you trace and analyze an author's argument.

Checklist for Analyzing an Author's Argument

- ☐ Does the author present a clear argument?
- ☐ Is the argument supported by evidence?
- ☐ Is the evidence believable?
- ☐ Does the author use sound reasoning to develop the argument?

Content-Area Vocabulary

These words appear in the selections that follow. You may also encounter them in other content-area texts.

- **decibels** (des´ ə bəlz) *n.* units for measuring the relative loudness of sounds
- **marsh** (märsh) *n.* low land that is permanently or temporarily under water
- **ecology** (ē käl´ə jē) *n.* study of the relationships among plants, animals, and people and their surroundings

462 Types of Nonfiction

? What should we learn?

Have students relate details about the problems identified in each text to community issues.

Differentiated Instruction for Universal Access

Reading Support
Give students reading support with the appropriate version of the *Reader's Notebooks*:

L2 L3 *Reader's Notebook*

L1 *Reader's Notebook: Adapted Version*

EL *Reader's Notebook: English Learner's Version*

Keeping It Quiet

from *Prentice Hall Science Explorer*

A construction worker uses a jackhammer; a woman waits in a noisy airport; a spectator watches a car race. All three experience noise pollution. In the United States alone, 40 million people face danger to their health from noise pollution.

> The writer identifies a problem in the opening paragraph.

People start to feel pain at about 120 decibels. But noise that "doesn't hurt" can still damage your hearing. Exposure to 85 decibels (a kitchen blender) can slowly damage the hair cells in your cochlea. As many as 9 million Americans have hearing loss caused by noise. What can be done about noise pollution?

> Supporting facts and statistics explain specific dangers and identify the extent of the problem.

The Issues

What Can Individuals Do?

Some work conditions are noisier than others. Construction workers, airport employees, and truck drivers are all at risk. Workers in noisy environments can help themselves by using ear protectors, which can reduce noise levels by 35 decibels.

> The writer proposes some solutions to the problem.

Many leisure activities also pose a risk. A listener at a rock concert or someone riding a motorbike can prevent damage by using ear protectors. People can also reduce noise at the source. They can buy quieter machines and avoid using lawnmowers or power tools at quiet times of the day. Simply turning down the volume on headphones for radios and CD players can help prevent hearing loss in young people.

Reading for Information: Textbook Article **463**

PROFESSIONAL DEVELOPMENT William G. Brozo, Ph. D.

APPLY THE STRATEGY

Turn-to-Your-Neighbor After reading, ask students "What is the central point the author makes about noise pollution?" Before eliciting responses, tell students to *turn to their neighbor and discuss* an answer. Walk around the room monitoring conversations. After a minute, open the floor to students' ideas. Maintain silence after a comment to encourage other comments, and ask students to respond to each other. To extend the discussion, have students form groups and think of an additional way noise pollution affects them and how to eliminate it. Using a *fishbowl* approach, gather the other students around a particular group to observe their conversation and ask additional questions; then put another group in the fishbowl.

For more of William G. Brozo's strategies, see his Professional Development essay, pp. 406c–406d.

463

⑫ **Autobiography**

1. Have students reread the bracketed passage. **Ask:** Fifty years ago, what did most parents want their boys to grow up to be? How does this compare to what Baker as a boy wanted to be?
Answer: Most parents wanted their boys to grow up to be president. Baker, however, wants to be a garbage man.

2. **Ask** the Autobiography question.
Possible response: The details reveal that Russell is more interested in doing what he finds interesting than in being "successful."

3. **Ask** students why they think Baker included the information in this passage in his autobiography.
Possible response: It gives readers a glimpse of his priorities and interests; it is humorous.

Spiral Review

Author's Point of View

1. Remind students that they studied the concept of author's point of view in the Unit 3 Literary Analysis Workshop (pp. 408–419).

2. **Ask** the Spiral Review question.

Possible response: The author's humorous perspective shows that he wants to entertain as well as inform his readers.

Vocabulary
paupers (pô´ pərz)
n. people who are very poor

Autobiography
What does Baker reveal about himself with these details?

Ⓒ ⑫

Spiral Review
Author's Point of View What does the author's humorous perspective tell readers about his purpose for writing?

---

the material the Lord had given her to mold, she didn't overestimate what she could do with it. She didn't insist that I grow up to be President of the United States.

Fifty years ago parents still asked boys if they wanted to grow up to be President, and asked it not jokingly but seriously. Many parents who were hardly more than  still believed their sons could do it. Abraham Lincoln had done it. We were only sixty-five years from Lincoln. Many a grandfather who walked among us could remember Lincoln's time. Men of grandfatherly age were the worst for asking if you wanted to grow up to be President. A surprising number of little boys said yes and meant it.

I was asked many times myself. No, I would say, I didn't want to grow up to be President. My mother was present during one of these interrogations.[3] An elderly uncle, having posed the usual question and exposed my lack of interest in the Presidency, asked, "Well, what do you want to be when you grow up?"

I loved to pick through trash piles and collect empty bottles, tin cans with pretty labels, and discarded magazines. The most desirable job on earth sprang instantly to mind. "I want to be a garbage man," I said.

My uncle smiled, but my mother had seen the first distressing evidence of a bump budding on a log. "Have a little gumption, Russell," she said. Her calling me Russell was a signal of unhappiness. When she approved of me I was always "Buddy."

When I turned eight years old she decided that the job of starting me on the road toward making something of myself could no longer be safely delayed. "Buddy," she said one day, "I want you to come home right after school this afternoon. Somebody's coming and I want you to meet him."

When I burst in that afternoon she was in conference in the parlor with an executive of the Curtis Publishing Company. She introduced me. He bent low from the waist and shook my hand. Was it true as my mother had told him, he asked, that I longed for the opportunity to conquer the world of business?

My mother replied that I was blessed with a rare determination to make something of myself.

"That's right," I whispered.

"But have you got the grit, the character, the never-say-quit spirit it takes to succeed in business?"

---

3. interrogations (in ter ə´ gā´ shənz) *n.* situations in which a person is formally questioned.

Vocabulary Development　　　　　　　　　　　　　　　　Ⓒ **CCSS Language 6**

Word Forms
Expand students' vocabulary by helping them learn related forms of the selection vocabulary words. Give students a blank **Word Form Chart** (*Professional Development Guidebook*, p. 41),

with *gumption*, *paupers*, *crucial*, and *aptitude* in the correct columns. Work with the class to determine the more commonly used related forms, if any.

Noun	Verb	Adjective	Adverb
gumption			
paupers	pauperize		
crux		**crucial**	crucially
aptitude		aptitudinal	

My mother said I certainly did.

"That's right," I said.

He eyed me silently for a long pause, as though weighing whether I could be trusted to keep his confidence, then spoke man-to-man. Before taking a crucial step, he said, he wanted to advise me that working for the Curtis Publishing Company placed enormous responsibility on a young man. It was one of the great companies of America. Perhaps the greatest publishing house in the world. I had heard, no doubt, of the *Saturday Evening Post*?

Heard of it? My mother said that everyone in our house had heard of the *Saturday Post* and that I, in fact, read it with religious devotion.

Then doubtless, he said, we were also familiar with those two monthly pillars of the magazine world, the *Ladies Home Journal* and the *Country Gentleman*.

Indeed we were familiar with them, said my mother.

Representing the *Saturday Evening Post* was one of the weightiest honors that could be bestowed in the world of business, he said. He was personally proud of being a part of that great corporation.

My mother said he had every right to be.

Again he studied me as though debating whether I was worthy of a knighthood. Finally: "Are you trustworthy?"

My mother said I was the soul of honesty.

"That's right," I said.

The caller smiled for the first time. He told me I was a lucky young man. He admired my spunk. Too many young men thought life was all play. Those young men would not go far in this world. Only a young man willing to work and save and keep his face washed and his hair neatly combed could hope to come out on top in a world such as ours. Did I truly and sincerely believe that I was such a young man?

"He certainly does," said my mother.

"That's right," I said.

He said he had been so impressed by what he had seen of me that he was going to make me a representative of the Curtis Publishing Company. On the following Tuesday, he said, thirty freshly printed copies of the *Saturday Evening Post* would be delivered at our door. I would place these magazines,

⓭ ▼ Critical Viewing
How does your image of Russell Baker compare with this photograph of him with his sister? **[Compare and Contrast]**

✓ Reading Check
⓮ What job does Russell have?

No Gumption **477**

Differentiated Instruction   for Universal Access

EL **Background for English Learners**
Arrange students in groups, and have the groups review the maxims, or wise sayings, used by Russell's mother. Encourage students to explain in their own words what each maxim means. Remind students of the meanings of key words such as *early, rise,* and *succeed.* Then, invite students to share popular maxims used in their first languages, and write these on the board.

Enrichment for Gifted/Talented Readers
Arrange students in groups, and have them role-play Russell and his sister selling magazines to a client. Encourage students to make up their own elaborate dialogue. Have students take turns assuming each role. Afterward, ask students to explain how the activity improved their understanding of the characters.

⓭ Critical Viewing

Possible response: Baker describes himself as rather lazy and unmotivated at this time in his life, creating the mental impression of someone who might look unkempt. In the photograph, however, he appears neat, scrubbed, and pleasant. He describes himself as being less energetic than his sister, a comparison that some students might feel is reflected in the eyes and expression of the children in the photograph.

⓮ Reading Check

Answer: Russell has a job selling *The Saturday Evening Post.*

⓯ Autobiography

1. Remind students that an autobiography provides details that provide insight into the writer's actions and feelings at the time of the event being recounted. Read aloud the bracketed passage. Call attention to all of the details Baker provides to suggest that he has gone to a part of town where lots of people are likely to be present. Help students see the humor Baker creates by contrasting the amount of activity readers can imagine is taking place in this setting—people getting haircuts, buying food, refueling the car, getting a bite to eat—and Baker's lack of ability to capture the attention of a single person.

2. **Ask:** Why is Russell so unsuccessful at selling *The Saturday Evening Post*?
   Answer: He just stands on the street. He doesn't say anything or approach anyone.

3. **Ask** the Autobiography question.
   Answer: No, Russell wants to do things that interest him, while his mother wants him to do things that will lead to financial success. The mother wants her son to have the same comfortable life her brother has achieved, as a salesman, and that her own husband, Russell's father, did not achieve.

---

still damp with the ink of the presses, in a handsome canvas bag, sling it over my shoulder, and set forth through the streets to bring the best in journalism, fiction, and cartoons to the American public.

He had brought the canvas bag with him. He presented it with reverence fit for a chasuble.[4] He showed me how to drape the sling over my left shoulder and across the chest so that the pouch lay easily accessible[5] to my right hand, allowing the best in journalism, fiction, and cartoons to be swiftly extracted and sold to a citizenry whose happiness and security depended upon us soldiers of the free press.

The following Tuesday I raced home from school, put the canvas bag over my shoulder, dumped the magazines in, and, tilting to the left to balance their weight on my right hip, embarked on the highway of journalism.

We lived in Belleville, New Jersey, a commuter town at the northern fringe of Newark. It was 1932, the bleakest year of the Depression. My father had died two years before, leaving us with a few pieces of Sears, Roebuck furniture and not much else, and my mother had taken Doris and me to live with one of her younger brothers. This was my Uncle Allen. Uncle Allen had made something of himself by 1932. As salesman for a soft-drink bottler in Newark, he had an income of $30 a week; wore pearl-gray spats,[6] detachable collars, and a three-piece suit; was happily married; and took in threadbare relatives.

With my load of magazines I headed toward Belleville Avenue. That's where the people were. There were two filling stations at the intersection with Union Avenue, as well as an A&P, a fruit stand, a bakery, a barber shop, Zuccarelli's drugstore, and a diner shaped like a railroad car. For several hours I made myself highly visible, shifting position now and then from corner to corner, from shop window to shop window, to make sure everyone could see the heavy black lettering on the canvas bag that said *The Saturday Evening Post*. When the angle of the light indicated it was suppertime, I walked back to the house.

"How many did you sell, Buddy?" my mother asked.

"None."

"Where did you go?"

Autobiography
Does Russell have the same goals for himself that his mother has? Explain.

---

4. **chasuble** (chaz´ ə bəl) *n.* sleeveless outer garment worn by priests.
5. **accessible** (ak ses´ ə bəl) *adj.* available.
6. **spats** (spats) *n.* cloth or leather material that covers the upper part of shoes or ankles.

Vocabulary Development   Ⓒ **CCSS** Language 6

Vocabulary Reinforcement

To reinforce and assess students' comprehension of selection vocabulary words, give them sentences using the words in which the word may or may not be used correctly. Students must tell whether the use is correct and explain their answer. Use these sentences:

1. He has an *aptitude* for math and failed the first three quizzes.
   Answer: No, if he has ability for math, he would not have failed the first three quizzes.

2. The doctor could not remove her tonsils because they are *crucial* to a person's health.
   Answer: No, many people have their tonsils removed because tonsils are not critical to a person's health.

3. The students in the class showed *gumption* as they faced the overwhelming task of writing a research paper with excitement.
   Answer: Yes, *gumption* means "courage or enterprise."

"The corner of Belleville and Union Avenues."

"What did you do?"

"Stood on the corner waiting for somebody to buy a *Saturday Evening Post.*"

"You just stood there?"

"Didn't sell a single one."

"For God's sake, Russell!"

Uncle Allen intervened. "I've been thinking about it for some time," he said, "and I've about decided to take the *Post* regularly. Put me down as a regular customer." I handed him a magazine and he paid me a nickel. It was the first nickel I earned.

Afterwards my mother instructed me in salesmanship. I would have to ring doorbells, address adults with charming self-confidence, and break down resistance with a sales talk pointing out that no one, no matter how poor, could afford to be without the *Saturday Evening Post* in the home.

I told my mother I'd changed my mind about wanting to succeed in the magazine business.

"If you think I'm going to raise a good-for-nothing," she replied, "you've got another think coming." She told me to hit the streets with the canvas bag and start ringing doorbells the instant school was out next day. When I objected that I didn't feel any aptitude for salesmanship, she asked how I'd like to lend her my leather belt so she could whack some sense into me. I bowed to superior will and entered journalism with a heavy heart.

My mother and I had fought this battle almost as long as I could remember. It probably started even before memory began, when I was a country child in northern Virginia and my mother, dissatisfied with my father's plain workman's life, determined that I would not grow up like him and his people, with calluses on their hands, overalls on their backs, and fourth-grade educations in their heads. She had fancier ideas of life's possibilities. Introducing me to the *Saturday Evening Post,* she was trying to wean me as early as possible from my father's world where men left with lunch pails at sunup, worked with their hands until the grime ate into the pores, and died with a few sticks of mail-order furniture as their legacy. In my mother's vision of the better life there were desks

Autobiography
Why do you think Baker includes this conversation between himself and his mother?

17 ▲ Critical Viewing
Does this picture fit your idea of Baker's mother? Explain. **[Connect]**

Vocabulary
aptitude (ap´ tə tood)
n. talent; ability

18 ✓ Reading Check
How did Russell do on his first day of selling?

No Gumption **479**

---

16 Autobiography

1. **Ask** two students to read the dialogue between Baker and his mother.

2. Tell students to call out words to describe the mother's attitude. **Possible responses:** Words include *disgust* and *disbelief.*

3. **Ask** the Autobiography question.
   Answer: He includes it because it is funny. It points up how inept Baker is as a salesman. His mother's reaction makes it clear that she thinks her son could have sold all of the magazines easily if he had just made some effort to do so. It confirms her impression of Baker as behaving like a bump on a log: just being there and doing nothing.

17 Critical Viewing

Answer: Most students will say that the woman in the picture could be Baker's mother because the photograph is old and the woman looks strong-willed and serious.

18 Reading Check

Answer: He didn't sell even one magazine.

Differentiated Instruction for Universal Access

Support for Less Proficient Readers
Have students reread the paragraph at the top of page 478 that begins, "He had brought the canvas bag with him." Guide students to recognize the tone of exaggerated importance in this passage. Then, ask them why they think Baker presents information this way and what he really thinks about his impending responsibility. Help students to see that Baker attempts to entertain the reader through exaggeration; his description of the job contrasts with the comparative unimportance of the task itself.

Enrichment for Gifted/Talent Students
Have groups of three students reread the episode involving the man from the publishing company, Russell, and his mother. Then, ask them to collaborate to write a script that uses the dialogue included in this section. Have each student take the role of one of the three speakers and then practice acting out the scene. Finally, have groups present their dramatic interpretations to the rest of the class. Students should try to capture the humor of the scene in their dramas.

479

Possible responses: Some students might suggest that the magazine would be easy to sell because it is colorful and inviting. Others might suggest that it would be hard to sell a magazine or any unnecessary item at a time when so many people didn't have much money.

⑳ 🅱 **Connecting to the Big Question**

1. Remind students of the Big Question ("What should we learn?") and point out that Baker's mother tried to teach him about salesmanship after his first day selling magazines.

2. **Ask:** What does Baker need to learn in order to sell more copies of *The Saturday Evening Post?*
   Answer: Baker needs to learn how to make a good sales pitch.

3. **Ask:** What do we learn about Baker's personality from the way he interacts with people?
   Answer: We learn that he is timid when talking to strangers.

4. Finally, **ask** students how important it is for someone of Baker's type to learn salesmanship?
   Possible responses: It is important to learn how to deal with others; it is not necessary to learn salesmanship if you can earn a living in some other way.

⑲ ▼ **Critical Viewing**
Based on these covers, do you think *The Saturday Evening Post* would be easy to sell? Why? **[Take a Position]**

and white collars, well-pressed suits, evenings of reading and lively talk, and perhaps—if a man were very, very lucky and hit the jackpot, really made something important of himself— perhaps there might be a fantastic salary of $5,000 a year to support a big house and a Buick with a rumble seat⁷ and a vacation in Atlantic City.

And so I set forth with my sack of magazines. I was afraid of the dogs that snarled behind the doors of potential buyers. I was timid about ringing the doorbells of strangers, relieved when no one came to the door, and scared when someone did. Despite my mother's instructions, I could not deliver an engaging sales pitch. When a door opened I simply asked, "Want to buy a *Saturday Evening Post?*" In Belleville few persons did. It was a town of 30,000 people, and most weeks I rang a fair majority of its doorbells. But I rarely sold my thirty copies. Some weeks I canvassed the entire town for six days and still had four or five unsold magazines on Monday evening; then I dreaded the coming of Tuesday morning, when a batch of thirty fresh *Saturday Evening Posts* was due at the front door.

"Better get out there and sell the rest of those magazines tonight," my mother would say.

I usually posted myself then at a busy intersection where a traffic light controlled commuter flow from Newark. When the light turned red I stood on the curb and shouted my sales pitch at the motorists.

"Want to buy a *Saturday Evening Post?*"

One rainy night when car windows were sealed against me I came back soaked and with not a single sale to report. My mother beckoned to Doris.

"Go back down there with Buddy and show him how to sell these magazines," she said.

Brimming with zest, Doris, who was then seven years old, returned with me to the corner. She took a magazine from the bag, and when the light turned red she strode to the nearest car and banged her small fist against the closed window. The driver, probably startled at what he took to be a midget assaulting his car, lowered the window to stare, and Doris thrust a *Saturday Evening Post* at him.

---

7. **rumble seat** in the rear of early automobiles, a seat that could be folded shut.

Vocabulary Development   © **CCSS Language 6**

Vocabulary Reinforcement
Students will benefit from additional examples and practice with the selection vocabulary words. Reinforce their comprehension with "show-you-know" sentences. The first part of the sentence uses the vocabulary word in an appropriate context. The second part of the sentence clarifies the first. Model the strategy with this example for *gumption:*

The girl had gumption *for one so young; she could speak to perfect strangers with ease.*
Then give students these sentence prompts:

1. Passing the test was *crucial* for the student; _____. **Sample answer:** he would fail the course if he did not pass.
2. The girl had a natural *aptitude* for basketball; _____. **Sample answer:** she played well with little coaching or training.
3. The story is about two young men who lead very different lives: a prince and a *pauper;* _____. **Sample answer:** the prince lives in a grand palace, and the pauper has no place to live.

"You need this magazine," she piped, "and it only costs a nickel."

Her salesmanship was irresistible. Before the light changed half a dozen times she disposed of the entire batch. I didn't feel humiliated. To the contrary. I was so happy I decided to give her a treat. Leading her to the vegetable store on Belleville Avenue, I bought three apples, which cost a nickel, and gave her one.

"You shouldn't waste money," she said.

"Eat your apple." I bit into mine.

"You shouldn't eat before supper," she said. "It'll spoil your appetite."

Back at the house that evening, she dutifully reported me for wasting a nickel. Instead of a scolding, I was rewarded with a pat on the back for having the good sense to buy fruit instead of candy. My mother reached into her bottomless supply of maxims[8] and told Doris, "An apple a day keeps the doctor away."

By the time I was ten I had learned all my mother's maxims by heart. Asking to stay up past normal bedtime, I knew that a refusal would be explained with, "Early to bed and early to rise, makes a man healthy, wealthy, and wise." If I whimpered about having to get up early in the morning, I could depend on her to say, "The early bird gets the worm."

The one I most despised was, "If at first you don't succeed, try, try again." This was the battle cry with which she constantly sent me back into the hopeless struggle whenever I moaned that I had rung every doorbell in town and knew there wasn't a single potential buyer left in Belleville that week. After listening to my explanation, she handed me the canvas bag and said, "If at first you don't succeed . . ."

Three years in that job, which I would gladly have quit after the first day except for her insistence, produced at least one valuable result. My mother finally concluded that I would never make something of myself by pursuing a life in business and started considering careers that demanded less competitive zeal.

One evening when I was eleven I brought home a short "composition" on my summer vacation which the teacher had graded with an A. Reading it with her own school-teacher's eye, my mother agreed that it was top-drawer seventh grade

---

8. maxims (mak′ simz) *n.* wise sayings.

Autobiography
What do you learn about Russell based on his feelings about his sister's salesmanship?

 Reading Check 22
What skill does Doris have that Russell does not?

---

21 Autobiography

1. Remind students that writers choose details when they write an autobiography that will help readers understand the writer's feelings, actions, and personality traits. Have students reread the bracketed passage. **Ask:** Why do you think the author included these details about his sister Doris's salesmanship?
Possible response: The author may have included the details about Doris's salesmanship to contrast her character with his. It adds humor. It contrasts Russell's difficulty selling magazines, even after he's done it for a while, with Doris's ability to sell one the first time she tries, even though it is raining.

2. **Ask** the Autobiography question on this page.
Possible response: Russell's feelings about his sister's sales ability show that he admires his sister and is not a jealous or competitive person.

22 Reading Check

Answer: She has good sales skill and Russell does not.

㉓ Autobiography

Have a student read the bracketed passage on this page aloud. Then, **ask** the Autobiography question. **Possible response:** Baker thinks you don't need gumption to be a writer, so being a writer sounds like a perfect job. He loves to read, so he figures that he will enjoy writing.

ASSESS

Answers

Critical Thinking

Before students respond, you may wish to have them write a brief objective summary of the selection. As they answer the questions below, remind them to support their answers with evidence from the text.

1. (a) **Possible response:** Two expressions used by Baker are his mother's comments that he has a "lack of gumption" and is "a son who was content with Dick Tracy." (b) He does not make much effort to sell magazines because he's not interested and would rather be doing something he enjoys.

2. (a) She wants him to get started early in a successful career. (b) She wants him to succeed in business, not be a laborer. (c) Baker wants to do something he enjoys. His mother wants to make sure that he develops the skills he will need to live comfortably.

3. (a) **Possible response:** He explains that he goes to a busy part of town and just stands there with his magazines. He rings doorbells and is relieved when no one is home. (b) His sense of humor reveals that he can look back at his past failures without feeling embarrassed.

4. (a) Baker learns that he isn't a good salesman. He also discovers that writing may be a good career for him. (b) Learning about someone else's life can help us make wise decisions in our own life.

---

prose and complimented me. Nothing more was said about it immediately, but a new idea had taken life in her mind. Halfway through supper she suddenly interrupted the conversation.

"Buddy," she said, "maybe you could be a writer."

I clasped the idea to my heart. I had never met a writer, had shown no previous urge to write, and hadn't a notion how to become a writer, but I loved stories and thought that making up stories must surely be almost as much fun as reading them. Best of all, though, and what really gladdened my heart, was the ease of the writer's life. Writers did not have to trudge through the town peddling from canvas bags, defending themselves against angry dogs, being rejected by surly strangers. Writers did not have to ring doorbells. So far as I could make out, what writers did couldn't even be classified as work.

I was enchanted. Writers didn't have to have any gumption at all. I did not dare tell anybody for fear of being laughed at in the schoolyard, but secretly I decided that what I'd like to be when I grew up was a writer.

Autobiography
How would a career in writing have solved a problem that Baker had?

㉓

Critical Thinking

Cite textual evidence to support your responses.

© 1. **Key Ideas and Details (a)** From the passage, find two words or expressions that Baker uses to describe his traits as a young boy. **(b) Analyze:** How did those traits prevent Baker from being a good salesperson?

© 2. **Key Ideas and Details (a)** Why does Baker's mother get him a job as a newsboy? **(b) Infer:** What goals does Baker's mother set for him as a child? **(c) Compare and Contrast:** Compare Baker's own aims in life as a child with the goals his mother sets for him.

© 3. **Craft and Structure (a) Analyze:** Identify two examples that show Baker's sense of humor about his poor salesmanship. **(b) Connect:** What does his sense of humor about failure show about his personality?

© 4. **Integration of Knowledge and Ideas (a)** What does Baker learn about himself through the events he relates here? **(b)** How can learning about someone else's life help us to learn about our own experiences? *[Connect to the Big Question: What should we learn?]*

482 Types of Nonfiction

Vocabulary Development

Vocabulary Knowledge Rating
When students have completed reading and discussing "A Special Gift—The Legacy of 'Snowflake' Bentley" and "No Gumption," have them take out their **Vocabulary Knowledge Rating Chart.** Read the words aloud once more, and have students rate their knowledge of the words again in the After Reading column. Clarify any words that are still problematic. Have students write their own definitions

and examples or sentences in the appropriate column. Then, have students complete the Vocabulary Practice activities on the next page. Encourage students to use the words in further discussion and written work about this selection. Remind them that they will be accountable for these words on the **Selection Test** (*Unit 3 Resources,* pp. 112–114 or 115–117).

Comparing Biography and Autobiography

1. Key Ideas and Details (a) In a chart, list three details in the biography that show the writer researched Snowflake Bentley. For each, indicate what source she may have used.

Details	Possible Source

(b) Are there occasions in a biography when readers get opinions directly from the person who is the focus of the biography? Explain.

2. Craft and Structure (a) List two details in "No Gumption" that only Russell Baker could have known. **(b)** How would the narrative be different if Doris were telling the story?

Timed Writing

Explanatory Text: Essay

Compare and contrast what you learned about Snowflake Bentley with what you learned about Russell Baker. As you write, consider the differences between the genres of biography and autobiography and the sorts of information that each genre delivers. **(40 minutes)**

5-Minute Planner

1. Read the prompt carefully and completely.

2. Gather your ideas by jotting down answers to these questions:
   - Which person do you feel you understand better? Why?
   - How does the form—autobiography or biography—affect your ability to learn about each person?
   - How does the way the story is organized add to your understanding of the subject?

3. Review each selection. Take notes on the types of details, such as facts, descriptions, or plot events, that lead to insights about each subject. Use these notes as you write your comparison-and-contrast essay.

4. Reread the prompt, and then draft your essay.

A Special Gift—The Legacy of "Snowflake" Bentley • No Gumption **483**

483

- Writing 2.a, b, c, d; 4, 5
- Language 2.b

Introducing the Writing Assignment

Review the assignment and the criteria, using the instruction on the student page.

Connecting to Real-Life Writing

Point out these examples of how-to writing:

- Instruction booklets give directions on how to use appliances.
- Technical directions explain how to operate electronic devices.

 **Writing Workshop**
Work in Progress

If students have completed the Work-in-Progress assignments on pp. 439 and 459, suggest that they try to develop their Work-in-Progress ideas in a how-to essay.

Prewriting/Planning Strategies

Introduce the prewriting strategy, and have students apply it to gather ideas.

Six Traits Focus

✔ Ideas	Word Choice
✔ Organization	Sentence Fluency
Voice	Conventions

Writing Workshop

Write an Explanatory Text

Exposition: How-to Essay

Defining the Form A **how-to essay** is a written, step-by-step explanation of how to do or make something. For example, how-to essays can explain how to repair a bicycle or how to make organic brownies. You may use elements of a how-to essay to write instructions, technical documents, and explanations.

Assignment Write a how-to essay about a process that you know well enough to explain clearly. You should feature these elements:

✔ a *narrow, focused topic* that can be fully explained in the essay

✔ a *list of materials* needed

✔ multi-step directions explained in *sequential order*

✔ *illustrations* that help clarify the directions

✔ appropriate *technical terms* relating to your topic

✔ error-free writing, including *correct use of conjunctions*

To preview the criteria on which your how-to essay may be judged, see the rubric on page 489.

 Writing Workshop: *Work in Progress*

Review the work you did on pages 439 and 459.

Prewriting/Planning Strategies

Choose a topic. List activities you know well in categories such as *sports, assembly and repair,* and *cooking.* Choose one as your topic.

List and itemize. List materials and steps, using the chart as a model. Itemize each part and add specific details.

Making Banana Bread

List	Itemize

Preheat oven.
Mix dry ingredients.
Mix other ingredients.
Prepare bananas.
Ice the cake.

- 2 c. flour   • 1 t. baking soda   • 1/3 c. butter
- 1 c. sugar   • 1 t. cinnamon   • 1 egg
- 1 c. yogurt   • 2 bananas   • 1 t. vanilla

Bananas should be peeled and ripe. Mash them with vanilla and yogurt.

Writing

2.a. Introduce a topic clearly, previewing what is to follow; organize ideas, concepts, and information, using strategies such as definition, classification, comparison/contrast, and cause/effect; include formatting, graphics, and multimedia when useful to aiding comprehension.

2.d. Use precise language and domain-specific vocabulary to inform about or explain the topic.

4. Produce clear and coherent writing in which the development, organization, and style are appropriate to task, purpose, and audience.

5. With some guidance and support from peers and adults, develop and strengthen writing as needed by planning, revising, editing, rewriting, or trying a new approach, focusing on how well purpose and audience have been addressed.

Teaching Resources

The following resources can be used to enrich or extend the instruction.

All *Unit 3 Resources*
Writing Workshop, pp. 118, 119

All *Common Core Companion,*
pp. 202–212; 225–239

All *Professional Development Guidebook*
Rubrics for Self-Assessment: How-to Essay,
pp. 228–229

All *Graphic Organizer Transparencies*
Rubric for Self-Assessment: How-to Essay, p. 91

PHLit Online! All resources, including print and video, are also available online at www.PHLitOnline.com.

First Things First

Organization is the structure a writer chooses to achieve a desired effect. Use **chronological,** or step-by-step, organization when you write a how-to essay. A reader needs clear, well-organized directions in order to complete a task sucessfully. If the steps are out of order, or if they are unclear, he or she will have a difficult time following your directions.

Creating a List Make a list of all materials or ingredients needed. Organize these items in the order in which they will be used. Doing so will help the reader organize his or her own workspace. Then, list all of the steps in consecutive order—that is, the order in which they should be performed. Use numbers and spacing to make the steps easy to follow.

Clarifying Terms and Steps Once you have your lists, look for any specialized terms or steps that need an explanation. A step or term that is familiar to you may not be familiar to someone else. Make your explanations clear, concise, and easy to follow.

One Simple Plan

To organize your draft, use a chart like the one below. Add lines for materials and instructions as needed.

Title/Introduction _____	
Materials list	**Instructions**
☐ _____	1. _____
☐ _____	2. _____
☐ _____	3. _____
Conclusion _____	

Checking Your Organization Exchange your completed how-to chart with a classmate for a peer review. As you read your partner's chart, note whether each of the materials and instructions listed are clearly described and appear in a logical and easy-to-follow order. Provide feedback for your partner by suggesting possible edits for clarity or improved organization.

Applying Understanding by Design Principles

Clarifying Expected Outcomes: Using Rubrics

- Before students begin work on this assignment, have them preview the Rubric for Self-Assessment (p. 489) to know what qualities their essays must have. A copy of this rubric appears in the *Graphic Organizer Transparencies,* p. 91.

- Review the criteria in the Rubric with the class. Before students use the Rubric to assess their own writing, work with them to rate the Student Model (p. 488) using the Rubric.
- If you wish to assess students' how-to essays with either a 4-point or a 6-point scoring rubric, see *Professional Development Guidebook,* pp. 228–229.

First Things First

1. Introduce the writing skill, using the instruction on the student page.
2. Encourage students to use the strategies as they draft.

Teaching the Writing Skill

1. Remind students that the purpose of a piece of writing determines the best structure to follow. Be certain they understand that step-by-step, or sequential, organization is necessary in a how-to essay so that the reader can successfully complete the task.

2. Use a recipe as an illustration of listing materials in the order in which they will be used. **Ask:** What might happen if you first had to add eggs and butter but those ingredients appeared at the end of the list?
   Possible answer: It would be more difficult for the person trying to follow the recipe.
   Then, ask students to check that the list of materials in their draft reflects the order of use.

3. Ask students to underline specialized terms or steps in their drafts and then define each to help readers who are unfamiliar with the topic.

4. Have students exchange papers. Instruct the reader to put an X at any point the instruction is not clear or a step is missing. Point out to the class that it is easier for someone other than the writer to note missing steps.

PH WRITING COACH Grade 7

Students will find additional support for writing a how-to essay in chapter 12.

Prentice Hall EssayScorer

A writing prompt for this mode of writing can be found on the *Prentice Hall EssayScorer* at **www.PHLitOnline.com.**

Drafting Strategies

1. Introduce the drafting strategies.

2. Have students apply the strategies as they draft.

Teaching the Strategies

Remind students that they cannot assume that the reader knows anything about the topic. Ask the class to think about tying a shoe. If someone didn't know how to tie a shoe, what details would the writer have to include? List the details on the board and guide the class to add to that list. Then, ask students to apply the same approach to their essays.

Think Aloud: Model Organization

Say to students:

> Suppose I write the following instructions for a cake recipe: *Mix the dry ingredients and the wet ingredients together.* The reader will think all of the ingredients should be mixed at one time, which is not correct. I need to break up the steps to read: *First, mix the dry ingredients together. Next, mix the wet ingredients together. Finally, combine the two mixtures.* Now the reader will know exactly what to do.

Six Traits Focus

✔ Ideas	✔ Word Choice
✔ Organization	Sentence Fluency
Voice	Conventions

Revising Strategies

1. Introduce the revising strategies, using the instruction on the student page.

2. Have students apply the strategies as they revise.

Teaching the Strategies

1. Remind students that they should use transitional words and phrases between sentences.

2. Emphasize that students should use precise terms rather than vague words, such as *stuff*.

Six Traits Focus

✔ Ideas	✔ Word Choice
✔ Organization	Sentence Fluency
Voice	Conventions

486

Drafting Strategies

Add details to make your essay more precise. Look for places in your draft that need elaboration or clarification. Add details that show how much, how long, or how to complete a step.

Include helpful illustrations. To help readers follow your directions, include illustrations that clarify one or more steps. Add labels to simple line drawings, photographs, or diagrams to help explain your graphics. Place each illustration in the section of your draft that describes the step it shows.

Revising Strategies

Insert transitions. Time transitions indicate sequential order. They include words such as *first, later, next,* and *finally,* as well as phrases such as *in about an hour* or *when the glue has dried.* Review your draft and add transitions, as necessary, to clarify the order of events.

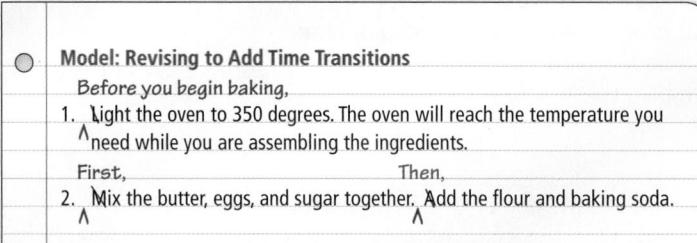

Model: Revising to Add Time Transitions

Before you begin baking,
1. Light the oven to 350 degrees. The oven will reach the temperature you need while you are assembling the ingredients.
First,   Then,
2. Mix the butter, eggs, and sugar together. Add the flour and baking soda.

Upgrade to technical vocabulary. When explaining a process, use appropriate technical terms associated with your topic. Technical words are more precise than general words. Because of this, technical words can make your writing less wordy and can minimize redundancy, or meaningless repetition. For example, in the items shown below, notice how the names of specific kitchen utensils use fewer words and are less repetitive than the general terms. Review your draft, circling all general terms. Replace the general terms with precise words that clarify the process while minimizing wordiness and redundancy.

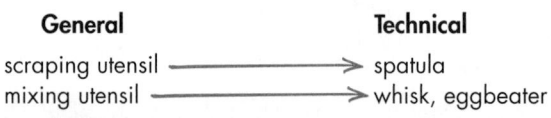

General	Technical
scraping utensil ⟶	spatula
mixing utensil ⟶	whisk, eggbeater

 **Common Core State Standards**

Writing

2.a. Introduce a topic clearly, previewing what is to follow; organize ideas, concepts, and information, using strategies such as definition, classification, comparison/contrast, and cause/effect; include formatting, graphics, and multimedia when useful to aiding comprehension.

2.b. Develop the topic with relevant facts, definitions, concrete details, quotations, or other information and examples.

2.c. Use appropriate transitions to create cohesion and clarify the relationships among ideas and concepts.

2.d. Use precise language and domain-specific vocabulary to inform about or explain the topic.

Language

3. Use knowledge of language and its conventions when writing, speaking, reading, or listening.

3.a. Choose language that expresses ideas precisely and concisely, recognizing and eliminating wordiness and redundancy.

Revising to Combine Sentences Using Conjunctions

Too many short sentences in a row can make your writing choppy—that is, your writing will seem to have a repetitive stop-start quality. Using conjunctions to combine sentences will help you create a smoother, more varied writing style.

Identifying Sentences to Combine Combine sentences that express similar ideas by using words that clarify the relationship between the ideas. Here are two common ways to combine sentences:

Use a coordinating conjunction, such as *and* or *but*.

CHOPPY: I really wanted to sleep. I had to walk my dogs.

COMBINED: I really wanted to sleep, **but** I had to walk my dogs.

Add a subordinating conjunction, such as *after* or *until*.

CHOPPY: You cannot read the book. I want a chance.

COMBINED: You cannot read the book **until** I get a chance.

Fixing Choppy Sentences To fix choppy sentences, rewrite them using the following method.

1. **Identify relationships between sentences.** Look for a series of related short sentences. Identify whether the ideas in the sentences are of equal importance or unequal importance.

2. **Combine sentences.** Combine sentences showing equal importance by using coordinating conjunctions. Use subordinating conjunctions to combine sentences of unequal importance.

Coordinating Conjunctions	Common Subordinating Conjunctions
and, or, so, for, but, nor, yet	after, although, as, as if, as long as, because, before, even though, if, in order that, since, so that, than, though, unless, until, when, whenever, where, wherever, while

PH WRITING COACH

Further instruction and practice are available in *Prentice Hall Writing Coach.*

Grammar in Your Writing

Read your draft aloud, highlighting any passages that sound choppy. Then, revise by combining sentences using the method described.

Strategies for Using Technology

Suggest that if students use a word processing program to draft their essays, they might want to use an automatic listing feature to help them organize their lists. As they add or remove steps, the feature will automatically renumber the remaining steps. Students can also use the revision tools on the *Writing and Grammar Interactive Text Online* at **www.pearsonsuccessnet.com.**

Revising to Combine Sentences Using Conjunctions

1. Introduce the grammar skill, using the instruction on the student page.

2. Discuss the rules and examples, as well as the strategies for improving choppy writing.

3. Have students follow the instruction under Grammar in Your Writing to fix choppy sentences in their drafts.

Teaching the Grammar Skill

1. Students may need help revising choppy sentences. Offer the following examples.

   Choppy: I am going to eat my dinner. Then, I will go to the library.

   Combined: After I eat my dinner, I will go to the library.

   Choppy: Not many people came to the party. The party was fun.

   Combined: Not many people came to the party, but it was fun.

2. Explain that coordinating conjunctions, such as *and* and *but*, combine two ideas of equal rank. *Example:* I went to the store and bought crackers.

3. Have students use conjunctions to revise the following sentences:

   • Come over to my house. Wait till I finish my homework. (**Possible response:** Come over to my house after I finish my homework.)

   • She thought the movie was thought provoking. She thought the movie was too long. (**Possible response:** She thought the movie was thought provoking, but too long.)

Think Aloud: Model Using Subordinating Conjunctions

Model the strategy of correctly using subordinating conjunctions, using the following "think aloud." Say to students:

   To combine ideas in my essay using subordinating conjunctions, I keep in mind that subordinating conjunctions join a main idea and a secondary idea. I can combine two choppy sentences, such as *I can't use the gym. I have to get a gym pass,* with a subordinating conjunction. I would write *I can't use the gym until I get a gym pass.* I have connected the two related ideas.

Student Model

Review the Student Model with the class, using the annotations to analyze the writer's use of the elements of a how-to essay.

Teaching From the Student Model

1. Explain that the student model is a sample and that essays may be longer.

2. **Ask** students how Danielle's opening paragraph interests readers in her topic. **Possible response:** by pointing out that volleyball is popular and that learning to serve will be useful

3. **Ask** students to evaluate Danielle's directions. Are there any points that are unclear or that use imprecise language? **Possible response:** The meaning of "square" toss is not immediately clear—*vertical* might better convey her idea.

4. Have students discuss the effectiveness of Danielle's conclusion. **Possible response:** It works well by summing up her point that this skill takes practice and by ending on an encouraging, enthusiastic note.

Connecting to Real–Life Writing

Tell students that many workplaces have internal, or in-house, publishing facilities for producing guidelines or instructional materials for employees. Point out that effective writing of this kind is often written in the style of a how-to essay. You may wish to obtain materials of this kind to share with students.

Student Model: Danielle Spiess, LaPorte, IN

 Common Core State Standards

Language
2.b. Spell correctly.

How to Serve Overhand in Volleyball

Volleyball is one of the most popular sports around. Knowing how to serve overhand will be useful if you ever decide to try out for a team. If you have ever seen anyone serve, it may look pretty easy, but it is not as easy as it looks. It takes a lot of practice!

To practice, you'll need a volleyball, a practice ball that is heavier than regulation balls, and a net.

1. To start off, use a volleyball that is heavier than normal. It will be more difficult at the beginning, but when you finally get your serve over, it will be a lot stronger. The regular volleyball is lighter, so you won't have to put as much force into your serve during games.

2. Next is the toss, probably the most important part of the serve. Throw the volleyball into the air. Try to get a high, square toss. If your toss is too low or off to one side, the ball will not go over the net the way you want it to. It might also go too far in front of you or behind you. If this happens, catch the volleyball and start over.

   It will take you a while to get the perfect toss. So, you may need extra practice to make sure you can toss the ball well enough to set up a good serve. Work with a partner to get your toss in the right zone—straight up and not too low.

3. The final step is hitting it over. You can use either an open or a closed hand. Using an open hand is easier because when a closed hand is used, you sometimes hit the volleyball off your knuckles. After you toss the ball, wait until your toss reaches its peak, and then hit it. The volleyball may not go over the first time, but soon you will get it.

   In volleyball, serving takes a lot of practice and a lot of effort, but it is a key skill for any serious player. As with any other athletic skill, set a goal for yourself. Then, just keep with it and don't give up!

Danielle focuses her essay on how to serve a volleyball.

This paragraph identifies the items necessary to complete the task.

Danielle explains why using a heavier ball is the best way to get started.

This paragraph clearly identifies the steps for tossing the ball.

Danielle explains all steps in sequential order.

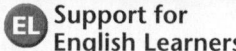

Differentiated Instruction for Universal Access

Strategy for Less Proficient Writers

Before the writing begins, work with students on their choice of topic. Encourage them to choose a topic that is very specific, for example, how to make a book cover, how to bake a potato in a microwave, how to tape a hockey stick, or how to set up a game of checkers. Encourage students to work in pairs and tell a partner how to do the task. Partners can raise questions when a step is not clear.

EL Support for English Learners

When students have chosen their topic, have them form lists of vocabulary that they will need for their essays. Encourage them to seek specific words for parts or steps in the process they plan to describe. Have them keep the list to refer to as they write.

Editing and Proofreading

Review your draft to eliminate errors in grammar, spelling, and punctuation. Use the **spell-check feature on your computer** to help you identify the correct spelling of words.

Focus on sentence fragments. A **sentence fragment** is a group of words that is incorrectly punctuated as a sentence. A fragment is missing a subject, a predicate, or both. Therefore, it does not express a complete thought. Proofread your essay to make sure all of your sentences are complete.

Publishing and Presenting

Consider one of the following ways to share your writing:

Give a demonstration. Use props to give a demonstration of the task you explain in your essay.

Make a class anthology. With classmates, combine your essays into a how-to reference booklet. Display the book in your school or local library, where people can use it.

Reflecting on Your Writing

Writer's Journal Jot down your answer to this question:
Which drafting strategy did you find most useful? Explain.

Spiral Review

Earlier in the unit, you learned about **conjunctions** (p. 438) and **prepositions and prepositional phrases** (p. 458). Check your use of conjunctions, prepositions, and prepositional phrases in your how-to essay.

PH | WRITING COACH
Further instruction and practice are available in *Prentice Hall Writing Coach*.

Rubric for Self-Assessment

Find evidence in your writing to address each category. Then, use the rating scale to grade your work.

Criteria	Rating Scale
	not very — very
Focus: How well have you focused your topic?	1 2 3 4 5
Organization: How clearly organized are the lists of materials and directions?	1 2 3 4 5
Support/Elaboration: How helpful are the illustrations?	1 2 3 4 5
Style: How appropriate are the technical terms?	1 2 3 4 5
Conventions: How correct is your grammar, especially your use of conjunctions?	1 2 3 4 5

Editing and Proofreading

1. Introduce the editing and proofreading focus, using the instruction on the student page.

2. Have students edit and proofread their narratives, correcting grammar, spelling, punctuation, and word choice. Make sure they check for errors of the type noted in the lesson focus and the Spiral Review.

Teaching the Editing Focus

Review fragments with students by presenting the following examples. Note that the examples contain subjects and verbs but do not express complete thoughts.

That I did yesterday.

As long as he is willing.

Until he gets here.

After the play was over.

Six Traits Focus

Ideas	Word Choice
Organization	Sentence Fluency
Voice	✔ Conventions

ASSESS

Publishing and Presenting

1. Have students hand out copies of their how-to essays so the audience can follow along as they perform their demonstration.

2. Suggest that students organize their anthologies into sections, such as sports, crafts, technical instructions, and recipes.

Reflecting on Your Writing

Suggest that students compare their first and final drafts to check for new insights that occurred to them during the writing process.

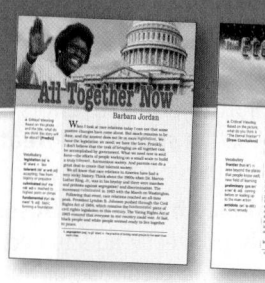 

✓ All Together Now • ✓✓ The Eternal Frontier
Lesson Pacing Guide

DAY 1 Preteach

- © Administer the Reading and Vocabulary Warm-ups (*Unit 3 Resources,* pp. 127–130 or 145–148) as necessary.
- • Introduce the Reading Skill: Classifying Fact and Opinion.
- © Introduce the Literary Analysis concept: Persuasive Essay.
- • Distribute copies of the graphic organizer for the Reading Skill (*Graphic Organizer Transparencies,* pp. 95–97).
- • Distribute copies of the graphic organizer for Literary Analysis (*Graphic Organizer Transparencies,* pp. 92–94).
- © Teach the selection vocabulary.
- © Introduce the Word Study skill.

DAYS 2–3 Preteach/Teach

- © Build background with the Background feature.
- • Develop thematic vocabulary and thematic thinking with Writing About the Big Question.
- • Prepare students to read with the Activating Prior Knowledge activities (TE).
- • Informally monitor comprehension while students read.
- • Use the Reading Check questions to confirm comprehension.
- • Develop students' ability to distinguish between fact and opinion using the Fact and Opinion questions.
- © Develop students' understanding of persuasive essays using the Persuasive Essay questions.
- © Reinforce vocabulary with the Vocabulary notes.
- © Reinforce unit focus standards using the Spiral Review prompts.

DAY 4 Assess

- • Assess students' comprehension and mastery of the skills by having them answer the Critical Thinking, Reading Skill, and Literary Analysis questions.
- © Have students complete the Vocabulary Practice activities.
- © Have students complete the Word Study activities.

DAY 5 Extend/Assess

- • Have students complete the Conventions lesson.
- © Have students complete the Writing activity and write a persuasive letter. (You may assign as homework.)
- © Extend learning by having students complete the Speaking and Listening activity, a public service announcement. As an alternative, assign them "The Titans Remember" or "The Price of Discovery" in *Reality Central.*
- • Administer Selection Test A or B (*Unit 3 Resources,* pp. 160–165 or 139–144).

© Common Core State Standards

Reading Informational Text
5. Analyze the structure an author uses to organize a text, including how the major sections contribute to the whole and to the development of the ideas.
8. Trace and evaluate the argument and specific claims in a text, assessing whether the reasoning is sound and the evidence is relevant and sufficient to support the claims.

Writing 1.a. Introduce claim(s), acknowledge alternate or opposing claims, and organize the reasons and evidence logically.
1.b. Support claim(s) with logical reasoning and relevant evidence, using accurate, credible sources and demonstrating an understanding of the topic or text, assessing whether the reasoning is sound and the evidence is relevant and sufficient to support the claims.

Speaking and Listening 4. Present claims and findings, emphasizing salient points in a focused, coherent manner with pertinent descriptions, facts, details, and examples.

Language 4.b. Use common, grade-appropriate Greek or Latin affixes and roots as clues to the meaning of a word.
6. Acquire and use accurately grade-appropriate general academic and domain-specific words and phrases; gather vocabulary knowledge when considering a word or phrase important to comprehension or expression.

Additional Standards Practice
***Common Core Companion,* pp. 122–123, 142–156**

Daily Block Scheduling
Each day in this Lesson Pacing Guide represents a 40–50 minute period. Teachers using block scheduling may combine days to revise pacing. In addition, teachers may differentiate and support core instruction by integrating components for extended and intensive support, as students require. See the Guide to Selected Leveled Resources (facing page).

Selection Support

"The Eternal Frontier" by Louis L'Amour

After You Read A: Reading—Recognize Opinion

Opinion	Clues
If that had been the spirit of man we would still be hunters and food gatherers,…	If that had been…

Graphic Organizer Transparencies
© Pearson Education, Inc. All rights reserved.

Graphic Organizer Transparencies

EL L1 L2 Reading: Graphic Organ...
pp. 95, 96 (partially filled i...

Also available for these selections:

L3 Literary Analysis: Graphic Organiz...
pp. 92, 93 (partially filled in)

EL L1 L2 Literary Analysis: Graphic
Organizer B, p. 94 (partiall...

EL L3 Reading: Graphic Organizer B,

PHLit Online!
www.PHLitOnline.com

Online

- complete narrated selection text
- a thematically related video with writing prompt
- an interactive graphic organizer
- highlighting feature
- access to all student print resources, adapted to individual student needs
- Spanish and English summaries
- adapted selection translations in Spanish

Backgrou...

Also avail...

Get Conne...
All videos...

Guide to Selected Leveled Resources

R T I **Tier 1** (students performing on level)	✓ **More Accessible** All Together Now	✓✓ **More Complex** The Eternal Frontier
Warm Up — Practice, model, and monitor fluency, working with the whole class or in groups.	Vocabulary and Reading Warm-ups B, *Unit 3 Resources,* pp. 145–146, 148	Vocabulary and Reading Warm-ups B, *Unit 3 Resources,* pp. 127–128, 130
Comprehension/Skills — Support and monitor comprehension and skills development, having students complete the activities, graphic organizers, and interactive prompts independently or as a class.	• *Reader's Notebook,* adapted instruction and summary **EL** *Reader's Notebook: English Learner's Version,* adapted instruction and summary • Reading Skill Graphic Organizer B, *Graphic Organizer Transparencies,* p. 97 • Literary Analysis Graphic Organizer B, *Graphic Organizer Transparencies,* p. 94	• *Reader's Notebook,* adapted instruction and full selection **EL** *Reader's Notebook: English Learner's Version,* adapted instruction and adapted selection • Reading Skill Graphic Organizer B, *Graphic Organizer Transparencies,* p. 97 • Literary Analysis Graphic Organizer B, *Graphic Organizer Transparencies,* p. 94
Monitor Progress **A** — Monitor student progress with the differentiated curriculum-based assessment in the *Unit Resources.*	• Selection Test B, *Unit 3 Resources,* pp. 163–165 • Open-Book Test, *Unit 3 Resources,* pp. 157–159	• Selection Test B, *Unit 3 Resources,* pp. 142–144 • Open-Book Test, *Unit 3 Resources,* pp. 136–138

R T I **Tier 2** (students requiring intervention)	✓ **More Accessible** All Together Now	✓✓ **More Complex** The Eternal Frontier
Warm Up — Practice, model, and monitor fluency in groups or with individuals.	• Vocabulary and Reading Warm-ups A, *Unit 3 Resources,* pp. 145–147 • *Reality Central,* "The Titans Remember" • *Hear It!* Audio CD	• Vocabulary and Reading Warm-ups A, *Unit 3 Resources,* pp. 127–129 • *Reality Central,* "The Price of Discovery" • *Hear It!* Audio CD (adapted text)
Comprehension/Skills — • Support and monitor comprehension and skills development, working in small groups or with individuals. • Pair students with more advanced peers and have them complete the writing activity in the *Real-World Writing Journal.* • As students complete the selection in the appropriate version of the *Reader's Notebook,* monitor comprehension frequently with group questions and individual instruction. • Model strategies while guiding students in completing the activities and prompts in the *Reader's Notebook,* as well as the graphic organizers. • Practice skills and monitor mastery with the *Reading Kit* worksheets.	• *Real-World Writing Journal,* Lesson 5, pp. 86–89 • *Reader's Notebook: Adapted Version,* adapted instruction and summary **EL** *Reader's Notebook: English Learner's Version,* adapted instruction and summary • Reading Skill Graphic Organizer A, *Graphic Organizer Transparencies,* p. 95 • Literary Analysis Graphic Organizer A, *Graphic Organizer Transparencies,* p. 92 • *Reading Kit,* Practice worksheets, pp. 124, 128, 134, 136, 144	• *Real-World Writing Journal,* Lesson 6, pp. 90–93 • *Reader's Notebook: Adapted Version,* adapted instruction and adapted selection **EL** *Reader's Notebook: English Learner's Version,* adapted instruction and adapted selection • Reading Skill Graphic Organizer A, *Graphic Organizer Transparencies,* p. 96 • Literary Analysis Graphic Organizer A, *Graphic Organizer Transparencies,* p. 93 • *Reading Kit,* Practice worksheets, pp. 124, 128, 134, 136, 144
Monitor Progress **A** — Monitor student progress with the differentiated curriculum-based assessment in the *Unit Resources* and in the *Reading Kit.*	• Selection Test A, *Unit 3 Resources,* pp. 160–162 • *Reading Kit,* Assess worksheets, pp. 125, 129, 135, 137, 145	• Selection Test A, *Unit 3 Resources,* pp. 139–141 • *Reading Kit,* Assess worksheets, pp. 125, 129, 135, 137, 145

TIER 3 Tier 3 intervention may require consultation with the student's special-education or dyslexia specialist. For additional support, see the Tier 2 activities and resources listed above.

One-on-one teaching Group work Whole class instruction Independent work **A** Assessment

For a complete guide to selection support, including support for Advanced students, see the Overview of Resources in the frontmatter.

✓ **All Together N**
✓✓ **The Eternal Fro**

"All-Together" Now
Barbara Jordan

RESOURCES FOR:
- **L1** Special-Needs Student
- **L2** Below-Level Students (
- **L3** On-Level Students (Tie
- **L4** Advanced Students (Tie
- **EL** English Learners
- **All** All Students

Prentice Hall
LITERATURE
Reader's Notebook

English Learner's Version

Differentiated
Instruction
for Universal Access

GRADE SEVEN

- **L2 L3** *Reader's Notebook*
- **L1** *Reader's Notebook: Adapte*
- **EL** *Reader's Notebook: English*
- **EL** *Reader's Notebook: Spanish*

490c

Critical Thinking

Before students respond, you may wish to have them write a brief objective summary of the selection. As they answer the questions below, remind them to support their answers with evidence from the text.

1. (a) L'Amour refers to outer space as the "eternal frontier." (b) **Possible response:** The frontier of space and the frontier of the West are both unknowns. They contain danger, beauty, mystery, and promise. Space is different from the West because its exploration requires complicated technology and great sums of money.

2. (a) He says we need leaders who are interested in exploring the frontier of outer space and who want to shape the future of humankind. (b) **Possible response:** Those leaders may vote for legislation and funding that support space travel.

3. (a) He compares the nay-sayers to babies who cling to their mothers. (b) **Possible responses:** This is not a fair evaluation because nay-sayers are drawing rational conclusions based on facts. The evaluation is fair because both nay-sayers and babies tend to cling to the safe and known.

4. (a) **Possible response:** The essay conveys the message that exploring outer space is our human destiny. (b) It is a positive message, because it paints a noble picture of humankind.

5. **Possible responses:** (a) Curiosity helps us explore the unknown by giving us a reason to keep looking beyond the familiar. (b) The desire to explore mysteries suggests that human beings have an innate urge to learn.

502

Vocabulary
impetus (im´ pə təs) *n.*
driving force

Yet we must not forget that along the way to outer space whole industries are springing into being that did not exist before. The computer age has arisen in part from the space effort, which gave great impetus to the development of computing devices. Transistors, chips, integrated circuits, Teflon, new medicines, new ways of treating diseases, new ways of performing operations, all these and a multitude of other developments that enable man to live and to live better are linked to the space effort. Most of these developments have been so incorporated into our day-to-day life that they are taken for granted, their origin not considered.

If we are content to live in the past, we have no future. And today is the past.

Critical Thinking

Cite textual evidence to support your responses.

1. **Key Ideas and Details (a)** What does L'Amour refer to as "the eternal frontier"? **(b) Compare and Contrast:** How might the "eternal" frontier be similar to and different from the western frontier that L'Amour writes about in his novels?

2. **Key Ideas and Details (a)** What kinds of leaders does L'Amour say we need now? Use examples from the essay to support your answer. **(b) Infer:** In which ways would those leaders support the cause of space travel?

3. **Key Ideas and Details (a)** To what does L'Amour compare the "nay-sayers" who are opposed to funding space exploration? **(b) Make a Judgment:** Do you think that is a fair evaluation? Why or why not?

4. **Integration of Knowledge and Ideas (a) Draw Conclusions:** What message about space does the essay convey? Which reasons best support L'Amour's claim? **(b) Evaluate:** Is the message positive? Explain.

5. **Integration of Knowledge and Ideas (a)** How does our curiosity help us to explore the unknown? **(b)** What can we learn from our desire to explore things that are a mystery? *[Connect to the Big Question: What should we learn?]*

502 Types of Nonfiction

Assessment Resources

Unit 3 Resources

L1 L2 EL **Selection Test A**, pp. 139–141. Administer Test A to less advanced readers.

L3 L4 EL **Selection Test B**, pp. 142–144. Administer Test B to on-level and more advanced students.

L3 L4 **Open-Book Test**, pp. 136–138. As an alternative, give the Open-Book Test.

All **Customizable Test Bank**

All **Self-tests**
Students may prepare for the **Selection Test** by taking the **Self-test** online.

PHLit Online! All assessment resources are available at **www.PHLitOnline.com**.

Reading Skill: Classifying Fact and Opinion

1. List two **facts** that L'Amour uses to support his argument about space exploration.

2. In a chart like the one shown, record three **opinions** L'Amour expresses in the essay. Then, list the clues that helped you identify each opinion.

Opinion	Clues

Literary Analysis: Persuasive Essay

© 3. **Craft and Structure** Identify one appeal to emotion and one appeal to reason that L'Amour uses in this **persuasive essay.**

© 4. **Key Ideas and Details** **(a)** What is the most convincing argument L'Amour makes? **(b)** Why is it convincing?

Vocabulary

© **Acquisition and Use** Answer each question by writing a complete sentence that includes the italicized vocabulary word. Explain your answer.

1. Was the western United States ever a new *frontier?*

2. Are *preliminary* plans the last plans a person makes?

3. Is eating dessert an *antidote* to feeling full after a heavy meal?

4. Is gravity one of the moon's *atmospheric* qualities?

5. Does your *destiny* lead you to a place you are meant to be?

6. Do some people need an *impetus* to start an assignment?

Word Study Use the context of the sentences and what you know about the **Latin root -peti-** to explain each answer.

1. When you *petition* a teacher, are you hoping for a response?

2. Can *competition* motivate a person to improve her skills?

Word Study

The **Latin root -peti-** means "to ask for, request, or strive after."

Apply It Explain how the word root -peti- contributes to the meanings of these words. Consult a dictionary if necessary.

repetitive
impetuous
appetite

The Eternal Frontier **503**

Reading Skill

1. **Possible responses:** In 1900, there were 144 miles of surfaced road in the United States, and now there are over 3,000,000.

2. **Possible response:** Opinion— There will always be the nay-sayers. . . . Clue Word—*always;* Opinion—If our world were to die tomorrow, that tiny vehicle would go on and on forever. . . . Clue Word—*forever;* Opinion— If we are content to live in the past, we have no future. Clue Word—*no.*

   For other sample answers, see *Graphic Organizer Transparencies,* **Reading Skill Graphic Organizer A,** p. 96, and the **Additional Answers** section.

Literary Analysis

3. **Possible response:** Appeal to emotion—It is our destiny to move out, to accept the challenge, to dare the unknown. Appeal to reason—The computer age has arisen in part from the space effort, which gave great impetus to the development of computing devices.

4. **Possible responses:** (a) Two convincing arguments are that space exploration is humankind's destiny and that space technology leads to other technologies that are beneficial in everyday life. (b) The first argument could be most convincing because it appeals to the human desire for progress and greatness. The second could be most convincing because it appeals to the desire for practicality.

Vocabulary
Acquisition and Use
Sample answers:

1. Yes, the western United States was a new frontier to those from the East and Europe who explored it.

2. No, preliminary plans are the earliest plans a person makes, not the last plans.

3. No, eating dessert is not an antidote to fullness because it makes you even more full.

4. No, gravity does not relate to the air, so it is not an atmospheric quality.

Word Study: Apply It
Sample answers: Something that is *repetitive* is asked for or requested over and over. Behavior that is *impetuous* involves striving without thinking about the effect. An *appetite* is the desire to request or strive after something such as food.

Answers continued

5. Yes, destiny, or the power that controls the future, leads you to where you are meant to be.

6. Yes, some people need an impetus to begin an assignment they don't want to do.

Word Study
Sample answers:

1. Yes. The root -peti- means "to ask for," so when you *petition,* you ask for a response.

2. Yes. The root -peti- means "to strive after." *Competition* involves striving after victory.

Conventions

1. Introduce the skill, using the instruction on the student page.

2. Discuss the examples in the chart.

Think Aloud: Model the Skill

Model the skill of identifying subjects and predicates. Say to students:

> This basic sentence helps me identify subjects and predicates: *The astronaut walked. Astronaut* is the simple subject. *Walked* is the simple predicate. These parts work similarly in a longer sentence: *The senior astronaut on duty walked quickly to the controls. Astronaut* is still the simple subject, so words describing the astronaut are part of the subject. *Walked* is still the simple predicate, so words that describe the walking are part of the predicate.

PH WRITING COACH Grade 7

Students will find instruction on and practice with subjects and predicates in Chapter 18, Sections 1 and 2.

Practice A

Sample answers:

1. laws (SS); caused (SP)
2. People (SS); have (SP)
3. Parents (SS); must teach (SP)
4. They (SS); should lead (SP)

Reading Application

Sample answers:

1. I (SS) <u>have</u> (SP) yet to find a racist baby.
2. Those <u>issues</u> (SS), however, <u>remain</u> (SP) crucial.
3. And <u>today</u> (SS) <u>is</u> (SP) the past.

Practice B

Sample answers:

1. Space can expand our minds.
2. Explorers travel into space.
3. Shuttles carry people to space.
4. Technology grows every day.
5. Scientists study many topics.

Writing Application

Sentences should show three circled simple subjects and predicates, with lines linking complete subjects and complete predicates.

Integrated Language Skills

All Together Now • The Eternal Frontier

Conventions: Subjects and Predicates

Every sentence has two parts—the **subject** and **predicate**—which together express a complete thought. The **subject** describes whom or what the sentence is about. The **predicate** is a verb that tells what the subject does, what is done to the subject, or what the condition of the subject is.

- A **simple subject** is the main noun or pronoun in a complete subject. A **complete subject** is a simple subject and all the words that modify it.
- A **simple predicate** is the main verb or verb phrase in a complete predicate. A **complete predicate** is a simple predicate and all the words that modify it.

Sentence	Simple Subject / Simple Predicate	Complete Subject / Complete Predicate
Lila walked quickly.	Lila / walked	Lila / walked quickly.
Lush green trees provided shade.	trees / provided	Lush green trees / provided shade.
The crashing of the waves soothed me.	crashing / soothed	The crashing of the waves / soothed me.

Practice A Circle the simple subject and underline the simple predicate in each sentence.

1. Civil rights laws caused many positive changes.
2. People in America still have a lot of work to do.
3. Parents must teach children tolerance.
4. They should lead by example.

 **Reading Application** In "All Together Now," identify the simple subject and simple predicate in three different sentences.

Practice B Write sentences, using each simple subject and predicate listed.

1. space, expands
2. explorers, travel
3. shuttles, carry
4. technology, grows
5. scientists, study

Writing Application Write three sentences on any topic. In each sentence, circle the simple subject and the simple predicate. Then, draw a line between the complete subject and the complete predicate.

PH WRITING COACH Further instruction and practice are available in *Prentice Hall Writing Coach*.

504 Types of Nonfiction

Writing

Argument Write a brief **persuasive letter** on one of the following topics from either "All Together Now" or "The Eternal Frontier."

- A letter to community leaders advising them on how people in the community can promote tolerance
- A letter to government leaders advising them about space travel

Demonstrate understanding of your topic as you draft:

- Clearly state your claim, or position. For example, "Promoting tolerance in our community would . . ." or "Space travel is important because . . ."
- Identify your goals, and use the texts or other reliable sources to explain the steps you suggest to meet them.
- Defend your claims with logical reasoning and relevant evidence.

Grammar Application Make sure you have written complete sentences that contain a subject and predicate.

Writing Workshop: *Work in Progress*

Prewriting for Exposition Make a two-column chart of everyday decisions. In the left column, list six recent choices you have made. In the right column, jot down one alternate decision for each item. Keep this Everyday Decisions chart in your writing portfolio.

Common Core State Standards

L.7.4.b, L.7.6; W.7.1.a, W.7.1.b; SL.7.4
[For the full wording of the standards, see page 490.]

Use this prewriting activity to prepare for the **Writing Workshop** on page 548.

Speaking and Listening

Comprehension and Collaboration In a small group, write a **public service announcement** (PSA) on one of the following topics:

- Promoting the fair treatment of all people
- Encouraging space travel

Follow these steps to complete the assignment.

- Give all group members a chance to speak, and listen to their ideas.
- Identify your audience, and support your claims with relevant details and descriptions that they will find logical and appealing.
- Use persuasive techniques, such as those shown in the chart on page 491.
- Share your PSA with the class, and request audience feedback.

PHLit Online!
www.PHLitOnline.com
- Interactive graphic organizers
- Grammar tutorial
- Interactive journals

Teaching Resources

Unit 3 Resources

L3 L4 EL **Integrated Language Skills: Grammar,** p. 154

L3 L4 EL **Support for Writing,** p. 155

L3 L4 **Support for Extend Your Learning,** p. 156

L4 **Enrichment,** pp. 135, 153

Enriched Online Student Edition
Available under After You Read for this selection:
All **Interactive Grammar Tutorial**
L3 **Internet Research Activity**

Professional Development Guidebook
Rubrics for Self-Assessment: Writing an Editorial, pp. 263–264

PHLit Online! All print and digital resources are available online at **www.PHLitOnline.com.** Online resources accessible to students are noted on the student page.

Writing

1. Review the assignment, using the instruction on the student page.
2. To guide students in writing an argument letter, give them **Support for Writing,** p. 155 in *Unit 3 Resources.*
3. To evaluate students' letters, use the rubrics for **Writing an Editorial,** pp. 263–264 in *Professional Development Guidebook.* In addition, you might evaluate letters based on the clarity with which they articulate a position, then identify steps to achieving it and likely challenges in doing so.

Grammar Application

Have students check their drafts to make sure all their sentences contain a subject and a predicate.

Six Traits Focus

	Ideas	Word Choice
✔	Ideas	Word Choice
✔	Organization	Sentence Fluency
	Voice	Conventions

PH WRITING COACH Grade 7

Students will find further instruction on and practice with persuasive writing in Chapter 9.

Writing Workshop
Work in Progress

Have students save their completed Everyday Decisions Charts in their portfolios. They will use the charts later as they continue this Work-in-Progress assignment (see p. 527). These assignments prepare them to complete the Writing Workshop assignment (see pp. 548–555).

Speaking and Listening

1. Review the assignment, using the instruction on the student page.
2. To support students' work on the assignment, have them complete the **Support for Extend Your Learning** page (*Unit 3 Resources,* p. 156).

505

✓ **The Real Story of a Cowboy's Life** •
✓✓ **Rattlesnake Hunt**

Lesson Pacing Guide

DAY 1 Preteach

- Ⓒ Administer the Reading and Vocabulary Warm-ups (*Unit 3 Resources,* pp. 166–169 or 184–187) as necessary.
- Introduce the Reading Skill: Classifying Fact and Opinion.
- Ⓒ Introduce the Literary Analysis concept: Word Choice and Diction.
- Distribute copies of the graphic organizer for the Reading Skill (*Graphic Organizer Transparencies,* pp. 98–100).
- Distribute copies of the graphic organizer for Literary Analysis (*Graphic Organizer Transparencies,* pp. 101–103).
- Ⓒ Teach the selection vocabulary.
- Ⓒ Introduce the Word Study skill.

DAYS 2–3 Preteach/Teach

- Ⓒ Build background with the Background feature.
- Develop thematic vocabulary and thematic thinking with Writing About the Big Question.
- Prepare students to read with the Activating Prior Knowledge activities (TE).
- Informally monitor comprehension while students read.
- Use the Reading Check questions to confirm comprehension.
- Develop students' ability to distinguish between fact and opinion using the Fact and Opinion questions.
- Ⓒ Develop students' understanding of word choice and diction using the Word Choice and Diction questions.
- Ⓒ Reinforce vocabulary with the Vocabulary notes.
- Ⓒ Reinforce unit focus standards using the Spiral Review prompts.

DAY 4 Assess

- Assess students' comprehension and mastery of the skills by having them answer the Critical Thinking, Reading Skill, and Literary Analysis questions.
- Ⓒ Have students complete the Vocabulary Practice activities.
- Ⓒ Have students complete the Word Study activities.

DAY 5 Extend/Assess

- Have students complete the Conventions lesson.
- Ⓒ Have students complete the Writing activity and write an adaptation. (You may assign as homework.)
- Ⓒ Extend learning by having students complete the Research and Technology activity, a help-wanted ad. As an alternative, assign them "Someone Has to Do It" or "Have No Fear" in *Reality Central.*
- Administer Selection Test A or B (*Unit 3 Resources,* pp. 178–183 or 199–204).

Ⓒ Common Core State Standards

Reading Informational Text
4. Determine the meaning of words and phrases as they are used in a text, including figurative, connotative, and technical meanings; analyze the impact of a specific word choice on meaning and tone.

Writing 3.d. Use precise words and phrases, relevant descriptive details, and sensory language to capture the action and convey experiences and events.
4. Produce clear and coherent writing in which the development, organization, and style are appropriate to task, purpose, and audience.
5. Develop and strengthen writing as needed by planning, revising, editing, and rewriting, focusing on how well purpose and audience have been addressed.
8. Gather relevant information from multiple print and digital sources, using search terms effectively.

Language 4.b. Use common, grade-appropriate Greek or Latin affixes and roots as clues to the meaning of a word.
6. Acquire and use accurately grade-appropriate general academic and domain-specific words and phrases; gather vocabulary knowledge when considering a word or phrase important to comprehension or expression.

Additional Standards Practice
***Common Core Companion,** pp. 129–156*

Daily Block Scheduling
Each day in this Lesson Pacing Guide represents a 40–50 minute period. Teachers using block scheduling may combine days to revise pacing. In addition, teachers may differentiate and support core instruction by integrating components for extended and intensive support, as students require. See the Guide to Selected Leveled Resources (facing page).

Guide to Selected Leveled Resources

R T I **Tier 1** (students performing on level)	✓ **More Accessible** The Real Story of a Cowboy's Life	✓✓ **More Complex** Rattlesnake Hunt
Warm Up Practice, **model,** and **monitor** fluency, working **with the whole class** or **in groups.**	**Vocabulary** and **Reading Warm-ups B,** *Unit 3 Resources,* pp. 166–167, 169	**Vocabulary** and **Reading Warm-ups B,** *Unit 3 Resources,* pp. 184–185, 187
Comprehension/Skills **Support** and **monitor** comprehension and skills development, having students complete the activities, graphic organizers, and interactive prompts **independently** or **as a class.**	• *Reader's Notebook,* adapted instruction and full selection **EL** *Reader's Notebook: English Learner's Version,* adapted instruction and adapted selection • **Reading Skill Graphic Organizer B,** *Graphic Organizer Transparencies,* p. 100 • **Literary Analysis Graphic Organizer B,** *Graphic Organizer Transparencies,* p. 103	• *Reader's Notebook,* adapted instruction and summary **EL** *Reader's Notebook: English Learner's Version,* adapted instruction and summary • **Reading Skill Graphic Organizer B,** *Graphic Organizer Transparencies,* p. 100 • **Literary Analysis Graphic Organizer B,** *Graphic Organizer Transparencies,* p. 103
Monitor Progress **Monitor** student progress with the differentiated curriculum-based assessment in the *Unit Resources.*	• **Selection Test B,** *Unit 3 Resources,* pp. 181–183 • **Open-Book Test,** *Unit 3 Resources,* pp. 175–177	• **Selection Test B,** *Unit 3 Resources,* pp. 202–204 • **Open-Book Test,** *Unit 3 Resources,* pp. 196–198
Assess/Screen • **Assess** student progress using Benchmark Test 6. • **Preassess** instructional needs using the Vocabulary in Context section of the test.	• **Benchmark Test 6,** *Unit 3 Resources,* pp. 227–234, including Vocabulary in Context diagnostic items	• **Benchmark Test 6,** *Unit 3 Resources,* pp. 227–234, including Vocabulary in Context diagnostic items

R T I **Tier 2** (students requiring intervention)	✓ **More Accessible** The Real Story of a Cowboy's Life	✓✓ **More Complex** Rattlesnake Hunt
Warm Up Practice, **model,** and **monitor** fluency **in groups** or **with individuals.**	• **Vocabulary** and **Reading Warm-ups A,** *Unit 3 Resources,* pp. 166–168 • *Reality Central,* "Someone Has to Do It" • *Hear It!* Audio CD (adapted text)	• **Vocabulary** and **Reading Warm-ups A,** *Unit 3 Resources,* pp. 184–186 • *Reality Central,* "Have No Fear" • *Hear It!* Audio CD
Comprehension/Skills • **Support** and **monitor** comprehension and skills development, working **in small groups** or **with individuals.** • **Pair** students with more advanced peers and have them complete the writing activity in the *Real-World Writing Journal.* • As students complete the selection in the appropriate version of the *Reader's Notebook,* **monitor** comprehension frequently with group questions and individual instruction. • **Model** strategies while guiding students in completing the activities and prompts in the *Reader's Notebook,* as well as the graphic organizers. • **Practice** skills and **monitor** mastery with the *Reading Kit* worksheets.	• *Real-World Writing Journal,* Lesson 7, pp. 94–97 • *Reader's Notebook: Adapted Version,* adapted instruction and adapted selection **EL** *Reader's Notebook: English Learner's Version,* adapted instruction and adapted selection • **Reading Skill Graphic Organizer A,** *Graphic Organizer Transparencies,* p. 98 • **Literary Analysis Graphic Organizer A,** *Graphic Organizer Transparencies,* p. 101 • *Reading Kit,* Practice worksheets, pp. 124, 130, 134, 138, 146	• *Real-World Writing Journal,* Lesson 8, pp. 98–101 • *Reader's Notebook: Adapted Version,* adapted instruction and summary **EL** *Reader's Notebook: English Learner's Version,* adapted instruction and summary • **Reading Skill Graphic Organizer A,** *Graphic Organizer Transparencies,* p. 99 • **Literary Analysis Graphic Organizer A,** *Graphic Organizer Transparencies,* p. 102 • *Reading Kit,* Practice worksheets, pp. 124, 130, 134, 138, 146
Monitor Progress **Monitor** student progress with the differentiated curriculum-based assessment in the *Unit Resources* and in the *Reading Kit.*	• **Selection Test A,** *Unit 3 Resources,* pp. 178–180 • *Reading Kit,* Assess worksheets pp. 125, 131, 135, 139, 147	• **Selection Test A,** *Unit 3 Resources,* pp. 199–201 • *Reading Kit,* Assess worksheets, pp. 125, 131, 135, 139, 147
Monitor Progress • **Assess** student progress using the Benchmark Test 6. • **Preassess** instructional needs using the Vocabulary in Context section of the test.	• **Benchmark Test 6,** *Unit 3 Resources,* pp. 227–234, including Vocabulary in Context diagnostic items	• **Benchmark Test 6,** *Unit 3 Resources,* pp. 227–234, including Vocabulary in Context diagnostic items

TIER 3 Tier 3 intervention may require consultation with the student's special-education or dyslexia specialist. For additional support, see the Tier 2 activities and resources listed above.

👥 One-on-one teaching 👥 Group work 👥 Whole class instruction 👤 Independent work A Assessment

For a complete guide to selection support, including support for Advanced students, see the Overview of Resources in the frontmatter.

✓The Real Story of a Cowboy's Life
✓✓Rattlesnake Hunt

RESOURCES FOR:

- **L1** Special-Needs Students
- **L2** Below-Level Students (Tier 2)
- **L3** On-Level Students (Tier 1)
- **L4** Advanced Students (Tier 1)
- **EL** English Learners
- **All** All Students

Vocabulary/Fluency/Prior Knowledge

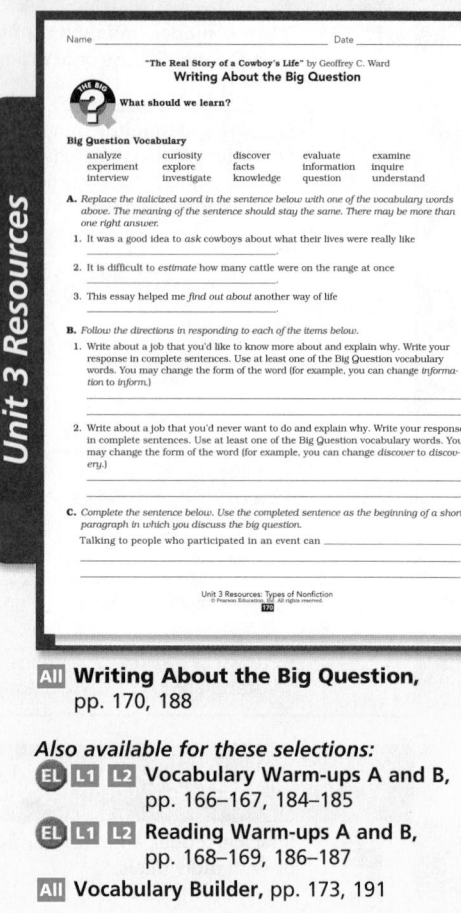

Unit 3 Resources

All Writing About the Big Question, pp. 170, 188

Also available for these selections:

EL **L1** **L2** Vocabulary Warm-ups A and B, pp. 166–167, 184–185

EL **L1** **L2** Reading Warm-ups A and B, pp. 168–169, 186–187

All Vocabulary Builder, pp. 173, 191

Reader's Notebooks

Pre- and postreading pages for both selections, as well as "The Real Story of a Cowboy's Life" appear in an interactive format in the Reader's *Notebooks*. Each *Notebook* is differentiated for a different group of learners. The selections in the Adapted and English Learner's versions are abridged.

- **L2** **L3** *Reader's Notebook*
- **L1** *Reader's Notebook: Adapted Version*
- **EL** *Reader's Notebook: English Learner's Version*
- **EL** *Reader's Notebook: Spanish Version*

©️ *Common Core Companion*

Additional instruction and practice for each Common Core State Standard

Selection Support

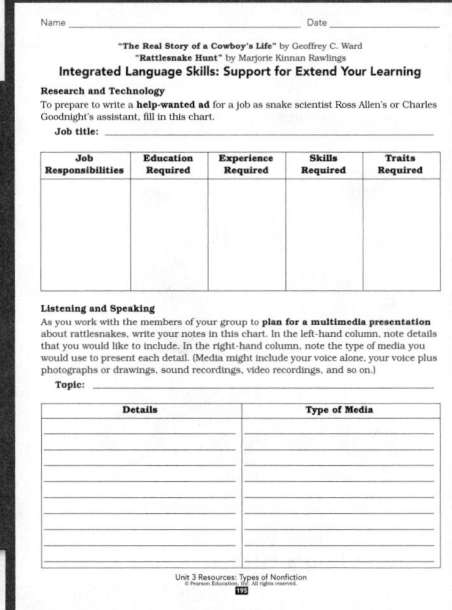

"The Real Story of a Cowboy's Life" by Geoffrey C. Ward
"Rattlesnake Hunt" by Marjorie Kinnan Rawlings

After You Read B: Literary Analysis—Diction

Technical Vocabulary	Formal Language	Informal Language

Graphic Organizer Transparencies
© Pearson Education, Inc. All rights reserved.
103

EL L3 Literary Analysis: Graphic Organizer B, p. 103

Also available for these selections:

EL L1 L2 Reading: Graphic Organizer A, pp. 98, 99 (partially filled in)

EL L3 Reading: Graphic Organizer B, p. 100

EL L1 L2 Literary Analysis: Graphic Organizer A, pp. 101, 102 (partially filled in)

Skills Development/Extension

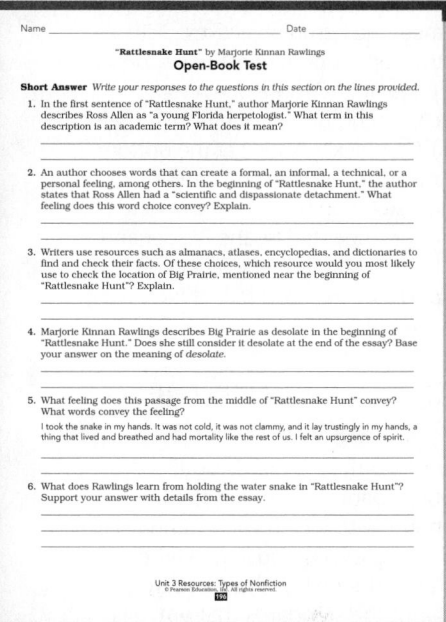

Name _____ Date _____

"The Real Story of a Cowboy's Life" by Geoffrey C. Ward
"Rattlesnake Hunt" by Marjorie Kinnan Rawlings

Integrated Language Skills: Support for Extend Your Learning

Research and Technology
To prepare to write a **help-wanted ad** for a job as snake scientist Ross Allen's or Charles Goodnight's assistant, fill in this chart.

Job title: _____

Job Responsibilities	Education Required	Experience Required	Skills Required	Traits Required

Listening and Speaking
As you work with the members of your group to **plan for a multimedia presentation** about rattlesnakes, write your notes in this chart. In the left-hand column, note details that you would like to include. In the right-hand column, note the type of media you would use to present each detail. (Media might include your voice alone, your voice plus photographs or drawings, sound recordings, video recordings, and so on.)

Topic: _____

Details	Type of Media

Unit 3 Resources: Types of Nonfiction
© Pearson Education, Inc. All rights reserved.
195

L3 L4 Support for Extend Your Learning, p. 195

Also available for these selections:

All Reading: Fact and Opinion, pp. 171, 189

All Literary Analysis: Word Choice and Diction, pp. 172, 190

L4 Enrichment, pp. 174, 192

EL L3 L4 Grammar, p. 193

EL L3 L4 Support for Writing, p. 194

Assessment

Name _____ Date _____

"Rattlesnake Hunt" by Marjorie Kinnan Rawlings

Open-Book Test

Short Answer *Write your responses to the questions in this section on the lines provided.*

1. In the first sentence of "Rattlesnake Hunt," author Marjorie Kinnan Rawlings describes Ross Allen as "a young Florida herpetologist." What term in this description is an academic term? What does it mean?

2. An author chooses words that can create a formal, an informal, a technical, or a personal feeling, among others. In the beginning of "Rattlesnake Hunt," the author states that Ross Allen had a "scientific and dispassionate detachment." What feeling does this word choice convey? Explain.

3. Writers use resources such as almanacs, atlases, encyclopedias, and dictionaries to find and check their facts. Of these choices, which resource would you most likely use to check the location of Big Prairie, mentioned near the beginning of "Rattlesnake Hunt"? Explain.

4. Marjorie Kinnan Rawlings describes Big Prairie as desolate in the beginning of "Rattlesnake Hunt." Does she still consider it desolate at the end of the essay? Base your answer on the meaning of *desolate*.

5. What feeling does this passage from the middle of "Rattlesnake Hunt" convey? What words convey the feeling?
   I took the snake in my hands. It was not cold, it was not clammy, and it lay trustingly in my hands, a thing that lived and breathed and had mortality like the rest of us. I felt an upsurgence of spirit.

6. What does Rawlings learn from holding the water snake in "Rattlesnake Hunt"? Support your answer with details from the essay.

Unit 3 Resources: Types of Nonfiction
© Pearson Education, Inc. All rights reserved.
196

All Open-Book Test, pp. 175–177, 196–198

Also available for these selections:

EL L1 L2 Selection Test A, pp. 178–180, 199–201

EL L3 L4 Selection Test B, pp. 181–183, 202–204

PHLit Online!
www.PHLitOnline.com

Online Resources: All print materials are also available online.

- complete narrated selection text
- a thematically related video with writing prompt
- an interactive graphic organizer
- highlighting feature
- access to all student print resources, adapted to individual student needs
- Spanish and English summaries
- adapted selection translations in Spanish

Get Connected! (thematic video with writing prompt)

Also available:

Background Video
All videos are available in Spanish.

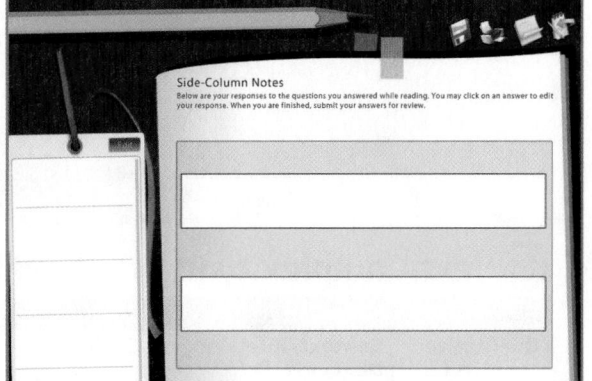

Writer's Journal (with graphics feature)

Also available:

Vocabulary Central (tools, activities, and songs for studying vocabulary)

❶ Leveled Texts

You may use either "The Real Story of a Cowboy's Life" or "Rattlesnake Hunt" to meet the lesson objectives. Skills instruction for both selections appears on page 507. Choose one selection to teach (or choose to teach both). The Text Complexity Rubric at the bottom of this page will help you determine which selection is more appropriate for your students. Use the Reader and Task Suggestions on the facing page to help all students read text of increasing complexity.

❷ ©️ Introducing the CCS Standards

Introduce the standards on the student page. (Note that the lesson element with which each standard is addressed is identified in parentheses after the text of the standard.) Call out the standards that you will cover with the selections, explaining to students what each requires and how they will address it as they work through the selection you have chosen. Standards labeled "Spiral Review" are introduced in the Literary Analysis Workshop for this unit.

Before You Read

The Real Story of a Cowboy's Life • Rattlesnake Hunt

❶ ©️ Leveled Texts

Build your skills and improve your comprehension of literary nonfiction with texts of increasing complexity.

Read **"The Real Story of a Cowboy's Life"** to experience what life was actually like in the early days of the West.

Read **"Rattlesnake Hunt"** to see how the author discovers her courage during an outdoor adventure.

❷ ©️ Common Core State Standards

Meet these standards with either **"The Real Story of a Cowboy's Life"** (p. 510) or **"Rattlesnake Hunt"** (p. 518).

Reading Informational Text
4. Determine the meaning of words and phrases as they are used in a text, including figurative, connotative, and technical meanings; analyze the impact of a specific word choice on meaning and tone. *(Literary Analysis: Word Choice and Diction)*

Writing
3.d. Use precise words and phrases, relevant descriptive details, and sensory language to capture the action and convey experiences and events. *(Writing: Adaptation)*
4. Produce clear and coherent writing in which the development, organization, and style are appropriate to task, purpose, and audience. *(Writing: Adaptation)*
5. Develop and strengthen writing as needed by planning, revising, editing, and rewriting, focusing on how well

purpose and audience have been addressed. *(Writing: Adaptation)*
8. Gather relevant information from multiple print and digital sources, using search terms effectively. *(Research and Technology: Help-wanted Ad)*

Language
4.b. Use common, grade-appropriate Greek or Latin affixes and roots as clues to the meaning of a word. *(Vocabulary: Word Study)*
6. Acquire and use accurately grade-appropriate general academic and domain-specific words and phrases; gather vocabulary knowledge when considering a word or phrase important to comprehension or expression. *(Vocabulary: Word Study)*

506 Types of Nonfiction

©️ Text Complexity Rubric: Leveled Texts

Text complexity is determined by both qualitative and quantitative measures. For this reason, the quantitative measure of a more complex selection may be lower than that of a more accessible selection.

		✓ **The Real Story of a Cowboy's Life**	✓✓ **Rattlesnake Hunt**
Qualitative Measures	**Context/Knowledge Demands**	Cowboy's life on the cattle trail; late 1800s U.S. 1 2 ③ 4 5	Fearful writer hunts rattlesnakes; Florida Everglades 1 2 3 ④ 5
	Structure/Language Conventionality	On-level vocabulary; colloquial diction 1 2 3 ④ 5	Some long sentences; formal and conversational diction 1 2 3 ④ 5
	Levels of Meaning/ Purpose/Concepts	Accessible concept (truth about cowboy's lives) 1 2 ③ 4 5	Accessible concept (overcoming fear) 1 2 ③ 4 5
Quantitative Measures	**Text Length**	Word Count: 1,208	Word Count: 1,981
	Lexile	1160L	1030L
Overall Complexity		✓ **More accessible**	✓✓ **More complex**

Reading Skill: Classifying Fact and Opinion

As you read nonfiction, be alert to the types of details a writer uses to support an idea. You can **classify** these details into two basic categories. A **fact** is information you can prove. An **opinion** is a judgment.

- **Fact:** The room measures ten feet by twelve feet.
- **Opinion:** Green is the best color for the room.

Be aware that some writers present opinions or beliefs as facts. To get to the truth, **use resources to check facts.**

Using the Strategy: Resources Chart

Use a chart like this one to identify information the writer presents. Then, indicate which resource could help you check the facts.

Resources	Statement in Text
almanac	
atlas or map	
biographical dictionary	
dictionary	
encyclopedia	
reliable Web site	

Literary Analysis: Word Choice, or Diction

A writer's word choice, or **diction,** is an important element of his or her writing. The words a writer uses can make writing seem difficult or easy, formal or informal. Diction includes not only individual words but also phrases and expressions the writer uses. The answers to these questions shape a writer's diction:

- *What does the audience already know about the topic?* The writer may have to define terms or use simpler language.
- *What feeling will this work convey?* Word choice can make a work serious or funny, academic or personal. The use of casual or formal language can make a work seem simple or complex.

As you read, notice how the author's word choice and diction affect the way you respond to a text.

Before You Read: The Real Story of a Cowboy's Life • Rattlesnake Hunt **507**

PHLit Online!
www.PHLitOnline.com

Hear It!
- Selection summary audio
- Selection audio

See It!
- Get Connected video
- Background video
- More about the author
- Vocabulary flashcards

Do It!
- Interactive journals
- Interactive graphic organizers
- Self-test
- Internet activity
- Grammar tutorial
- Interactive vocabulary games

❸ Reading Skill
Classifying Fact and Opinion

1. Introduce the skill, using the instruction on the student page.
2. Tell students that they will practice distinguishing facts and opinions as they read.

❹ Using the Strategy

Give students a copy of either **Reading Skill Graphic Organizer A** or **B** (*Graphic Organizer Transparencies,* pp. 98–100) to link statements to resources as they read. Use the examples in **Reading Skill Graphic Organizer A,** which is partially filled in, to model the process of completing the organizer.

❺ Literary Analysis
Word Choice, or Diction

1. Introduce the skill, using the instruction on the student page.
2. Tell students that they will analyze diction as they read.

Think Aloud: Model the Skill

Model a way of analyzing diction. Say to students:

> To analyze diction, I imagine someone saying the words on the page. Then I ask myself, "What does this person's voice sound like? Formal or informal, young or old, modern or traditional?" For example, the sentences *Hark! Who goes there?* and *Hey! Who's there?* have similar meanings, but use different words that create very different feelings. When you listen to diction, you will hear the writer's ideas more clearly.

Text Complexity: Reader and Task Suggestions

✓ The Real Story of a Cowboy's Life		✓✓ Rattlesnake Hunt	
Preparing to Read the Text	**Leveled Tasks**	**Preparing to Read the Text**	**Leveled Tasks**
• Using the Background information on p. 509, discuss the history of cowboys in America. • Preteach strategies for reading informal diction (p. 507). Also, explain that the essay mixes narration and quotations. • Guide students to use Multidraft Reading strategies (TE p. 509).	*Structure/Language* If students will have difficulty with language or structure, have them read to visualize the events of the drive. Then, have them reread, noting confusing examples of informal diction or jumps between narration and quotes. *Analyzing* If students will not have difficulty with language or structure, have them note ways in which the diction is used to contrast the narrator's voice with the cowboys'.	• Using the Background information on p. 517, discuss the dangers of studying rattlesnakes. • Preview and discuss examples of formal and informal diction. Use tone to contrast as you read examples aloud. • Guide students to use Multidraft Reading strategies (TE p. 517).	*Structure/Language* If students will have difficulty with diction, have them first read to track the author's confrontation with fear. Have them reread, listing examples of informal diction. *Evaluating* If students will not have difficulty with diction, have them note ways in which the author uses details to describe setting and emotion. Discuss how these details bring the narrator's experience to life.

① Writing About the Big Question

1. Review the assignment with the class.

2. Point out that learning history teaches us about the present by showing us how people in other times have faced similar situations.

3. Have students complete the sentence starter. Review responses as a class. (**Sample response:** The <u>facts</u> we can learn from historical accounts are important because they ensure that our understanding of the past is accurate.)

4. Remind students that their answers will help them think about the Big Question, "What should we learn?"

While You Read

Tell students that as they read, they should look for firsthand details that describe and explain the lives of cowboys, and then relate these details to their own lives.

② Vocabulary

1. Have students preview the selection vocabulary.

2. For each word, have students say the word aloud.

3. Then, use the word in a sentence that defines the word.

4. Finally, repeat your definitional sentence or a similar sentence with the word missing and have the class "fill in the blank" chorally. Here are some examples:

Something that is <u>ultimate</u> is final or last. We made six stops on the bus before arriving at school, our [students say "ultimate"] stop.

<u>Discipline</u> is strict control. For an army to succeed, its soldiers must be able to face combat and still maintain [students say "discipline"].

③ Word Study

1. Introduce the skill, using the instruction in the box.

2. Ask students to name a *-vers-* word that means "to go backwards." *(reverse)*

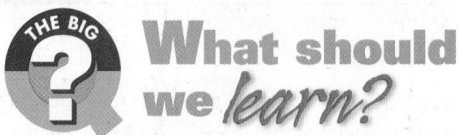 **What should we *learn?***

① Writing About the Big Question

"The Real Story of a Cowboy's Life" describes the duties and dangers that cowboys experienced in the 1800s. Use this sentence starter to develop your ideas about the Big Question.

The **facts** we can learn from historical accounts are important because _____.

While You Read Look for firsthand details that describe and explain the lives of cowboys. Then, consider which details in the text might be relevant to your life.

② Vocabulary

Read each word and its definition. Decide whether you know the word well, know it a little bit, or do not know it at all. After you read, see how your knowledge of each word has increased.

- **discipline** (dis´ ə plin´) *n.* strict control (p. 511) *When the captain slept, there was no <u>discipline</u> on the ship. disciplined v. disciplinary adj. disciplinarian n.*

- **gauge** (gāj) *v.* estimate or judge (p. 511) *She kept a straight face, and it was hard to <u>gauge</u> her reaction. gauged v. gauging v. gauge n.*

- **emphatic** (em fat´ ik) *adj.* expressing strong feeling (p. 511) *She was so <u>emphatic</u> that I believed her. emphatically adv. emphasize v. emphasis n.*

- **ultimate** (ul´ tə mit) *adj.* final (p. 512) *His <u>ultimate</u> goal was to become team captain. ultimately adv. ultimatum n.*

- **longhorns** (lôn´ hornz´) *n.* breed of cattle with long horns (p. 512) *<u>Longhorns</u> are common on ranches in Texas. longhorn n.*

- **diversions** (də vʉr´ zhənz) *n.* amusements (p. 513) *The park offered <u>diversions</u> for children and adults. divert v. diversion n. diversionary adj.*

③ Word Study

The **Latin root -vers-** means "to turn."

As this essay describes, cowboys enjoyed few **diversions**, or amusing activities that would turn their attention away from their work.

508 Types of Nonfiction

Vocabulary Development

Vocabulary Knowledge Rating

Create a **Vocabulary Knowledge Rating Chart** (*Professional Development Guidebook,* p. 33) for this selection. Include the selection vocabulary and the Big Question word that appears in the Writing About the Big Question sentence starter on this page. (The Big Question vocabulary is introduced on pp. 406–407).

Give students a copy of the chart. Read the words aloud, and have students mark their rating in the Before Reading column. Urge them to be alert to these words as they read and discuss the selection.

Tally how many students think they know a word to gauge how much instruction to provide. As students read and discuss the selection, point out the words and their context.

 **Vocabulary Central,** featuring tools, activities, and songs for studying vocabulary, is available online at **www.PHLitOnline.com.**

Geoffrey C. Ward
(b. 1940)

Author of

The Real Story of a
Cowboy's Life

Historian Geoffrey C. Ward strives to present an accurate portrayal of the past. He has written more than a dozen books about the United States and the people who played key roles in its growth. Ward's book *A First-Class Temperament*, about Franklin D. Roosevelt, won the 1989 National Book Critics Circle Award for biography. Ward has also written biographies of Mark Twain, Susan B. Anthony, Harry Truman, and Billy the Kid.

Screenwriter, Too In addition to his books, Ward has written or co-written more than a dozen screenplays for films, many of which have appeared on public television.

DID YOU KNOW ?

Ward teamed up with filmmaker Ken Burns to create the Emmy Award-winning PBS documentaries *The Civil War* and *Baseball*.

❹ BACKGROUND FOR THE ESSAY

Cowboys

American cowboys were most active from the Civil War through the 1890s. The meat industry was growing, but transportation was lacking. To get cattle to market, cowboys drove them—that is, forced them—to trudge long distances. When people hear the word *cowboy,* they think of a life of daring, romance, and adventure. As this essay shows, that may not be an accurate image.

The Real Story of a Cowboy's Life **509**

🔔 Daily Bellringer

For each class during which you teach this selection, have students complete one of the five Research activities for Week 17 in the *Daily Bellringer Activities* booklet.

❹ Background

Cowboys

Between 1866 and 1890, about 5,000,000 cattle were walked, or "driven," from Texas over the open ranges of Kansas, Nebraska, and other western states. The cattle grazed their way north to be sold in northern cities, where a profitable beef market had developed after the Civil War. Cattle drovers—men who contracted with the cattle owners to drive their herds north—were usually paid about $1 or $1.50 per head; cowboys, or trail hands—usually boys in their teens—earned about $25 to $40 a month. This lucrative business, and this legendary period in American history, virtually vanished in the 1890s, as settlers began using barbed wire to protect their homesteads.

Multidraft Reading

This icon ● marks natural pauses in the selection. To assist struggling readers and to deepen reading for all, assign the text in "chunks," following the icons, and apply multidraft reading protocols. For each reading, have students set the purpose indicated:

- **First reading**—identifying key ideas and details and answering any Reading Checks.
- **Second reading**—analyzing craft and structure and responding to the side-column prompts.
- **Third reading**—integrating knowledge and ideas, connecting to other texts and the world, and answering the end-of-selection questions.

For more guidance, refer to the *Classroom Strategies and Teaching Routines* card on multidraft reading.

Differentiated Instruction   Additional Instruction

ⓔⓛ Extended Support— English Learners
Have students complete the **Reading and Vocabulary Warm-ups**, *Unit 3 Resources*, pp. 166–169, before they read. Assign the prereading pages and the adapted selection in the *Reader's Notebook: English Learner's Version.* Then, have students listen to portions of the selection on the *Hear It!* **Audio CD.**

⎣1⎦ ⎣2⎦ Extended Support- Struggling Readers
Have students complete the **Reading and Vocabulary Warm-ups**, *Unit 3 Resources*, pp. 166–169, before they read. Assign the prereading pages and the adapted selection in the *Reader's Notebook: Adapted Version.* Then, have students listen to portions of the selection on the *Hear It!* **Audio CD** (adapted text).

Extended Support— Reluctant Readers
To build motivation and engagement before assigning the selection, have students read "Someone Has to Do It," a thematically related selection in *Reality Central.* Then, use the questions at the conclusion of the related selection to guide discussion.

For more about the author, practice with the selection vocabulary, or more background, go online at www.PHLitOnline.com.

1. Arrange students into small groups. Give them a copy of a **KWL chart** (see *Professional Development Guidebook,* p. 75), with the topic identified as *cowboys.*

2. Ask them to work together to complete the first two columns. In the Know column, they can write what they already know about cowboys. In the Want to Know column, they should write questions they have about cow-boys and how they lived.

Concept Connector ➡

Students will assess what they've learned after completing "The Real Story of a Cowboy's Life."

Whole-Class Activity

Before students begin reading, post a map that includes Texas, Oklahoma, Kansas, and Nebraska to help stu-dents see where the drives took place. Have students locate lower Texas and the rivers the cattle had to cross.

❷ **About the Selection**

This essay describes a cattle drive from the perspective of a real cow-boy who rode on one. It portrays the drive as a multifaceted, difficult expe-rience, full of conflict, danger, and reward, but not much glamour.

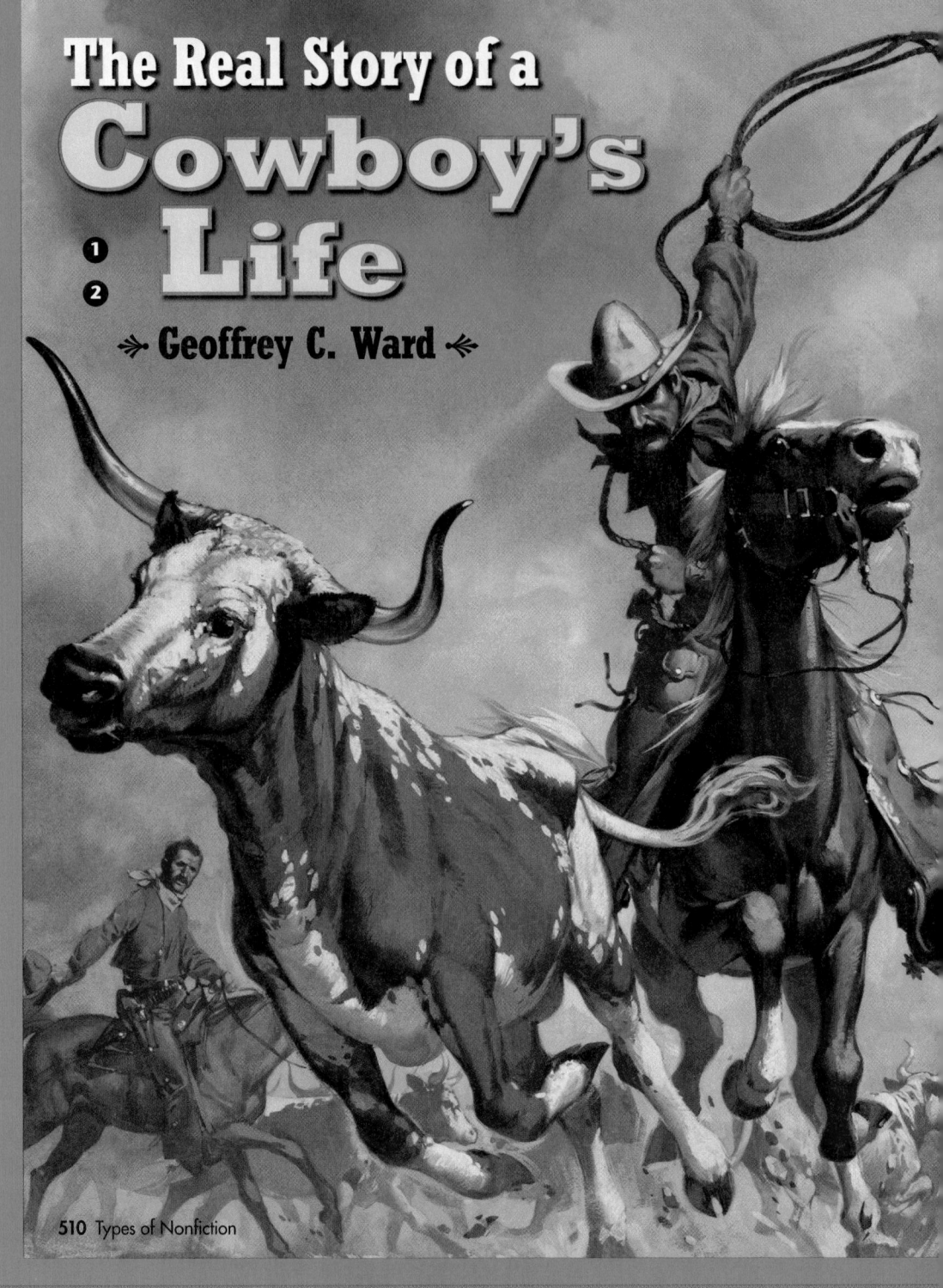

The Real Story of a
Cowboy's
❶ Life
❷
⇥ Geoffrey C. Ward ⇤

510 Types of Nonfiction

Vocabulary Development ⓒ **CCSS Language 6**

Thematic Vocabulary: The Big Question

As students are discussing "The Real Story of a Cowboy's Life," encourage them to use the thematic vocabulary presented in Introducing the Big Question, pp. 406–407. You might encourage them with sentence starters like these:

1. This essay provides some interesting <u>facts</u> and *information* about cowboys, such as . . .

2. Because modern life is so different, it's hard for me to *understand* why . . .

3. When I *evaluate* the cowboy's life, I find that they actually . . .

4. For example, I *question* whether the rules about guns . . .

5. I'd like to *discover* more about cowboys and . . .

A drive's success depended on discipline and planning. According to Teddy Blue,[1] most Texas herds numbered about 2,000 head with a trail boss and about a dozen men in charge—though herds as large as 15,000 were also driven north with far larger escorts. The most experienced men rode "point" and "swing," at the head and sides of the long herd; the least experienced brought up the rear, riding "drag" and eating dust. At the end of the day, Teddy Blue remembered, they "would go to the water barrel . . . and rinse their mouths and cough and spit up . . . black stuff. But you couldn't get it up out of your lungs."

They had to learn to work as a team, keeping the herd moving during the day, resting peacefully at night. Twelve to fifteen miles a day was a good pace. But such steady progress could be interrupted at any time. A cowboy had to know how to gauge the temperament of his cattle, how to chase down a stray without alarming the rest of the herd, how to lasso a steer using the horn of his saddle as a tying post. His saddle was his most prized possession; it served as his chair, his workbench, his pillow at night. Being dragged to death was the most common death for a cowboy, and so the most feared occurrence on the trail was the nighttime stampede. As Teddy Blue recalled, a sound, a smell, or simply the sudden movement of a jittery cow could set off a whole herd.

If . . . the cattle started running—you'd hear that low rumbling noise along the ground and the men on herd wouldn't need to come in and tell you, you'd know—then you'd jump for your horse and get out there in the lead, trying to head them and get them into a mill[2] before they scattered. It was riding at a dead run in the dark, with cut banks and prairie dog holes all around you, not knowing if the next jump would land you in a shallow grave.

Most cowboys had guns, but rarely used them on the trail. Some outfits made them keep their weapons in the chuck wagon to eliminate any chance of gunplay. Charles Goodnight[3] was still more emphatic: "Before starting on a trail drive, I made it a rule to draw up an article of agreement,

1. **Teddy Blue** Edward C. Abbot, a cowboy who rode in a successful trail drive in the 1880s.
2. **mill** *n.* slow movement in a circle.
3. **Charles Goodnight** cowboy who rode successful trail drives beginning in the 1860s.

Fact and Opinion
What resource could you use to check the size of Texas herds in the nineteenth century?

Vocabulary
discipline (dis′ ə plin′) *n.* strict control

gauge (gāj) *v.* estimate or judge

emphatic (em fat′ ik) *adj.* expressing strong feeling

5 ◄ **Critical Viewing**
How does this painting suggest the "real story" of a cowboy's life? **[Analyze]**

6  **Reading Check**
What are two dangers cowboys face?

The Real Story of a Cowboy's Life **511**

---

❸ Fact and Opinion

1. Read the first bracketed paragraph aloud. **Ask** students on what two factors a successful drive depends.
   Answer: It depended on discipline and planning.

2. **Ask** what facts illustrate the need for discipline and planning.
   Answer: Cattle numbered in the thousands, with only about a dozen men to herd them.

3. **Ask** the Fact and Opinion question.
   Answer: You might check the size of herds in an encyclopedia or on a reliable Web site.

4. Have students record these two facts in the appropriate row of their Resources Chart.

❹ Critical Thinking
Generalize

1. Have volunteers read aloud the second bracketed passage, continuing on to page 512. Then, **ask** students what each part of the passage describes.
   Answer: The first part describes a nighttime stampede, and the second part describes rules about guns on the trail.

2. **Ask** students *why* trail bosses had to have strict rules against gun use.
   Answer: They had to have strict rules to keep the cowboys from getting into fights. Living conditions on the trail probably made them irritable.

❺ Critical Viewing

Possible response: It shows a cowboy's life as hard but exciting.

❻ Reading Check

Answer: Two dangers cowboys faced were getting dragged to death and getting shot by another cowboy.

Fluency

Distribute copies of page 511 and pair students. Have partners take turns reading as listeners mark text with which readers struggle. Monitor the fluency of students' reading. Collect the marked up copies and review difficult features as a group. Look for these main problems:

- If students stumble over words such as *"point"* and *"swing,"* explain that the quotation marks highlight unusual meaning, not dialogue. Stress that in reading, the quotation marks can be ignored. Clarify, however, that

the indented text near the bottom of the page *is* a quotation. Model how to pause, then read the quotation as dialogue.

- If students stumble over the ellipsis on the page, clarify that these indicate omitted text but do not require a reading pause. The dashes that appear in the block quotation indicate a pause, like a comma. Model fluent reading of these unusual text features and have students echo, repeating until they are reading fluently.

PHLit Online!

This selection is available in interactive format in the **Enriched Online Student Edition**, at **www.PHLitOnline.com**, which includes a thematically related video with writing prompt and an interactive graphic organizer.

511

1. Identify the complete bracketed passage on the student page, then have one student read the part of Teddy Blue, and another student read the part of the narrator.

2. Have students identify a word used by the narrator that Teddy Blue might also use, and a word used by Teddy Blue that the narrator would not use.
   Answer: Teddy Blue might also use the word *nettlesome*. The narrator would not use the word *punkins*.

3. **Ask** students the Word Choice, or Diction, question.
   Possible responses: Both speakers' diction can be homespun and down-to-earth, but the narrator's diction is, in general, more formal. The narrator uses standard English ("Initially, the land immediately north of the Red River was Indian Territory. . . ."), while Teddy Blue uses conversational English ("it was sure a pretty sight. . . .").

Vocabulary
ultimate (ul´ tə mit) *adj.* final

longhorns (lôn´ hornz´) *n.* breed of cattle with long horns

Word Choice, or Diction ❼
A "jay-hawker" is a slang term for a thief. How does Blue's use of the term contribute to the meaning and feel of this passage?

---

❹ setting forth what each man was to do. The main clause stipulated[4] that if one shot another he was to be tried by the outfit and hanged on the spot, if found guilty. I never had a man shot on the trail." •

Regardless of its ultimate destination, every herd had to ford[5] a series of rivers—the Nueces, the Guadalupe, the Brazos, the Wichita, the Red.

A big herd of longhorns swimming across a river, Goodnight remembered, "looked like a million floating rocking chairs," and crossing those rivers one after another, a cowboy recalled, was like climbing the rungs of a long ladder reaching north.

"After you crossed the Red River and got out on the open plains," Teddy Blue remembered, "it was sure a pretty sight to see them strung out for almost a mile, the sun shining on their horns." Initially, the land immediately north of the Red River was Indian territory, and some tribes charged tolls for herds crossing their land—payable in money or beef. But Teddy Blue remembered that the homesteaders, now pouring onto the Plains by railroad, were far more nettlesome:

There was no love lost between settlers and cowboys on the trail. Those jay-hawkers would take up a claim right where the herds watered and charge us for water. They would plant a crop alongside the trail and plow a furrow around it for a fence, and then when the cattle got into their wheat or their garden patch, they would come cussing and waving a shotgun and yelling for damages. And the cattle had been coming through there when they were still raising punkins in Illinois.

The settlers' hostility was entirely understandable. The big herds ruined their crops, and they carried with them a disease, spread by ticks and called "Texas fever," that devastated domestic livestock. Kansas and other territories along the route soon established quarantine lines,[6] called "deadlines," at the western fringe of settlement, and insisted that trail drives not cross them. Each year, as settlers continued to move in, those deadlines moved farther west.

Sometimes, farmers tried to enforce their own, as John Rumans, one of Charles Goodnight's hands, recalled:

---

4. **stipulated** (stip´ yə lāt´ əd) *v.* stated as a rule.
5. **ford** (fôrd) *v.* cross a river at a shallow point.
6. **quarantine** (kwôr´ ən tēn) **lines** *n.* boundaries created to prevent the spread of disease.

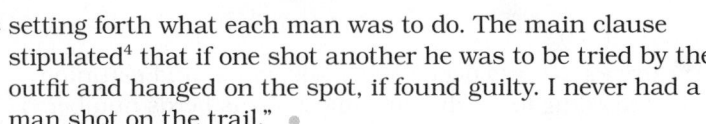

512 Types of Nonfiction

Vocabulary Development

Vocabulary Knowledge Rating
When students have completed reading and discussing "The Real Story of a Cowboy's Life," have them take out their **Vocabulary Knowledge Rating Chart** for this selection. Read the words aloud once more. Have students rate their knowledge of the words again in the After Reading column. Clarify any words that are still problematic. Have students write their own definition and example or sentence in the appropriate column.

Then have students complete the Vocabulary Practice activities at the end of the selection. Encourage students to use the words in further discussion and written work about the selection. Remind them that they will be accountable for these words on the **Selection Test**, *Unit 3 Resources*, pp. 178–180 or 181–183.

8 Critical Viewing

Possible response: They might wear hats to shield their heads and faces from the dust and sun.

9 Connecting to the Big Question

1. Discuss with students why it might be important to learn about dangers of another time.

2. Have students reread the bracketed text on page 513. **Ask:** What firsthand details does this paragraph reveal about the lives of cowboys? What does it reveal about how they solved problems? **Possible response:** The paragraph describes cowboys' experience of being threatened by settlers, and preparing to defend themselves and the cattle if needed. By being prepared but calm, they were able to solve the problem without violence.

3. **Ask:** What can you learn about the dangers facing cowboys from this recollection? How can learning this information be important and help you solve problems in today's world? **Possible response:** I can learn that cowboys sometimes faced real danger and threat from settlers. They tried to solve those threats without violence. In today's world, staying calm will also help me solve problems.

10 Reading Check

Possible response: The herds could ruin crops and carry disease as they traveled across settlers' land.

Some men met us at the trail near Canyon City, and said we couldn't come in. There were fifteen or twenty of them, and they were not going to let us cross the Arkansas River. We didn't even stop. . . . Old man [Goodnight] had a shotgun loaded with buckshot and led the way, saying: "John, get over on that point with your Winchester and point these cattle in behind me." He slid his shotgun across the saddle in front of him and we did the same with our Winchesters. He rode right across, and as he rode up to them, he said: "I've monkeyed as long as I want to with you," and they fell back to the sides, and went home after we had passed.

There were few diversions on the trail. Most trail bosses banned liquor. Goodnight prohibited gambling, too. Even the songs for which cowboys became famous grew directly out of doing a job, remembered Teddy Blue:

The singing was supposed to soothe [the cattle] and it did; I don't know why, unless it was that a sound they was used to would keep them from spooking at other noises. I know that if you wasn't singing, any little sound in the night—it might be just a horse shaking himself— could make them leave the country; but if you were singing, they wouldn't notice it.

The two men on guard would circle around with their horses on a walk, if it was a clear night and the cattle was bedded down and quiet, and one man would sing a

8 ▲ Critical Viewing
Why do you think cowboys, like those pictured, wear hats? **[Hypothesize]**

Vocabulary
diversions
(də vur´ zhənz) *n.* amusements

Reading Check

10 Why did the settlers want to stop the cowboys and their herd from coming through the land where they lived?

The Real Story of a Cowboy's Life **513**

Concept Connector

Writing About the Big Question
Have students compare their responses to the sentence starter they completed before reading the story with their ideas afterward. Ask them to explain whether their thoughts have changed.

KWL
Have students complete the last column of their KWL charts. As a class, evaluate what students learned in relation to the questions they had before reading.

Reading Skill Graphic Organizer
Ask students to review their completed graphic organizers. Then, have students share the graphic organizers they completed. Students can work in pairs to compare facts that could be checked in each resource. As they discuss their examples, remind students some facts can be verified in more than one resource.

Critical Thinking

Before students respond, you may wish to have them write a brief objective summary of the selection. As they answer the questions below, remind them to support their answers with evidence from the text.

1. He participated in several drives.

2. (a) Trail bosses commandeered the guns and set rules for behavior and responsibilities.
   (b) Someone who did not mind long hours and discomfort, a challenging and dangerous assignment, and many hours outdoors and away from family and community succeeded as a cowboy.

3. (a) The cattle ruined their crops and spread disease. (b) **Possible responses:** Their trails had been there long before the land was settled; going around settled areas made the drive longer; settlers claimed land where the herds used to water. (c) **Possible response:** Allowing settlers to charge for cattle drives across their land might be a fair solution.

4. **Possible responses:** Students might respond that the cowboys were more disciplined on the trail than they expected; that clashes with Native Americans were less common and those with settlers were more common. Students might also respond that the life was as dangerous and lonely as they thought.

5. **Possible responses:**
   (a) Careful planning, calm in periods of conflict, and tolerance of temporary discomfort can be useful in life today. (b) Information from others, whether current or in history, gives us access to other ideas and experiences beyond our own.

verse of song, and his partner on the other side of the herd would sing another verse; and you'd go through a whole song that way. . . . "Bury Me Not on the Lone Prairie" was a great song for awhile, but . . . they sung it to death. It was a saying on the range that even the horses nickered it and the coyotes howled it; it got so they'd throw you in the creek if you sang it. •

The number of cattle on the move was sometimes staggering: once, Teddy Blue rode to the top of a rise from which he could see seven herds strung out behind him; eight more up ahead; and the dust from an additional thirteen moving parallel to his. "All the cattle in the world," he remembered, "seemed to be coming up from Texas."

At last, the herds neared their destinations. After months in the saddle—often wearing the same clothes every day, eating nothing but biscuits and beef stew at the chuck wagon, drinking only water and coffee, his sole companions his fellow cowboys, his herd, and his horse—the cowboy was about to be paid for his work, and turned loose in town.

Critical Thinking

Cite textual evidence to support your responses.

1. **Key Ideas and Details** What qualifies Teddy Blue as a reliable source of information? Support your answer with details.

2. **Key Ideas and Details (a)** Identify two ways violence was kept down on the trail. **(b) Interpret:** Based on this information, what kind of person succeeded as a cowboy?

3. **Key Ideas and Details (a)** Why did settlers object to cattle coming through the land where they lived? **(b) Infer:** Why did cowboys object to going around settled areas? **(c) Make a Judgment:** What solution or compromise would have been most fair? Discuss your response with a classmate.

4. **Integration of Knowledge and Ideas Analyze:** How is the information presented about cowboys the same or different from what you have learned about cowboys or the American West in works of fiction or textbooks? Explain.

5. **Integration of Knowledge and Ideas (a)** What information from this article can you use in your own life? **(b)** Why might it be important to rely on information from others, rather than limiting our knowledge to things we experience ourselves? *[Connect to the Big Question: What should we learn?]*

514 Types of Nonfiction

Assessment Resources

Unit 3 Resources

L1 L2 EL Selection Test A, pp. 178–180. Administer Test A to less advanced readers.

L3 L4 EL Selection Test B, pp. 181–183. Administer Test B to on-level and more advanced students.

L3 L4 Open-Book Test, pp. 175–177. As an alternative, give the Open-Book Test.

All Customizable Test Bank

All Self-tests
Students may prepare for the **Selection Test** by taking the **Self-test** online.

All assessment resources are available at **www.PHLitOnline.com**.

Reading Skill: Classifying Fact and Opinion

1. Identify one **fact** and one **opinion** in the essay.
2. What resource would you use to check the distance between Canyon City and the Arkansas River?
3. How do both facts and opinions help the writer paint a full picture of his subject?

Literary Analysis: Word Choice, or Diction

4. **Craft and Structure** Review the author's **word choice,** or **diction,** by completing a chart like the one shown.

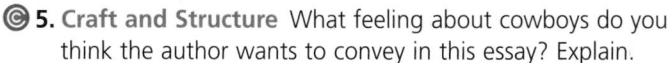

Technical Vocabulary	Formal Language	Informal Language

5. **Craft and Structure** What feeling about cowboys do you think the author wants to convey in this essay? Explain.

Vocabulary

Acquisition and Use For each item, write a sentence correctly using the words indicated.

1. diversions; long train rides
2. gauge; progress
3. ultimate; goal
4. discipline; grades
5. emphatic; message
6. longhorns; stampede

Word Study Use the context of the sentences and what you know about the **Latin root -vers-** to explain your answer to each question.

1. If you *reverse* direction, do you go the opposite way?
2. If you behave in a *subversive* manner, are you being supportive?

Word Study

The **Latin root -vers-** means "to turn."

Apply It Explain how the root **-vers-** contributes to the meanings of these words. Consult a print or online dictionary if necessary.

transverse
versatile
adversary

Word Study
Sample answers:
1. Yes. The root -vers- means "to turn" and *reverse* means to "turn back." If you turn back, you go the opposite way.
2. No. The root -vers- means "to turn" and *subversive* means in a way that "undermines or turns a government out of power." Behaving in this manner is not supportive to a government.

Word Study: Apply It
Sample answers: Something that is *transverse* lies crosswise to something else, or at a right-angle turn. Something that is *versatile* can turn into many different things or be used in many different ways. An *adversary* is someone who has turned against you.

Reading Skill

1. **Possible responses:** Fact—The cattle carried a disease spread by ticks called "Texas fever." Opinion—The cattle swimming across the river "looked like a million floating rocking chairs."
2. An atlas or a map could be used to check the distance between Canyon City and the Arkansas River.
3. The facts show what actually happened. The opinions show how the cowboys felt about what was happening.

Literary Analysis

4. **Possible responses:** Technical Vocabulary—quarantine lines, called "deadline"; Formal Language—Regardless of its ultimate destination. . . .; Informal Language—I've monkeyed as long as I want to with you.

   For other sample answers, see *Graphic Organizer Transparencies,* **Literary Analysis Graphic Organizer A,** p. 101, and the **Additional Answers** section.
5. **Possible response:** The author may have wanted to convey how difficult life as a cowboy was. He may have wanted the reader to feel both sympathy and respect for cowboys.

Vocabulary
Acquisition and Use
Sample answers:
1. On long train rides, good books are useful diversions.
2. On our hike up the mountain, we paused every hour to look at the map and gauge our progress.
3. My first goal is to run three miles, but my ultimate goal is to run a marathon.
4. If I use strict discipline in studying, I can achieve good grades.
5. The politician banged her hand on the podium to make her message more emphatic.
6. A stampede of longhorns would be dangerous and terrifying.

Skills instruction for the Reading Skill and Literary Analysis concepts appears on p. 507.

① 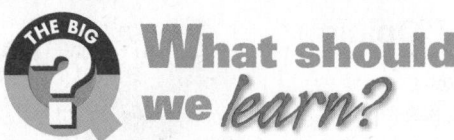 Writing About the Big Question

1. Review the assignment with the class.

2. Point out that facing obstacles such as fear can lessen those fears. Invite volunteers to share examples.

3. Have students complete the sentence starter. Review responses as a class. (**Sample response:** When we <u>evaluate</u> how we feel after trying something that scares us, we sometimes find that our feelings have changed because we know more.)

4. Remind students that their answers will help them think about the Big Question, "What should we learn?"

While You Read

Tell students that as they read, they should look for information Rawlings learns about rattlesnakes that helps her to gain courage.

② Vocabulary

1. Have students preview the selection vocabulary.

2. For each word, have students say the word aloud.

3. Then, use the word in a sentence that defines the word.

4. Finally, repeat your definitional sentence or a similar sentence with the word missing and have the class "fill in the blank" chorally. Here are some examples:

A place that is <u>desolate</u> is lonely and solitary. A deserted beach at six A.M. offers privacy but may feel [students say "desolate"].

A place that is <u>arid</u> is very dry. Desert air will dry your skin because it is so [students say "arid"].

③ Word Study

1. Introduce the skill, using the instruction in the box.

2. Ask students to name a *-sol-* word that describes the music played by the guitarist alone as the rest of the band waits. *(solo)*

① What should we *learn?*

Writing About the Big Question

In "Rattlesnake Hunt," the author learns to manage her fear of rattlesnakes. Use this sentence starter to develop your ideas about the Big Question.

> When we **evaluate** how we feel after trying something that scares us, we sometimes find that our feelings have changed because _____.

While You Read Look for things that Rawlings learns about rattlesnakes that help her to gain courage.

② Vocabulary

Read each word and its definition. Decide whether you know the word well, know it a little bit, or do not know it at all. After you read, see how your knowledge of each word has increased.

- **adequate** (ad´ i kwət) *adj.* sufficient (p. 518) *The filling meal was <u>adequate</u> before the hike. adequacy n. adequately adv.*

- **desolate** (des´ ə lit) *adj.* lonely; solitary (p. 519) *The mountain peak was <u>desolate</u>, but lovely. desolated v. desolation n.*

- **forage** (fôr´ ij) *n.* food for domestic animals (p. 519) *Hay is good <u>forage</u> for cows. foraged v. foraging v. forager n.*

- **translucent** (trans lōō´ sənt) *adj.* allowing some light through (p. 520) *The sun shone through the <u>translucent</u> window panes. translucency n. translucently adv.*

- **arid** (ar´ id) *adj.* dry and barren (p. 520) *No plants grew in the <u>arid</u> land. aridity n.*

- **mortality** (môr tal´ ə tē) *n.* condition of being mortal, or having to die eventually (p. 521) *Every living thing faces <u>mortality</u>. mortal adj. mortally adv. immortality n. immortal adj.*

③ Word Study

The **Latin root -sol-** means "alone."

Rawlings's hunting trip takes her into **desolate**, or lonely, territory.

516 Types of Nonfiction

Vocabulary Development

Vocabulary Knowledge Rating
Create a **Vocabulary Knowledge Rating Chart** (*Professional Development Guidebook,* p. 33) for this selection. Include the selection vocabulary and the Big Question word that appears in the Writing About the Big Question sentence starter on this page. (The Big Question vocabulary is introduced on pp. 406–407).

Give students a copy of the chart. Read the words aloud, and have students mark their rating in the Before Reading column. Urge them to be alert to these words as they read and discuss the selection.

Tally how many students think they know a word to gauge how much instruction to provide. As students read and discuss the selection, point out the words and their context.

Vocabulary Central, featuring tools, activities, and songs for studying vocabulary, is available online at **www.PHLitOnline.com.**

Meet
Marjorie Kinnan Rawlings (1896–1953)

Author of Rattlesnake Hunt

After starting out as a journalist, Marjorie Kinnan Rawlings quit and moved to a farm she bought in northern Florida. There, her experiences and close exposure to nature inspired her to write several novels, including the 1939 Pulitzer Prize–winning book, *The Yearling*. Her writing reflects an intimate understanding and appreciation of the outdoors.

A Disciplined Writer Rawlings devoted herself to writing but described it as "agony." She forced herself to type eight hours a day. Her daily goal was to produce at least six pages, although she would settle for three. She remained focused, refusing to let any outsiders interfere with her work. She felt that "living" with her characters was necessary in order to create a successful story.

DID YOU KNOW ?
When she worked on *The Yearling*, Rawlings prepared for key scenes by taking part in several bear hunts.

❹ BACKGROUND FOR THE ESSAY

Snakes

When people hear the word *snake*, they often react with fear, thinking of a dangerous and deadly creature. However, those who study and work with these sometimes poisonous reptiles have strategies for safety. In "Rattlesnake Hunt," you will see how professionals respect the potential danger of snakes while controlling their interactions with these reptiles.

Rattlesnake Hunt **517**

 Daily Bellringer
For each class during which you teach this selection, have students complete one of the five Research activities for Week 17 in the *Daily Bellringer Activities* booklet.

❹ Background
Snakes

The rattlesnake is one of the most common and feared snakes in North America. There are thirty species of rattlers, all of which possess a tail rattle, which the snake shakes to warn enemies. Most rattlesnakes average about five feet in length. Like other snakes, they lack ears. They detect prey (or predators) by using their jawbones to sense vibrations in the ground. Rattlesnakes also have heat-sensitive pits on their heads, which aid them in nighttime hunting. Rattlers can strike from any position, even while slithering along the ground. However, when approached by an intruder, rattlesnakes will typically issue a warning first, and, if not further disturbed, will retreat.

Multidraft Reading

This icon ● marks natural pauses in the selection. To assist struggling readers and to deepen reading for all, assign the text in "chunks," following the icons, and apply multidraft reading protocols. For each reading, have students set the purpose indicated:

- **First reading**—identifying key ideas and details and answering any Reading Checks.
- **Second reading**—analyzing craft and structure and responding to the side-column prompts.
- **Third reading**—integrating knowledge and ideas, connecting to other texts and the world, and answering the end-of-selection questions.

For more guidance, refer to the *Classroom Strategies and Teaching Routines* card on multidraft reading.

Differentiated Instruction   Additional Instruction

EL Extended Support— English Learners
Have students complete the **Reading and Vocabulary Warm-ups**, *Unit 3 Resources*, pp. 184–187, before they read. Assign the prereading pages for the selection in the *Reader's Notebook: English Learner's Version*. Then, have students listen to portions of the selection on the *Hear It!* Audio CD.

L1 L2 Extended Support- Struggling Readers
Have students complete the **Reading and Vocabulary Warm-ups**, *Unit 3 Resources*, pp. 184–187, before they read. Assign the prereading pages for the selection in the *Reader's Notebook: Adapted Version*. Then, have students listen to portions of the selection on the *Hear It!* Audio CD (adapted text).

Extended Support— Reluctant Readers
To build motivation and engagement before assigning the selection, have students read "Have No Fear," a thematically related selection in *Reality Central*. Then, use the questions at the conclusion of the related selection to guide discussion.

For more about the author, practice with the selection vocabulary, or more background, go online at **www.PHLitOnline.com**.

❶ Activating Prior Knowledge

1. Arrange students into small groups. Give them a copy of a **KWL chart** (see *Professional Development Guidebook*, p. 75), with the topic identified as *snakes*.

2. Ask them to work together to complete the first two columns. In the Know column, they can write what they already know about snakes. In the Want to Know column, they should write questions they have about snakes and their interactions with humans.

Concept Connector ➡

Students will assess what they've learned after completing "Rattlesnake Hunt."

Small-Group Activity

Explain to students that this essay discusses the author overcoming her fear of snakes through several encounters with them. Then, organize the class into small groups. Have each group pantomime a situation in which one of the group members is facing a fear. After practicing their pantomimes, students should present them to the class. Class members can try to identify the fear depicted in each pantomime.

❷ About the Selection

In this essay, the author shares her experiences of rattlesnake hunting near the Florida Everglades with an experienced herpetologist. At first, Rawlings is uneasy around snakes, but as she learns more about them she is able gradually to conquer her fears.

❸ Critical Viewing

Possible response: Students may say that the size and apparent strength of the snake would frighten them. Others might say that they would not be frightened, because the snake is fascinating and not terribly dangerous if one is careful around it.

Rattlesnake Hunt

❶
❷

Marjorie Kinnan Rawlings

❸ ▲ **Critical Viewing**
Would seeing a snake like this one frighten you? Why or why not? **[Connect]**

Vocabulary
adequate (ad′ i kwət) *adj.* sufficient

Ross Allen, a young Florida herpetologist,[1] invited me to join him on a hunt in the upper Everglades[2]—for rattlesnakes. Ross and I drove to Arcadia in his coupé[3] on a warm January day.

I said, "How will you bring back the rattlesnakes?"

"In the back of my car."

My courage was not adequate to inquire whether they were thrown in loose and might be expected to appear between our feet. Actually, a large portable box of heavy close-meshed wire made a safe cage. Ross wanted me to

---

1. **herpetologist** (hʉr′ pə täl′ ə jist) *n.* someone who studies reptiles and amphibians.
2. **Everglades** large region of marshes in southern Florida, about one hundred miles long and averaging fifty miles in width.
3. **coupé** (ko͞o pā′) *n.* small two-door automobile.

518 Types of Nonfiction

Vocabulary Development

Ⓒ **CCSS** Language 6

Thematic Vocabulary: The Big Question
As students are discussing "Rattlesnake Hunt," encourage them to use the thematic vocabulary presented in Introducing the Big Question, pp. 406–407. You might encourage them with sentence starters like these:

1. Despite her great fear, the author has *curiosity* about . . .

2. She hopes that learning *facts* about rattlesnakes will . . .

3. Ross Allen gives her a snake to *examine*, believing that . . .

4. As the author observes rattlesnakes, she *discovers* . . .

5. Her experience helps the author to *evaluate* . . .

write an article about his work and on our way to the unhappy hunting grounds I took notes on a mass of data that he had accumulated in years of herpetological research. The scientific and dispassionate detachment of the material and the man made a desirable approach to rattlesnake territory. As I had discovered with the insects and varmints,[4] it is difficult to be afraid of anything about which enough is known, and Ross' facts were fresh from the laboratory.

The hunting ground was Big Prairie, south of Arcadia and west of the northern tip of Lake Okeechobee. Big Prairie is a desolate cattle country, half marsh, half pasture, with islands of palm trees and cypress and oaks. At that time of year the cattlemen and Indians were burning the country, on the theory that the young fresh wire grass that springs up from the roots after a fire is the best cattle forage. Ross planned to hunt his rattlers in the forefront of the fires. They lived in winter, he said, in gopher holes, coming out in the midday warmth to forage, and would move ahead of the flames and be easily taken. We joined forces with a big man named Will, his snake-hunting companion of the territory, and set out in early morning, after a long rough drive over deep-rutted roads into the open wilds.

I hope never in my life to be so frightened as I was in those first few hours. I kept on Ross' footsteps, I moved when he moved, sometimes jolting into him when I thought he might leave me behind. He does not use the forked stick of conventional snake hunting, but a steel prong, shaped like an L, at the end of a long stout stick. He hunted casually, calling my attention to the varying vegetation, to hawks overhead, to a pair of the rare whooping cranes that flapped over us. In mid-morning he stopped short, dropped his stick, and brought up a five-foot rattlesnake draped limply over the steel L. It seemed to me that I should drop in my tracks.

"They're not active at this season," he said quietly. "A snake takes on the temperature of its surroundings. They can't stand too much heat for that reason, and when the weather is cool, as now, they're sluggish."

---

4. **varmints** (vär´ mənts) *n.* animals regarded as troublesome.

Rattlesnake Hunt **519**

Spiral Review
Author's Point of View What is the author's attitude toward snakes? Which words in this paragraph show her perspective on the topic?

Vocabulary
desolate (des´ ə lit) *adj.* lonely; solitary

forage (fôr´ ij) *n.* food for domestic animals

Fact and Opinion
What reference source could confirm the fact in the last paragraph about a snake's temperature?

 **Reading Check**
5 Why is the narrator going on a rattlesnake hunt?

Spiral Review

Author's Point of View

1. Remind students that they studied the concept of author's point of view in the Unit 3 Literary Analysis Workshop (pp. 408–419).

2. **Ask** the Spiral Review question.

   Possible response: The author is afraid of snakes. Some words that show this are "courage," "safe," "unhappy," and "afraid."

❹ Fact and Opinion

1. Remind students that facts can be proven or disproven and that students can use a variety of reference works to verify a fact. Unlike facts, opinions cannot be proven or disproven.

2. Explain that in this essay, the author holds a strong opinion about something; and that over the course of the essay, certain facts will persuade her to change that opinion. Then, **ask** students what strong opinion the author holds.
   Answer: She holds the opinion that snakes are always harmful.

3. **Ask** students to read the bracketed fact and tell how it might begin to alter the author's opinion.
   Answer: It might help her realize that during certain seasons or times of day, snakes are not dangerous.

4. **Ask** students the Fact and Opinion question.
   Answer: An encyclopedia or a science book about snakes might confirm this fact.

5. **Ask** students whether the author would feel the need to check this fact in a reference source, and why.
   Answer: No, she would not feel the need to check the fact in a reference source because her friend is a snake expert.

❺ Reading Check

Answer: She is going on the hunt because her friend wants her to write an article about his work.

Fluency

Distribute copies of pages 518–519 and pair students. Have partners take turns reading as listeners mark text with which readers struggle. Monitor the fluency of students' reading. Collect the marked up copies and review difficult features as a group. Look for these main problems:

• If students stumble over compound words such as *close-meshed* (p. 518), *snake-hunting* (p. 519), or *deep-rutted* (p. 519), explain that these words should be read as single terms,

with just the slightest pause between them. Show students how to cover one word in each compound term, read the separate word, then blend into a single term.

• If students have difficulty with the alliterative phrases the author uses on page 519, such as *cattle country, stout stick,* and *varying vegetation,* reread these phrases slowly, then have mixed fluency pairs read them aloud to each other until both partners are reading fluently.

519

⑥ Critical Thinking

Deduce

1. Have students reread the paragraph on p. 519 that begins " I hope never in my life to be so . . ." **Ask** students what the author is frightened of.
Answer: She is frightened of snakes, rattlesnakes in particular.

2. Have students read the bracketed text on p. 520. **Ask** them to identify the author's feelings and actions.
Answer: She feels faint and ill. She sweats. She cannot eat.

3. **Ask** students if the author's behavior fits with her overall beliefs.
Possible response: Yes, she is behaving like someone who believes that she is in terrible danger. She's sweating, she feels faint and ill, and she loses her appetite.

⑦ Critical Viewing

Answer: The snake looks big and fast, which would make it dangerous.

Vocabulary
translucent (trans loo´ sənt) *adj.* allowing some light through

arid (ar´ id) *adj.* dry and barren

⑥

⑦ ▼ **Critical Viewing**
What makes the snake in this photograph appear dangerous? **[Analyze]**

The sun was bright overhead, the sky a translucent blue, and it seemed to me that it was warm enough for any snake to do as it willed. The sweat poured down my back. Ross dropped the rattler in a crocus sack and Will carried it. By noon, he had caught four. I felt faint and ill. We stopped by a pond and went swimming. The region was flat, the horizon limitless, and as I came out of the cool blue water I expected to find myself surrounded by a ring of rattlers. There were only Ross and Will, opening the lunch basket. I could not eat. Will went back and drove his truck closer, for Ross expected the hunting to be better in the afternoon. The hunting was much better. When we went back to the truck to deposit two more rattlers in the wire cage, there was a rattlesnake lying under the truck.

Ross said, "Whenever I leave my car or truck with snakes already in it, other rattlers always appear. I don't know whether this is because they scent or sense the presence of other snakes, or whether in this arid area they come to the car for shade in the heat of the day."

The problem was scientific, but I had no interest.

That night Ross and Will and I camped out in the vast spaces of

520 Types of Nonfiction

Think Aloud

Fact and Opinion
Direct students' attention to the last full sentence on p. 521, which begins "'They pay no attention to a man. . . .'"Using a think-aloud process, model how to identify facts and prove or disprove them. Say to students:

I'm going to think aloud to show you how I would identify this statement as a fact and then evaluate the proof for it.

Ross makes a statement about snakes. I could verify this statement in a reference source, such as a science book. This tells me

that the statement is probably a fact. If I keep reading through the next sentence, I see that the text says that Ross provides the proof himself. He lets the snake come out and it crawls out of the hole and right past his legs. In this situation, the proof is in the text already in the form of direct observation by the author. If I want to be absolutely sure that the proof is true consistently, I might double-check a science book, too.

the Everglades prairies. We got water from an abandoned well and cooked supper under buttonwood bushes by a flowing stream. The camp fire blazed cheerfully under the stars and a new moon lifted in the sky. Will told tall tales of the cattlemen and the Indians and we were at peace.

Ross said, "We couldn't have a better night for catching water snakes."

After the rattlers, water snakes seemed innocuous[6] enough. We worked along the edge of the stream and here Ross did not use his L-shaped steel. He reached under rocks and along the edge of the water and brought out harmless reptiles with his hands. I had said nothing to him of my fears, but he understood them. He brought a small dark snake from under a willow root.

"Wouldn't you like to hold it?" he asked. "People think snakes are cold and clammy, but they aren't. Take it in your hands. You'll see that it is warm."

Again, because I was ashamed, I took the snake in my hands. It was not cold, it was not clammy, and it lay trustingly in my hands, a thing that lived and breathed and had mortality like the rest of us. I felt an upsurgence of spirit.

The next day was magnificent. The air was crystal, the sky was aquamarine, and the far horizon of palms and oaks lay against the sky. I felt a new boldness and followed Ross bravely. He was making the rounds of the gopher holes. The rattlers came out in the mid-morning warmth and were never far away. He could tell by their trails whether one had come out or was still in the hole. Sometimes the two men dug the snake out. At times it was down so long and winding a tunnel that the digging was hopeless. Then they blocked the entrance and went on to other holes. In an hour or so they made the original rounds, unblocking the holes. The rattler in every case came out hurriedly, as though anything were preferable to being shut in. All the time Ross talked to me, telling me the scientific facts he had discovered about the habits of the rattlers. •

"They pay no attention to a man standing perfectly still," he said, and proved it by letting Will unblock a hole while he stood at the entrance as the snake came out. It was exciting to

---

6. **innocuous** (in näk′ yōō əs) *adj.* harmless.

8 ▲ Critical Viewing
Snakes are often pictured in art and on artifacts such as this Native American basket. Why do you think that is so? **[Speculate]**

Vocabulary
mortality (môr tal′ ə tē) *n.* the condition of being mortal, or having to die eventually

10  Reading Check
How are the narrator's feelings changing?

Rattlesnake Hunt **521**

8 Critical Viewing
Possible response: Because snakes can be dangerous, people are interested in them. In some cultures, their danger may make them something that was honored or appealed to. In addition, because snakes are so common, people in many cultures have depicted them in art and artifacts.

9 Connecting to the Big Question

1. Point out that learning can help us disprove false assumptions. Share a pertinent experience and invite students to do the same.

2. Have students read the bracketed text in the middle of page 521.
Ask students: What does Rawlings learn here that helps her gain courage about snakes?
Possible response: She learns that snakes are not cold and clammy.

3. **Ask:** Why was it useful for Rawlings to learn what snakes feel like? What does this tell you about the importance of firsthand learning?
Possible response: She discovered for herself that something she found frightening wasn't actually unpleasant after all. Firsthand experience is a powerful way to learn.

10 Reading Check
Answer: Rawlings is becoming more confident and less fearful of snakes. The more exposure she has to them and the more she learns about them, the less fear she has.

Differentiated Instruction for Universal Access

Strategy for Less Proficient Readers
Help students relate to the selection by encouraging them to discuss situations in which they faced their fears or in which they learned that their preconceived notions—or opinions—about something were not accurate. Arrange students in groups, and have members take turns telling their stories. After each group member shares his or her story, have the group discuss what they learned from that person's experience.

EL Pronunciation for English Learners
Point out the word *surrounded* on page 520. Then, write the following word pairs on the board: *marrow / mallow* and *era / Ella.* Pronounce each in turn, and have students echo you. Then, call out words at random, and have a volunteer point to each on the board. Have the class judge the volunteer's success. Finally, have volunteers read the sentence in the text containing the word *surrounded.*

⑪ Fact and Opinion

1. Read the first bracketed paragraph aloud. Point out that in this passage, Ross is describing a process that occurs in nature.

2. **Ask** how scientists probably discovered this process.
   Answer: They probably discovered it by watching many snakes capture their prey.

3. **Ask** the Fact and Opinion question.
   Answer: He is stating a fact. I know this because he is describing a process that can be (or has been) proved.

▶ **Monitor Progress:** Ask students to name one common opinion about snakes, and one fact about snakes that contradicts this opinion.
   Possible response: Snakes are nasty (opinion); snakes are not cold (fact).

▶ **Reteach:** If students have difficulty stating an opinion or a fact, review with them the Fact and Opinion instruction on p. 507.

⑫ Word Choice, or Diction

1. Have students read the text beginning "As the sun mounted . . ." Remind students that different words convey different moods or feelings. Then, point out the words *mounted* and *moist Everglades earth.* **Ask** what kind of words these are and what feeling they give the sentence.
   Answer: They are descriptive words, giving the sentence a poetic feeling.

2. **Ask** students what the descriptive words mean literally.
   Answer: The sun is rising. It is warming the ground.

3. **Ask** the Word Choice, or Diction, question.
   Possible responses: "As the sun rose, it warmed the ground . . . "

Fact and Opinion
Is Ross stating fact or opinion in this paragraph? How do you know? ⑪

Word Choice, or Diction
How would you rephrase "as the sun mounted in the sky and warmed the moist Everglades" in less formal language? ⑫

---

watch the snake crawl slowly beside and past the man's legs. When it was at a safe distance he walked within its range of vision, which he had proved to be no higher than a man's knee, and the snake whirled and drew back in an attitude[7] of fighting defense. The rattler strikes only for paralyzing and killing its food, and for defense.

"It is a slow and heavy snake," Ross said. "It lies in wait on a small game trail and strikes the rat or rabbit passing by. It waits a few minutes, then follows along the trail, coming to the small animal, now dead or dying. It noses it from all sides, making sure that it is its own kill, and that it is dead and ready for swallowing."

A rattler will lie quietly without revealing itself if a man passes by and it thinks it is not seen. It slips away without fighting if given the chance. Only Ross' sharp eyes sometimes picked out the gray and yellow diamond pattern, camouflaged among the grasses. In the cool of the morning, chilled by the January air, the snakes showed no fight. They could be looped up limply over the steel L and dropped in a sack or up into the wire cage on the back of Will's truck. As the sun mounted in the sky and warmed the moist Everglades earth, the snakes were warmed too, and Ross warned that it was time to go more cautiously. Yet having learned that it was we who were the aggressors; that immobility meant complete safety; that the snakes, for all their lightning flash

---

7. attitude (at′ ə tōōd′) *n.* a position or posture of the body.

522 Types of Nonfiction

Vocabulary Development

Vocabulary Knowledge Rating

When students have completed reading and discussing "Rattlesnake Hunt," have them take out their **Vocabulary Knowledge Rating Chart** for this selection. Read the words aloud once more. Have students rate their knowledge of the words again in the After Reading column. Clarify any words that are still problematic. Have students write their own definition and example or sentence in the appropriate column.

Then, have students complete the Vocabulary Practice activities at the end of the selection. Encourage students to use the words in further discussion and written work about the selection. Remind them that they will be accountable for these words on the **Selection Test,** *Unit 3 Resources,* pp. 199–201 or 202–204.

in striking, were inaccurate in their aim, with limited vision; having watched again and again the liquid grace of movement, the beauty of pattern, suddenly I understood that I was drinking in freely the magnificent sweep of the horizon, with no fear of what might be at the moment under my feet. I went off hunting by myself, and though I found no snakes, I should have known what to do.

The sun was dropping low in the west. Masses of white cloud hung above the flat marshy plain and seemed to be tangled in the tops of distant palms and cypresses. The sky turned orange, then saffron. I walked leisurely back toward the truck. In the distance I could see Ross and Will making their way in too. The season was more advanced than at the Creek, two hundred miles to the north, and I noticed that spring flowers were blooming among the lumpy hummocks. I leaned over to pick a white violet. There was a rattlesnake under the violet.

If this had happened the week before, if it had happened the day before, I think I should have lain down and died on top of the rattlesnake, with no need of being struck and poisoned. The snake did not coil, but lifted its head and whirred its rattles lightly. I stepped back slowly and put the violet in a buttonhole. I reached forward and laid the steel L across the snake's neck, just back of the blunt head. I called to Ross:

"I've got one."

He strolled toward me.

"Well, pick it up," he said.

I released it and slipped the L under the middle of the thick body.

"Go put it in the box."

He went ahead of me and lifted the top of the wire cage. I made the truck with the rattler, but when I reached up the six feet to drop it in the cage, it slipped off the stick and dropped on Ross' feet. It made no effort to strike.

"Pick it up again," he said. "If you'll pin it down lightly and reach just back of its head with your hand, as you've seen me do, you can drop it in more easily."

I pinned it and leaned over. ●

⓭ LITERATURE IN CONTEXT

Language Connection

Scientific Words From Greek Origins

Ross Allen studies herpetology. The word *herpetology* comes from the Greek words *herpein*, meaning "to creep," and *logo*, meaning "word." Other scientific words derived from Greek and ending with the suffix *-ology* (meaning "science or theory of") include *biology*, the study of animals and plants; *anthropology*, the study of humans; *ichthyology*, the study of fish; and *paleontology*, the study of life forms from the past, especially fossils.

Connect to the Literature

How does the origin of the word *herpetology* explain why herpetologists study snakes?

⓮ ✓ Reading Check

What will a rattler do if it thinks it is not seen?

Rattlesnake Hunt **523**

⓭ Literature in Context

Language Connection The fear of snakes that Rawlings expresses in her essay has the scientific name *ophidiophobia*. This word comes from the Greek word *ophis*, meaning "snake," and *phobos*, meaning "fearing" or "fright." Many other fears, or *phobias*, also have scientific names that are derived from Greek. For example, *agoraphobia*, the fear of open spaces, comes from the Greek *agora*, which referred to an open marketplace. *Arachnophobia*, fear of spiders, is derived from the word *arachnid*, which comes from the Greek word for spiders, *arachne*. *Triskaidekaphobia*, the fear of the number thirteen, is from the Greek thirteen, *triskaideka*. *Hydrophobia* comes from the Greek prefix *hyd-*, meaning "water." *Hydrophobia* is also another name for rabies, which causes its victims' brains to fill with fluid.

Connect to the Literature Have students read the Literature in Context feature, and present the additional background information above. Then, **ask** the Connect to the Literature question: How does the origin of the word *herpetology* explain why herpetologists study snakes? If necessary, have students return to the side note to locate the word origin of *herpetology*.

Answer: The word herpetologist comes from a Greek word meaning "to creep," which suggests that these scientists study creatures that "creep," or move along the ground, such as snakes.

⓮ Reading Check

Possible response: It will lie quietly without revealing itself.

Concept Connector

? Writing About the Big Question
Have students compare their responses to the sentence starter they completed before reading the story with their ideas afterward. Ask them to explain whether their thoughts have changed.

KWL
Have students complete the last column of their KWL charts. As a class, evaluate what students learned in relation to the questions they had before reading.

Reading Skill Graphic Organizer
Ask students to review their completed graphic organizers. Then have students share the graphic organizers they completed. Students can work in pairs to compare facts that could be checked in each resource. As they discuss their examples, remind students that some facts can be verified in more than one resource.

← **523**

⑮ Word Choice, or Diction

1. Explain that when writing dialogue, authors often use informal expressions, or statements that a person might make in casual conversation.

2. Have students reread the text on p. 524, then respond to the Word Choice, or Diction, direction. **Possible response:** "I'm awfully sorry, . . . but you're pushing me a little too fast."

Critical Thinking

Before students respond, you may wish to have them write a brief objective summary of the selection. As they answer the questions below, remind them to support their answers with evidence from the text.

1. (a) She is invited by Ross Allen to write an article about his work. (b) She realizes that some of her views about snakes are incorrect, and she becomes willing to view snakes more objectively.

2. (a) Rawlings does not panic when she finds a rattlesnake under the violet she picks. She attempts to pick up the snake with the L-shaped prong. (b) She has conquered a fear.

3. **Possible response:** The essay shows that knowledge can help someone face his or her fears more objectively.

4. **Possible response:** Movies make rattlesnakes look dangerous and mean, but this story does just the opposite. Rawlins and the reader learn that rattlesnakes will not strike if a person stands still. We also learn that these snakes are slow and heavy animals. In the movies, rattlesnakes look fast and deadly.

5. **Possible responses:** (a) She views herself as more courageous, and she views nature as less dangerous. (b) Fear can keep us from exploring new places or topics, so if we conquer fear, we can go more places and learn more.

Word Choice, or Diction
On this page, find an example of an informal expression that is used by the author.

"I'm awfully sorry," I said, "but you're pushing me a little too fast."

He grinned. I lifted it on the stick and again as I had it at head height, it slipped off, down Ross' boots and on top of his feet. He stood as still as a stump. I dropped the snake on his feet for the third time. It seemed to me that the most patient of rattlers might in time resent being hauled up and down, and for all the man's quiet certainty that in standing motionless there was no danger, would strike at whatever was nearest, and that would be Ross.

I said, "I'm just not man enough to keep this up any longer," and he laughed and reached down with his smooth quickness and lifted the snake back of the head and dropped it in the cage. It slid in among its mates and settled in a corner. The hunt was over and we drove back over the uneven trail to Will's village and left him and went on to Arcadia and home. Our catch for the two days was thirty-two rattlers.

I said to Ross, "I believe that tomorrow I could have picked up that snake."

Back at the Creek, I felt a new lightness. I had done battle with a great fear, and the victory was mine.

Critical Thinking

> **Cite textual evidence to support your responses.**

© 1. **Key Ideas and Details (a)** Why does Rawlings go on the hunt? **(b) Infer:** Why do Rawlings's feelings about snakes change when she holds one?

© 2. **Craft and Structure (a)** Note two ways in which Rawlings shows that she has partly overcome her fears. **(b) Infer:** Why does the author announce at the end of the hunt that she has won a "victory"?

© 3. **Integration of Knowledge and Ideas Generalize:** What general truth does this essay suggest?

© 4. **Integration of Knowledge and Ideas Analyze:** How is the information presented about snakes the same as or different from information found in works of fiction, popular media, or textbooks? Support your answer with specific examples.

© 5. **Integration of Knowledge and Ideas (a)** In what ways does the hunt change how Rawlings thinks about nature and herself? **(b)** How does conquering our fears allow us greater freedom to learn about the world? *[Connect to the Big Question: What should we learn?]*

524 Types of Nonfiction

Assessment Resources

Unit 3 Resources

L1 L2 EL Selection Test A, pp. 199–201. Administer Test A to less advanced readers.

L3 L4 EL Selection Test B, pp. 202–204. Administer Test B to on-level and more advanced students.

L3 L4 Open-Book Test, pp. 196–198. As an alternative, give the Open-Book Test.

All Customizable Test Bank

All Self-tests
Students may prepare for the Selection Test by taking the Self-test online.

Reading Skill: Classifying Fact and Opinion

1. Identify one **fact** in the essay and one **opinion.**

2. What resource would you use to check the facts about a rattlesnake's vision?

3. How do both facts and opinions help the writer explain her experience with snakes?

Literary Analysis: Word Choice, or Diction

© 4. **Craft and Structure** Review the author's **word choice,** or **diction,** by completing a chart like the one shown.

Technical Vocabulary	Formal Language	Informal Language

© 5. **Craft and Structure** Reread the top of page 523. How do phrases like "the liquid grace of movement, the beauty of pattern" reflect the author's new attitude toward snake hunting?

© 6. **Integration of Knowledge and Ideas** What feeling about snakes and her own experience do you think the author wanted to convey in this essay? Explain.

Vocabulary

© **Acquisition and Use** For each item, write a single sentence correctly using the words indicated.

1. arid, farmer
2. mortality, medicine
3. desolate, midnight
4. adequate, light
5. forage, horse
6. translucent, marbles

Word Study Use the sentence context and your knowledge of the **Latin root -sol-** to explain your answer to each question.

1. How many people can play a game of *solitaire*?
2. If you seek *solitude*, do you want others around?

Word Study

The **Latin root -sol-** means "alone."

Apply It Explain how the root -sol- contributes to the meanings of these words. Consult a dictionary if necessary.

soliloquy
consolidate
soloist

Reading Skill

1. **Possible response:** Fact—Snakes pay no attention to a person standing perfectly still. Opinion—Snakes are disgusting.

2. You could use an encyclopedia or a science book about snakes.

3. The author's opinions show how she felt about snakes, and the facts show what she learned about snakes.

Literary Analysis

4. **Possible response:** Technical Vocabulary—herpetologist; data; Formal Language—I felt an upsurgence of spirit; The air was crystal, the sky was aquamarine . . .; Informal Language—I've got one; Well, pick it up.

   For other sample answers, see *Graphic Organizers Transparencies,* **Literary Analysis Graphic Organizer A,** p. 102, and the **Additional Answers** section.

5. **Possible response:** The author describes the snakes in a way that makes them a beautiful part of the environment, not something scary or dangerous. Now that she is not scared, the author can see more of the environment around her. She is not just looking at the ground seeing if a snake is there.

6. **Possible response:** She wanted to convey the feeling of fear most people have toward snakes and the feeling of pride she had in facing and overcoming that fear.

Vocabulary
Acquisition and Use

1. In an <u>arid</u> climate, a <u>farmer</u> might have to irrigate his crops.
2. Despite advances in <u>medicine</u>, <u>mortality</u> is still a reality that a person has to face eventually.
3. She found that the forest was <u>desolate</u> at <u>midnight</u> and felt terribly alone.
4. We didn't turn on any lamps because the sun offered <u>adequate</u> <u>light</u>.
5. The <u>horse</u> ate its <u>forage</u> as soon as we left the barn.
6. Some <u>marbles</u> are <u>translucent</u>, but others are so solid that no light shines through them.

Word Study
Sample answers:

1. The root -sol- means "alone," so <u>only one</u> person can play *solitaire*.
2. No. The root -sol- means "alone," so if you seek *solitude* you want to be the <u>only</u> one around.

Word Study: Apply It
Sample answers: A *soliloquy* is spoken by a theatrical character, while <u>alone</u> on the stage. To *consolidate* means to bring together parts that are separate, or <u>alone</u>. A *soloist* is a musician who plays <u>alone</u>.

Conventions

1. Introduce the skill, using the instruction on the student page.

2. Discuss the examples in the chart.

Think Aloud: Model the Skill

Say to students:

To identify a sentence's subject, I ask myself, "Who or what is this sentence about?" The answer is generally the subject of the sentence. If the sentence has a compound subject, the answer will include two or more nouns. To identify the predicate, I ask myself, "What words tells me what the subject does, what is done to the subject, or what the subject's condition is?" These words and the words that modify them are the predicate. If the sentence has a compound predicate, the answer will include two or more verbs.

PH WRITING COACH Grade 7

Students will find instruction on and practice with compound subjects and predicates in Chapter 18, Section 3.

Practice A

1. (comp. pred.) chased and lassoed
2. (comp. subj.) smell or sound
3. (comp. subj.) Teddy Blue and Charles Goodnight
4. (comp. pred.) cussed, threatened, and yelled

Reading Application

Sample answer: <u>Kansas</u> and <u>other territories</u> along the route soon established quarantines. . . .

Practice B
Sample answers:

1. <u>Vegetation, hawks, and whooping cranes</u> filled the landscape.
2. In the afternoon, we <u>picnicked and swam</u>.
3. <u>Cattlemen and Indians</u> hate snakes.
4. She <u>waits and watches</u> carefully until the snake emerges.
5. <u>Will and Ross</u> spent the afternoon hunting for rattlesnakes.

Writing Application
Sample answers: Socks and shoes were in a pile. She ate, drank, and rested at home. She and her brother cleaned up.

Integrated Language Skills

The Real Story of a Cowboy's Life • Rattlesnake Hunt

Conventions: Compound Subjects and Predicates

A **compound subject** contains two or more subjects that share the same verb. A **compound predicate** contains two or more verbs that share the same subject.

Both compound subjects and compound predicates are joined by conjunctions such as *and* and *or*.

Compound subject: *Bob* and *I* entertained at the talent show.

Compound predicate: We *clapped* and *laughed*.

Follow these rules for agreement with compound subjects:

Compound Subjects Joined With "and"	Compound Subjects Joined With "or"
Share the same verb and take the plural form	Take the form of the verb that agrees with the subject closest to the verb
Example: Jared and Willa *help* the customers.	**Example:** Jared or Willa *helps* the customers.

Practice A Identify the compound subject or compound predicate in each sentence.

1. Cowboys chased and lassoed steer.
2. A smell or sound could set off a herd.
3. Teddy Blue and Charles Goodnight were cowboys during the 1800s.
4. Homesteaders cussed, threatened, and yelled at the cowboys.

© Reading Application In "The Real Story of a Cowboy's Life," find a sentence with a compound subject or a compound predicate.

Practice B Write a sentence using each compound subject or compound predicate listed. Follow the rules for agreement.

1. vegetation, hawks, and whooping cranes
2. picnicked and swam
3. cattlemen and Indians
4. waits and watches
5. Will and Ross

© Writing Application Write two sentences using compound subjects and predicates. Review your sentences to ensure subject-verb agreement, and revise them as needed.

PH WRITING COACH Further instruction and practice are available in *Prentice Hall Writing Coach*.

Differentiated Instruction for Universal Access

Culturally Responsive Instruction: Standard English Learners

Language Focus If you have students who habitually use nonstandard English in academic discourse, explain that in standard English, the subject of a sentence is generally named only once, using either a noun or a pronoun, but not both. Provide students with the following paired sentence strips.

That man he is tall. / That man is tall.
The building it is crumbling. / The building is crumbling.
Raisha she busy. / Raisha is busy.

Have students identify the difference between statements in each pair. (In each pair, one statement doubles the subject with a pronoun. In the last pair, the verb is also omitted). Then, have students identify the Standard English sentence in each pair. Point out that while both statements can be understood to mean the same thing, Standard English is required in contexts such as schoolwork or office memos.

Writing

© **Informative Text** Write an **adaptation** of an incident that is described in the essay you read. Retell the incident for a new audience, such as a group of kindergarteners or a class of students learning English. Follow these steps:

- Choose an incident to retell and decide on an audience.
- Draft to reflect the needs and interests of your audience.
- Use precise words and sensory language to add life and immediacy to your description.
- Finally, revise to organize ideas logically, making sure you have met both your purpose and the needs of your audience.

Grammar Application Make sure to follow the rules of agreement for any compound subjects in your essay.

Writing Workshop: *Work in Progress*

Prewriting for Exposition Choose three sets of items from the Everyday Decisions chart in your writing portfolio. For each set, answer the following question: *What do these items have in common?* Save this Comparison Work in your portfolio.

Research and Technology

© **Build and Present Knowledge** Write a **help-wanted ad** for one of the following positions:

- A modern job involving cattle or horses
- A person to work with Ross Allen, the herpetologist

Before you write, use online search terms, such as *veterinarian, experience required,* and *scientist* to find related help-wanted ads to use as models.

- Notice the concise writing style of ads, and review what the ads cover, including job responsibilities, education, experience, skills, and personal traits the employer seeks.
- Use language that is appropriate for a business ad, including correct grammar and tone.
- Type your ad on a computer and use the spell-check feature.
- Add clip art or other visual displays to enhance key ideas, clarify a point, or add interest.
- Experiment with typefaces to emphasize main ideas.

 **Common Core State Standards**

W.7.3.d, W.7.4, W.7.5, W.7.8
[For the full wording of the standards, see page 506.]

Use this prewriting activity to prepare for the **Writing Workshop** on page 548.

www.PHLitOnline.com
- Interactive graphic organizers
- Grammar tutorial
- Interactive journals

The Real Story of a Cowboy's Life **527**

Writing

1. Review the assignment, using the instruction on the student page.
2. To give students guidance in writing this informative text, give them **Support for Writing,** page 194 in *Unit 3 Resources.*
3. To evaluate students' adaptations, use rubrics for **Generic (Holistic) Writing** rubrics, pages 256–257 in *Professional Development Guidebook.* In addition, you might evaluate adaptations based on their accuracy and their suitability for the specified audience.

Grammar Application

Have students check their drafts to make sure all their compound subjects follow the rules of agreement.

Six Traits Focus

Ideas	✔ Word Choice
Organization	Sentence Fluency
✔ Voice	Conventions

PH WRITING COACH Grade 7

Students will find further instruction on and practice with informative text in Chapter 5.

📖 Writing Workshop
Work in Progress

Have students save their completed questions and answers in their portfolios. They will use this information later as they complete the Writing Workshop assignment (see pp. 548–555).

Research and Technology

1. Review the assignment, using the instruction on the student page.
2. To support students' work on the assignment, have them complete the **Support for Extend Your Learning** page (*Unit 3 Resources,* p. 195).

Teaching Resources

Unit 3 Resources

L3 L4 **Integrated Language Skills: Grammar,** p. 193

L3 L4 EL **Support for Writing,** p. 194

L3 L4 EL **Support for Extend Your Learning,** p. 195

L4 **Enrichment,** pp. 174, 192

Enriched Online Student Edition
Available under After You Read for this selection:

All **Interactive Grammar Tutorial**

L3 **Internet Research Activity**

Professional Development Guidebook
Rubrics for Generic (Holistic) Writing, pp. 256–257

PHLit Online! All print and digital resources are available online at **www.PHLitOnline.com.** Online resources accessible to students are noted on the student page.

527

Using the Test Practice

In this two-page Test Practice, students apply the reading skill for the second half of Unit 3 to a passage of fiction and a passage of nonfiction.

Review this skill, classifying fact and opinion, and then administer the test. For more guidance, consult the *Classroom Strategies and Teaching Routines* card, **Formally Assessing Students.**

ASSESS

Answers

Answers With Explanations

1. **C**—The phrase "incredibly uncomfortable" represents an opinion. *Incorrect answers:* A—This is a fact that can be proved; B—This is a fact that can be proved; D—This is a fact that can be proved.

2. **D**—The details of a public event can be proved. *Incorrect answers:* A—Discomfort is a subjective judgment that cannot be proved; B—A fictional character's thoughts cannot be proved; C—Artistic greatness is a matter of opinion.

3. **D**—The number of paintings in a public exhbition can be proved. *Incorrect answers:* A—A fictional character's emotions cannot be proved; B—Eeriness is a subjective quality; C—This is the grandfather's opinion.

4. **C**—The number of paintings is a fact but their brilliance is a matter of opinion. *Incorrect answers:* A—The word *brilliant* prevents this statement from being completely factual; B—This sentence contains a provable fact (the number of paintings) so it is not simply an opinion; D—The sentence contains fact and opinion.

Writing for Assessment

Students should explain how they would verify the facts in this passage, naming at least two resources (tour guide to Boston, Boston subway map, history of Boston, encyclopedia article on Hopper, Museum of Fine Arts Web site) they could use to confirm that the facts are accurate.

528

Test Practice: Reading

Classifying Fact and Opinion

Fiction Selection

Directions: *Read the selection. Then, answer the questions.*

On Saturday morning, Rapha woke early. He was meeting his grandfather in Boston. To get there, he would take the Green Line, the oldest line in Boston's subway system. Rapha boarded the train at Woodland station. He thought the seats were incredibly uncomfortable. He was glad the ride would take only thirty minutes. He leaned back and thought about the day ahead.

In Boston, Rapha and his grandfather would have lunch before seeing the Edward Hopper exhibition at the Museum of Fine Arts. Rapha's grandfather believes that Edward Hopper is the greatest American artist. He says Hopper's work is dark and light at the same time and shows everyday America. To Rapha, Hopper's work seems eerie. However, he has seen only a few pieces. The exhibition will include ninety-two of Hopper's most brilliant paintings.

1. Which of these statements should be classified as an opinion?
   A. The Green Line is the oldest line in Boston's subway system.
   B. The train leaves from Woodland station.
   C. The seats on the train are incredibly uncomfortable.
   D. The ride to Boston takes thirty minutes.

2. Which statement can be proved?
   A. The seats on the train are incredibly uncomfortable.
   B. Rapha thought about the day ahead.
   C. Edward Hopper is the greatest American artist.
   D. The Museum of Fine Arts is hosting the exhibition.

3. Which statement should be classified as a fact?
   A. Rapha was glad the ride is short.
   B. Hopper's work seems eerie.
   C. Hopper's work is dark and light.
   D. Ninety-two paintings are on display.

4. Is the final sentence of the selection a fact or an opinion?
   A. It is a fact
   B. It is an opinion
   C. It is both a fact and an opinion
   D. It is neither a fact nor an opinion

Writing for Assessment

In a short paragraph, explain how you would verify the facts in this passage. Name at least two resources you could use to confirm that the facts are accurate.

528 Types of Nonfiction

Strategies for Test Taking

Tell students that when a reading comprehension test, or part of such a test, focuses on a specific skill such as "Classifying Fact and Opinion," they should keep that skill in mind when reading the passages. In this way, they will keep from wasting time on irrelevant details or characteristics of the passage.

For example, when reading this selection, the student does not need to ponder Rapha's grandfather's statement about the meaning of Hopper's work. He or she simply needs to know whether the statement is a fact or an opinion.

Nonfiction Selection

Directions: *Read the selection. Then, answer the questions.*

Georgia O'Keeffe is the greatest American artist. She was born in Sun Prairie, Wisconsin, in 1887. O'Keeffe loved experimenting with art as a child. Later, she studied art in college. For a while, she supported herself as a commercial artist. I don't believe this work suited her, though. After a while, she became an art teacher. She taught in schools around the country, winding up in the high plains of Texas.

O'Keeffe's move to the Southwest was wonderful for her. Many think it marked a turning point in her life as an artist. She said that the stark beauty of the land appealed to her. She began painting actively to capture her surroundings on canvas. She painted pictures of flowers, bleached animal bones, rolling hills, and clouds. I believe she did her best work during this period. Many of these paintings are included in museum collections around the world.

1. Which statement cannot be proved?
- **A.** Georgia O'Keeffe is the greatest American artist.
- **B.** O'Keeffe loved experimenting with art as a child.
- **C.** For a while, she supported herself as a commercial artist.
- **D.** Many think it marked a turning point in her life as an artist.

2. Which statement is an opinion?
- **A.** She was born in Sun Prairie, Wisconsin, in 1887.
- **B.** Later, she studied art in college.
- **C.** For a while, she supported herself as a commercial artist.
- **D.** I don't believe this work suited her.

3. Which detail can be supported but *not* proved?
- **A.** Georgia O'Keeffe is the greatest American artist.
- **B.** She was born in Sun Prairie, Wisconsin, in 1887.
- **C.** She studied art in college.
- **D.** She supported herself as a commercial artist.

4. Which statement is an opinion?
- **A.** She said that the stark beauty of the land appealed to her.
- **B.** She began painting actively to capture her surroundings on canvas.
- **C.** She painted pictures of flowers, bleached animal bones, rolling hills, and clouds.
- **D.** I believe she did her best work during this period.

Writing for Assessment

Connecting Across Texts

If the author of this passage and Rapha's grandfather were to meet, over what opinion might they disagree? Use details from both passages to write a brief response.

www.PHLitOnline.com
- Online practice
- Instant feedback

Test Practice: Reading **529**

Differentiated Instruction   for Universal Access

Strategy for Special-Needs Students

To help students distinguish between facts and opinions in standardized test passages and items, review common categories of facts: names, dates, places, actions, colors, sizes. Then, list common categories of opinions: beauty, value, quality. Ask volunteers to give other examples. Next, point out a few words and phrases that signal facts: "I know," "He did," "We went to."

Contrast these with examples of words and phrases that signal opinions: *good/bad, beautiful/ugly, easy/hard, I think,* and *I believe.* Finally, help students create several fact and opinion statements of their own, building on some of the words and phrases you have used as examples. If they make errors, carefully explain why something that might seem to be a fact or an opinion is actually the opposite.

Students may take the test in interactive format with instant feedback online at www.PHLitOnline.com.

529

Common Core State Standards

- Reading Informational Text 5, 9
- Language 4.b, d; 6

Reading Skill

1. Introduce the skill and chart.
2. Tell students they will analyze the structure and purpose of texts.

Think Aloud: Model the Skill

Say to students:

When I read a text, I examine how the information is organized and presented. For example, if I see a sign that has a heading "Warning!" above a bulleted list, I know that the bullets will list what I am being warned about. The information is easy to locate because I know how the text is structured.

Multidraft Reading

Have students follow a multidraft reading protocol.

- **First reading**—Have students read to identify key ideas and details.
- **Second reading**—Have students read to identify the structure of the text.
- **Third reading**—Have students read to integrate knowledge and ideas by connecting the text to the world, their own experiences, and other texts.

Content-Area Vocabulary

1. Have students say each word.
2. Next, use each word in a sentence that defines it.
3. Finally, repeat your definitional sentence or a similar sentence, omitting the word, and have the class "fill in the blank" chorally.

Reading for Information

Analyzing Functional Texts

Instruction Manual	Signs
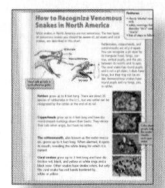	

Reading Skill: Structure and Purpose

When you **analyze the structure** of a text, you examine how the author shapes and organizes information. Doing so can help you to **locate information** and **understand the purpose**—what the text is meant to do. As you read the instruction manual and signs, consider how the structural features of each text relate to its purpose of giving information about snakes. Consider, too, that although the selections are about the same general topic, they emphasize different information based on their specific purposes.

The following chart lists some common structural features and the ways they support the purpose of a text.

Purpose	Category	Structural Features
to warn	sign	• Brief, easy-to-read text in large type • Large graphics
to teach	instruction manual	• Numbered lists that show step-by-step instructions • Labeled graphics that clarify important concepts

Content-Area Vocabulary

These words appear in the selections that follow. You may also encounter them in other content-area texts.

- **immobilize** (i mō′ bə līz′) *v.* prevent from moving
- **tourniquet** (toor′ ni kit) *n.* device that stops bleeding by putting pressure on a blood vessel

Common Core State Standards

Reading Informational Text
5. Analyze the structure an author uses to organize a text, including how the major sections contribute to the whole and to the development of the ideas.

9. Analyze how two or more authors writing about the same topic shape their presentations of key information by emphasizing different evidence or advancing different interpretations of facts.

Language
4.b. Use common, grade-appropriate Latin affixes and roots as clues to the meaning of a word.

4.d. Verify the preliminary definition of the meaning of a word or phrase.

6. Acquire and use accurately grade-appropriate general academic and domain-specific words and phrases; gather vocabulary knowledge when considering a word or phrase important to comprehension or expression.

 What should we learn?

Have students analyze the texts to locate information and understand purpose.

Differentiated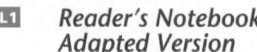
Instruction   for Universal Access

Reading Support
Give students reading support with the appropriate version of the *Reader's Notebooks:*

L2 L3 *Reader's Notebook*

L1   *Reader's Notebook: Adapted Version*

 Reader's Notebook: English Learner's Version

How to Recognize Venomous Snakes in North America

Most snakes in North America are not venomous. The two types of poisonous snakes you should be aware of, pit vipers and coral snakes, are described in this chart.

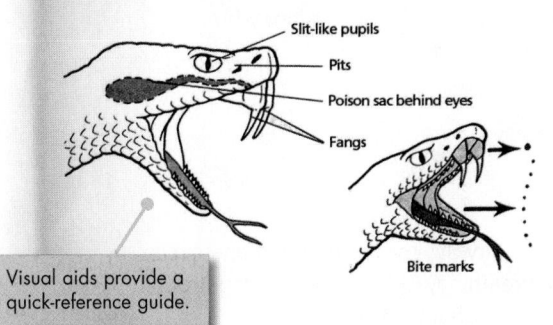

Slit-like pupils
Pits
Poison sac behind eyes
Fangs
Bite marks

Visual aids provide a quick-reference guide.

Rattlesnakes, copperheads, and cottonmouths are all *pit vipers*. You can recognize a pit viper by its triangular head, fangs, narrow, vertical pupils, and the pits between its nostrils and its eyes. The coral snake has round pupils and is not a pit viper; it does have fangs, but they may not be visible. Nonvenomous snakes have round pupils and no fangs, pits, or rattles.

Rattlers grow up to 8 feet long. There are about 30 species of rattlesnake in the U.S., but any rattler can be recognized by the rattles at the end of its tail.

Copperheads grow up to 4 feet long and have diamond-shaped markings down their backs. They vibrate their tails when angry, but have no rattles.

© Brian Kenney

Color photographs help the reader identify each type of snake.

The cottonmouth, also known as the water moccasin, grows up to 4 feet long. When alarmed, it opens its mouth, revealing the white lining for which it is named.

Coral snakes grow up to 3 feet long and have distinctive red, black, and yellow or white rings and a black nose. Other snakes have similar colors, but only the coral snake has red bands bordered by white or yellow.

Reading for Information: Instruction Manual **531**

About Instruction Manuals

1. Review the features listed in the Instruction Manual box on p. 531 with students. **Ask** the class to define the term *visual aids* in their own words.
   Possible response: Students may say that visual aids are pictures that provide information about the text on the page.

2. **Ask** students how the features help readers to better use or understand the contents of the manual. **Possible response:** The features help readers save time and locate important information easily.

Analyze Structure and Purpose

1. Review with students that the structure of a text refers to how the information in the text is presented and organized. Readers analyze text structure to confirm the purpose of the text and to locate information.

2. Draw students' attention to the structure of the page. Point out that, after a brief introduction, readers first learn about the general appearance of pit vipers. Then, further down the page, readers learn to distinguish between the different types of pit vipers before finally being presented with a venomous snake that is not a pit viper. **Ask** why the information is presented in this order.
   Answer: Information about similar species is grouped together.

Support for Less Proficient Readers

Explain any vocabulary that may be challenging for these students. Tell them that a sac is a "bag-like structure in some animals and plants." A *species* is a specific type of animal within a general family. Species of rattlesnakes include timber rattlers and sidewinders. While the word *pit* can refer to any slight indentation (as in the illustration), pits on snakes contain a heat-sensitive organ that helps the snake aim its strikes at warm-blooded animals.

Also, these students may find it difficult to track information on this page due to its layout.

Point out that the first paragraph refers to the page as a chart, and that as such, there are a variety of ways to read its text material. It is all right if the eye naturally skips ahead to items of interest. Explain that the paragraph that begins "Rattlesnakes, copperheads," does not constitute a right-hand column to be read after all the text on the left; it has been placed there only to accommodate the illustration.

1. Clarify that the page references in the text are to other parts of the First Aid manual from which it is excerpted.

2. Provide up-front vocabulary support for challenging words prior to reading. Tell students that *ABC* stands for "Airway-Breathing-Circulation," and *CPR* for "cardiopulmonary resuscitation."

3. Have students read "First Aid for a Snake Bite." Tell students to analyze the structure of the text in order to locate information and understand its purpose.

4. **Ask** students to identify the two parts of the manual.
   Answer: The top of the page is a bulleted list of guidelines about how to care for someone bitten by a snake. The second part of the page is a numbered list of instructions for helping the victim.

5. Ask students how having a numbered list of steps is helpful to the reader.
   Answer: The numbered list tells the reader exactly what to do and in what order.

6. Have students think about what they've learned about the features of an instruction manual. **Ask** students what features do not appear on this page and whether the page would benefit from including these features.
   Possible response: Visual aids do not appear on the page. The inclusion of illustrations for some of the steps for taking care of a snake-bite victim might make the information clearer.

First Aid for a Snake Bite

Follow these guidelines to care for someone bitten by a snake:

- Call 9-1-1 or the local emergency number.
- Wash the wound, if possible.
- **Immobilize** the affected part.
- Keep the affected area lower than the heart, if possible.
- Minimize the victim's movement. If possible, carry a victim who must be transported or have him or her walk slowly.
- Do not apply ice.
- Do not cut the wound.
- Do not apply a **tourniquet**.
- Do not use electric shock.

> This bulleted list describes how to respond to a victim of snake bite.

1. Check the victim's ABCs. Open the airway; check breathing and circulation. If necessary, begin rescue breathing, CPR, or bleeding control. (See the Emergency Action Guides on pages 199–210.)

2. If the victim is having breathing problems, keep his or her airway open. A conscious victim will naturally get into the position in which it is easiest to breathe.

3. Calm and reassure the victim. Anxiety aggravates all reactions.

4. Wash the bite with soap and water.

5. Remove any rings or constricting items, since the bitten area may swell.

6. Take steps to slow the rate at which the venom spreads in the victim's body. Have the victim lie still. Place the injured site below the level of the victim's heart and immobilize it in a comfortable position.

7. Look for signs of shock, such as decreased alertness or increased paleness. If shock develops, lay the victim flat, raise his or her feet 8 to 12 inches, and cover the victim with a coat or blanket. *Do not* elevate the bitten area, and *do not* place the victim in this position if you suspect any head, neck, back, or leg injury or if the position makes the victim uncomfortable. (See **Shock** on page 172.)

8. Stay with the victim until you get medical help.

> Numbered steps help readers follow the instructions for helping a snake-bite victim.

532 Types of Nonfiction

Vocabulary Development

© CCSS Language 6

First Aid Terms
Tell students that when reading manuals, they may encounter new words specific to the content of those manuals. Guide them to understand the meaning of the following first aid-related words that appear in this publication:

airway: an internal passageway through which air can reach the lungs from outside the body
rescue breathing: artificial respiration performed by a rescuer to restore breathing in an unconscious person
tourniquet: a cord tied around part of the body to limit blood flow to a specific area

State Park Warning Signs

Features:

- clearly printed text displayed in a public place
- large illustrations or other graphics
- concise language

A large illustration helps readers to quickly identify a rattlesnake.

RATTLESNAKES

Rattlesnakes may be found in this area. They are important members of the natural community, as they help keep rodent and other small animal populations under control. Rattlesnakes are not aggressive, but will strike to defend themselves if disturbed. Please give them distance and respect. Stay on designated trails. Be alert where you place your hands and feet.

The sign uses concise language to convey important information.

Reading for Information: Signs **533**

About Signs

1. Review the features listed in the Sign box on p. 533 with students. **Ask** the class to describe language that is *concise*.
   Answer: Concise language is language that is short and to the point.

2. **Ask** students to describe signs they have encountered.
   Possible response: Students may identify signs such as exit signs, parking signs, and signs with fire emergency instructions.

3. Talk to students about how best to read a sign. Suggest that it is important to first understand the purpose of the sign, then to analyze the specific features that tell more about the purpose.

Analyze Structure and Purpose

1. Review with students that the structure of a text refers to how the information in the text is presented and organized. Readers analyze structure to confirm the purpose of the text and to locate information. Make sure students understand that a sign in this context is a piece of text, even if much of the sign consists of labels or graphics.

2. Have students scan the sign and quickly describe it. Students should describe the sign as consisting of a large picture at top, a heading in large type, and a paragraph of text below.

3. **Ask** students to analyze the sign to decide what purpose the illustration serves. Suggest to students that the illustration may have two purposes.
   Answer: The illustration serves primarily to help people identify what a rattlesnake looks like. The bold nature of the picture also helps to serve as a warning.

4. **Ask** students to analyze the text. What is its purpose? What information does it provide?
   Answer: The purpose of the sign is to warn people about rattlesnakes. The sign says that rattlesnakes may be found in the area. It provides information about rattlesnakes and tips for avoiding rattlesnakes.

Fluency

Have students turn to the warning sign on p. 533. Tell students that a text such as this, which contains important information about possible danger, should be read at a deliberate pace. The phrasing of the read aloud should emphasize the important points. Model reading the text aloud, using a deliberate pace and clear phrasing. Then, have students read chorally or echo read.

Distribute copies of p. 533, and pair students. Have partners take turns reading the sign aloud. While one partner reads, the other should mark any words with which the reader has difficulty. Circulate to monitor the fluency of students' reading. Collect students' marked up copies of the page, and review difficult words and passages with the class.

1. Have students quickly scan the sign and tell what features of signs they recognize.
   Answer: Headings, illustrations, text that is linked to illustrations.

2. Tell students to read the two top lines. **Ask:** Why are these headings included on the sign?
   Possible response: The top line draws attention to the sign and signals that the sign is about telling the difference between something. The second line tells what is being compared. The lines help clarify the purpose of the sign.

3. Have students read the sign. Tell students to analyze the structure of the sign to locate information. Have students identify details from the sign.
   Answer: The sign provides information about non-venomous snakes and rattlesnakes. It provides detailed comparisons of the snakes' scales, eyes, heads, bodies, and tails.

4. Point out to students that the information in the sign appears in two columns, with information about non-venomous snakes in the first column and information about rattlesnakes in the second.
   Ask: How does this text structure help readers understand the information in the sign.
   Possible response: Because the purpose of the sign is to show the differences between the snakes, structuring the sign with the information side-by-side makes it easy to make the necessary comparisons.

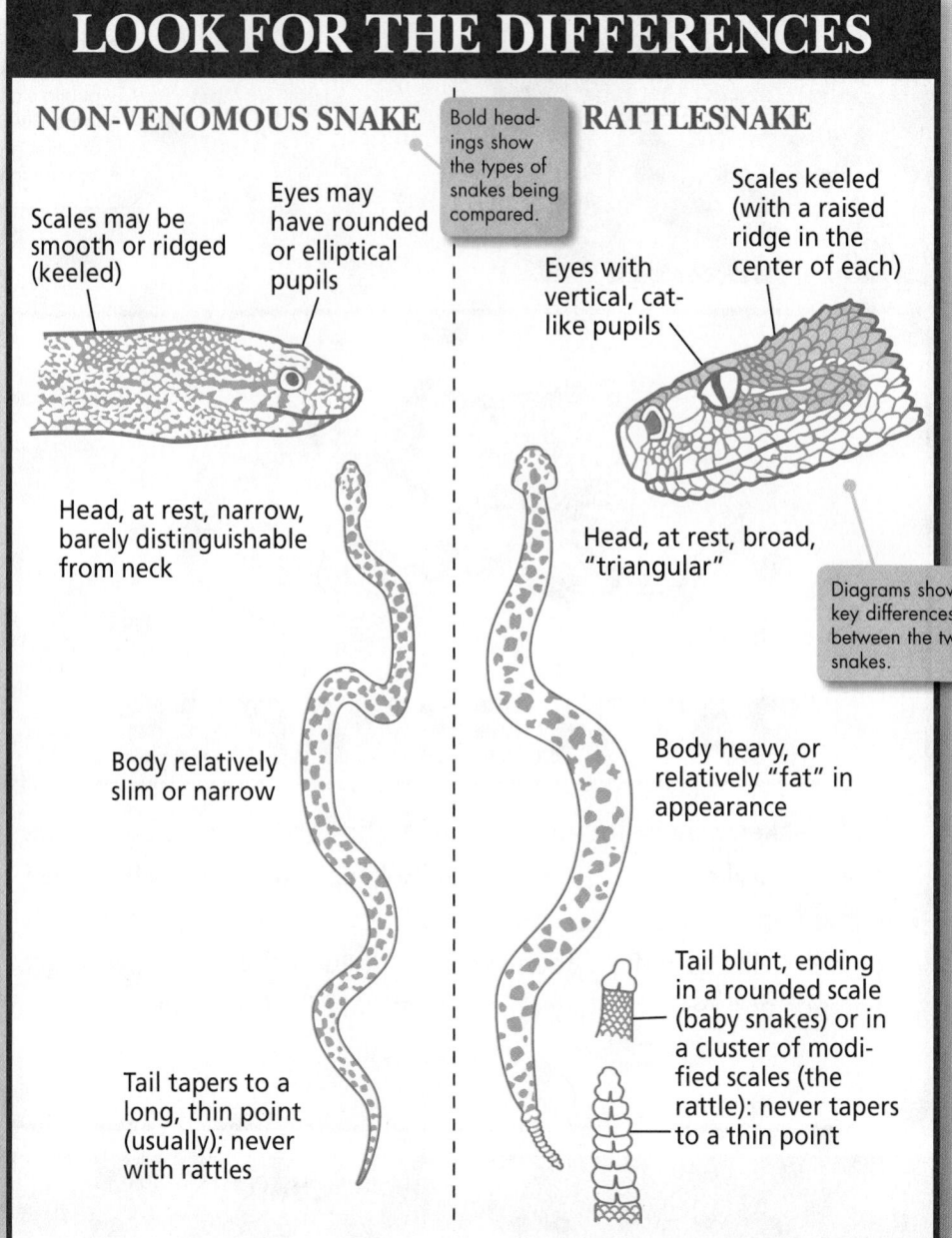

LOOK FOR THE DIFFERENCES

NON-VENOMOUS SNAKE | **RATTLESNAKE**

Bold headings show the types of snakes being compared.

Scales may be smooth or ridged (keeled)

Eyes may have rounded or elliptical pupils

Head, at rest, narrow, barely distinguishable from neck

Body relatively slim or narrow

Tail tapers to a long, thin point (usually); never with rattles

Scales keeled (with a raised ridge in the center of each)

Eyes with vertical, cat-like pupils

Head, at rest, broad, "triangular"

Diagrams show key differences between the two snakes.

Body heavy, or relatively "fat" in appearance

Tail blunt, ending in a rounded scale (baby snakes) or in a cluster of modified scales (the rattle): never tapers to a thin point

Think Aloud

Analyzing Text Structure

Model the skill of analyzing structure to locate information and establish purpose, using the following think aloud. Say to students:

When I see a sign such as this, my first thought is to figure out the purpose of the sign. To do so, I analyze the structure of the sign. I look at the headings, text, and illustrations. In the sign on this page, my eye is immediately drawn to the top heading, which tells me I'm going to be looking for differences. The next line of text tells me what I'm comparing: non-venomous snakes and rattlesnakes. I continue reading the sign and I see that the comparison is easy to make because of the design of the sign: the illustrations of the heads of the snakes and their bodies face each other. The text call-outs are clearly designed and laid out. Taking the time to analyze the structure of this sign helps me understand its contents better than if I just started reading bits of text here and there.

Comparing Functional Texts

1. Key Ideas and Details (a) What are some of the differences in **structure** and **purpose** between the instructional manual and the warning signs? **(b)** In what ways do structural features support the different purposes of each text?

Content-Area Vocabulary

2. (a) The word *immobilize* is based on the Latin root -*mov*-, which means "to move" and the prefix *im-*/*in-*, which means "without." Explain how the meaning of the word reflects the meanings of the two word parts. **(b)** Identify two other English words that are based on the root -*mov*-. Write the definition for each word. **(c)** Use a dictionary to verify your definitions.

⏱ Timed Writing

Explanatory Text: Essay

Audience
Remember that your readers may need to recall this information in an emergency. Your explanation should be clear, brief, and memorable.

In a short essay, explain how to effectively care for a snake-bite victim until help arrives. Include the most important information from the manual to support your response. (25 minutes)

Academic Vocabulary
When you *explain* a procedure or a process, you tell how to perform a task, using sequence words such as *before, first,* and *next.*

5-Minute Planner

Complete these steps before you begin to write:

1. Read the prompt carefully, noting the highlighted key words.

2. Review the section titled "First Aid for a Snake Bite" in the instruction manual. Jot down the most important and helpful information from both the bulleted list and the numbered list. **TIP** Focus on actions the reader *should* take. Do not focus on what the reader should not do or should do only in certain situations.

3. Review your notes, and identify the essential steps in caring for a snake-bite victim.

4. List the steps you identified in the order in which they should be performed. Then, use that list as the basis for your essay.

Comparing Functional Texts

1. (a) Signs are meant to warn, while instruction manuals are meant to teach. Signs include brief pieces of text in large type and large graphics. Instruction manuals include more detailed pieces of text, often in the form of lists. The graphics in an instruction manual are usually more detailed than those in signs. (b) The structural features of these two texts support the different purposes by using clearly marked lists, bulleted information, visual aids, step-by-step instructions, and large graphics.

2. (a) When you add the prefix *im-*, which means "without," to the word *mobilize,* which means "to move," the meaning becomes a verb meaning "to stop something from moving." (b) **Sample response:** *Motivate:* provide with a motive; cause to act. *Promote:* raise in rank, condition, or importance.

⏱ Timed Writing

1. Before students complete the activity, guide them in identifying and analyzing key words and phrases in the prompt, highlighted on the student page.

2. Work with students to draw up guidelines for their essays based on the key words:
   - **Focus** The writer should stay focused on the topic: how to care for a snake-bite victim.
   - **Organization** The writer should organize the explanation so that the steps needed to care for the victim are clear.
   - **Elaboration** The writer should be careful not to elaborate so much on the topic that the initial focus is lost.
   - **Style** The style should be clear and brief.

3. Have students use the 5-Minute Planner to structure their time.

4. Allow students 25 minutes to complete the assignment. Evaluate their work using the guidelines they have developed.

Common Core
State Standards

• Reading Literature 3
• Writing 9

❶ Comparing Humor

1. Introduce the skill, using the instruction on the student page.

2. Give students a copy of **Comparing Humor Graphic Organizer B** (*Graphic Organizer Transparencies,* p. 105). Tell them they will fill it in with comic details as they read.

Think Aloud: Model the Skill

Say to students:

Analyzing the humor of a work can help you understand its themes. Suppose I'm reading a humorous story about a businessman who is lost in the wilderness. If the story is funny because the businessman is ridiculously incompetent, I would suspect the author is making a point about how modern culture contrasts with nature. Understanding the point of the humor gives me greater insight.

Comparing Literary Works

**Alligator •
The Cremation
of Sam McGee**

❶ Comparing Humor

Humor is a type of writing that is meant to amuse readers. To entertain, authors may use one or more of these comic techniques:

• Present an illogical, inappropriate, improper, or unusual situation
• Contrast reality with the characters' mistaken views
• Exaggerate the truth, or exaggerate the feelings, ideas, and actions of characters
• Play with language by using funny names, nonsense words, humorous ways of speaking, or other forms of wordplay

While most humorists want to entertain the reader, many also write to convey serious messages. Humor usually reflects reality in some way, if only by turning reality upside down. In some humorous works, such as "Alligator," a writer observes a funny situation and captures it in words, managing to communicate the humor to readers. In other humorous works, such as "The Cremation of Sam McGee," the author begins with facts, but exaggerates them for comic effect.

Writers of humorous works often develop humor through the characters they present. In the essay "Alligator" and the narrative poem "The Cremation of Sam McGee," humorous characters are central to the selection. As you read, use a cluster diagram like the one shown to note comic details in the descriptions and actions of Aunt Belle in "Alligator" and Sam McGee in "The Cremation of Sam McGee."

Common Core
State Standards

Reading Literature
3. Analyze how particular elements of a story or drama interact.

Writing
9. Draw evidence from literary or informational texts to support analysis, reflection, and research.

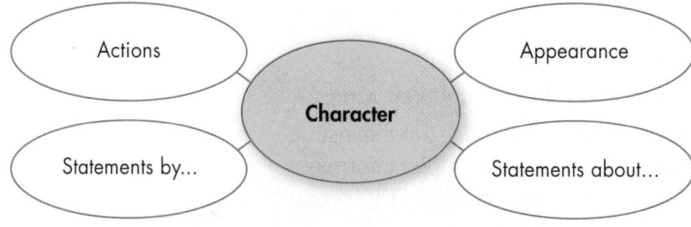

PHLit
Online!
www.PHLitOnline.com
• Vocabulary flashcards
• Interactive journals
• More about the authors
• Selection audio
• Interactive graphic organizers

536 Types of Nonfiction

Vocabulary Development

Vocabulary Knowledge Rating
Create a **Vocabulary Knowledge Rating Chart** (*Professional Development Guidebook,* p. 33) featuring the words glossed in the selections:

cattails (p. 539)   whimper (p. 543)
exultant (p. 540)   loathed (p. 544)
bellow (p. 540)

Give students a copy of the chart, and read the words aloud. Have students mark their rating of

each in the Before You Read column. To gauge how much instruction to provide, tally students who think they know each word.

Explain that the words are defined in the margin at the point where they appear in the selection. Urge students to be alert to these words as they read the selections. They will rate their knowledge again when they finish.

What should we *learn?*

Writing About the Big Question

In each of these selections, the narrator exaggerates the facts for humorous effect. Use these sentence starters to develop your ideas.

Our **curiosity** sometimes leads us to discover humor because we see _____.

Humor can help us gain insight by _____.

Meet the Authors

Bailey White (b. 1950)

Author of "Alligator"

Bailey White reads her humorous essays on *All Things Considered*, a program on public radio. She describes people and situations she encounters in and around Thomasville, Georgia, where she was born and lives today.

Juggling Two Careers White began writing when she was a teen. On graduation from Florida State University, she returned to Thomasville to teach first grade. During the twenty years she taught, she wrote in her spare time. Today, White pursues her writing career full time.

Robert Service (1874–1958)

Author of "The Cremation of Sam McGee"

Born in England and raised in Scotland, Robert Service went to Canada at age twenty to work for a bank. In the Yukon Territory, he met fur trappers and gold prospectors. Leaving the bank, Service traveled in the Arctic, where he observed the people and recorded his adventures. "The Cremation of Sam McGee" grew out of these experiences.

Alligator • The Cremation of Sam McGee **537**

---

❷ Writing About the Big Question

1. Introduce the assignment.
2. Ask students what it means to gain insight. Make the point that insights are often personal.
3. Have students complete the sentence starters. Review responses as a class. (**Sample response:** Our curiosity sometimes leads us to discover humor because we see unexpected aspects of life when we learn. Humor can help us gain insight by allowing us to see ourselves in a new way.)
4. Remind students that their answers will help them think about the Big Question.
5. Tell students to note as they read what characters learn.

Concept Connector ➡

Students will return to their sentence starters after reading.

Multidraft Reading

To assist struggling readers and to deepen reading for all, apply multidraft reading protocols. For each reading, have students set the purpose indicated:

- **First reading**—identifying key ideas and details and answering any Reading Checks.
- **Second reading**—analyzing craft and structure and responding to the side-column prompts.
- **Third reading**—integrating knowledge and ideas, connecting to other texts and the world, and answering the end-of-selection questions.

For more guidance, see the *Classroom Strategies and Teaching Routines* card on multidraft reading.

537

❶ Background

The American Alligator Alligators live in bodies of freshwater such as lakes, rivers, and swamps throughout the southeastern United States, in states such as Florida, Georgia, and Louisiana. They usually range in length from six to twelve feet (1.8 to 3.7 m), but they may grow up to nineteen feet (5.7 m), which could be closer to the size of the alligator in this essay.

❷ Activating Prior Knowledge

Have students name animals they consider frightening. **Ask** students to think about what might happen when a frightening animal turns out to be approachable and even humanlike.

Answer: Students might answer that the result can be humorous, since there is a contrast between the animal's frightening appearance or reputation, and its tameness.

❸ About the Selection

"Alligator" describes the years-long relationship between the narrator's aunt and an alligator that lives in a pond on her property. For some never-defined reason, Aunt Belle decides to "tame" the beast, and later teaches it to bellow on command. As woman and reptile grow older, their meetings become more subdued and a kind of bond develops between them as they seem to simply enjoy each other's company. The essay ends on an elegiac note as the alligator disappears, never to be seen again, and yet "an alligator" is sometimes heard by the narrator, now an adult, bellowing just as Aunt Belle's alligator did.

❶ ❷ ❸ ALLIGATOR

Bailey White

538 Types of Nonfiction

Ⓒ Text Complexity Rubric

Alligator		
Qualitative Measures	**Context/Knowledge Demands**	Rural Georgia wetlands; mid-1900s 1 ② 3 4 5
	Structure/Language Conventionality	First-person account with exaggerated and humorous description 1 2 ③ 4 5
	Levels of Meaning/ Purpose/Concepts	Accessible concept (sometimes adults do silly things) 1 2 ③ 4 5
Quantitative Measures	**Text Length**	Word Count: 605
	Lexile	890L

❹ ![THE BIG ?] **Connecting to the Big Question**

1. Remind students that children often learn by observing their elders.

2. **Ask** students: What are the children learning from Aunt Belle in this passage? **Answer:** They are learning about their aunt's character; she is brave and quirky. They are also learning that the behavior of wild animals is difficult to predict or analyze.

3. **Ask** students: Is everything we learn beneficial to us? Refer to the selection to explain your answer. **Answer:** No. For example, Aunt Belle is teaching the children to take chances around wild animals. This lesson is a potentially dangerous one, as it could lead to the children getting injured.

4. Tell students to look as they read for other lessons learned by the narrator.

❺ **Critical Viewing**

Possible responses: Some students may say that they would like to tame an alligator like this because they like exotic or dangerous animals. Other students will say no because the alligator looks large and dangerous.

I remember as a little child watching my Aunt Belle's wide rump disappear into the cattails and marsh grass at the edge of a pond as she crawled on her hands and knees to meet a giant alligator face to face. She was taming him, she said. We children would wait high up on the bank with our eyes and mouths wide open, hoping that the alligator wouldn't eat her up, but not wanting to miss it if he did.

Finally Aunt Belle would get as close to him as she wanted, and they would stare at each other for some minutes. Then my aunt would jump up, wave her arms in the air, and shout, "Whoo!" With a tremendous leap and flop the alligator would

❺
▲ **Critical Viewing**
Would you want to try to tame an alligator like this one? Why or why not? **[Connect]**

Vocabulary
cattails (kat′ tālz) *n.* tall reeds with furry spikes found in wetlands

Alligator **539**

© **Text Complexity: Reader and Task Suggestions**

Alligator

Preparing to Read the Text
- Using the Background note on p. 538, preview information about alligators.
- Review the bullet points on SE p. 536. Then encourage students to give examples of a real person they know who possesses some of these comic techniques.
- Guide students in using Multidraft Reading strategies (TE p. 537).

Leveled Tasks
Structure/Language If students will have difficulty with humorous language, have them first read to identify simple details about the alligator and its pond. Then, have them reread to note descriptive language they find confusing. Clarify the humor as needed.

Evaluating If students will not have difficulty with language, remind them that the author read this essay aloud. Have students note as they read passages that would be particularly humorous when read aloud. Discuss how changes in tone of voice would generate humor.

This selection is available in interactive format in the **Enriched Online Student Edition**, online at **www.PHLitOnline.com**, which includes an interactive graphic organizer.

Word Choice

1. Remind students that they studied the concept of word choice in the Unit 3 Literary Analysis Workshop (pp. 408–419).

2. **Ask** the Spiral Review question.

   Possible response: "Fast," "raising two diagonal waves," "haul," and "get situated."

❻ Humorous Essay

1. Review the bracketed passage with students. Have them note which parts, if any, make them laugh.

2. **Ask** students the Humorous Essay question.

   Possible responses: The description of the alligator's bellow as having "more authority than a lion's roar," is humorous because most people would find a lion's roar difficult to top. The image of Aunt Belle throwing the alligator a dead chicken is funny. She is treating the alligator like a pet. On the other hand, the fact that the alligator eats an entire dead chicken makes it clear that he isn't a cuddly animal doing tricks for treats.

❼ Critical Viewing

Possible response: The smile could make some students feel afraid. Other students might think it's funny that such a fearsome animal appears to be smiling.

540

Vocabulary

exultant (eg zult´ ´nt) *adj.* expressing great joy or triumph

bellow (bel´ ō) *v.* roar deeply

Spiral Review

Word Choice In this vivid description of the alligator, which words describe his motion?

Humorous Essay Which details make this paragraph funny?

❻

❼

▼ **Critical Viewing** This alligator appears to be smiling. Describe how its smile makes you feel. **[Connect]**

---

throw himself into the water. The little drops from that splash would reach all the way to where we were standing, and my aunt would come up the bank drenched and exultant. "I have to show him who's boss," she would tell us.

Later, Aunt Belle taught that alligator to bellow on command. She would drive the truck down to the edge of the pond and gun the engine. We would sit in the back, craning our necks to see him coming. He would come fast across the pond, raising two diagonal waves behind him as he came. He would haul himself into the shallow water and get situated just right. His back was broad and black. His head was as wide as a single bed. His tail would disappear into the dark pond water. He was the biggest alligator anyone had ever seen.

Then my aunt would turn off the engine. We would all stop breathing. The alligator would swell up. He would lift his head, arch his tail, and bellow. The sound would come from deep inside. It was not loud, but it had a carrying quality. It was like a roar, but with more authority than a lion's roar. It was a sound you hear in your bones. If we were lucky, he would bellow ten times. Then Aunt Belle would throw him a dead chicken.

The day came when she could just walk down to the pond and look out across the water. The alligator would come surging up to the bank, crawl out, and bellow.

540 Types of Nonfiction

Vocabulary Development

© **CCSS** Language 6

Vocabulary Reinforcement
To reinforce and assess students' comprehension of the selection vocabulary, give them sentences in which the word may or may not be used correctly. **Ask** students to say whether the usage is correct or not and to explain their answers. Use these sentences:

1. When my younger brother pulled on the *cattails,* the cats yowled loudly.
   Answer: No, *cattails* is not used correctly. They are plants, not the tails of cats.

2. *Cattails* make me sneeze because I am allergic to plants.
   Answer: Yes, *cattails* is used correctly.

3. My sister is *exultant* that she lost her race.
   Answer: No, *exultant* is not used correctly. When you lose a race, you do not express joy.

4. The teacher is *exultant* that her students aced their finals.
   Answer: Yes, *exultant* is used correctly. A teacher would be very happy if her students did well on their exams.

By this time he was very old. My aunt got old, too. Her children had all grown up. She got to where she was spending a lot of time down at the pond. She'd go down there and just sit on the bank. When the alligator saw her, he'd swim over and climb out. He never bellowed anymore. They would just sit and look at each other. After a while my aunt would walk back to the house. The alligator would swim out to where the water was deep and black, and float for a minute; then he'd just disappear, without even a ripple. That's how he did.

But one day he didn't come when Aunt Belle went to the pond. He didn't come the next day, or the day after. All that summer, Aunt Belle walked around and around the pond looking, listening, and sniffing. "Something as big as that, you'd know if he was dead, this hot weather," she'd say. Finally, she stopped going down to the pond.

But sometimes, on the nights of the full moon in springtime, I can hear an alligator bellow. It comes rolling up through the night. It's not loud, but it makes me sit up in bed and hold my breath. Sometimes I hear it ten times. It's a peaceful sound.

❽ Humorous Essay
Which details in this paragraph are probably exaggerated for effect? Explain.

Critical Thinking ©

1. **Key Ideas and Details (a)** According to the second paragraph of the essay, what were some early interactions between Aunt Belle and the alligator? **(b) Infer:** What does Aunt Belle mean when she says she has to "show him who's boss"?

2. **Craft and Structure (a)** What words and phrases does White use to describe the bellowing of the alligator? **(b) Speculate:** How would the story have been different if White had used a more realistic style to describe the scene?

3. **Integration of Knowledge and Ideas (a) Compare and Contrast:** How are the alligator and Aunt Belle similar at the end of the essay? **(b) Analyze:** How does the relationship between the alligator and Aunt Belle change over the years?

4. **Integration of Knowledge and Ideas (a)** What does the writer learn from her Aunt Belle? **(b)** Why do you think people sometimes use humor to convey a serious or touching message? *[Connect to the Big Question: What should we learn?]*

Cite textual evidence to support your responses.

Alligator **541**

541

❾ ❿ ⓫

The CREMATION of SAM McGEE

Robert Service

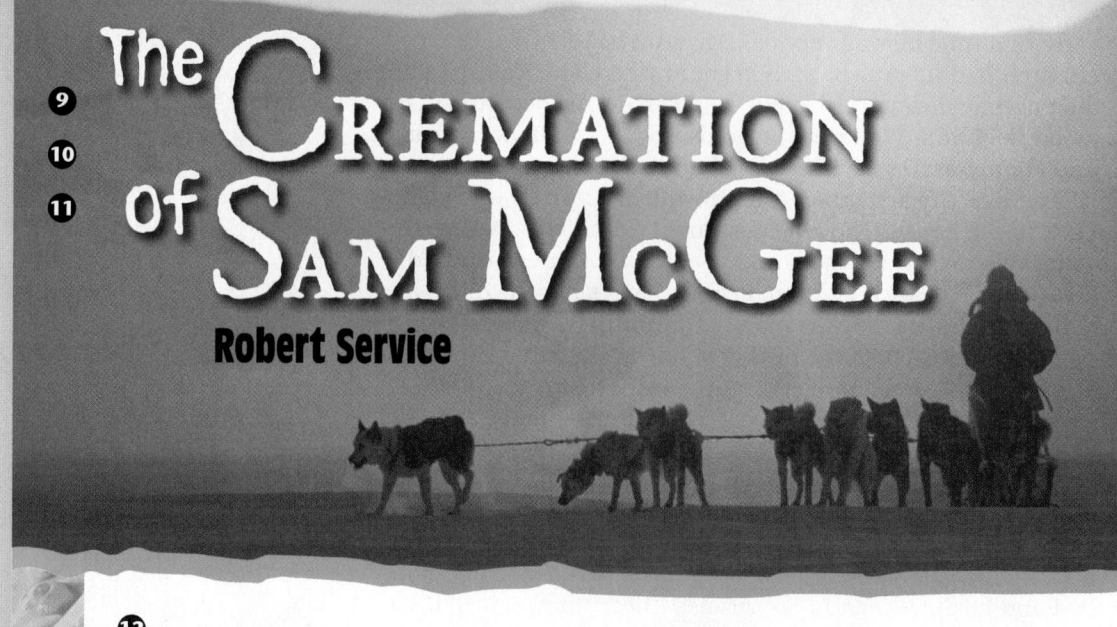

❾

❾ Background

The Klondike Gold Rush This poem is set in the Klondike Gold Rush, which began in the 1890s when George Carmack, Tagish Charlie, and Skookum Jim discovered gold on the Bonanza Creek. Word spread quickly after ships hauling gold from the Yukon reached Seattle and San Francisco. Because of the treacherous conditions in the region, miners had to prepare for the worst kinds of weather.

❿ Activating Prior Knowledge

Read aloud the following quotation: "The only society I like is that which is rough and tough—and the tougher the better. That's where you get down to bedrock and meet human people." Tell students that the man who said this also wrote the poem they are about to read. Ask students what they think the quotation means and if they agree with it. Have them keep the quotation and their response in mind as they read the poem.

Concept Connector ➡

Students will return to their ideas about the quotation after reading the poem.

⓫ About the Selection

Like a tall tale, the narrative poem "The Cremation of Sam McGee" tells a story using exaggeration, humor, and fantasy. Two prospectors, Sam and Cap, travel across the Yukon. Before he dies of cold, Sam asks Cap to cremate his remains. Cap fashions a crematorium from an abandoned ship on a frozen lake. Cap looks into the burning furnace, only to discover that Sam is alive and well—and warm at last.

⓬ Critical Viewing

Possible response: With few roads in the Arctic, sleds pulled by dogs that thrive in the harsh climate can most efficiently take people into the backcountry.

⓬

▲ **Critical Viewing** Why do you think people in the Arctic, like the men in this poem, travel by dog sled as pictured here? **[Hypothesize]**

Background In this poem, two men prospect for gold in Canada's Yukon Territory. Located just east of Alaska, where the temperature can reach −60°F, the area long attracted fortune hunters who came for its mineral wealth. Gold was discovered in the Klondike River region in the 1890s, and many people, including poet Robert Service, came to look for it.

> There are strange things done in the midnight sun
>   By the men who moil[1] for gold;
> The Arctic trails have their secret tales
>   That would make your blood run cold;
> 5   The Northern Lights have seen queer sights,
>   But the queerest they ever did see
> Was that night on the marge[2] of Lake Lebarge
>   I cremated Sam McGee.
>
> Now Sam McGee was from Tennessee,
>   where the cotton blooms and blows
> 10 Why he left his home in the South to roam
>   'round the Pole, God only knows.

---

1. **moil** (moil) *v.* toil and slave.
2. **marge** (märj) *n.* poetic word for the shore of the lake.

Ⓒ Text Complexity Rubric

The Cremation of Sam McGee		
Qualitative Measures	**Context/Knowledge Demands**	1890s Klondike Gold Rush; fantastic situation; cremation 1 2 ③ 4 5
	Structure/Language Conventionality and Clarity	Exaggeration and hyperbole; fantastic premise; formal syntax and challenging vocabulary 1 2 3 ④ 5
	Levels of Meaning/ Purpose/Concept Level	Implicit meaning; accessible concept (friendship is important, especially in hard times) 1 2 3 ④ 5
Quantitative Measures	**Text Length**	Word Count: 940
	Lexile	NP

He was always cold, but the land of gold
    seemed to hold him like a spell;
Though he'd often say in his homely way
    that "he'd sooner live in hell."

On a Christmas Day we were mushing our way
    over the Dawson trail.
Talk of your cold! through the parka's fold
    it stabbed like a driven nail.
15 If our eyes we'd close, then the lashes froze
    til sometimes we couldn't see;
It wasn't much fun, but the only one
    to whimper was Sam McGee.

And that very night, as we lay packed tight
    in our robes beneath the snow,
And the dogs were fed, and the stars o'erhead
    were dancing heel and toe,
He turned to me, and "Cap," says he,
    "I'll cash in this trip, I guess;
20 And if I do, I'm asking that you
    won't refuse my last request."

13
▲ **Critical Viewing**
What details of this image make it a good illustration for the poem? Explain. **[Evaluate]**

Vocabulary
whimper (hwim´ pər)
v. make low, crying sounds

15  Reading Check
Why is Sam McGee in the Arctic?

The Cremation of Sam McGee **543**

14 **Connecting to the Big Question**

1. Tell students that they can learn about the Yukon by reading this selection.
2. **Ask** students: What detail does the second stanza on this page tell you about the weather of the Yukon? **Answer:** It got so cold that your eyelashes could freeze together.
3. **Ask** students: What does the detail above tell us about the gold prospectors who traveled in the Yukon? **Answer:** They were willing to suffer a great deal of hardship to find gold.
4. Tell students to think about what else they are learning about the Yukon as they read.

15 **Reading Check**
Answer: Sam McGee is in the Arctic because he hopes to strike gold.

© **Text Complexity: Reader and Task Suggestions**

The Cremation of Sam McGee	
Preparing to Read the Text • Using the Background on p. 542, discuss information about the Klondike Gold Rush. • Explain that the poem uses dark humor to recount the dangers of life in the Yukon. Discuss why people sometimes want to present unpleasant events as funny. Use the instruction on p. 536 to link humorous techniques to dark humor. • Guide students in using Multidraft Reading strategies (TE p. 537).	**Leveled Tasks** *Structure/Language* If students will have difficulty with fantasy or exaggeration, have them first read to hear the poem's rhyme and rhythm. Then, have them reread to note details and descriptions that seem impossible. Clarify as needed. *Evaluating* If students will not have difficulty interpreting humorous language, have them note as they read lines with internal rhyme. Discuss how poetic syntax and rhyme create a sing-song quality that mocks the poem's supposedly serious events. Ask students to evaluate if the poem's dark humor is funny.

16 Humor

1. Remind students that exaggeration can be used to produce a particular effect, such as a smile or chuckle.

2. Read the bracketed text together as a class. **Ask** students to identify the exaggeration.
   Answer: "Chilled clean through to the bone" is exaggeration.

3. **Ask** students why they think Sam McGee is so cold, even colder than Cap.
   Answer: Sam McGee is from Tennessee, which has a mild climate, so he is unaccustomed to bitter cold.

4. Have a volunteer reread the bracketed text aloud. Then, **ask** the Humor question.
   Answer: McGee wants to be cremated so he will be warm at last.

Spiral Review

Word Choice

1. Remind students that they studied the concept of word choice in the Unit 3 Literary Analysis Workshop (pp. 408–419).

2. **Ask** the Spiral Review question.

   Possible response: The rhyming words give the poem rhythm and make it easier and more fun to read and listen to.

Humor 16
Why does McGee want to be cremated?

Spiral Review Word Choice Notice that there are rhyming words, such as *need* and *heed*, in the middle and end of alternating lines. How do these word choices affect the sound of the poem?

Vocabulary
loathed (lōthd) *v.* hated

17

Well, he seemed so low that I couldn't say no;
  then he says with a sort of moan:
"It's the cursed cold, and it's got right hold
  till I'm chilled clean through to the bone.
Yet 'tain't being dead—it's my awful dread
  of the icy grave that pains;
So I want you to swear that, foul or fair,
  you'll cremate my last remains."

25 A pal's last need is a thing to heed,
  so I swore I would not fail;
And we started on at the streak of dawn;
  but God! he looked ghastly pale.
He crouched on the sleigh, and he raved all day
  of his home in Tennessee;
And before nightfall a corpse was all
  that was left of Sam McGee.

There wasn't a breath in that land of death,
  and I hurried, horror-driven,
30 With a corpse half hid that I couldn't get rid,
  because of a promise given;
It was lashed to the sleigh, and it seemed to say:
  "You may tax your brawn[3] and brains,
But you promised true, and it's up to you
  to cremate those last remains."

Now a promise made is a debt unpaid,
  and the trail has its own stern code.
In the days to come, though my lips were dumb,
  in my heart how I cursed that load.
35 In the long, long night, by the lone firelight,
  while the huskies, round in a ring,
Howled out their woes to the homeless snows—
  O God! how I loathed the thing.
And every day that quiet clay
  seemed to heavy and heavier grow;
And on I went, though the dogs were spent
  and the grub was getting low;
The trail was bad, and I felt half mad,
  but I swore I would not give in;

---

3. **brawn** (brôn) *n.* physical strength.

544 Types of Nonfiction

Vocabulary Development
 Ⓒ **CCSS** Language 6

Connotations
Explain to students that the denotation of a word is its dictionary definition. The connotation of a word is the ideas or images connected with its meaning. Point out that words can have the same meanings but different connotations. Give students examples by writing *inexpensive* and *cheap* on the board. Read aloud the dictionary definitions. Then have students give the connotations. (Students might suggest *low–priced* for *inexpensive* and *shoddy* for *cheap*.) Conclude by having students give connotations of the word *inky* from line 52 of the poem. (Students might say *black, opaque,* and *stained.*)

40 And I'd often sing to the hateful thing,
        and it hearkened with a grin.

    Till I came to the marge of Lake Lebarge,
        and a derelict[4] there lay;
    It was jammed in the ice, but I saw in a trice
        it was called the "Alice May."
    And I looked at it, and I thought a bit,
        and I looked at my frozen chum;
    Then "Here," said I, with a sudden cry,
        "is my cre-ma-tor-eum."

45 Some planks I tore from the cabin floor,
        and I lit the boiler fire;
    Some coal I found that was lying around,
        and I heaped the fuel higher;
    The flames just soared, and the furnace roared—
        such a blaze you seldom see;
    And I burrowed a hole in the glowing coal,
        and I stuffed in Sam McGee.

    Then I made a hike, for I didn't like
        to hear him sizzle so;
50 And the heavens scowled, and the huskies howled,
        and the wind began to blow.
    It was icy cold, but the hot sweat rolled
        down my cheeks, and I don't know why;
    And the greasy smoke in an inky cloak
        went streaking down the sky.

    I do not know how long in the snow
        I wrestled with grisly fear;
    But the stars came out and they danced about
        ere again I ventured near;

---

4. **derelict** (der´ ə likt´) *n.* abandoned ship.

Humor

What problem, or conflict, does the speaker face?

18
Reading Check

What promise does the speaker keep?

---

17 ## Humor

1. Remind students that narrative poetry tells a story using poetic techniques and incorporating characters, plot, and setting.

2. Read the bracketed passage with students. **Ask** students to paraphrase each line. Remind students to use their own words but not to add any of their own ideas. **Possible response:** Every day the body seemed to get heavier. I kept going, although the dogs were exhausted and the food supply was running out. The trail was poor, and I felt half out of my mind, but I was determined not to give up. When I sang to the body, it smiled. One day, I came to the edge of Lake Lebarge, where I saw an old ship, called the "Alice May." I decided to use it to cremate the body.

3. **Ask** the Humor question. **Answer:** The speaker faces a conflict between keeping his promise and saving himself and his dogs.

18 ## Reading Check

Answer: The speaker keeps his promise to cremate Sam.

Differentiated
Instruction   for Universal Access

EL **Pronunciation for English Learners**

Some English learners may have difficulty pronouncing the initial "*th*" sound found in the words *thing, thought,* and *then* on this page. Assess students' ability by asking them to read lines 40, 43, and 44 out loud. Pair students with fluent English speakers. Assign the fluent speakers the task of modeling the correct pronunciation of the words.

Enrichment for Gifted/Talented Students

Explain to students that internal rhyme is the use of rhyming words in the same line, such as *sing* and *thing* in line 40 and *marge* and *Lebarge* in line 41. This rhyme adds to the overall rhyme scheme of the poem. Challenge students to write their own poems, incorporating internal rhyme.

⑲ Humor

Read the bracketed stanza with students. Then, **ask** the Humor question.

Answer: The sound of the simple, rhyming words is humorous. It's also funny and irreverent to refer to a body as "cooked."

Concept Connector

Have students return to their thoughts about the quotation on p. 542 and think about whether their ideas have changed.

⟵

ASSESS

Answers

Critical Thinking

Before students respond, you may wish to have them write a brief objective summary of the selection. As they answer the questions below, remind them to support their answers with evidence from the text.

1. (a) Sam hates the cold temperatures of the Yukon. (b) Sam wants to find gold.

2. (a) Cap is the speaker. Cap promises he will cremate Sam if Sam dies. (b) The speaker believes that promises are like "debts unpaid."

3. (a) The speaker finds Sam alive, well, and warm. (b) The poet probably expects you to be surprised and amused by the ending.

4. **Possible responses:**
   (a) The selection teaches that friendship is important, especially in harsh environments. It also teaches that it is important to keep your promises. (b) We often laugh at things that make us uncomfortable, like suffering or death. Thinking about why we laugh can offer insight into our emotional life.

Humor ⑲
How do the words "cooked" and "looked" create humor here?

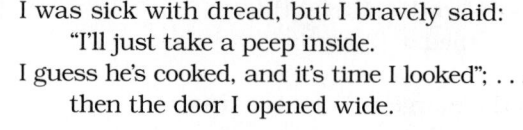

55 I was sick with dread, but I bravely said:
  "I'll just take a peep inside.
I guess he's cooked, and it's time I looked"; . . .
  then the door I opened wide.

And there sat Sam, looking cool and calm,
  in the heart of the furnace roar;
And he wore a smile you could see a mile,
  and he said: "Please close that door.
It's fine in here, but I greatly fear
  you'll let in the cold and storm—
60 Since I left Plumtree, down in Tennessee,
  it's the first time I've been warm."

There are strange things done in the midnight sun
  By the men who moil for gold;
The Arctic trails have their secret tales
  That would make your blood run cold;
65 *The Northern Lights have seen queer sights,*
  But the queerest they ever did see
Was that night on the marge of Lake Lebarge
  I cremated Sam McGee.

Critical Thinking

Cite textual evidence to support your responses.

1. **Key Ideas and Details (a)** What problem does Sam have with his surroundings? **(b) Deduce:** What prevents him from going home?

2. **Key Ideas and Details (a)** Who is the speaker, and what does he promise Sam? **(b) Interpret:** Why is the speaker determined to keep his promise? Use details from the poem to support your answer.

3. **Craft and Structure (a)** What does the speaker find when he opens the furnace door? **(b) Infer:** What reaction does the poet expect you to have to this unexpected occurrence?

4. **Integration of Knowledge and Ideas (a)** What does this selection teach about the Yukon and friendship through its use of humor? **(b)** What can we learn from the things that make us laugh? *[Connect to the Big Question: What should we learn?]*

Vocabulary Development

Vocabulary Knowledge Rating

When students have completed reading "Alligator" and "The Cremation of Sam McGee," have them take out the **Vocabulary Knowledge Rating Chart.** Read the words aloud once more, and have students rate their knowledge of the words again in the After Reading column. Clarify any words that are still problematic. Have students write their own definitions and examples or sentences in the appropriate column. Then, have students complete the Vocabulary activities on the next page. Encourage students to use the words in further discussion and written work about these selections. Remind them that they will be accountable for these words on the **Selection Test** (*Unit 3 Resources,* pp. 216–218 or pp. 219–221).

Comparing Humor

© **1. Craft and Structure** Complete a chart like the one shown to analyze the techniques each author uses to create humor.

	Humorous Scene	Details	Humorous Techniques
"Alligator"			
"The Cremation of Sam McGee"			

⏱ Timed Writing

Explanatory Text: Essay

Analyze which selection you think is more humorous: the essay "Alligator" or the poem "The Cremation of Sam McGee." Write a comparison-and-contrast essay, providing details from the selections to support your position. **(25 minutes)**

5-Minute Planner

1. Read the prompt carefully and completely.

2. Gather your ideas by jotting down answers to these questions:
   - What events from each selection amused you most?
   - Whom did you find funnier—Aunt Belle in "Alligator" or Sam McGee in "The Cremation of Sam McGee"?
   - Whom did you find more touching? Why?
   - What purpose might the authors have had beyond amusing you? Explain.
   - Which author would you choose to read again? Why?

3. Choose an organizational strategy. Use either the block method—discussing first one work, then the other—or the point-by-point method—discussing one point per work at a time—to compare elements such as the narrators, characters, and setting.

4. Reread the prompt, and then draft your essay.

ASSESS

Answers

Comparing Humor

As students complete their charts, remind them that "Humorous Scene" refers to an overall situation or event, "Details" include descriptions and what people say, and "Humorous Techniques" are described on page 536. For other sample answers, see *Graphic Organizer Transparencies*, **Comparing Humor Graphic Organizer A**, p. 106, and the **Additional Answers** section.

⏱ Timed Writing

1. Review the prompt with students.

2. Have students use the 5-Minute Planner to structure their time. Guide them in answering the bulleted questions. For example, point out that the third bulleted point might lead them to focus on which character they connected with the most.

3. Allow students 25 minutes to complete the assignment.

4. As students prewrite and draft, have them refer to their completed Comparing Humor Graphic Organizer.

Six Traits Focus

✔	Ideas		Word Choice
✔	Organization		Sentence Fluency
	Voice		Conventions

**Common Core
State Standards**

• Writing 2, 2.a, b, c, d, e; 4
• Language 1.c, 3.a

Introducing the Writing Assignment

Review the assignment and the criteria, using the instruction on the student page.

Richard Mühlberger on Comparison and Contrast

Show students Segment 3 on Richard Mühlberger on the *See It!* DVD or from this page on the **Enriched Student Online Edition** at **www.PHLitOnline.com.** Ask students what some of the challenges are in writing about an artist.

Writing Workshop
Work in Progress

If students have done the Work-in-Progress assignments on pp. 505 and 527, suggest that they consider developing their Work-in-Progress ideas into an essay.

What Do You Notice?

1. Have a volunteer read the quotation aloud. **Ask** students the first question: What do you notice about these sentences? (**Possible response:** The phrase *with it* is repeated several times.)

2. **Ask** students how the sentence structure contributes to the flow of the passage. (**Possible response:** The last three sentences begin with *with it*. This shift from usual word order emphasizes the phrase; the repetition adds rhythm.)

3. **Ask** the second question: How does the sentence structure and the repetition of certain words help to build ideas? (**Possible response:** The sentence structure and repetition emphasize Chief Dan George's central point: being loved is a universal necessity.)

4. Encourage students to apply their ideas about repetition and sentence structure to their own writing.

548

Writing Workshop

**Common Core
State Standards**

Writing
2. Write informative/explanatory texts to examine a topic and convey ideas, concepts, and information through the selection, organization, and analysis of relevant content.
2.a. Introduce a topic clearly, previewing what is to follow; organize ideas, concepts, and information, using strategies such as definition, classification, comparison/contrast, and cause/effect.
2.b. Develop the topic and relevant facts, definitions, concrete details, quotations, or other information and examples.
2.d. Use precise language and domain-specific vocabulary to inform about or explain the topic.
2.e. Establish and maintain a formal style.

Write an Explanatory Text

Exposition: Comparison-and-Contrast Essay

Defining the Form A **comparison-and-contrast essay** analyzes the similarities and differences between two or more related subjects. You might use elements of this form in persuasive essays, journals, and reviews.

Assignment Write a comparison-and-contrast essay that helps readers make a decision or see old things in a fresh way. Your essay should feature these elements:

• A *topic involving two or more things* that are neither nearly identical nor extremely different
• *Details illustrating both similarities and differences*
• *Clear organization* that highlights the points of comparison
• An *introduction* that grabs a reader's interest, and a strong, memorable *conclusion*
• Error-free writing, including *correct use of adjectives and adverbs*

To preview the criteria on which your comparison-and-contrast essay may be judged, see the rubric on page 555.

Writing Workshop: *Work in Progress*

Review the work that you did on pages 505 and 527.

WRITE GUY
Jeff Anderson, M.Ed.

What Do You Notice?

Sentence Structure

The following sentences are from Chief Dan George's "I Am a Native of North America." Read them several times.

You and I need the strength and joy that comes from knowing that we are loved. With it we are creative. With it we march tirelessly. With it, and with it alone, we are able to sacrifice for others.

Discuss these questions with a partner:

• What do you notice about these sentences?
• How does the sentence structure and the repetition of certain words help to build ideas?

Think about ways you might use structure to make your writing lively.

548 Types of Nonfiction

Reading-Writing Connection

To get a feel for comparison-and-contrast writing, read "Conversational Ballgames" by Nancy Masterson Sakamoto on page 432.

Teaching Resources

The following resources can be used to enrich or extend the instruction.

All *Unit 3 Resources*
   Writing Workshop, pp. 222–223

All *Common Core Companion,*
   pp. 202–212, 225–239; 333–338, 343–344

All *Professional Development Guidebook*
   Rubrics for Self-Assessment: Comparison-and-Contrast Essay, pp. 234–235

All *Graphic Organizer Transparencies*
   Rubric for Self-Assessment: Comparison-and-Contrast Essay, p. 108

All *See It!* DVD
   Richard Mühlberger

All resources, including print and video, are available online at
www.PHLitOnline.com.

Prewriting/Planning Strategies

Choose a topic. To choose a topic for your essay, use one of these strategies:

- **Quicklist** Fold a piece of paper in thirds lengthwise. In the first column, list recent choices you have made—for instance, products you have bought or activities you have completed. In the second column, next to each choice, write a precise descriptive phrase. In the third column, give an alternative to your choice.

  Example: polka-dot sweatshirt / playful, silly / team jacket
  Review your list, and choose the most interesting pairing to compare and contrast.

- **BUT Chart** Write the word BUT down the center of a piece of paper. On the left, list items with something in common. List differences among them on the right. Choose your topic from this list.

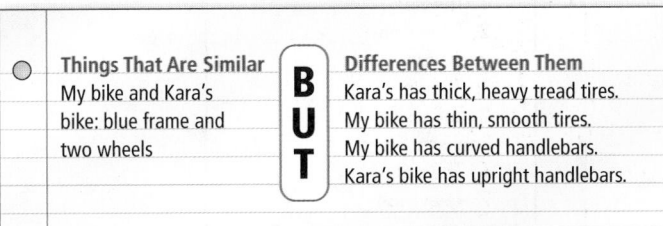

Get specific. You may find that your topic is too broad to cover in a brief essay. Use these strategies to narrow your topic.

- **Describe it** to someone who is not familiar with it.
- **Apply it,** explaining what you can do with it, on it, or to it.
- **Analyze it** by breaking it into parts.
- **Argue for or against it,** explaining good and bad points, while maintaining a formal style.

Circle details from your notes to create a focused topic.

Show similarities and differences. Focus on gathering details that show similarities and differences between your subjects. Use a Venn diagram to organize your details. Fill in details about one subject on the left side of the diagram and details about the other on the right side. Use the middle section to list common features.

Applying Understanding by Design Principles

Clarifying Expected Outcomes: Using Rubrics

- Before students begin work on this assignment, have them preview the Rubric for Self-Assessment (p. 555) to know what is expected. A copy of this rubric appears in the *Graphic Organizer Transparencies,* p. 108.
- Review the criteria in the Rubric with the class. Before students use the Rubric to assess their own writing, work with them to rate the Student Model (p. 554) using the Rubric.

- If you wish to assess student's autobiographical narratives with either a 4-point or a 6-point scoring rubric, see the *Professional Development Guidebook*, pp. 234–235.

Prewriting/Planning Strategies

1. Introduce the prewriting strategies, using the instruction on the student page.
2. Have students apply the strategies to choose a topic.

Teaching the Strategies

1. Tell students that in order to argue a strong point, they should be familiar with both of the items they will compare and contrast.
2. Suggest examples of products and activities students can compare, such as electronic devices, sports equipment, games, dances, food preparation, and crafts.
3. Have students offer possible topics suggested by the graphic organizer. (**Possible responses:** compare and contrast a mountain bike and a racing bike.)

Think Aloud: Model Narrowing a Topic

Say to students:

When I want to narrow my topic, I start by writing down a broad idea, such as "Vacations." Then, I ask myself what kinds of different vacations there are, such as beach vacations, winter vacations, unusual vacations, favorite vacations, and I make a chart. Then, I write a specific vacation under each category. For example, under "beach vacations," I would list the vacation my family took at the beach. I repeat the process to select another vacation that I can compare and contrast with the beach vacation. Now I have narrowed my topic.

Six Traits Focus

Ideas	✔	Word Choice	
✔	Organization	Sentence Fluency	
Voice		Conventions	

PH WRITING COACH   Grade 7

Students will find additional information on writing a comparison-and-contrast essay in Chapter 8.

Prentice Hall **EssayScorer**

A writing prompt for this mode of writing can be found on the *Prentice Hall EssayScorer* at www.PHLitOnline.com.

1. Introduce the drafting strategies, using the instruction on the student page.

2. Have students apply the strategies as they draft.

Teaching the Strategies

1. Discuss the two organizational methods. Suggest that students with more than three points of comparison use the block method of organization; students with three or fewer points should use the point-by-point method.

2. Direct students who are using the block method of organization to outline their draft with a separate list of details under each of the two items being compared. Outlines for students using the point-by-point method should be broken down into a list of features. Details about both items should be grouped with the appropriate feature.

3. Review the SEE strategy. Explain that if the main idea of a paragraph is difficult to identify, the paragraph may need to be rewritten. Suggest that students freewrite about their topic for several minutes to elaborate on their ideas.

4. Have students provide transitions between the following pairs of sentences.

   Skateboarding is my favorite sport. It can be dangerous. (**Possible response:** Skateboarding is my favorite sport. However, it can be dangerous.)

   Snow skiers have to be prepared for occasional spills. Water skiers fall sometimes. (**Possible response:** Like water skiers, snow skiers have to be prepared for occasional spills.)

Think Aloud: Model Using Transitions

Say to students:

I can use transitions to make the relationships between ideas clear. For example, if I want to compare my beach vacation to my winter vacation, I use transitions such as *like, also,* and *similar.* I write: "During my week at the beach, it rained all week. The weather *also* affected my winter vacation, because it snowed all week." Also, I can use transitions that contrast, such as *although, unlike,* or *however.* I can write, "However,

550

Drafting Strategies

Organize the body of your draft. Your essay should be easy for readers to follow and understand. There are two main ways to organize a comparison-and-contrast essay. Choose the one that is most appropriate to your topic and purpose.

- **Block Method** Present all the details about one of your subjects, then all the details about your next subject. This method works well if you are writing about more than two subjects or if your topic is complex.

- **Point-by-Point Method** Discuss one aspect of both subjects, then another aspect of both subjects, and so on.

Methods of Organization

Block Method
A. Theater
1. Amount of variety
2. Intensity
3. Realism
B. Television
1. Amount of variety
2. Intensity
3. Realism

Point-by-Point Comparison
A. Amount of Variety
1. Theater
2. Television
B. Intensity
1. Theater
2. Television
C. Realism
1. Theater
2. Television

Layer ideas using SEE. Often, the most interesting parts of an essay are the details you offer to support your main ideas. Use the SEE method to develop strong elaboration.

- **S**tate your main idea in every paragraph to stay on topic.

- **E**xtend the idea with an example that proves the main idea.

- **E**laborate by offering further details to describe your example.

Include formatting, graphics, and multimedia. Use headings to highlight the main sections in your paper. Graphics, such as charts and tables, or multimedia, such as a tape recording or slide show, can strengthen ideas and further comprehension.

Clarify relationships. Use words and phrases to show relationships between ideas. Transitions that show comparisons include *also, just as, like,* and *similarly.* Transitions that show contrasts include *although, but, however, on the other hand, whereas,* and *while.*

Common Core State Standards

Writing

2.a. Organize ideas, concepts, and information, using strategies such as definition, classification, comparison/contrast, and cause/effect; include formatting, graphics, and multimedia when useful to aiding comprehension.

2.b. Develop the topic and relevant facts, definitions, concrete details, quotations, or other information and examples.

2.c. Use appropriate transitions to create cohesion and clarify the relationships among ideas and concepts.

4. Produce clear and coherent writing in which the development, organization, and style are appropriate to task, purpose, and audience.

---

we were happier about the weather during the winter vacation, because we wanted to ski."

Six Traits Focus

✔	Ideas	✔	Word Choice
✔	Organization		Sentence Fluency
	Voice		Conventions

Writing and Grammar Interactive Textbook Online

Students can use the following tools at www.pearsonsuccessnet.com as they complete their comparison-and-contrast essays:

- Venn Diagram (Chapter 8.2)

- Word Bins: Transition Words (Drop-down menu)

Writers on Writing

Richard Mühlberger On Getting Readers Involved

Richard Mühlberger is the author of "What Makes a Rembrandt a Rembrandt?" (p. 413).

Whether you are writing comparison-and-contrast or another form of exposition, you need to keep the reader's interest and attention. Everyone involved in producing my book about Monet, the French Impressionist painter, knew before it was printed that it would be a success. Monet was the number one artist in popularity among adults. But the book was for middle-school students. My job was to get them involved in exploring Monet's art.

"I write with my audience in mind."
—Richard Mühlberger

Professional Model:

from *"What Makes a Monet a Monet?"*

Oscar-Claude Monet was born in Paris, France, on November 14, 1840. When he was five years old, his family moved to the seaside city of Le Havre. He went to school there, but he was not much of a student. He liked to draw irreverent caricatures of his teachers, who tried in vain to get him to concentrate on other subjects. Monet later confessed that he did not learn much in school except some spelling. "It seemed like a prison, and I could never bear to stay there, even for four hours a day, especially when the sunshine beckoned and the sea was smooth," he said.

Monet's favorite activity was wandering along the beaches, making caricatures of tourists. He usually pictured a person with a very small body and a very large head, exaggerating the nose or some other part of the face. He sold his caricatures for ten to twenty francs, more than what his teachers earned in a day!

I wanted to establish right away that Monet had only one interest in life—making art.

The word sunshine summarizes the essence of many of his paintings. Alone, that word may not compel a young person to read on. So I placed it in a context that makes the young artist sound like a maverick who might interest young readers.

My book does not contain a caricature by Monet so I had to come up with a description that would draw a picture in the reader's mind.

Richard Mühlberger on Getting Readers Involved

Review the passage on the student page with the class, using Richard Mühlberger's comments to deepen students' understanding about how to grab their readers' interest.

Teaching from the Professional Model

1. Show students Segment 4 on Mühlberger on the *See It!* DVD or from the link on this page in the **Enriched Online Student Edition** at ww.PHLitOnline.com.

2. Discuss how the author uses precise details to create a vivid portrait of Monet. **Ask** students to name several characteristics of Monet suggested by the details in Mühlberger's description. **Possible response:** restlessness, irreverence, nonconformity, closeness to nature.

Show or assign the video online at www.PHLitOnline.com.

Differentiated Instruction for Universal Access

Support for Less Proficient Writers
Make sure students are familiar with main ideas and topic sentences. Remind them that the topic sentence tells what the essay is about. Offer them examples of topic sentences, such as "Plays offer a kind of enjoyment movies do not."

EL Strategy for English Learners
Tell students that one way to come up with points of comparison is to ask questions about their topics. For example, if students were comparing bicycles, they might ask "Which one is more expensive?" Have students list several questions and then decide which points are most important to compare.

Support for Advanced Writers
Suggest that students approach comparisons differently by writing about one thing that appears different in changed circumstances. For example, students might compare an actor's personality with the personality of the character he or she plays on television or in the movies.

551

Revising Strategies

1. Introduce the revising strategies, using the instruction on the student page.
2. Have students apply the strategies as they revise.

Teaching the Strategies

1. Discuss the strategies for revising structure to heighten interest, using the following example:

   Figure skating is a lot more graceful than ice hockey. **Revision:** While ice hockey and figure skating are both sports, figure skating is more like ballet than a rough game of competition.

2. Have students revise the following passages to eliminate repetition.

   Serving a tennis ball takes practice. It takes practice to build up your arm strength. It also takes practice to perfect your aim. **Possible response:** Serving a tennis ball takes practice. Many hours of hitting the ball over the net are required to build up your arm strength and perfect your aim.

Think Aloud: Model Revising Sentences to Avoid Repetition

Model the strategy of revising sentences to avoid repetition, using the following "think aloud." Say to students:

I can revise sentences to avoid repeating information. One way to do so is to combine sentences. For example, instead of writing, *It rained at the beach. It rained for five straight days,* I would write, *It rained at the beach for five straight days.* With the revised sentence, I avoid repetition and combine the main ideas of the two old sentences. When reviewing your writing, look for ways to avoid repetition by combining sentences.

Six Traits Focus

✔ Ideas	✔	Word Choice
✔ Organization		Sentence Fluency
Voice	✔	Conventions

Revising Strategies

Heighten interest. Check your essay to make sure it grabs and holds your readers' attention. Use the following strategies:

- Sharpen your introduction to intrigue readers, encouraging them to read further. Consider including a strong image, a surprising comparison, or a thought-provoking question.
- Add details that are surprising, colorful, and important.
- Add headings, relevant graphics, or multimedia.
- Add language to emphasize similarities or differences.
- Rework your conclusion to add impact or leave readers with a lingering question. Be sure your conclusion makes the value of the comparison and contrast clear.

> **Model: Revising to Heighten Interest**
>
> When actors are filming a movie, they can do a retake if they forget a line or
> *The audience never gets to see or hear the hilarious*
> *verbal or physical mistakes of film actors.*
> if they "flub" it. In live theater, however, there are no second chances!
>   ∧

Avoid repetition. Check your writing for unnecessary repetition. Sometimes writers will repeat a point but add something slightly different the second time. Combine the two sentences to preserve your additional material while avoiding repetition and providing interest with sentence variety.

Repetitive: Lastly, the best thing about theater is it's real. What I mean is you see when people make mistakes. You see people being human by making mistakes every so often.

Combined: Lastly, the best thing about theater is it's human and real. What I mean is you see when people make mistakes.

Peer Review

Read your revised draft to a teacher or classmate. Ask whether you repeated information. Together, look for ways to make the writing clearer and less repetitive.

Common Core State Standards

Writing

2.e. Provide a concluding statement or section that follows from and supports the information or explanation presented.

4. Produce clear and coherent writing in which the development, organization, and style are appropriate to task, purpose, and audience.

5. With some guidance and support from peers and adults, develop and strengthen writing as needed by planning, revising, editing, rewriting, or trying a new approach, focusing on how well purpose and audience have been addressed.

Language

1.c. Place phrases and clauses within a sentence, recognizing and correcting misplaced and dangling modifiers.

3.a. Choose language that expresses ideas precisely and concisely, recognizing and eliminating wordiness and redundancy.

Strategies for Test Taking

Pay special attention to keywords in the prompt, such as *not, similarities,* and *differences.*

Revising Errors in Adjective and Adverb Usage

The common modifiers *just* and *only* often cause problems in both speaking and writing.

Identifying Errors in Adjective and Adverb Usage Usage problems with adjectives and adverbs typically occur when these words are placed incorrectly in a sentence or are confused because of similar meanings. When used as an adverb, *just* often means "no more than." When *just* has this meaning, place it right before the word it logically modifies.

Incorrect: Do you *just* want one brownie for dessert?

Correct: Do you want *just* one brownie for dessert?

The position of **only** can affect the entire meaning of a sentence.

Only he ate the cake. (Nobody else ate it.)

He *only* ate the cake. (He did nothing else with the cake.)

He ate *only* the cake. (He ate nothing else.)

Fixing Errors in Adjective and Adverb Usage To fix a usage problem with adjectives and adverbs, use one of the following methods.

1. **For *only*:** If the word is intended as an adverb meaning "no more than," place it right before the word it logically modifies.

2. **For *just*:** First, identify the intended meaning of the sentence. Then, position *just* in the sentence so that the meaning is clear.

3. **For other common problems:** See the chart or use a dictionary.

Commonly Confused Modifiers	
bad: (adjective) He was a *bad* skater.	**badly:** (adverb) I played *badly* at the recital.
fewer: answers "How many?" He had *fewer* questions.	**less:** answers "How much?" He drank *less* water today.

Grammar In Your Writing
Choose two paragraphs in your draft. Underline every sentence that contains one of the modifiers discussed or another modifier you think you may have used incorrectly. Fix any usage problems.

> **PH** **WRITING COACH**
>
> Further instruction and practice are available in *Prentice Hall Writing Coach*.

Revising Errors in Adjective and Adverb Usage

1. Introduce the grammar skill, using the instruction on the student page.

2. Discuss the rules and examples, as well as the strategies for fixing incorrect usage.

3. Have students follow the instruction under Grammar in Your Writing to correct errors in their drafts.

Teaching the Grammar Skill

1. Students may make errors in the usage of *just* and *only*. Have students revise the sentences in which the underlined word is placed incorrectly.

   I <u>only</u> ate a small piece of pie. (**Answer:** I ate <u>only</u> a small piece of piece of pie.)

   <u>Only</u> make one stop on the way home. (**Answer:** Make <u>only</u> one stop on the way home.)

   I <u>just</u> made two errors. (**Answer:** I made <u>just</u> two errors.)

   I have <u>just</u> this to say. (**Answer:** correct)

   I made <u>just</u> a mistake—that's all. (**Answer:** I <u>just</u> made a mistake—that's all.)

2. Ask students to determine which of the underlined modifiers is used correctly. Have them replace any incorrect modifiers.

   He did a <u>bad</u> job. (**Answer:** correct)

   She put <u>less</u> nuts in the cookies than the recipe called for. (**Answer:** fewer)

   I feel <u>good</u> about my performance. (**Answer:** correct)

   I would have liked <u>less</u> chili powder in the stew. (**Answer:** correct)

> **PH** **WRITING COACH** | Grade 7

Students will find practice with and guidance on adjectives and adverbs in Chapter 15.

Student Model

Review the Student Model with the class, using the annotations to analyze the writer's use of the elements of a narrative.

Teaching From the Student Model

1. Explain that the Student Model is a sample and that essays can be longer.

2. Have students read through the model and annotations. **Ask** students to identify the items being compared. **Answer:** live theater and television.

3. **Ask** students to identify the organization of the summary. **Answer:** point-by-point organization.

4. Have students identify the points of comparison the writer uses. **Answer:** the variety, intensity, and realism of television and live theater.

Writing Genres

Connecting to Real-Life Writing

Tell students that one way to make a well-informed decision is to compare and contrast. When businesses want to advertise a product, they ask an advertising agency to provide them with two or more ideas. By comparing and contrasting these ideas, a decision about which campaign will work best can be made. Discuss with students other occupations that would require comparison and contrast.

Student Model: Mackenzie Ames, Daytona Beach, FL

Stage vs. Set

Theater or television? If you are under eighteen, you more than likely said "television." Have you ever stopped to consider what the magical world of theater has to offer?

Anyone who has been to the theater can tell you that there is nothing like the feeling of sitting and watching people perform. Actors get something special out of theater, too. Knowing that hundreds of people are watching your every move creates a special kind of excitement.

There's also variety. In live theater, every show is different. When you watch a rerun on television, it's the exact same thing every time. With theater, you get a different experience every night. You can go to see the same show with a different cast or director and the performance will be totally different. Even if you go to a show with the same cast and director, it will be different. An actor might forget a line and improvise or suddenly decide to change the way he or she is playing a character in a scene. The audience never knows exactly what will happen.

Theater is also larger than the drama you see on television. I don't care how big a screen your television has, theater will always be BIGGER—the emotion more passionate, the voices louder, and the effect more profound. In theater, you have to project your voice and movements so that they carry to the back rows of the audience. In television, actors just need to be seen and heard by the cameras and microphones.

Lastly, the best thing about theater is it's human and real. You see when people make mistakes. On television, everything has to be perfect or they do a retake. You never see television actors miss a line or trip over their feet. Since there is no second chance in theater, everything is more spontaneous. When a performance takes an unexpected turn, the audience gets to see the professionalism of the actors as they respond to something new.

Next time you're channel surfing and there's nothing good on, why not take some time to check out what's playing in your community playhouse? Who knows? Maybe you'll discover a rising talent. Even better, maybe you'll decide you want to become an actor or actress after you see how thrilling a live production really is.

> In the first paragraph, Mackenzie introduces the comparison in a way that grabs the reader's attention. She compares things that are alike, yet different.

> Mackenzie develops her argument by including examples and explanations, using the point-by-point method of organization.

> In the final paragraph, Mackenzie offers a strong conclusion that challenges the reader to accept her point of view.

Editing and Proofreading

Review your draft to correct errors in grammar, spelling, and punctuation.

Focus on empty language. Review your work to delete words that do not add value or meaning. Consider cutting words such as *very* and *really* and clauses such as *I think, as I said,* and *you know.*

Publishing and Presenting

Consider one of the following ways to share your writing.

Be a consumer watchdog. If your essay contains information that is useful to consumers, form a Consumer Information Panel. Post your essays to a class blog or school Web site. Include links to reliable, related sites, such as government Web sites that focus on health and safety or consumer issues.

Submit it to a magazine. Submit your essay to a magazine that specializes in the subject you have chosen. You can find publishing information and an address in a recent edition of the magazine.

Reflecting on Your Writing

Writer's Journal Jot down your answer to this question:

What was the most important improvement you made when revising?

Rubric for Self-Assessment

Find evidence in your writing to address each category. Then, use the rating scale to grade your work.

Criteria	Rating Scale
	not very very
Focus: How clearly does the essay address two or more related subjects?	1 2 3 4 5
Organization: How effectively are points of comparison organized?	1 2 3 4 5
Support/Elaboration: How well do you use details to describe similarities and differences?	1 2 3 4 5
Style: How well have you used language that grabs the reader's interest?	1 2 3 4 5
Conventions: How correct is your grammar, especially your use of adjectives and adverbs?	1 2 3 4 5

© **Spiral Review**

Earlier in the unit, you learned about **subjects and predicates** (p. 504) and **compound subjects and predicates** (p. 526). Check the use of subjects and predicates in your comparison-and-contrast essay. Review your essay to be sure that each sentence contains at least one subject and predicate and that you have followed rules for agreement with compound subjects.

PH WRITING COACH

Further instruction and practice are available in *Prentice Hall Writing Coach.*

Strategies for Test-Taking

When taking a test that includes a comparison-and-contrast writing prompt, students should be able to support their compositions with both facts and opinions. Tell students that they should feel free to include opinions, but that they should also include support for them. For example, if a writer thinks one activity is more fun than another, he or she should give reasons for this opinion.

Editing and Proofreading

1. Introduce the editing and proofreading focus, using the instruction on the student page.

2. Have students edit and proofread their essays, correcting grammar, spelling, punctuation, and word choice. Make sure they look for errors of the type noted in the lesson focus and the Spiral Review.

Teaching the Editing Focus

1. Emphasize to students that vague words such as *really* will only clutter their writing and reduce its impact.

2. Have students suggest other examples of empty language. **Possible responses:** *a little, somewhat, I guess.*

Six Traits Focus

Ideas	Word Choice
Organization	Sentence Fluency
Voice	✓ Conventions

ASSESS

Publishing and Presenting

1. Students who choose to organize a consumer information panel may want to use tables or charts as visual aids.

2. Have students who want to submit their essays to a magazine consult with the reference librarian at the school or public library for suggestions of possible venues.

Reflecting on Your Writing

1. Have students compare their first drafts to their final papers to identify major revisions.

2. Suggest that students compare their Venn diagram from the prewriting stage with their final essays to identify any new insights they had during the writing process.

Words with Multiple Meanings

1. Introduce the skill, using the instruction on the student page.

2. Review the examples in the chart.

Think Aloud: Model the Skill

Model the skill of using words with multiple meanings. Say to students:

Lots of words have more than one meaning. To figure out which meaning of a word applies in a particular situation, I need to look for clues in the context, or surroundings. For example, when the context talks about keeping cool on a hot day, then *fan* means "device for moving air." When the context talks about liking baseball for a long time, then *fan* means "an enthusiastic admirer."

Practice A (p. 557)

Answers

1. a. small night-flying mammals

   b. wooden or metal sticks for hitting baseballs, softballs, etc.

2. a. in a particular place; here

   b. gift

3. a. related to 1/60 of a minute

   b. coming right after the first item in a sequence

4. a. portion left over; remainder

   b. time to refresh your energy

Vocabulary Workshop

Words With Multiple Meanings

A **multiple-meaning word** is a word that has more than one definition. Many words in English have multiple meanings; for example, *peach* can be defined as a color or a fruit. To determine the meaning intended in a sentence, you must consider the context, or the words surrounding the word. The following chart shows a multiple-meaning word used in two different sentences.

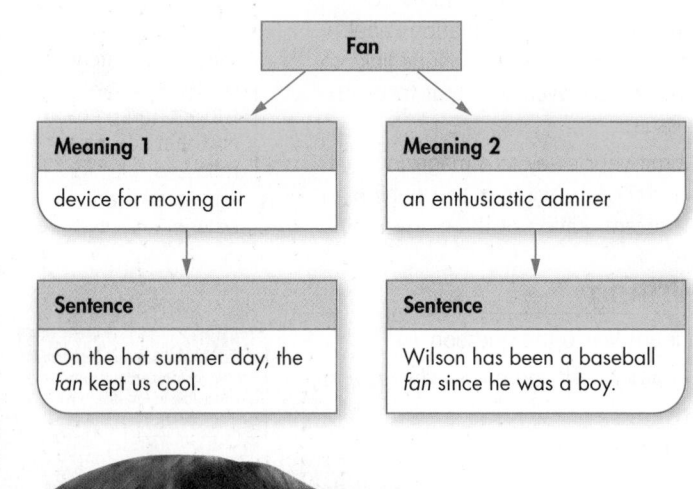

Fan

Meaning 1	Meaning 2
device for moving air	an enthusiastic admirer

Sentence	Sentence
On the hot summer day, the *fan* kept us cool.	Wilson has been a baseball *fan* since he was a boy.

556 Types of Nonfiction

 Common Core
State Standards

Language

4. Determine or clarify the meaning of unknown and multiple-meaning words and phrases based on grade 7 reading and content, choosing flexibly from a range of strategies.

4.a. Use context as a clue to the meaning of a word or phrase.

4.c. Consult general and specialized reference materials, both print and digital, to find the pronunciation of a word or determine or clarify its precise meaning or its part of speech.

4.d. Verify the preliminary determination of the meaning of a word or phrase.

Teaching Resources

Unit 3 Resources
Words with Multiple Meanings, pp. 224, 225

PHLit Online! **Vocabulary Central,** featuring definitions, audio pronunciations, Word Families, and activities, is online at **www.PHLitOnline.com.**

Practice A Write the meaning of each italicized word. Verify the meaning in a dictionary.

1. a. When the *bats* swooped down on my head, I let out a scream.
   b. I wish we could get new *bats* for our softball team this year.
2. a. Julian was not *present* to collect the prize he won.
   b. I decided to make my sister's birthday *present* this year.
3. a. The *second* hand on the clock ticked loudly.
   b. Liliana won *second* prize at the science fair.
4. a. We saved the *rest* of the cake for the next class.
   b. After running a mile in track, we all needed a *rest*.

Practice B For each word listed, write two sentences that use different meanings of the word. If necessary, look up the meanings in a dictionary.

1. kind   5. dash
2. object   6. season
3. express   7. desert
4. ring   8. seal

Activity Use a print or digital dictionary to learn about these words with multiple meanings: *power, degree, dynamite, file, patient*. Write each word on a separate notecard like the one shown. Fill in the left column of the notecard according to one of the word's meanings. Fill in the right-hand column according to another of the word's meanings. Then, trade note cards with a partner, and discuss the different meanings and uses of the words that each of you found.

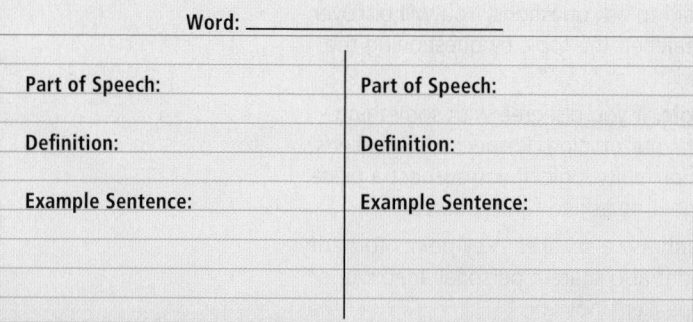

Word: _____	
Part of Speech:	**Part of Speech:**
Definition:	**Definition:**
Example Sentence:	**Example Sentence:**

PHLit Online!
www.PHLitOnline.com
• Author video: Writing Process
• Author video: Rewards of Writing

Comprehension and Collaboration
Work with two or three classmates to write a sentence that uses two different meanings of each of the following words. For example: *While we sat in a traffic jam, I was able to eat my breakfast of toast and* jam.

fair
long
last

Practice B
Sample answers:

1. Jo is a <u>kind</u> person who tries not to hurt anyone's feelings.
   The scientist invented a new <u>kind</u> of plastic.
2. A rock is a hard <u>object</u>.
   Do you approve of my remarks, or do you <u>object</u>?
3. Sometimes it is hard to <u>express</u> my true feelings.
   The <u>express</u> bus skips local stops and takes less time.
4. I heard the bells <u>ring</u>.
   She wore a gold <u>ring</u> on her finger.
5. A <u>dash</u> usually signals a longer pause than a comma.
   He ran the hundred-yard <u>dash</u>.
6. Spring is my favorite <u>season</u>.
   <u>Season</u> the food by adding salt.
7. Cactus grows in the <u>desert</u>.
   Stay by my side; please don't <u>desert</u> me now.
8. Luis used glue to <u>seal</u> the letter.
   The zookeeper threw a fish to the <u>seal</u>.

Activity
Provide students with notecards and dictionaries, and guide them in using the latter, if necessary. Divide the class into pairs or have students choose their own partners to complete the activity. Evaluate students' responses based on accuracy of definitions and parts of speech as well as appropriate word usage in the sample sentences.

Comprehension and Collaboration

Divide the class into groups of three or four students. Instruct groups to discuss the multiple meanings of each word before attempting to use two of those meanings in the same sentence. In evaluating students' responses, look for appropriate word usage to create sentences that make sense.

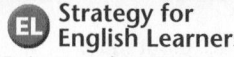

Differentiated
Instruction   for Universal Access

EL Strategy for English Learners
Point out that English words with multiple meanings sometimes have different pronunciations. For example, the word *object*, is stressed in the first syllable as a noun but in the second syllable as a verb. Offer more examples, and help students pronounce the words both ways and use them in sentences:

• **record** (ri kôrd´) *v.* write down
  record (rek´ərd) *n.* something written down
• **excuse** (ek skyo͞os´) *n.* apology; explanation to avoid blame
  excuse (ek skyo͞oz´) *v.* free from blame

Strategy for Advanced Learners
Note that while some words with multiple meanings have related meanings and origins, many do not. For example, *fan* meaning "device for moving air" comes from a Latin word for a device that forced air through grain to separate the useful parts, while *fan* meaning "enthusiastic admirer" is shortened from *fanatic*. Explain that words that are spelled the same but have different meanings and origins are called homographs and usually have separate entries in dictionaries. Have students use a dictionary to determine which italicized words in Practice A are homographs (all but *present*).

557

Learn the Skills

1. Introduce the workshop, including the activity on page 559.

2. Tell students to evaluate the evidence that a speaker provides. Make clear that they should be skeptical of speakers who include few facts or examples as support for their positions.

3. Have students consider whether the speaker appeals more to the audience's logic or feelings.

4. Remind students that the introduction and the conclusion are the most important parts of the speech.

5. To assess the speaker's evidence, use questions such as these: What kinds of evidence are used? Does the speaker supply enough evidence? What is the strongest evidence? Why?

6. Tell students to write questions and notes as they listen.

7. Explain that while students may not be able to question the speaker of a recorded presentation like a TV commercial, they can still list their questions or challenge claims. Tell them they might have to perform research to learn the answers.

8. Suggest that students ask questions to determine the credibility and relevance of information.

Communications Workshop

Evaluating a Persuasive Presentation

A **persuasive presentation** is similar to a persuasive composition. Its purpose is to persuade the listener to do, buy, or believe something. Use these strategies to assess persuasive presentations.

Learn the Skills

Use these strategies to complete the activity on page 559.

Evaluate content. Like its written counterpart, an effective persuasive presentation includes a clear statement of the speaker's position and relevant supporting evidence. Listen to every word of a persuasive presentation in order to explain the speaker's purpose. Evaluate whether the speaker is appealing to your emotions or using facts, statistics, and other information that can be proved.

Determine the speaker's attitude. Ask yourself these questions to determine how the speaker feels about his or her subject:

- Does the speaker appeal to emotion or to reason?
- Does he or she use words that convey strong images or associations?
- What do the speaker's body language and facial expressions suggest?
- What is the speaker's tone of voice?

Listen for a logical organization. Follow the argument from point to point. Listen for the connections between ideas. Also, listen for a convincing introduction and conclusion.

Listen for strong evidence. Be aware of the anecdotes, descriptions, facts, statistics, and specific examples that support the speaker's position. Is the support convincing? Why or why not?

Ask questions. Never be afraid to ask questions. You will discover how well the speaker has researched the topic by questioning the evidence.

Challenge bias or faulty logic. If you disagree with something the presenter has said, express your opinion. Respect the speaker's viewpoints if you identify bias or faulty logic. If you suspect a piece of evidence is wrong, challenge it by asking for its source.

Clarify and contribute. Paraphrase a speaker's key points to clarify what you have heard. You might also share a personal anecdote or observation that affirms the speaker's position.

Strategies for
Evaluating a Persuasive Presentation

Give students these additional strategies for evaluating a presentation:

- Encourage students to tap into their own experiences and knowledge as they respond to persuasive presentations.
- Instruct them to make notes or draw pictures that illustrate what they think or feel about a subject. Tell them to use their notes or sketches as prompts to share a point of view or experience relevant to the topic of the presentation.

- Suggest that they take notes about main points and supporting evidence in outline form to evaluate the organization of the argument. Guide students through how to structure their outlines.
- Encourage students to use their outlines as they formulate questions and opinions in response to the presentation.

Practice the Skills

© **Presentation of Knowledge and Ideas** Use what you have learned in this workshop to complete the following activity.

> **ACTIVITY: Evaluating a Persuasive Presentation**
>
> Watch a persuasive sales pitch, either live or in a recorded format.
> • Identify the speaker's message.
> • Evaluate if the speaker's purpose is to inform or influence the audience.
> • Explain how you felt listening to the message.
> • List questions that the speaker's claims raise for you.
> • Jot down notes about the presentation, such as the speaker's tone of voice, body language, and facial expressions.
> • Draw conclusions about the speaker's message by considering verbal and nonverbal cues.
> • Use the Assessment Guide to evaluate the presentation.

Use the Assessment Guide below to interpret the content and delivery of the persuasive presentation you watched.

Assessment Guide
What is the speaker's purpose behind this message?
Is the speaker's purpose to inform or influence the audience?
What does the speaker hope you will do after hearing the message?
What evidence does the speaker provide to support claims?
How could you research the speaker's claims?
On what points would you challenge the speaker?
How effective was the delivery of the presentation?
What can you conclude about the speaker's nonverbal and verbal communication, including tone of voice, gestures, and facial expressions?

© **Comprehension and Collaboration** Compare your findings with those of your classmates. As a group, discuss how you can use the strategies above to evaluate other messages, such as advertisements, commercials, and additional persuasive presentations. Then, evaluate various ways that media is used to influence and inform audiences.

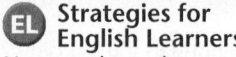

Differentiated Instruction for Universal Access

EL Strategies for English Learners

Have students demonstrate listening comprehension by summarizing and retelling the presentations they hear.
• Play a presentation on a familiar topic, suggesting they take notes as they listen.
• Encourage them to list key words and to seek clarification of terms as needed.
• Record important words on the board as students listen. Guide them in summarizing the general meaning, main points, and important details.

• Play another presentation, instructing students to take notes as they listen.
• Ask students to form small groups or work in pairs to summarize the general meaning, main points, and important details of the presentation, using their notes.

Practice the Skills

1. Review the assignment with students. Make sure they understand that a sales pitch is a line of talk designed to sell a product, service, or idea. Explain that the main purpose of a sales pitch is to influence, rather than inform, listeners.

2. Explain to students that they should use a copy of the Assessment Guide to evaluate their own presentation and the presentations made by classmates.

3. Before students give their presentations to the class, remind listeners to ask questions if any points are unclear. To maintain order, encourage them to raise their hands and wait to be acknowledged by the presenter before stating their questions. Suggest that students making presentations scan the classroom from time to time so they will notice any students who have questions.

Evaluate the Activity

1. Evaluate students' presentations on the basis of the speeches' accuracy and insightfulness, the speakers' delivery, and their use of questions and responses to ensure listeners' comprehension.

2. When the class discusses the presentations that were most persuasive, encourage students to make note of the features of those presentations that made them effective and to incorporate those techniques in their future presentations.

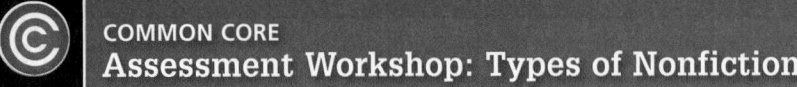
Cumulative Review

In this Common Core Assessment Workshop (pp. 560–565), students apply and reinforce their mastery of the Common Core Standards and the skills taught in Unit 3. The practice is divided into four sections, including a section of Performance Tasks addressing CCS Reading standards.

1. Before assigning each section, review the relevant Common Core State Standards and unit skills with students.

2. Set a time limit for the multiple-choice items in each section, allowing a little over one minute per question. Allow twenty minutes for any Timed Writing questions.

3. Administer each of the first three sections of the Cumulative Review (pp. 560–563).

4. Use the Performance Tasks on pages 564–565 to assess the depth of students' mastery of standards taught in the unit. Follow the suggestions on teacher pages 564–565 for assigning tasks and for supporting and evaluating student performance.

Reteaching Skills

1. For each practice, use the Reteach chart on the same page as the answers to determine which skills require reteaching, given the items students answered incorrectly.

2. Reteach these skills prior to assigning the **Benchmark Test** for the second half of Unit 3 (**Unit 3 Resources**, pp. 227–234). The Benchmark Test concludes instruction in the Unit skills.

Benchmark

Reteach skills as indicated by students' performance, following the Reteach charts included on pp. 561–563. Then, administer the end-of-Unit **Benchmark Test** (**Unit 3 Resources**, pp. 227–234). The Benchmark Test concludes instruction in the Unit skills. Follow the **Interpretation Guide** for the test (**Unit 3 Resources**, p. 235) to assign reteaching pages as necessary in the **Reading Kit.** Use the built-in tracking software at www.PHLitOnline.com to automatically assign these pages.

Cumulative Review

I. Reading Literature/Informational Text

Directions: *Read the passage. Then, answer each question that follows.*

Common Core
State Standards

RI.7.4, RI.7.6, RI.7.8; L.7.4.a; W.7.2.b
[For the full wording of the standards, see the standards chart in the front of your textbook.]

Dear City Council Members,

I am concerned about the dangers of bicycle riding in our city's neighborhoods. I ride my bike to school, and last week, I almost had a very serious accident. Because there are no bike lanes in my neighborhood, I was forced to ride in the street with cars. A car came around a corner fast, honked at me, and almost hit me. I swerved, fell off my bike, and hit my head on the curb. Luckily, I was wearing a helmet. Because I was so close to school, I was able to get help quickly. This incident serves as proof that major improvements to bicycle safety need to be implemented before a worse accident occurs.

The first and most important improvement is providing more bike lanes on neighborhood streets. After some research, I found that there have been many studies on the effectiveness of simply painting bike lanes onto existing streets. In one study, the city of Lakeland, only 100 miles away, spent two percent of their transportation safety budget on bike lanes. The results showed that the bicycle accident rate went down from 45 per year to only 18.

We also need to have driver education. In a questionnaire I sent to 50 of my classmates, they reported that it is common for drivers to honk or yell things like "Get out of the road!" at cyclists. Children are harassed by angry drivers for simply riding their bikes.

If the city could post yellow signs that have a "Bicycle Crossing" symbol, it would alert drivers that this is a bike route. The city currently has these signs posted on major roads. However, the signs are desperately needed in neighborhoods near schools. Young riders would feel safer going across these marked intersections.

Before we have any serious accidents involving children, the city needs to act now. The innocent act of children riding their bicycles is now loaded with angry drivers who take their <u>aggression</u> out at cyclists. This is unacceptable, and the city needs to step to the plate to change it.

Sincerely,
Priya Mandala

560 Types of Nonfiction

Differentiated Instruction   for Universal Access

Strategy for Less Proficient Readers

Point out to students that a full-page passage such as the letter on this page is not necessarily more difficult than a passage that is only one or two paragraphs long. Readers need to focus on one paragraph at a time and pause after each one to reflect on its main idea and important points before continuing. When reading standardized test passages, students can usually underline main ideas or jot notes in the margin to help themselves keep track of the content. Students may also want to number the paragraphs if they are not numbered in the test. Test items will often refer to information in a specific paragraph so that readers do not need to search through the entire selection for answers.

1. What is the **author's purpose** in this passage?

  A. to entertain readers

  B. to inform the public

  C. to explain a step-by-step process

  D. to persuade city officials

2. How does the use of **autobiographical details** in the first paragraph contribute to the argument?

  A. It tells the opinion of an expert.

  B. It makes the arguments weaker.

  C. It makes the writer appear more sincere.

  D. It makes the writer seem immature.

3. Which word in this sentence is an example of strong **word choice:** *However, these signs are desperately needed in neighborhoods near schools.*

  A. However

  B. needed

  C. neighborhoods

  D. desperately

4. Which of the following sentences demonstrates an **appeal to reason?**

  A. Because I was close to school, I was able to get help quickly.

  B. The results showed that the bicycle accident rate went down from 45 per year to only 18.

  C. The signs are desperately needed in neighborhoods near schools.

  D. Before we have any serious accidents involving children, the city needs to act now.

5. How does the writer **appeal to emotion?**

  A. She sends her letter directly to the City Council.

  B. She suggests solutions with facts to support her ideas.

  C. She cites a study conducted in Lakeland.

  D. She uses strong language to get her point across.

6. Why does the writer think driver education is necessary?

  A. Drivers get angry with children riding bicycles.

  B. The sidewalks are in poor condition for riding a bicycle.

  C. Streets around schools are used most by bicycle riders.

  D. The existing bicycle lanes are ignored by drivers.

7. Vocabulary Which word is closest in meaning to the underlined word <u>aggression</u>?

  A. danger

  B. changes

  C. anger

  D. difficulty

 Timed Writing

8. Make a list of the **author's main arguments.** In an essay, evaluate how well each **argument** is supported with **facts** or **opinions.** Cite evidence from the text to support your analysis.

GO ON

Reteach

Question	Pages to Reteach
1	491, 530
2	468
3	507
4	491
5	491
6	421, 441
7	—
8	491, 507

Answers continued

driver education; D—There are no bike lanes currently.

7. **C**—*Aggression* is the emotion felt by angry drivers, therefore the correct synonym is *anger*. *Incorrect answers:* A—Angry drivers create *danger*, but they feel *anger*; B—This word makes no sense in the sentence; D—The phrase "take out their difficulty" does not make sense.

Timed Writing

8. Students should make a list of the author's main arguments and explain how each one is supported with specific facts or opinions.

I. Reading Literature
Answers With Explanations

1. **D**—The author is trying to persuade city officials to take specific actions to improve bicycle safety. *Incorrect answers:* A—The selection is not an entertaining story; B—This letter is not addressed to the public; C—Although various actions are mentioned, no step-by-step process is explained.

2. **C**—Autobiographical details often strengthen a persuasive argument by making the writer seem more sincere. *Incorrect answers:* A—The details show that the writer is a member of the general public, not an expert; B—The autobiographical details do not weaken the argument; D—Although the details show that the writer is a student, they do not make the writer seem immature.

3. **D**—*Desperately* conveys an urgent situation and is a strong word choice. *Incorrect answers:* A—*However* is an adverb that lacks an intense impact; B—*Needed* is not a strong verb; C—*Neighborhoods* is not a vivid noun.

4. **B**—This sentence contains facts and figures that appeal to reason. *Incorrect answers:* A—The references to needing help and being near school create an emotional appeal related to a child in trouble; C—This statement gives an opinion; D—The reference to children is designed to appeal to a protective emotion.

5. **D**—Examples of strong language such as *very serious accident, harassed,* and *desperately* are included to appeal to emotion. *Incorrect answers:* A—Sending a request to the proper officials is not an appeal to emotion; B—Supporting proposed solutions with facts represents an appeal to reason; C—Citing a study is an appeal to reason.

6. **A**—The statement that driver education is necessary is followed by this evidence. *Incorrect answers:* B—The writer never states that the sidewalks are in poor shape; C—This fact prompts the writer to suggest signs around schools, not

561

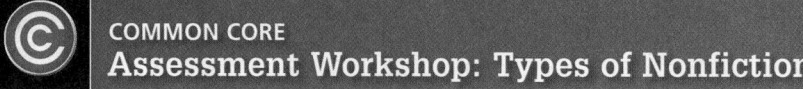
II. Reading Informational Text

Common Core
State Standards

RI.7.6; L7.1.c, L7.3.a
[For the full wording of the standards, see the standards chart in the front of your textbook.]

ASSESS/RETEACH

Answers

II. Reading Informational Text

Answers With Explanations

1. **C**—The writer lists solutions that will save the salamanders. *Incorrect answers:* A—The public does not need to help; B—Harm to people is not a concern; D—The life of the salamander is not discussed.

2. **B**—Paragraph 3 outlines this solution. *Incorrect answers:* A—The last paragraph states that people will continue to enjoy the pool; C—same explanation as for A; D—Divers will clean the bottom of the pool, not the salamanders.

3. **A**—This sentence describes the purpose: proposing solutions to protect the salamander population. *Incorrect answers:* B—This statement describes a procedure, not the purpose; C—same explanation as for B; D—same explanation as for B.

Reteach

Question	Pages to Reteach
1	462, 530
2	462
3	462, 530

The **Benchmark Tests** are available online at **www.PHLitOnline.com**.

II. Reading Informational Text

Directions: *Read the passage. Then, answer each question that follows.*

Salamander Population at Risk in Oasis Springs

The Agency for Natural Habitats recently discovered a rare species of salamander living in Oasis Springs, a popular spring-fed pool. We have found that the process used for cleaning the pool is endangering these creatures. To keep the water safe for swimmers, the pool staff currently uses an algae treatment of bleach and brushing. This treatment kills the salamanders. Therefore, we propose three solutions to preserve the salamander population and to keep the pool thriving.

First, we will remove salamanders from the pool for a special breeding program. Ten salamanders will be taken each month to reproduce. They will then be reintroduced into the pool. This program has been proven successful for other endangered species.

Our most important solution involves a new cleaning process. The pool will be cleaned without brushes or bleach. Divers will wipe the rocky bottom with special cloths. No soap products will be used.

Finally, specialists will visit the pool each week to inspect the water quality. An expert committee will then review the results.

These crucial steps will allow both salamanders and people to enjoy Oasis Springs for many years to come.

1. What is the **main purpose** of the passage?
   - **A.** to persuade the public to help to save the salamanders
   - **B.** to explain how to clean the spring-fed pool without harming people
   - **C.** to inform the public about the proposed steps to save the salamander population
   - **D.** to explore the life of the salamander population

2. Which is a **proposed solution?**
   - **A.** Ban swimming in the pool.
   - **B.** Clean the pool without using bleach.
   - **C.** Close the pool to the public.
   - **D.** Bring divers to clean the salamanders.

3. Which of the following sentences *best* shows the **author's purpose?**
   - **A.** Therefore, we propose three solutions to preserve the salamander population and to keep the pool thriving.
   - **B.** The pool will be cleaned without brushes or bleach.
   - **C.** An expert committee will then review the results.
   - **D.** Ten salamanders will be taken each month to reproduce.

562 Types of Nonfiction

Strategies for
Test Taking

Remind students that succeeding on a standardized reading comprehension test involves two steps: understanding the selection and answering the items correctly. If students feel that they fundamentally understand a selection after a first reading, they should go straight to the items. If they feel they know the answer to a given item right away, they should answer it.

If they are not sure of the answer, they should look back at the part of the selection referenced in the item. After answering all of the items, the student should reread the entire passage. By doing so, the student may notice a crucial detail or understand an important concept that he or she overlooked or misunderstood the first time through. Then he or she can revise any answers as necessary.

III. Writing and Language Conventions

Directions: *Read the passage. Then, answer the questions that follow.*

(1) Have some fun this weekend. (2) Learn how to catch a Frisbee® behind your back! (3) Decide where to catch the disc. (4) Run to that spot. (5) Next, take a step back with the foot that is on the same side as your catching hand. (6) Wrap your catching arm behind your back. (7) Bend your elbow. (8) Face your palm up, and point your thumb up. (9) The last step is to pinch your thumb to your fingers when the disc hits your hand. (10) Now, enjoy all of your friends' applause!

1. Which of these titles *best* supports the **topic** of the passage?

A. How to Catch a Disc at the Park
B. How to Teach Your Dog to Catch a Disc
C. How to Impress Your Friends
D. How to Catch a Disc Behind Your Back

2. Which of the following sentences placed after sentence 2 would *best* clarify the **multi-step directions?**

A. First, watch the disc when it is thrown.
B. Second, throw the disc to your partner.
C. Stand ten feet away from your partner.
D. First, scan the area for obstacles.

3. How should sentence 1 be revised to include a more informative **prepositional phrase?**

A. Have some fun and excitement this weekend.
B. Have some fun at the park this weekend.
C. Have some fun this weekend at school.
D. Have some fun this weekend and learn something new.

4. Which of the following revisions *best* combines sentence 3 and sentence 4 by using a **coordinating conjunction?**

A. Decide where you will catch the disk before you run to that spot.
B. Decide where you will catch the disk, and run to that spot.
C. Decide where you will catch the disk while you run to that spot.
D. Decide where you will catch the disk. In the meantime, run to that spot.

5. Which **transition** could the writer place in sentence 8 to clarify the instruction?

A. first
B. last
C. after
D. then

Assessment Workshop **563**

Differentiated
Instruction   *for Universal Access*

Strategy for English Learners

Point out to students that standardized tests often include how-to essays. To understand and answer questions about these essays, it is essential to master the definitions of prepositions and adverbs that relate to time order and spatial organization, such as *first, then, next, after, last, under, inside, beside, on top of, next to, over,* and *between*. Lists of these words are easily available in English language textbooks, workbooks, and Internet sites. Students should practice them.

III. Writing and Language Conventions

Answers With Explanations

1. **D**—This topic is clearly stated in sentence 2. *Incorrect answers:* A—The topic is not how to catch a disc at the park but behind your back; B—The essay does not mention this trick; C—Impressing friends is mentioned, but it is not the topic.

2. **A**—The player needs to see where the disc is thrown before deciding where to catch it. *Incorrect answers:* B—The focus of this passage is catching a disc; C—It makes no sense to say exactly where to stand before you decide where to catch the disc; D—This step would take place before the game begins.

3. **B**—*At the park* is a prepositional phrase that provides relevant information. *Incorrect answers:* A—This sentence does not contain a prepositional phrase; C—*At school* is a prepositional phrase, but it does not fit the context; D—same explanation as for A.

4. **B**—This revision combines the sentences with the coordinating conjunction *and*. *Incorrect answers:* A—This revision combines the sentences with a subordinating conjunction; C—same explanation as for A; D—This revision does not combine the sentences.

5. **D**—Step 8 is the next step after step 7, so it makes sense to begin it with *then*. *Incorrect answers:* A—This is not the first step in the sequence; B—This is not the last step in the sequence; C—*After* would have to be used in a phrase such as "After you do this," which would be too wordy.

Reteach

Question	Pages to Reteach
1	484
2	485
3	458
4	438, 487
5	486

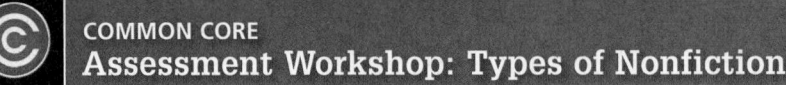

Performance Tasks

Assigning Tasks/Reteaching Skills

Use the chart below to choose appropriate Performance Tasks by identifying which tasks assess lessons in the textbook that you have taught. Use the same lessons for reteaching when students' performance indicates a failure to fully master a standard. For additional instruction and practice, assign the *Common Core Companion* pages indicated for each task.

Task	Where Taught/ Pages to Reteach	Common Core Companion Pages
1	410, 412, 421, 485, 526, 530	142–148, 279–286
2	410, 412, 441, 505, 530	142–148, 176–182
3	410, 412, 505	149–161, 279–286
4	462–466, 491, 558	169–175, 309–315
5	411–412, 507, 552	129–141, 316–322
6	408, 411, 421, 441, 459	109–121, 122–128, 316–322

Assessment Pacing

In assigning the Writing Tasks on this student page, allow a class period for the completion of a task. As an alternative, assign tasks as homework. In assigning the Speaking and Listening Tasks on the facing page, consider having students do any required preparation as a homework assignment. Then, allow a class period for the presentations themselves.

Evaluating Performance Tasks

Use the rubric at the bottom of this Teacher Edition page to evaluate students' mastery of the standards as demonstrated in their Performance Task responses. Review the rubric with students before they begin work so they know the criteria by which their work will be evaluated.

Performance Tasks

Directions: *Follow the instructions to complete the tasks below as required by your teacher.*

As you work on each task, incorporate both general academic vocabulary and literary terms you learned in this unit.

Common Core
State Standards

RI.7.2, RI.7.3, RI.7.4, RI.7.5, RI.7.6, RI.7.8; W.7.9.b; SL.7.3, SL.7.4; L.7.3.a
[For the full wording of the standards, see the standards chart in the front of your textbook.]

Writing

Task 1: Informational Text [RI.7.5; W.7.9.b]
Analyze Text Structure

Write an essay in which you analyze the structure an author uses to organize a work of literary nonfiction in this unit.

- Identify and describe the structure the author uses to organize the text you chose.
- Explain how the major sections contribute to the whole and to the development of the author's ideas.
- Cite evidence from the text to support your analysis, and present your ideas in an organized manner.
- Ensure that each sentence in your essay has a subject and predicate. Use conjunctions to combine choppy sentences that have related ideas.

Task 2: Informational Text [RI.7.5, W.7.9.b]
Analyze Structure and Purpose

Write an essay in which you explain the characteristics of two different types of nonfiction essays in this unit.

- Choose examples of two different types of essays—for example, a persuasive essay and a reflective essay.
- State which essays you chose and briefly explain their topics and purposes.
- Describe how information is organized or presented in each essay.

564 Types of Nonfiction

- Analyze the author's purpose for writing each essay, and evaluate the connection between that purpose and the essay's organization.
- Support the central idea in each paragraph with examples and details from the essays.
- Revise to eliminate unnecessary words. Confirm the spellings and meanings of words by consulting a dictionary.

Task 3: Informational Text [RI.7.6; W.7.9.b; L.7.3.a]
Determine an Author's Point of View

Write an essay in which you identify and analyze the author's point of view in a selection from this unit.

- Choose a selection in which the author presents a clear point of view on a topic. Explain which essay you chose, state the topic, and briefly describe the author's perspective.
- Analyze how the author presents his or her perspective by emphasizing certain evidence or by presenting an interpretation of facts.
- Conclude by telling whether or not you think the author conveys his or her perspective effectively. Support your opinion with examples from the text.
- Use appropriate transitions to create cohesion and to clarify the relationships among ideas.
- Vary your sentences, using coordinating or subordinating conjunctions accurately to combine sentences.

Performance Task Rubric: Standards Mastery	Rating Scale
Critical Thinking: How clearly and consistently does the student pursue the specific mode of reasoning or discourse required by the standard, as specified in the prompt (e.g., comparing and contrasting, analyzing, explaining)?	*not very* 1 2 3 4 5 *very*
Focus: How well does the student understand and apply the focus concepts of the standard, as specified in the prompt (e.g., development of theme or of complex characters, effects of structure, and so on)?	1 2 3 4 5
Support/Elaboration: How well does the student support points with textual or other evidence? How relevant, sufficient, and varied is the evidence provided?	1 2 3 4 5
Insight: How original, sophisticated, or compelling are insights the student achieves by applying the standard to the text(s)?	1 2 3 4 5
Expression of Ideas: How well does the student organize and support ideas? How well does the student use language, including word choice and conventions, in the expression of ideas?	1 2 3 4 5

Speaking and Listening

ⓒ Task 4: Informational Text [RI.7.8; SL.7.3]
Evaluate Arguments

Give an oral presentation in which you evaluate the author's argument in a nonfiction text in this unit. Share your presentation with a small group of classmates, then evaluate their assessments of the same text.

- Work as a group to choose the selection you will evaluate.
- As the basis for your presentation, write an essay in which you trace and evaluate the author's argument and specific claims in the text you chose. Include your assessment of the author's reasoning and evidence.
- Take turns presenting your evaluations to the group.
- Evaluate your classmates' arguments by considering their use of clear reasoning and relevant and sufficient evidence.
- Use precise language to express your ideas.

ⓒ Task 5: Informational Text [RI.7.4; SL.7.4]
Analyze the Impact of Word Choice

Give an oral presentation analyzing how word choice and diction impact meaning and tone in a work in this unit.

- Select a text, then choose a specific passage to use as the focus of your analysis. State which work you chose and why you chose it.
- Explain the tone of the selection—formal or informal, serious or funny, and so on.
- Show how the author's word choice affects your response to the text. Consider specific words, sentence length and style, and the feeling the work conveys. Include supporting examples.
- Consider how the author could have achieved a completely different effect by using different words or by putting sentences together in a different way.
- During your presentation, establish eye contact, speak with adequate volume, and pronounce your words clearly.

ⓒ Task 6: Informational Text
[RI.7.2, RI.7.3; SL.7.4]

Deliver a Response to Literature

Give an oral presentation of your response to one of the essays from this unit.

- Choose an essay that provoked a strong response in you—either positive or negative. State which work you chose.
- Explain the central idea or ideas that the author communicates in the essay. Then, describe your response by answering the following questions: *Do I agree with the author? Has the author provided solid support for his or her ideas? Has the author helped me look at something in a different way?*
- In your presentation, include descriptions, facts, and other details from the essay that support your ideas.

What should we learn?
At the beginning of Unit 3, you wrote a response to the Big Question. Now that you have completed the unit, write a new response. Discuss how your initial ideas have been either changed or reinforced. Cite specific examples from the literature in this unit, from other subject areas, and from your own life to support your ideas. Use Big Question vocabulary words (see p. 407) in your response.

Assessment Workshop **565**

Strategy for Less Proficient Readers
Assign a Performance Task, and then have students meet in groups to review the standard assessed in that task. Remind students of the selections or independent readings to which they have previously applied the standard. Have groups summarize what they learned in applying the standard and then present their summaries. Discuss, clarifying any points of confusion. After students have completed their tasks, have groups meet again to evaluate members' work. Encourage members to revise their work based on the feedback they receive.

EL Strategy for English Learners
For each assigned Performance Task, review the instructions with students. Clarify the meaning of any unfamiliar vocabulary, emphasizing routine classroom words such as *purpose, topic,* and *perspective,* and academic vocabulary such as *cite.*

Next, have students note ideas for their responses. Pair students, and have them review each other's notes, asking questions to clarify meaning and suggesting improvements. Encourage students to ask for your assistance in supplying English words or expressions they may require.

Supporting Speaking and Listening

1. Consider having students work with partners or in groups to complete Performance Tasks involving listening and speaking. For tasks that you assign for individual work, you may still wish to have students rehearse with partners, who can provide constructive feedback.

2. As students rehearse, have them keep in mind these tips:
   - Present findings and evidence clearly and concisely.
   - Observe conventions of standard English grammar and usage.
   - Be relaxed and friendly but maintain a formal tone.
   - Make eye contact with the audience, pronounce words clearly, and vary your pace.
   - When working with a group, respond thoughtfully to others' positions, modifying your own in response to new evidence.

Linking Performance Tasks to Independent Reading

If you wish to cover the standards with students' independent reading, adapt Performance Tasks of your choice to the works they have selected. (Independent reading suggestions appear on the next page.)

? What should we learn?

1. Remind students that the unit Big Question is "What should we learn?"

2. Have students complete their responses to the prompt on the student page. Point out that they have read selections in this unit about different approaches to learning and that they should draw on these selections in their responses. Remind them that they can also draw on their own experiences and what they have learned in other subject areas in formulating their answers.

Independent Reading

Titles featured on the Independent Reading pages at the end of each unit represent a range of reading, including stories, dramas, and poetry, as well as literary nonfiction and other types of informational text. Throughout, labels indicate the works that are CCSS Exemplar Texts. Choosing from among these featured titles will help students read works at increasing levels of text complexity in the grades 6–8 text complexity band.

Independent Reading and Pacing

See the Unit Overview and Pacing Plan, pp. 406a–406b, for suggestions on integrating independent reading with work in the Student Edition.

Using Literature Circles

A literature circle is a temporary group in which students independently discuss a book.

Use the guidance in the *Professional Development Guidebook*, pp. 47–49, as well as the teaching notes on the facing page, for additional suggestions for literature circles.

© Meeting Unit 3 CCS Focus Standards

Students can use books listed on this page to apply and to reinforce their mastery of the CCS Focus Standards covered in this unit. (The Focus Standards are introduced on pp. 408–411.)

Introducing Featured Titles

Have students choose a book or books for independent reading. Assist them by previewing the titles, noting their subject matter and level of difficulty. **Note:** Before recommending a work to students, preview it, taking into account the values of your community as well as the maturity of your students.

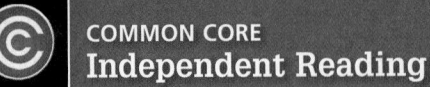

COMMON CORE
Independent Reading

Featured Titles

In this unit, you have read a variety of informational texts, including literary nonfiction. Continue to read on your own. Select books that you enjoy, but challenge yourself to explore new topics, new authors, and works of increasing depth and complexity. The titles suggested below will help you get started.

Informational Texts

Barrio Boy
by Ernesto Galarza

As a young boy in the early twentieth century, Galarza moved from a tiny Mexican village to a bustling Latino neighborhood in Sacramento. Follow him on his journey in this **memoir** of his early life.

Astronomy & Space
Edited by Phillis Engelbert   EXEMPLAR TEXT ©

Explore outer space in this three-volume **encyclopedia,** which includes a timeline, photographs, biographies, and a glossary of important words to know.

Discoveries: Finding Our Place in the World

This collection of **essays** explores four subject areas. In it, you will find "Stonehenge: Groundbreaking Discoveries," "Where on Earth Are You?" "From Bricks to Mortar to Cyberspace: Art Museums Online," and "Testing the Market."

Nonfiction Readings Across the Curriculum

This collection of **essays** and **stories** features writers such as Beverly Cleary, Gary Paulsen, Joe Namath, and more. Delve into its pages to find interesting observations about sports, literature, science, and social studies.

566 Nonfiction

Vincent van Gogh: Portrait of an Artist
by Jan Greenberg and Sandra Jordan
Yearling, 2003   **EXEMPLAR TEXT** ©

The painter Vincent van Gogh surprised the art world of the late nineteenth century with his broad brushstrokes, vivid colors, and dreamlike landscapes. Meet Van Gogh as a shy boy, an awkward young man, and an ambitious artist in this exciting **biography.**

Green Lantern's Book of Inventions
by Clare Hibbert

With a comic book superhero as your guide, learn about great inventions through the ages—from the wheel to the Internet—in this **nonfiction** book.

Literature

Child of the Owl
by Laurence Yep

When her father is hospitalized, twelve-year-old Casey is sent to live with her grandmother in the strange and unfamiliar world of Chinatown. This **novel** follows Casey as she learns to accept her new situation, drawing strength from family history and Chinese legend.

Slow Dance Heart Break Blues
by Arnold Adoff

In this collection of **poetry,** Adoff uses a hip-hop style and modern imagery to explore issues important to teenagers, such as love, loss, and identity.

© Text Complexity: Aligning Texts With Readers and Tasks

TEXTS	READERS AND TASKS
• *Astronomy & Space* • *Discoveries: Finding Our Place in the World* (Lexile: 860L)	**Below-Level Readers** Allow students to focus on reading for content, and challenge them to interpret multiple perspectives.
• *Nonfiction Readings Across the Curriculum* • *Vincent van Gogh: Portrait of an Artist* • *Slow Dance Heart Break Blues*	**Below-Level Readers** Challenge students as they read for content. **On-Level Readers** Allow students to focus on reading for content, and challenge them to interpret multiple perspectives. **Advanced Readers** Allow students to focus on interpreting multiple perspectives.
• *Child of the Owl* (920L) • *Barrio Boy* (Lexile: 1140L)	**On-Level Readers** Challenge students as they read for content. **Advanced Readers** Allow students to focus on reading for content, and challenge them to interpret multiple perspectives.

Preparing to Read Complex Texts

Attentive Reading As you read on your own, ask yourself questions about the text. The questions below, along with others that you ask as you read, will enrich your reading experience.

Common Core State Standards

Reading Literature/Informational Text
10. By the end of the year, read and comprehend literature, including stories, dramas, and poems, and literary nonfiction in the grades 6–8 text complexity band proficiently, with scaffolding as needed at the high end of the range.

When reading literary nonfiction, ask yourself...

- Who is the author? Why did he or she write the work?
- Is the author writing about a personal experience or a topic he or she has studied? In either case, what are my expectations about the work?
- Are the ideas the author expresses important? Why or why not?
- Did the author live at a different time and place than the present? If so, how does that affect his or her choice of topic and attitude?
- Does the author express beliefs that are very different from mine? If so, how does that affect what I understand and feel about the text?
- Does any one idea seem more important than the others? Why?
- What can I learn from this work?

Key Ideas and Details

- Does the author order ideas so that I can understand them? If not, what is unclear?
- Is the work interesting right from the start? If so, what has the author done to capture my interest? If not, why?
- Does the author give me a new way of looking at a topic? If so, how? If not, why?
- Is the author an expert on the topic? How do I know?
- Does the author use a variety of evidence that makes sense? If not, what is weak?
- Does the author use words in ways that are both interesting and clear? If so, are there any sections that I enjoy more than others? If not, why?

Craft and Structure

- Does the work seem believable? Why or why not?
- Do I agree or disagree with the author's arguments or ideas? Why or why not?
- Does this work remind me of others I have read? If so, in what ways?
- Does this work make me want to read more about this topic? Does it make me want to explore a related topic? Why or why not?

Integration of Ideas

Text Complexity: Reader and Task Support Suggestions

INDEPENDENT READING

Increased Support Suggest that students choose a book that they feel comfortable reading and one that is a bit more challenging. Pair a more proficient reader with a less proficient reader and have them work together on the more challenging text. Partners can prepare to read the book by reviewing questions on this student page. They can also read difficult passages together, sharing questions and insights. They can use the questions on the student page to guide after-reading discussion.

Increased Challenge Encourage students to integrate knowledge and ideas by combining the Big Question and the Unit Focus concepts in their approach to two or more featured titles

For example, students might consider the different kinds of knowledge the authors value in *Barrio Boy* and *Astronomy & Space*. In addition, students can focus on similarities and differences in the ways authors develop the main idea in works of literary nonfiction.

Preparing to Read Complex Texts

1. Tell students they can be attentive readers by bringing their experience and imagination to the texts they read and by actively questioning those texts. Explain that the questions they see on the student page are examples of types of questions to ask about works of literary nonfiction.

2. Point out that, like writing, reading is a "multidraft" process, involving several readings of complete works or passages, revising and refining one's understanding each time.

Key Ideas and Details

3. As an example, review and amplify the seventh bulleted item. **Ask:** What key ideas and details can you use to determine what you learned from a work?

Possible response: You might point to a new perspective or opinion on the subject or specific facts the author shares.

Craft and Structure

4. **Ask:** What details of craft and structure would you use to evaluate the author's evidence?

Possible response: You might point to the author's effective use of statistics or to the types of evidence provided.

Integration of Ideas

5. **Ask:** How would you determine whether a text seems believable?

Possible response: You might compare it to other works about the same topic or draw on your previous knowledge of the subject.

6. Finally, explain to students that they should cite key ideas and details, examples of craft and structure, or instances of the integration of ideas as evidence to support their points during a book discussion. After hearing the evidence, the group might reach a consensus or might agree to disagree.

Unit 4 Features Overview

Unit Genre and Big Question

In this unit, students will analyze poetry. As they read they will discuss responses to the unit Big Question: What is the best way to communicate?

Unit 4 Collections

Teach Collections are presented in leveled pairs. To teach the skills and meet the objectives, you need to assign only one collection in each pair.

Differentiate and Reinforce Choose the collection in a pair that is best suited for your students, based on the Text Complexity box shown on the next page. You may use the other collection to reinforce skills or provide enrichment.

Integrate Skills Each collection presents students with a reading strategy, a literary analysis concept, a vocabulary skill, and grammar instruction. Students can extend learning in the writing and extension activities.

Additional Unit Features

Ⓔ **Literary Analysis Workshop** Teach and model the Unit Focus standards. Spiral Review notes enable students to revisit these skills over the course of the unit.

Reading for Information Students analyze functional, expository, and argumentative texts and complete Timed Writing activities.

Comparing Literary Works Students study two literary works either within or across genres.

Test Practice: Reading This feature provides extra practice in utilizing reading skills to master assessments.

Writing Workshops Two writing workshops appear in each unit, along with rubrics and instruction in the writing process.

Assessment Workshop Cumulative Skill Review and Performance Tasks provide a range of assessment opportunities.

Independent Reading Students broaden their knowledge as they read longer works of increasing complexity.

THE BIG ? What is the best way to communicate?

Teaching From Technology

www.PHLitOnline.com

Enriched Online Student Edition
- full narration of selections
- interactive graphic organizers
- linked **Get Connected** and **Background** videos
- all worksheets and other student resources

Professional Development
- the *Professional Development Guidebook* online
- additional professional development articles by program authors

Planning, Assigning, and Monitoring
- software for online assignment of work to students, individually or to the whole class
- a system for tracking and grading student work

Instructional Resources

The booklet *Unit 4 Resources* supports Unit skills with pages of the following types:

▶ **Benchmark Tests** assess and monitor student progress at mid-Unit and at Unit's end.

▶ **Vocabulary and Reading Warm-ups** provide additional vocabulary support, based on Lexile rankings of words, for each selection. "A" Warm-ups are for students reading two grades below level. "B" Warm-ups are for students reading one grade below level.

▶ **Selection Support** These practice pages are available for each selection:

- Reading Skill
- Literary Analysis
- Writing About the Big Question
- Vocabulary
- Support for Writing
- Support for Extend Your Learning
- Enrichment

PHLit Online!
www.PHLitOnline.com

Hear It!
- Selection summary audio
- Selection audio
- BQ Tunes

See It!
- Author videos
- Big Question video
- Get Connected videos
- Background videos
- More about the authors
- Illustrated vocabulary words
- Vocabulary flashcards

Do It!
- Interactive journals
- Interactive graphic organizers
- Grammar tutorials
- Interactive vocabulary games
- Test practice

PHLit Online!

All worksheets and other student resources are also available online at www.PHLitOnline.com.

569

Ⓒ Text Complexity: Accessibility for Various Ability Levels

This chart gives a general text complexity rating to help you decide which collection in each leveled pair is more appropriate for your students. **Choose one collection in each pair, or choose to teach both.** You will meet the objectives for the pair when you teach either of the two collections. For additional guidance on factors that affect the complexity of each collection, see the Leveled Texts page for each collection set.

Accessibility for English Learners

 This icon indicates support for English learners at point of use in this Teacher's Edition.

	✓ **More Accessible**	✓✓ **More Complex**
Pair 1	Poetry Collection 1	Poetry Collection 2
Pair 2	Poetry Collection 3	Poetry Collection 4
Pair 3	Poetry Collection 5	Poetry Collection 6
Pair 4	Poetry Collection 7	Poetry Collection 8

Common Core State Standards

Unit 4 Focus Standards
• Reading Literature 4, 5

Additional Activities and Assessments
• Reading Literature 7
• Writing 2, 4, 6, 7, 9
• Speaking and Listening 1, 4, 5, 6
• Language 1, 4, 5, 6

	Week 1					Week 2					Week 3				
	1	2	3	4	5	1	2	3	4	5	1	2	3	4	5
Introduce the Unit Big Question (pp. 570–571).	●														
Introduce the unit form, poetry, using the Literary Analysis Workshop (pp. 572–575).	●														
Introduce the focus CCS standards for the unit and lead students in a close reading of exemplar texts. (pp. 574–581).	●	●													
Teach one collection from Pairing 1 (pp. 582–599).			●	●	●	●	●								
Teach one collection from Pairing 2 (pp. 600–619).							●	●	●	●	●				
Complete the Test Practice: Reading (pp. 620–621).									●						
Teach Reading for Information (pp. 622–627).										●					
Teach Comparing Literary Works (pp. 628–639).												●	●		
Have students complete the Writing Workshop (pp. 640–645).										●	●	●	●	●	
Administer **Benchmark Test 7** (*Unit 4 Resources*, pp. 120–125).														●	
Reteach skills, judging which skills to reteach by evaluating students' performance on **Benchmark Test 7**.															●

Independent Reading

Have students choose a full-length work from the Independent Reading feature at the end of the unit and read it while working on this unit.

Pacing Suggestions

• Have students read their chosen work for homework.

• Devote parts of class periods in each school week to Literature Circles in which students reading the same work discuss it.

	Week 4					Week 5					Week 6				
	1	2	3	4	5	1	2	3	4	5	1	2	3	4	5
Teach one collection from Pairing 3 (pp. 646–663).	●	●	●	●	●										
Teach one collection from Pairing 4 (pp. 646–683).						●	●	●	●	●					
Complete the Test-Practice: Reading (pp. 684–685).								●							
Teach Reading for Information (pp. 686–691).									●						
Teach Comparing Literary Works (pp. 692–697).										●	●				
Have students complete the Writing Workshop (pp. 698–705).								●	●	●	●	●			
Have students complete the Vocabulary Workshop (pp. 706–707).												●			
Have students complete the Communications Workshop (pp. 710–713).													●		
Have students complete the first three sections of the Assessment Workshop: Poetry (pp. 710–713).													●	●	●
Have students complete the selected Performance Tasks in the Assessment Workshop (pp. 714-715).														●	
Administer Benchmark Test 8 (*Unit 4 Resources,* pp. 227–234).														●	
Reteach skills, judging which skills to reteach by evaluating students' performance on **Benchmark Test 8.**															●

- Cover the focus standards with independent readings and abbreviate review of the focus standards with student-edition collections.

- Do not assign extension activities for collections (day 5 of main collection lessons), except as needed for full standards coverage.

- If students demonstrate reading proficiency, consider omitting Test Practice: Reading features in the unit.

Block and Daily Scheduling

The assignments and activities in this Unit planner are organized by week. You may adjust them to your daily or block schedule. The Time and Resource Managers for the selection set gives specific pacing suggestions, or you may use the comprehensive lesson planning support online at **www.PHLitOnline.com.**

Monitoring Progress

Diagnose Each pairing in the Unit contains a more accessible and a more complex collection of poems. To determine which collection in the pairing to assign, refer to students' results on the **Vocabulary in Context** section of **Benchmark Test 2,** *Unit 3 Resources,* pp. 240–242 (administered at the end of the previous Unit). Use the Interpretation Guide to interpret the results of the diagnostic portion of the test. **Note:** For the most accurate diagnosis of students who score in the middle range, administer the additional diagnostic questions online at **www.PHLitOnline.com.**

Preteach and Prepare As indicated by the diagnostic, prepare students for reading by assigning the **Vocabulary** and **Reading Warm-ups** for the collections you assign.

Teach Follow this Pacing Plan and use the resources to teach the skills and selections. For specific pacing suggestions and a list of resources, see the Time and Resource Manager and the Visual Guide to Featured Selection Resources preceding each pairing.

Classroom Management
For classroom management suggestions for using leveled texts in a mixed-ability classroom, see Harvey Daniels's professional development essay "Leveled Reading Selections," online at **www.PHLitOnline.com.**

Assess After students have completed the first half of the Unit, administer **Benchmark Test 7**. Administer **Benchmark Test 8** at the end of the Unit.

Intervention and Reteach After administering each test, use the **Interpretation Guide** for the tests to determine which reteaching pages, if any, you should assign from the *Reading Kit.* The appropriate pages are also available through the online Progress Monitoring software.

CLASSROOM STRATEGIES

Teaching Online Reading Comprehension **Donald J. Leu**

Online reading comprehension requires new reading skills.

Did you know that online reading comprehension requires new reading skills beyond those required for traditional offline reading comprehension? In fact, some of your lowest performing offline readers may actually be some of your best online readers (Leu, et al., 2007).

These new reading skills are often called new literacies. Mastery of these skills is essential to becoming fully prepared for the 21st century. Internet Workshop is a great vehicle to teach the new literacies of online reading comprehension.

What Are the New Literacies of Online Reading Comprehension?

The new literacies of online reading comprehension require distinctive reading skills (Leu, et al., 2007) in these areas:

Generating Important Questions We read online to find out the answer to a question. How can I become better at basketball? What is my favorite band doing now? When you are reading online, it is important to know how to ask good questions and how to refine your questions as you gather additional information.

Locating Information Once you have a question, you need to locate information online. Knowing how to use a search engine and infer meaning from the results page requires new reading skills. In fact, if you cannot locate information, you cannot read on the Internet.

Critically Evaluating Information After locating information, you need to evaluate it. Knowing how to evaluate the accuracy and validity of information becomes especially important online, where anyone may publish anything.

Synthesizing Information Online, we usually synthesize many short, separated units of information from multiple sites. This requires additional reading skills. Offline, these units are typically put together for us.

Communicating Information During online reading, we often communicate with others, seeking and sharing information using new tools such as IM, text messaging, wikis, blogs, and email. Each of these tools requires new skills.

Internet Workshop

Internet Workshop teaches these new literacies of online reading comprehension. It has three steps.

Develop an Information Challenge Activity. You first develop a question or a problem for students: Where does Lois Lowry get the

ideas for her novels? or, What themes typically appear in Gary Paulsen's writing? Why?

Have Students Complete the Research Activity. During the week, students can use the computer lab at school or work at home to investigate your question. Have them record the answer and bring it to class at the end of the week.

Conduct a Workshop Session. During a workshop session, have students share their answers and the online reading comprehension strategies used to complete the assignment. Post a running list of these effective online reading strategies.

Internet Workshop on Authors

I develop an Internet Workshop around each important, upcoming author and use it to conduct an author talk. Students do research about the author and exchange it in class. During the process, students also learn important online reading comprehension strategies, which they share with others.

Develop an Information Challenge Activity. One week before we read a selection from a new author, I provide students with an information challenge similar to this one:

Locate information on the Internet about Katherine Patterson. Find out all you can about this important author. Locate answers to these and other questions:

- *What was her childhood like? How did it influence her work?*
- *What topics does she often write about?*
- *What themes appear in her work?*

Find out everything! Record this information in your Internet Workbook. Be prepared to share everything that you discovered. Also, write down the most important reading strategies that you used so you can teach us what worked for you.

(An Internet Workbook is a spiral-bound notebook where information is recorded and evaluated with comments following each online reading assignment. Alternatively, a blog can be used by each student for these assignments.)

Have Students Complete the Research Activity. Allow students to complete the assignment at the school's computer lab or at home.

Conduct a Workshop Session. During this session, students do two things: (1) share their answers and (2) explain how they figured out each one. They discuss online reading strategies while offering their explanations. If students forget, ask them, "How did you figure that out?" Answering this prompt requires students to share the online reading strategies that proved most effective.

Donald J. Leu, Ph.D.

Donald J. Leu, Ph.D., is the Neag Endowed Chair in Literacy and Technology at the University of Connecticut. He is also Co-Director of the New Literacies Research Lab, a member of the Reading Hall of Fame, and a member of the International Reading Association Board of Directors.

Supporting Research

Leu, D. J., Jr. (2002). Internet workshop: Making time for literacy. *The Reading Teacher. 55,* 466-472.

Leu, D. J., Jr., Leu, D. D. & Coiro, J. (2004). *Teaching with the Internet: New literacies for new times* (4th ed.). Norwood, MA: Christopher-Gordon.

Leu, D. J., Zawilinski, L., Castek, J., Banerjee, M., Housand, B., Liu, Y., and O'Neil, M. (2007). What is new about the new literacies of online reading comprehension? In L. Rush, J. Eakle, & A. Berger, (Eds.). *Secondary school literacy: What research reveals for classroom practices.* (37-68). Urbana, IL: National Council of Teachers of English.

International Reading Association. (2001). *Integrating literacy and technology in the curriculum: A position statement of the International Reading Association.* Newark, DE: Author.

Common Core State Standards

- Speaking and Listening 1
- Language 6

Introducing the Big Question

1. Write the word *communication* on the board. Note that every communication involves three parts—a sender, a message, and a receiver. Then, have students read the introductory section on the student page.

2. **Ask:** Which of the communication media mentioned in the first paragraph (i.e., telephone, television, Internet) do you use the most? The least? Allow time for discussion.

3. **Ask** students: "What is the best way to communicate?" (**Possible responses:** by talking; on the Internet)

4. Tell students the poems in this unit show different ways to communicate. As students read, they should consider how the poems affect their first answers to the Big Question.

Exploring the Big Question

Collaboration: One-on-One Discussion

1. Introduce the activity, using the instruction on the student page.

2. Have students work individually to list examples. For example:

   - Why might someone film an event? **Sample response:** to make a documentary, to record the event for history.

   - What could a piece of music communicate? **Sample response:** A piece of music might communicate an emotion or a story.

3. Review the Big Question vocabulary on page 571, following the teaching suggestions. Have students use the vocabulary as they complete the activity on page 570.

Connecting to the Literature

Explain the Big Question strand in the unit, referring to the box at right.

What is the best way to *communicate?*

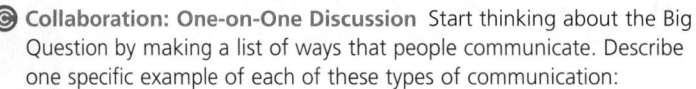

We **communicate** for different reasons and in different ways. Through communication, we can send a message to another person. The message may entertain or inform, and it may be made in person or transmitted through technology. We use telephones, television, and the Internet to send messages, videos, and music to many people or to those far away. We can also express ourselves through art, music, and photography. Sometimes, we read, or watch, or listen to communication created by someone else. With so many reasons and ways to communicate, we often have to choose the *best* way to express ourselves.

Exploring the Big Question

Collaboration: One-on-One Discussion Start thinking about the Big Question by making a list of ways that people communicate. Describe one specific example of each of these types of communication:

- telling stories
- transmitting messages through technology
- talking to friends or family members
- filming an event
- speaking in public
- creating music or art

Share your examples with a partner. With your partner, discuss which items on your lists are the best ways to communicate and why. Build on your partner's ideas, responding to each with related ideas of your own. Ask questions to make sure you have understood each other's points, and clarify your meaning as needed. Use the Big Question vocabulary in your discussion.

Connecting to the Literature Each reading in this unit will give you additional insight into the Big Question.

PHLit Online!
www.PHLitOnline.com

- Big Question video
- Illustrated vocabulary words
- Interactive vocabulary games
- BQ Tunes

Applying Understanding by Design Principles

The Big Question
Explain to students that they will continue to consider the Big Question as they work through the Unit.

- At the beginning of each selection, they will write a response to a Writing About the Big Question sentence starter.
- As they read the selection, they will look for details related to the Big Question.

- At the end of the selection, they will answer a Critical Thinking question that is related to the Big Question.
- Tell students that their goal will be to gain a deeper understanding of literature and a more sophisticated way of discussing the Big Question.

"Understanding by Design" is registered as a trademark with the Patent and Trademark Office by the Association for Supervision of Curriculum Development (ASCD). ASCD has not authorized, approved, or sponsored this work and is in no way affiliated with Pearson or its products.

Learning Big Question Vocabulary

Common Core State Standards

Speaking and Listening
1. Engage effectively in a range of collaborative discussions with diverse partners on grade 7 topics, texts, and issues, building on others' ideas and expressing their own clearly.

Language
6. Acquire and use accurately grade-appropriate general academic and domain-specific words and phrases; gather vocabulary knowledge when considering a word or phrase important to comprehension or expression.

© **Acquire and Use Academic Vocabulary** Academic vocabulary is the language you encounter in textbooks and on standardized tests. Review the definitions of these academic vocabulary words.

---

communicate (kə myōō′ ni kāt′) *v.* share thoughts or feelings

contribute (kən′ trib′ yōōt) *v.* add to; enrich

inform (in fôrm′) *v.* tell; give information about

media (mē′ dē ə) *n.* sources of information, such as newspapers, television, and the Internet

produce (prə dōōs′) *v.* make; create

react (rē akt′) *v.* respond to

speak (spēk′) *v.* use oral language

technology (tek näl′ ə jē) *n.* machines, equipment, and ways of doing things that are based on modern knowledge about science

transmit (trans mit′) *v.* send or give out

Use these words as you complete Big Question activities in this unit that involve reading, writing, speaking, and listening.

© **Gather Vocabulary Knowledge** Additional Big Question words are listed below. Categorize the words by deciding whether you know each one well, know it a little bit, or do not know it at all.

---

enrich	express	listen
entertain	learn	teach

Then, do the following:

1. Work with a partner to write each word on one side of an index card and its definition on the other side.
2. Verify the definitions by looking them up in a print or online dictionary and revising your cards as needed.
3. Place the cards with the words facing up in a pile.
4. Take turns drawing a word card, pronouncing the word and then using it in an original sentence.

Learning Big Question Vocabulary

Acquire and Use Academic Vocabulary

1. Introduce the academic vocabulary words in the first word bank on the student page. Have students preview the words.
2. For each word, have students say the word aloud. Then, use the word in a sentence that defines the word.
3. Finally, repeat your definitional sentence or a similar sentence, omitting the word, and have the class "fill in the blank" chorally.
4. Lead students in relating each word to issues of truth. Then, explain that they should use the words as they discuss the unit Big Question.

Gather Vocabulary Knowledge

1. Introduce the words in the second word bank to students. Explain that they will also use these Big Question words in discussing the unit Big Question.
2. With the class, review the steps in the activity on the student page. Have students complete the activity independently, with partners, or in small groups.
3. Before students complete the last step, review the words and their meanings as a class. (Definitions appear below on the left.) Then, have students complete their paragraphs.

Gather Vocabulary Knowledge: Definitions

enrich (en rich′) *v.* make better; improve

entertain (ent′ər tān′) *v.* please or amuse

express (ek spres′) *v.* say; show; communicate

learn (lʉrn) *v.* get knowledge or skills

listen (lis′ən) *v.* pay attention to

teach (tēch) *v.* give information or knowledge to others

❶ Elements of Poetry

1. Introduce the form, poetry, using the instruction on the student page.

2. Underscore the idea that in poetry, sound and meaning work together to capture feelings, experiences, and ideas in striking and imaginative ways. Have students recall some of their favorite poems and discuss what makes the poems striking and imaginative.

3. Stress that most poetry is arranged in lines and that lines are often arranged in stanzas. Note that stanzas usually work like paragraphs of prose, each expressing a key idea. Remind students to use punctuation and meaning, rather than line breaks, as a guide for when to pause in reading a poem.

4. Explain that refrains and other types of repetition are common in poetry partly because poetry has its origins in oral literature, which repetition makes easier to remember and recite. Point out that repetition not only stresses key ideas but can also add to the music of a poem.

5. Have students study the poem "Life" and the two boxed notes. Explain that a *peck* (line 3) is a large quantity and *foils* (line 9) are things that enhance by contrast. **Ask:** How does repetition, including the refrain, stress the poem's key ideas?

Sample response: The repetition of key words (*smile, joy, moan*) stresses the connection and contrast between the ideas in the two stanzas: life is more sorrow than joy; but the sorrow enhances the joy. The refrain "And that is life!" underscores the poet's view that both ideas are true about life.

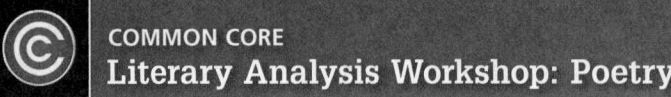

❶Elements of Poetry

Poetry uses the rhythms and sounds of words as well as their meanings to set the imagination in motion.

Poetry is a type of literature that uses the sounds, rhythms, and meanings of words to describe the world in striking and imaginative ways. Poetry comes in many forms, from structured traditional verse to contemporary poems that follow few rules. However varied their forms may be, many poems are made up of the same elements.

Lines and Stanzas Poetry is divided into **lines,** or groups of words. In some poems, the first word of each line is capitalized, even if it is not the beginning of a sentence. A sentence in a poem may stretch over several lines. The first one or two lines may *break,* or end, before the sentence is finished. However, good readers of poetry know that they should read the sentence as a whole, without pausing at the end of every line.

In many poems, lines are organized in units of meaning called **stanzas.** The lines in a stanza work together to express one key idea. A blank line, called a **stanza break,** signals that one stanza has ended and a new stanza is beginning.

As you read the poem below, think about the key idea in each stanza, and identify the relationship between ideas.

Refrains and Repetition Like a catchy song, a poem may repeat lines, either identically or with variations. A line or group of lines that is repeated at regular intervals in a poem is called a **refrain.** In a refrain, a poet reminds readers and listeners of a key idea, image, or event. Often, a refrain is repeated at the end of each stanza. A poet may also repeat lines with **variations**—changing one or more words with each repetition.

As you read the poem at the bottom of the page, notice how the poet uses repetition, including a refrain, to emphasize his key ideas.

"Life"
by Paul Laurence Dunbar

A crust of bread and a corner to sleep in,
A minute to smile and an hour to weep in,
A pint of joy to a peck of trouble,
And never a laugh but the moans come double;
    And that is life!

> This five-line **stanza** compares life's joys to its sorrows. Together, the lines **focus on one key idea:** Life has more sorrow than joy.

A crust and a corner that love makes precious,
With a smile to warm and the tears to refresh us;
And joy seems sweeter when cares come after,
And a moan is the finest of foils for laughter;
    And that is life!

> The **focus changes,** and a **new stanza** starts. Here, the speaker describes life's joys. The **key idea** is that sorrow intensifies joy.

Teaching Resources

- **All** *Common Core Companion,* pp. 41–66
- **All** *Unit 4 Resources,* pp. 7–22
- **All** *Professional Development Guidebook,* p. 32
- **All** *See It!* DVD
  Pat Mora, Segments 1 and 2
- **All** *Graphic Organizer Transparencies,* pp. 109, 110

- **All** **Enriched Online Student Edition**
- **L2 L3** *Reader's Notebook*
- **L1** *Reader's Notebook: Adapted Version*
- **EL** *Reader's Notebook: English Learner's Version*
- **L2 EL** *Hear It!* **Audio CD**
- **L1 EL** *Hear It!* **Audio CD** (adapted text)

PHLit Online! All resources, including print and video, are available online at www.PHLitOnline.com.

Sound Devices

❷ Rhythm and Meter Most poems have **rhythm,** or a beat, created by the stressed and unstressed syllables in words. To sustain a pattern of rhythm, or **meter,** a poet may arrange words and break lines at certain points.

Meter is measured in **feet,** or units of stressed and unstressed syllables. As you read the following lines, look for the pattern in the arrangement of stressed syllables (´) and unstressed syllables (˘). Feet are divided by slashes (/).

> Whĕn Í / sĕe bírch / ĕs bend /
> tŏ left / ănd ríght
> Ăcross / thĕ línes / ŏf stráight / ĕr
> dárk / ĕr tre´es,
> Ĭ like / tŏ think / sŏme bóy's /
> bĕen swíng / ĭng thém.
> (from "Birches," Robert Frost)

In this example, each foot consists of one unstressed syllable followed by one stressed syllable. This down-up, down-up rhythmic pattern fits the subject of an imagined boy swinging on the branches of trees.

Poets may break a metrical pattern for effect. For example, Frost shifts the accent to the first syllable in this line from "Birches": "Kicking his way down through the air to the ground." The shift emphasizes the boy's movement.

❸ Rhyme Some poems also contain **rhyme,** or the repetition of vowel and consonant sounds at the ends of words, as in *tin* and *pin*. In many poems, the rhymes follow a particular pattern, or **rhyme scheme.** In the following example, the first line rhymes with the third line, and the second line rhymes with the fourth line. This rhyme scheme is indicated by using a different letter for each rhyme sound: *abab*.

> **Rhyme Scheme**
>
> | How doth the little crocodile | **a** |
> | Improve his shining tail, | **b** |
> | And pour the waters of the Nile | **a** |
> | On every golden scale! | **b** |
>
> (from "How Doth the Little Crocodile," Lewis Carroll)

Additional Sound Devices

Poets may also use other sound devices to enhance mood and meaning in their poems.

- **Alliteration** is the repetition of consonant sounds in the beginnings of words, as in *slippery slope*.
- **Repetition** is the use of any element of language—a sound, word, or phrase—more than once.
- **Onomatopoeia** is the use of words that imitate sounds. *Splat, hiss,* and *gurgle* are all examples of onomatopoeia.

Literary Analysis Workshop **573**

❹ In This Section

Elements of Poetry

Analyzing Poetic Language

Analyzing Poetic Form and Structure

Close Read:
- Model Text
- Practice Text

After You Read

 Common Core State Standards

RL.7.4, RL.7.5
[For the full wording of the standards, see the standards chart in the front of your textbook.]

---

❷ Rhythm and Meter

1. Introduce rhythm and meter, using the instruction on the student page.

2. Write on the board this four-line stanza from Lord Byron's poem "The Destruction of Sennacherib." Omit the symbols and slashes. Have a volunteer mark the meter. **Ask:** What does the meter capture?

   Answer: It captures the sound of soldiers riding into battle.

   > ˘ ˘ / ˘ ˘ /
   > The Assyr / ian came down
   > ˘ ˘ / ˘ ˘ /
   > like a wolf / on the fold, /
   > ˘ ˘ / ˘ ˘ /
   > And his co / horts were gleam
   > ˘ ˘ / ˘ ˘ /
   > ing in pur / ple and gold; /
   > ˘ ˘ / ˘ ˘ /
   > And the sheen / of their spears
   > ˘ ˘ / ˘ ˘ /
   > was like stars / on the sea, /
   > ˘ ˘ / ˘ ˘ /
   > When the blue / wave rolls night
   > ˘ ˘ / ˘ ˘ /
   > ly on deep / Gal i lee.

❸ Rhyme

1. Introduce rhyme, using the instruction on the student page.

2. Clarify that a rhyme scheme is the pattern of rhyme at the ends of lines, and that lines ending with the same sound are assigned the same letter. Refer students to Byron's stanza and **ask:** What is this stanza's rhyme scheme?

   Answer: *aabb*

3. Review the examples of sound devices. **Ask** students to find examples of alliteration in the Byron stanza.

   Answer: Lines 2 and 3 use alliterated *g* and *s* sounds (*gleaming, gold; spears, stars, sea*).

❹ In This Section

Explain that in the remainder of this Literary Analysis Workshop, students will analyze poetry. After reviewing the concept, they will then see it applied to a Model text. Finally, they will apply what they have learned to some Practice texts.

Differentiated Instruction for Universal Access

Support for Special-Needs Students
Have students read the Learning About Poetry pages for these selections in the *Reader's Notebook: Adapted Version.* This version provides a basic-level introduction to poetry.

Support for Less Proficient Readers
Have students read the Learning About Poetry pages for these selections in the *Reader's Notebook.* This version provides a basic-level introduction to poetry.

EL Support for English Learners
Have students read the Learning About Poetry pages for these selections in the *Reader's Notebook: English Learner's Version.* This version provides a basic-level introduction to poetry.

Unit 4 Focus Standards

• **Reading Literature 4, 5**

These standards spiral through the unit.

❶ Analyzing Poetic Language

1. Introduce the concept of poetic language, using the instruction on the student page.

2. Review the information on denotation and connotation and discuss the examples in the chart. **Ask:** What connotations would the word *childish* have?

   Sample response: It would have negative connotations similar to *immature* or *babyish*.

3. Review the concept of imagery and the examples in the Sensory Imagery box. Have students provide images that appeal to the two remaining senses.

   Sample response: See the shiny green leaves. Touch the cold, crisp leaves.

4. Clarify that figurative language uses comparisons that are not meant to be taken literally. Have partners create original similes, metaphors, and personification, then exchange and label each other's examples.

   Sample response: *Simile*—The moon was like a bright coin in the sky. *Metaphor*—The moon was a bright coin in the sky. *Personification*—The moon smiled down on me.

❶Analyzing Poetic Language

Poetic language is specific, imaginative, and rich with emotion.

Common Core
State Standards
Reading Literature
4. Determine the meaning of words and phrases as they are used in a text, including figurative and connotative meanings; analyze the impact of rhymes and other repetitions of sounds on a specific verse or stanza of a poem or section of a story or drama.

Poetic language begins when a writer weaves together the images and associations called up by words and says something unique that could not be said in different words.

Shade of Meaning The **denotation** of a word is its literal, dictionary definition. The **connotation** consists of the ideas and feelings that the word brings to mind. The chart below lists several words that refer to dogs. Consider the differences in the words' connotations (printed in darker type).

Denotative and Connotative Meanings	
canine ⟶	dog
pooch ⟶	**friendly, lovable** dog
mongrel ⟶	**mean, ugly** mixed-breed dog

The technical term *canine* has a neutral connotation, neither positive nor negative. By contrast, the word *pooch* conveys positive feelings, while *mongrel* conveys negative feelings.

Imagery To create vivid word pictures, poets use **imagery,** or descriptions that appeal to the five senses. Imagery helps poets convey what they see, hear, smell, taste, or touch.

The example below appeals to the senses of taste, hearing, and smell.

Example: Imagery
Taste the green in the lettuce,
Hear the crunch of its freshness,
Smell its earth perfume.

Figurative Language To help readers share their perceptions and insights, poets may also use **figurative language,** or language that is not meant to be taken literally. Many types of figurative language are comparisons that show how things are alike in surprising ways. Three common types of figurative language are similes, metaphors, and personification.

A **simile** uses the word *like* or *as* to compare two seemingly unlike things.
  • *His hands were as cold as steel.*

A **metaphor** describes one thing as if it were something else.
  • *My chores were a mountain waiting to be climbed.*

Personification gives human qualities to a nonhuman subject.
  • *The fingertips of the rain tapped a steady beat on the windowpane.*

Vocabulary Development

Ⓒ CCSS Language 6

Domain-Specific Words: Poetry
Reinforce understanding of terms in poetry by having students choose the term in parentheses that correctly completes each sentence.

1. The word *crackle* is an example of (onomatopoeia, personification).
2. After the (stanza break, denotation), a new idea is introduced.
3. When I say that Jan is as sharp as a needle, I am using a (simile, refrain).
4. The poem had no pattern of rhythm; instead, it was written in (dramatic poetry, free verse).

5. To show the (meter, rhyme scheme), I marked the stressed and unstressed syllables.
6. The repeated *f* sounds in *funny face* are an example of (imagery, alliteration).
7. Since "The Highwayman" tells a story, it is (lyric poetry, narrative poetry).

   Answers: 1–onomatopoeia; 2–stanza break; 3–simile; 4–free verse; 5–meter; 6–alliteration; 7–narrative poetry

❷ Analyzing Poetic Form and Structure

Every form of poetry has its own structure.

Common Core State Standards

Reading Literature 5. Analyze how a drama's or a poem's form or structure contributes to its meaning.

There are many different forms of poetry. A poet chooses the form that best suits his or her intended meaning.

Narrative poetry tells a story in verse. Narrative poems have elements similar to those in short stories, such as plot and characters.

Haiku is a three-line Japanese form that describes something in nature. The first and third lines each have five syllables, and the second line has seven.

Free Verse poetry is defined by its lack of structure. It has no regular meter, rhyme, fixed line length, or specific stanza pattern.

Lyric poetry expresses the thoughts and feelings of a single speaker, often in highly musical verse.

Ballads are songlike poems that tell stories. They often deal with adventure or romance.

Concrete poems are shaped to look like their subjects. The poet arranges the lines to create a picture on the page.

Limericks are humorous, rhyming five-line poems with a specific rhythm pattern and rhyme scheme.

Look at the lyric poem below to see how the structural elements of rhythm, rhyme, and imagery help reinforce the poet's meaning.

Analysis of Lines from "Tiare Tahiti," Rupert Brooke		
Taü here, Mamua!	**a**	• The poem's meter emphasizes the commands "crown" and "come."
Crown the hair, and come away!	**b**	
Hear the calling of the moon,	**c**	• The *c* rhyme sound ties lines 3–5 together, reflecting their focus on the night's beauty. This focus is developed with **imagery**.
And the whispering scents that stray	**b**	
5 About the idle warm lagoon.	**c**	
Hasten, hand in human hand,	**d**	• The new *d* rhyme sound in lines 6–8 introduces a new idea: The speaker urges Mamua to come to the lagoon. The **alliteration** of the *h*, *w*, and *d* sounds reinforces this idea.
Down the dark, the flowered way,	**b**	
Along the whiteness of the sand,	**d**	
And in the water's soft caress,	**e**	• Lines 9–10 rhyme, interrupting the pattern of alternating end rhymes. The interruption shows that these lines express a key idea: Nature can ease the mind.
10 Wash the mind of foolishness,	**e**	
Mamua, until the day.	**b**	

Literary Analysis Workshop **575**

---

❷ Analyzing Poetic Form and Structure

1. Introduce poetic structure and form, using the instruction on the student page.

2. Review the different forms of poetry, and have students provide examples of each. Encourage students to preview some of the poems in this unit for more examples.

3. To illustrate free verse, have students turn to the poem "Life" on page 604. Help them recognize that the poem's line breaks are based entirely on meaning, or units of thought, rather than meter or stanza form.

4. Explain that Rupert Brooke wrote "Tiare Tahiti" on the South Pacific island of Tahiti. These lines are addressed to his girlfriend Mamua, pronounced with a final long *a* and thus rhyming with *away* in line 2. *Taü here* (line 1) is a term of endearment used in traditional Tahitian ceremonies; "crown the hair" (line 2) probably refers to donning flowers or a headdress for such a ceremony.

5. Review the bulleted points of analysis, emphasizing that each group of rhyming lines makes a different point. Explain that a lagoon is a shallow body of water separated from the sea by a reef or sandbar. **Ask:** What impression of the lagoon do the lines convey? What words and images convey this impression?

Sample response: It is a peaceful, beautiful place. The words *idle* and *warm* and the imagery of "whispering scents" and "the water's soft caress" help convey this impression.

❸ Close Read: Analyzing Structure and Meaning

1. Remind students that poetry usually conveys its meaning through language, sound, and structure.

2. Review the elements identified and defined in the chart.

3. Supply these stanzas by Emily Brontë and have students analyze them by citing one or more examples of each element in the chart.

   The night is darkening round me,
   The wild winds coldly blow;
   But a tyrant spell has bound me,
   And I cannot, cannot go.

   The giant trees are bending
   Their bare boughs weighed with snow;
   The storm is fast descending,
   And yet I cannot go.

   Possible response: The lines describe a powerful snowstorm that mesmerizes the speaker. Imagery in lines 1, 2, 5, 6, and 7 stresses the storm's power; *tyrant* in line 3, repeating *cannot* in line 4, and the repetition with variations in lines 4 and 8 stress the speaker's inability to seek shelter. The repetition, strong meter, intricate *abab cbcb* rhyme scheme, moaning long *o* in *cold* and the onomatopoeic *blow*, and alliteration in *wild winds* and *bare boughs* all help convey the mesmerizing nature of the storm.

4. Refer students to the model poem on page 577. Explain that details in the poem that illustrate each category on the chart are highlighted in the same color and that corresponding side-column annotations use corresponding colors.

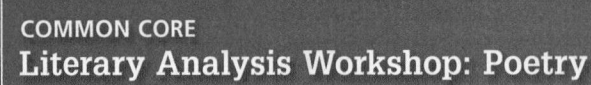

❸ Close Read: Analyzing Structure and Meaning

From sound to structure, each element of a poem helps to shape its meaning.

To analyze a poem, follow your ear and your imagination as well as the meanings of words.

- **Read the poem aloud.** Listen for sounds that repeat or that create strong contrasts. Then, reread the poem, thinking about how the sound patterns link ideas and reinforce meaning.

- **Read in complete sentences.** Do not pause at the end of a line unless it ends with a period or other punctuation mark. Instead, read for meaning.

- **Analyze poetic elements.** Follow the tips in the chart below.

Tips for Analyzing Structure and Meaning	
Word Choice • Use context or a dictionary to understand word **denotations** (literal meanings) and **connotations** (associated ideas and feelings). • Ask yourself what the connotations of key words show about the subject and the speaker (the voice that says the poem).	**Imagery** • Identify images—descriptions that appeal to one or more of the five senses. • Determine your emotional response to each. • Analyze ways in which images are connected and consider what they show about the poem's subject.
Figurative Language Identify **similes** (comparisons using *like* or *as*), **metaphors** (comparisons in which one thing is spoken of as if it were another), and **personifications** (comparisons giving human characteristics to a nonhuman subject).	**Sound Devices** • Identify any instances of **alliteration** (the repetition of sounds at the beginning of words), **onomatopoeia** (words with sounds that imitate what they name), **repetition** (the reuse of the same word or closely related words), and **rhyme** (the repetition of sounds at the end of words).
Structure Determine the poem's **form** and notice its patterns of elements such as **rhyme,** line breaks, and **stanzas.** • If the poem divides into stanzas, determine the main idea in each.	**Rhythm** • Identify the pattern of stressed and unstressed syllables in each line. • Consider how meter reinforces ideas. • Consider ways in which changes in the rhythm reinforce surprises or shifts in meaning.

Vocabulary Development

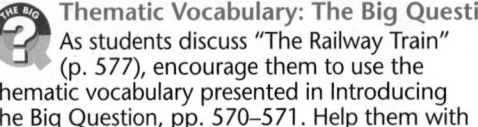

Thematic Vocabulary: The Big Question
As students discuss "The Railway Train" (p. 577), encourage them to use the thematic vocabulary presented in Introducing the Big Question, pp. 570–571. Help them with sentence starters such as these:

1. In "The Railway Train," Dickinson <u>communicates</u> . . .

2. Dickinson shows her excitement for the then-new <u>technology</u> of the train by . . .

3. Dickinson uses vivid images to <u>express</u> . . .

4. The image that <u>contributes</u> most to the impression of the train as an animal is . . .

5. The poem's rhythm <u>enriches</u> the meaning of the experience described by . . .

6. The repeated sounds at the start of words in the first two lines <u>produce</u> . . .

7. If you <u>listen</u> to lines . . .

 EXEMPLAR TEXT

❹ Model

About the Selection Emily Dickinson (1830–1886) lived a quiet life in Amherst, Massachusetts, growing increasingly secluded in her later days. Yet the poetry she wrote was daringly original. She is known for her individualistic use of punctuation and capitalization.

Dickinson lived during the Industrial Revolution, a time marked by the rapid expansion of cities, a great increase in the number of factories, and improved methods of transportation, including the growth of the railroad. During her lifetime, the citizens of Amherst debated whether to construct a train line to the town. This poem offers Dickinson's perceptions of a train.

"The Railway Train" by Emily Dickinson

❺ I like to see it lap the miles,
And lick the valleys up,
And stop to feed itself at tanks;
And then, prodigious, step

❻ 5 Around a pile of mountains,
And supercilious,[1] peer
In shanties by the sides of roads;
And then a quarry[2] pare

To fit its sides, and crawl between,
10 Complaining all the while
❼ In horrid, hooting stanza;
Then chase itself down hill

And neigh like Boanerges;[3]
Then, punctual as a star,
❽ 15 Stop—docile and omnipotent[4]—
At its own stable door.

---

1. **supercilious** (soo′ pər sil′ ē əs) *adj.* full of pride; haughty.
2. **quarry** (kwôr′ ē) *n.* a place where rock for building is mined; a pit or excavation dug in rock.
3. **Boanerges** (bō′ ə nʉr′ jēz′) *n.* a thunderously loud speaker (from the Bible).
4. **docile** (däs′ əl) and **omnipotent** (äm nip′ ə tənt) easy to train or manage and all-powerful.

---

❺ **Sound Devices** Alliteration emphasizes words that help to build an image of a speeding train.

❻ **Structure** Each stanza builds on the comparison of a train to an animal.

❼ **Sound Devices** The poet uses onomatopoeia to suggest the sound of a train's whistle.

❽ **Figurative Language** The words *neigh* and *stable* reinforce the comparison of the train to an animal. The train arrives at the station like a horse returning to its stable after a run.

Literary Analysis Workshop **577**

---

❹ Reading the Model

1. Discuss the About the Selection note. Explain that Dickinson is also known for her use of near, or inexact, rhyme, as in *far/more*.

2. Have students read the poem. Clarify as needed before reviewing the annotations.

❺ Sound Devices

1. Read aloud the annotation. **Ask:** What other alliteration does the first stanza contain?
   Possible response: repeating *s* sounds

2. **Ask:** Which stanzas use near rhyme?
   Answer: They all do: *up/step, peer/pare, while/hill, star/door.*

❻ Structure

Read aloud the annotation. **Ask:** What words help convey this comparison?
Possible response: "feed," "step," "supercilious," "and "peer"

❼ Sound Devices

Read aloud the annotation. **Ask:** What word in the last stanza is onomatopoeic?
Answer: *Neigh* is onomatopoeic.

❽ Figurative Language

1. Read aloud the annotation. **Ask:** Why is the comparison of a horse and a train appropriate?
   Possible response: It is appropriate because trains were replacing horses as a mode of transportation.

2. What simile does line 14 contain?
   Possible response: the simile "punctual as a star"

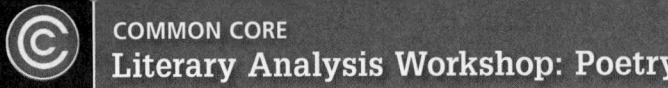
❾ Introducing the Independent Practice

1. Explain that students will analyze three poems by the same poet.

2. Discuss the About the Text notes, and have students read the poems (pp. 578–580). Then, direct them to go back through and respond to the side-column prompts. Conclude by having students answer the After You Read questions on page 581.

❿ Sound Devices

Ask the Sound Devices question.

Answer: It stresses the maestro's tremendous gratitude for the applause he receives.

⓫ Structure

Have students reread lines 6–8. **Ask** the Structure question.

Possible response: The topic shifts from the present—the maestro bowing after a performance—to the past of the maestro's youth.

⓬ Word Choice

Ask the Word Choice questions.

Possible response: It has connotations of capturing with difficulty but pleasure. It suggests that the son enjoyed his parents' music but could reproduce only bits of it.

⓭ Imagery

Ask the Imagery question.

Possible response: It stresses the warmth of his memory and his high opinion of the music he learned from his parents.

❾ Independent Practice

About the Text Born in El Paso, Texas, in 1942, Pat Mora enjoys writing about the Mexican American heritage of the Southwest. Bilingual and bicultural, she writes poetry in English and Spanish and often includes Spanish words and phrases in her English-language poems. "Maestro" was inspired by Mora's conversation with a music professor who conducts a local orchestra. In the conversation, he shared the childhood experiences that nourished his interest in music.

❿ **Sound Devices** What idea is emphasized by the repetition of the words "bows" and "again"?

⓫ **Structure** What shift in topic is marked by the stanza break between lines 6 and 7? Explain.

⓬ **Word Choice** What connotations does the word *snare* have? What do these connotations add to the image of the speaker playing music with his parents?

⓭ **Imagery** What does this final image convey about the speaker's memory of singing and playing music?

"Maestro" by Pat Mora

He hears her
when he **bows**.
❿ Rows of hands clap
again and again he bows
5 to stage lights and upturned faces
but he hears only his mother's voice

⓫ years ago in their small home
singing Mexican songs
one phrase at a time
10 while his father strummed the guitar
or picked the melody with quick fingertips.
Both cast their music in the air
⓬ for him to snare with his strings,
songs of lunas[1] and amor[2]
15 learned bit by bit.
She'd nod, smile, as his bow slid
note to note, then the trio
voz,[3] guitarra,[4] violín[5]
would blend again and again
⓭ 20 to the last pure note
sweet on the tongue.

1. **lunas** (lōō′ näs) *n.* Spanish for "moons."
2. **amor** (ä′ môr′) *n.* Spanish for "love."
3. **voz** (vōs) *n.* Spanish for "voice."
4. **guitarra** (gē tär′ rä) *n.* Spanish for "guitar."
5. **violín** (vē ō lēn′) *n.* Spanish for "violin."

578 Poetry

Vocabulary Development

Vocabulary Knowledge Rating

Create a **Vocabulary Knowledge Rating Chart** (*Professional Development Guidebook,* p. 33) with these words from the selections:

maestro   caress

Give students a copy. Read the words aloud. Have students mark their rating in the Before Reading column. Urge them to be alert to the words as they read and discuss the selections because they will rate their knowledge of the words again after they finish.

Tally how many students think they know the words to gauge how much instruction to provide. As students read, point out the words and their context.

About the Text In describing this poem, Pat Mora has said, "People who don't know the desert may find it bare and frightening. I wanted to show how the desert comforts me."

"The Desert Is My Mother" by Pat Mora

I say feed me.
She serves red prickly pear[1] on a spiked cactus.

I say tease me.
She sprinkles raindrops in my face on a sunny day.

5 I say frighten me.
She shouts thunder, flashes lightning.

I say hold me.
She whispers, "Lie in my arms."

I say heal me.
10 She gives me chamomile, oregano, peppermint.

I say caress me.
She strokes my skin with her warm breath.

I say make me beautiful.
She offers turquoise for my fingers,
15 a pink blossom for my hair.

I say sing to me.
She chants her windy songs.

I say teach me.
She blooms in the sun's glare,
20 the snow's silence,
the driest sand.

The desert is my mother.
El desierto es mi madre.
The desert is my strong mother.

---

1. prickly pear *n.* a species of cactus with sharp spines and an edible fruit.

(14) Imagery To what senses does this description appeal?

(15) Structure How does the speaker use repetition and line breaks to structure the poem? What does this structure suggest about the speaker and the desert?

(16) Figurative Language What type of figurative language does the speaker use? In what way does this figure of speech sum up the exchanges between the speaker and the desert in the preceding lines?

(14) Imagery
1. **Ask** the Imagery question.
   Answer: It appeals to the senses of sight, touch, and taste.
2. **Ask:** Who or what is serving the cactus to the speaker?
   Possible response: The desert is serving, or supplying, it.

(15) Structure
Have students study the beginnings of the first and second lines of the first nine stanzas. **Ask** the Structure questions.

Possible response: In the first line of each stanza, the speaker repeatedly uses "I say" to ask for something; in the rest of each stanza, a repeated "she," meaning the desert, responds. It suggests that the speaker is a child of the desert.

(16) Figurative Language
Ask the Figurative Language questions.

Possible response: A metaphor appears in both English and Spanish. It sums up the idea that the desert, like a mother, has always nurtured the speaker and is part of her heritage.

Literary Analysis Workshop **579**

Enriched Online Student Edition
To have students read the selection in interactive format, with narration and point-of-use interactive graphic organizers, go online at **www.PHLitOnline.com.**

⓱ Structure

1. Have students reread the poem, focusing on words that end in *-ing*. **Ask** the Structure question.

   Possible responses: It adds movement to the poem by creating the effect of dancing. It also shows the progress of the aunt from girlhood to old age.

2. **Ask:** What does the use of so many words ending in *-ing* suggest about the aunt?

   Possible response: She has been an active person, always dancing or moving.

⓲ Imagery

1. Have a student read aloud line 5. **Ask:** What does the imagery suggest about the aunt when she was a young girl in Mexico?

   Possible response: She was attractive and free spirited.

2. Refer students to the highlighted lines 6–8. **Ask** the Imagery question.

   Possible response: Words include "young woman" and "your long, blue dress swaying."

3. **Ask:** What does the imagery in lines 16–17 stress about the aunt?

   Possible response: She is still attractive to the speaker, who loves her very much.

⓳ Word Choice

Ask the Word Choice questions.

Possible responses: *Tottering* connotes being old and shaky. It contrasts with the vibrant, lively dancer of the past, described earlier in the poem.

Practice continued

About the Text In this poem, Pat Mora describes her aunt. Note how Mora inserts Spanish words into the poem. Think about why she might have chosen to do that.

⓱ Structure How does the repetition of words ending in *-ing* help structure the poem?

⓲ Imagery Which words help to create a vivid image of the young girl dancing?

⓳ Word Choice What are the connotations of the word *tottering*? What contrast does it establish between the aunt's movements when she was young and her movements now?

"Bailando"[1] by Pat Mora

I will remember you dancing,
spinning round and round
a young girl in Mexico,
your long, black hair free in the wind,
5 spinning round and round
a young woman at village dances
your long, blue dress swaying
to the beat of La Varsoviana,[2]
smiling into the eyes of your partners,
10 years later smiling into my eyes
when I'd reach up to dance with you,
my dear aunt, who years later
danced with my children,
you, white-haired but still young
15 waltzing on your ninetieth birthday,
more beautiful than the orchid
pinned on your shoulder,
tottering now when you walk
but saying to me, "Estoy[3] bailando,"
20 and laughing.

1. **Bailando** (bī län´ dō) *v.* Spanish for "dancing."
2. **La Varsoviana** (lä bär´ sō byä´ nä) *n.* a lively folk dance.
3. **Estoy** (es toī´) *adj.* Spanish for "I am."

Vocabulary Development

Vocabulary Knowledge Rating

When students have completed reading and discussing the poems, have them take out their **Vocabulary Knowledge Rating Chart** for these selections. Read the words aloud once more and have students rate their knowledge of the words again in the After Reading column. Clarify the words if still problematic.

Have students write their own definitions or examples in the appropriate column. Encourage students to use the words in further discussion and written work about this selection.

After You Read

Maestro • The Desert Is My Mother • Bailando

1. Key Ideas and Details (a) Explain what scene is described in lines 1–5 of "Maestro," citing details in support. **(b) Infer:** What does the speaker mean in saying "he hears only his mother's voice" (line 6)? **(c) Infer:** Which is more influential for him—his present audience or his childhood with his family? Explain.

2. Key Ideas and Details Analyze: What effect do the Spanish words contribute to the image of the speaker's childhood in the poem "Maestro"?

3. Craft and Structure (a) Cite: Find one image that appeals to the sense of touch, one that appeals to sight, and one that appeals to hearing in "The Desert Is My Mother." **(b) Analyze:** Do these images help paint an effective picture of the desert? Explain.

4. Key Ideas and Details (a) Infer: In the poem "Bailando," who describes the dancing? **(b) Analyze:** Describe three different times when the aunt dances. How are they connected? How are they different? **(c) Interpret:** What key point does the speaker make using these images of dancing?

5. Craft and Structure Interpret: How does the one-sentence, single-stanza structure of "Bailando" reinforce the ideas in the poem? Support your answer with details from the poem.

6. Craft and Structure (a) Find one example of the use of repetition in each of the three poems. **(b) Analyze:** Choose one of your examples and explain how the repetition conveys an idea or feeling or how it helps to structure the poem.

7. Craft and Structure (a) Analyze: Complete a Venn diagram to analyze **personification** in "The Desert Is My Mother." In one circle, list words that show the desert is like a woman. In the other, list words that describe it as a landscape.

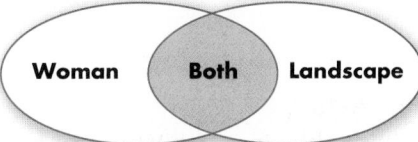

Woman **Both** **Landscape**

(b) Collaborate: Discuss your Venn diagram with a partner, and use your partner's feedback to guide you in revising your diagram.

8. Integration of Knowledge and Ideas (a) Interpret: Choose one of the poems and identify a lesson it suggests about life. **(b) Evaluate:** Explain how well this lesson applies to life generally, giving examples to support your evaluation.

Literary Analysis Workshop **581**

Answers

1. **Possible response: (a)** A musician bows after a performance. "Rows of hands clap," "stage lights," and "bows" suggest the scene. **(b)** He is remembering being young and listening to his mother singing while his father played guitar. **(c)** His childhood is more influential. He wouldn't be where he is today without his mother and father.

2. **Possible response:** They stress the maestro's close family ties and give the image a musical quality.

3. **(a) Possible response:** *Touch*—raindrops in my face; *Sight*—pink blossom; *Hearing*—windy songs. **(b)** Yes, they capture many aspects of the desert.

4. **Possible response: (a)** The dancer's niece describes it. **(b)** She dances as a young girl, a young woman, and an older woman with the speaker's children. **(c)** A beautiful, vibrant person remains special in old age.

5. **Possible response:** It captures the flow of the aunt's life and of the dancing.

6. **Possible response: (a)** *Bows* in the first poem; *I say* in the second; *spinning* in the third. **(b)** The repetition of *I say* creates a statement-and-response structure in which the desert always supplies something to fulfill the speaker's needs.

7. **Possible response: (a)** Left circle—*serves, shouts, whispers, strokes, offers, chants;* Right circle—*spiked cactus, sunny day, thunder and lightning, pink blossoms, windy, sun's glare, driest sand.* **(b)** Students should consider making changes based on their partner's ideas.

8. **Possible response: (a)** In the poem "Bailando," loved ones stay beautiful to us in spite of aging. **(b)** Students should support evaluations with examples.

Assessment Resources

The following resources can be used to assess students' knowledge and skills.

Unit 4 Resources

L1 L2 EL Selection Test A, pp. 17–19

L3 L4 EL Selection Test B, pp. 20–22

L3 L4 Open-Book Test, pp. 14–16

 Students may use the **Self-test**, online at **www.PHLitOnline.com**, to prepare for **Selection Test A** or **Selection Test B**.

Lesson Pacing Guide

DAY 1 Preteach

- ⓒ Administer the Reading and Vocabulary Warm-ups (*Unit 4 Resources,* pp. 23–26 or 41–44) as necessary.
- • Introduce the Reading Skill: Drawing Conclusions.
- ⓒ Introduce the Literary Analysis concept: Forms of Poetry.
- • Distribute copies of the appropriate graphic organizer for the Reading Skill (*Graphic Organizer Transparencies,* pp. 111–113).
- • Distribute copies of the appropriate graphic organizer for Literary Analysis (*Graphic Organizer Transparencies,* pp. 114–116).
- ⓒ Teach the selection vocabulary.
- ⓒ Introduce the Word Study skill.

DAYS 2–3 Preteach/Teach

- ⓒ Build background with the Background feature.
- • Develop thematic vocabulary and thematic thinking with Writing About the Big Question.
- • Prepare students to read with the Activating Prior Knowledge activities (TE).
- • Informally monitor comprehension while students read.
- • Use the Reading Check questions to confirm comprehension.
- • Develop students' ability to pull together several details to arrive at an overall meaning or understanding using the Drawing Conclusions questions.
- ⓒ Develop students' understanding of the forms of poetry using the Forms of Poetry questions.
- ⓒ Reinforce vocabulary with the Vocabulary notes.
- ⓒ Reinforce unit focus standards using the Spiral Review prompts.

DAY 4 Assess

- • Assess students' comprehension and mastery of the skills by having them answer the Critical Thinking, Reading Skill, and Literary Analysis questions.
- ⓒ Have students complete the Vocabulary Practice activities.
- ⓒ Have students complete the Word Study activities.

DAY 5 Extend/Assess

- • Have students complete the Conventions lesson.
- ⓒ Have students complete the Writing activity and write a lyric poem, concrete poem, or haiku. (You may assign as homework.)
- ⓒ Extend learning by having students complete the Speaking and Listening activity, a presentation. As an alternative, assign them "Thinking of You" or "Word on the Wire" in *Reality Central.*
- • Administer Selection Test A or B (*Unit 4 Resources,* pp. 35–40 or 56–61).

ⓒ **Common Core**
State Standards

Reading Literature
5. Analyze how a drama's or poem's form or structure contributes to its meaning.
7. Compare and contrast a written story, drama, or poem to its audio, filmed, staged, or multimedia version, analyzing the effects of techniques unique to each medium.

Writing 4. Produce clear and coherent writing in which the development, organization, and style are appropriate to task, purpose, and audience.
6. Use technology, including the Internet, to produce and publish writing.

Speaking and Listening
1.d. Acknowledge new information expressed by others and, when warranted, modify their own views.

Language 1.a. Explain the function of phrases and clauses in general and their function in specific sentences.
6. Acquire and use accurately grade-appropriate general academic and domain-specific words and phrases; gather vocabulary knowledge when considering a word or phrase important to comprehension or expression.

Additional Standards Practice
Common Core Companion, pp. 41–61

Daily Block Scheduling
Each day in this Lesson Pacing Guide represents a 40–50 minute period. Teachers using block scheduling may combine days to revise pacing. In addition, teachers may differentiate and support core instruction by integrating components for extended and extensive support as students require. See the Guide to Selected Leveled Resources (facing page).

Guide to Selected Leveled Resources

R T I **Tier 1** (students performing on level)		✓ **More Accessible**	✓✓ **More Complex**
		Poetry Collection 1	Poetry Collection 2
Warm Up	**Practice, model,** and **monitor** fluency, working with the whole **class** or **in groups**.	**Vocabulary** and **Reading Warm-ups B**, *Unit 4 Resources*, pp. 23–24, 26	**Vocabulary** and **Reading Warm-ups B**, *Unit 4 Resources*, pp. 41–42, 44
Comprehension/Skills	**Support** and **monitor** comprehension and skills development, having students complete the activities, graphic organizers, and interactive prompts **independently** or **as a class**.	• *Reader's Notebook*, adapted instruction and full selection **EL** *Reader's Notebook: English Learner's Version*, adapted instruction and adapted selection • **Reading Skill Graphic Organizer B**, *Graphic Organizer Transparencies*, p. 113 • **Literary Analysis Graphic Organizer B**, *Graphic Organizer Transparencies*, p. 116	• *Reader's Notebook*, adapted instruction and summary **EL** *Reader's Notebook: English Learner's Version*, adapted instruction and summary • **Reading Skill Graphic Organizer B**, *Graphic Organizer Transparencies*, p. 113 • **Literary Analysis Graphic Organizer B**, *Graphic Organizer Transparencies*, p. 116
Monitor Progress **A**	**Monitor** student progress with the differentiated curriculum-based assessment in the *Unit Resources*.	• **Selection Test B**, *Unit 4 Resources*, pp. 38–40 • **Open-Book Test**, *Unit 4 Resources*, pp. 32–34	• **Selection Test B**, *Unit 4 Resources*, pp. 59–61 • **Open-Book Test**, *Unit 4 Resources*, pp. 53–55

R T I **Tier 2** (students requiring intervention)		✓ **More Accessible**	✓✓ **More Complex**
		Poetry Collection 1	Poetry Collection 2
Warm Up	**Practice, model,** and **monitor** fluency in **groups** or **with individuals**.	• **Vocabulary** and **Reading Warm-ups A**, *Unit 4 Resources*, pp. 23–25 • *Reality Central*, "Thinking of You" • *Hear It!* Audio CD (adapted text)	• **Vocabulary** and **Reading Warm-ups A**, *Unit 4 Resources*, pp. 41–43 • *Reality Central*, "Word on the Wire" • *Hear It!* Audio CD
Comprehension/Skills	• **Support** and **monitor** comprehension and skills development, working in **small groups** or **with individuals**. • **Pair** students with more advanced peers and have them complete the writing activity in the *Real-World Writing Journal*. • As students complete the selection in the appropriate version of the *Reader's Notebook*, **monitor** comprehension frequently with group questions and individual instruction. • **Model** strategies while guiding students in completing the activities and prompts in the *Reader's Notebook*, as well as the graphic organizers. • **Practice** skills and **monitor** mastery with the *Reading Kit* worksheets.	• *Real-World Writing Journal*, Lesson 1, pp. 104–107 • *Reader's Notebook: Adapted Version*, adapted instruction and adapted selection **EL** *Reader's Notebook: English Learner's Version*, adapted instruction and adapted selection • **Reading Skill Graphic Organizer A**, *Graphic Organizer Transparencies*, p. 111 • **Literary Analysis Graphic Organizer A**, *Graphic Organizer Transparencies*, p. 114 • *Reading Kit*, Practice worksheets, pp. 150, 154, 160, 162, 168	• *Real-World Writing Journal*, Lesson 2, pp. 108–111 • *Reader's Notebook: Adapted Version*, adapted instruction and summary **EL** *Reader's Notebook: English Learner's Version*, adapted instruction and summary • **Reading Skill Graphic Organizer A**, *Graphic Organizer Transparencies*, p. 112 • **Literary Analysis Graphic Organizer A**, *Graphic Organizer Transparencies*, p. 115 • *Reading Kit*, Practice worksheets, pp. 150, 154, 160, 162, 168
Monitor Progress **A**	**Monitor** student progress with the differentiated curriculum-based assessment in the *Unit Resources* and in the *Reading Kit*.	• **Selection Test A**, *Unit 4 Resources*, pp. 35–37 • *Reading Kit*, Assess worksheets pp. 151, 155, 161, 163, 169	• **Selection Test A**, *Unit 4 Resources*, pp. 56–58 • *Reading Kit*, Assess worksheets, pp. 151, 155, 161, 163, 169

TIER 3 Tier 3 intervention may require consultation with the student's special-education or dyslexia specialist. For additional support, see the Tier 2 activities and resources listed above.

One-on-one teaching   Group work   Whole class instruction   Independent work   **A** Assessment

For a complete guide to selection support, including support for Advanced students, see the Overview of Resources in the frontmatter.

✓ Poetry Collection 1
✓✓ Poetry Collection 2

RESOURCES FOR:

- **L1** Special-Needs Students
- **L2** Below-Level Students (Tier 2)
- **L3** On-Level Students (Tier 1)
- **L4** Advanced Students (Tier 1)
- **EL** English Learners
- **All** All Students

Vocabulary/Fluency/Prior Knowledge

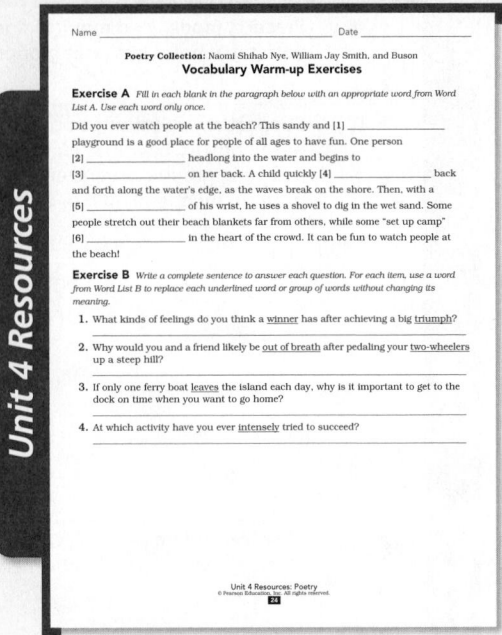

Unit 4 Resources

EL L1 L2 Vocabulary Warm-ups A and B,
pp. 23–24, 41–42

Also available for these selections:

EL L1 L2 Reading Warm-ups A and B,
pp. 25–26, 43–44

All Vocabulary Builder, pp. 30, 48

All Writing About the Big Question,
pp. 27, 45

- **L2 L3** *Reader's Notebook*
- **L1** *Reader's Notebook: Adapted Version*
- **EL** *Reader's Notebook: English Learner's Version*
- **EL** *Reader's Notebook: Spanish Version*

Reader's Notebooks

Pre- and postreading pages for both collections, as well as the selections in Poetry Collection 1, appear in an interactive format in the *Reader's Notebooks*. Each *Notebook* is differentiated for a different group of learners. The selections in the Adapted and English Learner's versions are abridged.

© *Common Core Companion*

Additional instruction and practice for each Common Core State Standard

Selection Support

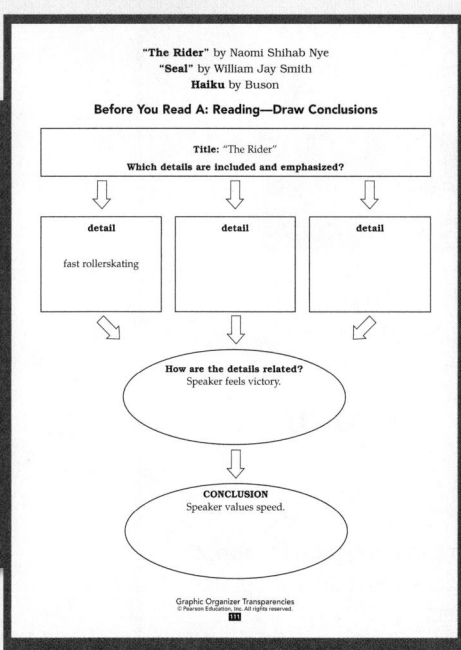

"The Rider" by Naomi Shihab Nye
"Seal" by William Jay Smith
Haiku by Buson

Before You Read A: Reading—Draw Conclusions

Title: "The Rider"
Which details are included and emphasized?

detail	detail	detail
fast rollerskating		

How are the details related?
Speaker feels victory.

CONCLUSION
Speaker values speed.

EL L1 L2 Reading: Graphic Organizer A, pp. 111, 112 (partially filled in)

Also available for these selections:

EL L3 Reading: Graphic Organizer B, p. 113

EL L1 L2 Literary Analysis: Graphic Organizer A, pp. 114, 115 (partially filled in)

EL L3 Literary Analysis: Graphic Organizer B, p. 116

Skills Development/Extension

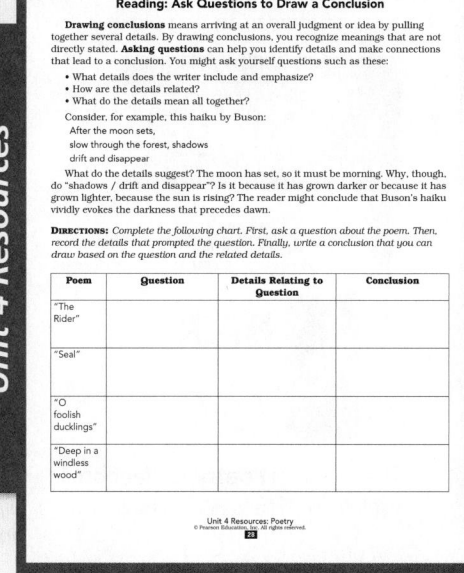

Name _____ Date _____

Poetry Collection: Naomi Shihab Nye, William Jay Smith, Buson
Reading: Ask Questions to Draw a Conclusion

Drawing conclusions means arriving at an overall judgment or idea by pulling together several details. By drawing conclusions, you recognize meanings that are not directly stated. **Asking questions** can help you identify details and make connections that lead to a conclusion. You might ask yourself questions such as these:

• What details does the writer include and emphasize?
• How are the details related?
• What do the details mean all together?

Consider, for example, this haiku by Buson:

After the moon sets,
slow through the forest, shadows
drift and disappear

What do the details suggest? The moon has set, so it must be morning. Why, though, do "shadows / drift and disappear"? Is it because it has grown darker or because it has grown lighter, because the sun is rising? The reader might conclude that Buson's haiku vividly evokes the darkness that precedes dawn.

DIRECTIONS: *Complete the following chart. First, ask a question about the poem. Then, record the details that prompted the question. Finally, write a conclusion that you can draw based on the question and the related details.*

Poem	Question	Details Relating to Question	Conclusion
"The Rider"			
"Seal"			
"O foolish ducklings"			
"Deep in a windless wood"			

All Reading: Drawing Conclusions, pp. 28, 46

Also available for these selections:

All Literary Analysis: Forms of Poetry, p. 29, 47

EL L3 L4 Grammar, p. 50

EL L3 L4 Support for Writing, p. 51

L3 L4 Support for Extend Your Learning, p. 52

L4 Enrichment, pp. 31, 49

Assessment

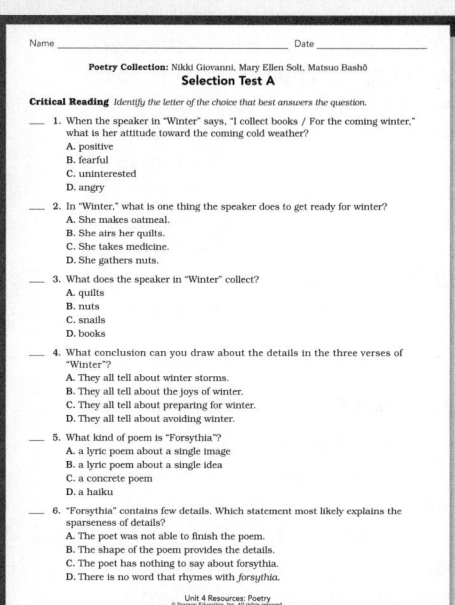

Name _____ Date _____

Poetry Collection: Nikki Giovanni, Mary Ellen Solt, Matsuo Bashō
Selection Test A

Critical Reading *Identify the letter of the choice that best answers the question.*

___ 1. When the speaker in "Winter" says, "I collect books / For the coming winter," what is her attitude toward the coming cold weather?
A. positive
B. fearful
C. uninterested
D. angry

___ 2. In "Winter," what is one thing the speaker does to get ready for winter?
A. She makes oatmeal.
B. She airs her quilts.
C. She takes medicine.
D. She gathers nuts.

___ 3. What does the speaker in "Winter" collect?
A. quilts
B. nuts
C. snails
D. books

___ 4. What conclusion can you draw about the details in the three verses of "Winter"?
A. They all tell about winter storms.
B. They all tell about the joys of winter.
C. They all tell about preparing for winter.
D. They all tell about avoiding winter.

___ 5. What kind of poem is "Forsythia"?
A. a lyric poem about a single image
B. a lyric poem about a single idea
C. a concrete poem
D. a haiku

___ 6. "Forsythia" contains few details. Which statement most likely explains the sparseness of details?
A. The poet was not able to finish the poem.
B. The shape of the poem provides the details.
C. The poet has nothing to say about forsythia.
D. There is no word that rhymes with *forsythia*.

EL L1 L2 Selection Test A, pp. 35–37, 56–58

Also available for these selections:

EL L3 L4 Selection Test B, pp. 38–40, 59–61

L3 L4 Open-Book Test, pp. 32–34, 53–55

Online Resources: All print materials are also available online.

• complete narrated selection text
• a thematically related video with writing prompt
• an interactive graphic organizer
• highlighting feature
• access to all student print resources, adapted to individual student needs
• Spanish and English summaries
• adapted selection translations in Spanish

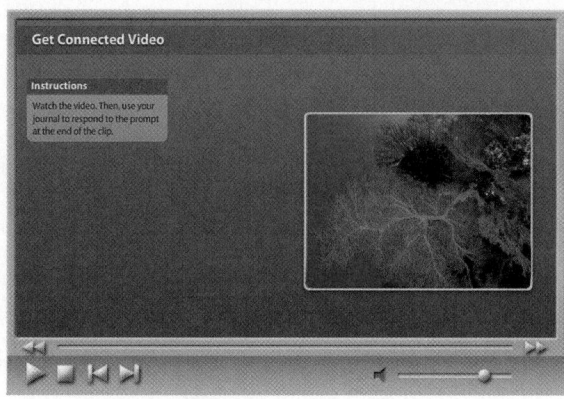

Get Connected! (thematic video with writing prompt)

Also available:

Background Video
All videos are available in Spanish.

Vocabulary Central (tools, activities, and songs for studying vocabulary)

Also available:

Writer's Journal (with graphics feature)

❶ Leveled Texts

You may use either Poetry Collection 1 or Poetry Collection 2 to meet the lesson objectives. Skills instruction for both selections appears on page 583. Choose one selection to teach (or choose to teach both). The Text Complexity Rubric at the bottom of this page will help you determine which selection is more appropriate for your students. Use the Reader and Task Suggestions on the facing page to help all students read text of increasing complexity.

❷ ⓒ Introducing the CCS Standards

Introduce the standards on the student page. (Note that the lesson element with which each standard is addressed is identified in parentheses after the text of the standard.) Call out the standards that you will cover with the selections, explaining to students what each requires and how they will address it as they work through the selection you have chosen. Standards labeled "Spiral Review" are introduced in the Literary Analysis Workshop for this unit.

Before You Read

Poetry Collection 1 • Poetry Collection 2

❶ ⓒ Leveled Texts

Build your skills and improve your comprehension of poetry with texts of increasing complexity.

The poems in **Poetry Collection 1** explore loneliness and nature.

The poems in **Poetry Collection 2** present ideas about animals, plants, and flowers.

❷ ⓒ Common Core State Standards

Meet these standards with either **Poetry Collection 1** (p. 586) or **Poetry Collection 2** (p. 594).

Reading Literature

5. Analyze how a drama's or poem's form or structure contributes to its meaning. (Literary Analysis: Forms of Poetry)

7. Compare and contrast a written story, drama, or poem to its audio, filmed, staged, or multimedia version, analyzing the effects of techniques unique to each medium. (Speaking and Listening: Presentation)

Writing

4. Produce clear and coherent writing in which the development, organization, and style are appropriate to task, purpose, and audience. (Writing: Lyric Poem, Concrete Poem, or Haiku)

6. Use technology, including the Internet, to produce and publish writing. (Writing: Lyric Poem, Concrete Poem, or Haiku)

Speaking and Listening

1.d. Acknowledge new information expressed by others and, when warranted, modify their own views. (Speaking and Listening: Presentation)

Language

1.a. Explain the function of phrases and clauses in general and their function in specific sentences. (Conventions: Infinitives and Infinitive Phrases)

6. Acquire and use accurately grade-appropriate general academic and domain-specific words and phrases; gather vocabulary knowledge when considering a word or phrase important to comprehension or expression. (Vocabulary: Word Study)

ⓒ Text Complexity Rubric: Leveled Texts

Text complexity is determined by both qualitative and quantitative measures. For this reason, the quantitative measure of a more complex collection may be lower than that of a more accessible collection.

		✓ **Poetry Collection 1**	✓✓ **Poetry Collection 2**
Qualitative Measures	**Context/Knowledge Demands**	Lyric poem, concrete poem, traditional haiku 1 ② 3 4 5	Lyric poem, concrete poem, traditional haiku 1 ② 3 4 5
	Structure/Language Conventionality and Clarity	On-level vocabulary; some terms not footnoted; mostly informal tone 1 ② 3 4 5	Subject-specific words in "Forsythia"; informal tone in "Winter"; haiku has formal but accessible tone 1 2 ③ 4 5
	Levels of Meaning/ Purpose/Concept Level	Accessible concept (images of bicycling, a swimming seal, and nature) 1 2 ③ 4 5	Challenging concept (images of winter preparations, forsythia blooming, and nature) 1 2 3 ④ 5
Quantitative Measures	**Text Length**	Word Count: 81, 111, 41	Word Count: 46, 10, 36
	Lexile	NP	NP
Overall Complexity		✓ **More accessible**	✓✓ **More complex**

Reading Skill: Drawing Conclusions

The techniques an author uses in poetry may require readers to think critically to determine meaning. **Drawing conclusions** means arriving at an overall meaning or understanding by pulling together several details. Drawing conclusions helps you recognize ideas that are not directly stated.

Asking questions like the ones that follow can help you identify details and make connections that lead to a conclusion.

- What details does the writer include and emphasize?
- How are the details related? Is there a pattern?
- What do the details mean all together?

Using the Strategy: Conclusions Map

Use a **conclusions map** like the one below to record details from the poems and draw conclusions from the details.

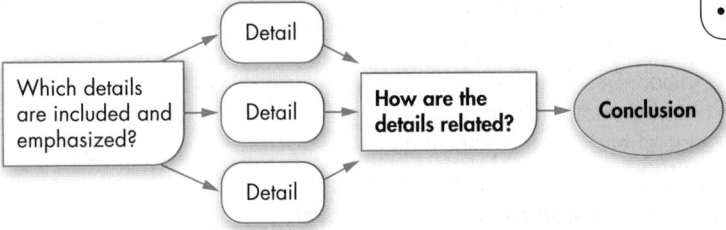

Literary Analysis: Forms of Poetry

There are many different **forms of poetry.** Each form has specific rules that guide the structure of a poem and contribute to its meaning.

- A **lyric poem** expresses the poet's thoughts and feelings about a single image or idea in vivid, musical language.
- In a **concrete poem,** the poet arranges the letters and lines to create a visual image that suggests the poem's subject.
- **Haiku** is a traditional form of Japanese poetry that is often about nature. The first line always has five syllables, the second line has seven syllables, and the third line has five syllables.

❸ Reading Skill
Drawing Conclusions

1. Introduce the skill, using the instruction on the student page.
2. Tell students that they will draw conclusions as they read.

❹ Using the Strategy

Give students a copy of either **Reading Skill Graphic Organizer A** or **B** (*Graphic Organizer Transparencies,* pp. 111–113) to draw conclusions as they read. Use the examples in **Reading Skill Graphic Organizer A**, which is partially filled in, to model the process of completing the organizer.

❺ Literary Analysis
Forms of Poetry

1. Introduce the skill, using the instruction on the student page.
2. Tell students that they will note poetic forms as they read.

Think Aloud: Model the Skill

Model a way to identify different forms of poetry. Say to students:

I use these reminders to help me identify different forms of poetry. A lyric poem is like a song lyric. It uses vivid, musical language. In a concrete poem, I can see the structure as I can see concrete blocks in a wall. The word *haiku* has five letters just as an actual haiku has five syllables in the first and third lines. Remembering a poem's form helps me know what to expect from its content.

© Text Complexity: Reader and Task Suggestions

✓ Poetry Collection 1		✓✓ Poetry Collection 2	
Preparing to Read the Text	**Leveled Tasks**	**Preparing to Read the Text**	**Leveled Tasks**
• Using the Background information on TE p. 585, discuss the history of the poetic forms of concrete poetry and haiku. • Ask students to think about how poets use figurative language to create vivid images. • Guide students to use Multidraft Reading strategies (TE p. 585).	*Levels of Meaning* If students will have difficulty understanding the poems' meanings, have them first read to identify the subject of each poem. Then, have them reread to identify language that describes these subjects. *Analyzing* If students will not have difficulty with the poems' meanings, have them read to identify vivid verbs used in the poems and to explain why the poets would have chosen these words.	• Using the Background information on TE p. 593, discuss the images associated with the seasons of winter and spring. • Ask students why a poet would arrange the lines of a poem in unusual ways. • Guide students to use Multidraft Reading strategies (TE p. 593).	*Levels of Meaning* If students will have difficulty with the poems' imagery, have them read to identify key images. Then, have them reread and describe the images based on language in the poems. *Evaluating* If students will not have difficulty with the poems' imagery, have them identify images that appeal to different senses and explain why a poet would use those images.

❶ ⁇ Writing About the Big Question

1. Review the assignment with the class.

2. Remind students that poetry communicates with vivid images rather than complete explanations of ideas.

3. Have students complete the sentence starters. Review responses as a class. (**Sample responses:** Writers might use poetry as a way to <u>communicate</u> because it allows them to focus on description instead of storytelling. Through poetry, writers can <u>express</u> their emotions.)

4. Remind students that their answers will help them think about the Big Question, "What is the best way to communicate?"

While You Read

Tell students that as they read, they should look for ways that the writers arrange words to create a picture or feeling.

❷ Vocabulary

1. Have students preview the collection vocabulary.

2. For each word, have students say the word aloud.

3. Then, use the word in a sentence that defines the word.

4. Finally, repeat your definitional sentence or a similar sentence with the word missing and have the class "fill in the blank" chorally. Here are some examples:

Something that is <u>luminous</u> gives off light. When we can see fish glowing in the dark water, we can call them [students say "luminous"].

A <u>swerve</u> is a curving motion, usually sudden. Anna avoided the tree by turning her bicycle, making a sudden [students say "swerve"].

❸ Word Study

1. Introduce the skill, using the instruction in the box.

2. Ask students to use the word *luminous* in a meaningful sentence. (**Sample answer:** Her face was *luminous* in the soft glow from the fireplace.)

Making Connections
Poetry Collection 1

The Rider •
Seal •
Haiku

⁇ What is the best way to *communicate?*

❶ Writing About the Big Question

In Poetry Collection 1, three poets use patterns of sounds and words to share their thoughts or observations. Use these sentence starters to develop your ideas about the Big Question.

> Writers might use poetry as a way to **communicate** because it allows them to _____.
> Through poetry, writers can **express** _____.

While You Read Look for ways that each writer arranges words to create a picture or feeling. Later, you can evaluate or judge each author's success in communicating meaning.

❷ Vocabulary

Read each word and its definition. Decide whether you know the word well, know it a little bit, or do not know it at all. After you read, see how your knowledge of each word has increased.

- **translates** (trans′ lāts) *v.* expresses the same thing in another form (p. 586) *I am not sure how well the thoughtful novel <u>translates</u> to the big screen.* translated *v.* translator *n.*

- **luminous** (loo′ mə nəs) *adj.* giving off light (p. 586) *The <u>luminous</u> moon stood out in the dark sky.* luminosity *n.*

- **minnow** (min′ ō) *n.* small fish (p. 589) *His tank was home to one <u>minnow</u> and three catfish.* minnows *n.*

- **swerve** (swʉrv) *n.* curving motion (p. 589) *With a <u>swerve</u>, the skater avoided hitting me.* swerve *v.* swerving *v.*

- **utter** (ut′ ər) *v.* speak (p. 589) *The shy boy refused to <u>utter</u> a word.* utterance *n.*

- **weasel** (wē′ zəl) *n.* small mammal that eats rats, mice, birds, and eggs (p. 590) *The <u>weasel</u> chased the rabbit but failed to catch it.* weaselly *adj.*

❸ Word Study

The **Latin root -*lum*-** means "light."

In "The Rider," the speaker sees flowers with **luminous,** or brightly lit, petals.

584 Poetry

Vocabulary Development

Vocabulary Knowledge Rating
Create a **Vocabulary Knowledge Rating Chart** (*Professional Development Guidebook,* p. 33) for this collection. Include the collection vocabulary and the Big Question words that appear in the Writing About the Big Question sentence starters on this page. (The Big Question vocabulary is introduced on pp. 570–571.)

Give students a copy of the chart. Read the words aloud, and have students mark their rating in the Before Reading column. Urge them to be alert to these words as they read and discuss the collection.

Tally how many students think they know a word to gauge how much instruction to provide. As students read and discuss the collection, point out the words and their context.

Meet the Authors

Naomi Shihab Nye

(b. 1952)

Author of "The Rider" (p. 586)

As a teenager, Naomi Shihab Nye probably felt the loneliness she describes in this poem. When Nye was fourteen, her family moved from Missouri to the Middle East. Though she now values learning about her Arab heritage, the move was not easy. Nye has published volumes of poetry as well as books for children.

William Jay Smith

(b. 1918)

Author of "Seal" (p. 588)

William Jay Smith was born in Winnfield, Louisiana. He has taught college students, written poetry and essays, translated Russian and French poetry, and even served in the Vermont State Legislature for two years. Like "Seal," many of Smith's poems show that poetry can be pure and simple—and fun.

Buson

(1716–1784)

Author of "Haiku" (p. 590)

Japanese poet Buson was not only a skilled writer of haiku, but also a talented painter. His love of color and interest in the visual world are reflected in much of his poetry. At age thirty-six, Buson became the "master" at the haiku school in Kyoto, Japan. When a student asked him to reveal the secret of haiku, Buson responded, "Use the commonplace to escape the commonplace."

Poetry Collection 1 **585**

 Daily Bellringer

For each class during which you teach this collection, have students complete one of the five Quick Write activities for Week 19 in the *Daily Bellringer Activities* booklet.

Background

- **"Seal"** Some historians trace the beginnings of concrete poetry all the way back to ancient Greece and the work of Apollinaire in his *Calligrammes.* Others say that one could read these ancient poems aloud and still appreciate their meaning, whereas a true concrete poem loses meaning without the visual layout.

- **Haiku** The Japanese form of haiku became popular in America during the mid-twentieth century. Interest had begun nearly a century earlier when trade with Japan began. Around 1900, that interest grew as Japanese poetry influenced American and British poets in the Imagist movement. As American soldiers returned from Japan after World War II, they also brought awareness of Japanese culture such as haiku. During the 1950s and 1960s, American poets began to write haiku in greater numbers, leading to the establishment of the American Haiku Society in 1968.

Multidraft Reading

To assist struggling readers and to deepen reading for all, apply multidraft reading protocols. For each reading, have students set the purpose indicated:

- **First reading**—identifying key ideas and details and answering any Reading Checks.
- **Second reading**—analyzing craft and structure and responding to the side-column prompts.
- **Third reading**—integrating knowledge and ideas, connecting to other texts and the world, and answering the end-of-selection questions.

For more guidance, refer to the *Classroom Strategies and Teaching Routines* card on multidraft reading.

For more about the author or practice with the selection vocabulary, go online at www.PHLitOnline.com.

❶ Activating Prior Knowledge

1. Prepare an **Anticipation Guide** (*Professional Development Guidebook,* p. 38) with the following statements:
   - Poetry is the best way to express one's deepest feelings.
   - Poetry is difficult to read and understand.
   - Poets see the world differently from other people.
   - Poetry focuses only on serious issues or deep thoughts.

2. Give students a copy of the prepared **Anticipation Guide** and have students mark their responses in the Me column. Have students discuss the statements in pairs or groups and mark the Guide again in the Group column.

3. For further guidance, use the *Classroom Strategies and Teaching Routines* card on **Anticipation Guides.**

Concept Connector ➡

Students will return to the **Anticipation Guide** after completing the poems in this collection.

Individual Activity

Tell students that text in poems often breaks out of the traditional column form. For example, some lines may be long or short, others may be shaped. Invite students to preview the poems to see the different shapes their lines form. Have students write a sentence telling how each poem's appearance affects their expectations about its content.

❷ About the Selections

In "The Rider," Naomi Shihab Nye wonders if one can ride fast enough to escape loneliness.

In the poem "Seal," William Jay Smith uses a seal's shape to describe the animal as it dives and swims through the water.

The three haiku by Buson express different images and feelings: a pond with ducks, a forest, and a setting moon. In addition to describing these images, the haiku express feelings of scorn, fear, and calm.

❶ ❷ The Rider
Naomi Shihab Nye

Vocabulary
translates (trans´ lāts)
v. expresses the same thing in another form
luminous (lōō´ mə nəs)
adj. giving off light

Forms of Poetry
Whose feelings does the poem express—"a boy's" or the speaker's? Explain.

A boy told me
if he rollerskated fast enough
his loneliness couldn't catch up to him,

5   the best reason I ever heard
for trying to be a champion.

❸   What I wonder tonight
pedaling hard down King William Street
is if it translates to bicycles.

10 A victory! To leave your loneliness
panting behind you on some street corner
while you float free into a cloud of sudden azaleas,
luminous pink petals that have
     never felt loneliness,
no matter how slowly they fell.

586 Poetry

Vocabulary Development
© **CCSS** Language 6

Thematic Vocabulary: The Big Question
As students are discussing "The Rider," "Seal," and "Haiku," encourage them to use the thematic vocabulary presented in Introducing the Big Question, pp. 570–571. You might encourage them with sentence starters like these:

1. The "The Rider," the poet *communicates* about azaleas by saying they are . . .

2. In "Seal," the seal's movements *communicate* . . .

3. In the haiku, the image of the windless forest helps to *transmit* a feeling of . . .

4. In "Seal," the shape that the poem forms on the page *contributes* . . .

◀ **Critical Viewing** What details of this photograph convey the feelings the poem describes? **[Analyze]**

❸ Forms of Poetry

1. Remind students that a lyric poem expresses the poet's thoughts and feelings about a single image or idea.

2. Point out that a lyric poem uses vivid, musical language to express ideas. Read the poem on page 586 aloud to students. Discuss how the combination of rhythm and word sounds makes the words sound like music.

3. Then, **ask** students to point out words or phrases in "Rider" that strike them as particularly vivid or musical.
   Possible response: Students may like the phrase "while you float free into a cloud of sudden azaleas" because it evokes an image of floating.

4. Have students reread the poem on page 586, focusing on the third stanza. Then, **ask** the Forms of Poetry question.
   Answer: Although the beginning of the poem focuses on the boy's idea about escaping loneliness, the speaker's feelings are expressed. It is the speaker who rides a bicycle really fast and imagines the falling cloud of flower petals.

❹ Critical Viewing

Answer: The bicycle appears blurry in the photograph, which suggests that it is moving really fast, just as the speaker does in the poem. The blurriness creates a feeling of motion as well as a dreamlike atmosphere.

PROFESSIONAL DEVELOPMENT | **Donald Leu**

▼ APPLY THE STRATEGY

Use Internet Workshops Develop an Internet Workshop session to practice effective online reading comprehension skills. Set students the task of learning why poets write poetry, using these steps:
1. Use a search engine to locate information about why poets write poetry. Have students find and read biographical information about specific poets.
2. Use your Internet Workbook to record

responses: (a) What are three reasons poets write poetry? (b) Which makes most sense? Why? (c) What reading strategies did you use for this task?

As students share findings, carefully note the reading skills students used online.
For more of Don Leu's strategies, see his Professional Development essay, pp. 570c–570d.

587

1. Point out that sometimes writers arrange words in a particular way in order to emphasize the ideas they want to communicate.

2. Have students read the first bracketed text on page 589.
   Ask students: What words end each line? What information do they communicate?
   Possible response: The ending words are *dives, zoom,* and *darts.* They communicate information about motion.

3. **Ask:** How does placing these words at the end of lines of varying length help to communicate the poet's ideas? Explain.
   Possible response: Placing them at the end of lines both draws readers' attention to them and also visually suggests motion through the uneven line length. The second line appears to be darting out from between the first and third lines.

588 Poetry

Vocabulary Development

Vocabulary Knowledge Rating
When students have completed reading and discussing the poems in this set, have them take out their **Vocabulary Knowledge Rating Chart** for the poems. Read the words aloud and have students rate their knowledge of the words again in the After Reading column. Clarify any words that are still problematic. Have students write their own definition and example or sentence in the appropriate column. Then, have students complete the Vocabulary Practice activities at the end of the selection. Encourage students to use the words in further discussion and written work about the poems. Remind them that they will be accountable for these words on the **Selection Test,** *Unit 4 Resources,* pp. 35–37 or pp. 38–40.

Seal

WILLIAM JAY SMITH

5

See how he dives
  From the rocks with a zoom!
    See how he darts
      Through his watery room
5   Past crabs and eels
      And green seaweed,
      Past fluffs of sandy
      Minnow feed![1]
        See how he swims
10   With a swerve and a twist,
      A flip of the flipper,
      A flick of the wrist!
      Quicksilver-quick,
      Softer than spray,
15   Down he plunges
      And sweeps away;
      Before you can think,
      Before you can utter
      Words like "Dill pickle"
20   Or "Apple butter,"
      Back up he swims
      Past Sting Ray and Shark,
      Out with a zoom,
      A whoop, a bark;
25   Before you can say
        Whatever you wish,
          He plops at your side
            With a mouthful of fish!

6

---

1. **feed** (fēd) *n.* tiny particles that minnows feed on.

Forms of Poetry

Why might the poet have arranged the lines of the poem this way?

Vocabulary

minnow (min ō) *n.* small fish

swerve (swʉrv) *n.* curving motion

Vocabulary

utter (ut´ ər) *v.* speak

7 ◀ **Critical Viewing**
What details in this photograph remind you of the poem? **[Analyze]**

6 **Forms of Poetry**

1. Have students look at the poem on page 589 as it appears on the page and discuss its shape before they begin to read. Then have them read the longer bracketed passage.

2. Draw students' attention to the lines of the poem, beginning with "See how he swims." Then **ask** students how the shape of the poem relates to its content. **Answer:** The shape of the poem mimics the shape of a swimming seal.

3. **Ask** students the Forms of Poetry question. **Answer:** The poet arranged the lines this way in order to suggest the shape of the seal. The shape of the poem illustrates the seal's actions, as described by the speaker.

▶ **Monitor Progress:** Ask students to identify what type of poem "Seal" is and to explain how they know.

▶ **Reteach:** If students have difficulty identifying why "Seal" is a concrete poem, lead students back to the description of the poetry forms on p. 583. Reinforce the idea of concrete poetry by asking students what shapes or forms the other poems in the set might have taken. Students may suggest a bicycle wheel for "The Rider" and a falling leaf for the haiku.

7 **Critical Viewing**

Answer: The seal in the photograph has a smooth, curvy shape, just like the lines of the poem. It is also darting and twisting as the poem describes a seal doing.

Concept Connector

Writing About the Big Question
Have students compare the sentence starters they completed before reading the collection with their ideas afterward. Ask them to explain whether their thoughts have changed.

Reading Skill Graphic Organizer
Ask students to review the graphic organizer in which they identified details and used them as the basis for their conclusions. Then, have students share the graphic organizers they completed and compare their findings.

Anticipation Guide
Have students return to their **Anticipation Guides** and respond to the statements again in the After Reading column. They may do this individually or in their original pairs or groups. Then, lead a class discussion, probing for what students have learned that confirms or invalidates each statement. Encourage students to cite specific details, quotations, or other evidence from the text to support their responses to each statement.

Spiral Review

Words and Phrases

1. Remind students that they studied the concept of words and phrases in the Unit 4 Literary Analysis Workshop (pp. 572–581).

2. **Ask** the Spiral Review question.

   Possible response: "Windless" is an essential word because nothing is moving.

❽ Draw Conclusions

1. **Ask** students what subject matter all three haiku share.
   Answer: All three haiku are about nature. Recall that traditional haiku are about nature.

2. Have students reread the first haiku. Then, **ask** the Draw Conclusions question.
   Possible response: The speaker is worried about the ducklings being eaten by the weasel.

ASSESS

Answers

Critical Thinking

Remind students to support their answers with evidence from the text.

1. (a) Rollerskating and bicycling are discussed in the poem. (b) They are both physical activities that involve wheels and speed.

2. (a) **Possible response:** *dives, zoom, swerve, twist, flip, flick, plunges, sweeps,* and *plops.*
   (b) **Possible response:** The mood is lively and lighthearted.

3. (a) The speaker warns the ducks about the weasel. (b) The speaker does not think the ducks are very wise.

4. ![icon] (a) Students' answers will vary, but should be supported.
   (b) **Possible response:** The form of a poem can communicate movement. For example, the way "Seal" looks on the page is like the movement a seal makes. Also the form of a poem can communicate how a person is feeling. "The Rider" communicates the thoughts of one person.

590

Spiral Review
Words and Phrases
Why is the "windless" detail essential to the central idea of the second haiku?

Vocabulary
weasel (wē′ zəl) *n.* small mammal that eats rats, mice, birds, and eggs

Draw Conclusions
What is the speaker in the first haiku worried about?

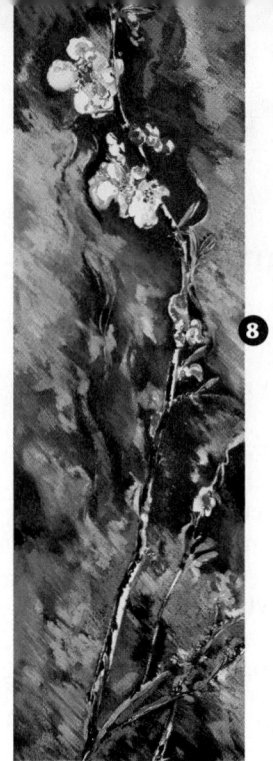

HAIKU
BUSON

❽ O foolish ducklings,
you know my old green pond is
watched by a **weasel**.

Deep in a windless
wood, not one leaf dares to move. . . .
Something is afraid.

After the moon sets,
slow through the forest, shadows
drift and disappear.

Critical Thinking

Cite textual evidence to support your responses.

© 1. **Key Ideas and Details (a)** What two sports are discussed in "The Rider"? **(b) Compare:** What do the two sports have in common?

© 2. **Craft and Structure (a)** Identify six words that describe the movement of the seal in "Seal." **(b) Infer:** How would you describe the mood or feeling that these words create?

© 3. **Key Ideas and Details (a)** In the first haiku, what does the speaker warn the ducklings about? **(b) Analyze:** How would you describe the speaker's attitude toward the ducks?

© 4. **Craft and Structure (a)** Which techniques or words help to convey ideas, pictures, or feelings most successfully?
(b) How does form or structure help to communicate a poem's meaning? Explain. *[Connect to the Big Question: What is the best way to communicate?]*

590 Poetry

Assessment Resources

Unit 4 Resources

L1 L2 EL **Selection Test A,** pp. 35–37. Administer Test A to less advanced students.

L3 L4 EL **Selection Test B,** pp. 38–40. Administer Test B to on-level and more advanced students.

L3 L4 **Open-Book Test,** pp. 32–34. As an alternative, give the Open-Book Test.

All **Customizable Test Bank**

All **Self-tests**
Students may prepare for the **Selection Test** by taking the **Self-test** online.

PHLit Online! All resources, including print and video, are available online at www.PHLitOnline.com.

After You Read
Poetry Collection 1

**The Rider •
Seal •
Haiku**

Reading Skill: Draw Conclusions

1. For each poem, ask a question that helps you **draw the conclusion** given. **(a)** The speaker in "The Rider" values speed. **(b)** The seal in "Seal" zooms around quickly. **(c)** The speaker in the haiku values nature.

Literary Analysis: Forms of Poetry

© 2. **Craft and Structure** In a chart like this one, check off the characteristics exhibited by each **poetic form.**

Poem	Characteristics of Poem				
	Musical language	Single image or idea	Thoughts of one speaker	Lines shaped like subject	Three lines; 17 syllables
The Rider (lyric)					
Seal (concrete)					
Haiku (haiku)					

© 3. **Craft and Structure** How is the form of each poem suited to the ideas each one conveys?

Vocabulary

© **Acquisition and Use** Rewrite each sentence using a vocabulary word from page 584.

1. The small brown mammal ate the eggs.
2. The shining moon was visible in the night sky.
3. The sled made a movement to turn at the bottom of the hill.
4. Frozen by stage fright, the actor could not speak a word.
5. Dan was able to speak the English word in Spanish.
6. John saw hundreds of tiny silver fish in the pond.

Word Study Use what you know about the **Latin root -lum-** to explain your answer to each question.

1. Is a *luminary* someone who is unknown?
2. When you switch on a light, does it *illuminate* the room?

Word Study

The **Latin root -lum-** means "light."

Apply It Explain how the root -lum- contributes to the meanings of these words. Consult a dictionary if necessary.
lumen
luminescence

Poetry Collection 1 **591**

Word Study

Sample answers:

1. No; A *luminary* is a person who "<u>radiates light</u>" or is famous.
2. Yes; The root -lum- means "light," and to *illuminate* means to <u>light</u> up.

Word Study: Apply It

Sample answers: A *lumen* is a unit of <u>light</u>. *Luminescence* is the emission of <u>light</u> by a means other than heat.

Reading Skill

1. **Possible responses:** (a) Taken together, what do the details about speed and movement mean? (b) How are the details about the seal's movements related? (c) What kinds of details about nature does the writer emphasize?

Literary Analysis

2. **Possible responses:** "The Rider"—Musical language, Single image or idea, Thoughts of one speaker; "Seal"—Lines shaped like subject; "Haiku"—Thoughts of one speaker, Three lines; 17 syllables.

 For other sample answers, see *Graphic Organizers Transparencies,* **Literary Analysis Graphic Organizer A,** p. 114, and the **Additional Answers** section.

3. **Possible response:** The form of "The Rider" alternates between short and long stanzas, giving a visual and rhythmic hint at the turning of a bicycle's wheels. The final, longer, stanza leaves readers feeling that the poem has sped up like a cyclist. The form of "Seal" mimics the shape and movements of a seal, supporting the poem's ideas. The compact haiku form allows for very focused meditations on natural scenes.

Vocabulary
Acquisition and Use
Sample answers:

1. The <u>weasel</u> ate the eggs.
2. The <u>luminous</u> moon was visible in the night sky.
3. The sled <u>swerved</u> at the bottom of the hill.
4. Frozen by stage fright, the actor could not <u>utter</u> a word.
5. Dan <u>translated</u> the English word into Spanish.
6. John saw hundreds of <u>minnows</u> in the pond.

591

Skills instruction for the Reading Skill and Literary Analysis concepts for this collection appears on p. 583.

❶ ? Writing About the Big Question

1. Review the assignment with the class.

2. Remind students that poetry can communicate by creating pictures in readers' minds.

3. Have students complete the sentence starters. Review responses as a class. (**Sample responses:** Writers might use poetry to <u>speak</u> to readers in a different way because the form offers great freedom. The descriptive language that poets use can <u>enrich</u> their writing because it communicates images so clearly.)

4. Remind students that their answers will help them think about the Big Question, "What is the best way to communicate?"

While You Read

Tell students that as they read, they should look for words and phrases that create pictures in their minds.

❷ Vocabulary

1. Have students preview the collection vocabulary.

2. For each word, have students say the word aloud.

3. Then, use the word in a sentence that defines the word.

4. Finally, repeat your definitional sentence or a similar sentence with the word missing and have the class "fill in the blank" chorally. Here are some examples:

Something that is <u>fragrant</u> has a strong but pleasant scent. When I smelled the scent of roses everywhere, I knew the flowers were very [students say "fragrant"].

A <u>telegram</u> is a short and usually important message sent by electronic code over wires. To wire someone a message is to send it by [students say "telegram"].

❸ Word Study

1. Introduce the skill, using the instruction in the box.

2. Ask students for a *-gram-* word that means a drawing such as a floor plan. (**Answer:** *diagram*)

592

? What is the best way to *communicate?*

❶ Writing About the Big Question

Each poem in Poetry Collection 2 describes an aspect of nature. Use these sentence starters to develop your ideas about the Big Question.

> Writers might use poetry to **speak** to readers in a different way because _____.

> The descriptive language that poets use can **enrich** their writing because it communicates _____.

While You Read Look for words and phrases in these poems that create pictures in your mind. Later, you can evaluate or judge each author's success in communicating meaning.

❷ Vocabulary

Read each word and its definition. Decide whether you know the word well, know it a little bit, or do not know it at all. After you read, see how your knowledge of each word has increased.

- **burrow** (bur′ ō) *v.* dig a hole for shelter (p. 594) *In the winter, turtles <u>burrow</u> in the mud under ponds.* burrow *n.*

- **forsythia** (fôr sith′ ē ə) *n.* shrub with yellow flowers that blooms in early spring (p. 595) *The <u>forsythia</u> blossoms were a welcome sign of spring.*

- **telegram** (tel′ ə gram) *n.* message transmitted by telegraph (p. 595) *The messenger delivered the <u>telegram</u> that arrived from overseas.*

- **fragrant** (frā′ grənt) *adj.* sweet-smelling (p. 596) *The flowers were colorful, but not very <u>fragrant</u>.* fragrance *n.* fragrantly *adv.*

❸ Word Study

The **Greek root *-gram-*** means "write," "draw," or "record."

In "Forsythia," a floral **telegram**, or coded message, announces the arrival of spring.

Vocabulary Development

Vocabulary Knowledge Rating

Create a **Vocabulary Knowledge Rating Chart** (*Professional Development Guidebook,* p. 33) for this collection. Include the collection vocabulary and the Big Question word that appears in the Writing About the Big Question sentence starters on this page. (The Big Question vocabulary is introduced on pp. 570–571.)

Give students a copy of the chart. Read the word aloud, and have students mark their rating in the Before Reading column. Urge them to be alert to this word as they read and discuss the collection.

Tally how many students think they know a word to gauge how much instruction to provide. As students read and discuss the collection, point out the words and their context.

All resources, including print and video, are available online at **www.PHLitOnline.com.**

Meet the Authors

Nikki Giovanni

(b. 1943)

Author of "Winter" (p. 594)

Many of Nikki Giovanni's poems highlight the major events in her life. In "Winter," however, she writes about a universal subject: the changing of the seasons. In addition to being a poet, Giovanni is a college professor who teaches both English literature and African American studies.

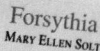
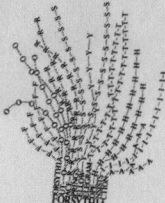

Mary Ellen Solt

(b. 1920)

Author of "Forsythia" (p. 595)

Mary Ellen Solt was born in Iowa. As a writer, she has devoted much of her energy to studying and creating concrete poetry. In the introduction to her book, *Concrete Poetry—A World View*, Solt writes, "[The reader] must now perceive the poem as an object and participate in the poet's act of creating it, for the concrete poem communicates first and foremost its structure."

Matsuo Bashō

(1644–1694)

Author of "Haiku" (p. 596)

Matsuo Bashō was born near Kyoto, Japan. He began studying poetry at an early age and became one of Japan's most famous poets. Along with writing poetry, Bashō taught poetry, served as a noble in the court, and lived in a monastery.

Poetry Collection 2 **593**

593

❶ Activating Prior Knowledge

1. Prepare an **Anticipation Guide** (see *Professional Development Guidebook*, p.38) with the following statements:

   • Poets write only about nature.

   • In poetry, nature is always beautiful and inspiring.

   • Nature poems are an excellent way to explore the world through words.

2. Give students a copy of the prepared **Anticipation Guide** and have them respond in the Me column. Have them discuss the statements in groups and mark the Guides again in the Group column.

3. For further guidance, use the *Classroom Strategies and Teaching Routines* card on **Anticipation Guides.**

Concept Connector ➡

Students will follow up on this activity after completing the poems in Collection 2.

Individual Activity

Tell students that, traditionally, nature has been a great inspiration to poets. Have students write a journal entry about an encounter with nature. What did they learn about nature and about themselves? Ask volunteers to share their thoughts.

❷ About the Selections

"Winter," by Nikki Giovanni, describes activities that help animals and people prepare for winter.

"Forsythia," by Mary Ellen Holt, is a concrete poem that uses letters and words to create an image of a growing plant.

The three haiku by Matsuo Bashō express different images and feelings and evoke surprise and wonder.

❸ Draw Conclusions

1. Read the poem aloud. Remind students to identify key details.

2. **Ask** the Draw Conclusions question.
   Answer: The activities are necessary to prepare to survive the approaching winter.

❶
❷ **WINTER**
NIKKI GIOVANNI

Vocabulary
burrow (bʉr´ ō) *v.* dig a hole for shelter

Draw Conclusions
Why are all the activities described in the poem necessary?

Frogs burrow the mud
snails bury themselves
and I air my quilts
preparing for the cold

5   Dogs grow more hair
❸ mothers make oatmeal
and little boys and girls
take Father John's Medicine[1]

Bears store fat
10   chipmunks gather nuts
and I collect books
For the coming winter

---

1. Father John's Medicine old-fashioned cough syrup.

594 Poetry

Vocabulary Development

Vocabulary Knowledge Rating
When students have completed reading and discussing the poems in the set, have them take out their **Vocabulary Knowledge Rating Chart** for the poems. Read the words aloud and have students rate their knowledge of words again in the After Reading column. Clarify any words that are still problematic. Have students write their own definition and example or sentence in the appropriate column. Then, have students complete the Vocabulary Practice activities at the end of the selection. Encourage students to use the words in further discussion and written work about the poems. Remind them that they will be accountable for these words on the **Selection Test,** *Unit 4 Resources,* pp. 56–58 or pp. 59–61.

Forsythia

MARY ELLEN SOLT

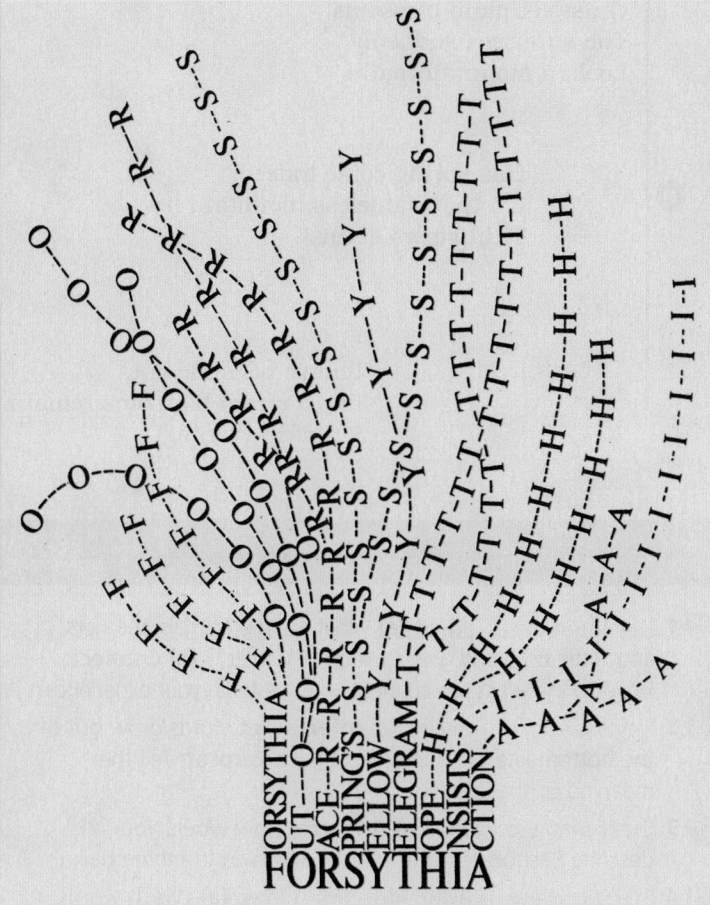

Vocabulary
forsythia (fôr sith´ ē ə) *n.* shrub with yellow flowers that blooms in early spring
telegram (tel´ ə gram) *n.* message transmitted by telegraph

Forsythia
Why might the poet have arranged the words and letters on the page in this way?

Poetry Collection 2 **595**

❻ Forms of Poetry

1. Review the elements of a haiku. Remind students that a haiku has seventeen syllables (five, seven, and five) and three lines. Often, haiku are about nature.

2. Read the three haiku aloud. Then, **ask** the Forms of Poetry question. **Answer:** All three poems have seventeen syllables and three lines. All are about nature, and all express a sense of wonder or surprise.

▶ **Monitor Progress:** Ask students to explain how a lyric poem, a concrete poem, and a haiku are different.

ASSESS

Answers

Critical Thinking

Before students respond, you may wish to have them write a brief objective summary of the collection. As they answer the questions below, remind them to support their answers with evidence from the text.

1. (a) They are preparing for winter. The animals are preparing nests, gathering food, and growing fur or storing fat. The people are taking medicine, making food, or gathering books. (b) Winter is cold, so people need blankets, food, and medicine. Animals need warm shelters and thick fur.

2. (a) The words include: *forsythia, out, race, spring's, yellow, telegram, hope, insists,* and *action.* (b) **Possible response:** The words suggest that forsythia blooms in early spring to announce spring's arrival.

3. **Possible response:** He feels respect for and is in awe of nature.

4. ⬤ **Possible responses:** (a) Students' answers will vary, but should be supported. (b) Students may or may not find the poems meaningful, but they should support their answers.

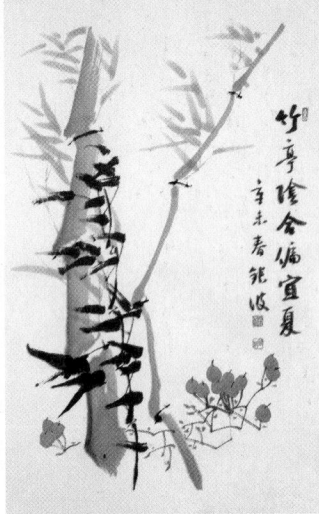

HAIKU
BASHŌ

On sweet plum blossoms
The sun rises suddenly.
Look, a mountain path!

❻

Has spring come indeed?
On that nameless mountain lie
Thin layers of mist.

Temple bells die out.
The fragrant blossoms remain.
A perfect evening!

Forms of Poetry
How are these three poems similar?

Vocabulary
fragrant (frā´ grənt) *adj.* sweet smelling

Critical Thinking

Cite textual evidence to support your responses.

© 1. **Key Ideas and Details (a)** What are the animals, mothers, and "little boys and girls" doing in "Winter"? **(b) Connect:** How do these actions connect with winter in your experience?

© 2. **Key Ideas and Details (a) Infer:** What words grow out of the bottom line of "Forsythia"? **(b) Interpret:** Tell the meaning of these lines.

© 3. **Craft and Structure (a) Analyze:** How would you describe Bashō's attitude toward nature in the three haiku?

© 4. **Integration of Knowledge and Ideas (a)** Which words convey pictures or feelings most successfully? **(b)** Do you think these poems are meaningful for people your age? Explain. *[Connect to the Big Question: What is the best way to communicate?]*

Unit 4 Resources

L1 L2 EL Selection Test A, pp. 56–58. Administer Test A to less advanced students.

L3 L4 EL Selection Test B, pp. 59–61. Administer Test B to on-level and more advanced students.

L3 L4 Open-Book Test, pp. 53–55. As an alternative, give the Open-Book Test.

All Customizable Test Bank

All Self-tests
Students may prepare for the **Selection Test** by taking the **Self-test** online.

PHLit Online! All resources, including print and video, are available online at www.PHLitOnline.com.

After You Read
Poetry Collection 2

Winter •
Forsythia •
Haiku

Reading Skill: Draw Conclusions

1. For each poem, ask a question that helps you **draw the conclusion** given. **(a)** The speaker in "Winter" accepts the changing seasons as part of the natural cycle of life. **(b)** Forsythia grows in a tangled, wild way. **(c)** The speaker in the three haiku values nature.

Literary Analysis: Forms of Poetry

Ⓒ **2. Craft and Structure** On a chart like the one shown, place a checkmark under each characteristic of the **poetic form** that applies.

Poem	Characteristics of Poem				
	Musical language	Single image or idea	Thoughts of one speaker	Lines shaped like subject	Three lines; 17 syllables
Winter (lyric)					
Forsythia (concrete)					
Haiku (haiku)					

Ⓒ **3. Craft and Structure** How is the form of each poem suited to the ideas each one conveys?

Vocabulary

Ⓒ **Acquisition and Use** Rewrite each sentence so it includes a vocabulary word from page 592 and conveys that same basic meaning.

1. A woodchuck tried to dig a hole under our tool shed.
2. Tim sent a message to let us know when he would arrive.
3. A row of yellow flowering bushes lines my driveway.
4. The sweet-smelling lilac bushes are my favorite.

Word Study Use what you know about the **Greek root -gram-** to explain your answer to each question.

1. Is a *diagram* useful if you want to show a stadium layout?
2. If you want to personalize your towels, could you get them *monogrammed*?

Word Study

The **Greek root -gram-** means "write," "draw," or "record."

Apply It Explain how the word root -gram- contributes to the meanings of these words. Consult a dictionary if necessary.

grammar
gramophone
hologram

Word Study: Apply It

Sample answers: *Grammar* is the system of rules used to <u>write</u> correctly. A *gramophone* is a player of sound that has been <u>recorded</u>. A *hologram* is a three-dimensional <u>draw</u>ing.

Reading Skill

1. **Possible responses:** (a) Taken together, what do the details about animals and people preparing for winter mean? (b) How are the words in the poem arranged? (c) Why does the speaker of the haiku celebrate blossoms, spring, and evening?

Literary Analysis

2. **Possible responses:** "Winter"— Musical language, Single image or idea, Thoughts of one speaker; "Forsythia"—Lines shaped like subject; "Haiku"—Thoughts of one speaker, Three lines; 17 syllables

   For other sample answers, see *Graphic Organizer Transparencies,* **Literary Analysis Graphic Organizer A, p. 115,** and the **Additional Answers** section.

3. "Winter" uses a repetitive structure that suits its content about repetitive action. "Forsythia" uses a shaped arrangement of words that suits its images of a plant and of movement. The spare haiku format suits the content of vivid snapshots of nature.

Vocabulary
Acquisition and Use
Sample answers:

1. A woodchuck tried to <u>burrow</u> under our tool shed.
2. Tim sent a <u>telegram</u> to let us know when he would arrive.
3. A row of <u>forsythia</u> lines my driveway.
4. The <u>fragrant</u> lilac bushes are my favorite.

Word Study
Sample answers:

1. Yes; The root -gram- means "draw," and *diagram* means "a simple <u>drawing</u> showing the layout of something."
2. Yes; The root -gram- means "write," and *monogrammed* means "identified with a label, usually of a person's initials." Monogrammed towels would be personalized.

Conventions

1. Introduce the skill, using the instruction on the student page.

2. Discuss the examples in the chart.

Think Aloud: Model the Skill

Model the skill of using infinitives and infinitive phrases. Say to students:

I can add action to sentences by using verb forms as nouns, adjectives, or adverbs. Suppose I want to write about growing food. I can use an infinitive as a noun to say "To grow food is our goal." I can also use an infinitive as an adjective, as in "I can always find some food to grow." I can use an infinitive as an adverb to say, "I am happy to grow food." In these examples, infinitives help readers imagine actions in the sentence.

PH WRITING COACH | Grade 7

Students will find instruction on and practice with infinitives and infinitive phrases in Chapter 19, Section 1.

Practice A

1. The rider wants _to ride (I) away from her loneliness._
2. _To swim (I) wild and free_ like a seal would be thrilling.
3. Weasels like _to eat (I) ducklings._
4. _To keep (I) perfectly still_ is difficult.

Reading Application
Sample answer:

"The Rider"—_To leave_ your loneliness panting behind you . . .

Practice B

Sample answers:

1. _to satisfy hunger;_ adverb; This answer is _to satisfy_ your request.
2. _to read by the fire;_ noun; Mrs. Bentley began _to read_ the rules.
3. _to see the flowers;_ adverb; I can't stand _to see_ people pay so much.
4. _to look at the path;_ adjective; The waiter asked us _to look_ at the menu.

Writing Application

Sample answer: "Winter"—Dogs grow more hair _to help them stay warm._

Integrated Language Skills

Poetry Collections 1 and 2

Conventions: Infinitives and Infinitive Phrases

An **infinitive** is a verb form that acts as a noun, an adjective, or an adverb. An infinitive usually begins with the word _to_.

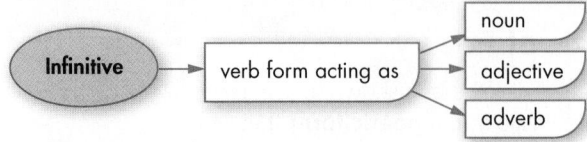

These example sentences show the infinitive in italics.

> **Examples:** _To learn_ is her goal. (noun)
> She is the one _to see._ (adjective)
> Everyone waited _to hear._ (adverb)

An **infinitive phrase** is an infinitive plus its own modifiers or complements. The examples show italicized infinitive phrases acting as different parts of speech.

> **Examples:** _To speak Spanish fluently_ is my goal. (noun)
> She is the one _to see for advice._ (adjective)
> Everyone waited _to hear the news._ (adverb)

Practice A Identify the infinitive and infinitive phrase in each sentence.

1. The rider wants to ride away from her loneliness.
2. To swim wild and free like a seal would be thrilling.
3. Weasels like to eat ducklings.
4. To keep perfectly still is difficult.

© Reading Application In "Poetry Collection 1," find a line of poetry that contains an infinitive. In your own words, explain what an infinitive phrase does.

Practice B Identify the infinitive phrase in each sentence. Determine the function each phrase performs in the sentence. Then, use each infinitive to write a new sentence.

1. In winter, mothers make oatmeal to satisfy hunger.
2. Some people like to read by the fire.
3. I can hardly wait to see the flowers bloom in spring.
4. He wants us to look at the path.

© Writing Application Choose a line in one of the poems in "Poetry Collection 2," and then rewrite it to include an infinitive.

PH WRITING COACH | Further instruction and practice are available in _Prentice Hall Writing Coach._

Poetry Collection 1

Poetry Collection 2

Extend the Lesson

Sentence Modeling

Choose the image given from or associated with the selection students have read:

> A victory! To leave your loneliness / panting behind you on some street corner / while you float free into a cloud of sudden azaleas . . . ("The Rider")
> To warm a room frozen by winter—that is a welcome comfort. (Poetry Collection 2)

Ask students what they notice about the lines. ("The Rider": An exclamation followed by an infinitive phrase explaining it; the connection between the two is made without the use of a verb. Poetry Collection 2: A sentence giving a contrast, followed by an exclamation giving the effect of the contrast.)

Have students imitate the lines in a sentence on a topic of their own choosing, matching each grammatical and stylistic feature discussed. Encourage them to include an infinitive or infinitive phrase. Collect the sentences, and share them with the class.

Writing

 **Poetry** Write a **lyric poem, concrete poem,** or **haiku** to share your thoughts in new, creative ways.

- Pick a subject that interests you. Write the subject in the center of a piece of paper, and create a cluster diagram around it.
- Brainstorm and list vivid descriptions, action words, thoughts, and feelings in a cluster diagram.
- Review the characteristics of each poetic form and decide which form is best suited to your topic. Then, use your notes to draft your poem in the form you have chosen. Add a creative title.
- Use one or more computer programs, such as a word-processing or drawing program, to write and format your poem. Use punctuation, line length, and arrangement to create a desired effect. Publish your poem by posting it on an approved Web site or in your classroom.

Grammar Application Check your writing to be sure you have correctly used all infinitives and infinitive phrases.

Writing Workshop: *Work in Progress*

Prewriting for Exposition For a problem-and-solution essay you may write, list three solutions that might solve a problem caused by cell phone use. Put this Solutions Lists in your writing portfolio.

Speaking and Listening

 Presentation of Ideas In the library or online, find a recording of a poet reading his or her own lyric poetry. Listen to one or more of the poems with a small group of classmates. Then, in a brief **presentation** to your group, tell what you like or do not like about the audio version in comparison with the written poem. Follow these steps to complete the assignment.

- Analyze the effects of hearing the words in comparison with reading them. Support your opinion with specific reasons and examples from the recording.
- Listen carefully to each person's opinions and weigh them against your own.
- With your group, acknowledge new information expressed and discuss whether or not your opinion changed after listening to other responses.

© **Common Core State Standards**

L.7.1.a, L.7.6; W.7.4, W.7.6; SL.7.1.d
[For the full wording of the standards, see page 582.]

Use this prewriting activity to prepare for the **Writing Workshop** on page 640.

www.PHLitOnline.com

- Interactive graphic organizers
- Grammar tutorial
- Interactive journals

Integrated Language Skills **599**

EXTEND/ASSESS

Writing

1. Review the assignment, using the instruction on the student page.
2. To guide students in writing a poem, give them **Support for Writing**, p. 51 in *Unit 4 Resources*.
3. To evaluate students' poems, adapt one of the rubrics for **Poem**, pp. 248–249 in *Professional Development Guidebook.*

Grammar Application

Have students check their drafts to make sure they have used infinitives and infinite phrases correctly.

Six Traits Focus

✔	Ideas	✔	Word Choice
	Organization		Sentence Fluency
✔	Voice		Conventions

PH **WRITING COACH** Grade 7

Students will find further instruction on and practice with description in Chapter 7.

Writing Workshop
Work in Progress

Have students save their completed Solutions Lists in their portfolios. They will use the lists later as they continue this Work-in-Progress assignment (see p. 619). These assignments prepare them to complete the Writing Workshop assignment (see pp. 640–645).

Speaking and Listening

1. Review the assignment, using the instruction on the student page.
2. To support students' work on the assignment, have students complete the **Support for Extend Your Learning** page (*Unit 4 Resources*, p. 52).

Teaching Resources

Unit 4 Resources
- **L3 L4 EL** Integrated Language Skills: Grammar, p. 50
- **L3 L4 EL** Support for Writing, p. 51
- **L3 L4** Support for Extend Your Learning, p. 52
- **L4** Enrichment, p. 49

Enriched Online Student Edition
Available under After You Read for this collection:
- **All** Interactive Grammar Tutorial
- **L3 L4** Internet Research Activity

Professional Development Guidebook
Rubrics for Self-Assessment: Poem: (rhyming), pp. 248–249

PHLit Online! All print and digital resources are available online at **www.PHLitOnline.com**. Online resources accessible to students are noted on the student page.

599

Lesson Pacing Guide

DAY 1 Preteach

- Ⓒ Administer the Reading and Vocabulary Warm-ups (*Unit 4 Resources,* pp. 62–65 or 80–83) as necessary.
- Introduce the Reading Skill: Draw Conclusions.
- Ⓒ Introduce the Literary Analysis concept: Figurative Language.
- Distribute copies of the appropriate graphic organizer for the Reading Skill (*Graphic Organizer Transparencies,* pp. 120–122).
- Distribute copies of the appropriate graphic organizer for Literary Analysis (*Graphic Organizer Transparencies,* pp. 117–119).
- Ⓒ Teach the selection vocabulary.
- Ⓒ Introduce the Word Study skill.

DAYS 2–3 Preteach/Teach

- Ⓒ Build background with the Background feature.
- Develop thematic vocabulary and thematic thinking with Writing About the Big Question.
- Prepare students to read with the Activating Prior Knowledge activities (TE).
- Informally monitor comprehension while students read.
- Use the Reading Check questions to confirm comprehension.
- Develop students' ability to pull together several details to arrive at an overall meaning or understanding using the Drawing Conclusions questions.
- Ⓒ Develop students' understanding of figurative language using the Figurative Language questions.
- Ⓒ Reinforce vocabulary with the Vocabulary notes.
- Ⓒ Reinforce unit focus standards using the Spiral Review prompts.

DAY 4 Assess

- Assess students' comprehension and mastery of the skills by having them answer the Critical Thinking, Reading Skill, and Literary Analysis questions.
- Ⓒ Have students complete the Vocabulary Practice activities.
- Ⓒ Have students complete the Word Study activities.

DAY 5 Extend/Assess

- Have students complete the Conventions lesson.
- Ⓒ Have students complete the Writing activity and write a metaphor. (You may assign as homework.)
- Ⓒ Extend learning by having students complete the Research and Technology activity, a scientific explanation. (You may assign as homework.) As an alternative, assign them "A Show of Strength" or "The Big Money" in *Reality Central.*
- Administer Selection Test A or B (Unit 4 Resources, pp. 74–79 or 95–100).

Ⓒ Common Core State Standards

Reading Literature 4. Determine the meaning of words and phrases as they are used in a text, including figurative and connotative meanings; analyze the impact of rhymes and other repetitions of sounds on a specific verse or stanza of a poem or section of a story or drama.

Writing 2. Write informative/explanatory texts to examine a topic and convey ideas, concepts, and information through the selection, organization, and analysis of relevant content.
2.d. Use precise language and domain-specific vocabulary to inform about or explain the topic. (*Writing: Metaphor*)
7. Conduct short research projects to answer a question, drawing on several sources.

Speaking and Listening 5. Include multimedia components and visual displays in presentations to clarify claims and findings and emphasize salient points. (*Research and Technology: Scientific Explanation*)

Language 1.a. Explain the function of phrases and clauses in general and their function in specific sentences. (*Conventions: Appositives and Appositive Phrases*)
6. Acquire and use accurately grade-appropriate general academic and domain-specific words and phrases.

Additional Standards Practice
Common Core Companion, pp. 41–61

Daily Block Scheduling
Each day in this Lesson Pacing Guide represents a 40–50 minute period. Teachers using block scheduling may combine days to revise pacing. In addition, teachers may differentiate and support core instruction by integrating components for extended and intensive support, as students require. See the Guide to Selected Leveled Resources (facing page).

Guide to Selected Leveled Resources

RTI Tier 1 (students performing on level)	✓ **More Accessible** *from* Poetry Collection 3	✓✓ **More Complex** Poetry Collection 4
Warm Up Practice, **model,** and **monitor** fluency, working with the **whole class** or **in groups.**	**Vocabulary** and **Reading Warm-ups B,** *Unit 4 Resources,* pp. 62–63, 65	**Vocabulary** and **Reading Warm-ups B,** *Unit 4 Resources,* pp. 80–81, 83
Comprehension/Skills **Support** and **monitor** comprehension and skills development, having students complete the activities, graphic organizers, and interactive prompts **independently** or **as a class.**	• *Reader's Notebook,* adapted instruction and full selection **EL** *Reader's Notebook: English Learner's Version,* adapted instruction and adapted selection • **Reading Skill Graphic Organizer B,** *Graphic Organizer Transparencies,* p. 122 • **Literary Analysis Graphic Organizer B,** *Graphic Organizer Transparencies,* p. 119	• *Reader's Notebook,* adapted instruction and summary **EL** *Reader's Notebook: English Learner's Version,* adapted instruction and summary • **Reading Skill Graphic Organizer B,** *Graphic Organizer Transparencies,* p. 122 • **Literary Analysis Graphic Organizer B,** *Graphic Organizer Transparencies,* p. 119
Monitor Progress **Monitor** student progress with the differentiated curriculum-based assessment in the *Unit Resources.*	• **Selection Test B,** *Unit 4 Resources,* pp. 77–79 • **Open-Book Test,** *Unit 4 Resources,* pp. 71–73	• **Selection Test B,** *Unit 4 Resources,* pp. 98–100 • **Open-Book Test,** *Unit 4 Resources,* pp. 92–94
Assess Screen **Assess** student progress using Benchmark Test 2.	• **Benchmark Test 7,** *Unit 4 Resources,* pp. 120–125	• **Selection Test 7,** *Unit 4 Resources,* pp. 120–125

RTI Tier 2 (students requiring intervention)	✓ **More Accessible** *from* Poetry Collection 3	✓✓ **More Complex** Poetry Collection 4
Warm Up Practice, **model,** and **monitor** fluency in **groups** or **with individuals.**	• **Vocabulary and Reading Warm-ups A,** *Unit 4 Resources,* pp. 62–64 • *Reality Central,* "A Show of Strength" • *Hear It!* **Audio CD** (adapted text)	• **Vocabulary and Reading Warm-ups A,** *Unit 4 Resources,* pp. 80–82 • *Reality Central,* "The Big Money" • *Hear It!* **Audio CD**
Comprehension/Skills • **Support** and **monitor** comprehension and skills development, working in **small groups** or **with individuals.** • **Pair** students with more advanced peers and have them complete the writing activity in the *Real-World Writing Journal.* • As students complete the selection in the appropriate version of the *Reader's Notebook,* **monitor** comprehension frequently with group questions and individual instruction. • **Model** strategies while guiding students in completing the activities and prompts in the *Reader's Notebook,* as well as the graphic organizers. • **Practice** skills and **monitor** mastery with the *Reading Kit* worksheets.	• *Real-World Writing Journal,* Lesson 3, pp. 112–115 • *Reader's Notebook: Adapted Version,* adapted instruction and adapted selection **EL** *Reader's Notebook: English Learner's Version,* adapted instruction and adapted selection • **Reading Skill Graphic Organizer A,** *Graphic Organizer Transparencies,* p. 120 • **Literary Analysis Graphic Organizer A,** *Graphic Organizer Transparencies,* p. 117 • *Reading Kit,* Practice worksheets, pp. 150, 156, 160, 164, 170	• *Real-World Writing Journal,* Lesson 4, pp. 116–119 • *Reader's Notebook: Adapted Version,* adapted instruction and summary **EL** *Reader's Notebook: English Learner's Version,* adapted instruction and summary • **Reading Skill Graphic Organizer A,** *Graphic Organizer Transparencies,* p. 121 • **Literary Analysis Graphic Organizer A,** *Graphic Organizer Transparencies,* p. 118 • *Reading Kit,* Practice worksheets, pp. 150, 156, 160, 164, 170
Monitor Progress **Monitor** student progress with the differentiated curriculum-based assessment in the *Unit Resources* and in the *Reading Kit.*	• **Selection Test A,** *Unit 4 Resources,* pp. 74–76 • *Reading Kit,* Assess worksheets pp. 151, 157, 161, 165, 171	• **Selection Test A,** *Unit 4 Resources,* pp. 95–97 • *Reading Kit,* Assess worksheets, pp. 151, 157, 161, 165, 171
Assess Screen **Assess** student progress using Benchmark Test.	• **Benchmark Test 7,** Unit 4 *Resources,* pp. 120–125	• **Selection Test A,** *Unit 4 Resources,* pp. 120–125

TIER 3 Tier 3 intervention may require consultation with the student's special-education or dyslexia specialist. For additional support, see the Tier 2 activities and resources listed above.

One-on-one teaching   Group work   Whole class instruction   Independent work   **A** Assessment

For a complete guide to selection support, including support for Advanced students, see the Overview of Resources in the frontmatter.

✓ Poetry Collection 3
✓✓ Poetry Collection 4

Life
Naomi Long Madgett

Loo-Wit
Wendy Rose

The Courage That My Mother Had
Edna St. Vincent Millay

Mother to Son
Langston Hughes

The Village Blacksmith
Henry Wadsworth Longfellow

Fog
Carl Sandburg
The fog comes on little...

RESOURCES FOR:

L1 Special-Needs Students

L2 Below-Level Students (Tier 2)

L3 On-Level Students (Tier 1)

L4 Advanced Students (Tier 1)

EL English Learners

All All Students

Vocabulary/Fluency/Prior Knowledge

Name _____ Date _____

Poetry Collection: Naomi Long Madgett, Wendy Rose, and Edna St. Vincent Millay
Reading Warm-up A

Read the following passage. Pay special attention to the underlined words. Then, read it again, and complete the activities. Use a separate sheet of paper for your written answers.

"What can we do that would entertain you?" Aunt Grace asked her niece she put away the dinner dishes.

Sandy plopped down on the sofa and checked the time on her <u>watch</u>. "Turn on the television, I guess."

Aunt Grace turned to hide her smile. *Kids! They have no idea of how to <u>amuse</u> themselves.*

Sandy moved some books on the coffee table so she could put her stocking-feet up. Thank goodness I'm staying only one night with my aunt, she thought. This place is such a bore. *Blam!* One of the books she had moved fell onto the floor. It was a photo album. Several loose photos slid out onto the carpet.

"Sorry!" Sandy exclaimed as she jumped down to gather up the photos. "Who's this?" she asked, staring at a wedding photo. The groom was dressed in a soldier's uniform.

Aunt Grace knelt down beside her. "That's my parents on their wedding day," she answered. "It's the only picture I have of them together, and I really <u>treasure</u> it. My dad was killed in the Vietnam war, about three months after this picture was taken."

"How sad," Sandy sympathized.

"My mom remarried four years later. Her second husband was your grandfather." Aunt Grace picked up a baby picture. The <u>infant</u> was dressed in a pink bunny suit. "This picture is of me," she said, laughing.

Aunt Grace turned pages in the album while telling family stories. Sandy learned how her grandmother had overcome many hardships to raise her two daughters. "She was a very strong woman," Aunt Grace said as she closed the album. "I admired her greatly and still do." She picked up a loose photo of her mom. "Here's a picture of her that I can <u>spare</u>. Would you like to have it?"

"I would, thank you," Sandy replied. Then she asked, "Do you have another album? I'd rather look at family photos <u>instead</u> of TV. Photographs are so much more interesting!"

1. Circle the word that tells what Sandy checked on her <u>watch</u>. Write a sentence that describes a watch.

2. Circle the word that is an antonym for <u>amuse</u>. Write the meaning of amuse.

3. Underline the words that tell what Aunt Grace <u>treasures</u>. Write about something you treasure.

4. Circle the word that is a synonym for <u>infant</u>. Use *infant* in a sentence.

5. Underline the words that tell what Aunt Grace has to <u>spare</u>. Describe something that you could not part with or spare.

6. Underline the words that tell what Sandy wanted to do <u>instead</u> of watching TV. Write about something you like to do instead of watching TV.

Unit 4 Resources: Poetry
© Pearson Education, Inc. All rights reserved.
A4

Unit 4 Resources

EL **L1** **L2** **Reading Warm-ups A and B,** pp. 64–65, 82–83

Also available for these selections:

EL **L1** **L2** **Vocabulary Warm-ups A and B,** pp. 62–63, 80–81

All **Writing About the Big Question,** pp. 66, 84

All **Vocabulary Builder,** pp. 69, 87

Reader's Notebooks

Pre- and postreading pages for both collections, as well as the selections in Poetry Collection 3 appear in an interactive format in the *Reader's Notebooks.* Each *Notebook* is differentiated for a different group of learners. The selections in the Adapted and English Learner's versions are abridged.

PRENTICE HALL LITERATURE
Reader's Notebook
English Learner's Version
Differentiated Instruction for Universal Access
GRADE SEVEN

L2 **L3** *Reader's Notebook*

L1 *Reader's Notebook: Adapted Version*

EL *Reader's Notebook: English Learner's Version*

EL *Reader's Notebook: Spanish Version*

PRENTICE HALL LITERATURE
Common Core Companion
STUDENT WORKBOOK • GRADE SEVEN

COMMON CORE EDITION ©

A Student workbook for Mastering the Common Core State Standards

Key Features
- Instruction and Practice for Common Core State Standards
- Writing Workshops
- Listening and Speaking Workshops
- Performance Tasks

ALWAYS LEARNING   PEARSON

© *Common Core Companion*

Additional instruction and practice for each Common Core State Standard

Selection Support

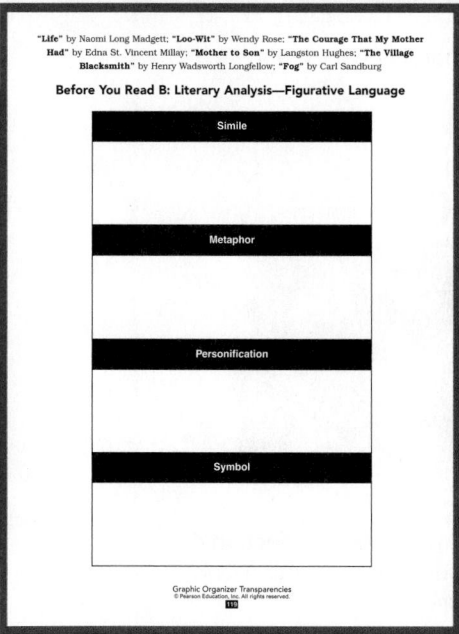

"Life" by Naomi Long Madgett; "Loo-Wit" by Wendy Rose; "The Courage That My Mother Had" by Edna St. Vincent Millay; "Mother to Son" by Langston Hughes; "The Village Blacksmith" by Henry Wadsworth Longfellow; "Fog" by Carl Sandburg

Before You Read B: Literary Analysis—Figurative Language

Simile
Metaphor
Personification
Symbol

EL L3 Literary Analysis: Graphic Organizer B, p. 119

Also available for these selections:

EL L1 L2 Literary Analysis: Graphic Organizer A, pp. 117, 118

EL L1 L2 Reading: Graphic Organizer A, pp. 120, 121 (partially filled in)

EL L3 Reading: Graphic Organizer B, p. 122

Skills Development/Extension

Name _____ Date _____

Poetry Collection: Naomi Long Madgett, Wendy Rose, Edna St. Vincent Millay
Literary Analysis: Figurative Language

Figurative language is language that is not meant to be taken literally. Writers use figures of speech to express ideas in vivid and imaginative ways. Common figures of speech include the following:

• A **simile** compares two unlike things using a word such as *like* or *as*.
• A **metaphor** compares two unlike things by stating that one thing is another thing. In an **extended metaphor**, several related comparisons extend over a number of lines.
• **Personification** gives human characteristics to a nonhuman subject.
• A **symbol** is an object, a person, an animal, a place, or an image that represents something else.

Look at this line from "Life." What figure of speech does the speaker use?
Life is but a toy that swings on a bright gold chain.
The speaker uses a metaphor to compare life to a toy, one "that swings on a bright gold chain."

DIRECTIONS: *As you read the poems in this collection, record the similes, metaphors, extended metaphors, personification, and symbols.*

Poem	Passage	Figurative Language
"Life"		
"Loo-Wit"		
"The Courage That My Mother Had"		

All Literary Analysis: Figurative Language, pp. 68, 86

Also available for these selections:

All Reading: Draw Conclusions, pp. 67, 85

L4 Enrichment, pp. 70, 88

EL L3 L4 Grammar, p. 89

EL L3 L4 Support for Writing, p. 90

L3 L4 Support for Extend Your Learning, p. 91

Assessment

Name _____ Date _____

Poetry Collection: Langston Hughes, Henry Wadsworth Longfellow, Carl Sandburg
Selection Test B

Critical Reading *Identify the letter of the choice that best completes the statement or answers the question.*

_____ 1. In "Mother to Son," what does the "crystal stair" represent?
   A. an easy life
   B. a hard life
   C. a satisfactory life
   D. a transparent life

_____ 2. What is the mother referring to in the following lines from "Mother to Son"?
   It's had tacks in it, / And splinters, / And boards torn up.
   A. repairs to be made
   B. successes of the past
   C. hopes for the future
   D. difficulties in life

_____ 3. What lesson does the mother in "Mother to Son" try to impart to her son?
   A. Rest when you grow weary.
   B. Strive to become wealthy.
   C. Keep going no matter what.
   D. Stay physically active.

_____ 4. Which phrase best captures the symbolic meaning of this line from "Mother to Son"?
   places with no carpet on the floor— / Bare.
   A. bare elegance
   B. lack of luxury
   C. street life
   D. easy comfort

_____ 5. What conclusion about the mother can you draw from the details in these lines from "Mother to Son"?
   For I'se still goin', honey, / I'se still climbin'.
   A. She is full of despair.
   B. She has not given up.
   C. She is becoming exhausted.
   D. She knows she will die soon.

_____ 6. What is Longfellow's attitude toward the blacksmith in "The Village Blacksmith"?
   A. deep admiration
   B. mild puzzlement
   C. slight annoyance
   D. lighthearted criticism

EL L3 L4 Selection Test B, pp. 77–79, 98–100

Also available for these selections:

EL L1 L2 Selection Test A, pp. 74–76, 95–97

L3 L4 Open-Book Test, pp. 71–73, 92–94

PHLit Online!
www.PHLitOnline.com

Online Resources: All print materials are also available online.

complete narrated selection text

a thematically related video with writing prompt

an interactive graphic organizer

highlighting feature

access to all student print resources, adapted to individual student needs

Spanish and English summaries

adapted selection translations in Spanish

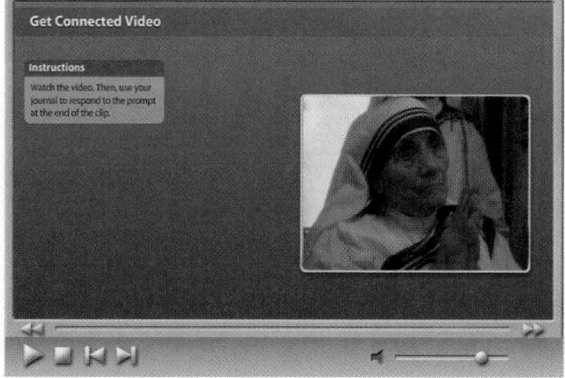

Get Connected! (thematic video with writing prompt)

Also available:

Background Video
All videos are available in Spanish.

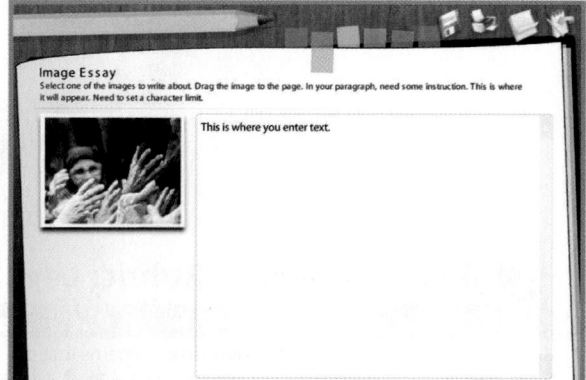

Writer's Journal (with graphics feature)

Also available:

Vocabulary Central (tools, activities, and songs for studying vocabulary)

600d

❶ Leveled Texts

You may use either Poetry Collection 3 or Poetry Collection 4 to meet the lesson objectives. Skills instruction for both selections appears on page 601. Choose one selection to teach (or choose to teach both). The Text Complexity Rubric at the bottom of this page will help you determine which selection is more appropriate for your students. Use the Reader and Task Suggestions on the facing page to help all students read text of increasing complexity.

❷ ⓒ Introducing the CCS Standards

Introduce the standards on the student page. (Note that the lesson element with which each standard is addressed is identified in parentheses after the text of the standard.) Call out the standards that you will cover with the selections, explaining to students what each requires and how they will address it as they work through the selection you have chosen. Standards labeled "Spiral Review" are introduced in the Literary Analysis Workshop for this unit.

Before You Read

❶ ⓒ Leveled Texts

Build your skills and improve your comprehension of poetry with texts of increasing complexity.

The poems in **Poetry Collection 3** explore the power of life, nature, and courage.

The poems in **Poetry Collection 4** express admiration for both people and nature.

❷ ⓒ Common Core State Standards

Meet these standards with either **Poetry Collection 3** (p. 604) or **Poetry Collection 4** (p. 613).

Reading Literature
4. Determine the meaning of words and phrases as they are used in a text, including figurative and connotative meanings; analyze the impact of rhymes and other repetitions of sounds on a specific verse or stanza of a poem or section of a story or drama. (*Literary Analysis: Figurative Language*)

Writing
2. Write informative/explanatory texts to examine a topic and convey ideas, concepts, and information through the selection, organization, and analysis of relevant content.
2.d. Use precise language and domain-specific vocabulary to inform about or explain the topic. (*Writing: Metaphor*)
7. Conduct short research projects to answer a question, drawing on several sources. (*Research and Technology: Scientific Explanation*)

Speaking and Listening
5. Include multimedia components and visual displays in presentations to clarify claims and findings and emphasize salient points. (*Research and Technology: Scientific Explanation*)

Language
1.a. Explain the function of phrases and clauses in general and their function in specific sentences. (*Conventions: Appositives and Appositive Phrases*)

6. Acquire and use accurately grade-appropriate general academic and domain-specific words and phrases; gather vocabulary knowledge when considering a word or phrase important to comprehension or expression. (*Vocabulary: Word Study*)

ⓒ Text Complexity Rubric: Leveled Texts

Text complexity is determined by both qualitative and quantitative measures. For this reason, the quantitative measure of a more complex collection may be lower than that of a more accessible collection.

		✓ Poetry Collection 3	✓✓ Poetry Collection 4
Qualitative Measures	**Context/Knowledge Demands**	Poems that use figurative language 1 ② 3 4 5	Classic poems that use figurative language 1 2 ③ 4 5
	Structure/Language Conventionality and Clarity	Mixture of long and short lines; some specific terminology (Loo-Wit); on-level vocabulary 1 ② 3 4 5	Conversational tone (Mother to Son); challenging vocabulary 1 2 ③ 4 5
	Levels of Meaning/ Purpose/Concept Level	Accessible concept (straightforward and explicit meaning) 1 2 ③ 4 5	Challenging concept (Comparisons require higher level of interpretation.) 1 2 ③ 4 5
Quantitative Measures	**Text Length**	Word Count: 40, 81, 166	Word Count: 100, 252, 21
	Lexile	NP	NP
Overall Complexity		✓ **More accessible**	✓✓ **More complex**

❸ Reading Skill: Draw Conclusions

In poetry, an author's techniques can add musicality and beauty to the work. To interpret meaning, **draw conclusions** after considering the details in a literary work. **Connecting the details** can help. For example, if the speaker in a poem describes beautiful flowers, bright sunshine, and happy children, you might conclude that he or she has a positive outlook. As you read, identify important details. Then, look at the details together to draw a conclusion about the poem's meaning.

❹ Literary Analysis: Figurative Language

Figurative language is language that is not meant to be taken literally. Writers use figures of speech to express ideas in vivid and imaginative ways. Common figures of speech include the following:

- A **simile** compares two unlike things by using the words *like* or *as.*
- A **metaphor** compares two unlike things by saying that one thing *is* another.
- In **personification,** a nonhuman subject is given human characteristics.
- A **symbol** is an object, person, animal, place, or image that represents something other than itself.

❺ Using the Strategy: Figurative Language Chart

As you read, refer to the chart below to identify figurative language.

Simile	Metaphor	Personification	Symbol
My love is like a red, red rose.	Life is a bowl of cherries.	The stars were dancing heel to toe.	dove = peace, harmony heart = love, romance

PHLit Online!
www.PHLitOnline.com

Hear It!
- Selection summary audio
- Selection audio

See It!
- Get Connected video
- Background video
- More about the author
- Vocabulary flashcards

Do It!
- Interactive journals
- Interactive graphic organizers
- Self-test
- Internet activity
- Grammar tutorial
- Interactive vocabulary games

❸ Reading Skill
Draw Conclusions

1. Introduce the skill, using the instruction on the student page.
2. Tell students that they will draw conclusions as they read.

❹ Literary Analysis
Figurative Language

1. Introduce the skill, using the instruction on the student page
2. Tell students that they will analyze figurative language as they read

Think Aloud: Model the Skill

Model a way to analyze figurative language. Say to students:

> To interpret figurative language, I first think about the images, or word pictures, that I associate with the language. For example, when I read the phrase "a bowl of cherries," I see a bowl of cherries. They look brightly colored and appealing. I use these ideas—*brightly colored* and *appealing*—to understand that the metaphor "life is a bowl of cherries" means "life is brightly colored and appealing" or more simply "life is good." I can use this same process to interpret similes, personification, and symbols.

❺ Using the Strategy

Give students a copy of either **Literary Analysis Graphic Organizer A** or **B** (*Graphic Organizer Transparencies,* pp. 117–119) to list and interpret figurative language as they read. Use the examples in **Literary Analysis Graphic Organizer A,** which is partially filled in, to model the process of completing the organizer.

© Text Complexity: Reader and Task Suggestions

✓ Poetry Collection 3		✓✓ Poetry Collection 4	
Preparing to Read the Text	**Leveled Tasks**	**Preparing to Read the Text**	**Leveled Tasks**
• Using the Background information on TE p. 603, discuss details that explain key items or places in the poems. • Ask students to think about different ways poets describe abstract qualities. • Guide students to use Multidraft Reading strategies (TE p. 603).	*Levels of Meaning* If students will have difficulty understanding the comparisons, have them first read to identify the ideas being described. Then, have them reread to identify the comparisons being made. *Analyzing* If students will not have difficulty with the comparisons, have them read to identify metaphors or personification. Then, have them explain why the poets chose to use the figurative language.	• Using the Background information on TE p. 611, discuss details in the poems. • Ask students why poets often write about simple, everyday things. • Guide students to use Multidraft Reading strategies (TE p. 611).	*Structure/Language* If students will have difficulty following the lines in the poems, have them read to identify punctuation within the poems. Then, have them reread to put ideas into their own words. *Evaluating* If students will not have difficulty understanding the poems, have them identify which poems rhyme and which do not. Ask them to explain why poets would choose to use rhyme in their poems.

601

❶ ❓ Writing About the Big Question

1. Review the assignment with the class.

2. Point out a symbol in the classroom, such as a green arrow indicating something acceptable or a stop sign indicating something unacceptable. Discuss reasons why such symbols might be effective ways to communicate.

3. Have students complete the sentence starter. Review responses as a class. (**Sample answer:** Sometimes, a comparison between seemingly unrelated things can <u>express</u> the idea that the two things have a secret resemblance.)

4. Remind students that their answers will help them think about the Big Question, "What is the best way to communicate?"

While You Read

Tell students that as they read, they should look for comparisons that inspire them to see things in a new way.

❷ Vocabulary

1. Have students preview the collection vocabulary.

2. For each word, have students say the word aloud.

3. Then, use the word in a sentence that defines the word.

4. Finally, repeat your definitional sentence or a similar sentence with the word missing and have the class "fill in the blank" chorally. Here is an example:

When someone <u>crouches</u>, he or she stoops or bends low. When Suki bends down to reach under her desk, we can say that she [students say "crouches"].

❸ Word Study

1. Introduce the skill, using the instruction in the box.

2. Have volunteers name adjectives. Ask the class to create adverbs by adding -ly. Then, ask students to define the new words. (**Sample answer:** *active; actively:* in an active manner)

Making Connections
Poetry Collection 3

Life •
Loo-Wit •
The Courage That My Mother Had

❓ What is the best way to *communicate?*

❶ Writing About the Big Question

The poets in Poetry Collection 3 make interesting comparisons among objects and ideas. Use this sentence starter to develop your ideas about the Big Question.

Sometimes, a comparison between seemingly unrelated things can **express** the idea that _____.

While You Read Look for comparisons that inspire you to see things in a new way.

❷ Vocabulary

Read each word and its definition. Decide whether you know the word well, know it a little bit, or do not know it at all. After you read, see how your knowledge of each word has increased.

- **fascinated** (fas´ ə nāt´ əd) *adj.* very interested (p. 604) *The <u>fascinated</u> child could not take her eyes off the twinkling lights. fascinate v. fascination n. fascinating v.*

- **prickly** (prik´ lē) *adj.* sharply pointed; thorny (p. 606) *She cried as she fell into the <u>prickly</u> bush. prickle n. prickled v. pricklier adj.*

- **crouches** (krouch´ əz) *v.* stoops or bends low (p. 607) *Rachel <u>crouches</u> to pick a flower. crouch v.*

- **unravel** (un rav´ əl) *v.* become untangled or separated (p. 607) *The ball of yarn began to <u>unravel</u>. unraveled v. unraveling v.*

- **dislodge** (dis läj´) *v.* leave a position or place (p. 607) *The books <u>dislodge</u> and fall off the shelf. dislodged v. dislodging v. lodger n.*

- **granite** (gran´ it) *n.* hard, gray rock (p. 608) *Many of New Hampshire's mountains are made of <u>granite</u>. granitic adj.*

❸ Word Study

The **Latin suffix -ly** means "like" or "in the manner of."

In "Loo-Wit," an old woman feels something **prickly**, like sharp points, on her neck.

Vocabulary Development

Vocabulary Knowledge Rating

Create a **Vocabulary Knowledge Rating Chart** (*Professional Development Guidebook,* p.33) for this collection. Include the collection vocabulary and the Big Question word that appears in the Writing About the Big Question sentence starter on this page. (The Big Question vocabulary is introduced on pp. 570–571.)

Give students a copy of the chart. Read the words aloud, and have students mark their rating in the Before Reading column. Urge them to be alert to these words as they read and discuss the collection.

Tally how many students think they know a word to gauge how much instruction to provide. As students read and discuss the collection, point out the words and their context.

Vocabulary Central, featuring tools, activities, and songs for studying vocabulary, is available online at **www.PHLitOnline.com.**

Meet the Authors

Naomi Long Madgett

(b. 1923)

Author of "Life" (p. 604)

Naomi Long Madgett first discovered poetry at the age of seven or eight, while reading in her father's study. She was most inspired by the poets Alfred, Lord Tennyson and Langston Hughes, though their styles are quite different. Madgett once said, "I would rather be a good poet than anything else." Her ambition to create good poetry has led her to write more than seven collections of poems.

Wendy Rose

(b. 1948)

Author of "Loo-Wit" (p. 606)

Wendy Rose was born in Oakland, California, to a Hopi father and a Scots-Irish-Miwok mother. In addition to being a poet, Rose is an anthropologist who has worked to protect Native American burial sites from developers. She is also a painter who has illustrated some of her own books. "Loo-Wit" is based on legends of the Cowlitz people of Washington State.

Edna St. Vincent Millay

(1892–1950)

Author of "The Courage That My Mother Had" (p. 608)

Edna St. Vincent Millay's mother was a hard-working nurse who encouraged her daughters to be independent and to love reading. Millay's mother had a powerful influence on young Edna, who grew up to be a widely published writer and political activist. Born in Rockland, Maine, Millay published her first poem at the age of fourteen. In 1923, she became the first woman to win the Pulitzer Prize for poetry.

Poetry Collection 3 **603**

 Daily Bellringer

For each class during which you teach this collection, have students complete one of the five Sentence Modeling activities for Week 20 in the *Daily Bellringer Activities* booklet.

Background

- **"Life"** Many watches, like the one in the poem, were once powered by a coiled spring that had to be wound by turning a knob. Over time, this spring wound down and the watch stopped. Before 1900, watches were often suspended on a chain and kept in one's pocket.

- **"Loo-Wit"** Mount St. Helens is a volcano just south of Seattle, Washington. On May 18, 1980, it erupted leaving 57 dead and a huge area of damage from explosions, forest fires, floods from melted snow, and hot ash. The poem personifies the volcano and its violent upheavals.

- **"The Courage That My Mother Had"** In many cultures, families pass down heirlooms, or items of special value. These items are often passed from one generation to the next on an older person's death, a marriage, or other life passage. This poem reflects on a different, non-material type of heirloom.

Multidraft Reading

To assist struggling readers and to deepen reading for all, apply multidraft reading protocols. For each reading, have students set the purpose indicated:

- **First reading**—identifying key ideas and details and answering any Reading Checks.

- **Second reading**—analyzing craft and structure and responding to the side-column prompts.

- **Third reading**—integrating knowledge and ideas, connecting to other texts and the world, and answering the end-of-selection questions.

For more guidance, refer to the *Classroom Strategies and Teaching Routines* card on multidraft reading.

For more about the author or practice with the selection vocabulary, go online at www.PHLitOnline.com.

❶ Activating Prior Knowledge

Write the following sentences on the board:

"Life can be like a/an _____."

"A volcano can be like a/an _____."

"Courage can be like a/an _____."

Ask students to complete the sentences and then explain their answers. Tell students that the poems they are about to read include comparisons that can help them think about the natural world and life in new ways.

Concept Connector ➡

Students will revisit their ideas after reading the collection.

Whole-Class Activity

Allow students five minutes to write an anecdote about a time when they witnessed a natural event, such as a snowstorm, a hurricane, or the eruption of a volcano. Then, draw a cluster chart on the board. As you draw, ask volunteers to call out the events they witnessed. As a class, figure out how each anecdote is connected to the other. Ask "What did you feel as you watched the event?" or "How are the events you described similar or different?"

❷ About the Selections

In "Life," the speaker explains that life is like a pocket watch that entertains an infant and then winds down.

In the poem "Loo-Wit," the eruption of Mount St. Helens is personified as an old woman waking up.

In "The Courage That My Mother Had," the speaker pays tribute to her late mother and wishes that she had her mother's strength and courage.

❸ Figurative Language

1. Review the four types of figurative language students often encounter in poetry—simile, metaphor, personification, and symbol.

2. Have students reread the poem "Life." Then **ask** them to identify the type of figurative language the poet uses. **Answer:** The poet uses a metaphor to describe life.

Life

Naomi Long Madgett

Vocabulary
fascinated (fas´ ə nāt´ əd) *adj.* very interested

Life is but a toy that swings on a bright gold chain
Ticking for a little while
To amuse a fascinated infant,
Until the keeper, a very old man,
5 Becomes tired of the game
And lets the watch run down.

604 Poetry

Vocabulary Development

© **CCSS** Language 6

Thematic Vocabulary: The Big Question
As students are discussing Poetry Collection 3, encourage them to use the thematic vocabulary presented in Introducing the Big Question, pp. 570–571. You might encourage them with sentence starters like these:

1. Edna St. Vincent Millay uses a piece of jewelry to *communicate* . . .
2. The speaker in "Life" wants to *contribute* an image of life losing energy like . . .
3. "Loo-Wit" *expresses* restlessness and anger by . . .
4. The poet in "Loo-Wit" *transmits* Native American culture by . . .

1. Explain that some ideas, such as *love*, are abstract or impossible to see or touch. One way to communicate abstract ideas is to compare them to something concrete that readers can imagine seeing or touching.

2. Have students reread the bracketed text on page 604. **Ask** students: What abstract idea does this poem describe? To what concrete objects is that idea compared? Does this comparison lead to new understanding for you? Explain.

   Possible response: The poem compares life with a watch and a toy. Yes; The comparison helps me think about life as less mysterious.

3. **Ask:** Do you enjoy poems that communicate by comparing unrelated objects or ideas? Do you think this is an effective way to communicate ideas? Explain.

   Possible response: If one of the ideas is familiar to me, I can use this to understand the other, unfamiliar, idea. If both ideas are unfamiliar to me, then I am just confused. In this case, it would be more effective if the writer just stated ideas directly.

Differentiated
Instruction for Universal Access

Strategy for Less Proficient Readers
To help students remember the types of figurative language, show them **Literary Analysis Graphic Organizer A** (*Graphic Organizer Transparencies*, p. 117). Students can use the partially completed organizer as a model for identifying figurative language on their own.

EL Strategy for English Learners
Allow students to listen to the recordings of these poems on the *Hear It!* **Audio CD.** Encourage students to listen more than once. At first, have them listen for meaning. Then, have students read the poems aloud as they listen, so that they can practice pronunciations and phrasings.

Strategy for Gifted/Talented Students
"The Courage That My Mother Had" (p. 608) reveals the respect the poet had for her mother. Invite students to think of a person they respect and to determine a symbol of that person. Have students use the symbol in a poem about the person. Allow students time to present their poems to the class.

PHLit Online!
This collection is available in interactive format in the **Enriched Online Student Edition,** at www.PHLitOnline.com, which includes a thematically related video with writing prompt and an interactive graphic organizer.

1. Help students infer the connections between the description of the woman and a volcanic eruption.

2. Tell students to reread lines 1–8 of the poem. Then, **ask** them what the tobacco might be or represent.
   Answer: The tobacco is probably the ash that a volcano spews before it erupts.

3. **Ask** students at what point they understood that the old woman in the poem was the volcano and to explain how they knew.
   Possible response: Students will probably say that the footnote about the poem's title helped them figure out the connection between the woman and the volcano.

❻ **Critical Viewing**

Possible response: Students may suggest lines 5–6, in which she spits tobacco, or lines 10–11, where she sprinkles ashes on the snow. They may also point to lines 51–52, in which she shakes the sky like a blanket. These lines provide visual images that match the picture of the smoke-filled sky in the photograph.

Loo-Wit

Wendy Rose

The way they do
this old woman
no longer cares
what others think
5 but spits her black tobacco
any which way
stretching full length
from her bumpy bed.
Finally up
10 she sprinkles ashes
on the snow,
cold buttes[2]
promise nothing
but the walk
15 of winter.
Centuries of cedar
have bound her
to earth,
huckleberry ropes
20 lay prickly
on her neck.
Around her
machinery growls,
snarls and plows
25 great patches
of her skin.

Vocabulary
prickly (prik´ lē) *adj.*
sharply pointed; thorny

❻ ▶ **Critical Viewing** Which lines of the poem best capture the action in this photograph? **[Assess]**

---

1. **Loo-Wit** name given by the Cowlitz people to Mount St. Helens, an active volcano in Washington State. It means "lady of fire."
2. **buttes** (byo͞ots) *n.* steep hills standing alone in flat land.

Vocabulary Development

Vocabulary Knowledge Rating
When students have completed reading and discussing the poems in this set, have them take out their **Vocabulary Knowledge Rating Chart** for the poems. Read the words aloud and have students rate their knowledge of words again in the After Reading column. Clarify any words that are still problematic. Have students write their own definition and example or sentence in the appropriate column. Then have students complete the Vocabulary Practice activities at the end of the selection. Encourage students to use the words in further discussion and written work about the poems. Remind them that they will be accountable for these words on the **Selection Test**, *Unit 4 Resources*, pp. 74–76 or 77–79.

She crouches
in the north,
her trembling
30 the source
of dawn.
Light appears
with the shudder
of her slopes,
35 the movement
of her arm.
Blackberries unravel,
stones dislodge;
it's not as if
40 they weren't warned.
She was sleeping
but she heard the boot scrape,
the creaking floor,
felt the pull of the blanket
45 from her thin shoulder.
With one free hand
she finds her weapons
and raises them high;
clearing the twigs from her
throat
50 she sings, she sings,
shaking the sky
like a blanket about her
Loo-wit sings and sings and
sings!

7

Vocabulary
crouches (krouch´ əz)
v. stoops or bends low
unravel (un rav´ əl)
v. become untangled or separated
dislodge (dis läj´) *v.*
leave a position
or place

Figurative Language
Which details does the
poet use to compare
the volcano to an old
woman?

Spiral Review
Repetition What
is the effect of the
repetition in the last
five lines of the poem?

❼ Figurative Language

1. Remind students that personification occurs when an inanimate object is given human characteristics. Tell students that in the case of "Loo-Wit," the volcano looks and acts like an old woman.

2. To support this idea, have students reread lines 27–53 on p. 607. **Ask** them to identify all the words that suggest human activity.
   Answer: The words include: *crouches, trembling, shudder, movement, sleeping, heard, felt, finds, raises, clearing, sings,* and *shaking.*

3. Read the bracketed text aloud, then **ask** students the Figurative Language question.
   Answer: Details include how the woman/volcano crouches and trembles before she raises her weapons and clears her throat and sings.

▶ **Monitor Progress:** Check that students can identify the type of figurative language used in "Loo-Wit" and can explain how they know.

▶ **Reteach:** If students have difficulty, reinforce the concept of figurative language by asking students what figurative language appears in "The Courage That My Mother Had." Make sure students see that the Millay poem uses simile and symbol. The speaker says that her mother's courage was like a rock. The mother's brooch is a symbol for what the speaker has lost.

Spiral Review

Repetition

1. Remind students that they studied the concept of repetition in the Unit 4 Literary Analysis Workshop (pp. 572–581).

2. **Ask** the Spiral Review question.
   Possible response: The repetition makes the last five lines more intense. Repetition also makes it seem like the explosion is lasting a long time.

Concept Connector

Reading Skill Graphic Organizer
Ask students to review the graphic organizer that identified figurative language. Then have students share the graphic organizers they completed and compare their findings.

Activating Prior Knowledge
Have students return to the sentence starters they completed in Activating Prior Knowledge and confirm or revise their statements. They may do this individually or in pairs or groups.

Then, lead a class discussion, probing for what students have learned that confirms or changes their ideas. Encourage students to cite specific details, quotations, or other evidence from the text to support their responses to each statement.

Writing About the Big Question
Have students compare their response to the sentence starter they completed before reading the collection with their ideas afterward. Ask them to explain whether their thoughts have changed.

1. Tell students that poets compress ideas into very few words, forcing readers to draw conclusions based on details and ideas in the poem.

2. Have students reread and summarize the third stanza of the poem. **Possible response:** The speaker wishes that her mother had left her courage, which she needs, rather than a brooch.

Note the comparison Millay makes between courage and a rock. **Ask** the Draw Conclusions question.
Answer: The detail of the rock shows that the speaker felt that her mother was truly strong and brave.

ASSESS

Answers

Critical Thinking

Before students respond, you may wish to have them write a brief objective summary of each poem. As they answer the questions below, remind them to support their answers with evidence from the text.

1. She uses the image of a pocket watch.

2. The scrape of a boot causes the eruption.

3. She would rather have her mother's character because it would help her survive and live more successfully.

4. **Possible response:** Figures of speech allow poets to make abstract ideas concrete and give nonhuman objects human qualities. Comparisons such as this help poets to make ideas more understandable.

The Courage That My Mother Had

Edna St. Vincent Millay

> The courage that my mother had
> Went with her, and is with her still:
> Rock from New England quarried;[1]
> Now granite in a granite hill.
>
> 5 The golden brooch[2] my mother wore
> She left behind for me to wear;
> I have no thing I treasure more:
> Yet, it is something I could spare.
>
> Oh, if instead she'd left to me
> 10 The thing she took into the grave!—
> **8** That courage like a rock, which she
> Has no more need of, and I have.

Vocabulary
granite (gran´ it) *n.*
hard, gray rock

Draw Conclusions
What detail in the third stanza shows how the speaker feels about her mother?

---

1. **quarried** (kwôr´ ēd) *adj.* carved out of the ground.
2. **brooch** (brōch) *n.* large ornamental pin.

Critical Thinking

Cite textual evidence to support your responses.

1. **Craft and Structure** In "Life," what image does Madgett use to describe life?

2. **Key Ideas and Details** **Analyze Causes and Effects:** According to the details in "Loo-Wit," what causes the volcano's eruption?

3. **Integration of Knowledge and Ideas** **Interpret:** In "The Courage That My Mother Had," why would the speaker rather have her mother's character than the physical item her mother left her?

4. **Integration of Knowledge and Ideas** How can a poet use figures of speech to communicate an idea in a new and different way? *[Connect to the Big Question: What is the best way to communicate?]*

608 Poetry

Assessment Resources

Unit 4 Resources

L1 L2 EL **Selection Test A,** pp. 74–76. Administer Test A to less advanced students.

L3 L4 EL **Selection Test B,** pp. 77–79. Administer Test B to on-level and more advanced students.

L3 L4 **Open-Book Test,** pp. 71–73. As an alternative, give the Open-Book Test.

All **Customizable Test Bank**

All **Self-tests**
Students may prepare for the **Selection Test** by taking the **Self-test** online.

PHLit Online! All assessment resources are available at **www.PHLitOnline.com**.

Reading Skill: Draw Conclusions

1. Use a graphic organizer like this one to connect details from the poem "Life" to reach the **conclusion** that is given.

Detail	Detail	Detail

Conclusion: The speaker believes that people lose interest in life as they grow older.

2. Which details from "Loo-Wit" support the conclusion that people are disturbing the mountain?

Literary Analysis: Figurative Language

Ⓒ 3. Craft and Structure (a) To what is life compared in "Life"? **(b)** Which type of **figurative language** does Madgett use?

Ⓒ 4. Craft and Structure Give three examples of **personification** in "Loo-Wit."

Ⓒ 5. Craft and Structure (a) What is a **symbol** for strength in "The Courage That My Mother Had"? **(b)** How do you know?

Vocabulary

Ⓒ Acquisition and Use Explain your answer to each question.

1. If a tree root is *dislodged*, is it still in the ground?

2. To *unravel* a ball of yarn, do you wind it around?

3. When a dog *crouches*, is he standing on his hind legs?

4. If Michael is *fascinated* by the show, is he bored?

5. If something is made of *granite*, will it break easily?

6. Would a bush that is *prickly* be pleasant to touch?

Word Study Use what you know about the **Latin suffix -ly** to explain your answer to each question.

1. If you speak a language *fluently*, do you speak it poorly?

2. Would it be wise to move *quickly* if you were late for school?

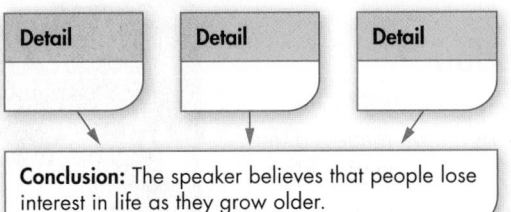

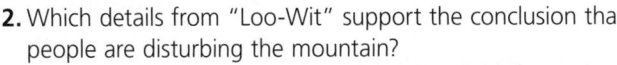

Word Study

The **Latin suffix -ly** means "like" or "in the manner of."

Apply It Explain how the suffix -ly contributes to the meanings of these words. Consult a dictionary if necessary.

haphazardly
proudly
rapidly

Reading Skill

1. Possible response:
Detail 1: a toy swings on a bright chain
Detail 2: The old man, once an infant, is tired and lets the watch wind down.
For other sample answers, see *Graphic Organizer Transparencies*, **Reading Skill Graphic Organizer A, p. 120,** and the **Additional Answers** section.

2. Details include the machinery that growls and plows the volcano's neck.

Literary Analysis

3. (a) Life is compared to a watch. (b) The comparison is a metaphor.

4. The volcano is personified as a woman who does not care what people think; who spits tobacco; who sprinkles ashes; who has skin that is irritated by machinery; who crouches and trembles; who raises her arms and her weapons; and who sings and shakes the sky.

5. (a) The rock is a symbol for strength. (b) The speaker compares her mother's courage to a rock, which is strong, sturdy, and resistant to change or movement.

Vocabulary
Acquisition and Use
Sample answers:

1. No; If a tree root is <u>dislodged</u>, it has been thrown out of the ground.

2. No; You unwind a ball of yard when you <u>unravel</u> it.

3. No; When a dog <u>crouches</u>, he is holding his or her body low to the ground, not standing on hind legs.

4. No; Someone who is <u>fascinated</u> is interested, not bored.

5. No; <u>Granite</u> is hard rock, so it would not break easily.

6. No; Something <u>prickly</u> is sharp and thorny so it would not be pleasant to touch.

Word Study: Apply It
Sample answers: Something done *haphazardly* is done in a haphazard, or careless, <u>manner</u>. Something that is done *proudly* is done in a proud <u>manner</u>. Something that is done *rapidly*, is done in a rapid, or fast, <u>manner</u>.

Word Study
Sample answers:

1. No; The suffix -ly means "in the manner of" and *fluently* means "in a fluent manner." A fluent speaker would speak well, not poorly.

2. Yes; The suffix -ly means "in the manner of" and moving in a quick <u>manner</u> is wise when you are late.

Skills instruction for the Reading Skill and Literary Analysis concepts for this collection appear on p. 601.

❶  Writing About the Big Question

1. Introduce the assignment.

2. Have students list ways to communicate admiration for someone, such as with an award nomination or a letter. Discuss why we want people to know they have made a difference in our lives.

3. Have students complete the sentence starter. Review responses as a class. **(Sample response:** Some writers choose to write poems about people who <u>enrich</u> their lives because they want to share their admiration with a wider audience.)

4. Remind students that their answers will help them think about the Big Question, "What is the best way to communicate?"

While You Read

Tell students they should look for words and images in each poem that communicate the speaker's feelings.

❷ Vocabulary

1. Have students preview the collection vocabulary.

2. For each word, have students say the word aloud.

3. Then, use the word in a sentence that defines the word.

4. Finally, repeat your definitional sentence or a similar sentence with the word missing and have the class "fill in the blank" chorally. Here is an example:

Someone who is <u>brawny</u> is strong and muscular. When you can see the muscles in Henrik's arms as he lifts the weights, you can say that Henrik is [students say "brawny"].

❸ Word Study

1. Introduce the skill, using the instruction in the box.

2. Point out the vocabulary word *sinewy.* Ask how -*y* affects its meaning and part of speech. (The suffix adds "having" to the noun *sinew,* turning it into an adjective: "having sinews.")

❓ What is the best way to *communicate?*

❶ Writing About the Big Question

In Poetry Collection 4, Langston Hughes and Henry Wadsworth Longfellow express admiration for people who have made a difference in their lives. Use this sentence starter to develop your ideas on the Big Question.

Some writers choose to write poems about people who **enrich** their lives because _____.

While You Read Look for words and images in each poem that communicate the speaker's feelings.

❷ Vocabulary

Read each word and its definition. Decide whether you know the word well, know it a little bit, or do not know it at all. After you read, see how your knowledge of each word has increased.

- **crystal** (kris´ təl) *adj.* made of clear, brilliant glass (p. 613) *Mother was very proud of her <u>crystal</u> glasses. crystal n. crystalize v.*

- **sinewy** (sin´ yo͞o wē) *adj.* tough and strong (p. 614) *With <u>sinewy</u> hands, he carved the stone. sinew n.*

- **brawny** (brôn´ ē) *adj.* strong and muscular (p. 614) *The piano mover had <u>brawny</u> arms. brawn n. brawnier adj.*

- **parson** (pär´ sən) *n.* minister (p. 615) *The <u>parson</u> had a deep voice that was easily heard in the rear pews. parsonage n.*

- **wrought** (rôt) *adj.* shaped by hammering (p. 615) *The fence was <u>wrought</u> iron.*

- **haunches** (hônch əz) *n.* upper legs and hips of an animal (p. 616) *The dog sat back on his <u>haunches</u>. haunch n.*

❸ Word Study

The **Greek suffix -*y*** means "marked by" or "having."

In his poem, Longfellow describes the village blacksmith's arms as **brawny,** or having strength.

Vocabulary Development

Vocabulary Knowledge Rating
Create a **Vocabulary Knowledge Rating Chart** (*Professional Development Guidebook,* p. 38) for this collection. Include the collection vocabulary and the Big Question word that appears in the Writing About the Big Question sentence starter on this page. (The Big Question vocabulary is introduced on pp. 570–571.)

Give students a copy of the chart. Read the words aloud, and have students mark their rating in the Before Reading column. Urge them to be alert to these words as they read and discuss the collection.

Tally how many students think they know a word to gauge how much instruction to provide. As students read and discuss the collection, point out the words and their context.

 **Vocabulary Central,** featuring tools, activities, and songs for studying vocabulary, is available online at www.PHLitOnline.com.

Langston Hughes

(1902–1967)

Author of "Mother to Son" (p. 612)

Langston Hughes published his first work just a year after his high school graduation. Though he wrote in many genres, Hughes is best known for his poetry. He was one of the main figures in the Harlem Renaissance, a creative movement among African Americans that took place in the 1920s in New York City.

Henry Wadsworth Longfellow

(1807–1882)

Author of "The Village Blacksmith" (p. 614)

Although his father wanted him to become a lawyer, Henry Wadsworth Longfellow chose to become a poet and college professor. Longfellow was part of a group of poets called the Fireside Poets, so named because families often gathered around their fireplaces, to read aloud poems such as "The Village Blacksmith."

Carl Sandburg

(1878–1967)

Author of "Fog" (p. 616)

The son of Swedish immigrants, Carl Sandburg was born in Illinois. Although he won the Pulitzer Prize in both poetry and history, he was not a typical scholar. By the time his first book appeared, he had tried many different occupations, including farm worker, stagehand, railroad worker, soldier, and cook.

Poetry Collection 4 **611**

Daily Bellringer

For each class during which you teach this collection, have students complete one of the five Sentence Modeling activities for Week 20 in the *Daily Bellringer Activities* booklet.

Background

- **"Mother to Son"** The poem refers to *tacks* and *landin's*. Tacks are small, sharp nails, such as might be used to attach carpet to flooring. "Landin's" are landings, which are the platforms between flights of stairs.

- **"The Village Blacksmith"** Blacksmiths like the one celebrated in this poem make or repair many different objects by heating iron and hammering it to shape it. The iron is softened by being heated in a forge or furnace. In Longfellow's time, blacksmiths were kept busy making everyday tools for homes and farms, as well as making horseshoes.

- **"Fog"** Like clouds, fog consists of tiny drops of water suspended in the air. It often forms over bodies of water, such as the harbor named in the poem. As air temperature rises through the day, the fog disappears.

Multidraft Reading

To assist struggling readers and to deepen reading for all, apply multidraft reading protocols. For each reading, have students set the purpose indicated:

- **First reading**—identifying key ideas and details and answering any Reading Checks.

- **Second reading**—analyzing craft and structure and responding to the side-column prompts.

- **Third reading**—integrating knowledge and ideas, connecting to other texts and the world, and answering the end-of-selection questions.

For more guidance, refer to the *Classroom Strategies and Teaching Routines* card on multidraft reading.

Differentiated Instruction for Universal Access

EL Extended Support— English Learners
Have students complete the **Reading and Vocabulary Warm-ups**, *Unit 4 Resources*, pp. 80–83, before they read. Assign the prereading pages in the *Reader's Notebook: English Learner's Version.* Then, have students listen to portions of the collection on the *Hear It!* **Audio CD.**

L1 L2 Extended Support— Struggling Readers
Have students complete the **Reading and Vocabulary Warm-ups**, *Unit 4 Resources*, pp. 80–83, before they read. Assign the prereading pages in the *Reader's Notebook: Adapted Version.* Then, have students listen to portions of the collection on the *Hear It!* **Audio CD** (adapted text).

Extended Support— Reluctant Readers
To build motivation and engagement before assigning the collection, have students read "The Big Money," a thematically related selection in *Reality Central.* Then, use the questions at the conclusion of the related selection to guide discussion.

PHLit Online!

For more about the author or practice with the collection vocabulary, go online at **www.PHLitOnline.com.**

Spiral Review

Figurative Language

1. Remind students that they studied the concept of figurative language in the Unit 4 Literary Analysis Workshop (pp. 572–581).

2. **Ask** the Spiral Review question. **Possible response:** The metaphor is the road looking like a gypsy's ribbon. The metaphor helps the reader visualize what the road looks like.

❼ Narrative Poems

1. Choose three volunteers to read. Have the first volunteer read the first stanza on this page. **Ask** students: Who arrived at the inn? **Answer:** Soldiers arrived at the inn.

2. Have the second volunteer read the second stanza. **Ask** students: What did the soldiers do to Bess? **Answer:** They gagged her and tied her up to her bed.

3. Have the third volunteer read the third stanza. **Ask** students: What does Bess expect the highwayman to do? **Answer:** She expected him to come see her at midnight.

4. **Ask** students the Narrative Poems question. **Possible response:** Bess wants to warn the highwayman that the soldiers are waiting for him, but she is bound and gagged.

Spiral Review
Figurative Language
Identify the metaphor in this stanza. What effect does it have on the reader? ❼

Vocabulary
bound (bound) *v.* tied

Narrative Poems
What problem, or conflict, does Bess face?

Part Two

He did not come in the dawning. He did not come at noon;
And out of the tawny sunset, before the rise of the moon,
When the road was a gypsy's ribbon, looping the purple moor,
40   A redcoat troop came marching—
        Marching—marching—
King George's men[8] came marching, up to the old inn door.

They said no word to the landlord. They drank his ale instead
But they gagged his daughter, and bound her, to the foot of her narrow bed.
45   Two of them knelt at her casement, with muskets at their side!
There was death at every window;
        And hell at one dark window;
For Bess could see, through her casement, the road that he would ride.

They had tied her up to attention, with many a sniggering jest.[9]
50   They had bound a musket beside her, with the muzzle beneath her breast!
"Now, keep good watch!" and they kissed her. She heard the doomed man say—
Look for me by moonlight;
        Watch for me by moonlight;
I'll come to thee by moonlight, though hell should bar the way!

55   She twisted her hands behind her; but all the knots held good!
She writhed her hands till her fingers were wet with sweat or blood!
They stretched and strained in the darkness, and the hours crawled by like years,

---

8. King George's men soldiers serving King George of Great Britain.
9. sniggering (snig´ ər iŋ) **jest** sly joke.

Think Aloud

Vocabulary: Using Context
Direct students' attention to the word *musket* on page 632. Using the following "think aloud," model how to use context to infer the meaning of an unknown word. Say to students:

    I'm going to think aloud to show you how I would figure out the meaning of *musket* from its context.

    The two men who tie up Bess are Soldiers and they have *muskets* at their sides. I think a *musket* must be a weapon.

    As I continue reading, I learn in Line 60 that the *musket* also has a trigger. This makes me think that a *musket* must be a type of gun. Because the gun rests against Bess, I realize it must be larger than a pistol. I decide that a *musket* is a type of gun that resembles a rifle.

8

◄ **Critical Viewing**
What details of this
painting capture
the mood of the
poem? [Connect]

Till, now, on the stroke of midnight,
　　　Cold, on the stroke of midnight,
60　The tip of one finger touched it! The trigger at least was
　　hers!

The tip of one finger touched it. She strove no more for
　　the rest.
Up, she stood up to attention, with the muzzle beneath
　　her breast.
She would not risk their hearing; she would not strive
　　again;
For the road lay bare in the moonlight;
65　　　Blank and bare in the moonlight;
And the blood of her veins, in the moonlight, throbbed to
　　her love's refrain.

Tlot-tlot; tlot-tlot! Had they heard it? The horsehoofs ringing
　　clear;
Tlot-tlot, tlot-tlot, in the distance? Were they deaf that
　　they did not hear?
Down the ribbon of moonlight, over the brow of the hill,

Narrative Poems
How does line 60 build
suspense in the narra-
tive?

10

Reading
Check
What did the soldiers
do at the inn?

The Highwayman **633**

8 Critical Viewing
Possible responses: Students may
respond that the violent and tragic
mood of the poem is captured by the
twisted and agitated positions of the
rider and horse in the foreground of
the painting. Some students will also
point out that the action shown in
the painting closely parallels that of
the poem.

9 Narrative Poems
1. Have two volunteers read lines
   55–60 aloud, alternating lines.
2. Discuss Bess's actions after she is
   tied up. **Ask** students what her
   actions tell about her.
   Possible responses: She is not
   afraid to face danger; she loves
   the highwayman and will be
   faithful.
3. **Ask** the Narrative Poems question.
   Answer: Line 60 builds suspense
   because it tells the reader that
   Bess can fire the musket. It creates questions about what she
   will do next.

10 Reading Check
Answer: The soldiers took Bess
hostage. They tied her up and
used her as bait in a trap for the
highwayman.

Differentiated
Instruction　　for Universal Access

Enrichment for Special-Needs Students
Have each students sketch an illustration of one
of the main events on pp. 632–633: the soldiers'
arrival, their tying up Bess, or Bess hearing the
highwayman's horse returning before the soldiers hear it. Tell students to use a line or two
from the poem as a caption for the picture.
Conclude the activity by discussing with students why each event shown in their pictures is
important in the poem.

Enrichment for Gifted/Talented Students
Ask students to choose a stanza of the poem
that they perceive as particularly suspenseful.
Have students identify a literary device—such as
rhythm and rhyme, word choice, or repetition—
that helps create the feeling of suspense. Tell
students to jot down their responses and share
them in class discussion. Then guide students to
create a general list of effects that create suspense. Have students use the list as a guide in
writing their own suspenseful narrative poems
about a legend or other topic of their choice.

⑪ Narrative Poems

Ask the first Narrative Poems question. **Answer:** He does not know that Bess is the person who has been shot.

⑫ Narrative Poems

1. Remind students that there are various types of figurative language. For example, *personification,* in which a nonhuman subject is given human characteristics, and *simile,* a figure of speech that uses *like* or *as* to make a comparison. **Ask:** What other types of figurative language can you describe?
   Possible response: Students might say *metaphor,* which describes one thing as if it were something else, or *symbols,* things that stand for something else.

2. Call on a volunteer to read the bracketed stanza aloud as other students follow along. Then **ask** the Narrative Poems question. **Answer:** Metaphor is used in the stanza to point out a similarity between unlike things. The poet compares the moon to a "ghostly galleon" and the road to a "ribbon of moonlight."

Narrative Poems ⑪
What does the reader know that the high-wayman does not yet realize?

Narrative Poems ⑫
What type of figurative language is used in this stanza?

---

70 The highwayman came riding—
                      Riding—riding—
    The redcoats looked to their priming!¹⁰ She stood up,
        straight and still.

    Tlot-tlot, in the frosty silence! Tlot-tlot, in the echoing
        night!
    Nearer he came and nearer. Her face was like a light.
75 Her eyes grew wide for a moment; she drew one last deep
        breath,
    Then her finger moved in the moonlight,
                      Her musket shattered the moonlight,
    Shattered her breast in the moonlight and warned him—
        with her death.

    He turned. He spurred to the west; he did not know who
        stood
80 Bowed, with her head o'er the musket, drenched with her
        own blood!
    Not till the dawn he heard it, and his face grew gray to
        hear
    How Bess, the landlord's daughter,
                      The landlord's black-eyed daughter,
    Had watched for her love in the moonlight, and died in
        the darkness there.

85 Back, he spurred like a madman, shouting a curse to the
        sky,
    With the white road smoking behind him and his rapier
        brandished¹¹ high.
    Blood-red were his spurs in the golden noon; wine-red
        was his velvet coat;
    When they shot him down on the highway,
                      Down like a dog on the highway,
90 And he lay in his blood on the highway, with a bunch of
        lace at his throat.

    *And still of a winter's night, they say, when the wind is in
        the trees,*
    *When the moon is a ghostly galleon tossed upon cloudy
        seas,*

---

10. **priming** (prī´ min) *n.* explosive used to set off the charge in a gun.
11. **brandished** (bran´ dishd) *adj.* waved in a threatening way.

634 Poetry

Vocabulary Development   © CCSS Language 6

Compound Nouns
Remind students that a compound noun is a noun formed by combining two smaller words. Have students scan pp. 634–635, jotting down compound words. Give students several minutes; then list the compound nouns on the board. *(highwayman, moonlight, landlord, madman, highway, innyard)*

Invite students to come to the board and underline the two smaller words in each compound noun. If time remains, discuss how the two smaller words work together to make the meaning of the compound noun.

When the road is a ribbon of moonlight over the purple
    moor,
A highwayman comes riding—
                Riding—riding—
95 A highwayman comes riding, up to the old inn door.

Over the cobbles he clatters and clangs in the dark
    innyard.
He taps with his whip on the shutters, but all is locked
    and barred.
He whistles a tune to the window, and who should be
    waiting there
100 But the landlord's black-eyed daughter,
                Bess, the landlord's daughter,
Plaiting a dark red love knot into her long black hair.

Critical Thinking

1. **Key Ideas and Details** **(a)** At the beginning of the narrative, how does the highwayman tell Bess he has arrived? **(b) Infer:** What does this method of communication tell you about their relationship?

2. **Key Ideas and Details** **(a)** Identify three details that make the highwayman seem like a romantic figure. **(b) Compare and Contrast:** How do these details compare with the details about Tim the ostler? **(c) Infer:** How do you think the king's men learned where to find the highwayman?

3. **Integration of Knowledge and Ideas** **Draw Conclusions:** What do the last two stanzas suggest about the love between Bess and the highwayman?

4. **Integration of Knowledge and Ideas** **(a)** In what ways do Bess and the highwayman communicate their love for each other? Explain your answer. **(b)** Based on the details in this poem, what do you think the author would say is the best way to express love? [Connect to the Big Question: What is the best way to communicate?]

Cite textual
evidence to
support your
responses.

The Highwayman **635**

Differentiated
Instruction   for Universal Access

Culturally Responsive Instruction
Culture Focus Students may lack the background knowledge or context-building experiences necessary to fully comprehend the selection. Build background knowledge about Britain in the eighteenth century. Explain that cars had not yet been invented. People traveled dirt roads on horseback or in coaches. Locate England on a map. Then, explain that while the people in the British Isles speak English, as we do in America, there are often differences between the two dialects. You can use the examples of "bonny" and "lorry" to illustrate this point. Americans would be more likely to say "pretty" and "truck."

Concept Connector
Have students compare the response to the Writing About the Big Question they gave before reading "The Highwayman" with their ideas afterwards.

ASSESS
Answers

Critical Thinking
Before students respond, you may wish to have them write a brief objective summary of the poem. As they answer the questions below, remind them to support their answers with evidence from the text.

1. (a) They have a signal—a whistle. (b) The fact that they have a special signal indicates that they are very close and have known each other for some time.

2. (a) **Possible responses:** Students may cite the highwayman's fancy dress and weapons, his scorn for danger, his appearances by moonlight, and his love for Bess. (b) **Possible response:** Tim is the opposite of the highwayman: He is grubby, sneaky, possibly mad, and jealous. (c) Tim, the ostler, probably told the soldiers where to find the highwayman.

3. The last two stanzas suggest that the love between Bess and the highwayman continues beyond death.

4. (a) Bess and the highwayman communicate their love through sacrifice. Bess sends a message that will protect the highwayman even though she must die to do so. The highwayman expresses his grief for Bess publicly, even though doing so allows the soldiers to discover him and kill him. (b) The author seems to suggest that acting selflessly is the true expression of love.

635

⑬ Background

Baseball

Baseball is a sport played between two teams of nine players each. The goal is to score runs by hitting a ball with a bat. Players who successfully hit the ball run around a series of bases arranged at the corners of a diamond. Defensive players try to stop hitters from scoring runs by tagging them with the ball or catching a hit ball in the air. The team with the most runs at the end of the game wins.

⑭ Activating Prior Knowledge

Have students brainstorm for challenges that kids face when entering a new neighborhood, school, and country. List students' ideas on the board. Discuss how new kids are able to meet these challenges. Lead students into the poem by telling them that the speaker is a new boy—not only in his Pennsylvania neighborhood but also in the United States.

Concept Connector ➡

Students will return to their ideas about being new after reading the poem.

⑮ About the Selection

In "How I Learned English" Gregory Djanikian speaks in the voice of an immigrant boy just arrived in Williamsport, Pennsylvania. The boy "learns English"—that is, starts to become one of the guys—after a ball knocks him in the forehead and he is able to join his teammates' merriment at his malapropism (ludicrous misuse of words), "Oh, my shin."

636 Poetry

Vocabulary Development

Word Forms

Expand students' vocabulary by helping them learn related forms of the selection vocabulary words. Both of the selection vocabulary words for "How I Learned English" have related forms. Give students a blank **Word Form Chart** (*Professional Development Guidebook*, p. 42) with *transfixed* and *writhing* in the correct columns. Work with the class, or have students work with a partner, to determine the related forms. Place an "X" in the box if there is no word form that fits there. Hold students accountable for integrating the related form of the words in their speaking and writing.

The final chart should look like the one shown.

Noun	Verb	Adjective	Adverb
writhe	writhe	writhing	writhingly
transfixion	transfix	transfixed	x

How I Learned English
Gregory Djanikian

It was in an empty lot
Ringed by elms and fir and honeysuckle.
Bill Corson was pitching in his buckskin[1] jacket,
Chuck Keller, fat even as a boy, was on first,
His t-shirt riding up over his gut,   5
Ron O'Neill, Jim, Dennis, were talking it up
In the field, a blue sky above them
Tipped with cirrus.[2]
            And there I was,
Just off the plane and plopped in the middle   10
Of Williamsport, Pa., and a neighborhood game,
Unnatural and without any moves,
My notions of baseball and America
Growing fuzzier each time I whiffed.[3]

So it was not impossible that I,   15
Banished to the outfield and daydreaming
Of water, or a hotel in the mountains,
Would suddenly find myself in the path
Of a ball stung[4] by Joe Barone.
I watched it closing in   20
Clean and untouched, transfixed
By its easy arc before it hit
My forehead with a thud.
            I fell back.
Dazed, clutching my brow,   25
Groaning, "Oh my shin, oh my shin,"
And everybody peeled away from me
And dropped from laughter, and there we were,
All of us writhing on the ground for one reason
Or another.   30

---

1. **buckskin** *adj.* yellowish-gray leather made from the hide of a deer.
2. **cirrus** (sir´ əs) *n.* high, thin clouds.
3. **whiffed** (hwift) *v.* struck out.
4. **stung** *v.* hit hard.

16 ◀ **Critical Viewing**
Which details in this photograph reveal that this player knows how to field a baseball? Explain. **[Analyze]**

Narrative Poems
What do you know so far about the main character?

Vocabulary
transfixed (trans fikst´) *adj.* rooted to the spot

writhing (rīth´ iŋ) *adj.* squirming, often in response to pain

18 ✓ Reading Check
What happens to the speaker when Joe hits a ball into the outfield?

---

16 Critical Viewing
Answer: Her eyes are on the ball, and she is positioned to catch it.

17 Narrative Poems

1. **Ask** students to read lines 9–14 to themselves. Then, make a list of phrases that describe the main character.
   Answer: He is "just off the plane"; he is in Williamsport, PA; he is playing baseball; he isn't very good at baseball; he is making a lot of "whiffs," or mistakes.

2. **Ask** the Narrative Poems question.
   Possible response: So far, we know that the main character is new to Williamsport, and that he isn't very good at playing baseball.

Connecting to the Big Question

1. Remind students of the Big Question.

2. **Ask** students: What happens when the narrator mistakenly says "shin" instead of "forehead"?
   Answer: Everyone laughs—even the narrator.

3. **Ask:** What does the narrator communicate nonverbally?
   Answer: He communicates that he is able to laugh at himself.

4. **Ask** students whether nonverbal communication is more or less effective than words.
   Possible response: It is less effective in communicating information, but more important in communicating personality.

5. Have students look for other instances of nonverbal communication as they read.

18 Reading Check
Answer: The ball hits the narrator in the head.

Ⓒ Text Complexity Rubric

How I Learned English	
Qualitative Measures	
Context/Knowledge Demands	Neighborhood baseball game; the recent past 1 ② 3 4 5
Structure/Language Conventionality	Straightforward diction; long poetic phrases 1 2 ③ 4 5
Levels of Meaning	Learning English; learning to be one of the group 1 2 ③ 4 5
Quantitative Measures	
Text Length	Word Count: 296
Lexile	NP

Reader and Task Suggestions

Preparing to Read the Text
- Using the Background information on TE p. 636, discuss the game of baseball.
- Ask students to think about the challenges of learning a new language in a new culture.
- Guide students to use Multidraft Reading strategies (TE p. 629) to deepen their comprehension.

Leveled Tasks
Structure/Language If students will have difficulty with long phrases, have them break them into smaller parts and paraphrase the smaller parts.

Analyzing If students will not have difficulty with language, have them read to answer this question: "How does the narrator's use of the phrase *Oh my shin* symbolize his experience on the team?"

Spiral Review

Figurative Language

1. **Remind** students that they studied the concept of figurative language in the Unit 4 Literary Analysis Workshop (pp. 572–581).

2. **Ask** the Spiral Review question. **Answer:** The simile tells readers that Joe Barone's hands are big and wide.

⑲ Narrative Poems

Read the bracketed stanza with students. Then, **ask** the Narrative Poems question.

Answer: You know the speaker is feeling better about baseball because he plays on till dusk, and describes himself as "doing all right."

ASSESS

Answers

Critical Thinking

Remind students to support their answers with evidence from the text.

1. (a) These details tell you that a baseball game is under way: One boy is pitching, another boy is on first, and three boys are talking in the field. (b) The speaker has trouble with the game because he is playing baseball for the first time.

2. (a) Joe Barone offers the speaker a hand up. (b) The speaker chooses to continue because he feels like one of the team.

3. **Possible response:** If he hadn't been hit in the head, the narrator might not have become friends with the other boys that day. The funny incident brought them together.

4. **Possible response:** Playing baseball could help the speaker learn English because as he plays he will listen to and communicate with people who are fluent in English.

5. (a) They laugh. They stamp the ground with their hands. Joe Barone offers the narrator a hand up and dusts him off. (b) These actions clearly communicate their acceptance of him.

Spiral Review
Figurative Language
What does the simile in ⑲ line 38 tell readers?

Narrative Poems
How do you know that the speaker's feelings about baseball have changed?

Someone said "shin" again,
There was a wild stamping of hands on the ground,
A kicking of feet, and the fit
Of laughter overtook me too,
35 And that was important, as important
As Joe Barone asking me how I was
Through his tears, picking me up
And dusting me off with hands like swatters,
And though my head felt heavy,
40 I played on till dusk
Missing flies and pop-ups and grounders
And calling out in desperation things like
"Yours" and "take it," but doing all right,
Tugging at my cap in just the right way,
45 Crouching low, my feet set,
"Hum baby" sweetly on my lips.

Critical Thinking

Cite textual evidence to support your responses.

1. **Key Ideas and Details** **(a)** What details in lines 1–9 tell you a baseball game is underway? **(b) Infer:** Why does the speaker have trouble with the game?

2. **Key Ideas and Details** **(a)** What help does Joe Barone offer the speaker in lines 35–38? **(b) Interpret:** Why does the speaker choose to continue playing?

3. **Key Ideas and Details** **Speculate:** How might the outcome of the day have been different for the speaker if he had not been hit in the head?

4. **Integration of Knowledge and Ideas** **Draw Conclusions:** Do you think playing baseball will help the speaker learn English? Why or why not?

5. **Integration of Knowledge and Ideas** **(a)** Name at least three nonverbal ways characters in this poem communicate. **(b)** Why are the players' actions more important to the speaker than words? *[Connect to the Big Question: What is the best way to communicate?]*

638 Poetry

Vocabulary Development

Vocabulary Knowledge Rating

When students have completed reading and discussing "The Highwayman" and "How I Learned English," have them take out their **Vocabulary Knowledge Rating Chart.** Read the words aloud once more and have students rate their knowledge of the words again in the After Reading column. Clarify any words that are still problematic. Have students write their own definition and example or sentence in the appropriate column. Then have students complete the Vocabulary Practice activities on the next page. Encourage students to use the words in further discussion and written work about these selections. Remind them that they will be accountable for these words on the **Selection Test,** *Unit 4 Resources,* pp. 112–114 or pp. 115–117.

Comparing Narrative Poems

1. Craft and Structure Narrative poems have many of the same elements as short stories. Use a chart like this one to find examples of short story elements in each poem.

Short Story Element	Highwayman	How I Learned English
Setting		
Characters		
Point of View		
Conflict (Problem to be solved)		
Outcome of conflict		

2. Craft and Structure (a) In each poem, identify a musical element and explain its effect. **(b)** In each poem, identify and interpret an instance of figurative language.

 Timed Writing

Explanatory Text: Essay

In an essay, explain how each poet creates contrasts between characters' points of view. Then, compare the effects the contrasts add—suspense, humor, and so on. **(40 minutes)**

5-Minute Planner

1. Read the prompt carefully and completely.

2. Gather your ideas by jotting down answers to these questions:

- Who narrates each poem? How is point of view developed?
- What different interests, motives, or perceptions do characters have?
- What important information do some characters know that others do not? What effect does this situation create?

3. Draw evidence from each poem, taking notes on similarities and differences. Use these notes as you write your essay.

4. Reread the prompt, and then draft your essay.

The Highwayman • How I Learned English **639**

Comparing Narrative Poems

1. "Highwayman": [row 1]: moonlight, inn; [row 2]: the highwayman, Bess, Tim; [row 3]: narrator/poet; [row 4]: soldiers are trying to capture robber; [row 5]: Both Bess and the highwayman die. "English": [row 1]: empty lot; [row 2]: Joe Barone and the narrator; [row 3]: Immigrant boy; [row 4]: The narrator wants to fit in; [row 5]: He feels like one of the boys. For another sample answer, see *Graphic Organizer Transparencies, Comparing Narrative Poems Organizer A,* p. 123.

2. **Possible response:** In "The Highwayman," the musical element of repeating words increases the suspense. In "How I Learned English," the musical element of the word "thud" adds humor.

Timed Writing

1. Review the prompt with students.

2. Have students use the 5-Minute Planner to structure their time. Guide them in answering the bulleted questions.

3. Allow students 40 minutes to complete the assignment.

4. As students prewrite and draft, have them refer to their completed **Comparing Narrative Poems Graphic Organizer.**

Six Traits Focus

	Ideas		Word Choice
✔	Organization	✔	Sentence Fluency
	Voice	✔	Conventions

Assessment Resources

Unit 4 Resources
L1 L2 EL **Selection Test A**, pp. 112–114.
L3 L4 EL **Selection Test B**, pp. 115–117.
L3 L4 **Open-Book Test**, pp. 109–111.

PHLit Online! All assessment resources are available at **www.PHLitOnline.com.**

Introducing the Writing Assignment

Review the assignment and the criteria.

Connecting to Real-Life Writing

Point out that problem-and-solution essays usually focus on real-life problems and the ways to solve them.

📖✏️ Writing Workshop
Work in Progress

If students have completed the Work-in-Progress assignments on pp. 599 and 619, suggest that they try to develop their Work-in-Progress ideas in a problem-and-solution essay.

Prewriting/Planning Strategy

1. Introduce the prewriting strategy, using the instruction and the graphic organizer on the student page.

2. Have students apply the strategy to choose a topic.

Six Traits Focus

✔ Ideas	Word Choice
Organization	Sentence Fluency
Voice	Conventions

Writing Workshop

Write an Argument

Argument: Problem-and-Solution Essay

Defining the Form A **problem-and-solution essay** identifies and explains a problem and offers one or more possible solutions to it. You might use elements of this type of writing in editorials, letters to authorities, and proposals.

Assignment Choose a problem with which you are familiar, and propose one or more solutions. Include these elements:

✔ a *thesis* that clearly states the problem

✔ an interesting *introduction*

✔ body paragraphs with *step-by-step solutions*

✔ *supporting details with facts and examples* to support each solution

✔ a strong *conclusion*

✔ error-free writing, including *correct use of participles*

To preview the criteria on which your essay may be judged, see the rubric on page 645.

 Writing Workshop: *Work in Progress*

Review the work you did on pages 599 and 619.

Prewriting/Planning Strategy

Identify a problem and possible solution. Think of problems that could inspire a strong essay. Consider problems in your town or city or in your school by reading local print or online newspapers or talking to other students. Once you decide on a problem, use a chart like this one to brainstorm for possible solutions.

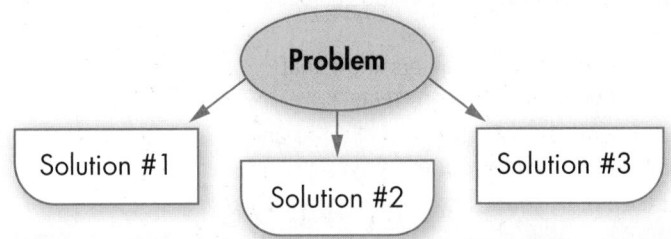

© Common Core
State Standards

Writing
1. Write arguments to support claims with clear reasons and relevant evidence.
1.a. Introduce claim(s), acknowledge alternate or opposing claims, and organize the reasons and evidence logically.
1.b. Support claim(s) with logical reasoning and relevant evidence, using accurate, credible sources and demonstrating an understanding of the topic or text.
7. Conduct short research projects to answer a question, drawing on several sources and generating additional related, focused questions for further research and investigation.

Teaching Resources

The following resources can be used to enrich or extend your instruction for the Writing Workshop.

All *Unit 4 Resources*
Writing Workshop: Writing for Assessment, pp. 118, 119

All *Common Core Companion,*
pp. 202–212, 232–239, 258–262; 333–342

All *Professional Development Guidebook*
Rubrics for Self-Assessment: Problem-and-Solution Essay, pp. 244, 245

All *Graphic Organizers*
Rubrics for Self-Assessment: Problem-and-Solution Essay, p. 168

 All resources are available online at **www.PHLitOnline.com**

Ideas	Conventions	Sentence Fluency	Voice	Organization	Word Choice

Making Your Ideas Convincing

Ideas make up the content of any piece of writing. You may have several thoughts about problems and solutions that come from your research and your own experience. To successfully persuade your readers, select the best ideas, then add convincing supporting details. Follow these tips to write a powerful essay.

Narrowing Your Focus After you choose a general problem for your essay, it is time to narrow the focus. If you write about a problem that is very broad, the solutions may be too complex. Break the problem down into smaller parts. Determine who your audience is. Then, imagine a part of the problem that your audience can help solve. To give focus to your ideas, write a thesis statement that clearly states the problem.

PH WRITING COACH

Further instruction and practice are available in *Prentice Hall Writing Coach.*

Explaining the Problem Your introduction should include a clear explanation of the problem. Use accurate, specific language when you explain your topic. While researching several sources, develop your ideas by answering the following questions before you write.

Who	What	When	Where	Why	How
Who is responsible for the situation?	What negative effects come from this problem?	When did the problem start?	Where is the problem most prevalent?	Why is this situation a problem now?	How did the problem develop over time?

Providing Elaboration To persuade readers that your solutions will be effective, you must provide relevant evidence and details that support each solution. Use the following techniques:

- Include accurate data, statistics, or research that supports your ideas. Quote expert opinions that favor your solutions.

- Interview people to gather anecdotes about the issue. Be sure to talk to people who know about your subject.

- Explain in detail exactly how and why your solution will be successful. Convince readers that the solution makes sense with step-by-step descriptions.

Writing Workshop **641**

Applying Understanding by Design Principles

Clarifying Expected Outcomes: Using Rubrics
- Before students begin work on this assignment, have them preview the Rubric for Self-Assessment (p. 645) to learn what qualities their problem-and-solution essay must have. A copy of this Rubric appears in the *Graphic Organizer Transparencies,* p. 127.
- Review the criteria in the Rubric with the class. Before students use the Rubric to assess their own writing, work with them to rate the Student Model (p. 644) using the Rubric.

- If you wish to assess students' problem-and-solution essays with either a 5-point or a 6-point scoring Rubric, see *Professional Development Guidebook,* pp. 244–245.

Making Your Ideas Convincing

1. Introduce the prewriting skill, using the instructions on the student page.

2. Have students follow the recommendations and use the questions in the chart to make their ideas convincing.

Teaching the Strategies

1. Help students practice narrowing topics to manageable length. **Ask** which of these problems would be best to address in a problem-and-solution essay appearing in the school newspaper, and have students explain their response:

   poor nutrition

   poor nutrition in restaurants

   poor nutrition in the school cafeteria

   (**Possible response:** The last; the others are too broad, and the last is the problem a student audience could do the most about.)

2. Once students have narrowed their own topic, have them use the questions on the chart to develop a clear explanation of the problem they will address. Note that every question on the chart may not apply to every problem, but students may be able to tweak a question to make it applicable. For example, for an essay about the problem of poor nutrition in the school cafeteria, a question more useful than the *Where* question on the chart might be *Which foods present the greatest problem?*

3. Have students list sources they plan to use to research their problem and its possible solutions. Remind students using the Internet to choose reliable Web sites.

PH WRITING COACH | Grade 7

Students will find additional support for writing a problem-and-solution essay in chapter 8.

641

Drafting Strategies

1. Introduce the drafting strategies, using the instruction and graphic organizer on the student page.
2. Have students apply the strategies as they draft their essays.

Teaching the Strategies

1. Tell students to include both an introduction and a conclusion to their essays. The introduction should capture readers' attention and clearly state the problem; the conclusion should restate the problem and inspire readers to accept the solution or solutions offered.
2. Remind students that the bodies of their essays should support their solution or solutions with reasons, statistics, examples, or other supporting details.

Think Aloud: Model Essay Openings

Stress that a good essay interests readers right from the start. Say to students:

A bold statement of the problem is one way to grab my readers' attention. For example, for a problem-and-solution essay about poor nutrition in the school cafeteria, I might open: *The unhealthy food in the school cafeteria has got to go!* A question will also grab attention; for example: *Isn't it time to stop serving unhealthy food in the school cafeteria?*

Six Traits Focus

	Ideas		Word Choice
✔	Organization		Sentence Fluency
✔	Voice		Conventions

Revising Strategies

1. Introduce the revising strategies, using the instruction and graphic organizer on the student page.
2. Have students apply the strategies as they revise.

642

Drafting Strategies

Introduce the problem. Begin your essay by stating your thesis, or main idea. Grab your readers' attention with a bold statement or question about the problem that you will address.

Develop your ideas. In the body of your essay, build your argument by presenting information. If you are presenting one solution, move through it step-by-step. If you are suggesting several possible solutions, arrange them in an order that makes logical sense. Treat each one separately and clearly. Use your ideas from the Writer's Toolbox to fully develop your ideas. Finally, craft a concluding statement that supports your thesis and leaves a memorable thought in readers' minds.

Revising Strategies

Use the present tense. To make a convincing argument, use the present tense when you present your supporting details. For example, if you are presenting the opinion of an expert, consider using the following style:

> **Weak:** The supervisor at the city water plant *stated* that he *will support* the Clean Water Act.

> **Better:** The supervisor at the city water plant *states* that he *supports* the Clean Water Act.

Peer Review

Ask a classmate to read your essay. Then, have him or her complete a response using the following format. Request that your reviewer be as specific as possible about any areas that need improvement. Use your peer reviewer's response to revise your problem-and-solution essay. If you are unclear about any feedback, ask your reviewer for clarification.

Peer Reviewer Questions	Yes or No	How can I improve my essay?
Can you identify the problem?		
Is my solution (or solutions) reasonable?		
Do I provide enough support for each solution I propose?		
Is my essay convincing?		
Does my conclusion inspire action?		

Common Core State Standards

Writing

1. Write arguments to support claims with clear reasons and relevant evidence.

1.c. Use words, phrases, and clauses to create cohesion and clarify the relationships among claim(s), reasons, and evidence.

1.e. Provide a concluding statement or section that follows from and supports the argument presented.

Language

1.c. Place phrases and clauses within a sentence, recognizing and correcting misplaced and dangling modifiers.

Teaching the Strategies

1. Explain that the present tense can lend a sense of urgency or immediacy to a problem, stressing that it is happening now and needs to be solved soon.
2. Allow students to choose a classmate as peer reviewer, or pair students yourself. Discuss ways in which students can improve their essays when the answer to a Peer Reviewer Question is *No*. For example, writers can offer more examples or statistics to show that a solution is reasonable or to make the essay convincing; or adjust the word choice to make the conclusion more inspiring.

Six Traits Focus

	Ideas		Word Choice
✔	Organization	✔	Sentence Fluency
	Voice	✔	Conventions

Revising Sentences Using Participles

To make your sentences flow smoothly, combine sentences using participles and participial phrases. A **participle** is a verb form that acts as an adjective, modifying a noun or pronoun. **Present participles** end in *-ing*. **Past participles** usually end in *-ed*, but may have an irregular ending, such as *-en* in *spoken*.

> past participle   noun
>
> She banged her fist against the <u>closed</u> <u>windows</u>.

A **participial phrase** consists of a participle and its modifiers. A **misplaced modifier** is placed far away from the word it describes.
> **Misplaced modifier:** <u>I</u> heard her voice listening to the song.
> **Solution:** Listening to the song, <u>I</u> heard her voice.

A **dangling modifier** is not logically connected to any word in the sentence.
> **Dangling modifier:** Raising the flag, the <u>wind</u> felt strong.
> **Solution:** Raising the flag, the <u>sailors</u> felt the strong wind.

Fixing Choppy Passages Using Participles To fix a choppy passage, identify sentences that can be combined. Then rewrite the passage using one or more of the following methods:

1. **Combine sentences using a present participle.**
   - ▶ **Example:** We arranged a tour. We would walk the grounds. We arranged a <u>walking</u> tour of the grounds.

2. **Combine sentences using a past participle.**
   - ▶ **Example:** The food is cooked. It will not spoil. The <u>cooked</u> food will not spoil.

3. **Combine Sentences using a participial phrase.**
   - ▶ **Example:** Marissa ate her food quickly. She was running late. <u>Running late,</u> Marissa ate her food quickly.

Grammar in Your Writing

Choose three paragraphs in your draft. Read the paragraphs aloud, highlighting any passages that sound choppy. Using one of the methods above, fix the choppy passages by combining sentences.

> **PH** WRITING COACH
> Further instruction and practice are available in *Prentice Hall Writing Coach*.

Strategies for *Using Technology in Writing*

Note that when students use a computer word-processing program to combine sentences as part of their revising, they may accidentally delete text they want to keep. Even if they print the text, mark revisions on the printout, and enter them later at the keyboard, they may still delete text accidentally. The best way to correct this problem is to make a backup copy of the file being revised. Then if text is lost, students can refer to the backup file or even copy the missing text and paste it into the file they are revising.

Revising Sentences Using Participles

1. Introduce the grammar skill, using the instruction on the student page.
2. Discuss the definitions and examples as well as the strategies for fixing the choppy passages.
3. Have students follow the instruction for Grammar in Your Writing to correct problems in their drafts.

Teaching the Strategies

1. Offer students these examples of participial phrases, all of which modify the noun *boy*. Note that participles in participial phrases can have objects as well as modifiers; in the last example, *race* is the object of *running*.

   Running swiftly, the mischievous boy snatched the woman's purse.

   Running down the street, the boy reached the bus before it left.

   Running the race, the boy finished in record time.

2. Caution students to place a participle or participial phrase close to the word it modifies in order to avoid ambiguous or dangling participles, in which the modified word is missing or unclear.

   Dangling: *Running swiftly, my ankle twisted.*

   Correct: *Running swiftly, I twisted my ankle.*

   Ambiguous: *Running swiftly, the audience watched the track star.*

   Clear: *The audience watched the track star running swiftly.*

Think Aloud: Model Revising Sentences Using Participles

Model how to combine sentences using participles. Say to students:

In a choppy passage where two sentences both say something about the same noun or pronoun, I can turn one sentence into a participle or participial phrase and use it to modify the noun in the other sentence. For example, in *The toast is burned. I threw it out*, I can turn the first sentence into the participle *burned* and use it to modify *toast* in the second sentence: *I threw the burned toast out.*

Student Model

Review the Student Model with the class, using the annotations to analyze the writer's use of the elements of a problem-and-solution essay.

Teaching from the Student Model

1. Note that Nicole organizes her essay into an introductory paragraph, a body of four paragraphs, and a conclusion.

2. Point out that Nicole introduces the problem with a question that immediately grabs readers' attention. **Ask** students how this approach makes the essay more effective. (**Possible responses:** It engages the reader as an active participant. It makes the reader identify with the problem, indicating that he or she may actually have experienced it.)

3. Point out the use of present-tense verbs that help make the essay more effective.

4. Note the many supporting details about ticket prices, anti-scalping laws, and scalping practices. **Ask** students where Nicole may have researched this information. (**Possible responses:** newspaper articles, government agencies, interviews with concert goers, reliable on-line Web sites)

5. Point out that Nicole ends each paragraph in the body of her essay by suggesting a solution to the problem elaborated in that paragraph. **Ask** which sentence in the conclusion sums up her solutions. (**Answer:** the last)

Connecting to Real-Life Writing

Point out that many jobs require people to identify problems and offer solutions in writing. Although the writing may take a shorter form than a full-length essay, the basic procedure will be the same: Define the problem and propose a solution or solutions.

Student Model: Nicole Eras, Cedarhurst, NY

Common Core State Standards

Language
2.b. Spell correctly.

Have you ever wanted to go to a concert or a big sporting event, and tried to get seats? You try to get them as soon as they go on sale and in the first two minutes, they're gone. Ticket brokers buy most of the seats right before anybody else can get to them and then they sell them at astronomical prices. This problem affects people of all ages, but especially teenagers. It is unfair and we should find a possible solution.

> Nicole introduces the problem in a clearly stated thesis.

This problem has shown up in a popular concert I saw recently. Ticket brokers have systems that allow them to buy big blocks of tickets in a short amount of time. Then they make their money reselling tickets. Brokers bought most of the tickets and sold them to people for about $360. When teenagers got their tickets in the mail, they saw the original cost on the ticket was $60! This is all illegal. It is unfair to teenagers who have a right to buy them at the original price. The performer of the concert has filed a lawsuit against these ticket brokers.

> In the body, she further explains the problem by providing detailed evidence.

Several states have anti-scalping laws. In New York State, for example, it is legal to buy tickets and resell them for $5 more or 10% more than the original price. This would make a $60 ticket cost $65 or $66, not $360. Brokers often sell them to people for more than three times the original cost! What makes it even worse is that the government doesn't really enforce this law. I say that the government should start enforcing it. Police should investigate the Web sites that ticket brokers use, and even arrest the people the police catch.

As part of the unfair broker system, there are also people who work for the brokers and buy the tickets in line at the concert and resell them there. These are the people you might meet at the concert who try to sell you $1000 seats. This is illegal, and I think that we should have police at these affairs to try to scout out these so-called workers.

> Nicole gives possible solutions to different parts of the problem she discusses.

In addition to the online broker system, which is mostly illegal, there are also licensed brokers. Licensed brokers are allowed to resell at a higher rate because they can charge a large service fee. They do this because they are allowed, and no one is stopping them. I think that this is not right. No one should rob people of their money. The only people who should be allowed to buy tickets are those who stand in line or get tickets from official vendors themselves.

So, the next time that you try to get tickets to a concert and they're either all sold out or available for a really high price, you now know why. You might think that it's unfair, unlawful, and just not right. If the police and other government officials would act, it would allow the REAL fans to enjoy seeing their favorite stars.

> She ends with a strong conclusion that reminds her readers of the seriousness of the problem and the need for a solution.

644 Poetry

Strategies for Test Taking

When taking a test that includes a problem-and-solution writing prompt, students should pay special attention to the clarity of their writing. Remind them to clearly state the problem and the solution or solutions they offer, supporting their ideas with ample evidence. Students should carefully organize their essays with cause-and-effect terms such as *because, therefore,* and *for that reason* that help make the relationships between ideas clear. Before submitting their essays, students should review them for overall coherence and unity.

Editing and Proofreading.

Focus on Spelling: Words With Suffixes Follow these spelling rules:

- If a one-syllable word ends in a vowel and a consonant, double the consonant before adding *-ed* or *-est*. (*hot* becomes *hottest*)
- If a word has more than one syllable and ends in one vowel followed by one consonant, and *if the accent is on the last syllable*, double the consonant before adding *-ed* or *-est*. (*patrol* becomes *patrolled*)
- If a word ends in a consonant followed by a silent *e*, drop the *e* before adding *-ing*. (*describe* becomes *describing*)
- If a word ends in *y*, change *y* to *i* before adding *-es* or *-ed*. (*ability* becomes *abilities*)

Publishing and Presenting

Prepare an advice column. Turn your essay into a question and answer, as if it appeared in an advice column. As a class, publish your columns under a collective name, such as *Ask Amanda* or *Dear Dan*.

Be a talk-show guest. With a partner, take on the role of a talk-show guest who has been asked to give advice about the problem addressed in your essay. Take turns being the host and the guest.

Reflecting on Your Writing

Writer's Journal Jot down your answer to this question:
How might you approach a problematic issue in the future?

Rubric for Self-Assessment

Find evidence in your writing to address each category. Then, use the rating scale to grade your work.

Criteria	Rating Scale				
	not very				*very*
Focus: How clearly does your thesis state the problem?	1	2	3	4	5
Ideas: How thoroughly do you explain the problem in an introduction?	1	2	3	4	5
Support/Elaboration: How developed is your support for each solution, including facts and examples?	1	2	3	4	5
Style: How persuasive is your language in the conclusion?	1	2	3	4	5
Sentence Fluency: How well do you avoid choppy sentences, especially by using participles and participle phrases?	1	2	3	4	5
Conventions: How correct is your spelling of words that contain suffixes?	1	2	3	4	5

Spiral Review
Earlier in the unit, you learned about **infinitives and infinitive phrases** (p. 598) and **appositives and appositive phrases** (p. 618). Make sure you have used them correctly in your essay.

Editing and Proofreading

1. Introduce the editing and proofreading focus, using the instruction on the student page.
2. Have students edit and proofread their narratives, correcting grammar, spelling, punctuation, and word choice. Make sure they check for errors of the type noted in the lesson focus and the Spiral Review.

Teaching the Editing Focus
Have students apply the spelling rules to these additional words:

fat + -est (**Answer:** fattest)

occur + -ed (**Answer:** occurred)

believe + -ing (**Answer:** believing)

family + -es (**Answer:** families)

Six Traits Focus

Ideas		Word Choice	
Organization		Sentence Fluency	
Voice		Conventions	✔

Publishing and Presenting

1. Have each student turn his or her essay into two letters. One letter, from a column reader, should ask for advice about the problem in the essay. The other letter should be a response offering "Dan's" or "Amanda's" solution.
2. Pair students to work as partners playing the roles of guest and host on a radio or TV talk show. The student portraying the guest should have his or her essay used as the basis of the discussion; when the other student takes on the guest's role, his or her essay should become the basis.

Reflecting on Your Writing

To prompt their journal writing, tell students to consider what this workshop showed them about identifying and explaining solutions to problems.

Differentiated Instruction
for Universal Access

Strategy for Special-Needs Students
Help students map out their essays using a graphic organizer. For a problem-and-solution essay with one solution, students should list the problem with an arrow pointing to the solution, listing the steps of the solution underneath it.

EL Strategy for English Learners
Pair English learners with students whose native language is English. Have the native English speaker complete his or her essay first, sharing it with the English learner. The student learning English should write his or her own essay, modeling it on his or her classmate's essay and addressing the same problem but offering a different solution.

Enrichment for Advanced Writers
Have students address a problem in the news and write their essays in the form of newspaper editorials. Each student should thoroughly research the issue and come up with a solution or solutions supported by facts, reasons, and examples. Encourage students to mail their efforts to newspapers for possible publication as guest editorials.

✓ Poetry Collection 5 • ✓✓ Poetry Collection 6
Lesson Pacing Guide

DAY 1 Preteach

- © Administer the Reading and Vocabulary Warm-ups (*Unit 4 Resources,* pp. 127–130 or 145–148) as necessary.
- Introduce the Reading Skill: Paraphrase.
- © Introduce the Literary Analysis concept: Sound Devices.
- Distribute copies of the appropriate graphic organizer for the Reading Skill (*Graphic Organizer Transparencies,* pp. 131–133).
- Distribute copies of the appropriate graphic organizer for Literary Analysis (*Graphic Organizer Transparencies,* pp. 128–130).
- © Teach the selection vocabulary.
- © Introduce the Word Study skill.

DAYS 2–3 Preteach/Teach

- © Build background with the Background feature.
- Develop thematic vocabulary and thematic thinking with Writing About the Big Question.
- Prepare students to read with the Activating Prior Knowledge activities (TE).
- Informally monitor comprehension while students read.
- Use the Reading Check questions to confirm comprehension.
- Develop students' ability to restate the author's words in their own words using the Paraphrase questions.
- © Develop students' understanding of sound devices using the Sound Devices questions.
- © Reinforce vocabulary with the Vocabulary notes.
- © Reinforce unit focus standards using the Spiral Review prompts.

DAY 4 Assess

- Assess students' comprehension and mastery of the skills by having them answer the Critical Thinking, Reading Skill, and Literary Analysis questions.
- © Have students complete the Vocabulary Practice activities.
- © Have students complete the Word Study activities.

DAY 5 Extend/Assess

- Have students complete the Conventions lesson.
- © Have students complete the Writing activity and write a paraphrase. (You may assign as homework.)
- © Extend learning by having students complete the Speaking and Listening activity, a poetry reading. As an alternative, assign them "Pay Days" or "The Music Mix" in *Reality Central.*
- Administer Selection Test A or B (*Unit 4 Resources,* pp. 139–144 or 160–165).

© Common Core State Standards

Reading Literature 4. Determine the meaning of words and phrases as they are used in a text, including figurative and connotative meanings; analyze the impact of rhymes and other repetitions of sounds (e.g., alliteration) on a specific verse or stanza of a poem or section of a story or drama.

Writing 9.a. Apply grade 7 Reading standards to literature.

Speaking and Listening 4. Use appropriate eye contact, adequate volume, and clear pronunciation.
6. Adapt speech to a variety of contexts and tasks, demonstrating command of formal English when indicated or appropriate.

Language 1.a. Explain the function of phrases and clauses in general and their function in specific sentences.
1.b. Choose among simple, compound, complex, and compound-complex sentences to signal differing relationships among ideas.
4.c. Consult general and specialized reference materials, both print and digital, to find the pronunciation of a word or determine or clarify its precise meaning or its part of speech.
5.b. Use the relationship between particular words to better understand each of the words.

Additional Standards Practice
Common Core Companion, *pp. 41–61*

Daily Block Scheduling
Each day in this Lesson Pacing Guide represents a 40–50 minute period. Teachers using block scheduling may combine days to revise pacing. In addition, teachers may differentiate and support core instruction by integrating components for extended and intensive support, as students require. See the Guide to Selected Leveled Resources (facing page).

Guide to Selected Leveled Resources

RTI **Tier 1** (students performing on level)	✓ **More Accessible** Poetry Collection 5	✓✓ **More Complex** Poetry Collection 6
Warm Up — Practice, **model**, and **monitor** fluency, working with the **whole class** or **in groups**.	**Vocabulary** and **Reading Warm-ups B**, *Unit 4 Resources*, pp. 127–128, 130	**Vocabulary** and **Reading Warm-ups B**, *Unit 4 Resources*, pp. 145–146, 148
Comprehension/Skills — **Support** and **monitor** comprehension and skills development, having students complete the activities, graphic organizers, and interactive prompts **independently** or **as a class**.	• *Reader's Notebook*, adapted instruction and full selection **EL** *Reader's Notebook: English Learner's Version*, adapted instruction and adapted selection • **Reading Skill Graphic Organizer B**, *Graphic Organizer Transparencies*, p. 133 • **Literary Analysis Graphic Organizer B**, *Graphic Organizer Transparencies*, p. 130	• *Reader's Notebook*, adapted instruction and summary **EL** *Reader's Notebook: English Learner's Version*, adapted instruction and summary • **Reading Skill Graphic Organizer B**, *Graphic Organizer Transparencies*, p. 133 • **Literary Analysis Graphic Organizer B**, *Graphic Organizer Transparencies*, p. 130
Monitor Progress — **Monitor** student progress with the differentiated curriculum-based assessment in the *Unit Resources*.	• **Selection Test B**, *Unit 4 Resources*, pp. 142–144 • **Open-Book Test**, *Unit 4 Resources*, pp. 136–138	• **Selection Test B**, *Unit 4 Resources*, pp. 163–165 • **Open-Book Test**, *Unit 4 Resources*, pp. 157–159

RTI **Tier 2** (students requiring intervention)	✓ **More Accessible** Poetry Collection 5	✓✓ **More Complex** Poetry Collection 6
Warm Up — Practice, **model**, and **monitor** fluency in **groups** or **with individuals**.	• **Vocabulary and Reading Warm-ups A**, *Unit 4 Resources*, pp. 127–129 • *Reality Central*, "Pay Days" • *Hear It!* Audio CD (adapted text)	• **Vocabulary and Reading Warm-ups A**, *Unit 4 Resources*, pp. 145–147 • *Reality Central*, "The Music Mix" • *Hear It!* Audio CD
Comprehension/Skills — • **Support** and **monitor** comprehension and skills development, working in **small groups** or **with individuals**. • **Pair** students with more advanced peers and have them complete the writing activity in the *Real-World Writing Journal*. • As students complete the selection in the appropriate version of the *Reader's Notebook*, **monitor** comprehension frequently with group questions and individual instruction. • **Model** strategies while guiding students in completing the activities and prompts in the *Reader's Notebook*, as well as the graphic organizers. • **Practice** skills and **monitor** mastery with the *Reading Kit* worksheets.	• *Real-World Writing Journal*, Lesson 5, pp. 120–123 • *Reader's Notebook: Adapted Version*, adapted instruction and adapted selection **EL** *Reader's Notebook: English Learner's Version*, adapted instruction and adapted selection • **Reading Skill Graphic Organizer A**, *Graphic Organizer Transparencies*, p. 131 • **Literary Analysis Graphic Organizer A**, *Graphic Organizer Transparencies*, p. 128 • *Reading Kit*, Practice worksheets, pp. 174, 178, 184, 186, 196	• *Real-World Writing Journal*, Lesson 6, pp. 124–127 • *Reader's Notebook: Adapted Version*, adapted instruction and summary **EL** *Reader's Notebook: English Learner's Version*, adapted instruction and summary • **Reading Skill Graphic Organizer A**, *Graphic Organizer Transparencies*, p. 132 • **Literary Analysis Graphic Organizer A**, *Graphic Organizer Transparencies*, p. 129 • *Reading Kit*, Practice worksheets, pp. 174, 178, 184, 186, 196
Monitor Progress — **Monitor** student progress with the differentiated curriculum-based assessment in the *Unit Resources* and in the *Reading Kit*.	• **Selection Test A**, *Unit 4 Resources*, pp. 139–141 • *Reading Kit*, Assess worksheets pp. 175, 179, 185, 187, 197	• **Selection Test A**, *Unit 4 Resources*, pp. 160–162 • *Reading Kit*, Assess worksheets pp. 175, 179, 185, 187, 197

TIER 3 Tier 3 intervention may require consultation with the student's special-education or dyslexia specialist. For additional support, see the Tier 2 activities and resources listed above.

One-on-one teaching 　Group work 　Whole class instruction 　Independent work 　Assessment

For a complete guide to selection support, including support for Advanced students, see the Overview of Resources in the frontmatter.

✓ Poetry Collection 5
✓✓ Poetry Collection 6

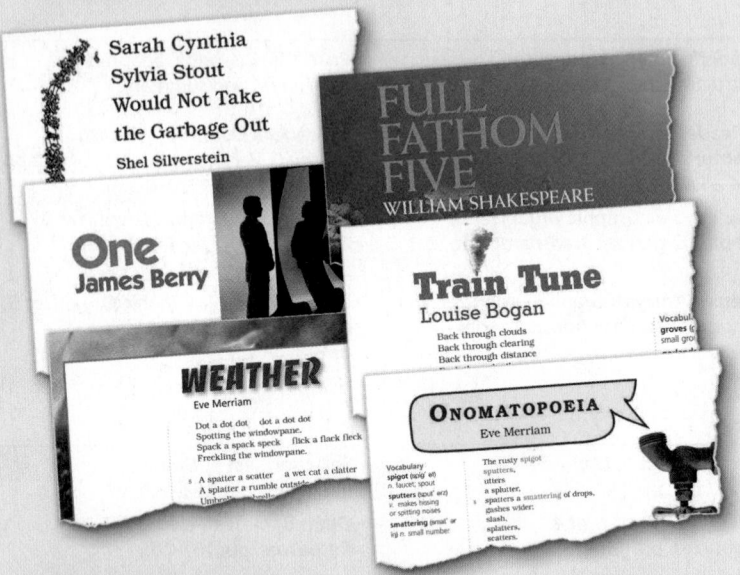

RESOURCES FOR:

- **L1** Special-Needs Students
- **L2** Below-Level Students (Tier 2)
- **L3** On-Level Students (Tier 1)
- **L4** Advanced Students (Tier 1)
- **EL** English Learners
- **All** All Students

Vocabulary/Fluency/Prior Knowledge

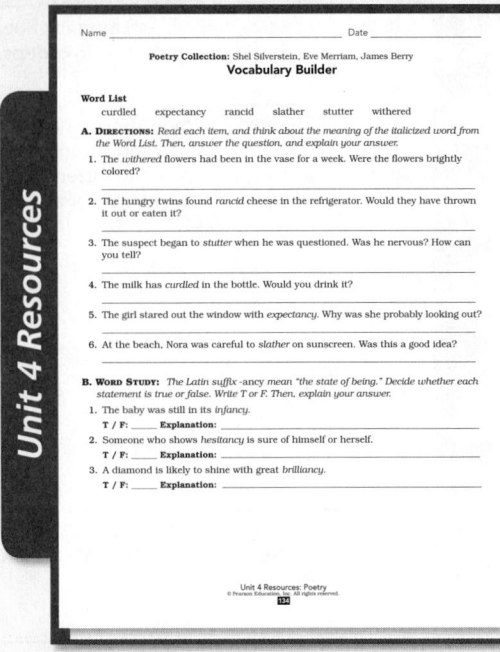

All **Vocabulary Builder,** pp. 134, 152

Also available for these selections:

EL **L1** **L2** **Reading Warm-ups A and B,**
pp. 129–130, 147–148

EL **L1** **L2** **Vocabulary Warm-ups A and B,**
pp. 127–128, 145–146

All **Writing About the Big Question,** pp. 131, 149

Reader's Notebooks

Pre- and postreading pages for both collections, as well as the selections in Poetry Collection 5 appear in an interactive format in the *Reader's Notebooks*. Each *Notebook* is differentiated for a different group of learners. The selections in the Adapted and English Learner's versions are abridged.

L2 **L3** *Reader's Notebook*

L1 *Reader's Notebook: Adapted Version*

EL *Reader's Notebook: English Learner's Version*

EL *Reader's Notebook: Spanish Version*

© *Common Core Companion*

Additional instruction and practice for each Common Core State Standard

Selection Support

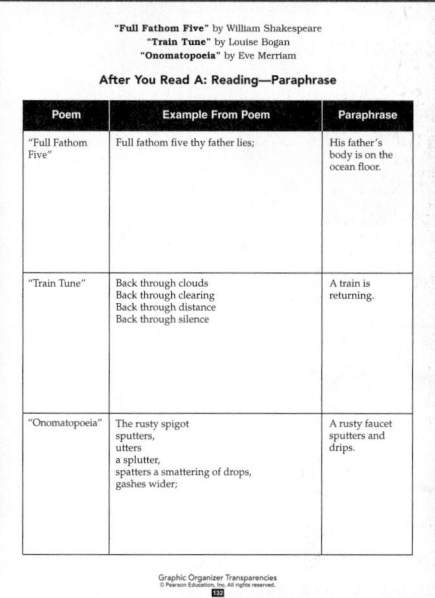

"Full Fathom Five" by William Shakespeare
"Train Tune" by Louise Bogan
"Onomatopoeia" by Eve Merriam

After You Read A: Reading—Paraphrase

Poem	Example From Poem	Paraphrase
"Full Fathom Five"	Full fathom five thy father lies;	His father's body is on the ocean floor.
"Train Tune"	Back through clouds Back through clearing Back through distance Back through silence	A train is returning.
"Onomatopoeia"	The rusty spigot sputters, utters a splutter, spatters a smattering of drops, gashes wider;	A rusty faucet sputters and drips.

EL L1 L2 Reading: Graphic Organizer A,
pp. 131, 132 (partially filled in)

Also available for these selections:

EL L3 Reading: Graphic Organizer B,
p. 133

**EL L1 L2 Literary Analysis: Graphic
Organizer A,** pp. 128–129

EL L3 Literary Analysis: Graphic Organizer B,
p. 130

Skills Development/Extension

Unit 4 Resources

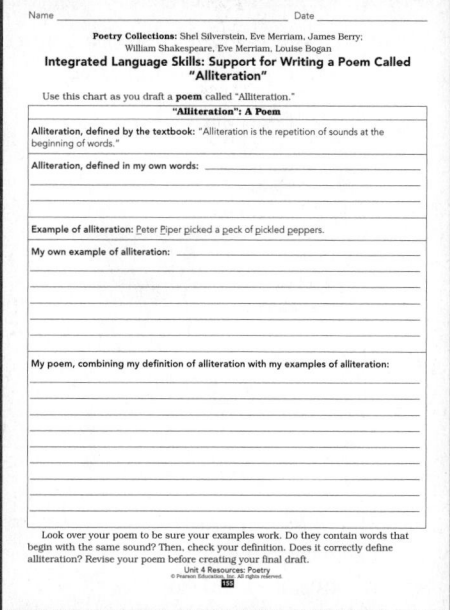

Name _____ Date _____

Poetry Collections: Shel Silverstein, Eve Merriam, James Berry;
William Shakespeare, Eve Merriam, Louise Bogan
**Integrated Language Skills: Support for Writing a Poem Called
"Alliteration"**

Use this chart as you draft a **poem** called "Alliteration."

"Alliteration": A Poem

Alliteration, defined by the textbook: "Alliteration is the repetition of sounds at the beginning of words."

Alliteration, defined in my own words: _____

Example of alliteration: Peter Piper picked a peck of pickled peppers.

My own example of alliteration: _____

My poem, combining my definition of alliteration with my examples of alliteration:

Look over your poem to be sure your examples work. Do they contain words that begin with the same sound? Then, check your definition. Does it correctly define alliteration? Revise your poem before creating your final draft.

EL L3 L4 Support for Writing, p. 155

Also available for these selections:

All Literary Analysis: Sound Devices,
pp. 133, 151

EL L3 L4 Grammar, p. 154

All Reading: Paraphrase, pp. 132, 150

L3 L4 Support for Extend Your Learning,
p. 156

L4 Enrichment, pp. 135, 153

Assessment

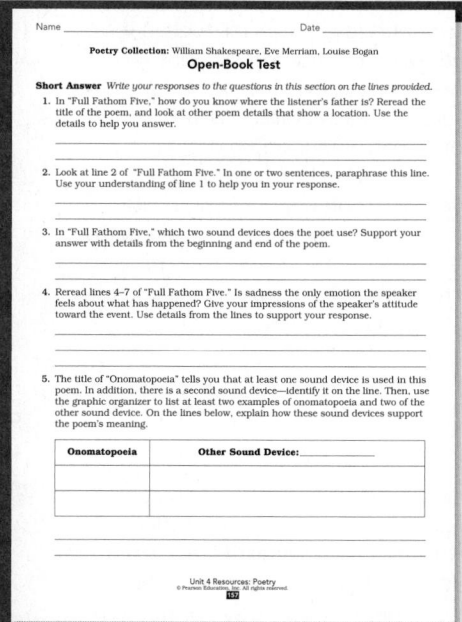

Name _____ Date _____

Poetry Collection: William Shakespeare, Eve Merriam, Louise Bogan
Open-Book Test

Short Answer *Write your responses to the questions in this section on the lines provided.*

1. In "Full Fathom Five," how do you know where the listener's father is? Reread the title of the poem, and look at other poem details that show a location. Use the details to help you answer.

2. Look at line 2 of "Full Fathom Five." In one or two sentences, paraphrase this line. Use your understanding of line 1 to help you in your response.

3. In "Full Fathom Five," which two sound devices does the poet use? Support your answer with details from the beginning and end of the poem.

4. Reread lines 4–7 of "Full Fathom Five." Is sadness the only emotion the speaker feels about what has happened? Give your impressions of the speaker's attitude toward the event. Use details from the lines to support your response.

5. The title of "Onomatopoeia" tells you that at least one sound device is used in this poem. In addition, there is a second sound device—identify it on the line. Then, use the graphic organizer to list at least two examples of onomatopoeia and two of the other sound device. On the lines below, explain how these sound devices support the poem's meaning.

Onomatopoeia	Other Sound Device: _____

L3 L4 Open-Book Test, pp. 136–138,
157–159

Also available for these selections:

EL L1 L2 Selection Test A, pp. 139–141,
160–162

EL L3 L4 Selection Test B, pp. 142–144,
163–165

PHLit Online!
www.PHLitOnline.com

Online Resources: All print materials are also available online.

- complete narrated selection text
- a thematically related video with writing prompt
- an interactive graphic organizer
- highlighting feature
- access to all student print resources, adapted to individual student needs
- Spanish and English summaries
- adapted selection translations in Spanish

Get Connected! (thematic video with writing prompt)

Also available:

Background Video
All videos are available in Spanish.

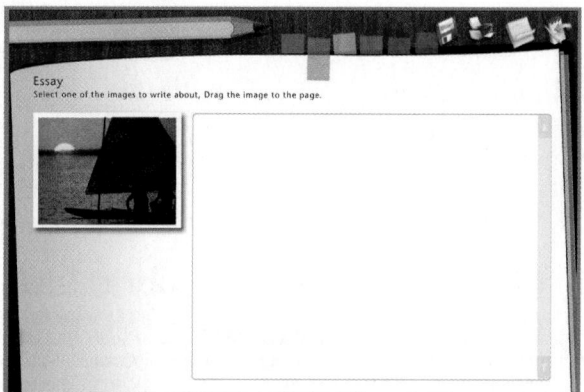

Writer's Journal (with graphics feature)

Also available:

Vocabulary Central (tools, activities, and songs for studying vocabulary)

Before You Read

❶ Leveled Text

You may use either Poetry Collection 5 or Poetry Collection 6 to meet the lesson objectives. Skills instruction for both selections appears on page 647. Choose one selection to teach (or choose to teach both). The Text Complexity Rubric at the bottom of this page will help you determine which selection is more appropriate for your students. Use the Reader and Task Suggestions on the facing page to help all students read text of increasing complexity.

❷ ⓒ Introducing the CCS Standards

Introduce the standards on the student page. (Note that the lesson element with which each standard is addressed is identified in parentheses after the text of the standard.) Call out the standards that you will cover with the selections, explaining to students what each requires and how they will address it as they work through the selection you have chosen. Standards labeled "Spiral Review" are introduced in the Literary Analysis Workshop for this unit.

❶ ⓒ Leveled Texts

Build your skills and improve your comprehension of poetry with texts of increasing complexity.

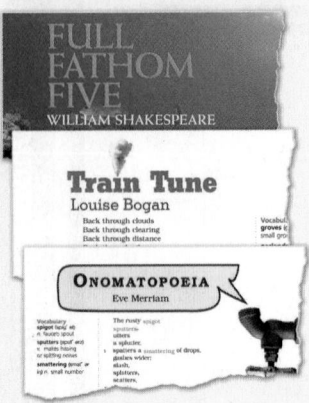

The poems in **Poetry Collection 5** explore responsibility, individuality, and the musicality of rain.

The poems in **Poetry Collection 6** present ideas of loss, rhythmic travel, and watery words.

❷ ⓒ Common Core State Standards

Meet these standards with either **Poetry Collection 5** (p. 650) or **Poetry Collection 6** (p. 658).

Reading Literature
4. Determine the meaning of words and phrases as they are used in a text, including figurative and connotative meanings; analyze the impact of rhymes and other repetitions of sounds on a specific verse or stanza of a poem or section of a story or drama. *(Reading Skill: Paraphrase; Literary Analysis: Sound Devices; Writing: Paraphrase)*

Writing
9.a. Apply grade 7 Reading standards to literature. *(Writing: Paraphrase)*

Speaking and Listening
4. Use appropriate eye contact, adequate volume, and clear pronunciation. *(Speaking and Listening: Poetry Reading)*

6. Adapt speech to a variety of contexts and tasks, demonstrating command of formal English when

indicated or appropriate. *(Speaking and Listening: Poetry Reading)*

Language
1.a. Explain the function of phrases and clauses in general and their function in specific sentences.

1.b. Choose among simple, compound, complex, and compound-complex sentences to signal differing relationships among ideas. *(Conventions: Independent and Subordinate Clauses)*

4.c. Consult general and specialized reference materials, both print and digital, to find the pronunciation of a word or determine or clarify its precise meaning or its part of speech. *(Writing: Paraphrase)*

5.b. Use the relationship between particular words to better understand each of the words. *(Writing: Paraphrase)*

ⓒ Text Complexity Rubric: Leveled Texts

Text complexity is determined by both qualitative and quantitative measures. For this reason, the quantitative measure of a more complex selection may be lower than that of a more accessible selection.

		✓ **Poetry Collection 5**	✓✓ **Poetry Collection 6**
Qualitative Measures	**Context/Knowledge Demands**	Contemporary and humorous poems; doing household chores, being unique, experiencing rain 1 ②️ 3 4 5	Poems from different time periods in varied styles 1 ②️ 3 4 5
	Structure/Language Conventionality	Some rhyme; sound devices; on-level vocabulary 1 ②️ 3 4 5	Challenging vocabulary repetition; sound devices 1 2 ③️ 4 5
	Levels of Meaning/Purpose/Concepts	Accessible concept (narrative and descriptive poems) 1 ②️ 3 4 5	Challenging concept (abstract) 1 2 ③️ 4 5
Quantitative Measures	**Text Length**	Word Count: 284, 83, 150	Word Count: 97, 29, 60
	Lexile	NP	NP
Overall Complexity		✓ **More accessible**	✓✓ **More complex**

Reading Skill: Paraphrase

When you **paraphrase,** you restate something in your own words. To paraphrase a poem, you must first understand it. Just as when you read prose in paragraphs, you should look for a poem's main idea and the details that support it. **Reading aloud according to punctuation** can help you identify complete thoughts in a poem. Observe the following rules when you read poetry:

- Keep reading when a line has no end punctuation.
- Pause at commas, dashes, and semicolons.
- Stop at periods, question marks, or exclamation points.

As you read, note the punctuation to help you paraphrase.

Literary Analysis: Sound Devices

Sound devices use the sound of words to create musical effects that appeal to the ear. These sound devices are used in poetry:

- **Onomatopoeia** is the use of words with sounds that suggest their meanings.
- **Alliteration** is the repetition of sounds at the beginnings of words.
- **Repetition** is the repeated use of words, phrases, or rhythms.

Using the Strategy: Sound Device Chart

The chart below gives examples of each type of sound device. As you read, notice the author's use of these devices in poetry.

Examples	
Onomatopoeia	The *shooshing* of skis
Alliteration	*maggie and millie and molly and may* Went down to the beach (to play one day)
Repetition	To the swinging and the ringing *Of the bells, bells, bells,* *Of the bells, bells, bells, bells*

PHLit Online!
www.PHLitOnline.com

Hear It!
- Selection summary audio
- Selection audio

See It!
- Get Connected video
- Background video
- More about the author
- Vocabulary flashcards

Do It!
- Interactive journals
- Interactive graphic organizers
- Self-test
- Internet activity
- Grammar tutorial
- Interactive vocabulary games

PRETEACH

❸ Reading Skill
Paraphrase

1. Introduce the skill, using the instruction on the student page.
2. Tell students that they will practice paraphrasing as they read.

❹ Literary Analysis
Sound Devices

1. Introduce and discuss the skill, using the instruction on the student page.
2. Tell students that they will interpret sound devices as they read.

Think Aloud: Model the Skill

Model a way to understand and interpret different sound devices in poetry. Say to students:

I use examples to help me remember different sound devices, such as *buzz* for onomatopoeia and *cracked/crushed* for alliteration. Repetition is just that, a word or phrase that is *repeated*. To help me interpret sound devices, I read the poem aloud and try to hear the sounds the poet created. Then, I ask myself, "What do these sounds make me think of?" I also try to figure out how the sounds support the poet's ideas.

❺ Using the Strategy

Give students a copy of either **Literary Analysis Graphic Organizer A or B** (*Graphic Organizer Transparencies,* pp. 128–130) to identify sound devices as they read. Use the examples in **Literary Analysis Graphic Organizer A,** which is partially filled in, to model the process of completing the organizer.

© Text Complexity: Reader and Task Suggestions

✓ Poetry Collection 5		✓✓ Poetry Collection 6	
Preparing to Read the Text	**Leveled Tasks**	**Preparing to Read the Text**	**Leveled Tasks**
• Use the Background information on TE p. 649 to prepare for reading the poems. • Ask students to think about ways poets make abstract images seem concrete. • Guide students to use Multidraft Reading strategies (TE p. 649).	*Structure/Language* If students will have difficulty with language, have them first read to identify vivid descriptive words. Then, have them reread to explain how this language helps convey the tone of the poems. *Evaluating* If students will not have difficulty with language, have them read to identify examples of sound devices. Then, have them explain how this language contributes to the rhythm of the poems.	• Using the Background information on TE p. 657, discuss details that provide important background context. • Ask students to think about ways in which a specific time period can be reflected in literature. • Guide students to use Multidraft Reading strategies (TE p. 657).	*Structure/Language* If students will have difficulty understanding language and structure, have them read to identify confusing passages and phrases. Then, have them reread to paraphrase these sections. *Analyzing* If students will not have difficulty with language and structure, have them read to identify an example of an abstract idea. Ask them to explain how the poet uses language to convey an abstract concept.

647

❶ Writing About the Big Question

1. Review the assignment with the class.

2. Remind students that music is an important way that people communicate ideas. Writers may use lyrics or may try to create sounds that suggest their ideas, feelings, or mood.

3. Have students complete the sentence starter. Review responses as a class. (**Sample response:** Poets and songwriters might use musical language in their work because it can <u>produce</u> emotional connections for readers.)

4. Remind students that their answers will help them think about the Big Question, "What is the best way to communicate?"

While You Read

Tell students that as they read, they should look for sounds that add to their enjoyment of the poems.

❷ Vocabulary

1. Have students preview the collection vocabulary.

2. For each word, have students say the word aloud.

3. Then, use the word in a sentence that defines the word.

4. Finally, repeat your definitional sentence or a similar sentence with the word missing and have the class "fill in the blank" chorally. Here are some examples:

   Something that is <u>withered</u> is dried up and shrunken. If leaves dry up and turn brown and brittle, they are [students say "withered"].

   When something is <u>rancid</u>, it is spoiled and smells bad. The milk Joseph left out in the sun spoiled and became [students say "rancid"].

❸ Word Study

1. Introduce the skill, using the instruction in the box.

2. Challenge students to add the suffix *-ency* to the word *absorb*, then to define the resulting word. (**Answer:** *absorbency*, the state of being able to absorb, or soak up, liquid)

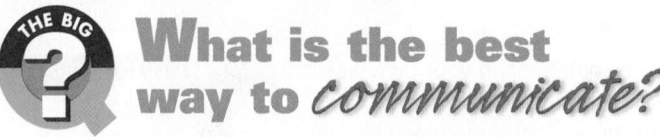

Making Connections
Poetry Collection 5

Sarah Cynthia Sylvia Stout Would Not Take the Garbage Out • One • Weather

What is the best way to *communicate?*

❶ Writing About the Big Question

Each poem in Poetry Collection 5 has a musical quality that helps bring an idea to life. Use this sentence starter to develop your ideas about the Big Question.

> Poets and song writers might use musical language in their work because it can **produce** _____ for readers.

While You Read Look for sounds that add to your enjoyment of the poem.

❷ Vocabulary

Read each word and its definition. Decide whether you know the word well, know it a little bit, or do not know it at all. After you read, see how your knowledge of each word has increased.

- **withered** (wi*th*´ ərd) *adj.* dried up (p. 651) *Raisins are <u>withered</u> grapes.* wither v.

- **curdled** (kʉrd´ 'ld) *adj.* rotten (p. 651) *After a hot day, milk in the broken thermos was <u>curdled</u>.* curdle v. curdling v.

- **rancid** (ran´ sid) *adj.* spoiled and smelling bad (p. 651) *Frozen food turned <u>rancid</u> during the blackout.* rancidness n.

- **expectancy** (ek spek´ tən sē) *n.* a feeling that something is about to happen (p. 652) *She awoke with a sense of <u>expectancy</u> on her birthday.* expectant adj. expectantly adv. expect v. expectation n.

- **stutter** (stut´ ər) *v.* speak in a hesitant or faltering way (p. 652) *Some people <u>stutter</u> when they are nervous.* stuttering v. stutterer n. stuttered v.

- **slather** (sla*th*´ ər) *v.* spread on thickly (p. 654) *Sunscreen works best when you <u>slather</u> it on.* slathered v.

❸ Word Study

The **Latin suffix -ancy** or **-ency** means "the state of being."

The narrator of "One" waits with **expectancy**, or in the state of expecting that something will happen.

648 Poetry

Vocabulary Development

Vocabulary Knowledge Rating

Create a **Vocabulary Knowledge Rating Chart** (*Professional Development Guidebook,* p. 33) for this collection. Include the collection vocabulary and the Big Question word that appears in the Writing About the Big Question sentence starter on this page. (The Big Question vocabulary is introduced on pp. 570–571.)

Give students a copy of the chart. Read the words aloud, and have students mark their rating in the Before Reading column. Urge them to be alert to these words as they read and discuss the collection.

Tally how many students think they know a word to gauge how much instruction to provide. As students read and discuss the collection, point out the words and their context.

Vocabulary Central, featuring tools, activities, and songs for studying vocabulary, is available online at **www.PHLitOnline.com.**

Meet the Authors

Shel Silverstein

(1932–1999)

Author of "Sarah Cynthia Sylvia Stout Would Not Take the Garbage Out" (p. 650)

Shel Silverstein was a cartoonist, composer, folk singer, and writer. He began writing poetry at an early age, before he had a chance to study any of the great poets. "I was so lucky that I didn't have anyone to copy," he has said. Silverstein is best known for two books of poetry, *Where the Sidewalk Ends* and *A Light in the Attic*. His poem "The Unicorn Song" was recorded by the Irish Rovers.

James Berry

(b. 1925)

Author of "One" (p. 652)

James Berry grew up in Jamaica, in a small village by the sea. He learned to read before he was four years old and began writing stories and poems when he got to school. In 1948, Berry moved to England, and soon after that, he began writing seriously. His poems include both English and Creole, the language he spoke growing up in Jamaica.

Eve Merriam

(1916–1992)

Author of "Weather" (p. 654)

Eve Merriam was born and raised in Philadelphia, Pennsylvania. Although she also wrote fiction, nonfiction, and drama, Merriam had a lifelong love of poetry. "I do think poetry is great fun," she said. "That's what I'd like to stress more than anything else: the joy of the sounds of language."

Poetry Collection 5 **649**

 Daily Bellringer

For each class during which you teach this collection, have students complete one of the five Revision activities for Week 22 in the *Daily Bellringer Activities* booklet.

Background

- **"Sarah Cynthia . . ."** Oatmeal and Cream of Wheat, mentioned in the poem, are grain-based cereals mixed with hot milk to form a paste, which gets rather sticky when cool. "Cellophane" is plastic wrap, while "green baloney" is lunch meat with mold on it. Finally, the Golden Gate is a famous bridge in San Francisco, California.

- **"Weather"** Rain forms as drops of water or ice high up in the clouds. Warm air melts the ice as it falls to the earth. Some raindrops are very big, almost 1/4 of an inch in diameter. Other raindrops are very small, barely 1/100 of an inch. The bigger the raindrop, the faster it falls. Bigger raindrops are also flatter in shape than small ones, due to air pressure as they fall. These bigger raindrops perhaps make a bigger splash as they hit a window.

Multidraft Reading

To assist struggling readers and to deepen reading for all, apply multidraft reading protocols. For each reading, have students set the purpose indicated:

- **First reading**—identifying key ideas and details and answering any Reading Checks.

- **Second reading**—analyzing craft and structure and responding to the side-column prompts.

- **Third reading**—integrating knowledge and ideas, connecting to other texts and the world, and answering the end-of-selection questions.

For more guidance, refer to the *Classroom Strategies and Teaching Routines* card on multidraft reading.

For more about the author or practice with the selection vocabulary, go online at **www.PHLitOnline.com.**

❶ Activating Prior Knowledge

Post the following sentences:

1. "_____ ," went the engine.
2. "_____ ," went the faucet.
3. "_____ !" went the jet plane.

Ask volunteers to complete the sentences and then explain how they chose their words (in all likelihood, they chose words that imitate sounds). Tell students that the poets in this collection use sounds and sound devices to set a mood for their poems.

Concept Connector ➡

Students will revisit their ideas after reading the collection.

Whole-Class Activity

Help students warm up for reading sound devices by saying tongue twisters. Post these: "Peter Piper picked a peck of pickled peppers"; "How much wood would a woodchuck chuck, if a woodchuck could chuck wood?" Help students identify the sound devices used, notably alliteration. Then, challenge students to invent new tongue twisters using sound devices.

❷ About the Collection

"Sarah Cynthia Sylvia Stout Would Not Take the Garbage Out" When a girl refuses to take out the garbage, it fills the house and reaches to the sky, delivering a gentle message about household responsibilities.

"One" juxtaposes the uniqueness and ordinariness of being human. The speaker asserts his unique traits along with his typically human moods and frailties.

"Weather" The poet describes rain from an indoor and outdoor perspective, using sound devices, such as onomatopoeia, alliteration, and repetition, to create a vivid image.

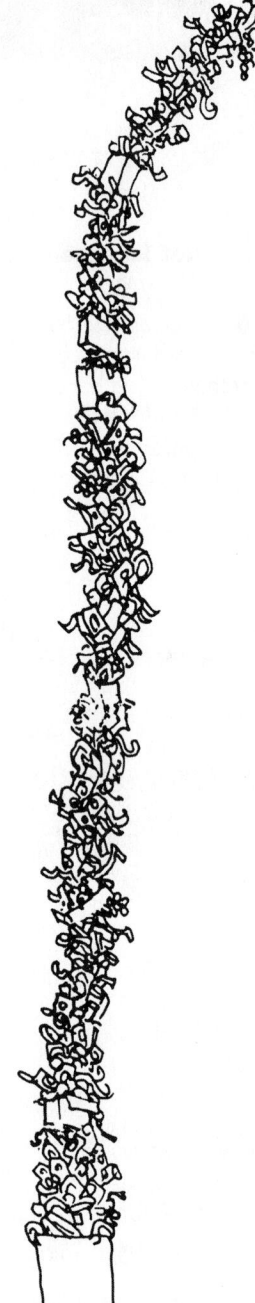

Sarah Cynthia
❶ Sylvia Stout
❷ Would Not Take
the Garbage Out

Shel Silverstein

Sarah Cynthia Sylvia Stout
Would not take the garbage out!
She'd scour[1] the pots and scrape the pans,
Candy[2] the yams and spice the hams,
5   And though her daddy would scream and shout,
She simply would not take the garbage out.
And so it piled up to the ceilings:
Coffee grounds, potato peelings,
Brown bananas, rotten peas,
10   Chunks of sour cottage cheese.
It filled the can, it covered the floor,
It cracked the window and blocked the door
With bacon rinds[3] and chicken bones,
Drippy ends of ice cream cones,
15   Prune pits, peach pits, orange peel,
Gloppy glumps of cold oatmeal,
Pizza crusts and withered greens,
Soggy beans and tangerines,
Crusts of black burned buttered toast,

---

1. **scour** (skour) *v.* clean by rubbing vigorously.
2. **candy** (kan´ dē) *v.* coat with sugar.
3. **rinds** (rīndz) *n.* tough outer layers or skins.

650 Poetry

Vocabulary Development   ©️ CCSS Language 6

Thematic Vocabulary: The Big Question

As students are discussing Poetry Collection 5, encourage them to use the thematic vocabulary presented in Introducing the Big Question, pp. 570–571. You might encourage them with sentence starters like these:

1. The attitude Sarah *expresses* toward garbage is . . .

2. If Sarah could *contribute* just five minutes a day . . .

3. The speaker of "One" asks readers to *listen* carefully to . . .

4. "Weather" *entertains* readers with elaborate . . .

5. The poem uses sounds to *transmit* . . .

20 Gristly bits of beefy roasts . . .
    The garbage rolled on down the hall,
    It raised the roof, it broke the wall . . .
    Greasy napkins, cookie crumbs,
    Globs of gooey bubble gum,
25 Cellophane from green baloney,
    Rubbery blubbery macaroni,
    Peanut butter, caked and dry,
    Curdled milk and crusts of pie,
    Moldy melons, dried-up mustard,
30 Eggshells mixed with lemon custard,
    Cold french fries and rancid meat,
    Yellow lumps of Cream of Wheat.
    At last the garbage reached so high
    That finally it touched the sky.
35 And all the neighbors moved away,
    And none of her friends would come to play.
    And finally Sarah Cynthia Stout said,
    "OK, I'll take the garbage out!"
    But then, of course, it was too late . . .
40 The garbage reached across the state,
    From New York to the Golden Gate.
    And there, in the garbage she did hate,
    Poor Sarah met an awful fate,
    That I cannot right now relate[4]
45 Because the hour is much too late.
    But children, remember Sarah Stout
    And always take the garbage out!

---

4. **relate** (ri lāt´) *v.* tell.

Vocabulary
withered (wi*th*´ ərd)
adj. dried up

Sound Devices
Which sound device
does the poet use in
line 24? Explain.

Vocabulary
curdled (kʉrd´
´ld) *adj.* rotten

rancid (ran´ sid)
adj. spoiled and
smelling bad

Spiral Review
Tone Which words
and phrases on this
page contribute to a
humorous, lighthearted tone? Explain.

4 ◄ **Critical Viewing**
The author drew
the cartoons that
accompany the poem.
How does the art
add to the poem's
humor? **[Assess]**

---

❸ Sound Devices

1. Talk about sound devices with students. Give examples of each one, for example, onomatopoeia: *zip, snap;* alliteration, *period, punctuation;* repetition: *hello, hello, hello.*

2. Read aloud line 24. Encourage students to use the definitions as you **ask** the Sound Devices question.
   Answer: In line 24, the poet uses alliteration—the *g* sound in *globs, gooey,* and *gum.*

3. Encourage students to record this example of alliteration on the Literary Analysis Graphic Organizer that they began on page 647.

Spiral Review

Tone

1. Remind students that they studied the concept of tone in the Unit 4 Literary Analysis Workshop (pp. 572–581).

2. **Ask** the Spiral Review question.
   Possible response: The phrases "gloppy glumps," "globs of gooey," and "rubbery blubbery" add to the humorous tone because they are funny-sounding, silly words.

❹ Critical Viewing

Possible response: The art reflects the humor of the exaggerated descriptions (hyperbole) that the author uses in the poem.

Differentiated

Instruction for Universal Access

**Strategy for
Less Proficient Readers**
Explain to students that hyperbole is a kind of exaggeration that makes a certain point or is used to create a specific effect. Give students this example of how Silverstein exaggerates the buildup of garbage: "And so it piled up to the ceilings: / Coffee grounds, potato peelings..." Then lead a discussion in which students respond to the following questions: Why does Silverstein use hyperbole in this poem? Is the use effective? Make sure students support their opinions.

**EL Support for
English Learners**
Some garbage items, such as pits (line 15) and lemon custard (line 30) may be unfamiliar to students, as may descriptions such as *gristly* (line 20). Encourage students to point out troubling words and descriptions in the poem. Have them work with partners who are proficient in English to decipher the items in question.

1. Remind students that paraphrasing a poem can help them understand the poet's ideas. Point out that the strategy of reading aloud according to punctuation can help students identify each complete thought in a poem.

2. Have students apply the strategy by reading aloud, according to punctuation, the last three lines in the third stanza. Then, **ask** the Paraphrase question.

3. **Possible response:** The commas help me see that "say" signals an example will follow.

⑥ **Connecting to the Big Question**

1. Point out that sometimes poets use the sounds of words in combination with their meaning to communicate ideas.

2. Have students read the bracketed text. **Ask** students: What words name sound actions? What words and sounds are repeated? Did you enjoy these sounds? Explain.
Possible response: The words *stutter* and *echoes* describe sound actions. The words *anybody* and *dressed up in* are repeated. The initial sound *m* is repeated; Students should support their response with specific details about the sounds.

3. **Ask:** Did the poet's use of sound help him communicate his ideas to you? Why or why not?
Possible response: The poet's use of sound helped me enjoy the poem, and so I became interested in the poet's ideas.

One
James Berry

Only one of me
and nobody can get a second one
from a photocopy machine.

Nobody has the fingerprints I have.
5 Nobody can cry my tears, or laugh my laugh
or have my expectancy when I wait.

But anybody can mimic my dance with my dog.
Anybody can howl how I sing out of tune.
And mirrors can show me multiplied
10 many times, say, dressed up in red
or dressed up in grey.

Nobody can get into my clothes for me
or feel my fall for me, or do my running.
Nobody hears my music for me, either.

15 I am just this one.
Nobody else makes the words
I shape with sound, when I talk.

But anybody can act how I stutter in a rage.
Anybody can copy echoes I make.
20 And mirrors can show me multiplied
many times, say, dressed up in green
or dressed up in blue.

Paraphrase
How does the punctuation help you understand the meaning of lines 9–11? **⑤**

Vocabulary
expectancy (ek spek´ tən sē) *n.* a feeling that something is about to happen
stutter (stut´ ər) *v.* speak in a hesitant or faltering way **⑥**

652 Poetry

Vocabulary Development

Vocabulary Knowledge Rating
When students have completed reading and discussing "Sarah Cynthia Sylvia Stout Would Not Take the Garbage Out," "Weather," and "One," have them take out their **Vocabulary Rating Chart** for this poetry collection. Read the words aloud once more and have students rate their knowledge of the words again in the After Reading column. Clarify any words that are still problematic. Have students write their own definition and example or sentence in the appropriate column. Then, have students complete the Vocabulary Practice activities at the end of the selection. Encourage students to use the words in further discussion and written work about these selections. Remind them that they will be accountable for these words on the **Selection Test,** *Unit 4 Resources,* pp. 139–141 or 142–144.

❼ Visual Connections

Whole-Class Activity

1. **Ask** students to describe what they see in the picture.
   Sample response: I see a man in front of three mirrors in which his reflection is repeated and distorted.

2. **Ask** students how they think the author of the poem would react to seeing himself reflected in these mirrors.
   Sample response: I think he would feel good seeing that, although the mirrors can imitate him, the reflections would never be exactly like him.

Small-Group Activity

1. Divide students into small groups. Tell them to imagine themselves in the picture and discuss what they might feel as they saw their reflections. Have them relate the ideas evoked by the image to the language in the poem.

2. Ask one student to summarize the group's ideas.

3. Record students' ideas on the board.

Individual Activity

1. As a class, briefly discuss the picture.

2. Ask students to write a short poem based on the picture.

3. Tell students to proofread and revise their poems in class or for homework.

4. Post the poems around the classroom and invite students to compare their poems to "One."

Concept Connector

Activating Prior Knowledge
Have students return to the sentences they completed in Activating Prior Knowledge and to revise them, using their awareness of sound devices. They may do this individually or in pairs or groups. Then, lead a class discussion, probing for what students have learned that suggests new word possibilities. Encourage students to cite specific details, quotations, or other evidence from the text to support their new ideas.

Writing About the Big Question
Have students compare their response to the sentence starter they completed before reading the collection with their ideas afterward. Ask them to explain whether their thoughts have changed.

Literary Analysis Graphic Organizer
Ask students to review the graphic organizers they completed to list examples of sound devices in the poetry collection. Then have students share the graphic organizers they did and the examples of sound devices that they identified.

PHLit Online!

"One" and "Weather" are available in interactive format in the **Enriched Online Student Edition**, at **www.PHLitOnline.com**, which includes a thematically related video with writing prompt and an interactive graphic organizer.

1. Read aloud the last stanza of "Weather" as students follow along. Remind students that sound devices create musical effects that are pleasant to hear.

2. Then, **ask** the Sound Devices question.

3. Allow students to use the definitions of various sound devices on p. 647 to help them answer. **Answer:** The poet uses onomatopoeia to describe a person in galoshes jumping into a rain puddle ("a puddle a jump puddle splosh"). She also uses repetition ("a puddle a jump a puddle a jump").

4. Encourage students to record these examples on their Literary Analysis Graphic Organizers.

ASSESS
Answers

Critical Thinking

As students answer the questions below, remind them to support their answers with evidence from the text.

1. (a) **Possible response:** Keep up with your work. (b) **Possible response:** The poem is funny and not preachy. I think the poet meant to entertain.

2. The speaker says that his fingerprints, tears, and laugh are unique.

3. (a) **Possible response:** Three made-up words in "Weather" are *juddle, luddle,* and *puddmuddle.* (b) These words bring a musical and rhythmic quality to the poem.

4. Students' responses will vary but should demonstrate an understanding of sound devices.

5. **Possible response:** The poets may have used musical sound devices to communicate the mostly lighthearted mood of their poems. Students may also point out that the music of poetry helps readers see connections and contrasts between the poet's ideas, and so helps convey meaning.

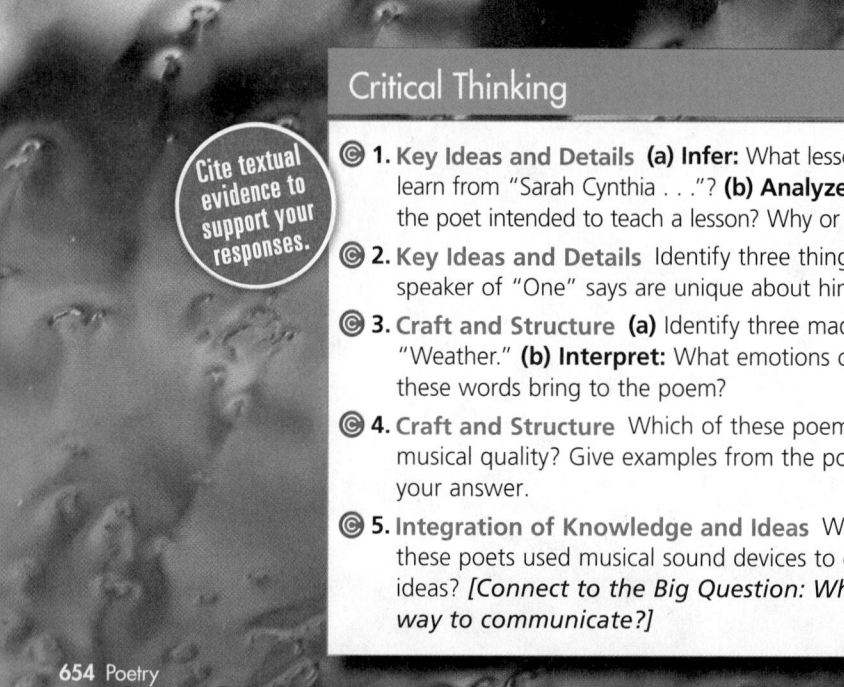

WEATHER
Eve Merriam

Dot a dot dot   dot a dot dot
Spotting the windowpane.
Spack a spack speck   flick a flack fleck
Freckling the windowpane.

5   A spatter a scatter   a wet cat a clatter
A splatter a rumble outside.
Umbrella umbrella umbrella umbrella
Bumbershoot barrel of rain.

Slosh a galosh   slosh a galosh
10   Slither and slather and glide
A puddle a jump a puddle a jump
A puddle a jump puddle splosh
A juddle a pump a luddle a dump a
Puddmuddle jump in and slide!

Vocabulary
slather (slath´ ər) *v.*
spread on thickly

❽ Sound Devices
Which sound devices does the poet use in the last stanza? Explain.

Critical Thinking

Cite textual evidence to support your responses.

1. **Key Ideas and Details** **(a) Infer:** What lesson might readers learn from "Sarah Cynthia . . ."? **(b) Analyze:** Do you think the poet intended to teach a lesson? Why or why not?

2. **Key Ideas and Details** Identify three things that the speaker of "One" says are unique about him.

3. **Craft and Structure** **(a)** Identify three made-up words in "Weather." **(b) Interpret:** What emotions or qualities do these words bring to the poem?

4. **Craft and Structure** Which of these poems has the most musical quality? Give examples from the poem to support your answer.

5. **Integration of Knowledge and Ideas** Why do you think these poets used musical sound devices to express their ideas? *[Connect to the Big Question: What is the best way to communicate?]*

654 Poetry

Assessment Resources

Unit 4 Resources

L1 L2 EL **Selection Test A,** pp. 139–141. Administer Test A to less advanced students.

L3 L4 EL **Selection Test B,** pp. 142–144. Administer Test B to on-level and more advanced students.

L3 L4 **Open-Book Test,** pp. 136–138. As an alternative, give the Open-Book Test.

All **Customizable Test Bank**

All **Self-tests**
Students may prepare for the **Selection Test** by taking the **Self-test** online.

PHLit Online! All assessment resources are available at **www.PHLitOnline.com.**

After You Read
Poetry Collection 5

Sarah Cynthia Sylvia Stout Would
Not Take the Garbage Out •
One • Weather

ASSESS/EXTEND

Answers

Reading Skill: Paraphrase

1. Write an example from each poem in which you read according to punctuation. **Paraphrase** each example.

Poem	Example From Poem	Paraphrase
Sarah Cynthia...		
Weather		
One		

Literary Analysis: Sound Devices

© **2. Craft and Structure (a)** Find two examples of **alliteration** in "Sarah Cynthia . . ." **(b)** How does alliteration add to the humor of the poem?

© **3. Craft and Structure (a)** Identify two examples of **repetition** in "One." **(b)** How does the repetition reinforce the poet's message?

© **4. Craft and Structure (a)** List two examples of **onomatopoeia** in "Weather" that imitate the sound of water. **(b)** How do these words help convey the author's ideas?

Vocabulary

© **Acquisition and Use** For each set of words, identify the word that does not belong and explain why.

1. shrunken   withered   swollen
2. rancid   fresh   stale
3. stutter   recite   swim
4. sweet   sour   curdled
5. slather   spread   uncover
6. expectancy   anticipation   boredom

Word Study Use what you know about the **Latin suffix -ancy** or **-ency** to explain your answer to each question.

1. Does an *emergency* require immediate attention?

2. Is the *relevancy* of an argument important to a judge?

Word Study

The **Latin suffix -ancy** or **-ency** means "the state of being."

Apply It Explain how the suffix *-ancy* or *-ency* contributes to the meanings of these words. Consult a dictionary if necessary.
militancy
hesitancy
consistency

Word Study
Sample answers:

1. Yes; An *emergency* is a <u>state</u> in which something emerges so quickly that it needs an immediate response.

2. Yes; An argument's *relevancy* is its <u>state of being</u> relevant, or important, to an issue.

Word Study: Apply It
Sample answers:

Militancy is the <u>state of being</u> militant. *Hesitancy* is the <u>state of being</u> hesitant. *Consistency* is the <u>state of being</u> consistent.

Reading Skill

1. **Possible responses:** "Sarah Cynthia"—lines 1–2; Sarah would not take out the trash; "One"—lines 1–3; I am unique and can't be photocopied; "Weather"—lines 1–4; Raindrops fall steadily on the windowpane, making spots on it.

   For other sample answers, see *Graphic Organizer Transparencies*, **Reading Skill Graphic Organizer A, p. 131**, and the **Additional Answers** section.

Literary Analysis

2. (a) **Possible responses:** Two examples of alliteration are *Prune pits, peach pits, orange peel* and *black burned buttered toast.* (b) **Possible responses:** Alliteration makes the poem fun to read.

3. (a) **Possible responses:** Two examples of repetition are *nobody* and *anybody.* (b) **Possible response:** The repetition reinforces the idea that, while anybody can imitate the speaker, nobody can *be* the speaker.

4. (a) **Possible responses:** Examples of onomatopoeia that imitate the sound of water include *splatter and slosh.* (b) They help readers hear the water, which makes them feel as if they are "inside" the world of the poem.

Vocabulary
Acquisition and Use
Sample answers:

1. <u>Swollen</u>; The other words describe something that has gotten smaller.

2. <u>Fresh</u>; The other words describe decomposing food.

3. <u>Swim</u>; The other words relate to speaking.

4. <u>Sweet</u>; The other words describe milk that has spoiled.

5. <u>Uncover</u>; The other words can describe actions that cover something with a liquid or paste.

6. <u>Boredom</u>; The other two words describe feelings of positive excitement.

PRETEACH

Skills instruction for the Reading Skill and Literary Analysis concepts for this collection appears on p. 647.

❶ ❓ Writing About the Big Question

1. Review the assignment with the class.

2. Remind students that a mood is an overall feeling, such as *excited* or *gloomy*. With students, generate examples of words and sounds that communicate mood.

3. Have students complete the sentence starters. Review responses as a class. (**Sample responses:** Sound can <u>entertain</u> us, but it can also express emotion. We can "<u>listen</u>" to words as we read by reading aloud.)

4. Remind students that their answers will help them think about the Big Question, "What is the best way to communicate?"

While You Read

Tell students that as they read, they should look for ways that the sounds of words add to the reading experience.

❷ Vocabulary

1. Have students preview the collection vocabulary.

2. For each word, have students say the word aloud.

3. Then, use the word in a sentence that defines the word.

4. Finally, repeat your definitional sentence or a similar sentence with the word missing and have the class "fill in the blank" chorally. Here are some examples:

> *A <u>spigot</u> is a faucet or spout. To run water so that you can wash the dishes, you must turn on the [students say "spigot"].*

> *<u>Groves</u> are small groups of trees. My neighbor has apple trees and pear trees growing in two small [students say "groves"].*

❸ Word Study

1. Introduce the skill, using the instruction in the box.

2. Challenge students to think of words ending in *-less*. Post these on the board and have the class define them.

656

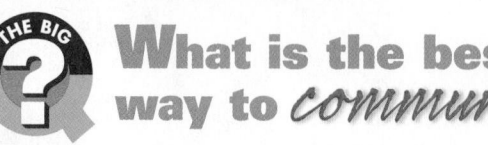

Making Connections
Poetry Collection 6

Full Fathom Five •
Train Tune •
Onomatopoeia

❓ What is the best way to *communicate?*

❶ Writing About the Big Question

In Poetry Collection 6, each poet uses sound to create an image or a certain mood in the poem. Use these sentence starters to develop your ideas about the Big Question.

> Sound can **entertain** us, but it can also express _____.
> We can **"listen"** to words as we read by _____.

While You Read Look for the ways that the sounds of the words add to your experience of reading the poems.

❷ Vocabulary

Read each word and its definition. Decide whether you know the word well, know it a little bit, or do not know it at all. After you read, see how your knowledge of each word has increased.

- **fathom** (fath´ əm) *n.* unit of length used to measure the depth of water (p. 658) *We guessed that the depth of the bay was four <u>fathoms</u>. fathom v.*

- **groves** (grōvz) *n.* small groups of trees (p. 659) *The farmer planted apple <u>groves</u>.*

- **garlands** (gär´ ləndz) *n.* wreaths of flowers and leaves (p. 659) *The holiday <u>garlands</u> looked real, but they were made of plastic.*

- **spigot** (spig´ ət) *n.* faucet; spout (p. 660) *The water from the dripping <u>spigot</u> made an annoying tapping sound.*

- **sputters** (sput´ ərz) *v.* makes hissing or spitting noises (p. 660) *On rainy days the engine <u>sputters</u>, then stops. sputter v. sputtering adj.*

- **smattering** (smat´ ər iŋ) *n.* small number (p. 660) *The little boy had a <u>smattering</u> of freckles on his nose. smatter v.*

❸ Word Study

The **Old English suffix** *-less* means "without."

In "Full Fathom Five," a king is believed to be lost in the **fathomless,** or bottomless, depths of the ocean.

656 Poetry

Vocabulary Development

Vocabulary Knowledge Rating

Create a **Vocabulary Knowledge Rating Chart** (*Professional Development Guidebook,* p. 33) for this collection. Include the collection vocabulary and the Big Question words that appear in the Writing About the Big Question sentence starters on this page. (The Big Question vocabulary is introduced on pp. 570–571).

Give students a copy of the chart. Read the words aloud, and have students mark their rating in the Before Reading column. Urge them to be alert to these words as they read and discuss the collection.

Tally how many students think they know a word to gauge how much instruction to provide. As students read and discuss the collection, point out the words and their context.

Meet the Authors

William Shakespeare

(1564–1616)

Author of "Full Fathom Five" (p. 658)

Many people regard William Shakespeare as the greatest writer in the English language. He wrote thirty-seven plays, many of which are still performed frequently today. They include *Romeo and Juliet, Hamlet,* and other classics. "Full Fathom Five" comes from *The Tempest,* one of Shakespeare's last plays.

Louise Bogan

(1897–1970)

Author of "Train Tune" (p. 659)

Louise Bogan was born in Livermore Falls, Maine, and attended the Girls' Latin School in Boston, where she developed an interest in poetry. During her writing career, Bogan became known for her compact use of language and for the traditional form of her poems. Because she was a very private person, Bogan struggled with her celebrity as a highly respected poet, critic, and lecturer.

Eve Merriam

(1916–1992)

Author of "Onomatopoeia" (p. 660)

Eve Merriam's fascination with words began at an early age. "I remember being enthralled by the sound of words," she said. This love, which led her to write poetry, fiction, nonfiction, and drama, is reflected in the poem "Onomatopoeia."

Poetry Collection 6 **657**

 Daily Bellringer

For each class during which you teach this collection, have students complete one of the five Revision activities for Week 22 in the *Daily Bellringer Activities* booklet.

Background

- **"Full Fathom Five"** Like other playwrights of his time, Shakespeare wrote his plays largely in verse. In addition, he also wrote many, many poems, including 154 sonnets. These 14-line poems had a rhyme pattern that defines what is now called the Shakespearean sonnet.

- **"Train Tune"** Train travel once formed an important part of American life. The transcontinental railroad had united the nation in 1869, and by the early 1900s, when Louise Bogan was growing up, trains were crisscrossing the nation to carry people and freight. Many of these trains offered sleeping cars and some even offered full service, top-quality restaurants and elegant living rooms in which travelers could socialize. For some, trains symbolize a more gracious and romantic time.

Multidraft Reading

To assist struggling readers and to deepen reading for all, apply multidraft reading protocols. For each reading, have students set the purpose indicated:

- **First reading**—identifying key ideas and details and answering any Reading Checks.

- **Second reading**—analyzing craft and structure and responding to the side-column prompts.

- **Third reading**—integrating knowledge and ideas, connecting to other texts and the world, and answering the end-of-selection questions.

For more guidance, refer to the *Classroom Strategies and Teaching Routines* card on multidraft reading.

For more about the author or practice with the selection vocabulary, go online at **www.PHLitOnline.com.**

❶ Activating Prior Knowledge

Post the following sentences:

1. "_____ ," went the engine.
2. "_____ ," went the faucet.
3. "_____ !" went the jet plane.

Ask volunteers to complete the sentences and then explain how they chose their words (in all likelihood, they chose words that imitate sounds). Tell students that the poets in this collection use sounds and sound devices to set a mood for their poems.

Concept Connector ➡

Students will revisit their ideas after reading the collection.

Individual Activity

Bring in several musical items, such as a cymbal or drum, tambourine, and toy xylophone. Then, have volunteers sound each, singly, then in unison. Have students write descriptions of each sound and of the unison.

❷ About The Selections

"Full Fathom Five": In this excerpt, a song from *The Tempest,* we learn that the young prince's father has drowned and has undergone a change on the sea floor. He has become part of the coral life there.

"Onomatopoeia": The poet uses sound devices to conjure the image of a sputtering faucet.

"Train Tune": Louise Bogan uses the repetition of "back" at the beginning of each line to evoke the chug of a moving train. The variation *Along love* (line 19) indicates a theme that Bogan treated often, the failure of love.

❸ Paraphrase

1. Remind students that reading aloud according to punctuation can help them identify and grasp the meaning of each complete thought in the poem.

2. Have students apply the strategy by softly reading aloud "Full Fathom Five." Then, **ask** the Paraphrase question.

3. **Answer:** You come to a complete stop after lines 6, 8, and 9.

❶ ❷ # FULL FATHOM FIVE

WILLIAM SHAKESPEARE

Background "Full Fathom Five" is from Shakespeare's *The Tempest*. In the play, a spirit named Ariel sings these lines to Prince Ferdinand, whose father, King Alonso, is thought lost in a shipwreck. Ariel describes the king's death, though later it is revealed that the king is still alive.

Vocabulary
fathom (fath´ əm)
n. unit of length used to measure the depth of water

❸

Paraphrase
After which lines do you come to a complete stop when reading?

Full fathom five thy father lies;
    Of his bones are coral made;
Those are pearls that were his eyes;
    Nothing of him that doth fade
5   But doth suffer a sea change
Into something rich and strange.
Sea nymphs hourly ring his knell;[1]
                    Ding-dong.
Hark! Now I hear them—ding-dong bell.

___

1. **knell** (nel) *n.* funeral bell.

658 Poetry

Vocabulary Development

Vocabulary Knowledge Rating
When students have completed reading and discussing "Full Fathom Five," "Onomatopoeia," and "Train Tune," have them take out their **Vocabulary Knowledge Rating Chart** for this poetry collection. Read the words aloud once more and have students rate their knowledge of the words again in the After Reading column. Clarify any words that are still problematic. Have students write their own definition and example or sentence in the appropriate column. Then, have students complete the Vocabulary Practice activities at the end of the selection. Encourage students to use the words in further discussion and written work about this poetry collection. Remind them that they will be accountable for these words on the **Selection Test**, *Unit 4 Resources,* pp. 160–162 or 163–165.

Train Tune

Louise Bogan

Back through clouds
Back through clearing
Back through distance
Back through silence

5   Back through groves
Back through garlands
Back by rivers
Back below mountains

④
10   Back through lightning
⑤   Back through cities
Back through stars
Back through hours

Back through plains
Back through flowers
15   Back through birds
Back through rain

Back through smoke
Back me through noon
Back along love
20   Back through midnight

Vocabulary

groves (grōvz) *n.* small groups of trees

garlands (gär´ ləndz) *n.* wreaths of flowers and leaves

Poetry Collection 6 **659**

④ Critical Thinking

1. Have students reread the bracketed text.
2. **Ask** students what kinds of things the speaker associates with riding a train.
   Possible response: The speaker associates certain types of weather, landscapes, times, and emotions with riding a train.

⑤ Connecting to the Big Question

1. Recall that the rhythm of a poem often contributes to its meaning.
2. Have students reread the poem on page 659. **Ask** students: How does the rhythm of this poem relate to the movement of a steam train such as the one pictured here? How does that rhythm affect your experience of reading the poem? Explain.
   Possible response: The poem's rhythm calls to mind the "Chug-a-chug" rhythm of a train like the one shown here. Hearing that rhythm while reading emphasizes the poem's ideas about train travel. It makes me "hear" a train in my mind as I read about trains.
3. **Ask:** Would the poem communicate effectively without the picture? Does it communicate more effectively when read silently or when heard aloud? Explain.
   Possible response: The poem would communicate effectively without the picture because the title draws the familiar picture of a train to mind. The poem communicates most effectively when heard aloud because reading aloud makes clear its natural rhythm.

Concept Connector

Activating Prior Knowledge
Have students return to the sentences they completed in Activating Prior Knowledge and complete them again, using their awareness of sound devices. They may do this individually or in pairs or groups. Then, lead a class discussion, probing for what students have learned that suggests new word possibilities. Encourage students to cite specific details, quotations, or other evidence from the text to support their new ideas.

Writing About the Big Question
Have students compare their response to the sentence starters they completed before reading the collection with their ideas afterward. Ask them to explain whether their thoughts have changed.

Literary Analysis Graphic Organizer
Ask students to review the graphic organizers they completed to list examples of sound devices in the poetry collection. Then have students share their graphic organizers and the examples of sound devices that they identified.

This collection is available in interactive format in the **Enriched Online Student Edition,** at **www.PHLitOnline.com,** which includes a thematically related video with writing prompt and an interactive graphic organizer.

Evaluate

1. **Ask** students to give examples of alliteration in the poem.
   Answer: The poet uses alliteration in the repetition of *s* sounds at the beginnings of words.

2. Have students reread the poem and evaluate the poet's use of alliteration. **Ask** how it adds to the poem.
   Possible response: The alliteration helps you hear water falling at varying speeds from the rusty spigot.

ASSESS

Answers

Critical Thinking

Before students respond, you may wish to have them write a brief objective summary of each poem. As they answer the questions below, remind them to support their answers with evidence from the text.

1. (a) **Possible response:** The father's bones have turned into coral and his eyes to pearls.
   (b) **Possible response:** The father seems to be changing from human form into a statue made of valuable ("rich") materials.

2. (a) Most lines are one or two words; a few lines are longer.
   (b) The short lines help the reader see and hear spurts of water.

3. **Possible response:** "Train Tune" has the most musical quality. As you read it, you can hear the chugging of the train.

4. (a) The speaker mentions love.
   (b) **Possible response:** Perhaps the speaker is remembering a love that has ended or died.
   (c) **Possible response:** Students may say that looking at someone else's responses broadened their understanding.

5. **Possible responses:**
   (a) "Train Tune" evoked the strongest response because it created a vivid image of train travel.
   (b) The repetition and rhythm of the poem contributes strongly to my response by helping me "hear" a train as I read.

ONOMATOPOEIA

Eve Merriam

Vocabulary

spigot (spig´ ət)
n. faucet; spout

sputters (sput´ ərz)
v. makes hissing
or spitting noises ❻

smattering (smat´ ər
iŋ) *n.* small number

The rusty spigot
sputters,
utters
a splutter,
5   spatters a smattering of drops,
gashes wider;
slash,
splatters,
scatters,
10   spurts,
finally stops sputtering
and plash!
gushes rushes splashes
clear water dashes.

Critical Thinking

Cite textual evidence to support your responses.

© 1. **Key Ideas and Details** **(a)** Name two changes that the speaker describes happening to the father in "Full Fathom Five." **(b) Interpret:** Why does the poet call these changes "rich and strange"?

© 2. **Craft and Structure** **(a)** Describe the length of the lines in the poem "Onomatopoeia." **(b) Analyze:** How do the line lengths contribute to the effect of the poem on the reader?

© 3. **Key Ideas and Details** Which of these poems has the most musical quality? Give examples from the poem to support your answer.

© 4. **Key Ideas and Details** **(a)** What emotion does the speaker mention in "Train Tune"? **(b) Speculate:** Why do you think the poet includes this detail? **(c) Discuss:** Share your responses with a partner. Then, discuss how talking about someone else's response did or did not change your answer.

© 5. **Integration of Knowledge and Ideas** **(a)** Which poem evokes the strongest response in you? Explain. **(b)** How do the sounds of the poem contribute to your response? *[Connect to the Big Question: What is the best way to communicate?]*

Assessment Resources

Unit 4 Resources

L1 L2 EL **Selection Test A**, pp. 160–162. Administer Test A to less advanced students.

L3 L4 EL **Selection Test B**, pp. 163–165. Administer Test B to on-level and more advanced students.

L3 L4 **Open-Book Test**, pp. 157–159. As an alternative, give the Open-Book Test.

All **Customizable Test Bank**

All **Self-tests**
Students may prepare for the **Selection Test** by taking the **Self-test** online.

 All assessment resources are available at **www.PHLitOnline.com.**

After You Read
Poetry Collection 6

Full Fathom Five • Train Tune • Onomatopoeia

Reading Skill: Paraphrase

1. In a chart like this one, write an example from each poem in which you read according to punctuation rather than stopping at the end of a line. Then, **paraphrase** each example.

Poem	Example From Poem	Paraphrase
Full Fathom Five		
Train Tune		
Onomatopoeia		

Literary Analysis: Sound Devices

2. Craft and Structure (a) What **sound device** is used in the title "Full Fathom Five"? **(b)** Find an example of another sound device in the poem.

3. Craft and Structure (a) Identify the **repetition** in "Train Tune." **(b)** What effect does this device have when you read the poem out loud?

4. Craft and Structure (a) Identify three words from "Onomatopoeia" that sound like falling water. **(b)** How do the sounds of the words help convey the author's meaning?

Vocabulary

Acquisition and Use For each set of words, identify the word that does not belong and explain why.

1. spigot   faucet   closet
2. sputters   creaks   opens
3. prairies   groves   orchards
4. fathom   depth   color
5. surplus   bit   smattering
6. garlands   wreaths   bushes

Word Study Use what you know about the **Old English suffix -less** to explain your answer to each question.

1. If a person is *friendless*, is he popular?

2. Would a *worthless* necklace be considered valuable?

Word Study

The **Old English suffix -less** means "without."

Apply It Explain how the suffix *-less* contributes to the meanings of these words. Consult a dictionary if necessary.

fearless
ceaseless
meaningless

Poetry Collection 6 **661**

Reading Skill

1. Possible responses: "Full Fathom Five"—lines 4–5; His whole body is transformed as it decays; "Train Tune"—lines 1–2; A train ride takes me through changing weather; "Onomatopoeia"—lines 1–2; The rusty spigot makes a sound that shows water will come out of it somehow.

For other sample answers, see *Graphic Organizer Transparencies*, **Reading Skill Graphic Organizer A**, p. 132, and the **Additional Answers** section.

Literary Analysis

2. (a) Alliteration is used in the title. (b) **Possible response:** Onomatopoeia is used for the sound of the bell: *Ding-dong.*

3. (a) Each line begins with *back*. (b) The repetition creates a steady rhythm as the reader reads the poem.

4. (a) *Gushes, rushes,* and *splashes* sound like falling water. (b) **Possible response:** The sounds of these words help the author convey the experience of hearing water.

Vocabulary
Acquisition and Use
Sample answers:

1. closet; The other words describe an outlet for water.
2. opens; The other words describe sounds.
3. prairies; The other words describe kinds of plantings.
4. color; The other words describe measures of depth.
5. surplus; The other words describe small amounts.
6. bushes; The other words describe plants arranged as decoration.

Word Study
Sample answers:

1. No; The suffix *-less* means "without" and *friendless* means "without friends." A person without friends is not popular.

2. No; The suffix *-less* means "without" and *worthless* means "without worth." Something without worth is not considered valuable.

Word Study: Apply It
Sample answers: Someone who is *fearless* is without fear. Something that is *ceaseless* is without cease, or is never ending. Something that is *meaningless* is without meaning.

Conventions

1. Introduce the skill, using the instruction on the student page.
2. Discuss the examples in the chart.

Think Aloud: Model the Skill

Say to students:

> Let's say I have the sentence *Dora broke her arm when she was nine.* If I read just the first clause—*Dora broke her arm*—it works all alone as a sentence. The second clause is incomplete. It doesn't tell what happened when she was nine.

PH **WRITING COACH** Grade 7

Students will find instruction on and practice with independent and subordinate clauses in Chapter 19, Section 2.

Practice A
Sample answers:
1. Ind: Miss Stout's house was a mess; Sub: because she would not take out the garbage
2. Ind: it begins to smell; Sub: If old food is not thrown away
3. Ind: it sounds like music. Sub: When raindrops fall
4. Ind: Every person is unique. Sub: since no two people are exactly alike.

Reading Application
Sample answer: Sub: And though her daddy would scream and shout; Ind: She simply would not take the garbage out. The first clause is dependent and modifies second clause. The second clause is the main clause of the sentence.

Practice B
Sample answers:
1. <u>Although the king had not died</u>, his family missed him.
2. <u>If a spigot becomes rusty</u>, the water may come out in a trickle.
3. <u>When you ride trains</u>, you often avoid traffic on highways.
4. The train whistle can startle you <u>if you allow it to</u>.

Writing Application
Sample answer: <u>When a poem is interesting</u>, it is memorable. This is often true <u>if the sounds of the words are unusual</u>. <u>Since she uses onomatopoeia</u>, I enjoy Merriam's poetry.

Integrated Language Skills

Poetry Collections 5 and 6

Conventions: Independent and Subordinate Clauses

Poetry Collection 5

A **clause** is a group of words with its own subject and verb. The two major types of clauses are *independent clauses* and *subordinate clauses.*

An **independent clause** has a subject and a verb and can stand by itself as a complete sentence. A **subordinate clause** has a subject and a verb but is only part of a sentence. It begins with a subordinating conjunction such as *although, but, because, since, when,* and *if.*

Poetry Collection 6

Comparing Two Kinds of Clauses	
Independent	**Subordinate**
S V He arrived this morning.	S V *if* he arrived this morning
S V The mosque has a golden dome.	S V *since* the mosque has a dome

Practice A Identify the independent and subordinate clauses in each sentence.

1. Miss Stout's house was a mess because she would not take out the garbage.
2. If old food is not thrown away, it begins to smell.
3. When raindrops fall, it sounds like music.
4. Every person is unique, since no two people are exactly like.

© Reading Application In Collection 5, find one sentence with an independent clause and one sentence with a subordinate clause. Explain the role of these clauses in the sentences.

Practice B Identify the subordinate clause in each sentence. Then, use the subordinate clause to write a new sentence.

1. Although the king had not died, Ariel sang of his death.
2. If a spigot becomes rusty, it can be difficult to turn.
3. When you ride trains, you see scenery.
4. The chugging of a train can lull you to sleep if you allow it to.

© Writing Application Write two sentences about what poetry means to you. Use two subordinate clauses.

PH **WRITING COACH** Further instruction and practice are available in *Prentice Hall Writing Coach.*

Extend the Lesson

Sentence Modeling

Choose the sentence given for the collection students have read:

> *She'd scour the pots and scrape the pans, / Candy the yams and spice the hams, / And though her daddy would scream and shout, / She simply would not take the garbage out.* ("Sarah Cynthia Sylvia Stout . . .")

> *Beneath the sea's curl / unable to speak or sing / Though ever he is surrounded by pearls / There lies the king.* (Poetry Collection 6)

Ask students what they notice. Elicit that a subordinate clause comes *before* the final independent clause. Then, ask what else they notice. ("Sarah Cynthia . . ."—The final independent clause carries the main point. Delaying the main point with the subordinate clause keeps reader's interest; Poetry Collection 6—Readers don't learn the subject of the sentence, *the king,* until the final clause.)

Have students write a sentence on a topic of their own choosing, matching each grammatical and stylistic feature discussed. Collect and share the sentences.

Writing

 **Informative Text** Write a **paraphrase** of one of the poems you read in either Poetry Collection 5 or 6.

- Read over each stanza of the original poem to identify the poet's main idea.
- Use a dictionary to define words you do not know. Replace these words with familiar synonyms, or words that have the same meaning.
- Restate the entire poem in your own words.
- Reread your paraphrase, making sure it has the same meaning as the original. Make revisions as necessary.

Grammar Application Check your writing to make sure you have correctly used main and subordinate clauses.

Writing Workshop: *Work in Progress*

Prewriting for Persuasion For a persuasive essay you might write, list three issues that affect you, your school, or your community. Next to each item, jot down why you would like this issue addressed. Put this Issues List in your writing folder.

Speaking and Listening

 **Presentation of Ideas** Present a **poetry reading** of one of the poems from Poetry Collection 5 or 6. Follow these tips as you prepare your reading:

- Rehearse your readings alone and with a small group.
- Be sure you are pronouncing each word correctly, and read according to the punctuation.
- Practice reading slowly and with expression in your voice. You may decide to emphasize certain words or ideas by raising or lowering the volume of your voice. Do not read with a sing-song tone. Be sure that your reading sounds natural.
- Speak clearly, and prepare to make eye contract periodically with your audience.
- Ask your classmates for feedback on your reading and make changes based on their suggestions.

After you have finished rehearsing, hold a reading for the class.

Common Core State Standards

L.7.1.a, L.7.1.b, L.7.4.c, L.7.5.b; W.7.9.a; SL.7.4, SL.7.6
[For the full wording of the standards, see page 646.]

Use this prewriting activity to prepare for the **Writing Workshop** on page 698.

www.PHLitOnline.com
- Interactive graphic organizers
- Grammar tutorial
- Interactive journals

Integrated Language Skills **663**

EXTEND / ASSESS

Writing

1. Review the assignment, using the instruction on the student page.

2. To guide students in writing their informative texts, give them **Support for Writing,** p. 155 in *Unit 4 Resources.*

3. To evaluate students' paraphrases, use the rubrics for **Generic (Holistic) Writing,** pp. 256–257 in *Professional Development Guidebook.* In addition, check to make sure that students looked up and replaced difficult words with more commonly used words, restated the poem in their own words, and retained the original meaning of the poem.

Grammar Application

Have students check their drafts to make sure they have used main and subordinate clauses correctly.

Six Traits Focus

✔	Ideas	✔	Word Choice
	Organization		Sentence Fluency
	Voice		Conventions

PH WRITING COACH Grade 7

Students will find further instruction on and practice with paraphrasing in Chapter 11.

Writing Workshop
Work in Progress

Have students save their completed Issues Lists in their portfolios. They will use the lists later as they continue this Work-in-Progress assignment (see p. 683). These assignments prepare them to complete the Writing Workshop assignment (see pp. 698–705).

Speaking and Listening

1. Review the assignment, using the instruction on the student page.

2. To support students' work on the assignment, have them complete the **Support for Extend Your Learning** page (*Unit 4 Resources,* p. 156).

663

COMMON CORE
Time and Resource Manager

✓ Poetry Collection 7 • ✓✓ Poetry Collection 8
Lesson Pacing Guide

DAY 1 Preteach

© Administer the Reading and Vocabulary Warm-ups (*Unit 4 Resources,* pp. 166–169 or 184–187) as necessary.

• Introduce the Reading Skill: Paraphrase.

© Introduce the Literary Analysis concept: Sound Devices.

• Distribute copies of the appropriate graphic organizer for the Reading Skill (*Graphic Organizer Transparencies,* pp. 134–136).

• Distribute copies of the appropriate graphic organizer for Literary Analysis (*Graphic Organizer Transparencies,* pp. 137–139).

© Teach the selection vocabulary.

© Introduce the Word Study skill.

DAYS 2–3 Preteach/Teach

© Build background with the Background feature.

• Develop thematic vocabulary and thematic thinking with Writing About the Big Question.

• Prepare students to read with the Activating Prior Knowledge activities (TE).

• Informally monitor comprehension while students read.

• Use the Reading Check questions to confirm comprehension.

• Develop students' ability to restate the author's words in their own words using the Paraphrase questions.

© Develop students' understanding of sound devices using the Sound Devices questions.

© Reinforce vocabulary with the Vocabulary notes.

© Reinforce unit focus standards using the Spiral Review prompts.

DAY 4 Assess

• Assess students' comprehension and mastery of the skills by having them answer the Critical Thinking, Reading Skill, and Literary Analysis questions.

© Have students complete the Vocabulary Practice activities.

© Have students complete the Word Study activities.

DAY 5 Extend/Assess

• Have students complete the Conventions lesson.

© Have students complete the Writing activity and write a poem. (You may assign as homework.)

© Extend learning by having students complete the Research and Technology activity, a survey. (You may assign as homework.) As an alternative, assign them "Follow Your Star" or "The Age Factor" in *Reality Central.*

• Administer Selection Test A or B (*Unit 4 Resources,* pp. 178–183 or 199–204).

© Common Core State Standards

Reading Literature 4. Determine the meaning of words and phrases as they are used in a text, including figurative and connotative meanings; analyze the impact of rhymes and other repetitions of sounds on a specific verse or stanza of a poem or section of a story or drama.

Writing 6. Use technology, including the Internet, to produce and publish writing and link to and cite sources as well as to interact and collaborate with others, including linking to and citing sources.
7. Conduct short research projects to answer a question, drawing on several sources and generating additional related, focused questions for further research and investigation.

Speaking and Listening 1.c. Pose questions that elicit elaboration and respond to others' questions and comments with relevant observations and ideas that bring the discussion back on topic as needed.

Language 1.b. Choose among simple, compound, complex, and compound-complex sentences to signal differing relationships among ideas.
5.b. Use the relationship between particular words to better understand each of the words.
6. Acquire and use accurately grade-appropriate general academic and domain-specific words and phrases.

Additional Standards Practice
Common Core Companion, pp. 41–61

Daily Block Scheduling
Each day in this Lesson Pacing Guide represents a 40–50 minute period. Teachers using block scheduling may combine days to revise pacing. In addition, teachers may differentiate and support core instruction by integrating components for extended and intensive support, as students require. See the Guide to Selected Leveled Resources (facing page).

Guide to Selected Leveled Resources

R T I Tier 1 (students performing on level)	✓ **More Accessible** Poetry Collection 7	✓✓ **More Complex** Poetry Collection 8
Warm Up — Practice, model, and monitor fluency, working with the whole class or in groups.	Vocabulary and Reading Warm-ups B, *Unit 4 Resources*, pp. 166–167, 169	Vocabulary and Reading Warm-ups B, *Unit 4 Resources*, pp. 184–185, 187
Comprehension/Skills — Support and monitor comprehension and skills development, having students complete the activities, graphic organizers, and interactive prompts independently or as a class.	• *Reader's Notebook*, adapted instruction and full selection **EL** *Reader's Notebook: English Learner's Version*, adapted instruction and adapted selection • Reading Skill Graphic Organizer B, *Graphic Organizer Transparencies*, p. 136 • Literary Analysis Graphic Organizer B, *Graphic Organizer Transparencies*, p. 139	• *Reader's Notebook*, adapted instruction and summary **EL** *Reader's Notebook: English Learner's Version*, adapted instruction and summary • Reading Skill Graphic Organizer B, *Graphic Organizer Transparencies*, p. 136 • Literary Analysis Graphic Organizer B, *Graphic Organizer Transparencies*, p. 139
Monitor Progress — Monitor student progress with the differentiated curriculum-based assessment in the *Unit Resources*.	• Selection Test B, *Unit 4 Resources*, pp. 181–183 • Open-Book Test, *Unit 4 Resources*, pp. 175–177	• Selection Test B, *Unit 4 Resources*, pp. 202–204 • Open-Book Test, *Unit 4 Resources*, pp. 196–198
Monitor Progress — • Assess student progress using Benchmark Test 8. • Preassess instructional needs using the Vocabulary in Context section of the test.	• Benchmark Test B, *Unit 4 Resources*, pp. 227–234, including Vocabulary in Context diagnostic items	• Benchmark Test B, *Unit 4 Resources*, pp. 227–234, including Vocabulary in Context diagnostic items

R T I Tier 2 (students requiring intervention)	✓ **More Accessible** Poetry Collection 7	✓✓ **More Complex** Poetry Collection 8
Warm Up — Practice, model, and monitor fluency in groups or with individuals.	• *Vocabulary and Reading Warm-ups A, Unit 4 Resources*, pp. 166–168 • *Reality Central*, "Follow Your Star" • *Hear It!* Audio CD (adapted text)	• *Vocabulary and Reading Warm-ups A, Unit 4 Resources*, pp. 184–186 • *Reality Central*, "Th Age Factor" • *Hear It!* Audio CD
Comprehension/Skills — • Support and monitor comprehension and skills development, working in small groups or with individuals. • Pair students with more advanced peers and have them complete the writing activity in the *Real-World Writing Journal*. • As students complete the selection in the appropriate version of the *Reader's Notebook*, monitor comprehension frequently with group questions and individual instruction. • Model strategies while guiding students in completing the activities and prompts in the *Reader's Notebook*, as well as the graphic organizers. • Practice skills and monitor mastery with the *Reading Kit* worksheets.	• *Real-World Writing Journal*, Lesson 7, pp. 128–131 • *Reader's Notebook: Adapted Version*, adapted instruction and adapted selection **EL** *Reader's Notebook: English Learner's Version*, adapted instruction and adapted selection • Reading Skill Graphic Organizer A, *Graphic Organizer Transparencies*, p. 134 • Literary Analysis Graphic Organizer A, *Graphic Organizer Transparencies*, p. 137 • *Reading Kit*, Practice worksheets, pp. 174, 178, 184, 188, 194	• *Real-World Writing Journal*, Lesson 8, pp. 132–135 • *Reader's Notebook: Adapted Version*, adapted instruction and summary **EL** *Reader's Notebook: English Learner's Version*, adapted instruction and summary • Reading Skill Graphic Organizer A, *Graphic Organizer Transparencies*, p. 135 • Literary Analysis Graphic Organizer A, *Graphic Organizer Transparencies*, p. 138 • *Reading Kit*, Practice worksheets, pp. 174, 178, 184, 188, 194
Monitor Progress — Monitor student progress with the differentiated curriculum-based assessment in the *Unit Resources* and in the *Reading Kit*.	• Selection Test A, *Unit 4 Resources*, pp. 178–180 • *Reading Kit*, Assess worksheets pp. 175, 179, 185, 189, 195	• Selection Test A, *Unit 4 Resources*, pp. 199–201 • *Reading Kit*, Assess worksheets, pp. 175, 179, 185, 189, 195
Monitor Progress — • Assess student progress using Benchmark Test 8. • Preassess instructional needs using the Vocabulary in Context section of the test.	• Benchmark Test B, *Unit 4 Resources*, pp. 227–234, including Vocabulary in Context diagnostic items	• Benchmark Test B, *Unit 4 Resources*, pp. 227–234, including Vocabulary in Context diagnostic items

TIER 3 Tier 3 intervention may require consultation with the student's special-education or dyslexia specialist. For additional support, see the Tier 2 activities and resources listed above.

One-on-one teaching   Group work   Whole class instruction   Independent work   A Assessment

For a complete guide to selection support, including support for Advanced students, see the Overview of Resources in the frontmatter.

✓ Poetry Collection 7
✓✓ Poetry Collection 8

RESOURCES FOR:

L1 Special-Needs Students

L2 Below-Level Students (Tier 2)

L3 On-Level Students (Tier 1)

L4 Advanced Students (Tier 1)

EL English Learners

All All Students

Vocabulary/Fluency/Prior Knowledge

Name _____ Date _____

Poetry Collection: Naomi Long Madgett, Wendy Rose, and Edna St. Vincent Millay
Reading Warm-up A

Read the following passage. Pay special attention to the underlined words. Then, read it again, and complete the activities. Use a separate sheet of paper for your written answers.

"What can we do that would entertain you?" Aunt Grace asked her niece as she put away the dinner dishes.

Sandy plopped down on the sofa and checked the time on her <u>watch</u>. "Turn on the television, I guess."

Aunt Grace turned to hide her smile. *Kids! They have no idea of how to <u>amuse</u> themselves.*

Sandy moved some books on the coffee table so she could put her stocking-feet up. *Thank goodness I'm staying only one night with my aunt,* she thought. *This place is such a bore. Blam!* One of the books had moved and fell onto the floor. It was a photo album. Several loose photos slid out onto the carpet.

"Sorry!" Sandy exclaimed as she jumped down to gather up the photos. "Who's this?" she asked, staring at a wedding photo. The groom was dressed in a soldier's uniform.

Aunt Grace knelt down beside her. "That's my parents on their wedding day," she answered. "It's the only picture I have of them together, and I really <u>treasure</u> it. My dad was killed in the Vietnam war, about three months after this picture was taken."

"How sad," Sandy sympathized.

"My mom remarried four years later. Her second husband was your grandfather." Aunt Grace picked up a baby picture. The <u>infant</u> was dressed in a pink bunny suit. "This picture is of me," she said, laughing.

Aunt Grace turned pages in the album while telling family stories. Sandy learned how her grandmother had overcome many hardships to raise her two daughters. "She was a very strong woman," Aunt Grace said as she closed the album. "I admired her greatly and still do." She picked up a loose photo of her mom. "Here's a picture of her that I can <u>spare</u>. Would you like to have it?"

"I would, thank you," Sandy replied. Then she asked, "Do you have another album? I'd rather look at family photos <u>instead</u> of TV. Photographs are so much more interesting!"

1. Circle the word that tells what Sandy checked on her <u>watch</u>. Write a sentence that describes a watch.

2. Circle the word that is an antonym for <u>amuse</u>. Write the meaning of <u>amuse</u>.

3. Underline the words that tell what Aunt Grace <u>treasures</u>. Write about something you treasure.

4. Circle the word that is a synonym for <u>infant</u>. Use <u>infant</u> in a sentence.

5. Underline the words that tell what Aunt Grace has to <u>spare</u>. Describe something that you could not part with or <u>spare</u>.

6. Underline the words that tell what Sandy wanted to do <u>instead</u> of watching TV. Write about something you like to do <u>instead</u> of watching TV.

EL **L1** **L2** **Reading Warm-ups A and B,** pp. 168–169, 186–187

Also available for these selections:

All **Writing About the Big Question,** pp. 170, 188

All **Vocabulary Builder,** pp. 173, 191

EL **L1** **L2** **Vocabulary Warm-ups A and B,** pp. 166–167, 184–185

Reader's Notebooks

Pre- and postreading pages for both collections, as well as the selections in Poetry Collection 7, appear in an interactive format in the *Reader's Notebooks.* Each *Notebook* is differentiated for a different group of learners. The selections in the Adapted and English Learner's versions are abridged.

L2 **L3** *Reader's Notebook*

L1 *Reader's Notebook: Adapted Version*

EL *Reader's Notebook: English Learner's Version*

EL *Reader's Notebook: Spanish Version*

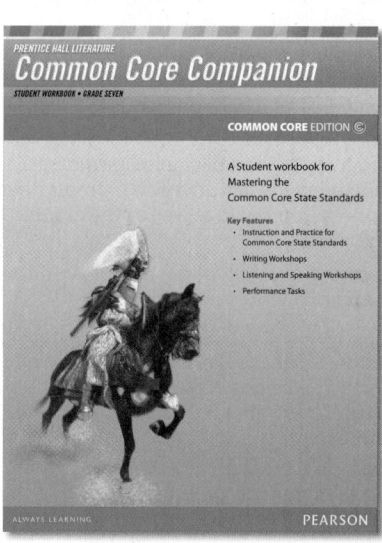

© Common Core Companion

Additional instruction and practice for each Common Core State Standard

Selection Support

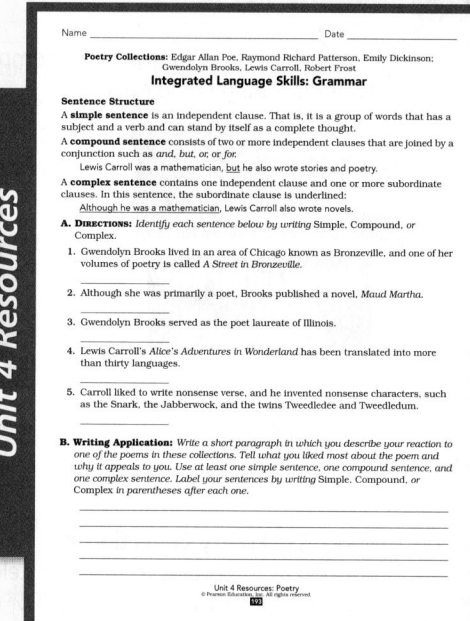

"Annabel Lee" by Edgar Allan Poe; **"Martin Luther King"** by Raymond Richard Patterson; **"I'm Nobody"** by Emily Dickinson; **"Father William"** by Lewis Carroll; **"Stopping by Woods on a Snowy Evening"** by Robert Frost; **"Jim"** by Gwendolyn Brooks

After You Read B: Literary Analysis—Rhythm and Rhyme

Poem	Rhyming Words

Graphic Organizer Transparencies

Unit 4 Resources

Skills Development/Extension

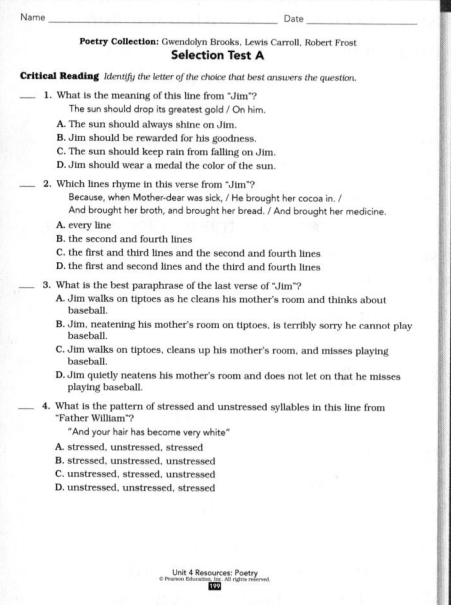

Name _____ Date _____

Poetry Collections: Edgar Allan Poe, Raymond Richard Patterson, Emily Dickinson; Gwendolyn Brooks, Lewis Carroll, Robert Frost
Integrated Language Skills: Grammar

Sentence Structure

A **simple sentence** is an independent clause. That is, it is a group of words that has a subject and a verb and can stand by itself as a complete thought.

A **compound sentence** consists of two or more independent clauses that are joined by a conjunction such as *and, but, or,* or *for.*

Lewis Carroll was a mathematician, <u>but</u> he also wrote stories and poetry.

A **complex sentence** contains one independent clause and one or more subordinate clauses. In this sentence, the subordinate clause is underlined:

<u>Although he was a mathematician,</u> Lewis Carroll also wrote novels.

A. DIRECTIONS: *Identify each sentence below by writing Simple, Compound, or Complex.*

1. Gwendolyn Brooks lived in an area of Chicago known as Bronzeville, and one of her volumes of poetry is called *A Street in Bronzeville.*

2. Although she was primarily a poet, Brooks published a novel, *Maud Martha.*

3. Gwendolyn Brooks served as the poet laureate of Illinois.

4. Lewis Carroll's *Alice's Adventures in Wonderland* has been translated into more than thirty languages.

5. Carroll liked to write nonsense verse, and he invented nonsense characters, such as the Snark, the Jabberwock, and the twins Tweedledee and Tweedledum.

B. Writing Application: *Write a short paragraph in which you describe your reaction to one of the poems in these collections. Tell what you liked most about the poem and why it appeals to you. Use at least one simple sentence, one compound sentence, and one complex sentence. Label your sentences by writing Simple, Compound, or Complex in parentheses after each one.*

Assessment

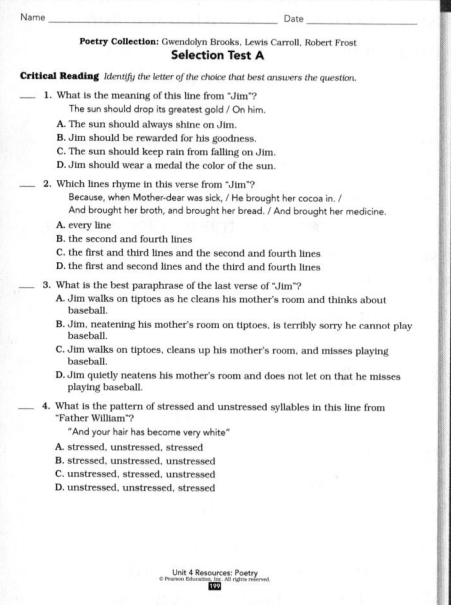

Name _____ Date _____

Poetry Collection: Gwendolyn Brooks, Lewis Carroll, Robert Frost
Selection Test A

Critical Reading *Identify the letter of the choice that best answers the question.*

___ 1. What is the meaning of this line from "Jim"?
The sun should drop its greatest gold / On him.
A. The sun should always shine on Jim.
B. Jim should be rewarded for his goodness.
C. The sun should keep rain from falling on Jim.
D. Jim should wear a medal the color of the sun.

___ 2. Which lines rhyme in this verse from "Jim"?
Because, when Mother-dear was sick, / He brought her cocoa in. / And brought her broth, and brought her bread. / And brought her medicine.
A. every line
B. the second and fourth lines
C. the first and third lines and the second and fourth lines
D. the first and second lines and the third and fourth lines

___ 3. What is the best paraphrase of the last verse of "Jim"?
A. Jim walks on tiptoes as he cleans his mother's room and thinks about baseball.
B. Jim, neatening his mother's room on tiptoes, is terribly sorry he cannot play baseball.
C. Jim walks on tiptoes, cleans up his mother's room, and misses playing baseball.
D. Jim quietly neatens his mother's room and does not let on that he misses playing baseball.

___ 4. What is the pattern of stressed and unstressed syllables in this line from "Father William"?
"And your hair has become very white"
A. stressed, unstressed, stressed
B. stressed, unstressed, unstressed
C. unstressed, stressed, unstressed
D. unstressed, unstressed, stressed

EL **L3** Literary Analysis: Graphic Organizer B, p. 139

Also available for these selections:

EL **L1** **L2** Reading: Graphic Organizer A, pp. 134–135 (partially filled in)

EL **L3** Reading: Graphic Organizer B, p. 136

EL **L1** **L2** Literary Analysis: Graphic Organizer A, pp. 137–138 (partially filled in)

EL **L3** **L4** Grammar, p. 193

Also available for these selections:

All Literary Analysis: Sound Devices, pp. 172, 190

All Reading: Paraphrase, pp. 171, 189

EL **L3** **L4** Support for Writing, p. 194

L3 **L4** Support for Extend Your Learning, p. 195

L4 Enrichment, pp. 174, 192

EL **L1** **L2** Selection Test A, pp. 178–180, 199–201

Also available for these selections:

EL **L3** **L4** Selection Test B, pp. 181–183, 202–204

L3 **L4** Open-Book Test, pp. 175–177, 196–198

PHLit Online!
www.PHLitOnline.com

Online Resources: All print materials are also available online.

- complete narrated selection text
- a thematically related video with writing prompt
- an interactive graphic organizer
- highlighting feature
- access to all student print resources, adapted to individual student needs
- Spanish and English summaries
- adapted selection translations in Spanish

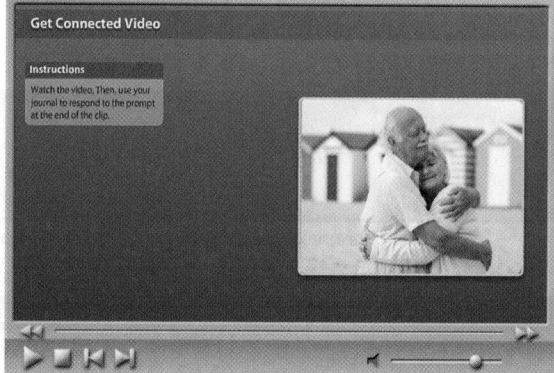

Get Connected! (thematic video with writing prompt)

Also available:

Background Video
All videos are available in Spanish.

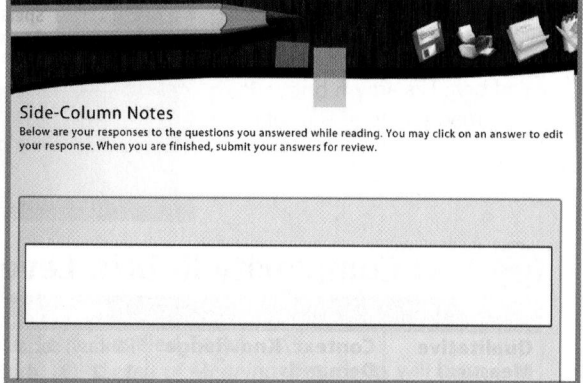

Writer's Journal (with graphics feature)

Also available:

Vocabulary Central (tools, activities, and songs for studying vocabulary)

6 ❓ Connecting to the Big Question

1. Point out one way to communicate big ideas is to list and describe specific examples of them.

2. Have students reread the bracketed text on page 670 that begins, "He came upon . . ." **Ask** students: What emotions does the poet name? What overall emotion does he communicate with his list of examples?
Possible response: He lists grief, rage, and love as examples of passion. The overall emotion is affirming: King's love helps the "suffering" earth, and although he has died, his spirit lives on ("he will come again").

3. **Ask:** How does the language of the poem help communicate this feeling?
Possible response: The repetitions and echoes in phrases such as "so deep, so wide" and "He could not turn aside"/"He would not turn around" add power and feeling to the poem.

7 Critical Viewing

Possible response: The expression on Martin Luther King's face shows his seriousness and determination.

Martin Luther King
Raymond Patterson

Background Martin Luther King, Jr. (1929–1968) was a great civil rights leader. He used nonviolent methods to help end legal discrimination against African Americans in the United States. Tragically, in 1968, while fighting for justice and equality, he was assassinated at the age of thirty-nine.

Vocabulary
passion (pash´ ən) *n.* strong feelings of love or hate

profound (prō found´) *adj.* deeply or intensely felt

7 ▶ **Critical Viewing**
What characteristics of Martin Luther King, Jr., does this photograph show? **[Infer]**

6 |
He came upon an age
Beset[1] by grief, by rage—

His love so deep, so wide,
He could not turn aside.

5 His passion, so profound,
He would not turn around.

8 |
He taught a suffering earth
The measure of man's worth.

For this he was slain,
10 But he will come again.

---

1. **Beset** (bē set´) *adj.* attacked from all sides; harassed.

670 Poetry

Vocabulary Development

Vocabulary Knowledge Rating
When students have completed reading and discussing "Annabel Lee," "Martin Luther King," and "I'm Nobody," ask them to take out their **Vocabulary Rating Chart** for this poetry collection. Read the words aloud once more, and have students rate their knowledge of the words again in the After Reading column. Clarify any words that are still problematic. Have students write their own definition and example or sentence in the appropriate column. Then tell them to complete the Vocabulary Practice activities at the end of the selection. Encourage students to use the words in further discussion and written work about these poems. Remind them that they will be accountable for these words on the **Selection Test**, *Unit 4 resources*, pp. 178–180 or 181–183.

Poetry Collection 7 **671**

Interpret

1. Direct students to reread lines 7–8 of the poem on page 670. **Ask** them what they think the lines mean.

   Answer: King taught a troubled society that every person is important and equal.

2. Have students reread the first six lines of the poem. **Ask** them how King taught people his important lesson.

   Answer: He refused to let grief and rage overcome love.

Concept Connector

Anticipation Guide

Have students return to their **Anticipation Guides** and respond to the statements again in the After Reading column. They may do this individually or in their original pairs or groups. Then, lead a class discussion, probing for what students have learned that confirms or invalidates each statement. Encourage students to cite specific details, quotations, or other evidence from the poems to support their responses to each statement.

Writing About the Big Question

Have students compare their responses to the sentence starters they completed before reading with their ideas afterward. Ask them to explain whether their thoughts have changed.

Reading Skill Graphic Organizer

Ask students to review the graphic organizers they used to help them paraphrase difficult lines as they read the assigned poems. Then have students share the graphic organizers they did and paraphrases they wrote.

Spiral Review
Connotation

1. Remind students that they studied the concept of connotation in the Unit 4 Literary Analysis Workshop (pp. 572–581).

2. **Ask** the Spiral Review question.

   Answer: The connotation of *nobody* is that it is a good thing to be.

❾ Critical Thinking
Analyze

1. Have students reread the last stanza and identify the comparison being made.
   Answer: "Somebody" is being compared to a frog.

2. **Ask** what the comparison says about "Somebodies."
   Answer: They are out in public; they make noise; they may presume to be important, but they're not.

ASSESS

Answers

Critical Thinking

Before students respond, you may wish to have them write a brief objective summary of each poem. As they answer the questions below, remind them to support their answers with evidence from the text.

1. (a) He is saddened by her death, but is determined to remain with her. (b) According to the speaker, their love will prevent the separation.

2. (a) King's passions were so strong that they propelled him to seek equality and justice. (b) **Possible response:** Dedication and passion enabled King to help many people and to convince others that his cause was just.

3. (a) People will banish her. (b) She is amused, because she thinks that being "somebody" is dreary. (c) The poem suggests that living in the public eye is "dreary."

4. **Possible response:** "Martin Luther King" expresses the most emotion toward its subject by conveying a vivid picture of the man.

672

Spiral Review
Connotation
What is the connotation of the word *nobody* in this poem?

Vocabulary
banish (ban' ish)
adj. send away

I'm Nobody
EMILY DICKINSON

I'm Nobody! Who are you?
Are you—Nobody—too?
Then there's a pair of us!
Don't tell! they'd banish us—you know!

5   How dreary—to be—Somebody!
❾   How public—like a Frog—
To tell your name—the livelong June—
To an admiring Bog!

Critical Thinking

Ⓒ **1. Key Ideas and Details (a)** In "Annabel Lee," how does the speaker react to Annabel Lee's death? **(b) Infer:** What will prevent the separation of the speaker's soul from Annabel Lee's soul?

Ⓒ **2. Key Ideas and Details (a) Interpret:** In "Martin Luther King," what does the poet mean by King's "passion, so profound"? **(b) Synthesize:** Using ideas from the poem, name two qualities that are important in a leader. Explain your answer.

Ⓒ **3. Integration of Knowledge and Ideas (a)** In "I'm Nobody," what does the speaker say will happen if it is revealed that she is "Nobody"? **(b) Infer:** How does the speaker feel about this consequence? **(c) Apply:** In what way does the poem suggest some of the difficulties celebrities face today?

Ⓒ **4. Integration of Knowledge and Ideas** Which of these poems do you think expresses the most emotion toward its subject? Explain. *[Connect to the Big Question: What is the best way to communicate?]*

Cite textual evidence to support your responses.

672 Poetry

Assessment Resources

Unit 4 Resources

L1 L2 EL **Selection Test A,** pp. 178–180. Administer Test A to less advanced students.

L3 L4 EL **Selection Test B,** pp. 181–183. Administer Test B to on-level and more advanced students.

L3 L4 **Open-Book Test,** pp. 175–177. As an alternative, give the Open-Book Test.

All **Customizable Test Bank**

All **Self-tests**
Students may prepare for the **Selection Test** by taking the **Self-test** online.

After You Read
Poetry Collection 7

Annabel Lee •
Martin Luther King •
I'm Nobody

Reading Skill: Paraphrase

1. Reread the following lines, and then **paraphrase** them.

   (a) "Annabel Lee": lines 9–10

   (b) "Martin Luther King": lines 1–2

   (c) "I'm Nobody": lines 5–8

2. Identify two words in these poems that you might look up in a dictionary to help you paraphrase meaning.

Literary Analysis: Sound Devices

3. **Craft and Structure** Do these poems have **rhythmic patterns**? Explain.

4. **Craft and Structure** Use a chart like this to analyze each poem's **rhyming patterns**.

Poem	Rhyming Words
Annabel Lee	
Martin Luther King	
I'm Nobody	

Vocabulary

Acquisition and Use An **analogy** shows a relationship between a pair of words. Use a word from the list on page 666 to complete each analogy. Your choice should make a word pair whose relationship matches that of the first two words.

1. enter : exit :: _____ : welcome
2. ate : consumed :: _____ : wanted
3. excellent : great :: _____ : intense
4. cat : feline :: _____ : relative
5. enjoying : smiling :: _____ : glaring
6. disinterest : indifference :: _____ : enthusiasm

Word Study Use the context of the sentences and what you know about the **Latin prefix im-** to explain your answer.

1. Is a U.S. *immigrant* someone who came to this country?

2. If someone is *imprisoned*, is that person free?

Word Study

The **Latin prefix im-** means "in," "into," or "toward."

Apply It Explain how the **prefix im-** contributes to the meanings of these words. Consult a dictionary if necessary.

imbue
implode
imperil

Poetry Collection 7 **673**

Reading Skill

1. **Possible responses:** (a) Annabel Lee was taken away from the speaker and put in a chamber for burial. (b) Martin Luther King was born in a time of trouble and turmoil. (c) It would be boring to be out in public, blathering to everyone all the time.

2. **Possible responses:** "Annabel Lee"—*bore* and *demons*; "Martin Luther King"—*grief* and *slain*; "I'm Nobody"—*dreary* and *bog*.

Literary Analysis

3. All three poems have rhythmic patterns, but "I'm Nobody" has a less regular rhythm than the others.

4. "Annabel Lee"—*ago, know; sea, Lee, me, we; chilling, killing; love, above; rise, eyes; side, bride;* "Martin Luther King"—*age, rage; wide, aside; profound, around; Earth, worth; be, free;* "I'm Nobody"— *you, too; Frog, Bog.*

For other sample answers, see *Graphic Organizer Transparencies,* **Literary Analysis Graphic Organizer A,** p. 137, and the **Additional Answers** section.

Vocabulary
Acquisition and Use
Sample answers:

1. banish
2. coveted
3. profound
4. kinsmen
5. envying
6. passion

Word Study
Sample answers:

1. Yes; The prefix *im-* means "into" and an *immigrant* is someone who has "come into the country."

2. No; The prefix *im-* means "into" and *imprisoned* means "put into prison." A person in prison is not free.

Word Study: Apply It

Sample answers: To *imbue* is to put a quality <u>into</u> something or someone. To *implode* is to collapse <u>in</u>wardly with great force. To *imperil* is to put something or someone <u>into</u> danger.

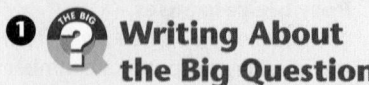

Skills instruction for the Reading Skill and Literary Analysis concepts for this collection appear on p. 665.

❶ ❓ Writing About the Big Question

1. Review the assignment with the class.

2. Remind students of ways that humor can communicate ideas, such as by making people laugh at themselves. Discuss why it might be important to use humor to communicate ideas.

3. Have students complete the sentence starter. Review responses as a class. (**Sample response:** Messages that <u>entertain</u> us can also <u>teach</u> us important lessons.)

4. Remind students that their answers will help them think about the Big Question, "What is the best way to communicate?"

While You Read

Tell students that as they read, they should consider how rhythm and rhyme affect the message of each poem.

❷ Vocabulary

1. Have students preview the collection vocabulary.

2. For each word, have students say the word aloud.

3. Then, use the word in a sentence that defines the word.

4. Finally, repeat your definitional sentence or a similar sentence with the word missing and have the class "fill in the blank" chorally. Here is an example:

> *When something happens <u>incessantly</u>, it happens without stopping. After ten days of constant rain, we can say that it has been raining [students say "incessantly"].*

❸ Word Study

1. Introduce the skill, using the instruction in the box.

2. Have students name adjectives, such as *common*, or adverbs, such as *commonly*. Challenge other students to add the prefix *un-* and define the new word.

Making Connections
Poetry Collection 8

Father William •
Stopping by Woods on a
Snowy Evening • Jim

❓ What is the best way to *communicate?*

❶ Writing About the Big Question

The poems in Poetry Collection 8 show different ways—some serious, some humorous—that poets communicate ideas about a memorable character or experience. Use this sentence starter to develop your ideas about the Big Question.

Messages that **entertain** us can also **teach** us _____.

While You Read Consider what lessons each poem may have to teach readers.

❷ Vocabulary

Read each word and its definition. Decide whether you know the word well, know it a little bit, or do not know it at all. After you read, see how your knowledge of each word has increased.

- **incessantly** (in ses′ ənt lē) *adv.* without stopping (p. 677) *He annoyed his friends by talking <u>incessantly</u> during the movie. incessant adj. cease v.*

- **uncommonly** (un käm′ ən lē) *adv.* remarkably (p. 677) *She was an <u>uncommonly</u> talented singer. uncommon adj. common adj.*

- **sage** (sāj) *n.* very wise person (p. 677) *The <u>sage</u> wisely advised daily exercise and the company of friends. sagest adj. sagacity n.*

- **supple** (sup′ əl) *adj.* able to bend easily; flexible (p. 677) *Rubber is a <u>supple</u> material. suppler adj. supplest adj.*

- **harness** (här′ nis) *n.* equipment used to drive a horse or to attach it to a vehicle (p. 679) *He bravely grabbed the <u>harness</u> of the runaway horse. harness v.*

- **downy** (dou′ nē) *adj.* soft and fluffy (p. 679) *The fur on the rabbit was <u>downy</u>. down n. downiest adj.*

❸ Word Study

The **Old English prefix un-** means "not."

In "Father William," a man is described as **uncommonly** large because it is not common for a person to be so big.

674 Poetry

Vocabulary Development

Vocabulary Knowledge Rating
Create a **Vocabulary Knowledge Rating Chart** (*Professional Development Guidebook*, p. 33) for this collection. Include the collection vocabulary and the Big Question words that appear in the Writing About the Big Question sentence starter on this page. (The Big Question vocabulary is introduced on pp. 570–571.)

Give students a copy of the chart. Read the words aloud, and have students mark their rating in the Before Reading column. Urge them to be alert to these words as they read and discuss the collection.

Tally how many students think they know a word to gauge how much instruction to provide. As students read and discuss the collection, point out the words and their context.

674

Lewis Carroll

(1832–1898)

Author of "Father William" (p. 676)

Lewis Carroll is the pen name of Charles Dodgson, a mathematics professor who was born in England. Under his pen name, Dodgson wrote *Alice's Adventures in Wonderland* and *Through the Looking Glass.* Like these classic novels, his poems are noted for their clever wordplay, nonsensical meanings, and delightfully zany worlds.

Robert Frost

(1874–1963)

Author of "Stopping by Woods on a Snowy Evening" (p. 678)

Robert Frost was born in San Francisco but moved across the country to New England when he was eleven. This region of the country proved to be inspirational for him as a writer. Frost's most popular poems describe New England country life and landscapes. Of these poems, "Stopping by Woods on a Snowy Evening" is considered one of his best. Frost won the Pulitzer Prize four times—more than any other poet.

Gwendolyn Brooks

(1917–2000)

Author of "Jim" (p. 680)

Gwendolyn Brooks began writing at the age of seven and published her first poem, "Eventide," at age thirteen. As an adult, Brooks wrote hundreds of poems, many of which focus on the African American experience. In 1950, she became the first African American to win a Pulitzer Prize.

Poetry Collection 8 **675**

Daily Bellringer

For each class during which you teach this collection, have students complete one of the five Research activities for Week 23 in the *Daily Bellringer Activities* booklet.

Background
"Father William"

The poem "Father William" appears in "Chapter 5: Advice from a Caterpillar" of *Alice's Adventures in Wonderland.* The stern Caterpillar, seated on a mushroom and smoking a hookah, asks Alice to recite "Father William" to test her memory. When Alice has finished, the Caterpillar remarks rudely that the recitation "is wrong from beginning to end."

Multidraft Reading

To assist struggling readers and to deepen reading for all, apply multidraft reading protocols. For each reading, have students set the purpose indicated:

- **First reading**—identifying key ideas and details and answering any Reading Checks.
- **Second reading**—analyzing craft and structure and responding to the side-column prompts.
- **Third reading**—integrating knowledge and ideas, connecting to other texts and the world, and answering the end-of-selection questions.

For more guidance, refer to the *Classroom Strategies and Teaching Routines* card on multidraft reading.

Differentiated Instruction   Additional Instruction

EL Extended Support— English Learners

Have students complete the **Reading and Vocabulary Warm-ups,** *Unit 4 Resources,* pp. 184–187, before they read. Assign the prereading pages in the *Reader's Notebook: English Learner's Version.* Then, have students listen to portions of the collection on the *Hear It!* **Audio CD.**

L1 L2 Extended Support— Struggling Readers

Have students complete the **Reading and Vocabulary Warm-ups,** *Unit 4 Resources,* pp. 184–187, before they read. Assign the prereading pages in the *Reader's Notebook: Adapted Version.* Then, have students listen to portions of the collection on the *Hear It!* **Audio CD.**

Extended Support— Reluctant Readers

To build motivation and engagement before assigning the collection, have students read "The Age Factor," a thematically related selection in *Reality Central.* Then, use the questions at the conclusion of the related selection to guide discussion.

For more about the author or practice with the collection vocabulary, go online at **www.PHLitOnline.com.**

❶
❷ # Father William
Lewis Carroll

❸

❹ ▲ **Critical Viewing**
Read the poem to identify which group of lines this drawing illustrates. **[Analyze]**

Background This poem, which comes from *Alice's Adventures in Wonderland,* is an amusing conversation between a father and son. Lewis Carroll wrote it as a humorous spoof on a serious poem by Robert Southey. In this version, Carroll pokes fun at the false ideas society often has about the way older people speak and behave.

676 Poetry

"You are old, Father William," the young man said,
    "And your hair has become very white;
And yet you incessantly stand on your head—
    Do you think, at your age, it is right?"

5 "In my youth," Father William replied to his son,
    "I feared it might injure the brain;
But, now that I'm perfectly sure I have none,
    Why, I do it again and again."

"You are old," said the youth, "as I mentioned before.
10   And have grown most uncommonly fat;
Yet you turned a back-somersault in at the door—
    Pray, what is the reason of that?"

"In my youth," said the sage, as he shook his gray locks,
    "I kept all my limbs very supple
15 By the use of this ointment—one shilling[1] the box—
    Allow me to sell you a couple?"

"You are old," said the youth, "and your jaws are too weak
    For anything tougher than suet;[2]
Yet you finished the goose, with the bones and the beak—
20   Pray, how did you manage to do it?"
"In my youth," said his father, "I took to the law,
    And argued each case with my wife;
And the muscular strength, which it gave to my jaw
    Has lasted the rest of my life."

25 "You are old," said the youth, "one would hardly suppose
    That your eye was as steady as ever;
Yet you balanced an eel on the end of your nose—
    What made you so awfully clever?"

"I have answered three questions, and that is enough,"
30   Said his father. "Don't give yourself airs!
Do you think I can listen all day to such stuff?
    Be off, or I'll kick you downstairs!"

---

1. **shilling** (shil´iŋ) *n.* British coin.
2. **suet** (soō´it) *n.* fat used in cooking.

Vocabulary

incessantly (in ses´ ənt lē) *adv.* without stopping

uncommonly (un käm´ ən lē) *adv.* remarkably

sage (sāj) *n.* very wise person

supple (sup´ əl) *adj.* able to bend easily; flexible

Spiral Review
Connotation What idea does the poet convey by using the word *sage*?

Paraphrase
How would you paraphrase "Don't give yourself airs!"?

Differentiated Instruction for Universal Access

Support for Special-Needs Students
Have students listen to "Father William" on *Hear It!* **Audio CD.** Tell them to follow along in their books as they listen. Then divide the students into two groups to practice reading the poem aloud. Have students in one group read the part of the father, while the other group reads the part of the son. Point out how the rhythm and rhyme add to the humor of the poem. Have the groups come together to read the entire poem, each group reading the part they practiced.

Enrichment for Advanced Readers
Ask students to compare and contrast the portrayal of the sons in "Father William" and "Jim." Suggest that they consider topics such as how the reader learns about each character, the personality traits of the characters, and each character's perspective of a parent. Have students write essays or share their ideas orally with the class.

This collection is available in interactive format in the **Enriched Online Students Edition,** at **www.PHLitOnline.com,** which includes a thematically related video with writing prompt and an interactive graphic organizer.

The deeper meaning of "Stopping by Woods on a Snowy Evening" is indicated in the final stanza. The speaker realizes that he or she has a long life and many things to do before dying. In this poem, sleep is a metaphor for death.

678 Poetry

Vocabulary Development

Vocabulary Knowledge Rating

When students have completed reading and discussing "Jim," "Father William," and "Stopping by Woods on a Snowy Evening," have them take out their **Vocabulary Rating Chart** for this poetry collection. Read the words aloud once more, and ask students to rate their knowledge of the words again in the After Reading column. Clarify any words that are still problematic. Have students write their own definition and example or sentence in the appropriate column. Then tell them to complete the Vocabulary Practice activities at the end of the selection. Encourage students to use the words in further discussion and written work about this selection. Remind them that they will be accountable for these words on the **Selection Test,** *Unit 4 Resources,* pp. 199–201 or 202–204.

⑥ Stopping by Woods on a Snowy Evening

ROBERT FROST

Background A poem may contain several levels of meaning. In "Stopping by Woods on a Snowy Evening," the speaker is a traveler passing through the winter countryside. On one level, his journey may be regarded simply as a trip through the woods. As you read the poem, however, look for a deeper meaning that relates to a journey through life.

⑦
Whose woods these are I think I know.
His house is in the village, though;
He will not see me stopping here
To watch his woods fill up with snow.

5 My little horse must think it queer
To stop without a farmhouse near
Between the woods and frozen lake
The darkest evening of the year.

He gives his harness bells a shake
10 To ask if there is some mistake.
⑧ The only other sound's the sweep
Of easy wind and downy flake.

The woods are lovely, dark, and deep,
But I have promises to keep,
15 And miles to go before I sleep,
And miles to go before I sleep.

Rhythm and Rhyme
In lines 1–8, which lines end with rhyming words?

Vocabulary
harness (här´ nis) *n.* equipment used to drive a horse or attach it to a vehicle
downy (dou´ nē) *adj.* soft and fluffy

Poetry Collection 8 **679**

---

1. Read aloud the first stanza on page 679 as students follow along. Then, **ask** students to identify the three end words that rhyme.
   Answer: *know, though, snow*

2. Write the letters a, a, b, a in a column on the board. Point out that the letters show the rhyming pattern for the stanza.

3. Repeat the process for the second stanza. Then, **ask** students to identify the end words that rhyme.
   Answer: *queer, near, year*

4. **Ask** the Rhythm and Rhyme question.
   Answer: In each stanza, lines 1, 2, and 4 end with rhyming words.

▶ **Monitor Progress:** Have students read the final stanza and tell which lines rhyme. (All the lines rhyme.)

▶ **Reteach:** If students have difficulty identifying rhymes, divide the class in two groups and read lines 1–4 aloud. Have one group read all the lines whose last word has a long o sound and the other group read the single line (3) whose last word has a long e sound. Then, ask which lines in the stanza end with rhyming words. (Lines 1, 2, and 4)

⑦ Connecting to the Big Question

1. Clarify that poets communicate through the meaning of words and the sounds the words create or suggest.

2. Have students reread the second bracketed passage on page 679. **Ask** students: What sounds does Frost describe? What rhythm and rhyme does he use? Describe it.
   Possible response: Frost describes the sounds of his harness bells, the light wind, and the snow falling. The lines rhyme *aaba, bbcb, ccdc, dddd.* The poem's rhythm is very musical.

3. **Ask:** Does Frost use rhythm and rhyme effectively in these lines to communicate his ideas? Explain.
   Possible response: Yes, the rhythm of the lines reinforces the sound of harness bells. Its regularity helps the reader feel the meditative mood of the poem.

Concept Connector

Anticipation Guide
Have students return to their **Anticipation Guides** and respond to the statements again in the After Reading column. They may do this individually or in their original pairs or groups. Then, lead a class discussion, probing for what students have learned that confirms or invalidates each statement. Encourage students to cite specific details, quotations, or other evidence from the poems to support their responses to each statement.

Writing About the Big Question
Have students compare their response to the sentence starter they completed before reading the collection with their ideas afterward. Ask them to explain whether their thoughts have changed.

Reading Skill Graphic Organizer
Ask students to review the graphic organizers they used to help them paraphrase difficult lines as they read the assigned poems. Then have students share their own graphic organizers and paraphrases.

1. Copy lines 5–6 of "Jim" on the board.

2. Have students tell you how to mark the stressed and unstressed syllables. Encourage them to use the example on p. 665 as a guide.

3. **Ask** students the Rhythm and Rhyme question.
   Answer: The even number syllables (two, four, and so on) are stressed.

ASSESS

Answers

Critical Thinking

Before students respond, you may wish to have them write a brief objective summary of each poem. As they answer the questions below, remind them to support their answers with evidence from the text.

1. (a) "Gray locks" and "fat" describe Father William's appearance. (b) Father William seems too old and too large to be able to stand on his head or do back-somersaults.

2. (a) The speaker has stopped to watch the snow fall and appreciate the woods' quiet beauty. (b) The loveliness and dark isolation of the scene capture the speaker's attention.

3. (a) The phrases "fill up with snow," "between the woods and frozen lake," "darkest evening," "gives his harness bells a shake," and "sweep of easy wind and downy flake" describe sights and sounds. (b) **Possible responses:** The poem has a quiet and thoughtful mood.

4. (a) The boy brings his mother food, drink, and medicine when she is ill. (b) Jim gives up a baseball game.

5. **Possible response:** On a snowy night, there are few people around, just as in life one is often alone. On a snowy night, there are obstacles to travel and visibility, and these mirror the obstacles of life. On a snowy night, there is beauty as in life.

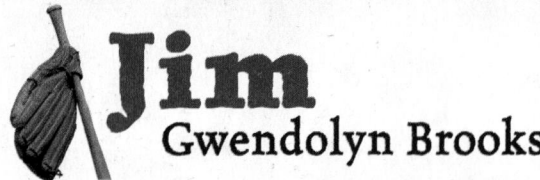

Jim
Gwendolyn Brooks

There never was a nicer boy
Than Mrs. Jackson's Jim.
The sun should drop its greatest gold
On him.

5 Because, when Mother-dear was sick,
9 He brought her cocoa in.
And brought her broth, and brought her bread.
And brought her medicine.

And, tipping,[1] tidied up her room.
10 And would not let her see
He missed his game of baseball
Terribly.

Rhythm and Rhyme
Which syllables are stressed in lines 5–6?

---

1. **tipping** (tip´ in) *v.* tiptoeing.

Cite textual evidence to support your responses.

Critical Thinking

C 1. **Key Ideas and Details (a)** In "Father William," what details from the poem describe Father William's appearance? **(b) Analyze:** How does his appearance make his actions seem especially surprising?

C 2. **Key Ideas and Details (a)** In "Stopping by Woods on a Snowy Evening," why has the speaker stopped? **(b) Infer:** What about the place captures his attention?

C 3. **Craft and Structure (a)** What words in Frost's poem describe sights and sounds? **(b) Apply:** What is the mood, or feeling, of the poem?

C 4. **Key Ideas and Details (a)** In "Jim," what tasks does the boy perform for his mother? **(b) Infer:** What detail tells you that Jim is not selfish?

C 5. **Integration of Knowledge and Ideas** Why do you think the author of "Stopping by Woods on a Snowy Evening" uses a snowy night to communicate the idea of the journey through life? Explain. *[Connect to the Big Question: What is the best way to communicate?]*

Assessment Resources

Unit 4 Resources

L1 L2 EL **Selection Test A**, pp. 199–201. Administer Test A to less advanced students.

L3 L4 EL **Selection Test B**, pp. 202–204. Administer Test B to on-level and more advanced students.

L3 L4 **Open-Book Test**, pp. 196–198. As an alternative, give the Open-Book Test.

All **Customizable Test Bank**

All **Self-tests**
Students may prepare for the **Selection Test** by taking the **Self-test** online.

PHLit Online! All assessment resources are available at **www.PHLitOnline.com**.

After You Read
Poetry Collection 8

Father William •
Stopping by Woods on a
Snowy Evening • Jim

ASSESS/EXTEND

Answers

Reading Skill: Paraphrase

1. Reread the following lines, and then **paraphrase** them.

   (a) lines 13–16 of "Father William"

   (b) lines 11–12 of "Stopping by Woods on a Snowy Evening"

   (c) lines 3–4 of "Jim"

2. Identify two words in these poems that you might look up in a dictionary to help you paraphrase meaning.

Literary Analysis: Sound Devices

3. Craft and Structure **(a)** Do the poems have **rhythmic patterns**? Explain. **(b)** Which poem has the most interesting rhythm? Explain.

4. Craft and Structure Use a chart like this to analyze **rhyme.**

Poem	Rhyming Words
Father William	
Stopping by Woods…	
Jim	

Vocabulary

Acquisition and Use Answer each question by writing a complete sentence that includes the italicized vocabulary word.

1. If a car alarm wails *incessantly*, is it annoying?

2. What qualities does a person need to be considered a *sage*?

3. How can exercise help give you a *supple* body?

4. Why are you likely to remember an *uncommonly* good meal?

5. Is burlap considered a *downy* material?

6. Why would a parachutist need a *harness*?

Word Study Use the context of the sentences and what you know about the **Old English prefix un-** to explain your answer.

1. Are people persuaded by *unconvincing* arguments?

2. If you are *unfit* for service, are you likely to do a good job?

Word Study

The **Old English prefix un-** means "not."

Apply It Explain how the prefix *un-* contributes to the meanings of these words. Consult a dictionary if necessary.

unpredictable
unintended
uninformed

Poetry Collection 8 **681**

Reading Skill

1. Possible responses: (a) When I was young, I stayed flexible by using this ointment. One box costs one shilling. Let me sell you two boxes. (b) The only other sound in the woods is made by a gentle breeze and fluffy snowflakes. (c) Jim should receive the highest honor.

2. Possible responses: "Father William"—*locks, airs.* "Stopping by Woods on a Snowy Evening"—*downy, harness.* "Jim"—*broth, tidied.*

Literary Analysis

3. (a) No, "Jim" does not have a regular pattern of stressed and unstressed syllables. (b) **Possible response:** "Jim" is interesting because its rhythm is irregular so you cannot read in a sing-song way.

4. "Father William"—*said, head; white, right; son, none; brain, again; before, door; fat, that; locks, box;* and so on; "Stopping by Woods . . ."—*know, though, snow; here, queer, near, year; lake, shake, mistake, flake; sweep, deep, keep, sleep;* "Jim"—*Jim, him; in, medicine; see, Terribly.*

For other sample answers, see *Graphic Organizer Transparencies,* **Literary Analysis Graphic Organizer A,** p. 138, and the **Additional Answers** section.

Vocabulary
Acquisition and Use
Sample answers:

1. Yes; A car alarm that wails <u>incessantly</u> would be annoying because it would continue without pause.

2. A person needs experience and wisdom to be considered a <u>sage</u>.

3. Exercise that involves stretching can help give you a <u>supple</u> body by making you flexible.

4. An <u>uncommonly</u> good meal will be remembered for being unusually and especially satisfying.

5. No; Burlap is scratchy, not soft and <u>downy</u>.

6. A parachutist would need a <u>harness</u> to attach the parachute to his or her body.

Word Study
Sample answers:

1. No; The prefix *un-* means "not" and *unconvincing* means "not convincing." Arguments that are <u>not</u> convincing will not persuade people.

2. No; The prefix *un-* means "not" and *unfit* means "not fit." A person who is <u>not</u> fit will not do a good job.

Word Study: Apply It
Sample answers: Something *unpredictable* is <u>not</u> predictable. Something *unintended* is <u>not</u> intended. Someone who is uninformed is <u>not</u> informed.

Co...
1. I
   i
2. D

Thi...

Say ...

Reading Skill

1. Introduce the skill, using the instruction on the student page.
2. Review the chart.
3. Tell students they will determine the main idea as they read.

Think Aloud: Model the Skill

Say to students:

When I read a text, I look for the main idea—the idea that all details in a text add up to. For example, if I read that attendance at football games is rising and that more football gear sold last year than the year before, I realize that these details add up to one main idea: football is growing in popularity. To help me get at a main idea, I paraphrase, or put words and phrases in the text into my own words.

Multidraft Reading

Have students follow a multidraft reading protocol.

- **First reading**—Have students read to identify key ideas and details.
- **Second reading**—Have students read to identify the structure of the text.
- **Third reading**—Have students read to integrate knowledge and ideas by connecting the text to the world, their own experiences, and other texts.

Content-Area Vocabulary

1. Have students say each word.
2. Next, use each word in a sentence that defines it.
3. Finally, repeat your definitional sentence or a similar sentence, omitting the word, and have the class "fill in the blank" chorally.

PH...
Stud...
prac...
Cha...

Pra...
Ans...
1. si...
2. c...

Rea...
San...
Simp...
The ...
Com...
was ...
Lee-...
aph...

Pra...
San...
1. W...
   fi...
2. R...
   b...
   th...
3. D...
   w...
   v...
4. A...
   th...

Wr...
San...
A g...
is sn...
it is ...
nee...
coul...
be a...

682

Reading for Information

Analyzing Expository Texts

Magazine Article

Educational Song

Reading Skill: Determine the Main Idea

The **main idea** is the central point or message conveyed in a passage or text. **Details** are the facts and examples that develop, or support, the main idea. One way to determine the main idea of a passage or text is through **paraphrasing,** or restating in your own words. When you paraphrase sentences or paragraphs, you retell all the details, but replace, combine, or rearrange words in a way that shows your understanding. Paraphrasing passages can help you to understand how they develop main ideas.

As you read, identify words that can be replaced or combined. Use a chart like the one shown to help you paraphrase.

Sentence or Passage	Replacement Words	Paraphrase
Rap is about words, but rhythm makes them more powerful.	rhythm = beat more powerful = stronger but = although	Although words are the point of rap, its beat makes it stronger.

Content-Area Vocabulary

These words appear in the selections that follow. You may also encounter them in other content-area texts.

- **composition** (käm´ pə zish´ ən) *n.* work of music, art, or literature
- **innovative** (in´ə vā´ tiv) *adj.* original; using new ideas or methods
- **junction** (juŋk´ shən) *n.* point where two or more things are joined

686 Poetry

What is the best way to communicate?

Have students look for how the writers give information and entertain as they read.

Features:

- content intended for informational or leisure reading
- illustrations or photographs that accompany the text
- text that may be written for a general or specific audience

The Rhythms of Rap

Kathiann M. Kowalski

Rap is about society; some songs get notoriety. But do your feet tap, when you hear rap?

Lots of rap tracks make you move along with them. Rap is about words, but rhythm makes them more powerful.

"Rhythm is the feeling of movement in time," explains Miami University (OH) music professor Chris Tanner. "Rhythm is the term we use in music for dividing time. Music can't exist without rhythm." In other words, one sound with no break is just noise. Play a sequence of notes for a certain time each, and you get music.

As music moves forward in time, your brain notes the duration of individual sounds and groups them together into bunches that let you perceive rhythm in the music. It could be the hammering lyrics of a rap artist. Or, it could be the beginning of Beethoven's *Fifth Symphony*: "Bum, bum, bum, bummm. Bum, bum, bum, bummm."

Saying Their Songs

Rap as a popular music style started

Odyssey Magazine   March, 2002

in the late 1970s. But, notes music professor Adam Krims at the University of Alberta, "In some form or another, this kind of music has been around for about 250 years. It continues very old practices of rhyming and rhythm among African Americans."

> The author provides historical details to support her main ideas.

Rap's style of rhythmic delivery sets it apart from talking or other styles of *declamatory* (words recited with music) delivery. "In rap, you're not just talking," notes Krims, "You're really foregrounding [bringing up front] the rhythmic aspects of what you're doing."

It's somewhat like the difference between reading a textbook and reading Dr. Seuss's *Green Eggs and Ham* aloud. However, stresses Krims, "Rap actually takes a lot of practice to do even slightly well." Effective rhythmic phrasing really draws listeners into the lyrics of an MC ("MC" is the same as "emcee" and stands for "master of ceremonies"—a name rap artists commonly use).

Often an MC works with words' natural

Reading for Information: Magazine Article **687**

About Magazines

About Magazines

1. Review the features listed in the box on p. 687.
   Ask the class to define *leisure reading*.
   Possible response: Leisure reading is reading you do for your own enjoyment.

2. **Ask** students to discuss what types of magazines they like to read and why.
   Possible response: Students may say that they like to read fashion or music magazines for leisure and news magazines for information.

Determine the Main Idea

1. Remind students that the main idea of a text is the central point or message. Emphasize that the main idea must be supported by facts and details.

2. Have students read "The Rhythms of Rap" and the callout notes that identify important elements of the article.

3. Read aloud the first callout note and point out how photographs are used to illustrate the article. Explain that teams of magazine writers and photographers are often assigned to cover stories so that the text and visuals closely match each other. Point out that photographs can help provide clues to the main idea of an article.

4. **Ask** what the purpose of the article's opening paragraph is.
   Answer: This paragraph mimics the rhyming lyrics of a rap song while indirectly introducing the article's topic. Point out that the topic is not stated directly until the second paragraph and not supported until the third.

Differentiated Instruction   for Universal Access

Strategy for Special-Needs Students
The sophisticated prose style and advanced vocabulary that the author uses may be challenging for students. However, the underlying message about music is quite accessible. To illustrate the article's points about rhythm in general, and rap in particular, play recordings as needed. Both dirges and fast marches such as Sousa's are readily available on CD in many libraries. Students may also enjoy listening to the opening of Beethoven's Fifth Symphony, as well as the 1970s disco song, "A Fifth of Beethoven."

Strategy for Less Proficient Readers
To students already familiar with the features of magazine articles, explain that the writing in professional and scholarly journals is closely related. Have them explore such journals and report to the class on key differences. Tell students to include a point-for-point comparison with magazines in their presentations. For example, journal articles are typically longer, are written for a more narrow audience, and are less oriented to current events. Also, the graphics may be sparse and consist of labeled diagrams rather than full-color photographs.

Determine the Main Idea

1. Check for comprehension.
   Ask students to **identify** the topic of the article.
   Answer: The article's topic concerns how the rhythmic basis of rap accounts for its appeal. The article also explains how the rhythms of rap are deeply rooted in musical tradition and history.

2. Enhance comprehension by having students use their paraphrase charts as needed. If a given sentence or paragraph is challenging, guide students to replace its words with ones with which they are more comfortable. If students have difficulty using their charts, verbally model the process of paraphrasing.

emphasis. Other times, the artist may deform words. "You purposely deliver them in a way that's a little perverse," explains Krims. So instead of "California," an MC might say "Californ-eye-ay."

In the Background

Sampling serves up yet more rhythms in rap. "Sampling is taking a little bit of music from another source," says Krims. Sampling may be the artist's own **composition**. It may be a segment from another popular song or even a classical piece.

The musician then makes a "loop" of the segment, which means that it's played over and over. Sampling adds background melody and harmony. Each bit of sampling also adds its own rhythms to a rap song.

The Beat Goes On

Underlying rap and almost all music is its pulse, or beat. "There are all kinds of rhythms going on in a *Sousa* march, but what do people march to?" says Tanner. It's not the rhythmic phrasing of the melody. Instead, he says, "They move their feet to the underlying pulse of the music."

Rap and other popular music forms often spell out the beat explicitly with drums. "Any popular music that we're used to usually has that characteristic," notes Tanner. "That's why it's fun to dance to. In fact, popular music is often designed for movement."

"Meter is simply organizing pulses into a regular cyclical pattern," adds Tanner. Instead of an endless series of beats, the musician may play cycles of "ONE, two, Three, four." This meter, known as "common time," stresses the first beat most. The third beat gets slight emphasis, too. Meter sets up a hierarchy, which the listener's brain can then remember and anticipate. That makes it possible for

you to tap your foot or clap in time with the music.

Tempo is how fast a piece of music delivers its meter. Too slow, and a rap song sounds like a *dirge*, or funeral song. Too fast, and the brain can't perceive individual sounds. The music becomes one big blur. Choose a tempo that's just quick enough, and listeners want to move with the music. Speed it up slightly or slow it down in places, and listeners respond to the music's different moods.

What Makes It Cool?

Hearing rhythm patterns in a song, listeners form expectations of what comes next. If music doesn't give enough for listeners to form those expectations, it sounds chaotic and grating. If music gets too predictable, however, it becomes boring.

Sophisticated rap music provides an **innovative** mix that satisfies and sometimes surprises listeners' expectations. With lyrics, an MC might stop in the middle of a line or give some offbeat accents. Sampling or the drum track may stress different notes than those that would usually be emphasized in the meter—a technique called *syncopation*.

Revel in the rhythms of your favorite music. Innovative rhythms not only move music forward in time, but they also make rap—and many other types of music—cool.

> The final paragraph states one of the main ideas of the article.

Vocabulary Development
© **CCSS** Language 6

Musical Terms
Tell students that when reading magazine articles, they may encounter new words specific to their subject matter. Guide students to understand the meaning of the following music-related terms that appear in the article:

- *phrasing:* a *phrase* is a short musical passage; *phrasing* refers to the organization and structure of these phrases
- *classical piece:* a musical composition intended and arranged for formally trained musicians who play traditional instruments
- *harmony:* the compatibility of sounds or, more specifically, the progression of musical chords
- *melody:* a tune made up of a succession of musical notes
- *lyrics:* the words in a song

SCHOOLHOUSE ROCK
Conjunction Junction

Music & Lyrics: Bob Dorough
Performed by: Jack Sheldon
Animation: Phil Kimmelman and Associates

Conjunction Junction, what's your function?
Hooking up words and phrases and clauses.
Conjunction Junction, how's that function?
I got three favorite cars
That get most of my job done.
Conjunction Junction, what's their function?
I got "and," "but," and "or,"
They'll get you pretty far.

"And":
That's an additive, like "this and that."
"But":
That's sort of the opposite,
"Not this but that."
And then there's "or":
O-R, when you have a choice like
"This or that."
"And," "but," and "or,"
Get you pretty far.

Conjunction Junction, what's your function?
Hooking up two boxcars and making 'em run right.
Milk and honey, bread and butter, peas and rice.
Hey that's nice!
Dirty but happy, digging and scratching,
Losing your shoe and a button or two.
He's poor but honest, sad but true,
Boo-hoo-hoo-hoo-hoo!

The song opens with a question followed by a statement of the main idea.

This stanza provides examples of conjunctions and supports the main idea of the song.

Reading for Information: Educational Song **689**

About Educational Songs

1. Review the features listed in the Educational Song box on p. 689 with students. **Ask** the class to explain the difference between verse and prose.
   Answer: Prose is ordinary speech or writing that consists of sentences organized in paragraphs. Verse is poetry. It consists of lines of text that have definite rhythms and that use sound effects such as rhyme.

2. **Ask** students to list educational songs they know, even songs they may remember from when they were much younger.
   Possible response: Songs students identify will vary.

3. Talk to students about how best to approach song lyrics in print. Tell students that one useful strategy is to consider how the lyrics would be sung or performed.

Determine the Main Idea

1. Direct students' attention to the song title, "Conjunction Junction." **Ask** what clue the song title provides about the main idea.
   Possible response: The title includes the word *conjunction,* which is a grammar term. Because this is an educational song, the central message of this song may be to teach about conjunctions or other grammar elements.

2. Have students begin reading the poem. Tell them to analyze the text to determine the main idea. Remind students to retell parts of the text in their own words to help them understand key ideas.

3. **Ask** students to paraphrase the stanza in the middle of the page that begins with "And."
   Possible response: *And, but,* and *or* are three conjunctions. They serve to link related ideas, show opposites, or give choices.

Fluency

Tell students that although "Conjunction Junction" was meant to be sung and heard, reading it aloud also serves to help convey its meaning. Distribute copies of page 689, and pair students. Have students read the lyrics on the page aloud for fluency. Tell partners they can apportion the lyrics as they see fit. One partner may read the boldfaced lines, for example, while the other responds. Tell students to focus on achieving a pace or tempo that both entertains and communicates the content of the lyrics. Tell students to use punctuation to help them phrase the text. They should stop at end punctuation and pause at commas. Words in quotation marks should receive special emphasis. Have student pairs "perform" the song for the class.

Determine the Main Idea

1. **Ask** students to identify the conjunctions in the first stanza on p. 690, and what purpose these conjunctions serve, according to the lyric.
   Answer: The stanza mentions the conjunctions *or* and *nor*. These conjunctions are used to relate choices.

2. **Ask** students to paraphrase the lines "Conjunction Junction, what's your function? / Hooking up phrases and clauses that balance."
   Possible response: Conjunctions are used to link phrases and clauses that relate connected ideas.

3. **Ask** students to state the main idea of the song.
   Possible response: Conjunctions, which are words that link words or phrases that are related, are an essential part of the English language.

Conjunction Junction, what's your function?
Hooking up two cars to one
When you say something like this choice:
"Either now or later"
Or no choice:
"Neither now nor ever"
Hey that's clever!
Eat this or that, grow thin or fat,
Never mind, I wouldn't do that,
I'm fat enough now!

Conjunction Junction, what's your function?
Hooking up phrases and clauses that balance, like:
Out of the frying pan and into the fire.
He cut loose the sandbags,
But the balloon wouldn't go any higher.
Let's go up to the mountains,
Or down to the sea.
You should always say "thank you,"
Or at least say "please."

> This stanza repeats the main idea of the song, and then provides additional examples as supporting details.

Conjunction Junction, what's your function?
Hooking up words and phrases and clauses
In complex sentences like:

Conjunction Junction, what's your function?
Hooking up cars and making 'em function.
Conjunction Junction, how's that function?
I like tying up words and phrases and clauses.
Conjunction Junction, watch that function.
I'm going to get you there if you're very careful.
Conjunction Junction, what's your function?
I'm going to get you there if you're very careful.
Conjunction Junction, what's your function?
I'm going to get you there if you're very careful.

Think Aloud

Main Idea

Model the skill of determining the main idea, using the following "think aloud." Say to students:

> I know that the main idea of a text is its central message. I also know that the main idea of a text needs to be supported by details and examples. After reading the first page of the song, I have determined that the topic is conjunctions. What I want to determine now is the main idea: What important point is the song making about conjunctions?

To determine this main idea, I paraphrase the first lines on this page. I paraphrase "Conjunction Junction, what's your function?" as "What is the purpose of conjunctions?" "Hooking up two cars to one" is a little tricky, but I realize that this phrase is a figure of speech. Just as train cars are hooked together by couplings, I realize that words are connected by conjunctions. I paraphrase this line as "Conjunctions connect ideas." By paraphrasing, I have found the main ideas of the song.

Comparing Expository Texts

1. Craft and Structure (a) Explain the differences in the way each text organizes and develops main ideas and supporting details. Give an example from each text. **(b)** Do you think either type of text is better suited for educating readers about a topic? Explain your response.

Content-Area Vocabulary

2. (a) Determine the verb forms of *composition* and *innovative*. **(b)** Use all four words in a brief paragraph about music.

⏱ Timed Writing

Explanatory Text: Paraphrase

> **Format**
> The prompt gives specific directions about the length of the assignment.

Choose either the magazine article or the educational song and paraphrase it. Use your own words to emphasize the same points as the source selection. Your paraphrase should be no longer than the original text.
(30 minutes)

> **Academic Vocabulary**
> When you *emphasize* a point in your writing, you stress its importance through word choice and details.

5-Minute Planner

Complete these steps before you begin to write:

1. Read the prompt. Look for highlighted key words.

2. Decide which text you are going to paraphrase, the magazine article or the educational song.

3. Read through the text and identify any unfamiliar words. Jot down a few synonyms, or words with similar meanings, that you can use in your paraphrase to replace those words.

4. Closely reread each section of the magazine article or song lyrics, and note the main ideas and supporting details. Jot down phrases that you can use to express the author's points in your own words.

Comparing Expository Texts

1. (a) A magazine article provides information about a topic in a narrative, with explanations and quotations. A magazine article often states a main idea and then follows with supporting details. For example, the statement "Rap is about words, but rhythm makes them more powerful" is a main idea. This is followed by a supporting detail, "Rhythm is the term we use in music for dividing time." Song lyrics provide information in a more creative way that requires more interpretation by the reader. In a song, the title often gives clues to what the main idea is. For example, "Conjunction Junction." The song then repeats the main idea, such as in the lyrics "Conjunction Junction, how's that function? Hooking up words and phrases." The supporting detail explains what a conjunction is: "*And, but, and or*/get you pretty far."
(b) Possible response: A magazine article might be better suited for a topic that readers already find interesting. Song lyrics might be better suited for a topic, such as grammar, that people might not take an interest in unless they are persuaded.

2. (a) The verb forms of the words *composition* and *innovative* are *compose* and *innovate.* **(b) Sample response:** It is not easy to compose good songs. A good song is familiar, but innovative at the same time. The best songwriters try to innovate whenever they write a composition.

⏱ Timed Writing

1. Before students complete the activity, guide them in identifying and analyzing key words and phrases in the prompt, highlighted on the student page.

2. Work with students to draw up guidelines for their essays based on the key words:

   • **Focus** The writer should stay focused on paraphrasing the main idea of the text.

   • **Organization** The writer should first present the original text, then give the paraphrase.

   • **Elaboration** The writer should be careful not to elaborate so much that the initial focus is lost.

   • **Style** The style should be clear.

3. Have students use the 5-Minute Planner to structure their time.

4. Allow students 30 minutes to complete the assignment. Evaluate their work using the guidelines they have developed.

Common Core State Standards

• Reading Literature 4
• Writing 1

❶ Comparing Imagery

1. Introduce and discuss the skill, using the instruction on the student page.
2. Discuss the chart.
3. Give students a copy of **Comparing Imagery Organizer B**, *Graphic Organizer Transparencies,* p. 141. Tell them they will fill it in with examples of images that appeal to the senses as they read.

Think Aloud: Model the Skill

Model the skill of using imagery. Say:

How do you think a poet comes up with a vivid description? Suppose I'm writing a poem about this classroom. I want to appeal to my readers' sense of sight.

Let's say I think the lighting in the room is interesting. Now I need to describe that lighting. A few adjectives will do the job—the question is which ones to choose. Some words that come to mind are *flickering, blazing,* and *shining.* The word I choose determines the image the reader will picture. By creating an image with words, I can convey my observations.

❶ Comparing Imagery

In poetry, an **image** is a word or phrase that appeals to one or more of the five senses. Writers use **imagery** to bring poetry to life with descriptions of how their subjects look, sound, feel, taste, and smell. Look at these examples:

- The phrase "the sweet, slippery mango slices" appeals to the senses of taste and touch.
- The phrase "glaring lights and wailing sirens" appeals to the senses of sight and hearing.

Writers also create **mood** through their use of images, words, and descriptive details. Mood is the feeling created in the reader by a literary work or passage. The mood of a work may be described with adjectives such as *joyous, gloomy, cozy,* or *frightening.*

To fully appreciate images and mood in a poem, determine the meaning of any unfamiliar words that the poet uses—including words the poet has made up. Also, pay close attention to the connotations of words—their emotional associations—as well as to their figurative, or nonliteral, meanings.

Both "Miracles" and "in Just—" contain images that appeal to the senses. On a chart like the one shown, track the images in the two poems. After you read, use your chart to help you compare the authors' use of imagery.

Common Core State Standards

Reading Literature
4. Determine the meaning of words and phrases as they are used in a text, including figurative and connotative meanings; analyze the impact of rhymes and other repetitions of sounds on a specific verse or stanza of a poem or section of a story or drama.

Writing
1. Write arguments to support claims with clear reasons and relevant evidence.

Sense	Images	
	"Miracles"	"in Just—"
Sight		
Hearing		
Touch/Movement		
Taste		
Smell		

www.PHLitOnline.com
- Vocabulary flashcards
- Interactive journals
- More about the authors
- Selection audio
- Interactive graphic organizers

Vocabulary Development

Vocabulary Knowledge Rating

Create a **Vocabulary Knowledge Rating Chart** (*Professional Development Guidebook,* p. 33) featuring the vocabulary words glossed in the selections:

exquisite (p. 695) *distinct* (p. 695)

Give students a copy of the chart, and read the words aloud. Have students mark their rating of each in the Before You Read column. To gauge how much instruction to provide, tally the number of students who think they know each word.

Explain that the words are defined in the margin at the point where they appear in the selection. Urge students to be alert to these words as they read and discuss the selections. They will rate their knowledge again when they finish.

Vocabulary Central, featuring tools, activities, and songs for studying vocabulary, is available online at **www.PHLitOnline.com.**

What is the best way to *communicate?*

Writing About the Big Question

In both of these selections, the writers use imagery to paint vivid pictures in the minds of readers. Consider how descriptive language can help readers "see" exactly what the writer sees. Use these sentence starters to develop your ideas.

Descriptive words can **enrich** a piece of writing because _____.

When writing **produces** a picture in the mind of a reader, the reader can understand _____.

Meet the Authors

Walt Whitman (1819–1892)
Author of "Miracles"

Walt Whitman worked at many occupations during his life. He was a carpenter, teacher, and newspaper reporter. During the Civil War, he nursed his wounded brother and other soldiers.

The Father of American Poetry In 1855, Whitman published the first edition of *Leaves of Grass*—poems that no established publisher would touch. In this book, Whitman abandoned regular rhyme and rhythm in favor of free verse, which followed no set pattern. Now considered a masterpiece, the book led critics to regard Whitman as the father of American poetry.

E. E. Cummings (1894–1962)
Author of "in Just—"

Edward Estlin Cummings first published a collection of poetry in the early 1920s. The work stood out, among other reasons, because of Cummings's original use of language and unusual punctuation, capitalization, and word spacing. In fact, the author's name usually appears the way he wrote it, with no capitals—as e. e. cummings.

A Sense of Humor Cummings often wrote poems that were playful and humorous. These poems reflected his attitude that "the most wasted of all days is one without laughter."

Miracles • in Just— **693**

Teaching Resources

The following resources can be used to enrich, extend, or differentiate the instruction.

- **All** *Unit 4 Resources,* pp. 205–212
- **All** *Graphic Organizer Transparencies,* pp. 140–143
- **All** *Common Core Companion,* pp. 41–53; 191–201
- **All** **Enriched Online Student Edition**

All resources, including print and audio, are available online at www.PHLitOnline.com.

---

2 **Writing About the Big Question**

1. Introduce the assignment.
2. Lead the class in a discussion of descriptive words. **Ask** each student to choose one word to describe him- or herself. Write some of the strongest words on the board (*athletic, hyper, bookish*) and label the list "Descriptive Words."
3. Have students complete the first sentence starter. Review responses as a class. (**Sample response:** Descriptive words can <u>enrich</u> a piece of writing because *they help the reader "see" what the writer is describing.*)
4. Have students complete the second sentence starter on their own.
5. Tell students that as they read, they should notice how the poets communicate through careful word choice.

Concept Connector ➤

Students will return to their sentence starters after reading.

Multidraft Reading

To assist struggling readers and to deepen reading for all, apply multidraft reading protocols. For each reading, have students set the purpose indicated:

- **First reading**—identifying key ideas and details and answering any Reading Checks.
- **Second reading**—analyzing craft and structure and responding to the side-column prompts.
- **Third reading**—integrating knowledge and ideas, connecting to other texts and the world, and answering the end-of-selection questions.

For more guidance, see the *Classroom Strategies and Teaching Routines* card on **Multidraft Reading.**

❶ Background

Whitman's Notebooks

Walt Whitman carried notebooks so that he could jot down observations, ideas, and impressions of the world. More than forty of his notebooks have survived. In early notebooks, Whitman recorded ideas for potential articles. Later notebooks contain drafts of poems and descriptions of historical events. Among the latter is a description of New York City the day after President Lincoln was assassinated.

❷ Activating Prior Knowledge

1. Pair students and ask each group to come up with a definition of the word "miracle." Circulate through the room to assess that each group has come up with a definition, but allow each group to keep their responses private.

2. Ask each group to write down three examples of miracles they have read or heard about.

3. Ask students if they have ever personally witnessed a miracle.

Concept Connector ➡

Students will return to their ideas about miracles after reading the poem.

❸ About the Selection

In "Miracles," the speaker expresses the belief that life is miraculous by noting the small things that people take for granted. These things include many natural phenomena, such as forests, oceans, and the cycle of day and night.

Miracles
Walt Whitman

694 Poetry

ⓒ Text Complexity Rubric: Leveled Texts

		✓ **Miracles**	✓✓ **in Just**
Qualitative Measures	**Context/Knowledge Demands**	Impressions of the world; life experience demands 1 ② 3 4 5	Neighborhood in America on an early spring day 1 2 ③ 4 5
	Structure/Language Conventionality and Clarity	Formal; mixture of long and short lines; on-level vocabulary; imagery 1 2 ③ 4 5	Unconventional use of grammar, spelling, language, punctuation, and line length 1 2 3 ④ 5
	Levels of Meaning/ Purpose/Concepts	Accessible concept (life is miraculous) 1 ② 3 4 5	Challenging concept (unique style) 1 2 3 ④ 5
Quantitative Measures	**Text Length**	Word Count: 230	Word Count: 64
	Lexile	NP	NP
Overall Complexity		✓ **Accessible**	✓✓ **Challenging**

5 Why, who makes much of a miracle?
As to me I know of nothing else but miracles,
Whether I walk the streets of Manhattan,
Or dart my sight over the roofs of houses toward the sky,
5 Or wade with naked feet along the beach just in the edge
   of the water,
Or stand under trees in the woods,
Or talk by day with any one I love . . .
Or sit at table at dinner with the rest,
Or look at strangers opposite me riding in the car,
10 Or watch honeybees busy around the hive of a summer
   forenoon
Or animals feeding in the fields,
Or birds, or the wonderfulness of insects in the air,
Or the wonderfulness of the sundown, or of stars shining
   so quiet and bright,
Or the exquisite delicate thin curve of the new moon in
   spring;
15 These with the rest, one and all, are to me miracles,
The whole referring, yet each distinct and in its place.

To me every hour of the light and dark is a miracle,
Every cubic inch of space is a miracle,
Every square yard of the surface of the earth is spread
   with the same,
20 Every foot of the interior swarms with the same.

To me the sea is a continual miracle,
The fishes that swim—the rocks—the motion of the
   waves—
the ships with men in them,
What stranger miracles are there?

Critical Thinking

© **1. Key Ideas and Details (a)** List events that the speaker calls miracles. **(b) Infer:** Why is the sea a "continual miracle"?

© **2. Integration of Knowledge and Ideas** Why do you think Whitman decided to use poetry to describe the beauty around him? *[Connect to the Big Question: What is the best way to communicate?]*

Cite textual evidence to support your responses.

---

4 ◄ **Critical Viewing**
Identify a line in the poem that relates to this painting. Explain your choice. **[Connect]**

Imagery
Which image in the first seven lines appeals to the sense of touch?

Vocabulary
exquisite (eks´ kwiz it)
adj. beautiful in a delicate way
distinct (di stiŋkt´)
adj. separate and different

Miracles **695**

© Text Complexity: Reader and Task Suggestions

Miracles		in Just	
Preparing to Read the Text	**Leveled Tasks**	**Preparing to Read the Text**	**Leveled Tasks**
• Using the Background information on TE p. 694, discuss the value of recording thoughts in a notebook. • Ask students to think about the impression conveyed by long-running sentences in a poem. • Guide students to use Multidraft Reading strategies (TE p. 693).	*Structure/Language* If students will have difficulty with language, have them first read to locate end punctuation throughout the poem. Then, have them reread, paraphrasing the long sentences into several shorter sentences. *Analyzing* If students will not have difficulty with language, have them identify imagery as they read. Then, have them note the images that develop the poem's concept.	• Using the Background information on TE p. 696, discuss Cummings's unusual style. • Ask students why a poet would create and use new and unusual words. • Guide students to use Multidraft Reading strategies (TE p. 693).	*Structure/Language* If students will have difficulty with language, have them first read to identify complete ideas. Then, have them reread, adding more traditional spelling and punctuation as they paraphrase sections of the poem. *Evaluating* If students will not have difficulty with language, ask them to identify language used to describe the characters and their actions. Ask students to explain the effect this language has on the reader.

❻ Background

Cummings's Unique Style

Cummings is known for his deviation from grammatical conventions. He uses unconventional capitalization, spacing, and spelling in his poems. While some say that these techniques allow his poems to be "heard," others counter that they make the poems challenging to read.

❼ Focusing Reading

Cummings has a special affinity for quirky characters, such as the balloonman. Ask students to think of peculiar characters they know from films, radio, television, or comics. Have students briefly explain what makes these characters interesting. Tell students to think about what the balloonman adds to the poem as they read.

ASSESS

Answers

Critical Thinking

Remind students to support their answers with evidence from the text.

1. (a) Children's reactions to the distant whistle of a balloonman. **Possible response:** (b) Unusual words make the reader slow down and pay attention to the language of the poem. These made-up words also add to the fun of the poem because they are silly sounding.

2. **Possible response:** Writers of fiction and poetry should break the rules of grammar if it helps them create a more effective story or poem. In "in Just—" Cummings breaks the rules about how text should appear on the page, but the result is pleasing. The words seem to skip, which is a wonderful way to communicate the feeling of a spring day.

---

❻ ❼ ❽

in Just—   E. E. Cummings

in Just—
spring   when the world is mud-
luscious the little
lame balloonman

5   whistles   far   and wee

and eddieandbill come
running from marbles and
piracies and it's
spring

10   when the world is puddle-wonderful

the queer
old balloonman whistles
far   and   wee
and bettyandisbel come dancing

15   from hop-scotch and jump-rope and

it's
spring
and
the

20   goat-footed

balloonMan   whistles
far
and
wee

696 Poetry

Cite textual evidence to support your responses.

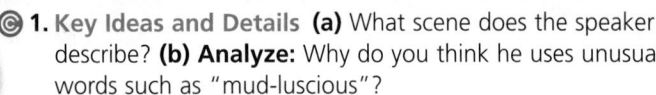

Critical Thinking

© **1. Key Ideas and Details (a)** What scene does the speaker describe? **(b) Analyze:** Why do you think he uses unusual words such as "mud-luscious"?

© **2. Craft and Structure** Cummings breaks many language conventions. When do you think it is OK for a writer to break grammatical rules? *[Connect to the Big Question: What is the best way to communicate?]*

Vocabulary Development

Vocabulary Knowledge Rating

When students have completed reading and discussing "Miracles" and "in Just—," have them take out their **Vocabulary Knowledge Rating Chart**. Read the words aloud once more and have students rate their knowledge of the words again in the After Reading column. Clarify any words that are still problematic. Have students write their own definition and example or sentence in the appropriate column. Then, have students complete the Vocabulary Practice activities on the next page. Encourage students to use the words in further discussion and written work about these selections. Remind them that they will be accountable for these words on the **Selection Test** (*Unit 4 Resources,* pp. 216–218 or 219–221.)

After You Read

Miracles • in Just—

Comparing Imagery

1. Craft and Structure Give an example from each poem of an **image** that appeals to each of the following senses: **(a)** hearing; **(b)** touch. Explain the meaning, including connotations, of key words in each image.

2. Craft and Structure (a) Using a chart like the one shown, identify and explain sight images in each poem. Explain the meaning, including connotations, of key words in each image. **(b)** Which poem has more vivid sight images?

Miracles	in Just—
Image:	Image:
Effect:	Effect:

Timed Writing

Argument: Recommendation

Write an essay that recommends one of the two poems to someone your age. Choose the poem that you believe provides more effective examples of imagery. Include details from the text to support your claim. **(40 minutes)**

5-Minute Planner

1. Read the prompt carefully and completely.

2. Gather your ideas by jotting down answers to these questions:
   - What do you find fascinating or distinctive about the imagery in the poem you are recommending?
   - Which images are most meaningful to you?
   - In what ways is the imagery in the poem you chose more effective than the imagery in the other poem?

3. Review the graphic organizer you completed as you read the poems to help you address the questions above.

4. Reread the prompt, and then draft your essay.

Miracles • in Just— **697**

Comparing Imagery

1. **Possible responses:** (a) The birds and honeybees in "Miracles" and the balloonman's whistle in "in Just—" appeal to the sense of hearing. (b) Wading with naked feet in "Miracles" and the "mudlusciousness" in "in Just—" appeal to the sense of touch. The meanings of answers will vary, but answers should show an understanding of how the poets develop each image.

2. **Possible response:**
(a) "Miracles"—*exquisite delicate thin curve of the new moon in spring;* This image describes the moon; the effect is to make the moon seem miraculous. "in Just—" —*the/goat-footed/balloonMan whistles;* This image creates a silly effect as it describes a man with goat feet. (b) Students may say that "Miracles" has the more numerous and varied visual images. Students should support their answers with examples from their charts.

Timed Writing

1. Review the prompt with students.

2. Have students use the 5-Minute Planner to structure their time. Guide them in answering the bulleted questions. For example, before students answer the bulleted questions, have them write down the first images that come to mind when they think of the poems. Suggest that those might be the most meaningful images to them.

3. Allow students 40 minutes to complete the assignment.

4. As students prewrite and draft, have them refer to their completed **Comparing Imagery Graphic Organizer.**

Six Traits Focus

✔	Ideas	✔	Word Choice
✔	Organization		Sentence Fluency
	Voice		Conventions

Assessment Resources

Unit 4 Resources

L1 L2 EL **Selection Test A,** pp. 216–218

L3 L4 EL **Selection Test B,** pp. 219–221

 All assessment resources are available at www. PHLitOnline.com.

Common Core State Standards

• Writing 1, 1.a, b, c, d, e
• Language 2

Introducing the Writing Assignment

Review the assignment and the criteria, using the instruction on the student page.

Pat Mora on Supporting a Point

Show students Segment 3 on Pat Mora on the *See It!* DVD or from this page in the **Enriched Online Student Edition**, at **www.PHLitOnline.com**. Discuss Mora's comment that she writes because she is a reader. Encourage students to talk about the effect their reading has on their own writing.

Writing Workshop
Work in Progress

If students have completed the Work-in-Progress assignments on pp. 663 and 683, suggest that they consider developing their Work-in-Progress ideas in a persuasive essay.

What Do You Notice?

1. Have a volunteer read the quotation aloud.

2. **Ask** the following question: How would you describe the writer's word choice and his message? (**Possible response:** The writer's choice of simple, time-related words helps him get his message across. His first statement is one that most readers would agree with. His second statement forces the reader to reconsider the first statement from a new perspective.)

3. Urge students to review their word choice and revise in ways that support a persuasive message.

Writing Workshop

Write an Argument

Exposition: Persuasive Essay

Defining the Form A **persuasive essay** presents arguments for or against a particular position. You might use elements of this form of writing in editorials or reviews.

Assignment Write a persuasive essay that persuades readers to share your point of view on an issue about which you feel strongly. Your persuasive essay should feature the following elements:

✔ a *clear statement of your position* on an issue that has more than one side

✔ the *context* surrounding the issue

✔ *persuasive evidence* and *logical reasoning* that support your claims

✔ language that *appeals to both reason and emotion*

✔ an *appropriate organizational structure* for an argument

✔ statements that *acknowledge opposing views and offer counterarguments*

✔ error-free writing, including *proper sentence structure*

To preview the criteria on which your persuasive essay may be judged, see the rubric on page 705.

Writing Workshop: *Work in Progress*

Review the work you did on pages 663 and 683.

WRITE GUY
Jeff Anderson, M.Ed.

What Do You Notice?

Word Choice

The following sentences are from Louis L'Amour's "The Final Frontier." Read them several times.

If we are content to live in the past, we have no future. And today is the past.

With a partner, discuss the writer's word choice and message. Then, think about ways you can convey a message effectively in your writing.

 Common Core State Standards

Writing
1. Write arguments to support claims with clear reasons and relevant evidence.
1.a. Introduce claim(s), acknowledge alternate or opposing claims, and organize the reasons and evidence logically.
1.b. Support claim(s) with logical reasoning and relevant evidence, using accurate, credible sources and demonstrating an understanding of the topic or text.

Reading-Writing Connection
To get the feel for persuasion, read "The Eternal Frontier" by Louis L'Amour, on page 500.

Teaching Resources

The following resources can be used to enrich or extend the instruction.

All *Unit 4 Resources*
   Writing Workshop, pp. 222, 223

All *Common Core Companion,*
   pp. 191–198; 339–342

All *Professional Development Guidebook*
   Rubrics for Self-Assessment: Persuasive Essay, pp. 230–231

All *Graphic Organizer Transparencies*
   Rubric for Self-Assessment: Persuasive Essay, p. 144

All *See It!* **DVD**
   Pat Mora

 All resources, including video, are also available online at **www.PHLitOnline.com**.

Prewriting/Planning Strategies

Hold a roundtable. With a group, hold a roundtable discussion of problems in your school. Raise as many different issues as possible. Jot down topics that spark strong feelings in you. Choose from these subjects for your essay topic.

Make a quick list. Fold a piece of paper in thirds lengthwise. In the first column, write issues and ideas that interest you. In the second column, write a descriptive word for each idea. In the third column, give an example that supports your description. Make sure each issue has an opposing side. Choose the issue or idea that interests you most.

Issues and Ideas	Descriptive Word	Examples
Cafeteria food	tasteless	macaroni and cheese
Water pollution	scary	streams polluted by fertilizer runoff
New playground	needed	child hurt on slide

Narrow your focus. Evaluate your topic to be sure you can fully and effectively discuss it. For example, the topic "violence in the media" would cover violence on news reports, in movies, and on television. To write an effective persuasive essay, you should consider focusing on violence in one medium, not all three.

Gather evidence to support your position. Conduct research either in the library, on the Internet, or by interviewing experts on your topic. Gather the following types of support from accurate, credible sources:

Facts: statements that can be proved true

Statistics: facts presented in the form of numbers

Anecdotes: brief stories that illustrate a point

Quotations from Authorities: statements from leading experts

Examples: facts, ideas, or events that support a general idea

Anticipate counterarguments. Make a list of the arguments people might have against your position. For each, identify a response that you can use to address the issues in your essay.

Writing Workshop **699**

Applying Understanding by Design Principles

Clarifying Expected Outcomes: Using Rubrics
- Before students begin work on this assignment, have them preview the Rubric for Self-Assessment (p. 705) to know what qualities their essays must have. A copy of this rubric appears in *Graphic Organizer Transparencies*, p. 144.
- Review the criteria in the Rubric with the class. Before students use the Rubric to assess their own writing, work with them to rate the Student Model (p. 704) using the Rubric.
- If you wish to assess students' persuasive essays with either a 4-point or a 6-point scoring rubric, see *Professional Development Guidebook*, pp. 230–231.

Prewriting/Planning Strategies

1. Introduce the prewriting strategies.
2. Have students apply the strategies to choose a topic.

Teaching the Strategies

1. Help students explore possible topics by suggesting that they brainstorm for events that affect the school or the community.
2. Explain to students that they should identify their position before they begin drafting. Once students have conducted research, they might change their position. They may then rewrite the statement of their position.
3. Draw a five-column chart on the board labeling the columns *Facts, Statistics, Quotations, Anecdotes* and *Examples*. Take a position on a topic, and then generate examples of each kind of evidence.

Think Aloud: Model Choosing an Issue

Say to students:

When I want to choose a topic for a persuasive essay, I need to make sure it is an issue that is open to debate. A thesis such as *Exercise is good for people* would not be a strong topic, since most people agree that exercise benefits people's health. However, a thesis such as *Yoga is the best form of exercise* would offer more for me to write about. I could present reasons for my opinion and also address counterarguments.

Six Traits Focus

✔	Ideas		Word Choice
✔	Organization		Sentence Fluency
	Voice		Conventions

Students will find additional information on writing a persuasive essay in Chapter 9.

Prentice Hall EssayScorer

A writing prompt for this mode of writing can be found in the *Prentice Hall EssayScorer* at **www.PHLitOnline.com**.

Drafting Strategies

1. Introduce the drafting strategies, using the instruction on the student page.

2. Have students apply the strategies as they draft.

Teaching the Strategies

1. Review how to elaborate on an idea. Present this idea to students: *It's important for students to feel connected to their school.* Ask students to suggest ideas that support that statement and help answer the question *Why?* (**Possible responses:** Students who feel a connection with their school may participate in more activities, behave in a way that reflects well on their school, and get more from attending school.)

2. Review the pyramid with students. Remind them that the conclusion usually restates the thesis statement.

3. Have students revise the following phrase providing as many forceful alternatives as possible.

   a serious problem

   Possible responses: devastating problem, catastrophe, disaster, harrowing predicament

Think Aloud: Model Paying Attention to Precise Terms

Say to students:

When I am writing a formal document, I pay more attention to precision. For instance, if I am writing a letter to the editor of a newspaper, I will be careful to make precise references. I would write: *In your editorial titled "Pollution in Our Backyards" on p. 4 of the October 10, 2007 issue of* The News-Record, *you neglected to mention that one way to reduce the use of chemicals on grass is to spot-treat problem areas.* The reference to the specific article shows that I have paid attention to being precise.

Six Traits Focus

✓	Ideas	✓	Word Choice
✓	Organization		Sentence Fluency
✓	Voice		Conventions

700

Drafting Strategies

Common Core State Standards

Writing
1.c. Use words, phrases, and clauses to create cohesion and clarify the relationships among claim(s), reasons, and evidence.
1.d. Establish and maintain a formal style.
1.e. Provide a concluding statement or section that follows from and supports the argument presented.

Develop and support your thesis statement. To keep your position clear to your readers, review your notes and develop a *thesis statement*—one strong sentence that sums up your argument. Include this statement in your introduction.

Organize to emphasize your arguments.
As you draft, present the supporting evidence you have gathered, starting with your least important points and building toward your most important ones. Use transitional words and phrases to unify your writing and show the relationships among your ideas. Address opposing concerns and counterarguments directly—do not avoid them. Delete information that does not support or add anything to your argument. Write a powerful conclusion that follows the logic of the evidence and supports your argument. Consider the method shown in the pyramid.

- Introduction and thesis
- First set of arguments
- Supporting details
- Concerns and counterarguments
- Statements proving opposition is weak or incorrect
- Strongest argument
- Supporting details
- Conclusions

Choose precise words. Forceful language helps convey your point and builds support for your position. Create a speaker's voice by using precise, lively words that will stir readers' emotions and appeal to their sense of reason.

> **Vague:** a *good* candidate
>
> **Precise:** a *trustworthy* candidate
> an *intelligent* candidate

Appeal to your audience. Use words that your audience will understand. If you are writing for teenagers, use informal language, but avoid slang and maintain standard English. If you are writing to a government official, use a formal style and serious language. Also, choose words that add interest and encourage readers to continue reading.

Writers on Writing

Pat Mora On Supporting a Point

Pat Mora is the author of "Maestro" (p. 578), "The Desert Is My Mother" (p. 579), and "Bailando" (p. 580).

When I was a university administrator, a friend mentioned that her daughter, Gabriela, wanted writing advice. I've always liked to write letters, so I wrote a persuasive essay as a letter to Gabi. The letter/essay became part of my collection *Nepantla: Essays from the Land in the Middle*. From the time I was in high school, I was intrigued by essays, perhaps because I like seeing how writers express their beliefs convincingly.

"I write because I'm a reader."
— Pat Mora

Professional Model:

from *"To Gabriela, A Young Writer"*

I know that the society we live in and that the movies, television programs, and commercials we see, all affect us. It's not easy to learn to judge others fairly, not because of the car they drive, the house they live in, the church they attend, the color of their skin, the language they speak at home. It takes courage to face the fact that we all have ten toes, get sleepy at night, get scared in the dark. Some families, some cities, some states, and even some countries foolishly convince themselves that they are better than others. And then they teach their children this ugly lie. It's like a weed with burrs and stickers that pricks people.

How are young women who are African American, Asian American, American Indian, Latinas, or members of all the other ethnic groups supposed to feel about themselves? Some are proud of their cultural roots. . . .

I played with different human similarities. Humans have arms and eyes. There's something so basic about the words "ten toes," though.

The right comparison, or metaphor, is like a shortcut to the reader's feelings and imagination. We all know the discomfort of stickers.

Here and throughout, I'm building my argument by using lists of examples to support my thesis. I'm building a case.

Pat Mora on Supporting a Point

Review the passage on the student page with the class, using Pat Mora's comments to deepen students' understanding about how to strengthen arguments.

Teaching From the Professional Model

Show students Segment 4 on Pat Mora on the *See It!* DVD or from this page in the **Enriched Online Student Edition** at www.PHLitOnline.com. Discuss the author's comments on the quoted passage. Note how concrete language ("ten toes") and simile ("like a weed") add to the power of an argument.

Show or assign the video online at www.PHLitOnline.com.

Strategies for
Focusing an Essay

Tell students that even professional writers often need help focusing their ideas. Point out that Pat Mora chooses to direct her writing to a friend's daughter rather than writing for a general audience. By choosing a particular audience for one's work, a writer may find it easier to focus his or her thoughts and to decide what to include in an essay.

Revising Strategies

1. Introduce the revising strategies, using the instruction on the student page.
2. Have students apply the strategies as they revise.

Teaching the Strategies

1. After students have highlighted their main points, have them skim their essays to determine if their argument is clear and if the order in which they present their points results in a compelling case.
2. Have students combine the following sentences to emphasize the connection between ideas.

   Jaywalking does not seem like a major offense. Jaywalking can cause serious accidents.
   (**Possible response:** Although jaywalking may not seem like a major offense, it can cause serious accidents.)

   The governor spoke out against water pollution. He also worked to pass a bill that taxed polluters.
   (**Possible response:** The governor not only spoke out against water pollution, but also worked to pass a bill that taxed polluters.)

Think Aloud: Model Adding Supporting Points

Say to students:

   In a persuasive essay, every detail or example I add strengthens my argument. Suppose my main argument is that chemicals should not be used on backyard lawns. As one supporting point, I have written, *Chemicals are bad for lawns because they run off into the rivers and streams.* I should add another supporting point to help people understand the importance of this point. I could add a sentence such as, *Chemicals affect all forms of wildlife.* Now my reader understands that animals and plants will also be affected.

Six Traits Focus

✔	Ideas		Word Choice
✔	Organization	✔	Sentence Fluency
	Voice		Conventions

Revising Strategies

Highlight your main points. To check your organization, highlight each main point. Then, use one or more of these strategies:

- If a reader needs to know one main point in order to understand a second one, make sure the first main point comes *before* the second.
- If one main point means the same as another, combine them, or combine the paragraphs in which they appear.
- If one main point is stronger than the others, move it to the end of your essay.

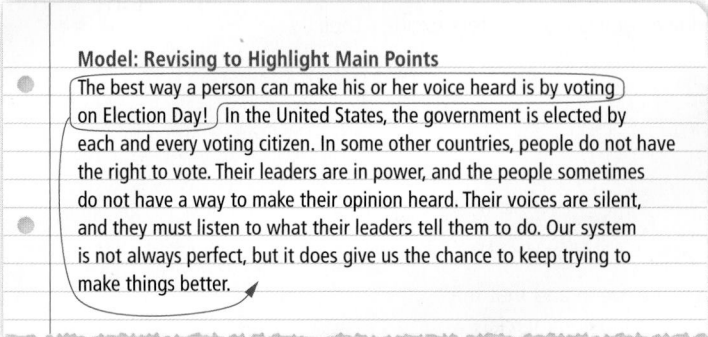

Model: Revising to Highlight Main Points

The best way a person can make his or her voice heard is by voting on Election Day! In the United States, the government is elected by each and every voting citizen. In some other countries, people do not have the right to vote. Their leaders are in power, and the people sometimes do not have a way to make their opinion heard. Their voices are silent, and they must listen to what their leaders tell them to do. Our system is not always perfect, but it does give us the chance to keep trying to make things better.

Combine sentences to show connections. To improve your writing, combine short, choppy sentences to stress the connections between ideas.

Similar Ideas: The town permits skating on the lake. We don't have the money to open a rink.

Combined: The town permits skating on the lake ***because*** we don't have the money to open a rink.

Opposing Ideas: The food is better heated. Most classrooms do not have microwave ovens.

Combined: The food is better heated, ***but*** most classrooms do not have microwave ovens.

Peer Review

Read your draft to a group of peers. Ask if the order of your main points is logical. Consider their responses as you revise.

 Common Core State Standards

Writing
1.c. Use words, phrases, and clauses to create cohesion and clarify the relationships among claim(s), reasons, and evidence.

Language
2. Demonstrate command of the conventions of standard English capitalization, punctuation, and spelling when writing.

Strategies for Using Precise Words

Tell students that they should review each sentence in their drafts to see if they can add adjectives or adverbs to make the sentence more forceful. They should also check to be sure their verbs are precise and strong.

WRITER'S TOOLBOX

| **Sentence Fluency** | Voice | Organization | Word Choice | Ideas | Conventions |

Revising Fragments and Run-on Sentences

The most basic sentence contains a single **independent clause**—a group of words including a subject and a verb and expressing a complete idea.

Fixing Sentence Fragments

A **fragment** is a group of words that does not express a complete thought. It is often missing a subject, a verb, or both.

Fragments: I'll read my report. As long as you read yours, too.

To fix a fragment, first identify the incomplete sentence. Then, make a complete sentence out of it.

Corrected: I'll read my report as long as you read yours, too.

Fixing Run-on Sentences

A **run-on sentence** occurs when two or more independent clauses are joined without proper punctuation.

Run-on: We dove into the water, we swam fast.

To fix run-ons with sentence combining, use the following methods:

- Use punctuation to correctly indicate where ideas end.

  Corrected: We dove into the water. We swam fast.

- Use a comma and a coordinating conjunction such as *and, or, so,* or *but* to express ideas of equal importance.

  Corrected: We dove into the water, and we swam fast.

- Use a semicolon and a subordinating conjunctions to show the relationship between ideas.

  Corrected: We dove into the water; then, we swam fast.

> **PH WRITING COACH**
> Further instruction and practice are available in *Prentice Hall Writing Coach.*

Common Subordinating Conjunctions				
after although as	as long as because before	even though if since	so that though unless	until when where

Grammar in Your Writing

Choose a paragraph in your draft and circle any fragments or run-ons you find. Fix these sentence errors using the methods above.

Revising Fragments and Run-On Sentences

1. Introduce the grammar skill, using the instruction on the student page.

2. Discuss the rules and examples, as well as the strategies for fixing incorrect usage.

3. Have students follow the instruction under Grammar in Your Writing to correct errors in their drafts.

Teaching the Grammar Skill

Have students correct the following fragments and run-on sentences.

The dog running down the street. (**Possible response:** The dog was running down the street.)

We will have lunch. When he arrives. (**Possible response:** We will have lunch when he arrives.)

He drove the car around the block, he parked it. (**Possible response:** He drove the car around the block and parked it.)

They saw the movie. That was playing at the mall. (**Possible response:** They saw the movie that was playing at the mall.)

The landscape was stunning, the weather was too hot. (**Possible response:** The landscape was stunning, but the weather was too hot.)

Differentiated Instruction for Universal Access

EL Strategy for English Learners

Languages other than English may have different conventions for composing a complete sentence. Some English-language learners may need help understanding the concept of a sentence fragment or a run-on sentence. In Spanish, for example, sentences that might be considered run-ons in English are perfectly acceptable, especially in formal or academic writing.

As you review the grammar lesson with students, make sure English learners have a good grasp of what constitutes a fragment or a run-on sentence.

Review the Student Model with the class, using the annotations to analyze the writer's use of the elements of a persuasive essay.

Teaching From the Student Model

1. Explain that the Student Model is a sample and that essays can be longer.

2. Have students read through the model and the annotations. Ask students to identify the statement of position in this essay. (**Answer:** Everyone who is eligible should take advantage of the right to vote.)

3. Discuss how Amanda clearly supports her argument. Then, have students identify two items of support in the text. (**Possible response:** the second and fourth sentences in the second paragraph)

4. Ask students to identify the opposing arguments Amanda addresses. (**Answer:** She addresses the excuse of not knowing enough about the candidates.) Note how the use of the expression *eenie, meenie, miney, mo* grabs your attention by dramatizing the confusion of people who aren't sure how to choose.

5. Point out the concluding paragraph, and discuss how Amanda ends the composition with a strong statement for voting.

Connecting to Real-Life Writing

Tell students that people are likely to use persuasive writing or speaking in many instances in the workplace. People who write advertisements must write persuasively, and politicians are known for their persuasive speeches. In addition, people who work for corporations need to write proposals to persuade their superiors to accept and move ideas forward. Discuss with students these and other occupations and situations that would require persuasive writing.

Student Model: Amanda Wintenburg, Daytona Beach, FL

Decide the Future

To you, voting may seem like just a waste of time, just a mere piece of paper with boxes on it, that you have to go through to mark which person you want for that particular job. But to me, it's something more, much more. . . it's your chance to decide the future. Everyone who is eligible should take advantage of the right to vote.

I'm not the only one who thinks voting should be a top priority for people. For years, companies and organizations have supplied numerous reminders and reasons to explain when and why you vote. You've seen the commercials; they've all told us about it. Although there is no financial profit in convincing people to vote, money is being spent to make sure it happens. That should tell you something.

Eenie, meenie, miney mo, . . . maybe you don't want to vote because you feel as if you don't know enough about the candidates to make an informed decision. However, newspapers, television broadcasts, performance records—all these fact-based sources of information are available to the interested voter who wants to make a responsible choice. Find out what the candidates have been doing and what they plan to do. Make your decision based on information.

In many countries, voting is not an option. In countries with kings and queens, leaders are born into their positions. In other countries, the leaders take control rather than being voted into a leadership role. Often leaders who are not elected can be corrupt or tyrannical, because the people can't remove them from power. We are citizens of a free country in which we have the right to vote. Whether or not the system works perfectly, it is better than a system with no voting. Vote because you can. Remind yourself that not everyone is as lucky.

If you don't vote, you have less control over your own life. Voting is your chance to make your voice heard. It's your chance to decide the future.

In the opening paragraph, Amanda points out the two "sides" to the voting issue. She follows with her thesis statement.

This evidence supports the idea that voting matters.

Here, Amanda identifies and addresses readers' concerns and counterarguments.

Amanda reminds readers that not everyone has the right to vote. She uses language that appeals to both reason and emotion.

Editing and Proofreading

Review your draft to correct errors in spelling, grammar, and punctuation.

Focus on Punctuation: Be sure to use the correct end mark for each kind of sentence in your essay. Use a period at the end of a statement, a question mark at the end of a question, and an exclamation mark at the end of a statement that indicates strong feeling. In addition, use a dash for additional emphasis or to offset important information.

Publishing and Presenting

Consider one of the following ways to share your writing:

Give a speech. Use your persuasive essay as the basis for a speech that you give to your classmates.

Submit a newspaper article. Many local newspapers will publish well-written persuasive essays if they appeal to the newspaper's audience. Submit your composition and see what happens.

Reflecting on Your Writing

Writer's Journal Jot down your answer to this question:
What part of the writing process was most challenging? Explain.

Spiral Review
Earlier in the unit, you learned about **independent and subordinate clauses** (p. 662) and **sentence structures** (p. 682). Review your essay to be sure that you have used a variety of sentence structures and have formed each kind correctly.

PH WRITING COACH
Further instruction and practice are available in *Prentice Hall Writing Coach*.

Rubric for Self-Assessment

Find evidence in your writing to address each category. Then, use the rating scale to grade your work.

Criteria	Rating Scale
	not very very
Focus: How clearly is your position stated?	1 2 3 4 5
Organization: How organized is your argument or judgment?	1 2 3 4 5
Support/Elaboration: How persuasive is your evidence?	1 2 3 4 5
Style: How well do you balance language to appeal to reason and emotion?	1 2 3 4 5
Conventions: How correct is your grammar, especially your use of independent clauses?	1 2 3 4 5

Editing and Proofreading

1. Introduce the editing and proofreading focus, using the instruction on the student page.

2. Have students edit and proofread their essays, correcting grammar, spelling, punctuation, and word choice. Make sure they look for errors of the type noted in the lesson focus and the Spiral Review.

Teaching the Editing Focus

Provide the following example of correctly punctuated sentences:
Statement: We left the restaurant at nine o'clock.
Question: Will you be coming with us?
Exclamation: I can't believe I did that!
Using a Dash for Emphasis: I'll meet you at the restaurant at noon—please be on time because I have an important meeting after lunch.

Six Traits Focus

Ideas	Word Choice
Organization	Sentence Fluency
Voice	✔ Conventions

ASSESS

Publishing and Presenting

1. If students decide to present their essays as speeches, encourage them to copy the main points on note cards and practice giving the speech without reading directly from the cards. Suggest that students read the essays to a partner to identify sentences that are too long for a speech.

2. Remind students who want to submit their essays to a local paper that they will need to present a typed, proofread copy for submission.

Reflecting on Your Writing

Suggest that students compare their various drafts to identify any new insights they had during the writing process.

Strategies for Test-Taking

- When responding to a persuasive essay prompt, be especially careful to take into account any argument suggested in the prompt against your position.

- List details that support your argument, but also anticipate counterarguments by jotting down reasons opposing your position. Be sure to address these in your essay. Review your draft, add details if necessary, and substitute precise words.

Connotation and Denotation

1. Introduce the skill, using the instruction on the student page.
2. Review the examples in the chart.

Think Aloud: Model the Skill

Model the skill of connotation and denotation. Say to students:

Words with the same denotation often have different connotations that create positive, neutral, or negative impressions. *Postpone*, for example, gives the neutral impression of putting something off because of factors beyond one's control, but *procrastinate* is more negative, suggesting that the task being put off is unpleasant and that the person putting it off is shirking his or her responsibilities.

Practice A
Answers
1. sound
2. holler
3. obtain
4. discontinue
5. intelligent
6. alert

Vocabulary Workshop

Connotation and Denotation

The **denotation** of a word is its dictionary meaning. A word's **connotations** are the ideas associated with that word. Those ideas and feelings might be positive or negative. Understanding connotations can help you to choose the right words in your writing. The following chart shows an example of three words with the same denotation and different connotations. Notice the various shades of meaning among the three words.

Word	Denotation	Connotation	Example Sentence
postpone	to put off until a later time	to reschedule, usually due to something out of one's control	We had to *postpone* the party because the hostess became ill.
delay		to hold off on something for a short amount of time	The heavy morning traffic will *delay* the city's buses.
procrastinate		to put something off that is undesirable by doing another thing	I *procrastinate* every day by watching television before doing my homework.

Practice A Each of the following words has a positive, neutral, or negative connotation. For each word pair, identify which word has a more positive connotation. If necessary, use a dictionary to check each word's denotation.

1. noise, sound
2. screech, holler
3. grab, obtain
4. discontinue, quit
5. brainy, intelligent
6. aware, alert

Teaching Resources

Unit 4 Resources
  Connotation and Denotation, pp. 224, 225

PHLit Online! **Vocabulary Central,** featuring definitions, audio pronunciations, Word Families, and activities, is online at **www.PHLitOnline.com.**

Practice B Sometimes connotations of words can help you see degrees of meaning. For example, the words *large* and *enormous* have the same basic meaning, but *enormous* implies greater size than *large*. Rewrite each of the following sentences by replacing the italicized word. The new word should have the same denotation but a connotation that implies a greater degree of the original word. If necessary, use a dictionary or a thesaurus to help you.

PHLit Online!
www.PHLitOnline.com
- Illustrated vocabulary words
- Interactive vocabulary games
- Vocabulary flashcards

1. The coach was *angry* after the team's poor performance.
2. My little sister loves to *bother* me when I have friends over.
3. We *eat* our lunch as soon as we sit down at the table.
4. The marching band from Southern California was *good*.
5. My mother was *happy* when I told her my grade on the test.
6. The weather in the desert is *hot*.
7. The rides at the amusement park were *fun*.
8. My cousin from Georgia is *nice*.
9. I drank a *large* glass of water after the race.
10. After playing a game of "fetch," my dog was *tired*.

Activity Each of the following words has neutral connotations. Use a thesaurus to find synonyms, or words with a similar meaning, for each word. Find at least one synonym with positive connotations and one synonym with negative connotations. Use a graphic organizer like the one shown to organize your synonyms. The first one has been completed as an example.

difficult   aged   calm   brave   humble

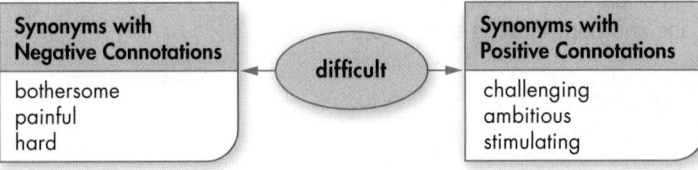

Synonyms with Negative Connotations
bothersome
painful
hard

difficult

Synonyms with Positive Connotations
challenging
ambitious
stimulating

Comprehension and Collaboration
Work with a partner to write two separate paragraphs about a fictional inventor. One partner's paragraph should describe the inventor as a visionary. The other's should describe the inventor as a dreamer. When you have finished writing, exchange paragraphs and discuss how the connotations of the words *visionary* and *dreamer* influenced your descriptions of the inventor.

Vocabulary Workshop **707**

Common Core State Standards

• Speaking and Listening 2, 3

Learn the Skills

1. Introduce the workshop, including the activity on page 709.

2. Review the different purposes media can have. Explain that when the purpose of a message is to persuade, the implicit message often differs from the explicit one. For example, the explicit message of an ad for hand cream may be that the cream relieves itching and soreness, but the implicit message is that people who use hand cream are glamorous.

3. Tell students to analyze both their emotional and intellectual responses to images and sounds.

4. Remind students to question broad generalizations such as "Everybody knows...."

5. Explain how word choice contributes to the message's overall tone.

6. Remind students that the way a product appears on television might not be the same way it looks up close.

7. Discuss how different voices can inspire emotional reactions to an ad. The reassuring voice of a familiar spokesperson makes an ad's claims seem more believable.

Evaluating Media Messages and Advertisements

Media messages and advertisements appear on television, the Internet, and radio. To ensure you understand and respond appropriately to these messages, critically evaluate them, using the strategies in this workshop.

Learn the Skills

Use these strategies to complete the activity on page 709.

Determine the purpose. Identify the purpose, or goal, of the message. Some messages are meant to inform, to persuade, or to entertain. Some messages are attempts to sell you something or to convince you to do something.

Analyze images and sounds. Think critically about what you see and hear. Some images are designed to sell instead of to inform. Notice how the mood created by music and sounds influences your decisions.

Challenge the claims and evidence. Analyze the accuracy of the claims. Consider whether the reasoning is logical and whether sufficient and relevant evidence supports the claims.

Identify propaganda techniques. To effectively analyze logic, be alert to techniques involving faulty reasoning.

- **Slant and Bias:** Beware of any message that presents only one side of a many-sided issue.

- **Bandwagon Appeal:** Beware of messages that suggest you will feel left out if you do not do or buy something.

- **Spokespersons:** Ask yourself whether the spokesperson has the knowledge to back up his or her claims.

Analyze the use of language. Advertisers use language to appeal to certain groups of people. Formal language makes messages seem more accurate. Informal language and popular slang appeal to a young audience.

Interpret visual techniques. Lighting can draw attention to specific parts of an image or set a mood. Camera angles can influence the way you view an image. Special visual effects can change an existing image to increase appeal or interest.

Common Core State Standards

Speaking and Listening
2. Analyze the main ideas and supporting details presented in diverse media and formats and explain how the ideas clarify a topic, text, or issue under study.
3. Delineate a speaker's argument and specific claims, evaluating the soundness of the reasoning and the relevance and sufficiency of the evidence.

Strategies for
Evaluating Media Messages

Give students these additional strategies for evaluating advertisements:

- Encourage students to ask questions about any elements of a message that seem confusing.
- Help students distinguish between fact and opinion. Explain that while facts are more objective than opinions, advertisements often rely heavily on emotional appeals.

- Guide students in creating a two-column chart to record facts and opinions for each message. Instruct them to count the totals for each column as they evaluate a message.
- Ask students to consider the audience of the advertisement. Explain that advertisers design messages that appeal to particular groups of people.

Practice the Skills

Presentation of Knowledge and Ideas Use what you have learned in this workshop to complete the following activity.

ACTIVITY: Evaluate Media Advertisements

Watch three television commercials. Then, follow the steps below.

• Identify the message and interpret the purpose of each commercial.
• Ask questions about the evidence that supports a claim.
• Explain how each commercial makes you feel.
• List memorable details from each commercial, such as special effects, camera angles, lighting, and music.
• Use the Interpretation Guide to interpret the advertisements.

Use the Interpretation Guide to analyze the content of each commercial.

Interpretation Guide

Visual Techniques
Which techniques does the advertisement include? Briefly explain each.
☐ camera angles   ☐ special effects
☐ special lighting   ☐ other visual

Sound Techniques
Which techniques does the advertisement include? Briefly explain each.
☐ music
☐ special effects
☐ other techniques

Messages
What is the message? How can you tell?

Claims and Evidence
Does the advertisement make claims about the product? If so, what are they? What evidence does the advertisement give? Is the evidence relevant? Is there enough reasonable evidence to support the claims? Explain.

Purpose
What is the purpose of the advertisement?

Comprehension and Collaboration Compare your findings with those of your classmates. As a group, interpret how visual and sound techniques influence the message in an advertisement.

Practice the Skills

1. Review the assignment with students. Make sure they ask questions about the evidence that supports a claim. Tell students to analyze how each visual and sound technique supports the advertisement's message.

2. Explain to students that they should use a copy of the Interpretation Guide to evaluate their own presentation and the presentations made by classmates.

3. Before students give their presentations to the class, remind listeners to ask questions if any points are unclear. To maintain order, encourage them to raise their hands and wait to be acknowledged by the presenter before stating their questions. Suggest that students making presentations scan the classroom from time to time so they will notice any students who have questions.

Evaluate the Activity

1. Evaluate students' interpretations on the basis of their accuracy and insightfulness in identifying the message and purpose of each commercial.

2. When the class discusses the evaluations that were the most thorough, encourage students to make note of the features of those presentations that made them effective and to incorporate those techniques in their future presentations.

Differentiated Instruction for Universal Access

Strategies for Special-Needs Students

Guide students in responding orally to information presented in the print, electronic, or visual media they wish to evaluate.

• Review the explanation of media messages on page 708 to reinforce concept attainment.
• Help students examine the advertisements, pointing out important features.
• Ask students to respond orally to questions such as "What information did I learn?" and "How did the advertisement make me feel?"

• Provide sentence starters to reinforce students' understanding, such as "The advertisement tells about...."
• Guide students in using the Interpretation Guide to analyze the use of visual and sound techniques.

Cumulative Review

In this Common Core Assessment Workshop (pp. 710–715), students apply and reinforce their mastery of the Common Core State Standards and the skills taught in Unit 4. The practice is divided into four sections, including a section of Performance Tasks addressing CCS Reading standards.

1. Before assigning each section, review the relevant Common Core State Standards and unit skills with students.

2. Set a time limit for the multiple-choice items in each section, allowing a little over one minute per question. Allow twenty minutes for any Timed Writing questions.

3. Administer each of the first three sections of the Cumulative Review (pp. 710–713).

4. Use the Performance Tasks on pages 714–715 to assess the depth of students' mastery of standards taught in the unit. Follow the suggestions on teacher pages 714–715 for assigning tasks and for supporting and evaluating student performance.

Reteaching Skills

1. For each practice, use the Reteach chart on the same page as the answers to determine which skills require reteaching, given the items students answered incorrectly.

2. Reteach these skills prior to assigning the **Benchmark Test** for the second half of Unit 4 (*Unit 4 Resources*, pp. 227–234). The Benchmark Test concludes instruction in the Unit skills.

Benchmark

Reteach skills as indicated by students' performance, following the Reteach charts included on pp. 711–713. Then, administer the end-of-unit **Benchmark Test** (*Unit 4 Resources*, pp. 227–234). The Benchmark Test concludes instruction in the Unit skills. Follow the **Interpretation Guide** for the test (*Unit 4 Resources*, p. 238) to assign reteaching pages as necessary in the *Reading Kit*. Use the built-in tracking software at www.PHLitOnline.com to automatically assign these pages.

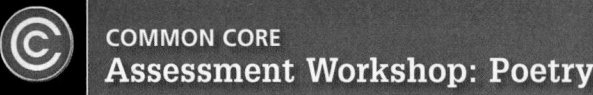

Cumulative Review

Common Core State Standards

RL.7.2, RL.7.4, RL.7.5; L.7.4.a; W.7.2
[For the full wording of the standards, see the standards chart in the front of your textbook.]

I. Reading Literature

Directions: *Read the passage. Then, answer each question that follows.*

I Wandered Lonely as a Cloud
by William Wordsworth

I wandered lonely as a cloud
That floats on high o'er vales[1] and hills,
When all at once I saw a crowd,
A host, of golden daffodils;
5   Beside the lake, beneath the trees,
Fluttering and dancing in the breeze.

Continuous as the stars that shine
And twinkle on the milky way,
They stretched in never-ending line
10   Along the margin of a bay:
Ten thousand saw I at a glance,
Tossing their heads in <u>sprightly</u> dance.

The waves beside them danced; but they
Outdid the sparkling waves in glee;
15   A poet could not but be gay,
In such a jocund[2] company;
I gazed—and gazed—but little thought
What wealth the show to me had brought:

For oft, when on my couch I lie
20   In vacant or in pensive[3] mood,
They flash upon that inward eye
Which is the bliss of solitude;
And then my heart with pleasure fills,
And dances with the daffodils.

---

1. **o'er vales** over valleys.
2. **jocund** *adj.* cheerful.
3. **pensive** *adj.* deeply or seriously thoughtful.

710 Poetry

Strategy for Less Proficient Readers
Point out to students that the poem uses old-fashioned poetic language that may seem difficult at first. To understand the vocabulary, students should first look for footnotes such as those that appear on page 712. Then they should try using context clues. For example, line 4 refers to a "host, of golden daffodils." This meaning of *host* may be unfamiliar to students: it does not mean someone who welcomes guests. Luckily, the poem itself provides the definition in line 3:

"a crowd,/ A host . . . ." *Host* means the same thing as *crowd*. Then have students look at the phrase "the margin of a bay" in line 10. Ask them what a *margin* usually refers to in their experience. (the margin of a piece of paper) Then have them figure out what the margin of a bay, or body of water, might be. (its edge) Encourage students to work through the rest of the poem, to gain a basic understanding of its meaning. If they fail to figure out a specific word, they should move on. They do not need to comprehend each word in order to grasp the overall meaning.

1. Which of the following are characteristics of a **lyric poem** such as this one?

   A. seventeen syllables; focuses on nature
   B. single image or idea; musical language
   C. letters and lines create a visual image
   D. no regular rhyme; no stanza pattern

2. Which of the following passages contains a **simile?**

   A. I wandered lonely as a cloud
   B. They stretched in never-ending line
   C. The waves beside them danced
   D. And then my heart with pleasure fills

3. What type of **figurative language** does Wordsworth use in lines 4–6?

   A. symbol
   A. personification
   A. metaphor
   A. simile

4. Which of the following lines contains the **sound device** of alliteration?

   A. I wandered lonely as a cloud
   B. Along the margin of a bay
   C. Outdid the sparkling waves in glee
   D. And dances with the daffodils.

5. Which lines **rhyme** in the second stanza?

   A. lines 7 and 8
   B. lines 8 and 9
   C. lines 8 and 10
   D. lines 10 and 11

6. Which of the following lines contains the most vivid **imagery?**

   A. lines 13 and 14
   B. lines 15 and 16
   C. lines 17 and 18
   D. lines 19 and 20

7. What **image** does Wordsworth **repeat** throughout the poem?

   A. sparkling waves
   B. shining stars
   C. dancing flowers
   D. lonely clouds

8. Which best summarizes the **main idea** of the poem?

   A. The speaker recalls the image of the daffodils, which comforts him when he is lonely or sad.
   B. The speaker compares the daffodils to his constant loneliness.
   C. The speaker thinks about the relationship between humans and nature.
   D. The speaker wanders through the fields and comments on nature's beauty.

9. **Vocabulary** Which word is closest in meaning to the underlined word <u>sprightly</u> in line 12?

   A. shiny
   B. energetic
   C. wilting
   D. moist

 Timed Writing

10. Identify one **simile, metaphor,** or example of **personification** used in the poem. In an essay, **explain** how the **figure of speech** contributes to the overall meaning of the poem.

GO ON ➔

Assessment Workshop **711**

Reteach

Question	Pages to Reteach
1	575, 583
2	601
3	601
4	647
5	665
6	692
7	692
8	647, 665, 686

Answers continued

energetically. *Incorrect answers:* A—A dance is not shiny; C—The daffodils are alive, not wilting; D—A dance is not moist.

 Timed Writing

10. Students should identify one simile, metaphor, or example of personification and explain how it contributes to the overall meaning.

I. Literary Skills

Answers With Explanations

1. **B**—These are characteristics of lyric poetry. *Incorrect answers:* A—These are characteristics of haiku; C—These are characteristics of a concrete poem; D—These are characteristics of free verse.

2. **A**—This is a simile because the poet is comparing two unlike things: a person and a cloud. *Incorrect answers:* B—Nothing is being compared in this line; C—This is personification: waves are performing a human action; D—Same explanation as for B.

3. **B**—The daffodils fluttering and dancing is personification. *Incorrect answers:* A—The daffodils have no clear symbolic meaning; C—There is no implied comparison between the daffodils and anything else; D—The daffodils are not compared to anything.

4. **D**—The *d* in *dances* and the *d* in *daffodils* alliterate. *Incorrect answers:* A—Initial sounds are not repeated in this line; B—Same explanation as for A; C—Same explanation as for A.

5. **C**—*Way* and *bay* rhyme. *Incorrect answers:* A—*Shine* and *way* do not rhyme; B—*Way* and *line* do not rhyme; D—*Bay* and *glance* do not rhyme.

6. **A**—The image of the daffodils dancing more gleefully than the sparkling waves is very vivid. *Incorrect answers:* B—These lines describe emotions, not images; C—These lines describe thoughts, not images; D—These lines create a picture, but it is not vivid.

7. **C**—The image of dancing flowers appears in lines 6, 12, 14, and 24. *Incorrect answers:* A—This image appears only in line 14; B—This image appears only in line 7; D—This image appears only in line 1.

8. **A**—The poet clearly states this main idea in the final stanza. *Incorrect answers:* B—The daffodils are joyous, not lonely; C—The poem is more about the beauty of nature; D—This is the main idea of the first part of the poem, not the whole poem.

9. **B**—The daffodils are dancing

711

II. Reading Informational Text

Answers With Explanations

1. **D**—Setting up the conditions of the filter is a key step because otherwise the filter will not fulfill its desired function. *Incorrect answers:* A—There is no need to open junk mail when setting up the filter; B—This is a benefit of setting up the filter, not a step in setting it up; C—You do this after setting up the filter.

2. **C**—Paraphrasing is the best way to ensure full understanding. *Incorrect answers:* A—If you skip the difficult words, you will not be able to understand Step 4; B—This is the first step to understanding Step 4, but it will not help you gain a full understanding; D—This will not help you fully understand the step.

3. **A**—The tips give useful advice. *Incorrect answers:* B—The tips give additional hints, not summaries; C—The tips do not illustrate the steps; D—The tips do not clarify the steps; they build on them.

4. **C**—The filter will prevent junk e-mail from getting through. *Incorrect answers:* A—The writer assumes that the reader is familiar with junk e-mail; B—This is the purpose of the final tip, not the whole passage; D—There is no information on sending e-mail.

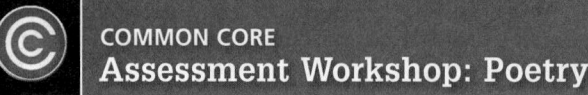

II. Reading Informational Text

Directions: *Read the passage below. Then, answer each question that follows.*

Common Core
State Standards

RI.7.5; W.7.1; L.7.1, L.7.3
[For the full wording of the standards, see the standards chart in the front of your textbook.]

How to Set up an E-mail Filter

An e-mail filter sorts your e-mail, deletes unwanted junk mail, and helps you avoid e-mail scams. Follow these steps to make your e-mail inbox easier to navigate and to avoid opening annoying junk e-mails.
Step 1 Open your e-mail account and locate the "Tools," "Filters," or "Options" menu items. Usually, these are listed at the top of the screen.
Step 2 Once you have found the filters option, click on "New" to build a new folder. **TIP:** Name the folder "Junk Mail" so it is easy to find.
Step 3 Set up the rules, or conditions, for the filter. The rules are the conditions the e-mail must meet for it to take the action you want. **TIP:** One rule you can make is to send e-mails from unknown senders to your new folder. This means any message from a sender that is not listed in your address book will be sorted.
Step 4 Specify the action you want the filter to implement. Filters can sort e-mails in a folder, delete them, or take other actions your provider lists. **TIP:** If your filter sends unwanted e-mails to a folder, be sure to check it periodically to see if a wanted e-mail has been filtered out.
Step 5 Click "OK" or "Save" to save your new folder. **TIP:** Add new filters for different uses, such as organizing school, work, or family events.

1. Which of the following is a **key step** in setting up your e-mail filter?
   A. opening your junk mail first
   B. avoiding Internet scams
   C. checking your junk mail folder for wanted e-mails
   D. setting up the conditions of the filter

2. What is the *best* way to fully understand Step 4?
   A. Skip the difficult words.
   B. Look up the technical words or phrases.
   C. Put the language into your own words.
   D. Make a list of technical words.

3. What **purpose** do the tips after each step serve?
   A. They give advice.
   B. They summarize the main points.
   C. They provide illustrations.
   D. They clarify difficult concepts.

4. What is the **main purpose** of the passage?
   A. to inform you of junk e-mail
   B. to advise you how to organize your e-mails
   C. to inform you how to get rid of junk e-mail forever.
   D. to advise you how to send emails to different groups of people

712 Poetry

Reteach

Question	Pages to Reteach
1	622
2	686
3	—
4	—

Strategies for Test Taking

Remind students that in many standardized tests, key terms are bolded in the items. For example, item 3 on this page asks for the **purpose** of the tips. This is different from asking about the **content** of the tips. Tell them that knowing what kind of answer they are looking for will help them eliminate incorrect responses and find the right answer.

III. Writing and Language Conventions

Directions: *Read the passage. Then, answer each question that follows.*

(1) Many students, including myself, depend on our cell phones to talk with our parents. (2) Every day I hear from my mother what time she will pick me up. (3) The problem is that Mr. Galindo wants to ban cell phones from school. (4) The solution is simple. (5) We should be allowed to bring our cell phones to school, but we will only use them when school is over. (6) Yes, calls will be missed. (7) They can be returned after school. (8) This way everyone wins.

1. Which sentence could the writer add to explain Mr. Galindo's **main problem** with cell phones in school?

  A. Students do not pay attention during class because they are text messaging.
  B. Cell phone ring tones are annoying.
  C. Students will miss calls during the day.
  D. Students spend too much money on new cell phones and ring tones.

2. Which argument could the writer use to *best* strengthen the proposed **solution?**

  A. We will only check our messages or make calls in between classes.
  B. We will keep our phones on silent mode, and return only the important calls.
  C. We will keep our phones locked in our lockers until the last bell.
  D. Cell phones are useful in emergencies.

3. Which revision combines sentence 6 and sentence 7 with a **past participle?**

  A. Calls will be missed and can be returned after school.
  B. Students can return calls after school.
  C. Missed calls can be returned after school.
  D. After school, you can return your calls.

4. Which revision of sentence 2 includes an **infinitive?**

  A. Every day I hear from my mother the time she will pick me up.
  B. Every day my mother tells what time she will pick me up.
  C. Every day my mother calls to tell me what time she will pick me up.
  D. Every day my mother calls before she picks me up.

5. What is the *best* way for the writer to add more information to sentence 3 by using an **appositive?**

  A. The problem, declared today, is that Mr. Galindo wants to ban all cell phones from school.
  B. The problem is that Principal Galindo wants to ban all cell phones from school.
  C. The problem is that Mr. Galindo, our principal, wants to ban all cell phones from school.
  D. The problem is that Mr. Galindo wants to ban all cell phones from Arthur High School.

Assessment Workshop **713**

Performance Tasks

Assigning Tasks/Reteaching Skills

Use the chart below to choose appropriate Performance Tasks by identifying which tasks assess lessons in the textbook that you have taught. Use the same lessons for reteaching when students' performance indicates a failure to fully master a standard. For additional instruction and practice, assign the *Common Core Companion* pages indicated for each task.

Task	Where Taught/ Pages to Reteach	Common Core Companion Pages
1	572–577, 583	54–66, 279–286
2	574, 576, 601, 692	41–53, 279–286
3	575, 583	54–66, 279–286
4	576, 647, 665	41–53, 316–322
5	574, 576, 601, 692	41–53, 298–304
6	574–576, 647, 665, 692	41–53, 316–322

Assessment Pacing

In assigning the Writing Tasks on this student page, allow a class period for the completion of a task. As an alternative, assign tasks as homework. In assigning the Speaking and Listening Tasks on the facing page, consider having students do any required preparation as a homework assignment. Then, allow a class period for the presentations themselves.

Evaluating Performance Tasks

Use the rubric at the bottom of this Teacher Edition page to evaluate students' mastery of the standards as demonstrated in their Performance Task responses. Review the rubric with students before they begin work so they know the criteria by which their work will be evaluated.

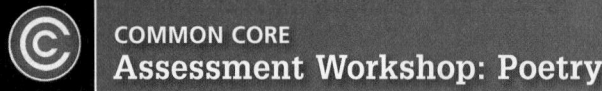

Performance Tasks

Directions: *Follow the instructions to complete the tasks below as required by your teacher.*

As you work on each task, incorporate both general academic vocabulary and literary terms you learned in this unit.

 Common Core State Standards

RL.7.4, RL.7.5; W.7.9.a; SL.7.1, SL.7.4; L.7.1, L.7.2
[For the full wording of the standards, see the standards chart in the front of your textbook.]

Writing

Task 1: Literature [RL.7.5; W.7.9.a]
Analyze a Poem's Form and Structure

Write an essay in which you analyze the form and structure of a poem in this unit.

- Plan to analyze the following elements of your chosen poem: rhyme, rhythm and meter, line length, stanza divisions, punctuation, capitalization, and spacing. Explain how these elements, both individually and together, contribute to the poem's meaning and effect.

- Revise your work to correct any run-on sentences or sentence fragments. Place phrases and clauses within sentences to clarify the relationships between ideas. Finally, correct misplaced or dangling modifiers.

- Publish your finished essay in the classroom library. Include a copy of the original text of the poem.

Task 2: Literature [RL.7.4; W.7.9.a]
Analyze Word Choice

Write an essay in which you use the literal and implied meanings of words to help you interpret a poem in this unit.

- Choose a poem that features powerful words and images.

- Note examples of figurative language—such as similes, metaphors, and personification—and imagery that appeals

to the five senses. Analyze the impact of each example.

- Cite evidence from the poem to support your analysis.

- As you edit, make sure you have used correct punctuation, including commas to separate items in a series.

Task 3: Literature [RL.7.5; W.7.9.a]
Compare and Contrast Forms of Poetry

Write an essay in which you compare and contrast two poetic forms.

- Plan your essay by determining the characteristics that define these poetic forms: lyric poetry, concrete poetry, and haiku. Choose two forms to compare and contrast in your essay.

- Pick one or more poems in each form.

- In your essay, compare the characteristics of each form, giving examples of each characteristic from the poems you have chosen.

- For each characteristic you discuss, explain how it contributes to the meaning of the poem.

- Include your topic sentence in the introductory paragraph. Organize the body of your compare-and-contrast essay to clearly show comparisons and contrasts. Use details from the poems to support your ideas.

714 Poetry

Performance Task Rubric: Standards Mastery	Rating Scale				
	not very				*very*
Critical Thinking: How clearly and consistently does the student pursue the specific mode of reasoning or discourse required by the standard, as specified in the prompt (e.g., comparing and contrasting, analyzing, explaining)?	1	2	3	4	5
Focus: How well does the student understand and apply the focus concepts of the standard, as specified in the prompt (e.g., development of theme or of complex characters, effects of structure, and so on)?	1	2	3	4	5
Support/Elaboration: How well does the student support points with textual or other evidence? How relevant, sufficient, and varied is the evidence provided?	1	2	3	4	5
Insight: How original, sophisticated, or compelling are insights the student achieves by applying the standard to the text(s)?	1	2	3	4	5
Expression of Ideas: How well does the student organize and support ideas? How well does the student use language, including word choice and conventions, in the expression of ideas?	1	2	3	4	5

Speaking and Listening

 ## Task 4: Literature [RL.7.4; SL.7.4]
Analyze the Impact of Sound Devices
Give an oral presentation of an essay in which you analyze the impact of sound devices in a poem in this unit.

- Analyze the impact of rhyme and other sound devices, such as repetition or alliteration, in a poem in this unit. Consider how the sound devices affect mood, meaning, and tone in the poem.
- Organize your key points and support them with examples from the poem.
- Before your presentation, consult a print or online dictionary to find the pronunciations of unknown words.
- Deliver your presentation to the class. Use appropriate eye contact, adequate volume, and clear pronunciation.

Task 5: Literature [RL.7.4; SL.7.1]
Lead a Discussion About Word Choice
Lead a small-group discussion about the effects of word choice in a poem from this unit.

- Choose a poem to use as the basis for your discussion. Prepare by jotting down examples of specific words in the poem and noting their figurative or connotative meanings.
- Ask someone in your group to read the poem aloud. Then, allow group members to share their opinions and ideas about word choice in the poem. Follow general rules for discussion, taking turns speaking.
- Pose questions and respond to others' questions. Acknowledge new information and adjust your own ideas in response if necessary.

- Use formal English and academic vocabulary to discuss the poem.

Task 6: Literature [RL.7.4; SL.7.4]
Respond to Poetry
Present an oral response to one of the poems in this unit.

- Choose a poem that you feel is particularly effective. Determine the most important idea or message the poet conveys in the poem.
- Analyze the impact of word choice, imagery, figurative language, structure, and sound devices in the poem.
- Formulate your personal response to the poem. Ask yourself questions such as these: *Do the connotations of specific words make me feel a certain way? What pictures do I see in my mind when I read this line? What is the effect of rhyme or rhythm when I read the poem aloud?*
- Organize your response logically. State your opinion clearly in your introduction. Establish eye contact with your audience, and speak with adequate volume.

What is the best way to communicate?
At the beginning of Unit 4, you wrote a response to the Big Question. Now that you have completed the unit, write a new response. Discuss how your initial ideas have either been changed or reinforced. Cite specific examples from the literature in this unit, from other subject areas, and from your own life to support your ideas. Use Big Question vocabulary words (see p. 571) in your response.

Assessment Workshop **715**

Supporting Speaking and Listening

1. Consider having students work with partners or in groups to complete Performance Tasks involving speaking and listening. For tasks that you assign for individual work, you may still wish to have students rehearse with partners, who can provide constructive feedback.

2. As students rehearse, have them keep in mind these tips:
   - Present findings and evidence clearly and concisely.
   - Observe conventions of standard English grammar and usage.
   - Be relaxed and friendly but maintain a formal tone.
   - Make eye contact with the audience, pronounce words clearly, and vary your pace.
   - When working with a group, respond thoughtfully to others' positions, modifying your own in response to new evidence.

Linking Performance Tasks to Independent Reading

If you wish to cover the standards with students' independent reading, adapt Performance Tasks of your choice to the works they have selected. (Independent reading suggestions appear on the next page.)

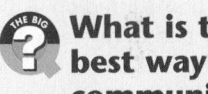 ### What is the best way to communicate?

1. Remind students that the unit Big Question is "What is the best way to communicate?"

2. Have students complete their responses to the prompt on the student page. Point out that they have read selections in this unit about different approaches to communication and that they should draw on these selections in their responses. Remind them that they can also draw on their own experiences and what they have learned in other subject areas in formulating their answers.

Differentiated Instruction for Universal Access

Strategy for Less Proficient Readers
Assign a Performance Task, and then have students meet in groups to review the standard assessed in that task. Remind students of the selections or independent readings to which they have previously applied the standard. Have groups summarize what they learned in applying the standard and then present their summaries. Discuss, clarifying any points of confusion. After students have completed their tasks, have groups meet again to evaluate members' work. Encourage members to revise their work based on the feedback they receive.

EL Strategy for English Learners
For each assigned Performance Task, review the instructions with students. Clarify the meaning of any unfamiliar vocabulary, emphasizing routine classroom words such as *fragments*, *characteristics*, and *response*, and academic vocabulary such as *interpret*.

Next, have students note ideas for their responses. Pair students, and have them review each other's notes. Encourage students to ask for your assistance in supplying English words or expressions they may require.

Independent Reading

Titles featured on the Independent Reading pages at the end of each unit represent a range of reading, including stories, dramas, and poetry, as well as literary nonfiction and other types of informational text. Throughout, labels indicate the works that are CCSS Exemplar Texts. Choosing from among these featured titles will help students read works at increasing levels of text complexity in the grades 6–8 text complexity band.

Independent Reading and Pacing

See the Unit Overview and Pacing Plan, pp. 570a–570b, for suggestions on integrating independent reading with work in the Student Edition.

Using Literature Circles

A literature circle is a temporary group in which students independently discuss a book.

Use the guidance in the *Professional Development Guidebook*, pp. 47–49, as well as the teaching notes on the facing page, for additional suggestions for literature circles.

© Meeting Unit 4 CCS Focus Standards

Students can use books listed on this page to apply and to reinforce their mastery of the CCS Focus Standards covered in this unit. (The Focus Standards are introduced on pp. 572–575.)

Introducing Featured Titles

Have students choose a book or books for independent reading. Assist them by previewing the titles, noting their subject matter and level of difficulty. **Note:** Before recommending a work to students, preview it, taking into account the values of your community as well as the maturity of your students.

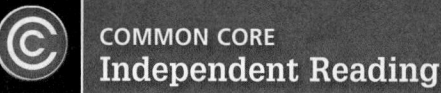

COMMON CORE
Independent Reading

Featured Titles

In this unit, you have read a wide variety of poems by many different poets. Continue to read on your own. Select works that you enjoy, but challenge yourself to explore new poets and works of increasing depth and complexity. The titles suggested below will help you get started.

Literature

It Doesn't Always Have to Rhyme
by Eve Merriam

This **poetry** collection is full of playful poems about poetry, including "How to Eat a Poem," "Metaphor," and a selection found in this unit, "Onomatopoeia."

The Poetry of Robert Frost: The Collected Poems
by Robert Frost   EXEMPLAR TEXT ©

Many readers admire Robert Frost's writing for how it captures a single thought or moment in a way that is personal but also universal. This **poetry** collection includes many of Frost's most popular poems.

When I Dance
by James Berry

This **poetry** collection pulses with the different rhythms of life in England and the Caribbean. In it, you will find the poem "One," which is also a selection in this unit.

My Own True Name
by Pat Mora

This **poetry** collection is divided into three sections: "Blooms" are poems about love and happiness, "Thorns" are poems about difficult times, and "Roots" are poems about family and home.

716 Poetry

The Music of Dolphins
by Karen Hesse

After a plane crash, the main character in this **novel** is raised by dolphins until the Coast Guard finds her. Mila "the Dolphin Girl" learns to speak, but she longs to return to the sea.

Informational Texts

Discoveries: Pushing the Boundaries

In this book, you can read about many different ways to communicate. The **nonfiction articles** in this collection include "The Samurai of Feudal Japan" and "Challenging Assumptions."

This Land Was Made for You and Me: The Life and Songs of Woody Guthrie
by Elizabeth Partridge   EXEMPLAR TEXT ©

During the Great Depression of the 1930s, folksinger Woody Guthrie wandered the nation, meeting workers and writing songs. In addition to a **biography** of Guthrie, this book includes photographs, posters, letters, and drawings.

© Text Complexity: Aligning Texts With Readers and Tasks

TEXTS	READERS AND TASKS
• *When I Dance* • *The Music of Dolphins*	**Below-Level Readers** Allow students to focus on reading for content, and challenge them to interpret multiple perspectives.
• *It Doesn't Always Have to Rhyme* • *My Own True Name* • *This Land Was Made for You and Me: The Life and Songs of Woody Guthrie*	**Below-Level Readers** Challenge students as they read for content. **On-Level Readers** Allow students to focus on reading for content, and challenge them to interpret multiple perspectives. **Advanced Readers** Allow students to focus on interpreting multiple perspectives.
• *Discoveries: Pushing the Boundaries*	**On-Level Readers** Challenge students as they read for content. **Advanced Readers** Allow students to focus on reading for content, and challenge them to interpret multiple perspectives.

Preparing to Read Complex Texts

Attentive Reading As you read poetry on your own, ask yourself questions about the text. The questions below, along with others that you ask as you read, will help you understand and appreciate poetry.

 **Common Core State Standards**

Reading Literature/Informational Text
10. By the end of the year, read and comprehend literature, including stories, dramas, and poems, and literary nonfiction in the grades 6–8 text complexity band proficiently, with scaffolding as needed at the high end of the range.

When reading poetry, ask yourself...

- Who is the speaker of the poem? What kind of person does the speaker seem to be? How do I know?
- What is the poem about?
- If the poem is telling a story, who are the characters and what happens to them?
- Does any one line or section state the poem's theme, or meaning, directly? If so, what is that line or section?
- If there is no direct statement of a theme, what details help me to see the poem's deeper meaning?

 **Key Ideas and Details**

- How does the poem look on the page? Is it long and rambling or short and concise? Does it have long or short lines?
- Does the poem have a formal structure or is it free verse?
- How does the form affect how I read the poem?
- How many stanzas form this poem? What does each stanza tell me?
- Do I notice repetition, rhyme, or meter? Do I notice other sound devices? How do these techniques affect how I read the poem?
- Even if I do not understand every word, do I like the way the poem sounds? Why or why not?
- Do any of the poet's word choices seem especially interesting or unusual? Why?
- What images do I notice? Do they create clear word-pictures in my mind? Why or why not?
- Would I like to read this poem aloud? Why or why not?

Craft and Structure

- Has the poem helped me understand its subject in a new way? If so, how?
- Does the poem remind me of others I have read? If so, how?
- In what ways is the poem different from others I have read?
- What information, ideas, or insights have I gained from reading this poem?
- Do I find the poem moving, funny, or mysterious? How does the poem make me feel?
- Would I like to read more poems by this poet? Why or why not?

Integration of Ideas

Independent Reading **717**

 Text Complexity: Reader and Task Support Suggestions

INDEPENDENT READING

Increased Support Suggest that students choose a book that they feel comfortable reading and one that is a bit more challenging. Pair a more proficient reader with a less proficient reader and have them work together on the more challenging text. Partners can prepare to read the book by reviewing questions on this student page. They can also read difficult passages together, sharing questions and insights. They can use the questions on the student page to guide after-reading discussion.

Increased Challenge Encourage students to integrate knowledge and ideas by combining the Big Question and the Unit Focus concepts in their approach to two or more featured titles.

For example, students might consider the different ways that people communicate in *The Music of Dolphins* and *Discoveries: Pushing the Boundaries*. In addition, students can focus on similarities and differences in the ways different poets use form and poetic devices to create meaning.

Preparing to Read Complex Texts

1. Tell students they can be attentive readers by bringing their experience and imagination to the texts they read and by actively questioning those texts. Explain that the questions they see on the student page are examples of types of questions to ask about poems.

2. Point out that, like writing, reading is a "multidraft" process, involving several readings of complete works or passages, revising and refining one's understanding each time.

Key Ideas and Details

3. As an example, review and amplify the fifth bulleted item. **Ask:** What key ideas and details can help you find a poem's deeper meaning?

   Possible response: You might point to the overall tone of the poem or look for metaphors, similes, or symbolism.

Craft and Structure

4. **Ask:** What details of craft and structure would you use to analyze each stanza?

   Possible response: You might find imagery or figurative language within each stanza or look for repetition or rhyme and other sound devices in stanzas.

Integration of Ideas

5. **Ask:** How would you determine how a poem made you feel?

   Possible response: You might evaluate whether the message of the poem was positive or negative or whether its images were appealing or unappealing.

6. Finally, explain to students that they should cite key ideas and details, examples of craft and structure, or instances of the integration of ideas as evidence to support their points during a poetry discussion. After hearing the evidence, the group might reach a consensus or might agree to disagree.

717

Unit 5 Features Overview

Unit Genre and Big Question

In this unit, students will analyze works of drama. As they read they will discuss responses to the unit Big Question: Do others see us more clearly than we see ourselves?

Unit 5 Selections

Teach Use the selections in this unit to teach the unit skills and meet the unit objectives.

Differentiate and Reinforce Use the information in the Text Complexity box on the next page to guide your teaching of the selections.

Integrate Skills Each selection presents students with a reading strategy, a literary analysis concept, a vocabulary skill, and grammar instruction. Students can extend learning in the writing and extension activities.

Additional Unit Features

Ⓒ Literary Analysis Workshop Teach and model the Unit Focus standards. Spiral Review notes enable students to revisit these skills over the course of the unit.

Reading for Information Students analyze functional, expository, and argumentative texts and complete Timed Writing activities.

Comparing Literary Works Students study two literary works either within or across genres.

Test Practice: Reading This feature provides extra practice in utilizing reading skills to master assessments.

Writing Workshops Two writing workshops appear in each unit, along with rubrics and instruction in the writing process.

Assessment Workshop Cumulative Skill Review and Performance Tasks provide a range of assessment opportunities.

Independent Reading Students broaden their knowledge as they read longer works of increasing complexity.

THE BIG ? Do others *see* us more clearly than we *see* ourselves?

Teaching From Technology

Enriched Online Student Edition
- full narration of selections
- interactive graphic organizers
- linked **Get Connected** and **Background** videos
- all worksheets and other student resources

Professional Development
- the *Professional Development Guidebook* online
- additional professional development articles by program authors

Planning, Assigning, and Monitoring
- software for online assignment of work to students, individually or to the whole class
- a system for tracking and grading student work

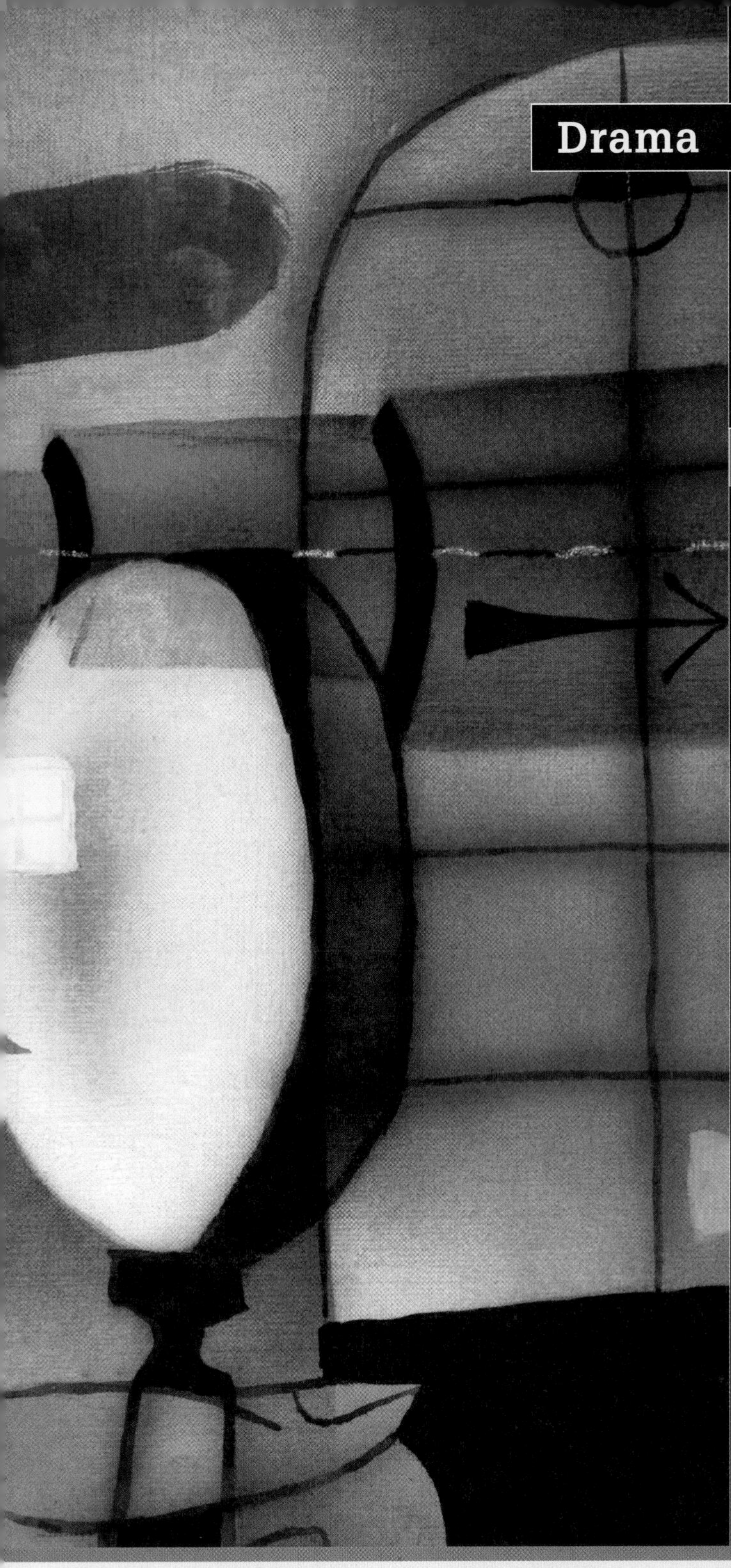

Unit

5

Drama

719

PHLit Online!
www.PHLitOnline.com

Hear It!
- Selection summary audio
- Selection audio
- BQ Tunes

See It!
- Author videos
- Big Question video
- Get Connected videos
- Background videos
- More about the authors
- Illustrated vocabulary words
- Vocabulary flashcards

Do It!
- Interactive journals
- Interactive graphic organizers
- Grammar tutorials
- Interactive vocabulary games
- Test practice

Instructional Resources

The booklet *Unit 5 Resources* supports Unit skills with pages of the following types:

▶ **Benchmark Tests** assess and monitor student progress at mid-Unit and at Unit's end.

▶ **Vocabulary and Reading Warm-ups** provide additional vocabulary support, based on Lexile rankings of words, for each selection. "A" **Warm-ups** are for students reading two grades below level. "B" **Warm-ups** are for students reading one grade below level.

▶ **Selection Support** These practice pages are available for each selection:
- Reading Skill
- Literary Analysis
- Writing About the Big Question
- Vocabulary Builder
- Support for Writing
- Support for Extend Your Learning
- Enrichment

PHLit Online!

All worksheets and other student resources are also available online at **www.PHLitOnline.com**.

© Text Complexity: Accessibility for Various Ability Levels

This chart gives a general accessibility rating to help you determine the depth of the prereading and reading support that you will need to provide students for each selection. For additional guidance on factors that affect the accessibility of each selection, see the Text Complexity Rubrics and Reader and Task Suggestions on selection-opening pages.

Accessibility for English Learners

 This icon indicates support for English learners at point of use in this Teacher's Edition.

	✓ Accessible
Act I	A Christmas Carol: Scrooge and Marley
Act II	A Christmas Carol: Scrooge and Marley
Drama Selection	The Monsters Are Due on Maple Street

Common Core State Standards

Unit 5 Focus Standards
- Reading Literature 2, 5

Additional Activities and Assessments
- Reading Literature 3, 7
- Writing 1, 2, 6, 7, 8
- Speaking and Listening 6
- Language 1, 2, 4, 6

	Week 1					Week 2					Week 3				
	1	2	3	4	5	1	2	3	4	5	1	2	3	4	5
Introduce the Unit Big Question (pp. 720–721).	●														
Introduce the unit form, drama, using the Literary Analysis Workshop (pp. 722–725).	●														
Introduce the focus CCS standards for the unit and lead students in a close reading of exemplar texts. (pp. 726–735).	●	●													
Teach *A Christmas Carol: Scrooge and Marley,* Act 1 (pp. 736–771).			●	●	●	●	●								
Teach *A Christmas Carol: Scrooge and Marley,* Act 2 (pp. 772–809).							●	●	●	●	●				
Complete the Test Practice: Reading (pp. 810–811).										●					
Teach Reading for Information (pp. 812–817).										●					
Teach Comparing Literary Works (pp. 818–823).											●	●			
Have students complete the Writing Workshop (pp. 824–829).										●	●	●	●	●	
Administer **Benchmark Test 9** (*Unit 5 Resources,* pp. 84–89).														●	
Reteach skills, judging which skills to reteach by evaluating students' performance on **Benchmark Test 9.**															●

Independent Reading

Have students choose a full-length work from the Independent Reading feature at the end of the unit and read it while working on this unit.

Pacing Suggestions

- Have students read their chosen work for homework.
- Devote parts of class periods in each school week to Literature Circles in which students reading the same work discuss it.

	Week 4					Week 5					Week 6				
	1	2	3	4	5	1	2	3	4	5	1	2	3	4	5
Teach *The Monsters are Due on Maple Street* (pp. 834–856).	●	●	●	●	●										
Complete the Test-Practice: Reading (pp. 860–861).						●									
Teach Reading for Information (pp. 862–865).							●								
Teach Comparing Literary Works (pp. 866–877).								●	●						
Have students complete the Writing Workshop (pp. 878–885).									●	●	●	●	●		
Have students complete the Vocabulary Workshop (pp. 886–887).												●			
Have students complete the Communications Workshop (pp. 890–893).												●			
Have students complete the first three sections of the Assessment Workshop: Drama (pp. 894–895).											●	●	●		
Have students complete the selected Performance Tasks in the Assessment Workshop (pp. 894–895).												●			
Administer Benchmark Test 10 (*Unit 5 Resources*, pp. 134–142).												●			
Reteach skills, judging which skills to reteach by evaluating students' performance on **Benchmark Test 10.**															●

- Cover the focus standards with independent readings and abbreviate review of the focus standards with student-edition selections.

- Do not assign extension activities for selections (day 5 of main selection lessons), except as needed for full standards coverage.

- If students demonstrate reading proficiency, consider omitting Test Practice: Reading features in the unit.

Block and Daily Scheduling

The assignments and activities in this Unit planner are organized by week. You may adjust them to your daily or block schedule. The Time and Resource Managers for each selection set gives specific pacing suggestions, or you may use the comprehensive lesson planning support online at www.PHLitOnline.com.

Monitoring Progress

Diagnose Refer to students' results on the **Vocabulary in Context** section of **Benchmark Test 8**, *Unit 4 Resources*, pp. 232–234 (administered at the end of the previous Unit). Use the **Interpretation Guide** to interpret the results of this diagnostic portion of the test. **Note:** For the most accurate diagnosis of students who score in the middle range, administer the additional diagnostic questions online at www.PHLitOnline.com.

Preteach and Prepare As indicated by the diagnostic, prepare students for reading by assigning the **Vocabulary** and **Reading Warm-ups** for each selection.

Teach Follow this Pacing Plan and use the resources to teach the skills and selections. For specific pacing suggestions and a list of resources, see the Time and Resource Manager and the Visual Guide to Featured Selection Resources preceding each selection.

> *Classroom Management*
> For classroom management suggestions for using leveled texts in a mixed-ability classroom, see Harvey Daniels's professional development essay "Leveled Reading Selections," online at www.PHLitOnline.com.

Assess After students have completed the first half of the Unit, administer **Benchmark Test 9.** Administer **Benchmark Test 10** at the end of the Unit.

Intervention and Reteach After administering each test, use the **Interpretation Guide** for the tests to determine which reteaching pages, if any, you should assign from the *Reading Kit.* The appropriate pages are also available through the online Progress Monitoring software.

CLASSROOM STRATEGIES

Questioning Literary Fiction **Doug Buehl**

> Literary fiction is predominantly an *indirect* method of delivering messages. As readers, it is often up to *us* to figure out just what a story is telling us.

What's the point of this story? Of course, stories entertain us and provide indispensable moments of pleasure and diversion. Stories are also a timeless vehicle for sharing ideas, insights, and understandings with each other. A well-told story can illustrate a truth, prompt reflection and introspection, stimulate discussion, challenge preconceptions, refine our thinking, inspire and move us to action, and change how we understand ourselves and our world. Unlike works of nonfiction, literary fiction (short stories, novels, drama) is predominantly an *indirect* method of delivering messages. As readers, it is often up to *us* to figure out just what a story is telling us. What might this story mean to its author? And what might this story mean to us?

"Wondering" Through Text

What do you wonder as you read? Undoubtedly, your mind is buzzing with questions like "I wonder why she did that?" or "I wonder what will happen next?" How can we work with students so that they too adopt inquiring frames of mind as readers? Students need ongoing opportunities to formulate their own questions. And they need to develop the habit of using texts to try to resolve things they are wondering about. Reader-generated questioning strategies play a significant role in comprehension instruction (Duke and Pearson, 2002).

Reading as Inquiry

Tracking Thinking The following activities prompt students to track the questions that surface for them as readers, and reinforce that asking questions is a natural component of trying to understand an author's message.

1. **Sticky Notes.** Ask students to monitor things they are wondering as they read. Students affix sticky notes to the page with their questions. Some of their questions will be satisfactorily addressed by the author, but others will likely be open to interpretation. Students share their sticky notes with partners or in cooperative groups.

2. **Thick and Thin Questions.** Introduce the concept of thin questions (raised for clarification: *I wonder what* covetous *means?*) and thick questions (pondering ideas and developing interpretations: *I wonder why Marley calls Scrooge "an old sinner"?*). Ask students to code their questions as thick or thin, and talk about their efforts to figure out answers.

3. **Before/During/After Charts.** Provide students with a three-column graphic organizer to record the questions on their minds before reading (based on a preview of the selection), questions that emerged while reading, and questions they still have after reading. Unresolved questions provide the gist for further conversation and interpretation. Students discuss their questions with partners or in groups.

Deeper Questioning

As students gain experience with generating questions about their reading, instruction can take them deeper into examining literary fiction. The revised Bloom's Taxonomy (Anderson & Krathwohl, 2001) provides an excellent framework for cueing students to ask themselves questions for each level of thinking.

Remembering-level questions focus on elements of basic story grammar and remind students to check their ability to follow the story.

Understanding-level questions emphasize the dynamics of the story, especially tracking the characters and conflict.

Applying-level questions prompt students to connect a story to their personal life experiences and use their background knowledge to begin to develop interpretations.

Analyzing-level questions ask students to notice author's craft and to read through a "literary lens."

Evaluating-level questions involve critical reading and sensitivity to author perspective and attitudes.

Creating-level questions ask students to consider the meaning they have constructed about a selection.

Level of Thinking	Focusing Questions
Creating	Why is the author telling me this story? What theme or idea might the author be exploring? What does this story mean to me?
Evaluating	Who is the author and how might author perspective have influenced the telling of this story? What does the author's choice of words indicate about what the author might be thinking? What emotions does the author elicit?
Analyzing	What literary devices does the author use, and what seems to be the purpose for using them?
Applying	How can I connect this story to my life and experiences? Why might the author have the characters say or do that? What point might the author be making about the characters' actions?
Understanding	How do the characters interact with each other? How do the characters feel about each other? How do characters' feelings and interactions change? How does the author use conflict in this story? How does the author resolve this conflict?
Remembering	Who are the characters? Where does the story take place? What are the major events of the story? What is the sequence of these events? What event initiates the action of the story?

Modeled Strategy

See pp. 834 and 868 for point-of-use notes modeling these strategies.

Teacher Resources

- *Professional Development Guidebook*
- *Classroom Strategies and Teaching Routines* cards

Log on as a teacher at **www.PHLitOnline.com** to access a library of all Professional Development articles by the Contributing Authors of Pearson Prentice Hall *Literature*.

Doug Buehl

Doug Buehl is a teacher, author, and national literacy consultant. His 33 years with the Madison Metropolitan School District, in Madison, Wisconsin, included experiences as a reading teacher and district adolescent literacy support teacher.

Supporting Research

Anderson, L. & Krathwohl, D. (Eds.). (2001). *A taxonomy for learning, teaching, and assessing: A revision of Bloom's taxonomy of educational objectives.* New York: Longman.

Beck, I., McKeown, M., Hamilton, R., & Kucan, L. (1997). *Questioning the author: An approach for enhancing student engagement with text.* Newark, DE: International Reading Association.

Buehl, D. (2007). Questioning literary fiction. *On WEAC.* Madison, WI: Wisconsin Education Association Council. Available online: http://www.weac. org/News/2007-08/nov07/reading-room.htm.

Duke, N. & Pearson, P. D. (2002). Effective practices for developing reading comprehension. In A. Farstrup and S. Samuels, *What research has to say about reading instruction,* 3rd ed. (pp. 205–242).

Newark, DE: International Reading Association.

Common Core State Standards

- Speaking and Listening 1
- Language 6

❶ Introducing the Big Question

1. When we look in the mirror, we see a reflection of our surface features. **Ask:** Is there also a "mirror" that reflects our inner features? Have students read the introduction on page 720.

2. Read the Big Question aloud. **Ask:** Does the answer depend on the identity of the other person? Are there some people who know you better than others? **Possible response:** Yes, close friends and family know us better than acquaintances.

3. Students will read dramas that have to do with self-exploration. As students read, they should consider how the dramas affect their first answers to the Big Question.

❷ Exploring the Big Question

Collaboration: Group Discussion

1. Introduce the activity, using the instruction on the student page.

2. Have students list examples. If students have difficulty with the fourth and fifth bullets, prompt ideas with questions:

   - Has someone known you were sad even if you were hiding it? **Sample response:** Yes, my mom can always tell when I'm sad.

   - Can you think of a time when someone had to make a hard decision? **Sample response:** My friend had to decide whether to tell on her sister.

3. Review the Big Question vocabulary on page 721. Have students use the vocabulary as they complete the activity on page 720.

Connecting to the Literature

Explain the Big Question strand in the unit, referring to the box at right.

720

---

❶ Do others *see* us more clearly than we *see* ourselves?

We are constantly learning about ourselves through our experiences and our interactions with others. Sometimes we feel that another person truly knows and understands us. Other times, however, we might suspect that someone is making an assumption about us based on appearance or other factors. To see ourselves and others clearly, it helps to reflect on the unique characteristics of each person. Our individual qualities and beliefs about ourselves influence how others see us and how we react to the people around us.

❷ Exploring the Big Question

© **Collaboration: Group Discussion** Start thinking about the Big Question by making a list of ways you form impressions about other people and ways that other people form impressions about you. Describe one specific example of each of the following:

- A judgment based on appearance

- A judgment influenced by prejudice, or bias

- An insight about the way another person treats you or others

- A time another person seemed to understand your thoughts

- A perception based on another person's reaction to a difficult situation

  Share your examples with a small group. Discuss whether or not each situation helped someone see another person clearly. Use the Big Question vocabulary in your discussion.

Connecting to the Literature Each reading in this unit will give you additional insight into the Big Question.

www.PHLitOnline.com
- Big Question video
- Illustrated vocabulary words
- Interactive vocabulary games
- BQ Tunes

720 Drama

Applying Understanding by Design Principles

The Big Question
Explain that students will continue to consider the Big Question as they work through the Unit.
- At the beginning of each selection, they will write a response to a Writing About the Big Question sentence frame.
- As they read the selection, they will look for details related to the Big Question.

- At the end of each selection, they will answer a Critical Thinking question that is related to the Big Question.
- Tell students that their goal will be to gain a deeper understanding of literature and a more sophisticated way of discussing the Big Question.

"Understanding by Design" is registered as a trademark with the Patent and Trademark Office by the Association for Supervision of Curriculum Development (ASCD). ASCD has not authorized, approved, or sponsored this work and is in no way affiliated with Pearson or its products.

❸ Learning Big Question Vocabulary

Acquire and Use Academic Vocabulary Academic vocabulary is the language you encounter in textbooks and on standardized tests. Review the definitions of these academic vocabulary words.

---

appreciate (ə prē′ shē āt′) *v.* be thankful for

assumption (ə sump′ shən) *n.* act of accepting something as true without proof

bias (bī′ əs) *n.* a slanted viewpoint

characteristic (kar′ ək tər is′ tik) *n.* trait; feature

define (dē fīn′) *v.* describe; explain

focus (fō′ kəs) *n.* central point; topic

identify (ī den′ tə fī′) *v.* recognize; point out

ignore (ig nôr′) *v.* pay no attention to

Use these words as you complete Big Question activities in this unit that involve reading, writing, speaking, and listening.

Gather Vocabulary Knowledge Additional Big Question words are listed below. Categorize the words by deciding whether you know each one well, know it a little bit, or do not know it at all.

---

appearance	perception	reflect
image	perspective	reveal
	reaction	

Then, do the following:

1. Work with a partner to determine and write each word's definition.
2. Verify definitions by looking them up in a print or online dictionary and revising as needed.
3. Then, for each word, write an original sentence about how we see ourselves and others. Provide enough information so the meaning of each word is clear.
4. Exchange sentences with your partner to see if he or she agrees with your main points and your use of the vocabulary words.

Introducing the Big Question **721**

**Common Core
State Standards**

Speaking and Listening
1. Engage effectively in a range of collaborative discussions with diverse partners on grade 7 topics, texts, and issues, building on others' ideas and expressing their own clearly.

Language
6. Acquire and use accurately grade-appropriate general academic and domain-specific words and phrases; gather vocabulary knowledge when considering a word or phrase important to comprehension or expression.

---

❸ Learning Big Question Vocabulary

Acquire and Use Academic Vocabulary

1. Introduce the academic vocabulary words in the first word bank on the student page. Have students preview the words.

2. For each word, have students say the word aloud. Then, use the word in a sentence that defines the word.

Gather Vocabulary Knowledge

1. With the class, review the steps in the activity on the student page. Have students complete the activity independently, with partners, or in small groups.

2. Before students complete the last step, review the words and their meanings as a class. (Definitions appear below on the left.) Then, have students complete their paragraphs.

Gather Vocabulary Knowledge: Definitions

appearance (ə pir′ əns) *n.* way a person or thing looks or seems
image (i′ mij) *n.* a visual representation of something
perception (pər sep′ shən) *n.* a mental image
perspective (pər spek′ tiv) *n.* a mental view or prospect

reaction (rē ak′ shən) *n.* a response to some stimulus
reflect (ri flekt′) *v.* to throw back light or sound
reveal (ri vēl′) *v.* to open up to view

721

❶ The Elements of Drama

1. Introduce the form, drama, using the instruction on the student page.

2. Stress that drama shares many elements with fiction, described in the second paragraph. Explain that in drama, the term *action* is frequently used for all the events of the plot.

3. Underscore that the biggest difference between drama and fiction is that drama is written to be performed. Note, however, that there are many smaller differences, including differences in format. Fiction is generally written in paragraphs; the script of a stage play consists of stage directions and dialogue, with labels to show which character is speaking. Mention that italics are often used for the stage directions to distinguish them from the dialogue.

4. Point out that the Elements of Drama chart gives more information about the elements of drama discussed in the last paragraph on the page. As you review the chart, clarify that *stage left* and *stage right* are the opposite of left and right to the audience because the terms refer to the actors' left and right as they face the audience.

5. **Ask:** What props might you include in a scene set in a classroom?

   Sample answer: I might include chalk, desks, and textbooks.

6. Discuss additional elements on the chart, making sure students are familiar with all terms used.

❶The Elements of Drama

A drama is a story that is meant to be performed.

A **drama,** or **play,** is a story that is performed for an audience. Some dramas are presented live on a stage, while others are recorded on film. No matter what the form, a drama brings to life the words of its author, the **playwright.**

Drama is similar to fiction in many ways. Like fiction, drama focuses on **characters,** made-up people who interact in a particular **setting,** or environment. The characters are caught up in a struggle, or **conflict.** This drives the **plot**—a series of actions that build to a **climax.** The climax is the highest point of tension. The action then winds down in a **resolution.**

Unlike fiction, drama is meant to be performed. Instead of *reading* a playwright's words, audiences see and hear actors speak the words.

The written text of a drama is called a **script.** A script consists of **dialogue,** the words spoken by the actors, and **stage directions,** the playwright's instructions about how the drama should be performed. **Acts** are the units of action in a drama. Acts are often divided into parts called **scenes.**

Elements of Drama	
Stage Directions	Stage directions are the playwright's instructions about how to perform the drama. They tell how actors should speak and move, and give details about lighting, sound effects, and costumes. These abbreviations are often used in stage directions: **C:** center stage **D:** downstage (nearest to audience) **U:** upstage (farthest from audience) **L:** stage left (audience's right) **R:** stage right (audience's left)
Dialogue	Dialogue is conversation between or among characters.
Set/Scenery	*Set* and *scenery* are terms used to describe the construction onstage that suggests the time and place of the action. A set may look like an actual place, or it may merely suggest a place.
Props	Props are small movable items, such as a doctor's clipboard or a student's notebook, that actors use to make their actions look realistic.
Acts and Scenes	Acts and scenes are the basic units of action in a drama. A full-length drama may consist of several acts, each of which may contain any number of scenes.

722 Drama

Teaching Resources

All *Common Core Companion,* pp. 28–40, 54–66

All *Unit 5 Resources,* pp. 7–22

All *Professional Development Guidebook,* p. 33

All *See It!* DVD
Laurence Yep, Segments 1 and 2

All *Graphic Organizer Transparencies,* pp. 145, 146

All **Enriched Online Student Edition**

L2 L3 *Reader's Notebook*

L1 *Reader's Notebook: Adapted Version*

EL *Reader's Notebook: English Learner's Version*

L2 EL *Hear It!* Audio CD

L1 EL *Hear It!* Audio CD (adapted text)

PHLit Online! All resources, including print and video, are available online at www.PHLitOnline.com.

② Changing Forms of Drama

Early Drama The earliest known written dramas came to us from the ancient Greeks. The Greeks divided drama into two basic categories that we still use today: **comedy** and **tragedy.**

Comedy	• features ordinary people in funny or ridiculous situations • usually has a happy ending • is meant to entertain, but also may point out human weaknesses and the faults of a society
Tragedy	• shows the downfall of the main character, known as the **tragic hero** • the tragic hero may be an admirable person with a fault that brings about his or her destruction • the hero might also be an ordinary person destroyed by an evil force in society

The biggest difference between a comedy and a tragedy is the way that the story ends. Comedies end in happy events, such as reunions or weddings. Tragedies end in sad events, such as deaths or partings.

After the great plays of the ancient Greeks, drama went into a decline that lasted more than one thousand years. It bloomed again during the time of English playwright William Shakespeare (1564–1616). Shakespeare and his fellow dramatists wrote both comedies and tragedies.

Drama Today The modern period has seen a tremendous growth in dramatic writing, and this growth has brought change—even in the meaning of the term *drama.* Contemporary plays and films that treat serious subjects tend to be called *dramas* now, rather than *tragedies.* These serious works are different from contemporary comedies, which, as expected, are lighter and more entertaining.

An even more important change is the way different media have altered people's experience with drama. For several thousand years, people saw dramas in only one way: live. Today, the world of drama is not limited to the stage. Here are some other common types of dramas:

- **Screenplays** are the scripts for films. They include camera angles and can allow for more scene changes than a stage play.
- **Teleplays** are scripts written for television. They contains elements similar to those in a screenplay.
- **Radio plays** are written to be performed as radio broadcasts. They include sound effects and do not require a set.

Literary Analysis Workshop **723**

---

③ In This Section

The Elements of Drama

Analyzing Drama

Close Read: Understanding Elements of Drama
- Model Text
- Practice Text

After You Read

 Common Core State Standards

RL.7.3, RL.7.5
[For the full wording of the standards, see the standards chart in the front of your textbook.]

---

② Changing Forms of Drama

1. Introduce the forms, using the instruction on the student page.

2. Discuss the two traditional forms of drama, comedy and tragedy, and the fact that the term *drama* is today often used to mean any serious play. Have students provide examples of plays that they have read or seen performed, and tell them to indicate which qualify as comedies and which as tragedies or dramas.

3. Explain that the early plays of the Greeks and Shakespeare are called verse dramas because most or all of their dialogue is in the form of poetry. Mention that Shakespeare often included songs in his plays and that Greek dramas were spectacles of song and dance. Note that today's plays are rarely verse dramas, but some, called musicals, do contain singing and dancing. Encourage students to discuss any musicals they have seen live or on television.

4. Stress that movies and television shows with plots (as opposed to news programs and the like) are also forms of drama. Tell students that the scripts of films are called screenplays and the scripts of television shows are called teleplays.

③ In This Section

Explain that in the remainder of this Literary Analysis Workshop, students will analyze the elements of drama. After reviewing the concept, they will then see it applied to the elements of drama in a Model text. Finally, they will apply what they have learned to a Practice text.

Differentiated Instruction for Universal Access

Support for Special-Needs Students
Have students read **Learning About Drama** in the *Reader's Notebook: Adapted Version.* This version provides a basic-level introduction to drama.

Support for Less Proficient Readers
Have students read **Learning About Drama** in the *Reader's Notebook.* This version provides a basic-level introduction to drama.

EL **Support for English Learners**
Have students read **Learning About Drama** in the *Reader's Notebook: English Learner's Version.* This version provides a basic-level introduction to drama.

Common Core State Standards

Unit 5 Focus Standards
• **Reading Literature 3, 5**

These standards spiral through the unit.

❶ Analyzing Drama

1. Introduce the concept of analyzing drama, using the instruction on pages 724–725.

2. Clarify that most full-length plays written for the stage are divided into acts, which are further divided into scenes. Note that some modern playwrights use only scenes, not acts. Explain that screenplays and teleplays follow special formats, and they too generally have just scenes, not acts.

3. Review the concepts of external and internal conflicts. Clarify that the main character facing the conflict is called the protagonist; if the conflict is with another character, that character is often called the antagonist. Note that not all external conflicts are between two characters; the protagonist may struggle against society, for example, or against an aspect of nature. Have students give examples of external and internal conflicts in some of the plays or films that they have read or seen.

4. Stress the distinction of showing, not telling. Readers of a play can be told information in stage directions, but an audience watching the play does not know what the stage directions say. Instead, the audience must figure out everything about the play from what is shown on stage. If a character is mean and petty, the audience must be shown those traits through the character's words and actions. If a setting is eerie or scary, the audience must be shown that through elements such as scenery, lighting, background music, and sound or other special effects.

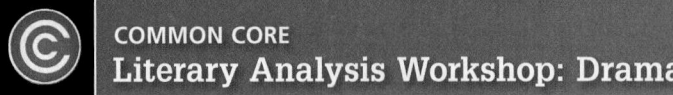

❶ Analyzing Drama

Drama has its own unique way of telling stories about characters.

Common Core State Standards

Reading Literature 3. Analyze how particular elements of a story or drama interact (e.g., how setting shapes the characters or plot).
Reading Literature 5. Analyze how a drama's or poem's form or structure (e.g., soliloquy, sonnet) contributes to its meaning.

Structure in Drama The **structure,** or framework, of a drama affects the way the audience or reader finds meaning in the performance or script. The following is a typical structure for a three-act drama.

Act I	The characters, setting, and **conflict,** or problem, are introduced in the **exposition.**
Act II	In the **rising action,** the main character, or **protagonist,** tries to solve the conflict, but faces obstacles that prevent an easy solution.
Act III	The **climax,** or highest point of interest, represents a turning point in the drama. During the **falling action,** the plot moves toward the **resolution** of the conflict.

Of course, not all dramas follow a three-act structure. Many classic dramas, including most works by the Ancient Greeks and by Shakespeare, consist of five acts. One-act plays, on the other hand, contain a single act. Some one-act plays are divided into multiple scenes.

Conflict in Drama Dramatic action is driven by **conflict,** or struggle. There are two types of conflict in drama. **External conflict** occurs between a character and an outside force, such as another character. **Internal conflict** occurs within the mind of a character,

as when a character is torn between opposing feelings or goals.

> **Examples: External Conflict**
> • Two young people want to marry, but their parents will not allow it.
> • A family must flee their war-torn country.
>
> **Examples: Internal Conflict**
> • A girl must decide if she should turn in her friend, who has committed a crime.
> • A man struggles to overcome a violent past.

Action: Showing, Not Telling
Drama is moved forward entirely by spoken dialogue and physical action. Audiences who watch a play or film are not *told* what is happening. Rather, they are *shown* what happens. For example, the audience may recognize conflict by hearing anger in an actor's voice or seeing tension in his body. As a drama unfolds, various elements work together to bring the story to life. A dimly lit stage may create an emotional effect; one character's tone of voice may make another character respond in a certain way.

Obviously, the experience of reading a drama differs from that of seeing it performed. Readers experience a script more fully if they imagine the setting described in the stage directions and the way the actors' voices and movements bring the dialogue to life.

724 Drama

Vocabulary Development

© **CCSS Language 6**

Domain-Specific Words: Drama

Reinforce understanding of terms in drama by having students choose the term in parentheses that correctly completes each sentence.

1. The actress memorized her lines using a (script, dialogue) of the play.
2. The (playwright, protagonist) appeared on stage in every scene.
3. The character playing a cheerleader used a baton as a (set, prop).
4. There were three scenes in the (act, stage directions).

5. Some performers stood back from the audience but others were (upstage, downstage).
6. The tragic hero delivered a memorable (soliloquy, monologue) to the character playing her father.
7. The show was a (comedy, tragedy); its goal to make everyone laugh.
8. The hero's struggle to make a decision was an (internal, external) conflict.

Answers: 1–script; 2–protagonist; 3–prop; 4–act; 5–downstage; 6–monologue; 7–comedy; 8–internal

724

Character Development In drama, two elements are key to the development of character: stage directions and dialogue. These are the tools with which a playwright can create believable and interesting dramatic stories. Playwrights use **stage directions** to tell how characters speak, move, and interact with other characters. Playwrights create **dialogue** to reveal character in several ways.

- A character may directly express private thoughts, feelings, and conflicts in a speech.
- Personality traits may be revealed as a character interacts with other characters.
- A character may comment on another character.

In addition, playwrights may have characters deliver different types of speeches.

- A **monologue** is a long, uninterrupted speech spoken by one character to another.
- A **soliloquy** is a speech in which a character is alone and reveals private thoughts. Sometimes a soliloquy is spoken to the audience. Other times, the character is speaking only to himself or herself.
- An **aside** is a comment made by a character to the audience. It is not meant to be heard by the other characters.

To engage the audience and reader, playwrights create **complex characters** who resemble real people. Complex characters are involved in complicated relationships. Sometimes they are pulled in many directions because of difficult situations and problems.

Complex characters change as a play progresses.

Theme in Drama As in most other literary genres, drama conveys **themes,** or insights about life and human nature. The words and actions of the characters point to a drama's theme.

Examples of Theme in Drama

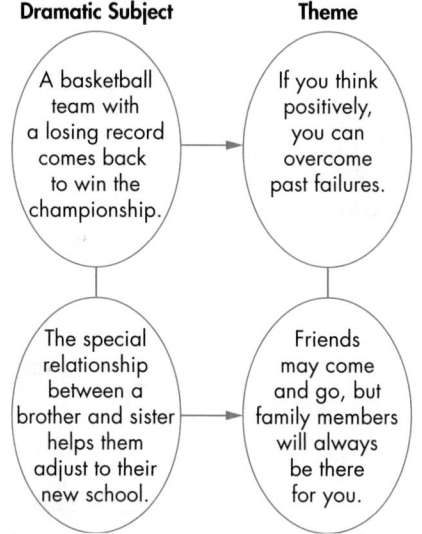

Dramatic Subject	Theme
A basketball team with a losing record comes back to win the championship.	If you think positively, you can overcome past failures.
The special relationship between a brother and sister helps them adjust to their new school.	Friends may come and go, but family members will always be there for you.

The various elements of a drama work together to convey its theme. To determine and analyze the theme of a drama, notice how the characters respond to conflicts and decide whether they change or grow as a result of their experiences. Consider how the setting—the time and place of the action—impacts characters or events. Finally, look for central ideas that are emphasized throughout the drama through the words and actions of the characters. Considering all of these elements will lead you to the central insight in a dramatic work.

5. Remind students that while readers of a drama are able to learn about a character through both dialogue and stage directions, an audience does not know the stage directions. It is up to the actor portraying the character to follow the stage directions and to play the role in a way that makes the audience understand the character.

6. Discuss the ways dialogue and actions can reveal character. **Ask:** What sort of character is a teenaged boy who shoves a smaller boy for no reason and says, "Get outta my way, bozo"?

   Possible response: He is a nasty bully.

7. Review the three special types of speech or dialogue. Clarify that a character need not be truly alone onstage in delivering a soliloquy but just has to act as if he or she is alone. Distinguish between an aside and a soliloquy by stressing that a soliloquy is a speech; an aside is just a brief comment.

8. Stress that drama, like other forms of literature, conveys theme. Explain that the details of drama, including characters' traits and behavior, the conflicts they face, and the outcome of those conflicts, point to theme. **Ask:** What might be the theme of a drama about an ambitious person who steps on others to reach the top of her field and in the end finds she has no friends left?

   Possible response: Excessive ambition can lead to unhappiness. It is lonely at the top.

❷ Close Read: Understanding Elements of Drama

1. Remind students that in the script, or written text, of a drama, plot, conflict, characters, and setting are conveyed through stage directions and dialogue.

2. Review the Key Elements of Drama chart, making sure students understand each element. Clarify that the stage directions give instructions about how to *stage,* or perform, the drama. In an actual performance, the audience must understand plot, conflict, characters, and setting through the staging—characters' movements, scenery, and so on—as well as from the dialogue.

3. Divide the class into groups. Provide this scene outline: *Bob, who has a crush on Jenn, does not want her to know he works after school at a store. One day, while he is at work, she comes in to shop.* Have each group work together to turn this outline into a dramatic scene that includes stage directions and dialogue.

Sample response:

SCENE: A supermarket. BOB is on a ladder, shelving cans, when he spots JENN. As she nears, he whisks off his store hat and apron and jumps from the ladder.

JENN: Hey, Bob, fancy meeting you here.

BOB: Yeah, I was just buying some—er—beef jerky for the guys.

MRS. SIMS, a cranky elderly customer, interrupts them.

MRS. SIMS: Young man, where do you keep the denture cream?

BOB *(nervously):* Sorry, ma'am, I don't work here.

MRS. SIMS: Of course you do! I've seen you here dozens of times!

4. Refer students to the Model text on page 727. Explain that details in the text that illustrate each category on the chart are highlighted in the same color and corresponding side-column annotations use corresponding colors.

❷Close Read: Understanding Elements of Drama

In drama, as in other genres, plot, characters, and setting propel the action forward.

The following elements are your keys to understanding a drama and its theme.

Key Elements of Drama	
Plot/Action Plot is the sequence of events in a drama. Look for details that reveal • the passage of time; • the importance of specific events; • the ways that characters grow or change.	**Characters** Characters in drama are described through stage directions and dialogue. As you read, look for details that reveal a character's • appearance and background; • personality traits; • attitudes toward other characters; • private thoughts and feelings.
Conflict Conflict in drama can be external or internal. As you read, look for clues about possible conflicts, including • stage directions and dialogue that describe a character's fears or worries; • dialogue that expresses strong feelings; • challenging situations.	**Stage Directions** Stage directions give clues about the characters and tell how the drama should be performed. As you read, look for instructions about • characters' movements, facial expressions, and tones of voice; • the props and scenery; • lighting and sound effects.
Setting A drama usually has a specific setting that may have a strong effect on the characters and plot. As you read, consider • the time and place of the action; • details that describe the physical environment; • details that make the environment challenging or dangerous.	**Dialogue** Dialogue refers to the words spoken by the characters. As you read, look for dialogue that • reveals a character's thoughts and feelings; • moves the action forward; • reveals the conflict.

726 Drama

Think Aloud

Theme

To model the skill of using dialogue and stage directions to understand drama, use the following "think aloud." Say to students:

When I read a play, the first thing I do is examine the opening stage directions. I look for a Cast of Characters to find out who the play is about. I identify the setting and pay attention to any background information. I use the stage directions to help myself picture the opening scene.

As I continue reading, I use the stage directions that tell performers how to speak and move to give me insight into the characters. I also consider what the dialogue reveals about plot, conflict, characters, and setting. For example, if Jo tells Lou, "Since you moved to town last week, I wondered if you'd be at this party," and the stage directions say she speaks shyly, I can tell that the characters are at a party, that Lou just moved to town, that Jo likes him, and that she is shy or feels shy with him.

EXEMPLAR TEXT

Model

3 **About the Text** This excerpt is from the drama *Sorry, Wrong Number* by Lucille Fletcher. This popular play has been performed on stage, as a movie, and as a radio play.

---

from *Sorry, Wrong Number* by Lucille Fletcher

[SCENE: *As curtain rises, we see a divided stage, only the center part of which is lighted and furnished as* **Mrs. Stevenson's** *bedroom. Expensive, rather fussy furnishings. A large bed, on which* **Mrs. Stevenson,** *clad in bed-jacket, is lying. A night-table close by, with phone, lighted lamp, and pill bottles. A mantle, with clock, R. A closed door, R. A window, with curtains closed, rear. The set is lit by one lamp on night-table. It is enclosed by three flats. Beyond this central set, the stage, on either side, is in darkness.*

Mrs. Stevenson *is dialing a number on the phone, as curtain rises. She listens to phone, slams down receiver in irritation.*

As she does so, we hear sound of a train roaring by in the distance. She reaches for her pill bottle, pours herself a glass of water, shakes out pill, swallows it, then reaches for the phone again, dials number nervously.]

Sound: *Number being dialed on phone: Busy signal.*

Mrs. Stevenson *(A querulous, self-centered neurotic.):* Oh—dear! *(Slams down receiver, dials* **Operator.***)*

[SCENE: *A spotlight, L. of side flat, picks up out of peripheral darkness, figure of* **1st Operator,** *sitting with headphones at a small table. If spotlight not available, use flashlight, clicked on by* **1st Operator,** *illuminating her face.*]

Operator: Your call, please?

Mrs. Stevenson: Operator? I've been dialing Murray Hill 4-0098 now for the last three-quarters of an hour, and the line is always busy. But I don't see how it could be that busy that long. Will you try it for me, please?

Operator: Murray Hill 4-0098? One moment, please. [SCENE: *She makes gesture of plugging in call through a switchboard.*]

Mrs. Stevenson: I don't see how it could be busy all this time. It's my husband's office. He's working late tonight, and I'm all alone here in the house. My health is very poor—and I've been feeling so nervous all day….

---

4 **Setting** The stage directions describe a woman's "fussy" bedroom surrounded by darkness. This setting creates a somewhat unsettling feeling.

5 **Plot/Action** The action in the play will center on the character's attempts to make a phone call.

6 **Characters** Mrs. Stevenson is described in the stage directions as "querulous," or irritable, and "neurotic." We can assume that she is easily upset.

7 **Stage Directions** In the stage directions, the playwright gives specific suggestions for lighting this scene.

8 **Dialogue** Mrs. Stevenson's speech reveals her conflict. She is frightened because she is alone and unable to reach someone by phone.

Literary Analysis Workshop **727**

---

3 Reading the Model

1. Discuss the About the Text note. Explain that *Sorry, Wrong Number* is a suspenseful drama about a woman who overhears a murder plot because of crossed wires on the telephone.

2. Have students read the excerpt (p. 727). Discuss it, clarifying as needed, before reviewing the annotations.

4 Setting

Read aloud the Setting annotation. **Ask:** What does the word *expensive* suggest about the woman living in this setting?

Possible response: She is rich.

5 Plot/Action

Read aloud the Plot/Action annotation. Explain that the play is set at a time when making phone calls was harder than it is today and often involved using operators. There were no area codes or call waiting, and phone numbers began with exchanges like *Murray Hill*, or *MU, 4.*

6 Characters

Read aloud the Characters annotation. **Ask:** What do the details in the stage directions suggest about Mrs. Stevenson's health?

Possible response: They suggest she is either ill or a hypochondriac and is bedridden.

7 Stage Directions

Read aloud the Stage Directions annotation. Remind students to use the stage directions to help them picture the scene.

8 Dialogue

Read aloud the Dialogue annotation. **Ask:** If you were playing Mrs. Stevenson, how would you speak the highlighted lines?

Sample response: I would speak them angrily or nervously.

9 Setting

1. Read aloud the setting annotation and the bracketed text.

2. **Ask:** What stage technique does the playwright use to indicate that this is a new scene?

   Possible response: The playwright shows the audience that this is a new scene by turning on a spotlight on a part of the stage, revealing a man sitting at a desk.

10 Stage Directions

1. Read aloud the stage directions annotation and the bracketed text.

2. Have students sketch the stage setting on a blank sheet of paper to help them visualize the scene.

3. **Ask:** Why does the playwright suggest that the director use a three-sided screen?

   Possible response: The three-sided screen is used to appear as a phone booth.

11 Plot/Action

1. Have three volunteers each take a part and read the bracketed text.

2. Then, read aloud the Plot/Action annotation. **Ask:** Who are George and the 1st Man and what are they planning?

   Possible response: George and the 1st Man appear to be assassins. They have been hired to kill a woman at the request of their "client."

3. Then, **ask:** How does this scene build tension and move the plot forward?

   Possible response: This scene builds tension because Mrs. Stevenson is overhearing their conversation to kill someone. This will undoubtedly make her even more nervous than she already is.

© EXEMPLAR TEXT

Model continued

9 Setting Stage directions indicate and describe changes in scene and setting.

10 Stage Directions The playwright suggests a way to stage this scene.

11 Plot/Action Dialogue builds tension and suspense and moves the action forward.

OPERATOR: Ringing Murray Hill 4-0098…. (SOUND: *Phone buzz. It rings three times. Receiver is picked up at other end.*)

9 [SCENE: *Spotlight picks up figure of a heavyset man, seated at desk with phone on right side of dark periphery of stage. He is wearing a hat. Picks up phone, which rings three times*]

MAN: Hello.

MRS. STEVENSON: Hello…? *(A little puzzled)* Hello. Is Mr. Stevenson there?

MAN: *(into phone, as though he had not heard.)* Hello…. *(Louder)* Hello.
[SCENE: *Spotlight on left now moves from* OPERATOR *to another man,* GEORGE. *A killer type, also wearing a hat, but standing as in a phone booth. A three-sided screen may be used to suggest this.*]

2ND MAN: *(slow, heavy quality, faintly foreign accent).* Hello.

1ST MAN: Hello, George?

GEORGE: Yes, sir.

MRS. STEVENSON: *(louder and more imperious, to phone).* Hello. Who's this? What number am I calling, please?

1ST MAN: We have heard from our client. He says the coast is clear for tonight.

GEORGE: Yes, sir.

1ST MAN: Where are you now?

GEORGE: In a phone booth.

1ST MAN: OK. You should know the address. At eleven o'clock the private patrolman goes around to the bar on Second Avenue for a beer. Be sure that all the lights downstairs are out. There should be only one light visible from the street. At eleven-fifteen a subway train crosses the bridge. It makes a noise in case her window is open and she should scream.

MRS. STEVENSON: *(shocked).* Oh—HELLO! What number is this, please?

GEORGE: OK. I understand.

1ST MAN: Make it quick. As little blood as possible. Our client does not wish to make her suffer long.

GEORGE: A knife OK, sir?

1ST MAN: Yes. A knife will be OK. And remember—remove the rings and bracelets and the jewelry in the bureau drawer. Our client wishes it to look like simple robbery.

GEORGE: OK—I get— [SCENE: *Spotlight suddenly goes out on* GEORGE.] *(SOUND: A bland buzzing signal)*

Independent Practice

⑫ **About the Selection** Laurence Yep's novel *Dragonwings* is about Moon Shadow, a Chinese boy who becomes deeply involved in his father's quest to build an airplane. More than twenty years after writing the novel, Yep created an hour-long dramatic version of the story. Following are an excerpt from the novel, narrated by Moon Shadow, and a scene from the drama.

from the novel *Dragonwings* by Laurence Yep

⑬ I do not know when I fell asleep, but it was already way past sunrise when I woke up. The light crept through the cracks in the walls and under the shutters and seemed to delight especially in dancing on my eyes. Father lay huddled, rolled up in his blanket. He did not move when the knock came at our door. I was still in my clothes because it was cold. I crawled out of the blankets and opened the side door.

The fog lay low on the hill. Tendrils drifted in through the open doorway. At first I could not see anything but shadows, and then a sudden breeze whipped the fog away from the front of our barn. Hand Clap stood there as if he had appeared by magic. He bowed.

"There you are." He turned and called over his shoulder. "Hey, everybody, they're here."

⑭ I heard the clink of harness and the rattle of an old wagon trying to follow the ruts in the road. Toiling up the hill out of the fog was Red Rabbit, and behind him I saw Uncle on the wagon seat. The rest of the wagon was empty—I suppose to give Red Rabbit less of a load to pull. Behind the wagon came the Company, with coils of ropes over their shoulders and baskets of food. I ran down the hill, my feet pounding against the hard, damp earth. I got up on the seat and almost bowled Uncle over. For once Uncle did not worry about his dignity but caught me up and returned my hug.

⑬ **Characters** What does Moon Shadow's description suggest about his father's condition? What details give you this idea?

⑭ **Setting** Describe the setting in your own words. How could staging create this same effect?

Literary Analysis Workshop **729**

---

⑫ **Introducing the Independent Practice**

1. Explain that students will examine a dramatic adaptation and the novel on which it is based to help them better understand the elements of drama.

2. Discuss the About the Selection note, and have students read the selections. Then, direct them to go back through and respond to the side-column prompts. Conclude by having students answer the After You Read questions on page 735.

⑬ **Characters**

1. Have students reread the first paragraph, including the highlighted section. **Ask:** Through which character's eyes do we see the scene and father? Is that personal impression likely to be retained in a dramatic adaptation?

   Possible response: We see them through the eyes of the narrator, Moon Shadow. No, plays are less personal than first-person narratives.

2. **Ask** the Characters questions.

   Possible response: It suggests he is exhausted or ill. Details include him lying huddled and not moving when someone knocks.

⑭ **Setting**

1. Have students reread the rest of the page, including the highlighted portion in the last paragraph. **Ask:** Who or what does Red Rabbit seem to be?

   Answer: Red Rabbit is the horse pulling the wagon.

2. **Ask** the Setting question.

   Sample response: The setting is foggy and eerie. Staging might use smoke to create the fog and sound effects for the clink of the harness and rattle of the wagon.

PHLit Online!

Enriched Online Student Edition
To have students read the selection in interactive format, with narration and point-of-use interactive graphic organizers, go online at **www.PHLitOnline.com**.

15 Conflict

1. Have students reread the dialogue between Moon Shadow and Uncle, including the highlighted exchange. **Ask:** What is "that thing" to which Uncle refers?

   Answer: It is the father's supposed flying machine.

2. **Ask:** Why is the narrator, Moon Shadow, glad to see the other men?

   Possible response: They can help in the difficult task of getting the flying machine to the top of the hill.

3. **Ask** the Conflict question.

   Possible response: Uncle has criticized or been opposed to the father's attempts to build a flying machine.

4. **Ask:** What past conflict to which Uncle refers helps explain his assistance today, in spite of his feelings about the flying machine?

   Possible response: Uncle's son has apparently robbed the narrator and his father, and because of that, Uncle feels a sense of obligation to them.

COMMON CORE
Literary Analysis Workshop: Drama

Practice continued

15 Conflict What conflict does the conversation between Moon Shadow and Uncle reveal?

"Ouch," he said, and pushed me away. He patted himself lightly on his chest. "I'm not as young as I used to be."

Then Hand Clap, Lefty, and White Deer crowded around.

"Am I ever glad you're here," I said. "Poor Father—"

Uncle held up his hands. "We know. That's why we came."

"But how? Why?" I was bursting with a dozen questions all at once.

15 "Why, to help you get that thing up to the top of the hill," Uncle said. "Why else would we close up our shop and take a boat and climb this abominable hill, all on the coldest, wettest day ever known since creation?"

"But you don't believe in flying machines."

"I still don't," Uncle said sternly. "But I still feel as if I owe you something for what was done to you by that man who once was my son.[1] I'll be there to haul your machine up the hill, and I'll be there to haul it back down when it doesn't fly."

"We were all getting fat anyway," White Deer said, "especially Uncle."

1. **man who once was my son** Black Dog, who robbed the narrator and his father.

730 Drama

Differentiated
Instruction   for Universal Access

Support for Special-Needs Students
Have students read the adapted version of *Dragonwings* in the *Reader's Notebook: Adapted Version.* They may also listen to the adapted version on the *Hear It!* **Audio CD** (adapted text). Then, have them complete the questions and activities in the Student Edition.

Support for Less Proficient Readers
Have students read *Dragonwings* in the *Reader's Notebook.* After students finish the selection in the *Reader's Notebook* have them complete the questions and activities in the Student Edition.

EL Support for English Learners
Have students read *Dragonwings* in the *Reader's Notebook: English Learner's Version.* English learners may also read the selection as they listen to the recorded version on the *Hear It!* **Audio CD.** Then, have them complete the questions and activities in the Student Edition.

16 **From the dramatization of _Dragonwings_ by Laurence Yep**

RED RABBIT a horse that pulls the company's laundry wagon **UNCLE BRIGHT STAR** another laundry owner **WHITE DEER** the third laundry owner	**MOON SHADOW** the narrator of the story **MISS WHITLAW** owner of a stable in San Francisco where the narrator and his father live **WINDRIDER** Moon Shadow's father

Scene 9 _Piedmont, later that day outside the stable._

MOON SHADOW: September twenty-second, Nineteen-ought-nine.

Dear Mother. I have bad news. We are going to lose **17** Dragonwings before father can fly it. Black Dog stole all we have, and the landlord will not give us an extension on our rent. So we'll have to move and leave Dragonwings behind. We have asked Miss Whitlaw for help, but her new house has taken up all of her money. And even if Uncle would speak to us, he has probably spent all he has on rebuilding his laundry.

[UNCLE BRIGHT STAR and MISS WHITLAW enter from L.]

MISS WHITLAW: I could have gotten down from the wagon by myself.

UNCLE BRIGHT STAR: Watch gopher hole.

MISS WHITLAW: I'm younger than you.

MOON SHADOW: Uncle, Miss Whitlaw!

MISS WHITLAW: How are you?

18 _[Shaking MOON SHADOW's hand. WINDRIDER enters from U. He now wears a cap.]_

WINDRIDER: Come to laugh, Uncle?

UNCLE BRIGHT STAR: I came to help you fly your contraption.

MOON SHADOW: But you don't believe in flying machines.

17 **Conflict** From this letter, which is performed as a monologue, what do you learn about the conflict the characters face? Is the conflict external or internal?

18 **Stage Directions** What is the meaning of "U" in the stage directions?

Literary Analysis Workshop **731**

---

16 ## Cast of Characters

Note that the text on this page begins the adaptation of _Dragonwings_ as a drama. The Cast of Characters would ordinarily appear at the start of the play, not before Scene 9. **Ask:** What valuable background information does the Cast of Characters provide?

Possible response: It explains who the characters are and clarifies the relationship between Moon Shadow, Miss Whitlaw, and Windrider.

17 ## Conflict

1. Have a student play the role of Moon Shadow, reading aloud the first highlighted passage. Stress that Moon Shadow is reading aloud a letter that he is writing home to his mother. **Ask:** What element of the novel does the device of the letter read aloud help capture?

   Possible response: It captures the novel's first-person narrative by Moon Shadow.

2. **Ask** the Conflict questions.

   Possible response: Moon Shadow and his father have suffered a serious setback in their struggle to fly Dragonwings because they were robbed and have no money for rent. The conflict is external.

18 ## Stage Directions

Have students examine the second highlighted passage. **Ask** the Stage Directions question.

Answer: It means upstage, or the part of the stage farthest from the audience.

Vocabulary Development © CCSS Language 6

 Thematic Vocabulary: The Big Question

As students are discussing the excerpts from _Dragonwings,_ encourage them to use the thematic vocabulary presented in Introducing the Big Question, pp. 720–721. You might use sentence starters such as these:

1. Uncle's opinion of Moon Shadow's <u>appearance</u> is . . .
2. Moon Shadow <u>appreciates</u> Uncle's help because . . .
3. One <u>characteristic</u> shared by Windrider and Moon Shadow is . . .
4. Uncle makes the <u>assumption</u> that Dragonwings will . . .
5. Moon Shadow is surprised by Windrider's <u>reaction</u> to the crash because . . .
6. The reason Windrider's <u>perspective</u> changes after the crash is . . .

⑲ Characters

1. Have a student play the role of Uncle Bright Star to read aloud the first highlighted passage. **Ask:** How does Uncle Bright Star seem to feel about Moon Shadow?

   Possible response: He seems to feel affection for Moon Shadow.

2. **Ask:** From what you learned earlier, why do you think Moon Shadow is thin and ragged?

   Possible response: He has not been eating well because he and his father have lost their money.

3. **Ask** the Characters question.

   Possible response: He thinks the project is doomed but will help because of the affection he feels for Moon Shadow and his father.

⑳ Stage Directions

1. Read aloud the highlighted stage directions. Clarify, if necessary, that *pantomiming* means "making the motions of doing something but not actually doing it."

2. **Ask** the two Stage Directions questions.

   Possible responses: The characters are supposed to be pulling the flying machine up the hill. The audience would see them making the motions of pulling the machine; there is no machine onstage.

㉑ Dialogue

1. Have students attempt to perform in unison the chant beginning on page 731. Clarify that Uncle Bright Star and the others are using a rhythmic work chant just as Uncle did when he worked on building a railroad. Workers, soldiers, and others use similar chants or songs to help them establish a rhythm when they are doing manual labor in groups, marching in groups, and so on.

2. **Ask** the Dialogue questions.

   Possible responses: They create the effect of the group laboring together on a difficult task. It supports the illusion that they are really hauling a flying machine up the hill.

Practice continued

⑲ **Characters** Based on this speech, how does Uncle Bright Star feel about the attempt at flight?

⑳ **Stage Directions** What is supposed to be happening at this point in the drama? What would the audience see, as described in the stage directions?

㉑ **Dialogue** What effect do the call-and-response speeches of Uncle Bright Star and the others create? How does this dialogue support the illusion that is being created onstage?

⑲ **Uncle Bright Star:** And I'll haul that thing back down when it doesn't fly. Red Rabbit and me were getting fat anyway. But look at how tall you've grown. And how thin. And ragged. *[Pause.]* But you haven't broken your neck which was more than I ever expected.

Miss Whitlaw: As soon as I told your uncle, we hatched the plot together. You ought to get a chance to fly your aeroplane.

Uncle Bright Star: Flat purse, strong backs.

Windrider: We need to pull Dragonwings to the very top.

Uncle Bright Star: That hill is a very steep hill.

Windrider: It has to be that one. The winds are right.

Uncle Bright Star: Ah, well, it's the winds.

Windrider: Take the ropes. *[Pantomimes taking a rope over his shoulder as he faces the audience.]* Got a good grip?

⑳ **Others:** *[Pantomiming taking the ropes.]* Yes, right, etc.

Windrider: Then pull.

[They strain. **Moon Shadow** *stumbles but gets right up. Stamping his feet to get better footing, he keeps tugging.]*

Moon Shadow: *[Giving up.]* It's no good.

Uncle Bright Star: Pull in rhythm. As we did on the railroad.[1] *[In demonstration,* **Uncle Bright Star** *stamps his feet in a slow rhythm to set the beat and the others repeat. The rhythm picks up as they move.]*

Ngúng, ngúng.
Dew gùng

Others: Ngúng, ngúng.
Dew gùng

Uncle Bright Star: *[Imitating the intonation of the Cantonese.]* Púsh, púsh.
㉑ Wòrk, wòrk.

Others: Púsh, púsh.
Wòrk, wòrk.

Uncle Bright Star: Seen gà,
Gee gá.

---

1. **railroad** Uncle Bright Star had helped dig tunnels through the mountains for the railroad.

Differentiated Instruction — for Universal Access

Enrichment for Advanced Readers

Have students imagine that they are Moon Shadow experiencing the scenes of greeting Uncle Bright Star and Miss Whitlaw as they arrive, pulling the flying machine up the hill, and watching as his father flies the machine. Ask students to finish the letter that Moon Shadow began writing to his mother on page 730. In their letters, students should put themselves in the place of Moon Shadow and describe in detail all that happens in this scene. Students' letters should describe the arrival of Uncle Bright Star and Miss Whitlaw, ways in which the circumstances have changed, things his father is able to accomplish, and Moon Shadow's feelings about the situation. Allow time for students to write and revise their letters. After students have completed their letters, give them an opportunity to share with the class what they have written.

[*High rising tone on the last syllable.*]

OTHERS: Seen gá,
Gee gá.

[*High rising tone on the last syllable.*]

UNCLE BRIGHT STAR: Get rìch,
Go hóme.

OTHERS: Get rìch,
Go hóme.

[*MOON SHADOW, WINDRIDER, UNCLE BRIGHT STAR and
MISS WHITLAW arrive D.*]

MOON SHADOW: [*Panting.*] We made it. Tramp the grass
down in front.

[*WINDRIDER stands C as the others stamp the grass. They
can't help smiling and laughing a little.*]

WINDRIDER: That's enough.

MOON SHADOW: [To *MISS WHITLAW.*] Take that propeller.

[*MISS WHITLAW takes her place before the right propeller
with her hands resting on the blade. MOON SHADOW takes
his place beside the left propeller. WINDRIDER faces U., his
back to the audience.*]

MISS WHITLAW: Listen to the wind on the wings.

UNCLE BRIGHT STAR: It's alive.

WINDRIDER: All right.

[*MOON SHADOW and MISS WHITLAW pull down at the
propellers and back away quickly. We hear a motor
cough into life. Propellers begin to turn with a roar.*]

UNCLE BRIGHT STAR: [*Slowly turning.*] What's wrong? Is it just
going to roll down the hill?

[*MISS WHITLAW crosses her fingers as they all turn to
watch the aeroplane.*]

MISS WHITLAW: He's up!

[*WINDRIDER starts to do his flight ballet.*]

MOON SHADOW: [*Pointing.*] He's turning.

UNCLE BRIGHT STAR: He's really flying.

Setting What do Moon
Shadow and the others
do to create the illusion
of a grassy hilltop?

Stage Directions
How do the actions
described in the stage
directions add
excitement as the action
builds to a climax?

Literary Analysis Workshop **733**

© CCSS Language 6

22 Setting

1. Have students reread the highlighted lines. **Ask:** What does the
   stage direction about panting
   suggest about Moon Shadow?

   Possible response: It suggests
   that he is doing hard labor.

2. **Ask** the Setting question.

   Possible response: They stamp
   the stage, as if they were flattening the tall grass on the hill.

23 Stage Directions

Ask the Stage Directions question.

Possible response: They indicate
that Moon Shadow and Miss Whitlaw
are setting the flying machine in
motion, building to the climax where
everyone will learn if the flying
machine really can fly.

Vocabulary Development

Word Forms

Expand students' vocabulary by helping them
learn related forms of several words appearing
on pages 732 and 733. Give students a blank
Word Form Chart (*Professional Development
Guidebook,* p. 42) with
stamp, wonderingly, and
addresses in the correct
columns. Work with the
class, or have students
work with a partner, to
determine the related
forms. The final chart

should look like the one shown.

Hold students accountable for integrating
the related forms of the words into their speaking and writing.

Noun	Verb	Adjective	Adverb
stamper	**stamp**	stampable	
wonderer	wonder		**wonderingly**
address, addresser	**addresses**	addressable addressed	

733

24 Plot/Action

1. Have volunteers perform the dialogue in the bracketed section while another student reads the stage directions. **Ask** the Plot/Action question.

   Possible response: They indicate that Windrider should move as if maneuvering the flying machine and that the others move and speak as if they are watching him do it.

2. Point out that even if the play called for something resembling a flying machine to appear onstage, it would still be a special-effects illusion. **Ask:** By calling for an imaginary machine and pantomimed actions and forcing the audience to imagine the machine, what theme or idea might Yep be stressing?

   Possible response: We are all capable of imagining wonderful things.

25 Dialogue

1. Read aloud Moon Shadow's soliloquy. **Ask:** How has the use of a soliloquy like this helped the author turn his novel into a play?

   Possible response: It provides a way of conveying the feelings of the novel's first-person narrator directly to the audience, almost as if he is narrating the play.

2. **Ask** the two Dialogue questions.

   Possible responses: It tells of the temporary success and then crash of Dragonwings and of Windrider's survival and injury; it also reveals Moon Shadow's expectation that his father would not give up flying. He might express admiration and wonder in the first part of the speech, concern and fear as he describes the accident, and finally relief that only the plane was wrecked.

26 Characters

1. Have students reread the last highlighted passage. **Ask:** If you were directing the play, what tone would you tell the actor playing Windrider to use to capture Windrider's feelings here?

   Sample response: I might tell the actor to use an affectionate, yet fearful, tone.

2. **Ask** the Characters question.

   Possible response: He shows that he has learned that his obsession for flying has kept him from knowing his son. He is now choosing to spend time on earth with Moon Shadow, rather than actively pursue his dream of flight.

734

Practice continued

Plot/Action How do the stage directions and dialogue help create the illusion that Windrider and Dragonwings are flying?

Dialogue What important information does this soliloquy reveal about the flight and what happened afterward? What emotions might Moon Shadow experience during this speech?

26 Characters What change and growth does Windrider show in this monologue?

MISS WHITLAW: I never thought I'd see the day. A human up in the sky. Off the ground.

[They turn and tilt their heads back.]

24 MISS WHITLAW: *[Cont'd.]* Free as an eagle.

UNCLE BRIGHT STAR: *[Correcting her.]* Like dragon.

MOON SHADOW: Father, you did it. *[Wonderingly.]* You did it.

[The aeroplane roars loudly overhead. MOON SHADOW as adult steps forward and addresses the audience.]

MOON SHADOW: I thought he'd fly forever and ever. Up, up to heaven and never come down. But then some of the guy wires[2] broke, and the right wings separated. Dragonwings came crashing to earth. Father had a few broken bones, **25** but it was nothing serious. Only the aeroplane was wrecked. Uncle took him back to the laundry to recover. Father didn't say much, just thought a lot—I figured he was busy designing the next aeroplane. But when Father was nearly well, he made me sit down next to him.

WINDRIDER: Uncle says he'll make me a partner if I stay. So the western officials would have to change my immigration class. I'd be a merchant, and merchants can bring their wives here. Would you like to send for Mother?

MOON SHADOW: *[Going to WINDRIDER.]* But Dragonwings?

WINDRIDER: When I was up in the air, I tried to find you. You were so small. And getting smaller. Just disappearing from sight. *[Handing his cap to MOON SHADOW.]* Like you were **26** disappearing from my life. *[He begins his ballet again.]* I knew it wasn't the time. The Dragon King[3] said there would be all sorts of lessons.

[MOON SHADOW turns to audience as an adult.]

MOON SHADOW: We always talked about flying again. Only we never did. *[Putting on cap.]* But dreams stay with you, and we never forgot.

[WINDRIDER takes his final pose. A gong sounds.]

---

2. **guy wires** wires that help to steady the plane's two sets of wings.

3. **Dragon King** In Chinese legends, most dragons are not evil creatures. Earlier in the story, Windrider relates a dream sequence in which he was given his name by the Dragon King and learned he had once been a flying dragon.

734 Drama

Differentiated Instruction   for Universal Access

Strategy for Special-Needs Students
Help students learn how to ask questions to draw meaning from the story. Present them with the following questions: Why do Uncle Bright Star and Miss Whitlaw come to help Windrider and Moon Shadow? What is Windrider able to accomplish because he has help? Lead students to answer these questions and discuss their relevance to the story's main idea.

Strategy for Advanced Readers
Stories have different levels of meaning. The surface meaning of this selection is simply a man's striving to achieve his dream. Deeper meanings come from evaluating the motivations of characters and determining symbols and themes. Have students write short essays about symbols and themes in the story. Ask students to evaluate the characters' motives in the excerpt from *Dragonwings* and think about why Windrider chose not to fly again. Give students time in class to write and revise their essays about the deeper meanings.

After You Read

Dragonwings

1. **Key Ideas and Details (a)** In the novel excerpt, how does Uncle plan to get the flying machine up the hill? **(b) Compare:** In the scene from the drama, what helps the audience grasp how Dragonwings will be moved?

2. **Key Ideas and Details (a) Interpret:** What does Moon Shadow mean at the end of the scene when he says, "dreams stay with you, and we never forgot"? **(b) Analyze:** What **theme** does this statement reveal?

3. **Key Ideas and Details Infer:** Based on the **dialogue,** how would you describe the character of Uncle Bright Star? Give specific examples.

4. **Key Ideas and Details Connect:** What qualities do you see in Moon Shadow that he may not see in himself?

5. **Key Ideas and Details Connect:** What evidence suggests that Moon Shadow does not know Uncle as well as he thinks he does?

6. **Craft and Structure Analyze:** If *Dragonwings* were a three-act play, in which act do you think you would find the excerpt you read? Explain.

7. **Integration of Knowledge and Ideas (a)** In a chart like the one shown, list examples of dialogue under the heading that reveals its use.

To Show Action	To Reveal Thoughts and Feelings	To Describe Setting
"Take that propeller"	"When I was up in the air, I tried to find you . . . Like you were disappearing from my life."	"That hill is a very steep hill."

(b) Collaborate: Compare charts with a partner. How have your ideas changed as a result of seeing other responses?

Literary Analysis Workshop **735**

Answers

1. **Possible response: (a)** He will use Red Rabbit, the horse. **(b)** The actors' pantomime and remarks help the audience grasp what is happening.

2. **Possible response: (a)** Even though he and his father never built another flying machine, they still dreamed about doing it. **(b)** Dreams endure, and so does the bond between parent and child.

3. **Possible response:** He is gruff on the outside but affectionate on the inside. Although he is practical—not a dreamer like Windrider—he has a strong sense of duty and loyalty to those he cares about. Evidence includes lines such as "I came to help you fly your contraption" and "And I'll haul the thing back down when it doesn't fly."

4. **Possible responses:** Faithfulness; Moon Shadow stays with Windrider even when the others believe Dragonwings will never fly. Perseverance; he never gives up the dream of flying.

5. **Possible response:** He is astonished when Uncle Bright Star shows up to help haul the machine up the hill.

6. **Possible response:** It would be in the third act. The conflict is resolved when we learn the outcome of the flight, and the final remarks by Moon Shadow tie up loose ends and are clearly a conclusion.

7. **Possible response: (a)** Col. 1: "We need to pull Dragonwings to the very top." Col. 2: "But you haven't broken your neck which was more than I ever expected." Col. 3: "Tramp the grass down in front." **(b)** Students should explain any changes in their understanding based on the ideas of their partner.

Assessment Resources

The following resources can be used to assess students' knowledge and skills.

Unit 5 Resources

L1 L2 EL **Selection Test A,** pp. 17–19

L3 L4 EL **Selection Test B,** pp. 20–22

L3 L4 **Open Book Test,** pp. 14–16

PHLit Online! Students may use the **Self-test,** online at www.PHLitOnline.com, to prepare for **Selection Test A** or **Selection Test B.**

✓ **A Christmas Carol: Scrooge and Marley, Act I**
Lesson Pacing Guide

DAY 1 Preteach

- Administer the Reading and Vocabulary Warm-ups (*Unit 5 Resources,* pp. 23–26) as necessary.
- Introduce the Reading Skill: Purpose for Reading.
- Introduce the Literary Analysis concept: Dialogue.
- Distribute copies of the appropriate graphic organizer for the Reading Skill (*Graphic Organizer Transparencies,* pp. 147–148).
- Distribute copies of the appropriate graphic organizer for Literary Analysis (*Graphic Organizer Transparencies,* pp. 149–150).
- Teach the selection vocabulary.
- Introduce the Word Study skill.

DAYS 2–3 Preteach/Teach

- Build background with the Background feature.
- Develop thematic vocabulary and thematic thinking with Writing About the Big Question.
- Prepare students to read with the Activating Prior Knowledge activities (TE).
- Informally monitor comprehension while students read.
- Use the Reading Check questions to confirm comprehension.
- Develop students' ability to set and monitor their purpose for reading using the Purpose for Reading questions.
- Develop students' understanding of dialogue using the Dialogue questions.
- Reinforce vocabulary with the Vocabulary notes.
- Reinforce unit focus standards using the Spiral Review prompts.

DAY 4 Assess

- Assess students' comprehension and mastery of the skills by having them answer the Critical Thinking, Reading Skill, and Literary Analysis questions.
- Have students complete the Vocabulary Practice activities.
- Have students complete the Word Study activities.

DAY 5 Extend/Assess

- Have students complete the Conventions lesson.
- Have students complete the Writing activity and write a letter. (You may assign as homework.)
- Extend learning by having students complete the Research and Technology activity, making costume plans. (You may assign as homework.) As an alternative, assign them "How Attitude Helps" and "Happiness: A Two-Way Street" in *Reality Central.*
- Administer Selection Test A or B (*Unit 5 Resources,* pp. 38–40 or 41–43).

Common Core State Standards

Reading Literature 3. Analyze how particular elements of a story or drama interact. *(Literary Analysis: Dialogue)*
5. Analyze how a drama's or poem's form or structure contributes to its meaning. *(Literary Analysis: Dialogue)*

Writing 1. Write arguments to support claims with clear reasons and relevant evidence.
1.a. Introduce claim(s), acknowledge alternate or opposing claims, and organize the reasons and evidence logically.
1.b. Support claim(s) with logical reasoning and relevant evidence, using accurate, credible sources and demonstrating an understanding of the topic or text.
1.c. Use words, phrases, and clauses to create cohesion and clarify the relationships among claim(s), reasons, and evidence.
7. Conduct short research projects to answer a question, drawing on several sources and generating additional related, focused questions for further research and investigation.

Language 1. Demonstrate command of the conventions of standard English grammar and usage when writing or speaking.
2. Demonstrate command of the conventions of standard English capitalization, punctuation, and spelling when writing.
4.b. Use common grade-appropriate Greek or Latin affixes and roots as clues to the meaning of a word.
6. Acquire and use accurately grade-appropriate general academic and domain-specific words and phrases.

Additional Standards Practice
Common Core Companion, *pp. 28–35, 54–61*

Daily Block Scheduling
Each day in this Lesson Pacing Guide represents a 40–50 minute period. Teachers using block scheduling may combine days to revise pacing. In addition, teachers may differentiate and support core instruction by integrating components for extended and intensive support, as students require. See the Guide to Selected Leveled Resources (facing page).

Guide to Selected Leveled Resources

R T I Tier 1 (students performing on level)
A Christmas Carol: Scrooge and Marley, Act I

Warm Up	**Practice, model,** and **monitor** fluency, working with the **whole class** or **in groups**.	**Vocabulary** and **Reading Warm-ups B,** *Unit 5 Resources,* pp. 23–24, 26
Comprehension/Skills	**Support** and **monitor** comprehension and skills development, having students complete the activities, graphic organizers, and interactive prompts **independently** or **as a class**.	• *Reader's Notebook,* adapted instruction and full selection **EL** *Reader's Notebook: English Learner's Version,* adapted instruction and adapted selection • **Reading Skill Graphic Organizer B,** *Graphic Organizer Transparencies,* p. 148 • **Literary Analysis Graphic Organizer B,** *Graphic Organizer Transparencies,* p. 150
Monitor Progress	**A** **Monitor** student progress with the differentiated curriculum-based assessment in the *Unit Resources.*	• **Selection Test B,** *Unit 5 Resources,* pp. 41–43 • **Open-Book Test,** *Unit 5 Resources,* pp. 35–37

R T I Tier 2 (students requiring intervention)
A Christmas Carol: Scrooge and Marley, Act I

Warm Up	**Practice, model,** and **monitor** fluency **in groups** or **with individuals**.	• **Vocabulary and Reading Warm-ups A,** *Unit 5 Resources,* pp. 23–25 • *Reality Central,* "How Attitude Helps" and "Happiness: A Two-Way Street" • *Hear It!* **Audio CD (adapted text)**
Comprehension/Skills	• **Support** and **monitor** comprehension and skills development, working **in small groups** or **with individuals**. • **Pair** students with more advanced peers and have them complete the writing activity in the *Real World Writing Journal.* • As students complete the selection in the appropriate version of the *Reader's Notebook,* **monitor** comprehension frequently with group questions and individual instruction. • **Model** strategies while guiding students in completing the activities and prompts in the *Reader's Notebook,* as well as the graphic organizers. • **Practice** skills and **monitor** mastery with the *Reading Kit* worksheets.	• *Real-World Writing Journal,* Lessons 1–2, pp. 138–145. • *Reader's Notebook: Adapted Version,* adapted instruction and adapted selection **EL** *Reader's Notebook: English Learner's Version,* adapted instruction and adapted selection • **Reading Skill Graphic Organizer A,** *Graphic Organizer Transparencies,* p. 147 • **Literary Analysis Graphic Organizer A,** *Graphic Organizer Transparencies,* p. 149 • *Reading Kit,* Practice worksheets, pp. 200, 204, 210, 212, 218
Monitor Progress	**A** **Monitor** student progress with the differentiated curriculum-based assessment in the *Unit Resources* and in the *Reading Kit.*	• **Selection Test A,** *Unit 5 Resources,* pp. 38–40 • *Reading Kit,* Assess worksheets, pp. 201, 205, 211, 213, 219

TIER 3 Tier 3 intervention may require consultation with the student's special-education or dyslexia specialist. For additional support, see the Tier 2 activities and resources listed above.

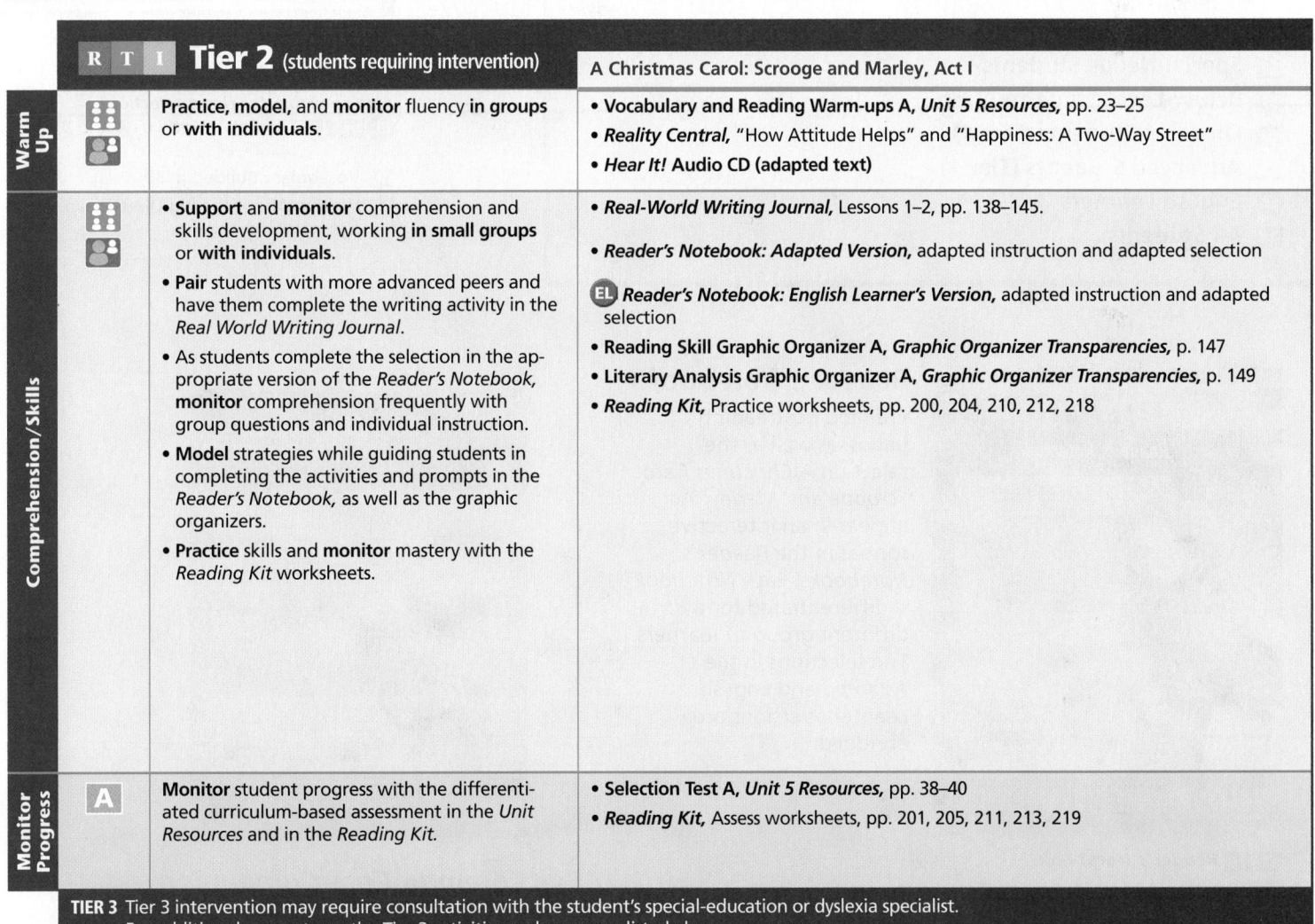

One-on-one teaching   Group work   Whole class instruction   Independent work   A Assessment

For a complete guide to selection support, including support for Advanced students, see the Overview of Resources in the frontmatter.

✓ A Christmas Carol: Scrooge and Marley, Act I

RESOURCES FOR:

- **L1** Special-Needs Students
- **L2** Below-Level Students (Tier 2)
- **L3** On-Level Students (Tier 1)
- **L4** Advanced Students (Tier 1)
- **EL** English Learners
- **All** All Students

Vocabulary/Fluency/Prior Knowledge

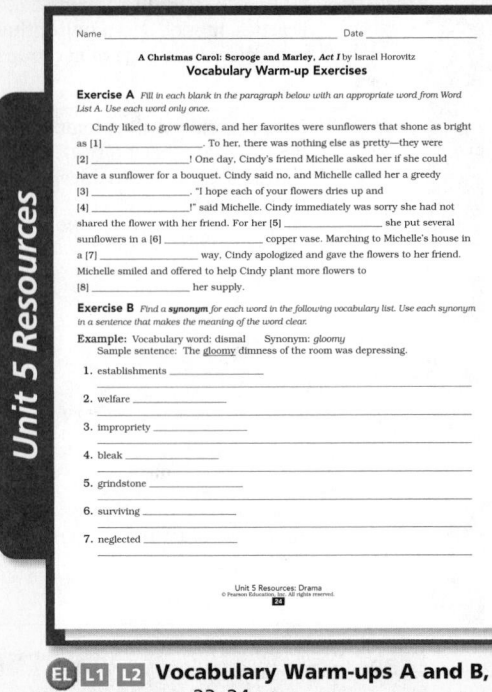

EL L1 L2 Vocabulary Warm-ups A and B, pp. 23–24

Also available for these selections:

EL L1 L2 Reading Warm-ups A and B, pp. 25–26

All Vocabulary Builder, p. 30

All Writing About the Big Question, p. 27

- **L2 L3** *Reader's Notebook*
- **L1** *Reader's Notebook: Adapted Version*
- **EL** *Reader's Notebook: English Learner's Version*
- **EL** *Reader's Notebook: Spanish Version*

Reader's Notebooks

Pre- and postreading pages, as well as the selection A *Christmas* Carol: *Scrooge and Marley,* Act I, appear in an interactive format in the *Reader's Notebooks.* Each *Notebook* is differentiated for a different group of learners. The selections in the Adapted and English Learner's versions are abridged.

© *Common Core Companion*

Additional instruction and practice for each Common Core State Standard

Selection Support

A Christmas Carol: Scrooge and Marley, Act I by Israel Horovitz

Before You Read A: Reading—Setting a Purpose

Element in Work	What Is Suggested About the Work?
Title	Story takes place at Christmas time
Pictures	Story takes place in the nineteenth century
Organization, Structure, Literary Form	drama
Beginnings of passages	Stage directions set the scene.

EL L1 L2 Reading: Graphic Organizer A, p. 147 (partially filled in)

Also available for these selections:

EL L3 Reading: Graphic Organizer B, p. 148

EL L1 L2 Literary Analysis: Graphic Organizer A, p. 149 (partially filled in)

EL L3 Literary Analysis: Graphic Organizer B, p. 150

Skills Development/Extension

A Christmas Carol: Scrooge and Marley, Act I by Israel Horovitz
Enrichment: Social Services

In Act I of *A Christmas Carol: Scrooge and Marley*, two men visit Scrooge's office to collect money for the needy. Scrooge refers to prisons, workhouses, the treadmill, and the Poor Law—all of which were used in nineteenth-century England to deal with people who were poverty-stricken. In the United States, more than 150 years after the events of *A Christmas Carol*, poverty is still a major problem. What do government and private agencies do today to try to help people in need?

A. DIRECTIONS: *Do research in a library, in a telephone directory, or on the Internet to find answers to the following questions.*

1. People whose earnings fall below the poverty line may be eligible to receive food stamps from the federal government. Where is the nearest office of the food-stamp agency in your area?

2. People in need may receive food, clothing, and shelter from organizations such as the Salvation Army. Where is the nearest Salvation Army center in your area? Where is the nearest soup kitchen? Is there another agency in your area that provides food, shelter, and clothing? If so, what is its name, and where is it located?

3. When people lose their home as a result of a fire, the American Red Cross often finds temporary shelter for them. Where is the nearest Red Cross office in your area?

4. Many senior citizens suffer from loneliness because they are unable to get around easily. Where is the nearest center providing services to senior citizens in your area?

5. Groups of people in communities often work together to help relieve the effects of poverty and hunger. Describe a group effort in your community. Who sponsors it? What is its mission?

B. DIRECTIONS: *Think about Ebenezer Scrooge's character in Act I of A Christmas Carol: Scrooge and Marley and his attitude toward people in need. Then, describe how you think Scrooge would react to one of the social services you learned about in doing your research for the first part of this activity. Would Scrooge be surprised by the service? Why or why not?*

L4 Enrichment, p. 31

Also available for these selections:

All Reading: Purpose for Reading, p. 28

All Literary Analysis: Dialogue, p. 29

EL L3 L4 Grammar, p. 32

EL L3 L4 Support for Writing, p. 33

L3 L4 Support for Extend Your Learning, p. 34

Assessment

A Christmas Carol: Scrooge and Marley, Act I by Israel Horovitz
Selection Test B

Critical Reading *Identify the letter of the choice that best completes the statement or answers the question.*

___ 1. In Act I of *A Christmas Carol: Scrooge and Marley*, what purpose might you set for reading as you scan the list of "People in the Play" and see characters with such names as Portly Do-Gooder, The Ghost of Christmas Past, Fezziwig, and A Corpse?
   A. to complete a task
   B. to make a decision
   C. to gain understanding
   D. to be entertained

___ 2. In Act I of *A Christmas Carol: Scrooge and Marley*, what purpose might you set after reading this opening passage, spoken by Scrooge?
   They owe me money and I will collect. I will have them jailed, if I have to.
   A. to be inspired
   B. to gain understanding of a character
   C. to take action or make a decision
   D. to learn about a subject

___ 3. Suppose your purpose for reading Act I of *A Christmas Carol: Scrooge and Marley* is to be entertained. Which elements of the text would contribute to that purpose?
   A. the title
   B. the captions
   C. the photographs
   D. the stage directions

___ 4. What is the purpose of Marley's speech at the beginning of Act I, Scene 1, of *A Christmas Carol: Scrooge and Marley?*
   A. to present himself as the Ghost of Christmas Past
   B. to introduce the character of Scrooge to the audience
   C. to explain why he and Scrooge were once partners
   D. to tell Scrooge what to expect on Christmas Eve

___ 5. Which line of dialogue best describes Scrooge's nephew's ideas about Christmas?
   A. "Christmas a 'humbug.' Uncle? I'm sure you don't mean that."
   B. "[Christmas is] when men and women seem to open their shut-up hearts freely."
   C. "Don't be angry, Uncle. Come! Dine with us tomorrow."
   D. "I'll keep my Christmas humor to the last. So a Merry Christmas, Uncle!"

EL L3 L4 Selection Test B, pp. 41–43

Also available for these selections:

L3 L4 Open-Book Test, pp. 35–37

EL L1 L2 Selection Test A, pp. 38–40

Online Resources: All print materials are also available online.

- complete narrated selection text
- a thematically related video with writing prompt
- an interactive graphic organizer
- highlighting feature
- access to all student print resources, adapted to individual student needs
- Spanish and English summaries
- adapted selection translations in Spanish

Background Video

Also available:

Get Connected! (thematic video with writing prompt)
All videos are available in Spanish.

Vocabulary Central (tools, activities, and songs for studying vocabulary)

Also available:

Writer's Journal (with graphics feature)

❶ Drama Selection

You may use *A Christmas Carol,* Act 1 to meet the lesson objectives. Skills instruction for this selection appears on page 737. Use the Reader and Task Suggestions on the facing page to help all students read text of increasing complexity.

❷ ⓒ Introducing the CCS Standards

Introduce the standards on the student page. (Note that the lesson element with which each standard is addressed is identified in parentheses after the text of the standard.) Call out the standards that you will cover with the selections, explaining to students what each requires and how they will address it as they work through the selection you have chosen. Standards labeled "Spiral Review" are introduced in the Literary Analysis Workshop for this unit.

Before You Read

A Christmas Carol: Scrooge and Marley, Act 1

❶ ⓒ Drama Selection

Build your skills and improve your comprehension of drama with texts of increasing complexity.

Read **A Christmas Carol: Scrooge and Marley, Act 1** to find out what happens when a mean and selfish man is forced to revisit key events from his past.

❷ ⓒ Common Core State Standards

Meet these standards with **A Christmas Carol: Scrooge and Marley, Act 1** (p. 740).

Reading Literature
3. Analyze how particular elements of a story or drama interact. (*Literary Analysis: Dialogue*)
5. Analyze how a drama's or poem's form or structure contributes to its meaning. (*Literary Analysis: Dialogue*)

Writing
1. Write arguments to support claims with clear reasons and relevant evidence. **1.a.** Introduce claim(s), acknowledge alternate or opposing claims, and organize the reasons and evidence logically. **1.b.** Support claim(s) with logical reasoning and relevant evidence, using accurate, credible sources and demonstrating an understanding of the topic or text. **1.c.** Use words, phrases, and clauses to create cohesion and clarify the relationships among claim(s), reasons, and evidence. (*Writing: Letter*)
7. Conduct short research projects to answer a question, drawing on several sources and generating additional

related, focused questions for further research and investigation. (*Research and Technology: Costume Plans*)

Language
1. Demonstrate command of the conventions of standard English grammar and usage when writing or speaking. (*Conventions: Interjections*)
2. Demonstrate command of the conventions of standard English capitalization, punctuation, and spelling when writing. (*Conventions: Interjections*)
4.b. Use common grade-appropriate Greek or Latin affixes and roots as clues to the meaning of a word. (*Vocabulary: Word Study*)
6. Acquire and use accurately grade-appropriate general academic and domain-specific words and phrases; gather vocabulary knowledge when considering a word or phrase important to comprehension or expression. (*Vocabulary: Word Study*)

736 Drama

ⓒ Text Complexity Rubric

A Christmas Carol: Scrooge and Marley, Act 1		
Qualitative Measures	**Context/Knowledge Demands**	Nineteenth-century London 1 2 3 ④ 5
	Structure/Language Conventionality and Clarity	Numerous long sentences with embedded phrases and clauses; challenging vocabulary, some covered in footnotes 1 2 3 ④ 5
	Levels of Meaning/ Purpose/Concept Level	Accessible concept (a miser learns generosity and kindness) 1 2 ③ 4 5
Quantitative Measures	**Text Length**	Word Count: 7,319
	Lexile	NP
Overall Complexity		✓ **Accessible**

Reading Skill: Purpose for Reading

Setting a purpose gives you a focus as you read. You may set one or more of these purposes:

- To learn about a subject
- To be entertained
- To gain understanding
- To take action or make a decision
- To be inspired
- To complete a task

To help you set a purpose, **preview a text before reading.** Look at the title, the pictures, the captions, the organization, and the beginnings of passages to help you determine your reason for reading the text.

Using the Strategy: Previewing Chart

Use a chart like the one shown to jot down details you notice as you preview. Then, use your notes to set your purpose.

Element in Work	What Is Suggested About the Work?
Title	
Pictures	
Organization, Structure, Literary Form	
Beginnings of Passages	

Literary Analysis: Dialogue

Dialogue is a conversation between characters. In a play, dialogue serves several key functions. When the play is viewed as a performance, the characters are developed entirely through dialogue. Their word choices and speech patterns give us clues to their personalities. Dialogue also advances the plot and develops the conflict.

In the script of a dramatic work, you can tell which character is speaking by the name that appears before the character's lines. Look at this example:

Mrs. Perez. Come on, kids! We're leaving.

Jen. Wait for me! *Please* wait for me!

❸ Reading Skill
Purpose for Reading

1. Introduce the skill, using the instruction on the student page.
2. Tell students that they will practice setting a purpose as they read.

❹ Using the Strategy

Give students a copy of either **Reading Skill Graphic Organizer A** or **B** (*Graphic Organizer Transparencies,* pp. 147–148) to preview the text before they read. Use the examples in **Reading Skill Graphic Organizer A**, which is partially filled in, to model the process of completing the organizer.

❺ Literary Analysis
Dialogue

1. Introduce the skill, using the instruction on the student page.
2. Tell students they will practice understanding dialogue as they read.

Think Aloud: Model the Skill

Model a way to understand dialogue. Say to students:

> To help me read and understand dialogue, I use the name labels to tell me which character is speaking. Then, I read the dialogue aloud in that character's voice. For example, look at Scrooge's first line on page 741. I know from his description that he is a mean, grumpy man, so I try to sound like one as I read: "They owe me money and I will collect." Hearing the dialogue helps me get to know the characters.

Text Complexity: Reader and Task Suggestions

A Christmas Carol: Scrooge and Marley, Act I	
Preparing to Read the Text • Use the Background note on TE p. 739 to discuss Victorian society and literature. • Discuss with students why reading a play is a unique experience, pointing out that a play is presented almost entirely as dialogue. • Guide students to use Multidraft Reading strategies (TE p. 739).	**Leveled Tasks** *Structure/Language* If students will have difficulty reading a play, have them first read to identify the various components of a dramatic text. Then, have them reread, taking notes to explain the function of those components. *Analyzing* If students will not have difficulty reading a play, have them note punctuation that would influence how lines are spoken. Then, have them choose some of those lines to read for the class, illustrating how the written text suggests performance choices.

737

❶ Writing About the Big Question

1. Review the assignment with the class.

2. Present to students the situation in which a friend treats another friend badly. Ask students what the first friend might discover in reflecting on his or her actions.

3. Have students complete the sentence starter. Review responses as a class. (**Sample response:** When we <u>reflect</u> on our actions toward others, we can learn how those actions affected others and whether we would want to be treated the same way.)

4. Remind students that their answers will help them think about the Big Question, "Do others see us more clearly than we see ourselves?"

While You Read

Tell students that as they read, they should consider how Scrooge treats other people and how they treat him in return.

❷ Vocabulary

1. Have students preview the selection vocabulary.

2. For each word, have students say the word aloud.

3. Then, use the word in a sentence that defines the word.

4. Finally, repeat your definitional sentence or a similar sentence with the word missing and have the class "fill in the blank" chorally. Here are some examples:

Someone who is <u>morose</u> is gloomy and ill-tempered. My brother is in such a bad mood that I call him [students say "morose"].

Someone who is among the <u>destitute</u> is among the extremely poor. When people lost their homes and money in the Great Depression, they were among the [students say "destitute."]

❸ Word Study

1. Introduce the skill, using the instruction in the box.

2. Ask students to give another -grat- word that means "thankful for." (*grateful*)

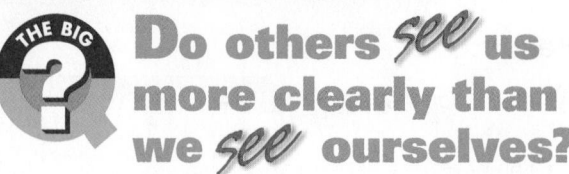

❶ Writing About the Big Question

In Act 1 of *A Christmas Carol*, Ebenezer Scrooge is visited by a ghost who warns him to change his mean, selfish behavior toward others. Use this sentence starter to develop your ideas about the Big Question.

When we **reflect** on our actions toward others, we can learn _____.

While You Read Consider how Scrooge sees himself and how others see him.

❷ Vocabulary

Read each word and its definition. Decide whether you know the word well, know it a little bit, or do not know it at all. After you read, see how your knowledge of each word has increased.

- **implored** (im plôrd´) *v.* begged (p. 742) *His mother <u>implored</u> him to be careful. implore v. imploring v. imploringly adv.*

- **morose** (mə rōs´) *adj.* gloomy; ill-tempered (p. 744) *The movie was so sad, the audience was <u>morose</u> by the end. morosely adv.*

- **destitute** (des´ tə tōōt´) *n.* people living in complete poverty (p. 747) *People donated food to the <u>destitute</u>. destitute adj. destitution n.*

- **void** (void) *n.* emptiness (p. 752) *The hot, dry desert was a lifeless <u>void</u>. void adj. devoid adj.*

- **conveyed** (kən vād´) *v.* made known; expressed (p. 754) *His tightly clenched fists <u>conveyed</u> anger. convey v. conveyable adj. conveyance n.*

- **gratitude** (grat´ i tōōd´) *n.* thankful appreciation (p. 764) *The small gift filled her with <u>gratitude</u>. gratuity n. ingratitude n.*

❸ Word Study

The **Latin root -grat-** means "thankful" or "pleasing."

In this play, Bob Cratchit expresses his **gratitude**, or thankfulness, for a day off from work on Christmas.

738 Drama

Vocabulary Development

Vocabulary Knowledge Rating
Create a **Vocabulary Knowledge Rating Chart** (*Professional Development Guidebook*, p. 33) for this selection. Include the selection vocabulary and the Big Question word that appears in the Writing About the Big Question sentence starter on this page. (The Big Question vocabulary is introduced on pp. 720–721.)

Give students a copy of the chart. Read the words aloud, and have students mark their rating in the Before Reading column. Urge them to be alert to these words as they read and discuss the selection.

Tally how many students think they know a word to gauge how much instruction to provide. As students read and discuss the selection, point out the words and their context.

Meet
Israel Horovitz
(b. 1939)

Author of
A CHRISTMAS CAROL:
SCROOGE AND MARLEY

Israel Horovitz was born in Wakefield, Massachusetts. As a teenager, he did not like books by Charles Dickens. As he got older, however, he came to appreciate Dickens's style and stories. Now, Horovitz refers to Dickens as "a masterful storyteller." He imagines that if Dickens were alive today, the Englishman would be "our greatest television writer, or perhaps screenwriter."

Thoughts About *A Christmas Carol* As Horovitz adapted Dickens's novel into a play, he thought about which character was his favorite. The answer may surprise you: It is Scrooge, who reminds Horovitz of his own father.

DID YOU KNOW?
Horovitz is the author of more than fifty plays and screenplays. He is also an actor.

❹ BACKGROUND FOR THE PLAY
Economic and Social Change

A Christmas Carol is set in England during the nineteenth century, a time of rapid industrial growth. In this booming economy, the wealthy lived in luxury, but the poor and the working class suffered. Charles Dickens's novel, from which this drama was adapted, shows sympathy for the situation of the poor and suggests a way it might be changed.

EBENEZER SCROOGE

A Christmas Carol: Scrooge and Marley, Act I **739**

❹ Background
Economic and Social Change

The Victorian age, a time of tremendous social and economic change in England, refers to the time period in which Queen Victoria reigned (1837-1901). The literature of this period reflects these changes and is often characterized by its humanitarian impulses and moralistic messages. Of all the remarkable Victorian novelists, Charles Dickens (1812-1870) is often considered the greatest because of his ability to bring a variety of characters to life. Dickens is known for his attacks on institutions and his commentary on social evils, which were often presented in a humorous, or at least an entertaining, way.

Multidraft Reading

To assist struggling readers and to deepen reading for all, assign the text in "chunks" and apply multidraft reading protocols. For each reading, have students set the purpose indicated:

- **First reading**—identifying key ideas and details and answering any Reading Checks.
- **Second reading**—analyzing craft and structure and responding to the side-column prompts.
- **Third reading**—integrating knowledge and ideas, connecting to other texts and the world, and answering the end-of-selection questions.

For more guidance, refer to the *Classroom Strategies and Teaching Routines* card on multidraft reading.

739

❶ Activating Prior Knowledge

Explain to students that in Act 1 of *A Christmas Carol,* a man revisits four key episodes from his past and learns something important from each scene he witnesses. Have each student divide a sheet of paper into four panels. Then, ask them to imagine that they are being escorted on a journey to four key scenes from their past. Instruct each student to make a sketch of each scene or summarize it in words. Finally, ask each student to add a sentence for each panel to tell what lesson can be learned from that scene.

Concept Connector ➡

Students will return to this activity after completing Act I.

Whole–Class Activity

Explain to students that tone of voice, inflection, volume, and tempo are several ways to express emotion through the voice. Write the following sentences on the board:

I want to go home.

Can you please help me?

Then have volunteers read each sentence aloud three times, following these guidelines: first, read as if they were desperate; then, read as if they were calm; and finally, read as if they were angry. Lead the class in a discussion about how changing the voice alters the emotional meaning conveyed in a sentence.

❷ About the Selection

In Act 1 of *A Christmas Carol,* we meet the stingy Ebenezer Scrooge on Christmas Eve. Scrooge proclaims the holiday a "humbug." That night, Ebenezer is visited by the ghost of his business partner, Jacob Marley, who warns of the coming of three spirits whose visits can save Scrooge from a terrible fate. As Marley predicts, the first of the spirits arrives to escort Scrooge on a journey to his past. Scrooge's hard heart begins to soften as he sees himself as a lonely young boy and then as a young man at a turning point in his life. At the end of Act I, Ebenezer Scrooge has returned to his bed, where he will soon be visited by a second spirit.

❶ ❷ A CHRISTMAS CAROL:
SCROOGE AND MARLEY

ISRAEL HOROVITZ
from *A CHRISTMAS CAROL*
by CHARLES DICKENS

JACOB MARLEY, a specter
EBENEZER SCROOGE, not yet dead, which is to say still alive
BOB CRATCHIT, Scrooge's clerk
FRED, Scrooge's nephew
THIN DO-GOODER
PORTLY DO-GOODER
SPECTERS (VARIOUS), carrying money-boxes
THE GHOST OF CHRISTMAS PAST
FOUR JOCUND TRAVELERS
A BAND OF SINGERS
A BAND OF DANCERS
LITTLE BOY SCROOGE
YOUNG MAN SCROOGE
FAN, Scrooge's little sister
THE SCHOOLMASTER
SCHOOLMATES
FEZZIWIG, a fine and fair employer
DICK, young Scrooge's co-worker
YOUNG SCROOGE
A FIDDLER
MORE DANCERS
SCROOGE'S LOST LOVE

SCROOGE'S LOST LOVE'S DAUGHTER
SCROOGE'S LOST LOVE'S HUSBAND
THE GHOST OF CHRISTMAS PRESENT
SOME BAKERS
MRS. CRATCHIT, Bob Cratchit's wife
BELINDA CRATCHIT, a daughter
MARTHA CRATCHIT, another daughter
PETER CRATCHIT, a son
TINY TIM CRATCHIT, another son
SCROOGE'S NIECE, Fred's wife
THE GHOST OF CHRISTMAS FUTURE, a mute Phantom
THREE MEN OF BUSINESS
DRUNKS, SCOUNDRELS, WOMEN OF THE STREETS
A CHARWOMAN
MRS. DILBER
JOE, an old second-hand goods dealer
A CORPSE, very like Scrooge
AN INDEBTED FAMILY
ADAM, a young boy
A POULTERER
A GENTLEWOMAN
SOME MORE MEN OF BUSINESS

740 Drama

Think Aloud

Purpose for Reading
You may wish to use the Purpose for Reading question on the student page as an occasion to model the process of setting a purpose for reading. Use the following "think aloud":

To preview this play, I first read the title. "A Christmas Carol" tells me that the story probably takes place during the Christmas season, which is a season of inspiration for many. The description of Ebenezer Scrooge

reads "not yet dead, which is to say still alive." This is an unusual description, which tells me the story may be funny. When I scan the pages, I notice pictures of people dressed in clothing of an earlier time. All of this information helps me choose a purpose—to be entertained and perhaps instructed.

❸ ACT 1

THE PLACE OF THE PLAY Various locations in and around the City of London, including Scrooge's Chambers and Offices; the Cratchit Home; Fred's Home; Scrooge's School; Fezziwig's Offices; Old Joe's Hide-a-Way.

THE TIME OF THE PLAY The entire action of the play takes place on Christmas Eve, Christmas Day, and the morning after Christmas, 1843.

SCENE 1

[*Ghostly music in auditorium. A single spotlight on* JACOB MARLEY, D.C. *He is ancient; awful, dead-eyed. He speaks straight out to auditorium.*]

MARLEY. [*Cackle-voiced*] My name is Jacob Marley and I am dead. [*He laughs.*] Oh, no, there's no doubt that I am dead. The register of my burial was signed by the clergyman, the clerk, the undertaker . . . and by my chief mourner . . . Ebenezer Scrooge . . . [*Pause; remembers*] I am dead as a doornail.

[*A spotlight fades up, Stage Right, on* SCROOGE, *in his countinghouse,[1] counting. Lettering on the window behind* SCROOGE *reads: "SCROOGE AND MARLEY, LTD." The spotlight is tight on* SCROOGE's *head and shoulders. We shall not yet see into the offices and setting. Ghostly music continues, under.* MARLEY *looks across at* SCROOGE; *pitifully. After a moment's pause*] I present him to you: Ebenezer Scrooge . . . England's most tightfisted hand at the grindstone, Scrooge! a squeezing, wrenching, grasping, scraping, clutching, covetous, old sinner! secret, and self-contained, and solitary as an oyster. The cold within him freezes his old features, nips his pointed nose, shrivels his cheek, stiffens his gait; makes his eyes red, his thin lips blue; and speaks out shrewdly in his grating voice. Look at him. Look at him . . .

[SCROOGE *counts and mumbles.*]

SCROOGE. They owe me money and I will collect. I will have

---

1. **countinghouse** office for keeping financial records and writing business letters.

Purpose for Reading
Based on the images, title, and other information you can quickly preview, what is your purpose for reading this play?

❺  Reading Check
Where and when does this drama take place?

A Christmas Carol: Scrooge and Marley, Act 1 **741**

1. Read the first two sentences of Marley's dialogue on page 742 aloud. Point out how the repetition of the word "sole" dramatically creates an image of a man who has no one in his life except his business partner, Scrooge.

2. Then, have students **interpret** the lines that begin with "But Scrooge was not . . ." and end where Marley pauses again in disgust.
   Answer: Scrooge worked on the day of Marley's funeral, and did not actually mourn his death.

3. Have students consider the attitude with which Marley describes his old partner, Scrooge. Then, **ask** students the Dialogue question.
   Possible response: Marley's words suggest that he is very unhappy, sarcastic, and judgmental. He is also very angry with Scrooge, even though Marley was probably just like his old partner at one time.

Dialogue
What do these lines reveal about Marley's character?

❻

Vocabulary
implored (im plôrd´) *v.* begged

them jailed, if I have to. They owe me money and I will collect what is due me.

[MARLEY *moves towards* SCROOGE; *two steps. The spotlight stays with him.*]

MARLEY. [*Disgusted*] He and I were partners for I don't know how many years. Scrooge was my sole executor, my sole administrator, my sole assign, my sole residuary legatee,[2] my sole friend and my sole mourner. But Scrooge was not so cut up by the sad event of my death, but that he was an excellent man of business on the very day of my funeral, and solemnized[3] it with an undoubted bargain. [*Pauses again in disgust*] He never painted out my name from the window. There it stands, on the window and above the warehouse door: Scrooge and Marley. Sometimes people new to our business call him Scrooge and sometimes they call him Marley. He answers to both names. It's all the same to him. And it's cheaper than painting in a new sign, isn't it? [*Pauses; moves closer to* SCROOGE] Nobody has ever stopped him in the street to say, with gladsome looks, "My dear Scrooge, how are you? When will you come to see me?" No beggars implored him to bestow a trifle, no children ever ask him what it is o'clock, no man or woman now, or ever in his life, not once, inquire the way to such and such a place. [MARLEY *stands next to* SCROOGE *now. They share, so it seems, a spotlight.*] But what does Scrooge care of any of this? It is the very thing he likes! To edge his way along the crowded paths of life, warning all human sympathy to keep its distance.

[*A ghostly bell rings in the distance.* MARLEY *moves away from* SCROOGE, *now, heading D. again. As he does, he "takes" the light:* SCROOGE *has disappeared into the black void beyond.* MARLEY *walks D.C., talking directly to the audience. Pauses*]

The bell tolls and I must take my leave. You must stay a while with Scrooge and watch him play out his scroogey

---

2. **my sole executor** (eg zek´ yoo tər), **my sole administrator, my sole assign** (ə sin´), **my sole residuary legatee** (ri zij´ oo er´ ē leg´ ə tē´) legal terms giving one person responsibility to carry out the wishes of another who has died.

3. **solemnized** (säl´ əm nīzd´) *v.* honored or remembered. Marley is being sarcastic.

742 Drama

Vocabulary Development

© **CCSS** Language 6

Thematic Vocabulary: The Big Question
As students are discussing *A Christmas Carol: Scrooge and Marley, Act 1,* encourage them to use the thematic vocabulary presented in Introducing the Big Question, pp. 720–721. You might encourage them with sentence starters like these:

1. It takes Scrooge a while to *identify* . . .

2. As each ghost makes its *appearance*, Scrooge must . . .

3. He wants to *ignore* . . .

4. Still, each ghost forces Scrooge to *focus* on . . .

5. Because of his experience, Scrooge's *perceptions* . . .

life. It is now the story: the once-upon-a-time. Scrooge is busy in his counting house. Where else? Christmas eve and Scrooge is busy in his counting-house. It is cold, bleak, biting weather outside: foggy withal: and, if you listen closely, you can hear the people in the court go wheezing up and down, beating their hands upon their breasts, and stamping their feet upon the pavement stones to warm them . . .

[*The clocks outside strike three.*]

Only three! and quite dark outside already: it has not been light all day this day.

[*This ghostly bell rings in the distance again.* MARLEY *looks about him. Music in.* MARLEY *flies away.*]

SCENE 2

[*N.B.* MARLEY'*s comings and goings should, from time to time, induce the explosion of the odd flash-pot. I.H.*]

[*Christmas music in, sung by a live chorus, full. At conclusion of song, sound fades under and into the distance. Lights up in set: offices of Scrooge and Marley, Ltd.* SCROOGE *sits at his desk, at work. Near him is a tiny fire. His door is open and in his line of vision, we see* SCROOGE'*s clerk,* BOB CRATCHIT, *who sits in a dismal tank of a cubicle, copying letters. Near* CRATCHIT *is a fire so tiny as to barely cast a light: perhaps it is one pitifully glowing coal?* CRATCHIT *rubs his hands together, puts on a white comforter*[4] *and tries to heat his hands around his candle.* SCROOGE'*s* NEPHEW *enters, unseen.*]

SCROOGE. What are you doing, Cratchit? Acting cold, are you? Next, you'll be asking to replenish your coal from my coal-box, won't you? Well, save your breath, Cratchit! Unless you're prepared to find employ elsewhere!

NEPHEW. [*Cheerfully; surprising* SCROOGE] A merry Christmas to you, Uncle! God save you!

SCROOGE. Bah! Humbug![5]

---

4. **comforter** (kum´ fər tər) *n.* long, woolen scarf.
5. **Humbug** (hum´ bug´) *interj.* nonsense.

⑦ ▼ Critical Viewing
How does this portrayal of Scrooge by actor George C. Scott compare with the image you picture as you read? [**Compare and Contrast**]

✓ Reading Check
⑨ What was Marley's relationship to Scrooge?

⑦ Critical Viewing
Answer: The image matches the description of Scrooge as someone who is unkind, bitter, and unfriendly.

⑧ Critical Thinking
Compare and Contrast

1. Explain to students that authors often use comparison and contrast to emphasize the similarities or differences between people, places, things, ideas, and so on.

2. Have students read the bracketed passage. Then, **ask** them to describe the atmosphere outside of Scrooge's offices.
   Answer: The Christmas music makes the atmosphere cheerful and festive.

3. Next, have students identify words and phrases that describe Scrooge's offices.
   Answer: Words and phrases such as *tiny, dismal tank, barely,* and *pitifully glowing coal* describe the offices and Cratchit's work space.

4. **Ask** students to compare and contrast the atmospheres described in the passage and explain why Scrooge's offices seem more dismal than they would if the story took place at any other time of year.
   Answer: It is cold and it is Christmastime both inside and outside; however, the light and cheery atmosphere outside contrasts sharply with the dark, cold, and depressing mood inside.

⑨ Reading Check
Answer: Marley was Scrooge's business partner.

▶ Critical Viewing
Bob Cratchit heats his hands over a candle flame in his office. What does this action tell you about the setting? **[Infer]**

Vocabulary
morose (mə rōs′) *adj.*
gloomy; ill-tempered

NEPHEW. Christmas a "humbug," Uncle? I'm sure you don't mean that.

SCROOGE. I do! Merry Christmas? What right do you have to be merry? What reason have you to be merry? You're poor enough!

NEPHEW. Come, then. What right have you to be dismal? What reason have you to be morose? You're rich enough.

SCROOGE. Bah! Humbug!

NEPHEW. Don't be cross, Uncle.

SCROOGE. What else can I be? Eh? When I live in a world of fools such as this? Merry Christmas? What's Christmas-time to you but a time of paying bills without any money; a time for finding yourself a year older, but not an hour richer. If I could work my will, every idiot who goes about with "Merry Christmas" on his lips, should be boiled with his own pudding, and buried with a stake of holly through his heart. He should!

NEPHEW. Uncle!

SCROOGE. Nephew! You keep Christmas in your own way and let me keep it in mine.

744 Drama

NEPHEW. Keep it! But you don't keep it, Uncle.

SCROOGE. Let me leave it alone, then. Much good it has ever done you!

NEPHEW. There are many things from which I have derived good, by which I have not profited, I daresay. Christmas among the rest. But I am sure that I always thought of Christmas time, when it has come round—as a good time: the only time I know of, when men and women seem to open their shut-up hearts freely, and to think of people below them as if they really were fellow-passengers to the grave, and not another race of creatures bound on other journeys. And therefore, Uncle, though it has never put a scrap of gold or silver in my pocket, I believe that it has done me good, and that it will do me good; and I say, God bless it!

[*The* CLERK *in the tank applauds, looks at the furious* SCROOGE *and pokes out his tiny fire, as if in exchange for the moment of impropriety.* SCROOGE *yells at him.*]

SCROOGE. [*To the clerk*] Let me hear another sound from you and you'll keep your Christmas by losing your situation. [*To the nephew*] You're quite a powerful speaker, sir. I wonder you don't go into Parliament.[6]

NEPHEW. Don't be angry, Uncle. Come! Dine with us tomorrow.

SCROOGE. I'd rather see myself dead than see myself with your family!

NEPHEW. But, why? Why?

SCROOGE. Why did you get married?

NEPHEW. Because I fell in love.

SCROOGE. That, sir, is the only thing that you have said to me in your entire lifetime which is even more ridiculous than "Merry Christmas"! [*Turns from* NEPHEW] Good afternoon.

NEPHEW. Nay, Uncle, you never came to see me before I married either. Why give it as a reason for not coming now?

SCROOGE. Good afternoon, Nephew!

---

6. **Parliament** (pär′ lə mənt) national legislative body of Great Britain, in some ways like the United States Congress.

Dialogue
How does this exchange between Scrooge and his nephew show the contrast between the two characters?

Reading Check
What invitation does Scrooge's nephew offer?

⓬ Dialogue

1. Assign the parts of Scrooge and Nephew in the bracketed passage, which continues onto page 746, to two students. Have them read their parts silently, think about how their characters should sound and act, and then read the dialogue aloud. **Ask** other students to summarize the conversation. **Answer:** Scrooge yells at Cratchit and threatens to fire him. Then he makes a sarcastic comment to his nephew. The nephew invites Scrooge to Christmas dinner, but Scrooge refuses and insults his family. The nephew continues to be friendly but Scrooge asks him to leave.

2. **Ask** students the Dialogue question.
   Answer: The discussion shows that the nephew is kind and forgiving by asking Scrooge to dinner. Scrooge shows that he is rude and thoughtless by making a sarcastic remark suggesting his nephew go into Parliament and by refusing dinner and insulting his nephew's family.

⓭ Reading Check

Answer: Scrooge's nephew invites Scrooge to Christmas dinner.

Differentiated Instruction for Universal Access

EL Support for English Learners

Help students understand some of the difficult words on these pages. Point out the following words:

dismal: gloomy, sad (744)
derived: received, gotten (745)
resolute: determined, decided (746)
trial: act of trying (746)
homage: honor, respect (746)

Work with students to use context clues to determine the meanings of these words and any other words they find difficult.

Enrichment for Advanced Readers

Students might enjoy reading parts of the novella *A Christmas Carol* by Charles Dickens, on which this play is based. Explain that a novella is a short novel. Have each student write an essay discussing the similarities and differences between the original and the adaptation, including whether the adaptation captures the mood of the novella and is true to its characters and action.

745

⓵ Dialogue

1. Before students read the second bracketed passage, tell them to imagine they are in the nephew's place and have just made a kind offer to Scrooge, only to be insulted and rebuffed. Have them consider how they would feel and what they might say to Cratchit as they leave.

2. After they read the bracketed lines, ask students if their imagined response would have been different from the nephew's.

3. **Ask** students the Dialogue question.
   Possible response: Students might say that the nephew is a man of honor and discipline. Even when he is bullied and insulted by his uncle, he remains calm and charitable.

▶ **Monitor Progress** Ask students to describe the nephew's reaction to Scrooge and his words to Cratchit.

▶ **Reteach** If students are having difficulty answering the question, act out the nephew's bracketed lines. Help students to notice that the nephew stops himself before saying something rude to Scrooge. Instead, he wishes Scrooge a merry Christmas.

Dialogue
What can you infer about the nephew's character from his words to Cratchit?

⓬ **NEPHEW.** I want nothing from you; I ask nothing of you; why cannot we be friends?

SCROOGE. Good afternoon!

NEPHEW. I am sorry with all my heart, to find you so resolute. But I have made the trial in homage to Christmas, and I'll keep my Christmas humor to the last. So A Merry Christmas, Uncle!

SCROOGE. Good afternoon!

NEPHEW. And A Happy New Year!

SCROOGE. Good afternoon!

NEPHEW. [*He stands facing* SCROOGE.] Uncle, you are the most . . . [*Pauses*] No, I shan't. My Christmas humor is intact . . . [*Pause*] God bless you, Uncle . . . [NEPHEW *turns and starts for the door; he stops at* CRATCHIT'S *cage.*] Merry Christmas, Bob Cratchit . . .

CRATCHIT. Merry Christmas to you sir, and a very, very happy New Year . . .

⓮ **SCROOGE.** [*Calling across to them*] Oh, fine, a perfection, just fine . . . to see the perfect pair of you: husbands, with wives and children to support . . . my clerk there earning fifteen shillings a week . . . and the perfect pair of you, talking about a Merry Christmas! [*Pauses*] I'll retire to Bedlam![7]

NEPHEW. [*To* CRATCHIT] He's impossible!

CRATCHIT. Oh, mind him not, sir. He's getting on in years, and he's alone. He's noticed your visit. I'll wager your visit has warmed him.

NEPHEW. Him? Uncle Ebenezer Scrooge? Warmed? You are a better Christian than I am, sir.

CRATCHIT. [*Opening the door for* NEPHEW; *two* DO-GOODERS *will enter, as* NEPHEW *exits*] Good day to you, sir, and God bless.

NEPHEW. God bless . . . [*One man who enters is portly, the other is thin. Both are pleasant.*]

CRATCHIT. Can I help you, gentlemen?

---

7. **Bedlam** (bed´ ləm) hospital in London for the mentally ill.

746 Drama

Vocabulary Development
ⓒ **CCSS** Language 6

Word Analysis
Direct students' attention to the word *intact* in the third line of the bracketed passage on p. 746. Tell students that they can determine the meaning of this word and others like it by analyzing its parts. Explain that the prefix *in-* means "not." Students may recognize this meaning in words such as *invisible* and *inactive*. The second syllable of the word is the Latin root *-tact-* meaning "touch," as in *contact*. Ask students to suggest a meaning for *intact*. Then, read the definition: untouched, especially by something that may do harm; unimpaired. Guide students to see that the nephew has kept his good spirits intact in spite of Scrooge's harmful words.

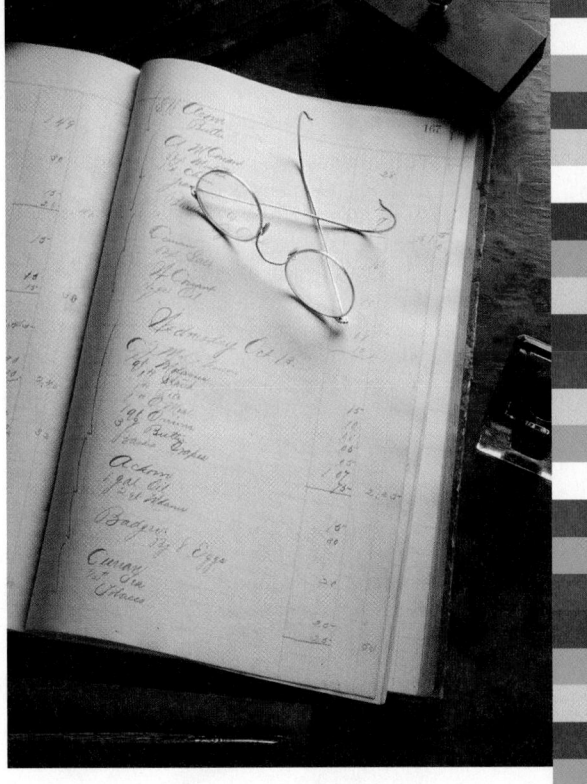

THIN MAN. [*Carrying papers and books; looks around* CRATCHIT *to* SCROOGE] Scrooge and Marley's, I believe. Have I the pleasure of addressing Mr. Scrooge, or Mr. Marley?

SCROOGE. Mr. Marley has been dead these seven years. He died seven years ago this very night.

PORTLY MAN. We have no doubt his liberality[8] is well represented by his surviving partner . . . [*Offers his calling card*]

SCROOGE. [*Handing back the card; unlooked at*] . . . Good afternoon.

THIN MAN. This will take but a moment, sir . . .

PORTLY MAN. At this festive season of the year, Mr. Scrooge, it is more than usually desirable that we should make some slight provision for the poor and destitute who suffer greatly at the present time. Many thousands are in want of common necessities; hundreds of thousands are in want of common comforts, sir.

SCROOGE. Are there no prisons?

PORTLY MAN. Plenty of prisons.

SCROOGE. And aren't the Union workhouses still in operation?

THIN MAN. They are. Still. I wish that I could say that they are not.

SCROOGE. The Treadmill[9] and the Poor Law[10] are in full vigor, then?

THIN MAN. Both very busy, sir.

SCROOGE. Ohhh, I see. I was afraid, from what you said at

Vocabulary
destitute (des´ tə tōōt´)
n. people living in complete poverty

 Reading Check
16
Who do the thin man and the portly man want to help?

8. **liberality** (lib´ ər al´ i tē) generosity.
9. **the Treadmill** (tred´ mil´) kind of mill wheel turned by the weight of people treading steps arranged around it; this device was used to punish prisoners.
10. **the Poor Law** the original 16th-century Poor Laws called for overseers of the poor in each neighborhood to provide relief for the needy. The New Poor Law of 1834 made the workhouses in which the poor sometimes lived and worked extremely hard and unattractive.

A Christmas Carol: Scrooge and Marley, Act 1 **747**

15 Critical Thinking
Speculate

1. Read aloud and clarify the footnotes on page 747, explaining that poor people and prisoners were used as workers.

2. **Ask** students how Scrooge replies to the request for charity.
   Answer: He asks if the Treadmill and the Poor Laws are still in force.

3. Have students **interpret** Scrooge's remark.
   Possible response: Scrooge believes that these institutions provide for the poor.

4. Challenge students to **speculate** on Scrooge's likely reaction to the request for charity, and to explain their thinking.
   Possible response: He will refuse the request because he thinks that the poor should work for any help they receive.

16 Reading Check

Answer: The men want Scrooge to make a donation for the poor.

Fluency

Distribute copies of pages 746–747, and pair students. Have listeners mark text with which their reading partners struggle. Circulate to monitor students' fluency, then collect the marked up pages. Review difficult words and passages, such as these:

• If students struggle to transition between stage directions and dialogue, point out the changes in typeface that cue readers to the different types of text. Model how to change the tone of your voice as you move through each type of text.

• If students stumble over the ellipses, point out that these marks indicate interrupted or incomplete dialogue. Have fluent readers model how to reflect the slight hesitation that the ellipses indicate.

• Point out that in dialogue, characters often speak in incomplete sentences. If students have difficulty reading such text fluently, help them complete the sentences for full comprehension, then reread the text as written.

Social Studies Connection In England in 1601, church communities, which were known as parishes, were given the responsibility of caring for the poor. One way they did this was to build workhouses to employ the able-bodied. Over time, these workhouses became places that drew all ages and types of people, including criminals, the infirm, and the insane. As in jails, authorities had the power to decide when to release inhabitants to work and when to forbid them to do so.

The Poor Law Amendment of 1834 disqualified the healthy who lived in their own homes from receiving public assistance, and required anyone seeking relief to live in the workhouses in harsh and degrading conditions. The changes were intended not to alleviate poverty but to discourage the needy from seeking parish relief.

Connect to the Literature

1. Have students read the Literature in Context feature, and present the additional background above. Then, **ask** students to identify lines that reveal how Scrooge feels about the poor.
   Answer: " . . . they cost enough: and those who are badly off must go there." and "If they would rather die, they had better do it, and decrease the surplus population."

2. **Ask** students the Connect to the Literature question.
   Answer: Scrooge has no compassion for the poor and seems to feel that the workhouses are adequate for them since they are a "surplus population" who do not contribute anything meaningful to society.

Social Studies Connection

Union Workhouses

In Victorian England, many people who were poverty-stricken, orphaned, old, or sick lived in workhouses. On a typical day, workers woke at 5 A.M. and spent ten hours doing physical labor, such as crushing stones, sewing, cleaning, and milling corn. Bedtime was 8 P.M. There was not enough food to eat. Typically, breakfast was a piece of bread; dinner was a piece of bacon and a piece of bread or a potato; supper was a piece of bread and a piece of cheese.

Connect to the Literature

Why does Scrooge think the workhouses are adequate?

---

first, that something had occurred to stop them from their useful course. [*Pauses*] I'm glad to hear it.

PORTLY MAN. Under the impression that they scarcely furnish Christian cheer of mind or body to the multitude, a few of us are endeavoring to raise a fund to buy the Poor some meat and drink, and means of warmth. We choose this time, because it is a time, of all others, when Want is keenly felt, and Abundance rejoices. [*Pen in hand; as well as notepad*] What shall I put you down for, sir?

SCROOGE. Nothing!

PORTLY MAN. You wish to be left anonymous?

SCROOGE. I wish to be left alone! [*Pauses; turns away; turns back to them*] Since you ask me what I wish, gentlemen, that is my answer. I help to support the establishments that I have mentioned: they cost enough: and those who are badly off must go there.

THIN MAN. Many can't go there; and many would rather die.

SCROOGE. If they would rather die, they had better do it, and decrease the surplus population. Besides— excuse me—I don't know that.

THIN MAN. But you might know it!

SCROOGE. It's not my business. It's enough for a man to understand his own business, and not to interfere with other people's. Mine occupies me constantly. Good afternoon, gentlemen!
[SCROOGE *turns his back on the gentlemen and returns to his desk.*]

PORTLY MAN. But, sir, Mr. Scrooge . . . think of the poor.

SCROOGE. [*Turns suddenly to them. Pauses*] Take your leave of my offices, sirs, while I am still smiling.

[*The* THIN MAN *looks at the* PORTLY MAN. *They are undone. They shrug. They move to the door.* CRATCHIT *hops up to open it for them.*]

Vocabulary Development   ⓒ CCSS Language 6

Selection Vocabulary Reinforcement

To reinforce and assess students' comprehension of selection vocabulary words, give them sentences using the words in which the word may or may not be used correctly. Students must tell whether the use is correct and explain their answer. Use these sentences:

1. David *implored* a new flower bed.
   Answer: No, people dig and plant flower beds. They don't beg them.
2. Since losing the championship game, he has looked *morose* and spoken very little.

Answer: Yes, someone who has lost an important game might feel gloomy.
3. We should find shelter, food, and clothes for these people and not leave them *destitute*.
   Answer: Yes, those without shelter, food, or clothes may be considered destitute.
4. I want to express my sincere *gratitude* for your help.
   Answer: Yes, *gratitude* is an appropriate response to receiving help.

THIN MAN. Good day, sir . . . [*To* CRATCHIT] A merry Christmas to you, sir . . .

CRATCHIT. Yes. A Merry Christmas to both of you . . .

PORTLY MAN. Merry Christmas . . .

[CRATCHIT *silently squeezes something into the hand of the* THIN MAN.]

THIN MAN. What's this?

CRATCHIT. Shhhh . . .

[CRATCHIT *opens the door; wind and snow whistle into the room.*]

THIN MAN. Thank you, sir, thank you.

[CRATCHIT *closes the door and returns to his workplace.* SCROOGE *is at his own counting table. He talks to* CRATCHIT *without looking up.*]

SCROOGE. It's less of a time of year for being merry, and more a time of year for being loony . . . if you ask me.

CRATCHIT. Well, I don't know, sir . . . [*The clock's bell strikes six o'clock.*] Well, there it is, eh, six?

SCROOGE. Saved by six bells, are you?

CRATCHIT. I must be going home . . . [*He snuffs out his candle and puts on his hat.*] I hope you have a . . . very very lovely day tomorrow, sir . . .

SCROOGE. Hmmm. Oh, you'll be wanting the whole day tomorrow, I suppose?

CRATCHIT. If quite convenient, sir.

SCROOGE. It's not convenient, and it's not fair. If I was to stop half-a-crown for it, you'd think yourself ill-used, I'll be bound?

[CRATCHIT *smiles faintly.*]

CRATCHIT. I don't know, sir . . .

SCROOGE. And yet, you don't think me ill-used when I pay a day's wages for no work . . .

18

▼ **Critical Viewing**
Compare this actor's portrayal of Cratchit with the one on page 744. Which looks more like your idea of Cratchit? Explain. **[Compare and Contrast]**

19 ✓ Reading Check

How does Scrooge feel about Christmas?

A Christmas Carol: Scrooge and Marley, Act 1 **749**

749

Connecting to the Big Question

1. Tell students to imagine that one friend is excited about an upcoming school trip and the other is dreading the trip. Then ask students why it might be hard for each friend to understand the other's point of view.

2. Have students read the bracketed text on pages 749–750. **Ask** students: How does Scrooge treat Cratchit as Christmas approaches? How does Cratchit treat Scrooge?
Possible response: Cratchit treats Scrooge with courtesy and respect while trying to share his warm feelings about Christmas. Scrooge treats Cratchit grumpily and rudely as he refuses to consider any happiness related to Christmas.

3. **Ask:** Do you think that Cratchit sees Scrooge clearly? Explain.
Possible response: No, he thinks that he can talk Scrooge into being more positive. If he saw Scrooge clearly, he wouldn't keep trying to wish him a merry Christmas.

21 **Critical Viewing**

Answer: The actor playing Cratchit seems frightened and might speak in a small, timid voice to convey his fear of Scrooge. The actor playing Scrooge looks angry and is likely to use a loud, sharp tone to convey his displeasure with Cratchit.

21 ▶ **Critical Viewing**
Describe the tone of voice that each actor might use to play the scene pictured here. **[Speculate]**

CRATCHIT. It's only but once a year . . .

SCROOGE. A poor excuse for picking a man's pocket every 25th of December! But I suppose you must have the whole day. Be here all the earlier the next morning!

CRATCHIT. Oh, I will, sir. I will. I promise you. And, sir . . .

SCROOGE. Don't say it, Cratchit.

CRATCHIT. But let me wish you a . . .

SCROOGE. Don't say it, Cratchit. I warn you . . .

CRATCHIT. Sir!

SCROOGE. Cratchit!

[CRATCHIT *opens the door.*]

CRATCHIT. All right, then, sir . . . well . . . [*Suddenly*] Merry Christmas, Mr. Scrooge!

[*And he runs out the door, shutting same behind him.* SCROOGE *moves to his desk; gathering his coat, hat, etc. A* BOY *appears at his window. . . .*]

BOY. [*Singing*] "Away in a manger . . ."

[SCROOGE *seizes his ruler and whacks at the image of the* BOY *outside. The* BOY *leaves.*]

SCROOGE. Bah! Humbug! Christmas! Bah! Humbug! [*He shuts out the light.*]

A note on the crossover, following Scene 2:

[SCROOGE *will walk alone to his rooms from his offices. As he makes a long slow cross of the stage, the scenery should change. Christmas music will be heard, various people will cross by* SCROOGE, *often smiling happily.*]

There will be occasional pleasant greetings tossed at him.

SCROOGE, *in contrast to all, will grump and mumble. He will snap at passing boys, as might a horrid old hound.*

In short, SCROOGE'S *sounds and movements will define him in contrast from all other people who cross the stage: he is the misanthrope,[11] the malcontent, the miser. He is* SCROOGE.

11. **misanthrope** (mis´ ən thrōp´) *n.* person who hates or distrusts everyone.

750 Drama

Vocabulary Development

© CCSS Language 6

Word Forms

Expand students' vocabulary by helping them learn related forms of the selection vocabulary words. Four of the words have related forms. Give students a blank **Word Form Chart** (*Professional Development Guidebook,* p. 42), with *implored, morose, destitute,* and *conveyed* in

the correct columns. Work with the class to determine the related forms. The final chart should look like the one shown.

Noun	Verb	Adjective	Adverb
	implore, implored		imploringly
moroseness		morose	morosely
destitution		destitute	
conveyance or conveyor	convey, conveyed		

750

This statement of SCROOGE'S *character, by contrast to all other characters, should seem comical to the audience.*

During SCROOGE'S *crossover to his rooms, snow should begin to fall. All passers-by will hold their faces to the sky, smiling, allowing snow to shower them lightly.* SCROOGE, *by contrast, will bat at the flakes with his walking-stick, as might an insomniac swat at a sleep-stopping, middle-of-the-night swarm of mosquitoes. He will comment on the blackness of the night, and, finally, reach his rooms and his encounter with the magical specter:[12]* MARLEY, *his eternal mate.]*

---

12. **specter** (spek´ tər) *n.* ghost.

Dialogue
What do you learn about Scrooge through his words as he shuts out the light and through the description of him as he walks home?

 **Reading Check**
Why is Cratchit taking a day off?

A Christmas Carol: Scrooge and Marley, Act 1 **751**

1. After students read the bracketed passage, which begins at the bottom of page 750, have them summarize the scene.
   Answer: Scrooge leaves his office and walks alone to his home, grumbling and snapping at other people along the way.

2. Point out that the passage is intended to contrast Scrooge's mood with his surroundings in order to make his personality stand out. Ask students to identify details that show this contrast.
   Answer: Scrooge's words "Bah! Humbug!" and grumbling contrast with the pleasant greetings of others. He also walks alone while others are gathered in groups.

3. **Ask** students the Dialogue question.
   Answer: Scrooge is alone and speaks to no one except to grumble or snap, suggesting that he not only loathes the Christmas season but is also mean, miserable, and possibly lonely.

23 Critical Thinking

Infer

1. Ask students to imagine they know Scrooge and consider how they would describe him to others.
   Possible responses: Students might say Scrooge is mean, grouchy, or hateful and that they either dislike or feel sorry for him.

2. Read the bracketed passage which begins on page 751, aloud. Ask students to paraphrase it to explain its meaning.
   Possible response: The description shows Scrooge to be so different from the other people that he seems funny to the audience.

3. Point out that the actions and dialogue in the drama are the author's way of describing Scrooge. **Ask** students why the author might want Scrooge to appear comical.
   Possible responses: The play might not be fun to watch if Scrooge was taken seriously. The author might want to entertain the audience by making fun of someone who is unlikeable.

24 Reading Check

Answer: Cratchit is taking a day off because it is Christmas.

Differentiated Instruction for Universal Access

Culturally Responsive Instruction:
Culture Focus Students may lack the background knowledge or context-building experiences necessary to fully comprehend the selection. At this point in the students' reading, build additional background about the Christmas season in which the play is set. Point out the many references to Christmas traditions such as caroling, saying "Merry Christmas," and inviting friends and family to special holiday meals. Discuss and provide images or descriptions of Christmas traditions with which students may not be familiar, such as gift giving (including charitable donations), decorating a tree, and making a special effort to be kind to others. Many cultures do not celebrate Christmas, but almost all have special occasions or seasons that feature some of the traditions discussed. Invite students to share their knowledge and experience of holiday occasions and cultural traditions in their home culture or family's country of origin.

1. Have students use **Graphic Organizer B** (*Graphic Organizer Transparencies,* p. 148) to preview Scene 3.

2. Point out that an important part of a play's structure is the way the dialogue is arranged. **Ask** students how this structure can suggest what will happen in this scene.
   Answer: The names make it easy to see quickly which characters play important roles in the scene.

3. **Ask** students to speculate about the situation shown in the photograph on p. 755.
   Possible responses: Students might suggest that the person standing is Marley's ghost and the one kneeling is Scrooge. They might speculate that Scrooge is begging Marley for mercy.

4. After previewing the scene, have students share their ideas.
   Possible responses: Students may note that Marley will talk to Scrooge, that Scrooge seems upset, and that Marley is dead, so his ghost might be issuing some type of warning to Scrooge.

5. **Ask** students the Purpose for Reading question.
   Possible response: To find out what will happen to Scrooge, the reader could find out who speaks with Scrooge, study the picture, and skim the dialogue and action.

Vocabulary
void (void) *n.* emptiness

Purpose for Reading
Preview Scene 3. If your purpose were to find out what happens next to Scrooge, what details would you look for in the scene?

---

25 SCENE 3

SCROOGE. No light at all . . . no moon . . . that is what is at the center of a Christmas Eve: dead black: void . . .

[SCROOGE *puts his key in the door's keyhole. He has reached his rooms now. The door knocker changes and is now* MARLEY'S *face. A musical sound; quickly: ghostly.* MARLEY'S *image is not at all angry, but looks at* SCROOGE *as did the old* MARLEY *look at* SCROOGE. *The hair is curiously stirred; eyes wide open, dead: absent of focus.* SCROOGE *stares wordlessly here. The face, before his very eyes, does deliquesce.[13] It is a knocker again.* SCROOGE *opens the door and checks the back of same, probably for* MARLEY'S *pigtail. Seeing nothing but screws and nuts,* SCROOGE *refuses the memory.*]

Pooh, pooh!

[*The sound of the door closing resounds throughout the house as thunder. Every room echoes the sound.* SCROOGE *fastens the door and walks across the hall to the stairs, trimming his candle as he goes; and then he goes slowly up the staircase. He checks each room: sitting room, bedrooms, slumber room. He looks under the sofa, under the table: nobody there. He fixes his evening gruel on the hob,[14] changes his jacket.* SCROOGE *sits near the tiny low-flamed fire, sipping his gruel. There are various pictures on the walls: all of them now show likenesses of* MARLEY. SCROOGE *blinks his eyes.*]

Bah! Humbug!

[SCROOGE *walks in a circle about the room. The pictures change back into their natural images. He sits down at the table in front of the fire. A bell hangs overhead. It begins to ring, of its own accord. Slowly, surely, begins the ringing of every bell in the house. They continue ringing for nearly half a minute.* SCROOGE *is stunned by the phenomenon. The bells cease their ringing all at once. Deep below* SCROOGE, *in the basement of the house, there is the sound of clanking, of some enormous chain being dragged across the floors; and now up the stairs. We hear doors flying open.*]

---

13. **deliquesce** (del´ i kwes´) *v.* melt away.
14. **gruel** (groo´ əl) **on the hob** (häb) thin broth warming on a ledge at the back or side of the fireplace.

752 Drama

Think Aloud

Author's Purpose
Direct students' attention to the stage directions and dialogue at the bottom of page 752 and the top of page 753. Use the following "think aloud" to model the process of identifying the author's purpose (introduced on page 99). Say to students:

I know that *stage directions* and *dialogue* are the main tools that a playwright uses to achieve a purpose. So, I will look at the details the author includes to determine what he is trying to do. Details in the stage directions, such as the pictures changing, the bells ringing, the clanking of a chain, the doors flying open, and the appearance of a ghost, all seem to contribute toward a suspenseful, scary mood. Scrooge's lines of dialogue seem to indicate his disbelief in what he is seeing and hearing. I think the author's purpose here is to create a mood so scary that even Scrooge, who is normally very rational and difficult to impress, will begin to doubt his senses.

Bah still! Humbug still! This is not happening! I won't believe it!

[MARLEY'S GHOST *enters the room. He is horrible to look at: pigtail, vest, suit as usual, but he drags an enormous chain now, to which is fastened cash-boxes, keys, padlocks, ledgers, deeds, and heavy purses fashioned of steel. He is transparent.* MARLEY *stands opposite the stricken* SCROOGE.]

How now! What do you want of me?

MARLEY. Much!

SCROOGE. Who are you?

MARLEY. Ask me who I was.

SCROOGE. Who were you then?

MARLEY. In life, I was your business partner: Jacob Marley.

SCROOGE. I see . . . can you sit down?

MARLEY. I can.

SCROOGE. Do it then.

MARLEY. I shall. [MARLEY *sits opposite* SCROOGE, *in the chair across the table, at the front of the fireplace.*] You don't believe in me.

SCROOGE. I don't.

MARLEY. Why do you doubt your senses?

SCROOGE. Because every little thing affects them. A slight disorder of the stomach makes them cheat. You may be an undigested bit of beef, a blot of mustard, a crumb of cheese, a fragment of an underdone potato. There's more of gravy than of grave about you, whatever you are!

[*There is a silence between them.* SCROOGE *is made nervous by it. He picks up a toothpick.*]

Humbug! I tell you: humbug!

[MARLEY *opens his mouth and screams a ghosty, fearful scream. The scream echoes about each room of the house. Bats fly, cats screech, lightning flashes.* SCROOGE *stands and walks backwards against the wall.* MARLEY *stands and screams again. This time, he takes his head and lifts it*

Dialogue
Based on this dialogue, what is Scrooge's attitude toward Marley's Ghost?

27 **Reading Check**
What does Scrooge see in the door knocker?

A Christmas Carol: Scrooge and Marley, Act 1 **753**

---

26 **Dialogue**

1. Have students summarize what they know about Scrooge and explain whether they think he is a spiritual person or believes in life beyond the grave.
   Possible response: Since Scrooge thinks only about money and does not care about others' feelings or needs, he probably doesn't think about or have an interest in spiritual affairs.

2. Then, **ask** them to speculate about how Scrooge will react to a visit from a ghost.
   Possible response: Scrooge will probably deny the ghost exists, think it is a trick, or will treat the ghost as badly as he does everyone else.

3. Have students read the bracketed passage, and then **ask** them the Dialogue question.
   Answer: Though he acknowledges Marley's presence and appears to be somewhat frightened of him, Scrooge's attitude is one of disbelief or a refusal to believe.

4. **Ask** students how Scrooge's reaction to Marley is consistent with his character.
   Answer: Since Scrooge thinks only of money and values it above all else, it makes sense that he would not believe in something as far removed from worldly possessions as a ghost.

27 **Reading Check**

Answer: He sees Marley's face in the door knocker.

Differentiated Instruction for Universal Access

Strategy for Less Proficient Readers
Check students' comprehension of this scene and its significance by asking the following questions: 1. What is Marley dragging? (cashboxes, keys, padlocks, ledgers, deeds, and heavy purses made of steel) 2. How are those objects related to Scrooge's life? (They are the items he uses in his business.) 3. What reason does Scrooge give for not believing in Marley's ghost? (He says that his visions are probably the result of stomach problems.) Discuss each answer with the students while encouraging them to speculate about the significance of the items.

1. Marley used these heavy items during life to earn money and now they weight his spirit in death. 2. The items symbolize what is most important to Scrooge. 3. Scrooge may not want to believe that there are such things as ghosts or punishment after death for one's deeds in life. Hold a brief question-and-answer session as a class, encouraging students to answer each other's questions.

1. After students read the bracketed lines beginning "I do. I must," tell them that something significant has happened: Scrooge has acknowledged the existence of Marley's ghost. Now he wants to know why the ghost has come to him. **Ask** students what they think Marley will say.
Possible response: Marley will explain the reason for his visit to Scrooge.

2. Point out that up until now, the drama has provided background information about Scrooge. This question sets up the conflict that will begin to drive the plot. Then, **ask** the Purpose for Reading question.
Possible response: Scrooge's question makes the reader want to learn the answer, and although the reader is still being entertained, the purpose at this point might be to learn what will happen next.

29 Critical Thinking

Interpret

1. Read aloud the bracketed passage that begins "It is required." Then, **ask** students what Marley means by saying, "I wear the chain I forged in life. I made it link by link, and yard by yard."
Answer: Marley's spirit is bound by a chain that represents his misdeeds in life—his obsession with making money, his mistreatment of others, and his lack of compassion.

2. Ask students to interpret the meaning of the following: "Or would you know, you, Scrooge, the weight and length of the strong coil you bear yourself? It was full as heavy and long as this, seven Christmas Eves ago. You have labored on it, since."
Possible response: Scrooge has lived as Marley did, only he's been doing it for seven additional years so the chain he is forging is even longer and heavier.

3. Then, **ask** students why they think Scrooge is so frightened of the chains.
Possible response: Students might suggest that Scrooge thinks that he too will end up wearing heavy chains like Marley's ghost.

754

---

from his shoulders. His head continues to scream. MARLEY'S *face again appears on every picture in the room: all screaming.* SCROOGE, *on his knees before* MARLEY.]

Mercy! Dreadful apparition,[15] mercy! Why, O! why do you trouble me so?

MARLEY. Man of the worldly mind, do you believe in me, or not?

SCROOGE. I do. I must. But why do spirits such as you walk the earth? And why do they come to me?

MARLEY. It is required of every man that the spirit within him should walk abroad among his fellow-men, and travel far and wide; and if that spirit goes not forth in life, it is condemned to do so after death. [MARLEY *screams again; a tragic scream; from his ghosty bones.*] I wear the chain I forged in life. I made it link by link, and yard by yard. Is its pattern strange to you? Or would you know, you, Scrooge, the weight and length of the strong coil you bear yourself? It was full as heavy and long as this, seven Christmas Eves ago. You have labored on it, since. It is a ponderous chain.

[*Terrified that a chain will appear about his body,* SCROOGE *spins and waves the unwanted chain away. None, of course, appears. Sees* MARLEY *watching him dance about the room.* MARLEY *watches* SCROOGE; *silently.*]

SCROOGE. Jacob. Old Jacob Marley, tell me more. Speak comfort to me, Jacob . . .

MARLEY. I have none to give. Comfort comes from other regions, Ebenezer Scrooge, and is conveyed by other ministers, to other kinds of men. A very little more, is all that is permitted to me. I cannot rest, I cannot stay, I cannot linger anywhere . . . [*He moans again.*] my spirit never walked beyond our countinghouse—mark me!—in life my spirit never roved beyond the narrow limits of our moneychanging hole; and weary journeys lie before me!

SCROOGE. But you were always a good man of business, Jacob.

MARLEY. [*Screams word "business"; a flash-pot explodes with him.*] BUSINESS!!! Mankind was my business. The

---

15. **apparition** (ap′ ə rish′ ən) *n.* ghost.

754 Drama

28
Purpose for Reading
What purpose for reading might Scrooge's question suggest to readers?

29

Vocabulary
conveyed (kən vād′) *v.* made known; expressed

30

Vocabulary Development   © **CCSS** Language 6

Expressive Vocabulary
To help students discuss Marley's plight and to broaden their expressive vocabulary, encourage them to use the following words as they discuss the selection: *acquire, involve,* and *attitude.*
Have them complete these sentence starters:

1. In life Marley worked to *acquire* . . .
2. In life Marley did not *involve* himself in . . .
3. In death, Marley has a new *attitude* about . . .

common welfare was my business; charity, mercy, forbearance, benevolence, were, all, my business. [SCROOGE *is quaking.*] Hear me, Ebenezer Scrooge! My time is nearly gone.

SCROOGE. I will, but don't be hard upon me. And don't be flowery, Jacob! Pray!

MARLEY. How is it that I appear before you in a shape that you can see, I may not tell. I have sat invisible beside you many and many a day. That is no light part of my penance. I am here tonight to warn you that you have yet a chance and hope of escaping my fate. A chance and hope of my procuring, Ebenezer.

SCROOGE. You were always a good friend to me. Thank'ee!

MARLEY. You will be haunted by Three Spirits.

SCROOGE. Would that be the chance and hope you mentioned, Jacob?

MARLEY. It is.

SCROOGE. I think I'd rather not.

MARLEY. Without their visits, you cannot hope to shun the path I tread. Expect the first one tomorrow, when the bell tolls one.

SCROOGE. Couldn't I take 'em all at once, and get it over, Jacob?

MARLEY. Expect the second on the next night at the same hour. The third upon the next night when the last stroke of twelve has ceased to vibrate. Look to see me no more. Others may, but you may not. And look that, for your own sake, you remember what has passed between us!

31 ▲ **Critical Viewing**
How do the actors' gestures and positions reinforce the emotion of the scene? **[Connect]**

32 ☑  Reading Check

Why does Marley visit Scrooge?

A Christmas Carol: Scrooge and Marley, Act 1 **755**

30 **Critical Viewing**
Assess

1. Read aloud the bracketed passage beginning at the bottom of page 754. **Ask** students to summarize what Marley is trying to communicate to Scrooge.
   Possible response: Marley is trying to warn Scrooge that he needs to change his ways or he will end up like Marley.

2. **Ask** students what methods Marley uses to convey his message.
   Answer: He describes the torments his spirit has endured. He lists the actions he did not take when alive.

3. **Ask** students if they think that Marley is equipped to warn Scrooge, and if they think his warning will be successful.
   Possible response: Marley certainly has the personal experience with which to warn Scrooge, and his passionate tone seems likely to make an impression. Still, given how hardened Scrooge is, it may take more than just Marley's warning to change Scrooge's behavior.

31 **Critical Viewing**

Answer: Marley's hands and his standing position emphasize the importance of his words, while Scrooge's hands and kneeling posture suggest that he is imploring Marley for help.

32 **Reading Check**

Answer: Marley visits Scrooge to warn him to change his life and to tell him that three spirits will be visiting him soon.

Differentiated
Instruction for Universal Access

EL **Support for English Learners**
Read aloud Marley's lines at the top of page 755, with expression. Clarify that Marley is saying that the concerns he lists should have been his "business" while he was alive. Make sure English learners understand what these concerns represent; you may want to relate the terms to life today to make them more relevant.
mankind: all people
welfare: health, happiness, and well-being
charity: goodwill toward people; generous acts

mercy: kindness shown to those who need it most
forbearance: patience
It may also be helpful to read aloud and discuss Marley's next speech on p. 755. Clarify that Marley's *penance,* or punishment, is for his spirit to be weighted down by heavy chains. This punishment is his *fate:* After death, Marley's spirit must pay for Marley's actions in life. To save Scrooge from a similar fate, Marley has *procured,* or arranged for, visits to Scrooge from three spirits.

755

1. **Ask** students to summarize what they have read so far in this scene.
Answer: Marley visits Scrooge and explains Scrooge's fate, but also gives him hope for changing it. Marley informs Scrooge that he will be visited one at a time by three spirits.

2. After students have read the bracketed section, **ask** them to answer the Purpose for Reading question.
Possible response: Students' questions may include, Will any ghosts visit Scrooge? Why will they visit? What will they do with Scrooge, and will their actions change him?

3. Point out to students that they satisfied their previous purpose of learning about Marley's visit and have now found another purpose for reading—to find answers to these new questions.

33

Purpose for Reading
What questions do you have about what will happen to Scrooge? Read on to answer your questions.

MARLEY *places his head back upon his shoulders. He approaches the window and beckons to* SCROOGE *to watch. Outside the window, specters fly by, carrying money-boxes and chains. They make a confused sound of lamentation.* MARLEY, *after listening a moment, joins into their mournful dirge. He leans to the window and floats out into the bleak, dark night. He is gone.*]

SCROOGE. [*Rushing to the window*] Jacob! No, Jacob! Don't leave me! I'm frightened! [*He sees that* MARLEY *has gone. He looks outside. He pulls the shutter closed, so that the scene is blocked from his view. All sound stops. After a pause, he re-opens the shutter and all is quiet, as it should be on Christmas Eve. Carolers carol out of doors, in the distance.* SCROOGE *closes the shutter and walks down the stairs. He examines the door by which* MARLEY *first entered.*] No one here at all! Did I imagine all that? Humbug! [*He looks about the room.*] I did imagine it. It only happened in my foulest dream-mind, didn't it? An undigested bit of . . . [*Thunder and lightning in the room; suddenly*] Sorry! Sorry!

[*There is silence again. The lights fade out.*]

SCENE  4

[*Christmas music, choral, "Hark the Herald Angels Sing," sung by an onstage choir of children, spotlighted, D.C. Above,* SCROOGE *in his bed, dead to the world, asleep, in his darkened room. It should appear that the choir is singing somewhere outside of the house, of course, and a use of scrim[16] is thus suggested. When the singing is ended, the choir should fade out of view and* MARLEY *should fade into view, in their place.*]

34

MARLEY. [*Directly to audience*] From this point forth . . . I shall be quite visible to you, but invisible to him. [*Smiles*] He will feel my presence, nevertheless, for, unless my senses fail me completely, we are—you and I—witness to the changing of a miser: that one, my partner in life, in business, and in eternity: that one: Scrooge. [*Moves to staircase, below* SCROOGE] See him now. He endeavors to pierce the

---

16. **scrim** (skrim) *n.* see-through fabric used to create special effects in the theater.

Think Aloud

Vocabulary: Context Clues
Instruct students to find the words *lamentation* and *mournful dirge* in the first italicized section on p. 756. Use a think-aloud process to model how to use context to determine the meaning of these words. You might say:

I'm going to think aloud to show you how I would figure out the meanings of *lamentation* and *mournful dirge* from their context.

In this scene, many ghosts who suffer like Marley are floating about in the air. They are making sounds of *lamentation* while they fly. Since Marley is so miserable, I imagine that these spirits are unhappy, too, and are making sounds of grief. *Lamentation* might be some type of weeping or moaning. In the sentence, the words *mournful dirge* restate the word *lamentation*, so they must have similar meanings. To mourn is to grieve, so a *mournful dirge* must be sad sounds made by suffering souls.

darkness with his ferret eyes.[17] [*To audience*] See him, now. He listens for the hour.

[*The bells toll.* SCROOGE *is awakened and quakes as the hour approaches one o'clock, but the bells stop their sound at the hour of twelve.*]

SCROOGE. [*Astonished*] Midnight! Why this isn't possible. It was past two when I went to bed. An icicle must have gotten into the clock's works! I couldn't have slept through the whole day and far into another night. It isn't possible that anything has happened to the sun, and this is twelve at noon! [*He runs to window; unshutters same; it is night.*] Night, still. Quiet, normal for the season, cold. It is certainly not noon. I cannot in any way afford to lose my days. Securities come due, promissory notes,[18] interest on investments: these are things that happen in the daylight! [*He returns to his bed.*] Was this a dream?

[MARLEY *appears in his room. He speaks to the audience.*]

MARLEY. You see? He does not, with faith, believe in me fully, even still! Whatever will it take to turn the faith of a miser from money to men?

SCROOGE. Another quarter and it'll be one and Marley's ghosty friends will come. [*Pauses; listens*] Where's the chime for one? [*Ding, dong*] A quarter past [*Repeats*] Half-past! [*Repeats*] A quarter to it! But where's the heavy bell of the hour one? This is a game in which I lose my senses! Perhaps, if I allowed myself another short doze . . .

MARLEY. . . . Doze, Ebenezer, doze.

[*A heavy bell thuds its one ring; dull and definitely one o'clock. There is a flash of light.* SCROOGE *sits up, in a sudden. A hand draws back the curtains by his bed. He sees it.*]

SCROOGE. A hand! Who owns it! Hello!
[*Ghosty music again, but of a new nature to the play. A strange figure stands before* SCROOGE—*like a child, yet at the same time like an old man: white hair, but unwrinkled skin, long, muscular arms, but delicate legs and feet. Wears*

---

17. **ferret eyes** a ferret is a small, weasel-like animal used for hunting rabbits; this expression means to stare continuously, the way a ferret hunts.
18. **promissory** (pram′ i sôr′ ē) **notes** written promises to pay someone a certain sum of money.

A Christmas Carol: Scrooge and Marley, Act 1 **757**

Dialogue
What important information in Marley's opening speech will influence the rest of the play?

Spiral Review
Conflict How do details about the setting work together to increase the tension?

Reading Check
35
Why is Scrooge confused when he wakes up?

757

36 **Dialogue**

1. **Ask** students how the Scrooge they have come to know speaks to others.
   Answer: He is blunt and rude.

2. **Point out** that Scrooge is about to meet and talk with the first of three spirits. Then, have students read the bracketed section.

3. **Ask** students how Scrooge treats the Ghost.
   Answer: Scrooge is extremely polite.

4. **Ask** students to respond to the Dialogue question.
   Answer: At the beginning of the play, Scrooge is a bully. With his polite words to the Ghost, Scrooge seems to acknowledge that he is not the most important or powerful being in the room.

▶ **Monitor Progress** Have students study Scrooge's language in his bracketed dialogue, and then identify the polite words and expressions he uses.

▶ **Reteach** If students have difficulty seeing the change represented in the dialogue, have two students read the section as though they are performing it on stage. Instruct the reader of Scrooge's lines to speak in a humble, slightly nervous tone. Then, **ask** students to contrast Scrooge's new tone with the way he spoke to his nephew and to Cratchit.
   Answer: Scrooge was rude to his nephew and Cratchit but is nice to the Ghost of Christmas Past.

---

white tunic; lustrous belt cinches waist. Branch of fresh green holly in its hand, but has its dress trimmed with fresh summer flowers. Clear jets of light spring from the crown of its head. Holds cap in hand. The Spirit is called PAST.]

Are you the Spirit, sir, whose coming was foretold to me?

PAST. I am.

MARLEY. Does he take this to be a vision of his green grocer?

SCROOGE. Who, and what are you?

PAST. I am the Ghost of Christmas Past.

SCROOGE. Long past?

PAST. Your past.

36 **SCROOGE.** May I ask, please, sir, what business you have here with me?

PAST. Your welfare.

SCROOGE. Not to sound ungrateful, sir, and really, please do understand that I am plenty obliged for your concern, but, really, kind spirit, it would have done all the better for my welfare to have been left alone altogether, to have slept peacefully through this night.

PAST. Your reclamation, then. Take heed!

SCROOGE. My what?

PAST. [*Motioning to* SCROOGE *and taking his arm*] Rise! Fly with me! [*He leads* SCROOGE *to the window.*]

SCROOGE. [*Panicked*] Fly, but I am a mortal and cannot fly!

PAST. [*Pointing to his heart*] Bear but a touch of my hand here and you shall be upheld in more than this!

[SCROOGE *touches the spirit's heart and the lights dissolve into sparkly flickers. Lovely crystals of music are heard. The scene dissolves into another. Christmas music again*]

Dialogue
Based on this dialogue, how has Scrooge been affected by what has happened to him so far?

Vocabulary Development

© **CCSS** Language 6

Word Analysis

Direct students' attention to the word *reclamation* on p. 758. Tell them that a good way to decipher the meaning of an unfamiliar word is to figure out what part of speech it is and to break it into parts. Explain that *–tion* is a common noun suffix; it turns a word into a noun. The verb form of *reclamation* is *reclaim*. Point out that the prefix *re-* can mean "back," as in *repay,* or it can mean "again," as in *redo.* Ask students to explain the meaning of the familiar word *claim* that makes up the second part of the word. (to ask for or take as one's own) Guide students to develop a meaning for *reclaim.* (to take back) Help students to see that *reclamation* is the act of reclaiming, and in the context of the drama, indicates that Scrooge will be given the opportunity to take back his soul, or his ability to live life as a decent human being.

SCENE 5

[SCROOGE *and the* GHOST OF CHRISTMAS PAST *walk together across an open stage. In the background, we see a field that is open; covered by a soft, downy snow: a country road.*]

SCROOGE. Good Heaven! I was bred in this place. I was a boy here!

[SCROOGE *freezes, staring at the field beyond.* MARLEY'S *ghost appears beside him; takes* SCROOGE'S *face in his hands, and turns his face to the audience.*]

MARLEY. You see this Scrooge: stricken by feeling. Conscious of a thousand odors floating in the air, each one connected with a thousand thoughts, and hopes, and joys, and care long, long forgotten. [*Pause*] This one—this Scrooge— before your very eyes, returns to life, among the living. [*To audience, sternly*] You'd best pay your most careful attention. I would suggest rapt.[19]

[*There is a small flash and puff of smoke and* MARLEY *is gone again.*]

PAST. Your lip is trembling, Mr. Scrooge. And what is that upon your cheek?

SCROOGE. Upon my cheek? Nothing . . . a blemish on the skin from the eating of overmuch grease . . . nothing . . . [*Suddenly*] Kind Spirit of Christmas Past, lead me where you will, but quickly! To be stagnant in this place is, for me, unbearable!

PAST. You recollect the way?

SCROOGE. Remember it! I would know it blindfolded! My bridge, my church, my winding river! [*Staggers about, trying to see it all at once. He weeps again.*]

PAST. These are but shadows of things that have been. They have no consciousness of us.

[*Four jocund travelers enter, singing a Christmas song in four-part harmony—"God Rest Ye Merry Gentlemen."*]

SCROOGE. Listen! I know these men! I know them! I remember the beauty of their song!

Reading Check

Who appears to Scrooge during Scene 4?

---

19. rapt (rapt) *adj.* giving complete attention; totally carried away by something.

---

③⑦ Critical Thinking

Analyze

1. Remind students that in drama, authors use dialogue as one method of revealing the traits, moods, or changes in a character. Have them read the bracketed passage.

2. Then, **ask** students to describe Scrooge's feelings at this point. **Answer:** He is upset by this reminder of the past.

3. **Ask** students to identify details in the dialogue that reveal Scrooge's emotions. **Answer:** Past says that Scrooge's lip is trembling and asks about a tear on his cheek. Scrooge cannot bear to stand still in this place.

4. Point out to students that Scrooge also staggers and weeps. **Ask** them why he might want to see all of the place at once. **Possible responses:** Students might suggest that Scrooge has mixed feelings about his boyhood home; he finds it painful to be there, but he also can't wait to see all of the places that were part of his childhood.

③⑧ Reading Check

Answer: The Ghost of Christmas Past appears to Scrooge in Scene 4.

Strategy for Special-Needs Students
Explain to students that the Ghost of Christmas Past is taking Scrooge on a trip through his life, highlighting important events. To help students comprehend the events and keep track of the sequence of events in Scrooge's life, provide copies of the **Timeline Graphic Organizer** (*Graphic Organizer Transparencies,* p. 216). Students should begin their timelines with Scrooge's boyhood home and add more information as they read on.

Support for Less Proficient Readers
Make certain students are following the action by discussing the events and time changes on these pages. Explain that the Ghost of Christmas Past visits Scrooge at one o'clock in the morning and takes him on a journey. Ask students where the characters have gone. (The ghost takes Scrooge to a place where Scrooge lived in the past.) Point out that it is now daytime in the past. Tell students that Scrooge is deeply moved by returning to this place, but Past explains that what they see no longer exists in reality.

1. Ask students to **identify** what the author attempts to emphasize by describing the merry carolers outside the schoolhouse.
Answer: The joy of the carolers at Christmas emphasizes Scrooge's loneliness as a child.

2. **Ask** students what this tells them about why Scrooge is so angry and bitter about Christmas now.
Possible response: His sadness over being left alone on Christmas as a child might have turned to anger later.

3. Have students read the first bracketed passage on page 760. **Ask** them what made Scrooge think of the singing boy.
Answer: He saw himself as a boy.

4. Explain that Scrooge now remembers himself as a boy and can identify with the boy he heard singing. **Ask** students the Dialogue question.
Answer: Scrooge was stingy before, but the lines show that he now wishes that he had given something to the boy he heard singing earlier in the play.

Dialogue
How do these lines reveal that a change is taking place in Scrooge?

PAST. But, why do you remember it so happily? It is Merry Christmas that they say to one another! What is Merry Christmas to you, Mr. Scrooge? Out upon Merry Christmas, right? What good has Merry Christmas ever done you, Mr. Scrooge? . . .

SCROOGE. [*After a long pause*] None. No good. None . . . [*He bows his head.*]

PAST. Look, you, sir, a school ahead. The schoolroom is not quite deserted. A solitary child, neglected by his friends, is left there still.

[SCROOGE *falls to the ground; sobbing as he sees, and we see, a small boy, the young* SCROOGE, *sitting and weeping, bravely, alone at his desk: alone in a vast space, a void.*]

SCROOGE. I cannot look on him!

PAST. You must, Mr. Scrooge, you must.

SCROOGE. It's me. [*Pauses; weeps*] Poor boy. He lived inside his head . . . alone . . . [*Pauses; weeps*] poor boy. [*Pauses; stops his weeping*] I wish . . . [*Dries his eyes on his cuff*] ah! it's too late!

PAST. What is the matter?

SCROOGE. There was a boy singing a Christmas Carol outside my door last night. I should like to have given him something: that's all.

39 **PAST.** [*Smiles; waves his hand to* SCROOGE] Come. Let us see another Christmas.

[*Lights out on little boy. A flash of light. A puff of smoke. Lights up on older boy*]

SCROOGE. Look! Me, again! Older now! [*Realizes*] Oh, yes . . . still alone.

[*The boy—a slightly older* SCROOGE —*sits alone in a chair, reading. The door to the room opens and a young girl enters. She is much, much younger than this slightly older* SCROOGE. *She is, say, six, and he is, say, twelve. Elder* SCROOGE *and the* GHOST OF CHRISTMAS PAST *stand watching the scene, unseen.*]

40 **FAN.** Dear, dear brother, I have come to bring you home.

Vocabulary Development

© **CCSS** Language 6

Selection Vocabulary Reinforcement
Students will benefit from additional examples and practice with the selection vocabulary words. Reinforce their comprehension with "show-you-know" sentences. The first part of the sentence uses the vocabulary word in an appropriate context. The second part of the sentence clarifies the first. Model the strategy with this example for *implored*:

The stranger *implored* me for some bread; then he begged my mom for water.

Then give students these sentence prompts, and coach them in creating the clarification part.
1. The little girl *implored* her mother for some candy; _____.
2. Your cousin seems *morose*; _____.
3. The people we helped were *destitute*; _____.
4. He seemed to drift into a *void*; _____.
5. Her voice *conveyed* her joy; _____.
6. Today you showed your *gratitude*; _____.

BOY. Home, little Fan?

FAN. Yes! Home, for good and all! Father is so much kinder than he ever used to be, and home's like heaven! He spoke so gently to me one dear night when I was going to bed that I was not afraid to ask him once more if you might come home; and he said "yes" . . . you should; and sent me in a coach to bring you. And you're to be a man and are never to come back here, but first, we're to be together all the Christmas long, and have the merriest time in the world.

BOY. You are quite a woman, little Fan!

[*Laughing; she drags at boy, causing him to stumble to the door with her. Suddenly we hear a mean and terrible voice in the hallway, Off. It is the* SCHOOLMASTER.]

SCHOOLMASTER. Bring down Master Scrooge's travel box at once! He is to travel!

FAN. Who is that, Ebenezer?

BOY. O! Quiet, Fan. It is the Schoolmaster, himself!

[*The door bursts open and into the room bursts with it the* SCHOOLMASTER.]

SCHOOLMASTER. Master Scrooge?

BOY. Oh, Schoolmaster. I'd like you to meet my little sister, Fan, sir . . .

[*Two boys struggle on with* SCROOGE'S *trunk.*]

FAN. Pleased, sir . . . [*She curtsies.*]

SCHOOLMASTER. You are to travel, Master Scrooge.

SCROOGE. Yes, sir. I know sir . . .

[*All start to exit, but* FAN *grabs the coattail of the mean old* SCHOOLMASTER.]

BOY. Fan!

SCHOOLMASTER. What's this?

FAN. Pardon, sir, but I believe that you've forgotten to say your goodbye to my brother, Ebenezer, who stands still now

Purpose for Reading
What questions do you have about Scrooge's family? Read on to see if they are answered.

41 ✓ Reading Check
Where is Scrooge when his sister arrives to take him home?

1. Have students read the bracketed passage. **Ask** them what they learned about Scrooge's past. **Answer:** Scrooge had a cheerful, kind sister he loved and who loved him. He also appears to have had a harsh, unkind father.

2. **Ask** students if anything about the event seems odd. **Possible response:** Students might notice that a six-year-old is coming to bring her older brother home and that their father is not present. They also may note that Fan had to ask her father to allow Scrooge to come home.

3. **Ask** students the Purpose for Reading question. **Possible response:** Why was Scrooge left at school until his sister asked to have him come home? Is Scrooge's nephew Fan's son? Where is Fan now?

4. Point out that they will continue reading to find answers to their questions.

41 **Reading Check**

Answer: He is at his boyhood boarding school.

Differentiated Instruction for Universal Access

Support for Special-Needs Students
Help students stay oriented in the story by reminding them that Scrooge and Past are watching but cannot involve themselves in the action. Point out that Scrooge speaks near the top of p. 762, but only Past can hear him. Then have students name each of the different characters in the scene that begins on p. 761 and explain each character's relationship to Scrooge. Have them consider how Scrooge must have felt about each person he watched. (He might have felt love for Fan, sadness for himself, fear of his father and the schoolmaster.)

EL **Vocabulary for English Learners**
Help students understand words on pages 760–761 that may be unfamiliar to them. When possible, use pictures, pantomime, and facial expressions to explain meanings. For example, to explain *harmony* you could play a clip of musical harmony. For *solitary,* you might move to a place in the room where you are sitting alone. For *vast,* you might show a picture of wide open space, and for *void,* the inside of an empty box. Other pictures that might be helpful are of a *coach* and a *trunk.*

1. Ask students to read the bracketed passage to themselves. Have
   them summarize what they learn
   in their own words.
   Answer: The nephew who
   invited Scrooge to Christmas dinner is the son of Scrooge's
   beloved sister, Fan.

2. Direct students' attention to
   Scrooge's lines at the beginning
   of the passage. Point out that
   these words are uncharacteristic
   of the Scrooge they met earlier in
   the play. Then, **ask** the Dialogue
   question.
   Answer: This scene reveals that
   Scrooge has a gentle side and
   that he once had love in his
   heart.

3. Have students contrast Scrooge's
   feelings for Fan with those he
   seemed to have for his nephew
   and Cratchit.
   Answer: Scrooge seems to have
   opposite feelings for Fan and the
   two men.

4. Have students consider what they
   know now about Scrooge's
   nephew, and **ask** them whether
   they are surprised by Scrooge's
   attitude toward him.
   Possible response: Students
   might be surprised that Scrooge
   does not treat his nephew better
   considering how much he loved
   Fan.

Dialogue
What surprising aspect
of Scrooge's character
does this scene reveal?

awaiting it . . . [*She smiles, curtsies, lowers her eyes.*]
pardon, sir.

SCHOOLMASTER. [*Amazed*] I . . . uh . . . harumph . . . uhh . . .
well, then . . . [*Outstretches hand*] Goodbye, Scrooge.

BOY. Uh, well, goodbye, Schoolmaster . . .

[*Lights fade out on all but* BOY *looking at* FAN; *and* SCROOGE
and PAST *looking at them.*]

SCROOGE. Oh, my dear, dear little sister, Fan . . . how I
loved her.

PAST. Always a delicate creature, whom a breath might have
withered, but she had a large heart . . .

SCROOGE. So she had.

PAST. She died a woman, and had, as I think, children.

SCROOGE. One child.

PAST. True. Your nephew.

SCROOGE. Yes.

PAST. Fine, then. We move on, Mr. Scrooge. That warehouse,
there? Do you know it?

SCROOGE. Know it? Wasn't I apprenticed[20] there?

PAST. We'll have a look.

[*They enter the warehouse. The lights crossfade with them,
coming up on an old man in Welsh wig:* FEZZIWIG.]

SCROOGE. Why, it's old Fezziwig! Bless his heart; it's Fezziwig,
alive again!

[FEZZIWIG *sits behind a large, high desk, counting. He lays
down his pen; looks at the clock: seven bells sound.*]

Quittin' time . . .

FEZZIWIG. Quittin' time . . . [*He takes off his waistcoat and
laughs; calls off*] Yo ho, Ebenezer! Dick!

[DICK WILKINS *and* EBENEZER SCROOGE—*a young man version—enter the room.* DICK *and* EBENEZER *are* FEZZIWIG's *apprentices.*]

---

20. **apprenticed** (ə pren´ tist) *v.* receiving instruction in a trade as well as food and housing or
wages in return for work.

Think Aloud

Draw Conclusions

Draw students' attention to young Scrooge's
last words to the Schoolmaster. Use the following "think aloud" process to model drawing
conclusions (introduced on p. 583):

When I read this line, in which young
Scrooge mumbles to Schoolmaster, I think
that he was a timid boy. If I reread the
school scene from page 760, I see many
clues to Scrooge's timidity. For example,
Past says, "He was a solitary child, neglected
by his friends." I see that the young boy

cried alone at his desk. Even at twelve, he
sits alone. He frantically shushes Fan, so
Schoolmaster won't hear them. Facing
Schoolmaster, he stumbles, unsure of what
to say. I can use these details, plus my own
experience with frightening situations, to
conclude that young Scrooge was shy and
afraid of people. The contrast with Fan, who
despite her youth, speaks to her older
brother and Schoolmaster with confidence,
confirms my conclusions about Scrooge.

SCROOGE. Dick Wilkins, to be sure! My fellow-'prentice! Bless my soul, yes. There he is. He was very much attached to me, was Dick. Poor Dick! Dear, dear!

FEZZIWIG. Yo ho, my boys. No more work tonight. Christmas Eve, Dick. Christmas, Ebenezer!
[*They stand at attention in front of* FEZZIWIG; *laughing*]
Hilli-ho! Clear away, and let's have lots of room here! Hilli-ho, Dick! Chirrup, Ebenezer!
[*The young men clear the room, sweep the floor, straighten the pictures, trim the lamps, etc. The space is clear now. A fiddler enters, fiddling.*]
Hi-ho, Matthew! Fiddle away . . . where are my daughters?

[*The fiddler plays. Three young daughters of* FEZZIWIG *enter followed by six young male suitors. They are dancing to the music. All employees come in: workers, clerks, housemaids, cousins, the baker, etc. All dance. Full number wanted here. Throughout the dance, food is brought into the feast. It is "eaten" in dance, by the dancers.* EBENEZER *dances with all three of the daughters, as does* DICK. *They compete for the*

43 ▲ **Critical Viewing**
Based on this photograph, what kind of a man is Fezziwig? **[Infer]**

44  Reading Check
Who is Fezziwig?

A Christmas Carol: Scrooge and Marley, Act 1 **763**

---

1. Read the first bracketed passage aloud. **Ask** students to paraphrase Young Scrooge's words. **Possible response:** Fezziwig is the best. If I ever have my own business, I'm going to treat my workers as well as he does.

2. Have students identify words in the dialogue that reveal how Young Scrooge feels about Fezziwig.
   Answer: Words include "best, best, the very and absolute best," "wonderful lesson," and "master."

3. Then, **ask** students to respond to the Dialogue question.
   Answer: The dialogue reveals that Young Scrooge greatly admired and respected Fezziwig.

46 **Critical Thinking**

Analyze

1. Have students read the second bracketed passage, which continues on page 765. Then, **ask** them why the Past asks Scrooge these questions.
   Answer: The Past wants Scrooge to think carefully and explain his own memories and current feelings.

2. **Ask** students how these memories appear to affect Scrooge.
   Answer: The memories seem to make Scrooge regret the way he treated his clerk, Cratchit.

3. Have students identify clues that support their answer to the previous question.
   Answer: Scrooge praises Fezziwig and appears to compare himself to the man when he mentions his wish to speak to Cratchit.

764

Vocabulary
gratitude (grat´ i tŏōd´) *n.* thankful appreciation

Dialogue
What does this dialogue reveal about Scrooge's feelings for Fezziwig?

45

46

---

daughters, happily, in the dance. FEZZIWIG *dances with his daughters.* FEZZIWIG *dances with* DICK *and* EBENEZER. *The music changes:* MRS. FEZZIWIG *enters. She lovingly scolds her husband. They dance. She dances with* EBENEZER, *lifting him and throwing him about. She is enormously fat. When the dance is ended, they all dance off, floating away, as does the music.* SCROOGE *and the* GHOST OF CHRISTMAS PAST *stand alone now. The music is gone.*]

PAST. It was a small matter, that Fezziwig made those silly folks so full of gratitude.

SCROOGE. Small!

PAST. Shhh!

[*Lights up on* DICK *and* EBENEZER]

DICK. We are blessed, Ebenezer, truly, to have such a master as Mr. Fezziwig!

YOUNG SCROOGE. He is the best, best, the very and absolute best! If ever I own a firm of my own, I shall treat my apprentices with the same dignity and the same grace. We have learned a wonderful lesson from the master, Dick!

DICK. Ah, that's a fact, Ebenezer. That's a fact!

PAST. Was it not a small matter, really? He spent but a few pounds[21] of his mortal money on your small party. Three or four pounds, perhaps. Is that so much that he deserves such praise as you and Dick so lavish now?

SCROOGE. It isn't that! It isn't that, Spirit. Fezziwig had the power to make us happy or unhappy; to make our service light or burdensome; a pleasure or a toil. The happiness he gave is quite as great as if it cost him a fortune.

PAST. What is the matter?

SCROOGE. Nothing particular.

PAST. Something, I think.

SCROOGE. No, no. I should like to be able to say a word or two to my clerk just now! That's all!

---

21. **pounds** (poundz) *n.* money used in Great Britain at the time of the story.

764 Drama

Think Aloud

Vocabulary: Dictionary Use
Direct students' to the word *aspirations* in the Woman's dialogue in the middle of p. 765. Use a think-aloud process to model how to use a dictionary to choose the best definition for the word. You might say:

I would like to look for the definition of *aspirations* in the dictionary. The first definition is "the expulsion of breath in speech." The Woman refers to Scrooge's nobler aspirations, so I don't think breathing fits here. The second definition is "the pronunciation of a consonant with an aspirate." That's also about breathing.

The third definition begins with an abbreviation, *Med.* The dictionary guide tells me that *Med.* means "medicine," and the entry is about removing liquids or gases with an aspirator. That isn't what we are looking for. The last definition is "a strong desire to achieve something noble." The Woman mentions the word *nobler.* Her statement means that she has seen the Man give up his nobler, decent goals. This definition must therefore be the correct one.

[EBENEZER *enters the room and shuts down all the lamps. He stretches and yawns. The* GHOST OF CHRISTMAS PAST *turns to* SCROOGE *all of a sudden.*]

PAST. My time grows short! Quick!

[*In a flash of light,* EBENEZER *is gone, and in his place stands an* OLDER SCROOGE, *this one a man in the prime of his life. Beside him stands a young woman in a mourning dress. She is crying. She speaks to the man, with hostility.*]

WOMAN. It matters little . . . to you, very little. Another idol has displaced me.

MAN. What idol has displaced you?

WOMAN. A golden one.

MAN. This is an even-handed dealing of the world. There is nothing on which it is so hard as poverty; and there is nothing it professes to condemn with such severity as the pursuit of wealth!

WOMAN. You fear the world too much. Have I not seen your nobler aspirations fall off one by one, until the master-passion, Gain, engrosses you? Have I not?

SCROOGE. No!

MAN. What then? Even if I have grown so much wiser, what then? Have I changed towards you?

WOMAN. No . . .

MAN. Am I?

WOMAN. Our contract is an old one. It was made when we were both poor and content to be so. You are changed. When it was made, you were another man.

MAN. I was not another man: I was a boy.

WOMAN. Your own feeling tells you that you were not what you are. I am. That which promised happiness when we were one in heart is fraught with misery now that we are two . . .

Dialogue
What personal change in Scrooge does this dialogue show?

48  Reading Check

What does the woman tell Scrooge about himself?

Draw Conclusions

1. Read aloud the full bracketed passage beginning on page 766.
Ask students to describe the comments by Scrooge and Man.
Possible response: First, the two characters say the same thing, "Please, I . . . I . . . ." Then, Scrooge repeats "No!" while Man says "Goodbye."

2. **Ask** to compare the two characters' comments and explain what each reflects about its speaker's attitude toward the situation.
Answer: The shared comment shows that both men are unsure of how to handle the situation. Man's parting remark suggests that he is unwilling or unable to say anything to change the situation. Scrooge's repeated "NO!" suggests that the older man wants to change the outcome of the situation.

3. **Ask** students to draw conclusions about what Scrooge has learned about his younger self from the scene.
Possible response: Scrooge learns that he's been too passive and too self-absorbed. He learns that he gave up something precious because he couldn't see past himself.

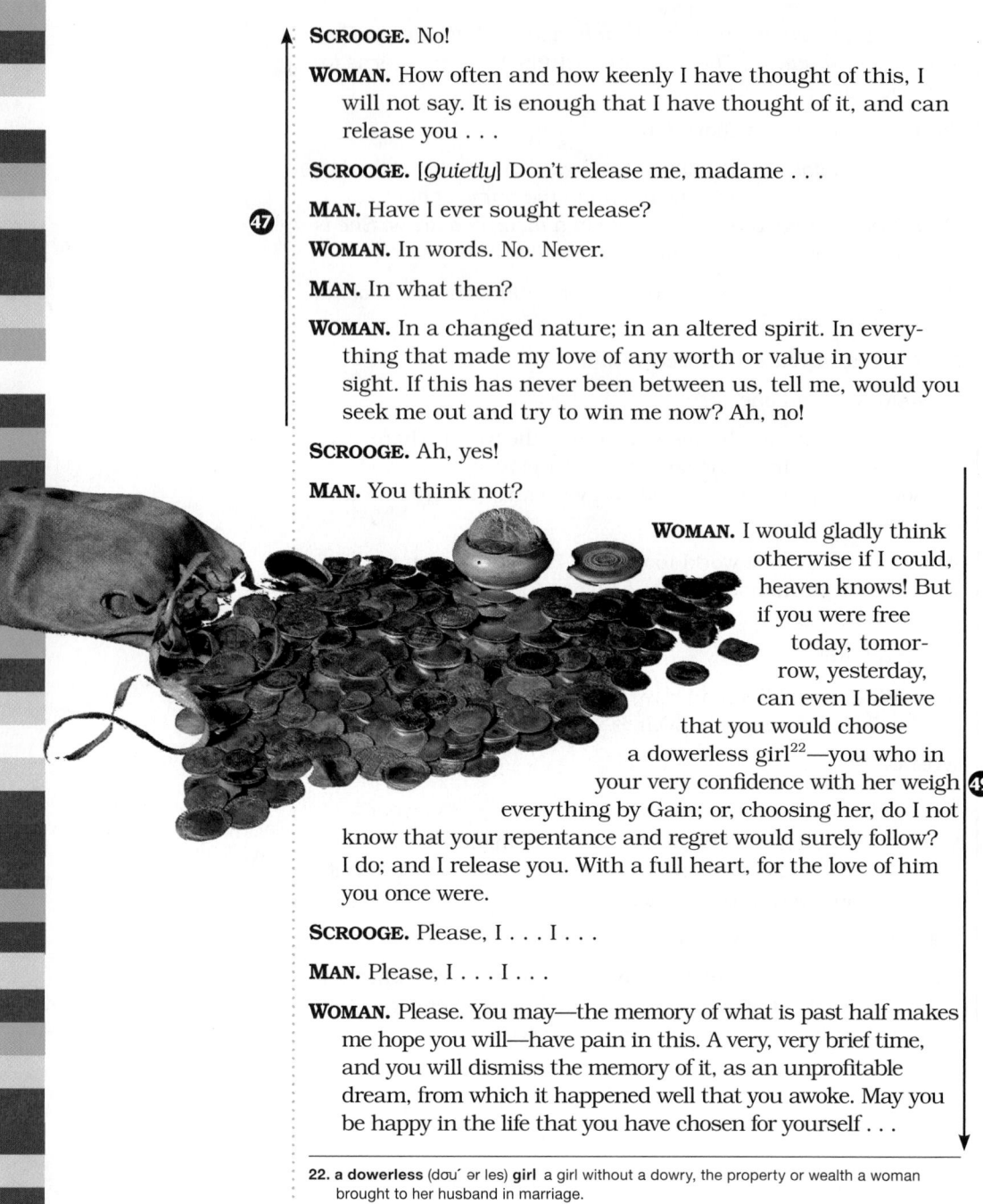

SCROOGE. No!

WOMAN. How often and how keenly I have thought of this, I will not say. It is enough that I have thought of it, and can release you . . .

SCROOGE. [*Quietly*] Don't release me, madame . . .

47 **MAN.** Have I ever sought release?

WOMAN. In words. No. Never.

MAN. In what then?

WOMAN. In a changed nature; in an altered spirit. In everything that made my love of any worth or value in your sight. If this has never been between us, tell me, would you seek me out and try to win me now? Ah, no!

SCROOGE. Ah, yes!

MAN. You think not?

WOMAN. I would gladly think otherwise if I could, heaven knows! But if you were free today, tomorrow, yesterday, can even I believe that you would choose a dowerless girl²²—you who in your very confidence with her weigh **49** everything by Gain; or, choosing her, do I not know that your repentance and regret would surely follow? I do; and I release you. With a full heart, for the love of him you once were.

SCROOGE. Please, I . . . I . . .

MAN. Please, I . . . I . . .

WOMAN. Please. You may—the memory of what is past half makes me hope you will—have pain in this. A very, very brief time, and you will dismiss the memory of it, as an unprofitable dream, from which it happened well that you awoke. May you be happy in the life that you have chosen for yourself . . .

22. **a dowerless** (dou´ ər les) **girl** a girl without a dowry, the property or wealth a woman brought to her husband in marriage.

766 Drama

Vocabulary Development

Vocabulary Knowledge Rating
When students have completed reading and discussing Act I of *A Christmas Carol,* have them take out their **Vocabulary Knowledge Rating Chart** for this selection. Read the words aloud once more and have students write their own definitions or examples in the appropriate column. Then have students complete the Vocabulary Practice activities at the end of the selection. Encourage students to use the words in further discussion and written work about this selection. Remind them that they will be accountable for these words on the **Selection Test,** *Unit 5 Resources,* pp. 38–40 or pp. 41–43.

SCROOGE. No!

WOMAN. Yourself . . . alone . . .

SCROOGE. No!

WOMAN. Goodbye, Ebenezer . . .

SCROOGE. Don't let her go!

MAN. Goodbye.

SCROOGE. No!
[*She exits.* SCROOGE *goes to younger man: himself.*]
You fool! Mindless loon! You fool!

MAN. [*To exited woman*] Fool. Mindless loon. Fool . . .

SCROOGE. Don't say that! Spirit, remove me from this place.

PAST. I have told you these were shadows of the things that have been. They are what they are. Do not blame me, Mr. Scrooge.

SCROOGE. Remove me! I cannot bear it!
[*The faces of all who appeared in this scene are now projected for a moment around the stage: enormous, flimsy, silent.*]
Leave me! Take me back! Haunt me no longer!

[*There is a sudden flash of light: a flare. The* GHOST OF CHRISTMAS PAST *is gone.* SCROOGE *is, for the moment, alone onstage. His bed is turned down, across the stage. A small candle burns now in* SCROOGE'S *hand. There is a child's cap in his other hand. He slowly crosses the stage to his bed, to sleep.* MARLEY *appears behind* SCROOGE, *who continues his long, elderly cross to bed.* MARLEY *speaks directly to the audience.*]

MARLEY. Scrooge must sleep now. He must surrender to the irresistible drowsiness caused by the recognition of what was. [*Pauses*] The cap he carries is from ten lives past: his boyhood cap . . . donned atop a hopeful hairy head . . . askew, perhaps, or at a rakish angle. Doffed now in honor of regret.[23] Perhaps even too heavy to carry in his present state of weak remorse . . .

---

23. **donned . . . regret** To *don* and *doff* a hat means to put it on and take it off, *askew* means "crooked," and *at a rakish angle* means "having a dashing or jaunty look."

Dialogue
What do you learn about Scrooge's past from the dialogue here?

**Reading Check**
Why does the woman leave Scrooge?

A Christmas Carol: Scrooge and Marley, Act 1 **767**

Have students read the bracketed passage. **Ask** them the Purpose for Reading question.
Possible response: Students might say that they look forward to seeing whether Scrooge's behavior will change. Students might say that their purpose for reading Act 2 is to be entertained and inspired.

ASSESS

Answers

Critical Thinking

Before students respond, you may wish to have them write a brief objective summary of the selection. As they answer the questions below, remind them to support their answers with evidence from the text.

1. (a) Scrooge sees himself as a young boy lonely in a school-room; as an older boy whose sister has come for him at boarding school; as a young man celebrating Christmas Eve with his employer; and as an older man whose fiancée is leaving him.
(b) **Possible responses:** Scrooge's isolation and mistreatment at school lead to his contempt for others; the loss of his sister leads to bitterness; the loss of his fiancée leads to distrust in love.

2. (a) Scrooge values money.
(b) No, he is lonely and bitter because he has forsaken humanity for greed.

3. (a) Scrooge is moved by scenes from his past and says he would like to make amends to people in the present. (b) **Possible response:** In the present, Scrooge treats people harshly, but in the future, he might make an effort to build friendly relationships with others.

4. (a) His past experiences have shaped and hardened him into the man he is today. (b) **Possible responses:** Some might say that no one should be excused for behaving as Scrooge does. Others might express sympathy for him.

5. **Possible response:** The people in Scrooge's past show how his behavior has made them feel.

Purpose for Reading
How does this speech by Marley influence your purpose for reading Act 2?

[SCROOGE *drops the cap. He lies atop his bed. He sleeps. To audience*]
He sleeps. For him, there's even more trouble ahead. [*Smiles*] For you? The play house tells me there's hot cider, as should be your anticipation for the specter Christmas Present and Future, for I promise you both. [*Smiles again*] So, I pray you hurry back to your seats refreshed and ready for a miser—to turn his coat of gray into a blazen Christmas holly-red. [*A flash of lightning. A clap of thunder. Bats fly. Ghosty music.* MARLEY *is gone.*]

Critical Thinking

Cite textual evidence to support your responses.

1. **Key Ideas and Details (a)** What scenes from his past does Scrooge visit? **(b) Draw Conclusions:** How does each event contribute to his current attitude and personality?

2. **Key Ideas and Details (a) Deduce:** What does Scrooge value in life? **(b) Draw Conclusions:** Do his values make Scrooge a happy man? Explain.

3. **Key Ideas and Details (a) Connect:** What hints suggest to you that Scrooge may change for the better?
(b) Speculate: In the future, how might Scrooge's interactions with others differ from his interactions in the present?

4. **Integration of Knowledge and Ideas (a) Deduce:** What effects have Scrooge's past experiences had on the person he has become? **(b) Evaluate:** Based on Scrooge's past experiences, do you think he should be excused for his current attitude and behavior? Explain.

5. **Integration of Knowledge and Ideas** How do the people in Scrooge's past reveal his own behavior to him?
[Connect to the Big Question: Do others see us more clearly than we see ourselves?]

768 Drama

Assessment Resources

Unit 5 Resources

L1 L2 EL Selection Test A, pp. 38–40. Administer Test A to less advanced readers.

L3 L4 EL Selection Test B, pp. 41–43. Administer Test B to on-level and more advanced students.

L3 L4 Open-Book Test, pp. 35–37. As an alternative, give the Open-Book Test.

All Customizable Test Bank

All Self-tests
Students may prepare for the **Selection Test** by taking the **Self-test** online.

PHLit Online! All assessment resources are available at www.PHLitOnline.com.

Reading Skill: Purpose for Reading

1. What clues in the title helped you to preview the content of the play?
2. **(a)** What is your **purpose for reading** this play? **(b)** How might your purpose be different if you were reading a nonfiction play about life in the workhouses of Victorian England?

Literary Analysis: Dialogue

© 3. **Craft and Structure** Complete a chart like the one shown by identifying important examples of dialogue. **(a)** For each line of **dialogue** in the first column, use the second column to tell what it means. **(b)** In the third column, tell why this dialogue is important for advancing the action of the play or developing characters.

What Does It Say?	What Does It Mean?	Why Is It Important?

Vocabulary

© **Acquisition and Use** Rewrite the following sentences so that each includes a vocabulary word from the list on page 738 and retains the same basic meaning it has here.

1. Jack's gloomy expression showed that he had lost the game.
2. Her sudden inheritance meant that she would no longer live among the poor.
3. Ted's helpful gesture made me feel thankful.
4. The party helped to ease the emptiness I was feeling.
5. The grin on Dr. Jackson's face expressed his relief.
6. We begged the guard not to close the gate.

Word Study Use the context of the sentences and what you know about the **Latin root -grat-** to explain your answer.

1. If a friend helped you out of a bind, would you feel *grateful*?
2. Would *congratulations* be in order if you failed an exam?

Word Study

The **Latin root -grat-** means "thankful" or "pleasing."

Apply It Explain how the root -grat- contributes to the meanings of these words. Consult a dictionary if necessary.

gratuity
ingrate
gratis
gratification

Reading Skill

1. The words *Christmas Carol* along with the people's names suggest that the play is an inspiring Christmas story about two men.

2. **(a) Possible response:** Some might wish to be entertained, others to be inspired, and some may mention both purposes. **(b)** One might read a nonfiction play to learn about a subject or to gain understanding.

Literary Analysis

3. **Possible response:** [col 1]: "Let me hear another sound from you and you'll keep your Christmas by losing your situation." [col 2]: Scrooge threatens Cratchit with the loss of his job for agreeing with his nephew. [col 3]: It shows what a bully Scrooge is.
For other sample answers, see *Graphic Organizer Transparencies,* **Literary Analysis Graphic Organizer A,** p. 149, and the **Additional Answers** section.

Vocabulary
Acquisition and Use
Sample answers:

1. Jack's <u>morose</u> expression showed unhappiness about losing the game.

2. Her sudden inheritance gave her enough money so that she was no longer <u>destitute</u>.

3. Ted's thoughtful gift filled me with <u>gratitude</u>.

4. The party helped me to stay busy and fill the <u>void</u> I was feeling.

5. The grin on Dr. Jackson's face <u>conveyed</u> his relief.

6. We <u>implored</u> the guard not to close the gate, begging her to let us in.

Word Study
Sample answers:

1. Yes; The root -*grat*- means "thankful" and *grateful* means "thankful." You would feel <u>thankful</u> to a friend that helped you.

2. No; The root -*grat*- means "pleasing" and *congratulations* are expressions of pleasure. If you failed an exam, you wouldn't be <u>pleased</u>.

Word Study: Apply It
Sample answers: A *gratuity* is a small gift or amount of money given in <u>thanks</u>. An *ingrate* is someone who is not <u>thankful</u> for help. To get something *gratis* means to get it for free, often as a way of saying <u>thank you</u>. *Gratification* is the state of being <u>pleased</u>.

Conventions

1. Introduce the skill, using the instruction on the student page.
2. Discuss the examples in the chart.

Think Aloud: Model the Skill

Model the skill of using interjections. Say to students:

Interjections can help me add excitement to sentences by showing my feelings. For example, I can show excitement with "Wow! You did extremely well on the quiz. I'm proud of you." I can show disappointment with "Oh boy, you did not do well on the quiz." If I write these sentences on the board, I use an exclamation mark after *Wow!* to show excitement, but a comma after *Oh boy,* to show a more subdued reaction.

PH WRITING COACH | Grade 7

Students will find further instruction on and practice with interjections in Chapter 17, Section 2.

Practice A

1. Hey
2. Wow
3. Yikes
4. Humph

Reading Application
Sample answer:

1. Bah! The emotion is disgust.
2. Mercy! The emotion is fear.

Practice B
Sample answers:

1. Yikes! Who are you and what do you want?
2. Hey! Go away and leave me alone.
3. No! I do not want any more visitors.
4. Ugh! Take me away from here; this is too painful to watch.

Writing Application
Sample answer:

1. Hey, Wow, Oh
2. Well, Yikes, Oh
3. Well, Hey, Yikes
4. Wow, Boy, Oh

Students should note that the meanings of the sentences stay about the same, but the intensity varies with the strength of the interjection.

Integrated Language Skills

A Christmas Carol: Scrooge and Marley, Act 1

Conventions: Interjections

An **interjection** is a part of speech that expresses a feeling, such as pain or excitement.

An interjection may be set off with a comma or an exclamation point. Interjections are used to add emphasis to your writing. When writing dialogue, use interjections to make the language sound more realistic.

Pain: Ouch! I hit my toe.
Excitement: Wow, Melissa can certainly run fast!

The chart lists some common interjections.

Wow	Whew	Well	Hey
Huh	Oh	Oops	Boy
Hmmm	Yikes	Yuck	Ugh

Practice A Identify the interjection in each sentence.

1. Hey, it is snowing outside!
2. Wow! Don't the carolers sound wonderful?
3. Yikes! It is cold in here!
4. Humph, I suppose you want to go home now!

Reading Application Find at least two different interjections in *A Christmas Carol: Scrooge and Marley*, Act 1. For each, indicate the emotion it expresses.

Practice B Add an interjection and appropriate punctuation to help express emotion in each sentence.

1. Who are you and what do you want?
2. Go away and leave me alone.
3. I do not want any more visitors.
4. Take me away from here; this is too painful to watch.

Writing Application Compare your responses with a partner, and, together, provide three interjections for each sentence above. Explain how the meaning and intensity of the sentence changes in each case.

PH WRITING COACH Further instruction and practice are available in *Prentice Hall Writing Coach*.

770 Drama

Extend the Lesson

Sentence Modeling

Use the sentences below to model:

Mercy! Dreadful apparition, mercy! Why, O! why do you trouble me so?

Remind students of the grammar lesson on interjections. Ask students what they notice about the sentences. Elicit from them that the sentences include several interjections. Then ask what else students notice. (The first interjection sets the fearful tone, and each successive interjection raises the tension and fear of Scrooge's experience. The closing question becomes a plea.)

Have students imitate the sentences in sentences on a topic of their own choosing, matching each grammatical and stylistic feature discussed. Collect the sentences, and share them with the class.

Writing

Argument Write a **letter** to Scrooge, telling him what he is missing in life by being cranky and negative with the people around him. Start your letter with a salutation, or greeting. Then, support the main points of your argument with clear reasons and evidence. Conclude with a closing and your signature.

- Present a balanced argument by carefully organizing the body of the letter. Fully support each claim with valid reasons and text evidence before moving on to the next one. Use transitional phrases like "another issue is . . ." or "in addition" to help unify the main argument—that there are many things Scrooge is missing.
- If you handwrite your letter, write legibly.

(For a model of a friendly-letter format, see p. R26.)

Grammar Application Check your writing to be sure your use of interjections is correct.

Writing Workshop: *Work in Progress*

Prewriting for Research For a multimedia report you may write, list four ideas in response to one of these general topics: locations around the world, nature and wildlife, or sports and athletes. Save this Ideas List in your writing portfolio.

Research and Technology

Build and Present Knowledge Prepare **costume plans** for this play. With a small group, research the clothing worn during the Victorian period in England.

- Use the Internet and library resources to gather information, photos, sketches, and descriptions.
- Determine what types of clothing different characters would have worn, based on their social positions.
- Research what kinds of clothing people wore for different seasons. Find out about the fabrics and materials that were available during the time period.

Use the information you find to plan costumes for two different characters in *A Christmas Carol.* In your plan, show or describe the types of clothing, including the colors and fabrics. Include pictures or sketches with your descriptions.

Common Core State Standards

L.7.1, L.7.2; W.7.1, W.7.1.a, W.7.1.b, W.7.1.c, W.7.7
[For the full wording of the standards, see page 736.]

Use this prewriting activity to prepare for the **Writing Workshop** on page 824.

www.PHLitOnline.com

- Interactive graphic organizers
- Grammar tutorial
- Interactive journals

Integrated Language Skills **771**

Teaching Resources

Unit 5 Resources
- L3 L4 EL **Integrated Language Skills: Grammar,** p. 32
- L3 L4 EL **Support for Writing,** p. 33
- L3 L4 **Support for Extend Your Learning,** p. 34
- L4 **Enrichment,** p. 31

Enriched Online Student Edition
Available under After You Read for this selection:
- All **Interactive Grammar Tutorial**
- L3 L4 **Internet Research Activity**

Professional Development Guidebook
Rubrics for Self-Assessment: Letter, pp. 236–237

PHLit Online! All print and digital resources are available online at **www.PHLitOnline.com.** Online resources accessible to students are noted on the student page.

Answers

Writing

1. Review the assignment, using the instruction on the student page.
2. To guide students in writing this argument, provide them with **Support for Writing,** p. 33 in the *Unit 5 Resources.*
3. To evaluate students' letters, use the rubrics for letter, pp. 236–237 in *Professional Development Guidebook.* In addition, you might evaluate how well students stated their ideas to Scrooge and how well they supported their opinions.

Grammar Application

Have students check their drafts to make sure they have used interjections correctly.

Six Traits Focus

✓	Ideas	✓	Word Choice
✓	Organization	✓	Sentence Fluency
	Voice		Conventions

PH WRITING COACH Grade 7

Students will find further instruction on and practice with friendly letters in Chapter 12.

Writing Workshop
Work in Progress

Have students save their completed Ideas Lists in their portfolios. They will use the lists later as they continue this Work-in-Progress assignment (see p. 809). These assignments prepare them to complete the Writing Workshop assignment (see pp. 824–829).

Research and Technology

1. Review the assignment, using the instruction on the student page.
2. To support students' work on the assignment, have students complete the **Support for Extend Your Learning** page (*Unit 5 Resources,* p. 34).

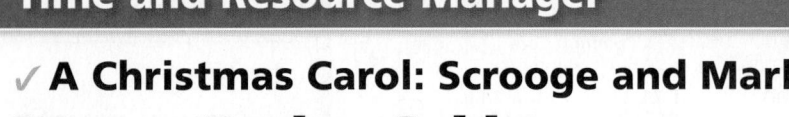
✓ **A Christmas Carol: Scrooge and Marley, Act II**
Lesson Pacing Guide

DAY 1 Preteach

- ⓒ Administer the Reading and Vocabulary Warm-ups (*Unit 5 Resources*, pp. 44–47) as necessary.
- Introduce the Reading Skill: Purpose for Reading.
- ⓒ Introduce the Literary Analysis concept: Stage Directions.
- Distribute copies of the appropriate graphic organizer for the Reading Skill (*Graphic Organizer Transparencies*, pp. 151–152).
- Distribute copies of the appropriate graphic organizer for Literary Analysis (*Graphic Organizer Transparencies*, pp. 153–154).
- ⓒ Teach the selection vocabulary.
- ⓒ Introduce the Word Study skill.

DAYS 2–3 Preteach/Teach

- ⓒ Build background with the Background feature.
- Develop thematic vocabulary and thematic thinking with Writing About the Big Question.
- Prepare students to read with the Activating Prior Knowledge activities (TE).
- Informally monitor comprehension while students read.
- Use the Reading Check questions to confirm comprehension.
- Develop students' ability to set and monitor a purpose for reading using the Purpose for Reading question.
- ⓒ Develop students' understanding of stage directions using the Stage Directions questions.
- ⓒ Reinforce vocabulary with the Vocabulary notes.
- ⓒ Reinforce unit focus standards using the Spiral Review prompts.

DAY 4 Assess

- Assess students' comprehension and mastery of the skills by having them answer the Critical Thinking, Reading Skill, and Literary Analysis questions.
- ⓒ Have students complete the Vocabulary Practice activities.
- ⓒ Have students complete the Word Study activities.

DAY 5 Extend/Assess

- Have students complete the Conventions lesson.
- ⓒ Have students complete the Writing activity and write a tribute. (You may assign as homework.)
- ⓒ Extend learning by having students complete the Speaking and Listening activity, a dramatic monologue. As an alternative, assign them "Called Out" in *Reality Central.*
- Administer Selection Test A or B (*Unit 5 Resources,* pp. 59–61 or 62–64).

ⓒ **Common Core State Standards**

Reading Literature 3. Analyze how particular elements of a story or drama interact. *(Literary Analysis: Spiral Review)*
5. Analyze how a drama's or poem's form or structure contributes to its meaning. *(Literary Analysis: Stage Directions)*

Writing 2. Write informative/explanatory texts to examine a topic and convey ideas, concepts, and information through the selection, organization, and analysis of relevant content.
9. Draw evidence from literary or informational texts to support analysis, reflection, and research.

Speaking and Listening 6. Adapt speech to a variety of contexts and tasks, demonstrating command of formal English when indicated or appropriate.

Language 1. Demonstrate command of the conventions of standard English grammar and usage when writing or speaking.
2. Demonstrate command of the conventions of standard English capitalization, punctuation, and spelling when writing.
4.b. Use common grade-appropriate Greek or Latin affixes and roots as clues to the meaning of a word.
6. Acquire and use accurately grade-appropriate general academic and domain-specific words and phrases; gather vocabulary knowledge when considering a word or phrase important to comprehension or expression.

Additional Standards Practice
Common Core Companion, *pp. 28–40, 54–66*

Daily Block Scheduling
Each day in this Lesson Pacing Guide represents a 40–50 minute period. Teachers using block scheduling may combine days to revise pacing. In addition, teachers may differentiate and support core instruction by integrating components for extended and intensive support, as students require. See the Guide to Selected Leveled Resources (facing page).

Guide to Selected Leveled Resources

R T I Tier 1 (students performing on level)

A Christmas Carol: Scrooge and Marley, Act II

Warm Up	Practice, model, and monitor fluency, working with the whole class or in groups.	Vocabulary and Reading Warm-ups B, *Unit 5 Resources,* pp. 44–45, 47
Comprehension/Skills	Support and monitor comprehension and skills development, having students complete the activities, graphic organizers, and interactive prompts independently or as a class.	• *Reader's Notebook,* adapted instruction and full selection EL *Reader's Notebook: English Learner's Version,* adapted instruction and adapted selection • Reading Skill Graphic Organizer B, *Graphic Organizer Transparencies,* p. 152 • Literary Analysis Graphic Organizer B, *Graphic Organizer Transparencies,* p. 154
Monitor Progress	Monitor student progress with the differentiated curriculum-based assessment in the *Unit Resources.*	• Selection Test B, *Unit 5 Resources,* pp. 62–64 • Open-Book Test, *Unit 5 Resources,* pp. 56–58
Assess/Screen	Assess student progress using Benchmark Test 2.	• Benchmark Test 9, *Unit 5 Resources,* pp. 84–89

R T I Tier 2 (students requiring intervention)

A Christmas Carol: Scrooge and Marley, Act II

Warm Up	Practice, model, and monitor fluency in groups or with individuals.	• Vocabulary and Reading Warm-ups A, *Unit 5 Resources,* pp. 44–46 • *Reality Central,* "Called Out" • *Hear It!* Audio CD (adapted text)
Comprehension/Skills	• Support and monitor comprehension and skills development, working in small groups or with individuals. • Pair students with more advanced peers and have them complete the writing activity in the *Real-World Writing Journal.* • As students complete the selection in the appropriate version of the *Reader's Notebook,* monitor comprehension frequently with group questions and individual instruction. • Model strategies while guiding students in completing the activities and prompts in the *Reader's Notebook,* as well as the graphic organizers. • Practice skills and monitor mastery with the *Reading Kit* worksheets.	• *Real-World Writing Journal,* Lesson 3, pp. 146–149 • *Reader's Notebook: Adapted Version,* adapted instruction and adapted selection EL *Reader's Notebook: English Learner's Version,* adapted instruction and adapted selection • Reading Skill Graphic Organizer A, *Graphic Organizer Transparencies,* p. 151 • Literary Analysis Graphic Organizer A, *Graphic Organizer Transparencies,* p. 153 • *Reading Kit,* Practice worksheets, pp. 200, 206, 210, 214, 220
Monitor Progress	Monitor student progress with the differentiated curriculum-based assessment in the *Unit Resources* and in the *Reading Kit.*	• Selection Test A, *Unit 5 Resources,* pp. 59–61 • *Reading Kit,* Assess worksheets, pp. 201, 207, 211, 215, 221
Assess/Screen	Assess student progress using Benchmark Test.	• Benchmark Test 9, *Unit 5 Resources,* pp. 84–89

TIER 3 Tier 3 intervention may require consultation with the student's special-education or dyslexia specialist. For additional support, see the Tier 2 activities and resources listed above.

One-on-one teaching   Group work   Whole class instruction   Independent work   A Assessment

For a complete guide to selection support, including support for Advanced students, see the Overview of Resources in the frontmatter.

5 Critical Viewing

Answer: Because Scrooge is expecting another ghost, this character is probably the Ghost of Christmas Present.

6 Purpose for Reading

1. Have students use their graphic organizers to preview pp. 776–777. **Ask** them how the stage directions appear to differ from the dialogue.
   Answer: The lines of dialogue are short, but the stage directions are long and probably include more details than the dialogue.

2. Tell students that they can read most dialogue fairly quickly without missing any important information; a longer speech, such as Scrooge's on the bottom of p. 777, may take longer, because some of the words are unfamiliar.

3. **Ask** the Purpose for Reading question.
   Answer: The many details in these stage directions are probably important for understanding the scene, so they should be read carefully.

4. Have students read the bracketed text silently, and then **ask** if their reading rate changed while completing this section.
   Possible response: Students might say that they read slowly at first to gain a sense of the sounds being heard and action taking place. Then, they may have picked up speed while reading through the list of foods as they are easy to envision. Finally, they may have slowed again to catch all of the action.

---

5 ▶ Critical Viewing
Based on your knowledge of the play so far, whom do you expect this character to be? Explain. **[Hypothesize]**

Purpose for Reading
At what rate would you read these stage directions? Why?

6

---

clock strike one and, when he awakes expecting my second messenger, there will be no one . . . nothing. Then I'll have the bell strike twelve. And then one again . . . and then nothing. Nothing . . . [*Laughs*] nothing will . . . astonish him. I think it will work.

[*The bell tolls one.* SCROOGE *leaps awake.*]

SCROOGE. One! One! This is it: time! [*Looks about the room*] Nothing!

[*The bell tolls midnight.*]

Midnight! How can this be? I'm sleeping backwards.

[*One again*]

Good heavens! One again! I'm sleeping back and forth! [*A pause.* SCROOGE *looks about.*] Nothing! Absolutely nothing!

[*Suddenly, thunder and lightning.* MARLEY *laughs and disappears. The room shakes and glows. There is suddenly spring-like music.* SCROOGE *makes a run for the door.*]

MARLEY. Scrooge!

SCROOGE. What?

MARLEY. Stay you put!

SCROOGE. Just checking to see if anyone is in here.

[*Lights and thunder again: more music.* MARLEY *is of a sudden gone. In his place sits the* GHOST OF CHRISTMAS PRESENT—*to be called in the stage directions of the play,* PRESENT—*center of room. Heaped up on the floor, to form a kind of throne, are turkeys, geese, game, poultry, brawn, great joints of meat, suckling pigs, long wreaths of sausages, mince-pies, plum puddings, barrels of oysters, red hot chestnuts, cherry-cheeked apples, juicy oranges, luscious pears, immense twelfth cakes, and seething bowls of punch, that make the chamber dim with their delicious steam. Upon this throne sits* PRESENT, *glorious to see. He bears a torch, shaped as a Horn of Plenty.*[1] SCROOGE *hops out of the door, and then peeks back again into his bedroom.* PRESENT, *calls to* SCROOGE.]

---

1. **Horn of Plenty** a horn overflowing with fruits, flowers, and grain, representing wealth and abundance.

Think Aloud

Vocabulary: Context Clues
Direct students' attention to the word *scabbard* in the stage directions on p. 777. Use a think-aloud process to model how to use context to infer the meaning of an unfamiliar word. Say to students:

> I'm going to think aloud to show you how I would interpret the meaning of the word *scabbard* using context clues.

The stage directions state that the *scabbard* girdles the Ghost's middle, so it must be attached to his waist. Then, the sentence says the *scabbard* is without a sword and restates the word *scabbard* with the word *sheath*. Since a sword is held in a sheath at a person's side, then I think a *scabbard* is a *sheath*—a covering for a sword.

PRESENT. Ebenezer Scrooge. Come in, come in! Come in and know me better!

SCROOGE. Hello. How should I call you?

PRESENT. I am the Ghost of Christmas Present. Look upon me.

[PRESENT *is wearing a simple green robe. The walls around the room are now covered in greenery, as well. The room seems to be a perfect grove now: leaves of holly, mistletoe and ivy reflect the stage lights. Suddenly, there is a mighty roar of flame in the fireplace and now the hearth burns with a lavish, warming fire. There is an ancient scabbard girdling the* GHOST'S *middle, but without sword. The sheath is gone to rust.*]

You have never seen the like of me before?

SCROOGE. Never.

PRESENT. You have never walked forth with younger members of my family; my elder brothers born on Christmases past.

SCROOGE. I don't think I have. I'm afraid I've not. Have you had many brothers, Spirit?

PRESENT. More than eighteen hundred.

SCROOGE. A tremendous family to provide for! [PRESENT *stands*] Spirit, conduct me where you will. I went forth last night on compulsion, and learnt a lesson which is working now. Tonight, if you have aught to teach me, let me profit by it.

PRESENT. Touch my robe.

[SCROOGE *walks cautiously to* PRESENT *and touches his robe. When he does, lightning flashes, thunder claps, music plays. Blackout*] ❽

Vocabulary
compulsion (kəm puľ shən) *n.* driving, irresistible force

❽ ✓ Reading Check
Who visits Scrooge in Scene 1?

A Christmas Carol: Scrooge and Marley, Act 2 **777**

777

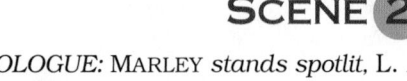

SCENE 2

[*PROLOGUE:* MARLEY *stands spotlit, L. He speaks directly to the audience.*]

MARLEY. My ghostly friend now leads my living partner through the city's streets.

[*Lights up on* SCROOGE *and* PRESENT]

See them there and hear the music people make when the weather is severe, as it is now.

[*Winter music. Choral group behind scrim, sings. When the song is done and the stage is re-set, the lights will fade up on a row of shops, behind the singers. The choral group will hum the song they have just completed now and mill about the streets,*[2] *carrying their dinners to the bakers' shops and restaurants. They will, perhaps, sing about being poor at Christmastime, whatever.*]

PRESENT. These revelers, Mr. Scrooge, carry their own dinners to their jobs, where they will work to bake the meals the rich men and women of this city will eat as their Christmas dinners. Generous people these . . . to care for the others, so . . .

[PRESENT *walks among the choral group and a sparkling incense*[3] *falls from his torch on to their baskets, as he pulls the covers off of the baskets. Some of the choral group become angry with each other.*]

MAN #1. Hey, you, watch where you're going.

MAN #2. Watch it yourself, mate!

[PRESENT *sprinkles them directly, they change.*]

MAN #1. I pray go in ahead of me. It's Christmas. You be first!

❾ **MAN #2.** No, no, I must insist that YOU be first!

MAN #1. All right, I shall be, and gratefully so.

MAN #2. The pleasure is equally mine, for being able to watch you pass, smiling.

MAN #1. I would find it a shame to quarrel on Christmas Day . . .

---

2. **mill about the streets** walk around aimlessly.
3. **incense** (in´ sens) *n.* any of various substances that produce a pleasant odor when burned.

Vocabulary
severe (sə vir´) *adj.*
harsh

Purpose for Reading
At what rate would you read dialogue such as this? Why?

Vocabulary Development

ⓒ **CCSS** Language 6

Word Analysis
Direct students' attention to the word *audience* at the beginning of Scene 2. **Ask** them to define the word. (An audience is a group of people who listen to or watch a presentation.) Tell students that the root of the word *audience* is *–aud-*, meaning "to hear." **Ask** them how the meaning of the root word relates to the meaning of the word *audience.* (Students should note that members of an audience hear a performance.) Then, **ask** students to list other words that use the same root word. (Students may suggest words such as *auditorium, auditory,* and *audition.*)

MAN #2. As would I.

MAN #1. Merry Christmas then, friend!

MAN #2. And a Merry Christmas straight back to you!

[*Church bells toll. The choral group enter the buildings: the shops and restaurants; they exit the stage, shutting their doors closed behind them. All sound stops.* SCROOGE *and* PRESENT *are alone again.*]

SCROOGE. What is it you sprinkle from your torch?

PRESENT. Kindness.

SCROOGE. Do you sprinkle your kindness on any particular people or on all people?

PRESENT. To any person kindly given. And to the very poor most of all.

SCROOGE. Why to the very poor most?

PRESENT. Because the very poor need it most. Touch my heart . . . here, Mr. Scrooge. We have another journey.

[SCROOGE *touches the* GHOST'S *heart and music plays, lights change color, lightning flashes, thunder claps. A choral group appears on the street, singing Christmas carols.*]

SCENE

[MARLEY *stands spotlit in front of a scrim on which is painted the exterior of* CRATCHIT'S *four-roomed house. There is a flash and a clap and* MARLEY *is gone. The lights shift color again, the scrim flies away, and we are in the interior of the* CRATCHIT *family home.* SCROOGE *is there, with the* spirit *(*PRESENT*), watching* MRS. CRATCHIT *set the table, with the help of* BELINDA CRATCHIT *and* PETER CRATCHIT, *a baby, pokes a fork into the mashed potatoes on his highchair's tray. He also chews on his shirt collar.*]

SCROOGE. What is this place, Spirit?

PRESENT. This is the home of your employee, Mr. Scrooge. Don't you know it?

SCROOGE. Do you mean Cratchit, Spirit? Do you mean this is Cratchit's home?

Stage Directions
What information in these stage directions adds to the effectiveness of the scene?

✓ Reading Check
⑪ What does the Ghost of Christmas Present show Scrooge?

---

⑩ Stage Directions
Have students read the second bracketed passage. Then, **ask** them the Stage Directions question.
Possible response: Students might suggest that the church bells are sounds that remind people of Christmas. They may also note that the street becomes quiet as though Christmas has brought peace to the area.

⑪ Reading Check
Answer: The Ghost shows Scrooge poor people celebrating and preparing for Christmas.

Differentiated Instruction   for Universal Access

Enrichment for Advanced Readers
Tell students that the word *carol* is from the French and originally referred to a ring dance accompanied by singing. By the sixteenth century, *carol* had come to mean a Christmas song of joy.

Ask students to name any Christmas carols they know. (Students might mention "Silent Night, " "O Little Town of Bethlehem," or "God Rest Ye Merry Gentlemen.") Then use the following questions for discussion:

1. Why has the playwright included carolers? (Students might say that the carolers remind Scrooge and the audience of the triumph of joy and kindness over gloom and selfishness. They add to the festive atmosphere of Christmas.)
2. Why do you think Dickens titled his story *A Christmas Carol*? (Students might note that his story celebrates Christmas joy as carols do.)

779

Vocabulary
meager (mē´ gər) *adj.* small in amount; of poor quality

⓬

PRESENT. None other.

SCROOGE. These children are his?

PRESENT. There are more to come presently.

SCROOGE. On his meager earnings! What foolishness!

PRESENT. Foolishness, is it?

SCROOGE. Wouldn't you say so? Fifteen shillings⁴ a week's what he gets!

PRESENT. I would say that he gets the pleasure of his family, fifteen times a week times the number of hours a day! Wait, Mr. Scrooge. Wait, listen and watch. You might actually learn something . . .

MRS. CRATCHIT. What has ever got your precious father then? And your brother, Tiny Tim? And Martha warn't as late last Christmas by half an hour!

[MARTHA *opens the door, speaking to her mother as she does.*]

MARTHA. Here's Martha, now, Mother! [*She laughs. The* CRATCHIT CHILDREN *squeal with delight.*]

BELINDA. It's Martha, Mother! Here's Martha!

PETER. Marthmama, Marthmama! Hullo!

⓭

BELINDA. Hurrah! Martha! Martha! There's such an enormous goose for us, Martha!

MRS. CRATCHIT. Why, bless your heart alive, my dear, how late you are!

MARTHA. We'd a great deal of work to finish up last night, and had to clear away this morning, Mother.

MRS. CRATCHIT. Well, never mind so long as you are come. Sit ye down before the fire, my dear, and have a warm, Lord bless ye!

BELINDA. No, no! There's Father coming. Hide, Martha, hide!

[MARTHA *giggles and hides herself.*]

MARTHA. Where? Here?

PETER. Hide, hide!

---

4. **Fifteen shillings** a small amount of money for a week's work.

Purpose for Reading
How does Mrs. Cratchit's use of language affect your reading rate? Explain.

780 Drama

BELINDA. Not there! THERE!

MARTHA *is hidden.* BOB CRATCHIT *enters, carrying* TINY TIM *atop his shoulder. He wears a threadbare and fringeless comforter hanging down in front of him.* TINY TIM *carries small crutches and his small legs are bound in an iron frame brace.*]

BOB AND TINY TIM. Merry Christmas.

BOB. Merry Christmas my love, Merry Christmas Peter, Merry Christmas Belinda. Why, where is Martha?

MRS. CRATCHIT. Not coming.

BOB. Not coming: Not coming upon Christmas Day?

MARTHA. [*Pokes head out*] Ohhh, poor Father. Don't be disappointed.

BOB. What's this?

MARTHA. 'Tis I!

BOB. Martha! [*They embrace.*]

TINY TIM. Martha! Martha!

MARTHA. Tiny Tim!

[TINY TIM *is placed in* MARTHA'S *arms.* BELINDA *and* PETER *rush him offstage.*]

BELINDA. Come, brother! You must come hear the pudding singing in the copper.

TINY TIM. The pudding? What flavor have we?

PETER. Plum! Plum!

TINY TIM. Oh, Mother! I love plum!

[*The children exit the stage, giggling.*]

MRS. CRATCHIT. And how did little Tim behave?

BOB. As good as gold, and even better. Somehow he gets thoughtful sitting by himself so much, and thinks the

⓮ ▲ Critical Viewing
Based on this picture, how would you describe the relationship between Tiny Tim and his father? **[Infer]**

⓰  Reading Check
Why does Martha hide?

A Christmas Carol: Scrooge and Marley, Act 2 **781**

⓮ Critical Viewing
Answer: Cratchit carries Tiny Tim on his shoulder playfully, suggesting a warm, friendly relationship between the two.

⓯ Background

Christmas Goose and Plum Pudding

Goose has been a part of Christmas feasts since the Middle Ages, particularly among the English. Of the Cratchits' Christmas goose, Dickens says in his novel, "There never was such a goose . . . . Its tenderness and flavor, size and cheapness, were the themes of universal admiration."

Early accounts of English plum pudding being eaten for the holidays date from the reign of Queen Anne in the early 1700s. The pudding was made of thickened mutton broth, brown bread, raisins, and spices. Today's plum pudding is a dark, firm, rounded dessert, made with breadcrumbs, shortening, eggs, spices, chopped nuts, and dried and candied fruits—but no plums. During Dickens's time, a proper Christmas pudding could take three days to make. Everyone in the household helped prepare the ingredients and stir the pudding. The mixture was then tied tightly in a cloth or pressed into a bowl and lowered into a kettle of boiling water for at least six hours.

⓰ Reading Check
Answer: Martha hides because her younger siblings want to surprise their father.

⑰ Stage Directions

1. Remind students that novels can convey meaning through lengthy, detailed descriptions, but that actors on stage must rely on their speech and actions.

2. Have students read the bracketed dialogue that begins at the bottom of p. 781. Then, **ask** them the Stage Directions question.
Possible response: The pause would make Cratchit seem thoughtful for a moment and help set a somber mood.

3. Then, **ask** students how the sound of Tim's crutch might give the audience a clue for understanding Cratchit's final words "one would never know."
Possible response: The crutch would remind the audience of Tim's poor health and suggest that the child is not growing stronger but weaker.

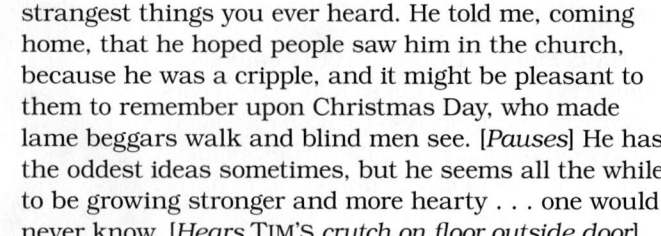

Stage Directions
Why is the pause in Bob's speech important here?

⑰ strangest things you ever heard. He told me, coming home, that he hoped people saw him in the church, because he was a cripple, and it might be pleasant to them to remember upon Christmas Day, who made lame beggars walk and blind men see. [*Pauses*] He has the oddest ideas sometimes, but he seems all the while to be growing stronger and more hearty . . . one would never know. [*Hears* TIM'S *crutch on floor outside door*]

⑮ **PETER.** The goose has arrived to be eaten!

BELINDA. Oh, mama, mama, it's beautiful.

MARTHA. It's a perfect goose, Mother!

TINY TIM. To this Christmas goose, Mother and Father I say . . . [*Yells*] Hurrah! Hurrah!

OTHER CHILDREN. [*Copying* TIM] Hurrah! Hurrah!

[*The family sits round the table.* BOB *and* MRS. CRATCHIT *serve the trimmings, quickly. All sit; all bow heads; all pray.*]

BOB. Thank you, dear Lord, for your many gifts . . . our dear children; our wonderful meal; our love for one another; and the warmth of our small fire—[*Looks up at all*] A merry Christmas to us, my dear. God bless us!

ALL. [*Except* TIM] Merry Christmas! God bless us!

TINY TIM. [*In a short silence*] God bless us every one.

All freeze. Spotlight on PRESENT *and* SCROOGE]

SCROOGE. Spirit, tell me if Tiny Tim will live.

PRESENT. I see a vacant seat . . . in the poor chimney corner, and a crutch without an owner, carefully preserved. If these shadows remain unaltered by the future, the child will die.

SCROOGE. No, no, kind Spirit! Say he will be spared!

PRESENT. If these shadows remain unaltered by the future, none other of my race will find him here. What then? If he be like to die, he had better do it, and decrease the surplus population.

⑱ [SCROOGE *bows his head. We hear* BOB'S *voice speak* SCROOGE'S *name.*]

782 Drama

782

BOB. Mr. Scrooge . . .

SCROOGE. Huh? What's that? Who calls?

BOB. [*His glass raised in a toast*] I'll give you Mr. Scrooge, the Founder of the Feast!

SCROOGE. Me, Bob? You toast me?

PRESENT. Save your breath, Mr. Scrooge. You can't be seen or heard.

MRS. CRATCHIT. The Founder of the Feast, indeed! I wish I had him here, that miser Scrooge. I'd give him a piece of my mind to feast upon, and I hope he'd have a good appetite for it!

BOB. My dear! Christmas Day!

MRS. CRATCHIT. It should be Christmas Day, I am sure, on which one drinks the health of such an odious, stingy, unfeeling man as Mr. Scrooge . . .

⑲ ▲ Critical Viewing
Why might a director stage the scene this way, with Tiny Tim standing on the table? **[Interpret]**

⑳  **Reading Check**
What is wrong with Tiny Tim?

A Christmas Carol: Scrooge and Marley, Act 2 **783**

⑱ **? Connecting to the Big Question**

1. Point out that sometimes people gain insights gradually. Something gets their attention, but it may take them a while to completely figure out their reaction. Discuss ways that people might show an initial reaction through body language or facial expression.

2. Have students read the bracketed text that runs from p. 782 to p. 783. **Ask** students: What does Scrooge do in response to Present's call for Tiny Tim to hurry up and die? What does he do when Bob toasts him? What insights do these reactions suggest? **Possible responses:** Scrooge bows his head in response to Present. He shows surprise in response to Bob's toast. The first insight is in realizing that he might once have said what Present says. The second insight is in realizing that, unlike him, some people are generous even to those who have treated them badly.

3. **Ask:** Do you think Present's remark at the bottom of page 782 shows that Present sees Scrooge clearly? Do you think that Scrooge sees himself clearly in Present's remark? **Possible response:** Yes, Present's remark is a perfect description of Scrooge's attitudes. Yes, when Scrooge bows his head in response to Present's remark, he shows that he too sees himself in the remark.

⑲ Critical Viewing

Possible response: Some students might say that placing Tiny Tim on the table highlights his importance in the play as the character who most captures Scrooge's heart.

⑳ Reading Check

Answer: He is crippled and sick.

783

Compare and Contrast

1. Ask for volunteers to read the first bracketed text, which begins on p. 783. Assign the roles of Bob, Mrs. Cratchit, and Scrooge. You may want to have students reread the lines as though they were performing on stage to better express each character's tone.

2. Then **ask** students to compare and contrast Bob's attitude about Scrooge with Mrs. Cratchit's. **Answer:** Bob has a forgiving, benevolent attitude while Mrs. Cratchit's is aggravated and critical.

3. **Ask** students to explain why the characters feel the way they do about Scrooge and which character they agree with most. **Possible responses:** Bob is very kind and appreciates the job Scrooge has given him. Mrs. Cratchit is sorry that her husband must tolerate an "odious" man like Scrooge. Students might identify with Bob, because they know how unhappy Scrooge is, or they might agree with Mrs. Cratchit because Scrooge treats Bob so badly.

㉒ Critical Viewing

Answer: In modern times, Martha would probably play a guitar.

㉓ Stage Directions

1. **Ask** students to describe the scene's mood and find examples from the text to support their ideas. **Possible response:** Students might say the family's closeness and politeness is warm and sentimental. They might also note that Tim's poor health gives the scene a somber, sad feeling.

2. Read the bracketed section on pp. 784–785 aloud to students. Then, **ask** the Stage Directions question. **Possible response:** Tim is small and unwell, so having him sing about a tiny lost child intensifies the touching, emotional mood of the scene.

㉒ ▼ Critical Viewing
Martha plays a lute like this one while her family sings. If this play were set in modern times, what instrument would Martha probably play? **[Apply]**

Stage Directions
What does the song— and its subject—add to the mood of the scene?

784 Drama

SCROOGE. Oh, Spirit, must I? . . .

MRS. CRATCHIT You know he is, Robert! Nobody knows it better than you do, poor fellow!

BOB. This is Christmas Day, and I should like to drink to the health of the man who employs me and allows me to earn my living and our support and that man is Ebenezer Scrooge . . .

MRS. CRATCHIT. I'll drink to his health for your sake and the day's, but not for his sake . . . a Merry Christmas and a Happy New Year to you, Mr. Scrooge, wherever you may be this day!

SCROOGE. Just here, kind madam . . . out of sight, out of sight . . .

BOB. Thank you, my dear. Thank you.

SCROOGE. Thank you, Bob . . . and Mrs. Cratchit, too. No one else is toasting me, . . . not now . . . not ever. Of that I am sure . . .

BOB. Children . . .

ALL. Merry Christmas to Mr. Scrooge.

BOB. I'll pay you sixpence, Tim, for my favorite song.

TINY TIM. Oh, Father, I'd so love to sing it, but not for pay. This Christmas goose—this feast—you and Mother, my brother and sisters close with me: that's my pay—

BOB. Martha, will you play the notes on the lute, for Tiny Tim's song.

BELINDA. May I sing, too, Father?

BOB. We'll all sing.

[*They sing a song about a tiny child lost in the snow—probably from Wordsworth's poem.* TIM *sings the lead vocal; all chime in for the chorus. Their song fades under, as the* GHOST OF CHRISTMAS PRESENT *speaks.*]

㉑

㉓

Vocabulary Development © CCSS Language 6

Word Forms
Expand students' vocabulary by helping them learn related forms of the selection vocabulary words. All the words for Act II of *A Christmas Carol* have related forms. Give students a blank **Word Form Chart** (*Professional Development Guidebook*, p. 42), with *astonish, compulsion, severe, meager,* and *audible* in the correct columns. Work with the class to determine the related forms. The final chart should include the words shown.

Noun	Verb	Adjective	Adverb
astonishment	**astonish**	astonishing	astonishingly
compulsion	compel	compulsive, compulsory	compulsively
severity		**severe**	severely
meagerness		**meager**	meagerly
audibility		**audible**	audibly

PRESENT. Mark my words, Ebenezer Scrooge. I do not present the Cratchits to you because they are a handsome, or brilliant family. They are not handsome. They are not brilliant. They are not well-dressed, or tasteful to the times. Their shoes are not even waterproofed by virtue of money or cleverness spent. So when the pavement is wet, so are the insides of their shoes and the tops of their toes. These are the Cratchits, Mr. Scrooge. They are not highly special. They are happy, grateful, pleased with one another, contented with the time and how it passes. They don't sing very well, do they? But, nonetheless, they do sing . . . [*Pauses*] think of that, Scrooge. Fifteen shillings a week and they do sing . . . hear their song until its end.

SCROOGE. I am listening. [*The chorus sings full volume now, until . . . the song ends here.*] Spirit, it must be time for us to take our leave. I feel in my heart that it is . . . that I must think on that which I have seen here . . .

PRESENT. Touch my robe again . . .

[SCROOGE *touches* PRESENT'S *robe. The lights fade out on the* CRATCHITS, *who sit, frozen, at the table.* SCROOGE *and* PRESENT *in a spotlight now. Thunder, lightning, smoke. They are gone.*]

SCENE 4

[MARLEY *appears* D.L. *in single spotlight. A storm brews. Thunder and lightning.* SCROOGE *and* PRESENT *"fly" past,* U. *The storm continues, furiously, and, now and again,* SCROOGE *and* PRESENT *will zip past in their travels.* MARLEY *will speak straight out to the audience.*]

MARLEY. The Ghost of Christmas Present, my co-worker in this attempt to turn a miser, flies about now with that very miser, Scrooge, from street to street, and he points out partygoers on their way to Christmas parties. If one were to judge from the numbers of people on their way to friendly gatherings, one might think that no one was left at home to give anyone welcome . . . but that's not the case, is it? Every home is expecting company and . . . [*He laughs.*] Scrooge is amazed.

A Christmas Carol: Scrooge and Marley, Act 2 **785**

Spiral Review
Character What point is the Ghost of Christmas Present trying to impress upon Scrooge as he describes the Cratchits?

25 ✓ Reading Check
What does Scrooge observe the Cratchits doing?

Spiral Review
Character

1. Remind students that they studied the concept of character in the Unit 5 Literary Analysis Workshop (pp. 722–735).
2. **Ask** the Spiral Review question.

   Possible response: The Ghost is telling Scrooge that having a family and loving other people makes people happier than being pretty, stylish, smart, or rich.

24 ### Connecting to the Big Question

1. Remind students of the toast the Cratchits made to Mr. Scrooge on page 783 and again on page 784. Discuss how the Cratchit family appears to readers and to Scrooge.
2. Have students read the second bracketed passage on page 785. **Ask** students: Does Scrooge gain any insight in this scene? How can you tell?
   Possible response: Yes, he gains insight into the fact that family and love are more important than money. His comments that he's ready to go and that he needs to think about what he's seen show that he's gained insight.
3. **Ask:** Do you think Scrooge's insights throughout the scene at the Cratchits help him to see himself more clearly? Explain.
   Possible response: Yes, in seeing his behavior reflected by Present and contrasted by the Cratchits, Scrooge sees himself more clearly.

25 ### Reading Check
Answer: He observes them toast him and sing carols before dinner.

Differentiated Instruction for Universal Access

Strategy for Special-Needs Students

Review with students the meanings of the stage directions, such as *D.C., U.R., D.L.,* and *U.* (*downstage center, upstage right, downstage left,* and *upstage*) Make certain they understand that downstage refers to the front half of the stage while upstage pertains to the rear of the stage. Have students review the stage directions at the beginning of Scene 4 and draw diagrams that show the positions of the characters.

EL ### Vocabulary for English Learners

Students may encounter unfamiliar expressions. Discuss the following expressions with students along with any others they find unclear.

1. *piece of one's mind* (p. 783, bottom): tell a person why you are angry with him or her
2. *drinks the health of* (p. 783, bottom): make a toast in honor of someone
3. *for your sake, for his sake* (p. 784, middle): *sake* in this context means "benefit"
4. *take our leave* (p. 785, middle): leave, go away

1. Have students preview Scene 4, using their graphic organizers as a guide for determining their reading rate. **Ask** volunteers for suggestions about a possible rate. **Possible response:** Students might note that they will read the opening section carefully, since it seems dense with information, and they will read most of the dialogue at a quicker pace.

2. Read the first bracketed section aloud for students, which begins on p. 785. Show your reading rate for the stage directions that begin and end the section. Pause and inflect the many phrases as necessary to help students follow Marley's long sentences.

3. **Ask** students the Purpose for Reading question.
   Answer: The stage directions summarize events by describing the actions of Scrooge and Present, so it is important to read them carefully. Marley also relates important information about the action in the play. He also speaks in long sentences with many clauses and phrases, which should be read slowly and carefully.

4. **Ask** a volunteer to summarize the stage directions and Marley's dialogue.
   Answer: Present takes Scrooge on many flights. The great number of Christmas partygoers and their various destinations surprise Scrooge. Present ends the travels at Nephew's home.

Purpose for Reading
Why is it important to read the change of scene carefully? **26**

[SCROOGE *and* PRESENT *zip past again. The lights fade up around them. We are in the* NEPHEW'S *home, in the living room.* PRESENT *and* SCROOGE *stand watching the* NEPHEW: FRED *and his wife, fixing the fire.*]

SCROOGE. What is this place? We've moved from the mines!

PRESENT. You do not recognize them?

SCROOGE. It is my nephew! . . . and the one he married . . .

[MARLEY *waves his hand and there is a lightning flash. He disappears.*]

FRED. It strikes me as sooooo funny, to think of what he said . . . that Christmas was a humbug, as I live! He believed it!

WIFE. More shame for him, Fred!

FRED. Well, he's a comical old fellow, that's the truth.

WIFE. I have no patience with him.

FRED. Oh, I have! I am sorry for him; I couldn't be angry with him if I tried. Who suffers by his ill whims? Himself, always . . .

SCROOGE. It's me they talk of, isn't it, Spirit?

FRED. Here, wife, consider this. Uncle Scrooge takes it into his head to dislike us, and he won't come and dine with us. What's the consequence?

WIFE. Oh . . . you're sweet to say what I think you're about to say, too, Fred . . .

FRED. What's the consequence? He don't lose much of a dinner by it, I can tell you that!

WIFE. Ooooooo, Fred! Indeed, I think he loses a very good dinner . . . ask my sisters, or your bachelor friend, Topper . . . ask any of them. They'll tell you what old Scrooge, your uncle, missed: a dandy meal!

27

FRED. Well, that's something of a relief, wife. Glad to hear it! [*He hugs his wife. They laugh. They kiss.*] The truth is, he misses much yet. I mean to give him the same chance every year, whether he likes it or not, for I pity him. Nay, he is my only uncle and I feel for the old miser . . . but, I tell you,

786 Drama

Think Aloud

Vocabulary: Context Clues
Direct students' attention to the word *consequence* that appears twice in Fred's dialogue. Using a think-aloud process, model how to use context to infer the meaning of this word. Say to students:

I'm going to think aloud to show you how to use context clues to determine a meaning for the word *consequence*. Fred

asks the question, "What's the *consequence*?" Then he and his wife answer the question, indicating that the *consequence* is missing dinner. If Scrooge did not attend his nephew's party, then he would miss dinner. Not attending is the cause and missing dinner is the effect, so a *consequence* must be an *effect* or a *result* of one's actions.

wife: I see my dear and perfect mother's face on his own wizened cheeks and brow: brother and sister they were, and I cannot erase that from each view of him I take . . .

WIFE. I understand what you say, Fred, and I am with you in your yearly asking. But he never will accept, you know. He never will.

FRED. Well, true, wife. Uncle may rail at Christmas till he dies. I think I shook him some with my visit yesterday . . . [*Laughing*] I refused to grow angry . . . no matter how nasty he became . . . [*Whoops*] It was HE who grew angry, wife! [*They both laugh now.*]

SCROOGE. What he says is true, Spirit . . .

FRED AND WIFE. Bah, humbug!

FRED. [*Embracing his wife*] There is much laughter in our marriage, wife. It pleases me. You please me . . .

WIFE. And you please me, Fred. You are a good man . . . [*They embrace.*] Come now. We must have a look at the meal . . . our guests will soon arrive . . . my sisters, Topper . . .

FRED. A toast first . . . [*He hands her a glass.*] A toast to Uncle Scrooge . . . [*Fills their glasses*]

WIFE. A toast to him?

FRED. Uncle Scrooge has given us plenty of merriment, I am sure, and it would be ungrateful not to drink to his health. And I say . . . Uncle Scrooge!

WIFE. [*Laughing*] You're a proper loon,[5] Fred . . . and I'm a

Reading Check

What scenes does the Ghost of Christmas Present show Scrooge?

---

5. **a proper loon** a silly person.

A Christmas Carol: Scrooge and Marley, Act 2 **787**

1. Have students explain what is happening to the Present as time passes and why.
   Answer: Present is growing old very quickly because he only lives for one day.

2. Point out that nearly all of Christmas Day has passed. Then read the first bracketed line aloud and **ask** students to answer the Stage Directions question.

3. **Possible response:** By tolling the time 11:45, the clock emphasizes the urgency of Present's final words.

30 **Critical Thinking**

Connect

1. Draw students' attention to the second bracketed passage. **Ask** them to recall where they read these words earlier in the play.
   Answer: In speaking to the men who come to his office asking for money for the poor, Scrooge suggests that if the poor can go to workhouses and prisons, they do not need charity.

2. Point out that this is one of several instances in the play where the dialogue echoes something Scrooge has said earlier. Guide students to see how this technique connects to the plot of the work. Explain that by using Scrooge's own words to reply to him, the ghosts give Scrooge a taste of his own medicine.

Vocabulary
audible (ô′ də bəl) *adj.*
loud enough to be heard

Stage Directions **29**
Why is the clock on stage important to the action?

proper wife to you . . . [*She raises her glass.*] Uncle Scrooge! [*They drink. They embrace. They kiss.*]

SCROOGE. Spirit, please, make me visible! Make me audible! I want to talk with my nephew and my niece!

[*Calls out to them. The lights that light the room and* FRED *and wife fade out.* SCROOGE *and* PRESENT *are alone, spotlit.*]

PRESENT. These shadows are gone to you now, Mr. Scrooge. You may return to them later tonight in your dreams. [*Pauses*] My time grows short, Ebenezer Scrooge. Look you on me! Do you see how I've aged?

SCROOGE. Your hair has gone gray! Your skin, wrinkled! Are spirits' lives so short?

PRESENT. My stay upon this globe is very brief. It ends tonight.

SCROOGE. Tonight?

PRESENT. At midnight. The time is drawing near!

[*Clock strikes 11:45.*]

Hear those chimes? In a quarter hour, my life will have been spent! Look, Scrooge, man. Look you here.

[*Two gnarled baby dolls are taken from* PRESENT'S *skirts.*]

SCROOGE. Who are they?

PRESENT. They are Man's children, and they cling to me, appealing from their fathers. The boy is Ignorance; the girl is Want. Beware them both, and all of their degree, but most of all beware this boy, for I see that written on his brow which is doom, unless the writing be erased. [*He stretches out his arm. His voice is now amplified: loudly and oddly.*]

30

SCROOGE. Have they no refuge or resource?

PRESENT. Are there no prisons? Are there no workhouses? [*Twelve chimes*] Are there no prisons? Are there no workhouses?

[*A* PHANTOM, *hooded, appears in dim light,* D., *opposite.*] Are there no prisons? Are there no workhouses?

[PRESENT *begins to deliquesce.* SCROOGE *calls after him.*]

Vocabulary Development

Graphic Organizers
Have students analyze the words *refuge* and *resource* using a **Cluster Diagram** (*Graphic Organizer Transparencies*, p. 209). Fill in the organizer to show the following information: definition, characteristics, and examples. Then, work with students to complete information about *refuge* and *resource*.

Refuge

Definition: shelter or protection from danger; a place that provides protection; something to which one may turn for help or relief

Characteristics: helpful, necessary, may be lifesaving

Examples: homes, schools, churches, families, friends

Resource

Definition: a source of help; a supply that can be drawn upon when needed

Characteristics: available, useful, helpful

Examples: education, skills, necessary supplies such as food or water, money saved, strength, people

SCROOGE. Spirit, I'm frightened! Don't leave me! Spirit!

PRESENT. Prisons? Workhouses? Prisons? Workhouses . . .

[*He is gone.* SCROOGE *is alone now with the* PHANTOM, *who is, of course, the* GHOST OF CHRISTMAS FUTURE. *The* PHANTOM *is shrouded in black. Only its outstretched hand is visible from under his ghostly garment.*]

SCROOGE. Who are you, Phantom? Oh, yes, I think I know you! You are, are you not, the Spirit of Christmas Yet to Come? [*No reply*] And you are about to show me the shadows of the things that have not yet happened, but will happen in time before us. Is that not so, Spirit? [*The* PHANTOM *allows* SCROOGE *a look at his face. No other reply wanted here. A nervous giggle here.*] Oh, Ghost of the Future, I fear you more than any Specter I have seen! But, as I know that your purpose is to do me good and as I hope to live to be another man from what I was, I am prepared to bear you company. [FUTURE *does not reply, but for a stiff arm, hand and finger set, pointing forward.*] Lead on, then, lead on. The night is waning fast, and it is precious time to me. Lead on, Spirit!

[FUTURE *moves away from* SCROOGE *in the same rhythm and motion employed at its arrival.* SCROOGE *falls into the same pattern, a considerable space apart from the* SPIRIT. *In the space between them,* MARLEY *appears. He looks to* FUTURE *and then to* SCROOGE. *He claps his hands. Thunder and lightning. Three* BUSINESSMEN *appear, spotlighted singularly: One is D.L.; one is D.R.; one is U.C. Thus, six points of the stage should now be spotted in light.* MARLEY *will watch this scene from his position,* C. SCROOGE *and* FUTURE *are* R. *and* L. *of* C.]

FIRST BUSINESSMAN. Oh, no, I don't know much about it either way, I only know he's dead.

SECOND BUSINESSMAN. When did he die?

FIRST BUSINESSMAN. Last night, I believe.

SECOND BUSINESSMAN. Why, what was the matter with him? I thought he'd never die, really . . .

FIRST BUSINESSMAN. [*Yawning*] Goodness knows, goodness knows . . .

Stage Directions
The stage direction calls for Future to stretch out his hand. How does this action add to the drama of the scene?

Spiral Review
Character What valuable information does Scrooge reveal about himself?

Reading Check 32
What warning does the Ghost of Christmas Present give Scrooge?

A Christmas Carol: Scrooge and Marley, Act 2 **789**

Infer

1. Have three students each read aloud a part of the first bracketed passage, which begins on p. 789. Then, **ask** students whom the men are talking about in the passage.
   Answer: The men are talking about Scrooge.

2. **Ask** students what clues led them to make an inference about the topic of the conversation.
   Possible responses: The fact that they are in the future is a clue, and they might say that the words "money to money" and "cheap funeral" suggest references to Scrooge.

3. **Ask** students why the Ghost wants Scrooge to witness his own funeral.
   Possible response: The Ghost wants Scrooge to see that no one will be sorry to see him die if he does not change his ways.

34 **Critical Viewing**

Answer: The Ghost of Christmas Present speaks and is colorful and inviting, while the Ghost of Christmas Future is bleak, dark, and eerie.

34 **Critical Viewing**
How does the Ghost of Christmas Future differ from the other ghosts? **[Contrast]**

790 Drama

THIRD BUSINESSMAN. What has he done with his money?

SECOND BUSINESSMAN. I haven't heard. Have you?

FIRST BUSINESSMAN. Left it to his Company, perhaps. Money to money; you know the expression . . .

THIRD BUSINESSMAN. He hasn't left it to me. That's all I know . . .

FIRST BUSINESSMAN. [*Laughing*] Nor to me . . . [*Looks at* SECOND BUSINESSMAN] You, then? You got his money???

SECOND BUSINESSMAN. [*Laughing*] Me, me, his money? Nooooo!

[*They all laugh.*]

THIRD BUSINESSMAN. It's likely to be a cheap funeral, for upon my life, I don't know of a living soul who'd care to venture to it. Suppose we make up a party and volunteer?

SECOND BUSINESSMAN. I don't mind going if a lunch is provided, but I must be fed, if I make one.

FIRST BUSINESSMAN. Well, I am the most disinterested among you, for I never wear black gloves, and I never eat lunch. But I'll offer to go, if anybody else will. When I come to think of it, I'm not all sure that I wasn't his most particular friend; for we used to stop and speak whenever we met. Well, then . . . bye, bye!

SECOND BUSINESSMAN. Bye, bye . . .

THIRD BUSINESSMAN. Bye, bye . . .

[*They glide offstage in three separate directions. Their lights follow them.*]

SCROOGE. Spirit, why did you show me this? Why do you show me businessmen from my streets as they take the death of Jacob Marley. That is a thing past. You are future!

35 [JACOB MARLEY *laughs a long, deep laugh. There is a thunder clap and lightning flash, and he is gone.* SCROOGE *faces* FUTURE, *alone on stage now.* FUTURE *wordlessly stretches*

33

Vocabulary Development   © CCSS Language 6

Selection Vocabulary Reinforcement
Students will benefit from additional examples and practice with the selection vocabulary words. Reinforce their comprehension with "show-you-know" sentences. The first part of the sentence uses the vocabulary word in an appropriate context. The second part of the sentence—the "show-you-know" part—clarifies the first. Model the strategy with this example for *astonish*:

Your clean room will *astonish* your mother; she'll be shocked not to see the usual disaster.

Then, give students these sentence prompts, and coach them in creating the clarification part:

1. She feels a *compulsion* to wash her hands; _____.

2. His illness is *severe*; _____.

3. We ate only a *meager* breakfast; _____.

4. We want the music to be *audible* in the rear of the concert hall; _____.

out his arm-hand-and-finger-set, pointing into the distance, U. There, above them. Scoundrels "fly" by, half-dressed and slovenly. When this scene has passed, a woman enters the playing area. She is almost at once followed by a second woman; and then a man in faded black; and then, suddenly, an old man, who smokes a pipe. The old man scares the other three. They laugh, anxious.]

FIRST WOMAN. Look here, old Joe, here's a chance! If we haven't all three met here without meaning it!

OLD JOE. You couldn't have met in a better place. Come into the parlor. You were made free of it long ago, you know; and the other two ain't strangers [*He stands; shuts a door. Shrieking*] We're all suitable to our calling. We're well matched. Come into the parlor. Come into the parlor . . . [*They follow him D. SCROOGE and FUTURE are now in their midst, watching; silent. A truck comes in on which is set a small wall with fireplace and a screen of rags, etc. All props for the scene.*] Let me just rake this fire over a bit . . .

[*He does. He trims his lamp with the stem of his pipe. The FIRST WOMAN throws a large bundle on to the floor. She sits beside it crosslegged, defiantly.*]

FIRST WOMAN. What odds then? What odds, Mrs. Dilber? Every person has a right to take care of themselves. HE always did!

MRS. DILBER. That's true indeed! No man more so!

FIRST WOMAN. Why, then, don't stand staring as if you was afraid, woman! Who's the wiser? We're not going to pick holes in each other's coats, I suppose?

MRS. DILBER. No, indeed! We should hope not!

FIRST WOMAN. Very well, then! That's enough. Who's the worse for the loss of a few things like these? Not a dead man, I suppose?

MRS. DILBER. [*Laughing*] No, indeed!

FIRST WOMAN. If he wanted to keep 'em after he was dead, the wicked old screw, why wasn't he natural in his lifetime? If he had been, he'd have had somebody to look after him

Stage Directions
If you were staging this play, how could you make people appear to "fly" by?

36 Reading Check
What does Scrooge think the spirit is showing him?

---

35 Stage Directions

1. Have students read the first bracketed passage, which begins on p. 790. Then, direct their attention to the line that describes "scoundrels" flying by, and **ask** students to respond to the Stage Directions question. **Possible response:** Students might suggest using ropes to swing actors across the stage, while others might prefer using projectors to display actors on an overhead screen.

2. Remind students that early in Act II, Marley delighted in the prospect of surprising Scrooge by shifting time back and forth. Then, **ask** students why showing flying people might be important. **Possible response:** Students might say that magical occurrences like flying people would affect Scrooge more strongly than anything common or ordinary.

36 Reading Check

Answer: Scrooge thinks that the spirit is showing him businessmen discussing the death of Jacob Marley.

Differentiated Instruction for Universal Access

Support for Less Proficient Readers
Check students understanding of the funeral scene by asking these questions:

1. Do the businessmen speak of Scrooge respectfully or carelessly? What are some examples that show this? (They speak carelessly, such as when the second man says, "I thought he'd never die, really . . ." on p. 789, or when they all laugh on p. 790.)

2. Why might each man attend the funeral? (The First will go to enjoy the company of the others, the Second wants a free lunch, and

the Third seems to pity Scrooge because no one else will attend—p. 790.)

3. How do Scrooge's words at the bottom of p. 790 reveal that the funeral is for him and not Marley? (The funeral takes place in the future and Marley's funeral already occurred.)

If students have difficulty with the questions, assign the roles of First, Second, and Third Businessmen to three of them and have them read the dialogue that begins at the bottom of p. 789. Then, have students summarize their reading.

1. Read aloud the first bracketed passage, which begins on p. 791. **Ask** students to summarize the events that led to First Woman's speech.
   Answer: Someone has died and the woman is taking his things.

2. Read aloud First Woman's final remark on p. 791. Then, **ask** students the Purpose for Reading question.
   Possible response: She asks why Scrooge didn't behave more naturally while alive. This directs me to read to find out if she knew Scrooge when he was alive.

3. Have students **speculate** about the woman's identity.
   Possible response: Students may suggest that the woman is a thief, that she worked in Scrooge's house, or that she worked for the people who prepared Scrooge's body.

4. Tell students they will read further to confirm or revise their ideas.

Purpose for Reading
What question about the characters directs your purpose for reading this dialogue?

37

when he was struck with Death, instead of lying gasping out his last there, alone by himself.

MRS. DILBER. It's the truest word that was ever spoke. It's a judgment on him.

FIRST WOMAN. I wish it were a heavier one, and it should have been, you may depend on it, if I could have laid my hands on anything else. Open that bundle, old Joe, and let me know the value of it. Speak out plain. I'm not afraid to be the first, nor afraid for them to see it. We knew pretty well that we were helping ourselves, before we met here, I believe. It's no sin. Open the bundle, Joe.

FIRST MAN. No, no, my dear! I won't think of letting you being the first to show what you've . . . earned . . . earned from this. I throw in mine.

[*He takes a bundle from his shoulder, turns it upside down, and empties its contents out on to the floor.*]

It's not very extensive, see . . . seals . . . a pencil case . . . sleeve buttons . . .

FIRST WOMAN. Nice sleeve buttons, though . . .

FIRST MAN. Not bad, not bad . . . a brooch there . . .

OLD JOE. Not really valuable, I'm afraid . . .

FIRST MAN. How much, old Joe?

OLD JOE. [*Writing on the wall with chalk*] A pitiful lot, really. Ten and six and not a sixpence more!

FIRST MAN. You're not serious!

OLD JOE. That's your account and I wouldn't give another sixpence if I was to be boiled for not doing it. Who's next?

MRS. DILBER. Me! [*Dumps out contents of her bundle*] Sheets, towels, silver spoons, silver sugar-tongs . . . some boots . . .

38

OLD JOE. [*Writing on wall*] I always give too much to the ladies. It's a weakness of mine and that's the way I ruin myself. Here's your total comin' up . . . two pounds-ten . . . if you asked me for another penny, and made it an open question, I'd repent of being so liberal and knock off half-a-crown.

FIRST WOMAN. And now do MY bundle, Joe.

792 Drama

Think Aloud

Vocabulary: Dictionary Use
Some dictionary definitions may be incomprehensible to students. Model how to choose the best definition for an unfamiliar word using a think-aloud process. Direct students' attention to the word *liberal* in Old Joe's dialogue on p. 792. Then, say to students:

> This word may be unfamiliar, so I am going to find its definition. We'll need to consider the context in which *liberal* is used because the dictionary has several definitions for it.

In the story, Old Joe complains that he pays ladies too much, but says he won't be so *liberal* if Mrs. Dilber complains. That means he won't give her as much money.

Let's look at the definitions: 1. following political views that promote social progress. No, that doesn't have anything to do with giving too much. 2. generous. *Generous* means "giving" so this one might work. 3. not literal. 4. tolerant. 5. not conservative. None of the last three relate to giving, so in this case, *liberal* means "generous."

OLD JOE. [*Kneeling to open knots on her bundle*] So many knots, madam . . . [*He drags out large curtains; dark*] What do you call this? Bed curtains!

FIRST WOMAN. [*Laughing*] Ah, yes, bed curtains!

OLD JOE. You don't mean to say you took 'em down, rings and all, with him lying there?

FIRST WOMAN. Yes, I did, why not?

OLD JOE. You were born to make your fortune and you'll certainly do it.

FIRST WOMAN. I certainly shan't hold my hand, when I can get anything in it by reaching it out, for the sake of such a man as he was, I promise you, Joe. Don't drop that lamp oil on those blankets, now!

OLD JOE. His blankets?

FIRST WOMAN. Whose else's do you think? He isn't likely to catch cold without 'em, I daresay.

OLD JOE. I hope that he didn't die of anything catching? Eh?

FIRST WOMAN. Don't you be afraid of that. I ain't so fond of his company that I'd loiter about him for such things if he did. Ah! You may look through that shirt till your eyes ache, but you won't find a hole in it, nor a threadbare place. It's the best he had, and a fine one, too. They'd have wasted it, if it hadn't been for me.

OLD JOE. What do you mean 'They'd have wasted it?'

FIRST WOMAN. Putting it on him to be buried in, to be sure. Somebody was fool enough to do it, but I took it off again . . .

[*She laughs, as do they all, nervously.*]

If calico[6] ain't good enough for such a purpose, it isn't good enough then for anything. It's quite as becoming to the body. He can't look uglier than he did in that one!

SCROOGE. [*A low-pitched moan emits from his mouth; from the bones.*] OOOOOOOooooooOOOOOooooooOOOOOOOOO ooooooOOOOOOooooooOO!

---

6. **calico** (kal′ i kō) *n.* coarse and cheap cloth.

Stage Directions
How do the stage directions help you picture the action in this scene?

Reading Check
Whose possessions are these people selling?

A Christmas Carol: Scrooge and Marley, Act 2 **793**

---

38 Stage Directions

1. Have students read the bracketed dialogue, which begins on p. 792. Then, **ask** a volunteer to summarize what is happening in this section.
   Answer: The women and one man are selling their stolen goods to Old Joe.

2. Point out that the dialogue explains what items have been stolen and how much they are worth. Then, **ask** the Stage Directions question.
   Possible response: The stage directions are necessary for explaining the characters' movements, since they don't tell us in their dialogue.

3. Have volunteers reread the section aloud, omitting the stage directions. Instruct remaining students to listen, but not to read along. Then, discuss whether they would still understand the story without the stage directions.

39 Reading Check

Answer: The people are selling Scrooge's possessions.

Differentiated Instruction for Universal Access

Strategy for Special-Needs Students
Ask students to describe Old Joe, First Woman, Mrs. Dilber, and First Man. Then, explain that even though these characters are thieves, they come off as better people than Scrooge. Help students to understand by explaining that even though the people are thieves, they are poor and their misdeeds are motivated by a need for survival. Clarify also that Scrooge seems meaner because he mistreated these people when he was alive.

Enrichment for Gifted/Talented Students
Have students review this scene with the thieves and pawnbroker. Then, ask them to write songs or narrative poems about the events. Challenge students to incorporate a rhyme scheme into their poems or songs. Encourage them to use other poetic devices with which they are familiar, such as alliteration, simile, and metaphor. Tell them to focus on capturing the action and emotion presented in this scene, as well as the characters' personality traits. Ask volunteers to read aloud their poems or perform their songs for the class.

793

1. Ask students to reread the first bracketed passage. Point out that Scrooge and Future are no longer watching the thieves. Scrooge is now standing in front of his own corpse, pleading with Future, who once again points but does not speak.

2. **Ask** students the Stage Directions question.
Possible responses: Students might note that the Spirit's silence adds to the gloom and despair of the scene. They may also mention that the silence makes the scene more frightening.

3. **Ask** students why they think Future is silent. **Possible responses:** The future hasn't happened yet. Future can't shape what will happen, only Scrooge can do that.

▶ **Monitor Progress** Have students compare the Ghosts of Christmas Present and Future.

▶ **Reteach** Remind students that the Spirit wants to emphasize the most undesirable results of Scrooge's actions and will not give Scrooge the comfort of a verbal response. You might have students imagine how unnerving it would be to see something as ghastly as Scrooge has viewed and not have the comfort of hearing your companion, who is showing you these things, say a single word.

41 Critical Viewing

Possible responses: Students might say that the director placed the actors on the stage floor to emphasize their humble social status. The characters are positioned in a way that shows how close the family is and how they have drawn together since Tiny Tim's death. The actors' somber faces show their heavy mood.

Stage Directions
What is the effect of the spirit's silence?

41 ▶ **Critical Viewing**
Why might a director choose to place the actors playing the Cratchits this way? What do their positions reveal about the family? **[Analyze]**

794 Drama

OLD JOE. One pound six for the lot. [*He produces a small flannel bag filled with money. He divvies it out. He continues to pass around the money as he speaks. All are laughing.*] That's the end of it, you see! He frightened every one away from him while he was alive, to profit us when he was dead! Hah ha ha!

ALL. HAHAHAHAhahahahahahah!

SCROOGE. OOOoooOOOoooOOOoooOOOooo OOoooOOoooOOOooo! [*He screams at them.*] Obscene demons! Why not market the corpse itself, as sell its trimming??? [*Suddenly*] Oh, Spirit, I see it, I see it! This unhappy man—this stripped-bare corpse . . . could very well be my own. My life holds parallel! My life ends that way now!

[SCROOGE *backs into something in the dark behind his spotlight.* SCROOGE *looks at* FUTURE, *who points to the corpse.* SCROOGE *pulls back the blanket. The corpse is, of course,* SCROOGE, *who screams. He falls aside the bed; weeping.*]

Spirit, this is a fearful place. In leaving it, I shall not leave its lesson, trust me. Let us go!

40 [FUTURE *points to the corpse.*]

Spirit, let me see some tenderness connected with a death, or that dark chamber, which we just left now, Spirit, will be forever present to me.

[FUTURE *spreads his robes again. Thunder and lightning. Lights up, U., in the* CRATCHIT *home setting.* MRS. CRATCHIT *and her daughters, sewing*]

42 TINY TIM'S VOICE. [*Off*] And He took a child and set him in the midst of them.

SCROOGE. [*Looking about the room; to* FUTURE] Huh? Who spoke? Who said that?

MRS. CRATCHIT. [*Puts down her sewing*] The color hurts my eyes. [*Rubs her eyes*] That's better. My eyes grow weak sewing by candlelight. I shouldn't want to show your father weak eyes when he comes home . . . not for the world! It must be near his time . . .

Vocabulary Development

©CCSS Language 6

Expressive Vocabulary
To help students broaden their expressive vocabulary encourage them to use the following words as they discuss the changes they see in Scrooge: *responds, require, plead, trigger,* and *survive.* Have them complete these sentence starters.

1. Scrooge *responds* to what he has seen by . . .
2. The Ghost of Christmas Future seems to think that Scrooge will *require* . . .
3. In this scene, we see Scrooge *plead* with the Ghost about . . .
4. Seeing his own corpse seems to *trigger* . . .
5. This scene also suggests that Tiny Tim did not *survive* because . . .

PETER. [*In corner, reading. Looks up from book*] Past it, rather. But I think he's been walking a bit slower than usual these last few evenings, Mother.

MRS. CRATCHIT I have known him walk with . . . [*Pauses*] I have know him walk with Tiny Tim upon his shoulder and very fast indeed.

PETER. So have I, Mother! Often!

DAUGHTER. So have I.

MRS. CRATCHIT. But he was very light to carry and his father loved him so, that it was not trouble—no trouble. [BOB, *at door*] And there is your father at the door.

[BOB CRATCHIT *enters. He wears a comforter. He is cold, forlorn.*]

PETER. Father!

BOB. Hello, wife, children . . .

[*The daughter weeps; turns away from* CRATCHIT.]

Children! How good to see you all! And you, wife. And look at this sewing! I've no doubt, with all your industry,

43 ☑ Reading Check

Whose corpse does Scrooge see?

A Christmas Carol: Scrooge and Marley, Act 2 **795**

Differentiated Instruction for Universal Access

Strategy for Less Proficient Readers

Help students see the contrast in the characters' reactions to the two deaths in this scene. Review with them the reactions Scrooge witnesses to his own death. (Scrooge sees businessmen casually discussing his death, his money, and whether they have any reason to attend his funeral. He also sees thieves discussing his poor treatment of others and showing no remorse for selling items stolen from his home.) Ask students why they think Scrooge wants to see kind, tender reactions to a death. (He wants to know that people do grieve when someone they love dies.) Point out that the Cratchits are deeply saddened by the loss of Tiny Tim. Have students define what qualities in Scrooge and Tiny Tim account for the differences in people's reactions to their respective deaths. (Scrooge is stingy, thoughtless, rude, and unfriendly. Tiny Tim is caring, lively, and cheerful.) Have students discuss why it is important for Scrooge to see these scenes and how they will affect him. (These scenes point out to Scrooge what an odious person he is and may encourage him to help the Cratchits in any way he can.)

---

42 Critical Thinking

Infer

1. Read aloud the bracketed passage beginning at the bottom of page 794. **Ask** students to describe the scene.
   Possible response: The Cratchits are gathered together, waiting for Mr. Cratchit to come home.

2. Point out the line spoken by Tiny Tim's Voice. **Ask** students if Tiny Tim is present at the Cratchit's house.
   Answer: No, his line is spoken from off-stage.

3. Point out Peter's remark that his father has been walking a bit slower than usual and Mrs. Cratchit's reply. **Ask** students why Mrs. Cratchit pauses in her reply.
   Answer: She is hesitant to mention Tiny Tim's name or to call up the image of the boy on his father's shoulder.

4. Challenge students to infer what has happened to Tiny Tim.
   Possible response: He has died.

43 Reading Check

Answer: Scrooge sees his own corpse.

1. Read the bracketed dialogue aloud to students. Then, **ask** the Purpose for Reading question. **Answer:** Scrooge's nephew expressed his sympathy for the Cratchit's loss, gave Bob his card, and offered to help in any way he could.

2. Have students speculate about ways Scrooge's nephew could help the Cratchits. **Possible response:** Students might say that he could help Bob find a new job.

3. Tell students they will continue reading to confirm or revise their ideas.

we'll have a quilt to set down upon our knees in church on Sunday!

MRS. CRATCHIT. You made the arrangements today, then, Robert, for the . . . service . . . to be on Sunday.

BOB. The funeral. Oh, well, yes, yes, I did. I wish you could have gone. It would have done you good to see how green a place it is. But you'll see it often. I promised him that I would walk there on Sunday, after the service. [*Suddenly*] My little, little child! My little child!

ALL CHILDREN. [*Hugging him*] Oh, Father . . .

BOB. [*He stands*] Forgive me. I saw Mr. Scrooge's nephew, who you know I'd just met once before, and he was so wonderful to me, wife . . . he is the most pleasant-spoken gentleman I've ever met . . . he said "I am heartily sorry for it and heartily sorry for your good wife. If I can be of service to you in any way, here's where I live." And he gave me this card.

PETER. Let me see it!

BOB. And he looked me straight in the eye, wife, and said, meaningfully, "I pray you'll come to me, Mr. Cratchit, if you need some help. I pray you do." Now it wasn't for the sake of anything that he might be able to do for us, so much as for his kind way. It seemed as if he had known our Tiny Tim and felt with us.

MRS. CRATCHIT. I'm sure that he's a good soul.

BOB. You would be surer of it, my dear, if you saw and spoke to him. I shouldn't be at all surprised, if he got Peter a situation.

MRS. CRATCHIT. Only hear that, Peter!

MARTHA. And then, Peter will be keeping company with someone and setting up for himself!

PETER. Get along with you!

BOB. It's just as likely as not, one of these days, though there's plenty of time for that, my dear. But however and whenever we part from one another, I am sure we shall none of us forget poor Tiny Tim—shall we?—or this first parting that was among us?

Purpose for Reading
What plot information does this dialogue provide about a possible future for the Cratchits?

44

Vocabulary Development

Ⓒ **CCSS** Language 6

Multiple Meanings

Tell students that the word *industry* is a noun that has several different but related meanings—they all have to do with either work or effort. Have students read Bob Cratchit's lines at the bottom of p. 795 and suggest a meaning for the word *industry* as it is used there. (hard work; diligence) Ask students to use the word in sentences that relate to themselves. Then, explain that *industry* can have a very general meaning that refers to commercial manufacturing and sales of goods and services as a whole. It can also refer to a certain type of business that employs people, such as the fitness industry or the car manufacturing industry. Ask students to provide examples of other industries. (logging, construction, computer, publishing, music, and so on)

ALL CHILDREN. Never, Father, never!

BOB. And when we recollect how patient and mild he was, we shall not quarrel easily among ourselves, and forget poor Tiny Tim in doing it.

ALL CHILDREN. No, Father, never!

LITTLE BOB. I am very happy, I am, I am, I am very happy.

[BOB *kisses his little son, as does* MRS. CRATCHIT, *as do the other children. The family is set now in one sculptural embrace. The lighting fades to a gentle pool of light, tight on them.*]

SCROOGE. Specter, something informs me that our parting moment is at hand. I know it, but I know not how I know it.

[FUTURE *points to the other side of the stage. Lights out on* CRATCHITS. FUTURE *moves slowing, gliding.* SCROOGE *follows.* FUTURE *points opposite.* FUTURE *leads* SCROOGE *to a wall and a tombstone. He points to the stone.*]

Am I that man those ghoulish parasites[7] so gloated over? [*Pauses*] Before I draw nearer to that stone to which you point, answer me one question. Are these the shadows of things that will be, or the shadows of things that MAY be, only?

45 ▼ **Critical Viewing**
Why do you think the sight of this tombstone terrified Scrooge? **[Connect]**

Reading Check

48 What has happened to Tiny Tim?

---

7. **ghoulish parasites** (gōōl′ ish par′ ə sits) man and women who stole and divided Scrooge's goods after he died.

A Christmas Carol: Scrooge and Marley, Act 2 **797**

Differentiated Instruction for Universal Access

Culturally Responsive Instruction

Culture Focus Students may lack the background knowledge or context-building experiences necessary to fully comprehend the selection. At this point in the students' reading, build additional background about funerals. Point out the reference to "the service." Explain that in many cultures, a funeral includes a religious service. The service may be held in a house of worship, such as a church or temple. Prayers may be recited and people may speak of the person who has died. In addition, part of the service may take place at a cemetery, or burial ground, which is typically a park-like place with grass and trees. Many cultures have different ways to observe funerals, but almost all have rituals and traditions associated with the passage into death. Invite students to share their knowledge and experience of such cultural traditions in their home culture or family's country of origin.

---

45 Critical Viewing

Possible response: Scrooge is frightened of spending eternity in Marley's condition, and the stone probably reminds him of his unbearable fate.

46 Critical Thinking

Infer

1. Read the bracketed passage aloud, and **ask** the students how they feel about Tiny Tim as they hear about him through the dialogue.

    Possible responses: Students might say they feel sad or sorry that he died. They might also say that he was a good model for how to behave.

2. **Ask** students how Bob describes Tiny Tim.

    Answer: Tiny Tim was patient and mild-mannered.

3. Have students infer how the memory of Tiny Tim will serve his family.

    Answer: The memory of Tiny Tim's gentle character may bring peace to his brothers and sisters.

47 Critical Thinking

Interpret

1. Read aloud the second bracketed passage, which continues onto p. 798. Then, **ask** why it is important for Scrooge to know whether the visions are shadows of things that will happen or of things that might happen.

    Answer: His hopes are based on the possibility that he can change the future by changing his behavior.

2. Ask students to speculate about whether Scrooge will get a second chance. Tell them to check their predictions as they read on.

48 Reading Check

Answer: Tiny Tim has died.

797

49 Stage Directions

1. **Ask** students to identify the only form of communication Future has offered and to describe its effect.
   Answer: Future points at objects, stressing their significance to Scrooge.

2. Have students read the bracketed passage that begins, "Spirit!" and note that the stage directions indicate Future's response to Scrooge's pleas. Then, **ask** the Stage Directions question.
   Answer: The Spirit's hand wavers and then trembles.

3. If students struggle to answer the question, use the Think Aloud note on p. 798 to support them.

4. **Ask** students to imagine that Future says "yes" or "no," rather than gesturing. Then, **ask** how the silent actions build suspense.
   Possible response: The gestures build the tension and suspense because they don't give Scrooge a definite answer.

50 Critical Thinking

Interpret

1. Read aloud the bracketed passage that begins "I will honor". Then, **ask** students what Scrooge means by the first sentence.
   Answer: Scrooge means he will honor kindheartedness and charity by being kindhearted and charitable all year round.

2. Reread the rest of the passage, and **ask** students to paraphrase its meaning.
   Answer: Scrooge will hold his whole life dear, including the Past, Present, and Future, and will keep in mind the lessons he learned from these times. He wonders if he can change the Spirit's prediction by changing his actions.

3. **Ask** students why Scrooge has made so many promises.
   Possible responses: Perhaps he has had a change of heart or perhaps he has made these promises to avoid the horrible end shown to him by the Ghost of Christmas Future.

[FUTURE *points to the gravestone.* MARLEY *appears in light well U. He points to grave as well. Gravestone turns front and grows to ten feet high. Words upon it:* EBENEZER SCROOGE: *Much smoke billows now from the grave. Choral music here.* SCROOGE *stands looking up at gravestone.* FUTURE *does not at all reply in mortals' words, but points once more to the gravestone. The stone undulates and glows. Music plays, beckoning* SCROOGE. SCROOGE *reeling in terror*]

Oh, no. Spirit! Oh, no, no!

[FUTURE'S *finger still pointing*]

Spirit! Hear me! I am not the man I was. I will not be the man I would have been but for this intercourse. Why show me this, if I am past all hope?

[FUTURE *considers* SCROOGE'S *logic. His hand wavers.*]

Oh, Good Spirit, I see by your wavering hand that your good nature intercedes for me and pities me. Assure me that I yet may change these shadows that you have shown me by an altered life!

[FUTURE'S *hand trembles; pointing has stopped.*]

I will honor Christmas in my heart and try to keep it all the year. I will live in the Past, the Present, and the Future. The Spirits of all Three shall strive within me. I will not shut out the lessons that they teach. Oh, tell me that I may sponge away the writing that is upon this stone!

[SCROOGE *makes a desperate stab at grabbing* FUTURE'S *hand. He holds firm for a moment, but* FUTURE, *stronger than* SCROOGE, *pulls away.* SCROOGE *is on his knees, praying.*]

Spirit, dear Spirit, I am praying before you. Give me a sign that all is possible. Give me a sign that all hope for me is not lost. Oh, Spirit, kind Spirit, I beseech thee: give me a sign . . .

[FUTURE *deliquesces, slowly, gently. The* PHANTOM'S *hood and robe drop gracefully to the ground in a small heap. Music in. There is nothing in them. They are mortal cloth. The* SPIRIT *is elsewhere.* SCROOGE *has his sign.* SCROOGE *is alone. Tableau. The lights fade to black.*]

Vocabulary
intercedes (in′tər sēdz′) *v.* makes a request on behalf of another

50 Stage Directions
What action described in the stage directions gives Scrooge hope that he may change the future?

Think Aloud

Predicting
Explain that to answer the Stage Directions question on page 798, students will have to make a prediction, a skill introduced on page 217. To reinforce that process, use the following "think aloud":

When I read the stage direction that says *"His hand wavers,"* I realize that it holds an important clue about how Scrooge's question will be answered. When I read on, I see that the next stage directions says *"FUTURE'S hand trembles; pointing has stopped."* The

words *wavers* and *trembles* suggest hesitation on FUTURE'S part, so I think that maybe there's a chance Scrooge is right about being able to change the future. I can predict that Scrooge will find a way to change his actions and thus change his future. As I read the rest of Scene 4, I see that Scrooge asks for a sign and that the stage directions say that he gets that sign. Now I am really sure that Scrooge will find a way to change his future. I will read further to see if my prediction is correct.

SCENE

[*The end of it.* MARLEY, *spotlighted, opposite* SCROOGE, *in his bed, spotlighted.* MARLEY *speaks to audience, directly.*]

MARLEY. [*He smiles at* SCROOGE:] The firm of Scrooge and Marley is doubly blessed; two misers turned; one, alas, in Death, too late; but the other miser turned in Time's penultimate nick.[8] Look you on my friend, Ebenezer Scrooge . . .

SCROOGE. [*Scrambling out of bed; reeling in delight*] I will live in the Past, in the Present, and in the Future! The Spirits of all Three shall strive within me!

MARLEY. [*He points and moves closer to* SCROOGE'S *bed.*] Yes, Ebenezer, the bedpost is your own. Believe it! Yes, Ebenezer, the room is your own. Believe it!

SCROOGE. Oh, Jacob Marley! Wherever you are, Jacob, know ye that I praise you for this! I praise you . . . and heaven . . . and Christmastime! [*Kneels facing away from* MARLEY] I say it to ye on my knees, old Jacob, on my knees! [*He touches his bed curtains.*] Not torn down. My bed curtains are not at all torn down! Rings and all, here they are! They are here: I am here: the shadows of things that would have been, may now be dispelled. They will be, Jacob! I know they will be!

[*He chooses clothing for the day. He tries different pieces of clothing and settles, perhaps on a dress suit, plus a cape of the bed clothing: something of color.*]

I am light as a feather, I am happy as an angel, I am as merry as a schoolboy. [*Yells out window and then out to audience*] Merry Christmas to everybody! Merry Christmas to everybody! A Happy New Year to all the world! Hallo here! Whoop! Whoop! Hallo! Hallo! I don't know what day of the month it is! I don't care! I don't know anything! I'm quite a baby! I don't care! I don't care a fig! I'd much rather be a baby than be an old wreck like me or Marley! (Sorry, Jacob, wherever ye be!) Hallo! Hallo there!

[*Church bells chime in Christmas Day. A small boy, named* ADAM, *is seen now* D.R., *as a light fades up on him.*]

---

8. **in Time's penultimate nick** just at the last moment.

Purpose for Reading
Why might you read this speech by Scrooge quickly?

 **Reading Check**
What promises does Scrooge make?

799

Media Connection Charles Dickens's novel *A Christmas Carol* has been produced for audiences in several different forms, such as drama, stage, public readings (beginning with Dickens's own readings and progressing to modern radio performances), and film. Each production has its own special qualities, such as the musical version titled *Scrooge*, starring Albert Finney and Alec Guinness, which was released on film in 1970.

On television, Mister Magoo, a popular cartoon character, appeared in Scrooge's role in 1962. Later, *Mickey's Christmas Carol*, featuring the Disney characters, appeared in the early 1980s. The versions are many and varied. Some attempt to follow the original tale faithfully, while others give the story a twist by using children's characters or setting it in a modern time period. Dickens's timeless themes of Christmas and choosing loving kindness over greed contribute to the story's adaptability and to audiences' ability to relate to its message.

Connect to the Literature Have students examine the graphics in the Literature in Context feature. Present the additional background information above. Then, have students speculate about which scenes the Scrooge actors are depicting in each picture. Note that the photo from the version with Reginald Owen shows a scene from the end of the story after Scrooge has had his change of heart. **Ask** the Connect to the Literature question: Which of these actors best portrays Scrooge as you imagine him from your reading? Explain.

Possible responses: Students might say that the Scrooge they imagine looks more frightening than those in the cartoon and Muppet versions, but that Alistair Sim appears as old and unlikable as they would expect a Scrooge character to be.

---

53 **LITERATURE IN CONTEXT**

Media Connection

The Many Faces of Scrooge
The part of Ebenezer Scrooge has been played by many different actors over the years.

1983 Scrooge McDuck

1951 Alistair Sim

1938 Reginald Owen

1962 Mister Magoo

1992 Michael Caine

Connect to the Literature

Which of these actors best portrays Scrooge as you imagine him from your reading? Explain.

Hey, you boy! What's today? What day of the year is it?

ADAM. Today, sir? Why, it's Christmas Day!

SCROOGE. It's Christmas Day, is it? Whoop! Well, I haven't missed it after all, have I? The Spirits did all they did in one night. They can do anything they like, right? Of course they can! Of course they can!

ADAM. Excuse me, sir?

SCROOGE. Huh? Oh, yes, of course, what's your name, lad?

[SCROOGE *and* ADAM *will play their scene from their own spotlights.*]

54

ADAM. Adam, sir.

800 Drama

Vocabulary Development   © **CCSS** Language 6

Expressive Vocabulary
To help students broaden their expressive vocabulary, encourage them to use the following words as they analyze the favorable changes in Scrooge's character: *respond, require, plead, trigger,* and *survive.* Have them complete these sentence starters:

1. One might expect others to *respond* to Scrooge's changes . . .

2. Scrooge will now *require* . . .
3. Scrooge will no longer need to *plead* for . . .
4. For Scrooge, Christmas Day will now *trigger* . . .
5. The old Scrooge did not *survive* the . . .

SCROOGE. Adam! What a fine, strong name! Do you know the poulterer's[9] in the next street but one, at the corner?

ADAM. I certainly should hope I know him, sir!

SCROOGE. A remarkable boy! An intelligent boy! Do you know whether the poulterer's have sold the prize turkey that was hanging up there? I don't mean the little prize turkey, Adam. I mean the big one!

ADAM. What, do you mean the one they've got that's as big as me?

SCROOGE. I mean, the turkey the size of Adam: that's the bird!

ADAM. It's hanging there now, sir.

SCROOGE. It is? Go and buy it! No, no, I am absolutely in earnest. Go and buy it and tell 'em to bring it here, so that I may give them the directions to where I want it delivered, as a gift. Come back here with the man, Adam, and I'll give you a shilling. Come back here with him in less than five minutes, and I'll give you half-a-crown!

ADAM. Oh, my sir! Don't let my brother in on this.

[ADAM *runs offstage.* MARLEY *smiles.*]

MARLEY. An act of kindness is like the first green grape of summer: one leads to another and another and another. It would take a queer man indeed to not follow an act of kindness with an act of kindness. One simply whets the tongue for more . . . the taste of kindness is too too sweet. Gifts—goods—are lifeless. But the gift of goodness one feels in the giving is full of life. It . . . is . . . a . . . wonder.

[*Pauses; moves closer to* SCROOGE, *who is totally occupied with his dressing and arranging of his room and his day. He is making lists, etc.* MARLEY *reaches out to* SCROOGE:]

ADAM. [*Calling, off*] I'm here! I'm here!

[ADAM *runs on with a man, who carries an enormous turkey.*]

Here I am, sir. Three minutes flat! A world record! I've got the poultryman and he's got the poultry! [*He pants, out of breath.*] I have earned my prize, sir, if I live . . .

---

9. poulterer's (pōl′ tər ərz) *n.* British word for a store that sells poultry.

Stage Directions Why does having a spotlight of both Scrooge and Adam add drama to the scene?

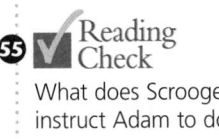

55 Reading Check

What does Scrooge instruct Adam to do?

A Christmas Carol: Scrooge and Marley, Act 2 **801**

54 Stage Directions

1. Read aloud the stage direction that begins the bracketed passage. **Ask** students to describe the stage. **Possible response:** The stage will be dark, except for two spotlights that will shine separately on the characters of Scrooge and Adam.

2. Have students read aloud the rest of the bracketed passage. **Ask** them to describe the mood of the scene. **Possible response:** The mood is festive, with Scrooge happy to share his wealth and Adam amazed to be receiving such treatment.

3. **Ask** students the Stage Directions question. **Possible response:** Lighting only Scrooge and Adam heightens the emotions of the two characters and adds drama to the scene.

55 Reading Check

Answer: He instructs Adam to buy the prize turkey from the poulterer's.

Differentiated Instruction for Universal Access

EL Support for English Learners

Students might encounter common words and phrases in the dialogue that cannot be translated literally and may be unfamiliar. Point out that on p. 801 Scrooge uses the word *prize* to describe a turkey. Explain that *prize* in this case refers to something highly desirable. However, Adam uses *prize* to mean "reward." Have students read Scrooge's line farther down the page that includes the phrase, "in earnest." Explain that to be in earnest is to be truthful or honest. Then, have them read Adam's line that refers to his brother. Tell them that to be "in on" something means "to know about it." Have students paraphrase both Scrooge's and Adam's lines with their new understanding of "in earnest" and "in on it."

801

1. Instruct students to preview the final four pages of the play. Remind them to notice the density and length of each section of dialogue and the stage directions along with the complexity of the sentences.

2. Have students read the bracketed passage that continues onto p. 803. Instruct them to notice the mood in the play and the continuing change in Scrooge's character. Then, **ask** them to describe the mood and the change in Scrooge.
   Answer: The mood is still joyful and Scrooge is in such high spirits that he gives Adam and the Man good tips for their trouble.

3. **Ask** the Purpose for Reading question. **Possible responses:** Students might say that Scrooge's giddy mood, the short sentences, and their curiosity about what Scrooge will do next make them want to continue reading at a rapid but comfortable pace.

Purpose for Reading
The positive change in Scrooge is becoming more noticeable. Will your reading rate change from here until the end of the act? Why or why not?

[*He holds his heart, playacting.* SCROOGE *goes to him and embraces him.*]

SCROOGE. You are truly a champion, Adam . . .

MAN. Here's the bird you ordered, sir . . .

SCROOGE. Oh, my, MY!!! look at the size of that turkey, will you! He never could have stood upon his legs, that bird! He would have snapped them off in a minute, like sticks of sealingwax! Why you'll never be able to carry that bird to Camden-Town. I'll give you money for a cab . . .

MAN. Camden-Town's where it's goin', sir?

SCROOGE. Oh, I didn't tell you? Yes, I've written the precise address down just here on this . . . [*Hands paper to him*] Bob Cratchit's house. Now he's not to know who sends him this. Do you understand me? Not a word . . . [*Handing out money and chuckling*]

MAN. I understand, sir, not a word.

SCROOGE. Good. There you go then . . . this is for the turkey . . . [*Chuckle*] and this is for the taxi. [*Chuckle*] . . . and this is for your world-record run, Adam . . .

ADAM. But I don't have change for that, sir.

SCROOGE. Then keep it, my lad. It's Christmas!

ADAM. [*He kisses* SCROOGE'S *cheek, quickly.*] Thank you, sir. Merry, Merry Christmas! [*He runs off.*]

MAN. And you've given me a bit overmuch here, too, sir . . .

SCROOGE. Of course I have, sir. It's Christmas!

MAN. Oh, well, thanking you, sir. I'll have this bird to Mr. Cratchit and his family in no time, sir. Don't you worry none about that. Merry Christmas to you, sir, and a very happy New Year, too . . .

[*The man exits.* SCROOGE *walks in a large circle about the stage, which is now gently lit. A chorus sings Christmas music far in the distance. Bells chime as well, far in the distance. A gentlewoman enters and passes.* SCROOGE *is on the streets now.*]

SCROOGE. Merry Christmas, madam . . .

802 Drama

Vocabulary Development

Vocabulary Knowledge Rating
When students have completed reading Act II of *A Christmas Carol*, have them take out their **Vocabulary Knowledge Rating Chart** for this selection. Read the words aloud once more, and have students write their own definitions or examples in the appropriate column. Then have students complete the vocabulary practice activities at the end of the selection. Encourage students to use the words in further discussion and written work about this selection. Remind them that they will be accountable for these words on the **Selection Test**, *Unit 5 Resources*, pp. 59–61 or 62–64.

57 **Critical Viewing**

Possible response: Students might say that the colorful costumes and lively movement reflect Scrooge's shift from a dull, plodding life to one bursting with vitality. They also might note that Scrooge is surrounded by children, and he is clearly enjoying their company.

58 **Reading Check**

Answer: Scrooge wants the turkey delivered to the Cratchits.

WOMAN. Merry Christmas, sir . . .

[*The portly businessman from the first act enters.*]

SCROOGE. Merry Christmas, sir.

PORTLY MAN. Merry Christmas, sir.

SCROOGE. Oh, you! My dear sir! How do you do? I do hope that you succeeded yesterday! It was very kind of you. A Merry Christmas.

PORTLY MAN. Mr. Scrooge?

SCROOGE. Yes, Scrooge is my name though I'm afraid you may not find it very pleasant. Allow me to ask your pardon. And will you have the goodness to—[*He whispers into the man's ear.*]

PORTLY MAN. Lord bless me! My dear Mr. Scrooge, are you serious!?!

57 ▲ **Critical Viewing**
How do the color and movement in this photo convey Scrooge's new attitude? [**Analyze Cause and Effect**]

58  Reading Check
Where does Scrooge want the turkey delivered?

A Christmas Carol: Scrooge and Marley, Act 2 **803**

Instruction for Universal Access

Enrichment for Gifted/Talented Students
Clarify that Scrooge is giving the turkey to the Cratchits as a sort of Christmas gift, or bonus. Explain that the custom of giving such holiday gifts comes from a tradition of the English church. On the day after Christmas, church alms boxes are opened so that the money can be distributed to the poor. Through the years, the tradition grew to include public servants and employees, who took small earthenware boxes around to collect tips and year-end-bonuses. Each box had a slit in the top to admit coins.

At the end of the day, the boxes were broken and the money distributed.

Tell students that the custom of giving gifts of money to public servants and employees has continued, but now it happens before Christmas.

Conduct a debate in which one group acts as the "old" Scrooge and argues against giving Christmas bonuses and the other acts as the "new" Scrooge and argues in favor of the practice.

1. Review with students Scrooge's past encounters with his nephew, Fred. Have them recall how poorly Scrooge treated Fred and how forgiving the nephew was. **Ask** students to imagine they are Scrooge and whether they would have the nerve to approach their nephew now. Have them explain why or why not.
Possible responses: Some might say that they would be too embarrassed to approach another person after acting the way Scrooge once did. Others might feel that since Fred has never shown any anger toward Scrooge, they would have no reluctance in meeting with him.

2. Read the first bracketed passage aloud and **ask** students to answer the first Stage Directions question.
Answer: Scrooge seems to feel uncertain and even anxious about how Fred will react to his appearance, but finally shows his determination not to give up on his chance to make amends.

60 **Stage Directions**

1. Discuss with students the passage of time in the play. Make certain they understand that the story began on Christmas Eve and it is now the day after Christmas.

2. Read the second bracketed passage aloud. **Ask** students to identify the day that Cratchit appears in the office.
Answer: It is the day after Christmas.

3. Point out that in a play, audiences often rely on lighting to suggest the changes in time from day to night. Then, **ask** the second Stage Directions question.
Possible responses: Students might suggest that white lights in the background dim to darkness and then brighten gradually. Others might mention using colored lights to suggest sunset and sunrise.

804

Stage Directions
What do Scrooge's actions tell you about his feelings at this point?

Stage Directions **60**
How could lighting be used to show the passage of time?

SCROOGE. If you please. Not a farthing[10] less. A great many back payments are included in it, I assure you. Will you do me that favor?

PORTLY MAN. My dear sir, I don't know what to say to such munifi—

SCROOGE. [*Cutting him off*] Don't say anything, please. Come and see me. Will you?

PORTLY MAN. I will! I will! Oh I will, Mr. Scrooge! It will be my pleasure!

SCROOGE. Thank'ee, I am much obliged to you. I thank you fifty times. Bless you!

[*Portly man passes offstage, perhaps by moving backwards.* SCROOGE *now comes to the room of his* NEPHEW *and* NIECE. *He stops at the door, begins to knock on it, loses his courage, tries again, loses his courage again, tries again, fails again, and then backs off and runs at the door, causing a tremendous bump against it. The* NEPHEW *and* NIECE *are startled.* SCROOGE, *poking head into room*]

Fred!

NEPHEW. Why, bless my soul! Who's that?

NEPHEW AND NIECE. [*Together*] How now? Who goes?

SCROOGE. It's I. Your Uncle Scrooge.

NIECE. Dear heart alive!

SCROOGE. I have come to dinner. May I come in, Fred?

NEPHEW. *May you come in???!!!* With such pleasure for me you may, Uncle!!! What a treat!

NIECE. What a treat, Uncle Scrooge! Come in, come in!

[*They embrace a shocked and delighted* SCROOGE: FRED *calls into the other room.*]

NEPHEW. Come in here, everybody, and meet my Uncle Scrooge! He's come for our Christmas party!

[*Music in. Lighting here indicates that day has gone to night and gone to day again. It is early, early morning.* SCROOGE *walks alone from the party, exhausted, to his offices, opposite*

10. **farthing** (fär´ *thin*) *n.* small British coin.

804 Drama

Vocabulary Development

Dictionary Use
Help students choose the correct dictionary definition for the word *obliged*. Read aloud Scrooge's line on p. 804: "Thank'ee, I am much obliged to you. I thank you fifty times. Bless you!" Tell students that dictionaries sometimes include example sentences within their definitions to show the different ways a word might be used. Then, read the following dictionary entry for *oblige* aloud:

1. to limit or restrict. 2. to make indebted or grateful: *We are obliged to you for your benevolence.* 3. to do a favor for: *The actor obliged us by giving another performance.*

Guide students to see that the sentence in the second definition parallels the one Scrooge uses. Help them list synonyms for the word such as *grateful, thankful, appreciative, gratified,* and *indebted.* Then, ask students to use the word *obliged* in a sentence to share with the class.

side of the stage. He opens his offices. The offices are as they were at the start of the play. SCROOGE *seats himself with his door wide open so that he can see into the tank, as he awaits* CRATCHIT, *who enters, head down, full of guilt.* CRATCHIT, *starts writing almost before he sits.*]

SCROOGE. What do you mean by coming in here at this time of day, a full eighteen minutes late, Mr. Cratchit? Hallo, sir? Do you hear me?

BOB. I am very sorry, sir. I am behind my time.

SCROOGE. You are? Yes, I certainly think you are. Step this way, sir, if you please . . .

BOB. It's only but once a year, sir . . . it shall not be repeated. I was making rather merry yesterday and into the night . . .

SCROOGE. Now, I'll tell you what, Cratchit. I am not going to stand this sort of thing any longer. And therefore . . .

[*He stands and pokes his finger into* BOB'S *chest.*]

I am . . . about . . . to . . . raise . . . your salary.

BOB. Oh, no, sir, I . . . [*Realizes*] what did you say, sir?

SCROOGE. A Merry Christmas, Bob . . . [*He claps* BOB'S *back.*] A merrier Christmas, Bob, my good fellow! than I have given you for many a year. I'll raise your salary and endeavor to assist your struggling family and we will discuss your affairs this very afternoon over a bowl of smoking bishop.[11] Bob! Make up the fires and buy another coal scuttle before you dot another i, Bob. It's too cold in this place! We need warmth and cheer, Bob Cratchit! Do you hear me? DO . . . YOU . . . HEAR . . . ME?

[BOB CRATCHIT *stands, smiles at* SCROOGE: BOB CRATCHIT *faints. Blackout. As the main lights black out, a spotlight appears on* SCROOGE: C. *Another on* MARLEY: *He talks directly to the audience.*]

MARLEY. Scrooge was better than his word. He did it all and infinitely more; and to Tiny Tim, who did NOT die, he was a second father. He became as good a friend, as good a master, as good a man, as the good old city knew, or any other good old city, town, or borough in the good old world.

---

11. **smoking bishop** hot sweet orange-flavored drink.

Stage Directions
What information in the stage directions might be funny to audiences? Why?

Reading Check
What has Scrooge promised to give Bob?

A Christmas Carol: Scrooge and Marley, Act 2 **805**

61 **Stage Directions**

1. When students reach the bottom of p. 805, **ask** them why Scrooge is acting the way he is and how Bob is interpreting his employer's behavior.
   Answer: Scrooge is trying to surprise Bob, and Bob thinks he is being reprimanded.

2. Instruct students to read the second bracketed passage, and then **ask** them to answer the Stage Directions question.
   Possible responses: Students might think that Scrooge's joyful playacting to fool Bob is funny. Others might see Bob's surprise and final reaction as especially humorous.

▶ **Monitor Progress Ask** students why Bob Cratchit would be fearful of Scrooge's response to his being late.

▶ **Reteach** Point out the dramatic irony in this scene, and then reread the passage aloud while students visualize the action. **Ask** students to identify one moment that they find humorous.
Possible responses: Students may choose any moment described in the stage directions.

62 **Reading Check**

Answer: Scrooge has promised to give Bob a raise in salary.

Concept Connector

Activating Prior Knowledge
Have students discuss how Scrooge responds to the challenges he faces in the play and then review the characters and challenges they listed before reading the selection. Ask them to compare and contrast Scrooge's response to challenges with those of the other characters.

Writing About the Big Question
Have students compare their response to the sentence starter they completed before reading the selection with their ideas afterward. Ask them to explain whether their thoughts have changed.

Reading Skill Graphic Organizer
Ask students to review the graphic organizers they completed to set a purpose for reading. Then have students share the graphic organizers they did, tell whether they satisfied the purpose they set for reading, and explain why or why not.

Critical Thinking

Before students respond, you may wish to have them write a brief objective summary of the selection. As they answer the questions below, remind them to support their answers with evidence from the text.

1. (a) He learns the size of the Cratchit family and about Tiny Tim's illness. (b) He seems drawn to the caring young boy. (c) He is beginning to care more about people than money.

2. (a) Scrooge's belongings are stolen after he dies. (b) He learns that he must respect others in order for them to respect him.

3. (a) He is happy because he learns the value of love and human companionship. (b) **Possible response:** Scrooge's actions suggest that he has taken the lessons to heart. His Christmas generosity shows that he is considering others and that he now enjoys giving.

4. **Possible response:** Some students might say that they do the right thing because Scrooge is making a real effort to change. Others might say that Cratchit and Fred should demand an apology.

5. **Possible responses:** (a) He learns how his behavior affects others and how they view him as a result. (b) He begins to treat others more kindly and with greater generosity.

And it was always said of him that he knew how to keep Christmas well, if any man alive possessed the knowledge. [*Pauses*] May that be truly said of us, and all of us. And so, as Tiny Tim observed . . .

TINY TIM. [*Atop* SCROOGE'S *shoulder*] God Bless Us, Every One . . .

[*Lights up on chorus, singing final Christmas Song.* SCROOGE *and* MARLEY *and all spirits and other characters of the play join in. When the song is over, the lights fade to black.*]

Critical Thinking

Cite textual evidence to support your responses.

1. **Key Ideas and Details (a)** In Scene 3, what does Scrooge learn about the Cratchit family? **(b) Analyze:** Why does Scrooge care about the fate of Tiny Tim? **(c) Draw Conclusions:** In what way is Scrooge changing?

2. **Key Ideas and Details (a)** In Scene 4, what happens to Scrooge's belongings in Christmas future? **(b) Draw Conclusions:** What does Scrooge learn from this experience?

3. **Key Ideas and Details (a) Analyze:** Why is Scrooge happy at the end of the play? **(b) Evaluate:** How well does he live up to his promise to learn his "lessons"?

4. **Integration of Knowledge and Ideas Take a Position:** Do you think Cratchit and Scrooge's nephew do the right thing by forgiving Scrooge immediately? Explain, using details from the play to support your answer.

5. **Integration of Knowledge and Ideas (a)** What does Scrooge learn from the opportunity to watch his own life? **(b)** How does he change his behavior to reflect his new insight? *[Connect to the Big Question: Do others see us more clearly than we see ourselves?]*

806 Drama

Assessment Resources

Unit 5 Resources

L1 L2 EL **Selection Test A,** pp. 59–61. Administer Test A to less advanced readers.

L3 L4 EL **Selection Test B,** pp. 62–64. Administer Test B to on-level and more advanced students.

L3 L4 **Open-Book Test,** pp. 56–58. As an alternative, give the Open-Book Test.

All **Customizable Test Bank**

All **Self-tests**
Students may prepare for the **Selection Test** by taking the **Self-test** online.

PHLit Online! All assessment resources are available at www.PHLitOnline.com.

After You Read

A Christmas Carol: Scrooge and Marley, Act 2

Reading Skill: Purpose for Reading

1. Which did you read more quickly: the dialogue or the stage directions? In your answer, explain how your **purpose** affected your reading rate.

2. When you read long speeches with difficult words, what happens to your reading rate? Explain.

Literary Analysis: Stage Directions

ⓒ 3. **Craft and Structure** Reread the **stage directions** at the beginning of Scene 1. Then, complete a chart like the one shown to record the information the directions reveal.

Characters on Stage	Movement of Characters	Description of Lighting	Description of Sound	Other Special Effects

ⓒ 4. **Craft and Structure** Which stage direction in Scene 4 is especially effective in making the scene mysterious? Explain.

Vocabulary

ⓒ **Acquisition and Use** Answer each question, then explain your answer.

1. When you speak, do you want your voice to be *audible*?
2. Would it *astonish* you if an elephant sang?
3. Would you take cover if a *severe* storm were approaching?
4. Can a family with a *meager* income build a large, fancy house?
5. Would you *intercede* if two friends were arguing?
6. Would a person with a *compulsion* to save money give away a million dollars?

Word Study Use the context of the sentences and what you know about the **Latin prefix *inter-*** to explain your answers.

1. Is an *international* crisis one that occurs between two states?
2. Does an *intermission* usually occur at the start of a play?

Word Study

The **Latin prefix *inter-*** means "between" or "among."

Apply It Explain how the prefix *inter-* contributes to the meanings of these words. Consult a dictionary if necessary.

interplanetary
interpersonal
interject

A Christmas Carol: Scrooge and Marley, Act 2 **807**

Word Study

Sample answers:
1. No. The prefix *inter-* means "between," but an *international* crisis would occur <u>between</u> two nations.
2. No. The prefix *inter- means* "between," so an *intermission* would occur <u>between</u> two parts of a play.

Word Study: Apply It

Sample answers: *Interplanetary* means <u>between</u> planets. Something *interpersonal* is <u>between</u> persons. To *interject* is to speak <u>between</u> someone else's speech.

Reading Skill

1. **Possible response:** Students might say that when they needed to gather information (as in the stage directions), they read slowly, and when they were enjoying the play, they read more quickly.

2. **Possible response:** Students might say that they read long speeches with difficult vocabulary slowly and carefully to improve their understanding of the text.

Literary Analysis

3. On Stage—Scrooge, Marley; Movement—Marley moves close to the sleeping Scrooge; Lighting—spotlights on Scrooge and Marley, lightning flashes, candle, colors change; Sound—choral music, thunder, ghostly music, Marley laughs and speaks; Special Effects—flame shoots from Marley's hand.

   For other sample answers, see *Graphic Organizer Transparencies,* **Literary Analysis Graphic Organizer A,** p. 153, and the **Additional Answers** section.

4. The direction that describes Ghost of Christmas Future as a phantom creates mystery. This spirit does not speak but points to communicate. Future's silence is eerie and leaves Scrooge and the audience with unanswered questions.

Vocabulary
Acquisition and Use
Sample answers:
1. Yes, I want my voice to be <u>audible</u> so that people can hear me speaking.
2. Yes, it would <u>astonish</u> me if an elephant sang because I know that elephants cannot sing.
3. Yes, I would take cover from a <u>severe</u> storm because it would be a very dangerous storm.
4. No, large houses are too expensive for people with <u>meager</u> incomes.
5. Yes, I would <u>intercede</u> to stop two friends if they were arguing.
6. No, a person with a <u>compulsion</u> to save money would not give away a million dollars because he or she would feel a need to keep the money.

807

Conventions

1. Introduce the skill, using the instruction on the student page.
2. Discuss the examples in the chart.

Think Aloud: Model the Skill

Model the skill of correcting double negatives. Say to students:

Double negatives can confuse people. Suppose I write on the board: *Never shut off no lights when you leave the classroom.* You might not be sure if I mean always turn off the lights or never turn off the lights. If I remove one of the negatives, I can write: *Never shut off any lights when you leave the classroom.* Now my meaning is clear and you know exactly what to do: leave the lights on.

PH WRITING COACH Grade 7

Students will find further instruction on and practice with double negatives in Chapter 20, Section 4.

Practice A
Sample answers:

1. Marley said that Scrooge would not be afraid of anything now.
2. correct
3. correct
4. His meanness did not have any effect on the spirit of his nephew.

Reading Application
Sample answers:

They don't sing very well, do they? You do not recognize him? I have no patience with him.

Practice B
Sample answers:

1. Scrooge did not want to go anywhere with Christmas Past, but knew he must.
2. The thieves believed that nobody cared anything for Scrooge.
3. The Cratchits mourned that Tiny Tim would not be a part of their lives anymore.
4. Once changed, Scrooge would not let anything stop his acts of kindness.

Writing Application
Sample answer:

At the beginning of Act 2, Scrooge is never kind to anyone. He does not see a reason to be kind.

Integrated Language Skills

A Christmas Carol: Scrooge and Marley, Act 2

Conventions: Double Negatives

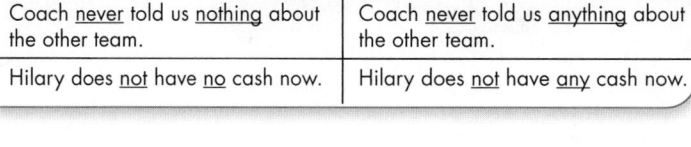

> **Double negatives** are two negative words used when only one is needed in Standard English.

Examples of negative words are *nothing, not, never,* and *no.* You can correct a double negative by revising the sentence.
This chart shows double negatives and ways to correct them.

Double Negative	Corrected Sentence
Coach <u>never</u> told us <u>nothing</u> about the other team.	Coach <u>never</u> told us <u>anything</u> about the other team.
Hilary does <u>not</u> have <u>no</u> cash now.	Hilary does <u>not</u> have <u>any</u> cash now.

Practice A Identify and revise the sentences that contain double negatives. Write "correct" for those sentences without double negatives.

1. Marley said that Scrooge would not be afraid of nothing now.
2. No one could show him anything surprising.
3. He was not aware the Cratchits survived on almost nothing.
4. His meanness did not have no effect on the spirit of his nephew.

© Reading Application In *A Christmas Carol: Scrooge and Marley,* Act 2, Scene 1, find three sentences that contain negative words.

Practice B Rewrite each sentence to correct the double negative.

1. Scrooge did not want to go nowhere with Christmas Past but knew he must.
2. The thieves believed that nobody cared nothing for Scrooge.
3. The Cratchits mourned that Tiny Tim would not be a part of their lives no more.
4. Once changed, Scrooge would not let nothing stop his acts of kindness.

© Writing Application Write two sentences about *A Christmas Carol: Scrooge and Marley,* Act 2, using the words *not* and *never.* Avoid using a double negative.

PH WRITING COACH Further instruction and practice are available in *Prentice Hall Writing Coach.*

808 Drama

Writing

Argumentative Text Respond to the play by writing a **tribute,** or expression of admiration, to the changed Scrooge. Your tribute may share brief stories from the drama that show how Scrooge has transformed his life. It may also reflect on the events or experiences that caused Scrooge to change. As you draft, identify the new traits that make Scrooge worthy of a tribute, and include evidence from the play to support your analysis. Conclude by giving your opinion of the play and providing your own insights about whether there is a lesson that everyone can learn from Scrooge's story.

Grammar Application Check your writing to be sure you have corrected any double negatives.

Writing Workshop: *Work in Progress*

Prewriting for Research For each topic on your Ideas List, jot down a creative idea for using a visual or audio aid for use in a research report you may write. Save this Multimedia List in your writing portfolio.

Speaking and Listening

Presentation of Ideas Think about Scrooge's experiences with one of the ghosts. Then, write and present a **dramatic monologue** that shares Scrooge's thoughts.

- As you draft your monologue, write as Scrooge from the first-person point of view, using the word *I*.
- Include stage directions to indicate gestures and emotions.
- Punctuate your monologue correctly. Use a colon after the speaker's name and brackets to set off stage directions. Use commas and dashes in the monologue to indicate pauses and changes in thought.

As you prepare to present your monologue, consider these tips:

- Project your voice so that everyone can hear you.
- Follow stage directions that tell how to move or speak.
- As you rehearse, read the monologue several different ways. Try pausing at suitable moments, speaking at different speeds where a tempo change makes sense, and raising and lowering your voice for effect. Decide which techniques work and use these in your final presentation.

Common Core State Standards

L.7.1, L.7.2, L.7.4.b, L.7.6; W.7.2, W.7.9; SL.7.6
[For the full wording of the standards, see page 772.]

Use this prewriting activity to prepare for the **Writing Workshop** on page 824.

www.PHLitOnline.com
- Interactive graphic organizers
- Grammar tutorial
- Interactive journals

Writing

1. Review the assignment, using the instruction on the student page.
2. To guide students in writing their argumentative texts, give them **Support for Writing,** p. 54 in *Unit 5 Resources*
3. To evaluate students' work, look for the following:
   - student understanding of the text
   - complete and accurate response to the assignment
   - adequate support and/or examples from the text
   - correct grammar and mechanics

Grammar Application

Have students check their drafts to make sure they have corrected any double negatives.

Six Traits Focus

✓ Ideas	✓ Word Choice
✓ Organization	Sentence Fluency
✓ Voice	Conventions

PH WRITING COACH Grade 7

Students will find further instruction on and practice with persuasive writing in Chapter 9 and on responses to literature in Chapter 10.

Writing Workshop
Work in Progress

Have students save their completed Multimedia Lists in their portfolios. They will use the lists later as they complete the Writing Workshop assignment (see pp. 824–829).

Speaking and Listening

1. Review the assignment, using the instruction on the student page.
2. To support students' work on the assignment, have students complete the **Support for Extend Your Learning** page (*Unit 5 Resources,* p. 55).

Teaching Resources

Unit 5 Resources

L3 L4 EL Integrated Language Skills: Grammar, p. 53

L3 L4 EL Support for Writing, p. 54

L3 L4 Support for Extend Your Learning, p. 55

L4 Enrichment, p. 52

Enriched Online Student Edition
Available under After You Read for this selection:

All Interactive Grammar Tutorial

L3 L4 Internet Research Activity

ASSESS

Answers

Answers With Explanations

1. **D**—This is the purpose of reading most plays. *Incorrect answers:* A—The play is building suspense rather than informing the audience; B—A persuasive essay, not a play, would have this purpose; C—A nonfiction book or article, not a play, would have this purpose.

2. **B**—The characters do not state their motivations or emotions, but readers can infer much by studying the characters' actions and words. *Incorrect answers:* A—This information could be found by skimming; C— This information could be found by skimming; D—This information could be found by skimming.

3. **A**—Since the stage directions refer to the object, the next part of the play will probably reveal what it is. *Incorrect answers:* B—The first stage directions state David's age; C—The publication date would be listed earlier in the play; the time when it was written is probably not specified; D—This would have been stated in the stage directions when Erykah first entered if the playwright intended to provide this information.

4. **B**—Stage directions are important and should be read slowly. *Incorrect answers:* A—Stage directions are not conversational; dialogue is; C—Readers might be tempted to rush over stage directions in order to get to exciting plot developments, but this would be a mistake; D—Stage directions do not contain the author's main message.

810

Test Practice: Reading

Purpose for Reading

Fiction Selection

Directions: *Read the selection. Then, answer the questions.*

[*A single spotlight on* DAVID, *a young man in his early twenties. He appears stern and anxious as he hunches over his desk, hard at work. A MAN is seen leaving stage left.*]

David. [*fiercely*] No more interruptions!

[ERYKAH *enters stage right and approaches* DAVID *from behind. Her hands are behind her back. She is holding an object that we cannot see.*]

Erykah. [*cheerfully, in a Jamaican accent*] Hello, David!

David. [*annoyed*] What is it? [*He turns, smiles.*] Oh, Erykah. It's you.

Erykah. I'm sorry to interrupt. I can come back . . .

David. No, no. Come, sit down. For you, there is always time.

1. What is the most likely purpose a reader would have for reading this passage?
   A. to learn about a subject
   B. to make a decision
   C. to be informed
   D. to be entertained

2. For what purpose might you choose to read the play from which this scene comes slowly and carefully?
   A. to find out what happens next
   B. to analyze its characters
   C. to find a specific scene
   D. to discover when a character first appears

3. What question might a reader hope to answer by reading on?
   A. What is Erykah holding?
   B. How old is David?
   C. When was this play written?
   D. What is Erykah wearing?

4. At what rate should you read the stage directions, and why?
   A. Quickly, to give the impression of conversation.
   B. Slowly, in case action is revealed that is not shown in the dialogue.
   C. Quickly, in case something exciting happens next.
   D. Slowly, to figure out the author's main message.

Writing for Assessment

In a short paragraph, describe two different purposes a person might have for reading the play from which this passage comes. Discuss the reading rate that would best suit each purpose and identify key details from the text that support each idea.

Writing for Assessment

In their responses, students should describe two different purposes for reading the play and discuss the appropriate rate for each giving key details that support each idea.

Strategies for Test Taking

Remind students that when taking a test that is narrowly focused on one skill or a few skills, such as this test, they should first think about the instruction they have received related to that skill. In this case, after mentally reviewing some of the standard purposes for reading, students should remember what they learned about previewing a text to assess its suitability to the reader's purpose. Then, they should answer the test questions about purpose for reading as they apply to the selection in the test.

Nonfiction Selection

Directions: *Read the selection. Then, answer the questions.*

The Development of Stanislavsky's Method

The Stanislavsky Method, also known as "the method," is a style of acting developed by Konstantin Stanislavsky in the early twentieth century. Stanislavsky, an actor and producer, believed that actors should not *appear* to feel a certain way but should instead recreate the emotions of their characters for themselves. His method became popular during his lifetime and is still used by some actors today.

Using Stanislavsky's Method

To use Stanislavsky's method, actors concentrate on feeling the same emotions their characters experience. For example, if an actor wants to appear happy on stage, she might recall a time when she felt happy in real life. Focusing on that feeling, according to Stanislavsky, helps an actor capture the emotions of a character more realistically.

1. What is the *best* way to preview this passage?
   - **A.** Read the text.
   - **B.** Read the headings.
   - **C.** Reread and take notes.
   - **D.** Carefully read each word.

2. What can you learn from a close reading of the passage?
   - **A.** how actors use "the method"
   - **B.** which plays Stanislavsky produced
   - **C.** where and when "the method" was first used
   - **D.** why actors might not want to use "the method"

3. What might be a purpose for reading this passage?
   - **A.** to be entertained
   - **B.** to find information about auditioning
   - **C.** to understand an acting technique
   - **D.** to be persuaded to see a play

4. You should read this passage at about the same rate as you would read—
   - **A.** a comic book.
   - **B.** a letter from a friend.
   - **C.** an encyclopedia article.
   - **D.** a folk tale.

Writing for Assessment

Connecting Across Texts

Why might the actors playing David and Erykah benefit from reading the description of Stanislavsky's method? Using details from both passages, explain your answer in a few sentences.

www.PHLitOnline.com
- Online practice
- Instant feedback

Test Practice: Reading **811**

Answers With Explanations

1. **B**—Reading headings is a standard previewing technique. *Incorrect answers:* A—Reading the text takes place after previewing the text; C—Rereading and taking notes takes place after previewing; D—The technique of previewing involves looking at a few key elements in order to get a quick overview of a selection; it does not require reading every word.

2. **A**—The second paragraph tells how to use "the method." *Incorrect answers:* B—This information is not contained in the selection; C—These precise details are not contained in the selection; D—Drawbacks of "the method" are not discussed.

3. **C**—The selection describes an acting technique. *Incorrect answers:* A—The selection is informative, not entertaining; B—The passage does not contain information about auditioning; D—The selection is not persuasive and does not focus on a single play.

4. **C**—Like an encyclopedia article, this informational selection should be read slowly and carefully. *Incorrect answers:* A—Comic books can be read quickly; B—Letters from friends can be read quickly; D—Folk tales are easy to understand; they can be read more quickly than informational articles.

Writing for Assessment

In their responses, students should explain that since the emotions of David and Erykah are clearly an important part of the play, and since these emotions (anxiety, irritation, cheerfulness, etc.) are common ones, the actors could prepare for the roles by remembering times they felt these emotions and using their memories to enact the emotions realistically on stage.

Common Core State Standards

- Reading Informational Text 6
- Language 6
- Writing 1.b, 9

Reading Skill

1. Introduce the skill, using the instruction on the student page.

2. Review the chart.

Think Aloud: Model the Skill

Say to students:

When I read a review, I ask questions about the author's perspective, or the attitudes, beliefs, and experiences that shape the author's statements. If a review of a movie I want to see is bad, I'll determine what kind of movies the critic likes. If he dislikes a lot of movies I like, I might not give much consideration to the critic's opinion. Recognizing the author's perspective can help me understand the text as a whole.

Multidraft Reading

Have students follow a multidraft reading protocol.

- **First reading**—Have students read to identify key ideas and details.

- **Second reading**—Have students read to identify the structure of the text.

- **Third reading**—Have students read to integrate knowledge and ideas by connecting the text to the world, their own experiences, and other texts.

Content-Area Vocabulary

1. Have students say each word.

2. Next, use each word in a sentence that defines it.

3. Finally, repeat your definitional sentence or a similar sentence, omitting the word, and have the class "fill in the blank" chorally.

812

Reading for Information

Analyzing Argumentative and Expository Texts

Review	Review	Radio Interview

Reading Skill: Identify the Author's Perspective

In a review, the author makes a claim or gives his or her opinion about a work. In an interview, the guest speaks from his or her own experiences and knowledge. In each case, you are getting one person's perspective, or point of view. When you **identify an author's perspective,** you gain an understanding of the reasons behind his or her arguments, opinions, and statements. As you read, use a chart like this one to **trace the development of the author's** (or speaker's) **perspective.**

Statement	Perspective
"A new take on an old classic always offers fresh insights."	The writer approaches classic story adaptations with a positive attitude.
"A retelling of a classic story can never live up to the original."	The writer approaches classic story adaptations with a negative attitude.

Content-Area Vocabulary

These words appear in the selections that follow. You may also encounter them in other content-area texts.

- **cast** (kast) *n.* the actors in a movie, television show, or play

- **adaptation** (ad´ ap tā´ shən) *n.* something that is produced by changing the original version

- **ensemble** (än säm´ bəl) *n.* all of the actors who participate in a performance

812 Drama

 Common Core State Standards

Reading Informational Text
6. Determine an author's point of view or purpose in a text and analyze how the author distinguishes his or her position from that of others.

Language
6. Acquire and use accurately grade-appropriate general academic and domain-specific words and phrases; gather vocabulary knowledge when considering a word or phrase important to comprehension or expression.

Writing
1.b. Support claim(s) with logical reasoning and relevant evidence, using accurate, credible sources and demonstrating an understanding of the topic or text.
9. Draw evidence from literary or informational texts to support analysis, reflection, and research.

? **Do others see us more clearly than we see ourwselves?**

As students read, have them look for the authors' insights into others.

Differentiated Instruction for Universal Access

Reading Support
Give students reading support with the appropriate version of the *Reader's Notebooks:*

L2 L3 *Reader's Notebook*

L1 *Reader's Notebook: Adapted Version*

EL *Reader's Notebook: English Learner's Version*

A Christmas Carol
TNT

(Sun., Dec. 5, 8 p.m. ET)
Picks & Pans: Television
Full text: COPYRIGHT
1999 Time, Inc.

So you muttered "humbug" when you spied yet another version of *A Christmas Carol* on the TV schedule. Don't feel guilty. It doesn't take a spiritual descendant of Ebenezer Scrooge to notice that the Charles Dickens classic has been adapted nearly to death. (Two years ago, there was even a Ms. Scrooge.)

> The tone in the opening of the review hints at the author's perspective.

But TNT's *Carol* would be worth watching if only for the lead performance of Patrick Stewart. The ex-skipper of *Star Trek: The Next Generation* has been giving staged, one-man readings of *A Christmas Carol* for 10 years, and his approach to Scrooge is consistently interesting and intelligent. Early on, Stewart seems to be speaking on the misanthropic diatribes straight from Scrooge's flinty heart, rather than reciting thoroughly familiar quotations. And when Scrooge offers a boy a one-shilling tip, Stewart has the reformed miser feel a pang of the old parsimony.

> The author reveals his feelings about the lead actor and his previous work.

People Weekly, Dec. 6, 1999

…this *Carol* feels more like Masterpiece Theatre than seasonal merchandise…

Filmed in England with a solid supporting **cast** (including Richard E. Grant as Bob Cratchit and Joel Grey as the Spirit of Christmas Past), this *Carol* feels more like Masterpiece Theatre than seasonal merchandise–except when the filmmakers embellish Scrooge's nocturnal visions with gratuitous special effects.

Bottom line: Old story well told.
–Terry Kelleher

> The review ends with a summary of the critic's opinion.

Identify the Author's Perspective

1. **Ask** students to identify the elements of the production that are judged by the critic.
   Answer: The critic judges all aspects of the production, including the actors, the director, the set designer, and the technical crew.

2. **Ask** students to identify a positive and a negative comment in the review.
   Possible response:
   Positive comment: "But Wicks has introduced a modicum of restraint into the Happy English populace, reducing the play's saccharine content considerably and making *A Christmas Carol* a more palatable holiday treat for adults and children."
   Negative comment: "In prior productions, the play's singing Londoners seemed positively hopped up on Christmas cheer . . ."

3. **Ask** students whether this critic gives a positive or negative review of the production.
   Answer: He gives an overall positive review of the production.

4. **Ask** students where he includes a statement of his judgment.
   Answer: He includes his judgment in the first sentence of the review and also in the last paragraph of the review.

Toned-down *Christmas Carol* has more spirit

by John Sousanis

Special to *The Oakland Press*

Director Debra Wicks has tinkered with Meadow Brook's recipe for *A Christmas Carol* just enough to make the old holiday fruitcake seem fresh. To be sure, Wicks's changes are subtle. Meadow Brook is still producing the Charles Nolte **adaptation** of Charles Dickens's Christmas classic that has been a mainstay of local theater for most of the last two decades.

The audience still is serenaded by a band of merry carolers in the lobby before the show. With its giant revolving set pieces and big bag of special effects, the production's script, set and costumes are unchanged from these many Christmases past.

But ironically, Wicks has infused the show with new energy by calming everything down a bit. In prior productions, the play's singing Londoners seemed positively hopped up on Christmas cheer to the point where one feared for the life of anyone not bubbling over with the spirit of the season.

Against this unebbing Yuletide, it was easy to forgive Scrooge of all his bah-hum-bugging. If only he had seen fit to give Tiny Tim a good spanking, we might all have enjoyed Christmas a little more. But Wicks has introduced a modicum of restraint into the Happy English populace, reducing the play's saccharine content considerably and making *A Christmas Carol* a more palatable holiday treat for adults and children.

Peter Hicks's set design for the show is, as always, enormous and gorgeous: Scrooge's storefront on a busy London street revolves to reveal the interior of the businessman's office and home, then opens on itself, providing the frame for scenes from Scrooge's boyhood, young adulthood and, of course, his potential end.

Meadow Brook's technical crew executes its stage magic without a hitch: Ghosts materialize and dematerialize in thick fogs and bolts of bright light, speaking to Scrooge in electronically altered voices and freezing the action onstage with a wave of their otherworldly hands.

The cast members take on multiple roles populating busy London in one scene, then visiting poor Scrooge in his dreams of Christmas Then, Now and Soon.

Standouts in the huge **ensemble** include John Biedenbach as Scrooge's put-upon assistant Bob Cratchit, Jodie Kuhn Ellison as Cratchit's fiercely loyal wife and Mark Rademacher, who pulls double duty as the Spirit of Christmas Present (the beefiest role in the play) and as a determined charity worker.

Scott Crownover, paying only passing attention to his English accent, takes an energetic turn as Scrooge's nephew, Fred, and Tom Mahard and Geoffrey Beauchamp have fun with a handful of roles they've been performing for years. Newcomer Sara Catheryn Wolf, fresh from three seasons at the Hilberry Theatre Company, provides an ethereal Spirit of Christmas Past.

The biggest change for longtime fans of the spectacle, however, is the replacement of Booth Coleman as Scrooge. Dennis Robertson's debut as the man in need of serious Christmas redemption is in perfect keeping with Wicks's toned-down production. If he's not quite as charismatic a miser as Coleman, Robertson is a much darker, even scarier Scrooge, which makes his ultimate transformation into an unabashed philanthropist that much more affecting.

All in all, *A Christmas Carol* is what it always has been: A well-produced, grand-scale event that is as much pageant as play. And like a beautifully wrapped gift under a well-decorated tree, it suits the season to a tee.

The critic's point of view is affected by the fact that he has seen past productions.

This title offers clues about the author's perspective on the subject.

814 Drama

Think Aloud

Vocabulary: Context Clues
Direct students' attention to the word *saccharine* on this page. Using a think-aloud process, model how to use context to infer the meaning of an unknown word. Say to students:

In the sentence, *saccharine* is used to describe the presentation of Dickens's story in this play. Earlier in the review, the reviewer mentioned that previous productions have been a little too merry and bubbly. Now, the play is less saccharine. So does *saccharine* mean "bubbly and full of energy"? The critic says that because the play is less saccharine, it is now a more "palatable treat" for audiences. My guess then is that *saccharine* is the food equivalent of "bubbly and merry." It probably means "sweet." If I look in the dictionary, I can confirm my guess. *Saccharine* means "syrupy sweet."

Charles Dickens's *A Christmas Carol:* A Radio Interview

Philip V. Allingham, Faculty of Education, Lakehead University, Thunder Bay, Ontario

Published with the kind permission of The Canadian Broadcasting Corporation, Thunder Bay (ON) Regional Station.

Lisa Laco, Host: Well we're going to talk about

Charles Dickens right now because Charles Dickens is ever foremost in our minds this week as we get ready to read Charles Dickens' *A Christmas Carol* this weekend here in Thunder Bay. When he was about ten years old poverty forced him to take a job in a factory to provide for his family. Now he was so ashamed of his time there that he never told anyone about it, but he couldn't hide the secret totally.

> Background information provides clues about the guest's point of view.

According to Philip the experience surfaces in the actions and the attitudes of many of Charles Dickens' [characters], especially in Ebenezer Scrooge from *A Christmas Carol*. Philip Allingham is a professor in the Faculty of Education at Lakehead University in Thunder Bay; he's also a Dickens scholar. CBC reporter Cathy Alex asked him what inspired Charles Dickens to write *A Christmas Carol*.

Philip V. Allingham: He was fascinated by German ghost stories; in fact, he had written himself one in the middle of *Pickwick Papers* in 1836. In the fall of 1843 he was invited to go to Manchester, where he saw a good deal of urban poor, . . . other social ills. He and a number of other Victorian reformers including Cobden and Disraeli[1] were to speak and so he heard all the tales of horror in industrial society. He saw a great deal of it; he stayed with his sister whom he loved very much—remember Scrooge's relationship with his sister. And his sister had a little boy who was lame; he probably had what we call now Pot's disease, tuberculosis of the bone, if you can imagine. So there is Tiny Tim, who was originally by the way called "Tiny Fred" after Dickens' younger brother, but "Tiny Fred" doesn't really make it does it. So in proof he corrected that to "Tiny Tim." He also put in the famous "God bless us, everyone!"—it wasn't in the original manuscript. And I think he was also interested in trying to help the ragged schools that were trying to educate poor children at night. These children worked in factories

---

1. **Cobden and Disraeli** Richard Cobden (1804–1865), British politician known for defense of free trade; Benjamin Disraeli (1804–1881); British novelist and politician known for defense of landowners.

Radio Interview

Features:

- content broadcast over radio or Internet
- a discussion between a host and a guest
- a question-and-answer format
- text intended for a listening audience

About Radio Interviews

1. Review the features listed in the box on page 815. **Ask** the class to discuss the type of people usually interviewed on the radio.
   Possible response: Students may name popular bands as well as celebrities and important figures in the business world.

2. **Ask** students to discuss why guests may agree to participate in a radio interview.
   Possible response: Students may mention that guests want to promote a project of theirs or talk about a subject that interests them.

3. Talk to students about how to read a radio interview. As they read suggest that they ask themselves what the interviewer is interested in finding out.

Identify the Author's Perspective

1. Have students read the portion of the radio interview on p. 815 and the side notes that point to important elements. Tell students that for the purposes of the interview, they should consider Philip V. Allingham as the author.

2. **Ask** students to give examples of the information Professor Allingham provides about Charles Dickens.
   Answer: He discusses Charles Dickens's relationship with his sister, his nephew, and brother, his interest in ghost stories, and his interest in helping schools for the poor.

3. **Ask** them what point he is making with this information.
   Answer: He is showing that a number of factors in Dickens's life influenced the writing of *A Christmas Carol*.

4. Have students summarize Allingham's perspective on the story and on Dickens.
   Possible response: He seems very interested in Dickens and sees the story as a reflection of Dickens's own life. He thinks the story is a masterpiece.

5. Point out that the guest on the radio is not a celebrity, but a literary scholar. **Ask** students how this information will affect an audience listening to the interview.
   Possible response: Because the radio guest is a professor and "Dickens scholar," the audience is likely to listen with respect to what he has to say about this topic.

Fluency

Tell students that radio reviews are meant to be heard. How fluently the questions are posed and how fluently they are answered will affect whether the listener understands and enjoys the interview. Ask students to think about radio broadcasts or Internet podcasts they have heard. Tell them to think about how the participants spoke.

Distribute copies of pages 815–816, and have students work in groups of threes. Have the students take turns "conducting" the radio interview, with each student taking one of the roles. Tell students to concentrate on the fluency of their pacing, intonation, and expression. While one students reads, the others should mark any words with which the one reading has difficulty. Circulate to monitor the fluency of students' reading. Collect students' marked up copies of the page, and review difficult words and passages with the class.

Identify the Author's Perspective

1. **Ask** students how Allingham explains the popularity of Dickens' *A Christmas Carol* in his own day.
   Answer: Although many people couldn't afford to buy it or go see it, it became popular by "word of mouth."

2. Remind students that an author's perspective includes his or her background knowledge. **Ask** students what Allingham's explanations shows about his perspective.
   Possible response: He has a great deal of background knowledge about the time during which Dickens lived.

3. **Ask** students to explain why Allingham thinks *A Christmas Carol* has remained a classic.
   Answer: He thinks it bears the qualities of a fairy tale, and is filled with realistic characters that readers can relate to. He also praises Dickens's mastery of good dialogue and storytelling.

4. **Ask** students to sum up Allingham's perspective on Dickens and his work.
   Possible response: Allingham sees Dickens as a great and fascinating author and sees his works as great achievements.

during the daytime. And so all of these things were fermenting in his mind and, like a great Coleridgian[2] dream, *A Christmas Carol* was born.

Alex: How successful was *A Christmas Carol* when it first came out, with respect to the public? How did they take to this novel?

Allingham: Everybody loved it, but everybody couldn't afford it. It was five shillings: Bob Cratchit earns only about three times that each week. So this is a huge chunk of lower middle class income; the working poor would have been locked out of it entirely. But it was very popular by word of mouth. People I think borrowed it off one another. The poor people could see it in the theaters; after half-time, they could pay a very small amount and get into the theaters and at least get the essence of the dialogue and the characters. . . .

Alex: What would Charles Dickens have been like in that period? I mean, how popular would he have been in the 1840s in England and around the world?

Allingham: His popularity grew as his ability to take on larger issues, write larger books, extend his range grew. I think his readings had a great deal to do with his popularity, so that he became a physical presence to people outside the metropolis. He was the Victorian stage; he was the Victorian sage; he was the great entertainer. He was, you know, Ringo Starr and Leonardo DiCaprio and Margaret Atwood all wrapped up in one. . . .

Alex: What do you think makes *A Christmas Carol* such a classic, that it could live on for 160 years and still resonate today the same way it would have when Dickens first wrote it?

Allingham: Well, first of all from a literary perspective it's a masterpiece

> The speaker responds to the question from the point of view, or perspective, of a Dickens scholar.

of controlled tone. We have this absolute sense, this conviction of the narrator in his relationship to us; all the [characters] are just right, in that they are very Dickensian and fully realized in a short amount of space, partly because he gets, he has this wonderful ear for dialogue for the way different people sound. And there is, of course, the timeless fairy tale quality to it that everybody has remarked on. It is, it's a remarkable change of heart for the curmudgeon miser affected by a recognition of the importance of his past and instead of trying to bury it he has to come to terms with it, even if some of it was unpleasant, which is very much a Dickens autobiographical slant on things, working in the blacking factory, hiding the secret from his family. You know, they never knew about that and he was called "The Little Gentlem'n" by the boys who worked there because they initially didn't like him at all. They realised he came from a different social class. And that sensitive little boy, that little boy died during that experience really and was reborn as a man who was determined to be terribly tough and make it. And, you see, that's the other side of Ebenezer Scrooge. All these are really just extensions of Dickens himself. So it has all kinds of critical interest for scholars, but it's also just this wonderful, heart-warming story with people that we feel we know extremely well.

Laco: Dr. Philip Allingham teaches in the Faculty of Education at Lakehead University in Thunder Bay. Speaking there with our reporter, Cathy Alex.

---

2. **Coleridgian** (1772–1834) Reference to Samuel Taylor Coleridge, British poet, best known for his fantastical poem, "The Rime of the Ancient Mariner."

Think Aloud

Identifying the Author's Perspective
Model the skill of identifying the author's perspective. Say to students:

When I identify the author's perspective, I gain an understanding of the reasons behind the author's opinions and statements. As I read the radio interview, I ask myself, what is Dr. Allingham's perspective? He has a lot of interesting things to say about Dickens and *A Christmas Carol.* In each case, he reveals great knowledge of Dickens's life and his time period. He has many positive things to say about Dickens and his work. I realize that part of his perspective is that of a scholar—someone who studies a subject deeply and knows much about it. I see that he has a great love for Dickens and Dickens's writing. His explanations of the connections between Dickens's life and his work are convincing. At the same time, I realize that another scholar might have a different evaluation of Dickens's work. By analyzing an author's perspective, I form my own opinions about his work.

Comparing Argumentative and Expository Texts

© **1. Key Ideas and Details** **(a)** Identify the author's perspective in each of the reviews of *A Christmas Carol* and the speaker's perspective in the radio interview. **(b)** In what ways are the perspectives similar? **(c)** In what ways do the perspectives differ? **(d)** How might a particular medium, such as a radio interview, achieve a more powerful impact than a written review? Explain.

Content-Area Vocabulary

2. (a) Remove the suffix *-tion* from the word *adaptation*. Using a print or an online dictionary, explain how removing the suffix reveals a different word that is a different part of speech. **(b)** Then, use the words *adaptation* and *adapt* in sentences that show their meaning.

🕐 Timed Writing

Analytic Text: Essay

Format
The prompt gives specific directions about the type of information to include in your essay.

In an essay, trace the perspective of the author of "Toned-Down *Christmas Carol* Has More Spirit." Support your response by providing details, words, and phrases from the text that give clues to Sousanis's point of view. Be sure to explain how each clue helps reveal his perspective. (25 minutes)

Academic Vocabulary
When you *support* your response, you provide evidence that helps show that your response is true or reasonable.

5-Minute Planner

Complete these steps to write your essay:

1. Carefully read the writing prompt, noting the highlighted key words.

2. Gather information for your response. Reread the review and jot down details, words, and phrases that hint at the author's perspective on the subject.

3. Look over the evidence you've gathered and choose the strongest points. Mark these points with a checkmark, and, for each, make notes about how it helps reveal the author's perspective.

4. Refer to your notes as you write your essay.

Reading for Information **817**

Comparing Argumentative and Expository Texts

1. **(a)** The author's perspective in *A Christmas Carol* is that although the story is retold year after year, the TNT show is worth seeing because of what actor Patrick Stewart brings to the lead performance. In the radio interview, Professor Allingham praises Dickens's contribution to the literary world and discusses why the story has remained a classic all these years. **(b)** The texts are similar in that they are based upon opinions and experiences—both the critic and the professor are in their element, and share information with their respective audiences that is likely to interest them. **(c)** **Possible responses:** The radio interview is different from the print review because the interview is a series of questions and answers, rather than the discourse of one person. It also differs in that the radio interview is positive in nature, complimenting the work of Charles Dickens, rather than criticizing it. The review offers a more critical perspective from the author. **(d)** **Possible response:** A radio interview can achieve a more powerful impact than a written review because a radio interview allows the listener to hear the feelings expressed by the interviewee.

2. **(a)** When you take the *-tion* suffix away from the word *adaptation*, you get the word *adapt*. (The dictionary shows that you have to take away the "a," too.) It is a verb that means "to change (something) to fit a different purpose," instead of a noun that means "something that is produced by changing the original version." **(b)** **Sample response:** He wrote an adaptation of the short story for our school play.

🕐 Timed Writing

1. Before students complete the activity, guide them in identifying and analyzing key words and phrases in the prompt, highlighted on the student page.

2. Work with students to draw up guidelines for their essays based on the key words:

   • **Focus** The writer should clearly define the author's perspective.

   • **Organization** The writer should present ideas and the support for each in logical order.

   • **Elaboration** The writer should gather details, words, and phrases from the original text to trace the author's perspective, explaining how each supports the response.

   • **Style** The style should be clear and formal.

3. Have students use the 5-Minute Planner to structure their time.

4. Allow students 25 minutes to complete the assignment. Evaluate their work using the guidelines they have developed.

❶ Comparing Characters

1. Introduce and discuss the skill.
2. Discuss the character wheel.
3. Give students a copy of **Comparing Characters Organizer B,** (*Graphic Organizer Transparencies,* p. 156). Tell them that they will fill it in with details as they read.

Think Aloud: Model the Skill

To get students started in analyzing characters, use the following "think aloud." Say to students:

> To understand literary characters, I can imagine spending some time with the character in my own world. I can imagine having lunch with Scrooge. He might be complaining that eating lunch was a waste of time. He would probably nag me to get back to my desk and do some work. Fezziwig would probably be a better companion. He might bring some food to share, or tell a few jokes.

Comparing Literary Works

from A Christmas Carol: Scrooge and Marley, Act 1, Scene 2; Act 1, Scene 5

❶ Comparing Characters

A **character** is a person who takes part in a literary work. In a drama, characters are built largely through their words and actions. When a drama is presented on the stage, characters are played by actors.

- Like main characters in stories and novels, main characters in dramas have traits that make them unique. These may include qualities such as dependability, intelligence, and selfishness.
- Like other fictional characters, those in dramas have *motives,* or reasons, for acting the way they do. For example, one character may be motivated by love, but another may be motivated by fear.

In drama, one way to develop a character is through a **foil,** a character whose behavior and attitude contrast with those of the main character. With a foil, audiences can see *good* in contrast with *bad,* or *joy* in contrast with *sadness.* When you read a drama, note what each character says and does, and find the reactions these words and actions spark in others. Notice what these things reveal to you about the characters' traits and motives.

These two excerpts from *A Christmas Carol: Scrooge and Marley* show two employers reacting to the celebration of Christmas. As you read, use a character wheel like the one shown to analyze each character. Draw conclusions about whether these characters can be classified as foils. Then, make connections across the texts by comparing the characters' reactions to the celebration.

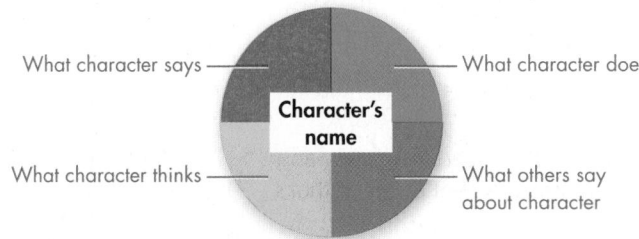

What character says — Character's name — What character does

What character thinks — What others say about character

www.PHLitOnline.com

- Vocabulary flashcards
- Interactive journals
- More about the authors
- Selection audio
- Interactive graphic organizers

818 Drama

Vocabulary Development

Vocabulary Knowledge Rating

Create a **Vocabulary Knowledge Rating Chart** (*Professional Development Guidebook,* p. 33) featuring the words glossed in the selections:

 snuffs (p. 820) *suitors* (p. 821)
 fiddler (p. 821)

 Give students a copy of the chart, and read the words aloud. Have students mark their rating of each in the Before You Read column.

To gauge how much instruction to provide, tally the students who think they know each word. Explain that the words are defined in the margin at the point where they appear in the selection. Urge students to be alert to these words as they read the selections. They will rate their knowledge again when they finish.

Vocabulary Central, featuring tools, activities, and songs for studying vocabulary, is available online at www.PHLitOnline.com.

Do others *see* us more clearly than we *see* ourselves?

Writing About the Big Question

As Bob Cratchit's boss, Ebenezer Scrooge is very different from the person he was when he worked for Fezziwig. Use this sentence starter to develop your ideas about the Big Question:

When we **reflect** on our lives, we may see differences in ourselves over time based on _____.

Meet the Authors

Charles Dickens (1812–1870)

Author of *A Christmas Carol*

English author Charles Dickens's early life was difficult. When he was a boy, his father went to prison, and young Charles had to work long hours pasting labels on bottles to earn money.

Writing As a young man, Dickens taught himself shorthand and got a job as a court reporter. In his early twenties, Dickens began to publish humorous stories. People liked his writing, and he was able to earn a living as a writer. Some of his novels are *David Copperfield, Hard Times,* and *Nicholas Nickleby.* One of his most well-known works is *A Christmas Carol,* which was published in 1843.

Israel Horovitz (b. 1939)

Author of *A Christmas Carol: Scrooge and Marley*

Israel Horovitz is a well-known playwright who lives in New York City with his wife. Horovitz is the author of more than fifty plays. His plays have introduced such actors as Al Pacino and Richard Dreyfus. *A Christmas Carol: Scrooge and Marley* was first produced in Baltimore, Maryland, in 1978.

Finding Inspiration in Tragedy Shortly after the attacks of September 11, 2001, Horovitz wrote a play about the event. The play, *3 Weeks After Paradise,* reflects his experiences during the tragedy and includes family photos and films.

from A Christmas Carol: Scrooge and Marley **819**

Teaching Resources

- **All** *Unit 5 Resources,* pp. 65–81
- **All** *Graphic Organizer Transparencies,* pp. 155–158
- **All** Enriched Online Student Edition
- **All** *Common Core Companion,* pp. 28–35, 67–68; 279–296

- **All EL** *Hear It!* Audio CD

All resources, including print and audio, are available online at www.PHLitOnline.com.

♦ Daily Bellringer

For each class during which you will teach this selection, have students complete one of the five Vocabulary activities for Week 27 in the *Daily Bellringer Activities* booklet.

② Writing About the Big Question

1. Introduce the assignment.
2. Lead the class in a discussion of how people change over time. Ask students what was important to them when they were ten years old. List a few responses on the board. What do they think will be important to them when they are twenty, or thirty, or fifty?
3. Have students complete the sentence starter. Review responses as a class. **(Sample response:** When we reflect on our lives, we may see differences in ourselves over time based on *what is important to us, who our friends are, and how we spend our time.*)
4. Tell students that as they read, they should think about how the characters are changing and how that change influences the way other people see them.

Concept Connector ➡

Students will return to their sentence starters after they read.

♦ Multidraft Reading

To assist struggling readers and to deepen reading for all, apply multidrarft reading protocols. For each reading, have students set the purpose indicated:

- **First reading**—identifying key ideas and details and answering any Reading Checks.
- **Second reading**—analyzing craft and structure and responding to the side-column prompts.
- **Third reading**—integrating knowledge and ideas, connecting to other texts and the world, and answering the end-of-selection questions.

For more guidance, see the *Classroom Strategies and Teaching Routines* card on multidraft reading.

For more about the authors and practice with the selection vocabulary, go online at www.PHLitOnline.com.

❶ Background

A Christmas Carol The play *A Christmas Carol: Scrooge and Marley* is based on Charles Dickens's classic story "A Christmas Carol."

❷ Activating Prior Knowledge

Prepare an **Anticipation Guide** (*Professional Development Guidebook,* p. 38) with the following statements.

- Christmas is the best holiday.
- No one should have to work during the holidays.
- People's feelings about the holidays reveal their personalities.

Give students a copy of the prepared **Anticipation Guide** and have students mark their responses in the Me column. Have students discuss the statements in pairs and mark the Guides again in the Group column.

Concept Connector ➡

Students will return to the **Anticipation Guides** after reading.

❸ About the Selection

In the first scene, Cratchit is eager to go home to his family for Christmas. Scrooge thinks it is unreasonable for Cratchit to take off Christmas. Cratchit is unable to contain his holiday cheer. The second scene is a flashback to a Christmas Eve when Scrooge was working for Fezziwig. Fezziwig shuts the office early and sets up a party. Scrooge dances with his boss's daughters and wife.

❹ Character

1. Remind students that characters reveal their attitudes through their words, movements, and actions.

2. Have two students read the first six lines of dialogue in the scene. Then **ask** the Character question. **Answer:** Scrooge asks Cratchit if he will want the whole day off on Christmas. He tells Cratchit that he is displeased by the request.

❺ Critical Viewing

Answer: The actor is dressed in somber clothing that matches Scrooge's joyless approach to life.

from

A CHRISTMAS CAROL:

SCROOGE AND MARLEY

❶
❷
❸

ISRAEL HOROVITZ
from *A CHRISTMAS CAROL* by CHARLES DICKENS

ACT 1, SCENE ❷

Vocabulary
snuffs (snufs) *v.* extinguishes; puts out

Character
What details here show how Scrooge feels about the holiday?

❹

▶ **Critical Viewing**
In what ways does this actor's costume reflect Scrooge's character traits?

❺

CRATCHIT. I must be going home . . . [He snuffs out his candle and puts on his hat.] I hope you have a . . . very very lovely day tomorrow, sir . . .

SCROOGE. Hmmm. Oh, you'll be wanting the whole day tomorrow, I suppose?

CRATCHIT. If quite convenient, sir.

SCROOGE. It's not convenient, and it's not fair. If I was to stop half-a-crown for it, you'd think yourself ill-used, I'll be bound?

[CRATCHIT *smiles faintly.*]

CRATCHIT. I don't know, sir . . .

SCROOGE. And yet, you don't think me ill-used when I pay a day's wages for no work . . .

CRATCHIT. It's only but once a year . . .

SCROOGE. A poor excuse for picking a man's pocket every 25th of December! But I suppose you must have the whole day. Be here all the earlier the next morning!

CRATCHIT. Oh I will, sir. I will. I promise you. And, sir . . .

SCROOGE. Don't say it, Cratchit.

820 Drama

Ⓒ Text Complexity Rubric

from A Christmas Carol: Scrooge and Marley		
Qualitative Measures	**Context/Knowledge Demands**	Victorican England 1 2 ③ 4 5
	Structure/Language Conventionality and Clarity	Conversational dialogue includes incomplete sentences and outdated expressions 1 2 3 ④ 5
	Levels of Meaning/ Purpose/Concepts	Accessible concept (classic story of the man who hates Christmas) 1 2 ③ 4 5
Quantitative Measures	**Text Length**	Word Count: 495
	Lexile	NP
Overall Complexity		✓ **Accessible**

CRATCHIT. But let me wish you a . . .

SCROOGE. Don't say it, Cratchit. I warn you . . .

CRATCHIT. Sir!

SCROOGE. Cratchit!

[CRATCHIT *opens the door.*]

CRATCHIT. All right, then, sir . . . well . . . [*Suddenly*] Merry Christmas, Mr. Scrooge!

[*And he runs out the door, shutting same behind him.*]

ACT 1, SCENE 5

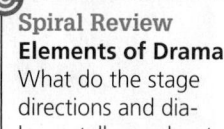

FEZZIWIG. Yo ho, my boys. No more work tonight. Christmas Eve, Dick. Christmas, Ebenezer!

[*They stand at attention in front of* FEZZIWIG; *laughing*] Hilli-ho! Clear away, and let's have lots of room here! Hilli-ho, Dick! Chirrup, Ebenezer!

[*The young men clear the room, sweep the floor, straighten the pictures, trim the lamps, etc. The space is clear now. A* **fiddler** *enters, fiddling.*]

Hi-ho, Matthew! Fiddle away . . . where are my daughters?

[*The fiddler plays. Three young daughters of* FEZZIWIG *enter followed by six young male* **suitors**. *They are dancing to the music. All employees come in: workers, clerks, housemaids, cousins, the baker, etc. All dance. Full number wanted here. Throughout the dance, food is brought into the feast. It is "eaten" in dance, by the dancers.* EBENEZER *dances with all three of the daughters, as does* DICK. *They compete for the daughters, happily, in the dance.* FEZZIWIG *dances with the daughters.* FEZZIWIG *dances with* DICK *and* EBENEZER. *The music changes:* MRS. FEZZIWIG *enters. She lovingly scolds her husband. They dance. She dances with* EBENEZER, *lifting him and throwing him about. She is enormously fat. When the dance is ended, they all dance off, floating away, as does the music.*]

PAST. It was a small matter, that Fezziwig made those silly folks so full of gratitude.

Spiral Review
Elements of Drama
What do the stage directions and dialogue tell you about Cratchit's personality? Explain.

Character
What details here show how Fezziwig feels about the holiday?

Vocabulary
fiddler (fid′ lər) *n.* person who plays a fiddle, or violin

suitors (so͞ot′ ərz) *n.* men who court a woman or seek to marry her

8 **Reading Check**
What does Scrooge warn Cratchit not to say?

Text Complexity: Reader and Task Suggestions

A Christmas Carol: Scrooge and Marley, Act I	
Preparing to Read the Text	**Leveled Tasks**
• Use the Background note on TE p. 820 to explain the connection between the play and Charles Dickens. • Ask students to point out how sentences in dialogue sometimes differ from those in prose narration. • Guide students to use Multidraft Reading strategies (TE p. 819).	***Structure/Language*** If students will have difficulty understanding selection sentences, have them first read to identify repeated punctuation in the text. Then, have them reread, noting how the punctuation might influence the actors' delivery of the lines. ***Analyzing*** If students will not have difficulty with selection sentences, have them read to explain how the punctuation in dialogue might contribute to characterization. As a class, discuss their responses.

Spiral Review
Elements of Drama
1. Remind students that they studied the concept of stage directions in the Unit 5 Literary Analysis Workshop (pp. 722–735).
2. **Ask** students the Spiral Review question. **Possible response:** Cratchit is stubborn and scared of Scrooge. The dialogue and stage directions show he is stubborn because he doesn't give up on his desire even though Scrooge tells him not to say the words. The dialogue and stage directions tell us he is scared of Scrooge because he says it and then runs out of the room.

6 Character
1. Review what students learned earlier about characters that are foils.
2. Have one student read the lines spoken by Fezziwig and another read the stage directions in parentheses.
3. Then **ask** students the Character question.

   Answer: Fezziwig's words and actions show how much he enjoys the holiday. He tells everyone to stop working as he sets up the feast and dancing. He expresses his excitement with expressions such as "Hilli-ho!"

7 Critical Thinking
Analyze

Ask students to contrast the feelings and events of this scene with Act 1, Scene 2, on p. 820.
Answer: This scene, unlike Act 1, Scene 2, celebrates Christmas with food and dancing. In Act 1, Scene 2, Scrooge is unwilling to celebrate Christmas or let his employee do so.

8 Reading Check
Possible response: Scrooge doesn't want Cratchit to wish him a Merry Christmas.

PHLit Online!
This selection is available in interactive format in the **Enriched Online Student Edition**, at **www.PHLitOnline.com**, which includes an interactive graphic organizer.

Have students return to their Anticipation Guides and respond to the statements again in the After Reading column. Encourage students to cite specific details, quotations, or other evidence from the text to support their responses to each statement.

ASSESS

Answers

Critical Thinking

Remind students to support their answers with evidence from the text.

1. (a) Cratchit wishes Scrooge a Merry Christmas. (b) **Possible responses:** Cratchit can't contain his joy; or Cratchit wants to see how his boss will react. (c) **Possible response:** It shows that Cratchit is a good man who enjoys the holiday and wants his boss to do so, too.

2. (a) Students will probably agree that Scrooge will work during the holiday because he seems to think it unfair that employees should not work on Christmas Day. (b) **Possible response:** It does seem fair because everyone deserves to have a day off. Even if not everyone celebrates the holiday, everyone will be happier.

3. (a) Fezziwig has a loving relationship with his daughters. (b) He calls his daughters to the party and dances with them.

4.  **Possible responses:** The scenes reveal that Scrooge has changed over time. He wasn't always a tightfisted, joyless person. As a young man, he knew how to relax and have a good time. (b) **Possible response:** When did he change? Did something happen to make him change? (c) **Possible response:** Cratchit's overwhelming emotion is pity. Cratchit shows he is not afraid of Scrooge when he insists on sharing a "Merry Christmas" with his boss.

SCROOGE. Small?

PAST. Shhh!?

[Lights up on DICK *and* EBENEZER.]

DICK. We are blessed, Ebenezer, truly, to have such a master as Mr. Fezziwig!

YOUNG EBENEZER. He is the best, best, the very and absolute best! If ever I own a firm of my own, I shall treat my apprentices with the same dignity and the same grace. We have learned a wonderful lesson from the master, Dick!

DICK. Ah, that's a fact, Ebenezer. That's a fact!

Critical Thinking

Cite textual evidence to support your responses.

1. **Key Ideas and Details (a)** What does Cratchit say to Scrooge as Cratchit leaves? **(b) Infer:** Why do you think he says this—against Scrooge's wishes? **(c) Generalize:** What do you think this action shows about Cratchit?

2. **Key Ideas and Details (a) Infer:** Do you think Scrooge will work on Christmas day? Why or why not? **(b) Make a Judgment:** Do you think that a boss should be required to give employees a day off for a holiday that is not celebrated by everyone? Explain.

3. **Key Ideas and Details (a) Infer:** What kind of relationship do you think Fezziwig has with his daughters? **(b) Support:** What examples illustrate this opinion?

4. **Integration of Knowledge and Ideas (a)** What changes in Scrooge do these scenes reveal? **(b)** What questions would you ask to learn more about the changes? **(c)** How do you think Cratchit regards the older Scrooge—with fear or pity? *[Connect to the Big Question: Do others see us more clearly than we see ourselves?]*

822 Drama

Vocabulary Development

Vocabulary Knowledge Rating
When students have completed reading and discussing these scenes from *A Christmas Carol: Scrooge and Marley,* have them take out their **Vocabulary Knowledge Rating Chart**. Read the words aloud once more and have students rate their knowledge of the words again in the After Reading column. Clarify any words that are still problematic. Have students write their own definition and example or sentence in the appropriate column. Then have students complete the Vocabulary Practice activities on the next page. Encourage students to use the words in further discussion and written work about these selections. Remind them that they will be accountable for these words on the **Selection Test,** (*Unit 5 Resources,* pp. 76–78 or pp. 79–81).

Comparing Characters

1. Key Ideas and Details (a) How would you describe Scrooge? **(b)** What details from the play support your ideas?

2. Key Ideas and Details (a) How would you describe Fezziwig? **(b)** What details from the play support your ideas?

3. Craft and Structure Complete a chart like the one below to compare each character's traits and motives.

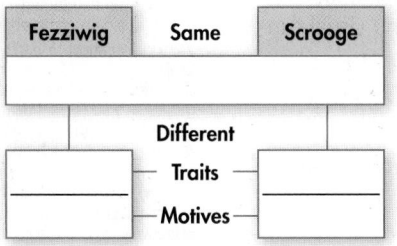

4. Key Ideas and Details (a) In what ways does Fezziwig act as a foil to Scrooge? **(b)** Why is Fezziwig's character important to the play?

Timed Writing

Explanatory Text: Essay

Make connections across the texts to compare and contrast Fezziwig and Scrooge. In an essay, discuss how each character's actions and words help the playwright make a point about Scrooge and his behavior. **(40 minutes)**

5-Minute Planner

1. Read the prompt carefully and completely.

2. Gather your ideas by jotting down answers to these questions:
- Why does each character act as he does?
- What do audiences learn about Scrooge because of Fezziwig?

3. Review each scene and take notes on Fezziwig's and Scrooge's words and actions. Then, draw conclusions about the differences between the two men. Use these notes as you write your comparison-and-contrast essay.

4. Reread the prompt, and then draft your essay.

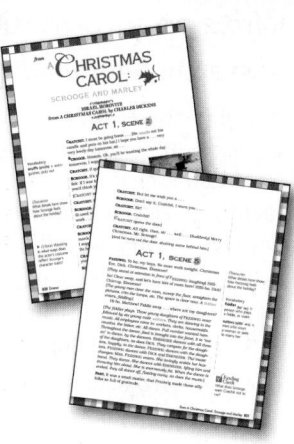

from A Christmas Carol: Scrooge and Marley **823**

Comparing Characters

1. (a) **Possible responses:** Scrooge was once a young man who enjoyed the Christmas holiday, but now he is an old miser who hates the holiday. (b) He grumbles about paying Cratchit on Christmas Day and warns Cratchit not to wish him a Merry Christmas.

2. (a) Fezziwig is a joyful, loving man who enjoys Christmas. (b) Fezziwig ends the workday early to start the Christmas celebration. He treats his employees as if they were part of his family.

3. **Same:** both are employers; **Fezziwig: Traits:** generous, fun, loving; **Motives:** He wants everyone to have a good time, wants to enjoy himself on the holiday. **Scrooge: Traits:** miserly, grumpy, withholding; **Motives:** He wants to make money, does not want others to enjoy themselves

4. For another sample answer, see **Literary Analysis Transparency A,** p. 168, *Graphic Organizer Transparencies.*

Timed Writing

1. Review the prompt with students.

2. Have students use the 5-Minute Planner to structure their time. Guide them in answering the bulleted questions. For example, point out that the second bulleted point might lead them to focus on how Scrooge has betrayed his past self.

3. Allow students 40 minutes to complete the assignment.

4. As students prewrite and draft, have them refer to their completed **Comparing Characters Graphic Organizer.**

Six Traits Focus

✔ Ideas	Word Choice
✔ Organization	Sentence Fluency
Voice	Conventions

Introducing the Writing Assignment

Review the assignment on the student page.

Connecting to Real-Life Writing

Point out to students that the basic elements of a multimedia report are often incorporated into research reports and TV news reports.

 **Writing Workshop**
Work in Progress

If students have completed the Work-in-Progress assignments on pp. 771 and 809, suggest that they try to develop their Work-in-Progress ideas in a multimedia report.

TEACH

Prewriting/Planning Strategy

1. Introduce the prewriting strategy.
2. Have students apply the strategy to gather details.

Six Traits Focus

✔	Ideas		Word Choice
✔	Organization		Sentence Fluency
	Voice		Conventions

Writing Workshop

Write an Informative Text

Research: Multimedia Report

Defining the Form Presentations that include videos, slides, photographs, maps, music, or sound effects capture your attention. A presentation that uses information from both print and non-print sources is called a **multimedia report.** You might use elements of this type of writing in documentaries and research.

Assignment Create a multimedia report about a topic that interests you and that presents opportunities for audio and visual support. Your report should feature the following elements:

✔ a *focused topic* that can be covered in the time and space allotted

✔ a *clear and logical organization* that presents a main idea

✔ well-integrated *audio and visual features* from a variety of sources

✔ use of *formatting and presentation techniques* for visual appeal

✔ *effective pacing* with *smooth transitions* between elements

✔ error-free writing, including *correct usage of frequently confused words*

To preview the criteria on which your multimedia report may be judged, see the rubric on page 829.

 Writing Workshop: *Work in Progress*

Review the work you did on pages 771 and 809.

Prewriting/Planning Strategy

Flip through magazines. Scan credible magazines that explore areas you find interesting, such as travel, the arts, or sports. List possible topics and note creative ways to engage your audience. Beyond typical print sources, use multimedia sources such as reliable sites on the Internet, video documentaries, maps, photographs, music, sound, and film clips. Consider whether you will be able to find information in both print and nonprint sources, for example, by typing your topic into a search engine. Then, choose a topic.

© **Common Core State Standards**

Writing

2. Write informative/explanatory texts to examine a topic and convey ideas, concepts, and information through the selection, organization, and analysis of relevant content.

2.a. Introduce a topic clearly, previewing what is to follow; organize ideas, concepts, and information, using strategies such as definition, classification, comparison/contrast, and cause/effect; include formatting, graphics, and multimedia when useful to aiding comprehension.

7. Conduct short research projects to answer a question, drawing on several sources and generating additional related, focused questions for further research and investigation.

8. Gather relevant information from multiple print and digital sources, using search terms effectively; assess the credibility and accuracy of each source.

Teaching Resources

The following resources can be used to enrich or extend the instruction.

All *Unit 5 Resources*
Writing Workshop, pp. 82–83

All *Common Core Companion,*
pp. 202–212, 245–276; 323–324; 333–342

All *Professional Development Guidebook*
Rubrics for Self-Assessment: Multimedia Report, pp. 240–241

All *Graphic Organizer Transparencies*
Rubric for Self-Assessment: Multimedia Report, p. 159

PHLit Online! All resources are available online at **www.PHLitOnline.com.**

Focus on Ideas

Your **ideas** will help you create an interesting and enjoyable multimedia report. After you have chosen your topic, look for ways to sustain your audience's interest. Make sure your ideas are original and that you have learned as much as you can about your topic.

Narrowing Your Topic If you have chosen a broad topic, like sports, narrow your topic to focus on a specific aspect. For example, focus on a favorite team, a memorable event in sports, or a specific sport you like to play. Use a chart like the one shown to help you narrow your topic.

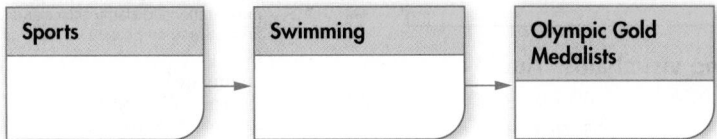

Sports → Swimming → Olympic Gold Medalists

Be sure that your topic can be covered in the allotted time and space. Once you have defined your topic and purpose, generate ideas for making that topic interesting to your audience. Ask yourself these questions:

- What do I want to say about my topic?
- Why should my audience care about my topic?
- How can I share my enthusiasm for my topic?
- Is there anything that my audience may not understand?

Connecting Your Ideas Think of past presentations you have seen. What has made them successful or unsuccessful? In other words, what makes an audience want to pay attention?

Gather as many ideas as you can regarding visual and audio aids. Research each idea and choose the ones that will work best with your topic. For example, if you are focusing on sports, you might use a video clip of a game or interview. If your topic relates to science, you might show a clip of a documentary or provide charts to support your research. Keep your content, audience, and purpose in mind as you choose your multimedia aids.

> **PH WRITING COACH**
>
> Further instruction and practice are available in *Prentice Hall Writing Coach*.

Writing Workshop **825**

Applying Understanding by Design Principles

Clarifying Expected Outcomes: Using Rubrics

- Before students begin work on this assignment, have them preview the Rubric for Self-Assessment (p. 829) to know what is expected. A copy of this rubric appears in *Graphic Organizer Transparencies*, p. 159.
- Review the criteria in the Rubric with the class. Before students use the Rubric to assess their own writing, work with them to rate the Student Model (p. 828) using the Rubric.

- If you wish to assess students' multimedia reports with either a 4-point or a 6-point scoring rubric, see the *Professional Development Guidebook*, pp. 240–241.

Focus on Ideas

1. Introduce the writing skill, using the instructions on the student page.
2. Discuss the graphic organizer and the questions.
3. Have students follow the instructions to develop their ideas.

Teaching the Writing Skill

1. Explain to the class that presenting new ideas or presenting ideas in a new way keeps an audience interested. Tell the class that very few people pay attention to something that they have seen and heard several times. To illustrate presenting ideas in a new way, ask how many students pay attention to a commercial that they have seen many times. Ask the class if they pay attention to a commercial they are seeing for the first time. Then, ask the students to brainstorm for one unique or novel way of getting an audience's attention using multimedia.

2. Remind students that they must narrow their topic so that they can understand it. Ask the class to tell you whether the following topics are narrow enough for a good multimedia report:

World War II	(too broad)
The Best Bowlers of the Twentieth Century	(probably narrow enough)
British Fashions of the 1970s	(probably narrow enough)
Jazz	(too broad)

3. Tell students that once they have started researching and learning about their topic, they will be able to further narrow the topic.

4. Remind students that they have to work with the materials available to them. Although an interview with an Olympic gold medalist would be a wonderful addition to a multimedia presentation, it is not likely that a student will be able to conduct one. However, there are historical interviews available on the Internet that students might be able to use, as long as they respect copyright laws.

> **PH WRITING COACH** | Grade 7
>
> Students will find additional support for creating a multimedia report in chapter 11.

Drafting Strategies

1. Introduce the drafting strategies on the student page.
2. Have students apply the strategies as they draft.

Teaching the Strategies

1. Draw students' attention to the example of a script, noting that it specifies visuals and sound effects as well as the narrator's words.
2. Show students examples of spreadsheets and charts to give them ideas for organizing and presenting information. Explain how spacing and design can enhance the appearance of documents.

Six Traits Focus

✔	Ideas		Word Choice
✔	Organization		Sentence Fluency
	Voice		Conventions

Revising Strategy

1. Introduce the revising strategy on the student page.
2. Have students apply the strategy as they revise.

Teaching the Strategies

Have students choose appropriate transitional words from the chart on the student page to join the sentences in the following pair:

Whales are endangered./
Some people continue to hunt them.

(**Possible response:** Whales are endangered, *yet* some people continue to hunt them.)

I did not feel bad when my team lost./
They had made it to the postseason for the first time in years.

(**Possible response:** I did not feel bad when my team lost. *After all,* they had made it to the postseason for the first time in years.)

Six Traits Focus

	Ideas	✔	Word Choice
	Organization		Sentence Fluency
	Voice		Conventions

826

Drafting Strategies

Write a script. Plan every word and action in your multimedia presentation by writing a script. Use index cards to help organize your ideas. Include any words that you will speak and any stage directions that make actions and effects clear. Note when you will use each visual or audio aid.

> Card 1
>
> Visual 1: Documentary clip of a cooking show
>
> Script: The clip I am going to show now explains how to prepare a turkey for Thanksgiving. As you will see, all of the materials are carefully laid out to make the process easier.
>
> Actions: Press play on DVD player

Incorporate your audio and visual aids. Audio aids, such as interviews or music, can set a mood and provide information. **Visual aids,** such as spreadsheets, maps, or charts, can organize large amounts of information, making it easier to present.

Use appropriate software to design additional information, and plan to display information on posters, on computer monitors, or as handouts. Use headings, spacing, and design features to enhance the appearance of your report.

Revising Strategy

Use effective transitions. Read the final sentence of each paragraph. Then, read the opening sentence of the next paragraph. If one or both sentences clearly show the relationship between paragraphs, underline them. If you do not find a relationship, add a transitional word, phrase, or sentence to link them together. Use this tip as you revise.

To add to an idea or show sequence, use . . .	*also, and, next, equally important, furthermore, first, second, third, likewise, still, too, another, besides*
To add contrast to ideas, use . . .	*alternatively, despite, although, yet, but, conversely, instead, nor, on the other hand, however, otherwise, regardless*
To give examples or clarify ideas, use . . .	*after all, in other words, certainly, for example, such as*
To show cause and effect of ideas, use . . .	*as a result, because, for that reason, since, so that, therefore, to do this, due to*

Common Core State Standards

Writing
2.a. Introduce a topic clearly, previewing what is to follow; organize ideas, concepts, and information, using strategies such as definition, classification, comparison/contrast, and cause/effect; include formatting, graphics, and multimedia when useful to aiding comprehension.
2.c. Use appropriate transitions to create cohesion and clarify the relationships among ideas and concepts.
6. Use technology, including the Internet, to produce and publish writing.

Speaking and Listening
5. Include multimedia components and visual displays in presentations to clarify claims and findings and emphasize salient points.

Language
1. Demonstrate command of the conventions of standard English grammar and usage when writing or speaking.

Revising to Avoid Common Usage Problems

Identifying Common Usage Problems When you choose the wrong word in your writing, you can confuse readers or lead them to question the care you take with your work. The sets of words presented here are frequently confused:

- **Accept,** a verb, means "to take what is offered" or "to agree to."
- **Except,** a preposition, means "leaving out" or "other than."

  Verb: She **accepted** her award graciously.

  Preposition: Everyone **except** Anabelle went to the movie.

- **Affect,** a verb, means "to influence" or "to cause a change in."
- **Effect,** usually a noun, means "result."

  Verb: Lack of sleep can **affect** your ability to concentrate.

  Noun: What is the **effect** of getting too much sleep?

Fixing Common Usage Problems To fix a usage problem, first identify words that you often confuse. Then, correct your error using one of the following methods.

1. Identify the word's part of speech and its use in the sentence.
2. Determine the meaning you want to convey.
3. Consult a dictionary or a language handbook for clarification, then choose the correct word.

PH WRITING COACH

Further instruction and practice are available in *Prentice Hall Writing Coach.*

Grammar in Your Writing

Choose three paragraphs in your draft. Underline each sentence that contains one of the words discussed on this page or another word you suspect you may have used incorrectly. Fix any usage problems using one of the methods described.

Other Commonly Confused Words

advice: noun, "an opinion"
advise: verb, "to give an opinion"

in: preposition, refers to position
into: preposition, suggests motion

beside: preposition, "at the side of"
besides: preposition, "in addition to"

farther: adjective, refers to distance
further: adjective, "additional" or "to a greater extent"

Revising to Avoid Common Usage Problems

1. Introduce the grammar skill, using the instruction on the student page.
2. Discuss the rules and examples, as well as the strategies for fixing incorrect usage.
3. Have students follow the instruction under Grammar in Your Writing to correct errors in their drafts.

Teaching the Grammar Skill

Students often make errors when using commonly confused words. Have them determine whether the following sentences contain any errors in usage and, if so, correct them.

The accountant adviced his client not to invest in the new company. (**Answer:** incorrect: The accountant advised his client not to invest in the new company.)

Tonya sat beside me at the movie (**Answer:** correct)

We will discuss the topic farther tomorrow. (**Answer:** incorrect: We will discuss the topic further tomorrow.)

He went into the furthest reaches of the cave. (**Answer:** incorrect: He went into the farthest reaches of the cave.)

He went in the hallway. (**Answer:** incorrect: He went into the hallway.)

Student Model

Review the Student Model with the class, using the annotations to analyze the writer's use of the elements of a multimedia report.

Teaching from the Student Model

1. Explain that the Student Model is a sample and that reports may be longer. Point out that although the model is not complete, it can be used as a guide for scripting and organizing reports.

2. Have students read through the model and annotations. Have students examine the elements or features that are identified, analyze the effects of these elements on the report, and consider how to apply these in their own report.

3. Ask students to identify the information presented in the visual aids. Then, have them discuss how the information enhances the presentation. (**Possible response.** The presentation includes slides of the gray whale and the California coastline. This information enables the audience to picture the animal and the setting.)

4. Ask students to identify the sound effects and the purpose they serve. (**Possible response:** The whale song adds to our knowledge of the whale; the sound of waves crashing brings the setting alive.)

Connecting to Real-Life Writing

Tell students that multimedia reports are used frequently in such workplaces as accounting offices, banks, stock brokerages, and government agencies. By researching a topic or a proposed project and presenting the information in an organized fashion, businesspeople are able to make educated decisions and to train employees. Discuss in class some work situations in which multimedia reports might be needed.

Student Model:
Shane Larkin and Ian Duffy, Williamston, MI

Common Core State Standards

Writing
6. Use technology, including the Internet, to produce and publish writing and link to and cite sources as well as to interact and collaborate with others.

Zia

Slide 1
Visual: Title and Author Slide: *Zia*, by Scott O'Dell
Script: This presentation is about the book *Zia* by Scott O'Dell. *Zia* is a sequel to the book *Island of the Blue Dolphins* and shares some of the same characters. Instead of dolphins, though, Zia and her brother see gray whales, like those heard here.

> The writers have chosen a topic that can be well covered in the time allotted to their report.

Slide 2
Visual: Whale
Sound: Whale song
Script: Reading this book got us very interested in the study of whales and how they adapt to the world around them.

Slide 3
Visual: Setting Slide
Sound: Ocean waves crashing against beach
Script: The setting of *Zia* is the southern coast of California during the Spanish colonial era. The action takes place in several locations. This is a picture of the California coast.

> The writers' choice of visual is both dramatic and appropriate to their topic, audience, and purpose.

Video 1: Video clip of whale scanning for food
Script: From reading this book and doing a small amount of research, we discovered many ways whales can adapt to these kinds of harsh environments. Several of the toothed whales shoot a jet of water at the ocean floor. They use this jet to stir up prey hiding in the sand. These whales also have very flexible necks that help them scan the ocean floor for food.

> The writers use bold-face heads and other appropriate formatting to present the organization of their report clearly.

Slide 4
Visual: Arctic shoreline
Sound: Ocean waves crashing against beach
Script: Other characteristics can help a whale live in a harsh environment. The bowhead, for instance, has several interesting physical features that allow it to live in the Arctic all the time.

> Sound effects such as this enhance the presentation.

Sound: Whale song
Script: We learned a lot about whales by reading *Zia* and doing our research, but this is only the beginning. This book has inspired us to continue our research to learn more about these amazing creatures and their adaptations to the environment.

Strategies for
Test Taking

When preparing a multimedia report as part of a take-home test, students should include as many media sources as they can, yet make sure that their topics are focused and that their visual and audio aids enhance the presentation. Before giving his or her presentation, each student should practice at home in front of a mirror or with a partner to be sure the presentation flows smoothly.

Editing and Proofreading

Review your draft to eliminate errors in grammar, spelling, and punctuation.

Focus on presentation copies. To avoid distracting your audience with mistakes, run a spelling and grammar check on any visuals you present. Be careful, however, because spell-checkers do not catch mistakes in homophones such as *there, their,* and *they're*. You must catch these errors yourself. In addition, check the layouts of slides or handouts to be sure information is clear and error-free.

Publishing and Presenting

Consider one of the following ways to share your writing:

Present your report. Perform your multimedia report for your classmates. Ask them to evaluate what they see and hear.

Post your work. Post your report to an approved Web site. Add links to your online sources and, if possible, invite and respond to comments.

Reflecting on Your Writing

Writer's Journal Jot down your answer to these questions:

What was the most effective visual aid or audio aid you used in your presentation? Why?

Rubric for Self-Assessment

Find evidence in your writing to address each category. Then, use the rating scale to grade your work.

Criteria	Rating Scale
	not very very
Focus: How clearly focused is your topic?	1 2 3 4 5
Organization: How logical is your organization?	1 2 3 4 5
Support/Elaboration: How effective are your audio and visual features?	1 2 3 4 5
Style: How smooth are the transitions between elements?	1 2 3 4 5
Conventions: How correct is your word usage?	1 2 3 4 5
Ideas: Does your report have a specific purpose with original ideas?	1 2 3 4 5

Spiral Review

Earlier in the unit, you learned about **interjections** (p. 770) and **double negatives** (p. 808). Check the use of interjections in your multimedia report. Review your essay to be sure that you have corrected any sentence that contains a double negative.

Editing and Proofreading

1. Introduce the editing and proofreading focus, using the instruction on the student page.
2. Have students edit and proofread their narratives, correcting grammar, spelling, punctuation, and word choice. Make sure they check for errors of the type noted in the lesson focus and the Spiral Review.

Teaching the Editing Focus

Have students brainstorm for other common homophones. **Possible responses:** *piece / peace, sum / some, meat / meet, real / reel, hole / whole, tale / tail, too / two, right / write*

Six Traits Focus

Ideas		Word Choice	
Organization		Sentence Fluency	
Voice		Conventions	✔

ASSESS

Publishing and Presenting

1. Suggest that students practice delivering their presentations beforehand, using appropriate gestures and expressions.
2. Suggest that students who want to present their reports outside their schools write a letter introducing themselves and their project to the appropriate official such as a head librarian, school principal, or club president.
3. Work with students to find approved Web sites that relate to their topics.

Reflecting on Your Writing

Suggest that students revisit their notes and various drafts to identify what they might do differently when they next write a multimedia report.

Strategies for Less Proficient Writers

Explain to students that the visual and audio aids they use in their presentations must enhance the presentation, provide additional information, and pique interest. After students have chosen their topic, have them preview various visual aids and write brief descriptions of how each serves a purpose.

Strategies for English Learners

Tell students that they will need to introduce the visual aids they use in their reports. Point out the introductions in the Student Model, and have students use those as models for their own reports. They might also describe the information presented in the aids. Have students practice with partners to refine their introductions.

✓ The Monsters Are Due on Maple Street
Lesson Pacing Guide

DAY 1 Preteach

- Ⓒ Administer the Reading and Vocabulary Warm-ups (*Unit 5 Resources,* pp. 91–94) as necessary.
- • Introduce the Reading Skill: Summarize.
- Ⓒ Introduce the Literary Analysis concept: Characters' Motives.
- • Distribute copies of the appropriate graphic organizer for the Reading Skill (*Graphic Organizer Transparencies,* pp. 162–163).
- • Distribute copies of the appropriate graphic organizer for Literary Analysis (*Graphic Organizer Transparencies,* pp. 160–161).
- Ⓒ Teach the selection vocabulary.
- Ⓒ Introduce the Word Study skill.

DAYS 2–3 Preteach/Teach

- Ⓒ Build background with the Background feature.
- • Develop thematic vocabulary and thematic thinking with Writing About the Big Question.
- • Prepare students to read with the Activating Prior Knowledge activities (TE).
- • Informally monitor comprehension while students read.
- • Use the Reading Check questions to confirm comprehension.
- • Develop students' ability to present only the main ideas and most important details in a brief statement.
- Ⓒ Develop students' understanding of characters' motives using the Characters' Motives questions.
- Ⓒ Reinforce vocabulary with the Vocabulary notes.
- Ⓒ Reinforce unit focus standards using the Spiral Review prompts.

DAY 4 Assess

- • Assess students' comprehension and mastery of the skills by having them answer the Critical Thinking, Reading Skill, and Literary Analysis questions.
- Ⓒ Have students complete the Vocabulary Practice activities.
- Ⓒ Have students complete the Word Study activities.

DAY 5 Extend/Assess

- • Have students complete the Conventions lesson.
- Ⓒ Have students complete the Writing activity and write a a summary. (You may assign as homework.)
- Ⓒ Extend learning by having students complete the Research and Technology, a film version activity. (You may assign as homework.) As an alternative, assign them "Pushing Buttons" in *Reality Central.*
- • Administer Selection Test A or B (*Unit 5 Resources,* pp. 106–108 or 109–111).

Ⓒ Common Core State Standards

Reading Literature 2. Determine a theme or central idea of a text and analyze its development over the course of the text; provide an objective summary. *(Reading Skill: Summarizing)*
3. Analyze how particular elements of a story or drama interact.
5. Analyze how a drama's or poem's form or structure (e.g., soliloquy, sonnet) contributes to its meaning.
7. Compare and contrast a written story, drama, or poem to its audio, filmed, staged, or multimedia version, analyzing the effects of techniques unique to each medium.

Writing 2.b. Develop the topic with relevant facts, definitions, concrete details, quotations, or other information and examples.
2.c. Use appropriate transitions to create cohesion and clarify the relationships among ideas and concepts.
6. Use technology, including the Internet, to produce and publish writing.
9.a. Apply *grade 7 Reading standards* to literature.

Language 2. Demonstrate command of the conventions of standard English capitalization, punctuation, and spelling when writing.
4.b. Use common, grade-appropriate Greek or Latin affixes and roots as clues to the meaning of a word.

Additional Standards Practice
Common Core Companion, pp. 28–35, 54–61

Daily Block Scheduling
Each day in this Lesson Pacing Guide represents a 40–50 minute period. Teachers using block scheduling may combine days to revise pacing. In addition, teachers may differentiate and support core instruction by integrating components for extended and intensive support, as students require. See the Guide to Selected Leveled Resources (facing page).

Guide to Selected Leveled Resources

RTI Tier 1 (students performing on level)

The Monsters Are Due on Maple Street

Warm Up

Practice, model, and **monitor** fluency, working with the **whole class** or **in groups**.

Vocabulary and **Reading Warm-ups B,** *Unit 5 Resources,* pp. 91–92, 94

Comprehension/Skills

Support and **monitor** comprehension and skills development, having students complete the activities, graphic organizers, and interactive prompts **independently** or **as a class**.

- *Reader's Notebook,* adapted instruction and full selection
- **EL** *Reader's Notebook: English Learner's Version,* adapted instruction and adapted selection
- **Reading Skill Graphic Organizer B,** *Graphic Organizer Transparencies,* p. 163
- **Literary Analysis Graphic Organizer B,** *Graphic Organizer Transparencies,* p. 161

Monitor Progress

A

Monitor student progress with the differentiated curriculum-based assessment in the *Unit Resources.*

- **Selection Test B,** *Unit 5 Resources,* pp. 109–111
- **Open-Book Test,** *Unit 5 Resources,* pp. 103–105

RTI Tier 2 (students requiring intervention)

The Monsters Are Due on Maple Street

Warm Up

Practice, model, and **monitor** fluency **in groups** or **with individuals**.

- **Vocabulary and Reading Warm-ups A,** *Unit 5 Resources,* pp. 91–93
- *Reality Central,* "Pushing Buttons"
- *Hear It!* Audio CD (adapted text)

Comprehension/Skills

- **Support** and **monitor** comprehension and skills development, working **in small groups** or **with individuals.**
- **Pair** students with more advanced peers and have them complete the writing activity in the *Real World Writing Journal.*
- As students complete the selection in the appropriate version of the *Reader's Notebook,* **monitor** comprehension frequently with group questions and individual instruction.
- **Model** strategies while guiding students in completing the activities and prompts in the *Reader's Notebook,* as well as the graphic organizers.
- **Practice** skills and **monitor** mastery with the *Reading Kit* worksheets.

- *Real-World Writing Journal,* Lesson 4, pp. 150–153
- *Reader's Notebook: Adapted Version,* adapted instruction and adapted selection
- **EL** *Reader's Notebook: English Learner's Version,* adapted instruction and adapted selection
- **Reading Skill Graphic Organizer A,** *Graphic Organizer Transparencies,* p. 162
- **Literary Analysis Graphic Organizer A,** *Graphic Organizer Transparencies,* p. 160
- *Reading Kit,* Practice worksheets, pp. 224, 228, 232, 234, 240

Monitor Progress

A

Monitor student progress with the differentiated curriculum-based assessment in the *Unit Resources* and in the *Reading Kit.*

- **Selection Test A,** *Unit 5 Resources,* pp. 106–108
- *Reading Kit,* Assess worksheets, pp. 225, 229, 233, 235, 241

TIER 3 Tier 3 intervention may require consultation with the student's special-education or dyslexia specialist. For additional support, see the Tier 2 activities and resources listed above.

One-on-one teaching **Group work** **Whole class instruction** **Independent work** **A Assessment**

For a complete guide to selection support, including support for Advanced students, see the Overview of Resources in the frontmatter.

✓ The Monsters Are Due on Maple Street

RESOURCES FOR:

- **L1** Special-Needs Students
- **L2** Below-Level Students (Tier 2)
- **L3** On-Level Students (Tier 1)
- **L4** Advanced Students (Tier 1)
- **EL** English Learners
- **All** All Students

Vocabulary/Fluency/Prior Knowledge

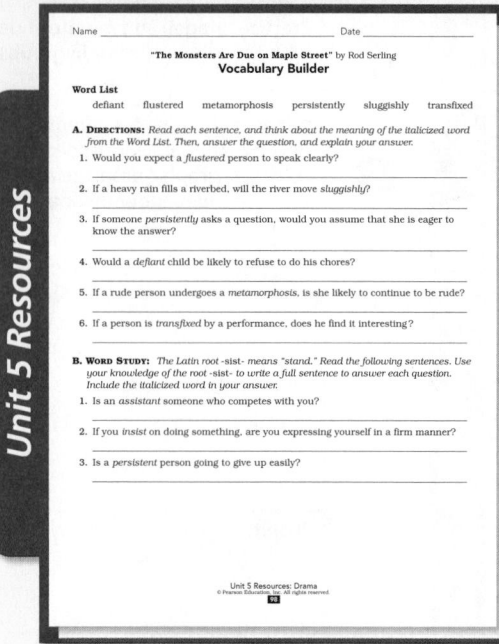

All **Vocabulary Builder,** p. 98

Also available for these selections:

- **EL** **L1** **L2** Reading Warm-ups A and B, pp. 93–94
- **EL** **L1** **L2** Vocabulary Warm-ups A and B, pp. 91–92
- **All** Writing About the Big Question, p. 95

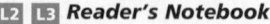

- **L2** **L3** *Reader's Notebook*
- **L1** *Reader's Notebook: Adapted Version*
- **EL** *Reader's Notebook: English Learner's Version*
- **EL** *Reader's Notebook: Spanish Version*

Reader's Notebooks

Pre- and postreading pages, as well as the selection *"The Monsters Are Due on Maple Street,"* appear in an interactive format in the *Reader's Notebooks.* Each *Notebook* is differentiated for a different group of learners. The selections in the Adapted and English Learner's versions are abridged.

© *Common Core Companion*

Additional instruction and practice for each Common Core State Standard

Selection Support

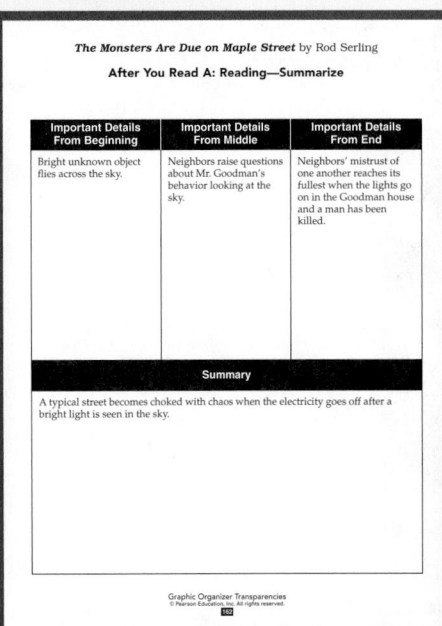

The Monsters Are Due on Maple Street by Rod Serling

After You Read A: Reading—Summarize

Important Details From Beginning	Important Details From Middle	Important Details From End
Bright unknown object flies across the sky.	Neighbors raise questions about Mr. Goodman's behavior looking at the sky.	Neighbors' mistrust of one another reaches its fullest when the lights go on in the Goodman house and a man has been killed.

Summary

A typical street becomes choked with chaos when the electricity goes off after a bright light is seen in the sky.

EL L1 L2 Reading: Graphic Organizer A, p. 162 (partially filled in)

Also available for these selections:

EL L3 Reading: Graphic Organizer B, p. 163

EL L1 L2 Literary Analysis: Graphic Organizer A, p. 160 (partially filled in)

EL L3 Literary Analysis: Graphic Organizer B, p. 161

Skills Development/Extension

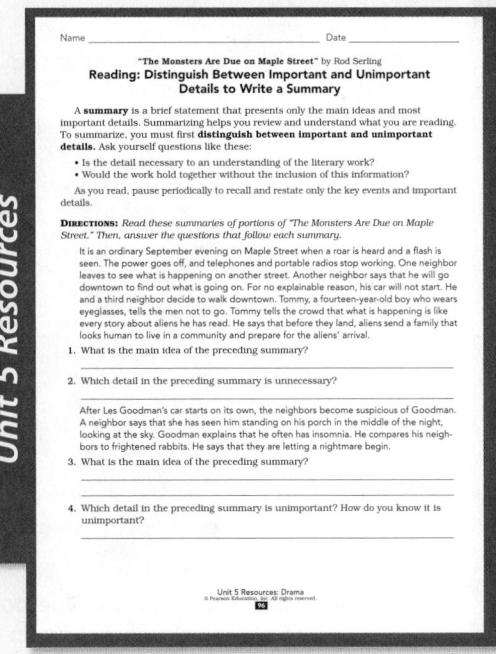

Name _____ Date _____

"The Monsters Are Due on Maple Street" by Rod Serling
Reading: Distinguish Between Important and Unimportant Details to Write a Summary

A **summary** is a brief statement that presents only the main ideas and most important details. Summarizing helps you review and understand what you are reading. To summarize, you must first **distinguish between important and unimportant details.** Ask yourself questions like these:

• Is the detail necessary to an understanding of the literary work?
• Would the work hold together without the inclusion of this information?

As you read, pause periodically to recall and restate only the key events and important details.

DIRECTIONS: *Read these summaries of portions of "The Monsters Are Due on Maple Street." Then, answer the questions that follow each summary.*

It is an ordinary September evening on Maple Street when a roar is heard and a flash is seen. The power goes off, and telephones and portable radios stop working. One neighbor leaves to see what is happening on another street. Another neighbor says that he will go downtown to find out what is going on. For no explainable reason, his car will not start. He and a third neighbor decide to walk downtown. Tommy, a fourteen-year-old boy who wears eyeglasses, tells the men not to go. Tommy tells the crowd that what is happening is like every story about aliens he has read. He says that before they land, aliens send a family that looks human to live in a community and prepare for the aliens' arrival.

1. What is the main idea of the preceding summary?

_____

2. Which detail in the preceding summary is unnecessary?

_____

After Les Goodman's car starts on its own, the neighbors become suspicious of Goodman. A neighbor says that she has seen him standing on his porch in the middle of the night, looking at the sky. Goodman explains that he often has insomnia. He compares his neighbors to frightened rabbits. He says that they are letting a nightmare begin.

3. What is the main idea of the preceding summary?

_____

4. Which detail in the preceding summary is unimportant? How do you know it is unimportant?

_____

All Reading: Summarize, p. 96

Also available for these selections:

All Literary Analysis: Characters' Motives, p. 97

EL L3 L4 Grammar, p. 100

EL L3 L4 Support for Writing, p. 101

L3 L4 Support for Extend Your Learning, p. 102

L4 Enrichment, p. 99

Assessment

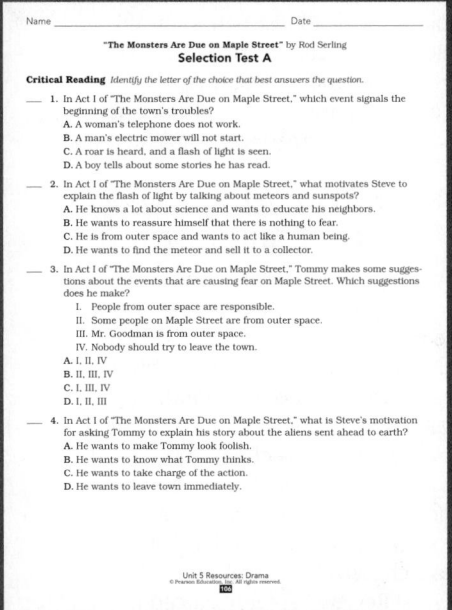

Name _____ Date _____

"The Monsters Are Due on Maple Street" by Rod Serling
Selection Test A

Critical Reading *Identify the letter of the choice that best answers the question.*

____ 1. In Act I of "The Monsters Are Due on Maple Street," which event signals the beginning of the town's troubles?
A. A woman's telephone does not work.
B. A man's electric mower will not start.
C. A roar is heard, and a flash of light is seen.
D. A boy tells about some stories he has read.

____ 2. In Act I of "The Monsters Are Due on Maple Street," what motivates Steve to explain the flash of light by talking about meteors and sunspots?
A. He knows a lot about science and wants to educate his neighbors.
B. He wants to reassure himself that there is nothing to fear.
C. He is from outer space and wants to act like a human being.
D. He wants to find the meteor and sell it to a collector.

____ 3. In Act I of "The Monsters Are Due on Maple Street," Tommy makes some suggestions about the events that are causing fear on Maple Street. Which suggestions does he make?
I. People from outer space are responsible.
II. Some people on Maple Street are from outer space.
III. Mr. Goodman is from outer space.
IV. Nobody should try to leave the town.
A. I, II, IV
B. II, III, IV
C. I, II, III, IV
D. I, II, III

____ 4. In Act I of "The Monsters Are Due on Maple Street," what is Steve's motivation for asking Tommy to explain his story about the aliens sent ahead to earth?
A. He wants to make Tommy look foolish.
B. He wants to know what Tommy thinks.
C. He wants to take charge of the action.
D. He wants to leave town immediately.

EL L1 L2 Selection Test A, pp. 106–108

Also available for these selections:

EL L3 L4 Selection Test B, pp. 109–111

L3 L4 Open-Book Test, pp. 103–105

PHLit Online!
www.PHLitOnline.com

Online Resources: All print materials are also available online.

- complete narrated selection text
- a thematically related video with writing prompt
- an interactive graphic organizer
- highlighting feature
- access to all student print resources, adapted to individual student needs
- Spanish and English summaries
- adapted selection translations in Spanish

Background Video

Also available:

Get Connected! (thematic video with writing prompt)
All videos are available in Spanish.

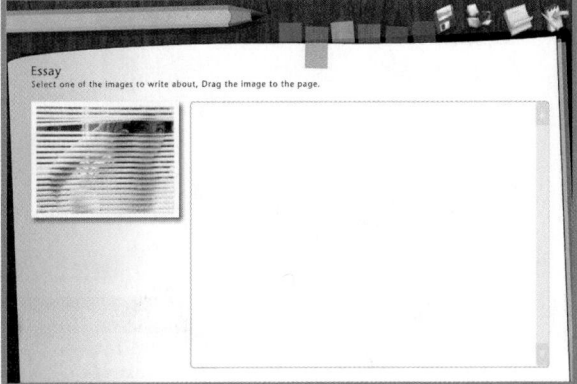

Writer's Journal (with graphics feature)

Also available:

Vocabulary Central (tools, activities, and songs for studying vocabulary)

❶ Drama Selection

You may use "The Monsters Are Due on Maple Street" to meet the lesson objectives. Skills instruction for this selection appears on page 831. Use the Reader and Task Suggestions on the facing page to help all students read text of increasing complexity.

❷ Ⓒ Introducing the CCS Standards

Introduce the standards on the student page. (Note that the lesson element with which each standard is addressed is identified in parentheses after the text of the standard.) Call out the standards that you will cover with the selections, explaining to students what each requires and how they will address it as they work through the selection you have chosen. Standards labeled "Spiral Review" are introduced in the Literary Analysis Workshop for this unit.

Before You Read

The Monsters Are Due on Maple Street

❶ Ⓒ Drama Selection

Build your skills and improve your comprehension of drama with texts of increasing complexity.

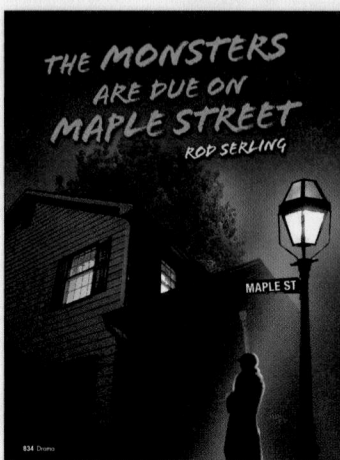

Read **The Monsters Are Due on Maple Street** to find out what happens when a group of frightened neighbors become suspicious of one another.

❷ Ⓒ Common Core State Standards

Meet these standards with **The Monsters are Due on Maple Street** (p. 834).

Reading Literature

2. Determine a theme or central idea of a text and analyze its development over the course of the text; provide an objective summary. *(Reading Skill: Summarize)*

3. Analyze how particular elements of a story or drama interact. *(Literary Analysis: Characters' Motives)*

7. Compare and contrast a written story, drama, or poem to its audio, filmed, staged, or multimedia version, analyzing the effects of techniques unique to each medium. *(Research and Technology: Film Version)*

Spiral Review: RL.7.5

Writing

2.b. Develop the topic with relevant facts, definitions, concrete details, quotations, or other information and examples. **2.c.** Use appropriate transitions to create cohesion and clarify the relationships among ideas and concepts. *(Writing: Summary)*

6. Use technology, including the Internet, to produce and publish writing. *(Writing: Summary)*

9.a. Apply *grade 7 Reading standards* to literature. *(Writing: Summary)*

Language

2. Demonstrate command of the conventions of standard English capitalization, punctuation, and spelling when writing. *(Conventions: Sentence Functions and Endmarks)*

4.b. Use common, grade-appropriate Greek or Latin affixes and roots as clues to the meaning of a word. *(Vocabulary: Word Study)*

830 Drama

Ⓒ Text Complexity Rubric

The Monsters Are Due on Maple Street		
Qualitative Measures	**Context/Knowledge Demands**	Small-town America, the 1950s 1 2 ③ 4 5
	Structure/Language Conventionality and Clarity	Conversational diction (dialogue), vernacular (everyday language); some subject-specific vocabulary (production terms) 1 2 3 ④ 5
	Levels of Meaning/ Purpose/Concepts	Accessible concept (conflicts among neighbors) 1 2 ③ 4 5
Quantitative Measures	**Text Length**	Word Count: 5,849
	Lexile	NP
Overall Complexity		✓ **Accessible**

❸ Reading Skill: Summarize

A **summary** is a brief statement that presents only the central ideas and most important details of a text. Summarizing helps you review and understand what you are reading.

To summarize, you must first **distinguish between important and unimportant** details. Ask yourself questions like the following:

- Is this detail necessary for my understanding of the literary work?
- Would the literary work hold together without this information?

As you read, pause periodically to recall and restate only the key events and important details.

❹ Literary Analysis: Characters' Motives

A **character's motives** are the reasons for his or her actions. Motives are usually related to what a character wants, needs, or feels. A character's motives may affect the way events unfold in a plot. For example, a character who wants to keep a secret may try to mislead other characters.

To identify characters' motives, examine the way they speak, think, and respond to situations and to other characters. Then, ask yourself why they behave as they do.

❺ Using the Strategy: Character Web

As you read, use a graphic organizer like the one shown to explore each character's motives.

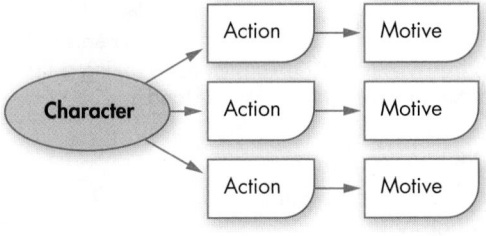

Before You Read: The Monsters Are Due on Maple Street **831**

PHLit
Online!
www.PHLitOnline.com

Hear It!
- Selection summary audio
- Selection audio

See It!
- Get Connected video
- Background video
- More about the author
- Vocabulary flashcards

Do It!
- Interactive journals
- Interactive graphic organizers
- Self-test
- Internet activity
- Grammar tutorial
- Interactive vocabulary games

❸ Reading Skill
Summarize

1. Introduce the skill, using the instruction on the student page.
2. Tell students that they will practice summarizing as they read.

❹ Literary Analysis
Characters' Motives

1. Introduce the skill, using the instruction on the student page.
2. Tell students that they will note characters' motives as they read.

Think Aloud: Model the Skill

Model a way to analyze characters' motives. Say to students:

> We look at people's motives in real life just as we discuss characters' motives in literature. Someone who is motivated by love might spend hours preparing a special meal for his wife's birthday. When I read a screenplay, I look at characters' actions the same way. I also study stage directions for hints about motivation. For example, a character who speaks "persistently" might be motivated by the need to persuade listeners. Understanding a character's motives helps me understand his or her words and actions.

❺ Using the Strategy

Give students a copy of either **Literary Analysis Graphic Organizer A or B** (*Graphic Organizer Transparencies*, pp. 160–161) to record clues about characters' motives as they read. Use the examples in **Literary Analysis Graphic Organizer A**, which is partially filled in, to model the process of completing the organizer.

© Text Complexity: Reader and Task Suggestions

The Monsters Are Due on Maple Street	
Preparing to Read the Text	**Leveled Tasks**
• Use the Background note on TE p. 833 to discuss the Cold War and Communism. • Ask students how playwrights make dialogue sound realistic. • Guide students to use Multidraft Reading strategies (TE p. 833).	*Structure/Language* If students will have difficulty understanding selection vocabulary, have them first read to identify technical terms in the stage directions. Then, have them reread, taking notes on what they think the terms mean. Discuss their notes, and provide clarification. *Analyzing* If students will not have difficulty with selection vocabulary, have them read to identify how the stage directions help create tone. Then, have them explain whether the tone shifts. As a class, discuss their responses.

❶ Writing About the Big Question

1. Review the assignment with the class.

2. Describe a situation in which a store window is cracked, but no one knows how. Ask students to name some possible explanations. Highlight or offer an ordinary and entirely unthreatening explanation, such as that a bird flew into the window.

3. Have students complete the sentence starter. Review responses as a class. (**Sample response:** Fear can influence our <u>perception</u> of others by causing us to imagine frightening motivations where none may exist.)

4. Remind students that their answers will help them think about the Big Question, "Do others see us more clearly than we see ourselves?"

While You Read

Tell students that as they read, they should consider how the neighbors' reactions toward one another change as their fears increase.

❷ Vocabulary

1. Have students preview the selection vocabulary.

2. For each word, have students say the word aloud.

3. Then, use the word in a sentence that defines the word.

4. Finally, repeat your definitional sentence or a similar sentence with the word missing and have the class "fill in the blank" chorally. Here are some examples:

    A <u>metamorphosis</u> is a change of form. When a caterpillar goes into a cocoon and comes out a butterfly, it has had a [students say "metamorphosis"].

    An action that is done <u>persistently</u> is done firmly and steadily. When you gradually make your way from one end of a crowded room to the other end, we can say that you moved [students say "persistently"].

❸ Word Study

1. Introduce the skill, using the instruction in the box.

2. Ask students which -sist- word could mean "to help stand." (assist)

832

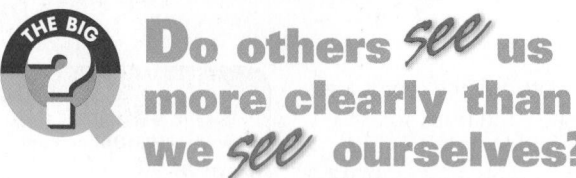

The Monsters Are Due on Maple Street

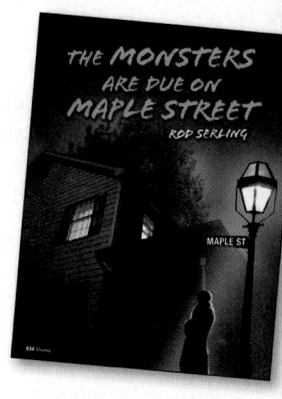

THE MONSTERS
ARE DUE ON
MAPLE STREET
ROD SERLING

MAPLE ST

❶ Do others *see* us more clearly than we *see* ourselves?

❶ Writing About the Big Question

In *The Monsters Are Due on Maple Street*, mysterious events cause neighbors to become frightened and fearful. Use this sentence starter to develop your ideas about the Big Question:

Fear can influence our **perception** of others by _____.

While You Read Consider whether the neighbors are able to see themselves clearly.

❷ Vocabulary

Read each word and its definition. Decide whether you know the word well, know it a little bit, or do not know it at all. After you read, see how your knowledge of each word has increased.

- **transfixed** (trans fikst´) *adj.* fascinated (p. 836) *He was transfixed by the TV show about penguins. transfix v.*

- **flustered** (flus´ tərd) *adj.* nervous; confused (p. 838) *The flustered bus driver took many wrong turns. fluster v.*

- **sluggishly** (slug´ ish lē) *adv.* as if lacking energy (p. 838) *The tired hikers walked sluggishly down the trail. sluggish adj. sluggishness n.*

- **persistently** (pər sist´ ənt lē) *adv.* firmly and steadily (p. 839) *The dog scratched persistently at the door. persistent adj. persist v. persistence n.*

- **defiant** (dē fī´ ənt) *adj.* boldly resisting (p. 840) *The defiant colonists demanded independence. defiantly adv. defy v. defying v.*

- **metamorphosis** (met´ ə môr´ fə sis) *n.* change of form (p. 843) *We witnessed the metamorphosis of a caterpillar into a butterfly. metamorphic adj. metamorphoses n. pl.*

❸ Word Study

The **Latin root -sist-** means "stand."

In this screenplay, a teen defends his opinion **persistently**, or by taking a firm stand.

832 Drama

Vocabulary Development

Vocabulary Knowledge Rating

Create a **Vocabulary Knowledge Rating Chart** (*Professional Development Guidebook*, p. 33) for this selection. Include the selection vocabulary and the Big Question word that appears in the Writing About the Big Question sentence starter on this page. (The Big Question vocabulary is introduced on pp. 720–721.)

Give students a copy of the chart. Read the words aloud, and have students mark their rating in the Before Reading column. Urge them to be alert to these words as they read and discuss the selection.

Tally how many students think they know a word to gauge how much instruction to provide. As students read and discuss the selection, point out the words and their context.

Vocabulary Central, featuring tools, activities, and songs for studying vocabulary, is available online at www.PHLitOnline.com.

Meet
Rod Serling
(1924–1975)

Author of

THE MONSTERS ARE DUE ON MAPLE STREET

Rod Serling once said that he did not have much imagination. This is an odd statement from a man who wrote more than 200 television scripts.

Quick Success Serling did not become serious about writing until he was in college. Driven by a love for radio drama, he earned second place in a national script contest. Soon after, he landed his first staff job as a radio writer. Serling branched out into writing for a new medium—television—and rocketed to fame.

DID YOU KNOW?

In the 1950s and 1960s, television censors banned scripts that appeared to question American society.

④ BACKGROUND FOR THE SCREENPLAY

The Cold War

This screenplay was written during the Cold War (1946–1989), a period when the United States and the communist Soviet Union were engaged in a nuclear arms race. Fear led to suspicion, and many people in the United States were accused of being communist spies. In much the same way, Serling's characters suspect and accuse one another in *The Monsters Are Due on Maple Street.*

MAPLE ST

The Monsters Are Due on Maple Street **833**

For each class during which you teach the selection, have students complete one of the five Revision or Research activities for Weeks 28–29 in the *Daily Bellringer Activities* booklet.

④ Background

The Cold War The Cold War began when Soviet dictator Joseph Stalin refused to accept the Marshall Plan, which aimed to stabilize Europe's economy after World War II. His refusal spawned great anti-Communist sentiment in the United States. The House Un-American Activities Committee (HUAC) held many hearings in which prominent Hollywood actors and directors were interrogated about their involvement with the Communist Party. Many were blacklisted from the movie and television industry because of their alleged involvement with the Communists. In much the same way, Serling's characters "blacklist" one another in *The Monsters Are Due on Maple Street.*

▌ Multidraft Reading

To assist struggling readers and to deepen reading for all, assign the text in "chunks," and apply multidraft reading protocols. For each reading, have students set the purpose indicated:

- **First reading**—identifying key ideas and details and answering any Reading Checks.
- **Second reading**—analyzing craft and structure and responding to the side-column prompts.
- **Third reading**—integrating knowledge and ideas, connecting to other texts and the world, and answering the end-of-selection questions.

For more guidance, refer to the *Classroom Strategies and Teaching Routines* card on multidraft reading.

For more about the author, practice with the selection vocabulary, and more background, go online at **www.PHLitOnline.com.**

❶ Activating Prior Knowledge

Tell students that you have just heard a rumor about a plan to extend the school day. As students respond, do not try to calm their fears. Instead, allow them to protest for a minute or two. Then, tell them that you made up the rumor. Explain that their emotional response to your statement is similar to that of characters in the selection, who react to rumors when their everyday lives are interrupted by a bright flash of light.

Concept Connector ➡

Students will reconsider their ideas after reading *The Monsters Are Due on Maple Street.*

Small-Group Activity

To help students visualize the actions of the play, have them act out one or more scenes for the class. Have them work together to cast the characters, block out their movements, and practice the readings.

❷ About the Selection

This screenplay explores the effects of prejudice and suspicion. After a bright unknown object flashes across the sky, the astonished neighbors on Maple Street discover that the electricity in their homes is gone, their cars will not start, and they cannot make telephone calls. As the neighbors gather, Tommy, a fourteen-year-old boy, describes stories he has read about such flying objects and strange occurrences. He tells his neighbors that in these stories, a family is always "sent ahead"—a family that appears to be human. As neighbors begin to accuse one another of being aliens, the small crowd transforms itself into a mob. Suddenly, they hear footsteps approaching in the darkness. With a single shot, Charlie causes more hysteria and violence by killing his neighbor Pete Van Horn, who had gone to the next street for help.

Meanwhile, the camera cuts to a shot of a metal spacecraft. In it, two figures discuss how their job is made easy. After all, the neighbors of Maple Street are their own worst, and most dangerous, enemies.

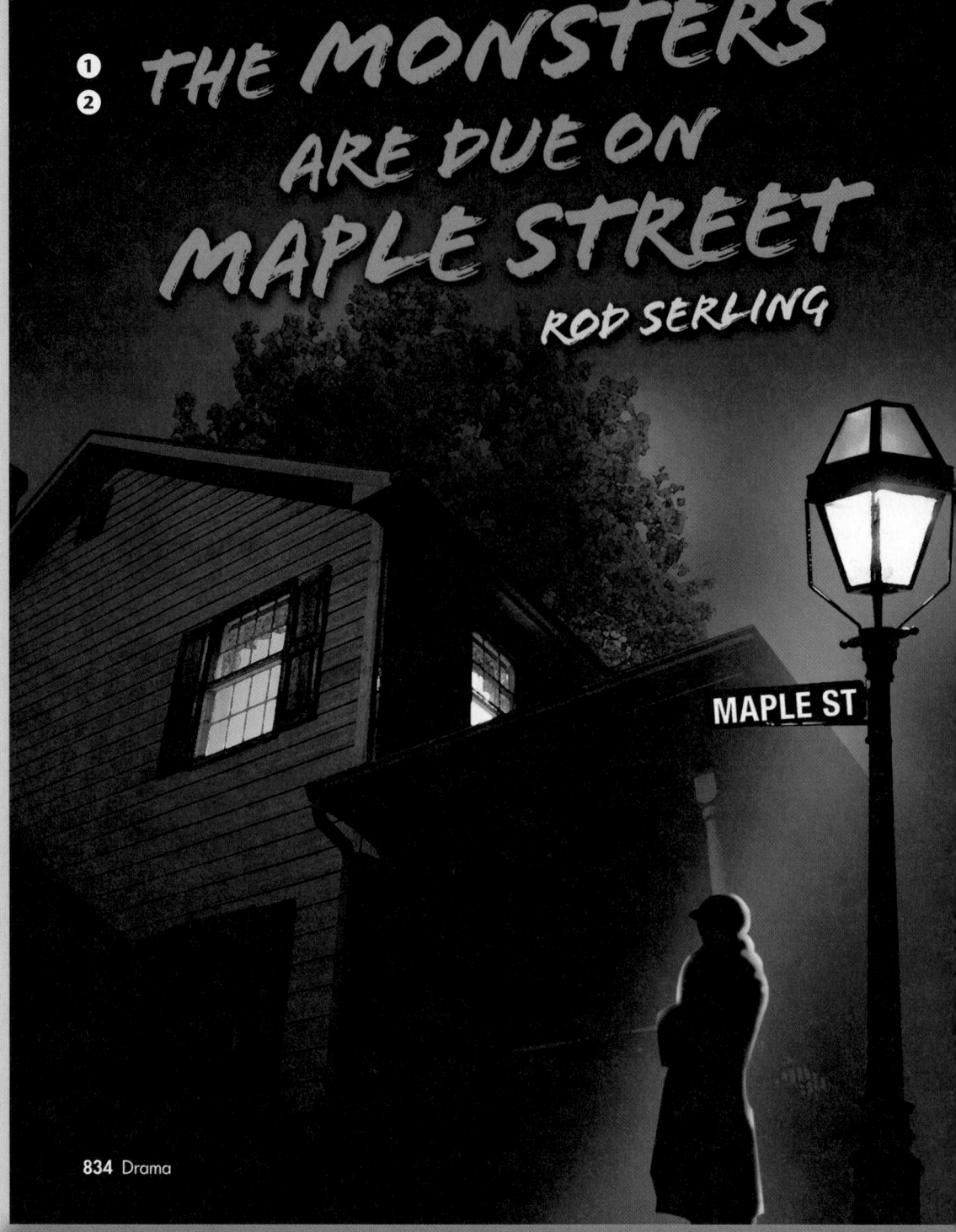

❶
❷ # THE MONSTERS ARE DUE ON MAPLE STREET

ROD SERLING

MAPLE ST

834 Drama

PROFESSIONAL DEVELOPMENT **Doug Buehl**

APPLY THE STRATEGY

Focus Reading Introduce the play by noting that authors often use the way characters interact with each other to communicate ideas. Ask students to focus on "How do characters feel about each other and interact with each other?" as they read the first two pages of the play. Then, ask students to share with a partner places in the play that show character interactions (children laughing and buying ice cream, women gossiping, and so forth.) Next, have students continue to read Act 1, and focus on "How do feelings and interactions change in the play?" and "How does the author introduce conflict in the play?" Have them use sticky notes to identify places where changes begin to occur and when conflicts begin to surface.

For more of Doug Buehl's strategies, see the Professional Development essay, pp. 720c–720d

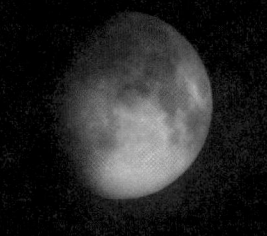

CHARACTERS

NARRATOR   FIGURE ONE   FIGURE TWO

RESIDENTS OF MAPLE STREET

STEVE BRAND   WOMAN   MAN TWO
CHARLIE'S WIFE   DON MARTIN   PETE VAN HORN
MRS. GOODMAN   SALLY (TOMMY'S MOTHER)   CHARLIE
MRS. BRAND   LES GOODMAN   TOMMY   MAN ONE

ACT 1

[*Fade in on a shot of the night sky. The various nebulae and planet bodies stand out in sharp, sparkling relief, and the camera begins a slow pan across the Heavens.*]

NARRATOR'S VOICE. There is a fifth dimension beyond that which is known to man. It is a dimension as vast as space, and as timeless as infinity. It is the middle ground between light and shadow—between science and superstition. And it lies between the pit of man's fears and the summit of his knowledge. This is the dimension of imagination. It is an area which we call The Twilight Zone.

[*The camera has begun to pan down until it passes the horizon and is on a sign which reads "Maple Street." Pan down until we are shooting down at an angle toward the street below. It's a tree-lined, quiet residential American street, very typical of the small town. The houses have front porches on which people sit and swing on gliders, conversing across from house to house.* STEVE BRAND *polishes his car parked in front of his house. His neighbor,* DON MARTIN, *leans against the fender watching him. A Good Humor man rides a bicycle and is just in the process of stopping to sell some ice cream to a couple of kids. Two women gossip on the front lawn. Another man waters his lawn.*]

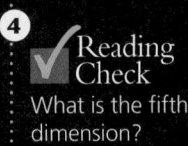

④ ✓ Reading Check

What is the fifth dimension?

The Monsters Are Due on Maple Street **835**

---

③ **Critical Thinking**
Analyze

1. Explain that the narrator's speech is the one that Rod Serling used to introduce each episode of *The Twilight Zone,* although the words varied somewhat from one season to the next. Then, read the speech aloud, using a serene but dramatic voice. **Ask** students what feelings the narrator's words stir up in them.
   Possible response: The narrator's words arouse feelings of suspense, tension, and expectation.

2. Next, have a volunteer read the first stage direction. **Ask** students to identify the kinds of directions these notes contain.
   Answer: They contain camera directions, set directions, and character placement.

3. **Ask** students how these details aid the reader.
   Answer: The directions allow readers to picture in their minds the setting of the story—what they would see on the screen if they were watching instead of reading.

4. **Ask** students how the "realm" described in the story's setting contrasts with the one described in the narrator's commentary.
   Answer: The setting of the story is very familiar and known, whereas the realm described by the narrator is totally unknown.

5. Write the words *known* and *unknown* on the board. **Ask** students how they think the known and the unknown will interact in this story.
   Possible responses: They will clash. The unknown will "invade" the known. The known will become the unknown, and vice versa.

④ **Reading Check**
Answer: The fifth dimension is a realm of the imagination.

1. Remind students that summarizing includes identifying the main ideas and most important details of a text.

2. Have students read aloud the bracketed text, including the stage directions and the parts of the narrator, Steve, Don, and Mrs. Brand. Then, **ask** students to summarize what has just happened.
   Answer: A bright object has just whizzed across the sky, and the neighbors wonder what it was.

3. Point out that in their summary of this event, students included only the most important detail. They did not, for example, say that Steve had been polishing his car.

4. **Ask** the Summarize question.
   Answer: It is an important detail, because it is a very unusual event and because it affects the behavior of the Maple Street residents.

Summarize
Do you think the flash of light is an important or unimportant detail? Explain.

❺

Vocabulary
transfixed (trans fikst) *adj.* fascinated

NARRATOR'S VOICE. Maple Street, U.S.A., late summer. A tree-lined little world of front porch gliders, hop scotch, the laughter of children, and the bell of an ice cream vendor.

[*There is a pause and the camera moves over to a shot of the Good Humor man and two small boys who are standing alongside, just buying ice cream.*]

NARRATOR'S VOICE. At the sound of the roar and the flash of light it will be precisely 6:43 P.M. on Maple Street.

[*At this moment one of the little boys,* TOMMY, *looks up to listen to a sound of a tremendous screeching roar from overhead. A flash of light plays on both their faces and then it moves down the street past lawns and porches and rooftops and then disappears.*

Various people leave their porches and stop what they're doing to stare up at the sky. STEVE BRAND, *the man who's been polishing his car, now stands there* transfixed, *staring upwards. He looks at* DON MARTIN, *his neighbor from across the street.*]

❺ **STEVE.** What was that? A meteor?

DON. [*Nods*] That's what it looked like. I didn't hear any crash though, did you?

STEVE. [*Shakes his head*] Nope. I didn't hear anything except a roar.

MRS. BRAND. [*From her porch*] Steve? What was that?

STEVE. [*Raising his voice and looking toward porch*] Guess it was a meteor, honey. Came awful close, didn't it?

MRS. BRAND. Too close for my money! Much too close.

[*The camera pans across the various porches to people who stand there watching and talking in low tones.*]

NARRATOR'S VOICE. Maple Street. Six-forty-four P.M. on a late September evening. [*A pause*] Maple Street in the last calm and reflective moment . . . before the monsters came!

[*The camera slowly pans across the porches again. We see a man screwing a light bulb on a front porch, then getting down off the stool to flick the switch and finding that nothing happens.*

Another man is working on an electric power mower. He plugs in the plug, flicks on the switch of the power mower, off and on, with nothing happening.

❻

836 Drama

Vocabulary Development

ⓒ **CCSS** Language 6

Words From Visual Media
Introduce students to some of the camera terminology used in the play. Present the following words and definitions to students.
- *pan:* to rotate or move a camera to follow an action
- *close-up:* a camera shot taken at very close range
- *medium shot:* a camera shot from a medium distance, or showing subjects from the waist up

- *long shot:* a camera shot that shows the subject from top to bottom, or head to toe
- *angle shot:* a shot in which an angle lens is used to give a feeling of exaggeration
- *full shot:* the same as a long shot
- *dissolve:* occurs when an image blurs and melts away

Through the window of a front porch, we see a woman pushing her finger back and forth on the dial hook. Her voice is indistinct and distant, but intelligible and repetitive.]

WOMAN. Operator, operator, something's wrong on the phone, operator!

[MRS. BRAND *comes out on the porch and calls to* STEVE.]

MRS. BRAND. [*Calling*] Steve, the power's off. I had the soup on the stove and the stove just stopped working.

WOMAN. Same thing over here. I can't get anybody on the phone either. The phone seems to be dead.

[*We look down on the street as we hear the voices creep up from below, small, mildly disturbed voices highlighting these kinds of phrases:*]

VOICES.

Electricity's off.

Phone won't work.

Can't get a thing on the radio.

My power mower won't move, won't work at all.

Radio's gone dead!

[PETE VAN HORN, *a tall, thin man, is seen standing in front of his house.*]

VAN HORN. I'll cut through the back yard . . . See if the power's still on on Floral Street. I'll be right back!

[*He walks past the side of his house and disappears into the back yard.*

The camera pans down slowly until we're looking at ten or eleven people standing around the street and overflowing to the curb and sidewalk. In the background is STEVE BRAND'S *car.*]

STEVE. Doesn't make sense. Why should the power go off all of a sudden, and the phone line?

DON. Maybe some sort of an electrical storm or something.

CHARLIE. That don't seem likely. Sky's just as blue as anything. Not a cloud. No lightning. No thunder. No nothing. How could it be a storm?

Characters' Motives
Why do the characters come out of their homes?

Reading Check
What strange event occurs just before Maple Street loses electricity?

---

❽ Humanities

Woman On Telephone As Seen Through Window, by William Low, oil on paper

William Low was born and raised in New York City, where he continues to make art. After a childhood spent watching the city from his father's Chinese laundry, Low went on to study art first at the city's High School of Art and Design and later at the Parsons School of Design. Many of Low's paintings and illustrations, like *Woman on telephone as seen through window,* reflect the artist's interest in architecture and light.

1. **Ask:** How does the light in the painting reflect the eerie mood developing on Maple Street?
   Answer: The light is unnaturally bright for what is clearly night-time.

2. **Ask:** How does the image of the woman on the phone relate to the problem facing the residents of Maple Street?
   Answer: In the story, the phones are dead. The woman in the painting might be trying to tell someone about a problem she has, but in the story she would be unable to make this call.

❾ Critical Viewing

Answer: With its warm, cozy house and starry night sky, this image gives the viewer the impression that life on Maple Street is calm, quiet, and serene.

❿ Critical Thinking

Interpret

1. As students read the first bracketed passage on this page, have them pay special attention to the way the crowd responds to each new development. Draw students' attention to descriptive phrases in the stage directions, such as "murmur softly in wonderment and question."

2. **Ask** what these phrases suggest about how the people seem to feel when the woman reports her malfunctioning radio.
   Answer: They seem to feel confused and curious.

3. **Ask** how this mood changes, and what causes it to change.
   Answer: When Steve can't get his car started, the mood changes to one of intense interest, and perhaps the beginnings of fear.

❽

Woman on telephone as seen through window, William Low, Courtesy of the artist

❾ ▲ **Critical Viewing**
What impression does this illustration convey about life on Maple Street? **[Analyze]**

Vocabulary
flustered (flus′ tərd)
adj. nervous; confused

sluggishly (slug′ ish lē)
adv. as if lacking energy

WOMAN. I can't get a thing on the radio. Not even the portable.

[*The people again murmur softly in wonderment and question.*]

CHARLIE. Well, why don't you go downtown and check with the police, though they'll probably think we're crazy or something. A little power failure and right away we get all flustered and everything.

STEVE. It isn't just the power failure, Charlie. If it was, we'd still be able to get a broadcast on the portable.

[*There's a murmur of reaction to this.* STEVE *looks from face to face and then over to his car.*]

STEVE. I'll run downtown. We'll get this all straightened out.

[*He walks over to the car, gets in it, turns the key. Looking through the open car door, we see the crowd watching him from the other side.*

STEVE *starts the engine. It turns over* sluggishly *and then just stops dead. He tries it again and this time he can't get it to turn over. Then, very slowly and reflectively, he turns the key back to "off" and slowly gets out of the car.*

The people stare at STEVE. *He stands for a moment by the car, then walks toward the group.*]

STEVE. I don't understand it. It was working fine before . . .

DON. Out of gas?

STEVE. [*Shakes his head*] I just had it filled up.

WOMAN. What's it mean?

CHARLIE. It's just as if . . . as if everything had stopped. [*Then he turns toward* STEVE.] We'd better walk downtown.

[*Another murmur of assent at this.*]

STEVE. The two of us can go, Charlie. [*He turns to look back at the car.*] It couldn't be the meteor. A meteor couldn't do this.

⓫ [*He and* CHARLIE *exchange a look, then they start to walk away from the group.*]

838 Drama

Thematic Vocabulary: The Big Question
As students are discussing *The Monsters Are Due on Maple Street,* encourage them to use the thematic vocabulary presented in Introducing the Big Question, pp. 720–721. You might encourage them with sentence starters like these:

1. The neighbors become frightened by the *appearance* of . . .
2. Because of their fear, they begin to *ignore* . . .
3. Instead, they *define* people by . . .
4. All of a sudden, everyone's *reactions* are . . .
5. The neighbors are driven by a *perception* that . . .

We see TOMMY, *a serious-faced fourteen-year-old in spectacles who stands a few feet away from the group. He is halfway between them and the two men, who start to walk down the sidewalk.*]

TOMMY. Mr. Brand . . . you better not!

STEVE. Why not?

TOMMY. They don't want you to.

[STEVE *and* CHARLIE *exchange a grin, and* STEVE *looks back toward the boy.*]

STEVE. Who doesn't want us to?

TOMMY. [*Jerks his head in the general direction of the distant horizon*] Them!

STEVE. Them?

CHARLIE. Who are them?

TOMMY. [*Very intently*] Whoever was in that thing that came by overhead.

[STEVE *knits his brows for a moment, cocking his head questioningly. His voice is intense.*]

STEVE. What?

TOMMY. Whoever was in that thing that came over. I don't think they want us to leave here.

[STEVE *leaves* CHARLIE *and walks over to the boy. He kneels down in front of him. He forces his voice to remain gentle. He reaches out and holds the boy.*]

STEVE. What do you mean? What are you talking about?

TOMMY. They don't want us to leave. That's why they shut everything off.

STEVE. What makes you say that? Whatever gave you that idea?

WOMAN. [*From the crowd*] Now isn't that the craziest thing you ever heard?

TOMMY. [*Persistently but a little intimidated by the crowd*] It's always that way, in every story I ever read about a ship landing from outer space.

Characters' Motives
Why does Tommy warn Charlie and Steve not to leave?

Vocabulary
persistently (pər sist′ ənt lē) *adv.* firmly and steadily

 **Reading Check**

What happens when Steve tries to start his car?

The Monsters Are Due on Maple Street **839**

⓫ Characters' Motives

1. **Ask** students whether they have ever interrupted a focused conversation among a group of adults, or tried to stop a course of action that had been determined by a group of adults. Have students think about their motives for doing so. Were their motives strong or weak?
   Possible response: Most students will say they had strong motives.

2. Next, have volunteers read the first bracketed passage which begins on p. 838. **Ask** the Characters' Motives question.
   Answer: Tommy is afraid that if Charlie and Steve leave, "they" will become angry.

3. **Ask** students whether they believe Tommy's fear is a strong motivator or a weak one, and how they know.
   Answer: Tommy's fear is a strong motivator, because it takes courage to interrupt a group of determined adults.

4. Distribute copies of **Literary Analysis Graphic Organizer B** (*Graphic Organizer Transparencies,* p. 161), or have students create their own version. Then, ask them to write Tommy's name in the top oval and to list his first action and its motive in the appropriate places. Have students complete the graphic organizer as they read.

⓬ Reading Check

Answer: The car starts to turn over, but then stops dead.

839

⑬ Characters' Motives

1. After students read the first bracketed passage, which begins on p. 839, have them think about how the characters might be feeling. Point out that the people are probably nervous and unsure of what is happening. **Ask** students what Tommy believes, and why. **Answer:** He believes that "they" don't want anyone to leave, because that is how it always is in the stories he reads.

2. Discuss with students how the context in which Tommy's comments are made gives them greater weight than if he had made them under more normal circumstances. **Ask** students why Tommy is increasingly intimidated as he continues to argue his point. **Possible responses:** He feels intimidated because the adults' responses are so intense. Some of them, such as Steve, seem to be taking him seriously, while others are growing annoyed with him.

3. **Ask** how Tommy's mother attempts to intervene. **Answer:** She tells him to stop talking.

4. **Ask** the Characters' Motives question. **Possible responses:** She is afraid that the crowd will grow too aggressive in their jeering and mocking; she is embarrassed by Tommy's naive ideas.

▶ **Monitor Progress:** Check to make sure students understand why the characters say what they say, such as the woman suggesting Tommy be sent to bed.

▶ **Reteach:** If students have difficulty identifying the characters' motives, have them reread the bracketed text and then act it out. Help students to understand that the crowd is getting nervous. Point out that the woman thinks Tommy has foolish ideas or that she might be afraid that they are true.

840

Characters' Motives
Why does Tommy's mother want him to stop talking?

Vocabulary
defiant (dē fī´ ənt)
adj. boldly resisting

---

⑬

WOMAN. [*To the boy's mother,* SALLY, *who stands on the fringe of the crowd*] From outer space, yet! Sally, you better get that boy of yours up to bed. He's been reading too many comic books or seeing too many movies or something.

SALLY. Tommy, come over here and stop that kind of talk.

STEVE. Go ahead, Tommy. We'll be right back. And you'll see. That wasn't any ship or anything like it. That was just a . . . a meteor or something. Likely as not—[*He turns to the group, now trying to weight his words with an optimism he obviously doesn't feel but is desperately trying to instill in himself as well as the others.*] No doubt it did have something to do with all this power failure and the rest of it. Meteors can do some crazy things. Like sunspots.

DON. [*Picking up the cue*] Sure. That's the kind of thing—like sunspots. They raise Cain[1] with radio reception all over the world. And this thing being so close—why, there's no telling the sort of stuff it can do. [*He wets his lips, smiles nervously.*] Go ahead, Charlie. You and Steve go into town and see if that isn't what's causing it all.

[STEVE *and* CHARLIE *again walk away from the group down the sidewalk. The people watch silently.*

TOMMY *stares at them, biting his lips, and finally calling out again.*]

TOMMY. *Mr. Brand!*

[*The two men stop again.* TOMMY *takes a step toward them.*]

TOMMY. Mr. Brand . . . please don't leave here.

[STEVE *and* CHARLIE *stop once again and turn toward the boy. There's a murmur in the crowd, a murmur of irritation and concern as if the boy were bringing up fears that shouldn't be brought up; words which carried with them a strange kind of validity that came without logic but nonetheless registered and had meaning and effect. Again we hear a murmur of reaction from the crowd.*

TOMMY *is partly frightened and partly* defiant *as well.*]

TOMMY. You might not even be able to get to town. It was that way in the story. Nobody could leave. Nobody except—

---

1. raise Cain badly disturb.

840 Drama

Vocabulary Development © CCSS Language 6

Word Forms

Expand students' vocabulary by helping them learn related forms of the selection vocabulary words. The two selection vocabulary words on pp. 839 and 840, for example, have related word forms. Give students a blank **Word Form Chart** (*Professional Development Guidebook,* p. 42), with *persistently* and *defiant* in the correct columns. Work with the class, or have students work in pairs, to determine the related forms. The final chart should look like the one shown.

Hold students accountable for integrating the related forms of the words into their speaking and writing.

Noun	Verb	Adjective	Adverb
persistence	persist	persistent	**persistently**
defiance	defy	**defiant**	defiantly

STEVE. Except who?

TOMMY. Except the people they'd sent down ahead of them. They looked just like humans. And it wasn't until the ship landed that—

[*The boy suddenly stops again, conscious of the parents staring at them and of the sudden hush of the crowd.*]

SALLY. [*In a whisper, sensing the antagonism of the crowd*] Tommy, please son . . . honey, don't talk that way—

MAN ONE. That kid shouldn't talk that way . . . and we shouldn't stand here listening to him. Why this is the craziest thing I ever heard of. The kid tells us a comic book plot and here we stand listening—

[STEVE *walks toward the camera, stops by the boy.*]

STEVE. Go ahead, Tommy. What kind of story was this? What about the people that they sent out ahead?

TOMMY. That was the way they prepared things for the landing. They sent four people. A mother and a father and two kids who looked just like humans . . . but they weren't.

[*There's another silence as* STEVE *looks toward the crowd and then toward* TOMMY. *He wears a tight grin.*]

STEVE. Well, I guess what we'd better do then is to run a check on the neighborhood and see which ones of us are really human.

[*There's laughter at this, but it's a laughter that comes from a desperate attempt to lighten the atmosphere. It's a release kind of laugh. The people look at one another in the middle of their laughter.*]

CHARLIE. There must be somethin' better to do than stand around makin' bum jokes about it.

[*Rubs his jaw nervously*] I wonder if Floral Street's got the same deal we got. [*He looks past the houses.*] Where is Pete Van Horn anyway? Didn't he get back yet?

[*Suddenly there's the sound of a car's engine starting to turn over. We look across the street toward the driveway of* LES GOODMAN'S *house. He's at the wheel trying to start the car.*]

Summarize
Do you think Steve's comment will prove to be important as the story develops? Why or why not?

 **Reading Check**
What does Tommy say about the people who were sent from outer space?

---

⑭ Summarize

1. Remind students that they should keep the main idea in mind as they consider which details are important. Important details are those that help support the main idea of a text.

2. Read the bracketed passage. **Ask** students to paraphrase Steve's comment.
   Possible response: We should look each other over to make sure we're all human.

3. **Ask** the Summarize question on this page.
   Possible response: Yes, Steve's comment will prove important. The crowd's silence and laughter before and after the comment suggest that Steve has voiced an actual fear, one that will probably influence the behavior of the already-nervous crowd.

⑮ Reading Check

Answer: Tommy says that they look like humans, but aren't really; and that they were sent ahead to prepare things for the spaceship landing.

Differentiated Instruction *for Universal Access*

Strategy for Less Proficient Readers

After students have read the opening pages and made predictions about the story, have them set a purpose for reading based on what they know and expect to find out. Remind students to take the title into consideration when they set purposes. Suggest that students jot down any questions they have that might be answered by the text. Tell them to keep these questions in mind as they read. Have them stop periodically to answer the questions and to record any other questions the text elicits.

Strategy for Gifted/Talented Students

Tell students to analyze the initial events of this selection. Then, have each use his or her imagination to put together an ongoing newscast about the flash of light and the events that follow. Tell them to include the time and place as well as information about specific characters to provide updates on the crisis and to speculate on the resolution. Have students practice their newscasts, and then allow time to present their newscasts to the rest of the class.

⓰ Humanities

Overview Of Family Walking Dog On The Street,
by William Low, oil on paper

In traveling around his native city of New York, William Low often takes photographs of buildings. He uses these, along with his vivid imagination, to create vibrant urban scenes. Low incorporates his strong mathematical skills to create compositions, such as *Overview of family walking dog on the street,* in which the image is viewed from an unusual perspective but still makes sense.

1. **Ask:** How does the view from above reflect the drama?
   Answer: The drama suggests that creatures from outer space are watching Maple Street.

2. **Ask:** If the family walking the dog lived on Maple Street, how might they feel at this point in the drama? Would they be walking their dog? Explain.
   Answer: If the family lived on Maple Street, they'd probably feel afraid and so stay inside.

⓱ Critical Viewing

Answer: Students might say that although the bright colors of the houses contrast with the eerie threatening mood of this scene, they do match the mood at the beginning of the screenplay.

⓲ Summarize

1. Read the stage direction at the beginning of the bracketed passage (p. 841). **Ask** students how the directions let us know that one important event is ending, and another is beginning.
   Answer: The stage direction says *We look across the street.* This shift in attention and location suggests that the story is moving on to another event.

2. Have volunteers read the remaining bracketed text. Then, **ask** the Summarize question.
   Possible response: The car's mysterious behavior seems to cast suspicion on the car's owner, Les Goodman.

3. Have students **identify** one detail in this passage that is *not* crucial to the unfolding of the story.
   Possible response: The detail of smoke coming out of the car's exhaust is not crucial to the story.

842

Overview of family walking dog on the street, William Low, Courtesy of the artist

⓱ ▲ **Critical Viewing**
How do the colors in this illustration contrast with the mood of the drama? Explain. **[Compare and Contrast]**

⓲

Summarize
Why might this detail about a car starting be important?

SALLY. Can you get it started, Les? [*He gets out of the car, shaking his head.*]

GOODMAN. No dice.

[*He walks toward the group. He stops suddenly as behind him, inexplicably and with a noise that inserts itself into the silence, the car engine starts up all by itself.* GOODMAN *whirls around to stare toward it.*

The car idles roughly, smoke coming from the exhaust, the frame shaking gently.

GOODMAN'S *eyes go wide, and he runs over to his car. The people stare toward the car.*]

MAN ONE. He got the car started somehow. He got his car started!

[*The camera pans along the faces of the people as they stare, somehow caught up by this revelation and somehow, illogically, wildly, frightened.*]

WOMAN. How come his car just up and started like that?

842 Drama

Vocabulary Development

© **CCSS** Language 6

Word Analysis

1. Post the following words: *inexplicably* (p. 842), *inserts* (p. 842), *incisive* (p. 843), *intruded* (p. 843). Circle the prefix *in-.*
2. Explain that this prefix can mean "in, into, toward," or "no, not, without."
3. Have students write a definition for each word. Ask students to underline the part of each definition that shows how the prefix *in-* is used in that word.
   Possible responses: *inexplicably:* in a way that can<u>not</u> be explained or accounted for;

inserts: puts or fits <u>into</u> something else; *incisive:* cutting <u>into</u>; *intruded:* pushed or forced <u>into</u>

4. Explain that when a word begins with *l,* the prefix *in-* becomes *il-.* Ask students which of the two meanings of *in-* applies in the case of *illogically,* and why.
   Answer: The meaning "not, no, without" applies, because *illogically* means "in a manner lacking or without logic."

hours of the morning sta
looking up at the sky. [*Sh*
That's right, looking up a
waiting for something. [*A*
something.

[*There's a murmur of reaction*

We cut suddenly to a group
toward them, they back awa

GOODMAN. You know really .
what I'm guilty of? [*He la*
what's the penalty for ins
the humor, leaves his voic
said it was insomnia. [*A*
shouts.*] I said it was inso
frightened rabbits, you. *Y*
that? You're sick people—
know what you're startin
me tell you—this thing yo
you. As God is my witnes
begin here that's a night

ACT 2

[*We see a medium shot of th*
On the side table rests an u
into the scene, a glass of mil
on the table, lights the cand
table, picks up the glass of r

MRS. GOODMAN *comes th*
in hand. The entry hall, wit
behind her.

Outside, the camera slow
in little knots of people who
At the end of each conversa
MAN'S *house. From the vari*
but no electricity, and there
kets the whole area, disturt
voices of the people as they
over to one group where CH
GOODMAN'S *house.*

SALLY. All by itself. He wasn't anywheres near it. It started all by itself.

[DON *approaches the group, stops a few feet away to look toward* GOODMAN'S *car and then back toward the group.*]

DON. And he never did come out to look at that thing that flew overhead. He wasn't even interested. [*He turns to the faces in the group, his face taut and serious.*] Why? Why didn't he come out with the rest of us to look?

CHARLIE. He always was an oddball. Him and his whole family. Real oddball.

DON. What do you say we ask him?

[*The group suddenly starts toward the house. In this brief fraction of a moment they take the first step toward performing a* metamorphosis *that changes people from a group into a mob. They begin to head purposefully across the street toward the house at the end.* STEVE *stands in front of them. For a moment their fear almost turns their walk into a wild stampede, but* STEVE'S *voice, loud, incisive, and commanding, makes them stop.*]

STEVE. Wait a minute . . . wait a minute! Let's not be a mob!

[*The people stop as a group, seem to pause for a moment, and then much more quietly and slowly start to walk across the street.* GOODMAN *stands alone facing the people.*]

GOODMAN. I just don't understand it. I tried to start it and it wouldn't start. You saw me. All of you saw me.

[*And now, just as suddenly as the engine started, it stops and there's a long silence that is gradually intruded upon by the frightened murmuring of the people.*]

GOODMAN. I don't understand. I swear . . . I don't understand. What's happening?

DON. Maybe you better tell us. Nothing's working on this street. Nothing. No lights, no power, no radio. [*And then meaningfully*] Nothing except one car—yours!

[*The people pick this up and now their murmuring becomes a loud chant filling the air with accusations and demands for action. Two of the men pass* DON *and head toward* GOODMAN, *who backs away, backing into his car and now at bay.*]

Vocabulary
metamorphosis
(met´ ə mour´ fə sis) *n.*
change of form

Spiral Review
Elements of Drama
What do these stage directions suggest about Steve's personality?

Reading Check
What happens to Goodman's car?

The Monsters Are Due on Maple Street **843**

843

㉑ Summarize

1. Explain that students can det__ mine which details are impor__ by asking themselves if the d__ is necessary to understand th__ main idea.

2. Remind students that in the l__ scene, Tommy was the target__ the crowd's growing aggress__ and that in this scene, Les Goodman is. Have students r__ the bracketed text. Then, as__ Summarize question on this p__ **Possible response:** First, hi__ won't start. Then, after he ge__ out of it, it mysteriously does__ start. The crowd begins to qu__ tion why nothing works exce__ Les's car. They advance towa__ Les, who retreats to his porc__

3. **Ask** students why the events surrounding Les and his car a__ important to the story. **Possible response:** They increase the fear and hysteri__ the crowd and trigger its tra__ mation into a mob.

㉙ Critical Viewing

Possible response: Students might point out that when a person cannot see in the dark, other senses become heightened. For example, a common noise might seem strange, and the feel of a gentle breeze might be more noticeable. These heightened sensations add to people's natural feeling of vulnerability in the darkness.

㉚ Connecting to the Big Question

1. Remind students of their reaction when you described a cracked store window. Point out that fear often causes us to overreact. Discuss why students think this is so.

2. Have students read the bracketed text on pages 848–849, beginning with "Go ahead, what's my wife said?" **Ask** students: How do the neighbors view Steve at this point in the play? How does their fear affect their attitude toward their neighbor? **Possible response:** They view Steve as highly suspicious. Their fear has led them to doubt even his most ordinary actions.

3. **Ask:** Do you think the neighbors see Steve clearly? Explain. **Possible response:** No. Their fear has entirely distorted their view of Steve, such that they think he is an alien from outer space because he spends hours working on a radio that no one has seen.

㉙ ▲ Critical Viewing Why does night's darkness, shown in this illustration, make the people of Maple Street more fearful? **[Hypothesize]**

[*We see a long shot of* STEVE *as he walks toward them from across the street.*]

STEVE. Go ahead, what's my wife said? Let's get it all out. Let's pick out every idiosyncrasy of every single man, woman, and child on the street. And then we might as well set up some kind of kangaroo court.[3] How about a firing squad at dawn, Charlie, so we can get rid of all the suspects? Narrow them down. Make it easier for you.

㉚

DON. There's no need gettin' so upset, Steve. It's just that . . . well . . . Myra's talked about how there's been plenty of nights you spent hours down in your basement workin' on some kind of radio or something. Well, none of us have ever seen that radio—

[*By this time* STEVE *has reached the group. He stands there defiantly close to them.*]

㉛

CHARLIE. Go ahead, Steve. What kind of "radio set" you workin' on? I never seen it. Neither has anyone else. Who you talk to on that radio set? And who talks to you?

---

3. **kangaroo court** unofficial court that does not follow normal rules.

Think Aloud

Summarize

Direct students' attention to the events of Act 2 beginning on page 845 and continuing through the line "Now the crowd gathers around them" on page 851. Then, use the following "think aloud" to model summarizing those events:

I know that to summarize this passage, I need to identify the key events in this part of the story. When I think back on Act 2 so far, I think the key events are the following: Charlie and the other neighbors grow suspicious of Steve; a shadowy figure appears down the street; Charlie shoots the figure. I would include each of these key events in a summary because each event moves the story along. I would not include a detail such as the woman's stifled cry. Even though it heightens the story's suspense, it does not advance the plot.

STEVE. I'm surprised at you, Charlie. How come you're so dense all of a sudden? [*A pause*] Who do I talk to? I talk to monsters from outer space. I talk to three-headed green men who fly over here in what look like meteors.

[STEVE'S *wife steps down from the porch, bites her lip, calls out.*]

MRE. BRAND. Steve! Steve, please. [*Then looking around, frightened, she walks toward the group.*] It's just a ham radio set, that's all. I bought him a book on it myself. It's just a ham radio set. A lot of people have them. I can show it to you. It's right down in the basement.

STEVE. [*Whirls around toward her*] Show them nothing! If they want to look inside our house—let them get a search warrant.

CHARLIE. Look, buddy, you can't afford to—

STEVE. [*Interrupting*] Charlie, don't tell me what I can afford! And stop telling me who's dangerous and who isn't and who's safe and who's a menace. [*He turns to the group and shouts.*] And you're with him, too—all of you! You're standing here all set to crucify—all set to find a scapegoat[4]—all desperate to point some kind of a finger at a neighbor! Well now look, friends, the only thing that's gonna happen is that we'll eat each other up alive—

[*He stops abruptly as* CHARLIE *suddenly grabs his arm.*]

CHARLIE. [*In a hushed voice*] That's not the only thing that can happen to us.

[*Cut to a long shot looking down the street. A figure has suddenly materialized in the gloom and in the silence we can hear the clickety-clack of slow, measured footsteps on concrete as the figure walks slowly toward them. One of the women lets out a stifled cry. The young mother grabs her boy as do a couple of others.*]

TOMMY. [*Shouting, frightened*] It's the monster! It's the monster!

[*Another woman lets out a wail and the people fall back in a group, staring toward the darkness and the approaching figure.*]

---

4. **scapegoat** person or group blamed for the mistakes or crimes of others.

Characters' Motives
What do you think Steve is feeling at this point?

Characters' Motives
What explains the characters' fearful actions here?

33 Reading Check
What does Steve have in his basement?

The Monsters Are Due on Maple Street **849**

---

31 Characters' Motives

1. Have several students read the bracketed passage aloud beginning with "Go ahead, Steve" at the bottom of p. 848, each taking a different part. Encourage them to use dramatic expression that is appropriate to the text.

2. **Ask** students to describe the tone of Steve's first speech ("I'm surprised at you, Charlie . . . .")
   Answer: The tone of this speech is sarcastic.

3. **Ask** students how Steve's tone changes in the third speech ("Charlie, don't tell me . . . .").
   Answer: His tone becomes angry and accusatory.

4. **Ask** the Characters' Motives question.
   Possible response: Steve is feeling frustrated, angry, and perhaps a bit fearful. He feels as if he is losing a battle.

32 Characters' Motives

1. Read aloud the third bracketed passage, beginning with *He stops abruptly* and continuing onto p. 850. Then, **ask** the second Characters' Motives question.
   Answer: The characters' fearful actions are prompted by the approach of a shadowy figure.

2. Have students identify some of the characters' specific actions.
   Answer: Charlie grabs Steve's arms. One or two women let out a cry. Tommy's mother grabs him. Tommy shouts. The group falls back into the shadows. Don Martin brings out his gun.

3. **Ask** students how the appearance of the figure alters the way the neighbors interact with one another.
   Answer: They have stopped arguing among themselves and have momentarily banded together in their fear.

33 Reading Check

Answer: Steve has a ham radio set in his basement.

③④ Critical Viewing

Answer: The light at the top of the image brings to mind the flash of light at the beginning of the drama. The single light at the center of the darkness reinforces the fear of the unknown that grips the neighbors of Maple Street.

③⑤ Characters' Motives

1. Have three students read the exchange between Don, Steve, and Charlie. **Ask** students how Steve feels about the gun. **Possible response:** He thinks it is pointless and can only make the situation more dangerous for the neighbors.

2. **Ask** who is siding with whom. **Answer:** Charlie is siding with Don.

3. **Ask** the Characters' Motives question. **Answer:** He pulls the gun from Steve's hands because he wants action, not more talk. He is afraid and wants to use the gun against the approaching figure, which he believes to be a monster.

③④ ▲ **Critical Viewing**
How does this image help communicate the ideas of the play? **[Connect]**

Characters' Motives
Why does Charlie pull the shotgun from Steve's hands?

We see a medium group shot of the people as they stand in the shadows watching. DON MARTIN *joins them, carrying a* ③② *shotgun. He holds it up.]*

DON. We may need this.

STEVE. A shotgun? [*He pulls it out of* DON'S *hand.*] Good Lord—will anybody think a thought around here? Will you people wise up? What good would a shotgun do against—

③⑤ [*Now* CHARLIE *pulls the gun from* STEVE'S *hand.*]

CHARLIE. No more talk, Steve. You're going to talk us into a grave! You'd let whatever's out there walk right over us, wouldn't yuh? Well, some of us won't!

[*He swings the gun around to point it toward the sidewalk. The dark figure continues to walk toward them.*

The group stands there, fearful, apprehensive, mothers clutching children, men standing in front of wives. CHARLIE *slowly raises the gun. As the figure gets closer and closer he suddenly pulls the trigger. The sound of it explodes in the stillness. There is a long angle shot looking down at the figure, who suddenly*

Vocabulary Development

© **CCSS** Language 6

Selection Vocabulary Reinforcement
To reinforce and assess students' comprehension of selection vocabulary words, give them these sentences. Students must tell whether the word is used correctly.

1. The calm, soothing music made me feel *flustered.* **Answer:** No, soothing music would not make a person feel nervous or confused.

2. The energetic dancers leaped *sluggishly* across the stage. **Answer:** No, energetic dancers would not move as if they were lacking energy.

3. The alarm clock beeped *persistently* until George turned it off. **Answer:** Yes, alarm clocks do beep firmly and steadily until they are turned off.

4. It was *defiant* of Jen to be home ten minutes before her curfew. **Answer:** No, to be home before a curfew is not to resist the curfew.

5. Each spring, I am awed by the garden's *metamorphosis.* **Answer:** Yes, a garden changes in the spring when flowers bloom and grow.

lets out a small cry, stumbles forward onto his knees and then falls forward on his face. DON, CHARLIE, *and* STEVE *race forward over to him.* STEVE *is there first and turns the man over. Now the crowd gathers around them.*]

STEVE. [*Slowly looks up*] It's Pete Van Horn.

DON. [*In a hushed voice*] Pete Van Horn! He was just gonna go over to the next block to see if the power was on—

WOMAN. You killed him, Charlie. You shot him dead!

CHARLIE. [*Looks around at the circle of faces, his eyes frightened, his face contorted*] But . . . but I didn't know who he was. I certainly didn't know who he was. He comes walkin' out of the darkness—how am I supposed to know who he was? [*He grabs* STEVE.] Steve—you know why I shot! How was I supposed to know he wasn't a monster or something? [*He grabs* DON *now.*] We're all scared of the same thing. I was just tryin' to . . . tryin' to protect my home, that's all! Look, all of you, that's all I was tryin' to do. [*He looks down wildly at the body.*] I didn't know it was somebody we knew! I didn't know—

[*There's a sudden hush and then an intake of breath. We see a medium shot of the living room window of* CHARLIE'S *house. The window is not lit, but suddenly the house lights come on behind it.*]

WOMAN. [*In a very hushed voice*] Charlie . . . Charlie . . . the lights just went on in your house. Why did the lights just go on?

DON. What about it, Charlie? How come you're the only one with lights now?

GOODMAN. That's what I'd like to know.

[*A pause as they all stare toward* CHARLIE.]

GOODMAN. You were so quick to kill, Charlie, and you were so quick to tell us who we had to be careful of. Well, maybe you had to kill. Maybe Peter there was trying to tell us something. Maybe he'd found out something and came back to tell us who there was amongst us we should watch out for—

[CHARLIE *backs away from the group, his eyes wide with fright.*]

Summarize
How do you know that Pete Van Horn's death is an important detail?

 **Reading Check**
Who shoots Pete Van Horn?

The Monsters Are Due on Maple Street **851**

36 Summarize

1. **Ask** students what has happened. **Answer:** Charlie has shot Pete Van Horn, thinking he was an alien.

2. Have students read the first bracketed passage. Then, **ask** the Summarize question. **Possible response:** You can tell this is an important detail because of the characters' extreme reactions to the event.

3. **Ask** how this event is different from all those that came before. **Answer:** It is different because it is much more serious. All the earlier events helped feed the crowd's growing fear, whereas this one is a tangible—and irreversible—result of that fear.

37 Critical Thinking

Analyze

1. Have students read the second bracketed passage. Point out to students that Goodman's tone has changed now that Charlie is a suspect. **Ask** students to describe this change and to explain why it has occurred. **Answer:** Goodman is now accusatory rather than defensive. In order to direct suspicion away from himself, he has joined the mob in targeting Charlie.

2. Point out that so far, Tommy, Steve, Les Goodman, and Charlie have all been objects of the mob's suspicions. **Ask** how this constant shift in suspicions affects the overall feel of the drama. **Answer:** With every shift, the tension of the drama is heightened. Like a camera swinging crazily from subject to subject, this constant shift gives a dizzying, chaotic feel to the drama.

38 Reading Check

Answer: Charlie shoots Pete Van Horn.

Differentiated Instruction for Universal Access

Enrichment for Advanced Readers
Suggest that students read additional works by Rod Serling. You may wish to use *Authors in Depth*, Grade 7, which contains the following selections:
• from *About Writing for Television* (nonfiction, p. 124)
• from *Requiem for a Heavyweight* (drama, p. 126)
• "The Mirror Image" (fiction, p. 136)

After students read two or more of these selections, have them form discussion groups to compare and contrast the ideas presented in the works. Students should take notes in their discussions to gather ideas for essay topics. Then, have students write essays comparing and contrasting the ideas and themes in these works and *The Monsters Are Due on Maple Street.*

851

1. Have students read the long stage direction to themselves. Then, **ask** why the residents of Maple Street have become so violent.
   Answer: Their fear has reached a fever pitch. Their behavior is almost totally determined by the mob mentality.

2. Have several volunteers read the remaining bracketed text aloud continuing onto p. 853. Then, **ask** the Characters' Motives question.
   Answer: Charlie's own fear motivates him to claim that he knows who the monster is. One person is already dead, and he doesn't want himself or his wife to become the second casualty.

3. Encourage students to draw a conclusion about the central feeling or desire that motivates most of the characters in the drama.
   Answer: Fear or the desire for self-preservation motivates most of the characters.

Characters' Motives
What motivates Charlie to claim that he knows who the monster is? Explain.

CHARLIE. No . . . no . . . it's nothing of the sort! I don't know why the lights are on. I swear I don't. Somebody's pulling a gag or something.

[*He bumps against* STEVE, *who grabs him and whirls him around.*]

STEVE. *A gag?* A gag? Charlie, there's a dead man on the sidewalk and you killed him! Does this thing look like a gag to you?

[CHARLIE *breaks away and screams as he runs toward his house.*]

CHARLIE. No! No! Please!

[*A man breaks away from the crowd to chase* CHARLIE. *We see a long angle shot looking down as the man tackles* CHARLIE *and lands on top of him. The other people start to run toward them.* CHARLIE *is up on his feet, breaks away from the other man's grasp, lands a couple of desperate punches that push the man aside. Then he forces his way, fighting, through the crowd to once again break free, jumps up on his front porch. A rock thrown from the group smashes a window alongside of him, the broken glass flying past him. A couple of pieces cut him. He stands there perspiring, rumpled, blood running down from a cut on the cheek. His wife breaks away from the group to throw herself into his arms. He buries his face against her. We can see the crowd converging on the porch now.*]

VOICES.

It must have been him.

He's the one.

We got to get Charlie.

[*Another rock lands on the porch. Now* CHARLIE *pushes his wife behind him, facing the group.*]

CHARLIE. Look, look I swear to you . . . it isn't me . . . but I do know who it is . . . I swear to you, I do know who it is. I know who the monster is here. I know who it is that doesn't belong. I swear to you I know.

GOODMAN. [*Shouting*] What are you waiting for?

Vocabulary Development

Word Analysis

1. Point out the prefix *con-* in *converging* on this page. Tell students that in this word, the prefix *con-* means "with, together." To *converge* means to "come together at a point."

2. Direct students' attention to the same prefix in *contorted* on p. 851. Explain that the word part *tort* means "to twist." Then, **ask** students to combine the meaning of *con-* with the meaning of *tort* to come up with a meaning for *contorted*.

Possible response: *Contorted* must mean "twisted together." When a person's face is *contorted,* his or her features must be twisted together.

3. Ask students to apply the meaning of *con-* in definitions or explanations of these words:
   conjoin (to join together)
   consolidate (to bring or put together)
   confide (to trust someone with something)

WOMAN. [*Shouting*] Come on, Charlie, come on.

MAN ONE. [*Shouting*] Who is it, Charlie, tell us!

DON. [*Pushing his way to the front of the crowd*] All right, Charlie, let's hear it!

[CHARLIE'S *eyes dart around wildly.*]

CHARLIE. It's . . . it's . . .

MAN TWO. [*Screaming*] Go ahead, Charlie, tell us.

CHARLIE. It's . . . it's the kid. It's Tommy. He's the one!

[*There's a gasp from the crowd as we cut to a shot of* SALLY *holding her son* TOMMY. *The boy at first doesn't understand and then, realizing the eyes are all on him, buries his face against his mother.*]

SALLY. [*Backs away*] That's crazy! That's crazy! He's a little boy.

WOMAN. But he knew! He was the only one who knew! He told us all about it. Well, how did he know? How could he have known?

[*The various people take this up and repeat the question aloud.*]

VOICES.

How could he know?

Who told him?

Make the kid answer.

DON. It was Charlie who killed old man Van Horn.

WOMAN. But it was the kid here who knew what was going to happen all the time. He was the one who knew!

[*We see a close-up of* STEVE.]

STEVE. Are you all gone crazy? [*Pause as he looks about*] Stop.

[*A fist crashes at* STEVE'S *face, staggering him back out of the frame of the picture.*

There are several close camera shots suggesting the coming of violence. A hand fires a rifle. A fist clenches. A hand grabs the hammer from VAN HORN'S *body, etc. Meanwhile, we hear the following lines.*]

Summarize
What details show that Charlie finds it hard to say who to blame?

 Reading Check

According to Charlie, who is the monster?

---

40 Summarize

1. Have students read the second bracketed passage silently. Then, **ask** the Summarize question. **Answer:** Charlie's stuttering shows that it is difficult for him to say who is to blame.

2. **Ask:** Whom does Charlie blame? **Answer:** He blames Tommy.

   Ask students what earlier event or scene is connected to this one. **Answer:** This event is connected to the scene in which Tommy first hypothesizes about aliens.

3. Guide students to see how the plot has spiraled back to an earlier event, but with a greatly intensified atmosphere. Point out that, in effect, these two related events serve as bookends for the other major events in the story.

41 Reading Check

Answer: According to Charlie, Tommy is the monster.

Fluency

Distribute copies of pages 852–853 and pair students. Have listeners mark text with which readers struggle. Circulate to monitor students' fluency, and then collect the marked-up pages. Review difficult words and passages. Watch for these trouble spots:

- If students struggle with unconventional punctuation, such as repeated ellipsis points, explain the author's unusual use of the marks. Rather than indicating omitted text, the ellipsis points indicate an incomplete thought or sentence. Model how to pause slightly at the ellipsis points and have students echo to develop fluency.

- If students stumble over the dashes, point out that these marks also indicate interrupted or incomplete thoughts, but also show leaps from one idea to another. Have fluent readers model how to reflect the slight hesitation that the dashes indicate. Invite other students to echo their classmates until all are reading fluently.

1. Discuss with students the hysteria and frenzy of the scene. Explain that at this point in the narrative, the specific details that contribute to the chaos—such as Man One's opinion that Steve and Charlie are in cahoots—are not crucial to the reader's or viewer's understanding of what is going on. Rather, the overall *impression* of division and conflict is what the author wants to convey.

2. Read the first bracketed stage direction aloud. Then, **ask** students the Summarize question. **Possible responses:** The detail about the flashing lights is important in that it reflects the chaos that is occurring and may heighten it somewhat. However, this detail is not significant to the development of the plot. The chaos would continue to occur with or without the flashing lights.

43 **Critical Thinking**

Compare and Contrast

1. Have students read the second bracketed passage. Then, have them turn to p. 835 and reread the opening camera shot of Maple Street.

2. **Ask** students to compare the way the viewer first sees Maple Street and the way it appears now. **Answer:** Students should note that Serling gives instructions for the same camera angles, but the content of the setting is much different. Maple Street in the beginning of the screenplay was calm and happy. Now, the camera shows pandemonium and the chaos of the neighborhood.

Summarize
Is the detail about lights going on and off in various homes important? Why or why not?

DON. Charlie has to be the one—Where's my rifle—

WOMAN. Les Goodman's the one. His car started! Let's wreck it.

MRS. GOODMAN. What about Steve's radio—He's the one that called them—

MRS. GOODMAN. Smash the radio. Get me a hammer. Get me something.

STEVE. Stop—Stop—

CHARLIE. Where's that kid—Let's get him.

MAN ONE. Get Steve—Get Charlie—They're working together.

[*The crowd starts to converge around the mother, who grabs the child and starts to run with him. The crowd starts to follow, at first walking fast, and then running after him.*

We see a full shot of the street as suddenly CHARLIE'S *lights go off and the lights in another house go on. They stay on for a moment, then from across the street other lights go on and then off again.*]

MAN ONE. [*Shouting*] It isn't the kid . . . it's Bob Weaver's house.

WOMAN. It isn't Bob Weaver's house. It's Don Martin's place.

CHARLIE. I tell you it's the kid.

DON. It's Charlie. He's the one.

[*We move into a series of close-ups of various people as they shout, accuse, scream, interspersing these shots with shots of houses as the lights go on and off, and then slowly in the middle of this nightmarish morass of sight and sound the camera starts to pull away, until once again we've reached the opening shot looking at the Maple Street sign from high above. The camera continues to move away until we dissolve to a shot looking toward the metal side of a space craft, which sits shrouded in darkness. An open door throws out a beam of light from the illuminated interior. Two figures silhouetted against the bright lights appear. We get only a vague feeling of form, but nothing more explicit than that.*]

FIGURE ONE. Understand the procedure now? Just stop a few of their machines and radios and telephones and lawn

Vocabulary Development

Vocabulary Knowledge Rating
When students have finished reading and discussing *The Monsters Are Due on Maple Street*, have them take out their **Vocabulary Knowledge Rating Chart** for this selection. Read the words aloud once more and have students rate their knowledge of the words again in the After Reading column. Clarify any words that are still problematic. Have students write their own definition and example or sentence in the appropriate column. Then, have students complete the Vocabulary Practice activities at the end of the selection. Encourage students to use the words in further discussion and written work about the selection. Remind them that they will be accountable for these words on the **Selection Test**, *Unit 5 Resources,* pp. 106–108 or 109–111.

mowers . . . throw them into darkness for a few hours, and then you just sit back and watch the pattern.

FIGURE TWO. And this pattern is always the same?

FIGURE ONE. With few variations. They pick the most dangerous enemy they can find . . . and it's themselves. And all we need do is sit back . . . and watch.

FIGURE TWO. Then I take it this place . . . this Maple Street . . . is not unique.

FIGURE ONE. [*Shaking his head*] By no means. Their world is full of Maple Streets. And we'll go from one to the other and let them destroy themselves. One to the other . . . one to the other . . . one to the other—

LITERATURE IN CONTEXT

Media Connection

Onscreen Aliens

For many years, filmmakers have imagined beings from outer space. Here are a few examples of movie aliens.

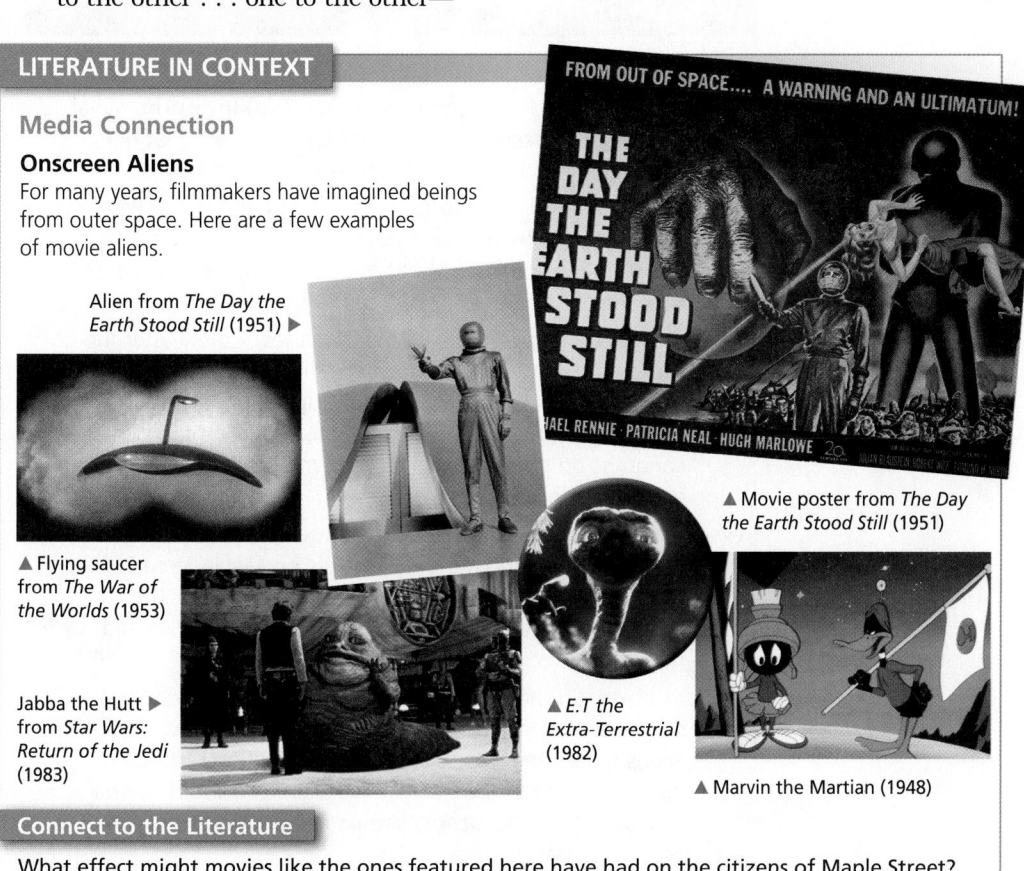

Alien from *The Day the Earth Still* (1951) ▶

▲ Flying saucer from *The War of the Worlds* (1953)

Jabba the Hutt ▶ from *Star Wars: Return of the Jedi* (1983)

▲ Movie poster from *The Day the Earth Stood Still* (1951)

▲ *E.T the Extra-Terrestrial* (1982)

▲ Marvin the Martian (1948)

FROM OUT OF SPACE.... A WARNING AND AN ULTIMATUM!

THE DAY THE EARTH STOOD STILL

MICHAEL RENNIE · PATRICIA NEAL · HUGH MARLOWE

Connect to the Literature

What effect might movies like the ones featured here have had on the citizens of Maple Street?

Critical Thinking

Before students respond, you may wish to have them write a brief objective summary of the selection. As they answer the questions below, remind them to support their answers with evidence from the text.

1. (a) They gang up on him and accuse him of being an imposter. (b) He and his family did not come out to look at the strange object in the sky. A neighbor has noticed that he goes outside in the early morning hours to stare at the sky. (c) It suggests that people are scapegoating one another because of their fear.

2. (a) Charlie cannot see well and thinks a monster is approaching. (b) Their thinking is unclear.

3. (a) Charlie accuses Tommy in order to place the mob's attention on someone else. (b) They want to blame someone. If they can figure out who is responsible, they will feel more secure. (c) The people's prejudices and attitudes lead them to destroy themselves.

4. (a) **Possible response:** The monsters are the residents themselves. (b) Encourage students to discuss the possibility that there is more than one answer to this question.

5. **Possible responses:** (a) The neighbors become quickly suspicious of each other and are quick to make accusations out of fear. (b) The aliens can see the distrust among the residents of Maple Street and can see how easily it can tear their neighborhood apart. (c) The perspective of the aliens is more clear-eyed because it is from the outside and not clouded by fear.

[*Now the camera pans up for a shot of the starry sky and over this we hear the* NARRATOR'S *voice.*]

NARRATOR'S VOICE. The tools of conquest do not necessarily come with bombs and explosions and fallout. There are weapons that are simply thoughts, attitudes, prejudices—to be found only in the minds of men. For the record, prejudices can kill and suspicion can destroy and a thoughtless frightened search for a scapegoat has a fallout all its own for the children . . . and the children yet unborn. [*A pause*] And the pity of it is . . . that these things cannot be confined to . . . The Twilight Zone!

Critical Thinking

Cite textual evidence to support your responses.

© 1. **Key Ideas and Details (a)** How do the people on Maple Street single out Les Goodman in Act I? **(b) Interpret:** What qualities of his cause the reaction? **(c) Deduce:** What does this suggest about what is really happening on Maple Street?

© 2. **Key Ideas and Details (a)** Why does Charlie shoot Pete Van Horn? **(b) Infer:** What does the crowd's response to this shooting suggest about how clearly they are thinking? Cite at least two examples to support your response.

© 3. **Key Ideas and Details (a)** Who accuses Tommy after the shooting, and why? **(b) Connect:** Why are people prepared to believe such an accusation? **(c) Support:** How do the events of the play support this statement: "The tools of conquest do not necessarily come with bombs and explosions and fallout"?

© 4. **Integration of Knowledge and Ideas (a) Draw Conclusions:** Who are the monsters on Maple Street? **(b) Discuss:** Share your responses with a partner. Then, discuss how hearing someone else's responses did or did not change your answers.

© 5. **Integration of Knowledge and Ideas (a)** How do the neighbors regard each other in the story? **(b)** How do the aliens regard the residents of Maple Street? **(c)** Whose perspective is more clear-eyed? Explain. [*Connect to the Big Question: Do others see us more clearly than we see ourselves?*]

856 Drama

Assessment Resources

Unit 5 Resources

L1 L2 EL **Selection Test A,** pp. 106–108. Administer Test A to less advanced readers.

L3 L4 EL **Selection Test B,** pp. 109–111. Administer Test B to on-level and more advanced students.

L3 L4 **Open-Book Test,** pp. 103–105. As an alternative, give the Open-Book Test.

All **Customizable Test Bank**

All **Self-tests**
Students may prepare for the **Selection Test** by taking the **Self-test** online.

PHLit Online! All assessment resources are available at **www.PHLitOnline.com.**

The Monsters Are Due on Maple Street

Reading Skill: Summarize

1. At the beginning of the play, the electricity goes off, and phones and radios stop working. Are these important or unimportant details? Explain your answer.

2. Summarize the play using a chart like the one shown.

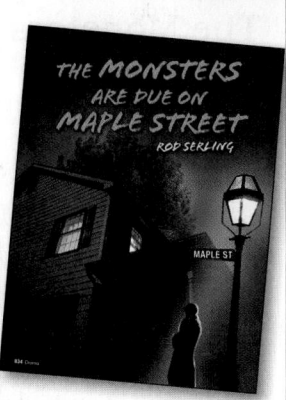

Important Details From Beginning	Important Details From Middle	Important Details From End
Summary:		

Literary Analysis: Characters' Motives

3. Key Ideas and Details Explain the **character's motives** in each of these examples: **(a)** Pete Van Horn walks from his neighborhood to the next one. **(b)** Charlie shoots Pete Van Horn. **(c)** Goodman accuses Charlie of being one of the others.

4. Key Ideas and Details What is the motivation of Figure One? How does his motivation shape the plot?

Vocabulary

Acquisition and Use Write a single sentence using both words.

1. transfixed; film
2. flustered; teacher
3. sluggishly; engine
4. persistently; nagged
5. defiant; teenager
6. metamorphosis; tadpole

Word Study Use the context of the sentences and what you know about the **Latin root -sist-** to explain your answer.

1. Is an *assistant* someone who will not help you?
2. If you *insist* on doing something, are you expressing yourself in a firm manner?

Word Study

The **Latin root -sist-** means "stand."

Apply It Explain how the root *-sist-* contributes to the meanings of these words. Consult a dictionary if necessary.

consistent
resistance
subsist

Reading Skill

1. These are important details because they lead to the events that follow. The story would not make sense if these details were left out.

2. Beginning—There is a flash across the sky; the electricity goes out; Tommy suggests that aliens may be responsible. Middle—Les Goodman's car starts on its own; the crowd decides that Les may be a monster; it is revealed that Steve has a radio in his basement, and the crowd's suspicions shift to him; Charlie shoots a shadowy figure who turns out to be Pete Van Horn. End—The crowd accuses Charlie; Charlie accuses Tommy; the street dissolves into chaos; two aliens review the "procedure" used to get humans to destroy one another.

   For other sample answers, see *Graphic Organizer Transparencies,* **Reading Skill Graphic Organizer A,** p. 162, and the **Additional Answers** section.

Literary Analysis

3. **Possible responses:** Pete Van Horn—motivated by curiosity, wants to find out why the electricity is out. Charlie—motivated by fear, wants to protect himself from the "monster." Goodman—motivated by fear, wants people to stop suspecting him.

4. Figure One is motivated by the desire to conquer Earth; his motivation starts the actions of the plot.

Vocabulary

Acquisition and Use
Sample answers:

1. Henry was <u>transfixed</u> by the <u>film</u> about life on Mars.
2. The <u>teacher</u> became <u>flustered</u> when she lost her grade book.
3. If your car moves <u>sluggishly</u>, you may want to check the <u>engine</u>.
4. Tara <u>nagged</u> her mother every day and quite <u>persistently</u> for a new bike.

Word Study
Sample answers:

1. No; The root *-sist-* means "to stand," and an *assistant* is someone who helps, such as by <u>standing</u> nearby.
2. Yes; The root *-sist-* means "to stand," and to *insist* means to "<u>stand</u> by your ideas."

Answers continued:

5. The <u>defiant</u> <u>teenager</u> refused to stop despite a direct request to do so.
6. The <u>metamorphosis</u> of a <u>tadpole</u> into a frog is fascinating.

Word Study: Apply It
Sample answers: *Consistent* action stays, or "<u>stands</u>," the same over time. During *resistance,* people <u>stand</u> up for their ideas, even against attack. To *subsist* is to stay alive, to <u>stand</u> alive.

Conventions

1. Introduce the skill, using the instruction on the student page.
2. Discuss the examples in the chart.

Think Aloud: Model the Skill

Model the skill of identifying sentence types and choosing correct end marks. Say to students:

Using different sentence types adds variety to my writing. For example, I can say, "Why is that costume so fragile?" or "Don't touch that costume!" Both sentences convey similar information, but they serve different functions and also reflect different moods. The first sentence can convey curiosity, frustration, or even wonder, while the second conveys alarm. The first asks a question, so I must end with a question mark. The second ends with an exclamation point because it is an imperative.

PH WRITING COACH   Grade 7

Students will find further instruction on and practice with sentence functions and end marks in Chapter 25, Section 1.

Practice A
Sample answers:

1. to make a statement
2. to ask a question
3. to call out or exclaim
4. to give a command
5. to make a statement

**Reading Application
Sample answers:**

1. declarative: At the sound of the roar and the flash of light it will be precisely 6:43 P.M. on Maple Street.
2. interrogative; What was that?
3. imperative; Just stay right where you are, Steve.
4. exclamatory; It's the monster!

Practice B
Sample answers:

1. The flash of light surprises people.
2. What caused the loss of electricity?
3. Start your car, Les.
4. Watch out, Pete!

**Writing Application
Sample answer:** The power outage frightens the people on Maple Street. What could be the problem? Stay inside, everyone, until we figure it out. What a horrible experience!

858

Integrated Language Skills

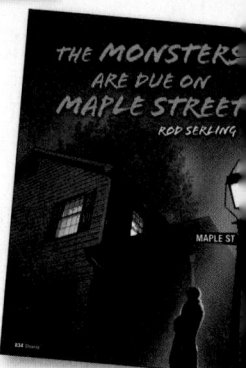

The Monsters Are Due on Maple Street

Conventions: Sentence Functions and Endmarks

> Sentences are classified into four categories based on their **function.** Each type of sentence calls for its own specific punctuation mark(s).

Catagory	Function	Endmark	Example
Declarative	to make statements	.	Our cat chased a squirrel up a tree.
Interrogative	to ask questions	?	Where did I put my jacket?
Imperative	to give commands	. or !	Put your books away. Don't touch that stove!
Exclamatory	to call out or exclaim	!	That's a great idea!

Practice A Identify the function of each sentence below.

1. The neighbors came out of their homes.
2. What caused them to be afraid?
3. There are monsters on the street!
4. Don't jump to conclusions about people.
5. Pete went to see if the next street had electricity.

Ⓒ **Reading Application** In *The Monsters Are Due on Maple Street*, find one declarative sentence, one interrogative sentence, one imperative sentence, and one exclamatory sentence.

Practice B Follow the directions to write a sentence that performs the indicated function.

1. Make a statement about the flash of light on Maple Street.
2. Ask a question about the loss of electricity in the neighborhood.
3. Issue a command to Les Goodman about his car.
4. Call out a warning to Pete Van Horn as he approaches his neighbors in Act 2.

Ⓒ **Writing Application** Write four sentences about events that take place in *The Monsters Are Due on Maple Street*. Use one declarative sentence, one interrogative sentence, one imperative sentence, and one exclamatory sentence.

PH WRITING COACH   Further instruction and practice are available in *Prentice Hall Writing Coach*.

Extend the Lesson

Sentence Modeling

Use the sentences below as models:

> *Go ahead, what's my wife said?*
> *It's Tommy. He's the one!*

Remind students of the grammar lesson on sentence functions and end marks. Ask students what they notice about the sentences as a group. Elicit from them that the three sentences have different functions and end with different end marks. Then, ask what else students notice.

(The first sentence includes both imperative and interrogative elements. The second and third sentences are very short, which makes the exclamation in the third sentence more powerful.)

Have students imitate the sentences in sentences on a topic of their own choosing, matching each grammatical and stylistic feature discussed. Collect the sentences and share them with the class.

Writing

 **Informative Text** Write a **summary** of Act 1 or 2 of the screenplay.

- Include only the main ideas and most significant details.

- Use your own words, except when including quotations.

- Be sure your summary reflects the act's underlying meaning, or theme, not just the superficial details. Relay facts, not personal reactions.

- Use effective transitions between sentences to unify important ideas. For example, you might use words like *next*, *finally*, *at first*, and *however* to link events.

Type your summary using a word processing program. Use the spell-check feature to make sure that your spelling is accurate.

Grammar Application Check to be sure you have correctly punctuated your writing.

Writing Workshop: *Work in Progress*

Prewriting for Exposition For a cause-and-effect essay, make a list of three questions you have that begin with the word *Why*. The subject of each sentence is a *cause*. The answers to each question are *effects*. Keep this Question List in your writing portfolio.

Research and Technology

 **Build and Present Knowledge** Plan how you would prepare a **film version** of any scene from the screenplay. Consider how you could use the medium to portray the scene in a unique way. Follow these steps to complete the assignment:

- List the events that occur in the scene.
- Plan the camera angles that will best illustrate the action.
- Consider using special sound or lighting effects.
- Think about the background and interests of your audience.
- Organize the details and sequence of your film to make it interesting and exciting to your audience.

If a camera is available and you have the time, film the scene.

Compare and contrast your filmed version of the scene with the original screenplay version.

 **Common Core State Standards**

L.7.2, L.7.4.b; W.7.2.b, W.7.2.c, W.7.6, W.7.9.a
[For the full wording of the standards, see page 830.]

Use this prewriting activity to prepare for the **Writing Workshop** on page 878.

www.PHLitOnline.com

- Interactive graphic organizers
- Grammar tutorial
- Interactive journals

Integrated Language Skills **859**

Writing

1. Review the assignment, using the instruction on the student page.

2. To guide students as they write their informative texts, give them **Support for Writing**, p. 101 in *Unit 5 Resources.*

3. To evaluate students' reports, use the rubrics for summaries, pp. 246–247 in *Professional Development Guidebook.*

Grammar Application

Have students check their drafts to make sure they have used correct punctuation.

Six Traits Focus

✔ Ideas	Word Choice
✔ Organization	Sentence Fluency
Voice	Conventions

PH WRITING COACH | Grade 7

Students will find further instruction on and practice with summarizing in Chapter 11.

 Writing Workshop
Work in Progress

Have students save their completed Question Lists in their portfolios. They will use the lists later as they complete the Writing Workshop assignment (see pp. 878–885).

Research and Technology

1. Review the assignment, using the instruction on the student page.

2. To support students' work on the assignment, have students complete the **Support for Extend Your Learning** page (*Unit 5 Resources,* p. 102).

Teaching Resources

Unit 5 Resources
L3 L4 EL Integrated Language Skills: Grammar, p. 100
L3 L4 EL Support for Writing, p. 101
L3 L4 Support for Extend Your Learning, p. 102
L4 Enrichment, p. 99

Enriched Online Student Edition
Available under After You Read for this selection:
All Interactive Grammar Tutorial
L3 L4 Internet Research Activity
Professional Development Guidebook
Rubrics for Self-Assessment: Summary, pp. 246–247

PHLit Online! All print and digital resources are available online at **www.PHLitOnline.com.**
Online resources accessible to students are noted on the student page.

Using the Test Practice

In this two-page Test Practice, students apply the reading skill for the second half of Unit 5 to a passage of fiction and a passage of nonfiction.

Review this skill and summary, and then administer the test. For more guidance, consult the *Classroom Strategies and Teaching Routines* card Formally Assessing Students.

ASSESS

Answers

Answers With Explanations

1. **B**—The orange glow is a crucial detail since it prompts the rest of the action. *Incorrect answers:* A—This minor detail does not belong in a summary; C—The fact that the cat seems frightened is important, but the fact that Carrie lets her cat out for the night is not; D—The color of the door is insignificant.

2. **A**—This answer summarizes the information in each of the three sentences in paragraph 1. *Incorrect answers:* B—This summarizes only the last sentence in the paragraph; C—This summarizes only the second sentence; D—This is a conclusion drawn from the third sentence in the paragraph.

3. **B**—Carrie worries that she may get into trouble, but the passage does not state that she often gets into trouble. *Incorrect answers:* A—This detail is important because it suggests danger; C—This summarizes what the character is doing in this paragraph; D—This is important characterization.

4. **A**—Pointing out that a character is taking an unnecessary risk builds suspense. *Incorrect answers:* B—In itself, this fact does not build suspense; C—This detail describes the action in this paragraph rather than adding suspense; D—This is an offhand comment that does not build suspense.

5. **D**—The summary must first mention the existence of the strange glow so that the other details make sense. *Incorrect answers:* A—This detail would come at the end of the summary; B—This detail does not belong in the summary

860

Test Practice: Reading

Summarize

Fiction Selection

Directions: *Read the selection. Then, answer the questions.*

(1) A strange orange glow shone through the cracks in the toolshed walls. Carrie was troubled by the spooky light she noticed as she opened the pale blue back door to let her cat out for the night. Miss Kitty, who usually sprang for freedom as soon as the door opened, hung back hesitantly.

(2) Creeping carefully but nervously toward the shed, Carrie had the feeling her curiosity might get her into trouble. Mom and Dad were scheduled to return soon from a meeting at school, and she knew she should wait and let them explore the cause of the light. Patience had never been one of her strongest virtues, though.

1. Which detail from paragraph 1 should be included in a summary?
   A. The shed walls were cracked.
   B. An orange glow shone from the shed.
   C. Carrie let her cat out for the night.
   D. The back door was a pale blue color.

2. Which of the following is the *best* one-sentence summary of paragraph 1?
   A. A spooky light in the shed frightened Carrie and her cat.
   B. A light in the shed frightened Miss Kitty, who usually went out at night.
   C. When Carrie opened the door to let the cat out, she saw a light in the shed.
   D. Miss Kitty's behavior made it clear that something scary was in the shed.

3. What detail does *not* belong in a summary of paragraph 2?
   A. Carrie is not waiting for her parents.
   B. Carrie is often in trouble.
   C. Carrie is creeping towards the shed.
   D. Carrie is not a patient person.

4. What key detail adds suspense to paragraph 2?
   A. Carrie knew she should wait.
   B. Mom and Dad had a meeting at school.
   C. Carrie crept carefully but nervously toward the tent.
   D. Patience had never been one of her strongest virtues.

5. Which detail should come first in a summary of the entire selection?
   A. Carrie knew she should wait.
   B. Carrie opened the door of the shed.
   C. Carrie's cat hung back from the door.
   D. Carrie saw a strange orange glow.

Writing for Assessment

Write a one-sentence summary of paragraph 2. Be sure to include only the most important ideas and details.

860 Drama

at all; it is a prediction; C—This belongs in the middle of the summary.

Writing for Assessment

Students should write a one-sentence summary of paragraph 2. The summary should contain only the most important ideas and details, including the fact that Carrie crept toward the shed even though she knew she should wait for her parents to return before investigating.

Strategies for
Test Taking

Tell students that sometimes standardized tests require students to summarize an entire selection in just one sentence. This task can be a challenging one. The sentence must include all of the information important to understanding the selection in just a few words. One way to meet the challenge is to perform the task in steps. Tell students they can start by writing a one-paragraph summary. Then, they can summarize that paragraph in just two sentences. Last, they can summarize the most important information in just one sentence.

Nonfiction Selection

Directions: *Read the selection. Then, answer the questions.*

(1) Imagine trying to find your tent in a packed campground after a long day at a nearby music festival. With thousands of campers spread out across the field, it could take hours—unless you live in Europe and have a new cellphone-activated tent.

(2) Launched recently by one of Europe's largest telecommunications companies, this tent has a special gray antenna rising from its center, and its edges are lined with luminous ribbing. When a tent owner sends a text message to a special phone number, the antenna flashes, and the entire tent glows bright orange.

(3) Although the tents are not yet available for sale in the United States, American camping retailers are interested in incorporating the technology into their equipment. Soon, campers around the world might more easily find their way "home to their domes"—so long as everyone else doesn't run out and buy one too!

1. Which of these details should *not* be included in a summary of paragraph 1?
A. A cellphone activates the tent.
B. The tents are available in Europe.
C. Music festivals can be long.
D. Locating a tent may be difficult.

2. What is the *best* one-sentence summary of paragraph 1?
A. Campers attend crowded music festivals with thousands of other campers.
B. Campers with cellphone-activated tents can locate their campsites easily.
C. European campers have trouble finding their tents in crowded fields.
D. Campers can buy cellphone-activated tents.

3. A summary of paragraph 2 should include the detail that each tent—
A. is a popular choice for campers.
B. has a special phone number.
C. was manufactured in Europe.
D. has a gray, flashing antenna.

4. Which detail should *not* be included in a summary of paragraph 3?
A. American campers are not yet able to buy these special tents.
B. The tents will be available to campers around the world.
C. American retailers want to incorporate the technology into their equipment.
D. If everyone buys a glowing tent, they will not be so useful.

Writing for Assessment

Connecting Across Texts
Imagine that the glowing light in the first passage is caused by the tent described in the second passage. Write a three-sentence summary of the first passage, incorporating this new information.

www.PHLitOnline.com
• Online practice
• Instant feedback

Test Practice: Reading **861**

861

Common Core State Standards

- **Reading Informational Text 6, 9**
- **Language 6**

Reading Skill

1. Introduce the skill and the chart.

2. Tell students they will learn how to determine bias and stereotyping.

Think Aloud: Model the Skill

Say to students:

When I read, I keep an eye out for instances of bias and stereotyping. Suppose I'm reading an article on a new car. If the article is written by someone who works for the car company, the person might unfairly favor his or her company's product—a case of bias. If a person engages in bias or stereotyping, I am inclined to mistrust his or her entire argument.

● Multidraft Reading

Have students follow a multidraft reading protocol.

- **First reading**—Have students read to identify key ideas and details.

- **Second reading**—Have students read to identify the structure of the text.

- **Third reading**—Have students read to integrate knowledge and ideas by connecting the text to the world, their own experiences, and other texts.

Content-Area Vocabulary

1. Have students say each word.

2. Next, use each word in a sentence that defines it.

3. Finally, repeat your definitional sentence or a similar sentence, omitting the word, and have the class "fill in the blank" chorally.

862

Reading for Information

Analyzing Argumentative Texts

Editorial

Editorial

Common Core State Standards

Reading Informational Texts
6. Determine an author's point of view or purpose in a text and analyze how the author distinguishes his or her position from that of others.
9. Analyze how two or more authors writing about the same topic shape their presentations of key information by emphasizing different evidence or advancing different interpretations of facts.

Language
6. Acquire and use accurately grade-appropriate general academic and domain-specific words and phrases; gather vocabulary knowledge when considering a word or phrase important to comprehension or expression.

Reading Skill: Identify Bias and Stereotyping

In persuasive writing, authors provide evidence to support their claims. As a good reader, you should **assess that evidence, deciding if it is adequate and accurate.** When judging a text, look for bias and stereotyping. A **bias** is a leaning toward a certain position. A **stereotype** unfairly suggests that all members of a group are exactly the same. The following chart gives examples and explanations of bias and stereotyping.

	Example	How It Works
Bias	"He *won* the election with his plans for reform." "He *stole* the election with a web of empty promises."	Two writers describe the same event differently, based on their personal feelings.
Stereotyping	"All teenagers are lazy."	The writer makes an unsupported claim about a group of people in order to sway readers' opinions.

Content-Area Vocabulary

These words appear in the selections that follow. You may also encounter them in other content-area texts.

- **derring-do** (der´ iŋ dōō´) *n.* daring deeds

- **lobbying** (läb´ ē iŋ) *v.* trying to influence the members of a lawmaking group

- **junket** (jun´ kit) *n.* a trip paid for with the public's money

---

Do others see us more clearly than we see ourselves?

Have students consider as they read how believable each viewpoint is.

Differentiated Instruction for Universal Access

Reading Support
Give students reading support with the appropriate version of the *Reader's Notebook:*

L2 L3 *Reader's Notebook*

L1 *Reader's Notebook: Adapted Version*

EL *Reader's Notebook: English Learner's Version*

> The title of the editorial suggests the author's point of view.

Veteran Returns, Becomes Symbol

Editorial in the *Minneapolis Star and Tribune*, January 19, 1998

John Glenn went into orbit in 1962 and took America's hearts soaring with him. Who better to fire the nation's imagination again about the promise of space exploration?

NASA has done itself and its cause great good by announcing that Glenn, the astronaut-turned-U.S. senator, will fly into space once more. Though Glenn has represented Ohio in the Senate for five terms and run for president once, many Americans still consider his name synonymous with the nation's manned space program.

At a time when all astronauts were esteemed as America's best and brightest, Glenn stood out. Though not the first American in space, nor the one to seize the space-race prize—a moon landing—Glenn possessed an appeal that surpassed that of his peers.

Just as Glenn's orbital heroics inspired America when he was a young man, by joining the shuttle crew in October at age 77, he can inspire the nation again. He can reignite curiosity about the benefits and challenges for humankind that lie beyond Earth. He can let a watchful public share vicariously[1] his delight at leaving Earth's bounds once more.

> The author uses persuasive language that appeals to the emotions.

And he can again be an exemplar for his generation—a generation already setting new standards for vigor and productivity past age 70. Glenn's flight should dramatically demonstrate that age is no limit to derring-do, nor to service to one's country.

Volunteering for a space ride isn't an option for most septuagenarians.[2] But many of Glenn's contemporaries are also volunteering, lending a hand to the young, old, sick and needy in their own communities. As America honors Glenn's past and future career in space, let the nation also take grateful note of the good works senior citizens are doing here on the ground.

> The editorial concludes with a memorable sentence.

Editorial

Features:

- leisure reading
- writer's opinion on a current issue
- persuasive language
- text written for a general or a specific audience

---

1. **vicariously** (vī kerʹ ē əs lē) *adv.* Indirectly; through the experience of another; by sympathy or imagination.
2. **septuagenarians** (sepʹ tŏŏ ə jə nerʹ ē ənz) *n.* Persons between the ages of 70 and 80.

About Editorials

1. Review the features listed in the Editorial box on page 863 with students. **Ask** the class to discuss the difference between an editorial and a news article.
   Answer: Editorials express the opinion of a writer on a particular topic, while news articles are strictly based on facts.

2. Talk to students about how to read editorials. Suggest that they analyze the author's perspective to determine a purpose for writing and evaluate the author's supporting evidence.

Identify Bias and Stereotyping

1. Have students read the editorial on page 863 and the side notes that point to important elements.

2. Point out that the persuasive language used in the editorial can help readers easily identify the author's perspective on the topic.
   Ask students to identify the author's perspective.
   Answer: The language in the editorial suggests that the author is in favor of John Glenn's returning to space once again.

Differentiated Instruction   for Universal Access

Strategy for Less Proficient Readers

Students may not be familiar with editorials as a genre. Review the features of editorials in more depth with these students. Make sure they understand that they are not reading the kind of article they would find on the news pages of a newspaper. Emphasize that the editorial is providing an opinion, although it does contain facts and details. Also make sure less proficient readers understand that the subject of the editorial is an event that had not yet taken place when the editorial was written.

Enrichment for Advanced Readers

Have students conduct research to find out what happened regarding John Glenn's return to space. Have them find out if Glenn's ride aboard the space shuttle actually took place. Then, have students reread the two editorials and report back to the class whether the ride, if it indeed took place, had positive results, as predicted in the first editorial, or was indeed simply a "junket," as claimed by the second editorial.

1. **Ask** students how the perspective of the second editorial differs from that of the first.
   Answer: The two authors disagree. The second editorial criticizes John Glenn and his desire to return to space at such an old age.

2. Tell students that a stereotype does not have to be stated explicitly in writing; it can be implied. **Ask** students if they can identify an implied stereotype in the editorial.
   Answer: The author draws attention to Glenn's age constantly, implying that the older generation shouldn't consider going into space because they have nothing to offer any space program.

3. **Ask** students if there is bias present in the second editorial.
   Answer: Yes, the author does not view John Glenn's achievements favorably.

The title of the editorial clearly states the author's point of view.

The Wrong Orbit: Senator Has No Legitimate Business Blasting into Space

Editorial in The *Kansas City Star*, January 20, 1998

Most Americans think of political lobbying as something done by special interest groups trying to curry favor with lawmakers to affect some legislation. Not so in the case of Sen. John Glenn and his former employer, the National Aeronautics and Space Administration.

Glenn, a Democratic senator from Ohio, has lobbied NASA for some time in hope of returning to space. Glenn, who will turn 77 in July, was the first American to orbit the Earth.

He plans to retire from the Senate, but for his next engagement he wants to strap on a space suit under the pretense of scientific merit. Glenn says his space jaunt would help the space program understand the effects of weightlessness on the aging human form. (C'mon, Senator, it's doubtful even you believe that, so don't expect anyone else to.)

There are much better uses for the taxpayers' money than Glenn's planned junket in space via the Discovery mission in October. Besides, as the senator ought to

The author uses persuasive language that appeals to the emotions.

know, workers in the space program are being laid off around the country due to downsizing at NASA. And there's something questionable, if not downright indecent, about a U.S. senator who has been a NASA ally in Congress, calling on the space agency for a favor. Whether on this planet or another, a quid pro quo[1] is the same.

John Glenn became a hero after his pioneering space flight, and he parlayed that status into what was said to be a successful political career. His political career was jeopardized by his involvement in the Keating Five scandal, and he became excessively shrill this year during committee hearings as the Senate defender of the Democratic presidential fund-raising debacle.[2]

Certainly, there are times when good science and good politics mix, as happened with the launch of the U.S. space program as part of the space race with the former Soviet Union.

But Glenn's proposed junket in space is neither good science nor good politics.

The author concludes by firmly restating his or her opinion.

---

1. **quid pro quo** (kwid prō kwō) *n.* Latin phrase meaning "this for that"; a thing given or done in exchange for another.
2. **Keating Five . . . fund-raising debacle** (di bä´ kəl) *n.* The Keating Five were five senators, including John Glenn, who received contributions from Charles Keating, a businessman under criminal investigation. In 1997, the Senate and the Justice Department investigated White House fund-raising practices.

864 Drama

Think Aloud

Making Inferences
Model the skill of identifying bias, using the following "think aloud." Say to students:

This is an editorial, so I know it will include opinions. If the author supported Glenn's trip into space, he or she would not have called the rationale for the trip a "pretense." Also, the author implies that Glenn is lying about the rationale. I can't tell if this is true because the author hasn't included facts to support this accusation. However, I can tell from the parenthetical comment that the author is passionate about this point. Finally, the author notes only negative points in Glenn's political career. The author doesn't include any other facts about Glenn's career in politics. In addition, I'm not sure that the points mentioned really are negative—the author's comments that the events were a "scandal" and a "debacle" may simply be his or her opinions.

Comparing Argumentative Texts

1. Key Ideas and Details (a) Identify differences between the arguments made in each editorial. **(b)** Identify instances of **bias** and **stereotyping** in each editorial.

Content-Area Vocabulary

2. (a) Remove the suffix *-ing* from the word *lobbying*. Using a print or an online dictionary, explain how removing the suffix reveals a different word that is a different part of speech. **(b)** Use the words *lobbying* and *lobby* in sentences that show their meaning.

⏱ Timed Writing

Argumentative Text: Evaluation

Format
The prompt gives directions about what to write and the type of information to include.

Choose one of the editorials about John Glenn's plans to travel in space, and write an evaluation of the piece. Tell whether the author successfully argued and supported his or her claims. Use details from the text to support your answer. (30 minutes)

Academic Vocabulary
When you *support* your answer, you provide details, examples, and facts to show that your answer is reasonable and logical.

5-Minute Planner

Complete these steps to write your evaluation:

1. Read the writing prompt carefully from start to finish. Be sure that you fully understand the assignment. **TIP** When reading a prompt, look for verbs such as "choose," "write," and "tell." These words are often important to understanding what you are being asked to do.

2. Gather information for your evaluation by rereading the editorial that you have chosen to evaluate. Jot down the author's claims and details that support each claim.

3. Determine whether the author's supporting details are based in fact or opinion, whether they are biased or unbiased, and whether they include emotional language. Use this information to decide if you are persuaded to accept the author's claims.

4. Use your notes about the author's claims to keep your thoughts focused as you write your evaluation.

Comparing Argumentative Texts

1. (a) **Answer:** The first editorial supports Glenn's decision while the second does not. The writer of the second editorial focuses more on personal feelings and opinions than on fact. The editorials also differ in how they present Glenn's role in politics and his missions in space.
(b) **Answer:** In the first editorial, the writer's perspective can be viewed as biased because it portrays Glenn in a glowing manner without full support. The statement regarding astronauts as "America's best and brightest" can be viewed as a reverse stereotype. In the second editorial, the writer seems to be biased against Glenn returning to space because of his age. Though it is not stated directly, the writer implies that the older generation does not belong in space by calling attention to Glenn's age.

2. (a) When you take the *-ing* suffix away from the word *lobbying*, you get the word *lobby*. *Lobby* is a verb that means "to act in order to influence public officials." It is also a noun that means "a group of people working to influence public officials," as well as "a large entry room or foyer."
(b) **Sample response:** We were lobbying to get the new law passed. We met our friends in the lobby of the theater.

⏱ Timed Writing

1. Before students complete the activity, guide them in identifying and analyzing key words and phrases in the prompt, highlighted on the student page.

2. Work with students to draw up guidelines for their evaluations based on the key words:

   • **Focus** The writer should clearly state an evaluation.

   • **Organization** The ideas should be logically organized.

   • **Elaboration** The writer should include details from the editorial, showing how each supports his or her evaluation.

   • **Style** The style should be clear and formal.

3. Have students use the 5-Minute Planner to structure their time.

4. Allow students 30 minutes to complete the assignment. Evaluate their work using the guidelines they have developed.

Common Core State Standards

- Reading Literature 5
- Writing 2, 2.b

---

❶ Comparing Dramatic Speeches

Dramatic Speeches

1. Introduce and discuss the skill.

2. Give students a copy of **Comparing Dramatic Speeches Organizer B**, (*Graphic Organizer Transparencies*, p. 165). Tell them that they will fill it in with what they learn about the characters and how they learned it.

Think Aloud: Model the Skill

Model the skill of analyzing dramatic speeches. Say to students:

> To help me analyze a monologue or dialogue, I can imagine the scene as if it were a movie. Instead of just reading the lines, I can try to imagine how the actors would speak them, what the actors' faces would look like, and what emotions they would be trying to convey.

> Imagining how a character looks and feels during a dramatic dialogue can help you understand that character.

❶ Comparing Dramatic Speeches

Dramatic speeches are spoken by characters in a play. These speeches can move the action forward and reveal more about the characters. Dramatic speeches are an important part of the structure, or organization, of a drama. There are two main types of dramatic speeches:

- **Dialogue** is conversation between or among characters in a drama. It reveals characters' traits and helps develop conflict.

- **Monologues** are long, uninterrupted speeches that are spoken by a single character. They reveal the private thoughts and feelings of the character.

The following selections are both dramatic speeches. The excerpt from *Grandpa and the Statue* is a dialogue, and *My Head Is Full of Starshine* is a monologue. Both provide information and details about the characters. Some details are told directly through the words a character speaks. For example, a character may say, "I am happy." Other details are supplied indirectly. For example, if a character constantly disagrees with others, you can infer that he or she is angry or argumentative. As you read, use a chart like the one below to record what you learn about the main characters in these dramatic speeches.

Common Core State Standards

Reading Literature
5. Analyze how a drama's or poem's form or structure contributes to its meaning.

Writing
2. Write informative/explanatory texts to examine a topic and convey ideas, concepts, and information through the selection, organization, and analysis of relevant content.
2.b. Develop the topic with relevant facts, definitions, concrete details, quotations, or other information and examples. *(Timed Writing)*

	Grandpa and the Statue	My Head Is Full of Starshine
Main Characters		
Description of Characters		
How I Learned About Characters		

Online!
www.PHLitOnline.com

- Vocabulary flashcards
- Interactive journals
- More about the authors
- Selection audio
- Interactive graphic organizers

Vocabulary Development

Vocabulary Knowledge Rating

Create a **Vocabulary Knowledge Rating Chart** (*Professional Development Guidebook,* p. 33) featuring the words glossed in the selections:

peeved (p. 871)	rummaging (p. 875)
practical (p. 875)	potential (p. 875)

Give students a copy of the chart, and read the words aloud. Have students mark their rating of each in the Before You Read column.

To gauge how much instruction to provide, tally the students who think they know each word. Explain that the words are defined in the margin at the point where they appear in the selection. Urge students to be alert to these words as they read the selections. They will rate their knowledge again when they finish.

Online! **Vocabulary Central,** featuring tools, activities, and songs for studying vocabulary, is available online at **www.PHLitOnline.com.**

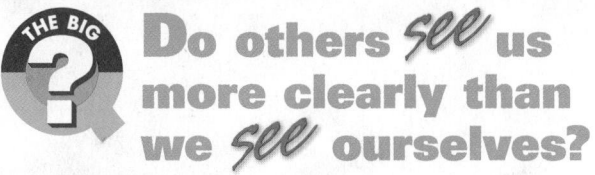

Do others *see* us more clearly than we *see* ourselves?

Writing About the Big Question

In each of these selections, what characters say reveals a lot about them. Use this sentence starter to develop your ideas.

The best way to **appreciate** someone is to _____.

Meet the Authors

Arthur Miller (1915–2005)

Author of *Grandpa and the Statue*

Arthur Miller is considered among the finest American playwrights. Most of his plays focus on the problems of ordinary people. Born in New York City, Miller was unable to finish high school because of the Depression. In 1934, he convinced the University of Michigan to accept him as a student anyway.

Promising Playwright In 1947, Miller saw his first play, *All My Sons,* open on Broadway. *Death of a Salesman* (1949), perhaps his most famous play, won a Pulitzer Prize and made Miller internationally famous. *Grandpa and the Statue* was originally written as a radio drama in 1944.

Peg Kehret (b. 1936)

Author of *My Head Is Full of Starshine*

Before Peg Kehret began writing books for children, she wrote radio commercials, plays, and stories for magazines.

Animal Lover Kehret is a longtime volunteer for animal welfare causes and has won an award for her work with animals. For years, she and her husband traveled around the United States so that Kehret could speak at schools and libraries. The couple traveled in a motor home so that their pets could go with them.

from Grandpa and the Statue • My Head Is Full of Starshine **867**

Daily Bellringer

For each class during which you will teach this selection, have students complete one of the five Sentence Combining activities for Week 30 in the *Daily Bellringer Activities* booklet.

② Writing About the Big Question

1. Introduce the assignment.

2. Lead the class in a discussion of the different ways you can learn about another person. Make a list of responses on the board. (**Possible responses:** *from what he says, from how he acts, from the way he dresses, from who his friends are, from how he spends his time*)

3. Have students complete the sentence starter. Review responses as a class. (**Sample response:** The best way to <u>appreciate</u> someone is to *pay attention to what is unique in the person's words and actions.*)

4. Tell students that as they read, they should think about how characters reveal their personality, and ask themselves if the character is aware of the impression he or she is making.

Concept Connector ➡

Students will return to their sentence starters after reading.

Multidraft Reading

To assist struggling readers and to deepen reading for all, apply multidraft reading protocols. For each reading, have students set the purpose indicated:

• **First reading**—identifying key ideas and details and answering any Reading Checks.

• **Second reading**—analyzing craft and structure and responding to the side-column prompts.

• **Third reading**—integrating knowledge and ideas, connecting to other texts and the world, and answering the end-of-selection questions.

For more guidance, refer to the *Classroom Strategies and Teaching Routines* card on multidraft reading.

867

❶ Background

A Method of Characterization

Characterization is the way in which a writer creates and develops a character. Since human relationships are an essential part of people's lives, one way that a writer develops a character is by showing how the character interacts with other people, especially in conversation.

❷ Activating Prior Knowledge

Use the **Vocab-o-Gram** strategy (*Professional Development Guidebook,* p. 39) to introduce students to vocabulary in the selection and to make predictions about the selection. Put the following words on the board or on an overhead:

Statue of Liberty	fund
subscribed	immigrants
dime	visualize
Roman numbers	rooming house
register	welcome
disgrace	swindle

Then, give students the **Vocab-o-Gram Chart** (*Professional Development Guidebook,* p. 40) and have them place the words in appropriate categories and make predictions about the story. Have students discuss and explain their word placements, reasons, and predictions.

Concept Connector ➡

Students will follow up on this activity after completing "Grandpa and the Statue."

❸ About the Selection

In this excerpt from a radio play, Sheean visits Monaghan to persuade him to contribute to the fund to build a base for the Statue of Liberty. Monaghan—the only person in the neighborhood who has not contributed—refuses to give a dime, unwilling to believe the statue exists. Sheean takes him to the warehouse where the unassembled pieces of the statue are stored, yet Monaghan still refuses, claiming the statue is broken and the fund is a swindle. Exasperated, Sheean leaves Monaghan to make his own way back to the neighborhood.

868 Drama

PROFESSIONAL DEVELOPMENT	Doug Buehl

▼ APPLY THE STRATEGY

Questioning Distribute Before/During/After Questioning Charts. Ask students to read the title of the radio play and examine the photo and think about something they might be wondering, such as "I wonder what Grandpa has to do with the Statue of Liberty?" Instruct students to write two questions they are wondering about in the first column (Before). Provide time for a brief partner share of these "before" questions. Then, ask students to read the radio play and record (in the middle "during" column) five questions that surface as they read. Ask students to talk about their questions with a partner, and discuss which of their questions they were able to answer, and which remain unanswered. Solicit both types from the class. After discussion, ask students to record two significant unresolved questions that they still have.

For more of Doug Buehl's strategies, see the Professional Development essay, pp. 720c–720d.

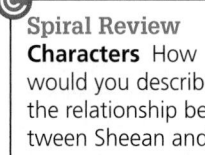

from Grandpa and the STATUE

ARTHUR MILLER

SHEEAN. [*Slight brogue*[1]] A good afternoon to you, Monaghan.

MONAGHAN. How're you, Sheean, how're ya?

SHEEAN. Fair, fair. And how's Mrs. Monaghan these days?

MONAGHAN. Warm. Same as everybody else in summer.

SHEEAN. I've come to talk to you about the fund, Monaghan.

MONAGHAN. What fund is that?

SHEEAN. The Statue of Liberty fund.

MONAGHAN. Oh, that.

SHEEAN. It's time we come to grips with the subject, Monaghan.

MONAGHAN. I'm not interested, Sheean.

SHEEAN. Now hold up on that a minute. Let me tell you the facts. This here Frenchman has gone and built a fine statue of Liberty. It costs who knows how many millions to build. All they're askin' us to do is contribute enough to put up a base for the statue to stand on.

MONAGHAN. I'm not . . . !

SHEEAN. Before you answer me. People all over the whole United States are puttin' in for it. Butler Street is doin' the same. We'd like to hang up a flag on the corner

---

1. brogue (brōg) *n.* Irish accent.

◀ **Critical Viewing**
What can you see in this photograph that you do not usually see in pictures of the Statue of Liberty? **[Analyze]**

Spiral Review
Characters How would you describe the relationship between Sheean and Monaghan? Explain.

✓ Reading Check
What does Sheean want from Monaghan?

from Grandpa and the Statue **869**

© **Text Complexity Rubric**

from **Grandpa and the Statue**	
Qualitative Measures	
Context/Knowledge Demands	Immigrants' attitudes toward the Statue of Liberty 1 2 ③ 4 5
Structure/Language Conventionality and Clarity	Conversational dialogue with nonstandard spellings 1 2 ③ 4 5
Levels of Meaning/ Purpose/Concepts	Accessible (friends have different perspectives) 1 2 ③ 4 5
Quantitative Measures	
Text Length	Word Count: 1,037
Lexile	NP

Reader and Task Suggestions

Preparing to Read the Text
- Use the Background note on TE p. 868 to discuss how writers develop characters.
- Use the Think Aloud activity on TE p. 872 to discuss dramatic speeches.
- Guide students to use Multidraft Reading strategies (TE p. 867).

Leveled Tasks
Knowledge Demands If students will have difficulty with knowledge demands, have them first read to identify dramatic speeches. Have them reread, noting character details that are revealed in the speeches.

Analyzing If students will not have difficulty with knowledge demands, have them read and suggest appropriate physical gestures that could accompany the characters' dialogue.

❻ Critical Viewing

Answer: To Monaghan, the statue appears to be broken and so not worth contributing to.

❼ Dramatic Speeches

1. Have students read the bracketed speeches. Point out that some of the speeches are short (a few words) and some are longer (several longer sentences). Explain to students that a dramatic speech does not have to be long and complicated in order to reveal something important about a character.

2. **Ask** students to notice how many of the sentences on page 870 are questions.
   Answer: There are six questions on this page.

3. Point out that questions and responses are an efficient way of revealing characters' concerns, ideas, feelings, and beliefs.

4. **Ask** the Dramatic Speeches question.
   Answer: These lines reveal that Monaghan is a hard and practical man who believes only what he sees with his own eyes. He is suspicious by nature, even cynical, and tight with his money.

❻ ▲ **Critical Viewing**
Why might Monaghan be unwilling to contribute after seeing these pieces of the statue? **[Infer]**

Dramatic Speeches
What characteristics of Monaghan do the lines of dialogue on this page reveal?

❼

saying—"Butler Street, Brooklyn, is one hundred per cent behind the Statue of Liberty." And Butler Street is a hundred per cent subscribed except for you. Now will you give us a dime, Monaghan? One dime and we can put up the flag. Now what do you say to that?

MONAGHAN. I'm not throwin' me good money away for somethin' I don't even know exists.

SHEEAN. Now what do you mean by that?

MONAGHAN. Have you seen this statue?

SHEEAN. No, but it's in a warehouse. And as soon as we get the money to build the pedestal they'll take it and put it up on that island in the river, and all the boats comin' in from the old country will see it there and it'll raise the hearts of the poor immigrants to see such a fine sight on their first look at this country.

MONAGHAN. And how do I know it's in this here warehouse at all?

SHEEAN. You read your paper, don't you? It's been in all the papers for the past year.

MONAGHAN. Ha, the papers! Last year I read in the paper that

870 Drama

Vocabulary Development   ©️ CCSS Language 6

Thematic Vocabulary: The Big Question
As students are discussing the interaction between Sheean and Monaghan, encourage them to use the Big Question vocabulary presented on pp. 720–721. You might encourage them with sentence starters like these:

1. Based on one bad experience, Monaghan makes the *assumption* that . . .

2. It is difficult to *identify* with Monaghan's . . .

3. My *perception* of Sheean is that . . .

4. My *reaction* to these characters may be based on . . .

5. The way Sheean won't give up may *reveal* . . .

they were about to pave Butler Street and take out all the holes. Turn around and look at Butler Street, Mr. Sheean.

SHEEAN. All right. I'll do this: I'll take you to the warehouse and show you the statue. Will you give me a dime then?

MONAGHAN. Well . . . I'm not sayin' I would, and I'm not sayin' I wouldn't. But I'd be more likely if I saw the thing large as life, I would.

SHEEAN. [Peeved] All right, then. Come along.

[*Music up and down and out*]

[*Footsteps, in a warehouse . . . echo . . . they come to a halt.*] Now then. Do you see the Statue of Liberty or don't you see it?

MONAGHAN. I see it all right, but it's all broke!

SHEEAN. *Broke!* They brought it from France on a boat. They had to take it apart, didn't they?

MONAGHAN. You got a secondhand statue, that's what you got, and I'm not payin' for new when they've shipped us something that's all smashed to pieces.

SHEEAN. Now just a minute, just a minute. Visualize what I'm about to tell you, Monaghan, get the picture of it. When this statue is put together it's going to stand ten stories high. Could they get a thing ten stories high into a four-story building such as this is? Use your good sense, now Monaghan.

MONAGHAN. What's that over there?

SHEEAN. Where?

Vocabulary
peeved (pēvd) *adj.*
irritated; annoyed

❽ ▼ Critical Viewing
What tools and equipment might be needed to reassemble the statue?
[Draw Conclusions]

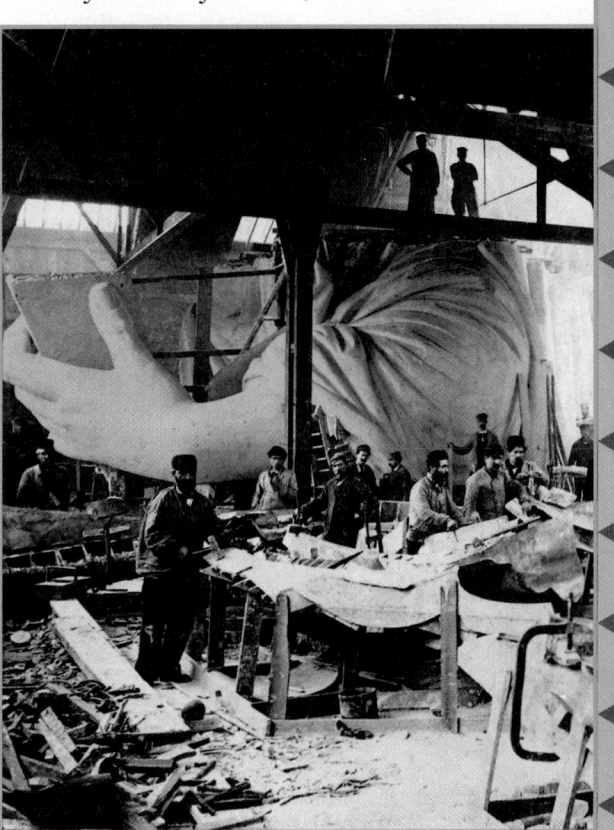

from Grandpa and the Statue **871**

1. Have students read the bracketed dramatic speech.

2. **Ask** students how the story Monaghan tells in his dramatic speech helps explain his attitude toward the statue.
   Possible response: Monaghan had a very negative experience when he first arrived in America, so when he thinks of immigrants landing he thinks of crime, swindling, and bitterness. A safe room would have been more important to him than a statue.

⑪ **THE BIG ? Connecting to the Big Question**

1. Remind students that people don't always carefully consider what they say. People sometimes speak from anger or another strong emotion.

2. **Ask** students: What is Monaghan revealing in the speeches he delivers on this page? **Possible response:** He was robbed when he first arrived in the United States, and this event made him feel unwelcome.

3. **Ask** students: Is Monaghan choosing his words carefully?
   Answer: No, he is angry and is likely yelling the first thing that comes to mind.

4. **Ask** students: Does Monaghan realize how he is coming across?
   Possible response: Probably not. He probably feels that the story about the robbery makes him sympathetic and that his arguments about the Roman numerals sound well reasoned.

5. Encourage students to look for further examples of characters' perceptions of themselves—or failure to perceive themselves.

MONAGHAN. That tablet there in her hand. What's it say? July Eye Vee (IV) MDCCLXXVI . . . what . . . what's all that?

SHEEAN. That means July 4, 1776. It's in Roman numbers. Very high class.

MONAGHAN. What's the good of it? If they're going to put a sign on her they ought to put it: Welcome All. That's it. Welcome All.

SHEEAN. They decided July 4, 1776, and July 4, 1776, it's going to be!

MONAGHAN. All right, then let them get their dime from somebody else!

SHEEAN. Monaghan!

MONAGHAN. No, sir! I'll tell you something. I didn't think there was a statue but there is. She's all broke, it's true, but she's here and maybe they can get her together. But even if they do, will you tell me what sort of a welcome to immigrants it'll be, to have a gigantic thing like that in the middle of the river and in her hand is July Eye Vee MCDVC . . . whatever it is?

SHEEAN. That's the date the country was made!

MONAGHAN. The divil with the date! A man comin' in from the sea wants a place to stay, not a date. When I come from the old country I git off at the dock and there's a feller says to me, "Would you care for a room for the night?" "I would that," I sez, and he sez, "All right then, follow me." He takes me to a rooming house. I no sooner sign me name on the register—which I was able to do even at that time—when I look around and the feller is gone clear away and took my valise[2] in the bargain. A statue anyway can't move off so fast, but if she's going to welcome let her say welcome, not this MCDC. . . .

SHEEAN. All right, then, Monaghan. But all I can say is, you've laid a disgrace on the name of Butler Street. I'll put the dime in for ya.

MONAGHAN. Don't connect me with it! It's a swindle, is all it is. In the first place, it's broke; in the second place, if

___

2. **valise** (və lēs´) *n.* small suitcase.

872 Drama

Think Aloud

Dramatic Speeches
Direct students' attention to Sheean's line: "They decided July 4, 1776, and July 4, 1776, it's going to be!" on this page. Model how to analyze a line of dialogue for clues about character. Say to students:

I'm going to think aloud to show you how I would analyze this line of dialogue. The first thing I notice is that the line ends in an exclamation point. That means the character is speaking with force. Quickly scanning backward, I can see that this is one of the first times the author used an exclamation point for one of Sheean's lines. This suggests that this line is said with more feeling than most of the others up to this point in the dialogue. I decide that means Sheean lost patience with Monaghan right at this point. If that's true, Sheean will probably never see Monaghan's side of the argument, and the two men will never reach an agreement. I will keep reading to see if my analysis is on target.

they do put it up it'll come down with the first high wind that strikes it.

SHEEAN. The engineers say it'll last forever!

MONAGHAN. And I say it'll topple into the river in a high wind! Look at the inside of her. She's all hollow!

SHEEAN. I've heard everything now, Monaghan. Just about everything. Good-bye.

MONAGHAN. What do you mean, good-bye? How am I to get back to Butler Street from here?

SHEEAN. You've got legs to walk.

MONAGHAN. I'll remind you that I come on the trolley.

SHEEAN. And I'll remind you that I paid your fare and I'm not repeating the kindness.

MONAGHAN. Sheean? You've stranded me!

[Music up and down]

Dramatic Speeches
List three adjectives you would use to describe Monaghan based on this dialogue.

Critical Thinking ©

© **1. Key Ideas and Details (a)** Why does Monaghan object to the Roman numbers on the tablet the statue holds? **(b) Connect:** Do you agree with him? Explain why or why not.

© **2. Key Ideas and Details (a) Infer:** Judging from the dialogue, how do you think that Sheean and Monaghan know each other? **(b) Speculate:** Do you think that they are good friends? Why or why not?

© **3. Key Ideas and Details (a) Summarize:** List three excuses that Monaghan gives for not giving a dime to Sheean. **(b) Predict:** Do you think Monaghan will ever give money for the pedestal? Explain.

© **4. Integration of Knowledge and Ideas (a)** What does Sheean learn about Monaghan from their conversation? Use details to explain. **(b)** Do you think it is good to learn the truth about someone even if it makes you like him or her less? Explain. *[Connect to the Big Question: Do others see us more clearly than we see ourselves?]*

Cite textual evidence to support your responses.

---

⑫ Dramatic Speeches

Ask the Dramatic Speeches question. **Possible responses:** *cranky, irritable, stingy,* and *unpatriotic.*

Concept Connector ▬▬▬

Have students return to their **Vocab-o-grams.** Ask them to explain whether any of their predictions were fulfilled and if so, how.

◄─────────────

ASSESS

Answers

Critical Thinking

Before students respond, you may wish to have them write a brief objective summary of the selection. As they answer the questions below, remind them to support their answers with evidence from the text.

1. (a) Monaghan objects to the Roman numerals because he does not understand them. (b) **Possible response:** Roman numerals connect a modern monument with the noble classical monuments of the past, so they seem to belong on an important work like the Statue of Liberty.

2. (a) **Possible responses:** Sheean and Monaghan live in the same neighborhood. (b) They are probably not good friends—just neighbors.

3. (a) Monaghan says the statue is broken, secondhand, hollow, too weak to stand in the wind, and a swindle. (b) **Possible response:** No, it is unlikely that Monaghan will ever contribute.

4. (a) **Possible response:** He learns how stubborn his neighbor is. For example, Monaghan argues that the statue is broken or poorly constructed, even though experts have stated otherwise in the newspaper. Sheean also learns Monaghan was robbed on the day he arrived in the United States. (b) **Possible response:** Learning the truth about someone is valuable even if it makes you like him or her less. There is little value in liking someone you don't really know.

Monologues Monologues are dramatic speeches told by a single character. Monologues can be included in a longer work, like a drama or a play. Other monologues stand alone as a single dramatic speech, like the monologue "My Head Is Full of Starshine." Monologues are used to reveal the inner thoughts and feelings of a character. Since monologues are told in the first person, the audience gets to hear directly what the speaker is feeling and thinking. Monologues are used to characterize the person speaking because readers learn the inner thoughts of the speaker.

14 Activating Prior Knowledge

Use the **Vocab-o-Gram** strategy (*Professional Development Guidebook,* p. 39) to help students make predictions about selection elements. Put the following words on the board or overhead:

starshine	practical
makes a list	library fines
rummaging	birthday poem
daydream	paying attention
write an essay	float out the window

Then give students the Vocab-o-Gram chart (**Professional Development Guidebook**, p. 40) and have them work in groups to place the words in appropriate categories and make predictions. Have students discuss or explain their word placements, their reasons, and their predictions.

Concept Connector ➤

Students will follow up on this activity after completing the monologue.

15 About the Selection

"My Head Is Full of Starshine" is a monologue about the differences between the narrator and her friend Pam. The narrator is a daydreamer and a creative writer, but she is also forgetful and disorganized. Pam, on the other hand, is practical, organized, down to earth, and loves science. The two friends are opposites, but they both appreciate and accept the other for who they are. The friends understand that it is okay and good to be different.

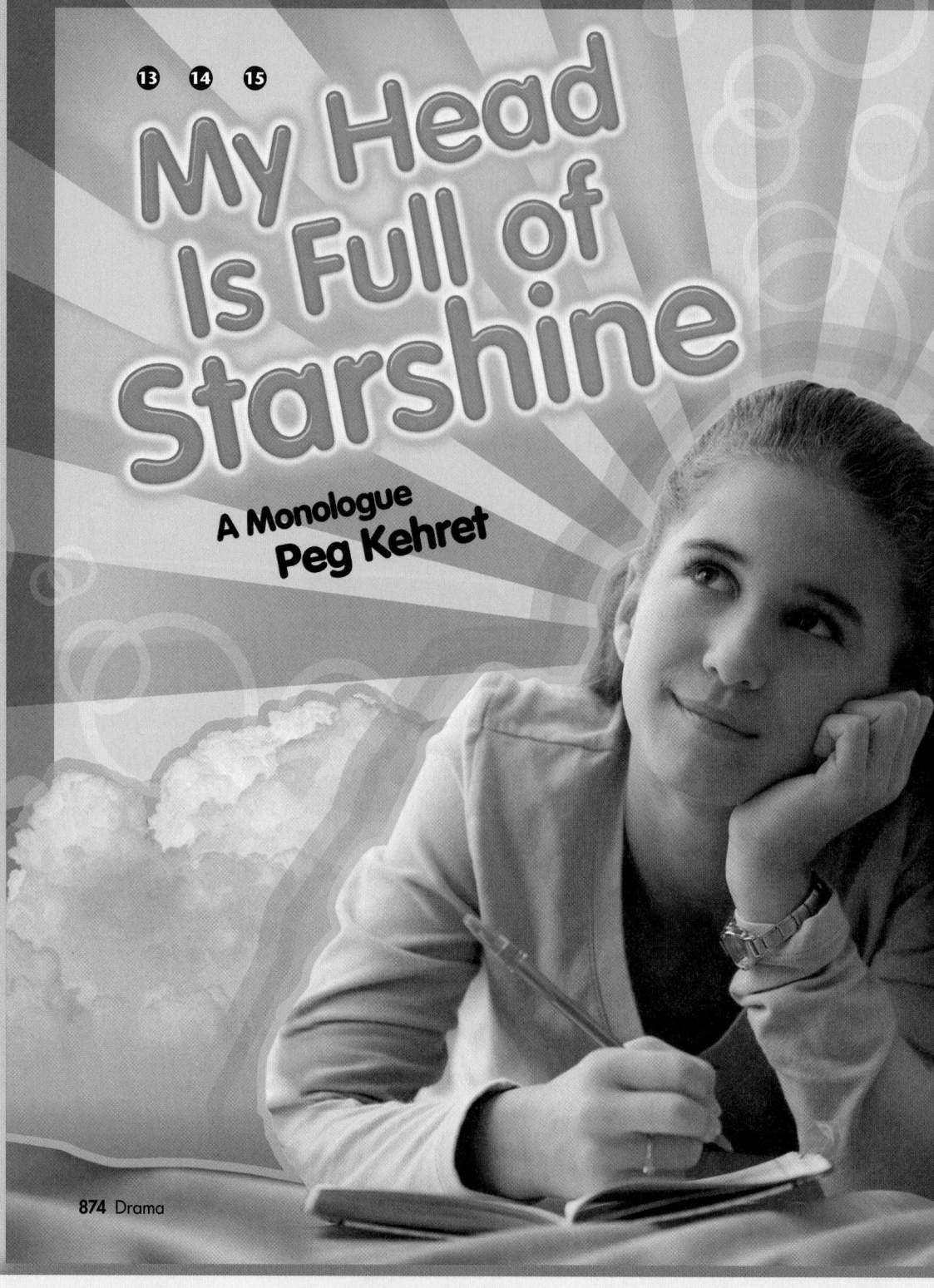

13 **14** **15**

My Head Is Full of Starshine

A Monologue
Peg Kehret

874 Drama

Vocabulary Development

Vocabulary Reinforcement
Students will benefit from additional examples and practice with the selection vocabulary words. Reinforce their comprehension with "show-you-know" sentences. The first part uses the vocabulary word in an appropriate context. The second part of the sentence—the "show-you-know" part—clarifies the first.

Give students these sentence starters. Coach them in creating the "show-you-know" part:

1. It wasn't *practical* to go to the movies on a school night; _____ _____

(**Sample response:** we'd have to leave in the middle to get to bed on time.)
2. My aunt was always *rummaging* through her purse; _____ _____ (**Sample response:** she could never find what she was looking for right away.)
3. The music teacher saw Lily's *potential*; _____ _____ (**Sample response:** she told Lily's parents that the girl would play wonderfully if she had proper training.)

My friend, Pam, says my head is full of starshine. She laughs when she says it. What she really means is that she doesn't always understand the poems I write, but she's glad that I write them.

She means she recognizes that I'm not like her, but it's OK for me to be different.

Pam is practical. Every night before she goes to sleep, Pam makes a list of what she needs to do the next day. She puts down items like return library books and hem dress for Margo's party on Saturday. When the list is made, she numbers the items in order of importance. If it's critical, it's Number One. Pam has never had to pay an overdue fine at the library and when Saturday arrives, her dress will not only be hemmed, it will be washed, ironed, and ready to wear.

I have a long history of library fines. Twenty cents here, fifty cents there. I'm always amazed to notice that a book is overdue. It just never seems like three weeks could go by so quickly. When Saturday comes, I'll be rummaging frantically through my closet, hoping to find something decent to wear to the party. But I wrote a birthday poem for Margo that I like a lot. It took me two days; I think Margo will like it, too.

My mother often wonders aloud why I can't be more like Pam. Just once, according to my mother, it would be nice to know more than twenty-four hours in advance that your child is performing in a school concert. I always forget to bring home the notices, or else I write something on the back and stick them in my desk. Either way, Mom doesn't get them in time to make plans.

On my last report card, Mr. Evans, my science teacher, wrote that I am not working up to my potential. He said I tend to daydream, instead of paying attention in class. I have to admit that's true, especially when we were learning about insects. Pam found the unit on insects fascinating. Too fascinating, if you ask me. One day she sat beside me in the cafeteria and announced that ladybugs eat aphids, spider mites, white-flies and mealybugs.

I said, "Yuck."

Pam continued blissfully on, informing me that ladybugs eat several times their own weight in insects every day. I put down my peanut butter sandwich and told Pam that the conversation was not very appetizing, but she was so excited about ladybugs that she didn't even hear me. She just babbled

Dramatic Speeches
What clue tells you this is a monologue and not a dialogue?

Vocabulary
practical (prak´ ti kəl) *adj.* levelheaded; efficient; realistic

rummaging (rum´ ij iŋ) *v.* searching through

potential (pō ten´ shəl) *n.* possibility; capability

Spiral Review
Characters Is it surprising that Pam and the speaker are close friends? Why or why not?

Reading Check
What does Mr. Evans say about the speaker?

My Head Is Full of Starshine **875**

16 Dramatic Speeches
1. Remind students that monologues have one speaker and dialogues have two.
2. Have a volunteer read the first paragraph of the selection.
   Ask students who is speaking.
   Answer: Pam's friend, a middle school student
3. **Ask** the Dramatic Speeches question.
   Possible responses: the use of the first person; the lack of quotations and labels for the speaker

17 Connecting to the Big Question
1. Remind students that what we say may reveal things about our character.
2. **Ask** students: What is the speaker revealing about her character in this passage?
   Possible response: She is admitting that she is disorganized.

Spiral Review
Characters
1. Remind students that they studied the concept of characters in the Unit 5 Literary Analysis Workshop (pp. 722–735).
2. **Ask** students the Spiral Review question.
   Possible response: No, it is not surprising. Opposites attract; people sometimes look for traits in others that they wish they had.

18 Reading Check
Answer: Mr. Evans says the speaker isn't working up to her potential.

Text Complexity Rubric

My Head Is Full of Starshine	
Qualitative Measures	
Context/Knowledge Demands	Contemporary, a young girl's thoughts 1 ② 3 4 5
Structure/Language Conventionality	Conversational; monologue 1 2 ③ 4 5
Levels of Meaning/ Purpose/Concept Level	Accessible (differences between friends) 1 2 ③ 4 5
Quantitative Measures	
Text Length	Word Count: 673
Lexile	900L

Reader and Task Suggestions

Preparing to Read the Text
- Use the Background note on TE p. 874 to discuss monologues.
- Review the SE reading note on TE p. 875 about Dramatic Speeches to discuss the selection's structure.
- Guide students to use Multidraft Reading strategies (TE p. 867).

Leveled Tasks
Structure/Language If students will have difficulty with the selection's structure, have them read to identify details about the character's personality. Have them reread, noting how point of view contributes to characterization.

Analyzing If students will not have difficulty with the selection's structure, have them read to explain why the selection does or does not seem like a dramatic text. As a class, discuss their responses.

875

⓳ Dramatic Speeches

1. Read aloud the bracketed paragraph with students. Point out to students that the author is reemphasizing the speaker's love for creativity and the speaker's dislike of the scientific.

2. **Ask** the Dramatic Speeches question.
   Answer: The speaker has a vivid and creative imagination.

Concept Connector

Have students return to the predictions they made on the two **Vocab-o-Gram** charts for these selections. After reading both selections, ask students to refine their ideas. Review the vocabulary and clarify any words by returning to the selection or using reference works.

ASSESS

Answers

Critical Thinking

Before students respond, you may wish to have them write a brief objective summary of the selection. As they answer the questions below, remind them to support their answers with evidence from the text.

1. (a) **Possible response:** Pam returns library books on time. The speaker returns them late. Pam gets A's in science. The speaker gets A's in English. (b) The speaker does not mind because she knows Pam is her friend and accepts her. (c) The speaker and Pam have a strong friendship.

2. (a) The speaker is comfortable with herself and glad that she is a daydreamer, except that it costs her money in library fines. (b) The actor could stand confidently straight to show that she is comfortable with herself, and her tone could be strong and happy to show that she likes who she is.

3. **Possible response:** Even though Pam and the speaker have different interests, they are each passionate about what they like. It's possible that they appreciate that enthusiasm in each other.

---

on about how even the ladybug larvae eat insects and how a company in California collects the ladybugs and sells them to fruit growers, to eat the aphids off the fruit trees. I finally moved to a different table, but by then my appetite was gone.

Pam got an A in science. I only get As in English. Some kids moan and complain whenever they have to write an essay or a story, but I love assignments like that. I have a whole notebook full of ideas for stories and poems that I intend to write someday. I also have a list of good titles. My favorite title is "Magic Mud in Kansas City," but so far I haven't been able to think of a story to go with it.

I will, though. I always do. Usually it happens when I least expect it, like when I'm sitting in science class trying not to get sick as I listen to how certain animals eat their young. When Mr. Evans talks about gross things like that, I pretend my chair is a flying carpet, and I watch myself float out the window, up past the flagpole and over the trees. Sometimes I pretend that I fly beyond the moon, to a different galaxy, where I meet wonderful creatures with purple beards who ride on giant rabbits.

Maybe Pam is right. My head is full of starshine. Except for those library fines, I'm glad it is.

Dramatic Speeches
What do the details in this passage tell you about the speaker?

⓳

Cite textual evidence to support your responses.

Critical Thinking

© 1. **Key Ideas and Details** (a) **Compare and Contrast:** Which details from the text show how Pam is different from the speaker? (b) **Infer:** How does it make the speaker feel when Pam tells her that she has a head full of starshine? (c) **Draw Conclusions:** What does this detail tell you about their friendship?

© 2. **Key Ideas and Details** (a) **Analyze:** What does the last paragraph reveal about the speaker's feelings about herself? (b) **Speculate:** How do you think an actor playing the role of the speaker could use body language and vocal tone to express these feelings?

© 3. **Integration of Knowledge and Ideas** Even though they are quite different, Pam and the speaker are friends. What do you think they see in each other? Explain. *[Connect to the Big Question: Do others see us more clearly than we see ourselves?]*

876 Drama

Vocabulary Development

Vocabulary Knowledge Rating

When students have completed reading and discussing "Grandpa and the Statue," and "My Head Is Full of Starshine," have them take out their **Vocabulary Knowledge Rating Chart**. Read the words aloud once more and have students rate their knowledge of the words again in the After Reading column. Clarify any words that are still problematic. Have students write their own definition and example or sentence in the appropriate column. Then, have students complete the Vocabulary Practice activities on the next page. Encourage students to use the words in further discussion and written work about these selections. Remind them that they will be accountable for these words on the **Selection Test** (*Unit 5 Resources*, pp. 123–125 or 126–128).

Comparing Dramatic Speeches

1. Craft and Structure (a) Rewrite these lines of dialogue as a monologue delivered by Sheean. **(b)** Rewrite these lines of the monologue as a dialogue between the speaker and Pam. **(c)** Share your chart with a partner.

from Grandpa and the Statue	As a Monologue
SHEEAN. I've come to talk to you about the fund, Monaghan. MONAGHAN. What fund is that? SHEEAN. The Statue of Liberty Fund. MONAGHAN. Oh, that.	

from My Head Is Full of Starshine	As a Dialogue
She means she recognizes that I'm not like her, but it's OK for me to be different.	

2. Craft and Structure (a) Can you learn more about a character from a monologue or from a dialogue? Explain. **(b)** Can you learn more about a character in a play or in a story told by a narrator? Explain.

⏱ Timed Writing

Explanatory Text: Essay

Compare and contrast a dramatic speech given by each speaker. In an essay discuss how these dramatic speeches shape your attitude toward the characters. **(35 minutes)**

5-Minute Planner

1. Read the prompt carefully and completely.
2. Gather your ideas by answering these questions:
   • Which ideas in the speeches are familiar to you?
   • Which character do you feel you know best? Why?
3. Review each selection and take notes on the differences between the way the two speeches are presented. Use these notes as you write your essay.
4. Reread the prompt, and then draft your essay.

Comparing Dramatic Speeches

1. **Sample response:** (a) I told Monaghan that I was there to talk to him about the fund and he acted like he didn't know what I was talking about. (b) SPEAKER: What do you mean when you say, "my head is full of starshine"? PAM: I know that you're not like me, but it's okay for you to be different from me. Another sample response can be found on **Comparing Dramatic Speeches Organizer A** (p. 166 in *Graphic Organizer Transparencies*).

2. (a) **Possible response:** Some students may think that you can learn more from a monologue because you learn the speaker's thoughts and feelings firsthand. Others may feel that you learn more from a dialogue because you get to see a character interact with other characters. (b) **Possible response:** Some students may feel you can learn more about a character in a story told by a narrator because the narrator is often omniscient and knows everything that is going on.

⏱ Timed Writing

1. Review the prompt with students.

2. Have students use the 5-Minute Planner to structure their time. Guide them in answering the bulleted questions. For example, point out that the second bulleted point might lead them to focus on what is revealed by someone expressing their private thoughts and feelings in a journal versus what is revealed by people having a public dialogue.

3. Allow students 35 minutes to complete the assignment.

4. As students prewrite and draft, have them refer to their completed **Comparing Dramatic Speeches Graphic Organizer.**

Six Traits Focus

✔ Ideas	Word Choice	
✔ Organization	Sentence Fluency	
Voice	Conventions	

Unit Genre and Big Question

In this unit, students will analyze tales in the oral tradition. As they read they will discuss responses to the unit Big Question: Community or individual—which is more important?

Unit 6 Selections

Teach Selections are presented in leveled pairs. To teach the skills and meet the objectives, you need to assign only one selection in each pair.

Differentiate and Reinforce Choose the selection in a pair that is best suited for your students, based on the Text Complexity box shown on the next page. You may use the other selection to reinforce skills or provide enrichment.

Integrate Skills Each selection presents students with a reading strategy, a literary analysis concept, a vocabulary skill, and grammar instruction. Students can extend learning in the writing and extension activities.

Additional Unit Features

Ⓒ Literary Analysis Workshop Teach and model the Unit Focus standards. Spiral Review notes enable students to revisit these skills over the course of the unit.

Reading for Information Students analyze functional, expository, and argumentative texts and complete Timed Writing activities.

Comparing Literary Works Students study two literary works either within or across genres.

Test Practice: Reading This feature provides extra practice in utilizing reading skills to master assessments.

Writing Workshops Two writing workshops appear in each unit, along with rubrics and instruction in the writing process.

Assessment Workshop Cumulative Skill Review and Performance Tasks provide a range of assessment opportunities.

Independent Reading Students broaden their knowledge as they read longer works of increasing complexity.

THE BIG ? Community or individual—which is more important?

898

Teaching From Technology

www.PHLitOnline.com

Enriched Online Student Edition
- full narration of selections
- interactive graphic organizers
- linked **Get Connected** and **Background** videos
- all worksheets and other student resources

Professional Development
- the *Professional Development Guidebook* online
- additional professional development articles by program authors

Planning, Assigning, and Monitoring
- software for online assignment of work to students, individually or to the whole class
- a system for tracking and grading student work

Themes in the Oral Tradition

PHLit Online!
www.PHLitOnline.com

Hear It!
- Selection summary audio
- Selection audio
- BQ Tunes

See It!
- Author videos
- Big Question video
- Get Connected videos
- Background videos
- More about the authors
- Illustrated vocabulary words
- Vocabulary flashcards

Do It!
- Interactive journals
- Interactive graphic organizers
- Grammar tutorials
- Interactive vocabulary games
- Test practice

899

Instructional Resources

The booklet *Unit 6 Resources* supports Unit skills with pages of the following types:

▶ **Benchmark Tests** assess and monitor student progress at mid-Unit and at Unit's end.

▶ **Vocabulary and Reading Warm-ups** provide additional vocabulary support, based on Lexile rankings of words, for each selection. "A" Warm-ups are for students reading two grades below level. "B" Warm-ups are for students reading one grade below level.

▶ **Selection Support** These practice pages are available for each selection:
- Reading Skill
- Literary Analysis
- Writing About the Big Question
- Vocabulary
- Support for Writing
- Support for Extend Your Learning
- Enrichment

PHLit Online!
All worksheets and other student resources are also available online at www.PHLitOnline.com.

© Text Complexity: Accessibility for Various Ability Levels

This chart gives a general text complexity rating to help you decide which selection in each leveled pair is more appropriate for your students. **Choose one selection in each pair, or choose to teach both.** You will meet the objectives for the pair when you teach either of the two selections. For additional guidance on factors that affect the complexity of each selection, see the Leveled Texts page for each selection set.

Accessibility for English Learners

 This icon indicates support for English learners at point of use in this Teacher's Edition.

	✓ More Accessible	✓✓ More Complex
Pair 1	Icarus and Daedalus	Demeter and Persephone
Pair 2	Tenochtitlan: Inside the Aztec Capital	Popocatepetl and Ixtlaccihuatl
Pair 3	Sun and Moon in a Box	How the Snake Got Poison
Pair 4	The People Could Fly	All Stories Are Anansi's

899

Common Core State Standards

Unit 6 Focus Standards
• Reading Literature 2

Additional Activities and Assessments
• Reading Literature 3
• Writing 1, 2, 3
• Speaking and Listening 1, 4
• Language 2, 3, 4, 5, 6

	Week 1					Week 2					Week 3				
	1	2	3	4	5	1	2	3	4	5	1	2	3	4	5
Introduce the Unit Big Question (pp. 900–901).	●														
Introduce the unit form, oral tradition, using the Literary Analysis Workshop (pp. 902–905).	●														
Introduce the focus CCS standards for the unit and lead students in a close reading of exemplar texts. (pp. 904–911).	●	●													
Teach one selection from Pairing 1 (pp. 912–933).			●	●	●	●	●								
Teach one selection from Pairing 2 (pp. 934–957).							●	●	●	●	●				
Complete the Test Practice: Reading (pp. 958–959).									●						
Teach Reading for Information (pp. 960–965).										●					
Teach Comparing Literary Works (pp. 966–981).												●	●		
Have students complete the Writing Workshop (pp. 982–987).										●	●	●	●	●	
Administer **Benchmark Test 11** (*Unit 6 Resources*, pp. 120–125).														●	
Reteach skills, judging which skills to reteach by evaluating students' performance on **Benchmark Test 11.**															●

Independent Reading

Have students choose a full-length work from the Independent Reading feature at the end of the unit and read it while working on this unit.

Pacing Suggestions
• Have students read their chosen work for homework.
• Devote parts of class periods in each school week to Literature Circles in which students reading the same work discuss it.

	Week 4					Week 5					Week 6				
	1	2	3	4	5	1	2	3	4	5	1	2	3	4	5
Teach one selection from Pairing 3 (pp. 988–1005).	●	●	●	●	●										
Teach one selection from Pairing 4 (pp. 1006–1025).					●	●	●	●	●						
Complete the Test-Practice: Reading (pp. 1026–1027).								●							
Teach Reading for Information (pp. 1028–1033).									●						
Teach Comparing Literary Works (pp. 1034–1039).										●	●				
Have students complete the Writing Workshop (pp. 1040–1049).									●	●	●	●	●		
Have students complete the Vocabulary Workshop (pp. 1050–1051).												●			
Have students complete the Communications Workshop (pp. 1052–1053).													●		
Have students complete the first three sections of the Assessment Workshop: Oral Tradition (pp. 1054–1057).												●	●	●	
Have students complete the selected Performance Tasks in the Assessment Workshop (pp. 1058–1059).													●		
Administer Benchmark Test 12 (*Unit 6 Resources,* pp. 227–232).													●		
Reteach skills, judging which skills to reteach by evaluating students' performance on **Benchmark Test 12.**															●

- Cover the focus standards with independent readings and abbreviate review of the focus standards with student-edition selections.

- Do not assign extension activities for selections (day 5 of main selection lessons), except as needed for full standards coverage.

- If students demonstrate reading proficiency, consider omitting Test Practice: Reading features in the unit.

Block and Daily Scheduling

The assignments and activities in this Unit planner are organized by week. You may adjust them to your daily or block schedule. The Time and Resource Manager for each selection set gives specific pacing suggestions, or you may use the comprehensive lesson planning support online at **PHLitOnline.com.**

Monitoring Progress

Diagnose Each main selection pairing in the Unit contains a more accessible and a more complex selection. To determine which selection in each pairing to assign, refer to students' results on the **Vocabulary in Context** section of **Benchmark Test 10,** *Unit 5 Resources,* pp. 140–142 (administered at the end of the previous Unit). Use the **Interpretation Guide** to interpret the results of the diagnostic portion of the test. **Note:** For the most accurate diagnosis of students who score in the middle range, administer the additional diagnostic questions online at **www.PHLitOnline.com.**

Preteach and Prepare As indicated by the diagnostic, prepare students for reading by assigning the **Vocabulary** and **Reading Warm-ups** for the selections you assign.

Teach Follow this Pacing Plan and use the resources to teach the skills and selections. For specific pacing suggestions and a list of resources, see the Time and Resource Manager and the Visual Guide to Featured Selection Resources preceding each selection pairing.

Classroom Management
For classroom management suggestions for using leveled texts in a mixed-ability classroom, see Harvey Daniels's professional development essay "Leveled Reading Selections," online at **www.PHLitOnline.com.**

Assess After students have completed the first half of the Unit, administer **Benchmark Test 11.** Administer **Benchmark Test 12** at the end of the Unit.

Intervention and Reteach After administering each test, use the **Interpretation Guide** for the tests to determine which reteaching pages, if any, you should assign from the *Reading Kit.* The appropriate pages are also available through the online Progress Monitoring software.

Editing Is Important **Jeff Anderson**

> Editing is much more than a step at the end of the writing process.

"**B**ut my teacher last year said don't worry about editing." Have you ever heard this? I reply, "Worrying about something and caring about it aren't the same thing. If we worry too much, we won't write. If we don't care, though, our readers get confused." Understanding of standard English usage helps students comprehend when reading and shape prose when composing. At the same time, to keep students engaged in the reading and writing processes, we invite them to read and write authentic texts. They begin developing the skills to edit for grammar and mechanics as they read and write, but the question remains: How can we help students develop more power and control over their writing using and writing authentic text?

Editing Is More Than Just One Step

Many students think of editing as merely a step at the end of the writing process. While editing is indeed that, it is much more. Editing—especially the grammar and mechanics we edit for—helps bolster our writing at every step of the writing process. It is with the conventions of our language that we communicate with each other. For example, capital letters tell readers something about a word, and it behooves readers and writers to understand the effect of capital letters, commas, and apostrophes, as both receivers and composers of information.

Use Reading and Rereading to Highlight Editing

Use Reading to Teach Writing Usually editing focuses on correcting mistakes. Students also need to highlight correct usage to become familiar with the grammatical patterns and usage of standard English. Literature gives us endless opportunities to be exposed to beautiful and correct grammar and mechanics that we will later edit for when we write. But how do we enhance our reading experiences to highlight grammar and mechanics?

- Keep a list of language patterns that are introduced and discussed in your class.
- Reread selections or sections of a selection to find a convention applied in an authentic context.
- Keep a list of how a mark of punctuation or grammatical convention is used in texts that are read.
- Add to the list(s) as understanding deepens.

Activities that promote tracking and articulating the patterns of our language are a first step toward successful editing. Students also need to be familiar with what effectively edited writing looks like. Once we have helped students highlight these patterns within their reading, they can then identify and modify these patterns in their own writing.

Use Writing to Teach Grammar and Editing It's a simple truth: When students write, they become better writers. Writing also helps students see how editing and grammar can help them communicate their thoughts and feelings.

Often we make the mistake of waiting until writing is finished to edit because we don't want to interfere with idea generation and drafting. In fact, struggling writers often can't write because they are too worried about making mistakes. But we don't have to wait until the entire assignment is complete to edit. We want to shape meaning as we write, too. It's part of writing, not just a separate step.

Here is how I use writing to teach grammar and editing:

- Students must write. It can be as little as a few paragraphs for any assignment. Students now have something to edit.

- Before we edit, the class and I review the patterns of English we have been discussing while reading literature. We focus in on what conventions students need to enhance this or their next writing assignment.

Students are now ready to edit. I start my students with an express-lane edit.

Try an Express-Lane Edit

Why do we want to use the express lane at the grocery store? It saves time. That's the idea behind the express-lane edit. We can edit our papers as we write them. When our writing time comes to an end for the day, why not stop a few minutes early and read or reread what we have written so far? To help hone students' editing eyes, we can have them look for targeted items in their papers.

- Create a shopping list of items to edit. Keep it short. We want it to be quick, so we would not want more than one or two things on our shopping list.

- Students draw a two-column chart at the bottom of their draft. The left side of the chart is labeled "Shopping List," and the right side is labeled "Receipt."

- In the Shopping List column, students list conventions we are learning. For example, "Use capital letters to show proper nouns (specific names of people and places)." This is the place to reteach and clarify.

- In the Receipt box, students note anything they did involving the conventions and articulate why they did it.

- Students silently reread their papers looking for correct examples of the convention as well as things they may change. (If they haven't used the convention, they are expected to add a sentence or two using the convention.) The key is to look for only one or two items.

Modeled Strategy
See pp. 984 and 1000 for point-of-use notes modeling these strategies.

Teacher Resources
- *Professional Development Guidebook*
- *Classroom Strategies and Teaching Routines* cards

Log on as a teacher at **www.PHLitOnline.com** to access a library of all Professional Development articles by the Contributing Authors of Pearson Prentice Hall *Literature*.

Jeff Anderson

Jeff Anderson has written two books and numerous articles on teaching grammar and editing in context. NCTE honored him with the Paul and Kate Farmer *English Journal* Writing Award in 2006. He continues to work in classrooms and do staff development for teachers.

Supporting Research

Anderson, Jeff. (2005). *Mechanically inclined: Building grammar, usage, and style into writer's workshop.* Portland: Stenhouse.

Graham, Steve and Delores Perin. (2007). *Writing next.* New York: Carnegie Foundation.

Murray, Donald. (2003). *A writer teaches writing.* Boston: Heinle.

Weaver, Constance. (1996). *Teaching grammar in context.* Portsmouth: Heinemann.

 Common Core
State Standards

- Speaking and Listening 1
- Language 6

❶ Introducing the Big Question

1. Discuss with students familiar sayings that address the primacy of the group over the individual or vice versa, such as "There is no *I* in *team*" and "A chain is as strong as its weakest link."

2. Have a volunteer read the intrductory section on the student page aloud. **Ask** students to think of situations in which the needs, desires, and goals of individuals and their community are at odds. **Possible response:** a community ordinance against noise.

3. **Ask** students the Big Question: "Community or individual—which is more important?" **Possible response:** Community, because more people are involved.

4. Explain that the selections in this unit consider both individual and community. Urge students to keep the Big Question in mind as they read.

❷ Exploring the Big Question

Collaboration: One-on-One Discussion

1. Introduce the activity, using the instruction on the student page.

2. Have students work individually to list examples. If students have difficulty with the third and fourth bullets, prompt ideas with questions:
   - Can you think of a volunteer job that helps a community? **Sample response:** Volunteer fireman.
   - What kinds of decisions does the mayor make? **Sample response:** The mayor can raise taxes or get laws passed.

3. Review the Big Question vocabulary on page 901, following the teaching suggestions. Have students use the vocabulary as they complete the activity on page 900.

Connecting to the Literature

Explain the Big Question strand in the unit, referring to the box at right.

900

---

❶ *Community* or *individual*— which is more important?

In many parts of our lives, we celebrate the individual—encouraging people to reach their personal best and to pursue their own dreams. Each individual has unique qualities and beliefs. However, an individual may also be part of a family or group that shares common cultural beliefs, traditions, or customs. Even these families and groups are part of a larger community.

Communities help individuals by providing services, support, and opportunities. Yet, sometimes the rights or desires of an individual may conflict with those of his or her community. In these cases, it can be difficult to find a fair solution.

❷ Exploring the Big Question

© **Collaboration: One-on-One Discussion** Start thinking about the Big Question by making a list of conflicts between individuals and their communities. Describe one specific example of each of the following situations:

- A school rule that students do not believe is fair
- A situation in which one family member does not want to do what the rest of the family is doing
- A sacrifice that one person is asked to make in order to help many others
- A decision made by someone in power that affects a large group of people

Share your examples with a partner. For each example, discuss whether the interests of the community or the individual seem more important. Use the Big Question vocabulary in your discussion.

Connecting to the Literature Each reading in this unit will give you additional insight into the Big Question.

900 Themes in the Oral Tradition

www.PHLitOnline.com

- Big Question video
- Illustrated vocabulary words
- Interactive vocabulary games
- BQ Tunes

Applying Understanding by Design Principles

The Big Question
Explain to students that they will continue to consider the Big Question as they work through the Unit.

- At the beginning of each selection, they will write a response to a Writing About the Big Question sentence starter.
- As they read the selection, they will look for details related to the Big Question.

- At the end of the selection, they will answer a Critical Thinking question that is related to the Big Question.
- Tell students that their goal will be to gain a deeper understanding of literature and a more sophisticated way of discussing the Big Question.

"Understanding by Design" is registered as a trademark with the Patent and Trademark Office by the Association for Supervision of Curriculum Development (ASCD). ASCD has not authorized, approved, or sponsored this work and is in no way affiliated with Pearson or its products.

Learning Big Question Vocabulary

Common Core State Standards

Speaking and Listening

1. Engage effectively in a range of collaborative discussions with diverse partners on *grade 7 topics, texts, and issues,* building on others' ideas and expressing their own clearly.

Language

6. Acquire and use accurately grade-appropriate general academic and domain-specific words and phrases; gather vocabulary knowledge when considering a word or phrase important to comprehension or expression.

Acquire and Use Academic Vocabulary Academic vocabulary is the language you encounter in textbooks and on standardized tests. Review the definitions of these academic vocabulary words.

common (käm´ ən) *adj.* shared; public

community (kə myoo´ nə tē) *n.* group living in a particular area

culture (kul´ chər) *n.* customs of a group or community

diversity (də vur´ sə tē) *n.* variety

duty (doot´ ē) *n.* responsibility

environment (en vī´ rən mənt) *n.* surroundings

individual (in´də vij´ oo əl) *n.* single person or thing

team (tēm) *n.* group with a common goal

tradition (trə dish´ ən) *n.* custom, as of a group or culture, handed down

unify (yoo´ nə fī´) *v.* bring together as one

unique (yoo nēk´) *adj.* one-of-a-kind

Use these words as you complete Big Question activities in this unit that involve reading, writing, speaking, and listening.

Gather Vocabulary Knowledge Additional Big Question words are listed below. Categorize the words by deciding whether you know each one well, know it a little bit, or do not know it at all.

custom	family	group
ethnicity		

Then, do the following:

1. Discuss the meaning of each word with a partner. Then, verify each meaning using a dictionary.

2. Next, use each word in an original paragraph that gives examples of what community and individuality mean to you. Provide context clues for every vocabulary word you use.

3. Remember that context clues might be definitions, synonyms, antonyms, examples, or explanations.

4. Finally, take turns reading your paragraph with a partner. If, during the readings, the meaning of any Big Question word is still unclear, work with your partner to clarify it.

Introducing the Big Question **901**

❸ Learning Big Question Vocabulary

Acquire and Use Academic Vocabulary

1. Introduce the academic vocabulary words in the first word bank on the student page. Have students preview the words.

2. For each word, have students say the word aloud. Then, use the word in a sentence that defines the word.

Gather Vocabulary Knowledge

1. With the class, review the steps in the activity on the student page. Have students complete the activity independently, with partners, or in small groups.

2. Before students complete the last step, review the words and their meanings as a class. (Definitions appear below on the left.) Then, have students complete their paragraphs.

Show the Big Question video, online at **www.PHLitOnline.com.**

Gather Vocabulary Knowledge: Definitions

culture (kul´chər) *n.* customs of a group or community

custom (kus´təm) *n.* accepted practice

ethnicity (eth nis´ə tē) *n.* racial or cultural background

family (fam´ə lē) *n.* people related by blood

group (groop) *n.* collection or set

❶ Elements of Folk Literature

1. Introduce the form, folk literature, using the instruction on the student page.

2. Explain that even after writing was invented, many people could not read and write; instead, they composed and transmitted stories orally. Stress that folk literature is the product of this oral tradition. Its authors are usually not professional writers but anonymous, or unknown, people. Today, however, some professional writers retell folk literature or create stories modeled on those of folk literature.

3. Stress that folk literature reflects the cultural perspective of the storyteller and provides valuable information about his or her culture. **Ask:** Who might find this information especially valuable?

   Possible response: Historians, anthropologists, or people interested in their own cultural heritage might find it especially useful.

4. Note that in spite of being culturally specific, folk literature also expresses themes that are universal. Read aloud the example of a universal theme and mention one or two others, such as the need to respect nature or the conflict between generations.

5. Have students examine the chart showing characteristics of folk literature from around the world. **Ask:** Based on what you have learned, what other characteristics might you add to this chart?

   Possible responses: It was originally composed in the oral tradition; folk literature includes myths, legends, folk tales, and fables; it may simply aim to entertain.

❶ Elements of Folk Literature

Folk literature is a genre of writing that has its roots in the oral tradition.

The Oral Tradition Stories were told long before reading and writing began. These stories were handed down through the ages by word of mouth. The sharing of stories by word of mouth is called the **oral tradition.**

Folk literature is a genre of writing that originated in the oral tradition. Once writing and books were invented, the stories were collected and retold in print. Myths, legends, folk tales, and fables are all forms of folk literature.

The Importance of the Storyteller

Stories in the oral tradition were created thousands of years ago. No one knows for sure who the first storytellers were. As stories were passed down, new storytellers added and changed details. These details reflected the storyteller's roots and **cultural perspective,** or view of the world. That viewpoint was shaped by the storyteller's background and experiences.

Theme is the central idea, message, or insight about life that a story conveys.

Some works of folk literature have **universal themes**—themes that are repeated across many cultures and over many time periods. They express insights into life and human nature that many people understand and find important. The struggle of good against evil is an example of a universal theme.

Other works of folk literature—especially fables—present their theme in the form of a **moral.** A moral is a lesson about life that is stated directly, usually at the very end of the work.

Purposes of Folk Literature The **purpose** of a piece of literature is the reason it was written. The purpose of some forms of folk literature may be to explain or teach. For example, a myth may explain a natural phenomenon, and a fable may teach a lesson about life. Other types of folk literature may have the simple purpose of entertaining readers.

```
        ┌─────────────────────────────────────┐
        │  Folk Literature from Around the World │
        └─────────────────────────────────────┘
```

| May convey **universal themes** that people from many cultures and time periods understand. | Explores the **customs, values, and beliefs** of the culture in which the works were created. | May **teach** a lesson or **explain** something in nature. |

902 The Oral Tradition

❷ Forms of Folk Literature

Myths are tales that relate the actions of gods, goddesses, and the heroes who interact with them. Many cultures have their own collections of myths, or **mythology.**

Legends are traditional stories based on real-life events. As these stories are told and retold, fact often changes to fiction, and the characters often become larger than life.

Tall tales often focus on a central hero who performs impossible feats.

Folk tales may deal with real people or magical characters. They reflect the values and beliefs of the culture in which they were created.

Fables are brief stories or poems that often feature animal characters who act and speak like humans. They usually end with a moral that is directly stated.

Epics are long narrative poems important to the history of a nation or culture. They tell of a larger-than-life hero who goes on a dangerous journey, or **quest.**

❹ In This Section

Elements of Folk Literature

Determining Themes in Folk Literature

Examining Structure and Theme

Close Read: Story Development and Theme
• Model Text
• Practice Text

After You Read

 Common Core State Standards

RL.2
[For the full wording of the standards, see the standards chart in the front of your textbook.]

❸ Characteristics of Folk Literature

Here are some common characteristics you will see as you read folk literature.

Characteristic	Definition	Often Featured In...
Heroes and heroines	Larger-than-life figures who overcome obstacles or participate in exciting adventures	Myths Legends Epics
Quest	A journey filled with adventure that the hero or heroine goes on to achieve an important goal	Myths Legends Epics
Trickster	A clever character who can fool others but often gets into trouble	Folk tales Fables
Personification	A type of figurative language in which nonhuman subjects are given human qualities	Myths Fables
Hyperbole	A type of figurative language that uses exaggeration, either for comic effect or to express strong emotion	Tall tales Myths Epics
Dialect	Language spoken by people in a particular region or group	Tall tales Folk tales

Literary Analysis Workshop **903**

❷ Forms of Folk Literature

1. Introduce the forms, using the instruction on the student page.

2. Explore students' knowledge of folk literature by inviting them to name examples of the six forms.

3. **Sample response:** A famous legend tells of George Washington chopping down a cherry tree; some famous tall tales feature John Henry and Paul Bunyan.

❸ Characteristics of Folk Literature

1. Review the chart, pointing out that the first two rows list types of characters common in folk literature. **Ask:** Who are some folk heroes, heroines, or tricksters that you have read or heard about?

   Sample response: King Arthur of English legends; Coyote of Native American folk tales.

2. Clarify the pronunciation of hyperbole (hī pur′ bə lē). Provide these examples of the language uses defined in the last three rows of the chart:

   • Personification: *John Henry's hammer sang out.*

   • Hyperbole: *John Henry had the strength of twenty men.*

   • Dialect: *John Henry said, "Afore I let that steel drill whup me, I'd die with a hammah in my hand."*

❹ In This Section

Explain that in the remainder of this Literary Analysis Workshop, students will analyze an important element of folk literature, theme. After reviewing the concept, they will then see it applied in an analysis of a Model text. Finally, they will apply what they have learned to two Practice texts.

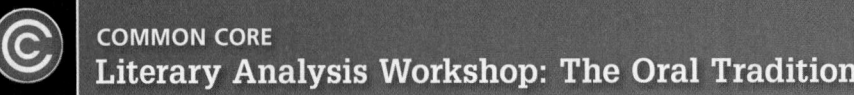

❶ Determining Themes in Folk Literature

1. Introduce the concept of theme, using the instruction on the student page.

2. Review the concept of stated themes, using the moral at the end of "The Lion and the Mouse" as an example. **Ask** how the events of the fable support its moral.

   Possible response: The mouse performs an act of kindness for the lion, and the lion later repays the mouse by showing it kindness.

3. Review with students the concept of an implied theme. Note that while fables often have a single stated theme or moral, "The Lion and the Mouse" also has an implied theme. **Ask:** What theme is implied by the fable's two contrasting characters?

   Possible response: The small and weak can sometimes help the big and strong.

4. Stress that universal themes arise from experiences and values that human beings share in many times and places: growing up, aging, quarreling, deciding whom to trust, and so on. Note that many universal themes are also expressed in proverbs, or wise, memorable sayings. **Ask:** Can you think of sayings that express ideas similar to the themes in the bulleted list?

   Possible response: "Beauty is only skin deep" expresses an idea similar to the second theme; "The grass is always greener on the other side" expresses an idea similar to the third.

❶ Determining Themes in Folk Literature

Folk literature expresses themes—insights about life and human nature.

Folk literature is rich with humor, adventure, romance, suspense, and drama. At the same time, it is the themes of these stories that have made them meaningful to readers of many generations and cultures.

Stated Themes Themes in folk literature take different forms. Sometimes, the theme is directly stated at the end of the story as a moral, or lesson. For example, look at the retelling of Aesop's fable, "The Lion and the Mouse."

> **Example: The Lion and the Mouse**
> A tiny mouse accidentally crossed paths with a ferocious lion. The lion was about to eat the mouse, when the mouse pleaded with the lion to let him go. "If you do, I promise to help you one day," the mouse said. The mighty lion doubted he would ever need the help of a tiny mouse, but he let the mouse go. One day, the lion became trapped in a hunter's net. The little mouse heard the lion's roars and came to his aid. In a few minutes, the mouse had gnawed his way through the net, setting the lion free.
>
> ***Moral:*** *One act of kindness often leads to another.*

Implied Themes As in other literary genres, themes in folk literature are sometimes implied, or suggested, rather than stated. Clues to these themes lie in the details that describe setting, characters, and plot. Stories with implied themes require the reader to analyze the details to see what they reveal about the deeper meaning of the story.

Universal Themes A universal theme is an insight or lesson that appears in literature across cultures and throughout different periods in history. These themes are "universal" because they express ideas that are meaningful to most people. Here are a few universal themes that are commonly found in folk literature. They reflect ideas that have been understood for many generations.

• Goodness is eventually rewarded.
• Inner beauty is more important than outward appearance.
• Those who always want more are never satisfied.
• Cleverness and courage can overcome brute strength.
• Those who plan carefully now can avoid problems in the future.

Vocabulary Development
CCSS Language 6

Expressions Based on Literary Allusions
Explain that some fables are so famous that allusions, or references, to them have become expressions. Give these examples and origins, and have students explain what each expression means.

1. She says she didn't want the prize she didn't win, but that's *sour grapes.* **Original Fable:** A fox longs to eat grapes it cannot reach and finally stops jumping for them, saying they were sour anyway.

2. Some forecasters *cry wolf* whenever there is a slim chance of rain. **Original Fable:** A bored shepherd boy keeps falsely crying out that a wolf is attacking the sheep, only to have his cries ignored when a wolf really attacks.

3. If I stop working nights, I'll *kill the goose that lays the golden egg.* **Original Fable:** A couple with a goose that lays a golden egg each day kill it to get at the gold they think is inside but find none there.

Possible response: 1–falsely pretending that something you cannot have is no good; 2–give a false alarm; 3–ruin something very profitable.

② Examining Structure and Theme

The **structural elements** of a work of folk literature contribute to its theme.

Folk literature of various types contains structural elements that contribute to the development of theme. As you read, look for these elements.

Repetition Folk literature often features the repetition of events, dialogue, descriptions, and sound patterns. Repetition adds rhythm to the text. It can also help build suspense and emphasize main ideas. For example, in the well-known tale of "The Three Little Pigs," the following lines of dialogue are repeated three times.

> **Example: Repetition**
>
> "Little pig, little pig, let me come in."
>
> "Not by the hair of my chinny chin chin."
>
> "Then I'll huff, and I'll puff, and I'll blow your house in."

Patterns Many works of folk literature share a common pattern, or repeated element. For example, many stories begin and end with such familiar phrases as "Once upon a time" and "They lived happily ever after." Another common structural element found in folk literature is the pattern of three. Many stories feature three important characters, three wishes, or three tasks.

Archetypes An archetype is an element that occurs regularly in literature from around the world and

throughout history. Oral storytellers have used archetypes to convey such universal themes as the power of love or the importance of bravery. Here are some common archetypes found in folk literature:

Plot	• a dangerous journey • a struggle between a good character and an evil one • an explanation of how something came to be
Characters	• a brave hero • trickster, or wise fool • talking animals
Ideas	• magic in the normal world • hero or heroine helped by supernatural forces • evil disguised as good

Flat Characters Folk literature often features characters who seem to have only one main trait, such as kindness, cruelty, wisdom, or foolishness. Such characters are **flat,** or one-sided. They are not like real people, who usually have many different sides to their personalities. Flat characters can help storytellers express important themes. For example, in "Snow White," the evil queen remains evil throughout the tale, while Snow White herself remains kind and good. Together, these opposing characters help develop the theme that kindness is stronger than cruelty.

Literary Analysis Workshop **905**

② **Examining Structure and Theme**

1. Introduce structure, using the instruction on the student page.

2. Discuss repetition. Underscore that repetition contributes to theme by emphasizing main ideas and key details. **Ask:** Why else might a work originating in the oral tradition use repetition?

   Answer: Repetition creates a rhythm that makes a story easier to remember and recite.

3. Discuss the patterns and archetypes found in folk literature. Have students identify examples of some of the archetypes listed on the chart.

   Sample responses: Stories about Snow White and Sleeping Beauty feature good and evil characters; Native American myths of Coyote and Southern folk tales of Brer Rabbit include tricksters and talking animals.

4. Stress that a flat character displays only one or two traits and does not change or grow. Have students think about characters they named to illustrate the archetypes on the chart. **Ask:** Which of these characters are flat, and what are their main traits?

   Sample responses: Snow White and Sleeping Beauty are beautiful and good; Coyote and Brer Rabbit are clever or tricky.

5. Remind students that in this Workshop they will read a model analysis of folk literature and then perform their own analyses.

COMMON CORE
Literary Analysis Workshop: The Oral Tradition

❸ Close Read: Story Development and Theme

1. Remind students that a work's theme is its message or insight about life.

2. Review the elements of story development defined in the chart. To illustrate how different elements work together to convey a theme, offer a plot in which a heroine on a quest for truth must overcome three obstacles as she crosses a dangerous landscape until she finally reaches a hidden mine and digs up the diamond that is Truth. Based on these story traits, the theme might be *Truth is difficult to find, but very valuable.*

3. Write this theme on the board: *Patience and persistence are eventually rewarded.* Have students work in groups to outline a tale that conveys this theme, supplying traits or elements from each of the chart's first four sections.

   Sample response: *Plot*—two animals hope to see inside a princess's tower; the dog tries to enter, to no avail, but the cat waits years for a tree to grow high enough so that she can climb up and enter from it; *Characters*—a foolish, hasty dog and a patient, persistent cat; *Repetition and Patterns*—the dog disguises himself three times but is always turned back at the tower gate; *Setting*—a high tower and its surrounding gardens

4. Refer students to the model text on page 907. Explain that details in the text that illustrate each category on the chart are highlighted in the same color and corresponding side-column annotations use corresponding colors.

---

❸ Close Read: Story Development and Theme

All types of folk literature share traits that contribute to story development and theme.

Folk tales, fables, legends, and myths have different elements that make them distinct. However, all folk literature shares certain qualities, or traits. As you read folk literature, notice details that help develop the story. Think about how the story's development helps express a theme.

Plot

Plot is the sequence of events in a story. In folk literature, the plot often has twists and turns. It frequently develops around one of these ideas:

- a journey, or quest, that includes a series of challenges or tests;
- the physical transformation of a character;
- a character who wears a disguise to hide his or her identity.

Repetition and Patterns

The use of repetition and patterns in folk literature helps unify a story, move it toward its end, and reveal the theme. As you read, look for

- the repetition of dialogue and descriptions;
- patterns of three;
- plot patterns, such as the breaking of a magic spell or a competition between two characters.

Characters

The characters in folk literature may have special skills or powers, or may display only one main trait. As you read, notice

- characters with exaggerated talents, magical abilities, or superhuman powers;
- animal characters with human traits;
- characters with one-sided personalities.

Setting

In folk literature, consider how certain common settings affect story development. These settings include

- challenging or threatening landscapes;
- severe or unexpected weather;
- supernatural worlds.

Theme

Theme is the central message of a story. As you read,

- look for a statement that expresses a moral;
- think about what lessons the characters learn or how a character changes or is transformed;
- notice how repetition and patterns work to keep the story moving toward its central message.

Vocabulary Development

© CCSS Language 6

Domain-Specific Words: Literature
Reinforce comprehension of the literary terms in parentheses by having students choose the term that best completes each statement.

1. The fable states its (moral, implied theme) at the end.
2. Since Pandora has just one main trait, curiosity, she is a (flat character, trickster).
3. The importance of bravery is (an archetype, a universal theme).
4. A fox disguising himself as a sheep in order to steal a lamb illustrates the (archetype, oral tradition) of evil disguised as good.
5. Pecos Bill, whose feats include riding a tornado and using a rattlesnake as a lasso, is a typical hero of a (tall tale, fable).
6. Saying the young African prince Sundiata pulled up a tree with his bare hands is an example of (personification, hyperbole).

Answers: 1–moral; 2–flat character; 3–universal theme; 4–archetype; 5–tall tale; 6–hyperbole

❹ Model

About the Text Aesop's fables have been enjoyed for centuries, but the fact is that no one knows for sure who composed these stories. According to traditional belief, Aesop was a Greek slave who lived during the sixth century B.C. However, some scholars doubt his existence.

"The Travelers and the Bear"
from *Aesop's Fables*
retold by Jerry Pinkney

❺ Two men were traveling through the forest together on a lonely trail. Soon they heard a sound up ahead as if heavy feet were trampling through the underbrush.

"It could be a bear!" one whispered with alarm, and quickly as he could, he scrambled up a tall tree. He had barely reached the first branch when a huge brown bear thrust aside the bushes and stepped out onto the path.

Hugging the trunk with both arms, the first traveler refused to lend a hand to his terrified companion, who threw himself on the ground and prepared for death. ❻

The bear lowered its great head and sniffed at the man, ruffling his hair with its nose. Then, to the amazement of both men, the fierce beast walked away.

❼ The first traveler slid down from his tree. "Why, it almost looked as if the bear whispered something in your ear," he marveled.

"It did," said the second traveler. "It told me to choose a better companion for my next journey."

Misfortune is the true test of friendship.

---

❺ **Setting** The forest is a typical threatening setting in folk literature. The words *lonely* and *heavy* suggest that the travelers may encounter something dangerous.

❻ **Plot** Surprising events, such as the departure of the bear, are a common element of story development in folk literature.

❼ **Theme** A combination of details—the threat of the bear, the refusal of the first traveler to help his companion, and the bear's advice—develop the story and reveal the theme. As in many fables, the theme is stated directly as a moral at the end of the story.

❹ Model

1. Discuss the About the Text note. Explain that there are many legends about Aesop's identity. Often he is portrayed as a slave who won his freedom and became the adviser or storyteller to a king.

2. Have students read the fable. Discuss it, clarifying as needed, before reviewing the annotations.

❺ Setting

Read aloud the Setting annotation and the highlighted text. **Ask:** In what other fables or tales is the forest a dangerous place?

Sample response: "Little Red Riding-Hood," "Hansel and Gretel"

❻ Plot

Read aloud the Plot annotation. Explain that dangerous events are also common in folk literature. **Ask:** What dangerous event occurs in this fable?

Possible response: A bear appears out of nowhere.

❼ Theme

1. **Ask:** What main traits does the man who climbs the tree display?

   Possible response: He displays cowardice and disloyalty.

2. Read aloud the highlighted moral and the Theme annotation. Have a student explain how the fable's details lead to its moral.

   Possible response: It shows a cowardly man not coming to the aid of his friend and thereby failing the test of friendship.

Literary Analysis Workshop **907**

1. Explain to students that they will examine structural elements for help in determining the theme of the Independent Practice selections.

2. Discuss the About the Selections note, and have students read the selections. Then, direct them to go back through and respond to the side-column prompts. Conclude by having students answer the After You Read questions on page 911.

9 Character

1. Have students examine the first highlighted passage. **Ask:** Are the characters of Grasshopper and his mom well developed?

   Answer: No, they are not.

2. **Ask** the Character question.

   Answer: The characters are flat.

10 Plot

Ask the Plot question.

Possible response: It is similar because the challenge seems nearly impossible; it is different because homework is rarely a challenge in folk literature.

11 Theme

1. Read the highlighted moral. **Ask** the Theme question.

   Possible responses: He procrastinates. He calls his enormous project "one small thing."

2. Explain that one of Aesop's tales features a grasshopper who idles the summer away and then has no food for winter. The moral of that fable is *Do not procrastinate.* **Ask:** Is that also the moral of this tale?

   Possible response: No, this story's theme focuses on the different concerns of parents and children. Grasshopper does not seem to have learned a lesson.

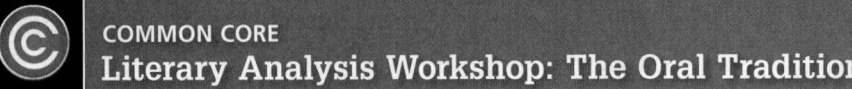

8 Independent Practice

About the Selections The following stories by author Jon Scieszka are twisted versions of traditional folk literature. Even though Scieszka tells these stories in a humorous way, the stories still contain many of the common traits found in traditional folk literature.

"Grasshopper Logic" from *Squids Will Be Squids* by Jon Scieszka and Lane Smith

9 **Character** What common characteristic of fables describes the characters of Grasshopper and his mom?

9 One bright and sunny day, Grasshopper came home from school, dropped his backpack, and was just about to run outside to meet his friends.

"Where are you going?" asked his mom.

"Out to meet some friends," said Grasshopper.

"Do you have any homework due tomorrow?" asked his mom.

"Just one small thing for History. I did the rest in class."

"Okay" said Mom Grasshopper. "Be back at six for dinner."

Grasshopper hung out with his friends, came home promptly at six, ate his dinner, then took out his History homework.

His mom read the assignment and freaked out.

10 **Plot** How does Grasshopper's assignment compare to the challenges that are often featured in folk literature?

10 "Rewrite twelve Greek myths as Broadway musicals. Write music for songs. Design and build all sets. Sew original costumes for each production."

"How long have you known about this assignment?" asked Mom Grasshopper, trying not to scream.

"I don't know," said Grasshopper.

11 **Theme** How does Grasshopper's behavior in the fable contribute to the idea expressed in the moral?

11 **Moral**
There are plenty of things to say to calm a hopping mad grasshopper mom. "I don't know" is not one.

---

908 The Oral Tradition

Vocabulary Development

Vocabulary Knowledge Rating

Create a **Vocabulary Knowledge Rating Chart** (*Professional Development Guidebook,* p. 33) with these words from the selections:

   promptly   pathetic   spell   bragged

Give students a copy. Read the words aloud. Have students mark their rating in the Before Reading column. Urge them to be alert to these words as they read and discuss the selections because they will rate their knowledge of the words again after they finish.

To gauge how much instruction to provide, tally how many students think they know a word. As students read, point out the words and their context.

"The Other Frog Prince" from *The Stinky Cheese Man and Other Fairly Stupid Tales* by Jon Scieszka and Lane Smith

⑫ Once upon a time there was a frog. One day when he was sitting on his lily pad, he saw a beautiful princess sitting by the pond. He hopped in the water, swam over to her, and poked his head out of the weeds.

"Pardon me, O beautiful princess," he said in his most sad and pathetic voice. "I wonder if you could help me."

The princess was about to jump up and run, but she felt sorry for the frog with the sad and pathetic voice.

So she asked, "What can I do to help you, little frog?"

⑬ "Well," said the frog. "I'm not really a frog, but a handsome prince who was turned into a frog by a wicked witch's spell. And the spell can only be broken by the kiss of a beautiful princess."

The princess thought about this for a second, then lifted the frog from the pond and kissed him.

⑭ "I was just kidding," said the frog. He jumped back into the pond and the princess wiped the frog slime off her lips.

The End.

---

⑫ Patterns What does the familiar opening suggest about how the plot will unfold?

⑬ Plot What does the author want readers to believe will happen next in the story? What elements of folk literature does the author use to make readers believe this?

⑭ Theme This outcome puts a humorous twist on this famous fairy tale. Based on the outcome, how would you state the story's theme?

---

⑫ Patterns

1. Read aloud the highlighted sentence. **Ask** the Patterns question.

   Possible response: It suggests that the plot will be that of a typical folk tale.

2. **Ask:** How does the title of the fable counteract the effect of the opening sentence?

   Possible response: It suggests that the story will be different from the typical tale of the frog prince.

⑬ Plot

Have a volunteer read aloud the highlighted text. Then, **ask** the Plot questions.

Possible responses: The princess will kiss the frog and break the spell, turning him back into a handsome prince. Elements include the wicked witch, magic spell, handsome prince, transformation, and talking animal.

⑭ Theme

1. Have a student read aloud the last highlighted passage. **Ask:** How did you react to the frog's final words?

   Sample responses: I was not surprised; I found it funny but was also a little disgusted by the slime.

2. **Ask** the Theme question.

   Possible responses: The romance and magic of fairy tales are not realistic. Sometimes a frog is just a frog.

Differentiated Instruction   for Universal Access

Support for Special-Needs Students
Have students read the adapted version of these selections in the *Reader's Notebook: Adapted Version.* They may also listen to the adapted version on the *Hear It!* **Audio CD** (adapted text). Then, have them complete the questions and activities in the Student Edition.

Support for Less Proficient Readers
Have students read these selections in the *Reader's Notebook.* After students finish the selections in the *Reader's Notebook,* have them complete the questions and activities in the Student Edition.

EL Support for English Learners
Have students read the adapted version of these selections in the *Reader's Notebook: English Learner's Version.* English learners may also read the selections as they listen to the recorded version on the *Hear It!* **Audio CD.** Then, have them complete the questions and activities in the Student Edition.

PHLit Online!

Enriched Online Student Edition
To have students read the selection in interactive format, with narration and point-of-use interactive graphic organizers, go online at **www.PHLitOnline.com.**

15 Character

1. Have a student read aloud the highlighted passage. **Ask:** In creating the character of BeefSnakStik®, what aspect of modern life are the authors poking fun at?

   Possible response: They are poking fun at junk food and its ingredients.

2. **Ask:** Why do you think the authors include the registered trademark symbol in one character's name?

   Possible response: It adds to the humor because it is so unusual in a story; it also stresses the commercial nature of the product.

3. **Ask** the Character question.

   Possible response: They are flat characters, they boast, and they are talking nonhumans. Instead of a talking animal, though, BeefSnakStik® is a talking snack food.

16 Theme

1. Have a student read the moral aloud. **Ask** the Theme question.

   Possible response: Duckbilled Platypus brags about all his unusual natural characteristics; BeefSnakStik® counters with mostly artificial ingredients that seem even more unusual.

2. **Ask:** Besides the stated moral, what additional themes does this modern fable conveys?

   Possible response: Ingredients in some processed foods are very strange. Artificial ingredients are replacing natural ingredients to an alarming degree.

Practice continued

15

Character How are Duckbilled Platypus and BeefSnakStik® similar to and different from the characters that typically appear in fables?

16

Theme What details in the story contribute to the development of the idea expressed in the moral?

"Duckbilled Platypus vs. BeefSnakStik®" *from Squids Will Be Squids* **by Jon Scieszka and Lane Smith**

"I have a bill like a duck and a tail like a beaver," bragged Duckbilled Platypus.

15

"So what?" said BeefSnakStik®. "I have beef, soy protein concentrate, and dextrose."

"I also have webbed feet and fur," said Duckbilled Platypus.

"Who cares?" said BeefSnakStik®. "I also have smoke flavoring, sodium erythorbate, and sodium nitrite."

16

"I am one of only two mammals in the world that lay eggs," said Duckbilled Platypus.

"Big deal," said BeefSnakStik®. "I have beef lips."

Moral

Just because you have a lot of stuff, don't think you're so special.

Vocabulary Development

Vocabulary Knowledge Rating

When students have completed reading and discussing these selections, have them take out their **Vocabulary Knowledge Rating Chart** for these selections. Read the words aloud once more and have students rate their knowledge of the words again in the After Reading column. Clarify any words that are still problematic. Have students write their own definitions or examples in the appropriate column. Encourage students to use the words in further discussion and written work about these selections.

After You Read

from the Works of Jon Scieszka and Lane Smith

1. **Key Ideas and Details** (a) **Summarize:** Summarize the plot of each story, making sure not to include your own opinions or judgments. (b) **Analyze:** Which of the stories has a surprise ending?

2. **Key Ideas and Details** (a) **Infer:** Why does Grasshopper call his History assignment "small." (b) **Generalize:** What makes the details of the assignment so funny?

3. **Key Ideas and Details** (a) **Describe:** What tone of voice does the frog use with the princess? (b) **Compare:** Does the frog have the same attitude or tone of voice as BeefSnakStik®? Explain. (c) **Interpret:** What makes these characters funny?

4. **Key Ideas and Details** (a) **Describe:** What is the argument between Duckbilled Platypus and BeefSnakStik® about? (b) **Draw Conclusions:** Why is neither one of these characters likely to win this argument?

5. **Key Ideas and Details** (a) **Analyze:** What makes the moral or lesson of each tale funny? Cite details in support of your answer. (b) **Evaluate:** In your opinion, which story is the funniest, and why?

6. **Craft and Structure** (a) **Interpret:** Explain the attitude toward life and literature that the fables reflect. (b) **Apply:** Is one type of reader likelier than other types to appreciate this attitude? Explain.

7. **Integration of Knowledge and Ideas** (a) **Compare:** Compare the style of Scieszka's fables with the style of a traditional fable with which you are familiar. (b) **Evaluate:** Which type of fable do you prefer? Explain.

8. **Craft and Structure** (a) In a chart like the one shown, list examples of hyperbole and personification in each story.

Fable/Fairy Tale	Hyperbole	Personification
Grasshopper Logic		
The Other Frog Prince		
Duckbilled Platypus vs. BeefSnakStik®		

(b) **Collaborate:** Discuss your chart with a classmate. Explain how your understanding of each fable has grown.

Literary Analysis Workshop **911**

911

✓ **Icarus and Daedalus •**
✓✓ **Demeter and Persephone**
Lesson Pacing Guide

DAY 1 Preteach

- Ⓒ Administer the Reading and Vocabulary Warm-ups (*Unit 6 Resources,* pp. 23–26 or 41–44) as necessary.
- Introduce the Reading Skill: Cause and Effect.
- Ⓒ Introduce the Literary Analysis concept: Myth.
- Distribute copies of the appropriate graphic organizer for the Reading Skill (*Graphic Organizer Transparencies,* pp. 171–173).
- Distribute copies of the appropriate graphic organizer for Literary Analysis (*Graphic Organizer Transparencies,* pp. 174–176).
- Ⓒ Teach the selection vocabulary.
- Ⓒ Introduce the Word Study skill.

DAYS 2–3 Preteach/Teach

- Ⓒ Build background with the Background feature.
- Develop thematic vocabulary and thematic thinking with Writing About the Big Question.
- Prepare students to read with the Activating Prior Knowledge or Focusing Reading activities (TE).
- Informally monitor comprehension while students read.
- Use the Reading Check questions to confirm comprehension.
- Develop students' ability to identify the connections between the cause and effect in the passage using the Cause-and-Effect questions.
- Ⓒ Develop students' understanding of myth using the Myth questions.
- Ⓒ Reinforce vocabulary with the Vocabulary notes.
- Ⓒ Reinforce unit focus standards using the Spiral Review prompts.

DAY 4 Assess

- Assess students' comprehension and mastery of the skills by having them answer the Critical Thinking, Reading Skill, and Literary Analysis questions.
- Ⓒ Have students complete the Vocabulary Practice activities.
- Ⓒ Have students complete the Word Study activities.

DAY 5 Extend/Assess

- Have students complete the Conventions lesson.
- Ⓒ Have students complete the Writing activity and write a myth. (You may assign as homework.)
- Ⓒ Extend learning by having students complete the Speaking and Listening, a debate activity. As an alternative, assign them "The Great Dress Debate" or "Commanding the Weather" in *Reality Central.*
- Administer Selection Test A or B (*Unit 6 Resources,* pp. 35–40 or 56–61).

Ⓒ Common Core State Standards

Reading Literature 2. Determine a theme or central idea of a text and analyze its development over the course of the text; provide an objective summary of the text.

Writing 3. Write narratives to develop real or imagined experiences or events using effective technique, relevant descriptive details, and well-structured event sequences.
3.a. Engage and orient the reader by establishing a context and point of view and introducing a narrator and/or characters; organize an event sequence that unfolds naturally and logically.
3.b. Use narrative techniques, such as dialogue, pacing, and description, to develop experiences, events, and/or characters.

Speaking and Listening 1.a. Come to discussions prepared, having read or researched material under study; explicitly draw on that preparation by referring to evidence on the topic, text, or issue to probe and reflect on ideas under discussion.
1.c. Pose questions that elicit elaboration and respond to others' questions and comments with relevant observations and ideas that bring the discussion back on topic as needed. *(Speaking and Listening: Debate)*

Language 2. Demonstrate command of the conventions of standard English capitalization, punctuation, and spelling when writing.
4.b. Use common grade-appropriate Greek or Latin affixes and roots as clues to the meaning of a word.

Additional Standards Practice
Common Core Companion, pp. 15–22

Daily Block Scheduling
Each day in this Lesson Pacing Guide represents a 40–50 minute period. Teachers using block scheduling may combine days to revise pacing. In addition, teachers may differentiate and support core instruction by integrating components for extended and intensive support, as students require. See the Guide to Selected Leveled Resources (facing page).

Guide to Selected Leveled Resources

RTI Tier 1 (students performing on level)

			✓ More Accessible **Icarus and Daedalus**	✓✓ More Complex **Demeter and Persephone**
Warm Up		**Practice, model,** and **monitor** fluency, working with the **whole class** or **in groups.**	Vocabulary and Reading Warm-ups B, *Unit 6 Resources,* pp. 23–24, 26	Vocabulary and Reading Warm-ups B, *Unit 6 Resources,* pp. 41–42, 44
Comprehension/Skills		**Support** and **monitor** comprehension and skills development, having students complete the activities, graphic organizers, and interactive prompts **independently** or **as a class.**	• *Reader's Notebook,* adapted instruction and full selection **EL** *Reader's Notebook: English Learner's Version,* adapted instruction and adapted selection • **Reading Skill Graphic Organizer B,** *Graphic Organizer Transparencies,* p. 173 • **Literary Analysis Graphic Organizer B,** *Graphic Organizer Transparencies,* p. 176	• *Reader's Notebook,* adapted instruction and summary **EL** *Reader's Notebook: English Learner's Version,* adapted instruction and summary • **Reading Skill Graphic Organizer B,** *Graphic Organizer Transparencies,* p. 173 • **Literary Analysis Graphic Organizer B,** *Graphic Organizer Transparencies,* p. 176
Monitor Progress	A	**Monitor** student progress with the differentiated curriculum-based assessment in the *Unit Resources.*	• **Selection Test B,** *Unit 6 Resources,* pp. 38–40 • **Open-Book Test,** *Unit 6 Resources,* pp. 32–34	• **Selection Test B,** *Unit 6 Resources,* pp. 59–61 • **Open-Book Test,** *Unit 6 Resources,* pp. 53–55

RTI Tier 2 (students requiring intervention)

			✓ More Accessible **Icarus and Daedalus**	✓✓ More Complex **Demeter and Persephone**
Warm Up		**Practice, model,** and **monitor** fluency in **groups** or **with individuals.**	• *Vocabulary and Reading Warm-ups A,* Unit 6 Resources, pp. 23–25 • *Reality Central,* "The Great Dress Debate" • *Hear It!* Audio CD (adapted text)	• *Vocabulary and Reading Warm-ups A,* Unit 6 Resources, pp. 41–43 • *Reality Central,* "Commanding the Weather" • *Hear It!* Audio CD
Comprehension/Skills		• **Support** and **monitor** comprehension and skills development, working **in small groups** or **with individuals.** • **Pair** students with more advanced peers and have them complete the writing activity in the *Real World Writing Journal.* • As students complete the selection in the appropriate version of the *Reader's Notebook,* **monitor** comprehension frequently with group questions and individual instruction. • **Model** strategies while guiding students in completing the activities and prompts in the *Reader's Notebook,* as well as the graphic organizers. • **Practice** skills and **monitor** mastery with the *Reading Kit* worksheets.	• *Real-World Writing Journal,* Lesson 1, pp. 156–159 • *Reader's Notebook: Adapted Version,* adapted instruction and adapted selection **EL** *Reader's Notebook: English Learner's Version,* adapted instruction and adapted selection • **Reading Skill Graphic Organizer A,** *Graphic Organizer Transparencies,* p. 171 • **Literary Analysis Graphic Organizer A,** *Graphic Organizer Transparencies,* p. 174 • *Reading Kit,* Practice worksheets, pp. 244, 248, 254, 256, 262	• *Real-World Writing Journal,* Lesson 2, pp. 160–163 • *Reader's Notebook: Adapted Version,* adapted instruction and summary **EL** *Reader's Notebook: English Learner's Version,* adapted instruction and summary • **Reading Skill Graphic Organizer A,** *Graphic Organizer Transparencies,* p. 172 • **Literary Analysis Graphic Organizer A,** *Graphic Organizer Transparencies,* p. 175 • *Reading Kit,* Practice worksheets, pp. 244, 248, 254, 256, 262
Monitor Progress	A	**Monitor** student progress with the differentiated curriculum-based assessment in the *Unit Resources* and in the *Reading Kit.*	• **Selection Test A,** *Unit 6 Resources,* pp. 35–37 • *Reading Kit,* Assess worksheets, pp. 245, 249, 255, 257, 263	• **Selection Test A,** *Unit 6 Resources,* pp. 56–58 • *Reading Kit,* Assess worksheets, pp. 245, 249, 255, 257, 263

TIER 3 Tier 3 intervention may require consultation with the student's special-education or dyslexia specialist. For additional support, see the Tier 2 activities and resources listed above.

One-on-one teaching   Group work   Whole class instruction   Independent work   A Assessment

For a complete guide to selection support, including support for Advanced students, see the Overview of Resources in the frontmatter.

6 Cause and Effect

1. Have students reread the bracketed passage, which begins on p. 916.

2. **Ask:** What has happened to Daedalus?
   Answer: He has been imprisoned by the king.

3. **Ask** the Cause and Effect question.
   Answer: Daedalus wants to escape from the island, and he has been watching the sea-gulls. He sees that flying is the only way to escape.

▶ **Monitor Progress:** Review students' graphic organizers to check their understanding of cause-and-effect relationships.

▶ **Reteach:** If students are having difficulty analyzing cause-and-effect relationships, show them the partially completed **Reading Skill Graphic Organizer A** (*Graphic Organizer Transparencies* p. 171) to help them clear up misconceptions and correct their work.

7 Myth

1. Ask a volunteer to read aloud the second bracketed passage. **Ask** students what Daedalus taught his son to do.
   Answer: Daedalus taught Icarus to fly.

2. Point out that Daedalus also tried to teach Icarus a lesson. Then, **ask** the Myth question.
   Answer: Daedalus tried to teach Icarus to be cautious when flying.

3. **Ask** students to speculate what lesson the myth will teach.
   Possible responses: The myth may teach a lesson about moderation or about the dangers of being overconfident.

© **Spiral Review**

Theme

1. Remind students that they studied the concept of theme in the Unit 6 Literary Analysis Workshop (pp. 902–911).

2. **Ask** the Spiral Review question.

   Possible response: The universal theme is that children should listen to their parents.

Cause and Effect
Why does Daedalus make wings out of feathers? ⑥

Myth
What lesson does Daedalus try to teach Icarus? ⑦

© **Spiral Review**
Theme What universal theme involving parents and their children is hinted at in the paragraph beginning, "For Icarus, these cautions…"?

Vocabulary

aloft (ə lôft′) *adv.* high up; flying; in the air

vacancy (vā′ kən sē) *n.* emptiness; unoccupied position

reel (rēl) *v.* spin; whirl

sustained (sə stānd′) *adj.* supported

captivity (kap tiv′ i tē) ⑧ *n.* imprisonment

---

by waving his arms he could winnow[5] the air and cleave it, as a swimmer does the sea. He held himself **aloft**, wavered this way and that with the wind, and at last, like a great fledgling,[6] he learned to fly.

Without delay, he fell to work on a pair of wings for the boy Icarus, and taught him carefully how to use them, bidding him beware of rash adventures among the stars. "Remember," said the father, "never to fly very low or very high, for the fogs about the earth would weigh you down, but the blaze of the sun will surely melt your feathers apart if you go too near."

For Icarus, these cautions went in at one ear and out by the other. Who could remember to be careful when he was to fly for the first time? Are birds careful? Not they! And not an idea remained in the boy's head but the one joy of escape.

The day came, and the fair wind that was to set them free. The father bird put on his wings, and, while the light urged them to be gone, he waited to see that all was well with Icarus, for the two could not fly hand in hand. Up they rose, the boy after his father. The hateful ground of Crete sank beneath them; and the country folk, who caught a glimpse of them when they were high above the treetops, took it for a vision of the gods—Apollo,[7] perhaps, with Cupid[8] after him.

At first there was a terror in the joy. The wide **vacancy** of the air dazed them—a glance downward made their brains **reel**.

But when a great wind filled their wings, and Icarus felt himself **sustained**, like a halcyon bird[9] in the hollow of a wave, like a child uplifted by his mother, he forgot everything in the world but joy. He forgot Crete and the other islands that he had passed over: he saw but vaguely that wingèd thing in the distance before him that was his father Daedalus. He longed for one draft of flight to quench the thirst of his **captivity**: he stretched out his arms to the sky and made towards the highest heavens.

Alas for him! Warmer and warmer grew the air. Those arms, that had seemed to uphold him, relaxed. His wings wavered, drooped. He fluttered his young hands vainly—he was falling—and in that terror he remembered. The heat of the sun

---

5. **winnow** (win′ ō) *v.* beat, as with wings.
6. **fledgling** (flej′ liŋ) *n.* young bird.
7. **Apollo** (ə päl′ ō) *n.* the Greek god of music, poetry, and medicine; identified with the sun.
8. **Cupid** (kyōō′ pid) *n.* in Roman mythology, the god of love, son of Venus.
9. **halcyon** (hal′ sē ən) **bird** *n.* legendary sea bird, which the ancient Greeks believed could calm the sea by resting on it.

Vocabulary Development

Vocabulary Knowledge Rating
When students have completed reading and discussing "Icarus and Daedalus," have them take out their **Vocabulary Knowledge Rating Chart.** Read the words aloud once more and have students rate their knowledge of the words again in the After Reading column. Clarify any words that are still problematic. Have students write their own definition and example or sentence in the appropriate column. Then, have students complete the Vocabulary Practice activities at the end of the selection. Encourage students to use the words in further discussion and written work about this selection. Remind them that they will be accountable for these words on the **Selection Test,** *Unit 6 Resources*, pp. 35–37 or 38–40.

He fluttered
his young
hands vainly—
he was falling...

Connecting to the Big Question

1. Have students read the third bracketed passage on page 918, beginning "But when a great wind . . ." **Ask** students: How does Icarus feel in this moment? How do these emotions keep him from hearing his father?
Possible response: Icarus feels overwhelming joy to be flying. He is so distracted by his joy that he forgets all his father's warnings about flying.

2. **Ask:** Do you understand why Icarus ignores his father? Explain. How will Icarus' individual action likely affect the community that he and his father form in this moment?
Possible response: It's understandable that Icarus is amazed and distracted by the joy of flying. Still, given the warnings he has received, it's likely that both he and his father are going to suffer because of that distraction.

Concept Connector

Vocab-o-Gram
Have students return to their **Vocab-o-Gram** charts and re-examine the ideas that they recorded. Then, lead a class discussion, probing for what students have learned that confirms or invalidates their predictions about the story.

Writing About the Big Question
Have students compare their response to the sentence starter they completed before reading the selection with their ideas afterward. Ask them to explain whether their thoughts have changed.

Reading Skill Graphic Organizer
Ask students to review the graphic organizers they completed to analyze cause-and-effect relationships while reading. Then, have students share their graphic organizers.

Have students read silently the bracketed passage which begins on p. 918. Then, **ask** the Cause and Effect question.
Answer: The sun melts the wax from Icarus' wings.

ASSESS
Answers

Critical Thinking

Before students respond, you may wish to have them write a brief objective summary of the selection. As they answer the questions below, remind them to support their answers with evidence from the text.

1. (a) He is in a tower prison on an island. (b) He designs the Labyrinth and makes wings.

2. (a) Icarus is Daedalus's son. (b) Daedalus reveals his cautious nature and his love for his son.

3. (a) Do not fly too high, near the sun, or too low, near the water. (b) **Possible response:** Icarus is irresponsible. To him, having fun is more important than safety.

4. (a) Icarus feels joyful forgetfulness, like a bird or a child. Daedalus is concerned about the mechanics of flying. (b) The difference reveals that Icarus is young and immature, and Daedalus is mature, scientific, and disciplined.

5. (a) **Possible responses:** Many students may say that Daedalus is not responsible because he warned Icarus. Some students may think that Daedalus should have been firmer with his son. (b) Students should share and discuss their responses, noting how their ideas have changed.

6. **Possible responses:** (a) He is enjoying flying high. (b) He drowns. (c) Often, others are hurt when an individual puts his or her own desires before everything else. Sometimes, as in this case, the individual is also hurt.

---

had melted the wax from his wings; the feathers were falling, one by one, like snowflakes; and there was none to help.

He fell like a leaf tossed down the wind, down, down, with one cry that overtook Daedalus far away. When he returned, and sought high and low for his poor boy, he saw nothing but the birdlike feathers afloat on the water, and he knew that Icarus was drowned.

The nearest island he named Icaria, in memory of the child; but he, in heavy grief, went to the temple of Apollo in Sicily, and there hung up his wings as an offering. Never again did he attempt to fly.

Critical Thinking

Cite textual evidence to support your responses.

© 1. **Key Ideas and Details** (a) Where is Daedalus when the story begins? (b) **Analyze:** In what ways does Daedalus show how clever he is?

© 2. **Key Ideas and Details** (a) Who is Icarus? (b) **Infer:** What does Daedalus reveal about himself through his words to Icarus?

© 3. **Key Ideas and Details** (a) Summarize the warning Daedalus gives Icarus. (b) **Infer:** What do Icarus's actions reveal about his character?

© 4. **Key Ideas and Details** (a) **Compare and Contrast:** Compare and contrast Icarus's experience of flying with Daedalus's experience. (b) **Evaluate:** What does this difference reveal about their characters? Explain.

© 5. **Integration of Knowledge and Ideas** (a) **Take a Position:** Does Daedalus share any responsibility for Icarus's fall? Why or why not? (b) **Discuss:** Share your answer with a classmate. How has your answer grown or changed?

© 6. **Integration of Knowledge and Ideas** (a) Why does Icarus ignore his father's advice? (b) What is the result of Icarus's actions? (c) What happens when an individual puts his or her own desires before everything else? *[Connect to the Big Question: Community or individual—which is more important?]*

920 Themes in the Oral Tradition

Assessment Resources

Unit 6 Resources

L1 L2 EL **Selection Test A,** pp. 35–37. Administer Test A to less advanced students.

L3 L4 EL **Selection Test B,** pp. 38–40. Administer Test B to on-level and more advanced students.

L3 L4 **Open-Book Test,** pp. 32–34. As an alternative, give the Open-Book Test.

All **Customizable Test Bank**

All **Self-tests**
Students may prepare for the **Selection Test** by taking the **Self-test** online.

All assessment resources are available at **www.PHLitOnline.com.**

Icarus and Daedalus

Reading Skill: Cause and Effect

1. Answer these questions to analyze **cause-and-effect** relationships in the myth:

    (a) What happens to Icarus at the end of the myth? Why?

    (b) What happens to Daedalus? Why?

2. What effect does the sun have in the myth?

Literary Analysis: Myth

3. **Key Ideas and Details** What superhuman qualities does Daedalus possess?

4. **Craft and Structure** Complete a chart like the one shown to describe the lessons the **myth** teaches through each character.

Character	Lesson	How Taught
Icarus		
Daedalus		

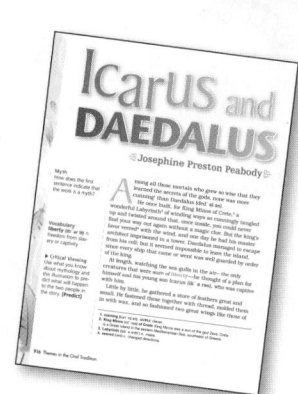

Vocabulary

Acquisition and Use For each item, write a single sentence using the words indicated.

1. vacancy; hole
2. sustained; noise
3. liberty; prisoner
4. aloft; eagle
5. reel; boxer
6. captivity; animals

Word Study Use context and what you know about the **Latin root -vac-** to explain your answer to each question.

1. Is it wise to *evacuate* a town if a powerful hurricane is approaching?
2. If you *vacate* your house, do you stay at home?

Word Study

The **Latin root -vac-** means "empty."

Apply It Explain how the root -vac- contributes to the meanings of these words. Consult a dictionary if necessary.

vacation

vacuous

vacuum

Icarus and Daedalus **921**

Reading Skill

1. (a) Icarus drowns because he has flown too close to the sun and melted his wings. (b) Daedalus hangs up his wings because he is grief-stricken that his son Icarus was killed while flying.

2. **Possible response:** The sun has a deadly effect. Icarus dies because the sun melts his wings.

Literary Analysis

3. Daedalus knows the secrets of the gods—especially those related to building and design.

4. **Possible response:** Icarus's Lesson—take warnings of danger seriously; How Taught—through Icarus's death; Daedalus's Lesson—it's dangerous to outwit fate using the secrets of the gods; How Taught—through Icarus's death.

    For other sample answers, see *Graphic Organizer Transparencies,* **Literary Analysis Graphic Organizer A,** p. 174, and the **Additional Answers** section.

Vocabulary
Acquisition and Use
Sample answers:

1. The <u>vacancy</u> in Abby's gaze revealed a <u>hole</u> in her understanding.

2. The <u>sustained</u> <u>noise</u> of the drill hurt my ears as it went on and on.

3. A <u>prisoner</u> has no <u>liberty</u> to move or travel.

4. An <u>eagle</u> has giant wings to keep it <u>aloft</u>.

5. The <u>boxer</u> began to <u>reel</u> after being hit over and over.

6. In a zoo, <u>animals</u> are kept in <u>captivity</u>.

Word Study
Sample answers:

1. Yes; The root -vac- means "empty." It would be wise to *evacuate* a town, or make it <u>empty</u>, before a hurricane.

2. No; The root -vac- means "empty." When you *vacate* your home, you leave it <u>empty</u>.

Word Study: Apply It

Sample answers: A *vacation* is <u>empty</u> of work or responsibility. Someone who is *vacuous* is <u>empty</u> of serious ideas or intelligence. A *vacuum* is a space completely <u>empty</u> of air and matter.

Skills instruction for the Reading Skill and Literary Analysis concepts for this selection appears on p. 913.

❶ Writing About the Big Question

1. Review the assignment with the class.

2. Ask students to imagine they are putting on a play in a public space. Brainstorm with them for the kinds of decisions they would have to make. Discuss problems that could occur if decisions are not carefully made.

3. Have students complete the sentence starter. Review responses as a class. (**Sample response:** When making a decision that will affect the greater <u>community</u>, a person is responsible for everyone's safety.)

4. Remind students that their answers will help them think about the Big Question, "Community or individual— which is more important?"

While You Read

Tell students that as they read, they should consider how others suffer to satisfy the desires of Pluto and Demeter.

❷ Vocabulary

1. Have students preview the selection vocabulary.

2. For each word, have students say the word aloud.

3. Then, use the word in a sentence that defines the word.

4. Finally, repeat your definitional sentence or a similar sentence with the word missing and have the class "fill in the blank" chorally. Here is an example:

> *When someone <u>defies</u> an order, he or she disobeys it. If your sister stays out past her curfew, we can say that she* [students say "defies"] *it.*

❸ Word Study

1. Introduce the skill, using the instruction in the box.

2. Tell students that a *domicile* is a building in which people live. Ask them to name several kinds of *domiciles* (houses, apartments, etc.)

| Making Connections | Demeter and Persephone |

❶ Writing About the Big Question

In "Demeter and Persephone," the characters of Demeter and Pluto indulge their own desires at the expense of others. Use this sentence starter to develop your ideas about the Big Question.

> When making a decision that will affect the greater **community,** a person is responsible for _____.

While You Read Consider how others suffer to satisfy the desires of Pluto and Demeter.

❷ Vocabulary

Read each word and its definition. Decide whether you know the word well, know it a little bit, or do not know it at all. After you read, see how your knowledge of each word has increased.

- **defies** (dē fīz′) *v.* resists or opposes boldly or openly (p. 926) *She <u>defies</u> the law by driving too fast. defy v. defiant adj.*

- **monarch** (man′ ərk) *n.* ruler, like a king or queen (p. 926) *The people bowed before the <u>monarch</u>. monarchy n.*

- **dominions** (də min′ yəns) *n.* governed countries or territories (p. 927) *Canada and Australia were once <u>dominions</u> of the British empire. dominion n.*

- **intervene** (in′ tər vēn′) *v.* come between as an influence to help settle an action or argument (p. 927) *My mother will often <u>intervene</u> in the fights between my brothers. intervention n.*

- **realm** (relm) *n.* kingdom (p. 928) *The entire <u>realm</u> was saddened by the king's death.*

- **abode** (ə bōd′) *n.* home; residence (p. 930) *The governor's residence was an elegant <u>abode</u>. abide v.*

❸ Word Study

The **Latin root -*dom-*** means "master" or "building."

Pluto snatches Persephone and takes her to his underground **dominions,** the territories he rules.

Vocabulary Development

Vocabulary Knowledge Rating

Create a **Vocabulary Knowledge Rating Chart** (*Professional Development Guidebook,* p. 33) for this selection. Include the selection vocabulary and the Big Question word that appears in the Writing About the Big Question sentence starter on this page. (The Big Question vocabulary is introduced on pp. 900–901).

Give students a copy of the chart. Read the words aloud, and have students mark their rating in the Before Reading column. Urge them to be alert to these words as they read and discuss the selection.

Tally how many students think they know a word to gauge how much instruction to provide. As students read and discuss the selection, point out the words and their context.

Vocabulary Central, featuring tools, activities, and songs for studying vocabulary, is available online at **www.PHLitOnline.com.**

▲ White's "Demeter and Persephone" appears in this treasury of myths and legends.

Author of
DEMETER AND PERSEPHONE

Anne Terry White, who was born in Ukraine (then part of Russia), was one of the leading writers of nonfiction for children. White's first two books were *Heroes of the Five Books,* a look at figures of the Old Testament, and *Three Children and Shakespeare,* a family discussion of four of Shakespeare's plays. She wrote them to introduce her own children to great works of literature.

A Life of Learning In addition to being a writer, White was an editor, a translator, and an authority on ancient Greece. She shares this knowledge in her retelling of the myth of Demeter and Persephone.

DID YOU KNOW?
White wrote books about the stars, rocks, rivers, archaeology, and mountains in her "All About" series.

❹ BACKGROUND FOR THE MYTH
Seasonal Changes
Ancient Greeks explained the changing seasons with the story of "Demeter and Persephone." Today, scientists explain these changes differently. The Earth completes one revolution around the sun during the course of a year. As the Earth travels, its tilt causes different parts of its surface to receive more of the sun's light. In regions getting more sunlight, it is summer. In areas getting less sunlight, it is winter.

Demeter and Persephone **923**

❹ Daily Bellringer
For each class during which you teach this selection, have students complete one of the five Quick Write activities for Week 31 in the *Daily Bellringer Activities* booklet.

❹ Background
Seasonal Changes "Demeter and Persephone" has several characteristics of myths, as enumerated on p. 913. The story explains a natural occurrence: it tells why seasons change. It contains gods and goddesses with human traits. It explores universal themes (of want and plenty, love and loss), and it explains the world in human terms.

Multidraft Reading

To assist struggling readers and to deepen reading for all, assign the text in "chunks" and apply multidraft reading protocols. For each reading, have students set the purpose indicated:

- **First reading**—identifying key ideas and details and answering any Reading Checks.
- **Second reading**—analyzing craft and structure and responding to the side-column prompts.
- **Third reading**—integrating knowledge and ideas, connecting to other texts and the world, and answering the end-of-selection questions.

For more guidance, refer to the *Classroom Strategies and Teaching Routines* card on multidraft reading.

For more about the author, practice with the selection vocabulary, or more background, go online at **www.PHLitOnline.com.**

❶ Activating Prior Knowledge

1. Use the **Vocab–o–Gram** strategy (*Professional Development Guidebook*, p. 39) to help students make predictions about selection elements. Put the following words on the board or overhead:

Mt. Aetna	realm of the
Pluto	dead
defies	river nymph
giants	Zeus
harvest	pomegranate

2. Then, give students the **Vocab–o–Gram** chart and have them place the words in appropriate categories and make predictions about the story. Have students discuss or explain their word placements, their reasons, and their predictions.

Concept Connector ➡

Students will re–examine their ideas after completing the story.

Small-Group Activity

Have students work in groups to create a narrated pantomime of part of this myth. You may wish to assign each group a different part, such as the beginning through Persephone's capture. Ask one student in each group to be the narrator. This person should read aloud or paraphrase the part of the myth that the group has chosen or been assigned. Students who take the roles of gods and goddesses should use facial expressions and gestures to convey their characteristics.

❷ About the Selection

"Demeter and Persephone" explains Earth's seasons. Pluto, king of the underworld, kidnaps Persephone and carries her away. Demeter, goddess of the harvest, becomes angry and makes the Earth infertile. Zeus asks for Persephone's release. Persephone must return to Pluto for four months of every year. These months are known as winter. When Persephone is home, the soil is fertile and productive.

924

❶ ❷ DEMETER AND PERSEPHONE

Anne Terry White

❸ **D**eep under Mt. Aetna, the gods had buried alive a number of fearful, fire-breathing giants. The monsters heaved and struggled to get free. And so mightily did they shake the earth that Pluto, the king of the underworld, was alarmed.

924 Themes in the Oral Tradition

Vocabulary Development

© **CCSS** Language 6

Thematic Vocabulary: The Big Question
As students are discussing "Demeter and Persephone," encourage them to use the thematic vocabulary presented in Introducing the Big Question, pp. 900–901. You might encourage them with sentence starters like these:

1. In this myth, many *individuals* act . . .
2. Still, Aphrodite and Eros do work as a *team* to . . .
3. Because Pluto falls in love with Persephone, a *family* is . . .
4. Demeter's angry actions change the entire *environment*, making it . . .
5. Finally, Zeus gets involved to save the *community*, even though . . .

Demeter and Persephone **925**

❸ **Critical Thinking**

Speculate

1. Have students read the bracketed opening lines of the story on p. 924.

2. **Ask** students to paraphrase the lines.
   Possible response: The gods buried terrible monsters under Mt. Aetna. The monsters' struggles to get out shook the world. Pluto, king of the underworld, was worried by the shaking.

3. **Ask** students to speculate on why Pluto is alarmed by the shaking.
   Possible response: He might be afraid that the monsters will get out. He might be afraid that his kingdom, the underworld, will be damaged.

4. Have students guide you as you draw a picture of Mt. Aetna with the monsters beneath it, and then Pluto in his underworld kingdom beneath that. **Ask** students to speculate on what could happen to Pluto's kingdom if the monsters shook Mt. Aetna hard enough to break free and get out.
   Possible response: It could expose Pluto's kingdom so that it was no longer underground.

Differentiated

Instruction   for Universal Access

Strategy for Special-Needs Students

Students may have trouble keeping track of the different characters in this myth. Create a checklist of the following characters from the story, and give each student a copy: Pluto, Aphrodite, Eros, Persephone, Demeter, River nymph, Zeus, and Hermes. Then, guide students as they reread the selection. Each time a character is introduced or developed, have students pause in their reading. Instruct students to put a checkmark on the list next to the character's name.

Discuss the character's traits and actions and what other characters think of him or her. Explain to students that some of this information may not be directly stated in the story and that they may have to infer information about some characters from their dialogue and actions. Encourage students to use graphics to make notes about each character next to his or her name on the list. When students' lists are complete, display them for the rest of the class.

PHLit Online!

This selection is available in interactive format in the **Enriched Online Student Edition**, at **www.PHLitOnline.com,** which includes a thematically related video with writing prompt and an interactive graphic organizer.

925

4 ❓ **Connecting to the Big Question**

1. Describe two small children, one of whom grabs the other's toys.
   Ask students how the second child probably feels.
   Possible response: The other child probably feels hurt or angry.

2. Have students read the first bracketed passage on page 926.
   Ask students: How does Persephone suffer here because Pluto wants to satisfy his desires?
   Possible response: She is taken from her mother and she is badly frightened.

3. **Ask:** Does Pluto have the right to take Persephone from her community against her will? Explain. If Persephone wanted to go, would it be right for her to leave her community behind?
   Possible response: No. No one has the right to take someone from his or her community without permission. If Persephone wanted to go, it might be all right for her to leave her community, depending on her mother's need for her.

Vocabulary
defies (dē fīz´) *v.* resists or opposes boldly or openly
monarch (man´ ərk) *n.* ruler, like a king or queen

She saw Pluto as he drove around with his coal-black horses...

"They may tear the rocks asunder and leave the realm of the dead open to the light of day," he thought. And mounting his golden chariot, he went up to see what damage had been done.

Now the goddess of love and beauty, fair Aphrodite (af´ rə dīt´ ē), was sitting on a mountainside playing with her son, Eros.[1] She saw Pluto as he drove around with his coal-black horses and she said:

"My son, there is one who **defies** your power and mine. Quick! Take up your darts! Send an arrow into the breast of that dark **monarch**. Let him, too, feel the pangs of love. Why should he alone escape them?"

At his mother's words, Eros leaped lightly to his feet. He chose from his quiver[2] his sharpest and truest arrow, fitted it to his bow, drew the string, and shot straight into Pluto's heart.

The grim King had seen fair maids enough in the gloomy underworld over which he ruled. But never had his heart been touched. Now an unaccustomed warmth stole through his veins. His stern eyes softened. Before him was a blossoming valley, and along its edge a charming girl was gathering flowers. She was Persephone (pər sef´ ə nē), daughter of Demeter (di mēt´ ər), goddess of the harvest. She had strayed from her companions, and now that her basket overflowed with blossoms, she was filling her apron with lilies and violets. The god looked at Persephone and loved her at once. With one sweep of his arm he caught her up and drove swiftly away.

"Mother!" she screamed, while the flowers fell from her apron and strewed the ground. "Mother!"

And she called on her companions by name. But already they were out of sight, so fast did Pluto urge the horses on. In

1. **Eros** (er´ äs) in Greek mythology, the god of love; identified by the Romans as Cupid.
2. **quiver** (kwiv´ ər) case for arrows.

4

5

Think Aloud

Cause and Effect
Draw students' attention to the paragraph on p. 927, beginning "That year was the . . . " Use the following "think aloud" process to reinforce the skill of identifying cause and effect:

When I read the first sentence, I see that it describes an effect—it was the cruelest year mankind had known. I ask myself, "What caused this effect?" Then I think back on what I have read so far. I remember that Demeter is upset that her daughter Persephone is gone. I also remember that

Demeter is the goddess of the harvest. Still, I ask myself, "Why is Demeter punishing the land for her daughter's disappearance?" Then I remember that she blames the land. Because of Demeter's anger at the land, she makes it infertile. I know that sometimes effects become causes, so I ask myself, "What happens because the land is infertile?" The story tells me that everyone is hungry. I will keep reading to find more causes and effects.

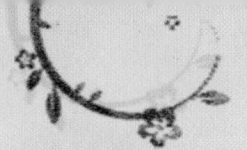
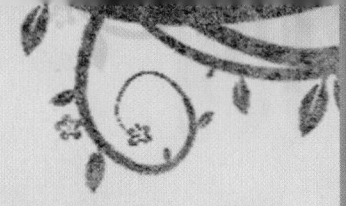

a few moments they were at the River Cyane.[3] Persephone struggled, her loosened girdle[4] fell to the ground, but the god held her tight. He struck the bank with his trident.[5] The earth opened, and darkness swallowed them all—horses, chariot, Pluto, and weeping Persephone.

From end to end of the earth Demeter sought her daughter. But none could tell her where Persephone was. At last, worn out and despairing, the goddess returned to Sicily. She stood by the River Cyane, where Pluto had cleft the earth and gone down into his own dominions.

Now a river nymph[6] had seen him carry off his prize. She wanted to tell Demeter where her daughter was, but fear of Pluto kept her dumb. Yet she had picked up the girdle Persephone had dropped, and this the nymph wafted[7] on the waves to the feet of Demeter.

The goddess knew then that her daughter was gone indeed, but she did not suspect Pluto of carrying her off. She laid the blame on the innocent land.

"Ungrateful soil!" she said. "I made you fertile. I clothed you in grass and nourishing grain, and this is how you reward me. No more shall you enjoy my favors!"

That year was the most cruel mankind had ever known. Nothing prospered, nothing grew. The cattle died, the seed would not come up, men and oxen toiled in vain. There was too much sun. There was too much rain. Thistles[8] and weeds were the only things that grew. It seemed that all mankind would die of hunger.

"This cannot go on," said mighty Zeus. "I see that I must intervene." And one by one he sent the gods and goddesses to plead with Demeter.

But she had the same answer for all: "Not till I see my

---

3. **River Cyane** (sī an) a river in Sicily, an island just south of Italy.
4. **girdle** (gʉrd´ əl) *n.* belt or sash for the waist.
5. **trident** (trīd´ ənt) *n.* spear with three points.
6. **river nymph** (nimf) *n.* goddess living in a river.
7. **wafted** (wäft´ əd) *n.* carried.
8. **thistles** (this´ əlz) *n.* stubborn, weedy plants with sharp leaves and usually purplish flowers.

Myths
What details in this paragraph reveal that the story is a myth?

Vocabulary
dominions (də min´ yəns) *n.* governed countries or territories
intervene (in tər vēn´) *v.* come between as an influence to help settle an action or argument

6 ✓ Reading Check
Who is Pluto?

Demeter and Persephone **927**

⑤ Myth

1. **Read** the bracketed paragraph which begins on p. 926, with students. Call on a volunteer to explain what happens.
   Answer: Pluto overpowers Persephone and brings her to the underworld.

2. Have students identify a fantastical element in the paragraph.
   Answer: Pluto's opening the Earth is a fantastical element.

3. **Ask** students the Myth question.
   Answer: The speed of the horses, who travel faster than sound, and Pluto's striking the river bank with a trident to open the Earth tell you that the story is a myth.

⑥ Reading Check

Answer: Pluto is the god who rules the underworld.

Differentiated Instruction for Universal Access

Support for Less Proficient Students

To give students a context for the story and to model how to analyze cause-and-effect relationships, show them **Reading Skill Graphic Organizer A** (*Graphic Organizer Transparencies* p. 172). The partially completed graphic organizer will give students insight into the process of cause and effect. They can use it as a model for analyzing cause-and-effect relationships as they read.

EL Strategy for English Learners

Students may be unfamiliar with some words and phrases in this selection. Before students read, use gestures and drawings to introduce and clarify such unfamiliar words and phrases as "tear asunder," "dark monarch," "stole through his veins," "strewed the ground," "kept her dumb," "sweet pulp," and "fare you well." Have student partners take turns using the words and phrases in sentences.

❼ Critical Thinking

Analyze Causes and Effects

1. **Ask** a volunteer to explain the condition Zeus puts on Persephone's return.
   Answer: As long as she has not tasted food in the realm of the dead, she may return to her mother forever.

2. Have students read the bracketed passage, which continues onto p. 929.

3. Remind students that where there is an effect, there is a cause. Then, **ask** what the effect will be of Persephone's consumption of four pomegranate seeds.
   Answer: She cannot leave the underworld once and for all.

▶ **Monitor Progress:** If students have trouble identifying cause-and-effect relationships, review their Reading Skill Graphic Organizers.

▶ **Reteach:** Use the partially completed **Reading Skill Graphic Organizer A** (*Graphic Organizer Transparencies*, p. 172) to help them clear up misconceptions.

Vocabulary
realm (relm)
n. kingdom

 ❼

daughter shall the earth bear fruit again."

Zeus, of course, knew well where Persephone was. He did not like to take from his brother the one joyful thing in his life, but he saw that he must if the race of man was to be preserved. So he called Hermes[9] to him and said:

"Descend to the underworld, my son. Bid Pluto release his bride. Provided she has not tasted food in the realm of the dead, she may return to her mother forever."

Down sped Hermes on his winged feet, and there in the dim palace of the king, he found Persephone by Pluto's side. She was pale and joyless. Not all the glittering treasures of the underworld could bring a smile to her lips.

"You have no flowers here," she would say to her husband when he pressed gems upon her. "Jewels have no fragrance. I do not want them."

When she saw Hermes and heard his message, her heart leaped within her. Her cheeks grew rosy and her eyes

---

9. **Hermes** (hur´ mēz) a god who served as a messenger.

Vocabulary Development

Vocabulary Knowledge Rating

When students have completed reading and discussing "Demeter and Persephone," have them take out their **Vocabulary Knowledge Rating Chart.** Read the words aloud once more and have students rate their knowledge of the words again in the After Reading column. Clarify any words that are still problematic. Have students write their own definition and example or sentence in the appropriate column. Then, have students complete the Vocabulary Practice activities at the end of the selection. Encourage students to use the words in further discussion and written work about this selection. Remind them that they will be accountable for these words on the **Selection Test**, *Unit 6 Resources*, pp. 56–58 or 59–61.

Mythology Connection

Gods and Goddesses

The ancient Greeks and Romans had different names for their gods and goddesses. In the diagram below, the Roman name for the god or goddess is given in parentheses. In their traditions, each god and goddess had control or power in a different area.

Poseiden (Neptune)
god of the sea

Zeus (Jupiter)
ruler of gods and men

Hera (Juno)
goddess of marriage

Demeter (Ceres)
goddess of agriculture

Hades (Pluto)
god of the underworld

Hermes (Mercury)
messenger of the gods

Aphrodite (Venus)
goddess of beauty

Ares (Mars)
god of war

Athena (Minerva)
goddess of wisdom

Persephone (Proserpina)
goddess of springtime

Connect to the Literature **Why do you think that ancient peoples told stories about gods and goddesses such as Demeter and Persephone?**

---

sparkled, for she knew that Pluto would not dare to disobey his brother's command. She sprang up, ready to go at once. Only one thing troubled her—that she could not leave the underworld forever. For she had accepted a pomegranate[10] from Pluto and sucked the sweet pulp from four of the seeds.

With a heavy heart Pluto made ready his golden car.[11] He helped Persephone in while Hermes took up the reins.

"Dear wife," said the King, and his voice trembled as he spoke, "think kindly of me, I pray you. For indeed I love you truly. It will be lonely here these eight months you are away.

10. **pomegranate** (päm′ ə gran′ it) *n.* round fruit with a red leathery rind and many seeds.
11. **car** (kär) *n.* chariot.

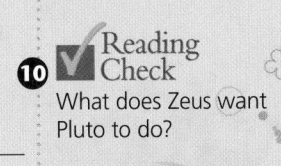

Reading Check

What does Zeus want Pluto to do?

Demeter and Persephone **929**

Concept Connector

Vocab-o-Gram

Have students return to their **Vocab-o-Gram** charts and re-examine the ideas that they recorded. Then, lead a class discussion, probing for what students have learned that confirms or invalidates their predictions about the story.

Writing About the Big Question

Have students compare their response to the sentence starter they completed before reading the selection with their ideas afterward. Ask them to explain whether their thoughts have changed.

Reading Skill Graphic Organizer

Ask students to review the graphic organizers they completed to analyze cause-and-effect relationships while reading. Then, have students share their graphic organizers.

---

❽ Literature in Context

Gods and Goddesses In Greek mythology, Zeus, Poseidon, and Hades (Pluto) were brothers. Each one took one realm of the universe as his responsibility: the sky, the sea, and the underworld, respectively. Zeus had the most power. As the story goes, of all his siblings only Zeus was saved from being swallowed by his father as a baby. When he grew up, Zeus forced his father to vomit up his brothers and sisters.

Connect to the Literature
Have students read the Literature in Context feature, and present the additional background information above. Then, **ask** the Connect to the Literature question: Why do you think that ancient peoples told stories about gods and goddesses such as Demeter and Persephone?
Possible answers: Ancient people needed ways to explain natural phenomena and to understand human behavior, and these stories helped.

❾ Critical Thinking

Speculate

1. Read the bracketed passage with students. **Ask** students what natural phenomenon the myth explains.
   Answer: The myth explains why Earth has different seasons.

2. Invite students to consider how the outcome of the myth would be different if Persephone had not tasted the pomegranate seeds.
   Possible responses: Most students will probably say that Persephone would leave the underworld forever, and people could grow crops all year. Others may say that Persephone would take pity on Pluto and return for a visit of her own free will.

❿ Reading Check

Answer: Zeus wants Pluto to set Persephone free so that she may return to her mother.

Critical Thinking

Before students respond, you may wish to have them write a brief objective summary of the selection. As they answer the questions below, remind them to support their answers with evidence from the text.

1. (a) Pluto falls in love with Persephone when he is struck by Eros's arrow. (b) Pluto's nickname suggests that he views the world with suspicion and anger.

2. (a) She blames the land for her daughter's disappearance and makes it infertile. (b) **Possible responses:** Some students may say that Demeter's actions are justifiable because she has lost someone she loves. Others may say that her actions are not justifiable because innocent people will suffer as a result. (c) After discussing their responses, some students may see the validity in one of the responses given in (b) above.

3. (a) Zeus intervenes and, in an attempt to save humankind, instructs Pluto to return Persephone. (b) **Possible responses:** Persephone might become more grateful for what she has; Pluto might become more loving; Demeter might become less vengeful.

4. (a) When Persephone goes home, spring, summer, and fall occur. When she returns to Pluto, it is winter. (b) When Persephone returns to the underworld, Demeter grieves and vegetation dies. When Persephone returns to her mother, Demeter's joy brings life back to the fields.

5.  **Possible responses:** (a) Winter overtakes the world. (b) Humankind has to endure winter each year because Pluto could not resist Persephone, Persephone could not resist the pomegranate, and Demeter could not control her temper.

And if you think mine is a gloomy palace to return to, at least remember that your husband is great among the immortals. So fare you well—and get your fill of flowers!"

Straight to the temple of Demeter at Eleusis, Hermes drove the black horses. The goddess heard the chariot wheels and, as a deer bounds over the hills, she ran out swiftly to meet her daughter. Persephone flew to her mother's arms. And the sad tale of each turned into joy in the telling.

So it is to this day. One third of the year Persephone spends in the gloomy abode of Pluto—one month for each seed that she tasted. Then Nature dies, the leaves fall, the earth stops bringing forth. In spring Persephone returns, and with her come the flowers, followed by summer's fruitfulness and the rich harvest of fall.

⑨

Vocabulary
abode (ə bōd′) *n.* home; residence

Cite textual evidence to support your responses.

Critical Thinking

© 1. **Key Ideas and Details (a)** Why did Pluto take Persephone to his kingdom? **(b) Analyze:** What does Pluto's nickname, "the grim King," suggest about his emotional outlook on the world?

© 2. **Key Ideas and Details (a)** What does Demeter do when she discovers her daughter is lost? **(b) Make a Judgment:** Do you think her actions were justifiable? Why or why not? **(c) Discuss:** Share your answer with a classmate. How has your response grown or changed?

© 3. **Key Ideas and Details (a)** How is Persephone reunited with her mother? **(b) Speculate:** How might their experiences in this myth change each of the three main characters?

© 4. **Key Ideas and Details (a)** How does nature change as Persephone moves between Earth and the underworld? **(b) Synthesize:** How do the powerful emotions of the main characters account for the changing of the seasons?

© 5. **Integration of Knowledge and Ideas (a)** What was the consequence of Demeter's actions? **(b)** How did humankind suffer as a result of one individual's impulses? *[Connect to the Big Question: Community or individual—which is more important?]*

930 Themes in the Oral Tradition

Assessment Resources

Unit 6 Resources

L1 L2 EL Selection Test A, pp. 56–58. Administer Test A to less advanced students.

L3 L4 EL Selection Test B, pp. 59–61. Administer Test B to on-level and more advanced students.

L3 L4 Open-Book Test, pp. 53–55. As an alternative, give the Open-Book Test.

All Customizable Test Bank

All Self-tests
Students may prepare for the **Selection Test** by taking the **Self-test** online.

PHLit Online! All assessment resources are available at **www.PHLitOnline.com.**

Reading Skill: Cause and Effect

1. Answer these questions to analyze **cause-and-effect** relationships in the myth:
   (a) What happens to Persephone at the end of the myth? Why? **(b)** What happens to Demeter? Why?

2. Describe the effect of the giants struggling to get free at the beginning of the myth.

Literary Analysis: Myth

© 3. **Key Ideas and Details** What human qualities does Pluto possess?

© 4. **Craft and Structure** Complete a chart like the one shown to describe the lessons the **myth** teaches through each character.

Character	Lesson	How Taught
Demeter		
Persephone		
Pluto		

Vocabulary

© **Acquisition and Use** For each item, write a single sentence using the words indicated.

1. realm; distant
2. intervene; argument
3. monarch; ancient
4. dominions; powerful
5. defies; stubborn
6. abode; family

Word Study Use the context of the sentences and what you know about the **Latin root -dom-** to explain your answer to each question.

1. If you behave in a *domineering* manner, are you being humble?
2. If a building *dominates* a city skyline, is it hard to see?

Word Study

The **Latin root -dom-** means "master" or "building."

Apply It Explain how the root *-dom-* contributes to the meanings of these words. Consult a dictionary if necessary.

domain
dominant
predominate

Reading Skill

1. (a) Persephone returns to Earth because Zeus intervenes with Pluto to release her. (b) Demeter is deprived of her daughter for four months out of the year because Persephone has eaten pomegranate seeds in the under-world.

2. Pluto becomes alarmed and goes aboveground to see what damage has been done to his realm.

Literary Analysis

3. **Possible response:** Pluto possesses human emotions, such as love and sadness. Like a human king, he inspires respect and fear.

4. Demeter's Lesson—show restraint; How Taught—through Zeus's mercy toward humankind and Persephone's return; Persephone's Lesson—do not give into temptation; How Taught—she must return to the underworld for one month for each pomegranate seed she ate; Pluto's Lesson—love is a powerful emotion; How Taught—through his feelings for Persephone

   For other sample answers, see *Graphic Organizer Transparencies,* **Literary Analysis Graphic Organizer A,** p. 175, and the **Additional Answers** section.

Vocabulary
Acquisition and Use
Sample answers:

1. She is queen of a <u>distant</u> and far away <u>realm</u>.

2. Please <u>intervene</u> in the <u>argument</u> so that a compromise can be reached.

3. In <u>ancient</u> times, people were often ruled by a <u>monarch</u>.

4. <u>Powerful</u> kings ruled <u>dominions</u> around the world.

5. My mother thinks my sister Lori is <u>stubborn</u> when she <u>defies</u> the rules.

6. Come see my <u>family</u> at our <u>abode</u>.

Word Study
Sample answers:

1. No; The root *-dom-* means "master." Someone who is *domineering* acts as a <u>master</u> and so is not humble.

2. No; The root *-dom-* means "master." A building that *dominates* the skyline is "<u>master</u>" of that view—it is easy to see.

Word Study: Apply It
Sample answers:

A *domain* is a subject or place over which one has <u>mastery</u>. Something that is *dominant* is <u>master</u> of or in control of its surroundings. If something *pre-dominates*, it is <u>master</u> in importance or power.

Conventions

1. Introduce the skill, using the instruction on the student page.

2. Discuss the examples in the chart.

Think Aloud: Model the Skill

Say to students:

I use commas and colons to show relationships between ideas. For example when I introduce a list of items, I use the strong pause indicated by a colon, as in this sentence: *Joan packed everything she needed for the hike: water bottle, compass, rope, and sun block.* Without the colon, my sentence won't make sense.

PH WRITING COACH Grade 7

Students will find instruction on and practice with colons, semicolons, hyphens, dashes, and brackets in Chapter 25, Sections 3, 5, 7, and 8.

Practice A

Sample answers: Dashes set off the aside about Icarus. Parentheses are used to include information about King Minos. A semicolon is used to join the parts of the compound sentence.

Reading Application
Sample answers:

He fluttered his young hands vainly—he was falling—and in that terror he remembered. / . . .none was more cunning than Daedalus (ded' əl əs). / He forgot Crete and the other islands that he had passed over: he saw but vaguely that winged thing in the distance before him that was his father Daedalus. / The heat of the sun had melted the wax from his wings; the feathers were falling, one by one, like snowflakes; and there was none to help.

Practice B

Sample answer: Aphrodite—her beauty is legendary—urged her son to pierce Pluto's heart with an arrow of love. He swooped down from the sky; he snatched Persephone and descended deep into the ground.

Writing Application

Sample answer: The story of Demeter (di mēt' ər) is an upsetting one. It shows all-consuming love at its worst. Demeter is so angry—her daughter has been kidnapped—that she punishes the entire world.

Integrated Language Skills

Icarus and Daedalus • Demeter and Persephone

Conventions: Punctuation Marks

Review the chart to learn the functions of several common **punctuation marks**.

Punctuation / Usage	Example
colon (:) A *colon* introduces information that defines, explains, or provides a list of what is referred to before.	Lily brought many toys to the beach: buckets, shovels, balls, and floats.
semicolon (;) *Semicolons* are used in compound sentences.	We spent all morning riding our bikes; then we had a picnic.
hyphen (-) A *hyphen* is used to join two or more separate words into a single word.	Billy ordered a double-scoop, bubble-gum-flavored ice cream.
dash (—) *Dashes* are used to set off information that interrupts a thought.	On our way to the cinema—it had just opened—we stopped for gas.
bracket ([ ] ( )) A commonly used type of bracket is the parenthesis. Parentheses provide information that could be left out of a sentence without changing its meaning.	My brother Raf (the shyest person in our family) declined to make a speech at the party.

Practice A Identify each punctuation mark in this paragraph, and explain its function.

Daedalus and his son Icarus—a lively young boy—were trapped on Crete. King Minos was fickle (among other character flaws) and would imprison his loyal subjects on a whim. Daedalus fastened feathers together; he molded them in with wax to make wings.

Reading Application In "Icarus and Daedalus," find one sentence that contains dashes, one that contains parentheses, one that contains a colon, and one that contains a semicolon.

Practice B Rewrite the paragraph below, using punctuation, so that each sentence makes sense.

Aphrodite her beauty is legendary urged her son to pierce Pluto's heart with an arrow of love. He swooped down from the sky he snatched Persephone and descended deep into the ground.

Writing Application Write a brief paragraph about the myth you read, using each of the following types of punctuation at least once: hyphen, dash, parentheses, colon, and semicolon.

PH WRITING COACH Further instruction and practice are available in *Prentice Hall Writing Coach*.

Extend the Lesson

Sentence Modeling

Choose the sentence given from the selection students have read:

The hateful ground of Crete sank beneath them; and the country folk, who caught a glimpse of them when they were high above the treetops, took it for a vision of the gods—Apollo, perhaps, with Cupid after him. ("Icarus and Daedalus")

But she had the same answer for all: "Not till I see my daughter shall the earth bear fruit again." ("Demeter and Persephone")

Ask students what they notice about the sentence. Elicit from them the types of punctuation in the sentence. Then ask what else students notice. ("Icarus and Daedalus": A subordinate clause forces readers to pause before finding out what the country folk did. "Demeter and Persephone": The first independent clauses creates context in advance of the second clause.)

Have students imitate the sentence in a sentence on a topic of their own choosing, matching each grammatical and stylistic feature discussed.

Writing

© **Narrative Text** You may have wondered why leaves change colors in the fall or what causes an earthquake. Write a short **myth** that explains a natural phenomenon that fascinates you. The following tips will help you.

- Think of a natural phenomenon and a creative explanation for its occurrence.
- Limit the number of characters to keep the story simple.
- Develop your characters by describing their appearance and actions and by showing how they relate to other characters.
- Plan the action of your story by identifying a problem and its solution.

Grammar Application Check your writing to be sure you have used punctuation correctly.

Writing Workshop: *Work in Progress*

Prewriting for Workplace Writing For a business letter that you might write, imagine you are planning an elaborate party. Develop a Wish List of five places where you would like to hold the party. Keep the Wish List in your writing portfolio.

Speaking and Listening

© **Comprehension and Collaboration** With a small group, conduct a **debate.** If you read "Icarus and Daedalus," debate whether or not Daedalus shares any responsibility for Icarus' fall. If you read "Demeter and Persephone," debate whether or not Demeter was justified in changing the weather on Earth. Each side should prepare an argument and material to support the argument.

- Appoint a leader for your debate team and choose a person to act as a moderator, or discussion leader.
- Before the debate, consider what the opposing arguments might be and prepare counterarguments to address them.
- Volunteer your own opinions and make contributions to your team. Cite evidence that is logical and supported by your reading.
- Respond directly to questions and pose your own.
- After the debate, meet with your group to provide constructive feedback about how well speakers conveyed logical ideas.

© **Common Core State Standards**

L.7.2, L.7.4.b; W.7.3.a, W.7.3.b; SL.7.1.a, SL.7.1.c
[For the full wording of the standards, see page 912.]

Use this prewriting activity to prepare for the **Writing Workshop** on page 982.

PHLit Online!
www.PHLitOnline.com
- Interactive graphic organizers
- Grammar tutorial
- Interactive journals

Teaching Resources

Unit 6 Resources
- L3 L4 EL **Integrated Language Skills: Grammar,** p. 50
- L3 L4 EL **Support for Writing,** p. 51
- L3 L4 **Support for Extend Your Learning,** p. 52
- L4 **Enrichment,** p. 49

Enriched Online Student Edition
Available under After You Read for this selection:
- All **Interactive Grammar Tutorial**
- L3 L4 **Internet Research Activity**

Professional Development Guidebook
Rubrics for Self-Assessment: Short Story, pp. 226–227

PHLit Online! All print and digital resources are available online at www.PHLitOnline.com. Online resources accessible to students are noted on the student page.

Writing

1. Review the assignment, using the instruction on the student page.
2. To guide students in writing their narrative texts, give them the **Support for Writing,** p. 51 in *Unit 6 Resources.*
3. To evaluate students' myths, use the rubrics for **Short Story,** pp. 226–227 in the *Professional Development Guidebook.*

Grammar Application

Have students check their drafts to make sure they have used punctuation correctly.

Six Traits Focus

✔ Ideas		Word Choice
✔ Organization		Sentence Fluency
✔ Voice		Conventions

PH WRITING COACH   Grade 7

Students will find further instruction on and practice with myths in Chapter 2 and with fiction narrative texts in Chapter 6.

Writing Workshop
Work in Progress

Have students save their completed Wish Lists in their portfolios. They will use the lists later as they continue this Work-in-Progress assignment (see p. 957). These assignments prepare them to complete the Writing Workshop assignment (see pp. 982–987).

Speaking and Listening

1. Review the assignment, using the instruction on the student page.
2. To support students' work on the assignment, have students complete the **Support for Extend Your Learning** page (*Unit 6 Resources,* p. 52).

933

✓ **Tenochtitlan: Inside the Aztec Capital •**
✓✓ **Popocatepetl and Ixtlaccihuatl**

Lesson Pacing Guide

DAY 1 Preteach

- Ⓒ Administer the Reading and Vocabulary Warm-ups (*Unit 6 Resources,* pp. 62–65 or 80–83) as necessary.
- • Introduce the Reading Skill: Cause and Effect.
- Ⓒ Introduce the Literary Analysis concept: Legend and Fact.
- • Distribute copies of the appropriate graphic organizer for the Reading Skill (*Graphic Organizer Transparencies,* pp. 177–179).
- • Distribute copies of the appropriate graphic organizer for Literary Analysis (*Graphic Organizer Transparencies,* pp. 180–182).
- Ⓒ Teach the selection vocabulary.
- Ⓒ Introduce the Word Study skill.

DAYS 2–3 Preteach/Teach

- Ⓒ Build background with the Background feature.
- • Develop thematic vocabulary and thematic thinking with Writing About the Big Question.
- • Prepare students to read with the Activating Prior Knowledge activities (TE).
- • Informally monitor comprehension while students read.
- • Use the Reading Check questions to confirm comprehension.
- • Develop students' ability to identify the connections between cause and effect using the Cause-and-Effect questions.
- Ⓒ Develop students' understanding of legend and fact using the Legend and Fact questions.
- Ⓒ Reinforce vocabulary with the Vocabulary notes.
- Ⓒ Reinforce unit focus standards using the Spiral Review prompts.

DAY 4 Assess

- • Assess students' comprehension and mastery of the skills by having them answer the Critical Thinking, Reading Skill, and Literary Analysis questions.
- Ⓒ Have students complete the Vocabulary Practice activities.
- Ⓒ Have students complete the Word Study activities.

DAY 5 Extend/Assess

- • Have students complete the Conventions lesson.
- Ⓒ Have students complete the Writing activity and write a description. (You may assign as homework.)
- Ⓒ Extend learning by having students complete the Speaking and Listening activity, a persuasive speech. As an alternative, assign them "Restoring Cities From the Ground Up" or "What It Takes to Lead" in *Reality Central.*
- • Administer Selection Test A or B (*Unit 6 Resources,* pp. 74–79 or 95–100).

Ⓒ Common Core State Standards

Reading Literature 2. Determine a theme or central idea of a text and analyze its development over the course of the text; provide an objective summary of the text.
9. Compare and contrast a fictional portrayal of a time, place, or character and a historical account of the same period as a means of understanding how authors of fiction use or alter history.

Writing 1.a. Introduce claim(s), acknowledge alternate or opposing claims, and organize the reasons and evidence logically.
1.b. Support claim(s) with logical reasoning and relevant evidence, using accurate, credible sources and demonstrating an understanding of the topic or text.
2. Write informative/explanatory texts to examine a topic and convey ideas, concepts, and information through the selection, organization, and analysis of relevant content.
2.b. Develop the topic with relevant facts, definitions, concrete details, quotations, or other information and examples.

Speaking and Listening 4. Present claims and findings, emphasizing salient points in a focused, coherent manner with pertinent descriptions, facts, details, and examples; use appropriate eye contact, adequate volume, and clear pronunciation.

Language 2. Demonstrate command of the conventions of standard English capitalization, punctuation, and spelling when writing.
2.a. Use a comma to separate coordinate adjectives.
4.b. Use common grade-appropriate Greek or Latin affixes and roots as clues to the meaning of a word.

Additional Standards Practice
Common Core Companion, pp. 15–22

Daily Block Scheduling
Each day in this Lesson Pacing Guide represents a 40–50 minute period. Teachers using block scheduling may combine days to revise pacing. In addition, teachers may differentiate and support core instruction by integrating components for extended and intensive support, as students require. See the Guide to Selected Leveled Resources (facing page).

Guide to Selected Leveled Resources

R T I **Tier 1** (students performing on level)		✓ **More Accessible** Tenochtitlan: Inside the Aztec Capital	✓✓ **More Complex** Popocatepetl and Ixtlaccihuatl
Warm Up	Practice, model, and monitor fluency, working with the whole class or in groups.	Vocabulary and Reading Warm-ups B, *Unit 6 Resources,* pp. 62–63, 65	Vocabulary and Reading Warm-ups B, *Unit 6 Resources,* pp. 80–81, 83
Comprehension/Skills	Support and monitor comprehension and skills development, having students complete the activities, graphic organizers, and interactive prompts independently or as a class.	• *Reader's Notebook,* adapted instruction and full selection EL *Reader's Notebook: English Learner's Version,* adapted instruction and adapted selection • Reading Skill Graphic Organizer B, *Graphic Organizer Transparencies,* p. 179 • Literary Analysis Graphic Organizer B, *Graphic Organizer Transparencies,* p. 182	• *Reader's Notebook,* adapted instruction and summary EL *Reader's Notebook: English Learner's Version,* adapted instruction and summary • Reading Skill Graphic Organizer B, *Graphic Organizer Transparencies,* p. 179 • Literary Analysis Graphic Organizer B, *Graphic Organizer Transparencies,* p. 182
Monitor Progress A	Monitor student progress with the differentiated curriculum-based assessment in the *Unit Resources.*	• Selection Test B, *Unit 6 Resources,* pp. 77–79 • Open-Book Test, *Unit 6 Resources,* pp. 71–73	• Selection Test B, *Unit 6 Resources,* pp. 98–100 • Open-Book Test, *Unit 6 Resources,* pp. 92–94
Assess/Screen A	Assess student progress using Benchmark Test 2.	• Benchmark Test 11, *Unit 6 Resources,* pp. 120–125	• Benchmark Test 11, *Unit 6 Resources,* pp. 120–125

R T I **Tier 2** (students requiring intervention)		✓ **More Accessible** Tenochtitlan: Inside the Aztec Capital	✓✓ **More Complex** Popocatepetl and Ixtlaccihuatl
Warm Up	Practice, model, and monitor fluency in groups or with individuals.	• Vocabulary and Reading Warm-ups A, *Unit 6 Resources,* pp. 62–64 • *Reality Central,* "Restoring Cities from the Ground Up" • *Hear It!* Audio CD (adapted text)	• Vocabulary and Reading Warm-ups A, *Unit 6 Resources,* pp. 80–82 • *Reality Central,* "What It Takes to Lead" • *Hear It!* Audio CD
Comprehension/Skills	• Support and monitor comprehension and skills development, working in small groups or with individuals. • Pair students with more advanced peers and have them complete the writing activity in the *Real-World Writing Journal.* • As students complete the selection in the appropriate version of the *Reader's Notebook,* monitor comprehension frequently with group questions and individual instruction. • Model strategies while guiding students in completing the activities and prompts in the *Reader's Notebook,* as well as the graphic organizers. • Practice skills and monitor mastery with the *Reading Kit* worksheets.	• *Real-World Writing Journal,* Lesson 3, pp. 164–167 • *Reader's Notebook: Adapted Version,* adapted instruction and adapted selection EL *Reader's Notebook: English Learner's Version,* adapted instruction and adapted selection • Reading Skill Graphic Organizer A, *Graphic Organizer Transparencies,* p. 177 • Literary Analysis Graphic Organizer A, *Graphic Organizer Transparencies,* p. 180 • *Reading Kit,* Practice worksheets, pp. 244, 250, 254, 258, 264	• *Real-World Writing Journal,* Lesson 4, pp. 168–171 • *Reader's Notebook: Adapted Version,* adapted instruction and summary EL *Reader's Notebook: English Learner's Version,* adapted instruction and summary • Reading Skill Graphic Organizer A, *Graphic Organizer Transparencies,* p. 178 • Literary Analysis Graphic Organizer A, *Graphic Organizer Transparencies,* p. 181 • *Reading Kit,* Practice worksheets, pp. 244, 250, 254, 258, 264
Monitor Progress A	Monitor student progress with the differentiated curriculum-based assessment in the *Unit Resources* and in the *Reading Kit.*	• Selection Test A, *Unit 6 Resources,* pp. 74–76 • *Reading Kit,* Assess worksheets, pp. 245, 251, 255, 259, 265	• Selection Test A, *Unit 6 Resources,* pp. 95–97 • *Reading Kit,* Assess worksheets, pp. 245, 251, 255, 259, 265
Assess/Screen A	Assess student progress using Benchmark Test.	• Benchmark Test 11, *Unit 6 Resources,* pp. 120–125	• Benchmark Test 11, *Unit 6 Resources,* pp. 120–125

TIER 3 Tier 3 intervention may require consultation with the student's special-education or dyslexia specialist. For additional support, see the Tier 2 activities and resources listed above.

One-on-one teaching Group work Whole class instruction Independent work A Assessment

For a complete guide to selection support, including support for Advanced students, see the Overview of Resources in the frontmatter.

✓Tenochtitlan: Inside the Aztec Capital
✓✓Popocatepetl and Ixtlaccihuatl

MEXICAN LEGEND

Popocatepetl and Ixtlaccihuatl

JULIET PIGGOTT WOOD

TENOCHTITLAN: INSIDE THE AZTEC CAPITAL
Jacqueline Dineen

RESOURCES FOR:
- **L1** Special-Needs Students
- **L2** Below-Level Students (Tier 2)
- **L3** On-Level Students (Tier 1)
- **L4** Advanced Students (Tier 1)
- **EL** English Learners
- **All** All Students

Vocabulary/Fluency/Prior Knowledge

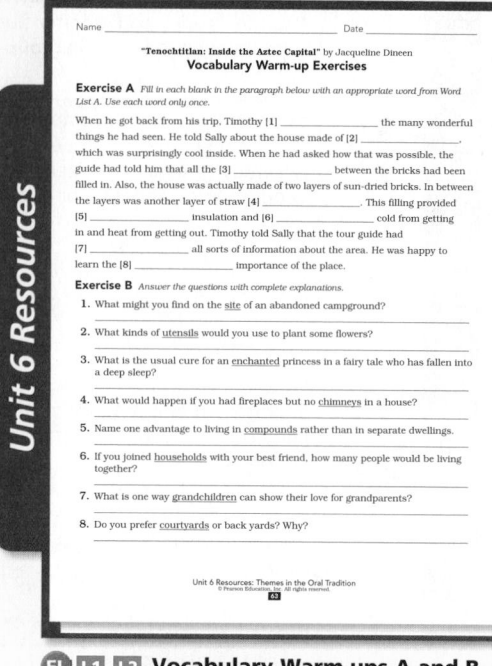

Unit 6 Resources

Name _____ Date _____

"Tenochtitlan: Inside the Aztec Capital" by Jacqueline Dineen
Vocabulary Warm-up Exercises

Exercise A *Fill in each blank in the paragraph below with an appropriate word from Word List A. Use each word only once.*

When he got back from his trip, Timothy [1] _____ the many wonderful things he had seen. He told Sally about the house made of [2] _____, which was surprisingly cool inside. When he had asked how that was possible, the guide had told him that all the [3] _____ between the bricks had been filled in. Also, the house was actually made of two layers of sun-dried bricks. In between the layers was another layer of straw [4] _____. This filling provided [5] _____ insulation and [6] _____ cold from getting in and heat from getting out. Timothy told Sally that the tour guide had [7] _____ all sorts of information about the area. He was happy to learn the [8] _____ importance of the place.

Exercise B *Answer the questions with complete explanations.*

1. What might you find on the <u>site</u> of an abandoned campground?
_____
2. What kinds of <u>utensils</u> would you use to plant some flowers?
_____
3. What is the usual cure for an <u>enchanted</u> princess in a fairy tale who has fallen into a deep sleep?
_____
4. What would happen if you had fireplaces but no <u>chimneys</u> in a house?
_____
5. Name one advantage to living in <u>compounds</u> rather than in separate dwellings.
_____
6. If you joined <u>households</u> with your best friend, how many people would be living together?
_____
7. What is one way <u>grandchildren</u> can show their love for grandparents?
_____
8. Do you prefer <u>courtyards</u> or back yards? Why?
_____

Unit 6 Resources: Themes in the Oral Tradition
© Pearson Education, Inc. All rights reserved.

EL **L1** **L2** **Vocabulary Warm-ups A and B,** pp. 62–63, 80–81

Also available for these selections:
EL **L1** **L2** **Reading Warm-ups A and B,** pp. 64–65, 82–83
All **Vocabulary Builder,** pp. 69, 87
All **Writing About the Big Question,** pp. 66, 84

Reader's Notebooks

Pre- and postreading pages for both selections, as well as "Tenochtitlan: Inside the Aztec Capital" appear in an interactive format in the *Reader's Notebooks.* Each *Notebook* is differentiated for a different group of learners. The selections in the Adapted and English Learner's versions are abridged.

- **L2** **L3** *Reader's Notebook*
- **L1** *Reader's Notebook: Adapted Version*
- **EL** *Reader's Notebook: English Learner's Version*
- **EL** *Reader's Notebook: Spanish Version*

© *Common Core Companion*

Additional instruction and practice for each Common Core State Standard

Selection Support

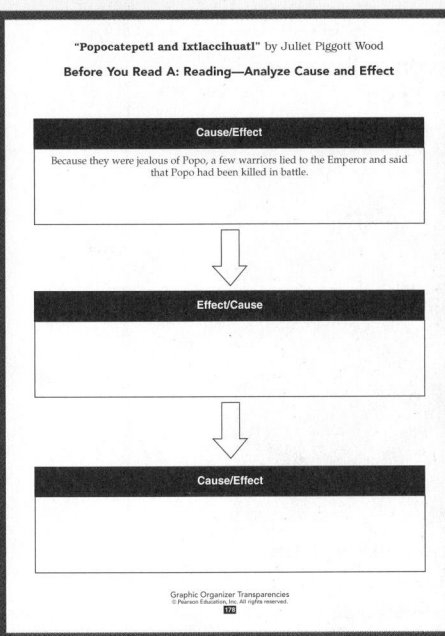

Graphic Organizer Transparencies

EL **L1** **L2** **Reading: Graphic Organizer A,** pp. 177, 178

Also available for these selections:

EL **L1** **L2** **Literary Analysis: Graphic Organizer A,** pp. 180, 181

EL **L3** **Literary Analysis: Graphic Organizer B** p. 182

EL **L3** **Reading: Graphic Organizer B** p. 179

Skills Development/Extension

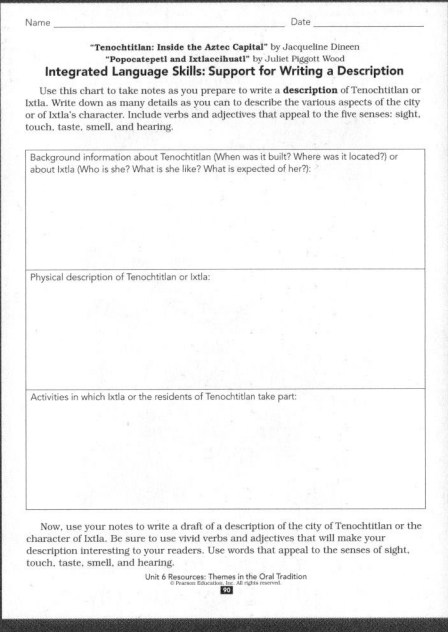

Unit 6 Resources

EL **L3** **L4** **Support for Writing,** p. 90

Also available for these selections:

All **Literary Analysis: Legend and Fact** pp. 68, 86

EL **L3** **L4** **Grammar,** p. 89

All **Reading: Cause and Effect** pp. 67, 85

L3 **L4** **Support for Extend Your Learning,** p. 91

L4 **Enrichment,** pp. 38, 56

Assessment

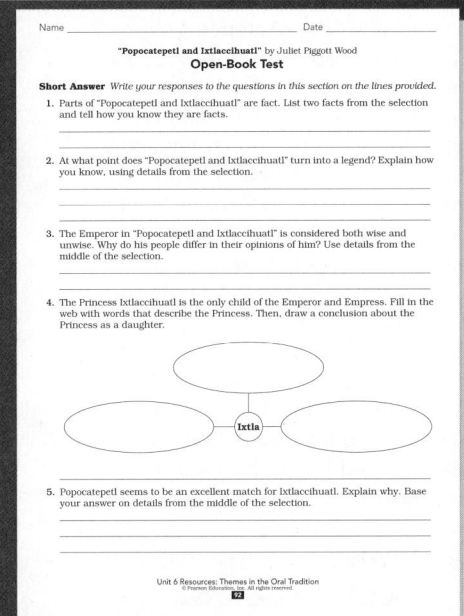

L3 **L4** **Open-Book Test,** pp. 71–73, 92–97

Also available for these selections:

EL **L1** **L2** **Selection Test A,** pp. 74–76, 95–97

EL **L3** **L4** **Selection Test B,** pp. 77–79, 98–100

PHLit Online!
www.PHLitOnline.com

Online Resources: All print materials are also available online.

- complete narrated selection text
- a thematically related video with writing prompt
- an interactive graphic organizer
- highlighting feature
- access to all student print resources, adapted to individual student needs
- Spanish and English summaries
- adapted selection translations in Spanish

Get Connected! (thematic video with writing prompt)

Also available:

Background Video
All videos are available in Spanish.

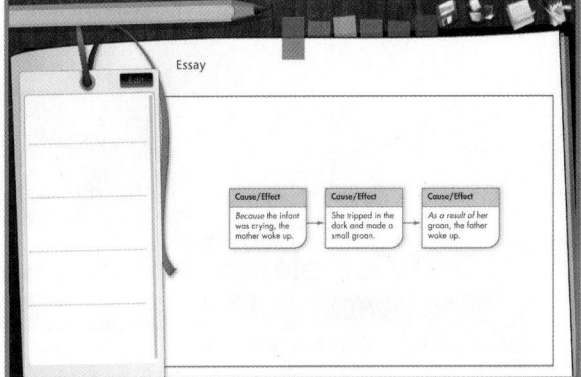

Writer's Journal (with graphics feature)

Also available:

Vocabulary Central (tools, activities, and songs for studying vocabulary)

❶ Leveled Texts

Skills instruction for both "Tenochtitlan: Inside the Aztec Capital" and "Popocatepetl and Ixtlaccihuatl" appears on p. 935. To meet CCSS RL.7.9, have students read both selections and compare them, following the Literary Analysis instruction on p. 935 and using the Writing activity on p. 957. To meet the other lesson objectives, you may choose to focus on just one of the selections. The Text Complexity Rubric at the bottom of this page will help you determine which selection is more appropriate for your students. Use the Reader and Task suggestions on the facing page to help all students read text of increasing complexity.

❷ ⓒ Introducing the CCS Standards

Introduce the standards on the student page. (Note that the lesson element with which each standard is addressed is identified in parentheses after the text of the standard.) Call out the standards that you will cover with the selections, explaining to students what each requires and how they will address it as they work through the selection you have chosen. Standards labeled "Spiral Review" are introduced in the Literary Analysis Workshop for this unit.

**Tenochtitlan: Inside the Aztec Capital •
Popocatepetl and Ixtlaccihuatl**

Before You Read

❶ ⓒ Leveled Texts

Build your skills and improve your comprehension of fiction and literary nonfiction with texts of increasing complexity.

Read **"Tenochtitlan: Inside the Aztec Capital"** to learn about life in the ancient Aztec city of Tenochtitlan.

Read **"Popocatepetl and Ixtlaccihuatl"** to learn what happens when a selfish emperor interferes with true love.

❷ ⓒ Common Core State Standards

Meet these standards with either **"Tenochtitlan: Inside the Aztec Capital"** (p. 938) or **"Popocatepetl and Ixtlaccihuatl"** (p. 946).

Reading Literature
9. Compare and contrast a fictional portrayal of a time, place, or character and a historical account of the same period as a means of understanding how authors of fiction use or alter history. *(Literary Analysis: Legend and Fact; Writing: Description and Comparison)*

Spiral Review: RL.2

Writing
1.a. Introduce claim(s), acknowledge alternate or opposing claims, and organize the reasons and evidence logically.
1.b. Support claim(s) with logical reasoning and relevant evidence, using accurate, credible sources and demonstrating an understanding of the topic or text. *(Speaking and Listening: Persuasive Speech)*

2. Write informative/explanatory texts to examine a topic and convey ideas, concepts, and information through the selection, organization, and analysis of relevant content.

2.b. Develop the topic with relevant facts, definitions, concrete details, quotations, or other information and examples. *(Writing: Description)*

Speaking and Listening
4. Present claims and findings, emphasizing salient points in a focused, coherent manner with pertinent descriptions, facts, details, and examples; use appropriate eye contact, adequate volume, and clear pronunciation. *(Speaking and Listening: Persuasive Speech)*

Language
2. Demonstrate command of the conventions of standard English capitalization, punctuation, and spelling when writing. **2.a.** Use a comma to separate coordinate adjectives. *(Conventions: Commas)*

4.b. Use common, grade-appropriate Greek or Latin affixes and roots as clues to the meaning of a word. *(Vocabulary: Word Study)*

934 Themes in the Oral Tradition

ⓒ Text Complexity Rubric: Leveled Texts

Text complexity is determined by both qualitative and quantitative measures. For this reason, the quantitative measure of a more complex selection may be lower than that of a more accessible selection.

		✓ Tenochtitlan: Inside the Aztec Capital	✓✓ Popocatepetl and Ixtlaccihuatl
Qualitative Measures	**Context/Knowledge Demands**	Aztecs; ancient Mexico 1 2 ③ 4 5	Volcanic mountains are explained; Aztec society 1 2 3 ④ 5
	Structure/Language Conventionality and Clarity	Subject-specific vocabulary; formal language; mostly short sentences; subheadings 1 2 3 ④ 5	Challenging vocabulary; some long and ornate sentences; fantastic descriptions; formal diction; flashback 1 2 3 ④ 5
	Levels of Meaning/ Purpose/Concept Level	Explicit purpose (describe life in Tenochtitlan); accessible concept (learn about other cultures) 1 2 ③ 4 5	Allegory (human story explains nature); challenging concept (don't interfere with true love) 1 2 3 ④ 5
Quantitative Measures	**Text Length**	Word Count: 1,052	Word Count: 2,566
	Lexile	870L	870L
Overall Complexity		✓ **More accessible**	✓✓ **More complex**

❸ Reading Skill: Cause and Effect

A **cause** is an event or situation that produces a result. An **effect** is the result produced. In a story or an essay, each effect may eventually become a cause for the next event. This results in a cause-and-effect chain that propels the action forward.

As you read, think about the causes and effects of events. If you do not clearly see the cause-and-effect relationships in a passage, **reread to look for connections** among the words and sentences.

Some words that identify causes and effects are *because, due to, for this reason,* and *as a result.*

❹ Using the Strategy: Cause-and-Effect Chain

Notice the clue words in this **cause-and-effect chain**.

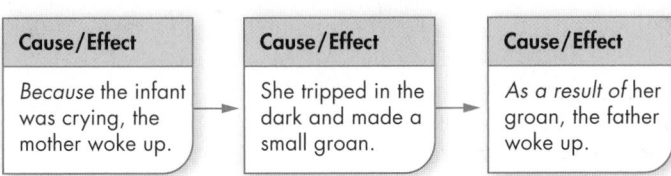

Cause/Effect	Cause/Effect	Cause/Effect
Because the infant was crying, the mother woke up.	She tripped in the dark and made a small groan.	*As a result of* her groan, the father woke up.

❺ Literary Analysis: Legend and Fact

A **legend** is a traditional story about the past. A **fact** is something that can be proved to be true. Before legends were written down, they were passed on orally. Legends are based on facts that have grown into fiction in the many retellings over generations.

Every culture has its own legends to immortalize famous people. Most legends include these elements:

- a human who is larger than life
- fantastic elements
- roots or basis in historical facts
- events that reflect the culture that created the story

As you read, compare and contrast the historical facts about the ancient Aztec city of Tenochtitlan with a legend about that same city.

Before You Read: Tenochtitlan: Inside the Aztec Capital • Popocatepetl and Ixtlaccihuatl **935**

❸ Reading Skill
Cause and Effect

1. Introduce the skill, using the instruction on the student page.
2. Tell students they will practice identifying causes and effects as they read.

❹ Using the Strategy

Give students a copy of either **Reading Skill Graphic Organizer A** or **B** (*Graphic Organizer Transparencies,* pp. 177–179) to identify cause-and-effect chains as they read. Use the examples in **Reading Skill Graphic Organizer A,** which is partially filled in, to model the process of completing the organizer.

❺ Literary Analysis
Legend and Fact

1. Introduce the skill, using the instruction on the student page.
2. Tell students that they will compare legends and facts as they read.

Think Aloud: Model the Skill

Model a way to identify elements of legends. Say to students:

> To help me remember the elements of legends, I think of a simple legend from my community. Brian was an amazing football quarterback. Over time, people said that Brian never missed a pass and never lost a game. These weren't true facts about Brian, but people were so excited by Brian's success that they made it bigger and bigger in their minds. Eventually, Brian was a legend. When I read legends, I look for what may have originally been the facts and what has been added.

© Text Complexity: Reader and Task Suggestions

✓ Tenochtitlan: Inside the Aztec Capital		✓✓ Popocatepetl and Ixtlaccihuatl	
Preparing to Read the Text	**Leveled Tasks**	**Preparing to Read the Text**	**Leveled Tasks**
• Using Background on p. 937, relate the origins of modern Mexico City to the Aztec city in the essay. • Urge students to use subheadings to guide their understanding of difficult vocabulary. (Differentiated Instruction, TE p. 939) • Guide students to use Multidraft Reading strategies (TE p. 937).	*Structure/Language* If students will have difficulty with language, have them first read to identify amazing details about the ancient city. Then, have them reread, noting vocabulary or sentences they find confusing. *Evaluating* If students will not have difficulty with language, have them note ways in which the author uses subject-specific descriptive language to create a vivid image of the Aztec city and its achievements.	• Using Background on p. 945, discuss the role of the oral tradition in ancient Aztec culture. • Review strategies for reading formal language and complex diction, such as using punctuation to isolate accessible chunks. • Guide students to use Multidraft Reading strategies (TE p. 945).	*Structure/Language* If students will have difficulty with language, have them read to learn how Popo's and Ixtla's love story ends. Have them reread, identifying confusing sentences and clauses. *Analyzing* If students will not have difficulty with language, have them note as they read ways in which the author uses diction to capture the legend's historical voice.

935

❶ Writing About the Big Question

1. Review the assignment with the class.

2. Name and describe a common community effort, such as to clean up a park or to get rid of graffiti. Ask students who might participate in such an effort and who might benefit from it.

3. Have students complete the sentence starter. Review responses as a class. (**Sample response:** When people work together for a <u>common</u> cause, they can help not only themselves but <u>others</u>.)

4. Remind students that their answers will help them think about the Big Question, "Community or individual— which is more important?"

While You Read

Tell students that as they read, they should look for details that show how the Aztecs worked to benefit the entire community.

❷ Vocabulary

1. Have students preview the selection vocabulary.

2. For each word, have students say the word aloud.

3. Then, use the word in a sentence that defines the word.

4. Finally, repeat your definitional sentence or a similar sentence with the word missing and have the class "fill in the blank" chorally. Here are some examples:

> *Outskirts* are a part of a city far from the city center. It takes me an hour to get to work because I live far away, in the city's [students say "outskirts"].

> *Goblets* are large bowl-shaped drinking containers without handles. Kings and queens often drank from large golden [students say "goblets"].

❸ Word Study

1. Introduce the skill, using the instruction in the box.

2. Post this sentence: *The safety measures are <u>outdated</u>.* Then, ask students what *outdated* means (**Possible response:** "outside the date"; not suited to the present).

936

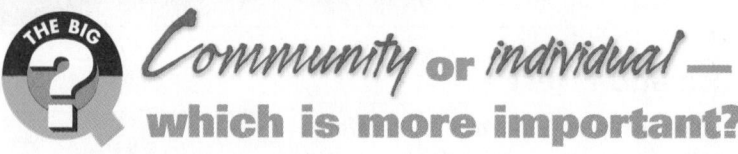

Community or individual— which is more important?

❶ Writing About the Big Question

"Tenochtitlan: Inside the Aztec Capital," describes how the Aztecs designed their city to prevent crop damage and protect against flooding. Use this sentence starter to develop your ideas about the Big Question.

> When people work together for a **common** cause, they can help not only themselves but _____.

While You Read Look for details that show how the Aztecs worked to benefit the entire community.

❷ Vocabulary

Read each word and its definition. Decide whether you know the word well, know it a little bit, or do not know it at all. After you read, see how your knowledge of each word has increased.

- **causeways** (kôz´ wāz´) *n.* roads across wet ground or shallow water (p. 939) *High waves washed away the causeways.* *causeway n.*

- **irrigation** (ir´ ə gā´ shən) *n.* the act of supplying water to land or crops (p. 940) *Irrigation makes farming possible in dry regions.* *irrigate v. irrigated v. irrigating v.*

- **nobility** (nō bil´ ə tē) *n.* people with a high rank in society (p. 940) *The nobility threw fancy parties.* *noble adj. nobleness n. nobly adv.*

- **outskirts** (out´ skurtz´) *n.* parts of a district far from the center of a city (p. 941) *The mall is on the outskirts of the city.*

- **reeds** (rēdz) *n.* tall, slender grasses that grow in marshy land (p. 941) *The reeds blew in the wind.* *reedy adj. reedier adj.*

- **goblets** (gäb´ lits) *n.* bowl-shaped drinking containers without handles (p. 942) *We broke two goblets during Thanksgiving dinner.* *goblet n.*

❸ Word Study

The **Old English prefix** *out-* means "outside" or "more than."

This article describes how poor people built their homes on the **outskirts,** or areas outside the center, of an ancient Aztec city.

936 Themes in the Oral Tradition

Vocabulary Development

Vocabulary Knowledge Rating

Create a **Vocabulary Knowledge Rating Chart** (*Professional Development Guidebook*, p. 33) for this selection. Include the selection vocabulary and the Big Question word that appears in the Writing About the Big Question sentence starter on this page. (The Big Question vocabulary is introduced on pp. 900–901.)

Give students a copy of the chart. Read the words aloud, and have students mark their rating in the Before Reading column. Urge them to be alert to these words as they read and discuss the selection.

Tally how many students think they know a word to gauge how much instruction to provide. As students read and discuss the selection, point out the words and their context.

Vocabulary Central, featuring tools, activities, and songs for studying vocabulary, is available online at **www.PHLitOnline.com**.

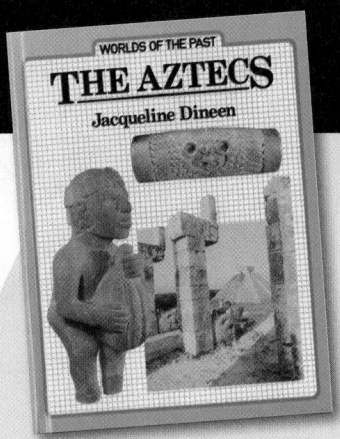

WORLDS OF THE PAST
THE AZTECS
Jacqueline Dineen

▲ "Tenochtitlan: Inside the Aztec Capital" appears in Dineen's book *The Aztecs.*

Meet
Jacqueline Dineen

Author of
TENOCHTITLAN:
INSIDE THE AZTEC CAPITAL

Jacqueline Dineen began her career as an editor for an educational publisher in London before she turned to writing children's books. She has written books on a variety of subjects, including science, history, and geography. Among them are *Lift the Lid on Mummies, The Early Inventions,* and *Food From the Sea.*

Text and Images In "Tenochtitlan: Inside the Aztec Capital," Dineen uses a skillful mix of description, eyewitness accounts, maps, photographs, and art to give readers a sense of what it took to build the city.

DID YOU KNOW?
Dineen has written more than eighty books.

❹ BACKGROUND FOR THE ESSAY

The Origins of Mexico City

Mexico City, the capital of Mexico, was built on the ruins of the ancient Aztec city of Tenochtitlan. The city itself sat on an island in the center of a lake called Texcoco. Over the years, the lake was slowly drained to make room for the growing city. Because Mexico City is located on a drained lakebed, the effects of earthquakes have been severe. The city is slowly sinking several inches a year. "Tenochtitlan: Inside the Aztec Capital" presents factual information about the people and activities of the legendary city.

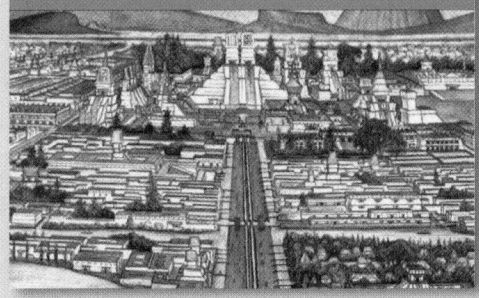

Tenochtitlan: Inside the Aztec Capital **937**

🖊 Daily Bellringer

For each class during which you teach this selection, have students complete one of the five Sentence Modeling activities for Week 32 in the *Daily Bellringer Activities* booklet.

❹ Background
Origins of Mexico City

Tenochtitlan saw monumental construction in A.D.100–200, when it became the largest and most densely populated urban center in the Americas. Astute use of natural resources, growth in agricultural production, technological innovation, and trading systems help explain the city's development and expansion. At its height, Tenochtitlan was the sixth largest city in the world.

Multidraft Reading

To assist struggling readers and to deepen reading for all, assign the text in "chunks" and apply multidraft reading protocols. For each reading, have students set the purpose indicated:

- **First reading**—identifying key ideas and details and answering any Reading Checks.
- **Second reading**—analyzing craft and structure and responding to the side-column prompts.
- **Third reading**—integrating knowledge and ideas, connecting to other texts and the world, and answering the end-of-selection questions.

For more guidance, refer to the *Classroom Strategies and Teaching Routines* card on multidraft reading.

Differentiated
Instruction   Additional Instruction

EL Extended Support— English Learners
Have students complete the **Reading and Vocabulary Warm-ups,** *Unit 6 Resources,* pp. 62–65, before they read. Assign the prereading pages and the adapted selection in the *Reader's Notebook: English Learner's Version.* Then, have students listen to portions of the selection on the *Hear It!* **Audio CD.**

L1 L2 Extended Support— Struggling Readers
Have students complete the **Reading and Vocabulary Warm-ups,** *Unit 6 Resources,* pp. 62–65, before they read. Assign the prereading pages and the adapted selection in the *Reader's Notebook: Adapted Version.* Then, have students listen to portions of the selection on the *Hear It!* **Audio CD** (adapted text).

Extended Support— Reluctant Readers
To build motivation and engagement before assigning the selection, have students read "Restoring Cities from the Ground Up," a thematically related selection in *Reality Central.* Then, use the questions at the conclusion of the related selection to guide discussion.

PHLit Online!
For more about the author, practice with the selection vocabulary, or more background, go online at www.PHLitOnline.com.

❶ Activating Prior Knowledge

1. Assign students to small groups. Give students a copy of a **KWL chart** (*Professional Development Guidebook,* p. 75), with the topic identified as "Tenochtitlan." Ask them to work together to complete the first two columns. In the Know column, they can write what they know or something they learned reading the background information on the previous page. In the Want to Know column, they should write questions they have about the ancient Aztec capital.

2. For further guidance, see the *Classroom Strategy and Teaching Routines* card for **Using a Graphic Organizer.**

Concept Connector ➡

Students will assess what they've learned after completing "Tenochtitlan: Inside the Aztec Capital."

Whole-Class Activity

Have students sketch a map of their community in the style of the map on this page. Tell students to include waterways and geographical features, in addition to streets. Display the completed maps in the classroom. Then, lead a discussion about the similarities and differences in the layout of Tenochtitlan and students' communities.

❷ About the Selection

"Tenochtitlan: Inside the Aztec Capital" gives a brief overview of the city of Tenochtitlan and the lives of its inhabitants. The selection contains heads that break up the text and can help students find information on specific topics.

❶ TENOCHTITLAN:
❷ INSIDE THE AZTEC CAPITAL
Jacqueline Dineen

938 Themes in the Oral Tradition

Vocabulary Development

© **CCSS Language 6**

Thematic Vocabulary: The Big Question
As students are discussing "Tenochtitlan: Inside the Aztec Capital," encourage them to use the thematic vocabulary presented in Introducing the Big Question, pp. 900–901. You might encourage them with sentence starters like these:

1. The Aztec *community* was . . .
2. The *environment* at Tenochtitlan led the Aztecs . . .
3. People rich and poor shared the *common* goals of . . .
4. Everyone worked as a *team* in order to . . .
5. Most Aztec *families* lived in . . .

The Lake City of Tenochtitlan

The city of Tenochtitlan[1] began on an island in the middle of a swampy lake. There the Aztecs built their first temple to Huitzilopochtli.[2] The place was given the name Tenochtitlan, which means "The Place of the Fruit of the Prickly Pear Cactus." Later on the name was given to the city that grew up around the temple. The Aztecs rebuilt their temples on the same site every 52 years, so the first temple eventually became the great Temple Mayor[3] that stood at the center of the city.

The city started as a collection of huts. It began to grow after 1385, while Acamapichtli[4] was king. The Aztecs were excellent engineers. They built three causeways over the swamp to link the city with the mainland. These were raised roads made of stone supported on wooden pillars. Parts of the causeways were bridges. These bridges could be removed to leave gaps and this prevented enemies from getting to the city. Fresh water was brought from the mainland to the city along stone aqueducts.[5]

Inside the City

The Spaniards' first view of Tenochtitlan was described by one of Cortés's[6] soldiers, Bernal Diaz: "And when we saw all those towns and level causeway leading into Mexico, we were astounded. These great towns and buildings rising from the water, all made of stone, seemed like an enchanted vision."

By that time Tenochtitlan was the largest city in Mexico. About 200,000 people lived there. The houses were one story high and had flat roofs. In the center of the city was a large square. The twin temple stood on one side, and the king's palace on another. Officials' houses made of white stone also lined the square. There were few roads. People traveled in canoes along canals.

Floating Gardens

Tenochtitlan was built in a huge valley, the Valley of Mexico, which was surrounded by mountains. Rivers flowed from the

---

1. **Tenochtitlan** (tä nôch′ tēt län′) *n.* ancient Aztec capital located in what is now Mexico City.
2. **Huitzilopochtli** (wēt sē lō pōch′ tlē)
3. **Mayor** (mä yōr′) *adj.* (Sp.) main.
4. **Acamapichtli** (ä kä mä pēch′ tlē)
5. **aqueducts** (ak′ wə dukts′) *n.* large bridgelike structures made for bringing water from a distant source.
6. **Hernando Cortés** (er nän′ dō kōr tes′) Spanish adventurer (1485–1547) who conquered what is now central and southern Mexico.

Tenochtitlan: Inside the Aztec Capital **939**

---

❸ ◄ Critical Viewing
What features of the city described in the text are shown on this map? [Connect]

Vocabulary
causeways (kôz′wāz′) *n.* roads across wet ground or shallow water

Legend and Fact
How might the Spaniards' reactions to their first sight of Tenochtitlan have sparked the beginning of a legend?

❺ Reading Check
Who built the city of Tenochtitlan?

---

❸ Critical Viewing
Answer: The temples, lake, canals, and causeways linking the city with the mainland are shown on the map.

❹ Legend and Fact

1. Remind students how legend and fact are connected: legends are based on facts that have grown into fiction as they are passed from generation to generation.

2. Read Diaz's description of Tenochtitlan with students. Point out that Diaz reports the Spaniards were "astounded" by their first view of Tenochtitlan. **Ask** students why the Spaniards may have felt this way. **Possible response:** The design and architecture of the city may have been far superior to anything they had seen before.

3. Then, **ask** the Legend and Fact question. **Possible response:** The astounding things that the Spaniards saw might have led them to exaggerate and therefore sparked the beginning of a legend.

❺ Reading Check
Answer: The Aztecs built the city of Tenochtitlan.

Differentiated
Instruction *for Universal Access*

Strategy for Less Proficient Readers
To help less proficient readers understand the selection, explain that the writer uses heads to organize information. Have students list the heads and write brief summaries of the information contained under each. After students finish reading the selection, have them combine their summaries to make a summary of the whole article.

Enrichment for Advanced Readers
Point out that the selection gives a brief overview of the city of Tenochtitlan and the lives of its inhabitants. Challenge students to find out more about one aspect of ancient Aztec life. Students might focus on the engineering used to build Tenochtitlan, how the city was planned, or what became of it. Invite students to share their findings with the class.

PHLit Online!
This selection is available in interactive format in the **Enriched Online Student Edition**, at **www.PHLitOnline.com**, which includes a thematically related video with writing prompt and an interactive graphic organizer.

❻ Cause and Effect

1. Ask a volunteer to read the bracketed paragraph aloud. **Ask:** What dangers did the northern lakes pose to the city?
Possible responses: They could damage the crops and cause flooding.

2. Then, **ask** the Cause and Effect question.
Answer: The Aztecs built an embankment to keep salt water out of the irrigation system and to protect Tenochtitlan from floods.

3. **Ask** students to explain whether the answers they gave are causes or effects. How do they know?
Possible response: They are causes. The word *reasons* in the question shows that it asks about causes. Causes are reasons why something happened.

▶ **Monitor Progress:** Review students' graphic organizers to check their identification of cause-and-effect relationships.

▶ **Reteach:** If students are having difficulty identifying cause-and-effect relationships, show them the partially completed **Graphic Organizer A** (*Graphic Organizer Transparencies,* p. 177) to help them clear up misconceptions and correct their work.

❼ ⸮ Connecting to the Big Question

1. Display food items and explore their origin with students. Point out that food producers and consumers become a community.

2. Have students read the bracketed text on page 940. **Ask** students: How did the Aztecs get food for everyone in the community?
Possible response: Food came from farming and from outside the city.

3. **Ask:** In what ways did adding more people—more individuals—cause problems for the community?
Possible response: To grow sufficient food, the Aztecs had to drain and create more farmland.

940

Cause and Effect ❻
What are two reasons the Aztecs built an embankment?

940 Themes in the Oral Tradition

---

mountains into Lake Texcoco, where Tenochtitlan stood. The lake was linked to four other shallow, swampy lakes. The land around the lakes was dry because there was very little rain. The Aztecs dug ditches and piled up the earth to make islands in the shallow parts of the lake. These chinampas, or swamp gardens, could be farmed. The ditches carried water into larger canals that were used for irrigation and as waterways to the city.

Texcoco and the lake to the south contained fresh water, but the northern lakes contained salt water, which was no good for irrigation. The Aztecs built an embankment[7] 10 miles long to keep out the salt water and also to protect the city from flooding.

Feeding the People
Archaeologists think that when Tenochtitlan was at its greatest, about one million people lived in the Valley of Mexico. That included Tenochtitlan and the 50 or 60 city-states on the mainland surrounding the lakes. Food for all these people had to come from farming.

Historians are not sure how many people in Tenochtitlan were farmers, but they think it may have been between one third and one half of the population. The rest were the nobility, craftspeople, and others. Each chinampa was only big enough to grow food for one family. Most people in Tenochtitlan depended on food from outside the city.

As the city grew, more and more land was drained for farming and for building. Farmers had no tools except simple hoes and digging sticks, but the loose soil was fertile and easy to turn. The main crop was corn, but farmers also grew tomatoes, beans, chili peppers, and prickly pears. They grew maguey cactus for its fibers and to make a drink called pulque. Cacao trees were grown in the hottest areas. The seeds were used for trading and to make a chocolate drink.

Inside an Aztec Home
There were big differences between a rich Aztec home and a poor one. The nobles' houses were like palaces. They were one story high and built around

❼

❽

7. **embankment** (em bank′ mənt) *n.* wall of earth built to keep water back.

Vocabulary Development

Vocabulary Knowledge Rating
When students have completed reading and discussing "Tenochtitlan: Inside the Aztec Capital," have them take out their **Vocabulary Knowledge Rating Chart**. Read the words aloud once more and have students rate their knowledge of the words again in the After Reading column. Clarify any words that are still problematic. Have students write their own definition and example or sentence in the appropriate column. Then, have students complete the Vocabulary Practice activities at the end of the selection. Encourage students to use the words in further discussion and written work about this selection. Remind them that they will be accountable for these words on the **Selection Test,** *Unit 6 Resources,* pp. 74–76 or 77–79.

a courtyard. Each of the four sides contained four or five large rooms. The courtyards were planted with flower and vegetable gardens. Some houses on the island in the center of the city were built of adobe—bricks made from mud and dried in the sun. Adobe is still used for building in Mexico today. These grand houses and palaces were whitewashed so that they shone in the sun. The Spanish soldier Bernal Diaz described buildings that looked like "gleaming white towers and castles: a marvelous sight."

There is very little evidence about the buildings in Tenochtitlan and hardly any about the poor people's houses. What we do know has been pieced together from scattered historical records such as documents that record the sale of building sites on the chinampa gardens. All of the poorer people's homes were built on the chinampas on the outskirts of the city. Because the chinampas would not take the weight of stone, houses had to be built of lighter materials such as wattle-and-daub. This was made by weaving reeds together and then plastering them with mud. We know that the outskirts of the city were divided into groups of houses inside walled areas, or compounds. A whole family lived in each compound. The family consisted of a couple, their married children, and their grandchildren. Every married couple in the family had a separate house of one or two rooms. All the

Spiral Review
Central Idea How does the author support the idea that the homes of rich and poor Aztecs were very different?

Vocabulary
outskirts (out skʉrtz´) *n.* parts of a district far from the center of a city
reeds (rēdz) *n.* tall, slender grasses that grow in marshy land

❾ ▼ Critical Viewing
What details in this picture suggest the Aztecs' daily activities? **[Analyze]**

Tenochtitlan: Inside the Aztec Capital **941**

Spiral Review
Central Idea

1. Remind students that they studied the concept of central idea in the Unit 6 Literary Analysis Workshop (pp. 902–911).

2. **Ask** the Spiral Review question.

Possible response: The author uses details to describe the differences between the richer and poorer people's homes. Richer people's houses were at the center of the city, while the poorer people's were on the outskirts. Richer people's houses were made of adobe, while the poorer people's were made of wattle -and -daub.

❽ Critical Thinking
Compare and Contrast

1. Have students read the bracketed passage, which begins on p. 940.

2. Then, **ask** students to identify differences between the houses of the rich and houses of the poor. **Answer:** The rich lived in houses that were like palaces. They were large and surrounded by courtyards planted with flower and vegetable gardens. Some nobles' houses were made of adobe and whitewashed, so they shone in the sun. The poor lived with their families in small one- or two-room huts that were part of a compound. Built on the chinampas, the huts were made of lighter building materials, such as wattle-and-daub.

❾ Critical Viewing

Possible response: The pile of corn on cobs and the bowls of corn kernels suggest that one daily activity was shucking corn.

Concept Connector

KWL Chart
Have students complete the last column of their **KWL charts.** They may do this individually or in their original pairs or groups. As a class, discuss what questions have been answered and what new questions have emerged.

Writing About the Big Question
Have students compare their response to the sentence starter they completed before reading the selection with their ideas afterward. Ask them to explain whether their thoughts have changed.

Reading Skill Graphic Organizer
Ask students to review the graphic organizers they completed to analyze cause-and-effect relationships while reading. Then have students share their graphic organizers.

Critical Thinking

Before students respond, you may wish to have them write a brief objective summary of the selection. As they answer the questions below, remind them to support their answers with evidence from the text.

1. (a) **Possible response:** In the shallow part of Lake Texcoco, the Aztecs made chinampas, which could be farmed. (b) The chinampas allowed the people of Tenochtitlan to produce more of their own food. Each chinampa produced enough food to feed one family.

2. (a) **Possible response:** The island environment separated the people of Tenochtitlan from the people on the mainland. (b) The Aztecs dealt well with this element. They built causeways to link the city with the mainland.

3. **Possible responses:** The author uses factual information about the Aztecs' environment to show their achievements in agriculture and engineering. She uses factual information about houses to compare and contrast the lives of the rich and poor.

4. **Possible response:** Individuals helped to build the canals, causeways, and chinampas that benefited the entire community.

---

houses opened onto an outdoor patio that belonged to the whole family.

Outside the house, the families often kept turkeys in pens. The turkeys provided eggs and meat. There was also a beehive for honey. Most families had a bathhouse in the garden.

Furniture and Decoration

Aztec houses were very plain inside. Everyone slept on mats of reeds that were spread on the dirt floor at night. Families had cooking pots and utensils made of clay. There were goblets for pulque and other drinks, graters for grinding chilis, and storage pots of various designs. Reed baskets were also used for storage. Households had grinding stones for grinding corn into flour. There was also a household shrine with statues of the gods.

The houses had no windows or chimneys, so they must have been dark and smoky from the cooking fire. There were no doors, just an open doorway. Even the palaces had open doorways with cloths hanging over them.

Vocabulary
goblets (gäb´ lits) *n.* bowl-shaped drinking containers without handles

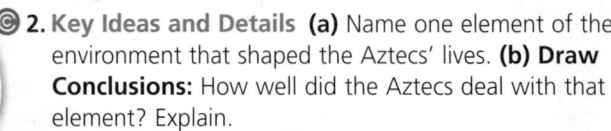

Critical Thinking

Cite textual evidence to support your responses.

1. **Key Ideas and Details (a)** Describe one way the Aztecs shaped their environment to suit their needs. **(b) Make a Judgment:** How did this improve their lives?

2. **Key Ideas and Details (a)** Name one element of the environment that shaped the Aztecs' lives. **(b) Draw Conclusions:** How well did the Aztecs deal with that element? Explain.

3. **Craft and Structure Analyze:** How does the author use factual information to present a clear picture of ancient Aztec life?

4. **Integration of Knowledge and Ideas** How did each individual's efforts contribute to the good of the Aztec community? *[Connect to the Big Question: Community or individual—which is more important?]*

Assessment Resources

Unit 6 Resources

L1 L2 EL Selection Test A, pp. 74–76. Administer Test A to less advanced students.

L3 L4 EL Selection Test B, pp. 77–79. Administer Test B to on-level and more advanced students.

L3 L4 Open-Book Test, pp. 71–73. As an alternative, give the Open-Book Test.

All Customizable Test Bank

All Self-tests
Students may prepare for the **Selection Test** by taking the **Self-test** online.

 All assessment resources are available at www.PHLitOnline.com.

Reading Skill: Cause and Effect

1. What might have **caused** the Aztecs to remove the bridges from the causeways?

2. Reread the essay to find an **effect** for each of these causes:
   (a) The city of Tenochtitlan was built on a lake.
   (b) The city grew.
   (c) Aztec houses had no windows or chimneys.

Literary Analysis: Legend and Fact

3. **Key Ideas and Details (a)** Identify three **facts** from the essay. **(b)** Identify two predictions or assumptions made by archaeologists that are likely to be true but cannot be proved.

4. **Integration of Knowledge and Ideas** Use the chart below to explain what facts in this essay could be used to create an interesting **legend** about Tenochtitlan.

Facts from the essay	Possible use in a legend

Vocabulary

Acquisition and Use Answer each of the following questions.

1. What type of buildings might you find on the *outskirts* of a modern city?

2. Where do *reeds* grow?

3. What might you do with a set of *goblets*?

4. When might it be useful to build a *causeway*?

5. In what way is *irrigation* useful to farmers?

6. Why would you expect members of the *nobility* to live in fancy homes?

Word Study Use the context of the sentences and what you know about the **Old English prefix *out-*** to explain your answers.

1. If you *outbid* me, did you bid more or less than I did?

2. What do you risk by engaging in an activity that has been *outlawed*?

Word Study

The **Old English prefix *out-*** means "outside" or "more than."

Apply It Explain how the prefix *out-* contributes to the meanings of these words. Consult a dictionary if necessary.

outcast
outnumber
outpatient

Word Study
Sample answers:
1. More; The prefix *out-* means "more than" and *outbid* means "bid more than."
2. The prefix *out-* means "outside" and *outlawed* means "outside, or against, the law." Engaging in an outlawed activity risks arrest.

Word Study: Apply It
Sample answers: An *outcast* lives <u>outside</u> a group or community. To *outnumber* is to have <u>more</u> people than another group. An *outpatient* gets care <u>outside</u> or without staying the night in a hospital.

Reading Skill

1. Approaching enemies might have caused the Aztecs to remove the bridges.

2. **Possible response:** (a) The Aztecs had water for irrigation. (b) There were more people to feed. (c) The houses were dark and smoky.

Literary Analysis

3. **Possible responses:** (a) The Aztecs built three causeways over the swamp; Tenochtitlan was built in a huge valley; Water flowed along stone aqueducts from the mainland to Tenochtitlan. (b) About one million people lived in the Valley of Mexico when Tenochtitlan was at its height; Between one third and one half of the people in Tenochtitlan were farmers.

4. **Possible responses:** Article Facts—Tenochtitlan means, "The Place of the Fruit of the Prickly Pear Cactus;" the Aztecs rebuilt their temples on the same site every 52 years; Use for Legend— One day, the cactus fruit takes human form and marries an Aztec princess.

   For other sample answers, see *Graphic Organizer Transparencies,* **Literary Analysis Graphic Organizer A,** p. 180, and the **Additional Answers** section.

Vocabulary
Acquisition and Use
Sample answers:
1. You would find homes on the <u>outskirts</u> of a modern city.
2. <u>Reeds</u> grow in swamps.
3. You might serve drinks in <u>goblets</u>.
4. A <u>causeway</u> would be useful to connect an island to nearby land.
5. <u>Irrigation</u> helps farmers get water for their plants.
6. Members of the <u>nobility</u> live in fancy houses because they have high rank and are probably wealthy.

Skills instruction for the Reading Skill and Literary Analysis concepts for this selection appears on p. 935.

❶ ⓧ **Writing About the Big Question**

1. Review the assignment with the class.

2. Ask students to name chores that different family members are responsible for in their homes. Discuss what duty, or responsibility, family members have to each other.

3. Have students complete the sentence starter. Review responses as a class. <u>Tradition</u> and <u>duty</u> to one's community sometimes require a person to put his or her own needs last.)

4. Remind students that their answers will help them think about the Big Question, "Community or individual— which is more important?"

While You Read

Tell students that as they read, they should look for details that suggest the Emperor does not consider the future results of his actions.

❷ Vocabulary

1. Have students preview the selection vocabulary.

2. For each word, have students say the word aloud.

3. Then, use the word in a sentence that defines the word.

4. Finally, repeat your definitional sentence or a similar sentence with the word missing and have the class "fill in the blank" chorally. Here are some examples:

When a vote is <u>unanimous,</u> all of the voters agree. If everyone votes for Yoshi to be captain, his election is [students say "unanimous"].

To be <u>routed</u> is to be totally defeated. When our soccer team lost the game 10–0, we said we had been [students say "routed"].

❸ Word Study

1. Introduce the skill, using the instruction in the box.

2. Ask students to suggest a *uni-* word that means "the only one of a kind." *(unique)*

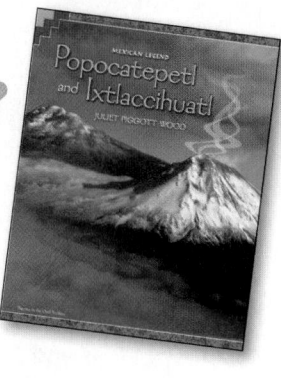

Community or *individual—* **which is more important?**

❶ Writing About the Big Question

In "Popocatepetl and Ixtlaccihuatl," an Aztec princess is expected to sacrifice true love in order to assume her responsibilities as ruler of a kingdom. Use this sentence starter to develop your ideas about the Big Question.

> **Tradition** and **duty** to one's community sometimes require a person to _____.

While You Read Look for details that suggest the Emperor does not consider the future results of his actions.

❷ Vocabulary

Read each word and its definition. Decide whether you know the word well, know it a little bit, or do not know it at all. After you read, see how your knowledge of each word has increased.

- **shortsightedness** (short´ sīt´ id nəs) *n.* condition of not considering the future effects of something (p. 948) *Her shortsightedness left her unprepared for the storm.* shortsighted *adj.* shortsightedly *adv.*

- **feebleness** (fē´ bəl nəs) *n.* weakness (p. 949) *His feebleness did not stop the old man from walking his beloved dog.* feeble *adj.* feebly *adv.* feebler *adj.*

- **decreed** (di krēd´) *v.* officially ordered (p. 949) *The Queen decreed the day a holiday.* decree *v.* decreeing *v.*

- **relished** (rel´ isht) *v.* enjoyed; liked (p. 950) *Her grandmother relished time alone with a good book.* relish *v.* relish *n.*

- **unanimous** (yoo nan´ ə məs) *adj.* based on complete agreement (p. 951) *Beth was elected president by a unanimous vote.* unanimously *adv.* unanimity *n.*

- **routed** (rout´ əd) *v.* completely defeated (p. 952) *The king's men routed the invaders.* rout *v.*

❸ Word Study

The **Latin prefix** *uni-* means "having or consisting of only one."

In this legend, the Aztec warriors are **unanimous,** or sharing one opinion, about who is responsible for their victory.

---

944 Themes in the Oral Tradition

Vocabulary Development

Vocabulary Knowledge Rating
Create a **Vocabulary Knowledge Rating Chart** (*Professional Development Guidebook,* p. 33) for this selection. Include the selection vocabulary and the Big Question words that appear in the Writing About the Big Question sentence starter on this page. (The Big Question vocabulary is introduced on pp. 900–901.)

Give students a copy of the chart. Read the words aloud, and have students mark their rating in the Before Reading column. Urge them to be alert to these words as they read and discuss the selection.

Tally how many students think they know a word to gauge how much instruction to provide. As students read and discuss the selection, point out the words and their context.

Vocabulary Central, featuring tools, activities, and songs for studying vocabulary, is available online at **www.PHLitOnline.com.**

Meet
Juliet Piggott Wood
(1924–1996)

Author of
Popocatepetl
and Ixtlaccihuatl

Juliet Piggott Wood discovered her love for learning about different cultures while living in Japan, where her grandfather was a legal advisor to Prince Ito. Wood's interest in Japan inspired her to produce several books on Japanese history and folklore. Her fascination with one culture led to research about others. She went on to co-author a book retelling famous fairy tales from around the world.

Far and Wide In World War II, Wood served in England in the Women's Royal Naval Service. Her experience in that war may have influenced her to write about other military battles, especially the legendary Aztec battle described in her book on Mexican folk tales. Clearly a person with many talents, Wood expanded her nonfiction list with a work on famous regiments in Queen Alexandra's Royal Army Nursing Corps.

> **DID YOU KNOW?**
> Wood co-authored a book retelling famous fairy tales from around the world.

❹ BACKGROUND FOR THE LEGEND

The Oral Tradition

The oral tradition is the collection of songs, stories, and poems that are passed from generation to generation by word of mouth. People used the traditional stories to communicate shared beliefs and to explain their world. In "Popocatepetl and Ixtlaccihuatl," you will see how the storyteller shares Aztec beliefs through a tale about teenagers who fall in love.

Popocatepetl and Ixtlaccihuatl **945**

❹ Daily Bellringer

For each class during which you teach this selection, have students complete one of the five Sentence Modeling activities for Week 32 in the *Daily Bellringer Activities* booklet.

❹ Background

Oral Tradition Aztec legends treat the origins not only of Tenochtitlan's volcanic mountains but also of the city itself. According to legend, the god Quetzalcoatl told the people to build their capital city in the place where they would see an eagle holding a snake in its claw while perched atop a cactus growing out of a rock. Hundreds of years passed before a group of people saw just such an eagle. Unfortunately, the rock from which the cactus grew was in the middle of a lake. Believing that they had received a signal from Quetzalcoatl, the Aztecs began the long and difficult process of filling the lake to create a building site for their city.

Multidraft Reading

To assist struggling readers and to deepen reading for all, assign the text in "chunks" and apply multidraft reading protocols. For each reading, have students set the purpose indicated:

- **First reading**—identifying key ideas and details and answering any Reading Checks.
- **Second reading**—analyzing craft and structure and responding to the side-column prompts.
- **Third reading**—integrating knowledge and ideas, connecting to other texts and the world, and answering the end-of-selection questions.

For more guidance, refer to the *Classroom Strategies and Teaching Routines* card on multidraft reading.

Differentiated Instruction   Additional Instruction

EL Extended Support— English Learners
Have students complete the **Reading and Vocabulary Warm-ups,** *Unit 6 Resources,* pp. 80–83, before they read. Assign the prereading pages and the adapted selection in the *Reader's Notebook: English Learner's Version*. Then, have students listen to portions of the selection on the *Hear It! Audio CD.*

L1 L2 Extended Support— Struggling Readers
Have students complete the **Reading and Vocabulary Warm-ups,** *Unit 6 Resources,* pp. 80–83, before they read. Assign the prereading pages and the adapted selection in the *Reader's Notebook: Adapted Version*. Then, have students listen to portions of the selection on the *Hear It! Audio CD* (adapted text).

Extended Support— Reluctant Readers
To build motivation and engagement before assigning the selection, have students read "What It Takes to Lead," a thematically related selection in *Reality Central*. Then, use the questions at the conclusion of the related selection to guide discussion.

For more about the author, practice with the selection vocabulary, or more background, go online at www.PHLitOnline.com.

❶ Activating Prior Knowledge

1. Assign students to small groups. Give students a copy of a **KWL chart** (*Professional Development Guidebook*, p. 75), with the topic identified as Legend. Ask them to work together to complete the first two columns. In the Know column, they can write what they know or something they learned reading the background information on the previous page. In the Want to Know column, they should write questions they have about legends.

2. For further guidance, use the *Classroom Strategies and Teaching Routines* card, **Using a Graphic Organizer.**

Concept Connector ➡

Students will assess what they've learned after completing "Popocatepetl and Ixtlaccihuatl."

Individual Activity

Suggest that interested students find illustrations of weapons that the Aztecs used in battle: wooden clubs, machetes, javelins, throwing boards, slings, bows and arrows, spears set with obsidian fragments, and lances.

❷ About the Selection

"Popocatepetl and Ixtlaccihuatl" is a legend that explains the origin of two volcanoes near present–day Mexico City. A powerful Emperor in the Aztec capital of Tenochtitlan has only one child, the beautiful princess Ixtla. Although she loves a brave warrior named Popo, the Emperor has forbidden them to marry. Although Popo eventually wins the right to marry Ixtla, the jealousies of others keep them apart. Heartbroken, Ixtla dies. Popo builds two stone pyramids outside the city. He buries Ixtla near the peak of one and takes his place atop the taller, watching over Ixtla's body for the rest of his days. The two volcanoes stand as reminders of the two lovers who dreamed of always being together.

MEXICAN LEGEND

❶ Popocatepetl
❷ and Ixtlaccihuatl

JULIET PIGGOTT WOOD

946 Themes in the Oral Tradition

Vocabulary Development

© **CCSS** Language 6

Thematic Vocabulary: The Big Question

As students are discussing "Popocatepetl and Ixtlaccihuatl," encourage them to use the thematic vocabulary presented in Introducing the Big Question, pp. 900–901. You might encourage them with sentence starters like these:

1. The Aztecs told this story to explain why their *environment* included . . .
2. It is a story of jealousy and *family* . . .
3. The *individual* wishes of Popocatepetl and Ixtlaccihuatl . . .
4. The story shows that the Aztec *culture* valued . . .
5. Aztecs believe that the two volcanoes *unify* . . .

Before the Spaniards came to Mexico and marched on the Aztec capital of Tenochtitlan[1] there were two volcanoes to the southeast of that city. The Spaniards destroyed much of Tenochtitlan and built another city in its place and called it Mexico City. It is known by that name still, and the pass through which the Spaniards came to the ancient Tenochtitlan is still there, as are the volcanoes on each side of that pass. Their names have not been changed. The one to the north is Ixtlaccihuatl [ēsʹ tlä sēʹ wätʹ əl] and the one on the south of the pass is Popocatepetl [pôʹ pô kä teʹ petʹ əl]. Both are snowcapped and beautiful, Popocatepetl being the taller of the two. That name means Smoking Mountain. In Aztec days it gushed forth smoke and, on occasion, it does so still. It erupted too in Aztec days and has done so again since the Spaniards came. Ixtlaccihuatl means The White Woman, for its peak was, and still is, white.

Perhaps Ixtlaccihuatl and Popocatepetl were there in the highest part of the Valley of Mexico in the days when the earth was very young, in the days when the new people were just learning to eat and grow corn. The Aztecs claimed the volcanoes as their own, for they possessed a legend about them and their creation, and they believed that legend to be true.

There was once an Aztec Emperor in Tenochtitlan. He was very powerful. Some thought he was wise as well, whilst others doubted his wisdom. He was both a ruler and a warrior and he kept at bay those tribes living in and beyond the mountains surrounding the Valley of Mexico, with its huge lake called Texcoco [tä skōʹ kō] in which Tenochtitlan was built. His power was absolute and the splendor in which he lived was very great.

It is not known for how many years the Emperor ruled in Tenochtitlan, but it is known that he lived to a great age. However, it was not until he was in his middle years that his wife gave him an heir, a girl. The Emperor and Empress loved the princess very much and she was their only child. She was a dutiful daughter and learned all she could from her father about the art of ruling, for she knew that when he died she would reign in his stead in Tenochtitlan.

1. **Tenochtitlan** (tä nochʹ tēt länʹ) the Aztec capital, conquered by the Spanish in 1521.

❸ ◄ **Critical Viewing**
Why do you think volcanoes like these inspired ancient peoples? **[Speculate]**

❺ Reading Check
Explain the meaning of each mountain's name.

❸ **Critical Viewing**
Possible Response: The volcanoes' size probably inspired ancient people, but mostly eruptions that could cause incredible damage, likely inspired people with their potential power.

❹ **Critical Thinking**

Analyze

1. Ask students to explain what kind of information they have read in the story so far.
   Possible response: The author has given background information.

2. Read aloud the bracketed text as students follow along. Pause at the paragraph change.

3. Point out that the phrase, "There was once," is similar to "Once upon a time." Then, **ask** students to describe the transition that the phrase signals.
   Answer: The phrase, "There was once" signals that the background to the story is finished and the legend will begin.

❺ **Reading Check**

Answer: Popocatepetl means Smoking Mountain because the mountain gushed smoke often. Ixtlaccihuatl means White Woman because the mountain has a permanent snow cap.

Differentiated Instruction for Universal Access

Support for Special-Needs Students
Remind students that legends often give insight into the cultures from which they came. Instruct students to point out passages that suggest beliefs, values, and attitudes of Aztec culture. For example, the text on p. 947 suggests that the Aztecs believed that effective rulers were very rich and held absolute power. Draw a web diagram on the board around the topic *Beliefs, Values,* and *Attitudes.* Guide students in filling in examples. Suggest that students copy the diagram and add to it as they read.

EL Support for English Learners
To increase students' understanding, discuss and clarify terms used to describe characters in the legend, such as *wisdom, delighted, serious, studious, selfishness,* and *shortsightedness.* Write these terms on the board, and give students a simple definition of what each term means. Give examples from your own experience. Then challenge students to give examples of their own. Collect students' ideas in a web around each term.

This selection is available in interactive format in the **Enriched Online Student Edition,** at **www.PHLitOnline.com,** which includes a thematically related video with writing prompt and an interactive graphic organizer.

1. Have students review what they know about Ixtla's life up to this point.
   Possible response: She has lived a happy life, in a great palace, surrounded by friends and family who love her.

2. Have students read the Cause and Effect question to themselves. Remind students that a cause is an event or situation that produces a result. **Ask:** What result is identified in this question? **Answer:** Ixtla is serious.

3. Now, call on volunteers to read the first bracketed passage aloud. Then, **ask** the Cause and Effect question.
   Answer: The heavy responsibilities that Ixtla will have and her father's forbidding her to marry cause her to be serious.

7 **Critical Thinking**

Infer

1. Have students reread the bracketed paragraph, which continues on p. 949.

2. Draw students' attention to the characterization of the relationship between Ixtla and Popo in the first sentence. Discuss why their relationship is described as unfortunate but moderately happy.
   Answer: Their relationship is unfortunate and only moderately happy because they are unable to marry.

3. Have students use the information provided in the paragraph, as well as their own knowledge or experience, to make an inference about Ixtla's relationship with her father.
   Answer: She disagrees with her father's position, but she is an obedient daughter and cannot imagine acting against his wishes.

Vocabulary
shortsightedness
(short´ sit´ id ness)
n. condition of not considering the future effects of something

6

Cause and Effect
What causes Ixtla to be serious?

Her name was Ixtlaccihuatl. Her parents and her friends called her Ixtla. She had a pleasant disposition and, as a result, she had many friends. The great palace where she lived with the Emperor and Empress rang with their laughter when they came to the parties her parents gave for her. As well as being a delightful companion Ixtla was also very pretty, even beautiful.

Her childhood was happy and she was content enough when she became a young woman. But by then she was fully aware of the great responsibilities which would be hers when her father died and she became serious and studious and did not enjoy parties as much as she had done when younger.

Another reason for her being so serious was that she was in love. This in itself was a joyous thing, but the Emperor forbade her to marry. He wanted her to reign and rule alone when he died, for he trusted no one, not even his wife, to rule as he did except his much loved only child, Ixtla. This was why there were some who doubted the wisdom of the Emperor for, by not allowing his heiress to marry, he showed a selfishness and shortsightedness towards his daughter and his empire which many considered was not truly wise. An emperor, they felt, who was not truly wise could not also be truly great. Or even truly powerful.

The man with whom Ixtla was in love was also in love with her. Had they been allowed to marry their state could have been doubly joyous. His name was Popocatepetl and Ixtla and his friends all called him Popo. He was a warrior in the service of the Emperor, tall and strong, with a capacity for gentleness, and very brave. He and Ixtla loved each other very much and while they were content and even happy when they were together, true joy was not theirs because the Emperor continued to insist that Ixtla should not be married when the time came for her to take on her father's responsibilities.

This unfortunate but moderately happy relationship between Ixtla and Popo continued for several years, the couple pleading with the Emperor at regular intervals and the Emperor remaining constantly adamant. Popo loved Ixtla no less for her father's stubbornness and she loved him no less while she studied, as her father

948 Themes in the Oral Tradition

Think Aloud

Vocabulary: Context Clues
Direct students' attention to the word *siege* in the middle of the text on p. 949. Using a think–aloud process, model how to use context to infer the meaning of an unfamiliar word. Say to students:

I'm going to think aloud to show you how I would figure out the meaning of *siege* from its context.

In this paragraph, *siege* is being used to describe the situation that the Emperor

bribes the warriors to change. The warriors can end the *siege* only by defeating the enemy tribesmen, who have come nearer and nearer to Tenochtitlan. We know from the previous paragraph that the Emperor's enemies want to "enter and lay waste to Tenochtitlan." All this makes me think that *siege* refers to the enemy tribesmen's having surrounded Tenochtitlan in preparation for attacking it.

demanded she should do, the art of ruling in preparation for her reign.

When the Emperor became very old he also became ill. In his <u>feebleness</u> he channeled all his failing energies towards instructing Ixtla in statecraft, for he was no longer able to exercise that craft himself. So it was that his enemies, the tribes who lived in the mountains and beyond, realized that the great Emperor in Tenochtitlan was great no longer, for he was only teaching his daughter to rule and not ruling himself.

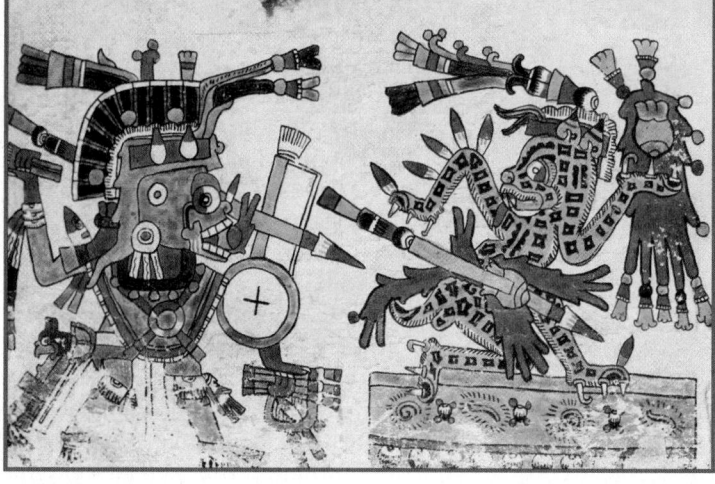

The tribesmen came nearer and nearer to Tenochtitlan until the city was besieged. At last the Emperor realized himself that he was great no longer, that his power was nearly gone and that his domain was in dire peril.

Warrior though he long had been, he was now too old and too ill to lead his fighting men into battle. At last he understood that, unless his enemies were frustrated in their efforts to enter and lay waste to Tenochtitlan, not only would he no longer be Emperor but his daughter would never be Empress.

Instead of appointing one of his warriors to lead the rest into battle on his behalf, he offered a bribe to all of them. Perhaps it was that his wisdom, if wisdom he had, had forsaken him, or perhaps he acted from fear. Or perhaps he simply changed his mind. But the bribe he offered to whichever warrior succeeded in lifting the siege of Tenochtitlan and defeating the enemies in and around the Valley of Mexico was both the hand of his daughter and the equal right to reign and rule, with her, in Tenochtitlan. Furthermore, he <u>decreed</u> that directly he learned that his enemies had been defeated he would instantly cease to be Emperor himself. Ixtla would not have to wait until her father died to become Empress and, if her father should die of his illness or old age before his enemies were vanquished,

Cause and Effect
What was one effect of the Emperor's becoming old and ill?

Vocabulary
feebleness (fē′ bəl nəs) *n.* weakness

decreed (di krēd′) *v.* officially ordered

9 Reading Check
What does the Emperor forbid Ixtla to do?

Popocatepetl and Ixtlaccihuatl **949**

8 Cause and Effect

1. **Ask** students who will succeed the Emperor as ruler of Tenochtitlan.
   Answer: Ixtla will succeed the Emperor.

2. Point out that at one point the Emperor begins to spend all his time instructing Ixtla in statecraft. **Ask:** What prompts him to do this?
   Possible response: He does so because he has become old and ill; he knows he does not have much time left.

3. Have students read the bracketed paragraph. Then, **ask** the Cause and Effect question. Remind students that an effect is the result produced by an event or situation.
   Answer: Because he was old and ill, the Emperor could not lead his fighting men into battle.

▶ **Monitor Progress:** Review students' graphic organizers to check their identification of cause–and–effect relationships.

▶ **Reteach:** If students are having difficulty identifying cause–and–effect relationships, show them the partially filled-in graphic organizer (*Graphic Organizer Transparencies,* p. 178) to help them clear up misconceptions and correct their work.

9 Reading Check
Answer: The Emperor forbids Ixtla to marry.

Fluency

Distribute copies of pages 948–949, and pair students. Have listeners mark text with which their reading partners struggle. Circulate to monitor students' fluency, then collect the marked up pages. Review difficult words and passages, such as these:

- If students struggle with the Aztec names, model how to use pronunciation keys (p. 947) as a guide. Pronounce each name and have students echo. Discuss the shortened form of the names and agree on a pronunciation for these.

- If students stumble over embedded clauses, clarify that readers should pause before and after such clauses, and should modulate their voices to show that the clauses are secondary. Have fluent readers model how to reflect the slight hesitations that the surrounding commas indicate.

- Acknowledge that the text on these pages flows around the images. If students struggle to track text due to its visual layout, urge them to trace the text with a finger as they read.

Connecting to the Big Question

1. Describe the situation of an excited child that runs into a room, knocking over a lamp and breaking it. Ask students what the child was thinking.

2. Have students read the bracketed text on pages 949–950. **Ask** students: What details suggest that the Emperor has not considered the results of his bribe?
Possible response: Details include that the text suggests the Emperor acted without wisdom or from fear. Also, the bribe contains specifics that make no sense for an Emperor to offer, such as that he give his empire to the victor and would immediately stop being emperor.

3. **Ask:** Do you think the Emperor's bribe is good for any of the individuals involved? Do you think it is good for the community? Explain.
Possible response: The bribe might be good for the individual who is the victor. It is almost certainly not good for the community because it puts the future of the empire in the hands of chance.

⓫ Critical Viewing

Possible answer: The warriors in the picture carry some of the kinds of weapons described in the story.

Vocabulary
relished (rel´isht) **⓾**
v. enjoyed; liked

⓫ ▼ Critical Viewing
How does this picture relate to the details of the battle in the story? **[Connect]**

950 Themes in the Oral Tradition

---

he further decreed that he who overcame the surrounding enemies should marry the princess whether he, the Emperor, lived or not.

Ixtla was fearful when she heard of her father's bribe to his warriors, for the only one whom she had any wish to marry was Popo and she wanted to marry him, and only him, very much indeed.

The warriors, however, were glad when they heard of the decree: there was not one of them who would not have been glad to have the princess as his wife and they all relished the chance of becoming Emperor.

And so the warriors went to war at their ruler's behest, and each fought trebly[2] hard for each was fighting not only for the safety of Tenochtitlan and the surrounding valley, but for the delightful bride and for the right to be the Emperor himself.

Even though the warriors fought with great skill and even though each one exhibited a courage he did not know he possessed, the war was a long one. The Emperor's enemies were firmly entrenched around Lake Texcoco and Tenochtitlan by the time the warriors were sent to war, and as battle followed battle the final outcome was uncertain.

The warriors took a variety of weapons with them; wooden clubs edged with sharp blades of obsidian,[3] obsidian machetes,[4] javelins which they hurled at their enemies from troughed throwing boards, bows and arrows, slings and spears set with obsidian fragments, and lances, too. Many of them carried shields woven from wicker and covered in tough hide and most wore armor made of thick quilted cotton soaked in brine.

The war was long and fierce. Most of the warriors fought together and in unison, but some fought alone. As time went on natural leaders emerged and, of these, undoubtedly Popo was the best. Finally it was he, brandishing his club and shield,

⓬

---

2. **trebly** (treˊ blē) *adv.* three times as much; triply.
3. **obsidian** (əb sidˊ ē ən) *n.* hard, usually dark-colored or black, volcanic glass.
4. **machetes** (mə shetˊ ēz) *n.* large, heavy-bladed knives.

Vocabulary Development

© **CCSS** Language 6

Word Forms

Expand students' vocabulary by helping them learn related forms of the Vocabulary Builder words. Three of the Vocabulary Words for "Popocatepetl and Ixtlaccihuatl" have related word forms. Give students a blank **Word Form Chart** (*Professional Development Guidebook*, p. 42), with *decreed*, *unanimous,* and *routed* in the correct columns. Work with the class to determine the related forms. Hold students accountable for integrating the related forms of the words into their speaking and writing.

Noun	Verb	Adjective	Adverb
decree	**decreed**	decreed	
unanimity		**unanimous**	unanimously
rout	**routed**	routed	

who led the great charge of running warriors across the valley, with their enemies fleeing before them to the safety of the coastal plains and jungles beyond the mountains.

The warriors acclaimed Popo as the man most responsible for the victory and, weary though they all were, they set off for Tenochtitlan to report to the Emperor and for Popo to claim Ixtla as his wife at last.

But a few of those warriors were jealous of Popo. Since they knew none of them could rightly claim the victory for himself (the decision among the Emperor's fighting men that Popo was responsible for the victory had been unanimous), they wanted to spoil for him and for Ixtla the delights which the Emperor had promised.

These few men slipped away from the rest at night and made their way to Tenochtitlan ahead of all the others. They reached the capital two days later, having traveled without sleep all the way, and quickly let it be known that, although the Emperor's warriors had been successful against his enemies, the warrior Popo had been killed in battle.

It was a foolish and cruel lie which those warriors told their Emperor, and they told it for no reason other than that they were jealous of Popo.

When the Emperor heard this he demanded that Popo's body be brought to him so that he might arrange a fitting burial. He knew the man his daughter had loved would have died courageously. The jealous warriors looked at one another and said nothing. Then one of them told the Emperor that Popo had been killed on the edge of Lake Texcoco and that his body had fallen into the water and no man had been able to retrieve it. The Emperor was saddened to hear this.

After a little while he demanded to be told which of his warriors had been responsible for the victory but none of the fighting men before him dared claim the successful outcome of the war for himself, for each knew the others would refute him. So they were silent. This puzzled the Emperor and he decided to wait for the main body of his warriors to return and not to press the few who had brought the news of the victory and of Popo's death.

Legend and Fact
What does the account of the battle suggest about the Aztecs' attitudes toward war?

Vocabulary
unanimous (yōō nan′ ə məs) *adj.* based on complete agreement

Reading Check
13 What is the outcome of the battle?

Popocatepetl and Ixtlaccihuatl **951**

12 Legend and Fact
1. Call on volunteers to read aloud the bracketed paragraph, which begins on p. 950.
2. Remind students that a legend is a traditional story that is based on fact. Then, **ask** the Legend and Fact question.
   Possible response: The Aztecs were a warrior society. War was an important activity that they prepared for and one that won individuals a certain status in society.

13 Reading Check
Answer: With Popo leading the great charge, the Emperor's warriors end the siege of Tenochtitlan and drive the enemies away.

Differentiated Instruction for Universal Access

Strategy for Less Proficient Readers
To give students a context for the story and to model how to identify cause-and-effect relationships, show them **Reading Skill Graphic Organizer A** (*Graphic Organizer Transparencies,* p. 178). The partially completed graphic organizer will give students insight into the process of noting connections among words and sentences to identify causes and effects. They can use it as a model for analyzing cause-and-effect relationships as they read.

Enrichment for Gifted/Talented Students
Ask students to think about which events in "Popocatepetl and Ixtlaccihuatl" push the plot toward a tragic ending. One such event, for example, is the Emperor's decision to use his daughter to bribe the warriors. Have students brainstorm for ideas to generate a new version of the story set in modern times. Ask them to dramatize the new story and present it to the class.

⑭ Literature in Context

Social Studies Connection The Aztecs settled on a small, swampy island in Lake Texcoco. They built small floating gardens known as "chinampas." The gardens were made of cane, but eventually became permanent plots of land. The Tenochtitlans were able to grow plenty of food on these islands. Building the islands also helped drain some of the main island, giving the Aztecs sturdier, drier land on which to build their city. The main island increased in size, as did the strength and power of the Aztec empire.

Connect to the Literature

Have students read the Literature in Context feature, and present the additional background information above. Then, **ask** the Connect to the Literature question.

Possible response: Students may say that the Emperor's rewards were appropriate because they would encourage all of his warriors to fight extra-hard. Others may say that the reward system encouraged too much competition among the warriors, or that it was unfair to Ixtla and Popo, who had long wanted to marry each other.

⑮ Critical Thinking

Support

1. Call on a volunteer to read aloud the bracketed paragraph. Tell students to listen carefully. **Ask** them to identify the cause of Ixtla's death.
   Answer: Ixtla died "of a broken heart."

2. Write the above answer on the board. **Ask** students to give evidence from the passage to support it.
   Possible responses: Ixtla fell ill as soon as she heard that Popo was dead. Neither the doctors nor her parents could help her. The narrator reports that there was no name for Ixtla's illness "unless it was the illness of a broken heart."

---

⑭ **LITERATURE IN CONTEXT**

Social Studies Connection

Tenochtitlan

Archaeologists believe that at one time, more than 200,000 people lived in Tenochtitlan, the Aztec capital city in the middle of the giant lake Texcoco. Approximately one half of the population were farmers. Much of the farming was done on small island gardens surrounding the city. People living in Tenochtitlan depended on food the farmers grew outside the city. They also depended on water from outside the city, which was carried to the city by a system of aqueducts.

Because of its location and dependence on outside food and water, the city would have been helpless in the face of a siege. With no way to get in or out to get food, a siege would soon lead to starvation.

Connect to the Literature

Based on the situation, do you think the rewards offered by the Emperor in this story were appropriate? Explain.

952 Themes in the Oral Tradition

Then the Emperor sent for his wife and his daughter and told them their enemies had been overcome. The Empress was thoroughly excited and relieved at the news. Ixtla was only apprehensive. The Emperor, seeing her anxious face, told her quickly that Popo was dead. He went on to say that the warrior's body had been lost in the waters of Lake Texcoco, and again it was as though his wisdom had left him, for he spoke at some length of his not being able to tell Ixtla who her husband would be and who would become Emperor when the main body of warriors returned to Tenochtitlan.

But Ixtla heard nothing of what he told her, only that her beloved Popo was dead. She went to her room and lay down. Her mother followed her and saw at once she was very ill. Witch doctors were sent for, but they could not help the princess, and neither could her parents. Her illness had no name, unless it was the illness of a broken heart. Princess Ixtlaccihuatl did not wish to live if Popocatepetl was dead, and so she died herself.

The day after her death Popo returned to Tenochtitlan with all the other surviving warriors. They went straight to the palace and, with much cheering, told the Emperor that his enemies had been routed and that Popo was the undoubted victor of the conflict.

The Emperor praised his warriors and pronounced Popo to be the new Emperor in his place. When the young man asked first to see Ixtla, begging that they should be married at once before being jointly proclaimed Emperor and Empress, the Emperor had to tell Popo of Ixtla's death, and how it had happened.

Popo spoke not a word.

He gestured the assembled warriors to follow him and together they sought out the few jealous men who had given the false news of his death to the Emperor. With the army of warriors watching, Popo killed each one of them in single combat with

⑮

Vocabulary Development

Vocabulary Knowledge Rating
When students have completed reading and discussing "Popocatepetl and Ixtlaccihuatl," have them take out their **Vocabulary Knowledge Rating Chart.** Read the words aloud once more and have students rate their knowledge of the words again in the After Reading column. Clarify any words that are still problematic. Have students write their own definition and example or sentence in the appropriate column. Then, have students complete the Vocabulary Practice activities at the end of the selection. Encourage students to use the words in further discussion and written work about this selection. Remind them that they will be accountable for these words on the **Selection Test,** *Unit 6 Resources,* pp. 95–97 or 98–100.

his obsidian studded club. No one tried to stop him.

That task accomplished Popo returned to the palace and, still without speaking and still wearing his stiff cotton armor, went to Ixtla's room. He gently lifted her body and carried it out of the palace and out of the city, and no one tried to stop him doing that either. All the warriors followed him in silence.

When he had walked some miles he gestured to them again and they built a huge pile of stones in the shape of a pyramid. They all worked together and they worked fast while Popo stood and watched, holding the body of the princess in his arms. By sunset the mighty edifice was finished. Popo climbed it alone, carrying Ixtla's corpse with him. There, at the very top, under a heap of stones, he buried the young woman he had loved so well and for so long, and who had died for the love of him.

That night Popo slept alone at the top of the pyramid by Ixtla's grave. In the morning he came down and spoke for the first time since the Emperor had told him the princess was dead. He told the warriors to build another pyramid, a little to the southeast of the one which held Ixtla's body and to build it higher than the other.

He told them too to tell the Emperor on his behalf that he, Popocatepetl, would never reign and rule in Tenochtitlan. He would keep watch over the grave of the Princess Ixtlaccihuatl for the rest of his life.

The messages to the Emperor were the last words Popo ever spoke. Well before the evening the second mighty pile of stones was built. Popo climbed it and stood at the top, taking a torch of resinous pine wood with him.

Vocabulary
routed (rout′ əd) *v.*
completely defeated

17 Reading Check
What does Popo ask the Emperor when he returns?

⑱ Legend and Fact

1. **Ask** students what a fact is.
   Answer: A fact is something that can be proved true.

2. Have students read the bracketed text. Then, **ask** the Legend and Fact question.
   Answer: Volcanoes are real. You know because you can observe them. You can also confirm their existence in a specific location by consulting reference materials.

⑲ Critical Viewing

Possible answer: In the story, Popocatepetl stands next to Ixla's grave and holds a torch. The smoke from his torch is similar to the smoke that comes from the mountain in the picture.

ASSESS
Answers

Critical Thinking

Before students respond, you may wish to have them write a brief objective summary of the selection. As they answer the questions below, remind them to support their answers with evidence from the text.

1. (a) Ixtla's father will not let them. (b) **Possible response:** Both are serious and kind and want the best for Tenochtitlan.

2. (a) He does not want to rule without Ixtla. (b) The Aztecs admired honesty, bravery, and loyalty.

3. (a) Both accounts illustrate the city's size by describing it in terms of the vast natural surroundings, such as mountains and lakes. (b) The legend describes the inner thoughts and feelings of the characters who are larger than life and perform extraordinary deeds.

4. (a) **Possible response:** The story suggests that love is a powerful emotion that should not be suppressed. (b) **Possible response:** Yes, people today should recognize the strength and importance of love.

5. **Possible responses:**
   (a) The Emperor's decision that Ixtla could not marry was better for him, but not the community. (b) Yes, an individual's needs should not damage the community.

954

And when he reached the top he lit the torch and the warriors below saw the white smoke rise against the blue sky, and they watched as the sun began to set and the smoke turned pink and then a deep red, the color of blood.

So Popocatepetl stood there, holding the torch in memory of Ixtlaccihuatl, for the rest of his days.

The snows came and, as the years went by, the pyramids of stone became high white-capped mountains. Even now the one called Popocatepetl emits smoke in memory of the princess whose body lies in the mountain which bears her name.

Legend and Fact
Are the volcanoes real? How do you know?

⑲ ▶ **Critical Viewing**
What details in this photo are similar to the details of Popo's actions in the story? **[Analyze]**

⑱

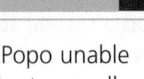

Critical Thinking

Cite textual evidence to support your responses.

1. **Key Ideas and Details (a)** Why are Ixtla and Popo unable to marry? **(b) Analyze:** What qualities make the two well matched?

2. **Key Ideas and Details (a)** Why does Popo refuse to become emperor and rule in Tenochtitlan? **(b) Draw Conclusions:** Based on this legend, what traits do you think the Aztecs admired?

3. **Key Ideas and Details Compare and Contrast:** How do the factual account and the legend convey the size and magnificence of Tenochtitlan and the Aztec empire? **Analyze:** What elements are present in the legend that you would not find in a factual account?

4. **Integration of Knowledge and Ideas (a) Interpret:** What lesson does the legend suggest? **(b) Evaluate:** Can this lesson be applied in modern times?

5. **Integration of Knowledge and Ideas (a)** Was the Emperor's decision at the story's beginning better for the individual or the community? **(b)** Is it ever important to consider the needs of a community over the needs of an individual? Explain. *[Connect to the Big Question: Community or individual—which is more important?]*

954 Themes in the Oral Tradition

Assessment Resources

Unit 6 Resources
L1 L2 EL Selection Test A, pp. 95–97. Administer Test A to less advanced students.

L3 L4 EL Selection Test B, pp. 98–100. Administer Test B to on-level and more advanced students.

L3 L4 Open-Book Test, pp. 92–94. As an alternative, give the Open-Book Test.

All Customizable Test Bank

All Self-tests
Students may prepare for the **Selection Test** by taking the **Self-test** online.

PHLit Online! All assessment resources are available at **www.PHLitOnline.com**.

Reading Skill: Cause and Effect

1. Reread the legend to find an **effect** for each of these **causes**.

(a) The Emperor does not allow his daughter to marry.

(b) The Emperor spends all his time teaching Ixtla statecraft.

(c) The warriors lie to the Emperor about Popo's death.

(d) Ixtla hears that Popo is dead.

2. According to the legend, what **causes** the volcano to smoke?

Literary Analysis: Legend and Fact

3. Key Ideas and Details Identify two **facts** in this story. How do you know that they are facts?

4. Integration of Knowledge and Ideas Use the chart below to help you identify which events in this **legend** might have been based on historical events.

Events from Legend	Possible Historic Connection

Vocabulary

Acquisition and Use Answer each question and then explain your answer.

1. If something is *decreed*, is it undecided?

2. If a vote is *unanimous*, does everyone agree?

3. If one's enemies have been *routed*, have the enemies won?

4. Is *shortsightedness* useful when making decisions for the future?

5. Would *feebleness* prevent a person from exercising?

6. If you *relished* the last book you read, did you enjoy it?

Word Study Use the context of the sentences and what you know about the **Latin prefix uni-** to explain your answers.

1. How many wheels does a *unicycle* have?

2. If two people speak in *unison*, do they speak at the same time?

Word Study

The **Latin prefix uni-** means "having or consisting of only one."

Apply It Explain how the prefix *uni-* contributes to the meanings of these words. Consult a dictionary if necessary.

unity
unilateral
uniform

Popocatepetl and Ixtlaccihuatl **955**

Reading Skill

1. **Possible responses:** (a) Ixtla does not experience true joy. (b) His enemies realize that the Emperor is no longer powerful. (c) The Emperor demands that the body be brought to him for burial. (d) Ixtla dies of a broken heart.

2. Popocatepetl's torch, still burning in memory of Ixtla, causes the volcano to smoke.

Literary Analysis

3. **Possible response:** Two facts are that Ixtlaccihuatl and Popocatepetl are volcanic mountains, and Popocatepetl means "smoking mountain." You know they are facts because they can be proved to be true.

4. **Possible response:** Events—the siege of Tenochtitlan; the successful defense of the city; Connection—The legend could be based on an actual siege and defense.

For other sample answers, see *Graphic Organizer Transparencies,* Literary Analysis Graphic A, p. 181, and the **Additional Answers** section.

Vocabulary
Acquisition and Use
Sample answers:

1. No; If something has been decreed, it is not undecided but rather has been officially ordered.

2. Yes; If a vote is unanimous, everyone has voted for the same result.

3. No; If one's enemies have been routed, the enemies have been defeated and have lost.

4. No; Shortsightedness fails to consider the future.

5. Yes; Feebleness is weakness, which could make exercising difficult.

6. Yes; If you relished something, you enjoyed it very much.

Word Study
Sample answers:
1. The prefix *uni-* means "one," so a *unicycle* has one wheel.
2. Yes; The prefix *uni-* means "one" and *unison* means "together, at one time."

Word Study: Apply It
Sample answers: *Unity* means the state of being one. A *unilateral* decision is made by one person alone. A *uniform* is an outfit of identifying clothes that is the one correct way to dress.

Conventions

1. Introduce the skill, using the instruction on the student page.
2. Discuss the examples in the chart.

Think Aloud: Model the Skill

Model the skill of using commas. Say to students:

Commas give me choices of how to form sentences. Look at this example: "Madelyne got ready; The guests arrived." I can combine the sentences by adding *and* after "ready." I can also use a comma to rewrite the two sentences as one: "As Madelyne got ready, the guests arrived."

PH WRITING COACH Grade 7

Students will find instruction on and practice with commas in Chapter 25, Sections 2.

Practice A

1. *shallow, swampy;* separates adjectives
2. *causeways, irrigation ditches, and;* separates words in a series
3. *city, the;* used after an introduction
4. *the lake, but they were;* joining parts of a compound sentence

Reading Application
Sample answer:

1. The twin temple stood on one side, and the king's palace stood. . . . (joins independent clauses).
2. . . . four other shallow, swampy lakes (separates adjectives).
3. . . . the nobility, craftspeople, and others (separate words in a series).

Practice B
Sample answers:

1. In the great city of Tenochtitlan, there once lived a stubborn and foolish Emperor.
2. His daughter fell in love with a great warrior, but the Emperor would not allow them to marry.
3. Because of his stubbornness, he lost his daughter, his greatest warrior, and the respect of his subjects.

Writing Application
Sample answer:

Popo and Ixtla are in love, but they cannot be together. They are brave, loyal, and devoted. The story says, "His power was absolute. . . ." However, he is selfish.

956

Integrated Language Skills

Tenochtitlan: Inside the Aztec Capital • Popocatepetl and Ixtlaccihuatl

Conventions: Commas

A **comma** signals a brief pause. A *semicolon* signals a stronger separation than a comma.

Using Commas	Example
Use a comma before a conjunction that joins independent clauses in a compound sentence.	John thought he was late, and he rushed through the parking lot.
Use a comma after an introductory word, phrase, or clause.	If you go to the play, how will you get your homework finished?
Use commas to separate three or more words, phrases, or clauses in a series.	The café offered fruit juice, iced tea, and sparkling water.
Use a comma to separate adjectives of equal rank.	We received a warm, joyful welcome from our neighbors.

Practice A Explain how the comma in each sentence is used.

1. Tenochtitlan rose from the center of a shallow, swampy lake.
2. Workers in Tenochtitlan built causeways, irrigation ditches, and stately homes.
3. In the center of the city, the homes of the nobility lined a large square.
4. Many people built swamp gardens in the lake, but they were only big enough to grow food for one family.

© **Reading Application** In "Tenochtitlan: Inside the Aztec Capital," find three sentences that contain commas and explain how each comma is used.

Practice B Rewrite the following sentences, inserting commas as necessary.

1. In the great city of Tenochtitlan there once lived a stubborn and foolish Emperor.
2. His daughter fell in love with a great warrior but the Emperor would not allow them to marry.
3. Because of his stubbornness he lost his daughter his greatest warrior and the respect of his subjects.

© **Writing Application** Write five sentences about two people who are in love. At least one of the sentences should be a compound sentence, one should contain items in a series, and one should include a direct quotation.

PH WRITING COACH Further instruction and practice are available in *Prentice Hall Writing Coach*.

Extend the Lesson

Sentence Modeling

Choose the sentence given for the selection students have read:

The main crop was corn, but farmers also grew tomatoes, beans, chili peppers, and prickly pears. ("Tenochtitlan: Inside the Aztec Capital")

The Aztecs claimed the volcanoes as their own, for they possessed a legend about them and their creation, and they believed that legend to be true. ("Popocatepetl and Ixtlaccihuatl")

Ask students what they notice about the sentence. Have students identify any commas and explain their use. Then ask what else students notice. ("Tenochtitlan: Inside the Aztec Capital": The sentence has two independent clauses, joined by a conjunction. "Popocatepetl and Ixtlaccihuatl": The sentence has two independent clauses, and a dependent clause.)

Have students imitate the sentence in a sentence on a topic of their own choosing, matching each grammatical and stylistic feature discussed.

Writing

Common Core State Standards

L.7.2, L.7.2.a; RL.7.9; W.7.1.a, W.7.1.b, W.7.2, W.7.2.b; SL.7.4

[For the full wording of the standards, see page 934.]

Informative Text Write a short **description** of the ancient city of Tenochtitlan based on the selections. Review "Tenochtitlan" and "Popocatepetl and Ixtlaccihuatl." Jot down details about the time, place, and overall environment of the city, as well as details about the lives of its inhabitants. Refer to your notes as you draft your description.

Next, draw on your notes to write a brief **comparison** of the selections. Identify the common historical elements that the article and the legend refer to. Finally, explain the ways in which the legend adapts or alters historical fact.

Grammar Application Check your writing to be sure you have correctly used commas, especially after introductory words, phrases, or clauses and to separate adjectives of equal rank.

Writing Workshop: *Work in Progress*

Prewriting for Workplace Writing Choose one of the locations from the Wish List in your portfolio and write a brief sentence stating your purpose for writing to that specific service provider. Save this Purpose Sentence in your writing portfolio.

Use this prewriting activity to prepare for the **Writing Workshop** on page 982.

Speaking and Listening

Presentation of Ideas Deliver a **persuasive speech** based on your reading. If you read "Tenochtitlan," your goal is to persuade authorities that building a city in the middle of a lake is a good idea. If you read "Popocatepetl and Ixtlaccihuatl," your goal is to persuade the Emperor to allow Popo and Ixtla to marry.

- On a note card, write your position and a short statement explaining the reasons for your position.

- List the main points that support your position on additional cards. Use solid evidence, including facts, statistics, and quotations from authorities, to overcome opposing views.

- Jot down phrases that will remind you of your points, rather than writing complete sentences.

- Refer to your note cards as you deliver your speech.

- As you deliver your speech, establish eye contact, adjust your volume, and pronounce each word clearly.

www.PHLitOnline.com
- Interactive graphic organizers
- Grammar tutorial
- Interactive journals

Integrated Language Skills **957**

Writing

1. Review the assignment, using the instruction on the student page.

2. To guide students in writing their informative texts, give them the **Support for Writing**, p. 90 in *Unit 6 Resources.*

3. To evaluate students' descriptions, use one of the **Descriptive Essay** rubrics, pp. 220–221 in *Professional Development Guidebook.*

Grammar Application

Have students check their drafts to make sure they have used commas correctly.

Six Traits Focus

Ideas		Word Choice	✔
Organization	✔	Sentence Fluency	
Voice		Conventions	

PH WRITING COACH Grade 7

Students will find further instruction on and practice with informational texts in Chapters 8 and 11.

Writing Workshop
Work in Progress

Have students save their completed Sentences in their portfolios. They will use the sentences later as they complete the Writing Workshop assignment (see pp. 982–987).

Speaking and Listening

1. Review the assignment, using the instruction on the student page.

2. To support students' work on the assignment, have students complete the **Support for Extend Your Learning** page (*Unit 6 Resources,* p. 91).

Teaching Resources

Unit 6 Resources

- L3 L4 EL **Integrated Language Skills: Grammar,** p. 89
- L3 L4 EL **Support for Writing,** p. 90
- L3 L4 **Support for Extend Your Learning,** p. 91
- L4 **Enrichment,** pp. 70, 88

Enriched Online Student Edition

Available under After You Read for this selection:
- All **Interactive Grammar Tutorial**
- L3 L4 **Internet Research Activity**

Professional Development Guidebook
Rubrics for Self-Assessment: Descriptive Essay, pp. 220–221

All print and digital resources are available online at **www.PHLitOnline.com.** Online resources accessible to students are noted on the student page.

In this two-page Test Practice, students apply the reading skill for the first half of Unit 6 to a passage of fiction and a passage of nonfiction.

Review this skill, cause and effect, and then administer the test. For more guidance, consult the *Classroom Strategies and Teaching Routines* card, *Formally Assessing Students.*

ASSESS

Answers

Answers With Explanations

1. **A**—Sentence 1 clearly indicates that Lisa has her camera ready to photograph a whale. *Incorrect answers*: B—Phil never asks for or uses the camera; C—Lisa hopes to become a marine biologist, not a photographer; D—Lisa is ready to take a picture, which suggests that the camera is not broken.

2. **D**—Lisa drags Phil whale watching because it is her birthday. *Incorrect answers*: A—Phil did not ask Lisa; she asked him; B—Lisa asked him to go, and at first he had no interest in whales; C—Lisa, not Phil, wants to be a marine biologist.

3. **C**—*Result* and *effect* are synonyms; this phrase signals a cause-and-effect relationship. *Incorrect answers*: A—*Now* signals a sequential relationship; B—The verb *had seen* signals an event in the past; D—This phrase signals a spatial relationship.

4. **C**—Phil says "Wow!" and Lisa takes many photos of the whale. *Incorrect answers*: A—Lisa's purpose was to take photographs of a whale, and she fulfills it; B—Phil is annoyed before he sees the whale; afterward, he thinks the experience is great; D—Neither is too tired to appreciate seeing the whale.

Writing for Assessment

In their responses, students should describe the cause-and-effect chain leading from Lisa's seeing the dolphins when she is five years old to Phil and Lisa's whale-watching years later.

958

Test Practice: Reading

Cause and Effect

Fiction Selection

Directions: *Read the selection. Then, answer the questions.*

Lisa clutched her camera, afraid of missing the moment when a whale would soar out of the water. She had seen dolphins playing in the ocean when she was five years old. As a result, Lisa dreamed of one day becoming a marine biologist. Now, in honor of her thirteenth birthday, she had dragged her older brother Phil whale watching. "I'm freezing! Why do we have to whale-watch in the winter?" Phil said. Lisa glanced at Phil, who was dripping with ocean water. Over his shoulder, she noticed a massive shape rising out of the water. Phil turned and followed her gaze. "Wow!" he said in a stunned voice. "That whale is so cool! This is great." Lisa smiled at her brother's amazement as she happily snapped photos of the humpback whale.

1. Lisa has her camera ready because—
   A. she wants to photograph a whale.
   B. her brother needs to borrow it.
   C. she hopes to be a photographer.
   D. the camera might be broken.

2. What caused Phil to go whale watching?
   A. He wants a photograph of a whale, and he has convinced Lisa to come.
   B. His parents asked him to go, and he loves whales.
   C. He wants to be a marine biologist, and he has to do a science project.
   D. It is Lisa's birthday, and she wants him to go.

3. Which phrase in the story signals a cause-and-effect relationship?
   A. Now,
   B. had seen
   C. As a result
   D. Over his shoulder,

4. What effect does seeing the whale have on Phil and Lisa?
   A. Phil is glad he came, but Lisa is disappointed.
   B. Phil is annoyed that he is wet, but Lisa is thrilled to get a photograph.
   C. Both Phil and Lisa are excited to see the whale.
   D. Both Phil and Lisa are too tired to appreciate seeing the whale.

Writing for Assessment

Write a paragraph describing the cause-and-effect chain leading from Lisa's seeing dolphins when she is five years old to Phil and Lisa's whale-watching years later.

Strategies for Test Taking

Remind students that sometimes cause-and-effect relationships are signaled by words and phrases such as *as a result, therefore, as an effect,* and *because,* and sometimes these relationships are implied. The author uses the phrase "as a result" to signal the cause-and-effect relationship between Lisa's seeing dolphins and Lisa's deciding to become a marine biologist. The author does not state that Phil is cold because he is soaked. The author signals the second relationship by putting the sentence about Phil dripping with ocean water right after his statement that he is freezing. (Point out that a statement about an event is often followed by a statement about its effect or its cause.) The reader must also use common sense and prior knowledge to identify implied cause-and-effect relationships. For example, readers know that getting soaked with ocean water in the middle of winter will make someone very cold.

Nonfiction Selection

Directions: *Read the selection. Then, answer the questions.*

During summers off the coast of Alaska, long hours of sunshine warm the icy waters. Microscopic water plants begin to bloom, and tiny marine animals flock to the warming waters to feed on them. The tiny animals, in turn, lure giant humpback whales to the waters.

Humpbacks eat these tiny animals, but they also eat larger fish, such as sardines and mackerel. In fact, humpback whales spend most of their time eating because they need an enormous amount of food to remain active and warm. Each whale eats between 4,500 and 5,000 pounds of food each day!

As autumn nears, the days grow shorter, causing the water to cool. Food is not as plentiful in the cooler water. Because of this, the humpback whales move to warmer waters, traveling past California toward Hawaii. There they stay until summer days call them northward.

1. What is the effect of longer hours of sunshine?
  A. Microscopic plants begin to bloom.
  B. Whales create a bubble net.
  C. Humpback whales swim toward Hawaii.
  D. Sardines and mackerel are plentiful.

2. Why do humpback whales spend so much time eating?
  A. Food takes a long time to consume.
  B. Hunting takes a lot of energy.
  C. They require a lot of food to stay active and warm.
  D. They need to eat as much as they can before the waters cool.

3. The water cools because—
  A. the days grow shorter as autumn nears.
  B. the whales eat lots of fish in the water.
  C. winds blow colder air over the ocean.
  D. the days are longer in summer.

4. What is the *main* reason humpback whales leave the waters of Alaska?
  A. The sun shines for more hours per day as autumn nears.
  B. Fewer fish are in the water after the whales have been there.
  C. The whale's food supply is not as plentiful in the cooler water.
  D. The humpback whales always spend the winter near Alaska.

Writing for Assessment

Connecting Across Texts

In the first passage, Phil asks why he and Lisa can only whale-watch in the winter. Use details from both passages to explain the cause-and-effect relationship that answers his question. In your response, explain where Lisa and Phil might be.

www.PHLitOnline.com
- Online practice
- Instant feedback

Test Practice: Reading **959**

Answers With Explanations

1. **A**—In sentence 1, the author states that sunshine warms the icy waters, and in sentence 2, the author states that microscopic plants begin to bloom. The reader can infer that the first event is the cause of the second. *Incorrect answers*: B—There is no reference to this in the passage; C—This occurs when the water becomes colder in the fall; D—The passage implies that tiny plants and animals, not sardines and mackerel, increase as the water warms.

2. **C**—This cause-and-effect relationship is stated in paragraph 2. *Incorrect answers*: A—If the food took a long time to consume, the whales could not eat so much each day; B—The whales would not spend so much time hunting for food if the primary reason for the food was to sustain hunting; D—This is neither stated nor implied.

3. **A**—This cause is stated in the first sentence of Paragraph 3. *Incorrect answers*: B—The whales' behavior has no effect on the water temperature; C—This is not the stated cause; D—Longer days warm the water.

4. **C**—This cause is stated in Paragraph 3. *Incorrect answers*: A—The sun shines for fewer hours as autumn approaches; B—Cool weather, not the whales' eating habits, reduces the number of fish; D—Humpback whales spend the winter in warmer waters, not in Alaska.

Writing for Assessment

In their responses, students should explain that in some locations, whales are present only in winter. Lisa and Phil must be in cooler waters near northern California, along the migration path.

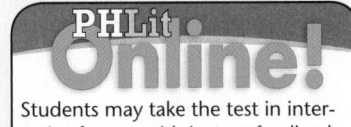
Students may take the test in interactive format with instant feedback online at **www.PHLitOnline.com**.

Differentiated

Instruction for Universal Access

EL **Strategy for English Learners**

To help English learners answer cause-and-effect questions, use the items on this page to review some of the terms related to causes and effects. Item 1 asks, "What is the effect?" This item is obviously asking for an effect. **Ask** for another way to word the same question. (**Answer:** "What is the result?") Next, point out that item 2 asks "Why" something happens. This is asking for a cause. Item 3 requires the examinee to complete a sentence ending with "because." This item is also looking for a cause. Item 4 asks "What is the main reason?" The reason for an event is its cause.

959

Reading for Information

Common Core State Standards

- Reading Informational Text 5
- Writing 2.a, c
- Language 4.c, 6

Analyzing Expository Texts

Textbook Article	Question and Answer

Reading Skill: Analyze Cause-and-Effect Organization

When you **analyze cause-and-effect organization,** you look at the way relationships between events are presented in a text. Some texts show how several events or conditions (causes) produce a single effect. Others show how a single event can have several effects. To understand how causes and effects are organized in a text, begin by identifying and analyzing cause-and-effect relationships. Ask questions like the ones shown to find relationships between events.

Questions for Analyzing Cause-and-Effect Relationships	
What happened?	Winter
Why did this happen? (**cause**)	Earth's axis tilted away from the sun.
What has happened or will happen as a result? (**effect**)	Sunlight hit our hemisphere less directly; the days were colder.

Content-Area Vocabulary

These words appear in the selections that follow. You may also encounter them in other content-area texts.

- **spectrum** (spek´trəm) *n.* the band of colors formed when a beam of light is passed through a prism or is broken up by some other means
- **wavelengths** (wāv´ leŋths´) *n.* (in physics) the distances between the tops of waves of energy, such as sound or light, that follow each other
- **stratosphere** (strat´ə sfir´) *n.* the part of Earth's atmosphere that extends from about seven miles above the surface to 31 miles

960 Themes in the Oral Tradition

Common Core State Standards

Reading Informational Text
5. Analyze the structure an author uses to organize a text, including how the major sections contribute to the whole and to the development of the ideas.

Writing
2.a. Introduce a topic clearly, previewing what is to follow; organize ideas, concepts, and information, using strategies such as definition, classification, comparison/contrast, and cause/effect.
2.c. Use appropriate transitions to create cohesion and clarify the relationships among ideas and concepts.

Language
4.c. Consult general and specialized reference materials, both print and digital, to find the pronunciation of a word or determine or clarify its precise meaning or its part of speech.
6. Acquire and use accurately grade-appropriate general academic and domain-specific words and phrases; gather vocabulary knowledge when considering a word or phrase important to comprehension or expression.

Reading Skill

1. Introduce the skill and table.
2. Tell students they will analyze cause-and-effect organization.

Think Aloud: Model the Skill

Say to students:

Identifying why things happen in a text is important to understanding the text as a whole. When I read, I look for cause-and-effect relationships to figure out why things happen. Why something happened is its cause. What happened is the effect. I also keep in mind that a single effect can have several causes. Also, the effect can be a cause of another effect. As I read, I keep careful track of all of these relationships.

Multidraft Reading

Have students follow a multidraft reading protocol.

- **First reading**—Have students read to identify key ideas and details.
- **Second reading**—Have students read to identify the structure of the text.
- **Third reading**—Have students read to integrate knowledge and ideas by connecting the text to the world, their own experiences, and other texts.

Content-Area Vocabulary

1. Have students say each word.
2. Next, use each word in a sentence that defines it.
3. Finally, repeat your definitional sentence or a similar sentence, omitting the word, and have the class "fill in the blank" chorally.

Community or individual— which is more important?

Have students consider how the information might benefit individuals and the community.

Differentiated Instruction *for Universal Access*

Reading Support
Give students reading support with the appropriate version of the *Reader's Notebooks:*

L2 L3 *Reader's Notebook*
L1 *Reader's Notebook: Adapted Version*
EL *Reader's Notebook: English Learner's Version*

The Seasons on Earth

from *Prentice Hall Science Explorer*

Most places outside the tropics and polar regions have four distinct seasons: winter, spring, summer, and autumn. But there are great differences in temperature from place to place. For instance, it is generally warmer near the equator than near the poles. Why is this so?

How Sunlight Hits Earth

Figure 1 shows how sunlight strikes Earth's surface. Notice that sunlight hits Earth's surface most directly near the equator. Near the poles, sunlight arrives at a steep angle. As a result, it is spread out over a greater area. That is why it is warmer near the equator than near the poles.

> Phrases such as *as a result* and *that is why* indicate cause-and-effect relationships.

Earth's Tilted Axis

If Earth's axis were straight up and down relative to its orbit, temperatures would remain fairly constant year-round. There would be no seasons. Earth has seasons because its axis is tilted as it revolves around the sun.

Notice in Figure 2 that Earth's axis is always tilted at an angle of 23.5° from the vertical. As Earth revolves around the sun, the north end of its axis is tilted away

Features:
- instructional reading
- headings and subheadings that organize material
- clearly identified concepts, ideas, or topics
- charts, diagrams, or other visuals
- text written for a student audience

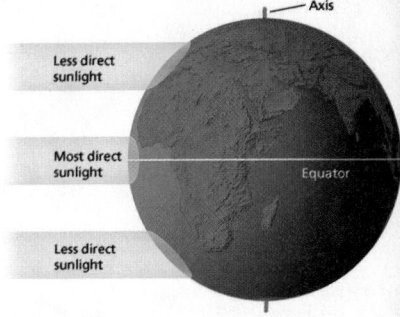

Figure 1 Sunlight Striking Earth's Surface Near the equator, sunlight strikes Earth's surface more directly and is less spread out than near the poles.

> This section of the article explains the cause-and-effect relationship shown in the diagrams.

from the sun for part of the year and toward the sun for part of the year.

Summer and winter are caused by Earth's tilt as it revolves around the sun. The change in seasons is not caused by changes in Earth's distance from the sun. In fact, Earth is farthest from the sun when it is summer in the Northern Hemisphere.

Differentiated Instruction — Additional Instruction

Vocabulary for Less Proficient Readers

There are several words and phrases on this page that could be challenging for students. Some are easier to grasp when defined in relationship with others.
- *tropics* and *equator:* The tropics are regions that lie neither too far north nor south of the equator, the imaginary line that circles the Earth at its midpoint.
- *polar regions* and *poles:* The polar regions are near the North or South Pole.

Enrichment for Advanced Readers

Earlier theories of astronomy offered far different models of Earth's rotation and revolution than those presented here. Have students research how people throughout history attempted to explain the change of seasons. Ask them to choose one theory and write a corresponding page from a textbook of the time. Encourage them to use diagrams, heads, and other features.

About Textbook Articles

1. Review the features listed in the Textbook Article box on page 961 with students. **Ask** students why headings and subheadings are important features.
   Answer: Headings and subheadings help show how the article is organized and provide a quick summary of the article.

2. Have students **explain** why charts, diagrams, or visuals might be especially important in a science textbook article.
   Possible response: Science textbook articles often explain why something in the natural or physical world occurs. Charts, diagrams, or visuals can show why things occur graphically, making it easier to understand the particular relationship.

3. Talk to students about how to read a textbook article. Suggest that textbook articles often focus on cause-and-effect relationships.

Analyze Cause-and-Effect Organization

1. Have students skim the title, heads, and any boldfaced items on the page to determine the subject and purpose of the text. Then, **ask** what the page is about.
   Possible response: The text explains the role of sunlight and the Earth's axis in causing seasons.

2. Have students identify the textbook's subject area, title, and publisher.
   Answer: Prentice Hall publishes the science textbook, *Science Explorer,* from which this excerpt is taken.

3. Have students read "The Seasons on Earth." Then, draw their attention to the organization of the page: there are three main sections of text, plus a caption.

4. Read the last annotation and have students follow its direction. Then, have students identify key words and phrases in the last three paragraphs on this page that offer clues to cause-and-effect relationships.
   Possible responses: Clue words are: *because, always, caused, not caused,* and *in fact.*

Analyze Cause-and-Effect Organization

1. Before they read this page, have students scan it for repeated words. After they have scanned the page, **ask** them which words appear many times.

   Answer: Terms such as *solstice, hemisphere, equinox,* and *axis* are repeated throughout.

2. Guide students to understand that this page, unlike the previous one, is really a single figure without any conventional text. Have students read the callout at the top of the page, then read the diagram and analyze how it illustrates the cause-and-effect relationship.

3. Have students read the remainder of "The Seasons on Earth." Then, have students connect the information in the text to their own lives. **Ask** them what changes in the length of daylight hours they notice in June, December, March, and September.

   Possible responses: Students living in the Northern Hemisphere will report that June contains the longest day, and December the shortest. March and September days fall midway between these extremes in their amounts of sunlight.

4. To check for comprehension, **ask** the question in the bottom diagram.

   Answer: The sun is at its maximum height above the horizon in June.

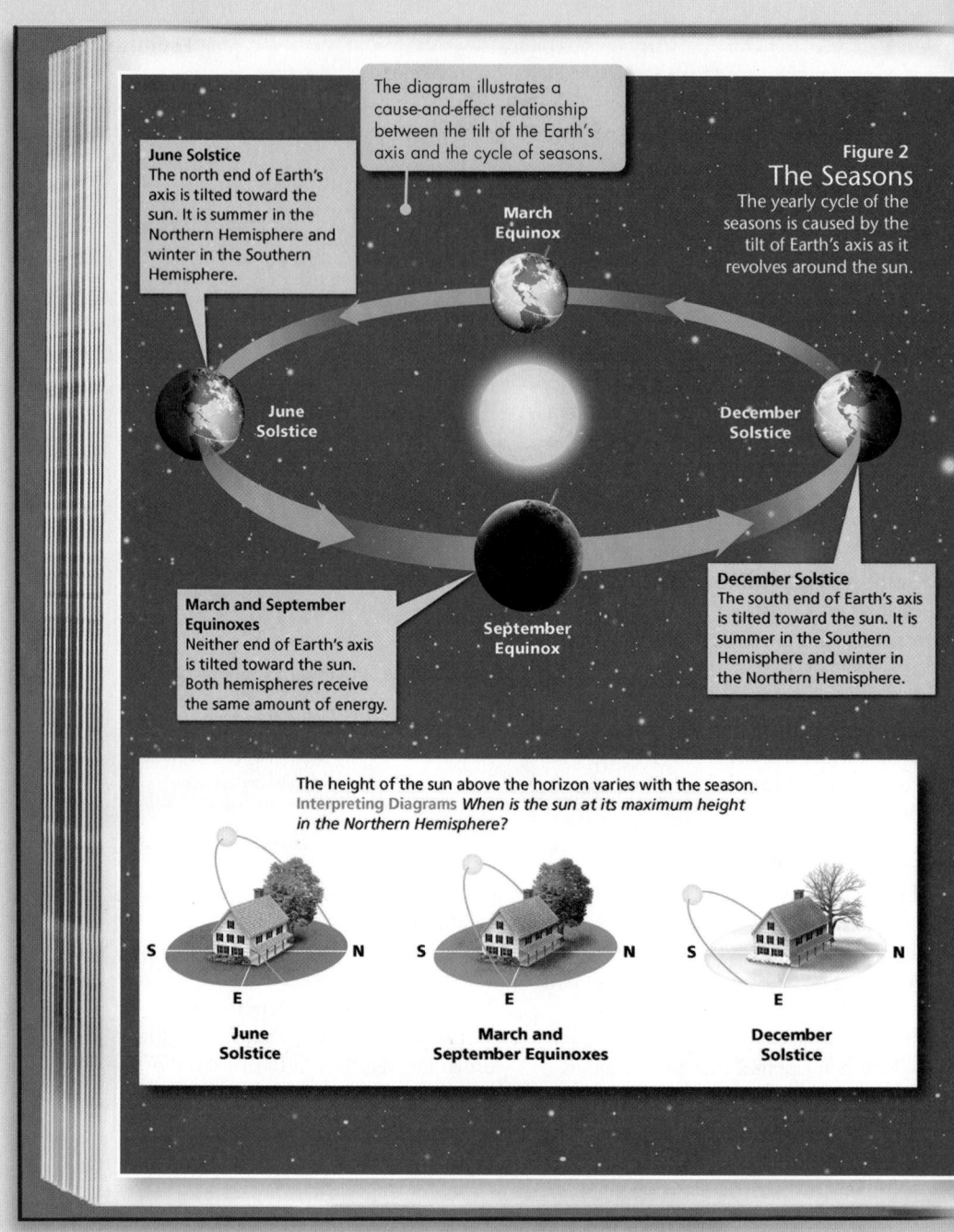

The diagram illustrates a cause-and-effect relationship between the tilt of the Earth's axis and the cycle of seasons.

Figure 2
The Seasons
The yearly cycle of the seasons is caused by the tilt of Earth's axis as it revolves around the sun.

June Solstice
The north end of Earth's axis is tilted toward the sun. It is summer in the Northern Hemisphere and winter in the Southern Hemisphere.

March Equinox

December Solstice

September Equinox

March and September Equinoxes
Neither end of Earth's axis is tilted toward the sun. Both hemispheres receive the same amount of energy.

December Solstice
The south end of Earth's axis is tilted toward the sun. It is summer in the Southern Hemisphere and winter in the Northern Hemisphere.

The height of the sun above the horizon varies with the season.
Interpreting Diagrams *When is the sun at its maximum height in the Northern Hemisphere?*

June Solstice

March and September Equinoxes

December Solstice

Vocabulary Development

© **CCSS** Language 6

Scientific Terms

Tell students that when reading textbooks, they will encounter new words specific to the subject area covered. Many textbooks include glossaries. Often textbooks will define such words the first time they are used. However, since the excerpt on these pages may assume a prior knowledge of relevant vocabulary, you may want to provide the meanings of the following astronomical and geographic terms.

- *solstice:* one of the two times each year when the sun is farthest from the equator
- *equinox:* one of the two times each year when the sun crosses the equator's plane and night and day are equal in length
- *hemisphere:* one half of the globe
- *axis:* a straight line through something; in the case of the Earth and other round objects, it is the center around which they rotate

What Gives the Sunrise and Sunset its Orange Glow?

GantDaily
March 11th, 2007
Meghan Holohan, Research at Penn State

The question-and-answer format outlines causes and effects.

In Key West, Florida, tourists flock to Mallory Square at the end of the day to watch the sun set. Street performers entertain waiting crowds with magic and vendors sell souvenirs of the daily sunset celebration. Flashes click as tourists try to capture the beautiful orange sun as it disappears behind the sparkling blue ocean.

In almost every location around the globe, the sky appears orange at sunrise and sunset. What causes this colorful phenomenon?

Sunlight is composed of a multicolored **spectrum**, just like a rainbow, explains Jon Nese, senior lecturer in meteorology at Penn State. Combined together, its different **wavelengths** are perceived as white light when they enter the Earth's atmosphere.

That atmosphere is made up of a mixture of gaseous molecules, mostly nitrogen and oxygen, with some water vapor and trace gases thrown in. These molecules, clumped more densely close to Earth where the atmosphere is thickest, create tiny obstacles for traveling light waves to navigate.

The light at the longest wavelengths—red, orange, and yellow—sails more easily over these atmospheric speed bumps, while the shorter

Reading for Information: Question and Answer **963**

About Question and Answer Texts

1. Review the features listed in the Question and Answer box on page 963 with students. **Ask** the class to discuss the benefits of a question and answer text format.
   Possible response: Students may say that the questions could target the readers' concerns and make it easy for them to find the answers that address them. They may also point out that this format is more straightforward and direct, making it easy for a general audience to understand.

2. **Ask** students to discuss why a question and answer text is easy to understand.
   Possible response: Good readers ask questions as they read, but a question and answer text provides the questions and answers directly, making it accessible.

3. Explain the structure of a question and answer text. Note that this particular passage contains a single question and one detailed answer, though question and answer texts can also contain multiple questions and answers.

Analyze Cause-and-Effect Organization

1. Tell students that they are likely to encounter question and answer texts in newspapers and magazines but may also view them on television talk shows, news programs, or podcasts.

2. Have students read the question and answer text on page 963 and the callouts that point to the organization of the text.

3. Point out that the author uses a cause-and-effect organization within the question and answer format. **Ask** students to analyze the purpose of this organization.
   Possible response: The author uses this organization to explain what causes the orange glow in sunrises and sunsets.

Fluency

Have students use the question-and-answer format to practice their fluency.

Distribute a photocopy of page 963 and pair students. Have the students read the text aloud, taking turns asking the question and then alternating reading paragraphs of the text that makes up the response. Remind students to pause at commas and stop briefly at periods in order to make their reading more fluent and convey meaning more accurately. While one student reads, the other should mark any words with which the one reading has difficulty. Circulate to monitor the fluency of students' reading. Collect students' marked up copies of the page, and review difficult words and passages with the class as a whole.

Analyze Cause-and-Effect Organization

1. Have students read page 964, which continues the answer to the question raised on the previous page.

2. **Ask** students to identify the cause of the yellowish-white appearance of sunshine at "solar noon."

   Answer: The sun is at its highest point in our sky. Its light reaches us most directly, passing through less atmosphere. The result is less scattering of the rays and a purer form of light, which is yellowish-white in color.

3. **Ask** students to explain the cause of the difference in the way sunsets appear in Key West and in heavily populated cities.

   Answer: The sun appears orange in Key West because of longer wavelengths at this time of day. It appears red in heavily populated cities as a result of pollution.

---

blue and violet rays get bounced left and right as they journey towards us, in a process called "scattering."

At "solar noon," when the sun appears at its highest point in the daytime sky, light reaches us most directly, passing through less atmosphere on the way, reducing the scattering effect. When the spectrum remains together, the light we see is the familiar yellowish-white look of sunshine.

But as the Earth turns during the day and the sun drops toward the horizon, sunbeams enter the atmosphere at a slant and pass through a denser swath of air before they reach us. "When the short rays at the violet and blue end of the spectrum are deflected out in all directions, they can't get to our eyes," Nese notes, "while the orange and red wavelengths dominate our perception of the sky's color."

> This paragraph begins an explanation of the cause of colorful skies.

While people in Key West almost always view orange sunsets, residents in heavily populated cities often see red. That's due to pollution in the air, says Nese. Older residents of Donora, Pennsylvania, a town on the outskirts of Pittsburgh, recall beautiful red sunsets at the height of coke production decades ago, due to the coal dust in the air.

Pollution particles are larger than the molecules of atmospheric gases, Nese explains. Even orange and yellow light waves have a hard time passing through. Red—which is composed of the longest wavelengths in the visible spectrum—is the most successful at streaming past the particles, creating a scarlet sky.

Volcanic activity can produce the same effect. In April of 1982, sunrises and sunsets were fiery red across most of the United States after the El Chichon volcano erupted in Mexico, spewing ash clear into the **stratosphere**. Red rays were the only visible light rays long enough to slice through the clouds of dense ash and sulfur dioxide.

> Here, the article points out another possible cause for red skies.

While science has unlocked the secrets of the sky's many shades, "to many, the scientific explanation is secondary," Nese admits.

"There's something magical, even mysterious, about it because the colors only appear near sunrise and sunset, and few people really understand why."

GantDaily Editor's Note: This article is part of the feature, "A Probing Question." Presented through the Pennsylvania State University, researchers answer questions on things to wake up the kid in you.

Think Aloud

Analyze Cause-and-Effect Organization
Model the skill of analyzing cause-and-effect organization using the following "think aloud." Say to students:

As I read this text, it seems clear that a cause-and-effect relationship is central to the selection. The question-and-answer format lends itself to the presentation of causes and effects. The question in this case describes an effect—the orange glow of the sun at sunrise and sunset—and asks about the cause. The answer text presents the cause of this effect under normal circumstances, as well as variations in it brought about by pollution and volcanic activity, either of which can cause the sky to appear reddish at different times of day.

Comparing Expository Texts

© **1. Craft and Structure (a)** Compare the **cause-and-effect organization** of the textbook article and the question-and-answer text. In which text do you find cause-and-effect relationships more clearly identified? **(b)** Which text cites more effects resulting from a single cause? Explain.

Content-Area Vocabulary

2. Consulting a specialized reference, such as a dictionary of earth science, find two scientific words in addition to *stratosphere* that are formed by adding a prefix to the root *-sphere-*. Define each of the three words and their prefixes, using a dictionary as needed.

Timed Writing

Explanatory Text: Essay

Format
The prompt directs you to write a brief essay. Therefore, you will need to express your ideas in three to five paragraphs.

Extend the chain of causes and effects in the textbook article by explaining how the cycle of seasons affects your area. Write a brief essay that explains some of the effects caused by changes in the weather and the number of daylight hours. (40 minutes)

Academic Vocabulary
When you *extend* an idea, you build on it or apply it to new situations.

5-Minute Planner

Complete these steps to write your explanation:

1. Carefully read the writing prompt. Look for key words shown in highlighted colors.

2. Reread the textbook article. As you read, find cause-and-effect relationships. **TIP** Make a list of words and phrases such as *because, as a result,* and *for this reason* that show relationships between ideas.

3. Jot down notes about how life in your area changes with the seasons. For example, wintry cold means more time indoors.

4. Organize your notes so that you can clearly see the relationships between causes and effects. Then, refer to your notes and your list of words and phrases as you draft your essay.

Comparing Expository Texts

1. (a) **Answer:** The textbook article presents cause-and-effect relationships in a way that makes them easy to identify. By supplementing the text with a diagram, a reader can clearly visualize the relationship between Earth's axis and our changing seasons. (b) **Answer:** The question-and-answer text goes into detail about the effects of light filtering through the atmosphere, so it cites several possible effects stemming from that cause.

2. (a) **Sample responses:** A *biosphere* is all parts of the earth that are capable of supporting life. The prefix *bio-* means "life" or "living things." The *hydrosphere* is water vapor in the atmosphere. The prefix *hydro-* means "water." A *hemisphere* is half of a sphere or globe. The prefix *hemi-* means "half."

Timed Writing

Before students complete the activity, guide them in identifying and analyzing key words and phrases in the prompt, highlighted on the student page.

Work with students to draw up guidelines for their brief essays based on the key words:

• **Focus** The writer should focus on the effects of local weather changes and the number of daylight hours during each season.

• **Organization** The writer should organize the essay by the cause-and-effect relationships presented.

• **Elaboration** The writer should use the textbook article to extend the cause-and-effect chain in the essay.

• **Style** The style should be clear and brief.

3. Have students use the 5-Minute Planner to structure their time.

4. Allow students 40 minutes to complete the assignment. Evaluate their work using the guidelines they have developed.

❶ Comparing Universal Themes

1. Introduce and discuss the skill, using the instruction on the student page.
2. Discuss the chart.
3. Give students a copy of **Comparing Epic Conventions Organizer B,** (*Graphic Organizer Transparencies,* p. 184). Tell them they will fill it in with details that will help them note epic conventions in both selections.

Think Aloud: Model the Skill

Model a way to understand epic conventions. Say to students:

To help me understand epic conventions, I think about comic books. Comic books are full of larger-than-life heroes, just like epics. Like epics, comic books often have universal themes, such as "Good triumphs over evil." I keep these ideas in mind as I read an epic, looking for examples of epic conventions.

Comparing Literary Works

The Voyage *from*
Tales from the Odyssey •
To the Top of Everest

❶ Comparing Universal Themes

A **universal theme** is a message about life that is expressed in many different cultures and time periods. Universal themes include concepts such as the value of courage and the danger of greed. You can identify the universal theme in a literary work by focusing on the main character, thinking about conflicts the character faces, and noticing the changes that come about as a result of those conflicts.

Universal themes are important ideas, so many cultures present these themes prominently in **epics**—stories or long poems about larger-than-life heroes. In many ways, an epic can be seen as a portrait of the culture that produced it. Ancient epics were recited as entertainment and passed down from storyteller to storyteller. Epics express a culture's values and its perspective on universal themes, such as bravery. Other **epic conventions,** or characteristics, are listed in the chart below.

Epics and their themes are an important part of the literature of different cultures. New generations often create works inspired by these epics. For example, it is not unusual to find an **allusion,** or reference, to the ancient Greek epic the *Odyssey* in a new adventure story. As you read these selections, use a chart like this to note the examples of epic conventions that help point toward a universal theme.

Epic Conventions	from *Tales from the Odyssey*	"To the Top of Everest"
dangerous journey		
characters who help	Goddesses Ino and Athena	
broad setting		
serious, formal style		

PHLit
Online!
www.PHLitOnline.com

• Vocabulary flashcards
• Interactive journals
• More about the authors

• Selection audio
• Interactive graphic organizers

Vocabulary Development

Vocabulary Knowledge Rating

Create a **Vocabulary Knowledge Rating Chart** (*Professional Development Guidebook,* p. 33) featuring the vocabulary words glossed in the selections:

impervious (p. 969)   designated (p. 976)
inflicted (p. 969)   saturation (p. 978)

Give students a copy of the chart, and read the words aloud. Have students mark their rating of each in the Before You Read column. To gauge how much instruction to provide, tally the number of students who think they know each word.

Explain that the words are defined in the margin at the point where they appear in the selection. Urge students to be alert to these words as they read and discuss the selections. They will rate their knowledge again when they finish.

Community or individual — which is more important?

❷ Writing About the Big Question

Both of these selections show that travel can enrich individuals and shape their views. Use this sentence starter to develop your ideas.

When individuals travel to other places, their **communities** can also benefit because _____.

Meet the Authors

Mary Pope Osborne (b. 1949)

Author of *Tales from the Odyssey*

Mary Pope Osborne has lived an adventurous life. As a child, she never stayed in one place for long. Her father was in the military, and the family moved seven times before Mary was fifteen. As a young adult, she explored sixteen Asian countries with friends, including Iraq, Iran, Afghanistan, Pakistan, India, and Nepal.

Pope Osborne did not begin to write until she was in her thirties. Today, she is best known for her series, *The Magic Tree House.* "I'm one of those very lucky people who absolutely loves what they do for a living," Pope Osborne says. "There is no career better suited to my eccentricities, strengths, and passions than that of a children's book author."

Samantha Larson (b. 1988)

Author of "To the Top of Everest"

In 2007, American Samantha Larson became the youngest person to climb the "Seven Summits"—the highest mountains on each of the seven continents. Larson climbed her first, Mount Kilimanjaro in Africa, at the age of 12. She finished her quest on May 17, 2007, when she successfully reached the top of Mt. Everest at the age of 18.

Larson says "Everest was much harder, longer, and higher" than the other peaks she had tackled in the past. "There were a lot of difficult moments," Larson recalls. "It was one big challenge, but I never gave up hope completely. Deep down I thought I would make it."

Tales from the Odyssey • To the Top of Everest **967**

❶ Background
The Gods and Goddesses of Ancient Greece

The ancient Greeks believed in more than one god. In fact, they believed in hundreds of gods and goddesses. Each one had his or her realm of influence. They shared the traits of humans—including jealousy and anger.

Many of the characters mentioned in this selection are gods and goddesses. Poseidon is the god of the sea, while Athena is the goddess of wisdom.

❷ Activating Prior Knowledge

1. Prepare an **Anticipation Guide** (see *Professional Development Guidebook*, pp. 36–38):
   - Struggling against someone who is more powerful than you are is pointless.
   - Human beings can only endure so much pain and suffering.
   - A story from ancient Greece isn't relevant to a modern student.

2. Give students a copy of the prepared Anticipation Guide and have students mark their responses in the Me column. Have students discuss the statements in pairs and mark the Group column.

Concept Connector ➡️

Students will return to the **Anticipation Guide** after reading.

❸ About the Selection

In this excerpt from *The Odyssey*, Odysseus endures a long trip across the ocean. Poseidon, who is apparently angry with Odysseus for blinding his son, the Cyclops, punishes Odysseus by trying to drown him in a series of storms. Several goddesses, including Athena, come to Odysseus' aid. The selection leaves him exhausted and sleeping on the beach.

❹ Critical Viewing

Answer: The goddess in the picture is much larger than the man, and she is surrounded by clouds like Mount Olympus. The man seems to be suffering a boat wreck at sea, so he may represent Odysseus.

---

❶ ❷ ❸

THE VOYAGE
from Tales from the Odyssey

MARY POPE OSBORNE

From *TALES FROM THE ODYSSEY BOOK #4: THE GRAY-EYED GODDESS* by Mary Pope Osborne. Copyright © 2003 by Mary Pope Osborne. Reprinted by permission of Hyperion Books for Children. All rights reserved.

968 Themes in the Oral Tradition

In the early morning of time, there existed a mysterious world called Mount Olympus. Hidden behind a veil of clouds, this world was never swept by winds, nor washed by rains. Those who lived on Mount Olympus never grew old; they never died. They were not humans. They were the mighty gods and goddesses of ancient Greece.

The Olympian gods and goddesses had great power over the lives of the humans who lived on earth below. Their anger once caused a man named Odysseus to wander the seas for many long years, trying to find his way home.

Almost three thousand years ago, a Greek poet named Homer first told the story of Odysseus' journey. Since that time, storytellers have told the strange and wondrous tale again and again. We call that story the Odyssey.

◀ **Critical Viewing**
In what ways does this image reflect the description of gods and goddesses in these three paragraphs? **[Connect]**

© Text Complexity Rubric

The Voyage *from* Tales of the Odyssey

Qualitative Measures	Context/Knowledge Demands	Ancient Greece; mythical situation 1 2 ③ 4 5
	Structure/Language Conventionality and Clarity	Straightforward myth with some fantastic elements; mostly short to moderate sentences; some formal diction 1 2 ③ 4 5
	Levels of Meaning/Purpose/Concept Level	Challenging concept (Can humans chart their own course even if gods act like people?) 1 2 3 ④ 5
Quantitative Measures	Text Length	Word Count: 1,021
	Lexile	800L

With his hands gripping the rudder, Odysseus skillfully guided his raft over the waves. He never slept. All night, he kept his eyes fixed on the stars that Calypso had told him to watch—the Pleiades and the Bear.

Day after day and night after night, Odysseus sailed the seas. Finally, on the eighteenth day, he saw the dim outline of mountains on the horizon.

As Odysseus steered his raft toward the shore, dark clouds gathered overhead. The water began to rise. The wind began to blow, until it was roaring over the earth and sea.

Has Poseidon discovered my raft? Odysseus wondered anxiously. *Does he now seek his final revenge?*

For many years, Poseidon, mighty ruler of the sea, had been angry with Odysseus for blinding his son, the Cyclops. Now it seemed he was trying to destroy Odysseus once again. The wind roared from the north, south, east, and west. Daylight plunged into darkness. Odysseus feared he was about to come to a terrible, lonely end.

Suddenly an enormous wave crashed down on Odysseus' raft. Odysseus was swept overboard and pulled deep beneath the sea. He struggled wildly to raise his head above the water and breathe.

When his head finally broke the surface, Odysseus saw his raft swiftly moving away across the water. He swam as fast as he could toward the wooden craft. He grabbed the timbers and pulled himself aboard.

Then, as the wind swirled the raft across the water, Odysseus saw an astonishing sight. A sea goddess was floating like a gull on top of the waves.

Seemingly impervious to the great storm, she floated near his raft and climbed aboard.

"My friend," she said, "I am Ino, the White Goddess, who guides sailors in storms. I know not why Poseidon is angry with you. But I know this: for all the torture he has inflicted upon you, he will not kill you. But you must leave your raft at once and swim for the shore. Take my veil, for it is enchanted. You will come to no harm as long as you possess it. As soon as you reach land, you must throw it back into the sea."

⑤

Vocabulary
impervious (im pur´ vē əs) *adj.* not affected by something

inflicted (in flikt´ əd) *v.* delivered something painful

Reading Check
⑥ Who climbs aboard Odysseus' raft?

Tales from the Odyssey **969**

⑤  **Connecting to the Big Question**

1. Point out that Odysseus seems to believe in his own importance as an individual because he fights tenaciously to survive.

2. **Ask** students who is traveling in this passage. **Answer:** Odysseus is taking a long journey across the sea.

3. **Ask** students if Odysseus is benefiting from his trip. **Answer:** No. The god Poseidon is creating a difficult, stormy passage for Odysseus, because he believes Odysseus blinded his son.

⑥ Reading Check

Answer: Ino climbs aboard Odysseus' raft.

© Text Complexity: Reader and Task Suggestions

The Voyage *from* Tales from the Odyssey

Preparing to Read the Text

- Using the Background on p. 968, preview information about ancient Greek gods.
- Discuss students' knowledge of Greek gods and goddesses and their human traits. Then, guide students in considering how such traits might influence godly actions toward people. For example, if gods experience human jealousy, they might want to punish humans.
- Guide students in using Multidraft Reading strategies (TE p. 967).

Leveled Tasks

Levels of Meaning If students will have difficulty with levels of meaning, have them first read to identify the dangers Odysseus survives. Then, have them reread to identify actions or traits of the gods that they find confusing. Clarify as needed.

Evaluating If students will not have difficulty interpreting meaning, have them note as they read ways that the author differentiates the personalities of the gods. Discuss as a class how each personality reflects human traits and how this helps or hinders Odysseus from controlling his fate.

This selection is available in interactive format in the **Enriched Online Student Edition,** online at **www.PHLitOnline.com,** which includes an interactive graphic organizer.

❼ Universal Themes

1. Challenge students to recall the epic conventions introduced on p. 966. Make a list on the board (*dangerous journey, characters who help, broad setting, formal style*).

2. Have a volunteer read the bracketed passage aloud.

3. **Ask** the Universal Theme question. **Answer:** In this passage, Athena is a good example of a character that helps.

Spiral Review

Theme

1. Remind students that they studied the concept of theme in the Unit 6 Literary Analysis Workshop (pp. 902–911).

2. **Ask** the Spiral Review question.

   Possible response: The sea makes Odysseus do whatever it wants.

Universal Themes
Which epic convention appears in this paragraph? ❼

Spiral Review
Theme What is Odysseus's relationship to the sea?

With these words, the White Goddess removed her enchanted veil and gave it to Odysseus. Then she disappeared back into the wild seas.

At that moment, a huge wave crashed down on Odysseus' raft, ripping it to pieces. Clutching Ino's veil, Odysseus pulled himself onto a wooden plank and rode it as if it were a horse. Then he dove down into the sea.

Suddenly, all the winds died down—except the north wind. Odysseus felt that Athena[1] was holding the other winds back, so he could swim safely and swiftly to some distant shore. For two days and two nights, with the north wind gently flattening the waves before him, he swam and floated on the calm sea.

On the third day, the north wind died away and the sea was completely calm. Odysseus saw land ahead. With a burst of joy, he swam toward the rocky shore.

In an instant, the wind and waves returned. With a thundering roar, sea spray rained down on him.

Odysseus struggled to keep his head above the churning water, seeking a place to go ashore.

Angry waves were pounding the reefs with great force. *I'll be dashed against the rocks if I try to swim ashore now,* he thought desperately.

But once again, Odysseus felt the presence of Athena. A giant wave picked him up and carried him over the rocks toward the beach. But before Odysseus could crawl ashore to safety, another wave dragged him back into the sea and pulled him under the water.

Odysseus swam desperately, escaping the waves pounding the shore. Soon he came to a sheltered cove. He saw a riverbank free of rough stones. As he swam toward the bank, he prayed to the gods to save him from the angry attack of Poseidon.

Suddenly the waves were still. But when Odysseus tried to haul himself ashore, his body failed him. He had been defeated by the storm. It had ripped his flesh and robbed his muscles of their strength. He was passing in and out of consciousness.

---

1. **Athena** *n.* goddess of wisdom and protector of Odysseus.

Vocabulary Development   © CCSS Language 6

Vocabulary Reinforcement
Students will benefit from additional examples and practice with the selection vocabulary words. Reinforce their comprehension with "show-you-know" sentences. The first part of the sentence uses the vocabulary word in an appropriate context. The second part of the sentence—the "show-you-know" part—clarifies the first.

Model the strategy with this example for *impervious*. Sarah was *impervious* to fads; she always had her own unique style of dress.

Then give students these sentence starters, and coach them in creating the "show-you-know" part:

1. Jack was *impervious* to his sister's pleas; _____
   _____.

2. A penalty was *inflicted* on the team by the referee; _____
   _____.

Gasping for breath, he pulled off Ino's veil and threw it back into the sea. Then he used his last bit of strength to drag himself out of the water and throw himself into the river reeds.

If I lie here all night, I shall die from the cold and damp, he thought. *If I go farther ashore and pass out in a thicket, wild beasts will devour me.* No matter what evils lay ahead, he knew he had to push on. On bleeding hands and knees, he crawled to a sheltered spot under an olive tree, a tree sacred to the goddess Athena.

Odysseus lay down in a pile of dead leaves. With his bloody hands, he spread leaves over his torn body. Like a farmer spreading ashes over the embers of his fire, he tried to protect the last spark of life within him.

Mercifully, the gray-eyed goddess slipped down from the heavens and appeared at his side. She closed his weary eyes and pulled him down into a sweet sleep that took away his pain and sorrow.

Universal Themes
Based on this paragraph, what trait do you think the ancient Greeks valued in heroes?

Critical Thinking

1. **Key Ideas and Details (a)** How does Odysseus react to the storm at sea? **(b) Generalize:** Choose three adjectives that describe Odysseus. **(c) Speculate:** Why do you think the goddesses help Odysseus?

2. **Key Ideas and Details (a) Make a Judgment:** Do you think Odysseus will survive his injuries? **(b) Support:** Find several passages in the text that support your answer.

3. **Integration of Knowledge and Ideas Infer:** How would you describe ancient Greek culture after reading this passage based on an ancient Greek myth?

4. **Integration of Knowledge and Ideas** Odysseus struggles mightily against beings more powerful than he is. Do you think his story can teach lessons to individuals, communities, or both? Explain your answer, using details from the text. *[Connect to the Big Question: Community or individual—which is more important?]*

> Cite textual evidence to support your responses.

Tales from the Odyssey **971**

8 Universal Themes

1. Choose a student to read the bracketed paragraph aloud.

2. **Ask** students to list adjectives that describe Odysseus. **Possible responses:** tenacious, tough, determined, and brave.

3. **Ask** the Universal Themes question. **Possible response:** The ancient Greeks valued a hero who wouldn't give up.

Concept Connector

Ask students to take out their **Anticipation Guides** and respond to the statements again in the After Reading column. Then, lead a class discussion to probe for ideas that students have learned that confirm or invalidate each statement. Encourage students to cite specific evidence from the text.

ASSESS

Answers

Critical Thinking

Before students respond, you may wish to have them write a brief objective summary of the selection.

1. (a) Odysseus reacts bravely to the storm at sea. (b) **Possible responses:** brave, strong, tenacious, tireless (c) **Possible responses:** because they admire how hard Odysseus is trying to survive; or they dislike what Poseidon is doing to Odysseus.

2. (a) Most students will predict that Odysseus will survive his injuries. (b) The goddess Ino says, "But I know this: for all the torture he has inflicted upon you, he will not kill you." Odysseus says, "he knew he had to push on." Athena grants Odysseus a sleep that takes away his pain and sorrow.

3. Greek culture seems harsh. The gods punish a good man who was trying to protect himself.

4. **Possible responses:** Odysseus' struggle can teach lessons to both individuals and communities. Individuals can learn about the importance of never giving up. Communities could learn a lesson about working together.

Instruction   for Universal Access

EL **Strategy for English Learners**

If students are having difficulty following the selection, they may find the story easier to understand if they hear it. Have them listen to the selection on the *Hear It!* **Audio CD,** while reading along.

Enrichment for Gifted/Talented Students

Have a group of students dramatize the action of the selection. Students can play the parts of the narrator, Poseidon, Odysseus, Ino, and Athena. Students may read from the book or construct their own scripts based on the selection. In addition to reading the dialogue and narration, encourage students to use body language and facial expressions that clearly show the characters' actions and emotions.

❾ Background

Blogs

The word "blog" is short for "Web log." It is a specialized kind of Web site that allows an individual or group to share a running log of events and personal insights with online audiences. Blogging first burst into popularity in 1999. As of December 2007, approximately 112 million blogs had been created.

❿ Activating Prior Knowledge

New Zealander Edmund Hillary (1919–2008) was one of the first climbers to reach the summit of Mount Everest. He said, "It is not the mountain we conquer, but ourselves." Lead students in a discussion about Hillary's quote. Ask students to work independently to come up with ways explorers enhance society in general.

Concept Connector ⟶
Students will return to their list after reading the selection.

⓫ About the Selection

Teenager Samantha Larson writes about her successful summit attempt on Mount Everest, beginning with pre-trip training and ending with her triumphant return to the United States. The selection was originally a blog, and it appears in diary format. The style is contemporary and chatty. Larson touches on the acclimatization process, which involves hiking between camps at different elevations on the mountain, and describes the Puja ceremony, during which a local Lama asks the mountain gods for permission to climb the mountain.

972 Themes in the Oral Tradition

ⓒ Text Complexity Rubric

To the Top of Everest		
Qualitative Measures	**Context/Knowledge Demands**	Mount Everest; mountain climbing 1 2 ③ 4 5
	Structure/Language Conventionality and Clarity	Blog format in casual style; mix of short and moderate sentences; some technical vocabulary 1 2 ③ 4 5
	Levels of Meaning/ Purpose/Concepts	Accessible concept (teen overcomes physical/dangerous challenge) 1 2 ③ 4 5
Quantitative Measures	**Text Length**	Word Count: 2,147
	Lexile	1080L

TO THE TOP OF EVEREST

Samantha Larson

9 **10** **11**

12 ◄ **Critical Viewing**
Which details in this photograph suggest Larson is about to go on a dangerous journey?

Friday, March 30, 2007

Here we go ⟶ Kathmandu!

Today is the day! Our bags are (nearly) packed and we're (just about) ready to go. I've got eleven hours to run around doing last minute errands before our plane takes off.

I arrived back in Long Beach from New York last Saturday, where I've been since our return from Cho Oyu. When I wasn't training by running, swimming at the pool, taking dance classes, or rock climbing, I was taking oboe lessons, French, and photography classes. Hopefully I'll be able to take some great pictures on this expedition!

It has been a very exciting week in all our general trip preparation mayhem, filled with lots of gear sorting and fedex package arrivals. But now my dad and I are pretty much all set to go.

See you in Kathmandu!

13 ✓ **Reading Check**
How did Larson train for her expedition?

To the Top of Everest **973**

---

12 **Critical Viewing**

Answer: Larson looks as if she is going on a dangerous journey because she is wearing gear that is suitable for extreme weather, including a down jacket, warm hat, and sunglasses. In addition, she is carrying a bag full of outdoor gear. The mountains are looming over her in the background.

13 **Reading Check**

Answer: She trained by running, swimming, dancing, and rock climbing. She also took photography classes.

© Text Complexity: Reader and Task Suggestions

To the Top of Everest	
Preparing to Read the Text • Using the Background note on p. 972, discuss blogs and their similarity to diary formats. • Explain that the selection recounts a teenager's attempt to overcome a great physical challenge. Discuss some dangers of mountain climbing and elevation. Then, guide students in applying this knowledge to understanding the author's challenges. • Guide students in using Multidraft Reading strategies (TE p. 967).	**Leveled Tasks** *Knowledge Demands* If students will have difficulty with knowledge demands, have them first use the dates to identify the sequence of events as they read. Then, have them reread to identify aspects of the physical experience or of feeling danger that they find confusing. *Evaluating* If students will not have difficulty with knowledge demands, have them note as they read ways that the blog format is similar to or different from a diary. Discuss how a blog makes the dangers and challenges of the trip seem real for readers.

⑭ Critical Viewing

Answer: A person would need to be brave to climb the ladder because it is extremely tall and has been set against a wall of ice.

⑭ ▼ Critical Viewing
Why would a person have to be brave to attempt the climb seen here? **[Deduce]**

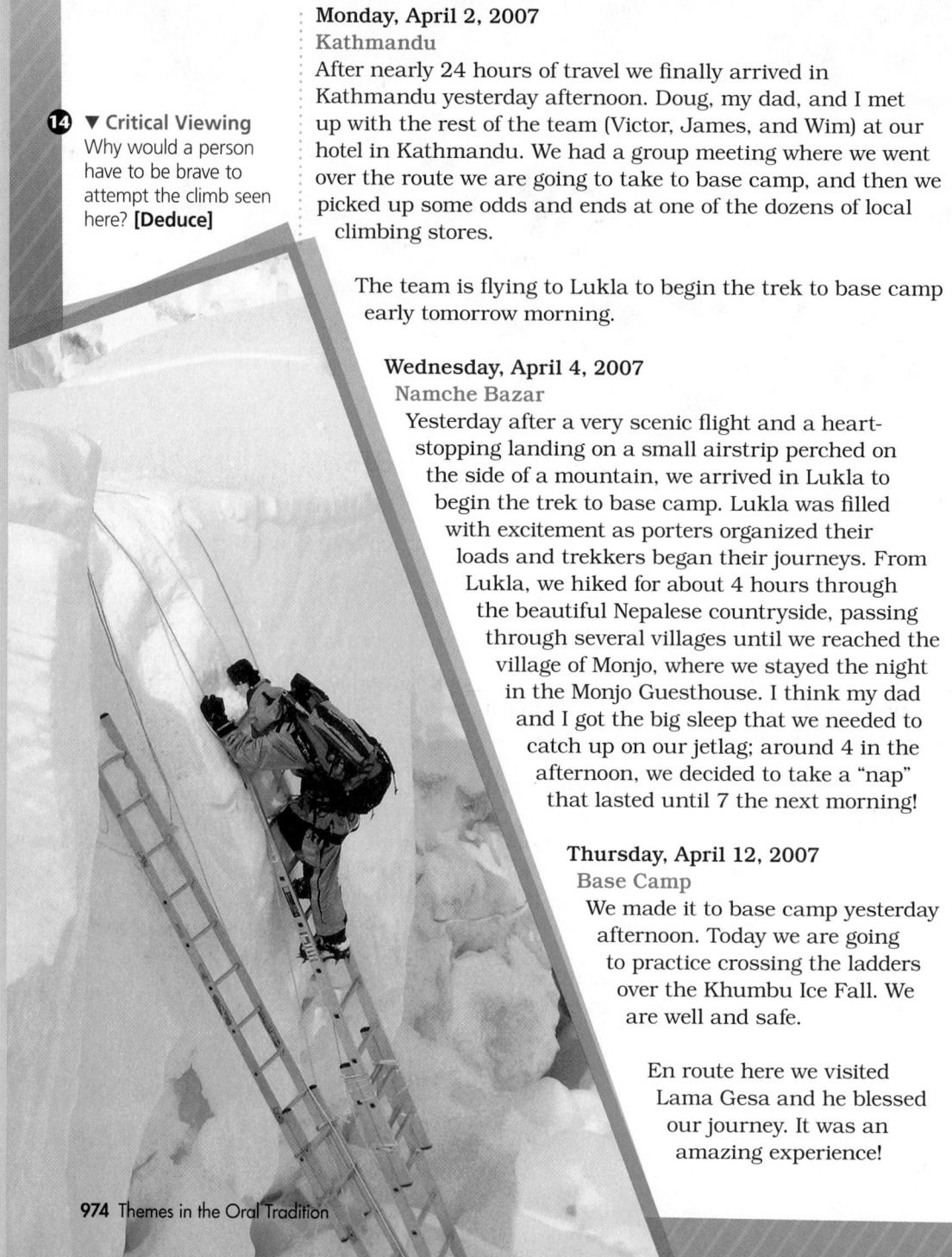

Monday, April 2, 2007
Kathmandu

After nearly 24 hours of travel we finally arrived in Kathmandu yesterday afternoon. Doug, my dad, and I met up with the rest of the team (Victor, James, and Wim) at our hotel in Kathmandu. We had a group meeting where we went over the route we are going to take to base camp, and then we picked up some odds and ends at one of the dozens of local climbing stores.

The team is flying to Lukla to begin the trek to base camp early tomorrow morning.

Wednesday, April 4, 2007
Namche Bazar

Yesterday after a very scenic flight and a heart-stopping landing on a small airstrip perched on the side of a mountain, we arrived in Lukla to begin the trek to base camp. Lukla was filled with excitement as porters organized their loads and trekkers began their journeys. From Lukla, we hiked for about 4 hours through the beautiful Nepalese countryside, passing through several villages until we reached the village of Monjo, where we stayed the night in the Monjo Guesthouse. I think my dad and I got the big sleep that we needed to catch up on our jetlag; around 4 in the afternoon, we decided to take a "nap" that lasted until 7 the next morning!

Thursday, April 12, 2007
Base Camp

We made it to base camp yesterday afternoon. Today we are going to practice crossing the ladders over the Khumbu Ice Fall. We are well and safe.

En route here we visited Lama Gesa and he blessed our journey. It was an amazing experience!

974 Themes in the Oral Tradition

Think Aloud

Vocabulary: Using Context

Direct students' attention to the word *Lama* on this page. Using a think-aloud process, model how to use context to infer the meaning of an unknown word. Say to students:

I'm going to think aloud to show you how I would figure out the meaning of the word *Lama* from its context.

In this sentence, *Lama* is used before another unfamiliar word—*Gesa*. Both words are capitalized, and that makes me think they could be a name like Joe Jones. It is also possible that *Lama* is an honorific like Doctor, Coach, or the "Father" we use to refer to a Catholic priest.

Reading on, I learn that Lama Gesa blessed the journey. That means he is a spiritual leader of some sort. I know *Lama* isn't a common term in the United States. Scanning back through the text, I see that Larson is writing from Kathmandu. I know that Kathmandu is the capital of Nepal, so I decide that a *Lama* is a spiritual leader in Nepal. I will read on to see if my definition is correct.

I am going to try and connect my laptop and charge it with my solar charger—we will see if that works.

More to follow.....

Monday, April 16, 2007
Rest Day

Yesterday we got an early start for our first time through the icefall. We left around 6:30 in the morning, with the idea that we would turn around 11—we did not necessarily have a destination in mind, it was more for acclimatization[1] and to get an idea of what the icefall was like. However, at 11 we were about half an hour from the top of the icefall, so we decided to just continue to the top.

It was quite fun climbing up the icefall. The ladders that we had to cross over crevasses[2] were especially exciting. I was pretty tired by the time we got back to base camp, but today was a rest day (our first), so I've had plenty of time to recover.

Tomorrow we are going up to camp one to spend the night. Camp one is about an hour further than we went yesterday. The next day we will go up to tag camp two and then come back down to base camp.

Thursday, April 19, 2007
Puja

The day before yesterday we all made it up to camp one to spend the night. This time we were able to get through the Khumbu Icefall an hour quicker than the last. We had a pretty good night at camp one; my dad and I both had a bit of a headache at first, but we were both able to eat and sleep well.

Camp one is at the start of the Western Cwm.[3] Yesterday, from camp one we continued up the Cwm to camp two. The cwm

---

1. **acclimatization** (ə klī′ mə tə zā′ shən) *n.* process of allowing the body to adjust to the climate, especially at high altitude.
2. **crevasses** (krə vas′ əz) *n.* deep cracks in ice or a glacier.
3. **Western Cwm** *n.* a broad valley at the base of Mount Everest

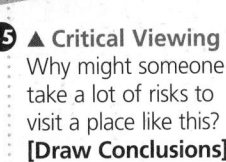

15 ▲ **Critical Viewing**
Why might someone take a lot of risks to visit a place like this? **[Draw Conclusions]**

16 **Universal Themes**
How is Lama Gesa's role in this selection similar to Athena's role in "The Voyage"?

17 Reading Check
How long did it take to travel to Kathmandu?

To the Top of Everest **975**

15 **Critical Viewing**
Answer: People may take risks to view a place like this because of its natural beauty.

16 **Universal Themes**
1. Remind students that Athena is a Greek goddess who helps protect Odysseus from the wrath of Poseidon in "The Voyage."
2. If necessary, **ask** students to use the dictionary or the Internet to look up the word "Lama." Write a class definition on the board. **Possible responses:** Lama is the title for a Tibetan religious teacher.
3. **Ask** the Universal Themes question. **Answer:** Lama Gesa plays the role of a "helpful person" in Larson's epic, which is the same role Athena plays in "The Voyage."

17 **Reading Check**
Answer: It took 24 hours to reach Kathmandu.

Fluency

Distribute copies of pages 974–975, and pair students. Have partners take turns reading paragraphs aloud. While one partner reads, the other should mark any words with which the one reading has difficulty. Circulate to monitor the fluency of students' reading. Collect students' marked up copies of the story, and review difficult words and passages with the class. Look for these problem spots:
• If students struggle with the word *Nepalese*

(p. 974), explain that the story takes place in Nepal. *Nepalese* is the adjective word form of *Nepal.*
• If students have difficulty with the many unfamiliar place names in the selection (*Kathmandu, Namche Bazar, Puja, Western Cwm*), model the pronunciation of each place name for students. Then try reading the selection chorally several times, until students' fluency increases.

Spiral Review

Central Idea

1. **Remind** students that they studied the concept of central idea in the Unit 6 Literary Analysis Workshop (pp. 902–911).

2. **Ask** the Spiral Review question.
   Possible response: The Sherpas know that climbing the mountain is dangerous and that they will need protection.

⑱ Universal Themes

1. **Ask** the Universal Themes question.
   Answer: We know that Larson and her team face great dangers because an area they had felt to be safe turned out to be unstable. She also refers frequently to the need to rest and recover from her physical activities at high altitude. She also mentions the need for good weather to reach the summit, which implies that the climb could be prohibitively dangerous during bad weather.

2. **Ask** students which epic convention appears in this entry.
   Answer: A dangerous journey.

---

is infamous for being very uncomfortably hot, but yesterday it was actually really nice. It was very beautiful, and we could see the summit of Everest, which we haven't been able to see since before we got to base camp. After we tagged camp two we came all the way back down to base camp. It was a long day, and we all returned pretty tired. However, it was nice to be back in base camp, and after dinner we watched Mission Impossible III on Ben's laptop (from the London Business School team). Unfortunately the power ran out about half way through, but I have been asked to charge up my laptop so we can finish tonight.

Today was the Puja, which is a ceremony that the Sherpas organize. A Lama comes up and performs many chants to ask the mountain gods for permission to climb the mountain, and to ask for protection. I had my ice ax and my crampons[4] blessed in the ceremony. As part of the ceremony, they also put out long lines of prayer flags coming out from the stupa where the ceremony was performed. Afterwards, they passed out lots of yummy treats.

While we were up at camp one, the shower tent was set up here at base camp. It's just a little bucket of water with a hose attached to it, but definitely 15 minutes of heaven.

Saturday, April 28, 2007
Base Camp

We are back at base camp! We came down from camp two yesterday, and arrived just in time for lunch. We were delayed a bit in the morning because we were radioed from base camp that there was a break in the icefall, and we didn't want to leave until we knew that the "ice doctors" had fixed up the route. As we came down, we found that the break was in a flat area known as the "football field" that we had previously designated as a "safe" area to take a little rest. And the whole shelf just collapsed!

Now that we have spent a night at camp three, we are done with the acclimatization process. We are going to take a few days for rest and recovery, and then we just wait for good weather to make a summit bid. We plan to go back down to Pengboche tomorrow so we can really get a good rest at lower altitude before our summit attempt.

---

4. **crampons** (kram´ pənz) *n.* metal plates with spikes that are attached to shoes to provide greater traction.

Spiral Review

Central Idea Why do you think the Sherpas organize a blessing ceremony?

⑱ Universal Themes

Which details in this entry show that Larson and her team face great dangers as they continue to climb?

Vocabulary
designated (dez´ ig nāt´ əd) *v.* identified; pointed out

Vocabulary Development   © CCSS Language 6

Words from Mountaineering

To reinforce and assess students' comprehension of the specialized vocabulary, give them sentences using the words in which the word may or may not be used correctly. Students must tell whether the use is correct and explain their answer.

1. The process of *acclimatization* can take several weeks. **Answer:** Yes. *Acclimatization* means "to allow your body to adjust to the climate." That process could take several weeks, especially on Everest.

2. A series of beautiful *crevasses* towered over my head. **Answer:** No. A *crevasse* is a "deep crack in ice or a glacier."

3. Wayne enjoyed wearing his *crampons* to bed on chilly nights. **Answer:** No. *Crampons* are spikey plates that attach to your shoes to provide traction for walking.

4. The *hypoxic* climber was short of breath and felt sick to her stomach. **Answer:** Yes, *hypoxic* means "having too little oxygen."

Here is what we have been up to these past few days:

4/23/07
Yesterday we all made it up to camp one for the night. We were joined by Tori from the London Business School team, because she wasn't feeling 100% when her team went up the day before.

Today we all came up to camp two. It was very hot coming up the Cwm this time, and we all had heavy packs because we had to bring up what we had left at camp one the last time we stayed there. It certainly made it a lot harder work!

4/24/07
Despite the fact that I caused us to get a later start than planned this morning (I had a particularly hard time getting out of my warm sleeping bag into the cold air) we accomplished our goal for the day. We went up the very first pitch of the Lhotse Face, and are now back at camp two for the evening.

4/26/07
Yesterday we went about halfway up the Lhotse face to camp three to spend the night. This was a new record for my dad and me, as our highest night ever! Camp three is at about 23,500 feet, and our previous highest night was at camp two on Cho Oyu, at 23,000 feet. We arrived at camp three around noon, and then had a lot of time to kill in our tents, as it wasn't really safe to go more than five feet outside the tent without putting on crampons and clipping into the fixed ropes. Thankfully, I had not yet reached a hypoxic[5] level where I couldn't enjoy my book.

Coming up the Lhotse Face was a bit windy, and some parts were pretty icy. It gets fairly steep, so I was glad to have my ascender, which slides up the rope, but not back down, so you can use it as a handhold to pull yourself up.

⓳

⓴ ✓ Reading Check
What did the Lama ask for during the Puja?

5. **hypoxic** (hī päk´ sik) *adj.* having too little oxygen.

To the Top of Everest **977**

⓳ **Connecting to the Big Question**

1. **Ask** students why Larson and her team must climb up and down from base camp, camp one, camp two, and camp three.
Answer: They are getting their bodies used to climbing at high elevation through a process of exercise and rest.

2. **Ask** students how this process affects the amount of time it takes to climb Mount Everest.
Answer: The process greatly adds to the amount of time people must spend on the mountain preparing for a climb.

3. **Ask** students to think of some positive and negative ways this long time spent on the mountain affects individuals and the community.
Possible responses: *positive effects:* For individuals, the process is good because it gets them to the top of the mountain in good health. For communities, the time spent on the mountain gives climbers time to learn more about Nepal, its customs and people. *negative effects:* For individuals, the long period of time spent on the mountain is bad because it keeps them away from home, adds cost to their travel, and can even lead to boredom. The community loses the climbers for an extended period of time.

⓴ **Reading Check**

Answer: The Lama asked the mountain gods for permission to climb the mountain, and for protection.

Differentiated Instruction for Universal Access

Culturally Responsive Instruction
Culture Focus Students may lack the background knowledge or context-building experiences necessary to fully comprehend the description of the Puja ceremony on p. 976. Before students read, build background knowledge about Nepal and Buddism. Locate Nepal on the globe and show photographs of its Sherpa people and extremely mountainous geography. Then, explain why people who live in these surroundings may treat the mountains with great respect. Point out that Larson and her team show respect for Buddist traditions while visiting Nepal. Lead a discussion about why they are so respectful.

1. Ask a student to read the entries for Friday, May 11, 2007, and Saturday, May 12, 2007, aloud to the class.

2. **Ask** the students what Larson and her team are doing on these days. **Answer:** They are waiting at base camp for a chance to climb to the summit. While they are waiting, they are exercising by doing day hikes. They are also testing their oxygen masks.

3. **Ask** students to describe Larson's tone in these entries. **Answer:** She sounds excited and slightly impatient.

4. **Ask** the Universal Themes question. **Answer:** She sounds excited about her summit attempt—even after enduring a long process of acclimatization. She is working to keep her fitness up. She describes herself as "a little restless" at base camp, which makes her sound ready to go.

21

Universal Themes
How do you know that Larson is willing to face challenges to meet her goal?

Vocabulary
saturation (sach´ ə rā´ shən) *n.* the state of being completely filled

---

Sunday, May 6, 2007
Back from Holiday
We're back at base camp from our little holiday down the mountain.

Now that we are back in base camp, we are just waiting till we can go for our summit attempt. The ropes are not yet fixed to the summit. Once the ropes are fixed, we hope there will soon be a good weather window.

Friday, May 11, 2007
Base Camp
We're still at base camp. Hopefully we'll be able to go up soon though.

We've tried to hold on to our fitness these past few days by doing some sort of activity each day. We've been ice climbing in a really neat cave near base camp, and we've also been on hikes up Pumori to Pumori base camp, and then up to camp one. Pumori is a 7145-meter mountain near Everest.

Saturday, May 12, 2007
Still at Base Camp
It looks like we're going to be able to go up soon for our summit attempt. Fingers crossed!

We've gotten our oxygen masks and tested them out. I was able to get my oxygen saturation back up to 100% this morning! After I turned off the oxygen, I only had a few seconds of being at pseudo sea-level before it went back down, though.

We're all getting a little restless hanging around base camp.

Monday, May 14, 2007
Camp 2
We finally started our summit push yesterday, making our way from base camp to camp two. We don't have internet access up here, but we were able to relay this information to our correspondents in New York via phone. We're taking a rest day today, and plan to press on tomorrow. If all goes well, we should summit on the 17th.

Think Aloud

Vocabulary: Using Context
Direct students' attention to the word *pseudo* on this page. Using a think-aloud process, model how to use context to infer the meaning of an unknown word. Say to students:

I'm going to think aloud to show you how I would figure out the meaning of *pseudo* from its context.

In this sentence *pseudo* is being used to describe the word *sea-level*. That doesn't offer much help, so I go back and read the full paragraph to broaden the context.

From the paragraph, I learn that Larson is trying out her new oxygen mask and manages to get her oxygen saturation up to 100%. Her tone in this passage is excited, so 100% oxygen saturation must be a good thing.

Then, she says, after she turns off the oxygen she remains at *pseudo sea-level* before her oxygen saturation goes down. I know Larson is not at sea-level. She is high in the mountains. So I guess that *pseudo* means "pretend" or "fake."

Thursday, May 17, 2007
Summit!
We made it to the top! Now all we have to do is get back down...

Wednesday, May 23, 2007
Back Home!
We've been in a big rush getting back home, and I haven't been able to update for awhile, as I have not had internet access. We woke up this morning at 16,000 feet in a village called Lobuche, and this evening my dad and I arrived back at sea-level in Long Beach! The rest of the team are celebrating in Kathmandu—my dad and I skipped out on the celebration to make it back in time for my brother Ted's college graduation in New York.

The day after we summitted, we came down from the South Col (camp 4) to camp 2. I was very tired at that point, but glad that we had all made it back safely lower on the mountain. It was amazing how after being to almost 30,000 feet, 20,000-foot camp 2 felt like it was nearly at sea-level!

The day after that, we came back down to base camp, where we received lots of warm hugs and congratulations. We only had one night back at base camp, as the next day (the 20th), we packed up our bags and headed down the valley. Base camp had a strange, empty feeling—it was sad to leave my little tent that had been my home for the past 2 months! My dad, Doug, Wim, and I were hoping to get a helicopter out of Lobuche on the 21st to save a little time, but Victor and

㉒ ✔ Reading
Check
How does Larson stay fit while waiting to go to the summit?

**We made it to the top!
Now all we have to do
is get back down...**

To the Top of Everest **979**

Differentiated
Instruction   **for Universal Access**

Strategy for Less Proficient Readers
To give students a context for the selection and to model how to identify and compare epic conventions, show them **Comparing Universal Themes, Graphic Organizer A** (*Graphic Organizer Transparencies*, p. 185). The completed graphic organizer will give students insight into epic conventions. They can use it as a model when they compare epic conventions in two such dissimilar works as "The Voyage" and "To the Top of Everest."

Enrichment for Advanced Readers
Ask students to compare and contrast how the theme of "person against nature" applies to "The Voyage" and "To the Top of Everest." Suggest that they consider topics such as the personality traits of the main characters, their respective ages and genders, and each character's ability to endure suffering. Have students write essays to express their ideas.

1. **Ask** the Universal Themes question. **Answer:** The fact that she is greeted by reporters who want to tell her story.

2. Remind students that Larson was just 18 years old when she reached the summit of Everest, and that she set a record.

3. **Ask** students if they feel that Larson is a hero. Lead a class discussion to explore some ideas.

ASSESS
Answers

Critical Thinking

Before students respond, you may wish to have them write a brief objective summary of the selection. As they answer the questions below, remind them to support their answers with evidence from the text.

1. (a) She gets into top physical shape. She also takes oboe lessons, and photography and French classes. (b) Because mountain climbing, especially at high elevations, is incredibly difficult. (c) She may take photographs. She may use her French to speak to other people who are climbing.

2. (a) About a month. (b) **Possible answers:** Hike up and down from different camps, ice climb, rest, read, watch movies, try out their oxygen masks (c) **Possible answers:** They must acclimatize to the altitude; the ropes are not yet fixed to the summit.

3. Climbers of many faiths would want to take part in the Puja ceremony because its purpose is to ask for permission to climb Everest, to ask for protection, and to bless the expedition.

4.  (a) **Possible responses:** Larson accomplishes a huge goal; she learns about a new country and the customs of the Nepalese people.
(b) **Possible responses:** Most students will feel that the community gains from Larson's experience. For example, by reading her blog.

---

23 **Universal Themes**
What details here suggest some people consider Larson and her team heroes?

James decided to walk down to the Lukla airstrip to fly out to Kathmandu on the 23rd. However, even though we awoke on the 21st to a beautiful, clear day in Lobuche, apparently there were clouds lower down the valley, so the helicopter couldn't fly in until the 23rd either. It was kind of hard waiting those two days in Lobuche. We were just an hour away from a hot shower and a big meal, if only those clouds would clear!

Once the helicopter landed in Kathmandu, I was greeted by a mob of journalists and cameramen. I was so surprised! After nearly 20 hours of travel, my dad and I landed at LAX[6] and were greeted by my family, and some more news people. Now we only have a few hours before we jump back on a plane to go to New York! I am very excited to see my mom and brother though.

Thank you everyone for all of your wonderful comments and your support!!!

---

6. **LAX** *n.* Los Angeles International Airport.

Critical Thinking

Cite textual evidence to support your responses.

1. **Key Ideas and Details** **(a)** What are some of the things Larson does to prepare for her journey before leaving home? **(b) Infer:** Why is it important to be in top physical shape? **(c) Deduce:** How might her other lessons and interests affect her trip?

2. **Key Ideas and Details** **(a)** How much time does Larson spend on the mountain before trying to reach the summit? **(b) Summarize:** List five things the team does with its time on the mountain before heading out for the summit. **(c) Deduce:** What prevents the team from trying to summit earlier?

3. **Integration of Knowledge and Ideas** **Speculate:** Why might climbers of many faiths want to take part in the Puja ceremony?

4. **Integration of Knowledge and Ideas** Climbing Mt. Everest takes an incredible amount of time, effort, and money. **(a)** How might a journey like Larson's enrich her as an individual? **(b)** Do you think the community also gains from her success? Explain. *[Connect to the Big Question: Community or individual— which is more important?]*

Vocabulary Development

Vocabulary Knowledge Rating
When students have completed reading and discussing "The Voyage" and "To the Top of Everest," have them take out their **Vocabulary Knowledge Rating Chart.** Read the words aloud once more and have students rate their knowledge of the words again in the After Reading column. Clarify any words that are still problematic. Have students write their own definition and example or sentence in the appro-

priate column. Then have students complete the Vocabulary Practice activities on the next page. Encourage students to use the words in further discussion and written work about these selections. Remind them that they will be accountable for these words on the **Selection Test** (*Unit 6 Resources*, pp. 112–114 or 115–117.)

After You Read

The Voyage *from* Tales
from the Odyssey •
To the Top of Everest

Comparing Universal Themes

1. Key Ideas and Details Compare and contrast Larson's voyage with Odysseus's.

	Odysseus	Samantha Larson
Journey undertaken		
Attitude of character		
Obstacles character must overcome		
Outcome		

2. Craft and Structure (a) Why might you include an allusion to the *Odyssey* if you were writing about Larson for your school paper? **(b)** Would you describe her as a "hero"? Explain.

3. Integration of Knowledge and Ideas One theme of the *Odyssey* is the triumph of bravery over power. Do you think "To the Top of Everest" expresses the same message? Why or why not? If not, how would you state its central idea?

⏱ Timed Writing

Explanatory Text: Essay

In an essay, compare and contrast the themes of the classic epic tale "The Voyage" with the modern account "To the Top of Everest." Explain how time and place influence the theme of each selection. (40 minutes)

5-Minute Planner

1. Read the prompt carefully and completely.

2. Jot down answers to these questions:
   - What is the universal theme of each selection?
   - How do the heroes overcome obstacles?
   - How does each form—epic tale or nonfiction blog—affect your response?

3. Take notes on which epic conventions are used in each selection. Record how the place and time influence the events. Then, jot down differences between the two selections.

4. Reread the prompt, and then draft your essay.

Assessment Resources

Unit 6 Resources

L1 L2 EL **Selection Test A,** pp. 112–114.

L3 L4 EL **Selection Test B,** pp. 115–117.

L2 **Open-Book Test,** pp. 109–111.

**PHLit
Online!** All assessment resources are available online at
www.PHLitOnline.com.

ASSESS

Answers

Comparing Universal Themes

1. **Possible responses:** Odysseus column—*journey:* across the ocean; *attitude:* tenacious struggle to survive; *obstacles:* storms created by Poseidon; *outcome:* positive because he survives. Samantha Larson column—*journey:* to the top of Mt. Everest; *attitude:* upbeat; *obstacles:* physical difficulties of climbing at high altitude *outcome:* positive—she makes it to the top and back safely.

2. (a) **Possible responses:** Some students will say yes, they would allude to the *Odyssey* because Larson has an epic voyage like Odysseus. Others will say no, because Larson doesn't suffer like Odysseus. (b) **Possible responses:** Some students will say Larson is a hero because she accomplishes a very difficult task. Others will say she isn't a hero because she climbs for her own enrichment. For example, she doesn't climb to benefit a charity.

3. **Possible responses:** Some students will feel that "the triumph of bravery over power" describes the theme of "To the Top of Everest." They may make the argument that the mountain is "power." If not, students might state the central idea of the blog as "the triumph of endurance over hardship" or "hard work pays off."

⏱ Timed Writing

1. Review the prompt with students.

2. Have students use the 5-Minute Planner to structure their time. Guide them in answering the bulleted questions. For example, point out that the first bulleted point might lead them to focus on what each story says about the challenges of life.

3. Allow students 40 minutes to complete the assignment.

4. As students prewrite and draft, have them refer to their completed **Comparing Universal Themes Graphic Organizer.**

Six Traits Focus

✔ Ideas	✔ Word Choice
✔ Organization	Sentence Fluency
Voice	Conventions

981

Common Core
State Standards

• Writing 2, 2.a, b, c, e, f; 4; 6
• Language 2.a, b; 3.a

Introducing the Writing Assignment

Review the assignment and the criteria.

Connecting to Real-Life Writing

Point out that the basic elements of a business letter are often incorporated into other types of writing.

• Memos use elements of a business letter.

 Writing Workshop
Work in Progress

If students have completed the Work-in-Progress assignments on pp. 933 and 957, suggest that they try to develop their Work-in-Progress ideas in a business letter.

Prewriting/Planning Strategy

1. Introduce the prewriting strategy, using the instruction and organizer on the student page.

2. Have students apply the strategy to organize the facts in their writing.

Six Traits Focus

✔	Ideas		Word Choice
✔	Organization		Sentence Fluency
	Voice		Conventions

Writing Workshop

Write an Informative Text

Workplace Writing: Business Letter

Defining the Form A **business letter** is a brief but formal written communication with a specific purpose. People write business letters to provide or request information, to express an opinion, or to issue a complaint. You might use elements of this form in memos, proposals, or letters to an author or newspaper.

Assignment Write a business letter requesting information from a company or an organization. Include these elements:

✔ standard *business letter format*

✔ a *clear statement* of your request

✔ *transitions* that unify your ideas

✔ *formal* and polite *language*

✔ an appropriate and logical *organizational structure*

✔ error-free writing, including the *correct use of commas*

To preview the criteria on which your business letter may be judged, see the rubric on page 987.

 Writing Workshop: *Work in Progress*

Review the work you did on pages 933 and 957.

Prewriting/Planning Strategy

Organize the facts. Briefly, state your purpose for writing. Then, jot down your contact information to ensure that the recipient can respond to your letter. Use the library, Internet, or customer service department to locate the recipient's name, title, and business address. Use an organizer like this to keep track of your information.

Company or Organization	Purpose for Writing	Contact Information	Details
Greenhaus Dance Company	To get information about the faculty	Name: Rita Moore Title: Director Address: 2 Main St., Chicago, IL 80808	I want to know the dance background of the various faculty members.

**Common Core
State Standards**

Writing
2. Write informative/explanatory texts to examine a topic and convey ideas, concepts, and information through the selection, organization, and analysis of relevant content.

2.a. Introduce a topic clearly, previewing what is to follow; organize ideas, concepts, and information, using strategies such as definition, classification, comparison/contrast, and cause/effect; include formatting, graphics, and multimedia when useful to aiding comprehension.

4. Produce clear and coherent writing in which the development, organization, and style are appropriate to task, purpose, and audience.

Teaching Resources

The following resources can be used to enrich or extend the instruction.

All *Unit 6 Resources*
Writing Workshop, pp. 118–119

All *Common Core Companion,*
pp. 202–212, 225–226, 245–252; 339–344

All *Professional Development Guidebook*
**Rubrics for Self-Assessment: Business
Letter,** pp. 265–266

All *Graphic Organizer Transparencies*
**Rubric for Self-Assessment: Business
Letter,** p. 187

 All resources are available online at **www.PHLitOnline.com.**

982

WRITER'S TOOLBOX

Organization	Word Choice	Ideas	Conventions	Sentence Fluency	Voice

Organizing a Letter

Organization is essential when writing a letter. The correct organization will give your letter credibility. Remember, you are writing to a business or organization that receives letters every day, so it is important to show that you have taken the time to use the correct format. Follow the tips below to organize your letter.

Choosing an Appropriate Format Follow this standard business letter format so the recipient can easily locate information.

- **Heading:** your address and the date of the letter
- **Inside Address:** the name and address that shows where the letter will be sent
- **Greeting:** the recipient's name, *Dear Sir, Dear Madam,* or *To Whom It May Concern,* followed by a colon
- **Body:** your purpose for writing
- **Closing:** *Sincerely,* or *Respectfully,* followed by a comma
- **Signature:** your full name and your signature above it

In **block format,** each part of the letter begins at the left margin. In **modified block format,** the heading, the closing, and the signature are indented to the center of the page. See a sample on page R27.

Getting to the Point Begin your letter by telling your reader why you are writing. You might begin with a phrase such as, *I am writing to you concerning,* or, *The reason for my letter is to request. . .* Once you have stated your purpose, give reasons why the business or organization should grant your request. Use a web to organize your thoughts.

I am a student leader at school.

I want to improve my own leadership skills.

Purpose: To receive information about summer leadership programs

I want to meet new people who are also interested in leadership opportunities.

I've heard great things through people who have attended your programs.

Applying Understanding by Design Principles

Clarifying Expected Outcomes: Using Rubrics

- Before students begin work on this assignment, have them preview the Rubrics for Self-Assessment (p. 987) to know what is expected. A copy of this rubric appears in *Graphic Organizer Transparencies,* p. 187.
- Review the criteria in the Rubrics with the class. Before students use the Rubrics to assess their own writing, work with them to rate the Student Model (p. 986) using the Rubrics.

- If you wish to assess students' business letters with either a 4-point or a 6-point scoring rubric, see the *Professional Development Guidebook,* pp. 265–266.

Organizing a Letter

1. Introduce the writing skill, using the instruction on the student page.
2. Discuss the standard business letter format given on the student page.
3. Have students follow the format as they draft.

Teaching the Writing Skill

1. Explain to students that proper organization—including only relevant information and putting it in correct order—is necessary when writing a business letter.
2. Guide students to understand that a business letter format can be understood as a form to be filled in. Once students understand the elements of a business letter, they can list them and use the list as a checklist for writing.
3. Review the elements of a business letter with students. You may wish to refer them to the Student Model on p. 986 to see examples of each element. Explain that each part of the letter has a purpose. For example, the inside address and greeting clearly identify the recipient. In addition, the format is a social convention, just as wearing a tie is in certain workplaces. Explain to students that their letters will be read with more respect if they follow the format.
4. Have students make a list of people to write to and their reasons for writing. Emphasize that their purpose should involve a concrete outcome, such as a refund or advice on a specific decision they wish to make.
5. When students have finished jotting down ideas, have them exchange papers with a partner. Have partners comment on each other's ideas, evaluating how interesting they are as well as how focused.
6. Suggest that students gather support for their main points using a web similar to the one shown on the student page.

PH WRITING COACH Grade 7

Students will find additional support for writing a business letter in chapter 12.

Drafting Strategies

1. Introduce the drafting strategies, using the instruction on the student page.

2. Have students apply the strategies as they draft.

Teaching the Strategies

Review the information on formatting a business letter. Note especially the use of a colon after the greeting. Note the following examples of formal and informal languange.

Informal	Formal
I bet	*I believe*
bogus	*counterfeit*
I get it	*I understand it*
hassle	*trouble, bother*
input	*contribution*
OK, okay	*all right*

Think Aloud: Model Using Appropriate Tone

Model the strategy of using the appropriate tone for a business letter, using the following "think aloud." Say to students:

When I am writing a business letter, I need to keep the tone formal and polite because I am probably writing to someone I do not know. The tone must be different from the informal tone I use to write an e-mail or note to one of my friends. For example, as I end my business letter, I do not write a phrase such as "Thanks!" I would write "Thank you for your time and attention," which is a more formal and respectful phrase.

Six Traits Focus

✔	Ideas		Word Choice
✔	Organization		Sentence Fluency
	Voice	✔	Conventions

Revising Strategies

1. Introduce the revising strategies, using the instruction on the student page.

2. Have students apply the strategies as they revise.

Teaching the Strategies

Remind students that the person who will read their business letter will likely not have much time to examine it, so they should eliminate all unnecessary details. Only essential information should be included.

Six Traits Focus

✔	Ideas	✔	Word Choice
✔	Organization		Sentence Fluency
✔	Voice		Conventions

984

Drafting Strategies

Use formal language. The tone of your letter should be friendly, yet serious and respectful. Remember, you are writing to a specific audience and for an intended purpose. You will not be using the same tone or language as you would in an e-mail to a friend or close relative. Use conventional English and avoid slang or a chatty, conversational style. You want your audience to take you seriously, especially if you expect your reader to grant your request.

Informal Language	Formal Language
I love your cooking show! It would be awesome if you could send me your tasty recipes!	I have always enjoyed cooking. I watch your show to learn new recipes and to learn about new foods and cooking techniques. I would appreciate it if you would share some of your recipes with me.

Develop the body. Use the web you made in your prewriting to develop the body of your letter. The body should elaborate and specify your request and should include supporting details. The business or organization must understand what you are requesting or why you are requesting it. Always end by thanking the recipient.

Link your ideas. An effective letter has unity—its details relate to a main idea. As you draft, use transitions between sentences to show how your ideas are related.

Revising Strategies

Eliminate irrelevant details. The details you include in your business letter should support your main points. Delete unnecessary information, including extra—but not key—details from your personal life. You are contacting a busy professional, so include only essential information. Also, revise any wordy or repetitive passages.

Relevant Detail: Our school's past attempts to start a recycling program have failed, because we have not had the necessary information or supplies to be successful.

Irrelevant Detail: My family and I reuse and recycle at home and I would like to continue this practice at school.

Check your tone. To maintain your formal tone, avoid slang, colloquialism, and contractions. Avoid personal references unless they are necessary to your request. Review your draft, replacing casual passages with more formal language.

Common Core State Standards

Writing

2.b. Develop the topic with relevant facts, definitions, concrete details, quotations, or other information and examples.

2.c. Use appropriate transitions to create cohesion and clarify the relationships among ideas and concepts.

2.e. Establish and maintain a formal style.

2.f. Provide a concluding statement.

Language

2.a. Use a comma to separate coordinate adjectives.

3.a. Choose language that expresses ideas precisely and concisely, recognizing and eliminating wordiness and redundancy.

PROFESSIONAL DEVELOPMENT | Jeff Anderson

APPLY THE STRATEGY

Express-Lane Editing After students have begun to draft, stop them when they have written about half a page. Say:

Readers expect us to follow certain patterns when we write letters. One convention that really helps communicate to our readers in business letters is capitalization. Let's do an express-lane edit of what we've written in our draft so far.

First, let's review the rules of capitalization. What do writers show with capitalization?

(Capitalization shows that a word is the name of a specific place or person—like a company or brand.)

As the discussion continues, have students record this information on their shopping lists. During revising, they will focus on the items they have listed.

For more of Jeff Anderson's strategies, see his Professional Development essay, pp. 900c–900d.

Revising Incorrect Use of Commas

A **comma** is a punctuation mark used to indicate a brief pause. The following examples illustrate some common misuses of commas.

Rule: Commas separate two adjectives in a series, but not the adjective from the noun.

Misused: My favorite drink is a cool, refreshing, lemonade.

Correct: My favorite drink is a cool, refreshing lemonade.

Rule: Commas do not separate parts of a compound subject.

Misused: After dinner, my friend Annie, and her sister Emma, left.

Correct: After dinner, my friend Annie and her sister Emma left.

Rule: Commas separate clauses that include both a subject and its verb, not parts of a compound verb.

Misused: The candidate looked out at the audience, and laughed.

Correct: The candidate looked out at the audience and laughed.

Rule: Commas do not separate parts of a compound object.

Misused: He made a sundae with whipped cream, and sprinkles.

Correct: He made a sundae with whipped cream and sprinkles.

PH | WRITING COACH
Further instruction and practice are available in *Prentice Hall Writing Coach*.

Fixing Incorrect Use of Commas Follow these rules:

1. Add a comma or commas:

- before a conjunction that separates two independent clauses in a compound sentence.
- to separate three or more words, phrases, or clauses.
- to separate adjectives of equal rank.
- to set off an introductory adverb clause.

2. Eliminate the comma:

- if it comes directly between the subject and the verb of a sentence.
- if it separates an adjective from the noun that follows it.
- if it separates a compound subject, verb, or object.

Grammar in Your Writing

Reread your letter, noting compound subjects, verbs, and objects. If necessary, revise the sentences using one of the methods above.

Revising Incorrect Use of Commas

1. Introduce the grammar skill.

2. Discuss the rules and examples, as well as the strategies for fixing incorrect usage.

3. Have students follow the instruction under Grammar in Your Writing to correct errors in their drafts.

Teaching the Grammar Skill

1. Students may make errors in the use of commas. Clarify the rule about using commas to separate adjectives of equal rank with examples that show the distinction between adjectives whose order could be switched without affecting the sense of the sentence and those that must appear in a specific order.

   three black cats but not *black three cats*

   fragrant, lush blossoms or *lush, fragrant blossoms*

   several provocative, complex questions or *several complex, provocative questions* but not *provocative several complex questions*

2. Have students identify the following sentences as correct or incorrect and make the necessary revisions.

   He nodded, and gave his answer. (**Answer:** incorrect; He nodded and gave his answer.)

   He bought an expensive, fountain pen. (**Answer:** incorrect; He bought an expensive fountain pen.)

   The lawyer and her assistant entered the courtroom. (**Answer:** correct)

   Three brown and white mountain goats scampered over to the stream, and began drinking. (**Answer:** incorrect; Three brown and white mountain goats scampered over to the stream and began drinking.)

   She went to the local hardware store and bought two fluorescent light bulbs and a wrench. (**Answer:** correct)

Student Model

Review the Student Model with the class, using the annotations to analyze the writer's use of the elements of a business letter.

Teaching From the Student Model

1. Explain that the Student Model is a sample and that business letters may be longer.

2. Have students read through the model and annotations. Have students examine the elements or features that are identified, analyze the effects of these elements on the letter, and consider how to apply these in their own letter.

3. Ask students what information should be added to Melissa's first paragraph. (**Answer:** She should have explained who she was (a sixth-grader) and who the trip was for (her class).

Connecting to Real-Life Writing

Explain to students that the ability to write a business letter is an important skill in all professional fields. Scientists, engineers, marketing professionals, and lawyers must frequently draft internal memos, as well as letters to clients, vendors, colleagues, or officials. Business letters are also required when applying to schools, for jobs, and when requesting information or registering a complaint.

Student Model: Melissa Gornto, Durham, NC

Common Core State Standards

Writing
6. Use technology, including the Internet, to produce and publish writing.

Language
2.b. Spell correctly.

Melissa Gornto
1436 Any Street
Durham, NC 27713

September 23, 2010

14th District Judicial Bar Board
Government Office Building, Office #33
67 Sherman Street
Durham, NC 27713

Dear Sir or Madam:

I am writing to you concerning financing for the trip that my classmates and I are taking to London. I see it as a great educational opportunity to learn about a different culture, history, and way of life. We do not know much about the British society, and this is a chance for us to find out the real information.

If you were to help us with the monetary grant, a weight would be lifted off our shoulders concerning the money issue. Using the money, we would be able to go to London, where we could see many things. We would be able to go to Buckingham Palace, Stonehenge, and Big Ben. This is also a great educational opportunity because it allows us to see the English way of life, including the different monetary system and the difference in speech. They may speak English, but that doesn't mean the words have the same sound or definition. So, if you will, look at this as a once-in-a-lifetime opportunity to learn many different things that aren't taught in schools.

Thank you for your time regarding this matter. Please take this trip into consideration and help us out. If you do, you won't have to worry about us not being grateful. This is an adventure my fellow classmates and I would love to go on. Once again, thank you for your time.

Sincerely,

Melissa Gornto
Melissa Gornto

Melissa uses block format in her business letter, setting all elements at the left margin.

Melissa clearly states her purpose.

Melissa uses friendly, yet formal language.

Strategies for
Test Taking: Computer Test Taking

- Share these strategies with students: Read directions carefully. They will explain how to answer a question. Remember that you may not be able to go back to a question and may not be able to change your answer.

Concentrate on answering the question you are working on. Then, move on to the next question.

- If you are having trouble with your computer, ask for help right away.

Editing and Proofreading

A letter with mistakes makes a poor impression and may signal that the writer is not serious in his or her request. Review your draft to eliminate errors in grammar, spelling, and punctuation.

Focus on spelling. Use the Internet or phone directories to verify that the name, title, and address of the recipient are spelled correctly. Carefully reread your letter to check for any other spelling errors.

Publishing and Presenting

Consider one of the following ways to share your writing:

Swap letters. Trade letters with a classmate. Read the letter carefully. Then, write a realistic response to the request for information.

Send your letter. Use e-mail or standard mail to send your request for information to the company or organization you have selected. Maintain the correspondence as needed. If you send your letter by standard mail, sign it and neatly write the address on the envelope before mailing.

Reflecting on Your Writing

Writer's Journal Jot down your answer to this question:

In the process of writing, what did you learn about the business or organization you chose?

Rubric for Self-Assessment

Find evidence in your writing to address each category. Then, use the rating scale to grade your work.

Criteria	Rating Scale
	not very very
Focus: How clearly have you stated your request?	1　2　3　4　5
Organization: How well have you organized your letter according to standard business format?	1　2　3　4　5
Support/Elaboration: How well do the details support your request?	1　2　3　4　5
Style: How formal and polite is your language?	1　2　3　4　5
Conventions: How correct is your grammar, especially your use of commas?	1　2　3　4　5
Organization: Does your letter follow the correct organizational pattern, and is the body written in a logical pattern?	1　2　3　4　5

Spiral Review

Earlier in the unit, you learned about **punctuation marks** (p. 932) and **commas** (p. 956). Check your letter to be sure that you have correctly used commas and other punctuation marks.

Editing and Proofreading

1. Introduce the editing and proofreading focus, using the instruction on the student page.

2. Have students edit and proofread their narratives, correcting grammar, spelling, punctuation, and word choice. Make sure they check for errors of the type noted in the lesson focus and the Spiral Review.

Teaching the Editing Focus

1. Remind students using computers not to depend completely on a spell-checker. A spell-checker will not catch all errors in the use of homophones or errors in names and addresses.

2. If students are handwriting their letters, remind them to write neatly and legibly for their readers' ease.

Six Traits Focus

Ideas	Word Choice
Organization	Sentence Fluency
Voice	✔ Conventions

ASSESS

Publishing and Presenting

Suggest that students who send their letters by regular mail use good-quality paper.

Reflecting on Your Writing

Suggest that students review their notes and drafts to identify any new information they learned about the company.

Strategies for Test Taking

Emphasize to students the importance of an overall plan for the test. Tell students to make sure they stick to their plan; it will help them manage their time and streamline the writing process. For instance, students should not spend time at the drafting stage worrying about the spelling of a certain word. The time for that will come during the editing and proofreading stages.

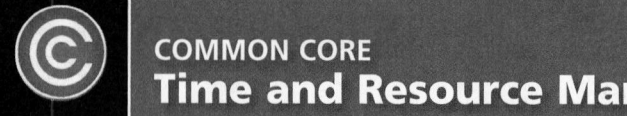

✓ **Sun and Moon in a Box** •
✓✓ **How the Snake Got Poison**
Lesson Pacing Guide

DAY 1 Preteach

- Ⓒ Administer the Reading and Vocabulary Warm-ups (*Unit 6 Resources*, pp. 127–130 or 145–148) as necessary.
- Introduce the Reading Skill: Compare and Contrast.
- Ⓒ Introduce the Literary Analysis concept: Cultural Context.
- Distribute copies of the appropriate graphic organizer for the Reading Skill (*Graphic Organizer Transparencies*, pp. 191–193).
- Distribute copies of the appropriate graphic organizer for Literary Analysis (*Graphic Organizer Transparencies*, pp. 188–190).
- Ⓒ Teach the selection vocabulary.
- Ⓒ Introduce the Word Study skill.

DAYS 2–3 Preteach/Teach

- Ⓒ Build background with the Background feature.
- Develop thematic vocabulary and thematic thinking with Writing About the Big Question.
- Prepare students to read with the Activating Prior Knowledge activities (TE).
- Informally monitor comprehension while students read.
- Use the Reading Check questions to confirm comprehension.
- Develop students' ability to understand an unfamiliar concept by using prior knowledge to compare and contrast using the Compare and Contrast questions.
- Ⓒ Develop students' understanding of cultural context using the Cultural Context questions.
- Ⓒ Reinforce vocabulary with the Vocabulary notes.
- Ⓒ Reinforce unit focus standards using the Spiral Review prompts.

DAY 4 Assess

- Assess students' comprehension and mastery of the skills by having them answer the Critical Thinking, Reading Skill, and Literary Analysis questions.
- Ⓒ Have students complete the Vocabulary Practice activities.
- Ⓒ Have students complete the Word Study activities.

DAY 5 Extend/Assess

- Have students complete the Conventions lesson.
- Ⓒ Have students complete the Writing activity and write a plot summary. (You may assign as homework.)
- Ⓒ Extend learning by having students complete the Speaking and Listening activity, a story. As an alternative, assign them "Rebuilding Communities" or "The Irresistible Urban Myth" in *Reality Central.*
- Administer Selection Test A or B (*Unit 6 Resources*, pp. 139–144 or 160–165).

Ⓒ **Common Core State Standards**

Reading Literature 2. Determine a theme or central idea of a text and analyze its development over the course of the text; provide an objective summary of the text.

Writing 2. Write informative/explanatory texts to examine a topic and convey ideas, concepts, and information through the selection, organization, and analysis of relevant content.
2.b. Develop the topic with relevant facts, definitions, concrete details, quotations, or other information and examples.
2.f. Provide a concluding statement or section that follows from and supports the information or explanation presented.
3. Write narratives to develop real or imagined experiences or events using effective technique, relevant descriptive details, and well-structured event sequences.
3.a. Organize an event sequence that unfolds naturally and logically.
3.b. Use narrative techniques, such as dialogue, pacing, and description, to develop experiences, events, and/or characters.

Speaking and Listening 4. Use appropriate eye contact, adequate volume, and clear pronunciation.

Language 2. Demonstrate command of the conventions of standard English capitalization, punctuation, and spelling when writing.
5.b. Use the relationship between particular words to better understand each of the words.
6. Acquire and use accurately grade-appropriate general academic and domain-specific words and phrases; gather vocabulary knowledge when considering a word or phrase important to comprehension or expression.

Additional Standards Practice
Common Core Companion, *pp. 15–22*

Daily Block Scheduling
Each day in this Lesson Pacing Guide represents a 40–50 minute period. Teachers using block scheduling may combine days to revise pacing. In addition, teachers may differentiate and support core instruction by integrating components for extended and intensive support as students require. See the Guide to Selected Leveled Resources (facing page).

Guide to Selected Leveled Resources

R T I **Tier 1** (students performing on level)	✓ **More Accessible** Sun and Moon in a Box	✓✓ **More Complex** How the Snake Got Poison
Warm Up **Practice, model,** and **monitor** fluency, working with the **whole class** or **in groups**.	**Vocabulary** and **Reading Warm-ups B,** *Unit 6 Resources,* pp. 127–128, 130	**Vocabulary** and **Reading Warm-ups B,** *Unit 6 Resources,* pp. 145–146, 148
Comprehension/Skills **Support** and **monitor** comprehension and skills development, having students complete the activities, graphic organizers, and interactive prompts **independently** or **as a class**.	• *Reader's Notebook,* adapted instruction and full selection **EL** *Reader's Notebook: English Learner's Version,* adapted instruction and adapted selection • **Reading Skill Graphic Organizer B,** *Graphic Organizer Transparencies,* p. 193 • **Literary Analysis Graphic Organizer B,** *Graphic Organizer Transparencies,* p. 190	• *Reader's Notebook,* adapted instruction and summary **EL** *Reader's Notebook: English Learner's Version,* adapted instruction and summary • **Reading Skill Graphic Organizer B,** *Graphic Organizer Transparencies,* p. 193 • **Literary Analysis Graphic Organizer B,** *Graphic Organizer Transparencies,* p. 190
Monitor Progress **A** Monitor student progress with the differentiated curriculum-based assessment in the *Unit Resources.*	• **Selection Test B,** *Unit 6 Resources,* pp. 142–144 • **Open-Book Test,** *Unit 6 Resources,* pp. 136–138	• **Selection Test B,** *Unit 6 Resources,* pp. 163–165 • **Open-Book Test,** *Unit 6 Resources,* pp. 157–159

R T I **Tier 2** (students requiring intervention)	✓ **More Accessible** Sun and Moon in a Box	✓✓ **More Complex** How the Snake Got Poison
Warm Up **Practice, model,** and **monitor** fluency **in groups** or **with individuals**.	• **Vocabulary and Reading Warm-ups A,** *Unit 6 Resources,* pp. 127–129 • *Reality Central,* "Rebuilding Communities" • *Hear It!* **Audio CD (adapted text)**	• **Vocabulary and Reading Warm-ups A,** *Unit 6 Resources,* pp. 145–147 • *Reality Central,* "The Irresistible Urban Myth" • *Hear It!* **Audio CD**
Comprehension/Skills • **Support** and **monitor** comprehension and skills development, working **in small groups** or **with individuals**. • **Pair** students with more advanced peers and have them complete the writing activity in the *Real-World Writing Journal.* • As students complete the selection in the appropriate version of the *Reader's Notebook,* monitor comprehension frequently with group questions and individual instruction. • **Model** strategies while guiding students in completing the activities and prompts in the *Reader's Notebook,* as well as the graphic organizers. • **Practice** skills and **monitor** mastery with the *Reading Kit* worksheets.	• *Real-World Writing Journal,* Lesson 5, pp. 172–175 • *Reader's Notebook: Adapted Version,* adapted instruction and adapted selection **EL** *Reader's Notebook: English Learner's Version,* adapted instruction and adapted selection • **Reading Skill Graphic Organizer A,** *Graphic Organizer Transparencies,* p. 191 • **Literary Analysis Graphic Organizer A,** *Graphic Organizer Transparencies,* p. 188 • *Reading Kit,* Practice worksheets, pp. 268, 272, 278, 280, 288	• *Real-World Writing Journal,* Lesson 6, pp. 176–179 • *Reader's Notebook: Adapted Version,* adapted instruction and summary **EL** *Reader's Notebook: English Learner's Version,* adapted instruction and summary • **Reading Skill Graphic Organizer A,** *Graphic Organizer Transparencies,* p. 192 • **Literary Analysis Graphic Organizer A,** *Graphic Organizer Transparencies,* p. 189 • *Reading Kit,* Practice worksheets, pp. 268, 272, 278, 280, 288
Monitor Progress **A** Monitor student progress with the differentiated curriculum-based assessment in the *Unit Resources* and in the *Reading Kit.*	• **Selection Test A,** *Unit 6 Resources,* pp. 139–141 • *Reading Kit,* Assess worksheets, pp. 269, 273, 279, 281, 289	• **Selection Test A,** *Unit 6 Resources,* pp. 160–162 • *Reading Kit,* Assess worksheets, pp. 269, 273, 279, 281, 289

TIER 3 Tier 3 intervention may require consultation with the student's special-education or dyslexia specialist. For additional support, see the Tier 2 activities and resources listed above.

One-on-one teaching **Group work** **Whole class instruction** **Independent work** **A Assessment**

For a complete guide to selection support, including support for Advanced students, see the Overview of Resources in the frontmatter.

✓ Sun and Moon in a Box
✓✓ How the Snake Got Poison

RESOURCES FOR:

L1 Special-Needs Students

L2 Below-Level Students (Tier 2)

L3 On-Level Students (Tier 1)

L4 Advanced Students (Tier 1)

EL English Learners

All All Students

Vocabulary/Fluency/Prior Knowledge

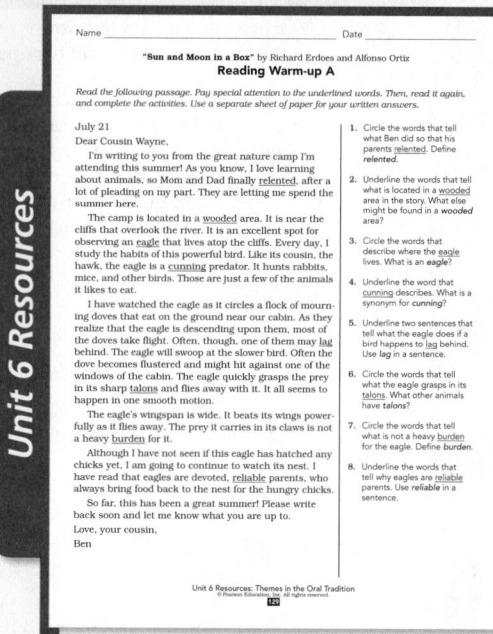

EL L1 L2 **Reading Warm-ups A and B,** pp. 129–130, 147–148

Also available for these selections:

EL L1 L2 **Vocabulary Warm-ups A and B,** pp. 127–128, 145–146

All **Writing About the Big Question,** pp. 131, 149

All **Vocabulary Builder,** pp. 134, 152

Reader's Notebooks

Pre- and postreading pages for both selections, as well as the selection "Sun and Moon in a Box," appear in an interactive format in the *Reader's Notebooks*. Each *Notebook* is differentiated for a different group of learners. The selections in the Adapted and English Learner's versions are abridged.

L2 L3 *Reader's Notebook*

L1 *Reader's Notebook: Adapted Version*

EL *Reader's Notebook: English Learner's Version*

EL *Reader's Notebook: Spanish Version*

© Common Core Companion

Additional instruction and practice for each Common Core State Standard

Selection Support

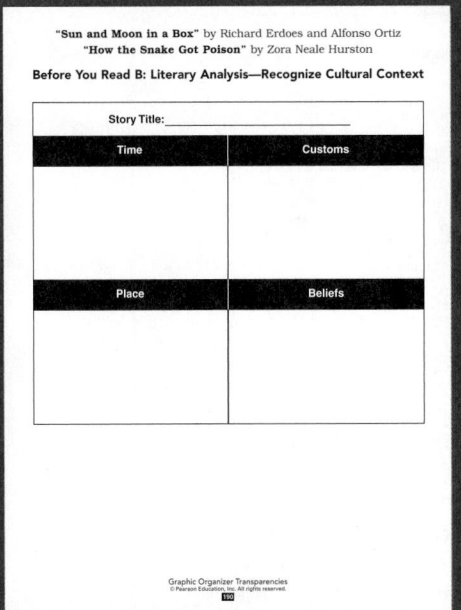

Graphic Organizer Transparencies (side tab)

EL **L3** **Literary Analysis: Graphic Organizer B,** p. 190

Also available for these selections:

EL **L1** **L2** **Literary Analysis: Graphic Organizer A,** pp. 188, 189 (partially filled in)

EL **L1** **L2** **Reading: Graphic Organizer A,** pp. 191, 192 (partially filled in)

EL **L3** **Reading: Graphic Organizer B,** p. 193

Skills Development/Extension

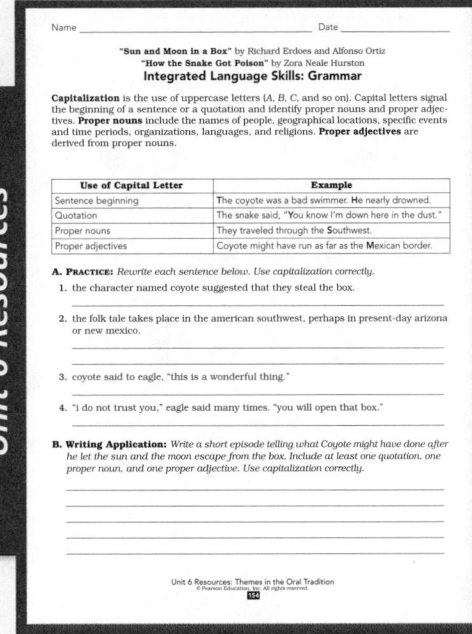

Unit 6 Resources (side tab)

EL **L3** **L4** **Grammar,** p. 57

Also available for these selections:

All **Literary Analysis: Cultural Context,** p. 133, 151

L4 **Enrichment,** pp. 135, 153

All **Reading: Compare and Contrast,** pp. 132, 150

EL **L3** **L4** **Support for Writing,** p. 155

L3 **L4** **Support for Extend Your Learning,** p. 156

Assessment

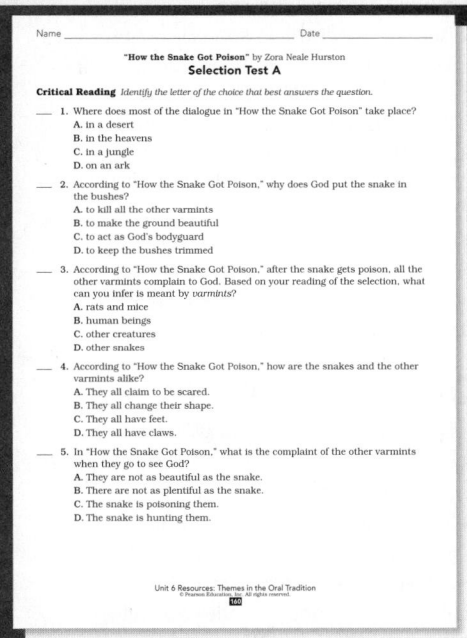

EL **L1** **L2** **Selection Test A,** pp. 139–141, 160–162

Also available for these selection:

EL **L3** **L4** **Selection Test B,** pp. 142–144, 163–165

L3 **L4** **Open-Book Test,** pp. 136–138, 157–159

PHLit Online!
www.PHLitOnline.com

Online Resources: All print materials are also available online.

- complete narrated selection text
- a thematically related video with writing prompt
- an interactive graphic organizer
- highlighting feature
- access to all student print resources, adapted to individual student needs
- Spanish and English summaries
- adapted selection translations in Spanish

Background Video

Also available:

Get Connected! (thematic video with writing prompt)
All videos are available in Spanish.

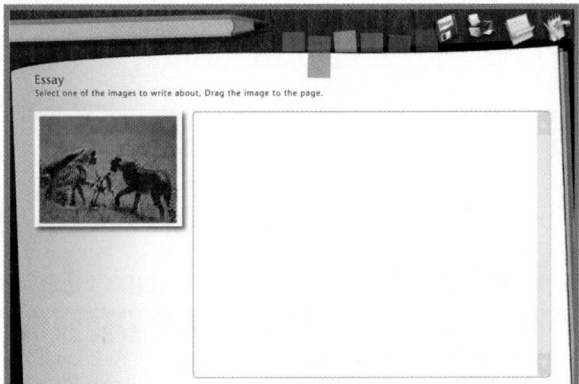

Writer's Journal (with graphics feature)

Also available:

Vocabulary Central (tools, activities, and songs for studying vocabulary)

❶ Leveled Texts

You may use either "Sun and Moon in a Box" or "How the Snake Got Poison" to meet the lesson objectives. Skills instruction for both selections appears on page 989. Choose one selection to teach (or choose to teach both). The Text Complexity Rubric at the bottom of this page will help you determine which selection is more appropriate for your students. Use the Reader and Task Suggestions on the facing page to help all students read text of increasing complexity.

❷ ⓒ Introducing the CCS Standards

Introduce the standards on the student page. (Note that the lesson element with which each standard is addressed is identified in parentheses after the text of the standard.) Call out the standards that you will cover with the selections, explaining to students what each requires and how they will address it as they work through the selection you have chosen. Standards labeled "Spiral Review" are introduced in the Literary Analysis Workshop for this unit.

Before You Read

Sun and Moon in a Box • How the Snake Got Poison

❶ ⓒ Leveled Texts

Build your skills and improve your comprehension of folk tales with texts of increasing complexity.

Read **"Sun and Moon in a Box"** to learn what happens when Eagle and Coyote borrow a sacred Native American box.

Read **"How the Snake Got Poison"** to find out how the snake learns to protect himself.

❷ ⓒ Common Core State Standards

Meet these standards with either **"Sun and Moon in a Box"** (p. 992) or **"How the Snake Got Poison"** (p. 1000).

Reading Literature
2. Determine a theme or central idea of a text and analyze its development over the course of the text; provide an objective summary of the text. *(Literary Analysis: Spiral Review; Writing: Oral Summary)*

Writing
2. Write informative/explanatory texts to examine a topic and convey ideas, concepts, and information through the selection, organization, and analysis of relevant content. **2.b.** Develop the topic with relevant facts, definitions, concrete details, quotations, or other information and examples. **2.f.** Provide a concluding statement or section that follows from and supports the information or explanation presented. *(Writing: Plot Summary)*

3. Write narratives to develop real or imagined experiences or events using effective technique, relevant descriptive details, and well-structured event sequences. **3.a.** Organize an event sequence that unfolds naturally and logically.

3.b. Use narrative techniques, such as dialogue, pacing, and description, to develop experiences, events, and /or characters. *(Speaking and Listening: Story)*

Speaking and Listening
4. Use appropriate eye contact, adequate volume, and clear pronunciation. *(Speaking and Listening: Story)*

Language
2. Demonstrate command of the conventions of standard English capitalization, punctuation, and spelling when writing. *(Conventions: Capitalization)*

5.b. Use the relationship between particular words to better understand each of the words. *(Vocabulary: Analogy)*

6. Acquire and use accurately grade-appropriate general academic and domain-specific words and phrases; gather vocabulary knowledge when considering a word or phrase important to comprehension or expression. *(Vocabulary: Word Study)*

988 Themes in the Oral Tradition

ⓒ Text Complexity Rubric: Leveled Texts

Text complexity is determined by both qualitative and quantitative measures. For this reason, the quantitative measure of a more complex selection may be lower than that of a more accessible selection.

		✓ **Sun and Moon in a Box**	✓✓ **How the Snake Got Poison**
Qualitative Measures	**Context/Knowledge Demands**	Traditional folk tale; Zuni history/culture 1 2 ③ 4 5	African American folk tale; 1930s Florida 1 2 3 ④ 5
	Structure/Language Conventionality and Clarity	Some subject-specific vocabulary, footnoted; simple sentences; straightforward narrative 1 2 ③ 4 5	Regionalisms; challenging diction; informal tone; straightforward narrative 1 2 3 ④ 5
	Levels of Meaning/ Purpose/Concept Level	Accessible concept (curiosity brings problems) 1 2 ③ 4 5	Challenging concept (animals talk to God) 1 2 3 ④ 5
Quantitative Measures	**Text Length**	Word Count: 830	Word Count: 408
	Lexile	630L	900L
Overall Complexity		✓ **More accessible**	✓✓ **More complex**

❸ Reading Skill: Compare and Contrast

- A **comparison** tells how two or more things are alike.
- A **contrast** tells how two or more things are different.

Often, you can understand an unfamiliar concept by using your prior knowledge to compare and contrast. For example, you may understand an ancient culture better if you look for ways it is similar to and different from your own culture. You might also find similarities and differences between a story told long ago and one that is popular today. To help you compare and contrast stories, ask questions such as the following:

- Does this character make me think of someone I know or someone I have encountered in books, television shows, or movies?
- Is this plot similar to one I have seen elsewhere?
- What traditions does this story emphasize that are similar to or different from my own?

❹ Literary Analysis: Cultural Context

Stories such as fables, folk tales, and myths are influenced by the **cultural context,** or background, customs, and beliefs, of the people who originally told them. Recognizing the cultural context will help you understand and appreciate what you read.

❺ Using the Strategy: Cultural Context Chart

Use a chart like the one shown to identify the cultural context of a literary work. Consider the impact that cultural context might have on the author's intended theme, or message about life.

Story Title	
Time	Customs
Place	Beliefs

PHLit Online!
www.PHLitOnline.com

Hear It!
- Selection summary audio
- Selection audio

See It!
- Get Connected video
- Background video
- More about the author
- Vocabulary flashcards

Do It!
- Interactive journals
- Interactive graphic organizers
- Self-test
- Internet activity
- Grammar tutorial
- Interactive vocabulary games

Before You Read: Sun and Moon in a Box • How the Snake Got Poison **989**

❸ Reading Skill
Compare and Contrast

1. Introduce the skill, using the instruction on the student page.
2. Tell students that they will practice comparing and contrasting as they read.

❹ Literary Analysis
Cultural Context

1. Introduce the skill, using the instruction on the student page.
2. Tell students that they will identify cultural context as they read.

Think Aloud: Model the Skill

Model a way to understand features of cultural context. Say to students:

To interpret cultural context, I think of examples from life. Today, many women work in the same fields as men. Many older women who wanted to work in professions such as medicine faced resistance even just forty years ago. It was a *custom* for many women to stay at home and mind the children. Today's customs reflect people's changing *beliefs* about women's roles. By keeping the ideas of *custom* and *belief* in mind as I read, I better understand fables, folk tales, and myths.

❺ Using the Strategy

Give students a copy of either **Literary Analysis Graphic Organizer A or B** (*Graphic Organizer Transparencies*, pp. 188–190) to identify aspects of cultural context as they read. Use the examples in **Literary Analysis Graphic Organizer A**, which is partially filled in, to model the process of completing the organizer.

© Text Complexity: Reader and Task Suggestions

✓ Sun and Moon in a Box		✓✓ How the Snake Got Poison	
Preparing to Read the Text	**Leveled Tasks**	**Preparing to Read the Text**	**Leveled Tasks**
• Using the Background on p. 991, review the features of folk tales and link these to the selection. • Discuss ways in which different cultures explain natural events (creation of the sun and moon) to future generations. • Guide students to use Multidraft Reading strategies (TE p. 991).	*Knowledge Demands* If students will have difficulty with knowledge demands, have them first read to identify the results of Coyote's curiosity. Have them reread to identify aspects of the folk tale's natural explanation they find confusing. *Analyzing* If students will not have difficulty with knowledge demands, have them note ways in which the author's description authenticates the folk tale's explanation.	• Using the Background note on p. 999, discuss dialect/vernacular and how these convey something about where the author is from. • Review strategies for reading dialect, such as trying different pronunciations. • Guide students to use Multidraft Reading strategies (TE p. 999).	*Structure/Language* If students will have difficulty with language, have them read to learn how God helps the snake solve his problem. Have them reread, identifying dialect they find confusing. *Analyzing* If students will not have difficulty with language, have them note ways in which the author uses diction to capture her community's regional voice. Read parts of the folk tale aloud to convey this voice.

989

Skills instruction for the Reading Skill and Literary Analysis concepts for this selection appears on p. 989.

❶ Writing About the Big Question

1. Review the assignment with the class.

2. Ask students what happens when one member of their family doesn't want to see the same movie as the others. Discuss ways people work to meet each other's needs.

3. Have students complete the sentence starter. Review responses as a class. (**Sample responses:** When the needs of the <u>individual</u> and the needs of the larger <u>group</u> are in conflict, it is helpful to compromise because then everyone gets what he or she needs.)

4. Remind students that their answers will help them think about the Big Question, "Community or individual—which is more important?"

While You Read

Tell students that as they read, they should look for details that suggest both the snake's needs and the varmints' needs are valid.

❷ Vocabulary

1. Have students preview the selection vocabulary.

2. For each word, have students say the word aloud.

3. Then, use the word in a sentence that defines the word.

4. Finally, repeat your definitional sentence or a similar sentence with the word missing and have the class "fill in the blank" chorally. Here is an example:

   <u>Immensity</u> is immeasurable largeness. We will never be able to explore all of outer space because of its [students say "immensity"].

❸ Word Study

1. Introduce the skill, using the instruction in the box.

2. Have students suggest another *-ity* word and challenge a partner to define it.

Making Connections | How the Snake Got Poison

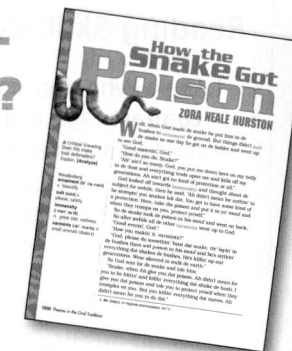

❓ Community or individual — which is more important?

❶ Writing About the Big Question

In "How the Snake Got Poison," God must figure out a solution to keep the snake from being killed by the varmints, and the varmints from being killed by the snake. Use this sentence starter to develop your ideas about the Big Question.

When the needs of the **individual** and the needs of the larger **group** are in conflict, it is helpful to _____ because _____.

While You Read Look for details that suggest both the snake's needs and the varmints' needs are important.

❷ Vocabulary

Read each word and its definition. Decide whether you know the word well, know it a little bit, or do not know it at all. After you read, see how your knowledge of each word has increased.

- **ornament** (ôr´ nə ment´) *v.* beautify (p. 1000) *I put lights in the tree to <u>ornament</u> the patio.* ornament *n.* ornamental *adj.* ornamentation *n.*

- **suit** (sŏot) *v.* please; satisfy (p. 1000) *As nice as they were, the flowers did not <u>suit</u> her.* suitable *adj.* suitability *n.* suitably *adv.*

- **immensity** (i men´ sə tē) *n.* great size; vastness (p. 1000) *The search team had to spread out because of the canyon's <u>immensity</u>.* immense *adj.* immensely *adv.*

- **varmints** (vär´ mənts) *n.* small animals (dialect) (p. 1000) *<u>Varmints</u> got into the grain silo to eat.* varmint *n.*

❸ Word Study

The **Latin suffix *-ity*** means "state," "quality," or "condition of."

In this folk tale, God looks toward **immensity.** The author uses this word to describe the enormous size of the universe.

Vocabulary Development

Vocabulary Knowledge Rating

Create a **Vocabulary Knowledge Rating Chart** (*Professional Development Guidebook,* p. 33) for the selection vocabulary words and for the thematic words in the Writing About the Big Question sentence starter on the student page.

Give each student a copy of the chart with the words on it. Read the words aloud, and have students mark their rating of each in the Before Reading column. When students have completed reading and discussing the selection, have them take out their **Vocabulary Knowledge Rating** charts for the story. Read the words aloud and have students rate their knowledge again in the After Reading column. Clarify any words that are still problematic. Then, have students complete the Vocabulary practice at the end of the selection.

 **Vocabulary Central,** featuring tools, activities, and songs for studying vocabulary, is available online at www.PHLitOnline.com.

Meet
Zora Neale Hurston
(1891–1960)

Author of

How the Snake Got Poison

Zora Neale Hurston, the daughter of a preacher and a schoolteacher, grew up in the small town of Eatonville, Florida. In 1925, Hurston headed to New York and became part of the Harlem Renaissance, a creative movement among African Americans.

Hurston's Career Hurston collected folklore in the southern United States and in Jamaica, Haiti, Bermuda, and Honduras. Her first book, *Jonah's Gourd Vine*, was published in 1934. Although Hurston's writing was popular, she was not able to make a living from it and died penniless. In 1973, author Alice Walker found Hurston's grave and placed a gravestone on the site.

❹ BACKGROUND FOR THE FOLK TALE

Dialect

Dialect is the form of a language that is spoken by people in a particular region or social group. It differs from standard English in pronunciation, grammar, word choice, and sentence structure. Dialect used in the retelling of a folk tale honors the oral tradition by helping the reader "hear" how the story was first told. The dialect in "How the Snake Got Poison" reflects its roots in African American folklore.

DID YOU KNOW?
Hurston studied anthropology at Barnard College and Columbia University, in New York.

How the Snake Got Poison **999**

🔔 Daily Bellringer
For each class during which you teach this selection, have students complete one of the five Revision activities for Week 34 in the *Daily Bellringer Activities* booklet.

❹ Background
Dialect
African American folklore had its origins in the oral tradition of community storytelling. In this story, some of the humor results from dialect, a nonstandard form of English spoken in a particular region. "How the Snake Got Poison" is a story the author first heard in her hometown of Eatonville, Florida. In the 1930s, Zora Neale Hurston returned home from New York City to collect tales she had heard as a child. Hurston retold them the way she remembered hearing them on the front porch of the local store.

Multidraft Reading

To assist struggling readers and to deepen reading for all, assign the text in "chunks" and apply multidraft reading protocols. For each reading, have students set the purpose indicated:

- **First reading**—identifying key ideas and details and answering any Reading Checks.
- **Second reading**—analyzing craft and structure and responding to the side-column prompts.
- **Third reading**—integrating knowledge and ideas, connecting to other texts and the world, and answering the end-of-selection questions.

For more guidance, refer to the *Classroom Strategies and Teaching Routines* card on multidraft reading.

Differentiated Instruction   Additional Instruction

EL Extended Support— English Learners
Have students complete the **Reading and Vocabulary Warm-ups**, *Unit 6 Resources*, pp. 145–148, before they read. Assign the prereading pages and the adapted selection in the *Reader's Notebook: English Learner's Version*. Then, have students listen to portions of the selection on the *Hear It!* **Online Audio CD.**

L1 L2 Extended Support— Struggling Readers
Have students complete the **Reading and Vocabulary Warm-ups**, *Unit 6 Resources*, pp. 145–148, before they read. Assign the prereading pages and the adapted selection in the *Reader's Notebook: Adapted Version*. Then, have students listen to portions of the selection on the *Hear It!* **Audio CD** (adapted text).

Extended Support— Reluctant Readers
To build motivation and engagement before assigning the selection, have students read "The Irresistible Urban Myth," a thematically related selection in *Reality Central*. Then, use the questions at the conclusion of the related selection to guide discussion.

PHLit Online!
For more about the author, practice with the selection vocabulary, or more background, go online at www.PHLitOnline.com.

999

❶ Activating Prior Knowledge

1. Prepare an **Anticipation Guide** (see *Professional Development Guidebook,* p. 38) with the following statements:

• The main purpose of any good folk tale is to entertain.

• You can't believe anything you read or hear in a folk tale.

• Folk tales are told and retold because they contain truths about people and the world.

• Folk tales are valuable because they reveal something about the people who tell them.

Concept Connector ➡

Students will follow up on this activity after completing the selection.

Small-Group Activity

Have students work in pairs to identify and share ideas on a topic about which they disagree. Partners should not try to persuade each other; they should simply explain their perspectives. As a class, discuss whether students were able to understand another perspective.

❷ About the Selection

This folk tale explains how the snake got poison and a rattle. In the tale, the snake goes to God to complain that it lacks protection from its enemies. When God gives the snake poison, the other animals complain that the snake is killing anyone that comes near it. Then, God gives the snake a bell (its rattle) to give other creatures fair warning when they approach.

❸ Critical Viewing

Possible response: Students may say that the snake does not look defenseless, in part because they know that rattlesnakes can be deadly.

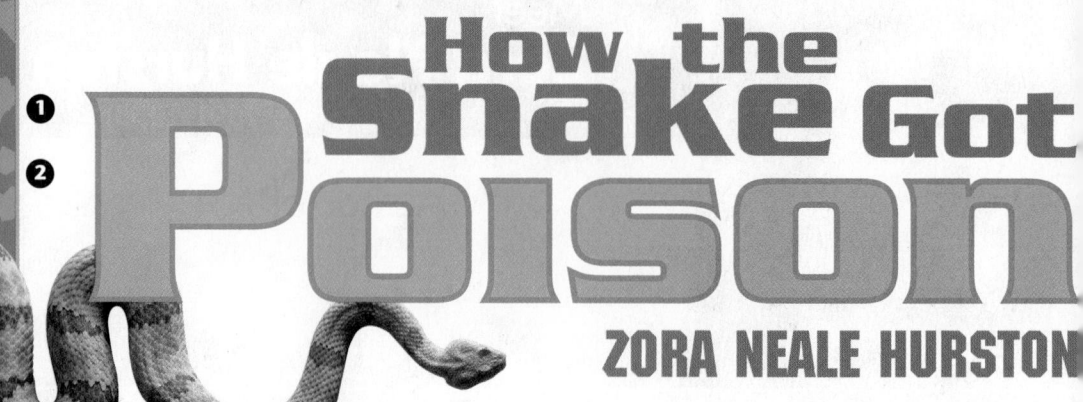

How the Snake Got Poison

ZORA NEALE HURSTON

❸ ▲ **Critical Viewing**
Does this snake look defenseless? Explain. **[Analyze]**

Vocabulary
ornament (ōr´ nə ment´) *v.* beautify

suit (sōōt) *v.* please; satisfy

immensity (i men´ sə tē) *n.* great size; vastness

varmints (vär´ mənts) *n.* small animals (dialect)

Well, when God made de snake he put him in de bushes to ornament de ground. But things didn't suit de snake so one day he got on de ladder and went up to see God.

"Good mawnin', God."

"How do you do, Snake?"

"Ah[1] ain't so many, God, you put me down here on my belly in de dust and everything trods upon me and kills off my generations. Ah ain't got no kind of protection at all."

God looked off towards immensity and thought about de subject for awhile, then he said, "Ah didn't mean for nothin' to be stompin' you snakes lak dat. You got to have some kind of a protection. Here, take dis poison and put it in yo' mouf and when they tromps on you, protect yo'self."

So de snake took de poison in his mouf and went on back. So after awhile all de other varmints went up to God.

"Good evenin', God."

"How you makin' it, varmints?"

"God, please do somethin' 'bout dat snake. He' layin' in de bushes there wid poison in his mouf and he's strikin' everything dat shakes de bushes. He's killin' up our generations. Wese skeered to walk de earth."

So God sent for de snake and tole him:

"Snake, when Ah give you dat poison, Ah didn't mean for you to be hittin' and killin' everything dat shake de bush. I give you dat poison and tole you to protect yo'self when they tromples on you. But you killin' everything dat moves. Ah didn't mean for you to do dat."

---

1. Ah dialect, or regional pronunciation, for "I."

1000 Themes in the Oral Tradition

PROFESSIONAL DEVELOPMENT | **Jeff Anderson**

▼ Apply the Strategy

Rereading for Grammar Ask students: "Why do you think Zora Neale Hurston chose to write her tale the way she did?" They may say she is trying to sound like someone talking—continuing the theme of oral tradition. Ask students to notice how she remains consistent in the rules she's breaking.

Next, discuss her use of commas in the selection. She uses them traditionally, in fact. Have students go back through the selection with a partner, noting the ways she uses commas (set off mild exclamations, names in direct address, dialogue, etc.).

Have students share all the patterns they see, and then help connect those patterns to the comma rules that govern the English language. Students may find a handbook helpful for this activity.

For more of Jeff Anderson's strategies, see the Professional Development essay, pp. 900c–900d

Social Studies Connection

The Harlem Renaissance

During the 1920s and '30s in New York City, a talented group of African American writers, artists, and musicians took part in a cultural movement that became known as the Harlem Renaissance.

Music

▶ Blues great Bessie Smith and musicians such as jazz legend Duke Ellington performed at the famous Cotton Club nightclub.

Zora Neale Hurston, Countee Cullen, and Langston Hughes brought the African American experience to life through their writing. ▼

Arts

Into Bondage, 1936 by Aaron Douglas. Corcoran Gallery of Art.

Literature

The photographs of James Van Der Zee and the paintings of Aaron Douglas captured the look and feel of the times. ▲

Connect to the Literature How did works like Hurston's folk tale, "How the Snake Got Poison," contribute to the Harlem Renaissance?

How the Snake Got Poison **1001**

---

❹ Literature in Context

Social Studies Connection At the end of World War I, the United States entered a period of economic growth and artistic freedom. One place where economic and artistic forces came together was the Harlem section of New York City, one of the largest African American communities in the United States.

Writer James Weldon Johnson is often credited with inspiring many writers of the Harlem Renaissance. He served as a mentor to struggling young writers such as Claude McKay and Countee Cullen. Cullen in turn became the editor of an important poetry magazine that published African American writers' poems.

Wealthy white writers and philanthropists were also influential for the projects of African American writers, painters, and musicians. Writer Carl Van Vechten and Charlotte Mason provided both financial and critical support for Zora Neale Hurston's folklore collecting and fiction writing.

Connect to the Literature

1. Have students read the Literature in Context feature, and present the additional background information above. Then, have students discuss why folk tales like "How the Snake Got Poison" are important. Guide students toward understanding that folk tales reveal the values of the cultures they come from and help preserve these cultures in memory.

2. **Ask** students the Connect to the Literature question: How did works like Hurston's folk tale "How the Snake Got Poison" contribute to the Harlem Renaissance? **Answer:** Folk tales like Hurston's preserve African American folklore. They preserve the sound of the way people talked and the way they told stories.

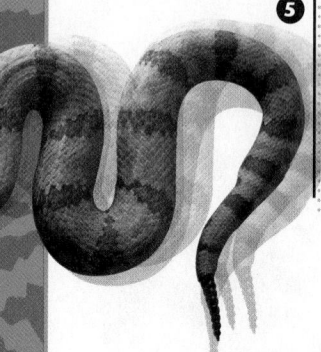

De snake say, "Lawd, you know Ah'm down here in de dust. Ah ain't got no claws to fight wid, and Ah ain't got no feets to git me out de way. All Ah kin see is feets comin' to tromple me. Ah can't tell who my enemy is and who is my friend. You gimme dis protection in my mouf and Ah uses it."

God thought it over for a while then he says:

"Well, snake, I don't want yo' generations all stomped out and I don't want you killin' everything else dat moves. Here take dis bell and tie it to yo' tail. When you hear feets comin' you ring yo' bell and if it's yo' friend, he'll be keerful. If it's yo' enemy, it's you and him."

So dat's how de snake got his poison and dat's how come he got rattles.

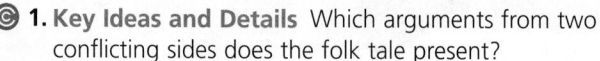

Critical Thinking

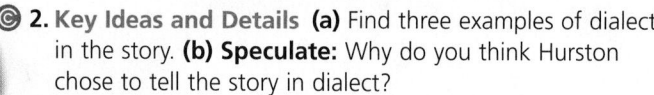

Cite textual evidence to support your responses.

1. **Key Ideas and Details** Which arguments from two conflicting sides does the folk tale present?

2. **Key Ideas and Details** (a) Find three examples of dialect in the story. (b) **Speculate:** Why do you think Hurston chose to tell the story in dialect?

3. **Key Ideas and Details** (a) In your notebook, describe the two arguments that the snake makes in the story. (b) **Analyze:** Tell whether you think each argument was effective and explain why you think so. (c) **Discuss:** Share your responses with a partner. Then discuss how looking at someone else's responses did or did not change your opinion.

4. **Key Ideas and Details** (a) What is God's final decision? (b) How does this decision affect both the snake and the varmints?

5. **Integration of Knowledge and Ideas** (a) **Analyze:** Explain why the varmints and the snake did not work out their problems together. (b) **Apply:** What might this situation reveal about people and their ways of interacting? (c) **Apply:** How does this story illustrate the concept of "balance of nature"?

6. **Integration of Knowledge and Ideas** (a) Why do the snake and varmints need protection from each other? (b) Why must a compromise be made to help settle this conflict between an individual and a group? *[Connect to the Big Question: Community or individual—which is more important?]*

| After You Read | How the Snake Got Poison | |

Reading Skill: Compare and Contrast

1. Use a Venn diagram like the one shown to **compare and contrast** the snake and the varmints at the beginning of the story. Think about how they look and their abilities.

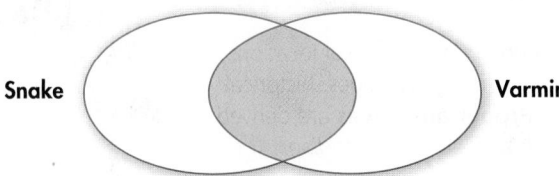

Snake — Varmints

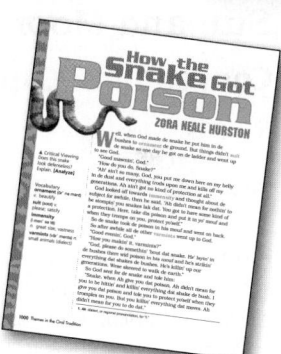

Literary Analysis: Cultural Context

2. **Craft and Structure** How does the author's use of **dialect** help you understand the **cultural context** of the story?

3. **Integration of Knowledge and Ideas** In the story, God says to the snake, "You got to have some kind of protection." What does this statement show about beliefs within the culture where the story originated?

Vocabulary

Acquisition and Use An **analogy** shows the relationship between a pair of words. Use a word from the vocabulary list on page 998 to complete each analogy. Your choice should make a word pair that matches the relationship between the first two words. Explain the relationship.

1. cold : hot :: _____ : smallness

2. ignore : neglect :: _____ : satisfy

3. critters : creatures :: _____ : vermin

4. hiking : trekking :: _____ : decorate

Word Study Use the context of the sentences and what you know about the **Latin suffix -ity** to explain your answer.

1. Can gentle stretching increase your *flexibility*?

2. Would your *mobility* be affected by a broken leg?

Word Study

The **Latin suffix -ity** means "state," "quality," or "condition of."

Apply It Explain how the suffix -ity contributes to the meanings of these words. Consult a dictionary if necessary.

probability
vanity
sincerity

How the Snake Got Poison **1003**

Reading Skill

1. Snake—defenseless; living on the ground without protection from other animals; he has no poison, rattle, legs, or claws; can only see feet; Varmints—can't see, smell, or hear the snake in the bushes; they step on the snake and kill its kind; Overlap—snake and varmints are both unable to see their enemies clearly; they accidentally kill too many of the other's kind.

For other sample answers, see *Graphic Organizer Transparencies*, **Reading Skill Graphic Organizer A**, p. 192, and the **Additional Answers** section.

Literary Analysis

2. The use of dialect helps readers understand that the folk tale comes from the African American oral tradition.

3. The comment suggests that fairness is important to the culture. Every creature, even the snake, is valued in the culture and deserves to be protected.

Vocabulary
Acquisition and Use
Sample answers:

1. *Immensity* and *smallness* are antonyms, as are *cold* and *hot*.

2. *Suit* and *satisfy* are synonyms, as are *ignore* and *neglect*.

3. *Critters* and *creatures* are synonyms, as are *varmints* and *vermin*.

4. *Ornament* and *decorate* are synonyms, as are *hiking* and *trekking*.

Word Study
Sample answers:

1. Yes; The suffix -ity means "condition of" and *flexibility* is the "condition of being flexible," which gentle stretching can create.

2. Yes; The suffix -ity means "condition of" and *mobility* is "the condition of being mobile." A broken leg would reduce mobility.

Word Study: Apply It
Sample answers: *Probability* is the condition of being probable, or likely. *Vanity* is the quality of being vain. *Sincerity* is the quality of being sincere.

Conventions

1. Introduce the skill, using the instruction on the student page.
2. Discuss the examples provided.

Think Aloud: Model the Skill

Model the skill of using capitalization. Write the sentences given below on the board. Say to students:

Capitalization helps me state ideas clearly by identifying the beginning of each new thought. I can also use capitalization to clearly identify character and place names. Look at this sentence: *mr. tyler said, "lateesha, the test will be on china."* Now look at it with capitals: *Mr. Tyler said, "Lateesha, the test will be on China."* The meaning is much clearer.

PH WRITING COACH Grade 7

Students will find instruction on and practice with capitalization in Chapter 26.

Practice A
Sample answers:

1. Richard Erdoes: person; German: location; Native American: group; America: location
2. Association on American Indian Affairs: organization; Alfonso Ortiz: person
3. "Sun and Moon in a Box": title; Zuni: group
4. Zunis: group; American Indian: group; Southwest: location

Reading Application
Sample answer:

1. "Let us fly over it," said Eagle.
2. "My chief, I cannot fly," said Coyote.
3. Eagle flew over the stream, and Coyote swam across.
4. They came to Kachina Pueblo.

Practice B
Sample answers:

1. In; African American; Zora Neale Hurston; Florida.
2. The; God; Snake.
3. To; God's; Snake; Good; God.
4. In; God; Snake.

Writing Application
Sample answer:

I read "Sun and Moon in a Box." The story is a Native American folktale. In it, Eagle says to his friend Coyote, "Good, let us stay together."

Integrated Language Skills

Sun and Moon in a Box • How the Snake Got Poison

Conventions: Capitalization

Capital letters signal the beginning of a sentence or quotation and identify proper nouns and adjectives.

Proper nouns include the names of people, geographical locations, specific events and time periods, organizations, languages, historical events and documents, and religions. **Proper adjectives** are derived from proper nouns, as in *France/French* and *Canada/Canadian*.

Sentence beginning: My dog ran away.
Quotation: I yelled, "Come back!"
Proper nouns: Michael, Queen Elizabeth, U.S. Constitution, Friday
Proper adjectives: Mexican, Jeffersonian, Irish

Practice A Identify the proper nouns and adjectives in each sentence, and tell what each names (geographic location, historical event, etc.) or describes.

1. Richard Erdoes is a German artist who became interested in Native American culture after moving to America.
2. As president of the Association on American Indian Affairs, Alfonso Ortiz did much to help his people.
3. Their story "Sun and Moon in a Box" retells a Zuni folk tale.
4. The Zunis are an ancient American Indian people who live in the Southwest.

© **Reading Application** In "Sun and Moon in a Box," find two sentences that contain quotations and two additional sentences that each contain a different type of proper noun.

Practice B Rewrite the following sentences, correcting the capitalization.

1. in this folk tale, african american writer zora neale hurston retells a story she first heard as a child in florida.
2. the story explains how god helped snake protect himself against other creatures.
3. to get god's attention, snake climbed a ladder and called, "good mawnin', god."
4. in the end, god settles on a compromise that meets the needs of both snake and the varmints.

© **Writing Application** Write three sentences about a folk tale you have read. In your sentences, use at least one quotation, one proper adjective, and two proper nouns.

PH WRITING COACH Further instruction and practice are available in *Prentice Hall Writing Coach*.

Extend the Lesson

Sentence Modeling

Choose the sentence given from the selection students have read:

"This is something wonderful," Coyote whispered to Eagle. ("Sun and Moon in a Box")
"How do you do, Snake?" ("How the Snake Got Poison")

Remind students of the lesson on capitalization. Ask students what they notice about the sentence. Elicit from them that the sentence includes one or more capitalized proper nouns. Then, ask what else students notice. ("Sun and Moon in a Box": The sentence refers to animal characters and uses the word *wonderful*, creating a sense of mystery. "How the Snake Got Poison": The sentence addresses an animal character in an almost comically formal way.)

Have students imitate the sentence in a sentence on a topic of their own choosing, matching each grammatical and stylistic feature discussed. Collect the sentences, and share them with the class.

Writing

Common Core
State Standards

L.7.2, L.5.b, L.7.6; RL.7.2;
W.7.2, W.7.2.b, W.7.2.f,
W.7.3, W.7.3.a, W.7.3.b; SL.4
[For the full wording of the
standards, see page 988.]

Informative Text Write a **plot summary** of either "Sun and Moon in a Box" or "How the Snake Got Poison."

- Take notes to describe each element of the folk tale: setting, major characters, main events, and final outcome.

- Use your notes to write your summary. Include one major event from the beginning, middle, and end of the story.

- Conclude your summary by stating a possible theme that logically supports the ideas you present.

Remember to remain objective, avoiding your personal reactions and including only the most important ideas and details.

Grammar Application Check your writing to be sure you have used correct conventions of capitalization.

Writing Workshop: *Work in Progress*

Prewriting for Research For a research report that you may write, list six ideas in response to one or more of the following topics: science, technology, society, or the environment. Save this Ideas List in your writing portfolio.

Use this prewriting activity to prepare for the **Writing Workshop** on page 1040.

Speaking and Listening

Comprehension and Collaboration With a partner, find five unusual facts about an animal. Include these facts in a **story** about the animal that does not reveal the animal's name. Present the story to your classmates, and ask them to guess the animal. Make your presentation entertaining and effective by using these ideas:

- Organize the plot of your story so that it unfolds naturally and is engaging and interesting to your readers.

- Include narrative techniques such as dialogue and description that help to develop your story characters and events.

- Create suspense by withholding certain details until later in the story.

- As you read, use facial expressions and body movements that enhance and support the story.

- Adjust your speaking rate, volume, and tone to suit the action of your story. Pronounce words clearly, and use appropriate expression.

- Make eye contact with your audience from time to time.

www.PHLitOnline.com
- Interactive graphic organizers
- Grammar tutorial
- Interactive journals

Integrated Language Skills **1005**

EXTEND/ASSESS

Writing

1. Review the assignment, using the instruction on the student page.

2. To guide students in writing an informative text, give them **Support for Writing**, p. 155 in the *Unit 6 Resources*.

3. To evaluate students' essays, adapt one of the **Summary** rubrics, pp. 246–247 in *Professional Development Guidebook.* Make sure that students' summaries include only the most important plot events and related details.

Grammar Application

Have students check their drafts to make sure they have capitalized correctly.

Six Traits Focus

✔ Ideas	Word Choice
✔ Organization	Sentence Fluency
Voice	Conventions

PH WRITING COACH Grade 7

Students will find further instruction on and practice with informational texts in Chapters 8 and 11.

Writing Workshop
Work in Progress

Have students save their completed Ideas Lists in their portfolios. They will use the lists later as they continue this Work-in-Progress assignment (see p. 1025). These assignments prepare them to complete the Writing Workshop assignment (see pp. 1040–1049).

Speaking and Listening

1. Review the assignment, using the instruction on the student page.

2. To support students' work on the assignment, have students complete the **Support for Extend Your Learning** page (*Unit 6 Resources*, p. 156).

Teaching Resources

Unit 6 Resources

[L3] [L4] [EL] **Integrated Language Skills: Grammar,** p. 154

[L3] [L4] [EL] **Support for Writing,** p. 155

[L3] [L4] **Support for Extend Your Learning,** p. 156

[L4] **Enrichment,** pp. 135, 153

Enriched Online Student Edition
Available under After You Read for this selection:
[All] **Interactive Grammar Tutorial**
[L3] [L4] **Internet Research Activity**

Professional Development Guidebook
Rubrics for Self-Assessment: Summary, pp. 246–247

All print and digital resources are available online at **www.PHLitOnline.com.**
Online resources accessible to students are noted on the student page.

1005

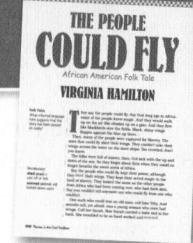

✓ **The People Could Fly** •
✓✓ **All Stories Are Anansi's**
Lesson Pacing Guide

DAY 1 Preteach

- © Administer the Reading and Vocabulary Warm-ups (*Unit 6 Resources,* pp. 166–169 or 184–187) as necessary.
- Introduce the Reading Skill: Compare and Contrast.
- © Introduce the Literary Analysis concept: Folk Tale.
- Distribute copies of the appropriate graphic organizer for the Reading Skill (*Graphic Organizer Transparencies,* pp. 194–196).
- Distribute copies of the appropriate graphic organizer for Literary Analysis (*Graphic Organizer Transparencies,* pp. 197–199).
- © Teach the selection vocabulary.
- © Introduce the Word Study skill.

DAYS 2–3 Preteach/Teach

- © Build background with the Background feature.
- Develop thematic vocabulary and thematic thinking with Writing About the Big Question.
- Prepare students to read with the Focusing Reading activities (TE).
- Informally monitor comprehension while students read.
- Use the Reading Check questions to confirm comprehension.
- Develop students' ability to understand an unfamiliar concept by using prior knowledge to compare and contrast using the Compare and Contrast questions.
- © Develop students' understanding of folk tales using the Folk Tale questions.
- © Reinforce vocabulary with the Vocabulary notes.
- © Reinforce unit focus standards using the Spiral Review prompts.

DAY 4 Assess

- Assess students' comprehension and mastery of the skills by having them answer the Critical Thinking, Reading Skill, and Literary Analysis questions.
- © Have students complete the Vocabulary Practice activities.
- © Have students complete the Word Study activities.

DAY 5 Extend/Assess

- Have students complete the Conventions lesson.
- © Have students complete the Writing activity and write a review. (You may assign as homework.)
- © Extend learning by having students complete the Speaking and Listening a television news report activity. As an alternative, assign them "The Ripple Effect" or "Trickster Appeal—Revealed!" in *Reality Central.*
- Administer Selection Test A or B (*Unit 6 Resources,* pp. 178–183 or 199–204).

© **Common Core State Standards**

Reading Literature 3. Analyze how particular elements of a story or drama interact.

Writing 1. Write arguments to support claims with clear reasons and relevant evidence.
1.a. Introduce claim(s), acknowledge alternate or opposing claims, and organize the reasons and evidence logically.
1.b. Support claim(s) with logical reasoning and relevant evidence, using accurate, credible sources and demonstrating an understanding of the topic or text.
2.a. Introduce a topic clearly, previewing what is to follow; organize ideas, concepts, and information, using strategies such as definition, classification, comparison/contrast, and cause/effect.
2.b. Develop the topic with relevant facts, definitions, concrete details, quotations, or other information and examples.
2.f. Provide a concluding statement or section that follows from and supports the information or explanation presented.

Speaking and Listening 4. Present claims and findings, emphasizing salient points in a focused, coherent manner with pertinent descriptions, facts, details, and examples; use appropriate eye contact, adequate volume, and clear pronunciation.

Language 2. Demonstrate command of the conventions of standard English capitalization, punctuation, and spelling when writing.
3.a. Choose language that expresses ideas precisely and concisely, recognizing and eliminating wordiness and redundancy.
4.b. Use common, grade-appropriate Greek or Latin affixes and roots as clues to the meaning of a word.

Additional Standards Practice
***Common Core Companion,** pp. 15–22*

Daily Block Scheduling
Each day in this Lesson Pacing Guide represents a 40–50 minute period. Teachers using block scheduling may combine days to revise pacing. In addition, teachers may differentiate and support core instruction by integrating components for extended and intensive support, as students require. See the Guide to Selected Leveled Resources (facing page).

Guide to Selected Leveled Resources

R T I Tier 1 (students performing on level)	✓ **More Accessible** The People Could Fly	✓✓ **More Complex** All Stories Are Anansi's
Warm Up Practice, model, and monitor fluency, working with the whole class or in groups.	Vocabulary and Reading Warm-ups B, *Unit 6 Resources,* pp. 166–167, 169	Vocabulary and Reading Warm-ups B, *Unit 6 Resources,* pp. 184–185, 187
Comprehension/Skills Support and monitor comprehension and skills development, having students complete the activities, graphic organizers, and interactive prompts independently or as a class.	• *Reader's Notebook,* adapted instruction and full selection **EL** *Reader's Notebook: English Learner's Version,* adapted instruction and adapted selection • Reading Skill Graphic Organizer B, *Graphic Organizer Transparencies,* p. 196 • Literary Analysis Graphic Organizer B, *Graphic Organizer Transparencies,* p. 199	• *Reader's Notebook,* adapted instruction and summary **EL** *Reader's Notebook: English Learner's Version,* adapted instruction and summary • Reading Skill Graphic Organizer B, *Graphic Organizer Transparencies,* p. 196 • Literary Analysis Graphic Organizer B, *Graphic Organizer Transparencies,* p. 199
Monitor Progress Monitor student progress with the differentiated curriculum-based assessment in the *Unit Resources.*	• Selection Test B, *Unit 6 Resources,* pp. 181–183 • Open-Book Test, *Unit 6 Resources,* pp. 175–177	• Selection Test B, *Unit 6 Resources,* pp. 202–204 • Open-Book Test, *Unit 6 Resources,* pp. 196–198
Assess/Screen • Assess student progress using Benchmark Test 2. • Preassess instructional needs using the Vocabulary in Context section of the test.	• Benchmark Test 12, *Unit 6 Resources,* pp. 227–234, including Vocabulary in Context diagnostic items	• Benchmark Test 12, *Unit 6 Resources,* pp. 227–234, including Vocabulary in Context diagnostic items

R T I Tier 2 (students requiring intervention)	✓ **More Accessible** The People Could Fly	✓✓ **More Complex** All Stories Are Anansi's
Warm Up Practice, model, and monitor fluency in groups or with individuals.	• Vocabulary and Reading Warm-ups A, *Unit 6 Resources,* pp. 166–168 • *Reality Central,* "The Ripple Effect" • *Hear It!* Audio CD (adapted text)	• Vocabulary and Reading Warm-ups A, *Unit 6 Resources,* pp. 184–186 • *Reality Central,* "Trickster Appeal—Revealed!" • *Hear It!* Audio CD
Comprehension/Skills • Support and monitor comprehension and skills development, working in small groups or with individuals. • Pair students with more advanced peers and have them complete the writing activity in the *Real-World Writing Journal.* • As students complete the selection in the appropriate version of the *Reader's Notebook,* monitor comprehension frequently with group questions and individual instruction. • Model strategies while guiding students in completing the activities and prompts in the *Reader's Notebook,* as well as the graphic organizers. • Practice skills and monitor mastery with the *Reading Kit* worksheets.	• *Real-World Writing Journal,* Lesson 7, pp. 180–183 • *Reader's Notebook: Adapted Version,* adapted instruction and adapted selection **EL** *Reader's Notebook: English Learner's Version,* adapted instruction and adapted selection • Reading Skill Graphic Organizer A, *Graphic Organizer Transparencies,* p. 194 • Literary Analysis Graphic Organizer A, *Graphic Organizer Transparencies,* p. 197 • *Reading Kit,* Practice worksheets, pp. 268, 274, 278, 282, 290	• *Real-World Writing Journal,* Lesson 8, pp. 184–187 • *Reader's Notebook: Adapted Version,* adapted instruction and summary **EL** *Reader's Notebook: English Learner's Version,* adapted instruction and summary • Reading Skill Graphic Organizer A, *Graphic Organizer Transparencies,* p. 195 • Literary Analysis Graphic Organizer A, *Graphic Organizer Transparencies,* p. 198 • *Reading Kit,* Practice worksheets, pp. 268, 274, 278, 282, 290
Monitor Progress Monitor student progress with the differentiated curriculum-based assessment in the *Unit Resources* and in the *Reading Kit.*	• Selection Test A, *Unit 6 Resources,* pp. 178–180 • *Reading Kit,* Assess worksheets, pp. 269, 275, 279, 283, 291	• Selection Test A, *Unit 6 Resources,* pp. 199–201 • *Reading Kit,* Assess worksheets, pp. 269, 275, 279, 283, 291
Assess/Screen • Assess student progress using Benchmark Test. • Preassess instructional needs using the Vocabulary in Context section of the test.	• Benchmark Test 12, *Unit 6 Resources,* pp. 227–234, including Vocabulary in Context diagnostic items	• Benchmark Test 12, *Unit 6 Resources,* pp. 227–234, including Vocabulary in Context diagnostic items

TIER 3 Tier 3 intervention may require consultation with the student's special-education or dyslexia specialist. For additional support, see the Tier 2 activities and resources listed above.

One-on-one teaching   Group work   Whole class instruction   Independent work   **A** Assessment
For a complete guide to selection support, including support for Advanced students, see the Overview of Resources in the frontmatter.

✓The People Could Fly
✓✓All Stories Are Anansi's

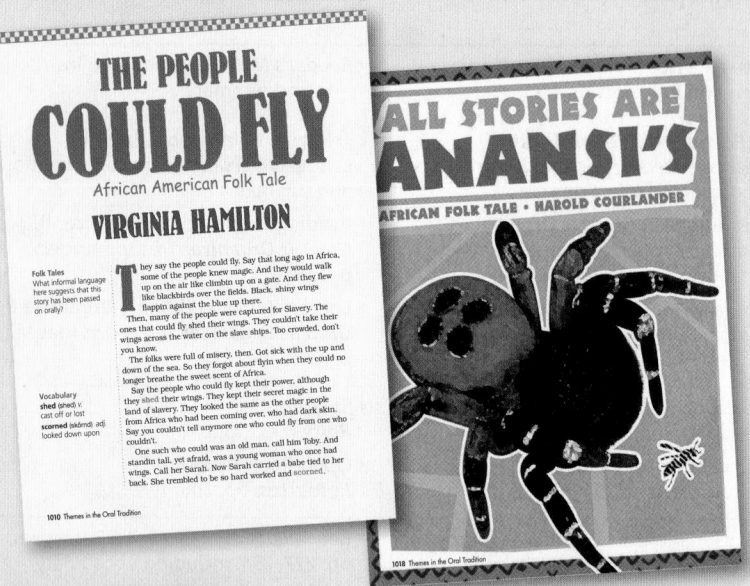

Vocabulary/Fluency/Prior Knowledge

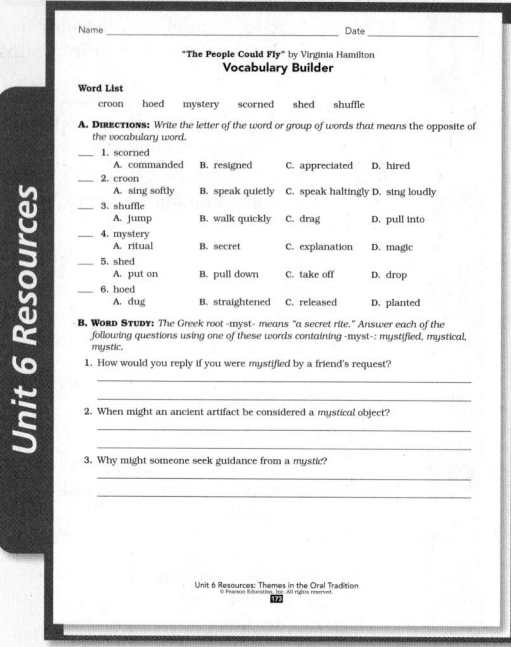

RESOURCES FOR:

L1 Special-Needs Students

L2 Below-Level Students (Tier 2)

L3 On-Level Students (Tier 1)

L4 Advanced Students (Tier 1)

EL English Learners

All All Students

All **Vocabulary Builder,** pp. 173, 191

Also available for these selections:

EL L1 L2 **Reading Warm-ups A and B,**
pp. 168–169, 186–187

EL L1 L2 **Vocabulary Warm-ups A and B,**
pp. 166–167, 184–185

All **Writing About the Big Question,**
pp. 170, 188

Reader's Notebooks

Pre- and postreading pages for both selections, as well as the selection "The People Could Fly," appear in an interactive format in the *Reader's Notebooks*. Each *Notebook* is differentiated for a different group of learners. The selections in the Adapted and English Learner's versions are abridged.

L2 L3 *Reader's Notebook*

L1 *Reader's Notebook: Adapted Version*

EL *Reader's Notebook: English Learner's Version*

EL *Reader's Notebook: Spanish Version*

© *Common Core Companion*

Additional instruction and practice for each Common Core State Standard

Selection Support

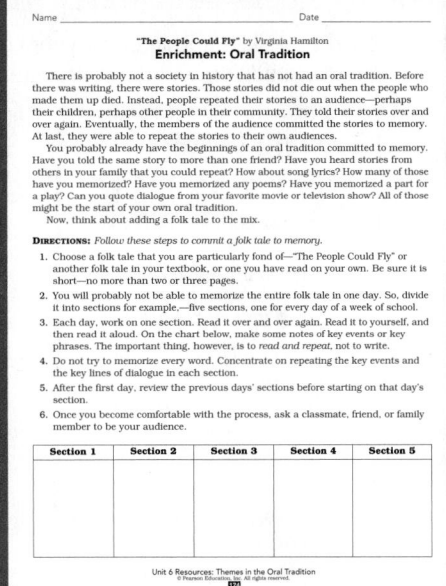

"All Stories Are Anansi's" by Harold Courlander

After You Read A: Literary Analysis—Folk Tales

Elements:	Good	Evil	Lesson	Theme
Examples:	The Sky God offering Anansi a fair price for the stories	All the animals being motivated by self-interest	Don't be overly trustful.	Brains are more effective than size or might.

Graphic Organizer Transparencies
© Pearson Education, Inc. All rights reserved.

Literary Analysis: Graphic Organizer A, pp. 197, 198

Also available for these selections:

EL L3 **Literary Analysis: Graphic Organizer B,** p. 199

EL L1 L2 **Reading: Graphic Organizer A,** pp. 194–195 (partially filled in)

EL L3 **Reading: Graphic Organizer B,** p. 196

Skills Development/Extension

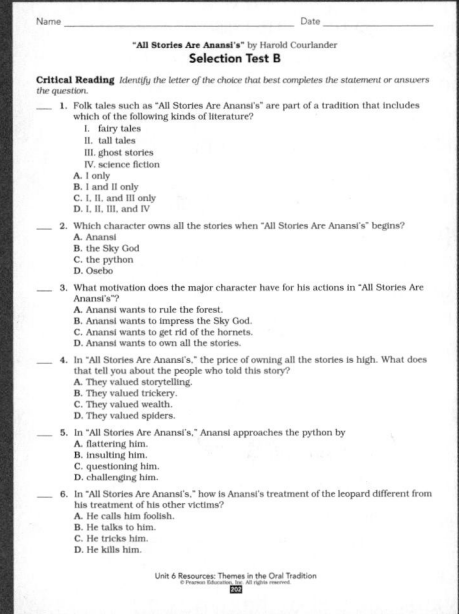

"The People Could Fly" by Virginia Hamilton

Enrichment: Oral Tradition

There is probably not a society in history that has not had an oral tradition. Before there was writing, there were stories. Those stories did not die out when the people who made them up died. Instead, people repeated their stories to an audience—perhaps their children, perhaps other people in their community. They told their stories over and over again. Eventually, the members of the audience committed the stories to memory. At last, they were able to repeat the stories to their own audiences.

You probably already have the beginnings of an oral tradition in your memory. Have you told the same story to more than one friend? Have you heard stories from others in your family that you could repeat? How about song lyrics? How many of those have you memorized? Have you memorized any poems? Have you memorized a part for a play? Can you quote dialogue from your favorite movie or television show? All of those might be the start of your own oral tradition.

Now, think about adding a folk tale to the mix.

DIRECTIONS: *Follow these steps to commit a folk tale to memory.*

1. Choose a folk tale that you are particularly fond of—"The People Could Fly" or another folk tale in your textbook, or one you have read on your own. Be sure it is short—no more than two or three pages.
2. You will probably not be able to memorize the entire folk tale in one day. So, divide it into sections for example,—five sections, one for every day of a week of school.
3. Each day, work on one section. Read it over and over again. Read it to yourself, and then read it aloud. On the chart below, make some notes of key events or key phrases. The important thing, however, is to *read and repeat*, not to write.
4. Do not try to memorize every word. Concentrate on repeating the key events and the key lines of dialogue in each section.
5. After the first day, review the previous days' sections before starting on that day's section.
6. Once you become comfortable with the process, ask a classmate, friend, or family member to be your audience.

Section 1	Section 2	Section 3	Section 4	Section 5

Unit 6 Resources: Themes in the Oral Tradition
© Pearson Education, Inc. All rights reserved.

L4 **Enrichment,** pp. 174, 192

Also available for these selections:

All **Literary Analysis: Folk Tale,** pp. 172, 190

EL L3 L4 **Grammar,** p. 193

EL L3 L4 **Support for Writing,** p. 194

L3 L4 **Support for Extend Your Learning,** p. 195

All **Reading: Compare and Contrast,** pp. 171, 189

Assessment

Name _____ Date _____

"All Stories Are Anansi's" by Harold Courlander

Selection Test B

Critical Reading *Identify the letter of the choice that best completes the statement or answers the question.*

_____ 1. Folk tales such as "All Stories Are Anansi's" are part of a tradition that includes which of the following kinds of literature?
   I. fairy tales
   II. tall tales
   III. ghost stories
   IV. science fiction
   A. I only
   B. I and II only
   C. I, II, and III only
   D. I, II, III, and IV

_____ 2. Which character owns all the stories when "All Stories Are Anansi's" begins?
   A. Anansi
   B. the Sky God
   C. the python
   D. Osebo

_____ 3. What motivation does the major character have for his actions in "All Stories Are Anansi's"?
   A. Anansi wants to rule the forest.
   B. Anansi wants to impress the Sky God.
   C. Anansi wants to get rid of the hornets.
   D. Anansi wants to own all the stories.

_____ 4. In "All Stories Are Anansi's," the price of owning all the stories is high. What does that tell you about the people who told this story?
   A. They valued storytelling.
   B. They valued trickery.
   C. They valued wealth.
   D. They valued spiders.

_____ 5. In "All Stories Are Anansi's," Anansi approaches the python by
   A. flattering him.
   B. insulting him.
   C. questioning him.
   D. challenging him.

_____ 6. In "All Stories Are Anansi's," how is Anansi's treatment of the leopard different from his treatment of his other victims?
   A. He calls him foolish.
   B. He talks to him.
   C. He tricks him.
   D. He kills him.

Unit 6 Resources: Themes in the Oral Tradition
© Pearson Education, Inc. All rights reserved.

EL L3 L4 **Selection Test B,** pp. 181–183, 202–204

Also available for these selections:

EL L1 L2 **Selection Test A,** pp. 178–180, 199–201

L3 L4 **Open-Book Test,** pp. 175–177, 196–198

PHLit Online!
www.PHLitOnline.com

Online Resources: All print materials are also available online.

- complete narrated selection text
- a thematically related video with writing prompt
- an interactive graphic organizer
- highlighting feature
- access to all student print resources, adapted to individual student needs
- Spanish and English summaries
- adapted selection translations in Spanish

Get Connected! (thematic video with writing prompt)

Also available:

Background video
All videos are available in Spanish.

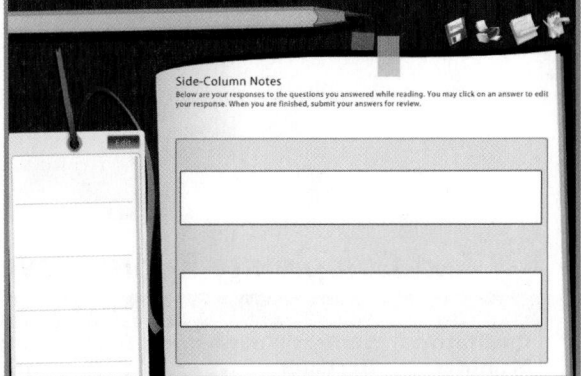

Writer's Journal (with graphics feature)

Also available:

Vocabulary Central (tools, activities, and songs for studying vocabulary)

❶ Leveled Texts

You may use either "The People Could Fly" or "All Stories Are Anansi's" to meet the lesson objectives. Skills instruction for both selections appears on page 1007. Choose one selection to teach (or choose to teach both). The Text Complexity Rubric at the bottom of this page will help you determine which selection is more appropriate for your students. Use the Reader and Task Suggestions on the facing page to help all students read text of increasing complexity.

❷ ⓒ Introducing the CCS Standards

Introduce the standards on the student page. (Note that the lesson element with which each standard is addressed is identified in parentheses after the text of the standard.) Call out the standards that you will cover with the selections, explaining to students what each requires and how they will address it as they work through the selection you have chosen. Standards labeled "Spiral Review" are introduced in the Literary Analysis Workshop for this unit.

Before You Read

The People Could Fly • All Stories Are Anansi's

❶ ⓒ Leveled Texts

Build your skills and improve your comprehension of folk tales in the oral tradition with texts of increasing complexity.

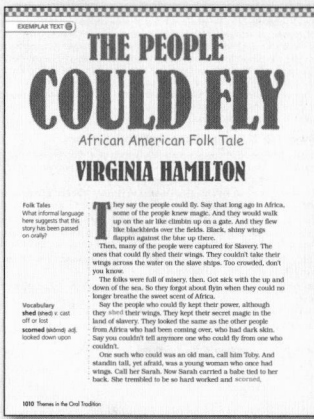

Read **"The People Could Fly"** to learn the story of enslaved Africans who find freedom in a unique way.

Read **"All Stories Are Anansi's"** to find out how Anansi earns the right to own all the stories in the world.

❷ ⓒ Common Core State Standards

Meet these standards with either **"The People Could Fly"** (p. 1010) or **"All Stories Are Anansi's"** (p. 1018).

Reading Literature
3. Analyze how particular elements of a story or drama interact. *(Literary Analysis: Folk Tale)*

Writing
1. Write arguments to support claims with clear reasons and relevant evidence. **1.a.** Introduce claim(s), acknowledge alternate or opposing claims, and organize the reasons and evidence logically. **1.b.** Support claim(s) with logical reasoning and relevant evidence, using accurate, credible sources and demonstrating an understanding of the topic or text. *(Writing: Review)*

2.a. Introduce a topic clearly, previewing what is to follow; organize ideas, concepts, and information, using strategies such as definition, classification, comparison/contrast, and cause/effect. **2.b.** Develop the topic with relevant facts, definitions, concrete details, quotations, or other information and examples. **2.f.** Provide a concluding statement or section that follows from and supports the

information or explanation presented. *(Speaking and Listening: Television News Report)*

Speaking and Listening
4. Present claims and findings, emphasizing salient points in a focused, coherent manner with pertinent descriptions, facts, details, and examples; use appropriate eye contact, adequate volume, and clear pronunciation. *(Speaking and Listening: Television News Report)*

Language
2. Demonstrate command of the conventions of standard English capitalization, punctuation, and spelling when writing. *(Conventions: Abbreviations)*

3.a. Choose language that expresses ideas precisely and concisely, recognizing and eliminating wordiness and redundancy. *(Writing: Review)*

4.b. Use common, grade-appropriate Greek or Latin affixes and roots as clues to the meaning of a word. *(Vocabulary: Word Study)*

1006 Themes in the Oral Tradition

ⓒ Text Complexity Rubric: Leveled Texts

Text complexity is determined by both qualitative and quantitative measures. For this reason, the quantitative measure of a more complex selection may be lower than that of a more accessible selection.

		✓ The People Could Fly	✓✓ All Stories Are Anansi's
Qualitative Measures	**Context/Knowledge Demands**	Folk tales, African American history; slavery 1 2 3 ④ 5	African folk tales, Ashanti culture 1 2 3 ④ 5
	Structure/Language Conventionality and Clarity	On-level vocabulary; simple sentences; informal language, nonstandard diction; African words 1 2 ③ 4 5	On-level vocabulary; medium-length sentences; embedded phrases/clauses; informal "oral" tone 1 2 3 ④ 5
	Levels of Meaning/ Purpose/Concept Level	Accessible concept (enslaved people escape) 1 2 ③ 4 5	Challenging concept (brains can outwit physical qualities) 1 2 3 ④ 5
Quantitative Measures	**Text Length**	Word Count: 1,206	Word Count: 1,061
	Lexile	450L	560L
Overall Complexity		✓ **More accessible**	✓✓ **More complex**

Reading Skill: Compare and Contrast

When you **compare and contrast**, you recognize similarities and differences. You can compare and contrast elements in a literary work by **using a Venn diagram** to examine character traits, situations, and ideas.

- First, reread the text to locate the details you will compare.
- Then, write the details on a diagram like the one below.

Recording these details will help you understand the similarities and differences in a literary work.

Using the Strategy: Character Diagram

As you read, use a Venn diagram to compare and contrast the characters of the folk tales that follow.

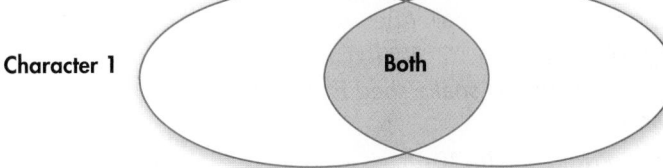

Character 1   Both   Character 2

Literary Analysis: Folk Tales

A form of fiction, a **folk tale** is a story that is composed orally and then passed from person to person by word of mouth. Though they originate in this **oral tradition,** most folk tales are eventually collected and written down. Similar folk tales are told by different cultures throughout the world, using common character types, plot elements, and themes. Folk tales often teach a lesson about life and clearly differentiate between good and evil. Folk tales are part of the oral tradition that also includes fairy tales, legends, myths, fables, tall tales, and ghost stories. As you read, notice how common elements of folk tales work together to give meaning to the story.

Before You Read: The People Could Fly • All Stories Are Anansi's **1007**

PRETEACH

❸ Reading Skill
Compare and Contrast

1. Introduce the skill, using the instruction on the student page.
2. Tell students that they will practice comparing and contrasting as they read.

❹ Using the Strategy
Give students a copy of either **Reading Skill Graphic Organizer A** or **B** (*Graphic Organizer Transparencies*, pp. 194–196) to compare and contrast as they read. Use the examples in **Reading Skill Graphic Organizer A**, which is partially filled in, to model the process of completing the organizer.

❺ Literary Analysis
Folk Tale

1. Introduce the skill using the instruction on the student page.
2. Tell students that they will note elements of folk tales as they read.

Think Aloud: Model the Skill

Model a way to identify elements of folk tales. Say to students:

To help me remember the characteristics of folktales, I think of a familiar American folktale like the story of Paul Bunyan, about the giant, strong, and generous lumberjack. I ask myself what the story tells me about the people who first told it—What did they think was important? I think that the story of Paul Bunyan tells me that the early Americans who first shared it valued strength, generosity, and hard work—the qualities and values of Paul Bunyan. Each time I read a folk tale, I try to answer this same question.

© Text Complexity: Reader and Task Suggestions

✓ The People Could Fly		✓✓ All Stories Are Anansi's	
Preparing to Read the Text	**Leveled Tasks**	**Preparing to Read the Text**	**Leveled Tasks**
• Using the Background on p. 1009, review the important role of folk tales in African American history. • Review strategies for reading nonstandard diction and informal language. • Guide students to use Multidraft Reading strategies (TE p. 1009).	*Structure/Language* If students will have difficulty with language, have them first read to identify how the slaves escape. Have them reread, identifying sentences, phrases, or words that they find confusing. *Analyzing* If students will not have difficulty with language, have them note ways in which the author uses nonstandard diction and informal language to create an inspiring tone for the tale.	• Using the Background note on p. 1017, discuss trickster tales and relate their features to the folk tale. • Review strategies for reading ornate sentences, such as removing embedded phrases and clauses. • Guide students to use Multidraft Reading strategies (TE p. 1017).	*Structure/Language* If students will have difficulty with language, have them first read to learn how Anansi outsmarts the other animals. Have them reread, identifying sentences they find confusing. *Evaluating* If students will not have difficulty with language, have them note ways in which the author uses language to create narrative style and how this style helps him craft Anansi's trickster qualities.

1007

❶ ❓ Writing About the Big Question

1. Review the assignment with the class.

2. Remind students that *unify* means "bring together." Explore experiences that many students in the class have shared, such as being involved in a school play or other event. Discuss how sharing the experience creates a connection.

3. Have students complete the sentence starter. Review responses as a class. (**Sample responses:** Stories can sometimes <u>unify</u> people who share a common struggle, because they stress what the people share rather than ways they are different.)

4. Remind students that their answers will help them think about the Big Question, "Community or individual—which is more important?"

While You Read

Tell students that as they read, they should consider how the idea of enslaved people flying to freedom may have inspired those who heard about it.

❷ Vocabulary

1. Have students preview the selection vocabulary.

2. For each word, have students say the word aloud.

3. Then, use the word in a sentence that defines the word.

4. Finally, repeat your definitional sentence or a similar sentence with the word missing and have the class "fill in the blank" chorally. Here are some examples:

   To <u>croon</u> is to sing or hum quietly and softly. To get the baby to stop crying, the father began to quietly sing, or [students say "croon"].

   To <u>shuffle</u> is to walk with dragging feet. Unwilling to come inside, my brother finally began to [students say "shuffle"] inside.

❸ Word Study

1. Introduce the skill, using the instruction in the box.

2. Using the word *mystery* as they explain, ask students to tell if they like *mystery* stories, and why.

❶ Writing About the Big Question

In "The People Could Fly," a character uses ancient African magic to free his people. Use this sentence starter to develop your ideas about the Big Question.

Stories can sometimes **unify** people who share a common struggle because _____.

While You Read Consider how the idea of enslaved people flying to freedom may have inspired a community of people.

❷ Vocabulary

Read each word and its definition. Decide whether you know the word well, know it a little bit, or do not know it at all. After you read, see how your knowledge of each word has increased.

- **shed** (shed) *v.* cast off or lost (p. 1010) *The snake <u>shed</u> its skin several times last year.* shedding *v.*

- **scorned** (skôrnd) *adj.* looked down upon (p. 1010) *Lisa was <u>scorned</u> by her teammates because of her refusal to come to practice.* scorn *v.* scornful *adj.* scornfully *adv.*

- **hoed** (hōd) *v.* weeded or loosened soil with a metal hand tool (p. 1011) *Lisa <u>hoed</u> the garden until she developed blisters.* hoe *v.* hoe *n.*

- **croon** (krōōn) *v.* sing or hum quietly and soothingly (p. 1011) *When you <u>croon</u> that lullaby, I get sleepy.* crooned *v.* crooning *v.* crooner *n.*

- **mystery** (mis´ tə rē) *n.* something unexplained, unknown, or kept secret (p. 1012) *Peter wanted to solve the <u>mystery</u> before he read the last chapter.* mysterious *adj.* mysteries *n.*

- **shuffle** (shuf´ əl) *v.* walk with dragging feet (p. 1013) *We heard the tired man <u>shuffle</u> down the hallway.* shuffling *v.* shuffled *v.* shuffler *n.*

❸ Word Study

The **Greek root -myst-** means "secret."

This folk tale tells a story about the African **mystery**, or secret, of people who could fly.

Vocabulary Development

Vocabulary Knowledge Rating

Create a **Vocabulary Knowledge Rating Chart** (*Professional Development Guidebook*, p. 33) for the selection vocabulary words and for the thematic words in the Writing About the Big Question sentence starter on the student page. Give each student a copy of the chart with the words on it. Read the words aloud, and have students mark their rating of each in the Before

Reading column. When students have completed reading and discussing the selection, have them take out their **Vocabulary Knowledge Rating** charts for the story. Read the words aloud and have students rate their knowledge again in the After Reading column. Clarify any words that are still problematic. Then, have students complete the Vocabulary practice at the end of the selection.

Vocabulary Central, featuring tools, activities, and songs for studying vocabulary, is available online at **www.PHLitOnline.com.**

Meet
Virginia Hamilton
(1936–2002)

Author of
THE PEOPLE
COULD FLY

"I started writing as a kid," Virginia Hamilton once said. "It was always something I was going to do." The author of countless novels, stories, and collections of African American folk tales, Hamilton has been called "America's most honored writer of books for children."

Stories of the Past Hamilton was raised in a house of gifted storytellers. She described her childhood as ideal, saying "I heard 'tells' every day of my life from parents and relatives." Some of those stories were about slavery, and most were about the past. As a result, the past came to play an important role in Hamilton's writing. She developed a unique style, combining elements of history, myth, legend, and dream to bring her stories to life.

DID YOU KNOW?
As a child, Hamilton was a cheerleader and captain of the girls' basketball team. She also ran track and sang in her school choir.

❹ BACKGROUND FOR THE FOLK TALE
African American Folk Tales

"The People Could Fly" is a freedom tale, a kind of folk tale that enslaved Africans told to keep their hopes alive, despite the hardships they faced. Like many freedom tales, "The People Could Fly" contains images of freedom and escape as well as many references to the original storyteller's native Africa.

The People Could Fly **1009**

❹ Daily Bellringer
For each class during which you teach this selection, have students complete one of the five Research activities for Week 35 in the *Daily Bellringer Activities* booklet.

❹ Background
Influence of African Folk Tales

Stories were important to Virginia Hamilton, whose family was descended from a man who escaped slavery. Hamilton grew up listening to tales told by her parents, aunts, and uncles. She first encountered traditional African folk tales on a visit to Africa in the early 1960s. They deeply influenced Hamilton's own writing. Her retellings of African and African American folk tales and her stories brim with imagery and magic that she borrowed from traditional African folk tales and stories.

Multidraft Reading

To assist struggling readers and to deepen reading for all, apply multidraft reading protocols. For each reading, have students set the purpose indicated:

- **First reading**—identifying key ideas and details and answering any Reading Checks.
- **Second reading**—analyzing craft and structure and responding to the side-column prompts.
- **Third reading**—integrating knowledge and ideas, connecting to other texts and the world, and answering the end-of-selection questions.

For more guidance, refer to the *Classroom Strategies and Teaching Routines* card on multidraft reading.

Differentiated Instruction   Additional Instruction

EL Extended Support— English Learners
Have students complete the **Reading and Vocabulary Warm-ups**, *Unit 6 Resources*, pp. 166–169, before they read. Assign the prereading pages and the adapted selection in the *Reader's Notebook: English Learner's Version*. Then, have students listen to portions of the selection on the *Hear It!* Audio CD.

L1 L2 Extended Support— Struggling Readers
Have students complete the **Reading and Vocabulary Warm-ups**, *Unit 6 Resources*, pp. 166–169, before they read. Assign the prereading pages and the adapted selection in the *Reader's Notebook: Adapted Version*. Then, have students listen to portions of the selection on the *Hear It!* Audio CD (adapted text).

Extended Support— Reluctant Readers
To build motivation and engagement before assigning the selection, have students read "The Ripple Effect," a thematically related selection in *Reality Central*. Then, use the questions at the conclusion of the related selection to guide discussion.

For more about the author, practice with the selection vocabulary, or more background, go online at **www.PHLitOnline.com**.

❶ Focusing Reading

Vocab-o-Gram

1. Use the **Vocab-o-Gram** strategy (*Professional Development Guidebook,* p. 39–40) to help students make predictions about selection elements. Post the following words and phrases:

people could fly	*"Kum . . .*
slave ships	*tambe."*
labored in the fields	*Overseer*
	under the whip

2. Then, have partners place the words in appropriate categories on the **Vocab-o-Gram** chart and make predictions. Discuss students' predictions.

3. For further guidance, use the **Classroom Strategies and Teaching Routines** card on using graphic organizers.

Concept Connector ➡

Students will re-examine their ideas after reading the story.

Individual Activity

Pause during the selection and ask individual students to use their own words to summarize the story so far.

❷ About the Selection

In "The People Could Fly," long ago in Africa, people knew how to fly. When they were enslaved, people lost their wings. Toby whispers magic words to help them fly. He finally flies away himself.

❸ Folk Tales

1. Remind students that folk tales were often passed down from generation to generation and repeated orally.

2. Read aloud with expression the bracketed passage. The author writes in an informal style, as if she were telling the story.

3. Then, **ask** the Folk Tales question. **Possible response:** The phrases "call him Toby" and "Call her Sarah" suggest that the names of these characters are not certain. Dropping the final *g*, as in "climbin," suggests spoken rather than written words.

THE PEOPLE COULD FLY

❶
❷ African American Folk Tale

VIRGINIA HAMILTON

Folk Tales
What informal language here suggests that this story has been passed on orally?

Vocabulary
shed (shed) *v.* cast off or lost

scorned (skôrnd) *adj.* looked down upon

They say the people could fly. Say that long ago in Africa, some of the people knew magic. And they would walk up on the air like climbin up on a gate. And they flew like blackbirds over the fields. Black, shiny wings flappin against the blue up there.

Then, many of the people were captured for Slavery. The ones that could fly shed their wings. They couldn't take their wings across the water on the slave ships. Too crowded, don't you know.

❸ The folks were full of misery, then. Got sick with the up and down of the sea. So they forgot about flyin when they could no longer breathe the sweet scent of Africa.

Say the people who could fly kept their power, although they shed their wings. They kept their secret magic in the land of slavery. They looked the same as the other people from Africa who had been coming over, who had dark skin. Say you couldn't tell anymore one who could fly from one who couldn't.

One such who could was an old man, call him Toby. And standin tall, yet afraid, was a young woman who once had wings. Call her Sarah. Now Sarah carried a babe tied to her back. She trembled to be so hard worked and scorned.

1010 Themes in the Oral Tradition

Vocabulary Development

Thematic Vocabulary: The Big Question

As students are discussing "The People Could Fly," encourage them to use the thematic vocabulary presented in Introducing the Big Question, pp. 900–901. You might encourage them with sentence starters like these:

1. All the people captured for slavery faced a *common* . . .

2. When their *families* were separated, they . . .

3. Still, Toby and Sarah were able to carry the *tradition* of . . .

4. Each *individual* that could fly helped the *group* left behind . . .

5. Telling the story was also important because it helped the *community* to . . .

From *The People Could Fly* by Virginia Hamilton, illustrated by Leo and Diane Dillon.

(4)

The slaves labored in the fields from sunup to sundown. The owner of the slaves callin himself their Master. Say he was a hard lump of clay. A hard, glinty[1] coal. A hard rock pile, wouldn't be moved. His Overseer[2] on horseback pointed out the slaves who were slowin down. So the one called Driver[3] cracked his whip over the slow ones to make them move faster. That whip was a slice-open cut of pain. So they did move faster. Had to.

Sarah hoed and chopped the row as the babe on her back slept.

Say the child grew hungry. That babe started up bawling too loud. Sarah couldn't stop to feed it. Couldn't stop to soothe and quiet it down. She let it cry. She didn't want to. She had no heart to croon to it.

"Keep that thing quiet," called the Overseer. He pointed his finger at the babe. The woman scrunched low. The Driver

---

1. **glinty** (glint′ ē) *adj.* shiny; reflecting light.
2. **Overseer** (ō′ vǝr sē′ ǝr) *n.* someone who watches over and directs the work of others.
3. **Driver** *n.* someone who forced (drove) the slaves to work harder.

Vocabulary

hoed (hōd) *v.* weeded or loosened soil with a metal hand tool

croon (krōōn) *v.* sing or hum quietly and soothingly

(5) **Reading Check**

What special gift do some of the people in this tale have?

The People Could Fly **1011**

Humanities

(4)

Illustration for *The People Could Fly* by Leo and Diane Dillon

Leo and Diane Dillon have been producing illustrations together since 1957. They pass artwork back and forth, with each artist adding details until the illustration is completed. Use these questions for discussion.

1. **Ask:** How does the illustration help you understand the title of the folktale?
   Answer: It shows that all the "People" from the title are African American. It shows that the people fly in some magical way, rather than by flapping wings or even arms.

2. **Ask:** How can you tell that this illustration was created for Virginia Hamilton's story?
   Answer: The caption tells readers this, but also the image shows events from the story: people are flying.

Reading Check

(5)

Answer: They can fly.

Differentiated Instruction   for Universal Access

Strategy for Less Proficient Readers
To help students compare and contrast, show them **Reading Skill Graphic Organizer A** (*Graphic Organizer Transparencies*, p. 194). The partially completed graphic organizer will give students insight into comparing and contrasting characters' actions and traits. Students may use it as a model for comparing and contrasting characters on their own.

Strategy for Special-Needs Students
Students may have difficulty reading and understanding written dialect, especially sentences that have no subjects. Tell students that the author chose to write in this manner in order to make the story sound like spoken language. To increase comprehension, have students listen to the story on *Hear It!* Audio CD.

EL Strategy for English Learners
Students learning English may find the informal language and dialect in this selection confusing. Make a simple chart. In the first column, list confusing sentences, phrases, and words that students identify in the selection. In the second column, provide standard English forms for words that are missing letters.

PHLit Online!

This selection is available in interactive format in the **Enriched Online Student Edition**, at **www.PHLitOnline.com** which includes a thematically related video with writing prompt and an interactive graphic organizer.

6 Compare and Contrast

1. Point out that the Overseer and the Driver are the villains in this story. **Ask** students to think of words to describe them.
   Possible response: Students may suggest words such as *brutal, cruel, rough,* and *mean.*

2. Next, **ask** students how they would describe Toby, the old man.
   Possible response: Students may say that Toby is caring, thoughtful, dependable, and kind.

3. Have students read the bracketed passage. **Ask** students the Compare and Contrast question.
   Answer: Unlike the Overseer, who is harsh and cruel toward Sarah, Toby is kind and supportive.

4. Challenge students to predict what effect Toby's "magic words" will have on Sarah. Students may suggest that Toby is casting a spell that will help Sarah fly to freedom.

Compare and Contrast
How does the Overseer's treatment of Sarah compare with Toby's treatment of her?

> The young woman lifted one foot on the air. Then the other. She flew clumsily at first...

Vocabulary
mystery (mis´ tə rē) *n.* something unexplained, unknown, or kept secret

cracked his whip across the babe anyhow. The babe hollered like any hurt child, and the woman fell to the earth.

The old man that was there, Toby, came and helped her to her feet.

"I must go soon," she told him.

"Soon," he said.

Sarah couldn't stand up straight any longer. She was too weak. The sun burned her face. The babe cried and cried, "Pity me, oh, pity me," say it sounded like. Sarah was so sad and starvin, she sat down in the row.

"Get up, you black cow," called the Overseer. He pointed his hand, and the Driver's whip snarled around Sarah's legs. Her sack dress tore into rags. Her legs bled onto the earth. She couldn't get up.

Toby was there where there was no one to help her and the babe.

"Now, before it's too late," panted Sarah. "Now, Father!"

"Yes, Daughter, the time is come," Toby answered. "Go, as you know how to go!"

He raised his arms, holding them out to her. *"Kum . . . yali, kum buba tambe,"* and more magic words, said so quickly, they sounded like whispers and sighs.

The young woman lifted one foot on the air. Then the other. She flew clumsily at first, with the child now held tightly in her arms. Then she felt the magic, the African mystery. Say she rose just as free as a bird. As light as a feather.

The Overseer rode after her, hollerin. Sarah flew over the fences. She flew over the woods. Tall trees could not snag her. Nor could the Overseer. She flew like an eagle now, until she was gone from sight. No one dared speak about it. Couldn't believe it. But it was, because they that was there saw that it was.

Say the next day was dead hot in the fields. A young man slave fell from the heat. The Driver come and whipped him. Toby come over and spoke words to the fallen one. The words of ancient Africa once heard are never remembered completely. The young man forgot them as soon as he heard them. They went way inside him. He got up and rolled over on the air. He

1012 Themes in the Oral Tradition

Concept Connector

Vocab-o-Gram
Have students return to their **Vocab-o-Grams** and review and verify or update their predictions.

Reading Skill Graphic Organizer
Ask students to review the graphic organizer in which they compared and contrasted two characters. Then have students share the graphic organizers they completed and compare their findings.

Writing About the Big Question
Have students compare their response to the sentence starter they completed before reading the selection with their ideas afterward. Ask them to explain whether their thoughts have changed.

rode it awhile. And he flew away.

Another and another fell from the heat. Toby was there. He cried out to the fallen and reached his arms out to them. *"Kum kunka yali, kum . . . tambe!"* Whispers and sighs. And they too rose on the air. They rode the hot breezes. The ones flyin were black and shinin sticks, wheelin above the head of the Overseer. They crossed the rows, the fields, the fences, the streams, and were away.

"Seize the old man!" cried the Overseer. "I heard him say the magic *words*. Seize him!"

The one callin himself Master come runnin. The Driver got his whip ready to curl around old Toby and tie him up. The slaveowner took his hip gun from its place. He meant to kill old, black Toby.

But Toby just laughed. Say he threw back his head and said, "Hee, hee! Don't you know who I am? Don't you know some of us in this field?" He said it to their faces. "We are ones who fly!"

And he sighed the ancient words that were a dark promise. He said them all around to the others in the field under the whip,

"*. . . buba yali . . . buba tambe. . . .*"

There was a great outcryin. The bent backs straightened up. Old and young who were called slaves and could fly joined hands. Say like they would ring-sing.[4] But they didn't **shuffle** in a circle. They didn't sing. They rose on the air. They flew in a flock that was black against the heavenly blue. Black crows or black shadows. It didn't matter, they went so high. Way above the plantation, way over the slavery land. Say they flew away to *Free-dom.*

And the old man, old Toby, flew behind them, takin care of them. He wasn't cryin. He wasn't laughin. He was the seer.[5] His gaze fell on the plantation where the slaves who could not fly waited.

---

4. **ring-sing** joining hands in a circle to sing and dance.
5. **seer** (sē´ ər) *n.* one who has supposed power to see the future; prophet.

7 ▲ **Critical Viewing**
What are some reasons why a person might wish to fly? **[Speculate]**

Vocabulary
shuffle (shuf´ əl) *v.* walk with dragging feet

9 ✓ Reading Check
What did Sarah do to escape the Overseer?

The People Could Fly **1013**

Ask the Compare and Contrast question.

Answer: Toby was once a slave who was in a position of weakness, and now he is a powerful seer who has led many slaves to freedom by reminding them how to fly.

▶ **Monitor Progress:** Clarify how the positions of Toby and the Overseer have changed in regard to one another.

▶ **Reteach:** If students struggle to compare and contrast Toby and the Overseer, use **Reading Skill Transparency A** (*Graphic Organizer Transparencies,* p. 194) to review how Toby and the Overseer are similar and different at the beginning and at the end of the story.

ASSESS

Answers

Critical Thinking

Before students respond, you may wish to have them write a brief objective summary of the selection. As they answer the questions below, remind them to support their answers with evidence from the text.

1. (a) **Possible response:** Students may suggest the words *abusive, unjust,* and *inhuman.* (b) **Possible response:** The insults of the Overseer, the whipping of Sarah and her child, and the Overseer's refusal to allow Sarah to feed and comfort her child are details that reveal the living conditions.

2. (a) Toby says *"Kum kunka yali, kum buba tambe."* (b) The author uses the African words to represent the free life to which the slaves hope to return.

3. (a) The people remember how to fly. (b) Flying stands for being free and living a free life.

4. (a) The slave owner is called Master. (b) The real "master" is Toby. (c) Students should give opinions they support with details from the story.

5. 🅱 **Possible response:** Freedom tales would likely have given enslaved or oppressed people hope that they too might one day "fly" to freedom.

Compare and Contrast How is Toby's position now different from his position at the beginning of the story? ⑩

"Take us with you!" Their looks spoke it but they were afraid to shout it. Toby couldn't take them with him. Hadn't the time to teach them to fly. They must wait for a chance to run.

"Goodie-bye!" The old man called Toby spoke to them, poor souls! And he was flyin gone.

So they say. The Overseer told it. The one called Master said it was a lie, a trick of the light. The Driver kept his mouth shut.

The slaves who could not fly told about the people who could fly to their children. When they were free. When they sat close before the fire in the free land, they told it. They did so love firelight and *Free-dom,* and tellin.

They say that the children of the ones who could not fly told their children. And now, me, I have told it to you.

Critical Thinking

Cite textual evidence to support your responses.

© 1. **Key Ideas and Details** (a) **Describe:** What words would you use to describe the living conditions of many African Americans during the time this story originated? (b) **Support:** Describe three details that help you understand these living conditions.

© 2. **Craft and Structure** (a) **Infer:** What are the "magic words" Toby says? (b) **Interpret:** Why do you think the author includes these words in the story?

© 3. **Key Ideas and Details** (a) What happens when Toby says the "magic words"? (b) **Draw Conclusions:** What do you think "flying" really means?

© 4. **Key Ideas and Details** (a) Who is called Master? (b) **Contrast:** Who is the real "master" in the story? (c) **Evaluate:** Do you think this folk tale inspires hope? Explain.

© 5. **Integration of Knowledge and Ideas** What effect might freedom tales, like this folk tale, have had on enslaved or otherwise oppressed people? *[Connect to the Big Question: Community or individual—which is more important?]*

1014 Themes in the Oral Tradition

Assessment Resources

Unit 6 Resources

L1 L2 EL **Selection Test A,** pp. 178–180. Administer Test A to less advanced students.

L3 L4 EL **Selection Test B,** pp. 181–183. Administer Test B to on-level and more advanced students.

L3 L4 **Open-Book Test,** pp. 175–177. As an alternative, give the Open-Book Test.

All **Customizable Test Bank**

All **Self-tests** Students may prepare for the **Selection Test** by taking the **Self-test** online.

PHLit Online! All assessment resources are available at **www.PHLitOnline.com.**

Reading Skill: Compare and Contrast

1. **Compare and contrast** the personalities of Toby and the Overseer. How are they similar? How are they different?

2. Use a Venn diagram to compare and contrast "The People Could Fly" with another story you have read in this book. In your diagram, include details about setting, plot, and characters.

Literary Analysis: Folk Tales

3. **Craft and Structure** Use a chart like the one shown to identify examples of the elements of **folk tales** that you find in this story and explain how they contribute to the meaning of the story.

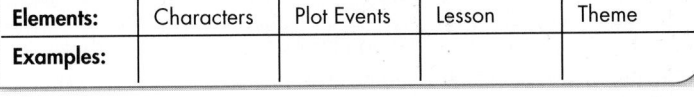

Elements:	Characters	Plot Events	Lesson	Theme
Examples:				

Vocabulary

Acquisition and Use For each item, write a single sentence correctly using the words indicated.

1. shuffle; dance
2. scorned; opinion
3. croon; lullaby
4. shed; leaves
5. hoed; planting
6. mystery; movie

Word Study Use the context of the sentences and what you know about the **Greek root -myst-** to explain your answer to each question.

1. Would a *mysterious* disappearance be easy to solve?
2. If I am *mystified* by your answer to my question, how might I respond?

Word Study

The **Greek root -myst-** means "a secret rite."

Apply It Explain how the root *-myst-* contributes to the meanings of these words. Consult a dictionary if necessary.

mystique
mystical
mysticism

Reading Skill

1. Toby is helpful, caring, careful, and powerful in an unexpected way. The Overseer is brutal, violent, and mean. Both men are leaders, but Toby leads quietly and effectively. The Overseer needs weapons in order to make people follow.

2. Students should complete their Venn diagrams with details about the setting, plot, and characters of both stories.

Literary Analysis

3. Characters—Sarah, Toby, the Master, the Overseer, the Driver; Plot Events—The Overseer whips Sarah; Toby helps Sarah fly to freedom; other slaves follow; Lesson—remembering your past will give you the strength to be free; Theme—freedom comes to those who remember how important it is. All the different elements of the story contribute to the meaning by adding information for the reader.

For other sample answers, see *Graphic Organizer Transparencies,* **Literary Analysis Graphic Organizer A,** p. 197, and the **Additional Answers** section.

Vocabulary
Acquisition and Use
Sample answers:

1. In this dance, you shuffle to slow your feet down to the beat of the music.

2. The man stated his opinion but was scorned by those who disagreed.

3. The mother will croon a lullaby to quietly sing her baby to sleep

4. Each year the big tree drops its leaves like a snake sheds its skin.

5. As part of the planting process, we hoed straight lines in the field.

6. The end of the movie was a mystery until the final scene.

Word Study
Sample answers:

1. No; The root *-myst-* means "secret." A *mysterious* disappearance involves a secret, or is hard to figure out or solve.

2. The root *-myst-* means "secret," so being *mystified* means "confused, as if the meaning is secret." A person who is mystified by an answer might ask for more information.

Word Study: Apply It
Sample answers: *Mystique* is an impression of mystery or secrecy. Something that is *mystical* has a meaning beyond human understanding, a meaning that could seem secret. *Mysticism* is the belief that connection to the divine comes in secret or unexpected ways, such as through a sudden insight.

Skills instruction for the Reading Skill and Literary Analysis concepts for this selection appears on p. 1007.

❶ 🅱 Writing About the Big Question

1. Review the assignment with the class.

2. Present this situation: One student in a group project does less work but takes the credit at the final presentation. Discuss how others in the group might feel.

3. Have students complete the sentence starter. Review responses as a class. (**Sample response:** When an <u>individual</u> uses others for personal gain, he risks their anger because they will feel unfairly treated.)

4. Remind students that their answers will help them think about the Big Question, "Community or individual— which is more important?"

While You Read

Tell students that as they read, they should look for details that show how Anansi gained others' trust.

❷ Vocabulary

1. Have students preview the selection vocabulary.

2. For each word, have students say the word aloud.

3. Then, use the word in a sentence that defines the word.

4. Finally, repeat your definitional sentence or a similar sentence with the word missing and have the class "fill in the blank" chorally. Here is an example:

   To <u>acknowledge</u> something is to recognize and admit it. When we recognized the skill of the other team, we had to [students say "acknowledge"] it.

❸ Word Study

1. Introduce the skill using the instruction in the box.

2. Have students use the word *acknowledge* in a meaningful sentence.

Making Connections | **All Stories Are Anansi's**

Community or *individual— which is more important?*

❶ Writing About the Big Question

In "All Stories Are Anansi's," Anansi the spider uses trickery to capture a hornet, a python, and a leopard. Use this sentence starter to develop your ideas about the Big Question.

When an **individual** uses others for personal gain, he risks _____ _____ because _____.

While You Read Look for details that show how Anansi gained the trust of those around him.

❷ Vocabulary

Read each word and its definition. Decide whether you know the word well, know it a little bit, or do not know it at all. After you read, see how your knowledge of each word has increased.

- **yearned** (yʉrnd) *v.* wanted very much (p. 1019) *I yearned for some hot chocolate on that cold winter night.* yearn *v.* yearning *n.*

- **gourd** (gôrd) *n.* hard-shelled fruit (p. 1020) *We drank water from a gourd.* gourds *n.*

- **python** (pī´ than´) *n.* large snake (p. 1020) *The python kills its prey by squeezing it.*

- **dispute** (di spyoot´) *n.* disagreement (p. 1020) *They had not spoken in several days because of a dispute.* dispute *v.* disputant *n.* disputable *adj.*

- **opinion** (ə pin´ yən) *n.* belief based on what seems true or probable (p. 1021) *His opinion was based on a book he read.* opinionated *adj.*

- **acknowledge** (ak näl´ ij) *v.* recognize and admit (p. 1022) *I acknowledge that you were right and I was wrong.* acknowledgement *n.* acknowledged *v.*

❸ Word Study

The **Old English root -know-** means "understand."

In this folk tale, the Sky God decrees that all storytellers must **acknowledge,** or understand and admit, that the tales they tell belong to Anansi.

1016 Themes in the Oral Tradition

Vocabulary Development

Vocabulary Knowledge Rating

Create a **Vocabulary Knowledge Rating Chart** (*Professional Development Guidebook,* p. 33) for this selection. Include the selection vocabulary and the Big Question word that appears in the Writing About the Big Question sentence starter on this page. (The Big Question vocabulary is introduced on pp. 900–901).

Give students a copy of the chart. Read the words aloud, and have students mark their rating in the Before Reading column. Urge them to be alert to these words as they read and discuss the selection.

Tally how many students think they know a word to gauge how much instruction to provide. As students read and discuss the selection, point out the words and their context.

Vocabulary Central, featuring tools, activities, and songs for studying vocabulary, is available online at **www.PHLitOnline.com.**

Meet
Harold Courlander
(1908–1996)

Author of
ALL STORIES ARE ANANSI'S

Harold Courlander is best known for his collections of folk tales from around the world. He once told an interviewer that his interest in folk tales arose from the rich multicultural environment in his hometown of Detroit, Michigan.

World Traveler During Courlander's career, he published more than thirty-five books. As he traveled around the world, he made sound recordings of the music and stories of African, African American, and Native American cultures. About his work, Courlander has said, "I think of myself primarily as a narrator. I have always had a special interest in using fiction and nonfiction narration to bridge communication between other cultures and our own."

DID YOU KNOW?
For five years, Courlander worked as a farmer. He was also a historian and a United Nations press officer.

❹ BACKGROUND FOR THE FOLK TALE

The Trickster in Folk Tales

"All Stories Are Anansi's" is a trickster tale. Typically, the trickster is an animal character, such as a spider, a fox, or a coyote, that tries to fool others. In some tales, he succeeds. In others, he himself is fooled. In American, African, and West Indian folklore, tricksters take advantage of larger and stronger animals through cunning or magic.

All Stories Are Anansi's **1017**

🔔 Daily Bellringer
For each class during which you teach this selection, have students complete one of the five Research activities for Week 35 in the *Daily Bellringer Activities* booklet.

❹ Background
Ashanti Trickster Tales

The trickster in this Ashanti folk tale is a spider named Anansi. Although Anansi is small, his strength lies in his wits. In the language of the Ashanti people, *Anansi* means "spider." The word *nan* means "to spin." Ashanti folk tales are known as *Ananisem*, which means "story" and which may or may not be about spiders.

Multidraft Reading

To assist struggling readers and to deepen reading for all, apply multidraft reading protocols. For each reading, have students set the purpose indicated:

- **First reading**—identifying key ideas and details and answering any Reading Checks.
- **Second reading**—analyzing craft and structure and responding to the side-column prompts.
- **Third reading**—integrating knowledge and ideas, connecting to other texts and the world, and answering the end-of-selection questions.

For more guidance, refer to the *Classroom Strategies and Teaching Routines* card on multidraft reading.

Differentiated Instruction   Additional Instruction

🆔 Extended Support— English Learners
Have students complete the **Reading and Vocabulary Warm-ups**, *Unit 6 Resources*, pp. 184–187, before they read. Assign the prereading pages and the adapted selection in the *Reader's Notebook: English Learner's Version*. Then, have students listen to portions of the selection on the *Hear It!* Audio CD.

L1 L2 Extended Support— Struggling Readers
Have students complete the **Reading and Vocabulary Warm-ups**, *Unit 6 Resources*, pp. 184–187, before they read. Assign the prereading pages and the adapted selection in the *Reader's Notebook: Adapted Version*. Then, have students listen to portions of the selection on the *Hear It!* Audio CD (adapted text).

Extended Support— Reluctant Readers
To build motivation and engagement before assigning the selection, have students read "Trickster Appeal— Revealed!"—a thematically related selection in *Reality Central*. Then, use the questions at the conclusion of the related selection to guide discussion.

For more about the author, practice with the selection vocabulary, or more background, go online at **www.PHLitOnline.com.**

❶ Activating Prior Knowledge
Vocab-o-Gram

1. Use the **Vocab-o-Gram** strategy (*Professional Development Guidebook*, p. 39–40) to help students make predictions about selection elements. Post the following words and phrases:

in the beginning	flew into the gourd
Spider yearned	python
owner of all the stories.	"even more foolish"
"My price is three things," the Sky God said.	Osebo the leopard
	"Tie this to your tail."
hornets	

2. Then, have partners place the words in appropriate categories on the **Vocab-o-Gram** chart and make predictions about the story. Have students discuss or explain their word placements, their reasons, and their predictions.

3. For further guidance, use the *Classroom Strategies and Teaching Routines* card on using graphic organizers.

Concept Connector ➡

Students will re-examine their ideas after reading the story.

Small-Group Activity

To help students visualize the efforts Anansi makes to purchase all the stories, have them act out one of his conquests. Tell them to work in small groups to cast the characters, block out their movements, create any props, and practice their lines.

❷ About the Selection

In this folk tale, Anansi, trickster figure and hero of many West African tales, seeks to own "all the stories known in the world." Anansi, the spider, goes to the Sky God who possesses all the stories. The Sky God agrees to sell Anansi the stories if Anansi will bring him the hornets, the great python, and the leopard. The tale describes how Anansi uses his brain to outwit these animals and capture them.

1018 Themes in the Oral Tradition

❶
❷
ALL STORIES ARE ANANSI'S
AFRICAN FOLK TALE • HAROLD COURLANDER

Vocabulary Development ©CCSS Language 6

Thematic Vocabulary: The Big Question
As students are discussing "All Stories Are Anansi's," encourage them to use the thematic vocabulary presented in Introducing the Big Question, pp. 900–901. You might encourage them with sentence starters like these:

1. This story explains the *tradition* that . . .
2. Anansi think that he will be the *individual* that . . .
3. He uses a *unique* method to get . . .
4. Still, all three methods have in *common* that . . .

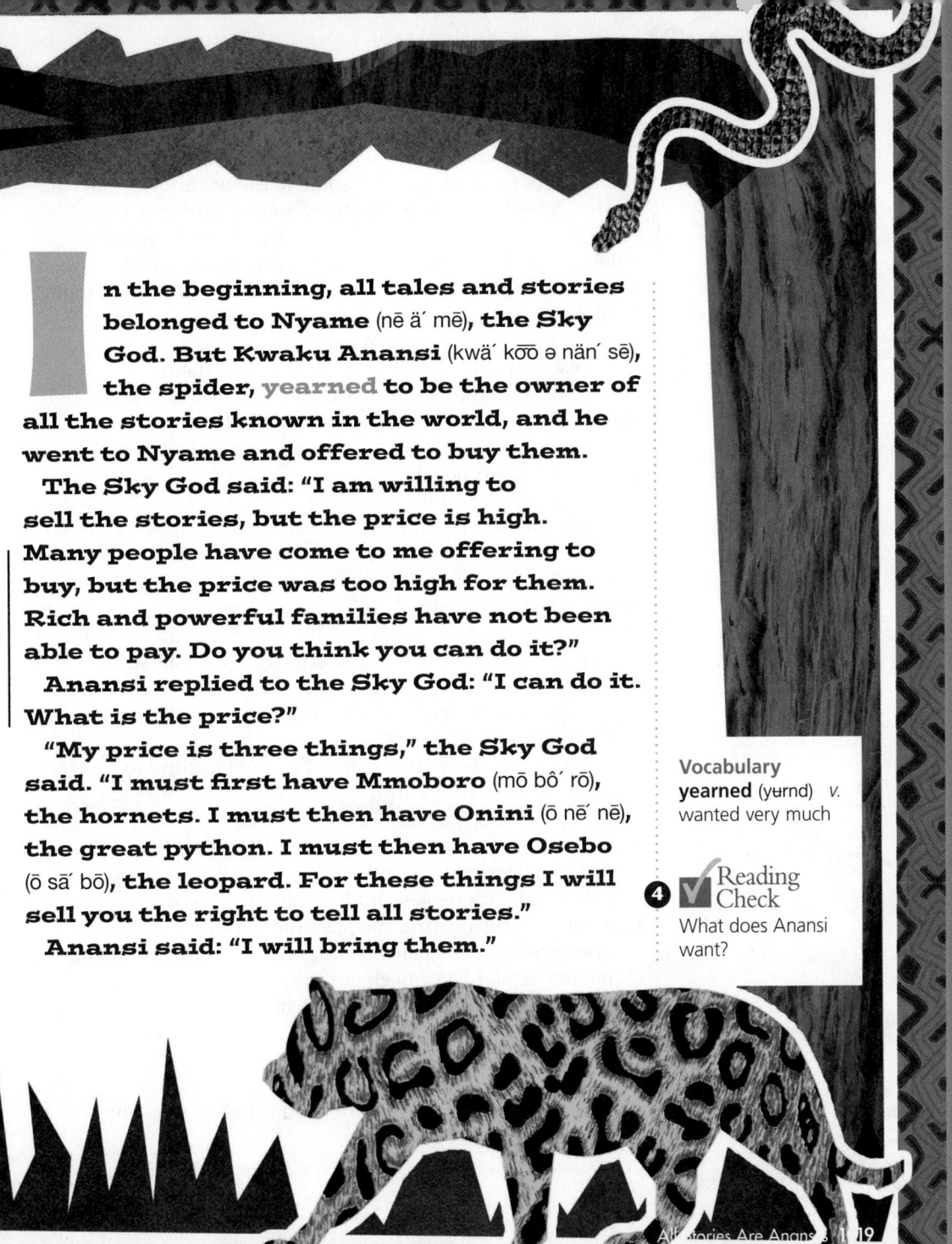

I n the beginning, all tales and stories belonged to Nyame (nē ä´ mē), the Sky God. But Kwaku Anansi (kwä´ kōō ə nän´ sē), the spider, **yearned** to be the owner of all the stories known in the world, and he went to Nyame and offered to buy them.

The Sky God said: "I am willing to sell the stories, but the price is high. Many people have come to me offering to buy, but the price was too high for them. Rich and powerful families have not been able to pay. Do you think you can do it?"

Anansi replied to the Sky God: "I can do it. What is the price?"

"My price is three things," the Sky God said. "I must first have Mmoboro (mō bô´ rō), the hornets. I must then have Onini (ō nē´ nē), the great python. I must then have Osebo (ō sā´ bō), the leopard. For these things I will sell you the right to tell all stories."

Anansi said: "I will bring them."

Vocabulary

yearned (yʉrnd) *v.* wanted very much

✓ **Reading Check**
What does Anansi want?

All Stories Are Anansi's 1019

1. Remind students that folk tales communicate the ideas and values that are important to people in a culture. For example, Anansi seems very bold when he tells the Sky God that he will pay the price for all the stories. Suggest to students that the Ashanti probably admire people who are brave and bold.

2. **Ask** students to identify the qualities Anansi demonstrates as he captures the hornets.
Answer: Anansi demonstrates intelligence, daring, and cunning when outsmarting the hornets.

3. **Ask** students the Folk Tale question.
Answer: The hornets' experience teaches readers and listeners not to follow someone blindly.

Vocabulary
gourd (gôrd) *n.* hard-shelled fruit

python (pī´ than´) *n.* large snake

dispute (di spyo͞ot´) *n.* disagreement

Folk Tale
What lesson does the hornets' experience teach?

⑤

He went home and made his plans. He first cut a gourd from a vine and made a small hole in it. He took a large calabash[1] and filled it with water. He went to the tree where the hornets lived. He poured some of the water over himself, so that he was dripping. He threw some water over the hornets, so that they too were dripping. Then he put the calabash on his head, as though to protect himself from a storm, and called out to the hornets: "Are you foolish people? Why do you stay in the rain that is falling?"

The hornets answered: "Where shall we go?"

"Go here, in this dry gourd," Anansi told them.

The hornets thanked him and flew into the gourd through the small hole. When the last of them had entered, Anansi plugged the hole with a ball of grass, saying: "Oh, yes, but you are really foolish people!"

He took the gourd full of hornets to Nyame, the Sky God. The Sky God accepted them. He said: "There are two more things."

Anansi returned to the forest and cut a long bamboo pole and some strong vines. Then he walked toward the house of Onini, the python, talking to himself. He said: "My wife is stupid. I say he is longer and stronger. My wife says he is shorter and weaker. I give him more respect. She gives him less respect. Is she right or am I right? I am right, he is longer. I am right, he is stronger."

When Onini, the python, heard Anansi talking to himself, he said: "Why are you arguing this way with yourself?"

The spider replied: "Ah, I have had a dispute with my wife. She says you are shorter and weaker than this bamboo pole. I say you are longer and stronger."

Onini said: "It's useless and silly to argue when you can find out the truth. Bring the pole and we will measure."

So Anansi laid the pole on the ground, and the python came and stretched himself out beside it.

"You seem a little short," Anansi said.

The python stretched further.

"A little more," Anansi said.

"I can stretch no more," Onini said.

"When you stretch at one end, you get shorter at the

---

1. **calabash** (kal´ ə bash´) *n.* large fruit that is dried and made into a bowl or cup.

Vocabulary Development

Vocabulary Knowledge Rating
When students have completed reading and discussing the selection, have them take out their **Vocabulary Knowledge Rating Chart** for the selection. Read the words aloud and have students rate their knowledge of words again in the After Reading column. Clarify any words that are still problematic. Have students write their own definition and example or sentence in the appropriate column. Then, have students complete the Vocabulary Practice activities at the end of the selection. Encourage students to use the words in further discussion and written work about the selection. Remind them that they will be accountable for these words on the **Selection Test**, *Unit 6 Resources,* pp. 199–201 or 202–204.

other end," Anansi said. "Let me tie you at the front so you don't slip."

He tied Onini's head to the pole. Then he went to the other end and tied the tail to the pole. He wrapped the vine all around Onini, until the python couldn't move.

"Onini," Anansi said, "it turns out that my wife was right and I was wrong. You are shorter than the pole and weaker. My opinion wasn't as good as my wife's. But you were even more foolish than I, and you are now my prisoner."

Anansi carried the python to Nyame, the Sky God, who said: "There is one thing more." Osebo, the leopard, was next. Anansi went into the forest and dug a deep pit where the leopard was accustomed to walk. He covered it with small branches and leaves and put dust on it, so that it was impossible to tell where the pit was. Anansi went away and hid. When Osebo came prowling in the black of night, he stepped into the trap Anansi had prepared and fell to the bottom. Anansi heard the sound of the leopard falling, and he said: "Ah, Osebo, you are half-foolish!"

When morning came, Anansi went to the pit and saw the leopard there.

"Osebo," he asked, "what are you doing in this hole?"

"I have fallen into a trap," Osebo said. "Help me out."

"I would gladly help you," Anansi said. "But I'm sure that if I bring you out, I will have no thanks for it. You will get hungry, and later on you will be wanting to eat me and my children."

"I swear it won't happen!" Osebo said.

"Very well. Since you swear it, I will take you out," Anansi said.

He bent a tall green tree toward the ground, so that its top was over the pit, and he tied it that way. Then he tied a rope to the top of the tree and dropped the other end of it into the pit.

"Tie this to your tail," he said.

Osebo tied the rope to his tail.

"Is it well tied?" Anansi asked.

"Yes, it is well tied," the leopard said.

"In that case," Anansi said, "you are not merely half-foolish, you are all-foolish." And he took his knife and cut the other

Vocabulary
opinion (ə pin′ yən) *n.* belief based on what seems true or probable

Compare and Contrast
What word does Anansi use to describe both the hornets and the python after he catches them?

7 Reading Check
How does Anansi catch the hornets and the python?

All Stories Are Anansi's **1021**

Concept Connector

Vocab-o-Gram
Have students return to their **Vocab-o-Grams** and compare their predictions to the setting, characters, and events of the story.

Reading Skill Graphic Organizer
Ask students to review the graphic organizers they completed while reading. Then, have students share the graphic organizers they completed and compare their findings.

Writing About the Big Question
Have students compare their response to the sentence starter they completed before reading the selection with their ideas afterward. Ask them to explain whether their thoughts have changed.

---

6 Compare and Contrast

1. Point out that repetition is important to this folk tale. Explain that the bracketed passage describes the second of three instances in which Anansi tricks and captures another animal.

2. **Ask** students to compare Anansi's attempt to trick the python with the way he tricked the hornets. **Answer:** When he tricked the hornets, Anansi played on the way hornets blindly follow a leader. Here, Anansi seems to be appealing to the python's sense of vanity. In both cases, however, Anansi outsmarts the other animal.

3. Ask students to reread the bracketed passage. Then, **ask** them the Compare and Contrast question. **Answer:** Anansi calls the hornets and the python "foolish."

4. **Ask** students if they agree with Anansi's assessment of the hornets and the python. **Possible response:** Students will probably agree that the hornets and the python were foolish to be captured so easily.

▶ **Monitor Progress:** Ask students to compare and contrast Anansi's reactions after he captures the hornets and later when he captures the python.

▶ **Reteach:** If students have trouble comparing and contrasting Anansi's reactions, guide students to the place in the text where Anansi captures the animals. Talk about how his reactions are similar or different each time.

7 Reading Check

Answer: He catches the hornets by convincing them that it is raining and telling them to hide in the gourd. He catches the python by telling it that his wife believes the python is shorter and weaker than a bamboo pole. When the python tries to prove the wife wrong, Anansi ties up the python.

Spiral Review

Theme

1. **Remind** students that they studied the concept of theme in the Unit 6 Literary Analysis workshop (pp. 902–911).

2. **Ask** the Spiral Review question.

   Possible response: A spider is not stronger than a python or a leopard. Anansi, the spider, beat both the python and the leopard with his cleverness.

ASSESS

Answers

Critical Thinking

Before students respond, you may wish to have them write a brief objective summary of the selection. As they answer the questions below, remind them to support their answers with evidence from the text.

1. (a) Students may infer that all the animals trusted Anansi. (b) Like humans, the animals are motivated by self-interest and their own wants.

2. (a) He thinks they are foolish and easily misled. (b) He calls them foolish. He is able to outwit them easily.

3. (a) The Sky God asks Anansi to bring the hornets, the python, and the leopard. (b) Anansi uses wit and cunning instead of physical powers to capture the animals. (c) His success reveals his resourcefulness and cleverness.

4. (a) **Possible response:** Anansi acts purely out of self-interest and will say anything to get his way. (b) **Possible response:** Students are likely to say that they disagree with such a self-serving code of conduct.

5.  **Possible response:** (a) In each case, he made it seem as if he were helping the other creatures to solve a problem. (b) No, he used his skill at getting others' trust to trick them. (c) No, it is wrong to use others for personal gain.

Spiral Review
Theme How does Anansi's story show that sometimes cleverness beats strength?

Vocabulary
acknowledge
(ak näl´ ij) *v.* recognize and admit

rope, the one that held the tree bowed to the ground. The tree straightened up with a snap, pulling Osebo out of the hole. He hung in the air head downward, twisting and turning. And while he hung this way, Anansi killed him with his weapons.

Then he took the body of the leopard and carried it to Nyame, the Sky God, saying: "Here is the third thing. Now I have paid the price."

Nyame said to him: "Kwaku Anansi, great warriors and chiefs have tried, but they have been unable to do it. You have done it. Therefore, I will give you the stories. From this day onward, all stories belong to you. Whenever a man tells a story, he must acknowledge that it is Anansi's tale."

In this way Anansi, the spider, became the owner of all stories that are told. To Anansi all these tales belong.

Critical Thinking

Cite textual evidence to support your responses.

1. **Key Ideas and Details (a) Infer:** What can you infer about the hornets, the python, and the leopard from the fact that they listen to Anansi? **(b) Interpret:** In what way do these animals resemble humans in their behavior?

2. **Key Ideas and Details (a) Infer:** What is Anansi's attitude toward the other animals? **(b) Support:** What details reveal this attitude?

3. **Key Ideas and Details (a)** What does the Sky God ask Anansi to do? **(b) Draw Conclusions:** Why is Anansi able to do what warriors and chiefs have failed to do? **(c) Apply:** What qualities or characteristics are revealed by his success?

4. **Integration of Knowledge and Ideas (a) Interpret:** How would you describe Anansi's personal code of behavior? **(b) Evaluate:** Do you approve or disapprove of Anansi's behavior? Explain.

5. **Integration of Knowledge and Ideas (a)** How did Anansi gain the trust of those around him? **(b) Analyze:** Are his accomplishments admirable? Explain. **(c) Evaluate:** Was Anansi justified in using the creatures for personal gain? Why or why not? *[Connect to the Big Question: Community or individual—which is more important?]*

Assessment Resources

Unit 6 Resources

L1 L2 EL **Selection Test A,** pp. 199–201. Administer Test A to less advanced students.

L3 L4 EL **Selection Test B,** pp. 202–204. Administer Test B to on-level and more advanced students.

L3 L4 **Open-Book Test,** pp. 196–198. As an alternative, give the Open-Book Test.

All **Customizable Test Bank**

All **Self-tests**
Students may prepare for the **Selection Test** by taking the **Self-test** online.

PHLit Online! All assessment resources are available at **www.PHLitOnline.com.**

All Stories Are Anansi's

Reading Skill: Compare and Contrast

1. **Compare and contrast** the hornets, the python, and the leopard. How are they similar? How are they different?

2. Use a Venn diagram to compare and contrast "All Stories Are Anansi's" with another story you have read in this book. In your diagram, include details about setting, plot, and characters.

Literary Analysis: Folk Tales

© 3. Craft and Structure Use a chart like the one shown to identify examples of the elements of **folk tales** that you find in this story and explain how they contribute to the meaning of the story.

Elements:	Characters	Plot Events	Lesson	Theme
Examples:				

Vocabulary

© Acquisition and Use For each item, write a single sentence correctly using the words indicated.

1. yearned; warmth
2. gourd; dip
3. python; grass
4. dispute; movie
5. opinion; chocolate
6. acknowledge; right

Word Study Use the context of the sentences and what you know about the **Old English root -know-** to explain your answer to each question.

1. If an actor is *unknown*, have many people heard of him?
2. If you are having computer problems, would it be useful to call someone with technical *know-how*?

Word Study

The **Old English root -know-** means "understand."

Apply It Explain how the root *-know-* contributes to the meanings of these words. Consult a dictionary if necessary

knowledge
unbeknownst

Reading Skill

1. The animals are different in that the hornets are afraid of rain, the python is vain, and the leopard is too trusting. They are similar in that all of the animals are bigger and stronger than Anansi, and yet all are tricked by Anansi.

2. Students' Venn diagrams should identify similarities and differences among the stories' settings, plots, and characters.

Literary Analysis

3. Characters—Anansi, Sky God, the hornets, the python, and the leopard; Plot Events—Anansi asks the Sky God to sell him all the stories of the world; the Sky God asks for the hornets, the python, and the leopard; Lessons—Don't be overly trustful; Learn to think for yourself; Theme—Brains are more effective than size or might.

For other sample answers, see *Graphic Organizer Transparencies,* **Literary Analysis Graphic Organizer A,** p. 198, and the **Additional Answers** section.

Vocabulary
Acquisition and Use
Sample answers:

1. The hornets <u>yearned</u> for a dry place where they could find <u>warmth</u>.

2. You can <u>dip</u> a hollowed <u>gourd</u> in water to fill it and get a drink.

3. Look at the <u>python</u> slithering through the <u>grass</u>.

4. We had a <u>dispute</u> about whether the <u>movie</u> was scary or not.

5. In my <u>opinion</u>, <u>chocolate</u> is the best dessert.

6. The Sky God must <u>acknowledge</u> that Anansi has earned the <u>right</u> to own all the stories.

Word Study
Sample answers:

1. No; The root *-know-* means "understand." Someone who is *unknown* is "not <u>understood</u>," so few would have heard of such an actor.

2. Yes; The root *-know-* means "understand," so someone with *know-how* <u>understands</u> how a computer works.

Word Study: Apply It
Sample answers: *Knowledge* is the possession of information that helps you <u>understand</u>. When something is *unbeknownst*, it is not known or <u>understood</u>.

Conventions

1. Introduce the skill, using the instruction on the student page.
2. Discuss the examples in the chart.

Think Aloud: Model the Skill

Model the skill of using abbreviations. Say to students:

Abbreviations offer me a way to conveniently and quickly communicate my meaning. For example, if I am taking notes or making a list, I may want to get my ideas down very quickly. Suppose I want to list all the states that border California. I can write NV, OR, and AZ. This is much faster and easier than writing Nevada, Oregon, and Arizona.

PH WRITING COACH Grade 7

Students will find instruction on and practice with abbreviations in Chapter 26.

Practice A
Sample answers:

1. ounce
2. feet
3. Road
4. Massachusetts

Reading Application

Sample answer: So they forgot about flyin when they could no longer breathe the sweet scent of Africa. (Afr.)

Practice B
Sample answers:

1. Mister
2. Indiana
3. United Nations
4. World War II
5. doctor of medicine

Writing Application
Sample answers:

1. revolutions per minute
2. government
3. manager
4. exempli gratia
5. kilometer
6. Senator

The People Could Fly • All Stories Are Anansi's

Conventions: Abbreviations

An **abbreviation** is a shortened form of a word or phrase, such as *Dr.* for *Doctor* or *Rd.* for *Road*.

Most abbreviations end with a period. Abbreviations are useful when taking notes or writing lists.

Instance	Example	Abbreviation
Common Titles	Captain	Capt.
Academic Degrees	Master of Business Administration	M.B.A.
States	Maryland	MD
Addresses	Street	St.
Traditional Measurements	foot	ft.
Metric Measurements	centimeter	cm

Most abbreviations should not be used in formal writing.

Practice A Correct these items by substituting the words that are represented by the abbreviations.

1. The overseer did not have one oz. of compassion for the hungry infant.
2. When Toby uttered the magic words, Sarah rose up 50 ft. in the air.
3. The overseer chased her down Hilltop Rd.
4. She was on her way to a new home in a free place, like Boston, MA.

Reading Application In "The People Could Fly" find a sentence containing a word that could be abbreviated in a list.

Practice B Identify the words that these abbreviations represent.

1. Mr.
2. Indianapolis, IN
3. U.N. press officer
4. WW II
5. M.D.

Writing Application Locate the meanings for these commonly used abbreviations: *rpm; govt.; mgr.; e.g.; km; Sen.* Then, write four sentences that each use one of the abbreviations correctly.

PH WRITING COACH Further instruction and practice are available in *Prentice Hall Writing Coach*.

Extend the Lesson

Sentence Modeling

Choose the sentence given for the selection students have read:

So they forgot about flyin when they could no longer breathe the sweet scent of Africa. ("The People Could Fly")

The python is four feet shorter than the pole, proving that Anansi is a fool. ("All Stories Are Anansi's")

Ask students what they notice about the sentence. Elicit from them the sentence includes a word that can be abbreviated. (The People Could Fly: Africa, Afr.; All Stories Are Anansi's: foot, ft.) Then, ask what else students notice. ("The People Can Fly": The sentence has a dependent clause that adds poetic detail. "All Stories Are Anansi's": The sentence has a dependent clause at the end that adds detail.)

Have students imitate the sentence in a sentence on a topic of their own choosing, matching each grammatical and stylistic feature discussed. Collect the sentences, and share them with the class.

Writing

Ⓒ Argument Write a **review** of "The People Could Fly" or "All Stories Are Anansi's" to argue whether others will enjoy the tale.

- First, review story elements, such as characters, description, dialogue, and plot, in order to choose your position.
- State your opinion, acknowledging that some readers may not agree with you. Then, support your ideas with details from the story. Organize an effective argument by giving your strongest reasons or evidence at the beginning.

Revise your word choice to use words that are precise and descriptive. For example, replace "good" with "entertaining" or "comical," or change "boring" to "simplistic" or "predictable."

Grammar Application Check your writing to be sure you have used abbreviations correctly.

Writing Workshop: *Work in Progress*

Prewriting for Research Choose two ideas from the Ideas List in your portfolio. For each topic, jot down three different types of resources that are likely to provide you with enough information for an in-depth report. Save this Resource List in your writing portfolio.

Speaking and Listening

Ⓒ Presentation of Ideas Prepare a **television news report** that provides a clear interpretation of story events.

- Get ready by summarizing the main points of the story.
- Organize your main points by beginning with the most important point or event. Follow these points with supporting ideas.
- Describe events in your own words. Include facts about when and where the incidents took place, using details from the story.
- Include an interview with an eyewitness—someone who saw events and can provide an on-the-scene reaction. In your report, use quotations to add credibility and bring the action to life.
- Conclude your report with an insight about the meaning of the events and the characters' actions.
- Present your news report to a small group. Speak clearly and vary your voice to emphasize key points.

Ⓒ Common Core State Standards

L.7.2, L.7.3.a; W.7.1, W.7.1.a, W.7.1.b, W.7.2.a, W.7.2.b, W.7.2.f; SL.7.4
[For the full wording of the standards, see page 1006.]

Use this prewriting activity to prepare for the **Writing Workshop** on page 1040.

PHLit
Online!
www.PHLitOnline.com
- Interactive graphic organizers
- Grammar tutorial
- Interactive journals

Integrated Language Skills **1025**

Teaching Resources

Unit 6 Resources
- L3 L4 EL **Integrated Language Skills: Grammar,** p. 193
- L3 L4 EL **Support for Writing,** p. 194
- L3 L4 **Support for Extend Your Learning,** p. 195
- L4 **Enrichment,** pp. 174, 192

Enriched Online Student Edition
Available under After You Read for this selection:
- All **Interactive Grammar Tutorial**
- L3 L4 **Internet Research Activity**

Professional Development Guidebook
Rubrics for Self-Assessment: Critique, pp. 250–251

PHLit Online! All print and digital resources are available online at **www.PHLitOnline.com.** Online resources accessible to students are noted on the student page.

Writing

1. Review the assignment, using the instruction on the student page.
2. To guide students in writing an argument, give them **Support for Writing,** p. 194 in *Unit 6 Resources.*
3. To evaluate students' reviews, adapt the **Critique** rubric, pp. 250–251 in *Professional Development Resources.* Make sure that students' reviews include a plot summary and a recommendation to other readers.

Grammar Application

Have students check their drafts to make sure they have used abbreviations correctly.

Six Traits Focus

✓ Ideas		Word Choice
✓ Organization		Sentence Fluency
✓ Voice		Conventions

PH WRITING COACH Grade 7

Students will find further instruction on and practice with reviews in Chapter 10.

Writing Workshop
Work in Progress

Have students save their completed Resource Lists in their portfolios. They will use the lists later as they complete the Writing Workshop assignment (see pp. 1040–1049).

Speaking and Listening

1. Review the assignment, using the instruction on the student page.
2. To support students' work on the assignment, have students complete the **Support for Extend Your Learning** page (*Unit 6 Resources,* p. 195).

In this two-page Test Practice, students apply the reading skill for the second half of Unit 6 to a passage of fiction and a passage of nonfiction.

Review this skill, compare and contrast, and then administer the test. For more guidance, consult the *Classroom Strategies and Teaching Routines* card, **Formally Assessing Students.**

ASSESS

Answers

Answers With Explanations

1. **C**—When the narrator expresses hope that they can all work on the play, both Jamal and Doug nod enthusiastically. *Incorrect answers:* A—Doug can't stand team sports; B—They only met last summer; D—They enjoy acting at camp, but there is no indication they hope to become actors.

2. **A**—Jamal wants to join the basketball tournament; Doug says that he can't stand team sports. *Incorrect answers:* B—The three boys share a cabin and act like friends; C—There is no reference to acting talent or lack of it; D—Doug is the one who wants to go swimming.

3. **D**—The narrator agrees with Jamal that basketball is fun; Doug says he can't stand team sports. *Incorrect answers:* A— Doug wants to swim; the narrator shows no interest in swimming; B—Jamal says that both he and the narrator are fast. C—All three boys are at camp.

4. **C**—The narrator shares an interest in basketball and acting with Jamal, but only an interest in acting with Doug. *Incorrect answers:* A—The narrator shares two interests with Jamal. B—The narrator has more in common with Jamal than Doug. D—The narrator and Doug share only an interest in acting.

Writing for Assessment

Students should write two or three sentences that summarize the similarities and differences between Jamal and Doug.

Test Practice: Reading

Compare and Contrast

Fiction Selection

Directions: *Read the selection. Then, answer the questions.*

As Jamal, Doug, and I left our cabin on the first day of camp, Jamal begged Doug and me to join the basketball tournament with him. "No way," said Doug. "I can't stand team sports! Let's go swimming instead."

"Come on," Jamal said to me, "You played basketball last year. We're not tall, but we're both fast. We'll be great together!"

"Okay," I said. "Basketball is fun. But I really hope we all work on the play together again this summer." Both Doug and Jamal nodded enthusiastically. We all met while acting in the camp play last summer, and I knew none of us would want to miss it this year.

1. What is one similarity between Jamal, Doug, and the narrator?
   A. They share a love of team sports.
   B. They have been friends for many years.
   C. They share an interest in acting.
   D. They hope to become actors.

2. One difference between Jamal and Doug is
   A. Jamal loves team sports; Doug does not.
   B. Doug is the narrator's friend, but Jamal is not.
   C. Doug is a talented actor, while Jamal gives weak performances.
   D. Jamal wants to go swimming, but Doug does not.

3. What is one similarity between the narrator and Jamal that Doug does not share?
   A. They both want to swim.
   B. They are both slow.
   C. They both go to camp.
   D. They both enjoy basketball.

4. Based on details in this passage, you can conclude that
   A. the narrator does not have much in common with Jamal.
   B. the narrator has qualities in common with both boys.
   C. the narrator has more in common with Jamal.
   D. the narrator has more in common with Doug.

Writing for Assessment

In a few sentences, summarize the similarities and differences between Doug and Jamal.

Strategies for Test Taking

Tell students that sometimes it can be confusing to keep track of similarities and differences in a passage that compares and contrasts more than two people, places, or things. One useful strategy is to create a compare-and-contrast chart on a piece of scratch paper. For example, the student could create one column for the narrator of this story, one column for Jamal, and one for Doug. Filling in each character's interests would make it much easier to answer items 1–4 correctly.

Nonfiction Selection

Directions: *Read the selection. Then, answer the questions.*

Equipment required for playing football includes helmets, mouthpieces, and a lot of thick padding. Because players often make physical contact, they must be well protected. They can wear up to ten pounds of gear during a game. The action in football is stop-and-go. A player holds the ball and runs, while others try to tackle him. Many football players are large and muscular. Their size makes it hard for opposing players to move them out of the way.

In soccer, players wear shorts, shirts, and stiff pads to protect their shins. Players mostly use their feet to move the ball, but they are allowed to use any body part other than their arms. They sometimes bounce the ball off their heads. The action in soccer is nonstop. Most soccer players are lean and muscular so that they can move quickly back and forth across the field.

1. According to the passage, in what way are football and soccer alike?
   A. Both require helmets.
   B. Both have non-stop action.
   C. Both are played by muscular athletes.
   D. Both require a lot of padding.

2. In contrast to soccer, football players—
   A. can hold the ball in their hands.
   B. never make contact with other players.
   C. wear pads to protect their shins.
   D. need very little gear.

3. Which statement is *most* accurate?
   A. Football requires players to be strong; soccer requires them to be aggressive.
   B. Football requires players to be strong; soccer requires them to be quick.
   C. Football is a team sport; soccer is an individual sport.
   D. Football is difficult to learn; soccer is easy.

4. What is the *best* title for this selection?
   A. Football and Soccer: What's the Difference?
   B. Stories From the School's Playing Fields
   C. How to Play Soccer and Football
   D. Why Football Is a Better Game than Soccer

Writing for Assessment

Connecting Across Texts
Which sport described in the second passage is Jamal more suited to play? Write a paragraph, using details from both selections to support your response.

www.PHLitOnline.com
- Online practice
- Instant feedback

Test Practice: Reading **1027**

Answers With Explanations

1. **C**—Both paragraphs mention the muscular nature of the players. *Incorrect answers:* A—Only football requires a helmet; B—Soccer has nonstop action, but football is stop-and-go; D—Football requires more padding.

2. **A**—Football players hold the ball and run, but soccer players cannot use their arms to move the ball. *Incorrect answers:* B—The passage states that football players make lots of contact with other players; C—Soccer players wear shin guards; D—Football players wear up to ten pounds of gear.

3. **B**—The passage states soccer players need to move quickly. *Incorrect answers:* A—The passage does not say that soccer players must be aggressive; C—Both are team sports; D—The passage does not discuss difficulties in learning to play these sports.

4. **A**—Since the passage focuses on differences between the two sports, this title is most appropriate. *Incorrect answers:* B—There are no stories about sports in this selection; C—The selection does not provide step-by-step instructions; D—The author does not express an opinion about which sport is better.

Writing for Assessment

Students should use details from both selections to support an opinion about which sport Jamal is better suited to play: football or soccer. Some students may say that because Jamal is fast but not tall, he is better suited to soccer than to football, since soccer requires speed but most football players are large. On the other hand, Jamal is good at basketball, which requires throwing a ball, as does football.

Differentiated
Instruction   for Universal Access

Strategy for Less Proficient Readers
Remind students that in many compare-and-contrast essays, all of the features of one person, place, or thing are described and then all of the features of a second person, place, or thing are described. In order to compare the things being contrasted, the reader needs to look back at both descriptions. For example, in the passage comparing and contrasting football and soccer, paragraph 1 describes football and paragraph 2 describes soccer. In order to compare the equipment used in the two sports, the reader needs to reread the beginning of each paragraph.

Students may take the test in interactive format with instant feedback online at **www.PHLitOnline.com**.

1027

Common Core State Standards

- **Reading Informational Text 6, 9**
- **Writing 1.a, b, e**

Reading Skill

1. Introduce the skill and review the charts.
2. Tell students they will learn how to analyze point of view.

Think Aloud: Model the Skill

Say to students:

All writers bring a particular point of view to their work. The purpose of an editorial is to state an opinion about a topic. When I read an editorial, I look for a clear statement of opinion, and I read to see if the writer of the editorial supports his or her point of view with facts and details. I also look to see if the editorial writer presents competing points of view. Addressing the concerns of people with other opinions makes the editorial more credible.

◆ Multidraft Reading

Have students follow a multidraft reading protocol.

- **First reading**—Have students read to identify key ideas and details.
- **Second reading**—Have students read to identify the structure of the text.
- **Third reading**—Have students read to integrate knowledge and ideas by connecting the text to the world, their own experiences, and other texts.

Content-Area Vocabulary

1. Have students say each word.
2. Next, use each word in a sentence that defines it.
3. Finally, repeat your definitional sentence or a similar sentence with the word missing and have the class "fill in the blank" chorally.

1028

Reading for Information

Analyzing Argumentative Texts

Editorial    Editorial

Reading Skill: Analyze Point of View

Editorials reflect a writer's **point of view,** or opinion, on an issue. An editorial writer develops his or her point of view using various techniques, such as including persuasive language or providing specific evidence. When writers with differing points of view write about the same subject, they may focus only on evidence that supports their argument. Use the chart to help you **analyze the authors' point of view** in the editorials that follow.

Techniques for Developing Point of View	Example
A clearly stated position	"School dress codes promote a sense of unity."
Supporting statistics, facts, and examples	"Students are more focused when distractions such as fashion choices are eliminated."
Persuasive techniques and language	"The self-confident manner of uniformed students makes a positive impression on visitors."
Arguments that address opposing views	"Some people believe that dress codes discourage individuality, yet there are many other creative outlets."
A concluding statement that reinforces the author's point of view	"Schools with dress codes shift the focus from fashion to education, which is exactly where it should be."

Content-Area Vocabulary

These words appear in the selections that follow. You may also encounter them in other content-area texts.

- **habitats** (hab´ ə tats) *n.* places where specific animals or plants naturally live or grow
- **vulnerable** (vul´ nər ə bəl) *adj.* open to attack
- **resources** (ri sôrs´ iz) *n.* any supplies that will meet a need

1028 Themes in the Oral Tradition

Common Core State Standards

Reading Informational Text

6. Determine an author's point of view or purpose in a text and analyze how the author distinguishes his or her position from that of others.

9. Analyze how two or more authors writing about the same topic shape their presentations of key information by emphasizing different evidence or advancing different interpretations of facts.

Writing

1.a. Introduce claims, and organize the reasons and evidence logically. **1.b.** Support claim(s) with logical reasoning and relevant evidence, demonstrating an understanding of the topic or text. **1.e.** Provide a concluding statement or section that follows from and supports the argument presented. *(Timed Writing)*

 Community or individual— which is more important?

Have students read the texts to analyze the differing points of view.

Differentiated Instruction for Universal Access

Reading Support
Give students reading support with the appropriate version of the *Reader's Notebooks:*

L2 L3 *Reader's Notebook*

L1 *Reader's Notebook: Adapted Version*

EL *Reader's Notebook: English Learner's Version*

Zoos: Joys or Jails?

Rachel F., San Diego, CA

Imagine your family lives in a luxurious mansion where all your needs are provided for. There are gardens and daily walks and all your favorite foods.

Suddenly, you're taken from your home and shipped to a place where people come from far and wide to ogle at you, thinking they are learning about your lifestyle. Sometimes, your captors force you to perform for thousands of people.

Your life has changed drastically. Welcome to the zoo!

Although the circumstances and reasons for animals being in zoos vary, its concept has faults many don't notice during their visit with the animals. Animals in many zoos are kept in areas that are much smaller than their natural **habitats**. As a result, animals behave differently than they would in their natural surroundings. Animals like big cats are accustomed to roaming territories of up to 10 square miles.

One of the best aspects of the zoo is its emphasis on education. Signs tell visitors about the animals and their behavior in the wild, but notice how the majority say the animals were born in the zoo. Unfortunately, the adaptive behavior due to small cages gives visitors a skewed perception of how the animals actually behave in the wild.

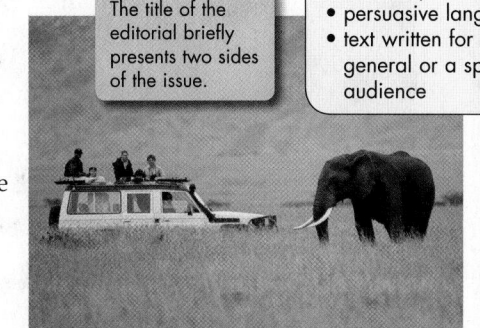

Although the idea of education to protect and preserve animals is excellent, is the zoo really setting a good example of treatment or representing the natural actions of these creatures?

Some advocates say that zoos protect and save endangered species. Despite today's advanced breeding techniques, animals raised in the zoo or other places of captivity are not learning the survival techniques they would in the wild. These animals would be very **vulnerable** if released and would encounter difficulties coping. Would it not be more beneficial to raise them in their natural habitat?

In this way scientists wouldn't face as many risks in reintroducing captive animals raised into the wild.

Helping endangered species in the wild gives them a better chance for survival and reproduction. Scientists should only revert to the zoo if the necessary funding or habitat for breeding is not available.

Editorial

Features:
- writer's opinion on an issue
- facts, statistics, and/or examples
- persuasive language
- text written for a general or a specific audience

The title of the editorial briefly presents two sides of the issue.

The most important point is presented first and is supported with statistics.

TEACH

About Editorials

1. Review the features listed in the box on page 1029. **Ask** students why persuasive language is used in editorials.
   Answer: Persuasive language is used to sway the readers to adopt the viewpoint of the writer.

2. **Ask** students what purpose facts and statistics serve in editorials.
   Answer: They support the opinion expressed in the editorial.

3. Talk to students about how to read an editorial. Point out that they need to look for details that support the writer's point of view.

Analyze Point of View

1. Before students read the editorial, point out that the title implies that different points of view will be discussed. **Ask** students why, aside from considerations of fairness, an author might choose this title.
   Possible response: The title draws readers' attention and makes them curious about the writer's opinion.

2. Point out that editorial writers often anticipate opposing arguments and counter them while in the course of making their arguments. **Ask** why such an organization might be easier for readers.
   Possible response: If the writer compares and contrasts two positions in an ongoing manner, then readers may more easily appreciate the flow of his or her argument.

3. Revisit the title of the editorial, and illustrate the skillful way the author organizes her comparisons. **Ask** students whether each paragraph describes a "joy" or a "jail."
   Answer: The first paragraph describes a joy, while the second describes a jail, and the third describes neither. The fourth paragraph describes a jail, the fifth both, and the sixth, while describing both, mostly describes jail-like conditions.

4. Return to the last four paragraphs and **ask** what clue words indicate that points of view are being contrasted.
   Answer: *But, although* and *despite* imply contrasts.

Differentiated Instruction   for Universal Access

Strategy for Special-Needs Students
Students may be challenged by the fact that the first three paragraphs of the editorial addresses readers directly, while no specific information about zoos is provided until the fourth. In addition, the editorial features rhetorical questions and concludes with an admonishment.
Help students understand that these elements of the editorial's style resemble those of a spoken argument. Remind students that the purpose of an editorial is to persuade readers, which is why they are often addressed directly.

Enrichment for Advanced Readers
Encourage students to use their critical thinking skills by developing arguments opposing those in the editorial, whether or not they personally agree with this viewpoint. For example, point out that if funding for zoos increased, habitats could be enlarged, but would the author's argument against zoos in general still be valid?
Have students share their opposing arguments once the class has finished reading the editorial.

1. **Ask** students what major goal the author assumes is common ground for all readers of the editorial.
   Possible response: She assumes that all readers want to help animals, especially endangered ones.

2. **Ask** students why an author writing persuasively may want to emphasize the common concerns of both sides of an argument.
   Possible response: The author shows that the contradictory positions are not as far apart as one might think, and that it is therefore easy for any reader to make the necessary leap to adopt a viewpoint that he or she formerly opposed.

3. Draw attention to the typical feature of editorials that is called out by the final annotation. **Ask** students to identify the real conclusion of the editorial's argument.
   Possible response: In the second-to-last paragraph the writer thinks that zoos cannot revere animals. Therefore, animals should be left in their natural habitats.

4. **Ask** students why the last paragraph is powerful.
   Possible response: The last paragraph contains more than the writer's opinion. It draws in the readers and challenges them to think about their actions.

Animals are not just brought to the zoo to protect their species, but also to provide entertainment. Many animals' lives will include performing for visitors. Four shows are performed every day at the San Diego Zoo. The zoo should be reserved for education and protecting endangered species, not an amusement park where animals are trained to perform.

Although the zoo is trying to be helpful in providing shows about the animals, it is harming those it intends to protect. The zoo has good intentions in its educational purposes, and in breeding endangered species, but animals shouldn't perform or be treated in a manner that could change their behaviors from how they act in the wild.

Though zoos are meant to be a joy to viewers and teach lessons about our earth, the zoo jails its inhabitants and passes on faulty knowledge. The wild animals in our world are a wonder, and they must be preserved. At the zoo they are treated with care, but they should be treated with reverence.

Next time you visit a zoo, look at the enclosure of the tigers and watch the seals balance a ball on their noses, and then think about what you are really learning from your day at the zoo.

> The editorial concludes with a strong, direct statement.

Vocabulary Development
CCSS Language 6

Zoological Terms
Guide students to understand the meaning of the following conservation-related words that appear in this editorial.

- *natural habitat:* specific areas where animals thrive in the wild
- *adaptive behavior:* actions that help animals survive in a given environment
- *survival techniques:* the skills animals use to hunt prey or to avoid becoming prey

KID TERRITORY:
Why Do We Need Zoos?

San Diego Zoo Staff

It's an interesting question that many people wonder about. Why have people created zoos, and why are they important now?

The idea of a zoo actually started a long time ago, in the ancient cultures of China, the Middle East, and then the Roman Empire. As people started to travel more, for longer distances to explore the unknown, they began to discover animals and plants that they had never seen or heard of before. They were fascinated by these amazing creatures. Travelers reported back to their communities and their leaders what they had seen. Rulers like emperors, sultans, and kings often wanted to prove how wealthy and powerful they were, to each other and to their subjects. One way to do that was to "collect" some of these animals, and allow people to come and see them. These collections were called menageries, and usually only the rich and powerful had them.

But that changed as time went on, and eventually it was countries and then individual cities that had collections of exotic animals for people to come and see, and they were no longer reserved only for wealthy rulers. Zoology is the study of animals, so these became zoological collections. You guessed it—that was then shortened to the word we use now: zoos.

Zoos open to the public

At first most zoos only had a limited number of animals, usually the ones people had heard about but never seen in person, like lions, bears, giraffes, hippos, and other big and impressive species. Then as zoos became more popular, and traveling to get animals became more possible, zoos started to represent animals from particular countries and parts of the world. Zoologists studied these animals to find out more about them: what they ate, how they grew, how they had young, and how they behaved, among other things. But zoos were open to the general public, too, so everyone could find out about animals.

Connecting with critters

Zoos today still serve that important purpose: they allow us to study and find out more about animals that we would not understand otherwise.

Reading for Information: Editorial **1031**

Editorial

Features:
- text written for newspapers, magazines, and online publications
- a particular point of view expressed by a writer
- strong arguments
- persuasive techniques

The title of the editorial clearly identifies the issue.

The author provides historical context for the issue.

About Editorials

1. **Ask** students to discuss the importance of establishing a point of view in an editorial.
   Answer: By establishing a point of view, writers not only stay focused but also reveal their opinions on a particular issue. A writer's point of view is developed and strengthened by stating their position, citing facts and examples, and using language that will appropriately persuade the reader.

2. Review the features listed in the Editorial box on page 1031 with students. **Ask** students why readers might enjoy reading editorials.
   Possible response: Students may say that editorials contain more than just facts. Editorials contain strong points of view and challenge readers to think more about a topic.

Analyze Point of View

1. Have students read the editorial on p. 1031 and the callouts that point out elements of persuasion that help make up the author's point of view.

2. Point out that the author establishes a point of view in the beginning of the editorial. **Ask** students to identify the author's point of view.
   Answer: The author believes that zoos are important for preserving wildlife and enabling people to see animals from around the world.

3. **Ask** students to discuss why the author provides a historical background on zoos.
   Answer: By providing a historical background on zoos, the writer explains how zoos were once a prize and privilege of the rich. With the onset of travel and exploration, people from all classes of society became interested in seeing animals they had never seen before. This background also informs the reader that zoos are much more than just a haven of caged animals; they are just as much a part of our history as they are a part of our culture.

1031

Analyze Point of View

1. **Ask** students to discuss an important purpose of zoos today, according to the author.
   Answer: Zoos allow scientists to study and inform us about wild animals from around the world.

2. **Ask** students to discuss how zoos help wildlife.
   Answer: Zoologists believe in animal conservation and do everything in their power to study each species and protect it from danger. Because humans are constantly displacing animals in the wild, the zoo has become a place of refuge for animals, especially those in danger of becoming extinct.

3. **Ask** students to discuss why the author mentions opposing arguments in the editorial.
   Possible response: Students may say that acknowledging opposing arguments actually strengthens the writer's point of view.

People are curious and want to know about the world around them, and that especially includes the animals and plants with which we share the Earth. In addition to studying animals in zoos, scientists are also able to go out to the countries where animals live and study them in the field, or their habitat. But most people cannot do that, so zoos allow them to see and connect with what would otherwise be unavailable to them.

Helping wildlife

These days we also have cable TV, though, and there are lots of wild animal shows that we can watch. So why still have zoos? One of the most important reasons is conservation. Humans are destroying the Earth's habitats at a very fast pace, in order to make space, food, and products for ourselves. But that leaves less and less room for animals and plants. Zoos and wildlife parks are places where we can protect species that are in trouble, so they don't disappear from the Earth completely.

People do have different opinions about that, though. Some people think that animals should not be kept by humans for any reason, and that if they go extinct, then that's the way it should be. Other people think that animals are precious **resources**, an important part of the Earth, and that we should do everything we can to protect them, especially since we are the ones putting them in danger in the first place. Some people feel that there is lots of wild space and that animals should only live there. Other people feel that there is very little wild space left, that animals are contained by humans in some way no matter where they are, and it is up to us to take care of them the best we can. It's a discussion that will probably go on for a long time, especially as more and more species become endangered.

> The author acknowledges opposing arguments.

There is another thing that zoos accomplish, which could be one of the most important of all. Zoos give people the opportunity to see animals in person, often up close, to watch them, realize how alike we are in many ways, to understand them, and to appreciate them. It's amazing to come almost face to face with an elephant or tiger, for example, to see how big it is, to feel its power, to look in its eyes; or to see an orangutan or gorilla amble right by you, holding its baby or playing chase with its brother or sister. It is said that people only love what they understand, and they only protect what they love. Zoos may be the last stand for wild species, the place where humans can grow to love them, and then work to protect them.

> The editorial concludes with a reinforcement of the author's point of view.

Think Aloud

Analyzing Point of View

Model the skill of analyzing point of view. Say to students:

> Because "Why Do We Need Zoos?" is an editorial, I know that a particular point of view will be expressed by the author or authors. To assess the editorial, I will have to analyze point of view. I am going to look for the following elements: a clearly stated position, supporting details, persuasive language, arguments that address opposing views, and a closing statement that reinforces the author's opinion. All of these elements are important to analyze. For example, the author may state an opinion, but if he or she doesn't support it with details and examples, the point of view will not be convincing. Also, if other points of view are not even acknowledged, I'll think that the author hasn't even considered other view-points. Finally, I'll expect persuasive language and an ending that may be emotional, and although these elements may be convincing, I won't allow them alone to sway me.

Comparing Argumentative Texts

1. **Key Ideas and Details (a)** Compare the **point of view** of each author on zoos. **(b)** Are the different points of view on the problem of extinction caused by disagreement over facts or by different interpretations of the same set of facts? Explain.

Content-Area Vocabulary

2. Use the words *habitats, vulnerable,* and *resources* in a paragraph in which you explain your opinion of zoos.

Timed Writing

Argument: Editorial

> **Format and Audience**
> The prompt gives specific directions about what to write and information about your audience. Therefore, write an essay that is four or five paragraphs long and uses clear, formal language.

> Write a brief editorial for a school newspaper about an issue that affects your community or the nation. For example: building affordable housing versus protecting animal habitats. Use supporting details to develop your argument. (35 minutes)

> **Academic Vocabulary**
> When you write and *develop* an argument, you introduce your ideas, provide supporting evidence, and conclude with a restatement of your most important ideas.

5-Minute Planner

Complete these steps to write your editorial:

1. Choose an issue that affects your community or the nation.

2. Write a sentence that clearly states your point of view.

3. Make notes that give reasons, facts, descriptions, and examples in support of your claims. **TIP** Including language that evokes positive or negative emotions can sway readers.

4. Scan the two editorials to get ideas about how to structure and develop your argument. Finalize your organizational plan.

5. Consult your notes as you write your editorial. Conclude with a final paragraph that summarizes your argument in memorable phrases.

Reading for Information **1033**

Comparing Argumentative Texts

1. (a) The two strongest points made by the author of the first editorial are that animals raised in captivity are not learning the survival techniques they would in the wild, and that animals should not be taught to do anything that would change their natural behavior. In the second editorial, the author's two strongest points include how much scientists have learned about animals in zoos and how zoos help protect endangered species. (b) **Possible response:** Students may say that the author of the first argument had the strongest case because the zoos are described in such a way that the reader cannot help but feel sorry for the animals. Most people think of zoos in a positive way, but this editorial makes you think about the treatment of wildlife, and whether or not we are really protecting them by keeping them caged and on display.

2. **Sample response:** Zoos are a good idea because they help save *vulnerable* animals. Some of these animals are losing their *habitats* in the wild and are endangered. We need to give zoos more *resources* to help save these animals.

Timed Writing

1. Before students complete the activity, guide them in identifying and analyzing key words and phrases in the prompt, highlighted on the student page.

2. Work with students to draw up guidelines for their editorial based on the key words:

   • **Focus** The writer should focus on a local or national issue.

   • **Organization** The writer should organize the editorial by establishing a strong point of view using supporting details and persuasive language.

   • **Elaboration** The writer should give ample reasons and facts that support his or her point of view.

   • **Style** The style should be clear and brief.

3. Have students use the 5-Minute Planner to structure their time.

4. Allow students 35 minutes to complete the assignment. Evaluate their work using the guidelines they have developed.

1033

Common Core State Standards

- Reading Literature 2, 3, 5
- Writing 2.b

❶ Comparing Tone and Theme

1. Introduce and discuss the skill.
2. Discuss the chart.
3. Give students a copy of **Comparing Tone and Theme Organizer B**, *Graphic Organizer Transparencies,* p. 201. Tell them they will fill it in as they read.

Think Aloud: Model the Skill

Get students thinking about how to identify the theme of a text. Say:

Your textbook says the theme is the main message and gives the example of "Love conquers all." Let's see if we can think of some stories with that theme.

We're probably looking for a love story. The "conquers all" part means it needs to have a happy ending. *Romeo and Juliet* is probably not going to work.

How about *Cinderella*? Love conquers the plotting of the evil stepsisters. Cinderella and Prince Charming "live happily ever after."

Once you identify a theme, work backwards to see if it fits.

---

❶ Comparing Tone and Theme

The **tone** of a literary work is the writer's attitude toward a subject. The tone can often be described in one word, such as *playful* or *serious.* Tone is produced by factors such as these.

- Word choice: The words a writer chooses may be formal or informal, fancy or simple, energetic or mournful. The connotations, or emotional associations, of words help to create tone.
- Sentence structure: Simple, direct sentences can add a conversational tone. Long, complex ones can create a dignified tone.

Because a writer's tone expresses an attitude towards the writer's subject, it can help convey a theme. The **theme** is the main message in a literary work—an insight about people or life. One example is "Love conquers all." Sometimes the author states the theme explicitly, or directly. More often, however, the theme is implied. To understand a text's theme, pay attention to the author's tone, as well as to the lessons that characters learn.

The poem "The Fox Outwits the Crow" and the fable "The Fox and the Crow" have similar characters, settings, and plots. However, the authors have different attitudes toward their subjects. As you read, use a chart like the one shown to analyze the tone and theme of each selection.

Common Core State Standards

Reading Literature

2. Determine a theme or central idea of a text and analyze its development over the course of the text.

3. Analyze how particular elements of a story or drama interact.

5. Analyze how a drama's or poem's form or structure contributes to its meaning.

Writing

2.b. Develop the topic with relevant facts, definitions, concrete details, quotations, or other information and examples. *(Timed Writing)*

	Details I Notice	What Details Show About Tone/Theme
Title: "The Fox and the Crow"	"Good day, Mistress Crow," he cried.	formal
Title:		

- Vocabulary flashcards
- Interactive journals
- More about the authors
- Selection audio
- Interactive graphic organizers

www.PHLitOnline.com

1034 Themes in the Oral Tradition

Vocabulary Development

Vocabulary Knowledge Rating

Create a **Vocabulary Knowledge Rating Chart (Professional Development Guidebook,** p. 33) featuring the vocabulary words glossed in the selections:

whiff (p. 1037)
hors d'oeuvres (p. 1037)
malice (p. 1037)

glossy (p. 1038)
surpass (p. 1038)
flatterers (p. 1038)

Explain that the words are defined in the margin at the point where they appear in the selection. Have students mark their rating of each in the Before You Read column.

Urge them to be alert to these words as they read and discuss the selections. Have students rate the words again after concluding reading. Clarify any words that remain problematic.

Vocabulary Central, featuring tools, activities, and songs for studying vocabulary, is available online at **www.PHLitOnline.com.**

Community or individual — which is more important?

Writing About the Big Question

Each of these selections ends with a moral, or life lesson, about how to get along with others. Use this sentence starter to develop your ideas about the Big Question.

A **common** difficulty in getting along with others is _____ because _____.

Meet the Authors

William Cleary (b. 1926)

Author of "The Fox Outwits the Crow"

William Cleary is a writer, composer, filmmaker, and poet who lives in Burlington, Vermont. He has written twelve books on spirituality, published five collections of religious music, and composed a musical comedy that was performed at the 1988 Olympics. He has retold eighty of Aesop's fables in verse.

Aesop (about 620–560 B.C.)

Author of "The Fox and the Crow"

People have enjoyed Aesop's fables for centuries. However, very little is known about the origin of these well-known tales—including who actually wrote them.

Many Theories Aesop may have been an enslaved person who lived on the Greek island of Samos, a spokesman who defended criminals in court, or an advisor for one of the Greek kings. The most widely held theory, however, is that Aesop was not an actual person at all. Rather, the theory holds, as the stories were told over and over in ancient Greece, people invented an imaginary author for them.

▲ Aesop as imagined by the Spanish painter Diego Velazquez, b. 1599

Teaching Resources

All *Unit 6 Resources*, pp. 205–221

All *Graphic Organizer Transparencies*, pp. 200–203

All Enriched Online Student Edition

All *Common Core Companion*, pp. 15–40, 54–66; 202–213

L2 **EL** *Hear It!* Audio CD

All resources, including print and audio, are available online at www.PHLitOnline.com.

Daily Bellringer

For each class during which you will teach this selection, have students complete one of the five Sentence Combining activities for Week 36 in the *Daily Bellringer Activities* booklet.

② Writing About the Big Question

1. Introduce the assignment.

2. Lead the class in a discussion of why people don't always get along. Write some of your students' best ideas on the board (*you find different things important, you don't share the same sense of humor, you are competing for the same things*).

3. Have students complete the sentence starter. Review responses as a class. (**Sample response:** A common difficulty in getting along with others is *you can't appreciate the other person's strengths* because *you are competing for the same things.*)

4. Tell students that as they read, they should think about whether the morals of the selections emphasize the importance of the individual or the community.

Concept Connector ➡

Students will return to their sentence starters after reading.

Multidraft Reading

To assist struggling readers and to deepen reading for all, apply multidraft reading protocols. For each reading, have students set the purpose indicated:

• **First reading**—identifying key ideas and details and answering any Reading Checks.

• **Second reading**—analyzing craft and structure and responding to the side-column prompts.

• **Third reading**—integrating knowledge and ideas, connecting to other texts and the world, and answering the end-of-selection questions.

For more guidance, see the *Classroom Strategies and Teaching Routine* card on multidraft reading.

PHLit Online!

For more about the authors, practice with the selection vocabulary, or more background, go online at www.PHLitOnline.com.

1035

❶ Background
Fables

A fable is a short tale that imparts a useful truth, or moral. William Cleary's poem is based on Aesop's fable. Both works teach a lesson about flattery, although in different tones.

❷ Activating Prior Knowledge

Have students think about what kind of fable they would be interested in writing and the moral it would impart.

Concept Connector ➡

Students will follow up on this activity after completing the poem.

❸ About the Selection

"The Fox Outwits the Crow" is a poetic version of Aesop's fable. It is written in rhyme and includes speech and imagery not usually associated with fables.

❶ ❷ ❸

The Fox Outwits the Crow
William Cleary

1036 Themes in the Oral Tradition

©️ Text Complexity Rubric

The Fox Outwits the Crow; The Fox and the Crow		
Qualitative Measures	**Context/Knowledge Demands**	Fables; opera singing 1 2 ③ 4 5
	Structure/Language Conventionality	Informal, casual, and humorous language; formal diction Some subject-specific vocabulary, footnoted 1 2 ③ 4 5
	Levels of Meaning/ Purpose/Concepts	Accessible concept (fox outwits crow) 1 2 ③ 4 5
Quantitative Measures	**Text Length**	Word Count: 142, 164
	Lexile	NP, 730L

One day a young crow snatched a fat piece of cheese
From the porch of a house made of stone,
Then she flew to the top of a Juniper Tree
To enjoy her good fortune alone.

But a fox passing by got a *whiff* of the cheese,
The best of his favorite *hors d'oeuvres,*
So he called to the crow, *Hey, you glamorous thing,*
Does your voice match your beautiful curves?

The crow was so pleased by the flattering words
She quickly took out a libretto,[1]
How fondly that fox will listen, she thought,
To hear how I caw in falsetto.[2]

She opened her mouth—and the cheese tumbled out,
Which the fox gobbled up full of *malice*
While he chuckled to think how that dim-witted crow
Could believe she was MARIA CALLAS.[3]

MORAL: Attending to flattery comes at a high price.

---

1. **libretto** (li bret′ ō) *n.* the text of an opera.
2. **falsetto** (fôl set′ ō) *n.* an artificially high voice.
3. **Maria Callas** (kal′ əs) (1923–1977) U.S. opera singer.

Critical Thinking

1. Key Ideas and Details (a) What does the crow think after the fox flatters her? **(b) Analyze:** What do her thoughts reveal about the crow?

2. Key Ideas and Details (a) To what does the poet compare the crow's voice? **(b) Support:** Why is this amusing?

3. Key Ideas and Details (a) Connect: How do the characters' actions support the moral? Explain. **(b) Evaluate:** Is this an easy or difficult lesson to learn? Explain.

4. Integration of Knowledge and Ideas (a) Who was more to blame—the crow or the fox? Explain. **(b)** Would you rather have someone like the crow or the fox in your community? Explain. *[Connect to the Big Question: Community or individual—which is more important?]*

Cite textual evidence to support your responses.

Vocabulary

whiff (hwif) *n.* smell; scent

hors d'oeuvres (ôr′ dɜrvz′) *n.* savory foods served as appetizers

malice (mal′ is) *n.* ill will

4 Tone
What details indicate that Cleary's attitude is playful?

---

4 Tone

1. Remind students that word choice and the use of rhythm and rhyme contribute to a writer's tone, or attitude.
2. **Ask** the Tone question. **Answer:** The poem has a lively rhythm, and Cleary uses humor in describing the encounter between the characters.

Critical Thinking

Before students respond, you may wish to have them write a brief objective summary of the selection. As they answer the questions below, remind them to support their answers with evidence from the text.

1. (a) She is pleased and flattered. (b) They show that she is vain.

2. (a) The fox compares the crow's voice to her "beautiful curves." (b) **Possible response:** A crow isn't usually thought to be the most attractive of birds.

3. (a) Believing the flattering words led the crow to lose her cheese. (b) **Possible response:** It is difficult because we all like to be praised.

4. (a) **Possible responses:** The fox has the motive of stealing, so he is guiltier than the crow. She is simply susceptible to flattery—as many people are. (b) Some students will say they would rather have the crow, because she is an innocent victim. Others will say they prefer the

---

C Text Complexity: Reader and Task Suggestions

The Fox Outwits the Crow; The Fox and the Crow	
Preparing to Read the Text	**Leveled Tasks**
• Using the Background note on p. 1036, review the features of fables, such as morals; using the Background note on p. 1038, discuss Aesop and the types of fables credited to him. • Review strategies for reading rhymed poetry, including when to pause during long sentences; review strategies for reading symbolism, for example, renaming each character with the name of its symbolic quality. • Guide students to use Multidraft Reading strategies (TE p. 1035).	***Levels of Meaning*** If students will have difficulty with levels of meaning, have them first read to identify the morals. Then, have them reread, noting everything they can about each character. As needed, help students link each character to a moral quality. ***Synthesizing*** If students will not have difficulty with levels of meaning, have them explain the moral of each selection in their own words. Then, have them give examples of how these morals might apply to the real world.

This selection is available in interactive format in the **Enriched Online Student Edition**, at **www.PHLitOnline.com**, which includes an interactive graphic organizer.

❺ Background

Aesop

Although very little is actually known about the true origins of Aesop's fables, he has been credited with over 600. Subjects include gratitude, the deceptiveness of appearances, and the necessity of thrift.

❻ Activating Prior Knowledge

As students read the fable and compare its tone to that of the poem, have them continue to think about what kind of fable they would be interested in writing, and its moral.

Concept Connector ➡

Students will follow up on this activity after completing the fable.

❼ About the Selection

"The Fox and the Crow" is a traditional version of the fable by Aesop. Note that in the first paragraph the fox is referred to by a proper name, which is explained in a footnote.

Critical Thinking

Before students respond, you may wish to have them write a brief objective summary of the selection. As they answer the questions below, remind them to support their answers with evidence from the text.

1. (a) The Fox flatters the Crow. (b) He stops flattering her and becomes disdainful.

2. (a) The Fox represents greed and trickery. The Crow represents vanity. (b) The Fox wants the cheese and resorts to trickery. The Crow lifts her head and caws after the Fox flatters her.

3. **Possible responses:** If people stopped believing in false flattery, there would be no reason to do it. That might create a better community.

---

❺ ❻ ❼ THE FOX AND THE CROW
AESOP

A Fox once saw a Crow fly off with a piece of cheese in its beak and settle on a branch of a tree. "That's for me, as I am a Fox," said Master Reynard,[1] and he walked up to the foot of the tree.

"Good day, Mistress Crow," he cried. "How well you are looking today: how glossy your feathers; how bright your eye. I feel sure your voice must surpass that of other birds, just as your figure does; let me hear but one song from you that I may greet you as the Queen of Birds."

The Crow lifted up her head and began to caw her best, but the moment she opened her mouth the piece of cheese fell to the ground, only to be snapped up by Master Fox. "That will do," said he. "That was all I wanted. In exchange for your cheese I will give you a piece of advice for the future—

MORAL: Do not trust flatterers."

---

1. **Master Reynard** (rĕn´ ərd) the fox in the medieval beast epic *Reynard the Fox*; therefore, a proper name for the fox in other stories.

Vocabulary
glossy (glôs´ ē) *adj.* smooth and shiny

surpass (sər pas´) *v.* be superior to

flatterers (flat´ ər ərz) *n.* those who praise a person insincerely

---

Critical Thinking

Cite textual evidence to support your responses.

1. Key Ideas and Details (a) How does the Fox persuade the Crow to drop the piece of cheese? **(b) Infer:** How does the Fox's attitude change when he gets the cheese?

2. Craft and Structure (a) Draw Conclusions: What human character traits do the animal characters in the fable represent? **(b) Support:** What details in the fable support your answer?

3. Integration of Knowledge and Ideas How could learning the moral of this story help people in communities get along better? *[Connect to the Big Question: Community or individual—which is more important?]*

Vocabulary Development

Vocabulary Knowledge Rating
When students have completed reading and discussing "The Fox Outwits the Crow" and "The Fox and the Crow," have them take out their **Vocabulary Knowledge Rating Chart.** Read the words aloud once more and have students rate their knowledge of the words again in the After Reading column. Clarify any words that are still problematic. Have students write their own definition and example or sentence in the appropriate column. Then have students complete the Vocabulary Practice activities on the next page. Encourage students to use the words in further discussion and written work about these selections. Remind them that they will be accountable for these words on the **Selection Test** (*Unit 6 Resources,* pp. 216–218 or 219–221.)

Comparing Tone and Theme

1. **Key Ideas and Details** Compare the tone of the fable "The Fox and the Crow" with that of the poem "The Fox Outwits the Crow" by completing a diagram like this one.

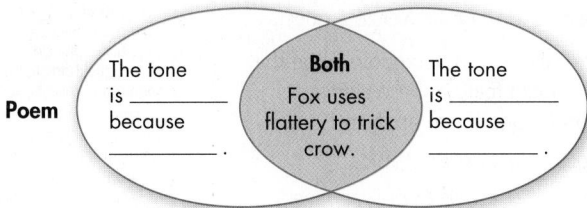

Poem

The tone is _____ because _____ .

Both

Fox uses flattery to trick crow.

The tone is _____ because _____ .

Fable

2. **Key Ideas and Details** Explain the theme of each selection in your own words.

3. **Craft and Structure** **(a)** Explain how the structure of the poem—its division into stanzas and use of rhyme—adds to its effect. **(b)** Are poems or fables better for teaching lessons? Why?

⏱ Timed Writing

Explanatory Text: Essay

In an essay, compare the relationship between tone and theme in each selection. **(40 minutes)**

5-Minute Planner

1. Read the prompt carefully and completely.

2. Reread and take notes on the tone of each selection. Support your ideas with concrete details and examples from the selections. Then, jot down whether the genre affected the tone. Finally, analyze the effect of tone on the theme. Gather your ideas by jotting down answers to these questions:

   - What is each writer's tone, or attitude, toward the characters?
   - In what ways did the genre affect the presentation of story events?
   - What is the theme of each selection?
   - Which selection illustrates its theme more effectively?

3. Reread the prompt, and then draft your essay.

The Fox Outwits the Crow • The Fox and the Crow **1039**

Comparing Tone and Theme

1. Students' responses should include references to the poetic structure of "The Fox Outwits the Crow" and its use of humor in contrast to Aesop's more formal, serious tone. Sample answers can also be found on **Comparing Tone and Theme Graphic Organizer A**, *Graphic Organizer Transparencies* p. 202.

2. **Possible responses:** Students should point out that the poem and the fable have the same theme. It can be stated as *don't listen to sweet talk; if something sounds too good to be true, it probably is;* or *those who listen to flattery lose their lunch.*

3. **Possible responses: (a)** The division into stanzas in which the viewpoint of the crow alternates with that of the fox helps the poet tell the fable from different perspectives. The rhyme helps create a whimsical tone. **(b)** The more serious, formal tone of the fable underlines the importance of learning a lesson. The humor and whimsy of the poem make learning a lesson seem secondary.

⏱ Timed Writing

1. Review the prompt with students.

2. Have students use the 5-Minute Planner to structure their time. Guide them in answering the bulleted questions. For example, point out that the first bulleted point might lead them to focus on whether it seems that the writer thinks the characters are funny or silly, or something else entirely.

3. Allow students 40 minutes to complete the assignment.

4. As students prewrite and draft, have them refer to their completed **Comparing Tone and Theme Graphic Organizer.**

Six Traits Focus

✔	Ideas	✔	Word Choice
✔	Organization		Sentence Fluency
	Voice		Conventions

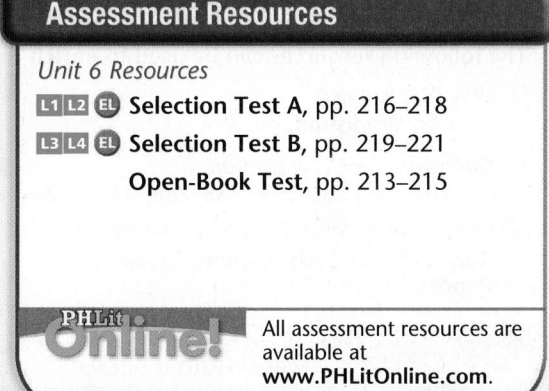

Assessment Resources

Unit 6 Resources

L1 L2 EL **Selection Test A,** pp. 216–218

L3 L4 EL **Selection Test B,** pp. 219–221

Open-Book Test, pp. 213–215

PHLit Online!

All assessment resources are available at **www.PHLitOnline.com.**

1039

Introducing the Writing Assignment

Review the assignment and the criteria, using the instruction on the student page.

Jon Scieszka on Research

Show students Segment 3 on Jon Scieszka on *See It! DVD*. Discuss Scieszka's comment about the research he did for *Time Warp Trio*.

 Writing Workshop
Work in Progress

If students have completed the Work-in-Progress assignments on pp. 1005 and 1025, suggest that they consider developing their Work-in-Progress ideas in a research report.

What Do You Notice?

1. Have a volunteer read the quotation aloud. **Ask** students the first question: What do you notice about the passage? (**Possible response:** Each sentence explains a piece of related legislation.)

2. Guide students in examining Barbara Jordan's use of dependent clauses. **Ask** them how the second clause in the first sentence builds on the first. (**Possible response:** It adds detail that emphasizes the importance of the legislation.)

3. **Ask** the second question: What factual evidence does the writer provide? (**Possible response:** She gives names and dates of the pieces of legislation.)

4. Encourage students to use dependent clauses for adding detail as they draft.

1040

Writing Workshop

Write an Informative Text

Research: Research Report

Defining the Form A **research report** analyzes information gathered from reference materials, observations, interviews, or other sources to present a clear and accurate picture of a topic or answer to a question.

Assignment Write a research report about a contemporary issue that interests or affects you. Your report should feature these elements:
✔ an overall *focused topic* or main idea to be analyzed
✔ *relevant and tightly drawn questions* on the topic
✔ a thesis statement with a *clear and accurate perspective*
✔ a *clear organization* and *smooth transitions*
✔ *appropriate facts* and *relevant details* to support main point
✔ visuals or media to support key ideas
✔ accurate, *complete citations* identifying research materials by means of *footnotes* or *bibliography*
✔ a strong *concluding statement*

To preview the criteria on which your research report may be judged, see the rubric on page 1049.

 Writing Workshop: *Work in Progress*

Review the work you did on pages 1005 and 1025.

WRITE GUY
Jeff Anderson, M.Ed.

What Do You Notice?

Facts and Details

The following passage is from Barbara Jordan's "All Together Now."

President Lyndon B. Johnson pushed through the Civil Rights Act of 1964, which remains the fundamental piece of civil rights legislation in this century. The Voting Rights Act of 1965 ensured that everyone in our country could vote.

Discuss these questions with a partner:
• What do you notice about the passage?
• What factual evidence does the writer provide?

Think about ways you can support your writing with research.

1040 Themes in the Oral Tradition

Teaching Resources

The following resources can be used to enrich or extend the instruction.

All *Unit 6 Resources*
 Writing Workshop, pp. 118–119

All *Common Core Companion,*
 pp. 202–212, 232–239, 258–284; 333–342

All *Professional Development Guidebook*
 Rubrics for Self-Assessment: Research Report, pp. 242–243

All *Graphic Organizer Transparencies*
 Rubric for Self-Assessment: Research Report, p. 204

All *See It!* DVD
 Jon Scieszka

 All resources, including print and video, are available online at www.PHLitOnline.com.

Prewriting/Planning Strategies

Watch and browse. Look through print, multimedia, and digital sources, such as recent magazines or newspapers, newscasts, and the Internet. List current events, issues, or subjects of interest and the questions they spark in you. Choose your topic from among these ideas.

After you choose your topic, make sure it is narrow enough to cover in a short report. For example, "illiteracy" is too broad a topic for a research paper. Narrow the topic by asking focused questions such as "How serious a problem is illiteracy in the United States?"

Use a variety of primary and secondary sources. Use both **primary sources** (firsthand or original accounts, such as interview transcripts and newspaper articles) and **secondary sources** (accounts that are not original, such as encyclopedia entries or an online library catalog) in your research.

Determine topics or key terms and check for them in indexes or type them into search engines. Prioritize information essential to your report. Collect relevant and objective, or neutral, information. Ensure the credibility and accuracy of each source. Crosscheck information from the Internet or an interview whenever possible by consulting printed sources.

Take notes. Use different strategies to take notes:

- Use index cards to create note cards and source cards. Write one note per card and note the source and page number.
- Photocopy articles and copyright pages; then highlight relevant information.
- Print articles from the Internet or copy them directly into a "notes" folder.

You will use these notes to help you write original text.

Record your research. Copying from sources without citing them is **plagiarism,** an act that has serious academic and legal consequences. Without giving credit to a source, you are stealing another person's words. It is important to use ethical practices when conducting research.

Whether you are paraphrasing, summarizing, or using a direct quotation, you must credit the source. You can give credit by writing a *bibliography*, a list of the print and nonprint sources you have used. Review pages R34–R35 to see the appropriate format for citing sources in a bibliography.

PHLit Online!
www.PHLitOnline.com

- Author video: Writing Process
- Author video: Rewards of Writing

Note Card

> **Education**
> Papp, p.5
>
> Only the upper classes could read.
>
> Most of the common people in Shakespeare's time could not read.

Source Card

> Papp, Joseph
> and Kirkland, Elizabeth
>
> **Shakespeare Alive!**
>
> New York: Bantam Books, 1988

Applying Understanding by Design Principles

Clarifying Expected Outcomes: Using Rubrics

- Before students begin work on this assignment, have them preview the Rubric for Self-Assessment (p. 1049) to know what is expected. A copy of this rubric appears in the *Graphic Organizer Transparencies,* p. 204.
- Review the criteria in the Rubric with the class. Before students use the Rubric to assess their own writing, work with them to rate the Student Model (pp. 1046–1048) using the Rubric.

- If you wish to assess students' autobiographical narratives with either a 4-point or a 6-point scoring rubric, see the *Professional Development Guidebook,* pp. 242–243.

Prewriting/Planning Strategies

1. Introduce the prewriting strategies.
2. Have students apply the strategies to choose a topic.

Teaching the Strategies

1. Tell students that they should attempt a search on the key words in the question. If the search turns up too many sources, students will need to further narrow their topic. If only a few sources appear, students will need to broaden their topic.
2. Students using the Internet should seek out articles by authors who are experts in their field. If students have doubts about the reliability of a source, they should check with a librarian.

Think Aloud: Model Avoiding Plagiarism

Say to students:

> I don't want other people to take credit for what I do, so I need to give credit to other people for their work, too. It's important to give credit for the information I use because that represents someone's time, thought, and work. I have to tell my readers where I got my information. For example, I read an article stating that people earn more money if they have a high school diploma. I write: *People who complete high school earn more money.* I need to add a citation showing that this information came from that article. By citing the article, I am giving credit to the people who did the work.

Six Traits Focus

✔ Ideas	Word Choice
✔ Organization	Sentence Fluency
Voice	Conventions

PH WRITING COACH Grade 7

Students will find additional information on writing a research report in Chapter 11.

Drafting Strategies

1. Introduce the drafting strategies, using the instruction on the student page.

2. Have students apply the strategies as they draft.

Teaching the Strategies

1. Tell students that a thesis statement presents an argument or a theory. The goal of writing a research report is to support the thesis with examples, facts, and details.

2. Call students' attention to the outline graphic format. Note that the outline moves from the general (main point) to the specific (supporting detail).

3. Remind students that they should have at least two supporting details for each main point in their outline. Additional subpoints added under the capital letters should be numbered with Arabic numerals.

Think Aloud: Model Using Graphics

Model using graphics to enhance a report, using the following "think aloud." Say to students:

I can use graphics to improve the impact of a research report. If I am writing a report about global warming, for instance, I might want to include a spreadsheet or chart that shows the decline in certain species over the last fifty years. In addition, I could add to my report's strength by preparing maps that show the current climate ranges in different countries compared to what they once were. When I use graphics, I make sure that they clarify and add to the written information I have prepared.

Six Traits Focus

✔	Ideas		Word Choice
✔	Organization		Sentence Fluency
	Voice		Conventions

Drafting Strategies

Develop a main idea or thesis. Review your prewriting notes to determine the overall focus of your report. Then, write a sentence that expresses your main idea. This sentence is called a **thesis statement.** As you draft, add facts, details, statistics, and examples that support and develop your thesis statement. **Thesis:** *Whales are among the most intelligent mammals on Earth.*

Supporting detail: *Whales have developed an elaborate series of sounds that serves as a language that allows them to communicate across vast stretches of water.*

Pose relevant questions. When you research, you may come up with more questions about your topic. The questions you ask yourself should be relevant to your thesis and tightly drawn. This means you should not stray too far from the perspective you convey in your report.

Make an outline. Group your prewriting notes by category. Use Roman numerals (I, II, III) to number your most important points. Under each Roman numeral, use capital letters (A, B, C) for the supporting details. Use your outline as a guide for developing your draft by turning your draft, notes into complete sentences. As you draft, review the data you have collected.

- Refer to the notes you made on index cards in the prewriting and researching stage.

- Confirm that the supporting details you include directly relate to the thesis statement.

- Delete any irrelevant information you have gathered.

Include visuals to support key ideas. Using charts or other visual aids allows you to present detailed information that might otherwise interrupt the flow of your report. In your writing, introduce the visual and explain its purpose. Direct readers to reference these aids as needed. To create visual aids, carry out these steps:

- Use databases and spreadsheets to organize, manage, and prepare information for your report.

- Clarify your charts, graphs, and tables by using headings and adding appropriate spacing.

- Vary the color and design of your visual aids as you display different types of information.

Provide a satisfying conclusion. Your conclusion should bring together your main ideas logically in a way that *proves* your thesis statement for the reader. For example, if your thesis is about the causes of the Civil War and the body of your report analyzes these causes in detail, your conclusion would show how these related causes combined to produce a war.

 Common Core State Standards

Writing

2.a. Include formatting, graphics, and multimedia when useful to aiding comprehension.

2.b. Develop the topic with relevant facts, definitions, concrete details, quotations, or other information and examples.

2.f. Provide a concluding statement or section that follows from and supports the information or explanation presented.

7. Conduct short research projects to answer a question, drawing on several sources and generating additional related, focused questions for further research and investigation.

9. Draw evidence from literary or informational texts to support analysis, reflection, and research.

Outline format

Thesis Statement
 I. First main point
   A. First supporting detail
   B. Second supporting detail
II. Second main point
   A. First supporting detail
   B. Second supporting detail

Writers on Writing

Jon Scieszka On Using Research in Fiction

Jon Scieszka is the author of "Grasshopper Logic" (p. 908) and "Duckbilled Platypus vs. BeefSnakStik®" (p. 910) from *Squids Will Be Squids* and "The Other Frog Prince" from *The Stinky Cheese Man and Other Fairly Stupid Tales* (p. 909).

Here's an early draft of the beginning of a *Time Warp Trio* novel. The Time Warp guys can travel anywhere in time. So to make their adventures come alive, I have to know every detail I can about the place and time they travel to—in this case, Italy hundreds of years ago.

I read everything I can find for at least a month before I start writing. I want to know what kind of food people of that time and place ate, how they brushed their teeth, what they wore for underwear.

"I do research . . . to learn about the history of stories."
— Jon Scieszka

Professional Model:

from *"Da Wild, Da Crazy, Da Vinci"*

"Ready! . . . Aim! . . ."

"Wait," yelled Sam. He fixed his glasses to ~~get~~ take a better look ~~around.~~ "~~I think~~ We're supposed to be in Italy." .

Fred, Sam, and I were standing with our backs to a steep, sandy hill. ~~In front of us sat~~ It looked like it could be Italy. But there was a ~~scary~~ strange-looking invention sitting in front of us— a wooden, flying-saucer-shaped thing, about as big as an ice cream truck.

~~But that~~ The size wasn't the scary part. The scary part was the guns sticking out of it. The even scarier part was knowing the word that usually comes after "Ready! Aim!"

"You're ~~both~~ lucky we didn't end up in a giant toilet," said Fred. "But now you better figure out what to do about those guns pointed our way."

All of the *Time Warp* books start in the middle of some action. I figured these would be two great action words that everyone knows.

The challenge in writing history-based fiction is to introduce the real history in a natural way. This tank really was one of Italian artist Leonardo da Vinci's inventions.

My characters set up the history for me. Here Fred mentions an invention we find out about later—the flush toilet.

Writing Workshop **1043**

Jon Scieszka on Using Research in Fiction

Teaching From the Professional Model

1. Show students Segment 4 on Jon Scieszka on the *See It! DVD* or from the link on this page online at **www.PHLitOnline**. Review the passage on the student page with the class, using Jon Scieszka's comments to deepen students' understanding about how to conduct effective research.

2. Review Scieszka's revisions. Note how he helps the reader visualize something they've never seen by comparing it to familiar images (flying saucer, ice cream truck). Discuss how students might apply this technique to their own writing.

Show or assign the video online at **www.PHLitOnline.com**.

Strategies for Technology

Students who use word-processing programs will find the copy-and-paste function useful. As they revise, they can reorganize, print, and preview a change. If they think the original was better, they can then revert to the original. To use the copy-and-paste functions, students should highlight the text to be copied. Then, they can access the Copy function by scrolling down under the Edit menu. They will need to place the cursor at the point where they want to paste the text, then click on Paste under the Edit menu. Remind students to delete the text from its original position after it has been pasted.

1043

Revising Strategies

1. Introduce the revising strategies, using the instruction on the student page.

2. Have students apply the strategies as they revise.

Teaching the Strategies

Review strategies for varying sentence length, such as using compound subjects and predicates, and introductory clauses. Have students combine the following pairs of choppy sentences:

Sharks terrify most people. Sharks seldom attack humans.
(**Possible response:** Although sharks terrify most people, they seldom attack humans.)

The koala's diet consists of eucalyptus leaves. The eucalyptus is an Australian evergreen.
(**Possible response:** The koala's diet consists of the leaves of the eucalyptus tree, an Australian evergreen.

Aristotle was a philosopher from ancient Greece. Plato was also a Greek philosopher.
(**Possible response:** Aristotle and Plato were both philosophers from ancient Greece.)

Think Aloud: Model Adding Transitions

Model the strategy of adding transitions to show cause and effect, using the following "think aloud." Say to students:

Suppose I am writing a research report about the invention of the elevator, and I want to show cause and effect. I include transition words to show how the elevator's development had an impact on other events. For instance, I can write, *As a result of the invention of the modern elevator, architects were able to design tall city buildings.* Here's another example: *Early elevators were used to haul freight. Therefore, the work of moving large objects from one place to another became easier and quicker.* By adding transitions that show cause and effect, I connect ideas for the reader.

Six Traits Focus

✔ Ideas	✔ Word Choice
✔ Organization	✔ Sentence Fluency
Voice	Conventions

Revising Strategies

Analyze your organization. Look over your draft and analyze your organization to see if it matches your outline. Stop at the end of each paragraph and refer to your outline. Follow these steps:

1. Mark each paragraph with the Roman numeral and capital letter from your outline and write a key word or phrase to identify the subject of the paragraph.

2. If all the paragraphs with the same Roman numeral are not next to each other, decide whether the change is an improvement. If it is not, correct it.

Check your facts. Read through your draft to verify that the facts, statistics, and quotations you cite are accurate. Don't rely on your memory—refer to the original source material as you work. With the exception of direct quotations, be sure you have written the information in your own words.

Vary sentence length. To add interest to your writing, vary the length of your sentences. Underline or highlight sentences in your draft in alternating colors so you can easily see differences in length. Then, review your color coding. Combine short, choppy sentences or break up longer sentences if there are too many of either.

> **Model: Revising to Vary Sentence Length**
> Basketball has been played in various forms for hundreds of years. The modern sport was introduced in 1891. An instructor at a YMCA was looking to keep his students active during the long New England winters.
>
> The basketball hoop was made from a peach basket. The basket had a closed bottom. Soon, the players realized that if they removed the bottom, the game could be played quicker.

Review

Ask a classmate, your teacher, or another adult to read your report to determine if the organization of your draft is clear. If your reader finds areas that require transitions, consider revising your draft by adding a word, phrase, or sentence that shows the connection between your paragraphs. Use transitions such as *at first, finally,* or *as a result* to show relationships between ideas.

Ask the reader for feedback as to whether or not you have supported your thesis statement adequately. Revise your report as needed based on your reviewer's comments.

Common Core State Standards

Writing

2.c. Use appropriate transitions to create cohesion and clarify the relationships among ideas and concepts.

5. With some guidance and support from peers and adults, develop and strengthen writing as needed by revising, focusing on how well purpose and audience have been addressed.

8. Assess the credibility and accuracy of each source; and quote or paraphrase the data and conclusions of others while avoiding plagiarism and following a standard format for citation.

Language

1. Demonstrate command of the conventions of standard English grammar and usage when writing.

Revising to Correct Use of Pronoun Case

Many pronouns change form according to usage. *Case* is the relationship between a pronoun's form and its use.

Personal Pronouns	
Nominative Case	**Objective Case**
I, we	me, us
you	you
he, she, it, they	him, her, it, them

Using Personal Pronouns Personal pronouns in the **nominative case** may be the subject of a verb or a predicate nominative—a noun or pronoun that renames the subject.

Subject: <u>She</u> plays soccer. Cassie and <u>I</u> play soccer, too.

Predicate Nominative: Beckham's biggest fans are Jenna and <u>I</u>.

Personal pronouns in the **objective case** have three uses: as a direct object, as an indirect object, and as the object of a preposition.

Direct Object: Jason invited Raf and <u>me</u> to the game.

Indirect Object: Paul had given <u>him</u> two extra tickets.

Object of a Preposition: All three of <u>us</u> were grateful to <u>him</u>.

Fixing Incorrect Use of Personal Pronouns Mistakes with pronouns usually occur when the subject or object is compound.

1. **To test a pronoun in a compound subject, use just the pronoun with the verb in the sentence.** For example, in the sentence, "Cassie and me play soccer," "me play" clearly sounds wrong. The nominative case *I* is needed.

2. **To test a pronoun in a compound object, use the pronoun by itself after the verb or preposition.** For example, in the sentence, "Jason invited Raf and I to the game," "Jason invited I" sounds wrong. The objective case *me* is needed.

Grammar in Your Writing

Choose two paragraphs in your draft. Underline every sentence that contains a pronoun as part of a compound subject or a compound object. Use the methods above to fix any pronouns used incorrectly.

> **PH** **WRITING COACH**
>
> Further instruction and practice are available in *Prentice Hall Writing Coach*.

Revising to Correct Use of Pronoun Case

1. Introduce the grammar skill, using the instruction on the student page.

2. Discuss the rules and examples, as well as the strategies for fixing incorrect usage.

3. Have students follow the instruction under Grammar in Your Writing to correct errors in their drafts.

Teaching the Grammar Skill

Students may make errors in case when using personal pronouns. Have students identify and fix any errors in the following sentences.

Mrs. Lee will drive Ben and she to the basketball game. (**Answer:** incorrect; Mrs. Lee will drive Ben and her to the basketball game.)

He and I both passed the swimming test. (**Answer:** correct)

The teacher gave her and me passes to the library. (**Answer:** correct)

The two best players on the team are him and Stanley. (**Answer:** incorrect; The two best players on the team are he and Stanley.)

Us five girls have been friends since first grade. (**Answer:** incorrect; We five girls have been friends since first grade.)

Differentiated
Instruction   for Universal Access

EL Strategies for English Learners

A strong thesis statement is crucial to a successful report. To help students achieve a strong opening, encourage them to test various forms of openings for their papers. Have students write a potential first sentence as a question or description, or encourage them to open with an impressive fact or quotation. Then, they can choose the strongest opening.

Strategies for Advanced Readers

Tell students that they must evaluate the sources of information they use for their research. They should consider the topic's relevance, author's credentials, publisher's respectability, and publication date. Provide students with several books, magazines, newspapers, and other sources on a particular topic, such as the intelligence of dolphins. Then, have students decide which sources are relevant and reliable.

Review the Student Model with the class, using the annotations to analyze the writer's use of the elements of a research report.

Teaching From the Student Model

1. Have students read through the model and annotations. Have students examine the elements or features that are identified, analyze the effects of these elements on the model, and consider how to apply these in their own writing.

2. Ask students to identify the thesis statement. (**Answer:** "My hypothesis is that an incubator can provide the right external conditions more effectively and efficiently.")

Student Model: Laura Agajanian, Santa Clara, CA

Hatching Chirpers

A hen's egg is an amazing thing. Sitting in the nest, it seems as if it is an inanimate, or lifeless, object, but it contains everything that is needed to make a chick. In order for the chick to grow inside the egg, however, the right external conditions are needed. Under normal circumstances, these conditions are provided by the hen. They can also be reproduced and regulated in an incubator. My investigation was to discover whether the hen or the incubator would more efficiently and effectively provide the right external conditions. My hypothesis is that an incubator can provide the right external conditions more effectively and efficiently. Let's find out.

A chicken egg should take about twenty-one days to incubate, or take form. During that time, the eggs must be kept warm. The ideal temperature is between 99 and 100 degrees Fahrenheit. In addition, the eggs must be rotated, or turned, every eight to twelve hours. If they remain in one position for longer than that, the chick can become stuck to one side of the egg and may not form properly (Johnson 14–16).

Usually, the temperature and the turning are handled by the hen that sits on the nest. She regulates the temperature of the eggs by getting off the nest or standing above the eggs if the eggs begin to get too warm. When they have had some time to cool, she gets back on the nest. The hen turns the eggs by poking at them with her beak until each egg rolls a little to one side, eventually turning from its original position (Scott).

An incubator performs these same functions. The temperature inside the incubator is measured and regulated by a thermostat that tells the heater when to turn on and when to turn off. In this way, the temperature of the eggs is kept at a constant 99 degrees. The eggs sit on a device that rolls them every eight hours. This device is controlled by an electronic timer. It is dependable because it is automatic and does not require a person to push a button for the eggs to turn. It is more efficient than a hen, because all the eggs get turned equally and consistently (Little Giant 2–6).

In the first paragraph, Laura identifies her main topic, the question she is investigating. In this science report, she provides a hypothesis— a proposition that the research will prove or disprove. This statement gives her perspective or viewpoint on the topic.

Accurate facts and details gathered through the formal research process are presented. Since these are specific statistics that a reader might want to check, the writer gives the source.

The report is organized to give balanced information about both methods being investigated—natural hatching and incubation.

Based on the fact that conditions in the incubator are more consistent and controlled, I concluded that an incubator sets the ideal conditions more efficiently, and I hypothesized that it would hatch eggs more effectively. To test my hypothesis, I observed four hens sitting on a total of twenty-four eggs and placed twenty-four eggs in an incubator. Each egg was marked with a small *x* so that I could observe how frequently and completely each egg was turned. Chart A shows specific observations over a twenty-five-day period.

Detailed information that would interrupt the flow of the report is presented in a separate chart for readers to reference as needed.

Chart A

Day	Incubator Observations	Nest Observations
Day 1	**6:45 AM:** After placing the turner in the incubator, I put the 24 eggs on the turner. The temperature leveled off at 100 degrees. The eggs have warmed up quickly. **5:33 PM:** The turner is working efficiently—eggs are tilted appropriately.	**7:10 AM:** After placing the 24 eggs on the nests in the cage, I put food and water in the cage. Then, I placed the hens in the cage. **6:01 PM:** All hens are on the eggs.
Day 5	X marks on the eggs show that eggs have made a complete turn.	X marks on the eggs show that the eggs were not turned completely since I last checked.
Day 10	The turner seems to be tilting the eggs efficiently—X marks show a complete turn.	X marks show that 18 eggs were turned, but 6 were not.
Day 15	The temperature of the eggs is at a steady 100 degrees.	Two hens have moved off the nest for a brief time. Temperature of the eggs right now is 97 degrees.
Day 25	The incubator has hatched thirteen out of the twenty-four eggs.	The hens have hatched ten out of the twenty-four eggs.

3. Note how the chart provides a clear side-by-side comparison that enables the reader to quickly and easily evaluate the two methods. Encourage students to think of visual aids and graphic organizers that might improve their reports.

4. Discuss Laura's conclusion. Note that rather than merely restating her thesis statement, her conclusion incorporates a surprising observation gleaned from her research ("maybe 'ideal' conditions are not required for a successful hatch"). Point out that by including new insights, students can heighten the impact of their conclusions.

Connecting to Real-Life Writing

Explain to students that writing reports is an essential skill in many careers. Scientists, historians, lawyers, teachers, doctors, office workers, and literary critics write reports. Remind students that the main objective of a research report is to provide the reader with accurate information. Discuss with students other careers that require research writing, and have students consider what kinds of information workers in those careers would need to research.

In general, the incubator eggs received much more consistent attention to their condition. The machine did not need to stop to eat or exercise, as the hens did. The marks on the eggs showed that the eggs under the hens did not always get completely turned. Sometimes, some of the eggs were turned and some were not. In addition, the hens sometimes left the nest for as long as an hour. When the temperature of the eggs was measured after a hen had been gone a long time, the egg temperature was sometimes as low as 97 degrees.

After twenty-five days, the hens had hatched ten out of the twenty-four eggs, and the incubator had hatched thirteen. The difference between the two numbers is not great enough to say that one way of incubating is more effective than the other. The incubator is definitely more efficient at delivering ideal conditions than the hens were. However, since the increased efficiency does not result in a higher number of hatches, maybe "ideal" conditions are not required for a successful hatch.

Bibliography

Johnson, Sylvia A. *Inside an Egg.* Minneapolis: Lerner Publications Company, 1982.

Kruse Poultry Feed. *Care and Feeding of Baby Chicks.*

Little Giant Instruction Manual for Still Air Incubator and Automatic Egg Turner. Miller Mfg. Co., So. St. Paul, MN, 1998.

Scott, Wyatt. Personal Interview. 1 Dec. 2000.

Selsam, Millicent E. *Animals as Parents.* Canada: George J. McLeod Limited, 1965.

Common Core State Standards

Writing

8. Follow a standard format for citation.

Laura concludes by explaining whether the research did or did not support her original hypothesis.

In the bibliography, the writer lists all the works from which she gathered information used in her report. Some teachers prefer a "Works Cited" list, which lists only the sources that are actually cited, or noted, in a research report.

Editing and Proofreading

Focus on citations. Cite the sources for quotations, factual information, and ideas that are not your own. Some word-processing programs have features that allow you to create footnotes and endnotes. If you are using MLA style, citations should appear in parentheses directly after the information cited. Include the author's last name and the relevant page number.

Example: *The Atlantic Ocean has a total area of 41.1 million square miles (Smith 676).*

Publishing and Presenting

Create a reference list. Following the format your teacher prefers, create a bibliography or Works Cited list of the information you used to write your research report. (For more information, see Citing Sources, pp. R34–R35.)

Give an oral presentation. Use your research report as the basis for an oral presentation on your topic. Keep your audience in mind and revise accordingly as you prepare your presentation.

Reflecting on Your Writing

Writer's Journal Jot down your answer to this question:
What research strategy did you find most useful?

Rubric for Self-Assessment

Find evidence in your writing to address each category. Then, use the rating scale to grade your work.

Criteria	Rating Scale
	not very · · · very
Focus: How clearly stated is your thesis?	1 2 3 4 5
Organization: How effective is your organization of information?	1 2 3 4 5
Support/Elaboration: How accurate and thorough are your supporting facts and details?	1 2 3 4 5
Style: How smooth are your transitions?	1 2 3 4 5
Conventions: How complete and accurate are your citations?	1 2 3 4 5

Spiral Review
Earlier in the unit, you learned about **capitalization** (p. 1004) and **abbreviations** (p. 1024). Check your research report to be sure that you have used both capitalization and abbreviations correctly.

PH **WRITING COACH**

Further instruction and practice are available in *Prentice Hall Writing Coach.*

Editing and Proofreading

1. Introduce the editing and proofreading focus, using the instruction on the student page.
2. Have students edit and proofread their essays, correcting grammar, spelling, punctuation, and word choice. Make sure they look for errors of the type noted in the lesson focus and the Spiral Review.

Teaching the Editing Focus
Review the use of citations in the Student Model, which consist of the author's name and the page numbers in parentheses.

Six Traits Focus

Ideas	Word Choice
Organization	Sentence Fluency
Voice	✔ Conventions

ASSESS

Publishing and Presenting

1. Review the bibliography in the Student Model, noting the proper usage of punctuation, italics, and so on. Emphasize the importance of consistency when listing citations in a bibliography. Students should choose one approved style and adhere to its conventions. If a style is required, the students must use that style.
2. Students planning oral presentations should practice their delivery in front of a peer and ask for feedback on their gestures and facial expressions. If presenting to a younger audience, students should use simple language and be sure to explain any technical terms.

Reflecting on Your Writing

Suggest that students review their note cards to evaluate sources and identify the most interesting facts they learned during their research.

Figurative Language

1. Introduce the skill, using the instruction on the student page. Clarify that *literal* language means precisely what it says, word for word; in *figurative* language, the actual meaning is different from the word-for-word meaning.

2. Review the examples in the chart.

Think Aloud: Model the Skill

Model the skill of identifying figurative language. Say to students:

Figurative language can make communication clearer as well as more interesting. A simile or metaphor often compares something abstract or otherwise hard to understand to something concrete or easier to understand. When I use an analogy, I'm trying to make something unfamiliar clearer by comparing it to something familiar.

Practice A
Answers

1. metaphor
2. simile
3. metaphor
4. simile
5. metaphor

Vocabulary Workshop

Figurative Language

Figurative language is language that is not meant to be taken literally. Most types of figurative language are based on imaginative comparisons, lending ordinary things extraordinary qualities. The use of figurative language makes writing vivid and expressive. Refer to this chart to see common types of figurative language and examples of each.

Type of Figurative Language	Example
Simile: a comparison of two apparently unlike things using *like, as, than,* or *resembles.*	The sky is <u>like</u> a patchwork quilt.
Metaphor: a description of one thing as if it were another.	The sky <u>is</u> a patchwork quilt.
Analogy: an extended comparison of relationships. An analogy shows how the relationship between one pair of things is like the relationship between another pair.	Walter lives like a sheet of paper blown along a windy street. He is carried this way and that way with no control of his direction.
Personification: a figure of speech giving human characteristics to a nonhuman subject.	The <u>sea</u> was <u>angry</u> that day, my friends.
Paradox: a statement, an idea, or a situation that seems contradictory but actually expresses a truth.	The more things change, the more they stay the same.
Idiom: an expression whose meaning differs from the meanings of its individual words.	It was raining cats and dogs last night.

Practice A Identify each instance of figurative language in these sentences as a *simile* or *metaphor.*

1. Because I studied for several nights, the quiz was a breeze.

2. The winter night was so quiet that every sound was as clear as a bell.

3. Ivan's dog is the sunshine of his life.

4. After shoveling snow for several hours, I slept like a log last night.

5. A ghost of a moon shone over the fields.

1050 Themes in Oral Tradition

Practice B Identify the *simile, metaphor, idiom,* or *analogy* in each sentence. Then, use context clues to explain the meaning of each.

1. Tyrone understands people very well; he reads them like a book.
2. I tried to get my friend to change his mind, but he was a mule.
3. Two peas in a pod, Simon and Jack liked exactly the same music.
4. Seeing the fascinating art in the museum sparked my interest in sculpture.
5. After she won the diving competition, Elana was as happy as a lark.
6. Learning the times tables is like riding a bike; once you learn it, you never forget it.
7. After losing the concert tickets, Kevin was as mad as a hornet.
8. Her hair was a cloud of snowy white.

PHLit Online!
www.PHLitOnline.com
- Illustrated vocabulary words
- Interactive vocabulary games
- Vocabulary flashcards

Activity With a partner, browse through a current magazine. Search through the articles to find at least two examples of each type of figurative language. Use a note card like the one shown to list the examples you have found. Then, explain the meaning of each simile, metaphor, analogy, and idiom. Use the context clues in the article to help your understanding.

Similes:	
Metaphors:	
Analogies:	
Personifications:	
Paradoxes:	
Idioms:	

Comprehension and Collaboration

With a partner, write a scene with dialogue between two characters, taking care to use no figurative language. Then, rewrite the dialogue, adding idioms, analogies, similes, and metaphor. Compare your scenes. Which one sounds more realistic? Why?

1051

**Common Core
State Standards**

• **Speaking and Listening 4, 5, 6**

Research Presentation

These guidelines will help you through the processes of conducting research, writing a report, and presenting it to an audience.

Learn the Skills

Use these strategies to complete the activity on page 1053.

Generate questions. Consider what you would like to discover about your topic. Pose relevant and concise questions to guide your research and help you to stay on topic.

Evaluate your sources. Prepare to use both print and electronic sources, such as databases, the Internet, and magazines. Evaluate the credibility, scope, and objectivity of each source.

• Is the source known for its correct facts?
• Does a Web site have *.edu* or *.org* at the end of the Web address?
• Does the publication date fall within the last three years?

Organize your information. Take notes from each source to answer your research questions. Include only the information that is meaningful to your topic. Use your notes to develop an outline.

Write the report. Organize the report to include an introduction, several body paragraphs, and a conclusion. Avoid **plagiarism** by paraphrasing instead of copying information directly from each source. Credit your sources by citing them at the end of your report on a Bibliography or Works Cited page.

Present your report. Practice your presentation using the following techniques.

• Use graphics, such as charts, graphs, photographs, or a slide-show to enhance the main points in your report.
• Credit sources by using phrases like "According to . . ." and "In the book by . . . ."
• Vary your speaking rate and pitch to engage and retain your listeners' interest. Pronounce words clearly and speak loudly enough for everyone to hear.
• Use a natural but serious tone. Speak in formal English. For example, avoid "filler" phrases, such as "you know." Make eye contact and use hand gestures to emphasize certain points.

**Common Core
State Standards**

Speaking and Listening

4. Present claims and findings, emphasizing salient points in a focused, coherent manner with pertinent descriptions, facts, details, and examples; use appropriate eye contact, adequate volume, and clear pronunciation.

5. Include multimedia components and visual displays in presentations to clarify claims and findings and emphasize salient points.

6. Adapt speech to a variety of contexts and tasks, demonstrating command of formal English when indicated or appropriate.

Learn the Skills

1. Introduce the workshop, including the activity on page 1053.

2. Have students create a chart with the questions *Who?, What?, When?, Where?, Why?,* and *How?* in the first box of each column. Ask them to fill in the chart as they research their topic.

3. Explain that students must decide on the best sources to use. For example, for a presentation on a famous painter, they might use a biography. For a presentation on how to paint portraits, they would rely on art books.

4. Tell students there are many methods of taking notes. Note cards, electronic bookmarking, cutting and pasting, and titled pages are all types of note taking.

5. Review plagiarism. Tell students it is better to cite too much information for a source than to plagiarize.

6. Remind students that visual aids can help illustrate, clarify, or synthesize information. They can also make a presentation more interesting to watch.

Strategies for
Developing a Research Presentation

Guide students through the process of choosing a topic for a research presentation.

• Explain that students should pick a main topic that is narrow enough to cover in the time they have to make the presentation. For example, a topic like "trees" is probably too broad to cover in a short time.
• At the same time, the topic should be broad enough to fill the time in an interesting way. For example, the topic "why tree leaves have veins" is too narrow to remain interesting for long.

• Tell students to make sure there is enough reliable information available on their topic. For example, the topic "keeping cockroaches as pets" might not have enough sources available.
• Advise students to choose a topic they find interesting. Explain that the research process will go faster if they want to learn more about the topic.

Practice the Skills

© **Presentation of Knowledge and Ideas** Use the skills you learned in this Workshop to complete the following activity.

ACTIVITY: Delivering a Research Report

Prepare a research presentation by following the steps below. Then, deliver the report to your class.

- Develop your major research question.
- Gather research and organize your report.
- Present your research report to your classmates.
- Use the Research Guide to plan your report.

Use a Research Guide like the one below to develop your presentation.

Research Guide

Major Research Question:

Brainstorm to list ideas that address the research topic:

Open-ended research questions:

1.   3.

2.   4.

Research plan: Jot down notes explaining your plan for researching each question.

Assessment of sources: Briefly demonstrate the reliability and credibility of each source. Then, explain why one source is more useful than another.

Synthesize the research: Draw conclusions about and summarize or paraphrase each source to synthesize the research.
Conclusions: _____ Summary: _____

Organize your research: Think about your purpose and audience when you organize your presentation.
Purpose of the research: _____ Audience: _____

© **Comprehension and Collaboration** At the end of your presentation, invite your audience to discuss, respond to, or ask questions about your presentation. Then, listen to your classmates present their reports. Interpret the purpose of each report by explaining the content, evaluating the delivery of the presentation, and asking questions or making comments about the evidence that supports the claims.

Practice the Skills

1. Review the assignment with students. Invite students to work in small groups to develop their major research question, brainstorming to narrow their topics. Students should perform the other steps individually.

2. Explain to students that they should use a copy of the Research Guide to gather their research and to organize their topics.

3. Before students give their presentations to the class, remind listeners to ask questions if any points are unclear. To maintain order, encourage them to raise their hands and wait to be acknowledged by the presenter before stating their questions. Suggest that students making presentations scan the classroom from time to time so they will notice any students who have questions.

Evaluate the Activity

1. Evaluate students' presentations on the basis of the scope of their topic, the quality of their research, and the organization of the presentation.

2. When the class discusses the presentations that were most informative, encourage students to make note of the features of those presentations that made them effective and to incorporate those techniques in their future presentations.

Differentiated Instruction for Universal Access

Strategies for Special-Needs Students

The task of developing a research report can be overwhelming when students think about the entire task. Help students by carefully breaking the research report into small steps.

- Ask students to develop their topic.
- Check that the topic is not too broad or too narrow.
- Make sure there is information available.
- Help students generate questions to guide their research on the topic.

- Guide students in determining the types of sources that are most appropriate for the topic.
- Ask them to research the topic using the Internet. Help them determine which key words to use during the search.
- Continually remind students to focus on the step of the process they are working on. Tell them to try not to worry about the other steps.

Cumulative Review

In this Common Core Assessment Workshop (pp. 1054–1059), students apply and reinforce their mastery of the Common Core State Standards and the skills taught in Unit 6. The practice is divided into four sections, including a section of Performance Tasks addressing CCS Reading standards.

1. Before assigning each section, review the relevant Common Core State Standards and unit skills with students.

2. Set a time limit for the multiple-choice items in each section, allowing a little over one minute per question. Allow twenty minutes for any Timed Writing questions.

3. Administer each of the first three sections of the Cumulative Review (pp. 1054–1057).

4. Use the Performance Tasks on pages 1058–1059 to assess the depth of students' mastery of standards taught in the unit. Follow the suggestions on teacher pages 1058–1059 for assigning tasks and for supporting and evaluating student performance.

Reteaching Skills

1. For each practice, use the Reteach chart on the same page as the answers to determine which skills require reteaching, given the items students answered incorrectly.

2. Reteach these skills prior to assigning the **Benchmark Test** for the second half of Unit 6 (*Unit 6 Resources*, pp. 227–232). The Benchmark Test concludes instruction in the Unit skills.

Benchmark

Reteach skills as indicated by students' performance, following the Reteach charts included on pp. 1055–1057. Then, administer the end-of-unit **Benchmark Test** (*Unit 6 Resources*, pp. 227–232). The Benchmark Test concludes instruction in the Unit skills. Follow the **Interpretation Guide** for the test (*Unit 6 Resources*, p. 238) to assign reteaching pages as necessary in the *Reading Kit.* Use the built-in tracking software at www.PHLitOnline.com to automatically assign these pages.

Cumulative Review

I. Reading Literature

Common Core
State Standards

RL.7.2; W.7.1.b; L.7.4.a
[For the full wording of the standards, see the standards chart in the front of your textbook.]

Directions: *Read the story. Then, answer each question that follows.*

Jack and the Beanstalk

Once upon a time, a boy named Jack lived with his widowed mother. There came a hard winter, and the two had little to eat. The woman said, "Jack, take the cow to market, and sell her. We need the money to buy food."

On his way to the market, Jack met a butcher who showed him some magical beans. Jack traded the cow for the beans, and proudly returned home. His mother was angered by Jack's foolishness and threw the beans out the window.

By the next morning, the beans had grown into an incredibly tall plant. Curious, Jack climbed the beanstalk and found a fine castle at the top. There, an old woman appeared and told him this story:

"Once, a knight lived in this castle with his lady and infant son. A monstrous giant grew jealous of their happiness. He killed the knight, but the lady and her son fled to the village where they remained hidden for many years. Jack, that lady is your mother. This castle is rightfully yours. To win it back, you must get the hen that lays golden eggs. Are you ready?"

"Yes, for my father's honor, it is my <u>duty</u>," Jack said.

Jack crept into the castle, and hid in a closet. He peered out of the huge keyhole. Soon he heard heavy steps and a voice like thunder crying out for his supper. It was the giant! The giant's head scraped the ceiling as he walked through the kitchen.

After he ate an enormous meal of meats and potatoes, the giant picked up an ordinary-looking brown hen and said to her, "Lay!" She instantly laid a golden egg. "Lay!" said the giant again. She laid another. This went on until the giant grew bored and fell fast asleep.

Jack crept out and tiptoed across the room. He grabbed the hen and ran like lightning. With a tremendous roar, the giant woke up and sprang after Jack. Quickly, Jack scrambled down the beanstalk. With the giant right behind him, Jack took his axe and chopped down the beanstalk. The giant fell with a crash and lay dead.

The old woman reappeared. "Jack, you have shown courage. Your inheritance is restored to you." So, Jack and his mother lived happily ever after in the castle with the hen that lays golden eggs.

Differentiated Instruction   for Universal Access

Strategy for Special-Needs Students

Remind students that when a story begins with the phrase "Once upon a time," it will most likely contain magical adventures and a heroine or hero who overcomes a big challenge. Rather than being surprised by talking animals or other supernatural characters, the reader needs to accept the world the author has created and then figure out what message the author is expressing. In the case of "Jack and the Beanstalk," Jack is used by the author to teach readers about the importance of being brave and meeting challenges, even though the challenge he meets would not occur in real life.

1. What type of story is "Jack and the Beanstalk"?
   A. a myth
   B. a folk tale
   C. a novel
   D. a play

2. What event in the **plot** happens first?
   A. Jack sells the cow.
   B. The beanstalk grows.
   C. The giant kills Jack's father.
   D. Jack snatches the hen that lays the golden eggs.

3. What **values** do Jack's actions reveal?
   A. He is not afraid of giants.
   B. He feels a sense of responsibility toward his family.
   C. He does not believe that beans can have magical powers.
   D. He thinks it is important to be quick and clever.

4. Stories such as this one often feature a character who helps the main character. Who helps Jack?
   A. nobody
   B. his mother
   C. the butcher
   D. the old woman

5. What **character trait** is most important, according to this story?
   A. intelligence
   B. kindness
   C. bravery
   D. gardening skills

6. What is the **theme** of the story?
   A. Butchers are not trustworthy.
   B. Good things come to those who wait.
   C. Giants are greedy.
   D. Courage will be rewarded.

7. What characteristic of the **oral tradition** is *not* shown in this story?
   A. wondrous events
   B. a message that is repeated across many cultures
   C. animal characters that behave like humans
   D. a brave hero

8. **Vocabulary** Which word or phrase is closest in meaning to the underlined word <u>duty</u>?
   A. expectation
   B. responsibility
   C. castle
   D. chore

 Timed Writing

9. Write a **review** of "Jack and the Beanstalk." In your review, tell whether or not it makes a good bedtime story. **Support** your opinions and ideas with **concrete details** and **examples** from the story.

GO ON

Reteach

Question	Pages to Reteach
1	905, 1007
2	
3	989
4	
5	
6	1034
7	1007
8	—
9	1025

Answers continued

8. **B**—Jack has a duty, or <u>responsibility</u>, to win back the castle. *Incorrect answers:* A—Jack has no expectation of regaining the castle until he talks to the old woman; C—Jack's duty is not a physical object; D—A duty is an obligation, not a job or chore.

 Timed Writing

9. Students should write a review in which they tell whether the story makes a good bedtime story and cite details to support their position.

I. Reading Literature
Answers With Explanations

1. **B**—This story is a folk tale because folk tales are about ordinary people, and Jack is an ordinary boy rather than a god or great hero. *Incorrect answers:* A—Myths are about gods and goddesses; C—Novels are long; this is a short tale; D—A play is written in a different format.

2. **C**—Jack's father was killed before the beginning of this story. *Incorrect answers:* A—This is the first event described in the story, but not the first event in the plot; B—This event occurs after Jack sells the cow; D—This event occurs near the end of the story.

3. **B**—Jack's words, "for my father's honor," reveals his sense of duty toward his family. *Incorrect answers:* A—This is a characteristic, not a value; C—Jack trades his cow for the beans, so he does believe in magic; D—While Jack possesses these qualities, he does not say they are important.

4. **D**—The old woman tells Jack how he can win back the castle. *Incorrect answers:* A—Jack is helped by someone; B—Jack's mother scolds him; she does not help him; C—The butcher tricks Jack out of the money he needs.

5. **C**—The old woman specifies that bravery wins Jack his inheritance. *Incorrect answers:* A—Although Jack is clever, it is his courage that brings his reward; B—Jack does not show kindness; D—Jack grows a giant beanstalk by accident.

6. **D**—Jack's courage in stealing the hen from the giant wins him his inheritance. *Incorrect answers:* A—The butcher is untrustworthy, but there is no life lesson about butchers as a group; B—Jack does not wait, he acts; C—This is a stereotype, not a theme.

7. **C**—The animals in this story do not speak or act like humans. *Incorrect answers:* A—This story has many wondrous events, such as the growth of the beanstalk; B—The message about the importance of bravery has been expressed in many cultures; D—Jack is a brave hero.

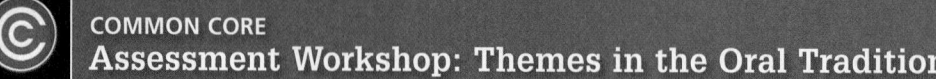

COMMON CORE
Assessment Workshop: Themes in the Oral Tradition

II. Reading Informational Text

Answers With Explanations

1. **B**—The author states this argument in the first paragraph. *Incorrect answers:* A—The author used to think this way until her daughter learned responsibility from looking after Coco; C—Anna was twelve when she got Coco; D—The author does not discuss this.

2. **A**—Anna used to dawdle on her way home from school, but now she runs home to take care of Coco. *Incorrect answers:* B—Although Anna now takes her dog for a walk each day, she used to take a longer walk home, so she may not be getting more exercise; C—There is no reference to new friends; D—It is not clear that Anna and her mother used to argue.

3. **D**—The author states this in the first sentence of the essay. *Incorrect answers:* A— This possible effect is not stated by the author; B—The author did this before allowing her daughter to keep the pet; C—The author does not list Anna's making her bed as one of the effects of their owning Coco.

4. **B**—In the last paragraph, the author provides numerous examples of how Anna has demonstrated responsibility since getting her dog. *Incorrect answers:* A—The author originally believed this, but changed her mind; C—The author does not state this belief; D—This opinion could be inferred, but it is never expressed.

Reteach

Question	Pages to Reteach
1	1028
2	913, 935, 960
3	913, 935, 960
4	1028

II. Reading Informational Text

Directions: *Read the passage. Then, answer each question that follows.*

Common Core
State Standards

RI.7.5, RI.7.6; L.7.2
[For the full wording of the standards, see the standards chart in the front of your textbook.]

Pet ownership is a wonderful way for children to learn responsibility. I didn't always think so, but then my daughter changed my mind.

Anna was four when she began asking for a dog. I always said no. Anna was the kind of child who "forgot" her homework and never made her bed. Whenever Anna asked for a dog, I'd tell her that she needed to be more responsible before I would feel comfortable putting her in charge of a living creature.

Then, one day a little dog followed Anna home. We put up signs, but nobody claimed the dog. It seemed like she was meant to be ours.

Anna was twelve when the lost dog we named Coco joined the family. I didn't expect her to take care of the dog without help, but I was pleasantly surprised. Anna used to <u>dawdle</u> on her way home from school, always taking the long way. Suddenly, she was running home to feed Coco and take her for a walk. Anna used to tease me for picking up garbage at the park. Now she carries a bag and a glove with her so she can pick up broken glass. She doesn't want Coco to cut her paws. More surprisingly, Anna has become more responsible about things that have nothing to do with Coco—things like getting dressed in the morning and remembering her homework. Anna isn't the only one who is happy that Coco followed her home. I'm happy too!

1. What is the **author's argument** at the beginning of the passage?
   A. Children should demonstrate responsibility before getting a pet.
   B. Owning a pet can teach responsibility.
   C. Twelve is too young to own a dog.
   D. Children should help around the house.

2. According to the passage, what is one **effect** of Anna getting a dog?
   A. She comes home more quickly.
   B. She gets more exercise.
   C. She makes new friends.
   D. She stops arguing with her mother.

3. What does the author say is one **effect** of allowing a child to own a pet?
   A. Your house will need frequent vacuuming.
   B. You will need to put signs up around the neighborhood.
   C. The child will make his or her own bed.
   D. The child will become more responsible.

4. What **point of view** does the author express at the end of the passage?
   A. Children should demonstrate responsibility before getting a pet.
   B. Owning a pet can teach responsibility.
   C. Children should help around the house.
   D. Coco is a sweet dog.

Strategies for
Test Taking

Often the anxiety surrounding test taking causes students to skim (or even skip) the instructions. Tell students that carefully reading the instructions for each section is essential to performing well. A misreading might cause them to answer every question in a section incorrectly.

III. Writing and Language Conventions

Directions: *Read the passage. Then, answer each question that follows.*

(1) October 3, 2010

(2) Dear Johnson Construction

   (3) Our baseball team has not replaced its uniforms in five years. (4) A $200 donation would allow us to purchase new shirts for each team member. (5) To show our thanks and gratitude we will put the name of your business on each shirt. (6) Spectators will see that you support an organization that gives kids something positive to do after school. (7) Please help support this talented Pleasantville team.

   (8) Thank you,

   (9) Joe Green

1. Which additional sentence would *best* state the author's **request**?
   A. The Pleasantville baseball team is in need of your financial support.
   B. We would appreciate it if you could donate team uniforms.
   C. Please, give us money.
   D. If you could donate your time and expertise, it would be greatly appreciated.

2. Which of the following revisions correctly uses a **colon**?
   A. October 3, 2010:
   B. Dear Johnson Construction:
   C. Please: help support this important Pleasantville tradition.
   D. Thank you:

3. Which elements of a **standard business letter** are missing from Joe's letter?
   A. inside address and sender's address
   B. inside address and closing
   C. closing and sender's address
   D. sender's address and postscript

4. Which of the following revisions correctly uses a **comma**?
   A. To show our thanks, and gratitude, we will put the name of your business on each shirt.
   B. To show our thanks and gratitude, we will put the name of your business on each shirt.
   C. To show, our thanks and gratitude, we will put the name of your business on each shirt.
   D. To show our thanks and gratitude we will put the name of your business, on each shirt.

STOP

III. Writing and Language Conventions

Answers With Explanations

1. **B**—The author wants the business to replace the worn-out team uniforms. *Incorrect answers:* A—This sentence states a general financial need, but it is not as specific a request as B; C—This is not the best request because it does not explain why the money is needed or what it will be used for; D—The writer is not asking for time or expertise.

2. **B**—In a business letter, there should be a colon after the salutation. *Incorrect answers:* A—The date does not require any punctuation marks after the year; C—No punctuation is necessary after "Please"; D—The comma after "Thank you" is correct.

3. **A**—The inside address and sender's address belong at the top of the letter. *Incorrect answers:* B—The inside address is missing, but the closing (Thank you,) is included; C—The sender's address is missing, but the closing is there; D—The sender's address is missing, but there is no need for a postscript.

4. **B**—There should be a comma after a long introductory phrase. *Incorrect answers:* A—There is no need for a comma between *thanks* and *gratitude*; C—There is no need for a comma after *show*; D—There should be a comma after *gratitude* but not after *business*.

Reteach

Question	Pages to Reteach
1	983
2	983
3	983
4	956, 985

Strategies for
Test Taking

Point out to students that when taking a standardized test that covers writing and language conventions, examinees should read the passage slowly, trying to identify errors in spelling, punctuation, capitalization, grammar, and usage. This way, when they get to the test items associated with the passage, they will already be familiar with many of the issues covered in the items and will be able to answer the questions more quickly and efficiently than if they had read the passage without this focus.

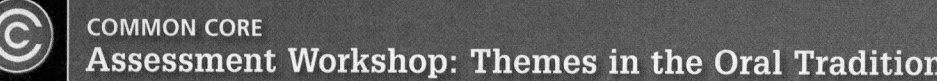

Performance Tasks

Assigning Tasks/Reteaching Skills

Use the chart below to choose appropriate Performance Tasks by identifying which tasks assess lessons in the textbook that you have taught. Use the same lessons for reteaching when students' performance indicates a failure to fully master a standard. For additional instruction and practice, assign the *Common Core Companion* pages indicated for each task.

Task	Where Taught/ Pages to Reteach	*Common Core Companion* Pages
1	935, 957, 989, 1007, 1040–1044	81–87, 279–286
2	904–907, 1034	15–27, 279–286
3	904–907, 966, 1034	15–27, 279–286
4	902–903, 1007, 1052–1053	28–40, 316–322
5	902–903, 905, 1007, 1052–1053	28–40, 316–322
6	902–906, 1034	15–27, 298–304

Assessment Pacing

In assigning the Writing Tasks on this student page, allow a class period for the completion of a task. As an alternative, assign tasks as homework. In assigning the Speaking and Listening Tasks on the facing page, consider having students do any required preparation as a homework assignment. Then, allow a class period for the presentations themselves.

Evaluating Performance Tasks

Use the rubric at the bottom of this Teacher Edition page to evaluate students' mastery of the standards as demonstrated in their Performance Task responses. Review the rubric with students before they begin work so they know the criteria by which their work will be evaluated.

Performance Tasks

Directions: *Follow the instructions to complete the tasks below as required by your teacher.*

As you work on each task, incorporate both general academic vocabulary and literary terms you learned in this unit.

Common Core State Standards

RL.7.2, RL.7.3, RL.7.9; W.7.9.a; SL.7.1, SL.7.4
[For the full wording of the standards, see the standards chart in the front of your textbook.]

Writing

Task 1: Literature [RL.7.9; W.7.9.a]
Analyze the Use of Historical Fact in Fiction and Nonfiction

Write an essay that compares and contrasts the use of facts in a work of fiction and a work of nonfiction.

- Explain that you will discuss similarities and differences in the use of facts in "Tenochtitlan: Inside the Aztec Capital" and "Popocatepetl and Ixtlaccihuatl."
- Identify at least three facts in the article and three facts in the legend. Explain at least two similarities and differences in the ways each author uses these facts. Consider the purpose each fact serves.
- Explain whether the author of the work of fiction has changed any facts. If so, identify how the fact was changed and the purpose for the change.
- Write a thesis statement summarizing your ideas.
- Support your thesis statement by citing specific details from the texts.
- Summarize your ideas in a conclusion.

Task 2: Literature [RL.7.2; W.7.9.a]
Analyze the Development of a Theme or Main Idea

Analyze a theme or main idea from one work of fiction in this unit and write an objective summary of that story.

- Choose one story from this unit to analyze. Identify a theme or main idea of that story.
- Write down how this theme or main idea is developed through characters' actions and story events.
- To make sure you understand the development of the idea, write an objective summary of the story.
- In your summary, use your own words to retell main ideas and story details.
- Include events from each part of the story to ensure completeness.
- Leave out minor ideas and details and avoid including personal opinions.
- Add transitions, such as *first, next,* and *finally,* to show the order of events.

Task 3: Literature [RL.7.2; W.7.9.a]
Analyze a Universal Theme

Identify a theme in a story and show how it is universal by identifying the same theme in other stories.

- Identify a universal theme of a story in this unit. Be sure that the theme contains a message about life that is found in other cultures and eras.
- Connect your universal theme to specific details from the story, including character traits, settings, conflicts, and the changes or results of these conflicts.
- Explain how the same theme can be found in other works you have read.

1058 Themes in the Oral Tradition

Performance Task Rubric: Standards Mastery	Rating Scale
Critical Thinking: How clearly and consistently does the student pursue the specific mode of reasoning or discourse required by the standard, as specified in the prompt (e.g., comparing and contrasting, analyzing, explaining)?	*not very* 1 2 3 4 5 *very*
Focus: How well does the student understand and apply the focus concepts of the standard, as specified in the prompt (e.g., development of theme or of complex characters, effects of structure, and so on)?	1 2 3 4 5
Support/Elaboration: How well does the student support points with textual or other evidence? How relevant, sufficient, and varied is the evidence provided?	1 2 3 4 5
Insight: How original, sophisticated, or compelling are the insights the student achieves by applying the standard to the text(s)?	1 2 3 4 5
Expression of Ideas: How well does the student organize and support ideas? How well does the student use language, including word choice and conventions, in the expression of ideas?	1 2 3 4 5

Speaking and Listening

 Task 4: Literature [RL.7.3; SL.7.4]

Analyze the Characters in a Folk Tale

Plan a presentation in which you analyze the characters and character development in a folk tale in this unit.

- Choose a folk tale from the unit and identify specific details about the characters, their personality traits, the conflicts they face, how the setting influences their choices, and what they learn as a result of their conflicts.
- Present your ideas, facts, details, and quotations in a clear, logical order.
- Extend the ideas in your presentation by discussing the ways in which the characters' behavior reflects the beliefs of the culture that produced the tale.
- Practice delivering your presentation, focusing on expression, pacing, volume, enunciation, and eye contact.

 Task 5: Literature [RL.7.3; SL.7.4]

Analyze the Plot in a Folk Tale

Plan a presentation in which you analyze the plot elements of a folk tale in this unit.

- Choose a folk tale from the unit and identify the main events in the plot.
- Identify the rising action, conflict, climax, falling action, and resolution.
- Discuss how events in the plot are influenced by other story elements, such as setting and characters.
- Present your ideas in a logical order.
- Include visual displays, such as plot diagrams, to clarify claims and emphasize important points.

 Task 6: Literature [RL.7.2; SL.7.1]

Analyze and Discuss Theme

Analyze a theme from a story in this unit and determine which customs and beliefs it reflects. Then, organize a discussion with a small group of classmates about the value of the story's message.

- Determine the theme of a story in this unit. Analyze how it is developed over the course of the story through plot events and characters' actions.
- List questions about customs and beliefs that arise as you analyze theme. Explore one question in your analysis. Conduct research as needed.
- Evaluate whether the story still contains a meaningful message for today's readers. Support your arguments with clear and relevant reasons.
- Discuss your findings with a small group. Be sure to come to the discussion having read the story and evaluated its message.
- Use vocabulary that accurately expresses your ideas.

 Community or individual— which is more important?

At the beginning of Unit 6, you wrote a response to the Big Question. Now that you have completed the unit, write a new response. Discuss how your initial ideas have either changed or been reinforced. Cite specific examples from the literature in this unit, from other subject areas, and from your own life to support your ideas. Use Big Question vocabulary words (see p. 901) in your response.

Assessment Workshop **1059**

Supporting Speaking and Listening

1. Consider having students work with partners or in groups to complete Performance Tasks involving speaking and listening. For tasks that you assign for individual work, you may still wish to have students rehearse with partners, who can provide constructive feedback.

2. As students rehearse, have them keep in mind these tips:
   - Present findings and evidence clearly and concisely.
   - Observe conventions of standard English grammar and usage.
   - Be relaxed and friendly but maintain a formal tone.
   - Make eye contact with the audience, pronounce words clearly, and vary your pace.
   - When working with a group, respond thoughtfully to others' positions, modifying your own in response to new evidence.

Linking Performance Tasks to Independent Reading

If you wish to cover the standards with students' independent reading, adapt Performance Tasks of your choice to the works they have selected. (Independent reading suggestions appear on the next page.)

 Community or individual—which is more important?

1. Remind students that the unit Big Question is "Community or individual—which is more important?"

2. Have students complete their responses to the prompt on the student page. Point out that they have read selections in this unit about different views of individuals and communities and that they should draw on these selections in their responses. Remind them that they can also draw on their own experiences and what they have learned in other subject areas in formulating their answers.

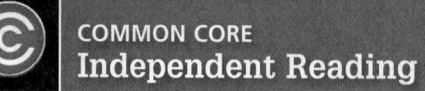
EXTEND

Independent Reading

Titles featured on the Independent Reading pages at the end of each unit represent a range of reading, including stories, dramas, and poetry, as well as literary nonfiction and other types of informational text. Throughout, labels indicate the works that are CCSS Exemplar Texts. Choosing from among these featured titles will help students read works at increasing levels of text complexity in the grades 6–8 text complexity band.

Independent Reading and Pacing

See the Unit Overview and Pacing Plan, pp. 900a–900b, for suggestions on integrating independent reading with work in the Student Edition.

Using Literature Circles

A literature circle is a temporary group in which students independently discuss a book.

Use the guidance in the *Professional Development Guidebook*, pp. 47–49, as well as the teaching notes on the facing page, for additional suggestions for literature circles.

Meeting Unit 6 CCS Focus Standards

Students can use books listed on this page to apply and to reinforce their mastery of the CCS Focus Standards covered in this unit. (The Focus Standards are introduced on pp. 902–905.)

Introducing Featured Titles

Have students choose a book or books for independent reading. Assist them by previewing the titles, noting their subject matter and level of difficulty. **Note:** Before recommending a work to students, preview it, taking into account the values of your community as well as the maturity of your students.

Featured Titles

In this unit, you have read a variety of literary works that originated in the oral tradition. Continue to read on your own. Select works that you enjoy, but challenge yourself to explore new writers and works of increasing depth and complexity. The titles suggested below will help you get started.

Literature

The People Could Fly: American Black Folktales
by Virginia Hamilton   **EXEMPLAR TEXT** ©

These twenty-four **folktales** celebrate the strength and resourcefulness of the people who survived slavery. The collection includes the selection "The People Could Fly," which is included in this unit.

Myths and Folktales Around the World
by Robert Potter

This collection includes traditional **myths and folktales** about famous figures, such as King Arthur, as well as new tales based on historical events, such as the sinking of the *Titanic*.

Trojan Horse
by David Clement-Davies

This modern retelling of the classic **myth** describes the clever use of a huge wooden horse in a bitterly fought battle to rescue the beautiful Helen of Troy.

The Adventures of Ulysses
by Bernard Evslin
Scholastic, 1969

In this modern interpretation of the classic **myth,** Ulysses and his men begin the journey home to Greece after conquering Troy—only to find they have angered the gods and must face many dangers along the way.

The Time Warp Trio: It's All Greek to Me
by Jon Scieszka

In this funny **novel,** Joe and his friends accidentally find themselves trapped in ancient Greece. With only a cardboard thunderbolt and painted apple as weapons, they must outwit the gods to survive the dangers of Hades and Mount Olympus.

Thirteen Moons on Turtle's Back
by Joseph Bruchac

The thirteen **poems** in this collection of myths and legends represent the thirteen moon cycles that make up the year in traditional Native American folklore.

Informational Texts

Around the World in a Hundred Years
by Jean Fritz

Jean Fritz uses a playful tone to explore the topic of explorers, like Columbus and Magellan, who ventured into unmapped territory from 1421 to 1522. This **nonfiction** book describes what happened when the explorers met the inhabitants of the lands they called "the Unknown."

The Great Fire
by Jim Murphy   **EXEMPLAR TEXT** ©

Using many personal accounts, Jim Murphy's **nonfiction** book tells the tale of Chicago's tragic Great Fire in 1871. This fascinating history tells how the fire began, how people responded, and how it was finally contained. Find out the true story behind one of the greatest disasters ever to be blamed on a cow.

1060 Themes in the Oral Tradition

Text Complexity: Aligning Texts With Readers and Tasks

TEXTS	READERS AND TASKS
• *The People Could Fly* • *The Time Warp Trio: It's All Greek to Me* (Lexile: 530L)	**Below-Level Readers** Allow students to focus on reading for content, and challenge them to interpret multiple perspectives.
• *Trojan Horse* (Lexile: 800L) • *The Adventures of Ulysses* (Lexile: 860L) • *Around the World in a Hundred Years* (Lexile: 1050L)	**Below-Level Readers** Challenge students as they read for content. **On-Level Readers** Allow students to focus on reading for content, and challenge them to interpret multiple perspectives. **Advanced Readers** Allow students to focus on interpreting multiple perspectives.
• *Thirteen Moons on Turtle's Back* • *The Great Fire* (Lexile: 1130L)	**On-Level Readers** Challenge students as they read for content. **Advanced Readers** Allow students to focus on reading for content, and challenge them to interpret multiple perspectives.

Preparing to Read Complex Texts

Attentive Reading As you read on your own, ask yourself questions about the text. The questions shown below and others that you ask as you read will help you learn and enjoy literature even more.

 **Common Core State Standards**

Reading Literature/Informational Text
10. By the end of the year, read and comprehend literature, including stories, dramas, and poems, and literary nonfiction in the grades 6–8 text complexity band proficiently, with scaffolding as needed at the high end of the range.

When reading texts from the oral tradition, ask yourself ...

- From what culture does this text come? What do I know about that culture?
- What type of text am I reading? For example, is it a myth, a legend, or a tall tale? What characters and events do I expect to find in this type of text?
- Does the text include the elements I expected? If not, how does it differ from what I expected?
- What elements of the culture do I see in the text? For example, do I notice beliefs, foods, or settings that have meaning for the people of this culture?
- Does the text teach a lesson or a moral? If so, is this a valuable lesson?

Key Ideas and Details

- Who is retelling or presenting this text? Do I think the author has changed the text from the original? If so, how?
- Does the text include characters and tell a story? If so, are the characters and plot interesting?
- What do I notice about the language used in the text? Which aspects seem similar to or different from the language used in modern texts?
- Does the text include symbols? If so, do they have a special meaning in the original culture of the text? Do they also have meaning in modern life?

Craft and Structure

- What does this text teach me about the culture from which it comes?
- What, if anything, does this text teach me about people in general?
- Does this text seem like others I have read or heard? Why or why not?
- Do I know of any modern versions of this text? How are they similar to or different from this one?
- If I were researching this culture for a report, would I include passages from this text? If so, what would those passages show?
- Do I enjoy reading this text and others like it? Why or why not?

Integration of Ideas

Independent Reading **1061**

 Text Complexity: Reader and Task Support Suggestions

INDEPENDENT READING

Increased Support Suggest that students choose a book that they feel comfortable reading and one that is a bit more challenging. Pair a more proficient reader with a less proficient reader and have them work together on the more challenging text. Partners can prepare to read the book by reviewing questions on this student page. They can also read difficult passages together, sharing questions and insights. They can use the questions on the student page to guide after-reading discussion.

Increased Challenge Encourage students to integrate knowledge and ideas by combining the Big Question and the Unit Focus concepts in their approach to two or more featured titles.

For example, students might consider the importance of individuals and community in *Trojan Horse* and *The Adventures of Ulysses*. In addition, students can analyze cause and effect in various myths.

Preparing to Read Complex Texts

1. Tell students they can be attentive readers by bringing their experience and imagination to the texts they read and by actively questioning those texts. Explain that the questions they see on the student page are examples of types of questions to ask about texts from the oral tradition.

2. Point out that, like writing, reading is a "multidraft" process, involving several readings of complete works or passages, revising and refining one's understanding each time.

Key Ideas and Details

3. As an example, review and amplify the fifth bulleted item. **Ask:** What key ideas and details would you cite as evidence that the story's lesson is valuable?

   Possible response: You might cite evidence that the moral applies to many different kinds of people or explain how the lesson applies to different characters in the story.

Craft and Structure

4. What details of craft and structure would you use to analyze the language used in the text?

   Possible response: You might point to the unique characteristics of the author's writing style or the author's use of devices such as figurative language.

Integration of Ideas

5. How would you choose which passages from the story to use in a research report about a particular culture?

   Possible response: You might look for sections that provide vivid details about the culture's people, traditions, or beliefs.

6. Finally, explain to students that they should cite key ideas and details, examples of craft and structure, or instances of the integration of ideas as evidence to support their points during a book discussion. After hearing the evidence, the group might reach a consensus or might agree to disagree.

1061

Resources

Student Edition Pages

Glossary

Big Question vocabulary appears in **blue type**. High-utility Academic vocabulary is <u>underlined</u>.

A

abode (uh BOHD) *n.* home; residence

acknowledge (ak NOL ihj) *v.* recognize and admit

acquainted (uh KWAYNT uhd) *adj.* familiar

adequate (AD ih kwiht) *adj.* enough; sufficient

adolescence (ad uh LEHS uhns) *n.* time when a young person is developing into an adult

aloft (uh LAWFT) *adj.* high up; flying; in the air

<u>**analyze**</u> (AN uh lyz) *v.* break down into parts and examine carefully

antidote (AN tih doht) *n.* remedy; cure

apparent (uh PAR uhnt) *adj.* seeming

appearance (uh PIHR uhns) *n.* how a person or thing looks or seems

<u>**appreciate**</u> (uh PREE shee ayt) *v.* be thankful for

approvingly (uh PROOV ihng lee) *adv.* consentingly

aptitude (AP tuh tood) *n.* talent; ability

arid (AR ihd) *adj.* dry and barren

<u>**assumption**</u> (uh SUHMP shuhn) *n.* belief or acceptance that something is true

astonish (uh STON ihsh) *v.* amaze

atmospheric (at muh SFEHR ihk) *adj.* having to do with the air surrounding Earth

<u>**attitude**</u> (AT uh tood) *n.* mental state involving beliefs, feelings, and values

audible (AW duh buhl) *adj.* loud enough to be heard

avid (AV ihd) *adj.* eager and enthusiastic

<u>**awareness**</u> (uh WAIR nehs) *n.* knowledge gained from one's own perceptions or from information

awe (aw) *n.* mixed feelings of fear and wonder

B

babbled (BAB uhld) *v.* murmured; talked foolishly or too much

ban (ban) *n.* an order forbidding something

banish (BAN ihsh) *v.* send away; exile

believable (bih LEE vuh buhl) *adj.* having the ability to draw out belief or trust

bellow (BEHL oh) *v.* roar deeply

<u>**bias**</u> (BY uhs) *n.* tendency to see things from a slanted or prejudiced viewpoint

bigots (BIHG uhts) *n.* narrow-minded, prejudiced people

blander (BLAND uhr) *adj.* more tasteless

bound (bownd) *v.* tied

brawny (BRAW nee) *adj.* strong and muscular

burrow (BUR oh) *v.* dig a hole for shelter

C

canyon (KAN yuhn) *n.* long narrow valley between high cliffs

captivity (kap TIHV uh tee) *n.* imprisonment; caught and held prisoner

cattails (KAT taylz) *n.* tall reeds with furry, brown spikes, found in marshes and swamps

causeways (KAWZ wayz) *n.* roads across wet ground or shallow water

<u>**challenge**</u> (CHAL uhnj) *v.* dare; a calling into question

<u>**characteristic**</u> (kar ihk tuh RIHS tihk) *n.* trait; feature

clusters (KLUHS tuhrz) *n.* numbers of things of the same sort that are grouped together; bunch

coax (kohks) *v.* use gentle persuasion

<u>**common**</u> (KOM uhn) *adj.* ordinary; expected

communal (kuh MYOON uhl) *adj.* shared by all

<u>**communicate**</u> (kuh MYOO nuh kayt) *v.* share thoughts or feelings, usually in words

<u>**communication**</u> (kuh myoo nuh KAY shuhn) *n.* activity of sharing information or speaking

<u>**community**</u> (kuh MYOO nuh tee) *n.* group of people who share an interest or who live near each other

compelled (kuhm PEHLD) *v.* forced

competition (kom puh TIHSH uhn) *n.* event or game in which people or sides attempt to win

compromise (KOM pruh myz) *n.* the settling of differences in a way that allows both sides to feel satisfied

compulsion (kuhm PUHL shuhn) *n.* driving, irresistible force

<u>**conclude**</u> (kuhn KLOOD) *v.* bring to a close; end

conflict (KON flihkt) *n.* clash or fight between opposing groups or people

consolation (KON suh LAY shuhn) *n.* something that comforts a disappointed person

conspired (kuhn SPYRD) *v.* planned together secretly

contradiction (KON truh DIHK shuhn) *n.* difference between two conflicting things that reveals only one is true

contraption (kuhn TRAP shuhn) *n.* strange device or machine

<u>**contribute**</u> (kuhn TRIHB yoot) *v.* add to; enrich

conveyed (kuhn VAYD) *v.* made known; expressed

conviction (kuhn VIHK shuhn) *n.* belief

<u>**convince**</u> (kuhn VIHNS) *v.* persuade; cause to accept a point of view

coveted (KUHV iht uhd) *v.* wanted; desired

croon (kroon) *v.* sing or hum quietly and soothingly

crouches (KROWCH uhz) *v.* stoops or bends low

crucial (KROO shuhl) *adj.* important; critical

crystal (KRIHS tuhl) *adj.* made of clear, brilliant glass

culminated (KUHL muh nayt uhd) *v.* reached its highest point or climax

culprit (KUHL priht) *n.* guilty person

<u>**culture**</u> (KUHL chuhr) *n.* collected customs of a group or community

cunning (KUHN ihng) *adj.* sly; crafty

cunningly (KUHN ihng lee) *adv.* cleverly

cupboard (KUHB uhrd) *n.* cabinet with shelves for cups, plates, and food

curdled (KUR duhld) *adj.* rotten

curiosity (kyur ee OS uh tee) *n.* desire to learn or know

custom (KUHS tuhm) *n.* accepted practice

D

dabbling (DAB lihng) *v.* wetting by dipping, splashing, or paddling in the water

danger (DAYN juhr) *n.* exposure to possible harm, injury, or loss

<u>**debate**</u> (dih BAYT) *v.* argue in an attempt to convince

deceive (dih SEEV) *v.* to make someone believe something that's not true

decreed (dih KREED) *v.* officially ordered

defiant (dih FY uhnt) *adj.* boldly resisting

defies (dih FYZ) *v.* resists or opposes boldly or openly

<u>**define**</u> (dih FYN) *v.* determine the nature of or give the meaning of

deserts (dih ZURTS) *v.* leaves, especially a military post

designated (DEHZ ihg nayt uhd) *v.* pointed out; marked

desire (dih ZYR) *n.* wish or want

desolate (DEHS uh liht) *adj.* lonely; solitary

desperate (DEHS puhr iht) *adj.* hopeless; very great desire or need

destiny (DEHS tuh nee) *n.* the seemingly inevitable succession of events; one's fate

destitute (DEHS tuh toot) *n.* people living in complete poverty

devastated (DEHV uh stayt uhd) *v.* destroyed; completely upset

devastating (DEHV uh stayt ihng) *adj.* destructive; overwhelming

dignitaries (DIHG nuh tehr eez) *n.* people holding high positions or offices

diplomats (DIHP luh mats) *n.* government employees who work with other nations

disagreement (DIHS uh GREE muhnt) *n.* difference or conflict between people or groups

discipline (DIHS uh plihn) *n.* training; self-control

<u>**discover**</u> (dihs KUHV uhr) *v.* find or explore

dislodge (dihs LOJ) *v.* force from a position or place

dismal (DIHZ muhl) *adj.* dark and gloomy

dispelled (dihs PEHLD) *v.* driven away; made to disappear

dispute (dihs PYOOT) *n.* disagreement

distinct (dihs TIHNGKT) *adj.* separate and different

distract (dih STRAKT) *v.* draw attention away

diversions (duh VUR zhuhnz) *n.* amusements

<u>**diversity**</u> (duh VUR suh tee) *n.* variety, as of groups or cultures

dominions (duh MIHN yuhnz) *n.* governed countries or territories

downy (DOW nee) *adj.* soft and fluffy

duty (DOO tee) *n.* responsibility; obligation

E

elaboration (ih lab uh RAY shuhn) *n.* adding of more details

elective (ih LEHK tihv) *n.* optional course

emerged (ih MURJD) *v.* came into view; became visible

emphatic (ehm FAT ihk) *adj.* felt or done with strong feeling

enrich (ehn RIHCH) *v.* make better; improve in quality

entertain (ehn tuhr TAYN) *v.* amuse; put on a performance

<u>**environment**</u> (ehn VY ruhn muhnt) *n.* surroundings; the natural world

envying (EHN vee ihng) *v.* wanting something that someone else has

epidemic (ehp uh DEHM ihk) *n.* outbreak of a contagious disease

equality (ih KWOL uh tee) *n.* social state in which all people are treated the same

ethnicity (ehth NIHS uh tee) *n.* racial or cultural background

evading (ih VAYD ihng) *v.* avoiding

<u>**evaluate**</u> (ih VAL yoo ayt) *v.* judge; determine the significance of

evaporated (ih VAP uh rayt uhd) *v.* changed from a liquid to a gas

evidence (EHV uh duhns) *n.* proof in support of a claim or statement

evidently (ehv uh DEHNT lee) *adv.* clearly; obviously

<u>**examine**</u> (ehg ZAM uhn) *v.* study in depth; look at closely

exertion (ehg ZUR shuhn) *n.* physical work

expectancy (ehk SPEHK tuhn see) *n.* that which is expected

expectations (ehks pehk TAY shuhnz) *n.* things looked forward to

expense (ehk SPEHNS) *n.* financial cost

experiment (ehk SPEHR uh mehnt) *n.* test to determine a result

<u>**explain**</u> (ehk SPLAYN) *v.* make plain or clear

<u>**explore**</u> (ehk SPLAWR) *v.* investigate; look into

express (ehk SPREHS) *v.* say or communicate a feeling

exquisite (EHKS kwih ziht) *adj.* beautiful in a delicate way

extenuating (ehk STEHN yoo ayt ihng) *adj.* giving a reason for; excusing

exultant (ehg ZUHL tuhnt) *adj.* expressing great joy or triumph

F

facts (fakts) *n.* accepted truths or reality

factual (FAK choo uhl) *adj.* based on or limited to what is real or true

falsely (FAWLS lee) *adv.* incorrectly; untruthfully

family (FAM uh lee) *n.* people related by blood or having a common ancestor

fascinated (FAS uh nayt uhd) *adj.* captivated

fathom (FATH uhm) *n.* unit of length used to measure the depth of water

feeble (FEE buhl) *adj.* weak; infirm

feebleness (FEE buhl nuhs) *n.* weakness

fiction (FIHK shuhn) *n.* something invented or imagined

fiddler (FIHD luhr) *n.* person who plays a fiddle, or violin

flatterers (FLAT uhr uhrz) *n.* those who praise a person insincerely

fluent (FLOO uhnt) *adj.* able to write with ease

flushed (fluhsht) *v.* drove from hiding

flustered (FLUHS tuhrd) *adj.* nervous; confused

focus (FOH kuhs) *n.* central point or topic of investigation

forage (FAWR ihj) *n.* food for domestic animals

formidable (FAWR muh duh buhl) *adj.* impressive

forsythia (fawr SIHTH ee uh) *n.* shrub with yellow flowers that blooms in early spring

fragrant (FRAY gruhnt) *adj.* sweet smelling

frontier (fruhn TIHR) *n.* the developing, often uncivilized, region of a country; any new field of learning

fundamental (FUHN duh MEHNT uhl) *adj.* basic; forming a foundation

furrowed (FUR ohd) *v.* wrinkled

G

garlands (GAHR luhndz) *n.* wreaths of flowers and leaves

garments (GAHR muhnts) *n.* clothes

gauge (gayj) *v.* estimate or judge

generate (JEN uhr ayt) *v.* create

globules (GLOB yoolz) *n.* drops of liquid

glossy (GLAWS ee) *adj.* smooth and shiny

goblets (GOB lihts) *n.* bowl-shaped drinking containers without handles

gourd (gawrd) *n.* a fruit; the dried shell is used as a cup

granite (GRAN iht) *n.* hard gray rock

gratitude (GRAT uh tood) *n.* thankful appreciation

group (groop) *n.* collection or set, as of people

groves (grohvz) *n.* small groups of trees

guidance (GY duhns) *n.* advice or assistance

gumption (GUHMP shuhn) *n.* courage; enterprise

guzzle (GUHZ uhl) *v.* drank greedily

H

harness (HAHR nihs) *n.* equipment used to drive a horse or attach it to a vehicle

haunches (HAWN chuhz) *n.* upper legs and hips of an animal

hexagons (HEHK suh gonz) *n.* six-sided figures

hind (hynd) *adj.* rear

hoarding (HAWR dihng) *v.* accumulating and storing a supply as a reserve

hoed (hohd) *v.* weeded or loosened soil with a metal hand tool

hors d'oeuvres (awr DUHRVZ) *n.* savory foods served as appetizers

huddled (HUHD uhld) *v.* crowded or nestled close together

I

identify (y DEHN tuh fy) *v.* recognize as being

ignorant (IHG nuhr uhnt) *adj.* not knowing facts or information

ignore (ihg NAWR) *v.* refuse to notice; disregard

ignored (ihg NAWRD) *v.* paid no attention to

image (IHM ihj) *n.* picture; representation

immensely (ih MEHNS lee) *adv.* a great deal; very much

immensity (ih MEHN suh tee) *n.* immeasurable largeness or vastness

impervious (ihm PUR vee uhs) *adj.* not affected by something

impetus (IHM puh tuhs) *n.* driving force

implored (ihm PLAWRD) *v.* begged

improvised (IHM pruh vyzd) *v.* composed or performed on the spur of the moment

improvising (IHM pruh vy zihng) *v.* making up or inventing on the spur of the moment

incessantly (ihn SEHS uhnt lee) *adv.* without stopping

indispensable (ihn dihs PEHN suh buhl) *adj.* absolutely necessary

individual (ihn duh VIHJ oo uhl) *n.* single person or thing

inflicted (ihn FLIHKT uhd) *v.* made someone suffer something painful or bad

inform (ihn FORM) *v.* tell; give information about

information (ihn fuhr MAY shuhn) *n.* knowledge gained through study or experience

initiation (ih nihsh ee AY shuhn) *n.* process by which one becomes a member of a group

inquire (ihn KWYR) *v.* ask in order to learn about

insight (ihn syt) *n.* ability to see the truth; an understanding

integration (ihn tuh GRAY shuhn) *n.* the end of separation of cultural or racial groups

intercedes (ihn tuhr SEEDZ) *v.* makes a request on behalf of another

intermixed (ihn tuhr MIHKST) *adj.* mixed together

interplanetary (ihn tuhr PLAN uh tehr ee) *adj.* between planets

interrupted (ihn tuh RUHPT uhd) *v.* broken into or upon a thought, discussion, etc.; not continuous

intervene (ihn tuhr VEEN) *v.* come between as an influence to modify, settle, or hinder some action or argument

interview (IHN tuhr vyoo) *v.* ask a series of questions of a person in order to gain information

intricate (IHN trih kiht) *adj.* complex; detailed

investigate (ihn VEHS tuh gayt) *v.* examine thoroughly

irrigation (ihr uh GAY shuhn) *n.* supplying water with ditches, canals, or sprinklers

J

justifies (JUHS tuh fyz) *v.* excuses; explains

K

kinsmen (KIHNZ muhn) *n.* male relatives

knowledge (NOL ihj) *n.* result of learning; awareness

L

laborious (luh BAWR ee uhs) *adj.* taking much work or effort

learn (lurn) *v.* gain knowledge or skills

legislation (lehj ihs LAY shuhn) *n.* law

liberty (LIHB uhr tee) *n.* freedom from slavery or captivity

listen (LIHS uhn) *v.* pay attention to; heed

loathed (lohthd) *v.* hated

longhorns (LAWNG hawrnz) *n.* breed of cattle with long horns

luminous (LOO muh nuhs) *adj.* giving off light

M

malice (MAL ihs) *n.* ill will

malicious (muh LIHSH uhs) *adj.* spiteful; hateful

manned (mand) *adj.* having human operators on board

meager (MEE guhr) *adj.* of poor quality; small in amount

media (MEE dee uh) *n.* collected sources of information, including newspapers, television, and the Internet

meek (meek) *adj.* timid; not showing anger

merely (MIHR lee) *adv.* no more than; and nothing else; simply

metamorphosis (meht uh MAWR fuh sihs) *n.* change of form

minnow (MIHN oh) *n.* small schooling fish

miracle (MIHR uh kuhl) *n.* a remarkable event or thing; marvel

misunderstanding (mihs uhn duhr STAN dihng) *n.* state where words or a point of view fail to be communicated

monarch (MON uhrk) *n.* hereditary rule, like a king or queen

morose (muh ROHS) *adj.* gloomy

mortality (mawr TAL uh tee) *n.* condition of being mortal, or having to die eventually

mourning (MAWR nihng) *n.* expression of grief, especially after someone dies

murmuring (MUR muhr ihng) *v.* making low, indistinct sounds

mystery (MIHS tuhr ee) *n.* something unexplained, unknown, or kept secret

N

neglected (nih GLEHKT uhd) *v.* failed to take care of

nobility (noh BIHL uh tee) *n.* people with a high rank in society

nonchalantly (NON shuh lahnt lee) *adv.* casually indifferent

O

obsession (uhb SEHSH uhn) *n.* extreme interest in something, which prevents you from thinking about anything else

obstacle (OB stuh kuhl) *n.* something in the way

ominous (OM uh nuhs) *adj.* threatening

opinion (uh PIHN yuhn) *n.* belief based on what seems true or probable

opposition (op uh ZIHSH uhn) *n.* state of being against

optimist (OP tuh mihst) *n.* someone who takes the most hopeful view of matters

ornament (AWR nuh muhnt) *v.* beautify

outcome (OWT kuhm) *n.* way something turns out

outskirts (OWT skurts) *n.* a district far from the center of a city

P

parallel (PAR uh lehl) *adv.* extending in the same direction and at the same distance apart

parson (PAHR suhn) *n.* minister

passion (PASH uhn) *n.* strong feelings of love, hate or fear

patriotic (pay tree OT ihk) *adj.* love and support for one's own country

paupers (PAW puhrz) *n.* people who are very poor

peasants (PEHZ uhnts) *n.* owners of small farms; farm laborers

peeved (peevd) *adj.* irritated; annoyed

penned (pehnd) *v.* locked up in a small enclosure

perceive (puhr SEEV) *v.* adopt a point of view; see

perception (puhr SEHP shuhn) *n.* the act of becoming aware of through one or more of the senses

perch (purch) *n.* roost for a bird; seat

perfunctorily (puhr FUHNGK tuh ruh lee) *adv.* done without care merely as a routine; superficially

perilous (PEHR uh luhs) *adj.* dangerous

permanent (PUR muh nuhnt) *adj.* lasting or intended to last forever

perpetual (puhr PEHCH yoo uhl) *adj.* constant; unending

persistently (puhr SIHS tuhnt lee) *adv.* firmly and steadily

perspective (puhr SPEHK tihv) *n.* point of view

pestering (PEHS tuhr ihng) *v.* annoying; bugging

plaited (PLAYT uhd) *adj.* braided

plausible (PLAW zuh buhl) *adj.* believable

porridge (PAWR ihj) *n.* soft food made of cereal boiled in water or milk

potential (puh TEHN shuhl) *n.* possibility; capability

practical (PRAK tih kuhl) *adj.* levelheaded; efficient; realistic

precaution (prih KAW shuhn) *n.* something you do to prevent something bad or dangerous from happening

preliminary (prih LIHM uh nehr ee) *adj.* coming before or leading up to the main action

presumptuous (prih ZUHMP choo uhs) *adj.* overconfident; arrogant

prickly (PRIHK lee) *adv.* sharply pointed; thorny

produce (pruh DOOS) *v.* make; create

profound (pruh FOWND) *adj.* deeply or intensely felt

promote (pruh MOHT) *v.* encourage; contribute to the growth of

proposal (pruh POH zuhl) *n.* plan; offer

python (PY thon) *n.* large snake

Q

quest (kwehst) *n.* a long search for something

question (KWEHS chuhn) *v.* challenge the accuracy of; place in doubt

R

rancid (RAN sihd) *adj.* spoiled and smelling bad

rash (rash) *adj.* too hasty

react (ree AKT) *v.* respond to; act with respect to

reaction (ree AK shuhn) *n.* response to an influence, action, or statement

readapted (ree uh DAPT uhd) *v.* gradually adjusted again

reality (ree AL uh tee) *n.* state or quality of being real or true

realm (rehlm) *n.* kingdom

reassuring (ree uh SHUR ihng) *adj.* having the effect of restoring confidence

reeds (reedz) *n.* tall, slender grasses that grow in marshy land

reel (reel) *v.* spin; whirl

reflect (rih FLEHKT) *v.* think about; consider

refugee (REHF yoo JEE) *n.* person who flees home or country to seek shelter from war or cruelty

refuse (REHF yooz) *n.* trash; waste

regretted (rih GREHT uhd) *v.* felt sorry about

relation (rih LAY shuhn) *n.* connection between two or more things

relented (rih LEHNT uhd) *v.* gave in

reliable (rih LY uh buhl) *adj.* dependable

relished (REHL ihsht) *v.* enjoyed; liked

remote (rih MOHT) *adj.* far away from anything else

repressive (rih PREHS ihv) *adj.* overly strict

reproach (rih PROHCH) *n.* disapproval; criticism

resilient (rih ZIHL yuhnt) *adj.* able to spring back into shape

resolution (rehz uh LOO shuhn) *n.* end of a conflict in which one or both parties is satisfied

resumed (rih ZOOMD) *v.* began again; continued

reveal (rih VEEL) *v.* make known; show

revived (rih VYVD) *v.* came back to life or consciousness

righteous (RY chuhs) *adj.* morally good and fair

routed (ROWT uhd) *v.* soundly defeated

rummaging (RUHM ihj ihng) *v.* searching through something

S

sage (sayj) *n.* very wise person

saluting (suh LOOT ihng) *v.* honor by performing an act or gesture

saturation (sach uh RAY shuhn) *n.* state of being completely filled

savored (SAY vuhrd) *v.* tasted or experienced with delight

scorned (skawrnd) *adj.* looked down upon

scowl (skowl) *v.* look at someone or something in an angry or disapproving way

sensitive (SEHN suh tihv) *adj.* easily hurt

sentimental (sehn tuh MEHNT uhl) *adj.* emotional; showing tender feeling

severe (suh VIHR) *adj.* harsh

shed (shehd) *v.* cast off or lose

shipments (SHIHP muhntz) *n.* the delivery or the act of sending goods

shortsightedness (shawrt SY tihd nuhs) *n.* lack of foresight

shuffle (SHUHF uhl) *v.* walk with dragging feet

simultaneously (sy muhl TAY nee uhs lee) *adv.* at the same time

sinewy (SIHN yoo ee) *adj.* tough and strong

slackening (SLAK uhn ihng) *adj.* easing; becoming less active

slather (SLATH uhr) *v.* spread on thickly

sluggishly (SLUHG ihsh lee) *adv.* as if lacking energy

smattering (SMAT uhr ihng) *n.* a small number

snuffs (snuhfs) *v.* extinguishes; puts out

solemn (SOL uhm) *adj.* serious; somber

speak (speek) *v.* use language; express in words

spectators (SPEHK tay tuhrz) *n.* people who watch

spied (spyd) *v.* watched secretly

spigot (SPIHG uht) *n.* faucet; spout

Glossary **R5**

spines (spynz) *n.* backbones

sputters (SPUHT uhrz) *v.* makes hissing or spitting noises

strategy (STRAT uh jee) *n.* set of plans used to gain success or achieve an aim

strive (stryv) *v.* struggle

struggle (STRUHG uhl) *n.* fight

stutter (STUHT uhr) *v.* speak in a hesitant or faltering way

suit (soot) *v.* please; satisfy

suitable (SOO tuh buhl) *adj.* appropriate

suitors (SOO tuhrz) *n.* men who court a woman or seek to marry her

summoned (SUHM uhnd) *v.* called together

supple (SUHP uhl) *adj.* able to bend easily; flexible

surpass (suhr PAS) *v.* be superior to

sustained (suh STAYND) *adj.* supported; maintained

swerve (swurv) *n.* curving motion

T

teach (teech) *v.* share information or knowledge

team (teem) *n.* group united in a common goal

technology (tehk NOL uh jee) *n.* practical application of science to business or industry

telegram (TEHL uh gram) *n.* message transmitted by telegraph

timid (TIHM ihd) *adj.* shy; fearful

tolerant (TOL uhr uhnt) *adj.* accepting; free from bigotry or prejudice

torrent (TAWR uhnt) *n.* flood

tradition (truh DIHSH uhn) *n.* custom, as of a social group or culture

transfixed (trans FIHKT) *adj.* fascinated

transformation (trans fuhr MAY shuhn) *n.* change

translates (trans LAYTS) *v.* expresses the same thing in another form

translucent (trans LOO suhnt) *adj.* allowing light through

transmit (trans MIHT) *v.* send or give out

truth (trooth) *n.* something supported by fact or reality

tumultuously (too MUHL choo uhs lee) *adv.* noisily and violently

twine (twyn) *n.* strong string or cord of strands twisted together

U

ultimate (UHL tuh miht) *adj.* final

unanimous (yoo NAN uh muhs) *adj.* based on complete agreement

uncommonly (uhn KOM uhn lee) *adv.* remarkably

unconsciously (uhn KON shuhs lee) *adv.* thoughtlessly

understand (uhn duhr STAND) *v.* grasp or reach knowledge with respect to something

understanding (uhn duhr STAN dihng) *n.* agreement; end of conflict

unify (YOO nuh fy) *v.* bring together as one

unique (yoo NEEK) *adj.* one of a kind

unravel (uhn RAV uhl) *v.* become untangled or separated

utter (UHT uhr) *v.* speak

V

vacancy (VAY kuhn see) *n.* emptiness; unoccupied position

varmints (VAHR muhnts) *n.* vermin

veranda (vuh RAN duh) *n.* open porch, usually with a roof

verge (vurj) *n.* edge; brink

vital (VY tuhl) *adj.* extremely important or necessary

void (voyd) *n.* emptiness

vowed (vowd) *v.* promised solemnly

W

weasel (WEE zuhl) *n.* small mammal that eats rats, mice, birds, and eggs

whiff (hwihf) *n.* smell; scent

whimper (HWIHM puhr) *v.* make low, crying sounds

withered (WIHTH uhr) *adj.* dried up

wonderment (WUHN duhr muhnt) *n.* feeling of surprise or astonishment

wonders (WUHN duhrz) *n.* things that cause astonishment; marvels

writhing (RYTH ihng) *adj.* squirming, often in response to pain

wrought (rawt) *v.* shaped; made; shaped by hammering

Y

yearned (yurnd) *v.* wanted very much

Spanish Glossary

El vocabulario de Gran Pregunta aparece en **azul**. El vocabulario académico de alta utilidad está <u>subrayado</u>.

A

abode / domicilio s. hogar; residencia

acknowledge / aceptar v. reconocer; admitir

acquainted / conocido adj. familiar

adequate / adecuado adj. bastante; suficiente

adolescence / adolescencia s. época de desarrollo en la que una persona joven se convierte en adulto

aloft / en vuelo adj. en lo alto; volando; en el aire

<u>**analyze / analizar**</u> v. separar las partes de un todo y examinar detenidamente

antidote / antídoto s. remedio; cura

apparent / aparente adj. simulado

appearance / apariencia s. aspecto o parecer de una persona o cosa

<u>**appreciate / apreciar**</u> v. estar agradecido

approvingly / con aprobación adv. con consentimiento

aptitude / aptitud s. talento; habilidad

arid / árido adj. seco; baldío

<u>**assumption / suposición**</u> s. creencia o aceptación de la existencia de algo

astonish / pasmar v. asombrar

atmospheric / atmosférico adj. relativo al aire que rodea la Tierra

<u>**attitude / actitud**</u> s. estado mental determinado por creencias, sentimientos y valores

audible / audible adj. lo suficiente-mente alto para que se pueda oír

avid / ávido adj. ansioso y entusiasmado

<u>**awareness / conciencia**</u> s. cono-cimiento adquirido por medio de la percepción o de información

awe / sobrecogimiento s. sentimien-tos encontrados de temor y asombro

B

babbled / balbuceó v. murmuró; habló sin saber o demasiado

ban / prohibición s. orden que impide algo

banish / desterrar v. expulsar; exiliar

believable / creíble adj. tener la habi-lidad de inculcar credibilidad o confianza

bellow / bramar v. rugir profundamente

bias / parcial s. tendencia a interpretar las cosas de manera sesgada o prejuiciosa

bigots / intolerantes s. personas de mentalidad cerrada, prejuiciosas

blander / insípido adj. sin sabor

bound/ sujeto v. atado

brawny / fornido adj. fuerte y musculoso

burrow / excavar v. cavar un hollo como refugio

C

canyon / cañón s. paso estrecho entre dos montañas

captivity / cautiverio s. encarcelami-ento; detenido como prisionero

cattails / espadañas s. plantas her-báceas de tallo alto con hojas en forma de espada que se encuentran en lugares húmedos

causeways / calzada elevada s. camino sobre terreno húmedo o agua poco profunda

<u>**challenge / desafiar**</u> v. retar; cuestionar

<u>**characteristic / característica**</u> s. rasgo; facción

clusters / grupos s. conjunto de cosas similares; montón

coax / convencer v. persuadir de manera sutil

common / común adj. ordinario; frecuente y muy sabido

communal / comunal adj. compartido por todos

<u>**communicate / comunicar**</u> v. compartir pensamientos o sentimientos, usualmente con palabras

<u>**communication / comunicación**</u> s. acto de compartir información o de hablar

<u>**community / comunidad**</u> s. grupo de personas que tienen un interés en común o que viven cerca el uno del otro

compelled / obligado v. forzado

competition / competencia s. evento o juego en que las personas o bandos pretenden ganar

compromise / solución s. convenio satisfactorio entre dos partes

compulsion / compulsión s. impulso irresistible

<u>**conclude / concluir**</u> v. terminar; finalizar

<u>**conflict / conflicto**</u> s. choque o lucha entre grupos opuestos

consolation / consolación s. algo que alivia la pena de una persona decepcionada

conspired / conspiró v. planeó de manera secreta

contradiction / contradicción s. diferencia entre dos cosas conflictivas que demuestra que sólo una es cierta

contraption / artilugio s. aparato o mecanismo extraño

<u>**contribute / contribuir**</u> v. agregar; enriquecer

conveyed / comunicó v. hizo saber; expresó

conviction / convicción s. creencia

<u>**convince / convencer**</u> v. persuadir; incitar a aceptar un punto de vista

coveted / codició v. quiso; deseó

croon / canturrear *v.* cantar o tararear silenciosa y dulcemente

crouches / acuclillar *v.* agacharse o doblarse a un nivel bajo

crucial / crucial *adj.* importante; crítico

crystal / cristal *adj.* hecho de vidrio claro y brillante

culminated / culminó *v.* alcanzó su punto más alto o clímax

culprit / inculpado *s.* persona culpable

culture / cultura *s.* conjunto de modos de vida y costumbres de un grupo o una comunidad

cunning / astuto *adj.* hábil; taimado

cunningly / astutamente *adv.* ingeniosamente

cupboard / gabinete *s.* mueble con repizas para tazas, platos y comida

curdled / cortado *adj.* podrido

curiosity / curiosidad *s.* deseo de aprender o saber

curiosity / curiosidad *s.* estado en el que se quiere aprender más sobre un tema

custom / costumbre *s.* lo que se hace comúnmente

D

dabbling / chapuzar *v.* zambullirse, sumergirse o patalear en el agua

danger / peligro *s.* exposición a posible daño, lesión o pérdida

debate / debate *v.* argumento que pretende convencer

deceive / engañar *v.* hacer a alguien creer lo que no es cierto

decreed / decretó *v.* creó un mandato oficial

defiant / desafiante *adj.* que resiste valientemente

defies / desafía *v.* que se resiste o se opone valientemente o de manera abierta

define / definir *v.* determinar la naturaleza o establecer el significado de algo

deserts / desertar *v.* dejar, abandonar, especialmente un puesto militar

designated / designó *v.* señaló; maró

desire / deseo *s.* acción de desear o querer

desolate / desolado *adj.* solo; solitario

desperate / desesperado *adj.* sin esperanzas; con gran deseo o necesidad

destiny / destino *s.* aparente secuencia de sucesos inevitables

destitute / indigentes *adj.* personas que viven en pobreza absoluta

devastated / devastado *adj.* destruido; completamente disgustado

devastating / devastador *adj.* destructivo; arrollador

dignitaries / dignatarios *s.* personas investidas de un cargo elevado

diplomats / diplomáticos *s.* empleados del gobierno que trabajan con otras naciones

disagreement / desacuerdo *s.* diferencia o conflicto entre dos grupos o personas

discipline / disciplina *s.* entrenamiento; autocontrol

discover / descubrir *v.* encontrar o explorar

dislodge / desplazar *v.* mover a la fuerza de una posición o lugar

dismal / lúgubre *adj.* oscuro y sombrío

dispelled / disipó *v.* alejó; hizo desvanecer

dispute / disputa *s.* desacuerdo

distinct / distinto *adj.* separado y diferente

distract / distraer *v.* apartar la atención

diversions / diversiones *s.* formas de entretenimiento

diversity / diversidad *s.* variedad de grupos o culturas

dominions / dominios *s.* países o territorios gobernados

downy / suave *adj.* blando y esponjoso

duty / deber *s.* responsabilidad; obligación

E

elaboration / elaboración *s.* unión de más detalles

elective / opción *s.* curso o decisión que se puede tomar

emerged / sobresalió *v.* apareció a la vista; se volvió visible

emphatic / enfático *adj.* que se siente o se hace con fuerza

enrich / enriquecer *v.* mejorar

entertain / entretener *v.* divertir; hacer una presentación

environment / medio ambiente *s.* lo que nos rodea; el mundo natural

envying / envidiando *v.* queriendo lo que otro posee

epidemic / epidemia *s.* proliferación de una enfermedad contagiosa

equality / igualdad *s.* estado de la sociedad en el que todas las personas se tratan de la misma manera

ethnicity / etnicidad *s.* origen cultural o racial

evading / evadiendo *v.* evitando

evaluate / evaluar *v.* juzgar; determinar el significado de algo

evaporated / evaporó *v.* cambió de líquido a gas

evidence / evidencia *s.* prueba que apoya un reclamo o argumento

evidently / evidentemente *adv.* claramente; obviamente

examine / examinar *v.* estudiar a fondo; observar detenidamente

exertion / esfuerzo *s.* trabajo físico

expectancy / expectativa *s.* lo que se espera

expectations / expectativas *s.* esperanzas de lo que viene

expense / gasto *s.* costo financiero

experiment / experimento *s.* prueba que determina un resultado

explain / explicar *v.* esclarecer o aclarar

explore / explorar *v.* investigar; examinar

express / expresar *v.* hablar de o comunicar un sentimiento

exquisite / refinado *adj.* hermoso y delicado

Student Edition Pages

extenuating / atenuar *v.* aliviar la gravedad de una situación

exultant / jubiloso *adj.* que expresa gran alegría o triunfo

F

facts / hechos *s.* la verdad o la realidad

factual / basado en hechos *adj.* basado en o limitado a lo que es real o verdadero

falsely / falsamente *adv.* de manera incorrecta o incierta

family / familia *s.* personas de relación consanguínea o que tienen un ancestro en común

fascinated / fascinado *adj.* encantado

fathom / braza *s.* unidad de longitud para medir la profundidad del agua

feeble / débil *adj.* flojo; enclenque

feebleness / debilidad *s.* falta de fuerza

fiction / ficción *s.* lo inventado o imaginado

fiddler / violinista *s.* persona que toca el violín

flatterers / alabadores *s.* personas que halagan a otra persona con poca sinceridad

fluent / fluido *adj.* que escribe con facilidad y soltura

flushed / expulsó *v.* obligó a salir de un lugar

flustered / nervioso *adj.* agitado; confuso

focus / enfoque *n.* punto central o tema de investigación

forage / forraje *s.* comida para animales domésticos

formidable / formidable *adj.* imponente; impresionante

forsythia / forsitia *s.* arbusto de flores amarillas que florece a principios de laprimavera

fragrant / fragante *adj.* que emana un aroma dulce

frontier / frontera *s.* región bajo desarrollo de un país; cualquier campo nuevo de aprendizaje

fundamental / fundamental *adj.* básico; que forma una base

furrowed / arrugar *v.* hacer pliegues

G

garlands / guirnalda *s.* corona de flores y hojas

garments / prendas *s.* ropa

gauge / medir *v.* estimar o juzgar

generate / spanish copy to come

globules / glóbulos *s.* gotas

glossy / lustroso *adj.* liso y brillante

goblets / copa *s.* envase para tomar que no tiene asas

gourd / mate *s.* fruta; la coraza seca se usa como taza

granite / granito *s.* piedra de color gris

gratitude / gratitud *s.* agradecimiento

group / grupo *s.* conjunto o agrupación, como de personas

groves / arboleda *s.* grupo pequeño de árboles

guidance / orientación *s.* consejo o asistencia

gumption / arrojo *s.* coraje; empuje

guzzle / engullir *v.* tragar atropelladamente

H

harness / arnés *s.* equipo que se usa para maniobrar un caballo o ajustarlo a un vehículo

haunches / ancas *s.* las patas posteriores de un animal

hexagons / hexágonos *s.* figuras de seis lados

hind / trasero *adj.* que está en la parte de atrás

hoarding / acaparando *v.* acumulando y almacenando provisiones como reservas

hoed / limpió con la azada *v.* cavó y removió tierra con una herramienta de metal

hors d'oeuvres / entremeses *s.* platillos sabrosos para picar antes de la comida

huddled / agrupado *v.* atestado o arrimado

I

identify / identificar *v.* reconocer como existente

ignorant / ignorante *adj.* que no sabe los hechos o que no tiene la información apropiada

ignore / ignorar *v.* hacer caso omiso; desconocer

ignored / ignoró *v.* no le prestó atención

image / imagen *n.* retrato; representación

immensely / inmensamente *adv.* de gran extremo; mucho

immensity / inmensidad *s.* cantidad inconmesurable o enorme

impervious / insensible *adj.* que no es afectado por algo

impetus / ímpetu *s.* fuerza motriz

implored / implorado *v.* suplicado

improvised / improvisó *v.* hizo o presentó de manera espontánea

improvising / improvisando *v.* creando o inventando espontáneamente

incessantly / incesante *adv.* sin parar

indispensable / indispensable *adj.* absolutamente necesario

individual / individuo *s.* una sola persona o cosa

inflicted / inflijió *v.* que ha causado sufrimiento o daño

inform / informar *v.* decir; dar información de algo

information / información *s.* conocimiento adquirido por medio de estudio o de la experiencia

initiation / iniciación *s.* proceso por el cual uno se convierte en miembro de un grupo

inquire / preguntar *v.* cuestionar con el fin de aprender

insight / perspicacia s. habilidad de ver la verdad; entendimiento

integration / integración s. fin de la separación cultural o de grupos raciales

intercedes / intercede v. actúa por otra persona

intermixed / mixto adj. compuesto de elementos diferentes

interplanetary / interplanetario adj. entre planetas

interrupted / interrumpido v. se refiere a un pensamiento o discusión que se ha detenido; sin continuidad

intervene / interviene v. que toma parte en una situación como influencia para modificar, resolver o estropear una acción o argumento

interview / entrevistar v. hacer una serie de preguntas a una persona con el fin de obtener información

intricate / intricado adj. complejo; detallado

investigate / investigar v. examinar a fondo

irrigation / irrigación s. suministro de agua a acequias, canales o regaderas

J

justifies / justifica v. que da escusas; explica

K

kinsmen / parientes s. familiares; en inglés se usan dos palabras diferentes para referirse a los hombres o a las mujeres que son miembros de la familia

knowledge / conocimiento s. el resultado de conocer; acción de tener presente

L

laborious / laborioso adj. que cuesta bastante trabajo o esfuerzo

learn / aprender v. obtener conocimiento o destrezas

legislation / legislación s. ley

liberty / libertad s. autonomía de la esclavitud o cautiverio

listen / escuchar v. prestar atención; atender

loathed / abominado v. odiado

longhorns / ganado longhorn s. tipo de ganado que se caracteriza por sus cuernos largos

luminous / luminoso adj. que despide luz

M

malice / malicia s. mala intención

malicious / malicioso adj. que tiene mala intención; odioso

manned / tripulado adj. que tiene un operador humano abordo

meager / exiguo adj. precario; escaso

media / medios de comunicación s. conjunto de fuentes de información incluyendo periódicos, televisión y la Internet

meek / manso adj. tímido; que no demuestra enfado

merely / meramente adv. no más de; y nada más; sencillamente

metamorphosis / metamorfosis s. en estado de cambio

minnow / pececillo s. pez pequeño

miracle / milagro s. suceso o cosa extraordinaria; maravilla

misunderstanding / malentendido s. estado en el que palabras o un punto de vista no logra ser comunicado

monarch / monarca s. dominio por carácter hereditario, como el de un rey o una reina

morose / lúgubre adj. sombrío

mortality / mortalidad s. condición de ser mortal, o de tener que morir en algún momento

mourning / luto s. expresión de pena, especialmente después de que alguien muere

murmuring / murmurando v. haciendo ruidos bajos e indescifrables

mystery / misterio s. algo inexplicable, desconocido o que se mantiene bajo secreto

N

neglected / descuidó v. no logró cuidar

nobility / nobleza s. personas de alto nivel en la sociedad

nonchalantly / con toda tranquilidad adv. despreocupado, con indiferencia

O

obsession / obsesión s. interés extremo en algo que previene pensar en cualquier otra cosa

obstacle / obstáculo s. algo que se interviene en el camino

ominous / siniestro adj. amenazante

opinion / opinión s. creencia basada en lo que parece ser cierto o probable

opposition / oposición s. estar en contra

optimist / optimista s. alguien que tiende a ver las cosas de la manera más favorable

ornament / adornar v. embellecer

outcome / resultado s. la manera en que algo se resuelve

outskirts / alrededores s. distritos lejos del centro de una ciudad

P

parallel / paralelo adj. que se extiende en la misma dirección y está separado siempre a la misma distancia

parson / pastor s. ministro

passion / pasión s. sentimientos fuertes de amor, odio o temor

patriotic / patriótico adj. sentir gran amor y apoyo por su país de origen

paupers / pobres s. gente necesitada

peasants / campesinos s. dueños de pequeñas fincas; trabajadores de fincas

peeved / molesto adj. irritado; fastidiado

penned / acorralado adj. encerrado en un área pequeña

perceive / percibir v. aceptar un punto de vista; ver

perception / percepción *s.* estar conciente por medio de uno o más sentidos

perch / percha *s.* palo para que los pájaros y aves se posen; asiento

perfunctorily / superficialmente *adv.* hecho sin mucho cuidado, como parte de una rutina

perilous / arriesgado *adj.* peligroso

permanent / permanente *adj.* duradero o que debe durar para siempre

perpetual / perpetuo *adj.* constante; sin fin

persistently / persistentemente *adv.* de manera firme y constante

perspective / perspectiva *s.* punto de vista

pestering / molestando *v.* fastidiando; irritando

plaited / entretejido *adj.* trenzado

plausible / plausible *adj.* creíble

porridge / gacha *s.* comida blanda compuesta de cereal hervido en agua o leche

potential / potencial *s.* posibilidad; capacidad

practical / práctico *adj.* sensato; eficiente; realista

precaution / precaución *s.* lo que se hace para prevenir que ocurra algo malo o peligroso

preliminary / preliminar *adj.* que viene antes o anticipando el acto principal

presumptuous / presumido *adj.* con exceso de confianza en sí mismo; arrogante

prickly / espinoso *adj.* puntiagudo; con espinas

produce / producir *v.* hacer; crear

profound / profundo *adj.* que se siente grave o intensamente

promote / promover *v.* animar; contribuir al crecimiento de algo

proposal / propuesta *s.* plan; oferta

python / pitón *s.* culebra de gran tamaño

Q

quest / búsqueda *s.* seguimiento extenso

question / cuestionar *v.* desafiar la precisión de algo; poner en duda

R

rancid / rancio *adj.* dañado y maloliente

rash / imprudente *adj.* muy precipitado

react / reaccionar *v.* responder; hacer algo al respecto

reaction / reacción *s.* respuesta a una influencia, acción o afirmación

readapted / se adaptó de nuevo *v.* se ajustó gradualmente otra vez

reality / realidad *s.* estado o calidad de ser real o verdadero

realm / dominio *s.* reino

reassuring / tranquilizante *adj.* que alivia o da confianza

reeds / cañas *s.* hierbas de tallo alto que crecen en pantanos

reel / girar *v.* dar vueltas; enrollar

reflect / refleccionar *v.* pensar en algo; considerar

refugee / refugiado *s.* persona que huye de su hogar o país en busca de asilo debido a la guerra o crueldad

refuse / basura *s.* desperdicios; desechos

regretted / arrepentirse *v.* sentir pesar por algo

relation / relación *s.* referencia, respeto

relented / cedió *v.* se dejó convencer

reliable / confiable *adj.* del que se puede depender

relished / deleitar *v.* causar placer; gozar; disfrutar

remote / remoto *adj.* muy lejos de cualquier cosa

repressive / represivo *adj.* altamente estricto

reproach / reproche *s.* desgracia, culpa

resilient / resistente *adj.* fuerte; que puede recobrar su estado original

resolution / resolución *s.* fin satisfactorio de un conflicto

resumed / recobrar *v.* volver al estado original

reveal / revelar *v.* hacer saber; demostrar

revived / revivió *v.* volvió a la vida o recobró consciencia

righteous / recto *adj.* que actúa de manera justa

routed / derrotó *v.* venció

rummaging / hurgando *v.* buscando entre cosas

S

sage / erudito *s.* sabio

saluting / homenajear *v.* honrar con un acto o gesto

saturation / saturación *s.* condición en la que se está completamente lleno

savored / saboreó *v.* degustó o apreció con placer

scorned / desdeñar *v.* menospreciar

scowl / fruncir el ceño *v.* mirar a alguien o algo con ira o desaprobación

sensitive / sensible *adj.* que se hiere con facilidad

sentimental / sentimental *adj.* que demuestra sentimientos compasivos

severe / severo *adj.* duro

shed / mudar *v.* perder o cambiar

shipments / remesa *s.* envío o acto de trasportar objetos

shortsightedness / falta de visión *s.* carencia de proyección en el futuro

shuffle / arrastrar *v.* caminar sin levantar los pies

simultaneously / simultáneo *adv.* al mismo tiempo

sinewy / vigoroso *adj.* recio y fuerte

slackening / aminorando *v.* relajando; volviéndose menos activo

slather / untar *v.* extender de manera generosa

sluggishly / perezosamente *adv.* sin energía

smattering / poquito *s.* cantidad pequeña

snuffs / extinguir *v.* apagar

solemn / solemne *adj.* serio; sombrío

speak / hablar *v.* usar lenguaje; expresar con palabras

spectators / espectadores *s.* personas que ven con atención

spied / espiar *v.* observar a escondidas

spigot / grifo *s.* llave; espita

spines / espinazo *s.* vértebras

sputters / chisporrotear *v.* hacer ruidos explosivos o sibilante

strategy / estrategia *s.* planes para alcanzar el éxito o lograr un objetivo

strive / esforzarse *v.* luchar

struggle / lucha *s.* pelea

stutter / tartamudear *v.* hablar sin fluidez o de manera entrecortada

suit / convenir *v.* ser placentero; satisfacer

suitable / adecuado *adj.* apropiado

suitors / pretendientes *s.* hombres que cortejan o buscan el matrimonio

summoned / convocar *v.* citar o llamar a una reunión

supple / ágil *adj.* que usa su cuerpo con facilidad y soltura

surpass / superar *v.* ser superior

sustained / sostenido *adj.* apoyado; mantenido

swerve / viraje *s.* movimiento en curva

T

teach / enseñar *v.* compartir información o conocimiento

team / equipo *s.* grupo unido por una meta en común

technology / tecnología *s.* aplicación práctica de las ciencias en negocios o en la industria

telegram / telegrama *s.* mensaje transmitido por telégrafo

timid / tímido *adj.* reservado, temeroso

tolerant / tolerante *adj.* que acepta; libre de resistencia o prejuicios

torrent / torrente *s.* inundación

tradition / tradición *s.* costumbre, de un grupo social o cultura

transfixed / embelesado *adj.* fascinado

transformation / transformación *s.* cambio

translates / trasladar *v.* mover de un lado al otro

translucent / translúcido *adj.* que permite pasar la luz

transmit / transmitir *v.* enviar o repartir

truth / verdad *s.* lo que se corrobora con hechos o la realidad

tumultuously / tumultuoso *adv.* de manera ruidosa y violenta

twine / bramante *s.* cordón delgado o grueso, con las hebras entretejidas

U

ultimate / último *adj.* final

unanimous / unánime *adj.* basado en un acuerdo total

uncommonly / extraordinariamente *adv.* fuera de lo común

unconsciously / inconscientemente *adv.* con poca consideración; sin pensarlo

understand / entender *v.* llegar a conocer y comprender algo

understanding / entendimiento *s.* acuerdo; fin de un conflicto

unify / unificar *v.* juntar para formar uno solo

unique / único *adj.* sin otro de su especie

unravel / desenmarañar *v.* desenredar o separar

utter / pronunciar *v.* articular

V

vacancy / vacante *s.* desocupado, vacío; cargo disponible

varmints / alimañas *s.* insectos

veranda / veranda *s.* porche descubierto, usualmente con techo

verge / borde *s.* orilla; límite

vital / vital *adj.* de extrema importancia o necesario

void / vacío *s.* desocupado

vowed / juró *v.* prometió solemnemente

W

weasel / comadreja *s.* mamífero pequeño que se alimenta de ratas, ratones, aves y huevos

whiff / olorcillo *s.* olor; aroma

whimper / quejido *v.* llanto, lamento

withered / marchitado *adj.* que se ha secado

wonderment / maravilla *s.* asombro

wonders / maravillas *s.* cosas que causan asombro

writhing / retorcido *adj.* contorcionado, usualmente a causa de dolor

wrought / forjó *v.* dio forma; fabricó; dio forma al martillar

Y

yearned / anhelar *v.* desear vehemente

Literary Terms

ALLITERATION *Alliteration* is the repetition of initial consonant sounds. Writers use alliteration to draw attention to certain words or ideas, to imitate sounds, and to create musical effects.

ALLUSION An *allusion* is a reference to a well-known person, event, place, literary work, or work of art. Allusions allow the writer to express complex ideas without spelling them out. Understanding what a literary work is saying often depends on recognizing its allusions and the meanings they suggest.

ANALOGY An *analogy* makes a comparison between two or more things that are similar in some ways but otherwise unalike.

ANECDOTE An *anecdote* is a brief story about an interesting, amusing, or strange event. Writers tell anecdotes to entertain or to make a point.

ANTAGONIST An *antagonist* is a character or a force in conflict with a main character, or protagonist.

See *Conflict* and *Protagonist.*

ARGUMENT See *Persuasion.*

ATMOSPHERE *Atmosphere,* or *mood,* is the feeling created in the reader by a literary work or passage.

AUTHOR'S ARGUMENT An *author's argument* is the position he or she puts forward, supported by reasons.

AUTHOR'S PURPOSE An *author's purpose* is his or her main reason for writing. For example, an author may want to entertain, inform, or persuade the reader. Sometimes an author is trying to teach a moral lesson or reflect on an experience. An author may have more than one purpose for writing.

AUTOBIOGRAPHY An *autobiography* is the story of the writer's own life, told by the writer. Autobiographical writing may tell about the person's whole life or only a part of it.

Because autobiographies are about real people and events, they are a form of nonfiction. Most autobiographies are written in the first person.

See *Biography, Nonfiction,* and *Point of View.*

BIOGRAPHY A *biography* is a form of nonfiction in which a writer tells the life story of another person. Most biographies are written about famous or admirable people.

Although biographies are nonfiction, the most effective ones share the qualities of good narrative writing.

See *Autobiography* and *Nonfiction.*

CHARACTER A *character* is a person or an animal that takes part in the action of a literary work. The main, or *major,* character is the most important character in a story, poem, or play. A *minor* character is one who takes part in the action but is not the focus of attention.

Characters are sometimes classified as flat or round. A *flat character* is one-sided and often stereotypical. A *round character,* on the other hand, is fully developed and exhibits many traits—often both faults and virtues. Characters can also be classified as dynamic or static. A *dynamic character* is one who changes or grows during the course of the work. A *static character* is one who does not change.

See *Characterization, Hero/Heroine,* and *Motive.*

CHARACTERIZATION *Characterization* is the act of creating and developing a character. Authors use two major methods of characterization—*direct* and *indirect.* When using direct characterization, a writer states the *characters' traits,* or characteristics.

When describing a character indirectly, a writer depends on the reader to draw conclusions about the character's traits. Sometimes the writer tells what other participants in the story say and think about the character.

See *Character* and *Motive.*

CLIMAX The *climax,* also called the turning point, is the high point in the action of the plot. It is the moment of greatest tension, when the outcome of the plot hangs in the balance.

See *Plot.*

COMEDY A *comedy* is a literary work, especially a play, which is light, often humorous or satirical, and ends happily. Comedies frequently depict ordinary characters faced with temporary difficulties and conflicts. Types of comedy include *romantic comedy,* which involves problems between lovers, and the *comedy of manners,* which satirically challenges social customs of a society.

CONCRETE POEM A *concrete poem* is one with a shape that suggests its subject. The poet arranges the

letters, punctuation, and lines to create an image, or picture, on the page.

CONFLICT A *conflict* is a struggle between opposing forces. Conflict is one of the most important elements of stories, novels, and plays because it causes the action. There are two kinds of conflict: external and internal.

An *external conflict* is one in which a character struggles against some outside force, such as another person. Another kind of external conflict may occur between a character and some force in nature.

An *internal conflict* takes place within the mind of a character. The character struggles to make a decision, take an action, or overcome a feeling.

See *Plot.*

CONNOTATIONS The *connotation* of a word is the set of ideas associated with it in addition to its explicit meaning. The connotation of a word can be personal, based on individual experiences. More often, cultural connotations—those recognizable by most people in a group—determine a writer's word choices.

See also *Denotation.*

COUPLET A *couplet* is two consecutive lines of verse with end rhymes. Often, a couplet functions as a stanza.

CULTURAL CONTEXT The *cultural context* of a literary work is the economic, social, and historical environment of the characters. This includes the attitudes and customs of that culture and historical period.

DENOTATION The *denotation* of a word is its dictionary meaning, independent of other associations that the word may have. The denotation of the word *lake,* for example, is "an inland body of water." "Vacation spot" and "place where the fishing is good" are connotations of the word *lake.*

See also *Connotation.*

DESCRIPTION A *description* is a portrait, in words, of a person, place, or object. Descriptive writing uses images that appeal to the five senses —sight, hearing, touch, taste, and smell.

See *Images.*

DEVELOPMENT See *Plot.*

DIALECT *Dialect* is the form of a language spoken by people in a particular region or group. Dialects differ in pronunciation, grammar, and word choice. The English language is divided into many dialects. British English differs from American English.

DIALOGUE A *dialogue* is a conversation between characters. In poems, novels, and short stories, dialogue is usually set off by quotation marks to indicate a speaker's exact words.

In a play, dialogue follows the names of the characters, and no quotation marks are used.

DICTION *Diction* is a writer's word choice and the way the writer puts those words together. Diction is part of a writer's style and may be described as formal or informal, plain or fancy, ordinary or technical, sophisticated or down-to-earth, old-fashioned or modern.

DRAMA A *drama* is a story written to be performed by actors. Although a drama is meant to be performed, one can also read the script, or written version, and imagine the action. The *script* of a drama is made up of dialogue and stage directions. The *dialogue* is the words spoken by the actors. The *stage directions,* usually printed in italics, tell how the actors should look, move, and speak. They also describe the setting, sound effects, and lighting.

Dramas are often divided into parts called *acts.* The acts are often divided into smaller parts called *scenes.*

DYNAMIC CHARACTER See *Character.*

ESSAY An *essay* is a short nonfiction work about a particular subject. Most essays have a single major focus and a clear introduction, body, and conclusion.

There are many types of essays. An *informal essay* uses casual, conversational language. A *historical essay* gives facts, explanations, and insights about historical events. An *expository essay* explains an idea by breaking it down. A *narrative essay* tells a story about a real-life experience. An *informational essay* explains a process. A *persuasive essay* offers an opinion and supports it. A *humorous essay* uses humor to achieve the author's purpose. A *reflective essay* addresses an event or experience and includes the writer's personal insights about the event's importance.

See *Exposition, Narration,* and *Persuasion.*

EXPOSITION In the plot of a story or a drama, the *exposition,* or introduction, is the part of the work that introduces the characters, setting, and basic situation.

See *Plot.*

EXPOSITORY WRITING *Expository writing* is writing that explains or informs.

EXTENDED METAPHOR In an *extended metaphor,* as in a regular metaphor, a subject is spoken or written of as though it were something else. However, extended metaphor differs from regular metaphor in that several connected comparisons are made.

See *Metaphor.*

EXTERNAL CONFLICT See *Conflict.*

FABLE A *fable* is a brief story or poem, usually with animal characters, that teaches a lesson, or moral. The moral is usually stated at the end of the fable.

See *Irony* and *Moral.*

FANTASY A *fantasy* is highly imaginative writing that contains elements not found in real life. Examples of fantasy include stories that involve supernatural elements, stories that resemble fairy tales, stories that deal with imaginary places and creatures, and science-fiction stories.

See *Science Fiction.*

FICTION *Fiction* is prose writing that tells about imaginary characters and events. Short stories and novels are works of fiction. Some writers base their fiction on actual events and people, adding invented characters, dialogue, settings, and plots. Other writers rely on imagination alone.

See *Narration, Nonfiction,* and *Prose.*

FIGURATIVE LANGUAGE *Figurative language* is writing or speech that is not meant to be taken literally. The many types of figurative language are known as *figures of speech.* Common figures of speech include metaphor, personification, and simile. Writers use figurative language to state ideas in vivid and imaginative ways.

See *Metaphor, Personification, Simile,* and *Symbol.*

FIGURE OF SPEECH See *Figurative Language.*

FLASHBACK A *flashback* is a scene within a story that interrupts the sequence of events to relate events that occurred in the past.

FLAT CHARACTER See *Character.*

FOIL A *foil* is a character whose behavior and attitude contrast with those of the main character.

FOLK TALE A *folk tale* is a story composed orally and then passed from person to person by word of mouth. Folk tales originated among people who could neither read nor write. These people entertained one another by telling stories aloud—often dealing with heroes, adventure, magic, or romance. Eventually, modern scholars collected these stories and wrote them down.

Folk tales reflect the cultural beliefs and environments from which they come.

See *Fable, Legend, Myth,* and *Oral Tradition.*

FOOT See *Meter.*

FORESHADOWING *Foreshadowing* is the author's use of clues to hint at what might happen later in the story. Writers use foreshadowing to build their readers' expectations and to create suspense.

FREE VERSE *Free verse* is poetry not written in a regular, rhythmical pattern, or meter. The poet is free to write lines of any length or with any number of stresses, or beats. Free verse is therefore less constraining than *metrical verse,* in which every line must have a certain length and a certain number of stresses.

See *Meter.*

GENRE A *genre* is a division or type of literature. Literature is commonly divided into three major genres: poetry, prose, and drama. Each major genre is, in turn, divided into lesser genres, as follows:

1. *Poetry:* lyric poetry, concrete poetry, dramatic poetry, narrative poetry, epic poetry

2. *Prose:* fiction (novels and short stories) and nonfiction (biography, autobiography, letters, essays, and reports)

3. *Drama:* serious drama and tragedy, comic drama, melodrama, and farce

See *Drama, Poetry,* and *Prose.*

HAIKU The *haiku* is a three-line Japanese verse form. The first and third lines of a haiku each have five syllables. The second line has seven syllables. A writer of haiku uses images to create a single, vivid picture, generally of a scene from nature.

HERO/HEROINE A *hero* or *heroine* is a character whose actions are inspiring or noble. Often heroes and heroines struggle to overcome the obstacles and problems that stand in their way. Note that the term *hero* was originally used only for male characters, while heroic female characters were always called *heroines.* However, it is now acceptable to use *hero* to refer to females as well as to males.

HISTORICAL CONTEXT The *historical context* of a literary work includes the actual political and social events and trends of the time. When a work takes place in the past, knowledge about that historical time period can help the reader understand its setting, background, culture, and message, as well as the attitudes and actions of its characters. A reader must also take into account the historical context in which the writer was creating the work, which may be different from the time period of the work's setting.

HUMOR *Humor* is writing intended to evoke laughter. While most humorists try to entertain, humor can also be used to convey a serious theme.

IDIOM An *idiom* is an expression that has a meaning particular to a language or region. For example, in "Seventh Grade," Gary Soto uses the idiom "making a face," which means to contort one's face in an unusual, usually unattractive way.

IMAGERY See *Images.*

IMAGES *Images* are words or phrases that appeal to one or more of the five senses. Writers use images to describe how their subjects look, sound, feel, taste, and smell. Poets often paint images, or word pictures, that appeal to the senses. These pictures help you to experience the poem fully.

INTERNAL CONFLICT See *Conflict.*

IRONY *Irony* is a contradiction between what happens and what is expected. There are three main types of irony. *Situational irony* occurs when something happens that directly contradicts the expectations of the characters or the audience. *Verbal irony* is something contradictory that is said. In *dramatic irony,* the audience is aware of something that the character or speaker is not.

JOURNAL A *journal* is a daily, or periodic, account of events and the writer's thoughts and feelings about those events. Personal journals are not normally written for publication, but sometimes they do get published later with permission from the author or the author's family.

LEGEND A *legend* is a widely told story about the past—one that may or may not have a foundation in fact. Every culture has its own legends—its familiar, traditional stories.

See *Folk Tale, Myth,* and *Oral Tradition.*

LETTERS A *letter* is a written communication from one person to another. In personal letters, the writer shares information and his or her thoughts and feelings with one other person or group. Although letters are not normally written for publication, they sometimes do get published later with the permission of the author or the author's family.

LIMERICK A *limerick* is a humorous, rhyming, five-line poem with a specific meter and rhyme scheme. Most limericks have three strong stresses in lines 1, 2, and 5 and two strong stresses in lines 3 and 4. Most follow the rhyme scheme *aabba.*

LYRIC POEM A *lyric poem* is a highly musical verse that expresses the observations and feelings of a single speaker. It creates a single, unified impression.

MAIN CHARACTER See *Character.*

MEDIA ACCOUNTS *Media accounts* are reports, explanations, opinions, or descriptions written for television, radio, newspapers, and magazines. While some media accounts report only facts, others include the writer's thoughts and reflections.

METAPHOR A *metaphor* is a figure of speech in which something is described as though it were something else. A metaphor, like a simile, works by pointing out a similarity between two unlike things.

See *Extended Metaphor* and *Simile.*

METER The *meter* of a poem is its rhythmical pattern. This pattern is determined by the number of *stresses,* or beats, in each line. To describe the meter of a poem, read it emphasizing the beats in each line. Then, mark the stressed and unstressed syllables, as follows:

Mў fáth | ĕr wás | tῆe fírst | tŏ héar |

As you can see, each strong stress is marked with a slanted line (´) and each unstressed syllable with a horseshoe symbol (˘). The weak and strong stresses are then divided by vertical lines (|) into groups called feet.

MINOR CHARACTER See *Character.*

MOOD See *Atmosphere.*

MORAL A *moral* is a lesson taught by a literary work. A fable usually ends with a moral that is directly stated. A poem, novel, short story, or essay often suggests a moral that is not directly stated. The moral must be drawn by the reader, based on other elements in the work.

See *Fable.*

MOTIVATION See *Motive.*

MOTIVE A *motive* is a reason that explains or partially explains a character's thoughts, feelings, actions, or speech. Writers try to make their characters' motives, or motivations, as clear as possible. If the motives of a main character are not clear, then the character will not be believable.

Characters are often motivated by needs, such as food and shelter. They are also motivated by feelings, such as fear, love, and pride. Motives may be obvious or hidden.

MYTH A *myth* is a fictional tale that explains the actions of gods or heroes or the origins of elements of nature. Myths are part of the oral tradition. They are composed orally and then passed from generation to generation by word of mouth. Every ancient culture has its own mythology, or collection of myths. Greek and Roman myths are known collectively as *classical mythology.*

See *Oral Tradition.*

NARRATION *Narration* is writing that tells a story. The act of telling a story is also called narration. Each piece is a *narrative.* A story told in fiction, nonfiction, poetry, or even drama is called a narrative.

See *Narrative, Narrative Poem,* and *Narrator.*

NARRATIVE A *narrative* is a story. A narrative can be either fiction or nonfiction. Novels and short stories are types of fictional narratives. Biographies and autobiographies are nonfiction narratives. Poems that tell stories are also narratives.

See *Narration* and *Narrative Poem.*

NARRATIVE POEM A *narrative poem* is a story told in verse. Narrative poems often have all the elements of short stories, including characters, conflict, and plot.

NARRATOR A *narrator* is a speaker or a character who tells a story. The narrator's perspective is the way he or she sees things. A *third-person narrator* is one who stands outside the action and speaks about it. A *first-person narrator* is one who tells a story and participates in its action.

See *Point of View.*

NONFICTION *Nonfiction* is prose writing that presents and explains ideas or that tells about real people, places, objects, or events. Autobiographies, biographies, essays, reports, letters, memos, and newspaper articles are all types of nonfiction.

See *Fiction.*

NOVEL A *novel* is a long work of fiction. Novels contain such elements as characters, plot, conflict, and setting. The writer of novels, or novelist, develops these elements. In addition to its main plot, a novel may contain one or more subplots, or independent, related stories. A novel may also have several themes.

See *Fiction* and *Short Story.*

NOVELLA A fiction work that is longer than a short story but shorter than a novel.

ONOMATOPOEIA *Onomatopoeia* is the use of words that imitate sounds. *Crash, buzz, screech, hiss, neigh, jingle,* and *cluck* are examples of onomatopoeia. *Chickadee, towhee,* and *whippoorwill* are onomatopoeic names of birds.

Onomatopoeia can help put the reader in the activity of a poem.

ORAL TRADITION *Oral tradition* is the passing of songs, stories, and poems from generation to generation by word of mouth. Folk songs, folk tales, legends, and myths all come from the oral tradition. No one knows who first created these stories and poems.

See *Folk Tale, Legend,* and *Myth.*

OXYMORON An *oxymoron* (pl. *oxymora*) is a figure of speech that links two opposite or contradictory words in order to point out an idea or situation that seems contradictory or inconsistent but on closer inspection turns out to be somehow true.

PERSONIFICATION *Personification* is a type of figurative language in which a nonhuman subject is given human characteristics.

PERSPECTIVE See *Narrator* and *Point of View.*

PERSUASION *Persuasion* is used in writing or speech that attempts to convince the reader or listener to adopt a particular opinion or course of action. Newspaper editorials and letters to the editor use persuasion. So do advertisements and campaign speeches given by political candidates. An *argument* is a logical way of presenting a belief, conclusion, or stance. A good argument is supported with reasoning and evidence.

See *Essay.*

PLAYWRIGHT A *playwright* is a person who writes plays. William Shakespeare is regarded as the greatest playwright in English literature.

PLOT *Plot* is the sequence of events in which each event results from a previous one and causes the next. In most novels, dramas, short stories, and narrative poems, the plot involves both characters and a central conflict. The plot usually begins with an *exposition* that introduces the setting, the characters, and the basic situation. This is followed by the *inciting incident,* which introduces the central conflict. The conflict then increases during the *development* until it reaches a high point of interest or suspense, the *climax.* The climax is followed by the *falling action,* or end, of the central conflict. Any events that occur during the *falling action* make up the *resolution* or *denouement.*

Some plots do not have all of these parts. Some stories begin with the inciting incident and end with the resolution.

See *Conflict.*

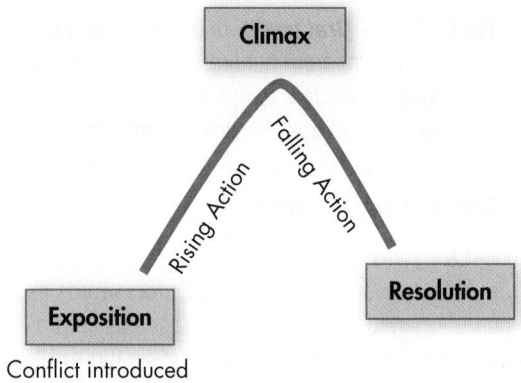

Conflict introduced

POETRY *Poetry* is one of the three major types of literature, the others being prose and drama. Most poems make use of highly concise, musical, and emotionally charged language. Many also make use of imagery, figurative language, and special devices of sound such as rhyme. Major types of poetry include *lyric poetry, narrative poetry,* and *concrete poetry.*

See *Concrete Poem, Genre, Lyric Poem,* and *Narrative Poem.*

POINT OF VIEW *Point of view* is the perspective, or vantage point, from which a story is told. It is either a narrator outside the story or a character in the story. *First-person point of view* is told by a character who uses the first-person pronoun "I."

The two kinds of *third-person point of view,* limited and omniscient, are called "third person" because the narrator

uses third-person pronouns such as *he* and *she* to refer to the characters. There is no "I" telling the story.

In stories told from the *omniscient third-person point of view,* the narrator knows and tells about what each character feels and thinks.

In stories told from the *limited third-person point of view,* the narrator relates the inner thoughts and feelings of only one character, and everything is viewed from this character's perspective.

See *Narrator.*

PROBLEM See *Conflict.*

PROSE *Prose* is the ordinary form of written language. Most writing that is not poetry, drama, or song is considered prose. Prose is one of the major genres of literature and occurs in fiction and nonfiction.

See *Fiction, Genre,* and *Nonfiction.*

PROTAGONIST The *protagonist* is the main character in a literary work. Often, the protagonist is a person, but sometimes it can be an animal.

See *Antagonist* and *Character.*

REFRAIN A *refrain* is a regularly repeated line or group of lines in a poem or a song.

REPETITION *Repetition* is the use, more than once, of any element of language—a sound, word, phrase, clause, or sentence. Repetition is used in both prose and poetry.

See *Alliteration, Meter, Plot, Rhyme,* and *Rhyme Scheme.*

RESOLUTION The *resolution* is the outcome of the conflict in a plot.

See *Plot.*

RHYME *Rhyme* is the repetition of sounds at the ends of words. Poets use rhyme to lend a songlike quality to their verses and to emphasize certain words and ideas. Many traditional poems contain *end rhymes,* or rhyming words at the ends of lines.

Another common device is the use of *internal rhymes,* or rhyming words within lines. Internal rhyme also emphasizes the flowing nature of a poem.

See *Rhyme Scheme.*

RHYME SCHEME A *rhyme scheme* is a regular pattern of rhyming words in a poem. To indicate the rhyme scheme of a poem, one uses lowercase letters. Each rhyme is assigned a different letter, as follows in the first stanza of "Dust of Snow" by Robert Frost:

The way a crow	*a*
Shook down on me	*b*
The dust of snow	*a*
From a hemlock tree	*b*

Thus, the stanza has the rhyme scheme *abab.*

RHYTHM *Rhythm* is the pattern of stressed and unstressed syllables in spoken or written language.

See *Meter.*

ROUND CHARACTER See *Character.*

SCENE A *scene* is a section of uninterrupted action in the act of a drama.

See *Drama.*

SCIENCE FICTION *Science fiction* combines elements of fiction and fantasy with scientific fact. Many science-fiction stories are set in the future.

SENSORY LANGUAGE *Sensory language* is writing or speech that appeals to one or more of the five senses.

See *Images.*

SETTING The *setting* of a literary work is the time and place of the action. The setting includes all the details of a place and time—the year, the time of day, even the weather. The place may be a specific country, state, region, community, neighborhood, building, institution, or home. Details such as dialects, clothing, customs, and modes of transportation are often used to establish setting. In most stories, the setting serves as a backdrop—a context in which the characters interact. Setting can also help to create a feeling, or atmosphere.

See *Atmosphere.*

SHORT STORY A *short story* is a brief work of fiction. Like a novel, a short story presents a sequence of events, or plot. The plot usually deals with a central conflict faced by a main character, or protagonist. The events in a short story usually communicate a message about life or human nature. This message, or central idea, is the story's theme.

See *Conflict, Plot,* and *Theme.*

SIMILE A *simile* is a figure of speech that uses *like* or *as* to make a direct comparison between two unlike ideas. Everyday speech often contains similes, such as "pale as a ghost," "good as gold," "spread like wildfire," and "clever as a fox."

SOUND DEVICES *Sound devices* are techniques used by writers to give musical effects to their writing. Some of these include *onomatopoeia, alliteration, rhyme, meter,* and *repetition.*

SPEAKER The *speaker* is the imaginary voice a poet uses when writing a poem. The speaker is the character who tells the poem. This character, or voice, often is not identified by name. There can be important differences between the poet and the poem's speaker.

See *Narrator.*

SPEECH A *speech* is a work that is delivered orally to an audience. There are many kinds of speeches suiting almost every kind of public gathering. Types of speeches include *dramatic, persuasive,* and *informative.*

STAGE DIRECTIONS *Stage directions* are notes included in a drama to describe how the work is to be performed or staged. Stage directions are usually printed in italics and enclosed within parentheses or brackets. Some stage directions describe the movements, costumes, emotional states, and ways of speaking of the characters.

STAGING *Staging* includes the setting, lighting, costumes, special effects, and music that go into a stage performance of a drama.

See *Drama.*

STANZA A *stanza* is a group of lines of poetry that are usually similar in length and pattern and are separated by spaces. A stanza is like a paragraph of poetry—it states and develops a single main idea.

STATIC CHARACTER See *Character.*

SURPRISE ENDING A *surprise ending* is a conclusion that is unexpected. The reader has certain expectations about the ending based on details in the story. Often, a surprise ending is *foreshadowed,* or subtly hinted at, in the course of the work.

See *Foreshadowing* and *Plot.*

SUSPENSE *Suspense* is a feeling of anxious uncertainty about the outcome of events in a literary work. Writers create suspense by raising questions in the minds of their readers.

SYMBOL A *symbol* is anything that stands for or represents something else. Symbols are common in everyday life. A dove with an olive branch in its beak is a symbol of peace. A blindfolded woman holding a balanced scale is a symbol of justice. A crown is a symbol of a king's status and authority.

SYMBOLISM *Symbolism* is the use of symbols. Symbolism plays an important role in many different types of literature. It can highlight certain elements the author wishes to emphasize and also add levels of meaning.

THEME The *theme* is a central message in a literary work. A theme can usually be expressed as a generalization, or a general statement, about human beings or about life. The theme of a work is not a summary of its plot. The theme is the writer's central idea.

Although a theme may be stated directly in the text, it is more often presented indirectly. When the theme is stated indirectly, or implied, the reader must figure out what the theme is by looking at what the work reveals about people or life.

TONE The *tone* of a literary work is the writer's attitude toward his or her audience and subject. The tone can often be described by a single adjective, such as *formal* or *informal, serious* or *playful, bitter* or *ironic.* Factors that contribute to the tone are word choice, sentence structure, line length, rhyme, rhythm, and repetition.

TRAGEDY A *tragedy* is a work of literature, especially a play, that results in a catastrophe for the main character. In ancient Greek drama, the main character is always a significant person—a king or a hero—and the cause of the tragedy is a tragic flaw, or weakness, in his or her character. In modern drama, the main character can be an ordinary person, and the cause of the tragedy can be some evil in society itself. The purpose of tragedy is not only to arouse fear and pity in the audience, but also, in some cases, to convey a sense of the grandeur and nobility of the human spirit.

TURNING POINT See *Climax.*

UNIVERSAL THEME A *universal theme* is a message about life that is expressed regularly in many different cultures and time periods. Folk tales, epics, and romances often address universal themes like the importance of courage, the power of love, or the danger of greed.

WORD CHOICE See *Diction.*

Tips for Literature Circles

As you read and study literature, discussions with other readers can help you understand and enjoy what you have read. Use the following tips.

- ## Understand the purpose of your discussion

  Your purpose when you discuss literature is to broaden your understanding of a work by testing your own ideas and hearing the ideas of others. Keep your comments focused on the literature you are discussing. Starting with one focus question will help to keep your discussion on track.

- ## Communicate effectively

  Effective communication requires thinking before speaking. Plan the points that you want to make and decide how you will express them. Organize these points in logical order and use details from the work to support your ideas. Jot down informal notes to help keep your ideas focused.

  Remember to speak clearly, pronouncing words slowly and carefully. Also, listen attentively when others are speaking, and avoid interrupting.

- ## Consider other ideas and interpretations

  A work of literature can generate a wide variety of responses in different readers. Be open to the idea that many interpretations can be valid. To support your own ideas, point to the events, descriptions, characters, or other literary elements in the work that led to your interpretation. To consider someone else's ideas, decide whether details in the work support the interpretation he or she presents. Be sure to convey your criticism of the ideas of others in a respectful and supportive manner.

- ## Ask questions

  Ask questions to clarify your understanding of another reader's ideas. You can also use questions to call attention to possible areas of confusion, to points that are open to debate, or to errors in the speaker's points. To move a discussion forward, summarize and evaluate conclusions reached by the group members.

  When you meet with a group to discuss literature, use a chart like the one shown to analyze the discussion.

Work Being Discussed:	
Focus Question:	
Your Response:	Another Student's Response:
Supporting Evidence:	Supporting Evidence:

Tips for Improving Reading Fluency

When you were younger, you learned to read. Then, you read to expand your experiences or for pure enjoyment. Now, you are expected to read to learn. As you progress in school, you are given more and more material to read. The tips on these pages will help you improve your reading fluency, or your ability to read easily, smoothly, and expressively.

Keeping Your Concentration

One common problem that readers face is the loss of concentration. When you are reading an assignment, you might find yourself rereading the same sentence several times without really understanding it. The first step in changing this behavior is to notice that you do it. Becoming an active, aware reader will help you get the most from your assignments. Practice using these strategies:

- Cover what you have already read with a note card as you go along. Then, you will not be able to reread without noticing that you are doing it.

- Set a purpose for reading beyond just completing the assignment. Then, read actively by pausing to ask yourself questions about the material as you read.

- Use the Reading Strategy instruction and notes that appear with each selection in this textbook.

- Stop reading after a specified period of time (for example, 5 minutes) and summarize what you have read. To help you with this strategy, use the Reading Check questions that appear with each selection in this textbook. Reread to find any answers you do not know.

Reading Phrases

Fluent readers read phrases rather than individual words. Reading this way will speed up your reading and improve your comprehension. Here are some useful ideas:

- Experts recommend rereading as a strategy to increase fluency. Choose a passage of text that is neither too hard nor too easy. Read the same passage aloud several times until you can read it smoothly. When you can read the passage fluently, pick another passage and keep practicing.

- Read aloud into a tape recorder. Then, listen to the recording, noting your accuracy, pacing, and expression. You can also read aloud and share feedback with a partner.

- Use *Hear It!* Prentice Hall Literature Audio program CDs to hear the selections read aloud. Read along silently in your textbook, noticing how the reader uses his or her voice and emphasizes certain words and phrases.

Understanding Key Vocabulary

If you do not understand some of the words in an assignment, you may miss out on important concepts. Therefore, it is helpful to keep a dictionary nearby when you are reading. Follow these steps:

- Before you begin reading, scan the text for unfamiliar words or terms. Find out what those words mean before you begin reading.

- Use context—the surrounding words, phrases, and sentences—to help you determine the meanings of unfamiliar words.

- If you are unable to understand the meaning through context, refer to the dictionary.

Paying Attention to Punctuation

When you read, pay attention to punctuation. Commas, periods, exclamation points, semicolons, and colons tell you when to pause or stop. They also indicate relationships between groups of words. When you recognize these relationships you will read with greater understanding and expression. Look at the chart below.

Punctuation Mark	Meaning
comma	brief pause
period	pause at the end of a thought
exclamation point	pause that indicates emphasis
semicolon	pause between related but distinct thoughts
colon	pause before giving explanation or examples

Using the Reading Fluency Checklist

Use the checklist below each time you read a selection in this textbook. In your Language Arts journal or notebook, note which skills you need to work on and chart your progress each week.

Reading Fluency Checklist

- ❏ Preview the text to check for difficult or unfamiliar words.
- ❏ Practice reading aloud.
- ❏ Read according to punctuation.
- ❏ Break down long sentences into the subject and its meaning.
- ❏ Read groups of words for meaning rather than reading single words.
- ❏ Read with expression (change your tone of voice to add meaning to the word).

Reading is a skill that can be improved with practice. The key to improving your fluency is to read. The more you read, the better your reading will become.

Types of Writing

Good writing can be a powerful tool used for many purposes. Writing can allow you to defend something you believe in or to show how much you know about a subject. Writing can also help you share what you have experienced, imagined, thought, and felt. The three main types of writing are argument, informative/explanatory, and narrative.

Argument

When you think of the word *argument,* you might think of a disagreement between two people, but an argument is more than that. An argument is a logical way of presenting a belief, conclusion, or stance. A good argument is supported with reasoning and evidence.

Argument writing can be used for many purposes, such as to change a reader's point of view or opinion or to bring about an action or a response from a reader.

There are three main purposes for writing a formal argument:

- to change the reader's mind
- to convince the reader to accept what is written
- to motivate the reader to take action, based on what is written

The following are some types of argument writing:

Advertisements An advertisement is a planned message meant to be seen, heard, or read. It attempts to persuade an audience to buy a product or service, accept an idea, or support a cause. Advertisements may appear in print, online, or in broadcast form.

Several common types of advertisements are public-service announcements, billboards, merchandise ads, service ads, and political campaign literature.

Persuasive Essay A persuasive essay presents a position on an issue, urges readers to accept that position, and may encourage a specific action. An effective persuasive essay

- Explores an issue of importance to the writer
- Addresses an issue that is arguable
- Uses facts, examples, statistics, or personal experiences to support a position
- Tries to influence the audience through appeals to the readers' knowledge, experiences, or emotions
- Uses clear organization to present a logical argument

Forms of persuasion include editorials, position papers, persuasive speeches, grant proposals, advertisements, and debates.

Informative/Explanatory

Informative/explanatory writing should rely on facts to inform or explain. Informative/explanatory writing serves some closely related purposes: to increase readers' knowledge of a subject, to help readers better understand a procedure or process, or to provide readers with an enhanced comprehension of a concept. It should also feature a clear introduction, body, and conclusion. The following are some examples of informative/explanatory writing:

Cause-and-Effect Essay A cause-and-effect essay examines the relationship between events, explaining how one event or situation causes another. A successful cause-and-effect essay includes

- A discussion of a cause, event, or condition that produces a specific result
- An explanation of an effect, outcome, or result
- Evidence and examples to support the relationship between cause and effect
- A logical organization that makes the explanation clear

Comparison-and-Contrast Essay A comparison-and-contrast essay analyzes the similarities and differences between or among two or more things. An effective comparison-and-contrast essay

- Identifies a purpose for comparison and contrast
- Identifies similarities and differences between or among two or more things, people, places, or ideas
- Gives factual details about the subjects
- Uses an organizational plan suited to the topic and purpose

Descriptive Writing Descriptive writing creates a vivid picture of a person, place, thing, or event. Most descriptive writing includes

- Sensory details—sights, sounds, smells, tastes, and physical sensations
- Vivid, precise language

- Figurative language or comparisons

- Adjectives and adverbs that paint a word picture

- An organization suited to the subject

Types of descriptive writing include descriptions of ideas, observations, remembrances, travel brochures, physical descriptions, functional descriptions, and character sketches.

Problem-and-Solution Essay A problem-and-solution essay describes a problem and offers one or more solutions to it. It describes a clear set of steps to achieve a result. An effective problem-and-solution essay includes

- A clear statement of the problem, with its causes and effects summarized for the reader

- The most important aspects of the problem

- A proposal of at least one realistic solution

- Facts, statistics, data, or expert testimony to support the solution

- A clear organization that makes the relationship between problem and solution obvious

Research Writing Research writing is based on information gathered from outside sources. A research paper—a focused study of a topic—helps writers explore and connect ideas, make discoveries, and share their findings with an audience. An effective research paper

- Focuses on a specific, narrow topic, which is usually summarized in a thesis statement

- Presents relevant information from a wide variety of sources

- Uses a clear organization that includes an introduction, body, and conclusion

- Includes a bibliography or works-cited list that identifies the sources from which the information was drawn

Other types of writing that depend on accurate and insightful research include multimedia presentations, statistical reports, annotated bibliographies, and experiment journals.

Workplace Writing Workplace writing is probably the format you will use most after you finish school. In general, workplace writing is fact-based and meant to communicate specific information in a structured format. Effective workplace writing

- Communicates information concisely

- Includes details that provide necessary information and anticipate potential questions

- Is error-free and neatly presented

Common types of workplace writing include business letters, memorandums, résumés, forms, and applications.

Narrative

Narrative writing conveys experience, either real or imaginary, and uses time to provide structure. It can be used to inform, instruct, persuade, or entertain. Whenever writers tell a of story, they are using narrative writing. Most narrative-writing types share certain elements, such as characters, a setting, a sequence of events, and, often, a theme. The following are some types of narration:

Autobiographical Writing Autobiographical writing tells a true story about an important period, experience, or relationship in the writer's life. Effective autobiographical writing includes

- A series of events that involve the writer as the main character

- Details, thoughts, feelings, and insights from the writer's perspective

- A conflict or an event that affects the writer

- A logical organization that tells the story clearly

- Insights that the writer gained from the experience

Types of autobiographical writing include personal narratives, autobiographical sketches, reflective essays, eyewitness accounts, and memoirs.

Short Story A short story is a brief, creative narrative. Most short stories include

- Details that establish the setting in time and place

- A main character who undergoes a change or learns something during the course of the story

- A conflict or a problem to be introduced, developed, and resolved

- A plot, the series of events that make up the action of the story

- A theme or message about life

Types of short stories include realistic stories, fantasies, historical narratives, mysteries, thrillers, science-fiction stories, and adventure stories.

Types of Writing **R25**

Writing Friendly Letters

Writing Friendly Letters

A friendly letter is much less formal than a business letter. It is a letter to a friend, a family member, or anyone with whom the writer wants to communicate in a personal, friendly way. Most friendly letters are made up of five parts:

✔ the heading

✔ the salutation, or greeting

✔ the body

✔ the closing

✔ the signature

The purpose of a friendly letter is often one of the following:

✔ to share personal news and feelings

✔ to send or to answer an invitation

✔ to express thanks

Model Friendly Letter

In this friendly letter, Betsy thanks her grandparents for a birthday present and gives them some news about her life.

---

11 Old Farm Road
Topsham, Maine 04011

April 14, 20—

Dear Grandma and Grandpa,

Thank you for the sweater you sent me for my birthday. It fits perfectly, and I love the color. I wore my new sweater to the carnival at school last weekend and got lots of compliments.

The weather here has been cool but sunny. Mom thinks that "real" spring will never come. I can't wait until it's warm enough to go swimming.

School is going fairly well. I really like my Social Studies class. We are learning about the U.S. Constitution, and I think it's very interesting. Maybe I will be a lawyer when I grow up.

When are you coming out to visit us? We haven't seen you since Thanksgiving. You can stay in my room when you come. I'll be happy to sleep on the couch. (The TV is in that room!!)

Well, thanks again and hope all is well with you.

Love,

Betsy

> The **heading** includes the writer's address and the date on which he or she wrote the letter.

> The **body** is the main part of the letter and contains the basic message.

> Some common **closings** for personal letters include "Best wishes," "Love "Sincerely," and "Yours truly."

Writing Business Letters

Formatting Business Letters

Business letters follow one of several acceptable formats. In **block format,** each part of the letter begins at the left margin. A double space is used between paragraphs. In **modified block format,** some parts of the letter are indented to the center of the page. No matter which format is used, all letters in business format have a heading, an inside address, a salutation or greeting, a body, a closing, and a signature. These parts are shown and annotated on the model business letter below, formatted in modified block style.

Model Business Letter

In this letter, Yolanda Dodson uses modified block format to request information.

Students for a Cleaner Planet
c/o Memorial High School
333 Veteran's Drive
Denver, CO 80211

January 25, 20—

Steven Wilson, Director
Resource Recovery Really Works
300 Oak Street
Denver, CO 80216

Dear Mr. Wilson:

Memorial High School would like to start a branch of your successful recycling program. We share your commitment to reclaiming as much reusable material as we can. Because your program has been successful in other neighborhoods, we're sure that it can work in our community. Our school includes grades 9–12 and has about 800 students.

Would you send us some information about your community recycling program? For example, we need to know what materials can be recycled and how we can implement the program.

At least fifty students have already expressed an interest in getting involved, so I know we'll have the people power to make the program work. Please help us get started.

Thank you in advance for your time and consideration.

Sincerely,

Yolanda Dodson

Yolanda Dodson

The **heading** shows the writer's address and organization (if any) and the date.

The **inside address** indicates where the letter will be sent.

A **salutation** is punctuated by a colon. When the specific addressee is not known, use a general greeting such as "To whom it may concern:"

The **body** of the letter states the writer's purpose. In this case, the writer requests information.

The **closing** "Sincerely" is common, but "Yours truly" or "Respectfully yours" are also acceptable. To end the letter, the writer types her name and provides a **signature.**

Writing Business Letters **R27**

21st-Century Skills

New technology has created many new ways to communicate. Today, it is easy to contribute information to the Internet and send a variety of messages to friends far and near. You can also share your ideas through photos, illustrations, video, and sound recordings. *21st Century Skills* gives you an overview of some ways you can use today's technology to create, share, and find information. Here are the topics you will find in this section.

- ✔ Blogs
- ✔ Social Networking
- ✔ Widgets and Feeds
- ✔ Multimedia Elements
- ✔ Podcasts
- ✔ Wikis

BLOGS

A **blog** is a common form of online writing. The word *blog* is a contraction of *Web log*. Most blogs include a series of entries known as *posts*. The posts appear in a single column and are displayed in reverse chronological order. That means that the most recent post is at the top of the page. As you scroll down, you will find earlier posts.

Blogs have become increasingly popular. Researchers estimate that 75,000 new blogs are launched every day. Blog authors are often called *bloggers.* They can use their personal sites to share ideas, songs, videos, photos, and other media. People who read blogs can often post their responses with a comments feature found in each new post.

Because blogs are designed so that they are easy to update, bloggers can post new messages as often as they like, often daily. For some people blogs become a public journal or diary, in which they share their thoughts about daily events.

Types of Blogs

Not all blogs are the same. Many blogs have a single author, but others are group projects. These are some common types of blog:

- ✔ Personal blogs often have a general focus. Bloggers post their thoughts on any topic they find interesting in their daily lives.

- ✔ Topical blogs focus on a specific theme, such as movie reviews, political news, class assignments, or health-care opportunities.

Web Safety

Always be aware that information you post on the Internet can be read by everyone with access to that page. Once you post a picture or text, it can be saved on someone else's computer, even if you later remove it.

Using the Internet safely means keeping personal information personal. Never include your address (e-mail or real), last name, or telephone numbers. Avoid mentioning places you can be frequently found. Never give out passwords you use to access other Web sites and do not respond to e-mails from people you do not know.

Student Edition Pages

Anatomy of a Blog

Here are some of the features you can include in a blog.

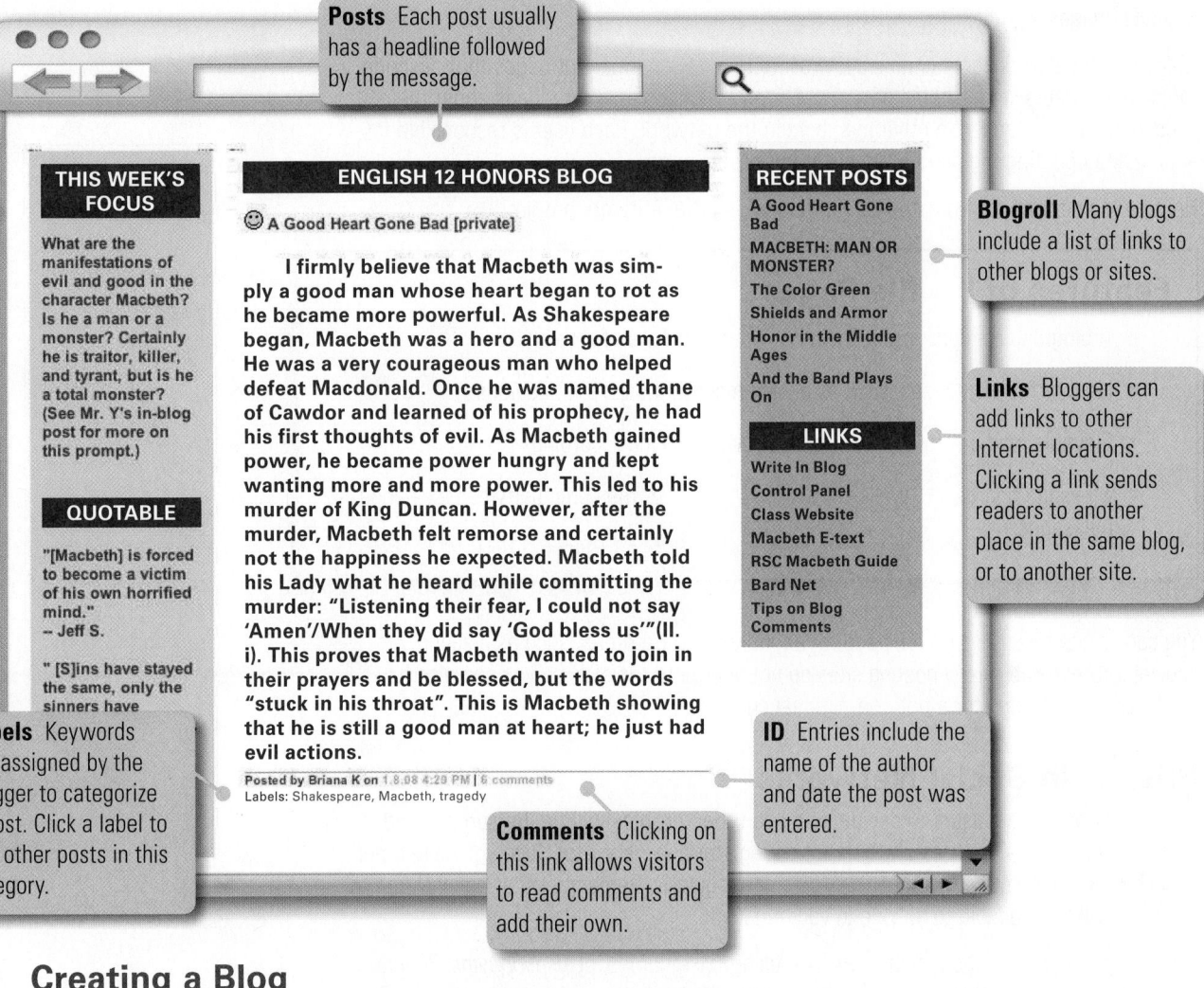

Posts Each post usually has a headline followed by the message.

THIS WEEK'S FOCUS

What are the manifestations of evil and good in the character Macbeth? Is he a man or a monster? Certainly he is traitor, killer, and tyrant, but is he a total monster? (See Mr. Y's in-blog post for more on this prompt.)

QUOTABLE

"[Macbeth] is forced to become a victim of his own horrified mind."
-- Jeff S.

" [S]ins have stayed the same, only the sinners have

Labels Keywords are assigned by the blogger to categorize post. Click a label to see other posts in this category.

ENGLISH 12 HONORS BLOG

☺ A Good Heart Gone Bad [private]

    I firmly believe that Macbeth was simply a good man whose heart began to rot as he became more powerful. As Shakespeare began, Macbeth was a hero and a good man. He was a very courageous man who helped defeat Macdonald. Once he was named thane of Cawdor and learned of his prophecy, he had his first thoughts of evil. As Macbeth gained power, he became power hungry and kept wanting more and more power. This led to his murder of King Duncan. However, after the murder, Macbeth felt remorse and certainly not the happiness he expected. Macbeth told his Lady what he heard while committing the murder: "Listening their fear, I could not say 'Amen'/When they did say 'God bless us'"(II. i). This proves that Macbeth wanted to join in their prayers and be blessed, but the words "stuck in his throat". This is Macbeth showing that he is still a good man at heart; he just had evil actions.

Posted by **Briana K** on 1.8.08 4:29 PM | 6 comments
Labels: Shakespeare, Macbeth, tragedy

RECENT POSTS

A Good Heart Gone Bad
MACBETH: MAN OR MONSTER?
The Color Green
Shields and Armor
Honor in the Middle Ages
And the Band Plays On

LINKS

Write In Blog
Control Panel
Class Website
Macbeth E-text
RSC Macbeth Guide
Bard Net
Tips on Blog Comments

Blogroll Many blogs include a list of links to other blogs or sites.

Links Bloggers can add links to other Internet locations. Clicking a link sends readers to another place in the same blog, or to another site.

ID Entries include the name of the author and date the post was entered.

Comments Clicking on this link allows visitors to read comments and add their own.

Creating a Blog

Keep these hints and strategies in mind to help you create an interesting and fair blog:

- ✔ Focus each blog entry on a single topic.

- ✔ Vary the length of your posts. Sometimes, all you need is a line or two to share a quick thought. Other posts will be much longer.

- ✔ Choose font colors and styles that can be read easily.

- ✔ Many people scan blogs rather than read them closely. You can make your main ideas pop out by using clear or clever headlines and boldfacing key terms.

- ✔ Give credit to other people's work and ideas. State the names of people whose ideas you are quoting or add a link to take readers to that person's blog or site.

- ✔ If you post comments, try to make them brief and polite.

SOCIAL NETWORKING

Social networking means any interaction between members of an online community. People can exchange many different kinds of information, from text and voice messages to video images.

Many social network communities allow users to create permanent pages that describe themselves. Users create home pages to express themselves, share ideas about their lives, and post messages to other members in the network. Each user is responsible for adding and updating the content on his or her profile page.

Here are some features you are likely to find on a social network profile:

Features of Profile Pages

- A biographical description, including photographs and artwork.

- Lists of favorite things, such as books, movies, music, and fashions.

- Playable media elements such as videos and sound recordings.

- Message boards, or "walls" in which members of the community can exchange messages.

You can create a social network page for an individual or a group, such as a school or special interest club. Many hosting sites do not charge to register, so you can also have fun by creating a page for a pet or a fictional character.

Privacy in Social Networks

Social networks allow users to decide how open their profiles will be. Be sure to read introductory information carefully before you register at a new site. Once you have a personal profile page, monitor your privacy settings regularly. Remember that any information you post will be available to anyone in your network.

Users often post messages anonymously or using false names, or *pseudonyms*. People can also post using someone else's name. Judge all information on the net critically. Do not assume that you know who posted some information simply because you recognize the name of the post author. The rapid speed of communication on the Internet can make it easy to jump to conclusions—be careful to avoid this trap.

Student Edition Pages

Tips for Sending Effective Messages

Technology makes it easy to share ideas quickly, but writing for the Internet poses some special challenges, as well. The writing style for blogs and social networks is often very conversational. In blog posts and comments, instant messages, and e-mails, writers often express themselves very quickly, using relaxed language, short sentences, and abbreviations. However, in a conversation, we get a lot of information from a speaker's tone of voice and body language. On the Internet, those clues are missing. As a result, Internet writers often use italics or bracketed labels to indicate emotions. Another alternative is using *emoticons*—strings of characters that give visual clues to indicate emotion:

:-) smile (happy)	:-(frown (unhappy)	;-) wink (light sarcasm)

Use these strategies to communicate effectively when using technology:

✔ Reread your messages. Before you click *Send,* read your message through and make sure that your tone will be clear to the reader.

✔ Do not jump to conclusions—ask for clarification first. Make sure you really understand what someone is saying before you respond.

✔ Use abbreviations your reader will understand.

WIDGETS AND FEEDS

A **widget** is a small application that performs a specific task. You might find widgets that give weather predictions, offer dictionary definitions or translations, provide entertainment such as games, or present a daily word, photograph, or quotation.

A **feed** is a special kind of widget. It displays headlines taken from the latest content on a specific media source. Clicking on the headline will take you to the full article.

Many social network communities and other Web sites allow you to personalize your home page by adding widgets and feeds.

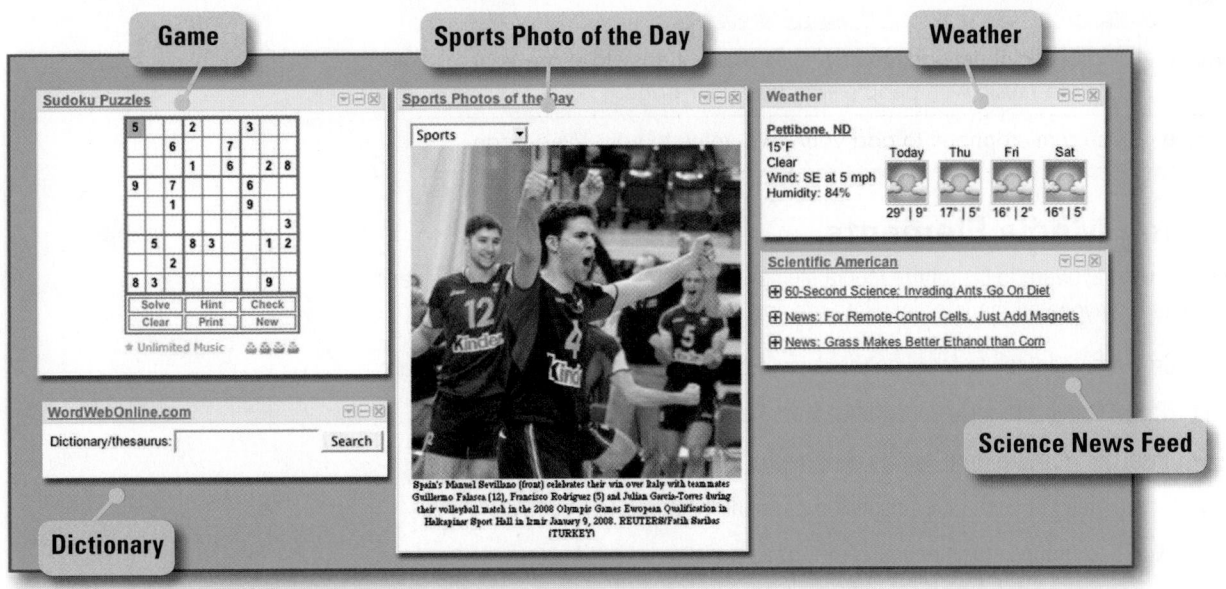

MULTIMEDIA ELEMENTS

One of the great advantages of communicating on the Internet is that you are not limited to using text only. When you create a Web profile or blog, you can share your ideas using a wide variety of media. In addition to widgets and feeds (see page R31), these media elements can make your Internet communication more entertaining and useful.

Graphics

Graphics	
Photographs	You can post photos taken by digital cameras.
Illustrations	Artwork can be created using computer software. You can also use a scanner to post a digital image of a drawing or sketch.
Charts, Graphs, and Maps	Charts and graphs can make statistical information clear. Use spreadsheet software to create these elements. Use Internet sites to find maps of specific places.

Video

Video	
Live Action	Digital video can be recorded by a camera or recorded from another media source.
Animation	Animated videos can also be created using software.

Sound

Sound	
Music	Many social network communities make it easy to share your favorite music with people who visit your page.
Voice	Use a microphone to add your own voice to your Web page.

Editing Media Elements

You can use software to customize media elements. Open source software is free and available to anyone on the Internet. Here are some things you can do with software:

✔ Crop a photograph to focus on the subject or brighten an image that is too dark.

✔ Transform a drawing's appearance from flat to three-dimensional.

✔ Insert a "You Are Here" arrow on a map.

✔ Edit a video or sound file to shorten its running time.

✔ Add background music or sound effects to a video.

PODCASTS

A **podcast** is a digital audio or video recording of a program that is made available on the Internet. Users can replay the podcast on a computer, or download it and replay it on a personal audio player. You might think of podcasts as radio or television programs that you create yourself. They can be embedded on a Web site or fed to a Web page through a podcast widget.

Creating an Effective Podcast

To make a podcast, you will need a recording device, such as a microphone or digital video camera, as well as editing software. Open source editing software is widely available and free of charge. Most audio podcasts are converted into the MP3 format. Here are some tips for creating a podcast that is clear and entertaining:

- ✔ Listen to several podcasts by different authors to get a feeling for the medium. Make a list of features and styles you like and also those you want to avoid.

- ✔ Test your microphone to find the best recording distance. Stand close enough to the microphone so that your voice sounds full, but not so close that you create an echo.

- ✔ Create an outline that shows your estimated timing for each element.

- ✔ Be prepared before you record. Rehearse, but do not create a script. Podcasts are best when they have a natural, easy flow.

- ✔ Talk directly to your listeners. Slow down enough so they can understand you.

- ✔ Use software to edit your podcast before publishing it. You can edit out mistakes or add additional elements.

WIKIS

A **wiki** is a collaborative Web site that lets visitors create, add, remove, and edit content. The term comes from the Hawaiian phrase *wiki wiki,* which means "quick." Web users at a wiki are both the readers and the writers of the site. Some wikis are open to contributions from anyone. Others require visitors to register before they can edit the content.

All of the text in these collaborative Web sites was written by people who use the site. Articles are constantly changing, as visitors find and correct errors and improve texts.

Wikis have both advantages and disadvantages as sources of information. They are valuable open forums for the exchange of ideas. The unique collaborative writing process allows entries to change over time. However, entries can also be modified incorrectly. Careless or malicious users can delete good content and add inappropriate or inaccurate information.

You can change the information on a wiki, but be sure your information is correct and clear before you add it. Wikis keep track of all changes, so your work will be recorded and can be evaluated by other users.

Parts of Speech

Nouns A **noun** is the name of a person, place, or thing. A **common noun** names any one of a class of people, places, or things. A **proper noun** names a specific person, place, or thing.

Common Nouns	*Proper Nouns*
writer	Francisco Jiménez

Use *apostrophes* with nouns to show ownership. Add an apostrophe and *s* to show the **possessive case** of most singular nouns. Add just an apostrophe to show the possessive case of plural nouns ending in *s* or *es*. Add an apostrophe and *s* to show the possessive case of plural nouns that do not end in *s* or *es*.

Pronouns A **pronoun** is a word that stands for a noun or for a word that takes the place of a noun. A **personal pronoun** refers to (1) the person speaking, (2) the person spoken to, or (3) the person, place, or thing spoken about.

	Singular	*Plural*
First Person	I, me, my, mine	we, us, our, ours
Second Person	you, your, yours	you, your, yours
Third Person	he, him, his, she, her, hers, it, its	they, them, their, theirs

A **demonstrative pronoun** directs attention to a specific person, place, or thing.

These are the juiciest pears I have ever tasted.

An **interrogative pronoun** is used to begin a question.

Who is the author of "Jeremiah's Song"?

An **indefinite pronoun** refers to a person, place, or thing, often without specifying which one.

Many of the players were tired.
Everyone bought something.

Verbs A **verb** is a word that expresses time while showing an action, a condition, or the fact that something exists. An **action verb** indicates the action of someone or something. A **linking verb** connects the subject of a sentence with a noun or a pronoun that renames or describes the subject. A **helping verb** can be added to another verb to make a single verb phrase.

Adjectives An **adjective** describes a noun or a pronoun or gives a noun or a pronoun a more specific meaning. Adjectives answer the questions *what kind, which one, how many,* or *how much.*

The articles *the, a,* and *an* are adjectives. *An* is used before a word beginning with a vowel sound.

A noun may sometimes be used as an adjective.

family home	*science* fiction

Adverbs An **adverb** modifies a verb, an adjective, or another adverb. Adverbs answer the questions *where, when, in what way,* or *to what extent.*

Prepositions A **preposition** relates a noun or a pronoun following it to another word in the sentence.

The ball rolled <u>under</u> the table.

Conjunctions A **conjunction** connects other words or groups of words. A **coordinating conjunction** connects similar kinds or groups of words. **Correlative conjunctions** are used in pairs to connect similar words or groups of words.

both Grandpa *and* Dad	*neither* they *nor* I

Interjections An **interjection** is a word that expresses feeling or emotion and functions independently of a sentence.

"Ah!" says he—

Phrases, Clauses, and Sentences

Sentences A **sentence** is a group of words with two main parts: a complete subject and a complete predicate. Together, these parts express a complete thought.

We read that story last year.

A **fragment** is a group of words that does not express a complete thought.

"Not right away."

Subject The **subject** of a sentence is the word or group of words that tells whom or what the sentence is about. The simple subject is the essential noun, pronoun, or group of words acting as a noun that cannot be left out of the complete subject. A **complete subject** is the **simple subject** plus any modifiers. In the following example, the complete subject is underlined. The simple subject is italicized.

<u>Pony express *riders*</u> carried packages for miles.

A **compound subject** is two or more subjects that have the same verb and are joined by a conjunction.

Neither the horse nor the driver looked tired.

Predicate The **predicate** of a sentence is the verb or verb phrase that tells what the complete subject of the sentence does or is. The **simple predicate** is the essential verb or verb phrase that cannot be left out of the complete predicate. A **complete predicate** is the simple predicate plus any modifiers or complements. In the following example, the complete predicate is underlined. The simple predicate is italicized.

Pony express riders <u>*carried* packages for miles.</u>

A **compound predicate** is two or more verbs that have the same subject and are joined by a conjunction.

She *sneezed and coughed* throughout the trip.

Complement A **complement** is a word or group of words that completes the meaning of the predicate of a sentence. Five different kinds of complements can be found in English sentences: *direct objects, indirect objects, objective complements, predicate nominatives,* and *predicate adjectives.*

A **direct object** is a noun, pronoun, or group of words acting as a noun that receives the action of a transitive verb.

We watched the *liftoff.*

An **indirect object** is a noun, pronoun, or group of words that appears with a direct object and names the person or thing that something is given to or done for.

He sold the *family* a mirror.

An **objective complement** is an adjective or noun that appears with a direct object and describes or renames it.

I called Meg my *friend.*

A **subject complement** is a noun, pronoun, or adjective that appears with a linking verb and tells something about the subject. A subject complement may be a *predicate nominative* or a *predicate adjective.*

A **predicate nominative** is a noun or pronoun that appears with a linking verb and renames, or explains the subject.

Kiglo was the *leader.*

A **predicate adjective** is an adjective that appears with a linking verb and describes the subject of a sentence.

Roko became *tired.*

Sentence Types There are four types of sentences:

1. A **simple sentence** consists of a single independent clause.
2. A **compound sentence** consists of two or more independent clauses joined by a comma and a coordinating conjunction or by a semicolon.
3. A **complex sentence** consists of one independent clause and one or more subordinate clauses.
4. A **compound-complex sentence** consists of two or more independent clauses and one or more subordinate clauses.

There are four functions of sentences:

1. A **declarative sentence** states an idea and ends with a period.
2. An **interrogative sentence** asks a question and ends with a question mark.
3. An **imperative sentence** gives an order or a direction and ends with either a period or an exclamation mark.
4. An **exclamatory sentence** conveys a strong emotion and ends with an exclamation mark.

Phrases A phrase is a group of words, without a subject and a verb, that functions in a sentence as one part of speech.

A **prepositional phrase** is a group of words that includes a preposition and a noun or a pronoun that is the object of the preposition.

near the town   with them

An **adjective phrase** is a prepositional phrase that modifies a noun or a pronoun by telling what kind or which one.

The house *on the corner* is new.

An **adverb phrase** is a prepositional phrase that modifies a verb, an adjective, or an adverb by pointing out where, when, in what manner, or to what extent.

Bring your saddle *to the barn.*

An **appositive phrase** is a noun or a pronoun with modifiers, placed next to a noun or a pronoun to add information and details.

The story, a *tale of adventure,* takes place in the Yukon.

A **participial phrase** is a participle modified by an adjective or an adverb phrase or accompanied by a complement. The entire phrase acts as an adjective.

Running at top speed, he soon caught up.

An **infinitive phrase** is an infinitive with modifiers, complements, or a subject, all acting together as a single part of speech. An infinitive is the verb form that starts with *to.*

I was happy *to sit down.*

Clauses A clause is a group of words with its own subject and verb. An **independent clause** can stand by itself as a complete sentence.

"I think it belongs to Rachel."

A **subordinate clause** has a subject and a verb but cannot stand as a complete sentence; it can only be part of a sentence.

"Although it was late"

Using Verbs, Pronouns, and Modifiers

Principal Parts A **verb** has four principal parts: the present, the present participle, the past, and the past participle.

Regular verbs form the past and past participle by adding *-ed* to the present form.

Present: walk   *Past:* walked

Present Participle: (am) walking   *Past Participle:* (have) walked

Irregular verbs form the past and past participle by changing form rather than by adding *-ed.*

Present: go   *Past:* went

Present Participle: (am) going   *Past Participle:* (have) gone

Verb Tense A **verb tense** tells whether the time of an action or condition is in the past, the present, or the future. Every verb has six tenses: *present, past, future, present perfect, past perfect,* and *future perfect.* The **present tense** shows actions that happen in the present. The **past tense** shows actions that have already happened. The **future tense** shows

actions that will happen. The **present perfect tense** shows actions that begin in the past and continue to the present. The **past perfect tense** shows a past action or condition that ended before another past action. The **future perfect tense** shows a future action or condition that will have ended before another begins.

Pronoun Case The **case** of a pronoun is the form it takes to show its use in a sentence. There are three pronoun cases: *nominative, objective,* and *possessive.* The **nominative case** is used to name or rename the subject of the sentence. The nominative case pronouns are *I, you, he, she, it, we, you, they.*

> *As the subject: She* is brave.
> *Renaming the subject:* The leader is *she.*

The **objective case** is used as the direct object, indirect object, or object of a preposition. The objective case pronouns are *me, you, him, her, it, us, you, them.*

> *As a direct object:* Tom called *me.*
> *As an indirect object:* My friend gave *me* advice.
> *As an object of a preposition:* She went without *me.*

The **possessive case** is used to show ownership. The possessive pronouns are *my, your, his, her, its, our, their, mine, yours, his, hers, its, ours, theirs.*

Subject-Verb Agreement To make a subject and a verb agree, make sure that both are singular or both are plural. Two or more singular subjects joined by *or* or *nor* must have a singular verb. When singular and plural subjects are joined by *or* or *nor,* the verb must agree with the closest subject.

> He *is* at the door.   They *drive* home.
> Either *Joe* or *you are* going.   Both *pets are* hungry.

Pronoun-Antecedent Agreement **Pronouns** must agree with their antecedents in number and gender. Use singular pronouns with singular antecedents and plural pronouns with plural antecedents. Many errors in pronoun-antecedent agreement occur when a plural pronoun is used to refer to a singular antecedent for which the gender is not specified.

> *Incorrect:* Everyone did their best.
> *Correct:* Everyone did his or her best.

The following indefinite pronouns are singular: *anybody, anyone, each, either, everybody, everyone, neither, nobody, no one, one, somebody, someone.* The following indefinite pronouns are plural: *both, few, many, several.* The following indefinite pronouns may be either singular or plural: *all, any, most, none, some.*

Modifiers The *comparative* and *superlative* degrees of most adjectives and adverbs of one or two syllables can be formed in either of two ways: Use *-er* or *more* to form a comparative degree and *-est* or *most* to form the superlative degree of most one- and two-syllable modifiers.

More and *most* can also be used to form the comparative and superlative degrees of most one- and two-syllable modifiers.

These words should not be used when the result sounds awkward, as in "A greyhound is *more* fast than a beagle."

Glossary of Common Usage

accept, except: *Accept* is a verb that means "to receive" or "to agree to." *Except* is a preposition that means "other than" or "leaving out." Do not confuse these two words.

> Aaron sadly *accepted* his father's decision to sell Zlata.
> Everyone *except* the fisherman had children.

affect, effect: *Affect* is normally a verb meaning "to influence" or "to bring about a change in." *Effect* is usually a noun, meaning "result."

among, between: *Among* is usually used with three or more items. *Between* is generally used with only two items.

bad, badly: Use the predicate adjective *bad* after linking verbs such as *feel, look,* and *seem.* Use *badly* whenever an adverb is required.

> Mouse does not feel *bad* about tricking Coyote.
> In the myth, Athene treats Arachne *badly.*

beside, besides: *Beside* means "at the side of" or "close to." *Besides* means "in addition to."

can, may: The verb *can* generally refers to the ability to act. The verb *may* generally refers to permission to act.

different from, different than: *Different from* is generally preferred over *different than.*

farther, further: Use *farther* when you refer to distance. Use *further* when you mean "to a greater degree or extent" or "additional."

fewer, less: Use *fewer* for things that can be counted. Use *less* for amounts or quantities that cannot be counted.

good, well: Use the predicate adjective *good* after linking verbs such as *feel, look, smell, taste,* and *seem.* Use *well* whenever you need an adverb.

its, it's: The word *its* with no apostrophe is a possessive pronoun. The word *it's* is a contraction for *it is.* Do not confuse the possessive pronoun *its* with the contraction *it's,* standing for "it is" or "it has."

lay, lie: Do not confuse these verbs. *Lay* is a transitive verb meaning "to set or put something down." Its principal parts are *lay, laying, laid, laid. Lie* is an intransitive verb meaning "to recline." Its principal parts are *lie, lying, lay, lain.*

like, as: *Like* is a preposition that usually means "similar to" or "in the same way as." *Like* should always be followed by an object. Do not use *like* before a subject and a verb. Use *as* or *that* instead.

of, have: Do not use *of* in place of *have* after auxiliary verbs like *would, could, should, may, might,* or *must.*

raise, rise: *Raise* is a transitive verb that usually takes a direct object. *Rise* is intransitive and never takes a direct object.

set, sit: *Set* is a transitive verb meaning "to put (something) in

a certain place." Its principal parts are *set, setting, set, set. Sit* is an intransitive verb meaning "to be seated." Its principal parts are *sit, sitting, sat, sat.*

than, then: The conjunction *than* is used to connect the two parts of a comparison. Do not confuse *than* with the adverb *then*, which usually refers to time.

that, which, who: Use the relative pronoun *that* to refer to things or people. Use *which* only for things and *who* for people.

when, where, why: Do not use *when, where,* or *why* directly after a linking verb such as *is*. Reword the sentence.

> *Faulty:* Suspense is *when* an author increases tension.
> *Revised:* An author uses suspense to increase tension.

who, whom: Use *who* only as a subject in clauses and sentences and *whom* only as an object.

Mechanics

Capitalization

1. Capitalize the first word of a sentence.
   > Young Roko glances down the valley.
2. Capitalize all proper nouns and adjectives.
   > Mark Twain   Amazon River   Thanksgiving Day
3. Capitalize a person's title when it is followed by the person's name or when it is used in direct address.
   > Doctor   General Khokhotov   Mrs. Price
4. Capitalize titles showing family relationships when they refer to a specific person, unless they are preceded by a possessive noun or pronoun.
   > Granny-Liz   Margie's mother
5. Capitalize the first word and all other key words in the titles of books, periodicals, poems, stories, plays, paintings, and other works of art.
   > from *Tom Sawyer*   "Grandpa and the Statue"
6. Capitalize the first word and all nouns in letter salutations and the first word in letter closings.
   > Dear Willis,   Yours truly,

Punctuation

End Marks

1. Use a **period** to end a declarative sentence, an imperative sentence, and most abbreviations.
2. Use a **question mark** to end a direct question or an incomplete question in which the rest of the question is understood.
3. Use an **exclamation mark** after a statement showing strong emotion, an urgent imperative sentence, or an interjection expressing strong emotion.

Commas   Use commas:

1. before the conjunction to separate two independent clauses in a compound sentence.
2. to separate three or more words, phrases, or clauses in a series.
3. to separate adjectives of equal rank. Do not use commas to separate adjectives that must stay in a specific order.
4. after an introductory word, phrase, or clause.
5. to set off parenthetical and nonessential expressions.
6. with places and dates made up of two or more parts.
7. after items in addresses, after the salutation in a personal letter, after the closing in all letters, and in numbers of more than three digits.

Semicolons   Use semicolons:

1. to join independent clauses that are not already joined by a conjunction.
2. to join independent clauses or items in a series that already contain commas.

Colons   Use colons:

1. before a list of items following an independent clause.
2. in numbers giving the time, in salutations in business letters, and in labels used to signal important ideas.

Quotation Marks

1. A **direct quotation** represents a person's exact speech or thoughts and is enclosed in quotation marks.
2. An **indirect quotation** reports only the general meaning of what a person said or thought and does not require quotation marks.
3. Always place a comma or a period inside the final quotation mark of a direct quotation.
4. Place a question mark or an exclamation mark inside the final quotation mark if the end mark is part of the quotation; if it is not part of the quotation, place it outside the final quotation mark.

Titles

1. Underline or italicize the titles of long written works, movies, television and radio shows, lengthy works of music, paintings, and sculptures.
2. Use quotation marks around the titles of short written works, episodes in a series, songs, and titles of works mentioned as parts of collections.

Hyphens   Use a **hyphen** with certain numbers, after certain prefixes, with two or more words used as one word, and with a compound modifier that comes before a noun.

Apostrophes   Use apostrophes:

1. to show the possessive case of most singular nouns.
2. to show the possessive case of plural nouns ending in *s* and *es*.
3. to show the possessive case of plural nouns that do not end in *s* or *es*.
4. in a contraction to indicate the position of the missing letter or letters.

Index of Skills

Boldface numbers indicate pages where terms are defined.

R46 Index of Skills

Vocabulary

Writing Strategies

Prewriting:

More Skills. . .
Critical Thinking

Index of Features

Writing Workshop: Work in Progress

Index of Authors and Titles

Notes: Page numbers in italics refer to biographical information. Nonfiction appears in red.

Acknowledgments

Grateful acknowledgment is made to the following for copyrighted material: *English—Language Arts Content Standards for California Public Schools* reproduced by permission, California Department of Education, CD Press, 1430 N Street, Suite 3207, Sacramento, CA 95814.

All Children's Hospital c/o Florida Suncoast Safe Kids Coalition "2006 Safe Kids "Walk This Way" Program" from *http://www.allkids.org/body.cfm?xyzpdqabc=0&id=396&action=detail&ref=28.* Copyrgiht © 2007 All Children's Hospital. All rights reserved. Used by permission.

Miriam Altshuler Literary Agency "Treasure of Lemon Brown" by Walter Dean Myers from *Boy's Life Magazine, March 1983.* Copyright © 1983, by Walter Dean Myers. Used by permission of Miriam Altshuler Literary Agency, on behalf of Walter Dean Myers.

American Broadcasting Music, Inc. "Conjunction Junction" composed by Jack Sheldon and Bob Dorough. Copyright © 1973 American Broadcasting Music, Inc. Used by permission.

American National Red Cross "How to Recognize Venomous Snakes in North America" Copyright © 1992 by The American National Red Cross. Courtesy of the American National Red Cross. All rights reserved in all countries. Used by permission.

Americas Magazine "Mongoose on the Loose" reprinted from *Americas,* a bimonthly magazine published by the General Secretariat of the Organization of American States in English and Spanish. Content may not be copied without written permission. Used by permission.

Arte Publico Press, Inc. "Maestro" is used with permission from the publisher of *Borders* by Pat Mora. (Houston: Arte Publico Press - | University of Houston © 1986). "Bailando" from Chants by Pat Mora. Used with permission from the publisher of *Chants* (Houston: Arte Publico Press - University of Houston copyright © 1985).

Atheneum Books for Young Readers, an imprint of Simon & Schuster "Papa's Parrot" from *Every Living Thing* by Cynthia Rylant. Text copyright © 1985 Cynthia Rylant. Used by permission of Atheneum Books for Young Readers, an imprint of Simon & Schuster Children's Publishing Division.

Bantam Books, a division of Random House, Inc. "The Eternal Frontier" from *Frontier* by Louis L'Amour, Photographs by David Muench, copyright © 1984 by Louis L'Amour Enterprises, Inc. Used by permission of Bantam Books, a division of Random House, Inc.

Susan Bergholz Literary Services "My First Free Summer" by Julia Alvarez, copyright © 2003 by Julia Alvarez. First published in *Better Homes and Gardens, August 2003.* Used by permission of Susan Bergholz Literary Services, New York, NY and Lamy, NM. All rights reserved.

Brandt & Hochman Literary Agents, Inc. "The Third Wish" from *Not What You Expected: A Collection of Short Stories* by Joan Aiken. Copyright © 1974 by Joan Aiken. Any electronic copying or redistribution of the text is expressly forbidden. Used by permission of Brandt & Hochman Literary Agents, Inc.

Brooks Permissions "Jim" Copyright © 1956 from *Bronzeville Boys and Girls* by Gwendolyn Brooks. Copyright © 1956 by Gwendolyn Brooks. Used by consent of Brooks Permissions.

Curtis Brown Ltd. "Two Haiku" ("O foolish ducklings…" and "After the moon sets…") first appeared in *Cricket Songs: Japanese Haiku,* published by Harcourt. Copyright © 1964 by Harry Behn. "Suzy and Leah" first published in *American Girl Magazine.* Copyright © 1993 by Jane Yolen. *Dragonwings by Laurence Yep from Theatre For Young Audiences: Around The World In 21 Plays.* Copyright © 1992 by Laurence Yep. First appeared in *American Theatre Magazine.* Now appears in *Norton Anthology of Children's Literature.* Used by permission of Curtis Brown, Ltd. CAUTION: Professionals and amateurs are hereby warned that *Dragonwings,* being fully protected under the copyright Laws of the United States of America, the British Empire, including the Dominion of Canada, and all other countries of the Universal Copyright and Berne Conventions, are subject to royalty. All rights, including professional, amateur, motion picture, recitation, lecturing, public reading, radio and television broadcasting, and the rights of translation into foreign languages, are strictly reserved. All inquiries for *Dragonwings* should be addressed to Curtis Brown Ltd.

CA Walk to School Headquarters "Walk to School" from *www.cawalktoschool.com.* Copyright © 2006 California Center for Physical Activity.

Canadian Broadcasting Corporation "Charles Dickens's A Christmas Carol: A Radio Interview" from *http://www.victorianweb.org/authors/dickens/xmas/pva303.html.* Originally broadcast on the Canadian Broadcasting Corporation (The Great Northwest, Dec. 4, 2000). Copyright © Canadian Broadcasting Corporation. Used by courtesy of Canadian Broadcasting Corporation.

Carus Publishing Company "The Rhythms of Rap" by Kathiann M. Kowalski from *Odyssey's March 2002 issue: Music: Why Do We Love It?* Copyright © 2002, Cobblestone Publishing, 30 Grove Street, Suite C, Peterborough, NH 03458. All rights reserved. Used by permission of Carus Publishing Company.

Chronicle Books "The Travelers and the Bear" by Jerry Pinkney from *Aesop's Fables.* Copyright © 2000 by Jerry Pinkney.

City of Melbourne Stormwater Management Web Page from *http://www.melbourneflorida.org/stormwater/howyoucanhelp.htm.* Copyright City of Melbourne.

City of Oceanside City of Oceanside Clean Water Program from *www.oceansidecleanwaterprogram.org/kids.asp.* Copyright © City of Oceanside. Used by permission.

ClearyWorks "The Fox Outwits the Crow" by William Cleary from *www.clearyworks.com.* Used by permission of William Cleary, Burlington, Vermont.

Code Entertainment "The Monsters are Due on Maple Street" by Rod Serling from *The Monsters Are Due On Maple Street.* Copyright © 1960 by Rod Serling; Copyright © 1988 by Carolyn Serling, Jodi Serling, and Anne Serling. Used by permission. CAUTION: Professionals and amateurs are hereby warned that "The Monsters are Due on Maple Street," being fully protected under

the copyright laws of the United States of America, the British Commonwealth countries, including Canada, and the other countries of the Copyright Union, is subject to royalty. All rights, including professional, amateur, motion picture, recitation, lecturing, public reading, radio, television and cable broadcasting, and the rights of translation into foreign languages, are strictly reserved. All inquiries should be addressed to Code Entertainment.

Don Congdon Associates, Inc. "All Summer In A Day" by Ray Bradbury, published in *The Magazine of Fantasy and Science Fiction, March 1954.* Copyright © 1954, copyright © renewed 1982 by Ray Bradbury. From *No Gumption* by Russell Baker. Copyright © 1982 by Russell Baker. Used by permission of Don Congdon Associates, Inc.

The Emma Courlander Trust "All Stories Are Anansi's" from *The Hat-Shaking Dance And Other Ashanti Tales From Ghana* by Harold Courlander with Albert Kofi Prempeh Copyright © 1957, 1985 by Harold Courlander. Used by permission of The Emma Courlander Trust.

Crystal Springs Uplands School Crystal Springs Uplands School Theatre Contract from *http://www.csus.com/pageprint.cfm?p=1212.* Copyright © Crystal Springs Uplands School. Used by permission of the Crystal Springs Uplands School and John Hauer, Theater Manager and Production & Design Teacher.

Dell Publishing, a division of Random House, Inc. "The Luckiest Time of All" from *The Lucky Stone* by Lucille Clifton. Copyright © 1979 by Lucille Clifton. Used by permission of Dell Publishing, a division of Random House, Inc.

Demand Media, Inc. "How to Download Ringtones for a Cell Phone" from *www.ehow.com.* Copyright © 1999-2007 eHow, Inc. Article used with the permission of eHow, Inc., www.ehow.com.

Dial Books for Young Readers, a division of Penguin Young Readers Group "The Three=Century Woman" copyright © 1999 by Richard Peck, from *Past Present, Perfect Tense* by Richard Peck. Used by permission of Dial Books for Young Readers, a division of Penguin Young Readers Group, a member of Penguin Group (USA) Inc., 345 Hudson Street, New York, NY 10014. All rights reserved.

Gregory Djanikian "How I Learned English" by Gregory Djanikian from *Falling Deeply Into America,* Carnegie Mellon University, Copyright © 1989. Used by permission of the author.

Dramatists Play Service Inc. "Sorry, Wrong Number" by Lucille Fletcher. Copyright © renewed 1976, Lucille Fletcher. All rights reserved.

Dutton Children's Books From "The Tale of Mandarin Ducks" by Katherine Paterson, copyright © 1990 by Katherine Paterson, text. Used by permission of Dutton Children's Books, A Division of Penguin Young Readers Group, A Member of Penguin Group (USA) Inc. All rights reserved.

Gulf Publishing Look for the Differences (park sign) from *A Field Guide To Snakes Of California* by Philip R. Brown. Copyright © 1997.

Farrar, Straus & Giroux, LLC "Seal" from *Laughing Time: Collected Nonsense* by William Jay Smith. Copyright © 1990 by William Jay Smith. "Train Tune" from *The Blue Estuaries* by Louise Bogan. Copyright © 1968 by Louise Bogan. Copyright renewed © 1996 by Ruth Limmer. Used by permission of Farrar, Straus & Giroux, Inc.

Joanna Farrell for the Estate of Juliet Piggott Wood "Popocatepetl and Ixtlaccihuatl" by Juliet Piggott from *Mexican Folktales.* Used by permission of Mrs. J.S.E. Farrell.

Food Security Learning Center Food Security Learning Center from *www.worldhungeryear.org.* Copyright © 2007. All rights reserved. Used by permission.

Estate of Mona Gardner "The Dinner Party" by Mona Gardner from *McDougal, Littell.* Copyright © 1942, 1970. Reprinted by permission.

Georgia Department of Transportation "Safe Routes to School: It's Happening in Metro Atlanta" from *http://www.atlantabike.org/srtsfrontpage.html.* Copyright © 2007. Used by permission of Georgia Department of Transportation, Atlanta Bicycle Campaign, and the Federal Highway Administration.

Golden Books, an imprint of Random House Children's Book "The Bride of Pluto"(retitled "Demeter and Persephone") from *The Golden Treasury of Myths and Legends* by Anne Terry White, illustrated by Alice and Martin Provensen, copyright © 1959, renewed copyright © 1987 by Random House, Inc. Used by permission of Golden Books, an imprint of Random House Children's Books, a division of Random House, Inc.

June Hall Literary Agency c/o PFD "One" from *When I Dance* by James Berry (Copyright © James Berry 1990) is reproduced by permission of PFD (www.pfd.co.uk) on behalf of James Berry.

Harcourt, Inc. Excerpt from "Seventh Grade" in *Baseball in April and Other Stories,* copyright © 1990 by Gary Soto. "Fog" from Chicago Poems by Carl Sandburg, copyright © 1916 by Holt, Rinehart and Winston and renewed copyright © 1944 by Carl Sandburg. This material may not be reproduced in any form or by any means without the prior written permission of the publisher. Used by permission of Harcourt, Inc.

Harcourt Education Limited "Tenochtitlan: Inside the Aztec Capital" from *The Aztecs: Worlds Of The Past* by Jacqueline Dineen. Used by permission of Harcourt Education.

HarperCollins Publishers, Inc. "Sarah Cynthia Sylvia Stout Would Not Take the Garbage Out" from *Where the Sidewalk Ends* by Shel Silverstein. Copyright © 2004 by Evil Eye Music, Inc. Used with permission from the Estate of Shel Silverstein and HarperCollins Children's Books. From *An American Childhood.* Copyright © 1987 by Annie Dillard. "How the Snake Got Poison" from *Mules and Men* by Zora Neale Hurston. Copyright © 1935 by Zora Neale Hurston. Copyright renewed © 1963 by John C. Hurston and Joel Hurston. Used by permission of HarperCollins Publishers.

HarperTrophy, an Imprint of HarperCollins Publishers Inc. From *Dragonwings* by Laurence Yep. Copyright © 1975 by Laurence Yep. Used by permission of HarperCollins Publishers.

Harvard University Press "I'm Nobody (#288)" by Emily Dickinson. Used by permission of the publishers and the Trustees of Amherst College from *The Poems Of Emily Dickinson,* Thomas H. Johnson, ed., Cambridge, Mass.: The Belknap Press of Harvard University Press, Copyright © 1951, 1955, 1979, 1983 by the President and Fellows of Harvard College.

Helmut Hirnschall "I am a Native of North America" by Chief Dan George from *My Heart Soars*. Copyright © 1974 by Clarke Irwin. Used by permission.

Edward D. Hoch "Zoo" by Edward D. Hoch, copyright © 1958 by King Size Publications, Inc.; © renewed 1991 by Edward D. Hoch. Used by permission of the author.

The Barbara Hogenson Agency, Inc. "The Night the Bed Fell" from *My Life and Hard Times* by James Thurber. Copyright © 1933, 1961 by James Thurber. Used by arrangement with Rosemary Thurber and The Barbara Hogensen Agency, Inc. All rights reserved.

Holiday House, Inc. Copyright © 2006 by Russell Freedman from "Freedom Walkers: The Story of the Montgomery Bus Boycott." All rights reserved. Used by permission of Holiday House, Inc.

Meghan Holohan "What Gives the Sunrise and Sunset Its Orange Glow" by Meghan Holohan from *www.gantdaily.com*. Used by permission of the author.

Henry Holt and Company, Inc. Excerpt from "My Dear Cousin Tovah" from *Letters From Rifka* by Karen Hesse. Copyright © 1992 by Karen Hesse. "Stopping by Woods on a Snowy Evening" from *The Poetry Of Robert Frost* edited by Edward Connery Lathem. Copyright © 1923, 1969 by Henry Holt and Company, copyright 1951 by Robert Frost. Used by permission of Henry Holt and Company, LLC. All rights reserved.

Houghton Mifflin Harcourt "Prayers of Steel" from The Complete Poems of Carl Sandburg, Revised and Expanded Edition, copyright © 1970, 1969 by Lilian Steichen Sandburg, Trustee, reprinted by permission of Houghton Mifflin Harcourt Publishing Company. The material may not be reproduced in any form or by any means without the prior written permission of the publisher.

Hyperion Books for Children "The Voyage" (including the Prologue) from *Tales From The Odyssey - Book Four: The Gray-Eyed Goddess* by Mary Pope Osborne. Copyright © 2003 by Mary Pope Osborne. Used by permission of Hyperion Books for Children. All rights reserved.

Information Please® "Fall of the Hindenburg" *www.infoplease.com*. Information Please® Database, Copyright © Pearson Education, Inc. All rights reserved. Used by permission.

Jacksonville Zoo and Gardens "Jacksonville Zoo & Gardens Leading the Charge in Northeast Florida to Save the Frogs!" from *http://www.jaxzoo.org/about/amphibianconservationpr.asp*. All content copyright © 2008 Jacksonville Zoo and Gardens. Special appreciation to Jacksonville Zoo & Gardens, Jacksonville, FL, for information on the frog crisis.

Japan Publications, Inc. "On sweet plum blossoms," "Has spring come indeed?" and "Temple bells die out" by Bashō from *One Hundred Famous Haiku* by Daniel C. Buchanan. Copyright © 1973. Used by permission of Japan Publications, Inc.

Stanleigh Jones "He-y, Come on O-ut!" by Shinichi Hoshi translated by Stanleigh Jones from *The Best Japanese Science Fiction Stories*. Reprinted with the permission of Stanleigh Jones.

The Estate of Barbara Jordan "All Together Now" by Barbara Jordan from *Sesame Street Parents*. Used by permission of Hilgers Bell & Richards Attorneys at Law for the Estate of Barbara Jordan.

The Kansas City Star "The Wrong Orbit: Senator Has No Legitimate Business Blasting Into Space" Kansas City Star Editorial from *The Kansas City Star, 1/20/98*. Used with permission of The Kansas City Star © Copyright 2007 The Kansas City Star. All rights reserved. Format differs from original publication. Not an endorsement.

Kinseido Publishing Co., Ltd. "Conversational Ballgames" by Nancy M. Sakamoto from *Polite Fictions: Why Japanese And Americans Seem Rude To Each Other*. Used by permission.

Alfred A. Knopf, Inc. "Mother to Son" from *The Collected Poems of Langston Hughes* by Langston Hughes, edited by Arnold Rampersad with David Roessel, Associate Editor. Copyright © 1994 by The Estate of Langston Hughes. Used by permission of Alfred A. Knopf, a division of Random House, Inc.

Alfred A. Knopf Children's Books "The People Could Fly" from *The People Could Fly: American Black Folktales* by Virginia Hamilton, copyright © 1985 by Virginia Hamilton, illustrations copyright © 1985 by Leo and Diane Dillon. Used by permission of Alfred A. Knopf, an imprint of Random House Children's Books, a division of Random House, Inc.

Barbara S. Kouts Literary Agency "The Bear Boy" by Joseph Bruchac from *Flying with the Eagle, Racing the Great Bear*. Copyright © 1993 by Joseph Bruchac. Used with permission.

Samantha Larson "Everest 2007" by Samantha Larson from *www.samanthalarson.blogspot.com*. Copyright © 2006 SamanthaLarson.com. Used by permission.

Little, Brown and Company, Inc. "The Real Story of a Cowboy's Life" (The Grandest Enterprise Under God 1865–1874) from *The West: An Illustrated History* by Geoffrey Ward. Little Brown and Company. Copyright © 1996 by The West Book Project, Inc. Used by permission.

Gina Maccoby Literary Agency "MK" from *Open Your Eyes* by Jean Fritz. Copyright © 2003 by Jean Fritz. Used by permission of The Gina Maccoby Literary Agency.

Naomi Long Madgett "Life" by Naomi Long Madgett from *One and the Many*, copyright © 1956; *Remembrances of Spring: Collected Early Poems*, copyright © 1993. Used by permission of the author.

Meriwether Publishing Ltd. "My Head is Full of Starshine" from Acting Natural by Peg Kehret, copyright © 1991 Meriwether Publishing Ltd. Used by permission.

Eve Merriam c/o Marian Reiner "Onomatopoeia" from *It Doesn't Always Have To Rhyme* by Eve Merriam. Copyright © 1964, 1992 Eve Merriam. Used by permission of Marian Reiner Literary Agency.

Edna St. Vincent Millay Society "The Courage That My Mother Had" by Edna St. Vincent Millay, from *Collected Poems*, HarperCollins. Copyright © 1954, 1982 by Norma Millay Ellis. All rights reserved. Used by permission of Elizabeth Barnett, literary executor.

William Morris Agency *A Christmas Carol: Scrooge and Marley* by Israel Horovitz. Copyright © 1994 by Fountain Pen, LLC. Used by permission of William Morris Agency, LLC on behalf of the Author. All rights reserved. CAUTION: Professionals and amateurs are hereby warned that "A Christmas Carol: Scrooge and Marley" is subject to a royalty. It is fully protected under the copyright laws of the United States of America and of all countries covered by the

William Morrow & Company, Inc., a division of HarperCollins "Winter" from *Cotton Candy On A Rainy Day* by Nikki Giovanni. Copyright © 1978 by Nikki Giovanni. Used by permission of William Morrow & Company, Inc., a division of HarperCollins Publishers, Inc.

Naomi Shihab Nye "The Rider" by Naomi Shihab Nye from *Invisible*. Used by permission.

Harold Ober Associates, Inc. "Stolen Day" by Sherwood Anderson from *This Week Magazine*. Copyright © 1941 by Sherwood Anderson. Copyright renewed © 1968 by Eleanor Copenhaver Anderson. Used by permission of Harold Ober Associates Incorporated.

ODYSSEY Magazine (Cobblestone Publishing) "A Special Gift—The Legacy of 'Snowflake' Bentley" by Barbara Eaglesham from *Odyssey's December 2002 Issue: Chilly Science: Ice and Snow,* Copyright © 2002, Carus Publishing Company. Published by Cobblestone Publishing, 30 Grove Street, Suite C, Peterborough, NH 03458. All rights reserved. Used by permission of the publisher.

Ama B. Patterson "Martin Luther King" by Raymond Richard Patterson. Used by permission of the Estate of Raymond R. Patterson.

Pearson Prentice Hall "Keeping It Quiet" from *Prentice Hall Science Explorer Sound and Light*. Copyright © 2005 by Pearson Education, Inc., or its affiliates. "The Seasons on Earth" from *Prentice Hall Science Explorer Astronomy*. Copyright © 2005 by Pearson Education, Inc., or its affiliates. Used by permission.

People Weekly "Picks & Pans: A Christmas Carol (TNT)" by Terry Kelleher from *People Weekly, December 6th, 1999, Vol.52*. People Weekly Copyright © 1999 All Rights Reserved Time Inc. Used by permission.

Perseus Books "Alligator" by Bailey White from *Mama Makes Up Her Mind And Other Dangers Of Southern Living*. Copyright © 1993 by Bailey White. Used by permission of Da Capo Press, a member of Perseus Books Group. All rights reserved.

Piñata Books, an imprint of Arte Publico Press "The Desert Is My Mother/El desierto es mi madre" is used with permission from the publisher of *My Own True Name* by Pat Mora. (Houston: Arte Publico Press - University of Houston copyright © 1985).

G. P. Putnam's Sons, a division of Penguin Group (USA) Inc. "Two Kinds" from *The Joy Luck Club* by Amy Tan, copyright © 1989 by Amy Tan. Used by permission of G.P. Putnam's Sons, a division of Penguin Group (USA) Inc.

Random House, Inc. "Melting Pot" from *Living Out Loud* by Anna Quindlen, copyright © 1987 by Anna Quindlen. Used by permission of Random House, Inc.

Marian Reiner, Literary Agent "Weather" from *Catch a Little Rhyme* by Eve Merriam. Copyright © 1966 by Eve Merriam. Copyright renewed © 1994 by Dee Michel and Guy Michel. Used by permission of Marian Reiner.

Wendy Rose "Loo-Wit" by Wendy Rose from *The Halfbreed Chronicles and Other Poems*. Copyright © 1985 by Wendy Rose. Used by permission.

Santa Rosa Plateau Ecological Reserve Rattlesnakes (park sign) from *http://www.californiaherps.com/images/signs/knowyour-snakessignmt306.jpg*.

Scholastic Inc. "The Great Fire" by Jim Murphy from *Scholastic Hardcover*. Copyright © 1995 by Jim Murphy. All rights reserved. Published by Scholastic Inc.

Scribner, a division of Simon & Schuster "Rattlesnake" from *Cross Creek* by Marjorie Kinnan Rawlings. Copyright © 1942 by Marjorie Kinnan Rawlings: copyright renewed © 1970 by Norton Baskin and Charles Scribner's Sons. From *Angela's Ashes* by Frank McCourt. Copyright © 1996 by Frank McCourt. Used by permission of Scribner, an imprint of Simon & Schuster Adult Publishing Group. All rights reserved.

Seaside Music Theater "Costume Rental Policy" from *www.seasidemusictheater.org*. Copyright © 2006 Seaside Music Theater. All rights reserved. Used by Permission.

Simon & Schuster, Inc. "A Day's Wait" from *Winner Take Nothing* by Ernest Hemingway. Copyright © 1933 Charles Scribner's Sons. Copyright renewed © 1961 by Mary Hemingway.

Simon & Schuster Books for Young Readers "The Fox and the Crow" from *The Fables of Aesop Selected, Told Anew and Their History Traced* by Joseph Jacobs. Copyright © 1964 Macmillan Publishing Company. Used by the permission of Simon & Schuster Books for Young Readers, an imprint of Simon & Schuster Children's Publishing Division.

Susan Solt "Forsythia" by Mary Ellen Solt from *Concrete Poetry: A World View*. Copyright © 1968 by Mary Ellen Solt. Copyright © 1970 by Mary Ellen Solt. All rights reserved. Used by permission.

John Sousanis "Toned-down 'Christmas Carol' has more spirit" by John Sousanis, from *The Oakland Press, November 29, 2000, Vol. 156, No. 280*. Copyright © 2000 The Oakland Press. Used by permission of John Sousanis.

Star Tribune "Veteran Returns, Becomes Symbol" (Original title "Astronaut Glenn: He Can Inspire America Again") from *Minneapolis Star Tribune, January 19, 1998*. Copyright © 1998 Star Tribune, Minneapolis, MN. Used by Permission.

The Statue of Liberty-Ellis Island Foundation, Inc. "Byron Yee: Discovering a Paper Son" from *http://www.ellisisland.org/immexp/wseix_3_3.asp?* Copyright © 2000 by The Statue of Liberty-Ellis Island Foundation, Inc. www.ellisisland.org. Used by permission.

Piri Thomas "Amigo Brothers" by Piri Thomas from *Stories from El Barrio*. Used by permission of the author.

Tribute Entertainment Media Group "Indian Grey Mongoose (Herpestes edwardsi)" from *www.wildinfo.com.* Used by permission of Tribute Entertainment Media Group.

The University of Georgia "On the Boardwalk" by Amanda E. Swennes from Outreach, Winter 2007. Copyright © 2007 by the University of Georgia. Used by permission. All rights reserved.

The University of Georgia Press "Volar: To Fly" from *The Latin Deli: Prose and Poetry.* Copyright by Judith Ortiz Cofer. Used by permission of the author and The University of Georgia Press.

University of Notre Dame Press From *Barrio Boy* by Ernesto Galarza. Copyright © 1971 by University of Notre Dame Press. Used by permission of the University of Notre Dame Press. All rights reserved.

The Vagabond School of the Drama "The Flat Rock Playhouse Apprentice Showcase ad Apprentice Application Form" from *www. flatrockplayhouse.org.* Used by permission.

Viking Penguin, Inc. From *What Makes a Rembrandt a Rembrandt?* by Richard Mühlberger. Copyright © 1993 by The Metropolitan Museum of Art. "The Other Frog Prince" by Jon Scieszka and Lane Smith from *The Stinky Cheese Man & Other Fairly Stupid Tales.* Text Copyright © Jon Scieszka, 1992. Illustration © Lane Smith, 1992. "Grasshopper Logic" from *Squids Will Be Squids: Fresh Morals, Beastly Fables* by Jon Scieszka, copyright © 1998 Jon Scieszka, text. Illustrations by Lane Smith © 1998. "Duckbilled Platypus vs. BeefSnakStik®" from *Squids Will Be Squids: Fresh Morals, Beastly Fables* by Jon Scieszka, copyright © 1998 Jon Scieszka, text. Illustrations by Lane Smith © 1998. "Sun and Moon in a Box (Zuni)" from *American Indian Trickster Tales* by Richard Erdoes and Alphonso Ortiz, copyright © 1998 by Richard Erdoes & The Estate of Alphonso Ortiz. Used by permission of Viking Penguin, a division of Penguin Young Readers Group, A member of Penguin Group (USA) Inc., 345 Hudson Street, New York, NY 10014. All rights reserved.

The Wylie Agency, Inc. "Grandpa and the Statue" by Arthur Miller. Copyright © 1945 by Arthur Miller. Used with permission of The Wylie Agency. CAUTION: Professionals and amateurs are hereby warned that *Grandpa and the Statue,* being fully protected under the copyright Laws of the United States of America, the British Empire, including the Dominion of Canada, and all other countries of the Universal Copyright and Berne Conventions, are subject to royalty. All rights, including professional, amateur, motion picture, recitation, lecturing, public readin g, radio and television broadcasting, and the rights of translation into foreign languages, are strictly reserved. All inquiries for *Grandpa and the Statue* should be addressed to The Wylie Agency, Inc.

Laurence Yep "Ribbons" by Laurence Yep from *American Girl magazine, Jan/Feb 1992.* Used by permission of the author.

The Young Authors Foundation, Inc. "Zoos: Joys or Jails?" by Rachel F. from *www.teenink.com.* Copyright © 2003 by Teen Ink, The 21st Century and The Young Authors Foundation, Inc. All rights reserved. Used by permission.

Robert Zimmerman "Life Without Gravity" by Robert Zimmerman from *Muse Magazine, April 2002.* © 2002 Carus Publishing Company. All rights reserved. Used by permission, author Zimmerman owns the rights.

Zoological Society of San Diego "Kid Territory: Why Do We Need Zoos?" from *http://www.sandiegozoo.org/kids/readaboutit_ why_zoos.html.* Copyright © Zoological Society of San Diego. Used by permission of the Zoological Society of San Diego.

Note: Every effort has been made to locate the copyright owner of material reproduced on this component. Omissions brought to our attention will be corrected in subsequent editions.

Credits

Photo Credits

Kobal Collection; **800:** l. Photofest; **800:** bl. Photofest; **800:** tl. Photofest; **803:** Ebenezer Scrooge celebrating in the Guthrie Theatre's 1994 production of *A Christmas Carol* adapted by Barbara Field. Photo credit: Michal Daniel.; **813:** Photofest; **819:** t. Bettmann/CORBIS; **819:** t. ©Michal Daniel, 2003; **820:** CBS/The Kobal Collection; **822:** ©Michal Daniel, 2003; **833:** b. Bettmann/CORBIS; **834:** l. istockphoto.com; **834:** l. istockphoto.com; **834:** Bkgrnd. istockphoto.com; **834:** m. CNAC/MNAM/Dist. RÈunion des MusÈes Nationaux / Art Resource, NY; **835:** tr. istock-photo.com; **838:** *Woman on telephone as seen through window,* William Low, Courtesy of the artist.; **839:** © Paul Loven/Getty Images; **842:** *Over view of family walking dog on the street,* William Low, Courtesy of the artist; **842:** *Over view of family walking dog on the street,* (detail) William Low, Courtesy of the artist; **847:** *Streetlight,* 1930, Constance Coleman Richardson, © Indianapolis Museum of Art, Gift of Mrs. James W. Fesler; **848:** Hans Wolf/Getty Images; **850:** William Whitehurst/CORBIS; **855:** tl. Getty Images; **855:** tr. John Springer Collection/CORBIS; **855:** bm. Photofest; **855:** br. Photofest; **855:** bl. Photofest; **867:** b. Courtesy of Peg Kehret; **867:** t. Sophie Bassouls/ CORBIS Sygma; **868:** David Nieves/ Hudson Valley Aerial Photography; **870:** Courtesy of the Library of Congress; **871:** MusÈ Bartholdi, Colmar, reprod. C. Kempf"; **872:** istock-photo.com/ Joshua Haviv; **874:** Inset. Jose Luis Pelaez Inc /Getty Images; **874:** Bkgrnd. istockphoto.com; **876:** istockphoto.com; **878:** b. Charles Gupton/CORBIS; **999:** b. ©The Stock Market/Paul Loven; **1000:** ©The Stock Market/Paul Loven;

Grade 7 Unit 6 898: © Hyacinth Manning /SuperStock; **903:** t. Courtesy of the Springville Museum of Art, Springville, Utah; **904:** PEANUTS reprinted by permission of United Feature Syndicate, Inc.; **907:** Rights and Permissions will add to their acknowledgement section; **907:** b. istockphoto.com; **908-909:** Rights and Permissions will add to their acknowledgement section; **915:** t. Courtesy of the Library of Congress; **917:** Private Collection/ The Bridgeman Art Library; **919:** Mary Evans Picture Library; **924:** bl. istockphoto.com/Nicholas Monu; **924:** m. istock-photo.com/Stefan Klein; **924:** bl. istockphoto.com/Christopher Steer; **924:** b. istockphoto.com/James Warren; **924:** istockphoto.com; **925:** bl. istockphoto.com/Lise Gagne; **925:** br. istockphoto.com/Nicholas Monu; **925:** t4. istockphoto.com; **925:**tr. istockphoto.com/Clint Spencer; **926:** bl. istockphoto.com/Mike Modine; **926-927:** istockphoto.com/Ryan Burke; **927:** rb. istockphoto.com/Nicholas Monu; **928:** t. istockphoto.com/Marcin Pa-ko; **928:** t. © Leeds Museums and Galleries (City Art Gallery) U.K.; **929:** 2. The Granger Collection, New York; **929:** 1. The Granger Collection, New York; **929:** 5. The Granger Collection, New York; **929:** 3. The Granger Collection, New York; **929:** 9. The Granger Collection, New York; **929:** 7. The Granger Collection, New York; **929:** 10. Massimo Listri/CORBIS; **929:** 6. Andrea Jemolo/CORBIS; **929:** 4. Andrea Jemolo/CORBIS; **929:** 8. Mimmo Jodice/CORBIS; **929:** Bkgrnd. Paul A. Souders/CORBIS; **930:** tl. ack-figure amphora depicting Demeter, Persephone and Apollo,/Museum of Fine Arts, Budapest, Hungary, / The Bridgeman Art Library International; **937:** t. Educational and Professional Publishing.; **938:** Charles & Josette Lenars/CORBIS; **940:** The Art Archive / National Anthropological Museum Mexico/Gianni Dagli Orti; **941- 942:** The Art Archive / National Anthropological Museum Mexico / Gianni Dagli Orti; **945:** t. By permission of Mrs. J.S.E. Farrell; **945:** Ullses Ruiz/epa/CORBIS; **946:** Daniel Aguiler/Reuters/CORBIS; **947:** Werner Forman/CORBIS; **948:** Private Collection/Bridgeman Art Library; **950:** The Art Archive /Museo Franz Mayer Mexico/Gianni Dagli Orti/The Picture Desk, Inc.; **951:** Museum fur Volkerkunde, Vienna, Austria/The Bridgeman Art Library; Nationality/copyright status: out of copyright; **952:** ©Charles & Josette Lenara/CORBIS; **953:** Biblioteca Nacional de Mexico, Mexico/Giraudon/The Bridgeman Art Library; **954:** Ullses Ruiz/epa/CORBIS; **962:** David Young-Wolff/PhotoEdit; **967:** t. **968:** From Mary Pope Osborne THE GRAY-EYED GODDESS copyright (c) 2003 by Mary Pope Osborne, cover illustration by Troy Howell. Reprinted by permission of Disney/Hyperion, an imprint of Disney Book Group LLC. All rights reserved; **991:** b. AP/Wide World Photos; **991:** t. ©Bassouls Sophie/CORBIS Sygma; **992:**Darren Bennett/Animals Animals; **994:** Ron Sanford/CORBIS;

995: bl. istockphoto.com; **999:** t. The Granger Collection, New York; **999:** b. © Paul Loven/Getty Images; **1000:** © Paul Loven/Getty Images; **1001:** tm. The Granger Collection, New York; **1001:** tl. Hulton Archive/ Getty Images Inc.; **1001:** m. Aaron Douglas, Into Bondage, 1936, 60 3/8 x 60 1/2, oil on canvas. In the collection of the Corcoran Gallery of Art, Washington, DC. Museum Purchase and Partial Gift of Thurlow Tibbs Jr., The Evans-Tibbs Collection. 1996.9; **1001:** tr. The Granger Collection, New York; **1001:** bmr. Bettmann/CORBIS; **1001:** tmr. Bettmann/CORBIS; **1001:** bml. Portrait of Langston Hughes (1902-1967) c. 1925, Winold Reiss, National Portrait Gallery, Washington, DC,USA/Art Resource, NY; **1001:** m. Aaron Douglas (1899-1979). Artist., 1953, Betsy Graves Reyneau, National Portrait Gallery, Smithsonian Institution/Art Resource, NY; **1001:** bl. The Granger Collection, New York; © Paul Loven/Getty Images; **1009:** t.Prentice Hall; **1009:** tr. istockphoto.com; **1011:** Book cover illustrated by Leo and Diane Dillon, © 1985 by Knopf Children, from THE PEOPLE COULD FLY (ILLUSTRATIONS ONLY) by Leo and Diane Dillon. Used by permission of Alfred A. Knopf, an imprint of Random House Children's Books, a division of Random House, Inc.; **1013:** tr. istockphoto.com/Sergey Surkov; **1017:** © 1966 by Michael Courlander; **1018:**Hans Christoph Kappel/Nature Picture Library; **1019:** t. istockphoto.com; **1019:** b. istockphoto.com; **1028:** t. Buddy Mays/CORBIS; **1029:** t. Ralph A. Clevenger/CORBIS; **1035:** t. Copyright 2004 The Burlington Free Press/Peter Huoppi; **1035:** b. Aesop, c. 1639-1640. Oil on canvas, Diego Rodriguez Velazquez, Scala/Art Resource, NY; **1040:** b. Image Source/SuperStock; **1043:** Prentice Hall

Staff Credits

The people who made up the Pearson Prentice Hall Literature team—representing design, editorial, editorial services, education technology, manufacturing and inventory planning, market research, marketing services, planning and budgeting, product planning, production services, project office, publishing processes, and rights and permissions—are listed below. Boldface type denotes the core team members.

Tobey Antao, **Margaret Antonini**, Rosalyn Arcilla, Penny Baker, James Ryan Bannon, Stephan Barth, **Tricia Battipede**, Krista Baudo, Rachel Beckman, Julie Berger, Lawrence Berkowitz, Melissa Biezin, **Suzanne Biron**, Rick Blount, **Marcela Boos**, **Betsy Bostwick**, Kay Bosworth, Jeff Bradley, Andrea Brescia, Susan Brorein, Lois Brown, **Pam Carey**, Lisa Carrillo, **Geoffrey Cassar**, Patty Cavuoto, Doria Ceraso, Jennifer Ciccone, Jaime Cohen, Rebecca Cottingham, Joe Cucchiara, Jason Cuoco, **Alan Dalgleish**, **Karen Edmonds**, **Irene Ehrmann**, Stephen Eldridge, Amy Fleming, Dorothea Fox, Steve Frankel, Cindy Frederick, Philip Fried, Diane Fristachi, Phillip Gagler, **Pamela Gallo**, Husain Gatlin, **Elaine Goldman**, Elizabeth Good, John Guild, Phil Hadad, Patricia Hade, Monduane Harris, Brian Hawkes, Jennifer B. Heart, Martha Heller, John Hill, Beth Hyslip, Mary Jean Jones, Grace Kang, Nathan Kinney, Roxanne Knoll, **Kate Krimsky**, Monisha Kumar, Jill Kushner, Sue Langan, Melisa Leong, Susan Levine, Dave Liston, **Mary Luthi**, **George Lychock**, **Gregory Lynch**, **Joan Mazzeo**, **Sandra McGloster**, Salita Mehta, Eve Melnechuk, Kathleen Mercandetti, Artur Mkrtchyan, Karyn Mueller, Alison Muff, Christine Mulcahy, Kenneth Myett, Elizabeth Nemeth, Stefano Nese, Carrie O'Connor, April Okano, Kim Ortell, Sonia Pap, Raymond Parenteau, Dominique Pickens, Linda Punskovsky, **Sheila Ramsay**, Maureen Raymond, Mairead Reddin, **Erin Rehill-Seker**, **Renee Roberts**, **Laura Ross**, Bryan Salacki, Sharon Schultz, Jennifer Serra, **Melissa Shustyk**, Rose Sievers, Christy Singer, Yvonne Stecky, **Cynthia Summers**, Steve Thomas, Merle Uuesoo, Roberta Warshaw, Patricia Williams, Daniela Velez

Additional Credits

Lydie Bemba, Victoria Blades, Denise Data, Rachel Drice, Eleanor Kostyk, Jill Little, Loraine Machlin, Evan Marx, Marilyn McCarthy, Patrick O'Keefe, Shelia M. Smith, Lucia Tirondola, Laura Vivenzio, Linda Waldman, Angel Weyant